ARCTIC OCEAN

Barents Sea

Laptev Sea

East Siberian Sea

Bering Strait

RUSSIAN FEDERATION

Bering Sea

Sea of Okhotsk

FINLAND
Helsinki
Tallinn
ESTONIA
Riga
LATVIA
Vilnius
LITHUANIA
Minsk
BELARUS
Kyiv
UKRAINE
Moscow

MOLDOVA
Chişinău
ROMANIA
SERBIA
Sofia
BULGARIA
Black Sea
Bucharest
Budapest

Astana

KAZAKHSTAN

Ulan Bator

MONGOLIA

DEMOCRATIC PEOPLE'S REPUBLIC OF KOREA

Sea of Japan

JAPAN

GREECE
Athens
Ankara
TURKEY
Nicosia
CYPRUS
Beirut
LEBANON
ISRAEL
Damascus
SYRIA
Amman
JORDAN
Baghdad
IRAQ

GEORGIA
Tbilisi
Yerevan
ARMENIA
Baku
AZERBAIJAN

Almaty
Bishkek
KYRGYZSTAN
Tashkent
UZBEKISTAN
Dushanbe
TAJIKISTAN
Asgabat
TURKMENISTAN

Beijing

PEOPLE'S REPUBLIC OF CHINA

Pyongyang
Seoul
REPUBLIC OF KOREA

Tokyo

Tehran
IRAN

Kabul
AFGHANISTAN
Islamabad

New Delhi

NEPAL
Kathmandu
Thimphu
BHUTAN

East China Sea

Tropic of Cancer

Cairo
EGYPT
Kuwait City
KUWAIT
BAHRAIN
Manama
QATAR
Doha
Abu Dhabi
UAE
Muscat
OMAN

Riyadh

SAUDI ARABIA

PALESTINIAN AUTONOMOUS AREAS

Red Sea

PAKISTAN

INDIA

BANGLADESH
Dhaka

MYANMAR
Pyinmana
Yangon

MACAO (CHINA)
Hanoi
HONG KONG (CHINA)

Taipei
TAIWAN

Khartoum
SUDAN

ERITREA
Asmara
San'a
YEMEN
DJIBOUTI

Addis Ababa
ETHIOPIA

Bay of Bengal

THAILAND
Bangkok
Vientiane
LAOS
VIET NAM
CAMBODIA
Phnom Penh

South China Sea

Manila

PHILIPPINES

Philippine Sea

NORTHERN MARIANA ISLANDS (USA)

PACIFIC OCEAN

GUAM (USA)

DEMOCRATIC REPUBLIC OF THE CONGO

UGANDA
Kampala
Nairobi
KENYA
RWANDA
Kigali
BURUNDI
Bujumbura
Dodoma
TANZANIA

SOMALIA
Mogadishu

Colombo
SRI LANKA
Sri Jayawardenepura

MALDIVES

Kuala Lumpur
Putrajaya
MALAYSIA
SINGAPORE

BRUNEI
Bandar Seri Begawan

PALAU

MARSHALL ISLANDS

FEDERATED STATES OF MICRONESIA

NAURU

KIRIBATI

Victoria
SEYCHELLES

Dar es Salaam

BRITISH INDIAN OCEAN TERRITORY (UNITED KINGDOM)

INDIAN OCEAN

Jakarta

INDONESIA

PAPUA NEW GUINEA

SOLOMON ISLANDS

TUVALU

Lubumbashi

COMOROS
Moroni
MAYOTTE (FRANCE)

CHRISTMAS ISLAND (AUSTRALIA)

COCOS ISLANDS (AUSTRALIA)

Dili
TIMOR-LESTE

Honiara

Port Moresby

TOKELAU (NEW ZEALAND)

WALLIS AND FUTUNA ISLANDS (FRANCE)
SAMOA
AMERICAN SAMOA (USA)

ZAMBIA
Lusaka
Lilongwe
Harare
ZIMBABWE

MALAWI

Antananarivo
MADAGASCAR
MAURITIUS
Port Louis
RÉUNION (FRANCE)

Mozambique Channel

AUSTRALIA

Coral Sea

VANUATU
Port Vila

NEW CALEDONIA (FRANCE)

FIJI
Suva
NIUE (NZ)
TONGA

BOTSWANA
Gaborone
Pretoria
Maputo
Mbabane
SWAZILAND
LESOTHO
Maseru
SOUTH AFRICA

MOZAMBIQUE

NORFOLK ISLAND (AUSTRALIA)

Canberra

Tasman Sea

NEW ZEALAND

Wellington

© Routledge, supplied by the Cartographic Unit, University of So...

Eastern Europe, Russia and
Central Asia
2009

Eastern Europe, Russia and Central Asia 2009

9th Edition

Routledge
Taylor & Francis Group

LONDON AND NEW YORK

Ninth edition 2009

ISBN13: 978-1-85743-473-6
ISBN10: 1-85743-473-0
ISSN 1470-5702

Editor: Dominic Heaney

Contributing Editor: Imogen Gladman

Regional Organizations Editors: Catriona Appeatu Holman, Helen Canton

Statistics Editor: Philip McIntyre

Assistant Editors: Kim Chamberlain, Catriona Marcham, Adrian Reynolds, Gareth Vaughan

Contributing Editor (Who's Who): Robert Elster

Associate Editor (Directory Research): James Middleton

Series Editor: Joanne Maher

Typeset in New Century Schoolbook

Typeset by Data Standards Limited, Frome, Somerset

Printed and bound in Great Britain by Polestar Wheatons, Exeter

FOREWORD

The ninth edition of EASTERN EUROPE, RUSSIA AND CENTRAL ASIA covers a period characterized by the increasing international assertiveness of the major power in the region, Russia, most notably exemplified by its military invasion of Georgia in August 2008, undertaken ostensibly to protect its citizens in the separatist territory of South Ossetia. The outgoing Russian President, Vladimir Putin, retained substantial power following his appointment to the positions of Chairman of both the Government and the de facto ruling party, United Russia, following the election of Dmitrii Medvedev to succeed him as Head of State. Meanwhile, prior to the conflict, Georgia underwent a period of heightened political instability that resulted in the premature resignation from office of President Mikheil Saakashvili, although his re-election, and the success of his allies at parliamentary polls, suggested that the reformist administration retained popular support. In Ukraine tensions between the executive and legislative branches continued to be exacerbated by proposals for constitutional reform, resulting in a prolonged political crisis and, for the second time in little more than a year, the scheduling of pre-term parliamentary elections. Meanwhile, the established regimes in Armenia, Azerbaijan and Belarus were among those in the region that continued their consolidation of power. As this edition went to press in late 2008 it was becoming evident that several countries in the region would be affected adversely by the consequences of the international economic downturn.

Chapters on each country are complemented by a General Survey, which presents in-depth analyses of various issues of significance to the region as a whole, including economic developments, international relations, environmental degradation, and poverty and social welfare, as well as essays dealing with specific sub-regional questions and developments. The politics of energy in the Caspian Sea region, separatism and Islamist militancy in the North Caucasus, and the politics of water in the Aral Sea region are among topics discussed.

Each country chapter also includes a detailed statistical survey and directory sections, all of which have been extensively updated and revised. De facto or de jure autonomous or sovereign territories are covered in some detail, as are all of the constituent units of the Russian Federation. The volume also includes an up-to-date Who's Who section, comprising the biographical details of men and women prominent in the region; and a section of Regional Information, which provides extensive coverage of international and regional organizations operating in Eastern Europe, Russia and Central Asia, comprehensive listings of research institutes engaged in the study of the region, a books bibliography, and a select bibliography of periodicals relevant to the area.

The Editors are grateful to all the contributors for their articles and advice, and to the numerous governments and organizations that have provided statistical and other information.

October 2008

ACKNOWLEDGEMENTS

The editors gratefully acknowledge the co-operation, interest and advice of all the authors who have contributed to the volume. We are also indebted to the many organizations connected with the region, particularly the national statistical offices. We owe special thanks to a number of embassies and ministries. In addition, we are grateful to Edward Oliver and to the University of Southampton Cartographic Unit, for preparing the maps that are included in this volume.

The editors gratefully acknowledge particular indebtedness for permission to reproduce material from the following sources: the United Nations' statistical databases and *Demographic Yearbook*, *Statistical Yearbook*, *Monthly Bulletin of Statistics*, *Industrial Commodity Statistics Yearbook* and *International Trade Statistics Yearbook*; the United Nations Educational, Scientific and Cultural Organization's *Statistical Yearbook* and Institute for Statistics database; the *Human Development Report* of the United Nations Development Programme; the Food and Agriculture Organization of the United Nations' statistical database; the statistical databases of the World Health Organization; the International Labour Office's statistical database and *Yearbook of Labour Statistics*; the World Bank's *World Bank Atlas*, *Global Development Finance*, *World Development Report* and *World Development Indicators*; the International Monetary Fund's statistical database, *International Financial Statistics* and *Government Finance Statistics Yearbook*; the World Tourism Organization's *Compendium* and *Yearbook of Tourism Statistics*; the US Geological Survey; and the International Telecommunication Union. We are also grateful to the International Institute for Strategic Studies, Arundel House, 13–15 Arundel Street, London WC2R 3DX, for the use of defence statistics from *The Military Balance 2008*.

HEALTH AND WELFARE STATISTICS: SOURCES AND DEFINITIONS

Total fertility rate Source: WHO Statistical Information System. The number of children that would be born per woman, assuming no female mortality at child-bearing ages and the age-specific fertility rates of a specified country and reference period.

Under-5 mortality rate Source: WHO Statistical Information System. Defined by WHO as the probability of a child born in a specific year or period dying before reaching the age of five, if subject to the age-specific mortality rates of that year or period.

HIV/AIDS Source: UNAIDS. Estimated percentage of adults aged 15 to 49 years living with HIV/AIDS. < indicates 'fewer than'.

Health expenditure Source: WHO Statistical Information System.
US $ per head (PPP)
International dollar estimates, derived by dividing local currency units by an estimate of their purchasing-power parity (PPP) compared with the US dollar. PPPs are the rates of currency conversion that equalize the purchasing power of different currencies by eliminating the differences in price levels between countries.
% of GDP
GDP levels for OECD countries follow the most recent UN System of National Accounts. For non-OECD countries a value was estimated by utilizing existing UN, IMF and World Bank data.
Public expenditure
Government health-related outlays plus expenditure by social schemes compulsorily affiliated with a sizeable share of the population, and extrabudgetary funds allocated to health services. Figures include grants or loans provided by international agencies, other national authorities, and sometimes commercial banks.

Access to water and sanitation Source: WHO/UNICEF Joint Monitoring Programme on Water Supply and Sanitation (JMP) (Mid-Term Assessment, 2004). Defined in terms of the percentage of the population using improved facilities in terms of the type of technology and levels of service afforded. For water, this includes house connections, public standpipes, boreholes with handpumps, protected dug wells, protected spring and rainwater collection; allowance is also made for other locally defined technologies. Sanitation is defined to include connection to a sewer or septic tank system, pour-flush latrine, simple pit or ventilated improved pit latrine, again with allowance for acceptable local technologies. Access to water and sanitation does not imply that the level of service or quality of water is 'adequate' or 'safe'.

Human Development Index (HDI) Source: UNDP, *Human Development Report* (2007/08). A summary of human development measured by three basic dimensions: prospects for a long and healthy life, measured by life expectancy at birth; knowledge, measured by adult literacy rate (two-thirds' weight) and the combined gross enrolment ratio in primary, secondary and tertiary education (one-third weight); and standard of living, measured by GDP per head (PPP US $). The index value obtained lies between zero and one. A value above 0.8 indicates high human development, between 0.5 and 0.8 medium human development, and below 0.5 low human development. A centralized data source for all three dimensions was not available for all countries. In some cases other data sources were used to calculate a substitute value; however, this was excluded from the ranking. Other countries, including non-UNDP members, were excluded from the HDI altogether. In total, 177 countries were ranked for 2005.

CONTENTS

THE CONTRIBUTORS

Shirin Akiner. School of Oriental and African Studies, University of London and Associate Fellow, Chatham House (Royal Institute of International Affairs), London.

John Anderson. University of St Andrews.

Anders Åslund. Senior Fellow, Peterson Institute for International Economics, Washingon, DC.

Annette Bohr. Chatham House (Royal Institute of International Affairs), London.

Aleh Cherp. Central European University, Budapest.

Tamara Dragadze. Writer and specialist on the former Soviet Union.

Jane Falkingham. Professor of Demography and International Social Policy at University of Southampton.

Matteo Fumagalli. Central European University, Budapest.

Philip Hanson. Emeritus Professor at University of Birmingham and Associate Fellow of the Russia and Eurasia Programme, Chatham House (Royal Institute of International Affairs), London.

Edmund Herzig. University of Oxford.

Michael Kaser. Emeritus Reader in Economics and Emeritus Fellow of St Antony's College, University of Oxford.

Taras Kuzio. Senior Transatlantic Fellow of the German Marshall Fund of the United States, and Adjunct Professor at the Institute for European, Russian and Eurasian Studies, Elliott School of International Affairs, George Washington University, Washington, DC.

Neil Melvin. Brussels School of International Studies, University of Kent.

Ruben Mnatsakanian. Central European University, Budapest.

Vladimer Papava. Georgian Foundation for Strategic and International Studies, Tbilisi.

Steven D. Roper. Eastern Illinois University, Charleston, IL.

Angus Roxburgh. Journalist, broadcaster and author.

Andrew Ryder. University of Portsmouth.

Andrei Smirnov. Journalist specializing in the North Caucasus.

George Tarkhan-Mouravi. Co-director, Institute for Policy Studies, Tbilisi.

Michael Tokmazishvili. Senior researcher, Foundation CASE-Transcaucasia, Tbilisi

Kai Wegerich. Wageningen University.

Toby Wight. Specialist in banking and economic development in Azerbaijan and the CIS.

Kenneth Wilson. University of Edinburgh.

Andrew Yorke. Political and economic analyst.

ABBREVIATIONS

Acad., Akad.	Academician; Academy
AD	anno domini
ADB	Asian Development Bank
Adm.	Admiral
admin.	administration
AH	Anno Hegirae
a.i.	ad interim
AID	(US) Agency for International Development
AIDS	acquired immunodeficiency syndrome
Alt.	Alternate
AM	Anno Mundi
AOb	Avtonomnyi Oblast (Autonomous Oblast)
AOk	Avtonomnyi Okrug (Autonomous Okrug)
approx.	approximately
ASEAN	Association of South East Asian Nations
asscn	association
assoc.	associate
ASSR	Autonomous Soviet Socialist Republic
asst	assistant
Aug.	August
auth.	authorized
Ave	Avenue
b.	born
BC	before Christ
Bd	Board
bd, blvd	Bulevardi, Boulevard
b/d	barrels per day
Bldg	Building
br.(s)	branch(es)
Brig.	Brigadier
BSE	bovine spongiform encephalopathy
BSEC	(Organization of the) Black Sea Economic Co-operation
BTC	Baku–Tbilisi–Ceyhan
bul., bulv.	bulvar (boulevard)
C	Centigrade
c.	circa; child, children
cap.	capital
Capt.	Captain
Cdre	Commodore
Cen.	Central
CEO	Chief Executive Officer
CFE	Treaty on Conventional Forces in Europe
Chair.	Chairman/woman
c.i.f.	cost, insurance and freight
CIS	Commonwealth of Independent States
C-in-C	Commander-in-Chief
circ.	circulation
cm	centimetre(s)
CMEA	Council for Mutual Economic Assistance
c/o	care of
Co	Company; County
Col	Colonel
Commdr	Commander
Corpn	Corporation
CPC	Caspian Pipeline Consortium
CPSU	Communist Party of the Soviet Union
CSCE	Conference on Security and Co-operation in Europe
Cttee	Committee
cu	cubic
cwt	hundredweight
d.	daughter(s)
Dec.	December
Dep.	Deputy
dep.	deposits
Dept	Department
devt	development
Dir	Director
DM	Deutsche Mark (German mark)
Dr	Doctor
dwt	dead weight tons
E	East; Eastern
EBRD	European Bank for Reconstruction and Development
EC	European Community
ECE	(United Nations) Economic Commission for Europe
ECO	Economic Co-operation Organization
Econ.	Economist; Economics

ECOSOC	(United Nations) Economic and Social Council
ECU	European Currency Unit
edn	edition
EEC	European Economic Community
EFTA	European Free Trade Association
e.g.	exempli gratia (for example)
eKv	electron kilovolt
e-mail	electronic mail
eMv	electron megavolt
Eng.	Engineer; Engineering
ESCAP	Economic and Social Commission for Asia and the Pacific
est.	established; estimate; estimated
et al.	et alii (and others)
etc.	et cetera
EU	European Union
excl.	excluding
exec.	executive
F	Fahrenheit
f.	founded
FAO	Food and Agriculture Organization
Feb.	February
FDI	foreign direct investment
FM	frequency modulation
fmrly	formerly
f.o.b.	free on board
Fr	Father
FRG	Federal Republic of Germany
Fri.	Friday
FRY	Federal Republic of Yugoslavia
FSB	Federalnaya sluzhba bezopasnosti (Federal Security Service)
ft	foot (feet)
g	gram(s)
GATT	General Agreement on Tariffs and Trade
GDP	gross domestic product
Gen.	General
GNI	gross national income
GNP	gross national product
Gov.	Governor
Govt	Government
grt	gross registered tons
ha	hectares
HE	His (or Her) Eminence; His (or Her) Excellency
HIV	human immunodeficiency virus
hl	hectolitre(s)
HM	His (or Her) Majesty
Hon.	Honorary (or Honourable)
hp	horsepower
HQ	Headquarters
HRH	His (or Her) Royal Highness
HSC	Harmonized System Classification
IAEA	International Atomic Energy Agency
ibid	ibidem (from the same source)
IBRD	International Bank for Reconstruction and Development (World Bank)
ICC	International Chamber of Commerce
ICFTU	International Confederation of Free Trade Unions
ICRC	International Committee of the Red Cross
IDA	International Development Association
i.e.	id est (that is to say)
ILO	International Labour Organization/Office
IMF	International Monetary Fund
in (ins)	inch (inches)
Inc	Incorporated
incl.	including
Ind.	Independent
INF	Intermediate-range Nuclear Forces
Ing.	Engineer
Insp.	Inspector
Int.	International
IRF	International Road Federation
irreg.	irregular
Is	Islands
IT	information and communication technology
Jan.	January

Jr	Junior
Jt	Joint
kg	kilogram(s)
KGB	Komitet Gosudarstvennoi Bezopasnosti (Committee for State Security)
kHz	kilohertz
km	kilometre(s)
ko'ch	ko'chasi (street)
kom.	komnata (room), komnaty (rooms)
küç	küçasi (street)
kv.	kvartira (apartment); kvartal (apartment block)
kW	kilowatt(s)
kWh	kilowatt hours
lb	pound(s)
Lt, Lieut	Lieutenant
Ltd	Limited
m	metre(s)
m.	married; million
Maj.	Major
Man.	Manager; managing
MDRI	multilateral debt relief initiative
mem.	member
MEV	mega electron volts
mfrs	manufacturers
Mgr	Monseigneur; Monsignor
MHz	megahertz
Mil.	Military
mm	millimetre(s)
Mon.	Monday
MP	Member of Parliament
MSS	Manuscripts
MW	megawatt(s); medium wave
MWh	megawatt hour(s)
N	North; Northern
n.a.	not available
nab.	naberezhnaya (embankment, quai)
Nat.	National
NATO	North Atlantic Treaty Organization
NCO	Non-Commissioned Officer
NGO	non-governmental organization
NMP	net material product
no.	number
Nov.	November
OAO	Otkrytoye aktsionernoye obshchestvo (Open jointstock company)
obl.	oblast (region)
Oct.	October
OECD	Organisation for Economic Co-operation and Development
OIC	Organization of the Islamic Conference
OOO	Obshchestvo s ogranichennoi otvetstvennostyu (Limited company)
OPEC	Organization of the Petroleum Exporting Countries
opp.	opposite
Org.	Organization
OSCE	Organization for Security and Co-operation in Europe
p.	page
p.a.	per annum
Parl.	Parliament(ary)
per.	pereulok (lane, alley)
Perm. Rep.	Permanent Representative
pl.	ploshchad, ploshcha (square)
PLC	Public Limited Company
POB	Post Office Box
pr.	prospect, prospekti (avenue)
Pres.	President
Prin.	Principal
Prof.	Professor
prov.	provulok (lane)
Pte	Private
p.u.	paid up
publ.	publication; published
Publr	Publisher
q.v.	quod vide (to which refer)
Rd	Road
reg., regd	register; registered
reorg.	reorganized
Rep.	Republic; Representative
res	reserve(s)
retd	retired
Rev.	Reverend
Rm.	Room
RSFSR	Russian Soviet Federative Socialist Republic
s.	son(s)
S	South; Southern
SARS	Severe Acute Respiratory Syndrome
SDR(s)	Special Drawing Right(s)
Sec.	Secretary
Secr.	Secretariat
Sen.	Senior
Sept.	September
SGP	Stability and Growth Pact
Soc.	Society
Sq.	Square
sq	square (in measurements)
SS	Saints
SSR	Soviet Socialist Republic
St	Saint; Street
START	Strategic Arms Reduction Treaty
str.	strada (street)
Sun.	Sunday
Supt	Superintendent
SWG	Special Working Group
tech., techn.	technical
tel.	telephone
TEU	twenty-foot equivalent unit
Thurs.	Thursday
Treas.	Treasurer
Tues.	Tuesday
TV	television
UK	United Kingdom
ul.	ulitsa (street)
UN	United Nations
UNAIDS	United Nations Joint Programme on HIV/AIDS
UNCTAD	United Nations Conference on Trade and Development
UNDP	United Nations Development Programme
UNEP	United Nations Environment Programme
UNESCO	United Nations Educational, Scientific and Cultural Organization
UNHCR	United Nations High Commissioner for Refugees
UNICEF	United Nations Children's Fund
Univ.	University
UNPA	United Nations Protected Area
UNWTO	United Nations World Tourism Organization
USA	United States of America
USAID	United States Agency for International Development
USSR	Union of Soviet Socialist Republics
VAT	value-added tax
Ven.	Venerable
viz.	videlicet (namely)
vol.(s)	volume(s)
vul.	vulitsa, vulytsa (street)
W	West; Western
Wed.	Wednesday
WFTU	World Federation of Trade Unions
WHO	World Health Organization
WTO	World Trade Organization
yr	year
ZAO	Zakrytoye aktsionernoye obshchestvo (Closed joint-stock company)

INTERNATIONAL TELEPHONE CODES

To make international calls to telephone and fax numbers listed in *Eastern Europe, Russia and Central Asia*, dial the international code of the country from which you are calling, followed by the appropriate country code for the organization you wish to call (listed below), followed by the area code (if applicable) and telephone or fax number listed in the entry.

	Country code	Time + GMT*
Armenia	374	+4
Azerbaijan	994	+5
Belarus	375	+2
Georgia	995	+4
Kazakhstan	7	+6
Kyrgyzstan	996	+5
Moldova	373	+2
Russia	7	+2 to +12
Tajikistan	992	+5
Turkmenistan	993	+5
Ukraine	380	+2
Uzbekistan	998	+5

* Time difference in hours + Greenwich Mean Time (GMT). The times listed compare the standard (winter) times. Some countries may adopt Summer (Daylight Saving) Times—i.e. + 1 hour—for part of the year.

EXPLANATORY NOTE ON THE DIRECTORY SECTION

The Directory section of each chapter is arranged under the following headings, where they apply:

THE CONSTITUTION

THE GOVERNMENT
HEAD OF STATE
CABINET/COUNCIL OF MINISTERS
MINISTRIES

PRESIDENT

LEGISLATURE

LOCAL GOVERNMENT

ELECTION COMMISSION

POLITICAL ORGANIZATIONS

DIPLOMATIC REPRESENTATION

JUDICIAL SYSTEM

RELIGION

THE PRESS

PUBLISHERS

BROADCASTING AND COMMUNICATIONS
TELECOMMUNICATIONS
RADIO
TELEVISION

FINANCE
CENTRAL BANK
STATE BANKS
DEVELOPMENT BANKS
COMMERCIAL BANKS
STOCK EXCHANGE
INSURANCE

TRADE AND INDUSTRY
GOVERNMENT AGENCIES
DEVELOPMENT ORGANIZATIONS
CHAMBERS OF COMMERCE
INDUSTRIAL AND TRADE ASSOCIATIONS
EMPLOYERS' ASSOCIATIONS
UTILITIES
STATE HYDROCARBONS COMPANIES
MAJOR COMPANIES
TRADE UNIONS

TRANSPORT
RAILWAYS
ROADS
INLAND WATERWAYS
SHIPPING
CIVIL AVIATION

TOURISM

CULTURE
NATIONAL ORGANIZATIONS
CULTURAL HERITAGE
SPORTING ORGANIZATIONS
PERFORMING ARTS
ASSOCIATIONS

EDUCATION
UNIVERSITIES

SOCIAL WELFARE
NATIONAL AGENCIES
HEALTH AND WELFARE ORGANIZATIONS

ENVIRONMENT
GOVERNMENT ORGANIZATIONS
ACADEMIC INSTITUTIONS
NON-GOVERNMENTAL ORGANIZATIONS

DEFENCE

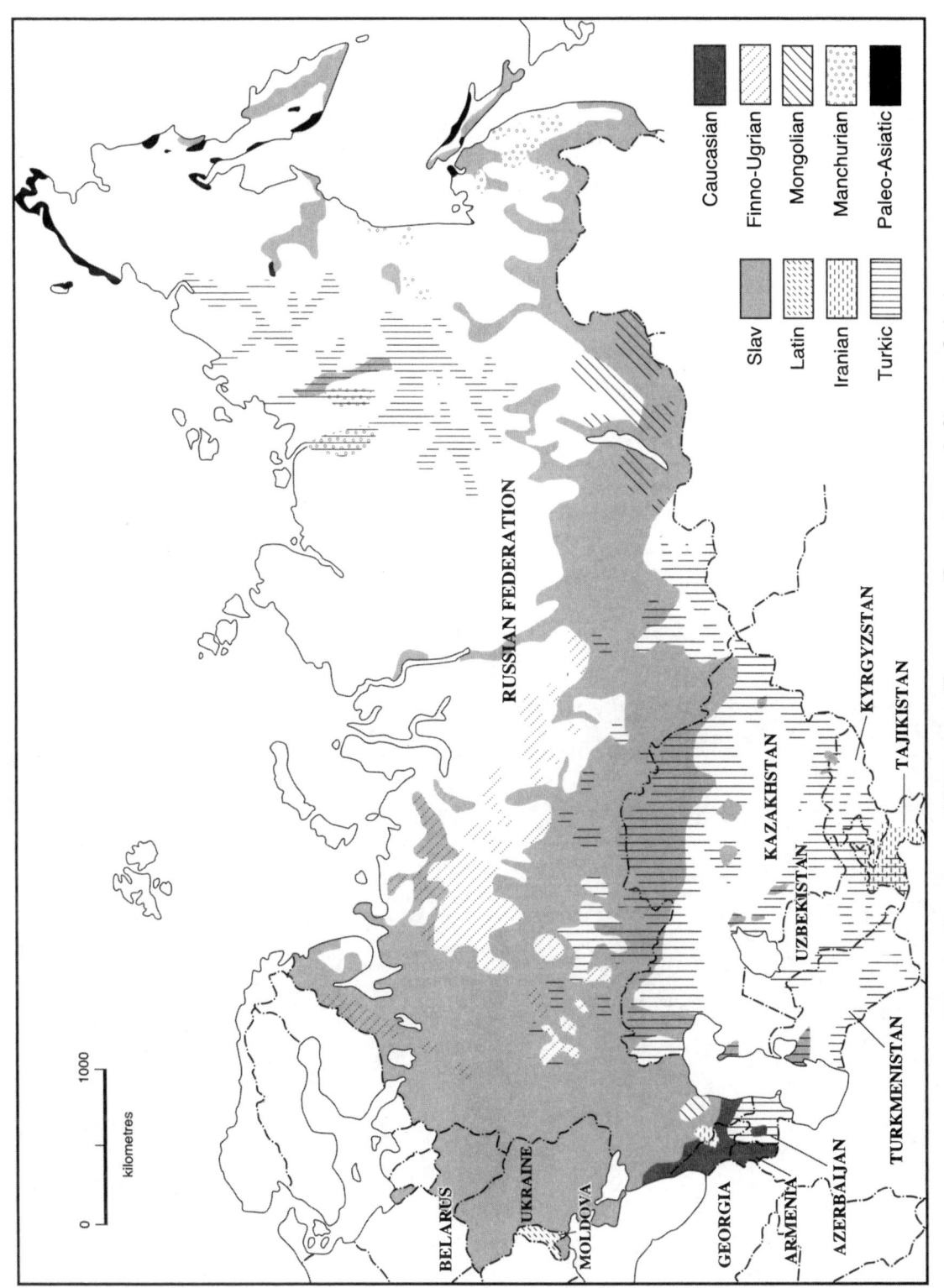

Ethnic Groups of Eastern Europe, Russia and Central Asia

PART ONE
General Survey

INTERNATIONAL RELATIONS OF RUSSIA AND THE COMMONWEALTH OF INDEPENDENT STATES

Dr TAMARA DRAGADZE

INTRODUCTION

During the course of 2008 the leadership in Russia has chosen to firm up its identity as a superpower, although only time will tell whether this is primarily for the benefit of its domestic public or for the outside world. For centuries Russians have been searching for their identity, something that continues to be reflected in their leaders' foreign policy, with a different theme seemingly coming to the fore each year. Some questions are perennial: are they still an Empire? Are they the leaders of Eurasia and, therefore, should they seek special alliances with countries in the East? Or should they show, in their unique way, that despite appearances, they are bona fide adherents of Western economic and political values and culture at home and abroad? Furthermore, in an age of self-conscious image making, there is an ongoing debate about how best to be effective in presenting the identity that the leadership in Russia has chosen, and also whether that choice is worthwhile in the long run.

The confusion created by events in 2008, such as deliberate displays of military might and the patronage of Venezuela, and the war in Georgia in August, has compounded the problems of analysis instigated by actions in the previous year. Let us remember that an almost surreal event had occurred in 2007—the poisoning with Polonium-210, in London, United Kingdom, of former FSB officer Aleksandr Litvinenko. Although the Russian Government denies involvement, the spectacular manner in which it took place had posed as many questions about Russia's internal politics as it did about the country's international relations. And was it to impress its future electors that this incident took place, to demonstrate Russia's regained competence to deal with enemies abroad? Throughout the past few years the linking of domestic political manoeuvring with international relations appears to have grown significantly stronger. The initiative to place a Russian flag on the Arctic seabed in August 2007 was imaginative and in the same month Russia's military air force had flown over the Pacific in a fashion not seen since the end of the Cold War around twenty years earlier. In late 2008, however, the proposed military exercises in the Caribbean Sea would surpass all previous activity by Russia in the region. Is the purpose of these acts to show the domestic public or the USA that Russia had become as combative as in the 'good old days' of the Soviet period? The war in Georgia, truculent in its attitude towards its past master, was deemed to be popular at home. Yet the strength of outside reaction, with its worrying economic consequences, had probably not been expected. So 2008 can be seen as a time when Russia reinvested its efforts to recreate for itself the status of a fearless superpower, although the pragmatism of its leadership suggests that this will not necessarily define the future direction of Russia's international behaviour. A more collaborative and yet not subservient relationship with the other powers might yet emerge.

As for the Commonwealth of Independent States (CIS), although it is 17 years since the Union Republics gained independence from the USSR in 1991, the CIS members still feel obliged to choose their international relations policies as a function of their relationship with the Russian Federation. More fundamentally, Russian–Georgian relations have reached such an all-time low in the past year that a nonsense was made of the CIS concept. Indeed, in August 2008 Georgia filed a case at the International Court of Justice, urging the court to prevent Russia from committing acts of 'ethnic cleansing' in those territories of Georgia then subject to Russia's control. For practical purposes, the remnants of the organization are divided between, on the one hand, Georgia and Ukraine (whose President, alone among the leadership of these states, has openly sympathised with the plight of Georgia) who form a kind of unity and, on the other hand, all the other CIS countries, which have defined their membership by an effort to maintain a display of harmony with Russia. Belarus continues to court fuller union with the Russian Federation, that reacts as a reluctant bride. Turkmenistan also has its own brand of relationship with both Russia and the other former Soviet countries. The ties of the CIS, which would define it as a recognisable entity, are therefore becoming more tenuous.

The aftershocks of the Russia–Georgia war will be felt for an indefinite period. Each country will be reviewing its identity as formerly Soviet and to what extent that entails an acceptance of the need to reassure Russia of its undying loyalty. Russia, in turn, will have to decide whether relying on the legacy left by Stalin (Iosif Dzhugashvili) is indeed to its own benefit.

Stalin created the basis of the statehood of the countries under review here, defining both their status and their borders. Some of his decisions were not without logic; it was easier than not for the status of a Union Republic, which had the symbolic trappings of independent statehood, to be conditional upon having a border with a non-Soviet country. So, Kazakhstan's border with China allowed it to qualify for Union Republic status, whereas Tatarstan, in the middle of the Volga country within Russia proper, did not.

Even Stalin, though, also had to bow to the inclination of Lenin (Vladimir Ulyanov) to humour those peoples, such as the Georgians, who had so vigorously sought for internationally recognized independent statehood during the years immediately following the end of the Russian Empire (1918–21). They repeated this, 70 years later, as soon as signs appeared that the USSR was collapsing too.

However, Stalin devised a hierarchy of symbolic degrees of self-government—some were 'autonomous republics' and others were 'autonomous regions (okrugs)'. Together with the lowlier Russian regions or provinces (oblasts and krais), the majority of these Soviet entities formed a giant Russian Soviet Federative Socialist Republic (RSFSR). The logic behind the creation of the 'sub-states' in the RSFSR, as well as those within the Union Republics, was that some kind of outward recognition had to be given to the dominant ethnic group in a given territory. Thus, the 'ethnicization' of territory became both a legal issue as well as a state of mind.

The way that borders were drawn for the Union Republics and the autonomous entities was mischievous and controversial. Some borders were drawn right through territories shared more or less by the same people; other places were parcelled into 'islands', where another republic had to be crossed before rejoining the main entity (such as the province of Naxçıvan, which was allocated to Azerbaijan, but which was separated from the remainder of the Republic by Armenian territory). Stalin's nationalities policy, therefore, left a series of time-bombs, which the post-Soviet states have had to reckon with and which have sorely affected their international relations and the image that they each project abroad.

In the Soviet regime of Leonid Brezhnev (1964–82), intellectuals were commissioned by the Communist Party's Central Committee to have another look at the tired concept of 'Soviet man' and demonstrate that this shared identity overrode nationality or ethnicity. It went without saying that the Russian language would be the language of choice of *homo sovieticus*, and that loyalty and admiration of Russia would be expressed naturally. Thus, a collective farm in Tajikistan might typically be called 'Kolkhoz Moscow', and this was interpreted as an affirmation of the Tajiks' affection.

Central command was ubiquitous. For example, all books for publication and dissertations for qualifications throughout the USSR had to have a Russian summary and censors in Moscow (the Soviet, as well as the Russian, capital) decided whether they could be passed. The contents were tailored accordingly, a fact not to be forgotten by those subordinate intellectuals turned leaders of local opinion in later years. In return, there was relative economic and political stability throughout the

USSR and the many nations were given enough leeway for their folklore and national cultures to thrive.

The ferocity of the independence movements in some of the Union Republics in the late 1980s, such as in the Baltic republics (Estonia, Latvia and Lithuania) and Georgia, took Mikhail Gorbachev by surprise after he had come to power in 1985 and allowed more genuine self-expression. For the rulers in Moscow to be labelled as oppressors and not as benefactors was not something the Soviet ear was used to hearing. Gorbachev sent troops to quell what he saw as one-off rebellions (such as to Tbilisi in Georgia in 1989 and Baku—Bakı in Azerbaijan in 1990), one of his greatest mistakes. To his credit, however, in comparison with the wars of independence fought several decades earlier against France and the United Kingdom, respectively, in Algeria or Kenya, for example, the Union Republics attained *de jure* independence with relative ease, in 1991.

Before independence, the realities of national sentiment had begun to make themselves known in the late 1980s, as did its uglier side. Violence broke out in Central Asia—against Meskhetians in Uzbekistan (June 1989), between Uzbeks and Kyrgyz in Osh, Kyrgyzstan (June 1990) and in the Caucasus (in Georgia over Abkhazia and South Ossetia; in Azerbaijan and Armenia over Nagornyi Karabakh, from 1988 onwards)—which a strong Soviet fist could not contain. In most cases intervention exacerbated the situation, since the Soviet army, when involved, usually took sides. Envoys from Moscow were not seen as trusted arbiters.

In December 1991 the rejected Slavs took matters into their own hands, forming an alliance of Russia, Ukraine and Belarus, thus signalling the end of the USSR. Mindful of its own large Russian population, Kazakhstan wanted to join the other three. Also, each Union Republic felt that it had, after all, contributed to the overall wealth of the USSR and wanted something back in return. A wider CIS was, therefore, formed to address this issue. With the acquiescence of the rest of the world, Russia declared itself the successor state to the USSR and the custodian and, soon after, heir of all its assets, including the embassies and the seat on the UN Security Council. The Russians themselves now contended that their own culture had been subsumed and repressed, since their own ways, despite being dominant in the USSR, had been camouflaged under the rubric of 'Soviet' rather than 'Russian'. The consequences for Russia were that: externally, Russia was seen by the other republics as being a mighty and therefore unequal partner, to be both feared and contained; and, internally, Russian nationalism was to become a leading political force.

RUSSIA

The 'doctrinal' basis for Russia's actions in 2008, as in recent years, is based on the 2000 revision of the Military Doctrine of the Russian Federation. This reflected on the undesirability of a 'mono-polar' world with one superpower (meaning the USA, without naming it, as the superpower capable of waging war unilaterally, without the sanction of the UN). This was contrasted with the alternative, the formation of a 'multi-polar' world, based on the equal rights of peoples and nations. This preference, which is of course shared by the European Union (EU), seeks to assure a balance between the national interests of states and an implementation of fundamental rules of international law.

In 2008, however, there has been a nuance in the interpretation of this approach. Whereas previously, in keeping with the more ancient view of its having a special mission, Russia offered to take on the role of creating a better balance of power for the sake of the world as a whole, the emphasis has shifted to a simple assertion that Russia is a superpower in its own right, regardless of how the rest of the world perceives it. Russia no longer argues that it will once again strengthen its position as a superpower because other institutions are failing to ensure international security (the effectiveness of the UN and the Organization for Security and Co-operation in Europe—OSCE—having been significantly weakened). No longer does Russia feel it must state that its mission is to assume the role of a counterbalance to a world monopoly of power and, as such, to take a leading role in making the world a safer place. Now it

states instead that Russia has its own interests and that is, in itself, enough to justify whatever it does to protect and promote them.

Previously, Russia had relied on the understanding of the rest of the world, or at least of political commentators, to be sympathetic towards its sense of insecurity, along its borders in particular. That is why it had the right to fear North Atlantic Treaty Organization (NATO) expansion. However, Russia no longer sees fit to present this argument, but is, rather, assertive of its own strength. Although this position has been evident for several years recently, it has now become dominant. To this end, Russia seeks six main objectives.

First, Russia seeks to rebuild its military might. Russia had abandoned the staggeringly high levels of military expenditure of the Soviet period. Yet it is apparently planning to increase its spending on defence by almost 50% in 2009–11, in 2009 by 25.7%, compared with the previous year, to 1,280,000m. roubles (US $51,300m.). The Russian parliament expected that by 2011 total defence expenditures would have increased by 45.6% compared with 2008, with much of the additional funding going towards improving the salaries and living conditions of military personnel. President Dmitrii Medvedev recently stated that Russia would make the modernization of its nuclear deterrent and armed forces a priority in the decade up to 2020. He said: 'We must ensure air superiority, precision strikes at land and sea targets, and timely deployment of troops. We are planning to launch large-scale production of warships, primarily, nuclear submarines with cruise missiles and multi-purpose attack submarines.' Federal budgets for this in 2008 increased by 20% compared to the previous year. Yet a declining population and the constraints of having a conscript, instead of a professional army, decrease the armed forces' viability. Foreign policy can, however, be targeted to stimulate the patriotism needed to compensate for this.

With the Russian economy no longer as dependent on arms exports as previously, those that are agreed can be directed so as to be used more overtly as a tool of international relations. The People's Republic of China purchased new weapons from Russia, leading to joint military exercises in 2007, which underlined both countries' desire to demonstrate their freedom from Western dependency. In 2008, however, these sales have been downscaled. Instead, Venezuela is providing the arena for Russia to display itself as a power with consequence, with large joint military exercises scheduled in the autumn. A generous loan of up to US $1,000m. for weapons purchases and military development is as conspicuous as the reasons for it are complex. Speculation is futile as to whether this action so close to the USA expresses an accusation that there has been too much of the latter's naval activity close to Russia (in the Black Sea). Prime Minister Vladimir Putin declared in a meeting with maverick President Hugo Chavez of Venezuela that, 'Latin America, of course, is becoming an obvious link in the chain making up a multipolar world. We will allocate more and more attention to this vector of our economics and foreign policy'.

The next year or so the pace of progress on international arms reduction treaties, which are still outstanding, will reveal whether Russia will focus on confirming its membership of the wider international community or focus more on establishing its superpower status on an even firmer footing. In past years, the Russian Government had not refrained from hard work, both at home and abroad, to refine in a positive way all the arms reduction treaties to which it is a signatory. Boris Yeltsin had a hard time getting the second Strategic Arms Reduction Treaty (START II) ratified by the already nationalist Duma; the treaty was finally ratified in 2000, under Putin's presidency, and, with the three parties supporting Putin merging in late 2006, forming a single, large presidential majority, such struggles in parliament have become obsolete. President Medvedev, who assumed office in May 2008, so far has no centre of independent decision-making capacity and, furthermore, the issuing of acts and decrees in 2007–08, which legitimize the use of force against the enemies of the State wherever they may be, have reflected the increasing influence of intelligence services and political figures who still believe that one promotes stability through the stifling of dissent.

One can also reflect on the relevance of the present negotiations for the Non-Proliferation Treaty on nuclear weapons, which also began with the USSR. The 1991 transformation of the USSR into several independent states included the implication that some Soviet nuclear bases now belonged to Belarus, Kazakhstan and Ukraine. They had to be cajoled into relinquishing this unexpected windfall in international stakes, while allowing Russia the right to retain its nuclear status. This was urged by the Western powers themselves. More recently, the assurances given to the Ukrainians by Russia—to protect them with their own nuclear capacity—were hardly welcomed, given Ukraine's overtures to NATO. It will be interesting to see whether Ukraine will invoke this agreement as a reason for demanding sympathy from the West, if there is any likelihood that Russia will flex its muscles in Ukraine any time soon. Likewise, the Conventional Forces in Europe (CFE) Treaty was first signed at the end of the Soviet era (in 1990). In an agreement specifically aimed at 'flank' reductions, on either side of the former Soviet borders, the CFE treaty subsequently became a bone of contention between the now independent border countries and Russia. Georgia used the CFE treaty as a convincing argument for requesting the removal of Russian bases on its territory, as did Moldova, nervous of Russia's support for the separatist enclave of Transnistria. The favouritism of the 'Russia first' policy of the US administration under President Bill Clinton (1993–2001) notwithstanding, base closure agreements were achieved, although they are still incomplete in 2008. A far more difficult problem for Russian CFE compliance is its seemingly unending struggles in the North Caucasus, in Chechnya and other neighbouring republics within the Russian Federation, which require a strong military presence. Nevertheless, there is evidence that there is still a powerful attempt by Russia to express an intrinsic part of its identity by attenuating its yearnings to become a superpower through sheer military might by also demonstrating the responsible attitude expected of a forward-looking player in the international community.

Second, Russia seeks to use its newly found economic power. The Russian economy grew by an annual average of some 6% in 1999–2005 or, cumulatively, by 65% (although 1999 was not a prosperous base to measure from). The phenomenal rise in petroleum wealth had allowed Russia to invest like never before in energy sources in the developing world, although state-owned Gazprom has so far been deliberately prevented from becoming a significant investor in strategic sectors in Europe. The importance given to economic clout, however, has also strengthened internally the role of the elusive band of 'oligarchs' who stand like an *eminence grise* behind Russia's present rulers and can therefore influence foreign policy. This phenomenon might even have brought in a measure of belated restraint in Russia's military actions in Georgia initiated on 7 August 2008. In late 2008 the Deputy Chairman of the Government and Minister of Finance Aleksei Kudrin forecast that Russian growth in 2009 would be around 5.7%, the worst performance since at least 2001, compared with the rate of growth of between 6.5%–7.5% forecast for 2008. Kudrin stated, 'Since 7 August investor confidence has plummeted. At least in part because of the Georgia crisis, Russian financial markets have lost nearly a third of their value, with losses in market capitalization of hundreds of billions of dollars.'

It follows that the supply of energy itself, rather than the wealth it generates, will be used as a more useful instrument of foreign policy. However, this approach, when used with Russia's immediate neighbours has hitherto tended to be at least partially counterproductive. In past years, Georgia has long been used to having gas supplies cut off by its large, northern neighbour to express displeasure, although at other times it has benefited from favourable pricing. A subcommittee of the US House of Representatives, on 25 July 2006, however, discussed policies that would help Georgia break its energy dependence on Russia. Since the August war, Azerbaijan has assured Georgia of gas supplies for the winter of 2008/09 even though it had not defended its neighbour openly. Likewise, long before 2008, Western Europe had already discussed reducing purchases of energy supplies from Russia when it punitively targeted Ukraine by withholding them. Even Armenia, the most loyal Russian ally in the whole of the Caucasus, north and south, was threatened with a dramatic increase in energy prices in 2006. This could mean either that there were cracks in the alliance between energy policy and foreign policy in Russia, or that, with the increased Russian economic presence in Armenia, Russia's foreign policy was becoming economy-driven and, thus, closer in nature to that attributed to the Administration of President George W. Bush in the USA. Reasons given by the World Trade Organization for its reluctance to accept Russia include the latter's misuse of energy supplies as an arbitrary weapon of foreign influence.

It has been evident throughout 2008, but especially since August, that the Russian Government has subtly divided the EU's states among themselves, largely along the lines of those who are more energy dependent on Russia and those that are not, and thus has successfully sabotaged a unified foreign policy in such obvious arenas such as Georgia's right to territorial integrity. This is no mean achievement. Furthermore, although Russia is affected (and to what extent is yet to be established) by the impact of global financial instability, it has been able to use its economic influence through lending to foreign banks or governments in urgent need of assistance, such as in the case of Iceland in October 2008, a point that will serve Russia's cause in further international developments.

Third, Russia has sought to act as a key player in international disputes. It reproached the US-led international community for having bypassed Russian offers to help with Iraq, the People's Democratic Republic of Korea (North Korea) and Iran. However, the credibility of Russia's peace-keeping role has been shaken by the violence used in Georgia, an issue it will undoubtedly debate behind closed doors in the coming months. A change of policy on its use of such force could ensue, if eventually it appeared regrettable that Russia were not able to capitalize internationally on its vast experience, from Soviet times, of relations with certain countries in the Arab and developing worlds, which it still maintains.

Fourth, Russia had been actively seeking to create an alternative axis—even if not militarily as yet—to the NATO dominated or sympathizing group of countries. In 2008, however, the tendency has been for Russia to go it alone and to rely on its own capacities, picking up any opportunities that come its way. Even nostalgic memories of Russia's socialist past have been used advantageously for responding to Venezuela's left-leaning leadership. Cold War nostalgia was also a factor that led the former Marxist leader of Nicaragua, Daniel Ortega, uniquely to side with Russia's tactics in Georgia, as his country became the first to join Russia in recognizing the formal independence from Georgia of South Ossetia and Abkhazia. Thoroughly disappointed with the former Warsaw Pact countries' rush to NATO and EU membership, and the latter organizations' willingness to take them in, Russia has had to look again at its destiny and advantages. Some observers in past years had keenly analysed events that could indicate the formation of a Russia-People's Republic of China-Iran axis, although it has now proved impossible to reach serious conclusions about this. Reciprocal visits between the leaders of Russia and the People's Republic of China, joint military exercises in 2005 with further ones in 2007 and a deal for Russian arms reportedly signed in 2004 and apparently worth more than US $2,000m., as well as increased energy exports, were all cited as evidence in support of claims for the existence of such an alliance. These activities have slowed down remarkably. Nevertheless, Russia and China both allegedly assisted Iran with weapons purchases. The People's Republic of China was keen to import Iranian energy, becoming its leading petroleum export market from 2004 onwards. Russia was involved in the controversial issue of developing Iran's nuclear capacity, a position it would be unlikely to relinquish to other players. Russia, the People's Republic of China and Iran share the same negative attitude to local aspirations for sovereignty: Russia towards Chechnya; China towards Taiwan; and Iran towards the occasional rumblings from Azeri ethnic groups around Tabriz, who would like to have closer ties with Azerbaijan to the north (with which country both Iran and Russia today have a far from easy relationship). Silence from these countries in response to Russia's action in Georgia was a poor reward from perceived allies. It is such a long way from this triangular relationship having any formally shared identity to compare with that of, say, the USA and Europe, that it has only speculative value. This does not mean that such a triangle could not conform some day to Russia's traditional and apt aspirations to be a bridge between East and West.

Fifth, Russia declares that it seeks to combat terrorism. This valuable role is one of the main restraining forces in the response of western democracies to perceived Russian aggression in the past year. The events of 11 September 2001 in the USA, and its Administration's interpretation and reaction, provided Russia with a window of opportunity to join the internationally accepted and lauded goal of combating global terrorism. Like the US Administration, Russia has not been required to give a precise definition of who constitutes a terrorist. Likewise, operations by the leaders of neighbouring countries (for example, in Central Asia), occasionally supported by Russia, against opposition forces are supposedly against terrorists. Russia's warm relations with some Arab countries notwithstanding, it was convenient to single out the resistance to Russian rule in Chechnya as constituting the ugly side of Islamic fundamentalism that could be presented as a threat to democracy and freedom. In a subtle way, as much to appease domestic opinion as to display shared reactions with the West, Russia hints that its heroic fight is in keeping with its mainly Christian identity. This year, although the action in Georgia was sometimes interpreted in the Arab world as a welcome reaction to US domination and a return to bi-polar international relations, this was followed by a more cautious reaction to Russian politics, given that the reportedly excessive use of force in Chechnya had alienated sections of opinion in the Arab and Muslim world. And innocent civilian Russian personnel have not escaped being kidnapped by extremists in those countries.

Finally, Russia, as stated by a clause in its Military Doctrine's list of threats, has the right to intervene in defence of Russian nationals threatened anywhere in the world. This explains its frenetic distribution of Russian passports to the local population in Abkhazia and South Ossetia, to the extent that elements of the Western media, including the major US newspaper *USA Today*, reported (incorrectly) that the Russian action was taken to defend Ossetians of Russian ethnicity. Indeed, the leadership sees itself as the defender of Slavic peoples (not just ethnic Russians beyond its borders, but also, for example, the Serbs), again particularly to please growing domestic Russian nationalism. Furthermore, the Moscow Patriarchate of the Orthodox Church, in a display of closeness to government foreign policy, from 2005 onwards has attempted, mostly unsuccessfully, to claim direct ownership of émigré Russian Orthodox parishes in several parts of Western Europe. Although 2007 saw the symbolic reintegration into the Moscow Patriarchate of one group of exiled churches (ROCOR, Russian Orthodox Church Outside Russia), the latter have insisted that they still be allowed to appoint their own clergy, thus resisting direct rule. The tasks of the Patriarchate are many, however, and the strengthening of its relationship with the Russian Federal Armed Forces as well as with the Ministry of Foreign Affairs is still being developed.

In conclusion, one must be mindful of an ongoing debate within and outside Russia, as to how much the apparent growth in influence of the *'siloviki'* (from a Russian word for power or force, *sila*, and denoting former security or military officials now on the rise) is likely to influence foreign policy in the future, presuming that their mindset is likely to be conservative, statist and nationalist, with a craving for superpower status. The global financial meltdown also highlights the importance of Russia's financial bosses and their capacity to counteract bold external political acts with necessary co-operation with their Western partners. Yet as far as the former CIS countries are concerned, the relationships from Soviet times that some *siloviki* still have, with their counterparts there, occasionally have been revived to influence internal political events, but they have not always succeeded, notably in Georgia so far. It might be the avowed desire of some Russian politicians to reconstitute the USSR, but that is unlikely, because of a combination of good Russian realism in some government quarters and the stance of the 'newly independent' states to maintain their sovereignty.

THE COMMONWEALTH OF INDEPENDENT STATES

The CIS is a sort of 'flag of convenience' to identify the former Union Republics of the USSR, without including the Baltic states. It will be interesting to see how long the international community will continue to refer to it as such. The importance of the CIS has fluctuated greatly over the past 17 years. Initially, it was almost a point of honour for Russia that the Union Republics should all become members. For example, when in 1992 Georgia's new leader, Eduard Shevardnadze, hesitated to join the CIS, in order to pursue instead a policy of 'active neutrality', he was brought to his knees and forced to join—without that, Russia would not have withdrawn its participation in the civil and ethnic wars raging within Georgia at the time. Then, as Western institutions and foreign ministries were drawn into providing aid and technical assistance, it was also easier for them to deal with these countries as a single group (for example, as with Technical Assistance to the CIS—TACIS). In the early days, too, it was Western policy to support the rouble as a single currency for the whole of the CIS, rather than to acquiesce to the wishes of those states, at first symbolic and then economic, to crown their new sovereignty with a national currency.

The pressures, from both Russia and the outside world, for the CIS to become a unified entity—more like a confederation—have not really succeed. There are so many reasons for this complex situation, and they have fluctuated over the years, that just a few can be mentioned here.

First, although bound by a common Soviet experience, there are no deep ties of affection between the former Union Republics. Stalin drew a border between the Tajiks and Uzbeks that was much neater than their past history had warranted, with the result that both peoples have competing claims to the ancient cities of Buxoro (Bukhara) and Samarqand. Armenia and Azerbaijan have a cease-fire, but are still technically at war. Georgia and Moldova have long resented Russia for giving their minorities Russian passports, with all the legal and military entitlements signified thereby, instead of encouraging them to abandon separatism and accept the principle of territorial integrity.

Second, as was mentioned above, Russia became the successor state to the USSR, in which all the Union Republics had seen themselves as stakeholders. They expected a redistribution of commonly held assets—military, foreign reserves and other—which for Russia was neither advantageous nor practical. Hence, Russia pressed for a body, the CIS, that could be seen to share the assets as before. The newly independent states, however, in their enjoyment of genuine sovereignty, preferred the idea of a clean break. This tug of war has not been conducive to constructing the CIS as a vigorous and united international body. In 2008, Russia's newly found voice as a superpower insists on these countries accepting they are part of their former master's sphere of influence, its 'near abroad', and that they cannot compare themselves to entirely sovereign nations elsewhere that have the right to pick and choose which superpower with which to align themselves. If there is one unifying factor for the so-called CIS, it is Russia's shadow which they all share.

Third, despite some potential economies of scale, which could have been derived from treating the whole CIS area as a single market, foreign investment has usually been tailored to suit each individual state, producing specialization and competition between them. There is no economic 'commonwealth'.

Fourth, each member of the CIS has pursued its own domestic political agenda and they each have opposition politicians who take refuge in one another's countries.

Finally, closer integration has been precluded for practical reasons alone (the geographical span of the CIS is vast and varied), with the international relations of Kazakhstan, which has a huge border with the People's Republic of China, hardly a mirror of those pursued by Moldova, on Romania's doorstep. Separate alliances between some countries of the CIS were made partly as a reflection of their relationships with Russia, as well as for greater co-operation among themselves. The dynamism of these bodies, however, has been almost as frail as that of the CIS and has tended to disintegrate almost as soon as it is really tested. In 2008 any meaning they might really have had of an important, symbolic kind, has faded. One example is

GUAM (Georgia, Ukraine, Azerbaijan and Moldova), set up in 1997. Ukraine's support of Georgia was as a sovereign neighbour, not as a member of GUAM. The other two countries were forced to be cautious. The transport route, avoiding Russia, that had stimulated the creation of GUAM (for a while too Uzbekistan had joined in, with, among other things, the transport of cotton in mind) never led to a special relationship with the rest of the Black Sea group of countries. Nor has GUAM achieved, as one body, relationships with Western organizations such as the EU or NATO. Interestingly, however, in May 2006 the GUAM countries met in Kyiv, Ukraine, to form the Organization for Democracy and Economic Development (ODED). This action derived partly from the elections of Western-orientated reformists in Georgia and Ukraine, which they did not want to go unnoticed by the rest of the world. The aims of the ODED are 'to promote democracy, the rule of law, human rights, economic development, security and stability', and more. Another aim mentioned is for the member states together achieving a sustainable supply of energy resources. Kyiv was to be the capital of the ODED. Its first president is Ilham Aliyev, the President of Azerbaijan. On 19 June 2007, the presidents of Lithuania, Poland and Romania attended the GUAM summit in Baku, together with the Vice-President of Bulgaria, the Vice-Speaker of the Estonian Parliament, the Latvian Minister of the Economy, heads of diplomatic missions in Azerbaijan and high-level representatives of UNESCO, the OSCE, Japan and the USA. The crisis of August 2008 has been a clarion call, however, that the dominant concern is everyone's relationship with Russia and little else.

In 2008 Kazakhstan holds the rotating presidency of the CIS, which, after Georgia announced its withdrawal from the organization during the conflict with Russia, comprises Russia, Belarus, Kazakhstan, Kyrgyzstan, Azerbaijan, Armenia, Moldova, Tajikistan and Uzbekistan. Ukraine is a founding and participating country but technically not a member state, as its parliament failed to ratify the membership documents. Turkmenistan holds associate status. The Russian minister appealed to Georgia to return to membership of the CIS, but little else pertinent to foreign relations was noted at its meeting in October 2008. Not that much recent activity, however, could be reported from the Minsk headquarters of the CIS either. The decision by Turkmenistan to downgrade its position from member to observer or associate member status in August 2005 has yet to have important consequences. However, in mid-August 2006 the summit of the Eurasian Economic Community (EURASEC) took place in Sochi, on the Russian Black Sea coast. The EURASEC (note the term 'Eurasia', which had become internationally reactivated only in the previous couple of decades) brought together six member states: Russia, its tagalong Belarus, Kazakhstan, Kyrgyzstan, Tajikistan and Uzbekistan. Military security agreements have little but symbolic usefulness. Not for the first time the creation of a customs union was discussed, but, more important was the focus on sharing an energy policy, which could have consequences for international relations elsewhere. Competition for privileges to access the natural gas and the petroleum reserves of Central Asia had become an active issue for the USA, both through investment and export-route planning. This kind of control has been contested by Russia and is a target of its superpower status policy.

Every step is keenly observed by the rest of the international community, for example the recent decision in Kazakhstan to export new energy through the Caspian route (and thus through Georgia to Turkey). Other gestures are also keenly watched, such as the recent growth of Turkmenistani-Latvian relations, following the presidents' mutual visits in October 2008. The recent growth rate of Turkmenistani-Latvian trade has exceeded that of Turkmenistan with Russia. In 2007 bilateral Turkmenistani-Latvian trade was worth a paltry US $1.7m., but it exceeded $58m. during the first six months of 2008.

Such actions have provided those Central Asian states that possess substantial hydrocarbons resources with leverage in the international community and with Russia. These hydrocarbons resources are courted by Russia, the West, Iran, South Asia and China, so there is a great deal of room for manoeuvre.

The three republics of the South Caucasus (Armenia, Azerbaijan and Georgia) had competed with each other to demonstrate their Western orientation, Armenia through its culture and its ties with a large foreign diaspora, and Georgia and Azerbaijan in a more overtly political way. In late 2008, of course, Georgia stands alone after its war with Russia. The election of a new US President in early November appeared unlikely to affect Georgia's preferred relationship with the USA, where its fate has figured in the election campaign. And Russian hopes of internal dissent bringing a change of political leadership in Georgia will hardly augur in a less obdurate policy. Neither is its isolated position completely without advantage. The executive board of the Asian Development Bank, representing countries from Japan and China to Turkmenistan and Uzbekistan, unanimously approved a US $40m. loan to Georgia at the lowest possible interest rate on 10 October 2008, the latest sign of Asian dissatisfaction with Russian military action there.

The fallout of the war for both of Georgia's South Caucasian neighbours has consequences for their own international relations. Armenia, despite the presence of Russian military bases on its soil that could be used to attack Georgia, has tried hard not to provoke Georgia, which, for geographical and geopolitical reasons, is its only viable route to the outside world. It is historically significant, however, that in 2008 Armenia and Turkey have held talks that could prove to be of some importance, given Georgia's present vulnerability as a transit route.

The consequences for Azerbaijan are also notable. Always a keen NATO participant in its 'Partnership for Peace' programme, it has had to use silence diplomatically. Furthermore, it now has had to reckon with Russian intervention in any military attempt to regain territory occupied by Armenia as a non-negotiable fact. However, the ongoing dispute over Nagornyi Karabakh has so far prohibited any meaningful co-operation between the three republics of the South Caucasus and restrained the region as a whole. For any regional meeting, Azerbaijani and Armenian non-governmental organization (NGO) representatives or traders are likely to continue to meet in Georgia (as a consequence, Tbilisi has become the neutral administrative centre for informal international representation for all the South Caucasus). The role of Russia as a mediator in any of the regional disputes is now even more difficult than before. Armenia signed every security agreement necessary to ensure that it enjoyed Russia's protection (Russian border guards patrol Armenia's frontiers with Russia as well as the Azerbaijani international border, which the fighting temporarily allocated to Armenian forces). It is uneasy, however, with a situation arising where its indebtedness to Russia could cause difficulties in its own pursuit of closer co-operation with NATO member Turkey, its southern neighbour, in the unlikely but yet possible scenario of historic impediments being overcome.

There is a sentiment of foreboding in the countries of the former Soviet Union, probably to the advantage of Russia. If in the past, all saw that Russia turned a blind eye to those CIS countries that ignored the Russian military doctrine not to tolerate foreign forces in its 'near abroad', when US bases were allowed on a temporary basis in Central Asia, or the US-trained Georgian troops tolerated in the Pankisi Gorge region of Georgia that borders Chechnya, the situation is now seen to be more threatening. Previously Russia had not exerted its self-allocated right to intervene wherever Russian passport-holders in the 'near abroad' were deemed to be badly treated. As a result, some CIS countries began to allow their citizens to hold dual nationality, which they had not permitted before. They had come to take it for granted that, as had always been the case in international relations with Russia over the centuries, its staying power was beyond question, but sometimes its bark was worse than its bite. Now, perhaps, it is the other way round.

CONCLUSION

Although Robert F. Kennedy, then a US senator, declared in 1966 that 'living in interesting times' was a curse, according to a Chinese proverb, that certainly does not apply when looking at the foreign policy of both Russia and of the newly independent states. The 'interesting times' give room for optimism. Russia has seemingly revealed its aspirations towards superpower status, whatever the cost, but at the same time it has had to become more responsive to domestic opinion, in a way never seen before. Nationalist pride is a wonderfully unifying dynamic in an uneven economy—the disparities in wealth in the Russian Federation are still dramatic—but such sentiment will not endure without visible increases in domestic wellbeing. Such improvements are likely to increase internal tolerance and in turn promote a new dynamic in co-operation with the rest of the world and remove the excuse of the other superpowers to expand into a wild polarization. As the economically struggling newly independent states themselves develop—at present they are the recipients of humanitarian aid—it will be interesting to see whether they can turn their attention away merely from strategies for their own survival to becoming themselves aid donors, with the astuteness and experience that their foreign policies will be able to sustain.

AN ECONOMIC SURVEY OF THE COMMONWEALTH OF INDEPENDENT STATES

Dr ANDERS ÅSLUND

OVERVIEW

The countries of the former USSR underwent immense economic upheavals after the USSR's chaotic collapse in late 1991. For almost a decade, the whole region was in crisis, with sharply falling output combined with 'hyperinflation' (defined as a monthly rate of inflation of more than 50%, lasting for at least one month). From 1999, however, the region experienced high economic growth. Monthly inflation had largely fallen to under 10%, and most property had been privatized. However, differentiation both among and within countries had increased greatly.

The Commonwealth of Independent States (CIS) comprises 12 countries: Armenia, Azerbaijan, Belarus, Georgia (which announced its decision to secede from the organization in August 2008), Kazakhstan, Kyrgyzstan, Moldova, Russia, Tajikistan, Turkmenistan, Ukraine and Uzbekistan—that is to say, the entire former USSR, with the exception of the three Baltic states of Estonia, Latvia and Lithuania (now members of the European Union—EU).

During the first decade of post-communist economic transformation, the pattern of economic reform was clear. The countries of Central Europe (the Czech Republic, Hungary, Poland and Slovakia) generally implemented early, radical and successful economic reforms, while the CIS member states pursued slower, more gradual and unsuccessful reforms. As a result, from 1989 until its lowest point preceding recovery, the aggregate official decline in gross domestic product (GDP) was 19% in Central Europe, 29% in Bulgaria and Romania, 44% in the Baltic states and 53% in the CIS. Moreover, the countries of Central Europe reached the nadir relatively early, in 1992, whereas the CIS states reached it in 1998. These falls in output were exaggerated by multiple statistical biases, but a reasonable assessment is that the real decline was about one-half of the official figure.

The conventional wisdom was that Central Europe pursued the correct course, while the CIS countries made mistakes, both economically and politically. Overall, this held true until 1998, the year of the Russian financial crisis. The CIS countries trailed behind those of Central and South-Eastern Europe, not only in terms of official economic growth, but also with regard to democracy, economic deregulation, financial stabilization and privatization—and there were strong positive correlations between all these factors.

From 1999, however, the situation changed completely. Most CIS countries recorded an impressive rate of economic growth in 2001–07; the unweighted average rate of growth was an impressive 9.2% per year, about twice the rate recorded in the Central European countries. Rates of growth varied, but not dramatically. The leading CIS countries in terms of growth were Azerbaijan, Armenia and Kazakhstan, all of which recorded annual GDP growth in excess of 10% in 2001–07, while the worst-performing was Kyrgyzstan, with growth of 4%.

Two major features distinguish the CIS countries from each other. The first is the contrast between market and non-market economies. Nine CIS countries (Armenia, Azerbaijan, Georgia, Kazakhstan, Kyrgyzstan, Moldova, Russia, Tajikistan and Ukraine) have undertaken substantial market reform, and by the mid-2000s all could be classified as market economies, with predominant private ownership and reasonable macroeconomic stability. In contrast, Belarus, Turkmenistan and Uzbekistan have not completed the transition to capitalism. Overall, they retain a Soviet economic system, even if the private sector in those countries has expanded. The second distinction is between rich and poor countries. Russia and Kazakhstan have both reached an economic level exceeding that of some Central European countries, whereas other CIS countries, in particular Kyrgyzstan, Moldova, Tajikistan and Uzbekistan, have become extremely poor.

None the less, after 1999 the rate of growth has persistently been high almost everywhere in the CIS. Obviously, simple recovery growth is one explanation. It is easier to utilize existing production capacity than to expand capacity, and after their large declines in output, many post-communist countries possessed ample excess capacity. Another reason for the recovery is the Russian financial crisis of August 1998, although exactly how this revitalized the region is disputed. First, the whole region undertook major currency devaluations, which made their exports highly profitable. Second, the crisis resulted in stringent budget constraints and reduced state largesse, thereby making it more profitable to produce than to rely on the extraction of state subsidies. Third, prices for commodities began to rise at about the same time, and the prices of CIS exports, such as energy and steel, soon increased dramatically. Finally, and perhaps most importantly, by about this time most CIS countries had finally accomplished the critical mass of market economy and private enterprise, and the market economy began to function.

INITIAL ECONOMIC UPHEAVALS

It is difficult to overestimate the severe economic shocks that shook the CIS countries in 1991. The Soviet economy was literally collapsing. The state could no longer control its finances, so public expenditure increased rapidly, while state revenue dwindled. As a result, the budget deficit widened hugely. The state regulated most prices, which resulted in a near-total shortage of most necessary consumer goods. The Soviet Government attempted to compensate for the lack of supplies by purchasing consumer goods with foreign credits, but the USSR lost its creditworthiness and was no longer able to service its debts; when the USSR collapsed, its international reserves totalled US $100m. As a consequence, the Government had to let the exchange rate float, and it subsequently went on to collapse. By December 1991 the average wage in Russia was just $6 per month. Since people could not use their earnings to buy anything, it made little sense to work. Supplies to state enterprises were also severely disrupted, which meant that output began to collapse as well. Despite price controls, the USSR recorded consumer price inflation of no less than 144% in 1991, and it was obvious that hyperinflation would erupt once prices were liberalized, which they had to be to make it possible for people and businesses to acquire supplies. The economic chaos had been caused by the Soviet partial economic reforms that had made the managers of state enterprises the masters of state corporations. Their interest was no longer to maximize production, but to enrich themselves, either by privatizing 'their' state companies to their own benefit or by selling their goods cheaply to a trading company owned by themselves.

All these economic problems were aggravated by the political situation. The very state, the USSR, was falling apart. Only Russia had ordinary state institutions in place. The other newly independent states had to build ministries and central banks, etc. Many new nations were initially preoccupied with nation- and state-building rather than economic transformation, and they lacked the knowledge and human resources for these tasks. The state ideology, communism, was collapsing, and few people knew how to go about constructing a market economy.

The general collapse had many other consequences. With the transition to market prices and liberalization of imports, most Soviet manufactures became more or less worthless, and the production of about one-half of them ceased almost instantly, since the quality was too poor to attract buyers. In particular, the large military industrial complex, which had previously accounted for as much as one-quarter of Soviet demand, dwindled, rendering the large military industry idle. Within the USSR, neither market prices nor transportation costs had played any role, but now they began to do so. Much of the manufacturing industry in remote places in Central Asia and the Caucasus became unprofitable. The Central Asian states had previously received a direct subsidy from the Soviet Government of about one-10th of their GDP, which was eliminated when the USSR ceased to exist. The terms of trade also changed markedly, with the producers of petroleum, natural gas and steel doing reasonably well, while the producers of armaments, agricultural goods and manufactures suffered.

In comparison with the collapse of other empires, little violence erupted after the Soviet collapse. The worst occurred in Tajikistan, which experienced a bloody civil conflict in 1992–97, leaving it far poorer than any other CIS country. Georgia also experienced civil conflict in the early 1990s, and two of its regions (Abkhazia and South Ossetia) were left beyond government control, jeopardizing the efficacy of the state. In 1992 Armenia and Azerbaijan fought an outright war over the Nagornyi Karabakh region, and Armenian forces continue to occupy approximately one-10th of the territory of Azerbaijan. Moldova experienced only limited warfare, but a significant part of that country, Transnistria, remained outside of the Moldovan Government's purview, causing havoc to its economic policy. Later, Russia's long-lasting war in Chechnya became the region's bloodiest conflict.

COMPLETE SYSTEMIC TRANSFORMATION

The essence of the Soviet economic system was central state control over the whole economy. The system was ruled by Marxist-Leninist doctrines, such as the public ownership of all means of production, central state planning, central state distribution and price controls. Money and finances played only a passive or subordinate role. Since the domestic economy was so thoroughly regulated, foreign trade had to be equally regulated, isolating the Soviet economy from market prices and trends. The strength of the Soviet economic system was that it mobilized all labour, raw materials and investment, while its weakness was that its extreme centralization led to low efficiency and minimal flexibility. Incentives for innovation and modernization were poor, and, guided by physical output targets, state enterprises were inclined to lower quality.

Toward the end of the USSR, a broad consensus had developed that the Soviet economy no longer worked and had to be replaced with a normal market economy with free prices, free markets and predominant private ownership. However, the changes that had to be made were huge, and their very dimensions were intimidating. In the end, politics was decisive. Democratic countries carried out more radical market reforms, while authoritarian regimes preferred gradual reforms, which allowed the incumbent rulers to retain power. As democratic transformation in the countries of the CIS was at best partial, reforms in these countries did not become very radical. Post-Soviet economic reforms were highly gradual, with a brief exception for the initial reforms in Russia, and perhaps in Kyrgyzstan.

The fundamental market reforms were to liberalize prices and markets. Russia did so in January 1992, and the other post-Soviet countries had little choice but to follow. The quintessence of liberalization was to move from a shortage of goods and services to a shortage of money, which is the predicament of capitalism. It also involved a shift from a sellers' market to a buyers' market, and the transfer of economic power from producers to consumers. At the beginning of the transition, all CIS countries undertook significant deregulation. However, most CIS countries opted for gradual and partial liberalization. There were strong reasons for such an approach. In December 1991 one metric ton of crude petroleum cost US $0.5 in the USSR, while the world market price was around $100. To allow the price to rise to the market level was inconceivable for most, and in order to keep domestic prices low, a thorough regulation of foreign trade was required. The unfortunate consequence was that a small but strong group of operators bought petroleum and other raw materials at low, state-controlled prices, then acquired export permits illicitly and sold the commodities abroad for huge sums, which were invested off shore.

FINANCIAL STABILIZATION

During the early transition, the means to economic growth was to control inflation. The situation was similar in all the former Soviet republics. They entered the transition with huge public expenditure, far higher than under Soviet rule, while tax revenue was in decline because of plummeting output and increased tax evasion. With the change of economic system, many taxes had to be altered, and high but ill-conceived value-added taxes were introduced, causing great disorder. The inevitable consequence was declining state revenue. The old socialist system had aspired to fiscal balance, but this was no longer a priority, and inflation was primarily restrained through price controls. Capitalism required a different institutional framework, transferring economic policy-making from the Central Committee of the Communist Party, the State Planning Committee and industrial ministries to the ministry of finance and central bank, which had to be strengthened to be able to control inflation.

For the first couple of years of transition, monetary policy was loose. The state issued huge credits at subsidized rates of interest. As a result, state credits were essentially gifts, and they fuelled inflation as well as corruption; new fortunes were based on cheap state credits. The old payments system had been handled by state banks, but a completely new, market-orientated payments system was required, and while this complicated process was taking place, massive arrears amassed between enterprises. The natural response was to issue more money to resolve the apparent shortage, but the effect of this was only to increase inflation further and to convince enterprises not to settle future bills.

One important reason for high inflation was that the old Soviet currency union, the 'rouble zone', persisted for almost two years. In effect, the central banks of all the CIS countries issued the same money freely, giving them a tremendous incentive to issue as much as possible to seize a disproportionate share of the common GDP, which was dwindling rapidly. Inevitably, the whole region began to compete in issuing the largest amounts of money, which almost guaranteed hyperinflation. Only after the collapse of the rouble zone in late 1993 were the elementary preconditions for macroeconomic stability created.

Thus, inflation became high and persistent. In all CIS countries, it increased rapidly at the outset of the transition, and, with little macroeconomic knowledge, the new governments were initially uncertain as to how to restrain it (with the exception of the reformist Russian Government). These countries experienced hyperinflation in 1993. The IMF took substantial responsibility for bringing about financial stabilization through austerity programmes and significant financing. Eventually, in 1994–96 the CIS countries launched serious stabilization efforts, and inflation was brought under control. Money had begun to operate in the CIS countries as in functioning market economies.

However, the early stabilization efforts were not entirely secure. They had relied far more on strict monetary policy than on fiscal adjustment. Budget deficits tended to be large and persistently amounted to about 9% of GDP until 1998 in Russia. The deficit was increasingly financed by credits from international financial institutions and the sale of bonds. Russian domestic bonds became very popular because they offered international investors enormous returns; however, these high yields had to be paid by the Russian Government, which became overwhelmed by the debt burden. In 1998 the situation became untenable. According to a World Bank assessment, total enterprise subsidies in Russia amounted to no less than 16% of GDP in 1998. The debt volume was excessive, and the Russian legislature was not inclined to accept new hardship. As a result, in August 1998 Russia defaulted on US $70,000m. of domestic treasury bills and was forced to implement a huge devaluation. Ordinary citizens lost most of their savings in multiple bank bankruptcies. The Russian financial crisis severely affected the entire country, and many observers concluded that the market economic experiment had failed in Russia.

In reality, however, the financial crash served to 'cleanse' Russia's market economy. When no financing was available, dubious public expenditures had to be reduced. Russia proved that it was able to balance the state budget primarily by reducing enterprise subsidies. Contrary to expectations, the financial crisis heralded Russia's return to economic growth. Several small CIS countries had already recorded substantial growth, notably Armenia, Georgia and Kyrgyzstan, but now the whole of the CIS had to adjust. The Russian financial collapse had several effects. The vital domestic market contracted, sharply reducing exports from other CIS countries. With the devaluation of the Russian rouble, almost all CIS countries had to adjust and devalue their currencies. The remaining CIS governments were alarmed by the Russian crash and decided to take all possible financial precautions, reducing public expenditure and improving payment discipline. As a result of their huge enterprise subsidies, the CIS countries could cut public expenditures drastically without any perceivable social suffering. On the contrary, their reduction facilitated growth, by eliminating barter and levelling the market. The sharp reduction of enterprise subsidies was probably a major cause of the rebound in economic growth in the CIS countries.

With some exceptions, such as the unreformed countries of Belarus, Uzbekistan and Tajikistan, by 2007 macroeconomic performance in the CIS had become impressive. From 2001 until 2006 the median rate of inflation in the CIS countries was less than 10%, and the average budget deficit was as little as 1% of GDP. The changes in macroeconomic policy that followed the Russian economic crisis prepared the way for high contemporaneous growth. In 2007, however, inflation surged to an average rate of more than 10%, and it was projected to reach 15% in 2008, owing to overheating at the end of a long economic boom, combined with inadequate exchange rate and monetary policies. Inflation in Ukraine, measured on a year-on-year basis, reached 31% in May 2008.

PRIVATIZATION

One of the most important and most controversial systemic changes has been privatization. It had become particularly necessary to restructure the predominant state-owned enterprises, since at the end of communist rule they were effectively controlled by their managers, many of whom were more interested in profiting from the sale of their companies' assets than in their management.

Most CIS countries undertook the mass privatization of large enterprises, while small enterprises were sold to their managers for nominal sums. Mass privatization in Russia, which was carried out in 1992–94, served as a model. Most shares were awarded to employees and managers, but some shares were given to the public, in exchange for freely distributed vouchers. After the initial mass privatization was completed, many large, valuable enterprises remained in state hands because their managers had resisted privatization, which would have diluted their control. Such companies tended to be sold to prominent businessmen close to the Government. The model was again Russian, the so-called 'loans-for-shares' privatizations of 1995–96, which transferred several major petroleum and metals companies to a number of prominent entrepreneurs. By the late 1990s privatization had resulted in considerable disillusionment. Ownership often appeared to be unjust and too dispersed to facilitate restructuring, and privatization had not brought about the desired economic growth. While privatization in the CIS countries had been belated, other reforms had tended to be even slower; enterprises were unable to thrive in a hostile environment, regardless of ownership.

In this sphere, too, the Russian financial crash brought about a transformation. As the value of everything declined, many state managers feared that their assets would become worthless, and numerous ineffective owners sold their companies to new entrepreneurs, who rapidly consolidated ownership. Consolidation began in industries producing lucrative export commodities, such as petroleum and steel, but it has also proceeded in the wireless telecommunications, food-processing and retail sectors. Domestic businessmen dominated in heavy industry, while foreign investment played a significant role in lighter industry. Consolidated industrial business groups, usually focusing on a few major branches of industry and always containing at least one bank, drove the economic recovery in the CIS countries. Particularly in Russia, Ukraine and Kazakhstan, the three largest economies, 'oligarchs' or prominent businesspeople became dominant, accounting for about one-half of industrial production. From 2000 Russian oligarchs swiftly extended their 'empires' to other CIS countries, especially in the petroleum and metals sectors, and large transnational companies, often with some 100,000 employees, were established in both Russia and Ukraine.

The relatively large number of US dollar billionaires in Russia (101 in 2008, according to the business publication *Forbes*) led to political protests. In 2003–07 the Russian Government effectively confiscated the once leading petroleum company, Yukos. Its main owner and chief executive, Mikhail Khodorkovskii, was arrested in October 2003 and sentenced to eight years' imprisonment for tax evasion. In the wake of the Yukos affair, large-scale renationalization took place in Russia, as state officials endeavoured to enhance the power of state enterprises as well as to enrich themselves. In Ukraine, the 'orange revolution' of November–December 2004 (which brought a new President, Viktor Yushchenko, to power) prompted a broad discussion of the possible reprivatization of companies sold to oligarchs close to the old regime, but by mid-2008 only two large enterprises had been renationalized and then reprivatized.

A major reason for the emergence of large oligarchic groups was the business climate: a large enterprise must have privileged access to the government in order to manage its business. Another reason is that emerging financial markets often do not function efficiently. Minority shareholders have the potential to cause trouble in corrupt courts, and major restructuring is required. The most successful businesspeople have tended to be those who consolidate their ownership, although after they have undertaken the main restructuring and require fresh capital, many tend to seek it on Western capital markets. The capital city of the United Kingdom, London, has become the financial centre for the CIS countries, and by 2007 many Russian and Ukrainian companies were listed on the London Stock Exchange.

Although privatization has often been blamed for the widespread corruption in CIS countries, this corruption is primarily caused by the extensive and arbitrary power of undemocratic governments. The centralization and rationalization of extortion has rendered corruption less cumbersome and more predictable. In many CIS countries, particularly in Central Asia and the Caucasus, the ruling family tends to play a major role in both business and government extortion, making the behaviour of the ruling family one of the main influences on the business climate. In the early 1990s organized crime was a serious problem, but it has since receded. By 2007 the main threat of crime came from the official law enforcement authorities. The CIS countries rank highly on all corruption indices, and corruption remains the main threat to economic development.

With regard to the extent of privatization, the capitalist post-communist economies are quite similar. According to estimates by the European Bank for Reconstruction and Development, in 2007 the private sector generated between 65% and 80% of GDP in these countries, with the exception of the slow reformer Tajikistan, where it created only 55% of GDP. The average for Central Europe is 79%, compared with 69% in the nine reformist CIS countries. In contrast, in Belarus and Turkmenistan only minimal privatization has taken place.

COMPLEX TRADE RELATIONS

Ever since the collapse of the USSR, the newly independent states have been trying to sort out their trade relations, but initially their mutual trade contracted for years. The CIS countries have found it very difficult to establish a functioning framework for free trade. The CIS was conceived by Russia, which has remained its guardian. It was inspired by the British

SEPARATISM AND ISLAMIST MILITANCY IN THE NORTH CAUCASUS

ANDREI SMIRNOV

INTRODUCTION

During Vladimir Putin's presidency (2000–08) the economic and political situation in Russia stabilized noticeably. High prices of energy resources and other raw materials on the world market have allowed the Russian economy to grow. Meanwhile, an increase in the central control over all governing institutions and major organs of the media has practically brought the influence of opposition forces to zero, in turn permitting one to speak of political stability, albeit one achieved by the creation of an authoritarian regime. However, in the North Caucasus, the reverse is the case; in that region, political stability and the control of the Russian state has deteriorated to such a degree that it would not be an exaggeration to say that the potential for a new war between insurgent forces and the state is a likely consequence.

In early 2000, during his election campaign for the presidency, Putin (then acting President) explained in an interview to journalists the reason for the second military campaign in the Chechen Republic (Chechnya) that he had instigated, as Chairman of the Government (that is, prime minister), in the previous year. (Following an earlier conflict in 1994–96, the Republic had been effectively autonomous, although a decision on its final status had been deferred.) Putin stated, 'I never doubted that Chechnya would limit itself to its own independence. It was clear that after [the neighbouring region of] Dagestan, the whole North Caucasus would separate [from Russia], then the Volga region, Tatarstan, Bashkortostan, [separatism] would go further to the heartland of Russia' (First Person, 2000). Hence, in Putin's opinion, the militant separatism that had first, following the dissolution of the USSR, found violent expression in Chechnya, had to be brought under control. By 2008 it was clear that the maintenance of the territorial integrity of the Russian Federation was still an unresolved issue, while the concern that militant separatism might spread from Chechnya to other regions of Russia has become a reality.

In order to assess the deep reasons for the ongoing destabilization that can be observed in the Caucasus today, some understanding of the historic context can be helpful. The North Caucasus was joined to Russia in the 19th century as a result of a long-lasting, bloody and fierce colonial war. Some historians consider this war to have continued for more than 100 years, although it is hard to pinpoint the exact dates of the beginning or the end of the Caucasian War, as the conflict had never been officially declared, and because fighting came to an end in different regions of the Caucasus at different times. By the end of the 19th century Russia had managed to break the resistance of the Caucasian peoples and to integrate the region into the tsarist empire, despite having suffered enormous casualties and substantial acts of reprisal. However, the Russian state disintegrated following the Soviet Revolution of 1917, and with the onset of civil war in Russia, an independent state known as the Confederation of Mountain Peoples was declared in the North Caucasus in 1918, and in 1920 an Islamic Emirate was proclaimed in Dagestan and Chechnya, in the northeastern Caucasus. However, once the Bolsheviks had strengthened their control over the state, with the establishment of the Union of Soviet Socialist Republics (USSR) in 1922, all attempts by the people of the Caucasus peoples to secede were suppressed, and Russian and Soviet domination over the region was restored. None the less, there remained considerable hostility to Russian rule in the region, particularly among the Chechens.

In 1944, during the Second World War, the Soviet Government decided to 'pacify' the Caucasus, apparently conclusively, deporting *en masse* to Siberia and Central Asia those Caucasian peoples that the Soviet leadership considered to be disloyal. Among those peoples deported were the Chechens, Ingush, Balkars, and Karachai. Other ethnic groups of the North Caucasus were spared. The Circassian peoples—the Kabardins, Cherkess, and Adyges (Adyghes)—essentially one people speaking almost the same language, were not considered dangerous both because they were scattered over three territories (the Kabardino-Balkar Republic—Kabardino-Balkariya, the Karachai-Cherkess Republic—Karachayevo-Cherkessiya and, further north, in the Adygei Autonomous Oblast—now the Republic of Adygeya) and because most of these peoples had been deported to Turkey at the end of the Caucasian War in 1864. The various ethnic groups that lived in the Republic of Dagestan were numerous and fragmented and thus could be easily controlled. The Osetiyans (Ossetians), a majority Christian people, living in North Osetiya (now the Republic of North Osetiya—Alaniya), had always been loyal to Russia and practically never put up armed resistance, with exception of some Muslim Osetiyans.

After the death of Stalin (Iosif Dzhugashvili) in 1953, the deported peoples were allowed to return to the Caucasus. The region was calm for more than three decades thereafter. As the USSR began to disintegrate in 1991, a wave of popular unrest in the Checheno-Ingush Republic brought to power Gen. Dzhohar Dudayev, who set a course for the complete separation of Chechnya from Russia as an independent state. The Russian Government refused to recognize Chechen independence, thereby causing a sharp political conflict between the federal authorities in Moscow and the Chechen Government, which later grew into an open armed confrontation.

Unlike the Chechens, the other peoples of the North Caucasus did not seek to break away from Russia. The regional policy of Russian President Boris Yeltsin, formulated in his well-known phrase 'Take as much sovereignty as you want', suited both the authorities and much of the population of the North Caucasus. Yeltsin's policy of encouraging greater local autonomy gave a significant degree of economic and political independence to the units (the federal subjects) of the Russian Federation, among them the republics of the North Caucasus. The Chechen separatists apart, nobody wanted a conflict with the federal state, and in 1992 Ingushetiya even separated itself from Chechnya to form a republic of its own, so as to dissociate itself from the secessionist policy of Dudayev.

THE SPREAD OF INSTABILITY ACROSS THE NORTH CAUCASUS

The ongoing Russian–Chechen conflict, however, was resulting in the gradual destabilization of the entire North Caucasus. From the time that it declared independence, the separatist Chechen 'Government' attempted to obtain the support of its neighbours in its confrontation with the federal authorities. The first programme and propaganda documents of the Chechen separatist regime described the North Caucasus as a unified region with its own specific requirements.

The Chechen leadership was perfectly aware that it needed to win support from other peoples of the Caucasus in order to carry out their plans for a complete separation from Russia or, even better, for them to break away from Russia alongside the Chechens. Russia would be much harder placed to clash with the whole Caucasus instead of Chechnya alone. Moreover, in the event that the entire North Caucasus seceded from the Russian Federation, the Chechens could be expected to have a leading role in any ensuing polity, both because of their status as the most numerous ethnic group of the region and because of the potential wealth of Chechnya.

The Confederation of the Peoples of the Caucasus (CPC) headed by Yusup Soslambekov, a Chechen, was set up in 1991, with the support of Dudayev. In 1992, the CPC was a major organizer of volunteer groups to support the separatists in Abkhazia who fought for the independence of Abkhazia from Georgia.

The CPC, which included most public leaders from all Caucasian republics, declared repeatedly that it would call the peoples of the Caucasus to fight against Russia if the latter took military action to retain control over Chechnya. However, when this happened in late 1994, the CPC quickly dissolved itself, and the Chechens did not receive any organized armed support from their neighbours. Instead, support was limited to the staging of peaceful protest rallies against the war in Chechnya in Kabardino-Balkariya and Ingushetiya and the absence of objections from the Governments of Adygeya and Dagestan to the arrival in their republics of refugees from Chechnya.

Only small groups of volunteers made their way to Chechnya from other parts of the Caucasus to fight against Russia, most notably a group from Karachayevo-Cherkessiya known as the 'Karachai Battalion', who numbered no more than 100. Other volunteers from Dagestan, Ingushetiya, and Kabardino-Balkariya fought alongside Chechen insurgents during the 1994–96 campaign. The total number of such volunteers is unknown but was relatively insubstantial. While public opinion in the Caucasus was undoubtedly in favour of Chechen independence, mass armed support remained a distant prospect.

The failure of their first military campaign in Chechnya forced the Russian leadership, in mid-1996, to sign a peace treaty with the separatist regime and to withdraw their troops from the Republic. The confrontation had not ended, however. Not recognized by the world at large, the independent 'Chechen Republic of Ichkeriya', as the separatist leaders styled their regime, found itself in political isolation, and the Russian Government did not hasten to render it any substantial assistance. Civil strife started in Chechnya between various militarized political groups. Both the Chechen Government and field commanders opposed to it tried to spread their influence across the North Caucasus. Their aims and methods were different, however. Aslan Maskhadov, the Chief of Staff of the Chechen insurgent army during the 1994–96 war, and who became the President of Chechnya following elections held in January 1997, preferred a moderate policy and was in contact with leaders of other republics of the North Caucasus, recognizing them as the heads of autonomous regions within Russia. In interviews that Maskhadov gave even during the second armed incursion of Russian troops into Chechnya (that commenced in 1999—see below), he repeatedly emphasized that he had never supported the secession of the entire North Caucasus from Russia and that he had even made the leaders of the neighbouring republics promise that they would not break away from Russia in the event that the Russian authorities recognized an independent Chechen Republic (*Moscow News*, 21 November 2000).

The field commanders opposed to Maskhadov, on the contrary, made every effort to stimulate support for separatism in other regions of the North Caucasus. The most influential commanders, Shamil Basayev and al-Khattab, the latter a native of Saudi Arabia who arrived in Chechnya to fight in 1995, organized a training camp for insurgents from other Caucasian republics near the Chechen village of Serzhen-Yurt. The exact number of trainees there is unknown, most of them were believed to come from Dagestan. It seems likely that the camp was created to form a Caucasian army that in future could start military operations against Russia across the entire North Caucasus. The political wing of this army, the Congress of the Peoples of Chechnya and Dagestan (CPCD), was headed by Basayev. It is quite possible that Basayev and his colleagues intended to use the CPCD eventually to unite all the separatist forces in the Caucasus, so as to spread their influence over the whole region.

Basayev and al-Khattab did not hesitate to intervene in the political situation in the regions neighbouring Chechnya. Islamists and separatists from Dagestan such as Adallo Aliyev, Bagaudin Magomedov, and Sirazhudin Ramazanov regularly visited Chechnya where they openly supported the separation of Dagestan from Russia and the creation of a unified independent Islamic state together with Chechnya. Armed raids were organized from Chechnya on Dagestan. In 1997 al-Khattab organized an attack on a garrison of Russian troops in the Dagestani city of Buinaksk in at attempt to force the Government of Dagestan to stop applying pressure on the inhabitants of two villages in the Republic, Karamakhi and Chabanmakhi, in which the rule of *Shari'a* (Islamic religious law) had been proclaimed.

Attempts to raise the whole Caucasus against Russia were not confined to Dagestan alone. A previous attempt, in 1998, to establish a guerrilla camp in Kabardino-Balkariya in 1998 had failed when the base was discovered and destroyed after a fierce fight with a small group of insurgents.

In August 1999 a combined party of Dagestanis and Chechens under the command of al-Khattab and Basayev commenced hostilities against Russian troops in the mountainous region of Dagestan bordering on Chechnya. Whatever the objectives of Basayev and al-Khattab, they clearly counted on the support of the Dagestani people. However, most Dagestanis distanced themselves from the conflict or supported the authorities.

The events of August–September 1999 led to the second armed invasion of the Russian armed forces into Chechnya from late September. Putin, as Chairman of the Russian Government, justified the renewal of conflict in the region with reference to the expansion of the separatist struggle from Chechnya to other regions of Russia. (Concerns about this issue had been heightened following a series of bombings, in which more than 200 people died, in Moscow, and other regions of Russia, which the Government stated had been committed by Chechen separatists.) Maskhadov's call for negotiations was ignored by the federal authorities, alongside any search for compromise or a non-military solution to the crisis.

The Russian armed forces had occupied practically the whole of Chechnya by the end of the winter of 1999/2000. Maskhadov proclaimed the beginning of a guerrilla war.

Many field commanders, most notably Basayev and al-Khattab, continued to insist on their idea of spreading the war all over the North Caucasus, but the disunity of the insurgents, Maskhadov's opposition, and the loss of rebel-controlled territory in Dagestan constrained the implementation of these plans. Many commanders and, above all, Maskhadov hoped that they would be able in the long run to repeat their success, to defeat the Russian army, and to force the Russian authorities into a resumption of negotiations. However, as the conflict continued, and despite the ability of the insurgents to inflict heavy casualties on the Russian armed forces, the prospect of a negotiated settlement deteriorated further.

In July 2002 the separatists held a large congress (Great Majlis) in the Chechen mountains to unite their forces, to overcome internal controversy, and to draw up a plan of future actions. As a result of the meeting, all of the rebel commanders confirmed that they recognized Maskhadov as the President of Chechnya, while Basayev was proclaimed the 'Military Amir'—that is, the military commander of the separatist armed forces. Basayev subsequently claimed that it was at this Majlis that the programme of expanding what he referred to as a *jihad* (holy war) across the entire North Caucasus, and of the mass involvement of other Caucasian peoples in the anti-Russian struggle had been decided (interview published at Kavkazcenter website, 9 January 2006).

Basayev's words are indirectly confirmed by the fact that attacks on police officers and Russian servicemen in Dagestan have increased markedly since 2002. More than 200 police officers and officials of the Federal Security Service (FSB) were killed in Dagestan in 2002–06, including such high-ranking officers as the head of the counter-intelligence department of the Dagestan branch of the FSB, Col Kamil Etinbekov, and a republican deputy interior minister, Magomed Omarov.

In 2005 the insurgents in Dagestan changed their tactics, choosing to launch frequent attacks and bombings against police and military patrols in urban areas, whereas previously they had undertaken targeted assassinations of those law enforcement officers in charge of fighting Islamist and insurgent groups.

The military expansion from Chechnya reached not only eastwards towards Dagestan but also in the western direction. In August 2003 Zarema Muzhakhoyeva, a Chechen woman sent to Moscow as a potential suicide bomber instead surrendered to the police. She gave the investigators the names of those who had sent her and informed them of the building in Baksan, Kabardino-Balkariya, in which they were hiding. Special units of the FSB and police then surrounded this building, but met fierce resistance and failed to capture the insurgents hidden there. It was soon discovered that Basayev had been among them (*Russkii Kuryer*, August 2003; *Kommersant-Vlast*, 29 September 2003; *Izvestiya*, 16 September 2003).

Having returned to Chechnya, Basayev issued a statement stating that, as a result of his secret voyage across the Caucasus, six military sectors of the common insurgent front had been created, namely: the Sunzha sector, in southern Ingushetiya; the Ingush sector, around the principal city in Ingushetiya, Nazran; the Alkhanchurt sector, in northern Ingushetiya; the Osetiyan sector; the Stavropol sector; and the Dagestan sector (grani.ru, 22 June 22 2004).

Meanwhile, field commanders from all over the Caucasus were gathering volunteers in forest camps for training in military operations outside Chechnya. The Chechen commander Ruslan Gelayev led a group across the border from Chechnya to Ingushetiya and established a camp near the mountain village of Arshty, gathering a group of Chechens and up to 120 Ingush, Kabardins and Karachai (grani.ru, 22 June 2004). After the dissemination of Basayev's statement, the insurgents ceased to hide their intention of extending the armed conflict beyond the borders of Chechnya.

In November 2003 a Chechen field commander explained the actions of the insurgents thus: 'Not only do we carry out raids to various areas in the Caucasus, but we also form local jamaats, insurgent groups, there. We are joined by a lot of Kabardins, Dagestanis, Karachai, Ingush, and even [Muslim] Osetiyans' (prima-news, 24 November 2003). In January 2004 the field commander Doku (Dokka) Umarov told the Ichkeriya website 'If the operations that we plan are successful, they can radically change the whole situation in the North Caucasus.' (grani.ru, 22 June 2004).

While the insurgents, who describe themselves as *mujahidin* ('holy warriors') called their groups jamaats to emphasize their Islamic identity, the rebel groups are, above all, set up for armed struggle against the official state authorities, and the extent to which they are permeated by Islamist ideology varies. Each jamaat is headed by an Amir (Commander) who makes decisions with the approval of a Shura (Council) comprising commanders of the smaller groups that make up the jamaat. Each Amir in turn is subordinate to the Military Amir of All Mujahidin of the North Caucasus—the post initially occupied by Basayev.

In mid-2004 the insurgents began to put their plans to expand the conflict into practice. On 21 June several hundred Chechen and Ingush insurgents launched a raid into Ingushetiya, the first large-scale combat operation mounted by rebels outside Chechnya. Basayev led this operation, but a significant role in its organization was also played by an Ingush commander who was variously known by the pseudonyms of Amir Magas, Ahmed Yevloyev or Ali Taziyev.

Soon after the raid into Ingushetiya, local insurgent groups made themselves known in many Caucasian regions. Online declarations named the leaders of the Dagestani rebels. Rappani Khalilov commanded the bands of Dagestanis fighting in Chechnya, while Rasul Makasharipov led the insurgency in the cities of Dagestan, as the head of a group called Shari'a Jamaat. The local insurgent group in Kabardino-Balkariya took the name of Jamaat Yarmuk. A little later, a group of local insurgent Muslims formed in North Osetiya—Alaniya, known by the Arabic name *Kataib-al-Khoul* ('Horror Battalion'). Jamaats were also formed in Karachayevo-Cherkessiya and in the majority ethnic-Russian region of Stavropol Krai.

Basayev continued to be Supreme Military Amir until July 2006 when he was killed; as such, he almost certainly coordinated if not guided the general course of the insurgency that had developed in the Caucasus since 2004.

The pace of development of the insurgent movement in the North Caucasus varied from region to region. The pace of growth of the guerrilla war depended on many factors, including the degree of support given by the local population, the number of fighting groups, counteractions by the Russian law enforcement agencies, the level of experience of rank-and-file fighters and their commanders, and the material resources available to the militants. It is also obvious that the activity in a particular region of the Caucasus also depended on the plans of the top military command of the insurgents based in Chechnya.

In early 2005 a new stage of preparations for spreading the conflict across the Caucasus commenced. Following the killing, in Chechnya, of Maskhadov in March, that faction of the separatists who supported a rapid extension of the war across the Caucasus became increasingly prominent. Abdul-Khalim Sadulayev, an Islamic preacher and a supporter of the formation of an Islamic state in Chechnya and the North Caucasus, succeeded Maskhadov as the 'President' of the separatist Chechen regime. The death of Maskhadov also effectively ruled out any possibility, however remote, of negotiations with the Russian authorities, and meant that the only means by which the insurgents could force the federal Government to sue for peace would be by extending the war from Chechnya across the Caucasus. As soon as he became the leader of the insurgents, Sadulayev declared that the conditions of peace that the insurgents would be prepared to offer Russia in the future would be far more demanding that those agreed in the Russian-Chechen peace agreements signed in 1996 and 1997.

In May 2005 Sadulayev issued a decree on the creation of a military 'Caucasian Front', encompassing all regions of the North Caucasus west of Chechnya, including Ingushetiya, North Osetiya—Alaniya, Kabardino-Balkariya, Karachayevo-Cherkessiya, Stavropol Krai and Krasnodar Krai. Sadulayev's decree announced the formation in each region of a 'sector' of the front, each of which was to be headed by a commander, who was expected to govern all operations of the insurgents in the area. The Chechen separatists declared that the commanders of rebel groups in Dagestan, Ingushetiya, Kabardino-Balkariya and Karachayevo-Cherkessiya had sworn an oath of loyalty to Sadulayev.

Five months after the declaration of this unified front was declared, the insurgents launched their first large-scale operation in the north-western Caucasus. On 13 October 2005 an estimated 100–200 insurgents attacked buildings of law enforcement agencies and military garrisons in the city of Nalchik, the capital of Kabardino-Balkariya. The attack was made in the daytime and was not entirely successful; indeed, the near failure of the raid led insurgents across the Caucasus to change their tactics, as discussed below.

COUNTERMEASURES IMPLEMENTED BY THE RUSSIAN AUTHORITIES

The Russian authorities were aware from the very beginning of the second military campaign in Chechnya that the insurgents might attempt to lead other peoples of the Caucasus against Russia. The Russian authorities, however, expected that their 'anti-terrorist operation' (as the post-1999 Chechen military campaign was officially referred to in its initial stages) would finish quickly, and thus ensure stability across the North Caucasus. In reality, the war in Chechnya proved to be unexpectedly prolonged. Although Russian troops had obtained control over practically all Chechen territory by the end of February 2000, once the insurgents had started a guerrilla war it soon became clear that the military campaign would endure for some considerable period. In February 2001 Putin placed the FSB in charge of military operations in Chechnya. In practice, the FSB started to exercise control not only over the counter-guerrilla activities but also over broader questions of Russian policy over Chechnya, and imposed a strict media blackout in the Republic. The purpose of this blackout was to conceal, as far as possible, the scale of the guerrilla war, as well as the punitive actions taken against the civilian population.

It was clear, however, that terror and military operations alone were not enough to overcome the guerrillas. The Kremlin realized that there was no other alternative than to 'chechenize' the conflict—that is, to establish local authorities loyal to the federal regime, who would themselves combat the insurgents—so as to strengthen the pro-Russian authorities in Chechnya. At the same time, the Russian leaders understood that separatists would respond to this policy by trying to spread the conflict beyond Chechnya.

In early May 2001 the heads of the security and military services of Russia, including FSB Director Nikolai Patrushev, Minister of Defence Sergei Ivanov and Minister of Internal Affairs Boris Gryzlov, visited the North Caucasus, in order to establish new tactics in the struggle against the insurgents. In particular, it was proposed that Russian military units and police officers loyal to the pro-Russian administration of Chechnya should start patrolling Chechen settlements jointly at night (gazeta.ru, 5 May 2001). Security officials discussed measures intended to make the Chechen police a credible force capable of resisting the guerrillas and of strengthening the pro-Russian authorities in the Republic. On 5 May Patrushev, Ivanov, and Gryzlov held another meeting in Yessentuki (Stavropol Krai) where, in addition to Chechen issues, they also 'discussed the prevention of terrorist acts in the North Caucasus, the situation with Wahhabism in Karachayevo-Cherkessiya and Kabardino-Balkariya, and security problems in the areas adjoining Chechnya, in particular, in Stavropol Krai' (Wahhabism is the generic term used by Russian officials to refer to Islamist rebels in the North Caucasus and elsewhere) (Radio Liberty, 5 May 2001). It thus appeared that the

Russian leaders' primary concern was that unrest might spread from Chechnya to the north-western Caucasus.

In June 2001 groups of investigators were sent to Karachayevo-Cherkessiya and Kabardino-Balkariya from the head office of the federal Ministry of Internal Affairs to help the local authorities find persons fighting in Chechnya on the side of insurgents and those being trained in the Serzhen-Yurt camp. On 16 August suspects accused of preparing a coup were arrested in both republics. Later on, these people were sentenced by court to long terms of imprisonment. Given that the trials were held *in camera* in a prison in Pyatigorsk (Stavropol Krai) and the accused never pleaded guilty, it could be assumed that the charges had been fabricated and that no coup had, in fact, been planned. In 2001 both Karachayevo-Cherkessiya and Kabardino-Balkariya were still quite stable regions without any clear sign of possible aggravation of the situation. It seems most likely that these arrests and detentions were preventive measures intended to serve as a deterrent against those who would like to join in armed struggle against Russia.

Meanwhile, the Russian authorities began preparing the legal basis for the start of large-scale reprisals in the Caucasus against Islamist fundamentalists, separatists, nationalists and sympathizers with Chechen independence, but above all against those devout younger Muslims whom the authorities regarded as an obvious potential source of support for guerrilla groups.

In 1999 Dagestan adopted legislation on the Struggle against Wahhabism that outlawed all Muslim organisations that did not recognize the authority of the official Islamic body in the Republic, the Spiritual Department of Muslims (SDM). Later, similar laws were adopted in other Caucasian republics. In 2002 a federal law on the Struggle against Religious and Political Extremism was approved.

Such laws gave a free hand to the secret services to arrest those who criticized government policy or who had views on religion that differed from those officially approved. Mass reprisals, falsified cases, and the abuse of power by the secret services and the police ensued. Whereas such measures had been expected to intimidate people, subsequent events showed that such policies made it easier for the insurgents to win the support of the population of the republics of the North Caucasus. As the insurgents became more active, so the reprisals became harsher, in turn bringing new supporters to the rebels.

In 2004 the insurgents mounted a number of successful operations in Ingushetiya and Chechnya, and on 1 September a group of terrorists sent by Basayev seized a school in the city of Beslan, North Osetiya—Alaniya, following which at least 331 hostages were killed, including 186 children. Such attacks made the federal authorities realize that it was impossible to suppress the insurgent movement in the Caucasus by force alone, and that a more flexible policy was needed. On 13 September Dmitrii Kozak, an official regarded as the most capable administrator among Putin's staff, was appointed as the presidential representative in the Southern Federal Okrug (District), a position that was based in Rostov-on-Don but included responsibility for all of the republics of the North Caucasus. Kozak announced the intention of implementing a 'carrot and stick' policy of incentives and disincentives in the Caucasus, stating that 'executive power and law enforcement agencies should act together so as to eradicate corruption and do away with terrorism alongside promoting social and economic development' (quoted in grani.ru, 24 September 2004). This dual policy meant that, while on the one hand, Kozak was to ensure that security services remained vigilant, on the other hand, he was also to supervise cash flows by means of which the presidential regime expected to cajole the North Caucasian republics, above all Chechnya, to remain under Russian rule. Simultaneously, an anti-terrorist commission was set up in each federal subject (territory) in the North Caucasus, including the local heads of security and military services, the head of the federal subject, and major ministers of the respective local government.

In late 2004 Russia's regional policy changed radically as democratic elections of regional leaders were abolished, with local leaders of executive power henceforth to be appointed by the central government. The autonomous status of the ethnic republics in the North Caucasus, as elsewhere, was thus effectively removed, while regional leaders lost what remained of their influence over the security services, which became subordinate directly to the federal authorities. The regional leaders in the North Caucasus effectively became managers, whose task was to improve the economic situation in their republics under the vigilant supervision of Kozak. Officials in the federal presidential administration believed that accelerated economic growth would help to restrain the spread of the influence of the insurgents across the region. Between 2005 and 2007 new regional leaders, generally regarded as loyal to Kozak, were appointed in several of the republics of the North Caucasus, including Kabardino-Balkariya, North Osetiya—Alaniya, Adygeya, and Chechnya. (Kozak was replaced by the former Minister of Justice and Prosecutor-General, Vladimir Ustinov, in May 2008.)

Those measures, however, did not inhibit the development of the insurgent movement in the Caucasus. Threats that direct federal rule would be introduced, made in an attempt to fortify local leaders, the maintenance of strict control over regional governments by federal officials, attempts to attract private investment to the Caucasus and an increase in appropriations from the central government budget to the region all failed to reduce the appeal of the insurgents. Moreover, the introduction by regional administrations of measures that could be interpreted as representing a flirtation with the precepts of Islam, such as the prohibition of public gambling or the sale of alcohol in Chechnya, Dagestan and Ingushetiya, appeared to be potentially counter-productive. In response to pressure from the federal authorities, Islamic officials, heads of the republican branches of the SDM and imams increased their criticism of the insurgents and their ideology in mosques, but to little avail.

The problems with the development of a political and ideological line that would help to decrease the growing social support of the insurgents in the republics of the North Caucasus republics compelled the Russian authorities to continue to rely mainly on force to achieve their objectives. Immediately after Basayev declared that a Caucasian Front had been founded, the Russian military command began moving reinforcements to the Caucasus.

In early 2005 more than 300,000 federal troops were stationed in the North Caucasus but, excepting 80,000–100,000 troops in Chechnya, all of them were scattered over a large territory, including regions dominated by ethnic Russians such as Rostov Oblast, Krasnodar Krai, and Stavropol Krai. In May of that year the military units started to congregate in the minority ethnic republics of the North Caucasus in preparation to fight insurgents. On 13 May the Commander of the federal interior ministry troops, Nikolai Rogozhkin, announced that the forces under his command were reinforced in the cities of Elista (Kalmykiya), Cherkessk (Karachayevo-Cherkessiya), Nalchik, and Sochi (Krasnodar Krai) (Interfax, 13 May 2005). In September units from the 58th Russian army, along with federal interior ministry troops, border guards, and air force units started unprecedented exercises in Kabardino-Balkariya, Dagestan, North Osetiya—Alaniya, Ingushetiya and Karachayevo-Cherkessiya. The North Caucasus Military District announced that the objective of the exercises was associated with the establishment of a unified command centre that would oversee special operations against illegal armed formations (*Izvestiya*, 20 September 2005).

Despite these exercises, the rebel attack on Nalchik in October 2005 caught the officials unprepared. The authorities had information in advance about plans for a rebel assault, but failed to take sufficient measures to prevent the offensive on the city.

Although the raid of the insurgents on Nalchik failed and the rebels suffered casualties, most of them managed to leave the city. The intended scenario of the authorities, in accordance with which insurgents would be blockaded into a settlement block and annihilated, which had been practised during exercises, failed to ensue. It became clear that the military skills of a great number of the troops in the North Caucasus left much to be desired.

Troops continued to be moved to the North Caucasus in 2006 and 2007. The creation of special mountain brigades for Dagestan and Karachayevo-Cherkessiya was accelerated. Military manoeuvres went on unabated for much of 2007.

At the same time, security services stepped up arrests of potential insurgents and other suspects in Ingushetiya, Dagestan, Chechnya, and North Osetiya—Alaniya. Such detentions frequently took the form of a kidnapping, involving the seizing of a suspect by masked men, and their subsequent detention in a military base, where the detainee would be interrogated in order to force either a confession of being an Islamist extremist or the revelation of information about insurgents

Attacks of insurgents against local police targets led the Russian authorities to send an increasing quantity of police officers from other regions of Russia to the North Caucasus. In 2006 temporary police departments composed exclusively of seconded officers were set up in Ingushetiya, similar in form to those that had existed in Chechnya since 2000, while special police units were relocated from the central regions of Russia to Dagestan, Kabardino-Balkariya, and Karachayevo-Cherkessiya.

The militarization of the North Caucasus and the russification of the police there more than anything else demonstrated the success of the insurgents. In 2006 it became clear that the regional anti-terrorist commissions could not establish effective methods with which to fight the insurgents. An All-Russian Anti-terrorist Committee headed by Patrushev was created. It included Igor Sechin, a senior adviser of Putin; Gen. Yurii Baluyevskii, Chief of the General Staff of the federal military; Minister of Internal Affairs Col-Gen. Rashid Nurgaliyev; Minister of Civil Defence, Emergencies and Clean-up Operations Col-Gen. Sergei Shoigu; the speakers of both Russian parliamentary chambers; and other members of the Government (RIA Novosti, 7 March 2006). Patrushev explained the creation of the Committee by the need 'to establish and utilize new approaches and methods to counter-act terrorism'. The FSB director had to admit that terrorism had become such a serious threat for Russia that 'all resources of the state and of society should be engaged' to fight it (RIA Novosti, 7 March 2006).

THE IDEOLOGY AND THE POLITICAL OBJECTIVES OF THE INSURGENTS

The broader political and security situation across the North Caucasus accentuates the difficulty of understanding the ideology and objectives of the insurgent movements there. While the motives of the Chechen separatists in their attempts to extend the war beyond Chechnya are evident, the motives of the people of the republics of the region that until very recently were considered peaceful and relatively stable are still somewhat unclear.

The Chechen insurgent leaders have formulated clearly what objectives they are trying to achieve spreading the war to the whole Caucasus.

Movladi Udugov, a key ideologist of Chechen separatism, described these objectives thus 'From the very beginning of military aggression, the Kremlin has set for itself the tasks of localizing the war within the borders of Chechnya, chechenizing the war as much as possible, splitting resistance forces...the Chechen side responded to this threat absolutely adequately by setting themselves the tasks of taking the war beyond Chechnya, making the war public and demonstrative as far as possible and the object of not imaginary but real international concern. Experience has shown that these tasks could be achieved only by taking the war beyond the territory of Chechnya.' (Chechenpress, Kavkaz-Center, 24 January 2005). In 2003 a Chechen field commander was even more direct, stating: 'As they (Russians) don't wish to negotiate with us, then we shall do what we can. And there is a lot we can do. The war will seize all the Caucasus from the Caspian to the Black Sea' (prima-news, 24 November 2003).

Thus, the main motive of the attempts of the insurgents to transform the entire Caucasus into a unified war zone has been to force Russia to start negotiations that would bring about the recognition of Chechen independence—the goal demanded since the time of Dudayev.

However, by the late 2000s the question is not only one of the recognition of the independence of Chechnya but also one of the whole North Caucasus. Armed insurgent groups demanding independence from Russia have sprung up in other republics, following the example of the Chechen separatists.

The peoples of the North Caucasus are united above all by the fact that the region was included in the Russian Empire by force and that, ever since the Russian conquest, the authorities have inflicted many humiliations upon the peoples of the region. The sympathy and desire to assist Chechens in their armed struggle was natural, therefore, when Russia launched a military invasion of Chechnya in 1994, even if, at that time, no other people sought full independence.

The situation changed dramatically during Putin's presidency. The increasing pressures upon Muslims in general and upon those of the Caucasus in particular, and the growing impossibility of defending civil rights by peaceful means have resulted in more and more people in the Caucasus coming to support armed struggle and separation from Russia. Different sources of radicalization have emerged, including: the notion, particularly prevalent among those that have received religious Islamic education abroad, that territories inhabited by Muslims ought not to be part of a non-Muslim state; the desire to avenge the humiliation associated with police interrogations; anger at the increasing level of harassment experienced by people from the Caucasus in cities of central Russia; and resentment at the abolition of elections for regional leaders. The historical memory of the Caucasus, of ancestors who long and furiously resisted the attempts of Russia to conquer them, is a unifying factor.

These motives alone would not have been sufficient in themselves for an insurgent movement to arise. That would require war experience, weapons and material resources and, above all, organization. It would have been impossible to start a war in the Caucasus without these conditions. It is these conditions that Basayev was persistently trying to create while travelling around the Caucasus in 2003–04. It would not be an exaggeration to say that owing to Basayev's vigorous efforts, the Chechen separatists managed in a short time to transform the prerequisites for an armed rebellion in the republics of the North Caucasus into a real armed resistance. Moreover, it is impossible to imagine that without the Chechen insurgents and such a leader as Basayev that all the guerrilla groups of the North Caucasus could have merged into one military organism that could co-ordinate their insurgent operations.

Islam has become the key cementing force of the Caucasian militancy. The revival of Islam in the North Caucasus after decades of domination by the atheistic communist ideology was another important reason for the fast development of armed resistance in the region. The emphasis on an Islamic ideology rather than on nationalism made it possible to avoid ethnic tensions between insurgents from different Caucasian republics and served as a unifying factor.

The purpose of all insurgents in the Caucasus, including the Chechens, is to build an Islamic state with the framework of *Shari'a* laws as the principal source of legislation. However, detailed analysis of the future framework of such a state leads to the conclusion that, despite their religious declarations, the Caucasian insurgents are striving, in reality, to create a democratic state, albeit one that has distinctively Islamic features.

In a declaration published online in early February 2006, Sadulayev said that elections in the North Caucasus would be carried out according to an Islamic principle that 'approximately adheres to the US system of elections' (apparently referring to the Electoral College by which the President is elected). In discussing a future Caucasian state, Sadulayev said that 'the peoples of the Caucasus have a common history, a common struggle for freedom and independence, a common religion, common ideals and values. In the future, there are plans for creating a Majlis-ul-Shura (National Council) of the Caucasus [and] a Council of Ulema (Council of Elders) of the Caucasus, and for creating a confederated state similar to the European Union'. Umarov, who became the head of the Caucasian and Chechen insurgents after the killing of Sadulayev in the summer of 2006, has also invariably emphasized the indissolubility of the concepts of Islam and freedom.

It should be noted in addition that the leaders of insurgent groups in other regions of the North Caucasus such as Dage-

stan, Ingushetiya, and Kabardino-Balkariya also invariably emphasize in their interviews that in case of negotiations with Russia, the powers of the negotiator on behalf of all Caucasian *mujahidin* will be given to the Supreme Amir of the whole Caucasus, who will be simultaneously the President of the Chechen Republic of Ichkeriya.

It is hard to say what such a polity might look like in reality, but clearly the Chechen separatists continue to play the key role in the formation of the ideology and political objectives of the pan-Caucasian insurgent movement. This means that, despite the widespread use of Islamic rhetoric, the main motivations behind the insurgency in the North Caucasus are ultimately political, rather than religious.

PRESENT AND PROSPECTIVE TACTICS OF THE INSURGENTS

While preparing the 2005 raid on Nalchik, the rebels stressed its political and military significance. Had the operation succeeded, as the similar raid of 2004 in Ingushetiya had, the Russian authorities might have been threatened with losing their control over the north-western Caucasus, losing international prestige and losing their influence in the South Caucasus, particularly in Georgia. By 2005 all these reasons combined to provide a reason for the federal authorities to seek a dialogue with the separatists.

The denial of civil rights to Muslims in Kabardino-Balkariya, which had been introduced in an attempt to prevent the revival of Islam in the region, had led to the formation of armed resistance groups. Nevertheless, the will to fight proved insufficient for the undertaking of a successful large-scale military operation. Intelligence about the raid having been leaked in advance, the badly trained and poorly armed rebels suffered great losses and finally failed in their aims. Only the slow response of the police and army troops and their inefficient co-ordination saved the insurgents from a crushing defeat on the morning of 13 October 2005, and the bulk of the rebels managed to escape.

However, even such an unsuccessful raid demonstrated that the situation in the North Caucasus had changed not to Russia's best advantage. Basayev told an interviewer: 'Even if we had lost all the *mujahidin* who took part in the Nalchik raid, this would have still been our victory.' As such, Basayev regarded that the very fact of the organization of such a large-scale attack as far as 150 km away from Chechnya was in itself a great success, demonstrating the weakness of Russia's control over the North Caucasus.

Less than three months after the attack on Nalchik, the Russian military command again began to talk about the likelihood of new rebel attacks. In January 2006 Lt-Gen. Sergei Topchii, deputy commander of the Russian interior ministry troops, told the Interfax news agency that his command anticipated a rebel attack in any of six North Caucasian territories: Krasnodar Krai; Karachayevo-Cherkessiya, Kabardino-Balkariya, North Osetiya—Alaniya, Ingushetiya, and Dagestan (newsru.com, 8 January 2006).

Topchii stated that special reserves totalling 13,000 troops had been formed for each of the five operational zones of the North Caucasus to respond quickly to an insurgency offensive. The reserves were to deploy to the conflict zone by air or by rail. Topchii stated that the primary task of the interior ministry forces would be to prevent any planned attacks by blocking escape routes that rebel groups could use to reach the lowland from the Great Caucasian Range, along the Russian–Azerbaijani and the Russian–Georgian borders. Special mountain units, which would co-ordinate their operations with border guard forces posted in the region, were to be established for this task.

The Russian generals usually regard the high mountain areas of the North Caucasus as representing the rear of the rebels' front. The mountain forests are the only place where the insurgents can secretly congregate in numbers big enough to start a large-scale offensive. Their lines of arms supplies and reinforcements also run along the foot of the Great Caucasian Range. It is clear to the Kremlin that federal agents must obtain control of the mountains in order to defeat the rebels.

Otherwise, large-scale attacks could be possible anywhere in the North Caucasus.

After the raid on Nalchik, Putin ordered that additional frontier posts be established in the mountainous regions of the North Caucasus. The first of seven new frontier posts designated in Kabardino-Balkariya was to open in early 2007 (Regnum, 28 December 2006), while new frontier posts were also to be set up in Dagestan, Ingushetiya, North Osetiya—Alaniya, and Karachayevo-Cherkessiya.

None the less, since the raid on Nalchik, despite the apprehensions of the law enforcement bodies, the rebels have abstained from carrying out large-scale operations, at least for an interim period. Instead, a policy of assaulting senior police officers in certain of the republics of the North Caucasus began, seemingly with the aim of demoralizing the local forces, so as to weaken Russian authority and cut the channels of information about armed rebel movements. During 2006 a large number of senior police officers in the North Caucasus were killed in such assaults, including: the first deputy interior minister of Ingushetiya, Dzhabrail Kostoyev; a deputy head of Dagestan's criminal investigation department, Magomed Magomedov; the commander of the Ingushetiyan special police unit, Musa Nalgiyev; and a district police chief in Kabardino-Balkariya, Mustafa Konokov.

Following the killing of both Sadulayev and Basayev in 2006, the security forces managed to capture and kill a number of commanders and militants in Chechnya and Dagestan. The federal anti-terrorist committee, headed by Patrushev, announced an amnesty, expecting rebels to feel demoralized and ready to surrender after the loss of their leaders.

However, this amnesty did not change the situation substantially. Umarov, a commander with substantial experience, now stood at the head of the Caucasian insurgency and was proclaimed as the new leader of the Chechen separatists. In 2007, under Umarov's guidance, insurgents all over the Caucasus utilized new tactics, with the goal of obtaining control over the mountainous areas. This would make possible the creation of a wider network of training camps at which young insurgents could learn to undertake large-scale attacks. More importantly still, insurgent control over the mountainous parts of the North Caucasus would permit the formation of an area that could be used as a 'springboard' from which assaults against big settlements on the plains could be launched. In summer 2007 the principal forces of the insurgents were concentrated in: the Buinaksk and Utsukulsk districts of Dagestan; the Nozhai-Yurt, Vedeno and Shatoi districts of Chechnya; the mountain forests near the villages of Yandiri, Galashki, Datykh and Ali-Yurt in Ingushetiya; and in the Elbrus district of Kabardino-Balkariya.

The attacks on military and police bases in Ingushetiya in the summer of 2007 indicated that the insurgents were training in new methods for future military operations. The incompetent responses to these attacks and the failures of counter-guerrilla measures, even when the forces of the state outnumber the insurgents, suggest that the insurgents may eventually enjoy success.

As for the strength of the insurgent movement, the official numbers are quite contradictory and range from several hundreds of armed separatists across the entire North Caucasus to 1,500 in Chechnya alone. The real numbers are hard to assess. None the less, taking into account the great sympathy that the people feel for the guerrillas, Umarov's claims to a Turkish newspaper in mid-2006 that he could mobilize a whole army in the Caucasus provided it were sufficiently financed, could have some basis in fact (Vakit, 5 July 2006).

MILITARY DEVELOPMENTS, 2007–08

In 2007–08 the North Caucasus continued to be subject to a low-level insurgency. Russian officials stopped talking about normalization of the situation, instead being obliged increasingly to focus on security concerns. Chechnya, where the end of the war was officially declared in 2006, has again become a stronghold of insurgents. Meanwhile, rebels came close to seizing control of neighbouring Ingushetiya, while rebel groups in other parts of the North Caucasus have succeeded in attracting a growing number of young members.

Despite the fact that, in 2007 and 2008, no large-scale rebel attacks, on the scale of those against Ingushetiya in 2004 or against Nalchik in 2005, occurred, the insurgency has achieved a limited success in some regions of the North Caucasus, and, in some areas, has even attempted to obtain power and to bring about a change in the political regime.

In late 2007 the insurgency changed its political structure and radicalized its ideology. The self-proclaimed authorities of the so-called 'Chechen Republic of Ichkeriya' were reformed on the basis of a 'Caucasus Emirate', an 'underground' organization intended to unite all rebel groups in the North Caucasus under the banner of *jihad* against the (non-Muslim) 'infidels' with the intention of establishing a state across the region based upon *Shari'a* law.

Meanwhile, the Russian authorities have continued to militarize the North Caucasus, sending further troops there, including special police units, from other regions of Russia, to strengthen the mountainous parts of the frontier with Georgia and Azerbaijan, and to invest more money in the ethnically defined republics of the Russian Federation in the hope that this will afford Russia greater security.

The military operations of insurgents have continued to comprise attacks against police officers and on individual military columns and, more rarely, the bombardments of military garrisons and raids on small settlements. The frequency of these attacks, however, is gradually increasing, although not at the same rate in all regions.

Dagestan

Attacks on police and FSB officers have increased markedly since 2002, when the local insurgents began their subversive operations. In 2005 and early 2006 it even appeared as though the policing structures of the Republic were close to collapse, although the law enforcement agencies ensured that this did not occur. Subsequently, so-called 'apartment wars' commenced when, having received intelligence on the location of certain insurgents, special units surrounded the insurgent group in an apartment or a private house prior to storming it. As a rule, the surrounded *mujahidin* offered fierce resistance and seldom allowed themselves to be captured. Over twenty such operations were undertaken in Dagestan in 2007, during the course of which 55 insurgents were killed (Regnum, 28 December 2007).

The increasing number of informants hired by the police and FSB in Dagestan and the growing casualties among insurgents reduced the frequency of their attacks there. During 2007–08 ordinary police officers, rather than federal military personnel or senior officers, were increasingly the victims of attack. In September 2007 the appointment of a new head of the FSB Department in Dagestan, Vyacheslav Shanshinyn, was rapidly followed by an important victory, when, on 17 September, the leader of the insurgents in the Republic, Khalilov, was killed in an operation in Novyi Sulak village near the town of Kizilyurt. (He was succeeded by Abu Majid.)

However, the law enforcement agencies continued to suffer casualties. According to Adalgerei Magomedtagirov, the Minister of Internal Affairs of Dagestan, a total of 46 FSB and police officers and Russian military personnel were killed and 83 wounded in the Republic during 2007. Feeling the increasing pressure of the police and special services, the insurgents began to move gradually to the mountains of central Dagestan. The insurgents felt especially free in the Untsukul district, while the village of Gimri and its surroundings, which in the 19th century had been the native land of the national heroes of Dagestan and leaders of the anti-Russian resistance, Imam Shamil and Imam Gazi-Magomed, became the centre of the insurgent movement in the Republic. Indeed, the authorities lost control both over Gimri and over the entire Untsukul district, where two district police chiefs were killed during 2007. On 15 December the Dagestani authorities announced the beginning of a 'counter-terrorist operation' in the village. Gimri was completely surrounded by army and police units, with full access to the village only being restored on 1 August 2008, although a garrison of 430 police officers and soldiers remained in place (RIA Novosti, 5 August 2008).

In early 2008 the law enforcement units conducted several operations to destroy rebel bases in the mountain woods of

Dagestan. Despite the ensuing casualties, these operations should be recognized as a success, in which more than 30 insurgents were killed.

None the less, the heads of the Dagestani Ministry of Internal Affairs and FSB remain outwardly pessimistic about the restoration of security. In April 2008 the republican Minister of Internal Affairs declared that large-scale attacks by guerrillas in various cities of Dagestan were quite possible, while the President of Dagestan, Mukhu Aliyev, and officials in Moscow have constantly criticized security officials in the Republic for their low efficiency.

It should be noted that the area of Dagestan in which insurgents operate is gradually expanding. Whereas previously, insurgents had mainly been active in three Dagestani cities (the capital, Makhachkala, Khasavyurt, and Buinaksk), by 2008 fighting had spread to many other areas. The southern regions of Dagestan, in particular the cities of Derbent and Dagestanskiye Ogni, became especially troublesome for the authorities in the summer of 2008. In late July Magomedtagirov announced that the real number of Islamist insurgents in southern Dagestan was far higher than the 150 estimated by the police (*Kavkazkii Uzel*, 24 July 2008). Earlier in the year he had named Makhachkala, Khasavyurt, Kizilyurt, Kizlyar, Buinaksk, Kaspiisk, and Derbent as potential targets of attack (Interfax, 30 April 2008).

Despite suffering casualties at the hands of law enforcement agencies, in mid-2008 it appeared that the insurgents were continuing to increase in strength in Dagestan and to expand the territory in which they were able to operate. Moreover, they also succeeded in locating and assassinating high-ranking police officers: the head of the police department in Buinaksk, Magomedarip Aliyev, was killed on 23 June, and the head of the organized crime department in Makhachkala, Magomed-Khabiba Abdul-Kadyrov, was shot dead on 29 July.

Chechnya

The insurgents in Chechnya lost many leading commanders and a great number of rank-and-file fighters in 2006–07. The police and federal army units conducted several operations against rebels in Groznyi, liquidating several small insurgent groups based there. The insurgents have traditionally suffered heavy casualties during the winter season, as the cold weather forces them to leave their remote mountain bases for settlements, where, hiding singly, they are more easily targeted.

Consequently, the insurgent commanders decided to withdraw as many fighters as possible to the mountains for permanent posting. Umarov described these tactics during a visit to a mountain base in Chechnya in 2007: 'As we know, the winter [in the Chechen mountains] is harsh, but despite this a *mujahid* should spend the winter in the forest . . . because in the forest, when you are armed, well-equipped . . . you are able to defend your honour when you have weapons and equipment close at hand. When a *mujahid* comes home unarmed in order to warm up or to sleep, the enemies can attack him and try to capture or to kill him. So in order to prevent such things, we should stay here, in the forest, and spend the winter there too' (from a video that was posted on the internet video-sharing website YouTube).

Russian army and police units attempted more than once, without success, to crush the largest insurgent squads hiding in the mountains of southern Chechnya during the winter of 2007/08. Fierce clashes occurred in January 2008 in the Kurchaloi, Nozhai-Yurt, and Vedeno districts, but attempts to capture or assassinate the insurgents failed.

In spring 2008 the insurgents began to reassert themselves. Their targets were mainly local police units reporting to Chechnya's pro-Russian President, Ramzan Kadyrov, rather than units of the Russian federal army. There seem to be several reasons for this. First, the armed formations and police officers answerable to Kadyrov are less well armed and trained than are the federal units. Second, the federal army units are unable to fight insurgents effectively without support from the local law enforcement agencies, meaning that the priority task for the insurgents is to destroy or weaken the latter. Third, strikes on the local law enforcement agencies represent an attack on the prestige of the local pro-Russian authorities because the insurgents need to demonstrate constantly, both to

Chechen civilians and to the international community, that it is they who continue to hold real power in Chechnya, and not those authorities answerable to the federal regime in Moscow.

The insurgents conducted several large-scale raids on Chechen villages in the foothill areas of the Republic during the spring and early summer of 2008. Attacks on the villages of Alkhazurovo in April and Benoi-Vedeno in June were of particular note, and several policemen were killed and the houses of several police officers set ablaze.

The exact number of insurgents in Chechnya is unknown, but, as of mid-2008, their activity was such to suggest that their number could be in excess of 1,000, allowing us to draw the conclusion that the Republic has the largest of all the insurgent groups existing in the North Caucasus.

Ingushetiya

Unlike Chechnya, where the insurgents have launched attacks almost solely in the mountain and foothill areas, those in Ingushetiya have attacked army and police personnel travelling in cars within large settlements. Those targeted were mostly local police officers and those sent from other regions of Russia to provide assistance to the Ingush authorities. According to official estimates, 70 military and police personnel were killed or wounded in Ingushetiya during the first six months of 2008 (Ingushetiya.ru, 21 July 2008), although the general reluctance of the authorities to reveal the extent of their casualties means that these numbers may be an underestimate. On 9 July insurgents raided the mountain village of Muzhichi and killed three persons connected with the security services. For a period in late July–early August at least one police officer, FSB officer or serviceman was killed or wounded every day in the Republic, and it appeared that the security forces had almost completely lost control. Late at night on 4 August rebel squads entered Nazran and attacked private houses belonging to the republican Prime Minister, Kharun Dzeitov, and the local imam, Khizir Tsoloev, having first blockaded mobile police posts. On the following day further attacks against police officers and on a police station in the village of Troitskaya ensued.

In Ingushetiya, as nowhere else in the Caucasus, the insurgents are close to obtaining control over the entire territory of the Republic.

North Osetiya—Alaniya

Whether there are insurgent groups in North Osetiya—Alaniya or not is a moot question. For example, when statements began to appear on the Kavkaz-Center website on behalf of an Osetiyan Muslim armed group calling itself *Kataib-al-Houl* (see above), the authorities of North Osetiya—Alaniya angrily denied the presence of the group in the Republic. In September 2006 Larisa Khabitsova, the Chairman of the North Osetiyan parliament, said 'We are deeply indignant at attempts to ascribe a certain mythical jamaat to the Osetiyan people . . . We do not have the environment for *mujahidin*. It is a blasphemy to make such statements about the people who had suffered as a result of the monstrous Beslan tragedy'.

However, violent acts attributable to insurgents have clearly happened in the region, pointing to the presence of an underground organization. For example, a hall of gambling slot machines was blown up in the republican capital, Vladikavkaz, in February 2006, and several armoured vehicles were targeted by bombs in regions near the border with Ingushetiya. In February 2008 it was announced that FSB special forces had conducted an operation against a small group of insurgents in the outskirts of the city of Mozdok (in the north of the republic). During the ensuing gun-battle an FSB officer and two insurgents were killed (RIA Novosti, 13 February 2008). The refusal to reveal the identity of the dead insurgents has given rise to speculation that they were Osetiyan, and that the disclosure of their names would serve as recognition of the fact that there are Osetiyans in the ranks of anti-Russian forces in the North Caucasus. This would be regarded as significant in as much as the Osetiyans, who are mostly Orthodox Christians, unlike most of the other peoples of the North Caucasus, have traditionally been considered the most loyal allies of Russia in the region.

The most high profile operation conducted by insurgents in North Osetiya—Alaniya in 2008 was the murder, on 7 March, of Col Mark Metsayev, Head of the republican Organized Crime Department.

Russian authorities are seriously afraid lest large-scale attacks or sabotage be carried out by insurgents in North Osetiya—Alaniya, the most important region strategically for Russia in the North Caucasus, and thus preventive police searches for possible insurgents have been conducted constantly in the region, while supervision of the administrative borders of North Osetiya—Alaniya with the adjacent republics of Ingushetiya, Chechnya and Kabardino-Balkariya was strengthened on several occasions in 2007–08.

Kabardino-Balkariya

After their unsuccessful attack on the capital of the Republic, Nalchik, in 2005, local insurgents in Kabardino-Balkariya have refrained from undertaking large-scale attacks. However, since spring 2008 attacks on police patrols and officers have become more frequent, particularly in the suburbs of Nalchik and in the area around Elbrus. A police post near Khasanya settlement, which is located around the road between Nalchik and the mountainous southern regions, has become a particular focus of attack, in part because this road has been a principal supply route for insurgents to bring weapons and food to their bases. In July 2008 the insurgents issued a press release in which they bragged that their constant shooting at the police post had compelled the authorities to remove it and to thereby permit unrestricted access to the road.

Karachayevo-Cherkessiya

Karachayevo-Cherkessiya is presently the most stable of all of the Republics of the Russian North Caucasus. It appears that the law enforcement agencies have managed to crush the local armed underground groups that began to rise there. On 5 September 2007 one of the local insurgent leaders, Rustam Ionov, was killed as he attempted to escape into neighbouring Georgia. In early 2008, following a number of operations in the south-west of the Republic and the elimination of Ionov's group, the federal director of the FSB, Nikolai Patrushev, announced that the Karachayevo Jamaat had been eradicated.

Nevertheless, the killing of three police patrol officers in the southern city of Karachayevsk in July 2008 suggests that it may be too early yet to say that the underground had been utterly destroyed in Karachayevo-Cherkessiya.

Stavropol Krai

Stavropol Krai is an area in the North Caucasus populated mainly by ethnic Russians, although there is one region, neighbouring Chechnya and Dagestan, inhabited principally by members of the Nogai ethnic group. A Muslim people subjected to mass killings by Russia during the Caucasian War in the 18th–19th centuries, the Nogai remain extremely aggressive toward the Russian authorities despite their small number today, and a certain number of them have joined insurgents in the North Caucasus. Consequently, the special services have increased their activity in the Nogai-inhabited district of Stavropol Krai, searching for participants in the armed underground. Several members of the so-called Nogai Battalion were killed in combat during 2007–08.

It remains unclear what kind of guerrilla operations could be conducted by insurgents in Stavropol Krai, a flat area. It seems that the only potential method of struggle in the Krai could be through the sabotage of industrial facilities, above all gas and oil pipelines. The major Bakı (Baku, Azerbaijan)–Novorossiisk (Krasnodar Krai) oil pipeline runs through Stavropol Krai, bringing oil from Azerbaijan and Kazakhstan to the seaport at Novorossiisk for subsequent export deliveries. Some acts of sabotage have already been carried out at oil industry facilities near the city of Neftekumsk, and a gas pipeline in the Krai was blown up in late June 2008.

Summary

As we can see, insurgents stepped up their activities in 2008 in all regions of the North Caucasus, albeit at a different scale in different areas. At the same time, their actions are quite similar. The insurgents in all the republics operate as a rule from mountain areas where they maintain their bases, and they target first of all local police officers.

IDEOLOGICAL RADICALIZATION AND THE DECLARATION OF THE CAUCASUS EMIRATE

Substantial changes were made in the military and political structure of the insurgent movement in the North Caucasus in the autumn of 2007. By the time that the leaders of the Chechen insurgents had decided to expand their zone of operations beyond the borders of Chechnya, the need to find a new separatist state-like formation to replace that hitherto provided by the structures of 'the Chechen Republic of Ichkeriya' had become increasingly urgent. Above all, it was impossible to explain to insurgents from Dagestan or Kabardino-Balkariya why they should fight, first and foremost, for the independence of Chechnya. In contrast to the insurgents in Chechnya, the insurgent groups in the other regions of the North Caucasus had, from the very beginning, professed allegiance to the establishment of an Islamic religious, rather than a secular, state. In addition, the Russian authorities have constantly sought to arouse the enmity of the other peoples of the Caucasus towards Chechens in their anti-insurgent propaganda. For example, after the raid on Nalchik in 2005, Russian state-controlled TV channels broadcast reports in which young inhabitants of Kabardino-Balkariya were seen to accuse Chechens of having perpetrated the attack. Any incidents of fighting, even without weapons, between Chechens and members of other ethnic groups of the Caucasus are widely covered, as a rule, by official Russian news agencies.

It was becoming more and more clear to insurgent commanders that a positive programme was called for, in order to strengthen the insurgent movement in the Caucasus. This programme would need to be evident to all peoples of the region, avoiding any use of nationalistic slogans. The idea to proclaim a Caucasus Emirate and to present this state as the ultimate goal of the struggle of all Caucasian insurgents had been finally determined by late 2007. Another important factor that induced the insurgents to give up the slogan of Chechen independence was that of financing their struggle. Radical Islamist organizations supporting *jihad* internationally are effectively the only external source of financial aid to the insurgents of the North Caucasus. Based on this reality, the insurgent leaders adopted militant Islamist rhetoric, declaring solidarity with all *mujahidin* of the world, with those who fight against the US troops in Iraq, with the Taliban in Afghanistan, with Islamist groups in Somalia, and so on. The commanders believed that this step would facilitate a greater access to funds donated by supporters of armed *jihad* across the Islamic world.

In October 2007 Umarov, in an online declaration, announced the formation of the Caucasus Emirate, stating 'I am announcing to all Muslims that I am at war against the infidels under the banner of Allah. This means that I, Amir of the Caucasian *Mujahidin*, reject all infidel laws that have been established in this world. I reject all laws and systems that the infidels have established on the land of the Caucasus. I reject and outlaw all names that the infidels use to split the Muslims. I outlaw all ethnic, territorial and colonial zones named the North Caucasian republics … We renounce all these names.' (Radio Marsho, 30 October 2007).

Instead, the insurgency announced the division of the North Caucasus into vilayets (the Arabic term for an administrative area). According to Umarov, rebels should now refer to Dagestan as the vilayet of Dagestan, Chechnya as the vilayet of Nokhchicho, Ingushetiya as the vilayet of Khyalgaicho, Osetiya as the vilayet of Iriston, Stavropol Krai as the vilayet of the Nogai Steppe, and Karachayevo-Cherkessiya and Kabardino-Balkariya together as the unified vilayet of Balkariya, Kabarda, and Karachai. The Caucasus Emirate was to be ruled by the Supreme Amir (that is, Umarov), who was to be the only source of power in this 'state'.

The Caucasus Emirate can be compared with the Islamic Emirate of Iraq, the state proclaimed by Sunni insurgents in Iraq in those areas of the country populated mainly by Sunni Muslims. The purpose of the proclamation of this Emirate was to offer to the Iraqis an alternative to the US-led occupation and to the pro-US Government. The Iraqi insurgents thought that the proclamation of the Emirate would enable them to seize power in Iraq quickly in the event that they succeeded in driving the US troops from the country. Similarly, the proclamation of an eventual Caucasus Emirate was intended to give a positive meaning to the struggle of the insurgents, beyond simply driving Russians and 'infidels' from the Caucasus, but to establish 'fair laws' under *Shari'a* that would, in the opinion of the insurgents, permit the establishment of peace and prosperity in the North Caucasus.

Movladi Udugov, the main ideologist of the insurgents, announced in an interview with the Czech Republic-based *Prague Watchdog* in mid-2008 that the insurgents had finally determined the purpose and the flag of the Emirate (that is, its identity as an Islamic state), stating: 'These are not just chosen symbols. They are driving belts of our struggle. . . They mobilize new forces, give motivation, and point the exact direction of movement. Today the fighters go into the villages—there's a different attitude between them and the villagers, and it works both ways. The fighters themselves are in a different position. Today when the *mujahidin* go into a village, they destroy the occupiers or their collaborators, but at the same time they carry out very serious ideological work with the local population. Nowadays they don't just arrive, strike, put the enemy to rout and withdraw. The fighters who enter a village and maintain permanent contact with the local residents require them to observe *Shari'a* law.' (*Prague Watchdog*, 1 August 2008).

Similarly, Umarov called for the establishment of *Shari'a* law in all places where *mujahidin* were located. The insurgents can attempt to establish adherence to their rules and laws where they are strong, such as among the mountains and foothills of Chechnya and the mountainous regions of Dagestan and Ingushetiya. It is particularly noticeable that the insurgents have become increasingly active in introducing elements of an Islamic state in Ingushetiya, where many gambling establishments, restaurants and liquor shops have been closed, prostitution has been driven underground, following threats and arson attacks by insurgents, and Ingush fortune-tellers and sorcerers have been killed by Islamist fundamentalists. Clearly, if the position of the insurgents were to strengthen in other regions of the Caucasus, the consequence would be the same: the Islamicization of public life.

COUNTERMEASURES OF THE RUSSIAN AUTHORITIES, 2007–08

In 2007–08 the Russian authorities continued their 'carrot and stick' policy of incentives and disincentives in the North Caucasus. It should be noted, however, that the Kremlin has lately focused more on the incentives. Transfers of money to the economies of the republics of the region have been growing, and various projects, in areas such as the development of agriculture, mountaineering, or sports, are a topic of constant discussion. The Russian Government is trying to create a new industrial base in Chechnya and to induce the growth of the economies of Dagestan and Ingushetiya. The greatest opportunities were seen in Chechnya. It seemed that the Republic could be pacified and the situation would stabilize under the control of Ramzan Kadyrov. However, in early 2008, as the rebels intensified their attacks in several republics, the federal authorities began to realize that the reconstruction of Chechnya had not affected support for the insurgency among the Chechen population and that young Chechen men were continuing to join the ranks of the rebels.

In mid-2008 a mass exodus of young men into the mountains was reported in Chechnya. In an interview with *Krasnaya Zvezda* newspaper given in May 2008, Maj.-Gen. Nikolai Sivak, the commander of the Russian forces in Chechnya, stated 'There is still an outflow of young people into the militants' ranks ... many of the militants we catch in the mountains are 20 years old at the most. This means that certain young lads fall victim to Wahhabi propaganda and, unfortunately, leave for the mountains'. (*Krasnaya Zvezda*, 20 May 2008)

Given Sivak's statement, we can speak, in essence, of the ideological failure of Ramzan Kadyrov's regime to attract the loyalty of young citizens. A similar failure is increasingly evident in the other republics of the North Caucasus, with more and more young people joining the rebels. The federal authorities are challenged by the necessity of forming a pro-Russian form of Islam in the Caucasus to provide an alternative to the existing Islam that is hostile towards Russia. The official Islamic clergy have, as yet, been unable to form any such viable ideology. While the spiritual or ideological leaders of the insurgents say that the (ethnically) Russian Muslim is their friend and the Chechen who serves the infidel Russians is their enemy, the official Islamic leaders in the Caucasus try to combine faith, which by definition does not recognize ethnic borders, with the traditions of a specific ethnic group, such as the Chechens or the Kabardin. This approach is doomed to failure from the start. Besides, it is unclear which of these types of Islam is, in reality, traditional to the Caucasus: that which urges submission to non-Muslim powers or that which urges war upon the 'infidels'. This latter style of Islam, like that professed by contemporary insurgents, was popular in the region during the Caucasian War in the 19th century, and it was only after Russia had conquered the Caucasus that this type of Islam was largely supplanted by a Sufism that remained detached from political processes and which emphasized individual self-improvement. Now that calls for separatism from Russia are again in fashion in the North Caucasus, it is the more fundamentalist form of Islam that is again in the ascendant.

Losing the ideological battle with the rebels, the Russian authorities continue to rely on force, above all by strengthening the police and FSB. In August 2008 Putin (who had returned to the office of federal prime minister earlier in the year, following the expiry of his second term as President) declared a new 'anti-terror' program, under which the funding of law enforcement agencies was increased sharply.

CONCLUSION AND PROSPECTS

The present situation in the North Caucasus can be called paradoxical in as much as the strength of the Russian army and police in the region does not correspond to the number and scale of rebel attacks. Such attacks are numerous, but still not so numerous as to make it necessary to constantly dispatch fresh military and police reinforcements to the region, which has, none the less, been occurring. At first sight, it would appear that the special police units, reinforced by interior ministry troops, can easily win at this level of guerrilla war. However, it is clear at the same time that the potential activity of insurgents goes far beyond the raids on mountain villages and attacks on police officers and army columns that they have conducted. The question is only when and how the insurgents intend to demonstrate this potential. In 2007–08 they have been marking time, abstaining from large-scale operations, even though it is understood that they have sufficient numbers to conduct them. It can be assumed that the insurgents are waiting for a favourable political moment before mounting a serious onslaught or simply awaiting a chance to make an unexpected surge. Meanwhile, the Russian authorities are making substantial efforts and spending huge amounts of money in attempts to restrain the rebels.

The plan of the federal authorities is two-fold: while the security forces hold the situation under control, the civil authorities will improve the economy and distract the youth from radical ideas. This approach has not worked so far and can hardly be expected to work in the short term. Sooner or later, Russian authorities will get tired or will be unable for economic reasons to maintain so many troops in the Caucasus on a permanent state of alert. It is then that the sporadic rebel attacks can be expected to turn into a large-scale war. The insurgents believe that their forces in different regions of the Caucasus will have, by that time, become equal in strength to those of the state, meaning that the insurgent movement would be able to launch simultaneous strikes all over the North Caucasus.

POLITICS OF ENERGY IN THE CASPIAN SEA REGION

Dr SHIRIN AKINER

GEOGRAPHY

The Caspian Sea is the largest inland sea in the world. With a surface area of approximately 371,000 sq km (143,244 sq miles), it is some five times bigger than Lake Superior, in Canada, which is the world's second largest landlocked stretch of water. It is larger, too, than open seas such as the Baltic Sea and the Persian (Arabian) Gulf. From north to south the Caspian Sea measures some 1,171 km (728 miles); its maximum width from east to west is about 435 km (measurements are subject to cyclical variation). The Sea, which contains six hydrocarbons basins, is supplied by several rivers. These include, in the north, the Volga, Ural and Emba, which together account for some 80% of the river water supplies to the Sea. In the west, the Kura and other rivers supply about 7% of river water, while in the south, the Iranian rivers account for a further 5%. The Caspian Sea has no outlets or tides, and salinity is low. In winter, the northern coastal waters can be frozen for several months. The Sea has a complex hydrogeology and divides naturally into three sections:

the shallow northern section, bordered by Kazakhstan and Russia, has a depth of 25 m, and reaches just 5 m in depth near the coast; this is being rapidly eroded by deposits from the Volga and other large rivers that flow into this section;

the central section, stretching between Azerbaijan and northern Turkmenistan, has a depth that varies in places from 170 m to 790 m;

the southern, deepest section, bordered by Iran and southern Turkmenistan, has a depth of between 334 m and 980 m, and is separated from the central stretch by the Apsheron Peninsula and a massive submarine ridge.

The water level in the Caspian Sea rises and falls in an irregular cycle that lasts between 50 and 170 years. During 1960–75 the level dropped very considerably, but throughout the 1980s it rose at an alarming rate (rising by more than 1.5 m over a period of 12 years), causing severe flooding along the southern coastline. This flooding gradually spread to the central section, inundating parts of the coasts of Azerbaijan, Russia (especially the Republic of Kalmykiya) and Turkmenistan. By the mid-1990s the level had begun to fall, and between 1996 and 2001 a decrease of some 0.5 m was recorded. However, in 2002 the waters of the Caspian began to rise again. It was expected that this trend would continue until 2013–15, increasing the level by some 80 cm. There were fears that low-lying lands would again be inundated, particularly along the coast of Azerbaijan.

The Caspian Sea has great economic and strategic significance. Apart from possessing significant hydrocarbons reserves, it has several other assets, including a great diversity of fish species. The most highly prized fish is the sturgeon, which produces the world-famous Beluga caviar. The Caspian Sea also provides an important maritime alternative to overland cargo routes between Russia and the Middle East. During the Soviet era transborder traffic across the Sea was severely restricted, but in the 1990s the littoral states (Azerbaijan, Iran, Kazakhstan, Russia and Turkmenistan) evinced new interest in developing transport links using barges and steamers. Concurrently, there was an upsurge in maritime piracy and smuggling, and stringent measures were required to police the Sea.

However, the Caspian basin is best known for its resources of oil (petroleum) and natural gas (a substantial proportion of which is located off shore). In the early 1990s many areas had not yet been fully explored. A decade later, more data were available, but it was still difficult to assess the full volume of the hydrocarbons reserves of the region, and estimates varied considerably. In 2008 Azerbaijan, Kazakhstan and Turkmenistan (on shore and off shore) collectively contained some 6,600m. metric tons (47,300m. barrels) of proven oil reserves (just under 4% of total world reserves) and some 7,210,000m. cu m of proven natural gas reserves (approximately 3.9% of total world reserves).

INVESTMENT, EXPLORATION AND DEVELOPMENT

Kazakhstan

Following the disintegration of the USSR, Kazakhstan was the first, and the most significant, recipient of foreign investment in the hydrocarbons sector among the member countries of the Commonwealth of Independent States (CIS). Three major areas for investment attracted Western energy companies: Tengiz, Karachaganak and Kashagan. The first major agreement, reached in May 1992, was with the US petroleum company Chevron Corporation, providing for the development of the huge Tengiz field on the Caspian's north-eastern littoral. A joint venture, Tengizchevroil (TCO), was established between Chevron and Kazakhstan to manage the project. Other petroleum companies later bought into the venture, and in 1999 the Government of Kazakhstan began to consider selling part of its shareholding in the consortium (then valued at between US $500m. and $1,000m.). In 2005 TCO produced 272,000 barrels per day (b/d) of crude petroleum and 3,400m. cu m of associated natural gas. In 2006 TCO announced plans to invest some $5,500m. in a Second Generation/Sour Gas Injection (SG/SGI) project to increase production capacity by 250,000 b/d. These developments helped raise production capacity to 540,000 b/d by mid-2008, with a target of some 18m. metric tons of crude petroleum for the whole year (compared with 13.9m. tons of crude in 2007).

Environmental concerns were a recurrent source of tension between TCO and the Government of Kazakhstan. The chief problem was the storage and disposal of sulphur. The oil from Tengiz contained toxic hydrogen sulphide, which was processed into inert yellow sulphur and stored in huge piles near the oil wells. In 2003 TCO was fined US $7m. for open-air sulphur storage (the original claim was for $71m., but this was reduced on appeal by the Supreme Court of Kazakhstan). TCO claimed that it was steadily reducing the amount of sulphur placed in storage and making every effort to dispose of it by selling it on to new markets. Nevertheless, in 2007 a new fine of $609m. (reduced by one-half on appeal) was imposed on TCO, again over the sulphur issue. The authorities in Kazakhstan insisted that TCO was not doing enough to deal with the problem, but a TCO spokesman claimed that the company was doing all it reasonably could and, moreover, had sold an unprecedented 2m. tons of the product in 2007, far above its 2006 figure.

Another massive project was initiated in 1992, when British Gas (now BG Group) and its partner, Azienda Generale Italiana Petroli SA (Agip SA, incorporated into Eni SpA in 1998), embarked on the redevelopment of the huge Karachaganak gas field in north-west Kazakhstan (with estimated gross reserves of 2,400m. barrels of condensate and 453,070m. cu m of gas). The field, which had been in production since 1984, was in urgent need of investment and modernization. The Karachaganak Petroleum Operating Co (KPO) was formed, with BG and Agip SA/Eni SpA as joint operators (each with a stake of 32.5%), and Chevron (20%) and LUKoil of Russia (15%) as junior partners. In 1997 the KPO partners signed a 40-year Final Production Sharing Agreement with the Government of Kazakhstan. Production from the redevelopment began in 2000. In September 2007 it was announced that the project, in its third phase, was within budget and on course to meet its target of doubling annual gas sales by 2012, to 16,000m. cu m, and of increasing annual liquid gas sales to 16.5m. metric tons.

The third large-scale project was the Kashagan field, located off shore some 75 km south of Atyrau. This was a new, hitherto undiscovered deposit. In 1993 the Caspian Shelf Consortium (a seven-member group, consisting of Agip, British Gas, British Petroleum—now BP, Mobil—now ExxonMobil—of the USA, Royal Dutch/Shell of the Netherlands and the United Kingdom, Statoil—now StatoilHydro—of Norway, and Total of France—the last of which subsequently merged with Petrofina, of Belgium, and Elf Aquitaine, of France, to become TotalFinaElf, then Total again in 2003) was created to explore an offshore area of 100,000 sq km in the north-eastern (Kazakhstani) sector of the Caspian Sea. In 1997, after having completed a four-year seismic survey, the group was dissolved, to be reformed as the North Caspian Project Consortium. In July 2000 a nine-member consortium, the Offshore Kazakhstan International Operating Company (OKIOC, known as the Agip Kazakhstan North Caspian Operating Company and, later, Agip KCO, before being renamed after the North Caspian Production Sharing Agreement—NCPSA), announced the discovery of large reserves of oil. In February 2001 the Kazakhstani Government selected Agip KCO (part of Eni SpA) as project operator for the field, but specified that the company would have to meet five obligations, including a commitment to commence oil extraction in 2005.

In the following years the structure of the NCPSA consortium underwent several changes. In 2001 BP and Statoil withdrew; their shares were redistributed among the remaining members, giving Eni-Agip (the field operator), Total-FinaElf, Royal Dutch/Shell, ExxonMobil and the BG Group 16.7% each, while the US-based Phillips Petroleum Company (ConocoPhillips from 2002) and Inpex (Japan) each held 8.3%. In 2003 the BG Group decided to sell its stake in the Kashagan project. Sinopec (China Petroleum and Chemical Corporation—the People's Republic of China's second largest petroleum and gas producer) and China National Offshore Oil Corporation (CNOOC—China's third largest petroleum company) each attempted to acquire one-half of BG's stake, but they were thwarted by the other consortium partners, which exercised pre-emptive rights to buy the shares. In April 2005 the sale of the BG Group's interest in the NCPSA was finally completed. (The deal was estimated to have earned BG approximately US $1,800m. before tax.) The Kazakhstani company KazMunaiGaz acquired one-half of the BG Group's stake, the remainder being sold to the other project partners. Following this deal, shareholdings in the NCPSA (which now included not only the Kashagan oilfield, but also recent offshore discoveries in Kalamkas, Kairan and Aktote) were as follows: Eni-Agip, TotalFinaElf, ExxonMobil and Royal Dutch/Shell each controlled 18.5%; ConocoPhillips held 9.3%; and Inpex and KazMunaiGaz each had 8.3%.

There were numerous delays. The extraordinarily difficult technical and environmental conditions in the Kashagan field meant that extra work was needed to meet safety requirements. It was announced that commercial production would be delayed until 2006, but this, too, proved to be unrealistic. A fine of some US $150m. was imposed for the delay. In 2007 it was confirmed that production would be postponed until late 2010. Cost estimates for the project had by now significantly increased, from $57,000m. to $136,000m. The Kazakhstani Government accused the operator of mismanagement and failure to meet contractual obligations. In late August 2007 the Government ordered the suspension of operations at Kashagan; a penalty (reportedly of some $10,000m.) was to be imposed for production delays to date. Soon after, Prime Minister Karim Masimov warned the Italian company that it must either fulfil its obligations or hand over management of the field to others. He also stated that Kazakhstan was no longer satisfied with its current share of 8.3%, without, however, specifying what would be deemed an acceptable stake. His most radical, and perhaps most significant, proposal was that KazMunaiGaz, the national gas and oil company, should become the joint operator of the Kashagan project, indicating that the fundamental objective was increased national control over hydrocarbons resources. Further complaints against the consortium management included serious environmental damage, estimated at $40,000m., and large-scale tax evasion (a criminal investigation was launched against some of the senior executives). Negotiations with Eni-Agip continued until the end of the year.

In January 2008 the Kazakhstan Minister of Energy and Mineral Resources, Sauat Mynbayev, announced that agreement had been reached on the following points: KazMunaiGaz increased its stake to 16.8%, placing it on an equal basis with other major shareholders; a new project operator was to replace Eni-Agip; and oil extraction was to be postponed until the end of 2011. KazMunaiGas was to pay the six foreign shareholders US $1,780m. for its new shares, once production

had commenced. Compensation due to Kazakhstan for the delay in production was set at $5,000m. (one-half the original estimate); investors would have the option of paying immediately or over a period of 40 years (the life of the project), in which case inflationary pressures would cause the final sum to rise dramatically. However, this agreement did not conclude the difficulties. A memorandum of understanding was signed in June 2008, which finalized the contractual changes made in January, but established a new production date, of 2013. The Kazakhstani side consequently demanded a number of concessions, including a new 'floating' royalties structure linked to global petroleum prices. The amended deal was expected to be incorporated into a new production-sharing agreement (PSA), although by October 2008 it had not yet been confirmed. A significant reshaping of the management of the project was envisaged, with separate divisions to assume responsiblity for offshore operations, shipping and refining. Many commentators thought Shell likely to manage Kashagan's offshore operations after 2013.

The desire expressed by the People's Republic of China to join the Kashagan consortium was not its first attempt to establish a presence in the Caspian basin. In 1997 the Government of Kazakhstan had awarded the China National Petroleum Corporation (CNPC—China's largest petroleum and gas company) exclusive negotiating rights for a contract to develop the Uzen field (Kazakhstan's largest after Tengiz), although for technical reasons it was unable to develop the project and later withdrew. Other acquisitions followed, however, including CNPC's majority shareholding in the Aktobe field in north-west Kazakhstan. In 2005 CNPC acquired the Canadian company PetroKazakhstan (formerly Hurricane Hydrocarbons) for US $4,200m. (see the Economy of Kazakhstan). In October 2006 China's state-controlled International Trust and Investment Corporation (CITIC), a multi-sector conglomerate, successfully concluded a deal (worth $1,900m.) to take over the Karazhanbas oilfield in western Kazakhstan. In 1997 this field had been acquired by the newly formed company Nations Energy (NE), based in Alberta, Canada, and listed on the Canadian stock exchange. Headed by an Indonesian, Hashim Djojohadikusumo, production in late 2004 averaged 50,000 b/d, but with modern technology it was estimated that output could be increased considerably.

Indian interest developed more slowly. In 1997 India's Oil and Natural Gas Corporation (ONGC) secured a licence to explore a 10,000-sq km area in the Pavlodar basin (northern Kazakhstan). There was little further activity until 2005, when ONGC's subsidiary, ONGC Videsh Ltd (OVL), signed a memorandum of understanding with KazMunaiGaz to undertake joint exploration in the Caspian Sea, with the aim of identifying opportunities for collaborative ventures. The first venture in the Caspian by the Republic of Korea (South Korea) was led by the state-run Korea National Oil Corporation (KNOC), heading a consortium that included SK Corporation, South Korea's largest petroleum refiner. In February 2005 the consortium signed agreements with KazMunaiGaz to develop a crude petroleum project in the offshore Zhambyl field.

In the 1990s it seemed possible that Russia would be excluded from hydrocarbons projects in the Caspian region. However, from 2000 Russian companies became more active in the region, making significant investments in the Caspian states and taking part in multinational consortia as well as bilateral joint ventures. In 2002 KazMunaiTeniz (a subsidiary of KazMunaiGaz) and two state-owned Russian petroleum companies, Rosneft and Zarubezhneft, signed a 55-year PSA for the Kurmangazy oilfield; in 2005 the PSA was revised to incorporate amendments to the tax provisions. Situated on the median line between the Russian and Kazakhstani sectors of the Caspian, Kurmangazy (reserves estimated at 1,000m. metric tons or 7,300m. barrels) was reckoned to be the fourth largest oilfield in Kazakhstan. The Kazakhstani-Russian partnership planned to invest US $66m. to develop the field. It was anticipated that commercial petroleum production would commence in 2012. The Khvalynskoye oilfield, likewise divided between the Russian and Kazakhstani sectors, was also the subject of a joint agreement; in March 2005 LUKoil and KazMunaiGaz announced plans to invest some $1,000m. in the development of this project.

The Spanish company Repsol became involved in the petroleum industry in Kazakhstan in 1997, when, in partnership with Enterprise Oil of the United Kingdom, it signed an agreement with Kazakhstan for the right to explore the Baiganinsk field in the north-west of the country. In mid-2006 Repsol expanded its operations in the Caspian basin with the acquisition of a 25% stake in the exploration company TOO Zhambai. Hitherto, this had been an equally shared joint venture between KazMunaiGaz and LUKoil, until the latter sold one-half of its share to Repsol; total project exploration costs were estimated at US $80m.

An alarming development for foreign companies in Kazakhstan was the Government's stringent new energy policy. In early 2008 it was clear that PSAs were to be gradually eradicated. However, it was officially stated that contractual obligations stipulated in existing PSAs would be honoured. In May it was announced that an oil export duty of US $109.9 per metric ton was to be imposed on all domestic producers; in September it was reported that duty was to increase almost two-fold in October. Kazakh officials initially assured Western companies that their operations would not be affected, as their production contracts could not be changed. However, within weeks the Minister of Finance, Bolat Zhamishev, was publicly supporting efforts to make all producers liable to export duties in order to maximize budget revenues and stabilize domestic supplies. Subsequently, KPO, the operator of the Karachaganak field, was compelled to pay the duty. In July attempts were made to extend the remit of the new law to TCO. Meanwhile, legal experts on all sides sought to resolve the situation amicably.

Azerbaijan

Western involvement in post-Soviet Azerbaijan began in earnest in 1994, when, after many delays, a BP-led consortium finally signed a US $8,000m. contract with the Government of Azerbaijan to develop the offshore Azeri, Chirag (Çıraǧ) and deep-water Guneshli (Güneşli) fields—collectively referred to as ACG—in the western (Azerbaijani) sector of the Caspian. In October 1995 the Azerbaijan International Operating Company (AIOC), a consortium of companies from Azerbaijan, Japan, Norway, Russia, Saudi Arabia, Turkey, the United Kingdom and the USA, was established to develop the offshore fields; it finally started producing petroleum for export in November 1997. In July 1999 BP Amoco (created through the merger of BP and Amoco of the USA—its name later reverting to BP) announced that gas resources of some 400,000m. cu m had been discovered in the offshore prospect of Shah Deniz (Şah Deniz), representing the first confirmed discovery of new energy resources in the region since the dissolution of the USSR. In July 1998 BP Azerbaijan had secured a 25% stake in the Inam field when it signed a 25-year PSA with the State Oil Company of the Azerbaijan Republic (SOCAR), which held 50% of the equity; the remaining 25% was acquired by Royal Dutch/Shell. Located some 40 km off shore, the Inam contract area covered 225 sq km. Preliminary estimates suggested that it contained 1,000m. barrels of crude petroleum, as well as natural gas; development costs were expected to reach at least $3,000m. In 2006 BP, the project operator, announced plans for the drilling of a second exploration well.

Meanwhile, KNOC began negotiating to acquire a 20% share of SOCAR's stake in Inam in 2006, the latest in a number of Asian companies to show interest in Caspian resources. The first Chinese company to succeed in acquiring a stake in the Azerbaijani sector of the Caspian was Sinopec, which in June 2003 concluded an agreement with SOCAR to become the operator of the consortium developing the Pirsaat field (with recoverable reserves estimated at 1.5m. metric tons), some 70 km south of Baku (Bakı), the Azerbaijani capital. Japanese involvement in Caspian hydrocarbons mainly took the form of participation in multilateral consortia, and was largely directed towards Kazakhstan. There was some Japanese involvement in Azerbaijan, generally in partnership with SOCAR. However, by the mid-2000s results had been disappointing, and had failed to yield commercially viable quantities of petroleum. A lack of links with export routes meant that India was unable to import crude petroleum from the Caspian Sea

region. In 2005 the Indian Oil Corporation, Bharat Petroleum and Hindustan Petroleum sought to remedy this by exploring ways of importing crude from Azerbaijan for processing in Indian refineries. Several methods were under consideration, including making use of the BTC (Baku–Tbilisi–Ceyhan) pipeline (which traverses Georgia—see below) to transport petroleum to Ceyhan, Turkey, for subsequent shipment through Israel or the Suez Canal. Other Indian companies (including OVL) were seeking to acquire stakes of some 5% in the ACG fields and in Shah Deniz. In 2007 a senior Israeli diplomat reaffirmed his country's interest in acquiring energy supplies from Azerbaijan; Israel was already a major recipient of oil from the BTC project, and the aim was to construct a new pipeline to link Ceyhan to that country.

Most major international petroleum companies were by this time involved in the development of the Azerbaijani sector of the Caspian Sea. Cumulatively, since 1994, foreign companies had invested US $1,000m. in exploration drilling, and a total of 48 wells had been drilled. The early 2000s were somewhat disappointing, with few new discoveries. In 2007, however, significant finds were announced. The proven reserves at the ACG field were increased by an additional 500m. metric tons of hydrocarbons, giving a total volume of 1,350,000m. tons. Production from the 25 wells at ACG already stood at 90,000 tons of oil per day; it was anticipated that annual production would rise to 43m. tons in 2008, and to 65m. tons by 2010. Estimated gas reserves at Shah Deniz were revised upwards, to 1,200,000m. cu m. Total gas production in 2010 was expected to amount to 22,600m. cu m.

Turkmenistan

Turkmenistan took longer than Kazakhstan and Azerbaijan to attract foreign investment to its petroleum and gas fields. However, in 1996 an agreement covering the development of three large offshore petroleum and gas deposits (Barinov, Livonov and Shafag) was concluded with Petronas, the Malaysian state energy company. An exploration and production-sharing agreement for petroleum fields in the Balkanabat (Nebit-Dag) region of western Turkmenistan was also reached with Monument Oil and Gas PLC of the United Kingdom. Other deals included a concession to the Argentine company Bridas, to develop the Keimir and Ak-Patlauk petroleum fields and, likewise, to prospect in south-eastern Turkmenistan (where the company discovered new gas deposits in the Yashlar area). In 1998 an agreement was signed with the National Iranian Drilling Company to drill four wells in the coastal region of Turkmenistan.

These projects encountered technical as well as political problems. Nevertheless, some companies were able to operate relatively successfully. In 2005 the Arab-British company Dragon Oil PLC was pumping about 1,600 b/d from the offshore Cheleken contract area (which included the Djeitun and Djigalybek fields). Petronas was also making progress, producing nearly 800 metric tons of petroleum and 500,000 cu m of natural gas each day from the offshore Ovez and Makhtumkuli fields (located in contract area Block 1).

In 2006 Petronas began commercial production of petroleum at the Dyarbekir field (part of the same contract area); by mid-year it had extracted some 40,000 metric tons. Under the terms of the 25-year PSA concluded in 1996 between Petronas and the Turkmenistani Government, 60% of the revenue was allocated to covering extraction costs and 40% was to be shared equally as profit. Another foreign company operating under a PSA in the offshore Turkmenistani sector was Danish Maersk, which had completed seismic tests on two contract blocks by 2006. Oil and gas companies from Russia, Ukraine, Germany, Canada and other states were also in discussion with the Government regarding joint projects to develop hydrocarbons resources in this sector of the Caspian Sea.

In 2007 Turkmenistan's new President, Gurbanguly Berdymuhamedov (elected in February following Saparmyrat Niyazov's death in late 2006), indicated that he intended to follow a more open policy with regard to the country's hydrocarbons resources. In June it was announced that two foreign energy companies, Chevron and the Russian-British TNK-BP, had been given permission to open representative offices in the Turkmenistani capital city, Aşgabat. Russian companies such as Gazprom, LUKoil and Itera were expected to expand their operations in the country. Dragon Oil was also optimistic about prospects for future projects in Turkmenistan; in June the oil complex that it had built on the Cheleken Peninsula was commissioned, and the Turkmenistani authorities granted permission for the construction of a facility for recycling petroleum gas. Dragon Oil's board chairman announced that the company was ready to invest an additional US $500m. in the country's oil and gas infrastructure.

Iran and Russia

The Russian and the Iranian sectors of the Caspian Sea remained largely undeveloped in the 1990s. However, in the following decade this situation began to change. Iran, in particular, implemented plans to explore possible reserves. In July 2005 Iran's Deputy Minister of Petroleum announced that the initial phase of offshore drilling would commence in May 2006, as part of a joint venture between Sadra of Iran and GVA of Sweden; the intended exploration area seemed to be in a section of the Caspian where jurisdiction was disputed with Azerbaijan (see Legal Status, below). In 2006 the Hong Kong-registered China Oilfield Services Ltd signed a three-year deal with Sadra (estimated at some US $33m.) for drilling, as well as for management and maintenance of the Alborz platform, which would be used in this operation. (The venture marked an expansion of already significant Chinese involvement in the energy sector in Iran.) Likewise, in 2006 Iran announced the discovery of 10 new blocks within its section of the Caspian; the size of petroleum reserves in these blocks had yet to be established. In a further development, Iran was in negotiation with Brazilian state oil company Petróleo Brasileiro, SA (Petrobras) about exploration rights in the Caspian.

Russia, too, began to increase its exploration of its sector of the Caspian. In 2006 LUKoil discovered a major petroleum and gas condensate field in the Yuzhno-Rakushechnaya structure, in the northern Caspian, 220 km from Astrakhan. Total reserves (possible and proven) of the new field were estimated to be 600m. barrels of petroleum and 33,960m. cu m of gas.

LEGAL STATUS

In the early 19th century, having annexed most of Transcaucasia and much of western Kazakhstan, Russia became the major power on the Caspian Sea. The Gulistan Pact (1813) and the Treaty of Turkmanchai (1828) allowed Persia (as Iran was known until 1935) some rights of access to the Sea, but gave Russia the exclusive right to maintain a fleet of warships. After the Bolshevik Revolution of 1917 these unequal arrangements (always much resented by Persia) were abrogated, being replaced in 1921 by the Persian-Soviet Friendship Treaty. In theory, this gave equal rights of access to the Sea to both countries (at this period, the only littoral states). In practice, the USSR continued to play the dominant role; this was scarcely surprising, given the relative strengths of the two countries and the fact that the USSR controlled all but the southern rim of the Caspian littoral. Subsequent agreements with Iran regarding the Sea were confined to such matters as the development of fish stocks and the protection of the environment. Soviet exploitation of the offshore petroleum and gas fields, located in the central and northern sections of the Sea, was not discussed: this was treated by both sides as a matter of Soviet domestic policy. There was, therefore, implicit recognition of a 'Soviet sector' in the Caspian Sea. However, neither the question of national sovereignty nor the delimitation of the Sea was raised in official exchanges between Iran and the USSR. Thus, there was no formal definition of the legal status of the Caspian Sea.

In December 1991, following the dissolution of the USSR, three new littoral states came into existence: Azerbaijan, Kazakhstan and Turkmenistan. This emphasized the lack of clarity, at national and international level, regarding the status of the Caspian Sea. There was no unanimity between the five littoral states as to what type of legal regime should apply (whether it should be subject to the law of the sea, of frontier lakes, of a condominium or of some other regime). Past practice (between Persia and the Russian Empire and, subsequently, between Persia/Iran and the USSR) had followed a condominium-type model of joint use and joint sovereignty.

Russia and Iran favoured a continuation of this approach, arguing that the Sea should be treated as an 'indivisible reservoir', the object of common use by all the littoral states, to be utilized with the agreement of all.

However, any common zone would, effectively, be under Russian control, since the Russian Federation maintained the only substantial military forces in the area. Moreover, such a regime would have excluded Western petroleum companies from any exploitation of resources and left the remaining littoral states as junior partners in Russian- and Iranian-led projects. This approach would have retained Russian domination of the region, since Russia could use its right of veto on the development of offshore petroleum resources to exert pressure on other governments. The proposed arrangement was, therefore, unacceptable to the newly emergent states of Azerbaijan, Kazakhstan and Turkmenistan. They put forward various proposals for the delimitation of the Sea into exclusive national sectors. This was to entail the demarcation of seven international boundaries between Iran and Azerbaijan; Azerbaijan and Russia; Russia and Kazakhstan; Kazakhstan and Turkmenistan; Turkmenistan and Iran; Azerbaijan and Turkmenistan; and Azerbaijan and Kazakhstan.

In November 1996, after lengthy negotiations, preliminary agreement was reached between all the states, except Azerbaijan, on the partial division of the Sea into national sectors. Each sector was to extend 45 nautical miles (75 km) from the coast, with the middle of the Sea to be preserved as a common economic zone, shared equally between the littoral states. Unilateral hydrocarbons-extraction projects in the central waters that were at, or about to reach, the development stage would be allowed to continue, but in future such enterprises were to be owned by joint-stock companies of the five states. Azerbaijan declined to accept this compromise, although it did agree to the creation of a Special Working Group (SWG) to develop a related convention. This body, comprising senior government officials and academics from all the littoral states, convened on a regular basis.

At the end of January 1997 a new issue arose that greatly complicated the situation. Turkmenistan laid claim to offshore petroleum fields that were already being developed on Azerbaijan's behalf by an international consortium. Both states insisted that the fields lay within their sovereign waters (although the whole question of 'sovereign waters' was still open to dispute, since no legal regime had yet been agreed for the Caspian). Turkmenistan's position was supported by neither Russia nor Iran; however, Russia did try to act as a mediator. Its role was somewhat compromised when, in July, two Russian petroleum companies, Rosneft and LUKoil, concluded an agreement with SOCAR to develop one of the disputed fields (known as Kyapaz by Azerbaijan and Serdar by Turkmenistan). The Russian companies later withdrew from the contract. Despite some diplomatic initiatives on both sides, relations between Azerbaijan and Turkmenistan remained tense. In mid-2001 Turkmenistan closed its embassy in Azerbaijan ostensibly owing to 'financial difficulties'; however, a more probable reason was the continuing dispute over the ownership of the Caspian hydrocarbons deposits. In early 2005, after a period of relative calm between the two states, the dispute was rekindled when Turkmenistan gave permission to the Canadian company Buried Hill Energy to develop blocks in the Serdar field, without having consulted Azerbaijan. That country responded angrily, insisting that the field formed part of its sector; there was then an impasse, with neither side prepared to make any concession to the other. After the death of President Niyazov of Turkmenistan in December 2006, relations between the two countries improved considerably. The Azerbaijani authorities expressed willingness to resolve the Kyapaz/Serdar dispute by developing the field jointly, a proposal that Turkmenistan announced it was prepared to accept. Further bilateral talks were held in September 2007. In early 2008, with the support of the European Union (EU) and the USA, Azerbaijan expressed interest in co-operating with Turkmenistan to construct a trans-Caspian pipeline. In May President Berdymuhamedov of Turkmenistan met his Azerbaijani counterpart in Baku (in the first such visit since 1996) and inaugurated the reopened Turkmenistani embassy. The Presidents of both countries spoke warmly of 'fraternal' relations and 'common interests', and the Turkmen side announced the cancellation of Azerbaijan's debt of US $44m. However, neither President was forthcoming on the issue of the proposed trans-Caspian pipeline. Nor was there any further progress on the issue of the disputed hydrocarbons fields.

In September 1998 the Minister of Foreign Affairs of Kazakhstan addressed the UN General Assembly and urged that a decision be reached on the legal status of the Caspian Sea. A summit meeting of the leaders of the Caspian littoral states, originally scheduled for March 2001, eventually took place in Aşgabat in April 2002. The stated aim of the summit was to decide on a legal regime for the Sea. Azerbaijan, Kazakhstan and Russia had, by this time, reached a common standpoint (largely owing to enthusiastic petitioning by Russian President Vladimir Putin's special envoy on Caspian issues, Viktor Kalyuzhnyi), based on the principle that the surface be used in common, but the seabed be divided into national sectors, corresponding to each country's coastline, along a median line. This division would award Kazakhstan approximately 29% of the Sea, Turkmenistan 21%, Azerbaijan 20%, Russia 16% and Iran 14%. However, Iran rejected the proposal, advocating, instead, an equal division of the seabed and the surface of the sea into national sectors, with each littoral state holding 20%. The Turkmenistani stance was less clear, but for the most part appeared to be close to that of Iran. There were indications from 2001 that the Iranian position might be modified, as officials began to advocate the adoption of a more flexible approach to Caspian issues. Nevertheless, despite much preparatory work, the April 2002 summit did not yield conclusive results. The assembled heads of state failed to sign any agreement; not even a joint declaration was produced.

Meanwhile, the SWG persevered with work on the preparation of a draft convention on the legal status of the Caspian Sea, and presented the results at its eighth session, held in Baku in February 2003. The document identified issues on which there was already common agreement, such as the need for the demilitarization of the Sea, free commercial shipping for the littoral states and protection of the environment. However, wide divergences of opinion on several vital questions remained. These were discussed at subsequent sessions of the SWG, which, after the Baku meeting, were held every few months, rather than, as previously, once a year. At the 17th session of the SWG, held in Tehran, the Iranian capital, in May 2005, it was announced that some 75%–80% of the outstanding legal issues had been resolved. The remaining points were, unsurprisingly, the most controversial. Two more meetings were held in 2005, and in March 2006 the 20th session was held in Moscow, the Russian capital. By this time, most of the issues concerning shipping, ecology and fishing had been agreed; the chief remaining area of contention was the division of the seabed. Azerbaijan, Russia and Kazakhstan had reached agreement, but Iran and Turkmenistan still had objections (see below). A Kazakhstani proposal for a Stability Pact in the Caspian Sea was also discussed at this meeting. The next session of the SWG was held in April 2007 in Aşgabat; the talks were cordial, with an emphasis on multilateral co-operation. A further meeting was held in Tehran in June, in preparation for the second summit meeting of the Presidents of the five littoral states, held in Tehran in mid-October.

Alongside the multilateral negotiations, there was also bilateral activity between the Caspian states aimed at resolving border issues. Kazakhstan and Russia had for some time been working towards a full resolution of boundary demarcation issues. On 13 May 2002 the leaders of the two countries signed an historic protocol setting out the geographical co-ordinates of the modified median line; this supplemented an agreement, reached in July 1998, on the bilateral demarcation of the seabed. A protocol on amendments to the 2002 document was agreed in January 2006. In September 2002 the Presidents of Azerbaijan and Russia had likewise signed a bilateral demarcation agreement. On the basis of these separate bilateral agreements, a trilateral document was signed on 14 May 2003. This, in effect, completed the division of the seabed in the northern Caspian into national sectors.

In the southern Caspian, no formal demarcation agreements had been concluded. Relations between Iran and Azerbaijan, and similarly between Azerbaijan and Turkmenistan, had been strained on a number of occasions, particularly in 2001–02. However, all parties made constructive efforts to resolve their differences, and by the end of 2003 senior officials were indicating that agreement had been reached in principle on an equitable tripartite division of the southern part of the Caspian Sea. In 2007 there were signs of new momentum in relations between Azerbaijan and Turkmenistan; in July a high-level delegation from the former country visited Aşgabat for talks that were reportedly cordial and constructive. Talks continued in 2008, but failed to resolve the outstanding problems.

PIPELINE POLITICS

The second issue that initially hindered the exploitation of the hydrocarbons resources of the Caspian basin was the lack of an adequate export infrastructure. In the past, oil and gas pipelines from the region were linked to the internal Soviet network. After the collapse of the USSR, Russia used the situation to exert political and economic leverage over the newly independent states. This was highly unsatisfactory, not only for these states, but also for foreign investors, who wanted to export hydrocarbons from the Caspian without the potential threat of Russian interference. However, there were several concerns regarding the construction of new pipelines. Principal factors were: the distance from world markets and the consequent high cost of such projects; environmental problems related to the export of petroleum through the Bosphorus; US sanctions against Iran; and regional instability that could threaten the transboundary transportation of hydrocarbons.

Azerbaijan

Three possible destinations were considered for pipelines from Baku's offshore petroleum fields: the Black Sea; the Mediterranean Sea; and the Persian Gulf. The distance to the Black Sea was shorter than that to the Mediterranean, but pipelines terminating on this coast would attract the major disadvantage of increasing petroleum-tanker traffic through the Bosphorus and the Dardanelles. The Turkish authorities were bound by the 1936 Montreux Convention to allow free passage for all merchant ships through the Straits of Marmara, but the traffic had reached such a volume that it could no longer be managed safely. Moreover, the constant movement of large tankers was causing severe environmental damage. The use of the Straits for the transportation of Caspian petroleum would further augment these problems.

There was strong competition between Iran, Russia and Turkey (the last supported by the West, in particular the USA) to secure pipeline routes that would cross their respective territories and, thus, yield lucrative transit fees. In October 1995, after months of campaigning by the concerned parties, and the personal intervention of US President Bill Clinton, it was finally announced that two routes to the Black Sea had been chosen for the initial 'early oil' stage (for the export of petroleum extracted prior to the main development of the ACG fields). The northern route, from Baku to Novorossiisk, would run into Russia, and the southern route, from Baku to Supsa, into Georgia. The latter route was the AIOC's preferred choice for the main export pipeline, although there were some who believed that, from an economic point of view, a route to the Persian Gulf would have been a more rational choice. However, that was not a feasible option while US sanctions against Iran remained in force.

'Early Oil' Routes

Baku–Novorossiisk (Krasnodar Krai, Russia): Selected as the northern 'early oil' route, and terminating on Russia's Black Sea coast, this pipeline became operational in November 1997. At 1,400 km, it was the longest of the Black Sea routes, but, geographically, the terrain was the easiest. However, the political risk associated with the pipeline remained very high, as a section of it ran through Groznyi, the principal city in the separatist Chechen—Nokchi Republic (Chechnya), which was at the heart of the armed hostilities with Russian federal forces in 1994–96, and again from

1999. In mid-1999 the Chechen section of the pipeline was closed, owing to violence and the threat of sabotage in the region. A new section of the pipeline, avoiding Chechnya, was completed in April 2000. Petroleum transit through the Baku–Novorossiisk pipeline increased from 2.6m. metric tons in 2004 to 4.1m. tons in 2005.

Baku–Supsa (Georgia): Selected as the southern 'early oil' route, this represented the shortest distance to the Black Sea, at some 830 km. It became operational in April 1999. It was upgraded in stages, expanding its capacity to 250,000 b/d by 2004.

Main Export Route

Baku–Tbilisi–Ceyhan (BTC): Despite concerns over its economic viability, this was selected as the route for the main export pipeline, which would cover a distance of 1,768 km, running from the Caspian Sea to the Mediterranean. In October 1998 the Governments of Azerbaijan, Georgia, Kazakhstan, Turkey and Turkmenistan signed the Ankara Declaration in support of this route, which was also favoured by the US Government. In November 1999 a further intergovernmental agreement on the construction of the pipeline was signed in İstanbul, Turkey; a financial agreement was signed in Washington, DC, in April 2000, and a detailed engineering study was initiated in 2001. There was strong pressure from the US Government to realize this project, but initially petroleum companies were seriously concerned as to whether the pipeline was commercially viable. It did not seem likely that Azerbaijan alone would be able to produce sufficient petroleum, and representatives of the Kazakhstani petroleum industry were reluctant to commit to the project. In early 2002, however, as the significant size of the recently discovered Kashagan deposit became clear, they showed greater enthusiasm. In May the British-based European Bank for Reconstruction and Development (EBRD) agreed to provide US \$300m. in funding (about 10% of the estimated cost of construction); the World Bank also indicated its willingness to support the project. The Baku–Tbilisi–Ceyhan Company (BTC Company), a BP-led multinational consortium—other shareholders were SOCAR, Chevron, Statoil, Türkiye Petrolleri Anonim Ortakliği (TPAO—of Turkey), ENI, Total, Itochu of Japan, Inpex, Conoco Phillips and Hess Amerada of the USA (now the Hess Corporation)—was formed to construct the pipeline, and an historic ceremony was held at the Baku terminal in September. However, from late 2002 a coalition of local and international non-governmental organizations, including Amnesty International, Campagna per la Riforma della Banca Mondiale, Friends of the Earth and WWF (formerly the World Wide Fund for Nature), launched a vigorous campaign to draw attention to the potential environmental dangers and human rights abuses that they believed were associated with the construction of the pipeline. As a result, the international financial organizations that had originally been prepared to support the project decided to await the outcome of further environmental- and social-impact assessments before making a final commitment to the release of funds. In November 2003 the EBRD and the International Finance Corporation (a member of the World Bank Group) agreed financing for the project, thereby not only removing this final uncertainty, but also, importantly, validating the undertaking with their seal of approval. Construction of the pipeline was completed in early 2005. The inauguration ceremony, held in May, was attended by the Presidents of Azerbaijan, Georgia, Kazakhstan and Turkey, as well as US Secretary of Energy Samuel W. Bodman. None the less, security, political and technical problems remained unresolved, and the project fell behind schedule by over one year and exceeded the original budget by 30% (the final cost was estimated at some \$4,000m.). The pipeline did not commence operations until May 2006, and the official launch of regular operations took place in Ceyhan in mid-July. Despite strict security surveillance, within weeks of the launch some 10 metric tons of petroleum had been illegally diverted from the pipeline. This emphasized the need for an ongoing review of the security situation. By late 2006 some 300,000 b/d of crude petroleum

were being pumped to the Mediterranean terminal; full throughput capacity of 1m. b/d was reached in 2008. Security problems remained, however. In early August 2008 an explosion in the Turkish stretch of the pipeline caused the temporary suspension of operations; Kurdish rebels claimed responsibility for the attack. Kazakhstan formally agreed to join the BTC project in June 2006, although the treaty was not ratified until May 2008. Initially, the agreement allowed for up to 500,000 b/d of Kazakhstani petroleum to be shipped from Aktau on the north Caspian to Baku by tanker, and there was speculation that a sub-sea Caspian oil pipeline to Baku might be constructed. However, this would not be economically viable until Kazakhstan had a large export surplus to commit to the route. Moreover, there were serious environmental objections to sub-sea pipeline projects; Russia and Iran were particularly opposed.

Proposed Future Routes from Azerbaijan

Baku–Armenia (along the Araks river valley)–Ceyhan: Geographically, this would have been the easiest route, but it involved political risks in crossing Armenia and eastern Turkey (although one group of supporters believed that it could encourage regional co-operation, referring to it as the 'Peace Line').

Baku–Iran–Ceyhan: This was technically and economically feasible, but unacceptable to Western investors while US sanctions against Iran remained in place.

Baku–Groznyi–Novorossiisk–Trabzon or Samsun or Zonguldak (Turkey)–Mediterranean Sea: This proposed pipeline could transport petroleum overland to the Russian Black Sea coast, then by tanker (or, eventually, pipeline) to a Turkish Black Sea port (such as Trabzon, Samsun or Zonguldak, or possibly a port to the west of İstanbul), then overland to a terminal on the Mediterranean coast. It would have the advantage of avoiding the Straits; moreover, both Turkey and Russia would profit from the transit fees. The main disadvantage was the cost of constructing the pipelines and the two new terminals required. There were also serious security concerns associated with crossing Chechen territory.

Baku–Groznyi–Novorossiisk–Burgas (Bulgaria, Black Sea coast)–Aleksandroupolis (Greece, Aegean coast): This route found favour with EU member states, but was initially difficult to fund. However, in March 2007 Russia, Bulgaria and Greece signed an agreement in the Greek capital, Athens, on the construction of the trans-Balkan pipeline, which was due for completion in 2011. The 285-km pipeline would have the capacity to pump 35m. metric tons of oil each year, with the potential to expand to 50m. metric tons. In May 2008 it was agreed that Kazakhstan would supply an extra 17m. metric tons of oil for transportation through the Burgas–Alexandroupolis pipeline.

Odesa–Brody: Other options for avoiding the Bosphorus included proposed routes via Constanța (Romania) to Trieste (Italy), and via the Odesa–Brody pipeline to Ukraine. The former did not progress beyond the preliminary proposal. However, the Odesa–Brody pipeline, part of Ukraine's Eurasian Oil Transport Corridor, was completed in mid-2002; the intention was to transport Caspian petroleum northward from Odesa to the Druzhba pipeline network at Brody for delivery to markets in Europe. The first consignment of Caspian petroleum (from the Tengiz field) was unloaded at Odesa in early August. However, the project stalled when Ukraine failed to secure sufficient volumes of Caspian petroleum to fill the pipe. Ukraine subsequently agreed to reverse the flow so that it could be used for Russian exports to the Black Sea, and in late 2004 the Russian-British company TNK-BP began pumping petroleum through the pipeline for delivery to Odesa. It was estimated that some 6.0m. metric tons of petroleum would be pumped through this pipeline in 2006, compared with 5.8m. tons in 2005. However, in 2005 the Ukrainian state oil company, Naftogaz Ukrainy, announced that it wanted to exploit the link as originally intended, to export Caspian petroleum to Europe, with effect from 2007; it claimed that the transit targets pledged under the 2004 contract had not been met. In May 2006 the President of Azerbaijan, İlham Aliyev, indicated that his Government might consider transporting some of its petroleum through the Odesa–Brody line.

Kazakhstan

Tengiz–Novorossiisk: The Caspian Pipeline Consortium (CPC) was created in 1992 as a joint venture between the Governments of Kazakhstan and Oman, acting through the Oman Oil Company. Subsequently, Azerbaijan and Russia joined the group, along with Western companies. The CPC initially proposed the construction of a pipeline from the Tengiz petroleum field on the northern littoral to the Russian Black Sea port of Novorossiisk. The original plan was to route the pipeline through Groznyi to the Black Sea. In July 1993 a more northerly course, via Dagestan, was agreed, in order to avoid Chechnya. Construction was delayed by a number of problems, including major disagreements over the ownership structure. In October 1995 the Government of Kazakhstan decided to terminate the original agreement and to relaunch the project in a new form. A revised share structure was finally accepted in May 1997, with Russia acquiring 24% of shares in the project, Kazakhstan 19% and Oman 7%, and with the remaining 50% to be shared between a number of foreign companies, headed by Chevron (with 15%). In November 1998 the first major contract for the implementation of the pipeline was signed in Moscow. The pipeline was opened in March 2001, and became fully operational in September. It was formally inaugurated in November, at a ceremony held near Novorossiisk, and attended by the Russian Minister of Energy, the Kazakhstani Minister of Energy and Natural Resources, and the US Secretary of Energy.

The CPC pipeline was originally designed for a throughput capacity of some 24m. metric tons per year, primarily from Tengiz. It would not be able to cope with the increased volumes that would start flowing as the enormous Kashagan field came on stream; other large fields such as Kurmangazy were also being developed and would eventually produce substantial flows. Accordingly, in April 2006 Russia and Kazakhstan agreed on a second phase of expansion to increase the pipeline's capacity from 560,000 b/d to 1.3m. b/d by 2011. The expansion (at an estimated cost of US $1.6m.) demanded extra pumping stations, as well as additional infrastructure at Novorossiisk, including an increase in crude petroleum storage capacity of 3.7m. barrels. At the same time, the management was restructured; a Russian, Vladimir Razdukhov (formerly of Zarubezhneft), was appointed Director-General. By 2007 the CPC pipeline (the main export conduit for TCO crude) was running close to full capacity. However, Russia continued to block plans for expansion, demanding a higher price. CPC shareholders, led by Chevron, made some concessions, and in May 2008 Russia and Kazakhstan jointly agreed to double the capacity of the pipeline by 2012, with expansion to be implemented in two stages.

Other Routes: Other export facilities were also used to transport Caspian petroleum. The first regular tanker shipments of crude petroleum from the Tengiz field in Kazakhstan began at the end of July 1997, delivering between 100,000 b/d and 150,000 b/d to the Black Sea terminals at Novorossiisk and Batumi (Adjara, Georgia). In July 2006 it was announced that Total, along with other members of the consortium developing Kashagan, would invest in a crude petroleum transport system that would include the use of a number of tankers. There were also 'swap deals' with Iran. In 1996 Kazakhstan agreed to ship crude petroleum across the Caspian for refining and distribution in northern Iran; in exchange, Iran assigned an equivalent amount of crude petroleum to Kazakhstan at a terminal in the Gulf or at one of its European storage facilities. The deal was suspended the following year because Iran's refineries refused to accept Kazakhstani petroleum, owing to its high sulphur content. In 2002, after the Iranian refineries had been upgraded, swaps were reinstated. By early 2003 Iran was importing about 50,000 b/d from Kazakhstan. Turkmenistan and Russia also operated swap deals with Iran. An upgraded pipeline running from the Iranian port of Neka on the Caspian Sea to the Rey refinery near Tehran was completed in Sep-

tember 2003. This had an initial capacity of 120,000 b/d, later scheduled to be upgraded to 370,000 b/d. However, the swaps mechanism remained a marginal option for Caspian exporters. By August 2006 the total volume of swaps with Iran (from Kazakhstan, Turkmenistan and Russia) stood at around 120,000 b/d. Construction of a pipeline from western Kazakhstan via Turkmenistan to Tehran, and then to Kharg Island in the Persian Gulf, was another option under consideration. TotalFinaElf conducted the feasibility study, but it seemed unlikely that there would be progress on this project in the near future.

In 1997 Kazakhstan also began transporting crude petroleum by rail to China. Later the same year the Canadian-owned PetroKazakhstan registered a joint venture with a Kazakhstani company to complete the construction of a rail transshipment terminal on the China–Kazakhstan border. Projects for oil pipelines were discussed at various times, but the cost of these ventures made them appear uneconomical in the 1990s. However, in China, as well as in Kazakhstan, political backing for the construction of such a network was given priority at the highest level. The first step towards the realization of a Kazakhstan–China link was the completion in 2002 of the Atyrau–Kenkiyak pipeline within Kazakhstan. It was envisaged that this would eventually become part of a transcontinental line that would stretch from the Caspian to the Dushanzi refinery in Xinjiang (western China). In May 2004 Kazakhstani President Nursultan Nazarbayev visited the Chinese capital, Beijing, and with his Chinese counterpart, Hu Jintao, signed an agreement on the construction of the cross-border section of this pipeline, to run from Atasu to Alashankou (a distance of 962 km). It was completed in December 2005 and became fully operational in mid-2006. The pipeline (jointly funded by China and Kazakhstan, at a cost of US $700m.) had an annual throughput of 10m. metric tons, carrying Kazakhstani oil, as well as Russian oil from the west Siberian oilfields. During the visit to Kazakhstan of President Hu in August 2007, the Chinese energy company CNPC signed an agreement with KazMunaiGaz for the inauguration of the second phase of the project, the extension of the Atasu–Alashankou pipeline by a further 700 km westward to the Caspian Sea; when completed, this would double the pipeline's capacity to 20m. metric tons of crude petroleum per year.

Prior to agreeing, in June 2006, to join the BTC project, Kazakhstan had intermittently expressed interest in an underwater link to Baku, and in 1998 had concluded an agreement with three Western companies (Royal Dutch/Shell, Mobil and Chevron) for a feasibility study on parallel oil and gas pipelines under the Caspian Sea to Azerbaijan. It was not until late 2002, however, that serious negotiations began on the construction of an oil pipeline from the Caspian port of Aktau to Baku. A framework agreement was concluded in March 2003. However, it was far from certain that the project would proceed. Russia and Iran, as well as local and international environmentalist groups, were firmly opposed to the construction of underwater pipelines in the Sea. The seabed is subject to frequent earthquakes and mud volcanoes. The risk of damage to such a line, leading to an environmental catastrophe, would be considerable.

Existing oil pipelines, meanwhile, continued to be used. The main western pipeline, which after upgrading was capable of transporting 310,000 b/d, ran 3,000 km from Atyrau to Samara (in the Volga region of Russia). The Kenkiyak–Omsk pipeline (of some 400 km) carried petroleum from the Aktyubinsk fields to a Siberian refinery.

Kazakhstan was also eager to diversify gas export routes. In 2007 the construction of a Kazakhstan–China gas pipeline was announced, with a scheduled completion date of 2010 being tentatively offered. Construction work commenced in the Almaty region of Kazakhstan in July 2008, with Kazakhstani and Chinese companies as co-project contractors. Meanwhile, KazTransGaz was to lay the 1,510 km Beyneu–Akbulak pipeline, with a first-phase capacity of 5,000m. cu m annually by mid-2011, and full capacity of 10,000m. cu m per year from 2014. It was planned that this would eventually link up with the Turkmenistan–China trans-Asian gas pipeline (see below).

Concurrently, another gas pipeline project was agreed between Kazakhstan, Russia and Turkmenistan. This envisaged the upgrading and additional construction of connecting sections of a pipeline that would run along the Caspian coast from Turkmenistan to Kazakhstan to link into the existing Central Asia-Centre pipeline to Russia. Uzbekistan would eventually join this network. This would allow Russia to increase imports of Central Asian gas, which currently amount to around 50,000m. cu m–90,000m. cu m per annum.

Turkmenistan

In the 1990s the main customers for Turkmenistani gas were other members of the CIS, such as Armenia, Azerbaijan, Georgia and Ukraine. However, these countries were unable to meet payments and fell deeply into arrears. By the end of 1995 Turkmenistan was owed a little under US $2,000m., and the establishment of export outlets to Europe, the Middle East and South Asia became a priority. Several projects were under consideration in the late 2000s, but most proposals were long term, with limited hope of implementation in the near future. The most promising development was a tripartite agreement with Kazakhstan and Russia, concluded in May 2007, which offered real and fairly rapid prospects for increasing Turkmenistan's gas export potential. It seemed probable that if this project was successfully completed, then it would reduce still further the likelihood of other pipeline projects being realized.

Turkmenistan–Iran–Turkey–Western Europe: This was the Turkmenistani Government's favoured option for an export route. In 1994 financing for the first segment of a 1,400-km gas pipeline was secured, and construction commenced. The Turkmenistan–Iran section (from Korpeje in western Turkmenistan to Kord Koy in northern Iran) became operational in December 1997. Originally, it had an annual capacity of 8,000m. cu m, but this was later upgraded to 12,400m. cu m–14,000m. cu m. In June 2007, according to official Turkmenistani sources, some 4,125m. cu m were exported via this route, an increase of 112% compared with the previous year. A second, and smaller Turkmenistan–Iran pipeline, from Artyk to Luftbud, was inaugurated in 2000, with a capacity of less than 1,000m. cu m. Some of the gas that Turkmenistan has been exporting to Iran—reportedly, some 8,000m. cu m of the total in 2006—is liquefied. The USA was initially opposed to an extension of this pipeline to Turkey and Europe, because of Iran's involvement, but abandoned its objections in mid-1997. The project aroused international interest, with companies such as Royal Dutch/Shell and the French company Sofregaz bidding for the construction contract. By 2006 no work had been undertaken, and the project was effectively moribund; in 2007 it seemed possible that the project might be revived, but by 2008 no firm progress had been made.

Trans-Asian Pipeline: Turkmenistan–People's Republic of China: In 1992 the Mitsubishi Corporation (of Japan) and CNPC began to undertake feasibility studies regarding the construction of a trans-Asian gas pipeline. In August 1995 they were joined by Esso China, a unit of Exxon Corporation (now ExxonMobil Corporation) of the USA. The intention was that the gas pipeline would terminate at a port on the Yellow Sea, with the possibility of subsequent shipment to Japan and, perhaps, South Korea. In early 1997 it was announced that Mitsubishi had formed a consortium, with Exxon and CNPC, to develop a pilot project for the trans-Asian gas pipeline, to connect gas fields in Uzbekistan and Turkmenistan with China's Pacific coast, via Kazakhstan and mainland China (with an estimated length of 6,130 km, and at an estimated cost of US $9,500m.). The project was technically viable, but the distance and difficult geographic conditions made it extremely costly and therefore unlikely to be realized in the short term.

A further attempt to construct a gas pipeline from Turkmenistan to China was launched in April 2006, when President Niyazov visited Beijing. While there, he signed an agreement with President Hu on the supply of Turkmenistani gas to China. It was expected that this would come from as yet undeveloped deposits near the Amu Dar'ya river. A Chinese-Turkmenistani working group was set up to conduct feasibility studies on the joint development of these deposits, and also on

the construction of a gas pipeline from Turkmenistan to western China, by way of Uzbekistan and Kazakhstan. In July 2007, during the visit of President Berdymuhamedov, Niyazov's successor, to China, CNPC signed a PSA with the Turkmenistani Government to develop the Bagtyyarlyk territory in the east of the country, on the right bank of the Amu Dar'ya; estimated reserves of natural gas at the site amounted to 1,700,000m. cu m. In the following month Berdymuhamedov inaugurated the construction of a trans-Asian gas pipeline to China; scheduled for completion in 2009, initially it would deliver 30,000m. cu m per year of Turkmenistani gas to Urumchi (Xinjiang). A second stage of the project would boost capacity to 50,000m. cu m per year by 2010. The total length of the projected pipeline was 7,000 km, but only some 190 km would cross Turkmenistan; thereafter it would run via Uzbekistan and Kazakhstan to China, where it would feed into the domestic network. In 2008 development of the Samandepe field (on the right bank of the Amu Dar'ya) was already under way. This would be the starting point of the Turkmenistan–Uzbekistan–Kazakhstan–China line. In June CNPC began construction of a gas-purification plant, with an annual capacity of 5,000m. cu m, to prepare gas for pumping into the new pipeline. Construction work on the pipeline was proceeding according to schedule.

Turkmenistan–Afghanistan–Pakistan: In May 1997 the US petroleum company Unocal and its strategic partner, the Saudi Arabian company Delta Nimir, signed a memorandum of agreement with the Turkmenistani Government, regarding projects for the construction of oil and gas pipelines from Turkmenistan's eastern gas fields to Pakistan, via Afghanistan (the estimated length of the pipeline was 1,043 km, and its estimated cost was US $1,900m.), with a possible extension to India. Bridas, which had previously put forward a similar proposal, continued to make preliminary preparations for construction, in the hope of participating in the project. However, distance, terrain, climatic conditions and, above all, the chronic instability in the region, made this route seem impractical. In 2002, however, following the US-led military intervention in Afghanistan from October 2001, and the collapse of that country's Taliban regime, hopes for a more peaceful and prosperous future began to revive. Consequently, there was renewed interest in the proposed pipeline. At a meeting held in Islamabad, Pakistan, in May 2002, the Presidents of Afghanistan, Pakistan and Turkmenistan agreed to pursue the project, and in July the Asian Development Bank provided funding for a feasibility study. In 2005 the project gained new impetus, and plans for implementing it were under active discussion. It was anticipated that construction would begin once agreement had been reached on the legal framework. However, at 2008 the matter was still pending.

Turkmenistan–Azerbaijan–Georgia–Turkey: In August 1999 Royal Dutch/Shell joined a consortium to build a Trans-Caspian Gas Pipeline under the Sea, from Turkmenistan to Azerbaijan, and on to Turkey. The company became a 'strategic partner' of Turkmenistan in developing the various gas deposits that were to be the main source of supply for the pipeline. On the eve of the signing ceremony, which took place in November, the President of SOCAR indicated that, although Azerbaijan was prepared to act as a transit country for Turkmenistani gas in the initial stages, in the longer term provision must also be made for the export of Azerbaijani gas via this route. This view was prompted by the fact that Azerbaijan had recently discovered substantial gas reserves in the offshore Caspian waters of Shah Deniz and expected to become a major exporter in its own right within a few years. In 2000 negotiations over how the pipeline's anticipated annual throughput should be divided resulted in serious disagreements between Azerbaijan and Turkmenistan. In February 2003 it was announced that work was to begin in 2004 on the construction of the 690-km pipeline from Baku via Tbilisi (Georgia) to Erzurum (Turkey), and the Trans-Caspian Gas Pipeline project was postponed indefinitely in March 2003, when Royal Dutch/Shell decided to reduce its activities in Turkmenistan. In 2007 there were hopes that the new Turkmenistani President,

Gurbanguly Berdymuhamedov, might revitalize the project, but by 2008 no firm commitment had been forthcoming (see above).

ENVIRONMENTAL PROBLEMS

Towards the end of the 1990s environmental problems in the Caspian basin began to attract increasing attention. Since the middle of the 20th century, and more particularly since the 1990s, the intensive economic exploitation of the Caspian Sea and adjacent coastal regions has resulted in serious environmental degradation. The socio-economic impact has also been very considerable, lowering standards of living and jeopardizing the quality of life of local communities. The worst problem is land-based pollution, which contaminates land, air and groundwater, and enters the Sea through waste water that is discharged either into the rivers that flow into the Sea, or directly into the Sea. The most severely contaminated areas are in the northern Caspian, which is bordered by densely populated, industrialized regions. The chief culprits are the heavy-industrial and military-industrial plants that are located within the catchment area of the Volga and discharge substantial quantities of hazardous pollutants, such as heavy metals and phenols. Further south, in Azerbaijan, industry (especially decaying Soviet-era equipment) is responsible for high levels of soil, air and water pollution in and around Baku and Sumqayıt. Pollution has also been responsible for the introduction of aggressive alien organisms into the Sea, some of which resulted in a depletion of the oxygen content of the water, thereby creating 'dead zones' in the Sea. Another dangerous new intruder was a tiny jellyfish, *Mnemiopsis leidyi*, probably introduced into the Caspian Sea in ballast water. It reproduces at an exponential rate. A voracious feeder, it devours zooplankton, the mainstay of the diet of the small fish that are in turn consumed by larger predators such as sturgeon and seal. The effect on the fishing industry was devastating; by mid-2001 hauls of some fish had reduced by one-half. Research on ways of eliminating these unwanted species without causing more harm to the environment was in progress.

The Caspian Sea is home to over 100 species of fish, some of which are unique to this habitat. Around 20 types of fish are harvested commercially, the most valuable being caviar-bearing sturgeon, and sprat and herring. Prior to the collapse of the USSR, the Caspian Sea had been the source of some 95% of the world's supply of caviar. In the 1990s, however, economic and social problems in the successor states had a highly detrimental impact on the sturgeon fishery. Private entrepreneurs were eager to maximize their profits, and this led to massive over-harvesting. There was also a dramatic growth in poaching, as heavily armed criminal groups established a hold on the profitable caviar trade. In 2001 the official retail price for caviar was US $2,000 per kg; the 'black' (unofficial) market price in Baku or Moscow was between $20 and $70 per kg. In just two decades, from the late 1970s to the late 1990s, officially recorded sturgeon catches declined rapidly from 30,000 metric tons to less than one-10th of that amount. The pressure on sturgeon stocks was further heightened by increasing levels of pollution. By the end of the decade there were fears that the sturgeon population had fallen below a sustainable level and that it was on the way to extinction. In response to this situation, in April 1998 the Convention on International Trade in Endangered Species of Wild Fauna and Flora (CITES) introduced strict controls for all species of sturgeon, requiring, among other things, the introduction of export permits and labelling of products. At a meeting of CITES held in Paris, France, in June 2001, Azerbaijan, Kazakhstan and Russia agreed to a voluntary moratorium on sturgeon-fishing in the Caspian for the rest of the year. Iran was not subject to these restrictions as it already had an effective management programme in place. Although Turkmenistan was not represented at the meeting, it was required to adhere to the agreement or would be subject to the prohibition of its caviar exports. Fixed export quotas were set for all five littoral states. Additionally, the former Soviet republics were required to establish a survey and management programme for the sturgeon fisheries, to regulate domestic trade, to implement a caviar-labelling sys-

tem and to increase efforts to combat poaching and illegal trade. By March 2002 they were considered to have fulfilled these undertakings so successfully that CITES lifted the ban on sturgeon-fishing. These figures were disputed by independent environmentalists, who believed that the sturgeon population had in fact declined, and that the beluga should be placed on the endangered-species list. In August 2003 Kazakhstan became the first littoral state to agree to the tagging of infant beluga, in order to monitor the survival rate. In 2006 it was reported that sturgeon numbers in the Caspian Sea were at their lowest recorded level. In April CITES gave Iran approval to export caviar (up to 44,370 kg), as the Persian sturgeon was the only species of the fish that was surviving reasonably well. However, a temporary suspension of caviar exports from Azerbaijan, Kazakhstan, Russia and Turkmenistan was imposed in order to protect other varieties of the endangered fish. In January 2007 CITES lifted the ban, though some restrictions were maintained. The Caspian states jointly agreed to reduce the catch quota for Beluga caviar by 29% compared with 2005 (the last year for which quotas had been approved), thereby agreeing to respect a combined export limit of 3,761 kg for the year.

The decline in Caspian fish stocks has taken place over a long period. The sudden death of thousands of seals in 2000 was, however, an unexpected development. The mammal (*Phoca caspica*), which winters along the northern coast on the exposed ice rim, is unique to the Caspian Sea. It takes eight years to become fully mature and can live for 50 years. Kazakhstani environmentalists blamed the petroleum industry for the seal deaths, but scientists believed cumulative poisoning by toxic elements, such as mercury, to be a more likely cause. Further seal deaths were reported in 2001; some 5,000 dead seals were washed ashore in Azerbaijan alone. In May 2006, once again, hundreds of sturgeon and seals were found dead on the shores of the Caspian Sea, this time near Kazakhstan's Kalamkas oilfield (under development by a consortium that included ENI, ConocoPhillips, ExxonMobil, Royal Dutch/Shell and Total). The suspected cause of the disaster was leaked crude petroleum. In early 2007 there was another spate of seal deaths; by June, some 1,000 dead seals had been found along the Kazakh coastline. Laboratory tests identified a form of canine distemper as the probable cause of death.

The Caspian littoral states made institutional and organizational progress towards the formulation of a joint approach to these problems with the signing in Kazakhstan of the Almaty Declaration on Environmental Co-operation in May 1994. The launching of the Caspian Environment Programme in May 1998, funded by the Global Environmental Facility and the EU, with additional support from the private sector, institutionalized a multi-sectoral plan of action to address environmental and bio-resource issues. In 1998–2002 transboundary analytical studies were produced, as well as strategic action programmes. The Convention on the Environmental Protection of the Caspian Sea was signed in November 2003 in Tehran. This historic document—the first post-Soviet agreement to which all the littoral states acceded—set legally binding rules for environmental good conduct. It was envisaged that this Convention would be fully incorporated into the eventual final treaty on the legal status of the Sea.

SECURITY CONCERNS

A disturbing development at the end of the 1990s was the militarization of the Sea. When the USSR disintegrated, the Soviet Caspian flotilla was divided equally between the four successor littoral states. Azerbaijan used its portion of the force as the basis for the development of an independent navy, but Kazakhstan and Turkmenistan ceded their shares to Russia, to operate as a joint flotilla under Russian command. Subsequently, Kazakhstan and Turkmenistan also began to develop independent capabilities. During the 1990s Azerbaijan, Kazakhstan and Turkmenistan received foreign military aid, in the form of equipment and training, to build up their naval strength. The modernization and upgrading of the Azerbaijani army and navy was carried out with assistance from Turkey and the USA. In 1993 Azerbaijan (along with

Armenia) had been put on the USA's list of proscribed destinations for munitions. In March 2002, however, this ban was lifted. Kazakhstan made initial progress towards the creation of a navy in 1998, when a rapid reaction force was established to protect the section of the Sea that fell within its national territory. In October 1999 President Niyazov of Turkmenistan decreed the establishment of a 'national service' for the development of his country's sector of the Caspian Sea—a sector that, the decree proclaimed, was 'an inalienable part of Turkmenistan'. In 2001, however, both Azerbaijan and Turkmenistan purchased speedboats from the USA in order to patrol the Caspian. Turkmenistan purchased 20 additional boats from Ukraine, including 40-metric-ton vessels capable of carrying large calibre guns. Meanwhile, Iran and Russia were also reinforcing their Caspian fleets.

The first military clash in the Caspian Sea in the post-Soviet period occurred in July 2001, when Iran initiated a confrontation with two Azerbaijani boats. The vessels, on lease to BP, were in a part of the Sea that was disputed by Azerbaijan and Iran; they were evicted from the area by an armed Iranian patrol boat, supported by military aircraft, prompting BP to suspend its petroleum exploration activities in the southern Caspian. Azerbaijan angrily denounced Iran's action. Coincidentally, in August the Turkish air force staged a display over Baku; the event had allegedly been planned a year in advance, but the timing implied Turkish readiness to defend Azerbaijani interests. High-level diplomacy between Azerbaijan and Iran in the following weeks helped to defuse the tension, and good relations were soon restored. However, concerns remained that such incidents might be repeated in the future unless the littoral states co-operated more closely. Meanwhile, the Kazakhstani Ministry of Defence announced plans to establish a Higher Naval School at Aktau.

At the beginning of August 2002 Russia staged large-scale military exercises in the Caspian, designed to demonstrate Russia's ability to combat such threats as terrorism and large-scale poaching. Azerbaijan and Kazakhstan also took part in the operations; Iran sent observers, but Turkmenistan declined to participate, citing its declared stance of neutrality. The Russian Minister of Defence, Sergei Ivanov, indicated that Russia might establish a permanent military force in the region to guarantee stability. In July 2005 President Putin reiterated Russia's readiness to work with the other Caspian littoral states to combat terrorism and drugs-trafficking. Russian officials proposed the establishment of a naval task force, similar to the Black Sea Force Group. It was envisaged that Russia's Caspian Sea flotilla, which was based in Astrakhan and comprised two frigates, 12 patrol ships and a number of smaller vessels, would play a major role in any such regional structure. Iran supported the initiative, acknowledging the need for a rapid reaction force in the Caspian. In January 2006 Ivanov stated that the proposed force would comprise members of defence ministries, border guards and special services. Its tasks would include protecting the Caspian countries from weapons proliferation, poaching and piracy, as well as ensuring the safety of energy supplies. He did not regard as yet unresolved border issues (notably in the southern Caspian) as an obstacle to the establishment of such a force. In 2007 Kazakhstan announced that it was developing a new concept for its navy, aimed at protecting its Caspian Sea strategic facilities. The programme of re-equipping the fleet and improving coastal infrastructure would be implemented in three phases, from 2007 to 2025. Plans for improving operations to combat sturgeon-poaching were also disclosed.

REGIONAL POLITICS

In the early 2000s the most obvious cause for concern in the Caspian basin was the war in Chechnya. Despite the destruction of Groznyi and the great loss of human life, neither the Chechens, intent on full independence, nor the Russian Government, determined to preserve the integrity of the Russian Federation, were prepared to contemplate compromise solutions. The desire to secure control over the export pipeline, with the economic and political power that it would give, was undoubtedly a major factor in the struggle. Conditions in the Republics of Dagestan and Kalmykiya, and in Astrakhan

Oblast, the other territories of the Russian Federation that bordered the Caspian Sea, were more stable, although the two Republics were among the most impoverished regions of Russia.

In 2003, following months of failing health, President Heydar Aliyev of Azerbaijan was replaced by his son, İlham, several weeks before his death. However, the dispute with Armenia over Nagornyi Karabakh had still not been resolved, and relations remained tense. In Georgia, a transit country, the situation was also fragile, and in the early 2000s the conflict with the separatist 'Republic of Abkhazia' remained an ongoing matter of concern. However, it was an internal uprising that forced President Eduard Shevardnadze from office, after alleged electoral malpractice by elements of the incumbent Government at legislative elections held in November 2003 prompted large-scale, although peaceful, public protests. In January 2004 Mikheil Saakashvili, a US-educated lawyer who had been a prominent leader of the so-called 'rose revolution', was elected President by a substantial majority. On 8 August 2008, coinciding with the inauguration of the Summer Olympic Games in Beijing, Georgia launched a military offensive in the separatist republic of South Ossetia. Russia immediately came to the aid of the Ossetians and, after a brief but brutal conflict, decisively routed the Georgian forces, prompting fears in the West that Russia's real motive was to disrupt oil supplies via the BTC pipeline. Russia denied this, but the regional situation remained tense and unpredictable.

In Kazakhstan, President Nazarbayev was still firmly in control. In May 2007 a constitutional amendment abolished restrictions on the number of terms that he could serve, thus effectively allowing him to stay in office for as long as he wished. In Turkmenistan, after the death of the long-serving leader Saparmyrat Niyazov in December 2006, Gurbanguly Berdymuhamedov was elected to the presidency in February 2007. Some in the West had expected that Azerbaijan, Kazakhstan and Turkmenistan, like Georgia, would want to reduce their ties with Russia; however, despite diversifying their foreign trade and diplomatic relations, all, in fact, maintained cordial relations with Russia. Kazakhstan in particular, which shares a long border with Russia, had important economic and defence links.

Iran maintained good relations with all the littoral states. Some Western analysts had initially feared that Iran would attempt to spread Islamist extremism throughout the Caspian basin. However, there was little evidence of this, and Iranian activities from the 1990s were directed primarily towards economic co-operation and the establishment of cultural contacts. The Caspian Sea Co-operation Zone (CSCZ), which included all five littoral states, was created, on Iran's initiative, in February 1992. Its aim was to provide a forum for the discussion of matters of common interest. However, the CSCZ did not succeed in playing a leading role regarding the delimitation of the Sea, nor was it actively involved in negotiations concerning the exploitation of the Sea's hydrocarbons resources. The CSCZ gradually ceded its role to the Economic Co-operation Organization, which includes a wider grouping of regional states (members comprise the former Soviet Central Asian states, Afghanistan, Azerbaijan, Iran, Pakistan and Turkey, but not Russia).

OUTLOOK

By 2008 the political and economic outlook for the Caspian basin was relatively promising. Major projects for the extraction and export of hydrocarbons were well under way. There was as yet no comprehensive treaty on the legal status of the Sea, but steady progress was being made towards the resolution of areas under dispute. The littoral states had jointly reached agreement on over 80% of the outstanding issues. In the northern part, Azerbaijan, Kazakhstan and Russia had concluded a trilateral agreement on the delimitation of the seabed. In the southern part, Azerbaijan, Iran and Turkmenistan were still in negotiation over inter-state boundaries, but seemed to be moving towards an agreement. Environmental problems continued to cause serious concern, but the 2003 Convention on the Environmental Protection of the Caspian Sea was a major achievement. This historic document, which set legally binding rules for environmental good conduct, was the first post-Soviet agreement to which all the Caspian states acceded. There was also progress on the creation of export facilities. The completion of the CPC and BTC pipelines meant that the short- and intermediate-term needs of petroleum producers were being met. In the longer term, other routes would be needed, such as the oil transit pipeline from Kazakhstan to China. Projects for other routes had been temporarily suspended, but it was widely anticipated that some of them (for example, from Kazakhstan to Iran) would be implemented in the future. Construction of a gas pipeline from Baku to Erzurum (the South Caucasus pipeline), running parallel to the BTC pipeline, commenced in 2003 and was completed in 2007. A gas pipeline from Turkmenistan to Iran was launched in 1997. The tripartite Kazakhstan–Russia–Turkmenistan Caspian gas pipeline project, announced in May 2007, seemed likely to be realized in a fairly short time. In 2008 a gas pipeline from Turkmenistan to China was under construction. Other pipeline projects (for example, via Afghanistan) were still under consideration, but had not progressed beyond feasibility studies. The domestic political situation in the littoral states was reasonably calm and stable. The business environment remained difficult; in particular, there was concern about the high levels of corruption in the new littoral states, despite efforts by national governments and international agencies to address this issue. Another concern was growing resource nationalism. In Kazakhstan in particular, this was resulting in legislation to increase government control over hydrocarbons projects and to squeeze the profit margins of foreign companies. Regional relations were still vulnerable, complicated by economic rivalry and—to a greater extent than had previously been the case—by military might. The conflict in Georgia in 2008 emphasized the fragility of the situation, demonstrating how rapidly local disputes could escalate into major military confrontation. Nevertheless, bilateral and multilateral co-operation was increasing, and overall, in comparison with other petroleum-rich regions of the world (for example, the Middle East, Latin America and West Africa), the Caspian basin remained relatively stable.

ENVIRONMENTAL DEGRADATION: PAST ROOTS, PRESENT TRANSITION AND FUTURE HOPES

Prof. ALEH CHERP and Prof. RUBEN MNATSAKANIAN

INTRODUCTION

The reforms of the Soviet system in the late 1980s were closely associated with environmental concerns. Politicians widely used environmental issues to challenge the existing political order and demand independence for the newly emerging nations. The old system, which was felt to be ineffective and unconcerned with public opinion, was considered to be the main cause of the widespread environmental degradation. Naturally, there were abundant hopes that the reforms would deliver environmental improvements almost immediately.

As with many other expectations, this one was not entirely fulfilled. Almost two decades later, reports of environmental problems abound and positive news is rare. In order to explain why it has proved increasingly difficult to tackle environmental problems in post-Soviet countries, this essay first examines some of their root causes, before evaluating the extent to which recent developments have been able to reverse them.

The authors argue that the interaction between people and the environment in northern Eurasia has always been of a specific character, distorted, but not radically altered, by socialism. The post-socialist transition provided many opportunities for environmental improvement, but also posed grave threats to the environment. Although the existing situation may not be as bleak as is often portrayed by the media, tremendous efforts will be required to ensure that environmental policies and management conform to international standards and protect the unique ecosystems of this part of the world.

The essay is divided into two principal parts: the first part deals with the historic roots of the existing environmental situation—in particular, the environmental legacy of the Soviet era; the second considers how the recent changes have influenced the nature of environmental risks and opportunities.

THE ENVIRONMENTAL LEGACY

The countries of the former USSR are located in northern Eurasia, which, with its harsh climate and natural conditions, has historically determined specific patterns of human settlement and activity. Vast swathes of land were unable to sustain a considerable human population and remained untouched well into the 20th century, and even beyond. Many of these tracts are home to fragile, unique ecosystems, for example, permafrost taiga (marshy, predominantly pine forest) and tundra (permafrost plains and wetlands), Lake Baikal in Eastern Siberia, and the steppe (dry grasslands). In large areas, such as the steppe of Central Asia and Southern Siberia, or tundra, only nomadic pastoral agriculture was possible, which did not encourage the creation of stable human settlements. In other territories, such as European Russia, Belarus and Ukraine, agriculture was high-risk, owing to the harsh winter climate and the short and unstable summer. At the same time, this vast territory holds a remarkable diversity and wealth of landscapes, ecosystems and minerals. Russian taiga contains roughly one-half of the world's boreal forests. The major rivers—Dniepr (Dnieper), Volga, Ob, Irtysh, Yenisei, Lena, Angara and Amur—have total annual flow that rivals that of all the other great rivers of the world. Even by the early 20th century the Apsheron Peninsula in Azerbaijan produced more than one-half of the world's petroleum, while the Caspian Sea has historically provided more than 90% of sturgeon and black caviar globally. If reserves of gas and coal, iron, magnesium, manganese, bauxite (aluminium), gold and platinum, and other ores and minerals are also taken into consideration, it is easy to claim that Russia and the USSR owned one of the greatest stocks of natural resources in the world. However, many of these abundant mineral resources could not be used until modern times because they required industrial means to extract and transport them to population and production centres.

Until the early 20th century much productive land, especially in the European part of the Russian Empire, was found in large estates and most of the rest in communal village property, the latter ensuring the survival of families in areas where there was a high risk of crop failure. The institution of private land ownership did not extend beyond a very narrow circle of noble landowners in European Russia, and was even less developed in the more traditional societies of Siberia and Central Asia. Most mineral resources were controlled and exploited by the state. Thus, for the majority of the population, the idea of privately owned agricultural or forested land was neither familiar nor particularly attractive. This attitude was reinforced by a strong dependence on foraging (for mushrooms, berries, fish, game, firewood and construction timber) and on the freely accessible forests and rivers for day-to-day food requirements.

Surrounded by vast territories of uncultivated land, people often perceived these as being of marginal value, representing 'wild nature', which had to be 'conquered' or 'tamed'. The Muscovite state further encouraged this 'frontier mentality' by promoting expansion into new areas: through the settlement of Siberia from the 16th century; the conquest of Central Asia and the Caucasus in the 19th century; the agrarian reforms of Prime Minister Petr Stolypin (1906–11), which encouraged the rural population to migrate from Central European Russia to Siberia and Central Asia; the ploughing of Kazakhstan's 'Virgin Lands' in the 1950s; the drainage of wetlands in the Polesie region of Belarus in 1966–90; and the vast irrigation projects to facilitate cotton production in Central Asia in the 1960s and 1970s.

Shortly after the Bolshevik Revolution of 1917, the Soviet Government became preoccupied with modernization and industrialization, with the aim of ending the economic underdevelopment of Russia. The notorious way in which the environment was treated during this period can be partially explained by the Bolsheviks' interpretation of Marxism, emphasizing the so-called labour theory of value, which claimed that undeveloped land has no economic worth.

The industrialization of the USSR was led by the highly centralized state bureaucracy and primarily reflected the interests of this bureaucracy, with little regard for local concerns. For example, in the 1960s, during the assessment of the ambitious plans to develop large-scale irrigation schemes in Central Asia in order to facilitate cotton production, it was noted that the Aral Sea (covering Kazakh and Uzbek territory) was likely to become desiccated. Although this enormous inland water body provided fish and other means of subsistence to large coastal communities, in national terms the cultivation of cotton in the region was deemed to be more important than the maintenance of the local fishing industry, given that fish could be obtained elsewhere in the USSR. Therefore, it was decided to proceed with the irrigation plans, compensating local communities by shipping fish from the Arctic and the Far East for processing. The end result was one of the largest anthropogenic environmental disasters of the 20th century, which inflicted tremendous suffering on former coastal inhabitants. Furthermore, the overall objectives of modernization were ideologically justified and, thus, often not subject to pragmatic analysis at all.

The inability of the state to halt environmental deterioration was further determined by its traditional suspicion of foreign 'capitalist' ideas. Environmental pollution was often considered to be purely a 'capitalist' problem, the existence of which was simply not possible in a well-functioning socialist society. This resulted in an unwillingness to learn from the experience of Western countries, and justified only marginal participation by the USSR in international environmental agreements.

At the same time, certain unique streams of thought directed some environmental efforts in Soviet Russia. The Bolsheviks, with their 'scientific' approach to social development, sought to recruit scientists to various government bodies. One of these scientists, Vladimir Vernadskii, led a government committee that sought to identify natural and other resources that could facilitate economic development. In the 1920s and 1930s Vernadskii developed the theory of the 'noosphere', based on the idea that humankind was becoming a 'geological force', transforming the earth into a system in which natural and anthropogenic factors would become equally important. A number of other scientists argued for the protection of certain ecosystems and landscapes for recreational, economic and scientific purposes. As a result, the USSR pioneered a unique network of nature protection reserves or *zapovedniky*. These were strictly protected territories, with largely undisturbed natural ecosystems useful for scientific observations.

However, the overall record of the USSR in creating viable environmental protection institutions was very poor. At the heart of the problem was the sector-based organization of the centrally planned economy, and the lack of checks and balances in the central government. The Soviet economy was managed by about 50 specialized ministries, each of which held an absolute monopoly within a particular branch of industry or agriculture. Any enterprise directly reporting to one of these ministries in the Russian and Soviet capital, Moscow, had little or no incentive to co-operate with local government or to consider local needs, including those relating to the environment.

Another important factor was the very high degree of militarization of the Soviet economy (Smith and Moomaw, 2000). In the military-industrial sector, production objectives had to be achieved without regard for the environmental, health or even economic consequences. Disregard for the environment and human health was reinforced by a system in which a significant proportion of the economy was operated by forced labour, through the infamous GULag (State Corrective Camps) system of the 1930s, 1940s and 1950s.

The Government tended to consider the environment as an industrial sector, and manage it through specialized authorities (for example, the Committee for Water Works, the Main Hunting Authority, the Ministry of Fisheries, the Committee for Meteorology—also responsible for air and water quality—etc.). The widely accepted myth that socialism was incompatible with environmental problems explains the absence of an overarching Ministry of the Environment, which could have co-ordinated these diverse functions. However, although such agencies were able to achieve certain results within their own 'sectors' (for example, by ensuring the protection of game or fish from poaching), they had no mandate to influence other ministries and sectors.

The problem was exacerbated by the lack of accountability in central government, where the Central Committee of the Communist Party was simultaneously responsible for all functions of society. Whenever any conflict of interest arose between the environment and development, the non-transparent, informal policy process would almost always result in economic interests prevailing, except in such plainly catastrophic situations as the accident at the Chornobyl (Chernobyl) nuclear reactor in Ukraine in April 1986. The lack of participatory decision-making procedures, the disregard for public opinion and the reliance on Moscow-based experts to evaluate problems added to the anti-environmental bias of most economic decisions.

Another environmentally important institutional factor was the lack of innovation under the centrally planned economy. It was easier for the state to operate large, stable enterprises, with constant levels of inputs and outputs. For example, in the Urals, until the mid-1990s several factories were still working with equipment received in reparations from Germany after the Second World War (1939–45). Thus, the introduction of any progressive, environmentally clean technologies or management practices was extremely rare in the USSR.

At the same time, it would be inaccurate to state that the environment was entirely disregarded in industrial and agricultural activities. The Soviet system attempted to deal with it by imposing planning and design rules, and co-ordination procedures, by means of which new developments were required to satisfy minimum environmental and public health criteria. Many of these rules are still in operation in post-Soviet countries.

Thus, the Soviet economy created a specific and unique pattern of environmental degradation. However, both positive and negative features of the Soviet environmental legacy can be identified.

The first feature, noted by many researchers, is the unique spatial pattern of environmental conditions. In some ecological disaster zones environmental degradation was quite unprecedented. High levels of water and air pollution were combined with the destruction of the landscape and ecosystems, and a deterioration in the local economy and in health. Notorious examples of environmental disaster zones include: the Aral Sea area; the areas surrounding the former Semipalatinsk nuclear test site in northern Kazakhstan; the areas around Norilsk in northern Siberia (Russia); industrial zones in the Kola Peninsula (north-western Russia) and the southern Urals (Russia); the Donbas region of south-eastern Ukraine; and the Sarasiya valley in Uzbekistan (Mnatsakanian, 1992).

At the same time, post-Soviet countries feature large areas where ecosystems are relatively intact. In some regions biodiversity is well protected, owing to lower population densities and restrictions on personal movement. The approach to biodiversity protection in the USSR benefited from the fact that the country retained sufficiently vast, and relatively untouched, ecosystems. The biodiversity protection areas of post-Soviet countries include: the unique wetlands of Belarus; beech and pine forests and alpine meadows in the northern Caucasus; vast areas of primary forest in northern and central Russia; untouched steppe at Askaniya-Nova in Ukraine; the Volga river delta in the Caspian Sea; the Lena river delta in northern Siberia; and Lake Baikal, the world's largest freshwater body (Pryde, 1995). There are also significant areas of relatively unspoiled countryside and traditional land use patterns.

The most notorious feature of the Soviet environmental legacy was the oversized heavy, especially military, industry, which resulted in tremendous environmental pressures. Another widely publicized environmental issue was the wastefulness of the socialist production processes, which resulted in one of the most intense levels of energy usage in the world. The centrally planned economy provided little or no incentive to conserve energy or raw materials or to minimize waste, with the result that the USSR 'generated waste on the scale of a highly industrialized country, but dealt with it in a fashion appropriate for a Third World nation' (Peterson, 1993).

Although the USSR largely managed to cope with most public health issues typical of low-income societies, the environmental issues encountered by the post-Soviet countries combine characteristics of both developed and developing countries. For example, some regions in Europe and the Urals are struggling to find appropriate methods for the disposal of radioactive waste, chemical weapons and extremely toxic missile fuel, whereas in many areas of Central Asia the predominant problem is that of providing a basic rural water supply and sanitation.

A number of urban environmental issues were caused by the pattern of urbanization in this part of the world. Cities in Russia were almost never self-governed centres of trade, crafts and entrepreneurship, but instead performed the role of military outposts and factory towns. The rapid industrialization of the first half of the 20th century strengthened this pattern. Soviet towns were typically provided with reasonable infrastructure and were free from slums. At the same time, the rapidly constructed cities provided bleak urban landscapes, dominated by concrete high-rise buildings and the almost ubiquitous pollution-emitting smokestacks of industrial facilities.

On the positive side, levels of consumer waste and motor vehicle congestion were lower in the USSR than in most developed countries. Priority was given to the development of public means of transportation, and private car-ownership was regarded as an unnecessary luxury. Systems for collecting, recycling and reusing consumer waste were also relatively well developed.

In summary, socialism left a mixed environmental legacy, unevenly distributed between the regions and successor states of the USSR. The roots of the most prominent environmental issues can be traced far back to the history of the Soviet state and beyond, and linked to specific interaction between the environment and society in the 'first developing country', stretching across the tundra, forests, steppe and deserts of northern Eurasia.

THE ENVIRONMENT AND TRANSITION

At the beginning of the reform process, popular opinion was sensitized to environmental problems, and closely associated these with the economic and political failures of socialism. Such high-profile events as the Chornobyl disaster served as a catalyst, encouraging the popular belief that the socialist system was unable to ensure environmental safety. Observing the relatively cleaner environment in the West led the majority to assume that free market and democratic reforms would deliver environmental improvements almost as a matter of course.

In the early reform period many environmental activists or individuals with 'green' programmes were elected to the first democratic parliaments of the countries of the region. Ministries tasked specifically with resolving environmental issues were created in all of the Soviet successor states. Environmental clauses were included in newly written constitutions, and framework laws on the environment were enacted. Many of the newly independent states participated in the Earth Summit, held in Rio de Janeiro, Brazil, in 1992, and enthusiastically joined the international environmental agreements developed during the 1990s. In particular, the newly independent states, especially Armenia, Georgia, Moldova and Ukraine, took part in the UN Economic Commission for Europe's (ECE) 'Environment for Europe' process (with its fifth Ministerial Meeting taking place in Kyiv, Ukraine, in 2003). As part of the framework for this process, the condition of the environment in the region was properly assessed, and National Environmental Action Plans (NEAPs) were drawn up.

However, it soon became clear that legitimization of environmental discourse and popular enthusiasm for environmental protection were, in themselves, insufficient to create viable institutions able to tackle the systemic causes of environmental degradation, as well as newly emerging threats. Many of the newly independent states were either politically unstable or found it very difficult to establish viable national institutions when confronted with political and economic challenges. The environment had soon almost disappeared from political agendas, and environmental activism declined, hastened by the rise of authoritarian tendencies.

Environmental protection agencies and laws created in the 1990s secured some degree of environmental monitoring of economic activities, the basics of the 'Polluter Pays Principle', as well as certain elements of public participation and access to environmental information. However, on the whole, they proved to be only marginally effective. In many of the USSR's successor states environmental regulations throughout the 1990s and the early 2000s failed to challenge the systemic causes of environmental degradation associated with the lack of integration of environmental concerns into economic decision-making, being largely based on Soviet concepts. Environmental protection institutions were further weakened by the corruption characteristic of the post-Soviet states. As a result, by 2002 the Environmental Sustainability Index (ESI), designed by the World Economic Forum, ranked the Commonwealth of Independent States (CIS) countries much lower than the countries of Central and South-Eastern Europe, in terms of their institutional capacity to ensure environmental sustainability (World Economic Forum *et al*, 2002). By 2005 the ESI recorded significant improvements for Russia and Ukraine and declines for Turkmenistan and Uzbekistan, while the positions of the remainder were largely unchanged (Esty *et al*, 2005). In 2008 the ESI recorded improvements for eight countries, which were substantial in some cases (for example, Tajikistan moved from 134th place to 79th, and Turkmenistan from 144th place to 85th).

Meanwhile, a significant reverse for environmental institution-building had been the disbandment of the Russian Ministry of the Environment in 2000, when all environmental responsibilities were transferred to the Ministry for Natural Resources. This measure was interpreted by many as undermining the fundamental principle of separation of control and management of environmental resources.

Some of the negative trends of environmental degradation succeeded in being reversed from the early 1990s. The most remarkable development was the rapid reduction in levels of air and water pollution in many areas, associated with the abrupt decline in industrial output. In most cases, however, this was a result of economic contraction, rather than the increasing effectiveness of environmental protection measures. In some newly independent countries the trend reversed as production levels recovered in the 2000s.

In the early 1990s it was widely believed that economic reform in the region would promote more efficient use of energy and resources, thereby reducing environmental problems. Indeed, in economically profitable sectors that managed to attract foreign investment such resource gains did occur, and the environmental impact per unit of production decreased. Unfortunately, this trend was counterbalanced by the shift to more resource-, energy- and pollution-intensive branches of industry (such as oil and gas production, gold-mining, and ferrous and non-ferrous metallurgy—EEA and UNEP, 2007). As a result of free market reforms, combined with economic globalization, many of the formerly state-subsidized manufacturing industries proved to be less competitive than more-polluting branches, associated with the extraction of raw materials. In order to increase the independence of their energy supplies, countries such as Belarus and Ukraine are considering constructing nuclear reactors (as in Belarus) and enhancing energy production from domestic sources, for example, wood, peat and brown coal (lignite), which could lead to significant problems for the environment, or the construction of hydropower plants on small rivers (Cherp *et al*, 2007).

As emissions of pollutants into the atmosphere decreased, the registered discharges of waste water also declined significantly. This was mostly associated with the decline in industrial and intensive agricultural activities. For example, in Georgia the use of fertilizers declined from 240 kg per ha–250 kg per ha in the late 1980s to around 10 kg per ha in 1994. The use of mineral fertilizers in Armenia declined to only some 3% of its previous levels (UNEP, 2002). Moldova, which in the Soviet times was notorious for its extensive use of fertilizers and pesticides, now hardly uses any agricultural chemicals, because of lack of funds. However, the safe storage and disposal of banned or obsolete pesticides remains an acute problem (Cherp *et al*, 2007). Overall, waste generation per head in Eastern Europe, Russia and Central Asia totals some 14 metric tons per year, compared with four tons in the countries of the European Union (EU). Moreover, significant amounts of hazardous waste are generated, but only a small fraction is managed in an environmentally safe manner. This adds to the existing problem of the legacy of hazardous waste dumps in the region (EEA and UNEP, 2007).

Some of the newly emerged environmental threats concern biodiversity. Encroaching on protected areas and ecosystems has taken many forms, such as illegal deforestation: ranging from impoverished people extracting timber from urban parks, botanical gardens and valuable forests for heating and cooking (for example, in Crimea, Ukraine, and the Caucasus—UNEP, 2003; Cherp *et al*, 2007), to the industrial-scale clearance of protected forests in Siberia and the Russian Far East for export to the People's Republic of China and Japan, or in Kareliya, Russia, for export to Finland and Western Europe. According to Greenpeace and the Russian Forest Programme, deforestation that was at least partly illegal accounted for 20% of all logging in Russia. A further threat to biodiversity has been the poaching of rare and endangered species on an unprecedented scale. In the early 2000s poaching in the Caspian Sea region led to curbs on the caviar trade, under the Convention on International Trade in Endangered Species of Wild Flora and Fauna. Post-independence, many nature reserves also suffered from military conflict in the proximity of biodiversity-rich areas (for example in the northern Caucasus, or Tigrovaya

Balka in Tajikistan). At the same time, there was a gradual return to wilderness in some areas, associated with the decline in agriculture and the abandonment of rural areas, and withdrawal from military bases and other remote outposts that the state was no longer able to maintain.

The effect of the transition on urban environmental problems has been uneven. Some cities benefited from the decline in pollution associated with declining industrial production, and some metropolitan centres experienced rapid expansion of the property market and the rejuvenation of historic centres and infrastructure. At the same time, the growth in private motor vehicle ownership threatens to reverse gains in air quality, which, according to the European Environment Agency (2002, 2007), remains one of the most challenging environmental problems in the region. Moreover, in many places crumbling infrastructure poses serious challenges to the health and well-being of urban dwellers, as well as to the efficient use of energy and water resources.

Attracting investment for infrastructure development has proved to be easier for major roads than for either local roads or for public transport. In urban areas some authorities are reallocating road space previously used by public transport to cater for the increases in private vehicles. The greater use of motor transport has been accompanied by an increase in energy use and in emissions of greenhouse gases, as well as other pollutants, exacerbated by old and poorly maintained vehicle fleets.

In Eastern Europe, Russia and Central Asia domestic energy consumption per head is higher than the EU average, and twice as high as the average for South-Eastern Europe (with comparable living standards). Household water consumption is significantly higher than EU averages, and distribution losses are high in the heating and water supply networks. In Russia, for example, heat loss during distribution is estimated to reach 20% in some regions. For water distribution, losses of 30%–50% are typical in many regions, and in some countries water distribution systems are close to collapse (EEA and UNEP, 2007).

The population of the ecological disaster zones probably fared worst as a result of reform. The CIS countries have generally been unable to fund large-scale environmental remediation or local development in areas such as those affected by the Chornobyl disaster, the nuclear testing at Semipalatinsk or the dessication of the Aral Sea. The population of such areas has entered a downward spiral of poverty, collapsing social structures, poor health and environmental degradation, from which it can only be rescued by means of concerted national and international efforts (UN, 2002).

CONCLUSIONS: ENVIRONMENTAL OPPORTUNITIES AND THREATS

This essay has attempted to provide an overview of environmental degradation in the CIS that is somewhat broader than the conventional picture presented by media reports. The first conclusion is that although socialism was responsible for many of the existing environmental problems in the region, its environmental legacy has not been entirely negative, and it was not the sole cause of the widespread 'frontier mentality', the suspicion of private ownership of land, and the low value placed by society on untouched areas of the environment.

The political and economic changes in the CIS have not yet significantly altered these systemic causes of environmental problems, although some progress has been made in increasing public participation, international co-operation, and the integration of environmental concerns into development decision-making. The process of transition presents significant opportunities for reversing environmental degradation, including administrative reforms and decentralization, social mobilization and democracy, and reduced subsidies to military and other heavy industries. Perhaps most significantly, the CIS countries have been more prepared than the USSR had been to accept international assistance, to learn from the experience of developed and developing countries, and to adhere to international environmental agreements. Many of these states, particularly Moldova, Russia and Ukraine, have been seeking to align their environmental legislation with that of the EU.

However, environmental threats associated with transition include: the reduced time-scales of decision-makers, who have shifted their focus to the resolution of immediate economic and social problems, rather than longer-term environmental issues; economic globalization, which is threatening traditional lifestyles and encouraging the growth of resource- and pollution-intensive industries; a dependence on external markets and a drive to overexploit natural resources; as well as political and social instability, and the marginalization of certain regions and groups.

As mentioned above, the changes to the overall environmental situation since independence have been mixed. While air and water pollution have tended to decline, pressures on undeveloped, biodiversity-rich regions have, in many instances, increased. Collapsing urban infrastructure and the rapid growth in private motor vehicle ownership might undo the positive changes in urban air quality in the near future. Moreover, there is generally insufficient human and financial capacity to clean up environmental disaster zones and support the sustainable development of communities living there.

The 2008 ESI used 25 indicators in six categories to evaluate the progress made towards achieving environmental sustainability in 149 countries, and thus provide an international overview of environmental sustainability. Although only three CIS states were ranked higher than 50th in 2008 (Russia, Georgia and Belarus), the positive progress made in the majority of states indicates that, despite the widely reported problems, the environment remains a significant and unique resource in the CIS. Untouched areas and unspoiled countryside have recreational, cultural, scientific and economic value, which can potentially be used to increase quality of life. The global value of such environmental assets as renewable fresh water, carbon sinks (boreal forests and peat soils) and diverse undisturbed ecosystems is increasing with time and may, once again, present a unique opportunity for sustainable development of this region and even affect the global environmental equilibrium.

Environmental institutions in the CIS also show signs of strengthening. If in the mid-1990s many environmental agencies were unwieldy and inefficient, by the 2000s they were gradually reforming to conform to international standards and serve sustainable development. Although popular interest has focused on environmental issues of immediate concern, such as environmental health, the interest in wider and global causes has also increased. Traditional connections with the environment, in the form of dependence on forests and rivers for food and other basic needs, are being revived and can be used within the newly established institutions of public participation to ensure wider support and responsibility for environmental protection in the countryside and small towns.

However, the latest developments in the region have clearly indicated that the environment is far from being a priority for most governments. On several occasions President Vladimir Putin of Russia (2000–08) observed that environmental considerations were blocking attractive investment opportunities. He also stated that environmental considerations had to be respected, unless they were used as a means for economic competition. This explains certain actions of his Government, such as the disbandment of the Russian Forest Service (which had operated continuously since the 17th century). It was also notable that after Putin entered office, not one national park or *zapovednik* was established. This reflected the Russian Government's approach towards environmental issues, in which economic matters had been prioritized. Nevertheless, in April 2006 Putin urged that the route of the planned East Siberia–Pacific Ocean oil pipeline be moved further away from the shores of Lake Baikal, citing environmental concerns. This gesture received widespread publicity in Russia, perhaps indicating that increasing environmental awareness might lead to environmental matters being given increased political importance. In a series of subsequent moves, however, the Russian Government demonstrated that it viewed environmental concerns merely as a tool for achieving economic and political ends. Thus, the concession for exploring for oil and natural gas in Sakhalin Oblast was taken away from an international consortium led by BP (of the United Kingdom) and Royal Dutch/Shell (of the Netherlands and the United Kingdom) purportedly on environmental grounds, but these apparent environmental concerns all but vanished once a majority stake in the development had been transferred to the state-owned Gazprom. Similarly, while the Russian authorities object to the construction of a pipeline on the Caspian seabed (to transport fuels from Central Asia to potential European markets), it is intending to lay a similar pipeline under the Baltic Sea in order to facilitate Russian natural gas exports to Germany. Although the high probability of leakages was the reason stated for the cessation of oil transportation through the Druzhba pipeline, it was notable that the flow ceased immediately following political and economic disputes between Russia and Lithuania, through which country the pipeline passes. Indeed, following the purchase, in 2006, of the Mažeikiai oil refinery in Lithuania by PKN Orlen of Poland, in preference to the Russian LUKoil, crude petroleum has been supplied to the plant only by sea, and not by way of the pipeline. Similarly, imports of wine to Russia from Georgia and Moldova were halted, apparently on the grounds of contamination, but in reality as a consequence of intense political disagreements between those countries and Russia. Other CIS states have been quick to adopt this disreputable use of an apparent concern for environmental matters as a mechanism for political manoeuvring, as evidenced by Belarusian protests over the Ignalina Nuclear Power Plant in Lithuania or in the Ukrainian–Romanian dispute over the proposed construction of a deep-water route, the Bystroe (Bâstroe) channel, in the Danube delta (Cherp *et al*, 2007). More recently, the Kazakhstani Government cited environmental concerns as a justification for attempts to take control of the large Kashagan oilfield in the Caspian Sea from a consortium led by the Italian company Agip-Eni.

In summary, in many countries and regions there are signs that the opportunities offered by the transition and by the positive legacies of the past can be wisely employed, and new threats averted, in order to reverse the pattern of environmental degradation that developed throughout much of the 20th century. The Global Environmental Outlook (Earthscan, 2002) outlined four main scenarios for global development: 'markets first' (economic globalization, with a primary focus on economic development); 'policy first' (economic globalization, with a focus on achieving environmental and social development objectives); 'security first' (regionalization, with a focus on economic development); and 'sustainability first' (development based on regionalized sustainability objectives and policies). As in other countries and regions of the world, the 'sustainability first' scenario would bring most opportunities for using the diverse resources of the countries of the CIS to benefit present and future generations. Unfortunately, the predominant dogma in the region appears, instead, to be 'markets first'.

BIBLIOGRAPHY

Cherp, A., Antypas, A., Cheterian, V., and Salnykov, M. *Environment and Security. Transforming Risks into Co-operation. The Case of Eastern Europe*. Geneva, United Nations Environment Programme (UNEP), United Nations Development Programme (UNDP), the North Atlantic Treaty Organization (NATO) and the Organization for Security and Co-operation in Europe (OSCE), 2007.

Cherp, A., Mnatsakanian, R., and Kopteva, I. 'Economic Transition and Environmental Sustainability: Effects of Economic Restructuring on Air Pollution in the Russian Federation', in *Journal of Environmental Management*. Vol. 68, 2003.

Earthscan. *Global Environmental Outlook*, No. 3. London, Earthscan, 2002.

Esty, D. C., Levy, M. A., Srebotnjak, T., and de Sherbinin, A. *Environmental Sustainability Index: Benchmarking National Environmental Stewardship*. New Haven, CT, Yale Center for Environmental Law and Policy, 2005.

European Environmental Agency (EEA). *Europe's Environment: The Third Assessment*. Copenhagen, EEA, 2002.

European Environmental Agency (EEA) and UNEP. *Sustainable Consumption and Production in South East Europe and Eastern Europe, Caucasus and Central Asia*. Copenhagen and Genenva, EEA and UNEP, 2007.

Mnatsakanian, R. *Environmental Legacy of the Former Soviet Republics*. Edinburgh, Centre for Human Ecology, 1992.

Peterson, D. J. *Troubled Lands: The Legacy of Soviet Environmental Destruction*. Boulder, CO, Westview Press, 1993.

Pryde, P. (Ed.). *Environmental Resources and Problems in the Former Soviet Union*. Boulder, CO, Westview Press, 1995.

Russian Forest Programme; internet www.forest.ru.

Shanin, T. *Russia as a 'Developing Society'*. Basingstoke, Macmillan, 1985.

Smith, W. D., and Moomaw, W. R. 'Making Peace with the Environment: Addressing the Military-Industrial Legacy in the Post-Soviet Era', in *Eastern Europe, Russia and Central Asia*. 1st Edn, London, Europa Publications, 2000.

United Nations. *The Human Consequences of the Chernobyl Nuclear Accident. A Strategy for Recovery*. New York, UN, 2002.

UNEP. *Caucasus Environmental Outlook 2002*. Tbilisi, New Media Tbilisi (for UNEP), 2002.

Caucasus Environmental Outlook 2003. Tbilisi, New Media Tbilisi (for UNEP), 2003.

World Economic Forum, Global Leaders of Tomorrow Environment Task Force and Yale Center for Environmental Law and Policy. *Environmental Sustainability Index (Main Report)*. New Haven, CT, Yale Center for Environmental Law and Policy, 2002.

POLITICS OF WATER IN CENTRAL ASIA

Dr KAI WEGERICH

INTRODUCTION

During the period of Soviet rule the Syr Dar'ya basin and parts of the Amu Dar'ya basin, both of which were located in territories of the USSR, were managed according to hydrological boundaries, irrespective of the administrative boundaries of the constituent Union Republics (SSRs). The basin approach allowed the construction of most reservoirs upstream, in Kyrgyzstan and Tajikistan, to facilitate irrigation in the downstream states of Kazakhstan, Turkmenistan and Uzbekistan. On the disintegration of the USSR in 1991 administrative boundaries became national boundaries, and water-management approaches became transnational in status. In the Amu Dar'ya and Syr Dar'ya basins the collapse of the Soviet system created new and very serious risks and security challenges for the independent states. These challenges involved the disintegration of the water, energy and food sectors and dependence on the now transboundary water-control and -management infrastructure.

River basins can be classified as common pool resources. These are resources that are utilized by two or more users. Ostrom *et al* (1994—see Bibliography) distinguish between two types of common pool resource problems: appropriation and provision. The appropriation problem of a common pool resource is related to the subtractability of the benefits consumed by one member from those available to others. Provision problems arise from the operation and maintenance of the resource delivery system. In post-Soviet Central Asia the new challenges concern both the allocation of water resources and the structures that provide the resources.

Since independence, much has been written on the potential for water wars in Central Asia. Indeed, Smith (1995) stated that 'Nowhere in the world is the potential for conflict over the use of natural resources as strong as in Central Asia'. Whereas in the period that immediately followed independence attention was focused on the potential disputes over water allocation among the riparian states, subsequent analysis of the Syr Dar'ya basin has focused on the conflicting upstream and downstream uses of water and the interdependence between energy and water. In the Syr Dar'ya basin, Kyrgyzstan, an upstream state, is economically and politically weak, but water-rich and with the necessary water control infrastructure. Thus Kyrgyzstan has significant influence in terms of water management. In this case, Kyrgyzstan's willingness to co-operate with the downstream riparian states, Kazakhstan and Uzbekistan, is crucial. In the Amu Dar'ya basin, conversely, the main emphasis has been on the allocation of resources, since the upstream states of Afghanistan, Kyrgyzstan and Tajikistan do not have the necessary control infrastructure. During the Soviet period the allocation of resources benefited the economically and politically strong, but water-poor, downstream riparian states of Uzbekistan and Turkmenistan. In terms of allocation or reallocation, the willingness of the two downstream states to co-operate has been of the utmost importance. However, various possibilities for funding the development of the pump stations in the basin drew attention to the problem of provision, which could potentially lead to tension between the downstream riparian states. In addition, Tajikistan planned to build a new dam (the Rogun dam) on the Vakhsh river to increase its hydropower production (Spoor and Krutov, 2003; Karaev, 2005). The dam would confer to Tajikistan increased control over an important tributary of the Amu Dar'ya, as a result of which the country could secure a more powerful position. In both basins the questions of allocation and provision remain problematic and need to be addressed. To understand the situation fully one has to consider the historical background of water management in the region.

THE SOVIET LEGACY

The Aral Sea basin covers about 1.8m. sq km and is located within six states: Afghanistan, and the five Central Asian republics (Kazakhstan, Kyrgyzstan, Tajikistan, Turkmenistan and Uzbekistan). With the exception of Kazakhstan, the Central Asian republics lie almost entirely within the Aral Sea basin. The basin can be described as a large drainage system, which terminates in the Aral Sea. The western and central parts are covered by plains (the Kara-Kum and Kyzyl-Kum deserts), while the eastern part contains large mountain ranges. The mountain ranges form the flow-generation zone for Central Asia's main rivers, the Amu Dar'ya and the Syr Dar'ya, which cross the deserts and flow to the Aral Sea. The Syr Dar'ya is the longer river. Measured from the Naryn headwater in Kyrgyzstan to the Sea, its length is 3,019 km, with a catchment area of 219,000 sq km. The Amu Dar'ya is the largest river in Central Asia. It is formed by the confluence of its main headwater tributaries, the Vakhsh and Pyanj rivers. The Vakhsh originates in the alpine regions of the Pamir Alai in the south-east of Kyrgyzstan. The Pyanj originates at the glacier in the Vakjdjir Pass, and forms the border between Afghanistan and Tajikistan. The total length of the Amu Dar'ya, from the head of the Pyanj river to the Aral Sea, is about 2,540 km, and it has a catchment area of 309,000 sq km. On their way to the Aral Sea both rivers not only cross international boundaries, but are also used as boundaries between states.

Under the Russian Empire the comparative advantage of the Aral Sea basin for cotton production had been recognized. Following assumption of Russian control over territories in the region in the mid-19th century, agricultural policies that encouraged the production of cotton were implemented. The establishment of Soviet power after 1917 did not bring a change in the economic specialization of the region. Under the so-called virgin lands policy, initiated by the Soviet leader Nikita Khrushchev in 1953, and the beginning of the 'hydraulic mission', the area under irrigation expanded further. By 1956 an additional 88.6m. ha of agricultural land were under cultivation in the USSR, mainly in Kazakhstan and Western Siberia (Russia). As part of the virgin lands project, Khrushchev promoted the idea of expanding the irrigated areas in Central Asia (Rumer, 1989). The Kara-Kum canal in Turkmenistan (length: 1,400 km, intake: 10 cu km–12 cu km) and the pumping stations bringing water to the Buxoro (discharge: 270 cu m/second, elevation: 57 m) and Qashqadaryo (discharge: 350 cu m/second, elevation: 170 m) viloyats (regions) of Uzbekistan give an indication of the dimension of the water-management constructions (Orlovsky and Orlovsky, 2002; O'Hara, 1997; Bucknall *et al*, 2001). The total area under irrigation in Central Asia increased from 4.5m. ha in 1965 to some 7.0m. ha in 1991. After independence the irrigated area increased even further, to 8.1m. ha (Spoor and Krutov, 2003).

During the Soviet era the Ministry of Land Reclamation and Water Resources of the USSR controlled the Central Asian water authorities. The institutions and interests of the Central Asian republics in resource utilization were subordinate to the central authority in Moscow, the Russian and Soviet capital, and to the greater interest of the USSR. According to Renger (1998), 'The ministries of the Central Asian republics were extensions of the ministry in Moscow. They were responsible for fulfilling the centralized plans and norms. Their role in decision-making was limited to providing data to the centre'. The subordination of the republics was two-fold: sectoral (with regard to irrigated agriculture) and national. Consequently, the utilization of the rivers did not correspond to the administrative boundaries and the interests of the administrative zones. As a result of the Soviet policy to increase cotton production in Central Asia, equal distribution of water between the riparian administrative units was not considered (see Table 1).

Table 1. Sources of river flows in the Aral Sea basin
(annual averages in cu km)

	Amu Dar'ya basin	Syr Dar'ya basin
Kazakhstan	—	2.4
Kyrgyzstan	1.6	27.6
Tajikistan	49.6	1.0
Turkmenistan	1.5	—
Uzbekistan	5.1	6.2
Afghanistan and Iran* . .	21.6	—
Total for the Aral Sea basin .	79.3	37.2

* Figures for Afghanistan are contested. In the early 2000s estimates of the country's contribution to the annual flow varied from 10 cu km to 20 cu km. Neither the Murghab and Hari rivers from Afghanistan nor the Tijen river from Iran contribute directly to the Amu Dar'ya, but could be considered as sub-basins.

Sources: PA Consortium Group and PA Consulting, 2002; UNECE, 2001; Ahmad and Wasiq, 2004.

Lange (2001) explained the sectoral subordination, stating that 'the water management infrastructure was designed for a unified purpose and placed where it made sense geologically'. Although this reasoning is correct for the Toktogul dam, located in Kyrgyzstan, in the Syr Dar'ya basin, it cannot be applied to the Nurek dam in Tajikistan (Wegerich *et al*, 2007). Within the basin framework, most dams and reservoirs were built upstream in the mountains of Kyrgyzstan and Tajikistan, whereas the irrigated areas were downstream in the valleys and in the steppes. The water-management constructions were built to facilitate irrigated agriculture in the downstream regions. In order to use the dams for agricultural purposes, water had to be released in the vegetation season to satisfy irrigation demands. The basin-management framework approach for the Syr Dar'ya had the benefit of permitting total control over water and efficient water management for irrigation. The basin-management framework for the Amu Dar'ya led to the construction of pumping stations in Turkmenistan that provided water for the Buxoro and Qashqadaryo viloyats of Uzbekistan, and also to the construction of the Tuyamuyun reservoir, located in Turkmenistan, to provide water for Xorazm and Qoraqalpog'iston in Uzbekistan and Daşoguz in Turkmenistan. Prior to the construction of the Buxoro pumping station, Buxoro received water from the Zerafshan river. The Zerafshan, however, has shared the fate of other small rivers in Central Asia. Such smaller rivers were tributaries of the Amu Dar'ya and Syr Dar'ya, but have ceased to be so, as a consequence of the expansion of irrigated areas in the smaller basins. This should have alerted the political authorities to the issue of environmental degradation in the region.

Table 2. Agreed annual water use limits in the Amu Dar'ya and Syr Dar'ya basins
(cu km)

	Amu Dar'ya basin*	Syr Dar'ya basin†
Kazakhstan	—	12.3
Kyrgyzstan	0.4	4.0
Tajikistan	9.5	2.5
Turkmenistan	22.0	—
Uzbekistan	29.6	19.7

* Figures agreed by Protocol 566 of the Scientific-Technical Council of the Ministry of Land Reclamation and Water Management of the USSR on 10 September 1987.

† Figures agreed by Protocol 413 of the Scientific-Technical Council of the Ministry of Land Reclamation and Water Management of the USSR on 7 February 1984.

Source: PA Consortium Group and PA Consulting, 2002.

The massive expansion of the irrigated area led to greater competition between the different administrative units. The increasing mistrust over water allocation and management between the Central Asian states prompted the Soviet authorities to create River Basin Organizations (each of which was frequently referred to by the acronym BVO, from the Russian designation—Basseinovoye Vodnoye Obyedineniye) for the Syr Dar'ya and the Amu Dar'ya. Since the entire catchment area of the Syr Dar'ya was within the USSR, it was possible to manage the river according to hydrological boundaries. In February 1984 the Scientific-Technical Council of the Soviet Ministry of Land Reclamation and Water Management decided on annual water-distribution limits for the Union Republics of the Syr Dar'ya basin. Limits were established for those in the Amu Dar'ya basin in September 1987 (see Table 2). With the setting of water limits, the former system of distributing water according to the demands of the administrative units (collective farms, districts, provinces and republics) was replaced by the 'adjusted water demand principle'. Under this system, requests for water were adjusted proportionately, according to the availability of water (Abdullaev, 2005).

It should be noted that Afghanistan did not participate in the 1987 meeting that determined allocations to the four Soviet republics in the Amu Dar'ya basin. Agreements between Afghanistan and the Soviet authorities in 1921, 1946 and 1958 focused on boundary issues, navigation and water quality. In 1977 Afghanistan sent a delegation to the Uzbek SSR to prepare a water-sharing agreement. Although the delegation hoped to claim an equal share of the river flow, no agreement on water allocation was reached (Qaseem Naimi, 2005). Hence, the limits set in 1987 ignored the claims of Afghanistan and assumed a utilization of 2.1 cu km (lower than the 3.9 cu km that was already being used in 1965). Overall, it is not evident whether the 2.1 cu km refers only to the direct tributaries (the Kunduz, the Pyanj and its tributaries) or whether it includes the rivers that flow from Afghanistan into Turkmenistan (the Hari and the Murghab).

In the Soviet system there were no significant disputes between upstream and downstream interests within the Central Asian republics. Upstream and downstream riparian units benefited through the regional approach, using water, energy and food as common pool resources. Owing to the focus on irrigation, the upstream water-management constructions in the Syr Dar'ya basin, such as dams and reservoirs, did not produce hydroelectric power during the winter season, when it was most needed in the upstream regions. The dams released water during the summer, when the downstream riparian administrative units needed it for agriculture. Kemelova and Zhalkubaev (2003) argue, with respect to the Syr Dar'ya basin, that, as compensation, 'Kazakhstan and Uzbekistan supplied Kyrgyzstan with a billion cu m of natural gas. Moreover, the USSR budget contributed roughly US \$600m. to Kyrgyzstan's budget annually'. It is not evident how this was regulated for the Tajik SSR.

POST-INDEPENDENCE PROBLEMS

With independence and the shift from a single administrative unit to independent states, the regional approach to water management that had hitherto existed was at risk. Nevertheless, shortly after independence in 1991, the Governments of the newly independent Central Asian states agreed to continue with the principles of water allocation that had prevailed in the USSR. The Almaty Agreement, signed in February 1992 by representatives of Kazakhstan, Kyrgyzstan, Tajikistan, Turkmenistan and Uzbekistan, acknowledged joint management of water resources. (Again, Afghanistan was excluded from the agreement.) 'Under the agreement the states retained their Soviet-period water allocations, refrained from project infringements on other states and promised an open exchange of information' (O'Hara, quoted in Horsman, 2001).

Although an agreement was reached in 1992, the international community recognized the potential for conflict over water issues. Smith's 1995 statement, cited in the introduction to this essay, was influenced primarily by concerns about the allocation of water resources, specifically with regard to the differences in allocation between upstream and downstream states. The focus on conflict in relation to the distribution of water between the riparian states was dominant until the early 2000s (UNESCO, 2000; Horsman, 2001). Subsequently, attention shifted to the conflicting uses of water upstream and downstream, and the interdependence of energy and water in the Syr Dar'ya basin (Weinthal, 2001; Chait, undated). By mid-2008 neither the allocation nor the provision problems had been solved for either basin. The national policies of all the Central Asian states have focused on independence rather than interdependence, thereby furthering the problems associated with common pool resources.

Amu Dar'ya Basin

In the Amu Dar'ya basin the issue of water allocation is based on two main concerns: the allocation of resources between the riparian states, and the quantity of water that should be allocated to the environment (i.e. the Aral Sea). Although the population figures (see Table 3) refer to entire countries, and not only to the provinces located in the Amu Dar'ya basin, they do raise doubts as to whether the allocation of water is equitable or adequate with regard to the possible future water demands of the riparian states.

Table 3. Population and irrigated areas of Amu Dar'ya basin riparian states

	Population (UN estimates, millions, 2004)	Irrigated Area ('000 ha, 1998)
Afghanistan	28.6	385*
Kyrgyzstan	5.2	22
Tajikistan	6.4	469
Turkmenistan	4.8	1,735
Uzbekistan	26.2	2,321

* Figure for 2004.

Sources: UN, *World Population Prospects: The 2004 Revision*; Dukhovny and Sokolov, undated (a); Zonn, 2001; Qaseem Naimi, 2005.

Had the riparian states changed their demand for water or were they anticipating such a change? Dukhovny and Sokolov (undated—a) state that the Government of Turkmenistan was to reduce the country's demand for irrigated agriculture by 19.5%. Nevertheless, Stanchin and Lerman (2006) show that Turkmenistan's agricultural area increased from 1,329,000 ha in 1990 to 1,843,000 ha in 2003. During the same period the country's total water use increased from 22,435 cu km to 27,958 cu km. Although the paper does not state explicitly that the overall increase comes from the Amu Dar'ya, it is very doubtful that it could have been achieved from only the smaller rivers (Murghab, Hari, Tedjen and Atrek) and that no additional water was taken from the Amu Dar'ya.

In addition, Turkmenistan had commenced the construction of an artificial reservoir, known as the Golden Age Lake, located in the Kara-Kum desert (Stone, 2008). Although Turkmenistan claimed that only drainage water would be used for the lake, Uzbekistan expressed concern that freshwater might also be used during its construction (International Crisis Group—ICG, 2002). After independence Tajikistan increased its area of irrigated land by 200,000 ha, and it intended to expand that area by a further 500,000 ha (ICG, 2002; Spoor and Krutov, 2003). In addition, Tajikistan added to its water requirements by decreasing livestock production and increasing the area of land allocated to wheat and rice production (FAO, undated). Although Uzbekistan also had the potential to expand its irrigated area, demand for water was expected to stabilize at the level recorded in the late 1990s (Dukhovny and Sokolov, undated—a). According to Sokolov (1999), 'approximately 634,400 additional ha are suitable for new irrigation developments, and water conservation would allow a limited expansion of irrigated areas, bringing the total irrigation potential to be estimated at 4.9m. ha'. The national food self-sufficiency strategies in Uzbekistan, which reallocated some irrigated areas from cotton to wheat production, could have led to water savings. However, the potential savings were nullified as a result of increased demand for water through leaching and the deterioration of the irrigation systems (Spoor and Krutov, 2003). In addition, studies in the Xorazm viloyat of Uzbekistan show that, following the land reforms, rice production increased, resulting in a higher demand for water (Wegerich, 2006—a). Furthermore, the reduction in funding for the operation and maintenance of the irrigation infrastructure in all the Central Asian states

caused the infrastructure to deteriorate and management control to decline (Scientific Information Center of the Inter-state Co-ordination Water Commission of Central Asia—SIC ICWC, 1999). All these different points suggest that more water was being used in agriculture.

In northern Afghanistan only 385,000 ha of land were under irrigation (Qaseem Naimi, 2005). There are differing estimates of the potential total area suitable for irrigation in northern Afghanistan, varying from 443,000 ha to 840,000 ha (Ahmad and Wasiq, 2004; Zonn, 2001). Zonn (2001) estimates that the annual water intake for agricultural requirements in northern Afghanistan could amount to 14.6 cu km. Conversely, Ahmad and Wasiq (2004) argue that northern Afghanistan's water requirements from the Amu Dar'ya basin might only amount to 5.8 cu km–6.0 cu km per year, and that such a level of diversion may be achieved only by 2024. Overall, it appears that all of the states in the region had either already increased, or were planning to increase, their demands for water. (Nevertheless, according to official BVO data, Tajikistan and Uzbekistan had decreased their demand for water.)

There appear to be substantial differences between the limits set in 1987 (see Table 2) and the published and unpublished data provided by the Amu Dar'ya BVO on water utilization in Uzbekistan (Wegerich, 2005)—see Table 4. According to unpublished data, Uzbekistan utilized substantially more water than had been officially stated, significantly exceeding the limits set by Protocol 566 of 1987 and the subsequent water-sharing agreements. Neither the official nor the unofficial BVO data indicate that Tajikistan and Turkmenistan had increased their water utilization, and there seems to be no evident explanation as to why the official BVO data do not show an increase for Tajikistan and Turkmenistan.

In addition, it is questionable whether water is continuing to reach the Aral Sea. Official BVO figures state that, on average, 6.1 cu km of water reached the Aral Sea annually between 1993 and 1999; unofficial data, however, suggest that no water reached the lake (Wegerich, 2005). The unofficial data seem to confirm the statement of Spoor and Krutov (2003), who argue that the desiccation of the Aral Sea that Micklin (1992) predicted for 2010 is already a reality.

Table 4. Water use in the Amu Dar'ya basin
(cu km)

	Official data (1993–99)	Unofficial data (1991–2001)*
Kyrgyzstan	0.2	n.a.
Tajikistan	7.3	7.0
Turkmenistan	21.5	20.6
Uzbekistan	21.6	42.8
Aral Sea	6.1	n.a.
Total	56.7	70.4

* Data on water extracted at intakes utilizing pumps.

Source: BVO Amu Dar'ya.

As a guiding principle for water allocation for the Central Asian rivers, SIC ICWC cites 'the countries' right to equitable and reasonable water use with regard to previous use' (Dukhovny, undated); this implies that the limits set during the Soviet period continue to be applied. However, Dukhovny and Sokolov (undated—b), cited by UNESCO, emphasize the temporary nature of the set water allocation, stating that 'the principles of water allocation that existed in Soviet times have been retained for the purpose of annual planning until new regional and national water management strategies can be developed and adopted'. This gives more space for renegotiation of water limits for the upstream countries. If renegotiations do take place, and Afghanistan can increase its allocated share, the question should be raised as to whether Afghanistan could effectively 'sell its legitimate share of the Amu Dar'ya water to downstream users, because it is not in a position to use that water at present' (Glantz, 2002).

In the mid-2000s the water-provision problem in the Amu Dar'ya was mainly based on the question of access to, and responsibility for, the pump stations and the downstream Tuyamuyun reservoir in Turkmenistan that provide water to Uzbekistan and, in the case of the reservoir, also to Turkmenistan. Uzbekistan and Turkmenistan came to a bilateral agreement in April 1996. According to this agreement, Uzbekistan pays to Turkmenistan US $11.4m. annually as land rent for the Buxoro and Qashqadaryo pump stations and for the water storage area of Tuyamuyun, and in addition covers all the operational and maintenance costs (which include visas for maintenance personnel and transport) (Wegerich, 2006—b). In the early 2000s the World Bank refused to finance a project designed to rehabilitate the pump station providing water for Qashqadaryo viloyat in Uzbekistan, because of the extraterritorial location of the pumping station and because Uzbekistan and Turkmenistan were unable to reach agreement over which of the two countries should benefit from the funds. A similar problem could potentially arise with the anticipated rehabilitation project for the pump station that provides water for Buxoro viloyat in Uzbekistan.

A provision problem could also arise with the current and proposed dams in Tajikistan. Currently, Tajikistan does not exercise full control over the water flow of the Vakhsh river, a tributary of the Amu Dar'ya. However, Tajikistan is planning to recommence the construction of the 3,600-MW Rogun dam, 100 km north-east of the country's capital, Dushanbe, which had commenced during the Soviet period, but which ceased during the civil war of the mid-1990s. The Government of Uzbekistan has been very critical of these proposals (Spoor and Krutov, 2003), because they would 'put [Tajikistan] firmly in control of the river' (ICG, 2002). Parshin (2003) argues that international financial institutions would not support Tajikistan's plans without the prior agreement of neighbouring states. Spoor and Krutov argue that 'taking into consideration the power relations [Uzbekistan] will never allow this [the construction of Rogun] to happen'. However, neither Spoor and Krutov nor the ICG report distinguish between different stages of the Rogun construction. It is not clear whether Uzbekistan would be opposed to the construction in general or to a particular height for the dam, either Stage I (225 m), Stage II (285 m) or Stage III (335 m) (Schmidt *et al*, 2006). Nevertheless, Dukhovny and Sorokin (2007) supported the Rogun dam project. Their concerns were about the operation of the dam, not its construction.

Although Tajikistan secured funding for Stage II from the Russian aluminium company RusAL (now RUSAL) in October 2004, Tajikistan's ambition is to construct the dam to Stage III, and therefore it hopes to secure funding from other countries interested in the hydropower produced, such as Iran. Until recently, Tajikistan was integrated into the regional electrical energy grid, centered in Tashkent, the capital of Uzbekistan. In order to bypass Uzbekistan, Tajikistan secured Chinese funding to build a South–North electric transmission line. In 2007 Tajikistan was already supplying 10m. kWh of electricity to Afghanistan (Abdrakhmanov, 2007).

Syr Dar'ya Basin

Although the post-Soviet Central Asian states agreed to share their water resources according to Soviet-era agreements, other regional institutions and practices, such as the exchange of food and energy, disappeared. Each of the newly independent republics established their own national strategies for energy and food security. Whereas downstream countries could divert water away from cash crop production to food crop production (as was the policy in Uzbekistan from the early 1990s), the small amount of water allocated to upstream Kyrgyzstan does not allow much flexibility. Any increase in demand for water for agricultural purposes in the upstream countries has the effect of reducing the availability of water for downstream users. Since independence the agricultural sector in Kyrgyzstan has become more important, and dominates the domestic economy. The agricultural sector accounted for 33.6% of gross domestic product (GDP) in 2007, according to preliminary official figures.

Like other Central Asian states, Kyrgyzstan privatized its state and collective farms; this privatization resulted in an increase in the number of agricultural water users. Whereas in 1990 there were some 450 state and collective farms, by 2002 the number of farms had increased to some 84,700, most of which were small in size (Spoor, 2004). On-farm irrigation structures became inter-farm structures; however, these

structures were not equipped to control the water use of small-scale farms. In addition to the problems of water distribution at the local level, small-scale subsistence farming changed the focus of agricultural production from livestock to crops (Baumann, 1999). This shift from livestock to food and cash crops led to increased water demands in Kyrgyzstan. Ul Hassan *et al* (2004) state that, based on evidence from sample areas, water limits 'no longer appear to be imposed as an operational parameter'. They conclude that 'this situation can be viewed as an indicator that Kyrgyzstan no longer perceives the institution of [water] limits as binding'. However, the disputes anticipated as a result of the water-allocation limits had not arisen by the late 2000s. Nevertheless, Abdullaev *et al* (2006) mention, in addition to the Syr Dar'ya, its small tributaries, which cross international boundaries in the Farg'ona (Fergana) valley. Hitherto, little attention had been paid to the smaller transboundary tributaries and the conflicts between upstream and downstream riparian states.

Disputes in which water played a significant role were based not on allocation issues, but on different uses of water in now competing sectors, such as water releases from the Toktogul reservoir for hydropower (Weinthal, 2001; Chait, undated). The tension between upstream and downstream riparian states resulted from the shift from operating the dams for downstream irrigation in the summer months to winter releases in order to increase the availability of energy upstream. The previous arrangements for water allocation ceased to function when Kazakhstan and Uzbekistan began to charge market prices for petroleum and gas supplies to Kyrgyzstan. Kyrgyzstan began to release water during the winter, to produce energy for its population. Although the use of water for energy production did not change the regional allocation of water, it has changed the availability of water at certain periods and therefore causes floods in downstream regions. In addition, owing to the high costs of operation and maintenance of the reservoir and Kyrgyzstan's poor economic situation, water facilities in the country are deteriorating. Kyrgyzstan began to demand payment from the downstream riparian states for the use of water from its reservoirs.

Pressure from the US Agency for International Development (USAID) resulted in the establishment of a barter agreement, thereby reinforcing the Soviet arrangements on energy (Lange, 2001; Weinthal, 2001). On 17 March 1998 the Governments of Kazakhstan, Kyrgyzstan and Uzbekistan adopted an interstate agreement on the use of the water and energy resources of the Syr Dar'ya river basin (Kasymova, 1999). According to this agreement, each riparian state is responsible for the operation and maintenance costs of the water infrastructure owned by it (Article VII). Nevertheless, the downstream riparian states agreed to purchase hydropower from Kyrgyzstan during the summer and sell other energy resources to Kyrgyzstan in the winter (Article IV). The agreement on how much energy the downstream riparian states purchase, and therefore how much water they should receive, is determined annually. Since the agreement was reached between the riparian states, the Interstate Commission for Water Coordination bulletin (ICWC bulletin) often shows the problems of implementing the agreement, with reference to downstream riparian Kazakhstan. Reasons given for the failure of the agreement are late signing and non-fulfilment on the part of Kazakhstan to take the requested electricity from Kyrgyzstan. However, as indicated by a World Bank report (2004), there is a difference between agreed and actual delivery of energy swaps on all sides, not only in Kazakhstan. Furthermore, all parties, including Uzbekistan, were late in signing the contract.

There are some problems with the interstate agreement. Even though the agreement makes reference to the whole Syr Dar'ya basin, in the individual articles there are only references to the flow from the Naryn-Syr Dar'ya Cascade. Hence all other tributaries below the cascade, and located in Uzbekistan, are excluded from the agreement. For Uzbekistan, not having to share these tributaries has benefits, since in a water-abundant year it allows it to avoid taking allocations from Toktogul altogether. Having annual agreements on energy swaps has two advantages for Uzbekistan. First, depending on the surface water availability forecast, Uzbekistan can decide whether it needs to negotiate with Kyrgyzstan. Second, Uzbekistan can follow a long-term strategy on water independence in the Syr Dar'ya basin by building its own reservoirs, which can be filled in winter with water from the upstream Kyrgyz reservoir. This water can then be released when it is needed in the summer months for agricultural production. Currently, Uzbekistan is expanding existing reservoirs and planning to construct new reservoirs in the Syr Dar'ya basin (Global Environment Facility, 2003).

Article VII of the March 1998 interstate agreement, which stipulates responsibility for operation and maintenance costs of water infrastructure, leaves the burden with the owner of the facility. This is quite different from the bilateral agreement between Uzbekistan and Turkmenistan, which leaves the burden with the main beneficiary (in this case Uzbekistan), and from the recent agreement between Kazakhstan and Kyrgyzstan in the Chu-Talas basin, which provides for cost-sharing in relation to upstream provision structures.

CONCLUSION

The basin studies of the Amu Dar'ya and Syr Dar'ya rivers show that neither the existing problems of allocation that were not resolved during the Soviet period (namely the allocation of water to the Aral Sea and to Afghanistan), nor the problems of provision that only came into existence because of the disintegration of the USSR have been resolved. In addition, the disintegration caused new allocation problems. The riparian states are no longer integrated in the issue-linkage approach that had incorporated food, energy and water. The policies of food self-sufficiency, developed since independence by all the individual riparian states, led to increased demand for water upstream and therefore put pressure on the downstream riparian states as well as on the Aral Sea.

Although all of the riparian states in the Syr Dar'ya basin participated in negotiations on water allocation in the past and agreed to the limits set in 1984, the evidence suggests that the limits will have to be renegotiated in order to reflect recent developments. Indeed, in the case of the Amu Dar'ya basin, not all of the riparian states were present when the utilization limits were set in 1987. In addition, before agreements can be reached on allocation, there should be agreement about the amount of water that Afghanistan contributes to the annual flow of the Amu Dar'ya. Any future increase in water allocation to Afghanistan would decrease the water availability for the existing main stakeholders, Uzbekistan and Turkmenistan. Such an increase in allocation to Afghanistan would put the downstream countries under pressure to change their current method of irrigation, and perhaps shift even further towards crops that demand less water, with the result that the income of these states would decrease. Uzbekistan and Turkmenistan did not fully privatize the agricultural sector, and retained significant state control over the cotton sector. Such a shift in agricultural policy could have serious implications for the political control of the downstream states. Furthermore, a shift from high-value cash crops (cotton) to low-value food crops (wheat) in the downstream riparian states would intensify existing difficulties in financing the water-provision infrastructure.

The disintegration of the USSR and the upgrading of administrative boundaries to national boundaries has had a severely negative impact on relations between the Central Asian republics and their water-sharing agreements. Although pledges were made in the past for closer co-operation and the UN was asked to establish a commission with the objective of giving UN status to the organizations involved in the Aral Sea basin, tension and mistrust between the riparian states remains.

The data presented for developments at national level gives rise to questions as to whether any international agreement on water allocation will be effective. None of the national water-management organizations have the means to monitor and enforce agreed limits at the lower levels of administration. In early 2005, at a workshop organized by the UN University of Peace in Almaty, the Afghan delegation recognized the problem of enforcement. A delegate stated: 'Politicians may decide on water allocation, but currently the farmers just take the water, when they have access to it' (Qaseem Naimi, 2005). Therefore, national governments must not only have the political will to agree on limits, they must also take responsibility and fund the day-to-day functioning of the water sector.

BIBLIOGRAPHY

Abdrakhmanov, A. 'Tajikistan Today: Economics and Politics at Home and Abroad', in *Central Asia and the Caucasus: Journal of Social and Political Studies*. 2007; internet www.ca-c.org/online/2007/journal_eng/cac-06/03.shtml#nazad42 (accessed July 2008).

Abdullaev, I. 'Improving Water Management by Better Water Distribution in the Tertiary Canals of Central Asia'. Case Study for E-Forum of the FAO/Netherlands Conference on Water for Food and Ecosystems: Make it Happen, 2005; internet ftp://ftp.fao.org/agl/emailconf/wfe2005/Better_water_distribution_CAsia.doc (accessed April 2008).

Abdullaev, I., Manthrithilake, H., and Kazbekov, J. 'Water Security in Central Asia: Troubled Future or Pragmatic Partnership?'. Paper presented at 'The Last Drop?: Water, Security and Sustainable Development in Central Eurasia', Institute of Social Studies, The Hague, (1–2 December) 2006.

Ahmad, M., and Wasiq, M. *Water Resource Development in Northern Afghanistan and its implication for Amu Darya Basin*. Working Paper No. 36, Washington, DC, World Bank, 2004.

Baumann, P. *Kyrgyz Republic, Agriculture Area Development Project, Social Diagnosis* (unpublished). 1999.

Bucknall, J., Klytchnikova, I., Lampietti, J., Lundell, M., Scatasta, M., and Thurman, M. *Irrigation in Central Asia: Where to Rehabilitate and Why*. Washington, DC, World Bank, 2001.

Chait, E. A. *Water Politics of Syr Darya Basin, Central Asia: Question of State Interests*; internet www.iwra.siu.edu/pdf/Chait.pdf, undated.

Dukhovny, V. *Transboundary Water and their Joint Use—Hydrological and Political Aspects*. Scientific Information Center of the Interstate Co-ordination Water Commission of Central Asia (SIC ICWC); internet www.cawater-info.net/library/eng/dukhovny5_eng.pdf, undated.

Dukhovny, V., and Sokolov, V. *Integrated Water Resources Management in the Aral Sea Basin*. Baku, SIC ICWC, undated (a).

Lessons on Cooperation Building to Manage Water Conflicts in the Aral Sea Basin. UNESCO; internet unesdoc.unesco.org/images/0013/001332/133291e.pdf, undated (b).

Dukhovny, V. and Sorokin, A. *Assessment of the Impact of Rogun Reservoir on Amudarya River Water Regime*. Tashkent, SIC ICWC, 2007; internet cawater-info.net/library/rus/rogun_at_amudarya_rus.pdf (accessed 4 September 2008).

Food and Agriculture Organization (FAO). *Statistical Database*; internet faostat.fao.org.

Glantz, M. *Water, Climate, and Development Issues in the Amudarya Basin*. Workshop report, Philadelphia, PA, Franklin Institute, 2002.

Global Environment Facility (GEF). *Draft regional policy, strategy, and action program for water and salt management*; internet www.cawater-info.net/library/eng/reports/report3.pdf, 2003.

Horsman, S. 'Water in Central Asia: Regional Co-operation or Conflict?' in Allison, R., and Jonson, L. (Eds), *Central Asian Security: The New International Context*. Washington, DC, Brookings Institute, and London, Royal Institute for International Affairs, 2001.

International Crisis Group. *Central Asia: Water and Conflict*, Asia Report No. 34. Osh/Brussels, International Crisis Group, 2002.

Interstate Commission for Water Coordination (ICWC). *ICWC Bulletin*; internet www.cawater-info.net/library/eng/icwc.

Karaev, Z. 'Water Diplomacy in Central Asia', in *Middle East Review of International Affairs*, Vol. 9, No. 1. 2005.

Kasymova, V. *National Constraining Factors to the Agreement on Water and Energy Use in the Syr Darya Basin*. Silver Spring, MD, USAID-EPIQ, 1999; internet www.dec.org/pdf_docs/PNACH123.pdf.

Kemelova, D., and Zhalkubaev, G. 'Water, Conflict, and Regional Security in Central Asia Revisited', in *New York University Environmental Law Journal*, Vol. 11, No. 2. 2003.

Lange, K. *Energy and Environmental Security in Central Asia: the Syr Darya*. Washington, DC, Center for Strategic and International Studies (CSIS), 2001; internet web.archive.org/web/20050212201901/http://www.csis.org/ruseura/cs010220lange.htm.

Micklin, P. 'The Aral Sea Crisis: Introduction to the Special Issue', in *Post-Soviet Geography*, Vol. 33, No. 5. 1992.

O'Hara, S. 'Irrigation and Land Degradation: Implications for Agriculture in Turkmenistan, Central Asia', in *Journal of Arid Environments*, Vol. 37, No. 1 (Sept.). 1997.

Orlovsky, N., and Orlovsky, L. 'Water Resources of Turkmenistan: Use and Conservation'. Paper presented at a workshop on water, climate and development issues in the Amu Dar'ya basin, Philadelphia, PA, 2002.

Ostrom, E., Gardener, R., and Walker, J. *Rules, Games, and Common-Pool Resources*. Ann Arbor, MI, University of Michigan Press, 1994.

PA Consortium Group and PA Consulting. *Transboundary Water and Related Energy Co-operation for the Aral Sea Basin Region of Central Asia*. Washington, DC, US Agency for International Development Regional Mission for Central Asia Office of Energy and Water, 2002.

Parshin, K. *Tajik Power Plans Still Tread Water*. New York, Open Society Institute, 2003; internet www.eurasianet.org/departments/business/articles/eav121503.shtml.

Putnam, E., and Mukhamadiev, B. 'In Focus: Hydropower in Central Asia—Prospects and Problems', in *Central Asian ESTH Hub Highlights*, Tashkent, US State Department Regional Environmental Hub for Central Asia, (Nov.) 2005; internet www.usembassy.uz/_includes/GetEmbassyFile.aspx?id=1505.

Qaseem Naimi, M. 'Conflict Prevention and the Politics of Central Asia Water Co-operation from the Point of View of Afghanistan'. Paper presented at a workshop, Almaty, University of Peace, Central Asia Programme, 2005.

Renger, J. *The Institutional Framework of Water Management in the Aral Sea Basin and Uzbekistan*. Brussels, European Union—TACIS Programme, 1998.

Rumer, B. Z. *Soviet Central Asia: A Tragic Experiment*. Boston, MA, Unwin Hyman, 1989.

Schmidt, R., Zambaga-Schulz, S., and Seibitz, M. 'Bankable Feasibility Study for Rogun HEP Stage 1 Construction Completion in Tajikistan', in Berga, L., *et al*, *Dams and Reservoirs, Societies and Environment in the 21st Century*. Abingdon, Routledge, 2006.

Scientific Information Center of the Interstate Co-ordination Water Commission of Central Asia (SIC ICWC). *Institutional, Technical and Financial Issues Facing the Irrigation Sector in the Central Asian Republics*, consultant report. Tashkent, SIC ICWC, 1999.

Smith, D. R. 'Environmental Security and Shared Water Resources in Post-Soviet Central Asia', in *Post-Soviet Geography*, Vol. 36, No. 6. 1995.

Sokolov, V. 'Integrated Water Resources Management in the Republic of Uzbekistan', in *Water International*, Vol. 24, No. 2 (Sept.). 1999.

Spoor, M. *Agricultural Restructuring and Trends in Rural Inequalities in Central Asia: A Socio-Statistical Survey*., Civil Societies and Movements Programme, paper number 13. Geneva, United Nations Research Institute for Social Development, 2004.

Spoor, M., and Krutov, A. 'The Power of Water in a Divided Central Asia', in *Perspectives on Global Development and Technology*, Vol. 2, No. 3–4. 2003.

Stanchin, I., and Lerman, Z. 'Water in Turkmenistan'. Conference paper presented at 'The Last Drop?: Water, Security and Sustainable Development in Central Eurasia', Institute of Social Studies, The Hague, (1–2 December) 2006. (Also available at the Hebrew University website as discussion paper No. 8.07; internet departments.agri.huji.ac.il/economics/lerman-turkmen-water.pdf).

Stone, R. 'A New Great Lake—or Dead Sea?', in *Science*, Vol. 320. 2008.

Ul Hassan, M., Starkloff, R., and Nizamedinkhodjaeva, N. *Inadequacies in the Water Reforms in the Kyrgyz Republic*. Research Report 81. Colombo, Sri Lanka, International Water Management Institute, 2004.

UN Economic Commission for Europe (UNECE). *Diagnostic Report for Preparation of the Regional Strategy of Rational and Efficient Use of Water Resources in Central Asia*. Geneva, UNECE, 2001.

UNESCO. *Water Related Vision for the Aral Sea Basin*. Paris, Presses Universitaires de France, 2000.

Wegerich, K. 'Wasserverteilung im Flusseinzugsgebiet des Amudarja. Offene und verdeckte Probleme-heute und in der Zukunft', in Neubert, S., Scheumann, W., van Edig, A., and Huppert, W. (Eds), *Integriertes Wasserressourcen-Management (IWRM): ein Konzept in die Praxis überführen*. Baden-Baden, Nomos-Verlag, 2005.

"Illicit' water: Un-accounted, But Paid For. Observations on Rent-Seeking as Causes of Drainage Floods in the Lower Amu Dar'ya'; internet www.ceres.wur.nl/Activities/2006_Wegerich_illicit_water.pdf, 2006 (a).

'Have your Cake and Eat it too. Problem Definitions in Central Asian Transboundary Rivers'. Conference paper presented at 'The Last Drop?: Water, Security and Sustainable Development in Central Eurasia', Institute of Social Studies, The Hague, (1–2 December) 2006 (b).

Wegerich, K., Olsson, O., and Froebrich, J. 'Reliving the past in a changed environment: Hydropower ambitions, opportunities and constraints in Tajikistan', in *Energy Policy*. Vol. 35, 2007.

Weinthal, E. 'Sins of Omission: Constructing Negotiating Sets in the Aral Sea Basin', in *Journal of Environment and Development*, Vol. 10, No. 1. 2001.

World Bank. *Water Energy Nexus in Central Asia: improving Regional Cooperation in the Syr Darya Basin*. Washington, DC, World Bank, 2004.

Zonn, I. 'Water Resources of Northern Afghanistan and their Future Use'. Paper presented at workshop on water, climate and development issues in the Amu Dar'ya basin, Philadelphia, PA, 2001.

POVERTY AND SOCIAL WELFARE IN THE COMMONWEALTH OF INDEPENDENT STATES

Prof. JANE FALKINGHAM

Revised for this edition by the Editor

INTRODUCTION

At independence in 1991, the new countries that had been part of the former USSR enjoyed relatively high levels of human development. Extensive social investment during the Soviet period meant that literacy was almost universal, and well above the rate in other countries with comparable levels of income per head, while life expectancy averaged 68 years. Unemployment was unheard of, and—at least officially—poverty did not exist. Few could have foreseen that the process of transition towards market economies and democratic governments would have such a high human cost. The virtual collapse of economic output in many countries following independence, along with 'hyperinflation', which eroded individual savings, resulted in a dramatic decline in living standards for many people. By 1996 about two-thirds of the population of Georgia had incomes below the official poverty line, while in Ukraine the rate was about one-half. The severity of the situation was emphasized by the reversal in life expectancy, primarily owing to increasing mortality among young and middle-aged men, reported in several major countries in the region. In 1995 male life expectancy in Russia was just 58 years, 10 years lower than male life expectancy in the People's Republic of China.

After 1998, however, there was some cause for optimism. The region as a whole enjoyed unprecedented economic stability after the Russian financial crisis of 1998. A return to positive economic growth was observed in almost every country of the region, and in some countries democratic elections had taken place, giving new impetus for reform, while ethnic tensions had also abated in many places.

However, significant progress in improving the material and social welfare of ordinary people remained elusive. At the beginning of the 21st century an estimated 50m. people continued to live in severe poverty in the region. Moreover, in some countries, the proportion of the population living in poverty had increased, despite economic growth, and inequality in income had continued to rise. Public services continued to experience hardship. Real spending on health and education remained low by international standards and in some cases had actually declined, despite economic growth. In many countries educational standards had fallen, as schools continued to lack basic supplies and infrastructure deteriorated.

There were also worrying signs of new hazards, with a rise in organized crime, increasing drugs use and an escalation of the HIV epidemic. According to the Joint UN Programme on HIV/AIDS (UNAIDS) and the World Health Organization (WHO), the number of people in Eastern Europe, Russia and Central Asia living with HIV had increased dramatically, reaching some 1.6m. by the end of 2007; this represented an increase of more than two-fold since 2001 (UNAIDS and WHO, 2007—see Bibliography). AIDS resulted in almost seven times as many deaths in 2007 (an estimated 55,000) as in 2001 (8,000). For many, the real objective of transition—improving the lives of the populace—remained a distant prospect and appeared to have taken second place to the imperative of economic growth.

This essay focuses on trends in the indicators of well-being in the countries of the former USSR since independence. The essay is divided into four sections, each dealing with a different aspect of welfare. The first section examines changes in national income and in expenditure on principal social sectors, including education and health. The second section discusses changes in material living conditions and the extent and depth of poverty in the region. It is increasingly recognized that material resources, or the lack thereof, reflect just one, albeit very important, dimension of poverty. The third section, therefore, looks at changes in indicators of health and access to health care services. Trends in education enrolment and attendance rates are discussed in the fourth and final section.

ECONOMIC GROWTH AND PUBLIC SPENDING

Following independence, the withdrawal of subsidies from Russia, the dismantling of the Council of Mutual Economic Assistance and the subsequent interruption of inter-republican trade within the former USSR, and the impact of tight government stabilization policies, all combined to result in a dramatic reduction in output across the region. In some areas, the severe economic impact accompanying the collapse of the USSR was further exacerbated by natural disasters and by armed conflicts and border disputes (for example, between Armenia and Azerbaijan, particularly in 1988–94; in South Ossetia and Abkhazia, Georgia, especially in 1989–94; in the Transnistria region of Moldova in 1991–92; in Tajikistan in 1992–97; and in the Farg'ona—Fergana—valley region of Kyrgyzstan, Tajikistan and Uzbekistan in 1989–91). All parts of the region experienced a marked contraction in output per head during the early 1990s, followed by recovery. From 1999 output increased in almost all the 12 countries of the Commonwealth of Independent States (CIS). However, despite this growth, the real value of gross domestic product (GDP) per head remained significantly lower than its pre-transition level. In the South Caucasus (Armenia, Azerbaijan and Georgia), where the decline in output was more extreme, and where recovery took place later, in the early 2000s GDP per head remained around 40% lower than its pre-transition level.

Although there were significant differences in experience between sub-regions, by 2006 per head GDP was, on average, in real terms, at around the same level as it had been in 1990, following a period of prolonged economic recovery in many of the CIS countries. However, the levels recorded in Ukraine (74.7% of the 1990 level, in real terms), Georgia (72.0%), Kyrgyzstan (70.1%), Moldova (59.7%) and particularly Tajikistan (50.9%) were markedly lower (UN Children's Fund—UNICEF, 2008). Only in Armenia (where GDP per head in 2006 was equivalent to 161.1% of the 1990 level, in real terms), Belarus (146.6%), Kazakhstan (134.4%) and Azerbaijan (125.6%) was GDP per head substantially larger than in 1990, while the achievement in 2006, for the first time, of Russian GDP per head greater than that recorded in 1990, reflected the prolonged recovery there. (No data were available for Turkmenistan.) According to revised estimates by the World Bank, in 2006 the Central Asian republic of Tajikistan recorded the lowest level of annual gross national income (GNI) per head among the countries of the region, at just US $390 (or $1,560, in terms of international purchasing-power parity, with figures adjusted to take into account differences in the cost of living) (World Bank, *World Development Indicators database*).

It is important to note that the above estimates reflect measured output only, and may overestimate the decline in output and underestimate subsequent economic growth, as they may exclude some, or all, informal sector activity. However, even after accepting that there may be measurement problems, it remains clear that the region had suffered a severe decline in economic output.

Furthermore, the ability of governments to respond to depressed economic activity by increasing public expenditure had been severely constrained, with a dwindling tax base and poor tax-collection rates. The level of general government spending as a percentage of GDP declined in many countries of the region. Since one of the aims of transition was to reduce the once all-encompassing role of the state, a decrease in government spending was to be expected. However, in a number of CIS countries, the proportion of government spending had become so low that the functioning of vital state services may have been impaired. Furthermore, it is important to remember that social spending comprised a diminishing share of a significantly reduced real GDP.

Once again, there were marked differences between sub-regions, with social spending being generally higher in the western CIS (Belarus, Moldova, Russia and Ukraine) than in the Caucasus and Central Asia (Kazakhstan, Kyrgyzstan, Tajikistan, Turkmenistan and Uzbekistan). Public expenditure on health and education was at critically low levels in Armenia (where spending in 2006 accounted for 1.1% and 2.7% of GDP, respectively), Georgia (1.8% and 3.0%) and Tajikistan (1.1% and 3.4%) (UNICEF, 2008). In comparison, most member governments of the Organisation for Economic Co-operation and Development (OECD) spend between 5% and 7% of GDP on health care. With the decline in government expenditure in the CIS region, private spending has necessarily increased. However, the introduction of charges for health care, textbooks and school lunches, together with the increasing cost of public transport, all mean that access to basic social services has been severely eroded, particularly in the poorest countries, and it is likely that this will be reflected in a deterioration of the indicators of human development over time.

INEQUALITY AND POVERTY

High levels of social expenditure and low wage differentials meant that the distribution of income within the USSR was significantly more egalitarian than in most market economies (Atkinson and Micklewright, 1992). Unfortunately, the decline in measured output during the 1990s discussed above was accompanied by large increases in inequality in household incomes across the region. Inequality in household incomes can be measured in terms of the Gini coefficient, where 0 indicates absolute equality of the population and 1 indicates absolute inequality. In the mid-1990s the average value for the OECD countries was 0.31. In 1989 all the republics of the USSR experienced a lower rate of inequality than in OECD. However, by 2007, according to the UN Development Programme (UNDP) Human Development Report, many of the former Soviet countries (most notably Georgia and Turkmenistan) displayed values close to the top of the OECD range (in 2007 the OECD country that displayed the greatest disparity in household incomes was the USA, with a Gini coefficient of 0.408). In 2007 the countries of the region that recorded the lowest income inequalities were Belarus and Ukraine.

Some increase in income inequality during transition was to be expected, as the market system allows rewards to be more closely associated with risk-taking, training, individual talent and effort. The emergence of open unemployment and the increasing inequality of income from sources other than employment further added to this trend. However, it is clear that the growth in inequality was far more rapid than anticipated, fuelled by a widespread failure to respect employment contracts, leading to the pervasive practice of wages being paid in arrears, especially for the less well-paid; and by the flawed privatization of public assets, leading to the concentration of wealth among very few people. The widening of the gap between those at the top and bottom of the scale resulted in an acute sense of relative deprivation for those left behind.

Trends in income inequality and poverty are closely linked, and it is not surprising that both absolute and relative poverty levels increased. As well as exacerbating the hardship of those groups traditionally thought of as being disadvantaged—pensioners, families with large numbers of children and single-parent families—the economic dislocation of transition also gave rise to new groups of poor, including the families of workers on leave without pay or with low pay (especially agricultural and public sector employees), the long-term unemployed, young people in search of their first job and a growing number of refugees, both economic refugees and persons displaced as a result of civil conflict.

A commonly used international definition of absolute poverty is survival on less than US $1 per person per day. This standard was developed by the World Bank in the 1980s, and was based on the average of the national poverty lines of 10 low-income countries, all of which were located wholly, or in part, within the tropics. In a 2000 report on poverty in Central and Eastern Europe and the CIS (see Bibliography), the World Bank argued that a higher poverty line was required for the region, given that its cooler climate necessitates additional expenditure on heat, winter clothing and food. A level of $2.15 a day was, therefore, interpreted as a low threshold. A higher threshold of $4.30 was also used, recognizing that what may be considered as a 'subsistence need' inevitably varies with the level of a country's development. Even the poorest households in the region incur expenses on basic services such as the post, child care and health care, and need to cover the running costs of at least some basic consumer durables, such as a television and/or a refrigerator.

At the end of a decade of transition, the World Bank estimated that 164m. people living in the countries of the former USSR were living in poverty, of whom over 50m. were living in extreme poverty (World Bank, 2000). One in five people were surviving on less than US $2.15 per day, compared with the rate of less than one in 25, recorded 10 years earlier. From 2000 significant progress was made in reducing poverty, and more recent estimates from the World Bank indicated that more than 40m. people moved out of poverty during 1998–2003 (World Bank, 2005). Much of this reduction occurred in the populous middle-income countries of Russia, Belarus, Ukraine and Kazakhstan, but improvements in poverty rates were recorded everywhere, with the notable exception of Georgia. Nevertheless, the problem of low living standards remained endemic (and even in the former Soviet Baltic states of Estonia, Latvia and Lithuania between one-fifth and one-third of the population were living on less than $4.30 per person per day). Absolute poverty was greatest, however, in Tajikistan, Moldova, Armenia and Kyrgyzstan. According to the World Bank, in Tajikistan 74% of the population lived in extreme poverty (less than $2.15 per person per day) in 2003. The corresponding figures, using the most recently available data, were: 70% in Kyrgyzstan; 50% in Armenia; 43% in Moldova; 21% in Kazakhstan; 9% in Russia; 5% in Estonia and around 2% in Belarus.

HEALTH AND POVERTY

Health is both a determinant and a dimension of poverty. Ill health and malnutrition are often causes of poverty or cause further hardship to households that are already poor. Illness in the primary or sole wage-earner, and the consequent loss of income, can undermine a poor household's ability to cope financially. In a consultation exercise conducted by the World Bank, ill health emerged as one of the main reasons cited by households as a cause of poverty. Payments for health services, in particular hospital care, can make the difference between whether a household is able to cope or not. However, poverty is also a cause of ill health. Poor people suffer from a multiplicity of deprivations, which translates into ill health. Most obviously, such people lack the financial resources to pay for food, clean water, adequate sanitation and health services, which constitute the principal inputs to producing good health. It is not only lack of income that causes the high level of ill health among poor people. The health facilities serving them are often dilapidated, inaccessible, inadequately stocked with basic medicines and run by poorly trained staff.

Under the Soviet system, entitlement to comprehensive and free, but inefficient, health care was universal, with excess human and physical infrastructure. Health-care utilization rates were high, and differences across groups, in terms of access to health services, were negligible. Indicators of population health were high by international standards. Tragically, from the 1990s there were remarkable reversals in both health and health care.

Mortality

The most fundamental measure of the well-being of a population is how long its members can expect to live. Life expectancy at birth is a hypothetical measure, calculating the number of years a man or woman could expect to live, on average, if they were exposed to the risk of dying at the prevailing age-specific mortality rates throughout their entire life. The measure is hypothetical as no one individual lives their entire life in one calendar year, and it is sensitive to short-term changes in mortality rates. During 1989–95 the health of the population deteriorated across much of the CIS, with declines in life expectancy in the majority of the countries of the region. Proportionately, the declines were most marked among men, particularly in the countries of the western CIS. For example, between 1989 and 1995 life expectancy for Russian males declined by almost six years, from 64.2 years in 1989 to 58.3 years in 1995. From the mid-1990s, however, mortality rates appeared to begin to improve, although in many countries life expectancy remained lower than was the case in 1989. For example, in 2006 life expectancy for Russian men remained just 60.4 years (thus 2.1 years of life had been added in the nine calendar years since 1995). In 2004 men in Kazakhstan could expect to live for an average of 60.5 years and men in Ukraine for 62.4 years. The 'mortality crisis' among Russian men attracted considerable attention (Chen *et al*, 1996; Cornia and Paniccia, 1995), with much being written about its causes, and its relationship with poverty, unemployment, depression and, especially, the abuse of alcohol (McKee, 1999; Shkolnikov *et al*, 2001; Walberg *et al*, 1998). However, by 2006 male life expectancy in Armenia, Azerbaijan, Georgia, Tajikistan, Turkmenistan and Uzbekistan exceeded the levels recorded in 1989.

Nutritional Status

There is a very real possibility that the level and depth of income poverty experienced by households within the region is affecting children's nutritional status, with subsequent long-term developmental consequences. The three standard indices of physical growth are: height-for-age (arrested growth reflects chronic undernutrition), weight-for-height (reflecting acute or recent malnutrition), and weight-for-age (the percentage underweight is a good overall indicator of the child population's nutritional health). In a healthy, well-nourished child population, it is expected that 2.3% of children will fall below two standard deviations of the reference population and will be classified as stunted, wasted or underweight.

The figures for seven CIS countries, including Russia, demonstrated that the nutritional status of children in the region was a major cause for concern (Falkingham, 2004). The percentage of children classified as stunted was significantly greater than the WHO standard of 2.3% in all instances. The rate of stunting in 2000 was 10.6% in Russia, 13.0% in Armenia and 19.6% in Azerbaijan. In Georgia, the rate was 11.7% in 1999, and in children aged between 0 and 35 months, the rate was 21.8% in Kyrgyzstan in 1997 and 21.1% in Uzbekistan in 2002. In Tajikistan the 2003 figure, of 36.2% (for children aged between six and 59 months), was a particular cause for concern, showing a deterioration compared with the rates recorded by previous nutritional surveys. Countries with high levels of material poverty, such as Tajikistan and Kyrgyzstan, generally also had more malnourished children, emphasizing the link between low income and poor health. Unless something is done to improve material living standards, it is likely that rates of malnutrition will increase, with a concomitant increase in morbidity as these children enter young adulthood.

Access to Health Care

An important determinant of good health is access to good-quality health care. After independence, health services in many countries deteriorated rapidly, owing to the imposition of severe financial constraints, exacerbated in some areas by extensive damage to infrastructure during armed conflict. It is clear that the widening gap between the health care budget and the actual costs of care resulted in both a decline in the quality of services and an increased burden on the household, both in terms of official charges and, more commonly, informal payments. There is a growing body of evidence that cost represents an important barrier to health care within the region. Indicators of financial barriers to health care in six CIS countries demonstrated that between 13% (in Russia) and 94% of respondents (in Georgia) were either unable to afford care, or compelled to borrow money or sell assets to obtain care, during the 1990s (Lewis, 2002). Payments for health care can cause households to fall into poverty; research by the World Bank suggested that 'catastrophic' health expenditure increased the proportion of the population within the region deemed to be poor by between 3% and 9% (World Bank, 2005).

EDUCATION

As with health, the countries of the CIS began the transition with an enviable record on education, with near-universal literacy. Attendance at school was compulsory between the ages of seven and 15, and there was also an extensive system of kindergartens for pre-school-age children, and technical and vocational schools for post-compulsory education. However, over the subsequent years there were serious reversals in several countries, and it is unlikely that the high literacy rates of the past will be sustained in future generations.

The impact of economic decline on education outcomes can be thought of as being three-fold (Falkingham, 2000). First, decreased access (and increased costs) may reduce enrolment rates. Parents who are unable to afford the cost of textbooks, uniforms, or even shoes, may simply withdraw their children from education altogether. Second, even if enrolled, children may not attend school regularly, either for the reasons given above, or because they are needed as family labour (working in the home looking after younger children, or working on family land or in the hired labour market to supplement household income). Finally, children may attend school, but may not benefit from the education. The teacher may be absent, owing to a second job, or—reflecting decreasing public finance for education—there may be no textbooks, it may be too cold to concentrate as a result of a lack of adequate heating, or the child may be anaemic and/or malnourished, and too lethargic to learn. There is very little evidence concerning learning outcomes, so discussion here focuses on trends in kindergarten, primary- and secondary-school enrolment and attendance.

One of the most worrying trends is the decline in the proportion of children aged between three and six years enrolled in pre-primary school education. Prior to independence, attendance at kindergartens was widespread. In the western CIS in 1989, over 60% of children in the relevant age-group were enrolled at kindergartens, rising to nearly 75% in Russia. Enrolment rates were lower in the Caucasus and Central Asia, but even there, with the exception of Azerbaijan and Tajikistan, over 30% of children were enrolled in pre-schools. After independence, rates declined dramatically in almost all of the CIS countries; declines were especially steep in the poorest countries, with pre-primary enrolment falling by 2006 to as little as 7.0% in Tajikistan and 12.4% in Kyrgyzstan (UNESCO, 2008). This was partly a result of the closure of enterprise-based (employer-provided) kindergartens. However, enrolment fell by more than the reduction in capacity, suggesting a decline in demand for kindergarten places, as well as their supply. Official statistics indicated that girls were disproportionately withdrawn from pre-school education compared with boys, especially in Tajikistan (Silova and Magno, 2004). Such trends were of concern, given the role that kindergartens can play in increasing household welfare, both in terms of freeing the parent to participate in other activities, specifically paid employment, and the developmental role of pre-school education and nutritional and health interventions (Klugman *et al*, 1997).

Primary education remains compulsory, and enrolment rates in basic education have generally remained high. However, there were worrying declines in enrolment in basic education in Belarus and, particularly, in Turkmenistan; data from UNICEF indicated that the equivalent of 86.7% of children aged between seven and 15 years were enrolled in school in Turkmenistan in 2006, compared with 90.0% in 2001 or 91.2% in 1989. Furthermore, enrolment rates reveal only part of the situation: there is a growing problem of declining attendance.

Outside Russia and Ukraine, post-compulsory education enrolment also decreased dramatically. Once again, the decline was most marked in the countries with higher levels of poverty. Worryingly for future levels of human capital and associated prospects for economic growth, between 1989 and 2005 the proportion of 15–18-year-olds attending general secondary schools declined by nearly one-half in Tajikistan, Turkmenistan and Uzbekistan (in the period to 2004 in the case of Turkmenistan, where no data for 2005 were available), while declines of around 10% were registered in Georgia (to 2004) and Kyrgyzstan.

In contrast, there was significant growth in higher education in all but three countries. The expansion of higher education was particularly rapid in Kyrgyzstan, where the proportion of 19–24-year-olds in tertiary education increased by more than two-fold (from 13% to 36%) between 1989 and 2004. Almost all of the growth in tertiary education was in the private sector, with a proliferation of private colleges in fields that were under-represented in the past, most notably business studies, economics and law. The quality of education provided varied enormously, and again cost presented a barrier to access for children from the poorest families.

In Kyrgyzstan, at the age of 15 years there was little difference in enrolment rates by sex or by income (Falkingham *et al*, 2002). However, enrolment subsequently declined dramatically. There was a tendency for boys from poor households, in particular, to leave school at 15, whereas for girls, and for boys from wealthier households, the trend did not begin until one year later. By the age of 21, the greatest distinction in enrolment data was influenced by income, rather than sex, with the poor being much less likely to continue in education than the non-poor.

With rising costs at both schools and colleges, it was difficult to resist the conclusion put forward by UNDP that the education systems in the CIS were beginning to reflect the increasing socio-economic stratification of these societies. Access to quality education had become confined substantially to those who could afford private fees and tuition. It was imperative that action was taken to ensure that the increasing poverty and stratification outlined above did not result in the re-emergence of illiteracy within the region and the cycle of deprivation and social exclusion that accompanies it.

CONCLUSION

The preceding sections have provided a gloomy picture of declining real incomes, growing poverty, stagnating life expectancy, rising child malnutrition and deteriorating educational status. Although from the beginning of the 2000s economic growth throughout the region demonstrated a positive trend, this alone was insufficient to reverse the decline in indicators of human development. In countries where disparities in incomes are large, it will be difficult substantially to increase the incomes of poor families in the short and medium term without some reduction in those income differences. This will necessitate tackling the vested interests that are holding back restructuring, stifling small-scale private enterprise and frustrating efforts to improve public-expenditure management. Action is also required to protect and build capabilities, so that the poor are able to take advantage of new income-generating opportunities. Moreover, there remains an urgent need to invest in schools and primary health-care facilities and to strengthen public-expenditure management systems to ensure equality of access for all.

BIBLIOGRAPHY

Atkinson, A. B., and Micklewright, J. *Economic Transformation in Eastern Europe and the Distribution of Income*. Cambridge, Cambridge University Press, 1992.

Bureau of Economic Analysis (BEA). *Russian Economic Trends*. Moscow, BEA, June 2003.

Chen, L., Wittgenstein, F., and McKeon, E. 'The Upsurge of Mortality in Russia: Causes and Policy Implications', in *Population and Development Review*, Vol. 22, No. 3. 1996.

Cornia, G., and Paniccia, R. 'The Demographic Impact of Sudden Impoverishment: Eastern Europe during the 1989–94 Transition'. Innocenti Occasional Papers, EPS 49. Florence, UNICEF Innocenti Research Centre, 1995.

Falkingham, J. 'From Security to Uncertainty: The Impact of Economic Change on Child Welfare in Central Asia'. Innocenti Working Paper, ESP 76. Florence, UNICEF Innocenti Research Centre, 2000.

'Inequality and Poverty in the CIS-7 Countries, 1989–2002', pp. 141–170, in Shiells, C. R., and Sattar, S. (Eds). *The Low-Income Countries of the Commonwealth of Independent States: Progress and Challenges in Transition*. Washington, DC, IMF and World Bank, 2004.

Falkingham, J., Namazie, C., and Siyam, A. 'Poverty and Vulnerability in the Kyrgyz Republic 1996–1998'. Mimeo paper. Washington, DC, World Bank, 2002.

Joint United Nations Programme on HIV/AIDS (UNAIDS) and World Health Organization (WHO). *AIDS Epidemic Update: December 2007*. Geneva, UNAIDS, 2007.

Klugman, J., *et al*. 'The Impact of Kindergarten Divestiture on Household Welfare', in Falkingham, J., Marnie, S., and Micklewright, J. (Eds). *Household Welfare in Central Asia*. Basingstoke, Macmillan, 1997.

Lewis, M. 'Informal Health Payments in Eastern Europe and Central Asia: Issues, Trends and Policy Implications', in Mossialos, E., Dixon, A., Figueras, J., and Kutzin, J. (Eds). *Funding Health Care: Options for Europe*. Buckingham, Open University Press, 2002.

McKee, M. 'Unravelling the Enigma of the Russian Mortality Crisis: A Review Essay on Charles M. Becker and David Bloom (Eds), *The Demographic Crisis in the Former Soviet Union* ', in *Population Development Review*, Vol. 25, No. 2. 1999.

Shkolnikov, V., McKee, M., and Leon, D. A. 'Changes in Life Expectancy in Russia in the 1990s', in *The Lancet*, Vol. 357. 2001.

Silova, I., and Magno, C. 'Gender Equity Unmasked: Democracy, Gender and Education in Central/Southeastern Europe and the Former Soviet Union', in *Comparative Education Review*, Vol. 48, No. 4. 2004.

UNDP. *Human Development Report*. New York, UNDP, Annual.

UNECE. *Economic Survey of Europe*. Geneva, UNECE, 2005.

UNICEF. *TransMONEE 2006*. Florence, UNICEF Innocenti Research Centre, 2006.

TransMONEE 2007. Florence, UNICEF Innocenti Research Centre, 2007.

TransMONEE 2008, Florence, UNICEF Innocenti Research Centre, 2008.

Walberg, P., McKee, M., Shkolnikov, V., Chenet, L., and Leon, D. A. 'Economic Change, Crime, and Mortality Crisis in Russia: A Regional Analysis', in *British Medical Journal*. August 1998.

World Bank. *Making Transition Work for Everyone*. Oxford, Oxford University Press, 2000.

Growth, Poverty and Inequality: Eastern Europe and the Former Soviet Union. Washington, DC, World Bank, 2005.

World Development Indicators database; internet sima-ext .worldbank.org/query (accessed 19 October 2007).

APPENDIX: THE RELIGIONS OF EASTERN EUROPE, RUSSIA AND CENTRAL ASIA

There is a vast array of religions, denominations and sects in the region, ranging from the many Christian churches to Islam, and from Buddhism to Judaism. A brief survey of the main groups follows.

CHRISTIANITY

The Christian religion is a monotheistic faith, which evolved from Judaism in the first century AD. Christianity is based on a belief in the divinity and teachings of Jesus Christ, the Messiah or Son of God, through whom salvation (deliverance from sin or a drawing closer to God) can be obtained. His followers established the institution of a single Church, originally based on the four leading cities of the Roman Empire: Antioch, Alexandria, Rome itself and Constantinople (from AD 330, the capital). Four distinct traditions emerged: the Syrian or Jacobite Church was based on Antioch; the Coptic Church was based on Alexandria; the Western, or Latin, Church was based on Rome and became known as the Roman Catholic Church (the Protestants sprang from this tradition too); and the Eastern, or Greek, Orthodox Church became centred on Constantinople (this is the tradition of most of the region's Orthodox Churches). Subsequent divisions resulted in the emergence of the Armenian Apostolic (sometimes referred to as Gregorian) Church and the Assyrian (sometimes referred to as Nestorian) Church of the East.

The Church also established the Christian era (a calendar of years denoted by *Anno Domini*), a reckoning that is now the most widely used international system and is in official use throughout the countries of Eastern Europe, Russia and Central Asia. Likewise, it was the Church that preserved the use of the ancient Roman, Julian calendar, which was used in the Russian Empire until the revolution. A reformed Gregorian calendar (in normal use now) was first introduced in 1582, but, because it was the initiative of Pope Gregory XIII, its adoption was initially resisted by non-Roman Catholic countries. For religious purposes, the Eastern Orthodox Church still uses a version of the old Julian calendar (and the Georgian Orthodox calendar is different again).

The Eastern Orthodox Church

The split (schism) in the Church that had become established in the old Roman Empire was formalized in 1054. The bishops of what had been the Latin-speaking West supported the authority of the Pope, the Roman patriarch, and the insertion of the *filioque* clause into the standard confession of faith, the Nicene Creed. (This claimed that the Holy Spirit, a constituent part of the triune deity, was a product of both the Father and the Son— *Logos*—not merely of the Father.) The bishops of the Greek-speaking Eastern Roman Empire, dominated by the Byzantine Patriarch of Constantinople (today still regarded as the Ecumenical Patriarch), rejected this, and the religious division of Europe into East and West became formal. The Eastern Orthodox Church continued to use the Greek alphabet, but had also added to the success of its missionary work among the 'barbarian' peoples, on the Byzantine borders, by introducing the Cyrillic alphabet (the invention of which is attributed to the ninth century Byzantine missionaries SS Cyril—Constantine—and Methodius) and a Slavonic liturgy. The powerful formative influence of the Church, particularly on culture, education and national identity, is still relevant today.

The Eastern Orthodox churches have a membership of some 200m., most of them in Eastern Europe and Russia. They are not formally linked, save in acknowledging the pre-eminence of the Ecumenical Patriarch (Bartholomeos I of Constantinople and New Rome, since 1991), who convened a meeting of 12 of the highest Eastern Orthodox patriarchs in the Turkish city of İstanbul (formerly Constantinople) during 1992. The Russian Orthodox Church (Moscow Patriarchate) is the largest ecclesiastical organization and also assumed jurisdiction, following the westward expansion of the USSR during the Second World War, over the Orthodox of Moldavia (Moldova), Transcarpathian Ukraine and Galicia. In the period leading up to the collapse of the USSR, and in the years that followed, however, it increasingly devolved power from the Moscow Patriarchate (which had been re-established in 1943, in an attempt to retain influence); for example, in 1989 the former Ukrainian Exarchate of the Moscow Patriarchate was re-formed as the Ukrainian Orthodox Church (Moscow Patriarchate) and granted a greater level of self-government. All the countries of the region have at least some Orthodox Christians.

Within the countries of Eastern Europe, Russia and Central Asia, there are missions of the Eastern Orthodox Patriarchs of Antioch and Alexandria, but the other main Orthodox Church is the Georgian Church. The Primate of the Georgian Orthodox Church, the Catholicos-Patriarch, also enjoys jurisdiction over several Russian and Greek communities, but, under the communists, the Church was restricted by the lack of its own seminary and by the limited instruction in Georgian devotional literature and liturgical traditions. After independence, this position was reversed.

With the liberalization of religion, religious groups increasingly demanded greater autonomy and a reversal of russification, resulting in, *inter alia*, the revival of the Ukrainian Autocephalous Orthodox Church (which had been suppressed and absorbed into the Moscow Patriarchate in 1930). There was also the return of those Orthodox who went into exile after the communists came to power (often forming rival hierarchies abroad) and after the secession of the Eastern-rite 'Greek' Catholics (see below), who had been forcibly amalgamated with the Orthodox, notably in Ukraine at the so-called Synod of Lviv in 1946. (Since the bishops of the Ukrainian Greek Catholic Church were at that time either imprisoned or living in exile, no bishops—and indeed very few members of the clergy of any description—were involved in the gathering, rendering it canonically illegitimate to the vast majority of those outside of the Soviet regime.)

The Old Believers (*Staroobryadtsi*) of the Russian Orthodox tradition, who rejected reforms of the 18th century, have long had an eminent role in Russian cultural and spiritual life. Old Believers are divided into two main branches: the *popovtsi* (which have priests) and the *bespopovtsi* (which reject the notion of ordained priests). Both branches are further divided into various groupings. The largest *popovtsi* group are those of the Belokrinitskii Concord, while another important group are those of the Beglopopovtsyi Concord.

The Roman Catholic Church

The Western, or Roman Catholic, Church was distinguished by its use of a liturgy in Latin, which is still referred to as the Latin Rite, although, in response to the Second Vatican Council (1962–65), most services were thenceforth conducted in the vernacular, and much of the liturgical practice associated with the rite was also substantially amended, with the introduction of what is sometimes referred to as the *Novus Ordo* form of the mass. The Latin Rite is not used by the adherents of the 'Greek' Catholic or 'Uniate' Church. This denomination is part of the Roman Catholic Church, but uses an Eastern or Byzantine Rite; their Orthodox predecessors had acknowledged the primacy of the Roman pontiff, the Pope—as well as the existence of Purgatory, the doctrine of the *filioque* and the use of unleavened bread for communion—but retained their traditional liturgies and ecclesiastical organization; these arrangements were, initially, instigated by the Synod of Brest (in present-day Belarus) in 1596. Not all Eastern Catholics use Byzantine Rites; there are some from non-Orthodox traditions. In the region there are the Armenian Catholics, Rusyn-Carpathian Catholics and some Chaldean (Nestorian) Catholics, who also retain their Oriental customs and rites (the remaining Uniates are the Maronites, the Syrian Catholics and the Coptic Catholics).

Protestant Churches

In the Reformation period of the 16th and 17th centuries some of the Western, or Catholic, Christians rejected the authority of the Roman pontiff, the Pope, and formed separate sects. Most of these groups (which subsequently became known as 'Protestants', from the Latin expressions *pro testare*—to bear witness to—and *protestatio*—the act of protesting—against ecclesiastical practices or dogma) relied to a greater extent on the authority of the Bible and often rejected the episcopal organization of the Church. The main denominations are: Lutheran Evangelicals (who define their faith by the Augsburg Confession of 1530); Calvinists and Presbyterians; Zwinglists; Baptists; Pentecostalists; and Unitarians. There are also communities of Seventh-day Adventists (distinguished among Christians by their observance of the Sabbath on Saturday), Methodists, Mennonites (mainly of German descent, they combine characteristics of the Baptists and the Religious Society of Friends—Quakers), Molokane ('milk-drinkers'—pacifists who broke away from Russian Orthodoxy, and who are mainly resident in the Caucasus) and many others.

Other Christian Churches

The Armenian Apostolic, or Gregorian, Church is one of the Monophysite churches, like the Coptic and Syrian Jacobite Churches. It separated from the rest of the Church when it rejected the authority of the Council of Chalcedon in 451. (The Monophysites maintain that there is a single, divine nature in the person of the incarnate Christ, whereas Chalcedon decreed that Christ had two natures, both human and divine.) There are significant Armenian communities in the region and abroad, quite apart from in Armenia itself. In the 1950s there was an acrimonious schism in the Church, between the Supreme Patriarchate and the Catholicosate of Cilicia (based in Beirut, Lebanon). In 1995, however, the Catholicos of Cilicia was chosen as the new Supreme Patriarch, with the support of the Armenian Government, in an effort to end the schism; he died in 1999.

Another ancient Christian sect that differed from the orthodox on the nature of Christ were the Nestorians (followers of a fifth-century Patriarch of Constantinople), some communities of whom live in the countries of Eastern Europe, Russia and Central Asia. The Nestorians once dominated Central Asia and much of the Middle East.

ISLAM

Islam means 'submission' or surrender to God. It is the preferred name for the monotheistic religion founded by its Prophet, Muhammad (AD 570–632), in Arabia. The unparalleled spread of the religion in its first centuries can be attributed to the concept of holy war (*jihad*), although this term is also used to describe a non-military, spiritual struggle.

The Five Pillars of the practice of Islam are: the Witness that 'there is no god but God' (*Allah*) and that 'Muhammad is His Prophet'; prayer, which takes place five times daily and includes recitation of set verses and prostration in the direction of the holy city of Mecca (Makkah), Saudi Arabia, and which is also performed in congregational worship at a mosque on Fridays (the Muslim holy day); almsgiving; fasting, which must take place during the hours of daylight for the whole of the ninth month, Ramadan (some exceptions are allowed); and the Pilgrimage (*hajj*) to Mecca, which is incumbent at least once in the lifetime of a Muslim, if this is feasible. The heart of Islam is contained in the Koran, which is considered to be the very Word of God as uttered to his Prophet, and therefore to be above criticism. This authority is supplemented by various traditions (*hadith*). To interpret the application of Islamic law (*Shari'a*) into everyday activity, four main schools of thought emerged, the main one in the region being the Hanafi. An ideal of the Islamic community (*umma*) is that the brotherhood of Muslims is its basis and that the religion is international and beyond tribal division. However, there has not been an unchallenged Muslim leader since the Prophet, and the last of the Caliphs (*khalifas* or 'successors' of Muhammad), who resided in Constantinople, had his office abolished by the Turkish Government in 1924.

Uzbekistan has the largest Muslim population in the region, although the other states in Central Asia, as well as Azerbaijan, are also predominantly Muslim. The North Caucasus, within Russia, is also an important Muslim region. In central Russia and Siberia there are large numbers of predominately Muslim Tatars, Chuvash and Bashkirs.

Muslims use a lunar calendar, which is about 10 days shorter than the solar calendar of the Gregorian reckoning. Islam dates its years from the *Hijra*—the flight of the Prophet Muhammad from Mecca to Medina, also in Saudi Arabia, so the year 1430 AH (*Anno Hegirae*) begins on AD 29 December 2008.

Sunni Muslims

Some 80% of the world's Muslims are Sunni, followers of 'the path' or customary way. They acknowledge the first four Caliphs as successors of Muhammad—Abu Bakr, 'Umar (Omar), 'Uthman (Othman) and 'Ali—and follow one of the four main schools of law. Other Muslims differ only in the interpretation of the true tradition (*sunna*). Except in the Iranian-influenced area of Azerbaijan, most of the region's Muslims are Sunni and of the Hanafi sect.

The theologians of the Salafi *ikhwan* ('brotherhood') maintain the strictest observance of the principle of monotheism, rejecting the veneration of holy men and holy places, and advocate the cleansing of Islam of late accretions and innovations. The 'Wahhabism' movement, as it is often described (and usually pejoratively in the post-Soviet states), was, within the USSR, primarily to be found in the Uzbek SSR, but was considered increasingly influential in Tajikistan at the beginning of the civil war (1992–97). There are also similar groups, which grew in influence and number in the 1990s and 2000s in the Russian North Caucasus, particularly in Chechnya, Dagestan, Ingushetiya and the Kabardino-Balkar Republic.

Shi'a Muslims

The Shi'a, or 'followers' of 'Ali (cousin of Muhammad and husband of Fatima, the Prophet's daughter), reject the first three Caliphs of Sunni Islam and assert that the fourth Caliph was the rightful successor of Muhammad. 'Ali's son, Husain, is the great Shi'ite martyr. 'Ali's name is added after Muhammad's in the confession of faith, but otherwise the fundamental beliefs of the Shi'a are broadly similar to those of the Sunnis. The Shi'a instituted an *imam*, rather than a caliph, as their spiritual 'leader'. Most Shi'ites are 'Twelvers' and recognize a succession of 12 Imams, the last disappearing in AD 878; this occluded or hidden Imam, it is believed, will return as the *Mahdi* ('guided one'). However, some Shi'ites—the Isma'ilis—are known as 'Seveners', because they believe that Isma'il, or one of his sons, was the seventh and last Imam, disappearing in AD 765. There were political reasons for the schism, but the Isma'ilis also have a more mystical faith. There are several sects. The main group in the region is in Kuhistoni Badakhshon Autonomous Viloyat in eastern Tajikistan, and they are Pamirs, followers of the Aga Khan (some Pamirs are Sunni).

Sufis

The Sufis are mystics, found in all branches of Islam since very early in the religion's history. Named on account of their woollen (*suf*) monastic robes, the Sufis tempered orthodox formalism and deism with a quest for complete identification with the Supreme Being and annihilation of the self (the existence of the latter is known as polytheism, *shirk*), although this sometimes approached pantheism. The Sufis verged on the edge of acceptability for some time, but became an important influence. They are organized into what are loosely known as 'brotherhoods' (*turuq* or, singular, *tariqa*). In Soviet Central Asia clandestine Sufi groups were responsible for bolstering the officially tolerated Islamic institutions; they were fiercely anti-communist. After the dissolution of the USSR, their influence became more apparent, not only in Central Asia but also in the eastern Caucasus. Thus, Sufis (mainly of the *Qadiriya tariqa*) were predominant in the religious establishment of secessionist Chechnya in the mid-1990s.

BUDDHISM

The number of Buddhists in Russia is uncertain, but there have been reports of up to 1m., mostly among the Buryats of Eastern

Siberia, the Tyvans, near the border with Mongolia, and the Kalmyks, to the west of the Caspian Sea. There are only small groups of Buddhist converts in Eastern Europe.

The founder of the faith, sometimes referred to as 'the Buddha', was a north Indian of the warrior caste, Siddhartha Gautama (usually ascribed the dates 563–483 BC). He renounced his privileges in the search for enlightenment, which he found under the Bo or Bodhi-tree; he understood the cycle of existence, the cycle of suffering and the way to Nirvana—the state of perfect peace believed to be achievable by the eradication of *kilesa* (mind-contaminants, such as avarice and anger). He had become a Buddha or 'enlightened one' and, with the support of a monastic following, taught his *Dharma* (law, virtue, right, religion or truth), which must be followed on a Middle Way between the extremes of sensuality and asceticism. Gautama taught a scheme of moral and spiritual improvement by which the endless round of existence could be escaped and Nirvana obtained. Sometimes described as agnostic, or even atheistic, this ignores the adoration of the Buddha himself. Furthermore, northern Buddhism, as practised in Siberia, has particularly retained and developed a belief in the hosts of celestial beings who can help. There are not only many Buddhas, but countless Bodhisattvas ('beings of enlightenment'), who have deferred their own Nirvana. The northern Buddhists describe themselves as of the Mahayana school, followers of the 'great vehicle' to Nirvana.

Buddhists use a lunar calendar. The Buddhist era is usually dated from the death of Gautama Buddha, nominally reckoned to be 544 BC, with AD 2009 approximately conterminous with 2553.

JUDAISM

Judaism is the oldest of the major monotheistic religions, and advocates a code of morality and civil and religious duties. Its holy book (which also serves as the Old Testament of the Christian Bible) is supported by ancient rabbinic writings (the Talmud) and by traditions, which are expounded by the rabbis, who are doctors of the law and leaders of the Jewish congregations, which meet in synagogues. There are two main Jewish communities, which observe distinct rituals but have no doctrinal differences. The predominant European group is the Ashkenazim; there are some Sephardim in the Caucasian and Central Asian countries. While both Christianity and Islam claim descent from, or to be the fulfilment of, Judaism, the Jews, as a race as well as a religious group, have long been the victims of prejudice. Anti-Semitism has a long history in the Christian Church, and the more recent Arab–Israeli conflict has bolstered anti-Semitic prejudice among the Islamic community. The Jews were formerly widespread throughout Eastern Europe and Russia. Their numbers, however, were substantially reduced during the Second World War, particularly in areas dominated by the Nazis. This holocaust (*shoah*) of the Jewish people was the most extreme manifestation of the anti-Semitism that was endemic in Central and Eastern Europe and in the Russian Empire. These traditional prejudices were not completely rejected (and, indeed, on occasion, were promoted) by the communist regimes, and, after the fall of these governments, anti-Semitism re-emerged strongly in some areas, despite the often small number of Jews. Emigration, usually to Israel, also reduced numbers, although a significant number of Jews were reported to have returned to Russia and Ukraine from Israel by the mid-2000s, while many Jews migrated from the post-Soviet states to Germany. Some Turkic peoples of the region, notably a small minority of Azeris, practise Judaism, surviving since the times of the Khazar (Hazar) kaganate, an empire to the north of the Caucasus that disappeared in the 11th century. There are also small communities of so-called Mountain Jews (also known as Tats or Dagchufuts), who speak a Persian language, in the Caucasus region, principally in Dagestan, Georgia and Azerbaijan. Central Asian Jews, who generally speak a form of Tajik, and live in Uzbekistan and Tajikistan, are also regarded as a distinct group.

The Jewish calendar is luni-solar and reckons years in the Era of Creation (*Anno Mundi*)—the year AM 5768 began at sundown on AD 29 September 2008.

OTHER RELIGIONS

Some traditional beliefs persist in Eastern Europe, Russia and Central Asia, including some shamanistic practices and ancestor worship. Shamanism is particularly prevalent in some regions of Siberia, while some aspects of the traditional animistic religion of the Finno-Ugric Mari people remain in the Republic of Marii-El, on the River Volga. There are also some small Zoroastrian communities, to the north of Iran. This ancient religion is sometimes described as dualistic, but believes in the ultimate triumph of the principle of good. It is thought to have influenced both Judaism and Christianity and was once the state religion of Persia (Iran). Some of the Kurdish people are Yazidis, most of whom live in Armenia and Georgia. They are sometimes known as 'Devil-worshippers', owing to a mistaken understanding of their belief in the redemption of Lucifer, the fallen angel or evil principle of Christian and Zoroastrian cosmology. The Yazidi beliefs are a synthesis of Zoroastrian, Nestorian Christian, Jewish and Muslim traditions.

PART TWO
Country Surveys

ARMENIA

Geography

PHYSICAL FEATURES

The Republic of Armenia is situated in the western South Caucasus, on the north-eastern border of Turkey. Its other borders are with Iran to the south, Azerbaijan to the east, Georgia to the north, and the Autonomous Republic of Naxçıvan (an Azerbaijani territory) to the south-west. The Republic of Armenia, which covers 29,743 sq km (11,484 sq miles), is the remnant of a much larger area of Armenian settlement that existed before the First World War and included many areas of eastern Turkey and other regions of the Caucasus, including Nagornyi Karabakh, in Azerbaijan.

The central physical feature of Armenia is Lake Sevan, a mountainous lake at an altitude of 1,924 m (6,313 ft), which is surrounded by high mountain ranges, reaching 4,090 m (13,419 ft) at Mt Aragats. The mountains are drained by numerous streams and rivers flowing into the River Araks (Aras, Araxes), which empties into the Caspian Sea. The Araks marks the south-western border of the country, and its basin forms a fertile lowland to the south of Yerevan called the Ararat plain.

CLIMATE

The climate is typically continental: dry, with large variations in temperature. Winters are cold, the average January temperature in Yerevan being -3°C (26°F), but summers can be very warm, with August temperatures averaging 25°C (77°F), although high altitude moderates the heat in much of the country. Precipitation is low in the Yerevan area (annual average, 322 mm), but much higher in the mountains.

POPULATION

At the 1989 census, 93.3% of the total de facto population of 3,287,677 were Armenians, 2.6% Azeri, 1.7% Kurds and 1.5% Russians, according to the official declaration of nationality (or ethnicity) required of Soviet citizens. Other ethnic groups included Ukrainians, Assyrians and Greeks. As a result of inter-ethnic tension, almost the entire Azeri population was reported to have left Armenia after the census was conducted, principally for Azerbaijan, and Armenian refugees entered Armenia from Azerbaijan. There are many Armenians in Georgia, and there are also important Armenian communities abroad, particularly in the USA, Russia and France. At the census of 2001 97.9% of the population were Armenians, 1.3% were Yazidis and 0.5% were Russians.

The official language is Armenian, the sole member of a distinct Indo-European language group. It is written in the Armenian script. Much of the population speak Russian as a

second language, and Kurdish is used in some broadcasting and publishing. Most of the population are adherents of Christianity, the largest denomination being the Armenian Apostolic Church. There are also Russian Orthodox, Protestant, Islamic and Yazidi communities.

The total population at the census of 10 October 2001 was 3,002,594. (However, this figure failed to take account of the migration of many Armenians in search of work abroad.) The estimated population at January 2008 was 3,230,100, giving a population density of 108.6 inhabitants per sq km. The capital is Yerevan, which had an estimated population of 1,103,800 at January 2006. Other important towns include Gyumri (formerly Leninakan), with an estimated 148,300 inhabitants at January 2006, and Vanadzor (formerly Kirovakan—105,500). In 2004 64% of the country's population lived in urban areas.

Chronology

c. 850 BC: Indo-European tribes, Chaldeans, occupied territory to the south of the Caucasus, destroying the ancient kingdom of Urartu (Ararat); these two peoples were the ancestors of the Armenians.

64: The Roman Empire secured its pre-eminence in the region with the final defeat of the Kingdom of Pontus, to which the Armenians had been allied; parts of Armenia eventually became a Roman province.

AD 117: The Emperor Hadrian retracted the borders of the Roman Empire back to the River Euphrates (that is, still including what was known as Lesser Armenia or Armenia

Minor), despite his predecessor Trajan's conquest of much territory to the east (Greater Armenia or Armenia Major).

c. 300: St Gregory the Illuminator began the conversion of Armenia, which became the first Christian state at a time of renewed struggle for dominance in the region, between the Empires of Rome and Persia (Iran).

451: The Fourth Council of Chalcedon condemned Monophysitism, isolating the Armenians from the rest of the Christian Church.

639: The first Arab raids on Armenia marked the beginning of Muslim influence in the area.

1071: The Seljuq Turk victory at the Battle of Manzikert (now Malazgirt, Turkey) confirmed the Eastern Roman ('Byzantine') expulsion from Armenia and its environs and the dominance of the Sultanate of Iconium (Konya) or Rum.

1375: Egypt's Mamelukes conquered the Armenian capital of Sis and ended the country's nominal independence.

1639: After many years of dispute, Armenia was partitioned between the Turkish Ottoman Empire (which secured the larger, western part) and the Persian Empire by the Treaty of Zuhab.

1828: Persia ceded Eastern Armenia to the Russian Empire by the Treaty of Turkmanchai.

1878: Russia gained the province of Kars from the Ottomans by the Congress of Berlin.

1915: The Ottoman massacres and persecution of Armenians, increasing since the 1890s, were at their most severe, rapidly depopulating Anatolian Armenia. More than 1m. Armenians were killed in the massacres of 1915–17.

22 April 1918: Proclamation of a Transcaucasian federation (Armenia, Azerbaijan and Georgia), following the collapse of tsarist rule and the Soviet signing of the Treaty of Brest-Litovsk.

28 May 1918: Turkish menaces caused the collapse of Transcaucasia and the proclamation of an independent Armenia, which was governed by the Armenian Revolutionary Federation (ARF—Dashnaktsutyun, also known as Dashnaks); Armenia was forced to cede territory around Kars to the Turks.

10 August 1920: The Treaty of Sèvres, between the Allied Powers and the Ottoman authorities, recognized an independent Armenia, but the Treaty was rejected by the new Turkish leader, Mustafa Kemal (Atatürk).

September 1920: Turkish troops invaded Armenia after the ARF Government intervened in Anatolia, concerned at the savage persecution of ethnic Armenians there.

29 November 1920: Proclamation of the Soviet Republic of Armenia, following the invasion of Bolshevik troops.

1921: A series of treaties led to the establishment of Nagornyi Karabakh as a mainly ethnic Armenian enclave within, and part of, Azerbaijan; Turkey recognized its borders with Soviet Transcaucasia.

December 1922: Armenia became a member of the Transcaucasian Soviet Federative Socialist Republic (TSFSR), which itself joined the Union of Soviet Socialist Republics (USSR).

December 1936: The new Soviet Constitution dissolved the TSFSR, and Armenia became a full Union Republic in its own name.

February 1988: The Nagornyi Karabakh Soviet (Council) passed a resolution demanding a transfer to Armenian jurisdiction. Armenians, led by a group of Yerevan intellectuals, the Karabakh Committee, demonstrated in support. The demands were followed by anti-Armenian violence in Sumqayıt, Azerbaijan.

December 1988: Northern Armenia, particularly the city of Leninakan (now Gyumri), was devastated by an earthquake.

September 1989: In response to mounting tensions over Nagornyi Karabakh, the Azerbaijani authorities commenced a blockade of energy and fuel supplies to Armenia. Turkey subsequently instigated a similar blockade of Armenia in support of Azerbaijan.

1 December 1989: The Armenian Supreme Soviet (Supreme Council, the republican legislature) declared Nagornyi Karabakh to be part of a unified Armenian Republic, following the end of direct rule in the enclave by the all-Union Government (since January) and the restoration of Azerbaijani authority.

January 1990: The all-Union Supreme Soviet declared that Armenia's December declaration was unconstitutional, whereupon the Armenian Supreme Soviet resolved that it had the power to veto central legislation.

May 1990: In the elections to the Armenian Supreme Soviet, the Armenian Pan-National Movement (APNM), the successor to the Karabakh Committee, became the largest single party, obtaining some 35% of the votes cast; the APNM leader, Levon Ter-Petrossian, was elected Chairman of the Supreme Soviet (republican Head of State).

23 August 1990: The Armenian SSR declared its sovereignty and changed its name to the Republic of Armenia.

March 1991: Armenia refused to participate in the referendum on the Union, having declined to join negotiations since late 1990.

August 1991: Vazgen Manukian resigned as premier, being replaced by Khosrov Haroutunian.

23 September 1991: The results of a referendum on secession held two days earlier (94.4% of the electorate participated and, of them, 99.3% voted in favour of secession) prompted the republican Supreme Council to declare Armenia an independent state.

16 October 1991: Ter-Petrossian remained Head of State after national elections for the post of President of the Republic.

10 December 1991: In a referendum, residents of Nagornyi Karabakh strongly favoured independence from Azerbaijan, although neither the poll, nor the 'Republic of Nagornyi Karabakh' that had been proclaimed in September received international recognition.

21 December 1991: Armenia signed the Almaty Declaration, by which it became a member of the Commonwealth of Independent States (CIS), the formation of which effectively dissolved the USSR.

2 March 1992: Armenia became a member of the UN. In the previous month Armenia had been admitted to the Conference on Security and Co-operation in Europe—CSCE, from December 1994 the Organization for Security and Co-operation in Europe—OSCE.

May 1992: Following months of full-scale conflict, Armenia and Azerbaijan negotiated a brief cease-fire, although Armenia claimed to have no control over the Nagornyi Karabakh militia, which had secured the whole enclave and a land 'corridor' to Armenia.

December 1992: President Ter-Petrossian declared a national state of emergency in Armenia.

February 1993: Following the resignation of Khosrov Haroutunian, Hrant Bagratian was appointed as Prime Minister.

30 April 1993: The UN Security Council, under Resolution 822, demanded that all Armenian forces immediately withdraw from Azerbaijani territory and that a cease-fire be observed. Further motions were adopted on 29 July (Resolution 853) and 14 October (Resolution 874).

24 May 1993: The Armenian Government agreed to a CSCE-negotiated peace plan for Nagornyi Karabakh. Azerbaijan also signed the plan, but it was not accepted by the Nagornyi Karabakh leadership until June.

22 November 1993: An Armenian currency, the dram, was introduced.

9–11 May 1994: Following protracted mediation by the CSCE and Russia, a new cease-fire agreement was signed by the Ministers of Defence of Armenia and Azerbaijan, and representatives of Nagornyi Karabakh. The agreement was formalized on 27 July.

October 1994: Armenia joined the North Atlantic Treaty Organization's (NATO) 'Partnership for Peace' programme.

5 July 1995: A referendum on a new Constitution was held: some 68% of those voting approved the document, which gave wider executive power to the President and reduced the number of seats in the legislature, the Azgayin Zhoghov (National Assembly), from 190 to 131, with effect from the next general election. In concurrent legislative elections, the Republican (Hanrapetutiun) bloc, a coalition led by the APNM, won 119 of the 190 elective seats.

24 July 1995: Hrant Bagratian was confirmed as premier by the new Azgayin Zhoghov.

22 September 1996: A presidential election was held, in which Ter-Petrossian obtained 51.8% of the votes cast. In November the Constitutional Court rejected opposition appeals that the election results be declared invalid.

4 November 1996: Bagratian resigned as Prime Minister; Armen Sarkissian was appointed in his place.

6 March 1997: Sarkissian resigned as Prime Minister, and was replaced by Robert Kocharian (hitherto the President of the 'Republic of Nagornyi Karabakh') on 20 March.

April 1997: The Azgayin Zhoghov ratified a treaty allowing Russia to maintain military bases in Armenia for a period of 25 years. In August Armenia and Russia signed a Treaty of 'Friendship, Co-operation and Mutual Understanding'.

3 February 1998: Ter-Petrossian resigned as President, following disputes within the Government over his support for an OSCE peace settlement for Nagornyi Karabakh, which entailed some withdrawal of Armenian forces. The Chairman of the Azgayin Zhoghov, Babken Ararktsian, resigned the following day.

30 March 1998: Robert Kocharian, who, as Prime Minister, had been acting President since Ter-Petrossian's resignation, was confirmed as President following a second round of voting in the presidential election, with 59.5% of the votes cast. Of the registered electorate, 68.1% voted.

10 April 1998: Armen Darbinian was appointed Prime Minister. In the same month President Kocharian met President Heydar Aliyev of Azerbaijan in Moscow, Russia, and agreed to recommence negotiations on Nagornyi Karabakh.

5 February 1999: New legislation, which provided for a 131-member legislature composed of 80 deputies elected by majority vote through single-mandate constituencies, with 51 chosen under a system of proportional representation, on the basis of party lists, was adopted.

May 1999: Vano Siradeghian, the Chairman of the APNM and a former Minister of the Interior, was arrested for his alleged participation in a number of political murders in the mid-1990s; his trial commenced in January 2000, and he fled the country in April.

30 May 1999: Legislative elections were held. The Unity bloc (Miasnutiun), an alliance of the Republican Party of Armenia (RPA) and the People's Party of Armenia (PPA), proved successful, winning a total of 55 seats in the Azgayin Zhoghov.

11 June 1999: Armen Darbinian was replaced as Prime Minister by the unofficial leader of the RPA and hitherto Minister of Defence, Vazgen Sarkissian (unrelated to former Prime Minister Armen Sarkissian).

27 October 1999: Five gunmen (who claimed no political allegiance) besieged the legislative chamber. Eight people were killed during the attack, including Prime Minister Vazgen Sarkissian and Karen Demirchian, the Chairman of the Azgayin Zhoghov. President Kocharian assumed control of the Government until a new Prime Minister could be assigned.

2 November 1999: Armen Khachatrian, a member of the PPA, was elected Chairman of the Azgayin Zhoghov. On the following day President Kocharian appointed Aram Sarkissian, the younger brother of the murdered premier, as the new Prime Minister.

12 May 2000: Andranik Markarian was appointed Prime Minister, replacing Sarkissian, who had been removed from

his post on 2 May. A cabinet reorganization subsequently took place.

25 January 2001: Both Armenia and Azerbaijan were formally admitted to the Council of Europe.

9 July 2001: Senior government officials reached an agreement with their Turkish counterparts providing for the establishment of a Turkish-Armenian Reconciliation Commission (TARC).

7 September 2001: The PPA left the Unity bloc and subsequently joined two opposition parties in demanding the resignation of President Kocharian.

14–15 September 2001: The Russian President, Vladimir Putin, visited Armenia and signed a 10-year economic agreement, which included proposals to transfer a number of state-owned enterprises to Russian ownership, in partial repayment of debts to Russia amounting to over US $90m.

5 April 2002: Some 10,000 people attended an opposition-sponsored protest against the closure of the country's only independent television station, A1+, which opposition parties claimed to be politically motivated. Demands were made for President Kocharian's resignation at a further large-scale protest held one week later, and demonstrations continued throughout April.

3 July 2002: Amendments to the electoral law provided for the election of 56 deputies by majority single-mandate constituencies, with the remaining 75 to be elected under a system of proportional representation, on the basis of party lists.

5 February 2003: Armenia became a full member of the World Trade Organization.

19 February and 5 March 2003: Following two rounds of voting, Kocharian was re-elected as President, with 67.5% of the votes cast in the run-off poll. There was strong international criticism of electoral procedure, and widespread protest demonstrations took place inside Armenia.

28 April 2003: Representatives from Armenia, Belarus, Kazakhstan, Kyrgyzstan, Russia and Tajikistan formally inaugurated the successor to the CIS Collective Security Treaty, the Collective Security Treaty Organization (CSTO). The membership agreement was ratified by the Azgayin Zhoghov in September.

25 May 2003: Legislative elections were held, in which the RPA obtained the largest number of seats in the Azgayin Zhoghov, followed by the Law-Governed Country Party of Armenia. The OSCE and opposition parties subsequently reported a number of electoral violations. A concurrent referendum on proposed constitutional amendments was declared invalid, after fewer than the requisite one-third of registered voters approved the proposals.

11 June 2003: The RPA, the Law-Governed Country Party of Armenia and the ARF signed an agreement on the formation of a new, coalition Government; RPA leader Andranik Markarian retained the premiership, and Artur Baghdasarian, the Chairman of the Law-Governed Country Party of Armenia, assumed the post of Chairman of the Azgayin Zhoghov. The new legislature was the first in 85 years not to include any communist representation. Members of the opposition Justice (Artarutiun) bloc and the National Unity Party boycotted the opening session of the Azgayin Zhoghov, and maintained their protest until September.

18 November 2003: Armen Sarkissian, the younger brother of the murdered premier Vazgen Sarkissian and of prominent opposition leader (and former premier) Aram Sarkissian, was sentenced to 15 years' imprisonment, having been found guilty of arranging and funding the murder of the Chairman of the board of Armenian Public Television and Radio, Tighran Naghdalian, in December 2002. It was claimed that the charges against him were politically motivated.

2 December 2003: Six men were sentenced to life imprisonment for the attack on the Azgayin Zhoghov in 1999 and on eight associated charges of murder; another was sentenced to 14 years' imprisonment.

3 February 2004: Opposition parties began a boycott of the Azgayin Zhoghov over the refusal to debate constitutional amendments that would permit a referendum of confidence in the President. The boycott ended in September 2005.

April–June 2004: A series of large-scale anti-Government protests took place, despite the precautionary detention of members of the opposition, and the widespread use of force and mass arrests in response to the demonstrations. Remonstrations from the international community followed in reaction to the Government's handling of the crisis.

8–10 September 2004: President Hojatoleslam Dr Sayed Muhammad Khatami of Iran undertook a state visit to Armenia, during which he and President Kocharian signed seven bilateral agreements.

28 September 2005: The Azgayin Zhoghov approved a number of proposed constitutional amendments, which were to be submitted to a national referendum in November, despite ongoing objections by the Justice bloc and the National Unity Party. The amendments had been approved by the Council of Europe's advisory body on constitutional issues, the European Commission for Democracy through Law (Venice Commission), in July.

27 November 2005: Some 93% of valid votes were cast in favour of the proposed constitutional amendments at a referendum, with a participation rate by the electorate of 65%. However, the results were strongly disputed by opposition parties, and public rallies of protest ensued. International observers also noted discrepancies in attendance figures.

12 May 2006: Artur Baghdasarian resigned as Chairman of the Azgayin Zhoghov, and his political party, the Law-Governed Country Party of Armenia, withdrew from the governing coalition, after he expressed opinions on foreign relations counter to government policy. However, several members resigned from that party, including the Minister of Urban Planning, Aram Haroutunian (who retained his post). Levon Mkrtchian of the ARF was subsequently appointed as Minister of Education and Science (in place of Sergo Yeritsian) and Hasmik Poghossian assumed the portfolio of Culture and Youth Affairs, succeeding Gevorg Gevorgian. Poghossian was nominated by the United Labour Party, which had agreed to co-operate with the government coalition. (A new bloc of members of parliament who had left the Law-Governed Country Party of Armenia was established in the legislature.)

1 June 2006: Tigran Torossian of the RPA was elected Chairman of the Azgayin Zhoghov.

22 July 2006: Minister of Defence Serge Sarkissian joined the ruling RPA and was elected as its Chairman. Sarkissian was perceived as a potential successor to President Kocharian.

31 July 2006: Official approval was granted for the establishment of a new party, Prosperous Armenia, led by Gagik Tsarukian, a wealthy businessman and supporter of President Kocharian.

December 2006: The Armenian authorities claimed to have suppressed a plot to stage a coup; Zhirair Sefilian, a former military commander during the 1991–94 war, was arrested as one of the founders of the newly formed Union of Armenian Volunteers organization, to which the plot was attributed.

25 March 2007: Prime Minister Markarian died suddenly, following a heart attack.

4 April 2007: Serge Sarkissian was appointed as the new Prime Minister, in an acting capacity. Later that month Col-

Gen. Mikhail Haroutunian, hitherto Chief of General Staff of the Armed Forces, was named as Sarkissian's successor as Minister of Defence.

12 May 2007: Elections to the 131-member Azgayin Zhoghov were held. The RPA secured 64 seats, attracting 33.9% of the votes; Prosperous Armenia won 25 seats and the ARF 16 seats.

8 June 2007: A new coalition Government, comprising the RPA, Prosperous Armenia and the ARF, was established; the RPA commanded 11 ministerial portfolios, while Prosperous Armenia and the ARF were each allocated three. Hovik Abrahamian, of the RPA, received the post of Deputy Prime Minister (while retaining the territorial administration portfolio).

10 October 2007: The US House of Representatives' Foreign Affairs Committee passed a non-binding resolution referring to the 1915 Ottoman massacre of Armenians as 'genocide', prompting strong criticism from the Turkish Government and from US President George W. Bush. However, a vote on the issue was subsequently postponed indefinitely.

19 February 2008: A presidential election was challenged by nine candidates; according to official results, Sarkissian secured 52.8% of the votes cast and Ter-Petrossian 21.5% of the votes. Ter-Petrossian (and other opposition candidates) immediately attributed the results to widespread falsification and demanded that the ballot be repeated, prompting his followers to stage mass protests in his support.

1 March 2008: President Kocharian declared a 20-day state of emergency, after continued protests by opposition supporters in Yerevan were violently suppressed by special police units and interior ministry forces; eight demonstrators were killed as a result of the operation. A number of associates of Ter-Petrossian were detained, and some 30 prominent opposition members were subsequently arrested on charges of precipitating the clashes with the police.

4 March 2008: Severe clashes between Armenian and Azerbaijani military units erupted in Nagornyi Karabakh; four members of the Azerbaijani armed forces were confirmed to have been killed, while Azerbaijan claimed that 12 Armenian soldiers had also died. Each country accused the other of initiating the hostilities. The OSCE 'Minsk Group' (established in 1992 to mediate a resolution) subsequently appealed to Armenia and Azerbaijan to abide by the cease-fire agreement.

8 March 2008: The Constitutional Court upheld the final official election results in favour of Sarkissian, rejecting an appeal by Ter-Petrossian.

21 March 2008: The RPA, Prosperous Armenia and the ARF, together with the Law-Governed Country Party of Armenia, signed an agreement providing for the formation of a coalition government.

9 April 2008: Serge Sarkissian was officially inaugurated as President; he immediately nominated Tigran Sarkissian, hitherto the Governor of the Central Bank of Armenia, as Prime Minister.

21 April 2008: A coalition administration was established; new ministerial appointments included that of Armen Gevorgian (who had no party affiliation) as Deputy Prime Minister and Minister of Territorial Administration. The reorganization also incorporated the creation of a new Ministry of Emergency Situations.

2 June 2008: President Sarkissian accepted the resignation of three ARF government ministers who had been elected to the party's bureau of officials, and appointed a further three members of the ARF in their stead.

6 June 2008: President Sarkissian met President Aliyev of Azerbaijan for discussions on the occasion of a CIS summit meeting in St Petersburg, Russia; the two Heads of State agreed that negotiations on the conflict in Nagornyi Karabakh should continue on the basis of proposals submitted by the OSCE Minsk Group in November 2007.

6 September 2008: Following confirmation that Turkish and Armenian delegations had met in Switzerland for informal discussions on bilateral relations in July, Turkish President Abdullah Gül accepted an invitation from President Sarkissian to attend a football match between their two countries in Yerevan (the first visit by a Turkish Head of State to Armenia). The Ministers of Foreign Affairs of Turkey, Armenia and Azerbaijan met in New York, USA, later in September to discuss Nagornyi Karabakh.

History

Dr EDMUND HERZIG

Revised for this edition by the Editorial Staff.

EARLY HISTORY

Armenia and the Armenians first emerge clearly in historical records of the first millennium BC. In c. AD 314 Armenia became the first state to adopt Christianity. About one century later it developed a distinct alphabet and literary language, and religion and language have remained central to Armenian national identity ever since. Apart from brief periods of independence, for most of its history Armenia formed a borderland and battleground between more powerful, neighbouring states based on the Iranian plateau, in Mesopotamia, in Anatolia or Constantinople (now İstanbul, Turkey) and, more recently, in Russia.

The Treaties of Amasya (1555) and Zuhab (1639) led to the partition of Armenia, with the larger, western part being allotted to the Turkish Osmanlı (Ottoman) Empire and the eastern region becoming part of the Persian (Iranian) Safavid Empire. This division resulted in the development of distinct eastern and western Armenian languages. In 1828 the Russian Empire gained Eastern (Persian) Armenia by the Treaty of Turkmanchai, and in 1878 the Congress of Berlin transferred much of Western (Ottoman) Armenia (Kars province) to Russian control. Over the centuries successive invasions and deportations, as well as the dynamics of international trade, in which Armenian merchants played an active role, resulted in the growth of an Armenian diaspora throughout Eastern Europe, the Middle East, the major commercial centres of Europe and the Indian Ocean, and, ultimately, North America.

In the late 19th century competing claims engendered by emerging Turkish and Armenian nationalism, coupled with the decline and dismemberment of the Ottoman Empire, led to increased tension, antagonism and conflict. This culminated in the 'genocide' of 1915, when the Ottoman authorities, fearing possible Armenian support for a Russian invasion, systematically deported or killed almost the entire Armenian population of Anatolia. Some 1.5m. Armenians were estimated to have been massacred during 1915–23. As a consequence, the diaspora communities of France, Lebanon, Syria and the USA expanded, and the memory of the genocide became a defining element in the Armenian identity.

Following the collapse of Russian imperial power in 1917, Eastern Armenia became part of the short-lived anti-Bolshevik Transcaucasian federation, which also included Azerbaijan and Georgia. Subsequently, on 28 May 1918, after the dissolution of the federation, Armenia became an independent republic. The Government, dominated by the Armenian Revolutionary Federation—Dashnaktsutyun (ARF—also known as the Dashnaks), had to contend with the problems of famine, a continuing Ottoman war and ethno-territorial disputes with Georgia and, more seriously, with Azerbaijan. Hopes that the future of an independent Armenia would be guaranteed by the Treaty of Sèvres, signed by the Allied Powers and the Ottomans on 10 August 1920, were quickly destroyed by the Bolsheviks' friendship treaty with the new Turkish leader, Mustafa Kemal (Atatürk), who rejected the Treaty. This was rapidly followed by a Turkish invasion of Armenia in September. In November the ARF Government resigned, preferring incorporation into the Union of Soviet Socialist Republics (USSR) to annihilation by the Turks.

Bolshevik forces having secured the country, the Soviet Republic of Armenia was officially proclaimed on 29 November.

The ARF was excluded from Armenian politics throughout the period of Soviet rule, but remained a major political force in the diaspora, where it continued to espouse the cause of an independent, non-communist Armenia. Following the dissolution of the USSR in 1991, the ARF returned to Armenia, once more to become an important force in the country.

SOVIET ARMENIA

The borders of Soviet Armenia were defined by a friendship treaty agreed in Moscow, Russia, in March 1921 and by the Treaty of Kars of October, under the terms of which the Bolsheviks ceded to Turkey the bulk of the Western Armenian territories that had been conquered by Imperial Russia. In addition, the Autonomous Republic of Naxçivan was established under Azerbaijan's jurisdiction. Nagornyi Karabakh (Gharabagh or, in Armenian, Artsakh) was also incorporated into Azerbaijan, although it was given the status of an autonomous oblast (region), in recognition of its mainly Armenian population. In December 1922 Armenia joined Azerbaijan and Georgia in the Transcaucasian Soviet Federative Socialist Republic. This was dissolved in December 1936, and Armenia became a full Union Republic of the USSR.

Armenia experienced rapid social and economic development during the Soviet period. Considerable advances were made in agriculture, industry, transport, education, health care, urban development and standards of living. This achievement was the more impressive given the extremely poor socio-economic conditions in Armenia at the beginning of the 1920s, but, as in other republics, the human and material costs of forced collectivization and industrialization were severe. Soviet rule brought security and stability to the truncated Armenia it had created and, to some extent, allowed the consolidation of Armenian national culture and identity through the promotion of the Armenian language and by the establishment of a number of cultural institutions. However, any significant nationalist expression was suppressed. The purges of 1936–38 and 1947–53 greatly reduced the ranks of the Communist Party of Armenia (CPA) and the republic's intelligentsia. The Armenian Apostolic Church was also persecuted severely.

THE NATIONALIST MOVEMENT

From the mid-1980s the policies of the new Soviet leader, Mikhail Gorbachev, perestroika (restructuring) and glasnost (openness), permitted Armenian nationalists to give open expression to their views. There was considerable popular support for their demands, and what began as a loyal movement protesting a few specific issues was rapidly transformed into a campaign for national liberation and independence. Among the concerns expressed were the perceived threat to the future of the Armenian language and the problem of environmental damage caused by Soviet mismanagement and neglect. However, the primary issue that galvanized the Armenian national movement was that of Nagornyi Karabakh, the majority Armenian population of which was expressing deep dissatisfaction with Azerbaijani rule. In late 1987 there was increasing pressure in both Nagornyi Karabakh and Armenia for the reopening of the issue of the status of the enclave. There were also outbreaks of violence between ethnic Armenian and Azeri (ethnic Azerbaijani) villages in the region itself. In February 1988 the Nagornyi Karabakh Regional Soviet (Council) passed an unprecedented resolution demanding a transfer to Armenian jurisdiction. In Armenia and in the Soviet capital, Moscow, Armenians demonstrated in support of the resolution. The number of participants in daily demonstrations in the Armenian capital, Yerevan, increased to hundreds of thousands within one week.

Initially, the Armenian people demonstrated against crimes committed against them before and during the period of Stalin's (Iosif Dzhugashvili's) rule (1924–53), corruption in the higher echelons of the communist parties of Armenia and Azerbaijan, and the maladministration of Nagornyi Karabakh. The protests were generally spontaneous and optimistic, and not antagonistic towards Azeri people in general. However, the mood in Armenia was transformed by anti-Armenian violence, in late February 1988, in the Azerbaijani town of Sumqayıt, in which, according to official reports, 26 Armenians died. This was followed by the exodus, often forced, of hundreds of thousands of Armenians from Azerbaijan and of Azeris from Armenia. The failure of local authorities to control the unrest led to the dismissal, in May, of the First Secretary of the CPA.

The demonstrations were organized by a number of Yerevan intellectuals, who formed a group, the Karabakh Committee, which included Levon Ter-Petrossian, Vazgen Sarkissian and Vazgen Manukian. Through strikes and demonstrations it forced the republican Government, in June 1988, to endorse Nagornyi Karabakh's demand for unification with Armenia, thus creating a major inter-republican crisis with Azerbaijan. In July the Presidium of the Supreme Soviet of the USSR rejected Nagornyi Karabakh's demands, bringing the Armenian national movement into direct confrontation with the Soviet authorities.

In December 1988 a strong earthquake occurred in northern Armenia, destroying the town of Spitak and badly damaging the republic's second largest city, Leninakan (now Gyumri). More than 25,000 people died and some 500,000 were left homeless. Earthquake relief work and reconstruction, far from generating national unity, became a political issue. The CPA Government and the nationalist opposition each accused the other of incompetence and corruption.

Also in December 1988 the central Soviet authorities in Moscow ordered the arrest of the Karabakh Committee and the following month effectively placed Nagornyi Karabakh under direct rule. The crisis, however, continued. There was a general strike in Stepanakert (Xankandi), the enclave's capital, in May to August 1989, and continuing mass demonstrations in Yerevan and Baku (Bakı), Azerbaijan, where, in January 1990, there were further anti-Armenian pogroms. In May 1989 the Karabakh Committee was released and renewed its campaign for the unification of Nagornyi Karabakh with Armenia. Although still fragmented, the opposition became better co-ordinated, forming the Armenian Pan-National Movement (APNM), which later became the party of government during the years of Levon Ter-Petrossian's presidency. By the end of 1989, with the decline of the communist system in Eastern Europe, demands for Armenian independence became stronger. In September Azerbaijan began a road, rail and pipeline blockade of Armenia, which remained in force thereafter, and caused immense damage to the Armenian economy, reducing energy supplies to a minimum and severely impeding the process of reconstruction following the earthquake.

From January 1990 until the attempted coup against Gorbachev in August 1991, there was an increasing alignment of the Russian and Soviet authorities with Azerbaijan against Armenia. Soviet security forces supported Azerbaijan's efforts to reimpose control over Nagornyi Karabakh and ethnic Armenian villages outside the enclave. Xankandi was effectively under siege, and a number of other Armenian settlements were subjected to sustained bombardment and forced depopulation. The conflict escalated markedly, with an increasing use of rockets, artillery, armoured vehicles and even aircraft. In early and mid-1990 there were also outbreaks

of fighting along Armenia's borders with both metropolitan Azerbaijan and Naxçıvan.

In Armenia the nationalist opposition retained the political initiative, with the APNM emerging as the strongest party in elections to the Armenian Supreme Soviet (Supreme Council) in May–July 1990, obtaining some 35% of the seats in the legislature. Levon Ter-Petrossian, the leader of the APNM, defeated Vladimir Movsissian, First Secretary of the CPA, to become Chairman of the Supreme Soviet. Vazgen Manukian, also a leader of the APNM, was appointed Chairman of the Council of Ministers (Head of Government). On 23 August the Supreme Soviet adopted a resolution on sovereignty, including the right to maintain armed forces. The Armenian SSR was renamed the Republic of Armenia.

The existence of illegal Armenian armed formations, and Armenia's refusal to enter into the negotiations between the Soviet republics on a new treaty of union, or to participate in the referendum on the renewal of the USSR, which took place in March 1991, were the main issues of contention between the all-Union authorities and the Armenian Government in that year. In May Ter-Petrossian accused the USSR of having 'declared war on Armenia'. However, the failed coup attempt against Gorbachev in Moscow in August was followed by an improvement in relations between the Soviet authorities and Armenia, to the detriment of relations between the central authorities and Azerbaijan.

INDEPENDENT ARMENIA

Armenia's referendum on secession from the USSR took place on 21 September 1991. According to official figures, 94.4% of the electorate participated, with 99.3% of votes cast in favour of Armenian independence. Two days later the Supreme Council declared Armenia to be an independent state. This was followed, on 16 October, by a presidential election. Six candidates participated in the election, which was won by Ter-Petrossian, with 87% of the total votes cast.

Armenia thus achieved independence relatively smoothly, in marked contrast to neighbouring Azerbaijan and Georgia. However, in late 1991 Ter-Petrossian's Government had some significant problems to resolve: first, the human and material costs of supporting the war effort of the Karabakh Armenians; second, the decline of the economy, owing to the dissolution of the USSR in December and the economic blockade imposed by Azerbaijan (and supported by Turkey); and, finally, the task of reconstruction following the earthquake.

Living standards in Armenia deteriorated considerably in the early 1990s, reducing much of the population to poverty and reliance on international aid and remittances from relatives working abroad. The severe energy shortage was only partially alleviated by the controversial reopening of the Medzamor nuclear power station in 1995 (it had been closed after the earthquake of 1988). Far from fulfilling people's hopes of a better life, the experience of independence left many Armenians disillusioned, impoverished and disaffected. According to some assessments, in the first 10 years of independence nearly 1m. Armenians (some 25% of the total population), largely men of working age, emigrated, mostly to Russia. However, the 2001 census revealed a total population of 3,002,594, representing a decrease of less than 300,000 compared with the figure recorded at the 1989 census. (According to official estimates, the population had increased to 3,230,100 by the beginning of 2008.)

In order to overcome these difficulties, Ter-Petrossian's Government pursued a programme of radical economic reform and developed generally moderate and pragmatic policies in other areas. The Government suffered internal upheaval, including the resignation as premier of Vazgen Manukian in August 1991 and of Khosrov Haroutunian in February 1993, and vigorous opposition in the Supreme Council and on the streets of Yerevan. Opponents described the regime as corrupt, incompetent and authoritarian. However, by the mid-1990s the Government appeared to have succeeded in gaining support, if not from the masses, at least from the new élite, comprising bureaucrats, local administrators and the entrepreneurs of the new market economy.

NAGORNYI KARABAKH

On the issue of Nagornyi Karabakh, President Ter-Petrossian was much more moderate in government than in opposition. Eventually, this cost him his office. Armenia provided substantial moral and material support for the separatists, but denied (although with little credibility) direct military involvement. By the mid-1990s the Armenian Government no longer demanded unification with the enclave, stating that it would accept any settlement that satisfied the Karabakh Armenians. It also resisted pressure to recognize the self-styled 'Republic of Nagornyi Karabakh', which was declared in September 1991, and which, following a referendum on 10 December, declared independence from Azerbaijan.

The nationalist opposition frequently criticized the Armenian Government for its lack of support of the Karabakh cause. Criticism was particularly strong following the launch of an intensive counter-offensive by Azerbaijani forces in June 1992, which resulted in several thousand people being expelled, exacerbating the already serious refugee crisis in Armenia. Armenia's international reputation also suffered following the massacre of Azerbaijani civilians at Xojali on 25 February 1992, and declined further in 1993, when two UN Security Council Resolutions (822 and 853) demanded an Armenian withdrawal from occupied Azerbaijani territory outside the enclave and the implementation of a cease-fire.

Internal critics and its own disclaimers notwithstanding, the Armenian Government's support for the Karabakh Armenians proved vital. In early May 1994 a cease-fire agreement was signed by the Ministers of Defence of Armenia and Azerbaijan, and representatives of Nagornyi Karabakh. By this time the Armenians had not only gained full control of the enclave, but also occupied extensive Azerbaijani territories outside its borders. There were some violations of the cease-fire, but not enough to prevent the agreement being formalized on 27 July. In September President Ter-Petrossian and the Azerbaijani President, Heydar Aliyev, reached agreement on some important provisions of a future peace treaty. Negotiations for a settlement had been in progress before the cease-fire, principally under the auspices of the Minsk Group of the Organization for Security and Co-operation in Europe (OSCE, until 1994 the Conference on Security and Co-operation in Europe—CSCE), with the support of the UN. The Minsk Group of the OSCE was the principal mediator throughout the 1990s and the early 2000s, although there were also intermittent bilateral negotiations. In December 1994 Russia became a permanent co-chair of the Minsk Group, which helped to bring its own mediation efforts more firmly into conformity with those of the OSCE, and in 1997 the USA and France joined Russia as co-chairs, adding to the Group's international significance.

A period of intense negotiation and increased international pressure on the parties to the conflict in 1996–97 resulted not in the resolution of the dispute, but in the emergence of a growing rift between the leaders of Armenia and Nagornyi Karabakh over the implementation of any agreement (either as a staged series of measures or a single comprehensive settlement). The same division was reflected within the Armenian Government and, ultimately, precipitated President Ter-Petrossian's forced resignation in February 1998. Ter-Petrossian's successor, Robert Kocharian, originated from Nagornyi Karabakh and, indeed, had been the President of the 'Republic of Nagornyi Karabakh' before he became Prime Minister of Armenia in 1997. Kocharian's Government, which included another Karabakh Armenian, the influential Minister of Internal Affairs and National Security, Serge Sarkissian, was more sympathetic to the interests of the Karabakh Armenians and maintained a close alliance with the President of the unrecognized republic, Arkadii Ghukassian (who was re-elected for a second term in 2002 and whose supporters retained a strong majority in the Karabakh parliament elected in June 2005). Certainly, President Kocharian was keen to avoid Ter-Petrossian's mistake of appearing to put pressure on the enclave's authorities to accept an unfavourable settlement. He supported Nagornyi Karabakh's demands for direct negotiations with the Azerbaijani Government and insisted on a package settlement to the conflict, while continuing the previous Government's policy of non-recognition of independence for Nagornyi Karabakh and

of stating that Armenia would accept any solution that was acceptable to the Karabakh Armenians. Nevertheless, both in Armenia and in Nagornyi Karabakh itself, critics of the leadership (from within the ruling coalitions, as well as from the opposition) continued to focus on the Karabakh issue and the danger of submitting to Azerbaijani and international pressure. In February 2001 the leading internal critic of Nagornyi Karabakh's President was silenced when Samuel Babaian, the enclave's former Minister of Defence and army Commander-in-Chief, was imprisoned for 14 years for instigating an attempt to assassinate Ghukassian.

In the mid-2000s the negotiations remained at an impasse. In addition to the central issue of the eventual constitutional status of Nagornyi Karabakh, among the most difficult questions to be resolved were: the arrangements for the 'Lachin (Laçin) corridor'—captured territory that provided an overland link between the enclave and Armenia; reciprocal arrangements to guarantee Azerbaijani communication with Naxçıvan through Armenian territory; guarantees for the security of the Armenians in Nagornyi Karabakh; and the return of Azeri refugees to the enclave. Meanwhile, the cease-fire remained subject to continuous minor violations, with frequent casualties resulting from sniper fire and occasional more serious hostilities. Opinion polls showed that the public continued to support a peaceful resolution, but were even less willing than the political leaders to make the necessary compromises. There was an increasing amount of bellicose rhetoric regarding Nagornyi Karabakh from both official and opposition figures in Azerbaijan, rhetoric that was further intensified following the election, in October 2003, of İlham Aliyev as President of Azerbaijan.

In January 2005 the Parliamentary Assembly of the Council of Europe (PACE) approved a controversial resolution regarding the region, which expressed concern at the large-scale ethnic expulsiun from Nagornyi Karabakh and the creation of mono-ethnic areas as a result of the conflict; the resolution clearly stated the unacceptability of the continuing occupation of Azerbaijani territory by Armenian forces. There was also concern within the international community over the annual competitive increases in the defence budgets of Armenia and Azerbaijan. In addition, Azerbaijan claimed to have concerns over the transfer of Russian military hardware from bases in Georgia to Armenia. (For more detailed coverage of recent developments in the de facto republic, see the separate section on the 'Republic of Nagornyi Karabakh' in the chapter on Azerbaijan.)

POLITICAL DEVELOPMENTS

In July 1995 President Ter-Petrossian's party succeeded in winning a second term in office, following the country's first post-Soviet general election. The pro-Government Republican (Hanrapetutiun) bloc secured 119 of the 190 seats in parliament, by this time known as the Azgayin Zhoghov (National Assembly). In a referendum held concurrently with the election, 68% of voters (56% of the electorate) supported a new Constitution, which, however, had been strongly opposed in the legislature and attracted international criticism for the excessive powers it granted the president. Constitutional reform remained on the agenda thereafter, and in May 2003 a referendum was held on comprehensive proposals for reform. Some 600,000 people voted in favour of the proposed amendments, fewer than the 700,000 required, so the Constitution remained unchanged. The failure to implement the changes had implications not only for domestic affairs, but also for Armenia's participation in the Council of Europe (to which it had acceded in January 2001), which required constitutional reform as a condition of membership. Eventually, in November 2005, a series of constitutional amendments were adopted in a referendum, again marred by accusations of the falsification of votes and procedural irregularities. Whatever the shortcomings of the process, however, the reforms did go some way to bringing Armenia's Constitution into line with international norms and were welcomed by Europe and the USA.

In September 1996 Ter-Petrossian was re-elected President, defeating Vazgen Manukian in the first round of voting, although he obtained only slightly more than the 50% of the votes required to avoid a second round. The elections and constitutional referendum of 1995 and 1996 were marred by electoral malpractice. The refusal of the Central Electoral Commission to register a large number of opposition parliamentary candidates, the Government's monopoly of television and radio broadcasts, and the falsification of results were among the most serious irregularities. Voters' choice was, in any case, significantly reduced by the suspension in December 1994 of the ARF. The narrow margin of victory and allegations of widespread abuses left the result open to question. Shortly after the election, opposition demonstrators stormed the parliament building, and the Government imposed martial law for a short period to restore order. Several unpopular ministers were replaced, but this was not sufficient to restore the credibility and legitimacy of President Ter-Petrossian and his Government.

In 1995–97 President Ter-Petrossian's Government attracted increasing criticism from both the domestic opposition and the international community for its authoritarianism and weak commitment to democracy. These criticisms and concerns continued into the 2000s, with all elections and referendums marred, to a greater or lesser extent, by malpractice, although Armenia's admission to the Council of Europe gave recognition to a degree of progress in the areas of democratization and human rights, as did its election to the UN's Commission on Human Rights in May 2001.

Levon Ter-Petrossian's political demise was precipitated in the latter part of 1997, when his disagreement with the leadership in Nagornyi Karabakh became clear, engendering divisions among his most senior ministers. The loss of the support of Prime Minister Kocharian, the Minister of Defence, Vazgen Sarkissian, and the Minister of Internal Affairs and National Security, Serge Sarkissian, as well as the defection of a large number of his parliamentary supporters to the recently formed Yerkrapah Union of Volunteers parliamentary faction (which was loyal to the Minister of Defence) were decisive in persuading Ter-Petrossian to resign in February 1998.

In the ensuing presidential election, the Prime Minister and acting President, Robert Kocharian, defeated Karen Demirchian, the First Secretary of the CPA for much of the 1970s and 1980s, with a large majority. The first post-Soviet change of president was achieved smoothly and within the framework of the Constitution (although Ter-Petrossian did not lose office through the electoral process).

Kocharian continued many of the policies of his predecessor, but with a less compromising position on the issue of Nagornyi Karabakh, a more strongly professed commitment to open and democratic Government (one of his first measures was to lift the suspension of the ARF), and certain differences of emphasis in foreign and economic policy (see below). The parliamentary elections of May 1999 were won by a new force in Armenian politics, the Unity bloc, the principal components of which were the Republican Party of Armenia (RPA), unofficially led by Vazgen Sarkissian, and the People's Party of Armenia (PPA) of Karen Demirchian. Following the elections, Sarkissian became Prime Minister, and Demirchian was elected the Chairman of the Azgayin Zhoghov. In October of the same year Sarkissian and Demirchian, as well as six other deputies and officials, were assassinated when gunmen (who claimed no political affiliation) infiltrated the legislative chamber. The loss of the two leaders left both the Unity bloc and the Government in temporary disarray.

The murdered premier's younger brother, Aram, was appointed Prime Minister in early November 1999, but tensions between the President and the Azgayin Zhoghov soon emerged. In May 2000 President Kocharian appointed Andranik Markarian, the leader of the RPA, as Prime Minister, and Serge Sarkissian as Minister of Defence, quelling parliamentary opposition for a time. Parliamentary politics remained fluid in the early 2000s, with new parties and groupings emerging and old ones declining or disappearing, together with numerous defections. Among the most significant developments were the dissolution of the Yerkrapah grouping, members of which formed the Republic (Hanrapetutiun) party in early 2001, and simmering differences between the RPA and the PPA, with the former generally supportive of Kocharian, and the latter becoming increasingly critical of both the Government and

its Unity bloc partner, leading to a split in September 2001. Thereafter, Kocharian's control over the political situation was more secure, with the opposition too fragmented to offer a serious challenge, threats of impeachment and efforts to emulate Georgia's 'rose revolution' of late 2003 notwithstanding. Kocharian won a second term of office in the second round of the presidential election held in March 2003, securing 67.5% of the votes cast. In the parliamentary elections held in May, the RPA emerged with the largest number of seats, receiving 32 mandates, followed by the Law-Governed Country Party of Armenia (with 18 seats), the Justice—Artarutiun bloc (a coalition of the Armenian Democratic Party, the National Democratic Party, the PPA and the Union of National Democrats), with 15 seats, and the ARF with 11 seats. The coalition of pro-Government parties, comprising the RPA, the Law-Governed Country Party of Armenia and the ARF, emerged as the clear winners, and subsequently formed a new Government under Markarian, although there were the usual, and well-founded, accusations that the elections had not been fairly conducted, followed by protracted protests and a boycott of parliament by opposition deputies.

In May 2006 Artur Baghdasarian resigned as Chairman of the Azgayin Zhoghov, and withdrew his Law-Governed Country Party of Armenia from the coalition. This was as a result of his outspoken views on foreign policy (pro-Western and pro-NATO) and, less recently, his criticism of the Government's management of the referendum. Markarian maintained that, contrary to the coalition agreement, Baghdasarian had not attempted to address these issues internally before making them public. Baghdasarian's actions were perceived to represent pre-electoral populist manoeuvring, in order to distance himself and his party from any unpopularity generated by the Government, and to establish him strongly as a contender. These developments were not unanimously supported by his party, however, some of whom defected to other parties and some of whom joined a newly established bloc in parliament, focusing on business issues. The small United Labour Party agreed to co-operate with the coalition and was allocated some senior official posts. Meanwhile, there was growing speculation that Serge Sarkissian would contest the presidency at the election in 2008, when Kocharian's second and final term was to expire. This possibility appeared more likely when Sarkissian joined Markarian's RPA in July 2006. Another major development in 2006 was the formation of the Prosperous Armenia party by Gagik Tsarukian, an influential businessman close to the governing regime.

In December 2006 the authorities claimed to have thwarted a plot to stage a coup, apparently organized by nationalists opposed to what they perceived to be the Armenian Government's concessionary stance towards Azerbaijan regarding the conflict in Nagornyi Karabakh. Zhirair Sefilian, a former military commander during the 1991–94 war, was arrested (and subsequently deported) as one of the founders of the recently formed Union of Armenian Volunteers, alleged to be behind the plot.

In February 2007 President Kocharian announced that legislative elections were to be held on 12 May. In March Prime Minister Markarian died unexpectedly, having suffered a heart attack; Serge Sarkissian was appointed in his stead in early April, and was also appointed as acting President of the RPA. Later that month Sarkissian's former portfolio, that of defence, was assumed by the hitherto Chief of General Staff of the Armed Forces, Col-Gen. Mikhail Haroutunian. All other members of the outgoing Government remained in office, pending the forthcoming parliamentary elections.

Legislative elections were held according to schedule on 12 May 2007. The ruling RPA won 64 of the 131 seats (90 of which were allocated through party list voting, and 41 through single-mandate voting), attracting 33.9% of the total number of votes. The Prosperous Armenia party and the ARF, both allies of the RPA, were placed second and third, with 25 seats (15.1% of the votes) and 16 seats (13.2%), respectively. Two opposition parties—the Law-Governed Country Party of Armenia and the Heritage Party—achieved the minimum 5% threshold required to secure parliamentary representation, winning nine seats (7.1% of the votes) and seven seats (6.0% of the votes), respectively. In a joint statement issued shortly after the elections, the OSCE and the International Election Observation Mission (IEOM), which was supported by the OSCE and several European institutions, commended the conduct of the polls, describing them as 'a further step towards European democratic values'. However, the IEOM noted that regulations to address issues such as possible vote-buying and inequality in conditions for campaigning had not been implemented effectively. The opposition accused the RPA and its allies of widespread vote-buying and other electoral irregularities, and four opposition groups, including Republic, filed appeals with the Constitutional Court, demanding that the election results be annulled and new elections be held. However, in June the Court rejected the appeals, and ruled that the results were valid.

The new Azgayin Zhoghov was inaugurated on 7 June 2007. President Kocharian reappointed Sarkissian to the position of Prime Minister, and the RPA, Prosperous Armenia and the ARF agreed to form a coalition Government, which controlled 105 of the 131 seats in the legislature. The new administration, comprising 11 members of the RPA, and three each of Prosperous Armenia and the ARF, was announced later that month; new ministers were appointed to only six of the 17 posts. Hovik Abrahamian of the RPA, who was known to be a close associate of President Kocharian, was appointed to the position of Deputy Prime Minister, while retaining the territorial administration portfolio. Sarkissian's decision to agree to form a power-sharing coalition, despite the RPA having secured an outright majority in the elections, was interpreted by some as an indication that the Prime Minister was trying to broaden his base of political support in advance of the 2008 presidential election to aid him in his candidacy.

The presidential poll was duly conducted on 19 February 2008; according to official results, Sarkissian secured 52.8% of the votes cast and Ter-Petrossian 21.5% of the votes. Although attacks against opposition campaigners and other incidences of violence had been reported shortly before the election, on the following day Council of Europe and OSCE observers issued a statement that the poll had been mostly conducted in accordance with international standards. Ter-Petrossian (and other opposition candidates) immediately attributed the results to widespread falsification and demanded that the ballot be repeated, prompting his followers to stage mass protests in his support; Ter-Petrossian claimed that he had been placed under house arrest. On 1 March President Kocharian declared a 20-day state of emergency (which included extensive restrictions on the media and public assembly), after opposition protesters in the capital, Yerevan, were violently dispersed by special police units and interior ministry forces, resulting in clashes in which some eight people were killed and many injured. A number of associates of Ter-Petrossian were detained, and some 30 prominent opposition members were subsequently arrested on charges of precipitating the clashes with the police. Ter-Petrossian urged the international community to condemn unequivocally the measures taken by the authorities, and deplored the limited response of observer missions to procedural violations. In early March the Azgayin Zhoghov voted in favour of removing the immunity from prosecution of four parliamentary deputies, who were charged with attempting to seize power through participation in the violent clashes. On 8 March the Constitutional Court upheld the final official election results, rejecting an appeal by Ter-Petrossian. Later that month the Azgayin Zhoghov approved the indefinite extension of restrictions on public gatherings imposed under the state of emergency, pending an investigation into the unrest. The non-governmental organization Human Rights Watch strongly criticized the restrictions as a violation of international obligations, and expressed objections to the subsequent detention of a number of opposition supporters who had demonstrated peacefully. On 9 April Serge Sarkissian was officially inaugurated as President; at the ceremony he pledged to seek reconciliation with his opponents. He immediately nominated Tigran Sarkissian, hitherto the Governor of the Central Bank of Armenia, as Prime Minister. In his previous office, Tigran Sarkissian had gained an international reputation as a successful reformer. Later in the month a new administration, retaining 10 of the incumbent ministers, was formed. New ministers included Armen Gevor-

gian as Deputy Prime Minister and Minister of Territorial Administration, Edvard Nalbandian as Minister of Foreign Affairs and Seyran Ohanian as Minister of Defence; the reorganization also incorporated the creation of a new Ministry of Emergency Situations.

In mid-April 2008 PACE adopted a resolution that demanded the conduct of an independent inquiry into the violence of 1 March, the immediate release of opposition supporters detained in the aftermath, and the annulment of restrictions on the right to stage public rallies and demonstrations. On 11 June (when some 70 opposition supporters remained in detention) the Azgayin Zhoghov voted in favour of lifting the restrictions. A mass opposition demonstration in support of Ter-Petrossian was conducted in Yerevan in late June, and was followed by a rally in Gyumri in early July. Later that month PACE agreed to allow the Armenian authorities six months to comply with the demands of the April resolution. Meanwhile, Ter-Petrossian had begun a campaign to demand an independent investigation into the violence in March and that Kocharian stand trial for crimes against the Armenian people. At the beginning of August, at a further rally in Yerevan, Ter-Petrossian officially announced the establishment of his Armenian National Congress, which constituted 16 opposition parties. In early September the RPA leadership increased pressure on the Chairman of the Azgayin Zhoghov, Tigran Torossian, to resign in favour of a long-term supporter of Kocharian, Hovik Abrahamian.

FOREIGN AFFAIRS

Armenia declared its independence in September 1991, but won international recognition only after the dissolution of the USSR in December of that year. Armenia was one of the original signatories of the Almaty Declaration, which established the Commonwealth of Independent States (CIS). Armenia was admitted to the CSCE in February 1992, and to the UN in March. On 15 May Armenia signed the CIS Collective Security Treaty in Tashkent, Uzbekistan, and in 1999 was one of only six CIS states to continue as a signatory of the agreement. In April 2003 the Treaty was formally superseded by the Collective Security Treaty Organization (CSTO). Armenia also signed many other CIS agreements aimed at achieving closer co-operation among member states.

Armenia's foreign policy aimed to normalize relations with all neighbouring countries. Armenian-Russian relations were especially strong, both countries having a particular interest in security and military co-operation, and viewing each other as strategic partners. Armenia needed a safeguard against a perceived Turkish threat and to gain equipment, training and expertise for its own armed forces, while Russia was interested in retaining control of the former Soviet external borders and in maintaining a forward air defence zone. In 1994 and 1995 a series of agreements was signed, giving Russia 25-year military basing rights in Armenia. Close military co-operation continued into the 2000s, with the implementation of a new, joint air defence system in May 2001. There were limits, however, on how far Armenia would persist in its relations with Russia; neither President Ter-Petrossian nor Kocharian favoured joining the Russia-Belarus Union, and Kocharian also rejected a proposal to make Russian Armenia's official second language. None the less, Armenia and Russia signed a 10-year economic co-operation programme in September of that year, during a visit to the country by the Russian President, Vladimir Putin, and the 2000s saw Russian interests, notably the state-owned gas company Gazprom, gain a growing stake in Armenia's energy sector. The Armenian Government reacted with caution to Russian military operations in Georgia, following an offensive on 8 August 2008 to support separatists in the South Ossetia region against attacks by Georgian forces (see the chapter on Georgia). The conflict in Georgia (Armenia's major supply route from abroad) inflicted considerable damage on the Armenian economy, including severe shortages of fuel and food. While most of the state-controlled media in Armenia was pro-Russian, many opposition and independent publications were viewed as being sympathetic to Georgia. Following Russia's official recognition of the separatist regions of South Ossetia and Abkhazia as independent states on 26 August, Presidents Sarkissian and Dmitrii Medvedev of Russia met in Sochi, Russia, on 2 September to discuss the situation in Georgia and proposed new, large-scale, bilateral co-operation projects between Russia and Armenia. On the following day, when the committee of the chiefs of the security councils convened in Yerevan; Russia sought the recognition of South Ossetian and Abkhazian independence by Armenia and other CSTO member states. (Sarkissian subsequently declared that his country was unable to recognize the independence of South Ossetia and Abkhazia while the issue of Nagornyi Karabakh remained unresolved.) Armenia officially assumed the presidency of the CSTO at a summit meeting on the situation in Georgia, convened in Moscow on 5 September; CSTO leaders issued a statement criticizing the military action of Georgia in South Ossetia.

Armenia also sought to diversify its foreign and security links, and in October 1994 joined NATO's 'Partnership for Peace' programme of military co-operation. Its membership remained, for the most part, passive until 2000, when Armenia began to take a more active interest, especially following the suicide attacks on mainland USA of 11 September 2001, which brought about an intensification of US and NATO security interests and funding in the Caucasus region. In June 2003 Armenia hosted NATO exercises for the first time, with the unprecedented participation of the Turkish military in exercises on Armenian territory; in 2004–05 Armenia dispatched peace-keepers to Iraq and the Serbian province of Kosovo and Metohija, and in June 2005 it followed Georgia and Azerbaijan in agreeing an 'Individual Partnership Action Plan' with NATO. In April 1996 Armenia, together with Azerbaijan and Georgia, signed an agreement on partnership and co-operation with the European Union (EU—the agreement came into force in 1999), and in June 2000 PACE accepted Armenia's application for membership. Kocharian emphasized the importance of the European orientation of the country's foreign policy, and this dimension was further strengthened in June 2004, when Armenia, Azerbaijan and Georgia were included in the EU's European Neighbourhood Policy. Meanwhile, Armenia became a full member of the World Trade Organization in February 2003.

Relations with the USA, a substantial donor to Armenia, became closer during the 1990s and 2000s, notwithstanding Armenia's continuing close relations with Russia; its concerns about the overall direction of US policy in the Caucasus and the Caspian Sea basin, which was viewed as inclining towards the interests of Azerbaijan and Turkey; and US displeasure at Armenia's friendly relations with Iran. In March 2006 a five-year compact, with funding of US $235m., was reached with the US-funded Millennium Challenge Corporation on poverty reduction proposals; the country programme was launched in September. In August 2007 the USA provided the Armenian armed forces with $3m. worth of military equipment for use by a special Armenian peace-keeping battalion, intended to facilitate the execution of operations jointly conducted with US and NATO forces.

Independent Armenia's relations with Iran generally remained cordial, despite tension during the conflict in Nagornyi Karabakh, when Armenian successes threatened to send many thousands of Azeri refugees into Iran. The two countries signed numerous commercial and cultural agreements, and there was increasing cross-border traffic. (There had been no crossing-point on the Armenian–Iranian border during the Soviet period.) In December 1995 a permanent bridge across the River Araks (Aras, Araxes) was completed, replacing a temporary structure that had hitherto linked the two countries, and in 2006 an improved highway to the border with Iran was under construction in Armenia. The electricity grids of both countries were also linked in 1997, and work commenced in 2004 on the construction of a 141-km cross-border natural gas pipeline. In 2006 agreement was reached on the construction of a US $90m. third power transmission line connecting the two countries (to allow for the increased electricity supplies to Iran, following the volume of gas that would flow from that country via the new pipeline). In September a trilateral arrangement was reached, whereby the communal grid was also to be extended to Georgia. The joint construction of two hydroelectric plants on the River Araks was also in progress.

In contrast, relations with Azerbaijan and Turkey, Armenia's most important neighbours, from an economic perspective, remained suspended owing to the Nagornyi Karabakh conflict. President Ter-Petrossian was criticized by the nationalist opposition for his pragmatic policy towards Turkey during the mid-1990s. He was accused of ignoring the historic issue of the 1915 'genocide' for the sake of contemporary economic and political benefits. This pragmatic policy was only partly successful. Although the approach was appreciated by Turkish officials and an informal dialogue was maintained, the Turkish Government insisted that the establishment of diplomatic relations and the opening of the border were conditional upon the resolution of the Nagornyi Karabakh issue. Moreover, the issues surrounding Turkey's potential candidacy for EU membership revived international pressure regarding that country's lack of official acknowledgement of the Armenian genocide. In December 2004, following an appeal from President Kocharian, the European Parliament issued a statement that Turkey should recognize that genocide had taken place in 1915–23, and open its borders; in September 2005 the European Parliament issued a further non-binding resolution, with the stronger implication that Turkey's refusal to recognize the killings as genocide could adversely affect membership negotiations.

A large proportion of the diaspora has resided in France, which has maintained a supportive stance towards Armenia with regard to Turkey. French President Jacques Chirac made a state visit to Armenia on 29 September–1 October 2006, during which he appealed once more for Turkey to recognize the 'genocide'. On 12 October the lower house (Assemblée nationale) of the French parliament voted to make it a criminal offence to deny the occurrence of genocide against the Armenians in 1915. Many members of the EU already felt that Turkey should acknowledge the nature of the historical event before being allowed to become a member of the union; however, this marked a further development. (The French Government apparently did not support the bill, however, and its passage into legislation would require the further support of the upper house—Sénat—and the President.) Critics surmised that the French authorities were citing the genocide issue politically, as a means of delaying or preventing Turkey's EU membership. This gesture certainly revived the urgency and exposure of the Armenian campaign.

The murder in the Turkish city, İstanbul, in January 2007 of Hrant Dink, a prominent ethnic-Armenian Turkish journalist who had received a six-month suspended sentence in October 2005 for writing about the 'Armenian genocide', further heightened the sensitivity of relations between the two countries. In October 2007 the US House of Representatives' Foreign Affairs Committee voted, by a margin of 27 to 21, in favour of a non-binding resolution that recognized the 1915 massacres of Armenians (see above) as 'genocide'. The congressional committee's approval of the measure came despite fierce lobbying against the resolution by US President George W. Bush, who argued that its adoption would inflict severe damage on US relations with 'a key ally in NATO and in the global war on terror'. The Turkish Government responded angrily to the vote, and, like Bush, warned that the resolution would cause much damage to US–Turkish relations. President Kocharian welcomed the results of the vote, expressing his hope that it would lead to full recognition by the USA of the 'Armenian genocide'. However, a debate and vote on the issue in the House of Representatives was subsequently postponed indefinitely.

Hopes of a rapprochement between Armenia and Turkey, after President Sarkissian's installation in April 2008, increased significantly when Turkish President Abdullah Gül accepted an invitation from President Sarkissian to attend the first football match between the national teams in Yerevan on 6 September (the first visit by a Turkish Head of State to Armenia). The Armenian Government additionally waived visa controls to allow Turkish football fans to travel to Armenia. The announcement followed confirmation by Turkish foreign ministry officials in July of speculation in the Turkish media that Turkish and Armenian delegations had met in Switzerland for informal discussions on bilateral relations. After the outbreak of hostilities between Russia and Georgia in early August (see above), Turkey had proposed the creation of a 'Caucasus Stability and Co-operation Platform' as a regional framework for negotiations. The visit was conducted cordially; in late September the Ministers of Foreign Affairs of Turkey, Armenia and Azerbaijan met in New York, USA, to discuss the question of Nagornyi Karabakh. It was also reported that Sarkissian had accepted a reciprocal invitation to attend a further football match between Armenia and Turkey, scheduled to take place in the Turkish capital in October 2009.

The Armenian Government's relations with the Armenian diaspora, which contributed significantly to aid programmes and to the finances of the Karabakh separatists, suffered in the mid-1990s. This was mainly owing to opposition in the diaspora to the 1994 suspension of the ARF, to the Ter-Petrossian Government's refusal to allow dual citizenship, and to what many viewed as the attempt to cultivate Armenian-Turkish relations at the expense of winning recognition of the 'genocide'. President Kocharian's Government developed policies to help foster and consolidate relations with the Armenian diaspora in all of these areas. One of the constitutional reforms adopted in 2005 was that dual citizenship be allowed. Improved homeland-diaspora relations brought tangible benefits in major investment in Armenia by diaspora organizations, most notably the US-based Lincy Foundation, which funded construction, road-building and cultural programmes worth US $170m. during 2000–04.

Economy

Dr EDMUND HERZIG

Revised for this edition by the Editorial Staff.

INTRODUCTION

Following the dissolution of the USSR in 1991, Armenia, like other former Soviet countries, was affected by a range of economic problems associated with the transition from a centralized, command economy to a market-orientated system. Armenia was particularly vulnerable following the collapse of the Soviet economic system as, in the Soviet period, it developed a primarily industrial economy, which was heavily dependent on inter-republican trade. In addition to the problems caused by the transition to a free-market system in the early 1990s, the Armenian economy was adversely affected by various other factors, not least the continuing costs of reconstruction after a severe earthquake in northern Armenia in December 1988. Equally serious was the cost of supporting the Karabakh Armenians' war effort in the disputed enclave (within Azerbaijan) of Nagornyi Karabakh, unofficially estimated at 30%–50% of the government budget before the May 1994 cease-fire. By 2000 Armenia was still contributing at least one-half of the funds for the annual budget of US $25m. of the unrecognized 'Republic of Nagornyi Karabakh'. An additional burden was the influx of refugees from both Nagornyi Karabakh and Azerbaijan. The imposition of a road, rail and pipeline blockade by Azerbaijan from September 1989, which was subsequently reinforced by Turkey, caused immense economic damage. Before this date almost 90% of Armenia's imports from other Soviet republics came via Azerbaijan. Furthermore, in the early 1990s political instability in neighbouring Georgia resulted in a prolonged energy crisis in Armenia; main trade routes, both to traditional markets and suppliers in the former USSR and to potential new markets in the West, were closed, impeding deliveries of urgent supplies. Unlike some countries of the former USSR, Armenia was not richly endowed with petroleum, gas or other readily marketable natural resources. Moreover, in the Soviet period it imported many of its food requirements. The fact that it was landlocked made integration into the world economy difficult, especially since the most obvious route to world markets—via Turkey—remained closed.

The combination of all these factors caused a severe economic decline in the early 1990s. Gross domestic product (GDP) in Armenia decreased, in real terms, by 52.4% in 1992 alone. At the beginning of 1994 it was calculated that the average Armenian was spending 80% of his or her income on food, an indication of very low living standards. A 1996 official survey of living conditions found that 55% of the population qualified as poor, and 28% as very poor. Official figures put the rate of unemployment at between 9% and 11% of the work-force in 1994–2003, but the actual rate was probably three times higher. At the end of the 1990s only some 35% of the population was in employment, and the poverty rate remained high. Basic social services, notably education and medicine, which were available to all in the Soviet period, were out of reach for a significant and growing proportion of the population, a particularly worrying development when the country's principal economic asset was its highly skilled and industrious work-force.

Social and economic pressures led to extensive emigration in the 1990s and 2000s, and many Armenians, especially the young and the well-qualified, went abroad (mainly to Russia) in search of work. Independent Armenia conducted its first census in October 2001, the results of which indicated that the de facto population stood at a little over 3.0m.—substantially lower than the total of 3.3m. recorded at the last Soviet census, held in January 1989. Remittances from relatives working abroad, contributions from the Armenian diaspora, as well as Western humanitarian aid, went some way towards alleviating the severe social problems caused by the economic decline. The Government's social welfare policy also underwent radical change, with successive legislation laying the foundations for a policy based on targeted, means-tested benefits for those deemed to be in greatest need. The large unofficial economy also made a significant contribution to many people's livelihood.

Recovery was, initially, slow. In 1994–2000 annual GDP growth averaged 5.4%, leaving real GDP in 2000 at only 63% of its 1989 level, but the recovery accelerated in the early 2000s. Annual growth in excess of 10% was recorded every year in the period 2001–07, and between 1999 and 2005 the proportion of the population living below the official poverty line declined from 55% to 35%.

ECONOMIC POLICY

In the early 1990s the Government implemented a radical economic-reform programme aimed at creating the legal, institutional and economic basis for a market economy. The reforms included the liberalization of prices, stabilization of the national currency, reduction of the budgetary deficit, promotion of privatization, and rationalization of the taxation system. These measures, assisted by the May 1994 cease-fire in the Nagornyi Karabakh conflict, allowed Armenia to become the first country among the Commonwealth of Independent States (CIS) to achieve growth in GDP.

President Levon Ter-Petrossian's Government (1991–98) pursued a privatization programme that was among the most radical in the former USSR. Privatization began with land and small-scale enterprises from 1991, and embraced housing in 1993. These early stages of the privatization process achieved a high level of success (by mid-1999 around 85% of small enterprises had been transferred to private ownership). The privatization of medium- and large-sized enterprises, initiated in 1995, proved to be more difficult and controversial, and the poor performance of privatized large-scale industries and utilities continued to be a source of public discontent and political friction in the 2000s. In the early 2000s Armenia, like several other CIS members, traded state assets in the defence and energy industries in exchange for its large debts to Russia, but, unlike in other states, this attracted only muted public criticism. Privatization resulted in a dramatic shift in employment patterns: in 2004 some 66% of the work-force were employed in the private sector, whereas in 1995 the figure remained below 50%.

Armenia experienced very high rates of inflation in the early post-Soviet years. Salary increases, price liberalization, shortages resulting from the economic blockade and the almost complete suspension of trade with other former Soviet territories all contributed to an increase in consumer prices. Until November 1993, when the Government introduced a national currency, the dram (see below), Armenia was adversely affected by Russia's financial and monetary policy. The average annual rate of increase in consumer prices was more than 5,000% in 1994, although this rate declined rapidly following the imposition of a strict monetary policy, and had stabilized at a very low rate by the late 1990s. The annual rate of consumer price inflation was less than 1% in 2000, although this rate had reached 6.5% by 2004. Although prices increased by just 0.6% in 2005, the inflation rate rose to 3.5% in 2006 and 4.5% in 2007. Progress was also made in reducing the budget deficit, which was equivalent to 56% of GDP in 1993 but which had declined to 1.9% of GDP by 2005. Revenue collection remained weak, and the deficit increased from 33,000m. drams in 2006 to 96,000m. drams in 2007, representing 3.0% of GDP. The IMF projected the deficit to remain high in 2008, at 80,600m. drams. In 2005 the IMF representative in Armenia described the Government's achievements as disappointing, and criticized the small contribution made to taxation by large-scale enterprises, thereby confirming public suspicions of informal deals between state officials and oligarchs. Small businesses and the public contribute most to taxation revenues, with value-added tax (VAT) accounting for almost 50% of tax revenue, according to statistics published by the Ministry of Finance.

In November 1993 Armenia, like several other post-Soviet states, was forced to introduce a new national currency when Russia refused to extend new rouble credits. (Armenia later also suffered the adverse effects of the Russian financial crisis of 1998.) The dram was introduced at a rate of 77 per US dollar, but it declined in value to convert at more than 400 to the dollar within one year, stabilizing at about that level in 1994–95, before decreasing further, to around 500 to the dollar at the end of 1997. Apart from the early rapid decline in value, the new currency could be considered one of the successes of government economic policy, which aimed to achieve economic competitiveness through a combination of a strong currency and low inflation. The value of the dram strengthened in 2004–06, from 548 drams to the dollar at mid-2004 to below 306 drams to the dollar at mid-2008, giving rise to fears that the strength of the currency might damage export capabilities.

Armenia's economic reforms achieved a relatively high degree of macroeconomic stability, and impressed the IMF, the World Bank and the European Bank for Reconstruction and Development (EBRD), all of which Armenia joined in 1992, and which, together with Russia and Western countries, extended major credits and technical assistance. Armenia's dependence on foreign creditors and donors meant that it had little choice but to adopt the economic policies that the international financial organizations recommended. In 2008 the US-based Heritage Foundation/*Wall Street Journal* Index of Economic Freedom placed Armenia 28th in the world, and ahead of all other CIS countries. At mid-2005 Armenia had accumulated some US $1,000.3m. in external debt, of which about 90% was owed to multilateral creditors (principally the World Bank and the IMF), and most of the rest to Russia and the USA. From 2002 some $94m. of Armenia's debt to Russia was cancelled in exchange for ownership stakes in state energy enterprises, but external debt still amounted to over 40% of GDP and 200% of fiscal revenues in that year. In 2006 external debt amounted to 16.5% of GDP, according to official figures.

Foreign investment was slow in coming to Armenia. The absence of commercially attractive natural resources, the economic blockade, corruption, bureaucracy, and opaque and changing laws and regulations outweighed the advanced state of economic reform and the availability of cheap skilled labour in the calculations of most potential investors. Direct investment totalled just US $25m. in 1995, increasing to $221m. in 1998, declining to $70m. in 2001 and recovering to $258m. in 2005. The importance of foreign investment, and of foreign economic relations more generally, was one of the more intensely debated issues in Armenian economic policy. President Levon Ter-Petrossian, like most Western analysts, considered that Armenia's only hope for sustained economic growth lay in dynamic trade relations with its neighbours in the region, since the domestic market was too small to stimulate growth and investment. From this perspective, the resolution of the Karabakh conflict and the lifting of the Turkish and Azerbaijani blockades were essential prerequisites for economic recovery. President Robert Kocharian (1998–2008) and others argued that it was corruption, excessive government bureaucracy and failure in the implementation of reforms that discouraged investment, and that if these problems were addressed, investment and growth would follow, irrespective of the blockades. Although growth was vigorous in the early 2000s, foreign direct investment remained limited, and proved controversial when foreign investors bought into major privatized enterprises and services. However, in mid-2006 Armenia received its first credit rating by two international risk-assessment firms. Although this indicated a medium level of creditworthiness and a relatively high risk in doing business, it was hoped that this form of international recognition would encourage international investment. Foreign direct investment increased substantially during 2007, representing a 58% increase year-on-year by the end of September. This was primarily because the communications sector attracted funds, accounting for almost 41% of all foreign investment in that period. Russian companies invested over 400% more funds into the economy than at the same point in the previous year.

AGRICULTURE

Armenia's agricultural potential is constrained by the relatively small extent of its agricultural land (1.4m. ha). Both during the Soviet period and thereafter, Armenia was heavily dependent on food imports (which accounted for 41% of the domestic market in 2000). The country's main agricultural products are fruits and vegetables grown in the fertile Ararat plain, and potatoes, grain, fodder and livestock from the uplands. Agriculture also provided the inputs for the food industry, which included important wine and cognac factories. The privatization of agricultural land in Armenia proceeded rapidly from 1991; by late 1992 approximately 90% of arable land was under private ownership. This had an immediate effect on production levels, which increased by a total of 15% in 1991. In the 1990s, however, the sector's progress was hampered by problems in land distribution, and in agricultural and market infrastructure. In 2000 these problems were exacerbated by severe drought. Nevertheless, with the industrial contraction of the early 1990s, agriculture and forestry came to occupy a very significant place in the national economy, accounting for 49% of GDP in 1993. With the beginnings of a recovery in the services and industrial sectors, agriculture's contribution to GDP narrowed to 19.1% by 2006. In that year some 46% of those employed worked in farming. Initial figures for 2007 showed agricultural GDP to have grown by 9.6%, with the output of crops increasing significantly. The first major foreign investment in the country's agricultural sector took place in 2005, when an Argentine-Armenian investor pledged to invest US $25m. in fruit production, on an area totalling 3,000 ha.

MINING AND ENERGY

Armenia possesses significant mineral resources, notably copper, gold and molybdenum, and a variety of building stones, including tuff (tufa). There are also deposits of mineral salt, calcium oxide and carbon. Some of these were extracted and processed in the Soviet period, but the mining industry was largely inactive throughout the 1990s, although it began to show signs of recovery at the end of the decade and, following privatization and foreign investment, achieved impressive growth in the mid 2000s.

The energy crisis was a major factor in Armenia's economic difficulties in the early 1990s. In the Soviet period, most of Armenia's energy requirements were imported in the form of natural gas from neighbouring Azerbaijan. However, this source was unavailable after Azerbaijan imposed its blockade in 1989. Following this, Armenia relied heavily on Turkmenistan and Russia for supplies of natural gas and petroleum, respectively. The only gas pipeline bypassing Azerbaijan traversed a region of Georgia where it was subject to frequent sabotage. Georgia's internal unrest and alleged deliberate diversion of natural gas intended for Armenia also interrupted supplies, as did Armenia's occasional failure to meet payment conditions. In February 2001 Armenia and Russia reached an agreement under the terms of which Russia was to cancel Armenia's gas arrears of US $7m., in return for obtaining a share of the infrastructure of the Armenian gas-distribution company for the Russian companies Gazprom and Itera. In 2003 Gazprom signed agreements with Armenia, which designated the Russian company as Armenia's predominant supplier of natural gas. Similar to other Gazprom customers, Armenia began to pay much higher gas prices from mid-2006. In March 2007 the first stage of a 140-km gas pipeline linking Armenia with Iran was opened. Initially, Iran will deliver some 400m. cu m of gas a year, but the intention is to increase volumes to up to 2,500m. cu m when the second phase of the project, linking the pipeline to Yerevan and providing the potential for the transshipment of gas, is complete.

In the early 1990s domestic energy production was limited to a number of hydroelectric plants, which provided around 68% of Armenia's electricity in 1993. By 2004 that proportion had declined to 33.4%, although there were plans significantly to extend Armenia's hydroelectric capacity. The country's only nuclear power plant, which was closed following the 1988 earthquake, was restarted in June 1995 and began generating later in the same year amid widespread international anxiety and protest. The Medzamor station was a VVER-440 pressurized-water reactor, of a different design to the Chornobyl (Chernobyl) reactor in Ukraine, which had failed in April 1986. Nevertheless, it was considered unsafe by many external specialists, owing to the absence of a containment dome and its location in an earthquake zone. By 2004 Medzamor was generating some 39.8% of Armenia's electricity. The Government came under pressure from the European Union (EU) to close the power station but, despite initial agreement, it resisted, claiming that the station could be operated safely until 2016, following extensive renovation, and demanding international funds to allow it to develop alternative sources of power generation. This impasse remained unresolved. In September 2003 financial control of the plant was transferred to Unified Energy System of Russia (RAO EES Rossii—in which the Russian Government held a majority share), for a period of five years, after that company took responsibility for the plant's arrears. During the course of bilateral discussions in April 2007 the Russian side indicated willingness to help Armenia build a new nuclear power plant, and subsequently President Kocharian suggested that it might be desirable for Armenia to build new nuclear power stations in the future.

In 2006 Armenia's hydroelectric, thermal and nuclear power stations generated 5,941m. kWh of electricity, and more than 1m. kWh was exported (including exports to Nagornyi Karabakh). Iran and Armenia linked their electricity grids in 1997, allowing trade in electricity to follow patterns of seasonal demand, and Armenia also exported electricity to Georgia (which also sought to connect its grid in 2006). In 2002 agreement was reached on the expansion of the exchange arrangement with Iran, and also on the construction of a hydroelectric plant on the River Araks (Aras, Araxes). In 2004 agreement was reached with the Japan Bank for International Co-operation on financing of US $150m. for the construction of a gas-fuelled thermal-power plant (intended to replace one at Hrazdan). By 2003 most of Armenia's electricity distribution system had been privatized, with a large part foreign-owned, and successful attempts by RAO EES Rossii to establish a dominant position in the market paralleled Gazprom's initiatives in the gas sector; in September 2005 the Armenian Government approved the sale of the Electricity Networks of Armenia distribution company to RAO EES Rossii, provided that it assumed responsibility for the previous owner's liabilities.

INDUSTRY

Industry was the dominant sector in Soviet Armenia's economy, accounting for 57% of net material product (NMP) in 1980 and employing nearly 40% of the work-force. Both heavy and light industry were largely dependent on inputs from other Soviet republics, notably energy from Azerbaijan and Russia, as well as catalysts and iron ore for metallurgy, and fabrics and leather for the garment and footwear industries. Armenia was also a major centre for the Soviet electronics industry, which relied on components from outside the republic, and which was integrated into the Soviet military-industrial complex. The main markets for all of these industries' products were other Soviet republics.

The collapse of the interdependent Soviet economy, therefore, affected Armenia's industrial sector acutely. However, it was the energy blockade that was the immediate cause of the collapse in industrial output in the early 1990s. The sector contracted by almost 50% in 1992 alone, with many of Armenia's 450 factories inoperative owing to lack of power. Industry recovered gradually, registering modest growth each year from 1994—with the exception of 1998, when Russia's financial crisis caused demand to contract (the average annual rate of growth was 2.4% in 1994–2000). Armenia's industrial growth was slower than that of most other CIS countries, and the continuing relative decline of the sector was indicated by the fact that in 2000 industry (excluding construction) contributed 22.0% of GDP, whereas it had contributed more than 40% in 1990; industrial output in 2000 was just over one-half the level recorded one decade before. However, in the early 2000s the pace of industrial growth accelerated, with improved performance in the diamond-cutting and -polishing, metals, woods, rubber, tobacco, mining, information technology, food-processing and alcoholic beverages sectors. According to the Asian Development Bank (ADB), industry's share of GDP was just 16.2% in 2006 (excluding construction), but industrial production increased by 15.2% in 2003 and by 17.0% in 2004. In 2006, however, the industrial sector (excluding construction) contracted by 4.6%.

SERVICES AND TRADE

The services sector, comprising trade, transport and communications, social and financial services, as well as construction, grew more rapidly than did either agriculture or industry during most of the 1990s. Between 1994 and 2000 trade's share of overall value-added rose from 4.5% to 10.0%; that of transport and communications increased from 4.2% to 7.8%; and that of construction increased from 6.7% to 11.1%. The contribution to GDP of the services sector as a whole (excluding construction) was 36.0% in 2006, according to the ADB. In the 2000s the large share of construction in GDP cast doubt on the sustainability of economic recovery. In 2006, in particular, the country experienced large-scale activity in the construction sector (primarily in Yerevan), when it contributed 28.7% of GDP.

Under Soviet rule, Armenia's economy was heavily dependent on trade, with imports and exports each equivalent to more than 50% of GDP in the 1980s. The vast majority of trade was with other Soviet republics (98% of exports and 79% of imports in 1980–90). In the Soviet period, Armenia's exports were dominated by light industrial goods, the production of which, like that of other industries, collapsed after independence. By the late 1980s Armenia already had a trade deficit, a problem that became increasingly serious in the 1990s. The deficit reached US $682m. in 1998, when the value of imports was more than three times the value of exports. In the early 2000s international trade expanded rapidly, particularly with non-CIS countries, and the balance improved dramatically, with the deficit declining to $368.8m. in 2002, largely owing to strong export growth (exports increased from $231.7m. in 1999 to $685.6m. in 2003); however, the trade deficit increased thereafter, reaching $1,206.5m. in 2006, according to official figures.

Russia remained Armenia's most important trading partner throughout the 1990s, but its position was steadily eroded; in 1995 Russia absorbed 33.1% of Armenian exports, but it accounted for only 12.2% of export trade by 2005. In 1998, for the first time, the member countries of the EU accounted for a higher percentage of Armenia's imports (28.7%) than did the CIS countries. This trend appeared to be stabilizing by the end of the decade, and by 2000 the CIS countries accounted for 20% of external trade, and the EU countries for 35%. A considerable proportion of the EU countries' share was attributable to trade with Belgium in precious stones, which Armenia imported uncut for subsequent re-export. Outside the EU, Israel was an important trading partner. Largely because of the blockades by Azerbaijan and Turkey, Iran became an increasingly important trading partner in the 1990s (as, to a lesser extent, did Georgia). The construction (completed in December 1995) of a permanent road bridge linking Armenia and Iran facilitated the further development of trade. There was also some limited indirect trade between both Turkey and Azerbaijan and Armenia via Georgia (as well as significant direct contraband trade in defiance of the blockades). The tariffs charged for transport through Georgia were high, however, while the new route to Iran was longer and more expensive than the old road and rail routes through Naxçıvan that had been closed by the blockade. In 2006 Armenia's principal import partners were Russia (accounting for 16.6% of imports), Belgium (7.2%), UAE (6.6%), USA (6.2%), Iran (6.1%) and Ukraine (5.0%). Its export partners were Germany (15.0%), Netherlands (12.9%), Russia (12.3%), Belgium (11.0%), Israel (8.9%), Switzerland (7.3%) and the USA (6.6%). Official figures, however, do not capture the unrecorded trade with neighbours such as Georgia, Turkey and Azerbaijan. Most analysts consider the volume of such trade to be considerable.

An important objective for Armenia during the 1990s and early 2000s was securing membership of the World Trade Organization, to which it acceded in February 2003.

PROSPECTS

After independence, Armenia made strong progress in its transition towards a market economy, although it incurred significant social costs in the process. After more than 15 years of independence macroeconomic stability had been achieved, and most sectors of the economy were registering steady growth. The continuing blockade by both Azerbaijan and Turkey constrained the growth of trade, but proved less damaging than many had predicted. For a country with such a weak domestic market as Armenia, most analysts judged that integration into the larger regional economy was essential to attract and retain investment and talent, both foreign and domestic. Economic performance in the first half of the 2000s suggested that the potential for growth, despite the ongoing blockade, was greater than had been anticipated, and that routes through Georgia and Iran, as well as air routes, could partially offset its effects. Nevertheless, it remained the case that Armenia's economic prospects would improve significantly if the Karabakh conflict could be resolved and the borders with Turkey and Azerbaijan—especially the former—reopened. In the absence of a resolution of the conflict, Armenia could enhance its economic prospects by further developing efficient institutions, and clear and consistently applied laws and regulations, while implementing measures to combat corruption, bureaucracy and favouritism. The Government introduced programmes to combat these problems in the early 2000s, but most commentators assessed the measures implemented as being, at best, only partly effective. In the early 2000s the country's economic development gained momentum and appeared less fragile, and the benefits of growth began to be felt more widely in society. Economic progress was cited by an IMF report in May 2008, with praise for sound fiscal and monetary policies, concomitant with exchange rate flexibility. Although the economy remained under threat from a worsening global outlook and increased inflationary pressure, the IMF cited positive short-term prospects for Armenia.

Statistical Survey

Principal source: National Statistical Service of the Republic of Armenia, 0010 Yerevan, Republic Sq., Government House 3; tel. (10) 52-42-13; fax (10) 52-19-21; e-mail info@armstat.am; internet www.armstat.am.

Area and Population

AREA, POPULATION AND DENSITY

Area (sq km)	29,743*
Population (census results)†	
12 January 1989	3,287,677
10 October 2001	
Males	1,407,220
Females	1,595,374
Total	3,002,594
Population (official estimates at 1 January)‡	
2006	3,219,200
2007	3,222,900
2008	3,230,100
Density (per sq km) at 1 January 2008	108.6

* 11,484 sq miles (including inland water, totalling 1,278 sq km).

† Figures refer to de facto populations, although the methodology for calculating the relationship between *de jure* and de facto populations was amended for the 2001 census, and later figures are, therefore, not strictly comparable with those for 1989; the *de jure* total population for 2001 was 3,213,011.

‡ Figures include persons temporarily absent (475,200 at 1 January 1999).

POPULATION BY ETHNIC GROUP*
(permanent inhabitants, 2001 census)

	Number	%
Armenian	3,145,354	97.89
Yazidi	40,620	1.26
Others	27,037	0.84
Total	3,213,011	100.00

* According to official declaration of nationality; figures refer to *de jure* population.

MARZER (PROVINCES)
(1 January 2007)

Marz (Province)	Area (sq km)	Estimated population	Density (per sq km)	Capital
Yerevan City .	227	1,104,900	4,867.4	Yerevan
Aragatsotn . .	2,753	140,000	50.9	Ashtarak
Ararat . . .	2,096	275,100	131.3	Artashat
Armavir . .	1,242	280,200	225.6	Armavir
Gegharkunik .	5,348	239,600	44.8	Gavar
Kotayk . . .	2,089	276,200	132.2	Hrazdan
Lori . . .	3,789	282,700	74.6	Vanadzor
Shirak . . .	2,681	281,300	104.9	Gyumri
Syunik . . .	4,506	152,900	33.9	Kapan
Tavush . . .	2,704	134,200	49.6	Ijevan
Vayots Dzor .	2,308	55,800	24.2	Yeghegnadzor
Total . . .	29,743	3,222,900	108.4	—

PRINCIPAL TOWNS
(estimated population at 1 January 2006)

Yerevan (capital) .	1,103,800	Etchmiadzin . . 56,700
Gyumri* . . .	148,300	Hrazdan (Razdan) . 52,800
Vanadzor† . . .	105,500	Kapan 45,600

* Known as Leninakan between 1924 and 1991.
† Known as Kirovakan between 1935 and 1992.

BIRTHS, MARRIAGES AND DEATHS*

	Registered live births		Registered marriages		Registered deaths	
	Number	Rate (per 1,000)	Number	Rate (per 1,000)	Number	Rate (per 1,000)
1999 . .	36,502	9.6	12,459	3.3	24,087	6.3
2000 . .	34,276	9.0	10,986	2.9	24,025	6.3
2001 . .	32,065	10.0	12,302	3.8	24,003	7.5
2002 . .	32,229	10.1	13,682	4.3	25,554	8.0
2003 . .	35,793	11.2	15,463	4.8	26,014	8.1
2004 . .	37,520	11.7	16,975	5.3	25,679	8.0
2005 . .	37,499	11.7	16,624	5.2	26,379	8.2
2006 . .	37,639	11.7	16,887	5.2	27,202	8.5

* Rates for 1999–2000 are calculated from unrevised population estimates.

Expectation of life (years at birth, WHO estimates): 68.7 (males 64.9; females 72.2) in 2006 (Source: WHO, *World Health Statistics*).

ECONOMICALLY ACTIVE POPULATION
(annual averages, '000 persons)

	2004	2005	2006
Agriculture, hunting and forestry .	507.0	507.5	504.3
Fishing	0.1	0.1	0.2
Mining and quarrying	6.9	7.0	7.6
Manufacturing	111.5	114.3	110.5
Electricity, gas and water supply .	21.2	18.9	22.8
Construction	33.3	34.6	29.7
Wholesale and retail trade; repair of motor vehicles, motorcycles and personal household goods .	103.2	108.9	105.9
Hotels and restaurants . . .	3.9	5.7	7.7
Transport, storage and communications	46.5	49.7	48.6
Financial intermediation . . .	5.6	6.1	6.6
Real estate, renting and business activities	18.3	19.1	23.3
Public administration and defence; compulsory social security . .	29.1	28.2	34.9
Education	100.5	98.7	100.8
Health and social work . . .	49.8	50.6	48.8
Other community, social and personal service activities . .	44.8	48.4	40.8
Total employed	1,081.7	1,097.8	1,092.4
Registered unemployed . . .	114.8	98.0	88.9
Total labour force	1,196.5	1,195.8	1,181.3

Source: ILO.

Health and Welfare

KEY INDICATORS

Total fertility rate (children per woman, 2006)	1.3
Under-five mortality rate (per 1,000 live births, 2006) . .	24
HIV (% of persons aged 15–49, 2005)	0.1
Physicians (per 1,000 head, 2006)	3.7
Hospital beds (per 1,000 head, 2006)	4.4
Health expenditure (2005): US $ per head (PPP)	270
Health expenditure (2005): % of GDP	5.4
Health expenditure (2005): public (% of total)	32.9
Access to water (% of persons, 2004)	92
Access to sanitation (% of persons, 2004)	83
Human Development Index (2005): ranking	83
Human Development Index (2005): value	0.775

For sources and definitions, see explanatory note on p. vi.

Agriculture

PRINCIPAL CROPS
('000 metric tons)

	2004	2005	2006
Wheat	299.9	265.7	149.7
Barley	131.1	110.8	49.5
Maize	19.3	14.1	8.4
Potatoes	576.4	564.2	539.5
Cabbages and brassicas . .	93.8	107.2	125.0*
Tomatoes	229.5	234.9	278.0*
Cauliflowers and broccoli . . .	6.2	5.6	6.5*
Cucumbers and gherkins . . .	60.3	64.4	76.0*
Dry onions	42.8	48.8	57.0*
Garlic	7.3	8.7	10.0*
Carrots and turnips	14.4	17.1	20.0*
Watermelons	112.9	117.8	134.9
Apples	56.0†	85.7*	77.0*
Pears	21.3†	35.4*	32.0*
Apricots	5.4†	29.5	27.0*
Peaches and nectarines . . .	11.4†	62.0	56.0*
Plums and sloes	11.0†	60.0	54.0*
Grapes	148.9	164.4	201.4

* FAO estimate.
† Unofficial figure.

Aggregate production ('000 metric tons, may include official, semi-official or estimated data): Total cereals 460.0 in 2004, 399.2 in 2005, 215.6 in 2006; Total roots and tubers 576.4 in 2004, 564.2 in 2005, 539.5 in 2006; Total pulses 5.2 in 2004, 4.3 in 2005, 4.0 in 2006; Total vegetables (incl. melons) 719.9 in 2004, 775.1 in 2005, 885.1 in 2006; Total fruits (excl. melons) 262.5 in 2004, 480.4 in 2005, 473.4 in 2006.

Source: FAO.

LIVESTOCK
('000 head, year ending September)

	2004	2005	2006
Horses	13	12	12
Asses, mules or hinnies . . .	7	7	7
Cattle	566	573	592
Pigs	85	89	138
Sheep	580	557	549
Goats	48	47	43
Rabbits	22	18	21
Chickens*	4,740	4,590	4,675
Turkeys*	284	272	280

* FAO estimates.

Source: FAO.

LIVESTOCK PRODUCTS
('000 metric tons)

	2004	2005	2006*
Cattle meat	33	34	35
Sheep meat	7	8	8
Pig meat	9	9	10
Chicken meat	4	5	5
Cows' milk	536	557	570
Sheep's milk	16	16*	22
Hen eggs	31*	29	29
Wool: greasy	1	1	1

* FAO estimate(s).

Source: FAO.

Forestry

ROUNDWOOD REMOVALS
('000 cubic metres, excluding bark)

	2004	2005	2006
Sawlogs, veneer logs and logs for sleepers	6	4	5
Fuel wood	59	39	60
Total	65	43	65

Source: FAO.

Fishing

(metric tons, live weight)

	2004	2005*	2006
Capture	218	250	350
Common carp	26	30	42
Crucian carp	40	45	63
Freshwater fishes . . .	49	56	80
Trouts	62	72	100
Whitefishes	35	40	55
Aquaculture	813	739	1,056*
Common carp	216	200	300*
Crucian carp	45	40	53*
Silver carp	229	200	300*
Trouts	320	296	400*
Total catch	1,031	989	1,406*

* FAO estimate(s).

Source: FAO.

Mining

	2003	2004	2005
Copper concentrates (metric tons)*	18,068	17,700†	16,256
Molybdenum concentrates (metric tons)*	2,763	2,950†	3,030
Silver ores (kg)*†	4,000	4,000	4,000
Gold ores (kg)*	1,800	2,100	1,400
Salt ('000 metric tons) . . .	32	32	35

* Figures refer to the metal content of ores and concentrates.
† Estimated production.

Source: US Geological Survey.

Industry

SELECTED PRODUCTS
('000 metric tons, unless otherwise indicated)

	2004	2005	2006
Wheat flour	147	140	n.a.
Wine ('000 hectolitres) . . .	62	68	38
Beer ('000 hectolitres) . . .	88	108	126
Soft drinks ('000 hectolitres) . .	362	320	n.a.
Cigarettes (million)	2,720	3,020	2,825
Wool yarn—pure and mixed (metric tons)	58	57	n.a.
Cotton yarn—pure and mixed (metric tons)	54	n.a.	n.a.
Woven cotton fabrics ('000 sq metres)	236	143	240
Woven woollen fabrics ('000 sq metres)	n.a.	1	n.a.
Carpets ('000 sq metres) . . .	29	27	27
Cement	501	605	625
Electric energy (million kWh) .	6,030	6,317	5,941

Finance

CURRENCY AND EXCHANGE RATES

Monetary Units
  100 louma = 1 dram.

Sterling, Dollar and Euro Equivalents (30 May 2008)
  £1 sterling = 602.94 drams;
  US $1 = 305.52 drams;
  €1 = 473.80 drams;
  1,000 drams = £1.66 = $3.27 = €2.11.

Average Exchange Rate (drams per US $)
  2005   477.69
  2006   416.04
  2007   342.08

Note: The dram was introduced on 22 November 1993, replacing the Russian (formerly Soviet) rouble at a conversion rate of 1 dram = 200 roubles. The initial exchange rate was set at US $1 = 14.3 drams, but by the end of the year the rate was $1 = 75 drams. After the introduction of the dram, Russian currency continued to circulate in Armenia. The rouble had been withdrawn from circulation by March 1994.

STATE BUDGET
(million drams)

Revenue	2004	2005	2006
Tax revenue	250,119	304,257	359,715
Value-added tax	117,903	146,783	165,912
Excises	40,657	38,638	39,858
Enterprise profits tax . . .	32,011	46,557	65,329
Income tax	20,413	26,616	35,469
Customs duties	12,483	16,490	18,323
Fixed payments	11,742	12,963	15,074
Other taxes	14,977	16,207	19,733
Government duty	16,925	17,275	18,986
Non-tax incomes	12,394	29,218	32,638
Capital revenue	9,094	12,366	15,996
Other revenue	13,718	9,825	12,286
Total	302,249	372,941	439,620

Expense by economic type*	2004	2005	2006
Current expenditure	262,813	310,050	349,776
Wages	24,241	33,242	40,191
Interest	9,835	9,933	9,025
Subsidies	18,074	16,484	19,874
Current transfers	50,146	76,624	89,532
Goods and services . . .	160,517	173,767	191,154
Capital expenditure	60,619	71,928	89,228
Net crediting	n.a.	13,191	15,974
Total	323,432	395,169	454,978

*Excluding lending minus repayments (million drams): 10,539 in 2004; 13,109 in 2005; 17,636 in 2006 (preliminary).

Outlays by function of government	2004	2005	2006
General public services . . .	36,573	43,421	49,068
Defence	52,316	64,414	78,294
Public order and safety . . .	24,588	33,263	40,203
Education and science . . .	47,446	58,805	70,540
Health care	24,691	30,413	35,963
Social insurance	34,988	44,062	53,040
Culture, communication, religion and sport	8,486	10,412	13,597
Housing and community amenities	11,967	15,441	16,935
Fuel and energy production . .	9,552	10,759	1,544
Agriculture, fishing, forestry and waters	16,430	9,900	10,864
Industry and nature protection .	3,138	3,199	5,290
Transport and communications .	18,474	20,689	30,514
Other expenditures (transfer payments, debt obligations, etc.)	45,322	50,392	49,127
Total	333,970	395,169	454,978

2007 ('000 million drams): *Revenue:* Tax revenue 504.3 (Value-added tax 248.0, Excise duty 41.5, Corporation tax 75.5, Income tax 46.8, Customs duties 24.0, Other taxes, etc. 68.5); Non-tax revenue 19.6; Capital revenue 18.9; Total 542.8 (excl. grants 23.5). *Expenditure:* Current expenditure 455.9; Capital expenditure 183.3; Total 639.2 (excl. net lending 23.1) (Source: IMF, *Republic of Armenia: Sixth Review Under the Three-Year Arrangement Under the Poverty Reduction and Growth Facility—Staff Report; Press Release on the Executive Board Discussion; and Statement by the Executive Director for Republic of Armenia*—June 2008).

2008 ('000 million drams, projections): *Revenue:* Tax revenue 590.9; Non-tax revenue 9.0; Capital revenue 8.0; Total 608.0 (excl. grants 34.9). *Expenditure:* Current expenditure 514.4; Capital expenditure 182.9; Total 697.3 (excl. net lending 26.2) (Source: IMF, *Republic of Armenia: Sixth Review Under the Three-Year Arrangement Under the Poverty Reduction and Growth Facility—Staff Report; Press Release on the Executive Board Discussion; and Statement by the Executive Director for Republic of Armenia*—June 2008).

INTERNATIONAL RESERVES
(US $ million at 31 December)

	2005	2006	2007
IMF special drawing rights . .	10.18	13.96	9.60
Foreign exchange	659.30	1,057.96	1,649.49
Total	669.48	1,071.92	1,659.09

Source: IMF, *International Financial Statistics.*

MONEY SUPPLY
(million drams at 31 December)

	2005	2006	2007
Currency outside banks . .	144,311	211,469	326,016
Demand deposits at commercial banks	57,095	83,141	131,601
Total money (incl. others) . .	202,056	171,034	458,558

Source: IMF, *International Financial Statistics.*

COST OF LIVING
(Consumer Price Index; base: 2000 = 100)

	2003	2004	2005
Food (incl. non-alcoholic beverages)	114.4	125.8	126.8
Electricity, gas and other fuels .	102.1	103.8	106.0
Clothing (incl. footwear) . . .	102.8	101.8	99.7
Rent	100.7	116.6	132.8
All items (incl. others) . . .	109.2	116.3	117.0

2006 (base: 2000 = 100): Food (incl. non-alcoholic beverages) 132.0; All items (incl. others) 121.1.

2007 (base: 2000 = 100): Food (incl. non-alcoholic beverages) 140.9; All items (incl. others) 126.5.

Source: ILO.

NATIONAL ACCOUNTS
('000 million drams at current prices)

Expenditure on the Gross Domestic Product

	2004	2005	2006
Government final consumption expenditure	197.3	241.5	306.9
Private final consumption expenditure	1,570.4	1,706.7	1,922.1
Increase in stocks	19.4	8.4	4.3
Gross fixed capital formation .	455.3	657.7	870.4
Total domestic expenditure .	2,242.4	2,614.3	3,103.7
Exports of goods and services . .	522.5	604.0	576.7
Less Imports of goods and services	803.8	896.0	916.9
Statistical discrepancy* . . .	−53.1	−78.5	−98.5
GDP in market prices . . .	1,907.9	2,244.0	2,665.0

*Referring to the difference between the sum of the expenditure components and official estimates of GDP, compiled from the production approach.

Gross Domestic Product by Economic Activity

	2004	2005	2006
Agriculture and forestry . . .	431.1	421.5	473.5
Construction	297.2	487.4	711.5
Other industry*	366.3	422.1	402.8
Wholesale and retail trade; repair of motor vehicles, motorcycles and personal and household goods; hotels and restaurants .	222.3	245.1	280.5
Transport, storage and communications	113.8	124.6	156.0
Financial intermediation; real estate, renting and business activities; public administration and defence; other community, social and personal service activities	341.6	380.9	455.0
Sub-total	1,772.3	2,081.6	2,479.3
Less Imputed bank service charges	24.2	27.2	32.3
Gross value added in basic prices	1,748.1	2,054.3	2,447.0
Taxes, *less* subsidies on products .	159.9	189.7	218.0
GDP in market prices . . .	1,907.9	2,244.0	2,665.0

*Comprising mining and quarrying, manufacturing, electricity, gas and water.

Source: Asian Development Bank, *Key Indicators of Developing Asian and Pacific Countries.*

BALANCE OF PAYMENTS
(US $ million)

	2005	2006	2007
Exports of goods f.o.b.	1,004.9	1,025.5	1,200.2
Imports of goods f.o.b.	−1,592.8	−1,921.3	−2,807.1
Trade balance	−587.9	−895.9	−1,606.9
Exports of services	411.1	484.7	526.4
Imports of services	−531.1	−615.1	−718.3
Balance on goods and services	−707.9	−1,026.3	−1,798.8
Other income received	457.5	624.3	835.2
Other income paid	−325.0	−409.1	−536.4
Balance on goods, services and income	−575.4	−811.1	−1,500.0
Current transfers received . .	603.5	791.7	1,028.0
Current transfers paid	−79.9	−97.7	−99.4
Current balance	−51.7	−117.1	−571.4
Capital account (net)	73.3	86.4	138.8
Direct investment abroad . . .	−6.7	−3.1	3.4
Direct investment from abroad .	239.4	453.2	660.7
Portfolio investment assets . .	−2.7	−0.2	0.5
Portfolio investment liabilities .	1.1	9.4	−9.8
Other investment assets . . .	−170.7	−175.7	−197.8
Other investment liabilities . .	102.3	150.5	575.2
Net errors and omissions . . .	2.4	−16.1	−41.3
Overall balance	186.6	387.3	558.4

Source: IMF, *International Financial Statistics*.

External Trade

PRINCIPAL COMMODITIES
(distribution by HS, US $ million)

Imports c.i.f.	2004	2005	2006
Vegetable products	109.0	98.3	112.1
Cereals	72.6	53.7	60.7
Prepared foodstuffs; beverages, spirits and vinegar; tobacco and manufactured substitutes . .	112.7	145.9	163.8
Mineral products	209.4	297.4	366.0
Mineral fuels, mineral oils and products of their distillation; bituminous substances; mineral waxes	207.3	264.4	350.9
Products of chemical or allied industries	85.2	118.4	150.4
Textiles and textile articles . .	47.1	46.0	59.3
Natural or cultured pearls, precious or semi-precious stones, precious metals and articles thereof; imitation jewellery; coins	291.5	347.6	312.5
Base metals and articles thereof .	60.8	94.1	163.7
Machinery and mechanical appliances; electrical equipment; sound and television apparatus .	135.5	232.5	304.4
Nuclear reactors, boilers, machinery and mechanical appliances; parts thereof . .	69.1	156.6	168.6
Electrical machinery, equipment and parts; sound and television apparatus, and parts and accessories	66.4	75.9	135.8
Vehicles, aircraft, vessels and associated transport equipment .	92.5	151.8	196.6
Vehicles other than railway or tramway rolling-stock, and parts and accessories thereof .	90.4	146.6	195.7
Total (incl. others)	1,350.7	1,801.7	2,191.6

Exports f.o.b.	2004	2005	2006
Prepared foodstuffs; beverages, spirits and vinegar; tobacco and manufactured substitutes . .	69.2	96.9	95.1
Beverages, spirits and vinegar .	57.0	84.3	79.1
Mineral products	99.6	93.5	136.6
Ores, slag and ash	72.8	51.4	93.5
Textiles and textile articles . .	44.0	37.0	35.5
Non-knitted clothing and accessories	28.0	22.4	20.9
Natural or cultured pearls, precious or semi-precious stones, precious metals and articles thereof; imitation jewellery; coins	299.3	336.3	301.0
Base metals and articles thereof .	137.6	322.0	280.9
Iron and steel	70.5	243.7	167.6
Copper and articles thereof .	37.7	50.6	77.2
Aluminium and articles thereof	16.9	4.4	7.9
Machinery and mechanical appliances; electrical equipment; sound and television apparatus	21.9	28.0	20.8
Optical, photographic, measuring and medical instruments and apparatus; clocks and watches; musical instruments	7.1	4.9	22.7
Total (incl. others)	722.9	973.9	985.1

PRINCIPAL TRADING PARTNERS
(countries of consignment, US $ '000)

Imports c.i.f.	2004	2005	2006
Belgium	109,008	162,551	157,129
Bulgaria	11,038	11,709	19,423
China, People's Republic . .	13,379	27,173	52,547
Cyprus	18,929	10,554	9,632
France	17,979	39,668	37,147
Georgia	48,544	50,813	75,624
Germany	73,910	114,558	85,007
Greece	32,074	37,952	80,622
Iran	76,270	108,060	132,690
Israel	100,138	102,504	87,264
Italy	38,271	45,517	76,488
Luxembourg	41,287	24,213	2,234
Panama	54,051	70,767	75,453
Russia	179,679	268,484	364,775
Switzerland	46,085	86,106	85,264
Turkey	39,807	61,218	88,503
Ukraine	50,887	69,122	109,159
United Arab Emirates . . .	65,225	107,326	145,192
United Kingdom	106,776	91,176	79,326
USA	104,824	116,327	136,692
Total (incl. others)	1,350,698	1,801,736	2,191,613

Exports f.o.b.	2004	2005	2006
Belgium	107,929	124,598	108,846
Canada	8,232	11,482	11,133
China, People's Republic . .	21,750	9,245	464
Georgia	29,062	46,833	54,649
Germany	83,180	152,108	148,028
Iran	30,560	28,513	29,643
Israel	98,356	112,241	87,448
Italy	28,433	25,594	28,928
Netherlands	26,269	133,110	126,946
Russia	77,898	119,004	121,156
Switzerland	45,354	34,666	72,100
Ukraine	10,479	13,703	22,554
United Arab Emirates . . .	8,924	10,383	5,597
United Kingdom	1,194	419	7,618
USA	70,646	62,219	65,056
Total (incl. others)	722,912	973,921	985,108

Transport

RAILWAYS
(traffic)

	2004	2005	2006
Passenger journeys ('000)* . .	800	700	700
Passenger-km (million) . . .	30.0	26.6	27.7
Freight carried ('000 metric tons) .	2,629.6	2,612.3	2,719.6
Freight ton-km (million) . . .	678.2	654.1	668.0

* Rounded figures.

CIVIL AVIATION
(traffic)

	2004	2005	2006
Passengers carried ('000)* . .	1,100	1,200	1,200
Passengers-km (million) . . .	984.0	959.5	822.2
Freight carried ('000 metric tons) .	9.2	9.3	9.3
Cargo ton-kilometres ('000) . .	10.0	10.7	12.4

* Rounded figures.

Tourism

ARRIVALS BY NATIONALITY

	2004	2005	2006
Argentina	14,935	17,560	21,500
Brazil	5,412	6,465	7,014
Canada	13,588	15,795	19,840
CIS countries*	72,996	89,968	120,964
France	12,368	14,294	18,699
Germany	10,688	12,966	14,666
Iran	25,650	27,458	29,347
Japan	5,585	7,681	8,125
Lebanon	11,556	13,411	15,490
Syria	10,985	13,941	16,119
United Kingdom	5,988	8,124	8,559
USA	39,965	43,869	45,535
Total (incl. others)	262,959	318,563	381,136

* Comprising Azerbaijan, Belarus, Georgia, Kazakhstan, Kyrgyzstan, Moldova, Russia, Tajikistan, Turkmenistan, Ukraine and Uzbekistan.

Tourism receipts (US $ million, incl. passenger transport): 90 in 2003; 103 in 2004; 161 in 2005.

Source: World Tourism Organization.

Communications Media

	2003	2004	2005
Telephones ('000 main lines in use)	563.7	582.5	594.4
Mobile cellular telephones ('000 subscribers)	114.4	203.3	318.0
Personal computers ('000 in use)	103	200	n.a.
Internet users ('000)	140	150	161
Broadband subscribers . . .	—	1,000	2,000
Book production:*			
titles	1,025	970	991
copies ('000)	660	427	796
Newspapers:			
titles	120	170	177
total circulation ('000 copies) .	325	600	553
Periodicals:			
titles	77	112	120
total circulation ('000 copies) .	309	412	401

* Including brochures.

2000: Television receivers ('000 in use) 860.

2006: Internet users ('000) 172.8.

Source: partly International Telecommunication Union.

Education

(2004/05, public institutions, unless otherwise indicated)

	Institutions	Teachers	Students
Pre-primary	623*	7,585†	47,800*
General	1,427	41,700	471,300
Gymnasia and lyceums . .	35	313	10,500
Specialized secondary schools	83	2,671	27,800
State higher schools (incl. universities)	22	7,152	73,700

* December 2005.
† 1998/99.

Adult literacy rate (UNESCO estimates): 99.5% (males 99.7%; females 99.3%) in 2007 (Source: UNESCO Institute for Statistics).

Directory

The Constitution

The Constitution was approved by a national referendum held on 5 July 1995. Several constitutional amendments were approved by a referendum held on 27 November 2005. The following is a summary of the Constitution's main provisions:

GENERAL PROVISIONS OF CONSTITUTIONAL ORDER

The Republic of Armenia is an independent democratic state; its sovereignty is vested in the people, who execute their authority through free elections, referendums and local self-government institutions and officials, as defined by the Constitution. Referendums, as well as elections of the President of the Republic, the Azgayin Zhoghov (National Assembly) and local self-government bodies, are carried out on the basis of universal, equal, direct suffrage by secret ballot. Through the Constitution and legislation, the State ensures the protection of human rights and freedoms, in accordance with the principles and norms of international law. A multi-party political system is guaranteed. The right to property is recognized and protected. Armenia conducts its foreign policy based on the norms of international law, seeking to establish neighbourly and mutually beneficial relations with all countries. The official language is Armenian.

FUNDAMENTAL HUMAN AND CIVIL RIGHTS AND FREEDOMS

The acquisition and loss of citizenship are prescribed by law. Armenian citizens may hold dual citizenship. No one shall be subject to torture or cruel treatment. Every citizen has the right to freedom of movement and residence within the republic, as well as the right to leave the republic. Every citizen has the right to freedom of thought, speech, conscience and religion. The right to establish or join associations, trade unions, political organizations, etc., is guaranteed, as is the right to strike for protection of economic, social and labour interests.

Every citizen has the right to social insurance in the event of old age, disability, sickness, widowhood, unemployment, etc. Every citizen has the right to education. Education is provided free at elementary and secondary state educational institutions. Citizens belonging to national minorities have the right to preserve their traditions and to develop their language and culture. Everyone charged with a penal offence has the right to be presumed innocent until proved guilty. The advocacy of national, racial and religious hatred, and the propagation of violence and war, are prohibited.

THE PRESIDENT OF THE REPUBLIC

The President of the Republic ensures the observance of the Constitution and the effective operation of the legislative, executive and juridical authorities. The President is the guarantor of the independence, territorial integrity and security of the republic and is elected by citizens of the republic for a period of five years. Any person who has the right to participate in elections, has attained the age of 35 years, and has been a resident citizen of Armenia for the preceding 10 years is eligible for election to the office of President. No person may be elected to the office for more than two successive terms.

The President signs and promulgates laws adopted by the Azgayin Zhoghov, or returns draft legislation to the Azgayin Zhoghov for reconsideration; may dismiss the Azgayin Zhoghov and declare special elections to it, after consultation with the Prime Minister and the Chairman of the Azgayin Zhoghov; appoints and dismisses the Prime Minister, following approval by the Azgayin Zhoghov; appoints and dismisses the members of the Government, upon the recommendation of the Prime Minister; appoints civil service officials, in cases prescribed by law; establishes deliberation bodies; represents Armenia in international relations, co-ordinates foreign policy, concludes international treaties, signs international treaties ratified by the Azgayin Zhoghov, and ratifies agreements between governments; appoints and recalls diplomatic representatives of Armenia to foreign countries and international organizations, and receives the credentials of diplomatic representatives of foreign countries; recommends to the legislature the candidacy of the Procurator-General, the Chairman of the Central Bank and the Chairman of the Control Chamber; appoints four members of the Constitutional Court and the Chairman, if the Azgayin Zhoghov has failed to fill this position in the period prescribed; is the Supreme Commander-in-Chief of the Armed Forces; takes decisions on the use of the Armed Forces; grants titles of honour; grants amnesties to convicts; and is immune from prosecution.

THE AZGAYIN ZHOGHOV

Legislative power is executed by the Azgayin Zhoghov. The Azgayin Zhoghov comprises 131 deputies, elected for a five-year term. Any person who has attained the age of 25 years and has been a permanent resident and citizen of Armenia for the preceding five years is eligible to be elected a deputy.

The Azgayin Zhoghov deliberates and enacts laws; has the power to express a vote of 'no confidence' in the Government; confirms the state budget, as proposed by the Government; supervises the implementation of the state budget; elects its Chairman (Speaker) and two Deputy Chairmen; appoints the Chairman and Deputy Chairman of the Central Bank, upon the nomination of the President; and appoints five members and the Chairman of the Constitutional Court, upon the recommendation of the Chairman of the Azgayin Zhoghov.

At the suggestion of the President of the Republic, the Azgayin Zhoghov declares amnesties; ratifies or declares invalid international treaties; and declares war. Upon the recommendation of the Government, the Azgayin Zhoghov confirms the territorial and administrative divisions of the republic.

THE GOVERNMENT

Executive power is realized by the Government. The Prime Minister directs the current activities of the Government and co-ordinates the activities of the Ministers.

The Government presents the programme of its activities to the Azgayin Zhoghov for approval; presents the draft state budget to the Azgayin Zhoghov for confirmation, ensures implementation of the budget and presents a report on its implementation to the Azgayin Zhoghov; ensures the implementation of state policy; and takes measures to strengthen adherence to the laws, to ensure the rights and freedoms of citizens, and to protect public order and the property of citizens.

JUDICIAL POWER

The courts of general competence are the tribunal courts of first instance, the review courts, the Court of Cassation and the courts of appeal. There are also economic, military and other courts. The guarantor of the independence of judicial bodies is the President of the Republic. The Chairman of the Court of Cassation is the Head of the Council of Justice, and does not have the right to vote. The Council consists of up to nine judges, elected by secret ballot for a period of five years by the General Assembly of Judges; two legal scholars appointed by the President; and two legal scholars appointed by the Azgayin Zhoghov. The Constitutional Court is composed of nine members, of whom the Azgayin Zhoghov appoints five and the President of the Republic appoints four. The highest court of appeal is the Court of Cassation, the members of which are appointed by the President of the Republic, for life.

TERRITORIAL ADMINISTRATION AND LOCAL SELF-GOVERNMENT

The administrative territorial units of the Republic of Armenia are provinces (*marzer*) and communities (*hamaynker*). Marzer are comprised of rural and urban communities. Local self-government takes place in the communities. Bodies of local self-government, community elders and the community head (city mayor or head of village) are to be elected for a four-year term. The Government appoints and dismisses regional governors, who carry out the Government's regional policy and co-ordinate the performance of regional services by state executive bodies. The city of Yerevan holds the status of a community, with an elected mayor.

The Government

HEAD OF STATE

President: Serge Sarkissian (elected 19 February 2008, inaugurated 9 April 2008).

GOVERNMENT
(October 2008)

Prime Minister: Tigran Sarkissian.

Deputy Prime Minister and Minister of Territorial Administration: Armen Gevorgian.

Minister of Foreign Affairs: Edvard Nalbandian.

Minister of Defence: Seyran Ohanian.

Minister of Finance: Tigran Davtian.

Minister of Justice: Gevorg Danielian.

Minister of Energy and Natural Resources: Armen Movsissian.

Minister of Labour and Social Affairs: Arsen Hambardzumian.

Minister of Health Care: Harutyun Kushkian.

Minister of Agriculture: Aramayis Grigorian.

Minister of Environmental Protection: Aram Haroutunian.

Minister of the Economy: Nerses Yeritsian.

Minister of Education and Science: Spartak Seiranian.

Minister of Culture: Hasmik Poghossian.

Minister of Sport and Youth Affairs: Armen Grigorian.

Minister of Transport and Communications: Gurgen Sarkissian.

Minister of Urban Development: Vardan Vardanian.

Minister of Emergency Situations: Mher Shahgeldian.

Minister of Diaspora Affairs: Hranush Hacobian.

MINISTRIES

Office of the President: 0077 Yerevan, Marshal Baghramian Ave 26; tel. and fax (10) 52-23-64; e-mail press@president.am; internet www.president.am.

Office of the Prime Minister: 0010 Yerevan, Republic Sq., Govt Bldg 1; tel. (10) 52-03-60; fax (10) 15-10-35; internet www.gov.am/enversion/premier_2/primer_home.htm.

Ministry of Agriculture: 0010 Yerevan, Republic Sq., Govt Bldg 3; tel. and fax (10) 52-46-41; internet www.minagro.am.

Ministry of Culture: 0010 Yerevan, Republic Sq., Govt Bldg 3; tel. (10) 52-93-49; fax (10) 52-39-22; e-mail info@mincult.am; internet www.mincult.am.

Ministry of Defence: 0088 Yerevan, Proshian Settlement, G. Shaush St 60; tel. (10) 28-72-03; fax (10) 28-26-30; e-mail press@mil.am; internet www.mil.am.

Ministry of Diaspora Affairs: 0010 Yerevan, Vazgen Sarkissian St 26/1.

Ministry of the Economy: 0010 Yerevan, M. Mkrtchian St 5; tel. (10) 52-61-34; fax (10) 52-65-77; e-mail info@minted.am; internet www.mineconomy.am.

Ministry of Education and Science: 0010 Yerevan, Republic Sq., Govt Bldg 3; tel. and fax (10) 52-66-02; e-mail edu@edu.am; internet www.edu.am.

Ministry of Emergency Situations: Yerevan.

Ministry of Energy and Natural Resources: 0010 Yerevan, Republic Sq., Govt Bldg 2; tel. (10) 52-19-64; fax (10) 52-63-65; e-mail minenergy@minenergy.am; internet www.minenergy.am.

Ministry of Environmental Protection: 0010 Yerevan, Republic Sq., Govt Bldg 3; tel. (10) 52-10-99; fax (10) 58-54-69; e-mail info@mnp.am; internet www.mnp.am.

Ministry of Finance: 0010 Yerevan, Melik-Adamian St 1; tel. (10) 59-53-04; fax (10) 54-58-15; e-mail press@minfin.am; internet www.minfin.am.

Ministry of Foreign Affairs: 0010 Yerevan, Republic Sq., Govt Bldg 2; tel. (10) 52-35-31; fax (10) 54-39-25; e-mail info@armeniaforeignministry.com; internet www.armeniaforeignministry.com.

Ministry of Health Care: 0010 Yerevan, Republic Sq.; tel. (10) 58-24-13; fax (10) 15-10-97; e-mail pr@moh.am; internet www.moh.am.

Ministry of Justice: 0010 Yerevan, Vazgen Sarkissian St 3; tel. and fax (10) 58-21-57; e-mail info@moj.am; internet www.moj.am.

Ministry of Labour and Social Affairs: 0010 Yerevan, Republic Sq., Govt Bldg 3; tel. (10) 52-68-31; e-mail varduhii@mss.am; internet www.mss.am.

Ministry of Sport and Youth Affairs: 0010 Yerevan, Abovian 9; tel. 52-75-72; fax 52-65-29; e-mail minsportyouth@minsportyouth.am; internet www.minsportyouth.am.

Ministry of Territorial Administration: 0010 Yerevan, Republic Sq., Govt Bldg 2; tel. (10) 51-13-02; fax (10) 51-13-31; e-mail mta@mta.gov.am; internet www.mta.gov.am.

Ministry of Transport and Communications: 0010 Yerevan, Nalbandian St 28; tel. (10) 56-33-91; fax (10) 54-59-79; e-mail mtc@mtc.am; internet www.mtc.am.

Ministry of Urban Development: 0010 Yerevan, Republic Sq., Govt Bldg 3; tel. (10) 58-90-80; fax (10) 52-32-00; e-mail info@mud.am; internet www.mud.am.

President

Presidential Election, 19 February 2008

Candidates	Votes	% of votes
Serge Sarkissian	862,369	52.82
Levon Ter-Petrossian	351,222	21.51
Artur Baghdasarian	272,427	17.69
Vahan Hovhanissian	100,966	6.18
Vazgen Manukian	21,075	1.29
Others	24,607	1.51
Total	**1,632,666**	**100.00**

Legislature

Azgayin Zhoghov
(National Assembly)

0095 Yerevan, Marshal Baghramian St 19; tel. (10) 58-82-25; fax (10) 52-98-26; internet www.parliament.am.

Chairman: Hovik Abrahamian.

General Election, 12 May 2007

Parties	Party lists		
	% of votes	Seats	Total seats*
Republican Party of Armenia	33.91	41	64
Prosperous Armenia	15.13	18	25
Armenian Revolutionary Federation—Dashnaktsutyun	13.16	16	16
Law-Governed Country Party of Armenia	7.05	8	9
Heritage Party	6.00	7	7
Alliance	2.44	—	1
United Labour Party	4.39	—	—
National Unity Party	3.69	—	—
New Times Party	3.48	—	—
People's Party	2.74	—	—
Independents	—	—	9
Others	8.01	—	—
Total	**100.00**	**90**	**131**

* Including 41 seats filled by voting in single-member districts.

Local Government

Armenia is divided into 11 regions (marz—plural marzer), including the capital city, Yerevan. Each provincial governor (marzpet, or in the case of Yerevan, the mayor) is appointed by the Government to carry out regional administration. Following the constitutional referendum of November 2005, Yerevan changed status, becoming a community (*hamaynk*), with an elected mayor. The provinces are subdivided into 871 rural and, including Yerevan, 60 urban communities (*hamaynkner*). Local elections were held in September–October 2005.

CITY MARZ

Yerevan City Marz Administration: 0015 Yerevan, Argishti St 1; tel. (10) 51-41-87; fax (10) 58-39-64; e-mail info@yerevanmayoralty.am; internet www.yerevan.am; Mayor Yervand Zakharian.

MARZER

Aragatsotn Marz Administration: 0201 Ashtarak, Hanrapetoutioun St 4, Marzpetaran; tel. (232) 28-74-60; fax (232) 31-032; internet aragatsotn.region.am; Gov. Gabriyel Gezalian.

Ararat Marz Administration: 0701 Artashat, 23 August St 60, Marzpetaran; tel. and fax (235) 28-60-23; e-mail art-kar@kar.am; internet ararat.region.am; Gov. Vardges Hovakimyan.

Armavir Marz Administration: 0901 Armavir, Abovian St 71, Marzpetaran; tel. (237) 63-716; fax (237) 60-856; e-mail arm_kar@kar.am; internet armavir.region.am; Gov. Ashot Ghahramanyan.

Gegharkunik Marz Administration: 1201 Gavar, G. Lusavorichi St 36, Marzpetaran; tel. (264) 21-045; fax (264) 24-175; e-mail gav_kar@kar.am; internet gegharkunik.region.am; Gov. Nver Poghisian.

Kotayk Marz Administration: 2301 Hrazdan, Kentron Distr., Marzpetaran; tel. and fax (223) 23-663; e-mail kotayk_marz@mail.ru; internet kotayk.region.am; Gov. Kovalenko Shakhgaldian.

Lori Marz Administration: 2001 Vanadzor, Hayk Sq. 1, Marzpetaran; tel. (322) 46-192; fax (322) 22-877; e-mail inform_lori@yahoo.com; internet lori.region.am; Gov. Aram Kocharian.

Shirak Marz Administration: 3101 Gyumri, G. Nzhdeh St 16, Marzpetaran; tel. (312) 32-610; fax (312) 37-390; e-mail shirakmarzpetaran@yahoo.com; internet shirak.region.am; Gov. Lida Nanian.

Syunik Marz Administration: 3301 Kapan, G. Nzhdeh St 1, Marzpetaran; tel. (285) 62-010; fax (285) 62-443; e-mail kap_kar@kar.am; internet syunik.region.am; Gov. Surik Khachatrian.

Tavush Marz Administration: 4001 Ijevan, Sahmanadrutian Sq. 1, Marzpetaran; tel. (263) 32-356; fax (263) 32-203; internet tavush.region.am; Gov. Armen Ghularian.

Vayots Dzor Marz Administration: 3601 Yeghegnadzor, Shahumian St 5, Marzpetaran; tel. (281) 22-522; fax (281) 25-595; e-mail egeg_kar@kar.am; internet vdzor.region.am; Gov. Vardges Matevosian.

Election Commission

Central Electoral Commission (CEC): 0009 Yerevan, G. Kochar St 21a; tel. and fax (10) 54-35-23; e-mail cec@ielections.am; internet www.elections.am; Chair. Garegin Azarian.

Political Organizations

At January 2006 there were 74 duly registered parties in existence.

Armenian Christian Democratic Union (HDQM): 0010 Yerevan, Vardanants St 8a; tel. (10) 54-11-33; fax (10) 54-37-87; e-mail cduarm@yahoo.com; internet www.acdu.am; f. 1990; Chair. Khosrov Haroutunian.

Armenian Democratic Party: 0009 Yerevan, Koriun St 14; tel. and fax (10) 52-52-73; e-mail democracy@armenia.com; f. 1992 by elements of Communist Party of Armenia; contested the parliamentary election of 2003 as part of the Justice (Artarutiun) bloc; Chair. Aram Sarkissian.

Armenian Liberal Democratic Party (Ramgavar Azatagan—HRAK): 0070 Yerevan, Yervand Kochar St 19/6; tel. and fax (10) 57–23–97; e-mail hrak@arminco.com; internet www.hrak.am; f. 1991; centre-right; merged with Alliance (Dashink) Nov. 2007; Chair. Haroutiun Arakelian.

Armenian Pan-National Movement (APNM) (Haiots Hamazgaien Sharjoum–HHSh): 0010 Yerevan, Khanjian St 27; tel. (10) 57-04-70; f. 1989; Pres. Levon Ter-Petrossian; Chair. Ararat Zurabian.

Armenian Revolutionary Federation—Dashnaktsutyun (ARF) (Hai Heghapokhakan Dashnaktsutiun): 0010 Yerevan, Mher Mkrtchian St 30; tel. (10) 52-15-02; fax (10) 52-04-26; e-mail info@arf.am; internet www.arfd.am; f. 1890; formed the ruling party in independent Armenia, 1918–20; prohibited under Soviet rule, but continued its activities in other countries; permitted to operate legally in Armenia from 1991; suspended in December 1994; legally reinstated 1998; 40,000 mems; Chair. Hrant Markarian.

Heritage Party (Zharangutyun): 0002 Yerevan, Moscovian St 31; tel. (10) 53-69-13; fax (10) 53-26-97; e-mail info@heritage.am; internet www.heritage.am; f. 2002; national liberal party; Chair. RAFFI HOVHANISSIAN; Chair. of Bd ANAHIT BAKHSHIAN.

Law-Governed Country Party of Armenia (Orinats Yerkir—OY): 0009 Yerevan, Abovian St 43; tel. (10) 56-99-69; e-mail info@oek.am; internet www.oek.am; f. 1998; centrist; also known as the Rule of Law Party and the Legal State Party; absorbed the People's Democratic Party of Armenia in Nov. 2003; Head ARTUR BAGHDASARIAN; 41,000 mems.

Mighty Fatherland (Hzor Hayrenik): 0010 Yerevan, Tigran Mets Ave 9; tel. (10) 52-92-15; fax (10) 52-25-45; e-mail hzor_hayrenik@xter.net; f. 1997; Chair. VARDAN VARDAPETIAN; 11,500 mems.

National Democratic Party (AZhK): Yerevan, Paronyan St 11/4; tel. and fax (10) 56-21-50; e-mail ajk_info@web.am; internet www.ajk.am; f. 2001 following the division of the National Democratic Union; contested the 2003 parliamentary elections as part of the Justice (Artarutiun) bloc, but withdrew from the bloc in Dec. 2005; Leader SHAVARSH KOCHARIAN.

National Democratic Union (Azgayin Zhoghovrdavarakan Miutyun): 0001 Yerevan, Abovian St 12; tel. (10) 52-34-12; fax (10) 56-31-88; f. 1991; Chair. VAZGEN M. MANUKIAN.

National Revival Party (AV): Yerevan; f. 2005 by former mems of Republic (q.v.); Chair. of Bd ALBERT BAZEIAN.

National Unity Party (Azgayin Miabanutiun—MAK): c/o Azgayin Zhoghov, 0095 Yerevan, Marshal Baghramian St 19; tel. (10) 58-01-37; f. 1998; Chair. ARTASHES GEGHAMIAN.

New Times Party (Nor Zhamanakner): 0001 Yerevan, Tumanian St 8; tel. (10) 56-83-17; fax (10) 56-83-39; e-mail nor_jamanakner@yahoo.com; f. 2003; Chair. ARAM KARAPETIAN.

People's Party of Armenia (PPA) (Hayastani Zhoghovrdakan Kusaktsutyun—HzhK): Yerevan; e-mail hzhk@freenet.am; internet www.ppa.am; f. 1998; contested the general election of May 2003 as part of the Justice (Artarutiun) bloc; Leader STEPAN DEMIRCHIAN.

Prosperous Armenia (Bargavach Hayastan Kusaktsutyun—BHK): Yerevan, Myasnikian 1; tel. (10) 54-88-07; e-mail info@bhk.am; internet www.bhk.am; f. 2006; Leader GAGIK TSARUKIAN.

Republic (Hanrapetutiun): 0002 Yerevan, Mashtots Ave 37/30; tel. (10) 53-86-34; e-mail republic@arminco.com; f. 2001 by members of the Yerkrapah Union of Volunteers and fmr members of the Republican Party of Armenia; Leader ARAM SARKISSIAN.

Republican Party of Armenia (Haiastani Hanrapetakan Kusaktsutiun—RPA) (HHK): 0010 Yerevan, Melik-Adamian St 2; tel. (10) 58-00-31; fax (10) 50-12-59; e-mail hhk@hhk.am; internet www.hhk.am; f. 1990; national conservative party; Chair. SERGE SARKISSIAN.

United Communist Party of Armenia (Hayastani Miatsial Komunistakan Kusaktsutyun—HMKK): Yerevan; f. 2003 by the merger of seven pro-communist parties, including the Renewed Communist Party of Armenia, the Party of Intellectuals, the Communist Party of the Working People and the United Progressive Communist; First Sec. YURI MANUKIAN.

Diplomatic Representation

EMBASSIES IN ARMENIA

Belarus: 0028 Yerevan, N. Duman St 12–14; tel. (10) 27-56-11; fax (10) 26-03-84; e-mail armenia@belembassy.org; internet www.armenia.belembassy.org; Ambassador MARINA DOLGOPOLOVA.

Brazil: 0010 Yerevan, S. Yerevantzu 57; tel. (10) 50-02-10; fax (10) 50-02-11; e-mail brasembierevan@mre.gov.br; Ambassador RENATE STILLE.

Bulgaria: Yerevan, Nor Aresh, Sofia St 16; tel. (10) 45-82-33; fax (10) 45-46-02; e-mail bulembassy@arminco.com; internet www.mfa.bg/yerevan; Ambassador TODOR STAIKOV.

China, People's Republic: 0019 Yerevan, Marshal Baghramian St 12; tel. (10) 56-00-67; fax (10) 54-57-61; e-mail chiemb@arminco.com; internet am.chineseembassy.org; Ambassador HONG JIUYIN.

Egypt: Yerevan, Sepuhi St 6A; tel. (10) 22-01-17; fax (10) 22-64-25; e-mail egyemb@arminco.com; Ambassador WAHID GALAL.

France: 0015 Yerevan, Grigor Lusavorich St 8; tel. (10) 56-11-03; fax (10) 56-98-31; e-mail cad.erevan@diplomatie.gouv.fr; internet www.ambafrance-am.org; Ambassador SERGE SMESSOW.

Georgia: 0010 Yerevan, Aram St 42; tel. (10) 56-43-57; fax (10) 56-41-83; e-mail geoemb@netsys.am; internet www.armenia.mfa.gov.ge; Ambassador REVAZ GACHECHILADZE.

Germany: 0025 Yerevan, Charents St 29; tel. (10) 52-32-79; fax (10) 52-47-81; e-mail info@eriw.diplo.de; internet www.eriwan.diplo.de; Ambassador ANDREA WIKTORIN.

Greece: 0002 Yerevan, Demirchian St 6; tel. (10) 53-00-51; fax (10) 53-00-49; e-mail embassy@greekembassy.am; internet www.greekembassy.am; Ambassador IOANNIS KORINTHIOS.

India: 0019 Yerevan, Dzorapi St 50/2; tel. (10) 53-91-73; fax (10) 53-39-84; e-mail hoc@embassyofindia.am; internet www.indianembassy.am; Ambassador REENA PANDEY.

Iran: Yerevan, Budaghian St 1; tel. (10) 28-04-57; fax (10) 23-00-52; e-mail info@iranembassy.am; internet www.iranembassy.am; Ambassador SEYED ALI SAGHAEYAN.

Italy: 0010 Yerevan, Italiayi St 5; tel. (10) 54-23-35; fax (10) 54-23-41; e-mail segreteria.jerevan@esteri.it; internet www.ambjerevan.esteri.it; Ambassador MASSIMO CASSINELLI.

Kazakhstan: 0019 Yerevan, Marshal Baghramian 2-oi per. 1; tel. (10) 21-13-33; fax (10) 27-14-74; e-mail kazembassy@web.am; Ambassador AIYMDOC YE. BOZZHIGITOV.

Lebanon: 0010 Yerevan, Vardanants St 7; tel. (10) 52-65-40; fax (10) 52-69-90; e-mail libarm@arminco.com; Ambassador TONY BADAWI.

Lithuania: Yerevan, Noy 86; tel. (10) 74-19-64; fax (10) 74-19-63; Chargé d'affaires a.i. KĘSTUTIS STANKEVIČIUS.

Poland: 0010 Yerevan, Hanrapetutiun St 44A; tel. (10) 54-24-93; fax (10) 54-24-98; e-mail armpolemb@ct.futuro.pl; internet www.erewan.polemb.net; Ambassador TOMASZ KNOTHE.

Romania: Yerevan, Barbusse St 15; tel. (10) 27-53-32; fax (10) 22-75-47; e-mail ambrom@netsys.am; Ambassador RODINA CRINA PRUNARIU.

Russia: 0015 Yerevan, Grigor Lusavorichi St 13A; tel. (10) 56-74-27; fax (10) 56-71-97; e-mail info@rusembassy.am; internet www.armenia.mid.ru; Ambassador NIKOLAI V. PAVLOV.

Syria: 0019 Yerevan, Marshal Baghramian Ave 14; tel. (10) 52-40-36; fax (10) 54-52-19; e-mail syrem_ar@intertel.am; Chargé d'affaires a.i. ABDUL HAMID SALLOUM.

Turkmenistan: 0028 Yerevan, Kievian St 19; tel. (10) 22-10-29; fax (10) 22-21-32; e-mail serdar@arminco.com; Ambassador KHIDIR SAPARLIYEV.

Ukraine: 0037 Yerevan, Arabkir 29/5/1; tel. (10) 22-97-27; fax (10) 25-13-83; e-mail emb_am@mfa.gov.ua; internet www.mfa.gov.ua/armenia; Ambassador OLEKSANDR I. BOZHKO.

United Kingdom: 0019 Yerevan, Marshal Baghramian Ave 34; tel. (10) 26-43-01; fax (10) 26-43-18; e-mail enquiries.yerevan@fco.gov.uk; internet www.ukinarmenia.fco.gov.uk; Ambassador CHARLES LONSDALE.

USA: 0082 Yerevan, American Ave 1; tel. (10) 46-47-00; fax (10) 46-47-42; e-mail usinfo@usa.am; internet yerevan.usembassy.gov; Ambassador MARIE L. YOVANOVITCH.

Judicial System

A new judicial and legal system came into force in January 1999. The Supreme Court was replaced as the highest court of appeal by the Court of Cassation, and Appellate Courts replaced People's Courts. Members of the Court of Cassation were appointed by the President, for life. A constitutional referendum, held in November 2005, provided for the President to cede the chairmanship of the Council of Justice to the Chairman of the Court of Cassation; the Azgayin Zhoghov (National Assembly) was henceforth to appoint the Prosecutor-General; and the Council of Justice was to nominate the chairmen of all courts (including the Court of Cassation) and to draw up a list of proposed judges for approval by the President.

Constitutional Court

0019 Yerevan, Marshal Baghramian St 10; tel. (10) 58-81-40; fax (10) 52-99-91; e-mail armlaw@concourt.am; internet www.concourt.am. f. 1996; Chair. GAGIK HAROUTUNIAN.

Chairman of the Court of Cassation: HOVHANNES MANUKIAN, Yerevan, Hkorhrdaranayin St 6; tel. (10) 58-71-30; fax (10) 56-31-73.

Prosecutor-General: AGHVAN HOVSEPPIAN, 0010 Yerevan, V. Sarkissian St 5; tel. (10) 51-15-54; e-mail info@genpro.am; internet www.genproc.am.

Religion

The major religion is Christianity. The Armenian Apostolic Church is the leading denomination and was widely identified with the movement for national independence. There are also Russian Orthodox and Islamic communities, although the latter lost adherents as a result of the departure of large numbers of Muslim Azeris from the republic. Most Kurds are also adherents of Islam, although some are Yazidis. In 2006 10 religious organizations were registered in Armenia. (The Jehovah's Witness community was estimated to number 12,000, but failed to qualify for registration as its statutes were deemed to be in contravention of the Constitution.)

ADVISORY COUNCIL

Religious Council: Yerevan, c/o Department for National Minorities and Religious Affairs; tel. (10) 58-16-63; f. 2002 as a consultative council to advise the Government on religious affairs; was to comprise representatives of the Government, the Office of the Prosecutor-General, the Armenian Apostolic Church, and the Catholic and Protestant Churches.

CHRISTIANITY

Armenian Apostolic Church: Vagharshapat, Monastery of St Etchmiadzin; tel. (10) 28-57-37; fax (10) 15-10-77; e-mail holysee@ etchmiadzin.am; internet www.holyetchmiadzin.am; nine dioceses in Armenia, 29 dioceses and bishoprics in the rest of the world; 15 monasteries and three theological seminaries in Armenia; Supreme Patriarch KAREKIN II (Catholicos of All Armenians).

The Roman Catholic Church

Armenian Rite

Armenian Catholics in Eastern Europe are under the jurisdiction of an Ordinary. At 31 December 2006 there were an estimated 390,000 adherents within this jurisdiction.

Ordinary: Most Rev. NECHAN KARAKAHIAN (Titular Archbishop of Adana of the Armenian Rite), 3101 Gyumri, Atarbekian St 82; tel. (312) 22-115; fax (312) 34-959; e-mail armorda@gyurmi.am.

Latin Rite

The Apostolic Administrator of the Caucasus (responsible for Latin Rite Roman Catholics in Armenia and Georgia) is resident in Tbilisi, Georgia (q.v.).

JUDAISM

In the early 2000s the Jewish community numbered around 1,000, and was located principally in Yerevan.

Mordechay Navi Jewish Religious Community of Armenia: 0018 Yerevan, Nar-Dosi St 23; tel. (10) 57-16-77; fax (10) 55-41-32; e-mail burger_mc@rambler.ru; internet www.yehudim.am; Chief Rabbi of Armenia GERSH MEIR BURSHTEIN; Chair. of the Jewish Community in Armenia RIMMA VARJAPETYAN.

The Press

PRINCIPAL NEWSPAPERS

In 2004 170 newspaper titles were published in Armenia. In 2003 107 of 120 titles were published in Armenian. Those listed below are in Armenian except where otherwise stated.

Aravot (Morning): 0023 Yerevan, Arshakuniats Ave 2, 15th Floor; tel. (10) 56-89-68; fax (10) 52-87-52; e-mail news@aravot.am; internet www.aravot.am; f. 1994; daily; Editor A. ABRAMIAN; circ. 5,000.

Azg (The Nation): 0010 Yerevan, Hanrapetutiun St 47; tel. (10) 52-16-35; fax (10) 56-28-63; e-mail azg2@arminco.com; internet www .azg.am; f. 1990; daily; Editor HAGOP AVETIKIAN; circ. 3,000.

Delovoi Ekspress (Business Express): 0005 Yerevan, Tigran Metsi Ave 67A; tel. and fax (10) 57-31-25; e-mail editor@express.am; internet www.express.am; f. 1992; weekly; economic; in Russian; Editor EDUARD NAGDALIAN.

Golos Armenii (The Voice of Armenia): 0023 Yerevan, Arshakuniats Ave 2, 7th Floor; tel. (10) 52-77-23; fax (10) 52-89-08; e-mail gonline@press.arminco.com; internet www.golos.am; f. 1934 as *Kommunist*; 3 a week; in Russian; Editor F. NAKHSHKARIAN.

Grakan Tert (Literary Paper): 0019 Yerevan, Marshal Baghramian St 3; tel. (10) 52-05-94; e-mail gr_tert@freenet.am; f. 1932; weekly; organ of the Union of Writers; Editor NORAYR ADALIAN.

Haikakan Zhamanak (Armenian Times): 0016 Yerevan, Israelian St 37; tel. (10) 58-11-75; e-mail nikol@arminco.com; internet www .hzh.am; f. 1999; daily; Editor-in-Chief NIKOL PASHINIAN; circ. 6,000.

Haiots Ashkhar (Armenian World): Yerevan, Tumanian St 38; tel. (10) 53-32-11; fax (10) 53-88-65; e-mail hayashkh@arminco.com; f. 1997; daily; Editor G. MKRTCHIAN; circ. 3,500.

Iravunk (Right): 0002 Yerevan, Yeznik Koghbatsu St 50A; tel. (10) 53-27-30; fax (10) 53-41-92; e-mail info@iravunk.com; internet www .iravunk.com; f. 1989; twice weekly; opposition newspaper; Editor HAIK BABUKHANIAN; circ. 17,000.

Marzakan Haiastan (Sport Armenia): 0023 Yerevan, Arshakuniats Ave 5; tel. and fax (10) 52-62-41; f. 1956; weekly; sports; Editor S. MOURADIAN; circ. 3,000.

Novoye Vremya (New Times): 0023 Yerevan, Arshakuniats Ave 2, 3rd Floor; tel. (10) 52-69-46; fax (10) 52-73-62; e-mail nvremya@ arminco.com; internet www.nv.am; f. 1992; 3 a week; in Russian; Editor R. A. SATIAN; circ. 5,000.

Respublika Armenia (Hayastani Hanrapetutiun): 0023 Yerevan, Arshakuniats Ave 2, 9th Floor; tel. and fax (10) 54-57-00; e-mail ra@ arminco.com; internet www.ra.am; f. 1990; state-owned; twice weekly; in Russian; Editor YELENA KURDIYAN; circ. 3,000.

Vozny (Hedgehog): 0023 Yerevan, Arshakuniats Ave 2, 12th Floor; tel. (10) 52-63-83; f. 1954; Editor A. SAHAKIAN.

Yeter: Yerevan, A. Manukian St 5; tel. (10) 55-34-13; fax (10) 55-17-13; e-mail editor@eter.am; internet www.eter.am; weekly; independent; television and radio programming information; Editor G. KAZARIAN.

PRINCIPAL PERIODICALS

In 2003 77 periodicals were published, of which 51 were in Armenian. In 2004 112 periodicals were published.

168 zham (168 Hours): Yerevan, Pushkin St 3A; tel. (10) 58-48-31; fax (10) 52-29-58; e-mail info@168.am; internet www.168.am; f. 1994; weekly; opposition; news; Editor-in-Chief SATIK SEIRANIAN.

Armenia: Finance and Economy: 0023 Yerevan, Arshakuniats Ave 2A, 10th Floor; tel. (10) 54-48-97; e-mail armef@arminco.com; f. 1999; Editor-in-Chief MHER DAVOIAN.

Armenia Now: Yerevan; tel. (10) 53-24-22; e-mail info@ armenianow.com; internet www.armenianow.com; weekly; Editor-in-Chief JOHN HUGHES.

Aroghchapoutiun (Health): 0036 Yerevan, Halabian St 46; tel. (10) 39-65-36; e-mail mharut@dmc.am; f. 1956; quarterly; theoretical, scientific-methodological, organizational and practical journal of the Ministry of Health Care; Editor M. A. MURADIAN; circ. 2,000–5,000.

Avangard: 0023 Yerevan, Arshakuniats Ave 2A, 4th Floor; tel. (10) 54-89-18; e-mail avangard-1@rambler.ru; internet www.avangard .nt.am; f. 1923; Editor JULIETA MARTIROSSIAN.

Ayb-Fe: 0015 Yerevan, Grigor Lusavorichi St 15; tel. (10) 56-07-16; fax (10) 56-90-42; e-mail oratert@a1plus.am; internet www.a1plus .am; weekly; Editor PERCHUHI TATURIAN.

Chorord Ishkhanutiun/Chetvertaya Vlast (The Fourth Estate): Yerevan, Abovian St 12, Rm 105, Hotel Yerevan 105; tel. (10) 52-02-12; e-mail chiog@arminco.com; internet www.chi.am; monthly; in Armenian and Russian; Editor SHOGHER MATEVOSSIAN.

Garoun (Spring): 0015 Yerevan, Grigor Lusavorichi St 15; tel. (10) 56-29-56; e-mail garoun@garoun.am; internet www.garoun.am; f. 1967; monthly; independent; fiction, poetry and socio-political issues; Editor V. S. AYVAZIAN; circ. 1,500.

Gitutyun ev Tekhnika (Science and Technology): 0048 Yerevan, Komitasa Ave 49/3; tel. (10) 23-37-27; e-mail giteknik@rambler.ru; f. 1963; monthly; journal of the Research Institute of Scientific-Technical Information and of Technological and Economic Research; Dir S. AGAJANIAN; Editor H. R. KHACHATRIAN; circ. 1,000.

Hanrapetakan: Yerevan, Melik-Adamian St 2; tel. (10) 58-00-31; fax (10) 50-12-59; internet www.hhk.am; f. 2003; ideological, political and analytical journal of the Republican Party of Armenia; monthly.

Khorhrdaran (Parliament): Yerevan; tel. (10) 58-83-12; e-mail khorhrdaran@parliament.am; internet khorhrdaran.parliament .am; f. 2003; weekly; Editor HAMLET KHUBLARIAN.

Literaturnaya Armeniya (Literary Armenia): 0019 Yerevan, Marshal Baghramian St 3; tel. (10) 56-36-57; f. 1958; monthly; journal of the Union of Writers; fiction; in Russian; Editor A. M. NALBANDIAN.

New Yerevan Times: 0010 Yerevan, Arami St 3, 2nd Floor; tel. (10) 54-57-93; e-mail times@netsys.am; weekly; in English; Editor MARINA MKHITARIAN.

Nork: 0019 Yerevan, Marshal Baghramian St 3; tel. (10) 58-45-17; f. 1934; fmrly *Sovetakan Grakanutiun* (Soviet Literature); monthly; journal of the Union of Writers; fiction; in Russian; Editor F. MELOIAN.

Yerkir (Country): 0010 Yerevan, Hanrapetutiun St 30; tel. (10) 52-15-01; fax (10) 52-04-26; e-mail erkir@arminco.com; internet www .yerkir.am; f. 1991; weekly; organ of the ARF; also published in Lebanon; Editor-in-Chief SPARTAK SEYRANIAN; circ. 2,500.

NEWS AGENCIES

Arka News Agency: 0010 Yerevan, Pavstos Byuzand St 1/3; tel. (10) 52-21-52; fax (10) 52-40-80; e-mail arka@arminco.com; internet www .arka.am; f. 1996; economic, financial and political news; Russian and English.

Armenpress (Armenian News Agency): 0009 Yerevan, Isaahakian St 28, 4th Floor; tel. (10) 52-67-02; fax (10) 52-67-92; e-mail contact@ armenpress.am; internet www.armenpress.am; f. 1922 as state information agency, transformed into state joint-stock company in 1997; Armenian, English and Russian; Dir HRAYR ZORIAN.

Arminfo: 0009 Yerevan, Isaahakian St 28, 2nd Floor; tel. (10) 52-20-34; fax (10) 54-31-72; e-mail news@arminfo.am; internet www .arminfo.am; f. 1991 as Snark; name changed as above in 2001; Dir EMMANUIL MKRTCHIAN; Editor ALEKSANDR AVANISOV.

De Facto: Yerevan, Arshakuniats Ave 2, 9th Floor; tel. (10) 54-57-99; e-mail defacto@defacto.am; internet www.defacto.am; f. 2000; Editor KAREN ZAKHARIAN.

Mediamax Armenian News Agency: 0012 Yerevan, Marshal Baghramian St 31A; tel. (10) 54-54-31; fax (10) 54-54-37; e-mail news@mediamax.am; internet www.mediamax.am; Dir ARA TADE-VOSIAN; Editor-in-Chief DAVID ALAVERDIAN.

Noyan Tapan (Noah's Ark): 0009 Yerevan, Isaahakian St 28, 3rd Floor; tel. (10) 56-59-65; fax (10) 52-42-79; e-mail contact@noyan-tapan.am; internet www.nt.am; f. 1991; Dir TIGRAN HAROU-TUNIAN.

PRESS ASSOCIATION

Union of Journalists of Armenia: Yerevan, Pushkin St 3A; tel. (1) 56-12-76; fax (1) 56-14-47; e-mail www@internews.am; f. 1959; Dir ASTGHIK GEVORGIAN.

Publishers

Academy of Sciences Publishing House: 0019 Yerevan, Marshal Baghramian St 24G; Dir KH. H. BARSEGHIAN.

Arevik Publishing House: 0009 Yerevan, Terian St 91; tel. (10) 52-45-61; fax (10) 52-05-36; e-mail arevick@netsys.am; internet www .arevik.am; f. 1986; political, scientific, fiction for children, textbooks; Pres. DAVID HOVHANNES; Exec. Dir ASTGHIK STEPANIAN.

Haikakan Hanragitaran Hratarakchutioun (Armenian Encyclopedia Publishing House): 0001 Yerevan, Tumanian St 17; tel. (10) 52-43-41; fax (10) 52-27-33; e-mail encyclop@sci.am; internet www .encyclopedia.am; f. 1967; encyclopedias and other reference books; Editor H. M. AIVAZIAN.

Hayastan (Armenia Publishing House): 0009 Yerevan, Isaahakian St 28; tel. (10) 52-85-20; e-mail nunjan@hragir.aua.am; f. 1921; political and fiction; Dir VAHAGN SARKISSIAN.

Louys Publishing Co: 0009 Yerevan, Isaahakian St 28; tel. (10) 52-53-13; fax (10) 56-55-07; e-mail louys@arminco.com; f. 1955; textbooks; Dir H. Z. HAROUTUNIAN.

Nairi: 0009 Yerevan, Terian St 91; tel. and fax (10) 56-58-54; e-mail nairi_hrat@rambler.ru; f. 1991; fiction, science, translations and reference; Pres. HRACHIA TAMRAZIAN.

Tigran Mets (Tigran the Great) Publishing House: 0023 Yerevan, Arshakuniats St 2; tel. (10) 52-70-56; e-mail tigranmets2002@yahoo.com; fiction, poetry, science and children's books; Dir VREJ MARKOSSIAN.

Yerevan State University Publishing House: 0025 Yerevan, A. Manukian St 1; tel. (10) 55-55-70; fax (10) 55-46-41; e-mail pr-int@ysu.am; internet www.ysu.am; f. 1919; textbooks and reference books, history, literary criticism, science and fiction; Dir PERCH STEPANIAN.

Zangak-97: 0010 Yerevan, Vardanants St 8; tel. (10) 54-05-17; fax (10) 54-06-07; e-mail info@zangak.am; internet www.zangak.am; f. 2000; scientific works, school teaching manuals, literature for children, translations of foreign authors; Pres. SOKRAT MKRTCHIAN.

PUBLISHERS' ASSOCIATION

National Union of Armenian Publishers: 0009 Yerevan, Isahaakian St 28/22; tel. (10) 56-31-57; fax (10) 56-55-07; e-mail pubunion@gmail.com; f. 1999; Pres. SOS MOVSISSIAN.

Broadcasting and Communications

TELECOMMUNICATIONS

Armenia Telephone Co (ArmenTel): Yerevan, Azatutiun Ave 24; tel. (10) 54-91-00; fax (10) 28-98-88; internet www.armentel.com; f. 1995; 10% state-owned, 90% owned by VimpelCom (Russia); fixed line and mobile communications operator.

VivaCell: 0015 Yerevan, Argishti St 4/1; tel. (10) 56-87-77; fax (10) 56-92-22; e-mail info@vivacell.am; internet www.vivacell.am; f. 2004; mobile telecommunications provider; operated by K Telecom CJSC; Man. Dir RALPH YERIKIAN.

BROADCASTING

National Commission for Television and Radio (NCTR) (HRAH): 0002 Yerevan, Sarian St 22; tel. (10) 53-95-09; fax (10) 53-90-34; e-mail nctr@tvradio.am; internet www.tvradio.am; Dir GRIGOR AMALIAN.

Radio

Armenian Public Radio: 0025 Yerevan, A. Manukian St 5; tel. (10) 55-33-43; fax (10) 55-46-00; e-mail president@mediaconcern.am; internet www.armradio.am; domestic broadcasts in Armenian, Russian and Kurdish; external broadcasts in Armenian, Russian, Kurdish, Azerbaijani, Arabic, English, French, German, Spanish and Farsi; Dir-Gen. ARMEN AMIRIAN.

Television

Armenian Public Television: 0047 Yerevan, Hovsepian St 26; tel. (10) 65-15-00; fax (10) 65-24-40; internet www.armtv.com; state jt-stock co; Chair. of Council ALEKSAN HAROUTUNIAN; Exec. Dir ARMEN ARZUMANIAN.

Armenia TV: 0054 Yerevan, Yeghvard Ave 1; tel. (10) 36-69-25; fax (10) 36-68-52; e-mail mail@armeniatv.am; internet www.armeniatv .am; f. 1999; largest private television company in Armenia; transmits programming terrestrially, by cable and by satellite; Dir BAGRAT SARKISSIAN.

H2 (Armenian Second TV Channel): 0088 Yerevan, Ajapniak, Nazarbekian Distr., G. 3, Bl. 3/1; tel. (10) 39-88-31; fax (10) 39-56-40; e-mail h2@tv.am; internet www.tv.am; f. 1998; present name adopted 2005; Dir SAMVEL MAYRAPETIAN.

Shant TV: 0028 Yerevan, Kievian St 16, 10th Floor; tel. (10) 27-76-68; fax (10) 26-76-90; e-mail info@shanttv.am; internet www .shant-tv.com; f. 1994; private, independent; Pres. ARTHUR A. YEZEKIAN.

Finance

(cap. = capital; res = reserves; dep. = deposits; m. = million; brs = branches; amounts in drams, unless otherwise stated)

BANKING

Central Bank

Central Bank of the Republic of Armenia: 0010 Yerevan, Vazgen Sarkissian St 6; tel. (10) 58-38-41; fax (10) 52-38-52; e-mail mcba@cba .am; internet www.cba.am; f. 1993; state-owned; cap. 100.0m., res 22,355.5m., dep. 225,326.7m. (Dec. 2006); Gov. ARTUR JAVADIAN.

Commercial Banks

At the end of 2005 there were 21 commercial banks (with 269 branches) in operation in Armenia.

ACBA-Credit Agricole Bank CJSC: 0009 Yerevan, Byron St 1; tel. (10) 56-85-58; fax (10) 54-34-85; e-mail acba@acba.am; internet www .acba.am; f. 1996 as Agricultural Co-operative Bank of Armenia; name changed as above Sept. 2006; cap. 1,519.3m., res 4,231.1m., dep. 28,021.6m. (Dec. 2005); Gen. Man. STEPAN GISHIAN.

Ardshininvestbank (ASHIB) (Bank for Industry, Construction and Investment): 0015 Yerevan, Grigor Lusavorichi St 13; tel. (10) 52-85-13; fax (10) 56-74-86; e-mail office@ashib.am; internet www .ashib.am; f. 2003 with acquisition of banking business of Ardshinbank and partially acquired the assets of Armagrobank; 58.6% owned by Business Investments Centre Ltd (Armenia), 19.5% owned by Rasko Armenia; cap. 13,802.4m., res 3,625.7m., dep. 73,375.1m. (Dec. 2007); Chair. of Bd KAREN SAFARIAN; 54 brs.

Armbusinessbank (ABB): 0010 Yerevan, Vardanants St 13; tel. (10) 52-39-29; fax (10) 54-58-35; e-mail info@armbusinessbank.am; internet www.armbusinessbank.am; f. 1992; as Arminvestbank; name changed Aug. 2006; 35% owned by Ukrprombank (Ukraine), 35% owned by Alpha-Garant (Ukraine); cap. 5,000m. (Sept. 2007); Chair. of Bd ARA KIRAKOSSIAN.

Armenian Development Bank: 0015 Yerevan, Paronian St 21/1; tel. (10) 59-14-00; fax (10) 59-14-05; e-mail info@armdb.com; internet www.armdb.com; f. 1990; Chief Exec. KAREN SARKISSIAN.

Armenian Economy Development Bank (Armeconombank) (AEB): 0002 Yerevan, Amirian St 23/1; tel. (10) 53-20-07; fax (10) 53-89-04; e-mail bank@aeb.am; internet www.aeb.am; f. 1988; jt-stock co; corporate banking; cap. 2,333.3m., res 413.1m., dep. 29,367.8m. (Dec. 2006); 25% owned by the European Bank for Reconstruction and Development; Chair. of Bd SARIBEK SUKIASSIAN; CEO DAVIT SUKIASSIAN; 44 brs.

Armenian Import-Export Bank (Armimpexbank): 0010 Yerevan, Vazgen Sarkissian St 2; tel. (10) 58-99-06; fax (10) 56-59-58; e-mail office@impexbank.am; internet www.impexbank.am; f. 1992; 93.1% owned by CIE (United Kingdom); cap. 2,000m., res 338.0m., dep. 7,919.0m. (Dec. 2006); Chair. of Bd LEVON BARKHUDARIAN; CEO ARA ALEXANIAN; 5 brs.

Artsakhbank: 0028 Yerevan, Kievian St 3; tel. (10) 27-77-19; fax (10) 27-77-49; e-mail artsakhbank@ktsurf.net; internet www .artsakhbank.am; f. 1996; cap. 2,244.3m., res 393m., dep. 18,883.1m. (Dec. 2006); Chair. of Bd of Dirs HRATCH KAPRIELIAN; Chair. of Bd KAMO NERSISSIAN; 12 brs.

Converse Bank: 0010 Yerevan, Vazgen Sarkissian St 26/1; tel. (10) 51-12-00; fax (10) 51-12-12; e-mail marketing@conversebank.am; internet www.conversebank.am; f. 1993; 95% owned by Advanced Global Investments; cap. 1,296.3m., profits and res 9,318.6m., dep. 47,552.9m. (Aug. 2008); Dir-Gen. ARARAT GHUKASIAN; 16 brs (2008).

HSBC Bank of Armenia: 0009 Yerevan, Teryan St 66; tel. (10) 51-50-00; fax (10) 51-50-01; e-mail hsbc.armenia@hsbc.com; internet www.hsbc.am; f. 1996; 70% owned by HSBC Europe BV (Netherlands); cap. 2,437.6m., res −96.2m., dep. 70,702.4m. (Dec. 2006); Chief Exec. TIMOTHY SLATER; 4 brs.

InecoBank: 0001 Yerevan, Tumanian St 17; tel. (10) 56-37-25; fax (10) 54-51-66; e-mail inecobank@inecobank.com; internet www .inecobank.am; f. 1996; cap. 1,385.3m., res 2,252.1m., dep. 14,187.6m. (Dec. 2006); Chair. AVETIS BALOYAN.

Mellat Bank: 0010 Yerevan, Amirian St 6, POB 24; tel. (10) 58-13-54; fax (10) 54-08-85; e-mail mellat@mellatbank.am; internet www .mellatbank.am; f. 1995; wholly owned by Bank Mellat (Iran); cap. 3,522.1m., res 29.2m., dep. 5,397.8m. (Dec. 2006); Chair. and Gen. Dir MORTEZA BEHESHTIROUY.

Prometey Bank: 0010 Yerevan, Hanrapetutiun St 44/2; tel. (10) 56-20-36; fax (10) 54-57-19; e-mail intoperations@prometeybank.am; internet www.prometeybank.am; f. 1990; present name adopted 2001; cap. 3,700.0m., res 52.1m., dep. 3,817.6m. (Dec. 2006); Chair. of Bd EMIL SOGHOMONIAN.

Savings Bank

VTB Bank (Armenia): 0010 Yerevan, Nalbandian St 46; tel. (10) 58-04-51; fax (10) 56-55-78; e-mail headoffice@vtb.am; internet www .vtb.am; f. 1923 under the name Armsavingsbank; present name adopted 2006; owned by Bank VTB (Russia); cap. 13,906m., res 1,064m., dep. 36,243m. (Aug. 2008); Chair. VALERY V. OVSYANNIKOV; 81 brs.

Banking Union

Union of Banks of Armenia: 0009 Yerevan, Koriun St 19A; tel. and fax (10) 52-77-31; e-mail uba@uba.am; internet www.uba.am; f. 1995; oversees banking activity; Pres. STEPHEN GISHYAN; Exec. Dir SEYRAN SARGSYAN.

COMMODITY AND STOCK EXCHANGES

Armenian Stock Exchange (Armex): 0010 Yerevan, Mher Mkrtchian St 5B, 3rd & 4th Floors; tel. (10) 54-33-21; fax (10) 54-33-24; e-mail info@armex.am; internet www.armex.am; f. 2001; Exec. Dir ARMEN G. MELIKYAN.

Yerevan Adamand Commodity and Raw Materials Exchange: 0010 Yerevan, Agatangeghos St 6/1; tel. (10) 56-31-15; fax (10) 56-52-28; e-mail ycre@cornet.am; internet www.yercomex.am; f. 1990; Dir GRIGOR VARDIKIAN.

INSURANCE

In 2005 there were 23 licensed insurance companies in Armenia.

AHA Royal Insurance: 0010 Yerevan, Hanrapetutiun St 62/98; tel. (10) 52-67-30; fax (10) 52-67-40; e-mail aharoyal@insurer.am; internet www.insurer.am; f. 2004; insurance and reinsurance; Gen. Dir HRACHA I. KARAPETIAN.

Arajin Apahovagrakan: 0025 Yerevan, Charents St 1, 4th Floor; tel. (10) 57-51-18; fax (10) 55-94-73; e-mail info@arajin.am; f. 1995; general non-life insurance; Exec. Dir PAYLAK GHUKASSIAN.

Cascade Insurance and Reinsurance Co (CIRCO): 0033 Yerevan, Hrachya Kochari St 5/1; tel. (10) 27-87-76; fax (10) 27-82-21; e-mail info@cascadeinre.com; internet www.cascadeinsurance.am; f. 2004; 35% owned by the European Bank for Reconstruction and Development; Chief Exec. GARNIK TONOYAN.

Grand Insurance Co: 0002 Yerevan, Tumanian St 38; tel. (10) 56-03-92; fax (10) 51-28-23; f. 1999; Man. Dir ARTAK S. ANTONIAN.

IngoArmenia: 0010 Yerevan, Tpagrichneri St 8; tel. (10) 54-31-34; fax (10) 54-75-06; e-mail info@ingoarmenia.am; internet www .ingoarmenia.am; f. 1997; Exec. Dir LEVON ALTUNIAN.

London-Yerevan Insurance Co: 0015 Yerevan, Sarian St 26/3; tel. (10) 54-16-50; fax (10) 54-25-58; e-mail admin@london-yerevan.com; internet www.london-yerevan.com; f. 1998; wholly owned by Londongate Group (United Kingdom); Man. Dir SONA DALALIAN.

Sil Insurance Co: 0018 Yerevan, Tigran Mets Ave 39; tel. (10) 53-52-90; fax (10) 56-52-34; f. 2000; risk reinsurance; Exec. Dir HAYK BAGHRAMIAN.

State Insurance Armenia (Gosstrakh-Armenia): 0001 Yerevan, Hanrapetutiun St 76/3; tel. and fax (10) 56-06-89; e-mail info@ gosstrax-armenia.am; f. 2001; Russian-Armenian joint venture; insurance and reinsurance; Man. Dir VAHAN H. AVETISSIAN.

Trade and Industry

GOVERNMENT AGENCY

Armenian Development Agency (ADA): 0025 Yerevan, Charents St 17; tel. and fax (10) 57-01-70; e-mail info@ada.am; internet www .ada.am; f. 1998; foreign investment and export development; Gen. Dir Dr ROBERT HARUTIUNIAN.

CHAMBER OF COMMERCE

Chamber of Commerce and Industry of the Republic of Armenia: 0010 Yerevan, Khanjian St 11; tel. (10) 56-01-84; fax (10) 58-78-71; e-mail armcci@arminco.com; internet www.armcci .am; f. 1959; Chair. MARTIN SARGSYAN.

EMPLOYERS' ORGANIZATIONS

Armenian Business Small and Medium Entrepreneurship Association: 0010 Yerevan, Republic Sq., House of Unions 43; tel. (10) 56-31-50; fax (10) 56-02-29; e-mail invest@arminco.com; f. 1991; incl. Institute of Business Development and Human Resources, FOBIX Business Consulting Centre, Electronic Business Agency and Bankruptcy Protection Foundation; Pres. SEYRAN AVAGHIAN.

Armenian Union of Manufacturers and Businessmen (Employers) of Armenia—UMB(E)A: 0010 Yerevan, Agatanghegos St 5; tel. and fax (10) 56-29-21; e-mail umba@arminco.com; internet www.umba.am; f. 1996; Chair. ARSEN KHAZARIAN.

TRADE ASSOCIATIONS

Union of Merchants of Armenia: 0037 Yerevan, Azatutioun Ave 1/1; tel. (10) 25-28-54; fax (10) 25-91-76; e-mail merchants@netsys .am; f. 1993; reorganized 1999; Pres. TSOLVARD GEVORGIAN.

UTILITIES

Public Services Regulatory Commission of Armenia (PSRC): 0002 Yerevan, Sarian St 22; tel. (10) 52-25-22; fax (10) 52-55-63; e-mail info@psrc.am; internet www.psrc.am; f. 1997; fmrly Energy Commission of Armenia; Chair. ROBERT NAZARIAN.

Electricity

Electricity Networks of Armenia (ArmElNet—ENA): 0047 Yerevan, Armenakyian St 127; tel. (10) 54-21-63; fax (10) 54-36-83; e-mail elnet@arminco.com; internet www.ena.am; f. 2002; owned by Inter RAO UES (Russia); national electricity distributor comprising the four former regional electricity networks; Gen. Dir EUGENE GLADUNCHIK.

High Voltage Electric Networks (HV Networks): 0114 Yerevan, Zoravar Andranikian St 1; tel. (10) 72-00-10; fax (10) 72-01-21; e-mail hvn@arminco.com; f. 2003; comprises nine regions; Dir SAHAK ABRAHAMIAN.

International Energy Corpn CJSC: 0014 Yerevan, Adontsi St 10B; tel. (10) 24-50-99; fax (10) 24-51-99; e-mail mailmek@mek.am; internet www.mek.am; f. 2003; wholly owned by Inter RAO EES, a subsidiary of Unified Energy System of Russia; manages Hrazdan Thermal Power Plant, Sevan-Hrazdan Hydroelectric Power Plant cascade and Armenian Nuclear Power Plant; Gen. Dir MICHAEL MANTROV.

Operator of Electrical Energy System CJSC: 0009 Yerevan, Abovian St 27; tel. (10) 59-29-60; fax (10) 52-47-25; e-mail arm_eso@ freenet.am; f. 2003; assumed part of the function of former state monopoly Armenergo.

Gas

ArmRosGazProm—ARG: 0091 Yerevan, Tbilisi Highway 43; tel. (10) 29-48-10; fax (10) 29-47-28; e-mail inbox@armrusgasprom.am; internet www.armrusgasprom.am; f. 1997; Armenian-Russian joint-stock co; 26% state-owned, 68% owned by Gazprom (Russia); sole natural gas producer in Armenia; Exec. Dir KAREN KARAPETIAN.

Water

Yerevan Djur—Veolia Armenia (YD): 0025 Yerevan, Abovian St 66A; tel. (10) 56-13-26; fax (10) 56-93-57; e-mail office@yerevandjur .am; f. 2005; provides water and sewerage services to Yerevan municipality; managed by Générale des Eaux (France); Gen. Man. SERGE POPOFF.

MAJOR COMPANIES

Legislation to privatize state enterprises was enacted in July 1992. By September 2003 7,178 small firms and 1,789 medium-sized and large firms had been privatized, and the private sector was reported to generate more than 80% of national gross domestic product. The following is a selection of the principal industrial companies operating in Armenia.

Chemicals

Vanadzor Chimprom: 2001 Vanadzor, Vardanants St 47/6; privatized in 1999; fmrly owned by ZNGS-Prometey of Russia; comprises complex of Vanadzor chemical factories and thermal electrical plant; produces carbide, corundum, ammonite, acetate thread and melamine; Dir-Gen. ALEKSANDR SNEGIRIOV.

Electrical Goods

Armelektromash (Armenian Scientific-Production Electronic Machinery Association): 0083 Yerevan, Manandian St 41; tel. (10) 46-09-45; fax (10) 42-16-79; e-mail info@armelectromash.ru; internet www.armelectromash.ru; f. 1940; fully privatized in 2003; manufactures synchronous generators, transformers and industrial goods; Gen. Man. SEYRAN G. MATEVOSIAN.

Armenmotor: 0018 Yerevan, M. Khorenatsi St 28; tel. (10) 52-97-50; fax (10) 56-39-91; e-mail armmotor@netsys.am; internet www.armenmotor.am; f. 1928; manufacture and sale of motors, generators, pumps, electric meat mincers and ceiling fans; Pres. KARLOS PETROSSIAN; 2,000 employees.

Food and Beverages

Ashtarak Kat: 0069 Yerevan, Dro St 13; tel. (10) 24-98-12; fax (10) 24-54-30; e-mail info@ashtarakkat.com; internet www.ashtarak-kat.com; f. 1995; leading producer of dairy and ice-cream products; Man. Dir KHACHATUR ATANESSIAN.

Yerevan Brandy Company: 0082 Yerevan, Isakov Ave 2; tel. (10) 54-00-00; fax (10) 58-77-13; e-mail info@yerevan-brandy-company.com; internet www.ybc.am; f. 1887; subsidiary of the Pernod Ricard Group (France); Pres. and Gen. Dir PIERRE LARRETCHE; Gen. Man. JEAN-FRANÇOIS ROUCOU; 500 employees.

Information Technology

Leda Systems: 0014 Yerevan, Tigran Mets Ave 49; tel. (10) 55-95-83; fax (10) 55-95-89; e-mail info@leda-design.com; f. 1995; mixed-signal and analogue intellectual property design and development; Chief Exec. VAHRAM MOURADIAN; 110 employees.

Viasphere Technopark: 0026 Yerevan, Arshakuniats Ave 41; tel. (10) 44-21-88; fax (10) 44-89-02; e-mail viasphere@viasphere.am; internet www.viasphere.com/technopark; f. 2001; wholly owned subsidiary of venture fund Viasphere International (USA); commercial technological park based on the premises of the former Transistor semi-conductor plant, providing facilities, infrastructure and support services to local start-up companies and overseas subsidiaries; Pres. and CEO ANTHONY MOROIAN; Man. Dir Dr ARAM VARDANIAN.

Metals

Akhtala Ore Mining and Processing Co: 0019 Yerevan, Marshal Baghramian Ave 24B; tel. (10) 54-55-38; fax (10) 54-55-39; e-mail metalking@europe.com; copper concentrate; wholly owned by Metal Prince Co (Romania); undergoing investment and modernization programme; Pres. SEROP DER-BOGHOSSIAN.

Ararat Gold Recovery Co (AGRC): 0010 Yerevan, Khanjian St 19; tel. (10) 54-22-70; fax (10) 54-58-36; e-mail agrc@arminco.com; f. 1998; acquired by GeoProMining Ltd in 2008; mines and processes ore; operates at the Sotsk (Zod) and Megradzor fields as well as at Ararat; Dir VARDAN VARDANIAN.

ARMENAL: 0051 Yerevan, Griboyedov St 25; tel. (10) 23-05-70; fax (10) 28-68-87; e-mail armenal@armenal.am; internet www.rusal.ru/armenal_factory.aspx; f. 1950 as Kanaker Aluminium Factory—KanAZ; wholly owned by RUSAL (Russia); produced 10,476 metric tons of foil in 2003; Gen. Dir SERGEI BOROVIK.

Armenian Copper Programme (ACP): Yerevan, Khanjian St 19; tel. (10) 54-01-85; fax (10) 54-01-86; e-mail info@acp.am; internet www.copper.am; f. 1997; fmrly Manes yev Vallex, name changed in 2002; operates the sole copper smelter in Caucasus region at Alaverdy; affiliate companies include the Mining and Metallurgy Institute CJSC; Chair. Dr VALERI MEDZHLUMIAN; 800 employees.

Armzoloto (Armgold): 0051 Yerevan, Komitas Ave 49; tel. (10) 23-68-10; special state enterprise; gold-deposit prospecting, gold mine and open-deposit development; Man. ALEXANDR BEGLAROV.

Pure Iron Plant: 0053 Yerevan, Artsakh Ave 75; tel. (10) 47-42-60; e-mail pureiron@netsys.am; 48% owned by Cronimet (Germany); f. 1995; ferro-alloys, including ferro-molybdenum and metal powders; Dir GENIK KARAPETIAN.

Zangezur Copper-Molybdenum Combine (ZCMC): 3309 Kajaran, Syunik, Lenagortsneri St 18; tel. (285) 32-499; fax (285) 32-846; e-mail zcmc@arminco.com; f. 1951; re-opened in 1994; privatized in 2004; 60% owned by Cronimet (Germany), 15% owned by Pure Iron Plant; Man. Dir MAXIM HAKOBIAN.

Precious Stones and Jewellery

Diamond Co of Armenia (DCA): Yerevan; tel. (10) 58-99-93; fax (10) 54-39-16; e-mail dca@arminco.com; f. 1997; owned by Farfano Corpn (United Kingdom); Chief Exec. GAGIK ABRAHAMIAN.

Shoghakn Diamond Processing Co: 2223 Kotaik, Nor Hajen; tel. (224) 28-25-92; fax (224) 28-17-69; e-mail diamonds@shoghakn.am; internet www.shoghakn.am; f. 1971; privatized in 2000; owned by Lev Levaev Diamonds Ltd (Israel); cutting and polishing of diamonds; Dir SERGEY KASPARIAN; 408 employees (2007).

Yerevan Jewellery Plant: 0023 Yerevan, Arshakuniats Ave 12; tel. (10) 52-53-21; fax (10) 52-57-13; e-mail sales@yerjewel.com; internet www.yerjewel.com; f. 1950; produces jewellery and ornaments from precious metals and gems; also tools and jewellery-production equipment; Pres. ARMEN E. GRIGORIAN; 2,000 employees (2007).

Textiles and Clothing

Garun: 0023 Yerevan, Briusov St 26; tel. (10) 56-17-23; fax (10) 52-99-81; e-mail yenok@freenet.am; f. 1936; produces outdoor clothing; Pres. GOHAR ENOKIAN.

Tosp: 0065 Yerevan, Tichina St 2; tel. (10) 74-24-72; fax (10) 74-21-43; e-mail tosp@arminco.com; f. 1947; manufactures knitted textiles, underwear; Pres. SUREN BEKIRSKI; 840 employees.

Miscellaneous

Apaven: 0010 Yerevan, Abelian St 6/1, POB 22; tel. (22) 35-01-60; e-mail apaven@apaven.am; internet www.apaven.am; f. 1993; freight forwarding co; Gen. Dir ARSEN GHAZARIAN.

Ararat Cement: 0602 Ararat, Shahumian St 5; tel. (238) 44-279; fax (238) 41-737; e-mail info@araratcement.am; internet www.araratcement.am; f. 1982; owned by Multigroup; Gen. Man. LEVON HAMBARDZUMIAN.

Flash Co: Yerevan, Y. Koghbatsu St 30; tel. (10) 58-28-84; fax (10) 58-28-84; e-mail info@flashltd.am; internet www.flashltd.am; f. 1995; imports and distributes petroleum and diesel; Pres. BARSEGH BEGLARIAN.

Horizon 95: 0002 Yerevan, Amirian St 26; tel. (10) 53-88-52; fax (10) 53-88-47; e-mail horizon@horizon.am; internet www.horizon.am; fmrly First Construction Board of Yerevan's Industrial Engineering Trust; civil and industrial construction; Chair. GAGIK GALSTIAN.

Shen Concern: 0086 Yerevan, Shiraki St 2/2; tel. (10) 42-45-47; fax (10) 46-01-01; e-mail info@shenconcern.com; internet www.shenconcern.com; f. 1995; fmrly Armresourceinmex; produces and sells construction materials; Pres. SAMVEL BEGLARIAN.

TRADE UNIONS

At 1 January 2006 some 743 trade-union organizations were registered with the Ministry of Justice.

Confederation of Trade Unions of Armenia: 0010 Yerevan, Vazgen Sarkissian St 26; tel. (10) 58-36-82; fax (10) 54-33-82; e-mail boris@xar.am; Chair. MARTIN HAROUTUNIAN.

Transport

RAILWAYS

In 2005 there were 731 km of railway track in Armenia. There are international lines to Iran and Georgia. In November 2004 it was agreed that rail transport between Russia and Armenia would be restored in 2005, with the co-operation of Georgia; the restoration of the Kavkaz (Russia)–Poti (Georgia) ferry route, with its railway facility, in January 2005 was also expected greatly to enhance the speed of cargo transport across the region. In August 2008 the Government announced that repairs had commenced on a 12-km railway line (hitherto closed) that would link Gyumri with Kars, in eastern Turkey.

Armenia Railways: 0005 Yerevan, Tigran Mets Ave 50; tel. (10) 52-04-28; fax (10) 57-36-30; e-mail arway@mbox.amilink.net; f. 1998; managed by Russian Railways; Pres. ARARAT KHRIMIAN.

Yerevan Metro: 0033 Yerevan, Marshal Baghramian St 76; tel. (10) 27-45-43; fax (10) 27-24-60; e-mail papiev@netsys.am; f. 1981; 12.1 km, with 10 stations (2005); Gen. Dir VAHAGN HAKOPIAN.

ROADS

In 2005 there were an estimated 10,296 km of roads in Armenia. As a result of the closure of Azerbaijan's and Turkey's borders with Armenia, the Kajaran highway linking Armenia with Iran emerged as Armenia's most important international road connection; in December 1995 a permanent road bridge over the Araks (Aras, Araxes) river was opened.

CIVIL AVIATION

Zvartnots International Airport, 15 km west of Yerevan, is the main national airport; there are also international airports in Gyumri (Shirak) and Yerebuni (also near Yerevan).

Civil Aviation Department: 0042 Yerevan, Zvartnots Airport; tel. (10) 28-57-68; fax (10) 28-53-54; e-mail gayane.davtyan@aviation .am; internet www.aviation.am; f. 1933; Dir ARTYOM MOVSESIAN.

Armavia: 0042 Yerevan, Zvartnots Airport; tel. (10) 54-08-10; fax (10) 54-08-10; e-mail info@u8.am; internet www.u8.am; f. 1996; operates flights to destinations in Europe and Asia; Gen. Dir NORAIR BELLUIAN; 480 employees.

Tourism

Following secession from the USSR, tourism severely declined, although by the late 1990s some European firms were beginning to introduce tours to the country. According to the World Tourism Organization, tourism receipts amounted to US $161m. in 2005, compared with just $45m. in 1997. Armenia received an estimated 381,136 tourist arrivals in 2006. The major tourist attractions were the capital, Yerevan; Artashat, an early trading centre on the 'Silk Road'; and medieval monasteries. There was, however, little accommodation available outside the capital.

Tourism Armenia: 0010 Yerevan, 1 Proshian St 9; tel. (10) 53-45-01; fax (10) 52-25-83; e-mail tic@arminco.com; internet www .tourismarmenia.org; f. 1998; tourist information centre; Chair. KAREN GRIGORIAN.

Armenian Tourism Development Agency (ATDA): 0010 Yerevan, Nalbandian St 3; tel. (10) 54-23-03; fax (10) 54-47-92; e-mail help@armeniainfo.am; internet www.armeniainfo.am; f. 2001; Dir NINA HOVNANIAN.

Culture

NATIONAL ORGANIZATIONS

Ministry of Culture: see The Government (Ministries).

CULTURAL HERITAGE

In 2004 there were 95 museums (which were attended by a total of 750,100 visitors in that year), 24 theatres (attended by 340,000 people) and 1,058 libraries.

E. Charents State Museum of Literature and Art: Yerevan, Aram St 1; tel. (10) 58-16-51; f. 1921; history of Armenian literature (18th–20th century), theatre, cinema and music; Dir H. BAKCHINIAN.

History Museum of Armenia: 0010 Yerevan, Republic Sq.; tel. (10) 58-38-61; fax (10) 56-53-22; e-mail musuem@xter.net; internet www .historymuseum.am; f. 1919; 400,000 exhibits tracing the history and culture of Armenia from pre-historic times; Dir ANELKA GRIGORIAN.

Matenadaran Institute of Ancient Armenian Manuscripts: 0009 Yerevan, Mashtots Ave 53; tel. (10) 58-32-92; internet www .matenadaran.am; f. 1920; 17,000 manuscripts and 300,000 archival documents on Armenian history, medieval science, culture and art; Dir SEN AREVSHATIAN.

National Film, Photo and Audio Archive of Armenia (Filmadaran): 0052 Yerevan, Tbilisi Shosse 25A; tel. (10) 28-54-06; e-mail info@filmadaran.org; internet www.filmadaran.org; Dir GAREGIN ZAKOIAN.

National Gallery of Armenia: 0010 Yerevan, Aram St 1; tel. and fax (10) 58-08-12; e-mail galleryarmenia@yahoo.com; internet www .gallery.am; f. 1921; Western European, Armenian, Russian and Oriental art; Dir PARAVON MIRZOIAN.

National Library of Armenia: 0009 Yerevan, Terian St 72; tel. (10) 58-42-59; fax (10) 52-97-11; e-mail nla@arm.r.am; internet www.nla .am; f. 1919; over 6.2m. vols; Dir DAVIT SARGISSIAN.

Yerevan Contemporary Art Museum: Yerevan, Mashtots Ave 7; tel. (10) 53-53-59; fax (10) 56-48-51; e-mail harutmus@freenet.am; Dir H. S. IGITIAN.

SPORTING ORGANIZATIONS

National Committee of Physical Education and Sports: Yerevan, Abovian St 9; tel. (10) 52-86-01; e-mail sportarm@yahoo.com; governmental body; Chair. ISHKHAN ZAKARIAN.

National Olympic Committee of Armenia: 0001 Yerevan, Abovian St 9; tel. (10) 52-86-01; fax (10) 54-57-89; e-mail armnoc@ arminco.com; internet www.armnoc.am; unites 32 national federations of Olympic events and four national federations of non-Olympic events; Pres. GAGIK TSARUKIAN; Gen. Sec. ARMEN GRIGORIAN.

PERFORMING ARTS

Armenian A. Spendariyan National Academic Opera and Ballet Theatre: 0002 Yerevan, Tumaniyan St 54; tel. and fax (10) 52-02-41; e-mail info@opera.am; internet www.opera.am; Artistic Dir GEGHAM GRIGORIAN.

Armenian Philharmonic Orchestra: 0002 Yerevan, Mashtots Ave 46, Aram Khachaturian Concert Hall; tel. (10) 56-49-14; fax (10) 56-49-65; e-mail apo@arminco.com; internet www.apo.am; Artistic Dir EDUARD TOPJIAN.

Armenian State Academic Choir: Yerevan, Pushkin St 60; tel. (10) 58-63-03; f. 1936; Dir Prof. HOVANNES TCHEKIDJIAN.

H. Ghaplanian Yerevan Drama Theatre: 0009 Yerevan, Isaahakian St 28; tel. (10) 52-44-23; e-mail info@ydt.am; internet www.ydt .am; f. 1967; Dir ARMEN KHANDIKIAN.

National Chamber Orchestra of Armenia: 0025 Yerevan, Isaahakian St 1, Komitas Chamber Music Hall; tel. and fax (10) 52-67-18; e-mail ncoa@arminco.com; internet www.ncoa.am; f. 1961 as the Armenian State Chamber Orchestra; Artistic Dir and Principal Conductor ARAM GHARABEKIAN; Exec. Dir ARMEN ARABIAN.

A. Spendiarov Opera and Ballet National Academic Theatre: 0002 Yerevan, Tumanian St 54; tel. (10) 58-63-11; fax (10) 52–79–92; e-mail opera@arminco.com; Dir GEGHAM GRIGORIAN.

K. S. Stanislavsky State Drama Theatre: Yerevan, Abovian St 7; tel. (10) 56-91-99; fax (10) 52-62-67; e-mail grigoryan@netsys.am; Dir A. S. GRIGORYAN.

Yerevan Chamber Theatre: Yerevan, Mashtots Ave 58; tel. (10) 56-60-70; fax (10) 56-63-78; e-mail erkat@arminco.com; internet www.erkat.am; Dir A. H. YERNJAKIAN.

ASSOCIATIONS

Benevolent Fund for Culture Development: 0001 Yerevan, Tumanian St 5; tel. and fax (10) 56-21-31; e-mail mzbh@arminco .com; f. 1999; carries out cultural, educational and other charitable activities; Chair. SAMVEL MESROPIAN; Co-ordinator GOHAR SARKISSIAN.

Hamazkayin Armenian Cultural and Educational Society: 0002 Yerevan, Mashtots Ave 37/14; tel. (10) 53-39-49; e-mail hamazg@netsys.am; internet www.hamazkayin.com; f. 1928; international headquarters based in Cairo, Egypt; Dir LILIT KALSDIAN.

Union of Architects of Armenia: Yerevan, Marshal Baghramian Ave 17; tel. (10) 56-15-06.

Union of Artists of Armenia: 0001 Yerevan, Abovian St 16; tel. (10) 56-47-24; fax (10) 56-48-51; e-mail aghamyan@yahoo.com; f. 1932; Pres. KAREN AGHAMIAN.

Union of Writers of Armenia: 0019 Yerevan, Marshal Baghramian Ave 3; tel. (10) 56-38-11; fax (10) 56-18-31; e-mail wua@freenet .am; internet www.wua.am; f. 1934.

Education

Education is free and compulsory at primary and secondary levels. Until the early 1990s the general education system conformed to that of the centralized Soviet system. Extensive changes were subsequently made, with greater emphasis placed on Armenian history and culture. Armenia adopted an 11-year system of schooling in 2001/02, and in 2006 confirmed that it would be extended to 12 years. In 2004 total enrolment at pre-school establishments was equivalent to 19.8% of the relevant age-group. Primary enrolment in 2005 was equivalent to 90.7% of the age-group, while the comparable ratio for secondary enrolment was 87.9%. Most instruction is in Armenian, although Russian is widely learnt as a second language. In 2005/06 some 98.6% of students in general education schools were taught in Armenian, while for 1.2% Russian was the main language of instruction. In 2004/05 73,700 students were enrolled at one of the 22 higher education institutes (including universities). Current expenditure on education and science was 70,540m. drams in 2006 (15.5% of total state expenditure).

UNIVERSITIES

Russian-Armenian (Slavonic) State University: 0051 Yerevan, Hovsep Emin St 123; tel. (10) 27-50-52; fax (10) 28-97-01; e-mail rectorat@rau.am; internet www.rau.am; f. 1997 according to a convention between the Armenian and Russian Governments; university is under jurisdiction of the authorities of both countries; 11 faculties; 1,600 students; Rector ARMEN DARBINIAN.

State Engineering University of Armenia: 0009 Yerevan, Terian St 105; tel. (10) 27-70-52; fax (10) 28-97-01; e-mail info@seua.am; internet www.seua.am; f. 1991; fmrly Yerevan Polytechnic Institute (f. 1933); 12 departments; 1,000 teachers; 11,000 students; regional campuses in Goris, Gyumri, Kapan and Vanadzor; Rector VOSTANIK Z. MARUKHIAN.

Yerevan State Institute of Economics: 0025 Yerevan, Nalbandian St 164; tel. (10) 58-55-66; fax (10) 52-88-64; e-mail ysine@ysine .am; internet www.ysine.am; f. 1975; 5 faculties; 326 teachers; 5,600 students; Rector G. KIRAKOSSIAN.

Yerevan State Medical University: 0025 Yerevan, Koriun St 2; tel. (10) 58-25-32; e-mail info@ysmu.am; internet www.ysmu.am; f. 1922; teaching in Armenian, English and Russian; 4 faculties; 806 teachers; 4,700 students (2007); Rector GOHAR P. KYALIAN.

Yerevan State University: 0025 Yerevan, A. Manukian St 1; tel. (10) 55-52-40; fax (10) 55-46-41; e-mail rector@ysu.am; internet www .ysu.am; f. 1919; language of instruction: Armenian; Russian and English teaching also available for foreign students; 20 faculties; 1,250 teachers; 12,000 students at main campus; 1,000 students at Ijevan branch; Rector ARAM H. SIMONIAN.

OTHER INSTITUTIONS

Armenian Centre for National and International Studies: 0033 Yerevan, Yerznkian St 75; tel. (10) 52-87-80; fax (10) 52-48-46; e-mail root@acnis.am; internet www.acnis.am; independent strategic research centre focusing on foreign and public policy issues; Founding Dir RAFFI K. HOVHANISSIAN.

Social Welfare

In the 1990s the escalation in the conflict with Azerbaijan and the collapse of the USSR encouraged a large number of refugees to flee to Armenia, creating new demands on the social welfare system at a time of restricted government revenue, a situation that was exacerbated by the adaptation to a market economy and the economic blockade imposed on the country by neighbouring Azerbaijan and Turkey. In the 1990s much of Armenia's expenditure on health and welfare services was directed towards the survivors of the earthquake in northern Armenia in December 1988. A US $150m., three-year reconstruction programme commenced in 1999. In August 2003 the Government approved a Poverty Reduction Strategy, dependent on US $1,200m. pledged in external loans and grants, providing for social benefits to be increased by 400% over a period of 12 years.

In October 1991 the Armenian branch of the former USSR Pension Fund was reorganized into the Pension Fund of Armenia and further renamed the State Fund of Social Insurance. In 2005 533,288 people were in receipt of state pensions; in 2004 70.6% of pensions were provided on account of old age. At 1 January 2008, following the Government's approval of an increase in the state pension in August 2007, the average old-age pension amounted to some 23,390 drams per month (compared with 13,900 drams in 2007). In 2008 the retirement age was 63 years for men, and 61.5 years for women.

In 1995 the Armenian Government adopted a programme for the development and reform of the health care system between 1996 and 2000, and the system was subsequently fully decentralized. In March 1996 the Medical Care Act was adopted, which authorized the provision of funding from a number of sources (from state and municipal budgets, medical insurance or private payments by patients). Two years later all state-owned health care establishments were transformed into joint-stock companies. In 2006 there were 3.7 physicians and 4.4 hospital beds per 1,000 inhabitants in Armenia. In 2006 average life expectancy at birth was 68.7 years (males 64.9 years; females 72.2 years). Of state budget expenditure in 2006, 35,963m. (7.9% of expenditure) was allocated to health and 53,040m. (11.7%) to social insurance.

GOVERNMENT AGENCIES

Ministry of Labour and Social Affairs: see The Government (Ministries).

National Health Care Agency: Ministry of Health Care, 0010 Yerevan, Republic Sq., Govt Bldg 3; tel. (10) 58-24-13; fax (10) 15-10-97; Head ARA TER-GRIGORIAN.

State Social Security Service: 0010 Yerevan, Nalbandian St 13; tel. (10) 52-45-74; fax (10) 51-14-46; e-mail inter@sif.am; internet www.sif.am; f. 1991 as State Fund of Social Insurance; Chair. Prime Minister of Armenia.

HEALTH AND WELFARE ORGANIZATIONS

Armenian General Benevolent Union (AGBU): 0070 Yerevan, A. Manukian St 9; tel. (10) 52-22-50; fax (10) 51-22-52; e-mail agbu@ arminco.com; internet www.agbu.org; f. 1989; educational, cultural and humanitarian projects; Dir ASHOT GHASARIAN.

Armenian Red Cross Society (ARCS): 0015 Yerevan, Paronian St 21; tel. (10) 53-83-67; fax (10) 58-36-30; e-mail redcross@redcross.am; internet www.redcross.am; f. 1920; 11 regional and 62 community branches; Pres. Dr MKHITAR MNATSAKANIAN.

Armenian Relief Society: Yerevan, Nalbandian St 116/24; tel. (10) 56-75-13; e-mail ars@arminco.com; internet www.ars.1910.org; f. 1991; assists those needing medical and mental-health treatment; 18,000 mems.

Armenian Volunteer Corps: Yerevan, Hanrapetutiun St 62, Apt 108; tel. (10) 54-00-37; fax (10) 54-09-63; e-mail info@avc.am; internet www.armenianvolunteer.org; f. 2001; facilitates skilled diaspora Armenians to participate in the development of the country by working in Armenia for service terms lasting between one month and one year; Dir ANOUSH TATEVOSSIAN.

Caritas Armenia: Gyurmi, V. Sarkissian 8, Alley 3; tel. (312) 37-201; fax (312) 32-749; e-mail caritas@cararm.am; internet www .caritasarm.am; Roman Catholic welfare org.; Pres. Archbishop NECHAN KARAKAHIAN; Sec.-Gen. GAGIG TARASIAN.

National Institute of Health (NIH): 0051 Yerevan, Komitas Ave 49/4; tel. (10) 23-71-34; fax (10) 23-45-37; e-mail doumanian@nih.sci .am; internet www.niharm.am; f. 1963; independent org. financed by the Ministry of Health Care; Dir Prof. DERENIK H. DOUMANIAN.

UNICEF Armenia Branch: 0010 Yerevan, Adamian St 14; tel. (10) 58-01-74; fax 54-38-10; e-mail yerevan@unicef.org; internet www .unicef.org/armenia; f. 1994; Communication Officer EMIL SAHAKIAN.

Unison: 0002 Yerevan, Demirchian St 36; tel. (10) 52-21-70; fax (10) 22-64-70; e-mail unison@unison.am; internet www.unison.am; f. 2002; non-governmental org. for the support of people with special needs, including the disabled, the elderly, the homeless and orphans; Pres. RASMILA ALAVERDIAN; Dir ARMEN ALAVERDIAN.

The Environment

In the 1990s Yerevan experienced particularly severe pollution as a result of its high concentration of industrial enterprises and the surrounding mountains, which confined emissions. The influx of refugees and the shortage of fuel resulting from the conflict with Azerbaijan increased environmental degradation. In addition, the reopening of the Medzamor nuclear power station in mid-1995 raised fears of environmental damage. According to the terms of an agreement signed with the European Union (EU) in April 1996, the power station was to be closed by 2004. The agreement had depended, however, on the construction of adequate alternative energy facilities, and in mid-2004 the Government extended the facility's operating licence until 2016. The declining water level of Lake Sevan was also a cause for concern. A 10-year water management programme was drafted in 2001, to be funded by contributions from the World Bank and the German Government.

NATIONAL AGENCIES

Ministry of Environmental Protection: see The Government (Ministries); includes Bio-resources Management Agency, Geology Agency, Hydrometeorological and Environment Monitoring Agency, Mineral Resources Agency, Water Resources Management Agency.

Ministry of Agriculture: see The Government (Ministries).

State Committee of Water System of Territorial Administration: Yerevan, Vardananats St 13A; tel. (10) 54-09-09; fax (10) 54-06-03; e-mail scws@netsys.am; internet www.scws.am; f. 2001; Chair. ANDRANIK ANDREASSIAN.

ACADEMIC INSTITUTES

Armenian Centre for Scientific and Technological Information (ACSTI): 0051 Yerevan, Komitas Ave 49/3; tel. (10) 23-67-74; fax (10) 23-80-29; e-mail info@acsti.am; internet www.acsti .am; f. 1961; includes the Republic Science and Technology Library (RSTL); collates information and maintains databases, provides information support; publishes monthly magazine (Gitutyun ev Technika), books, directories and CD-ROMs, etc.; organizes exhibitions, conferences and presentations; Dir SIMON A. AGHAJANIAN.

National Academy of Sciences of the Republic of Armenia: 0019 Yerevan, Marshal Baghramian Ave 24; tel. (10) 52-70-31; fax (10) 56-92-81; e-mail academy@sci.am; internet www.sci.am; f. 1943; Pres. RADIK M. MARTIROSIAN.

Centre for Ecological-Noosphere Studies: 0025 Yerevan, Abovian St 68; tel. (10) 56-93-31; fax (10) 58-02-54; e-mail ecocentr@sci.am; internet www.ecocentre.am; f. 1989; carries out scientific and research activities; Dir Dr ARMEN K. SAGHATELIAN; Dep. Dir Dr ROBERT H. REVAZIAN.

Institute of Botany: 0063 Yerevan, Ajarian 1, Avan 63; tel. (10) 62-17-81; fax (10) 56-92-81; e-mail botanyinst@sci.am; f. 1939; Dir ZHIRAYR H. VARDANIAN.

Institute of Geological Sciences: 0019 Yerevan, Marshal Baghramian Ave 24A; tel. (10) 52-44-26; fax (10) 52-23-44; e-mail hrshah@sci.am; f. 1935; geological and environmental research; Dir ARKADIY S. KARAGHANIAN.

Institute of Hydroecology and Ichthyology: 0019 Yerevan, Marshal Baghramian Ave 24D/907, Rm 1112; tel. (10) 56-85-54; fax (10) 56-94-11; e-mail rhovan@sci.am; f. 1923; researches hydrobiology and fishery management; Dir Dr BARDUGH K. GABRIELIAN.

Institute of Zoology: 0014 Yerevan, Sevak St 7; tel. (10) 28-14-70; fax (95) 28-13-60; e-mail zool@sci.am; f. 1943; Dir GEORGII H. BOYAGHCHIAN.

Scientific Centre for Agronomy and Plant Protection: 1101 Etchmiadzin, Issy-le-Moulino 1; tel. (231) 53-454; e-mail su@pochta.ru; f. 1926; Dir HRACHYA V. HOVSEPYAN; Dep. Dir SUREN P. SEMERJYAN.

Scientific Centre of Hydrometeorology and Ecology: State Dept of Hydrometeorology, Arshakuniats Ave 46/1; tel. (10) 44-66-11; Dir K. H. HAIRAPETIAN.

Scientific Research Institute of Environmental Hygiene and Occupational Toxicology: 0001 Yerevan, Tumanian St 8; tel. (10) 58-24-13; fax (10) 15-10-97; researches environmental pollution and toxic wastes; Dir VLADIMIR L. KOGAN.

NON-GOVERNMENTAL ORGANIZATIONS

Armenian Ecological Benevolent Foundation: 0001 Yerevan; tel. (10) 61-48-51; e-mail dovlatian@yahoo.com; Pres. ARMEN DOVLATIAN.

Armenian Ecotourism Association (ARMECAS): 0033 Yerevan, H. Hakobian St 2/22; tel. and fax (10) 27-87-28; e-mail zhanna@netsys.am; internet www.ecotourismarmenia.com; f. 1998; Pres. ZHANNA GALIYAN.

Armenian Nature Protection Union: Yerevan, Charents St 8; tel. (10) 55-67-78; e-mail anpuorg@freenet.am; f. 1976; Pres. EDUARD YAVRUYAN.

Association for Sustainable Human Development: 0010 Yerevan, Khanjian St 33/18; tel. and fax (10) 52-23-27; e-mail ashd@freenet.am; internet users.freenet.am/~ashd; f. 1996; promotes sustainable development; Chair. KARINE DANIELIAN.

Ecology Fund of Armenia: Yerevan, Komitas Ave 49, Rms 302–304; tel. (10) 23-69-00; fax (10) 22-30-58; Pres. BORIS MEHRABIAN.

Ecoteam: 0001 Yerevan, Abovian St 22A/53; tel. (10) 52-92-77; e-mail ecoteam@freenet.am; internet www.users.freenet.am/~ecoteam; f. 1996; energy and environmental NGO and information centre; Pres. ARTASHES SARKISSIAN.

EDEM Plant Protection Union: Yerevan, Komitas St 58, Apt 53; tel. (10) 23-41-83; Pres. ARAMIS KHACHIKIAN.

Environmental Public Advocacy Centre (EPAC): 0025 Yerevan, Charents St 1, 3rd Floor; tel. (10) 57-49-86; e-mail info@epac.am; internet www.epac.am; f. 1997; represents the environmental interests of individuals, groups, public and other organizations; publishes quarterly newspaper; Pres. AIDA ISKOIAN.

Environmental Survival Ecological Union: 0019 Yerevan, Marshal Baghramian Ave 24D/908; tel. and fax (10) 52-38-30; e-mail esu@sci.am; f. 1997; Pres. Dr EVILINA GHUKASSIAN.

Green Union of Armenia: 0093 Yerevan, Mamikoniants St 47/13; tel. (10) 28-14-11; fax (10) 25-76-34; e-mail armgreen@ipia.sci.am; f. 1985; approx. 6,000 mems; Pres. HAKOB SANASARYAN.

Union of Armenian Ecologists: 0019 Yerevan, Marshal Baghramian St 24D, Rm 1108; tel. (10) 56-85-54; e-mail grignan@sci.am; Pres. RAFAEL HOVHANISSIAN.

Defence

Following the dissolution of the USSR in December 1991, Armenia became a member of the Commonwealth of Independent States and its collective security system, which was formally transformed into a regional defence organization, the Collective Security Treaty Organization (CSTO), in April 2003. The country also began to establish its own armed forces. The armed forces were estimated to number 42,080, as assessed at November 2007, including an army of 38,945 and an air force of 3,135. There was also a paramilitary force of an estimated 4,748. Military service is compulsory and lasts for two years (a law was passed in 2002, however, providing for a 42-month alternative civilian service). There were approximately 3,170 Russian troops on Armenian territory at November 2007. The budget for 2007 allocated an estimated 97,900m. drams to defence. In 1994 Armenia joined the North Atlantic Treaty Organization's 'Partnership for Peace' programme of military co-operation. In December 2005 Armenia's 'individual partnership action plan' with that body was approved, envisaging large-scale military reforms.

Commander-in-Chief of the Armed Forces: President of the Republic.

Chief of General Staff of the Armed Forces: Col-Gen. YURI G. KHACHATUROV.

Bibliography

Abrahamian, L. *Armenian Identity in a Changing World*. Costa Mesa, CA, Mazda Publishers, 2006.

Adalian, R. P. (Ed.). *Armenia and Karabakh Factbook*. Washington, DC, Armenia Assembly of America, 1996.

Auron, Y. *The Banality of Indifference: Zionism and the Armenian Genocide*. New Brunswick, NJ, Transaction Publishers, 2000.

Balakian, P. *The Burning Tigris: a History of the Armenian Genocide*. London, Pimlico, 2005.

Bloxham, D. *The Great Game of Genocide: Imperialism, Nationalism and the Destruction of the Ottoman Armenians*. Oxford, Oxford University Press, 2005.

Bournoutian, G. *A History of the Armenian People*. 2 vols. Costa Mesa, CA, Mazda Publishers, 1993.

Chorbajian, L., Dionabedian, P., and Mutafian, C. *The Caucasian Knot: the History and Geopolitics of Nagorno-Karabagh*. London, Zed Books, 1994.

de Waal, T. *Black Garden: Armenia and Azerbaijan Through Peace and War*. New York, and London, New York University Press, 2003.

Herzig, E. M., and Kurkchiyan, M. *The Armenians: Past and Present in the Making of National Identity*. Abingdon, RoutledgeCurzon, 2005.

Hewson, R. H. *Armenia: a Historical Atlas*. Chicago, IL, University of Chicago Press, 2000.

Hovannisian, R. G. (Ed.). *The Armenian People: from Ancient to Modern Times*. 2nd edn, 2 vols. New York, St Martin's Press, 2004.

Ishkanian, A. *Democracy Building and Civil Society in Post-Soviet Armenia*. Abingdon, Routledge, 2008.

Kirakossian, A. J. (Ed.). *The Armenian Massacres 1894–96: U.S. Media Testimony*. Detroit, IL, Wayne State University Press, 2004.

The Armenian Massacres, 1894-1896: British Media Testimony. Dearborn, Armenian Research Center, University of Michigan-Dearborn, 2008.

Lang, D. M. *The Armenians: a People in Exile*. London, Unwin Paperbacks, 1988.

Libaridian, G. L. *The Challenge of Statehood: Armenian Political Thinking Since Independence*. Watertown, MA, Blue Crane Books, 1999.

Masih, J. R., and Krikorian, R. O. *Armenia: at the Crossroads*. Amsterdam, Harwood Academic Publishers, 1999.

Matossian, M. K. *The Impact of Soviet Policies in Armenia*. Leiden, E. J. Brill, 1962.

Minassian, G. *Géopolitique de l'Arménie*. Paris, Ellipses Marketing, 2005.

Mouradian, C.-S. *De Staline…Gorbachev: histoire d'une république Sovietique: l'Armenie*. Paris, Editions Ramsay, 1990.

Panossian, R. *The Armenians: From Kings and Priests to Merchants and Commissars*. New York, Columbia University Press, 2006.

Suny, R. G. *Armenia in the Twentieth Century*. Chicago, IL, Scholar's Press, 1983.

Looking Towards Ararat: Armenia in Modern History. Bloomington and Indianapolis, IN, Indiana University Press, 1993.

Walker, C. *Armenia: the Survival of a Nation*. 2nd edn. London, Routledge, 1990.

Walker, C. J. (Ed.). *Armenia and Karabagh: the Struggle for Unity*. London, Minority Rights Publications, 1991.

Also see the Select Bibliography.

AZERBAIJAN

Geography

PHYSICAL FEATURES

The Azerbaijan Republic is situated in the eastern South Caucasus, on the western coast of the Caspian Sea. There are international borders with Iran to the south, with Armenia to the west, with Georgia to the north-west and, to the north across the Caucasus, with the Russian Republic of Dagestan. The Naxçıvan (Nakhchivan) Autonomous Republic is part of Azerbaijan, although it is separated from the rest of the country by Armenian territory. The enclave lies to the west of metropolitan Azerbaijan, with Iran to the south and west and Armenia to the north and east. There is a short border with Turkey at the north-western tip of Naxçıvan. Azerbaijan also includes the former Nagorno-Karabakh Autonomous Oblast (Nagornyi Karabakh), which lies in the south-west of the country. It is largely populated by ethnic Armenians. Armed conflict over the status of Nagornyi Karabakh began in 1989, and by October 1993 Azerbaijan had lost control of about one-fifth of its own territory, including all of Nagornyi Karabakh, to Armenian militia. Nagornyi Karabakh, Upper or Mountainous Karabakh (Dağlik Karabağ in Azerbaijani), is known as Art-sakh in Armenian. The historical region of Azerbaijan also includes northern regions of Iran, where there is a significant ethnic Azeri population. The country covers an area of 86,600 sq km (33,400 sq miles), 10% of which is forested. Nagornyi Karabakh covers 4,400 sq km of the total area and Naxçıvan 5,500 sq km.

The greater part of Azerbaijan is dominated by the lowlands around two rivers; the River Kura flows from the north-west into the Caspian Sea, and its tributary, the Araks (Aras, Araxes), runs along the border with Iran. North of the Kura lies the main axis of the Greater Caucasus mountain range, the traditional boundary between Asia and Europe. This mountain range extends along the northern border of the country into north-east Azerbaijan and ends in the Apsheron Peninsula, a promontory in the Caspian Sea, which has significant petroleum reserves. Numerous mountain rivers flow into the Kura basin from the mountains of the Lesser Caucasus in the south-west. South of the mouth of the Kura, the Caspian littoral around the town of Lenkoran forms the Lenkoran plain.

CLIMATE

The Kura plain has a hot, dry, temperate climate with an average July temperature of 27°C (80°F) and an average January temperature of 1°C (34°F). Average annual rainfall on the lowlands is 200 mm–300 mm, but the Lenkoran plain, noted for its subtropical climate, normally receives between 1,000 mm and 1,750 mm.

POPULATION

According to the 1999 census, at which the total population was 7,953,438, Azeris formed the largest ethnic group (90.6% of the total population), followed by Lazs (Lezghis—2.2%), Russians (1.8%) and Armenians (1.5%). There were also small numbers of Talish, Avars, Turks, Tatars, Ukrainians, Sakhurs, Georgians, Kurds, Tats, Jews, Udins and others. Armenians predominate in Nagornyi Karabakh and Azeris in Naxçıvan. After the outbreak of the conflict in Nagornyi Karabakh, many Armenians fled the country. Large numbers of Azeri refugees from the enclave entered Azerbaijan proper. The official

language is Azerbaijani, one of the South Turkic group of languages. In 1989 27% of Azeris claimed to have a good knowledge of Russian, but fewer than 2% of Russians and 1% of Armenians in the republic claimed fluency in Azerbaijani. According to government sources, by the end of the 1990s Azerbaijani was spoken by 95% of the population. In 1992 parliament chose to abandon the Cyrillic alphabet (in use since 1939) and restore a variant of the Latin script. A presidential decree abolishing the use of Cyrillic for official and business purposes came into force on 1 August 2001. Religious adherence corresponds largely to ethnic origins: almost all ethnic Azerbaijanis are Muslims, some 70% being Shi'ite and 30% Sunni. There are also Christian communities, mainly representatives of the Russian Orthodox and Armenian Apostolic denominations.

At 1 January 2007 the total estimated population was 8,532,700, giving a population density of 98.5 inhabitants per sq km. The capital is Baku (Bakı), which had an estimated population of 1,893,300 at the beginning of 2007. It is located on the coast of the Caspian Sea, near the southern shore of the Apsheron Peninsula. Other major cities include Ganca, an industrial town in the north-west of the country, in the foothills of the Lesser Caucasus (with an estimated population of 307,500 inhabitants at 1 January 2007), and Sumqayıt, a port on the Caspian Sea to the north of Baku (with an estimated 268,800 inhabitants). Naxçıvan town is the capital of the eponymous Autonomous Republic, and had an estimated 70,400 inhabitants at 1 January 2007. The chief town in Nagornyi Karabakh is Xankandi (Khankendi—Stepanakert), with a population of 53,000 at 1 January 2007.

Chronology

625 BC–585 BC: The Medes, under their ruler Cyaxares, with his capital at Ecbatana (now Hamadan, Iran), became a major power in the territories west of the River Tigris.

550: Cyrus II ('the Great') of Persia (Iran) conquered the kingdom of Media (Mada) and united the Medes and the Persians.

323: After the death of Alexander III ('the Great') of Macedon, who had conquered the Persian Empire, the satrap Atropates established an independent state in northern Media.

AD 637: The Persian Empire of the Sassanians, which had ruled Atropatene Media (from which is derived the name of Azerbaijan) since the third century AD, was conquered by the Arabs, under the Caliph 'Umar (Omar); the islamicization of the area began.

11th century: The assimilation of Turkic settlers by the previous population was to produce the Azeri people, distinct from the Persic people of modern Iran.

1502: The Safavids, an Azeri dynasty, assumed control of the Persian Empire.

1828: By the Treaty of Turkmanchai, following years of increasing Russian influence, Persia conceded the partition of Azerbaijan; territory to the north of the River Araks (Araxes, Aras) became part of the Russian Empire.

c. 1900: The province of Azerbaijan was a major producer of petroleum, attracting increasing Slav immigration.

1911: The Müsavat (Equality) party was founded, superseding the Himmat (Endeavour) party, formed by intellectuals in 1903–04. Müsavat was a left-wing, nationalist movement, similar to the 'Young Turks' of the Ottoman Empire.

1917: The Russian Revolution impelled Müsavat and the Bolsheviks to assume control in Baku (Bakı), although Müsavat withdrew from this administration shortly afterwards and established the Transcaucasian legislature.

22 April 1918: A Bolshevik and left-Menshevik soviet (council) was established in Baku; a Transcaucasian federation (Azerbaijan with Armenia and Georgia) was proclaimed, following the Soviet signing of the Treaty of Brest-Litovsk.

28 May 1918: The collapse of Transcaucasia forced Azerbaijan to establish its own Government. Subsequently, Müsavat began negotiations with the Turks; the Red Army was prevented from attempting to occupy Baku by a British military presence.

September 1918: The British left Baku, leaving anti-Bolshevik forces in charge, but were implicated in the execution of the Bolshevik leaders involved in the previous governments; this was accompanied by a massacre of Armenians.

November 1918: The British reoccupied Baku, but did not favour an independent Müsavat regime's close links with Turkey (an ally of the Central Powers in the First World War); the United Kingdom did recognize a coalition Government in the following month.

August 1919: British forces left Baku, withdrawing to Persia.

28 April 1920: Following the occupation of Baku by the Red Army, a Soviet Republic of Azerbaijan was proclaimed.

March 1921: In a friendship treaty, the Turks and Soviet Russia agreed that the enclave of Naxçıvan (Nakhchivan) should fall under the jurisdiction of Azerbaijan.

June 1921: The arbitrating Soviet Bureau of Transcaucasian Affairs (Kavburo) voted to recommend the union of Nagornyi Karabakh (a predominantly ethnic Armenian enclave within Azerbaijan) with the Soviet Republic of Armenia, but the Soviet leader Stalin (Iosif Dzhugashvili) enforced the reversal

of this decision; in 1923 Nagornyi Karabakh was granted the status of an autonomous oblast (region) within Azerbaijan.

October 1921: The Treaty of Kars agreed the borders of the Soviet Republics of Azerbaijan, Armenia and Georgia with Turkey, and the status of Nagornyi Karabakh and Naxçıvan as territories of Azerbaijan.

December 1922: The Soviet Socialist Republic (SSR) of Azerbaijan became a member of the Transcaucasian Soviet Federative Socialist Republic (TSFSR), which itself became a constituent member of the Union of Soviet Socialist Republics (USSR).

December 1936: The TSFSR was dissolved, and the Azerbaijan SSR became a full Union Republic.

1937–38: Purges of the local communists included Azerbaijan's leader, Sultan Mejit Efendiyev.

1946: Following a protest to the UN by Iran, Allied pressure forced the USSR to end its attempts to integrate Iranian Azerbaijan with Soviet Azerbaijan.

1969: Heydar Aliyev became First Secretary of the Communist Party of Azerbaijan (CPA) and the republic's leader.

October 1987: Aliyev was dismissed, owing to corruption in government and in the party.

February 1988: Nagornyi Karabakh's attempts to be transferred to Armenian jurisdiction caused increased inter-ethnic tension, culminating in anti-Armenian riots in Sumqayıt, in which 32 people were killed.

12 January 1989: The local authorities in Nagornyi Karabakh were suspended, and the oblast was placed under the administration of a Special Administrative Committee (SAC), responsible to the all-Union Council of Ministers.

September 1989: A general strike secured the official recognition of the nationalist opposition movement, the Popular Front of Azerbaijan (PFA), established earlier in the year.

23 September 1989: Under increasing popular pressure, the Supreme Soviet (Supreme Council—legislature) of Azerbaijan effectively declared the republic's sovereignty and imposed an economic blockade on Armenia (Soviet troops maintained the Baku–Yerevan rail link).

November 1989: The SAC for Nagornyi Karabakh was replaced by a republican Organizing Committee, dominated by ethnic Azerbaijanis.

1 December 1989: The Armenian Supreme Soviet declared Nagornyi Karabakh to be part of a 'unified Armenian republic', a claim that was termed unconstitutional by the all-Union Supreme Soviet the following month.

January 1990: The PFA were prominent in attacks on government and party buildings, on Armenians and on the border posts with Iranian Azerbaijan; PFA demonstrators also attempted to declare the secession of Naxçıvan from the USSR. Soviet troops evacuated non-Azeris from Baku and enforced a state of emergency, amid some violence. On 20 January Abdul Vezirov was replaced by Ayaz Niyaz oğlu Mutalibov as First Secretary of the CPA.

18 May 1990: Mutalibov was appointed Chairman of the Supreme Soviet (republican Head of State).

September 1990: In the elections to the Azerbaijan Supreme Soviet (postponed from February), the CPA, by this time resolved on the Nagornyi Karabakh issue, won some 80% of the seats; the opposition PFA, which had campaigned with other groups as the Democratic Alliance, alleged irregularities in the conduct of the elections and criticized the state of emergency.

5 February 1991: The Supreme Soviet convened, with the opposition deputies grouped as the Democratic Bloc of Azerbaijan.

17 March 1991: Azerbaijan participated in the Soviet referendum on the renewal of the Union; official results were that 93.3% of those who had voted (75.1% of the electorate) favoured remaining in the USSR, although in Naxçıvan only 20% supported this; the opposition claimed that only some 20% of the electorate had voted.

30 August 1991: Following the failure of a coup attempt in the Soviet and Russian capital, Moscow, and large anti-Government demonstrations, the Supreme Soviet of Azerbaijan voted in favour of claiming independence.

2 September 1991: Nagornyi Karabakh declared itself a republic.

8 September 1991: Mutalibov won 84% of the votes cast at elections to an executive presidency, which were boycotted by the opposition.

18 October 1991: The Supreme Soviet enacted legislation effecting the declaration of independence of 30 August. Later that month the PFA persuaded the Government and the Supreme Soviet to delegate some legislative powers to a smaller body, the Milli Majlis (National Assembly).

10 December 1991: In a referendum, residents of Nagornyi Karabakh voted overwhelmingly for independence; the Azerbaijani authorities considered the poll irregular, and the Karabakh Armenians secured no international recognition.

21 December 1991: President Mutalibov signed the Almaty Declaration, by which Azerbaijan became a founding member of the Commonwealth of Independent States (CIS).

6 January 1992: The new 'parliament' of Nagornyi Karabakh, elected on 28 December 1991, proclaimed the region's independence. In the same month President Mutalibov declared Nagornyi Karabakh to be under direct presidential rule.

February 1992: Azerbaijan was admitted to the Conference on Security and Co-operation in Europe (CSCE, now the Organization for Security and Co-operation in Europe—OSCE).

March 1992: President Mutalibov resigned, owing to military reversals in Nagornyi Karabakh. (He was replaced on an interim basis by Yagub Mamedov.) In the same month CIS troops were withdrawn from the area as Armenian forces began to achieve some success against Azerbaijan. Azerbaijan became a member of the UN.

May 1992: By the time Armenia and Azerbaijan negotiated a short-lived cease-fire, the Nagornyi Karabakh militia had secured control over the whole enclave and a land 'corridor' along the Lachin valley to Armenia. The Supreme Council voted to reinstate Mutalibov as President, but he was deposed after one day in office; this effective coup by the PFA was reinforced by the suspension of the Supreme Soviet and the transfer of its powers to the Milli Majlis.

7 June 1992: Abulfaz Elchibey (*né* Aliyev), leader of the PFA, was elected President of Azerbaijan by direct vote. Azerbaijan launched a counter-offensive in Nagornyi Karabakh.

August 1992: The Nagornyi Karabakh legislature declared a state of martial law; a State Defence Committee replaced the enclave's Government.

October 1992: Azerbaijan and Russia signed a Treaty of Friendship, Co-operation and Mutual Security. In the same month the Milli Majlis voted to withdraw Azerbaijan from the CIS.

February 1993: Col Surat Husseinov, who had successfully commanded Azerbaijani forces in the conflict over Nagornyi Karabakh, withdrew to Ganca, prompting allegations by President Elchibey that he was planning a military coup against

the Government. Husseinov was subsequently dismissed from his posts and expelled from the PFA.

April 1993: President Elchibey declared a three-month state of emergency. Azerbaijan withdrew from CSCE-sponsored negotiations, in protest at a large-scale Armenian offensive.

May 1993: Azerbaijan approved a peace plan formulated by Russia, Turkey and the USA, and negotiated by the CSCE; it was not accepted by the Nagornyi Karabakh leadership until June.

4 June 1993: President Elchibey ordered a punitive attack in Ganca by the Azerbaijani army on a unit still loyal to their rebel leader, Col Surat Husseinov. Over 60 people were killed. Husseinov assumed control of the town.

15 June 1993: Heydar Aliyev, the former CPA leader, was elected Chairman of the Milli Majlis. Shortly afterwards, President Elchibey fled to Naxçıvan.

25 June 1993: The Milli Majlis voted to transfer, on an acting basis, the majority of President Elchibey's powers to Aliyev and to impeach Elchibey. Three days later Husseinov's troops, having marched to Baku, pledged allegiance to acting President Aliyev.

1 July 1993: Aliyev nominated Husseinov as Prime Minister and Supreme Commander.

23 August 1993: Alikram Gumbatov, leader of the so-called 'Talysh-Mugan Autonomous Republic' (proclaimed during the Husseinov revolt of June), based in Lankaran, fled the city after his headquarters were attacked by PFA supporters. He was sentenced to death in 1996; the sentence was later commuted to life imprisonment.

1 September 1993: The Milli Majlis endorsed the results of a referendum, in which 97.5% of participants voted in favour of President Elchibey's impeachment.

20 September 1993: A resolution for Azerbaijan to rejoin the CIS was adopted by the Milli Majlis; the country was officially admitted on 24 September.

3 October 1993: Heydar Aliyev was elected President of Azerbaijan, with 98.8% of the votes cast.

14 October 1993: Resolution 874, adopted by the UN Security Council, endorsed the CSCE's schedule for implementing Resolutions 822 and 853, adopted earlier in the year and demanding, *inter alia*, an immediate cease-fire and the withdrawal of Armenian units from Azerbaijani territory.

27 October 1993: In reaction to CSCE cease-fire proposals, Armenia and Nagornyi Karabakh agreed to the schedule for the withdrawal of ethnic Armenian militia from Azerbaijani territory, but Azerbaijan rejected it as the CSCE plan did not envisage Armenian withdrawal from the Lachin corridor.

November 1993: The 'Minsk Group', established by the CSCE, organized a peace conference in Minsk, Belarus, on the issues concerning Nagornyi Karabakh.

May 1994: Azerbaijan joined the North Atlantic Treaty Organization's (NATO) 'Partnership for Peace' programme of military co-operation.

9–11 May 1994: Following protracted mediation by the CSCE and Russia, a new cease-fire agreement was finally signed by the Ministers of Defence of Azerbaijan and Armenia and representatives of Nagornyi Karabakh. The agreement was formalized on 27 July.

20 September 1994: Azerbaijan's state petroleum company and an international consortium signed an agreement establishing the Azerbaijan International Operating Company (AIOC), which was to develop Azerbaijani petroleum reserves.

29 September 1994: The Deputy Chairman of the Milli Majlis and the presidential security chief were assassinated, allegedly by members of special militia forces attached to the Ministry of Internal Affairs (known as OPON).

2 October 1994: In protest at the arrests of his men, the OPON military chief, Rovshan Javadov, attacked the offices of the Procurator-General, prompting President Aliyev to declare a state of emergency in Baku and Ganca.

5 October 1994: Husseinov was dismissed as Prime Minister, following allegations of a coup attempt in Ganca, reportedly led by a relative; he was replaced as premier by Fuad Kuliyev.

13–14 March 1995: A decree disbanding the special militia forces prompted violent OPON protests; in the ensuing clashes with government troops on 17 March, at least 70 people, including Javadov, were killed. The PFA was accused of involvement in the insurrection and its activities were temporarily suspended.

12 November 1995: Elections to the new, 125-member Milli Majlis were held. Only eight of the country's official parties were permitted to participate, and, of these, only two, the PFA and the National Independence Party (NIP), were opposition parties. At the same time, a reported 91.9% of the electorate approved a new state Constitution in a nation-wide referendum; the country became the Azerbaijan Republic. Further rounds of voting for seats in the Milli Majlis were held on 26 November, 4 February 1996 and 18 February—the overwhelming majority of deputies elected were supporters of President Aliyev and his New Azerbaijan Party (NAP).

14 April 1996: Mutalibov and the former defence minister, Rahim Gaziyev, were arrested in Moscow, accused of plotting to overthrow the Azerbaijani Government (Mutalibov escaped extradition owing to ill health).

19 July 1996: Following accusations of economic mismanagement by President Aliyev, Fuad Kuliyev resigned as premier. Three other ministers were dismissed on charges of corruption. The First Deputy Prime Minister, Artur Rasizade, was appointed to head the Government; his appointment was confirmed in November.

24 November 1996: A presidential election in Nagornyi Karabakh was won by Robert Kocharian, already the de facto republican Head of State, with some 86% of the votes cast; the election was condemned by Azerbaijan and the OSCE as a hindrance to the peace process.

January 1997: Many opponents of Aliyev's regime were arrested, following allegations of unsuccessful coup attempts, usually involving Mutalibov and Husseinov (the latter was extradited from Russia in March).

20 March 1997: Kocharian resigned the presidency of Nagornyi Karabakh upon his appointment as Prime Minister of Armenia; he was succeeded, on an acting basis, by Artur Tovmassian, the speaker of the legislature.

1 September 1997: Arkadii Ghukassian obtained some 90% of the votes cast in the Nagornyi Karabakh presidential election (he was inaugurated on 8 September).

16 October 1997: President Aliyev and President Ter-Petrossian of Armenia agreed to an OSCE proposal for a staged resolution of the conflict in Nagornyi Karabakh. Ter-Petrossian resigned in February 1998 following criticism of his moderate approach to the crisis.

12 November 1997: Despite security concerns, the AIOC officially began the first exports of petroleum from the Caspian Sea, along the pipeline running from Baku to Novorossiisk, Russia, via the separatist Russian republic of Chechnya. As a result of conflict in Chechnya from late 1999, a new section of the pipeline, avoiding the republic, was completed in March 2000.

29 April 1998: President Aliyev met the new Armenian President, Kocharian, at the CIS summit in Moscow, where it was agreed to resume negotiations on Nagornyi Karabakh.

11 October 1998: Aliyev was re-elected as President with 77.6% of the total votes cast; the opposition protested against the legitimacy of the elections, in the conduct of which international observers noted a number of irregularities. Seven days later, Aliyev was inaugurated for a second term. Rasizade was confirmed as premier on 23 October.

December 1998: The Milli Majlis approved a revised Constitution for Naxçivan, endorsed by the Naxçivan legislature, which defined the enclave as 'an autonomous state' within Azerbaijan.

16 February 1999: The Supreme Court sentenced Surat Husseinov to life imprisonment for his involvement in the October 1994 coup attempt. Also in February it was reported that Azerbaijan was not to renew its membership of the CIS Collective Security Treaty.

17 April 1999: A new pipeline, transporting crude petroleum from Baku to Supsa, Georgia, was inaugurated.

July 1999: Having been awarded observer status at NATO in June, Azerbaijan sent 30 troops to the Serbian province of Kosovo, the Federal Republic of Yugoslavia, as part of a NATO peace-keeping force.

18 November 1999: At a summit meeting of the OSCE, held in İstanbul, Turkey, an agreement was signed by the Presidents of Azerbaijan, Georgia, Kazakhstan, Turkey and Turkmenistan, on the construction of a pipeline to transport petroleum from Baku, via Tbilisi, Georgia, to the Turkish port of Ceyhan.

22 March 2000: Arkadii Ghukassian, the President of Nagornyi Karabakh, was seriously wounded by gunmen in the territory's capital, Stepanakert. Over 20 people were arrested in connection with the incident, including Nagornyi Karabakh's former Minister of Defence, Samuel Babaian, who was later found guilty of complicity in the attempted assassination.

5 November 2000: Parliamentary elections were held. The NAP retained its majority; the two main opposition parties, Müsavat and the NIP, failed to secure any seats. Following allegations of electoral irregularities, in mid-November up to 10,000 people attended rallies to protest against the results.

25 January 2001: Azerbaijan was formally admitted to the Council of Europe.

23 July 2001: An armed Iranian patrol ship and military aircraft expelled a research vessel that was exploring potential oilfields in a disputed area of the southern Caspian Sea. The Iranian Government claimed that, since the maritime borders had not yet been agreed by all the nations surrounding the Caspian Sea, no country had the right to conduct petroleum-exploration operations.

1 August 2001: A presidential decree came into immediate force, according to which the Azerbaijani language was to use a form of the Latin, rather than the Cyrillic, script.

24–26 January 2002: President Aliyev paid a state visit to Russia, at which seven bilateral agreements were signed, the most significant of which granted the Russian armed forces the right to use the Soviet-constructed Qabala radar station for a period of 10 years, while recognizing it as the property of Azerbaijan. Meanwhile, on 25 January, in recognition of Azerbaijan's support for the US-led campaign to combat international terrorism (initiated following large-scale terrorist attacks on the USA on 11 September 2001), US President George W. Bush signed a waiver to Section 907 of the Freedom Support Act, which barred direct US state aid to Azerbaijan while that country maintained its economic blockade of Armenia. The waiver was subsequently renewed.

11 August 2002: Ghukassian was re-elected as President of Nagornyi Karabakh, securing 88.4% of the votes cast. The rate of participation by the electorate was some 75%.

24 August 2002: A referendum was held on proposed amendments to the Constitution, which would, *inter alia*, eliminate election by proportional representation, and allow for the transfer of power from the president to the prime minister (a presidential appointee), rather than the chairman of the Milli Majlis, in the event of the former's inability to govern. According to official results, 96% of the votes cast by 84% of the electorate were in favour of the amendments. Protests over allegations of fraud and procedural violations followed.

23 September 2002: The Presidents of Azerbaijan and Russia signed a bilateral agreement on the delimitation of the Caspian Sea, based on the principle that the surface be used in common, but the seabed be divided into national sectors, corresponding to each country's coastline, along a median line; a similar agreement had already been signed between Russia and Kazakhstan. A trilateral agreement was signed on 14 May 2003.

21 April 2003: President Aliyev collapsed during a televised speech. In July he was admitted to a hospital in Turkey, owing to heart problems.

27 May 2003: The Milli Majlis approved a new electoral code, in conformity with the amendments approved in the referendum held in August, despite an opposition boycott.

4 August 2003: The Milli Majlis, meeting in emergency session, approved the appointment of the ailing President's son, İlham Aliyev, as Prime Minister, following his nomination by his father. Two days later, İlham Aliyev undertook a leave of absence, in order to campaign for the presidential election due to take place in October; former premier Artur Rasizade became acting Prime Minister. Opposition demonstrations subsequently took place in protest against these developments.

20 September 2003: During opposition rallies held in advance of the presidential election, there were violent clashes with the security forces, resulting in hundreds of injuries.

2 October 2003: It was announced that Heydar Aliyev was to withdraw his candidacy for the presidential election, in favour of his son.

15 October 2003: At the presidential election, İlham Aliyev was elected as the country's new President, obtaining some 80% of the votes cast. Members of the opposition alleged that widespread electoral violations had taken place, including intimidatory practices, and international observers declared the elections to have been neither free nor fair. Subsequent protests by the opposition were violently repressed by the authorities.

31 October 2003: İlham Aliyev was inaugurated as President. Subsequently, the Milli Majlis approved his reappointment of Rasizade as premier; the majority of the former Cabinet of Ministers were also reappointed.

12 December 2003: The death of Heydar Aliyev was announced and a state funeral was held three days later.

6 February 2004: President İlham Aliyev made a state visit to Russia, during which he and his Russian counterpart, Vladimir Putin, signed the 'Moscow Declaration', reaffirming bilateral agreements between the two countries.

23 July 2004: President Aliyev dismissed the long-standing Minister of National Security, Namik Abbasov; he was replaced by Lt-Gen. Eldar Akhmed Makhmudov. Several other senior officials in the ministry were also subsequently dismissed, and replaced by appointees from the Ministry of Internal Affairs, in what was regarded by some as a purge.

22 October 2004: Seven prominent opposition activists, who had been detained on charges of inciting violence following the presidential election in 2003, were sentenced to between 30 months' and five years' imprisonment. Following international pressure, they were released in March 2005.

17 December 2004: Municipal elections were held, in which the NAP won 64.7% of the votes cast; many of the major opposition parties boycotted the poll. The OSCE stated that the elections had not met democratic norms.

21 May 2005: A public demonstration to urge free and fair legislative elections was suppressed by the authorities. Demonstrations were permitted from June, as part of the pre-election campaign. Regular demonstrations were duly held by opposition groupings throughout the subsequent months, a number of which were again suppressed (sometimes violently) for taking place in unsanctioned locations.

25 May 2005: An inauguration ceremony for the completion of the construction of the Baku–Tbilisi–Ceyhan (BTC) oil pipeline was conducted in Azerbaijan; the first petroleum to traverse the pipeline was pumped in June 2006.

17–20 October 2005: The exiled leader of the Azerbaijan Democratic Party, Rasul Quliyev, attempted to return to Azerbaijan prior to participating in legislative elections, but his aircraft was denied entry, and he was temporarily detained upon landing in Simferopol, Ukraine. Many supporters in Azerbaijan were detained pre-emptively in order to prevent protest action. The Minister of Economic Development, Farhad Aliyev, and his brother were arrested on suspicion of conspiring to overthrow the Government in support of Quliyev; Ali Insanov, the Minister of Public Health, and several other senior officials were also implicated in the plot.

6 November 2005: The NAP secured 56 mandates in legislative elections, independent candidates (largely also supporters of the Government) received 43 seats, the Freedom (Azadlıq) bloc obtained six, and the Civic Solidarity Party and Fatherland Party (Ana Vatan) won two each; the results from 10 constituencies were annulled subsequently by the Constitutional Court. (This was the first election held since the adoption of amendments to the Constitution in August 2003, which had eliminated proportional representation from the process.) The election was deemed by international observers to have failed to meet democratic norms. Opposition protest demonstrations ensued, until prohibited by the authorities.

2 December 2005: The newly constituted Milli Majlis convened for the first time, electing Oktai Asadov of the NAP as its Chairman. President Aliyev subsequently effected a minor reorganization of the Cabinet of Ministers, including the creation of two new portfolios: those of Emergency Situations and Defence Industries.

6 February 2006: Col-Gen. Kamaladdin Heydarov, hitherto Chairman of the State Customs Committee, was appointed as the inaugural Minister of Emergency Situations.

17 February 2006: The Freedom bloc realigned, as some of its members, primarily Müsavat, diverged from the joint agreement to boycott the new parliament in protest at the alleged falsification of the November election.

4 March 2006: A criminal investigation against the President of electricity supplier Barmek-Azerbaijan was initiated on charges of abuse of office, embezzlement and the failure of the company to meet its commitments on investment, after having reached an illicit agreement with Farhad Aliyev. Numerous officials of the company were subsequently held in detention.

18 April 2006: Avaz Alekperov was dismissed as Minister of Finance (having held that office for nearly seven years); he was replaced by Samir Sharifov, hitherto the Director of the State Oil Fund (SOFAZ).

26 April–1 May 2006: President Aliyev made his first official visit to the USA.

13 May 2006: In repeat elections for the 10 constituencies in which the results had been annulled, the NAP secured five seats in the legislature, three independent candidates obtained seats and the Justice Party (Adalat) and the Civic Solidarity Party received one each.

18 May 2006: Abbas Abbasov, who had served as First Deputy Prime Minister for 14 years, tendered his resignation.

23 May 2006: The leaders of Georgia, Ukraine, Azerbaijan and Moldova met in Kyiv, Ukraine, to revive the regional GUAM organization, renaming it the Organization for Democracy and Economic Development–GUAM.

25 June 2006: A congress of the traditionalist faction of the Azerbaijan National Independence Party elected Ayaz Rustamov as its Chairman. (The party had divided into two factions in January; the other faction remained under the chairmanship of Ali Aliyev.) The former faction received official registration in March, the latter did not.

25 July 2006: The former head of the Criminal Investigation Department of the Ministry of the Interior, Haci Mammadov, confessed to having murdered opposition journalist Elmar Husseinov in March 2005, at the order of Farhad Aliyev. Twenty of Mammadov's associates were subsequently arrested, some of whom were already under suspicion for various abductions and murders.

10 December 2006: In a referendum concerning a de facto Constitution in Nagornyi Karabakh, 83% of those who participated voted in support of the document, which proclaimed the territory as a 'sovereign democratic' state.

March 2007: Construction of the Baku–Tbilisi–Erzurum gas pipeline was completed.

9 June 2007: After meeting on the sidelines of a CIS summit meeting in St Petersburg, Russia, President Aliyev and his Turkmenistani counterpart, Gurbanguly Berdymuhamedov, agreed to the reopening of the Turkmenistani embassy in Baku.

19 July 2007: A presidential election was conducted in Nagornyi Karabakh. Bako Sahakian emerged victorious, with 85.1% of the votes cast; the rate of participation was reported at 77%.

14 October 2007: Local elections were held in Nagornyi Karabakh.

7 March 2008: Severe clashes erupted in Nagornyi Karabakh; five members of the Azerbaijani armed forces were confirmed to have been killed. The OSCE Minsk Group subsequently appealed to Armenia and Azerbaijan to abide by the cease-fire agreement.

14 March 2008: A non-binding resolution, submitted by Azerbaijan, reaffirming its territorial integrity and demanding the withdrawal of all ethnic Armenian forces, was adopted by the UN General Assembly.

2 June 2008: The Milli Majlis approved amendments to the electoral code; the main opposition parties, which regarded these as further benefiting the authorities, and had demanded the implementation of reforms to end the ruling party's control of election commissions, subsequently announced a boycott of the forthcoming presidential election.

6 June 2008: President Aliyev met the newly elected Armenian President, Serge Sarkissian, for discussions on the occasion of a CIS summit meeting in St Petersburg; the two Heads of State agreed that negotiations on the issue of Nagornyi Karabakh would continue on the basis of proposals submitted by mediators of the Minsk Group in November 2007.

3 September 2008: Following the outbreak of conflict in Georgia in early August (see the chapter on Georgia), US Vice-President Dick Cheney visited Azerbaijan as part of a regional tour; amid concern over the security of the BTC and Baku–Tbilisi–Erzurum pipelines, Cheney announced the US Administration's intention of ensuring the free passage of oil and natural gas from the Caspian Basin.

16 September 2008: President Aliyev visited Moscow to discuss the impact of the conflict in Georgia with his Russian counterpart, President Dmitrii Medvedev.

17 September 2008: Campaigning for the presidential election, which was due to be contested by seven candidates on 15 October, officially began; the NAP conducted a rally near Baku, which, it was reported, local public sector workers were ordered to attend.

15 October 2008: İlham Aliyev was elected to a second term of office, obtaining 88.7% of the votes cast in the presidential election, according to provisional official results. Although the poll was contested by a further six candidates, the main opposition parties had organized an electoral boycott; nevertheless, voter turn-out was officially recorded at 75.6%.

History

ANDREW YORKE

Revised for this edition by Dr MATTEO FUMAGALLI

INTRODUCTION

Present-day Azerbaijan occupies an area that has been inhabited for at least 3,000 years, and probably for far longer. However, in the modern era Azerbaijan has existed as an independent state for just two short periods: in 1918–20 and since October 1991. The country formed part of Persia for much of its history, although Turkic tribes from Central Asia had become a significant presence by the 11th century. Consequently, the Azerbaijani language came to be dominated by Turkic rather than Persian influences. In the 19th century Azerbaijan experienced Russian domination, and was subsequently absorbed into the USSR. However, an area south of the Araks (Aras, Araxes) river, which was also Azeri-populated, remained under Persian influence and now forms part of northern Iran. As a result, Azeri (ethnic Azerbaijani) nationalists regard Azerbaijan as a nation divided by the great powers of Russia and Persia.

Islam replaced Orthodox Christianity in the territory that now constitutes Azerbaijan, following Arab domination in the seventh, eighth and ninth centuries AD. Traditions of mysticism in the region made its people particularly receptive to the Shi'a branch of Islam that remains dominant in the country. This was an important factor in setting Azerbaijan apart from Ottoman Turkey, where adherence was to the Sunni doctrine.

As the Persian Empire crumbled in the early 19th century, Russia came to dominate Azerbaijan as far south as the Araks river. However, the first major Russian incursion came under Tsar Peter (Petr) I ('the Great') in 1722, when Russian forces occupied Baku (Bakı) and other towns, until the reassertion of control by Persia in 1735. From the 1780s the peoples of the south Caucasus (Armenia, Azerbaijan and Georgia) began to seek protection from Russia against an increasingly aggressive Persia. Owing to its history of Persian dominance and adherence to Islam, Azerbaijan was least inclined to regard Russia as a protector, but its nobles were unable to form a united front against the great power to the north. In the early 1800s Georgia was annexed by Russia under Alexander (Aleksandr) I, prompting the Azeris to turn to Persia for help. Following Russian victories in wars against Persia in 1804–13 and 1826–28, however, the territory came under Russian control.

Initially, Russia treated Azerbaijan merely as a military outpost, rather than a region with economic potential, and Azeris were effectively divested of their rights and property. In the 1840s, partly to counter a growing level of Ottoman sympathy in the region, Azeris were granted the same rights as Russian subjects, and some property was restored to Azeri nobles. Russian interest in the region accelerated rapidly, following the discovery of large reserves of petroleum and the denationalization of the industry in 1872. This led to an influx of Russians and Western entrepreneurs, who provided the expertise necessary to develop the petroleum industry. By the early 20th century Baku was a leading source of the world's petroleum. However, Azeris benefited little from the resultant wealth, and by the end of the 1870s only 13% of the country's petroleum industry was Azeri-owned. The majority of the profits from the sector were divided between two European companies: the Swedish Nobel brothers and the Royal Dutch company, which bought the local operations of the French Rothschilds and of the British company Shell shortly after the turn of the century. Despite the infrastructural improvements by the leading petroleum companies, Azerbaijan remained a low priority for Russia, and only became connected to Russia's vastly expanded rail network in 1890.

Baku developed rapidly as an urban centre, and attracted an influx of ethnic Armenians, who chiefly worked as merchants, industrial managers and Russian government administrators. Azeris became a minority in Baku (accounting for just 10% of the working class population in 1907), largely holding menial jobs (for which they had to compete with immigrants from Iran, Russia and Turkey) and consigned to poverty, while the majority of Azeris were confined to the impoverished country-side. Resentment at their position in society and at the growing numbers of non-Azeris (especially Armenians) in the country led to riots and violent ethnic clashes in 1905.

The oppressive political environment in Baku meant that Azeri nationalism first flourished in European cities, such as Paris, France. However, the rapid urbanization that took place in Baku in the early 20th century encouraged the growth of an Azeri intelligentsia with a growing sense of national awareness. This new class was represented first by the Himmat (Endeavour) party, formed by intellectuals in 1903–04. Himmat was superseded in 1911 by the nationalist Müsavat (Equality) party, which openly advocated independent statehood for Azerbaijan. In 1915 the party's armed wing, the Difay, proclaimed a 'Republic of Azerbaijan' in Ganca (Gyanja or Yelizavetpol), which was repressed by Russian troops a few weeks later.

The final collapse of imperial Russia following the October 1917 revolution provided Azerbaijan with its first experience of real independence. Although the 'Baku Bolsheviks', who were predominantly ethnic Russian or Armenian, declared a Soviet Government in November 1917, on 28 May 1918 Islamic nationalists declared an Azerbaijan People's Democratic Republic, effectively ending the authority in Azerbaijan of the fragile Transcaucasian Federation, proclaimed in the previous month, and incorporating Armenia, Azerbaijan and Georgia. Once again, the north-western city of Ganca became the parallel centre of power in the country. In Baku, meanwhile, a council (soviet), comprising a number of commissars, had been created under the leadership of the Armenian Bolshevik Anastas Mikoian. The commissars formed an executive committee, with de facto authority, but allowed the former district council to establish a provisional government under Stepan Shaumian, a moderate Armenian.

With Ottoman Turkish assistance, an International Islamic Army was formed in Ganca, made up of some 7,000 élite troops and 14,000 volunteers. It entered Baku in September 1918, leading to clashes with Baku's Armenian population. A new Government was formed, dominated by the Müsavat Party, which ruled, in coalition with minor parties, in five successive Governments. The British military presence in Baku withdrew in September, after the collapse of the Baku Soviet, although the British were implicated in the execution of 26 commissars, in an incident that would form part of Soviet martyrology and help to define the identity of Soviet Azerbaijan. The Turkish army subsequently occupied the country, until it was forced to withdraw following its defeat in the First World War. In November the British declared Azerbaijan under provisional British rule, and in December 1918 the first multi-party elections in Azerbaijan's history were held to a Müsavat-dominated parliament. Meanwhile, the Bolsheviks began to win the support of left-wing factions in parliament and to smuggle arms from Russia.

SOVIET RULE

The British forces withdrew in August 1919, apparently believing that the Bolsheviks would be driven out of Azerbaijan by an ascendant Turkey. Independent Azerbaijan was thus left increasingly vulnerable to attack by Soviet forces, which were consolidating their hold over a Russia that had been torn apart by civil war. On 1 April 1920 the last Müsavat-dominated Government stood down, and the party's leadership took refuge in Tbilisi, Georgia. Armed Bolshevik forces took to the streets and proclaimed a Provisional Azerbaijani Military Revolutionary Committee. On 28 April the Soviet Red Army finally marched into Azerbaijan. It met little resistance, as much of the 30,000-strong Azerbaijani army was engaged in efforts to quell an uprising by ethnic Armenians in the enclave of Nagornyi Karabakh. By September the state of Azerbaijan had effectively been absorbed into the country that in 1922 became known as the Union of Soviet Socialist Republics (USSR).

In 1921 Azerbaijan was incorporated into a Transcaucasian Federated Republic (from 1922 the Transcaucasian Soviet Federative Socialist Republic—TSFSR), together with Georgia and Armenia. However, the republic was riven with tensions, and was abolished with the introduction of the so-called 'Stalin' Constitution (named after the Soviet Leader, Iosif Dzhugashvili) in 1936. Thereafter, the Azerbaijan Soviet Socialist Republic (SSR) became a full Union Republic.

Throughout the 1920s and 1930s the Soviet leadership attempted to nurture a Soviet Azerbaijani identity, while persecuting nationalists and intellectuals who were opposed to communist rule. Religious leaders were persecuted, and mosques were closed. The Azerbaijani people suffered as much as other Soviet peoples as a result of Stalin's policies of consignment to the prison and labour camps of the GULag (State Corrective Camps) system, the forced collectivization of agriculture between 1929 and 1935, and the 'Great Purges' of the late 1930s. (The islands of Nargen and Kum-Zirya became notorious prison colonies.) By 1940 approximately 120,000 Azerbaijanis had died as a result of repression. The purges and other repressive measures were co-ordinated by the First Secretary of the Communist Party of Azerbaijan (CPA), Mir Jafar Baghirov, although it was reputedly an appeal to Stalin by Baghirov that prevented Azeris sharing the fate of other Caucasian peoples deported towards the end of the Second World War (1939–45) in punishment for supposed collaboration with Nazi Germany.

However, Soviet rule did lead to a marked improvement in literacy rates and industrial development, and, at least until the Second World War, Baku was a location that benefited from Stalin's rapid industrialization programme. Subsequently, the penetration of German forces deep into the north Caucasus prompted Stalin to seek alternative sources of energy, particularly in Russian Siberia, at a safer distance from foreign invasion.

Stalin's death in 1953 and his replacement by a collective leadership, which included Nikita Khrushchev, marked the end for Baghirov, who was executed in 1956. The same political 'thaw' that took place in the Russian and Soviet capital, Moscow, was felt in Azerbaijan, with the introduction of greater political freedoms and the rehabilitation of the victims of Stalin's rule. The economy also demonstrated an improvement in the 1960s, particularly in the sectors of agriculture and construction. Nevertheless, even in the 1970s purchasing power in the republic was just one-half of the Union average, indicating that the population was failing to benefit from much of its oil wealth.

In 1969 Heydar Aliyev took over from Imam Mustafayev, who had been accused of corruption, as First Secretary of the CPA. Aliyev had previously been head of the KGB (Committee for State Security) in the exclave of Naxçıvan (Nakhchivan), and had played an important role in the Soviet security services during the Second World War. In 1982 Aliyev was appointed to the Political Bureau (Politburo) of the Communist Party of the Soviet Union (CPSU) by the party's General Secretary, Yurii Andropov. None the less, in 1987 he fell victim to a corruption investigation launched by the reformist CPSU General Secretary Mikhail Gorbachev. Aliyev, however, insisted that he had resigned from the CPSU for health reasons, rather than waiting to be expelled. In 1988 he returned to his home territory of Naxçıvan, where he founded the New Azerbaijan Party (NAP—Yeni Azerbaijan), which was to become the vehicle for his future political resurgence.

NAGORNYI KARABAKH

The disputed territory of Nagornyi Karabakh (Dağlik Karabağ in Azerbaijani, Artsakh in Armenian), located within Azerbaijani territory close to the border with Armenia, fuelled independence movements in both Armenia and Azerbaijan, and the failure of the Soviet authorities to control the situation contributed to the demise of the Union. The status of the enclave has proved an issue of contention for both newly independent states, hampering trade, deterring foreign investors and continuing to pose the threat of renewed conflict.

Contrary to the assertions of some nationalists, the dispute over Nagornyi Karabakh is relatively recent. Although conflicts took place in the territory in previous centuries, as was the case elsewhere in the south Caucasus, the first real inter-ethnic conflict in the enclave did not occur until the early 20th century. The majority of ethnic Armenians had as their homeland Anatolia (now in Turkey) and Syria, with a relatively small community in the lands of the present-day Republic of Armenia. This situation was to change when imperial Russia identified the Armenians as a potential source of support against the Ottoman Turks. Russia encouraged ethnic Armenians to settle in the south Caucasus, and over 500,000 did so in the first half of the 18th century. Russia also appears to have encouraged the activities of the extreme nationalist Armenian Revolutionary Federation (ARF—Dashnaktsutyun, also known simply as Dashnaks), which began to stage attacks against the Ottomans in eastern Anatolia in the early 1890s.

The first inter-ethnic clashes erupted in 1905, a time of political turmoil in St Petersburg (the Russian capital between 1712 and 1918). In February the murder by Dashnaktsutyun of a Muslim businessman in Baku led to violent clashes between Azeris and Armenians, which left over 300 dead. Similar confrontations quickly erupted in Yerevan, Armenia, where ethnic Azeris were murdered by armed Armenians. In August 1905 Dashnaktsutyun launched an attack in the Karabakh city of Shushi (Şuşa), leaving some 200 Azeris and 100 Armenians dead. In Baku, Himmat responded with a general strike aimed at forcing the Russian overlords to act to restore order. Despite attempts by the Russian Governor-General to put an end to the disorder, in November further sporadic violence was reported in Ganca and elsewhere. In mid-1906 a further Russian initiative to quell the unrest only led to an intensification of the two communities' conflict, in anticipation of the arrival of the Russians. Following three weeks of serious violence, in July Russia succeeded in regaining control, although the violence had claimed up to 10,000 lives.

During the interregnum between the collapse of imperial Russia and the imposition of Soviet control in the Caucasus, attempts were made to grant Nagornyi Karabakh independence under a joint presidency. However, the inter-ethnic violence continued in an increasingly extreme form. In 1918 the region became a battleground, in which Armenian forces seeking to incorporate it into their territory repelled Turkish-backed Azeri forces. The arrival of British forces in Azerbaijan prevented the complete takeover of Karabakh by Armenia. In January 1919 the British Governor-General appointed an Azeri landowner, Khosrovebek Sultanov, as Governor of Nagornyi Karabakh. However, Sultanov's offer of a cease-fire went unheeded, and Armenia retook much of the territory. Finally, in May 1920 the area came under Red Army control.

Nagornyi Karabakh was awarded to Azerbaijan in 1921, and acquired autonomous status in 1923. During the ensuing years of Soviet rule, Armenians campaigned unsuccessfully to have the Nagorno-Karabakh Autonomous Oblast transferred from Azerbaijani control. During the 'thaw' of the 1960s thousands of Karabakh Armenians sent a petition to the Kremlin, claiming that Azerbaijan was neglecting the region, and there were at least two incidents of related violence. However, the Karabakh issue was not to pose a genuine challenge to Soviet authority until 1988.

As in other Soviet republics, the political and economic freedoms introduced by Gorbachev as part of his campaign for glasnost (openness) and perestroika (restructuring) were accompanied by a growth of interest in national identities. In February 1988 the Armenian-dominated Nagornyi Karabakh Soviet demanded that the territory be transferred to the jurisdiction of the Armenian SSR. These demands prompted violent attacks against Azeri settlements in Karabakh, as well as organized attacks against ethnic Armenians in the industrial city of Sumqayıt. Further clashes led to the exodus of Azeris from Nagornyi Karabakh and Armenia, and of ethnic Armenians from the rest of Azerbaijan. In mid-1988 both the Armenian Supreme Soviet and the Nagornyi Karabakh Soviet declared that the territory had seceded from Azerbaijan and had been integrated with Armenia. A new, recently legalized party, the Popular Front of Azerbaijan (PFA), subsequently became an organ of Azeri nationalist sentiment, insisting that Azerbaijan's territorial integrity be preserved. Mass protests began in Baku and other cities, leading to hundreds of arrests by Soviet troops. After much prevarication in Moscow, Soviet troops finally intervened in Nagornyi Karabakh in early 1989, when the Soviet leadership imposed direct rule in the region. Nevertheless, tensions remained high, and Azerbaijan introduced an economic blockade of Armenia in September. In January 1990 Soviet troops finally entered Baku, which had become the scene of violent protests and pogroms, and over 120 protesters were killed. This incident was a major factor contributing to the alienation of Azeris from the USSR. Meanwhile, in the south of the country, there were further PFA-inspired uprisings, demanding greater access to relatives living in northern Iran. A semblance of order was finally restored at the end of January, after leading PFA members had been arrested and a new leader of Azerbaijan, Ayaz Niyaz oğlu Mutalibov, had been imposed by the Soviet authorities.

In August 1990 the Azerbaijani legislature voted to abolish the autonomous status of Nagornyi Karabakh; in September 1991 Nagornyi Karabakh responded by declaring the region a 'provisional republic'. By 1992 the situation had escalated into a state of full-scale conflict. During an ill-prepared military campaign hundreds of Azerbaijani troops were killed by the better-organized Armenian militia, and civilian casualties numbered in the thousands. Arguably the most notorious massacre of the war took place at Xojali (Khojali), north-east of Xankandi (Stepanakert, the principal city in the territory), in February 1992, when an Armenian assault was launched on the town, in which hundreds of Azeris had been resettled; approximately 485 Azeris were killed in the attack. By the end of February the Nagornyi Karabakh military controlled the entire enclave. The Nagornyi Karabakh forces also obtained control of other territories within Azerbaijan outwith the boundaries of the former Autonomous Oblast, including those regions between Nagornyi Karabakh and Armenia.

Mutalibov's successor Abulfaz Elchibey (*né* Aliyev), who was elected President of Azerbaijan in June 1992, made a number of unsuccessful attempts to retake the territory by force, and following intensive international mediation, a cease-fire was finally announced by the Russian Minister of Defence, Pavel Grachev, in May 1994, and was formalized in July. It has held subsequently, albeit with frequent border violations and some exchanges of fire. The Nagornyi Karabakh conflict resulted in between 1m. and 1.5m. refugees and internally displaced persons, and at least 30,000 deaths. Negotiations for a final settlement to the conflict continued under the auspices of the Organization for Security and Co-operation in Europe (OSCE), led by a 'troika' comprising representatives of France, Russia and the USA. The President elected in late 2003, İlham Aliyev, claimed to hold an uncompromising position on sovereignty over the region, although negotiations did resume in 2004.

In January 2005 the OSCE acquiesced to an Azerbaijani request that it monitor settlements in which it was claimed that the Armenian authorities had purposefully settled some 23,000 ethnic Armenians. A resolution was adopted by the Parliamentary Assembly of the Council of Europe in the same month, describing the occupation of Azerbaijani territory as a 'grave violation', and averring that the conflict had led to 'ethnic expulsion and the creation of mono-ethnic areas which resemble the terrible concept of ethnic cleansing'. The resolution also stated that the Azerbaijani leadership should establish contact with the secessionist leadership and refrain from any use of force. Potential recourse to the International Court of Justice was proposed, should negotiations fail to resolve the dispute. However, the increasing state wealth derived from the hydrocarbons sector allowed the Azerbaijani Government to continue to increase its defence budget, which was estimated at US $657m. in 2007, compared with $138m. in 2003. Azerbaijan justified this development by claiming that Russia was transferring military resources to Armenia from military bases that it was closing in Georgia. A presidential election held in Nagornyi Karabakh in July 2007, which was won by the former head of the local security service, Bako Sahakian, with 85% of votes, failed to result in any significant change in the ongoing conflict. Despite optimistic comments from the OSCE 'Minsk Group' (which was intended to encourage a peaceful, negotiated resolution to the conflict) about progress in a number of areas (including the political status of the region) and even a possible breakthrough in the negotiations, the prospects for this remained poor in 2008, partly owing to the fact that both countries held presidential elections and neither of the incumbents wanted to endanger his political base. Following Kosovo's declaration of independence from Serbia in February 2008, in the following month Azerbaijan presented a draft resolution before the UN General Assembly demanding the return of Nagornyi Karabakh and all Armenian-occupied territories to Azerbaijan. In early March severe clashes erupted in Nagornyi Karabakh; five members of the Azerbaijani armed forces were confirmed to have been killed, while Azerbaijan claimed that a number of Nagornyi Karabakh soldiers had also died. On 14 March the resolution reaffirming Azerbaijan's territorial integrity and demanding the withdrawal of all Armenian forces was adopted by the UN General Assembly, by 39 votes in favour and seven opposing, although 100 states abstained, and Russia, France and the USA were among those opposed. (For more detailed coverage of recent developments in the region, see the separate section on Nagornyi Karabakh.)

EARLY INDEPENDENCE

In August 1991 an abortive coup against Gorbachev (by that time President of the USSR) by hardliners in Moscow led to large pro-independence demonstrations in Azerbaijan, which also demanded Mutalibov's resignation. By the end of the month the Azerbaijani Supreme Soviet had voted in favour of independence from the USSR. Presidential elections held in the following month led to Mutalibov being re-elected unopposed, owing to an opposition boycott. Independence was formalized by the Azerbaijani Supreme Soviet in October, and took effect upon the dissolution of the USSR in December 1991.

The outcry that followed the events at Xojali forced Mutalibov's resignation in March 1992. After a failed interim presidency by Yagub Mamedov, and an unsuccessful attempt by Mutalibov to recover his position, the nationalist PFA seized power in a coup in May. In June the leader of the PFA, Abulfaz Elchibey, a philologist with nationalist views, was elected President. However, he too failed to bring about a military resolution to the war in Nagornyi Karabakh, and his Government had a threatening aspect, owing to the appointment of Iskander Hamidov, leader of the Azeri branch of a Turkish paramilitary group, as Minister of Internal Affairs. Elchibey was ousted in June 1993 by a maverick military garrison, under Col Surat Husseinov (who had commanded Azerbaijani forces in the conflict over Nagornyi Karabakh), which Elchibey had attempted to disband. Elchibey subsequently fled to Naxçıvan, and the Milli Majlis (National Assembly—as the legislature was now known) awarded the acting presidency to the former Soviet-era leader, Heydar Aliyev, who had, by this

time, been recalled from Naxçıvan and appointed parliamentary Chairman (speaker). In order to avoid confrontation with Husseinov, Aliyev duly appointed him Prime Minister.

THE ALIYEV ERA

Aliyev's first months in power were characterized by an assertion of control over the PFA and other opposition parties. Probably at the instigation of Husseinov, the Ministers of Defence, of Foreign Affairs and of Internal Affairs in the previous Government were imprisoned. Elchibey's removal from power was confirmed by a nation-wide referendum in August 1993, in which 98% of participants expressed 'no confidence' in the ousted President. This was followed by a victory for Aliyev in the presidential election held in October, in which he secured 99% of the votes cast. (The two candidates who stood against him were largely political unknowns.) In a further measure against the opposition, the Milli Majlis, under Chairman Rasul Quliyev, adopted a law on military censorship, which forbade the publication of any information deemed to damage the reputation of either the state or the President.

However, Aliyev experienced revolt in September–October 1994, after gunmen assassinated both the deputy speaker of parliament and Aliyev's head of security. The Procurator-General, Ali Omarov, a close ally of Husseinov, accused the Deputy Minister of Internal Affairs, Rovshan Javadov, of being responsible for the attack, and arrested members of the special police attached to the Ministry of Internal Affairs (known as OPON). Javadov responded by dispatching members of OPON to the Procuracy, where they kidnapped Omarov and released their colleagues. In response, Aliyev declared a state of emergency. There were suspicions that Husseinov and former President Mutalibov had co-ordinated the entire affair, possibly with Russian support. Both Omarov and Husseinov were subsequently dismissed from their positions, and the latter fled to Russia to avoid charges of treason.

In March 1995 Aliyev experienced further discord, when a presidential decree disbanding OPON prompted violent confrontation between the army and members of the OPON militia, as a result of which more than 50 people, including Javadov, were killed. Hundreds of people were arrested in the aftermath of the insurrection, among them the Minister of Internal Affairs. The PFA, which was accused of involvement in the incident, was temporarily banned.

In November 1995 the country held its first multi-party elections to the 125-member Milli Majlis. The majority of seats (60%) were won by Aliyev's NAP, and only two opposition parties, the PFA and the National Independence Party (NIP), led by Etibar Mamedov, were able to secure representation in the Milli Majlis. The voters also overwhelmingly approved a new Constitution, which granted wide-ranging powers to the President, including the right to appoint the Prime Minister and members of the Cabinet of Ministers, the Prosecutor-General, and the Supreme Court and Constitutional Court judges. The international community criticized the voting as having been neither free nor fair.

In August 1996 Quliyev published an accusatorial critique of Aliyev in a Russian journal. The following month Quliyev resigned as speaker, and fled to the USA. His parliamentary immunity from prosecution was removed in March 1998, and the Prosecutor-General subsequently launched criminal proceedings against Quliyev, who was charged with large-scale embezzlement during his tenure as head of a petroleum refinery. His replacement as parliamentary Chairman was an Aliyev loyalist, Murtuz Aleskerov.

In October 1998 Aliyev won a second term in office, securing 76% of the votes cast in the presidential election. Once again, the international community condemned the election. Five major opposition parties united to form the Movement for Democratic Elections and Electoral Reform (MDEER) prior to the election. As it approached, the MDEER announced a boycott, in protest at the Government's perceived attempts to manipulate issues such as the composition of the Central Electoral Commission (CEC) and media coverage, and staged mass rallies in the capital, some of which led to clashes with the police. However, Etibar Mamedov fared well in the election, and claimed to have evidence that would compel Aliyev to progress to a second round of voting. None the less, the CEC subsequently announced Aliyev as the first-round winner, although it failed to provide a district-by-district analysis of the results.

Shortly afterwards, Aliyev was affected by his first major health problems since the heart attack that he claimed had prompted his resignation as First Secretary of the CPA in 1987. In subsequent years he received regular treatment at hospitals in both Turkey and the USA. Eventually, in April 2003 Aliyev collapsed while giving a televised speech, and spent much of the following months in hospital. For some time, Aliyev's deteriorating health had prompted speculation about his likely successor, and in August 2002 constitutional amendments had been adopted by referendum, providing for the prime minister to assume the role of acting president, pending new elections, in the event of the incumbent President's death or incapacitation. However, Aliyev's collapse led to uncertainties about the anticipated outcome of the presidential election scheduled to take place on 15 October 2003. Heydar Aliyev's son, İlham, was clearly his chosen successor, and was appointed Prime Minister at the beginning of August 2003, with the overwhelming approval of the Milli Majlis. Apparently with the intention of insuring against the possibility that the incumbent President might not be well enough to stand as a candidate in the presidential election, İlham Aliyev also put forward his candidacy (with Artur Rasizade consequently becoming acting premier), and in early October Heydar Aliyev released a statement announcing his withdrawal from the election.

Owing to widespread doubts that the forthcoming election would be held under free and fair conditions, few observers had believed that any candidate from the opposition had a real chance of winning. These doubts were compounded by the fact that the opposition delayed uniting behind a single presidential candidate. Of the main challengers from the opposition, former parliamentary speaker Rasul Quliyev, leader of the Democratic Party of Azerbaijan, and former President Ayaz Mutalibov (in exile in Russia) had been disqualified, as they did not satisfy residency criteria. Thus, the main opposition candidates appeared to be İsa Qambar, the Chairman of Müsavat, and Etibar Mamedov.

İlham Aliyev was declared the victor in a single round of voting on 15 October 2003, with some 79.5% of the votes cast, although there were widespread allegations of electoral malpractice. Qambar was the second-placed candidate, with 12.1% of the votes cast. Opposition protests at the declared results ensued and were violently repressed; the opposition forces, led by Qambar, proved insufficiently strong or cohesive, and lacked the international support, to achieve the same results as those of the 'rose revolution', which took place in Georgia in November (see the chapter on Georgia). The subsequent detention and trial of many opposition figures was strongly criticized by the Council of Europe, the USA and others. (Aliyev tried to mitigate this criticism by releasing some other detainees who had been identified as political prisoners, such as Hamidov and Husseinov, and proposing legislative reform. In January 2004 the European Social Charter on human rights was approved by the Milli Majlis.) Frequent infringements of both religious and press freedom were also related to the Government's suppression of the political opposition, with the registration of one Islamic group contentiously being withdrawn (resulting in its eviction from the Juma Mosque in Baku in June 2004 and the enforced replacement of its leader, a high-profile human rights campaigner and an openly avowed opposition supporter).

THE PRESIDENCY OF İLHAM ALIYEV

Following his inauguration on 31 October 2003, İlham Aliyev reappointed Rasizade (whose loyalty to the President has been occasionally questioned) as Prime Minister, together with several members of the outgoing Council of Ministers. The death of Heydar Aliyev was announced in mid-December. Meanwhile, as İlham Aliyev gained control of the political situation, he consolidated his position. In February 2004 he dismissed Nadir Akhmedov (who had been regarded as having stifled competition and maintained high prices within the telecommunications sector) as Minister of Communications.

In April he appointed a new Minister of Foreign Affairs, Elmar Mammedyarov, and in July Namik Abbasov was removed from the influential post of Minister of National Security after a decade in office. (There was speculation that he might have represented a serious rival for power.) Abbasov's successor and several other principal members of the Ministry of National Security were recruited from the Ministry of Internal Affairs, in what was regarded by some as a purge. It was perceived that İlham Aliyev was keen to implement political restructuring, but was proceeding with caution so as not to jeopardize stability or support. Local elections took place on 17 December, but failed to meet democratic norms, according to the OSCE. Three of the four largest opposition parties boycotted the elections, in protest at obstacles to campaigning, pressure imposed by the authorities, and the imprisonment of several of their leaders. The NAP won 64.7% of the votes cast, and independent candidates received 31.1%.

In response to international pressure regarding the fair management of the legislative elections due in late 2005, the Government approved 43 amendments to electoral legislation in May (although not key changes stipulated by the Council of Europe); released a number of high-profile political prisoners in March and June; and opened the way for exiled politicians to participate in the elections (simultaneously withdrawing their political immunity and threatening them with arrest on their return). The informal ban on public rallies that had been in place since the unrest that followed the presidential election in 2003 was removed in June 2005 (following the detention of numerous attempted demonstrators the preceding month), although permission for such rallies was restricted to outlying locations. Thousands took the opportunity to participate in demonstrations over the following months, and the opposition began to reconfigure itself, recovering from the fragmentation that had followed its suppression in 2003. Nevertheless, the harassment of opposition journalists, politicians, religious leaders and organizations also increased, and conflict surrounded the opposition demonstrations. In March 2005 Elmar Husseinov, the prominent founder and Editor-in-Chief of the opposition periodical *Monitor*, was murdered.

In order to participate in the legislative elections from a position of strength, many opposition parties united into blocs, and many independent candidates formed alliances; however, the only parties to submit a sufficient number of candidates to qualify for broadcast time on national media were the ruling NAP, the Azerbaijan Liberal Party, the Freedom (Azadlıq) bloc and the New Policy (Yeni Siyaset—YeS) bloc. As the first elections to follow the constitutional changes approved in 2002, they were the first in which candidates were campaigning for single-mandate seats, rather than via the system of proportional representation. Also for the first time, the Central Electoral Commission voted to proceed with a symbolic ballot in the 125th district, encompassing areas of Nagornyi Karabakh (a seat that had previously remained vacant in the legislature). Another development prior to the legislative elections was the emergence of several youth groups, which modelled themselves on those that had helped to bring about political change in the Federal Republic of Yugoslavia, Georgia and Ukraine; New Thinking (Yeni Fikir) was among the most prominent of these new groups. The authorities initially responded by mobilizing young supporters of their own, but subsequently detained the leaders of New Thinking on conspiracy charges related to the Armenian intelligence services. In August 2006 the leaders received prison sentences of four and seven years; appeals were denied.

The opposition parties did not necessarily attract the support of the general population: several long-standing opposition figures were mistrusted for their association with the conflict of the early years of national independence, and others for fomenting violence and instability in 2003; nor had the security forces displayed any signs of disloyalty to the incumbent regime. It was widely perceived that the international community was attempting to encourage democratic reforms, in order to avoid jeopardizing the country's stability, especially given the security concerns surrounding the vital Baku–Tbilisi (Georgia)–Ceyhan (Turkey) or BTC petroleum pipeline, which had been inaugurated in May 2005, and would be reluctant to support public unrest.

However, the Government asserted its authority by pre-emptively tackling an alleged coup in October 2005. Rasul Quliyev, the exiled leader of the Azerbaijan Democratic Party, was turned away from the country as he tried to return in order to participate in the elections, and was temporarily detained at his detour destination of Simferopol, Ukraine, at the request of the Azerbaijani Government. Allegations emerged of a complex network, whereby former Minister of Finance Fikret Yusifov had transferred funding from Quliyev to the incumbent Minister of Economic Development, Farhad Aliyev, as part of a plot to seize power. Farhad Aliyev and the Minister of Public Health, Ali Insanov, were dismissed from office and arrested, as were numerous of Farhad Aliyev's acolytes (one of whom subsequently committed suicide in detention). Farhad Aliyev's brother Rafiq, the Chairman of Azpetrol, and several other prominent businessmen were also implicated. Repercussions from this alleged plot continued to surface even after the elections took place and into the following year. In March 2006 the President of the electricity supplier Barmek-Azerbaijan was accused of failing to honour the company's commitment to invest in the distribution network, under an agreement reached with Farhad Aliyev; numerous arrests followed once again, and the state was to reclaim ownership of the two utilities concerned. (A similar course of events occurred in relation to the Netherlands-based operator of Azerbaijan Aluminium.) Furthermore, in July a confession emerged to the murder of the journalist Elmar Husseinov in the previous year (see above), alleging that Farhad Aliyev had requested the task. Some observers felt that all allegations were an elaborate method merely of suppressing a potential rival. Meanwhile, Heydar Babayev, a long-term rival of Farhad Aliyev, was appointed as his successor.

Following the legislative elections held on 6 November 2005, international observers stated that, notwithstanding some improvements, the polls had again failed to meet democratic standards. Opposition parties held several public demonstrations in protest at the conduct of the poll, but these were eventually violently dispersed and further gatherings prohibited. The results from 10 constituencies were annulled, leaving the NAP with 56 mandates, independent candidates (widely accepted also to be loyal to the ruling party) with 43 seats and the Freedom bloc with six seats; the Fatherland (Ana Vatan) Party and Civic Solidarity Party also each received two places. Repeat elections were held in May 2006, in which results were similarly apportioned.

President İlham Aliyev consolidated his power with the further replacement of members of the old guard within the regime. The long-standing Chairman of the legislature was replaced, and another alleged rival of Farhad Aliyev, Col-Gen. Kamaladdin Heydarov, was appointed to the newly created portfolio of Minister of Emergency Situations in February 2006. The long-standing Minister of Labour and Social Security was also dismissed in February, the Minister of Finance was replaced in April, and the First Deputy Prime Minister of the previous 14 years resigned in May, reducing gradually the figures inherited from Heydar Aliyev. A newly created portfolio was that of Defence Industries, further accentuating the emphasis on defence in the country, both in terms of strategic relations with the North Atlantic Treaty Organization (NATO) and the USA, as well as for the purpose of intimidating Armenia, and attempting to support the manufacturing industry. It was observed that many of the new cabinet appointments to posts of significance were derived from members of the energy industry. Perhaps the most noticeable feature of İlham Aliyev's tenure has been the generational shift, whereby the old guard has gradually been replaced by a younger, Baku-based élite. His return to the presidency in the election scheduled for 15 October 2008 was widely considered to be all but certain. If anything, it was expected that the main challenges would emerge after a likely victory, since the second term would be, according to the present Constitution, Aliyev's last in office. The issue of securing his succession (if he decides to relinquish power) prompted a new wave of speculation, including the possibility that he may transfer power to his wife, Mehriban Aliyeva, also a politician.

Meanwhile, opposition parties and allegiances continued to fracture, and one of the first co-operative blocs ever to have been formed, Freedom, faltered over its policy of boycotting legislative functions in response to the perceived fraudulence of the electoral process. Led by Qambar, Müsavat broke away from the Freedom bloc in February 2006, contributing to a further splintering and weakening of the opposition. Oppressive actions against opposition politicians and members of the media continued, with violent attacks and tenuous judicial investigations. Following amendments, adopted in June 2008, to the electoral legislation, which they regarded as benefiting the authorities, the main opposition parties announced a boycott of the presidential election scheduled for 15 October. On that date Aliyev was overwhelmingly re-elected, as had widely been expected, to a further term of office.

FOREIGN RELATIONS

Azerbaijan's foreign policy has historically been defined by its relations with the three regional powers on or close to its borders: Iran, Russia and Turkey. Following the collapse of the USSR, relations with the USA also came to play an important role. Azerbaijan's first post-communist President, Ayaz Mutalibov, was widely regarded as being controlled by the Soviet, and later Russian, authorities, and his successors worked to strengthen the country's independence.

Mutalibov's immediate successor, Abulfaz Elchibey, regarded Turkey as Azerbaijan's chief ally. Elchibey was influenced by pan-Turkic ideology and favoured the cultivation of relations with Turkey, at the expense of relations with Iran and Russia. However, Elchibey's somewhat erratic leadership style meant that although Turkey may initially have offered its support, it was likely to have welcomed his succession by the more pragmatic Heydar Aliyev.

Foreign policy priorities under Heydar Aliyev were generally more balanced than those under his predecessor. İlham Aliyev soon embarked on a series of state visits following his inauguration in 2003, visiting Belgium, France, Georgia, Germany, Greece, Kazakhstan, Poland, Romania, Russia, Turkey, Ukraine and Uzbekistan within his first year in office, reiterating and reinforcing existing co-operation. He also received various senior delegations, and appeared to be universally accepted as the legitimate successor to his father within the international community.

A more conciliatory approach from the Russian side, particularly under the presidency of Vladimir Putin (2000–08), helped to stabilize bilateral relations. In particular, two events removed significant obstacles to the development of friendly Russian-Azerbaijani relations. First, in September 2002 the two sides signed a bilateral agreement on the division of their Caspian petroleum reserves. Second, in October an agreement came into effect, whereby Russia would pay for its continued use of the Qabala radar installation located on Azerbaijani territory. Nevertheless, Russia's continued supply of military assistance to Armenia hindered the cultivation of closer ties. Azerbaijan reacted angrily to the withdrawal of Russian equipment from military bases in Georgia, because that equipment was to be transferred to the Russian base situated in Gyumri, Armenia. İlham Aliyev demonstrated the continuing importance of Azerbaijan's relations with Russia by visiting the Russian capital, Moscow, in February 2004 and signing a set of bilateral agreements referred to as the 'Moscow Declaration'. However, Azerbaijan objected to Russian military exercises held in co-operation with Armenia near the Azerbaijani border in 2004, and Russia's impartiality as a mediator between the two countries was questioned. President Putin visited Azerbaijan in February 2006, with the emphasis of diplomatic relations primarily on economic and energy co-operation. It was alleged that tension was generated between the two countries in 2006 over Azerbaijan's reluctance to endorse or participate in Russia's proposed joint naval force for the Caspian Sea, CasFor, intended to comprise personnel from the five Caspian states. In addition, Azerbaijan reacted to Gazprom's decision to increase the price of natural gas exports to the country by threatening to turn to Turkmenistan for alternative supplies and to reduce oil exports through Russian pipelines. However, Russia's strategy to thwart US-supported efforts to establish alternative export routes resulted in a subsequent softening of its stance towards Azerbaijan and offering of concessionary prices. In early July 2008 a meeting between the new Russian President, Dmitrii Medvedev, and İlham Aliyev in Baku was followed by a declaration of friendship between the two nations; it was announced that Gazprom was to commence discussions on the purchase of large volumes of Azerbaijani gas at market prices. Following the outbreak of conflict in Georgia in early August (see the chapter on Georgia), US Vice-President Dick Cheney visited Azerbaijan as part of a regional tour; amid concern over the security of the BTC and Baku–Tbilisi–Erzurum (Turkey—BTE) pipelines, Cheney announced the US Administration's intention of ensuring the free passage of oil and natural gas from the Caspian Basin. At a regional energy conference, conducted in Baku in early September, the Azerbaijani Minister of Industry and Energy pledged continued support for the US-supported Nabucco natural gas project.

Relations with Turkey remained strong under the administrations of both Heydar and İlham Aliyev, and the construction of the BTC petroleum pipeline and of the BTE gas pipeline (completed in early 2007) were expected to help to further strengthen the relationship between the two countries. In 2005 a new railway project was announced, which would create a 258-km international corridor linking Kars, in north-east Turkey, with Tbilisi (via Akhalkalaki, Georgia) and Baku. This route was to replace a railway route to Turkey, via Armenia, used during the Soviet period, that had fallen into disuse as a result of the closure of the borders of both Azerbaijan and Turkey with Armenia. The effect of such a project could be to transform Azerbaijan into a regional traffic hub; naturally, Armenia held strong objections. Construction of the US $600m. railway line began in late 2007 and was scheduled for completion in 2009. An application was made to the European Commission to include the railway line in its TRACECA transport corridor (linking Europe, the Caucasus and Central Asia), as the route could potentially extend on to Kazakhstan and China.

Heydar Aliyev attempted to improve relations with Iran, which had been seriously undermined during Elchibey's pro-Turkish presidency. Given that the dominant Islamic doctrine in both countries is Shi'a, in addition to their common history and the fact that up to 20m. ethnic Azeris live in Iran, there is a potential for improved relations. However, in reality, these factors have served to contribute to tensions. Iran is wary of the ethnic Azeri population to the north, while Azerbaijan has accused Iran of fomenting unrest among its Shi'ite Muslim community. In particular, the Azerbaijani Government accused Iran of offering support to radical Islamist elements in the village of Nardaran, which became a focus for protests against the Heydar Aliyev regime in 2002–03. However, it was over the issue of the delimitation of the Caspian Sea that relations reached their nadir in July 2001, when Iran sent military patrol boats to threaten Azerbaijani survey vessels operating in the disputed sector of the Sea. Iran claims a 20% territorial share of the Caspian, whereas Azerbaijan, Kazakhstan and Russia, which signed a trilateral agreement on the delimitation of their respective sectors in May 2003, believe that the seabed should be divided into national sectors, corresponding to each country's coastline, according to the so-called median line principle; according to this principle, Iran would be left with less than 14% of the seabed. Relations improved after 2001, with mutual visits by government delegations and the planned construction of a gas pipeline linking the two countries. However, a bilateral agreement on the division of the Caspian Sea remained a remote prospect. In August 2004 President Hojatoleslam Dr Sayed Muhammad Khatami of Iran made the first state visit to Azerbaijan of an Iranian Head of State in a decade, signing 10 bilateral accords and pledging a further increase in energy supplies to Naxçıvan. President İlham Aliyev made a reciprocal visit to Iran in January 2005, signing further agreements and obtaining permission for an Azerbaijani consulate in the city of Tabriz in Iran, previously denied by the authorities. Strategic relations continued with the new regime elected in Iran later that year, amid a policy of the consolidation of allegiances by that country, in the face of increasingly bellicose statements from the USA with regard to the development of Iran's nuclear industry and apparent support for international militant Islamist groups, and the

potential for UN sanctions. (A minor diplomatic incident occurred in March 2006, following a large-scale World Azerbaijani Congress, held in Baku, at which certain nationalist speakers appealed for the unification of 'South Azerbaijan'—meaning an area in the north of Iran—with the rest of Azerbaijan. Objections were lodged by both the Iranian Ministry of Foreign Affairs and the Ambassador.)

The failure to reach agreement over the legal status of the Caspian Sea also posed an obstacle to relations with Turkmenistan, which sought an overarching agreement based on the median line principle, but with modifications that would allow it to lay claim to some of Azerbaijan's oilfields in the middle of the Caspian. Relations improved under Turkmenistan's new President, Gurbanguly Berdymuhamedov; in June 2007 Azerbaijan and Turkmenistan announced a plan to bolster bilateral co-operation, including the proposed joint exploration of a disputed offshore gas field, known as Kyapaz in Azerbaijan and as Serdar in Turkmenistan, building on earlier moves by Azerbaijani officials in 2006 to mend relations with Turkmenistan and to purchase Turkmenistani gas instead of the more expensive Russian supplies. The announcement came two days after President İlham Aliyev and his Turkmenistani counterpart held talks on the sidelines of a CIS summit meeting, during which they agreed to the reopening of the Turkmenistani embassy in Baku, which had been closed since 2001. Relations between the two countries appeared to improve even further in 2008, when closer energy and economic co-operation was announced.

Relations with the USA were complicated by the ambiguity of US policy in the south Caucasus. On the one hand, the US Department of State has tended to follow a pro-Azerbaijan line, in support of US petroleum interests in the Azerbaijani sector of the Caspian Sea, although a strong pro-Armenian lobby exists within the US Congress. The economic sanctions imposed by the USA against Azerbaijan in 1992, under Section 907 of the Freedom Support Act (preventing direct US state aid to Azerbaijan while that country maintained an economic blockade of Armenia), were suspended in early 2002 to facilitate bilateral co-operation in US-led efforts to combat international militant Islamist terrorism, following the suicide attacks on the USA of 11 September 2001. Azerbaijan received praise from the USA for its anti-terrorism efforts. In January 2004 the Government participated in an agreement with the USA on preventing the proliferation of weapons of mass destruction, in support of which it was to receive some US $10m. to strengthen border control measures. (However, in 2003 Azerbaijan announced proposals to ban the presence of foreign military bases on its territory.) Following the cessation of operations at a major airbase in Uzbekistan in 2005, Azerbaijan's role as an air transit route for the supply of Afghanistan also acquired increased significance for the USA. In April 2006 President İlham Aliyev made an official visit to the USA, meeting President George W. Bush.

In September 2004 'Co-operative Best Effort' military exercises, scheduled to take place in Azerbaijan, were cancelled by NATO, when the Government refused to issue visas for five Armenian participants, following national demonstrations of protest. (Azerbaijan had declined to participate in similar exercises the previous year, held in Armenia.) In the same month İlham Aliyev submitted a formal request to the Council of Europe to expel Armenia from its membership on the basis that it was occupying illegally the territory of another country, and made a similar declaration to the UN General Assembly. In November 2006 Azerbaijan formalized an Action Plan agreed with the European Union (EU), with regard to the EU's European Neighbourhood Policy of rapprochement and development, which offered aid, and improved political and trade co-operation, in exchange for political and economic reforms; an agreement on energy co-operation was also signed. At the same time, strains over the human rights situation in the country remained.

In addition to its membership of the Commonwealth of Independent States (CIS), Azerbaijan was a founding member of the GUAM grouping, a loose alliance of former Soviet states (Georgia, Ukraine, Azerbaijan, Moldova), drawn together by a pro-USA and anti-Russian orientation. From its inception in 1997, the grouping struggled to find common ground or achieve any meaningful co-operation. After the election of Putin as Russian President, several factors diminished the significance and viability of GUAM: first, the new, pro-Russian orientation of Moldova and Ukraine; second, the improved relations between the USA and Russia; third, the vacillation of Uzbekistan, which was a member in 1999–2005; and fourth, the fact that Russia has arguably adopted a more pragmatic approach to relations with the former Soviet republics. None the less, GUAM showed signs of renewed activity from 2003, amid reports of US support for the grouping, and in September 2004 it formed its own Parliamentary Assembly. In 2005 it was agreed that an electronic database for the dissemination of information on terrorism and organized crime was to be established in Baku, with US funding. In May 2006 the leaders of the four member states met in Kyiv, Ukraine, and agreed on renaming the body the Organization for Democracy and Economic Development–GUAM, with the intention of establishing a free trade zone between their countries. In September President Viktor Yushchenko of Ukraine further consolidated

relations during his first official visit to Azerbaijan, with the signing of seven bilateral co-operation agreements; he also sought Azerbaijan's assistance in reclaiming the purpose of the under-utilized Odesa–Brody pipeline for the transport of Caspian petroleum to Western Europe (bypassing Russia), rather than its current default usage of transporting Russian petroleum to Black Sea destinations. Azerbaijan's rise in international prominence was highlighted in 2007 by discussions (later abandoned) concerning the possible use of the Azerbaijani radar station in Gabala (about 250 km north-west of Baku), currently leased by Russia. It was expected that İlham Aliyev would continue to balance Azerbaijan's foreign policy conduct, maintaining good relations with both Russia's new President, Dmitrii Medvedev, and the incoming new US Administration in early 2009. Co-operation with the USA was to continue to strengthen in the areas of both energy and security, although Azerbaijan was expected to make efforts to remain uninvolved in the dispute between neighbouring Iran and the USA.

Economy

TOBY WIGHT

Revised for this edition by Dr MATTEO FUMAGALLI

INTRODUCTION

In the early years of independence after 1991 the Azerbaijan Republic was faced with many serious handicaps: a stagnant economy, with a poor infrastructure both in terms of physical assets and weak institutions; a corrupt and ageing leadership, ill-prepared for the difficulties of transition to a post-Soviet economy and society; political instability and anti-Russian riots in 1992, leading to many deaths and a deep hostility towards Russia (which would be damaging to future relations); the continuing bitter dispute with Armenia surrounding the ethnically Armenian enclave within Azerbaijani territory of Nagornyi Karabakh; and widespread social discontent and malaise, exacerbated by the heavy influx of large numbers of refugees displaced by this conflict.

It was not an auspicious beginning to a new chapter in the country's history, and, as elsewhere in the former Soviet Union, for the vast majority of the population conditions quickly deteriorated. Unemployment and poverty spread rapidly as many state-owned enterprises (SOEs) collapsed, and 'hyperinflation' took hold of the economy. Distinguishing Azerbaijan from some of the other former Soviet republics were the country's extensive resources—of petroleum, natural gas, iron ore, non-ferrous minerals, alumina and timber. In addition, the country has fertile land for agriculture, particularly in the temperate southern regions. However, these resources could not be properly exploited to ease the difficult transition period, owing to inadequate investment in the preceding Soviet period, and to continuing political and social instability within the country, which deterred any significant new foreign investment.

In the years following independence, Azerbaijan sought to maximize its political and economic potential. Throughout the 1990s the emphasis in all aspects of government policy was on stability: in politics, in the economy, and in society at large. Given the upheavals of its recent history, and the unresolved conflict with Armenia, this was a necessary and largely successful objective. For the economy, however, this became synonymous with stagnation, with agriculture and the rest of the non-petroleum sector failing to achieve any significant progress, and many sectors declining further.

Latterly, especially since the death in 2003 of Heydar Aliyev—the former communist ruler, who had led the country since independence—the economy, and society as a whole, became somewhat less restricted. Externally, Azerbaijan has a close political and strategic relationship with Turkey, which has stabilized and underpinned its position in an otherwise

difficult and unstable part of the world. It has also enabled Azerbaijan—situated far from its main markets in the west—to exploit more fully its export potential. Domestically, as a result of the development of petroleum and gas resources, economic growth has begun to increase rapidly, with greater prosperity beginning to extend, albeit slowly, beyond the oil sector. Exploitation of petroleum and gas reserves set the direction for the economy for the foreseeable future, generating vast export earnings and government revenues. The country has comparatively little external debt, and thus has relative independence in its utilization of revenues.

More negatively, poverty remains extensive, and almost one-half of the population lives below the national poverty line. Unemployment is high, especially in rural areas, where job opportunities have all but disappeared. Other structural problems remain to be solved, for example in the banking sector, which is weak and underdeveloped. Although high income from petroleum exports brings many benefits, it also brings many problems, notably in terms of a strong exchange rate, which damages the competitiveness of other businesses, as well as a lack of incentive to diversify the economy, generate employment, and distribute the country's wealth.

ECONOMIC POLICY

Structural and economic reform, to enable the transition from a planned to a market economy, has been slow and arduous. For many years after independence, progress was restrained by political instability, the Nagornyi Karabakh conflict, and a lack of commitment and resources. Some progress was made in the privatization of small and medium-sized enterprises (SMEs), land reforms, and other areas, but the development of properly functioning institutions and a stable regulatory environment remained a distant prospect.

From 2004, however, the reform programme accelerated, and further progress was achieved, notably in a new Banking System Law and a new Accounting Law, which provided for the introduction of International Financial Reporting Standards, and various programmes to promote economic development in the regions of Azerbaijan. These included the State Programme on Poverty Reduction and Economic Development and the State Programme on the Socio-Economic Development of the Regions of Azerbaijan for 2004–08.

None the less, other areas remained in need of reform, including the mostly bankrupt SOEs; the development of the non-petroleum sector, and economic diversification in general; the business environment, corporate governance, and transparency; and the weak and underdeveloped banking system. The banking sector has never been able to provide the necessary credit for the growth of new businesses, and, according to the European Bank for Reconstruction and Development (EBRD), weakness in the sector 'represents a significant risk to Azerbaijan's economic prospects in the medium term'.

The creation of an efficient physical infrastructure is also critical to economic development. The transport system, particularly the road network and international corridors, such as the main road linking Russia in the north to Iran in the south, is in urgent need of improvement, as is the infrastructure for power generation, and the system for energy pricing and the collection of revenues. Increased oil revenues have brought a degree of modernization to the country's infrastructure, including the Baku–Tbilisi (Georgia)–Kars (Turkey) rail network, construction of which was inaugurated in late 2007, with completion of the project anticipated by 2010. More remains to be done to improve road links (mostly disrupted by the Nagornyi Karabakh conflict), as well as the telecommunications network, although the mobile sector is rapidly expanding.

The economy remains dominated by the petroleum sector, and the experience of some other oil-rich countries—where reliance on such revenues at the expense of non-oil activities has often been harmful—provides a cautionary example. In 2006 the oil sector provided 93% of all export earnings, 50% of the country's gross domestic product (GDP) and 55% of budget revenue. The performance of the non-oil sector in Azerbaijan has been impressive in recent years, with output increasing strongly and exports also expanding rapidly. In reality, much of this performance has been due to high prices for other commodity exports, and to rapid growth in oil-related activities such as construction, transport, and services. Thus, the economy remains highly vulnerable to any decline in oil prices or eventual downturn in production. With oil output expanding, and likely to continue rapidly to do so over the next few years, the economic outlook may—in the absence of suitable policies to diversify the economy—become more precarious.

Development of activities unrelated to and independent of the petroleum sector is therefore of great importance. Such activities include agriculture and agribusiness (processing and packaging), the production of construction materials, the expansion of telecommunications, small-scale manufacturing, and possibly tourism, centred on the mountainous region in the north of the country. In all these activities, development is most likely to be led by privately owned SMEs. The Government (like most governments) lacks the ability and the resources to lead this type of development, and in any case is still struggling with reforms of its SOEs; foreign investment in these areas, although not insignificant, is deterred by political uncertainties, as well as by the availability of more attractive opportunities in the oil sector.

Unfortunately, however, SMEs are not yet able to meet this challenge. The business environment in which they operate is hampered by excessive bureaucracy, an unreliable legal system, lack of transparency (close but opaque links between businesses, political figures, and banks), and limited access to medium- and long-term finance based on business criteria rather than personal connections.

More positively, the Government's own financial position is relatively strong, supported by a high level of tax revenues from the petroleum sector. However, ineffective financial controls at the old SOEs mean that they are still a major drain on the state budget, although steps are being taken to restrict the budgets of these enterprises and to make them more accountable in their use of public funds. It could also be argued that, as major employers, the SOEs perform a useful social function of retaining labour for which there would be no alternative employment. Until these enterprises are reformed and new employment opportunities are created (another remote prospect), they will continue to be a heavy burden.

Elsewhere, progress has been made in broadening and strengthening the tax base, and in controlling non-state enterprise expenditure. Government debt is low, and thus debt-servicing absorbs relatively little expenditure. The main positive factor has been the rapid increase in petroleum revenues during the 2000s, which has enabled the Government to devote resources to necessary infrastructure projects such as

electricity, water, irrigation and road transport. In the short term, this could result in budgetary deficits being recorded, in contrast to the surpluses recorded in most recent years, but, given the underlying strength of the Government's financial position, this would not in itself present a major problem. Of far greater concern is the limited capacity of the economy to absorb high levels of expenditure (for example, on the shortage of skilled labour and other resources, many of which have to be imported), which is likely to have significant inflationary consequences.

In its monetary and exchange rate policies, the Government has faced the unusual quandary of a high rate of inflation, simultaneously combined with a strong exchange rate for the national currency, the new manat, as the currency was redenominated in January 2006 (the exchange rate being 1 manat = US $0.825 at the end of May 2008). This is potentially very harmful to domestic businesses trying to export to foreign markets, or trying to compete with a flood of relatively cheap imported goods on the home market. For some years the Government tried to restrain the exchange rate, but, given the sustained inflow of export earnings and high levels of foreign investment, this meant heavy intervention in the foreign exchange market. This, in turn, resulted in a rapid increase in money supply, which, combined with higher public spending, led to a high rate of inflation (with a rate of 16.9% recorded in 2007, with inflation of 20.3% forecast for 2008, before an anticipated decline to around 14% in 2009).

Partly to counter this development, the authorities have allowed further appreciation in the exchange rate of the manat, thereby enabling foreign goods to be imported more cheaply. In view of previous weakness in the exchange rate (between 1997 and 2004), the non-petroleum sector should be able to cope with some upward pressure, although its capacity to adjust would be improved by structural reforms (as of the banking system), and a more competitive environment (with less business done on the basis of personal contacts and more on the basis of price and quality). However, inflationary pressure on the exchange rate is likely to remain strong in the near future, and the ability of businesses to cope with this remains to be seen. The combination of inflation and a strong exchange rate was expected to result in a real effective appreciation of the manat of about 35% in 2008–09.

BANKING AND FINANCE

To a large extent, the weakness of the banking sector has been at the centre of the weakness of the economy as a whole for a large part of the post-independence period. The sector is dominated by the state-controlled International Bank of Azerbaijan, which accounts for about 50% of total assets. The rest of the banking system is characterized by a series of negative features, including excess capacity, with about 45 privately owned banks accounting for the remaining 50% of total assets in a relatively small economy. Loan and deposit concentrations are high, and bank liquidity is fairly poor, rendering banks vulnerable to any sudden large-scale withdrawal of deposits. Capitalization is weak, and roughly one-quarter of all banks do not meet the minimum capital requirement of US $5m. Poor lending decisions have resulted in a high level of non-performing loans. Dominance of the sector by one bank, a poor loan portfolio and undercapitalization have led to a lack of confidence in the system as a whole, with potential depositors justifiably afraid of losing their money. Thus, banks are unable to attract deposits except at extremely high rates of interest, which they are then obliged to pass on to borrowers. Typical deposit terms are also short (usually between six and nine months), which further limits the ability of banks to make the medium- and long-term loans that are essential for many enterprises. The banking system, therefore, would benefit from a strong, or at least a stable, exchange rate, since the risk of borrowers with earnings in manats defaulting on US dollar-denominated loans would be correspondingly lower. Since 2007 the National Bank of Azerbaijan has adopted a series of measures aimed at strengthening the banking sector, resulting in the growth of outstanding credit in 2007 (a rise of 98% year on year) and the lengthening of the loan portfolio. At the same time, the low share of household deposits suggests that a large part of the population prefers to keep cash outside banks. Overall, some progress is visible, although this still falls short of a structural reform of the sector.

PETROLEUM AND NATURAL GAS

The principal characteristic of the hydrocarbons sector is a high and rapidly increasing level of output and export earnings. As noted above, this is by no means a wholly beneficial development for the economy, and much will depend on how the authorities exploit these resources and invest the proceeds. However, the prevailing trend is positive, and petroleum and natural gas production will remain the basis for economic development for the foreseeable future.

Petroleum production in Azerbaijan has increased from 315,000 barrels per day (b/d) in 2004 to 870,000 b/d in 2007, and production in 2008 was targeted further to increase, to 1,000,000 b/d. The majority of output comes from the Azeri-Chirag (Çırağ)-Guneshli (Güneşli) or ACG field in the Caspian Sea. Total production is expected to reach 1.2m. b/d by 2010, of which over 80% will be derived from the ACG field. This project is operated by the Azerbaijan International Operating Company (AIOC), a 10-member international consortium led by BP (of the United Kingdom) and in which the State Oil Company of the Azerbaijan Republic (SOCAR—the other major production company in Azerbaijan) also holds a 10% stake. The AIOC accounts for most of the current increase in production from new fields, while the ACG field accounts for the majority of total proven oil reserves, currently estimated at 700m. barrels. Further reserves may be discovered and exploited in future years, but recent exploration efforts have been unsuccessful. Thus, on the basis of production plans at 2006, output from the ACG field will start to decline from 2015, and could be exhausted by around 2024.

Historically, petroleum exports from Azerbaijan have been transported via the Northern Export Route to Novorossiisk on the Russian Black Sea coast, or through Georgia to the Black Sea port of Supsa. In 2005 the 1,768-km Baku–Tbilisi–Ceyhan (BTC) petroleum pipeline, running from Azerbaijan through Georgia and Turkey to Ceyhan, on the Mediterranean coast, was completed, providing the country with a major strategic export outlet, avoiding Russian territory and the increasingly crowded Bosphorus strait. Deliveries through the pipeline commenced in 2006, and greatly increased the country's export capacity as well as reducing its vulnerability to factors outside its control (political differences with Turkey are unlikely given the close relationship between the two countries). Moreover, the BTC pipeline may potentially transport oil from western Kazakhstan (another country in which energy production is increasing substantially), generating additional income from transit fees for Azerbaijan.

Azerbaijan has enormous proven natural gas reserves of 45,130,000m. cu ft, equivalent to 250 years of annual production in the mid-2000s. However, this production is for domestic consumption, in addition to which the country imports substantial quantities. Almost all domestic output is derived from old offshore fields operated by SOCAR, but most future output growth is likely to be drawn from the giant Shah Deniz (Şah Deniz) field being developed by BP and other companies. Once the necessary infrastructure is in place, annual production is expected to increase to around 500,000m. cu ft, which will leave the country self-sufficient, with significant spare production available for export. The new 690-km South Caucasus Gas Pipeline (SCP), following the course of the BTC pipeline to Erzurum in Turkey, has been constructed specifically by the Shah Deniz gas consortium to transport natural gas from that field to the Turkish market.

These two major infrastructure projects (BTC and SCP) have significantly improved the country's economic and strategic position, by enabling a substantial increase in oil and gas exports, reducing dependence on Russia to the north, and strengthening ties with Turkey, its major ally, to the west. Another possible outlet for channelling Azerbaijani (and Turkmenistani) gas from the Caspian is the proposed Nabucco pipeline, which would transport natural gas to Western Europe. This US-supported project has been met with strong opposition from the Russian Government, and some European

countries have already agreed participation in Russia's rival South Stream Project instead.

Future earnings will depend on levels of production, and on international prices for oil and gas, but even under pessimistic assumptions the Government will receive large sums of money. The task of managing these inflows to the maximum benefit of the population as a whole is likely to be difficult. The Long-Term Strategy for the Management of Oil and Gas Revenues, published in 2004, provides for the division of earnings between the State Oil Fund of the Republic of Azerbaijan (SOFAZ—established in 1999, to receive the Government's share of profits from oil and gas development and to provide a home for current oil wealth, to be shared with future generations) and the state budget, and in the immediate future it is expected that current spending, on social and infrastructural needs, will take priority. However, this trend is likely to be modified, as capacity constraints restrict the Government's budget and inflationary pressures accumulate, and a higher proportion of earnings will be retained for investment.

AGRICULTURE

Overall, agriculture (accounting for a 7.5% of GDP in the first half of 2008, according to the London, United Kingdom-based Economist Intelligence Unit—EIU, or 6.2% according to the State Statistical Committee of the Azerbaijan Republic, and expected to decline by as much as one-half in 2009) appears increasingly marginal to Azerbaijan's economy, and contributes only around 8% of export revenue. The agricultural sector is generally unproductive, badly organized, and hampered by poor roads and communications, and by obsolete or non-existent mechanization. It also suffers from the competition provided by cheap imports, a problem exacerbated by the strong exchange rate, and by export subsidies on many imported goods. Imports of cheap food, wheat, and other commodities provide a benefit to the large sections of the population living on very low incomes, but the strong currency has a mixed effect on the development of domestic farming. Imports of fertilizers, machinery and other goods are cheaper than they would be otherwise, but, even so, many farms cannot compete with the low cost of imported goods. The collapse in July 2006 of the World Trade Organization's Doha Development Round (multilateral negotiations on the liberalization of international trade, held in the Qatari capital) was also likely to be harmful to future prospects.

The lack of commercial experience of many enterprises, which have not yet adapted to international business methods, plus the inability to obtain medium- or long-term finance from the banks, and the absence of reliable sources of finance are major handicaps in this sector. Some progress has been made by organizations such as the EBRD and other development institutions, but a great deal of investment is still needed in such areas as training, packaging, marketing and distribution.

INDUSTRY AND CONSTRUCTION

The extractive industry nearly monopolizes the country's industrial output, accounting for 70% of GDP in 2007, according to the EIU, compared with 60% in 2005 and 20% in 1991. (Official data attributed 52.8% of GDP to the sector in 2007, and 39.4% in 2005.) At the same time, the construction sector in Azerbaijan continues to demonstrate strong growth, creating demand for basic construction materials such as concrete, pipes and tubing. Although production is currently almost exclusively for the domestic market, as the sector develops, more opportunities may arise for exports to other rapidly growing countries in the region. The existence of a strong domestic market, in areas such as road-building, oil production, and commercial property development in Baku, will help local companies to acquire the necessary skills and competitiveness to compete in the foreign export market. The construction sector boomed especially in the late 1990s and early 2000s owing to the construction of the main pipelines, but slowed in recent years when these projects were completed.

FOREIGN TRADE AND EXTERNAL FINANCE

Once Azerbaijan began to conduct its own foreign transactions (which were previously combined with those of the rest of the USSR) after independence in 1991, the country consistently experienced an annual deficit on its current account. These deficits were typically very large, averaging 30% of GDP a year over the period 1996–2005. This turned to a small surplus in 2005 (1.3% of GDP), and increased rapidly, to 18% of GDP (US $3,707m.), in 2006, as a result of the long-awaited opening of the BTC pipeline; an even greater surplus of US $24,500m. (54.7% of GDP) was projected for 2008. Imports have consisted largely of high-value capital equipment needed for the exploitation of the country's hydrocarbon resources, but demand has grown at a slower rate than exports, as major projects, for which import of capital goods was necessary, have reached completion. The majority of imports were providing the country with the necessary basis with which to continue its development for the future (unlike imports of consumer goods, which would have no long-term benefit for the economy).

Total export earnings were expected to increase from US $13,000m. in 2006 to about $25,900m. in 2008, reflecting the increase in production of, and the continuing growth of world prices for, oil and gas. Although imports of investment goods required in other areas of the economy, such as transport and construction, will continue, a shortage of foreign exchange with which to pay for these imports is unlikely to be a problem. Azerbaijan's external debt remained modest, owing to the Government's cautious approach to foreign borrowing (8% of GDP, or $2,400m. in 2007). Debt-servicing (principal and interest payments as a proportion of current account earnings) is projected to remain at around, or below, 2% in the short term, a level that should be easily sustainable.

Given recent surpluses on the balance of payments, the National Bank has accumulated a high level of international reserves, estimated at US $4,400m. in June 2008. However, the large majority of hard currency earnings (estimated to total some $2,480m. at the end of 2007) are kept in SOFAZ.

OUTLOOK AND CONCLUSIONS

The prospects for Azerbaijan appear promising: oil production and exports have generated strong economic growth, which, in 2006 and 2007, was among the strongest in the world (34.5% and 25.7%, respectively). Although forecast to decelerate in 2008 and 2009 (to 17.0% and 10.5%, respectively), growth will remain strong. Impetus has been provided by new energy export routes, most notably the BTC pipeline. The two main challenges will be to maintain macroeconomic stability and to ensure that benefits from increased oil revenue are redistributed to the wider population, beyond the narrow élite circles.

In the campaign for the presidential election scheduled for October 2008, the Government has begun spending larger amounts of oil and gas revenues on health-care, wages, education, and infrastructure. Serious problems remain, and could pose a threat to sustained development. Structural reforms, particularly in business and in banking, are urgently needed if the non-oil sector of the economy is to receive the support and resources necessary for expansion and is, eventually, to reduce dependence on exports of oil and gas.

Economic diversification and employment creation through the growth of SMEs, particularly in rural areas, also remain urgent priorities. The creation of sustainable employment will be crucial to tackling the country's widespread poverty. The investment climate has to be improved significantly, and the often arbitrary laws and regulations need to be restructured and enforced, if private sector investment is to be adequate and well-directed. If these problems can be effectively addressed, and if regional political harmony, as well as the price and production levels of petroleum, can be maintained, the underlying outlook for Azerbaijan should remain highly favourable.

Statistical Survey

Source (unless otherwise stated): State Statistical Committee of the Azerbaijan Republic, 1136 Baku, İnşaatçılar pr.; tel. (12) 438-64-98; fax (12) 438-24-42; e-mail sc@azstat.org; internet www.azstat.org.

Area and Population

AREA, POPULATION AND DENSITY

Area (sq km)	86,600*
Population (census results)†	
12 January 1989	7,021,178
27 January 1999	
Males	3,883,155
Females	4,070,283
Total	7,953,438
Population (official estimates at 1 January)	
2005	8,347,300
2006	8,436,400
2007	8,532,700
Density (per sq km) at 1 January 2007	98.5

* 33,400 sq miles.

† Figures refer to *de jure* population. The *de facto* total at the 1989 census was 7,037,867.

ETHNIC GROUPS
(permanent inhabitants, 1999 census)

	Number ('000)	%
Azeri	7,205.5	90.6
Lazs (Lezghi)	178.0	2.2
Russian	141.7	1.8
Armenian	120.7	1.5
Talish	76.8	1.0
Others	230.7	2.9
Total	**7,953.4**	**100.0**

AUTONOMOUS REPUBLIC
(estimated population at 1 January 2007)

	Area (sq km)	Population	Population density (per sq km)
Naxçıvan	5,500	379,500	69.0

PRINCIPAL TOWNS
(estimated population at 1 January 2007)

Bakı (Baku, the capital) . . .	1,893,300	Naxçıvan . . .	70,400
Ganca*	307,500	Yevlakh . . .	54,700
		Xankandi	
Sumqayıt . . .	268,800	(Stepanakert) .	53,000
Mingəçevir . . .	95,500	Lankaran . . .	48,500
Şirvan†	69,600	Ağdam	39,500

* Known as Kirovabad between 1935 and 1989.
† Known as Ali-Bayramlı between 1938 and 2008.

BIRTHS, MARRIAGES AND DEATHS

	Registered live births		Registered marriages		Registered deaths	
	Number	Rate (per 1,000)	Number	Rate (per 1,000)	Number	Rate (per 1,000)
1999	117,539	14.9	37,382	4.8	46,295	5.9
2000	116,994	14.8	39,611	5.0	46,701	5.9
2001	110,356	13.8	41,861	5.2	45,284	5.7
2002	110,715	13.8	41,661	5.2	46,522	5.8
2003	113,467	14.0	56,091	6.9	49,001	6.0
2004	131,609	16.1	62,177	7.6	49,568	6.1
2005	141,901	17.2	71,643	8.7	51,962	6.3
2006	148,946	17.8	79,443	9.5	52,248	6.2

Expectation of life (years at birth, WHO estimates): 64 (males 62; females 66) in 2006 (Source: WHO, *World Health Statistics*).

ECONOMICALLY ACTIVE POPULATION
(ISIC major divisions, annual average, '000 persons)

	2004	2005	2006
Agriculture, hunting and forestry	1,502.7	1,510.0	1,548.0
Fishing	3.3	3.8	4.3
Mining and quarrying	41.9	42.2	45.0
Manufacturing	181.2	188.7	195.0
Electricity, gas and water supply	39.8	39.7	40.2
Construction	190.6	194.4	222.8
Wholesale and retail trade; repair of motor vehicles, motorcycles and household goods . . .	630.7	638.8	650.4
Hotels and restaurants . .	12.4	14.2	22.0
Transport, storage and communications	190.5	191.5	201.8
Financial intermediation . . .	13.1	13.2	13.4
Real estate, renting and business activities	100.0	100.6	106.7
Public administration and defence; compulsory social security . .	269.7	270.5	271.2
Education	330.8	335.3	339.4
Health and social work . .	174.6	177.2	180.5
Other community, social and personal service activities . .	127.3	129.5	131.7
Extra-territorial organizations and bodies	0.5	0.6	0.6
Total employed	3,809.1	3,850.2	3,973.0*
Unemployed	55.9	56.3	53.9
Total labour force	3,865.0	3,906.5	4,026.9

* Of which number males accounted for 2,054.1, and females 1,918.9.

2007 (working–age population, '000): Agriculture 1,556; Industry 284; Government 273; Total (incl. others) 4,014; Unemployed 281; Total labour force 4,295 (Source: IMF, *Republic of Azerbaijan: Statistical Appendix—July 2008*).

Health and Welfare

KEY INDICATORS

Total fertility rate (children per woman, 2006) . . .	1.7
Under-five mortality rate (per 1,000 live births, 2006) . .	89
HIV (% of persons aged 15–49, 2005)	0.10
Physicians (per 1,000 head, 2006)	3.6
Hospital beds (per 1,000 head, 2006)	8.1
Health expenditure (2005): US $ per head (PPP)	193
Health expenditure (2005): % of GDP	3.9
Health expenditure (2005): public (% of total)	24.8
Access to water (% of persons, 2004)	77
Access to sanitation (% of persons, 2004)	54
Human Development Index (2005): ranking	98
Human Development Index (2005): value	0.746

For sources and definitions, see explanatory note on p. vi.

Agriculture

PRINCIPAL CROPS
('000 metric tons)

	2004	2005	2006
Wheat	1,573.0	1,527.0	1,460.3
Rice (paddy)	10.2	8.3	5.1
Barley	349.9	368.9	399.7
Maize	152.9	151.4	145.9
Potatoes	930.4	1,083.1	999.3
Sugar beet	56.8	36.6	167.2
Hazelnuts	5.5	28.0	24.6
Cottonseed	83.4	120.7	80.0
Cabbages and other brassicas	92.4	96.9	100.2
Tomatoes	425.0	437.7	442.0
Cucumbers and gherkins . . .	151.1	159.8	171.3
Dry onions	163.4	177.4	184.2
Garlic	19.9	21.1	23.9
Watermelons*	355.3	363.8	362.1
Oranges	19.2	19.3	19.5
Apples	137.3	163.1	178.4
Pears	27.2	41.5	31.9
Apricots	6.8	16.2	18.7
Peaches and nectarines . .	6.7	16.0	16.8
Plums	14.7	21.5	18.9
Grapes	54.9	79.7	94.1
Tobacco (leaves)	6.5	7.1	4.8
Cotton (lint)	52.1	75.9	50.0

* Including melons, pumpkins and squash.

Aggregate production ('000 metric tons, may include official, semi-official or estimated data): Total cereals 2,086.6 in 2004, 2,056.2 in 2005, 2,011.6 in 2006; Total nuts 13.9 in 2004, 45.5 in 2005, 40.6 in 2006; Total pulses 26.9 in 2004, 29.3 in 2005, 28.9 in 2006; Total roots and tubers 930.4 in 2004, 1,083.1 in 2005, 999.3 in 2006; Total vegetables (incl. melons) 1,400.1 in 2004, 1,456.9 in 2005, 1,584.2 in 2006; Total fruits (excl. melons) 478.2 in 2004, 704.3 in 2005, 753.4 in 2006.

Source: FAO.

LIVESTOCK
('000 head, year ending September)

	2004	2005	2006
Horses	71	69	70
Asses, mules or hinnies . . .	45	46	46
Cattle	2,007	2,077	2,148
Buffaloes	309	303	299
Pigs	23	23	21
Sheep	6,887	7,105	7,304
Goats	601	593	578
Chickens	16,928*	17,553*	18,276†
Turkeys	617*	700*	760

* Unofficial figure.
† FAO estimate.

Source: FAO.

LIVESTOCK PRODUCTS
('000 metric tons)

	2004	2005	2006
Cattle meat	69.1	71.5	75.6
Sheep meat	40.7	41.9	43.6
Pig meat	1.6	1.6	1.6
Chicken meat	32.3	34.7	35.0
Cows' milk	1,188.6	1,226.1	1,272.7
Hen eggs	46.4	49.0	45.7
Wool: greasy	12.3	13.1	13.6

Source: FAO.

Forestry

ROUNDWOOD REMOVALS
('000 cubic metres, excl. bark)*

	1998	1999	2000
Sawlogs, veneer logs and logs for sleepers	3,200	3,200	3,500
Pulpwood	3,200	3,200	3,500
Other industrial wood	—	—	100
Fuel wood	6,200	6,200	6,400
Total	12,600	12,600	13,500

* Unofficial figure(s).

2001–06: Production as in 2000 (FAO estimates).

Source: FAO.

Fishing

(metric tons, live weight)

	2004	2005	2006
Capture	9,258	9,001	3,983
Azov sea sprat	8,897	8,637	3,667
Aquaculture	184	114	110
Total catch	9,442	9,115	4,093

Source: FAO.

Mining

	2005	2006	2007*
Crude petroleum (million metric tons)	22.2	32.3	41.6
Natural gas ('000 million cu metres)	5.7	6.1	11.0

* Preliminary figures.

Source: IMF, *Republic of Azerbaijan: Statistical Appendix* (July 2008).

Industry

SELECTED PRODUCTS
('000 metric tons, unless otherwise indicated)

	2000	2001	2002
Wheat flour	234	370	251
Wine ('000 hectolitres)	77	76	73
Beer ('000 hectolitres) . . .	71	116	125
Mineral water ('000 hectolitres)	21	30	56
Soft drinks ('000 hectolitres) . .	478	442	564
Cigarettes	2,362	6,808	6,296
Cotton yarn—pure and mixed (metric tons)	700	2,000	1,300
Woven cotton fabrics ('000 metres)	1,000	3,000	3,000
Footwear, excluding rubber ('000 pairs)	122	220	339
Cement	251	523	848
Sulphuric acid	52	10	19
Caustic soda (Sodium hydroxide)	30	27	25
Bricks (million)	10	12	24
Electric energy (million kWh)	18,699	18,969	19,543
Jet fuels	580	543	507
Motor spirit (petrol)	357	598	610
Kerosene	175	81	143
Gas-diesel (distillate fuel) oil . .	1,957	1,562	1,593
Lubricants	229	34	21
Residual fuel oil (Mazout) . . .	4,072	2,648	2,569

Source: mostly UN, *Industrial Commodity Statistics Yearbook*.

2004 ('000 metric tons, unless otherwise indicated): Cement 1,427.5; Motor spirit (petrol) 852.4; Kerosene 646.8; Gas-diesel (distillate fuel) oil 1,789.1; Residual fuel oil (Mazout) 2,520.8; Finished cotton fabrics ('000 sq m) 4,038; Electric energy ('000 million kWh) 21.7.

2005 ('000 metric tons, unless otherwise indicated): Cement 1,537.9; Motor spirit (petrol) 906.2; Kerosene 747.1; Gas-diesel (distillate fuel) oil 2,101.1; Residual fuel oil (Mazout) 3,060.7; Finished cotton fabrics ('000 sq m) 3,099.0; Electric energy ('000 million kWh) 22.9.

2006 ('000 metric tons, unless otherwise indicated): Cement 1,604.5; Motor spirit (petrol) 1,042.3; Kerosene 737.2; Gas-diesel (distillate fuel) oil 2,095.1; Residual fuel oil (Mazout) 2,825.4; Finished cotton fabrics ('000 sq m) 3,083.0; Electric energy ('000 million kWh) 24.0.

Finance

CURRENCY AND EXCHANGE RATES

Monetary Units
100 gopik = 1 new Azerbaijani manat.

Sterling, Dollar and Euro Equivalents (30 May 2008)
£1 sterling = 1.628 new manats;
US $1 = 0.825 new manats;
€1 = 1.279 new manats;
10 new manats = £6.14 = $12.12 = €7.82.

Average Exchange Rate (Azerbaijani manats per US $)
2005   0.9454
2006   0.8934
2007   0.8581

Note: The Azerbaijani manat was introduced in August 1992, initially to circulate alongside the Russian (formerly Soviet) rouble, with an exchange rate of 1 manat = 10 roubles. In December 1993 Azerbaijan left the rouble zone, and the manat became the country's sole currency. The manat was redenominated from 1 January 2006, with 1 new unit of currency (new manat) equivalent to 5,000 of the old currency. Figures in this survey are given in terms of the new manat, where possible.

STATE BUDGET
(million new manats)

Revenue	2005	2006	2007*
Tax revenue	1,902	3,341	5,634
Value-added tax	600	738	1,179
Excises	141	187	403
Taxes on profits	355	1,361	2,458
Taxes on income . . .	317	407	589
Taxes on international trade	205	239	287
Social security contributions .	198	294	551
Other	85	115	167
Non-tax revenue	938	1,499	2,152
Tax credits for energy subsidies .	292	408	163
Total	3,132	5,248	7,949

Expenditure	2005	2006	2007*
Current expenditure . . .	2,281	3,442	4,595
Wages and salaries . . .	580	745	1,086
Goods and services . . .	716	1,285	1,854
Transfers to households . .	640	884	1,297
Subsidies	28	41	161
Oil fund operating expenditures	2	1	4
Other purposes	7	66	0
Energy-related subsidies . .	292	408	163
Interest	16	13	30
Investment expenditure and net lending	558	1,693	2,761
Total	2,839	5,135	7,356

Outlays by functions of government†	2005	2006	2007*
General public services . . .	168	403	469
Defence	288	641	811
Public order and safety . . .	206	279	431
Agriculture	96	132	248
Housing and community amenities	40	61	92
Health	115	162	257
Recreation, culture and religion .	51	67	95
Education	373	479	723
Social protection	305	341	595
Public works, transport and communications	260	966	2,000
Other economic services and expenditures	171	193	256
Total	2,073	3,724	5,976

* Preliminary figures.
† Including net acquisition of non-financial assets.

Source: IMF, *Republic of Azerbaijan: Statistical Appendix (July 2008)*.

INTERNATIONAL RESERVES
(US $ million at 31 December)

	2005	2006	2007
IMF special drawing rights . .	13.91	15.43	10.13
Reserve position in IMF . .	0.01	0.02	0.08
Foreign exchange	1,163.82	2,484.93	4,262.91
Total	1,177.74	2,500.38	4,273.12

Source: IMF, *International Financial Statistics*.

MONEY SUPPLY
(million new manats at 31 December)

	2005	2006	2007
Currency outside banks . .	547.44	1,311.35	2,713.51
Demand deposits at commercial banks	202.80	527.84	907.85
Total money (incl. others) . .	750.24	1,839.57	3,621.71

Source: IMF, *International Financial Statistics*.

COST OF LIVING
(Consumer Price Index; base: 2000 = 100)

	2004	2005	2006
Food (incl. tobacco)	120.9	134.1	150.2
Fuel	109.6	243.4	212.3
Clothing	110.0	108.5	122.9
All items (incl. others) . . .	113.9	124.7	134.9

2007: Food (incl. tobacco) 174.6; All items (incl. others) 157.7.

Source: ILO.

NATIONAL ACCOUNTS
(million new manats at current prices)

Expenditure on the Gross Domestic Product

	2005	2006	2007*
Government final consumption expenditure	1,305	2,306	3,714
Private final consumption expenditure	5,277	6,138	7,442
Changes in stocks	27	30	−30
Gross fixed capital formation .	5,173	5,568	5,523
Total domestic expenditure .	11,782	14,042	16,649
Exports of goods and services .	7,877	12,489	19,296
Less Imports of goods and services	6,621	7,279	8,060
Statistical discrepancy . . .	−516	−505	−1,000
GDP in purchasers' values .	12,523	18,746	26,884

* Preliminary figures.

Gross Domestic Product by Economic Activity

	2005	2006	2007*
Agriculture and fishing . . .	1,146	1,329	1,565
Extractive industries . . .	5,284	9,534	15,014
Oil and gas extraction . . .	5,278	9,526	15,000
Processing	813	1,082	1,348
Oil and gas processing . .	243	566	753
Electricity, gas and water . .	94	116	221
Construction	1,172	1,446	1,802
Transport and communications .	933	1,243	1,526
Trade	832	1,107	1,485
Social services	1,305	1,866	2,085
GDP at factor cost . . .	11,576	17,722	25,044
Indirect taxes *less* subsidies . .	946	1,025	1,840
GDP in purchasers' values .	12,523	18,746	26,884

* Preliminary figures.

Source: IMF, *Republic of Azerbaijan: Statistical Appendix* (July 2008).

BALANCE OF PAYMENTS
(US $ million)

	2005	2006	2007
Exports of goods f.o.b.	7,649.0	13,014.6	21,269.3
Imports of goods f.o.b.	−4,349.9	−5,269.3	−6,045.0
Trade balance	3,299.1	7,745.3	15,224.3
Exports of services	683.0	939.9	1,247.5
Imports of services	−2,653.0	−2,863.2	−3,378.6
Balance on goods and services	1,329.1	5,821.9	13,093.3
Other income received	201.8	280.0	327.8
Other income paid	−1,847.4	−2,960.6	−5,407.2
Balance on goods, services and income	−316.6	3,141.3	8,013.9
Current transfers received . .	626.2	748.2	1,313.4
Current transfers paid	−142.3	−182.0	−308.4

—continued	2005	2006	2007
Current balance	167.3	3,707.6	9,018.9
Capital account (net) . . .	40.9	−3.8	−2.8
Direct investment abroad . .	−1,220.8	−705.5	−285.6
Direct investment from abroad	1,679.9	−584.0	−4,748.9
Portfolio investment assets . .	−47.8	−34.4	−110.9
Portfolio investment liabilities .	78.3	22.3	84.5
Other investment assets . .	−1,365.3	−1,416.7	−2,687.8
Other investment liabilities . .	953.7	612.9	874.6
Net errors and omissions . .	−125.7	−255.9	−360.7
Overall balance	160.5	1,342.6	1,781.3

Source: IMF, *International Financial Statistics*.

External Trade

PRINCIPAL COMMODITIES
(US $ million)

Imports c.i.f.	2004	2005	2006
Vegetable products . . .	232.0	171.9	201.7
Prepared foodstuffs, beverages, spirits and vinegar; tobacco and manufactured substitutes . .	113.8	194.5	273.2
Mineral products	507.1	641.0	779.8
Products of chemical or allied industries	132.9	183.8	249.2
Base metals and articles thereof	611.2	489.3	615.6
Machinery and mechanical appliances; electrical equipment; sound and television apparatus	1,084.6	1,402.9	1,547.3
Vehicles, aircraft, vessels and associated transportation equipment	242.0	420.9	877.8
Miscellaneous manufactured articles	151.5	163.6	86.7*
Total (incl. others)	3,515.9	4,211.2	5,267.6

Exports f.o.b.	2004	2005	2006
Vegetable products	n.a.	193.6	156.3
Mineral products	2,973.8	3,338.6	5,392.7
Products of the chemical industry	n.a.	131.8	193.0
Vehicles, aircraft, vessels and associated transportation equipment	144.0	272.3	84.8*
Total (incl. others)	3,615.5	4,347.2	6,372.2

*Excluding railway or tramway rolling stock, ships and air-transport facilities.

PRINCIPAL TRADING PARTNERS
(US $ million)

Imports c.i.f.	2004	2005	2006
China, People's Repub. . . .	145.5	173.8	222.5
France	120.1	121.8	55.8
Georgia	14.5	45.5	49.2
Germany	198.5	256.3	403.8
India	47.0	55.9	57.4
Iran	45.3	76.3	85.9
Italy	106.7	94.6	124.6
Japan	127.1	70.6	188.2
Kazakhstan	236.7	95.3	127.3
Netherlands	152.7	160.4	90.9
Russia	569.4	717.2	1,181.6
Singapore	8.9	384.9	6.2
Sweden	66.6	72.4	84.4
Turkey	225.0	313.0	385.0
Turkmenistan	114.4	242.9	369.0
Ukraine	170.4	226.3	317.5
United Kingdom	421.8	385.0	453.8
USA	131.9	151.3	197.9
Uzbekistan	79.7	99.8	27.5
Total (incl. others)	3,515.9	4,211.2	5,267.6

Exports f.o.b.	2004	2005	2006
Bulgaria	49.3	100.9	6.3
China, People's Repub. . .	31.7	99.2	6.4
Croatia	109.2	176.9	3.6
France	66.9	406.7	347.5
Georgia	188.9	208.4	285.3
Germany	37.6	34.8	9.0
Greece	20.2	95.7	182.0
Iran	153.5	166.5	295.9
Israel	323.7	195.1	684.8
Italy	1,614.9	1,315.7	2,845.4
Romania	82.3	119.1	80.1
Russia	209.8	285.4	344.3
Singapore	2.8	123.1	34.0
Spain	5.6	76.0	52.8
Tajikistan	46.5	78.9	130.9
Turkey	182.6	276.0	388.1
Turkmenistan . . .	143.4	273.6	9.5
USA	26.0	43.2	91.9
Total (incl. others)	3,615.5	4,347.2	6,372.2

Transport

RAILWAYS

	2004	2005	2006
Passengers carried ('000) . .	5,241	5,492	5,816
Passenger-km (million) . . .	789	878	959
Freight carried (million metric tons)	20.7	26.2	29.7
Freight ton-km (million) . . .	7,536	9,628	10,910

ROAD TRAFFIC
(vehicles in use at 31 December)

	2004	2005	2006
Passenger cars	438,964	479,447	548,979
Buses	20,991	26,735	27,474
Lorries and vans	80,918	90,852	97,395
Motorcycles and mopeds . .	4,993	3,562	3,408

SHIPPING
Merchant Fleet
(registered at 31 December)

	2005	2006	2007
Number of vessels	295	300	302
Total displacement ('000 grt) . .	672.8	692.9	708.4

Source: Lloyd's Register-Fairplay, *World Fleet Statistics*.

International Sea-borne Freight Traffic
('000 metric tons)

	1997	1998	1999
Goods loaded	7,128	7,812	7,176

Source: UN, *Monthly Bulletin of Statistics*.

Sea-borne imports ('000 metric tons): 5,118 in 2000; 7,029 in 2001; 7,853.4 in 2002.

Sea-borne exports ('000 metric tons): 703 in 2000; 996.3 in 2001; 1,057.3 in 2002.

CIVIL AVIATION
(traffic on scheduled services)

	2004	2005	2006
Passengers carried ('000) . . .	1,094	1,211	1,336
Passenger-km (million) . . .	1,450	1,588	1,686
Total ton-km (million)	315	310	290

Tourism

FOREIGN TOURIST ARRIVALS

Country of residence	2004	2005	2006
Georgia	405,500	396,391	386,180
Iran	270,657	207,105	161,504
Russia	496,050	387,368	460,801
Turkey	71,609	70,755	69,974
Total (incl. others)	1,348,655	1,177,277	1,193,742

Tourism receipts (incl. passenger transport, US $ million): 70 in 2003; 79 in 2004; 100 in 2005.

Source: World Tourism Organization.

Communications Media

	2004	2005	2006
Telephones ('000 main lines in use)	1,013.4	1,094.2	1,188.7
Mobile cellular telephones ('000 subscribers)	1,456.5	2,242.0	3,323.5
Personal computers ('000 in use) .	149	195	n.a.
Internet users ('000)	408	679	829
Broadband subscribers . . .	900	2,200	2,200

1999: Daily newspapers (number) 15; Daily newspapers (circulation) 80,000; Non-daily newspapers (number) 329; Non-daily newspapers (circulation) 122,000.

2000: Television receivers ('000 in use) 2,000; Book production (titles, incl. pamphlets) 400.

2005: Facsimile machines (number of units) 5,237; Newspapers and magazines sent by post 17.3m.

Sources: UN, *Statistical Yearbook*, UNESCO, *Statistical Yearbook*, and International Telecommunication Union.

Education

(2006/07, unless otherwise indicated)

	Institutions	Teachers	Students
Pre-primary*	1,758	10,947	109,925
General (primary and secondary) .	4,538	177,738	1,537,273
Specialized secondary education institutions	60	7,049	56,872
Higher	42	14,358	129,141

* Figures for state institutions only, 2004/05.

Adult literacy rate (UNESCO estimates): 99.4% (males 99.7%; females 99.1%) in 2007 (Source: UNESCO Institute for Statistics).

Directory

The Constitution

A new Constitution was endorsed by 91.9% of the registered electorate in a national referendum, held on 12 November 1995. The following is a summary of the Constitution's main provisions, including amendments to the status of Naxçıvan approved by the Milli Majlis (National Assembly) in December 1998.

GENERAL PROVISIONS

The Azerbaijan Republic is a democratic, secular and unitary state. State power is vested in the people, who implement their sovereign right through referendums and their directly elected representatives. No individual or organization has the right to usurp the power of the people. State power is exercised on the principle of the division of powers between the legislature, the executive and the judiciary. The supreme aim of the state is to ensure human and civil rights and freedoms. The territory of the Azerbaijan Republic is inviolable and indivisible. Azerbaijan conducts its foreign policy on the basis of universally accepted international law. The state is committed to a market economic system and to freedom of entrepreneurial activity. Three types of ownership—state, private and municipal—are recognized; natural resources belong to the Azerbaijan Republic. The state promotes the development of art, culture, education, medical care and science, and defends historical, material and spiritual values. All religions are equal by law; the spread of religions that contradict the principles of humanity is prohibited. The state language is Azerbaijani, although the republic guarantees the free use of other languages. The capital is Baku (Bakı).

MAJOR RIGHTS, FREEDOMS AND RESPONSIBILITIES

Every citizen has inviolable, undeniable and inalienable rights and freedoms. Every person is equal before the law and the courts, regardless of sex, race, nationality, religion, origin, property and other status, and political or other convictions. Every person has the right to life. Any person charged with a penal offence is considered innocent until proven guilty. Every person has the right to freedom of thought, speech, conscience and religion. Everyone has the right to protect their national and ethnic affiliation. No one is to be subject to torture or the degradation of human dignity. The mass media are free, and censorship is prohibited. Every person has the right to freedom of movement and residence within the republic, and the right to leave the republic. The right to assemble publicly is guaranteed, and every person has the right to establish a political party, trade union or other organization; the activity of unions that seek to overthrow state power is prohibited. Citizens of the Azerbaijan Republic have the right to participate in the political life of society and the state, and the right to elect and to be elected to government bodies, and to participate in referendums. Every person has the right to health protection and medical aid, and the right to social security in old age, sickness, disability, unemployment, etc. The state guarantees the right to free secondary education.

THE LEGISLATURE

The supreme legislative body is the 125-member Milli Majlis. Deputies are elected by universal, equal, free, direct suffrage, and by secret ballot, for a five-year term. Any citizen who has reached the age of 25 years is eligible for election, with the exception of those possessing dual citizenship, those performing state service, and those otherwise engaged in paid work, unless employed in the creative, scientific and education sectors. The instigation of criminal proceedings against a deputy, and his or her detention or arrest, are only permitted on the decision of the Milli Majlis, on the basis of a recommendation by the Prosecutor-General. The Milli Majlis adopts legislation, constitutional laws and resolutions; ratifies or denunciates treaties, agreements and conventions; ratifies the state budget; gives consent to declare war, on the recommendation of the President of the Republic; confirms administrative and territorial divisions; and declares amnesties. Upon the nomination of the President, the Milli Majlis is authorized to approve the appointment of the Prime Minister and the Prosecutor-General; appoint and dismiss members of the Constitutional Court and Supreme Court; and appoint and dismiss the Chairperson of the National Bank. It also has the power to express a vote of no confidence in the Government; to call a referendum; to initiate impeachment proceedings against the President, on the recommendation of the Constitutional Court; and to introduce draft legislation and other issues for parliamentary discussion.

EXECUTIVE POWER

The President, who is directly elected for a term of five years, is Head of State and Commander-in-Chief of the Armed Forces. Executive power is held by the President, who acts as guarantor of the independence and territorial integrity of the republic. Any university graduate aged 35 years or over, who has the right to vote, has been a resident of the republic for the preceding 10 years, has never been tried for a major crime, and who is exclusively a citizen of the Azerbaijan Republic is eligible for election to the office of President. The President appoints and dismisses the Cabinet of Ministers, headed by the Prime Minister, which is the highest executive body.

The President calls legislative elections; concludes international treaties and agreements, and submits them to the Milli Majlis for ratification; signs laws or returns draft legislation to the Milli Majlis for reconsideration; proposes candidates for the Constitutional Court, the Supreme Court and the Economic Court, and nominates the Prosecutor-General and the Chairman of the National Bank; appoints and recalls diplomatic representatives of Azerbaijan to foreign countries and international organizations, and receives the credentials of diplomatic representatives; may declare a state of emergency or martial law; and grants titles of honour.

The President enjoys immunity from prosecution during his or her period in office. In the event that the President commits a grave crime, he may be removed from office on the recommendation of the Supreme Court and the Constitutional Court, and with the approval of the Milli Majlis.

THE JUDICIARY

Judicial power is implemented only by the courts. Judges are independent and are subordinate only to the Constitution and the law; they are immune from prosecution. Trials are held in public, except in specialized circumstances.

The Constitutional Court is composed of nine members, appointed by the Milli Majlis on the recommendation of the President. It determines, among other things, whether presidential decrees, resolutions of the Milli Majlis and of the Cabinet of Ministers, laws of the Naxçıvan Autonomous Republic, and international treaties correspond to the Constitution; and decides on the prohibition of the activities of political parties. The Supreme Court is the highest judicial body in administrative, civil and criminal cases; the Economic Court is the highest legal body in considering economic disputes.

THE NAXÇIVAN AUTONOMOUS REPUBLIC

The Naxçıvan Autonomous Republic forms an autonomous state that is an inalienable part of the Azerbaijan Republic. It has its own Constitution, which must not contravene the Constitution and laws of Azerbaijan. Legislative power in Naxçıvan is vested in the 45-member Ali Majlis (Supreme Assembly), which serves a five-year term, and executive power is vested in the Cabinet of Ministers. The Ali Majlis elects a Chairman from among its members, as the highest official in the Naxçıvan Autonomous Republic. The Ali Majlis is responsible for the budget; the approval of economic and social programmes; and the approval of the Cabinet of Ministers. The Ali Majlis may dismiss its Chairman and express no confidence in the Cabinet of Ministers. Justice is administered by the courts of the Naxçıvan Autonomous Republic.

LOCAL SELF-GOVERNMENT

Local government in rural areas and towns, villages, and settlements is exercised by elected municipalities.

RIGHTS AND LAW

The Constitution has supreme legal force. Amendments and additions may only be introduced following a referendum.

The Government

HEAD OF STATE

President: İLHAM HEYDAR OĞLU ALIYEV (inaugurated 31 October 2003).

CABINET OF MINISTERS
(September 2008)

Prime Minister: ARTUR TAHIR OĞLU RASIZADE.

First Deputy Prime Minister: YAGUB ABDULLA OĞLU AYYUBOV.

Deputy Prime Minister: ELCHIN ILYAS OĞLU EFENDIYEV.

Deputy Prime Minister: ABID QOCA OĞLU SHARIFOV.

Deputy Prime Minister: ALI SAMIL OĞLU HASANOV.

Minister of Public Health: OGTAY KAZIM OĞLU SHIRALIYEV.

Minister of Foreign Affairs: ELMAR MAHARRAM OĞLU MAMMEDYAROV.

Minister of Agriculture: ISMET DURSUN OĞLU ABBASOV.

Minister of Internal Affairs: Col RAMIL IDRIS OĞLU USUBOV.

Minister of Culture and Tourism: ABULFAZ MURSAL OĞLU KARAYEV.

Minister of Education: MISIR CUMAYIL OĞLU MARDANOV.

Minister of Communications and Information Technology: ALI MAMMAD OĞLU ABBASOV.

Minister of Finance: SAMIR RAUF OĞLU SHARIFOV.

Minister of Justice: FIKRET FARRUKH OĞLU MAMMADOV.

Minister of Labour and Social Protection: FIZULI HASAN OĞLU ALEKPEROV.

Minister of National Security: Lt-Gen. ELDAR AKHMED OĞLU MAKHMUDOV.

Minister of Defence: Col-Gen. SAFAR AKHUNDBALA OĞLU ABIYEV.

Minister of Defence Industries: YAVAR TALIB OĞLU JAMALOV.

Minister of Emergency Situations: Col-Gen. KAMALADDIN FATTAH OĞLU HEYDAROV.

Minister of Industry and Energy: NATIQ AĞA AMI OĞLU ALIYEV.

Minister of Taxation: FAZIL ASAD OĞLU MAMMADOV.

Minister of Youth and Sport: AZAD ARIF OĞLU RAHIMOV.

Minister of Economic Development: HEYDAR AYDIN OĞLU BABAYEV.

Minister of Ecology and Natural Resources: HUSSEIN SEYID OĞLU BAGHIROV.

Minister of Transport: ZIYA ARZUMAN OĞLU MAMMADOV.

MINISTRIES

Office of the President: 1066 Baku, İstiklal küç. 19; tel. (12) 492-17-26; fax (12) 492-35-43; e-mail office@apparat.gov.az; internet www.president.az.

Office of the Prime Minister: 1066 Baku, Lermontov küç. 68; tel. (12) 492-66-23; fax (12) 492-91-79; e-mail nk@cabmin.gov.az; internet www.cabmin.gov.az.

Ministry of Agriculture: 1016 Baku, Azadlıq meydani 1; tel. (12) 493-53-55; internet agro.gov.az.

Ministry of Communications and Information Technology: 1000 Baku, Zarifa Aliyeva küç. 33; tel. (12) 498-58-38; fax (12) 498-79-12; e-mail mincom@mincom.gov.az; internet www.mincom.gov.az.

Ministry of Culture and Tourism: 1000 Baku, Azadlıq meydani 1, House of Government, 3rd Floor; tel. (12) 493-43-98; fax (12) 493-56-05; e-mail mugam@culture.gov.az.

Ministry of Defence: 1139 Baku, Azarbaycan pr.; tel. (12) 439-41-89; fax (12) 492-92-50.

Ministry of Defence Industries: Baku; e-mail info@mdi.gov.az; internet www.mdi.gov.az.

Ministry of Ecology and Natural Resources: 1073 Baku, Bahram Agayev küç. 100A; tel. (12) 492-59-07; fax (12) 439-84-32; internet eco.gov.az.

Ministry of Economic Development: 1006 Baku, Niyazi küç. 23; tel. (12) 492-41-10; fax (12) 492-58-95; e-mail office@economy.gov.az; internet www.economy.gov.az.

Ministry of Education: 1008 Baku, Xatai pr. 49; tel. (12) 496-06-47; fax (12) 496-34-83; e-mail office@min.edu.az; internet edu.gov.az.

Ministry of Emergency Situations: Baku.

Ministry of Finance: 1022 Baku, Samed Vurghun küç. 83; tel. (12) 493-30-12; fax (12) 498-79-69; e-mail office@maliyye.gov.az; internet maliyye.gov.az.

Ministry of Foreign Affairs: 1009 Baku, S. Qurbanov küç. 4; tel. (12) 596-90-00; fax (12) 498-84-80; e-mail press-service@mfa.gov.az; internet www.mfa.gov.az.

Ministry of Industry and Energy: 1012 Baku, Hasanbek Zardabi küç. 88; tel. (12) 498-78-56; fax (12) 598-16-78; e-mail pressa@mie.gov.az; internet www.mie.gov.az.

Ministry of Internal Affairs: 1005 Baku, Gusi Hajiyev küç. 7; tel. (12) 492-57-54; fax (12) 498-22-85; internet mia.gov.az.

Ministry of Justice: 1000 Baku, İnşaatçılar pr. 1; tel. (12) 430-01-16; fax (12) 430-09-81; e-mail contact@justice.gov.az; internet www.justice.gov.az.

Ministry of Labour and Social Protection: 1009 Baku, S. Asgarov küç. 85; tel. (12) 596-50-23; fax (12) 596-50-22; e-mail mlspp@mlspp.gov.az; internet www.mlspp.gov.az.

Ministry of National Security: 1006 Baku, Parlament pr. 2; tel. (12) 493-76-22; fax (12) 495-04-91; e-mail cpr@mns.gov.az; internet mns.gov.az.

Ministry of Public Health: 1014 Baku, Kicik Deniz küç. 4; tel. (12) 493-29-77; fax (12) 493-07-11; e-mail moh@alexd.baku.az.az; internet sehiyye.gov.az.

Ministry of Taxation: 1073 Baku, Landau küç. 16; tel. (12) 403-89-70; fax (12) 403-89-71; e-mail info@taxes.gov.az; internet www.taxes.gov.az.

Ministry of Transport: 1010 Baku, Uzeyir Hajibeyov küç. 72/4; tel. (12) 430-99-41; e-mail office@mintrans.az; internet mot.gov.az.

Ministry of Youth and Sport: 1072 Baku, Olimpiya küç. 4; tel. (12) 465-64-42; fax (12) 465-64-38; e-mail mys@mys.gov.az; internet mys.gov.az.

President

Presidential Election, 15 October 2008*

Candidates	Votes	% of votes
İlham Heydar oğlu Aliyev (New Azerbaijan Party)	3,232,259	88.73
İqbal Fehruz Ağa-Zada (Azerbaijan Hope Party)	104,279	2.86
Fazil Qazanfar Mustafayev (Great Revival Party)	89,985	2.47
Qüdrat Müzaffar Hasanqulıyev (United Azerbaijan Popular Front Party)	83,037	2.28
Qulamhüseyn Surxay Alibayli (Independent)	81,120	2.23
Others	52,194	1.43
Total	3,642,874	100.00

* Provisional results.

Legislature

Milli Majlis
(National Assembly)

1152 Baku, Parlament pr. 1; tel. (12) 439-97-50; fax (12) 493-49-43; e-mail azmm@meclis.gov.az; internet www.meclis.gov.az.

Chairman: OKTAI ASADOV.

General Election, 6 November 2005*

Parties and blocs	Seats
New Azerbaijan Party	61
Independents	46
Freedom bloc†	6
Civic Solidarity Party	3
Fatherland Party	2
Others	7
Total	125

* Including the results of repeat elections, held in 10 districts on 13 May 2006, in which the original results had been annulled, following confirmation of irregularities.

† Electoral bloc comprising the Azerbaijan Democratic Party, the Azerbaijan Popular Front Party and the Equality Party.

Local Government

For the purposes of local government, Azerbaijan has 74 administrative districts (rajons). The country also includes one Autonomous Republic (also termed an autonomous state), the exclave of Naxçıvan. These subdivisions incorporated the territory of the former autonomous oblast of Nagornyi Karabakh, which remained outside of central Government control in late 2008. There was some disruption to local government following the attempted secession of Nagornyi Karabakh and its occupation of some surrounding districts (for details, see section on autonomous territories). At municipal elections, held in December 2004, the New Azerbaijan Party won 64.7% of votes cast. By-elections and elections to newly-formed self-administrative bodies were held on 6 October 2006 in 603 municipalities. Further local elections were conducted on 14 October 2007.

CAPITAL CITY

Baku City Council: Baku, İstiqlaliyyat küç. 4; tel. (12) 492-63-11; e-mail bakumayor@box.az; internet www.bakucity.az; Mayor HACIBALA İBRAHIM OĞLU ABUTALIBOV.

OTHER PRINCIPAL CITIES

Ganca City Council: Ganca; Mayor ELDAR AZIZOV.

Lankaran City Council: 4200 Lankaran, Ş. Axundov küç. 33; tel. (171) 5-27-27; e-mail lankaran@aztelekom.net; internet www.lankaran.az; Mayor SÜLEYMAN SURXAY OĞLU MIKAYILOV.

Mingaçevir City Council: Mingaçevir.

Naxçıvan City Council: Naxçıvan; Mayor VASIV TALIBOVUN.

Şirvan City Council: 1800 Şirvan; tel. (197) 5-13-73.

Sumqayıt City Council: Sumqayıt; internet www.sumqayit-ih.gov.az; Mayor VAQIF QADIR OĞLU ALIYEV.

Election Commission

Central Electoral Commission: 1000 Baku, Rasul Rza küç. 3; tel. (12) 493-60-08; fax (12) 493-43-40; e-mail office@cec.gov.az; internet www.cec.gov.az; f. 1998; Chair. MAZAHIR PANAHOV.

Political Organizations

Azerbaijan Democratic Party (Azarbaycan Demokrat Partiyası): 1000 Baku, Sabayel Rayon, Acad. A. Alizade küç. 13; tel. (12) 496-07-22; fax (12) 496-18-61; e-mail adp2005@mail.ru; f. 1991; formed part of the Freedom bloc at legislative elections in 2005; Chair. SARDAR JALAL OĞLU MAMMADOV.

Azerbaijan Democratic Reforms Party (Azarbaycan Demokratik İslahatlar Siyasi Partiyasi): 1001 Baku, Bunyat Sardarov 17/2; tel. (12) 437-15-76; fax (12) 437-15-77; e-mail demreforms@party.az; internet www.demreforms.org; f. 2005; Chair. ASIM MOLLAZADE.

Azerbaijan Hope Party (Azarbaycan Ümid Partiyası): 1000 Baku, Qanub küç. 19/29; tel. (12) 496-65-48; f. 2001; Chair. İQBAL FEHRUZ AĞA-ZADA.

Azerbaijan Islamic Party (Azarbaycan İslam Partiyası—AİP): 1000 Baku; tel. (12) 491-86-45; fax (12) 491-83-88; e-mail AIP@azer.net; f. 1992; officially proscribed since 1995; forms part of the Union of Pro-Azerbaijanist Forces; Chair. MOVSUM SAMADOV.

Azerbaijan National Democratic Party (Azarbaycan Milli Demokrat Partiyası): 1000 Baku; tel. (12) 494-89-37; f. 1993; nationalist; fmrly associated with the prohibited Grey Wolves (Boz Gurd) mıltıa; Leader İSKANDAR MEJID OĞLU HAMIDOV.

Azerbaijan National Independence Party (ANIP) (Azarbaycan Milli İstiqlal Partiyası—AMIP): 1000 Baku, Nasimi rayon, Mirqasımov küç. 4; tel. (12) 441-53-09; e-mail nipa@azeri.com; f. 1992; centre-right; supports liberalization of the economy and strengthening of democratic institutions; opposed to administration of İlham Aliyev; formed part of the New Policy bloc in 2005; the party split into two rival factions in Jan. 2006: one (radical) headed by ALI ALIYEV, which joined the reconfigured Freedom bloc in 2006; and the other in support of ETIBAR MAMEDOV, headed by AYAZ RUSTAMOV, which was formally registered with the authorities.

Azerbaijan Social Democratic Party (Azarbaycan Sosial Demokrat Partiyası—ASDP): 1014 Baku, 28 May küç. 3/11; tel. (12) 493-33-78; fax (12) 498-79-03; e-mail asdp@bakililar.az; f. 1989; formed part of the New Policy (Yeni Siyaset) bloc for the legislative elections of 2005; Co-Chair. ARAZ ALIZADEH, AYAZ MUTALIBOV; 5,672 mems (2002).

Civic Solidarity Party (Vatandaş Hamrayliyi Partiyası): Baku, Abdulkarim Alizada küç. 9; tel. and fax (12) 493-71-45; internet www.vhp.az; f. 1992; Chair. SABIR RUSTAMKHANLI.

Equality Party (Müsavat) (Müsavat Partiyası): 1025 Baku, Darnagül qasabasi 30/97; tel. (12) 448-23-82; fax (12) 448-23-84; e-mail info@musavat.org; internet www.musavat.org; f. 1992 as revival of party founded in 1911 and in exile from 1920; withdrew from the Freedom bloc (formed in advance of legislative elections in 2005) in Feb. 2006; Chair. İSA QAMBAR; Gen. Sec. VURGUN EYYUB.

Fatherland Party (Ana Vatan Partiyası—AVP): 1000 Baku, Aziz Aliyev küç. 3; tel. (12) 493-82-92; f. 1992; supports administration of İlham Aliyev; represents interests of Naxçıvan Autonomous Republic in Azerbaijan; Leader FAZAIL AGAMALIYEV.

Justice Party (Adalat) (Adalat Partiyası): 1000 Baku, Nasimi rayon, Ceyhun Hacıbayli küç. 2; tel. (12) 440-85-23; e-mail adalat@azinternet.com; f. 2001; mem. of the Democratic Azerbaijan alliance; Leader İLYAS İSMAYILOV; 21,000 mems.

New Azerbaijan Party (NAP) (Yeni Azarbaycan Partiyası—YAP): 1000 Baku, Bül-Bül pr. 13; tel. (12) 493-84-25; fax (12) 498-59-71;

e-mail secretariat@yap.org.az; internet www.yap.org.az; f. 1992; Chair. ILHAM HEYDAR OĞLU ALIYEV.

New Generation Azerbaijan Communist Party (CPA) (Yeni Nasil Azarbaycan Kommunist Partiyası—AKP): 1073 Baku, A. Agayev küç. 1; tel. (12) 423-71-46; e-mail alesker-khalilov@rambler.ru; internet www.kommunist.az; Azerbaijan Communist Party disbanded Sept. 1991, re-established Nov. 1993; Chair. ALESKER KHALILOV.

Popular Front Party of Azerbaijan (PFPA) (Azarbaycan Xalq Cabhasi Partiyası—AXCP): 1152 Baku, Milli Majlis, Mehti Hussein küç. 2; tel. (12) 498-07-94; e-mail axcp@axcp.org; f. 1989; formed part of the Freedom bloc formed prior to 2005 legislative elections; Chair. ALI KERIMLI.

United Azerbaijan Popular Front Party (Bütöv Azarbaycan Xalq Cabhasi Partiyası—BAXCP): 1000 Baku, 12-ci Aşırım küç. 70A; tel. (12) 492-96-23; fax (12) 461-29-42; e-mail qudrat@hasanquliyev.com; f. 2003 by fmr mems of reformist wing of Azerbaijan Popular Front Party; Leader QÜDRAT MÜZAFFAR HASAN-QULIYEV.

Diplomatic Representation

EMBASSIES IN AZERBAIJAN

Belgium: 1073 Baku, Suleyman Dadaşov 19; tel. (12) 437-37-70; Ambassador FRANK GEERKENS.

Bulgaria: 1069 Baku-34, Oktai Kerimov küç. 34; tel. (12) 441-43-81; fax (12) 440-81-82; e-mail balkan@bg.embassy.in-baku.com; internet www.mfa.bg/baku; Ambassador IVAN K. PALCHEV.

China, People's Republic: 1000 Baku, Khagani küç. 67; tel. (12) 493-65-87; fax (12) 498-00-10; e-mail chinaemb@azeurotel.com; Ambassador ZHANG HAIZHOU.

Egypt: 1000 Baku, Hasan Aliyev küç. 7; tel. (12) 498-79-06; fax (12) 498-79-54; e-mail emb.egypt@azeuro.net; Ambassador YOUSSEF AHMED IBRAHEM ASH-SHARKAWY.

France: 1000 Baku, Rasul Rza küç. 7, POB 36; tel. (12) 490-81-00; fax (12) 490-81-01; e-mail ambafranbakou@azerin.com; internet www.ambafrance.az; Ambassador GABRIEL KELLER.

Georgia: 1073 Baku, Yasamal rayon, section 523, S. Dadashev küç. 29; tel. (12) 497-45-60; fax (12) 497-45-61; e-mail embgeo@azeurotel.com; internet www.az.mfa.gov.ge; Ambassador NIKOLOZ NATBILADZE.

Germany: 1005 Baku, Nizami küç. 340, ISR Plaza; tel. (12) 465-41-00; fax (12) 498-54-19; e-mail zreg@bakudiplo.org; internet www.baku.diplo.de; Ambassador Dr PEER STANCHINA.

Greece: 1004 Baku, Icheri Şeher, Kichik Gala küç. 86/88; tel. (12) 492-46-80; fax (12) 492-48-35; e-mail greekemb@azeurotel.com; Ambassador DIMIDIS TEMISTOKLES.

India: 1069 Baku, Sabayel rayon, Oktay Karimov küç. 31/39; tel. (12) 447-41-86; fax (12) 447-25-72; e-mail eibaku@adanet.az; Ambassador B. R. MUTHU KUMAR.

Iran: 1000 Baku, B. Sadarov küç. 4; tel. (12) 492-64-53; fax (12) 498-07-33; e-mail iranemb@azerin.com; Ambassador NASIR HAMIDI ZARE.

Iraq: 1000 Baku, Khagani küç. 9; tel. (12) 498-14-47; fax (12) 498-14-37; e-mail iraqyia@azeri.com; Ambassador ARSHAD OMAR ISMAYIL.

Israel: 1065 Baku, Izmir küç. 1033, Hyatt Tower III, 7th Floor; tel. (12) 490-78-81; fax (12) 490-78-92; e-mail info@baku.mfa.gov.il; internet baku.mfa.gov.il; Ambassador ARTHUR LENK.

Italy: 1004 Baku, Icheri Şeher, Kichik Gala küç. 44; tel. (12) 497-51-33; fax (12) 497-52-02; e-mail ambasciata.baku@esteri.it; internet www.ambbaku.esteri.it; Ambassador GIAN-LUIGI MASCIA.

Japan: 1065 Baku, Izmir küç. 1033, Hyatt Tower III, 6th Floor; tel. (12) 490-78-18; fax (12) 490-78-20; e-mail japan@emb.baku.az; Ambassador TADAKHIRU ABE.

Kazakhstan: 1110 Baku, X. Aliyev küç. 882/82; tel. (12) 465-62-48; fax (12) 465-62-49; e-mail embassyk@azdata.net; Ambassador SERIK D. PRIMBETOV.

Korea, Republic: 1000 Baku; internet aze.mofat.go.kr.

Latvia: 1065 Baku, J. Jabbarli küç. 44; tel. (12) 436-67-78; fax (12) 436-67-79; e-mail embassy.azerbaijan@mfa.gov.lv; Ambassador MIHAILS POPKOVS.

Libya: 1000 Baku, H. Javid pr. 520, apt 20; tel. (12) 493-23-65; fax (12) 498-12-47; e-mail libyabak@azerin.com; Chargé d'affaires a.i. MUHAMMAD AL-GILEDI JABIR.

Lithuania: 1000 Baku, Istiglaliyat küç. 15; tel. (12) 498-71-91; fax (12) 493-03-48; e-mail amb.az@urm.lt; Ambassador KĘSTUTIS KUDZMANAS.

Moldova: 1073 Baku, H. Javid pr. 520, Block 12; tel. (12) 510-15-38; fax (12) 403-52-91; e-mail baku@mfa.md; Ambassador ION ROBU.

Norway: 1000 Baku, Nizami küç. 340, ISR Plaza, 11th floor; tel. (12) 497-43-25; fax (12) 497-37-98; e-mail emb.baku@mfa.no; internet www.norway.az; Ambassador JON RAMBERG.

Pakistan: 1000 Baku, Atatürk pr. 30; tel. (12) 436-08-39; fax (12) 436-08-41; e-mail parepbaku@artel.net.az; Ambassador ABDUL HAMID.

Poland: 1000 Baku, Icheri Şeher, Kichik Gala küç. 2; tel. (12) 492-01-14; fax (12) 492-02-14; e-mail embpol@azeurotel.com; internet www.baku.polemb.net; Ambassador KRYSZTOF KRAJEWSKI.

Qatar: 1000 Baku, pr. Aliyev; tel. (12) 496-78-00; fax (12) 496-78-01.

Romania: 1000 Baku, Hasan Aliyev küç. 125A; tel. (12) 465-63-78; fax (12) 456-60-76; e-mail rom_amb_baku@azdata.net; Ambassador NICOLAE URECHE.

Russia: 1022 Baku, Bakixanov küç. 17; tel. (12) 498-60-16; fax (12) 498-14-16; e-mail embrus@azdata.net; internet www.embrus-az.com; Ambassador VASILII N. ISTRATOV.

Saudi Arabia: 1073 Baku, S. Dadashov küç. 44/2; tel. (12) 497-23-05; fax (12) 497-23-02; e-mail najdiahbaku@azereurotel.com; Ambassador ALI HASAN JAFAR.

Switzerland: 1000 Baku, Rasul Rza küç. 11/28–30; tel. (12) 598-53-14; fax (12) 498-15-43; e-mail baku.vertretung@eda.admin.ch; internet www.eda.admin.ch/baku; Ambassador ALAIN GUIDETTI.

Turkey: 1000 Baku, Khagani küç. 27; tel. (12) 444-73-20; fax (12) 444-73-55; e-mail bakube@artel.net.az; Ambassador HUSEYIN AVNI KARSLI.

Turkmenistan: Baku; tel. (12) 440-99-00; fax (12) 61-39-69.

Ukraine: 1069 Baku, Y. Vezirov küç. 49; tel. (12) 449-40-95; fax (12) 449-40-96; e-mail emb_az@mfa.gov.ua; internet www.mfa.gov.ua/azerbaijan; Ambassador BORYS P. KLIMCHUK.

United Kingdom: 1010 Baku, Khagani küç. 45; tel. (12) 497-51-88; fax (12) 492-27-39; e-mail generalenquiries.baku@fco.gov.uk; internet www.britishembassy.az; Ambassador Dr CAROLYN BROWNE.

USA: 1007 Baku, Azadlıq pr. 83; tel. (12) 498-03-36; fax (12) 465-66-71; internet azerbaijan.usembassy.gov; Ambassador ANNE E. DERSE.

Uzbekistan: 1021 Baku, Patamdart, 1-chi Şosesi, 9-chi tor 437; tel. (12) 497-25-49; fax (12) 497-25-48; e-mail embuzb@azeronline.com; Ambassador ISMATILLA R. ERGASHEV.

Judicial System

The judicial system in Azerbaijan is implemented by the following courts: regional (municipal) courts; the Court on Grave Crimes; the Military Court on Grave Crimes; local economical courts; the Economic Court on Disputes arising from International Agreements; the Supreme Court of Naxçıvan Autonomous Republic; the Court of Appeal; the Economic Court; the Supreme Court.

Supreme Court
(Azarbaycan Respublikasi Ali Mahkamasi)
1601 Baku, Z. Xalilov küç. 540; tel. (12) 493-18-37; fax (12) 493-11-68; e-mail sudaba_hasanova@supremecourt.gov.az; internet www.supremecourt.gov.az.

The highest judicial body in civil, criminal, administrative and other cases, referring to the activity of the general courts; judges are nominated by the President of the Republic and confirmed in office by the Milli Majlis.

President: SÜDABA CAMŞID QIZI HASANOVA.

Office of the Prosecutor-General (Baş Prokurorluğu): 1001 Baku, Nigar Rafibayli küç. 7; tel. (12) 492-30-32; fax (12) 493-03-35; e-mail info@genprosecutor.gov.az; internet www.genprosecutor.gov.az; Prosecutor-General ZAKIR BEKIR OĞLU QARALOV.

Constitutional Court
(Azarbaycan Republikasi Konstitusiya Mahkamasi)
1005 Baku, Genjler meydani 1; tel. (12) 492-88-41; fax (12) 492-97-66; e-mail inter.dept@constitutional-court-az.org; internet www.constitutional-court-az.org.

f. 1998; comprises a Chairman and eight judges, who are nominated by the President and confirmed in office by the Milli Majlis for a term of office of 15 years. Only the President, the Milli Majlis, the Cabinet of Ministers, the Procurator-General, the Supreme Court and the legislature of the Naxçıvan Autonomous Republic are permitted to submit cases to the Constitutional Court.

Chairman: FARHAD SAHIB OĞLU ABDULLAYEV.

Religion

ISLAM

The majority (some 70%) of Azerbaijanis are Shi'ite Muslims; most of the remainder are Sunni (Hanafi school). In 1944 the Soviet authorities established a Spiritual Board of Muslims of the Caucasus, with spiritual jurisdiction over the Muslims of Armenia, Georgia and Azerbaijan. The Chairman of the Board, which is based in Baku, is normally a Shi'ite, while the Deputy Chairman is usually a Sunni. The severe restrictions on religious activity during the Soviet period were liberalized following Azerbaijani independence in 1991.

Spiritual Board of Muslims of the Caucasus: 1000 Baku; Chair. Sheikh ul-Islam Haci ALLASHUKUR PASHEZADE.

CHRISTIANITY

The Roman Catholic Church

A Mission was established in October 2000, and the first Roman Catholic Church in Azerbaijan was consecrated in March 2008, in Baku. There were an estimated 390 adherents at 31 December 2006.

Superior: Rev. JÁN ČAPLA, 1069 Baku, Teimur Aliyev küç. 69B/1; tel. (12) 562-22-55; fax (12) 436-09-43; e-mail parish@catholic.baku.az.

The Russian Orthodox Church (Moscow Patriarchate)

Bishop of Baku and the Caspian Region: ALEKSANDR, 1010 Baku, Ş. Azizbekova küç. 205; tel. (12) 440-43-52; fax (12) 440-04-43; e-mail baku@eparchia.ru.

The Press

PRINCIPAL NEWSPAPERS

In Azerbaijani, except where otherwise stated.

525-ci Qazet/525-ya Gazeta: 1033 Baku, Ş. Mustafayev küç. 27/121; tel. (12) 466-67-98; fax (12) 466-25-20; e-mail 525@azdata.net; internet www.525ci.com; f. 1992; 5 a week; in Azerbaijani, English and Russian; Editor-in-Chief RASHAD MAJID.

Ayna/Zerkalo (Mirror): 1138 Baku, Sharifzadeh küç. 1; tel. and fax (12) 497-71-23; e-mail gazeta@zerkalo.az; internet www.ayna.az; internet www.zerkalo.az; f. 1990; daily; independent; Azerbaijani and Russian edns; Editor-in-Chief ELCIN SIXLINSKI; circ. 4,500 (daily).

Azadliq (Freedom): 1000 Baku, Khagani küç. 33; tel. (12) 498-90-81; fax (12) 498-78-18; e-mail mail@azadliq.com; internet www.azadliq.az; f. 1989; weekly; independent; organ of the Azerbaijan Popular Front; in Azerbaijani and Russian; Editor-in-Chief GANIMAT ZAKHIDOV.

Azarbaycan/Azerbaijan: 1073 Baku, Matbuat pr. 529/4, tel. (12) 438-20-87; fax (12) 439-43-23; internet www.azerbaijan.news.az; f. 1991; 5 a week; publ. by the Milli Majlis; in Azerbaijani and Russian; Editor-in-Chief BAKHTIYAR SADIGOV.

Azernews: 1002 Baku, S. Askerova küç. 85; tel. (12) 494-93-73; fax (12) 495-85-37; e-mail azernews@azeurotel.com; internet www.azernews.net; f. 1997; weekly; in Azerbaijani, Russian and English; in association with AssA-Irada news agency; Editor-in-Chief FAZIL ABBASOV; circ. 5,000–6,000.

Bakı Xabar (Baku News): 1000 Baku, Kicik Qala küç. 128; internet www.baku-xeber.com; f. 2003; newspaper of the Azerbaijan Democratic Party; 6 a week; Editor-in-Chief AYDIN QULIYEV; circ. 5,000 (2007).

Bakinskii Rabochii (The Baku Worker): 1146 Baku, Matbuat pr. 529; tel. (12) 438-00-29; e-mail bakrab@azerin.com; internet www.br.az; f. 1906; 5 a week; govt newspaper; in Russian; Editor I. VEKILOVA.

Baku Sun: 1073 Baku, İnşaatçılar pr. 2; tel. and fax (12) 497-55-32; e-mail chief@bakusun.baku.az; internet www.bakusun.az; f. 1998; weekly; in English; free of charge; Dir DMITRIY KUKLIN.

Bizim Asr: 1141 Baku, A. Alekperov küç. 83/23; tel. (12) 497-88-99; fax (12) 497-88-98; e-mail bizim_asr@media-az.com; internet bizimasr.media-az.com; f. 1999.

Bizim Yol (Our Way): Baku; tel. (12) 418-91-79; e-mail info@bizimyol.org; internet www.bizimyol.org; f. 2003; independent; weekly; associated with the Popular Front Party of Azerbaijan; Editor-in-Chief BAHADDIN HAZIYEV.

Day: Baku; e-mail editor@day.az; internet www.day.az; online only; in Russian and English.

Echo (Ekho): 1138 Baku, Sharifzadeh küç. 1; tel. (12) 497-51-74; fax (12) 447-41-50; e-mail gazeta@echo-az.com; internet www.echo-az.com; daily; in Russian; Editor-in-Chief RAUF TALISHINSKYI; circ. 10,000.

Ekspress (The Express): 1000 Baku, Khagani küç. 20B/43; tel. (12) 498-08-63; e-mail express@azeronline.com; internet www.express.com.az; Editor QAZANFAR BAYRAMOV.

İstiqlal (Independence): 1014 Baku, 28 May küç. 3–11; tel. (12) 493-33-78; fax (12) 498-75-55; e-mail istiklal@ngonet.baku.az; 4 a month; organ of the Azerbaijan Social Democratic Party; Editor ZARDUSHT ALIZADEH; circ. 5,000.

Respublıka (Republic): 1146 Baku, Matbuat pr. 529; tel. (12) 438-01-14; fax (12) 438-01-31; e-mail resp@azdata.net; internet www.respublica.news.az; f. 1996; daily; govt newspaper; Editor-in-Chief T. AHMADOV; circ. 5,500.

Sharg (The East): 1000 Baku, Matbuat pr. 529; tel. (12) 447-37-80; fax (12) 439-00-79; e-mail sharq@azerin.com; internet www.sherg.az.

Xalq Qazetı (Popular Gazette): 1000 Baku, Bül-Bül pr. 18; tel. (12) 493-02-80; fax (12) 498-85-29; e-mail webmaster@xalqqazeti.com; internet www.xalqqazeti.com; f. 1919; fmrly *Kommunist*; 6 a week; organ of the Office of the President; Editor HASAN HASANOV.

Yeni Azerbaijan (A New Azerbaijan): 1000 Baku; tel. (12) 439-82-27; fax (12) 497-53-04; internet www.yeniazerbaycan.com; f. 1993; weekly; organ of the New Azerbaijan Party; Editor ALGYSH MUSAYEV; circ. 2,493.

Yeni Müsavat (A New Equality): 1000 Baku; tel. (12) 498-00-61; e-mail ymusavat@azeronline.com; independent; pro-opposition; Editor-in-Chief AZAR AYHAN (acting).

Yezhednevnye Novosti (The Daily News): 1000 Baku, Terlan Aliyarbekov küç. 43; tel. and fax (12) 492-12-24; e-mail alpha@azeri.com; internet www.alpha.azeri.com; in Russian; Editor EMIL ASADOV; circ. 14,000.

OTHER PRINCIPAL PERIODICALS

Caspian Business News (CBN): 1000 Baku, Safaroğlu küç. 219B; tel. (12) 493-31-89; fax (12) 497-24-78; e-mail media@cbnmail.com; f. 2000; weekly; in English.

Dialog (Dialogue): 1000 Baku; f. 1989; fortnightly; in Azerbaijani and Russian; Editor R. A. ALEKPEROV.

Iki Sahil: 1025 Baku, A. Akhundov 22; tel. (12) 490-49-89; internet www.ikisahil.com; f. 1965; weekly; organ of the New Baku Oil-Refining Plant; Editor-in-Chief V. RAHIMZADEH; circ. 2,815.

Kirpi (Hedgehog): 1046 Baku, Matbuat pr. 529; tel. (12) 432-18-18; f. 1952; fortnightly; satirical; Editor A. M. AIVAZOV.

Literaturnyi Azerbaijan (Literary Azerbaijan): 1001 Baku, Khagani küç. 25; tel. (12) 493-51-00; e-mail sima@azeri.com; f. 1931; monthly; journal of the Union of Writers of Azerbaijan; fiction; in Russian; Editor-in-Chief M. F. VEKILOV.

Ulus (The Nation): 1000 Baku; tel. (12) 492-27-43; 2 a week; Editor TOFIK DADASHEV.

Vyshka—Oil (Oil Derrick): 1073 Baku, Matbuat pr. 529; tel. and fax (12) 439-96-97; e-mail medina@vyshka.com; internet vyshka.com; f. 1928; weekly; independent; in Russian; Editor M. E. GASANOVA.

NEWS AGENCIES

Azadinform Information Agency: 1000 Baku, F. Amirov küç. 1; tel. (12) 498-48-59; fax (12) 498-47-60; e-mail azadinform@azerin.com; internet azadinform.az; f. 1998; independent information agency; Chief Editor ASEF HAJIYEV.

AzarTAc—Azarbaycan Dövlat Teleqraf Agentlıyı (Azerbaijan State Telegraph Agency—AzerTAg): 1000 Baku, Bül-Bül pr. 18; tel. (12) 493-59-29; fax (12) 493-62-65; e-mail azertac@azdata.net; internet www.azertag.gov.az; f. 1920; provides information in Azerbaijani, Russian and English; Dir-Gen. ASLAN ASLANOV.

Azeri Press Agency (APA): 1001 Baku, İstiqlal küç. 31; tel. (12) 596-33-57; fax (12) 596-31-94; e-mail apa@azeurotel.com; internet www.apa.az; f. 2004; in Azerbaijani, Russian and English; Dir-Gen. VUSALA MAHIRGIZI.

Bilik Dünyasi Information Agency: 1000 Baku, D. Aliyev küç. 241/22; tel. (12) 493-55-61; fax (12) 498-18-41; e-mail bd@azdata.net.

Media-Press: 1141 Baku, A. Alekperov küç. 83/23; tel. (12) 497-07-05; fax (12) 497-88-98; e-mail news@mediapress.media-az.com; internet mediapress.media-az.com; f. 1999; owned by Media Holding; independent; Gen. Dir VUGAR GARADAGLY.

Trend Information-Analytical Agency: 1601 Baku, Fizuli küç. 69; tel. (12) 497-31-72; fax (12) 497-30-89; e-mail infotrend@azdata.net; internet www.trend-az.com; f. 1995; in Azerbaijani, Russian and English; Dir-Gen. INGILAB AKHMEDOV.

Turan İnformasıya Agentlıyı: 1000 Baku, Khagani küç. 20/56; tel. (12) 598-42-26; fax (12) 598-38-17; e-mail turan@azeurotel.az; internet www.turaninfo.com; f. 1990; independent news agency; in Azerbaijani, Russian and English; Dir MEHMAN ALIYEV.

PRESS ASSOCIATIONS

Azerbaijan Journalists' Confederation (AJK): 1000 Baku, Khagani küç. 33; tel. (50) 335-27-95; fax (12) 498-78-18; e-mail hasret@akjib.org; f. 2002; 15 member organizations; Gen. Sec. AZER H. HASRET.

Azerbaijan Press Council (Azerbaycan Metbuat Surasi): 1010 Baku, Nizami küç. 121/11; tel. and fax (12) 498-27-48; f. 2003; mediates disputes between the media and the authorities; acts as a self-regulatory body for the print media; Chair. AFLATUN AMASHOV.

Publishers

Azarbaycan Ensiklopediyasi (Azerbaijan Encyclopedia): 1004 Baku, Boyuk Gala küç. 41; tel. (12) 492-87-11; fax (12) 492-77-83; e-mail azenciklop@ctc.net.az; f. 1965; encyclopedias and dictionaries; Gen. Dir I. O. VELIYEV.

Azarneshr State Publishing House: 1005 Baku, Gusi Hajiyev küç. 4; tel. (12) 492-50-15; f. 1924; Dir A. MUSTAFAZADE; Editor-in-Chief A. KUSEINZADE.

Elm Azerbaijani Academy of Sciences Publishing House: 1000 Baku; scientific books and journals.

Gyanjlik (Youth): 1005 Baku, Gusi Hajiyev küç. 4; books for children and young people; Dir E. T. ALIYEV.

Ishyg (Light): 1601 Baku, Gogol küç. 6; illustrated publs; Dir G. N. ISMAILOV.

Madani-maarif Ishi (Education and Culture): 1073 Baku, Matbuat pr. 529; tel. (12) 432-79-17; Editor-in-Chief ALOVSAT ATAMALY OĞLU BASHIROV.

Medeniyyat (Culture) Publishing House: 1146 Baku, Matbuat pr. 146; tel. (12) 432-98-38; Dir SHAKMAR AKPER OĞLU AKPERZADE.

Sada: 1004 Baku, Boyuk Gala küç. 28; tel. (12) 492-75-64; fax (12) 492-98-43; reference.

Shur: 1000 Baku; tel. (12) 492-93-72; f. 1992; Dir GASHAM ISA OĞLU ISABEYLI.

Broadcasting and Communications

TELECOMMUNICATIONS

Azercell Telecom: 1139 Baku, Tbilisi pr. 61A; tel. (12) 496-70-07; fax (12) 430-05-68; internet www.azercell.com; f. 1996; jt-venture co between the Ministry of Communications and Information Technology and Fintur Holdings B.V. (Netherlands); Gen. Dir ESRA TAN.

Azerfon: 1102 Baku, Alatava küç. 2; tel. (12) 444-07-30; fax (12) 444-07-31; internet www.narmobile.az; f. 2005; provides mobile cellular communications under the Narmobile brand name; CEO GUIDO HELBICH.

AzTelecom Production Asscn: 1122 Baku, Tbilisi pr. 3166; tel. (12) 430-26-30; fax (12) 493-17-87; e-mail aztelekom@aztelekom.net; internet www.aztelekom.net; national monopoly fixed-line telecommunications operator; f. 1992; owned by the Ministry of Communications and Information Technology; privatization pending; Dir MUHAMMAD MAMEDOV.

Bakcell: 1000 Baku, U. Hajibeyov küç. 24; tel. (12) 498-94-44; fax (12) 498-92-55; e-mail bakcell@bakcell.com; internet www.bakcell .com; f. 1994; mobile telecommunications service provider; wholly owned by GTIB (Israel); Gen. Man. HAIM MAIMON.

RADIO AND TELEVISION

National Television and Radio Council (Milli Televiziya va Radio Şurası): 1000 Baku, Nizami küç. 105; tel. (12) 98-36-59; fax (12) 98-76-68; e-mail office@ntrc.gov.az; internet www.ntrc.gov.az; f. 2003; regulatory body, comprising nine members, six of whom are presidential appointees; Chair. NUSHIRAVAN MAGERRAMLI.

Azerbaijan Television and Radio Broadcasting Co: 1011 Baku, Mehti Hussein küç. 1; tel. (12) 492-72-53; fax (12) 439-54-52; internet www.aztv.az; f. 1956; closed jt-stock co.

Azerbaijan National Television (AzTV): 1011 Baku, Mehti Hussein küç. 1; tel. (12) 492-38-07; fax (12) 497-20-20; e-mail alishanov@aztv.az; internet www.aztv.az; f. 1956; programmes in Azerbaijani, English and Russian; one channel; Chair. ARIF ALISHANOV.

Azerbaijan National Radio: 1011 Baku, Mehti Hussein küç. 1; tel. (12) 492-87-68; fax (12) 439-72-48; internet www.aztv.az; f. 1926; broadcasts in Azerbaijani, Arabic, English and Turkish; two channels and one international broadcasting studio; Head MOVLUD SULEIMAN.

Public Television and Radio Broadcasting Co (İctimiai Televizya va Radiyo Yayımları Şirkati—ITV): Baku; tel. (12) 431-17-37; fax (12) 430-24-26; e-mail info@itv.az; internet www.itv.az; f. 2005; created from the second channel of the state broadcasting co (AzTV2); broadcasts in Azerbaijani and Armenian; Gen. Dir ISMAYIL OMAROV.

ANS Independent Broadcasting and Media Co (Azerbaijan News Service): 1073 Baku, Matbuat pr. 28/11; tel. (12) 497-72-67; fax (12) 498-94-98; e-mail ans@ans.az; internet www.ans.az; f. 1999; independent; broadcasts ANS-TV (f. 1990) and NAS-CHM Radio (f. 1994); Pres. VAHID MUSTAFAYEV.

Lider TV and Radio: 1141 Baku, A. Alekperov küç. 83/23; tel. (12) 497-88-99; fax (12) 497-87-77; e-mail mail@media-az.com; internet www.lidertv.com; f. 2000.

Regional Television Network of Azerbaijan (RTNA): Sumqayıt, Qarabağ Cinema, c/o Dunya TV; f. 2005; includes seven regional channels: Alternativ TV in Ganca; Mingaçevir TV; Xayal TV in Quba; Dunya TV in Sumqayıt; Lankaran TV; Simurq TV in Tovuz; and Aygun TV in Zaqatala.

Finance

(cap. = capital; res = reserves; dep. = deposits; m. = million; brs = branches; amounts in new manats, unless otherwise stated)

BANKING

Central Bank

National Bank of Azerbaijan: 1014 Baku, R. Behbutov küç. 32; tel. (12) 493-11-22; fax (12) 493-55-41; e-mail mail@nba.az; internet www .nba.az; f. 1992; central bank and supervisory authority; cap. 10m., res 5.9m., dep. 1,449.3m. (Dec. 2006); Chair. ELMAN RUSTAMOV.

State-owned Banks

International Bank of Azerbaijan: 1005 Baku, Nizami küç. 67; tel. (12) 493-00-91; fax (12) 493-40-91; e-mail ibar@ibar.az; internet www.ibar.az; f. 1992 to succeed br. of USSR Vneshekonombank; 50.2% owned by the Ministry of Finance; carries out all banking services; cap. 59.3m., res 18.9m., dep. 1,518.5m. (Dec. 2006); Chair. of Bd JAHANGIR F. HAJIYEV; 36 brs.

Kapital Bank: 1014 Baku, Fizuli küç. 71; tel. (12) 493-66-30; fax (12) 493-79-05; e-mail office@kapitalbank.az; internet www.kapitalbank .az; f. 2000 by merger; present name adopted 2005; cap. 12.0m., res 3.5m., dep. 104.4m. (Dec. 2006); Chair. RAUF RZAYEV; 87 brs.

Other Banks

At 1 August 2005 there were 43 banks operating in Azerbaijan, including two state-owned banks and 17 banks supported by foreign capital.

Amrahbank: 1000 Baku, Y. Safarov küç. 111; tel. (12) 497-88-60; fax (12) 497-88-63; e-mail info@amrahbank.com; internet www .amrahbank.com; f. 1993; cap. 6.8m., dep. 20.5m., total assets 29.4m. (Dec. 2006); Pres. YUNUS ILDIRIMZADEH; Chair. MAHMUD AGAMALIYEV.

AtaBank: 1010 Baku, Shamsi Badalbeyli küç. 102; tel. (12) 497-87-00; fax (12) 498-74-47; e-mail atabank@atabank.com; internet www .atabank.com; f. 1994; cap. 8.5m., dep. 53.0m. (Dec. 2006); Chair. of Supervisory Bd VUQAR ISMAYILOV.

Azarbaycan Sanaye Banki (Azerbaijan Industry Bank): 1005 Baku, Azarbaycan pr. 3; tel. (12) 493-50-67; fax (12) 493-84-50; e-mail contact@asb.az; internet www.asb.az; f. 1996; fmrly Capital Investment Bank; present name adopted Nov. 2006; cap. 7.8m., res 1.4m., dep. 14.9m. (Dec. 2006); Pres. ABDULBARI GUZAL; Chair. of Bd of Dirs AHMET YEMAN.

Azerdemiryolbank: 1008 Baku, Qarabağ küç. 31; tel. (12) 440-24-29; fax (12) 496-09-77; e-mail damir@azerdemiryolbank.az; internet www.azerdemiryolbank.com; f. 1992; cap. 7.2m., res 3.8m., dep. 42.9m. (Dec. 2006); Chair. of Bd ROMAN AMIRJANOV; 25 brs.

Azerigazbank: 1073 Baku, Landau küç. 16; tel. (12) 497-50-17; fax (12) 498-96-15; e-mail azerigazbank@azerigazbank.com; internet www.azerigazbank.com; f. 1992; jt-stock investment bank; cap. 12.0m., res 1.5m., dep. 112.3m. (Dec. 2007); Chair. AZER F. MOVSUMOV; 5 brs.

Azer-Turk Bank: 1005 Baku, Islam Seferli küç. 5; tel. (12) 497-43-16; fax (12) 598-37-02; e-mail atb@azerturkbank.biz; internet www .azerturkbank.biz; f. 1995; 46% owned by Türkiye Cumhuriyeti Ziraat Bankasi AS (Turkey); 46% owned by Agrarkredit; cap. 7.0m., dep. 16.8m. (Dec. 2006); Chair. MEMMED MUSAYEV; Gen. Man. MEHMET SAMI ACAROZMEN.

Bank of Baku: 1069 Baku, Atatürk pr. 40/42; tel. (12) 447-00-55; fax (12) 498-82-78; e-mail root@bankofbaku.com; internet www .bankofbaku.com; f. 1994; merged with Ilkbank in Feb. 2005; 40% owned by NAB DIS Ticaret (Turkey); 28.9% owned by Azpetrol Holding; cap. 6.8m., res 1.7m., dep. 57.1m. (Dec. 2006); Chair. of Bd SHAHRAM M. OROMI; 7 brs.

Bank Respublika: 1000 Baku, Khagani küç. 21; tel. (12) 598-08-00; fax (12) 598-08-80; e-mail info@bankrespublica.az; internet www .bankrespublica.az; f. 1992; cap. 12.6m., res 2.2m., dep. 208.8m. (Dec. 2007); Chair. of Exec. Bd KHADIJA HASANOVA.

Bank Silk Way: 1000 Baku, Nizami küç. 86; tel. (12) 498-60-56; fax (12) 498-97-01; e-mail azalbank@azalbank.az; internet www .azalbank.az; f. 1994 as Azalbank; name changed as above 2008; cap. 5m., dep. 10.4m., total assets 15.0m. (Dec. 2006); Chair. of Bd MAMADOV TEYMUR MAMED; 8 brs.

Bank Standard: 1005 Baku, H. Hadjiyev küç. 4; tel. (12) 497-10-71; fax (12) 498-07-78; e-mail bank@bankstandard.com; internet www .bankstandard.com; f. 1995; present name adopted 2004; cap. 15.0m., res 8.5m., dep. 179.8m. (Dec. 2006); Chief Exec. SALIM KRIMAN.

DEBUT Bank: 1025 Baku, Babek pr. 16; tel. (12) 496-45-51; fax (12) 496-45-60; e-mail info@debutbank.az; internet www.debutbank.az; f. 1994; cap. 25,000m. old manats, res 2,881.1m. old manats, dep. 22,441m. old manats (Dec. 2005); Pres. ANAR GARIBOV.

Günay Bank: 1001 Baku, Zergerpalan küç. 87, 5/4; tel. (12) 498-04-55; fax (12) 498-14-39; e-mail info@gunaybank.com; internet www .gunaybank.com; f. 1992; cap. 8.6m., res 0.4m., dep. 9.6m. (Dec. 2006); Pres. AHAD SHIRINOV; 1 br.

Rabitabank: 1001 Baku, B. Sardarov küç. 1; tel. (12) 492-57-61; fax (12) 497-11-01; e-mail rb@rabitabank.com; internet www .rabitabank.com; f. 1993; jt-stock commercial bank; operates mainly in telecommunications sector; cap. 23,135m. old manats, res 6,613m. old manats, dep. 124,986m. old manats (Dec. 2005); Chair. of Sup. Bd ZAKIR NURIYEV; 9 brs.

Unibank Commercial Bank: 1022 Baku, Raşid Behbudov küç. 57; tel. (12) 498-22-44; fax (12) 498-09-53; e-mail bank@unibank.az; internet www.unibank.az; f. 2002 by merger; cap. 6.6m., res 0.6m., dep. 90.0m. (Dec. 2006); Chair. and Chief Exec. FAIG HUSEYNOV; 8 brs.

United Credit Bank: 1025 Baku, N. Rafiyev küç. 49; tel. (12) 490-06-41; fax (12) 490-05-22; e-mail ucb@ucb.az; internet www.ucb.az; f. 1996; 81.39% owned by United Business Co Ltd; Chair. of Bd AZAD ISKENDEROV.

Association

Azerbaijan Association of Banks: 1001 Baku, B. Sardarov küç. 1; tel. (12) 497-58-29; fax (12) 497-15-15; e-mail bank_assoc@azeurotel .com; f. 1990; co-ordinates banking activity; Pres. ZAKIR NURIYEV; 47 mems.

STOCK EXCHANGE

Baku Stock Exchange (Bakı Fond Birjasi): 1000 Baku, Bül-Bül pr. 19; tel. (12) 498-85-22; fax (12) 493-77-93; e-mail info@bse.az; internet www.bse.az; f. 2000; Pres. ANAR AKHUNDOV.

INSURANCE

At January 2005 there were 30 insurance companies operating in Azerbaijan.

Ataşgah Insurance Co: Baku, Sabir küç. 3; tel. (12) 497-81-82; fax (12) 492-97-65; e-mail ateshgah@ateshgah.com; internet www .ateshgah.com; f. 1996; 30% owned by State Oil Co of Azerbaijan, 30% owned by Atlantic Reinsurance Co, 19% owned by Lukoil Azerbaijan; Man. ROBERT BRUNDRETT.

AZAL-siğorta: 1000 Baku, Khagani küç. 1/4; tel. (12) 598-39-50; fax (12) 598-38-02; e-mail azalsigorta@azalsigorta.com; internet www .azalsigorta.com; f. 1995; Man. Dir NIYAZI IMANOV.

Azergarant: 1001 Baku, H. Aslanov küç. 115/18; tel. (12) 493-81-65; fax (12) 493-81-02; e-mail azergarant@azdata.net; f. 1993; Pres. Dr ALEKPER MAMEDOV; Gen. Dir FAIG HUSSEINOV.

Azersiğorta: 1014 Baku, Füzuli 69; tel. (12) 495-95-64; fax (12) 495-94-69; e-mail azersigorta@azeuro.net; Dir MEMMED MEMMEDOV.

Beynalxalq Sığorta Şirkati (International Insurance Co): 1065 Baku, J. Jabbarli küç. 40C, IIC Bldg; tel. (12) 596-22-02; fax (12) 596-22-12; e-mail iic@iic.az; internet www.iic.az; f. 2002; universal insurance co; wholly owned subsidiary of the International Bank of Azerbaijan; Dir FEYRUZ NOVRUZOV.

Günay Anadolu Siğorta: 1005 Baku, Terlan Aliyarbekov küç. 3; tel. (12) 498-13-56; fax (12) 498-13-60; e-mail office@gunaysigorta .in-baku.com; internet insurancegunayanadolu.com; f. 1992; Gen. Man. ALOVSET GOJAYEV.

MBask Insurance Co: 1095 Baku, Azi Aslanov küç. 90/9; tel. (12) 498-91-90; fax (12) 498-10-62; e-mail office@mbask.com; f. 1992; 30% owned by the European Bank for Reconstruction and Development (United Kingdom); 7 brs; Chair. of Bd of Dirs JAMIL MALIKOV.

MOST Insurance Co: 1073 Baku, H. Javid pr. 15/21; tel. (12) 497-37-60; fax (12) 433-08-58; Dir KAMAL MIRSAHIB OĞLU IBRAHIMOV.

Trade and Industry

GOVERNMENT AGENCY

Azerbaijan Export and Investment Promotion Foundation: 1000 Baku, U. Hajibeyov küç. 40, Government House; tel. (12) 598-

01-47; fax (12) 598-01-52; e-mail office@azerinvest.com; internet www.azerinvest.com; f. 2003 under the Ministry of Economic Development.

CHAMBER OF COMMERCE

Chamber of Commerce and Industry: 1001 Baku, İstiklal küç. 31/33; tel. (12) 492-89-12; fax (12) 497-19-97; e-mail expo@chamber .baku.az; Pres. SULEYMAN BAYRAM OĞLU TATLIYEV.

INDUSTRIAL AND TRADE ASSOCIATIONS

National Confederation of Entrepreneurs' (Employers') Organizations of Azerbaijan (Azarbaycan Respublikasi Sahibkarlar—İşagötüranlar—Taşkilatları Milli Konfederasiyasi—ASK): 1002 Baku, S. Askerova küç. 85; tel. (12) 494-90-16; fax (12) 494-99-76; e-mail aazerenterprise@artel.net.az; internet www.ask.org.az; f. 1999; Pres. ALEKPER MAMEDOV.

UTILITIES

Electricity

AliBayramlıelektrikşebeke (Ali Bayramlı Electricity Network): 1800 Şirvan; f. 2001; comprises the Azerbaijani electricity network's southern zone; managed by Bakı Yüksakgarginlikli Elektroavadanlıq (BYGEA—Baku High Voltage Electrical Equipment Co).

Azerenerji: 1005 Baku, A. Alizade küç. 10; tel. (12) 493-73-58; fax (12) 498-55-23; state-owned jt-stock co; power generation and transmission company; Pres. ETIBAR S. PIRVERDIYEV.

Bakı Elektrikşebeke (Baku Electricity Network): 1008 Baku, Kazumzada 20; tel. (12) 440-44-04; fax (12) 440-22-26; e-mail info@ bakuelektrikshebeke.az; internet www.bakuelektrikshebeke.az; f. 2001.

Bayva-Enerji: 2000 Ganca, Ruzigar Gasimov küç. 10; tel. and fax (22) 56-97-40; e-mail bayva-qerbenerji@mail.ru; f. 2002 as Ganjaelektrikşebeke; comprising the Azerbaijani electricity distribution network's western zone; managed by Bakı Yüksakgarginlikli Elektroavadanlıq (BYGEA—Baku High Voltage Electrical Equipment Co); Gen. Dir RAMIZ AGAMALIYEV.

Naxçıvan Electrikşebeke (Naxçıvan Electricity Network): 7000 Naxçıvan; f. 2001; state-owned open jt-stock co; approximately 60% of electricity imported from Iran.

Gas

AzeriGaz: 1025 Baku, Yusif Safarov küç. 23; tel. (12) 490-42-52; fax (12) 490-42-55; e-mail azer_bayramov@azerigaz.com; f. 1992; transport, distribution, sale, compression and storage of natural gas; Chair. ALIKHAN MELIKHOV; 13,000 employees.

PETROLEUM

Azerbaijan's petroleum reserves were estimated to total some 7,000m. barrels at the end of 2004. Some 95% of petroleum extraction was in offshore fields in the Caspian Sea. In September 1994 Azerbaijan signed an agreement with 11 foreign petroleum companies, which, together with the State Oil Company of the Azerbaijan Republic (SOCAR), made up the Azerbaijan International Operating Company (AIOC—see below). The agreement allowed for the exploration and development of three offshore fields containing an estimated 511m. tons of petroleum and 55,000m. cu m of natural gas. Production began in December 1997. Further production-sharing agreements were signed from 1995.

State Hydrocarbons Company

State Oil Co of the Azerbaijan Republic (SOCAR): 1000 Baku, Neftchilar pr. 73; tel. (12) 492-17-89; fax (12) 497-11-67; e-mail info@ socar.az; internet www.socar.az; f. 1992; production and exploration activities, oversees refining and capital construction; owns Azerneftyag and Azerneftyanayag refineries; Pres. ROVNAG ABDULLAYEV; Vice-Pres. KHOSHBAKHT YUSIFZADE; 67,000 employees.

Other Major Producers and Distributors

Agip Azerbaijan: 1000 Baku, 340 Nizami küç., ISR Plaza; tel. (12) 497-22-12; fax (12) 497-22-07; e-mail eros.agostinelli@ agipazerbaijan.com; operate the offshore Kurdashi fields; member of the ENI Group (Italy).

Azerbaijan International Operating Co (AIOC): 1003 Baku, Neftchilar pr. 2, Villa Petrolea; tel. (12) 491-21-02; fax (12) 475-96-02; e-mail bayatltf@bp.com; f. 1994 as a consortium of: SOCAR (q.v.); British Petroleum (United Kingdom); Devon Energy, ExxonMobil and Unocal (USA); Itochu and Inpex (Japan); Statoil (Norway); Türkiye Petrolleri (Turkey); and the Delta Hess alliance (Saudi Arabia–USA); exploration and development of offshore petroleum reserves; Pres. DAVID WOODWARD.

Azpetrol Group BV: 1004 Baku, Mirza Mansur küç. 63/65; tel. (12) 497-69-74; fax (12) 497-68-64; e-mail azpetrol@1azpetrol.com; internet www.azpetrol.com; f. 1997; comprises Azpetrol Ltd, and Azpetrol Refinery SRL and Azpetrol SRL (both based in Moldova); participates in the joint ventures A&D and Azen Oil Co BV; owned by Azpetrol International Holdings BV; 4,000 employees; Dir-Gen. HUSEYNAGA RAHIMOV.

BP Caspian Sea Petroleum: 1003 Baku, Neftchilar pr. 2, Villa Petrolea; tel. (12) 497-90-00; fax (12) 497-96-02; e-mail hallg@bp.com; f. Dec. 1998 by merger of Azerbaijani interests of British Petroleum (United Kingdom) and Amoco (USA); operator of Azeri, Chirag, Deepwater Guneshli oilfields; operator of Shah Deniz gas field; operator of Inam oil field; operator of Araz Alov Sharg (suspended); Pres. BILL SCHRADER; Country Man. DOUGLAS HILL; 1,234 employees.

Chevron Khazar Ltd: 1010 Baku, Khagani küç. 45A; tel. (12) 497-88-00; fax (12) 497-88-04; e-mail ismm@chevron.com; f. 1998; subsidiary of Chevron (USA); Chevron Corpn acquired Unocal Corpn in 2005; Chevron holds a 8.9% stake in the Baku–Tbilisi (Georgia)–Ceyhan (Turkey) (BTC) pipeline project and a 10.3% stake in the Azerbaijan International Operating Co (AIOC—q.v.); Man. J. CONNOR.

Delta Hess: 1033 Baku, Izmir küç., Hyatt Tower 2; tel. (12) 497-60-81; fax (12) 497-23-19; e-mail deltahess@azdata.net; f. 1998; owned by Amerada Hess Corpn (USA) and Delta Oil Central Asia Ltd (Saudi Arabia); 20% shareholder in the Garabakhli-Kursangli production-sharing agreement, 2.72% shareholder in the Azeri-Chirag-Guneshli project and equity holder in the Baku–Tbilisi, Georgia–Ceyhan, Turkey (BTC) petroleum pipeline; Country Man. TOM SPRINGALL.

Devon Energy Caspian Corpn (DECC): 1000 Baku, Nizami küç. 96; tel. (12) 497-10-79; fax (12) 498-48-83; subsidiary of Devon Energy Corpn (USA); 5.6% shareholder in the Azeri-Chirag-Guneshli project; Pres. GREGORY MESSNER.

ExxonMobil Ventures Azerbaijan: 1004 Baku, Nizami küç. 96/300; tel. (12) 498-24-60; fax (12) 498-24-72; subsidiary of ExxonMobil (USA); Gen. Man. DREW GOODBREAD.

Itochu Oil Exploration (Azerbaijan): 1033 Baku, Izmir küç., Hyatt Tower 2; tel. (12) 490-75-60; fax (12) 490-75-62; e-mail cieco@itochuoil.in-baku.com; f. 1996; 100% owned by Itochu Corpn (Japan); member of the AIOC (q.v.) and shareholder in the Azeri-Chirag-Guneshli project; Gen. Man. KOTARO MORISHITA.

LUKoil Baku: 1004 Baku, Taghiyev küç. 13; tel. (12) 492-32-35; fax (12) 493-48-30; e-mail office@lukoil.baku.az; subsidiary of LUKoil (Russia); in Dec. 2004 completed purchase of the LukAgip jt venture from partner ENI (Italy); Gen. Dir FIKRAT ALIYEV.

Petroleum Geo-Services: 1004 Baku, Vagif Mustafa-Zadeh küç. 6–10; tel. (12) 497-43-45; internet www.pgs.com; f. 1991; collates geophysical data for the petroleum and gas industries; Dir HASSAN AKHMADOV; 1,800 employees.

Shell Business Development Central Asia: 1033 Baku, Bul pr. 30; tel. (12) 498-92-04; fax (12) 498-92-03; most of Shell's interests in Azerbaijan sold to National Oil Co of South Korea in Aug. 2007.

Statoil Caspian Region: 1010 Baku, Nizami küç. 96; tel. (12) 497-73-40; fax (12) 497-79-44; internet www.statoil.com; f. 1972; subsidiary of Statoil (Norway); Country Man. GEORGE GUNDERSEN.

Total Azerbaijan: 1000 Baku, Nizami küç. 340; tel. (12) 497-83-80; fax (12) 497-13-35; e-mail jean-claude.nawrot@total.com; internet www.total.com; subsidiary of Total (France/Belgium); Gen. Man. JEAN-CLAUDE NAWROT.

TPAO/TPOC/TP BTC (Türkiye Petrolleri Anonim Ortakliği): 1000 Baku, Nizami küç. 340; tel. (12) 498-95-26; fax (12) 498-14-35; e-mail info@tpao-az.com; f. 1994; involved in four Exploration-, Development- and Production-sharing Agreements, including Azeri-Chirag-Guneshli (6.75%), Shah Deniz (9%), Kur Dashi (5%) and Alov (10%); shareholder in the Baku–Tbilisi, Georgia–Ceyhan, Turkey (BTC) Main Export Pipeline (6.53%) and the South Caucasus Natural Gas Pipeline Project (SCP) (9%); Country Man. MEMET ALI KAYA.

MAJOR COMPANIES

By the early 2000s the majority of small enterprises were in the private sector. Most of the remaining larger state enterprises were to be privatized in the next phase of the privatization programme.

Azeraluminium (Azeral): 5000 Sumqayıt, Metallurgiya küç. 1; tel. (18) 642-98-60; fax (18) 642-98-61; e-mail info@azeral.com; internet www.azeral.com; f. 2000 from Sumqayıtalvanmetal (Sumgait Non-ferrous Metals), Gancaclinozem Aluminium Production Association (Ganca) and Daşkesan alunite plant; jt-stock co managed by Fondel Metal Participations BV of the Netherlands 2001–05.

Azerbaijan Electronics (AZEL): 1022 Baku, Raşid Behbutov küç. 71; tel. (12) 497-40-40; fax (12) 497-40-42; e-mail newmail@azel.net; internet www.azel.net; f. 1991; leading provider of computer and office equipment and consumer electronics in Azerbaijan and the south Caucasus.

Azerbaijan Rolled Pipes Manufacture (Azerboru): 5000 Sumqayıt, Sulh küç. 1; tel. and fax (418) 642-00-06; e-mail info@azerpipe.com; internet www.azerpipe.com; f. 1952; manufactures rolled pipes, building materials and drilling equipment for the petroleum industry; partly owned by Targol Investment (United Kingdom); Dir-Gen. AZIM AZIMOV; 3,250 employees.

AzerEnerji: 1005 Baku, Abdulkarim Alizada pr. 10; tel. (12) 492-31-09; fax (12) 492-63-55; e-mail azerenerji@azerenerji.com; f. 1993; constructs and installs power stations and electric facilities; seven subsidiary entities; Pres. ETIBAR PIRVERDIYEV; 700 employees.

Azerikhimia (Azerbaijan Chemicals Co): 5000 Sumqayıt, Samad Vurgun küç. 86; tel. (164) 5-94-01; fax (164) 5-98-17; e-mail root@qoch.sumgait.az; f. 1992; state-owned; chemical, pharmaceutical and plastic products; Pres. MEJIB KERIMOV; 10,300 employees.

Azerkontrakt (Azercontract): 1141 Baku, A. Alekperov küç. 83/23; tel. (12) 439-39-90; fax (12) 439-91-76; e-mail state@azcon.baku.az; state contract co; Pres. MIRI AHAD OĞLU GAMBAROV.

Azersun Holding: 2084 Baku, Heydar Aliyev pr. 94; tel. (12) 496-60-01; fax (12) 447-19-06; e-mail info@azersun.com; internet www.azersun.com; f. 1992; jt-stock co; production of canned meat and vegetables, tea- and vegetable oil-processing and packaging; packaging (incl. cardboard manufacture), distribution, transportation and warehousing; construction, banking and insurance; Pres. ABDOLBARI GUZEL; 3,000 employees.

Azertrans: 1001 Baku, İstiklal küç. 31; tel. (12) 492-07-05; fax (12) 492-54-71; f. 1992; provides tanker offload and rail facilities in Baku and Sangaçal; freight forwarding and transport; 10 affiliated cos; subsidiary of Azpetrol; Gen. Man. ELCHIN GULAMOV.

Azinmash (Azerbaijan Petroleum Engineering Research and Design Institute): 1029 Baku, Aras küç. 4; tel. and fax (12) 567-08-88; e-mail office@azinmash.azeri.com; internet www.azinmash.az; f. 1930; designs and manufactures equipment for petroleum and natural-gas industries; organizes patents and licences; prospecting; state-owned; Dir RAUF DJAVADOVICH DJABAROV.

Azneftkimyamash: 1110 Baku, Hasan Aliyev küç. 57; tel. (12) 441-17-16; fax (12) 441-17-23; e-mail azneftkimyamash@azdata.net; internet www.azneftkimyamash.com; f. 1936; open jt-stock co; designs and produces petroleum- and gas-related equipment; consists of 18 affiliated stock companies, including 14 machine-building plants; Chair. ALI YUSIF KARAKHANOV; 6,000 employees.

Bakinskii Rabochii (Baku Workers') Engineering Co: 1034 Baku, Proletarski küç. 10; tel. (12) 425-93-75; fax (12) 425-93-82; f. 1900; produces equipment for the petroleum industry, including pumping units and pipe transporters; state-owned; Dir MAMED AKPER OĞLU VELIYEV; 1,200 employees.

Baku Chinar Refrigerators Joint Stock Company: 1029 Baku, Narimanov küç. 4; tel. and fax (12) 496-64-73; e-mail cinar@azeronline.com; internet www.cinar-az.com; manufactures refrigerators; Dir MIRAKBAR MIRBABA SHUKUROV.

Improtex Group: 1000 Baku, Azi Aslanov küç. 115; tel. (12) 498-02-27; fax (12) 493-29-97; e-mail management@improtex.az; internet www.improtex.az; f. 1991; holding group, which includes IMAIR (see Civil Aviation), Improtex Commerce (distributor), Improtex Motors (importer), Improtex Trading (consumer-electronics retailer), Improtrans (transportation and logistics), and Improtex Travel (tour operator); Pres. VUGAR ALAKBAROV; approx. 1,200 employees.

Kaspmornefteflot (KMNF) (Caspian Maritime Oil Fleet): 1025 Baku, Telnov küç. 13; tel. (12) 490-62-36; fax (12) 490-62-37; e-mail frd@kmnf.baku.az; provides services for petroleum and natural gas production in the Caspian Sea, including construction, exploration, maintenance and transportation services; subsidiary of the State Oil Co of the Azerbaijan Republic—SOCAR; 318 vessels.

Milk-Pro Ltd (M-Pro): 1025 Baku, Mechanicheskaya küç. 4; tel. (12) 490-40-54; fax (12) 490-12-62; e-mail mpro@intrans.az; internet www.mpro-az.ru; f. 1991; produces dairy and juice products; Dir MOVSUM SHIKHIYEV.

SAF Ltd: 4002 Guba, Haydar Aliyev pr. 227; tel. (12) 433-23-42; fax (12) 431-66-49; e-mail safquba@aztelecom.net5; privatized in 1991; fmrly Quba canning factory; primary food-processing co; produces and exports fruit juice, jam and pickles; owns and produces the SAF brand; Dir ELMAN MIRZAKHANOV.

SINAM Ltd: 1141 Baku, F. Agayev küç. 9; tel. (12) 510-11-00; fax (12) 439-26-33; e-mail info@sinam.net; internet www.sinam.net; f. 1994; provides system integration services and support, software application and development and multimedia products; Pres. ELCHIN ALIYEV.

Ulduz: 1029 Baku, Khalglar Dostlugu Khiyabani küç. 1; tel. (12) 467-31-81; fax (12) 467-53-34; manufactures communications equipment; Dir ADIL MAMED OĞLU MAGERRAMOV.

Yeni BEMZ (Baku Electro-Mechanical Engineering Plant): 1029 Baku, Narimanov, Kondalan küç. 3; tel. and fax (12) 47-35-83; e-mail azema2002@rambler.ru; f. 1946; jt-stock co; undergoing privatization; manufactures electric motors for the mechanical engineering, mining and petroleum industries; Gen. Dir JAVID GASHIMOV; 230 employees.

TRADE UNIONS

Confederation of Azerbaijan Trade Unions (AHIK): 1000 Baku, Genjler meydani 3; tel. and fax (12) 492-72-68; e-mail ahik@ azerin.com; 1.3m. mems; Chair. SATTAR MEHBALIYEV.

Trade Union of Oil and Gas Industry Workers: 1033 Baku, Aga Neymatulla küç. 39; tel. (12) 467-69-53; fax (12) 447-15-85; e-mail oilunion@online.az; f. 1906; 161 local orgs in the petroleum and gas sectors; 67,900 mems (2003); Chair. JAHANGIR ALIYEV.

Transport

RAILWAYS

In 2005 there were 2,122 km of railway track, of which 1,270 km were electrified. The majority of total freight traffic is carried by the railways. Railways connect Baku with Tbilisi (Georgia) and Makhachkala (Dagestan, Russia). The rail link between metropolitan Azerbaijan and the Naxçıvan Autonomous Republic, and that to Yerevan (Armenia) have been suspended, owing to Azerbaijan's economic blockade of Armenia. An international line links Naxçıvan with Tabriz (Iran). In late 2007 construction began on a new 258-km railway line, linking Kars, in north-east Turkey, with Tbilisi (via Akhalkalaki, Georgia) and Baku; the project was scheduled for completion in 2009. There is an underground railway in Baku.

Azerbaijani Railways (ADDY): 1010 Baku, Dilara Aliyeva küç. 230; tel. (12) 498-44-67; fax (12) 498-85-47; e-mail info@addy.gov.az; internet addy.gov.az; f. 1992.

Baku Metro (Bakı Metropoliteni): 1073 Baku, H. Javid pr. 33A; tel. (12) 490-00-00; fax (12) 497-53-96; e-mail akhmedov_tagi@metro.gov .az; internet www.metro.gov.az; f. 1967; 20 stations on two lines (30 km); Gen. Man. TAGI M. AKHMEDOV.

ROADS

In 2004 the total length of roads in Azerbaijan was 25,021 km, of which 6,928 km were main roads; 92.6% of the road network was paved.

SHIPPING

Shipping services on the Caspian Sea link Baku with: Astrakhan, Russia; Türkmenbaşi (formerly Krasnovodsk), Turkmenistan; and the Iranian ports of Bandar Anzali and Bandar Nowshar. At 31 December 2007 the Azerbaijani merchant fleet comprised 302 vessels, with a combined displacement of 708,360 grt.

Baku Sea Port: 1010 Baku, U. Hajibeyov küç. 72; tel. (12) 493-67-74; fax (12) 493-36-72; e-mail port@sea.baku.az.

Shipowning Company

Caspian Shipping Company (Caspar): 1005 Baku, M. Rasulzade küç. 5; tel. (12) 493-20-58; fax (12) 493-53-39; internet www.caspar .baku.az; transports crude petroleum and petroleum products; operates cargo and passenger ferries; fleet of 69 vessels; Pres. A. A. BASHIROV.

CIVIL AVIATION

There are five airports in Azerbaijan, of which Heydar Aliyev Airport at Baku is the largest. Naxçıvan has its own airport.

Civil Aviation Administration: 1004 Baku, Heydar Aliyev International Airport; tel. (12) 492-90-98; fax (12) 437-49-41; e-mail hq@ caa.gov.az; Dir ARIF MAMMADOV.

Azerbaijan Airlines (AZAL) (Azerbaijan Hava Yollari): 1000 Baku, Azadlıq pr. 11; tel. (12) 493-44-34; fax (12) 498-52-37; e-mail azal@azal.baku.az; f. 1992; formerly Azalavia; state airline operating scheduled and charter passenger and cargo services to Africa, the CIS, Europe, South-East Asia and the Middle East; Gen. Dir JAHANGIR ASKEROV.

IMAIR Airlines: 1000 Baku, Hazi Aslanov küç. 115; tel. (12) 493-41-71; fax (12) 493-27-77; e-mail root@imair.com; internet www.imair .com; f. 1995; independent airline operating international regular scheduled and charter passenger and cargo services, mainly within the CIS region; Pres. FIZOULI ALEKPEROV.

Turan Air: 1010 Baku, 28 May küç. 68/64; tel. (12) 498-94-31; fax (12) 498-94-34; e-mail root@turan-air.com; internet www.turan-air .com; f. 1994; operates scheduled and charter passenger and cargo services, mainly within the former USSR; Gen. Dir VAGIF ISKENDEROV.

Tourism

Tourism is not widely developed. However, there are resorts on the Caspian Sea, including the Ganjlik international tourist centre, on the Apsheron Peninsula, near Baku, which has four hotels as well as camping facilities. There were 1,177,277 tourist arrivals in 2005, when receipts from tourism totalled US $100m. The number of tourist arrivals increased to 1,193,742 in 2006.

Dept of Tourism of the Ministry of Culture and Tourism: 1004 Baku, Neftchilar pr. 65; tel. (12) 492-87-13; fax (12) 492-98-41; e-mail tourism@myst.co-az.net; Head TEYMUR MEHDIYEV.

Culture

NATIONAL ORGANIZATIONS

Ministry of Culture and Tourism: see The Government (Ministries); organizes International Hari Bül-Bül Folk Festival, Kara Karayev International Festival of Modern Music, Musical September in Baku International Festival.

Ministry of Youth and Sport: see The Government (Ministries).

Autonomous Republic of Naxçıvan

Ministry of Culture of the Naxçıvan Republic: 7000 Naxçıvan, pr. 1; tel. (136) 4-22-52; Minister NIZAM IBRAHIM OĞLU HAJIYEV.

CULTURAL HERITAGE

At the end of 2006 there were 168 museums and 4,021 public libraries in the country.

Azerbaijan R. Mustafayev State Museum of Fine Arts: 1001 Baku, Niyazi küç. 9–11; tel. (12) 492-57-89; fax (12) 492-67-69; e-mail adim@science.az; f. 1924; Dir A. R. ASRAFILOV.

Baku Museum of Education: 1001 Baku, Niyazi küç. 11; tel. (12) 492-04-53; f. 1940; library of 52,000 vols; Dir T. Z. AHMEDZADE.

Baku State University Scientific Library: 1148 Baku, Z. Khalilova küç. 23; tel. (12) 439-06-21; fax (12) 498-33-76; e-mail sara_ibragimova@yahoo.com; internet www.bsu.az/ studentskitabxana.en.html; f. 1919; 2.5m. vols; publishes monthly newsletter and quarterly journals; Dir SARA IBRAGIMOVA.

Central Scientific Library of the Azerbaijan National Academy of Sciences: 1143 Baku, H. Javid pr. 31; tel. (12) 438-60-17; e-mail mail@csl-az.com; internet www.csl-az.com; f. 1925; 2.5m. vols; Dir A. ALIYEVA-KENGERLI.

Central State Archives of Literature and Art: 1106 Baku, Z. Bunyadov pr. 3; tel. (12) 462-96-53; e-mail marxiv@azintex.com; Dir MAARIPH ABI OĞLU TEYMUROV.

J. Jabbarli State Theatre Museum: 1004 Baku, Neftchilar pr. 123A; tel. (12) 493-40-98; Dir NURIDA GAMIDULLA KIZI NURULLAYEVA.

M. F. Akhundov Azerbaijan National Library: 1000 Baku, Khagani küç. 29; tel. (12) 493-40-03; fax (12) 498-08-22; e-mail anl@aznet.org; internet www.anl.az; f. 1923; 4.5m. vols; Dir KERIM TAHIROV.

Mähämmäd Füzuli Institute of Manuscripts of the National Academy of Sciences: 1001 Baku, İstiklal küç. 8; tel. and fax (12) 492-31-97; e-mail manuscript@dcacs.ab.az; internet www.science .az/en/manuscript/index.htm; f. 1950; manuscripts and historical documents relating to the history, philology and ethnology of Azerbaijani and other Muslim peoples; Dir MAMMAD MUSA OĞLU ADILOV.

Museum of the History of Azerbaijan of the Azerbaijan Academy of Sciences: 1005 Baku, H. Z. Tagiyev küç. 4; tel. (12) 493-36-48; fax (12) 498-52-11; internet www.science.az/en/ azhistorymuseum/index.htm; f. 1920; 120,000 exhibits on the history of the Azerbaijani people from ancient times; Dir NAILA MAMEDALI GIZI VALIKHANLI.

Nizami Ganjavi State Museum of Azerbaijani Literature: 1001 Baku, İstiklal küç. 53; tel. (12) 492-18-64; internet www.science.az/ en/literaturemuseum/index.htm; f. 1939; 76,000 exhibits on the history of Azerbaijani literature; Dir RAFAEL BABA OĞLU HUSEYNOV.

State Museum of Azerbaijani Musical Culture: 1000 Baku, R. Behbudov küç. 5; tel. (12) 498-81-84; fax (12) 498-69-72; e-mail musculture@azdata.net; internet www.musicmuseum.az; f. 1967; Dir ALLA BAYRAMOVA.

State Museum Palace of Shirvan-Shah: 1000 Baku, Icheri Şeher, Kichik Gala küç. 76; tel. (12) 492-83-04; fax (12) 492-29-10; f. 1964; historical and architectural museum and national park; Dir DADASHEVA SEVDA.

Autonomous Republic of Naxçıvan

J. Mamedkuluzade State Museum of Literature: 7000 Naxçıvan; tel. (136) 4-39-42; Dir SUBHI FARRUKH OĞLU KANKARLI.

Naxçıvan State Museum: 7000 Naxçıvan, Nizami küç. 31; tel. (136) 4-23-69; Dir Isfandiyar Mir Ismayil oğlu Asadullayev.

Xankandi (Stepanakert)

Xankandi (Stepanakert) Museum of the History of Nagornyi Karabakh: 2600 Xankandi, Gorkii küç. 4.

SPORTING ORGANIZATION

National Olympic Committee of Azerbaijan: 1072 Baku, Olimpiya küç. 5; tel. (12) 465-13-23; fax (12) 465-42-25; e-mail noc-aze@noc-aze.org; internet www.noc-aze.org; Pres. İlham Heydar oğlu Aliyev; Gen. Sec. Prof. Agadjan Abiyev.

PERFORMING ARTS

Drama, Opera, Dance

At the end of 2006 there were 31 professional theatres.

F. Amirov State Song and Dance Ensemble: 1001 Baku, İstiklal küç. 2; tel. (12) 497-62-31; f. 1936; Dir Agaverdi A. Pashayev.

State Academic Drama Theatre: 1000 Baku, Fizuli meydani; tel. (12) 494-49-19; fax (12) 494-35-66; f. 1873; Dir Qadirov Hiabbas Qulu oğlu.

State Academic M. F. Axundov Opera and Ballet Theatre: 1000 Baku, Nizami küç. 95; tel. (12) 493-16-51; f. 1959; Dir Akif Taran oğlu Melikov.

S. Vurgun State Theatre of Russian Drama: 1000 Baku, Khagani küç. 7; tel. (12) 493-40-48; e-mail rdt@azdata.net; internet www.rusdrama-az.com; f. 1920; Dir Marat Farrukh oğlu Ibrahimov.

Uns Theatre (Communication Theatre): Baku, Neftchilar pr. 69; f. 2006; non-commercial; aims to revitalize and modernize Azerbaijani theatrical traditions; Head Prof. Nargiz Pashayeva.

Music

Ganca State Philharmonia Chamber Orchestra: 2000 Ganca, M. Abbaszade küç.; tel. (22) 2-53-21; Artistic Dir. Rasim Isa oğlu Bagirov.

U. Hajibekov State Symphony Orchestra: 1001 Baku, İstiklal küç. 2; tel. (12) 493-75-37; f. 1938; Artistic Dir Rauf Abdullayev.

K. Karayev State Chamber Orchestra: 1001 Baku, İstiklal küç. 2; tel. (12) 492-51-53; Artistic Dir Yashar Abdulkhalig oğlu Imanov.

M. Magomayev Philharmonia: 1001 Baku, İstiklal küç. 2; tel. (12) 492-51-53; Dir Rafiq Hussein oğlu Seidzede.

State Brass Band: 1000 Baku; tel. (12) 494-90-40; Artistic Man. Nazim Magerram oğlu Aliyev.

Autonomous Republic of Naxçıvan

State Musical Drama Theatre: 7000 Naxçıvan, A. Djavad küç. 2; tel. (136) 25-89; Dir Mamed Tahir oğlu Gummatov.

State Philharmonia: 7000 Naxçıvan; tel. (136) 5-68-98; Dir Mamed Tahir oğlu Gumbatov.

ASSOCIATIONS

Azerbaijan Musicians' Union: 1000 Baku, A. Aliyev küç. 9; tel. (12) 492-67-04; fax (12) 498-13-30; Chair. Farhad Shamsi oğlu Badalbeyli.

Azerbaijan Society of Cultural Relations with Countrymen Abroad—Vatan (Fatherland): 1001 Baku, İstiklal küç. 27; tel. (12) 492-60-66; fax (12) 492-55-82; f. 1987; cultural organization for developing contacts with Azerbaijanis in other countries; Chair. Elchin Efendiyev.

Society for Contemporary Music (Yeni Musiqi): 1141 Baku, Haqverdiyev küç. 3A/32; tel. (12) 439-06-70; fax (12) 438-76-01; Pres. Prof. Faraj Karayev.

Union of Artists of Azerbaijan: 1000 Baku, Khagani küç. 19; tel. (12) 493-62-30; Chair. Farhad Kurban oğlu Khalilov.

Union of Writers of Azerbaijan: 1000 Baku, Khagani küç. 25; tel. (12) 493-66-40; Chair. Anar Rasul oğlu Rzayev.

Education

Under Soviet rule, a more extensive education system was introduced, and the level of literacy was greatly increased, from 8.1% in 1926 to 97.3% in 1989. Education is officially compulsory between the ages of six and 17 years. Primary education begins at the age of six years. Secondary education, comprising a first cycle of five years and a second cycle of two years, begins at the age of 10. In 2005/06 22.1% of children of the relevant age attended pre-primary schools. In the same year total net enrolment at primary schools was 84.8% of the relevant age group; the comparable ratio for secondary enrolment

was 77.8%. The main language of instruction is Azerbaijani, but there are also Russian-language schools and some teaching in Georgian and Armenian. From 1992 a Turkic version of the Latin alphabet was used in Azerbaijani-language schools (replacing the Cyrillic script). Almost all secondary schools use Azerbaijani as the language of instruction, and the percentage of pupils taught in Russian had declined to 6.7% by 2004/05. In higher education technical subjects were often taught in Russian, but there were demands for the greater use of Azerbaijani. There are 27 state-supported institutions of higher education, including the Azerbaijan State Petroleum Academy, which trains engineers for the petroleum industry, and 15 private universities. In 2006/07 there were 129,141 students in higher education. Government expenditure on education was estimated at 723m. new manats in 2007, representing 12.1% of total state spending.

UNIVERSITIES

Azerbaijan Medical University: 1022 Baku, Bakikhanov küç. 23; tel. (12) 495-43-24; fax (12) 440-27-70; e-mail admin@amu.edu.az; internet amu.edu.az; f. 1930; fmrly N. Narimanov Medical University; 6 faculties; 2,000 teachers; 7,186 students; Rector Ahliman Tapdiq oğlu Amiraslanov.

Azerbaijan State Economic University: 1001 Baku, İstiklal küç. 6; tel. (12) 437-10-86; fax (12) 492-59-40; e-mail aseu@aseu.az; internet www.aseu.az; f. 1929; current name and status adopted in 2000; 5 faculties; Rector Shamsaddin H. Haciyev.

Azerbaijan State Oil Academy (ASOA/ADNA): 1010 Baku, Azadlıq pr. 20; tel. (12) 493-45-57; fax (12) 498-29-41; e-mail ihm@adna.baku.az; internet www.adna.baku.az; f. 1920; training and scientific research; 7 faculties; Rector Prof. Siyavuş F. Qarayev.

Azerbaijan Technical University (AzTU): 1073 Baku, Hüseyn Cavid pr. 25; tel. (12) 438-33-43; fax (12) 438-32-80; e-mail aztu@aztu.org; internet www.aztu.az; f. 1950; 8 faculties; 835 teachers; 6,141 students; Rector Prof. Havar Amir oğlu Mammadov.

Baku State University (Bakı Dovlat Universiteti): 1148 Baku, Z. Khalilov küç. 23; tel. (12) 439-08-58; fax (12) 498-33-76; e-mail bsu@bsu.az; internet www.bsu.az; f. 1919; 16 faculties; 1,330 teachers; 14,850 students; Rector Abel Mammadali Maharramov.

Caucasus University (Qafqaz Universiteti): 1010 Baku, Baku-Sumqayıt Şosesi 16-km; tel. (12) 448-28-62; fax (12) 448-28-61; e-mail admin@qafqaz.edu.az; internet www.qafqaz.edu.az; f. 1993; instruction in Azerbaijani and Turkish; private; four faculties; Rector Dr Ahmad Sanıç.

Khazar University: 1096 Baku, Mehseti küç. 11; tel. (12) 421-79-27; fax (12) 498-93-79; e-mail contact@khazar.org; internet www.khazar.org; f. 1991; private; main language of instruction is English; six schools; 145 teachers; 1,500 students; Pres. Prof. Hamlet Isaxanli.

Social Welfare

Azerbaijan has a comprehensive social security system, which aims to ensure that every citizen receives at least a subsistence income and that health care and education are freely available. The system aims to cover all groups of the population. The social benefits are financed by three extra-budgetary funds, the Social Protection Fund, the Employment Fund and the Disabled Persons' Fund. The Social Protection Fund receives transfers from the republican budget as well as contributions from employers and employees, and the Employment Fund is financed by social-insurance contributions from employers. In 2006 there were 8.1 hospital beds for every 1,000 inhabitants in Azerbaijan. In 2008, according to Ministry of Health estimates, Azerbaijan had 36 physicians for every 10,000 people, with the number declining significantly outside the capital; medical facilities in remote regions were reported to be severely inadequate. According to the Minister of Health, some 94.5m. new manats were allocated to the upgrade and construction of medical institutions in 2008 (compared with 58.4m. new manats in 2007). In 2007 government expenditure on health was estimated at 257m. new manats (representing 4.3% of total state spending), and expenditure on social protection 595m. new manats (representing 10.0% of spending). On 6 January 2004 the Milli Majlis approved the European Social Charter of the Council of Europe, concerning human rights.

In 2006 life expectancy at birth was estimated to be 62 years for men and 66 years for women. The official retirement age is 62 for men and 57 for women. The extra-budgetary Social Protection Fund provides for old-age, disability and survivor pensions. Some 1.2m. people were receiving pensions at the beginning of 2008, according to official figures, of whom 821,000 were old-age pensioners. In 2008 the average monthly old-age pension totalled 62.9 new manats.

NATIONAL AGENCIES

Ministry of Labour and Social Protection (see The Government—Ministries): **Employment Fund:** 1000 Baku; f. 1991; extrabudgetary govt fund; pays for vocational training.

State Social Protection Fund: 1122 Baku, H. Zardabi pr. 80; tel. (12) 434-60-18; fax (12) 434-55-87; e-mail info@sspf.gov.az; internet www.sspf.gov.az; f. 1992; extra-budgetary govt fund; Chair. SALIM MUSLUMOV.

Ministry of Public Health: see The Government (Ministries).

State Committee for Refugees and Internally Displaced Persons: 1122 Baku, Tbilisi pr. 57; tel. (12) 430-09-25; fax (12) 431-51-36; e-mail info@refugees-idps-committee.gov.az; internet www.refugees-idps-committee.gov.az; Chair. Deputy Prime Minister ALI SAMIL OĞLU HASANOV.

State Oil Fund of the Republic of Azerbaijan (SOFAZ): 1014 Baku, Bül-Bül pr. 20; tel. (12) 498-77-53; fax (12) 498-76-53; e-mail office@oilfund.az; internet www.oilfund.az; f. 1999; Exec. Dir SAMIR ŞARIFOV.

HEALTH AND WELFARE ORGANIZATIONS

Azerbaijan Red Crescent Society: 1022 Baku, S. Vurgun küç. 112; tel. (12) 493-84-81; fax (12) 493-15-78; e-mail redcrescent@redcrescent.az; internet www.redcrescent.az; Pres. NOVRUZALI ASLANOV.

Azerbaijani League for the Defence of the Rights of Children: 1009 Baku, Mirzagi Aliyeva küç. 130/33; tel. (12) 948-81-42; e-mail league@box.az; f. 1990; Dir YUSIF BAKIROV.

Caritas Azerbaijan: 1069 Baku, Telymur Aliyev küç. 69B/1; tel. and fax (12) 462-22-55; e-mail parish@cathol.baku.az; Roman Catholic welfare org.; f. 2003; Dir Fr JOSEPH PRAVDA.

International Rescue Committee (IRC): 1141 Baku, A. Alekperov küç. 5, bl. 565, 2nd floor; tel. (12) 403-24-47; fax (12) 434-01-96; e-mail office@theirc.az; f. 1994.

Relief International (RI): 1000 Baku, Gorki küç. 50; tel. (12) 498-42-76; fax (12) 497-37-56; e-mail relief@baku.org; internet www.ri.org; delivers medical supplies and equipment and provides relief services; Dir SAMIR MAMEDOV.

United Nations Children's Fund (UNICEF Azerbaijan): 1073 Baku, S. Dadashev küç. 24; tel. (12) 492-30-13; fax (12) 492-24-68; e-mail baku@unicef.org; f. 1993; Country Dir HANAA SINGER.

United Nations World Food Programme: 1001 Baku, UN 50th Anniversary küç., UN House 3; tel. (12) 493-80-96; fax (12) 493-82-06; e-mail wfp.baku@wfp.org; Country Dir LYNNE MILLER.

The Environment

Considerable environmental damage has resulted from exploitation of the petroleum and gas resources of the Caspian Sea, and from the development of industrial areas in the east of the country. Baku and Sumgayıt (the Apsheron Peninsula) are particularly affected and are major sources of atmospheric, soil and marine pollution. In addition, excessive use of chemicals in agriculture has had a negative impact. Some regulation, including a Law on the Protection of the Environment, was introduced in 1992–93. The European Commission and the Global Environment Facility initiated a Caspian Environment Programme in the five Caspian littoral states, to combat pollution and the rising water level; seven towns and 35 populated areas had already become submerged in Azerbaijan, owing to this problem. There were significant concerns over the environmental impact of major pipeline construction projects under way in the Caucasus, particularly the Baku–Tbilisi (Georgia)–Ceyhan (Turkey) petroleum pipeline, which was inaugurated in 2005.

In 2005 there were 13 nature reserves (with a total area of 200.8 ha) and seven national parks (117.7 ha) in Azerbaijan. Expenditure on protection and maintenance related measures and projects in 2004 was 140,321m. manats.

GOVERNMENT ORGANIZATIONS

Ministry of Ecology and Natural Resources: see The Government (Ministries).

State Committee for Improvement of Soil and Water Economy: 1016 Baku, Azadlıq meydani 1; tel. (12) 493-61-54; fax (12) 493-

11-76; e-mail irriqation@azdata.net; f. 1923; Chair. AKHMED JUMA OĞLU AKHMEDZADE.

State Committee for Material Resources: 1016 Baku, Government House; tel. (12) 493-75-35; fax (12) 493-56-76.

ACADEMIC INSTITUTES

Azerbaijan National Academy of Sciences: 1141 Baku, Ağayev küç. 9; tel. and fax (12) 492-35-29; e-mail info@science.az; internet www.science.az; Pres. MAHMUD KERIM OĞLU KERIMOV; institutes incl.:

Central Botanical Garden: 1073 Baku, Badamdar şosesi 40; tel. (12) 438-11-72; e-mail cbg@lan.ab.az; internet www.aznabatat.com; f. 1934; Dir ORUC VELI İBADLI.

Institute of Botany: 1073 Baku, Badamdar şosesi 40; tel. (12) 439-32-30; fax (12) 439-33-80; e-mail botanica@baku.ab.az; internet www.science.az/en/botany/index.htm; f. 1936; Dir SALIM HUSEYINPHASA OĞLU MUSAYEV.

Azerbaijan Research Institute of Energetics and Energy Design: 1012 Baku, H. Zardabi pr. 94; tel. (12) 432-80-76; fax (12) 431-60-47; e-mail energy_acentre@bakililar.az; f. 1941; publishes *Problems of Power Engineering* (quarterly); Dir RAUF ISMAYIL OĞLU MUSTAFAYEV.

Azerbaijan Research Institute of Water Economy: 1012 Baku, Tbilisi pr. 69A; tel. (12) 431-69-90; f. 1961; Dir Dr ELCHIN SURKHOI OĞLU GAMBAROV.

National Centre on Climate Change and Ozone: 1154 Baku, Haydar Aliyev pr. 50, Ministry of Ecology and Natural Resources, National Hydrometeorological Dept; tel. (12) 498-27-95; fax (12) 441-56-85; e-mail climoz@online.az; f. 1995; Head MIRZAKHAN MANSIMOV.

Scientific Research Institute for Plant Protection: 2000 Ganca, Aziz Aliyev küç. 57; tel. and fax (222) 57-47-94; f. 1959; Pres. Dr CIDIQE RZA GIZI MAMEDOVA.

Non-Governmental Organizations

Azerbaijan Green Movement (AGM) (DZA): 1001 Baku, İstiklal küç. 47/17; tel. (850) 329-93-91; e-mail guseynovafk@azdata.org; f. 1989; sustainable life association; Contact FARIDA GUSEINOVA.

Caspian Environment Programme Thematic Centre: 1016 Baku, Uzeir Hadjibeyov küç. 40/108; tel. (12) 497-17-85; fax (12) 497-17-86; e-mail caspian@caspian.in-baku.com; internet www.caspianenvironment.org; Scientific Liaison Officer VLADIMIR VLADYMYROV.

Ecolex Environmental Law Centre (ELC): 1000 Baku, Bül-Bül pr., Ecoclub Bldg; tel. (12) 447-41-19; e-mail ecolex@azdata.net; internet ecolex.aznet.org; f. 2000; non-commercial org.; Man. SAMIR ISAYEV.

Ecosphere Social-Ecology Centre: 1006 Baku, Lermontov küç. 3/61; tel. (12) 492-43-48; e-mail ecosfera@azeurotel.com; internet ecocaucasus.org; f. 1999; humanitarian org., focusing on education, health care and environmental protection; Chair. FIRUZA SULTAN-ZADEH.

Defence

After gaining independence in 1991, Azerbaijan began forming a national army. As assessed at November 2007, this numbered 66,740 (an army of 56,840, a navy of 2,000 and air defence forces of 7,900). The country has a share of the former Soviet Caspian Flotilla. Military service is for 17 months (but may be extended for ground forces). The Ministry of Internal Affairs controls a militia of an estimated 10,000 and a border guard of an estimated 5,000; in 2006 the country's rapid reaction police regiment was also transferred to the immediate jurisdiction of the ministry. As a member of the Commonwealth of Independent States (CIS), Azerbaijan's naval forces operate under CIS (Russian) control. In May 1994 Azerbaijan joined the North Atlantic Treaty Organization's 'Partnership for Peace' programme. Defence expenditure in the 2007 state budget was estimated at 811m. new manats.

Chief of the General Staff: Col-Gen. NEDZHMEDDIN HUSSEIN OĞLU SADYKHOV.

AUTONOMOUS TERRITORIES

Constitutionally, Azerbaijan is described as a unitary state, but two territories had special status from the 1920s. The exclave of Naxçıvan (Nakhchivan) has the status of an Autonomous Republic and Nagornyi Karabakh formerly had that of an Autonomous Oblast.

The regional assembly of the Nagorno-Karabakh Autonomous Oblast, which had a majority ethnic Armenian population, proclaimed a 'Republic of Nagornyi Karabakh' on 2 September 1991. Following a referendum and elections to a 'parliament', the independence of the Republic of Nagornyi Karabakh was declared on 6 January 1992. All such pronouncements were declared invalid by the Azerbaijani authorities. However, local forces gradually gained control of the region and secured a de facto independence. In addition to territory linking Nagornyi Karabakh with Armenia, other parts of Azerbaijan proper were occupied.

AUTONOMOUS REPUBLIC OF NAXÇIVAN

Naxçıvan lies to the west of metropolitan Azerbaijan, separated from it by Armenian territory, which forms the northern and eastern borders of the exclave. Naxçıvan runs from the north-west to the south-east, following the course of the River Araks (Aras, Araxes), which forms its border with Turkey (at the north-west tip of the republic, on the Ararat plain) and with Iran. Its territory rises from the fertile lowlands of the Araks valley through the forested flanks of the Lesser Caucasus to the north. Naxçıvan covers an area of some 5,500 sq km (2,124 sq miles). Most of the population are ethnic Azerbaijani (Azeri), although at one time there was a sizeable Armenian community (comprising 45%–50% of the population in 1919), but this only provided some 5% of the total by the 1989 census. The chief town and capital is also called Naxçıvan, and is sited on the Araks. At 1 January 2007 the population of the Autonomous Republic of Naxçıvan was estimated at some 379,500, while that of Naxçıvan city was 70,400.

With the disintegration of the Ottoman and Russian Empires at the end of the First World War, conflicting historical claims to different areas exacerbated ethnic tensions and the process of forming nation states. Although Azerbaijan apparently surrendered its claims to Naxçıvan in 1920, it never became part of Soviet Armenia. In 1921 it became recognized as part of Azerbaijan: the Soviet-Turkish Treaty of March granted Azerbaijani jurisdiction; and the October Treaty of Kars, which finally established the borders of Turkey and Soviet Transcaucasia, effectively made Russia and Turkey the international guarantors of Naxçıvan's status. This fact, and the decline in the numbers of the ethnic Armenian population under Soviet rule, rendered renewed Armenian claims to the republic in the late 1980s and early 1990s largely rhetorical (there was a short-lived threat from Armenian militia in mid-1992). Naxçıvan was affected by the economic blockade on Armenia, however, and had

to rely on air links with Azerbaijan proper or on road routes through Iran.

Naxçıvan provided a source of strong support both for the nationalists who emerged in the late 1980s and for Heydar Aliyev, leader of Azerbaijan in 1969–87 and in 1993–2003. In 1990 nationalist demonstrators seized buildings of the ruling Communist Party in Naxçıvan and attempted to declare the republic's secession from the USSR. This protest was suppressed, but the authorities continued to experience demonstrations and outright challenges along the border with Iran. In March 1991 Azerbaijan participated in the Soviet referendum on the renewal of the USSR; some 93.3% of those who voted favoured remaining in the Union, but in Naxçıvan support was only some 20%. The leader of the nationalist Popular Front of Azerbaijan, Abulfaz Elchibey (*né* Aliyev), was a native of Naxçıvan, as was Heydar Aliyev, who had retired to his home after his dismissal from office in 1987. Aliyev formed his New Azerbaijan Party in Naxçıvan, and in September 1991 was elected Chairman of the local Supreme Soviet. He again became involved in national politics in 1993, replacing Elchibey as President of Azerbaijan in that year. Elchibey, meanwhile, took refuge in the exclave, and remained in effective internal exile until 1997, when he was permitted to return to Baku and active opposition politics until his death in 2000. The Azerbaijani Milli Majlis (National Assembly) approved a revised Constitution for Naxçıvan in December 1998, which was endorsed by the republic's legislature, and which defined the exclave as an 'autonomous state' within Azerbaijan. The highest official in the republic is the Chairman of the Ali Majlis (Supreme Assembly).

Chairman of the Ali Majlis (Supreme Assembly of the Autonomous Republic of Naxçıvan): Vasif Yusif oğlu Talibov, 7000 Naxçıvan; tel. (136) 44-01-01; fax (136) 44-01-01; e-mail ali-hasanov@mail.ru.

'REPUBLIC OF NAGORNYI KARABAKH'

Nagornyi Karabakh, Upper or Mountainous Karabakh (Dağlik Karabağ in Azerbaijani, Artsakh in Armenian), is on the north-eastern slopes of the Lesser Caucasus. The region lies in the south-west of Azerbaijan; Nagornyi Karabakh's own south-western border, near the town of Laçın (Lachin) in Azerbaijan proper, is separated from the international frontier with Armenia only by a narrow strip of land along the Akera valley. The terrain consists of lowland steppe and heavily forested mountainsides, with much of the territory rising above the tree line, reaching 3,724 m (12,218 ft) at Mt Gyamysh. The old autonomous region covers an area of 4,400 sq km (1,698 sq miles), but the forces of the 'Republic of Nagornyi Karabakh' actually occupy some 7,059 sq km or just over 8% of the territory of the Azerbaijan Republic. Historically, the Armenian population claims dominance in Şaumyan, on the north-western borders of the enclave, and in a wider 'Northern Nagornyi Karabakh', which stretches up as far as the town of Ganca (Gyanja, known as Gandzak by the Armenians—formerly Kirovabad). Following the troubles of the late 1980s and early 1990s, however, most ethnic Armenians had been expelled from areas still under the control of the Azerbaijani Government, and Azeris had been expelled from the territories occupied by the Nagornyi Karabakh forces (Nagornyi Karabakh, the districts of Cabrayil, Kelbecer, Qubadlı, Laçın and Zangilan and most of the districts of Ağdam and Fizuli). In 1989, at the time of the last Soviet census, the population of the Autonomous Oblast was 189,085, of whom 77% were ethnic Armenians and 22% Azeris. Even then, full

account had not been taken of the disruption caused by refugees from ethnic disputes, and this situation was exacerbated by the open conflict of the early 1990s. A census was held on 18–27 October 2005 by the de facto authorities, the preliminary results of which estimated the number of permanent inhabitants at 137,743. The population consisted almost entirely of ethnic Armenians. There were also small numbers of Russians in the region, as well as Ukrainians, Belarusians, Greeks, Tatars and Georgians. The capital and chief town is Xankandi (Khankendi—Stepanakert).

The Armenian principalities of Artsakh acknowledged Persian (Iranian) pre-eminence during the Middle Ages. Nagornyi Karabakh came under formal Russian control in the first decades of the 19th century, with the 1813 treaty between Russia and Persia being signed near the Karabakh village of Gulistan. The collapse of the Russian Empire of 1917 provoked Turkish intervention in Transcaucasia, to the detriment of the Armenian population, which suffered considerable loss of life in 1918–20. With the establishment of Bolshevik power, the Soviet Bureau of Transcaucasian Affairs (Kavburo) advised on the status of the autonomous protectorate. It recommended the union of Nagornyi Karabakh with the Soviet Republic of Armenia, but Stalin (Iosif Dzhugashvili) reversed the decision, and the enclave formally came under the jurisdiction of Azerbaijan on 5 July 1921, with Shushi (Şuşa) as its first capital. The borders of Soviet Transcaucasia and the status of Nagornyi Karabakh and Naxçıvan as territories of Azerbaijan were guaranteed by treaty with Turkey, at Kars, in October. Nagornyi Karabakh secured a distinct status within Azerbaijan when it was declared an autonomous oblast in 1923.

The Soviet state did not tolerate open discontent, although there were appeals to the all-Union authorities to permit the union of Nagornyi Karabakh with Armenia in 1945, 1966 and 1977. There were also periods of ethnic tension, notably in 1967–68. From the mid-1980s, with a reformist Soviet leadership in power, the pressure to re-examine the status of Nagornyi Karabakh increased. However, the authorities persisted in their refusal to address the issue. This resulted in large-scale demonstrations by Armenians in Nagornyi Karabakh and violence between ethnic Armenian and Azeri villages in the enclave. In February 1988 the Nagornyi Karabakh Soviet adopted a resolution demanding a transfer to Armenian jurisdiction, provoking anti-Armenian riots in Azerbaijan and much violence. Continued Armenian lobbying and unrest elicited a reaction from ethnic Azeris, with protests and rallies spreading to Kirovabad and other towns in November—in that month alone 14,000 ethnic Armenians fled Azerbaijan. Similar tensions and violence caused some 80,000 Azeris to leave Armenia in the same period. Many of these migrations were the result of forcible deportations.

On 12 January 1989 the Oblast's authorities were suspended, and the region was placed under the jurisdiction of a Special Administrative Committee (SAC), responsible to the all-Union Council of Ministers. The imposition of direct rule, however, did little to alleviate tensions. Widespread public discontent forced the Azerbaijani authorities to recognize the nationalist opposition movement and to declare the sovereignty of the republic. In September they imposed an economic blockade of Armenia. In November the SAC was replaced by a republican Organizing Committee, mainly consisting of Azeris. This provoked the Armenian Supreme Soviet to declare on 1 December that the enclave was part of a 'unified Armenian republic'; the economic blockade was reimposed, and there was violence in Nagornyi Karabakh and on the Armenian–Azerbaijani border. In January 1990 the all-Union Supreme Soviet deemed the Armenian declaration of December 1989 to be unconstitutional, but the Armenian legislature declared the primacy of its own legislation. In August 1990 the Azerbaijani legislature resolved to abolish the autonomous status of Nagornyi Karabakh.

A state of emergency was imposed in Nagornyi Karabakh in early 1991, but Soviet troops failed to contain the increasing violence. There were also allegations of these troops aiding Azerbaijani attempts to expel ethnic Armenians from border areas. Meanwhile, in July the increasing activity of ethnic Armenian paramilitary units led the Soviet leader, Mikhail Gorbachev, to insist on their disarmament. However, by the end of the year, following the formation of the Commonwealth of Independent States (CIS) and Gorbachev's resignation, the USSR had ceased to exist. Despite Russian and Kazakhstani efforts to mediate an agreement (the initiative foundered after an aircraft carrying Azerbaijani and Russian negotiators crashed or was shot down), nationalist activism and violence continued to escalate. Moreover, with Azerbaijan moving towards claiming independence, a joint session of the Supreme Soviet of the Nagorno-Karabakh Autonomous Oblast and the district soviet of Shaumyan declared a 'Republic of Nagornyi Karabakh' on 2 September. In December a referendum indicated overwhelming support for independence, and, following a general election on 28 December, a new 'parliament' formally proclaimed the independence of the Republic of Nagornyi Karabakh on 6 January 1992. The polity gained no international recognition, even from Armenia, which also renounced any territorial claims against Azerbaijan in March and denied that it had any control over the Nagornyi Karabakh Self-Defence Forces.

By 1992 sporadic clashes had developed into full-scale conflict. Stepanakert was, effectively, under siege by Azerbaijani forces and Shushi by Armenian paramilitaries. In January the President of Azerbaijan, Ayaz Mutalibov, placed the region under direct presidential rule, and the Conference on Security and Co-operation in Europe (CSCE, later the Organization for Security and Co-operation in Europe—OSCE) began attempts to mediate a solution to the conflict. The following month the Nagornyi Karabakh Self-Defence Forces attacked the town of Xojali, defeating Azerbaijani troops and killing many civilians. The militia continued to gain territory, in May seizing control of the towns of Shushi (thus ending the bombardment of Stepanakert) and, in Azerbaijan proper, Laçın. By the end of the month, when a short-lived cease-fire was negotiated, the Karabakh military was in control of the whole enclave and of a 'corridor' across the Laçın valley to Armenia.

There was a massive counter-offensive by Azerbaijani forces in June–October 1992, resulting in the exodus of several thousand people. In August the Nagornyi Karabakh legislature declared a state of martial law, with a State Defence Committee replacing the enclave's government. Its Chairman was Robert Kocharian, a member of the ruling faction, closely linked to the party of President Levon Ter-Petrossian of Armenia. Meanwhile, despite the latter's constant disclaimers of direct involvement, Armenian help was certainly important in resisting Azerbaijani attempts to close the Laçın corridor. However, in mid-1992 government forces did reoccupy

almost one-half of the territory of the Republic of Nagornyi Karabakh, mainly in the north. This, in turn, led the Armenians to accuse Azerbaijan of receiving covert assistance from Turkey. Other sources attributed Azerbaijani success to improved morale after the de facto coup of the nationalists and the election of their leader, Abulfaz Elchibey, as President in June. Furthermore, the new commander and presidential plenipotentiary in Karabakh, Col Surat Husseinov, could bolster the regular army with forces equipped at his own expense.

In 1993 the Azerbaijani forces again lost ground, weakened by domestic political divisions. In early February Husseinov withdrew his forces from the occupied northern Karabakh town of Mardakert to Ganca, for reasons that remain unclear. Certainly the move provided the Self-Defence Forces of Nagornyi Karabakh with the opportunity to embark on their own counter-offensive. By March they were occupying Azerbaijani territory outside the borders of the enclave, to the south (Fizuli) and to the west (Kelbecer). The Nagornyi Karabakh militias continued to make advances, seizing Ağdam in July and Fizuli in August. Although they made no permanent claim on territory outside the existing borders, and withdrew from some villages in Qubadlı, by October the ethnic Armenian forces had reached the Iranian border. By this time, the forces of Nagornyi Karabakh had occupied about one-fifth of Azerbaijani territory.

These advances caused widespread international concern. The UN approved Resolution 822 on 30 April 1993 (demanding an immediate cease-fire and the withdrawal of Armenian units from Azerbaijani territory), Resolution 853 on 29 July (condemning all hostilities and reiterating the demand for withdrawal, notably from Ağdam), and Resolution 874 on 14 October (endorsing a CSCE schedule for the implementation of Resolutions 822 and 853). This last resolution also acknowledged the Karabakh Armenians as a separate party in the conflict, although the Azerbaijan and Nagornyi Karabakh leaderships held their first direct negotiations in August. The weight of international opinion also encouraged Armenia to urge moderation on the Nagornyi Karabakh leadership. Continuing efforts by the CSCE, led by the 'Minsk Group' of interested parties, and a parallel initiative by Russia culminated in an agreement, the Bishkek Declaration, signed in Kyrgyzstan on 5 May 1994. A cease-fire came into effect one week later, and the agreement was formalized by the military authorities on 27 July. A political solution remained elusive, but the cease-fire, by and large, persisted. Prisoner-of-war exchanges took place in May 1995. By mid-1998 continuing OSCE efforts to mediate a settlement had caused the fall of President Ter-Petrossian and the accession of a less compromising Government in Armenia. This administration supported the Karabakh preference for a 'package' peace settlement, one which would not require Nagornyi Karabakh to relinquish its military advantages and security guarantees in advance of resolving the issue of its status. However, negotiations subsequently stalled, despite intensive international mediation.

In December 1994 the Nagornyi Karabakh Supreme Council introduced the institution of a presidency; Kocharian was elected by the Council as the first President of Nagornyi Karabakh on 22 December. In April–June 1995 elections were held to the republican legislature, which was renamed the Azgayin Zhoghov (National Assembly) in March 1996 and consisted of 33 members. On 24 November 1996 Kocharian secured an electoral mandate for remaining in the presidency, obtaining some 86% of the votes cast. On 20 March 1997, however, Kocharian was appointed Prime Minister of Armenia (he was elected President of Armenia on 30 March 1998). Arkadii Ghukassian was elected as the new President of Nagornyi Karabakh on 1 September 1997, with 88.9% of the votes cast. On 22 March 2000 Ghukassian was seriously wounded by gunmen in Stepanakert. The former republican Minister of Defence, Samuel Babaian, was subsequently found guilty of organizing the attack, in an attempt to carry out a coup. Further parliamentary elections were held on 18 June. On 11 August 2002 a presidential election took place; Ghukassian was re-elected to the presidency, with about 89.0% of the votes cast. The rate of voter participation was some 75%.

The worst border skirmishes for several years were reported in mid-2003, prompting fears of a resumption of the conflict, particularly given uncertainties over the political continuity of Azerbaijan's leadership in the months preceding the presidential election scheduled for October; however, both sides sought to avoid renewed military activity, although the newly elected President, İlham Aliyev, presented an aggressive stance, at least rhetorically, with regard to the territory. There were further violations of the cease-fire agreement in March 2005, resulting in fatalities on both sides. In legislative elections held in the region on 19 June, without international or Azerbaijani recognition, the majority of votes were cast in favour of pro-Government parties; an opposition candidate was reported to have been seriously assaulted by senior military officers following the elections. Talks on resolving the dispute over Nagornyi Karabakh had resumed between the Armenian and Azerbaijani sides in 2004, and continued in 2005–06.

After a bilateral summit, held in February 2006 in the French capital, Paris, and attended by the Armenian and Azerbaijani heads of state and other high-ranking government representatives, failed to produce any tangible results, Azerbaijani President Aliyev threatened, in March, to withdraw from the negotiation process unless progress was soon made. A subsequent summit meeting, held in Bucharest, Romania, similarly failed to end in agreement in June. Further talks in the Russian capital, Moscow, in January 2007 were also unsuccessful, although a representative of the Azerbaijani Ministry of Foreign Affairs declared that both sides had agreed to persevere with negotiations in the hope of reaching agreement before long. The Armenian and Azerbaijani foreign ministers both addressed the UN General Assembly in October on the subject of Nagornyi Karabakh. The former insisted that the Assembly was not the appropriate forum for a debate on this issue, since it was being dealt with under the auspices of the OSCE. The latter, however, contested that OSCE-orchestrated talks had failed to yield any positive results, and, as a result, that Azerbaijan was subject to 'the continued occupation by Armenia of a significant part...of [its] internationally recognized territories'.

A referendum on a draft constitution for Nagornyi Karabakh was conducted on 10 December 2006. According to official results, the Constitution, which described Nagornyi Karabakh as a sovereign and democratic state, was endorsed by some 98.6% of voters; the European Union and OSCE rejected the outcome of the referendum. A presidential election was held on 19 July 2007; the rate of voter participation was reported at 77%. Bako Sahakian, the former head of the Nagornyi Karabakh security service, secured a convincing victory with 85.1% of the votes, defeating four other candidates. Sahakian was installed on 7 September, and nominated Arayik Harutiunian, the leader of the Azat Hayrenik party (which had been represented in the Government since the 2005 elections) as Prime Minister. Harutiunian's nomination was approved on 3 September, and a new Government was formed later that month. At local elections, which were held on 14 October 2007, a company director, Vazgen Mikaelian, won the poll for Mayor of Stepanakert by about 84% of votes cast. The rate of voter participation was estimated at 62.8%.

In November 2007 the representatives of France, the Russian Federation and the USA chairing the OSCE Minsk Group, meeting on the occasion of the OSCE Ministerial Council in Madrid, Spain, jointly proposed to Azerbaijan and Armenia a number of basic principles for the peaceful settlement of the conflict; these were founded on the provisions of the Helsinki Final Act, including those related to refraining from the threat or use of force, the territorial integrity of states, and the equal rights and self-determination of peoples. In early March 2008 severe clashes between Armenian forces and Azerbaijani military units erupted in Nagornyi Karabakh; five members of the Azerbaijani armed forces were confirmed to have been killed, while Azerbaijan claimed that a number of Armenian soldiers had also died. Armenia denied accusations by the Azerbaijan Government that it had initiated the hostilities to divert attention from domestic political tension, and issued counter-accusations of responsibility. The OSCE Minsk Group subsequently appealed to Armenia and Azerbaijan to abide by the cease-fire agreement. On 14 March a non-binding resolution, submitted by Azerbaijan, reaffirming its territorial integrity and demanding the withdrawal of all Armenian forces, was adopted by the UN General Assembly, by 39 votes in favour and seven opposing (and 100 abstentions); in addition to Armenia, countries that rejected the resolution included France, the Russian Federation and the USA. Following the first visit by a Turkish Head of State to Armenia in early September, it was announced that the Ministers of Foreign Affairs of Turkey, Armenia and Azerbaijan would meet in New York, USA, later that month to discuss the issue of Nagornyi Karabakh.

President of the 'Republic of Nagornyi Karabakh': BAKO SAHAKIAN, Xankandi, 20 February St 3; tel. and fax (1) 4-52-22; e-mail ps@president.nkr.am; internet www.president.nkr.am.

Prime Minister of the 'Republic of Nagornyi Karabakh': ARAYIK HARUTIUNIAN, Xankandi; tel. and fax (1) 4-22-86; internet www.karabakh.net.

Chairman of the Azgayin Zhoghov (National Assembly) of the 'Republic of Nagornyi Karabakh': ASHOT GULIAN, Xankandi; tel. (1) 4-32-21.

Mayor of Stepanakert: VAZGEN MIKAELIAN, Xankandi; tel. (1) 4-46-33.

Bibliography

Broers, L. (Ed.). *The Limits of Leadership: Elites and Societies in the Nagorny Karabakh Peace Process*. London, Conciliation Resources, 2005.

Chorbajian, L. (Ed.). *The Making of Nagorno-Karabakh*. London, Palgrave, 2001.

Chorbajian, L., Donabedian, P., and Mutafian, C. *The Caucasian Knot: The History and Geopolitics of Nagorno-Karabagh*. London, Zed Books, 1994.

Coppieters, B. (Ed.). *Contested Borders in the Caucasus*. Brussels, Vubpress, 1996.

Cox, C. *Ethnic Cleansing in Progress: War in Nagorno-Karabakh*. Zurich, Institute for Religious Minorities in the Islamic World, 1993.

Croissant, M. P. *The Armenia–Azerbaijan Conflict*. Westport, CT, Praeger, 1998.

Fawcett, L. *Iran and the Cold War: The Azerbaijan Crisis of 1946*. Cambridge, Cambridge University Press, 1992.

Goldenburg, S. *The Caucasus and Post Soviet Disorder*. London, Zed Books, 1995.

Hasanli, J. *At The Dawn of the Cold War: the Soviet-American Crisis over Iranian Azerbaijan, 1941–1946*. Lanham, MD, Rowman & Littlefield, 2006.

Ismailzade, F. *Russia's Energy Interests in Azerbaijan: A Comparative Study of the 1990s and the 2000s*. London, Global Market Briefings, 2006.

Martin, R. J. *The Economy and Foreign Relations of Azerbaijan*. London, Royal Institute of International Affairs, 1996.

Najman, B., Pomfret, R., and Raballand, G. (Eds). *The Economics and Politics of Oil in the Caspian Basin: The Redistribution of Oil Revenues in Azerbaijan and Central Asia*. Abingdon, Routledge, 2007.

Shaffer, B. *Borders and Brethren: Iran and the Challenge of Azerbaijani Identity*. Cambridge, MA, MIT Press, 2002.

Swietochowski, T. *Russian Azerbaijan 1905–1920: the Shaping of National Identity in a Muslim Community*. Cambridge, Cambridge University Press, 1985.

Azerbaijan: Legacies of the Past and the Trials of Independence. Abingdon, Routledge, 2006.

Torjesen, S., Overland, I., and Umland, A. (Eds). *International Election Observers in Post-Soviet Azerbaijan: Geopolitical Pawns or Agents of Change?* Stuttgart, Ibidem-Verlag, 2007.

Van Der Leeuw, C. *Azerbaijan: a Quest for Identity*. Richmond, Curzon, 1999.

de Waal, T. *Black Garden: Armenia and Azerbaijan Through Peace and War*. New York, New York Univ. Press, 2003.

Wakeman-Linn, J. *Managing Oil Wealth: the Case of Azerbaijan*. Washington, DC, IMF, 2004.

Walker, C. (Ed.). *Armenia and Karabagh: The Struggle for Unity*. London, Minority Rights Publs, 1991.

Willerton, J. *Patronage and Politics in the USSR*. Cambridge, Cambridge University Press, 1992.

Also see the Select Bibliography.

BELARUS

Geography

PHYSICAL FEATURES

The Republic of Belarus is situated in north-eastern Europe. Historically, it was also known as Belorussia, White Russia or White Ruthenia. It is bounded by Latvia and Lithuania to the north-west, by Poland to the west, by Ukraine to the south and by Russia to the east. It covers an area of 207,595 sq km (80,153 sq miles).

The land is a plain with numerous lakes, swamps and marshes. There is an area of low hill country north of Minsk (Miensk), but the highest point, Mount Dzerzhinskii (Dzieržynski), is only 346 m (1,135 feet) above sea-level. The southern part of the country is a low, flat marshland. Forests covered some 34% of the territory in 1994, according to estimates by the UN Food and Agriculture Organization (FAO). The main rivers are the Dnepr (Dnieper), which flows south to the Black Sea, and the Pripyat or Prypiać (Pripet), which flows eastwards, to the Dnepr, through a forested, swampy area known as the Pripyat Marshes.

CLIMATE

The climate is of a continental type, with an average January temperature, in Minsk, of −5°C (23°F) and an average for July of 19°C (67°F). Average annual precipitation is between 560 mm and 660 mm.

POPULATION

Of a total population, at the 1999 census, of 10,045,237, some 81% were ethnic Belarusians, 11% Russians, 4% Poles and 2% Ukrainians. There were also small numbers of Jews, Tatars, Roma (Gypsies), Lithuanians and other ethnic groups. From 1990 the official language of the republic was Belarusian, an Eastern Slavonic language written in the Cyrillic script (there is also a Belarusian version of the Latin alphabet). This, and the long domination of the area by Russia, complicates the naming and transliteration of places and people. Russified versions of names are often the most familiar. Following a referendum in May 1995, Russian was reinstated as an official language. At the 1999 census, only 37% of Belarusians spoke Belarusian as their first language, and the remainder spoke Russian, although a far greater percentage regarded Belarusian to be their native language.

The major religion is Christianity, the Eastern Orthodox Church and the Roman Catholic Church being the largest groupings. There are also small Muslim and Jewish communities.

At 31 December 2007 the total population was estimated at 9,689,800, giving a density of 46.7 people per sq km. In 2006 72.4% of the population lived in urban areas. The capital is Minsk, which is situated in the centre of the country. Minsk was also declared to be the headquarters of the Commonwealth of Independent States (CIS). UN estimates indicated that it had a population of 1,805,000 in mid-2007. Other important towns are Gomel (Homiel—with an estimated population of 480,000 at January 2001), in the south-east of the country, Mogilev (Mahilou, 360,600), near the eastern border with Russia, Vitebsk (Viciebsk, 341,500), in the north-east, and, near the border with Poland, Grodno (Horadnia, 307,100) and Brest (Bieraście, 291,400), in the south-west.

Chronology

c. 878: Kievan (Kyivan) Rus, the first unified state of the Eastern Slavs, was founded, with Kyiv (Kiev, now in Ukraine) as its capital.

c. 988: Vladimir, ruler of Kievan Rus, converted to Orthodox Christianity.

10th century: The principality of Polotsk (Polatsak or Połacak) became the main centre of power on Belarusian territory, rivalling Kiev and Novgorod for predominance within Rus.

1054: The death of Yaroslav I ('the Wise') signalled the dissolution of the Kievan state into rival principalities, the main ones in Belarus being those of Polotsk and Turov (Turau).

1240–63: Rule of Mindaugas (Mindouh), in Novogrudok (Navahradak), who formed the Grand Duchy of Lithuania (Litva) and Rus. His state covered the western territories of Rus, including Minsk (Miensk), Vitebsk (Viciebsk) and Polotsk, and eastern Lithuania. Orthodox Slavs predominated

in the state and a precursor of Belarusian was the official language. The capital was later moved to Vilnius.

1386: Marriage of Jagiełło (Jahaila; baptized Władysław in 1386) of Lithuania and Jadwiga (Hedwig) of Poland established the union of the two states; subsequent treaties ensured Litva and Rus remained an autonomous Grand Duchy under Poland.

1569: The Grand Duchy of Litva, Rus and Samogitia (the latter—the 'lowlands', in western Lithuania—having been added in the 15th century) surrendered its separate status in the Union of Lublin, as part of an attempt to strengthen the Jagiellonian Polish-Lithuanian state, which was threatened by Sweden, the Ottoman Turks and the Russians.

1596: The Union of Brest ('Lithuanian' Brest or Brest-Litovsk) secured the allegiance of part of the Eastern Orthodox Church for the Pope, the head of the Roman Catholic Church; the creation of this 'Greek Catholic' or 'Uniate' Church was part of a process of attempting to catholicize the confessionally mixed Polish state.

1696: Old Belarusian was replaced by Polish as the language of official documentation in the Grand Duchy.

1772: Parts of Belarus were incorporated into the Russian Empire (the ruler of which had been proclaimed 'Tsar of all the Russias' in 1721) at the First Partition of Poland.

1793: Second Partition of Poland; acquisition by Russia of the rest of Belarus.

1839–40: The tsarist authorities intensified russification in the North-Western Territories, as Belarusian lands were known: the Greek Catholic Church was disbanded and the terms Belarus and Belarusian were banned.

1861: Emancipation of the serfs throughout the Russian Empire.

1902: The Belarusian Revolutionary (later Socialist) Hramada was founded; it became the leading Belarusian nationalist organization.

1 August 1914: Russia entered the First World War against Germany, Turkey and Austria-Hungary (the Central Powers); the tsarist military headquarters was based in Mogilev (Mahilou); from 1915 western Belarus was occupied by the Germans.

2 March (New Style 15 March) 1917: Abdication of Tsar Nicholas II after demonstrations and strikes in Petrograd (St Petersburg), the imperial capital.

5 August (18 August) 1917: A Rada (Council) was proclaimed in Belarus, following the assembly of a 'national council' in the previous month; the Rada was predominantly Socialist Revolutionary in nature, aiming for an autonomous republic under the Petrograd Provisional Government.

15 November (28 November) 1917: Bolshevik troops arrived in Minsk from Petrograd, where Lenin (Vladimir Ulyanov) and his Bolshevik allies had assumed power; the Bolsheviks took control of the city against little resistance.

28 December 1917 (10 January 1918): An All-Belarusian Congress proclaimed Belarus a democratic republic and refused to recognize Bolshevik power on Belarusian territory; the Bolsheviks disbanded the Congress, but it elected a Rada, which continued to work in secret.

14 February (Old Style 1 February) 1918: The Gregorian Calendar took effect in the Bolshevik territories.

21 February 1918: Bolshevik troops were forced to withdraw, as German forces occupied Minsk.

3 March 1918: By the Treaty of Brest-Litovsk, Soviet Russia ceded much territory to Germany, including Belarus, and recognized Ukrainian independence.

25 March 1918: The Belarusian Rada declared the independence of the state, as the Belarusian National Republic, but it only achieved limited autonomy under German military rule.

23 December 1918: Following the collapse of German power, the Russian communist leadership decided a Soviet Socialist Republic (SSR) should be established in the largely reoccupied Belarus.

1 January 1919: Proclamation of an independent Belarusian SSR.

February 1919: The Bolsheviks replaced the Belarusian SSR with a short-lived Lithuanian-Belarusian SSR ('Litbel'—in recognition of their common history).

March 1919: Polish armies invaded Belarus, Lithuania and Ukraine.

11 July 1920: Soviet troops recaptured Minsk; on the following day, by the Treaty of Moscow, the Soviet regime recognized Lithuanian independence and subsequently ceded some Belarusian territory; the Belarusian SSR was re-established in the following month.

16 January 1921: Soviet Russia recognized the Belarusian SSR and signed an alliance with the nominally independent state.

18 March 1921: Poland retained about one-third of Belarus, in the west, by the Treaty of Rīga, which formally concluded the Soviet–Polish War.

30 December 1922: Four Soviet Union Republics proclaimed the Union of Soviet Socialist Republics (USSR), of which the Belarusian SSR was a constituent and nominally independent member.

1924: The Belarusian SSR was almost doubled in size when the territories of Vitebsk and Mogilev were formally transferred from Russian jurisdiction.

October 1926: Gomel (Homiel) was transferred from Russia to the Belarusian SSR.

1933: The Soviet Government ordered mass arrests of Belarusian officials and party members; furthermore, the peasantry were enduring much hardship during the forcible collectivization of agriculture.

September 1939: The Soviet army occupied western Belarus (Polish since 1921), in accordance with the Treaty of Non-Aggression with Germany (the Nazi-Soviet Pact), signed in August.

3 November 1939: The communists ensured that the new territories (which increased the Belarusian SSR by one-half in area) voted for incorporation into the USSR.

22 June 1941: The Germans invaded the USSR.

28 June 1941: Minsk was occupied by German forces; a 'puppet' regime under Ivan Yermachenko was subsequently established.

December 1943: At an Allied conference in Tehran, Iran, the USSR insisted that it should not only have all of Belarus and Ukraine, but its western border should be along the Oder (Odra) river.

4 July 1944: Soviet troops recaptured Minsk; during the war about one-quarter of the population of Belarus died (pre-1941 population levels were not regained until 1970) and massive damage was done throughout the republic.

1946–48: A mass purge of the Communist Party of Belarus (CPB) resulted in the replacement of many ethnic Belarusian officials by Russians.

October 1980: Piotr Masherau, First Secretary of the CPB since 1965, was killed in suspicious circumstances, apparently after an argument with Leonid Brezhnev, General Secretary of the all-Union Communist Party.

April 1986: An explosion occurred at a nuclear reactor in Chornobyl (Chernobyl), Ukraine, 12 km south of the Belarusian border, which resulted in discharges of radioactive material; much of the 30-km exclusion zone around the disaster site was in Belarus and over 20% of the republic was severely affected.

June 1989: The Belarusian Popular Front (BPF) held its inaugural congress in Vilnius, Lithuania. In February 1990 a BPF rally in Minsk was attended by some 150,000 protesters, demanding extra funds to deal with the consequences of the Chornobyl disaster.

28 January 1990: The Supreme Soviet (Supreme Council) enacted a law replacing Russian as the official language with Belarusian.

4 March 1990: For the elections to the republican Supreme Soviet, the BPF was obliged to join the Belarusian Democratic Bloc; although the Bloc won about one-quarter of the seats decided by popular ballot, the CPB still controlled some 84% of the total number of seats in the legislature.

27 July 1990: The Supreme Soviet, after increasing popular pressure, declared the state sovereignty of Belarus (claiming the right to form its own armed forces, issue its own currency and conduct its own foreign policy), but rejected the possibility of secession.

17 March 1991: In the all-Union referendum on the future of the USSR, 83% of the citizens of the Belarusian SSR voted for a reformed Soviet federation, the highest proportion in any republic outside Central Asia.

25 August 1991: Following the collapse of an attempted coup in Moscow (the Russian and Soviet capital), the Supreme Soviet of Belarus adopted a declaration of independence; the communist leadership resigned and the CPB was suspended.

19 September 1991: Stanislau Shushkevich, a reformist, was formally elected as Chairman of the Supreme Soviet (Head of State); the name of the state was changed to the Republic of Belarus.

8 December 1991: The leaders of Belarus, Russia and Ukraine met near Brest and agreed to form a Commonwealth of Independent States (CIS) to replace the USSR; the headquarters of the organization was to be in Minsk. On 21 December the leaders of 11 Soviet republics, including Belarus, signed a protocol, the Almaty Declaration, on the formation of the CIS.

20–22 July 1992: A series of agreements between Belarus and Russia advocated increased co-operation and seemed to envisage some sort of confederation. The USA agreed to provide Belarus with US $59m., in order to assist with the removal of the former Soviet nuclear weapons located on its territory to Russia. The last remaining nuclear warhead was removed from Belarus in November 1996.

3 February 1993: The Supreme Council approved adherence to the Treaty on the Non-Proliferation of Nuclear Weapons and ratified the first Strategic Arms Reduction Treaty (START 1). The following day the Supreme Council voted to end the suspension of the CPB, which had been in force since August 1991.

26 January 1994: Shushkevich was dismissed from office by the Supreme Council. Vyacheslau Kuznetsou, the First Deputy Chairman of the legislature, became acting Head of State.

28 January 1994: Mechislau Gryb, a pro-Russian conservative, was elected the new Chairman of the Supreme Council.

30 March 1994: A new Constitution, providing for a presidential republic came into effect, following its approval by the Supreme Council earlier in the month.

10 July 1994: In the second round of voting in the presidential election (the first round was on 23 June) Alyaksandr Lukashenka, the head of the Supreme Council's anti-corruption committee and a supporter of closer integration with Russia, received 85% of the votes cast. He was inaugurated as the first President of Belarus on 20 July.

January 1995: Belarus joined the 'Partnership for Peace' programme of military co-operation of the North Atlantic Treaty Organization (NATO).

14 May 1995: The results of a referendum enhanced presidential authority, restored Russian as an official language and approved a change to the state symbols and closer integration with Russia. The first round of parliamentary elections was held.

28 May 1995: After a second round of elections, only 119 deputies had been elected to the 260-member Supreme Council. Another two rounds of voting, on 29 November and 10 December, brought the total number of new deputies to a quorate 198; the CPB obtained the largest number of seats, followed by the Agrarian Party (AP), the United Civic Party of Belarus (UCP) and the Party of People's Accord.

2 April 1996: Despite nationalist protests, President Lukashenka and the Russian President, Boris Yeltsin, signed a Treaty on the Formation of a Community of Sovereign Repub-

lics, which expressed the intention of closer integration and eventual confederation; opposition rallies were dispersed by police.

9 August 1996: President Lukashenka formally proposed a referendum on constitutional amendments to enhance his powers and extend his term of office (to 2001), after an increasing number of confrontations with parliament (the Constitutional Court ruled that the results of such a referendum were not legally binding, but the President revoked this decision by decree).

18 November 1996: Mikhail Chigir, who had been Lukashenka's premier, was replaced by Syargey Ling following criticism by Chigir of the referendum.

24 November 1996: Voting in the referendum on changes to the Constitution indicated substantial support for the President, despite drafts of the amendments being unavailable to the public and reports of widespread irregularities; the impeachment proceedings against Lukashenka initiated by 75 parliamentary deputies were, therefore, halted.

27 November 1996: The amended Constitution was published and came into immediate effect; it provided for a bicameral Natsionalnoye Sobraniye (National Assembly), the lower house of which, a 110-member Palata Predstaviteley (House of Representatives), was established the previous day by the majority in the old Supreme Council. Fifty deputies denounced the referendum results and declared themselves the legitimate legislature; the Chairman of the Constitutional Court and several other judges subsequently resigned in protest at the imposition of the constitutional changes.

13 December 1996: The President approved legislation inaugurating the new upper house of parliament, the 64-member Soviet Respubliki (Council of the Republic), consisting of regional representatives and presidential appointees.

8 January 1997: The deputies of a continuing 'Supreme Council' formed a 'shadow' cabinet, chaired by Genadz Karpenka.

2 April 1997: Presidents Lukashenka and Yeltsin signed the Treaty of Union between Belarus and Russia and initialled the Charter of the Union.

10 November 1997: The BPF initiated a petition campaign, known as Charter-97, with the aim of forcing new elections.

22–29 June 1998: Bulgaria, France, Germany, Greece, Italy, Japan, Poland, the United Kingdom and the USA withdrew their ambassadors from Belarus, in protest at the breach of international law involved in the effective eviction of the staff of 22 embassies housed in a residential compound outside Minsk. Subsequently, the European Union (EU) and the USA banned President Lukashenka and his ministers from entering their territory. In December Lukashenka gave assurances that, henceforth, he would comply with international agreements, and all ambassadors had returned to Minsk by September 1999.

2 November 1998: The Parliamentary Assembly of the Russia-Belarus Union voted for the creation of a unified parliament, to consist of two chambers.

15 December 1998: A new law was approved by the Palata Predstaviteley, effectively banning candidates with a police record or fine from standing in local elections to be held in April 1999. Numerous opposition candidates who had incurred fines for participating in anti-Government demonstrations were, thus, excluded.

10 January 1999: The Central Electoral Commission of the former Supreme Council scheduled a presidential election for May, in accordance with the 1994 Constitution. Despite the arrest of its Chairman, Viktar Ganchar, the Commission registered two candidates, the exiled leader of the BPF, Zyanon Paznyak, and the former premier, Chigir.

27 January 1999: President Lukashenka decreed that political parties, trade unions and other organizations must re-register by July; those failing to do so were to be disbanded. By September only 17 of the 28 existing official parties had been re-registered, owing to the imposition of stringent minimum levels of membership.

6 April 1999: The Chairman of the 'shadow' cabinet died. He was replaced on 21 April by Gryb, who was officially elected to the post in November.

6–16 May 1999: The Central Electoral Commission of the former Supreme Council was unable to organize fixed polling stations for the presidential election, which neither the Government nor the international community recognized as valid.

22 July 1999: Syamyon Sharetski, the leader of the AP and the former Chairman of the Supreme Council, fled to Lithuania to seek support, following his election as acting 'Head of State' by the former Supreme Council.

September 1999: Nine independent newspapers were closed down by the Government, amid a climate of increased government control and the 'disappearances' of several opposition figures, including Ganchar, from May.

17 October 1999: Up to 20,000 demonstrators participated in an anti-Government Freedom March. Leading opposition officials were among the 90 protesters arrested.

8 December 1999: A Union Treaty was signed between Russia and Belarus which, ultimately, intended to merge the two countries.

18 February 2000: Ling resigned as Prime Minister. Parliament subsequently approved Uladzimir Yermoshin, hitherto the Governor (Mayor) of Minsk, as his replacement.

15 March 2000: Up to 25,000 people took part in a second Freedom March in Minsk.

25 April 2000: The joint Council of Ministers of Belarus and the Russian Federation met for the first time.

19 May 2000: Chigir was convicted of abuse of office and received a three-year suspended prison sentence. The verdict, which was condemned as politically motivated by the international community, was overturned by the Supreme Court in December, pending a reinvestigation of the evidence, on the grounds that there had been legal irregularities during the trial.

15 and 29 October 2000: Despite boycotts by a number of opposition parties, elections to the Natsionalnoye Sobraniye were held. The Organization for Security and Co-operation in Europe (OSCE) declared the elections to be neither free, nor fair and the international community refused to recognize the results. After a second round of voting, 56 seats remained to be allocated, and further elections were scheduled for 18 March 2001.

9 September 2001: A presidential election was held; Lukashenka was re-elected, claiming 76% of the votes cast. However, international observers reported that the election was subject to serious irregularities, and the USA refused to recognize the results. Lukashenka was sworn in for a second term of office on 20 September; he appointed a new premier, Genadz Navitsky, on 1 October.

23 July 2002: Chigir was given a three-year, suspended prison sentence, following his trial on charges of tax evasion.

14 August 2002: At negotiations in Moscow, between Presidents Lukashenka and Vladimir Putin of Russia, the latter proposed dramatic changes to the two countries' proposed Union, suggesting the creation of a unified, federal state, with common parliamentary and presidential elections to be held in 2003–04, and the adoption of the Russian rouble as a common currency. Lukashenka, however, rejected the proposals, which he considered to represent a threat to Belarusian sovereignty.

24 September 2002: The Parliamentary Assembly of the Council of Europe (PACE) established a 10-member commission to investigate the disappearances of high-profile political figures in Belarus.

20 February 2003: The Parliamentary Assembly of the OSCE recognized the Belarusian National Council as legitimate. Meanwhile, travel bans on senior Belarusian officials, imposed by EU countries and the USA in November 2002, were withdrawn in April 2003.

17 April 2003: The UN Commission for Human Rights passed a resolution urging the Government to investigate the disappearances of opposition figures and the alleged implication of senior government officials in politically motivated executions.

28 April 2003: Representatives from Armenia, Belarus, Kazakhstan, Kyrgyzstan, Russia and Tajikistan formally inaugurated a new regional defence grouping known as the Collective Security Treaty Organization (CSTO).

10 July 2003: President Lukashenka dismissed a number of government officials, including Prime Minister Navitsky. The First Deputy Prime Minister, Syarhey Sidorsky, was appointed Prime Minister, initially on an acting basis. Navitsky was subsequently appointed Chairman of the Soviet Respubliki. Further appointments to the Government were made on 6 August.

19 February 2004: President Lukashenka accused Russia of supporting 'terrorism at the highest level' following the suspension of gas supplies (hitherto provided at a heavily subsidized rate) by the Russian company, Gazprom, to Belarus, following Belarus's failure to pay energy debts and accusations that Belarus had illegally siphoned gas supplies from pipelines across its territory. Although a compromise agreement was eventually reached, the dispute was considered to have stalled progress towards the proposed currency union with Russia.

28 April 2004: PACE approved two reports that criticized human rights abuses in Belarus. Senior government officials were accused of having been directly involved in the disappearances of several opposition figures.

24 July 2004: The Belarusian authorities closed the offices of the Russian state television company in Minsk, after the channel had broadcast footage of demonstrations held to protest against the 10th anniversary of Lukashenka's inauguration as President.

28 September 2004: The EU imposed prohibitions on the rights of four senior officials to travel to the Union, in response to the failure of the Belarusian authorities to conduct thorough investigations into the abuses reported by the Council of Europe earlier in the year, and the USA announced that it would impose similar restrictions.

17 October 2004: According to official results, some 90.3% of the registered electorate participated in a constitutional referendum seeking to abolish limits on the number of terms that a President was permitted to serve; the proposed amendment was approved by 77.3% of voters. In concurrent parliamentary elections, for which the rate of participation was reportedly 90.1%, no supporters of the opposition obtained representation. The opposition staged demonstrations in Minsk in the days following the polls, but these were subject to strong police pressure and failed to influence the results. Elections were repeated in two constituencies on 31 October.

30 December 2004: Mikhail Marinich, a former Mayor of Minsk and Minister of External Economic Affairs, who had attempted to stand against Lukashenka in the 2001 presidential election, was convicted of theft through abuse of office and sentenced to five years' imprisonment. Marinich's arrest in

April had caused widespread protests and was widely regarded as politically motivated. (In April 2006 Marinich was released on parole.)

25 March 2005: A rally to demand the resignation of Lukashenka, held on the anniversary of the foundation of the Belarusian People's Republic in 1918 and attended by up to 1,500 people, was dispersed by police, with several demonstrators reportedly injured.

1 June 2005: Prominent opposition politicians Mikalay Statkevich and Pavel Sevyarynets were sentenced to three years' corrective labour (subsequently reduced to two) for organizing demonstrations against Lukashenka in 2004.

28 July 2005: The Government of Poland recalled its ambassador to Belarus, owing to a diplomatic crisis that originated from perceived political interference by the Belarusian authorities in the activities of the Union of Poles of Belarus, a non-governmental organization representing the ethnic Polish minority in Belarus. The Polish ambassador returned to Minsk in October.

2 October 2005: A congress of opposition groups nominated civil society activist Alyaksandr Milinkevich as their single candidate to stand against Lukashenka in the presidential election scheduled for 2006.

19 March 2006: President Lukashenka won 83% of the votes cast in a presidential election, according to official figures; Milinkevich received 6%, but strongly disputed the outcome. The other two candidates did not receive more than 5%. Mass opposition protests were held in response to the conduct of the election and the official results. The Supreme Court subsequently rejected requests from two of the opposition candidates to invalidate the results.

8 April 2006: Lukashenka was inaugurated into his third term in office. On 17 April Prime Minister Sidorsky was reappointed to office.

10 April 2006: The EU imposed a visa ban on 30 Belarusian officials that it deemed responsible for the flawed conduct of the presidential election and the violent suppression of subsequent opposition protests. On 13 April PACE appealed to the Belarusian authorities to hold a repeat presidential election. In the following month the additional measure of 'freezing' the financial assets of Lukashenka and 35 others was passed by the EU. Also in May the US Administration imposed a visa ban on senior officials and in the following month introduced financial sanctions against 10 officials.

5 May 2006: A government reorganization included the appointment of Viktar Bura as a Deputy Prime Minister.

13 July 2006: One of the opposition candidates in the presidential election, Alyaksandr Kazulin, was sentenced to five-and-a-half years' imprisonment on charges of hooliganism and disorderly conduct related to events from his presidential campaign.

7 January 2007: The Russian Government suspended oil supplies through Belarus, in response to the imposition of a levy on Russian oil passing through Belarusian territory (following the introduction of an export duty by Russia). Supplies were resumed three days later when Belarus agreed to lift the transit duty and Russia in turn reduced its duty on oil exports.

14 January 2007: Local government elections were conducted. According to the Central Electoral Commission, voter turn-out was some 79.2% of the electorate. Opposition leaders again protested that the authorities had perpetrated gross malpractice, while the USA and EU declared that the elections had failed to meet democratic standards.

10 March 2007: A large opposition demonstration was staged with official authorization (on the anniversary of the creation of the Belarusian National Republic in 1918). Opposition leaders declared that some 10,000 supporters had attended the rally and that some 100 had been arrested.

14 September 2007: The military branch of the Supreme Court imposed sentences of between seven and 10 years on four Belarusian army officers, who were convicted of espionage after allegedly passing to Poland information on military facilities operated jointly by Russia and Belarus.

2 October 2007: Vadim Popov was elected, by an overwhelming majority, by the Palata Predstaviteley, to serve as its Chairman, replacing Vladimir Konoplev, who had resigned on grounds of ill health. (Popov had previously held this post in 2000–04.)

14 October 2007: An authorized rally, attended by some 5,000 opposition supporters, was staged in Minsk to demand that the Government meet 12 conditions that had been stipulated by the European Commission in November 2006 for Belarus's access to greater aid and trade co-operation within the European Neighbourhood Policy.

13 November 2007: The US Administration introduced additional financial sanctions, blocking the assets belonging to Belarus's largest state-owned company, Belneftekhim (Belarusian State Oil and Chemical Concern), on the grounds that it was controlled by Lukashenka, and, in addition, announced that it intended to impose similar measures against other Belarusian enterprises unless the authorities released political prisoners.

17 November 2007: A new organization, White Rus, chaired by Minister of Education Alyaksandr Radzkow, was officially established to consolidate support for Lukashenka prior to legislative elections due to take place in late 2008.

10 January 2008: Special police violently dispersed an unauthorized demonstration of about 3,000 in Minsk, which had been organized in protest at a new presidential decree restricting small-business activities; a number of participants who were arrested received fines or brief terms of imprisonment

7 March 2008: The Belarusian Government recalled its ambassador in the USA for consultations; the US Administration subsequently complied with Belarus's request that the US ambassador leave the country, and the number of staff in both embassies was reduced. The suspension of relations followed the USA's extension of sanctions, owing to the Belarus Government's continued failure to release Kazulin. In May Belarus expelled a further 10 US diplomats from the country.

28 June 2008: The Soviet Respubliki adopted a new media law imposing increased restrictions on media outlets; its introduction attracted criticism from the OSCE.

4 July 2008: A bomb exploded at a concert held in Minsk to commemorate the official Independence Day, injuring 54 people. A number of opposition activists were subsequently arrested, including former members of a nationalist organization banned in 1999 known as the Belarusian Union of Military Personnel. Several days later Lukashenka removed the State Secretary of the Security Council and the head of the presidential administration, on the grounds that they had failed to prevent the attack.

15 August 2008: Owing to the ill health of the Minister of Finance, Lukashenka appointed Andrei Kharkovets (hitherto Deputy Minister of Finance) to the post.

16 August 2008: Kazulin (who had already been allowed briefly to leave prison in February to attend his wife's funeral) was temporarily released for the funeral of his father-in-law; it was announced that he had been granted a pardon by Lukashenka. He subsequently declared that he accepted his release but not the pardon (on the grounds that the sentence had been unjust).

5 September 2008: In response to the release of Kazulin and other political prisoners, the US Administration announced the suspension of sanctions against two of the main companies belonging to Belneftekhim for a period of six months; the USA and the EU indicated that a further relaxation of the sanctions and visa restrictions in force against Belarus was conditional on the conduct of legislative elections scheduled for later in the month.

28 September 2008: Elections were held to the Palata Predstaviteley, in which no opposition representatives obtained election; 103 of the 110 elected deputies were nominally independent.

History

Dr ANDREW RYDER

EARLY HISTORY

The area of present-day Belarus was inhabited by Slavs from at least the ninth century. At the end of the 13th century Belarus constituted the core of a Grand Duchy of Lithuania and Rus, formed from Belarusian and Lithuanian lands. The Grand Duchy, in which Old Belarusian was the state language, united with Poland in the 16th century. Belarusian lands remained under Polish control until the partitions of Poland of 1772–95, when they became part of the Russian Empire. In the 19th century there was a growth of national consciousness among Belarusian intellectuals, but attempts to assert a Belarusian national identity were opposed by the tsarist authorities, which considered the Belarusian language to be a dialect of Russian and refused to accept the concept of a Belarusian nation. Although Belarus had a distinct culture and a distinct language, the national movement did not gather significant popular support.

SOVIET BELARUS

With the collapse of tsarist authority, in July 1917 a Belarusian national council, or Rada, was formed in Minsk (Miensk). However, the declaration of a Belarusian republic on 28 December, by an All-Belarusian Congress, had no lasting significance. Bolshevik forces loyal to the newly established regime of Lenin (Vladimir Ulyanov) in Petrograd (St Petersburg—then the Russian capital) seized power in Minsk in November, and dissolved the Congress at the end of December. Bolshevik troops withdrew when German forces occupied the city in February 1918. German occupation was formalized by the Treaty of Brest-Litovsk, signed by Germany and the Soviet regime in March, in the city of Brest (Bieraście). The Treaty ceded Russian control of a large swathe of western territory, running from the Baltic to the Black Sea, including Belarus. On 25 March Belarus again declared its independence, as the Belarusian National Republic (BNR), but achieved only limited autonomy under German military rule.

After Germany's defeat in November 1918, the Treaty of Brest-Litovsk was abrogated and German troops began to withdraw. Meanwhile, the Bolshevik Government of the newly created Russian Soviet Federative Socialist Republic (RSFSR) had changed its policy towards Belarus. The communist leadership had been unwilling to recognize the existence of a Belarusian nation and its right to self-determination, but it now seemed to want to create a semi-independent socialist Belarusian republic, as one in a series of 'buffer' states separating Soviet Russia from Germany and Central Europe. Accordingly, Bolshevik troops entered Belarus as the Germans withdrew, and a Belarusian Soviet Socialist Republic (SSR) was proclaimed on 1 January 1919.

In mid-January 1919 the Russian Communist Party (Bolsheviks)—RCP(B)—urged that the new SSR, as well as other newly established Soviet republics, be absorbed by the RSFSR. This scheme was soon replaced by a proposal for a military union of the two. In March, however, the Belarusian SSR was merged with Lithuania, then also under communist control, to form a new SSR, known as 'Litbel'. The new republic lasted less than one month, before Polish troops invaded in April 1919, occupied most of its territory, and declared Belarus part of Poland. Until 1921 control of Belarus passed back and forth between Soviet and Polish forces. Minsk was retaken by Soviet forces in July 1920 and one month later the Belarusian SSR was re-established. Finally, in March 1921, the Treaty of Rīga was signed, which allocated the western one-third of Belarusian lands to Poland, while in the east the Belarusian SSR was firmly established.

BELARUS IN THE USSR

Nominal independence did not give Belarus control over its own affairs. The Government of the Belarusian SSR was controlled by the Communist Party of Belarus (CPB), which was no more than a branch of the RCP(B)—which later became the Communist Party of the Soviet Union (CPSU). Government and state bodies of the RSFSR increasingly assumed responsibility for Belarusian affairs. However, the Belarusian SSR was permitted to enter into diplomatic relations with other countries and to conclude treaties with other states. This ambiguous situation was resolved on 30 December 1922 when the Union of Soviet Socialist Republics (USSR) was proclaimed, with the Belarusian SSR as one of six founding members. Belarusian affairs were now largely controlled by the all-Union authorities in Moscow.

Initially, the Belarusian SSR embraced the area around Minsk and territories extending south to the border of Ukraine. Under Soviet rule, the borders of Belarus were expanded three times. In 1924 Vitebsk (Viciebsk) and Mogilev (Mahiloŭ) provinces were transferred from Russia to Belarus. In 1926 Gomel (Homiel) province was also transferred from Russia. In 1939 the area of the republic was substantially increased when western Belarus, under Polish control since 1921, was annexed by the USSR under the terms of the Nazi-Soviet Pact and made part of the Belarusian SSR.

Belarus suffered severely under Soviet rule. In the early 1930s, during the programme of forced collectivization, many peasants were killed or deported. During the 1930s political repression engulfed the entire republic. Intellectual and political leaders suffered disproportionately, with most of the Belarusian cultural and political élite executed or imprisoned. During the Second World War the SSR was occupied by Nazi German forces during 1941–44. Up to 2.2m. people were estimated to have died in Belarus during the war, representing some 25% of the population. The republic did not reach its pre-1941 population level until 1970. As much as 80% of the republic's housing was damaged and much of its industrial capacity and transport system was destroyed. The war caused significant ethnic changes in Belarus. The large Jewish population was almost eradicated by the Nazis, and many Poles left the newly incorporated region of western Belarus to live in Poland. Thus, post-war Belarus had a high proportion of Belarusians in the population, although large-scale immigration by ethnic Russians after 1945 undermined Belarusian dominance.

Despite the destruction wreaked during the Second World War, when it became independent, the Belarusian SSR was one of the most prosperous areas in the USSR, and one of the most politically conservative. The closest to a reform movement was a move to protect the Belarusian language: in 1989 29.9% of the population spoke only Russian, and over 50% of the remainder spoke Russian fluently. More importantly, only 20.8% of pupils were taught in Belarusian, and there were no Belarusian-language schools in any of the Republic's major cities. No other nationality of republican status in the USSR had such a high proportion of nationals unable to speak their own language, or such a high proportion of nationals speaking Russian. The main proponent of the Belarusian language was the Belarus Popular Front (BPF), founded in June 1989, in Vilnius, Lithuania. The movement comprised a mix of politicians and intellectuals with a variety of different political agendas. Their efforts succeeded when the Supreme Soviet (Supreme Council—the legislature) adopted Belarusian as the state language on 28 January 1990, and mandated its use in education (these policies were later revoked by the legislature in 1995 when Russian was restored as an official language alongside Belarusian). The 1999 census revealed that only 37% of Belarusians spoke Belarus in everyday life; the rest spoke Russian).

In addition to the language issue, severe radiation 'fall-out' in April 1986 from the Chornobyl (Chernobyl) disaster, caused by an explosion in a Ukrainian nuclear reactor just south of the border with Belarus prompted increased activity by environmental groups. However, overt political opposition or public criticism of the Government or of Communist Party policies was firmly stifled.

The BPF was not permitted to campaign in elections to the Belarusian Supreme Soviet and local councils on 4 March 1990. Instead, BPF candidates joined other opposition groups in the Belarusian Democratic Bloc, which won approximately one-quarter of the 310 seats decided by popular vote (an additional 50 seats were allocated to CPB delegates). However, the Supreme Soviet was overwhelmingly dominated by deputies loyal to the CPB leadership, and the BPF faction had only about 30 seats.

Despite limited numbers, the BPF deputies initially seemed to have considerable influence in the new legislature. They successfully campaigned for a declaration of state sovereignty, which the Supreme Soviet adopted on 27 July 1990. It asserted the right of the Republic to organize its own armed forces, create a national currency and manage its own domestic and foreign policies, but it remained largely symbolic, and there was little popular support for independence. A referendum on the future of the Union was held in March 1991: 83% of voters supported a 'renewed union', the highest proportion in any Union Republic outside Central Asia.

INDEPENDENT BELARUS

The leadership of the CPB supported the communist 'State Committee for the State of Emergency' (SCSE) that had instigated the attempted coup in Moscow in August 1991. Following the collapse of the coup, Nikolai Dementei (Mikalai Dzemyantsei), First Secretary of the CPB and Chairman of the Supreme Soviet, was forced to resign. On 25 August the Supreme Soviet declared the formal independence of Belarus, gave the 1990 Declaration of State Sovereignty constitutional force, and temporarily suspended the activities of the CPB and the CPSU in Belarus. Dementei was replaced as Chairman of the Supreme Soviet by Stanislau Shushkevich, a centrist politician known for his criticism of government negligence in the aftermath of the Chornobyl disaster. On 19 September he was formally elected to the post (equivalent to head of state) by the Supreme Soviet, which voted to rename the country the Republic of Belarus. Belarusian independence was confirmed on 8 December 1991, when Belarus signed the Minsk Agreement (together with Russia and Ukraine), which established the Commonwealth of Independent States (CIS) and effectively dissolved the USSR. The headquarters of the new organization was to be in Minsk.

Shushkevich was not part of the communist *apparat* (although he remained a member of the CPB until August 1991) and had no strong links with any major political movement. This left him disadvantaged in the Supreme Council which was dominated by conservatives, and the BPF remained weak. Confronted by the legislature's continued hostility towards reform, he became more closely associated with the opposition BPF and its allies. He was increasingly marginalized, and replaced, on 28 January 1994, by a conservative former police chief, Mechislau Gryb (Myacheslau Hryb), who supported closer integration with Russia.

THE LUKASHENKA PRESIDENCY

A new post-communist constitution was not adopted by the Supreme Council until 15 March 1994, after the rejection of two earlier versions. It came into effect on 30 March. Based substantially on the Soviet-era Constitution, the Constitution provided for a directly elected executive President, thereby more readily facilitating a return to authoritarian rule.

Presidential elections were held in June–July 1994. After two rounds of voting, Alyaksandr Lukashenka, the former head of the Supreme Council's anti-corruption commission, was elected as President of Belarus on 10 July, with some 47.1% of the votes in the first round of voting, and 85% of the votes cast in the second round. Lukashenka's victory consolidated power among the conservatives, who advocated closer relations with Russia, the supremacy of central over local authority and the primacy of the executive, as opposed to the legislature, in determining policy and action. The democratic opposition was increasingly marginalized as President Lukashenka, exploited the power that the unreconstructed state apparatus provided.

In May 1995 elections to a new 260-member Supreme Council were held, accompanied by a referendum on increasing the powers of the presidency, closer integration with Russia, making Russian a state language and on restoring a version of the Soviet-era republican flag. The electorate overwhelmingly supported the referendum proposals. Although 61% participated in the first round of voting in the general election on 14 May, making it legally valid, only 18 candidates obtained the necessary simple majority of votes cast to secure election, and 242 seats in the legislature remained vacant. The state-owned media provided little coverage of the elections and the operating licence of the country's only private television station was suspended. In the second round of voting, on 28 May, 101 more seats were filled, but the Supreme Council remained inquorate. Subsequent elections took place on 29 November and 10 December, after which 198 deputies had been elected, 24 more than the two-thirds quorum required to allow parliament to function. The remaining 62 vacancies were ostensibly the result of low participation rates in certain electoral districts, areas in which the BPF had its strongest support, and were not finally filled until 1996. As a consequence, the BPF had no representation in the Supreme Council.

In the intervening period, the paralysis of the legislature enabled the President to arrogate more powers to himself. Lukashenka rapidly asserted control over the state-owned media, and responsibility for the security services was transferred from parliament to the President. The latter were largely unchanged from the Soviet era and they continued to be known as the Committee for State Security (KGB). They were split into two branches: one responsible for criminal affairs, the other for intelligence and state security. Lukashenka also created a new agency, the Control Service of the Office of the President, to deal with economic crime. At the same time actions were taken to outlaw or render impotent opposition and independent representative bodies.

After taking power, Lukashenka gradually expanded his control over the country, first in the political sphere, but later also in the social sphere. In mid-1996 confrontations between Lukashenka and parliament became increasingly frequent. In May the Supreme Council started investigating alleged human rights abuses, and in July Syamyon Sharetski, the parliamentary speaker, asked the Constitutional Court to examine the legality of several presidential decrees. In response, in early August the President proposed a referendum, to be held in November, on constitutional amendments extending his term of office until 2001, giving him extensive powers of appointment, and allowing him to rule by decree. The Supreme Council would be replaced with a bicameral National Assembly (Natsionalnoye Sobraniye). Although the Constitutional Court ruled that the results would not be legally binding, President Lukashenka decreed the ruling void, provoking fierce criticism.

Voting for the referendum began on 9 November 1996. Widespread violations of electoral law were reported. The Organization for Security and Co-operation in Europe (OSCE) refused to send monitors, and the Council of Europe declared that the amended Constitution did not comply with

European standards. Independent radio stations were closed down and some 200,000 copies of *Nasha Niva*, an independent weekly publication that was the country's oldest non-state newspaper, were confiscated. The Chairman of the Central Electoral Commission, Viktar Ganchar, refused to approve the referendum results and was dismissed shortly afterwards by Lukashenka. (Three years later, in mid-September 1999, Ganchar disappeared, following further opposition activity, and was never found.) The Chairman of the Council of Ministers (the Prime Minister), Mikhail Chigir, who had been appointed in July 1994, criticized the referendum, and was replaced by his deputy, Syargey Ling. A motion to impeach the President was submitted to the Constitutional Court by 75 Supreme Council deputies. However, support for impeachment rapidly dwindled and the Court abandoned further action after the referendum results appeared. According to official figures, some 84% of the electorate took part in the referendum, 70.5% of whom voted for the President's proposals. The referendum also contained three proposals from the Supreme Council, designed to curtail the President's power, but only 7.9% of voters supported them. The amended Constitution was published on 27 November 1996 and came into immediate effect. Over 100 Supreme Council deputies declared their support for the President. They passed legislation abolishing the Supreme Council and establishing the 110-member Palata Predstaviteley (House of Representatives), the lower chamber of the new Natsionalnoye Sobraniye. Existing deputies were invited to join the new legislature and their terms in office were confirmed for four years. Many opposition leaders refused to recognize the new institution, but deputies who refused to join had their terms curtailed to only two months.

The 64-member upper house, the Soviet Respubliki (Council of the Republic), convened for the first time in January 1997, with eight members appointed by the President and 56 elected by the seven regional (oblast) councils. The Council of Europe suspended Belarus's 'guest' status, citing the lack of democracy in the new political structures.

On 15 and 29 October 2000 parliamentary elections were again held, despite opposition demands for a boycott; of the 562 candidates contesting the 110 seats available, only 60 were not supporters of Lukashenka. About one-half of the prospective opposition candidates were denied permission to register. Official figures showed that over 60% of the electorate voted, but unofficial estimates suggested that the participation rate was as low as 40%, technically rendering the poll invalid. The OSCE, the Council of Europe and the European Parliament criticized the elections, and the USA refused to recognize the results.

In advance of the presidential election scheduled to take place in September 2001, opposition parties tried to ensure that votes cast against Lukashenka would not be divided between several candidates, selecting Uladzimir Gancharyk (Hancharyk), the leader of the Federation of Trade Unions of Belarus, to oppose Lukashenka.

The election was held on 9 September 2001, and, according to official figures, Lukashenka was returned to power with 75.7% of the votes cast, although many observers disputed the results. Gancharyk was credited with 15.7% of the votes (however, the opposition claimed that Lukashenka had received only 47% of the votes, and Gancharyk 41%, which would have forced a second round of voting). After the election, Lukashenka moved quickly to penalize organizations and individuals that had supported the opposition. Gancharyk was forced to resign as Chairman of the Federation of Trade Unions of Belarus, and the Government banned the automatic deduction and payment of union dues from salaries. The USA again refused to recognize the election results, and there were widespread allegations of electoral malpractice. However, the EU stated that diplomatic isolation would neither benefit the Belarusian people, nor contribute to the strengthening of democratic development, and announced that Western Governments needed to reassess their policies towards Belarus.

At the end of May 2004 the Government announced that elections to the Palata Predstaviteley would take place on 17 October, to be followed on 18 November by indirect elections to the Soviet Respubliki. Support for the organized opposition remained weak; it now consisted of three broad groupings: Five

Plus, an alliance of opposition parties; the European Coalition, favouring EU membership rather than federation with Russia; and Young Belarusians, a youth bloc. These groups vowed to nominate two common opposition candidates in each electoral district (in case one should be disqualified by the electoral commission). Nominees from the opposition groupings were to be selected on the basis of popularity, regardless of party or coalition affiliation. Trade union organizations and the Liberal Democratic Party of Belarus also vowed to present candidates in each district. However, no representatives of opposition groupings were elected to the Palata Predstaviteley.

President Lukashenka has suppressed the opposition by means of arrests, intimidation and, in some cases, disappearances. The former Prime Minister, Mikhail Chigir was placed in pre-trial detention at the end of March 1999; his trial for abuse of office commenced in January 2000. He was eventually convicted of embezzlement, and, in May, given a three-year suspended prison sentence. The human rights group Amnesty International and the US embassy in Belarus criticized the trial, claiming it was politically motivated. Chigir appealed against the sentence, which was overturned by the Supreme Court in December 2000, although the Court returned the case to the prosecutor's office for further investigation. In early 2002 Chigir was charged with tax evasion, and was given a three-year suspended prison sentence in late July. In January 2000 the Council of Europe issued a statement condemning Belarus's position on human rights, democracy and the rule of law. However, in March 2001 Prime Minister Uladzimir Yermoshin insisted that the Government recognized 'constructive opposition', but would not tolerate opposition that constituted a threat to the 'Belarusian state'.

Lukashenka has also steadily diminished the freedom of the press. Although there is no formal law on censorship, the media and non-governmental organizations (NGOs) are controlled by a series of nebulous laws. One such law forbids defamation of the President, a term that is broadly defined. (In 2003, for example, a newspaper editor was fined for satirizing the 2001 presidential election campaign.) Those found guilty can be sentenced to up to six years' imprisonment. Under Article 57 of the Civil Code, NGOs and other organizations can be closed down after a single violation of the law, including a violation of their charter. In April 2003 the Palata Predstaviteley passed legislation allowing the authorities to close down any political party or NGO that failed to ensure the maintenance of law and order during a demonstration or caused 'large-scale damage' (which can include disruption to traffic). After his re-election in 2001 Lukashenka further tightened his hold over the country's cultural and political institutions. In early 2002 he replaced the editors of leading literary magazines with government-approved editors, and ordered history textbooks to be rewritten. He suggested that teachers should be 'active propagandists' of state policy, and demanded the removal of teachers who did not support state policies. In mid-February 2004 the President ordered the Ministry of Justice to strengthen control over political parties, unions, and community organizations, claiming that special measures were necessary ahead of the forthcoming parliamentary elections. In March the Government announced new, more stringent, principles for handling emergency situations and civil defence. Also in that month Anatol Liabedzka, the Chairman of a small opposition party, the United Civic Party of Belarus, was arrested on charges of slandering the President.

At various times, Lukashenka has claimed that Belarus's political institutions are under threat from external forces. For example, in July 2004 he stated that Russia was supporting opposition groups in Belarus, claiming that some US $180,000 had been sent from Moscow in support of two opposition leaders, Mikhail Marinich and Valery Frolov, a former general, who subsequently participated in an anti-Government demonstration to mark the 10th anniversary of Lukashenka's accession to the presidency. The arrest of Marinich generated an unexpected outcry within the country. Between 3 and 21 June 2004 three deputies (including Frolov) of the very small opposition group Republic staged a hunger strike to demand Marinich's release, and in mid-June up to 80,000 vendors, market traders and small business owners participated in a strike to demand Marinich's release and the implementation of changes to the electoral code.

However, at the end of June 2004 the Government announced new rules giving the KGB the right to assign secret service agents to any enterprise, regardless of ownership. In early August the Supreme Court decreed that a political party, the Belarusian Party of Labour, should be abolished. This measure attracted widespread condemnation from the OSCE, the EU and the USA. In July, meanwhile, the Government revoked the licence of the country's only private university, the European Humanities University, in Minsk, and ordered it to vacate its premises. The University, which professed to have no political affiliation, had operated for more than 10 years, supported by fees and charitable donations from abroad. The OSCE office in Minsk was directly affiliated with the University, and the EU, the USA and other countries also provided support. At issue was the high number of foreign visitors. Despite attracting international condemnation, the closure of the University formed part of a broader drive against NGOs in the period preceding the legislative elections of 2004. Such closures were made possible by the use of the 'administrative warning' system, which permits the Government to shut down any organization or media outlet that receives two or more administrative warnings in a 12-month period. By issuing one warning, the Government can impose indirect censorship on those organizations it deems harmful. Organizations have been closed for a variety of minor reasons: one organization was shut down for using the word 'organization' in its name rather than the officially approved 'association'. Television and radio outlets are controlled by the state, which views them as tools for promoting state ideology, and the opposition is denied access to broadcast media (in the past, the media has broadcast statements accusing the opposition of being 'parasites', and compared one opposition leader to a Nazi collaborator). In March 2004, after Russian newspapers and magazines became increasingly critical of the Lukashenka administration, the Belarusian Government suggested that foreign periodicals would be subjected to government approval before they could be sold in the republic. Publications violating Belarusian media laws would be banned. In addition, the Government can close foreign news agencies and the offices of foreign broadcasters and expel their correspondents if it feels that they are reporting events in the country in a biased manner—as happened to the All-Russian State Television and Broadcasting Company (of Russia) after it reported a demonstration in Minsk in late July 2004 (see Foreign and Defence Policy). In early 2003 three Russian radio stations broadcasting in Belarus lost their transmitter facilities, and the rebroadcasting facilities of Russian television stations were restricted.

The Government has harassed NGOs and opposition parties in other ways, announcing, for example, its intention to close the offices of parties and organizations located in residential buildings, based on legislation approved in 2004. Most opposition party offices are based in private apartments, because the Government owns most of the office space in the country and refuses to rent it to opposition organizations. The Government has also announced plans to monitor internet use, limiting content and access to various sites.

Religious freedom has similarly been compromised. By 2004 the Government officially recognized 26 religious organizations, not all of which had the right to practise on a nation-wide basis. It provides financial support for the Belarusian Orthodox Church (of the Moscow Patriarchate—to which about 80% of believers are affiliated—although more than one-half of the population identifies itself as atheist), and in June 2003 signed a co-operation agreement with the Church. Religious affairs are managed by a State Committee on Religious Affairs and Nationalities, answerable to the Cabinet of Ministers. Religious communities must register to receive recognition, and to do so they must have a legal place of worship that can serve as an address. In 2000, following the adoption of a new housing code in 1999, religious groups had to register or re-register their properties with the local authorities. Several denominations and congregations that had been practising for years were subsequently refused registration. Controls over legal places of worship allowed the Government to ban informal study groups and Bible readings held in private residences. In late 2002 both legislative chambers approved new legislation on religion, which restricted the spread of unapproved and non-traditional denominations, and strongly favoured the Belarusian Orthodox Church.

The Lukashenka regime's exercise of control is illustrated by its response to nationalist demonstrations. Although Lukashenka claims to support the Belarusian language, nationhood, and national identity, he has suppressed demonstrations of those who differ in their interpretation of language and ethnic identity, such as, in March 2008, during an unofficial gathering commemorating the 90th anniversary of the creation of the first Belarusian state. Consequently, nationalist demonstrations have been associated with the opposition movement, while the proportion of the press that is published in Belarusian has declined sharply.

None the less, although indications of dissent continued, such as in early 2008 when small traders in Minsk and elsewhere staged strike action to protest against a requirement that they re-register with the authorities, President Lukashenka seems to remain popular, particularly as a result of the energy dispute with Gazprom in 2003–04 and subsequent years (see Foreign Policy). In early 2008 Belarus officially had 15 political parties. However, this included only parties officially registered with and licensed by the authorities. Moreover, in a speech in May, Lukashenka insisted that Belarusian society did not need proper political parties, but instead was based on four foundations: trade unions, councils of deputies, youth organizations, and veterans' organizations. Prior to the 2006 presidential election, Lukashenka's opponents hoped that the electorate would emulate Ukraine's 'orange revolution' of late 2004, when a reformist leadership obtained power. After the banners at an opposition demonstration were confiscated by police, one demonstrator waved his denim shirt around his head; denim banners subsequently became the symbol of the opposition, prompting hopes of a so-called 'denim revolution'. Most of the opposition united around Alyaksandr Milinkevich, who had no party affiliation, although a second opposition candidate, Alyaksandr Kazulin, also contested the poll against Lukashenka. Kazulin, a former rector of the Belarusian State University, was dismissed from his post in 2003 on political grounds. During the presidential campaign opposition candidates and their supporters were subject to repeated harassment, including by the police; Kazulin was assaulted by members of the security service who had disabled his car. Television reports suggested that the attack had been staged by foreign journalists to discredit the President. The KGB announced the discovery of an alleged plot to discredit the results, involving fake exit polls and bombings.

In the event, Lukashenka officially won an outright victory of 83.0% of the votes on 19 March 2006. Milinkevich supporters claimed that he had won over 30%, and that Lukashenka had failed to reach the 50% threshold necessary for an outright win after the first round of voting. After the results were announced, between 20,000 and 30,000 protesters gathered in October Square in central Minsk to support the opposition, despite Lukashenka's threat that protesters would have 'their necks broken like ducklings'. The protesters attempted to establish a tent settlement in the capital, as had been done in central Kyiv, Ukraine, in 2004, but after hundreds of arrests, the camp was stormed by police on 24 and 25 March and dispersed; Kazulin was again violently beaten. Following the pattern of former elections, Lukashenka swiftly neutralized his opponents: Milinkevich was arrested and briefly imprisoned, and Kazulin was arrested and sentenced to five-and-a-half years' imprisonment for leading a post-election protest and insulting the President (on official charges of 'hooliganism and incitement to mass disorder'). In addition, the Belarusian authorities accused Latvian diplomats of distributing pornography within Belarus, prompting an international dispute. Suppression of the freedom of speech continued; most notably, the weekly publication *Nasha Niva* was informed by the Minsk city authorities that its presence in the capital was 'no longer appropriate'. This followed the arrest and imprisonment of its editor for ten days, for the crime of swearing in public after being detained by police during post-election protests. Following the election, EU foreign ministers imposed a visa ban on 31 of the foremost Belarusian officials, including Lukashenka, noting that additional names could be added. Those officials banned were deemed to be directly responsible for the 'violation of international electoral standards'. The USA also banned the entry of leading Belarusian government officials and financial assets were frozen.

In October 2007 Vladimir Konoplev, one of Lukashenka's closest allies, who had held several prominent positions over the previous ten years, resigned as Chairman of the Palata Predstaviteley on grounds of ill health. However, his resignation coincided with a new economic situation resulting from increases in the cost of energy, and it was thought that it would provide an opportunity to refresh senior officials in advance of the 2008 legislative elections. He was succeeded by Vadim Popov, his predecessor as Chairman. In August 2008, following the temporary release of Kazulin from prison to permit his attendance at the funeral of his father-in-law (Kazulin had also been freed from detention briefly in February to attend his wife's funeral); it was announced that he had been granted a pardon by Lukashenka, and that he would not return to gaol. Kazulin subsequently declared that he accepted his release, but could not accept the presidential pardon, as he continued to regard his sentence as having been unjust.

In the campaign for the legislative elections, held on 28 September 2008, the opposition again found itself marginalized. Although Belarus had several political parties, they remained small and limited in influence: only 10% of the incumbent deputies belonged to a political party. Officially, all politicians are entitled to air time on radio and television, and to coverage in the press, but opposition candidates are limited to statements of no more than '4,000 characters', and they must be submitted for approval in advance of publication. In early September 2008 some 279 candidates were registered to contest the forthcoming elections, including 26 representatives of pro-Government parties and 63 opposition representatives. However, according to provisional results, no representatives of the opposition obtained election to the Palata Predstaviteley.

CHORNOBYL AND PUBLIC HEALTH

The Chornobyl nuclear accident of 1986 had a lasting impact on Belarus. Following the initial evacuation, some 210,000 people were resettled in subsequent years. As a result of the incident, 9,343 people were classified as invalids, and some 1,571,000 were classified as living on contaminated land; 282 rural settlements were closed. The number of affected people, about 1.8m., represented almost 20% of the country's population. The worst-affected regions were Gomel and Mogilev oblasts (regions).

Some 43,500 sq km of Belarusian land (just over 20%) has been classified as contaminated, although as much as 90% of the territory of the Republic was affected in the immediate aftermath of the explosion. Many people were not told they were living in contaminated areas until 1989, and some 1.5m. people still live in contaminated regions. Owing to the natural decay of radioactive material, it is estimated that radiation in affected areas will have declined by about 55% by 2046, and by 90% in the most severely affected areas. The issue of the resettlement and redevelopment of formerly polluted areas, as radiation levels decline, is only gradually being addressed.

FOREIGN POLICY

Since 1994 Belarus's foreign policy has been characterized by a series of international disputes. A variety of alleged threats, foreign interference in domestic affairs and political disputes were identified, allowing the Lukashenka regime to claim that it was defending the country, as well as the national way of life and standard of living, against foreign aggression. The regime has presented itself to its citizens as an embattled defender of a neo-socialist, 'socially orientated' development policy. As a consequence, Belarus has become increasingly isolated internationally. By 2000 the country had poor relations with international financial institutions, including the World Bank, the IMF and the European Bank for Reconstruction and Development (EBRD), although the IMF produces annual economic reviews, and the EBRD continues to make loans to the private sector, most recently, at the end of 2007, financing the creation of a bank to support small- and medium-sized

enterprises. Belarus has tenuous relations with the OSCE, which the Government has repeatedly criticized for interfering in the country's domestic affairs, and with the EU, while its relationship with Russia, Belarus's closest ally, is often increasingly turbulent. In addition, the Government has feuded with neighbouring states. The so-called 'orange revolution' in Ukraine at the end of 2004, which brought a new President to power (see the chapter on Ukraine), left the country still more isolated, since the Lukashenka regime had become concerned with containing any influence that the events in Ukraine might have on the domestic political scene. Post-independence, foreign policy had, on the whole, been dominated by a failed project of union with Russia, which would have ensured cheap energy supplies for the republic and safeguarded industry and employment. In the aftermath of the conflict between Russia and Georgia in early August 2008, Lukashenka, after several days of silence, declared support for Russia at a meeting with President Dmitrii Medvedev in Sochi, Russia. The Belarus Government subsequently announced that it was to sign an agreement with Russia on a unified air defence system later that year. Nevertheless, following a resolution endorsed by Medvedev on 26 August, officially recognizing the Georgian separatist regions of South Ossetia and Abkhazia as independent states, Lukashenka indicated that Belarus would not extend recognition.

As one of four nuclear powers created by the collapse of the USSR, Belarus signed the Lisbon Protocol to the Treaty on Nuclear Weapons in May 1992, committing it to transfer its nuclear weapons to Russia by 1999. The republican Supreme Council ratified the Treaty on Conventional Forces in Europe (CFE) on 4 February 1993, and on the next day adhered to the Treaty on the Non-Proliferation of Nuclear Weapons. Ratification was accompanied by US $65m. in aid from the USA and a further $10m. to help dismantle its nuclear weapons. Under the CFE, Belarus destroyed 2,171 tanks, 1,420 armoured carriers and 167 aircraft, and in November 1996 the last nuclear warheads were transferred to Russia.

Belarus signed a preliminary partnership and co-operation agreement with the EU in March 1995, but as the Lukashenka regime became increasingly autocratic, relations with the EU deteriorated. After the November 1996 referendum and the abolition of the Supreme Council, the EU refused to recognize the new legislature. Relations between the EU and Belarus steadily worsened. In June 1998 residents of a diplomatic compound near Minsk were evicted after the Belarusian Government announced that the compound needed urgent repairs. Ambassadors from the EU and the USA left the country, as did ambassadors from Bulgaria, Japan and Poland. In July the EU and the USA responded by banning Lukashenka and government ministers and officials from visiting their countries. Eventually, in mid-January 1999 ambassadors from five EU states returned to Belarus, and by September all ambassadors had returned, although relations between Belarus and Western Governments remained uneasy.

The actions of the Lukashenka Government were severely criticized by many official and non-governmental bodies, including the European Parliament, the International Helsinki Foundation for Human Rights and the OSCE, for the apparent disregard for the democratic process and the observance of human rights. In February 1998 the OSCE opened an advice and monitoring mission in Belarus, in order to promote democratization and monitor human rights in the country. The mission was initially tolerated by the Government, but from 2000 relations deteriorated. In April 2002 the acting head of the mission was compelled to leave the country, after the authorities refused to renew his visa, and in October the last remaining foreign member of the organization's staff left the country. In response to the effective closure of the mission, Norway, the USA, and all the EU member states (with the exception of Portugal) imposed a travel ban on President Lukashenka and seven other high-ranking government officials. In November Lukashenka was refused a visa to travel to the Czech Republic to participate in a meeting of the North Atlantic Treaty Organization's (NATO) Euro-Atlantic Partnership Council. However, in December Belarus agreed to permit the OSCE to establish a new mission office in Minsk, and in April 2003 the travel bans were lifted. Prior to the 2008 legislative elections, the Belarusian authorities allowed the OSCE to station election observers in the country, while accepting an equal number from the CIS member states.

Diplomatic interaction with Western powers remains poor. In August 2004 the US Congress passed a resolution demanding that the Belarusian Government uphold democracy, allow political freedoms and guarantee free elections. In response, the Government refused to issue visas to four US senators who were attempting to visit the country on a fact-finding mission. Relations with the EU also suffered. In May 2004, after absorbing 10 new member states (including three immediate neighbours of Belarus: Latvia, Lithuania and Poland), the EU made public a strategy for dealing with the Union's 'new neighbours', expressing the intention of creating 'a ring of friends'. However, the strategy excluded Belarus.

A dispute with Poland arose in 2004, after the Belarusian authorities accused a Polish diplomat of trying to recruit a Belarusian military officer to spy for Poland, leading to the cancellation of a planned visit to Poland by the Belarusian Prime Minister. Some 400,000 ethnic Poles live in Belarus, and they became the subject of Belarusian harassment. After Ukraine's 'orange revolution' in late 2004, President Lukashenka accused the Polish Government of trying to foment political revolution in Belarus. In July 2005 the headquarters of the Union of Poles in Belarus (UPB), an organization with over 20,000 members, based in the town of Grodno, was seized by the Belarusian authorities and the newly elected leadership replaced, after it failed to meet with the approval of the Belarusian authorities. This led the Polish Government to withdraw its ambassador to Belarus. The Belarusian authorities later reinstated the former President of the UPB. They also closed the country's main Polish-language newspaper, replacing it with a new government-edited newspaper of the same name. The Polish and Lithuanian Governments protested to the EU and urged it to revoke low tariff status for Belarusian goods, which could cost the republic up to US $120m. in lost sales to EU member states. Following the 2006 presidential elections, the EU and the USA banned entry to key Belarusian officials, particularly those connected with the elections.

At the beginning of 2008 the Belarusian authorities declared their readiness to co-operate with the EU, but this was not followed by any meaningful dialogue. Although President Lukashenka held several meetings with Western leaders, his foreign policy and domestic policies remained essentially the same. Neither the EU nor the USA supported the abolition of the UN post of Special Rapporteur on Human Rights in Belarus, which took effect from mid-2007, and in June the EU formally withdrew Belarus from the EU Generalized System of Preferences, which had offered tariff reductions on Belarusian goods exported to the Union. Perhaps more importantly, the USA intensified sanctions against Belarus in November, 'freezing' US assets of the largest state-owned firm Belneftekhim. The petrochemical concern and some 40 affiliated companies employs some 120,000 people, generates 30% of the Belarus's industrial production, and is responsible for 35% of exports. Belarus responded by demanding that the USA reduce the quantity of staff at its embassy in Minsk to be equal to the number of staff working at the Belarusian embassy in Washington, DC, USA. In March the US Administration complied, but then in May, the Belarusian authorities demanded further reductions in US diplomats, when sanctions were expanded to all the subsidiaries of Belneftekhim. Another indication of the country's growing international isolation was reflected in the declining number of visitors to and from the country. The number of Belarus nationals entering Poland as tourists declined from over 1m. in 2000–03 to just 106,347 in 2005, following Poland's accession to the EU in 2004, and was likely to decline further after Poland joined the Schengen Agreement on intra-EU movement at the end of 2007. Similarly, the number of Poles crossing the Belarus–Polish border fell significantly in 2004.

Belarus and Russia established formal diplomatic relations in June 1992, and in July 1993 the two states signed a declaration on economic integration. Although in April 1994 they concluded an agreement on an eventual currency union, Belarus finally introduced its own currency, the Belarusian rouble, in May 1995. Shortly afterwards, in April 1996, Belarus and Russia signed a Treaty on the Formation of a Community of Sovereign Republics, which provided for military, economic and political co-operation. Initially, co-operation was limited to military and border matters. On 2 April 1997 Lukashenka and Russian President Boris Yeltsin signed a Treaty of Union and initialled a Charter of Union, which was intended to lead towards a single currency, joint defence policy and, eventually, political unification. The charter was signed on 23 May of that year and ratified by the Russian and Belarusian legislatures in the following month. A Union Parliament, consisting of 36 members from the legislature of each country, was convened shortly afterwards.

Declarations of deeper union became an annual occurrence. In December 1998 an outline union accord was signed, and in December 1999 a more formal agreement was signed, creating a Union of the Russian Federation and Belarus. It was confirmed by the Russian State Duma (the lower house of the Russian legislature) one week later and ratified in January 2000. The agreement was modelled on the EU's Treaty on European Union, providing for unified customs, tariffs, and taxes, and the introduction of a single currency at the beginning of 2005. The establishment of a bicameral supranational legislature was envisaged; the upper chamber was to comprise 36 members from each state, the lower to comprise 25 members from Belarus and 75 from Russia. Neither country was to have the right to withdraw from the Union other than by means of a referendum. Yeltsin's successor as President of Russia, Vladimir Putin (2000–08), was less committed to the Union than was Yeltsin.

By mid-2002 Belarus had negotiated prices for the supply on natural gas from Russia (upon which country Belarus is almost entirely dependent for energy supplies), equivalent to Russian domestic prices charged in the region of Russia that neighbours Belarus. The main gas pipelines from Russia to Central and Western Europe cross Belarus, and the country's leadership assumed that the country was vital to Russia's economy in supplying energy to the EU. However, relations with Russia frequently became strained during the 2000s, with supplies of energy to Belarus being halted by the Russian state-controlled company Gazprom on various occasions, often in response to demands by Russia that Belarus pay higher prices for the supply of gas, and increases in transit fees charged by Belarus (see the essay on the Economy). However, while Gazprom (which is largely state-owned) has become an agent of Russian foreign policy, the distinction between Gazprom and the Russian Government has generally allowed official relations between Russia and Belarus to remain cordial.

In June 2002 Putin rejected the creation of a supranational body, as proposed in the union agreements signed with Yeltsin, and rejected the idea of reviving any association similar to the USSR. He proposed instead that the Union proceed on the basis of a unified federal state, according to which the constituent administrative units of Belarus would effectively be incorporated into the Russian Federation. According to a draft constitution for the Union state, finalized in March 2003, the Union was to comprise two sovereign states, with executive powers vested in the governing body, the Supreme State Council. The Union state would not levy its own taxes, but would rely on transfers from the member countries. The lower chamber of the Union legislature would be able to pass legislation only if more than three-quarters of its members voted in favour, and would be consulted on the appointment of a Union prime minister.

The foreign trade and customs regimes of the two countries were to be aligned by 2005, and transport, energy and telecommunications were to be harmonized. Belarus was to adopt the Russian rouble at the beginning of 2005; plans anticipated the creation of a 'union rouble' by 2008. In March 2004 it was announced that Belarus would not be ready for currency union by 2005, and the project was effectively abandoned. Despite the collapse of the union scheme, some aspects went ahead, including the close collaboration of the Belarus and Russian armed forces, the harmonization of customs, and a change in the assessment of VAT on exports and imports to Russia to match Russian practice. However, despite the apparent abandonment of the Union project, in early 2007, when it was announced that a tax would be imposed on exports of oil and refined products from Belarus, Russian authorities announced that Russian customs and tax inspectors would be stationed on Belarus's western border, calling it the 'external border of the Union state'.

DEFENCE

In mid-1992 Belarus assumed nominal control of former Soviet troops still on its territory, although these troops remained under joint CIS-Russian command. It was announced that Belarus was to form its own armed forces. However, ethnic Belarusians constituted only 20% of the staff at the republican Ministry of Defence and fewer than 30% of officers in the Belarusian armed forces, the remainder being mainly ethnic Russians. Moreover, the 1992 agreement on co-operation between Russia and Belarus ceded effective control over the country's military technology and production to Russia. Under Soviet rule, Belarus had one of the highest concentrations of military personnel in the former USSR—one per 43 civilians. Forces totalled 250,000 personnel, of which as many as one-third were officers. By 2004 the total number of officers and enlisted men was down to 72,940. That year, according to official sources, military spending equalled approximately 1.0% of GDP. In March 2003 Lukashenka announced that the air and air defence forces were to be re-equipped within six to 12 years.

Belarus's adherence to the Treaty on Collective Security (the 'Tashkent Agreement'), signed by six CIS states in May 1992, initially provoked controversy, some claiming that it contradicted the Constitution, but in April 1993 the Supreme Council voted to authorize Shushkevich to sign the Agreement, after imposing conditions on Belarusian inclusion in the pact. The most notable of these was the stipulation that Belarusian troops were not to serve outside the country and that no foreign troops were to be stationed in Belarus without the consent of the Government. The proposal was rejected by Shushkevich and the BPF, on the grounds that it would commit Belarus to participate in armed conflicts in Russia and elsewhere in the CIS and violate the 1990 declaration of state sovereignty, which committed Belarus to neutrality. Shushkevich initially refused to sign the Tashkent Agreement, but yielded in December 1993, thereby losing BPF support.

In connection with the proposed union with Russia, in February 2000 Lukashenka announced that the two countries would create a new military grouping of several hundred thousand troops, in response to the eastward expansion of NATO. In January it was also announced that the Governments of Belarus and Russia were to establish a joint defence-financial-industrial group and the Russian Government approved a plan to develop the group, 'Defence Systems', consisting of the Russian financial-industrial group of the same name and some Belarusian enterprises. Military co-operation intensified, with Russia completing an early-warning radar system along the country's western border, manned by Russian personnel. There were also plans to integrate the Belarusian and Russian air defence systems into one combined regional system. Despite erratic relations with Russia, such defence interaction continued to develop. By 2004 Belarus had been equipped with new anti-aircraft defences, provided by Russia, and Belarus had come to play a significant role in Russia's western defence. In August 2008, when Poland announced that it would allow NATO missile bases on its territory, the Russian authorities stated that they might review military co-operation with Belarus, but emphasized that nuclear weapons would not be stationed in Belarus.

CONCLUSION

After independence was formally declared in 1991, relations with Russia dominated the political agenda. Economic and constitutional reform was repeatedly delayed, initially by the Supreme Council, and later by President Lukashenka, and from 1996 the country reacquired many of the features of a command economy. The legal system lost its independence, and freedom of speech and assembly were eliminated. The Government exercised tight control over the media, cultural organizations, NGOs, political parties and religious groups. The EBRD characterized commercial and financial regulations as weak, and the international human rights organization Freedom House noted that human rights in Belarus were only slightly better observed than those in Turkmenistan (which had perhaps the worst human rights record in the CIS). The accession of Poland, Latvia, and Lithuania to NATO and to the EU, and Ukraine's 'orange revolution' at the end of 2004 left Belarus geopolitically isolated. Consequently, economic survival depends largely on ever closer co-operation with Russia. However, as Russia has developed a more aggressive foreign policy, relations with Russia became increasingly erratic. None the less, President Lukashenka remains a consummate politician. Despite his authoritarian rule, he appears to remain popular, particularly among the rural population and among those who remember the excesses of Soviet rule. Some give him credit for sponsoring a revival of the Belarusian language and traditions. He continues to present himself as a defender of a Belarusian 'way of life' against hostile outsiders, and portrays himself as a protector of Belarusian freedoms and living standards.

According to the Constitution, Lukashenka was due to relinquish office at the end of his term in 2006. However, a referendum, held in October 2004, approved constitutional amendments allowing him to contest another term. Unsurprisingly, he officially achieved a resounding victory in March 2006, officially gaining 83.0% of the popular vote. By mid-2008 it appeared that Lukashenka had firmly stifled any opposition to his regime, forestalling a 'denim revolution'. He could claim to have contained unemployment, in contrast to neighbouring Poland, Latvia, and Lithuania; to have reduced poverty; to have supported broad economic growth; and to have avoided the extreme inequalities in wealth that have appeared in Russia and Ukraine. President Lukashenka himself does not appear to have accumulated a large personal fortune, nor do members of his family, in contrast to other CIS leaders. However, his main source of economic support, subsidized energy from Russia, is now gone; his main group of supporters is in decline; and the economic prospects for the country are uncertain. President Lukashenka has not created a party base, but instead rules through the security services and the civil administration. Although his hold on the country appears to be secure, the lack of an organized political force to support him renders him vulnerable to sudden change. It remains to be seen, therefore, if he can retain his firm hold on power.

Economy

Dr ANDREW RYDER

INTRODUCTION

Belarus has few natural resources. Upon independence, its economy depended heavily on the former Soviet military-industrial complex. Agriculture suffered from structural defects and the after-effects of the 1986 Chornobyl (Chernobyl) disaster in Ukraine. Nevertheless, following the dissolution of the USSR at the end of 1991, restructuring occurred slowly, due to the leadership's reluctance to encourage the transition to a market economy. Instead, from 1994 the Government attempted to create what it termed a 'socially orientated market economy', with state-controlled prices, a limited private sector, extensive directed subsidies, artificially low unemployment, and a dominant, essentially unreformed state sector.

It is difficult to gauge Belarus's economic performance, both under Soviet rule and after independence. The lack of a responsive pricing mechanism, Soviet accounting practices, and the Soviet method of deriving measures of national income (national income produced and net material product—NMP) obscured economic reality. Within the former USSR, Belarus was a high-income Union Republic. Industrial output per head was 14.5% greater than the all-Union average, and throughout the 1980s the rate of increase in inward investment was substantially above the USSR average. In the 1970s and 1980s rates of return on investment also appeared to be substantially higher (18%–19%) than the all-Union average, and rates of increase of labour productivity were consistently the highest in the USSR.

Changing trade relations among the countries of the former USSR and a shift to world market prices altered the Republic's terms of trade after 1991. The leaders of newly independent Belarus had difficulty coming to terms with adjusted measures of economic performance, which showed Belarus to be less prosperous than had been imagined. Estimates by the World Bank, calculated by using exchange rates as a conversion factor, showed that gross national income (GNI) per head was just US $2,070 in 1995. As recently as 2001, per-head GDP was only $1,241.6, although by 2006 it had risen to approximately $3,800.

Since 1993 Belarus has had a persistent trade deficit. This was because Belarus repeatedly accumulated a high debt for energy imports from Russia, which was cancelled periodically after Belarus made concessions to Russia (see Mining and Energy).

After 1991, high rates of inflation, the retention of state control of prices and wages, and the existence of several different exchange rates made it difficult to measure economic performance. Officially, Belarus successfully made the adjustment to a post-Soviet economy, but the calculation of official gross domestic product (GDP) remains unreliable. By the end of 1995 GDP had fallen to 51% of the 1989 level, according to some estimates. Subsequently, GDP officially increased each year, although measurement was complicated by high inflation and a declining exchange rate. The calculation of GDP can be biased upwards by underestimating inflation and overestimating the value of goods sold at controlled prices (28% of consumer goods in 2004). Thus, the IMF noted that, although the assessment of GDP was flawed, real growth appeared to have taken place in the early 2000s. By the end of 2007 GDP had officially reached 144% of the 1989 level.

ECONOMIC POLICY

Since 1994 the Government has aimed to implement a socially orientated market economy. This means that the state controls over three-quarters of the economy through centrally mandated wage targets; directing bank loans to key sectors and firms regardless of their solvency; administering controls on prices and profit margins; and through legislation that allows the Government to overturn management decisions in any firm that is partially state-owned or was formerly state-owned. Privatization has been slow. Before 1994 the Government flirted with privatization, but postponed reform in favour of maintaining social stability. The introduction of the socially orientated market economy from 1994 caused economic policy to become an explicitly political instrument. The Government returned to the 'command and control' economy, with fixed prices and wages, and fixed growth targets for GDP. A main aim of government policy was to preserve and protect large Soviet-era enterprises and farms.

In April 1994 the Government began implementing a voucher privatization programme, the first auctions for which were to be held in July. One-half of the shares in enterprises to be privatized were to be distributed to voucher holders, and the remainder were to be sold. However, when he took office in July, President Alyaksandr Lukashenka suspended the programme. It was reorganized and later approved, but the private investment funds meant to manage the vouchers had their licences suspended in early 1995. In February 1996 all private enterprises were required to re-register with the authorities and the privatization of smaller enterprises was suspended in March that year. After 1994 the Government identified 960 large-scale enterprises that were not to be privatized, on the grounds of national interest. The privatization of large enterprises requires the approval of the workers' collective. Normally, privatization can only commence if the process is initiated by the labour force. If the labour force and the authorities cannot reach an agreement, the decision is made by the President, the Government or the relevant ministry, depending on the size of the firm. Small-scale privatization also stalled, although by 2007, some 82% of all retail turnover was in the private or co-operative sector, which accounted for 88% of all retail firms. In the restaurant sector, however, state ownership accounted for almost 40% of the total.

The Government again required a registration and relicensing procedure for the private sector, introduced in March 1999. Privatization through sale to foreign firms was hindered by a law stipulating that no more than 50% of a state-owned industrial enterprise could be sold to private sector owners, and any sale of stock worth US $40,000 or more had to be approved by the President. Price controls were extended to the private sector in October 1999 and private companies were required to pay salaries that conformed to government guidelines. Moreover, all enterprises in which the Government retained as little as one share were subject to a so-called 'golden share' regulation, which allowed the President to issue a decree giving the Government effective control of the firm, even if this had not been anticipated when the firm was privatized. Initially, it applied mainly to firms connected with defence. In March 2004 the scope of the provision was expanded by a presidential decree, allowing the Government to intervene in the management of any firm in which it had once held a share, regardless of whether it still owned any capital in the firm. As a result, privatization was, effectively, a meaningless process. However, government authorities insisted that the 'golden share' regulation was only exercised in exceptional circumstances. The 'golden share' law was finally revoked in March 2008, having been used 38 times. A presidential decree in April called for extensive privatization, and it was rumoured that 30% or more of state owned firms would be sold. As well, the Government passed a law on mortgages for the first time, establishing preconditions for issuing credit, and regulating claims. Allied to a move towards greater privatization, the Government sought and obtained a sovereign credit rating from US ratings agency Standard and Poor's, which gave the country a 'B+' rating for foreign currency paper, and a 'BB' rating for rouble denominated paper. Moody's Corporation of the USA gave a similar rating. However many 'privatizations' consisted of little more than a change in the nominal structure of the firm (corporatization), from a state-owned company to a joint stock enterprise in which all shares were owned by the state.

Despite these conditions, privatization has advanced, albeit extremely slowly: by the end of 2006 1,092 large firms had been privatized (compared with 1,010 in 2003), and 3,024 small firms had been transferred to private ownership (compared with 2,547 in 2000), according to the IMF. However, since the beginning of the 2000s virtually all privatizations of large firms have involved their conversion into joint stock companies. In 2007, in a major development following almost a decade of discussion, the Government agreed to sell one-half of the national natural gas supplier, Beltransgaz, to the Russian state-controlled company Gazprom in four annual tranches, thereby creating a joint Russia-Belarus gas-transit organization. By the end of January 2003 almost 50% of GDP was officially produced in the private sector, including some 1,500 large enterprises corporatized since 1991, but remaining under state ownership. (However, the European Bank for Reconstruction and Development—EBRD—subsequently estimated that just 25% of GDP was attributable to the private sector.) In 2007 some 47.6% of employment was officially in the domestically owned private sector, 50.9% in the state sector, 2.7% in firms with part-foreign ownership, and 1.5% in foreign-owned firms. A more accurate indicator of the importance of the private sector was the ownership of fixed assets: 62.1% were state-owned at the beginning of 2007, and 37.1% in the private sector, with an additional 0.8% foreign-owned. Private industry remains concentrated in particular branches of the economy: construction materials, light industry and food processing and production. A substantial amount of economic activity also takes place in the unofficial sector. According to some estimates, it was as much as 40% at the beginning of the 2000s, but by 2004 the IMF estimated the share of the informal economy at 10%–11% of GDP, and suggested that it was concentrated mainly in agriculture and internal trade.

An indication of the growth potential of the private sector can be seen among mostly privately owned small- and medium-sized enterprises (SMEs). However, since 2000 output by SMEs has fallen by about 25% when adjusted for inflation. Restrictions limit the number of people who can be employed by an individual businessman, interest rates on loans to the private sector are higher than those to the public sector, and few banks lend to the sector. Taxation is biased against profitable firms, and the pervasive powers of the Government constitute another lever of control over the business and political activities of small-business owners and managers, discouraging them from criticizing government policies. Despite this, the number of small enterprises reached 35,638 by the end of 2006, of which 32,545 were privately-owned, and the country had 191,815 registered private entrepreneurs, compared with just over 180,000 in 2001, and accounted for 8.8% of GDP. In 2006 SMEs employed almost 10% of the labour force, accounting for almost 20% of the output of goods and services in the national economy and almost one-quarter of total turnover in the general retail and service sector, with an overall profit rate of 13.3%. However, they are unevenly distributed throughout the country, with just over 46% located in Minsk City and 12.5% in Minsk Oblast. Privately owned firms produced 82.3% of output in the SME sector, and foreign-owned firms an additional 10.4% in 2004. Although a substantial proportion of SMEs are in catering and retailing, in 2006 they included industrial firms (22.3%), construction (11.7%), and financial services. Employment in the sector is difficult to measure due to its ambiguous definition, but in that year the number employed (as opposed to owners in the SME sector) accounted for 18% in construction, 20% in retail trade, 14% in industry, but just 2.3% in agriculture. However, at the end of 2006 some 25.6% of all SMEs were loss-making. A new law, entering into effect at the beginning of 2008, required all so-called individual enterprises and sole traders to re-register, and to turn their businesses into micro-enterprises or some other corporate form. This meant that many would be forced into a higher tax bracket. Enterprises which did not change would be allowed to employ a maximum of three employees, all of whom had to be close relatives. New restrictions were placed on the items they could import and sell, and a government spokesman suggested that it was wrong for market traders to import goods for foreign currency and sell them while the country's light industry was in crisis. When the law came into

force, a business organization, Perspektiva, organized protests in Minsk, which were forcibly dispersed by police. Private firms have repeatedly suffered from excessive inspection and control measures, such as visits from the fire service and sanitary agencies, leading to a large number being fined, although surveys in 2008 indicated that the number of inspections declined sharply between 2004 and 2006. Bribery remains pervasive, particularly among larger firms, and during 2002–2006 levels of corruption appeared to have increased. Bribery is most common in trade, catering and construction, all of which are characterized by small privately owned firms. Moreover, although private businesses support freer trade, the elimination of wage and price controls, greater privatization, and the privatization of banking, they are ill-equipped to cope with true market conditions and a more competitive and open economy. The result is what the IMF has described as a dual economy, consisting of a dominant, state-owned sector, characterized by large industrial enterprises that are essentially unreformed since communist times, and a small private sector, embracing some industry, but concentrated mainly in the retail and services sectors, alongside private farm markets which, as was the case in the Soviet era, exist alongside large state-owned farms.

EMPLOYMENT AND SOCIAL AFFAIRS

According to official figures, in 2007 some 27.4% of the workforce was engaged in industry, 14.0% in trade and services, 9.9% in agriculture, 10.3% in education, 8.2% in construction, 7.5% in health care and social welfare, 7.6% in transport and communications and the remainder in other sectors. According to the IMF, employment in the services sector increased from 38% of the total labour force in 1990 to 51.4% at the end of 2006, although this was a low proportion compared with other transition economies. Moreover, the share of employment in financial intermediation, real estate and transport has stagnated. Since independence, unemployment has remained low, never exceeding 3% of the labour force, and by 2007 it had fallen to only 1%. Low unemployment is partly the result of a government policy of subsidizing faltering industries at the expense of profitable ones, with a predictable effect on the budgetary deficit. It also reflects the contraction of the labour force, which decreased in size, so that it was only 80.3% of its 1989 level by the end of 2006. While the population of working age has grown by almost 200,000 since 2000, the absolute number of people who are economically active has contracted by almost 100,000, although the number has increased slightly since the end of 2003. In late 2000 the Ministry of Labour estimated that the rate of unemployment was actually between 5% and 8%, and in 2002 the IMF and other international organizations estimated that unemployment was at least eight percentage points higher than officially recorded. In 2006 the IMF estimated that less than 50% of those eligible applied for benefits, which averaged only about 10% of the average wage. The measurement of unemployment is compounded by the widespread late payment of wages and by the practice of granting leave of absence to employees without pay or with reduced pay. Unemployment is also low because the Labour Code of 1999 makes it difficult for employers to dismiss staff and restricts the use of short-term contracts. Consequently, in 2003 the IMF found that some 80% of job losses were the result of the employee's request or the result of a joint agreement between the employee and employer. Another contribution to low unemployment is the increasing tendency for young people to spend more time in education. Since the 1990/91 academic year, enrolment in higher education has increased from 188,600 to 414,000 in 2007/08.

Employment in state-owned firms accounts for 50.9% of the total, compared with 73.9% in 1990, however, this understates the role of the state sector: private sector enterprises include those in which all the shares are wholly owned by the state, and quasi-state entities such as collective farms. Wage rates are regulated by the Government. In US dollar terms, labour costs in Russia decreased by 20% between 1993 and 2000, but increased by 130% in Belarus, or by over 230%, according to the official exchange rate. In mid-2008 domestic observers suggested that earnings in Belarus were the third highest in the CIS countries.

During the presidential election campaign in 2001, Lukashenka promised to increase the average monthly wage from its 2000 level of US $89 to $250 by the end of 2005. Despite devaluation of the rouble, monthly wages were close to $250 in early 2006, and at the beginning of 2008 it was reported that the average wage had reached $396. During 1995–2004 wages increased by 10.6% per year in US dollar terms, and by 12.4% in terms of the national currency. Overall, between 1995 and 2004 real wages increased by 170%, but productivity increased by just 80%, and while wages increased by 82%, in real terms, during 2004–07 industrial output increased by only 55%. The policy of increasing wages means that firms have to spend profits on higher salaries, rather than new investment, with the result that in most branches of industry, old machinery has not been modernized or replaced. Despite wage increases, incomes remain low, and in 2008 it was reported that one-fifth of the country's pensioners (some 550,000) continued to work, compared with 4% in the previous year.

The proportion of people living in poverty (defined as living below the subsistence level budget) had declined to 27.1% by the end of 2003, and just 11.1% by 2007. However, despite wage increases, in 2007 51.3% of household spending went towards food, indicating the low disposable income of the population. Prior to the 2008 legislative elections, the Government has announced that the average monthly wage will reach US $700 by 2010.

Belarus has the lowest level of income inequality among all the CIS and transition states, and one of the lowest levels of income inequality in the world. However, in the early 2000s, according to the World Values Survey, collated by the International Network of Social Scientists, life satisfaction within Belarus was among the lowest in the CIS and transition countries. Moreover, pronounced differences in living standards and poverty levels persist within Belarus. Wages in Minsk were more than one-quarter higher than the national average, and in some sectors more than twice the average, while those in cities and large towns were higher than those in rural areas.

An additional problem confronting the labour force is the *propiska* (permit) system, a legacy from the days of the USSR. People have to register with the authorities in order to live in most towns and cities, and without being registered they are unable to obtain housing or work; however, without a job it is often difficult to register. There is strong evidence of a geographical mismatch between job vacancies and unemployed.

Apart from the increase in the minimum wage, there is no overall programme in place to address poverty. Instead, the Government has implemented a series of untargeted benefits, such as price controls, child support and subsidies for housing and agriculture. The state pension, although increased in recent years, remains low, but higher than unemployment benefits, which prompted many older workers to retire when confronted with possible unemployment.

FINANCE

In late 1991 Belarus assumed 4.13% of the total debt of the former USSR, which it later transferred to Russia in exchange for Belarus's share of Soviet assets. The authorities were reluctant to abandon the Russian rouble. In early 1992 shortages of currency led to a requirement that substantial payments be made by cheque, rather than cash, and the Government introduced currency coupons for use in state stores. The coupons were given a value of 10 Russian roubles, and 10%–15% of salaries were paid in coupons. After much discussion between 1992 and 1995, a Belarusian proposal for monetary union with Russia was rejected because the proposed conversion undervalued the Russian rouble and threatened Russian economic reforms. Consequently, in May 1992 Belarus introduced the Belarusian rouble (rubel), which became the country's sole legal tender.

In 1995 President Lukashenka nationalized the country's leading private currency exchange and transferred supervision of the central bank from the legislature to his office. In March 1998, at the time of the Russian financial crisis, the value of the currency collapsed. Exchange rate controls were imposed and the central bank lost its vestigial independence. These measures prompted warnings from the World Bank and the IMF. Both institutions suspended lending to Belarus in the mid-1990s, insisting that significant economic reform had to come first. However, in April 2001 the IMF restored its relations with Belarus, and has since produced annual monitoring reports on the economy.

Prices are regulated by the Government through the Price Committee of the Ministry of the Economy. By late 2000 controls existed for 30% of producer goods sold, and prices for the remaining 70% were set by manufacturers, within government limits. Consequently, many firms failed to make a profit, and many activities were driven into the unofficial economy. At the end of 2007 the Government announced the relaxation of some price controls exempting some firms and individual entrepreneurs from price limits, and expanded the list of uncontrolled goods. In an attempt to attract foreign investment, the Government created six Free Economic Zones, which allow tax exclusions, but these have had limited success. In 2008, as part of an attempt to support the economies of rural areas and small towns, it was announced that businesses operating in rural areas would receive tax holidays from 2008 to 2012, being exempted from taxes on real estate, contributions to innovation funds, customs duties, and VAT on technical equipment. In addition, from 1 April 2008, enterprises operating in localities with a population of under 50,000 were exempted from the profit tax. Foreign investors were to be exempted from payment of customs duties and VAT on imports of technical equipment.

Until September 2000 Belarus had several exchange rates for the rouble which comprised official cash and non-cash rates, a market-cash rate, a 'black market' rate and a parallel interbank market rate. The official rate was set by the central bank. The Russian currency devaluation of August 1998 compounded the problems of the Belarusian currency, which had devalued earlier in the year. In 1999 the Government instituted a 'sliding peg' devaluation of the official rate. From the beginning of 2000 a redenominated currency was introduced, one new rouble being equivalent to 1,000 old roubles. By April 2000 the exchange rate to the dollar was some 475,000 roubles (or 475 redenominated roubles), although on the open market the currency was worth approximately 40% of the official rate. However, although the National Bank of Belarus established a single exchange rate in September 2000, black market exchanges have persisted. In mid-2008 the official rate of the rouble was 2,146 to the dollar, virtually unchanged since 2006.

Since independence, inflation has been a persistent feature of the economy, reaching an annual rate of 2,219% in 1994, before declining to 27.5% in 1995. After 1996 it increased again, to an annual rate of 293.8% in 1998, before declining slowly. In 2006 it was officially just 6.6%, despite global increases in fuel and commodity prices, but rose to 12.1% in 2007, and reached almost 20% in the first half of 2008.

The banking system remains essentially unreformed. In 2006 there were 30 banks, with a total of 421 branches: nine were completely foreign-owned (one, Atombank, was bought by a Ukrainian bank in 2007), another seven were more than 50% foreign-owned; and 27 had some form of foreign participation. Eleven banks had been founded since the beginning of 2000. Five banks operated only in one of the country's Free Economic Zones. Of the six largest banks, five were state-owned, and only one, Priorbank, had been privatized. Over 50% of the shares in Priorbank were sold to Raiffeisen Bank of Austria in 2001, and in January 2003 Raiffeisen Bank acquired the remainder. The sector is characterized by extensive state intervention. The four largest state-controlled banks service specific sectors, and are compelled to lend regardless of the actual risk. Lending limits exist, but appear to be poorly enforced. In recent years directed lending has grown, reaching 3.4% of GDP in 2004. Bank risk has generally been concentrated in the three largest banks: Belarusbank, Belagroprombank and Belpromstroibank, which are all state-owned, although in July 2007, the Government ordered five 'authorized' banks to provide subsidized loans to manufacturing firms to enable them to 'secure a timely purchase' of agricultural products. At the end of the first quarter of 2007 the country's six largest banks accounted for 86.5% of all bank capital. Although the share of non-performing loans in total lending has decreased substantially since 2002, this was mainly owing to the cancellation of loans. Belarusbank and Belagroprombank had benefited from repeated capital infusions, which reached 1.6% of GDP in 2003. Several sectors, particularly agriculture, have benefited from interest rates on loans that are substantially below the rate of inflation. In 2004 most loans to collective farms were cancelled, and the overall real interest rate on loans remained low. International financial institutions have repeatedly expressed concern about the high level of foreign currency loans, arguing that many were made to firms with very limited access to foreign currency, creating the risk of default problems should the value of the Belarusian rouble decrease significantly against other currencies. Not surprisingly, foreign observers consider the banking sector unsound. In mid-2008 Standard and Poor's argued that Belarusian banks suffered from a high concentration of assets and a high degree of state involvement which could lead to excessive risks. Moreover, foreign asset cover was low, and at the end of 2002 central bank foreign-currency reserves were equivalent to just 0.8% of one month's spending on imports. Subsequently, however, reserves increased three-fold, totalling more than US $1,383m. at the end of 2006. Despite this, in 2008 the Government announced plans to sell a small amount of shares (10%–15%) in the country's largest bank, Belarusbank, to foreign investors, and at the beginning of 2008 created a national system of deposit insurance.

Subsidies are a prominent feature of economic management: in 2005 subsidies and transfers equalled almost 20% of GDP, and subsequently remained high. In 2000 the IMF estimated that direct and indirect subsidies, together, equalled some 10% of GDP, although this understated the total, since it excluded tax arrears and other liabilities. Direct subsidies, provided by the state budget, were equivalent to about 2% of GDP, while indirect and extra-budgetary subsidies were equivalent to some 8%. One of the largest single subsidies was for energy, particularly natural gas. Between 2001 and 2006 directed loans increased 10-fold.

Consumer subsidies operate through price controls, the underpricing of rents and utilities, and various types of cross-subsidy. From April 2001, in response to pressure from the IMF, the Government reduced the number of categories of 'socially important' goods that were subject to price controls. The share of controlled prices in the consumer price index decreased to 20%–22% by the end of 2001, compared with 50% at the end of 1998, but by 2004 had again risen to 28%. Recent increases in energy costs have not been passed on to consumers, further distorting the economy, and despite price increases, cost coverages remain low for urban services, including rent, heating, water, sewage and waste disposal. Housing subsidies have enabled housing costs to remain low, but between 2000 and 2006, they increased almost three-fold in terms of their share of household expenditure, to almost 9%, while the share of foodstuffs in total spending went down to 51.3% of household budgets in 2007, falling from 62.7% in 1995. In addition, enterprises were (and are) required to support medical services, social services, child care and housing, as they did during the Soviet era. Petroleum refineries have been ordered to provide energy resources to farm enterprises during sowing and harvesting campaigns. Arrears on wage, tax and energy payments peaked in 2000, but still remained substantial in the mid 2000s, rising after 2005. Inter-enterprise arrears also remained high, although they had declined from the peak level recorded in 2000. Year-end energy debts of enterprises decreased to the equivalent of 4.8% of GDP at the end of 2005, from a peak of 16.3% in 2000, but in 2006 rose again, equalling 14.3% of GDP at the end of that year.

Officially, Belarus had a budget deficit estimated at just 0.7% of GDP in 2005. The budget had a surplus of 1.4% in 206, but this did not include considerable off-budget transfers and subsidies, often referred to as 'quasi-fiscal activities', including directed loans and loan subsidies. The planned deficit for 2008 was expected to reach 1.9% of GDP; however, a feature of Belarusian economic management is that budgetary sleight of hand at the end of the year often turns a small deficit into a surplus. Given the high level of subsidies in the economy, it is not surprising that, despite extensive tax reforms over the previous 10 years, Belarus had the highest tax burden of the CIS countries, with total tax revenue equivalent to over 45% of GDP in 2004. If other off-budget government funding was taken into account, the level of tax burden was closer to 50% of GDP, and reached 51.6% of GDP in the first half of 2007. The tax burden is unequally distributed, falling most heavily on profitable enterprises. This has discouraged new investment and retarded economic growth. In 2007 the World Bank released a report saying that Belarus had the world's most complicated tax system. Using an average firm, the Bank found that the tax burden equalled 144.4% of profits, and required 148.5 working days for calculations. The Government and international financial observers have repeatedly agreed on the need to reduce taxes, and announced a general overhaul of the tax system; however, despite some reforms in 2004, taxes remain high and complex. International financial organizations noted that Belarus continued to rely on taxes that have been abolished in other transition states, particularly the turnover tax and numerous extra-budgetary 'innovation funds'. Moreover, not only are tax arrears a persistent feature of the Belarusian system of state finance, but exemptions, reschedulings and tax forgiveness were applied differentially to preferred enterprises or sectors, such as agriculture. In 2008 the Government announced plans further to reduce taxation, streamline the tax system, and cut taxes on stock profits, with the aim of encouraging more foreign and private sector investment.

AGRICULTURE

Until the early 1970s the Belarusian economy was mainly agricultural. In 1990 the contribution of agriculture to GDP was estimated at 24.0%, but had fallen to 7.5% in 2006 and 7.4% in 2007, according to official statistics; according to the IMF, agriculture and forestry accounted for 9.3% of GDP in 2006. By the end of 2006 the share of the work-force employed in agriculture had declined sharply, from 19.1% in 1990 to 10.2% of the total. About two-thirds of those employed in the sector worked on collective farms. Overall, the proportion of the rural population in the country's total population has declined from 33.2% in 1990 to 26.6% at the end of 2007, falling by about 750,000, almost 20%. Since much of the land is poor and the climate is severely continental, animal husbandry and hardier crops predominate. Under Soviet rule, major products included flax, potatoes, buckwheat, rye, meat and dairy products, and, from the early 1980s, sugar beet. Other important crops included barley and animal fodder. Oats, millet, hay and tobacco were grown in small amounts.

Agriculture in Belarus was devastated by radioactive 'fall-out' from the accident at the Chornobyl nuclear power station in Ukraine in 1986. Official estimates claimed that about 20% of Belarusian territory suffered contamination. By 1992 some 257,000 ha of agricultural land, just over 4% of the country's total, had been removed from use, as had 1,340,000 ha of forests, about 15% of the total.

Rural poverty is widespread. Farm workers' wages are well below those of the general population. At the end of 2005 only 70% of dwellings in rural areas had running water, only 65% had sewerage, only 54% had central heating, only 41% had hot water, and only 56% had indoor bathrooms or showers (versus 90%–95% for dwellings in urban areas). Many agricultural workers are paid in goods instead of money, and virtually all rely on household plots. From the late 1990s the Government attempted to raise rural incomes by increasing the purchasing price of output more rapidly than the rate of inflation, but in January 2002 Lukashenka announced that the state would only raise purchase prices for farm products to compensate for the rate of inflation (although since then annual increases in agricultural prices have exceeded the inflation rate). He added that the sector needed to reduce production costs by 25% through better organization and work discipline.

Production of grain and other crops declined sharply after independence. Animal husbandry suffered, and meat production declined by 42% between 1990 and 2005, but increased to 66.6% by the end of 2007. Overall, agricultural GDP declined by an annual average of 0.9% in 1993–2003, according to World Bank estimates. However, from 2000 the sector's contribution to GDP increased steadily, in contrast to other transition countries. By 2007 production had recovered to 90% of 1989 levels, following several years of growth. However, there was a change in the type of foodstuffs produced, with a decline in the quantities of meat, eggs, milk and dairy products produced, and increased production of fruit and vegetables. Grain production has slowly recovered from lows reached in the mid-1990s, but the mix of grains has changed: rye, buckwheat, oat and barley all decreased significantly, but there have been sharp increases in production of triticale, wheat, maize, and rape seed, suggesting the widespread introduction of new kinds of seeds and new varieties of crops.

From 1999 household plots of up to 1 ha could be privately owned. From the mid-1990s the private sector dominated production of some commodities, including 95% of fruit, 85% of potatoes and 75% of vegetables. In the mid-2000s household plots accounted for about 10.5% of agricultural land, but produced about 40% of gross agricultural output (33.5% in 2007, according to official figures, but this ignores output consumed by farmers themselves). Although the number of private farms increased from 1992 (when there were 792, accounting for just 0.2% of agricultural land), by 2006 there were fewer than 2,200 privately owned family farms, down from a peak of over 3,000 in the late 1990s.

Agriculture remains unreformed. At the beginning of the 1990s Belarus had about 2,500 state and collective farms; 15 years later most remained essentially unchanged. Assistance to farming has profoundly destabilized the national economy. The sector has been starved of investment capital, and is characterized by persistent wage arrears. At the end of 2003 some 1,444 of the country's 2,500 agricultural enterprises were loss-making, and more than one-third were bankrupt. After the cancellation of bank debts in 2004, the sector showed a return of 7.5%, and of 8.1% in 2005, and the number of loss-making enterprises fell to just 370 and to only 14 in 2005, but investment remained low, despite increasing sharply in 2004–05, to reach around two-fifths of the level recorded in 1990. However, by 2007 profitability in the sector had fallen (5.1% in 2006) and loss-making farms had grown in number. The rural population accounts for a substantial proportion of President Lukashenka's support. As part of his social contract, he implicitly guaranteed to preserve the sector in its existing form and to protect workers from massive economic upheavals. Loans continue to be made at notional rates of interest, and have helped to raise the country's fiscal deficit by several percentage points.

Agriculture is still managed centrally, with district and regional production targets for farms; all farms must make deliveries to state procurement agencies; and there are fixed price-procurement quotas for all the major crops and livestock products. Profits are strictly controlled. In the case of some products, commercial sales do not take place, owing to the need to fulfil production quotas. In late 1999 publicly owned farms sold about 85% of their output to the state or to state-owned processing firms, and private farms nearly two-thirds. According to the IMF, at the end of 1999 even household plots sold 20% of their output to state purchasers and processors, and another 35% to local collective farms. State agencies supply nearly all fertilizer, farm machinery, construction materials and fuel, and prices are controlled for fertilizers, pesticides, leasing machinery, drainage and veterinary medicines.

In 2007 state support to agriculture equalled about 2% of GDP. About one-third of all investment in agriculture comes from the state. Despite the costs to the economy and the risks to the banking system, the policy of farm subsidies remains popular. The Government has repeatedly announced plans to reform the sector. At one point, Lukashenka suggested that existing collective and co-operative farms be merged to form agro-combines, a proposal first suggested in the late 1970s. However, the most popular type of reform seems to involve merging collective farms with industrial enterprises, so that farm losses can be covered.

MINING AND ENERGY

The provision of cheap energy supplies has formed the basis of the Lukashenka regime's economic policy. For over a decade, Lukashenka successfully argued that Belarus should receive Russian gas at a substantially discounted price. The argument used was two-fold. First, the planned union between Russia and Belarus would make the two countries effectively one, and, therefore, Belarus should pay no more for fuel than Russian regions. Second, Belarus is the main transit route for Russian petroleum and natural gas to Western Europe. Until the mid-2000s tensions between Russia and Ukraine left Russian firms with effectively no option but to rely on Belarusian pipelines. A 'gas war' between Ukraine and Russia, and political upheavals in Ukraine in 2004 (see the chapter on Ukraine) substantially increased Russian dependence on Belarus as a transit country for petroleum and gas.

Two petroleum pipelines run through Belarus, both built during the Soviet period: the Druzhba (Friendship) pipeline along the southern border; and the Soyuz (Union) pipeline along the northern border. To complement the pipelines, two refineries were built. One was located at Mozyr (Mazyr), where the Druzhba pipeline split into two sections (one going towards Hungary and Slovakia, and the other towards Poland and Germany). The second refinery was sited at Polotsk (Polacak), where the Soyuz pipeline split into two (one line going to Poland, and the second to Ventspils, Latvia). Two gas pipelines also traverse the country: one Soviet-era pipeline, which is the property of the (until 2007) state-owned firm Beltransgaz, and the other, the Yamal pipeline, built and owned by the Russian firm Gazprom.

Belarus depends almost entirely on imported energy, producing less than 10% of its energy needs from domestic resources. Peat was traditionally used to produce electricity and for domestic heating, particularly in rural areas. However, after the Chornobyl disaster, peat was widely contaminated, and could not be burned to produce electric power. Small deposits of petroleum and natural gas had been found and exploited, although output declined from the 1970s; petroleum production stabilized in the late 1980s at approximately 2.0m. barrels per year and annual production of natural gas remained at between 200m. cu m and 300m. cu m in the early 2000s (about 1.2% of consumption in 2004). Although there are some deposits of brown coal (lignite) and other minerals, few are commercially exploitable. This level of dependence on imports is no different from that of Belarus's western neighbours, all of which have successfully coped with a shift to world energy prices. However, instead of reforming the domestic economy so as to be able to pay higher prices for energy imports, the regime has relied on cheap energy to reduce the need to undertake fundamental reforms, making possible the survival of inefficient and unprofitable firms, and allowing a higher standard of living than might otherwise be the case.

Heavy dependence on energy imports is the main cause of the persistent trade deficit. In 2006 some 16.0% of domestic electricity consumption was met through imports, and the cost of electricity imports was US $122.49m., compared with $99.9m. in the previous year. Annual imports of electricity have increased, by almost one-third in 2004–06, after falling (from one-quarter of consumption in 2001), and natural gas consumption has grown by 18% since 2001, and by 11% since 2003, although since 2004 growth has slowed down. Industry consumes around one-half of all electricity. Despite problems in paying for electricity imports, the transmission system suffers high losses which have increased over time (amounting to 12.4% of total output in 2006) and consumption of electricity has generally increased since the mid-1990s.

While petroleum is mainly processed and re-exported, most natural gas is consumed locally. In the 1980s many power stations were converted to use natural gas, to allow the USSR to consume its domestic gas output. In 2006 73.4% of natural gas consumption was used in electricity generation (and almost 99% of gas consumed was imported). Nevertheless, Belarus has made few efforts to restrict energy consumption or to promote energy conservation. As electricity consumption has grown, gas consumption registered an even faster increase.

From 1993 Belarus repeatedly fell behind in its energy payments, and defaulted several times on payments for gas. After the proclamation of the union treaty signed with Russia in April 1996, the country benefited from subsidized energy prices. The persistent energy debt became a major source of tension between Russia and Belarus, leading to the abandonment of monetary union and the proposed political union of the two countries. In exchange for low prices, the authorities had to cede control over principal assets. After Belarus first defaulted on gas payments in 1993, a 30% share in the Mozyr petroleum refinery was transferred to Russia, in exchange for a 10.8% stake in the petroleum firm Slavneft, leading to liquidation of the debt. When arrears accrued again in 1996–99, the Belarusian and Russian Governments concluded agreements allowing the repayment of debts by barter, using food, technical resources and manufactured goods. However, by the end of January 2000 Belarus's gas debt to Russia was still a little over US $200m. The Belarusian authorities demanded that Russia sell its energy still more cheaply. In January Gazprom announced that the price of gas (already reduced from $50 per 1,000 cu m to $30 per 1,000 cu m in March 1999) would be further reduced, by 10%, a concession that was related to the union treaty. In 2002, in connection with a plan for currency union, the Russian Government announced that Belarus would receive gas and transportation services at domestic Russian prices (identical to those in the Smolensk region that neighbours Belarus), leading to lower prices for both gas and electricity imports from Russia. However, the agreement covered only 10,600m. cu m of gas, or 59.8% of domestic consumption in that year.

The deal committed Belarus to establishing a joint venture with Russia to transport natural gas through Belarus, by transferring to Russian ownership a stale in the national gas pipeline monopoly, Beltransgaz. This led to a five-year standoff between Russian and Belarusian authorities. By late October 2002 Gazprom threatened to terminate supplies to the country. After inter-governmental negotiations Belarus announced that it would buy additional gas supplies, at the higher, although still subsidized, price of US $36. In December the Belarusian Government sold its remaining stake in Slavneft.

From 2004 Russia used energy pricing as part of a more aggressive foreign policy, employing a kind of energy diplomacy to extend its economic and political influence in Belarus. Gazprom has gradually increased the price of natural gas sold to Belarus, and the price of petroleum has also been increased, substantially reducing the country's foreign currency earnings. In preparation for the proposed sale of Beltransgaz, the Government transformed it into a joint-stock company in April 2003. (This required a legislative amendment, since the firm was designated for state ownership.) However, as the deadline for the sale of Beltransgaz approached (and as the deadline for Belarus's adoption of the Russian rouble neared), the Belarusian authorities baulked at the proposed purchase price. The Belarusian authorities valued the firm at some US $5,000m., while Gazprom valued it at no more than $580m. As the sale stalled and gas debts mounted, Gazprom announced that from 1 January 2004 it would supply gas to Belarus at the higher price paid by Ukraine. The Belarusian Government refused to accept the increase, and Gazprom stopped supplying gas to the country, forcing Belarus to rely on short-term contracts with other Russian suppliers. By mid-February Belarus had already accumulated substantial energy debts to those Russian suppliers. They and Gazprom accused the Belarusian authorities of making unauthorized use of gas from pipelines to meet their energy needs. Consequently, in mid-February Gazprom halted the supply of all gas running through the pipelines crossing Belarus. Observers suggested that the action was costing Gazprom as much as $10m. per day in lost revenue. Although the dispute was resolved, and flows of gas to and through the country resumed, Gazprom refused to supply any more gas to the Belarusian authorities. Belarus had to rely on short-term contracts, paying the same price that Gazprom had originally demanded. Finally, in June Gazprom agreed to supply the republic with 10,200m. cu m of gas (about two-thirds of its annual requirements) in the second half of 2004, at a price of $46.68 per 1,000 cu m. This was the price

Belarus had been demanding, slightly less than the price demanded by Gazprom, but more than Belarus had been paying before. In turn, Belarus said that it would charge a transit fee of $0.75 per 1,000 cu m, per 100 km, for transit through Beltransgaz pipelines, which were state-owned, and $0.46 for transit along Gazprom's own Yamal pipeline. This was less than the $1.02 Belarus had wanted to charge (which was the amount charged by Ukraine). This arrangement resolved what had become an 'energy war' between Russia and Belarus, but signalled the end of the proposed economic, political and currency unions between the two countries.

Despite ongoing energy disputes, cheap petroleum and natural gas, (sold to Belarus at well below the prices paid by European Union—EU member countries) allowed the republic to export refined petroleum products as well as manufactured goods to Western Europe at world market prices, taking advantage of the differentials between import and world prices, adding as much as 3% to GDP. In 2004, for example, the country imported petroleum products at an average of US $155 per metric ton and imported crude petroleum at an average price of $181 per ton, but exported products at an average price of $254. Fuel accounted for 21.7% of industrial output in 2005, chemical and petrochemical 11.3%, and electric power 6.2%. Between 2000 and 2005 output in the fuel sector rose by 10% annually (and by 23.1% in 2006), and that in the chemical and petrochemical industries by 6.5% annually (by 6.9% in 2006). Profit in the chemical and petrochemical sector reached 30.2% in 2005, but fell back to 27.2% in 2006, and in 2005 reached 29.9% in the fuel industry (29.3% in 2006). However, in November 2007 US sanctions were imposed against the largest state-owned firm, Belneftekhim, and its affiliates. It dominates output in the chemical and petrochemical sector, producing 30% of the country's total industrial output and generating 35% of exports. Moreover, the energy deficit remained unresolved, and at one point, Gazprom threatened to raise gas prices to $200 per 1,000 cu m, from the then current rate of $46.48 per 1,000 cu m, later announcing that it would compromise on price increases if Belarus ceded a 50% share of Beltransgaz. Agreement to pay a higher price of almost $100 per 1,000 cu m was finally reached on 31 December 2006, but subsequently, when Belarus was slow in implementing the sale of Beltransgaz, the dispute reignited. The dispute was finally resolved in May 2007, when Belarus agreed to sell 50% of Beltransgaz to Gazprom in four annual stages, each of 12.5%. The first sale was in June 2007, and the remaining three stages were to take place on 1 February in 2008, 2009, and 2010. In a concession to the Belarusian authorities, the firm was valued at $5,000m., but the agreement required the appointment of a new board, and ruled out the use of the 'golden share' policy. Additionally, the transit fee for gas passing through the Beltransgaz pipeline was raised from $0.75 to $1.45 per 1,000 cu m per 100 km, although gas transited through the Yamal pipeline was still to be charged only $0.46 per 1,000 cu m. Even after the agreement was implemented, Gazprom threatened to reduce by nearly one-half gas deliveries through the Republic unless Belarus paid all its remaining debt by 3 August 2007. The crisis was only averted after Belarus paid $456m. to Gazprom on 9 August, after receiving one week's extension of the deadline. Under the new agreement, gas prices are revised quarterly, rather than annually. Gazprom has insisted that prices charged to Belarus become the same as those charged to Western European consumers. In 2008 the gas price was set at $119 per 1,000 cu m in the first quarter, and $128 in the second. Government budget projections for 2009 forecast a price of $140. However, the gas agreement between Gazprom and Belarus did not specify a transparent method for negotiating gas price, and in mid-2008 Gazprom was proposing a price of $200 for 2009. In early 2007 a dispute also arose over the price of Russian oil sold to Belarus. Since the early 1990s Belarus has sold Russian oil and refined oil products on to third countries at world market prices, in recent years earning between $4,000m.–$5,000m. annually. Russian authorities announced that an export tax of $180 per ton would be imposed on all oil exports to Belarus. Belarus responded by imposing a 'transit service tax' of $45 per ton, designed to off-set the impact of the Russian tax. Russia demanded that Belarus remove the tax, calling it illegal, and saying it amounted to a trade war. On 7 January 2007 the flow of oil to Belarus was suspended, but resumed three days later, when Belarus and Russia agreed that Russia would impose an export tax of $53 per ton from 1 January 2007 on oil exported to Belarus and re-exported, or refined in the country and then sold abroad. Russian oil exported to Belarus for domestic use remained duty free. The tax was to be collected on oil and oil products as they were exported, and shared between Russia and Belarus, with Russia receiving 70% of the proceeds in 2007, 80% in 2008, and 85% in 2009. Russia also stated that if Belarus broke the agreement, it would unilaterally impose a tax of $180 per ton. In 2007 the tax was expected to return some $1,000m. to Russia and $1,500m. to Belarus, although Belarus's share was set to decline in subsequent years. In addition, oil prices increased by 34.6% in 2007.

By mid-2007 the impact of higher energy prices was beginning to be felt throughout the economy. The energy trade deficit reached US $901.1m. in August 2007, compared with $309m. in August 2006. The Government announced an increase in subsidies given to Belarusian oil refineries to guarantee their ability to process oil profitably, amounting to up to 130% of Russia's special duty. The Minister of Finance claimed that higher prices would cost the Government some $6,000m., and plans were announced to lend 150,000m. roubles to local governments to pay for fuel and oil. The Russian firm LUKoil announced that it would no longer process crude oil in Belarus due to higher costs. Schools and kindergartens were ordered to reduce electricity and heat consumption, and the Government announced that it was entering into negotiations with the People's Republic of China and Venezuela to guarantee alternative lines of credit and fuel supplies. The head of the secret services (which retained the Soviet designation of KGB) was replaced, as were the heads of Beltransgaz, the head of the country's two oil refineries, and the head of the Belarusian Oil Company. The head of the oil refineries was accused of embezzlement and other crimes. The heads of Belaz, a car manufacturer, and Dolomit, a large fertilizer manufacturer, were also replaced. According to news agencies, Lukashenka stated that 'the oil situation was now under [his] personal control'. In response to the ongoing energy crisis, in November 2007 the Government passed a law allowing the construction of a nuclear power station to be built with Russian technology and Russian assistance.

INDUSTRY

Industry (including transport and construction) contributed some 44.0% of total NMP in 1990 and 26.6% in 1994. In 2006 industry (excluding construction) accounted for 32.3% of GDP (compared with 27.8% in 1994), according to the IMF; construction accounted for 9.2%. (In 2006 official statistics put the share of industry at 27.6%, although that category excluded production from sensitive sectors.) In 2007 industry employed 26.4% of the labour force, and construction an additional 8.2%.

Until the early 1970s Belarus specialized in the processing of agricultural products. By the late 1980s the chemicals and machine-building industries were well developed, although light industry remained important. The construction of petroleum and natural gas pipelines across the republic fostered the development of industries that relied on cheap energy, and the construction of refineries stimulated the growth of industries relying on petroleum derivatives. Minsk became one of the most important centres of the Soviet microelectronics and computer industry. Major industrial enterprises tended to be concentrated in large cities, but smaller enterprises, processing agricultural and timber products, were distributed fairly evenly throughout the country. Since independence, industry has declined sharply in terms of output and profitability. In 2006 (with the exceptions of ferrous metallurgy; refrigerator and freezer manufacture; mineral fertilizer output; and cement production) spare capacity was at least 25% of total production capacity. In clothing and textiles and food processing, unused capacity was over one-half of the total, and in motorcycle production it was 85%.

Belarus was a leading producer of consumer durables in the USSR, including radio receivers, television sets, furniture and shoes, production of which far exceeded domestic demand. It was responsible for some 20% of Soviet motorcycle production (in 2005 the country produced just 6,000 units, down from 225,000 in 1990) and was a major producer of tractors and other agricultural machinery. Two factories, one producing self-propelled fodder harvesters in Gomel, and another producing the important chemical dimethyl terephthalate in Mogilev, dominated production of their respective products in the former USSR. However, Belarus depended on other parts of the former USSR for most basic products, and since independence, with the exception of tractors, the production of agricultural machinery has almost entirely disappeared.

At independence Belarus had a small steel industry: annual crude steel production averaged 1m. metric tons during the 1980s, and annual production of finished steel products remained fairly constant at some 700,000 tons. This industry depended entirely on imported raw materials, and satisfied only a small proportion of domestic demand. Steel production initially declined after 1991. However, the sector was subsequently extensively modernized. Since 1995, production in the iron and steel industry has expanded dramatically, reaching 2.3m. tons of steel and 301,000 tons of cast iron in 2006. Ferrous metallurgy became one of the most successful branches of industry in the country. In 2004 the sector showed a profit rate of 36.1%, making it Belarus's most profitable sector, although in 2006 this had fallen to 18.3%.

Many enterprises in Belarus produced materiel for the Soviet armed forces. With the collapse of the USSR, military orders almost halted, and attempts to convert to civil production were largely unsuccessful. In 1992 an estimated 120 large enterprises depended on military orders for survival, employing 370,000 people. Their closure would have had a severe impact on unemployment, hence the enthusiasm among many of the directors of such companies for an economic union with Russia, which would allow them to regain some of their pre-independence markets. From the mid-1990s the firms were partly sustained by the growing barter trade between Belarus and Russia, and in late January 2000 it was announced that the Belarusian and Russian Governments were to set up Defence Systems, a joint defence-financial-industrial group, comprising the Russian company of the same name and some Belarusian enterprises.

Industrial production declined sharply after independence, with manufacturing falling to just 61.% of 1989 levels by 1995, according to official statistics. Subsequently, measured in terms of output by value, it increased almost three-fold, to 172% of 1989 levels by the end of 2006. Production of many major industrial products has increased significantly in absolute terms, not just in monetary value, since the start of 2003. Despite IMF concerns about a tendency to overstate the value of industrial output, figures from previous years were regularly revised upwards. Prices of inputs are subsidized, product prices are controlled by the state, unsold inventories are not discounted, and a substantial proportion of exports are bartered for other goods. In 2003 the share of bartered goods in industry equalled 18.2% of GDP, and accounted for 70% of all domestic barter trade, although in 2004 the share of barter in the total economy declined to the equivalent of just 3.2% of GDP, the share of industry accounting for 56%. Between 1990 and 2002 entire sectors disappeared, such as the manufacture of cameras, cassette tape recorders and organic fertilizer applicators.

Overall investment also declined markedly after 1991. In comparison with other transition countries, foreign direct investment (FDI) remained low, and domestic investment remained insufficient. From late 1995 the Belarusian legal system and practice of law enforcement, particularly as related to FDI and private entrepreneurs, were described as flawed by the EBRD and, according to transition indicators published by the EBRD, Belarus has regressed in terms of reform. Legal statutes require significant improvement, and their effectiveness is weak. Laws are unclear and contradictory, independent legal advice is limited, courts are not independent and the administration of law is substantially deficient. Belarus remains among the least attractive of the transition countries for foreign investment and business. Per-head investment between 1989 and 2006 was only US $288, a rate exceeded by all but three other transition countries, and when measured in terms of GDP, FDI was the lowest of any transition country in 2006. By the end of 2006 only 1.4% of the work-force was employed in firms which were completely foreign-owned, and a further 2.7% were employed in firms with partial foreign ownership.

Although the number of industrial enterprises has grown from some 1,500 in 1990 to 2,343 at the end of 2006, employment and production remain concentrated in a few essentially unreconstructed large enterprises. Just 2% of enterprises employ over 1,000 employees, but account for 63.5% of all employment. More worryingly, despite increasing levels of investment, industry remains starved of capital. At the end of 2006, levels of amortization in the sector had reached 60.9% of fixed assets, and in the chemical and petrochemical sector were over 67%. Loss making firms are subsidized by profitable ones, preventing successful enterprises from investing in production facilities. In 2006, it was announced that just 15 large enterprises generated 28% of the total tax revenue of Belarus. Crucially, seven were in the oil and gas sector, including Beltransgaz, and three in the energy sector. Also included were the country's largest spirits distillery, a steel works, and a mobile cellular telecommunications operator.

TRADE

Since independence, Belarus has maintained Soviet-era trade relations with other CIS countries, particularly with Russia. Under Soviet rule, Belarus depended heavily on inter-republican trade, which accounted for 44.6% of GDP in 1989. After independence, it remained dependent on external trade, which equalled between 110% and 125% of GDP annually, by the beginning of the 2000s. The economic reality of trade was obscured by the Soviet pricing system, which undervalued the prices of raw materials (in comparison with world prices) in which the republic was deficient, but overvalued those for machinery, in which Belarus specialized. In terms of domestic prices, in 1989 Belarus had a positive inter-republican trade balance, of some 3,476m. roubles. However, when the World Bank used partial estimates of world market prices to calculate the trade balance, the republic recorded a trade deficit with other Union Republics, of 812m. roubles. The main factor in this disparity was the difference between the domestic price of Russian petroleum and the world market price. Since Belarus depended on Russia for supplies of petroleum, it was evident that shifting Belarus's trade to world prices would cause either a severe balance of payments crisis or an energy crisis. This unattractive choice was with Belarus's leaders from independence, when the World Bank estimated that, depending on the mix of exports and imports in any given year, the shift to world market prices could cause GDP to decline by 4%–7%.

Before 1991 Belarus appeared to have a negative balance in foreign (extra-Soviet) trade. In 1989 the foreign-trade deficit was 2,522m. roubles at domestic prices (at foreign prices it was only 668m. roubles, there being less distortion). In that year extra-Soviet trade accounted for 23.3% of all imports and 9.8% of total exports. That same year the republic was responsible for some 4% of the foreign trade of the USSR, and total foreign trade accounted for 7.4% of GDP. After 1991 the trade balance with non-CIS countries became positive and, with the exception of a deficit in the mid-1990s, generally remained positive. This was largely owing to the low price Belarus paid for imports of natural gas and petroleum from Russia. From 2001 increases in the global prices of petroleum and natural gas caused this price differential to widen. In 2004 Belarus paid an average price of US $14 below market prices for each barrel of Russian petroleum. (This price differential was some $5 greater than in 2001.) The refining margin on petroleum processed in the republic for sale to the West increased by $4.20 from 2001, to about $10.00 per barrel. Consequently, Belarus was able to pay for all petroleum imports, including those for domestic consumption, through sales of refined products abroad. However, this pricing advantage was substantially reduced in 2007, and was scheduled to be largely eliminated by 2010. Reflecting the trade based on re-exporting petroleum products, in 2006 mineral products accounted for 38.8% of imports, and chemical products 14.4%; mineral products contributed 33.3% of exports, and chemical products 12.6%.

In 1991 the republic's authorities asserted control over foreign trade from the all-Union authorities in Moscow. However, erratic progress towards a unified exchange rate, a unified import tariff system and the removal of impediments to exports commenced only in mid-1993. The country's trade remained concentrated in the CIS: in 2004 the CIS accounted for 63.5% of total trade turnover, 53.0% of total exports and 72.2% of imports. However, in 2007 the CIS accounted for just 57.1% of total trade turnover, despite an increase in total trade. Russia has consistently accounted for the bulk (86% in 2007; frequently more than 90% of the total) of CIS trade, and Ukraine makes up most of the rest. Dependence on subsidized fuel imports has resulted in a persistent trade deficit with Russia. Despite depending on Russia as a source of fuel, Belarus has slowly diversified the direction of its exports: in 2001–07 the proportion of exports going to the CIS declined from 60.7% to 46.0%. Belarus still exports a substantial share of its industrial production to the CIS countries, including refrigerators, television sets, tyres, tractors, bicycles, and trailers and semi-trailers. However, in 2007 Russia's share in overall trade fell to just over 49%, accounting for 36.6% of exports and 60% of imports.

Trading patterns are changeable. Since 2000 Germany has been the leading source of imports, followed by Poland. The direction of exports has varied, in 2005–06 the Netherlands, the United Kingdom, Poland and Germany were the leading non-CIS importers of Belarusian goods.

PROSPECTS

In 2008 Belarus was one of the few transition countries to have reversed the reform process, retreating from privatization and the use of market forces in economic management. It remained the only 'command and control' economy among the European transition states, and was described by the EBRD as remaining in the early stages of transition, an assessment unchanged since 1996. It was characterized as having a weak institutional environment for small- and medium-sized enterprises, and underdeveloped legal institutions and safeguards for investment. Government opposition to reform intensified after the financial crisis of 1998. The banking sector confronted extensive liabilities, owing to the provision of forced loans to enterprises and farms that were technically insolvent.

However, Belarus's economic performance has consistently exceeded the expectations of leading global institutions, including the IMF, the World Bank and the EBRD. To some extent, this was due to the over-measurement of output because of an underestimation of inflation, and to the use of controlled prices and arbitrary prices for manufactured goods. None the less, the economy recorded real growth from 2000. Financial conditions improved dramatically. Inflation declined sharply, enterprise arrears were reduced and non-performing loans cancelled. Incomes rose rapidly in real terms, and living standards improved. However, much of the improvement was linked to economic recovery and growth in Russia, Belarus's main trading partner. Belarus's economic growth rate was below the overall CIS average, and until 2005, inflation was the highest in the CIS. Industrial output and exports increased sharply, but again, the link with Russia was a key factor: imports of petroleum and gas from Russia were priced below world levels. This allowed Belarus to export refined petroleum products as well as manufactured goods to Western Europe at world market prices, taking advantage of the differentials between import and world prices, and adding as much as 3% to GDP. However, since the beginning of 2007 the situation has changed. Russia has increased the price of oil and gas, and claimed back a substantial share of the profits which had been made in exporting refined products to the West. Belarus's economy has been adversely affected, and future economic growth is uncertain.

Belarus remains strategically significant. Despite plans for new pipelines to deliver oil and gas to Western Europe, which will not pass through Belarus, it is the main transit route between metropolitan Russia and the Russian exclave of

Kaliningrad, and for Russian petroleum and gas deliveries to Western Europe. It is also the main overland road and rail route to Western Europe. A more aggressive Russian foreign policy over the last several years makes it unlikely that Belarus would be able to shift its political orientation towards the EU, even if there were a change of government, which seems unlikely at the present time. Following the election of Vladimir Putin as Russia's President in March 2000, the economic and political situation changed. President Putin was less interested in a Union than his predecessor, and has not been willing to extend energy subsidies to the Republic. Subsequently, EU accession for Latvia, Lithuania and Poland from 2004 meant that Belarus bordered member states of that organization. The EU had already compelled prospective members to strengthen their borders prior to EU membership, which had economic repercussions for border economies in Belarus, forcing the country to rely still more on the CIS for trade.

Despite his authoritarian rule, allegations of electoral fraud, and the preservation of a command-style economy, Lukashenka commands widespread popularity, and remains firmly in control. Belarusians witnessed the breakdown of government and local economies in the Russian Federation, and witnessed rapid growth in unemployment and a decline in living standards in Poland, Latvia and Lithuania. Belarusians experienced many of the same privations, but the rate of decline was slower and more controlled. Belarus does not display the wide contrast between wealth and poverty found in Russia. Nor does it display such striking concentrations of poverty and social exclusion as those found in Russia. Lukashenka made cheap energy prices a focus of his economic policy, which has made his regime vulnerable to external price fluctuations. His insistence on purchasing cheap energy from Russia led to repeated conflict with the

Russian Government and Russian gas suppliers, and was a fundamental factor in the collapse of the proposed currency union between Russia and Belarus. It was symptomatic of the failure of domestic reform: rather than reforming the economy so as to be able to afford energy imports at world market prices, as Belarus's neighbours have done, the regime continued to rely on low energy prices to protect unprofitable industries and resist substantive change. Economic dependence on Russia, particularly for imports of energy, has made Belarus increasingly vulnerable to Russian political influence and economic penetration. The price changes imposed by Gazprom were part of a broader policy shift implemented by the Russian authorities. The choice appeared to be a stark one between independence and union with Russia on the latter's terms. Despite this, there is still talk of some kind of economic union over the longer term. More important, perhaps, Belarus remains firmly within the Russian economic sphere, and Russian policy makers consider it to be part of their 'near abroad'. Close military co-operation and increasing Russian economic penetration would make any change in orientation towards Western Europe problematic.

Lukashenka has no party organization to maintain his support. Political opposition is diffuse and unco-ordinated. The press is tightly controlled, and the courts and the security services are controlled by the President. The end of the Lukashenka regime could leave a chaotic vacuum. This, together with his overall support for close ties with Russia, may be the main reason for continued Russian support, and appears to guarantee the continuation of the regime and its policies in the short to medium term. However, deteriorating economic conditions due to increased Russian energy prices may destabilize the country, and could, paradoxically, end in Belarus being forced out of Russia's orbit and towards the EU.

Statistical Survey

Source: mainly Ministry of Statistics and Analysis, 220070 Minsk, pr. Partizanski 12; tel. (17) 249-42-78; fax (17) 249-22-04; e-mail minstat@mail.belpak.by; internet www.belstat.gov.by.

Area and Population

AREA, POPULATION AND DENSITY

Area (sq km)	207,595*
Population (census results)†	
12 January 1989	10,151,806
16 February 1999	
Males	4,717,621
Females	5,327,616
Total	10,045,237
Population (official estimates at 31 December)	
2005	9,750,500
2006	9,714,500
2007	9,689,800
Density (per sq km) at 31 December 2007 . . .	46.7

* 80,153 sq miles.
† Figures refer to the *de jure* population. The *de facto* total was 10,199,709 in 1989.

POPULATION BY ETHNIC GROUP
(1999 census, % of total population)

Belarusian	81
Russian	11
Polish	4
Ukrainian	2
Others	2
Total	**100**

ADMINISTRATIVE DIVISIONS*
(31 December 2007; figures are rounded)

Oblasts (Regions)	
Brest (Bieraście)	1,435,100
Gomel (Homiel)	1,468,600
Grodno (Horadnia)	1,106,600
Minsk (Miensk)	1,461,800
Mogilev (Mahiloŭ)	1,129,600
Vitebsk (Viciebsk)	1,273,300
Capital City	
Minsk (Miensk)	1,814,800
Total	**9,689,800**

* The Belarusian names are given in parentheses after the more widely used Russian names, where they differ.

PRINCIPAL TOWNS*
(estimated population at 1 January 2001)

Minsk (Miensk, capital)	1,699,100	Borisov (Barysau) .	150,900
Gomel (Homiel) . .	480,000	Pinsk	131,100
Mogilev (Mahiloŭ) .	360,000	Orsha (Vorsha) .	124,000
Vitebsk (Viciebsk) .	341,500	Mozyr (Mazyr) .	110,700
Grodno (Horadnia) .	307,100	Novopolotsk .	102,100
Brest (Bieraście) . .	291,400	Soligorsk . .	101,900
Bobruysk (Babrujsk) .	221,400	Lida	100,000
Baranovichi (Baranavichy) . .	168,800		

* The Belarusian names are given in parentheses after the more widely used Russian names, where they differ.

Mid-2007 ('000, incl. suburbs, UN estimate): Minsk 1,805 (Source: UN, *World Urbanization Prospects: The 2007 Revision*).

BIRTHS, MARRIAGES AND DEATHS

	Registered live births		Registered marriages		Registered deaths	
	Number	Rate (per 1,000)	Number	Rate (per 1,000)	Number	Rate (per 1,000)
1998 . .	92,645	9.1	71,354	7.0	137,296	13.5
1999 . .	92,975	9.3	72,994	7.3	142,027	14.2
2000 . .	93,691	9.4	62,485	6.2	134,867	13.5
2001 . .	91,720	9.2	68,697	6.9	140,299	14.1
2002 . .	88,743	8.9	66,652	6.7	146,655	14.8
2003 . .	88,512	9.0	69,905	7.1	143,200	14.5
2004 . .	88,943	9.1	60,265	6.1	140,064	14.3
2005 . .	90,508	9.3	n.a.	n.a.	141,857	14.5

Source: partly UN, *Demographic Yearbook*.

Expectation of life (years at birth, WHO estimates): 68.8 (males 63.0; females 74.9) in 2006 (Source: WHO, *World Health Statistics*).

EMPLOYMENT

(monthly averages, '000 persons)*

	2004	2005	2006
Agriculture	473	458	444
Forestry	32	33	32
Industry†	976	974	969
Construction	237	261	267
Transport and communications .	268	268	265
Trade and related services‡ . .	251	260	263
Communal services . . .	177	184	187
Health and social services . .	304	308	310
Education, culture and science .	561	560	566
Banks and insurance . . .	57	59	60
Administration	84	86	86
Other activities	74	74	71
Total employed	3,494	3,525	3,520
Unemployed	83	68	52
Total labour force	3,577	3,593	3,572

* Excluding small non-state enterprises.
† Comprising manufacturing (except printing and publishing), mining and quarrying, electricity, gas, logging and fishing.
‡ Including material and technical supply and procurement.

Source: IMF, *Republic of Belarus: Statistical Appendix* (September 2007).

Health and Welfare

KEY INDICATORS

Total fertility rate (children per woman, 2006)	1.2
Under-5 mortality rate (per 1,000 live births, 2006) . . .	8
HIV/AIDS (% of persons aged 15–49, 2005)	0.3
Physicians (per 1,000 head, 2006)	4.8
Hospital beds (per 1,000 head, 2006)	11.2
Health expenditure (2005): US $ per head (PPP)	515
Health expenditure (2005): % of GDP	6.6
Health expenditure (2005): public (% of total)	75.8
Access to water (% of persons, 2004)	100
Access to sanitation (% of persons, 2004)	84
Human Development Index (2005): ranking	64
Human Development Index (2005): value	0.804

For sources and definitions, see explanatory note on p. vi.

Agriculture

PRINCIPAL CROPS

('000 metric tons)

	2004	2005	2006
Wheat	1,120.9	1,174.8	1,075.4
Barley	2,031.7	1,863.8	1,831.3
Maize	38.8	144.2	152.6
Rye	1,397.1	1,154.9	1,072.1
Oats	765.2	609.6	554.9
Buckwheat	11.9	7.3	5.1
Triticale (wheat-rye hybrid) .	1,216.0	1,121.5	978.3
Potatoes	9,902.2	8,185.0	8,329.4
Sugar beet	3,088.3	3,065.2	3,980.3
Dry beans	115.0	111.3	800.0
Dry peas	110.4	50.8	46.8
Walnuts*	12.0	12.0	12.5
Sunflower seed†	20.0	15.0	20.0
Rapeseed	142.9	149.9	115.0
Linseed	22.6	19.5	11.1
Cabbages and other brassicas .	573.4	529.8	568.6
Tomatoes	229.7	245.9	241.5
Cucumbers and gherkins . .	265.9	286.9	315.0
Dry onions	156.5	158.5	167.3
Carrots and turnips . . .	296.3	280.9	319.2
Apples	204.0	204.6	488.8
Pears	33.5	35.3	61.1
Plums	35.9	46.5	66.9
Sour (Morello) cherries . .	22.7	27.6	46.9
Sweet cherries*	11.0	12.0	12.0
Flax fibre	56.6	50.4	29.2

* FAO estimates.
† Unofficial figures.

Aggregate production ('000 metric tons, may include official, semi-official or estimated data): Total cereals 6,590.0 in 2004, 6,089.4 in 2005, 5,686.1 in 2006; Total roots and tubers 9,902.2 in 2004, 8,185.0 in 2005, 8,329.4 in 2006; Total pulses 425.8 in 2004; 331.2 in 2005, 238.2 in 2006; Total vegetables (incl. melons) 2,042.5 in 2004, 2,014.1 in 2005, 2,181.5 in 2006; Total fruits (excl. melons) 369.4 in 2004, 394.7 in 2005, 729.8 in 2006.

Source: FAO.

LIVESTOCK

('000 head at 1 January)

	2004	2005	2006
Horses	192	181	168
Cattle	3,924	3,963	3,980
Pigs	3,287	3,407	3,545
Sheep	63	59	53
Goats	63	66	68
Chickens	24,558	25,037	28,476

Source: FAO.

LIVESTOCK PRODUCTS

('000 metric tons)

	2004	2005	2006
Cattle meat	223.8	255.8	271.8
Sheep meat	1.8	1.2	1.0
Pig meat	298.9	321.0	345.9
Chicken meat	100.6	115.2	145.2
Cows' milk	5,124.1	5,650.1	5,869.9
Hen eggs	163.9*	172.4*	197.4†

* Unofficial figure.
† FAO estimate.

Source: FAO.

Forestry

ROUNDWOOD REMOVALS
('000 cubic metres, excl. bark)

	2003*	2004*	2005†
Sawlogs, veneer logs and logs for sleepers	2,304	3,676	3,771
Pulpwood	1,612	1,847	1,895
Other industrial wood	2,531	1,833	1,881
Fuel wood	1,097	1,266	1,170
Total	7,543	8,622	8,716

* Unofficial figures.
† FAO estimates.

2006: Figures assumed to be unchanged from 2005 (FAO estimates).

Source: FAO.

SAWNWOOD PRODUCTION
('000 cubic metres, incl. railway sleepers)

	2003*	2004*	2005†
Coniferous (softwood)	2,064	2,157	2,110
Broadleaved (hardwood)	239	570	557
Total	2,304	2,727	2,667

* Unofficial figures.
† FAO estimates.

2006: Figures assumed to be unchanged from 2005 (FAO estimates).

Source: FAO.

Fishing

(metric tons, live weight)

	2003	2004	2005*
Capture	6,925	890	900
Freshwater bream	393	164	160
Common carp	4,953	26	30
Crucian carp	497	188	190
Northern pike	336	125	130
Aquaculture	5,393	4,150	4,150
Common carp	3,386	3,207	3,207
Crucian carp	1,608	721	721
Total catch	12,318	5,040	5,050

* FAO estimates.

2006: Capture assumed to be unchanged from 2005 (FAO estimates).

Source: FAO.

Mining

('000 metric tons, unless otherwise indicated)

	2003	2004	2005
Crude petroleum	1,820	1,804	1,785
Natural gas (million cu metres)	254	245	228
Peat: for fuel	1,802	2,108	2,408

Source: US Geological Survey.

Industry

SELECTED PRODUCTS
('000 metric tons, unless otherwise indicated)

	2002	2003	2004
Refined sugar	666	n.a.	n.a.
Wheat flour	644	637	677
Ethyl alcohol ('000 hectolitres)	902	867	761
Other distilled alcoholic beverages('000 hectolitres)	1,885	1,682	1,512
Beer ('000 hectolitres)	2,026	2,056	2,272
Mineral water ('000 hectolitres)	1,900	1,873	1,777
Soft drinks ('000 hectolitres)	2,348	2,479	2,528
Cigarettes (million)	10,524	10,442	12,627
Bed linen, articles ('000)	3,690	3,253	3,959
Blouses, women's and girls' ('000)	1,315	1,158	1,151
Skirts, slacks and shorts for women and girls ('000)	2,706	2,792	3,420
Shirts, men's and boys' ('000)	2,230	1,923	1,858
Blankets ('000)	365	329	236
Carpets ('000 sq metres)	4,902	n.a.	n.a.
Footwear (excluding rubber, '000 pairs)	12,691	n.a.	n.a.
Plywood ('000 cu metres)	168	166	192
Paper and paperboard*	216.0	279.3	257.0
Benzene (Benzol)	34.5	n.a.	n.a.
Ethylene (Ethene)	121.2	n.a.	n.a.
Propylene (Propene)	69.7	n.a.	n.a.
Xylenes (Xylol)	50.7	n.a.	n.a.
Sulphuric acid (100%)	524	n.a.	n.a.
Nitrogenous fertilizers (a)*†	644.4	635.9	665.0
Phosphate fertilizers (b)*†	74.0	86.2	114.3
Potash fertilizers (c)*†	3,811.9	4,276.3	4,712.1
Non-cellulosic continuous fibres	130.7	125.4	n.a.
Cellulosic continuous filaments	11.5	11.0	n.a.
Soap	4.0	6.0	6.0
Rubber tyres: for agricultural and other off-road vehicles ('000)	156	183	231
Rubber tyres: for road motor vehicles ('000)	2,126	n.a.	n.a.
Rubber footwear ('000 pairs)	5,438	n.a.	n.a.
Quicklime	601	658	727
Cement	2,171	2,472	2,731
Domestic refrigerators ('000)	856	886	953
Radio receivers ('000)	47	31	21
Lorries (number)	16,544	n.a.	n.a.
Motorcycles ('000)	15	33	12
Bicycles ('000)	875	773	775
Watches ('000)	3,948	2,606	1,740
Electric energy (million kWh)	26,455	26,627	31,211

* Source: FAO.
† Production in terms of (a) nitrogen (N); (b) phosphorous pentoxide (P_2O_5); or (c) potassium oxide (K_2O).

Source (unless otherwise indicated): UN, *Industrial Commodity Statistics Yearbook*.

2005 (figures are rounded): Sausages ('000 metric tons) 257; Carpets ('000 sq metres) 7,400; Footwear ('000 pairs) 10,100; Particle board ('000 cu metres) 390; Paper ('000 metric tons) 69; Tyres for automobiles and agricultural machinery 3,052,000; Cement ('000 metric tons) 3,131; Tractors 41,500 units; Refrigerators and freezers 995,000 units; Television receivers 1,308,000 units; Bicycles (excl. children's) 438,000; Electric energy (million kWh) 31,000.

2006 (figures are rounded): Sausages ('000 metric tons) 278; Carpets ('000 sq metres) 7,000; Footwear ('000 pairs) 10,900; Particle board ('000 cu metres) 411; Paper ('000 metric tons) 63; Tyres for automobiles and agricultural machinery 3,563,000; Cement ('000 metric tons) 3,495; Tractors 49,200 units; Refrigerators and freezers 1,050,000 units; Television receivers 1,067,000 units; Bicycles (excl. children's) 458,000; Electric energy (million kWh) 31,800.

2007 (figures are rounded): Sausages ('000 metric tons) 273; Carpets ('000 sq metres) 6,700; Footwear ('000 pairs) 11,300; Particle board ('000 cu metres) 409; Paper ('000 metric tons) 57; Tyres for automobiles and agricultural machinery 4,792,000; Cement ('000 metric tons) 3,820; Tractors 59,600 units; Refrigerators and freezers 1,072,000 units; Television receivers 702,000 units; Bicycles (excl. children's) 374,000; Electric energy (million kWh) 31,800.

Finance

CURRENCY AND EXCHANGE RATES

Monetary Units
100 kopeks = 1 readjusted Belarusian rouble (rubel).

Sterling, Dollar and Euro Equivalents (30 May 2008)
£1 sterling = 4,211.4 readjusted roubles;
US $1 = 2,134.0 readjusted roubles;
€1 = 3,309.4 readjusted roubles;
10,000 readjusted Belarusian roubles = £2.37 = $4.69 = €3.02.

Average Exchange Rate (readjusted Belarusian roubles per US $)
2005   2,153.82
2006   2,144.56
2007   2,146.08

Note: The Belarusian rouble was introduced in May 1992, initially as a coupon currency, to circulate alongside (and at par with) the Russian (formerly Soviet) rouble. The parity between Belarusian and Russian currencies was subsequently ended, and the Belarusian rouble was devalued. In August 1994 a new Belarusian rouble, equivalent to 10 old roubles, was introduced. On 1 January 1995 the Belarusian rouble became the sole national currency, while the circulation of Russian roubles ceased. On 1 January 2000 a readjusted Belarusian rouble, equivalent to 1,000 of the former units, was introduced.

STATE BUDGET
('000 million roubles)

Revenue*	2002	2003	2004
Republican and local budget revenue:			
Tax revenue	6,263.4	9,333.6	12,660.5
Direct taxes on income and profits	1,684.5	2,369.0	3,538.8
Personal income tax . .	773.1	1,024.4	1,403.8
Profit tax	643.3	934.4	1,624.6
Enterprise income tax . .	136.8	173.3	233.3
Taxes on wage fund . . .	220.4	273.2	391.2
Taxes on goods and services .	3,311.7	4,837.2	6,401.7
Value-added tax . . .	2,165.1	2,894.8	3,814.6
Excises	592.0	837.8	1,121.6
Property tax	390.5	728.8	957.0
Other current revenue . . .	453.4	631.3	990.4
Capital revenue	21.8	15.7	27.0
Revenue from sales of assets .	21.5	13.9	24.1
Revenue of budgetary funds .	1,924.9	2,862.8	3,738.7
Sub-total	8,663.5	12,843.4	17,416.7
Social protection fund:			
Total revenue (incl. from state budget)	3,055.0	3,977.8	5,452.8
Less Transfers from the state budget	69.8	56.7	36.1
Total revenue	11,648.7	16,764.6	22,833.4

Expenditure	2002	2003	2004
Republican and local budget expenditure:			
Government administration .	251.6	381.5	565.7
Defence	259.9	376.9	472.2
Law, order and security . . .	461.0	654.1	920.7
Agriculture	178.8	520.3	766.6
Housing and communal services	612.4	940.9	1,174.7
Emergency funds, Chernobyl .	307.0	376.4	489.0
Education	1,738.1	2,343.1	3,020.0
Health, sports and physical education	1,270.1	1,809.8	1,410.3
Servicing of state debt . . .	154.2	175.7	209.8
Capital investment . . .	323.6	533.4	807.5
Expenditure of budgetary funds	1,805.2	2,619.7	3,579.5
Others	520.4	935.0	970.7
Unallocated	1,252.9	1,666.3	2,207.8
Sub-total	9,135.1	13,333.1	17,594.6
Less Transfers to the social protection fund	69.8	56.7	36.1
Social protection fund expenditure	3,061.4	3,987.8	5,262.1
Total expenditure	12,126.7	17,264.3	22,820.6

* Excluding receipts from privatization.

Source: IMF, *Republic of Belarus: Statistical Appendix* (June 2005).

General government totals ('000 million roubles): *Revenue:* 30,825 in 2005; 38,392 in 2006; 45,482 in 2007 (projection). *Expenditure* (cash basis): 31,257 in 2005; 38,010 in 2006; 45,043 in 2007 (Source: IMF, *Republic of Belarus: 2007 Article IV Consultation-Staff Report; Staff Supplement; Public Information Notice on the Executive Board Discussion; and Statement by the Executive Director for the Republic of Belarus*—September 2007).

INTERNATIONAL RESERVES
(US $ million at 31 December)

	2005	2006	2007
IMF special drawing rights . .	0.03	0.04	0.04
Reserve position in IMF . . .	0.03	0.03	0.03
Foreign exchange	1,136.56	1,162.96	4,266.24
Total	1,136.62	1,163.03	4,266.31

Source: IMF, *International Financial Statistics*.

MONEY SUPPLY
(million roubles at 31 December)

	2005	2006	2007
Currency outside banks . . .	2,016.41	2,818.35	3,323.21
Demand deposits at deposit money banks	2,928.49	4,203.46	5,415.17
Total money (incl. others) . .	4,945.79	7,023.21	8,739.94

Source: IMF, *International Financial Statistics*.

COST OF LIVING
(Consumer Price Index; base: 2000 = 100)

	2003	2004	2005
Food (incl. beverages)	267.6	320.1	358.2
Fuel and light	1,374.1	1,623.2	1,645.6
Clothing (incl. footwear) . . .	201.2	214.1	218.8
Rent	1,348.8	2,236.4	3,201.6
All items (incl. others) . . .	295.0	348.3	384.3

2006: Food (incl. beverages) 380.1; All items (incl. others) 411.2.

2007: Food (incl. beverages) 417.4; All items (incl. others) 445.9.

Source: ILO.

NATIONAL ACCOUNTS
('000 million roubles at current prices)

Expenditure on the Gross Domestic Product

	2005	2006	2007
Final consumption expenditure .	47,351.4	56,028.2	68,078.5
Households	33,827.0	40,803.1	50,247.6
Non-profit institutions serving households			
Government	13,524.4	15,225.1	17,830.9
Gross capital formation . .	18,518.4	25,511.4	31,893.6
Gross fixed capital formation .	17,253.6	23,511.2	29,590.3
Changes in inventories . . .	1,264.8	2,000.2	2,303.3
Total domestic expenditure	65,869.8	81,539.6	99,972.1
Exports of goods and services . .	38,908.7	47,608.8	59,314.2
Less Imports of goods and services	38,445.9	50,916.2	65,191.5
Statistical discrepancy . .	−1,265.5	1,034.8	1,992.4
GDP in market prices . . .	65,067.1	79,267.0	96,087.2
GDP at constant 2000 prices* .	13,118.9	14,423.0	n.a.

* Source: IMF, *International Financial Statistics*.

Gross Domestic Product by Economic Activity

	2004	2005	2006
Agriculture and forestry . . .	4,424	5,468	6,317
Industry*	14,007	18,509	21,865
Construction	3,234	4,500	6,271
Transport and communications .	4,829	6,172	7,318
Trade and catering	4,859	6,129	8,131
Material supply and procurement .	263	309	339
Housing and public utilities . .	2,154	2,498	3,102
Health care	1,785	2,311	2,712
Education, culture and science .	2,929	4,231	4,931
Other	4,352	5,821	6,948
GDP at factor cost	42,836	55,948	67,934
Taxes, *less* subsidies on products .	7,156	9,119	11,297
GDP in market prices . .	49,992	65,067	79,231

* Principally mining, manufacturing, electricity, gas and water.

Source: IMF, *Republic of Belarus: Statistical Appendix* (September 2007).

BALANCE OF PAYMENTS
(US $ million)

	2004	2005	2006
Exports of goods f.o.b.	13,942.2	16,108.8	19,838.1
Imports of goods f.o.b.	−16,126.1	−16,609.7	−22,236.5
Trade balance	−2,183.9	−500.9	−2,398.4
Exports of services	1,747.0	1,959.3	2,299.2
Imports of services	−1,058.4	−1,249.5	−1,486.9
Balance on goods and services	−1,495.3	208.9	−1,586.1
Other income received	157.6	283.4	244.6
Other income paid	−159.1	−227.7	−351.9
Balance on goods, services and income	−1,496.8	264.6	−1,693.4
Current transfers received . .	390.6	280.5	301.6
Current transfers paid . . .	−88.0	−111.4	−119.8
Current balance	−1,194.2	433.7	−1,511.6
Capital account (net)	49.3	40.5	70.5
Direct investment abroad . . .	−1.3	−2.5	−3.0
Direct investment from abroad .	163.8	305.0	354.0
Portfolio investment assets . .	3.2	−2.9	5.6
Portfolio investment liabilities .	59.6	−38.6	−24.7
Financial derivatives assets . .	n.a.	1.9	0.0
Financial derivatives liabilities .	n.a.	−2.2	−13.0
Other investment assets . . .	−151.4	−492.1	−136.8
Other investment liabilities . .	972.3	170.9	1,525.1
Net errors and omissions . . .	274.2	111.7	−250.0
Overall balance	175.5	525.5	16.2

Source: IMF, *International Financial Statistics*.

External Trade

PRINCIPAL COMMODITIES
(distribution by SITC, US $ million)

Imports c.i.f.	2002	2003	2004
Food and live animals . . .	898.5	1,016.7	1,325.9
Crude materials (inedible) except fuels	368.3	470.0	595.1
Mineral fuels, lubricants, etc. .	2,334.5	3,038.3	4,524.7
Petroleum, petroleum products and related materials	1,609.6	2,153.2	3,436.0
Gas, natural and manufactured .	566.3	719.2	973.3
Chemicals and related products	969.0	1,217.2	1,631.9
Basic manufactures	1,677.4	2,162.0	3,216.1
Textile yarn, fabrics, etc. . . .	266.3	322.2	403.3
Iron and steel	548.7	777.0	1,238.7
Machinery and transport equipment	2,018.2	2,581.8	3,774.8
Machinery specialized for particular industries . . .	249.7	377.6	584.6
General industrial machinery and equipment	332.6	474.0	697.1
Electric machinery, apparatus and appliances, etc.	375.9	503.2	756.2
Road vehicles	555.2	583.1	807.6
Miscellaneous manufactured articles	448.0	584.1	764.1
Total (incl. others)	9,092.3	11,558.0	16,345.4

Exports f.o.b.	2002	2003	2004
Food and live animals . . .	544.7	741.9	1,045.3
Crude materials (inedible) except fuels	389.4	432.3	515.4
Mineral fuels, lubricants, etc. .	1,624.4	2,194.1	3,697.8
Petroleum, petroleum products, etc.	1,605.0	2,150.5	3,596.7
Refined petroleum products .	1,478.8	1,960.6	3,295.7
Chemicals and related products	982.7	1,181.7	1,499.5
Fertilizers, manufactured . .	540.5	643.4	863.4
Potassium chloride	463.1	535.8	752.0
Basic manufactures	1,514.6	1,911.1	2,497.6
Textile yarn, fabrics, etc. . . .	381.2	448.6	513.7
Iron and steel	321.5	443.3	683.2
Other metal manufactures . .	249.5	330.2	445.4
Machinery and transport equipment	1,915.3	2,280.4	3,042.0
Machinery specialized for particular industries . . .	349.5	402.3	532.4
Electrical machinery, apparatus and appliances, etc.	388.7	500.6	637.6
Road vehicles	762.8	870.0	1,211.6
Lorries and special purposes motor vehicles	349.5	388.7	555.2
Miscellaneous manufactured articles	896.8	1,039.7	1,231.0
Clothing and accessories (excl. footwear)	292.1	340.9	400.7
Total (incl. others)	8,020.9	9,945.6	13,751.7

Source: UN, *International Trade Statistics Yearbook*.

2005 (US $ million): Total imports 16,708; Total exports 15,979.
2006 (US $ million): Total imports 22,351; Total exports 19,734.
2007 (US $ million): Total imports 28,693; Total exports 24,275.

PRINCIPAL TRADING PARTNERS
(US $ million)

Imports c.i.f.	2002	2003	2004
Brazil	104.5	89.2	97.0
China, People's Republic . . .	46.4	71.7	158.0
Czech Republic	54.2	74.4	111.0
France	94.8	116.3	165.0
Germany	693.0	820.6	1,081.0
Italy	215.1	283.9	300.4
Lithuania	109.3	154.2	175.5
Netherlands	84.0	93.3	118.6
Poland	221.7	348.4	474.9
Russia	5,922.3	7,601.9	11,142.5
Sweden	99.5	98.4	98.4
Ukraine	290.6	362.0	544.9
United Kingdom	67.7	79.3	128.3
USA	103.3	150.1	195.5
Total (incl. others)	9,092.3	11,558.0	16,345.4

Exports f.o.b.	2002	2003	2004
Brazil	89.4	113.4	146.4
China, People's Republic . . .	217.4	162.2	301.5
Denmark	26.2	105.8	131.1
Germany	347.9	421.1	502.8
Hungary	70.8	105.5	136.6
Italy	130.0	135.2	142.9
Latvia	520.1	344.3	326.0
Lithuania	256.7	264.9	356.2
Netherlands	279.0	413.8	924.4
Poland	273.3	434.1	728.7
Russia	3,977.1	4,879.8	6,462.9
Sweden	27.2	65.4	136.9
Ukraine	271.6	343.5	539.8
United Kingdom	493.7	938.3	1,147.5
USA	91.3	102.5	162.8
Total (incl. others)	8,020.9	9,945.6	13,751.7

Source: UN, *International Trade Statistics Yearbook*.

2005 (US $ million): *Imports:* Trade with CIS countries 11,142.5 (Moldova 72.3; Russia 10,118.2; Ukraine 893.9); Total (incl. others) 16,708. *Exports:* Trade with CIS countries 7,060.3 (Kazakhstan 183.5; Moldova 102.2; Russia 5,715.8; Ukraine 907.8); Total (incl. others) 15,979.

2006 (US $ million): *Imports:* Trade with CIS countries 14,511,7 (Moldova 81.1; Russia 13,099.1; Ukraine 213.7); Total (incl. others) 22,351. *Exports:* Trade with CIS countries 8,608,8 (Kazakhstan 259.4; Moldova 95.7; Russia 6,845.3; Ukraine 1,234.0); Total (incl. others) 19,734.

Transport

RAILWAYS
(traffic)

	2004	2005	2006
Passenger-km (million) . . .	13,893	10,351	9,968
Freight ton-km (million) . . .	40,331	43,559	45,723

ROAD TRAFFIC
(motor vehicles in use at 31 December)

	2001	2002	2004
Passenger cars	1,467,605	1,548,472	1,707,888
Buses and coaches	8,038	7,672	7,781
Road tractors	17,795	14,036	n.a.
Motorcycles and mopeds . . .	535,996	525,005	454,612

Source: IRF, *World Road Statistics*.

CIVIL AVIATION
(traffic on scheduled services)

	2004	2005	2006
Passenger-km (million) . . .	674	684	754
Total ton-km (million) . . .	49	59	92

Tourism

FOREIGN TOURIST ARRIVALS

Country of nationality	2004	2005	2006
Cyprus	1,179	940	956
Germany	8,542	7,402	9,973
Israel	2,515	3,120	1,829
Italy	4,533	5,090	4,910
Latvia	4,978	7,409	8,156
Lithuania	5,317	8,249	12,481
Netherlands	954	868	611
Poland	5,563	2,983	3,329
Russia	11,681	27,097	24,859
United Kingdom	5,222	8,208	3,092
USA	5,518	4,274	4,005
Total (incl. others)	67,297	90,588	89,101

Tourism receipts (US $ million, incl. passenger transport): 362 in 2004; 346 in 2005; 386 in 2006.

Source: World Tourism Organization.

Communications Media

	1998	1999	2000
Television receivers ('000 in use) .	3,300	3,400	3,500
Telephones ('000 main lines in use)	2,489.9	2,638.5	2,751.9
Facsimile machines (number in use)	19,472	23,847	26,925
Mobile cellular telephones (subscribers)	12,155	23,457	49,353
Internet users ('000)	7.5	50.0	180.0
Book production (incl. pamphlets):			
titles	6,073	6,064	7,686
copies ('000)	60,022	63,305	61,627
Daily newspapers:			
number	20	12	10
average circulation ('000) . .	1,559	1,094	1,101
Non-daily newspapers:			
number	560	578	600
average circulation ('000) . .	8,973	10,094	10,339
Other periodicals:			
number	318	331	354
average circulation ('000) . .	1,687	1,498	1,381

Radio receivers ('000 in use): 3,020 in 1997.

Telephones ('000 main lines in use): 2,862.4 in 2001; 2,967.2 in 2002; 3,071.3 in 2003; 3,175.9 in 2004; 3,284.3 in 2005.

Mobile cellular telephones ('000 subscribers): 138.3 in 2001; 462.6 in 2002; 1,118.0 in 2003; 2,239.3 in 2004; 4,098.0 in 2005.

Internet users ('000): 430.0 in 2001; 891.2 in 2002; 1,607.3 in 2003; 2,461.1 in 2004; 3,394.4 in 2005; 5,477.5 in 2006.

Broadband subscribers: 100 in 2003; 800 in 2004; 1,600 in 2005; 11,400 in 2006.

Sources: partly International Telecommunication Union; UNESCO, *Statistical Yearbook*.

Education

(2001/02, unless otherwise indicated)

	Institutions	Teachers	Students
Pre-primary	4,423	52,524	390,812
Primary (Grades 1–4) . . . } Secondary (Grades 5–11) . . }	4,187*	138,744	1,240,900*
Vocational and technical . .	248	14,772	138,593
Specialized secondary . . .	204*	12,748	154,100*
Higher	55*	21,684	383,000*
Institutions offering post-graduate studies	377	9,000	570,000

* 2005/06.

Source: partly Ministry of Education, Minsk.

Adult literacy rate (UNESCO estimates): 99.7% (males 99.8%; females 99.7%) in 2007 (Source: UNESCO Institute for Statistics).

Directory

The Constitution

A new Constitution came into effect on 30 March 1994. An amended version of the Constitution became effective on 27 November 1996, following a referendum held on 24 November. A constitutional referendum, held on 17 October 2004, removed the former two-term limit for presidential tenure. The following is a summary of the main provisions of the Constitution:

PRINCIPLES OF THE CONSTITUTIONAL SYSTEM

The Republic of Belarus is a unitary, democratic, social state based on the rule of law. State power is exercised on the principle of division of powers between the legislature, executive and judiciary, which are independent of one another. The Republic is bound by the principle of supremacy of law and ensures that its laws comply with universally acknowledged principles of international law. Property may be owned by the State or privately. The mineral wealth, waters and forests are the sole and exclusive property of the State. Land for agricultural use is the property of the State. All religions and creeds are equal before the law. The official languages are Belarusian and Russian. The Republic aims to make its territory a neutral, nuclear-free state. The capital is Minsk (Miensk).

THE INDIVIDUAL, SOCIETY AND THE STATE

All persons are equal before the law and entitled without discrimination to equal protection of their rights and legitimate interests. The State ensures the freedom, inviolability and dignity of the individual. No person may be subjected to torture or cruel, inhuman or humiliating treatment or punishment. Freedom of movement is guaranteed. The freedom of expression and public assembly, and the right to form public associations, including trade unions, are guaranteed. Citizens have the right to participate in the solution of state matters, both directly and through freely elected representatives. The State shall create the conditions necessary for full employment. The right to health care is guaranteed. Each person has the right to housing and to education. Everyone has the right to preserve his or her ethnic affiliation, to use his or her native language and to choose the language of communication.

THE ELECTORAL SYSTEM AND REFERENDUMS

Elections and referendums are conducted by means of universal, free, equal and secret ballot. Deputies are elected by direct ballot. National referendums may be called by the President of the Republic of Belarus, by the Natsionalnoye Sobraniye (National Assembly) or by no fewer than 450,000 citizens eligible to vote. Local referendums may be called by local representative bodies or on the recommendation of no less than 10% of the citizens who are eligible to vote and resident in the area concerned. Decisions adopted by referendum may be reversed or amended only by means of another referendum.

THE PRESIDENT

The President is Head of State, the guarantor of the Constitution, and of the rights and freedoms of its citizens. The President is elected for a term of five years by universal, free, equal, direct and secret ballot.

The President calls national referendums; calls elections to the Natsionalnoye Sobraniye and local representative bodies; dissolves the chambers of the Natsionalnoye Sobraniye, as determined by the Constitution; appoints six members to the Central Electoral Commission; appoints the Chairman of the Cabinet of Ministers (Prime Minister) with the consent of the Palata Predstavitaley (House of Representatives); appoints and dismisses Ministers and other members of the Government, and considers the resignation of the Government; appoints, with the consent of the Soviet Respubliki (Council of the Republic), the Chairmen of the Constitutional, Supreme and Economic Courts, the judges of the Supreme and Economic Courts, the Chairman of the Central Electoral Commission, the Prosecutor-General, the Chairman and members of the board of the National Bank, and dismisses the aforementioned, having notified the Soviet Respubliki; appoints six members of the Constitutional Court, and other judges; may chair meetings of the Government; conducts negotiations and signs international treaties, appoints and recalls diplomatic representatives; declares a state of emergency; has the right to abolish acts of the Government and to suspend decisions of local councils of deputies; forms and heads the Security Council of the Republic of Belarus; is the Commander-in-Chief of the Armed Forces; imposes, in the event of military threat or attack, martial law. In instances determined by the Constitution, the President may issue decrees which have the force of law. The President may be removed from office for acts of treason and other grave crimes, by a decision of the Natsionalnoye Sobraniye.

THE NATSIONALNOYE SOBRANIYE

The Natsionalnoye Sobraniye (National Assembly) is a representative and legislative body, comprising two chambers: the Palata Predstavitaley and the Soviet Respubliki. The term of the Natsionalnoye Sobraniye is four years. The Palata Predstavitaley comprises 110 deputies, who are elected by universal, equal, free, direct suffrage and by secret ballot. The Soviet Respubliki is a chamber of territorial representation with 64 members, consisting of eight deputies from every region and from the capital city, elected by deputies of local councils. Eight members of the chamber are appointed by the President. Any citizen who has reached the age of 21 years may become a deputy of the Palata Predstavitaley. Any citizen who has reached the age of 30 years, and who has been resident in the corresponding region for no less than five years, may become a member of the Soviet Respubliki. The chambers of the Natsionalnoye Sobraniye elect their Chairmen.

The Palata Predstavitaley considers draft laws and the interpretation of laws. The Palata Predstavitaley calls elections for the presidency; grants consent to the President concerning the appointment of the Chairman of the Cabinet of Ministers; accepts the resignation of the President; and together with the Soviet Respubliki, takes the decision to remove the President from office.

The Soviet Respubliki approves or rejects draft laws adopted by the Palata Predstavitaley; consents to appointments made by the President; elects six judges of the Constitutional Court and six members of the Central Electoral Commission; considers charges of treason against the President; takes the decision to remove the President from office; considers presidential decrees on the introduction of a state of emergency, martial law, and general or partial mobilization.

On the proposal of the President, the Palata Predstavitaley and the Soviet Respubliki may adopt a law, delegating to him legislative powers to issue decrees which have the power of a law. However, he may not issue decrees making alterations or addenda to the Constitution or to policy laws.

THE GOVERNMENT

Executive power is exercised by the Cabinet of Ministers. The Government is accountable to the President and responsible to the Natsionalnoye Sobraniye. The Chairman of the Cabinet of Ministers is appointed by the President with the consent of the Palata Predstavitaley. The Government formulates and implements domestic and foreign policy; submits the draft national budget to the President; and issues acts that have binding force.

THE JUDICIARY

Judicial authority is exercised by the courts. Justice is administered on the basis of adversarial proceedings and equality of the parties involved in the trial. Supervision of the constitutionality of enforceable enactments of the State is exercised by the Constitutional Court, which comprises 12 judges, of whom six are appointed by the President and six are elected by the Soviet Respubliki.

LOCAL GOVERNMENT

Citizens exercise local and self-government through local councils of deputies, executive and administrative bodies and other forms of direct participation in state and public affairs. Local councils of deputies are elected by citizens for a four-year term, and the heads of local executive and administrative bodies are appointed and dismissed by the President.

APPLICATION OF THE CONSTITUTION AND THE PROCEDURE FOR AMENDING THE CONSTITUTION

Amendments and supplements to the Constitution are considered by the chambers of the Natsionalnoye Sobraniye on the initiative of the President, or of no fewer than 150,000 citizens who are eligible to vote. The Constitution may be amended or supplemented via a referendum.

The Government

HEAD OF STATE

President: ALYAKSANDR R. LUKASHENKA (inaugurated 20 July 1994; re-elected 9 September 2001; re-elected 19 March 2006).

COUNCIL OF MINISTERS
(September 2008)

Chairman (Prime Minister): SYARHEY S. SIDORSKY.
First Deputy Prime Minister: ULADZIMIR I. SEMASHKA.

Deputy Prime Minister: IVAN M. BAMBIZA.

Deputy Prime Minister: ALYAKSANDR M. KASINETS.

Deputy Prime Minister: ANDREY U. KABYAKOW.

Deputy Prime Minister: VIKTAR P. BURA.

Minister of Agriculture and Food: SEMYON B. SHAPIRA.

Minister of Architecture and Construction: ALYAKSANDR SELYAZNYOU.

Minister of Communications and Information Technologies: MIKALAY PANTSYALEY.

Minister of Culture: ULADZIMIR F. MATVEICHUK.

Minister of Defence: Col-Gen. LEANID S. MALTSAW.

Minister of the Economy: MIKALAY P. ZAYCHANKA.

Minister of Education: ALYAKSANDR M. RADZKOW.

Minister of Emergency Situations: ENVER R. BARYYEW.

Minister of Energy: ALYAKSANDR AZYARETS.

Minister of Finance: ANDREY M. KHARKOVETS.

Minister of Foreign Affairs: SYARHEY M. MARTYNOW.

Minister of Forestry: PYOTR M. SYAMASHKA.

Minister of Health: VASIL I. ZHARKO.

Minister of Housing and Municipal Services: ULADZIMIR M. BELAKHVOSTOW.

Minister of Industry: ANATOLY M. RUSETSKY.

Minister of Information: ULADZIMIR U. RUSAKEVICH.

Minister of Internal Affairs: ULADZIMIR U. NAUMAU.

Minister of Justice: VIKTAR G. GOLOVANOU.

Minister of Labour and Social Protection: ULADZIMIR PATUP-CHYK.

Minister of Natural Resources and Environmental Protection: LYAVONTSY I. KHAROUZHYK.

Minister of Sports and Tourism: ALYAKSANDR U. HRIHORAW.

Minister of Statistics and Analysis: ULADZIMIR I. ZINOVSKY.

Minister of Taxes and Duties: HANNA K. DZEYKA.

Minister of Trade: ALYAKSANDR I. IVANKOW.

Minister of Transport and Communications: ULADZIMIR G. SOSNOVSKY.

Note: The following positions are also members of the Council of Ministers: Head of the Presidential Administration; President of the National Academy of Sciences; Chairman of the Management of the National Bank; and Chairmen of the following organizations: the Committee of State Control; the State Military-Industrial Committee; the Committee of State Security; the State Committee of Aviation; the Belarusian Republic Union of Consumer Societies; the State Committee of Border Troops; the State Committee of Science and Technology; and the State Customs Committee.

MINISTRIES

Office of the President: 220016 Minsk, vul. K. Marksa 38, Dom Urada; tel. (17) 222-35-03; fax (17) 222-30-20; e-mail press@president.gov.by; internet www.president.gov.by.

Office of the Council of Ministers: 220010 Minsk, vul. Savetskaya 11; tel. (17) 222-69-05; fax (17) 222-66-65; e-mail contact@government.by; internet www.government.by.

Ministry of Agriculture and Food: 220050 Minsk, vul. Kirava 15; tel. (17) 227-37-51; fax (17) 227-42-96; e-mail kanc@mshp.minsk.by; internet mshp.minsk.by.

Ministry of Architecture and Construction: 220048 Minsk, vul. Myasnikova 39; tel. (17) 227-26-42; fax (17) 220-74-24; tel. mas@mas.by; internet www.mas.by.

Ministry of Communications and Information Technologies: 220050 Minsk, pr. Nezavisimosti 10; tel. (17) 227-38-61; fax (17) 227-21-57; e-mail mpt@mpt.gov.by; internet www.mpt.gov.by.

Ministry of Culture: 220004 Minsk, pr. Pobeditelei 11; tel. (17) 203-75-74; fax (17) 223-90-45; e-mail admin@kultura.by; internet kultura.by.

Ministry of Defence: 220034 Minsk, vul. Kamunistychnaya 1; tel. (17) 297-12-12; fax (17) 289-19-74; internet www.mod.mil.by.

Ministry of the Economy: 220050 Minsk, vul. Bersona 14; tel. (17) 222-60-48; fax (17) 200-37-77; e-mail gen@plan.minsk.by; internet www.economy.gov.by.

Ministry of Education: 220010 Minsk, vul. Savetskaya 9; tel. (17) 227-47-36; fax (17) 200-84-83; e-mail root@minedu.unibel.by; internet www.minedu.unibel.by.

Ministry of Emergency Situations: 220050 Minsk, vul. Revolutsionnaya 5; tel. (17) 203-94-28; fax (17) 203-77-81; e-mail mcs@infonet.by; internet www.rescue01.gov.by.

Ministry of Energy: 220050 Minsk, vul. K. Marksa 14; tel. (17) 229-83-59; fax (17) 229-86-39; e-mail minsecretary@min.energo.net.by; internet www.minenergo.gov.by.

Ministry of Finance: 220048 Minsk, vul. Savetskaya 7; tel. (17) 227-27-26; fax (17) 222-45-93; e-mail web_mf@open.by; internet ncpi.gov.by/minfin.

Ministry of Foreign Affairs: 220030 Minsk, vul. Lenina 19; tel. (17) 227-29-22; fax (17) 227-45-21; e-mail mail@mfabelar.gov.by; internet www.mfa.gov.by.

Ministry of Forestry: 220039 Minsk, vul. Chkalova 6; tel. (17) 224-47-05; fax (17) 224-41-83; e-mail info@komleshoz.org; internet www.mlh.by.

Ministry of Health: 220048 Minsk, vul. Myasnikova 39; tel. (17) 222-60-33; fax (17) 222-62-97; e-mail mzrb@belcmt.by; internet minzdrav.by.

Ministry of Housing and Municipal Services: 220050 Minsk, vul. Bersona 16; tel. (17) 220-15-45; fax (17) 220-87-08; internet www.mjkx.gov.by.

Ministry of Industry: 220033 Minsk, pr. Partizansky 2; tel. (17) 224-95-95; fax (17) 224-87-84; e-mail minprom1@minprom.gov.by; internet minprom.gov.by.

Ministry of Information: 220004 Minsk, pr. Pobeditelei 11; tel. (17) 203-92-31; fax (17) 203-34-35; e-mail info@mininform.gov.by; internet www.mininform.gov.by.

Ministry of Internal Affairs: 220050 Minsk, vul. Gorodskoy Val 4; tel. (17) 218-78-08; fax (17) 226-12-47; e-mail admin@mvd.gov.by; internet mvd.gov.by.

Ministry of Justice: 220048 Minsk, vul. Kalektarnaya 10; tel. (17) 206-37-28; fax (17) 200-97-55; e-mail kanc@minjust.by; internet www.minjust.by.

Ministry of Labour and Social Protection: 220004 Minsk, pr. Pobeditelei 23, kor. 2; tel. (17) 206-38-84; fax (17) 222-49-30; e-mail press@mintrud.gov.by; internet mintrud.gov.by.

Ministry of Natural Resources and Environmental Protection: 220048 Minsk, vul. Kalektarnaya 10; tel. (17) 220-66-91; fax (17) 220-55-83; e-mail minproos@mail.belpak.by; internet minpriroda.by.

Ministry of Sports and Tourism: 220050 Minsk, vul. Kirava 8, kor. 2; tel. (17) 227-72-37; fax (17) 227-30-31; e-mail intersport@mst.by; internet www.mst.by.

Ministry of Statistics and Analysis: 220070 Minsk, pr. Partizansky 12; tel. (17) 249-42-09; fax (17) 249-22-04; e-mail minstat@mail.belpak.by; internet www.belstat.gov.by.

Ministry of Taxes and Duties: 220010 Minsk, vul. Savetskaya 9; tel. (17) 222-49-92; fax (17) 222-66-87; e-mail GNK@mail.belpak.by; internet www.nalog.by.

Ministry of Trade: 220050 Minsk, vul. Kirava 8, kor. 1; tel. and fax (17) 227-24-80; e-mail mintorgrb@mail.belpak.by; internet www.mintorg.gov.by.

Ministry of Transport and Communications: 220029 Minsk, vul. Chicherina 21; tel. (17) 234-11-52; fax (17) 239-42-26; e-mail mail@mintrans.by; internet www.mintrans.by.

President

Presidential Election, 19 March 2006

Candidates		Votes	%
Alyaksandr Lukashenka	. . . . .	5,501,249	83.0
Alyaksandr Milinkevich	. . . . .	405,486	6.1
Syarhey Gaydukevich	. . . . .	230,664	3.5
Alyaksandr Kazulin	. . . . .	147,402	2.2
Total*	. . . .	6,630,653	100.0

* Including invalid votes and votes cast against all candidates.

Legislature

NATSIONALNOYE SOBRANIYE
(National Assembly)

Soviet Respubliki (Council of the Republic)
220016 Minsk, vul. Krasnoarmeiskaya 4; tel. (17) 227-46-74; fax (17) 227-23-18; e-mail cr@sovrep.gov.by; internet www.sovrep.gov.by.

Chairman: GENADZ V. NAVITSKY.

The Soviet Respubliki is the upper chamber of the legislature and comprises 64 deputies. Of the total, 56 deputies are elected by regional councils (eight each from the six oblasts and the city of

Minsk) and eight deputies are appointed by the President of the Republic.

Palata Predstaviteley (House of Representatives)

220010 Minsk, vul. Savetskaya 11; tel. (17) 227-25-14; fax (17) 222-31-78; e-mail admin@gov.house.by; internet house.gov.by.

Chairman: VADIM A. POPOV.

General Election, 28 September 2008

Parties or groups	Seats
Independents	103
Communist Party of Belarus	6
Belarusian Agrarian Party	1
Total	**110**

Local Government

Belarus is divided into six regions (oblasts) and the capital city of Minsk (Miensk). The six regions, which are divided into districts (rayons), are based around the cities of Minsk, Grodno (Horadnia), Brest (Bieraście), Vitebsk (Viciebsk), Mogilev (Mahiloŭ) and Gomel (Homiel).

The head of local executive and administrative bodies, the chairman of the regional or city executive committee—Ispolkom, is appointed by the President. Local self-government is exercised by popularly elected councils, with four-year terms of office. Local elections took place on 14 January 2007.

CAPITAL CITY

Minsk City Administration: 220030 Minsk, pr. Nezavisimosti 8; tel. (17) 227-05-54; fax (17) 200-70-70; e-mail admin@minsk.gov.by; internet www.minsk.gov.by; Chair. of Council of Deputies MIKHAIL M. VASILYEVICH; Chair. of Exec. Cttee MIKHAIL YA. PAWLAW.

OBLASTS

Brest Oblast Administration: 224005 Brest, vul. Lenina 11; tel. (16) 221-23-32; fax (16) 223-47-73; e-mail contact@brest-region.by; internet www.brest-region.by; Chair. of Council ALYAKSANDR M. KOLEDA; Chair. of Exec. Cttee KONSTANTIN A. SUMAR.

Gomel Oblast Administration: 246050 Gomel, vul. Lenina 2; tel. (23) 274-06-24; fax (23) 274-51-19; e-mail oblisp-uip@mail.gomel.by; internet www.gomel-region.by; Chair. of Council VALERY S. SELITSKY; Gov. ALYAKSANDR S. YAKOBSON.

Grodno Oblast Administration: 230023 Grodno, vul. Ozheshko 3; tel. (15) 272-35-57; fax (15) 272-02-32; e-mail groblisp@mail.grodno .by; internet www.region.grodno.by; Chair. of Council ARKADY I. KAPUT; Chair. of Exec. Cttee ULADZIMIR E. SAVCHENKA.

Minsk Oblast Administration: 220030 Minsk, vul. Engelsa 4; tel. (17) 227-24-15; e-mail info@minsk-region.gov.by; internet www .minsk-region.gov.by; Chair. of Council SVETLANA M. GERASIMOVICH; Chair. of Exec. Cttee LEANID F. KRUPETS.

Mogilev Oblast Administration: 212030 Mogilev, vul. Pervomaiskaya 71, Dom Sovetov; tel. (22) 231-00-97; e-mail oblisp@mogilev.by; internet www.region.mogilev.by; Chair. of Council VLADIMIR I. PANTIUKHOV; Chair. of Exec Cttee BORIS V. BATURA.

Vitebsk Oblast Administration: 210010 Vitebsk, vul. Gogolya 6; tel. (21) 37-52-12; fax (21) 236-30-84; internet www.vitebsk-region .by; Chair. of Council ULADZIMIR KULAKOV; Chair. of Exec. Cttee ULADZIMIR ANDREICHENKO.

Election Commission

Central Commission of the Republic of Belarus for Elections and Referendums: 220010 Minsk, vul. Savetskaya 11, Dom Pravitelstva; tel. and fax (17) 227-19-03; e-mail centrizb@pmrb.gov.by; internet www.rec.gov.by; f. 1989; Chair. LYDIA M. YERMOSHINA.

Political Organizations

Following the Government's imposition of stringent measures for re-registration in January 1999, the number of political parties officially registered with the Ministry of Justice was reduced from 28 to 17. A number of unregistered parties operated, but were not permitted to participate in elections. In late 2008 there were 15 officially registered political parties operating in Belarus, of which the most important are listed below.

Assembly (Hramada)—Belarusian Social-Democratic Party (Belaruskaya Satsyal-demakratychnaya Partya 'Hramada'): 220095 Minsk, vul. Drozda 8/52; tel. and fax (17) 226-74-37; e-mail bsdggramada@tut.by; internet www.bsdp.org; f. 2005; the Belarusian Social Democratic Party (National Hramada), f. 1991, and the Belarusian Social-Democratic Hramada (f. 1998) merged in April 2005, although a dissenting faction of the Belarusian Social-Democratic Hramada remained; Chair. ALYAKSANDR KAZULIN.

Belarusian Agrarian Party (BAP) (Belaruskaya Agrarnaya Partya): 220073 Minsk, vul. Zakharava 31; tel. (17) 220-38-29; fax (17) 249-50-18; f. 1992; Leader MIKHAIL V. SHYMANSKI.

Belarusian Green Party (Belaruskaya Partya Zyaleny): 246023 Gomel, vul. Brestskaya 6; tel. (23) 47-08-08; fax (23) 247-96-96; e-mail bpz@tut.by; f. 1994 as Belarusian Greenpeace Party, present name adopted 1999; Leader ALEH A. NOVIKAU.

Belarusian Patriotic Party (Belaruskaya Patryatychnaya Partya): 220089 Minsk, vul. Papanina 7; tel. (17) 226-32-60; f. 1994; Leader MIKALAY D. ULAKHOVICH.

Communist Party of Belarus (CPB) (Kamunistychnaya Partya Belarusi): 220029 Minsk, vul. Chicherina 21; tel. (17) 293-48-88; fax (17) 232-31-23; f. 1996; Chair. TATSYANA H. HOLUBEVA.

Conservative Christian Party of the Belarusian National Front (CCP/BPF): 220005 Minsk, pr. Masherova 8; tel. (17) 285-34-70; e-mail bpfs@narod.ru; internet www.pbpf.org; f. 1999 as a breakaway faction of the BNF; Chair. ZYANON S. PAZNYAK.

Liberal Democratic Party of Belarus (Liberalna-Demakratychnaya Partya Belarusi): 220005 Minsk, vul. Platonava 22, 12th Floor; tel. and fax (17) 231-63-31; e-mail ldpb@infonet.by; internet www .ldpb.net; f. 1994; advocates continued independence of Belarus, increased co-operation with other European countries and eventual membership of the European Union, and expansion of the private sector; Leader SYARHEY V. HAYDUKEVICH; approx. 50,000 mems (2004).

Revival—Belarusian National Front (Belaruski Narodny Front 'Adradzhenniye'): 220005 Minsk, pr. Masherova 8; tel. and fax (17) 284-50-12; e-mail pbnf@pbnf.org; internet www.pbnf.org; f. 1993; fmrly the Belarusian Popular Front, name changed as above Dec. 1999; anti-communist movement campaigning for democracy, genuine independence for Belarus and national and cultural revival; Chair. LIAVON BARSHCHEUSKI.

Social-Democratic Party of Popular Accord (Satsial-Demakratychnaya Partya Narodnay Zhody): 220050 Minsk, vul. K. Marksa 10; tel. (29) 686-35-65; fax (23) 274-12-60; f. 1992; Leader SYARHEY U. ERMAK.

United Civic Party (UCP) (Abyadnanaya Hramadzyanskaya Partya): 220123 Minsk, vul. Khoruzhey 22; tel. and fax (17) 289-50-09; e-mail ucpb@ucpb.org; internet www.ucpb.org; f. 1995; liberal-conservative; Chair. ANATOL U. LIABEDZKA.

Diplomatic Representation

EMBASSIES IN BELARUS

Armenia: 220050 Minsk, vul. Kirava 17; tel. and fax (17) 227-51-53; e-mail armbelarusembassy@mfa.am; Ambassador OLEG YESAIAN.

Azerbaijan: 220029 Minsk, vul. Vostochnaya 133/167; tel. (17) 293-32-99; fax (17) 237-27-51; e-mail azoffice_minsk@avilink.net; Ambassador ALI NAGHIYEV.

Bulgaria: 220030 Minsk, pl. Svoboda 11; tel. (17) 328-65-58; fax (17) 328-65-59; e-mail embassy@bulgaria.by; internet www.mfa.bg/ minsk; Ambassador PETKO GANCHEV.

China, People's Republic: 220071 Minsk, vul. Brestyanskaya 22; tel. (17) 284-97-28; fax (17) 210-58-41; e-mail chinaemb_by@mfa.gov .cn; internet by.china-embassy.org; Ambassador WU HONGBIN.

Cuba: 220005 Minsk, vul. Krasnozvezdnaya 13; tel. (17) 200-03-83; fax (17) 200-23-45; e-mail embacuba@bnm.by; internet emba .cubaminrex.cu/belarus; Ambassador OMAR SENÓN MEDINA QUINTERO.

Czech Republic: 220030 Minsk, Muzykalny per. 1/2; tel. (17) 226-52-44; fax (17) 211-01-37; e-mail minsk@embassy.mzv.cz; internet www.mzv.cz/minsk; Chargé d'affaires JIŘÍ KARAS.

France: 220030 Minsk, pl. Svobody 11; tel. (17) 210-28-68; fax (17) 210-25-48; e-mail webmestreby@diplomatie.fr; internet www .ambafrance-by.org; Ambassador MIREILLE MUSSO.

Germany: 220034 Minsk, vul. Zakharava 26; tel. (17) 217-59-00; fax (17) 294-85-52; e-mail germanembassy@mail.belpak.by; internet www.minsk.diplo.de; Ambassador Dr GEBHARDT WEISS.

Holy See: 220050 Minsk, vul. Valadarskaga 6; tel. (17) 289-15-84; fax (17) 289-15-17; e-mail nuntius@catholic.by; internet nunciature .catholic.by; Apostolic Nuncio MARTIN VIDOVIĆ (Titular Archbishop of Nona).

India: 220090 Minsk, vul. Kaltsova 4, kor. 5; tel. (17) 262-93-99; fax (17) 262-97-99; e-mail amb@indemb.bn.by; internet www .indembminsk.org; Ambassador R. K. TYAGI.

Iran: 220049 Minsk, vul. Suvorava 2; tel. (17) 207-66-99; fax (17) 207-61-99; Ambassador ABDULHAMID FEKRI.

Israel: 220033 Minsk, pr. Partizansky 6A; tel. (17) 298-43-92; fax (17) 298-44-03; e-mail info@minsk.mfa.gov.il; Ambassador ZE'EV BEN ARIE.

Italy: 220004 Minsk, vul. Rakovskaya 16B; tel. (17) 220-29-69; fax (17) 306-20-37; e-mail ambasciata.minsk@esteri.it; internet www .ambminsk.esteri.it; Ambassador NORBERTO CAPPELLO.

Japan: 220004 Minsk, pr. Pobeditelei 23/1; tel. (17) 223-62-33; fax (17) 210-21-69; Chargé d'affaires a.i. NAOTAKE YAMASHITA.

Kazakhstan: 220029 Minsk, vul. Kuibysheva 12; tel. (17) 288-10-26; fax (17) 334-96-50; e-mail kazemb@nsys.by; internet www .kazembassy.by; Ambassador BOLAT G. ISKAKOV.

Kyrgyzstan: 220002 Minsk, vul. Starovilenskaya 57; tel. (17) 334-91-17; fax (17) 334-16-02; e-mail manas@nsys.by; internet kgembassy.by; Ambassador LIDIYA A. IMANALIYEVA.

Latvia: 220013 Minsk, vul. Doroshevicha 6A; tel. (17) 211-30-33; fax (17) 284-74-94; e-mail embassy.belarus@mfa.gov.lv; internet www .am.gov.lv/belarus; Ambassador MAIRA MORA.

Libya: 220000 Minsk, vul. Belaruskaya 4; tel. (17) 201-39-88; fax (17) 206-39-97; Ambassador ABDALLAH AL-MAGRAVI.

Lithuania: 220088 Minsk, vul. Zakharava 68; tel. (17) 285-24-48; fax (17) 285-33-37; e-mail amb.by@urm.lt; internet by.mfa.lt; Ambassador EDMINAS BAGDONAS.

Moldova: 220030 Minsk, vul. Belaruskaya 2; tel. (17) 289-14-41; fax (17) 289-11-47; e-mail minsk@mfa.md; Ambassador ION FILIMON.

Poland: 220034 Minsk, vul. Rumyantsava 6; tel. (17) 288-21-14; fax (17) 236-49-92; e-mail ambasada@minsk.polemb.net; internet www .minsk.polemb.net; Ambassador HENRIK LITWIN.

Romania: 220035 Minsk, zav. Maskvina 4; tel. (17) 203-77-26; fax (17) 211-21-63; e-mail romania@nsys.by; Chargé d'affaires a.i. DUMITRU BADEA.

Russia: 220002 Minsk, vul. Staravilenskaya 48; tel. (17) 250-36-66; fax (17) 250-36-64; e-mail kira1130@yahoo.com; internet www .belarus.mid.ru; Ambassador ALEKSANDR A. SURIKOV.

Serbia: 220034 Minsk, vul. Rumyantseva 4; tel. (17) 284-29-84; fax (17) 233-92-26; e-mail embassy.minsk@mfa.gov.yu; internet www .ambasadasrbije.info; Ambassador SRECKO DJUKIĆ.

Slovakia: 220034 Minsk, vul. Platonova 1B; tel. (17) 285-29-99; fax (17) 283-68-48; e-mail slovemb@iptel.by; internet www.mzv.sk/ minsk; Ambassador MARIÁN SERVÁTKA.

Syria: 220049 Minsk, vul. Suvorova 2; tel. (17) 280-37-08; fax (17) 280-72-00; e-mail syrembmin@yahoo.com; Ambassador FARUK TAKH.

Tajikistan: 220050 Minsk, vul. Kirava 17; tel. (17) 222-37-98; fax (17) 227-76-13; e-mail tajemb-belarus@mail.ru; Ambassador AMIRXON SAFAROV.

Turkey: 220050 Minsk, vul. Valadarskaya 6; tel. (17) 227-13-83; fax (17) 227-27-46; e-mail trembassy@forenet.by; Ambassador BIRNUR FERTEKLIGIL.

Turkmenistan: 220050 Minsk, vul. Kirava 17; tel. (17) 222-34-27; fax (17) 222-33-67; Ambassador ATA GUNDOGDIYEV.

Ukraine: 220002 Minsk, vul. Staravilenskaya 51; tel. (17) 283-19-90; fax (17) 283-19-80; e-mail emb_by@mfa.gov.ua; internet www .belarus.mfa.gov.ua/belarus; Ambassador IHOR D. LIKHOVYI.

United Kingdom: 220030 Minsk, vul. K. Marksa 37; tel. (17) 210-59-20; fax (17) 220-23-06; e-mail britinfo@nsys.by; internet www .britishembassy.gov.uk/belarus; Ambassador Dr NIGEL GOULD-DAVIES.

USA: 220002 Minsk, vul. Staravilenskaya 46; tel. (17) 210-12-83; fax (17) 234-78-53; e-mail webmaster@usembassy.minsk.by; internet www.usembassy.minsk.by; Chargé d'affaires a.i. JONATHAN MOORE.

Venezuela: 220000 Minsk; tel. (17) 226-07-88; fax (17) 220-20-19; e-mail embavenbel@gmail.com; Chargé d'affaires AMÉRICO DÍAZ NUÑEZ.

Judicial System

Supreme Court: 220030 Minsk, vul. Lenina 28; tel. (17) 226-12-06; fax (17) 227-12-25; e-mail scjustrb@pmrb.gov.by; f. 1923; Chair. VALENTIN SUKALO.

Supreme Economic Court: 220050 Minsk, vul. Valadarskaya 8; tel. (17) 227-16-41; fax (17) 220-20-85; e-mail bxc@court.by; internet www.court.by; Chair. VIKTAR S. KAMYANKOV.

Office of the Prosecutor-General: 220050 Minsk, vul. Internatsionalnaya 22; tel. and fax (17) 328-57-27; e-mail info@prokuratura .gov.by; internet www.prokuratura.gov.by; Prosecutor-General GRYGORY A. VASILEVICH.

Constitutional Court: 220016 Minsk, vul. K. Marksa 32; tel. and fax (17) 227-80-12; e-mail ksrb@user.unibel.by; internet ncpi.gov.by/ ConstSud; f. 1994; 12 mem. judges; Chair. PYOTR MIKLASHEVICH.

Religion

CHRISTIANITY

The major grouping is the Eastern Orthodox Church, but there are also an estimated 1.3m. adherents of the Roman Catholic Church. Of these, some 25% are ethnic Poles and there is a significant number of Catholics of the Eastern Rites.

The Eastern Orthodox Church

In 1990 Belarus was designated an exarchate of the Russian Orthodox Church (Moscow Patriarchate), known as the Belarusian Orthodox Church.

Belarusian Orthodox Church (Moscow Patriarchate): 220004 Minsk, vul. Osvobozhdeniya 10; tel. and fax (17) 223-25-05; e-mail orthobel@gin.by; 1,319 parishes (2004); Metropolitan of Minsk and Slutsk, Patriarchal Exarch of All Belarus His Eminence FILARET (VAKHROMEYEV).

The Roman Catholic Church

Although five Roman Catholic dioceses, embracing 455 parishes, had officially existed since the Second World War, none of them had a bishop. In 1989 a major reorganization of the structure of the Roman Catholic Church in Belarus took place. The dioceses of Minsk and Mogilev (Mahiloŭ) were merged, to create an archdiocese, and two new dioceses were formed, in Grodno (Horadnia) and Pinsk. At 31 December 2006 the Roman Catholic Church had an estimated 1,405,000 adherents in Belarus (about 13.7% of the population).

Bishops' Conference of Belarusian Catholics: 220030 Minsk, pl. Svobody 9; tel. (17) 226-61-27; fax (17) 226-90-92; internet www .catholic.by; Pres. Most Rev. ALEKSANDR KASZKIEWICZ Bishop of Grodno.

Archdiocese of Minsk and Mogilev: 220030 Minsk, ul. Revolutsionna 1A; tel. (17) 203-68-44; fax (17) 226-90-92; e-mail archdioces@ catholic.by; internet catholic.by; Archbishop Mgr TADEVUSH KANDRUSIEVICH.

Protestant Churches

Union of Evangelical Christian Baptists in the Republic of Belarus: 220107 Minsk, POB 25; tel. and fax (17) 295-67-84; e-mail office@baptist.by; internet www.baptist.by; f. 1989; Pres. NIKOLAY SINKOVETS.

ISLAM

There are small communities of Azeri and Tatar adherents of Islam. In 1994 the supreme administration of Muslims in Belarus, which had been abolished in 1939, was reconstituted. In mid-1998 there were some 4,000 Muslims and four mosques.

The Press

According to official figures, in 2002 there were 740 newspapers, 351 magazines and other periodicals and four information agencies in Belarus; 12 titles were published in a language other than Belarusian or Russian (primarily English, Polish or Ukrainian). Most daily newspapers are government-owned.

PRINCIPAL DAILIES

In Russian, except where otherwise stated. The Russian-based newspapers *Argumenty i Fakty* and *Komosomolskaya Pravda* (in a special edition, *Komsomolskaya Pravda v Belorusii*) also maintain a high rate of circulation in the country.

BDG Delovaya Gazeta (BDG Business Newspaper): 220039 Minsk, vul. Chekalova 12; tel. (17) 216-25-85; e-mail info@bdg.by; internet www.bdg.by; f. 1992; 2 a week; business affairs; suspended for three months in May 2003; subsequently printed in Smolensk, Russia; independent; in 2005 name changed from Belorusskaya Delovaya Gazeta (BDG), following a presidential decree restricting the use of certain words; Editor-in-Chief SVYATLANA KALONKINA.

Belaruskaya Niva (Belarusian Cornfield): 220013 Minsk, vul. B. Hmyalnitskaga 10A; tel. (17) 287-16-20; fax (17) 232-39-62; e-mail red@belniva.by; internet belniva.by; f. 1921; 5 a week; organ of the Cabinet of Ministers; in Belarusian and Russian; Editor E. SEMASHKO; circ. 34,021 (Aug. 2004).

Narodnaya Hazeta (The People's Newspaper): 220013 Minsk, vul. B. Hmyalnitskaga 10A; tel. (17) 268-28-70; fax (17) 268-25-29; e-mail info@ng.press.net.by; f. 1990; 5–6 a week; in Belarusian and Russian; Editor-in-Chief M. SHIMANSKY; circ. 90,000 (2000).

Narodnaya Volya (People's Will): Minsk; f. 1995; daily; independent; 5 a week; in Belarusian and Russian; Editor-in-Chief SVYATLANA KALONKINA; circ. 27,000.

Respublika (Republic): 220013 Minsk, vul. B. Hmyalnitskaga 10A; tel. (17) 287-16-15; fax (17) 287-16-12; e-mail info@respublika.info; internet www.respublika.info; 5 a week; publ. of Council of Ministers; in Belarusian and Russian; Editor ANATOLI I. LEMIASHONOK; circ. 101,000 (2005).

Sovetskaya Belorussiya (Soviet Belarus): 220013 Minsk, vul. B. Hmyalnitskaga 10A; tel. (17) 292-51-01; e-mail admin@sb.by; internet sb.by; 5 a week; Editor-in-Chief PAVEL I. YAKUBOVICH; circ. 400,000 (2004).

Vechernii Minsk (Evening Minsk): 220005 Minsk, pr. Nezavisimosti 44; tel. (17) 284-50-44; fax (17) 288-28-35; e-mail vm@nsys.by; internet newsvm.com; f. 1967; Editor SYARHEY SVERKUNOU; circ. 30,000 (2007).

Znamya Yunosti (Banner of Youth): 220013 Minsk, vul. B. Hmyalnitskaga 10A; tel. and fax (17) 267-16-84; e-mail zn@zn.by; internet www.zn.by; f. 1938; 5 a week; organ of the Ministry of Education; Editor-in-Chief ELENA PHILIPTCHIK; circ. 32,000 (2007).

Zvyazda (Star): 220013 Minsk, vul. B. Hmyalnitskaga 10A; tel. and fax (17) 287-19-19; e-mail info@zvyazda.minsk.by; internet www.zviazda.by; f. 1917; 5 a week; publ. by the National Assembly and the Cabinet of Ministers; in Belarusian; Editor ULADZIMIR B. NARKEVICH; circ. 32,000 (2008).

PRINCIPAL PERIODICALS

In Belarusian, except where otherwise stated.

Alesya: 220013 Minsk, pr. Nezavisimosti 77; tel. and fax (17) 232-20-51; e-mail magalesya@mail.ru; f. 1924; monthly; Editor TAMARA BUNTO; circ. 10,500 (2003).

Belarus: 220005 Minsk, vul. Zakharava 19; tel. (17) 284-80-01; f. 1930; monthly; publ. by the State Publishing House; journal of the Union of Writers of Belarus and the Belarusian Society of Friendship and Cultural Links with Foreign Countries; fiction and political essays; in Belarusian, English and Russian; Editor-in-Chief A. A. SHABALIN.

Belaruskaya Krynitsa (Belarusian Spring): 220065 Minsk, vul. Avakyana 38/59; tel. and fax (17) 220-67-56; e-mail b.krinica@tut.by; internet www.ibkby.com; f. 1991; monthly; journal of the Belarusian Public Organization of Social Development and Co-operation; Editor-in-Chief Dr PETR SILKO; circ. 5,000 (2006).

Chyrvonaya Zmena (The Red Rising Generation): 220013 Minsk, vul. B. Hmyalnitskaga 10A; tel. and fax (17) 232-21-03; f. 1921; weekly; Editor ALEKSANDR N. KARLUKIEVICH; circ. 5,000 (2000).

Gramadzyanin: Minsk; tel. (17) 229-08-34; fax (17) 272-95-05; publ. by the United Civic Party of Belarus.

Holas Radzimy (Voice of the Motherland): 220005 Minsk, pr. Nezavisimosti 44; tel. (17) 288-12-80; fax (17) 288-17-82; e-mail golas_radzimy@tut.by; f. 1955; weekly; articles of interest to Belarusians in other countries; Editor-in-Chief NATALIA SALUK.

Krynitsa (Spring): Minsk; tel. (17) 236-60-71; e-mail www.krynitsa@open.by; f. 1988; monthly; publ. by the state media holding, Literatura i Mastatstva; literary and cultural; Editor ALA KAPANELKA; circ. 2,100 (2001).

Kultura (Culture): 220029 Minsk, vul. Chicherina 1; tel. and fax (17) 289-34-66; e-mail kultura@tut.by; f. 1991; weekly; colour illustrated; incorporates *Mastatstva* (Arts); Editor-in-Chief LUDMILA KRUSHINSKAYA; circ. 4,000 (2005).

Litaratura i Mastatstva (Literature and Arts): 220034 Minsk, vul. Zakharava 19; tel. and fax (17) 284-66-73; e-mail LiM_new@mail.ru; internet www.lim.by/index.php?iss=1; f. 1932; weekly; Editor ANATOL KAZLOU; circ. 3,428 (2007).

Maladosts (Youth): 220034 Minsk, vul. Zakharava 19; tel. (17) 284-79-85; f. 1953; monthly; publ. by the state media holding, Literatura i Mastatstva; novels, short stories, essays, translations, etc., for young people; Editor-in-Chief R. BARAVIKOVA.

Narodnaya Asveta (People's Education): 220023 Minsk, vul. Makayenka 12; tel. (17) 267-64-69; fax (17) 267-62-68; e-mail n_asveta@tut.by; internet www.n-asveta.com; f. 1924; publ. by the Ministry of Education; Editor-in-Chief ALLA V. MASLAVA.

Nasha Niva (Our Cornfield): 220050 Minsk, POB 537; tel. (17) 284-73-29; e-mail nn@nn.by; internet www.nn.by; f. 1991; first founded in 1906; independent; weekly; Editor-in-Chief ANDREY SKURKO; circ. 2,500 (2007).

Neman (The River Nieman): 220005 Minsk, pr. Nezavisimosti 39; tel. (17) 284-85-24; e-mail neman@lim.by; f. 1945; monthly; publ. by

the state media holding, Literatura i Mastatstva; literary; fiction; in Russian; Editor-in-Chief A. ZHOUK.

Polymya (Flame): 220005 Minsk, vul. Zakharava 19; tel. (17) 284-80-12; e-mail polymya@bk.ru; f. 1922; monthly; publ. by the state media holding, Literatura i Mastatstva; literary; fiction; Editor-in-Chief S. I. ZAKONNIKOU.

Salidarnasts (Solidarity): Minsk; weekly; private; independent trade-union newspaper; Editor-in-Chief ALYAKSANDR STARYKEVICH.

Tovarisch (Comrade): 220005 Minsk, pr. Nezavisimosti 46A; tel. (17) 202-08-14; fax (17) 231-80-36; e-mail ck_pkb@anitex.by; internet pkb.promedia.minsk.by; f. 1994; weekly newspaper of the Party of Communists of Belarus; Editor-in-Chief SYARGEY V. VOZNYAK; circ. 6,000 (2001).

Vozhyk (Hedgehog): 220013 Minsk, pr. Nezavisimosti 77; tel. and fax (17) 232-12-40; f. 1941; fortnightly; satirical; Editor-in-Chief VLADIMIR SALAMAXA.

Vyaselka (Rainbow): 220004 Minsk, vul. Kalektarnaya 10; tel. (17) 220-91-90; fax (17) 220-92-61; f. 1957; bi-annual; popular, for 5–10-year-olds; Editor-in-Chief V. S. LIPSKY.

PRESS ASSOCIATIONS

Belarusian Association of Journalists (Belaruskaya Asatsyyatsyya Zhurnalistau): 220030 Minsk, pl. Svabody 17/304; tel. (17) 226-70-98; fax (17) 203-63-66; e-mail baj@baj.by; internet www.baj.ru; f. 1995; Chair. ZHANNA LITVINA.

Belarusian Union of Journalists: 220034 Minsk, vul. Rumyantsava 3; tel. and fax (17) 294-51-95; 3,000 mems; Chair. A. GEMESCHINOK.

NEWS AGENCIES

BelaPAN: tel. (17) 232-55-01; fax (17) 232-56-57; e-mail mail@belapan.com; internet www.belapan.com; in Belarusian, English and Russian; independent, commercial information company.

Belta—Belarusian Telegraph Agency: 220030 Minsk, vul. Kirava 26; tel. (17) 227-19-92; fax (17) 227-13-46; e-mail oper@belta.by; internet www.belta.by; f. 1918; Gen. Dir DMITRIY A. ZHUK.

Interfaks Zapad (Interfax-West): 222013 Minsk, vul. Brovki 3/2; tel. (17) 284-05-74; fax (17) 284-05-76; e-mail infportal@interfax.by; internet www.interfax.by; f. 1994; affiliated with Interfaks (Russia); regional bureau in Mogilev; online political and business news; publs. *Belarus Business Daily*, *Belarus News Wire*; Dir-Gen. VYACHESLAV ZENKOVICH.

Publishers

In 2000 there were 7,686 titles published in Belarus (62m. copies).

Belarus: 220600 Minsk, pr. Nezavisimosti 79; tel. (17) 223-87-42; fax (17) 223-87-31; f. 1921; social, political, technical, medical and musical literature, fiction, children's, reference books, art reproductions, etc.; Dir MIKHALAY KAVALEVSKY; Editor-in-Chief ELENA ZAKONNIKOVA.

Belaruskaya Entsiklopediya (Belarusian Encyclopedia): 220072 Minsk, vul. Akademicheskaya 15A; tel. and fax (17) 284-17-67; e-mail belen@mail.belpak.by; f. 1967; encyclopedias, dictionaries, directories and scientific books; Editor-in-Chief G. P. PASHKOV.

Belaruskaya Navuka (Belarusian Science): 220141 Minsk, Staroborisovsky trakt 40; tel. (17) 263-76-18; e-mail belnauka@infonet.by; f. 1924; scientific, technical, reference books, educational literature and fiction in Belarusian and Russian; Dir LUDMILA PIETROVA.

Belarusky Dom Druku (Belarusian Printing House): 220013 Minsk, pr. Nezavisimosti 79; tel. (17) 287-17-03; fax (17) 231-67-74; e-mail dom.pechati@bdp.minsk.by; f. 1917; social, political, children's and fiction in Belarusian, Russian and other European languages, newspapers and magazines; Gen. Dir ROMAN OLEINIK.

Belblankavyd: 220035 Minsk, vul. Timirazeva 2; tel. (17) 226-71-22; reference books in Belarusian and Russian; Dir VALENTINA MILOVANOVA.

Literatura i Mastatstva (Literary Fiction and Fine Arts): 220034 Minsk, vul. Zakhareva 19; tel. and fax (17) 284-84-61; internet www.lim.by; f. 2002; fiction in Belarusian and Russian; Dir ALES M. KARLIUKEVICH.

Narodnaya Asveta (People's Education): 220004 Minsk, pr. Pobeditelei 11; tel. and fax (17) 203-61-84; e-mail director@narasveta.by; f. 1951; scientific, educational, reference literature and fiction in Belarusian, Russian and other European languages; Dir LARISA MINKO.

Vysheyshaya Shkola (Higher School): 220048 Minsk, pr. Pobeditelei 11; tel. (17) 203-70-08; fax (17) 223-54-15; e-mail market@vshph.com; internet www.vshph.com; f. 1954; textbooks and science books for higher educational institutions; in Belarusian, Russian and other European languages; absorbed the Universitetskaye publishing house in 2002; Dir Anatol A. Zhadan; Editor-in-Chief Tetyana K. Maiboroda.

Yunatstva (Youth): 220600 Minsk, pr. Pobeditelei 11; tel. (17) 223-24-30; fax (17) 223-31-16; f. 1981; fiction and children's books; Dir Alyaksandr Komarovsky.

Broadcasting and Communications

TELECOMMUNICATIONS

BelCel: 22005 Minsk, vul. Zolotaya Gorka 5; tel. (17) 282-02-82; fax (17) 276-11-11; e-mail belcel@belcel.by; internet www.belcel.com.by; f. 1993; 50% owned by Cable and Wireless (United Kingdom); mobile telecommunications services; Gen. Dir Artem H. Orandzh; 23,000 subscribers (2003).

Beltelecom: 220030 Minsk, vul. Engelsa 6; tel. (17) 217-10-05; fax (17) 227-44-22; e-mail info@main.beltelecom.by; internet www.beltelecom.by; f. 1995; national telecommunications operator; Dir-Gen. Kanstantin Tsikar.

Best: 220030 Minsk, vul. Chervonoarmeiska 24; tel. (17) 295-99-99; e-mail info@best.by; internet www.best.by; f. 2004; 25% owned by Beltelecom; provides mobile cellular telecommunications services.

MTS Belarus: 222043 Minsk, pr. Nezavisimosti 95; tel. (17) 237-98-98; e-mail info@mts.by; internet www.company.mts.by; f. 2002; mobile cellular communications; 49% owned by Mobile TeleSystems (Russia); Dir-Gen. Andrei B. Rumyantsev; 465,500 subscribers (2004).

Velcom: 220002 Minsk, vul. Masherova 19; tel. (17) 222-49-01; fax (17) 206-62-52; e-mail pressa@velcom.by; internet www.velcom.by; f. 1999; mobile cellular telecommunications; 950,000 subscribers (2004); Gen. Dir Mikhail A. Batranets.

BROADCASTING

National State Television and Radio Company of Belarus (Belteleradiocompany): 220807 Minsk, vul. A. Makayenka 9; tel. (17) 264-88-43; fax (17) 264-81-82; e-mail pr@tvr.by; internet www.tvr.by; f. 1925; parent co of Belarusian Radio (q.v.) and Belarusian Television (q.v.); Chair. Uladzimir Matvyaychuk.

Radio

Belarusian Radio: 220807 Minsk, vul. Chyrvonaya 4; tel. (17) 239-58-10; fax (17) 284-85-74; e-mail radio-minsk@tvr.by; internet www.tvr.by; stations include Culture Channel, First National Channel (news), Radio Stalitsa (Capital Radio) and Radio Belarus (foreign service in Belarussian, Russian, German and English); Dir Uladzimir V. Deyakaw.

Television

Belarusian Television: 220807 Minsk, vul. A. Makayenka 9; tel. (17) 269-97-72; fax (17) 267-81-82; e-mail pr@tvr.by; internet www.tvr.by; f. 1956; Dir Uladzimir V. Isat.

Belarus-TV: 220807 Minsk, vul. A. Makayenka 9; tel. (17) 264-95-92; fax (17) 264-81-82; e-mail eksp@tvr.by; f. 2005; international satellite channel; Gen. Producer Viktar U. Mayuchy.

First National Channel: 220807 Minsk, vul. A. Makayenka 9; tel. (17) 233-45-01; fax (17) 264-81-82; main state news channel; also shows entertainment, sport, films etc.

LAD: 220807 Minsk, vul. A. Makayenka 9; tel. (17) 264-88-43; fax (17) 264-81-82; f. 2003; family channel; Gen. Producer Alyaksandr B. Semyarnyow.

ONT—Obshchenatsionalnoye Televideniye (Nation-wide TV): Minsk; tel. (17) 290-66-84; e-mail press@ont.by; internet www.ont.by; f. 2002; 51% state-owned; broadcasts nation-wide; Chair. Grigoriy L. Kisel.

TVS—Televizionnaya Veshchatelnaya Set (TBN—Television Broadcasting Network): 220072 Minsk, pr. Nezavisimosti 15a; tel. (17) 284-10-86; fax (17) 284-10-86; e-mail tbn@promedia.by; internet www.data.minsk.by/tbn; f. 1995; comprises 16 private television cos in Belarus's largest cities and an advertising co.

Finance

(cap. = capital; dep. = deposits; res = reserves; m. = million; brs = branches; amounts in readjusted Belarusian roubles, unless otherwise indicated)

BANKING

At October 2006 there were 30 commercial banks registered in Belarus.

Central Bank

National Bank of the Republic of Belarus: 220008 Minsk, pr. Nezavisimosti 20; tel. (17) 219-22-01; fax (17) 227-48-79; e-mail email@nbrb.by; internet www.nbrb.by; f. 1990; cap. 60,000.0m., res 644,278.7m., dep. 3,072,576.0m. (Dec. 2006); Chair. Petr P. Prakapovich; 6 brs.

Commercial Banks

Absolutbank: 220023 Minsk, pr. Nezavisimosti 95, POB 9; tel. (17) 237-07-02; fax (17) 264-24-43; e-mail root@absolutbank.by; internet www.absolutbank.by; f. 1993; closed jt-stock co; 53.78% owned by Theocritos Enterprises Ltd (Cyprus); 29.61% owned by Estudes Trading Ltd (Cyprus); cap. 16,257.4m., res 7,574.9m., dep. 54,678.9m. (Dec. 2007); Chair. Boris G. Cherednik; 3 brs.

Bank Moskva-Minsk (Moscow-Minsk Bank): 220002 Minsk, vul. Kamunistychnaya 49; tel. (17) 288-63-01; fax (17) 288-63-02; e-mail mmb@mmbank.by; internet www.mmbank.by; f. 2000; wholly owned by Bank of Moscow (Russia); cap. US $63.3m., dep. $518.4m., total assets $933.3m. (Aug. 2008); Gen.-Dir Dr Aleksandr Rakovets; 5 brs.

Belagroprombank: 220036 Minsk, pr. Zhukov 3; tel. (17) 218-57-77; fax (17) 218-57-14; e-mail belapb@belapb.by; internet www.belapb.by; f. 1991; 99.2% state-owned; cap. 1,578,600m., res 145,100m., dep. 1,020,000m. (Dec. 2006); Chair. Sergei N. Roumas; 118 brs.

Belarusbank: 220050 Minsk, vul. Myasnikova 32; tel. (17) 289-38-14; fax (17) 226-47-50; e-mail info@belarus-bank.by; internet www.belarus-bank.by; f. 1995 following merger with Sberbank (Savings Bank; f. 1922); cap. 1,130,923m., res −3,270m., dep. 10,478,582.0m. (Dec. 2006); Chair. Nadezhda A. Yermakova; 136 brs.

Belarusian Industrial Bank (Belarusskii industrialnyi bank): 220004 Minsk, vul. Melnikaite 8; tel. (17) 203-95-78; fax (17) 209-42-06; e-mail bib@bib.by; internet www.bib.by; f. 1991; cap. 15,859.7m., res 11,443.2m., dep. 60,823.1m. (Dec. 2007); Chair. of Bd Andrey Kireyev; 5 brs.

Belgazprombank: 220121 Minsk, vul. Pritytsky 60/2; tel. (17) 259-40-24; fax (17) 259-45-25; e-mail bank@bgpb.by; internet www.belgazprombank.by; f. 1990; present name adopted 1997; 48% owned by Gazprombank (Russia), 48% owned by OAO Gazprom (Russia), 10.6% owned by Beltransgaz; cap. 65,766m., dep. 834,246m., total assets 942,563m. (Dec. 2007); Chair. of Bd Viktar D. Babariko; 7 brs.

Belinvestbank—Belarusian Bank for Development and Reconstruction: 220002 Minsk, pr. Masherova 29; tel. (17) 289-28-99; fax (17) 289-35-22; e-mail corr@belinvestbank.by; internet www.belinvestbank.by; f. 2001 by merger; 66.0% owned by the State Committee for property; 15.6% owned by National Bank of the Republic of Belarus; universal bank; cap. 219,506m., res 21,095m., dep. 2,836,975m. (Dec. 2007)); Chair. of Bd Alyaksandr E. Rutkovsky; 18 brs.

Belpromstroibank (BPS-Bank): 220005 Minsk, Blvd Muliavin 6; tel. (17) 210-13-14; fax (17) 210-03-42; e-mail inbox@bpsb.by; internet www.bpsb.by; f. 1923; 90% privately owned; cap. 259,991m., res −245m., dep. 3,153,799m. (Dec. 2007); Dir-Gen. Galina P. Kukhorenko; 41 brs.

Belvnesheconombank: 220050 Minsk, vul. Myasnikova 32; tel. (17) 238-12-15; fax (17) 226-48-09; e-mail office@bveb.minsk.by; internet www.bveb.by; f. 1991; 53.2% owned by Vneshekonombank (Bank for Foreign Economic Affairs—Russia), 20.0% by National Cosmos Bank (Russia); cap. 226,947m., dep. 702,437m., total assets 823,807m. (Dec. 2006); Chair. of Bd Georgiy Yegorov; 26 brs.

ITI Bank (International Trade and Investment Bank): 220030 Minsk, vul. Savetskaya 12; tel. (17) 200-68-80; fax (17) 200-17-00; e-mail office@itibank.by; internet www.itibank.by; f. 1999; 42.7% owned by Daltotrade Ltd (Cyprus), 38.9% owned by National Bank of the Republic of Belarus; cap. 51,616.2m., dep. 255,090.2m. (Jan. 2008); Chair. Gennady S. Aleinikov; 5 brs.

Minski Tranzitnyi Bank (Minsk Transit Bank): 220033 Minsk, pr. Partizansky 6a; tel. (17) 213-29-00; fax (17) 213-29-09; e-mail cor@mtb.minsk.by; internet www.mtb.by; f. 1994; cap. US $50.3m., res $1.4m., dep. $45.9m. (Sept. 2008); Chair. of Bd Andrey K. Zhishkevich; 5 brs.

Paritetbank: 220090 Minsk, vul. Gamarnik 9/4; tel. (17) 288-32-50; fax (17) 228-38-37; e-mail info@paritetbank.by; internet www

.paritetbank.by; f. 1992; present name adopted 2004; 97.4% state owned; cap. 93,368m. (April 2007); res 964.3m., dep. 68,512.3m. (Dec. 2006); Chair. of Bd NATALYA ALEKSEYEVA; 17 brs.

Priorbank: 220002 Minsk, vul. V. Khoruzhey 31A; tel. (17) 289-90-87; fax (17) 289-91-91; e-mail info@priorbank.by; internet www .priorbank.by; f. 1989, present name since 1992; 63.05% owned by Raffeisen International Bank-Holding AG (Austria), 13.5% owned by the European Bank for Reconstruction and Development (United Kingdom); cap. 102,801m., res 374m., dep. 1,935,780m. (Dec. 2006); Chair. of Bd SERGEY A. KOSTYUCHENKO.

Trastbank: 220035 Minsk, vul. Ignatenka 11; tel. and fax (17) 250-43-88; fax (17) 228-52-31; e-mail root@trustbank.by; internet www .trustbank.by; f. 1994; jt-stock co; 37.4% owned by Delikates (Belarus), 35% owned by Libyan Arab Foreign Bank (Libya); fmrly Infobank, present name adopted Feb. 2005; cap. 14,501m., res 22,341.9m., dep. 94,675.5m. (Dec. 2006); Chair. IOSIF F. KARITSKY.

VTB Bank: 220004 Minsk, vul. Tsetkin K. 51; tel. (17) 306-26-36; fax (17) 306-26-37; e-mail info@vtb-bank.by; internet www.vtb-bank.by; f. 1996 as Slavneftebank; name changed as above 2007; 64.87% owned by VTB Bank (Russia); cap. 43,519m., dep. 354,410m., total assets 411,747m. (Dec. 2006); Chair. of Bd ULADZIMIR V. IVANOV; 6 brs.

BANKING ASSOCIATION

Association of Belarusian Banks: 220005 Minsk, vul. Smolyach-kova 9; tel. (17) 227-78-90; fax (17) 227-58-41; e-mail mail@abbanks .by; Chair. FELIX CHERNYAVSKY.

COMMODITY AND STOCK EXCHANGES

Belarusian Currency and Stock Exchange (Belorusskaya Valyutno-Fondovaya Birzha): 220013 Minsk, vul. Surganova 48 A; tel. (17) 209-41-03; fax (17) 209-41-10; e-mail bcse@bcse.by; internet www.bcse.by; f. 1998; currency and securities exchange trading organization, depository, clearing and information activities; value of trade US $8,934.5m. (2004); Gen. Dir PAVEL TSEKHANOVICH.

Belarusian Universal Commodity Exchange (BUTB): 220099 Minsk, vul. Kazintsa 2/200; tel. (17) 224-48-25; e-mail info@butb.by; internet www.butb.by; f. 2004; jt-stock co; trades in timber, metal and agricultural produce; Pres. ARKADII S. SALIKOV.

INSURANCE

AlVeNa: 220006 Minsk, vul. Mayakovskaya 14; tel. (17) 210-28-36; fax (17) 221-59-27; e-mail root@alvena.by; internet www.alvena.by; f. 1991; Belarusian-German jt-stock co; Dir-Gen. VIKTOR SIMONOV.

Bagach: 220104 Minsk, vul. Lynkova 19/1; tel. (17) 250-84-78; fax (17) 250-84-77; e-mail insure@bagach.gtp.by.

Belgosstrakh (Belarusian Republican Unitary Insurance Co): 220036 Minsk, vul. K. Libknekht 70; tel. (17) 259-10-21; fax (17) 213-08-05; e-mail bgs@belsonet.net; internet www.belgosstrakh.by; state-owned; Dir-Gen. VIKTAR I. SHOUST; 145 brs.

Belingosstrakh: 220050 Minsk, pr. Myasnikov 40; tel. (17) 203-58-78; fax (17) 217-84-19; e-mail bigs1@mail.belpak.by; f. 1992; non-life, property, vehicle and cargo insurance; Dir-Gen. ALYAKSANDR KHAMYAKOU.

Brolly: 220030 Minsk, vul. Uljanovskaya 31, POB 73; tel. (17) 210-46-33; fax (17) 222-48-71; e-mail brolly@brolly.by; internet www .brolly.by; f. 1994; offers 30 types of insurance; Gen. Dir VIKTOR A. LAVRUSHENKO.

Kupala: 220004 Minsk, vul. Nemiga 40; tel. (17) 200-80-71; fax (17) 200-80-13; e-mail office@kupala.by; internet www.kupala.by; f. 1993; affiliate of Wiener Städtische Allgemeine Versicherung AG (Austria); Dir-Gen. VIKTOR S. NOVIK.

TASK: 220005 Minsk, pr. Nezavisimosti 58/9; tel. (17) 225-11-24; fax (17) 296-68-35; e-mail info@task.by; internet www.task.by; f. 1991; partly state-owned; all forms of insurance; Gen. Dir I. I. VOLKOV .

INSURANCE ASSOCIATION

Belarusian Insurance Union (BIU) (Belaruskii Strakhovoi Soyuz): 220114 Minsk, pr. Nezavisimosti 169/905; tel. (29) 650-08-91; fax (17) 218-14-65; e-mail info@biu.by; internet www.biu.by; f. 1992; 56 mems; Pres. VIKTAR HOMYARCHUK.

Trade and Industry

GOVERNMENT AGENCIES

Belarusian Foreign Investment Promotion Agency: 220004 Minsk, pr. Pobeditelei 7; tel. (17) 203-40-36; fax (17) 203-07-78; e-mail ncm@icetrade.by; internet www.export.by; Dir BORIS SMOLKIN.

Belarusian Fund for the Financial Support of Entrepreneurs (BFFSE): 220048 Minsk, vul. Myasnikova 39; e-mail fund@belpak .minsk.by; f. 1996.

CHAMBER OF COMMERCE

Belarusian Chamber of Commerce and Industry (Belorusskaya Torgovo-promyshlennaya Palata): 220035 Minsk, pr. Pobeditelei 14; tel. (17) 226-91-27; fax (17) 226-98-60; e-mail mbox@cci.by; internet www.cci.by; f. 1952; brs in Brest, Gomel, Grodno, Mogilev and Vitebsk; Pres. ULADZIMIR N. BOBROV.

EMPLOYERS' ORGANIZATION

Business Union of Entrepreneurs and Employers (Biznes Soyuz Predprinimatelei i Nanimatelei): 220033 Minsk, vul. Fabrich-naya 22; tel. (17) 298-11-49; fax (17) 298-27-92; e-mail bspn-org@nsys .by; internet www2.bspn.nsys.by; f. 1990; Pres. GEORGY BADEY.

UTILITIES

Electricity

Belenergo/Belenerha (Belarusian Energy Co): 220030 Minsk, vul. K. Marksa 14; tel. (17) 218-23-59; fax (17) 218-26-39; e-mail belenergo@bel.energo.by; internet www.energo.by; f. 1995; restructuring pending; generation, transmission and distribution of electric power; includes six regional generation companies; Chair. SYARHEY BELY.

Gas

Beltopgaz: 220002 Minsk, vul. V. Khoruzhey 3; tel. (17) 288-23-93; fax (17) 284-37-86; e-mail admin@topgas.by; internet www.topgas .by; f. 1992; distributes natural gas to end-users.

Beltransgaz: 220040 Minsk, vul. Nekrasov 9; tel. (17) 280-01-01; fax (17) 285-63-36; e-mail mail@btg.by; internet www.btg.by; natural gas transportation and supply; underground gas storage; Dir VLADIMIR MAYAROU.

MAJOR COMPANIES

Chemicals

Belaruskali Production Amalgamation: 223710 Minsk Obl., Soligorsk, vul. Korzha 5; tel. (174) 23-72-03; fax (174) 23-71-65; e-mail info@kali.by; internet www.kali.by; f. 1970; produces potassium chloride and natrium chloride; Dir ANDREY BASHURA; 20,000 employees.

Dolomit: 211321 Vitebsk, vul. Tsentralnaya 23; tel. (212) 29-10-62; fax (212) 29-17-81; e-mail dolomit@vitebsk.by; internet www.dolomit .by; f. 1931; produces dolomite fertilizer; Gen. Dir IVAN P. BABAK; 1,500 employees.

Minsk Chemical Plant: 220024 Minsk, Serova 8; tel. (17) 277-19-14; fax (17) 278-01-07; produces a wide range of chemicals; Gen. Dir N. R. SIKALYUK.

Polymir Production Association: 211440 Vitebsk, Polotsky ray., Novopolotsk 5; tel. (21) 457-72-10; fax (21) 452-88-21; e-mail market@ polymir.vitebsk.by; f. 1968; chemical products; sales US $200m. (2001); Dir ALYAKSANDR V. BOROVSKY; 6,000 employees.

Electrical Goods

Atlant Incorporated Refrigerator Production (Minsk Refrigerator Plant): 220035 Minsk, pr. Pobeditelei 61; tel. (17) 203-46-14; fax (17) 203-96-97; e-mail info@atlant.com.by; internet www.atlant .by; f. 1959; production and export of refrigerators, automatic washing machines, small household appliances and industrial equipment; 13,000 employees.

Brest Electric Lamp Plant (BELP): 224020 Brest, vul. Moskovs-kaya 204; tel. (16) 242-45-93; fax (16) 242-60-78; e-mail box@lamp .belpak.brest.by; f. 1966; manufactures electric incandescent lamps for automobiles, medical use and general application; Dir G. S. TELESHOUK; 3,500 employees.

Brest Gas Appliance Plant: 224016 Brest, vul. Ordzhonikidze 22; tel. and fax (16) 227-62-47; e-mail mail@gefest.com; internet www .gefest.com; f. 1951; design and manufacture of domestic gas and electrical appliances; Gen. Dir ANATOLII V. MOROZOV; 3,080 employees.

Elektrodvigatel Plant: 212649 Mogilev, vul. Koroleva 8; tel. (222) 23-37-58; fax (222) 23-46-53; e-mail elmotorbkm@mail.ru; manufactures electrical motors; Dir SVYATOSLAV A. TITOV; 2,250 employees.

Elektromodule: 222310 Minsk, Molodechno, pr. Velikiy Gostinets 143; tel. (17) 737-45-14; fax (17) 735-26-87; f. 1970; jt-stock co; manufactures electric and electronic equipment; Gen. Dir I. I. DRA-GUN; 2,000 employees.

Integral Research and Production Corpn: 220108 Minsk, pl. Kazintsa 1; tel. (17) 278-26-26; fax (17) 278-16-22; e-mail dzum@ intergral.minsk.by; internet www.integral.by; f. 1963; manufactures semi-conductors, integrated circuits, telephones, counters; Pres. VIKTAR EMELYANOW; 15,000 employees.

Kalibr Production Co: 220815 Minsk, vul. Fabritsiusa 8; tel. (17) 222-13-75; fax (17) 222-07-28; e-mail marketing@kalibr.com; internet www.kalibr.com; f. 1962; state-owned; manufactures batteries, halogen lamps and televisions; Dir PETR D. KOVALEV; 1,500 employees.

Kamerton Plant: 225710 Pinsk, vul. Brestskaya 137; tel. (16) 534-15-80; fax (16) 534-18-84; e-mail box@camert.belpak.brest.by; f. 1979; state-owned; manufactures electronic wristwatches, resonators, and pedometers; Gen. Dir VASILIY M. OGIYEVICH; 1,000 employees.

Minsk V. I. Kozlov Electrical Plant: 220037 Minsk, vul. Uralskaya 4; tel. and fax (17) 230-32-93; fax (17) 230-80-80; e-mail info@metz.by; internet www.metz.by; f. 1956; manufactures transformers; Dir NIKOLAI M. BASARABA; 3,500 employees (2007).

Foodstuffs

Brestmyasomolprom (Brest Meat and Dairy Industrial Enterprise): 224621 Brest, vul. Karbysheva 119; tel. (162) 20-05-23; fax (162) 20-50-48; e-mail brestmmp@tut.by; f. 1975; state-owned; processes and produces meat and dairy products; Gen. Dir NIKOLAY M. YAZUBETS; 7,500 employees.

Vitebsk Meat and Dairy Industrial Regional Production Asscn: 210024 Vitebsk, pr. Gen. Beloborodova 2; tel. (21) 236-42-22; fax (21) 236-09-13; e-mail vp@mmp.belpak.vitebsk.by; jt-stock co; manufactures dairy products and processes meat; Pres. and Gen. Dir IVAN I. LOPATSO; 7,927 employees.

Metal-processing

Belarusian Metallurgical Plant (Belorusskii Metalurgicheskii Zavod—BMZ): 247210 Gomel Obl., Zhlobin, vul. Promyshlennaya 37; tel. (2334) 5-48-21; fax (2343) 2-47-05; e-mail ofwork@bmz.gomel .by; internet www.belsteel.com; f. 1984; steel-making, rolling and steel wire production; Gen. Dir NIKOLAI V. ANDRIYANOV.

Gomel Casting Plant (Gomelsky Zavod Litya i Normaley): 246010 Gomel, vul. Mogilevskaya 16; tel. (23) 259-60-44; fax (23) 259-42-13; e-mail zlinovs@yahoo.com; state-owned; produces and exports casting hardware; Man. Dir A. I. KAMKO; 4,826 employees.

Gomel Tsentrolit Foundry (Gomelskii liteinyi zavod 'Tsentrolit'): 246647 Gomel, vul. Barykina 240; tel. (232) 42-19-93; fax (232) 46-05-45; e-mail info@centrolit.com; internet www.centrolit.com; f. 1963; manufacture of various iron castings; Dir MIKHAIL SAIKOV; 1,700 employees.

Kirov Cutting-Machinery Plant: 220030 Minsk, vul. Krasnoarmeyskaya 21; tel. and fax (17) 227-14-44; state-owned; manufactures machine tools; Dir GENNADIY M. KOLESNIKOV; 2,500 employees.

Minsk Automatic Lines Plant: 220038 Minsk, vul. Dolgobrodskaya 18; tel. (17) 238-13-00; fax (17) 230-32-51; state-owned; produces iron castings and machine tools; Dir A. A. POTAPCHUK; 2,400 employees.

Minsk Bearing Plant (MKZ) Minskii podshipnikovyi zavod: 220026 Minsk, vul. Zhilunovicha 2; tel. (17) 295-14-11; fax (17) 295-15-01; e-mail mpz@mpz.com.by; internet www.mpz.com.by; f. 1950, jt-stock co from 1992; state-owned; production of spherical roller-bearings; Man. VALERY N. PENZA; 6,500 employees.

Stanko-Gomel—RUP Gomel S. M. Kirov Machine Tool Plant: 246050 Gomel, Internatsionalnaya 10; tel. (232) 74-15-43; fax (232) 74-04-98; e-mail stankogomel@tut.by; internet www.stankogomel .by; f. 1885; state-owned; production of metal-cutting machine tools; sales US \$10.6m. (2006); Gen. Dir VLADIMIR SOSNOVSKY; 1,400 employees (2007).

Vistan Vitebsk Machine-Tool Plant: 210627 Vitebsk, vul. Dmitrova 36/7; tel. (21) 236-49-31; fax (21) 236-31-53; e-mail vistan@vitebsk.net; state-owned; manufactures metal-cutting machine tools; Gen. Dir ULADZIMIR P. TURAVINOV; 2,000 employees.

Vizas: 210602 Vitebsk, pr. Frunze 83; tel. (21) 224-02-36; fax (21) 224-05-17; e-mail vz@vizas.belpak.vitebsk.by; internet www.belpak .vitebsk.by/vizas/english/index.htm; f. 1897; state-owned; manufactures tool and cutter grinders, special-purpose grinders, woodworking machinery, optical lens grinders, etc.; Dir-Gen. YEVGENY O. KISELEV; 1,700 employees.

Motor Vehicles and Components

Amkodor: 220013 Minsk, vul. P. Brovki 8; tel. (17) 292-43-42; fax (17) 288-20-85; e-mail kanz@amkodor.by; internet www.amkodor .by; f. 1991; jt-stock co; manufactures road-construction machinery, including front loaders and road rollers, snow-clearing machines and airfield sweepers; Gen. Dir ALEXANDER V. YANOVSKIY; 4,569 employees.

Borisov Avtogidrousilitel Plant (Borisovskii zavod 'Avtogidrousilitel'): 222120 Minsk Obl., Borisov, vul. Chapayeva 56; tel. (17) 773-14-19; fax (17) 773-15-44; e-mail ost@agu.by; internet www.agu.by; f. 1968; state-owned; manufactures hydraulic steering systems and

components for motor vehicles; Gen. Dir VASILII I. LAVNIK; 6,000 employees.

Belaz—Belarusian Autoworks: 222160 Zhodino, vul. Oktyabrya 40; tel. (17) 753-37-37; fax (17) 757-01-37; e-mail reklama@belaz .minsk.by; internet belaz.minsk.by; f. 1958; state-owned; manufactures heavy-load and off-road vehicles and consumer goods; Dir PIOTR PARKHOMCHIK; 8,000 employees.

Belshina (Belarus Tyre Works): 213824 Minsk Obl., Bobruisk, Minskoye shosse; tel. (225) 43-43-11; fax (225) 43-31-11; e-mail belshina@belshina.biz; internet www.belshina.biz; f. 1972; manufactures tyres for domestic and industrial use; Dir DMITRY KATERINICH; 12,000 employees.

Borisov Automobile and Tractor Electrical Plant (OAO-BATE) (Borisovskii zavod avtotraktornogo elektrooborudovaniya): 222120 Minsk Obl., Borisov, vul. Daumana 95; tel. (17) 774-49-80; fax (17) 773-45-51; e-mail info@starter.by; internet www.starter.by; f. 1958; open jt-stock co; manufactures starter-motors; Gen. Dir ANATOLIY KAPSKY; 4,765 employees.

Minsk Automobile Plant (MAZ): 220831 Minsk, vul. Sotsialisticheskaya 2; tel. (17) 216-96-98; fax (17) 246-07-33; e-mail maz@ads .belpak.minsk.by; internet www.maz.com.by; f. 1948; manufacture of trucks, trailers, buses, specialized vehicles and parts; sales US \$300m. (Dec. 1999); Dir VALENTIN A. GURINOVICH; 21,500 employees.

Minsk Motor Plant: 220046 Minsk, vul. Vaupshasov 4; tel. (17) 230-11-24; fax (17) 230-27-76; e-mail general@po-mmz.minsk.by; f. 1963; state-owned; design and manufacture of diesel engines and parts; aluminium-casting; sales US \$100m. (2003); Gen. Dir NIKOLAY I. LOBACH; 5,000 employees (10,000 incl. subsidiaries).

Minsk Tractor Plant (MTZ) (Minskii traktornyi zavod): 220009 Minsk, vul. Dolgobrodskaya 29; tel. (17) 230-18-62; fax (17) 230-85-48; e-mail sales@tractors.com.by; internet www.tractors.com.by; f. 1946; state-owned; manufacture, sale and export of tractors and parts, production of sheet steel; Gen. Dir ALYAKSANDR PUKHAVOI; 20,000 employees.

Mogilev S. M. Kirov Automobile Plant (MoAZ): 212601 Mogilev, pr. Vitebsky 5; tel. (22) 242-36-53; fax (22) 242-37-82; e-mail moaz@newmail.ru; internet www.moaz.ru; f. 1935; manufactures items and equipment for road construction, specialized vehicles and consumer goods; Dir ALYAKSANDR N. BUBELEV; 4,500 employees.

Mogilevtransmash Transport Engineering Plant: 212030 Mogilev, vul. Krupskaya 232; tel. and fax (22) 224-36-01; e-mail info@mztm.belpak.mogilev.by; f. 1982; state-owned; production and export of refrigerators, front-end loaders, trailers and truck-mounted cranes; Dir VALERY CHERTKOV; 4,000 employees.

Motovelo Corpn: 220033 Minsk, pr. Partizansky 8; tel. (17) 298-14-80; fax (17) 298-14-62; e-mail info@motovelo.com; internet www .motovelo.by; f. 1945; design and manufacture of small motorcycles and bicycles; Gen. Dir ANATOLY S. YAZVINSKY; 4,000 employees.

Natural Gas and Petroleum

Belneftekhim (Belarusian State Oil and Chemical Concern): 220116 Minsk, pr. Dzherzhinskaya 73; tel. (17) 271-79-01; fax (17) 271-94-10; internet www.belneftekhim.by; petrochemical complex comprising 84 cos; largest state-owned company; six largest subsidiaries, incl. Naftan (q.v.), Azot, Belshina (see Motor Vehicles and Components), Khimvolokno and Polymir (see Chemicals) were transformed into jt-stock cos in 2003, prior to privatization; Chair. VALERY KAZAKEVICH; 100,000 employees.

Naftan Industrial Group: 211440 Vitebsk Obl., Novopolotsk-1; tel. (214) 59-82-57; fax (214) 59-88-88; e-mail com@naftan.belpak .vitebsk.by; internet www.naftan.by; f. 1963; state-owned; petroleum refining; sales US \$840m. (1998); Gen. Dir VYACHESLAV V. YAKUSHEV; 4,500 employees.

Belorusneft Production Asscn: 246003 Gomel, vul. Rogachevskaya 9; tel. (232) 79-33-34; fax (232) 71-25-22; e-mail contact@beloil .by; internet www.beloil.by; f. 1964; state-owned; civil and industrial engineering, oilfield development, production of natural gas and consumer goods; Gen. Dir ALEKSANDR A. LYAKHOV; 7,900 employees.

Mozyr Oil Refinery (Mozyrskii neftepererabatyvayushchii zavod): 247760 Gomel Obl., Mozyr-11; tel. (2351) 7-38-97; fax (2351) 7-37-82; e-mail office@mnpz.by; internet www.mnpz.by; f. 1975; refines and produces diesel fuel, gasoline, jet fuel and heating oil fuel, bitumen, gases and technical sulphur; sales of US \$1,263.4m. (2004); Gen. Dir ANATOLI A. KUPRIYANOV.

Neftegazsystema: 246050 Gomel, POB 309; tel. and fax (23) 272-12-78; e-mail igorm@ogs.gomel.by; internet www.ogs.gomel.by; development and implementation of automated systems for pipeline operation; Dir VITALY A. NASHCHUBSKY.

Pharmaceuticals

Belmedpreparaty: 220001 Minsk, vul. Fabritsiusa 30; tel. and fax (17) 229-37-16; fax (17) 222-76-17; internet belmedpreparaty.com; f. 1929; medical and pharmaceutical products; Gen. Dir V. M. TSARENKOV; 2,700 employees.

Textiles and Clothing

Baranovichi Cotton Production Amalgamation: 225410 Brest Obl., Baranovichi, vul. Fabrichnaya 7; tel. (163) 47-55-61; e-mail bcpa@blakit.by; internet www.blakit.by; f. 1963; produces cotton fabrics (grey, bleached, uni-dyed, printed), yarns, bed-, child-, and table-linen and non-woven materials; Gen. Dir ALYAKSANDR V. SELIFONTOV; 4,100 employees.

Grodno Khimvolokno: 230026 Grodno, vul. Slavinskogo 4; tel. (152) 56-12-64; fax (17) 210-81-17; e-mail office@grodno-khim.by; internet www.grodno-khim.by; f. 1978; produces nylon six-cord fabric, nylon industrial yarn, polyester HMLS yarn and PA-6 granulated; Gen. Dir KONSTANTIN P. MAYANOV; 4,500 employees.

Kalinka Joint-Stock Co: 223710 Minsk Obl., Soligorsk, pr. Mira 32; tel. (174) 25-40-80; fax (174) 25-40-60; e-mail kalinkamarketing@ mail.ru; internet www.kalinka.by.com; f. 1981; manufactures clothing; Gen. Dir GALINA KALITSENA; 1,300 employees.

Kamvol: 220028 Minsk, vul. Mayakovskogo 176; tel. (17) 221-14-18; fax (17) 221-75-75; e-mail kamvol@tut.by; internet kamvol.at.tut.by; f. 1953 as state-owned Minsk Worsted Combine; current name adopted upon privatization in 1993; produces wool and cloth; Gen. Dir ANDREY A. MYTNIK; 1,850 employees.

Milavitsa: 220053 Minsk, vul. Novovilenskaya 28; tel. (17) 233-45-80; fax (17) 288-08-95; e-mail west_sales@milavitsa.by; internet milavitsa.com.by; f. 1908; jt-stock co; produces lingerie; sales US $32m. (2002); Dir DMITRY A. DITCHKOVSKY; 2,200 employees.

Mogoteks: 212781 Mogilev, vul. Grishina 87; tel. (22) 26-13-12; fax (22) 46-84-25; e-mail mogotex@mogilev.by; internet www.mogotex .com; produces a wide range of textiles; Gen. Dir VIKTOR MATIEVICH.

Orsha Linen Mill: 211030 Orsha, vul. Molodezhnaya 3; tel. and fax (21) 613-06-95; e-mail flax@linen.belpak.vitebsk.by; internet www .linenmill.by; f. 1930; produces linen fabrics and products; Dir V. SHATKOV; 8,000 employees.

Polese Industrial and Trading Amalgamation: Brest Obl., 225710 Pinsk, Pervomaiskaya 159; tel. (16) 535-39-08; fax (16) 533-09-05; e-mail box@belppto.belpak.brest.by; f. 1968; knitted products, wool and acrylic yarn; Gen. Dir A. P. GULEVICH; 6,500 employees.

Slavyanka Industrial Commercial Co: 213809 Bobruisk, vul. Sotsialisticheskaya 84; tel. (22) 512-98-50; fax (22) 512-97-76; e-mail slavianka@mail.ru; internet www.bobruisk.by/slavyanka; f. 1930; designs and manufactures clothing; Dir TEYMURAZ N. BOCHORISHVILI; 2,000 employees.

Slonim Worsted and Spinning Factory: 231800 Slonim, vul. Brestskaya 42; tel. and fax (15) 622-59-53; e-mail skpf@yarn.of.by; internet www.yarn.of.by; f. 1977; jt-stock co; produces wool knitting yarns; Pres. VIKTAR VARVASHEVICH; Dir VALENTINA VENSKOVSKAYA; 1,300 employees.

Sukno: 220121 Minsk, vul. Matusevicha 33; tel. (17) 216-93-98; fax (17) 253-99-55; e-mail sykno@sykno.belpak.minsk.by; internet www .belsukno.narod.ru; jt-stock co; produces fine-cloth fabrics; Dir NIKOLAI V. KUZMENKO; 2,000 employees.

Vitebsk Fashion Industry Classic Co (KIM) (Vitebskoye OAO 'Klassika Industrii Mody'): 210004 Vitebsk, vul. Gorkogo 42; tel. (212) 34-25-23; fax (212) 34-10-24; e-mail kim@kim.vitebsk.net; internet www.kim.vitebsk.net; f. 1931; jt-stock co; production and export of clothing; Gen. Dir GALINA F. ANICHKINA.

Wood Products

Borisovdrev: 222120 Minsk Obl., Borisov, vul. 30 Let VLKSM; tel. and fax (1777) 3-16-53; e-mail info@borisovdrev.com; internet www .borisovdrev.com; f. 1990; wood products; Gen. Dir ULADZIMIR A. TIHONOVICH; 1,300 employees.

Fandok: 213802 Mohilev Obl., Bobruisk, vul. Lenina 95; tel. and fax (225) 49-08-31; e-mail fandok@mebel.by; internet www.fandok.com; f. 1929; wood products.

Pinskdrev Industrial Woodworking Co: 225710 Brest Obl., Pinsk, vul. Chuklaya 1; tel. (165) 35-16-40; fax (165) 35-66-64; e-mail box@pinskdrev.by; internet www.pinskdrev.by; f. 1880; produces industrial and domestic furniture, plywood, particle board and matches etc.; Gen. Dir LORAN S. ARINICH; 4,500 employees.

Miscellaneous

Belarusrezinotekhnika: 213829 Mogilev Obl., Bobruisk, Minskoye shosse 102; tel. (22) 513-14-17; fax (22) 513-15-28; f. 1952; jt-

stock co; produces rubber products for industrial uses; Dir V. A. MOROZ; 2,500 employees.

Belcoopvneshtorg: 220611 Minsk, pr. Pobeditelei 17; tel. (17) 226-79-22; fax (17) 223-09-69; e-mail belkoopvnechtorg@mail.ru; import and export; Dir ULADZIMIR GAPANOVICH.

Belomo-Belarussian Optical-Mechanical Production Association: 220836 Minsk, vul. Makayenka 23; tel. (17) 263-55-47; fax (17) 263-75-57; e-mail belomo@belomo.by; internet www.belomo .by; f. 1957; manufactures guidance and observation equipment; Pres. VYACHESLAV A. BURSKY; 4,500 employees.

Bobruiskagromash: 213822 Mohilev Obl., Bobruisk, vul. Shinnaya 5; tel. (225) 43-45-52; fax (225) 43-86-83; e-mail info@agromash .by; internet www.agromash.by; f. 1974; produces agricultural machinery; Gen. Man. YEVGENII P. PAKHILKO; 2,200 employees.

Borisov Crystal Plant (Borisovskii khrustalnyi zavod): 222120 Minsk Obl., Borisov, vul. Tolstikova 2; tel. (177) 73-43-13; fax (177) 73-32-13; e-mail borisovcrystall@yandex.ru; internet www .borisovcrystall.by; f. 1898; sales US $8m. (2001); Dir V. N. IVANOV; 2,400 employees.

Minsk Electromechanical Plant (Minskii Elekmekhanicheskii zavod): 220600 Minsk, vul. Volgogradskaya 6; tel. (17) 267-60-80; fax (17) 267-23-22; e-mail memz@memzplant.com; internet www .memzplant.com; f. 1950; state-owned; manufactures heating equipment, household dryers, electric meters and metal fittings for furniture; Dir ALEKSANDR V. RYBKIN.

Minsk Watch Plant (Minskii chasovii zavod): 220043 Minsk, pr. Nezavisimosti 95; tel. (17) 280-19-30; fax (17) 280-45-21; e-mail luch@ luch.by; internet www.luch.by; f. 1954; jt-stock co; production and sale of mechanical and quartz watches; Gen. Dir L. N. MELESH; 1,500 employees.

Minskpromstroy: 220034 Minsk, Voiskovoy per. 12; tel. (17) 283-15-73; fax (17) 283-15-90; e-mail mps@mail.bn.by; internet www .minskpromstroy.by; f. 1946; jt-stock co; civil engineering and industrial construction; Dir V. S. NEKHAY; 2,000 employees.

Mogilevliftmash-Lift Producing Plant: 212798 Mogilev, pr. Mira 42; tel. (222) 26-15-12; fax (222) 47-42-06; e-mail liftmach@ liftmach.by; internet www.liftmach.by; Dir ULADZIMIR POLYAKOV; 4,000 employees.

Monolit Corpn: 210604 Vitebsk, vul. Gorkogo 145; tel. and fax (21) 234-22-66; fax (21) 234-33-53; e-mail mail@monolit.vitebsk.by; internet www.monolit.vitebsk.by; f. 1958; state-owned; manufactures ceramic capacitators, ferrite inductors and varistors; Dir NIKOLAI M. DUBROVSKY; 1,000 employees.

Polotsk–Steklovolokno: 211400 Vitebsk Obl., Polotsk, Promuzel Ksty; tel. (214) 41-57-69; fax (214) 43-02-89; e-mail commerce@glass .belpak.vitebsk.by; internet www.polotsk-psv.by; f. 1958; jt-stock co; manufacture of glass-fibre materials; Gen. Dir N. A. KOCHANOVSKY; 4,500 employees.

Shchuchin Avtoprovod (Shchunskii zavod 'Avtoprovod'): 231513 Grodno Obl., Shchuchin, vul. Sovetskaya 15; tel. (1514) 2-59-90; fax (1514) 2-69-27; internet www.avtoprovod.com; f. 1958; jt-stock co; production of cables and wires; Pres. A. I. SIMONOVICH.

Strommashina Mogilev Plant: 212648 Mogilev, vul. Pervomayskaya 77; tel. (22) 222-09-16; fax (22) 222-29-45; e-mail strommashina@hotbox.ru; internet strommashina.narod.ru; f. 1913; produces automated machinery for manufacturing building materials, bricks, pipes, tiles, etc.; Dir ULADZIMIR YA. SAKHANKO; 2,400 employees.

TRADE UNIONS

Automobile and Agricultural Machinery Workers' Union: 220126 Minsk, pr. Pobeditelei 21/1103; tel. (17) 203-82-04; fax (17) 203-84-27; e-mail acmbel7@mail.belpak.by; f. 1990; Leader VALERY KUZMICH.

Belarusian Congress of Democratic Trade Unions (BKDP): 220095 Minsk, vul. Yakubova 80/80, etazh 15/2; tel. (17) 214-89-05; fax (17) 249-31-79; e-mail bcdtu@mail.ru; internet www.bkdp.org; f. 1993; alliance of four independent trade unions; Pres. ALYAKSANDR YARASHUK; International Sec. OLEG PODOLINSKI; 9,500 mems (2007).

Belarusian Peasants' Union (Syalansky Sayuz): 220199 Minsk, vul. Brestskaya 64/327; tel. (17) 277-99-93; Chair. KASTUS YARMOLENKA.

Federation of Trade Unions of Belarus (FPB): 220126 Minsk, pr. Pobeditelei 21; tel. (17) 210-43-37; fax (17) 203-89-93; e-mail contact@fpb.by; internet www.fpb.by; f. 1990; Chair. LEANID P. KOZIK.

Transport

RAILWAYS

In 2000 the total length of railway lines in use was 5,512 km. Minsk is a major railway junction, situated on the east–west line between Moscow and Warsaw, and the north-west–south-east line linking Lithuania and Ukraine. There is an underground railway in Minsk, the Minsk Metro, which has two lines (total length 27.6 km in 2007), with 23 stations.

Belarusian State Railways (Belorusskaya Zheleznaya Doroga): 220745 Minsk, vul. Lenina 17; tel. (17) 225-44-00; fax (17) 227-56-48; internet www.rw.by; f. 1992; Pres. VLADIMIR ZHERELO.

Minsk Metro: 220030 Minsk, pr. Nezavisimosti 6; tel. (17) 219-50-09; fax (17) 200-51-22; e-mail metro@minsktrans.by; internet www .minsktrans.by; f. 1984; two lines (30 km) with 25 stations (2007); Dir NIKOLAI T. ANDREYEV.

ROADS

At 31 December 2004 the total length of roads in Belarus was 93,310 km (comprising 15,377 km of main roads and 66,094 km of secondary roads). Some 87% of the total network was hard-surfaced.

CIVIL AVIATION

Minsk has two airports.

State Committee for Aviation: 220065 Minsk, vul. Aerodromnaya 4; tel. (17) 222-53-93; fax (17) 222-77-28; e-mail gka@ivcavia.com; internet www.ivcavia.com; Chair. VADZIM MELNIK.

Belavia Belarusian Airlines: 220004 Minsk, vul. Nemiga 14; tel. (17) 220-24-24; fax (17) 220-23-83; e-mail info@belavia.by; internet www.belavia.by; f. 1993; state carrier since 1996; operates services in Europe and to the CIS and the Middle East; Dir-Gen. ANATOLY GUSAROV.

Gomelavia: 246011 Gomel, Gomel Airport; tel. (23) 253-53-58; fax (23) 253-02-00; e-mail gomelavia@gomelavia.com.com; internet www.gomelavia.com; f. 1944; state-owned; includes Gomel Airport and Gomelavia Airlines; Dir ANATOLY KIRSANOV.

Tourism

Tourism is not developed, although the Government has sought to promote Belarus as a destination for those interested in hunting a variety of animals and birds, and for those who wish to visit sites associated with World War II. According to the World Tourism Organization, there were 89,101 tourist arrivals in 2006, when receipts from tourism (including passenger transport) amounted to US $386m.

Belintourist: 220004 Minsk, pr. Pobeditelei 19; tel. (17) 226-98-40; fax (17) 203-11-43; e-mail out@belintourist.by; internet www .belintourist.by; f. 1992; national tour operator; Dir MARIA I. FILIPOVICH.

Culture

CULTURAL HERITAGE

Grodno State Historical-Archeological Museum: 230023 Grodno, vul. Zamkovaya 22; tel. and fax (15) 244-94-31; e-mail grodno_museum@tut.by; 165,000 exhibits; Dir Y. V. KITURKA.

Museum of Ancient Culture of the National Academy of Sciences: 220072 Minsk, vul. Surganava 1/2; tel. (17) 284-18-82; f. 1979; attached to the K. Krapiva Institute of the Study of Arts, Ethnography and Folklore; Prof. VIKTOR F. SCHMATOV.

National Archives of the Republic of Belarus: 220014 Minsk, pr. Nezavisimosti 116; tel. (17) 267-29-42; fax (17) 237-67-78; e-mail narb@infonet.by; internet archives.gov.by; f. 1927; under the Committee for Archives and Records Management of the Council of Ministers; 1 of 6 central archives; VIACHESLAV D. SELEMENEV.

National Art Museum of the Republic of Belarus: 220030 Minsk, vul. Lenina 20; tel. and fax (17) 227-71-63; fax (17) 206-68-44; e-mail nmmrb@tut.by; internet www.artmuseum.by; f. 1939; 25,000 exhibits; 6 brs; Dir ULADZIMIR I. PRAKAPTSOU.

National Library of Belarus: 220114 Minsk, pr. Nezavisimosti 116; tel. (17) 266-37-00; fax (17) 266-37-06; e-mail inbox@nlb.by; internet www.nlb.by; f. 1922; over 8.3m. vols; Dir Prof. ROMAN S. MATULSKI.

National Museum of the History and Culture of Belarus: 220030 Minsk, vul. K. Marksa 12; tel. and fax (17) 227-36-65; internet nacbibl.org.by/hist_cult/en; f. 1957; over 250,000 exhibits on the history of the Belarusian people; library; Dir PYOTR S. CHOTKO.

SPORTING ORGANIZATION

National Olympic Committee of the Republic of Belarus: 220050 Minsk, vul. Ya. Kolosa 2; tel. (17) 227-87-91; fax (17) 227-61-84; e-mail noc-rb@altolan.com; internet www.noc.by; Pres. ALYAKSANDR R. LUKASHENKA; Gen. Sec. GEORGII KATULIN.

PERFORMING ARTS

Belarusian State Academy of Arts: 220012 Minsk, pr. Nezavisimosti 81; tel. (17) 232-15-42; fax (17) 232-20-41; e-mail info@belam .by; internet belam.by.com; f. 1945; fmrly the State Theatrical and Arts Institute; training in drama, arts and applied arts; library of 83,5384 vols (2003); Rector Prof. Dr R. B. SMOLSKI.

Belarusian State Philharmonic Society: 220005 Minsk, pr. Nezavisimosti 50; tel. (17) 284-77-66; fax (17) 231-90-50; internet www.philharmonic.by; f. 1936; Dir ALYAKSANDR V. GARBAR.

M. Gorkii National Academic Drama Theatre of Belarus: 220050 Minsk, vul. Volodarskaya 5; tel. (17) 220-38-25; fax (17) 220-83-45; e-mail nadt@tut.by; internet www.rustheatre.nm.ru; f. 1932; Dir EDUARD GERASIMOVICH.

Ya. Kupala National Academic Theatre: 220030 Minsk, vul. Engelsa 7; tel. and fax (17) 227-60-81; e-mail general@ kupala-theatre.by; internet www.kupala-theatre.by; f. 1920; Dir MIKALAY M. KIRYCHENKA.

National Academic Bolshoi Ballet Theatre of Belarus: 220029 Minsk, Parizhskaya Kommuna 1; tel. and fax (17) 334-10-23; e-mail pr@balet.by; internet www.balet.by; f. 1933; Gen. and Artistic Dir VALENTIN YELIZARIEV.

National Academic Great Opera Theatre of Belarus: 220029 Minsk, Parizhskaya Kommuna pl. 1; tel. and fax (17) 334-10-41; fax (17) 334-07-72; e-mail belarus_opera@tut.by; internet www .belarusopera.com; f. 1933; restructured in 1996; Dir VALERY GEDROITS.

ASSOCIATIONS

Belarusian Cultural Fund: 220029 Minsk, 6B Kommunalnaya nab.; tel. (17) 283-28-26; fax (17) 234-42-03; e-mail bfk@tut.by; f. 1987; also publishes weekly newspaper (circ. 2,000); Pres. ULADZIMIR GILEP.

F. Skaryna Belarusian Language Society: 220034 Minsk, vul. Rumyantcava 13; tel. (17) 288-23-52; tel. and fax (17) 284-85-11; e-mail tbm@tbm.lingvo.minsk.by; internet www.tbm.org.by; f. 1989; publishes two weekly newspapers (Nasha Slova, circ. 4,500, and Novy Chas, circ. 2,000); Chair. ALIEH TRUSAU.

Union of Artists of Belarus: 220050 Minsk, vul. K. Marksa 8/21; tel. (17) 227-37-23; fax (17) 227-71-01; e-mail belartunion@solo.by; f. 1938; Chair. ULADZIMIR BASALYGA.

Education

In the early 1990s the Government began to introduce greater provision for education in the Belarusian language and more emphasis on Belarusian, rather than Soviet or Russian, history and literature. In 2001/02 27.7% of all pupils were taught in Belarusian, and 72.2% were taught in Russian (0.1% were taught in Polish). In 2005/06 total enrolment at pre-primary level included 89.8% of children in the relevant age-group. According to UNESCO, net enrolment at primary level in 2005/06 included 89.4% of children in the relevant age-group. Education is officially compulsory for nine years, but usually lasts for 11 years, between the ages of six and 17 years. Secondary education, beginning at the age of 10, lasts for seven years (Grades 5–11), comprising a first cycle of five years and a second of two years. Net enrolment at secondary level included 88.0% of children in the relevant age group in 2005/06. Gross enrolment at tertiary level was equivalent to 60.5% in 2004. In 1998 a programme of education reform was initiated. The programme, which was scheduled for completion in 2010, was to introduce compulsory education for 10 years and a general education lasting 12 years. In 2005/06 383,000 students were enrolled in higher education (equivalent to 393 per 10,000 inhabitants). Research was co-ordinated by the National Academy of Sciences of Belarus (see The Environment). Budgetary expenditure on education by all levels of government was 4,060,000m. readjusted roubles (equivalent to 16.6% of total spending) in 2005.

UNIVERSITIES

Belarusian State Agrarian Technical University: 220023 Minsk, pr. Nezavisimosti 99; tel. (17) 267-47-71; fax (17) 267-41-16; e-mail rektorat@batu.edu.by; internet www.batu.edu.by; f. 1954; fmrly Belarusian Institute of Mechanization of Agriculture; 6 faculties, 1 institute; 507 teachers; 10,000 students; Rector Prof. NIKOLAI KAZAROVETS.

Belarusian State Economic University: 220070 Minsk, pr. Partizansky 26; tel. (17) 209-88-88; fax (17) 249-10-59; e-mail umoms@bseu.by; internet www.bseu.by; f. 1933; fmrly Belarusian State Institute of Nat. Economy; 10 faculties, 1 br.; 1,300 teaching staff; 27,000 students; library of 1.5m. vols; Rector ULADZIMIR N. SHIMOV.

Belarusian State Technological University: 220050 Minsk, vul. Sverdlova 13A; tel. (17) 226-14-32; fax (17) 227-62-17; e-mail root@bstu.unibel.by; internet www.bstu.unibel.by; f. 1930; 10 faculties; 590 teachers; 11,000 students; Rector I. M. ZHARSKY.

Belarusian State University: 220030 Minsk, pr. Nezavisimosti 4; tel. (17) 226-59-40; fax (17) 209-53-32; e-mail bsu@bsu.by; internet www.bsu.by; f. 1921; 17 faculties, 5 institutes; 3,000 teachers; 24,000 students; Rector Prof. VASIL STRAZHEV.

Frantsisk Skaryna Gomel State University: 246019 Gomel, vul. Sovetskaya 104; tel. (23) 256-73-71; fax (23) 257-81-11; e-mail rogachevav@mail.ru; internet www.gsu.unibel.by; f. 1930; 12 faculties; 600 teachers; 11,500 students; Rector Prof. Dr A. V. ROGACHEV.

Grodno Ya. Kupala State University: 230023 Grodno, vul. Ozheshko 22; tel. (15) 244-85-78; fax (15) 244-06-19; e-mail int@grsu.by; internet www.grsu.by; f. 1940; 11 faculties; 696 teachers; 11,519 students; Rector Prof. SIARHEI MASKEVICH.

Minsk State Linguistic University: 220034 Minsk, vul. Zakharova 21; tel. (17) 288-15-44; fax (17) 294-75-04; e-mail info@mslu.by; internet www.mslu.by; f. 1948; teacher and interpreter training in 15 languages; international relations, public relations, cultural and management studies; 9 faculties; 665 teachers; 5,120 students; library of 1m. books and periodicals; Rector NATALYA P. BARANOVA.

Polotsk State University: 211440 Novopolotsk, vul. Blokhina 29; tel. (21) 455-63-40; fax (21) 445-42-63; e-mail admin4@psu.unibel.by; internet www.psu.unibel.by; f. 1968; 9 faculties; 500 teachers; 4,000 students; library of over 450,000 vols; Rector Prof. DMITRIY N. LAZOVSKY.

Social Welfare

From 1993 the social-security system was financed by two principal funds: the Social Security Fund (covering family allowances, pensions and sickness and disability benefits) and the Employment Fund (directing employment schemes, retraining projects and unemployment benefits). There were some 2.5m. pensioners in 2003. In 2005 government expenditure on social policies was 1,396,000m. readjusted roubles (equivalent to 5.7% of total spending). Social Protection Fund contributions amounted to 1,478,000m. roubles. In addition, local authorities subsidize housing and communal services for low income families and individuals (1,349,000m. roubles). In 2005, according to official statistics, wages increased by 21%, in real terms. Real pensions also increased, by 13%, in 2002, after increasing by 32% in 2004.

A variety of benefits, financed through the Chornobyl tax, are paid to victims of the accident at the Chornobyl (Chernobyl) power station in Ukraine in April 1986, and in May 2002 the World Bank announced that it was to provide funds of US $50m. to support those living in contaminated areas. There were 4.8 physicians and 11.2 hospital beds per 1,000 inhabitants in 2006. Government expenditure on health from the state budget was 3,183,000m. readjusted roubles in 2005 (equivalent to 13.0% of total expenditure).

GOVERNMENT AGENCIES

Belarusian Children's Fund: 220029 Minsk, pr. Nezavisimosti 31; tel. (17) 290-62-14; e-mail fund@bcf.by; internet www.bcf.by; Chair. ALYAKSANDR TRUKHAN.

Ministry of Health: see The Government (Ministries).

Ministry of Labour and Social Protection: see The Government (Ministries).

Chernobyl Committee of the Republic of Belarus: 220004 Minsk, pr. Masherava 23; tel. (17) 289-15-69; fax (17) 222-34-39; e-mail home@komchern.org.by; f. 1990; Pres. ULADZIMIR G. TSALKO.

Social Security Fund: 220029 Minsk, vul. Chicherina 21; tel. and fax (17) 334-30-61; e-mail korol@ssf.gov.by; internet www.ssf.gov.by; f. 1993 on the basis of the Pension Fund and the Social Insurance Fund; Gov. LYUDMILA T. BACHILO.

HEALTH AND WELFARE ORGANIZATIONS

Belarusian Charitable Fund 'For the Children of Chernobyl': 220029 Minsk, vul. Staravilenskaya 14; tel. (17) 234-12-15; fax (17) 234-34-58; e-mail bbf@charity.belpak.minsk.by; internet bbfchernobyl.iatp.by; f. 1990; charitable fund to aid the victims of the Chornobyl disaster; Chair. Prof. Dr GENNADY V. GRUSHEVOY.

Belarusian Red Cross: 220030 Minsk, vul. K. Marksa 35; tel. and fax (17) 227-14-17; e-mail brc@home.by; internet www.belredcross.org; Chair. Dr LYUDMILA POSTOIALKO; Sec.-Gen. Dr VASILY I. ZHARKO.

Belarusian Society for Blind Invalids: 220004 Minsk, vul. Amuratorskaya 7; tel. (17) 223-05-31; fax (17) 223-86-41; Pres. ANATOLIY I. NETUILKIN.

Belarusian Society of the Handicapped: 220012 Minsk, vul. Kalinina 7; tel. and fax (17) 280-00-96; Chair. ULADZIMIR P. POTAPENKO.

Caritas Belarus: 220004 Minsk, pr. Pobeditelei 3/22; tel. and fax (17) 227-51-02; e-mail caritask@nsys.by; Pres. ANDREI BARODZICH; Sec.-Gen. Fr MIKHAIL SAPEL.

Republic of Belarus Organization of Veterans: 220030 Minsk, vul. Ya. Kupali; tel. (17) 226-12-60; Pres. ANATOLIY N. NOVIKOV.

Society of the Deaf: 220030 Minsk, vul. Volodarskaha 12; tel. (17) 226-57-29; fax (17) 226-53-20; e-mail assdeaf@solo.by; f. 1931; Pres. SYARGEY P. SAPUTO.

The Environment

In 1990 Belarus declared itself an ecological disaster area and claimed that 2.2m. people lived in areas contaminated by radioactive matter, released as a result of the Chornobyl disaster. The Chornobyl nuclear power station is situated in Ukraine, very close to the Belarusian border. When an explosion occurred in April 1986, the radioactive discharge was carried by the prevailing winds across southern and western Belarus. The worst affected areas were Gomel and Mogilev oblasts, in the south and south-east of the country, comprising some 20% of Belarus' territory. The peaty soils and wetlands in these regions were particularly prone to contamination, since they easily absorbed radioactive particles. Later analyses suggested that the area contaminated was even greater than originally believed, including parts of Grodno and Vitebsk oblasts, and covering perhaps as much as 40% of the country.

GOVERNMENT ORGANIZATIONS

Ministry of Emergency Situations: see The Government (Ministries).

Ministry of Forestry: see The Government (Ministries).

Ministry of Natural Resources and Environmental Protection: see The Government (Ministries).

ACADEMIC INSTITUTES

National Academy of Sciences of Belarus: 220072 Minsk, pr. Nezavisimosti 66; tel. (17) 284-18-01; fax (17) 284-28-16; e-mail academia@mserv.bas-net.by; internet www.ac.by; f. 1929; Chair. MIKHAIL MYASNIKOVICH; institutes incl.:

'Ecomir' National Scientific-Technical Centre for Remote Environmental Diagnostics: 220012 Minsk, vul. Surganava 2; tel. and fax (17) 284-00-49; fax (17) 284-00-47; e-mail ecomir@open.by; f. 1990; Dir Dr ALEKSANDR A. KOVALYEV.

Forest Institute: 246654 Gomel, vul. Praletarskaya 71; tel. and fax (23) 253-14-23; fax (23) 253-53-89; e-mail forinst@server.by; f. 1930; Dir VIKTOR A. IPATYEV.

Institute of the Problems of the Use of Natural Resources and Ecology: 220114 Minsk, vul. Starabarysauski Trakt 10; tel. (17) 264-26-32; fax (17) 264-24-13; e-mail ipnrue@ns.ecology.ac.by; f. 1932; in the Dept of Chemical and Geological Sciences; environmental research; Dir ULADZIMIR F. LOGINOV.

Ecology Department, Belarusian National Technical University: 220027 Minsk, pr. Nezavisimosti 65; tel. (17) 232-74-26; fax (17) 232-74-26; e-mail bntu@bntu.by; internet www.bntu.by/faculty/fpre; f. 2002; environmental education and training; part of the faculty of Ecology and Natural Resources; Dir Prof. BORIS B. BOGATOV.

Bureau on Environmental Consultancy (BURENCO): 220123 Minsk, vul. Viery Charuzaj 16; tel. and fax (17) 234-71-57; e-mail burenco@user.unibel.by; f. 1996; implementation of Environmental Management Systems for industrial enterprises in Minsk; advice to government on environmental policy; EcoTeam project addresses the potential for energy saving in households; environmental education and teacher training; Dir ULADZIMIR KOLTUNOV.

Students National Ecocenter of Belarus (RECU): 220023 Minsk, vul. Makaenka 8; tel. (17) 264-11-68; e-mail root@swta.minsk.by; f. 1930; environmental forums and education; Dir Dr LIDIA A. KURGANOVA.

NON-GOVERNMENTAL ORGANIZATIONS

APB—Birdlife Belarus (Akhova Ptushak Batskaushchyny—APB): 220050 Minsk, POB 306; tel. (17) 263-01-30; fax (17) 263-06-

13; e-mail apb@tut.by; internet www.ptushki.org; f. 1998; Chief Exec. VIKTAR FENCHUK.

Association of Professional Ecologists: 220038 Minsk, vul. Botanicheskaya 5A; tel. and fax (17) 236-22-65.

Belarusian Ecological Union: 220030 Minsk, Lenina 15A; tel. (17) 227-87-96; fax (17) 226-59-42; unites various groups concerned with environmental issues.

Belarusian Green Party (Belaruskaya Partya Zyaleny): see Political Organizations.

Belovezhskaya Pushcha National Park Museum: 225063 Brest Obl., Kamenets Distr., Belovezhskaya Pushcha State National Park; tel. (1631) 56-267; fax (1631) 250-56; e-mail npbpby@rambler.ru; internet npbp.brest.by; f. 1960; works to preserve the European bison, and other flora and fauna; UNESCO world heritage site and biosphere reserve; Dir N. N. BAMBIZA.

MAB Berezinsky Biosphere Reserve: 211188 Vitebsk, Lepel Distr., Tsentralnaya 3; tel. (21) 322-63-44; fax (21) 322-63-42; e-mail bbsr@tut.by; internet www.berezinsky.com; f. 1978; a patchwork of boreal coniferous and broad-leafed forests, lakes, watercourses, marshlands, flood plains and represents one of the largest undrained peat bogs in Eastern Europe (11,000 ha); includes an environmental education centre and a nature museum; Dir VIKENTY E. KHMARO.

Chornobyl Socio-Ecological Union: 220000 Minsk, vul. Kropotkina 44–511; tel. (17) 234-22-41; fax (17) 283-25-52; e-mail sasha@by .glas.apc.org; f. 1990; concerned with social welfare of victims of the Chornobyl disaster and environmental remediation; campaigns on ecological issues; Pres. VASILY T. YAKAVENKA.

Green Class Belarusian National Association: 246028 Gomel, vul. Sovetskaya 106/65; tel. (23) 256-99-17; fax (23) 24423-52; e-mail greenway@karopa.belpak.gomel.by; internet www.friends-partners .org/ccsi/nisorgs/belarus/grnclass.htm; f. 1993 to disseminate environmental information; Pres. GENNADIY N. KAROPA.

Green Cross Belarus: 220030 Minsk, vul. Oktyabrskaya 16; 220007, POB 174; tel. (17) 227-79-54; fax 2(17) 227-57-80; e-mail gcb@greencross.by; internet www.greencross.by; f. 1989; present name adopted 1999; to raise ecological awareness and co-operation, especially with regard to education and health; offices in Gomel and Grodno; Exec. Dir VLADIMIR S. SHEVTSOV.

Defence

As assessed at November 2007, the total strength of Belarus's armed forces was an estimated 72,940, comprising ground forces of 29,600, an air force of 18,170, as well as 25,170 in centrally controlled units and Ministry of Defence staff. There is also a border guard numbering 12,000, which is controlled by the Ministry of Internal Affairs. Military service is compulsory and lasts for between nine and 12 months. Belarus joined the North Atlantic Treaty Organization's 'Partnership for Peace' programme of military co-operation in January 1995. The budget for 2007 allocated 1,130,000m. readjusted roubles to defence.

Chief of the General Staff: Lt-Gen. SERGEI P. GURULEV.

Bibliography

Balmaceda, M. M., et al. (Eds). *Independent Belarus: Domestic Determinants, Regional Dynamics, and Implications for the West.* Cambridge, MA, Harvard Univ. Press, 2002.

Butler, W. E. *Civil Code of the Republic of Belarus.* The Hague, London and New York, Kluwer Law International, 2000.

Danilovich, A. *Russian-Belarusian Integration: Playing Games Behind the Kremlin Walls.* Burlington, VT, Ashgate, 2006.

Demeš, P., Forbrig, J., Marples, D.R. (Eds). *Prospects for Democracy in Belarus.* Washington, DC, German Marshall Fund of the United States, 2006.

Feus, K. *The EU and Belarus.* London, Kogan Page, 2002.

Garnett, S. W., et al. (Eds). *Belarus at the Crossroad.* Washington, DC, Carnegie Endowment for International Peace, 2000.

Glantz, D. M. (Ed.) *Belorussia 1944: the Soviet General Staff Study.* London, Frank Cass, 2001.

Gross, J. *Revolution from Abroad: the Soviet Conquest of Poland's Western Ukraine and Western Belorussia.* revised edn, Princeton, NJ, Princeton Univ. Press, 2001.

Hawkes, M. *Belarus: the Mechanics of Repression, Obstacles to Free and Fair Elections in Belarus.* London, Article 19, 2001.

International Business Publications USA. *Belarus Business and Investment Opportunities Yearbook.* International Business Publications USA, 2002.

Belarus Recent Economic and Political Developments Yearbook (World Strategic and Business Information Library). International Business Publications USA, 2007.

Ioffe, G. V. *Understanding Belarus and how Western Foreign Policy Misses the Mark.* Lanham, Rowman & Littlefield Publishers, 2008.

Kipel, V., and Kipel, Z. *Byelorussian Statehood: Reader and Bibliography.* New York, Belarusian Institute of Arts and Sciences, 1988.

Korosteleva, E., et al (Eds). *Contemporary Belarus: Between Democracy and Dictatorship.* London, Routledge, 2003.

Lewis, A. (Ed.). *The EU and Belarus: Between Moscow and Brussels.* London, Federal Trust for Education and Research/Kogan Page, 2002.

Loftus, J. *The Belarus Secret.* St Paul, MN, Paragon House Publishers, 1998.

Lubachko, I. S. *Belorussia under Soviet Rule, 1917–1957.* Lexington, KY, Univ. of Kentucky Press, 1972.

Marples, D. R. 'Post-Soviet Belarus and the Impact of Chernobyl', in *Post-Soviet Geography.* Vol. 33, No. 7 (Sept.). 1992.

'Belarus Ten Years After Chernobyl', in *Post-Soviet Geography.* Vol. 36, No. 6. 1995.

Belarus: From Soviet Rule to Nuclear Catastrophe. London, Macmillan, 1996.

Belarus: A Denationalized Nation. Amsterdam, Harwood Academic, 1999.

The Lukashenka Phenomenon: Elections, Propaganda, and the Foundations of Political Authority in Belarus. Trondheim, Program on East European Cultures and Societies, 2007.

Martel, R. *Les Blancs-russes: Etude Historique, Geographique, Politique et Economique.* Paris, André Delpeuch, 1929.

Parker, S. *The Last Soviet Republic: Alexander Lukashenko's Belarus.* Victoria, BC, Trafford, 2007.

Silitski, V. *Historical Dictionary of Belarus.* Lanham, MD, Scarecrow Press, 2007.

Staliūnas, D. *Making Russians: Meaning and Practice of Russification in Lithuania and Belarus after 1863.* Amsterdam, Editions Rodopi, 2007.

Urban, M. *An Algebra of Soviet Power: Elite Circulation in the Belorussian Republic, 1966–86.* Cambridge, Cambridge Univ. Press, 1989.

Vakar N. *Belorussia: The Making of a Nation.* Cambridge, MA, Harvard Univ. Press, 1956.

White, S. and McAllister, I. *Belarus, Ukraine and Russia: East or West?* Aberdeen, Centre for the Study of Public Policy, University of Aberdeen, 2008.

Yafimava, K. *Post-Soviet Russian-Belarussian Relationships: the Role of Gas Transit Pipelines.* Stuttgart, Ibidem, 2007.

Zaprudnik, J. *Belarus: At a Crossroads in History.* Boulder, CO, Westview Press, 1993.

See also the Select Bibliography.

GEORGIA

Geography

PHYSICAL FEATURES

Georgia is situated in the western and central South Caucasus, on the southern foothills of the Greater Caucasus mountain range. There is a short frontier with Turkey to the south-west and a western coastline on the Black Sea. The northern border with the Russian Federation follows the axis of the Greater Caucasus, and includes borders with the republics, from east to west, of Dagestan, Chechnya, Ingushetiya, North Osetiya (Ossetia)—Alaniya, Kabardino-Balkariya and Karachayevo-Cherkessiya. To the south lies Armenia, and to the south-east, Azerbaijan. Georgia includes two Autonomous Republics (Abkhazia and Adjara) and formerly included an Autonomous Oblast, South Ossetia. The status of Abkhazia and South Ossetia remains in dispute. Georgia has an area of 69,700 sq km (26,911 sq miles), of which Abkhazia totals 8,600 sq km and the former Autonomous Oblast of South Ossetia 3,900 sq km.

Geographically, Georgia is divided by the Suram mountain range, which runs from north to south between the Lesser and Greater Caucasus mountains. To the west of the Surams lie the Rioni plains and the Black Sea littoral; to the east lies the more mountainous Kura basin. The Rion, flowing westwards into the Black Sea, and the Kura, flowing eastwards through Azerbaijan into the Caspian Sea, are the country's main rivers.

CLIMATE

The Black Sea coast and the Rioni plains have a warm, humid, subtropical climate, with over 2,000 mm of rain annually and average temperatures of 6°C (42°F) in January and 23°C (73°F) in July. Eastern Georgia has a more continental climate, with cold winters and hot, dry summers.

POPULATION

At the 1989 census, when the total de facto population was 5,443,359, 68.8% of the population were Georgians, 9.0% Armenians, 7.4% Russians, 5.1% Azeris, 3.2% Ossetians, 1.9% Greeks and 1.7% Abkhaz. After 1989 many non-ethnic Georgians emigrated as a result of inter-ethnic violence, notably Ossetians and Pontian Greeks. During the period of conflict in Abkhazia in 1992–93 more than 200,000 ethnic Georgians and others left the region. Some 50,000 refugees were resettled from 1996, but renewed hostilities in mid-1998 resulted in the departure of many of these; refugees began to return once again from March 1999. Ajars, ethnic Georgians who converted to Islam under Ottoman rule, were not counted separately in Soviet censuses from 1926, when they accounted for less than 4% of the population. Until 1944 there were also some 200,000 Meskhetian Turks in Georgia, who were of mixed Turkish and Georgian descent and predominantly Muslim. In

November 1944 they were deported *en masse* to Soviet Central Asia, and, although they were rehabilitated and granted the right to return to Georgia in 1968, few were actually permitted to leave Central Asia. Many were forced to flee Central Asia following inter-ethnic violence in 1989, but were refused permission by the Georgian authorities to resettle in their homelands; many of these Meskhetian Turks, who had settled in southern Russia, where they continued to experience discrimination, were granted asylum in the USA in 2004.

Most of the population are adherents of Christianity; the principal denomination is the Georgian Orthodox Church. Most Ossetians are Eastern Orthodox Christians. Islam is professed by the Abkhaz, Ajars, Azeris, Kurds and some Ossetians. There are also other Christian groups, and a small number of Jews. The official language is Georgian, a non-Indo-European language, which is written in the Georgian script.

At the census of 17 January 2002 (which did not take place in those areas of Abkhazia or South Ossetia not under Georgian government control), of the *de jure* population of 4,371,535, 83.8% were Georgians, 6.5% were Azeri, 5.7% were Armenian and 1.5% were Russian. At January 2008 the total population of the entire country was estimated at 4,382,100, and the average population density was 62.9 persons per sq km. The capital of Georgia is Tbilisi, which is situated in the south-east of the country, on the River Kura. In January 2008 its population was an estimated 1,106,700. Other important towns include the ports of Batumi (the capital of Adjara, with a population of 122,200) and Sukhumi (Sukhum, capital of Abkhazia, with an estimated population of 112,000 in 1994). The main town of western Georgia is Kutaisi, on the Rioni plains, with a population of some 190,100 in 2006. Another western city, Zugdidi, with a population of 172,200 in 2006, is the principal city of the historic province of Mingrelia.

Chronology

c. 299 BC–234 BC: Parnavaz (Farnavazi, Pharnabazus), traditionally the first king of an identifiably 'Georgian' state, reigned over eastern Georgia (anciently known as Iberia); his realm was centred on the province of Kartli, but he also came to dominate the kingdom in western Georgia (Egrisi—the area known as Colchis by the ancient Greeks).

64: The Roman general Pompey incorporated Colchis into the Empire and secured hegemony in Kartli-Iberia and Armenia; the Persian (Parthian—Iranian) Empire soon disputed this.

c. AD 328: St Nino began the evangelization of the Georgians; the king of Kartli-Iberia, Mirian III (Meribanes), adopted Christianity in 334.

523: Tsete, the ruler of Lazica (established in Egrisi in the previous century), accepted Orthodox Christianity; the territory soon returned to dependence on the Eastern Roman ('Byzantine') Empire.

580: The Persians abolished the Kartli-Iberian monarchy; the kingdom was effectively partitioned between the Byzantines (based at the old capital of Mtskheta) and the Sasanian Persians (located at the new capital a short distance away, Tbilisi).

645: Tbilisi fell to the Arabs; the presiding Prince of Kartli-Iberia was forced to acknowledge the Muslim Caliph as overlord.

888: The monarchy of Kartli-Iberia was restored by the Armenians, both kingdoms being ruled by branches of the Bagration family; there was also a kingdom in Egrisi, known as Abasgia (Abkhazia) or Abkhazeti.

1008: Bagrat III, King of Abkhazia, inherited the kingdom of Kartli-Iberia, uniting Egrisi and Kartli into a single Georgian kingdom ('Sakartvelo', the land of the Kartvelians or Georgians), with his capital at Kutaisi.

1089–1125: Reign of King David IV (the 'Builder'), who gained control of the remaining Georgian lands: the process began when he renounced the tribute to the Seljuq Turkish sultanate (1096); it was secured by the defeat of the Muslims at the Battle of Didgori (12 August 1121); and was symbolized by the final capture of Tbilisi, which became the royal capital (1122).

1184–1212: Reign of Queen Tamar; this marked the apogee of the independent medieval Georgian kingdom, which witnessed the work of the 'national bard', Shota Rustaveli, repulsed the Muslims and helped establish the Byzantine 'Empire' of Trebizond.

1223–45: Reign of Queen Rusudan, under whom Georgia was devastated by Mongol and Khwarazem raiders; the kingdom was fractured, and the Georgians became tributary to the Mongol rulers of the Persian Empire.

1314: Georgia was briefly reunited by Giorgi V (the 'Brilliant'), until the invasion of the Mongol leader, Timur (Tamerlane, 1370–1405).

1783: King Irakli (Erekle) II, of a reunited Kartli-Kakheti (1762–98), concluded the Treaty of Georgievsk with Russia, whereby his eastern kingdom surrendered responsibility for defence and foreign affairs, but retained internal autonomy.

18 December 1800: Tsar Paul (Pavel) I of Russia declared Kartli-Kakheti annexed outright to the Russian Empire, although the question of the continuance of the Bagration dynasty was left in abeyance—however, Giorgi XII, the last king of eastern Georgia, died before tsarist troops entered Tbilisi.

12 September 1801: The new Tsar, Alexander (Aleksandr) I, decreed the abolition of the kingdom of Kartli-Kakheti.

December 1803: Moving westwards, the Russians placed Samgrelo (Mingrelia) under the formal protection of the Empire.

1804: The last reigning Bagration, King Solomon II of Imereti (the main principality of western Georgia, based at Kutaisi), was forced to accept Russian sovereignty; he, and his title, died in 1810.

1809: Safar bey Sharvashedze placed his principality of Abkhazia under Russian protection.

1811: Mamia Gurieli placed the principality of Guria (western Georgia, on the Black Sea coast) under the protection of the Tsar; the Russians had also seized Sukhum-Kale and other cities from the Turks. In the same year the autocephaly of the eastern Georgian Orthodox Church was ended; a new exarchate was imposed on the western Georgian Church.

1828: The Treaty of Turkmanchai concluded the war between Russia and Persia, confirming Russian rule over the Georgians.

1864–65: Emancipation of the serfs, first in Tbilisi (Tiflis) province, then in Guria and Imereti (Kutaisi province).

1892: The first radical Marxist group, Mesami Dasi (Third Company), was formed; Iosif Dzhugashvili (Ioseb Jughashvili, later known as Stalin) became a member.

1899: The first Tbilisi committee of the All-Russian Social Democratic Labour Party (RSDLP) was formed, dominated by the Menshevik wing—the Bolsheviks of the main, Russian RSDLP were to include many prominent Georgians, notably Stalin and 'Sergo' Ordzhonikidze (Orjonikidze).

1 August 1914: Russia entered the First World War against Austria-Hungary, Germany and Ottoman Turkey.

2 March (New Style 15 March) 1917: Following the abdication of Tsar Nicholas (Nikolai) II, the Provisional Government nominated an executive in the South Caucasus (Transcaucasia), although its power was dependent upon the soviets (councils) established in Tbilisi and Baku (Azerbaijan).

November 1917: The Georgian Mensheviks and the Armenian leaderships denied the legitimacy of the new, Bolshevik, central Government and established a Transcaucasian Commissariat to assume temporary authority (an assembly, or Seim, convened in January 1918).

22 April 1918: The Transcaucasian Seim declared the independence of the Democratic Federative Republic of Transcaucasia.

26 May 1918: The Georgian leadership declared an independent Georgian state, allied to Germany.

July 1920: The British withdrew the last of their forces from Batumi, refusing to aid the Transcaucasian states militarily against Russia.

1921: The first Georgian Constitution was adopted.

25 February 1921: The Menshevik Government fled Tbilisi, which was occupied by the Red Army, under Ordzhonikidze; Georgia, the last of the Transcaucasian states to fall to the Bolsheviks, was subsequently declared a Soviet Socialist Republic (SSR).

10 December 1922: The Federal Union of SSRs of Transcaucasia (formed 12 March) was transformed into a single republic, the Transcaucasian Soviet Federative Socialist Republic (TSFSR); the TSFSR became a founder member of the Union of Soviet Socialist Republics (USSR) on 30 December.

28 August 1924: A widespread revolt, led by a coalition of opposition parties known as the Parity Committee, commenced; it failed and was followed by severe repression.

5 December 1936: The TSFSR was dissolved, and the Georgian, Armenian and Azerbaijani SSRs became full Union Republics.

1937: The leader of Georgia, Lavrenti Beria, assured Stalin, the Soviet leader, of his loyalty by conducting among the most severe of the Stalinist purges.

1941–45: The German–Soviet struggle during the Second World War had a severe effect on Georgia, although there was no fighting on its territory; the population declined from 3.5m. in 1939 to 3.2m. by 1945.

March 1953: Death of Stalin; most members of the Georgian leadership were subsequently dismissed.

March 1956: The anniversary of the death of Stalin (whose memory remained popular in Georgia) occasioned the first 'nationalist' demonstration since the 1920s, resulting in harsh suppression; there was great opposition that year to perceived 'russification'.

29 September 1972: Eduard Shevardnadze became head of the Communist Party of Georgia (CPG—serving until 1985, when he became Soviet Minister of Foreign Affairs).

14 April 1978: A public demonstration unexpectedly led to a constitutional amendment restoring Georgian as a state language.

9 April 1989: A number of people were killed in Tbilisi when soldiers dispersed a demonstration opposing Abkhazian secessionism and supporting Georgian independence.

July 1989: Several people were killed in Sukhumi (Sukhum, the capital of Abkhazia) during fighting; a state of emergency and curfew were imposed in the city.

November 1989: The Georgian Supreme Soviet (Supreme Council) declared the supremacy of Georgian over all-Union laws; the article in the Constitution safeguarding the CPG's monopoly on power was abolished.

December 1989: There were violent confrontations in South Ossetia, between Ossetians and Georgians, after demands that South Ossetia be made an autonomous republic and, eventually, be reunified with North Osetiya (part of the Russian Federation) were refused.

February 1990: The Georgian Supreme Soviet declared Georgia an 'annexed and occupied country'.

March 1990: The Supreme Soviet revoked the communist ban on opposition parties, at the behest of which the republican parliamentary elections were postponed.

25 August 1990: The Abkhazian Supreme Soviet voted to declare independence from Georgia and adopt the status of a full union republic; this declaration was pronounced invalid by the Georgian Supreme Soviet, and Georgian deputies in the Abkhazian legislature succeeded in reversing the declaration.

20 September 1990: The South Ossetian Supreme Soviet proclaimed the region's independence and state sovereignty within the USSR; this was declared unconstitutional by the Georgian Supreme Soviet.

30 September 1990: The more radical opposition parties rejected all Soviet institutions and conducted elections to a National Congress, in which only 51% of the electorate participated.

28 October 1990: In the first round of elections to the Georgian Supreme Soviet, the Round Table-Free Georgia coalition of pro-independence parties won some 64% of the votes cast (after the second round of voting, on 11 November, the coalition held 155 seats).

14 November 1990: Zviad Gamsakhurdia, leader of the Georgian Helsinki Union and of the victorious coalition, was elected Chairman of the Supreme Soviet; the state was renamed the Republic of Georgia.

11 December 1990: The Georgian parliament abolished South Ossetia's autonomous status, resulting in renewed violence in the region. The Soviet leadership annulled this decision in the following month.

31 March 1991: Having boycotted the all-Union referendum on continued federation (although polling stations were opened in South Ossetia and Abkhazia, both of which territories voted in favour of remaining within the USSR) and the negotiations on a new union treaty, the Georgian authorities conducted a republican referendum on independence, which was overwhelmingly supported.

9 April 1991: Georgia became the first republic to secede from the USSR, when the Supreme Soviet approved a decree formally restoring Georgian independence; six days later Gamsakhurdia was appointed to the new post of executive President of the Republic.

26 May 1991: Gamsakhurdia was directly elected to the presidency, with 85.6% of the votes cast.

September 1991: Following criticism of his reaction to the failed Soviet coup of August, and accusations of authoritarian rule, opposition parties united to demand Gamsakhurdia's resignation.

December 1991: The South Ossetian Supreme Soviet declared a state of emergency, following the dispatch of Georgian troops to the region; a second declaration of independence was adopted, as was a resolution, endorsed by a referendum held in January 1992, in favour of integration into the Russian Federation.

21 December 1991: Georgia sent observers to a meeting in Almaty, Kazakhstan, where the leaders of 11 former Union Republics of the USSR signed a protocol on the formation of the new Commonwealth of Independent States (CIS).

2 January 1992: President Gamsakhurdia was declared deposed by the opposition; he fled to Armenia four days later, and subsequently to Chechnya, Russia. A Military Council was formed, headed by Tengiz Kitovani and Jaba Ioseliani; this appointed Tengiz Sigua as premier.

10 March 1992: Shevardnadze was appointed Chairman of the State Council, which had recently replaced the Military Council.

24 June 1992: Shevardnadze and President Boris Yeltsin of Russia reached an agreement on the cessation of hostilities in South Ossetia; however, no political settlement was reached.

July 1992: Civil disturbance increased in violence, following repeated attempts by Gamsakhurdia and his supporters ('Zviadists') to regain control. In South Ossetia, where conflict was continuing, a cease-fire agreement was signed and peace-keeping monitors deployed. The Abkhazian legislature proclaimed the region's sovereignty as the 'Republic of Abkhazia'.

31 July 1992: Georgia became the last former Soviet Republic to be admitted to the UN.

11 August 1992: Zviadists kidnapped the Georgian Minister of Internal Affairs and other senior officials, who had been sent to western Georgia (Mingrelia) to negotiate the release of a deputy premier, taken hostage the previous month.

14 August 1992: Some 3,000 National Guard members arrived in Abkhazia, allegedly in an attempt to release the hostages; Abkhazian troops responded with a series of attacks, but the Georgian forces succeeded in capturing Sukhumi.

September 1992: Abkhazian forces launched a counter-offensive and gained control of all of northern Abkhazia; Shevardnadze claimed that secessionist forces were receiving military aid from Russia.

11 October 1992: Elections to the Supreme Council were participated in by an estimated 75% of the electorate; in direct elections held simultaneously, Shevardnadze was elected

Chairman, with 96% of the votes cast. The new parliament convened for the first time on 6 November.

6 August 1993: Sigua and the Council of Ministers resigned.

10 September 1993: A two-month state of emergency was declared (it ended on 20 February 1994), and a new administration, under Otar Patsatsia, was appointed. Shevardnadze forced parliament to accept these measures after offering his resignation (which was refused).

15 September 1993: Zviadist forces began an offensive to the west of Samtredia.

16 September 1993: Abkhazian forces launched numerous surprise attacks, breaking the UN cease-fire agreement of 27 July; Sukhumi was taken and government troops were defeated after 11 days of fighting.

30 September 1993: The last government troops were driven from Abkhazia (with the exception of the Kodori Gorge), and the region was declared to be separate from Georgia; ethnic Georgians were expelled from the region; others were killed by victorious troops.

2 October 1993: Zviadists captured the port of Poti and gained control of the railway line to Tbilisi, thereby blocking all rail traffic to the capital.

20 October 1993: The Supreme Council agreed that Georgia should join the CIS, which Shevardnadze had proposed a few days earlier. The next day Russian troops and supplies arrived in Georgia, and government forces were able to reopen supply lines, while Poti and other towns were soon recaptured. Georgia was formally admitted to the CIS on 3 December. Meanwhile, Gamsakhurdia and his supporters fled to Abkhazia.

1 December 1993: Georgian officials and Abkhazian separatists signed a UN-mediated eight-point peace 'memorandum'.

23 December 1993: The 'Republic of South Ossetia' adopted a new Constitution.

31 December 1993: Gamsakhurdia was killed, reportedly by his own hand, after being surrounded by government troops in western Georgia.

March 1994: Georgia joined the 'Partnership for Peace' programme of the North Atlantic Treaty Organization (NATO).

14 May 1994: The Georgian and Abkhazian Governments declared a full cease-fire agreement, under which a contingent of some 3,000 CIS (mainly Russian) peace-keepers were deployed in the region from June; this was in addition to the UN observer forces already in place. Nevertheless, hostilities recommenced.

26 November 1994: The Abkhazian legislature adopted a new Constitution, which declared the region to be a sovereign state; the speaker of the legislature, Vladislav Ardzinba, was appointed President, leading the Georgian Government to suspend peace negotiations.

March 1995: Georgia and Russia signed an agreement on the establishment of four Russian military bases in Georgia for a period of 25 years; however, it was not ratified.

July 1995: Discussions on a political settlement in South Ossetia began, under the supervision of the Organization for Security and Co-operation in Europe (OSCE).

24 August 1995: The Supreme Council adopted Georgia's new Constitution, the drafting of which had been prepared by a special commission appointed in 1992; the new Constitution provided for a strong executive presidency and a 235-member, unicameral Georgian Parliament (Sakartvelos Parlamenti).

29 August 1995: Shevardnadze survived an assassination attempt, sustaining only minor injuries. In early October the Minister of State Security, Igor Giorgadze, was named as the chief instigator of the plot, and warrants were issued for his arrest. In May 1996 Ioseliani, leader of the paramilitary

Rescue Corps (formerly Mkhedrioni, or Horsemen), was convicted of complicity in the assassination attempt.

25 September 1995: The Government introduced a new currency, the lari, which replaced the interim currency coupons introduced in April 1993 and subsequently became the sole legal tender.

5 November 1995: In the election to the restored post of President, Shevardnadze won 74.9% of the votes cast. In the parliamentary election, held simultaneously, Shevardnadze's Citizens' Union of Georgia (CUG) won 107 of the 235 seats.

11 December 1995: A new Council of Ministers was announced; the post of Minister of State replaced that of Prime Minister.

19 January 1996: At a meeting of CIS leaders in Moscow, Russia, it was agreed to impose an economic blockade of Abkhazia until it agreed to accept Georgian sovereignty.

10 November 1996: The Republic of South Ossetia, having introduced a presidential system of government, held elections for the post, which were won by Ludvig Chibirov.

23 November 1996: Elections to the Abkhazian National Assembly were held, despite national and international condemnation.

9 July 1997: Violent clashes occurred in the Kodori Gorge, and 20 people were reportedly killed.

17–19 November 1997: In UN-sponsored talks, it was decided to establish a joint co-ordinating council, comprising representatives of Georgia and Abkhazia, as well as delegates from Russia, the UN and the European Union (EU), to resolve the issues in Abkhazia.

December 1997: The South Ossetian parliament voted in favour of an independent South Ossetian republic within the CIS; negotiations scheduled to take place under Russian and OSCE supervision were cancelled.

9 February 1998: Shevardnadze survived a second assassination attempt; Zviadists were blamed for the attack, and in March Guram Absandze, a former finance minister, was extradited from Russia to stand trial. In August 2001 Absandze was sentenced to 17 years' imprisonment for his role in the failed attempt on Shevardnadze's life; seven other men also received prison sentences. However, Absandze was pardoned in April 2002.

25 May 1998: A cease-fire agreement was signed, following violent clashes in the Gali district of Abkhazia, a supposedly neutral zone, where many refugees had been resettled; some 30,000 refugees left the region once more.

26 July 1998: Nikoloz Lekishvili resigned as Minister of State. The entire cabinet subsequently resigned, with one exception. Vazha Lortkipanidze was confirmed as Minister of State in August.

27 April 1999: Georgia was admitted to the Council of Europe.

May 1999: Seventeen people were arrested following the discovery of a new conspiracy to overthrow the President. Georgia refused to sign the Collective Security Treaty of the CIS on its expiry.

3 October 1999: Ardzinba was re-elected as President of the Republic of Abkhazia, with 99% of the votes cast; the participation rate was 87.7%. A simultaneous referendum upheld the 1994 Constitution, and a State Independence Act was adopted by the legislature shortly afterwards.

14 November 1999: A second round of nation-wide legislative elections was held (the first had taken place on 31 October), in which the ruling CUG secured 41.9% of the votes cast and 130 seats. The Union for the Revival of Georgia bloc, comprising Zviadist parties, and the Industry Will Save Georgia bloc won 58 seats and 15 seats, respectively. Of the remaining seats, 17 were obtained by independents and two by the Georgian

Labour Party. One seat remained unfilled, and the mandates of 12 Abkhazian candidates were renewed, following the region's boycott of the election.

18–19 November 1999: At a summit meeting of the OSCE held in İstanbul, Turkey, Russia agreed to vacate two of its four military bases in Georgia by July 2001. Agreement was also reached by the Presidents of Azerbaijan, Georgia, Kazakhstan, Turkey and Turkmenistan on the construction of a pipeline (later known as the BTC pipeline) to carry petroleum from Baku, Azerbaijan, to Ceyhan, Turkey, via Tbilisi.

9 April 2000: Eduard Shevardnadze was re-elected as President for a further five-year term, with 79.8% of the votes cast; he was sworn in on 30 April. The OSCE expressed concern over violations in voting procedures and demanded an investigation.

11 May 2000: Parliament endorsed the appointment of Gia Arsenishvili as the new Minister of State, replacing Lortkipanidze.

14 June 2000: Georgia joined the World Trade Organization (WTO).

16 March 2001: At the conclusion of a UN-sponsored meeting in Yalta, Ukraine, delegations from Georgia and Abkhazia signed an agreement renouncing violence and permitting the safe return of refugees.

8 April 2001: The new South Ossetian Constitution, which designated Russian and Ossetian as the state languages, was approved in a referendum boycotted by the Georgian community in South Ossetia.

3 July 2001: The Government complained to Russia following the failure of its troops to vacate the Gudauta military base in Abkhazia by the agreed deadline of 1 July; Russia claimed the troops' continued presence to be necessary, since Georgia was unable to guarantee security at the base. Shevardnadze subsequently protested to the OSCE.

17 September 2001: President Shevardnadze resigned as Chairman of the CUG; the President's decision to retain the chairmanship while serving as President had long been regarded by critics as a violation of the Constitution.

1 November 2001: Shevardnadze dismissed the Government, following large-scale public demonstrations against the investigation by security officials of the independent television station Rustavi 2.

6 December 2001: Eduard Kokoyev (Kokoiti), a Russian citizen, was elected as the new South Ossetian President.

27 December 2001: Avtandil Jorbenadze was appointed as Minister of State to lead a new Government.

1 March 2002: During a CIS summit meeting, held in Almaty, Kazakhstan, President Shevardnadze and the Russian President, Vladimir Putin, agreed to amend the mandate of the CIS peace-keeping forces stationed in Abkhazia, to satisfy Georgian demands that they withdraw to a more northerly position, undertake policing duties, and include soldiers from CIS countries other than Russia.

24 May 2002: The Supreme Court ruled that the faction of the CUG that supported Shevardnadze was the group rightfully entitled to use the party's name, rather than an opposing 'reformist' faction, established by the former parliamentary Chairman, Zurab Zhvania. Zhvania set up a new party, the United Democrats, in the following month.

2 June 2002: Municipal elections took place, resulting in a serious reverse for the CUG, which failed to win any seats on Tbilisi City Council.

14 June 2002: The OSCE confirmed Russia's withdrawal from the Gudauta base, in Abkhazia.

29 June 2002: At a party congress, Jorbenadze was elected Chairman of the CUG, and Shevardnadze Honorary Chairman.

23 August 2002: Following the aerial bombardment of the Pankisi Gorge region by unmarked aircraft, Georgia accused Russia of an overt act of aggression, and announced that it would be prepared to utilize 'all possible means' to repel subsequent attacks, after one person died; Russia refused to accept responsibility for the attack.

25 August 2002: Some 1,000 government troops entered the Pankisi Gorge as part of an operation to reassert control over the area.

6 October 2002: At a CIS summit meeting in Chişinău, Moldova, Presidents Shevardnadze and Putin reached an agreement, according to which the two countries were to resume joint patrols of their common border, and seek to resolve border issues by diplomatic means. On 7 March 2003 the Presidents released a further statement, in which they agreed to expedite the repatriation of displaced persons to Abkhazia, and extend indefinitely the mandate of the CIS peace-keeping forces, until either Georgia or Abkhazia demanded their withdrawal.

21–22 November 2002: Georgia formally applied for membership of NATO at a summit meeting of the Alliance, held in Prague, Czech Republic.

2 November 2003: Legislative elections took place, amid reports of widespread electoral irregularities and falsification; Shevardnadze's For a New Georgia bloc was reported to have won the majority of the votes cast, followed by Aslan Abashidze's Democratic Union of Revival. (Abashidze was the self-styled 'Head of the Autonomous Republic of Adjara'.) Large-scale protest demonstrations led by Mikheil Saakashvili (the Co-Chairman of the pro-Western, opposition National Movement, formed in 2001), and supported by the parliamentary Chairman, Nino Burjanadze, and by Zhvania, ensued in response.

22 November 2003: Some 30,000 demonstrators seized the parliament building; Shevardnadze declared a nation-wide state of emergency.

23 November 2003: Shevardnadze resigned from the presidency. He was replaced, in an interim capacity, by Burjanadze. Two days later Jorbenadze and other key ministers also resigned from office. Zhvania was appointed as the interim Minister of State.

25 November 2003: The Supreme Court ruled that the results of the parliamentary elections were invalid.

4 January 2004: A new presidential election took place, in which Mikheil Saakashvili obtained 96.3% of the votes cast.

14 January 2004: A new national flag was adopted. Tamaz Nadareishvili resigned as Chairman of the Tbilisi-based 'parliament-in-exile' of Abkhazia. He was subsequently replaced by Teimur Mzhavia.

11 February 2004: Constitutional amendments were adopted and implemented, the most significant of which concerned the reintroduction of the post of Prime Minister and the capacity of the legislature to remove the Government following two consecutive votes of 'no confidence'.

17 February 2004: The new Government was approved by the legislature, with Zurab Zhvania as Prime Minister. (The interim Government had submitted its resignation on the inauguration of the new President on 25 January.)

28 March 2004: In new elections to the 150 parliamentary seats filled by proportional representation, the coalition of the National Movement-United Democrats won 135 seats, and the Rightist Opposition bloc won 15 seats. Of the 85 legislators elected on the basis of single-mandate constituencies, 74 of those elected in 2003 remained in place; one seat was vacant, while the remaining 10 seats, representing Abkhazia, were declared to be vacant on 30 April 2004.

5 May 2004: President Saakashvili imposed direct rule on Adjara, amid demonstrations against the Abashidze regime within the region; after negotiations with a Russian envoy, the following day Abashidze left Georgia, for Russia, under Saakashvili's offer of safe passage.

20 June 2004: Elections to a new republican unicameral legislature, the Supreme Council, took place in Adjara, in which the Saakashvili–Victorious Adjara party received some 75% of the votes cast and 28 of the 30 seats available; however, the ballot was regarded as having fallen short of international standards.

27 December 2004: A further reorganization of the Council of Ministers was effected (the first had taken place in May). Notable appointments included that of Irakli Okruashvili as Minister of Defence, and Giorgi Baramidze as Deputy Prime Minister with responsibility for European Integration; the Ministry of State Security, headed by Ivane Merabishvili, was merged with the Ministry of Internal Affairs.

12 January 2005: Following a disputed presidential election in Abkhazia on 3 October 2004 (which was unrecognized by Georgia or the international community), a repeat election was held, in which the two main candidates compromised by running jointly for the posts of President and Vice-President, with the powers of the latter to be augmented. Sergei Bagapsh was elected President, with Raul Khadzhimba (the candidate endorsed by Russia) as his deputy.

3 February 2005: Prime Minister Zurab Zhvania and a junior government official were discovered dead, apparently owing to poisoning from an accidental gas leak.

17 February 2005: The legislature approved a reorganized Council of Ministers, led by Zurab Noghaideli. Valeri Chechelashvili, hitherto ambassador to Russia, succeeded Noghaideli as Minister of Finance; Konstantine Kemularia, previously Chairman of the Supreme Court, became Deputy Prime Minister and Minister of Justice.

23 February 2005: Parlamenti endorsed constitutional amendments approved by referendum in November 2003, which provided for a reduction in the number of parliamentary deputies from 235 to 150; the measure was to take effect from the next legislative elections, scheduled to take place in 2008.

10 May 2005: President George W. Bush of the USA paid a state visit to Georgia. A hand grenade was thrown as he addressed a crowd, but failed to detonate.

25 May 2005: The BTC petroleum pipeline was officially inaugurated in Azerbaijan; the Georgian section of the pipeline was inaugurated on 12 October.

30 May 2005: Agreement was reached with the Russian Government, according to which it was to close the remaining two military bases that it maintained on Georgian territory by the end of 2008. Two months previously Parlamenti had approved a non-binding resolution demanding that Russia agree by 15 May a programme for the closure of the bases by 2006.

30 June 2005: Aleksi Aleksishvili was appointed as Minister of Finance, following the dismissal of Chechelashvili, amid allegations of bribery; Irakli Chogovadze succeeded Aleksishvili as Minister of Economic Development.

19 October 2005: Salomé Zurabishvili was dismissed from her position as Minister of Foreign Affairs; protest rallies by her supporters ensued, and she subsequently founded a political movement. She was succeeded by Gela Bezhuashvili.

22 December 2005: Gia Kavtaradze was appointed as Minister of Justice, in place of Kote Kemularia.

22 January 2006: Explosions on natural gas pipelines, and on an electricity power line supplying Georgia from Russia, severely disrupted energy provision in large parts of the country (and Armenia); Azerbaijan supplied some gas in an emergency capacity.

15 February 2006: Parlamenti approved a non-binding resolution recommending the withdrawal of Russian peace-keepers and their replacement by an international force.

31 March 2006: Agreement was reached on the final details for the withdrawal of Russian forces from two military bases in Georgia (although not the Gudauta base in Abkhazia) at a meeting in the Russian city of Sochi.

31 March 2006: The Conservative, Industrialists Will Save Georgia, New Conservative and Republican opposition parties commenced a parliamentary boycott, after the mandate of Valeri Gelashvili of the Republican Party was revoked (for business activities incompatible with his political work).

23 May 2006: The leaders of Georgia, Ukraine, Azerbaijan and Moldova met in Kyiv, Ukraine, to revive the regional GUAM organization, renaming it the Organization for Democracy and Economic Development—GUAM.

21 July 2006: Giorgi Khaindrava was dismissed as State Minister, responsible for Conflict Resolution after his increasing criticism of the Minister of Internal Affairs, Merabishvili. The Government was constitutionally obliged to re-form, as the additional appointment of a new Minister of the Environment was the sixth reassignment since its formation; the new Council of Ministers contained only two new members and was approved on 24 July.

25 July 2006: Some 1,000 Georgian troops were deployed in the nominally Georgian-controlled part of the Kodori Gorge in Abkhazia, in order to subdue a paramilitary group led by a former Governor of that area, Emzar Kvitsiani. Following the successful restoration of control, the Georgian-endorsed Abkhazian Government-in-exile transferred its base from Tbilisi to the region.

29 July 2006: Irakli Batiashvili, leader of the opposition Forward Georgia! movement, was detained and charged with conspiring to assist Kvitsiani in overthrowing the Georgian leadership.

6 September 2006: Police arrested 29 activists from the Samartlianoba (Justice) Party and affiliated organizations, associated with Giorgadze, 13 of whom were charged with plotting a coup in order to facilitate Giorgadze's return to the country.

27 September 2006: Four Russian military officers and 11 Georgian citizens were detained by Georgian security forces on suspicion of espionage activities. In response, the Russian Ambassador to Georgia was recalled and a partial evacuation of Russian personnel was initiated; the issue of visas to Georgian citizens was also suspended. On 2 October the detained officers were handed over to the OSCE. However, Russia continued to deport large numbers of ethnic Georgians.

5 October 2006: In municipal elections contested by six political groups, the ruling United National Movement (UNM—established by a merger of the National Movement and United Democrats in November 2004) secured a overwhelming victory, with 66.5% of the votes cast nation-wide. The voter participation rate was 51.8%.

10 November 2006: Okruashvili, who was reported as having made controversial comments regarding South Ossetia, was dismissed as Minister of Defence and appointed Minister of Economic Development; he was replaced in his former role by Davit Kezerashvili. (One week later Okruashvili resigned from the Government.)

12 November 2006: A presidential election was conducted in those areas of South Ossetia controlled by the separatist authorities. Kokoyev was overwhelmingly elected to a second term in office, reportedly attracting 98.1% of the votes cast. The poll coincided with a referendum, in which voters were asked whether or not South Ossetia should preserve its de facto independent status. Results released by the separatist election commission indicated that 99% of those who voted had cast their ballots in favour of independence from Georgia; voter turn-out was reported to be 95.2% of the registered electorate. However, what was termed an alternative election for a regional President was held concurrently in those South Ossetian territories that remained under the control of the Georgian state; this poll was reported to have been won by Dimitri Sanakoyev, a former rebel leader. A referendum held in these territories also expressed approval, by an overwhelming majority, for the commencement of negotiations with the central authorities in Tbilisi on the establishment of a federal Georgian state, of which South Ossetia would form a part.

1 December 2006: Sanakoyev was inaugurated as President in the part of South Ossetia under the control of the Georgian state and announced the formation of a parallel administration, based in Kurta, north of Tskhinvali (where the separatist authorities of South Ossetia were located).

4 March 2007: In Abkhazia, elections were conducted to the 35-member legislature; however, in the initial poll candidates were elected in only 18 constituencies. On the following day the Abkhazian election committee upheld the parliamentary elections as legitimate, on the grounds that 48% of the electorate had participated. On 18 March a second round of voting was held for the 17 seats not filled in the first round.

10 May 2007: Sanakoyev became head of the new Provisional Administration of South Ossetia, officially established under a resolution by Parlamenti on 8 May.

13 July 2007: President Saakashvili established a new Joint Control Committee, which was to initiate dialogue between all authorities for settlement of the conflict in South Ossetia.

6 August 2007: The Georgian authorities issued an announcement urging the international community to condemn an alleged incident, in which two military jets had entered Georgian airspace from Russia and launched a missile against its territory, which had failed to explode and had landed outside the village of Tsitelubani, near South Ossetia. The Russian Government strongly denied the allegations; however, international experts subsequently confirmed that at least one aircraft had violated Georgian airspace from Russia.

7 September 2007: A government reorganization, effected by Saakashvili at the end of August, was approved by Parlamenti; changes included the appointment of the hitherto Minister of Energy, Nikoloz Gilauri, as Minister of Finance.

27 September 2007: Okruashvili, who had accused Saakashvili of corruption and having planned to murder a prominent businessman, Arkadi (Badri) Patarkatsishvili, was arrested on charges of money laundering, precipitating, on the following day, a large anti-Government rally outside Parlamenti. In early October Okruashvili publicly announced that he had withdrawn the accusations of criminal behaviour he had made against Saakashvili. (He stated that he had been forced to retract the accusations while in detention, and left Georgia, subsequently securing asylum in France.)

7 November 2007: Following five days of demonstrations outside the parliamentary building in Tbilisi, which were organized by an opposition alliance to demand Saakashvili's resignation, special police violently dispersed protesters; later that day the Government declared a national state of emergency.

8 November 2007: Saakashvili announced that an early presidential election would be held on 5 January 2008, con-

currently with a referendum to determine whether legislative elections should be brought forward.

16 November 2007: The state of emergency was ended by parliamentary decree; on the same day Saakashvili dismissed Noghaideli and nominated Vladimer (Lado) Gurgenidze, hitherto the Chairman of the Bank of Georgia, to the premiership.

25 November 2007: Saakashvili resigned the presidency, as required by the Constitution, in order to campaign for the forthcoming election; Burjanadze replaced him in an interim capacity.

5 January 2008: Saakashvili was re-elected with 53.5% of votes cast; Levan Gachechiladze, the joint candidate of an alliance comprising nine main opposition parties, secured 25.7% of votes. At the concurrent referendum, some 79.9% of votes cast were in favour of bringing forward legislative elections to be conducted between March and May 2008.

10 January 2008: Patarkatsishvili (who had fled to the United Kingdom in December 2007, after claiming that the Georgian authorities were planning his assassination) was charged *in absentia* with conspiring to overthrow the Government. In early February 2008 Patarkatsishvili died unexpectedly at his British residence; medical investigations concluded that he had died from natural causes.

20 January 2008: Saakashvili was inaugurated. A reorganized administration, approved by Parlamenti at the end of January, included new Ministers of Justice and the Economy, and a new Prosecutor-General, but retained most of the significant figures of the previous administration.

6 March 2008: The Russian Government decided unilaterally to end an economic embargo that the CIS had imposed on Abkhazia in 1996.

12 March 2008: Parlamenti (which had in February approved legislation providing for legislative elections to be brought forward to May) adopted further constitutional amendments, which reduced the number of legislative deputies from 235 to 150, of whom 75 were to be elected on the basis of proportional representation and 75 in single-member constituencies. On 21 March Saakashvili issued a decree scheduling the forthcoming elections for 21 May.

16 April 2008: Following requests by South Ossetia and Abkhazia for legal recognition in March, the Russian Government announced that it was to establish legal connections with the separatist authorities in both regions; the Georgian Government condemned the decision as a violation of international law.

18 April 2008: In an apparent attempt to improve relations, Russian President Putin announced that postal and visa restrictions on Georgia would be lifted, and discussions initiated to end the embargo on exports of Georgian goods, including wine and mineral water.

21 April 2008: The Georgian Government accused Russia of violating its airspace, after a fighter jet shot down a Georgian reconnaissance drone over Abkhazia on the previous day. Russia denied the Georgian claim, stating that an Abkhazian military aircraft had carried out the attack.

4 May 2008: The separatist Abkhazian authorities announced that two unmanned Georgian reconnaissance drones had been shot down over the region; the Georgian Government denied the claim.

5 May 2008: Saakashvili appointed Eka Tkeshelashvili, who had been appointed as Prosecutor-General in January, as Minister of Foreign Affairs, replacing Davit Bakradze, who had resigned in April in order to lead the UNM list of candidates in the forthcoming elections.

21 May 2008: According to official results, the UNM secured 59.2% of votes cast on a party list basis and 119 seats overall in the legislative elections, while the Joint Opposition alliance won 17.7% of votes and 17 seats. Although international observers generally upheld the election results, the opposition again accused the authorities of extensive electoral malpractice, and announced a boycott of the new Parlamenti.

31 May 2008: Russia dispatched 400 troops to Abkhazia, with the stated intention of repairing a railway line; the Georgian Government formally protested at the measure, claiming that it represented a direct violation of its sovereignty and territorial integrity.

30 June 2008: A bomb exploded in Sukhumi (following two explosions in the town of Gagra on the previous day), prompting the Abkhazian authorities, which claimed that Georgian special forces had perpetrated the attacks with the aim of destabilizing the region, to announce the closure of the border between Abkhazia and the rest of Georgia.

1 August 2008: According to the South Ossetian separatist authorities, six people were killed in a Georgian bombardment of Tskhinvali. The Georgian Government claimed that South Ossetian forces had initiated the hostilities. Exchanges of fire between Georgian forces and South Ossetian militia subsequently continued.

7 August 2008: A cease-fire declared by Georgia with South Ossetia early that day was cancelled, and it was announced that Georgian troops were engaged in an 'operation to restore constitutional order' throughout the region. Georgia launched an unexpected offensive against South Ossetia, which included an intensive air bombardment of Tskhinvali.

8 August 2008: The Georgian Government announced that its troops had entered Tskhinvali and secured control of most of South Ossetia. Russia dispatched large numbers of troops through the Roki tunnel to South Ossetia, where they engaged in hostilities with Georgian forces at Tskhinvali, stating that it sought to protect its citizens and peace-keeping troops present in the region, and alleging that Georgia sought to commit 'genocide' against South Ossetians. Russian aircraft commenced bombardment of Georgian targets, including the port of Poti and the military base at Senaki.

9 August 2008: Parlamenti approved a presidential decree declaring a state of war with Russia, and martial law within Georgia. The Russian military claimed to have gained control of Tskhinvali, expelling the Georgian troops, while the Russian air force bombarded the town of Gori, 76 km west of the capital. Despite US condemnation of Russian military action, the UN Security Council for the third time failed to adopt a resolution on the conflict. Abkhazian separatist forces began military action against Georgian troops present in the Kodori Gorge.

11 August 2008: Russia accused Georgia of continuing to launch attacks on Tskhinvali, despite having declared a unilateral cease-fire. The Russian air force bombarded the outskirts of Tbilisi. Russia began to deploy troops against Georgian forces in Abkhazia.

12 August 2008: Russian President Dmitrii Medvedev ordered an end to Russia's military operation in Georgia, claiming that its aims had been achieved. Georgia and Russia agreed to a peace plan, mediated by French President Nicolas Sarkozy (on behalf of the EU), providing for an immediate cease-fire, the provision of humanitarian assistance, and the withdrawal of Russian troops to pre-conflict positions. Although Saakashvili, Medvedev and the separatist leaders of Abkhazia and South Ossetia subsequently signed the agreement, Russia failed to implement fully the withdrawal of troops as stipulated, prompting NATO to suspend formal contacts with the country.

14 August 2008: Parlamenti voted unanimously in favour of Georgia's withdrawal from the CIS. Georgia subsequently informed the CIS Executive Committee of the decision (although it was to remain part of the body for a further year, in accordance with regulations).

24 August 2008: In the first consignment of supplies by sea, a US warship transporting humanitarian aid arrived at the Georgian port of Batumi. (Poti continued to be occupied by Russian troops.)

26 August 2008: President Medvedev endorsed a resolution, which had been approved in both chambers of the Russian legislature, officially recognizing South Ossetia and Abkhazia as independent sovereign states. Georgia, the USA and EU condemned the decision. (By September Nicaragua was the only other state to have recognized the two regions as independent states.)

29 August 2008: Georgia formally suspended diplomatic relations with Russia, in protest at the continued Russian occupation of South Ossetia and Abkhazia, and security zones around the two regions. The Russian embassy in Tbilisi was subsequently closed.

4 September 2008: During a regional visit US Vice-President Dick Cheney announced a US pledge of US $1,000m. in reconstruction aid to Georgia.

8 September 2008: Following further negotiations with an EU delegation led by President Sarkozy in Moscow, Russia agreed on additional measures for the implementation of the August cease-fire plan, principally the withdrawal of all remaining forces from Georgian territory (apart from South Ossetia and Abkhazia) within 10 days of the deployment of EU monitors (scheduled for 1 October).

17 September 2008: Russia signed friendship and co-operation treaties with the leaders of South Ossetia and Abkhazia, pledging to support the two regions militarily; the treaties also formalized economic co-operation between Russia and the regions.

26 September 2008: Parlamenti approved legislation imposing a number of restrictions on non-Georgian citizens in Abkhazia and South Ossetia, to remain in effect until Georgian jurisdiction was restored.

1 October 2008: In accordance with the 8 September agreement, some 200 EU monitors were deployed in Georgia, and were to observe the envisaged withdrawal of Russian forces from the security zones around South Ossetia and Abkhazia by 10 October. (Russia had announced that it was to maintain a total of 7,600 troops within the two separatist regions.)

9 October 2008: The Council of CIS Foreign Ministers made the decision officially to suspend Georgia's membership. (Georgia's full withdrawal from the organization was expected to take place in August 2009).

History

GEORGE TARKHAN-MOURAVI

EARLY HISTORY

Introduction

The early archaeological cultures of the South Caucasus (the Kura-Arax and the Trialeti) demonstrate a high degree of sophistication, and from early ancient times Georgia occupied a place in occidental and oriental historiography, folklore and mythology. Parallel to the kingdom of western Georgia (Egrisi, or Colchis to the ancient Greeks), situated along the Black Sea coast, in southern and eastern Georgia another state of Kartli (anciently known as Iberia) united tribes speaking the Kartvelian language. Georgian historic tradition dates the first attempt to unite the country under King Parnavaz (Farnavazi, Pharnabazus) of Kartli at the beginning of the 3rd century BC. Georgia became a battlefield for the continuous rivalry of Persia (Iran) and the Eastern Roman (later 'Byzantine') Empire. Christianity was adopted in Georgia in AD 334, when King Mirian III of Kartli-Iberia (Meribanes, 284–361) followed the instruction of St Nino of Cappadocia; the Georgian alphabet was created for translating holy texts. The first Georgian inscriptions appeared in Jerusalem in the 5th century, followed soon after by the first known literary text, the *Martyrdom of St Shushanik*. At about the same time, King Vakhtang Gorgasali founded the future capital city of Tbilisi, and managed briefly to unite east and west Georgia.

In 645 Tbilisi fell to the Arabs, who dominated the area for two centuries, before being superseded by the Byzantines, and later by the Seljuq Turkish sultanate, in the 11th century. A new dynasty, the Bagrationi, gained control of Inner Kartli and the city of Uplistsikhe, and in 978 King Bagrat III Bagration became the first king of both Kartli and Abkhazia, that is to say of both eastern and western Georgia. The ascent to the throne of David IV (the 'Restorer' or 'Builder', 1089–1125) was marked by victory over the Muslim coalitions at the Battle of Didgori in 1121 and the recapture of Tbilisi. Under the reign of Queen Tamar (1178–1212), Georgia's statehood reached its peak, but it also developed the first signs of weakness. It fell to the invasions of Jelal-ed-Din in 1225–27, which were followed by a Mongol raid in 1235. Only in 1314 was Giorgi V (the 'Brilliant') able to reunite Georgia, but, soon after, the invasions of the Turco-Mongolian leader, Timur 'the Lame' (Tamerlane, 1370–1405), finally broke Georgia's resistance. With the fall of the Byzantine capital, Constantinople, in 1453, Georgia remained the only Christian stronghold in the region, surrounded by Muslim kingdoms, which relentlessly invaded the country. Georgia fragmented into a number of kingdoms and principalities (among the most important of which were Imereti, in the west, and Kartli and Kakheti, in the east). In despair, in 1783 King Irakli (Erekle) II of the reunified Kartli-Kakheti (1762–98) signed the Treaty of Georgievsk, under the terms of which the kingdom became a Russian protectorate. Nevertheless, when the Persians invaded Tbilisi in 1795, Russia showed no willingness to help. Irakli II's successor, Giorgi XII, continued to negotiate with Tsar Paul (Pavel) I of Russia, but, upon his death in December 1800, the Tsar immediately declared the annexation of eastern Georgia. The decree of his successor, Tsar Alexander (Aleksandr) I, of 12 September 1801, finalized the issue, abolishing the kingdom.

Under the Russian Empire (1801–1917)

Having annexed Kartli-Kakheti, the Russian Government exiled the heir, David, and the royal family to Russia, and continued expansion. In 1804 King Solomon II of Imereti (the main principality of western Georgia) was forced to accept Russian sovereignty; subsequently, in 1810, he was captured and deposed, and he died in exile, in Turkey, in 1815. The leaders of other, smaller principalities showed little resistance to Russian conquest. Subsequently, the autocephaly of the Georgian Orthodox Church was abolished, and the Russian exarchate was imposed. Successful wars with Turkey and Persia confirmed Russian rule over the South Caucasus, or Transcaucasia. Between 1811 and 1877 the Russian army captured Sukhum-Kale, Poti, Akhalkalaki, Akhaltsikhe and Batumi. None the less, frequent mishandling of sensitive issues and local traditions by the Russian administration caused uprisings throughout the 19th century. Forceful Russian expansion caused the Muslim peoples of the North Caucasus to resort to military resistance. Russian forces, supported by Georgian militia, finally won the Great Caucasian War, which ended in 1864–65. Many Caucasian Muslims (*muhajirs*), including Abkhazians, left for the Turkish Ottoman Empire, dramatically altering the demographic balance. Muslims from Akhaltsikhe (Meskheti) and Adjara also emigrated.

With the appointment of the first viceroy, Mikhail Vorontsov (1845–54), Georgia integrated more rapidly into the Russian Empire. At the same time, a political movement emerged, aimed at protecting national identity and headed by the prominent poet Ilia Chavchavadze. The 1860s were marked by the emancipation of the serfs in Georgia, as elsewhere in the Russian empire. This caused further social differentiation and economic disaster for the majority of peasants. The politicization of society increased, creating a favourable environment for the development of socialist ideas. The first radical Marxist group, Mesami Dasi (Third Company), was created in 1892. Seven years later the Tiflis (Tbilisi) committee of the All-Russian Social Democratic Labour Party was formed, dominated by a Menshevik, legalist wing, led by Noe Jordania. It was opposed by the Bolsheviks, among whom Stalin (Iosif Dzhugashvili, or Ioseb Jughashvili) gradually acquired a leading position. On 1 August 1914 Russia entered the First World War, and the Russian Army proceeded deep into Turkey, occupying Kars, Ardahan and Eastern Anatolia. Following the abdication of Tsar Nicholas (Nikolai) II in March 1917, the Provisional Government nominated an executive in Transcaucasia, the Special Transcaucasian Committee (Ozakom), its power restricted by soviets (councils), which were controlled in Georgia by Mensheviks. While the latter supported central Russian government and the prolongation of the war, the Bolsheviks demanded peace at any price, demobilization and revolution. When, in November, the Bolsheviks seized power in Petrograd (now St Petersburg), the Georgian Mensheviks, the Armenian Dashnaks and the Azeri Musavatists immediately responded by creating an executive body, the Transcaucasian Commissariat, and, later, the Seim (the legislature). Following the signature of the Brest-Litovsk Treaty on 3 March 1918, the Bolsheviks ceded the districts of Akhaltsikhe, Akhalkalaki, Ardahan, Batumi and Kars to Turkey, and the Russian-Caucasian army withdrew. Transcaucasia had no means to resist Turkish advancement, and an armistice was negotiated. Under Turkish pressure, an independent Federative Republic of Transcaucasia was proclaimed. Disagreements between Armenians, Azeris and Georgians put an end to the federation only five weeks later. On 26 May the Georgian Democratic Republic declared its independence.

First Republic (1918–21)

In June 1918 the Georgian Soviet (Council) was dissolved, and Noe Jordania became the Prime Minister of a social democratic administration. The Government implemented limited land reform and nationalized mines and railroads. After a Georgian Government was created, a special agreement was signed with the German General, Otto von Lossow, establishing a German protectorate. Shortly after that, another agreement was signed, with Turkey, which recognized the loss of Akhalkalaki and Akhaltsikhe. When, in November, Germany was defeated in the First World War, Georgia's pro-German orientation became a definite disadvantage, as the British emerged as the dominant power in the region. The dissatisfaction of the peasants and Bolshevik propaganda caused several uprisings, until in 1919–20 peasants were given full land-ownership rights, although the nobility retained significant amounts of land. Still, ethnocentric policies continued to feed tensions among the non-Georgian population. In December 1918, owing to a territorial dispute, the Armenian army moved into Georgia, which retaliated, following early Armenian successes. Further fighting on the Armenian border was halted by British forces. Later, the British decided to limit their presence in Baku (Bakı—Azerbaijan) and Batumi. The British Foreign Office supported Georgia's independence at the Paris Peace Conference in January 1919, where Georgia received de facto recognition by the Allied Powers. In the mean time, a serious military threat was presented by the Volunteer Army of Gen. Anton Denikin, which attacked Georgian forces in the Sochi region in February.

During 1920 the geopolitical situation changed dramatically. Civil war in Russia came to an end, and Soviet authority in the Caucasus, the Caucasian Bureau (Kavburo), was formally established by Russia, under the leadership of 'Sergo' Ordzhonikidze (Orjonikidze). When the Bolsheviks organized uprisings in South Ossetia and Abkhazia, the People's Guard responded with violence. In April the Red Army occupied Azerbaijan and proclaimed it a Soviet Republic, and the Soviet Republic of Armenia was declared in December. Georgia was left undefended against Soviet expansion when, in July, the British withdrew their forces. Russia signed a peace treaty with Georgia on 7 May. Nevertheless, Ordzhonikidze and his unyielding supporters in Baku continued to insist on invasion, and, with the assistance of Sergei Kirov, then the ambassador to Georgia, they prepared the Bolshevik network for the inevitable takeover. On 16 February a Revolutionary Committee was formed by Bolsheviks in Georgia. The 11th Red Army entered Georgia from the east, and other troops moved in from Armenia and from Sochi. The Georgian Republic was officially recognized by the Western powers at the beginning of 1921, and on 25 February the Georgian ambassador plenipotentiary presented his credentials in Paris, France; on the same day, however, Russian troops, led by Ordzhonikidze, entered Tbilisi, and Georgia's brief period of independence came to an end.

Soviet Georgia

With the fall of Tbilisi, the Menshevik Government retreated to Batumi without any serious resistance, finally fleeing to Europe on 16 March 1921. On 21 May Georgia's Bolshevik Government signed a treaty with the Russian Soviet Federative Socialist Republic (RSFSR), and Georgia became a Soviet Socialist Republic (SSR). Most of the leading members of the Menshevik Party who remained in the country were arrested in January 1922. The opposition began preparing an anti-communist revolt, the Mensheviks, in alliance with the other opposition parties, forming the so-called Parity Committee, in order to co-ordinate their efforts. Uprisings in Guria, Kakheti and Svaneti in 1922–23 were brutally suppressed. The Georgian Church was also persecuted, and its head, Patriarch Ambrosi (Khelaia), was arrested and imprisoned. In February 1923 the internal police (Cheka) arrested and shot leading conspirators. Nevertheless, a rebellion started on 28 August 1924, but initial success was short-lived, and was followed by widespread executions.

A number of autonomies were created. Turkey's interests were taken into account when the Autonomous SSR of Adjara (Ajaria, Ajara), populated mainly by Muslim Georgians, was officially established along religious lines in July 1921. Although a provisional Abkhazian SSR was declared in May, on 16 December a special contract of alliance was signed between Georgia and Abkhazia, which defined Abkhazia's somewhat ambiguous status as the 'Contractual' SSR of Abkhazia; however, this was subsequently abolished in 1931, and Abkhazia became an autonomous republic within Georgia. The South Ossetian Autonomous Oblast (region), with its capital at Tskhinvali, was created on 20 April 1922. The external borders of Georgia were also changed, and certain territories passed to Armenia, Azerbaijan and Russia. The economic structures of Armenia, Azerbaijan and Georgia were integrated, and in March of that year the three republics merged into a Federal Union of SSRs of Transcaucasia. Later, in December, it was further transformed into a single republic, the Transcaucasian Soviet Federative Socialist Republic (TSFSR), with Tbilisi as its capital. Georgia entered the USSR as part of the TSFSR on 30 December.

During 1925–26 the political atmosphere temporarily eased. Growth, both in agriculture and industry, was discernible. However, in 1927 the Soviet leadership, disappointed by the New Economic Policy, shifted from individual farming to collectivization, and ordered severe measures to suppress resistance. Repression in Georgia increased after 1931, when Lavrenti Beria became the First Secretary of the Transcaucasian Committee of the Communist Party. On 5 December 1936 the new Soviet Constitution (the 'Stalin' Constitution) was adopted. The TSFSR was dissolved, and Georgia became a 'sovereign' Union Republic, in its own right. Mass repression continued, progressively applied to different sectors of the population. Many Abkhaz experienced subjugation, and inhabitants of the Georgian mountains were forcibly moved to Abkhazia to colonize depopulated land.

In 1941 Adolf Hitler, the German leader, ordered an invasion of the USSR. Although the Germans did reach the North Caucasus, Georgia was spared from the fighting. Shortly after achieving his first military successes, Stalin ordered the deportation of entire peoples for alleged treason. In late 1944, for example, some 90,000 Muslims from Meskheti were deported to Central Asia, overnight, in cattle wagons. Georgian losses in the war were also enormous. Up to 600,000 Georgians fought in the war, and more than one-half that number perished. Georgian prisoners-of-war passed by the Allied Forces to the Soviet security police (People's Commissariat for Internal Affairs—NKVD) found themselves in even worse conditions in Soviet concentration camps. A new wave of purges followed in 1947–53. Stalin's death in March 1953, however, changed the distribution of power in the Kremlin.

After Stalin

With the death of Stalin, the Georgian leadership was immediately reshuffled by Beria, now the leading political figure. However, he soon fell victim to a conspiracy led by Nikita Khrushchev, part of the new collective leadership of the USSR, and further personnel changes followed. At a closed session of the 20th Congress of the Communist Party of the Soviet Union (CPSU), held on 25 February 1956, Khrushchev devoted his speech to uncovering the crimes of Stalin and his 'cult of personality'. Many Georgians, however, were unhappy with the criticism of Stalin, who had been an ethnic Georgian; in March students celebrating the anniversary of Stalin's birth were brutally dispersed, causing numerous casualties.

The economic reform carried out by Khrushchev brought privation and disaster to Georgia. His arrest was ordered, and Leonid Brezhnev replaced him as General Secretary of the CPSU. However, little changed while Vasilii Mzhavanadze continued in power as the First Secretary of the Communist Party of Georgia (CPG). His uninterrupted 19-year rule (1953–72) was characterized by the development of an extensive parallel economy and the criminalization of society. In 1972 the republican Minister of Internal Affairs, Eduard Shevardnadze, presented evidence to the Soviet leadership in Moscow (Russia) of widespread corruption at all levels of the Georgian party and state bureaucracy. On 29 September Shevardnadze succeeded Mzhavanadze as the leader of the CPG, and proceeded to launch unrelenting campaigns against so-called 'negative phenomena'.

As was the case elsewhere in the USSR, the dissident movement started in Georgia with the dissemination of 'samizdat' (self-published) literature. In April 1977 a young philologist, Zviad Gamsakhurdia, the son of one of Georgia's leading novelists, was arrested, together with several of his comrades, accused of conducting anti-Soviet activities. Prior to closed legal proceedings, a recording of Gamsakhurdia's recantation was broadcast on television, representing an important victory for the secret services, and a reverse for emerging Georgian dissent. After a new Soviet Constitution was adopted in October 1977, the Supreme Soviet of Georgia considered a draft republican constitution; in contrast to the Constitution of 1937, however, Georgian was no longer declared to be the state language. Following a demonstration of protest during the parliamentary session of 14 April 1978, the first such manifestation since 1956, Shevardnadze contacted the central authorities and obtained permission to amend the Constitution.

In 1982 Leonid Brezhnev died. The one-year rule of his successor, Yuri Andropov, was characterized by the launch of campaigns against corruption and alcoholism, and brought damage to the Georgian economy, which was strongly dependent upon the production of wine and alcoholic liquors. The subsequent death of the elderly Konstantin Chernenko, who succeeded Andropov, opened the way for the dramatic metamorphosis of perestroika (restructuring).

THE NATIONALIST MOVEMENT

With the ascent to power in 1985 of the new Soviet leader, Mikhail Gorbachev, the first steps of his policies of glasnost (openness) and perestroika, as his programme of gradual political and economic reform came to be known, brought immediate changes to the distribution of power in Georgia. At the beginning of July Shevardnadze was appointed Soviet Minister of Foreign Affairs, and his former deputy, Jumber Patiashvili, became First Secretary of the CPG.

Dissident and liberal ideas became combined with those of nationalism in the following years. One particularly sensitive area was the protection of the natural environment, which, being ideologically relatively safe, rapidly attracted the attention of the emerging political opposition. The most debated issues were proposed projects to construct a railway tunnel through the Caucasian range to link Vladikavkaz, in Russia, with Tbilisi, and to build the Khudoni hydroelectric power station on the Inguri (Enguri) river, although both were soon abandoned, partly owing to insufficient resources. Zviad Gamsakhurdia, a political outsider since his recantation, gradually gained unprecedented popularity, owing to his overtly anti-communist rhetoric and nationalist slogans. Dangerous tensions emerged inside Georgia, as nationalism was considered a growing threat by ethnic minorities. Abkhaz and Ossetians linked their hopes to support from Russia and the prolongation of the USSR, and demanded their incorporation into the Russian Federation, causing protests among ethnic Georgians. At the end of March and the beginning of April 1989 a number of demonstrations took place, initially directed against Abkhazian secessionism, but later extending to general demands for Georgian independence. On 9 April armed forces were used to disperse a group of protesters, as a result of which some 20 people died. National passions intensified, and in mid-1989 there were new, violent clashes in Sukhumi (Sukhum—the principal city in Abkhazia), and many casualties.

The actions of communist leaders further radicalized the national movement, already fully dominated by Gamsakhurdia. Elections to the Supreme Soviet (Supreme Council) of Georgia took place on 28 October and 11 November 1990, and brought victory to the nationalist, anti-communist Round Table-Free Georgia bloc, led by Gamsakhurdia, which obtained 64% of the votes cast, while the CPG took only 29%. Meanwhile, in September the South Ossetian Supreme Soviet had issued a unilateral declaration of sovereignty as a republic. South Ossetia boycotted the all-Georgian parliamentary elections, and, instead, parliamentary elections were held in that region on 9 December. The new parliament in the region's capital, Tskhinvali, immediately subordinated itself to the direct control of the all-Union authorities in Moscow; the Sakartvelos Parlamenti (Georgian Parliament) responded by abolishing the region's autonomy. Clashes began in and around Tskhinvali, and Gamsakhurdia, by that time Chairman of the Supreme Soviet, introduced a state of emergency. Fighting, with sporadic cease-fires, continued throughout 1991, and the continuous shelling of Tskhinvali and neighbouring Ossetian and Georgian villages, accompanied by a disastrous earthquake, left large areas in ruin.

When, in March 1991, a referendum on Gorbachev's concept of a renewed union treaty took place, Georgia refused to participate and, instead, held its own referendum on independence. Subsequently, the Georgian Supreme Soviet declared the country's independence on 9 April, thereby becoming the first republic to secede from the USSR. A few weeks later, on 26 May, Gamsakhurdia became the elected President of Georgia, with 86.5% of the votes cast.

INDEPENDENT GEORGIA

Although Gamsakhurdia secured the full support of the ethnic Georgian population, his nationalist rhetoric alienated him from both non-Georgians and the intelligentsia. His lack of managerial skills and haphazard personnel policies created enemies even among those who had been friends, such as the former Prime Minister, Tengiz Sigua, and the Minister of Defence, Tengiz Kitovani. His economic policies were even less successful, and the country gradually moved towards financial catastrophe. At the same time, most of the Soviet organizational legacy was preserved, and even the collective farms were retained under the euphemistic title of 'people's enterprises'. In August 1991 the attempted coup against Gorbachev in Moscow demonstrated Gamsakhurdia's lack of strength and unwillingness to adopt a clear position, provoking severe criticism from all sides. The opposition demanded Gamsakhurdia's resignation and accused him of authoritarian rule. Anti-Gamsakhurdia sentiments mounted after violence was used to disperse a demonstration by the opposition National Democratic Party. The Government gradually lost control of the military, and mass arrests of members of the opposition Mkhedrioni (Horsemen) militia, led by Jaba Ioseliani, only prolonged the crisis. Gamsakhurdia's rhetoric and policies, together with a general reluctance among Western powers to provoke Russia, caused full international isolation.

Georgia sent observers to a meeting held in Almaty, Kazakhstan, on 21 December 1991, at which the leaders of 11 former Union Republics of the USSR agreed to form the Commonwealth of Independent States (CIS). Georgia, however, refused to join the new structure. The same day, the Georgian opposition, led by Sigua and Kitovani, began concentrating tanks and other weaponry, received or purchased from the Soviet army, around the presidential residence in the centre of Tbilisi. On 22 December armed conflict began, causing significant casualties and severely damaging the surrounding area, while Gamsakhurdia and his Government sought refuge in the basement of the building. Ioseliani was released from prison, and the Mkhedrioni joined forces with Kitovani's troops. After 10 days of fluctuating success, the opposition succeeded in acquiring a significant amount of weaponry from Russia, and consequently tightened the siege. On 2 January 1992 Gamsakhurdia was declared deposed by the opposition. He fled first to Armenia, and then to Chechnya, in Russia. A Military Council was formed to replace the Government, headed by Kitovani and Ioseliani, with Sigua acting as premier.

POLITICAL DEVELOPMENTS

The Military Council encountered great difficulties in managing the country, and Gamsakhurdia's supporters (or 'Zviadists') organized armed resistance in western Georgia. In an attempt to increase their legitimacy, the former Soviet Minister of Foreign Affairs, Eduard Shevardnadze, was invited to Georgia as Chairman of the State Council, a structure created in March 1992 to replace the Military Council in legislative and executive matters. In October he was elected Chairman of the Supreme Council and Head of State, as emphatically as Gamsakhurdia had been one year previously. However, leading Georgia towards stability was a difficult task, as real control was held by the military leadership. Moreover, the country's integrity was threatened by civil war, and separatist conflicts in Abkhazia and South Ossetia. Former President Gamsakhurdia launched an offensive in September 1993, when Georgian forces were defeated by Abkhazian units supported by the Russian army and by volunteers from various regions of the North Caucasus. To prevent the partition of Georgia, in October Shevardnadze was forced to accept the assistance of Russian troops and to commit Georgia to entering the CIS. In early November Gamsakhurdia and his supporters fled to the mountains, after being defeated at their main base, Zugdidi, and Gamsakhurdia died shortly afterwards under mysterious circumstances, reportedly committing suicide. On 3 February 1994 Georgia and Russia signed a 10-year Treaty on Friendship, Good-Neighbourliness and Co-operation. One year later, a further agreement provided for the establishment of four Russian military bases in Georgia. Thus, Russia's dominant role in the region was acknowledged, although neither treaty was ever ratified.

On 24 August 1995 the Supreme Council adopted Georgia's new Constitution, providing for a strong executive presidency and a 235-seat, unicameral parliament. Five days later, Shevardnadze survived an assassination attempt. In early October the Minister of State Security, Igor Giorgadze, was named as the principal instigator of the plot, and he subsequently escaped to Russia by military aircraft. In May 1996 Ioseliani, the leader of the Mkhedrioni, was convicted of complicity in the assassination attempt. On 5 November 1995 Shevardnadze won 75% of the votes cast in a presidential election, and his Citizens' Union of Georgia (CUG) secured a decisive majority in Parlamenti. He immediately assumed full control, and attempted a new reorientation towards the West. This represented a turning-point in Georgian politics. Along with political stabilization, an economic revival began, and the rate of growth was over 10% annually in 1996–97. However, the Russian economic crisis of 1998 had dire consequences for the Georgian economy, causing growth to decelerate to a virtual standstill.

A new Government was announced in December 1995, with Nikoloz Lekishvili appointed Minister of State, a post that replaced that of Prime Minister; following his resignation in July 1998, he was replaced by Vazha Lortkipanidze. The parliamentary elections of October 1999, and the presidential election of April 2000, although far from fully democratic, demonstrated once more the strength of Shevardnadze's position against the fragmented opposition, which was mostly concentrated around the Chairman of the Adjaran Supreme Council and the leader of the Union for the Revival of Georgia, Aslan Abashidze. The CUG obtained 41.9% of the votes cast in the legislative elections, securing 130 of the 235 seats available in the legislature, and Shevardnadze was re-elected as President with 79.8% of the votes cast.

None the less, a significant problem for the Shevardnadze Government remained that of achieving a settlement of the conflict in Abkhazia, and returning the hundreds of thousands of people displaced as a result to their homes. Even more urgent was the need to improve the country's overall economic performance and to combat the overwhelming corruption that was destroying economic confidence. The President's family was widely believed to control the larger part of Georgia's scarce economic resources, and Shevardnadze's popularity declined significantly after 2000, as did that of the ruling party, the CUG, in which divisions increased between the older generation of former communist functionaries, and the younger and more energetic 'reformist' wing. As a result, the President resigned from the party's chairmanship. He also reorganized the Government, removing a number of reformists, and finally dismissed the entire cabinet at the beginning of November 2001. At the same time, the opposition was again closing ranks around Abashidze, although it lacked both unity and popularity, and Abashidze himself showed little activity.

Severe crises in both the Government and the governing political party were followed by significant changes to all branches of power. Nino Burjanadze replaced Zurab Zhvania as parliamentary speaker in November 2001, following which Zhvania gave open support to the opposition, resulting in a split within the CUG. In June 2002 the Minister of State appointed in December 2001, Avtandil Jorbenadze, was elected Chairman of the embattled CUG, but events had already served to demonstrate the party's dramatic loss of support. The CUG was unable to surpass the 4% threshold required to secure seats on Tbilisi City Council at the local government elections, held in early June 2002. Overall, despite numerous electoral violations (in particular, in the cities of Rustavi and Zugdidi), the elections demonstrated a shift in public sympathy towards the pro-US New Conservative Party, which had been established in 2000 by former members of the CUG, Levan Gachechiladze and Davit Gamkrelidze, and which represented business interests; the populist, leftist Georgian Labour Party, led by Shalva Natelashvili; and other reformist descendants of the CUG, led by the former Minister of Justice, Mikheil Saakashvili, and the former parliamentary Chairman, Zurab Zhvania, who established, respectively, the radical, nationalist National Movement and the more moder-

ate, centrist United Democrats, both of which were strongly pro-Western. As a result of an agreement between Natelashvili and Saakashvili, the latter was elected to the position of Chairman of the Tbilisi City Council in November 2002.

Meanwhile, in mid-October 2002 Shevardnadze and the Catholicos-Patriarch of the Georgian Orthodox Church, Ilia II, signed a constitutional agreement between the state and the Church, which was intended to regulate the legal relationship between the two sides and, in particular, provided for compensation for the moral and material damage experienced by the Church under Soviet rule. However, religious life in the country was far from harmonious. Although the majority of the population were adherents of the Orthodox Church, violence by extremist groups of Orthodox zealots toward confessional minorities marred the tradition of religious tolerance in the country, and drew protests from international human rights and religious freedom organizations.

The parliamentary and presidential elections, scheduled to take place in November 2003 and in 2005, respectively, posed a clear challenge to the opportunistic, corrupt Government of the ageing Shevardnadze, and his hold on power. Shevardnadze's term was due to end around 18 months after the legislative elections, and there was no clear scenario for a transfer of power that could maintain the status quo in the event that pro-Government parties lost these elections. Throughout 2002–03 preparations for the legislative elections increasingly influenced the political climate of Georgia. The pro-Shevardnadze CUG, under the leadership of Jorbenadze, began to consolidate support in order to improve its performance, becoming the core of the new political bloc, For a New Georgia, which attempted to use its administrative leverage to unite those opportunistic opposition elements that had declined in popularity over the preceding months, such as the Socialist Party of Georgia and the National Democratic Party of Georgia. There were political battles over voting arrangements, such as the composition of the Central Election Commission (CEC) and the creation of voter lists. In early June 2003 the main opposition parties, in an attempt to pressurize the Government, organized political rallies on electoral issues, while student associations mounted anti-Government actions, under the slogan 'Kmara' (Enough), formed along the model of the Serbian uprising in 2000, and reputedly with international support (e.g. from the prominent US philanthropist George Soros), at which demands were made for Shevardnadze's resignation. Meanwhile, the popular legislative Chairman, Nino Burjanadze, appealed to the US Administration to ensure that free and fair elections took place.

GEORGIA AFTER THE 'ROSE REVOLUTION'

The parliamentary elections held on 2 November 2003 represented a test of the willingness of the country's Government to proceed further in the process of democratic transition. International pressure mounted, demanding that the elections be held fairly, with an unending sequence of high-profile political visitors reiterating this demand. At the same time, it became clear that if the elections were to be held fairly, the ruling élite had next to no chance of winning, and would have to choose between fraud or an end to their privilege and power. Elections, when they finally took place, were perceived universally to have been fraudulent, even if the opposition's winning margin, according to the exit polls, was not high. The opposition, led by the triumvirate of Saakashvili, Burjanadze and Zhvania, worked to transform the frustration that electoral malpractice had created, together with the general dissatisfaction with the state of affairs in the country and endemic government corruption, into mass demonstrations that ultimately led to the resignation of President Shevardnadze on 23 November. The opposition leaders conducted a modern, politically-aware coup, by involving and invoking the international media in their activities. It was notable that, from the very beginning of the uprising, the West, and the USA in particular, explicitly demonstrated its dissatisfaction with the incumbent leadership and supported the victorious opposition.

Thus, in November 2003 Georgia moved to what some have labelled a 'post-post-Soviet' era. The events shattered the very basis of the post-Soviet establishment, and marked the emergence of a new generation of politicians, unburdened by the

Soviet legacy, and often more fluent in English than in Russian. On 4 January 2004 the election (with more than 96% of the votes cast) of the young, new President, Mikheil Saakashvili, took place. In February the post of Prime Minister was restored. Parliamentary elections were held successfully on 28 March, although observers reported an increase in procedural violations in comparison with the presidential election. The National Movement-United Democrats, together with their coalition partners, won the majority of the party-list votes (67.3%), while only one other political force, the Rightist Opposition (a coalition of the New Conservative Party and Industry Will Save Georgia), was able to pass the 7% barrier (with 7.5% of the party-list votes) required to achieve parliamentary representation. (In November 2004 the National Movement and United Democrats officially merged to form the United National Movement—UNM—headed by Saakashvili.)

Subsequently, dramatic events took place in Adjara, where confrontation with Aslan Abashidze reached its peak approximately 100 days after Saakashvili's inauguration as President on 25 January 2004. The Adjaran leader had armed his militia and vowed to fend off any attempt by the central Government to curb his regime. The culmination of tension took place when Abashidze issued an order to blow up three major bridges and train tracks linking Adjara with the rest of Georgia, under the pretext of unavoidable military intervention. This proved to be a tactical error, and, amid mass demonstrations in Batumi (the principal city in Adjara), soldiers in Abashidze's militia began to lay down their arms and to join the demonstrators. On 5 May Abashidze agreed to resign, following a meeting with the Russian envoy, Igor Ivanov, who also had been involved in Shevardnadze's resignation.

The resignation of the Adjaran autocrat advanced Saakashvili's position by creating the first step toward restoring Georgia's territorial integrity. Another very important consequence was that the central state regained control of much-needed tax funds from the strategic border crossing with Turkey, and the Batumi cargo port. New elections in Adjara followed on 20 June 2004; the National Movement, registered under the name of Saakashvili—Victorious Adjara, dominated the campaign, and secured 28 of the 30 parliamentary seats, while the Republican Party won the remaining two, prompting the latter's withdrawal from the ruling coalition. Subsequently, legislative changes largely reduced Adjara's autonomy to a formality.

Significant public support for the new Government provided favourable conditions for decisive reforms and actions, following a period of political stagnation, and a more unwavering pro-Western political orientation. However, the ensuing progress was not without some dramatic developments. On 3 February 2005 the Prime Minister, Zurab Zhvania, died in what some considered to be suspicious circumstances; his death was officially concluded to have been caused by carbon monoxide (CO) poisoning resulting from a domestic gas leak, although further examinations did not show the level of CO in his blood to be sufficiently high to cause death. Five days later, President Saakashvili nominated Zurab Noghaideli, a former Minister of Finance, as Zhvania's successor. However, the change of leadership did not remedy the fundamental lack of team spirit, co-ordination or shared reform strategy in the Government; this had been revealed frequently in controversial actions such as flawed privatization tenders and an attempt to sell the main natural gas pipeline passing through Georgia from the north to the Russian state-controlled monopoly Gazprom, which had been prevented following strong pressure from the USA.

Significant achievements were observed in economic and fiscal reform. Georgia's economy received a strong impetus from the construction of the Baku–Tbilisi–Ceyhan (Turkey—BTC) crude oil pipeline, which came on stream in late May 2006. Meanwhile, the South Caucasus gas pipeline started operations in January 2007. As a partner country in the project, Georgia was expected to receive 300m. cu m of natural gas, or 5% of the total flow from Azerbaijan en route to Erzurum, Turkey. Apart from the evident economic benefits, the pipelines added enormously to the geo-strategic importance of Georgia.

The new Government focused on stabilizing the economy, eliminating corruption, and bringing order to the budget. The first phase of stabilization yielded impressive results, with growth of around 6% in 2004, and just under 10% in the subsequent years. Indeed, despite the external shock associated with the economic blockade established by Russia (see Foreign Affairs, below), according to the IMF, the Georgian economy grew by 9.4% in 2006 and was projected to grow by 10% or more in 2007. Foreign direct investment also increased dramatically. Simplified tax legislation, introduced in 2004, and improved tax collection resulted in a sharp increase in budget revenues. The Government started addressing long-standing issues in the energy sector and implementing a strategic planning exercise by introducing a medium-term expenditure framework.

There were also notable achievements in policies: clearing pension and salary arrears; reform in the social assistance and pension system; and more government involvement in social protection for vulnerable groups. Radical reforms in school education, and the introduction of national examinations for university education could also be considered as constituting important progress. Religious minorities enjoyed more freedom, and a decrease in violence directed against them. The Government also made some advances in more intensively promoting the integration of regions populated by minority ethnic groups.

However, there were also some difficulties associated with the under-developed democratic and civic culture found in the country, and with the dangerous domination of a single political power. Consequently, although the law protecting freedom of speech in Georgia is considered strong by international standards, journalists and opposition groups claimed that legislation had not increased security for journalists. Authorities allegedly pressurized local media and used indirect measures to influence the content of published or broadcast material. Owing to a weak economic base and a small market, media outlets depend on subsidies linked to various economic and political interests. Media operating outside the capital are especially vulnerable. In particular, most broadcast stations rely on government support because of a lack of advertising revenue. A surprise development took place in the media market in August 2006, when the international media company News Corporation (owned by the Australian-born US citizen Rupert Murdoch) formally became a partner to Georgian Imedi Holding, after an agreement was signed reportedly involving some 30% of shares. This represented the first example of foreign investment in the Georgian media sector, with initial hopes that it could lead to the strengthening of its independence and diversity.

Particularly disturbing were the still frequent human rights abuses, and the lack of civil control over military and law-enforcement bodies, which led to numerous violations, in particular by police in places of detention and during arrests (by masked police officers), which were carried out with virtual impunity. Public outcry led to a high-profile court case and demands for the resignation of the Minister of Internal Affairs, Ivane Merabishvili, following the murder in January 2006 of a young banker, Sandro Girgvliani, by high-ranking police officers. Equally disturbing was the excessive brutality with which, in mid-March, riots in a Tbilisi prison were suppressed in a 'special operation' that left seven inmates dead and at least 17 injured. The judiciary continued to be subject to the strong influence of the executive branch, its powers having been radically eroded by the constitutional amendments of 2004. In a particularly striking case, four Supreme Court judges were dismissed in December 2005 in what seemed to be a political decision. The trial of opposition politician Irakli Batiashvili has also been subject to much criticism. In May 2007 Tbilisi City Court convicted Batiashvili on charges of providing 'intellectual assistance' to Emzar Kvitsiani, a rebel leader of a paramilitary group in the Kodori Gorge region of Abkhazia, and sentenced him to seven years' imprisonment.

Social protection expenditure increased from 7% of GDP in 2004 to 19% in 2007, and defence expenditure rose from an estimated 1.6% to 3.5% of GDP during 2004 alone, with a strong emphasis on increasing military numbers. The downsizing of the armed forces advocated in the late 1990s by the

International Security Advisory Board (ISAB) of Western advisers was reversed, in contradiction of previous statements by President Saakashvili that Georgia needed a small, efficient military able to inter-operate with troops of the North Atlantic Treaty Organization (NATO). In August 2006 President Saakashvili declared that Georgia should be ready to mobilize 100,000 reservists in 48 hours if necessary. The legal limit for the number of troops was also increased from 23,000 as of January 2006, to as high as 37,000 in July 2008. The rapid growth in the military budget also continued, and in July 2008 Parlamenti approved an amendment to the 2008 state budget, which envisaged the increase of the total funding of the Ministry of Defence to 1,395m. lari. According to the Stockholm International Peace Research Institute, Georgia throughout mid-2000s had the highest average growth rate of military spending in the world, although its overall military expenditure was still significantly smaller than that of its neighbours, Armenia and Azerbaijan.

Parlamenti, dominated by the UNM, routinely approved most of the legislative initiatives of the executive. The frustrated opposition announced on 7 April 2006 that it was to boycott parliamentary sessions, in an attempt to boost its influence in national politics. Four elements from the normally fractured opposition factions: the New Conservative Party; Industry Will Save Georgia; and the Democratic Front (uniting deputies from the Republican Party of Georgia and the Conservative Party of Georgia) joined forces to take part in the boycott and presented a list of demands to Parlamenti and President Saakashvili, which specified the resignation of Merabishvili, the investigation of the alleged employment of covert 'death squads' by the Ministry of Internal Affairs, and the complete reorganization of the ministry, as well as direct elections for mayors and regional governors.

The political opposition was disconcerted by President Saakashvili's unexpected decision to bring forward the date of local elections, scheduled to be held in December 2006, to 6 October, with less than six weeks' notice. Particular political importance was ascribed to the election of the mayor of Tbilisi, which accounted for one-third of the country's population. Previous legislation, adopted in 2005, stipulated that the capital city's mayor (who had hitherto been appointed by the President) was to be elected by the Tbilisi City Council (Sakrebulo, controlled by the UNM), rather than directly by voters, allowing the ruling party to strengthen its control over the city administration. This highly unpopular reversal of demands made by the National Movement (while in opposition to Shevardnadze) for the direct election of local government officials had revived political debate over Saakashvili's commitment to democratic reform. Additional controversy surrounded the restructuring of the CEC to include members with ties to the incumbent Government.

Five candidates contested the mayoralty on 6 October 2006, including the incumbent Mayor, Giorgi Ugulava, and Salomé Zurabishvili, former Minister of Foreign Affairs, subsequently leader of the opposition party Georgia's Way. The UNM won 34 of the 37 seats in the Tbilisi City Council, ensuring that Ugulava was re-elected to the post. The UNM received 77.1% of the votes cast throughout the country; Georgia's Way failed to meet the requisite threshold for representation on any local council, receiving just 1% of total votes cast. In October President Saakashvili announced the submission of a proposal to Parlamenti that the next presidential election be held simultaneously with legislative elections in 2008, some eight months in advance of its due date. This was perceived as an attempt to manipulate the elections' outcome, the democratic credentials of which were regarded as being under threat, as numerous misstatements, a poor human rights record, and strengthening authoritarian tendencies had led to a certain decline in the popularity of President Saakashvili and the ruling party.

However, by late 2007 no political opposition was strong enough to challenge the full political dominance of the governing élite, despite widespread frustration with the unsteady process of democratic reform. As a result, the only politician successfully to challenge Saakashvili's popularity was the Minister of Defence, Irakli Okruashvili, known for his 'hawkish' policies. In November 2006 Okruashvili was moved to a

less influential position to head the Ministry for Economic Development, and was replaced as Minister of Defence by Davit Kezerashvili. After a few days in the new position, Okruashvili resigned, and prepared to take a new role in the political opposition. One year later, in September 2007, he was arrested on charges of money-laundering, shortly after having announced the formation of a new party, the Movement for a United Georgia, and after having publicly accused Saakashvili of involvement in corruption and in plans to murder a prominent businessman. In October Okruashvili withdrew the accusations of criminal behaviour he had made against Saakashvili, and also confessed to criminal charges; soon afterwards, Okruashvili was released on bail, and was allowed to leave for Germany, where he repeated his previous accusations. (Eventually, after a Georgian court found Okruashvili guilty of embezzlement, and sentenced him *in absentia* to 11 years' imprisonment in March 2008, he obtained political asylum in France, which rejected the extradition demand by Tbilisi.) This scandal served further to incite widespread public dissatisfaction. While there was significant economic growth (from a rather low base), the incidence of poverty, and particularly of extreme poverty, has not changed much, while the gap between the new rich and the poor was growing. Based on the excessive concentration of presidential power, tensions between democratic and autocratic elements were never properly reconciled, and eventually led to mass protests in October–November 2007. In January 2007 Saakashvili had signed into force a series of constitutional amendments, stipulating that presidential and legislative elections were henceforth to be conducted simultaneously; this had the effect of bringing forward the next presidential election to late 2008 and extending the mandate of Parlamenti. The opposition, although objecting to the measure (which was widely viewed as an attempt to keep the ruling élite in power), had little leverage until protests were prompted by the scandal over the arrest of Okruashvili and the suspicious retraction of his accusations against Saakashvili, which few regarded as sincere. Another factor of change was related to the billionaire and co-owner (with Murdoch) of the most popular television channel, Imedi TV, Arkadi (Badri) Patarkatsishvili, who supported some of the opposition parties, having decided openly to oppose Saakashvili's Government; Imedi TV played a leading role in rallying protests. The arrest of Okruashvili and his short-lived retraction of the accusations shocked public opinion and emboldened the opposition, and mass protests were staged to demand Okruashvili's release and the reform of the presidential system. As the focus of demands shifted to a general anti-Government sentiment, a demonstration, held on 2 November, was attended by some 50,000 protesters, many of them travelling from the provinces. A 10-party opposition alliance, the National Council of the General Public Movement, presented joint demands to the Government and the President, foremost among which was a demand for the organization of early elections.

By 7 November 2007 the demonstrations had already lost much of their popularity, as the demands were hardly appealing to the public. On that day, however, the Government made the decision to disperse the gathered people, which resulted in police taking highly violent action using tear-gas, water cannons, rubber bullets and batons against basically peaceful protesters. Many protesters were hospitalized or arrested. The authorities declared a national state of emergency, under which all public gatherings were prohibited. Police seized control of the offices of Imedi TV, and all broadcasting channels other than those controlled by the state were closed. Not for the first time, Saakashvili increased his anti-Russian rhetoric, accusing some opposition leaders of collaborating with the Russian intelligence services, while three Russian diplomats were expelled from Georgia, accused of having instigated mass protests.

However, the violent action against peaceful protesters caused both domestic public outcry and international criticism, with many Western Governments and international organizations openly criticizing the disproportionate use of violence. As a result, the Government appeared to have little choice other than to make concessions to the opposition. On 8 November 2007 Saakashvili pledged that an early presidential election would be conducted on 5 January 2008 (which would hardly allow the opposition sufficient opportunity to prepare), and would be accompanied by a referendum to determine the timing of the legislative elections.

The state of emergency was officially ended on 16 November 2007, while most of those arrested during the turmoil were released; on the same day Saakashvili dismissed Noghaideli and nominated Vladimer (Lado) Gurgenidze, hitherto the Chairman of the Bank of Georgia, to the premiership. On 22 November Parlamenti endorsed the appointment of a largely unchanged Government. In accordance with the Constitution, Saakashvili resigned as President prior to the elections, and the Speaker of Parliament, Nino Burjanadze, became acting Head of State on 25 November.

The opposition coalition (now numbering nine parties) welcomed the initiative, and appeared able to present a joint candidate to contest the forthcoming presidential election; Levan Gachechiladze, a well known businessman and parliamentary deputy, was popular among younger voters but viewed with suspicion by many Western experts, due to his lack of political experience and strategy. Financial support was provided by Patarkatsishvili, before scandalous tapes revealing his intentions of post-elections violence discredited him as a possible political ally. In early January 2008 Patarkatsishvili, who, despite claiming that he was in danger of assassination, himself contested the presidential election, was charged *in absentia* with conspiring to overthrow the Government. A few weeks later, Patarkatsishvili unexpectedly died in the United Kingdom. (Despite immediate speculation that he had been assassinated, medical investigations concluded that he had died from natural causes.)

Both international and local observers noted numerous preelectoral violations, such as unfair use of mass media, and the abuse of administrative resources (including promises of, or actual increases of, salaries for teachers, higher pensions, distribution of vouchers, the employment programme) to secure public support. Four days after the disputed election on 5 January 2008, Saakashvili was declared by the CEC to have won about 53.5% of votes cast (despite Gachechiladze having taken the majority of votes in the capital); overall, Gachechiladze received 25.7% of votes. Ballot papers additionally included two plebiscites; a (non-binding, advisory) question on whether Georgia should join NATO received the support of some 77.0% of voters, while about 80% of votes were cast in favour of the legislative elections being conducted between March and May 2008.

The opposition continued to claim electoral malpractice, and opposition supporters demonstrated in Tbilisi on 13 January 2008, in protest at Saakashvili's re-election and to demand a recount of the results. Despite continuing protests, Saakashvili was inaugurated for a second term as President on 20 January. However, international support strengthened Saakashvili's standing, while his tactical skills subsequently proved useful in organizing legislative elections with much greater success. On 24 January, Saakashvili reorganized the Government, in an attempt to meet the demands of the opposition and the public, bringing into the administration some new professionals who were not affiliated formally with the ruling party. However, the opposition dismissed these changes as cosmetic, since the most unpopular figures in the Government, including Merabishvili as the Minister of Internal Affairs, retained their positions.

Legislative elections on 21 May 2008 resulted in a further victory of the ruling UNM, which secured 59.2% of votes cast on the basis of party lists, and enjoyed even greater success in the single-mandate constituencies. As a result, 119 deputies, of a total of 150, were members of the UNM. Five parties were admitted to Parlamenti. The opposition, apart from elected deputies of a small, newly established Christian Democratic Movement (which won about 8.7% of votes), headed by Giorgi Targamadze, refused to accept their parliamentary mandates, accusing the Government of further electoral malpractice.

Finally, instead of stability and democracy, as a result of political processes after November 2007, Georgia has a virtually single-party legislature fully controlled by the executive power, a weak and corrupt judiciary, and electronic media controlled by the incumbent Government. Also, since property rights remain insecure and justice arbitrary, there continued to be grounds for serious concern over the direction of reform. After initial unconditional support from the West, the state of democracy in Georgia began to attract increasing criticism, while the authoritarian tendencies of its leadership did not evoke the same positive appraisal on the part of international leaders as previously. The culmination of these tendencies found their ultimate realization before and during the conflict in August 2008 (see below).

INTER-ETHNIC CONFLICT

Inter-ethnic conflict dominated the internal politics of Georgia throughout the first half of the 1990s. Adjara was the least troubled of Georgia's self-governing regions. However, discontent increased in the early 1990s, as a result of proposals to abolish Adjaran autonomy and convert the Muslim population to Christianity, and relations between Aslan Abashidze and Eduard Shevardnadze continued to worsen.

Although comprising around 70% of the inhabitants of South Ossetia, the Ossetians, an Indo-European people, were considered to be relatively recent immigrants, and their autonomy to have been created artificially by Soviet power. Inter-ethnic relations deteriorated in 1989, as a result of Ossetian demands for reunification with North Osetiya (Ossetia), a nominally autonomous republic within the Russian Federation. Renewed violence began when the South Ossetian Supreme Soviet declared itself the 'Soviet Republic of South Ossetia' in December 1990, provoking legal conflict and, subsequently, the dispatch of Georgian police and paramilitary troops. Fighting continued until 24 June 1992, when Shevardnadze and the Russian President, Boris Yeltsin, signed the 'Agreement on the Principles of the Settlement of the Georgian–Ossetian Conflict between Georgia and Russia' aimed at ending the conflict, and introducing instruments such as a quadrilateral Joint Control Commission (JCC) peace-keeping force (comprising Georgians, South Ossetians, Russians and North Osetiyan representatives) to restore peace and maintain law and order in the zone of conflict.

A tense peace was established and no significant military action took place subsequently, although the issue of the future status of South Ossetia, active mediation by the Organization for Security and Co-operation in Europe (OSCE) notwithstanding, remained unresolved. In December 1997 the South Ossetian parliament voted, once again, in favour of independent status for the region, within the CIS. Nevertheless, economic relations between the two sides were developing, refugees had begun to return to their homes, people travelled more freely, and the prospects for a political solution continued to improve.

Throughout much of Shevardnadze's rule, the situation in South Ossetia gradually stabilized, with greater freedom of movement for the population and a tacit allowance for the separatist region to sustain its economy by trade, mainly involving the smuggling of various goods, such as petroleum products and alcohol from Russia, through the Roki tunnel. However, with the election in November 2001 of Eduard Kokoyev (Kokoiti), a Russian citizen strongly supported by the Russian authorities, as President of the self-proclaimed republic, relations became more strained, and a quick political solution became less probable. The majority of the residents of South Ossetia had been issued with Russian passports, thereby creating a pretext for Russian intervention in the interest of protecting its newly-created citizens. However, Saakashvili made the restoration of Georgia's territorial integrity a high political priority.

A further contentious development related to the decisive measures of the Georgian Government to curb smuggling and abolish the major venue for marketing the smuggled goods, the Ergneti market near Tskhinvali. Tensions were exacerbated by a greater inflow of weapons and armed groups into the region from Russia, while the central Georgian Government amassed interior ministry troops and established road blocks in an attempt to control these developments. For much of July and August 2004 clashes between the two sides led to dozens of casualties killed and wounded on both sides. In August the Georgian legislature adopted a non-binding decision to revoke the mandate of the Russian peace-keepers on the basis of their partisanship and to encourage international involvement in the peace-keeping effort. At the same time, Saakashvili appealed to world leaders to convene an international conference on the conflict, and requested that the USA, the European Union (EU) and the OSCE should participate in high-level negotiations, a position vehemently opposed by Russia. Georgian troops were withdrawn a few days later to the city of Gori, a short distance from the conflict zone, and an uneasy peace was established.

In late January 2005 President Saakashvili used a visit to the Council of Europe as an opportunity to address a session of the Parliamentary Assembly of the Council of Europe (PACE) and present proposals for the peaceful settlement of the conflict, which involved a power-sharing arrangement to allow South Ossetia broad autonomy. However, the proposal was immediately rejected by South Ossetia's President Kokoyev, who stated that Georgian proposals for broader autonomy were irrelevant, as 'South Ossetia has already determined its own status', while holding consultations with the Russian leadership in Moscow. Another effort was made by President Saakashvili in July, at an international conference in Batumi on the settlement of the Georgian–Ossetian conflict, where he announced that Georgia was ready to start talks on South Ossetia regaining its autonomous status, and disclosed further details of his plans for a three-stage conflict settlement. However, the South Ossetian leadership, which had already obstructed the conference, showed little enthusiasm, while Russia continued to consolidate its position in the breakaway region.

In July 2005 the legislature in South Ossetia voted to appoint a Russian citizen, Yurii Morozov—previously a commercial director at the Kursk petroleum company, with little, if any, relation to the region—as their new premier. Kokoyev proposed his own peace plan in December 2005. The three stages of his plan, not unlike the Georgian proposals, were: demilitarization, confidence-building and security guarantees; social and economic rehabilitation; and political settlement. It also called for a working group to elaborate a joint South Ossetian-Georgian conflict resolution plan. No resolution was achieved, however, mainly owing to mutual distrust and the lack of political will, combined with militarization on both sides.

None the less, certain positive developments followed a meeting of the UN-sponsored joint Co-ordinating Council in May 2006 in Tskhinvali. Agreement was reached on the establishment of a committee to merge the Georgian and Ossetian peace proposals for South Ossetia. In addition, the Council agreed on a list of projects that was later presented at the donors' conference that took place in Brussels, Belgium, in June. This first ever international donors' conference for South Ossetia yielded just over the expected €10m., a significant sum for the impoverished region—and all the more so given the Georgian Prime Minister's pledge to match it exactly and thus double the amount of assistance. The funds donated were intended to fund the rebuilding of essential infrastructure in the conflict zone and adjacent areas. However, the more belligerent statements by political figures on both sides continued to underscore the deep divisions between Georgia and the Ossetian separatists, giving little grounds for optimism.

Events took a rather unexpected turn on 12 November 2006, when two sets of presidential elections and status referendums were held in South Ossetia. The poll held in the territories controlled by the separatist regime in Tskhinvali overwhelmingly reconfirmed Kokoyev in office and reiterated the commitment of the region's population to separation from Georgia. The alternative poll, administered from the Georgian-controlled village of Eredvi in the zone of conflict, but in the settlements (on the territory of the former Autonomous Oblast of South Ossetia) under the control of Tbilisi, resulted in Dimitri Sanakoyev, an ethnic Ossetian with a record of military action against the Georgian authorities and of involvement with the previous separatist administration, being elected as an alternative President. Neither of these elections were recognized by the international community nor by the Georgian authorities, but, in an attempt to change the status quo peacefully, in May 2007 Parlamenti approved a resolution, based on an earlier (13 April) 'Law on the Creation of Appropriate Conditions for Peaceful Settlement of the Conflict in the

Former Autonomous Oblast of South Ossetia', establishing a new 'temporary administrative unit', of which Sanakoyev was duly appointed head. On 10 May he addressed the Parlamenti in his new capacity, stating that the Ossetian people's future was 'only within a democratic and stable Georgia'. The Georgian Government actively promoted the international recognition of Sanakoyev, with his administration located in the village of Kurta, around 5 km from Tskhinvali, as an equal participant in peace negotiations. A commission had been created to determine the legal status of South Ossetia within the Georgian state, although the Kokoyev-led administration categorically refused to take part in this process. Still, the main challenge for the new approach was to gain legitimacy for Sanakoyev's administration among Ossetians in those areas under the control of the separatist administration. Tension continued subsequently, with sporadic skirmishes and incidents of shooting preventing any normalization of the situation in the region. A particular issue of contention related to the use of water supplied by pipes that passed through territories controlled by both of the effective authorities in the region.

The security situation in and around South Ossetia (as well as Abkhazia) started to rapidly deteriorate after a NATO summit meeting, conducted in Bucharest, Romania, on 2–4 April 2008, where Georgia (and Ukraine) were refused the granting of the coveted Membership Action Plan (MAP), due to Russian pressure and the cautious attitude of some European nations (Germany and France, in particular).

In a surprising subsequent move, on 18 April 2008 outgoing Russian President Putin issued instructions to the Russian Government regarding the 'protection of the rights and interests of the peoples of Abkhazia and South Ossetia', declaring recognition of documents issued by the authorities of South Ossetia and Abkhazia, which would legalize the bodies of the secessionist governments, and effectively ascribe to the respective regions the same status as the internal regions of the Russian Federation. Relations between Tbilisi and Moscow, always tense, deteriorated sharply, after Georgia accused Russia of increasing interference in the affairs of South Ossetia and Abkhazia.

Tensions rose, when, in early July 2008, an explosion in the South Ossetian village of Dmenisi killed a separatist police chief, and a mine attack on a convoy transporting Sanakoyev injured three Georgian policemen near Tskhinvali. An incursion of four Russian aircraft over South Ossetia, on 8 July, became the first incident in which Russian Government openly confirmed its aircraft having entered Georgian airspace in order to avoid military confrontation. On 15 July Russia launched a large-scale military exercise, Kavkaz-2008, in the immediate vicinity of the Georgia's northern border. The Russian authorities referred to the exercise as a counter-terrorism measure, which was also aimed at preparing the troops for peace-keeping operations. Tensions escalated further, with sides in South Ossetia exchanging heavy artillery fire in early August. The South Ossetian leadership announced that it was prepared to bring in volunteers from the North Caucasus and Russia, while a Russian air-force Commander announced readiness to assist the Russian peace-keeping troops in South Ossetia if needed. After the completion of the Kavkaz-2008 military exercise on 2 August, Russian troops remained in their positions by the Georgian border. In a demonstration of preparations for war, the South Ossetian separatist authorities announced the start of evacuation of women and children to the neighbouring region of North Osetiya—Alaniya, within Russia.

When Kokoyev refused on 6 August 2008 to participate in bilateral peace talks with the Georgian authorities, as announced by the Russian chief negotiator in South Ossetia, Yurii Popov, it became clear that military confrontation was imminent. Exchanges of fire between the Georgian-controlled villages of Avnevi and Nuli and the Tskhinvali area became a dominant feature of the situation. Former Russian officer Anatolii Barankevich, head of the 'South Ossetian Security Council', announced that armed volunteers from Russia were travelling to South Ossetia to fight the Georgian invasion.

Although President Saakashvili was, on many occasions, urged by Western politicians not to be led into military confrontation with Russia, despite provocations, he failed to heed that advice. On 7 August 2008 the Georgian Government announced a cease-fire in order to defuse tension and offered to begin negotiations with the South Ossetian separatist regime. However, when, a few hours later, several Georgian-controlled villages came under heavy fire from the South Ossetian side, the Georgian Government announced that it was to take concerted military action 'to restore constitutional order' in South Ossetia. While the majority of international leaders were in Beijing, People's Republic of China, to attend the Olympic Games, war began in South Ossetia (see below).

The Abkhaz (an ethnic group related to the Circassians, a neighbouring people in the north-west Caucasus), having been decimated by migration to Turkey in the 1860s, constituted, before the outbreak of conflict, no more than 19% of the total population of Abkhazia, whereas Georgians represented approximately 46%. Following outbreaks of violence in the region from 1989 onwards, the violence intensified on 14 August 1992, when Georgian troops, ostensibly for the purpose of releasing hostages and protecting rail communications, entered Abkhazia and captured the capital, Sukhumi, forcing the Abkhazian leadership to evacuate. One month later Abkhazian forces, reportedly assisted by volunteers from Russia, launched a counter-offensive and occupied northern Abkhazia. In July 1993 Russia and the UN brokered a trilateral agreement providing for a cease-fire and demilitarization. However, in September Abkhazian forces launched an unexpected attack, taking Sukhumi and defeating the Georgian forces after 11 days of fighting. Georgian troops were driven from most parts of Abkhazia, excluding the Kodori Gorge, and large numbers of the Georgian population fled. On 14 May 1994 a cease-fire agreement was declared, providing for about 1,300 CIS (predominantly Russian) peace-keepers to be deployed in the border zone, in addition to UN military observers. Meanwhile, the Abkhazian legislature adopted a 'Republican' Constitution, declared sovereignty and appointed Vladislav Ardzinba as President. Under Georgian pressure, CIS leaders, meeting in Moscow in January 1996, imposed an economic blockade on Abkhazia. Relations improved slightly thereafter, but in May 1998 hostilities were resumed in the Gali district, where the Georgian population had begun to resettle, demonstrating the fragility of the peace. Negotiations continued, but the most sensitive issues, concerning Georgian refugees and the future status of Abkhazia, proved difficult to resolve. An additional concern was the activity of Georgian guerrillas, presumably supported by the Government, in Gali and the Kodori valley, which presented a permanent threat to both the Abkhazian population and the authorities. The revival of civil conflict in Chechnya, from late 1999, significantly altered the disposition of forces and interests in the region. While negotiations were proceeding at a slow pace, the fragility of peace in Abkhazia was demonstrated in August–September 2001 when, in addition to Georgian guerrillas, between 500 and 900 Chechen rebels were reported to have gathered in the Kodori Gorge to fight against the same Abkhazians that they had supported so strongly eight years previously. Clashes between Abkhazian forces and guerrillas followed throughout October, and military aircraft, apparently of Russian origin, bombed the Kodori Gorge region on 9 October.

In February 2002 the UN submitted a draft document on principles for the 'Distribution of Competences between Tbilisi and Sukhumi', which had been agreed between members of the UN Secretary-General's 'Group of Friends' on Georgia (comprising France, Germany, Russia, the United Kingdom and the USA), and which was to have served as a basis for negotiations. However, the Abkhazian party, under the 'hardline' premier Anri Dzhergenia, refused officially to receive the document. On 29 November Dzhergenia was dismissed by Ardzinba, appointing Gennadii Gagulia in his stead; none the less, the attitude toward the UN document did not change considerably. Meanwhile, Russia augmented its contacts with Abkhazia, issuing Russian passports and, on 25 December, unilaterally resuming railway connections from the Russian Black Sea port of Sochi to Tbilisi, via Sukhumi, thereby causing additional tensions in relations with Georgia. However, during a meeting between President Vladimir Putin of Russia and Shevardnadze, held on 7 March 2003 in Sochi, with the participation of Gagulia, it was agreed to co-ordinate the restoration of the railway connection through Abkhazia with the parallel return of internally displaced persons to Gali, Ochamchire and other regions of Abkhazia. The participants also decided to carry out several projects aimed at increasing energy production, through the rehabilitation of the Inguri hydroelectric power station and the construction of several new energy complexes. The Georgian Government was ready to compromise, in order to achieve at least symbolic progress in negotiations with the Abkhaz side, prior to the forthcoming parliamentary elections. As a result, in mid-2003 progress was already evident in negotiations over the return of refugees to the Gali region, and the overall situation appeared more positive.

The difficult change of leadership in Sukhumi that took place after the presidential election in October 2004 prompted a new political dynamic there. The first ever contested presidential election in Abkhazia was marred by the Russian Government's open support for one of the candidates, Raul Khadzhimba, who had a security service background. The incumbent 'President', Ardzinba, also supported Khadzhimba's candidature. When Abkhaz voters rejected Khadzhimba in favour of the more popular opposition leader Sergei Bagapsh, Abkhazia suffered two months of political crisis, which verged on the brink of mass violence. As Bagapsh announced his upcoming inauguration, Moscow exerted enormous direct pressure, sending officials to Sukhumi and closing the border, until an unexpected compromise was reached. A new election was held on 12 January 2005, which was effectively won by an alliance of the recent rivals, with Bagapsh becoming 'President' and Khadzhimba accepting the role of 'Vice-President'. However, Russia continued its controversial policy of explicit support for the secessionist region. Putin went so far as to meet both Bagapsh and South Ossetia's Kokoyev during his stay in the Black Sea resort of Sochi in April 2005. None of the secessionist leaders, backed by such a powerful patron, demonstrated any interest in discussing issues other than economic co-operation with the Georgian Government, or any inclination to relinquish their claims for independence.

Still, in March 2006 the Georgian authorities and those in Sukhumi agreed to resume bilateral consultations within the framework of the UN-sponsored Geneva process, and it was decided to revive the Georgian-Abkhaz Co-ordinating Council (which deals with security, economic, and refugee issues), which was reconvened in May for the first time since 2001. International developments continued, however, to influence the situation in Abkhazia. In particular, proposals under discussion within the UN for the eventual independence of the majority ethnic Albanian province of Kosovo from Serbia (a traditional ally of Russia) led the leadership of both Abkhazia and Russia to cite any such grant of independence as a precedent that could be applied to permit the recognition of Abkhazia's independence. Consequently, while Russia threatened to block any UN decision on Kosovo that would stipulate its independence, Russian President Putin has repeatedly drawn a parallel between the causes for independence in Kosovo and in Georgia's breakaway regions that are under Russian military protection. On the other hand, this led Georgia to look for ways to boost its claims over its secessionist regions, mainly through creating or strengthening alternative governments. In July 2006 a crisis erupted in the Kodori Gorge, a remote and mountainous stretch of Abkhazia under Georgian control. Emzar Kvtisiani, appointed as an envoy to the Kodori Gorge in 1999 by President Shevardnadze, in which capacity he had formed an armed militia known as Monadire (Hunters), issued an open challenge to the Georgian leadership, declaring that the Monadire would not permit government troops to move into the Gorge. The Government dispatched a large detachment of police and security forces to disarm the defiant paramilitary leader, and the mutiny quickly subsided, with Kvitsiani allegedly escaping to Sukhumi, and then to Russia. (The Monadire were disbanded officially in April 2005.) Whatever the reasons for this incident, it ended with the strengthening of Georgian control over the region, and the resumption of monitoring in the area by the UN observer mission. The crisis also prompted the relocation of the Abkhazian Government-in-exile (headed by Teimuraz Mzhavia), hitherto largely a formal structure based in Tbilisi, to Kodori, which was henceforth referred to officially as Upper Abkhazia. Notwithstanding the extremely negative response from the leadership of both Abkhazia and Russia, rapid construction and rehabilitation works were instituted in the village of Chkhalta in order to create the conditions for the officially sanctioned Government's operation.

However, on 11 March 2007 it was reported that a Russian helicopter had violated Georgian airspace and fired a missile at the building of the new administration in Chkhalta, accompanied by a barrage of rocket fire from neighbouring hills, causing an outcry from the Georgian authorities, although Russia denied any involvement in the attack. Several months later a joint fact-finding group of the UN Observer Mission in Georgia (UNOMIG) issued a report into what it termed 'the rocket firing incident'. While the report, prepared with Russian involvement, is somewhat inconclusive and does not directly name Russia as a perpetrator of the attack, it does state clearly that only an air-based missile could have been used in the attack, and that only a helicopter flying from Russian territory could have launched such a missile.

In the mean time, elections took place in Abkhazia in March 2007 to its separatist legislature, the 35-member 'National Assembly', as a result of which the position of the incumbent administration was strengthened. However, on 9 July 2007 the region's 'Prime Minister', Aleksandr Ankvab, was subject to an assassination attack, the fourth such attempt on his life in three years. As a close ally of Bagapsh, Ankvab also supported greater political distance from Russia, and this attempt on his life demonstrated the continuing volatility of the political situation in Abkhazia.

Apart from the developments in the Kodori Gorge, there have been other strains on Abkhaz–Georgian relations. The formation, by the Georgian leadership, of a 'patriotic' youth camp close to the administrative border with Abkhazia, in the village of Ganmukhuri, appeared to be a particularly sensitive issue. This latter event even caused strong criticism on the part of the UN Secretary-General, Ban Ki-Moon, who in mid-2007 urged the parties to avoid actions that would lead to additional tension in the region. A further development at this time that introduced considerable uncertainty was the announcement that the 2014 Winter Olympic Games are to be held in the Russian Black Sea resort of Sochi, near the border with Abkhazia. A proposal by Russia that Abkhazia could provide infrastructure for the Games was expected to represent a potentially destabilizing factor in the conflict.

Kosovo's declaration of independence from Serbia on 17 February 2008, and its subsequent recognition by major Western powers (opposed by Russia) precipitated a change of Russian policy in the Caucasus. A few weeks later a deputy chairman of the Russian Duma Committee on CIS and Compatriot Affairs suggested that it was time to move towards formal Russian recognition of the independence of Abkhazia and South Ossetia.

In March 2008 President Saakashvili announced a new peace proposal for Abkhazia, which was largely similar to the one presented in 2006, but with some new elements. In addition to the offer of 'unlimited autonomy', it also entailed: the creation of a Georgian-Abkhazian free economic zone in the Gali and Ochamchire districts of Abkhazia; amendment of the Georgian Constitution to create the post of Vice-President, which would be held by an Abkhaz; a veto right by Abkhazia on decisions of the central authorities that could negatively affect the region's constitutional status; and unspecified security guarantees. Also, Saakashvili demanded that the Abkhazian police force become gradually subsumed into the national police. Bagapsh immediately rejected Saakashvili's offer, describing it, or any reference to 'autonomy', as 'unacceptable' and as 'propaganda' issued prior to the NATO summit meeting in April. The Abkhazian Government declared no intention of embarking on any talks with Tbilisi on 'political issues', and ruled out talks on other issues while Georgian troops remained in the Kodori Gorge.

On 6 March 2008 Russia decided unilaterally to abolish the CIS-imposed trade embargo on Abkhazia introduced in 1996, and in April announced that legal relations were to be established with Abkhazia and South Ossetia. Amid strong protests from Georgia, and relatively half-hearted Western objections, both Abkhazian and Russian authorities began to accuse

Georgia of preparing a military intervention in Abkhazia. In April a Russian aircraft shot down an unmanned Georgian reconnaissance drone over Abkhazia, prompting renewed protests from Georgia. In early May Russia began to deploy additional forces of heavily armed peace-keepers and paratroopers in the area, arguing that this did not exceed the maximum quota of 3,000 peace-keeping troops. However, this was assessed by the Georgian Government as an act of aggression, while leading Western states condemned Russia's actions as constituting deliberate provocation. While there were some hopes after a visit of Georgia's UN ambassador, Irakli Alasania, to Sukhumi on 11–12 May, not long before the legislative elections in Georgia, nothing was achieved. On 15 May the UN General Assembly adopted a resolution recognizing the right of return of all refugees and internally displaced persons to Abkhazia. While Russia opposed the text proposed by Georgia, the USA voted for the resolution; most Western European states abstained. Delegations of EU and US officials subsequently visited Tbilisi and Sukhumi in attempts to diffuse tension and avert conflict, demonstrating a more active position in conflict resolution efforts. Nevertheless, at the end of May the Russian Government dispatched about 400 troops to repair a railway line south of Sukhumi, in an act that was denounced by Georgia as a further territorial violation, which was aimed at improving the transport infrastructure in Abkhazia in preparation for a military intervention. As tensions rose, on 30 June–1 July the Abkhazian authorities closed the region's border with the rest of Georgia, as further escalation appeared inevitable.

From their inception, the conflicts in Chechnya (1994–96 and from 1999) represented a serious threat to stability in Georgia. In August 1999 President Yeltsin requested consent to fly military missions to Chechnya from Russian bases in Georgia. Although this request was firmly rejected, Russia made further attempts to secure Georgian support in the conflict. Significant numbers of Chechen refugees moved across the Georgian–Russian border to the Pankisi Gorge, which had been traditionally home to an ethnic Chechen population. The Pankisi region became a permanent concern for the Georgian Government, owing to its limited control of the area and the increasing instability there, characterized by frequent kidnappings and drugs-trafficking. Accusations by Russia that Pankisi had become a base and training site for Chechen rebels were not formally substantiated by OSCE observers initially, but Georgia subsequently admitted the presence of Chechen militants there. According to official Georgian estimates, there were about 800 militants in the region in 1999–2002 (prior to the launch, in August–September 2002, of an operation to reassert control over the area—see below). Indeed, in July 2002 incursions into Georgia by Chechen militants brought Russia and Georgia to the brink of war.

From 2000 there were cases of the accidental shelling of Georgian villages by Russian aircraft, and there were fears that, following the suicide attacks on the mainland USA of 11 September 2001, the emerging internationalization of the fight against terrorism might serve as a pretext for the Russian military to attack Pankisi and thus further aggravate the situation there. Finally, following repeated accusations by the Russian side of the presence in the Pankisi Gorge of militants linked to the al-Qa'ida (Base) organization (held responsible for the attacks on the USA), in February–March 2002 the US Administration of George W. Bush resolved to assist the Georgian military in consolidating its capacity to undertake counter-terrorist operations, through the implementation of a special Train and Equip programme, with the allocation of US $64m. The principal group of US military instructors arrived in Georgia in May 2002, and trained several detachments of Georgian élite security forces, with a special focus on anti-terrorist operations. Nevertheless, Russian pressure on Georgia was mounting, and air raids and bombings of Georgian territory became increasingly frequent.

Tension increased further after Georgian border guards captured 15 Chechen militants trespassing on the Chechen–Georgian border, and refused to extradite all of them to Russia. As a result of increased external pressure, and in an attempt to subdue continued lawlessness in the Pankisi Gorge, at the end of August 2002 the Georgian authorities dispatched servicemen of the Ministries of Internal Affairs and of State Security to Pankisi Gorge, establishing checkpoints throughout the area, while the 'anti-criminal operation' was supported by army units. The troops re-established control over the Gorge and arrested several suspects, although the majority of Chechen militants were believed to have left the area in advance. Although the situation had begun to stabilize, on 11 September (symbolically linking the situation with the first anniversary of the suicide attacks on the USA) President Putin issued an ultimatum, stating that if Georgia did not implement immediate measures to improve the Pankisi security situation, Russian forces might consider unilateral military action. The resulting international criticism led Russia to moderate its position, while the success of the Georgian Government's security operation led to the gradual shift of the Pankisi issue to the periphery of bilateral relations with Russia. Some 2,000 Chechen refugees are estimated still to reside there, while the remainder had largely moved on to third countries.

On 11 July 2007 Parlamenti, after many years of delay, adopted legislation on the repatriation of the Muslim Meskhetians (often referred to as Meskhetian, or Akhaltsikh Turks). The Meskhetians are a Muslim Turkophone group deported from southern Georgia to Soviet Central Asia by the Soviet regime in 1944 on charges of treason through alleged collaboration with Germany and Turkey in the Second World War. One of the conditions for Georgia's admittance to the Council of Europe in 1999 was that the Meskhetians seeking to return to Georgia would be repatriated by 2011, and Georgian aspirations to further European integration were an important factor leading to the repayment of this outstanding moral debt. However, following the domestic political crisis in late 2007, the repatriation process was effectively suspended, and was not expected to be resumed soon in the aftermath of the Georgian–Russian conflict of August 2008.

FOREIGN AFFAIRS

Although Georgia declared its independence in April 1991, initially it had difficulty in securing international recognition. When Shevardnadze returned to Georgia in March 1992, however, the situation changed. In April Germany opened an embassy in Tbilisi, soon followed by the USA, Turkey and Russia. Georgia also started actively to seek participation in international organizations. After joining the Conference on Security and Co-operation in Europe (now the OSCE) in March 1992 and the Black Sea Economic Co-operation (now the Organization of the Black Sea Economic Co-operation), it finally become a member of the UN, the IMF and the World Bank in May–July 1992.

While trying to establish bilateral relations with all the newly independent states, Georgia avoided joining the CIS until the disastrous situation that resulted from defeat in Abkhazia obliged Shevardnadze to request membership in October 1993. Russia preserved four military bases in Georgia and participated in peace-keeping operations in both Abkhazia and South Ossetia, prompting Georgian politicians to accuse the Russian leadership of supporting secessionist forces and misusing military bases to destabilize its domestic situation. The Russian political élite, too, was dissatisfied with Georgia's gradual reorientation towards the West, its emerging role as an alternative transportation route for Caspian petroleum and with Georgia's unwillingness to become involved in the Russian–Chechen conflict. Moreover, although a bilateral Treaty on Friendship, Good-Neighbourliness and Co-operation was signed with Russia in February 1994, it was never ratified by the Russian Gosudarstvennaya Duma (State Duma—the lower chamber of Russia's parliament, the Federalnoye Sobraniye—Federal Assembly).

In the late 1990s Georgia increasingly sought to develop stronger relations with the West, and the USA provided significant assistance to Georgia at critical times. In March 1998 Georgia and the USA signed an agreement on military and security co-operation, reflecting the US commitment to the provision of special assistance to Georgia. Cordial relations were also established with the EU, as expressed by an agreement on partnership and co-operation, which was signed in April 1996. In April 1999 Georgia became a member of the

Council of Europe, and two months later, at a celebration in Luxembourg to mark the initiation of a partnership and co-operation treaty between the EU and the three South Caucasian states, Shevardnadze officially declared Georgia's intention to join the EU.

However, Georgia's relations with the Council of Europe were not without problems, as some of the obligations agreed on accession had not been met. In January 2005 PACE adopted a resolution advising Georgia, among other things, to: reconsider the recently adopted autonomous model for Adjara, in line with the rather critical opinion of its advisory body on constitutional issues, the European Commission for Democracy through Law (Venice Commission); accelerate the repatriation of the Muslim Meskhetian (Meskhetian Turk) population; ratify the Revised European Social Charter and the Framework Convention for the Protection of National Minorities; review the 'plea bargaining' system, which allowed some alleged offenders to use the proceeds of their crimes to buy their way out of prison, while creating the risk of its arbitrary, abusive and even politically motivated application; and, in particular, consult Council of Europe experts over recent constitutional amendments relating to the appointment of judges to the Supreme Court and the Constitutional Court, in order to ensure their compatibility with Council of Europe standards and principles. The majority of the recommendations were heeded, and, among other developments, Georgia finally ratified the Framework Convention in late 2005.

Although Georgia refused to renew its participation in the CIS Collective Security Treaty, it became an associate member of the NATO Parliamentary Assembly. In July 1997, moreover, Shevardnadze attended a NATO summit meeting held in Madrid, Spain, and participated in the work of the Euro-Atlantic Partnership Council (EAPC), and the Georgian Government openly expressed its willingness further to integrate into NATO. In November 2002 Georgia formally applied for membership of the Alliance at the NATO summit in Prague, Czech Republic: this intention was strongly endorsed two years later by the new Georgian Government at the June 2004 NATO summit in İstanbul, Turkey. An Individual Partnership Action Plan (IPAP) for Georgia was approved by the North Atlantic Council at the end of October 2004, and the process of Georgia's adjustment to NATO standards subsequently accelerated. In January 2005 the Alliance opened a liaison office in the Georgian Ministry of Defence. In May 2006 Parlamenti approved a resolution expressing support for Georgia's aspirations to NATO membership. Three weeks later NATO's Parliamentary Assembly adopted a resolution noting Georgia's 'significant progress' in implementing the goals set out in the IPAP and endorsing the initiation of an Intensive Dialogue—the next stage in co-operation—with Georgia. This was a step toward Georgia's intention to graduate to a Membership Action Plan, a decisive measure for fuller integration.

Georgia's participation in international peace-keeping efforts was an important part of its foreign policy. From 1999 Georgia dispatched peace-keeping troops to Bosnia and Herzegovina, and the Serbian province of Kosovo. Georgia also sent troops to Iraq, where around 850 mostly combat troops remained deployed in 2006, and to Afghanistan. In March 2007 Georgia declared that it had decided to raise further the number of its soldiers in Iraq to a 2,000-member contingent.

Co-operation with the neighbouring countries of Azerbaijan and Turkey increased in the 1990s, linked to common interests in both security and the transportation of petroleum from the Caspian Sea to the West. A pipeline to transport petroleum from Baku to the Georgian Black Sea port of Supsa began to operate in April 1999, and a project to construct two larger petroleum and natural gas pipelines, extending from the Caspian to Turkey, was under way. In late May 2003 construction work on the Georgian stretch of the vast Baku (Azerbaijan)–Tbilisi–Ceyhan (Turkey) petroleum (BTC) pipeline commenced, and was completed in early 2005. The pipeline became fully operational in May 2006, delivering the first petroleum shipments to the port of Ceyhan. This was to be followed by the construction of the Shah-Deniz (Baku–Erzurum) gas pipeline via Georgia to Turkey. Putting both pipelines into operation might help Georgia to escape its dependence on Russian energy supplies, a situation that had often been used to gain political leverage. (In early July 2005 Russian politicians approved an appeal to Russian Prime Minister Mikhail Fradkov, suggesting price increases on gas supplied by Russia to the supposedly hostile states of Estonia, Georgia, Latvia, Moldova and Ukraine, as well as to demand repayment of debts owed to Russia by these countries.) Overall, much of Georgia's future development appeared to be linked to international transportation projects, including the EU-sponsored Transport Corridor Europe–Caucasus–Asia (TRACECA—the 'Silk Road') agreement, which aimed to develop an East–West trade route, and seemed to be becoming reinvigorated after several years of slowdown. Among the latest developments were a highway linking Georgia with Armenia and Turkey, under construction as a part of the US Millennium Challenge programme, and the controversial (owing to Armenian objections) planned railway, connecting Kars in Turkey with Baku in Azerbaijan, via Akhalkalaki, agreement on the details of which was reached in October 2006. On 7 February 2007 Georgian President Saakashvili hosted President Ilham Aliyev of Azerbaijan and Turkish Prime Minister Reçep Tayyip Erdoğan in Tbilisi at a trilateral summit on strengthening regional co-operation, ending with the final agreement on the Baku–Kars railway. Construction of the project was estimated to cost about US $5,000m. and was scheduled to begin in late 2007, with completion expected by the end of 2009. The new route was to service a cargo capacity of 20m. metric tons per year.

When, in addition to the doubling of natural gas supply prices in January 2006, explosions in the Russian Republic of North Osetiya—Alaniya later that month severed two gas pipelines to Georgia, speculation emerged that Russia might be using energy for political leverage. Simultaneously, the electricity transmission line in Russia's southern Karachai-Cherkess Republic—also near the Georgian border—was brought down by an explosion. As a result, gas supplies to Georgia (and Armenia) were suspended, as was 25% of the electricity supply, once again highlighting the vulnerabilities created by an over-dependence on Russia for energy.

In what appeared to be another considerable reverse to the Georgian economy, a Russian ban on the import of Georgian wines began in late March 2006, on the basis of what were deemed insufficient hygiene methods. In May the Russian Government also banned the import of two popular brands of Georgian mineral water (Borjomi and Nabeghlavi), for allegedly failing to meet water purity standards. These evidently political decisions caused an extensive international reaction. The repercussions of the ban were such that Russian sanitary officials extended the offer of negotiations to lift the embargo some months later. However, the serious deterioration in general relations by October made the prospect of any imminent resolution unlikely.

The Georgian economy suffered a further reverse on 2 November 2006, when a Gazprom official announced that the Russian gas monopoly was to more than double its current price of natural gas in sales to Georgia, from US $110 to $230 per 1,000 cu m, beginning in January 2007. Georgia was forced to sign the consequent agreement, while it sought alternative sources to satisfy its growing energy needs.

Of the most sensitive issues in Georgian-Russian bilateral relations since independence, the withdrawal of Russian military bases occupied a prominent position. At an OSCE summit meeting, held in İstanbul, in November 1999, several important agreements were signed, including an agreement on the gradual removal of Russia's bases from Georgia, preparing the way for the introduction of new security arrangements. Technically, the agreement was a modification and clarification of the Conventional Forces in Europe (CFE) Treaty, setting limits on Russian troops in the Caucasus. The İstanbul protocol provided for the closure by July 2001 of two of the four Russian bases in Georgia: the Gudauta base, in Abkhazia, and the Vaziani base, near Tbilisi; withdrawal from the former was only completed in 2002. The protocol also provided for negotiations on the closures of the remaining two—in Akhalkalaki, in the majority ethnic Armenian-populated south-eastern region of Samtskhe-Javakheti, and in the autonomous province of Adjara, in south-west Georgia, both regions that were only weakly controlled by the central Government. Until May 2005,

Russia continued to request at least an 11-year transition period for the closure of the last two bases, owing to a lack of necessary funds, while Georgia demanded their closure within four years. The OSCE and PACE, as well as the EU and the USA, urged Russia to meet its obligations under the 1999 agreement, and this demand was further reiterated by world leaders at a NATO summit held in İstanbul in June 2004. Finally, on 30 May 2005, after Parlamenti threatened radical action, and prompted by mounting international pressure, the Ministers of Foreign Affairs of Russia and Georgia, meeting in Moscow, signed a joint statement regarding the 'cessation of functioning' of Russian military bases and other installations and the withdrawal of Russian forces from Georgia, to be completed in 2008. The withdrawal was already under way in 2006, but the schedule for the Tbilisi garrison was escalated significantly following the disputes in October (the agreement was finally ratified by the Russian State Duma and President Putin in that month). In addition, in a non-legally binding move, in July Parlamenti had demanded the immediate withdrawal of Russian peace-keeping troops from Abkhazia and South Ossetia, due to their inefficiency and bias, in a resolution supported by 144 deputies.

When Saakashvili came to power, it appeared that he and the Russian President had established a good working relationship, raising hopes for the settlement of various long-standing bilateral disputes. However, the brewing confrontation in South Ossetia put an abrupt end to the Georgian-Russian thaw. Putin pointedly announced that, contrary to his previous plans, he would not make a state visit to Georgia in late 2004, as had been initially anticipated. Although the Russian authorities had offered to mediate a solution to the crisis in South Ossetia, the Georgian leadership disputed their impartiality. The decision to withdraw military bases from Georgia offered a chance for improving bilateral relations, although the decision to strengthen the Russian military presence along Georgia's border with Chechnya demonstrated the readiness of Russia to use the unresolved conflict in Chechnya as a means of expressing concern about the alleged militant stronghold in Georgia's Pankisi Gorge, however unsubstantiated.

President Saakashvili travelled to meet his Russian counterpart in St Petersburg in June 2006. However, talks appeared not to have resolved any of the outstanding differences between the two countries. Matters deteriorated further with the closure by the Russians of the only Russian border crossing in South Ossetia recognized as legitimate by Georgia and the interception of a Russian diplomatic vehicle in South Ossetia by Georgian authorities. However, relations reached their nadir at the end of September, when the Georgian authorities detained four Russian officers and several Georgians on allegations of military espionage. Although the detainees were passed on to representatives of the OSCE within six days (for deportation), Russia responded with a broad range of measures: suspending visas, evacuating personnel (including its ambassador) from Georgia, blocking transport and mail, generating criminal investigations into Georgian individuals and businesses, and deporting hundreds of Georgians from the country (during which one death occurred). The Russian Ambassador, Vyacheslav Kovalenko, returned to Georgia in February 2007 as a first sign of improving relations. The meeting of Saakashvili and Putin at the informal summit of CIS leaders in St Petersburg in early June also brought certain expectations that positive changes would take place in bilateral relations, although this did not seem to happen at any rapid pace. However, the issuing of Russian visas to Georgian citizens resumed soon after his return, in a further positive development.

None the less, many other factors have served further to strain relations with Russia. While on a state visit to Washington, DC, USA, in January 2007, the Georgian interior minister, Merabishvili, revealed details to the US media about an incident in 2006 involving the smuggling of nuclear material within Georgia that had been disrupted in a joint operation of Georgian authorities and the US Central Intelligence Agency (CIA). According to the allegations, subsequently corroborated by officials in the US State Department, in January 2006 a Russian citizen from North Osetiya—Alaniya had travelled through the breakaway province of South Ossetia to deliver to a contact in Tbilisi around 100 g of enriched uranium, a small sample of the 2 kg of radioactive material to which he claimed to have access.

Meanwhile, Georgian and Russian negotiators have continuously failed to make a breakthrough in talks over Russia's possible accession to the World Trade Organization (WTO). Georgia, in exchange for its approval of Russia's WTO bid (which Georgia has withdrawn), is demanding that Russia legalize trade at the two border crossing points between Russia and the breakaway regions of Abkhazia and South Ossetia. On 6 August 2007 it was reported that what appeared to be two Russian SU-24 aircraft flown from northern Russia fired or dropped an air-to-surface anti-radar missile at Georgian territory, some 65 km west of Tbilisi. Georgia requested a thorough investigation, and the issue was to be considered by the UN Security Council, while Russia characteristically denied any involvement. (European investigators subsequently confirmed that Georgian airspace had been violated from Russia.)

As discussed above, the war in Chechnya was an important factor in Georgia's deteriorating relations with Russia, which accused it of supporting the Chechen militants' struggle for independence. Both political and economic pressure was applied, as Russia unilaterally introduced a visa regime with Georgia in December 2000, and also used its control of gas supplies as a political instrument. Although Georgian-Russian relations reached a nadir in September 2002, when Putin openly threatened Georgia with military action, Georgia had begun to benefit from US support following the arrival of US military advisers in early 2002. In the early 2000s Georgia's orientation toward the West, and especially towards the USA, strengthened, and US influence increased greatly. Georgia supported the US-led military action to remove the regime of Saddam Hussein in Iraq in early 2003, and subsequently agreed to dispatch troops to that country. Moreover, in March 2003 the Georgian legislature ratified an agreement granting members of the US military the right to enter Georgia without a visa and to diplomatic immunity (prompting strong protests from the Russian Gosudarstvennaya Duma). The expansion of a US military assistance programme provided Georgia with a much-needed boost as it promoted the country's integration into the Western security framework. The principal element here became the new Sustainment and Stability Operations Programme, worth approximately US $60m., an initiative intended to succeed the two-year Train and Equip programme that ended in April 2004. Four battalions, or some 2,000 soldiers, were being trained under the 16-month initiative. In addition to military assistance and other smaller aid packages, Georgia was to receive about $295m. through the US Millennium Challenge Account assistance programme, $100m. more than initially planned. The assistance was to focus on four priority sectors: the rehabilitation of infrastructure and roads in the Samtskhe-Javakheti region of southern Georgia; general infrastructure development in the country; the development of the agriculture and tourism sectors; and the rehabilitation of the main gas pipeline (north–south), which serves to support Georgia's gas system. However, the most visible sign of US support came with the rather symbolic visit to Georgia of US President George W. Bush in May 2005. This visit strongly emphasized the increasing US support for Georgia's democratization, along with Georgia's increased geopolitical involvement.

In what was regarded as a signal of support for Georgia's statehood, President Saakashvili was invited to Washington, DC, in July 2006, a few days after his strained meeting with Putin and 10 days before the Group of Eight (G8) countries' summit meeting in St Petersburg. The talks, which were held in the context of an increasingly urgent global power struggle over energy, emphasized US support for Georgia's Euro-Atlantic aspirations, and acknowledged the country's progress in democratic state-building. This support was further demonstrated when in March 2007 the US Congress approved a bill providing support and funding for Georgia's and Ukraine's membership of NATO.

Georgia's international standing depends strongly on US support, rooted in recent geopolitical developments and strategies. As President George W. Bush's global military restructuring plan for US forces is to establish new bases for US troops and equipment in Eastern European states, in order to provide a rapid response to unexpected threats, the security of the Black Sea region and the Caucasus has assumed increasing significance. Moving US forces and bases closer inevitably makes the region crucial, especially in conjunction with the Bush Administration's ambitious policy to promote democratic reform in the 'Greater Middle East', and with the strong emphasis placed on the importance of the petroleum transportation routes passing through the region. President Saakashvili's vigorously expressed intention to export democratic revolution to other countries of the post-Soviet space, and specifically to Belarus, was in accordance with such plans.

There was also increasing interest from the European institutions towards the Caucasus and Georgia. The appointment, in July 2003, of an EU Special Representative for the South Caucasus was a further step in the deepening of relations, which from June 2004 were framed by the new European Neighbourhood Policy (ENP) of the European Commission. The EU provides significant amounts of financial aid and technical assistance, and which visibly increased from 2003. Georgia, together with the EU experts, prepared an Action Plan under the ENP that was to serve as a framework for further co-operation.

The appointment in February 2006 of a new EU Special Representative for the South Caucasus, Peter Semneby of Sweden, marked the increased involvement of the EU in the region. Semneby's expanded mandate included: assisting Armenia, Azerbaijan and Georgia in implementing political and economic reforms; preventing conflicts in the region and contributing to the peaceful settlement of conflicts, including through promoting the return of refugees and internally displaced persons; and encouraging and supporting further co-operation between the states of the region, including on economic, energy and transport issues. Georgia's ENP Action Plan was adopted in November. Earlier in July it had been agreed to insert into the text of the plan for Georgia (and also Armenia) the wording: 'The EU takes note that [this country] has expressed its European aspirations.' This reference created significant hopes in the country that EU membership, although remote, was still a real possibility. The ENP Action Plan set the priorities of co-operation between the EU and Georgia for a period of five years. It focuses on such issues as the sustainability of economic growth and poverty reduction, business climate and governance, enhanced EU-Georgia trade relations, and co-operation in transport and energy, but also considers such sensitive political issues as conflict resolution. In May 2007 the Georgian Government adopted an ENP Action Plan Implementation Strategy for one year. The subsequent medium-term planning policy document of the Government, Basic Data and Directions for 2008–11, mentions the ENP Action Plan as one of the main sources for Georgia's strategic planning. In addition, the EU allotted €120m. to Georgia, envisaged for strategic plan implementation in 2007–10.

During the rising domestic tensions throughout late 2007, the international community continued to urge the Georgian leadership to proceed with democratic reforms, while expressing general support for Saakashvili's Government. At the same time, Saakashvili tried to blame hostile external forces for the turmoil, in early November accusing Russia of fomenting mass protests against him, and stirring instability in the country. A few days later, after the dispersion of the mass protest on 7 November, three diplomats at the Russian Embassy were declared *personae non gratae* and expelled from the country, prompting retaliatory action from Moscow. The Ministry of Internal Affairs of Georgia released documents supposedly confirming that a number of opposition figures had co-operated with the Russian intelligence, although such accusations were later abandoned.

When, following the suppression of mass demonstrations in November 2007 (see above), Saakashvili was obliged to announce an early presidential election on 5 January 2008, and the ending of the state of emergency, he also invited international observers to the country, in an attempt to legitimize the expected outcome. Hundreds of observers from the OSCE, Council of Europe, EU, and other organizations arrived to observe the presidential election. While many international observers noted pre-electoral violations and particularly breaches during the voting and vote-counting processes, the international reaction immediately afterwards was to congratulate Saakashvili on being elected in a poll that was considered a 'step forward', apparently due to the dislike of the risks related to the alternative opposition candidate, Gachechiladze. In some cases, Western and other leaders failed to wait even for votes to be counted before congratulating Saakashvili on his re-election.

Many international observers also welcomed as progress the legislative elections of May 2008, which, notwithstanding numerous violations, were undoubtedly won by the ruling UNM. As after the previous presidential poll, in the immediate aftermath of the elections, the assessments were relatively positive, while more thorough reports, such as those presented by the OSCE Office for Democratic Institutions and Human Rights (ODIHR), were much more critical.

One of the big failures of the incumbent Government just before the elections appeared to be the inability to obtain the much sought-after MAP at the NATO summit meeting of April 2008, owing mainly to the opposition of some European states such as Germany and France, as well as to increased pressure originating from Russia, notwithstanding strong support from the USA and most Eastern European member states. As minor compensation, Georgia (together with Ukraine) received a promise that it would eventually be admitted into NATO, while the MAP issue would be reconsidered at the next NATO summit in December. Even such modest success regarding Georgia's NATO aspirations infuriated the Russian leadership, and the Georgian-Russian relationship continued to deteriorate, exacerbated further by Russia's increased military presence in Abkhazia. As a strong demonstration of solidarity, US Secretary of State Condoleezza Rice, who visited Tbilisi in July, made a statement urging Russia to support Georgia in resolving conflicts with its breakaway regions, rather than fuel the already tense situation. According to later reports, Rice urged Saakashvili to avoid any military action in conflict regions and any direct confrontation with Russia, advice that was not heeded.

GEORGIAN–RUSSIAN WAR AND ITS AFTERMATH

On 7 August 2008, after bombarding Tskhinvali with artillery and rockets, Georgian troops began to advance towards the South Ossetian city and attempt to destroy part of the Roki tunnel connecting the breakaway region with North Osetiya—Alaniya, Russia. Georgian forces succeeded in damaging a significant bridge south of the Roki tunnel, intending to delay the advance of a convoy of tanks and armoured vehicles of the Russian 58th army, which were believed to have started entering Georgia through the tunnel, in a presumably premeditated response. Within hours, Georgian ground troops reached Tskhinvali and attacked buildings of the separatist administration in the city. Several hours later, the Georgian Government announced that its troops had secured control of most of South Ossetia. The Russian army rapidly attacked Georgian positions, bombarding Tskhinvali and surrounding areas occupied by Georgian troops. Russian military aircraft entered Georgian airspace, bombarding Georgian positions, firing missiles both against military targets outside South Ossetia, such as radar stations and military barracks, and against civilian targets, among them the villages of Variani and Kareli, and the city of Gori. Georgian anti-aircraft missiles succeeded in shooting down a number of Russian fighter jets, including a strategic bomber.

After several days of heavy fights and losses on both sides (including the wounding of the Commander of the Russian 58th army, Gen. Anatolii Khrulev), the Russian military, with its overwhelming military power and air domination, forced Georgian troops out of their positions, and took control not only of South Ossetia, but proceeded much further within Georgia, to the main east–west highway connecting Tbilisi with the Black Sea ports. At the same time Russian aircraft continued their bombardment of military and civil targets, using cluster bombs in the city of Gori and surrounding villages, and destroying a civilian radar device in Tbilisi that served its

airport. Georgian military bases at Vaziani, Marneuli and Bolnisi, all located within 50 km of Tbilisi, were attacked by Russian jets.

While the Russian Government attempted to justify invasion by the need to protect the Russian peace-keeping troops and citizens in South Ossetia, it also tried to pursue a change of Georgian leadership, as revealed in a telephone discussion between the Russian Minister of Foreign Affairs, Sergei Lavrov, and US Secretary of State Rice. Russian propaganda accused Georgia of having killed more than 2,000 civilians and numerous atrocities (although two weeks later only 134 civilian deaths could be documented). As an additional attempt to damage Georgia's public space and information channels, Georgia was exposed to 'cyber-attacks' that disabled access to numerous governmental websites.

While the Russian air force continued carrying out attacks against targets around South Ossetia and Tbilisi, its focus expanded to western Georgia, including Kopitnari airport near the city of Kutaisi, the military base in Senaki, the Black Sea port of Poti, and the Georgian-controlled villages of the Kodori Gorge in Abkhazia, together with its administrative centre, Chkhalta. The Russian Black Sea Fleet advanced from its permanent deployment in Sevastopol in Crimea, Ukraine, towards Abkhazia and Poti, sinking a number of Georgian military vessels, and preventing Georgian cargo ships from reaching Georgian Black Sea ports. Meanwhile, on 10 August 2008 Abkhazian forces, supported by Russian ground troops and aviation, launched an attack against the Kodori Gorge and secured control of the region. Russian ground forces advanced from out of Abkhazia into the cities of Zugdidi and Senaki, in north-western Georgia, then proceeded to Poti. Owing to the increased risk of attack on Tbilisi, Georgian troops were concentrated around the capital to protect it.

Reports emerged of 'ethnic cleansing', looting and burning of Georgian villages in South Ossetia and the surrounding area; this was confirmed by international human rights organizations, but also by a statement of South Ossetian President Kokoyev, published in the Russian media, in which he boasted of destroying all the Georgian villages of South Ossetia and pledged not to allow Georgians to return. Ossetian militias, together with Chechen volunteers, proceeded to loot and destroy villages controlled by the Russian army, in an atmosphere of total lawlessness.

While the attempts of the international community to act through the UN Security Council and other international bodies were vetoed by Russia, international condemnation of the Russian invasion achieved at least some results. On 12 August 2008, as head of the EU rotating presidency, French President Nicolas Sarkozy flew to Moscow. Under pressure, Russian President Dmitrii Medvedev agreed to sign a six-point cease-fire agreement that provided for the withdrawal of troops from both sides to their pre-conflict positions, an end to military actions, and free access for humanitarian aid. The details of the agreement were rather vague, and there was a controversial and poorly defined point on additional security measures that later became a subject of differing interpretations by the parties involved. On the same evening Sarkozy departed to Tbilisi, where Saakashvili also signed the document, after revising, with Russia's consent, the point concerning future international talks on the status of Abkhazia and South Ossetia.

Notwithstanding the signing of the cease-fire agreement, Russian military action continued, although at a reduced scale. Russian troops continued to loot and destroy Georgian military and civilian infrastructure. Much of the Georgian fleet based in Poti was sunk, and the administrative buildings looted. As late as 16 August 2008, days after the cease-fire officially entered into force, Russian air attacks continued against civilian targets. An important railway bridge, near the town of Kaspi, and other significant infrastructure was mined and destroyed, and several days later a train carrying fuel exports from Azerbaijan exploded, after striking a Russian mine. Forests in the Borjomi National Park were fire-bombed at several locations, causing widespread fire and devastation, while Turkish and Ukrainian planes sent to assist Georgia in fighting against the forest fires were denied permission to enter the required airspace by the Russian military. Russian ground troops entered the town of Akhalgori and other Georgian villages in the eastern part of the former South Ossetian Autonomous Oblast that had remained under Georgian control since 1991, bringing in South Ossetian police, and offering the local population Russian passports just as they had previously done in those territories under separatist control.

As a result of all these actions, more than 128,000 people from Georgian villages and towns became internally displaced, while about 30,000 of the Ossetian refugees began to return from Russia. Although some of the Georgian displaced persons were able to return to their homes in Gori and some villages further from South Ossetia's administrative border, the majority of the displaced people had to be settled in tents, kindergartens and schools, mainly in Gori and Tbilisi, and at September 2008 their future remained unclear. This was in addition to some 220,000 previously displaced people and returnees originating from the conflicts of the 1990s.

Meanwhile, the Russian leadership repeatedly violated its promises to begin the withdrawal of troops as envisaged by the 'Medvedev-Sarkozy' cease-fire agreement. On 17 August 2008 Medvedev once again promised Sarkozy that withdrawal would commence on the following day, but this did not ensue. Also on 17 August the German Chancellor Angela Merkel arrived in Tbilisi after talks with Medvedev, stressing again the urgency of Russian withdrawal, as well as stating German preparedness to contribute peace-keeping troops to the conflict zones, as stipulated in the cease-fire agreement.

On 19 August 2008 NATO foreign ministers conducted an emergency meeting on events in Georgia, reaching an agreement to deliver emergency aid to the country, support Georgia's reconstruction, and establish a NATO-Georgia commission. Once again it was repeated that Georgia would eventually join NATO, although no timetable was mentioned. On the following day Russia once again rejected a UN Security Council resolution on Georgia, drafted by France and based on the cease-fire agreement, demanding a withdrawal of all forces to positions held before 7 August and respect for Georgia's territorial integrity. Western powers continued to demand that Russia demonstrate its commitment to the cease-fire agreement, but to no avail, as Russian promises to withdraw to 'the zones of responsibility of the Russian peace-keepers' were routinely followed by statements that such withdrawal had already taken place, even though the Russian military maintained their presence in Poti and Senaki, far from any conflict zone, as well as controlling the main highway between Tbilisi and Gori.

In a demonstration of US support for Georgia, a US destroyer vessel arrived in Batumi on 24 August 2008, to deliver humanitarian assistance, while another US navy vessel was dispatched to the port of Poti. The Russian response was to move part of its Black Sea fleet to Sukhumi. In an unexpected move, on 26 August Russian President Medvedev endorsed a resolution recognizing the independence of South Ossetia and Abkhazia, which had just been approved by both chambers of the Russian legislature. Russia's decision was strongly disapproved of by all Western states, in particular the USA, where it was condemned not only by the incumbent Administration, but also by the two main candidates for the forthcoming presidential election.

On 28 August 2008 Parlamenti adopted a law instructing the Government to sever ties with Russia, in protest at the Russian occupation of Abkhazia and South Ossetia and the security zone around them, and at the recognition by Russia of the two separatist regions as independent states. On the following day the Georgian Government suspended diplomatic relations with Russia.

At the emergency EU summit meeting, held on 1 September 2008, in Brussels, Belgium, member nations warned Russia that its future ties with the bloc would depend on total adherence to a peace agreement to end the conflict in Georgia.

EU leaders strongly condemned Russia's move to recognize the independence of the rebel regions of South Ossetia and Abkhazia and urged other countries to avoid such a measure, but failed to introduce any sanctions against Russia, other than to freeze negotiations on a new EU-Russia agreement scheduled to begin on 15 September, in case the Russian Government failed to withdraw troops in accordance with the Medvedev-Sarkozy cease-fire agreement. There was also a decision adopted to dispatch an EU monitoring mission to Georgia, a promise of aid to Georgia and a pledge to create a special EU representative for the crisis.

In a further demonstration of support, US Vice President Dick Cheney travelled to Georgia on 4 September 2008, in a regional tour that also included Azerbaijan and Ukraine. Cheney's visit served to stress the depth of the USA's interests in Georgia, and he announced the US pledge to allocate US $1,000m. in reconstruction aid to Georgia. In addition, the IMF agreed to allocate credit of $750m. to Georgia, to support its financial system. Similar commitments to assist Georgia were expressed by the World Bank, the EU, and other big donors.

On 8 September 2008 three European leaders—the head of the rotating EU presidency, French President Nicolas Sarkozy, together with the President of the European Commission, José Manuel Barroso, and the EU High Representative for Common Foreign and Security Policy, Javier Solana—arrived in Moscow for talks with Russia's President Medvedev, in an attempt to pressure Russia into fulfilling its commitments. As a result, additional points to the Medvedev-Sarkozy cease-fire agreement were signed, and Russia undertook a responsibility to withdraw its military checkpoints from Poti and Senaki during the next seven days, and leave all of the 'core' Georgian territory (that is, other than Abkhazia and South Ossetia) by 11 October, provided that a sufficient number of EU and OSCE observers guaranteed that Georgia would not resume any military action. The Georgian Government, in its turn, was obliged to sign away the right to use force in either Abkhazia or South Ossetia, effectively relinquishing for the time being its sovereignty over the two separatist provinces.

Russia withdrew its troops from Poti and Senaki by mid-September 2008, but at the same time defied the West by establishing diplomatic relations with South Ossetia and Abkhazia, announcing plans to station some 3,800 regular troops in each of the secessionist regions, instead of the previous peace-keeping forces, and, on 17 September, signing friendship and co-operation treaties with the separatist authorities of South Ossetia and Abkhazia. In a rather biased interpretation of the Medvedev-Sarkozy cease-fire agreement, the Russian Government declared that it would not agree to allow stationing of international observers inside Abkhazia and South Ossetia. A NATO meeting took place on 15–16 September in Tbilisi, in a further demonstration of support for Georgia; however, NATO Secretary-General Jaap de Hoop Scheffer gave no indication as to whether Georgia would be offered a MAP at a summit meeting in December. At the same time, the EU formally approved the deployment of some 200 civilian monitors to Georgia, in order to replace Russian troops.

The August 2008 developments in Georgia came as a shock to much of the world, and threatened the global system of security. As a result of the conflict, Russia's international standing suffered considerably, while Georgia experienced severe damage. According to the most official recorded figures, 188 Georgian civilians died during the military action, together with 168 military personnel and 16 policemen. Pressure for the resignation of Saakashvili was expected to follow, while the future of plans for Georgia's integration into NATO remained uncertain, as did its relations with Russia and the secessionist regions of Abkhazia and South Ossetia.

Economy

Dr VLADIMER PAPAVA and Dr MICHAEL TOKMAZISHVILI

INTRODUCTION

Georgia began its transition period with low levels of income, slender fiscal resources, and weak institutional and administrative capacities, all of which were legacies of the communist period. In the 1990s internal wars and ethnic conflicts deepened economic problems. The wars in 1991–93 in South Ossetia and Abkhazia were followed by migration and a disruption and decline of the economy. As a result, the budget deficit increased, social and economic reforms were delayed, living standards declined, and hunger and poverty increased. In the mid-1990s internally displaced people made up 10% of the population of Georgia. Two-thirds of the population lived below the poverty line.

The situation was aggravated by institutional and political instability, ruined industries, lack of markets, and interrupted transport and communications. Georgia experienced the greatest economic decline among all the post-communist countries.

Between 1994 and 1998 the Government introduced a series of reforms to stabilize and liberalize the economy. The transition reforms entailed tremendous changes in fiscal and monetary policy, widespread privatization, price and trade liberalization, and new regulatory approaches. With these reforms implemented, Georgia's gross domestic product (GDP) grew rapidly, with the rate of growth reaching 11% in 1997.

Unfortunately, the period of economic revival was very short, and both state and market institutions remained underdeveloped. Before 2004 the economy grew at a very slow rate, and by 2003, the Georgian economy was only 73% its size in 1990.

During 1998–2003 period wages and pensions stagnated, with widespread poverty, and only a small élite segment of society benefiting from economic growth. Even worse, wages were decreasing in real terms. The official unemployment rate reached as high as 14%, and annual GDP growth was 3.0%–3.5%. Government inactivity and economic stagnation persisted for nearly seven years. Among the challenges experienced by the Government were an energy crisis, a budgetary crisis (related to the accumulation of substantial arrears of pensions' and wages' payments that resulted from the inability or unwillingness to collect taxes), and high rates of unemployment and poverty.

Economic stagnation was one of the reasons for the 'rose revolution' that removed the administration of Eduard Shevardnadze from office in November 2003. Mikheil Saakashvili's new Government, established following his election as President in January 2004, implemented radical social, political, and institutional changes. Since 2005 the main goals of the administration have been to establish fiscal discipline, restore the legal basis of the economy, reduce the scale of the shadow economy, and simplify regulations through the introduction of new laws on business. Corresponding changes then followed in the country's economic and social life. As such, Georgia has effectively embarked on building a new state since 2003, while assistance from the IMF was renewed in mid-2004 with the establishment of a new programme under the Fund's Poverty Reduction and Growth Facility.

MACROECONOMIC AND INSTITUTIONAL REFORMS

Most of Georgia's economic and social problems at the time of the rose revolution resulted from a combination of slender fiscal resources and the weak institutional and administrative capacity. Subsequently, the key challenges of the new post-revolutionary Government were to combat corruption and carry out institutional reforms.

The first step undertaken was civil service reform, focused on eliminating redundant agencies and a significant reallocation of personnel. The Government launched a radical reorganization, reducing bureaucracy and increasing both the responsi-

bility of government officials and their wages. At the same time, the number of institutions regulating, controlling and inspecting the private sector was reduced. Amendments to the Constitution have strengthened presidential powers. All this enabled the Government to start an effective fight against corruption, exemplified by the abolition of the traffic police and the expedited creation of a Western-style patrol police. As a consequence, the practice of bribery across the country's roads and highways was eliminated.

The combat of corruption and the implementation of institutional reforms helped to establish financial order in the country, yielding some significant increases in tax revenues and, as a consequence, the overcoming of the budgetary crisis. Some budgetary growth was achieved as a result of anti-corruption measures such as the arrest of former government officials and their relatives and their release upon payment of a 'price of liberty'. Officially, this was presented as constituting a repayment of stolen money and properties to the state. As a result, the post-revolutionary Government succeeded in paying off all accumulated debts to pensioners and public sector employees. The extrabudgetary accounts, which accumulated income from the sums paid by the accused, ensured that there was no transparency in spending; in early 2006, under pressure from the IMF, these accounts were abolished.

Perhaps the most successful policy reform has been that of economic liberalization. A new tax code has considerably simplified taxes. Before 2005 several types of income taxes had existed: a social tax (of 27%), medical insurance (3%), and employment tax (1%)—a total of 31% covered by employers in all. With effect from that year all these taxes were merged into one social payment of 20%, alongside a flat income tax (paid by employees) of 12%. As a result, the fiscal burden on entrepreneurs was reduced. At the same time, the administration of tax collection became more severe. These changes enabled the Government to increase the state budget several-fold; the tax-to-GDP ratio grew from 14.7% in 2000 to 25.8% in 2007. In 2007 the 20% social tax payable by employers was abolished while income tax was increased from 12% to 25%.

In mid-2008 a package of bills amending the Tax Code, under which the gradual reduction of some tax rates was envisaged, was submitted to Parliament. Over a five-year period starting from 2009, income tax would be reduced from 25% to 15% as follows: by one percentage point in 2009; by two percentage points during each of the next three years; and by three percentage points in the fifth year. The dividend tax would be gradually reduced during the same period, to zero from the current 10%. This reduction of tax rates would promote both business development and economic growth, while, in support of viticulture and winemaking, the excise on local wines would be abolished.

The customs reforms introduced in Georgia, which simplified procedures for importers and trade partners, have proved successful. The new customs code, introduced in 2007, replaced the previous 16 different types of duties with only three. The new duties are set at rates of zero, 5% and 12%, whereas those they replaced ranged from 1% to 25%. Reducing the import-tax base for agricultural goods and construction materials, as well as annulling import taxes for other goods, has made Georgia much more competitive.

The amnesty and legalization of non-declared tax liabilities and property was enacted in mid-2005, as part of the anti-corruption policy. This was a time-limited amnesty from June–September 2005, aimed at the legalization of hidden incomes.

Other reforms have reduced the quantity of official licences and permits required for various business activities, which had previously effectively created barriers to market entry. In 2005 a new law on licensing was adopted, following which, of the previous total of 950 licences and permits, only 150 remain. Licensing procedures were rationalized and the time taken to issue licences reduced. Additionally, the legal grounds for governmental intervention in businesses have been restricted.

A new, revolutionary, Labour Code has limited the rights of employees, and concomitantly substantially broadened those of employers. Although this may encourage businesses to develop, it also leaves employees unprotected.

Reforms implemented in 2005–06 made considerable strides in reversing policies that had previously stifled private initiative. Georgia's strategy was to establish a minimal state, and was oriented around a policy of terminating any state regulatory activity that enabled corruption and increased bureaucracy. These reforms mainly concerned the simplification of procedures required for business registration, with an emphasis on reducing the costs of excessive economic and administrative regulations. In the 'Doing Business 2007' report, published by the World Bank, Georgia's rank on the 'ease of doing business' indicator jumped from 100th place (of 155 economies surveyed) in 2006 to 37th (of 175), outstripping some EU countries, improving its ranking further in 2008 to 18th (of 178). As such, Georgia became one of the most rapidly reforming countries.

Despite this progressive movement toward economic liberalization, institutional changes yielded some negative effects. First, liberalization was accompanied by the hasty decision to abolish the anti-monopoly service in late 2004. As a result, new monopolies were formed. In late 2007 the Ministry of the Interior (which combines the police and domestic intelligence forces) was empowered to deal with the anti-monopoly regulation over domestic markets. Second, the State Department of Statistics, which before the rose revolution had been an independent agency accountable to the President, was incorporated into the Ministry of Economic Development, presenting perhaps the most palpable example of a conflict of interests. Consequently, official statistics presently play a political function to proclaim the annual improvement of the economy, particularly the official rate of inflation, which is dubiously low. Third, after the reorganization of some ministries and departments, most experienced employees were dismissed and replaced by younger officials with some international training. As a consequence, government ministries and departments have lost institutional memory.

No less important than institutional reforms, the large-scale privatization programme should be regarded as one of the key accomplishments of the post-revolutionary Governments. The completion of privatization and the minimum involvement of the state in economic matters are among the main priorities of Georgia's economic development.

The Georgian Government fully supported the entry of foreign capital into the economy during the wide-ranging privatization of state-owned enterprises that took place after the rose revolution. Among the largest investors are Russia, Kazakhstan, and the United Arab Emirates (UAE). Russian capital was invested in the Georgian banking system, electricity, and gold- and copper-mining and processing companies, while Kazakhstani involvement in the gas-distribution and oil-terminal sectors is substantial.

In 2008 the Government announced the establishment of a free economic zone (FEZ) around the port city of Poti, signing an agreement with the UAE-based Ras al Khaimah (RAK) Investment Authority, which also purchased 51% of the shares of the port at Poti, as the development company. It was anticipated that the opening of a FEZ would attract foreign investment. However, opponents of the scheme have argued that, considering that Georgia had embarked on liberalizing foreign trade more than ten years earlier, and that after the rose revolution business registration procedures had also been liberalized, the economic viability of setting up the FEZ would be uncertain.

In 2008 a so-called 'revolutionary' economic package of laws was developed with the main goal of turning Georgia into a global financial centre by offering tax exemptions to large international financial companies whose activity in Georgia does not exceed 10% of their financial turnover. This package also provided for a significant reorganization of the National Bank of Georgia (NBG), the central bank, by imposing a targeted inflation policy, in line with the authorities' commitment to keeping inflation to less than 10%.

Other projects stimulating economic development include the issuance of so-called 'cheap credits' for the development of small businesses, and of Eurobonds of US $500m. with a maturity period of five years in order to implement new power projects.

In parallel with liberalization and privatization, the question of property rights has become an area of contention for the post-revolutionary Government. The confiscations and temporary renationalization of property and assets initiated in late 2005–07, affected not only corrupt former officials, but also small and medium-sized businesses. This process meant that certain companies that had been privatized before the rose revolution were forcibly taken back by the Government, which then offered them for reprivatization. Moreover, extrajudicial decisions authorized the demolition of privately owned houses built before the rose revolution, the owners of which possessed all the requisite documents certifying both their ownership and legitimacy of construction. The only argument presented by the Government to support these actions was a desire to improve the image of the capital city, Tbilisi. Law enforcement agencies, including the Office of the Procurator-General and the Ministry of Internal Affairs, became involved in the process, reportedly pressuring the property owners to 'voluntarily' give up their property for the Government's benefit. Without formally pressing charges for possible infractions, the owners were reminded that they had received their licences or permissions for business through corrupt deals agreed with Shevardnadze-era officials. As way of recompense for these past errors, the owners then handed over their property to the state. These transfers were officially registered as gifts to the state, rather than as confiscated or expropriated properties. Business owners who thereby transferred their ownership of properties were not reimbursed.

These and other policies contributed to the unrest that began in November 2007, culminating in demonstrations that were violently suppressed by the Government. To quell the ensuing turmoil, President Saakashvili resigned and new presidential elections were called for January 2008, at which Saakashvili was re-elected.

ECONOMIC POLICY

In parallel with macroeconomic and institutional reforms, corruption and state involvement in the economy were reduced drastically, the investment climate improved, and the average annual rate of GDP growth reached 9.3% in 2004–07.

By 2008 the Georgian economy should be assessed as undergoing rapid development with moderately high inflation, the growth of foreign investment, and a low level of exports.

Privatization has attracted large-scale investments to the country. In 2002 flows of foreign direct investment (FDI) were equivalent to less than US $37 per head; in 2004 they amounted to $104, and by 2006 had further increased to $240. In addition, illicit gains made prior to the rose revolution were made legal. Much of this money has been invested in construction, financial activities and telecommunications, which in turn has made a positive impact on GDP growth.

Inflation began to increase in 2004, while the economic environment became more active and dynamic. In 2000–03 the annual rate of GDP growth averaged 4%, and the average annual rate of inflation was only 3.5%. These levels were a clear indicator of stagnation, and public expenditures also remained low.

In 2004–07 average annual GDP growth amounted to 8.3%, more than two times the level recorded in 2000–03, and the average annual rate of inflation increased to 11.1%, in 2004–07, more than three times the level recorded in 2000–03.

Several factors have been instrumental in precipitating this growth of inflation. First, the investment environment improved and transfer payments increased. A large-scale privatization programme and remissions received from abroad considerably exceeded (by up to 25%) the pace of GDP growth in 2004–07. Consequently, demand for the national currency kept growing, and its delivery to the financial markets brought about an increase in the money supply, which in turn created conditions for inflation. The stability of the national currency also became a cause for concern. The central bank, in implementing monetary policy, was forced to choose between either seeking to maintain inflation at the desired level or to ensure the stability of the exchange rate of the national currency. Second, budgetary revenues increased six-fold in 2004–07 (compared with 2000–03), although this also enabled the country to cover the previously accumulated domestic debts and also to increase salaries and pensions. Third, public sector salaries increased by 67% during 2004–06, while those in the private sector increased by an average of some 208%. Thus, conditions for inflation were created, further strained by international factors, such as an increase in the cost of energy resources, the declining value of the US dollar, and an increase of inflation in Georgia's principal trade partners; in Azerbaijan, Russia, Turkey and Ukraine inflation averaged around 10%. The upturn of inflation in Georgia was not, however, largely caused by internal monetary pressures, but was principally attributable to external pressures, including the Russian embargo introduced against Georgia (see History) in late 2005 and increases in prices of energy imported from Russia.

High inflation has also resulted in an increase in tax revenues, even though the value of these additional revenues is lower, in real terms. The Government has two sources of increased tax revenues: economic growth and high inflation. The NBG has issued certificates of deposit in order to reduce the money supply, and has intervened in the currency exchange market to cut inflation. However, it is impossible to regulate inflation fully if we take into account the rapid growth not only of budgetary revenues, but also of the budget deficit, which amounted to 5% of GDP in 2007.

Another serious challenge that has arisen since the imposition of the Russian economic embargo has concerned the current account deficit. Both exports and imports increased during 2002–07. Although the rate of growth of imports has been more rapid, the export-to-import cover ratio reduced gradually, and in 2007 reached 27.0%, compared with 46.5% in 2002. Consequently, while the trade deficit grew six-fold during 2002–07, the current account deficit grew by more than two-fold, reaching 19.0% of GDP.

FDI and transfers from abroad are the main sources of income to cover the deficit. During 2002–07 FDI increased by 6.6 times and transfers from abroad by 8.5 times. Rising energy prices and the increase of FDI are the main reasons for the growth in imports and the downturn in export potential.

THE ECONOMIC IMPACT OF THE RUSSIAN EMBARGO

Until 2004 Russia was Georgia's largest trade partner. After relations between the two countries deteriorated in the mid-2000s, Russia declined to third place, behind Turkey and Azerbaijan. The closure of the Russian market presented a great challenge to Georgia's economy, and resulted in substantial changes to its foreign-trade structure.

At the end of 2005 Russia restricted imports of Georgian fruits and vegetables, ostensibly due to sanitary regulations and the necessity of defending Russian consumers from counterfeits. (Politically, this move has been explained by a desire by Russia to restore its influence in Georgia and to impede the country's movement toward the North Atlantic Treaty Organization.) Relations with Russia were aggravated after the arrest of Russian officers on charges of espionage by Georgian authorities in 2006. In retaliation, Russia recalled its ambassador and began a partial evacuation of Russian diplomatic staff. Without giving any notice, Russia closed the only official border checkpoint between the two countries, at Verkhnyi Lars. Ethnic Georgians were expelled from Russia, transport and communications links between Russia and Georgia were closed (except for roads linking Russia with the separatist territories of Abkhazia and South Ossetia), and Russia stopped issuing visas to Georgian citizens. In October 2006, in response to these sanctions, Georgia threatened to block Russia's bid to join the World Trade Organization. In addition, in January 2007 Russia once more sharply increased the price of gas exports to Georgia.

The Russian embargo and transportation blockade have substantially reduced Georgian trade, thereby reducing the national income. According to various estimations the Russia embargo could reduce GDP growth of Georgia by between 0.5%

and 2.8% every year, before new markets (particularly for Georgian food and beverage products) are found.

The Russian–Georgian war of August 2008 represented another potentially severe setback to the Georgian economy. During the incursion of Russian air and land forces, civilian populations and infrastructure were bombed, with enduring consequences. However, the banking system, energy supply, and various private entities all successfully coped with the war shock, and the food market functioned without serious problems.

SECTORS OF THE ECONOMY

Agriculture

Agriculture has always been one of the key sectors of the Georgian economy. Since 1996 the share of agriculture in GDP has declined every year, reaching 12% in 2007, compared with 33% in 1996. In 1990–2007 total agricultural output, which principally comprises wheat, tobacco, vegetables, fruits and grapes, and tea, decreased substantially.

The main reason for this decline was the division of agricultural land into small plots after privatization, lack of funding, limited information about markets and new technologies, amortization of agricultural techniques and machinery, and the high prices and low quality of pesticides and mineral fertilizers.

Small farms produce more than four-fifths of total agricultural output; only 8%–10% of these products are for market. These farms operate mainly on a subsistence basis, and cannot create the conditions for economic growth. Moreover, only 19% of farms have privately owned machinery, and only 26% have mechanized production. Large farms produce only 10% of the total agricultural output, almost all of which is marketed.

Another problem is rural finance. The financial system focuses on short-term trade financing and does not serve the development of the agricultural sector. The primary agriculture and agro-processing sectors suffer from a limited supply of medium-term credit. Moreover, in eastern Georgia, obsolete irrigation systems and poor technical conditions reduce the efficiency of the sector.

Industry

Industry has grown substantially since the mid-2000s, with growth peaking, in real terms, at 14%, in 2007, since when growth has slowed.

Mining, chemicals, and food-processing are the main industrial sectors. The coal industry is well established. Manganese and non-metallic minerals, mineral fertilizers, synthetic materials and fibres, and pharmaceutical products are the main exports. The share of GDP attributed to the sector decreased from 11% in 1996 to 8% in 2003, due to energy shortages and lack of investment, but after privatization in 2005–07 its share reached 12%.

Food products include tea, wine, and brandy. Prior to the Russian embargo, wine was the largest export among agro-industrial products, accounting for 25% of the total, and the third largest export product overall, with 78% of the wine exported to Russia and 12% to Ukraine. Other important agricultural export goods are shelled hazelnuts (21%), mineral water (10%), refined sugar (9%), distilled alcoholic beverages (9%), non-alcoholic beverages (6%), and citrus fruits (5%).

Georgia has significant export potential for fruit and fruit concentrates. The climate is well suited to tobacco production, but Georgia lacks the skills and technologies for manufacturing, packing, and sorting for export. This is also true of wheat production.

In 2007 imported food products accounted for more than one-half of consumption. Such a strong dependence on imports is paradoxical for a country with such substantial resources for food production.

Energy

Despite the strategic importance of the energy sector, its share in industry has decreased, due to the rapid growth of other sectors. The sector suffers as a result of the poor conditions of power stations and the corrosion of gas-distribution networks, with associated losses, and the prevalence of corruption.

The sector experienced considerable progress during 2004–05. The electric-power engineering sector was reorganized and the collection of payments improved, thereby stabilizing the energy sector. The rehabilitation of hydro-electric generation works and of domestic gas pipelines had facilitated an increase in generation and supply. The local production of energy resources has increased, as has consumption.

Moreover, the combat of corruption in the energy sector resulted in the overcoming of the energy crisis: since the winter of 2006/07 the whole of Georgia has enjoyed a constant supply of electricity.

As the supply of energy has improved, the share of local resources in consumption has decreased. Privatization of the energy sector continues apace.

About 20 hydropower plants (HPPs) are privately owned, accounting for about one-third of installed capacity. The one-fifth share of the distribution companies owned by the state has been placed on the list of organizations to be privatized, excepting the Enguri HPP, one of the largest, which is located in the separatist territory of Abkhazia. Most of the gas-distribution companies are in poor financial condition, and not attractive for privatization.

Hydropower is the only potential export produced by the energy sector of Georgia. Natural gas is mainly supplied by Azerbaijan and Russia, and oil by Azerbaijan and Kazakhstan.

The current energy policy of Georgia, due to its tense relations with Russia, aims at providing energy stability through the use of alternative suppliers. In early 2007 the country began to receive gas from the Shah Deniz (Şah Deniz) field, the largest in Azerbaijani territory, in hopes of becoming independent of the politically unstable flows supplied by the Russian state-controlled company Gazprom.

Banking

In the 1990s, after the collapse of the USSR and Georgian independence, the development of the banking sector went through a troublesome period, being subject to the reform of the former Soviet system, recession, and concentration. Privatization began in 1994, when state-owned banks were transformed into joint stock companies. The first commercial banks were created from state banks. In 1996 a two-tier banking system was introduced, with international practices adapted to Georgian conditions. Stricter reserves requirements imposed by the national bank; assets, liabilities and risk management; and cases of licences being revoked, banks forced to close or being placed into liquidation all served as encouragements for banks to change their behaviour.

Despite the fact that Georgia's economy was closely associated and linked with that of Russia, the major Russian banking crisis of 1998 did not provoke the banking crisis that ensued in Georgia.

None the less, during 1998–99 the global economic crisis had a very significant effect on Georgia. Among the crises concerning banking, debt and exchange rates, only the latter developed rapidly. The Georgian currency, the lari, was permanently and sharply devaluated. Small banks experienced difficulties, after the deterioration in the exchange rate and the loss of value of the national currency encouraged consumers to withdraw deposits from the banks. To decrease broad money, the national bank increased the norm of reserve requirements for commercial banks from 12% to 16%. In consequence, the value of credits and rates of interest increased.

Although some commercial banks failed in this very difficult financial situation, a general banking crisis did not ensue, as 80% of deposits were invested in US dollars. Therefore, the withdrawal of consumer deposits affected only those in the national currency. The speculative rush to exchange national currency for foreign currency accelerated, and, as exchange rates fluctuated swiftly, a currency crisis developed. Thus, while the assets of commercial banks in national currency reduced, the large proportion of deposits held in foreign currency was preserved.

Moreover, the central bank offered short-term loans to commercial banks in order to support them through the difficulties, although it lacked the resources to assist all of the commercial banks that were in need of assistance. Some 13 banks were chosen to be issued credits so as to avoid bankruptcy. Until this time, the financial market had comprised a large number of small banks that were generally characterized by poor management, and, in many cases, held significant outstanding debts. None the less, as many such banks went bankrupt, the whole banking sector was not affected. Thus, while in 1998 more than 150 banks were deprived of their operating licence, more than 80% of clients' deposits were secure, and the crisis of the banking system within Georgia had been contained.

Until 2004 the banking sector developed slowly, with rapid development after the rose revolution, due to economic liberalization and an increase in FDI. Commercial bank assets, deposits, and loans all grew significantly. During 2004–06 bank assets tripled, as had been the case in 1997–2003. Commercial bank assets in 2009 were forecast at 60% of GDP. As around one-half of liquid assets are denominated in foreign currencies, the exchange rate is a significant factor in guaranteeing financial stability. Similarly, exchange rate fluctuation could increase credit risk. Along with attempts to restrict exchange rate spreads, the better management of expenditure will become a priority. Bank market concentration has increased, especially on the deposit market, which has always been more concentrated than the loan market, reflecting varying confidence in different banks. In early 2008 the six largest banks accounted for more than 80% of the bank market. In 2007 some 19 commercial banks were in operation, 13 of which were partially foreign-owned foreign capital investment. In total, 58% of the total capital assets of banks were held by foreign interests.

Other Sectors

In 2003–07 positive growth rates were recorded in every sector of the economy. The share of services (especially financial) in GDP increased rapidly, representing almost one-half of total GDP growth. Trade is still the largest sector, although the construction sector (of which pipeline construction only constitutes a small part) has been growing rapidly.

CONCLUSION AND PROSPECTS

In pursuit of economic transformation, the post-rose revolution Government initially demonstrated the political will to establish financial order and eradicate bribery and corruption, which allowed the country to overcome its budgetary and energy weaknesses and to enhance GDP growth.

Despite the external shock from the Russian economic embargo, subsequent economic growth has been strong, driven mainly by private capital inflows, which include a large element of FDI. While these inflows are welcome, and signal private sector confidence in the Georgian economy, they also give rise to macroeconomic imbalances. Georgia's current account deficit has increased substantially and was projected to increase further.

Large capital inflows also pose challenges for macroeconomic stabilization, with rapid budgetary growth creating inflationary pressures alongside a tight fiscal policy and the stated objective of ensuring that inflation remains under 10%. The pace of privatization and growth in investment experienced in the years that followed the rose revolution is unsustainable. By 2008 privatization was entering its final stages, meaning that FDI will decrease, thereby reducing the risk factors for high inflation. As local production will not be able to grow significantly and export opportunities are extremely limited, it will prove difficult to reduce the trade deficit. During the military conflict with Russia in August 2008, Georgia's economy proved resilient; if economic assistance is timely, Georgia will be able to overcome economic problems. In brief, Georgia has escaped a period of stagnation, and now faces the challenges of stabilization and the maintenance of moderately high economic growth.

Statistical Survey

Source (unless otherwise indicated): State Department for Statistics, 0115 Tbilisi, K. Gamsakhurdia 4; tel. (32) 33-05-40; fax (32) 93-89-36; e-mail info@statistics .gov.ge; internet www.statistics.ge.

Area and Population

AREA, POPULATION AND DENSITY

Area (sq km)	69,700*
Population (census results)†	
12 January 1989	5,400,841
17 January 2002‡	
Males	2,061,753
Females	2,309,782
Total	4,371,535
Population (official estimates at 1 January)§	
2006	4,401,300
2007	4,394,700
2008	4,382,100
Density (per sq km) at 1 January 2008	62.9

* 26,911 sq miles.
† Population is *de jure*. The *de facto* total at the 2002 census was 4,355,700.
‡ Those territories of the former autonomous oblast (district) of South Ossetia that remained outside Georgian government control, as well as those of the separatist 'Republic of Abkhazia', were not included in the census of 2002. It was estimated that around 230,000 people lived in these territories.
§ Including the territories not under the control of the central Government.

POPULATION BY ETHNIC GROUP
(2002 census result, excl. areas outside Georgian government control)

	Number ('000)	% of total population
Georgian	3,661.2	83.8
Azeri	284.8	6.5
Armenian	248.9	5.7
Russian	67.7	1.5
Ossetian	38.0	0.9
Kurdish	20.8	0.5
Others	50.1	1.1
Total (incl. others)	**4,371.5**	**100.0**

ADMINISTRATIVE DIVISIONS
(1 January 2008, '000, rounded figures*)

Territory	Population	Principal city†
Autonomous Republic . . .		
Adjara	380.2	Batumi (122.2)
Mkharebi (Regions)		
Guria	138.8	Ozurgeti (77.3)
Imereti	694.2	Kutaisi (188.6)
Kakheti	401.9	Telavi (70.0)
Kvemo Kartli	503.9	Rustavi (117.3)
Mtskheta-Mtianeti	118.1	Mtskheta (59.4)
Racha-Lechkumi and Kvemo-		
Svaneti	48.2	Ambrolauri (14.9)
Samegrelo-Zemo Svaneti‡ . .	469.6	Zugdidi (171.4)
Samstkhe-Javakheti	207.7	Akhaltsikhe (46.8)
Shida Kartli§	312.8	Gori (148.6)
Capital City		
Tbilisi	1,106.7	—

* These figures exclude the population of the 'Republic of Abkhazia'.
† With official estimate of population at 1 January 2008 ('000, rounded figures).
‡ Including population of Kodori Gorge (Upper Abkhazia).
§ Most of the territories of South Ossetia are included in Shida Kartli Mkhare.

PRINCIPAL TOWNS
(estimates at 1 January 2008, unless otherwise indicated)

Tbilisi (capital) . .	1,106,700	Marneuli* . . .		122,500
Kutaisi . . .	188,600	Batumi . . .	.	122,200
Zugdidi* . . .	171,400	Rustavi . . .	.	117,300
Gori* . . .	148,600	Gardabani* . . .		112,400

* Figures refer to the population of the municipality.

BIRTHS, MARRIAGES AND DEATHS

	Registered live births		Registered marriages		Registered deaths	
	Number	Rate (per 1,000)	Number	Rate (per 1,000)	Number	Rate (per 1,000)
2000 . .	48,800	11.0	12,870	2.9	47,410	10.7
2001 . .	47,589	10.8	13,336	3.0	46,218	10.5
2002 . .	46,605	10.7	12,535	2.9	46,446	10.7
2003 . .	46,194	10.7	12,696	2.9	46,055	10.6
2004 . .	49,572	11.5	14,866	3.4	48,793	11.3
2005 . .	46,512	10.7	18,012	4.1	42,984	9.9
2006 . .	47,795	10.9	21,845	5.0	42,255	9.6
2007 . .	49,287	11.2	24,891	5.7	41,178	9.4

Expectation of life (years at birth, WHO estimates): 69.9 (males 66.0; females 73.8) in 2006 (Source: WHO, *World Health Statistics*).

ECONOMICALLY ACTIVE POPULATION
(annual averages, '000 persons)*

	2003	2004	2005
Agriculture, hunting and forestry	995.6	962.4	947.8
Fishing	0.7	0.4	n.a.
Mining and quarrying	2.8	3.9	5.8
Manufacturing	88.8	90.8	89.8
Electricity, gas and water supply	19.8	20.7	23.4
Construction	40.1	42.1	43.1
Wholesale and retail trade; repair of motor vehicles and personal and household goods . . .	198.5	196.9	188.2
Hotels and restaurants . . .	16.6	18.7	16.3
Transport, storage and communications	76.9	74.3	69.3
Financial intermediation . . .	9.8	12.8	13.3
Real estate, renting and business activities	32.3	28.4	25.9
Public administration and defence; compulsory social security . .	91.4	86.8	81.8
Education	135.6	134.1	130.9
Health and social work . . .	49.0	54.8	58.0
Other community, social and personal service activities . .	45.2	42.7	38.2
Private households with employed persons	7.8	8.4	9.2
Extra-territorial organizations and bodies	3.5	4.4	3.3
Activities not adequately defined	0.1	1.4	0.3
Total employed	**1,814.5**	**1,783.3**	**1,744.6**
Unemployed	235.9	257.6	279.3
Total labour force	**2,050.4**	**2,041.0**	**2,023.9**
Males	1,081.7	1,069.7	1,074.4
Females	968.7	971.3	949.5

* Figures exclude employment in the informal sector, estimated to total about 750,000 persons at the end of 1997.

2006 ('000): Total employed 1,747.3; Unemployed 274.5; Total labour force 2,021.8.

2007 ('000): Total employed 1,704.3; Unemployed 261.0; Total labour force 1,965.3.

Health and Welfare

KEY INDICATORS

Total fertility rate (children per woman, 2006)	1.4
Under-5 mortality rate (per 1,000 live births, 2006) . . .	32
HIV/AIDS (% of persons aged 15–49, 2005)	0.2
Physicians (per 1,000 head, 2006)	4.7
Hospital beds (per 1,000 head, 2006)	3.7
Health expenditure (2005): US $ per head (PPP)	318
Health expenditure (2005): % of GDP	8.6
Health expenditure (2005): public (% of total)	47.0
Human Development Index (2005): ranking	96
Human Development Index (2005): value	0.754

For sources and definitions, see explanatory note on p. vi.

Agriculture

PRINCIPAL CROPS
('000 metric tons)

	2004	2005	2006
Wheat	185.8	190.1	160.0
Barley	61.4	65.4	47.3
Maize	410.6	421.3	217.6
Potatoes	419.5	432.2	208.3
Sunflower seed	22.3	22.3	10.7
Cabbages and other brassicas .	104.0	113.5*	53.0*
Tomatoes	116.0	126.5*	59.0*
Cucumbers and gherkins† . .	90.0	98.0	46.0
Dry onions	26.0	28.5*	13.5*
Watermelons	109.5	119.6	53.5
Oranges	38.2	122.4	137.0*
Apples	76.3	104.3	116.5*
Pears	25.4	35.7	40.0*
Sour (Morello) cherries . . .	12.4	20.0	22.0*
Peaches and nectarines . . .	2.9	10.2	12.0*
Plums and sloes	14.8	19.0	21.0*
Grapes	180.0	250.3	280.0*
Tea (made)	20.0	22.8	28.0*
Tobacco (leaves)	1.5	1.1	1.4

* FAO estimate.
† Unofficial figures.

Aggregate production ('000 metric tons, may include official, semi-official or estimated data): Total cereals 662.7 in 2004, 679.7 in 2005, 427.9 in 2006; Total nuts 14.7 in 2004, 30.9 in 2005, 32.0 in 2006; Total roots and tubers 419.5 in 2004, 432.2 in 2005, 208.3 in 2006; Total vegetables (incl. melons) 510.0 in 2004, 556.3 in 2005, 257.2 in 2006; Total fruits (excl. melons) 378.4 in 2004, 629.4 in 2005, 680.1 in 2006.

Source: FAO.

LIVESTOCK
('000 head at 1 January)

	2004	2005	2006
Horses	43.4	44.4	42.8
Cattle	1,242.5	1,250.7	1,260.4
Buffaloes	32.7	33.2	33.2*
Pigs	473.8	483.9	455.3
Sheep	628.8	689.2	719.8
Goats	93.4	115.7*	95.5
Chickens	8,500†	8,650*	6,850*
Turkeys	706†	705*	650*

* FAO estimate.
† Unofficial figure.

Source: FAO.

LIVESTOCK PRODUCTS
('000 metric tons)

	2004	2005	2006*
Cattle meat	49.8	49.2	47.0
Sheep meat	9.2	9.6	9.2
Pig meat	34.7	33.3	32.0
Chicken meat	15.2	16.9	16.5
Cows' milk	755.0	760.8	690.0
Hen eggs	15.0	15.3	11.3

* FAO estimates.

Source: FAO.

Forestry

ROUNDWOOD REMOVALS
('000 cubic metres, excl. bark)

	2003	2004	2005
Sawlogs, veneer logs and logs for sleepers	41.2	49.8	81.0
Other industrial wood	41.2	49.8	81.0
Fuel wood	367.3	443.3	453.9
Total	449.7	542.9	615.9

2006: Figures assumed to be unchanged from 2005 (FAO estimates).
Source: FAO.

SAWNWOOD PRODUCTION
('000 cubic metres, incl. railway sleepers)

	2003	2004*	2005†
Coniferous (softwood)	7.1	6.9	6.9
Broadleaved (hardwood) . . .	64.0	62.5	62.5
Total	71.1	69.4	69.4

* Unofficial figures.
† FAO estimates.

2006: Figures assumed to be unchanged from 2005 (FAO estimates).
Source: FAO.

Fishing

(metric tons, live weight)

	2004	2005*	2006*
Capture	2,951	3,000	3,000
Mullets	68	70	70
Surmullets	35	40	40
European anchovy	2,562	2,600	2,600
Sharks, rays, skates, etc. . .	31	35	35
Sea snails	65	70	70
Aquaculture	72	72	75
Total catch	3,023	3,072	3,075

* FAO estimates.

Source: FAO.

Mining

('000 metric tons, unless otherwise indicated)

	2003	2004	2005
Coal	8.0	8.0	8.0
Crude petroleum	139.7	97.6	66.7
Natural gas (million cu m) . .	17.8	6.1	14.8
Manganese ore	173.5	218.7	251.8
Cement	344.8	424.6	450.0*

* Estimated production.

Source: US Geological Survey.

Industry*

SELECTED PRODUCTS
('000 metric tons, unless otherwise indicated)

	2002	2003	2004
Refined sugar	47.9	91.8	n.a.
Wine ('000 hectolitres) . . .	201	231	n.a.
Beer ('000 hectolitres)	273	284	476
Vodka and liqueurs ('000 hectolitres)	21	26	62
Soft drinks ('000 hectolitres) . .	379	678	918
Mineral water ('000 hectolitres)	596	691	818
Cigarettes (million)	1,894	2,972	2,808
Mineral fertilizers	83.2	n.a.	n.a.
Synthetic ammonia	111.3	n.a.	n.a.
Residual fuel oil	12	13	14
Building bricks (million) . . .	6.0	9.0	9.0
Electric energy (million kWh) .	7,257	7,116	6,924

Source: mainly UN, *Industrial Commodity Statistics Yearbook*.

* Data for those areas of South Ossetia outside of central Government control and for the separatist 'Republic of Abkhazia' are not included.

Finance

CURRENCY AND EXCHANGE RATES

Monetary Units
100 tetri = 1 lari.

Sterling, Dollar and Euro Equivalents (30 May 2008)
£1 sterling = 2.850 lari;
US $1 = 1.444 lari;
€1 = 2.239 lari;
100 lari = £35.09= $69.25 = €44.66.

Average Exchange Rate (lari per US $)
2005   1.8127
2006   1.7804
2007   1.6075

Note: On 25 September 1995 Georgia introduced the lari, replacing interim currency coupons at the rate of 1 lari = 1,000,000 coupons. From April 1993 the National Bank of Georgia had issued coupons in various denominations, to circulate alongside (and initially at par with) the Russian (formerly Soviet) rouble. From August 1993 coupons became Georgia's sole legal tender, but their value rapidly depreciated. The transfer from coupons to the lari lasted one week, and from 2 October 1995 the lari became the only permitted currency in Georgia.

BUDGET
(million lari)*

Revenue†	2002	2003	2004
Tax revenue	1,054.7	1,186.8	1,811.2
Taxes on income	142.9	152.9	268.7
Taxes on profits	82.2	101.1	161.6
Value-added tax	404.6	406.8	628.2
Excise	86.7	100.1	163.8
Customs duties	59.0	70.3	100.1
Other taxes	114.0	128.0	134.1
Other current revenue . . .	80.6	86.1	274.4
Total‡	1,135.3	1,272.9	2,085.6

Expenditure§	2002	2003	2004
General state services	258.6	301.1	356.9
Defence	48.9	61.2	160.4
Civil order and security . . .	100.0	113.6	274.2
Education	166.6	164.1	289.1
Health	64.3	29.5	97.2
Social insurance and social care .	302.7	342.5	473.0
Recreation, culture, sports and religion	59.6	49.7	90.2
Fuel-energy services	16.9	36.8	78.8
Agriculture, forestry, fisheries and hunting	11.3	16.0	32.0
Transport and communications .	43.7	50.2	70.5
Other expenditures	336.9	445.2	489.9
Total	1,409.5	1,609.9	2,412.2

* Figures represent a consolidation of the State Budget (covering the central Government and local administrations) and extrabudgetary funds.
† Excluding grants received (million lari): 22.6 in 2002; 47.7 in 2003; 123.9 in 2004.
‡ Excluding extrabudgetary revenue (comprising the revenues of the Social Protection Fund, the Single State Employment Fund and the State Road Fund) (million lari): 165 in 2002; 254 in 2003; 337 in 2004.
§ Including net lending.

2005 (million lari): Total revenue (excl. grants) 3,152.7 (Tax revenue 2,411.5, Non-tax current revenue 321.8, Capital revenue 419.4); Grants received from abroad 104.6; Total expenditure and net lending 3,280.8 (Financial aid issued from state budget 176.7).

2006 (million lari): Total revenue (excl. grants) 4,235.5 (Tax revenue 3,149.4, Non-tax current revenue 521.7, Capital revenue 564.5); Grants received from abroad 194.3; Total expenditure and net lending 4,464.1 (Financial aid issued from state budget 217.3).

2007 (million lari): Total revenue (excl. grants) 5,915.6 (Tax revenue 4,391.1, Non-tax current revenue 880.7, Capital revenue 643.8); Grants received from abroad 116.9; Total expenditure and net lending 6,083.1 (Financial aid issued from state budget 178.6).

INTERNATIONAL RESERVES
(excl. gold, US $ million at 31 December)

	2005	2006	2007
IMF special drawing rights . .	1.02	0.90	14.80
Reserve position in the IMF . .	0.01	0.02	0.02
Foreign exchange	477.61	929.91	1,346.34
Total	478.64	930.83	1,361.16

Source: IMF, *International Financial Statistics*.

MONEY SUPPLY
(million lari at 31 December)

	2005	2006	2007
Currency outside banks . . .	736.28	827.36	1,152.07
Demand deposits	263.25	439.45	682.17
Total money (incl. others) . .	999.54	1,266.80	1,834.24

Source: IMF, *International Financial Statistics*.

COST OF LIVING
(Consumer Price Index for five cities*; base: December 2003 = 100)

	2005	2006	2007
Food and non-alcoholic beverages .	116.7	132.3	149.5
Alcoholic beverages and tobacco .	166.7	149.2	151.1
Clothing and footwear	104.7	107.6	100.3
Housing, utilities and other fuels .	110.7	135.3	167.5
Household furnishings and maintenance	106.2	107.9	119.4
Health	99.5	115.4	125.7
Transport	113.0	115.9	134.0
Education	96.1	98.2	101.9
Recreation and culture . . .	101.8	101.4	109.2
All items (incl. others) . . .	114.1	124.1	137.8

* Tbilisi, Kutaisi, Batumi, Gori and Telavi.

NATIONAL ACCOUNTS
(million lari at current prices)

National Income and Product

	2005	2006	2007
Compensation of employees . .	1,977.4	2,293.2	3,252.3
Net operating surplus	2,186.0	2,647.9	4,686.3
Net mixed income	4,923.2	5,680.5	4,927.0
Domestic primary incomes	9,086.6	10,621.6	12,865.6
Consumption of fixed capital . .	1,113.5	1,306.4	1,617.0
Gross domestic product (GDP) at factor cost	10,200.1	11,928.0	14,482.6
Taxes on production and imports .	1,481.7	1,919.5	2,587.6
Less Subsidies	60.8	57.6	71.6
GDP in market prices . . .	11,621.0	13,789.9	16,998.6
Primary incomes received from abroad	477.6	598.5	809.2
Less Primary incomes paid abroad	306.8	286.0	435.1
Gross national income (GNI) .	11,791.8	14,102.4	17,372.8
Less Consumption of fixed capital .	1,113.5	1,306.4	1,617.0
Net national income	10,678.3	12,796.1	15,755.7
Current transfers from abroad .	747.9	1,029.1	1,163.4
Less Current transfers paid abroad	98.5	111.7	129.1
Net disposable income . . .	11,327.7	13,713.4	16,790.0

EXPENDITURE ON THE GROSS DOMESTIC PRODUCT

	2005	2006	2007
Government final consumption expenditure	2,014.0	2,116.0	3,717.9
Private final consumption expenditure	7,780.2	10,855.9	12,014.0
Increase in stocks	630.1	731.1	1,077.0
Gross fixed capital formation . .	3,261.4	3,524.2	4,805.6
Total domestic expenditure .	13,685.6	17,227.3	21,614.5
Exports of goods and services . .	3,921.9	4,532.1	5,357.2
Less Imports of goods and services	5,992.7	7,862.6	9,815.3
Statistical discrepancy	6.0	−106.9	−157.8
GDP in market prices . . .	11,620.9	13,789.9	16,998.6
GDP at constant 1996 prices .	6,577.5	7,194.7	8,089.0

Gross Domestic Product by Economic Activity

	2005	2006	2007
Agriculture, forestry and fishing	1,716.4	1,544.3	1,596.8
Mining and quarrying	91.3	138.8	163.3
Manufacturing	998.7	1,194.3	1,435.3
Electricity, gas and water supply .	326.2	375.1	413.9
Processing of products by households	406.8	338.9	369.1
Construction	937.9	947.3	1,137.3
Wholesale and retail trade; repair of motor vehicles, motorcycles and personal and household goods	1,388.8	1,878.6	2,228.4
Hotels and restaurants . . .	330.3	317.4	370.1
Transport, storage and communications	1,443.0	1,594.5	1,828.2
Financial intermediation . . .	231.7	292.8	368.2
Real estate, renting and business activities*	620.6	788.6	890.1
Public administration and defence; compulsory social security . .	750.5	1,174.5	2,176.8
Education	385.2	511.2	551.7
Health and social services . . .	404.0	597.5	713.9
Other community, social and personal services	373.3	450.1	525.0
Private households with employed persons	9.6	10.2	11.1
Sub-total	10,414.2	12,154.1	14,779.2
Less Financial intermediation services indirectly measured .	129.7	107.3	163.4
Gross value added in basic prices	10,284.5	12,046.9	14,615.9
Taxes on products	1,397.3	1,800.6	2,454.3
Less Subsidies on products . .	60.8	57.6	71.6
GDP in market prices . . .	11,621.0	13,789.9	16,998.6

* Including imputed rent of owner-occupied dwellings.

BALANCE OF PAYMENTS
(US $ million)

	2005	2006	2007
Exports of goods f.o.b.	1,472.4	1,666.5	2,104.1
Imports of goods f.o.b.	−2,686.6	−3,685.9	−4,976.5
Trade balance	−1,214.2	−2,019.4	−2,872.4
Exports of services	711.1	900.9	1,136.3
Imports of services	−631.5	−727.0	−931.9
Balance on goods and services	−1,134.6	−1,845.5	−2,668.0
Other income received	263.3	339.5	490.2
Other income paid	−188.2	−170.6	−449.8
Balance on goods, services and income	−1,059.5	−1,676.6	−2,627.6
Current transfers received . .	351.2	504.1	663.8
Current transfers paid	−54.4	−63.0	−80.2
Current balance	−762.6	−1,235.5	−2,044.0
Capital account (net)	58.6	168.7	126.9
Direct investment abroad . . .	89.5	15.8	−74.5
Direct investment from abroad .	452.8	1,059.8	1,659.0
Portfolio investment assets . .	13.1	−2.2	−8.8
Portfolio investment liabilities .	2.5	117.8	34.2
Financial derivatives assets . .	—	—	1.2
Financial derivatives liabilities .	—	—	−0.2
Other investment assets . . .	−15.5	−45.7	−191.9
Other investment liabilities . .	123.6	193.6	738.4
Net errors and omissions . . .	18.6	58.4	−20.7
Overall balance	−19.4	330.7	219.6

Source: IMF, *International Financial Statistics*.

External Trade

PRINCIPAL COMMODITIES
(US $ million)

Imports	2005	2006	2007
Wheat	45.1	99.1	139.2
Sugar	78.2	65.6	90.5
Petroleum and petroleum oils	336.3	443.1	556.3
Petroleum gases and other gaseous hydrocarbons	90.8	213.1	293.7
Medicaments	92.5	114.5	144.0
Bars and rods of iron or non-alloy steel	14.6	33.1	71.9
Automatic data-processing machines	22.4	46.4	78.0
Transmission apparatus	27.1	58.7	105.2
Motor cars	178.5	295.3	369.7
Total (incl. others)	2,490.0	3,677.8	5,216.7

Exports	2005	2006	2007
Alcohol and other spirituous beverages	29.2	30.1	57.4
Edible fruits and nuts	70.3	56.6	65.1
Mineral or chemical fertilizers, nitrogenous	35.8	46.6	57.0
Portland cement	17.7	28.8	64.0
Copper ores and concentrates	36.4	79.5	79.2
Gold, unwrought or in semi-manufactured forms	34.7	49.4	69.4
Ferrous waste and scrap; remelting scrap ingots of iron or steel	84.2	72.4	96.9
Ferro-alloys	80.2	89.8	159.6
Motor cars	17.9	50.6	70.2
Total (incl. others)	865.5	936.2	1,240.2

PRINCIPAL TRADING PARTNERS
(US $ million)

Imports c.i.f.	2003	2004	2005
Armenia	11.2	26.2	39.3
Austria	11.3	22.3	19.0
Azerbaijan	93.7	156.4	233.4
Belgium	9.9	15.5	25.6
Brazil	11.2	23.7	33.0
Bulgaria	19.3	38.9	72.3
China, People's Repub.	23.2	28.9	46.7
France	55.7	63.2	97.3
Germany	82.8	151.1	206.8
Italy	36.5	61.6	64.4
Iran	7.0	15.2	26.0
Kazakhstan	9.8	21.4	11.6
Netherlands	23.8	34.6	53.1
Romania	10.5	14.0	40.7
Russia	161.1	257.8	384.3
Switzerland	14.3	26.1	17.5
Turkey	112.0	202.1	283.0
Turkmenistan	9.8	32.7	95.1
Ukraine	80.2	142.4	219.4
United Arab Emirates	19.8	46.7	73.0
United Kingdom	145.6	171.8	70.2
USA	90.7	110.9	146.8
Total (incl. others)	1,141.2	1,847.9	2,490.9

Exports f.o.b.	2003	2004	2005
Armenia	30.8	54.5	39.9
Azerbaijan	16.4	25.3	83.4
Bulgaria	0.1	15.6	42.8
Canada	0.2	3.7	35.6
France	4.9	9.6	11.5
Germany	9.8	15.9	28.5
Greece	5.2	7.3	10.4
India	6.4	6.0	2.3
Italy	8.7	11.6	33.6
Kazakhstan	4.3	7.6	9.8
Netherlands	9.9	9.8	11.3
Romania	1.0	1.3	8.8
Russia	83.9	104.5	153.9
Seychelles	0.0	2.1	12.6
Spain	7.0	9.5	14.2
Switzerland	33.3	17.8	3.2
Turkey	82.5	118.6	121.8
Turkmenistan	54.9	113.4	75.8
Ukraine	30.1	15.6	37.3
United Kingdom	27.9	31.7	31.9
USA	15.4	21.2	26.7
Total (incl. others)	461.4	647.0	866.2

2005 (US $ million, revised): Total imports 2,490.0; Total exports 865.5.

2006 (US $ million): Total imports 3,677.8 (Azerbaijan 318.5; Bulgaria 115.5; China, People's Republic 103.3; Germany 351.2; Italy 102.1; Russia 558.8; Ukraine 320.1; United Arab Emirates 109.1; USA 129.6); Total exports 992.5 (Armenia 73.6; Azerbaijan 92.2; Canada 45.4; Kazakhstan 15.4; Russia 75.7; Spain 16.6; Turkey 124.9; USA 58.9).

2007 (US $ million): Total imports 5,216.7 (Azerbaijan 382.0; Bulgaria 184.0; China, People's Republic 206.7; Germany 387.3; Russia 578.8; Turkey 727.9; Ukraine 574.9; United Arab Emirates 214.7; USA 203.9); Total exports 1,240.2 (Azerbaijan 137.3; Bulgaria 59.4; Germany 56.2; Russia 53.0; Turkey 171.8; Ukraine 94.2; USA 149.6).

Transport

RAILWAYS
(traffic)

	2002	2003	2004
Passengers carried (million)	2.1	2.2	3.0
Passenger-km (million)	400.6	387.4	614.0
Freight ('000 tons)	14,951.5	16,558.7	15,408.4
Freight net ton-km (million)	5,074.5	5,538.7	4,855.8

ROAD TRAFFIC
('000 motor vehicles in use)

	2001	2002	2003
Passenger cars	247.8	252.0	255.2
Buses	22.7	24.1	25.7
Lorries and vans	47.0	45.5	42.9
Total (incl. others)	319.6	323.6	325.0

SHIPPING

Merchant Fleet
(registered at 31 December)

	2005	2006	2007
Number of vessels	375	386	398
Total displacement ('000 grt)	1,091.9	1,129.3	1,048.4

Source: Lloyd's Register-Fairplay, *World Fleet Statistics*.

CIVIL AVIATION
(traffic on scheduled services)

	2002	2003	2004
Passengers carried ('000)* . . .	100	200	200
Passenger-km (million)	297.3	400.3	483.3
Total ton-km (million)	29	27	37

* Figures are rounded.

Tourism

FOREIGN TOURIST ARRIVALS

Country of residence	2004	2005	2006
Armenia	71,261	100,508	245,146
Azerbaijan	63,663	153,467	244,444
Germany	7,208	8,840	14,884
Greece	4,148	7,098	13,135
Israel	5,167	6,318	11,462
Russia	61,400	90,277	104,111
Turkey	74,700	109,796	192,436
Ukraine	14,721	12,431	29,163
United Kingdom	6,397	6,677	12,742
USA	9,609	12,928	16,622
Total (incl. others)	368,312	560,021	983,114

Tourism receipts (US $ million, incl. passenger transport): 172 in 2003; 209 in 2004; 288 in 2005.

Source: World Tourism Organization.

Communications Media

	2004	2005	2006
Telephones ('000 main lines in use) .	683.2	570.2	553.1
Mobile cellular telephones ('000 subscribers)	840.6	1,174.3	1,703.9
Internet users ('000)	175.6	271.4	332.0
Broadband subscribers ('000) . . .	1.9	2.4	27.0
Personal computers (in use, '000) .	192	n.a.	n.a.
Newspapers: titles	122	88	n.a.
Newspapers: circulation ('000) . .	600	400	n.a.

Radio receivers ('000 in use): 3,020 in 1997.

Television receivers ('000 in use): 2,590 in 2000.

Facsimile machines (number in use): 500 in 1996.

Book production (incl. pamphlets): 581 titles in 1996 (834,000 copies); 697 titles in 1999.

Sources: UN, *Statistical Yearbook*; UNESCO, *Statistical Yearbook*; and International Telecommunication Union.

Education

(2006/07 unless otherwise indicated)

	Institutions	Students†
Pre-primary schools	1,197	77,922
General education: schools (primary)* .	} 2,539	{ 322,249
General education: schools (secondary) .		313,739
General education: evening schools‡ .	14	n.a.
State secondary professional schools .	79	18,242
Private secondary professional schools .	26	6,658
State higher schools (incl. universities) .	18	110,846
Private higher schools (incl. universities)	148	29,961

* Including primary schools covering part of the secondary syllabus.
† Some figures are rounded.
‡ Data for 2005/06.

Teachers (2005/06 unless otherwise indicated): Pre-primary 7,783 (2004/05); Total in general day schools 68,992 (primary, basic 8,467, secondary 59,856); Total in secondary professional schools 4,673 (3,462 public, 1,211 private); Total in institutes of higher education 20,960 (13,288 in public institutions, 7,672 in non-state institutions).

Directory

The Constitution

A new Constitution was approved by the Georgian legislature on 24 August 1995; it entered into force on 17 October. The following is a summary of the Constitution's main provisions, as subsequently amended:

GENERAL PROVISIONS

Georgia is an independent, united and undivided state and a democratic republic.

All state power belongs to the people, who exercise this power through referendums, other forms of direct democracy and through their elected representatives. The State recognizes and defends universally recognized human rights and freedoms. The official state language is Georgian; in Abkhazia both Georgian and Abkhazian are recognized as state languages. While the State recognizes the exceptional role played by the Georgian Orthodox Church in Georgian history, it declares the complete freedom of faith and religion as well as the independence of the Church from the State. The capital is Tbilisi.

FUNDAMENTAL HUMAN RIGHTS AND FREEDOMS

Georgian citizenship is acquired by birth and naturalization. A Georgian citizen may not be a citizen of another state concurrently. Every person is equal before the law. No one may be subjected to torture or inhuman, cruel or humiliating treatment or punishment.

Freedom of speech and conscience are guaranteed. The mass media are free. The right to assemble publicly is guaranteed, as is the right to form public associations, including trade unions and political parties. Every citizen who has attained the age of 18 years has the right to participate in referendums and elections for state and local administrative bodies.

PARLAMENTI

Parlamenti (Sakartvelos Parlamenti, or the Georgian Parliament) is the supreme representative body. It is elected on the basis of universal, equal and direct suffrage by secret ballot, for a term of four years. It is composed of 235 members: 150 elected by proportional representation and 85 by majority vote in single-member constituencies. Under constitutional amendments adopted in March 2008, the number of deputies in Parlamenti was reduced from 235 to 150, with effect from early legislative elections in May: 75 were to be elected by proportional representation (with a minimum requirement of 5% of the votes cast to secure parliamentary representation) and 75 by majority vote in single-member constituencies. Any citizen who has attained the age of 25 years and has the right to vote may be elected to Parlamenti.

Parlamenti elects a Chairman and Deputy Chairmen (including one Deputy Chairman each from deputies elected in Abkhazia and Adjara), for the length of its term of office. Members of Parlamenti may unite to form parliamentary factions of no fewer than 10 members.

Following the creation of the appropriate conditions throughout the territory of Georgia and the formation of bodies of local self-government, Parlamenti will be composed of two chambers: the Council of the Republic and the Senate. The Council of the Republic will be composed of deputies elected according to the proportional system. The Senate will be composed of deputies elected in Abkhazia, Adjara and other territorial units of Georgia, and five members appointed by the President of Georgia.

THE PRESIDENT OF GEORGIA AND THE GOVERNMENT

The President of Georgia is Head of State and the head of executive power. The President is elected on the basis of universal, equal and direct suffrage by secret ballot, for a period of five years. The President may not be elected for more than two consecutive terms. Any citizen of Georgia who has the right to vote and who has attained the age of 35 years and lived in Georgia for no less than 15 years is eligible to be elected President.

The President of Georgia concludes international treaties and agreements and conducts negotiations with foreign states; with the consent of Parlamenti, appoints members of the Government and Ministers; is empowered to remove Ministers from their posts; submits to Parlamenti the draft state budget; declares a state of war, and concludes peace; declares a state of emergency; signs and promulgates laws; grants pardons; schedules elections to Parlamenti and other representative bodies; is the Commander-in-Chief of the Armed Forces, and appoints and dismisses military commanders.

The President enjoys immunity from arrest and criminal proceedings. In the event that the President violates the Constitution, betrays the State or commits other crimes, Parlamenti may remove him/her from office with the approval of the Constitutional Court or the Supreme Court.

Parlamenti appoints and dismisses a Prime Minister. Members of the Government may be removed from their posts by the President or by Parlamenti, or by two successive legislative votes expressing 'no confidence' adopted by a two-thirds' majority in Parlamenti. Ministries perform state management in specific spheres of state and public life.

JUDICIAL POWER

Judicial power is independent. Court proceedings are held in public (except for certain specified instances). It is prohibited to instigate criminal proceedings against a judge or to detain or arrest him, without the consent of the Chairman of the Supreme Court.

The Constitutional Court is the legal body of constitutional control. It is composed of nine judges, three of whom are appointed by the President, three elected by Parlamenti, and three appointed by the Supreme Court. The term of office of members of the Constitutional Court is 10 years.

The Supreme Court supervises legal proceedings in general courts and, as the court of first instance, examines cases determined by law. On the recommendation of the President of Georgia, the Chairman and judges of the Supreme Court are elected by Parlamenti for a period of at least 10 years.

The Procurator's Office is an institution of judicial power, which carries out criminal prosecution, supervises preliminary investigations and the execution of a punishment, and supports the state prosecution. On the recommendation of the President of Georgia, the Procurator-General is appointed by Parlamenti for a term of five years. Lower-ranking procurators are appointed by the Procurator-General.

The Government

HEAD OF STATE

President: MIKHEIL SAAKASHVILI (elected 4 January 2004; re-elected 5 January 2008; inaugurated 20 January 2008).

GOVERNMENT
(September 2008)

Prime Minister: VLADIMER GURGENIDZE.

Deputy Prime Minister and State Minister, responsible for European and Euro-Atlantic Integration: GIORGI BARAMIDZE.

State Minister, responsible for Regional Affairs: DAVIT TKESHELASHVILI.

State Minister, responsible for Diaspora Affairs: IULON GAGOSHIDZE.

State Minister, responsible for Reintegration: TEMUR IAKOBASHVILI.

Minister of Foreign Affairs: EKA TKESHELASHVILI.

Minister of Education and Science: GIORGI NODIA.

Minister of Economic Development: EKATERINE SHARASHIDZE.

Minister of Finance: NIKA GILAURI.

Minister of Defence: DAVIT KEZERASHVILI.

Minister of Internal Affairs: IVANE MERABISHVILI.

Minister of Justice: NIKA GVARAMIA.

Minister of Agriculture: BAKUR KVEZERELI.

Minister of Environmental Protection and Natural Resources: IRAKLI GVALADZE.

Minister of Energy: ALEXANDRE KHETAGURII.

Minister of Culture, the Protection of Monuments and Sport: NIKOLOZ VACHEISHVILI.

Minister of Refugee and Resettlement Affairs: TAMAR MARTIASHVILI.

Minister of Health, Labour, and Social Protection: ALEKSANDRE KVITASHVILI.

MINISTRIES

Office of the President: 0105 Tbilisi, P. Ingorovka 7; tel. (32) 99-00-70; fax (32) 99-88-87; e-mail secretariat@admin.gov.ge; internet www.president.gov.ge.

Chancellery of the Government: 0105 Tbilisi, P. Ingorovka 7; tel. (32) 92-22-43; fax (32) 92-10-69; e-mail primeminister@geo.gov.ge; internet www.government.gov.ge.

Office of the Deputy Prime Minister, State Minister, responsible for Euro-Atlantic Integration: 0105 Tbilisi, P. Ingorovka 7; tel. (32) 93-28-67; fax (32) 93-27-22; internet www.eu-nato.gov.ge.

Office of the State Minister, responsible for Diaspora Affairs: 0105 Tbilisi, P. Ingorovka 7.

Office of the State Minister, responsible for Regional Affairs: 0105 Tbilisi, P. Ingorovka 7.

Office of the State Minister, responsible for Reintegration: 0105 Tbilisi, P. Ingorovka 7; e-mail mg@smr.gov.ge; internet www.smr.gov.ge.

Ministry of Agriculture: 0179 Tbilisi, Kostava 41; tel. and fax (32) 93-23-25; e-mail ministry@maf.ge; internet www.maf.ge.

Ministry of Culture, the Protection of Monuments and Sport: 0108 Tbilisi, Sh. Rustaveli 37; tel. (32) 93-22-55; fax (32) 99-90-37; e-mail info@mcs.gov.ge; internet www.mcs.gov.ge.

Ministry of Defence: 0112 Tbilisi, Gen. Kvinitadze 20; tel. (32) 91-19-63; fax (32) 91-06-45; e-mail pr@mod.gov.ge; internet www.mod.gov.ge.

Ministry of Economic Development: 0108 Tbilisi, Chanturia 12; tel. (32) 93-16-33; fax (32) 92-15-34; e-mail ministry@econom.ge; internet www.economy.ge.

Ministry of Education and Science: 0102 Tbilisi, D. Uznadze 52; tel. (32) 95-70-10; fax (32) 91-04-47; e-mail pr@mes.gov.ge; internet www.mes.gov.ge.

Ministry of Energy: 0105 Tbilisi, Lermontov 10; tel. and fax (32) 98-31-94; internet www.minenergy.gov.ge.

Ministry of Environmental Protection and Natural Resources: 0114 Tbilisi, G. Gulua 6; tel. (32) 27-57-00; fax (32) 33-39-52; e-mail gmep@access.sanet.ge; internet www.moe.gov.ge.

Ministry of Finance: 0162 Tbilisi, I. Abashidze 70; tel. (32) 22-68-05; fax (32) 93-19-22; e-mail minister@mof.ge; internet www.mof.ge.

Ministry of Foreign Affairs: 0108 Tbilisi, Sh. Chitadze 4; tel. (32) 28-47-47; fax (32) 28-46-78; e-mail inform@mfa.gov.ge; internet www.mfa.gov.ge.

Ministry of Health, Labour and Social Protection: 0102 Tbilisi, K. Gamsakhurdia 30; tel. (32) 38-75-10; fax (32) 38-00-23; internet www.moh.gov.ge.

Ministry of Internal Affairs: 0114 Tbilisi, Gulua 10; tel. (32) 75-55-56; fax (32) 75-20-27; e-mail press_center@pol.ge; internet www.police.ge.

Ministry of Justice: 0146 Tbilisi, Sh. Rustaveli 30; tel. (32) 75-82-07; fax (32) 75-82-37; e-mail press@justice.gov.ge; internet www.justice.gov.ge.

Ministry of Refugees and Resettlement Affairs: 0180 Tbilisi, Ts. Dadiani 30; tel. (32) 92-13-05; fax (32) 92-14-27; e-mail presscentre@mra.gov.ge; internet www.mra.gov.ge.

President

Presidential Election, 5 January 2008

Candidates	Votes	%
Mikheil Saakashvili	1,060,042	53.47
Levan Gachechiladze	509,234	25.69
Arkadi (Badri) Patarkatsishvili . .	140,826	7.10
Shalva Natelashvili	128,589	6.49
David Gamkrelidze	79,747	4.02
Others	18,491	0.93
Total*	1,982,318	100.00

* Including invalid votes (2.29% of the total).

Legislature

Sakartvelos Parlamenti
(Georgian Parliament)

0118 Tbilisi, Rustaveli 8; tel. (32) 93-61-70; fax (32) 99-93-86; e-mail hdstaff@parliament.ge; internet www.parliament.ge.

Chairman: DAVIT BAKRADZE.
General Election, 21 May 2008

		Seats		
Parties and blocs	%*	A†	B†	Total
United National Movement . .	59.18	48	71	119
The Joint Opposition (National Council, New Rights)‡ . . .	17.73	15	2	17
Christian Democratic Movement .	8.66	6	—	6
Georgian Labour Party . . .	7.44	6	—	6
Republican Party of Georgia . .	3.78	—	2	2
Others	3.21	—	—	—
Total	100.00	75	75	150

* Percentage refers to the share of the vote cast for seats awarded on the basis of party lists.
† Of the 150 seats in the Sakartvelos Parlamenti, 75 (A) are awarded according to proportional representation on the basis of party lists, and 75 (B) are elected in single-mandate constituencies.
‡ An electoral alliance of nine parties.

Local Government

Georgia contains two nominally autonomous territories: the Autonomous Republics of Adjara and Abkhazia. The status of Abkhazia and the former Autonomous Oblast (region) of South Ossetia are both disputed (see section on the autonomous territories). The structures of local government were reformed during the 1990s. Those parts of the country under central government control are divided into nine mkharebi (regions—singular mkhare), headed by governors (trustees) appointed by the President, and the city of Tbilisi, headed by a mayor, who is elected by the City Council. Most of the disputed territory of South Ossetia is officially included in Shida Kartli Mkhare, although some parts of the former autonomous oblast are incorporated into other Mkharebi. A new 'temporary administrative unit', comprising those areas formerly in South Ossetia under government control, was additionally established in 2007, but Georgian control over these territories was lost during the armed conflict with Russia of August 2008. A second tier of local government comprises seven cities of special status and 60 districts (raions), and a third tier comprises a total of 966 villages and settlements. Local elections were held on 5 October 2006.

CAPITAL CITY

Tbilisi City Administration: Tbilisi; internet www.tbilisi.gov.ge; Mayor GIORGI UGULAVA; Chair. ZAZA BEGASHVILI.

MKHAREBI

Guria Mkhare Administration: 3500 Guria Mkhare, Ozurgeti, M. Kostava 1; tel. (296) 98-82-56; Governor RAMAZ NIKOLEISHVILI.

Imereti Mkhare Administration: 4600 Imereti Mkhare, Kutaisi, Rustaveli 3; tel. and fax (331) 41-585; e-mail businessaffairs@imereti.ge; internet www.imereti.ge; Governor AKAKI BOBOKHIDZE.

Kakheti Mkhare Administration: 2200 Kakheti Mkhare, Telavi; tel. (350) 99-67-03; e-mail kakheti_region@yahoo.com; Governor LEVAN BEZHASHVILI.

Kvemo Kartli Mkhare Administration: 3700 Kvemo Kartli Mkhare, Rustavi, Merab Kostava 20; tel. (34) 19-42-73; fax (34) 19-37-60; e-mail pr@kvemokartli.gov.ge; internet www.kvemokartli.gov.ge; Governor ZURAB MELIKISHVILI.

Mtskheta-Mtianeti Mkhare Administration: 3300 Mtskheta-Mtianeti Mkhare, Mtskheta; tel. (225) 99-90-40; internet www.mtskheta-mtianeti.gov.ge; Governor TSEZAR CHOCHELI.

Racha-Lechkumi and Kvemo Svaneti Mkhare Administration: 0400 Racha-Lechkumi and Kvemo Svaneti Mkhare, Ambrolauri, T. Mephe 1; tel. (203) 5-61; Governor OTAR SIRADZE.

Samegrelo-Zemo Svaneti Mkhare Administration: 2100 Samegrelo-Zemo Svaneti Mkhare, Zugdidi, Gamsakhurdia 45; tel. (315) 50-505; e-mail szs@szs.gov.ge; internet www.szs.gov.ge; Governor ZAZA GOROZIA.

Samtskhe-Javakheti Mkhare Administration: 0800 Samtskhe-Javakheti Mkhare, Akhaltsikhe, Davit Agmashenebeli 35; tel. (265) 21-434; fax (32) 91-19-21; Governor GIORGI KHACHIDZE.

Shida Kartli Mkhare Administration: 1400 Shida Kartli Mkhare, Gori; tel. (270) 71-874; internet www.shidakartli.ge; Governor LADO VARDZELASHVILI.

Election Commission

Central Electoral Commission of Georgia (CEC): 0108 Tbilisi, Rustaveli 29, 3rd Floor; tel. (32) 98-70-10; fax (32) 98-70-00; e-mail cec@cec.gov.ge; internet www.cec.gov.ge; Chair. LEVAN TARKHNISHVILI.

Political Organizations

In early 2008 some 190 political parties and alliances were registered with the Central Electoral Commission. The following were among the most prominent parties in Georgia at that time:

Christian Democratic Movement (CDM): 0162 Tbilisi, Faliashvili 63; tel. (32) 22–27–99; e-mail office@cdm.ge; internet www.cdm.ge; f. 2008; Chair. GIORGI TARGAMADZE.

Christian Democratic Union of Georgia: 0177 Tbilisi, Kazbegi 37; tel. (32) 48-20-01; fax (32) 48-20-04; e-mail cdu@cdu.ge; internet www.cdu.ge; f. 1990; centre-right; contested (subsequently annulled) 2003 legislative elections as mem. of the For a New Georgia bloc; Leader VAZHA LORTKIPANIDZE.

Citizens' Union of Georgia (CUG) (SMK): 0179 Tbilisi, Chavchavadze 55; tel. (32) 99-94-79; fax (32) 93-15-84; e-mail cug@access.sanet.ge; f. 1993; contested (subsequently annulled) 2003 legislative elections as mem. of the For a New Georgia bloc; Chair. AVTANDIL JORBENADZE.

Conservative Party of Georgia (Sakartvelos konservatorebi): 0108 Tbilisi, Kutateladze 4; tel. and fax (32) 28-12-25; e-mail kukava@parliament.ge; internet www.conservators.ge; f. 2001; Chair. ZVIAD DZIDZIGURI.

Freedom (Tavisupleba): Tbilisi; f. 2004 by a son of former President Zviad Gamsakhurdia; nationalist; Leader KONSTANTINE GAMSAKHURDIA.

Georgian Social Democratic Party: 0108 Tbilisi, Tskhra Aprilis 2; tel. (32) 99-95-50; fax (32) 98-42-57; f. 1990; contested (subsequently annulled) 2003 legislative elections as mem. of the Jumber Patiashvili-Unity bloc; Chair. Prof. JEMAL KAKHNIASHVILI.

Georgia's Way: 0108 Tbilisi, Rustaveli 40; f. 2006; Leader SALOMÉ ZURABISHVILI; Chair. of Political Council GIA TORTLADZE.

Green Party (Mtsvanta Partia): 0112 Tbilisi, D. Aghmashenebeli 182; tel. (32) 35-19-14; fax (32) 35-16-74; e-mail info@greensparty.ge; internet www.greensparty.ge; f. 1990; contested (subsequently annulled) 2003 legislative elections as mem. of the For a New Georgia bloc; Chair. GIORGI GACHECHILADZE.

Hope (Imedi): Tbilisi; f. 2006; opposition; supports exiled former minister Igor Giorgadze; Leader IRINA SARISHVILI-CHANTURIA.

Industry Will Save Georgia (Mretsveloba Gadaarchens Sakartvelos): 0105 Tbilisi, Marjvena Sanapiro 7; tel. (32) 94-09-81; f. 1999; contested 2004 legislative elections as mem. of Rightist Opposition bloc; Chair. ZURAB TKEMALADZE; Leader GIORGI TOPADZE.

Justice (Samartlianoba): 0108 Tbilisi, Rustaveli 24; tel. (32) 99-63-48; fax (32) 99-08-76; f. 2003; supports closer relations between Georgia and Russia; Chair. IGOR GIORGADZE (in exile).

Movement for a United Georgia: Tbilisi; f. 2007; Leader IRAKLI OKRUASHVILI.

National Forum: Tbilisi; f. 2006; Leader KAKHA SHARTAVA.

New Rights (Axali Memarjveneebi—Axlebi): 0114 Tbilisi, Bevreti 3; tel. (32) 72-21-01; fax (32) 72-38-58; e-mail ncp@ncp.ge; internet www .ncp.ge; f. 2001 as New Conservative Party; contested 2004 legislative elections as mem. of Rightist Opposition bloc; Chair. Dr DAVIT GAMKRELIDZE; Gen. Sec. DAVIT SAGANELIDZE.

People's Front of Georgia: 0105 Tbilisi, Pushkin 5; tel. (32) 93-17-10; f. 1989; Chair. NODAR NATADZE.

People's Party (Didgori): 0102 Tbilisi, D. Uznadze 56; tel. (32) 96-03-69; fax (32) 93-57-98; f. 1996; Chair. MAMUKA GIORGIADZE.

Republican Party of Georgia: 0108 Tbilisi, Griboyedov 13; tel. and fax (32) 92-00-58; e-mail republicans@republicans.ge; internet www.republicans.ge; f. 1995; absorbed Georgian Popular Front (f. 1989); politically, economically and socially liberal; Chair. DAVID USUPASHVILI.

Socialist Party of Georgia: 0105 Tbilisi, Leselidze 41; tel. (32) 93-10-21; fax (32) 93-27-09; e-mail spg@geo-plus.net; f. 1995; contested (subsequently annulled) 2003 legislative elections as mem. of the For a New Georgia bloc; Chair. IRAKLI MINDELI.

Union of Georgian Traditionalists: 0108 Tbilisi, Virsaladze 10; tel. (32) 98-39-55; f. 1990; contested (subsequently annulled) 2003 legislative elections as mem. of the Burjanadze-Democrats bloc; alliance with the National Democratic Party of Georgia announced in Dec. 2003; founded the People's Forum for Welfare and Democracy in 2005, to campaign for the direct election of city mayors and regional governors; Chair. AKAKI ASATIANI.

United National Movement (UNM): 0118 Tbilisi, Lesya Ukrainka 1; tel. (32) 92-30-84; fax (32) 92-30-91; e-mail info@unm.ge; internet www.unm.ge; f. Nov. 2004 by merger of National Movement and United Democrats; nationalist; Chair. MIKHEIL SAAKASHVILI; Sec.-Gen. ZURAB MELIKISHVILI.

Unity (Ertoba): 0105 Tbilisi, Tavisuplebis Moedani; tel. (32) 92-30-65; fax (32) 93-46-94; e-mail ertoba@post.com; f. 2001; contested (subsequently annulled) 2003 legislative elections as mem. of the Jumber Patiashvili-Unity bloc; Co-Chair. JUMBER PATIASHVILI, ALEKSANDER CHACHIA.

Diplomatic Representation

EMBASSIES IN GEORGIA

Armenia: 0102 Tbilisi, Tetelashvili 4; tel. (32) 95-17-23; fax (32) 96-42-87; e-mail armemb@caucasus.net; Ambassador HRACH SILVANIAN.

Azerbaijan: 0177 Tbilisi, Nutsubidze 47; tel. (32) 25-26-39; fax (32) 25-00-13; e-mail secretariat@azembassy.ge; internet www .azembassy.ge; Ambassador NAMIQ ALIYEV.

Bulgaria: 0102 Tbilisi, D. Aghmashenebeli 61; tel. (32) 91-01-94; fax (32) 91-02-70; e-mail bgembassy.georgia@gol.ge; internet www.mfa .bg/tbilisi; Ambassador VLADIMIR P. RADEV.

China, People's Republic: 0108 Tbilisi, Barnov 52, POB 224; tel. (32) 25-26-71; fax (32) 44-13-83; e-mail yfarm@access.sanet.ge; internet ge.china-embassy.org; Ambassador WANG KAIWEN.

Czech Republic: 0162 Tbilisi, Chavchavadze 37/6; tel. (32) 91-67-40; fax (32) 91-67-44; e-mail tbilisi@embassy.mzv.cz; internet www .mzv.cz/tbilisi; Ambassador IVAN JESTŘÁB.

Estonia: 0171 Tbilisi, Saburtalo, Likhauri 4; tel. (32) 36-51-22; fax (32) 36-51-38; e-mail tbilisisaatkond@mfa.ee; internet www.tbilisi .vm.ee; Ambassador TOOMAS LUKK.

France: 0108 Tbilisi, Gogebashvili 15; tel. (32) 99-99-76; fax (32) 95-33-75; e-mail ambafrance@access.sanet.ge; internet www .ambafrance-ge.org; Ambassador ERIC FOURNIER.

Germany: 0103 Tbilisi, Telavi 20, Sheraton Metekhi Palace Hotel; tel. (32) 44-73-00; fax (32) 44-73-64; e-mail info@tiflis.diplo.de; internet www.tiflis.diplo.de; Ambassador Dr PATRICIA FLOR.

Greece: 0179 Tbilisi, T. Tabldze 37D; tel. and fax (32) 91-49-70; e-mail grembgeo@access.sanet.ge; internet www.greekembassy.ge; Ambassador GEORGIOS CHATZIMIHELAKIS.

Holy See: 0108 Tbilisi, Jenti 40, Nutsubidze Plateau; tel. (32) 53-76-01; fax (32) 53-67-04; e-mail nuntius@access.sanet.ge; Apostolic Nuncio Most Rev. CLAUDIO GUGEROTTI (Titular Archbishop of Ravello).

Iran: 0160 Tbilisi, Zovreti 16; tel. (32) 98-69-90; fax (32) 98-69-93; e-mail iranemb@caucasus.net; Ambassador MOJTABA DAMIRCHILOU.

Israel: 0102 Tbilisi, D. Aghmashenebeli 61; tel. (32) 94-27-05; fax (32) 95-52-09; e-mail press@tbilisi.mfa.gov.il; internet tbilisi.mfa.gov .il; Ambassador SHABTAI TSUR.

Italy: 0108 Tbilisi, Chitadze 3A; tel. (32) 99-64-18; fax (32) 99-64-15; e-mail ambtbilisi@esteri.it; internet www.ambtbilisi.esteri.it; Chargé d'affaires a.i. VITTORIO SANDALLI.

Latvia: 0160 Tbilisi, Odessa 60; tel. (32) 24-48-58; fax (32) 38-14-06; e-mail embassy.georgia@mfa.gov.lv; Ambassador ANDRIS VILCANS.

Lithuania: 0162 Tbilisi, T. Abuladze 27; tel. (32) 91-29-33; fax (32) 22-17-93; e-mail amb.ge@urm.lt; internet ge.mfa.lt; Ambassador MEČYS LAURINKUS.

Netherlands: 0103 Tbilisi, Telavi 20, Sheraton Metekhi Palace Hotel; tel. (32) 27-62-00; fax (32) 27-62-32; e-mail tbi@minbuza.nl; internet www.dutchembassy.ge; Ambassador ONNO ELDERENBOSCH.

Poland: 0108 Tbilisi, Zubalashvili 19; tel. (32) 92-03-98; fax (32) 92-03-97; e-mail ambpolgruzja@access.sanet.ge; internet www.tbilisi .polemb.net; Ambassador JACEK MULTANOWSKI.

Romania: Tbilisi, Lvovi 7; tel. (32) 38-53-10; fax (32) 38-52-10; e-mail roembtbl@caucasus.net; Ambassador DAN MIHAI BÁRLIBA.

Switzerland: 0114 Tbilisi, Krtsanisi 11; tel. (32) 75-30-01; fax (32) 75-30-06; e-mail tif.vertretung@eda.admin.ch; internet www.eda .admin.ch/tbilisi; Ambassador Dr LORENZO AMBERG.

Turkey: 0162 Tbilisi, Chavchavadze 35; tel. (32) 25-20-72; fax (32) 22-06-66; e-mail tiblisbe@dsl.ge; Ambassador ERTAN TEZGOR.

Ukraine: 0160 Tbilisi, Oniashvili 75; tel. (32) 31-11-61; fax (32) 31-11-81; e-mail emb_ge@mfa.gov.ua; internet www.mfa.gov.ua/ georgia; Ambassador MYKOLA M. SPYS.

United Kingdom: 0105 Tbilisi, Tavisuplebis Moedani 4; tel. (32) 27-47-47; fax (32) 27-47-92; e-mail british.embassy.tbilisi@fco.gov.uk; internet www.britishembassy.gov.uk/georgia; Ambassador DENIS KEEFE.

USA: 0131 Tbilisi, G. Balanchine 11; tel. (32) 27-70-00; fax (32) 53-23-10; e-mail consulate-tbilisi@state.gov; internet georgia.usembassy .gov; Ambassador JOHN F. TEFFT.

Judicial System

Constitutional Court: 6000 Adjara, Batumi; tel. (222) 7-00-99; fax (222) 7-01-44; e-mail court@const.gov.ge; internet www.constcourt .gov.ge; f. 1996; consists of 9 members; Pres. GIORGI PAPUASHVILI.

Supreme Court
0110 Tbilisi, Zubalashvili 32; tel. (32) 93-12-62; fax (32) 92-08-76; e-mail reception@supremecourt.ge; internet www.supremecourt.ge; Chair. KONSTANTIN KUBLASHVILI.

Procurator-General: (vacant).

High Council of Justice: 0144 Tbilisi, Bochorma 12; tel. (32) 27-31-00; fax (32) 27-31-01; e-mail justice@caucasus.net; internet www .hcoj.gov.ge; f. 1997; 15-member council that co-ordinates the appointment of judges and their activities; Chair. Chairman of the Supreme Court KONSTANTIN KUBLASHVILI; Exec. Sec. VALERIAN TSERTSVADZE.

Religion

CHRISTIANITY

The Georgian Orthodox Church

The Georgian Orthodox Church is divided into 27 dioceses, and includes not only Georgian parishes, but also several Russian, Greek and Armenian Orthodox communities, which are under the jurisdiction of the Primate of the Georgian Orthodox Church.

Georgian Patriarchate: 0105 Tbilisi, Erekle II Moedani 1; tel. (32) 99-03-78; fax (32) 98-71-14; e-mail orthodox@patriarchate.ge; internet www.patriarchate.ge; Catholicos-Patriarch of All Georgia ILIA II.

The Roman Catholic Church

The Apostolic Administrator of the Caucasus for Roman Catholics of the Latin Rite is resident in Tbilisi. At 31 December 2006 there were some 50,000 adherents within the territory covered by the Administration (which includes Armenia in addition to Georgia).

Apostolic Administrator: Most Rev. GIUSEPPE PASOTTO (Titular Bishop of Musti), 0105 Tbilisi, G. Abesadze 6; tel. and fax (32) 99-60-50; e-mail ammapost@geo.net.ge.

ISLAM

The Meshketian population, which formerly constituted one of the principal Muslim groups in Georgia, was deported to Central Asia in 1944 at Stalin's behest. The principal Islamic communities in Georgia are those among the Ajars and Abkhaz (who are Sunni Muslims) and Azeris (who are Shi'ite).

The Press

PRINCIPAL NEWSPAPERS

In 2005 88 newspaper titles were printed. Those listed below appear in Georgian, except where otherwise stated.

Axali Taoba (New Generation): 0102 Tbilisi, D. Aghmashenebeli 89/24; tel. (32) 95-25-89; fax (32) 94-06-91; e-mail akhtao@geo.net.ge; internet www.opentext.org.ge/akhalitaoba; f. 1993; Editor Soso Goniashvili.

Axali Versia (New Possibility): 0154 Tbilisi, Agladze 39; tel. (32) 95-69-38; internet versia-online.com; Editor-in-Chief Aleko Tskitishvili.

Dilis Gazeti (Morning Newspaper): 0102 Tbilisi, Marjanishvili 5; tel. (32) 96-91-88; fax (32) 96-91-81; e-mail dilgazet@access.sanet.ge; Editor Manana Kartozia.

Droni (The Times): 0108 Tbilisi, Kostava 14; tel. (32) 99-56-54; e-mail newspdroni@usa.net; 2 a week; Editor-in-Chief Giorgi Chochishvili.

Georgia Today: 0179 Tbilisi, Irakli Abishidze 41/45; tel. (32) 91-48-92; fax (32) 91-72-75; e-mail info@georgiatoday.ge; internet www.georgiatoday.ge; f. 2000; weekly; in English; Gen. Man. George Sharashidze.

Georgian Messenger: 0162 Tbilisi, Barnov 28; tel. and fax (32) 93-91-69; e-mail gtze@messenger.com.ge; internet www.messenger.com.ge; f. 1990; daily; in English; Editor-in-Chief Zaza Gachechiladze.

Georgian Times: 0107 Tbilisi, Kikodze 12; tel. and fax (32) 93-44-05; e-mail geotimes@geotimes.ge; internet www.geotimes.ge; f. 1993; weekly, Mondays; in English, Georgian and Russian; Editor-in-Chief Zviad Pochkhua.

Iberia Spektri (Iberian Spectrum): 0105 Tbilisi, Machabeli 11; tel. (32) 98-73-87; fax (32) 98-73-88; Editor Irakli Gotsiridze.

Literaturuli Sakartvelo (Literary Georgia): 0105 Tbilisi, Gudiashvili Moedani 2; tel. (32) 99-84-04; internet www.opentext.org.ge/literaturulisakartvelo; weekly; organ of the Union of Writers of Georgia; Editor Tamaz Tsivtsivadze.

Respublika (Republic): 0196 Tbilisi, Kostava 14; tel. and fax (32) 93-43-91; f. 1990; weekly; independent; Editor J. Ninua; circ. 40,000.

Rezonansi (Resonance): 0102 Tbilisi, D. Aghmashenebeli 89/24; tel. (32) 37-79-69; fax (32) 95-06-42; e-mail resonance01@caucasus.net; internet www.resonance.ge; f. 1990; daily; Group Editor-in-Chief Zurab Matcharadze; circ. 7,000.

Sakartvelo (Georgia): 0196 Tbilisi, Kostava 14; tel. (32) 99-92-26; 5 a week; organ of the Georgian Parliament; Editor Sergo Janashia.

Shvidi Dghe (Seven Days): 0102 Tbilisi, Krilov 5; tel. (32) 94-35-52; fax (32) 95-40-76; e-mail dge7@caucasus.net; internet www.opentext.org.ge/7_dge/default.htm; f. 1991; weekly; Editor Koba Akhalbedashvili.

Svobodnaya Gruziya (Free Georgia): 0108 Tbilisi, Rustaveli 42; tel. (32) 93-11-58; e-mail new@caucasus.net; internet www.svobodnaya-gruzia.com; f. 1922 as *Zarya Vostoka* (Dawn of the East); present name adopted 1991; in Russian; Editor-in-Chief Tato Laskhishvili; circ. 5,000.

PRINCIPAL PERIODICALS

Dila (The Morning): 0196 Tbilisi, Kostava 14; tel. (32) 93-41-30; internet www.dila.ge; f. 1904; present name adopted 1947; fortnightly; illustrated; for 5-to-12 year-olds; Editor-in-Chief Dodo Tsivtsivadze; circ. 4,500.

Literaturnaya Gruziya (Literary Georgia): 0108 Tbilisi, Kostava 5; tel. (32) 99-06-59; fax (32) 22-47-37; e-mail abzianidze@hotmail.com; f. 1957; quarterly journal; politics, art and fiction; in Russian; Editor Prof. Zaza Abzianidze.

Metsniereba da Tekhnologiebi (Science and Technologies): 0108 Tbilisi, Rustaveli 52, Georgian Academy of Sciences; e-mail tech@gw.acnet.ge; internet www.acnet.ge/mectechnology; f. 1949; monthly; journal of the Georgian Academy of Sciences; popular; Editor V. Chavchanidze.

Nakaduli (Stream): 0108 Tbilisi, Kostava 14; tel. (32) 93-31-81; f. 1926; fmrly *Pioneri*; monthly journal of the Ministry of Education; illustrated; for 10-to-15-year-olds; Editor Manana Gelashvili; circ. 5,000.

Sakartvelos Metsnierebata Akademiis Moambe/Bulletin of Georgian Academy of Sciences: 0108 Tbilisi, Rustaveli 52; tel. (32) 99-75-93; fax (32) 99-88-23; e-mail bulletin@gw.acnet.ge; internet www.acnet.ge/moambe/index1.htm; f. 1940; 6 a year; in Georgian and English; Editor-in-Chief Thomas V. Gamkrelidze.

Saunje (Treasure): 0107 Tbilisi, Dadiani 2; tel. (32) 72-47-31; f. 1974; 6 a year; organ of the Union of Writers of Georgia; foreign literature in translation; Editor S. Nishnianidze.

Tsiskari (Dawn): 0107 Tbilisi, Khidis 1/29; tel. (32) 99-85-81; f. 1957; monthly; organ of the Union of Writers of Georgia; fiction; Editor Zaur Kalandia.

NEWS AGENCIES

Inter-Press: 0193 Tbilisi, M. Aleksidze 3; tel. (32) 99-67-72; fax (32) 93-56-39; e-mail ipcommerce@interpress.ge; internet www.interpressnews.ge; f. 2000; in Georgian, Russian and English.

Kavkasia-Press (Caucasus Press): 0108 Tbilisi, Rustaveli 42; tel. (32) 92-29-19; fax (32) 98-53-57; e-mail en-edit@caucasus.net.

Prime News Agency (PNA): 0105 Tbilisi, Leselidze 28; tel. (32) 92-32-63; fax (32) 93-91-35; e-mail info@primenewsonline.com; internet www.primenewsonline.com; f. 1997; news on Armenia, Azerbaijan and Georgia; Gen. Man. Demna Chagelishvili.

Sarke Information Agency: 0102 Tbilisi, D. Aghmashenebeli 54; tel. (32) 95-06-59; fax (32) 95-08-37; e-mail info@sarke.com; internet www.sarke.com; f. 1992; professional agency for economic and business news in Georgia; privately owned; Dir Valerian Khukhunashvili; Editor-in-Chief Victoria Gujelashvili.

JOURNALISTS' ASSOCIATIONS

Independent Association of Georgian Journalists: 0105 Tbilisi, Lermontov 10; tel. (99) 96-52-52; fax (32) 93-44-05; e-mail iagj@ip.osgf.ge; internet www.iagj.org.ge; f. 2000; Pres. Zviad Pochkhua.

Journalists' Federation of Georgia: 0105 Tbilisi, Erekle II Moedani 6; tel. (32) 98-24-47; e-mail foraf@geotvr.ge; Chair. Akaki Sikharulidze.

Publishers

Bakur Sulakauri Publishing: 0112 Tbilisi, D. Agmashenebeli 150; tel. and fax (32) 91-09-54; e-mail book@access.sanet.ge; internet www.sulakauri.ge; f. 1998; reference, fiction and children's literature; Dir Bakur Sulakauri.

Ganatleba (Education): 0164 Tbilisi, Chubinashvili 50; tel. (32) 95-50-97; f. 1957; educational, literature; Dir L. Khundadze.

Georgian National Universal Encyclopedia: 0108 Tbilisi, Rustaveli 52; Editor-in-Chief Z. Abashidze.

Khelovneba (Art): 0102 Tbilisi, D. Aghmashenebeli 179; f. 1947; Dir N. Jashi.

Merani (Writer): 0108 Tbilisi, Rustaveli 42; tel. (32) 99-64-92; fax (32) 93-46-75; e-mail hmerani@iberiapac.ge; f. 1921; fiction; Dir G. Gverdtsiteli.

Meridian Publishing Co: 0192 Tbilisi, Grmagele 22/10 a; tel. (32) 61-27-98; fax (32) 95-56-35; e-mail info@meridianpub.com; internet www.meridianpub.com; f. 1994; academic and schools; Editor-in-Chief Giorgi Gigineishvili.

Metsniereba (Sciences): 0160 Tbilisi, Gamrekeli 19; tel. and fax (32) 37-22-97; e-mail publicat@gw.acnet.ge; f. 1941; owned by Georgian Academy of Sciences; Dir David Kolotauri; Editor Cisana Kartozia.

Nakaduli (Stream): 0194 Tbilisi, Gamsakhurdia 28; tel. (32) 38-69-12; f. 1938; books for children and youth.

Sakartvelo (Georgia): 0102 Tbilisi, Marjanishvili 5; tel. (32) 95-42-01; f. 1921; fmrly *Sabchota Sakartvelo* (Soviet Georgia); political, scientific and fiction; Dir Jansul Gvinjilia.

Tbilisi State University Publishing House: 0128 Tbilisi, Chavchavadze 14; f. 1933; scientific and educational literature; Editor V. Gamkrelidze.

Broadcasting and Communications

TELECOMMUNICATIONS

Georgian National Communications Commission: 0177 Tbilisi, Al. Kazbegi 42; tel. (32) 92-16-67; fax (32) 92-16-25; e-mail post@gncc.ge; internet www.gncc.ge; f. 2000; Chair. Giorgi Arvel.

Geocell: 0102 Tbilisi, POB 48; tel. (32) 77-01-00; fax (32) 77-01-01; e-mail cc@geocell.com.ge; internet www.geocell.com.ge; f. 1996; mobile cellular communications.

Magti: 0186 Tbilisi, Jikia 5; tel. (32) 32-23-31; fax (32) 32-18-83; e-mail office@magtigsm.ge; internet www.magticom.ge; f. 1997; fmrly known as Magti GSM; name changed as above 2006; mobile cellular communications; launched 3G mobile services July 2006; Dir David Lee.

Telecom Georgia (Sakartvelos Telekomi): 0108 Tbilisi, Rustaveli 31; tel. (32) 44-19-19; fax (32) 44-29-29; e-mail tamta@telecom.ge; internet www.telecom.ge; f. 1994; provides international telecommunications services; 100% owned by Metromedia International Group Inc (USA); Gen. Dir Otar Zumburidze.

United Telecommunications Company of Georgia (United Telecom): 0107 Tbilisi, Tsinamdzgvrishvili 95; tel. (32) 99-55-99; fax (32) 00-10-55; e-mail unitedtelecom@utg.ge; fmrly Sakelektro-kavshiri; privatized in 2006; owned by Bank TuranAlem (Kazakhstan).

BROADCASTING
Television

Georgian Public Broadcasting: 0171 Tbilisi, Kostava 68; tel. and fax (32) 40-93-30; e-mail tamuna@gpb.geo; internet www.gpb.ge; f. 2005; comprises 2 television channels: Public TV (f. 1956) and Second Channel (f. 1971), and two radio stations: Public Radio (f. 1925) and Radio Two (f. 1995); Dir-Gen. TAMAR KINTSURASHVILI.

Adjara TV: 6000 Adjara, Batumi, M. Abashidze 41; tel. (222) 74-370; fax (222) 74-384; internet www.adjaratv.com; Chief Exec. TEA TSETSKHLADZE.

Imedi TV: 0159 Tbilisi, Lubliana 5; tel. (32) 91-93-12; fax (32) 91-90-41; e-mail info@imedi.ge; internet www.imedi.ge; partnership agreement concluded between Imedi Media Holding and News Corpn (USA) in Sept. 2006; Chair. (vacant); Man. Dir BIDZINA BARATASHVILI.

Mze TV (Sun TV): 0171 Tbilisi, Kostava 75B; tel. (32) 33-55-98; e-mail reklama@mze.ge; internet www.mze.ge; f. 2003; 78% owned by Rustavi 2; Dir ZAZA TANANASHVILI (acting).

Rustavi 2: 0177 Tbilisi, Vazha-Pshavela 45; tel. (32) 20-11-11; fax (32) 20-00-12; e-mail tv@rustavi2.com; internet www.rustavi2.com; f. 1994; independent; Gen. Dir KOBA DAVARASHVILI.

Radio

Georgian Public Broadcasting: see Television.

Radio Imedi: 0159 Tbilisi, Lubliana 5; e-mail info@radio-imedi.ge; internet www.radio-imedi.ge; f. 2001; national broadcasting, 24 hours; news; Dir IRAKLI KHETERELI.

Radio Sakartvelo (Radio Georgia): 0159 Tbilisi, Marshal Gelovani 2; tel. (32) 38-30-30; fax (32) 33-60-60; e-mail tamara@fortuna.ge; internet www.fortuna.ge; f. 1999; owns and operates 4 stations, incl. Radio Fortuna and Radio Fortuna Plus; popular and classical music; Gen. Dir GURAM CHIGOGIDZE.

Finance

(cap. = capital; res = reserves; dep. = deposits; m. = million; brs = branches; amounts in lari, unless otherwise indicated)

BANKING
Central Bank

National Bank of Georgia: 0105 Tbilisi, Leonidze 3–5; tel. (32) 99-65-05; fax (32) 99-93-46; e-mail info@nbg.gov.ge; internet www.nbg .gov.ge; f. 1991; cap. 15.0m., res 55.9m., dep. 1,003.8m. (Dec. 2006); Pres. and Chair. of Bd DAVID AMAGLOBELI (acting); 9 brs.

Other Banks

In 2007 some 19 commercial banks were in operation in Georgia.

Bank of Georgia (Sakartvelos Banki): 0105 Tbilisi, Pushkin 3; tel. (32) 44-44-44; fax (32) 44-42-47; e-mail welcome@bog.ge; internet www.bog.ge; f. 1991; present name adopted 1994; cap. 25.2m., res 281.7m., dep. 785.1m. (Dec. 2006); Chair. NICHOLAS ENUKIDZE; Chief Exec. IRAKLI GILAURI; 25 brs.

Bank Republic: 0179 Tbilisi, Gr. Abashidze 2; tel. (32) 92-55-55; fax (32) 92-55-44; e-mail info@republic.ge; internet www.republic.ge; f. 1991; 60% owned by Société Générale (France); cap. 22.0m., res 8.5m., dep. 278.8m. (Dec. 2006); Pres. LASHA PAPASHVILI; Gen. Dir GILBERT HIE.

Basisbank: 0103 Tbilisi, K. Tsamebuli 1; tel. (32) 92-29-22; fax (32) 98-65-48; e-mail info@basisbank.ge; internet www.basisbank.ge; f. 1993; cap. 5.0m., res 2.3m., dep. 62.2m. (Dec. 2006); Gen. Dir ZURAB TSIKHISTAVI.

Cartu Bank: 0162 Tbilisi, Chavchavadze 39A; tel. (32) 92-55-92; fax (32) 91-22-79; e-mail cartubank@cartubank.ge; internet www .cartubank.ge; f. 1996; cap. 54.7m., res 36.1m., dep. 82.6m. (Dec. 2006); Pres. GEORGE LOMAIA; Chair. of Bd GEORGE CHRDILELI; 5 brs.

Galt & Taggart Bank: 0108 Tbilisi, Chanturia 14; tel. (32) 92-23-76; fax (32) 92-24-33; e-mail bank@emporiki.ge; f. 1996 as International Commercial Black Sea Bank; name changed from Cascade Bank Georgia in 2007; owned by Bank of Georgia; cap. 9.7m., res 0.08m., dep. 5.3m. (Dec. 2005); Man. Dir IOANNIS PILINIS.

Investbank: 0108 Tbilisi, Lesya Ukrainka 3; tel. (32) 42-88-88; fax (32) 92-25-37; e-mail info@investbank.ge; internet www.investbank .ge; f. 2003; Gen. Dir IRAKLI KAKABADZE.

People's Bank of Georgia: 0162 Tbilisi, Chavchavadze 74; tel. (32) 91-22-45; fax (32) 93-64-68; e-mail info@peobge.com; internet www .peoplesbank.ge; f. 2002; cap. 10.0m., res 0.7m., dep. 64.8m. (Dec. 2005); Gen. Dir GIORGI GOGUADZE; 70 brs.

ProCredit Bank, Georgia: 0112 Tbilisi, David Agmashenebeli 154; tel. (32) 20-22-22; fax (32) 25-05-80; e-mail info@procreditbank.ge; internet www.procreditbank.ge; f. 1999; present name adopted 2003; 39% owned by Internationale Micro Investitionen AG (Germany); cap. 48.9m., res 6.3m., dep. 341.4m. (Dec. 2006); Chief Exec. PHILIPP POTT.

Standard Bank (Standartbank): 0162 Tbilisi, Chavchavadze 43; tel. (32) 50-77-01; fax (32) 50-77-07; e-mail mail@standardbank.ge; internet www.standardbank.ge; f. 2000; name changed from Agro-Business Bank (ABG) in 2005; development bank; cap. 12.6m., dep. 73.8m., total assets 98.1m. (Dec. 2006); wholly owned by the European Commission; Gen. Dir GEORGE KALANDARISHVILI; 61 brs.

TaoPrivatBank: 0119 Tbilisi, Tsereteli 114; tel. (32) 35-05-00; fax (32) 35-50-80; e-mail info@taobank.ge; internet www.taobank.ge; f. 1992; cap. 52.0m., dep. 9.8m. (July 2007); Chair. VLADIMER UGULAVA.

TBC Bank: 0102 Tbilisi, Marjanishvili 7; tel. (32) 77-70-00; fax (32) 77-27-74; e-mail info@tbcbank.com.ge; internet www.tbcbank.com .ge; f. 1992; 30.95% owned by International Finance Corpn (USA); cap. 5.4m., res 14.7m., dep. 819.8m. (Dec. 2006); Pres. of Bd of Dirs VAKHTANG BUTSKHRIKIDZE; 13 brs.

VTB Georgia (VneshTorgBank Georgia): 0108 Tbilisi, Chanturia 14; tel. (32) 50-55-05; fax (32) 99-91-39; e-mail info@vtb.com.ge; internet www.vtb.com.ge; f. 1995 as United Georgian Bank; name changed as above 2006; 53% owned by the VneshTorgBank Group (Russia); 19% owned by European Bank for Reconstruction and Development; cap. 41.0m., res 0.2m., dep. 287.9m. (Dec. 2006); Chair. of Supervisory Bd ZAZA SIORIDZE; Man. Dir IUZA TAVDIDISHVILI; 19 brs.

STOCK EXCHANGE

Georgian Stock Exchange: 0162 Tbilisi, Chavchavadze 74 A; tel. (32) 22-07-18; fax (32) 25-18-76; e-mail info@gse.ge; internet www .gse.ge; f. 1999; Chair. of Supervisory Bd GEORGE LOLADZE; Gen. Dir VAKHTANG SVANADZE.

INSURANCE

At the end of 2004 there were 14 insurance companies in Georgia.

State Insurance Supervision Service: 0164 Tbilisi, G. Chitaia 21; tel. (32) 95-64-89; fax (32) 95-71-42; e-mail isssg@inbox.ge; internet www.insurance.caucasus.net; f. 1997; provides state regulation of insurance activity; Dir ARCHIL TSERTSVADZE.

Aldagi Insurance Co: 0179 Tbilisi, Melikishvili 16; tel. (32) 92-44-11; fax (32) 29-49-05; e-mail aldagi@aldagi.com.ge; internet www .aldagi.com; f. 1990; 50% owned by Bank Republic; Chair. GURAM ASSATHIANY; Gen. Dir EVA IASHVILI.

Anglo-Georgian Insurance Co (AGIC): 0130 Tbilisi, I. Abashidze 29; tel. (32) 25-03-51; fax (32) 25-03-50; e-mail post@agic.com.ge; internet www.agic.com.ge; f. 1998 as a joint-stock co; all types of insurance; Gen. Dir FRANCIS MATHEW.

British-Caucasian Insurance Co: 0108 Tbilisi, Rustaveli 27; tel. (32) 98-89-98; fax (32) 25-28-08; e-mail bci@bci.ge; internet www.bci .ge; Dir RAMAZ KUKULADZE.

Europace: 0112 Tbilisi, Aghmashenebeli 150; tel. (32) 91-06-04; fax (32) 91-06-08; e-mail info@europace.com; internet www.europace.ge; f. 1998; fmrly Nabati Ltd; Dir VASIL AKHRAKHADZE.

Georgian Pension and Insurance Holding Co: 0162 Tbilisi, Chavchavadze 1/5; tel. (32) 92-01-20; internet www.gpih.ge; Gen. Dir PAATA GADZADZE.

Trade and Industry
GOVERNMENT AGENCIES

National Investment Agency: Invest In Georgia: 0108 Tbilisi, Chanturia 12; tel. (32) 43-34-33; fax (32) 98-27-55; e-mail info@ investingeorgia.org; internet www.investingeorgia.org; f. 2002 to promote foreign direct investment; Dir-Gen. OTAR NISHNIANIDZE.

State Property Management Agency: 0108 Tbilisi, Chanturia St; tel. (32) 99-74-16; e-mail info@privatization.ge; internet www .privatization.ge; responsible for divestment of state-owned enterprises.

CHAMBERS OF COMMERCE

Georgian Chamber of Commerce and Industry: 0179 Tbilisi, Chavchavadze 11; tel. (32) 23-00-45; fax (32) 23-57-60; e-mail info@ gcci.ge; internet www.gcci.ge; f. 1963; brs in Sukhumi and Batumi; Chair. JEMAL INAISHVILI.

Chamber of Commerce and Industry of the Autonomous Republic of Adjara: 6010 Adjara, Batumi, Melashvili 26; tel. (222) 728-41; fax (222) 728-42; e-mail cci@ajcci.ge; internet ajcci .ge; f. 2004; Pres. TENGIZ BAKURIDZE; Dir-Gen. IASON TSERTSVADZE.

TRADE ASSOCIATIONS

Agricultural Development Association of Georgia (ADA): 0102 Tbilisi, Doki 2; tel. (99) 58-86-28; e-mail ada@access.sanet.ge; Chair. ALEXANDER LAZASHVILI.

Association of Georgian Exporters: 0177 Tbilisi, Jikia 5; tel. (32) 24-43-02; fax (32) 24-43-03; e-mail gea@gepa.org.ge; Gen. Dir TAMAZ AGLADZE.

Employers' Association of Georgia: 0108 Tbilisi, R. Tabukashvili 15/4; tel. (32) 92-03-30; fax (32) 23-21-71; e-mail employer@gol.ge; Dir ELGUJA MELADZE.

Federation of Georgian Businessmen: 0105 Tbilisi, Gergeti 3; tel. (32) 94-04-72; fax (32) 92-30-15; e-mail admin@fgb.ge; internet www.fgb.ge; f. 2004; 150 mems; Pres. (vacant); Exec. Dir GIORGI ISAKADZE.

Small and Medium Enterprise Development Agency (SMEDA): 0162 Tbilisi, Kipshidze 7; tel. (32) 99-90-77; fax (32) 93-35-39; e-mail smeda@caucasus.net; internet www.abco.caucasus .net/smeda; f. 1994; Dir ALEXANDER GOGOBERIDZE.

UTILITIES

Regulatory Authorities

Georgian National Energy Regulation Committee (Semeki): 0177 Tbilisi, Al. Kazbegi 45; tel. (32) 24-10-40; fax (32) 24-10-42; e-mail mail@gnerc.org; internet www.gnerc.org; f. 1997; Chair. GURAM CHALAGASHVILI.

State Agency for the Regulation of Oil and Gas Resources (SAROGR): 0177 Tbilisi, Al. Kazbegi 45; tel. and fax (32) 25-33-11; e-mail sarogr@access.sanet.ge; internet www.sarogr.ge; f. 1999; Pres. ANDRIA KOTETISHVILI.

Electricity

In February 2007 Energo-Pro (Czech Republic) completed its purchase of 62.5% of Georgia's electricity distribution market, including six hydroelectric power plants (Ats, Dzevrula, Gumati, Lajanuri, Rioni and Shaori) and two distribution companies (UEDC and Energy Company of Adjara—ECA), with a total of 875,000 customers. The company pledged to invest US $285m. in the sector, including the construction of a new 100-MW hydroelectric plant.

Electricity System Commercial Operator (ESCO): 0177 Tbilisi, Al. Kazbegi 45; tel. (32) 31-14-70; fax (32) 31-17-49; e-mail office@esco .ge; internet www.esco.ge; f. 2006; state owned; scheduled for privatization; trades electricity and reserve capacity in order to maintain the balance of supply and demand; Gen. Dir BIDZINA CHKHONIA (acting).

Georgian State Electrosystem (GSE): 0105 Tbilisi, Baratashvili 2; tel. and fax (32) 20-17-00; internet www.gse.com.ge; f. 2002 by merger; operator of electricity transmission grid; state-owned; managed from March 2003 by ESBI Georgia, a subsidiary of ESBI International (Ireland); Gen. Dir SULKHAN ZUMBURIDZE.

Georgian United Energy Distribution Co (GUDC): 0107 Tbilisi, Lermontov 10; tel. (32) 93-13-84; f. 2002 by amalgamation of the majority of regional electricity cos, excluding the regions of Tbilisi, Adjara and Kakheti; privatized in 2006; owned by Energo-Pro (Czech Rep.); Dirs DEAN WHITE, GIVI VARDIASHVILI; 5,000 employees.

Kakhati Energy Distribution (KED): 2120 Samegrelo-Zemo Svaneti Mkhare, Zugdidi rajon, Kakhati; comprising eight distributors; owned by TBC Energy.

Sakenergo: 0105 Tbilisi, V. Vekua 1; tel. (32) 98-98-14; fax (32) 98-31-97; formerly state-owned energy supplier; in 1996 restructured into three cos (generation, transmission and distribution); further restructured in 1998, see Georgian United Energy Distribution Co and Sakenergogeneratsia; Gen. Dir VAZHA METREVELI.

Sakenergogeneratsia: 0105 Tbilisi, V. Vekua 1; tel. and fax (32) 98-98-13; f. 1996; state power-generating co; Gen. Dir G. BADURASHVILI.

Telasi: 0154 Tbilisi, Vani 3; tel. (32) 25-52-11; fax (32) 77-99-78; privatized in 1999; Tbilisi distribution grid; 412,000 customers; owns two hydroelectric plants and two gas-fuelled generation plants; Gen. Dir YURI PIMONOV.

Gas

Georgian Oil and Gas Corpn (GOGC): Tbilisi, Kakheti Highway 21; tel. (32) 24-40-40; fax (32) 24-40-42; e-mail public@gogc.ge; internet www.gogc.ge; f. 1997; state-owned; fmrly Georgian International Gas Corpn, reorganized in 2006, merged with Georgian International Oil Corpn and Saknavtobi; exclusive operator, owner,

user, disposer, and manager of natural and liquid gas imports and transit in Georgia; Gen. Dir ZURAB JANJGAVA.

KazTransGaz Tbilisi: 0194 Tbilisi, Mitskevich 18 A; tel. (32) 38-76-25; fax (32) 37-56-51; e-mail info@ktg-tbilisi.ge; internet www .tbilgazi.ge; fmrly Tbilgazi; gas distribution co for the Tbilisi region; privatized in 2006; 100% owned by KazTransGaz (Kazakhstan); Dir-Gen. GIORGI KOIAVA.

Water

Tbilisi Water Utility (Tbilisis Tskali): 0179 Tbilisi, M. Kostava 1st Alley 33; tel. (32) 48-71-10; scheduled for privatization; fmrly Tbiltskalkanali; water supply and sewerage system; Dir GIORGI GELBAKIANI.

MAJOR COMPANIES

Economic reforms from 1994 encouraged the development of the private sector. In early 1998 almost all small-scale enterprises were under private control and the privatization of medium- and large-scale enterprises was in progress. By the end of 1998 72% of medium-sized and large enterprises had been privatized.

Chemicals

Chiaturmanganese (Chiatura Manganese Mining and Processing Combine): 5500 Imereti Mkhare, Chiatura, Tsereteli 1; tel. (379) 5-25-35; fax (379) 55-023; f. 1880; jt-stock co; privatized in 2007; owned by Georgian Manganese, a subsidiary of Stemcor (United Kingdom); production of peroxide and manganese concentrates; functions in co-operation with Zestafoni Ferro-alloy Plant and Vartsikhe hydroelectric power plant; Gen. Dir ROLAND GOTSADZE; 2,500 employees.

Energy-Invest: 3702 Kvemo Kartli Mkhari, Rustavi, Mira 2; tel. (34) 17-09-09; fax (34) 17-09-09; e-mail info@energyinvest.ge; internet azot.energyinvest.ge; f. 1956; owner of several industrial plants including Rustavi Azoti (Nitrogen) Chemical Plant; produces ammonium nitrate and other fertilizers, oxygen and cosmetics; owned by Energy Invest; Gen. Dir GENO Z. MALAZONIA.

Electrical Goods

Ekrani: 0114 Tbilisi, Didi Kheivanis 3; tel. (32) 75-59-99; fax (32) 75-58-88; e-mail ekrani@caucasus.net; f. 1993; jt-stock co; mfrs of television sets and domestic electrical appliances; Man. Dir REVAZ TSULAIA.

Elmavalmshenebeli (Electrovozostroitel): 0141 Tbilisi, Guramishvili 84; tel. (32) 65-31-15; internet www.tevz.com; f. 1957; mfrs of direct-current long-haul industrial electric locomotives; privatized in 2005; 87% owned by Dema Computers (Russia); Principal Officer ZURAB TSINTSADZE; 1,500 employees.

Food and Beverages

Aromaproduct: 0192 Tbilisi, Guramishvili St 17; tel. (32) 61-42-91; fax (32) 61-33-56; e-mail info@aroma.ge; internet www.aroma.ge; f. 1958; production of fruit products, sauces and spices; Gen. Dir VLADIMIR GUGUSHVILI; 1,042 employees.

Georgian Wines and Spirits Co (GWS): 0162 Tbilisi, Chavchavadze 74A; tel. (32) 93-44-83; fax (32) 22-46-31; f. 1993; a subsidiary of Pernod Ricard Europe SA; leading producer and exporter of Georgian wine; Pres. LEVAN GACHECHILADZE.

Metals

Madneuli Copper and Gold Mines: 0112 Tbilisi, Aghmashenebeli Ave 154; tel. (32) 50-61-01; fax (32) 50-61-04; e-mail commercial@ madneuli.ge; internet www.madneuli.ge; f. 1994; scheduled for privatization; produces copper concentrate; Gen. Dir KOBA NAKOPIA; 788 employees.

Rustavi Iron and Steel Works: 3704 Kvemo Kartli Mkhare, Rustavi, Gagarin St 12; tel. and fax (34) 19-20-10; e-mail metalurg@gol.ge; f. 1956; seamless pipe mfrs; 51% owned by Metallurggasoilinvest; Gen. Dir NODARI GVAMBERIA; 700 employees.

Zestafoni Ferro-alloy Plant (Ferro JSC): 0102 Tbilisi, Aghmashenebeli 52; tel. (32) 91-09-16; fax (32) 92-31-48; e-mail info@ferro .ge; internet www.ferro.ge; jt-stock co; 73.12% owned by Stemcor (United Kingdom); 26.88% owned by DCM DECOmetal International Trading GmbH (Austria); Gen. Dir N. AMBOKADZE.

Petroleum and Natural Gas

Batumi Oil Refinery (Batumis Navtobgadamamushavebli Qarxana): 6000 Adjara, Batumi, Tamaris Dasaxleba; tel. (222) 3-21-55; f. 2000; scheduled for privatization; Gen. Dir VASIL JANGULASHVILI.

Georgia Pipeline Co: 0112 Tbilisi, Aghmashenebeli Ave 123; Vice-Pres. and Man. ROBERT MOORE.

Gruzneft (Georgian State Oil Co): 0115 Tbilisi, Kostava 65; tel. (32) 136-16-42; fax (32) 133-30-32; f. 1930; petroleum and gas exploration; petroleum production and refining; Gen. Dir GIORGI CHANTURIA; 6,000 employees.

Saknavtobi (Georgian National Oil Co): 0175 Tbilisi, Kostava 65; f. 1929; state-owned; petroleum and natural gas exploration and production; reorganized in 2006; Pres. VANO NAKAIDZE; 640 employees.

Miscellaneous

Borjomi Georgian Glass and Mineral Water Co: 0179 Tbilisi, Chavchavadze 26; tel. (32) 94-16-22; fax (32) 22-36-68; e-mail ggmw@ borjomi.com.ge; internet www.borjomi.com.ge; f. 1997; jt Georgian-Dutch-French venture; water-bottling and bottle-making facilities; Man. Dir JACQUES FLEURY.

Innovator Technology Systems: 0192 Tbilisi, T. Eristavi 1; tel. (32) 94-17-22; fax (32) 93-37-50; f. 1934; fmrly Tbilisi Lathe-Manufacturing Industrial Association; mfrs and exporters of new and used metal-working machine tools; Principal Officer ANZAR SHAUTUDZE; 1,107 employees.

Kutaisi Automobile Plant (KAZ): 4600 Imereti Mkhare, Kutaisi, Avtomashenebeli St 88; tel. (331) 7-26-95; fax (331) 0-10-81; e-mail autoplant@sanet.knet.ge; f. 1945; mfrs of freight containers and trailers, incl. Kamaz lorries; Dir TENGIZ SHUBLADZE; 1,300 employees.

Poti Shipyard: 4406 Samegrelo-Zemo Svaneti Mkhare, Poti, Davitaia 1; tel. and fax (39) 32-17-00; e-mail potishipyard@gol.ge; f. 1941; 51% acquired by RAK Investments (United Arab Emirates) in 2008; operations restricted as a consequence of military conflict between Russia and Georgia in Aug. 2008; shipbuilding and ship repairs; provides port services; Gen. Dir ALAN MIDDLETON; 550 employees.

Tbilaviamsheni (TAM) (Tbilisi Aircraft Manufacturing): 0136 Tbilisi, B. Khmelnitski 181; tel. (32) 70-84-12; fax (32) 70-88-38; e-mail info@tam.ge; internet www.tam.ge; f. 1941; name changed from Tbilisi Aircraft Factory in 2002; nine facilities, including metallurgical, mechanical, engraving, aircraft assembly and flight-testing; produces aircraft, agricultural equipment, bicycles and metal containers; Pres. and Chief Exec. PANTIKO TORDIA; 1,800 employees.

Tbilkhimpharmi: 0113 Tbilisi, Tsuladze 34; tel. (32) 77-85-86; e-mail info@tbilkhimpharmi.com.ge; internet www .tbilkhimpharmi.com.ge; f. 1934; jt-stock co; produces 40 types of drugs; largest pharmaceutical company in Georgia and one of the largest in the Caucasus; Gen. Dir TAMAZ SULUKHIA; 200 employees.

TRADE UNION CONFEDERATION

Amalgamation of Trade Unions of Georgia (GTUA): 0122 Tbilisi, Shartava 7; tel. (32) 38-29-95; fax (32) 22-46-63; e-mail gtua@geo.net.ge; internet wwww.gtuc.ge; f. 1995 as Confederation of Trade Unions of Georgia, name changed as above in 2000; comprises branch unions with a total membership of approx. 800,000; in February 2005 the association ceded 90% of its property to the state; following legislative amendments, all members were required to re-register; Chair. IRAKLI PETRIASHVILI.

Transport

RAILWAYS

In 2004 Georgia's rail network (including the sections within the secessionist republic of Abkhazia) totalled approximately 1,554 km. There are rail links with Azerbaijan, Armenia and Iran. Services on the railway line to Russia, along the Black Sea coast, have been disrupted and suspended as a result of the conflict in Abkhazia, although local services linking Abkhazia with the Black Sea region of Russia had been restored by the mid-2000s. In December 2004 an agreement was signed on the construction of a rail link between Kars, in Turkey, and Akhalkalaki, in Georgia, continuing to Azerbaijan, and the rehabilitation of the line between Akhalkalaki and Tbilisi.

The first section of the Tbilisi Metro was opened in 1966; by 2005 the system comprised two lines with 22 stations, totalling 26.4 km in length. Three extensions, totalling 15 km, were under construction; Tbilisi City Council's budget for 2006 allocated 16m. lari to the project.

Georgian Railway Co: 0112 Tbilisi, Tamar Mepis 15; tel. (32) 56-48-82; fax (32) 56-41-82; e-mail sag@railway.ge; internet www .railway.ge; f. 1872; Chair. and Dir-Gen. IRAKLI EZUGBAIA.

Tbilisi Metro (Tbilisi Metropolitena): 0112 Tbilisi, Tavisuplebis Moedani 2; tel. (32) 34-14-71; fax (32) 93-41-86; e-mail info@tbilmetro .com.ge; f. 1966; Gen. Dir ZURAB KIKALISHVILI.

ROADS

In 2004 the total length of roads in use was an estimated 20,247 km (including 1,474 km of main roads and 3,326 km of secondary roads). In that year 93.8% of the road network was paved.

SHIPPING

There are international shipping services to and from Black Sea and Mediterranean ports. The main ports are at Batumi and Poti.

Batumi Sea Port: 6003 Adjara, Batumi, Kutaisi 1; tel. (222) 76-261; fax (222) 76-958; e-mail bsport@batumiport.com; internet www .batumiport.com; operates five terminals: petroleum terminal, container terminal, railway ferry, dry cargo terminal and passenger terminal; privatized in 2006; owned by Greenoak Group (United Kingdom); Gen. Dir PHRIDON SURMANIDZE.

Georgian Ocean Shipping Co (OSCO): 0160 Tbilisi, Al. Kazbegi 12A; tel. (32) 25-18-95; fax (32) 25-18-97; e-mail osco@wanex.net; f. 1999; privatized in 2005; owns 15 petroleum product and chemical carrier tankers; Chair. GURAM DOLBAIA.

Poti Sea Port: 4401 Samegrelo-Zemo Svaneti Mkhare, Poti, D. Agmashenebeli 52; tel. (393) 20-660; fax (393) 22-888; e-mail administration@potiseaport.com; internet www.potiseaport.com; f. 1858; commercial port; Gen. Dir LASHA AKHALADZE.

CIVIL AVIATION

Georgia's primary airport is Tbilisi International Airport, Lochini. There are three other airports in operation in Batumi, Kutaisi and Senaki.

Civil Aviation Authority: 0160 Tbilisi, Al. Kazbegi 12; tel. (32) 93-30-92; fax (32) 99-74-80; e-mail inspect@access.sanet.ge; f. 2002; Dir GIORGI MZHAVANADZE.

Georgian Airways: 0108 Tbilisi, Rustaveli 12; tel. (32) 99-97-30; fax (32) 99-96-60; e-mail info@georgian-airways.com; internet www .georgian-airways.com; f. 1999; present name adopted 2004; privately owned; flights to various destinations in Europe and the Middle East; Chair. of Bd of Dirs TAMAZ GAIASHVILI.

Georgian National Airlines: 0119 Tbilisi, Bakradze 6; tel. (32) 35-58-02; fax (32) 35-58-01; e-mail info@national-avia.com; internet www.national-avia.com; f. 1998 as Air Bisec; present name adopted 2004; Pres. GIORGI KODUA.

Tourism

Prior to the disintegration of the USSR, Georgia attracted some 1.5m. tourists annually (mainly from other parts of the USSR). However, following the outbreak of civil conflict in the early 1990s in South Ossetia and Abkhazia, there was an almost complete cessation in tourism. Efforts to regenerate the sector were made in the late 1990s, with the historic buildings of Tbilisi and the surrounding area one of the primary attractions. According to the World Tourism Organization, there were 983,114 tourist arrivals in 2006, compared with 313,442 in 2003, and receipts from tourism (including passenger transport) totalled US $288m. in 2005.

Department of Tourism and Resorts of Georgia: 0162 Tbilisi, Chavchavadze 80; tel. (32) 22-61-25; fax (32) 29-40-52; e-mail georgia@tourism.gov.ge; internet www.tourism.gov.ge; forms part of the Ministry of Economic Development; Chair. SABA KIKNADZE.

Culture

NATIONAL ORGANIZATION

Ministry of Culture, the Protection of Monuments and Sport: see The Government (Ministries).

CULTURAL HERITAGE

In 2005 there were 111 museums in Georgia, with an annual attendance of 301,000 people.

Georgian Cultural Heritage Information Centre (GCHIC): 0108 Tbilisi, Kazbegi Ave 17, 2nd floor; e-mail info@heritage.ge; internet www.heritage.ge; non-governmental org.; Exec. Dir TSISIA KILADZE.

Georgian National Museum: 0105 Tbilisi, Purtseladze 3; tel. (32) 99-80-22; fax (32) 98-21-33; e-mail info@museum.ge; internet www .museum.ge; f. 2004 to unify eight of the most important museums in the country: Dmanisi Museum, G. Chitaia Open-Air Museum, I. Grishashvili Tbilisi History Museum (f. 1910), I. Javakhishvili Samtskhe-Javakheti History Museum, O. Lordkipanidze Vani Archeological Museum, Svaneti History-Ethnography Museum.

S. Amiranashvili Museum of Fine Arts: 0103 Tbilisi, L. Gudiashvili 1; tel. (32) 99-66-35; f. 1920 as the National Art Gallery of Georgia; part of the Georgian National Museum from 2004; 135,952 exhibits; Dir NODAR LOMOURI.

S. Janashia Museum of the History of Georgia: 0103 Tbilisi, Rustaveli 3; tel. (32) 99-80-22; fax (32) 98-21-33; f. 1919; part of the

Georgian National Museum from 2004; 1.2m. exhibits; library of over 250,000 vols; Dir L. A. CHILASHVILI.

Kutaisi State Museum of History and Ethnography: 4600 Imereti Mkhare, Kutaisi, Aghmashenebeli Moedani 1; tel. (331) 4-56-91; internet www.histmuseum.ge; f. 1922; attached to Georgian Academy of Sciences; 190,000 items; Dir M. V. NIKOLEISHVILI.

Modern Art Museum—National Picture Gallery: 0103 Tbilisi, Rustaveli 11; tel. (32) 93-16-52; f. 1920; 25,000 items; Dir TEIMURAZ GOTSADZE.

Museum of Archeology: 0181 Tbilisi, Aghmashenebeli; tel. (32) 52-13-05; archaeological material; library of over 150,000 vols.

National Library of Georgia: 0107 Tbilisi, Gudiashvili 5; tel. (32) 99-80-95; fax (32) 99-80-95; f. 1846; 16m. vols; Dir LEVAN BERDZENISHVILI.

Museum of Folklore and Applied Arts of Georgia: 0103 Tbilisi, Sololaki 11; tel. (32) 99-61-52; f. 1899; 10,000 exhibits; Dir MICHEIL KIKHNAVELIDZE.

Museum of Georgian Literature: 0103 Tbilisi, Chanturia 8; tel. (32) 99-20-73; f. 1929; 19th- and 20th-century Georgian literature; 125,000 exhibits; library of almost 12,000 vols; Dir I. A. ORJONIKIDZE.

State Museum of the Autonomous Republic of Abkhazia: 6600 Abkhazia, Sukhumi, pr. Leona 22; f. 1915; 100,000 exhibits; Dir A. A. ARGUN.

SPORTING ORGANIZATIONS

Georgian National Olympic Committee: 0102 Tbilisi, Aghmashenebeli 65; tel. (32) 95-30-79; fax (32) 95-38-29; e-mail geonoc@access.sanet.ge; internet www.geonoc.org.ge; Pres. GOGI TOPADZE (acting); Sec.-Gen. EMZAR ZENAISHVILI.

PERFORMING ARTS

In 2005 there were 41 theatres in Georgia, of which two provided opera and ballet, 30 provided drama and musical comedy, seven presented puppet shows and two were for youth productions.

Georgian Folk Theatre 'Nabadi': 0108 Tbilisi, Rustaveli 19; tel. (32) 98-99-91; e-mail nabaditheater@yahoo.com; internet www.nabadi.ge; f. 2004.

Griboyedov Russian Drama Theatre: 0107 Tbilisi, Rustaveli 2; tel. (32) 93-16-24; fax (32) 93-31-15; e-mail theatre@ip.osgf.ge; internet griboedovtheatre.ge; f. 1845; Dir AVTANDIL VARSIMASHVILI.

Marjanishvili State Academic Drama Theatre: 0102 Tbilisi, Marjanashvili 8; tel. (32) 95-35-82; fax (32) 95-40-01; e-mail eastern@caucasus.net; f. 1928 (in Kutaisi); Gen. Man. GAIOZ KANDELAKI; Artistic Dir OTAR MEGVINETUKHUTSESI.

Sh. Rustaveli State Academic Drama Theatre: 0108 Tbilisi, Rustaveli 17; tel. (32) 99-85-87; fax (32) 99-65-20; e-mail rustaveli.theatre@access.sanet.ge; f. 1879; Dir GIA TEVZADZE; Artistic Dir ROBERT STURUA.

N. Sulkhanishvili State Chorus Choir of Georgia: 0105 Tbilisi, Gorgasali 1; tel. (32) 72-27-25; f. 1947; Dir NATO MOISTSRAPISHVILI; Artistic Dir GIVI MUNJISHVILI.

Tbilisi V. Sarajishvili State Conservatoire: 0108 Tbilisi, Griboedov 8; tel. (32) 99-91-44; fax (32) 98-71-87; e-mail inter@conservatoire.edu.ge; internet www.conservatoire.edu.ge; f. 1917; Rector Prof. MANANA DOIJASHVILI.

Tbilisi Z. Paliashvili Opera and Ballet State Theatre: 0108 Tbilisi, Rustaveli 25; tel. and fax (32) 98-32-50; e-mail info@opera.ge; internet www.opera.ge; f. 1851; Gen. Dir DAVID SAKVARELIDZE.

ASSOCIATION

Union of Writers of Georgia: 0105 Tbilisi, Machabeli 13; tel. (32) 99-84-90; five regional Writers' Organizations.

Education

Education is free and compulsory for nine years, between the ages of six and 14. Free secondary education is available for the highest-achieving 30% of primary-school pupils. In 2005/06 pre-primary enrolment included 38.9% of children in the relevant age-group. Some 86.4% of children enrolled in pre-primary education in 2004/05 were instructed solely in Georgian. In 2005/06 primary enrolment included 89.1% of the relevant age-group, and the comparable ratio for secondary enrolment was 78.7%. In 2004/05 there were 1,816 secondary day schools, with a total enrolment of 565,900 pupils. In 2004/05 85.5% of primary- and secondary-school pupils were taught in Georgian-language schools, while 5.5% were taught in Russian-language schools, 5.4% in Azerbaijani-language schools and 3.5% in Armenian-language schools. There was also teaching in Abkhazian and Ossetian.

In addition to state institutions, many private institutions of higher education were opened after 1991; there were 146 in 2005/06. In 2005/06 there were 144,313 students enrolled at institutions of higher education (including universities). In 2005 8.8% of total consolidated budgetary expenditure (288.7m. lari) was allocated to education.

GOVERNMENT AGENCY

Ministry of Education and Science: see The Government (Ministries).

UNIVERSITIES

Abkhazian A. M. Gorkii State University: 6600 Abkhazia, Sukhumi, S. Zvanba 9; tel. (122) 2-25-98; f. 1985; 6 faculties; 3,800 students.

Georgian Technical University: 0175 Tbilisi, Kostava 77; tel. (32) 33-04-93; fax (32) 94-20-33; e-mail info@gtu.ge; internet www.gtu.edu.ge; f. 1922 (as Georgia Polytechnic Institute, renamed 1990); 10 faculties; 2,050 teachers; 28,000 students; Rector Prof. ARCHIL MOTSONELIDZE.

Gori State University (GSU): 1400 Shida Kartli Mkhare, Gori, Chavchavadze 53; tel. (270) 72-997; fax (270) 73-213; e-mail gori@ip.osgf.ge; f. 1998 on the basis of the Gori State Economic-Humanitarian Institute; 7 faculties; over 3,000 students; Rector GEDEVAN KHELAIA.

Kutaisi A. Tsereteli State University: 4600 Imereti Mkhare, Kutaisi, Tamar Mepis 55; tel. (331) 42-173; fax (331) 43-833; e-mail irpdd@sanetk.net.ge; internet ksu.gateway.ge; f. 1933; gained university status in 1990; 9 faculties; 380 teachers; 5,000 students; Rector Prof. Dr AVTANDIL NIKOLEISHVILI.

Rustaveli State University in Batumi: 6010 Adjara, Batumi, Ninoshvili 35; tel. (222) 71-780; fax (222) 71-786; e-mail info@bsu.edu.ge; internet www.bsu.edu.ge; f. 1935; 5 faculties; Rector VLADIMER BALADZE.

Tbilisi I. Javakhishvili State University: 0128 Tbilisi, Chavchavadze 1; tel. (32) 22-51-07; fax (32) 22-22-03; e-mail rec@tsu.ge; internet www.tsu.edu.ge; f. 1918; language of instruction is Georgian, with a Russian section in some faculties; the university underwent a far-reaching restructuring process from mid-2005; 6 faculties; 3 institutes; 1,659 teachers; 16,000 students; 8 brs; Rector Prof. GIORGI KHUBUA.

Tbilisi State Medical University: 0177 Tbilisi, Vazha-Pshavela 33; tel. (32) 39-18-79; fax (32) 39-22-84; e-mail iad@tsmu.edu; internet www.tsmu.edu; f. 1918; 8 faculties; 1,200 teachers; 4,300 students; 3 university hospitals; 29 clinics; Rector Prof. GEORGE MENABDE.

Social Welfare

Great pressures were placed on Georgia's social welfare system as a result of the civil and separatist conflicts in the early 1990s, when large numbers were killed, wounded or displaced, and by the renewed conflict in South Ossetia in August 2008.

At the end of 2005 there were 902,100 registered pensioners in Georgia; in 2004 the average monthly pension value was 20 lari. Under the existing 'pay-as-you-go' system, pensions are financed by the extrabudgetary Pension Fund (United State Social Safety Fund), which provides fixed-rate old-age pensions. However, the pensions system continued to accumulate arrears, and reform of the system was required urgently. In 2001 a plan was drawn up, as part of the country's Poverty Reduction and Economic Growth Programme, for the introduction, over a period of five years, of a programme to introduce a 'multi-pillar' pension system. The country's first private pensions insurance company, Georgian Pension Investment Holding (GPIH), was founded in May 2001, and aimed to offer (in addition to the existing, universal scheme) voluntary, non-state pensions insurance.

There are two further extrabudgetary funds: the Employment Fund, established in 1991, provides unemployment, sickness and maternity benefits; and a Health Fund was established in 1995. The Government aimed to privatize most health care facilities by 1998, although free medical care was to continue to be provided to the neediest sections of the population. In 2000 the Government adopted a state programme for a national health policy and a strategic plan for healthcare development in Georgia, according to which government spending on health care was to increase from 4% of GDP by 2005 to 6% of GDP by 2010. In 2006 there were 3.7 hospital beds and 4.7 doctors per 1,000 people. In 2006 the under-5 mortality rate was 32 per 1,000 live births. The 2004 budget allocated 19.6% of total consolidated expenditure (473.0m. lari) to social security, and a further 4.0% (97.2m. lari) to health care.

GOVERNMENT AGENCIES

Ministry of Health, Labour and Social Protection: see The Government (Ministries).

Georgian Health and Social Project Implementation Centre (GHSPIC): 0160 Tbilisi, Al. Kazbegi 23, Bldg 2, 5th Floor; tel. (32) 33-19-39; fax (32) 99-50-41; e-mail globalfund@caucasus.net; f. 1994; Dir MAMUKA JAPARIDZE.

State United Social Insurance Fund of Georgia (SUSIF): 0119 Tbilisi, Akaki Tsereteli 144; tel. (32) 69-54-11; fax (32) 69-00-20; e-mail info@susif.ge; internet www.susif.ge; f. 1996; ensures assignment and distribution of pensions, carries out state programmes of medical support, social protection, medical-social expertise, etc.; Chair. of Bd NINO OKRIBELASHVILI.

HEALTH AND WELFARE ORGANIZATIONS

CARE International (Georgia): 0162 Tbilisi, Chavchavadze 74 A; tel. (32) 29-19-41; fax (32) 29-43-07; e-mail caucasus@care.org.ge; internet www.care.org.ge; maintains 5 projects in Georgia, serving the needs of over 50,000 people, to overcome the causes of poverty; Country Dir JONATHON PUDDIFOOT.

Caritas Georgia: 0183 Tbilisi, Plateau Nutsubidze II 3A; tel. (32) 25-01-93; fax (32) 21-78-19; e-mail caritas-georgia@caritas.ge; internet www.caritas.ge; f. 1993; Roman Catholic welfare org.; Pres. Bishop GIUSEPPE PASOTTO; Sec.-Gen. Fr WITOLD SZULCZYNSKI.

Lazarus Georgian Patriarchate Charitable Foundation: 0105 Tbilisi, Erekle II Moedani 1; tel. (32) 98-73-00; fax (32) 93-51-99; e-mail lazarus@caucasus.net; internet www.lazarus.org.ge; f. 1994; implements humanitarian assistance programmes and co-ordinates humanitarian aid, principally to internally-displaced persons.

Red Cross Society of Georgia: 0102 Tbilisi, Krilov 15; tel. (32) 96-10-92; fax (32) 95-33-04; e-mail redcross@redcross.ge; internet www.redcross.ge; Pres. NANA KEINISHVILI.

United Nations Development Programme (UNDP): 0179 Tbilisi, Eristavi 9; tel. (32) 25-11-26; fax (32) 25-02-71; e-mail registry.ge@undp.org.ge; internet www.undp.org.ge; f. 1993; projects focus on democratic governance, environmental conservation, poverty reduction, and crisis prevention and recovery; 9 UN country team agencies are represented in Georgia; UNDP acts as the manager and main funding agency of the Resident Co-ordinator system; Representative ROBERT DERWYN WATKINS.

United Nations World Food Programme: 0162 Tbilisi, Chavchavadze 39A, 9th floor; tel. (32) 25-36-67; fax (32) 25-46-70; e-mail wfp.tbilisi@wfp.org; internet www.wfp.org; runs a Protracted Relief and Recovery operation, which provides assistance to over 200,000 people; sub-office in Kutaisi; Dir LOLA CASTRO.

The Environment

Georgia experienced environmental degradation as a result of conflict in the autonomous territories of Abkhazia and South Ossetia, and as a result of industrial pollution. Georgia is a member of the Black Sea environmental programme, which aims to improve the ability of Black Sea countries to manage the environment, to implement environmental legislation, and to promote ecologically sound investments.

GOVERNMENT ORGANIZATIONS

Ministry of Environmental Protection and Natural Resources: see The Government (Ministries).

State Department of Forest Management: 0186 Tbilisi, Mindeli 9; tel. (32) 30-43-76; fax (32) 32-05-49; Chair. MERAB DVALI.

State Department of Geology: 0162 Tbilisi, Mosashvili 24; tel. (32) 22-77-37; fax (32) 22-40-40; e-mail sandro@kheta.ge; f. 1925; Chair. ALEKSANDR G. TVALCHRELIDZE.

State Department of Protected Areas, Reserves and Hunting Farms: 0162 Tbilisi, Chavchavadze 84; tel. (32) 23-50-77; Chair. RAMAZ SHISHNIASHVILI.

ACADEMIC INSTITUTES

Georgian Academy of Sciences: 0108 Tbilisi, Rustaveli 52; tel. (32) 99-88-91; fax (32) 99-88-23; e-mail frg@gas.hepi.edu.ge; internet www.acnet.ge; Pres. THOMAS V. GAMKRELIDZE.

Attached institutes include:

Commission on Nature Conservation: 0193 Tbilisi, Z. Rukhadze 1; tel. (32) 99-88-91; fax (32) 99-88-23; Chair. L. K. GABUNIA.

Commission for Studying Productive Forces and Natural Resources: 0162 Tbilisi, Paliashvili 87; tel. (32) 22-32-16; fax (32) 22-20-46; e-mail keps@gw.acnet.ge; internet www.acnet.ge/geo/

prezidiumtan_arsebuli/index.html; f. 1978; attached to the Presidium of the Academy; Chair. Prof. IRAKLI ZHORDANIA.

A. Djanelidze Institute of Geology: 0193 Tbilisi, Aleksidze 1; tel. (32) 33-49-82; fax (32) 33-06-47; e-mail geolog@gw.acnet.ge; internet www.acnet.ge; f. 1925; Dir DAVID ZAKARAIA.

V. Gulisashvili Institute of Mountain Forestry: 0186 Tbilisi, Mindeli 9; tel. (32) 30-34-66; e-mail postmaster@forest.acnet.ge; Dir GIORGI GIGAURI.

Institute of Water Management and Engineering Ecology: 0162 Tbilisi, Chavchavadze 60; tel. (32) 22-40-94; fax (32) 22-74-01; e-mail root@hidroeco.acnet.ge; f. 1929; Dir TSOTNE E. MIRSKHOULAVA.

N. Ketskhoveli Institute of Botany: 0105 Tbilisi, Kojori 1; tel. (32) 99-77-46; fax (32) 98-82-76; e-mail botanins@gw.acnet.ge; f. 1933; also includes the Georgian Botanical Society; Dir ZAAL GAMTSEMLIDZE.

Scientific Research Centre for Radiobiology and Radiation Ecology: 0103 Tbilisi, Telavi 51; tel. (32) 77-55-91; fax (32) 93-35-23; e-mail kiazo@caucasus.net; internet www.radiobiology.org.ge; f. 1990; Dir G. L. ORMOTSADZE.

NON-GOVERNMENTAL ORGANIZATIONS

Caucasus Environmental NGO Network (CENN): 0105 Tbilisi, Betlemi 27; tel. (32) 75-19-03; fax (32) 75-19-04; e-mail info@cenn.org; internet www.cenn.org; f. 1998; fosters regional co-operation by means of improved communication among environmental organizations of Armenia, Azerbaijan and Georgia; produces monthly Caucasus Environment News e-bulletin.

Georgian Centre for the Conservation of Wildlife (GCCW): 0160 Tbilisi, POB 56; tel. (32) 32-64-96; fax (32) 53-74-78; e-mail office@gccw.org; internet www.gccw.org; f. 1994; non-profit, membership-based association; Dir RAMAZ GOKHELASHVILI.

Georgian Geoinformation Centre (G-Info): 0179 Tbilisi, Napareuli 14; tel. (32) 22-20-14; e-mail eis@ginfo.kheta.ge; f. 1994; creates geographical information systems and environmental databases.

Georgian Green Movement—Friends of the Earth (Sakartvelos Mtsvaneta Modzraoba—Dedamicis Megobrebi Sakartvelo): 0112 Tbilisi, Aghmashenebeli 182; tel. (32) 35-47-51; fax (32) 35-16-74; e-mail info@greens.ge; f. 1998; activist environmental group; non-political; affiliated with the Green Party of Georgia and the Asscn of Biofarmers of Georgia (ELKANA); Chair. NANA NEMSADZE; Exec. Dir RUSUDAN SIMONIDZE.

Green Alternative: 0162 Tbilisi, Chavchavadze 62, Entrance IV, 7th Floor; tel. (32) 22-16-04; fax (32) 22-38-74; e-mail greenalt@caucasus.net; internet www.greenalt.org; f. 2000.

Green Party (Mtsvanta Partia): see Political Organizations.

International Centre for Environmental Research: 0179 Tbilisi, Kostava 47/613; tel. and fax (32) 98-81-89; e-mail icfer@icfer.org; internet www.icfer.org; f. 1997 as Georgian Centre for Environmental Research; name changed as above in 2004; consultants on environment, agriculture and tourism; Dir GRIGORI ABRAMIA.

Regional Environmental Centre for the Caucasus (REC Caucasus): 0162 Tbilisi, Chavchavadze 74/901; tel. (32) 25-36-49; fax (32) 25-36-48; e-mail info@rec-caucasus.org; internet www.rec-caucasus.org; f. 2000 by the Govts of Armenia, Azerbaijan and Georgia, and the EU; independent, not-for-profit, non-advocacy foundation; Exec. Dir NATO KIRVALIDZE.

WWF Caucasus Programme Office: 0193 Tbilisi, Aleksidze 11, Georgian Academy of Sciences; tel. (32) 33-01-54; fax (32) 33-01-90; e-mail office@wwfcaucasus.ge; internet www.panda.org/caucasus; f. 1992; conservation of nature and biodiversity; Dir GIORGI SANADIRADZE.

Defence

Following the dissolution of the USSR in December 1991, Georgia began to create a unified army from the various existing paramilitary and other groups. A National Security Council (headed by the President) was established in early 1996 as a consultative body to co-ordinate issues related to defence and security. Compulsory military service lasts for 18 months. As assessed at November 2007, total armed forces numbered some 21,150: an army of 17,767, a navy of 495, an air force of 1,310 and a National Guard of 1,578. There were also paramilitary forces of 11,700. The separatist 'Republic of Abkhazia' and 'Republic of South Ossetia' have separate armed forces. A 1,500 member Joint Peace-keeping Force, comprising 500 Russian, Georgian and Ossetian troops, was established in 1992 to maintain a cease-fire in South Ossetia. A Commonwealth of Independent States (CIS) Peace-keeping Force of Russian troops in Abkhazia, numbering some 3,000, was established under a 1994 agreement. In addition, the UN Observer Mission in Georgia

(UNOMIG), created in 1993 for deployment in Abkhazia, comprised 129 military observers and 14 police officers, supported by 260 local and international staff, at the end of July 2008. Following conflict in Georgia in early August (see Recent History), a number of Russian troops remained in the country, concentrated in and around South Ossetia and Abkhazia, at the end of September. Under a peace agreement, reached on 8 September after mediation by the European Union (EU), all Russian forces were to be withdrawn from Georgian territory (apart from the separatist regions) within 10 days of the deployment of some 200 EU monitors, which commenced, as scheduled, on 1 October. However, the Russian Government announced that it was to maintain 3,800 troops each in Abkhazia and South Ossetia, and establish military bases in the regions.

In December 1993 Georgia became a member of the CIS and its collective security system; however, Georgia failed to renew its participation in the system upon its expiry in May 1999. In March 1994 Georgia joined the North Atlantic Treaty Organization's (NATO) 'Partnership for Peace' programme of military co-operation. In November 2004 Georgia became the first country to present an Individual Partnership Action Plan to NATO, in an effort to strengthen its relationship with the Alliance. From September 2006 the 'intensified dialogue' stage of negotiations on membership was launched. Under a bilateral agreement, signed in March 2006, Russia withdrew forces from Russian military headquarters in Tbilisi later that year and completed further withdrawals from bases in Akhalkalaki and Batumi by November 2007. In the early 2000s Georgia developed closer military links with the USA. In March 2005 Georgia dispatched 550 troops to assist in US-led operations in Iraq, in addition to some 300 troops already deployed there, guarding UN facilities. In March 2007 it was announced that Georgia's presence in Iraq was to be increased from 850 to 2,000. The 2007 budget allocated some 957m. lari to defence.

Chief of the General Staff: Brig.-Gen. Zaza Gogava.

AUTONOMOUS TERRITORIES

Georgia contains two Autonomous Republics, Abkhazia (Apsny) and Adjara (Ajaria), and one former Autonomous Oblast, South Ossetia. The status of both Abkhazia and South Ossetia remains disputed. Since 1995 the majority of South Ossetia, which was only partially under central government control, has been incorporated into Shida Kartli Mkhare (region), although in 2007 a new Provisional Administration, supported by the Government, was established in those areas of the former oblast under state control. In 2006, Georgian government forces obtained control of around 20% of the territory of Abkhazia, establishing their own administration in an area referred to as Upper Abkhazia. However, following armed conflict between Georgia and Russia in August 2008, it was reported that Georgia had lost control over the entire territories of South Ossetia and Abkhazia.

ABKHAZIA

Abkhazia (which for much of the Soviet period formed a nominally Autonomous Republic—ASSR—within the Georgian SSR) is situated in the north-west of Georgia and covers an area of 8,600 sq km. Formerly a colony of the Eastern Roman or 'Byzantine' Empire, Abkhazia was an important power in the ninth and 10th centuries, but it was later dominated by Georgian, Turkish and Russian rulers. In 1989 the total population was 537,000; in that year 17.8% of the population were Abkhazians, and 45.7% ethnic Georgians. During the conflict in 1992 and 1993 more than 200,000 ethnic Georgians and others left the region. Some 50,000 refugees were resettled from 1996, but many subsequently departed, following renewed hostilities. The language of the region is Abkhazian, a member of the North-Western group of Caucasian languages; according to the Constitution of Georgia, Georgian is also a recognized state language, although the Constitution of the Republic of Abkhazia recognizes Russian as a state language, alongside Abkhazian, but not Georgian. The capital of Abkhazia is Sukhumi (Sukhum, Sokhumi, Akua), with an estimated population of 112,000 in 1994.

In 1989 Abkhazians renewed a campaign for secession from the Georgian SSR, and in July 1992 the Abkhazian legislature proclaimed the 'Republic of Abkhazia'. In late September 1993, following a bloody civil war in which Georgian government troops were defeated, Abkhazian separatist forces officially declared the region liberated from Georgia, although this was not accepted by the central authorities. In May 1994 a full cease-fire agreement was signed, providing for the deployment of Commonwealth of Independent States (CIS) peace-keepers in the region; however, hostilities continued. On 26 November the Abkhazian legislature adopted a new Constitution, declaring the 'Republic of Abkhazia (Apsny)' to be a sovereign state, with an executive presidency. This was condemned by the Georgian Government, and protests were also voiced by the USA, Russia and the UN Security Council, all of which reaffirmed their recognition of Georgia's territorial integrity. Peace negotiations were subsequently suspended. In January 1996 the leaders of the CIS member states agreed to impose an economic embargo on Abkhazia until it agreed to accept Georgian sovereignty. Elections to the Abkhazian National Assembly were held on 23 November 1996 and to local councils on 14 March 1998, both of which were declared invalid by Georgian President Eduard Shevardnadze. On 3 October 1999 the incumbent President of the Republic, Vladislav Ardzinba, the sole candidate, was re-elected, obtaining 99% of the votes cast; the election was declared illegal by international observers. A referendum was held concurrently, in which 97% of the participants upheld the 1994 Constitution. The Abkhazian legislature subsequently adopted the State Independence Act. Despite this, negotiations between Georgia and Abkhazia resumed from 2000.

Local elections, held in Abkhazia on 10 March 2001, prompted condemnation from both the Georgian Government and the UN. None the less, at the conclusion of a UN-sponsored meeting in Yalta, Ukraine, in mid-March, delegations from both Georgia and Abkhazia agreed to permit the safe return of refugees. In early October a helicopter carrying members of the UN Observer Mission in Georgia (UNOMIG) was shot down by unidentified attackers, killing all nine people on board. The Abkhazian authorities blamed the Georgian Government for the subsequent escalation of violence in the region and accused the Georgian Government of carrying out subsequent aerial attacks on the Kodori Gorge, in Upper (Eastern) Abkhazia, which the Georgian side attributed to Russian military aircraft. Georgian troops were dispatched to the region in mid-October, although the UN deemed their deployment to be a violation of the 1994 cease-fire agreement. A protocol was signed by the Abkhazian and Georgian sides on 17 January 2002, according to which Georgia was to withdraw its troops by mid-April. Parliamentary elections, scheduled to take place in Abkhazia on 24 November 2001, were postponed until 2 March 2002, owing to the unstable security situation; the results of the elections were not recognized by international organizations. The Abkhazian premier, Anri Dzhergenia, was dismissed in December, and Gennadii Gagulia was appointed as

his replacement. In April 2003 a new Government, under Raul Khadzhimba, was appointed.

In March 2002 President Shevardnadze and the Russian President, Vladimir Putin, agreed to amend the mandate of the CIS peace-keepers stationed in Abkhazia, deploying them further north, along the Galidzga River. The amendments were condemned by the Abkhazian authorities. In late March several bombs exploded on a local train and in a port, killing one person and injuring 15; Abkhazia blamed the attacks on Georgian guerrillas. On 29 July the UN Security Council approved Resolution 1427, which demanded that the region begin negotiations on its progressive reintegration into Georgia, a proposal that was strongly opposed by the separatists; however, Russia's failure to employ its power of veto appeared to demonstrate a new tone of conciliation with Georgia. In late January 2003 Georgia refused to renew the mandate of the CIS peace-keepers in Abkhazia until, *inter alia*, the definition of the conflict zone was extended and the operation of a recently resumed railway link from the Russian Black Sea port of Sochi to Tbilisi, via Sukhumi, was halted. On 30 January the UN Security Council adopted Resolution 1462, which welcomed the reduction in tension in the Kodori region, but expressed regret at the lack of progress in reaching a political settlement on the status of Abkhazia. On 7 March Shevardnadze and Putin issued a joint statement, agreeing to expedite the repatriation of displaced persons to Abkhazia, prior to the resumption of the Sochi–Sukhumi–Tbilisi railway service and the renovation of the region's Inguri hydroelectric plant. In addition, they agreed to extend indefinitely the mandate of the CIS peace-keeping forces.

At the beginning of August 2002 the Abkhazian National Assembly adopted amendments to the Constitution, enabling Abkhazian citizens to hold dual citizenship. Some 60% of the region's population had already acquired Russian passports, following the adoption of amendments to the law on citizenship by the Russian legislature.

It is generally accepted that Russia conducts some trade with Abkhazia (despite sanctions imposed by the CIS), permitting the import of petroleum, flour and sugar, and the export of citrus fruits, fish, wine and timber. Some revenue is generated by continued Russian tourism.

Following the removal of Eduard Shevardnadze from power in Georgia in late 2003, there were strong demands for the resignation of Tamaz Nadareishvili as Chairman of the Abkhazian parliament-in-exile (which was based in Tbilisi); he was accused of corruption. Nadareishvili eventually resigned in January 2004 and died in August. Teimuraz (Temur) Mzhavia, a member of the new Georgian President Mikheil Saakashvili's National Movement, succeeded him as Chairman in mid-March.

On 9 June 2004 a prominent opponent of the separatist regime, Garri Ayba, was shot dead in Sukhumi; the legislature expressed concern at the increasing criminality in the region and appealed to Ardzinba to take action. Sergei Shamba, the Minister of Foreign Affairs, and the head of the State Security Service of the separatist regime submitted their resignations from office in response.

In an internationally unrecognized presidential election held on 3 October 2004, Raul Khadzhimba, the candidate endorsed by Ardzinba and supported by Russia, was initially declared the winner. However, following the processing of disputed results from the Gali region, Khadzhimba's rival, Sergei Bagapsh (the head of the Chernomorenergo energy company), was ultimately judged to have received the most votes, by a narrow margin. Khadzhimba disputed this result, demanding the annulment of the ballot. Following protest demonstrations by supporters of both candidates, an agreement was reached on 6 December, under the mediation of Russian officials, whereby the two candidates would participate jointly in a new election. In the repeat election held on 12 January 2005 Bagapsh was elected as President with some 90% of the votes cast; Khadzhimba was to be Vice-President (with augmented powers). Following Bagapsh's inauguration, he nominated Aleksandr Ankvab, a close ally, as Prime Minister. Ankvab survived assassination attempts in February and April. Despite Russia's apparent preference for Khadzhimba's candidacy, Bagapsh demonstrated continuity in the territory's policy of seeking a strategic union with Russia. In February President Saakashvili appointed Irakli Alasania, the head of the Tbilisi-based Abkhazian parliament-in-exile, as special envoy for negotiations with the separatist Abkhazian authorities, although the separatist regime refused to conduct talks with him on the basis that they did not recognize his official title as legitimate. (In order to overcome this difficulty, in March 2006 Saakashvili appointed Alasania as his assistant on Abkhazian conflict issues instead.)

Meanwhile, in September 2004 the railway line from Sukhumi to Moscow was fully reopened for the first time in 11 years, in accordance with the bilateral agreements made in Sochi in March 2003. However, this generated tension between Georgia and Russia, since the process of returning displaced persons to the Gali district, which had been agreed at the same time, had failed to be completed. In mid-2005 the Georgian authorities indicated that they might cease to link the railway project with the return of displaced persons, and agreement was reached in July that a feasibility survey should be conducted by Abkhazian, Georgian and Russian specialists on the condition of a 200-km stretch of the railway in the region. The survey was postponed, however, when the Abkhazian authorities refused to allow the Georgian representatives entry to the region. Negotiations progressed as far as the signing of an agreement on a Black Sea Railways consortium by separatist Abkhazian, Armenian, Georgian and Russian parties in May 2006. However, the implementation of a transportation moratorium on Georgia, by Russia, in October did not bode well for future developments. Moreover, the Abkhazian Government claimed to feel strongly threatened by the funding by international donors of Georgia's increasing military strength.

In July 2006 a paramilitary group, *Monadire* (Hunters), led by the former Georgian representative in the Kodori Gorge region during President Shevardnadze's term, Emzar Kvtisiani, declared that it would not disband, as the Minister of Defence had decreed it should. The group refused to relinquish its right to defence against Abkhazian forces, but was described as criminal by members of the Government. In response, the Georgian authorities deployed 1,000 troops to the area, and the rebels were effectively disbanded. Russia and the Republic of Abkhazia claimed that this action violated the 1994 cease-fire agreement, although Georgia categorized it as a police mission. (UNOMIG noted 13 violations of the cease-fire agreement by the Georgian side and two by the Abkhazians.) As a result of the mission, the Georgian authorities resolved to transfer the base of the exiled Abkhazian Government to upper Kodori (the only part of Abkhazia under Georgian control) from Tbilisi, and announced emergency aid and reconstruction plans for the local airport and the main road linking the Gorge to the rest of the region, in order to address local resentments. (Saakashvili also declared that any foreign diplomats seeking to visit the illegitimate authorities in Sukhumi, should also visit this Government in Chkhalta, as the official administrative centre of the region.) As a result, the region participated in local elections on 5 October, for the first time.

On 13 October 2006 the UN Security Council adopted Resolution 1716 expressing its concern with regard to the actions of Georgia in the Kodori Valley in July, and acknowledging the important role of the CIS peace-keeping force in the Georgian–Abkhazian conflict zone. The mandate of the observer mission was extended once more, until April 2007. The US Ambassador to the UN clarified that his Government regarded Georgian actions in Kodori to have been the country's sovereign right (provided they were enacted within the mandate of the cease-fire).

On 11 February 2007 elections were held to Abkhazia's 169 local council seats. On 4 March some 108 candidates contested the elections for the 35-member separatist legislature; however, the initial poll produced an outright victor in only 18 constituencies. On the following day the Abkhazian Central Election Committee upheld the parliamentary elections as legitimate, on the grounds that 48% of the electorate had participated, comfortably surpassing the rate of participation of 25% required to render the process valid. The Georgian Government denounced both ballots as illegal, while the international community also rejected their legitimacy. On 18 March a second round of voting was held for the 17 seats not filled in the first round; turn-out was reported to be 47% of the electorate.

In mid-March 2007 three military helicopters made a series of aerial bombings in the Kodori Gorge area of Georgian-controlled Upper Abkhazia, although no casualties ensued. Both the Russian and the Abkhazian authorities denied any involvement in the attacks, although some reports stated that the helicopters had entered the territory from Russian airspace. Following the announcement in July that Russia was to host the 2014 Winter Olympic Games in the Black Sea resort of Sochi, reports that Russian enterprises intended to import materials for the construction of sports facilities from Abkhazia (with considerable potential benefit to the local economy) prompted strong protests from Georgian officials.

On 6 March 2008 the Russian Government announced its decision (which was strongly condemned by Georgia) unilaterally to end the economic embargo that the CIS had imposed on Abkhazia in 1996. Later in March 2008 the Georgian Government presented a new peace proposal for Abkhazia, offering 'unlimited autonomy' to the region; Bagapsh (whose alternative proposal, based on the principle of recognition of Abkhazia as an independent state, had been declared unacceptable by Georgia) rejected the plan. In April the Georgian Government accused Russia of violating its airspace, after a fighter jet shot down a Georgian reconnaissance drone over Abkhazia. Russia denied the Georgian claim, stating that an Abkhazian military aircraft had carried out the attack. In early May the Abkhazian authorities announced that two unmanned Georgian reconnaissance drones had been shot down over the region; the Georgian Government denied the claim. On 15 May the UN General Assembly adopted a resolution, proposed by Georgia, recognizing the right of return of all refugees and internally displaced persons to Abkhazia. At the end of that month the Georgian Government formally protested at Russia's dispatch, without the consent of Georgia, of some 400 troops to Abkhazia to repair disused railway track, claiming that it represented a direct violation of its sovereignty and territorial integrity. (Nevertheless, the Russian troops continued repairs for two months, withdrawing from Abkhazia at the end of July.) On 30 June a bomb exploded in Sukhumi (following two similar incidents in the town of Gagra on the previous day), prompting the Abkhazian separatist authorities, which claimed that Georgian special forces had perpetrated the attacks to destabilize the region, to announce the closure of the border between the territories they controlled and the rest of Georgia. A German-mediated peace plan, which was to begin with direct negotiations between representatives of the Georgian Government and the Abkhazian authorities in Berlin, Germany, was rejected by Abkhazia (reportedly at the instigation of Russia) at the end of July.

On 9 August 2008, following the onset of hostilities concentrated in South Ossetia (see below), the Abkhazian separatists declared that their forces had commenced military action to expel Georgian troops from the Kodori Gorge. Two days later Russia announced that some 9,000 Russian troops had been dispatched to Abkhazia; on 12 August Abkhazian forces, with Russian support, were reported to have regained control of the Kodori Gorge. In early September the Russian Government announced plans to maintain 3,800 troops in each of Abkhazia and South Ossetia. Bagapsh stated that, although willing to continue to accept UN observers, he opposed the deployment of European Union (EU) monitors in Abkhazia (as stipulated under the terms of an EU-mediated peace plan). On 21 August a mass demonstration was staged in Abkhazia to urge the Russian Government to recognize the region's independence. Following Russia's official recognition of South Ossetia and Abkhazia as independent states on 26 August, a friendship and co-operation treaty, signed by the leaders of the two separatist Republics and the Russian President on 17 September, committing Russia to military support, was ratified by the Abkhazian National Assembly on 24 September. Bagapsh confirmed that two Russian military bases would be established in the region, one at Gudauta and one at Ochamchire, and announced that the security of Abkhazia's border with Georgia would be strengthened.

Note: the following representatives of the officially recognized Abkhazian Government were formerly based in Chkhalta, and their remit only extended, de facto, over those regions of Upper (Eastern) Abkhazia under the control of the Georgian authorities. However, following the conflict of August 2008, these regions, in common with the remainder of the territory, reverted to the control of the internationally unrecognized 'Republic of Abkhazia'.

Chairman of the Council of Ministers of the Autonomous Republic of Abkhazia: MALKAS AKYSHBAIA; internet www .abkhazia.gov.ge.

Chairman of the Supreme Council of the Autonomous Republic of Abkhazia: MALKHAZ AKISHBAIA.

President of the 'Republic of Abkhazia': SERGEI BAGAPSH, 6600 Abkhazia, Sukhumi; tel. (122) 2-46-35; fax (122) 2-71-17; internet www.abkhaziagov.org.

Prime Minister of the 'Republic of Abkhazia': ALEKSANDR ANKVAB, 6600 Abkhazia, Sukhumi; tel. (122) 2-46-32; e-mail premier@abkhazia.info.

Speaker of the 'National Assembly of the Republic of Abkhazia': NUGZAR N. ASHUBA, 6600 Abkhazia, Sukhumi; tel. (122) 2-76-84.

AUTONOMOUS REPUBLIC OF ADJARA

The Autonomous Republic of Adjara was established on 16 July 1921. It is situated in the south-west of Georgia, on the border with Turkey, and covers an area of 3,000 sq km. In January 2006 the population was estimated to be 377,200. The Ajars are a Georgian people, who adopted Islam while Adjara was under Ottoman rule. The Ajars have an unwritten language, Ajar, which is closely related to Georgian, but has been strongly influenced by Turkish. The capital of Adjara is Batumi, with an estimated population of 122,100 at January 2006.

In the late 1980s the Georgian nationalist movement questioned the region's autonomous status. In April 1991 Aslan Abashidze, a senior government official in Tbilisi of noble Adjaran descent, was appointed Chairman of the Adjaran Supreme Soviet (regional legislature). Abashidze's party, the All-Georgian Union of Revival, secured the majority of the parliamentary seats in Adjara in the November 1995 elections, a victory suspected by many to be in return for Abashidze's support for Eduard Shevardnadze in the national presidential election, held simultaneously. Elections to the Adjaran Supreme Council were held on 22 September 1996, when the majority of seats (some 83%, according to official results) were won by an alliance of the All-Georgian Union of Revival and Shevardnadze's Citizens' Union of Georgia, amid further allegations of electoral irregularities. Abashidze was re-elected Chairman of the Council. Relations between the region and the central authorities deteriorated somewhat thereafter, as the Adjarans claimed that the Georgian Government was attempting to increase its control over the republic. In October 1999 relations deteriorated further, when Adjara refused to release prisoners pardoned by Shevardnadze under an amnesty. Abashidze also criticized the legislative elections held in Georgia in October and November, and subsequently relinquished his parliamentary mandate, ostensibly owing to fear of assassination in Tbilisi; his seat was awarded to another member of his party. Abashidze was to have stood as a candidate in the Georgian presidential election of April 2000, but he withdrew his candidacy the day before it took place. On 18 April the Georgian Parlamenti voted to amend the Constitution, officially to register Adjara as an Autonomous Republic. In June the Adjaran Supreme Council endorsed amendments to its Constitution, and in July 2001 it voted to rename itself the Parliament of the Autonomous Republic of Adjara. Following elections in late 2001, the Parliament was reformed on a bicameral basis. The 35-member Council of the Republic was elected by proportional representation, while seven of the Senate's 10 members were elected by majority vote. Abashidze was directly elected to the new post of Head of the Autonomous Republic (leader of the executive) on 4 November. In 2003 Adjara withheld its tax contribution to Georgia's central budget, claiming that it had not received its share of budgetary spending; this was one of the factors leading to the suspension of IMF lending to Georgia.

Despite previous conflicts with Shevardnadze, Abashidze allied himself firmly with Shevardnadze in the dispute over the national legislative elections of November 2003, sending hundreds of supporters to Tbilisi to oppose the anti-Government protesters gathered there. Abashidze's Democratic Union of Revival would have been the second-placed party in the national elections had the election results ultimately been declared valid. Following Shevardnadze's resignation on 23 November, Abashidze declared a state of emergency in Adjara and pledged that the region would boycott the new presidential election scheduled to take place in January 2004, although he subsequently bowed to international pressure and permitted polling to take place. As a result of the overthrow of the national regime, and the inauguration of Mikheil Saakashvili as President, opposition groups to those which participated in the 'rose revolution' became active in Adjara, in spite of efforts at repression from the authorities.

Conflict with the administration of Saakashvili arose in mid-March 2004 prior to fresh national legislative elections, as the Adjaran security services attempted to prevent members of the national Government from moving freely and campaigning in the territory. The Georgian Minister of Finance was briefly detained on 13 March, and Saakashvili was prevented from entering Adjara on the following day. He issued Abashidze with an ultimatum to recognize the authority of the central Government; when this was ignored, he went on to impose an economic blockade on the region. Abashidze responded by declaring a renewed state of emergency and a curfew. However, in talks held on 18 March, under Russian mediation, Abashidze agreed, *inter alia*, to allow the holding of free and fair elections in Adjara, subject to the withdrawal of Georgian troops from neighbouring areas and an end to the transport restrictions imposed by Saakashvili. The state of emergency was suspended, as agreed, and legislative elections proceeded as part of the nation-wide ballot on 28 March.

On 6 April 2004 the Adjaran Parliament confirmed the appointment of Rostom Dzhaparidze, co-Chairman of Abashidze's political party, as the new Chairman of the Adjaran Council of Ministers.

Following the deployment of Georgian troops on territory neighbouring Adjara for military exercises, on 2 May Abashidze ordered two bridges linking Adjara with the rest of Georgia to be blown up and railway lines dismantled, arguing that this was a defensive move. Saakashvili reiterated his earlier ultimatum that illegal groups in Adjara be disarmed and that the region return within the framework of the Georgian Constitution. Widespread demonstrations against Abashidze occurred, with many officers of authority either joining the protesters or refusing to act against them. Following discussions with the Chairman of the Russian Security Council, Igor Ivanov, Abashidze finally resigned from office on 5 May 2004 and flew to Russia, with assurances of immunity from prosecution. Saakashvili immediately imposed presidential rule on Adjara, and on 6 May the Georgian legislature voted to approve the President's authority to dismiss the Parliament and Government of the Autonomous Republic of Adjara and to schedule new elections. On the same day the Adjaran Supreme Council voted to abolish the position of the Head of the Republic, scheduled new parliamentary elections and dissolved itself. (Immunity from prosecution was extended to armed groups that surrendered their weapons within seven days.) Levan Varshalomidze was appointed as the head of an interim council to rule the region in the mean time. The Council reduced the number of governing ministries from 18 to five. Many former figures of authority were detained and prosecuted. Elections to the new republican unicameral legislature, also known as the Supreme Council, took place on 20 June, although they were regarded to have fallen short of international standards. The Saakashvili—Victorious Adjara party (the local branch of Saakashvili's National Movement) received some 75% of the votes cast and 28 of the 30 seats in the Supreme Council.

On 1 July 2004 the Georgian Parlamenti approved legislation on the Status of the Autonomous Republic of Adjara, whereby the President of Georgia was empowered to dismiss the Adjaran Government, dissolve the parliament and annul legislation approved by that body; the law also stipulates which ministries the Government may comprise, officially reducing their number and excluding those of security or defence. On 20 July the new Supreme Council elected Mikhail Makharadze as its Chairman; Levan Varshalomidze was the sole candidate for Chairman of the Government. The property of Abashidze was subsequently confiscated by the state, on the basis that it had been obtained by means of corruption.

In January 2005 the Parliamentary Assembly of the Council of Europe issued a resolution commending the peaceful reintegration of Adjara, but declaring the region to be an inadequate model of autonomy, on the basis that the leader of the republic should be directly elected (rather than selected by the President of Georgia for the approval of the Adjaran parliament). Economic hardship continued to characterize the region, with an unemployment rate of some 18%, and 64% of the population living below the poverty line; severe electricity shortages deterred potential investors. However, the Government rapidly processed plans for the privatization of the area's assets (primarily the port and shipping company) and its power station, in order to facilitate investment and development. In December a warrant was issued for the arrest of Abashidze on charges of abuse of office, terrorist offences and embezzlement, regardless of claims that he had resigned under a negotiated guarantee of immunity from prosecution. (In January 2007 a court in Batumi sentenced Abashidze to 15 years' imprisonment *in absentia* and imposed a fine of US $57m., on charges of corruption and abuse of office.)

In 2006 the national Constitutional Court was relocated to Batumi in order to consolidate the integration of the region. Widespread redevelopment was undertaken in that year in order to restore the potential of the area for tourism; however, this involved the eviction of Abkhazian refugees who had occupied some former hotels for more than 10 years (although they received some compensation). In mid-December Parlamenti adopted constitutional amendments on the status on Adjara, which provided for the extension of the mandate of the Supreme Council to allow the next parliamentary elections to take place in late 2008 (rather than in June of that year). The Georgian President was henceforth required to appoint a Chairman of the Council of Ministers on the basis of consultations with the factions of the Supreme Council, and was no longer empowered to dismiss or appoint judges, nor be involved in the activities of the High Council of Justice. The amendments were signed into force by Saakashvili in January 2007.

On 30 July 2008 the Supreme Council adopted amendments to the region's electoral code, prior to forthcoming legislative elections, scheduled to take place on 4 October: the Council was to be reduced from 30 to 18 deputies, of whom six were to be elected in single-mandate constituencies and 12 by proportional representation on the basis of party lists; the minimum proportion of votes required for parties to obtain representation on this basis was reduced from 7% to 5%; and the composition of the local Central Election Commission (CEC) was reformed to include opposition representatives. On 9 August, following the outbreak of conflict in South Ossetia and other parts of Georgia (see below), the CEC indefinitely postponed the elections; in early September they were rescheduled for 3 November. By that time, eight political parties had registered to contest the elections; however, the local branch of the Republican Party declared that it would not participate in the poll, citing the post-conflict crisis and continuing presence of Russian troops in the country.

Chairman of the Council of Ministers of the Autonomous Republic of Adjara: LEVAN VARSHALOMIDZE, 6010 Batumi, Gamsakhurdia 10; tel. (222) 72-006; fax (222) 77-300; e-mail info@adjara .gov.ge; internet www.adjara.gov.ge.

Chairman of the Supreme Council of the Autonomous Republic of Adjara: MIKHEIL MAKHARADZE, Batumi; e-mail info@sca.ge; internet www.sca.ge.

SOUTH OSSETIA

The South Ossetian Autonomous Oblast (region) was established on 20 April 1922. It is situated in the north of Georgia and borders the Russian Republic of North Osetiya (Ossetia)—Alaniya. It covers an area of 3,900 sq km. In 1989 the population was 99,000, although the subsequent conflict resulted in the displacement of as many as 30,000 refugees. In 1979 66.4% of the population were Ossetians and 28.8% Georgians. The Ossetians are an Iranian (Persian) people, a minority of whom adopted Islam from the Kabardins. (The majority of Ossetians are Orthodox Christians.) The national language is Ossetian, a member of the North-Eastern group of Iranian languages. The principal city in the region is Tskhinvali.

The Regional Council (oblast soviet) adopted a declaration of sovereignty on 20 September 1990 and proclaimed the territory the 'Soviet Democratic Republic of South Ossetia'. The region's autonomous status was abolished by the Georgian Supreme Soviet on 11 December, and most territories of the former Autonomous Oblast were subsequently merged with adjoining areas to form an administrative region, Shida Kartli Mkhare (region). Jurisdiction of the region was then disputed, amid continuing conflict. A second declaration of independence was issued in December 1991, supported by a referendum held in the region in January 1992. Following the ousting of President Zviad Gamsakhurdia in January, the Georgian Military Council released the South Ossetian leader and reformed the system of local government. Tension in the area eased. In July a cease-fire agreement was reached and a Russian-led peace-keeping force was deployed in the region. The self-styled 'Republic of South Ossetia' introduced a new Constitution on 23 December 1993 and held elections in April 1994. (However, reports suggested that separatists had at no stage gained control over the full territorial extent of the former Autonomous Oblast, but that political control over the territory was characterized by the existence of discrete areas controlled either by supporters of the central Government in Tbilisi, or of the separatist 'Republic', a situation that continued to prevail until 2008.) In July 1995 discussions on a political settlement began, under the aegis of the Organization for Security and Co-operation in Europe (OSCE). The new Georgian Constitution, approved by the national legislature on 24 August, referred to the territory of South Ossetia as Tskhinvali. South Ossetian and Georgian leaders signed a Memorandum on Security and Mutual Understanding on 16 May 1996. In September a presidential system of government in the 'Republic' was introduced; a presidential election was held on 10 November and won by Ludvig Chibirov, who obtained some 65% of the votes cast. In September 1997 and June 1998 agreements providing for economic assistance to the region and the safe return of refugees were signed by Georgian President Eduard Shevardnadze and Chibirov. The status of the region was to be determined after the return of the refugees; Shevardnadze proposed the creation of a federation of states, including South Ossetia, but the South Ossetian parliament continued to favour the creation of an independent republic within the Commonwealth of Independent States. In May 1999 legislative elections were held. The Communist Party obtained some 39% of the votes cast, but neither the Georgian authorities nor the OSCE recognized the results. Dimitri Sanakoyev was appointed Prime Minister in mid-June 2001, following the resignation of Merab Chigoyev. Negotiations with the Georgian Government, on reconstruction and the status of the region, were held in September, but no agreement was reached. A presidential election took place on 18 November, and the two leading candidates, Eduard Kokoyev (Kokoiti), a Russian-based businessman, and the parliamentary Chairman, Stanislav Kochiyev, subsequently proceeded to a second round of voting. The 'run-off' election finally took place on 6 December, having been postponed when Chibirov's son reportedly led a detachment of police officers to the parliament building in protest at the first-round results. Kokoyev secured 55% of the votes cast in the second round, and was subsequently confirmed as President. Kokoyev advocated unification with North Osetiya—Alaniya and associate membership of the Russian Federation, following recognition of South Ossetian independence. In July 2003 Kokoyev purged

his Government (allegedly pre-empting a possible coup), thus undermining both the political power and business connections of several high-ranking figures, and strengthening his own position, which had previously been regarded as tenuous. In September he appointed Igor Sanakoyev, a Russian citizen, as Prime Minister, after dismissing the Government in the previous month for its failure to fulfil the budget, amid allegations of corruption. Kokoyev's Unity Party won a majority of seats in legislative elections held on 23 May 2004.

On 31 May 2004 the national Georgian Government dispatched some 300 servicemen to a key checkpoint at the border with Russia in South Ossetia, to reinforce its efforts to curb smuggling and illegal trade in goods and weapons. However, both the South Ossetian and Russian authorities regarded the action as threatening. Skirmishes ensued over the following months, involving numerous casualties and injuries, and a cease-fire agreement, made on 13 August, was not observed. On 19 August Georgian forces stormed and occupied three strategic hills near Tskhinvali, supposedly to neutralize a 'third force' of mercenaries who had been allegedly sabotaging the cease-fire; control of that area was then ceded to the peace-keeping forces. The most pressing demand from all sides was the demilitarization of the conflict zone. Georgia sought the greater internationalization of the peace-keeping forces in the region, with less emphasis on their Russian component, and the establishment of border and customs posts at the Roki tunnel, between South Ossetia and North Osetiya—Alaniya, which was reportedly the main conduit for contraband traded in Georgia. However, like the Abkhazian authorities, the authorities loyal to Kokoyev in South Ossetia rejected proposals for peace, announced by Georgian President Mikheil Saakashvili at the UN General Assembly in September, in which the President announced proposals for what were termed the fullest and broadest forms of autonomy; the proposals were likewise dismissed when subsequently presented at the Parliamentary Assembly of the Council of Europe in January 2005 and in mid-2005, despite wide-ranging, internationally funded commitments to economic investment and rehabilitation.

Analysts observed that the campaign by the Georgian authorities to eradicate the thriving trade in contraband in the region had been counter-productive, in that, where successful, it had caused a loss of local employment and income (even if illegal), thus exacerbating resentment against the Georgian Government and increasing economic dependence on Russia, which reacted by providing funding and assistance programmes. The situation was worsened by the revelation of a smuggling network comprising senior regional members of the Georgian police force in March 2005. In July the extent to which Russian involvement in regional affairs had developed was demonstrated by the appointment of a premier, a minister of defence and a chief of staff by the separatist Republic, all of whom originated from regions of Russia remote from the Caucasus. Meanwhile, kidnappings and other incidences of lawlessness in the region continued to take place regularly.

At events to mark the anniversary of the declaration of secession by the Republic, in September 2005, a large deployment of military troops and hardware was paraded, in breach of international demilitarization and limitation agreements; a treaty of friendship and bilateral co-operation was signed between the unrecognized regimes in South Ossetia and Abkhazia, and an agreement reached with the leader of North Osetiya—Alaniya on the creation of a commission on special relations and further political and economic co-operation (with the aim of eventual unification). The Georgian legislature reacted by drafting a resolution threatening to demand the immediate withdrawal of Russian peace-keeping detachments from both South Ossetia and Abkhazia. In February 2006 Parlamenti, the Georgian legislature, adopted a resolution demanding the replacement of the Russian peace-keepers with international forces. At a donor conference of the OSCE in June, some €10m. was committed towards post-conflict infrastructural reconstruction for the region, which the Georgian authorities pledged to match. In October a programme for the economic rehabilitation of the region was launched formally by an OSCE-led steering committee.

In July 2006 the Secretary of the separatist National Security Council, Oleg Alborov, was killed by an incendiary device at his home. Five days later two people were killed and two injured by another such device at the home of the head of a militia formation affiliated to the separatist Ministry of Defence. (In September a military helicopter carrying the Georgian Minister of Defence was shot at and damaged by rebel South Ossetian forces.) In advance of presidential elections scheduled to be held later in the year, in August the separatist authorities began issuing internal passports, which, in spite of their lack of international validity, would be required in order to vote in the elections; Georgian citizens would be required to renounce their citizenship in order to obtain one. The distribution by the separatist authorities of Russian passports within South Ossetia was also reported to have become widespread by the mid-2000s.

At the presidential election, which was conducted in those areas of South Ossetia controlled by the separatist authorities on 12 November 2006, Kokoyev was overwhelmingly elected to a second term in office, reportedly attracting 98.1% of the votes cast. The poll coincided with a referendum (again unrecognized by the international community), in which voters were asked whether or not the Republic should preserve its de facto independent status. Results released by the South Ossetian election commission indicated that some 99% of those who voted had cast their ballots in favour of independence from Georgia; voter turn-out was reported to be 95.2% of the registered electorate. However, what was termed an alternative election for a regional President, organized by the newly established Union of the National Salvation for Ossetians (UNSO), was held concurrently in those South Ossetian territories that remained under the control of the Georgian state; the poll was won by UNSO's leader, Dimitri Sanakoyev, a former separatist prime minister, reportedly with 96% of votes cast. A referendum held in these territories also expressed approval, by an overwhelming majority, for the commencement of negotiations with the central authorities in Tbilisi on the establishment of a federated Georgian state, of which South Ossetia would form a part.

Sanakoyev was inaugurated on 1 December 2006 and announced the formation of a local administration, based in Kurta, north of Tskhinvali. He subsequently appointed the head of the Georgian-backed central election commission, Uruzmag Karkusov, as premier, and a number of ministers, including Uruzmag's brother, Jemal Karkusov (previously in the separatist administration), as Minister of the Interior. On 8 May 2007, following discussions between Sanakoyev and representatives of the Georgian Government, Parlamenti adopted a resolution (based on draft legislation approved in April) providing for the establishment of a Provisional Administration of South Ossetia; Sanakoyev was officially appointed its head on 10 May, thereby giving his position official recognition. The regions of South Ossetia under the control of the Provisional Administration subsequently underwent a programme of infrastructural rehabilitation with support from the national authorities. President Saakashvili established a new state commission, chaired by the Georgian Prime Minister, for the determination of South Ossetia's status, which was convened for the first time on 24 July. The European Union (EU) and OSCE expressed support for the Georgian initiative, which was to conduct dialogue on settlement of the conflict between representatives of all political forces and local groups.

From early 2008 peace-keeping officials reported an increasing number of minor cease-fire violations in South Ossetia, and a general increase in tension was reported in the region. In March the Russian Government announced that it was to establish legal relations with the separatist authorities in both South Ossetia and Abkhazia. In early July Sanakoyev's personal vehicle came under fire; although he was uninjured. In mid-July the Russian authorities acknowledged that four Russian Air Force planes had entered airspace over South Ossetia, claiming that the purpose of the mission was to deter Georgia from flying unmanned military reconnaissance drones over the region. In early August tensions intensified, with various incidents of crossfire and shelling reported to have resulted in a number of deaths. Following continued exchanges of fire, by 7 August the conflict between Georgian troops and South Ossetian militia had intensified; and Georgian troops commenced a concerted offensive, including an aerial bombardment, against Tskhinvali. On 8 August the Georgian Government announced that its troops had entered the

city and had secured control of most of South Ossetia, and stated that its purpose in escalating military action had been to 'restore constitutional order' in the region. In response, Russia sent a substantial deployment of troops into South Ossetia, purportedly to protect the security of Russian citizens resident there (the allocation of Russian passports to residents of those regions of South Ossetia controlled by the separatists having been ongoing). The Russian President Dmitrii Medvedev, and other senior administration officials, accused Georgia of seeking to perpetrate 'genocide' against the ethnic Ossetian population, and alleged that up to 2,000 people had been killed as a result of the Georgian attack on Tskhinvali. On the following day, after a concerted counter-offensive, the Russian military (supported by volunteer militias, particularly from the Chechen Republic) claimed to have gained control of Tskhinvali and repulsed the Georgian troops; the separatists also gained control of those regions formerly part of the South Ossetian Autonomous Oblast that had remained under Georgian control, most notably around the town of Akhalgori. Looting, retaliatory attacks against ethnic Georgians, and burning of Georgian villages were subsequently reported by human rights organizations. Despite a cease-fire agreement, reached on 12 August, Russian troops remained deployed in strategic areas of Georgia, including locations far from South Ossetia and the adjacent security zone.

On 26 August 2008 President Medvedev announced that Russia officially recognized South Ossetia and Abkhazia as independent states. Although Kokoyev had declared that he sought for South Ossetia to be admitted to the Russian Federation, and to merge with the Russian federal subject of North Osetiya—Alaniya, following the repudiation of this stance by the Russian authorities, Kokoyev subsequently withdrew from this position, instead emphasizing that he wished South Ossetia to exist as an independent state. On 17 September Russia signed friendship and co-operation treaties with the leaders of South Ossetia and Abkhazia, pledging to support the regions militarily and economically. By that time, other than Russia, Nicaragua was the only state to have announced recognition of the independence of South Ossetia and Abkhazia. On 26 September the Georgian parliament approved legislation imposing a number of restrictions on non-Georgian citizens in Abkhazia and South Ossetia, to remain in effect until Georgian jurisdiction was restored. (However, as Georgia had effectively lost control of both regions, it appeared unlikely that this law would have any direct effect.) Under a further EU-mediated peace agreement, reached on 8 September, the deployment of EU monitors commenced in Georgia on 1 October, although it remained unclear as to whether these troops would be permitted to enter South Ossetia or Abkhazia, rather than the 'buffer zones' established around both territories in August, while a substantial deployment of Russian troops was to remain in each region. Human rights organization Amnesty International reported that continuing attacks against ethnic Georgians, both in South Ossetia and the adjacent zone, prevented the return to the region of several thousand people displaced by the conflict.

Note: the following representatives of the officially recognized Provisional Administration of South Ossetia were formerly based in Kurta, and their remit only extended, de facto, over those regions of South Ossetia under the control of the Georgian authorities. However, following the conflict of August 2008, these regions, in common with the remainder of the territory, came under the control of the internationally unrecognized 'Republic of South Ossetia'.

President of the Provisional Administration of South Ossetia: DIMITRI SANAKOYEV; internet www.soa.ge.

Prime Minister of the Provisional Administration of South Ossetia: URUZMAG KARKUSOV.

President of the 'Republic of South Ossetia': EDUARD J. KOKOYEV (KOKOITI), 7300 Shida Kartli Mkhare, Tskhinvali.

Prime Minister and Chairman of the Council of Ministers of the 'Republic of South Ossetia': YURII MOROZOV, 7300 Shida Kartli Mkhare, Tskhinvali, Engels 21; tel. (44) 5-50-52; fax (44) 5-47-63; internet www.cominf.org.

Speaker of the Parliament of the 'Republic of South Ossetia': ZNAUR GASSIYEV, 7300 Shida Kartli Mkhare, Tskhinvali.

Note: for details of the regional administration of Shida Kartli Mkhare, which officially incorporates the majority of territories proclaimed as the 'Republic of South Ossetia', see Local Government.

Bibliography

Allen, W. E. D. *A History of the Georgian People from the Beginning Down to the Russian Conquest in the Nineteenth Century*. London, Paul, 1932; New York, Barnes and Noble, 1971.

Areshidze, I. *Democracy and Autocracy in Eurasia: Georgia in Transition (Eurasian Political Economy and Public Policy Studies)*. Ann Arbor, MI, Michigan State University Press, 2007.

Avalov, Z. *The Annexation of Georgia to Russia*. New York, Chalidze Publications, 1982.

Aves, J. *Path to National Independence in Georgia 1987–1990*. London, School of Slavonic and East European Studies, 1991.

Georgia: From Chaos to Stability. London, Royal Institute of International Affairs, 1996.

Blandy, C. W. *Pankisskoye Gorge: Residents, Refugees and Fighters*. Camberley, Royal Military Academy Conflict Studies Research Centre, 2002.

Braund, D. *A History of Colchis and Transcaucasian Iberia*. Oxford, Clarendon Press, 1994.

Chervonnaya, S. *Conflict in the Caucasus: Georgia, Abkhazia and the Russian Shadow*. Glastonbury, Gothic Image Publications, 1995.

Coppieters, B. et al. *Georgians and Abkhazians: The Search for a Peace Settlement*. Köln, Bundesinstitut für ostwissenschaftliche und internationale Studien, 1998.

Cornell, S. E. *Georgia after the Rose Revolution: Geopolitical Predicament and Implications for U.S. Policy*. Carlisle, PA, Strategic Studies Institute, US Army War College, 2007.

Diuk, N., and Karatnycky, A. *New Nations Rising: The Fall of the Soviets and the Challenge of Independence*. New York, and Chichester, John Wiley and Sons, 1993.

Ekedahl, Carolyn M., and Goodman, Melvin A. *The Wars of Eduard Shevardnadze*. London, C. Hurst and Co, 1997.

Gachechiladze, R. *The New Georgia: Space, Society, Politics*. London, UCL Press, 1995.

Goltz, T. *Georgia Diary: A Chronicle of War And Political Chaos in the Post-Soviet Caucasus*. Armonk, NY, M. E. Sharpe, 2006.

Hewitt, G. *The Abkhazians: A Handbook*. New York, St Martin's Press, 1999.

Hin, J. *Ethnic and Civic Identity: Incompatible Loyalties? The Case of Armenians in Post-Soviet Georgia*. Amsterdam, Netherlands Geographical Studies, 2003.

Jones, S. 'The Establishment of Soviet Power in Transcaucasia: the Case of Georgia 1921–28', in *Soviet Studies*. Vol. 40, No. 4, 1982.

Katz, R. S. *The Georgian Regime Crisis of 2003–04: A Case Study of Post-Soviet Media Representation Of Politics, Crime and Corruption*. Stuttgart, Ibidem-Verlag, 2006.

Lang, D. M. *The Last Years of the Georgian Monarchy, 1658–1832*. New York, Columbia University Press, 1957.

A Modern History of Georgia. London, Weidenfeld and Nicolson, 1962.

Lynch, D. *The Conflict in Abkhazia: Dilemmas in Russian 'Peace-keeping' Policy*. London, Royal Institute of International Affairs, 1998.

Mikaberidze, A. *Historical Dictionary of Georgia*. Lanham, MD, Scarecrow Press, 2007.

Pelkmans, M. *Defending the Border: Identity, Religion, And Modernity in the Republic of Georgia (Culture and Society After Socialism)*. Ithaca, NY, Cornell University Press, 2006.

Rayfield, D. *The Literature of Georgia*. Oxford, Clarendon Press, 1995.

Reisner, O. 'The Tergdaleulebi–Founders of the Georgian National Identity', in Löb, L. (Ed.), *Forms of Identity in European History*. Szeged, 1995.

Sammut, D., and Cvetkovski, N. *The Georgia—South Ossetia Conflict*. London, Verification Technology Information Centre, 1996.

Suny, R. G. *The Making of the Georgian Nation*. 2nd edn, Bloomington, IN, Indiana University Press, 1994.

Wheatley, J. *Georgia from National Awakening to Rose Revolution: Delayed Transition in the Former Soviet Union*. Aldershot, Ashgate, 2005.

Also see the Select Bibliography.

KAZAKHSTAN

Geography

PHYSICAL FEATURES

The Republic of Kazakhstan is a landlocked country in Central Asia, the western extremity of which reaches into Europe. It extends some 1,900 km (1,200 miles) from the Volga river in the west to the Altai mountains in the east, and about 1,300 km (800 miles) from the Siberian plain in the north to the Central Asian deserts in the south. Western geographers considered Kazakhstan to be the northernmost of five Central Asian republics, but Soviet geographers, for historical reasons, did not include it in their concept of Central Asia.

To the south Kazakhstan borders Turkmenistan, Uzbekistan and Kyrgyzstan. To the east there is a 1,700-km frontier with the People's Republic of China. The long northern border is with Russia. In the south-west there is a 2,320-km coastline on the Caspian Sea. The total area is 2,724,900 sq km (1,049,150 sq miles), over four-fifths the size of India (but with only 2% of the population).

The relief is extremely varied. A northern belt dominated by steppes is separated by the hilly uplands of central Kazakhstan from the semi-desert and desert to the south (part of the Kzyl-Kum—Red Sands—desert falls within the borders of the country). Lowlands account for more than one-third of the territory, mountainous regions cover nearly one-fifth and hilly plains and plateaus occupy the rest of the country. The western regions are dominated by the lowlands of the Caspian Depression, which is drained by the River Ural. To the east of the western lowlands is the vast Turan Plain, much of which is sparsely inhabited desert. The flat north-central regions are the beginning of the Western Siberian Plain; to the south of the Plain are the hilly uplands of central Kazakhstan. On the eastern and south-eastern borders there are high mountain ranges.

Northern Kazakhstan possesses relatively good water resources, being dominated by numerous lakes and two large river systems. In the west the Ural and the Emba drain into the Caspian Sea. In the centre of the country the Irtysh, which rises in the north-east, and its tributaries flow north, across Siberia, Russia, to empty into the Arctic Ocean. There is a shortage of water in the south, however, the only substantial river in the area being the Syr Dar'ya, which rises in Kyrgyzstan, in the Tien Shan mountain range, and used to empty into the Aral Sea. The waters of the Syr Dar'ya were extensively used for irrigation from the 1960s, causing serious desiccation of the Aral Sea, the northern part of which is in Kazakhstan.

The Aral Sea became one of the world's most serious areas of environmental disaster. Without the in-flow from the Syr Dar'ya and, except in years of exceptionally high rainfall, without that from the Amu Dar'ya either, the Sea shrank at an ever-increasing rate. By the late 1990s it had lost almost one-half of its original area (to comprise almost 40,000 sq km), the surface level had fallen by 20 m (66 ft) and the volume reduced by over 800 cu km. For many years the favoured solution for alleviating the water shortage in the southern belt and in the southern Central Asian countries, and thereby lessening the demands on the Syr Dar'ya, was to divert the waters of the rivers that rose in central Kazakhstan (at its most extreme, the scheme aimed at the so-called reversal of the Siberian rivers; that is, to make them flow southwards rather than northwards). The demise of the USSR seemed to end the likelihood of this scheme being realized. Attempts then concentrated on stabilizing the level of the Sea, to prevent any further deterioration.

CLIMATE

The climate is of a strongly continental type, but there are wide variations throughout the territory. Average temperatures in January range from −18°C (0°F) in the north to −3°C (27°F) in the south. Winters are long in the north, lasting from late

October until mid-April. In July average temperatures are 19°C (66°F) in the north, although the north-east of the country tends to be slightly warmer, and 28°–30°C (82°–86°F) in the south. Levels of precipitation are equally varied. Average annual rainfall in mountainous regions reaches 1,600 mm (63 ins), whereas in the central desert areas it is less then 100 mm. There are strong winds throughout the year, especially in the north, west and central regions; the dry *sukhovei* is particularly harmful to agriculture.

POPULATION

According to the census of 1999, at which the total population was 14,953,126, Kazakhs formed the largest ethnic group in the republic, accounting for 53.4% of the population, outnumbering the ethnic Russian population (30.0%—having formed the majority at the 1979 census, and accounted for 37.8% of the population at the 1989 census), owing primarily to increased emigration by ethnic Russians and immigration by Kazakhs from other, mainly former Soviet, states. By 1 January 2004, according to official estimates, Kazakhs constituted some 57.2% of the population and ethnic Russians some 27.2%, according to official estimates. Other major ethnic groups were Ukrainians (3.1%), Uzbeks (2.7%) and Germans (1.6%). There were also Tatars and small numbers of Uigurs, Koreans (deported from the Soviet Far East in the late 1930s), Belarusians, Azeris and Turks.

Kazakh, a member of the Central Turkic group of languages, replaced Russian as the official language in September 1989. Since 1940 it has been written in a Cyrillic script of 42 characters. A Latin script was used from 1928, and the Arabic script up until that time. The predominant religion is Islam, most Kazakhs being Sunni Muslims of the Hanafi school. Other ethnic groups have their own religious communities, notably the (Christian) Eastern Orthodox Church, which is attended mainly by Slavs.

The total population at 1 January 2008 was estimated to be 15,565,647. The large areas of desert accounted for the low population density of 5.7 inhabitants per sq km. In 2001 some 56.3% of the population lived in urban areas. In November 1997 the city of Akmola was officially declared the capital. The city is located in the centre-north of the country, in the heart of the so-called 'Virgin Lands' (for which, from the 1950s, it was renamed under Soviet rule, as Tselinograd). In May 1998 it was renamed Astana ('Capital' in Kazakh), and it was declared open on 10 June; the city's population was estimated at 328,000 in mid-2001, or 466,235, if the suburbs were taken into consideration. Astana replaced as capital the largest city, Almaty (Alma-Ata), with an estimated population of 1,209,000 at mid-2007, which was situated in the extreme south-east of the country, on a seismic fault. Other important towns include Karaganda, an industrial city in central Kazakhstan (with a population of 436,900 at the census of 1999), and Chimkent (360,100) and Taraz (formerly Jambul—330,100) in the south of the coun-try, near the border with Uzbekistan. The main urban centres, however, are in the north-east: Ust-Kamenogorsk (311,000), Pavlodar (300,500) and Semipalatinsk (269,600). The main port on the Caspian Sea is Atyrau (formerly Guriyev—142,500).

Chronology

6th century: Turkic tribes began to settle in the area of modern Kazakhstan, which was on the western borders of their empire.

1219: The Mongols conquered the area, destroying the urban culture of the south, which had emerged in the 10th century. The Golden and White Hordes (Tatars) became the dominant powers of the region.

***c.* 1511–23:** Kasym Khan established himself as leader of a loose confederation of steppe tribes, the Kazakh Orda (Horde). Some unity continued under his successor, Tahir, but did not persist.

1645: Guriyev (now Atyrau), on the Caspian Sea, was acquired by the Russian Empire, which by this time bordered the territories of the Kazakh Hordes (the Little, the Middle and the Great).

1731: Under pressure from the Oirot Mongols, the Khan of the Little Horde (in the west, near the Caspian) was granted the protection of the Russian Tsar.

1740: The Khans of the Middle Horde (in the north and east of modern Kazakhstan) gained Russian protection.

1742: Part of the Great Horde, to the south of the other Hordes, secured the protection of the Russian Empire from the Oirot Mongols (although in 1758 the Oirots were defeated by the Chinese Manzhou—Manchu Empire, which became the ruler of the rest of the Great Horde).

1822: The absorption of the Kazakhs into the Russian Empire began with the territory of the Middle Horde, which was divided into Russian administrative units, while Russian military jurisdiction was imposed for criminal offences and Kazakhs were forbidden to acquire serfs.

1824: The same process was implemented in the territory of the Little Horde and, despite some revolts and resistance, was followed by new taxation demands and strictures, such as Kazakhs being denied the right to cultivate land.

1847: The Great Horde lost its independence, when it was required to pledge its allegiance to the Russian Empire. The following year the last Khan of the Middle Horde was formally deposed.

1854: Foundation of the Russian garrison town of Vernoye (now Almaty).

1861: The emancipation of the serfs in the Russian Empire witnessed the first large influx of Slav settlers to Kazakh territory.

1895: A Russian commission set aside more land of the nomadic Kazakhs for settlement by Slav cultivators.

1906–12: Agrarian reforms implemented under Russian Prime Minister Petr Stolypin allowed another large influx of Slav (mainly Russian and Ukrainian) settlers, provoking Kazakh nationalism and resentment.

1916: An attempt to impose labour and military service on the non-Russian peoples of the Empire occasioned a widespread revolt by the Kazakhs; the rebellion was savagely crushed by the Governor-General of Turkestan, who resolved to drive the nomads from their lands.

1917: With the collapse of tsarist authority in the Russian Revolutions, three Kazakh Conferences were held in Orenburg (now in Russia), although their narrow nationalism failed to attract widespread support. Kazakhstan became fiercely con-tested by the Red Army, the 'Whites' and the Kazakh nation-alists of the Alash Orda (led by Ali Bukeikhanov and Ahmed Bayturshin).

26 August 1920: Following the communist victory in the Civil War, the Russian authorities established a Kyrgyz Autono-mous Soviet Socialist Republic (ASSR), as a constituent unit of the Russian Federation. The ASSR had its capital in Orenburg (the Russians called the Kazakhs 'Kyrgyz' or 'Kyrgyz-Kazakhs' and knew the Kyrgyz as 'Kara-Kyrgyz').

1925: The Kyrgyz ASSR was renamed the Kazakh ASSR.

1928: The Arabic script was replaced by a Latin script for the written Kazakh language.

1929: The communist authorities decided on the collectiviza-tion and the resettlement of nomads in Kazakhstan; this provoked fierce resistance, and subsequent famine.

1930: Qoraqalpog'iston (Karakalpakstan) was detached from the Kazakh ASSR although it remained part of the Russian Federation. The region was incorporated into Uzbekistan in 1936.

1940: A modified Cyrillic alphabet, with 42 characters, was introduced for the Kazakh language.

1944: The Soviet leader, Stalin (Iosif Dzhugashvili), ordered the deportation to Kazakhstan and Siberia of many peoples who had attracted his suspicion, including some 400,000 Chechens, 200,000 Crimean Tatars, 75,000 Ingush and 40,000 Balkars. Many of the Volga Germans had already been deported, mainly to Kazakhstan. Despite the rehabilita-tion of significant numbers of these peoples in 1957, many remained in Kazakhstan.

1954: A Kazakh was replaced as First Secretary of the Com-munist Party of Kazakhstan (CPK) by an ethnic Russian, together with a Russian Second Secretary, Leonid Brezhnev (later Soviet leader, 1964–82), who himself became leader of the CPK in 1955–56. The official encouragement of ploughing 'Virgin Lands' began; the scheme continued until 1960 and Kazakhstan accounted for almost 60% of the extra land farmed throughout the USSR.

1961–62: There was a major influx of Kazakh and Uigur refugees from the People's Republic of China.

1964: Dinmukhamed Kunayev, who had briefly succeeded Brezhnev as First Secretary of the CPK in 1956, returned to the post, later becoming the first Kazakh in the Politburo of the all-Union Party.

1984: Nursultan Nazarbayev was appointed Chairman of the Council of Ministers, the republican premier.

16 December 1986: The first nationalist riots experienced by the new Soviet leader, Mikhail Gorbachev, took place in Almaty, after Kunayev was dismissed for corruption and replaced by an ethnic Russian, Gennadii Kolbin.

June 1989: Nazarbayev was appointed First Secretary of the CPK. An outbreak of ethnic violence in the western town of

Novyi Uzen, when Kazakh youths attacked Lezgins, was followed by sporadic violence over a period of several months.

September 1989: Among other reforms, the Supreme Soviet (Supreme Kenges or Supreme Council, the republican parliament) enacted a law making Kazakh the official language of the republic; Russian remained the 'language of inter-ethnic communication'—this law was upheld by the Constitution of January 1993.

February 1990: Nazarbayev was elected Chairman of the republican Supreme Soviet.

25 March 1990: Elections to the republican Supreme Soviet took place, with the CPK retaining a majority in the legislature, despite some political reforms; in the following month parliament elected Nazarbayev to the new post of President.

25 October 1990: Kazakhstan declared itself to be a sovereign state.

17 March 1991: In the referendum on the preservation of the Union, 94.1% of those who voted (88.2% of the electorate) favoured Kazakhstan remaining in the USSR.

18–21 August 1991: An attempted *coup d'état* in Moscow, Russia (the Soviet capital), failed, signalling the final dismantling of institutionalized communist authority in the USSR; the effective increase of authority for republican leaders enabled President Nazarbayev to ban nuclear testing at Semipalatinsk. In the same month Kazakhstan announced its first programme for the privatization of enterprises.

October 1991: Sergei Tereshchenko, an ethnic Ukrainian, was appointed Chairman of the Council of Ministers (Prime Minister).

1 December 1991: Nazarbayev was confirmed in office as President of Kazakhstan by direct election; he was the sole candidate and won 98.8% of the votes cast.

16 December 1991: The Supreme Soviet declared the independence of Kazakhstan, the last Union Republic to do so.

21 December 1991: At a meeting in Almaty the leaders of 11 Union Republics signed a protocol on the formation of a new Commonwealth of Independent States (CIS), thereby dissolving the USSR.

March 1992: Kazakhstan became a member of the UN.

June 1992: Some 5,000 opposition supporters demonstrated in Almaty against the continued dominance of government by former communists. Four months later the three main nationalist groups, Freedom (Azat), the Republican Party and the December National Democratic Party (Dzheltoksan), united to form the Republican Party—Azat.

28 January 1993: Following lengthy public consultations, the Supreme Kenges enacted a new Constitution.

15 November 1993: Kazakhstan introduced its own currency, the tenge.

December 1993: The Supreme Kenges announced its imminent dissolution, in preparation for new elections; it then proceeded to grant the President additional powers in the interim and to ratify the Treaty on the Non-Proliferation of Nuclear Weapons. The dissolution had been precipitated by 43 deputies resigning their mandates.

25 December 1993: Kazakhstan, unable to afford the maintenance of the former Soviet space programme alone, agreed that Russia should lease the Baikonur facilities; the city of Baikonur was subsequently transferred to Russian jurisdiction, for an initial period of 20 years from 1995.

7 March 1994: A general election to the Supreme Kenges took place.

May 1994: Kazakhstan joined the North Atlantic Treaty Organization's (NATO) 'Partnership for Peace' programme of military co-operation.

October 1994: The Government tendered its resignation, having been criticized by President Nazarbayev for the slow pace of economic reform. The President subsequently appointed Akezhan Kazhegeldin to chair a new Council of Ministers.

11 March 1995: Following the findings of the Constitutional Court, which had ruled in the previous month that the results of the general election of 1994 were null and void, President Nazarbayev dissolved parliament and proceeded to rule by decree. The Council of Ministers tendered its resignation but was later reinstated, with few changes.

29 April 1995: A nation-wide referendum was held on the extension of President Nazarbayev's term of office until 1 December 2000. A total of 95.4% of participants, representing 91% of the electorate, voted in favour.

30 August 1995: A new Constitution was approved by 89.1% of the electorate in a referendum; it took effect on 6 September, replacing the Supreme Kenges with a bicameral Parliament (comprising a 47-member Senate and a 67-member Majlis or Assembly) and the Constitutional Court with a Constitutional Council.

September 1995: A presidential decree confirmed that Akmola (formerly Tselinograd) would become the new capital.

5 December 1995: Elections were held to the Senate.

9 December 1995: In elections to the lower chamber of the legislature, the Majlis, candidates obtained the requisite number of votes in only 43 of the 67 constituencies, necessitating further elections in the remaining constituencies on 23 December.

22 September 1997: Prime Minister Kazhegeldin departed for medical treatment in Switzerland; despite being exonerated of alleged financial malpractice in August, his reputation had been undermined by earlier Russian media reports that he had admitted involvement with the former Soviet state security service (KGB) in the late 1980s.

10 October 1997: Nurlan Balgymbayev, hitherto President of the state hydrocarbons company, KazakhOil, and considered an opponent of privatization, was appointed Prime Minister; he formed a new, smaller Government.

8 November 1997: Akmola was inaugurated as the new capital by President Nazarbayev.

6 May 1998: A presidential decree was issued, changing the name of Akmola to Astana (meaning 'capital'); it was officially opened on 10 June.

6 July 1998: The Presidents of Kazakhstan and Russia signed a treaty agreeing the demarcation of seabed claims in the northern part of the Caspian Sea.

8 October 1998: Parliament adopted a number of constitutional amendments and a revised date for the presidential election (originally scheduled for 2000), which was brought forward to January 1999.

10 January 1999: Nazarbayev was re-elected as President with 81.0% of the votes cast in an election in which 86.3% of the registered electorate took part. The Organization for Security and Co-operation in Europe (OSCE) refused to monitor the election, judging it to be an unfair contest, owing, in part, to a ruling that had debarred certain candidates, including Kazhegeldin. President Nazarbayev was sworn in on 20 January and he announced a new government structure two days later, which included six new ministries and seven new agencies, to replace former state committees.

5 July 1999: A Russian craft exploded when launching from the Baikonur space centre at Turatam, dispersing potentially toxic debris over central Kazakhstan. A further incident occurred in October, prompting officials to prohibit Russia from using the facilities. In November Russia agreed to pay outstanding rental fees of US $115m., and the restriction was removed in February 2000.

1 October 1999: Balgymbayev resigned as Prime Minister and returned to his former position as President of KazakhOil. Kasymzhomart Tokayev was confirmed as his successor on 12 October.

10 October 1999: Elections to an expanded, 77-member Majlis (as well as those to municipal and local councils) were held. 'Run-off' elections to the Majlis were held on 24 October and 26 December, as a result of which Fatherland (Otan), a pro-presidential coalition, obtained 23 seats. Independent candidates secured 34 seats.

27 June 2000: A law was passed granting President Nazarbayev, as the first President of Kazakhstan, certain guarantees and rights, which were to remain in force even after the expiry of his term of office.

6 September 2001: Kazhegeldin, who had been tried *in absentia* on charges of abuse of power, bribery and the illegal possession of weapons, was sentenced to 10 years' imprisonment, amid allegations that the trial had been politically motivated.

18 November 2001: A number of prominent political and business figures, including the Akim (Governor) of Pavlodar Oblast, Ghalymzhan Zhakiyanov, and a Deputy Prime Minister, Oraz Zhandosov, announced the formation of a new, reformist political party, the Democratic Choice of Kazakhstan (DCK). Zhakiyanov and Zhandosov subsequently left their government posts, following accusations of disloyalty.

27 November 2001: A pipeline to carry petroleum from the country's Tengiz oilfield to Novorossiisk, Krasnodar Krai, on Russia's Black Sea coast, was inaugurated.

14 December 2001: President Nazarbayev signed the Comprehensive Nuclear Test Ban Treaty, following its ratification by both houses of Parliament.

28 January 2002: Tokayev announced the resignation of his Government. Tokayev was succeeded as Prime Minister by Imangali Tasmagambetov, and a new Government was formed, to which four new ministers were appointed.

16 March 2002: Following divisions with the DCK, the founding congress of a new party, Bright Road (Ak Zhol), established by Dzhandosov, took place.

13 May 2002: An agreement was signed with Russia on the equal division of three oilfields in the northern Caspian, augmenting the 1998 accord on the delimitation of the Sea. A trilateral agreement was signed between Azerbaijan, Kazakhstan and Russia on 14 May 2003.

15 July 2002: President Nazarbayev passed a new law on political parties, amid widespread opposition. The legislation required political parties to have at least 50,000 members in order to qualify for registration; all parties were required to re-register by April 2003.

2 August 2002: Opposition leader Zhakiyanov was sentenced to seven years' imprisonment, following charges of abuse of office and embezzlement. Human rights organizations expressed concern at the severity of the sentence, which the opposition claimed was politically motivated.

8 October 2002: Partial elections to the Senate were held.

30 March 2003: A US businessman was indicted under the 1977 US Foreign Corrupt Practices Act (which prohibits US companies or individuals from bribing foreign officials in order to secure an agreement), for allegedly using financial incentives to persuade prominent Kazakhstani politicians to award important contracts to US petroleum companies. Nazarbayev and Balgymbayev were among those alleged to have received money and gifts totalling US $78m. from James H. Giffen, a

former adviser to Nazarbayev. (Giffen was later indicted by a US federal court on charges of corrupt business practices.)

28 April 2003: Representatives from Armenia, Belarus, Kazakhstan, Kyrgyzstan, Russia and Tajikistan formally inaugurated the successor to the Collective Security Treaty, a new regional defence organization known as the Collective Security Treaty Organization (CSTO).

19 May 2003: Tasmagambetov's Government won a vote of 'no confidence' over its handling of agrarian reform. None the less, on 11 June Tasmagambetov announced the resignation of his Government, claiming that some votes had been falsified.

13 June 2003: Parliament approved the nomination of Danial Akhmetov, a former Governor of Pavlodar Oblast, as Prime Minister. Several ministers in the previous administration were subsequently re-appointed to the Government.

20 June 2003: Parliament adopted a controversial new land code, with amendments proposed by Nazarbayev, providing for the private ownership of land.

4 July 2003: Nazarbayev signed a number of laws confirming the delimitation of Kazakhstan's borders with Kyrgyzstan, Turkmenistan and Uzbekistan.

25 October 2003: The pro-presidential Mutual Help (Asar) party was founded by Darigha Nazarbayeva, the eldest daughter of President Nursultan Nazarbayev.

10 January 2004: A series of legislative amendments signed by President Nazarbayev, replacing the death penalty with life imprisonment, were published in the official press.

19 September and 3 October 2004: In two rounds of parliamentary elections, Fatherland won a majority of seats in the Majlis, with 42 mandates; 18 independent candidates were elected, and Aist, an electoral bloc comprising the Agrarian Party of Kazakhstan and the Civic Party of Kazakhstan, won 11 seats. Mutual Help obtained four mandates, while Bright Road and the Democratic Party of Kazakhstan each obtained one seat. The electoral proceedings were criticized by opposition activists and several foreign observers, including the OSCE.

6 December 2004: President Nazarbayev issued a decree instructing the Central Election Commission to establish procedures for the elections of local Governors (Akims) in villages, several oblasts and the cities of Astana and Almaty.

18 January 2005: President Nazarbayev and President Vladimir Putin of Russia signed a treaty defining the 7,500 km land border with Russia.

11 February 2005: A court order was issued dissolving the DCK, which had declared the Government to be illegitimate and urged a campaign of non-violent civil disobedience in December 2004.

29 June 2005: Legislation was approved by the Majlis, which, *inter alia*, required all religious organizations and communities to be registered with the state authorities.

July 2005: Nazarbayev and the Chinese President, Hu Jintao, signed an agreement on the establishment of a strategic partnership between their two countries.

19 August 2005: Partial elections to the Senate took place. Fatherland won 10 of the 16 seats contested, three seats were won by other pro-Nazarbayev parties and three by independents.

September 2005: Former parliamentary Chairman Zharmakhan Tuyakbai, leader of the opposition movement For a Just Kazakhstan, was elected the movement's sole presidential candidate.

November 2005: Zamanbek Nurkadilov, a member of For a Just Kazakhstan and a former Akim of Almaty City and Almaty Oblast, died following a shooting incident. Nurkadilov had been found guilty in June of defaming the President; in late December an official investigation found that he had committed suicide.

4 December 2005: Nazarbayev was re-elected to the presidency with 91.2% of the votes cast. Five candidates participated in the election, but his closest rival, Tuyakbai, won just 6.6%. Some 76.8% of the electorate participated in the poll. Although CIS observers declared the election to have been free and fair, representatives of the OSCE stated that international standards of democracy had not been met.

11 January 2006: Nazarbayev was inaugurated and the Government resigned, in accordance with the Constitution.

15 January 2006: Zhakiyanov was released from prison.

18 January 2006: Nazarbayev's nomination of Akhmetov as premier was unanimously accepted by Parliament; Akhmetov's new, largely unchanged Government was approved by the President the following day. Natalya Korzhova was appointed Minister of Finance.

13 February 2006: Three men, including Altynbek Sarsenbayev, one of the leaders of the opposition party Real Bright Road (Naghyz Ak Zhol—formed in 2005 after a split in Bright Road), were killed in Almaty; a special commission was set up to investigate the murders, which many believed to have been politically motivated.

21 February 2006: It was revealed that five members of the National Security Committee (KNB) and the head of administration of the Senate, Erzhan Utembayev, had been detained in connection with Sarsenbayev's death. The head of the KNB resigned the following day. A protest rally was held in Almaty later in the month, at which demonstrators demanded that the authorities end the persecution of opposition politicians and bring Sarsenbayev's murderers to trial. In March Utembayev allegedly confessed to having organized the killing of Sarsenbayev.

19 April 2006: Nazarbayev appointed Karim Masimov, a long-term ally who had been appointed as Deputy Prime Minister in January, to the additional post of Minister of the Economy and Budgetary Planning. (He was replaced in this latter position by Aslan Musin in October.)

21 June 2006: The Majlis passed a series of controversial amendments designed to increase the regulation of media outlets. The proposed changes gave rise to strong criticism within Kazakhstan, as well as from the OSCE, but were adopted by the Senate on 29 June. They were signed into law by the President on 4 July.

4 July 2006: At an extraordinary Fatherland party congress in Astana, the party merged with Darigha Nazarbayeva's Mutual Help party, thus strengthening support for President Nazarbayev in the Majlis.

28 September 2006: Nazarbayev made an official visit to Washington, DC, for talks with US President George W. Bush, during which he was praised for transforming Kazakhstan into a 'free nation'.

4 October 2006: President Nazarbayev completed a government reorganization.

30 December 2006: The Civic Party and the Agrarian Party also merged with Fatherland, which was renamed Light Of The Fatherland (Nur Otan).

8 January 2007: Akhmetov tendered his resignation as Prime Minister; it was reported that Nazarbayev had criticized him for poor organization and budget planning.

10 January 2007: The Majlis voted to approve the President's nomination of Masimov as Prime Minister. On the following day Musin was appointed as Deputy Prime Minister (retaining the portfolio of the economy and budget planning), while Akhmetov became Minister of Defence.

18 May 2007: Parliament approved extensive constitutional amendments, proposed by President Nazarbayev, strengthening the powers of an expanded Majlis, which was henceforth to approve prime ministerial appointments. The presidential term of office was reduced from seven to five years (with effect from 2012). An additional amendment removed the restriction limiting the incumbent President to two terms in office.

1 June 2007: The Kazakhstani ambassador to Austria and son-in-law of President Nazarbayev, Rakhat Aliyev, was arrested in Austria, after the Kazakhstani Government issued an arrest warrant against him in May for his alleged involvement in the kidnapping of two banking associates. (In January 2008 Aliyev, who had been granted asylum in Austria, was sentenced to 20 years' imprisonment *in absentia* on charges of kidnapping.)

20 June 2007: President Nazarbayev dissolved the Majlis and announced that legislative elections were to be brought forward to 18 August (two years earlier than scheduled).

18 August 2007: At the elections the presidential party, Light Of The Fatherland, won 88.4% of votes cast, securing all 98 contested seats in the enlarged 107-member Majlis. None of the other six parties participating in the poll achieved the 7% minimum of votes required to secure representation in the chamber; the newly established National Social-Democratic Party (NSDP) received 4.5% and Bright Road 3.1% of votes. The leaders of the NSDP, Bright Road and the Communist People's Party refused to acknowledge the results and demanded that the poll be repeated. The CIS declared that it was satisfied with the organization of the elections; however, the OSCE announced that, despite some improvements, the poll had failed to meet international standards.

20 August 2007: In accordance with the amended Constitution, the Assembly of Nations of Kazakhstan (which represents the country's minority ethnic groups) elected the remaining nine deputies to the Majlis.

2 September 2007: A reorganized Government was approved at the first session of the new Parliament; most of the incumbent ministers retained their posts. Umirzak Shukeyev, hitherto Akim of Southern Kazakhstan Oblast, became Deputy Prime Minister, succeeding Musin, who was elected Chairman of the Majlis.

29 October 2007: Yerbol Orynbayev, formerly a close aide to the Prime Minister, was appointed as a Deputy Prime Minister.

13 November 2007: A new Minister of Finance, Bolat Zhamishev, was appointed, succeeding Natalya Korzhova, while Vladimir Bozhko, hitherto First Deputy Chairman of the KNB, replaced the incumbent Minister of Emergency Situations, who had been dismissed over his suspected involvement in a corrupt land agreement during his tenure as Akim of Almaty.

30 November 2007: At an OSCE meeting in Madrid, Spain, Kazakhstan secured approval to assume the rotating chairmanship of that body in 2010, despite criticism by OSCE monitors of the conduct of the elections held in August and continuing international concerns over the human rights situation in the country.

19 February 2008: Vladimir Shkolnik, formerly deputy head of the presidential administration, replaced Galym Orazbakov as Minister of Industry and Trade.

29 February 2008: The opposition party Real Bright Road changed it name to Freedom (Azat), following a party congress. Bulat Abilov was elected as party Chairman.

22 May 2008: Newly installed Russian President Dmitrii Medvedev made his first official visit to Kazakhstan, where he met President Nazarbayev for discussions on bilateral co-operation.

4 October 2008: Elections were held to fill one-half of the 32 indirectly elected seats in the Senat; the Central Election Commission announced that the rate of voter participation was 97.6%.

History

Dr SHIRIN AKINER

THE FORMATION OF KAZAKHSTAN

Kazakhstan, in its modern form as a unified political entity, came into being after the establishment of Soviet rule. In 1920 the Kyrgyz (that is, Kazakh) Autonomous Soviet Socialist Republic (ASSR) was created, within the jurisdiction of the Russian Federation. The Kazakhs were then known to the Russians as Kyrgyz, or Kyrgyz-Kazakhs, to distinguish them from the unrelated Cossacks. As a result of the 1924–25 National Delimitation of Central Asia, some Kazakh-populated areas were transferred to the jurisdiction of the territory, which, in 1925, was formally renamed the Kazakh ASSR. In 1930 the Karakalpak region (now in Uzbekistan, as the Republic of Qoraqalpog'iston) was detached from the republic. In 1936 Kazakhstan was elevated to the status of a full Union Republic, becoming the Kazakh Soviet Socialist Republic (SSR). Despite some redrawing of the borders, therefore, the main contours of Kazakhstan remained those that had been mapped out in the early Soviet period. With the collapse of the USSR, on 16 December 1991 the territory declared its independence as the Republic of Kazakhstan. It joined 10 (later 11) other former Union Republics in the Commonwealth of Independent States (CIS), by the Almaty Declaration of 21 December, and was admitted to the UN as a member state in March 1992.

THE PEOPLES OF KAZAKHSTAN

Independent Kazakhstan was a multi-ethnic country. At the beginning of the 1990s the population numbered some 16.5m., and encompassed over 100 ethnic groups. The two largest groups were the Kazakhs (39.7% of the total population according to the 1989 census) and the Russians (37.8%). Other groups of significant size included non-indigenous peoples, such as Germans, Ukrainians and Koreans. The census of 1999 revealed that the population had declined to 14.9m., of which almost 8m. (53.4%) were Kazakhs and only some 4.5m. (30.0%) were Russians. This change in the ethnic balance was the result of such factors as the immigration of Kazakhs from other countries (mainly other Soviet successor states, but also including the return of several thousand from Iran and Mongolia, descendants of those who fled the Russian Revolution and Civil War) and the mass emigration of non-Kazakhs, especially Russians. In 2008 the population was estimated at 15.6m.; the ethnic balance had changed little since 1999.

KAZAKHS

The Kazakhs are a Turkic people, descendants of nomadic tribes who settled on the territory of present-day Kazakhstan in the sixth century AD, or possibly earlier. The region lay on the ancient transcontinental 'Silk Road', a network of trade routes that linked China, Persia (Iran) and Transoxiana (roughly the area of modern Uzbekistan). During the 10th century a strong urban culture developed in the south, although further to the north nomadic pastoralism remained the dominant way of life. In the early 13th century Kazakhstan was conquered by the Mongols, and the cities of the south, such as Otrar and Taraz, were destroyed. Trade links were eventually revived, but the urban centres never fully regained their previous levels of prosperity and sophistication.

The 14th and 15th centuries were marked by power struggles, most of which were centred on the southern belt. Mongol princes from the Golden and White Hordes fought among themselves, and also with Uzbek and Nogai contenders, for control of the region. This strife resulted in migration, as whole tribes changed allegiance and moved from one area to another. There was a period of relative stability in the early 16th century, when one warlord, Kasym Khan, succeeded in uniting the main tribes (such as the Kipchaks, Naimans, Usuns and Dulats) under his rule (from approximately 1511 to 1523). From this time it is possible to speak of a Kazakh nation, despite the fact that after Kasym's death the internecine

struggles were renewed, as too were the campaigns against Central Asian fiefdoms in the south. By the beginning of the 17th century three major groupings had emerged among the Kazakhs, each under the leadership of its own khan (leader): the Great Horde (Ulu Zhuz), the territory of which lay to the south-east, between the Aral Sea and Lake Balkhash; the Middle Horde (Orta Zhuz), which controlled the central zone, further north, between the Irtysh and the Tobol rivers; and the Little Horde (Kishi Zhuz), with territory to the north of the Caspian Sea, between the Emba and the Ural rivers. These Hordes were further divided into tribes and clans. There was a highly developed awareness of genealogy, since lineage determined both place in society and rights to pasture land. This feature of Kazakh society survived the later tsarist and Soviet periods.

The Kazakh aristocracy adopted Islam during the 14th and 15th centuries. Turkestan, a city in the far south, was the home of Ahmad Yasavi (who died in the middle of the 12th century), one of the greatest Sufi mystics. His influence did much to encourage the spread of Islam in the region. By the 14th century his burial place had become a highly revered shrine (three pilgrimages to this site were supposed to equal the Pilgrimage—*hajj*—to Mecca). In 1397 the Mongol ruler, Timur (Tamerlane), built a mausoleum over Yasavi's tomb and, later, several of the khans of the Middle and Little Hordes were buried there. The nomadic tribes in the north, however, had little contact with Islam. They were probably not fully converted until the 19th century, when, under the Russian tsarist administration, Tatar Muslim missionaries were sent to the region. A number of mosques were built during this period, but, although the Kazakhs became, by their own standards, sincere believers, they were not very devout by conventional measures. They incorporated many elements of customary law (adat) and animism into Islam, creating a fusion of different traditions that was uniquely Kazakh.

The Kazakh Hordes came under Russian domination because they were constantly under attack from their neighbours, particularly the Oirot Mongols. Thus, during the 18th century the Kazakhs gradually had recourse to Russian protection: the Little Horde in 1731; the Middle Horde in 1740; and part of the Great Horde in 1742 (the rest of this Horde was to come under Manzhou—Manchu rule and remained part of China). Russian influence in the steppes grew ever stronger until, eventually, the entire region was under Russian control (with the exception of the area that fell within the Chinese Empire). After a gradual policy of limiting the powers of the khans and the introduction of the Russian administrative system under Tsar Alexander I (1801–25), the last Khan of the Middle Horde was deposed in 1848. A Russian garrison named Vernoye (Faithful) was established in the far east of the territory in 1854; this town, renamed Alma-Ata (later Almaty), was to become the capital of the Kazakh SSR and, until 1997, of independent Kazakhstan.

Traditionally, Kazakh culture was rooted in the nomadic way of life, expressed in the crafts and skills of daily life, as well as in the oral epics that encapsulated the history and philosophy of the people. The advent of the Russians opened the way to the ideas and opportunities of a (comparatively) developed European society. The majority of the Kazakh élite was highly responsive and came genuinely to admire Russian culture. A number of Kazakhs received an excellent education in St Petersburg and other Russian cities. A member of one of the prominent families, Shokan Valikhanov (1835–65), served as an officer in the imperial army and wrote numerous scholarly works in Russian. The first of several Russian-Kazakh schools was opened in 1841. Scholars such as Ibraj Altynsarin (1841–89) played an active role in the development of the Kazakh literary language (which was written in the Arabic script until 1928), as well as in the general process of educational reform. Likewise, Abay Kunanbayev (1845–1904), a poet and prose writer, is widely considered to be the father of Kazakh literature. It was because of the pioneering efforts of this generation that, by the turn of the century, the Kazakhs were better educated and more politically aware than the other peoples of Central Asia.

Nomadism first came under threat in the second half of the 19th century, when large numbers of Russian settlers moved into northern Kazakhstan, took possession of the local population's traditional pasture lands and obstructed the routes of migration. This mass invasion of their territory was the cause of considerable resentment among the Kazakhs. It culminated in the fierce, though unsuccessful, uprising of 1916, which was triggered by the introduction of a draft for labour units, even though the Kazakhs had traditionally been exempt from military service. More than 50,000 tribesmen on the steppes and in the Farg'ona (Fergana) valley took part in the revolt, which was brutally suppressed.

Soon after, the February 1917 Revolution caused the collapse of tsarist power and, under Ali Bukeikhanov, a semi-independent Kazakh state, known as Alash Orda, was formed. However, the Kazakhs were soon brought under Bolshevik control, initially as part of the Russian Federation, although they were acknowledged as one of the nationalities of the USSR. It was under the communists that the second and decisive onslaught on the nomadic way of life took place, through the collectivization campaign of the 1930s. It has been estimated that just under one-half of the Kazakh population died from starvation and other problems caused by collectivization during this period (by 1959 the Soviet Kazakh population, then totalling 3.6m., some 347,000 fewer than in 1926, had still not recovered from these losses; within Kazakhstan itself there were only 2.8m. Kazakhs). Subsequently, there was a demographic recovery and by the 1980s the Kazakhs once again became the largest ethnic group in their own republic. In addition to the numerical recovery of the population, Kazakh representation in the republican government and party institutions began to increase as, after the 1950s, a new generation of urbanized, educated Kazakhs emerged. In the 1990s, after independence, there was a revival of interest in the cultural legacy of nomadism, but it was no longer a living tradition. However, the great majority of Kazakhs still lived in rural areas, mostly in the less-developed southern belt. They tended to be conservative and culturally far removed from the highly educated, Europeanized, Russian-speaking Kazakhs of the urban centres.

SLAVS

Slavs first began to settle in Kazakhstan in large numbers in the second half of the 19th century. The majority were farmers; there was a vast influx of land-hungry peasants after the emancipation of the serfs, in 1861, and the authorities continued to set aside large tracts of land for Russian and Ukrainian settlers, disrupting nomadic life and forcing many Kazakhs eastwards into Chinese territory. There were also industrial labourers who came to work in the nascent mining industry, as well as military personnel (including Cossack detachments) and a large civilian infrastructure. By 1926 the Russians already constituted nearly 20% (1.3m.) of the total population of Kazakhstan, and the Ukrainians accounted for a further 13% (860,000). While the Kazakh population was decreasing, the influx of Slavs continued during the 1930s and reached a peak during the Second World War (1939–45), when many industries and academic institutions were relocated to Kazakhstan. The 'Virgin Lands' scheme of Nikita Khrushchev (Soviet leader in 1953–64), which aimed to increase grain production by ploughing large areas of the steppe, brought new Slav settlers to the region in the 1950s and early 1960s. By 1970 there were 5.5m. Russians and 933,000 Ukrainians in Kazakhstan. Both groups continued to expand, although at a slower rate than previously, with far less immigration to increase numbers. These population trends were only reversed in the 1990s, owing to the political changes arising from the demise of the USSR. By the 1999 census there were some 547,000 Ukrainians in Kazakhstan (representing some 3.7% of the population).

Post-independence, as in the 19th century, the Slavs remained concentrated in the northern belt, particularly in the eastern corner of the country, where most of the industrial centres were located. They were well represented in parliament (in the early 1990s it was claimed by some Kazakhs that over one-half of the deputies were Slavs) and several of them held prominent positions in government. The Cossacks and other nationalist groups sometimes demanded autonomy, but, at least in the early years of independence, the majority of the Slav population seemed prepared to remain part of Kazakhstan. If they had decided to press for partition, either to form their own state or to seek reunification with Russia, it was unlikely that the Kazakhs would have been able to resist this pressure. However, many Russians chose to return to Russia and by August 1998 more than 2m. had left Kazakhstan.

'PUNISHED PEOPLES'

On the eve of the Second World War, and during the War itself, many thousands of Volga Germans, Crimean Tatars, Koreans, Greeks, Chechens, Ingush and other peoples were deported to Kazakhstan from other parts of the Union. In the post-war period they gradually succeeded in gaining acceptance in Kazakhstani society and some came to hold high public office. However, by the beginning of the 1990s a number of these groups were either beginning to return to their pre-deportation homes or seeking repatriation to their original homelands abroad. In 1989 the German population in Kazakhstan numbered just under 1m. (5.8% of the total population), but many subsequently emigrated to Germany, reducing the number to 353,000 (2.4%) by 1999 and some 237,600 by the beginning of 2004, although the numbers of ethnic Germans emigrating annually had declined since the mid-1990s. The reasons for their departure were varied, but the primary causes were undoubtedly their hope for a more secure economic future in Germany, as well as concern over what they perceived to be an inherent instability in Kazakhstan. By contrast, the Koreans (numbering just under 100,000 in 1999) seemed determined to remain and were extremely active in business ventures involving partnerships with the Republic of Korea (South Korea). Other groups of deportees had relatively limited opportunities to leave and there was little discernible reduction in their numbers during the early 1990s.

Some of the smaller groups did, however, make an impact on politics in Kazakhstan. The Kazakhstani Poles, for example, were the result of successive phases of political exile from 1831, and many of the descendants of the earliest exiles did not, in the 1990s, exhibit much evidence of their Polish identity. Nevertheless, in the early 1990s many of them applied for repatriation to Poland, claiming that they feared persecution on religious grounds, if not immediately, then at some time in the future. Poland, at that time, did not have the welfare resources to devote to the settlement of repatriates, and adopted delaying tactics: a case-by-case approach, and slow processing of applications. The Roman Catholic Church in Poland tacitly supported this approach, and organized fundraising to build churches for the Kazakhstani Poles. In September 1998 a mutual co-operation agreement was signed between Kazakhstan and the Vatican. The need to reassure the Kazakhstani Poles that their religious future was secure was undoubtedly one of the motives for concluding this agreement.

NATIONAL AWAKENING

The revival of Kazakh nationalism began during the period of glasnost or *aygilik* (openness), initiated by the Soviet leader, Mikhail Gorbachev (1985–91). Complaints about lack of school instruction in the Kazakh language led to a decree of March 1987, which recommended improvements in the teaching of both Kazakh and Russian—an indication of the authorities' constant awareness of having to balance the demands and anxieties of both the major ethnic groups. In September 1989 the Supreme Soviet declared Kazakh to be the official language, although Russian was to be the language of inter-ethnic communication and all officials dealing with the public were to know both languages. This ruling was later embodied in the new Constitution of January 1993. The issue did seem to cause some increases in inter-ethnic tension, but, generally, it seemed to have been economic hardship that encouraged actual incidents in the Soviet period (notably the 1989 riot in Novyi Uzen). However, the return of many Russians to their homeland in the 1990s was in part attributed to concern for the future of their children, since reductions in Russian tuition in secondary schools made it increasingly difficult for Russian children educated in Kazakhstan to proceed to higher education in Russia. Moreover, even fluent Kazakh-speakers encountered difficulties when using their language for 'official' purposes.

In independent Kazakhstan the Government remained cautious of any nationalist group, discouraging extremists such as the radical party Alash (founded in 1999) or Slav groups, such as Yedinstvo (Unity) and Lad. Yet Kazakhs were increasingly dominant in the state, which fuelled ethnic Russian fears. This was a reversal of the situation in the late 1980s, when many Kazakhs feared that Russians were dominating the state and party apparatus. Under the First Secretary of the Communist Party of Kazakhstan (CPK), Dinmukhamed Kunayev (1956–86), Kazakhs had reached the highest positions of state in the republic, but often as a result of nepotism and corruption. Gorbachev's dismissal of Kunayev and many of his supporters, therefore, as part of his anti-corruption campaign (part of the perestroika or *qayta qurilis*, restructuring, initiative), was interpreted by some as anti-Kazakh. In December 1986 there was a violent nationalist protest in Almaty, in reaction to the announcement that the party's new First Secretary was to be an ethnic Russian, Gennadii Kolbin (1986–89). Kolbin continued with his reforms, although he also recommended that institutions be established to ensure fair ethnic representation in the administration. The problem was only really resolved by the appointment of Nursultan Nazarbayev, an ethnic Kazakh, to the CPK leadership, in June 1989.

Nazarbayev was careful to allay the fears of the Slavs and won their confidence partly because of his obvious support for the Union in the last years of the USSR. The Supreme Soviet (Supreme Kenges or Supreme Council) did make a declaration of sovereignty in October 1990, and Nazarbayev was an advocate of economic sovereignty. However, in the referendum on the continuation of the Union, in March 1991, there was an overwhelming vote in favour of the federation. Although the question asked of voters in Kazakhstan was slightly different to the standard one, 94.1% of the votes cast (88.2% of those eligible voted) supported the renewal of the USSR. Kazakhstan was ready to sign the new Union Treaty in August, but the event was forestalled by the attempted coup in Moscow (the Soviet, and Russian, capital). On 20 August Nazarbayev openly condemned the coup and, as it collapsed, he led the communist resignations and ordered the depoliticization of state institutions. Nevertheless, Kazakhstan signed the Treaty of the Economic Community in October and committed itself to a new Union in November. It had still not declared its independence when the leaders of the Slav republics resolved on a CIS and the effective dissolution of the USSR. The Supreme Soviet declared the independence of the country on 16 December, before it was admitted to the CIS as a founder member by the Almaty Declaration of 21 December.

In 1994 there was sporadic unrest among the Russian minority. The March elections to the Supreme Kenges, in which 59% of successful candidates were ethnic Kazakhs and only 28% ethnic Russians, led to allegations of discrimination against the Slav population (although, in fact, the ratio of Kazakh–Russian representation in the Supreme Kenges did not deviate very greatly from that in the country as a whole). In March 1995, in an attempt to address the problem of inter-ethnic relations in the country, President Nazarbayev established the Assembly of Nations of Kazakhstan, a forum representing minority ethnic groups, with the status of a 'consultative presidential body'. The decision to move Kazakhstan's capital from Almaty to the industrial city of Akmola (formerly Tselinograd and, from May 1998, Astana), in the north of Kazakhstan, was perceived by some observers to be a strategic move to undermine Russian influence in the north of the country, where Russians far outnumbered Kazakhs. However, President Nazarbayev's policy of maintaining close relations with Russia helped allay Slav anxieties. In May 2008 a celebration of Astana's 10th anniversary as the nation's capital was attended by leaders from many countries. Meanwhile, the Kazakh authorities were seeking to resolve new challenges for the capital, notably of energy sustainability and demographic sustainability.

THE POLITICAL STRUCTURES OF INDEPENDENT KAZAKHSTAN

The first post-independence constitution was adopted on 28 January 1993; a new Constitution was adopted by national referendum on 30 August 1995 and was amended in October 1998. The country has a presidential system of government, with separate executive, legislative and judicial bodies. During the early years of independence the executive branch of government consolidated its pre-eminence. This tendency was repeated in local government, which retained a considerable degree of autonomy, even under the Constitution of 1995. As in Russia, at the local level there was an initial lack of clarity between the functions of the legislative bodies (soviets, councils or maslikhat) and the executive bodies (previously known as the ispolkom, then the akimiyat). The latter grew increasingly powerful in the last years of the Union and the early years of independence, and came to report directly to the President, bypassing both the local councils and the ministries of the central Government.

PRESIDENTIAL POWER

In December 1991 Nursultan Nazarbayev became the first elected President of Kazakhstan, initially for a five-year term, with extensive personal powers, which included the authority to appoint and dismiss officials at all levels and to issue decrees counteracting parliamentary legislation. In 1995 his term of office was extended until 2000, as the result of a referendum, although, in the event, a presidential election was held in 1999 (see below). Nazarbayev had been appointed to the post of Chairman of the Council of Ministers (Head of Government) of Kazakhstan in 1984, then to that of First Secretary of the CPK in 1989. He introduced political and administrative reforms in September 1989, including the introduction of extra executive duties for the Chairman of the Supreme Soviet (the republican legislature). He was duly elected to this post in February 1990 and was, therefore, de facto, the republican Head of State. On 1 December 1991 he was the sole candidate in elections to the presidency, in which he obtained 98.8% of the votes cast. He played a prominent role in all-Union politics in the last years of the Soviet regime, and came to be regarded by many as one of the most active and internationally respected of the post-Soviet presidents. Nazarbayev was considered to be an astute negotiator, capable of toughness as well as flexibility. One of his greatest assets was his ability to maintain the political balance between the Russian and Kazakh factions. Thus, although his authoritarian (albeit relatively benign) style of government did not encourage the growth of multi-party democracy, it did act as a stabilizing force in the country and the region.

In 1995, along with the adoption of the new Constitution, President Nazarbayev's tenure was extended by nation-wide referendum, thereby removing the need for an election. Constitutional amendments, approved in October 1998, included provisions for the extension of the presidential term of office (from five to seven years) and the abolition of the upper age limit for presidential candidates (previously set at 65 years of age). In January 1999 Nazarbayev was re-elected to a further term of office, receiving more than 80% of the votes cast; the runner-up was the Communist Party candidate, Serikbolsyn Abdildin, who received less than 12% of the votes. The election was monitored by over 130 international observers. It was generally agreed that the voting took place without any gross violations, although there were many shortcomings in the pre-electoral procedures. For this reason, the Organization for Security and Co-operation in Europe (OSCE) declined to take part in the official monitoring process. One of the main causes for concern was the debarring of presidential candidates, including the former Prime Minister, Akezhan Kazhegeldin. Regarded as the only serious rival to the incumbent President, he was disqualified in November 1998 on account of a minor legal technicality. Kazhegeldin left Kazakhstan in 1999, to live in self-imposed exile in Europe. In April 1999 he was charged with tax evasion; further charges were later brought against him. His trial *in absentia* began in August 2001, and in early September the Supreme Court found him guilty of abuse of power, tax evasion and the illegal possession of weapons. He was sentenced to 10 years in prison; in addition, a substantial fine was imposed and his property was confiscated.

In June 2000 a law was passed by both houses of Parliament, granting President Nazarbayev extraordinary powers and privileges, which were to remain in force after the expiry of his existing term of office. The bill prompted criticism from the opposition, some of whom blamed the country's rampant corruption and economic mismanagement on a system of government that focused on one person—the President. Nazarbayev stressed that he did not intend to be a President for life. However, in 2003 it was confirmed that he would stand again for office. According to the Constitution, a person may not be elected president more than twice in succession. Nevertheless, Nazarbayev was deemed eligible to stand in the next presidential election, on the grounds that he had been first elected to office before the adoption of the 1995 Constitution. Moreover, in 1995 his tenure had been extended by referendum, not by election.

In August 2005 it was announced that the presidential election, anticipated for January 2007, was to be brought forward to December 2005. The unexpected change of date left the opposition with very little time to organize their campaigns. Nevertheless, five candidates succeeded in registering as contestants. Although Nazarbayev was generally regarded as the most likely winner, Zharmakhan Tuyakbai, the candidate standing on behalf of the opposition alliance 'For a Just Kazakhstan', was seen by some as a serious contender. The Nazarbayev campaign, widely covered in the press, emphasized his achievements in economic and social policy and held out a vision of future progress and prosperity. Opposition candidates complained of harassment and obstruction. The independent media allegedly experienced intimidation and persecution, including the illegal seizure of printed material and the forced closure of newspapers. As anticipated, Nazarbayev was re-elected for another seven-year term, winning over 90% of the votes. There was again criticism of the electoral proceedings both from domestic commentators and from some foreign monitors, including the OSCE observer mission. Yet no one seriously doubted that Nazarbayev would have won, no matter how rigorously the election had been conducted, since he unquestionably enjoyed the confidence of a large sector of the population.

In May 2007 further amendments to the Constitution were introduced, with the aim of transforming the political system from a presidential to a presidential-parliamentary system. One change was the reduction of the presidential term of office from seven to five years (as it had been prior to 1998), with effect from 2012, after the expiry of the current presidential mandate. However, the new ruling would not affect President Nazarbayev, since all limitations on his term of tenure were removed, allowing him to remain in office for as long as he wished. Other changes included an increase in the number of elected deputies and an expansion of parliamentary powers, primarily through greater consultation and agreement. Thus, for example, prime ministerial appointments would have to be approved by a majority of the members of the Majlis (Assembly). Opposition politicians were critical of these new measures, regarding them as a means of vesting yet more power in President Nazarbayev. However, most Western government officials and commentators took a more positive view of the amendments and there was little negative reaction.

THE LEGISLATURE

The legislative body that Kazakhstan inherited from the Soviet era was the Supreme Kenges. Elections to the 360-member parliament had been held on 25 March 1990—many candidates were unopposed and the system of reserving seats for CPK-affiliated candidates was still in existence. In December 1993, having enacted a new Constitution on 28 January, parliament declared itself dissolved. It granted President Nazarbayev additional legislative powers until after the general election, which was held on 7 March 1994. Kazakhstan's

first free multi-party elections were held amid reports by international observers of irregularities, particularly allegations of discrimination against the Russian population (75% of the 754 candidates who registered were ethnic Kazakhs, and it was suggested that ethnic minority candidates had been obstructed from registering). Supporters of Nazarbayev secured a significant majority in the new Supreme Kenges, which was reduced in size to 177 seats.

Like its predecessor, the new Supreme Kenges was critical of the Government, in particular regarding the slow pace of economic reforms. In early 1995 the Supreme Kenges refused to approve the draft budget, because of the social hardships that the proposed economic measures would create. In April the impending political impasse was supplanted by a constitutional crisis, however, when the Constitutional Court declared the result of the 1994 elections to be null and void, owing to 'procedural infringements'. Parliament was dissolved and the President effectively ruled by decree pending the introduction of a new Constitution and a general election, which was held in December.

Under the terms of the new Constitution, approved at a referendum held at the end of August 1995, the Supreme Kenges was to be replaced by a bicameral Parliament, with a 47-member upper chamber, the Senate, and a directly elected 67-member lower chamber, the Majlis (Assembly). The new constitutional arrangements were, in many ways, inadequate and in some instances unnecessarily cumbersome. President Nazarbayev proposed a number of constitutional changes in his annual 'state of the nation' address to Parliament in September 1998. After initial opposition, Parliament finally accepted the amendments in October, although not entirely as the President had originally proposed. The reforms as enacted included: the extension of the presidential term of office from five to seven years; the extension of the mandates of the Senate (from four to six years) and of the Majlis (from four to five years); the raising of the minimum age for a presidential candidate from 35 to 40 years and the abolition of the upper age limit; and a reduction of the threshold for parties and movements to secure representation in parliamentary elections from 10% to 7% of the votes cast.

The first elections to the reformed bicameral Parliament were held in late 1999, with partial elections to the (now 39-member) Senate taking place in September, and elections to the Majlis in October. Of the 77 deputies now comprising the Majlis, 67 were elected in single-mandate constituencies and the remaining 10 by party lists. Only 20 seats were filled in the first round of direct elections, and a second round was held later in the month. A third round of voting took place in December, after three results were declared invalid. The Fatherland Republican Political Party (Otan) won 23 seats (securing over 30% of the popular vote); the Civic Party of Kazakhstan, 13; and the CPK and the Agrarian Party of Kazakhstan each won three. Pro-government independents and non-party 'business' groups accounted for 34 of the remaining seats. As in previous elections, there were many reports of irregularities and violations of the electoral law.

In July 2002 a controversial law on the regulation of political parties was approved, which included a requirement that parties seeking re-registration (a necessary precondition for political activity) should have branches in each of the country's regions, and a minimum of 50,000 members, instead of 3,000 as had previously been the case. The next elections to the Majlis were scheduled for 2004, and elections to the Senate for 2005. Very few of the existing political parties were able to comply with the new criteria. By mid-2004 only 12 parties had been re-registered and were therefore eligible to participate in the forthcoming parliamentary elections. These included 'semi-opposition' parties such as Bright Road—Democratic Party of Kazakhstan (Ak Zhol), as well as openly pro-presidential parties such as Mutual Help Republican Political Party (Asar), Fatherland and the newly founded Democratic Party of Kazakhstan (DPK). The Communist People's Party of Kazakhstan, a splinter group of the CPK (and strongly anti-CPK), was also registered in time to take part in the elections to the Majlis, held on 19 September and 3 October.

In the main cities an electronic voting system was introduced for the September–October 2004 elections; elsewhere the traditional system of voting was retained. Only 56.7% of the electorate participated in the first round, and 45.2% participated in the second round. Results for party-list seats and 45 single-mandate constituencies were announced on 23 September 2004, but in 22 single-mandate constituencies a second round of 'run-off' elections was scheduled. The final results showed that, as anticipated, the pro-presidential Fatherland party obtained a substantial majority, winning 42 (seven party-list seats and 35 in single-mandate constituencies) of the 77 seats. The Aist bloc, comprising the Agrarian Party of Kazakhstan and the Civic Party of Kazakhstan, which was also supportive of the President, won 11 seats (including one party-list seat). Mutual Help obtained four seats (including one on the basis of party lists). Bright Road was the only (mildly) opposition party to win a party-list seat; the pro-presidential DPK won one single-mandate seat, while 18 single-mandate seats were won by independents. The electoral proceedings were criticized by opposition activists and a number of foreign observers, including the OSCE. Elections to the Senate, originally scheduled for December 2005, were brought forward to August; as anticipated, pro-presidential candidates secured a large majority. Following the constitutional amendments adopted in May 2007 (see above), on 20 June the Majlis was dissolved and parliamentary elections were scheduled for August, two years earlier than planned. Under the amended Constitution, the Majlis was increased in size to 107 deputies, of whom 98 were to be directly elected on party lists, while the remaining nine members were to be elected by the Assembly of Nations of Kazakhstan (which, established in 1995, attained constitutional status). The Senate henceforth comprised 47 deputies, with the number of members appointed by the President increasing to 15.

The elections to the Majlis on 18 August 2007 were monitored by observers from the CIS, OSCE and other international organizations. From the outset, there were allegations that the renamed Light Of The Fatherland (Nur Otan—officially chaired by President Nazarbayev since July), had an unfair advantage in terms of media coverage and in the bias of local officials. The rate of participation by voters was about 64.6% (compared with 56.8% in 2004). Light Of The Fatherland won 88.4% of the votes cast, securing all 98 contested seats in the Majlis. None of the other six parties contesting the poll achieved the 7% minimum of votes required to secure representation in the chamber; the newly established NSDP (see below) received 4.5% and Bright Road 3.1% of votes. The leaders of the NSDP, Bright Road, and the Communist People's Party refused to acknowledge the results and demanded that the poll be repeated. The CIS declared that it was satisfied with the organization of the elections, while the OSCE noted improvements compared with previous polls, but again criticized some aspects of the proceedings. On 20 August the Assembly of Nations of Kazakhstan elected the remaining nine deputies to the Majlis. Later that month President Nazarbayev adopted a decree appointing the additional eight deputies to the Senate.

POLITICAL PARTIES

Prior to independence, the only legal political party in Kazakhstan (as elsewhere in the USSR) was the Communist Party. In the early 1990s, however, a number of new movements and parties began to emerge. Most were very small and broadly supportive of the Government; there was little genuine opposition. By 2000 there were some 20 political organizations (parties, movements and pressure groups). The main parties were the Agrarian Party of Kazakhstan, the Civic Party of Kazakhstan, the CPK (a remnant of the Soviet-era Communist Party), Fatherland, the People's Congress of Kazakhstan and the Republican People's Party of Kazakhstan (founded by former Prime Minister Kazhegeldin).

In November 2001 a new opposition party, the Democratic Choice of Kazakhstan (DCK), was launched, the leaders of which were predominantly of a younger generation than the incumbent leadership. Several held senior positions in the administration, including Oraz Zhandosov, a Deputy Prime Minister, Mukhtar Ablyazov, a former Minister of Energy, Industry and Trade, and Ghalimzhan Zhakiyanov, Akim

(Governor) of Pavlodar Oblast (region). Democratic in orientation, the party's programme included demands for the decentralization of power, independence of the media and an intensification of the fight against corruption. However, internal divisions soon became evident. In early 2002 Zhandosov created a separate party, Bright Road, which espoused policies similar to those of the pro-presidential Fatherland party and was regarded by some as an attempt to diminish the impact of the DCK. Following the adoption in July of the law on political parties, all parties were required to re-register. Most were unable to satisfy the onerous new requirements and thus failed to secure registration, significantly reducing the number of parties that were able to participate in elections. Among those that did successfully re-register were Fatherland, the CPK and the Civic Party of Kazakhstan.

In 2003 another pro-presidential party appeared, Mutual Help (Asar), founded by the President's daughter, Darigha Nazarbayeva. It rapidly attracted a large membership, obtaining supporters from a broad social and demographic base. It aimed to promote the national tradition of co-operation and interaction between different ethnic groups. Centrist in orientation, it supported the reforms initiated by President Nazarbayev. By August 2004, prior to the parliamentary elections, 12 parties had been registered with the Ministry of Justice, mostly pro-presidential in orientation (see above).

In February 2005 the fragile opposition was weakened by the dissolution of the DCK, following a court case that found the party guilty of insulting the President, after it urged a campaign of civil disobedience in late 2004. Later in 2005 leading opposition figures, such as former information minister Altynbek Sarsenbayev, were found guilty of issuing defamatory statements and ordered to pay substantial fines. Meanwhile, strains surfaced within Bright Road, and in April a splinter party, Real Bright Road (Naghyz Ak Zhol), was formed, led by Bulat Abilov, Zhandosov and Sarsenbayev. Later that year the DCK re-emerged under Asylbek Kozhakhmetov, with the new name of Forward (Alga!). Over 62,000 supporters of Forward signed a petition demanding that the party be registered, but in February 2006 this was rejected by the legal authorities on the grounds of procedural irregularities; the party's leadership contested the ruling, but in June it was upheld by the Supreme Court. In a separate development, in August 2005 a new opposition coalition, For a Just Kazakhstan, led by Tuyakbai, was granted official registration, and became eligible to nominate candidates to take part in elections. Real Bright Road (which was registered in March 2006) became a member of the bloc. Also in 2005 Mutual Help and the DPK formed a tactical alliance. In July 2006 Mutual Help merged with Fatherland, creating an even stronger pro-presidential party.

In late December 2006 Fatherland, which now had a registered membership of almost 500,000, merged with the Civic Party (160,000 members) and the Agrarian Party (102,000 members), and the new entity was renamed Light Of The Fatherland (Nur Otan—an echo of 'Nursultan', the forename of the President). Collectively, it now controlled some 90% of the parliamentary seats. Subsequently, several ministers and senior officials joined the party. On 4 July 2007, at a special meeting of the party, President Nazarbayev formally assumed leadership, as permitted by recent amendments to the Constitution. Meanwhile, the party's political council was enlarged but those who were known to be close to Rakhat Aliyev, President Nazarbayev's disgraced son-in-law (see below) withdrew. Another pro-presidential bloc, the Kazakhstan Centre-Right Homeland (Atameken) Party, with a combined membership of 170,000, was formed in January 2007 by the merger of Homeland (Atameken), the Compatriot (Sootechestvennik) Party, the Alash People's Party and the National Federation of Kazakh Farmers. However, none of the grouping's constituent parties subsequently obtained official registration. In late May the party Kazakhstan's National Unity was formed by a group of public organizations that disapproved of the new constitutional amendments; however, this, too, failed to obtain registration.

Further mergers took place in preparation for the elections to the Majlis, scheduled for August 2007. In July the pro-presidential Justice Democratic Party (Adilet) merged with the moderately oppositional Bright Road; Alikhan Baymenov remained at the head of the enlarged Bright Road, while Maksut Narikbayev, the former Adilet leader, joined the rank of his deputies. A more strongly oppositional party, the National Social-Democratic Party (NSDP), was formed in January 2007 by Tuyakbai, the former presidential candidate; its deputy head was Amirzhan Kosanov (previously a senior figure in the Republican People's Party of Kazakhstan). In July 2007 the Real Bright Road party formed a coalition with the NSDP (which had already attracted a substantial following of some 140,000 registered members). Some members of the opposition party Forward also favoured joining the NSDP, but the majority rejected this proposal, and Forward was not granted registration. Of the eight officially registered parties, only the CPK refused to participate in the elections, citing objections to the overall introduction of the party-list proportional representation system. In mid-July the Central Electoral Commission completed the registration of the candidate lists of the seven parties contesting the elections, which took place on 18 August (see above). In February 2008 the manoeuvring of Kazakhstan's political parties became yet more complex, when Real Bright Road adopted the name Azat (Freedom), despite the fact that an organization of that name already existed. The original Azat party declared its intention to challenge the legality of the move by Real Bright Road, which sought to register with the Ministry of Justice under its new name.

POLITICAL CHANGES AND SCANDALS

Less than a decade after independence, scandals involving the Kazakhstani political establishment began to impinge on the public domain. In 2001 allegations surfaced in the press claiming that more than US $1,000m. in state funds were being held in Swiss banks in President Nazarbayev's name. In addition, the President's son-in-law, Aliyev, the Deputy Chairman of the National Security Committee (KNB), was publicly accused of abuse of office, corruption and the manipulation of the mass media. The leaders of the newly founded DCK expressed their support for his being charged. Aliyev resigned from the KNB, but was almost immediately appointed deputy chief of the Presidential Guard. In January 2002 he was sent to Austria as ambassador to that country and to the OSCE. Shortly afterwards, Prime Minister Kasymzhomart Tokayev, who had become embroiled in the accusations and counter-accusations, tendered his resignation; he was subsequently appointed Minister of Foreign Affairs and Secretary of State in the new Government of Imangali Tasmagambetov, a former Deputy Prime Minister.

In June 2003 Tasmagambetov, too, resigned. According to official sources, he left his post owing to the alleged falsification of the results of a parliamentary vote of confidence linked to the proposed introduction of a new land code, which was to provide for the privatization of agricultural land; it was claimed that Tasmagambetov had been unaware of the fraud. In accordance with the Constitution, the entire Government duly resigned. The new Prime Minister, confirmed in office on 13 June, was Danial Akhmetov, a former Akim of Pavlodar Oblast. Some two-thirds of the members of the previous Government were subsequently reappointed.

While these government reorganizations were taking place, pressure on the opposition increased. In mid-2002 two leaders of the DCK, Ablyazov and Zhakiyanov, were given long prison sentences, following charges of financial irregularities and abuse of office. Many commentators believed that the charges were politically motivated. In May 2003 Ablyazov was pardoned and released, but Zhakiyanov continued to be held and a further charge was brought against him in September that year. In August 2004 his conditions of detention were slightly improved when he was moved from prison to a closed settlement, to be held under house arrest. His supporters continued to campaign for his release and collected 1m. signatures on a petition to be submitted to the President. He was eventually released on parole in January 2006, after serving half of his sentence.

Two sudden deaths caused yet more concern. In November 2005 Zamanbek Nurkadilov, formerly a senior figure in central and regional government, but latterly an outspoken critic of

President Nazarbayev, died in mysterious circumstances. According to press reports, bullet wounds were found in his head and chest. The police investigation concluded that he had committed suicide, but some opposition figures claimed that he had been murdered. However, others believed the claims to be part of a campaign to discredit Nazarbayev prior to the presidential election. In February 2006 there was another fatal incident. Altynbek Sarsenbayev, once a political ally of the President, had held senior government posts and served as ambassador to Russia in 2002–03; however, in 2004 he joined the opposition and became a leader of the Bright Road party (and subsequently of Real Bright Road). His body, along with those of his driver and bodyguard, were found riddled with bullets, their hands tied behind their backs, on a roadside near Almaty. Some suggested that the killing was linked to the deceased's business activities, but others insisted that it was politically motivated. Senior members of the administration and the National Security Committee came under suspicion; 10 people were eventually arrested and went on trial in mid-June. One of the defendants, a former interior ministry official, told the court that the murder had been planned by Senate Chairman Nurtai Abykayev and the former head of the National Security Committee, Nurtai Dutbayev, as part of a plot to overthrow President Nazarbayev. At the end of August the court sentenced the 10 defendants. Yerzhan Utembayev (the former head of the Senate administration) received a 20-year prison term, and Rustam Ibragimov, a former official of the interior ministry, received the death sentence (which was commuted to a sentence of life imprisonment, owing to the moratorium on capital punishment.)

In January 2007 there was an unexpected reorganization of the Government, in which Karim Masimov replaced Akhmetov as Prime Minister. An economist by training, Masimov (an ethnic Uighur) had studied and worked in the People's Republic of China, and also had ties with Russia—both strategic partners for Kazakhstan. Priority tasks for the new Prime Minister included securing membership of the World Trade Organization (WTO—Kazakhstan had applied to join in 1996) and the rotational chairmanship of the OSCE. In November 2007, after intensive campaigning, and despite opposition from some member states, it was confirmed that Kazakhstan would assume the chairmanship of the OSCE for a period of one year in 2010. Another important new appointment was that of Marat Tazhin as Minister of Foreign Affairs. Tazhin also had a background in economics and had studied abroad, in the United Kingdom. More recently, his experience had been in national security and within the presidential administration. Akhmetov, meanwhile, was awarded the defence portfolio. In mid-February 2007 the new Government presented its programme in parliament. Issues relating to public and private sector economic development received particular attention.

Scandal involving the President's family again attracted considerable media attention. As had frequently been the case, it centred on Rakhat Aliyev, the husband of the President's eldest daughter. For some time unsubstantiated reports had been circulating regarding his very extensive business interests. It was alleged that he was involved in extortion, racketeering and various other criminal activities. These accusations were vigorously denied by his friends and relations, and in February 2007 Aliyev was sent to Vienna, Austria's capital city, for a second tour of duty as Kazakhstan's ambassador to that country and the OSCE. However, in May court proceedings were opened against him in Astana for his alleged role in the disappearance (and possibly murder) of senior personnel at Nurbank, one of Kazakhstan's leading banks. Aliyev was a major shareholder in Nurbank and his son was the first deputy chairman of the bank's board. Aliyev was relieved of his post but remained in Vienna, from where he launched an impassioned attack on President Nazarbayev, condemning the constitutional amendments and representing himself as a champion of the opposition. He later retracted his criticisms and apologized in person to Nazarbayev. Meanwhile, an international warrant was issued for his arrest and he was briefly detained by the Austrian police, before being released on bail. In June his wife divorced him, apparently without his prior knowledge. Aliyev sought political asylum in Austria, where criminal charges against him had been abandoned, though the Kazakhstani authorities continued to demand his extradition. He was tried *in absentia*, and on 15 January 2008 one of Almaty's district courts imposed a 20-year sentence of imprisonment for his involvement in the creation of an organized criminal group, misappropriation of property and abductions of officials from the bank he controlled. His alleged accomplices, several of whom were also in hiding in Austria, also received long sentences. In late March, at a second trial *in absentia*, a military court sentenced Aliyev to another 20 years' imprisonment for illegal possession of armaments and ammunition, misappropriation of property and planning a coup. Aliyev, who was still claiming asylum in Austria, retaliated by offering to give evidence in the protracted US corruption trial of a former associate of President Nazarbayev, James Giffen, regarding allegations that Nazarbayev and other senior Kazakh officials accepted bribes from US businesses to receive lucrative oil contracts in the 1990s (see Economy).

MEDIA AND NON-GOVERNMENTAL ORGANIZATIONS

In the early 1990s the Kazakhstani media, compared with other states in Central Asia, were relatively free. However, from 2000 restrictive pressures were noticeably increased. Journalists who expressed criticism of the Government were subjected to both official and unofficial harassment, including physical attacks, and arrests for alleged tax violations and other financial irregularities. The most high profile case was that of Sergei Duvanov, a journalist known for his coverage of human rights issues and an outspoken critic of the country's leadership. In October 2002 he was charged with the rape of a minor and subsequently given a prison sentence. However, his supporters insisted that he was innocent and accused the authorities of falsifying the evidence. In November 2003 a draft law on the media was presented to Parliament for scrutiny. (The existing media law had been passed in 2000, and amended in 2002.) The new bill included proposals that, if accepted, would increase state control over the press and severely limit freedom of expression. However, after strong protests from foreign and national bodies, and a court ruling that the law would violate the Constitution, the Government withdrew it. A new draft was submitted in August 2004 that offered some concessions, such as provisions for limiting the state's right to own controlling shares in media companies and guarantees to preserve freedom of speech. The fine imposed on the independent newspaper *Soz* (Word) in February 2005, for publishing claims that the National Security Committee had harassed opposition activists, was an indication that criticism of official bodies was not to be undertaken lightly. Four other independent Kazakhstani newspapers (including *Epokha*, affiliated to Bright Road) complained that the authorities were illegally confiscating their publications and intercepting shipments in transit. In May 2006 it was announced that Khabar, Kazakhstan's leading semi-independent television company, was to be brought under full government control; there had already been a reshuffle of senior management in the state-owned television company. Amendments to the media law, putting journalists under tighter state control and making registration harder for news outlets, were passed by both houses of Parliament in June and were signed into law in early July. Journalists and opposition activists protested publicly about these actions, which they regarded as authoritarian and restrictive. Foreign organizations also criticized the bill, characterizing it as being contrary to the development of a free media in Kazakhstan.

Non-governmental organizations (NGOs) also came under pressure. In March 2005 Prosecutor-General Rashid Tusupbekov stated that the activities of all foreign NGOs would be monitored, in connection with intensified efforts to combat economic crime, and particularly illegal cash transactions. Draft legislation aimed at strengthening state control over NGOs was passed by Parliament in June and submitted to President Nazarbayev for ratification. The new measures were strongly criticized by the Confederation of NGOs of Kazakhstan, and by other representatives of civil society both domestically and abroad. Nazarbayev consequently referred the

matter to the Constitutional Court, which ruled that the proposed legislation contravened the Constitution and should be rejected.

Religious organizations complained of increasing restrictions on their activities. At first it was mainly new communities and missionary groups who experienced problems. However, in 2008 a new Law on Religion was under consideration that would introduce strict limitations on all religious bodies. In July the Roman Catholic Archbishop based in Astana, Tomasz Peta, issued a statement expressing the hope that religious freedom would be preserved 'according to the spirit of the current law from 1992'. A final draft of the legislation was expected to be approved by President Nazarbayev by the end of 2008.

SECURITY

In the immediate aftermath of the dissolution of the USSR, Western Governments were concerned about the fate of the Soviet-era nuclear arsenal that Kazakhstan had inherited. This issue was resolved when Kazakhstan declared its commitment to becoming a non-nuclear state. In 1992 the country ratified the first Strategic Arms Reduction Treaty (START 1) and became a signatory to the Treaty on the Non-Proliferation of Nuclear Weapons in December 1993. By April 1995 all nuclear warheads in Kazakhstan had been transferred to Russia; remaining intercontinental ballistic missile units were dismantled by mid-1996. The country's role as a nuclear test-site was not, however, over: in September 1998 the Academy of Sciences of Kazakhstan concluded an agreement with the USA to carry out two underground nuclear explosions, one at Semipalatinsk and the other at the USA's test-site in Nevada, in order to refine the monitoring techniques used to distinguish between bomb tests and natural seismic events. In July 2000 the Semipalatinsk nuclear facility was finally closed, and in late 2001 Kazakhstan ratified the Comprehensive Nuclear Test Ban Treaty. On 8 September 2006 the foreign ministers of Kazakhstan, Kyrgyzstan, Tajikistan, Turkmenistan and Uzbekistan met in Semipalatinsk to sign an historic treaty creating a zone free of nuclear weapons in Central Asia. In June 2007 Astana hosted the third meeting of the Global Initiative to Combat Nuclear Terrorism (launched at the G8 summit in St Petersburg by the US and Russian Presidents in 2006) where proposals for inclusion in the organization's work were presented.

New security concerns emerged during the 1990s and early 2000s. One was the massive upsurge in drugs-trafficking, a result of the exponential growth in the illegal production of drugs in Afghanistan; Kazakhstan took an active part in co-ordinated regional programmes to combat this problem. In 2006 Kazakhstani law enforcement agencies uncovered a total of 10,500 drug-related crimes and seized 25 metric tons of various drugs, including over 500 kg of heroin; 4,500 drug sellers were convicted and criminal investigations were launched against eight corrupt anti-narcotics officers. In 2007 the Kazakhstani police continued to make large drugs hauls, including consignments of over 50 kg of heroin. The situation was exacerbated by the increase in the flow of synthetic drugs reaching Kazakhstan from Europe.

Another security concern was the rise in extremist Islamism. Previously, Kazakhs had held a reputation for being relatively unobservant or secularized Muslims. However, in the late 1990s radical groups began to appear; members were blamed for acts of terrorism and a number were arrested. In August 2004, for example, 16 people were arrested in the south of Kazakhstan and charged with terrorism on religious grounds. A transnational radical Islamist organization, Hizb-ut-Tahrir al-Islami (Party of Islamic Liberation—Hizb-ut-Tahrir), was banned in Kazakhstan in March 2005 because, according to the Office of the Prosecutor-General, its activities aimed 'to change the constitutional system, destroy sovereignty and the country's territorial integrity'; several members of Hizb-ut-Tahrir were arrested later that year. In July the Pakistani authorities claimed that 17 suspected militants from the Islamist al-Qa'ida (Base) organization killed by security forces close to the Afghan border were citizens of Kazakhstan. Meanwhile, within Kazakhstan there were ongoing arrests of alleged members of other extremist Islamist organizations accused of disseminating radical ideology with the aim of establishing an Islamic caliphate. In January 2006 some 16 members of the Jamaat (Society) of Mujaheddin, a group reportedly linked to al-Qa'ida, were charged with terrorist activities and given lengthy prison sentences. In late 2006 the authorities increased pressure on the organization, suppressing foreign contacts and arresting local leaders. Computers, printing equipment and large amounts of religious extremist literature were seized during these operations. In 2007 official sources reported that thousands of Hizb-ut-Tahrir members were voluntarily presenting themselves to the National Security Committee and surrendering extremist literature.

FOREIGN AFFAIRS

Historically, Kazakhstan was a nodal point in the Eurasian trade networks, a crossroads for the east–west and north–south routes. Later, especially after the region's incorporation into the tsarist empire, the links with Russia assumed ever greater importance until, during the Soviet period, Kazakhstan was virtually sealed off from China and Iran. All foreign political and economic relations were conducted through, and by, the central authorities in the Soviet and Russian capital, Moscow. It was only after the collapse of the USSR that Kazakhstan was able to develop an independent foreign policy. From the outset, the Kazakhstani Government stressed that it would not be drawn into any exclusive political grouping, but would maintain good relations with all its neighbours, likewise with the wider international community. It became a member of the UN on 2 March 1992, and subsequently joined the main UN funds, programmes and special agencies, as well as the main international financial institutions. Kazakhstan was also a member of a number of collective security organizations, including the CIS, the North Atlantic Co-operation Council (subsequently the Euro-Atlantic Co-operation Council), the North Atlantic Treaty Organization's (NATO) 'Partnership for Peace' programme and the OSCE.

One of Kazakhstan's principal relationships was with Russia. This was not surprising, given that Kazakhstan shared a border of some 7,500 km with its northern neighbour, as well as having a large Slav population. Ties between the two countries were driven by vital mutual interests in many areas, including trade, investment, transport, defence and security. Relations were conducted through bilateral channels as well as multilateral structures. In 1998 the Presidents of Kazakhstan and Russia concluded a bilateral Treaty of Eternal Friendship and Co-operation. That same year the two states reached agreement on the bilateral demarcation of their sectors of the Caspian seabed; in May 2002 a protocol (somewhat amended in 2006) set out the geographical co-ordinates of the modified median line. This provided the basis for the joint development and exploitation of the oilfields that straddled the Kazakhstani-Russian sectors. These included the Kurmangazy field (with reserves estimated at 1,000m. metric tons or 7,300m. barrels), which was reckoned to be the fourth largest deposit in Kazakhstan. In 2005 the two states ratified the treaty on the demarcation of their common land border. Accords signed in 2006 included an agreement (long under negotiation) on the renting of four military training and testing grounds to Russia. It was also announced that Kazakhstan and Russia were planning a single system of observation satellites. Trade between the two countries was growing rapidly; in 2006 it was expected to have exceeded US $10,000m., in part owing to buoyant co-operation in the oil and gas sector.

In late May 2008 the new Russian President, Dmitrii Medvedev, visited Kazakhstan, in his first official visit abroad, which was interpreted by many Kazakhstanis as an acknowledgement of the country's fundamental role within the CIS. Substantive discussions were held on economic integration (see below) and on peaceful co-operation in space, notably on the use of the Global Navigation Satellite System. Within the framework of this meeting, an agreement was concluded between the Russian bank Vneshekonombank ('Bank for Foreign Economic Affairs') and the Kazakhstan Development Bank, whereby the Russian bank was to extend credit of up to US $300m. to its Kazakhstani partners. The credit, to be repaid

within 15 years, was to be used to finance purchases of Russian industrial equipment and to implement joint Russian-Kazakh projects in Kazakhstan.

An issue that caused some friction between the two states in the 1990s was that of the terms and conditions for use of the Soviet-era space centre, located in Baikonur, in southern Kazakhstan, but operated by Russia. In 1994 Kazakhstan agreed to lease it to Russia for a 20-year period. Subsequently, there were reports that Russia would terminate operations at the space centre, largely owing to the high cost of rent (US $115m. per year). However, in November 2003 the Russian Aerospace Agency announced that there were no such plans and that, on the contrary, Baikonur played a vital part in Russia's space programme. An amicable settlement of outstanding differences was reached, and in June 2005 President Vladimir Putin of Russia visited Kazakhstan to celebrate the 50th anniversary of the founding of the Baikonur centre. Agreement was reached on extending the Russian lease until 2050. Plans for collaborative projects were revealed, including the launch of a communications satellite and construction of a light space-rocket complex. In June 2006, in the presence of the two Heads of State, the first Kazakh satellite, 'Kazsat 1', was launched; however, in June 2008 contact with the satellite was lost. The launch of 'Kazsat 2' was scheduled for 2009. There were other operational problems. In July 2006 a rocket, carrying 18 satellites belonging to Belarus, Russia, Italy, the USA and Colombia, and some 86,500 kg of fuel, crashed shortly after it had been launched from Baikonur. The accident happened over an uninhabited area; there were no casualties or damage to infrastructure. In accordance with the Kazakhstani-Russian intergovernmental agreement covering such eventualities, a joint task force was established to investigate the causes of the crash. In November of the same year the Russian side promised to pay damages amounting to more than $1m. In September 2007 there was a similar accident with a Russian Proton rocket; further launches were suspended pending investigations. (For Kazakhstani-Russian multilateral ties within the framework of the Eurasian Economic Community and other regional organizations, see below.)

The People's Republic of China was another strategic partner. The interest was reciprocated by the Chinese Government and there were exchanges of high-level official delegations, as well as numerous trade, cultural and scientific missions. Both sides were eager to revive the ancient 'Silk Road', in modern form. At the beginning of the 1990s road, rail and air links, as well as a direct telephone line, already connected Almaty and Urumqi (Urumchi), the capital of Xinjiang Uigur Autonomous Region, a Chinese province with a Kazakh population of over 1m. There were plans to upgrade these links in the near future, so as to facilitate the eventual integration of the Chinese and Central Asian transportation and communications networks. A bilateral agreement to develop 'long-term neighbourly and stable relations' was signed by the leaders of the two countries in late 1995. At the end of July 1996 a source of considerable tension was removed when China announced that it had conducted its last nuclear test explosion. The issue of the demarcation of parts of the China–Kazakhstan border (still unresolved at the time of the collapse of the USSR) was finally settled to the satisfaction of both Governments in 1999. Some progress was also made on reaching agreement regarding the utilization of trans-boundary water resources. China announced plans to draw off some 10% of the flow of the Cherny Irtysh river by 2010 (some 1,000m. cu m of water per year); a joint commission was established in 2000 to monitor the situation. However, experts remained concerned that the Cherny Irtysh–Karamay canal, under construction as part of a plan to develop western China, might have a harmful effect on adjacent areas of Kazakhstan. Significant Chinese investment in the Kazakhstani energy sector began in 1997 and continued to increase thereafter.

In May 2004, during President Nazarbayev's visit to China, an interstate agreement was signed on the construction of a petroleum pipeline to connect the two countries. Within Kazakhstan, the first section of this project had been initiated in 2002, and by 2004 a significant part of the proposed pipeline was already operational. The 998-km cross-border section, running from Atasu (Kazakhstan) to Alashankou (China) was completed in December 2005, and became operational in May 2006. The burgeoning co-operation in trade, transport and energy (see Economy) between the two countries was strengthened by a strategic energy partnership signed in July 2005 during a visit by Chinese President Hu Jintao to Kazakhstan. It was subsequently announced that the two states aimed to increase bilateral trade to US $10,000m. annually (increasing the existing level twofold). Co-operation in security was also identified as a priority, particularly the fight against separatism, religious extremism and terrorism. In August 2003 China and Kazakhstan jointly hosted co-ordinated military exercises of member states of the international Shanghai Co-operation Organization (SCO—formerly the Shanghai Five, see below). Co-operation in this area was enhanced by the creation of an SCO Anti-Terrorist Centre in 2004 (see below).

Frequent high-level exchanges took place between Kazakhstan and China. In April 2008, during a visit to China, Prime Minister Masimov met President Hu, who stressed the importance that China accorded to its relationship with Kazakhstan. Masimov emphasized the need to increase co-operation, especially in investment, finance, energy, agriculture and infrastructure construction, and also reiterated ongoing support for the foreign-affairs policies of the Chinese Government. In June it was announced that Eurasian Natural Resources Corporation (ENRC), the holding company of a Kazakhstan-based natural resources group, had won the tender for the China Gateway Project. This was to involve several elements, including the construction of some 300 km of railway in South-East Kazakhstan (eventually to be operated by ENRC), extending to Khorgos on the Kazakhstan-Chinese border, which was designed to increase cargo volumes between Kazakhstan and China by some 30m. metric tons per year. In all, the project was to cost an estimated US $900m., the largest ever private investment in Kazakhstan's transport infrastructure. Construction was scheduled to begin by the end of 2008, with operations expected to commence in 2012. ENRC's concession to operate the railway was to continue until 2036.

Kazakhstan's third strategic relationship was with the USA. In May 1992 President Nazarbayev made an official visit to Washington, DC (one of his first trips outside the former USSR). Agreements were signed that laid the foundations for the development of economic, technical, and cultural ties between the two countries. Despite US concerns about Kazakhstan's sometimes faltering progress towards democracy, the relationship remained strong. US companies were among the largest investors in Kazakhstan, particularly in the oil and gas sector (see Economy).

Following the suicide attacks on the USA, attributed to the al-Qa'ida organization of Osama bin Laden, on 11 September 2001, Kazakhstan demonstrated its support for the US-led 'war on terror' by opening its airspace to US military aircraft and allowing emergency landings to be made on its territory. After the US-led coalition's removal of Saddam Hussain as President of Iraq in early 2003, Kazakhstan also sent a contingent of 27 technical staff to that country as part of the post-war coalition to stabilize and rebuild it. A number of troops were injured and one man was killed in Iraq in January 2005. In May the Kazakhstani Minister of Defence, Mukhtar Altynbayev, repeated a demand (first made in 2004) for the withdrawal of Kazakhstani troops from Iraq. However, this demand was generally regarded as representing a personal opinion, rather than an expression of state policy. Co-operation with the West in defence and security matters was strengthened by military assistance and joint operations. In March 2003 the Kazakhstani Ministry of Defence announced that the USA was to assist in building up Kazakhstan's navy, by supplying military ships for its Caspian Sea fleet. Deliveries of cargo aircraft and helicopters were also envisaged in the future. In July Kazakhstani airborne troops and units of the Kazakhstani peace-keeping battalion, Kazbat, were joined by British and US troops in operation 'Steppe Eagle 2003', a week of military manoeuvres in Almaty Oblast. Similar exercises were repeated in the following years. In February 2006 representatives from the US Central Command visited Kazakhstan to plan the exercise and examine the venue. They also visited the Kazbat peacekeeping battalion. In May US Vice-President Dick Cheney visited Kazakhstan and

signed three accords, including a co-operation agreement on the prevention of illegal smuggling of nuclear material and a memorandum of mutual understanding on economic development. President Nazarbayev made an official visit to Washington, DC, in September, when he met US President George W. Bush. In mid-2008 Kazakhstan held a large-scale military exercise, involving over 900 troops and emergency personnel, to simulate a terrorist siege at a nuclear research facility near Almaty. The initiative was part of a 'Global Initiative to Combat Nuclear Terrorism', aimed at preventing the use of radioactive materials by terrorists, which had been jointly endorsed by the USA and Russia during a summit in 2006. Kazakhstan was the first state to volunteer to hold the anti-nuclear terrorism exercise. In parallel with such initiatives with Western partners, Kazakh-Russian military co-operation continued to deepen. In July 2008 it was announced that a programme of joint military exercises, to be held on the territories of both states, was scheduled for 2009–11.

Kazakhstan joined the NATO 'Partnership for Peace' programme of military co-operation in 1994, and thereafter regularly participated in its various training operations. A NATO information centre was established in Astana in 2004, and in February 2005 a major NATO forum was held in Almaty. The Kazakhstani Deputy Minister of Defence indicated that the participation of Kazakhstani armed forces in NATO events would be expanded. There was speculation in some circles that NATO might seek to establish a base in Kazakhstan, but in October 2005 this was denied by Robert Simmons, NATO special representative for the Caucasus and Central Asia, during his visit to the region. However, in order to improve relations with the Central Asian countries, NATO appointed a special representative for communications and co-operation, to be based in Kazakhstan. Kazakhstan's relationship with NATO was further strengthened by the adoption of an Individual Partnership Action Plan (IPAP), signed in January 2006. In February 2007 it was announced that NATO and Kazakhstan would expand ties within the IPAP framework.

Despite Kazakhstan's ties with the West, and in particular with the USA, it also maintained good relations with Iran. During the Soviet period a few thousand Kazakhs had fled to Iran and subsequently settled there. However, there had been little official contact between the two countries. When Kazakhstan became an independent state, both sides were eager to establish good neighbourly relations. Plans to build a pipeline through Iran were not feasible while the US Government maintained a hostile attitude towards Iran's regime but exchange agreements with Iran provided a conduit for Kazakhstani petroleum exports. (For more information on the politics of energy, see the article by the same author on energy in the Caspian Sea region in Part One—General Survey.)

Trade with Iran was not initially a priority. However, from 2002 this began to change. In 2004 Kazakhstan undertook to export at least 1m. metric tons of grain to Iran annually. Iran was also eager to purchase 'unlimited' amounts of Kazakhstani steel. The two sides agreed to open trade centres in their respective states. In July 2005 Iran's First Vice-President, Muhammad Reza Aref, visited Kazakhstan to conduct talks with Kazakhstani officials and to attend the SCO summit (at which Iran was granted the status of observer member). Although no major agreements were announced, the results of the discussions were deemed to be positive. In mid-October 2007 President Nazarbayev made an official visit to Tehran to attend the summit meeting of the Caspian littoral states and also to boost bilateral relations with Iran. Several important agreements were concluded between the two countries.

The emerging relationship with India was given political impetus by the visit of Hamid Ansari, Vice-President of India, to Kazakhstan in April 2008, when he met senior Kazakhstani officials. Discussions focused on prospects for increasing bilateral trade and expanding economic co-operation, particularly in the hydrocarbons sector (a priority concern for India). Co-operation in higher education was also discussed, particularly in terms of an exchange of Indian professionals to study in Kazakhstan and Kazakhstanis to study in India. President Nazarbayev was scheduled to make a reciprocal visit to India in November 2008.

Relations with the neighbouring Central Asian states were initially complicated by economic rivalry and competition for foreign aid. However, bilateral ties were gradually strengthened. In 2007 Kazakhstan was enjoying good relations with all the Central Asian states. Diplomatic, commercial and security ties with Uzbekistan had improved markedly after the landmark reciprocal visits of the two Presidents in 2006. Kazakhstani-Uzbekistani trade reached US $703.8m. in that year, and was expected to increase substantially in the future. Relations with Kyrgyzstan were supported by growing Kazakhstani investment in the country. In April 2007 the formation of a $120m. Kyrgyzstani-Kazakhstani investment fund was announced ($100m. to be provided by Kazakhstan, the remainder by Kyrgyzstan). A similar joint investment fund was established in September for Tajikistan. Kazakhstan extended humanitarian assistance to both countries. During the unusually harsh winter of 2007–08 Kazakhstan provided aid amounting to $1.5m. to assist in relieving the extreme energy and food shortages in Tajikistan. Similarly, in April 2008, when Kazakhstan introduced a ban on grain exports, deliveries to Kyrgyzstan were exempted and continued as scheduled. Relations with Turkmenistan also improved, after the election of President Gurbanguly Berdymuhamedov in February of that year. In May it was announced that direct flights between the two countries, suspended more than a decade previously, would be resumed. Future joint projects included the building of road, rail and pipeline links.

At an institutional level, economic, as well as cultural and social links, were strengthened with 'core' CIS members in March 1996, with the signature of the so-called Quadripartite Treaty, aimed at developing closer integration, and eventually a customs union, between Belarus, Kazakhstan, Kyrgyzstan and Russia; Tajikistan joined the body in 1998. In October 2000, at a meeting of Heads of State, held in Astana, it was decided to transform this organization into the Eurasian Economic Community (EURASEC). Although it was emphasized that the aims of the new organization would be mainly economic (see Economy), it was interpreted by some as progress towards the creation of a 'Eurasian Union', a project first mooted by President Nazarbayev in 1994; political opinion in Uzbekistan was especially critical of this development, warning that it could lead to renewed 'Russian hegemony'. Nevertheless, in 2005 Uzbekistan joined EURASEC, which simultaneously merged with the Central Asian Co-operation Organization (CACO). One of the priorities for the enlarged organization was to complete the formalities required to create a legal basis for a customs union, initially between Belarus, Kazakhstan and Russia, that had been proposed in the mid-1990s but not as yet achieved. In 2006 the project was revitalized and at the summit meeting of EURASEC Heads of State Council in October 2007 documents providing for a legal framework for the union were signed. In January 2008, three years earlier than anticipated, Belarus, Russia and Kazakhstan signed agreements that completed the process of forming the Customs Union of the three countries. Tajikistani Prime Minister Akil Akilov confirmed that his country was eager to join the Customs Union; Kyrgyzstan and Uzbekistan also remained committed to future membership.

In 2003–04 there were efforts to enhance CIS economic integration through the creation of a Single Economic Space (SES), encompassing Belarus, Russia, Ukraine and Kazakhstan. The so-called 'orange revolution' in Ukraine in late 2004 (see the chapter on Ukraine) slowed the pace of negotiations, but did not disrupt the project. In May 2005, following his visit to Kazakhstan, the Ukrainian President, Viktor Yushchenko, appeared eager to pursue co-operation within the framework of the SES; President Nazarbayev emphasised that such co-operation would be beneficial for both countries and would facilitate the transport of hydrocarbons from Kazakhstan to Ukraine. In 2006 no discernible progress was made with this project and by 2007 it had been effectively abandoned. However, during President Medvedev's visit to Astana in May 2008, Nazarbayev proposed reviving the project, but this time without the participation of Ukraine and Belarus, which were regarded as obstacles to integration. Nazarbayev urged Russia to consider a comprehensive bilateral agreement on co-opera-

tion and integration in order to facilitate greater economic convergence; further discussions on the matter were planned.

In security matters, Kazakhstan, as a member of the CIS Collective Security Treaty Organization (CSTO), continued to participate in joint operations. Under the aegis of the CSTO, a Rapid Reaction Force was established to defend the southern borders of the CIS against external attack: the primary targets were identified as terrorism, drugs-smuggling and Islamist fundamentalism. The core unit was the anti-terrorism centre, which opened in Bishkek, Kyrgyzstan, in August 2001. Kazakhstan's commitment to the CSTO and to the development of military partnership with its member states remained a fundamental part of its national security strategy. This was emphasized by Minister of Defence (and former Prime Minister) Akhmetov in April 2007, when he outlined Kazakhstan's new military doctrine and commented that 'a priority for the country is participation in the CSTO'. He elaborated further that Kazakhstan would participate in forming a coalition within this organization in order 'to fulfil our goals and tasks within the CSTO'. However, he reaffirmed the country's intention to continue 'actively working in the military and political spheres within the Shanghai Co-operation Organization' and stressed that it attached 'serious attention to strengthening and improving co-operation with the USA and NATO'.

Kazakhstan's new military doctrine also set out the aims and principles of its participation in peace-keeping operations abroad and defined the role of its peace-keeping brigade, Kazbrig (a subdivision of Kazbat). Kazakhstan's fledgling navy likewise came under review. In 2007 a new strategy was announced aimed at developing defence capabilities to protect the country's coastal infrastructure and strategically important facilities in the Caspian Sea. A three-phase programme was initiated, to run until 2025. The acquisition of new ships and weapons would form part of the general military procurement plan. It was envisaged that small tonnage military cutters would be constructed by Zenith, a local company.

Kazakhstan was a founder member and regular participant in summit meetings of the Heads of State of the so-called Shanghai Five. This informal structure, which, besides Kazakhstan, comprised China, Kyrgyzstan, Russia and Tajikistan, aimed to resolve border issues and to promote confidence-building. At the summit meeting of June 2001, Uzbekistan joined the group, which was simultaneously transformed into the SCO. A separate document, the Shanghai Convention on Combating Terrorism, Separatism and Extremism, was signed, which provided a legal framework for increased regional co-operation in police operations and intelligence information gathering. In order to facilitate these efforts, an SCO anti-terrorism centre was inaugurated in June 2004, with headquarters in Tashkent, Uzbekistan. In July 2005, at an SCO heads of state summit meeting held in Astana, a counter-terrorism strategy was approved, together with an agreement on mutual assistance in emergency situations. India, Iran and Pakistan were granted official observer status at the SCO. The concluding declaration of the summit meeting included a statement noting that combat operations in Afghanistan were over, and requesting that the US-led coalition that had undertaken military action in that country provide a timetable for the withdrawal of its personnel from bases in Uzbekistan and Kyrgyzstan. This was widely regarded in the West as a provocative and hostile action. However, SCO member states insisted that they were merely calling for clarification of the situation. One of the benefits of the SCO was the boost it had given to regional trade. According to official data, trade between the member states in 2006 amounted to US $50,000m. At an SCO summit meeting, held in Shanghai in June of that year, President Putin proposed the formation of an SCO energy club, similar to OPEC; the initial reaction was positive and measures to study the practicalities of the project were initiated. In January 2007 Bolat Nurgaliyev, a senior Kazakhstani diplomat, became the first holder of the newly created post of Secretary-General of the SCO. The annual SCO summit meeting was held in Bishkek in August. One of the priorities to emerge was the need to expand co-operation with other international structures, such as the CIS, EURASEC and ASEAN, and to develop a dialogue with Afghanistan. At the next SCO summit meeting, held in the capital of Tajikistan, Dushanbe, at the end of August 2008, member states issued a declaration expressing support for 'the active role of Russia in promoting peace and co-operation in the region', following Russia's military action in Georgia earlier that month (see the chapter on Georgia), but emphasized the need to resolve conflict through peaceful dialogue.

In the early 1990s Kazakhstan joined two other regional structures. One was the Economic Co-operation Organization (ECO—founded originally by Iran, Pakistan and Turkey, and later enlarged to include all the independent Central Asian states, and also Azerbaijan and Afghanistan). The ECO continued to promote regional economic ties, but the implementation of major projects was hampered by limited financial resources. The other was the Turkic Summits, a series of high-level meetings between Turkey and the former Soviet Turkic states (namely Azerbaijan, Kazakhstan, Kyrgyzstan, Turkmenistan and Uzbekistan). Initiated in 1992, these meetings were held on an almost annual basis, in capitals of the member states. Initially the emphasis was on economic co-operation, particularly in the transport and energy sectors, but later issues such as the fight against terrorism and organized crime attracted increasing attention. After the seventh summit meeting in 2001, however, the Turkic Summits were suspended, before being relaunched in November 2006. In 2004 the security services of Azerbaijan, Kazakhstan, Kyrgyzstan and Turkey held a series of meetings on the conduct of joint anti-terrorism operations, and in July a formal agreement of co-operation in this field was signed.

In 1992 President Nazarbayev proposed the creation of an Asian equivalent of the OSCE, named the Conference on Interaction and Confidence-Building Measures in Asia (CICA). After 10 years of preparatory work, the first CICA summit was held in June 2002, in Almaty. It brought together representatives from the Middle East, South and South East Asia, including from some polities that had ongoing bilateral disputes, (for example, Iran, Israel and the Palestinian Autonomous Areas, India and Pakistan). The second meeting took place in June 2006. It was attended by 18 member states, while observer status was granted to the UN, the OSCE and the League of Arab States. Discussions focused on issues relating to stability and security in Asia. It was agreed that a CICA Secretariat should be established in Almaty. The Kazakhstani Government undertook to finance the first stage of its operations and the Secretariat began work almost immediately. In addition to the Kazakhstani diplomatic and administrative staff, eight states would be represented on a rotational basis.

Kazakhstan maintained relations with a wide range of other countries and regional structures. A Partnership and Co-operation Agreement was concluded with the European Union in 1995 and came into force in 1999. Good bilateral links were also fostered with Asian states, particularly Malaysia, Singapore, and the Republic of Korea (South Korea). Links with the Arab world were also strengthened. There were a number of reciprocal visits by high-level delegations, which paved the way for agreements on co-operation in trade, investment and joint projects. These included agreements with Egypt, Qatar and Syria. Relations with ex-Soviet states were likewise revived. In June 2006 the Kazakhstani legislature ratified a strategic partnership agreement with Azerbaijan, aimed at improving economic ties, as well as strengthening co-operation in the fight against terrorism, organized crime, drugs-trafficking and corrupt financial practices. Georgia also began to assume a strategic importance for Kazakhstan. In 2006 Kazakhstan was the third largest source of foreign direct investment in Georgia, with investment (from both the private and state sectors) totalling US $152m. in that year. In June 2007 the Kazakhstani Government agreed to construct a grain terminal (at a cost of $10m.) in the Georgian port of Poti on the Black Sea.

OUTLOOK

Kazakhstan's policy of encouraging international contacts, while maintaining a non-aligned stance, proved to be very effective. In 2008 the country continued to be regarded as one of the most stable and prosperous of the CIS states. It maintained diplomatic links with over 100 countries and was a member of numerous international and regional organizations. It had strong economic links with partners in Europe, North America and East Asia, and was also developing relations with countries such as Brazil and India. Its balanced foreign policy contributed to the efficacy of its leading role in the region.

Economy

Dr SHIRIN AKINER

INTRODUCTION

Kazakhstan encompassed approximately 20% of the arable land of the former USSR, although it represented only some 12% of the total territory. The country's extensive natural resources provided the base for a relatively diversified economy. However, years of central planning ensured that the economy developed into one that was highly dependent upon other Soviet republics, notably Russia, for supply lines and markets. With the failure of the Soviet economic system and the advent of full political independence in 1991, Kazakhstan began, cautiously, but with commitment, a programme of reform. The country had significant problems to overcome in the early 1990s, but the long-term prospects seemed secure, particularly with its natural advantages. By the end of the 1990s the main sectors of the economy were agriculture, heavy industry, construction and services. Gross domestic product (GDP) decreased at an annual average rate of 2.2% in 1990–2001. Thereafter this trend was reversed, and in 2001 GDP grew by 13.5%. In 2002–05 annual growth in excess of 9% was recorded. In 2006 Kazakhstan's GDP grew by 10.7% and totalled US $81,003m.; per head GDP amounted to $5,100. GDP increased by 8.9% in 2007, and was expected to increase by some 4.5% in 2008. Kazakhstan's dramatic economic growth during this decade (more than 75% in the previous seven years) was driven by high commodity prices and massive foreign investment, coupled with privatization and other market economic reforms.

ECONOMIC POLICY

Until December 1991 economic planning for Kazakhstan, as for the other Soviet republics, was carried out at Union level, in Moscow, Russia—the Soviet capital. The role of the republican governments was, primarily, to carry out the directives that they received from the centre. Scope for formulating policies within a given republic was extremely limited, because of the highly integrated nature of the Union economy as a whole. Detailed data were collected on a regular basis, but were transmitted to Moscow for full analysis. Several important areas of the economy, such as the military-industrial complex, transport, communications and major industrial plants, came directly under the jurisdiction of the all-Union authorities; the republican administrations had little, if any, knowledge of how they functioned. In Kazakhstan, strategically important facilities such as the nuclear testing site at Semipalatinsk and the Baikonur space centre were run almost exclusively by immigrant Slavs. In effect, they represented extra-territorial exclaves.

Thus, after gaining independence, one of the principal tasks for the Kazakhstani Government was to unravel the mysteries of its own economy. This involved taking direct charge of all sectors of the economy, including Baikonur, Semipalatinsk and other strategic facilities that had not hitherto been accessible to the republican administration. It also had the arduous task of data collection and analysis as, for the first time in history, it began to formulate its own economic policies. President Nursultan Nazarbayev was firmly committed to the process of reform, but mechanisms to implement the proposed changes were often lacking. Moreover, officials charged with the responsibility of implementing such programmes were often too conservative to sympathize with the task or too inexperienced to understand the nature of the transformation. Consequently, progress was slow. Training and technical assistance, particularly in the fields of central banking, taxation and economic and financial management, were provided by the IMF and other international bodies, as well as by some national governments (among them those of India, Japan, Turkey, the United Kingdom and the USA). However, technical capability in all the essential areas of economic planning remained very limited for several years.

The first stage of a privatization programme was launched in 1992, but the initial results were disappointing. The plan was excessively ambitious, and progress was impeded by the lack of basic technical and professional skills, together with public suspicion. Corruption and organized crime complicated the development of private enterprise, and a high level of bankruptcy further discredited the process. Nevertheless, although only 380 enterprises were privatized in 1992, some 6,000 small enterprises were sold to the private sector during the following year. Official support for privatization remained strong, and the second two-year stage of the programme was duly initiated in 1993. It proved to be more successful than the first. Its objective was to transfer the majority of state enterprises and farms to the private sector by one of three methods: privatization of small-scale enterprises by cash auctions; mass privatization of medium-sized and large enterprises by voucher and coupon auctions; and privatization of some 180 major enterprises via tenders on a case-by-case basis, usually to foreign investors. Of the small-scale enterprises offered for sale, about one-half, amounting to over 4,500 enterprises with a combined work-force of over 1m., were sold. These companies belonged mainly to the distribution and catering sectors. By the end of 1995 about 1,000 enterprises, with more than 400,000 employees, had been sold by mass privatization, which involved 169 Investment Privatization Funds. The establishment of an Enterprise Restructuring Agency in 1994 and a Rehabilitation Bank in 1995, together with the adoption of a new bankruptcy law in early 1995, resulted in substantial progress in enterprise restructuring during that year. The privatization of major enterprises attracted several international companies to the mining and metallurgy sector in the mid-1990s. Of particular significance was the acquisition of the giant Karmet steelworks near Karaganda by the international steel group, Ispat, in November 1995. In the same year a large stake in the copper conglomerate Kazakhmys was sold to Samsung (of the Republic of Korea—South Korea).

In January 1996 a new phase of privatization began. A law came into effect that abolished the preferential treatment of workers in the privatization of enterprises, and retained only two privatization methods: direct sales to investors and auctions. The privatization programme for 1996–98 included the auction of remaining state shares and of enterprises scheduled for privatization, but which remained unsold. The principle was that only the natural monopolies (such as energy, transport and water) should remain under state ownership. Kazakhstan became a major target for Western (and Japanese) investment, which by 1998 was the highest per head in the Commonwealth of Independent States (CIS). In that year the Government sold its 14.3% stake in a joint venture, the Offshore Kazakhstan International Operating Company, for US $500m. Other large-scale privatizations included the sale of a 90% stake in the Eastern Kazakhstan Copper and Chemical Plant to Samsung Deutschland GmbH for $6.3m. In total, 3,073 state enterprises were privatized in 1998. However, further privatization of selected major state assets was interrupted, owing to unfavourable market conditions. The programme was resumed in 1999, with stakes being offered in the national telecommunications company, Kazakhtelecom, the

Ust-Kamenogorsk metallurgy plant, and the petroleum producers AktobeMunaiGaz and MangistauMunaiGaz. In 2004 President Nazarbayev announced that some 90% of the Kazakhstani economy was privately owned, contributing about 65% of GDP.

Other economic reforms were also introduced in the early 1990s, often in response to specific situations, rather than as a result of long-term planning. Following the collapse of the USSR, there was serious economic dislocation. Essential industrial supplies were disrupted as republics, voluntarily or otherwise, reneged on contracts with partners within the Union. This prompted a negative series of events, with declining production, shortages, rising prices and, in some cases, unemployment. Agriculture, construction, and transport and communications, which had been vital contributors to GDP prior to Kazakhstan's independence, all suffered from the political and economic disruptions as the country struggled to make the transition to a market economy. In other areas, the indications were more promising. Extensive interest by foreign investors in the petroleum and natural gas sector, as well as an increase in exports of ferrous and non-ferrous metals, caused output in these commodities to increase. Furthermore, after limited success in 1994, the Government's stabilization programme helped to control inflation and make significant progress in enterprise restructuring. However, from 1997 the decline in world prices for Kazakhstan's principal exports led to major economic difficulties. In September 1998 a new Council on Economic Affairs was established by President Nazarbayev, specifically to counter the effects of the global economic crisis. These remedial measures were undermined by the financial crisis in Russia; this led to a contraction of 1.8% in that year.

Throughout the 1990s Kazakhstan maintained its determination to foster traditional links, and in March 1996 signed an agreement with Belarus and Russia, as well as Kyrgyzstan, on a common market and customs union. Closer economic integration within Central Asia was more actively encouraged, and in January 1994 Kazakhstan and Uzbekistan announced their intention to form a common market. Kyrgyzstan subsequently announced its support, and in July an agreement was reached between the three countries to form a trilateral economic and defence union, to be implemented by an Interstate Council (founded in February 1995). In March 1998 Tajikistan announced its intention to join, and in July of that year the four formally constituted themselves as the Central Asian Economic Union, which became known as the Central Asian Co-operation Organization (CACO) in 2001. Kazakhstan also joined a number of other regional organizations aimed at promoting economic co-operation, such as the Economic Co-operation Organization, the Eurasian Economic Community (EURASEC) and the Shanghai Co-operation Organization (SCO). In October 2005 CACO merged with EURASEC (see History).

The Kazakhstani Government had begun to advocate local control of republican economies towards the end of the Soviet period. However, after independence President Nazarbayev was a strong supporter of an integrated economic policy for the CIS. Moreover, the intimate relationship between the Russian and Kazakhstani economies meant that Kazakhstan had limited room for manoeuvre. Thus, when the Russian Government decided to implement price liberalization, Kazakhstan could only follow suit. Accordingly, in January 1992 the prices of all but some basic foodstuffs and essential services were deregulated. Public anger was such that some degree of control had to be reintroduced almost immediately. Salaries and social benefits were increased, and continued to be increased at regular intervals, but they were unable to keep pace with inflation. The most significant areas affected were fuel, staple foods (bread, milk and meat) and transportation costs (public and private). President Nazarbayev suggested a number of proposals for co-ordinating economic decision-making among the member states but remained firmly committed to the 'rouble zone'. The announcement by the Central Bank of Russia, in July 1993, that pre-1993 banknotes would no longer be legal tender was wholly unexpected. The measure was clearly designed to compel countries such as Kazakhstan either to introduce their own currency or to surrender their fiscal independence to Russia. The Kazakhstani Government was reluctant to adopt the former course in haste. However, the threat to stability from the vast stocks of old roubles in existence and the Russian demands, which proved too compromising for an independent state, required, on 15 November, the introduction of Kazakhstan's own currency, the tenge (which had already been printed, for such an eventuality).

The introduction of the tenge increased international optimism that Kazakhstan would be better able to control its economy and, importantly, its fiscal deficit. Despite extremely high inflation during 1992 (consumer prices increased by an annual average of 1,381%—largely caused by the monetary policies of Russia's Central Bank), which continued into the mid-1990s (with an average increase of 1,258% in 1994), the Government remained committed to improving the quality of, and its control over, public finances. A stabilization programme, introduced in January 1994 and assisted by a one-year stand-by arrangement from the IMF, initially foundered. Consequently, the exchange rate of the tenge depreciated by almost 600% in the first half of the year, and by June the monthly rate of inflation had reached 46%. In 1995, however, the annual average rate of increase in consumer prices was reduced to 176.2%, largely owing to a tightening of monetary and credit policies. In the late 1990s the annual rate of inflation slowed dramatically and by 1997 it had declined to 17.4%. This trend was maintained in subsequent years; in 2006 the rate of inflation was 8.6%, although it increased slightly, to 10.8% in 2007. Moreover, unemployment decreased steadily; the registered unemployment rate was 8.2% in 2006, falling to 7.3% in the second quarter of 2007. Meanwhile, wages rose consistently; the monthly average wage in 2006 was US $315 (compared with $248 in 2005). Budget revenues from personal income tax (levied at 10% in 2007) also increased substantially.

After independence, Kazakhstan rapidly accumulated foreign debt. According to the National Bank of Kazakhstan, between 1 January 1994 and 1 April 1998 direct national and state-guaranteed foreign debt increased by 89%, from US $1,765.6m. to $3,328.2m., and non-state-guaranteed foreign debt increased from $1,604.1m. to $4,328.2m.; payments due from Kazakhstani enterprises to foreign partners rose from $208m. to $1,113m. By the end of 1998 Kazakhstan's total external debt was estimated at $7,543m. Debt-servicing costs for that year were estimated at $539.7m. for direct and state-guaranteed foreign debt, and $1,458.6m. for non-government-guaranteed debt. The balance of payments continued to deteriorate; the current account deficit increased to $1,201.3m. Domestic finances were, likewise, in disarray: arrears of wages and salaries were estimated at around $550m. The move of the capital, with effect from late 1997, from Almaty to Akmola (renamed Astana in the following year) had not only been extremely expensive but had also, inevitably, proved disruptive. By mid-June 1998, only a few days after the official inauguration of that new capital, the economy was openly admitted to be in crisis.

There was serious disagreement over the reason for this state of affairs. The Prime Minister, Nurlan Balgymbayev, blamed it on the decline in world prices for Kazakhstan's main exports, and the effects of the economic collapse in South-East Asia in 1997–98, whereas President Nazarbayev attributed it to domestic incompetence and corruption. All were agreed, however, that urgent measures were necessary and an emergency programme was duly implemented. The collapse of the Russian rouble in August 1998 exacerbated the situation. Various measures refining the emergency programme followed. Thus, in mid-September a presidential decree ordered massive job reductions in the National Security Committee and other internal affairs and law-enforcement services. It was hoped that funds could be diverted to augment the customs service and so, hopefully, to increase the revenue flowing into the budget. Then, at the end of the month, there was announced what amounted to, in effect, a renationalization of bankrupt firms, reversing the existing policy of restricting state ownership to the natural monopolies. The recession persisted in 1999, and in April of that year, following a sharp decline in the value of the tenge against the US dollar, the Kazakhstani currency was 'floated' (made fully convertible) on the foreign exchange markets. The Government also under-

took a number of measures to strengthen the economy, such as the further privatization of large enterprises and export promotion. By the end of the decade Kazakhstan's external debt had been significantly reduced, partly owing to high global petroleum prices, and partly to careful macroeconomic policy. In April 2000 Nazarbayev announced that debts owed to the IMF had been repaid seven years ahead of schedule. In 2004 external debt was estimated at US $32,310m., equivalent to 85.1% of gross national income. Thereafter it began to rise again, mainly owing to borrowing by the banking sector; external debt totalled $43,429m. at the end of 2005, and $74,023m. at the end of 2006.

The Government realized the dangers of over-dependence on hydrocarbons and introduced measures to avoid this. In February 2002 Prime Minister Imangali Tasmagambetov emphasized the need to attract more investment in small and medium-sized businesses. He also urged the greater diversification of the economy and more movement of capital. In June 2003 a new Prime Minister, Danial Akhmetov, took office; like his predecessor, he continued to prioritize economic development. Also in 2003 the Strategy for Industrial and Innovation Development was officially launched, with the aim of expanding the non-petroleum sectors, in order to diversify the economy and reduce dependence on the oil sector.

Growth was supported by increased production in the hydrocarbons sector, and further stimulated by high petroleum prices. However, other sectors also recorded significant expansion. Public expenditure expanded and lending by banks rose dramatically. The property-related sector was particularly buoyant; by the end of 2004 it accounted for 18% of bank credit. In 2007 preparations to achieve compliance with World Trade Organization (WTO) requirements were progressing well, notably in legislation and enforcement practices. In mid-2008 Kazakhstan's economic performance suffered from the adverse effects of the sharp contraction of international credit markets. Inflation rose sharply, construction projects (significant in generating Kazakhstan's economic growth) were suspended. Government officials remained optimistic, but inevitably banks were affected by diminishing assets, a decreased number of international lenders and the legacy of over-generous loans made to the previously buoyant real estate sector. In view of such problems, it was expected that economic growth in 2008 would decline sharply, to less than 5%.

BANKING AND FINANCIAL INSTITUTIONS

In January 2001 a National Fund was created. Its aim was to guard against the adverse impact of sudden declines in petroleum prices, and to manage the country's wealth for the benefit of future generations. However, its management attracted criticism. In particular, there were concerns about the circumstances surrounding the creation of the Fund, which had originally been kept secret. Details were only revealed following a series of major political scandals, which implicated senior officials as well as President Nazarbayev's own family. The creation of an Oversight Committee to ensure greater transparency and accountability went some way towards dispelling suspicions of corruption. By the end of 2005 the Fund's assets were estimated at US $8,000m. In an effort to promote good practice, in October 2005 the Kazakhstani Government and several large energy companies joined the Extractive Industries Transparency Initiative (EITI), a voluntary, international scheme launched by British Prime Minister Tony Blair in 2002. More companies joined in 2006; by 2007 a total of 51 companies from the energy sector and 41 from the mining sector had signed up. In order to promote adherence to the principles of EITI, a new mechanism for governing the Fund was introduced, aimed at clarifying the scale and use of oil revenues. In the first quarter of 2007 these stood at $15,900m. (17% of GDP). Previously, the Fund had been kept in dollars, but it was diversified to include 15 other currencies; in 2007 the Fund comprised 48.5% in dollars, 27.9% in euros, 10.1% in pounds sterling and 8.8% in yen. Control of the Fund was 54% under the National Bank of Kazakhstan and 46% under external management.

One of the most notable developments in Kazakhstan in the 1990s was the emergence of a dynamic, highly competitive banking sector. In 2007 there were 34 commercial banks, the largest by far being the Kazkommertsbank (KKB—formed in 1991), BankTuranAlem and Halyk Bank (both created on the basis of privatized Soviet-era banks). Initially, the main emphasis had been on large-scale corporate lending. However, as the number of small and medium-sized businesses increased and personal incomes rose, the local population also began to turn to the banking system, triggering an increase in retail services. The banks expanded rapidly, extending their reach within the country and also abroad, building up foreign links and acquiring foreign strategic partners. In 2006 KKB and Halyk Bank launched highly successful initial public offerings (IPOs) on the London Stock Exchange, United Kingdom. Foreign banks (such as ABN Amro and ING of the Netherlands; Citibank of the USA; HSBC of the United Kingdom; and Credit Suisse of Switzerland) were also active in Kazakhstan and, together with local banks with foreign shareholdings, provided an important link to international capital markets. However, the pace of development was not without its problems. The regulatory framework in the financial sector was strengthened; measures introduced in 2004 included the creation of a Financial Supervision Agency. This was generally regarded as effective, but concerns remained that the system of bank management was being stretched beyond capacity. Another incipient problem was the accumulation of foreign indebtedness, which increased exposure to currency exchange risk and thus could endanger economic stability (the banking sector's external debts stood at US $33,300m. at the end of 2006).

In 2006 the Kazakhstani Government launched three important initiatives aimed at improving the country's competitiveness by promoting efficient corporate governance, transparency and accountability. The first new institution was the Samruk holding company, which was intended to serve as an active shareholder on behalf of the state in companies with a major state shareholding (for example, the national oil and gas company, KazMunaiGas, and the national railway company, Kazakhstan Temir Zholy). The second body was the Kazyna Fund for Sustainable Development; a joint-stock company, it was designed to strengthen industrial and innovative development. Kazyna's priorities were to facilitate the implementation of strategically important projects and to attract investment and management from transnational corporations. The third initiative was the creation of the Regional Financial Centre of Almaty (RFCA). A long-term project, similar in concept to the financial hubs in Singapore and Dubai, United Arab Emirates, it aimed at developing a full range of financial services that met international standards. It would also encourage growth by providing economic incentives and streamlining investment processes.

PETROLEUM AND NATURAL GAS

During the Soviet period the centre of Kazakhstan's petroleum industry was Guriyev (now Atyrau), on the north-eastern shore of the Caspian Sea. Petroleum production initially declined after independence. Crude petroleum output amounted to only 19.3m. metric tons in 1993 (it had been 25.5m. tons in 1988). However, from the mid-1990s Kazakhstan's success in attracting foreign investment in this sector brought about a significant recovery. Major production-sharing agreements and joint ventures were agreed with foreign partners. By mid-2005 accumulated foreign investments in Kazakhstan since independence totalled US $42,000m.; of this, foreign direct investment (FDI) amounted to some $23,200m. Almost one-third of the foreign investment (mainly from the USA, the United Kingdom and the Netherlands) was in oil and natural gas production. Output in this sector grew rapidly. In 2005 Kazakhstan produced 61.4m. metric tons of petroleum, of which 52.6m. tons were exported. According to official forecasts, oil production was expected to rise to 118m. tons in 2010 and 180m. tons in 2015; over the same period natural gas production was expected to rise to 45,000m. cu m. The exploration and development of the country's hydrocarbons wealth resulted in a significant upgrading of its reserves. In 2007 Kazakhstan had proven recoverable oil reserves of 39,800m. barrels (5,300m. tons). This was twice previous estimates;

moreover, with production constantly expanding, it was anticipated that this figure might be tripled over the next decade. Kazakhstan's natural gas reserves were estimated at 1,900,000m. cu m. The number of projects for oil and gas development was constantly increasing; in January 2006 some 224 projects were under contract, with more awaiting signature.

The bulk of Kazakhstan's known hydrocarbons reserves were found in three substantial deposits. First to attract foreign investment was the Tengiz field, located on the northern littoral of the Caspian, which was estimated to hold some 6,000m.–9,000m. barrels of recoverable petroleum. The field had been partially developed in the 1980s, but its full potential had not been realized. In 1990 the US Chevron Corporation (now ChevronTexaco) began negotiations with the Soviet Government, later continued with the Government of independent Kazakhstan, on the development of this field, and in 1993 the TengizChevroil (TCO) joint venture was formed between Chevron and the Kazakhstani authorities to implement the project. Other energy majors later joined the project. In 2005 TCO produced 272,000 barrels per day (b/d) of crude petroleum and 3,400m. cu m of associated gas. It was anticipated that petroleum production could be raised to over 540,000 b/d by 2010.

Karachaganak, a huge petroleum and gas condensate field in north-western Kazakhstan, was the second large joint venture. It accounted for over 40% of the country's total reserves, with estimated reserves of some 1,300,000m. cu m of natural gas and 650m. metric tons of gas condensate. It was discovered in 1979, but not fully developed during the Soviet period. In 1992 British Gas (later the BG Group) and Agip SA (of Italy) were awarded exclusive rights to negotiate a contract for the rehabilitation and development of the field, and in November 1997 BG and Agip, in partnership with Texaco and LUKoil of Russia, concluded a production-sharing agreement for the field. A multinational consortium was formed for the exploration and development of the Karachaganak field, the Karachaganak Integrated Organization—Karachaganak Petroleum Operating BV. In July 2006 Russian President Vladimir Putin and Nazarbayev signed a joint declaration on long-term co-operation in the processing and sale of gas from Karachaganak. It was announced that annual gas production from this field was expected to reach 25,000m. cu m. by 2012.

The third, and largest, deposit was Kashagan. In 1997 a multinational consortium, formed by European, US and Kazakhstani partners, signed an agreement to undertake seismic exploration in the northern Caspian. The Kashagan deposit was discovered in July 2000, some 75 km south of Atyrau. The project operator at that time was the Offshore Kazakhstan International Operating Company (OKIOC), renamed the Agip Kazakhstan North Caspian Operating Company (AgipKCO) in mid-2001; the project was known as the North Caspian Production Sharing Agreement (NCPSA—for further information see the essay by the same author on energy in the Caspian Sea region in Part One—General Survey).

Initially, the development of the hydrocarbons reserves of the Caspian Sea was complicated by the lack of an internationally recognized legal regime. During the Soviet period its status was covered by two treaties between the USSR and Iran, which effectively treated it as a trans-boundary lake. After the dissolution of the USSR, Russia and Iran wanted to keep this arrangement in force, or to replace it with a similar one in which all resources of the Caspian would be held in common. The three new successor states, Kazakhstan, Azerbaijan and Turkmenistan, wanted the Sea divided. In July 1998 Kazakhstan and Russia signed a pioneering bilateral agreement on the demarcation of their respective zones of the seabed. In May 2002 the leaders of the two countries signed a supplementary protocol setting out the geographic co-ordinates of the modified median line; this was further amended in 2006. A trilateral agreement was signed between Azerbaijan, Kazakhstan and Russia in May 2003. By 2007 considerable progress had been made in multilateral negotiations between the five littoral states. Over 80% of outstanding points of disagreement had been resolved, thus raising hopes that consensus agreement on a legal regime might be achieved, leading to a comprehensive demarcation of the Sea. (For further information see the essay by the same author on energy in the Caspian Sea region in Part One—General Survey.)

By the late 1990s foreign petroleum companies were becoming concerned by the growing propensity of the Kazakhstani Government to reinterpret contracts in such a way as to extract more revenue. In 2001 this resulted in a serious contractual dispute with TCO, and in November 2002 TCO decided not to implement the next phase of development until this matter had been resolved satisfactorily. In the mean time, Kazakhstan imposed a fine of US $70m. on TCO, for alleged damage to the environment, supposedly caused by the way in which it was storing more than 6m. metric tons of sulphur extracted from the petroleum. In January 2003 an uneasy settlement was reached, and TCO announced that it would proceed with the project as planned. A major expansion, worth an estimated $3,000m., was initiated. By the first half of 2005 the consortium (comprising ChevronTexaco with 50%, ExxonMobil of the USA and France with 25%, the Kazakhstani state oil and gas company KazMunaiGaz with 20% and the US-Russian joint venture LUKArco with 5%) was producing some 21% of Kazakhstan's crude petroleum and condensate output.

Other hydrocarbons joint ventures also experienced problems in their relationship with the Kazakhstani Government. In the Karachaganak oil- and gas-field, the consortium led by BG and ENI (which incorporated Agip in 1998) came close to suspending production in 2001, owing to the proposed imposition of 'double taxation' on exports of gas condensates from Kazakhstan to Russia. Eventually the issue was settled and production resumed; by mid-2005 Karachaganak was producing some 18% of Kazakhstani petroleum and condensate output. The NCPSA likewise encountered difficulties. In 2003 the consortium was informed that its exemption on paying value-added tax had been revoked; in addition, the ruling was backdated to 1999. The consortium regarded this as a violation of the terms of the production-sharing agreement signed in 1997. Further problems arose when the consortium sought to postpone production, which had originally been due to commence in 2005. There were complex technical issues to be addressed in the north Caspian. Apart from difficult environmental conditions (the shallow water is covered with ice for at least three months of the year), the Kashagan reservoir is highly fractured, with deep wells and high pressure. Moreover, it contains highly poisonous hydrogen sulphide and large quantities of sulphur, thus exceptional safety standards need to be applied. Consequently, the development plan had to be adjusted and the drilling programme re-planned. In February 2004, after lengthy negotiations, it was finally agreed that commercial petroleum extraction would probably begin in 2008; this was later revised to 2009. The fine imposed for this delay was some US $150m. In April 2005 the BG Group, one of the consortium partners, sold its 16.7% interest in the NCPSA. KazMunaiGaz bought one-half of the BG Group's stake; the remainder was sold to other project partners. As a result, ENI (the operator of the project), Total, ExxonMobil and the British-Dutch company Royal Dutch/Shell each acquired 18.5% of the shareholding, ConocoPhillips of the USA held 9.3%, and Inpex of Japan and KazMunaiGaz each held a 8.3% stake. In mid-2007 it was announced that production was expected to commence in late 2010. The Kazakhstani Government, already highly critical of the management of the project, decided to suspend operations at Kashagan and warned that a new operator might be appointed. Protracted negotiations with ENI followed. There was a partial settlement of outstanding issues in January 2008, including a significant increase in the shareholding of KazMunaiGaz. However, in June it was announced that production would be delayed until 2013. The Kazakhstani authorities subsequently demanded a number of changes to the structure and management of the project, and an amended deal was expected to be incorporated into a new production-sharing agreement (PSA), although by October 2008 it had not yet been confirmed. Meanwhile, in May 2008 it was announced that an oil export duty of $109.9 per metric ton would be imposed on all domestic producers. Official sources made it clear, however, that foreign companies would eventually be liable to this tax. Moreover, in September it was reported that duty was to increase almost two-fold in October.

In July the Karachaganak project had become the first to be required to pay the tax, albeit unwillingly. (For further information see the essay by the same author on energy in the Caspian Sea region in Part One—General Survey.)

Another problem for investors in Kazakhstan was the high level of corruption. International surveys of perceived corruption regularly ranked the country as markedly more corrupt than almost all the other CIS countries. In March 2003 the issue of bribery and corruption was emphasized when, following an extensive investigation, James H. Giffen, a close associate of President Nazarbayev, was arraigned in New York, USA, charged with violating the US Foreign Corrupt Practices Act (which prohibits US companies or individuals from using financial inducements to secure an agreement). He was accused of channelling illegal payments, worth more than US $78m., to the Swiss bank accounts of two senior Kazakhstani officials. The transactions were allegedly connected with the granting of contracts to US petroleum companies. One of the deals under investigation was the acquisition by Mobil (now ExxonMobil) of a stake in the Tengiz oilfield in 1996. Giffen's trial was repeatedly delayed and continued in 2008.

Despite such problems, the oil and gas wealth of Kazakhstan continued to attract investors. In July 2005 KazMunaiTeniz (a subsidiary of KazMunaiGaz) and the state-owned Russian petroleum companies Rosneft and Zarubezhneft signed a production-sharing agreement worth some US $23,000m. for the development of the Kurmangazy oilfield, located offshore on the border of the Russian and Kazakhstani sectors of the Caspian Sea. Output was expected to reach 600,000 b/d by the end of the decade. India's Oil and Natural Gas Corporation and an affiliate of the China National Petroleum Company (CNPC—of the People's Republic of China) made competing bids to buy Canadian-listed PetroKazakhstan, the third largest oil producer in Kazakhstan (the holdings of which included 12 oilfields, exploration licences in six areas and the Chimkent refinery). In October it was confirmed that the Chinese company's offer of $4,180m. had been accepted; shortly afterwards CNPC agreed to sell some of its shares to KazMunaiGaz. Accordingly, in July 2006 CNPC sold a 33% stake in PetroKazakhstan to KazMunaiGaz (reportedly at a cost of $55 per share); as part of this deal, the Kazakhstani state oil and gas company gained equal rights in the management of the Chimkent refinery. Also in July, KazMunaiGaz acquired a 50% stake in KazGerMunai (a Kazakh-German energy joint venture); the other 50% share was held by PetroKazakhstan. This series of transactions gave the Kazakhstani Government greater control over domestic oil supplies, but also increased China's hydrocarbons holdings in Kazakhstan. In 2008 LUKoil announced plans to exercise its pre-emptive right to acquire full control of the Kazakhstani company Turgai Petroleum, in which it already had a 50% stake. The remaining shares were owned by PetroKazakhstan, largely owned by the CNPC. The Kazakhstani authorities indicated that they would not oppose the deal. Turgai Petroleum, which in 2007 produced 3.5m. metric tons of petroleum, was valued at $1,700m. One of its main assets was the Kumkol field, containing some 177m. barrels of proven oil reserves. However, it seemed possible that LUKoil's bid for Turgai Petroleum was a tactical move to persuade CNPC to give LUKoil a stake in assets in third countries; in exchange it would abandon its pre-emptive right to purchase a 50% stake in Turgai Petroleum. It was anticipated that the matter would be resolved before the end of 2008.

PIPELINES AND REFINERIES

In the 1990s one of the main obstacles to the export of Kazakhstani petroleum was the limited nature of the routes to world markets. Consequently, the construction of new pipelines became a priority. The Caspian Pipeline Consortium (CPC) was formed in 1993 by the Governments of Kazakhstan and Oman; it was subsequently joined by the Governments of Azerbaijan and Russia, and a number of Western companies. The objective was the construction of a 1,568-km pipeline linking the Tengiz field with the Russian Black Sea port of Novorossiisk (in Krasnodar Krai), in order to enable exports to reach the European market. After numerous legal and technical difficulties the project finally got under way in the late 1990s, and petroleum began to flow through the pipeline in September 2001 (although it was not formally inaugurated until November). It had an initial capacity of some 560,000 b/d; this was to be upgraded in stages to 1.35m. b/d. The Atyrau–Samara pipeline, which connected to the Russian pipeline network, was also upgraded to carry 310,000 b/d. In 2002 construction of the 448-km Kenkiyak–Atyrau pipeline, linking the oilfields of western Kazakhstan with the Atyrau–Samara export pipeline to the north, was completed. A Kazakhstani company, MunaiTas (owned by KazMunaiGaz), held a 51% stake in the venture, and the remainder was held by a subsidiary of the CNPC. In July 2004 the European Bank for Reconstruction and Development (EBRD) announced that it had issued a loan of US \$81.6m. to refinance the debt incurred during construction. The Kenkiyak–Atyrau pipeline was part of an ambitious, multi-phased project that would eventually link western Kazakhstan with China. In May 2004, during a visit to the Chinese capital, Beijing, President Nazarbayev signed an interstate agreement with his Chinese counterpart on the construction of the cross-border stretch of the pipeline, to run from Atasu to Alashankou (a distance of some 1,300 km). This project complemented the Chinese acquisition of PetroKazakhstan (see above). The Atasu–Alashankou pipeline was completed in December 2005, and commercial operations commenced in mid-2006. The pipeline had an initial capacity of some 200,000 b/d, eventually to be increased to 400,000 b/d. In August 2007, during a visit by the Chinese President, Hu Jintao, to Kazakhstan, the CNPC signed an agreement with KazMunaiGaz for the inauguration of the second phase of the project, the extension of the Atasu–Alashankou pipeline 700 km westward to the Caspian Sea; when completed, this would increase capacity to 20m. metric tons of crude oil per year. Construction work on this project was under way in 2008.

In 2006 more than 65m. tons of crude petroleum and gas condensate were extracted in Kazakhstan, of which some 57m. tons were exported (over 4% higher than in 2005). A total of 24.4m. tons was carried by the CPC, 15.6m. tons by the Atyrau–Samara pipeline, 2.2m. tons by the Atasu–Alashankou pipeline and 9.6m. tons shipped through Aktau port; the remainder was transported by railway. It was anticipated that by 2015 the country would be producing 130m. tons annually, thus requiring additional export facilities. In 2007 feasibility studies were under way to determine the most commercially viable routes.

As with the petroleum sector, gas production was hindered by the poor pipeline infrastructure. Existing gas pipelines, like petroleum pipelines, all traversed Russia. The gas from Karachaganak was transported to the Orenburg processing plant in Russia, from where it was exported via the Russian pipeline system. In June 2002 a 10-year agreement was signed by the Kazakhstani and Russian Presidents to stimulate co-operation in the gas sector. The agreement included the creation of a joint venture, KazRosGaz, to transport Kazakhstani gas to Europe. In 2005 KazMunaiGaz and the Russian state-controlled Gazprom disclosed plans to create a joint venture to modernize the Orenburg processing plant in order to increase capacity. A formal agreement to this effect was signed in June 2007, to cover a 15-year period. Related agreements between Kaz-MunaiGaz and gas suppliers at the Karachaganak gasfield were also concluded. The Kazakhstani side undertook to provide some 5,000m. cu m of gas annually to the Orenburg plant. In May 2007, at a summit meeting of the leaders of Kazakhstan, Russia and Turkmenistan, it was announced that a draft agreement had been reached on the construction of a tripartite Caspian gas pipeline to link into the existing Central Asia–Central line of the Soviet era. Also in 2007, plans to construct a gas pipeline from western Kazakhstan to China were announced. Construction work commenced in mid-2008, and it was anticipated that it might be completed in 2010. (For further information see the essay by the same author on energy in the Caspian Sea region in Part One—General Survey.)

Post-independence, Kazakhstan had three main petroleum refineries: at Pavlodar in the east, Chimkent in the south and Atyrau on the Caspian. The Pavlodar plant received crude petroleum from western Siberian (Russian) oilfields, whereas the other two operated on domestic crude. After the collapse of the USSR, however, all three refineries were underused and the Kazakhstani Government sought investment for the renovation of the plants. In 2001 the Marubeni company of Japan embarked on the refurbishment of the Atyrau plant. The centre of the Kazakhstani petroleum industry, the small town of Atyrau, was experiencing rapid growth, as numerous foreign businessmen and technical personnel moved in to the region. In August 2002 the EBRD provided financing for the upgrading of the local airport to international standards. The Chimkent refinery was also scheduled for modernization.

AGRICULTURE

Kazakhstan is an important producer and exporter of agricultural products. During the Soviet era agriculture was the second largest sector of the economy. At the time of independence it accounted for over one-third of GDP. During the 1990s, however, agricultural production declined sharply. This was partly owing to political disruption, and the uncertainties that ensued but, more significantly, the result of the short-term consequences of economic reform. This could be attributed to shortages of inputs (for example, of fuel, feed and fertilizers), machinery and expertise, but also to adverse weather conditions. There was an urgent need for investment in new technologies, and in storage and transport facilities. The GDP of the agricultural sector decreased, in real terms, by an average of 4.2% per year in 1990–2003. However, in 1999 agricultural production recorded an increase for the first time since independence (of 27.3%) and further increases were recorded in the 2000s. Agriculture (including fisheries and forestry) provided employment for some 33.5% of the population in 2004, and accounted for around 5.8% of GDP in 2007.

The decline in production had some incidental benefits—in particular, the reduced demand for irrigation water from the Syr Dar'ya assisted the planned recovery of the northern part of the Aral Sea. The Sea, owing to the overuse of its feeder rivers in the last decades of Soviet power, had shrunk to about one-half of its original surface area, with a concurrent decline of some 20 m (66 ft) in its water level. However, the improvement in environmental conditions there was relative, and certainly far from sufficient to restore the Sea's once flourishing fisheries. With assistance from the World Bank, some restocking with fish had begun by the late 1990s. International financial institutions also financed projects to improve water management. In 2000 the Asian Development Bank (ADB) provided US \$40m. for irrigation and land improvement, and the World Bank also provided credits for irrigation and drainage projects and the building of a dam. By 2006, well ahead of schedule, the waters of the Aral Sea had been increased by millions of cubic metres. It was hoped that, at a later stage, a second dam would be created and that eventually it might be possible to use the Sea for the generation of hydroelectric power.

Grain production remained of crucial importance to the Kazakhstani economy. In the early 1990s approximately one-half of the land under cultivation was devoted to wheat, almost entirely under state supervision. This was a legacy of the Soviet 'Virgin Lands' scheme of the 1950s and early 1960s, whereby vast tracts of northern Kazakhstan were cultivated. After independence the total area under crop cultivation diminished. In 1999 15.2m. ha were sown (a reduction from 18.6m. ha in 1998); of this area, 11.3m. ha were under grain (compared with 16.0m. ha in 1998). By 2003 this had increased to 13.7m. ha. The main grain is wheat, particularly high quality durum (hard) wheat. Barley, millet and, in the south, rice are also cultivated. Marginal climatic conditions are largely responsible for fluctuations in the size of the harvest. Thus in 1998, for example, the wheat harvest fell to a disastrous low of 4.7m. metric tons; in 1999 the yield was much increased, at some 11.2m. tons, almost equal to that of the early 1990s. There were further reverses when, in 1999–2000, the country suffered a devastating infestation of locusts. This was largely occasioned by the failure of the Ministry of Agriculture to undertake pesticide spraying at the appropriate time. More than 4m. ha of arable land were damaged, causing a serious shortfall in the harvest. However, by 2002 production levels were again in line with average annual yields. Grain exports ranked among the country's leading export commodities and were a major source of convertible currency. The formation of a national grain market and the development of rail and port facilities helped to attract foreign investment in this sector. In 2006 Kazakhstan was the world's sixth largest grain producer; it aimed to occupy fifth place. Russia was the main destination for Kazakhstani grain, but Iran was a market of growing importance. Other customers included Belarus, Azerbaijan and Uzbekistan. To stimulate grain exports, in 2006 Kazakhstan announced plans to invest US $10m. in the construction of a grain terminal in Georgia's Black Sea port of Poti. In 2007 Kazakhstan's net grain harvest was 20.1m. tons of grain, a significant increase compared with 2006; the wheat yield was 16.6m. tons. Grain exports totalled 8m. tons in 2007; the eventual aim was to increase export volumes to 9m. tons. However, international food shortages had a secondary impact on Kazakhstan, triggering rising prices and deficits. Consequently, between April and the beginning of September 2008 the Kazakhstani authorities introduced a ban on wheat exports (excluding flour) to safeguard domestic supplies. However, Kyrgyzstan was exempted: the agreement to supply 50,000 metric tons of Kazakh grain was to be honoured.

Sugar beet, cotton and tobacco production were less significant, in terms of volume, than grain, but after the dissolution of the USSR they acquired a new significance and value. Foreign investors showed a particular interest in the tobacco industry. In 1993 Philip Morris, the US-based multinational, announced proposals for a joint venture for the production of cigarettes in Kazakhstan and a manufacturing plant was opened in May 2000. Cotton also received more attention. In southern Kazakhstan, the only region suitable for cotton production, fields were steadily enlarged from 1995 onwards. By 2004 220,000 ha were under cultivation. However, fertility declined, as a result of poor farming practices (lack of crop rotation, poor irrigation, etc.). Problems were compounded by locust infestations. In 2008 hail and other adverse weather conditions further exacerbated the situation. The state urged the introduction of remedial measures, but these were too expensive for small individual farmers, who began to form local unions in order to spread both costs and risk.

Cattle are raised mainly in the north and north-east of the country, sheep and camels in the south, and horses in the east. This sector is mainly orientated towards meat production. There is, however, significant output of milk and dairy products, including dried milk, butter and cheese. Wool (including the valuable astrakhan), camel hair and hides are, likewise, produced in large quantities. Animal husbandry was of major importance during the Soviet period. However, the relative importance of this sector declined after independence. As with grain production, from the early 1990s there was a massive decline in output, with livestock numbers falling to levels comparable with those of the period of collectivization in the early 1930s. Despite a partial recovery, by 2000 livestock breeding had not regained the importance that it had held prior to independence. In the 1990s attempts to restructure the agricultural sector were initiated, including the privatization of the national stock of cattle, horses and poultry. The ADB and the World Bank provided assistance through Farm Restructuring and Development and Agricultural Sector Development.

COAL AND METALS

Kazakhstan possesses large deposits of coal (it accounted for some 19% of Soviet coal production), petroleum and natural gas, and minerals such as chrome (some 90% of total Soviet reserves were located in Kazakhstan), copper, gold, lead, wolfram (tungsten) and zinc.

Most of the industrial base of the country is connected with the extraction and processing of these mineral resources. Industry (excluding construction) accounted for over one-third of GDP in the late 1980s. About one-fifth of the total work-force were employed in industry at that time. Post-independence, the basic infrastructure of industry remained sound, but equipment was generally old, inefficient and environmentally harmful, and there was a high degree of wastage, except in those enterprises that benefited from foreign investment. Overall, industrial production (including petroleum and gas and other, non-mining sectors) declined, in real terms, at an average annual rate of 3.5% in 1990–2003. Thereafter the trend was positive. In 2007 industry accounted for an estimated 38.8% of GDP; some 30% of the labour force was employed in this sector in 2005.

The Karaganda region is the main centre of the coal industry (in 2000 it had 13 mines producing high-quality coking coal); further north, Ekibastuz (the third largest coal basin in the former USSR), is also well developed, as are Turgai and Maikuben. In the Soviet era the republic produced far more coal than was needed for domestic consumption and had long been an exporter, mainly to the Volga region of Russia. Total coal production (hard coal and brown coal) declined from a peak of 143m. metric tons in 1988 to 86.9m. tons in 2004; this decrease in production was mainly the result of reduced demand and excess stocks. Poor safety standards were also a problem (some 30 people died in mining accidents in 2004). Although coal attracted less foreign interest than other energy sectors, there was some investment from Russian companies. Moreover, in 2004 the largest producer in Kazakhstan, accounting for some 35% of coal output, was a subsidiary of US Access Industries Incorporated. By 2006 coal production had risen again slightly, to 96.2m. tons. Russia is the main market for Kazakhstani coal, which is transported by rail from Pavlodar to western Siberia and the Urals (where there are plants designed to use such supplies).

Kazakhstan has world-class deposits of a wide range of metal ores, including the fourth largest reserves of manganese ore in the world (600m. tons), the third largest reserves of chromite ore and the eighth largest of iron ore (estimated at 16,600m. tons, 8% of global reserves). During the Soviet period this provided the basis for a highly developed ferrous and non-ferrous metallurgy sector. Important copper, zinc and lead works were located in the north-east of the country; the mining and processing of iron was based in the north, especially in the Kustanai and Karaganda regions. In 1992 a metal exchange was established in Kazakhstan. However, metals post-independence initially received less attention than hydrocarbons sector. This began to change in the late mid-1990s, when the Government encouraged the privatization of the metallurgy sector. In January 1996 Kazakhstan adopted new legislation on subsoil use, which addressed many of the concerns of foreign investors in the mineral sector. Substantial investments in new technology were made in 1995–97; there was also radical restructuring of management and production, resulting in a significant growth in output (in 1997 this amounted to 24% in the non-ferrous sector and 15% in the ferrous sector). By 1999 joint ventures involving the Government and strategic investors had been established in all the main metals enterprises. Production had increased for most metals, particularly for chromite, ferroalloys, manganese ore, pig-iron and refined lead. A signal success was the turnaround of the Karmet steel works, which in the mid-1990s appeared to be in terminal decline. In 1995 it was acquired by Ispat (part of the Mittal Steel group); by 2004, after significant investment, it was a thriving concern, producing 5.2m. metric tons of steel, with the prospect that this would eventually rise to 6m. tons or more. In 2006 one of the main producers of ferrous metallurgy in Kazakhstan was Mittal Steel. However, most of the metal production was destined for export, since domestic demand was still low, being restricted mainly to the construction industry and machine-building sector.

One of the first areas of interest for foreign mining groups was Kazakhstan's gold deposits, although by global standards these were small (total reserves estimated at about 800 metric tons). In 1993 the Bakyrchik mine (located in east Kazakhstan, and with estimated reserves of 350–400 tons) became the first gold-mining enterprise in the CIS to be wholly foreign-owned, and quoted on the London Stock Exchange; subsequently, however, there were production difficulties and changes in ownership, particularly in 1995–97. In April 1995 Placer Dome (based in Canada) announced plans to develop the Vasilkovskoye gold property, the largest field in Kazakhstan (located in north Kazakhstan, proven reserves of 370 tons, average grade at 2.8 grams per ton); it had been under development since

1979, but only 10% of the deposit had been extracted. However, the project became subject to various legal disputes and within six months the Canadian company had withdrawn from the venture. This prompted caution among foreign investors, leading to a degree of stagnation. By 2003 around 100 gold-mining licences had been awarded, but only about 35 companies were actively involved in development. Total production was around 10 tons per years.

Kazakhstan's copper reserves, ranked fourth in global terms, were a fundamental part of the Kazakhstani Government's large-scale privatization programme. In 1995 South Korean Samsung invested US $250m. into the huge Kazakh-mys plant, in return for a 42% stake in the company; the Kazakhstani Government retained 38% of the shares. By the end of the decade Kazakhmys had become one of the world's top 10 copper producers. In 2004 profits were $441.3m. on a turnover of $1,300m. At this stage Samsung withdrew from the company, selling its shares to the three Kazakhmys managers. In October 2005 it was listed on the London Stock Exchange. In 2006 Kazakhmys announced plans to invest up to $650m. in a new copper mine with total production capacity of around 160,000 metric tons.

Another important resource for Kazakhstan was its large reserves of uranium (1,610,000 metric tons, almost 20% of known global uranium reserves). However, in the 1990s uranium production was not a priority. In the following decade this changed and the industry acquired a new importance. In 2005 Kazakhstan was the world's fourth largest uranium producer, with an output of 4,300 tons (a 30% increase from 2004). In 2006 output had risen to 5,279 tons, pushing Kazakhstan into third place, behind Australia and Canada. The target for 2010 was 18,200 tons, which would make Kazakhstan the world's largest producer. In February 2007 Kazakhstan completed procedures for the ratification of an additional protocol with the International Atomic Energy Agency (IAEA), to report on activities such as the extraction of natural uranium that had not been included in previous agreements. However, Kazakhstani officials stressed that the country did not intend to create its own uranium enrichment facilities.

As part of its development strategy, KazAtomProm, Kazakhstan's national atomic company, created joint ventures with foreign partners. In 2004 a Russian company undertook to invest US $14.5m. in the construction of a uranium mine in southern Kazakhstan. Three other uranium projects were launched in 2006 with Russian partners, two to be sited in Kazakhstan (to produce fuel for Russian-designed nuclear reactors and to build a nuclear power plant) and one in Russia, at the International Uranium Centre in Siberia. The cost of the three projects was to be shared equally between the partners. The head of KazAtomProm emphasized that Kazakhstan did not seek to compete with Russia (which possessed huge uranium deposits of its own) in the nuclear field, but to work in different markets. China, meanwhile, evinced a growing interest in Kazakhstan's uranium reserves and nuclear technology. In 2005 an agreement was signed with a Chinese company to market processed uranium from Kazakhstan. In 2007 KazAtomProm and China Guangdong Nuclear Power Holding concluded a framework agreement aimed at strengthening co-operation in the production of nuclear fuel for Chinese power plants and at improving the resource base of China's developing nuclear power sector. Japan, a major importer of uranium (some 8,000 metric tons per year), had also identified Kazakhstan as an important partner in this field. In January 2006 KazAtomProm established a joint venture with two Japanese firms, the Sumitomo Corporation and the Kansai Electric Power Corporation. The project, known as Appak LLP, would extract uranium from the Mynkuduk mine, process it into pellets for use in nuclear energy plants at the Ulba Metallurgical Plant in eastern Kazakhstan, and market it in Japan and elsewhere; full commercial production (of some 1,000 tons of uranium per year) was scheduled for 2010. In January 2008 the expected date for the project to commence was brought forward to 2009. Nuclear Fuel Industries Ltd (based in Tokyo, Japan) was to process Kazakh uranium pellets and powder for use at stations run by Kansai Electric Power Co. The companies were to allocate up to 80,000m. yen to the project and, overall, investment in expanding uranium pro-

duction could reach several hundred billion yen. Expected profits over the 22-year lifetime of the enterprise were expected to amount to $830m. Projects such as these had the potential to increase Kazakhstan's share of Japanese uranium imports from around 1% to 30% or more. In April 2007 several agreements were signed between the two countries to increase co-operation in the production of civil nuclear energy, including the training of specialists in building light-water reactors.

Other metals being developed for export include molybdenum (used as an alloy in steel-making), of which Kazakhstan possesses the world's sixth largest proven reserves. In 2006 Kazakhstan opened its first molybdenum enrichment factory as part of the huge Stepnogorsk mining complex (in Northern Kazakhstan). The new venture, under the management of KazAtomProm, was expected to process 500,000 metric tons of molybdenum-containing ore annually. Initially, the factory's entire output would be for export. Titanium was another strategic resource that Kazakhstan was seeking to market. In February 2008 an agreement was concluded with French metals firm Eramet, whereby Kazakhstan was to supply titanium to the European Aeronautic Defence and Space Company (EADS) and its Airbus subsidiary, at a cost of €850m. over a period of 12 years. EADS also signed a memorandum of understanding with the Kazyna Sustainable Development Fund for a strategic partnership to develop Kazakhstan's aerospace industry and related services.

OTHER SECTORS

The construction industry, which had been a strong contributor to economic activity under the Soviet system, experienced an initial decline following the final collapse of the USSR. Construction had particularly benefited from investment associated with transfers from the all-Union Government. There was an added problem in the early months of independence, when the State Committee (later the Ministry) of the Economy did not assume responsibility for investment from the all-Union authorities (defunct since December 1991) until August 1992. Construction contributed 10.2% of GDP in 2007. Employment in the sector declined after independence, accounting for only 5.3% of the total by 2004. Construction activity tended to be concentrated in small, high-value projects, usually associated with the extractive industries. However, in the late 1990s the Government began to encourage investment, with infrastructure projects for pipelines and communications with countries apart from Russia, and with the building of the new capital, Astana.

The economic decline in the 1990s resulted in a serious deterioration of the country's transport infrastructure. Previously, there had been a well-developed transport system in Kazakhstan, which was important considering the sheer size of the country. However, it was orientated to Russia and often dependent on it and other former Soviet territories for spare parts. Thus, the railway system (the most important of the transport networks), apart from needing substantial basic investment and modernization, required spare parts, equipment and rolling stock from Russia and Ukraine. Likewise, the lorry fleet (numbering some 400,000 in 1992, but little more than 260,000 in 2003), upon which road transport was reliant, was affected by the rising cost and shortages of fuel, and the need for spare parts from Russia and Belarus. By the end of the decade, however, the situation was beginning to improve. The country participated in the September 1998 treaty designed to reactivate the ancient 'Silk Road', involving countries from Mongolia to the European Black Sea, and benefited from the associated European Union (EU) funds for the Transport Corridor Europe–Caucasus–Asia (TRACECA) project. Kazakhstan's existing facilities, notably its air links with Russia and Europe and with the other, southern Central Asian countries, helped make Almaty a hub for the Central Asian region.

In 2006 Kazakhstan adopted a long-term programme (up to 2015) for the development of the transport system. It envisaged the construction of 1,600 km of new railway lines and the electrification of existing lines, the repair of roads, and expansion of air and water transportation. A budget of US $30,000m. was allocated for the implementation of this project. The ADB and the EBRD agreed to finance the construction of motor roads in the Almaty region, and also to invest in a transport corridor between western China and Western Europe. In 2008 Kazakhstan's national railway company, Temir Zholy National Company, announced extensive plans to upgrade the country's railway network. A fibre-optic network was to be constructed, together with the main cargo routes. In all, the network was to span 4,700 km (2,920 miles). Construction was to be financed by a $105m. loan; of this, a 10-year loan for $55m. would come from the EBRD and a $50m. loan from commercial banks. It was anticipated that the network would be in operation by early 2010. An ambitious project for the future was proposed by President Nazarbayev in 2007, when he urged the construction of a 700-km canal between the Caspian and Black Seas, which would bypass along the Volga–Don Canal (1,700 km) and give the Central Asian states more rapid access to world markets.

The services sector, although less state-dominated, remained largely dependent on government expenditure. In 1992 it was estimated that services (mainly education and health) accounted for 26.5% of total employment. In 1994, excluding trade and catering (which involves procurement and material supply), services provided only 19.2% of GDP. Services, however, increased in importance during the course of the 1990s. Private retail outlets increased in number, and the services sector provided 48.2% of employment by 2002. This trend was maintained in the following years (with services accounting for 49.1% of employment in 2006, and 55.4% of GDP in 2007).

Other sectors continued to be revived and developed. One example of this was the maker of paper and packaging products, Kazakhstan Kagazy, which in July 2007 launched an IPO worth US $350m., with an anticipated value of $650m.–$750m. Another example was the military-industrial sector. In May 2008 Minister of Defence Danial Akhmetov confirmed Kazakhstan's aim to become a regional and international exporter of artillery systems. He emphasized the importance of a recent agreement with Israel, which stipulated 'as the main condition for purchasing new samples of military hardware' the requirement that all technical documentation be transferred to Kazakhstan. This included the new Israeli Nayza missile system, for which, as agreed, the necessary technical specifications had already been supplied to the Petropavlovsk heavy engineering plant in North Kazakhstan. The Nayza system had a range of 95 miles and could be used with different shells or missiles, making it highly marketable. Kazakhstan was also developing two new artillery systems, Aybat and Semser.

In the 1990s Kazakhstan's foreign trade declined, but showed strong recovery from 2000 onwards. In 2007 its main export commodities were mineral products (69.7%), and base metals (17.1%). The country's principal trading partners in that year were Russia, China, Germany, Italy and France. Russia's position as Kazakhstan's principal trading partner was underpinned by a multiplicity of political, commercial and institutional ties. Kazakhstan was also expanding economic links with the neighbouring Central Asian states, as well as with other ex-Soviet republics, particularly Georgia, where in 2006 Kazakhstan was the third largest foreign direct investor. Multilateral co-operation was strengthened by EURASEC, launched in 2001, of which Kazakhstan and Russia were both members (along with Belarus, Kyrgyzstan and Tajikistan, with Ukraine and Moldova as observers since 2002). Another important regional structure was the SCO. This too was formally established in 2001; membership comprised China, Kazakhstan, Kyrgyzstan, Russia, Tajikistan and Uzbekistan, with Mongolia, India, Iran and Pakistan as observers. One of the priorities for the SCO was to increase intra-regional economic co-operation; projects to improve transport and communications were aimed at achieving this goal. According to official data, trade between SCO member states in 2006 amounted to $50,000m. At the SCO summit meeting held in Shanghai, China, in June of that year Russia's President Putin proposed the formation of an SCO energy club, similar to the Organization of the Petroleum Exporting Countries (OPEC); the initial reaction was positive and steps to study the practicalities of the project were initiated. This proposal was discussed further at the SCO summit in Bishkek, Kyrgyzstan, in August 2007.

PROSPECTS

The decline in economic performance brought about by the disintegration of Soviet infrastructure and inter-republican trade had been overcome by the late 1990s. Kazakhstan's rich resource base, its sound record on structural reform and its clear commitment to safeguarding macroeconomic stability provided the impetus for dynamic economic growth. The country succeeded in attracting by far the largest share of FDI of any of the Central Asian states. In 2006 it attracted US $6,000m. The economy remained heavily dependent on the hydrocarbons sector, but government support for diversification was helping to encourage growth in other sectors, such as agriculture and metals. Foreign trade, particularly the export of strategic commodities, was increasing. Preparations for Kazakhstan's entry into the WTO were proceeding smoothly; by mid-2008 bilateral negotiations had been concluded with 20 member states of the Organization. The investment environment was more challenging than in the 1990s, and there were continuing problems in areas such as enterprise-restructuring. Nevertheless, international financial institutions were generally satisfied by the progress of reforms. Business confidence remained high, new markets and strategic partnerships were being developed and in 2008, despite some problems linked to the sharp contraction in credit markets, the international assessment of Kazakhstan's economic prospects remained positive.

Statistical Survey

Source (unless otherwise stated): Statistical Agency of the Republic of Kazakhstan, 050009 Almaty, Abai 125; tel. (727) 261-13-23; fax (7272) 242-08-24; e-mail stat@mail.online.kz; internet www.stat.kz.

Area and Population

AREA, POPULATION AND DENSITY

Area (sq km)	2,724,900*
Population (census results)	
12 January 1989†	16,464,464
25 February–4 March 1999	
Males	7,201,785
Females	7,751,341
Total	14,953,126
Population (official estimates at 1 January)	
2006	15,219,291
2007	15,396,878
2008	15,565,647
Density (per sq km) at 1 January 2008	5.7

* 1,049,150 sq miles.
† Figure refers to the *de jure* population. The *de facto* total was 16,536,511.

PRINCIPAL ETHNIC GROUPS
(1 January 2004, official estimates)

	Number	%
Kazakh	8,550,986	57.19
Russian	4,072,337	27.24
Ukrainian	469,397	3.14
Uzbek	409,770	2.74
German	237,643	1.59
Tatar	232,735	1.56
Uigur	223,039	1.49
Others	755,293	5.05
Total	14,951,200	100.00

ADMINISTRATIVE DIVISIONS
(1 January 2008, official estimates)

	Area (sq km)	Population	Density (per sq km)	Capital city
Oblasts				
Akmola . . .	146,200	747,208	5.11	Kokshetau
Aktobe . . .	300,600	703,433	2.34	Aktobe
Almaty . . .	224,000	1,642,324	7.33	Taldykorgan
Atyrau . . .	118,600	490,218	4.13	Atyrau
Eastern Kazakhstan .	283,200	1,416,393	5.00	Ust-Kamenogorsk
Jambul . . .	144,300	1,018,305	7.06	Taraz
Karaganda . .	428,000	1,341,507	3.13	Karaganda
Kostanai . .	196,000	894,157	4.56	Kostanai
Kyzyl-Orda . .	226,000	631,816	2.80	Kyzyl-Orda
Mangystau . .	165,600	407,248	2.46	Aktau
Northern Kazakhstan .	98,000	653,760	6.67	Petropavlovsk
Pavlodar . . .	124,800	746,216	5.98	Pavlodar
Southern Kazakhstan .	117,300	2,331,247	19.87	Chimkent
Western Kazakhstan .	151,300	615,290	4.07	Oral
Cities				
Almaty . . .	700	1,324,045	1,891.49	—
Astana (capital) .	300	602,480	2,008.27	—
Total . . .	2,724,900	15,565,647	5.71	—

PRINCIPAL TOWNS
(population at 1999 census)

Almaty (Alma-Ata) .	1,129,400		Petropavlovsk . .	203,500
Karaganda . .	436,900		Oral	195,500
Chimkent . .	360,100		Temirtau . . .	170,500
Taraz* . . .	330,100		Kyzyl-Orda . .	157,400
Astana† (capital) .	313,000		Aktau‡	143,400
Ust-Kamenogorsk .	311,000		Atyrau§ . . .	142,500
Pavlodar . . .	300,500		Ekibastuz . . .	127,200
Semipalatinsk . .	269,600		Kokchetau . .	123,400
Aktobe	253,100		Rudniy	109,500
Kostanai . . .	221,400			

* Formerly Jambul.
† Formerly Akmola, and prior to that, Tselinograd.
‡ Formerly Shevchenko.
§ Formerly Guriyev.

Mid-2007 ('000, incl. suburbs, UN estimate): Almaty (Alma-Ata) 1,209 (Source: UN, *World Urbanization Prospects: The 2007 Revision*).

BIRTHS, MARRIAGES AND DEATHS

	Registered live births		Registered marriages		Registered deaths	
	Number	Rate (per 1,000)	Number	Rate (per 1,000)	Number	Rate (per 1,000)
1999 . .	271,578	14.5	85,872	5.8	147,416	9.8
2000 . .	222,054	14.9	90,873	6.1	149,778	10.0
2001 . .	221,487	14.9	92,852	6.3	147,876	10.0
2002 . .	227,171	15.3	98,986	6.7	149,381	10.1
2003 . .	247,946	16.6	110,414	7.4	155,277	10.4
2004 . .	273,028	18.2	114,685	7.6	152,250	10.1
2005 . .	278,977	18.4	123,045	8.1	157,121	10.4
2006 . .	301,756	19.7	137,204	9.0	157,210	10.3

Expectation of life (years at birth, WHO estimates): 63.9 (males 58.6; females 69.5) in 2006 (Source: WHO, *World Health Statistics*).

ECONOMICALLY ACTIVE POPULATION
(labour force survey, annual averages, '000 persons)

	2002	2003	2004
Agriculture, forestry and fishing	2,380.2	2,462.6	2,406.0
Mining and quarrying	167.3	181.7	186.0
Manufacturing	503.7	506.4	519.8
Electricity, gas and water supply .	153.0	167.2	163.8
Construction	268.4	329.5	380.7
Wholesale and retail trade; repair of motor vehicles, motor cycles and personal and household goods	1,007.2	1,015.1	1,058.7
Hotels and restaurants . . .	56.5	70.2	82.0
Transport, storage and communications	503.7	503.9	519.7
Financial intermediation . . .	50.1	53.5	60.7
Real estate, renting and business activities	203.4	207.1	233.6
Public administration and defence; compulsory social security . .	280.4	318.2	334.7
Education	589.0	631.1	666.2
Health and social work . . .	292.6	299.7	318.7
Community, social and personal services	186.3	196.3	201.3
Households with employed persons	66.8	42.5	49.4
Extra-territorial organizations and bodies	0.3	0.3	0.5
Total employed	6,708.9	6,985.2	7,181.8
Unemployed	690.7	672.1	658.8
Total labour force	7,399.6	7,657.3	7,840.6

Source: ILO.

Total employed (labour force survey, annual averages, '000 persons): 7,261.0 in 2005; 7,403.7 in 2006.

Health and Welfare

KEY INDICATORS

Total fertility rate (children per woman, 2006)	2.2
Under-5 mortality rate (per 1,000 live births, 2006) . .	29
HIV/AIDS (% of persons aged 15–49, 2005)	0.1
Physicians (per 1,000 head, 2006)	3.9
Hospital beds (per 1,000 head, 2006)	7.8
Health expenditure (2005): US $ per head (PPP) . . .	306
Health expenditure (2005): % of GDP	3.9
Health expenditure (2005): public (% of total)	64.2
Access to water (% of persons, 2004)	86
Access to sanitation (% of persons, 2004)	72
Human Development Index (2005): ranking	73
Human Development Index (2005): value	0.794

For sources and definitions, see explanatory note on p. vi.

Agriculture

PRINCIPAL CROPS
('000 metric tons)

	2004	2005	2006
Wheat	9,936.9	11,198.4	13,500.0
Rice (paddy)	275.8	310.0*	320.0†
Barley	1,387.9	1,445.0*	1,800.0†
Maize	457.8	494.0*	495.0†
Rye	20.3	23.0*	25.0†
Oats	130.3	120.0*	165.0†
Millet	50.7	56.0*	65.0†
Buckwheat	52.4	58.0*	66.0†
Potatoes	2,260.6	2,520.8	2,361.6
Sugar beet	397.9	310.8	339.0
Dry beans	5.0*	5.0*	6.5†
Dry peas	31.6	30.0*	38.9†
Soybeans	46.7	45.0*	48.0*
Sunflower seed	265.5	267.4	268.0
Safflower seed	76.1	75.0†	75.0†
Seed cotton	467.1	465.0	435.4
Cabbages and other brassicas .	321.5	341.0*	320.0†
Tomatoes	490.9	516.0*	485.0†
Cucumbers and gherkins . .	260.0	275.0*	260.0†
Aubergines (Eggplants) . . .	48.3	50.0*	48.5†
Chillies and green peppers . .	73.5	77.0*	73.5†
Dry onions	327.3	345.0*	329.0†
Carrots and turnips . . .	236.4	250.0*	237.0†
Watermelons	666.9	703.5†	660.0†
Apples	148.9	170.0†	160.0†
Pears	16.8	15.0†	16.0†
Cherries	14.6	12.0†	13.0†
Plums and sloes . . .	7.8	8.0†	8.0†
Grapes	53.2	50.0†	29.0†
Tobacco (leaves)	14.3	14.0†	13.5†

* Unofficial figure.
† FAO estimate.

Aggregate production ('000 metric tons, may include official, semi-official or estimated data): Total cereals 12,333.8 in 2004, 13,728.0 in 2005, 16,461.6 in 2006; Total roots and tubers 2,260.6 in 2004, 2,520.8 in 2005, 2,361.6 in 2006; Total vegetables (incl. melons) 2,766.2 in 2004, 2,897.1 in 2005, 2,731.7 in 2006; Total fruits (excl. melons) 292.6 in 2004, 300.1 in 2005, 252.2 in 2006.

Source: FAO.

LIVESTOCK
('000 head, year ending September)

	2004	2005	2006
Horses	1,064.3	1,120.4	1,163.5
Asses, mules or hinnies* . . .	30.0	31.0	n.a.
Cattle	4,871.0	5,204.0	5,457.0
Buffaloes*	9.0	9.0	10.0
Camels	114.9	125.7	130.5
Pigs	1,368.8	1,292.1	1,281.9
Sheep	10,420.1	11,518.5†	12,183.5*
Goats	1,827.0	1,890.6†	2,151.0*
Chickens	24,773†	25,526†	26,100*
Turkeys	50†	80†	100*

* FAO estimate(s).
† Unofficial figure.

Source: FAO.

LIVESTOCK PRODUCTS
('000 metric tons)

	2004	2005	2006
Cattle meat	329.7	345.0*	370.0†
Sheep meat	101.6	110.0*	110.5†
Goat meat	7.7*	7.7*	10.0†
Horse meat	56*	55*	56†
Pig meat	198.6	200.0*	210.0†
Chicken meat	41.3	43.0*	50.0†
Cows' milk	4,504.0*	4,693.0	4,861.0†
Sheeps' milk	40.0*	42.0	50.0†
Goats' milk	12.8*	14.0	15.0†
Hen eggs	128.5*	139.4†	138.3†
Wool: greasy	28.5	30.4	32.4

* Unofficial figure.
† FAO estimate.

Source: FAO.

Forestry

ROUNDWOOD REMOVALS
(unofficial figures, cubic metres, excl. bark)

	2003	2004	2005
Sawlogs, veneer logs and logs for sleepers	103,920	216,800	513,600
Pulpwood	12,990	27,100	64,200
Other industrial roundwood . .	12,990	27,100	64,200
Fuel wood	170,900	202,000	210,000
Total	300,800	473,000	852,000

2006: Figures assumed to be unchanged from 2005 (FAO estimates).

Source: FAO.

SAWNWOOD PRODUCTION
(cubic metres, incl. railway sleepers)

	2003*	2004	2005*
Coniferous (softwood)	245,791	109,600	113,275
Broadleaved (hardwood) . . .	19,293	24,600	25,425
Total	265,084	134,200	138,700

* Unofficial figures.

2006: Figures assumed to be unchanged from 2005 (FAO estimates).

Source: FAO.

Fishing

('000 metric tons, live weight)

	2004	2005	2006
Capture	33.9	34.9	35.1
Freshwater bream	21.9	20.0*	17.2
Common carp	0.6	0.8	0.1
Crucian carp	1.4	2.4	2.2
Roaches	1.6	1.4	2.0
Asp	0.9	0.8*	0.8*
Northern pike	0.8	0.8	0.8
Wels (Som) catfish	0.9	1.8	1.9
Pike-perch	2.7	2.9	3.5
Aquaculture	0.6	1.1	0.5
Total catch	**34.5**	**36.0***	**35.7***

* FAO estimate.

Source: FAO.

Mining

('000 metric tons, unless otherwise indicated)

	2004	2005	2006
Hard coal . . . . . }	86,875	86,617	96,231
Brown coal (incl. lignite) . . }			
Crude petroleum*	50,672	50,870	54,339
Natural gas (million cu m) . .	22,102	24,973	26,382
Iron ore (gross weight) . .	20,303	19,471	22,263
Bauxite	4,706	4,815	4,884
Lead ore (metal content) . .	33	31	48
Zinc ore (metal content) . .	361	364	405
Manganese ore	2,318	2,233	2,531
Chromite	3,287	516	269
Silver ore (metal content, metric tons)	773,296	883,210	806,083
Gold (metal content, kg) . .	28,837	27,649	30,835
Asbestos	347	306	315

* Including gas condensate.

Industry

SELECTED PRODUCTS
('000 metric tons, unless otherwise indicated)

	2004	2005	2006
Wheat flour	2,126.6	2,756.0	2,849.9
Raw sugar	542.6	528.8	490.2
Wine ('000 hectolitres)	404	529	368
Beer ('000 hectolitres)	2,780	3,235	3,638
Cigarettes (million)	28,037.5	30,008.1	30,833.8
Woven cotton fabrics (metric tons)	20,301.9	35,530.2	56,459.6
Motor spirit (petrol)	1,927.5	2,359.2	2,345.3
Kerosene	294.3	248.7	313.6
Gas-diesel (distillate fuel) oils .	2,887.6	3,704.7	3,887.5
Residual fuel oils (Mazout) . .	2,708.4	3,549.9	3,333.1
Cement	3,662.0	4,181.2	4,880.2
Crude steel	5,372	4,477	4,245
Copper (unrefined, metric tons) .	445,268	418,356	427,723
Electric energy (million kWh) .	66,942.4	67,919.7	71,668.5

Finance

CURRENCY AND EXCHANGE RATES

Monetary Units
100 tein = 1 tenge.

Sterling, Dollar and Euro Equivalents (30 May 2008)
£1 sterling = 237.748 tenge;
US $1 = 120.470 tenge;
€1 = 186.825 tenge;
1,000 tenge = £4.21 = $8.30 = €5.35.

Average Exchange Rate (tenge per US $)
2005   132.88
2006   126.09
2007   122.55

Note: The tenge was introduced on 15 November 1993, replacing the old Russian (formerly Soviet) rouble at an exchange rate of 1 tenge = 500 roubles. On 18 November the rate was adjusted to 250 roubles per tenge. In April 1999 the tenge was allowed to 'float' on foreign exchange markets.

STATE BUDGET
(million tenge)

Revenue	2001	2002	2003
Tax revenue	635,792	752,785	947,251
Other current revenue	70,505	45,573	44,813
Capital revenue	25,363	9,494	12,502
Official transfers	233	—	—
Repayment of debt principal . .	12,719	13,308	17,690
Total	**746,612**	**821,160**	**1,022,256**

Expenditure	1999	2000	2001
General public services . . .	28,856	35,114	47,771
Defence	17,198	20,379	32,347
Public order and security . . .	32,507	47,738	63,681
Education	78,491	84,668	105,024
Health care	44,825	54,323	62,238
Social security and social assistance	159,064	171,065	186,641
Recreation and cultural activities .	12,237	17,487	18,076
Housing and communal services .	6,012	22,106	30,396
Economic affairs and services .	48,794	87,761	132,188
Agriculture, forestry, water management, fishing and environmental protection . .	6,944	11,441	23,113
Mining and minerals (excl. fuel), manufacturing and construction	2,867	7,191	4,558
Transport and communications .	12,865	37,804	41,651
Other purposes	19,442	35,541	37,764
Debt interest	19,442	35,541	37,764
Total	**447,426**	**576,182**	**716,126**

Revised expenditure totals (million tenge, rounded figures): Total expenditure (excluding lending minus repayments) 468,400 in 1999; 602,000 in 2000; 759,600 in 2001.

Expenditure in 2002 (million tenge, rounded figures): Total expenditure (excluding lending minus repayments) 834,200 (Defence 37,700; Social and cultural 416,500; Economic 123,800; Public administration 45,600).

Expenditure in 2003 (million tenge, rounded figures): Total expenditure (excluding lending minus repayments) 1,062,600 (Defence 47,500; Social and cultural 511,700; Economic 173,100; Public administration 63,900).

2004 (million tenge, rounded figures): Total revenue 1,286,700; Total expenditure (excluding lending minus repayments) 1,323,800 (Source: Asian Development Bank, *Key Indicators of Developing Asian and Pacific Countries*).

2005 (million tenge, rounded figures): Total revenue 2,098,500; Total expenditure (excluding lending minus repayments) 1,953,300 (Source: Asian Development Bank, *Key Indicators of Developing Asian and Pacific Countries*).

2006 (million tenge, rounded figures): Total revenue 2,338,100; Total expenditure (excluding lending minus repayments) 2,256,500 (Source: Asian Development Bank, *Key Indicators of Developing Asian and Pacific Countries*).

2007 (general government budget, '000 million tenge): Total revenue 3,767; Total expenditure (including net lending) 3,106 (Source: IMF, *Republic of Kazakhstan: 2008 Article IV Consultation—Staff Report; Staff Statement; and Public Information Notice on the Executive Board Discussion*—August 2008).

INTERNATIONAL RESERVES
(US $ million at 31 December)

	2005	2006	2007
Gold	985.5	1,376.2	1,852.5
IMF special drawing rights . .	1.2	1.3	1.4
Reserve position in IMF . . .	0.0	0.0	0.0
Foreign exchange	6,083.0	17,749.5	15,775.4
Total	7,069.7	19,127.0	17,629.3

Source: IMF, *International Financial Statistics.*

MONEY SUPPLY
(million tenge at 31 December)

	2005	2006	2007
Currency outside banks . . .	411,813	600,832	739,687
Demand deposits at commercial banks	381,364	663,600	756,591
Total money (incl. others) . .	799,440	1,281,549	1,532,688

Source: IMF, *International Financial Statistics.*

COST OF LIVING
(Consumer Price Index; base: 1995 = 100)

	2005	2006	2007
All items	301.7	327.6	363.0

Source: Asian Development Bank, *Key Indicators of Developing Asian and Pacific Countries.*

NATIONAL ACCOUNTS
('000 million tenge at current prices)

Expenditure on the Gross Domestic Product

	2005	2006	2007
Government final consumption expenditure	853.8	1,039.8	1,420.4
Private final consumption expenditure	3,784.4	4,669.9	5,801.3
Increase in stocks	228.1	378.1	707.9
Gross fixed capital formation . .	2,122.7	3,084.4	3,868.9
Total domestic expenditure .	6,989.0	9,172.2	11,798.5
Exports of goods and services .	4,064.2	5,223.0	6,352.3
Less Imports of goods and services	3,395.0	4,129.1	5,474.2
Sub-total	7,658.2	10,266.1	12,676.6
Statistical discrepancy	−67.7	−52.4	86.6
GDP in purchasers' values .	7,590.6	10,213.7	12,763.2

Gross Domestic Product by Economic Activity

	2005	2006	2007
Agriculture, forestry and fishing .	483.5	561.3	730.1
Mining and quarrying	1,198.9	1,646.6	1,926.9
Manufacturing	914.0	1,188.1	1,444.0
Electricity, gas and water . . .	148.3	183.8	222.0
Construction	595.0	1,001.2	1,273.7
Trade, restaurants and hotels .	897.9	1,164.7	1,573.9
Transport, storage and communications	896.8	1,178.8	1,422.1
Finance	245.8	475.5	796.8
Public administration	157.9	190.9	253.1
Other services	1,750.4	2,262.8	2,895.0
Sub-total	7,288.5	9,853.7	12,537.6
Import duties, less subsidies . .	467.8	665.8	839.5
Less Imputed bank service charges	165.7	306.0	614.0
GDP in purchasers' values .	7,590.6	10,213.7	12,763.2

Source: Asian Development Bank, *Key Indicators of Developing Asian and Pacific Countries.*

BALANCE OF PAYMENTS
(US $ million)

	2005	2006	2007
Exports of goods f.o.b.	28,300.6	38,762.1	48,349.1
Imports of goods f.o.b.	−17,978.8	−24,120.4	−33,208.4
Trade balance	10,321.8	14,641.7	15,140.7
Exports of services	2,228.4	2,807.6	3,552.1
Imports of services	−7,495.7	−8,719.6	−11,522.6
Balance on goods and services	5,054.5	8,729.7	7,170.2
Other income received	680.3	1,430.6	3,363.7
Other income paid	−6,377.2	−10,867.4	−15,508.1
Balance on goods, services and income	−642.4	−707.1	−4,974.1
Current transfers received . .	810.0	904.2	903.8
Current transfers paid	−1,223.5	−2,111.6	−3,113.4
Current balance	−1,055.8	−1,914.5	−7,183.7
Capital account (net)	14.0	32.7	−37.5
Direct investment abroad . .	145.9	387.4	−3,160.6
Direct investment from abroad .	1,971.2	6,223.6	10,259.4
Portfolio investment assets .	−5,157.1	−9,176.7	−4,162.6
Portfolio investment liabilities .	1,204.4	4,675.4	−439.0
Financial derivatives assets .	−119.7	−91.6	−614.0
Financial derivatives liabilities .	7.0	23.8	255.0
Other investment assets . .	−4,310.4	−8,022.2	−11,542.4
Other investment liabilities .	7,156.7	22,040.7	16,825.9
Net errors and omissions . .	−1,800.0	−3,104.0	−3,251.7
Overall balance	−1,943.8	11,074.6	−3,051.2

Source: IMF, *International Financial Statistics.*

External Trade

PRINCIPAL COMMODITIES
(US $ million)

Imports c.i.f.	2005	2006	2007
Prepared foodstuffs	741.1	1,082.6	1,435.4
Mineral products	2,322.8	3,375.3	4,275.6
Chemical products	1,337.0	1,638.6	2,129.8
Plastics and rubber	664.8	928.5	1,344.2
Base metals and articles thereof .	2,546.3	3,149.7	4,354.4
Machinery, mechanical appliances and electrical equipment . .	4,902.3	6,479.1	8,807.7
Transportation equipment . .	2,341.7	3,717.3	5,702.3
Total (incl. others)	17,352.5	23,676.9	32,756.4

Exports f.o.b.	2005	2006	2007
Vegetable products	456.5	837.0	1,783.2
Mineral products	20,553.3	27,510.9	33,276.1
Chemical products	899.1	1,553.2	1,839.4
Pearls, precious and semi-precious stones, and metals . . .	399.1	696.9	731.5
Base metals and articles thereof .	4,419.1	6,159.4	8,176.2
Total (incl. others)	27,849.0	38,250.4	47,755.3

Source: Asian Development Bank, *Key Indicators of Developing Asian and Pacific Countries.*

PRINCIPAL TRADING PARTNERS
(US $ million)

Imports c.i.f.	2001	2002	2003
Belarus	46.3	54.8	94.9
China, People's Republic . . .	172.0	313.0	523.7
Finland	71.4	73.4	97.2
France	141.6	110.2	196.9
Germany	490.2	586.2	734.2
Italy	268.9	219.1	250.2
Japan	142.0	164.6	212.0
Korea, Republic	110.6	110.2	114.6
Netherlands	85.4	87.5	127.6
Poland	61.3	74.7	117.2
Russia	2,891.9	2,548.8	3,282.1
Switzerland	67.6	60.2	61.7
Turkey	137.0	173.7	209.0
Ukraine	155.0	217.1	324.0
United Kingdom	249.4	259.7	248.6
USA	349.1	461.4	470.4
Uzbekistan	81.1	86.5	89.7
Total (incl. others)	6,446.0	6,584.0	8,408.7

Exports f.o.b.	2001	2002	2003
Bermuda	1,221.2	2,011.3	2,192.6
China, People's Republic . . .	659.6	1,023.0	1,653.1
Finland	56.1	48.8	108.9
Germany	501.8	220.3	146.4
Italy	956.3	904.2	1,013.1
Korea, Republic	43.4	48.9	55.5
Kyrgyzstan	87.0	108.6	156.4
Netherlands	144.2	123.6	186.1
Poland	164.2	320.5	201.0
Russia	1,759.5	1,497.8	1,967.9
Switzerland	408.7	792.4	1,679.9
Tajikistan	61.2	45.7	75.7
Turkey	74.2	97.4	99.2
Ukraine	490.2	291.5	426.2
United Kingdom	294.3	131.8	143.2
USA	159.0	116.9	99.1
Uzbekistan	150.2	101.0	137.9
Total (incl. others)	8,639.1	9,670.3	12,926.7

2004 (US $ million): *Imports c.i.f.:* China, People's Republic 758.2; France 313.7; Germany 1,053.1; Italy 426.5; Japan 398.2; Russia 4,812.6; Turkey 342.4; Ukraine 722.6; United Kingdom 301.1; USA 563.2; Total (incl. others) 12,779.6. *Exports f.o.b.:* China, People's Republic 1,967.3; France 1,468.2; Germany 212.8; Iran 712.0; Italy 3,109.0; Romania 32.7; Russia 2,838.1; Switzerland 3,760.4; USA 273.9; Total (incl. others) 20,095.2 (Source: Asian Development Bank, *Key Indicators of Developing Asian and Pacific Countries*).

2005 (US $ million): *Imports c.i.f.:* China, People's Republic 4,288.8; France 638.6; Germany 1,424.5; Italy 555.9; Japan 195.3; Netherlands 388.0; Russia 7,181.7; Turkey 505.9; Ukraine 733.9; United Kingdom 308.1; USA 592.1; Total (incl. others) 20,155.3. *Exports f.o.b.:* China, People's Republic 2,638.4; France 2,033.2; Germany 2,825.2; Iran 906.6; Italy 2,105.2; Romania 1,196.3; Russia 2,918.3; Switzerland 144.0; USA 1,058.7; Total (incl. others) 23,610.3 (Source: Asian Development Bank, *Key Indicators of Developing Asian and Pacific Countries*).

2006 (US $ million): *Imports c.i.f.:* China, People's Republic 5,226.7; France 923.4; Germany 1,999.4; Italy 874.1; Japan 259.9; Netherlands 447.5; Russia 9,352.2; Turkey 764.5; Ukraine 861.0; United Kingdom 426.5; USA 710.6; Total (incl. others) 27,082.4. *Exports f.o.b.:* China, People's Republic 3,279.3; France 2,236.5; Germany 3,716.8; Iran 1,119.2; Italy 3,144.6; Romania 1,403.6; Russia 3,357.0; Switzerland 149.0; USA 907.5; Total (incl. others) 29,730.7 (Source: Asian Development Bank, *Key Indicators of Developing Asian and Pacific Countries*).

2007 (US $ million): *Imports c.i.f.:* China, People's Republic 7,995.3; France 697.7; Germany 2,951.1; Italy 872.5; Netherlands 608.3; Russia 12,166.0; Turkey 1,188.1; Ukraine 1,082.6; United Kingdom 695.9; USA 828.3; Total (incl. others) 35,729.5. *Exports f.o.b.:* China, People's Republic 5,606.0; France 2,530.0; Germany 4,314.7; Iran 1,456.9; Italy 2,714.4; Romania 1,236.2; Russia 4,167.8; Switzerland 389.4; USA 1,172.7; Total (incl. others) 36,631.7 (Source: Asian Development Bank, *Key Indicators of Developing Asian and Pacific Countries*).

Transport

RAILWAYS
(estimated traffic)

	2004	2005	2006
Passenger-km (million) . . .	11,800	12,100	13,700
Freight net ton-km (million) . .	163,500	171,900	191,200

ROAD TRAFFIC
(motor vehicles in use at 31 December)

	2004	2005	2006
Passenger cars	1,204,100	1,405,300	1,745,000
Buses and coaches	62,894	65,698	75,042

SHIPPING

Merchant Fleet
(registered at 31 December)

	2005	2006	2007
Number of vessels	45	59	63
Total displacement (grt) . . .	43,486	64,932	54,291

Source: Lloyd's Register-Fairplay, *World Fleet Statistics*.

CIVIL AVIATION
(traffic on scheduled services)

	2001	2002	2003
Passengers carried ('000) . . .	884	1,036	1,275
Passenger-km (million) . . .	1,901	2,179	2,654
Total ton-km (million) . . .	44	53	94

Kilometres flown (million): 20 in 1996; 20 in 1997; 35 in 1998 (Source: UN, *Statistical Yearbook*).

Tourism

FOREIGN TOURIST ARRIVALS

Country of residence	2004	2005	2006
Armenia	4,684	5,765	7,220
Australia	1,614	2,040	2,385
Austria	1,433	1,964	2,422
Azerbaijan	37,179	67,030	49,417
Belarus	41,341	15,916	16,438
Canada	3,724	4,440	4,597
China, People's Republic . . .	76,806	85,696	117,279
France	3,834	4,712	5,893
Georgia	5,375	5,278	6,865
Germany	72,529	84,534	92,429
Hungary	1,502	2,261	2,965
India	5,868	6,160	7,197
Iran	11,331	9,659	9,474
Israel	3,427	4,737	5,166
Italy	6,996	8,462	9,640
Japan	2,681	3,171	4,222
Korea, Republic	9,311	10,412	13,450
Kyrgyzstan	1,091,923	851,568	1,018,524
Lithuania	2,639	4,122	4,641
Mongolia	3,878	7,707	9,676
Netherlands	5,375	6,576	6,978
Pakistan	2,602	1,944	2,623

Country of residence—*continued*	2004	2005	2006
Poland	3,551	4,491	5,669
Romania	1,428	1,580	2,606
Russia	1,628,823	1,405,543	1,385,964
Switzerland	1,121	1,580	1,832
Tajikistan	260,487	286,042	301,971
Turkey	42,064	58,034	88,070
United Kingdom	16,530	19,659	22,855
USA	19,513	25,346	26,077
Uzbekistan	767,162	1,266,401	1,352,879
Total (incl. others)	4,291,040	4,364,949	4,706,742

Tourism receipts (US $ million, incl. passenger transport): 638 in 2003; 803 in 2004; 809 in 2005.

Source: World Tourism Organization.

Communications Media

	2004	2005	2006
Telephones ('000 main lines in use)	2,550.0	2,708.0	2,928.0
Mobile cellular telephones ('000 subscribers)	2,447.0	5,398.0	7,830.4
Internet users ('000)	400.0	609.2	1,247.0
Broadband subscribers ('000) . .	2.0	3.0	30.5

Book production (titles, incl. pamphlets): 1,223 in 1999.

Book production (copies, 1996): 21,014,000.

Daily newspapers (1996): Titles 3; Average circulation 500,000.

Radio receivers ('000 in use, 1997): 6,470.

Television receivers ('000 in use, 2001): 5,440.

Sources: UNESCO, *Statistical Yearbook*; UN, *Statistical Yearbook*; International Telecommunication Union.

Education

(state educational institutions, 2005/06, unless otherwise indicated)

	Institutions	Students ('000)
Pre-primary	1,179	185.4
Primary *and* Secondary: general . .	8,157	2,824.6
Secondary: vocational	415	397.6
Professional-technical schools . . .	307	104.2
Higher	181	775.8

Note: In 2003/04 there were, additionally: 155 private primary and secondary-general schools, with 20,000 students; 179 private secondary-vocational schools, with 88,700 students; and 134 non-governmental higher education institutes, with 297,900 students.

Teachers: Pre-primary 15,412 in 2001/02; Primary 60,509 in 2002/03; Secondary—general 170,190 in 2002/03; Secondary—vocational 27,000 in 2005/06; Professional-technical schools 5,900 in 2005/06; Higher 43,400 in 2005/06.

Adult literacy rate (UNESCO estimates): 99.6% (males 99.8%; females 99.5%) in 2007 (Source: UNESCO Institute for Statistics).

Directory

The Constitution

The Constitution of the Republic of Kazakhstan was endorsed by 89% of the electorate voting in a national referendum on 30 August 1995, and was officially adopted on 6 September, replacing the Constitution of January 1993. A number of constitutional amendments were adopted on 8 October 1998 and on 18 May 2007. The following is a summary of the Constitution's main provisions:

GENERAL PROVISIONS

The Republic of Kazakhstan is a democratic, secular, law-based, unitary state with a presidential system of rule. The state ensures the integrity, inviolability and inalienability of its territory. State power belongs to the people, who exercise it directly through referendums and free elections, and also delegate the exercise of their power to state bodies. State power is separated into legislative, executive and judicial branches, with a system of checks and balances being applied.

Ideological and political diversity are recognized. State and private property are recognized. The state language is Kazakh. Russian is employed officially in state bodies and local government bodies on a par with Kazakh.

HUMAN AND CIVIL RIGHTS AND LIBERTIES

Citizenship of the Republic of Kazakhstan is acquired and terminated in accordance with the law. Citizenship of another state is not recognized for any citizen of Kazakhstan. The rights and liberties of the individual are recognized and guaranteed. No one may be subjected to discrimination on grounds of origin, sex, race, language, religious or other beliefs, or place of residence. No one may be subjected to torture, violence or other treatment or punishment that is cruel or degrading. Provision is made for the abolition of the death penalty. All are entitled to use their native language and practice their native culture. Freedom of speech and creativity are guaranteed. Censorship is prohibited. Citizens are entitled to assem-

ble and to hold demonstrations peacefully and without weapons. Defence of the republic is the duty and obligation of every citizen. Human and civil rights and liberties may be restricted only by law and only to the extent that is necessary to defend the constitutional system and to safeguard public order. Any action capable of disrupting inter-ethnic accord is deemed unconstitutional.

THE PRESIDENT OF THE REPUBLIC

The President of the Republic is the Head of State, who determines the main directions of the state's domestic and foreign policy and represents Kazakhstan domestically and internationally. The President is elected for a seven-year term by secret ballot on the basis of general, equal and direct suffrage. (Under the constitutional amendments of May 2007, the presidential term was reduced to five years, with effect from 2012.) A citizen of the republic by birth, who is at least 40 years of age, has a fluent command of the state language, and has lived in Kazakhstan for no less than 15 years, may be elected President.

The President: addresses an annual message to the people; schedules regular and extraordinary elections to Parliament; signs and promulgates laws submitted by the Senat (Senate), or returns draft legislation for further discussion; appoints the Prime Minister and relieves him of office, subject to the approval of the Majlis (Assembly); with the consent of the Senat, appoints to and relieves of office the Chairman of the National Bank, the Prosecutor-General and the Chairman of the National Security Committee; appoints and recalls the heads of diplomatic missions of the republic; decides on the holding of referendums; negotiates and signs international treaties; is supreme Commander-in-Chief of the armed forces; bestows state awards and confers honours; resolves matters of citizenship and of granting political asylum; in the event of aggression against the republic, imposes martial law or announces a partial or general mobilization; forms the Security Council, the Supreme Judicial Council and other consultative and advisory bodies.

The President may be relieved of office only in the event of his having committed an act of treason or if he exhibits a consistent incapacity to carry out his duties owing to illness. A decision on the President's early dismissal is adopted at a joint sitting of the chambers of Parliament by a majority of no less than three-quarters of the total number of deputies of each chamber. The question of dismissal of the President may not be raised at the same time as he is considering early termination of the authority of Parliament.

PARLIAMENT

Parliament is the supreme representative body of the republic, exercising legislative functions. It consists of two chambers, the Senat and the Majlis. The Senat comprises 47 members, of whom 32 are elected at joint sittings of the deputies of all representative bodies of the regions and the capital city, while 15 deputies are appointed by the President. The Majlis comprises 107 deputies, of whom 98 are elected by general, equal and direct suffrage and on a basis of party-list proportional representation. The remaining nine deputies are elected by the Assembly of Nations of Kazakhstan (a 350-member body representing the country's minority ethnic groups). The Senat's term is six years, and that of the Majlis is five years. One-half of the elected deputies in the Senat are subject to election every three years.

THE GOVERNMENT

The Government exercises the executive power of the republic and is responsible to the President. The Government drafts the main areas of the state's socio-economic policy, defence capability, security and public order, and orders their implementation; presents to Parliament the republican budget and the report of its implementation, and ensures that the budget is implemented; submits draft legislation to the Majlis and provides for the implementation of laws; organizes the management of state property; formulates measures for the pursuit of Kazakhstan's foreign policy; directs the activity of Ministries, State Committees and other central and local executive bodies. The Prime Minister, who is a member of the parliamentary majority party, proposes members of the Government, subject to the approval of the Majlis, organizes and directs the activity of the Government and is personally responsible for its work. A motion of 'no confidence' in a new Government may be approved by a simple majority of votes in the Majlis.

LOCAL STATE ADMINISTRATION GOVERNMENT

Local state administration is exercised by local representative and executive bodies, which are responsible for the state of affairs on their own territory. The local representative councils (maslikhat) express the will of the population and, bearing in mind the overall state interest, define the measures necessary to realize this will and monitor their implementation. Councils are elected for a five-year term by a secret ballot on the basis of general, equal and direct suffrage. The local executive bodies (akimiyat) are part of the unified system of executive bodies of Kazakhstan, and ensure that the general state policy of the executive authority is implemented in co-ordination with the interests and development needs of the corresponding territory. Each local executive body is headed by the Akim (Governor) of the corresponding administrative-territorial unit, who is appointed by the President after the approval of the appropriate maslikhat.

The Government

HEAD OF STATE

President: NURSULTAN A. NAZARBAYEV (elected indirectly 24 April 1990; elected unopposed 1 December 1991; term extended by referendum 29 April 1995; re-elected 10 January 1999; re-elected 4 December 2005; inaugurated 11 January 2006).

GOVERNMENT
(September 2008)

Prime Minister: KARIM K. MASIMOV.

Deputy Prime Ministers: UMIRZAK YE. SHUKEYEV, YERBOL T. ORYNBAYEV.

Minister of Foreign Affairs: MARAT M. TAZHIN.

Minister of Defence: DANIAL K. AKHMETOV.

Minister of Internal Affairs: BAURZHAN A. MUKHAMEJANOV.

Minister of Health: ANATOLII G. DERNOVOI.

Minister of Industry and Trade: VLADIMIR S. SHKOLNIK.

Minister of Culture and Information: MUKHTAR A. KUL-MUKHAMMED.

Minister of Tourism and Sport: TEMIRKHAN M. DOSMUKHANBETOV.

Minister of Education and Science: ZHANSEIT K. TUIMEBAYEV.

Minister of Environmental Protection: NURLAN A. ISKAKOV.

Minister of Agriculture: AKYLBEK K. KURISHBAYEV.

Minister of Transport and Communications: SERIK N. AKHMETOV.

Minister of Labour and Social Security: BERDIBEK M. SAPARBAYEV.

Minister of Finance: BOLAT B. ZHAMISHEV.

Minister of Emergency Situations: VLADIMIR K. BOZHKO.

Minister of the Economy and Budgetary Planning: BAKHYT T. SULTANOV.

Minister of Energy and Mineral Resources: SAUAT A. MYNBAYEV.

Minister of Justice: ZAGIPA YA. BALIYEVA.

MINISTRIES

Office of the President: 010000 Astana, Beibitshilik 11; tel. (7172) 32-13-99; fax (7172) 32-61-72; internet www.akorda.kz.

Office of the Prime Minister: 010000 Astana, Beibitshilik 11; tel. (7172) 32-31-04; fax (7172) 32-40-89; internet www.government.kz.

Ministry of Agriculture: 010000 Astana, pr. Abaya 49; tel. (7172) 32-37-63; fax (7172) 32-62-99; e-mail mailbox@minagri.kz; internet www.minagri.kz.

Ministry of Culture and Information: 010000 Astana, pr. Respubliki 24; tel. and fax (7172) 33-32-82; e-mail prmin@mininfo.katelco.kz; internet www.sana.gov.kz.

Ministry of Defence: 010000 Astana, Beibitshilik 51A; tel. and fax (7172) 33-78-89; internet www.mod.kz.

Ministry of the Economy and Budgetary Planning: 010000 Astana, pr. Pobedy 11; tel. (7172) 71-77-70; fax (7172) 71-77-12; e-mail info@minplan.kz; internet www.minplan.kz.

Ministry of Education and Science: 010000 Astana, Beibitshilik 11; tel. (7172) 75-20-27; fax (7172) 75-28-71; e-mail pressa@edu.gov.kz; internet www.edu.gov.kz.

Ministry of Emergency Situations: 010000 Astana, Beibitshilik 22; e-mail chs@emer.kz; internet www.emer.kz.

Ministry of Energy and Mineral Resources: 010000 Astana, Beibitshilik 37; tel. (7172) 31-71-33; fax (7172) 31-71-64; e-mail ministr@minenergo.kegoc.kz; internet www.minenergo.kz.

Ministry of Environmental Protection: 010000 Astana, Sol zhagalau, ui. Ministrigi 35-8/14; tel. (7172) 59-19-44; fax (7172) 59-19-73; internet www.nature.kz.

Ministry of Finance: 010000 Astana, pl. Respubliki 60; tel. (7172) 28-00-65; fax (7172) 32-40-89; e-mail info@minfin.kz; internet www.minfin.kz.

Ministry of Foreign Affairs: 010000 Astana, Tauelsizdik 31; tel. (7172) 72-05-18; fax (7172) 72-05-16; e-mail midrk@mid.kz; internet www.mfa.kz.

Ministry of Health: 010000 Astana, Moskovskaya 86; tel. and fax (7172) 31-73-27; e-mail zdrav@mz.gov.kz; internet www.mz.gov.kz.

Ministry of Industry and Trade: 010000 Astana, pr. Kabanbai Batyr 49, 'Transport Tauer'; tel. (7172) 29-90-00; fax (7172) 24-12-13; internet www.mit.kz.

Ministry of Internal Affairs: 010000 Astana, Manasa 4; tel. (7172) 34-36-01; fax (7172) 34-17-38; e-mail press@mvd.kz; internet www.mvd.kz.

Ministry of Justice: 010000 Astana, pr. Pobedy 45; tel. (7172) 39-12-13; fax (7172) 32-15-54; internet www.minjust.kz.

Ministry of Labour and Social Security: 010000 Astana, Manasa 2; tel. (7172) 71-28-51; fax (7172) 74-36-08; e-mail inter@enbek.kz; internet www.enbek.kz.

Ministry of Tourism and Sport: 010000 Astana, pr. Abai 33; tel. (7172) 753010; fax (7172) 753430; internet www.mts.gov.kz.

Ministry of Transport and Communications: 010000 Astana, pr. Kabanbai batyra 47; tel. (7172) 24-17-70; fax (7172) 24-11-70; e-mail janibek@mtc.gov.kz; internet www.mtk.gov.kz.

President

Presidential Election, 4 December 2005

Candidates	Votes	%
Nursultan A. Nazarbayev	6,147,517	91.15
Zharmakhan A. Tuyakbai	445,934	6.61
Others	150,816	2.24
Total	**6,744,267**	**100.00**

Legislature

Parliament is a bicameral legislative body, comprising the Senat and the Majlis (Assembly).

Majlis

010000 Astana, Parliament House; tel. (7172) 15-30-19; fax (7172) 33-30-99; e-mail www@parlam.kz; internet www.parlam.kz.

Chairman: ASLAN MUSIN.

General Election, 18 August 2007

Parties	Votes	%	Seats
Light Of The Fatherland (Nur Otan)	5,247,720	88.41	98
National Social-Democratic Party	269,310	4.54	—
Bright Road—Democratic Party of Kazakhstan (Ak Zhol) . . .	183,346	3.09	—
Village Kazakhstani Social-Democratic Party (Auyl) .	89,855	1.51	—
Communist People's Party of Kazakhstan	76,799	1.29	—
Party of Patriots of Kazakhstan .	46,436	0.78	—
Spirituality Party (Rukhaniyat) .	22,159	0.37	—
Total (incl. others)	5,935,625	100.00	107*

* Including nine deputies elected by the Assembly of Nations of Kazakhstan (a body representing the country's minority ethnic groups) on 20 August 2007.

Senat

010000 Astana, pr. Abaya 33, Parliament House; tel. (7172) 15-33-76; fax (7172) 33-31-18; e-mail smimazh@parlam.kz; internet www.parlam.kz.

Chairman: KASYM-ZHOMART K. TOKAYEV.

The 47-member Senat is the upper chamber of Parliament. Elections are held every three years for one-half of the 32 seats elected by special colleges (comprising members of local councils) in Kazakhstan's 14 regions and two cities; the term of office for members of the Senat is six years. Under constitutional amendments adopted on 18 May 2007, the number of deputies appointed by the President increased from seven to 15; the additional eight members were officially appointed to the Senat by presidential decree in August. Partial elections to the Senate were conducted on 4 October 2008.

Local Government

For the purposes of local government Kazakhstan is divided into 17 units: 14 oblasts (regions) and three cities. Of these, the city of Baikonur (formerly Leninsk), serving the space centre there, was transferred to Russian jurisdiction in August 1995, for a period of 20 years. Each region has an elected council (maslikhat), which is elected for a five-year term by secret ballot. Elections to local maslikhats took place in September–October 2003. In each unit, executive authority is represented by the akimiyat, headed by the Akim or Governor, who, under constitutional amendments approved on 18 May 2007, is appointed by the President of the Republic after the approval of the maslikhat of that region. Local elections took place, concurrently with legislative elections, on 18 August 2007.

CITIES

Almaty City Administration: 050000 Almaty; tel. (7272) 232-30-12; fax (727) 232-07-32; internet www.almaty.kz; Akim AKHMETZHAN S. YESIMOV.

Astana City Administration: 010000 Astana, Beibitshilik 11; tel. (7172) 55-64-14; fax (7172) 32-12-23; e-mail webmaster@astana.kz; internet www.astana.kz; Akim IMANGALI N. TASMAGAMBETOV.

OBLASTS

Akmola Oblast Administration: 020000 Akmola obl., Kokshetau, ul. Abaya 83; tel. (7162) 25-79-22; fax (7162) 25-55-11; internet www.akmo.kz; Akim ALBERT P. RAU.

Aktobe Oblast Administration: 030010 Aktobe, pr. Abulkhair-khana 40; tel. (7132) 53-22-65; fax (7132) 57-00-41; internet www.akto.kz; Akim YELEUSIN N. SAGINDIKOV.

Almaty Oblast Adminstration: 040000 Almaty obl., Taldykorgan, ul. Tauelsizdik 38; e-mail tkoblakimat@global.kz; internet www.almaty-reg.kz; Akim SERIK A. UMBETOV.

Atyrau Oblast Administration: 060000 Atyrau; tel. (7122) 25-45-01; fax (7122) 25-45-13; internet www.e-atyrau.kz; Akim BERGEI S. RYSKALIYEV.

Eastern Kazakhstan Oblast Administration: 070019 Eastern Kazakhstan obl., Ust-Kamenogorsk, ul. M. Gorkogo; tel. (7232) 24-

45-61; fax (7232) 26-13-63; e-mail ktokhmoldina@akimvko.gov.kz; internet www.akimvko.gov.kz; Akim ADYLGAZY S. BERGENEV.

Jambul Oblast Administration: 080000 Jambul obl., Taraz; tel. (7262) 23-18-22; fax (7262) 24-46-28; Akim BORIBAI B. ZHEKSEMBIN.

Karaganda Oblast Administration: 100008 Karaganda, bulv. Mira 39; tel. (7212) 41-10-11; fax (7212) 42-10-33; internet www.karaganda-region.kz; Akim NURLAN Z. NIGMATULIN.

Kostanai Oblast Administration: 110000 Kostanai, ul. Al-Farabi 66; tel. (7142) 57-50-57; fax (7142) 53-03-63; internet www.kostanay.kz; Akim SERGEI V. KULAGIN.

Kzyl-Orda Oblast Administration: 120000 Kzyl-Orda; tel. (7242) 26-21-44; fax (7242) 26-12-25; internet www.kyzylorda.kz; Akim BOLATBEK B. KUANDYKOV.

Mangystau Oblast Administration: 133000 Mangystau obl., Aktau, 14 mikro-raion 1; tel. (7292) 33-42-15; fax (7292) 43-45-52; e-mail akimmangistau@mail.kz; internet www.mangystau.kz; Akim KRYMBEK YE. KUSHERBAYEV.

Northern Kazakhstan Oblast Administration: 150000 Northern Kazakhstan obl., Petropavlovsk; tel. (7152) 46-41-25; fax (7152) 46-94-78; e-mail akimat@sko.kz; internet www.sko.kz; Akim SERIK S. BILYALOV.

Pavlodar Oblast Adminstration: 140000 Pavlodar; tel. (7182) 32-33-35; internet www.pavlodar.kz; Akim BAKYTZHAN A. SAGINTAYEV.

Southern Kazakhstan Oblast Administration: 160000 Southern Kazakhstan obl., Chimkent; tel. (7252) 53-74-73; fax (7252) 44-59-73; internet www.ontustik.kz; Akim NURGALI S. ASHIMOV.

Western Kazakhstan Oblast Administration: 090000 Western Kazakhstan obl., Oral; tel. (7112) 51-40-13; fax (7112) 51-06-26; e-mail zkue@nursat.kz; internet www.western.kz; Akim BAKTY-KOZHA S. IZMUKHAMBETOV.

CITY UNDER RUSSIAN JURISDICTION

Baikonur City Administration: 120513 Kzyl-Orda obl., Baikonur; Head of the Administration (Mayor) ALEKSANDR F. MEZENTSEV.

Election Commission

Ortalyk Sailau Komissiyasy (Central Election Commission): 010000 Astana, Beibitshilik 4; tel. (7172) 152210; fax (7172) 333388; e-mail info@election.kz; internet www.election.kz; Chair. KUANDYK TURGANKULOV.

Political Organizations

A new law was introduced in July 2002, which required all parties to have a minimum of 50,000 members from among all the country's regions in order to qualify for official registration. In 2007 the following eight parties were registered.

Bright Road—Democratic Party of Kazakhstan (Ak Zhol) (Kazakstan Demokratiyalyk Partiyasy Ak Zhol): 010000 Astana, Imanov 18/7; tel. (7172) 22-10-66; fax (7172) 22-14-50; e-mail oral@kepter.kz; internet www.akzhol.kz; f. 2002 by former members of the Democratic Choice of Kazakhstan; merged with Justice Democratic Party (Adilet) in 2007; Chair. ALIKHAN M. BAYMENOV; 175,862 mems (2007).

Communist Party of Kazakhstan (CPK) (Kazakstan Kommunistik Partiyasy): 010000 Astana, Beibitshilik 27/49; tel. and fax (727) 221-32-97; e-mail pravdakz@list.ru; f. 1937; suspended Aug. 1991, re-registered Aug. 1998 and March 2003; contested 2004 legislative elections in alliance with Democratic Choice of Kazakhstan, as the People's Opposition Union of Communists and DVK bloc; mem. of For a Just Kazakhstan opposition bloc formed in 2005; Chair. SERIKBOLSYN A. ABDILDIN; 54,246 mems (2007).

Communist People's Party of Kazakhstan (Kazakstan Kommunistik Khalyk Partiyasy): 010000 Astana, Zheltoksan 36A/37; tel. (7172) 32-24-61; internet www.knpk.kz; f. 2004 by fmr mems of the Communist Party of Kazakhstan; Sec. of the Central Cttee VLADISLAV B. KOSAREV; 90,000 mems (2004).

Light Of The Fatherland People's Democratic Party (Nur Otan) ('Nur Otan' Khalyktyk Demokratiyalyk Partiyasy): 050000 Almaty, Abylai khana 79; tel. (727) 279-78-00; fax (727) 279-40-66; e-mail partyotan@nursat.kz; internet www.ndp-nurotan.kz; f. 2006 by merger of Fatherland, Civic Party of Kazakhstan and Agrarian Party of Kazakhstan; supports administration of President Nazarbayev; Chair. NURSULTAN A. NAZARBAYEV; First Deputy Chair. BAKYTZHAN T. ZHUMAGULOV; 607,557 mems (2007).

National Social-Democratic Party (Zhalpyulttyk Sotsial Demokratiyalyk Partiyasy—ZhSDP): 050000 Almaty, Kabanbai batyr 58; tel. (727) 663-64-06; fax (727) 266-36-43; e-mail ocdp@mail.ru;

internet www.osdp.kz; f. 2006; contested 2007 legislative elections in coalition with Real Bright Road—Democratic Party of Kazakhstan (Naghyz Ak Zhol); Chair. ZHARMAKHAN A. TUYAKBAI; 140,000 mems (Jan. 2007).

Party of Patriots of Kazakhstan (PPK) (Kazakstan Patriottary Partiyasy): 050000 Almaty, Zhibek-zholy 76/318; tel. (7172) 22-98-34; fax (7172) 37-44-82; f. 2000; merged with the Union of Officers in 2004; Chair. GANI YE. KASYMOV; 172,000 mems (2007).

Spirituality Party (Rukhaniyat Partiyasy): 010000 Astana, Saryarka 5; tel. and fax (7172) 97-73-80; e-mail kazayelder@nursat.kz; internet www.rukhaniat.kz; f. 1995 as Renaissance Party of Kazakhstan; re-registered under new name 2003; supports Govt of President Nazarbayev; Chair. ALTYNSHASH K. JAGANOVA; 72,000 mems (2007).

Village Kazakhstani Social-Democratic Party (Auyl) ('Auyl' Kazakstandyk Sotsial-Demokratiyalyk Partiyasy): 010000 Astana, Beibitshilik 46/109; tel. and fax (7172) 31-71-57; internet auyl.by.ru; registered in 2002; seeks to strengthen government support for the agricultural sector; Chair. GANI A. KALIYEV; 61,043 mems (2006).

Diplomatic Representation

EMBASSIES IN KAZAKHSTAN

Afghanistan: 010000 Astana, Diplomatiyalyk kalashyk C-10; tel. (727) 224-29-46; fax (727) 224-30-25; e-mail aziz59@mail.ru; Ambassador AZIZ ARYANFAR.

Armenia: 050025 Almaty, Seyfulin 57/9; tel. and fax (727) 291-71-26; e-mail armeniaemb_kz@hotmail.com; Ambassador LEVON KHACHATRIAN.

Austria: 010000 Astana, Saryarka 6/1310, Arman Business Centre; tel. (727) 299-01-44; fax (727) 299-02-27; e-mail astana-ob@bmeia.gv .at; Ambassador URSULA FARINGER.

Azerbaijan: 010000 Astana, Diplomatiyalyk kalashyk C-14; tel. (7172) 24-15-81; fax (7172) 24-15-32; e-mail astana@azembassy.kz; Ambassador LATIF GANDILOV.

Belarus: 010000 Astana, Kenesary 35; tel. (7172) 32-48-29; fax (7172) 32-06-65; e-mail kazakhstan@belembassy.org; internet kazakhstan.belembassy.org; Ambassador VASILII I. HAPEYEV.

Belgium: 010000 Astana, Kosmonavtov 62; tel. (7172) 97-44-85; fax (7172) 97-78-49; e-mail embassy.astana@diplobel.fed.be; Ambassador CHRISTIAN MEERSCHMAN.

Brazil: 010000 Astana, Kabanbai Batyr 6/1; tel. (7172) 92-51-12; fax (7172) 92-51-17; e-mail brasembastana@mre.gov.br; Ambassador ESTRADA MEYER.

Bulgaria: 050000 Almaty, Gornyi Gigant, 8-oi Gvardeiskoi Divizii; tel. (727) 264-67-10; fax (727) 262-99-56; e-mail bulgarianembassy@ rambler.ru; internet www.mfa.bg/almaty; Ambassador NIKOLA F. BORISOV.

Canada: 050010 Almaty, Karasai Batyr 34; tel. (727) 250-11-51; fax (727) 258-24-93; e-mail almat@international.gc.ca; internet www .dfait-maeci.gc.ca/canadaeuropa/kazakhstan; Ambassador MARGARET SKOK.

China, People's Republic: 010000 Astana, pr. Kabanbai Batyr 37; tel. (7172) 79-35-70; fax (7172) 79-35-67; e-mail chinaemb_kz@mfa .gov.cn; internet kz.china-embassy.org; Ambassador ZHANG XIYUN.

Cuba: 010005 Astana, pr. Respublika 10/1; tel. and fax (7172) 22-14-19; e-mail embacuba@cubakaz.com; internet www.cubakaz.com; Ambassador TERESITA CAPOTE CAMACHO.

Czech Republic: 010000 Astana, Sary-Arka 6, Biznes-Tsentr Arman, 13th Floor; tel. (7172) 99-01-43; fax (7172) 99-01-42; e-mail astana@embassy.mzv.cz; internet www.mzv.cz/astana; Ambassador (vacant).

Egypt: 050010 Almaty, Muhammed Haidar Dulati 80; tel. (727) 269-15-93; fax (727) 291-10-22; e-mail egyptianemb_kz@yahoo.com; Ambassador ABDEL MAWJOOD AHMED AL-HABASHI.

France: 010000 Astana, Kosmonavtov 62; tel. (7172) 79-51-00; fax (7172) 79-51-01; e-mail ambafrance@mail.ru; internet www .ambafrance-kz.kz; Ambassador ALAIN COUANON.

Georgia: 010000 Astana, Diplomatiyalyk kalashyk C-4; tel. and fax (7172) 24-32-58; fax (7172) 24-34-26; e-mail geoembassy@mail.online .kz; Ambassador ZURAB SHURGHAIA.

Germany: 010000 Astana, Kosmonavtov 62; tel. (7172) 79-12-00; fax (7172) 79-12-13; e-mail info@astana.diplo.de; internet www.astana .diplo.de; Ambassador RAINER EUGEN SCHLAGETER.

Greece: 050020 Almaty, Kyz Zhibek 80, mer Kok-Tobe; tel. (727) 250-39-61; fax (727) 250-39-38; e-mail hellenic.embassy@ducatmail .com; Chargé d'affaires GEORGIOS PARTHENIOU.

Holy See: 010000 Astana, Zelenaya Alleya 20; tel. (7172) 24-12-69; fax (7172) 24-16-04; e-mail nuntius_kazakhstan@lycos.com; Apostolic Nuncio Most Rev. MIGUEL MAURY BUENDÍA (Titular Archbishop of Italica).

Hungary: 050000 Almaty, ul. Musabayeva 4, POB 166; tel. (727) 255-12-06; fax (727) 258-18-37; e-mail mission.ala@kum.hu; Ambassador JÁNOS NÉMETH.

India: 010000 Astana, pr. Kabanbai Batyr 6/1, Kaskad Business Centre, 5th Floor; tel. (7172) 92-57-10; fax (7172) 92-57-16; e-mail admn.astana@mea.gov.in; internet www.indembassy.kz; Ambassador ASHOK SAJJANHAR.

Iran: 050000 Almaty, ul. Luganskogo 31–33; tel. (727) 254-19-74; fax (7272) 254-27-54; e-mail iranembassy@itte.kz; Ambassador RAMIN MEHMAN PARAST.

Israel: 010000 Astana, ul. Auezova 8; tel. (7172) 68-87-38; e-mail info@almaty.mfa.gov.il; internet www.almaty.mfa.gov.il; Ambassador RAN ICHAY.

Italy: 010000 Astana, Kosmonavtov 62; tel. (7172) 24-33-90; fax (7172) 24-38-68; e-mail ambasciata.astana@esteri.it; internet www .ambastana.esteri.it; Chargé d'affaires BRUNO ANTONIO PASQUINO.

Japan: 010000 Astana, Chubar sh-a, Kosmonavtov 62; tel. (7172) 97-78-43; fax (7172) 97-78-42; internet www.kz.emb-japan.go.jp/jp/ index_r.htm; Ambassador TETSUO ITO.

Jordan: 010000 Astana; tel. (7172) 24-52-54; fax (7172) 24-52-53; Chargé d'affaires a.i. SULEIMAN ARABIAT.

Korea, Republic: 050000 Almaty, Jarkentskaya 2/77; tel. (727) 253-26-60; fax (727) 250-70-59; e-mail koreaemb-kz@mofat.go.kr; internet kaz.mofat.go.kr; Ambassador KIM IL-SOO.

Kyrgyzstan: 010000 Astana, Diplomatiyalyk kalashyk B-5; tel. (7172) 24-20-24; fax (7172) 24-24-12; e-mail kz@mail.online.kz; Ambassador JANUSH. RUSTENBEKOV.

Latvia: 010000 Astana, pr. Kabanbai Batyr 6/1/122, Kaskad Business Centre; tel. (7172) 92-53-16; fax (7172) 92-53-19; Ambassador RETS PLĒSUMS.

Lebanon: 010000 Astana, Riksos Prezident Hotel, kom. 5013; tel. (7172) 24-50-50; Chargé d'affaires a.i. VAZKEN KAVLAKIAN.

Libya: 010000 Astana, Karaotkel-2 sh-a, kot. 110; tel. (7172) 24-18-79; fax (7172) 24-27-57; e-mail libya@nursat.kz; Chargé d'affaires a.i. AHMED ADDEB.

Lithuania: 050059 Almaty, Iskanderova 15, Gornyi Gigant; tel. (727) 293-46-06; fax (727) 293-51-53; e-mail amb.kz@urm.lt; internet kz.mfa.lt; Ambassador ROMUALDAS KOZYROVIČIUS.

Malaysia: 050051 Almaty, Rubenshtein 9 A; tel. (727) 333-44-83; fax (727) 387-28-25; e-mail mwalmaty@nursat.kz; Ambassador Dato THAN TAI HING.

Mongolia: 050000 Almaty, Musabayev 1; tel. (727) 269-35-70; fax (727) 258-17-27; e-mail monkazel@kazmail.asdc.kz; Ambassador RAVDANGIIN KHATANBAATAR.

Netherlands: 010000 Astana, Kosmonavtov 62/3; tel. (7172) 55-54-50; fax (7172) 55-54-74; e-mail ast@minbuza.nl; Ambassador KLAAS VAN DER TEMPEL.

Oman: 010000 Astana, Chubar sh-a, Novostroitelnaya 3; tel. (7172) 24-18-61; fax (7172) 24-18-63; Ambassador AHMED BIN NASSER AL-MAHRIZI.

Pakistan: 050004 Almaty, Tulebayev 25; tel. (727) 273-15-02; fax (727) 273-13-00; e-mail parepalmaty@hotmail.com; Ambassador IRFAN-UR-REHMAN RAJA.

Poland: 050059 Almaty, Jarkent 9; tel. (727) 258-16-17; fax (727) 258-15-50; e-mail ambpol@mail.kz; internet www.almaty.polemb .net; Ambassador (vacant).

Romania: 050010 Almaty, Pushkin 97; tel. (727) 261-57-72; fax (727) 258-83-17; e-mail amb@rom.ricc.kz; Ambassador EMIL RAPCEA.

Russia: 010000 Astana, Barayev 4; tel. (7172) 22-24-83; fax (7172) 22-38-49; e-mail rfe@nursat.kz; internet www.rfembassy.kz; Ambassador MIKHAIL N. BOCHARNIKOV.

Saudi Arabia: 010000 Astana; tel. (727) 250-28-71; fax (727) 250-28-11; e-mail kzemb@mofa.gov.sa; Ambassador HISHAM BIN ABDEL-WAHAB ZARAA.

Slovakia: 010000 Astana, Mikroraion Karaotkel-2, 5; tel. (7172) 24-11-91; fax (7172) 24-20-48; e-mail zuastana1@post.sk; internet www .mzv.sk/astana; Ambassador Dr DUŠAN PODHORSKÝ.

South Africa: 010000 Astana, pr. Kabanbai Batyr 6/1; tel. (7172) 92-53-26; fax (7172) 92-53-29; e-mail administration@saembassy.kz; Ambassador BEKIZIZVE WISDOM GILA.

Spain: 010000 Astana, Kenesary 47/25; tel. (7172) 21-69-84; fax (7172) 20-03-17; e-mail emb.astana@maec.es; Ambassador SANTIAGO CHAMORRO Y GONZÁLEZ-TABLAS.

Tajikistan: 010000 Astana, Chubar sh-a, Marsovaya 15; tel. and fax (7172) 24-09-29; e-mail embassy_tajic@kepter.kz; Ambassador BAHROM M. KHOLNAZAROV.

Turkey: 050010 Almaty, Tole bi 29; tel. (727) 278-41-65; fax (727) 278-41-68; e-mail almatyturkbe@gmail.com; Ambassador TANER SEBEN.

Turkmenistan: 010000 Astana, Otyrar 64; tel. and fax (7172) 28-08-82; e-mail tm_emb@at.kz; Ambassador KURBANMUKHAMMED G. KASYMOV.

Ukraine: 010000 Astana, Auezova 57; tel. (7172) 32-60-42; fax (7172) 32-68-11; e-mail emb_kz@mfa.gov.ua; internet ukrembassy .kepter.kz; Ambassador MYKOLA F. SELIVON.

United Arab Emirates: 010000 Astana, pos. Zarechnyi, 70 let Oktyabrya 71; tel. (7172) 24-36-75; fax (7172) 24-36-76; e-mail emaratembassy_kz@yahoo.com; Ambassador IBRAHIM HASSAN SAIF.

United Kingdom: 010000 Astana, Kosmonavtov 62, RENCO bldg; tel. (7172) 55-62-00; fax (7172) 55-62-11; e-mail britishembassy@ mail.online.kz; internet www.britishembassy.kz; Ambassador PAUL BRUMMELL.

USA: 010010 Astana, Ak Bulak 4/23-22/3; tel. (7172) 70-21-00; fax (7172) 34-08-90; e-mail info@usembassy.kz; internet kazakhstan .usembassy.gov; Ambassador RICHARD E. HOAGLAND.

Uzbekistan: 050010 Almaty, Baribayeva 36; tel. (727) 291-02-35; fax (727) 291-10-55; Ambassador TURDIKUL S. BUTAYAROV.

Judicial System

Supreme Court of the Republic of Kazakhstan (Kazakhstan Respublikasynyn Zhogargy Soty): 010000 Astana, Levoberezhiye, Tayelsizdik 39; tel. (7172) 74-75-00; fax (7172) 74-78-13; e-mail ms@ supcourt.kz; internet www.supcourt.kz; Chair. KAYRAT A. MAMI.

Constitutional Council of the Republic of Kazakhstan (Kazakhstan Respublikasy Konstitutsiyalyk Keneci): 010000 Astana, Levoberezhiye, Tayelsizdik 39, Zhogargy Soty, Blok A; tel. (7172) 74-76-31; fax (7172) 74-76-51; internet www.constcouncil.kz; f. 1995; seven mems; Chair. IGOR I. ROGOV.

Prosecutor-General: RASHID T. TUSIPBEKOV, 010000 Astana, Seifullin 37; e-mail gp-rk@mail.online.kz; internet www.procuror.kz.

Religion

The major religion of the Kazakhs is Islam. They are almost exclusively Sunni Muslims of the Hanafi school. The Russian Orthodox Church is the dominant Christian denomination; it is attended mainly by Slavs. There are also Protestant Churches (mainly Baptists), as well as a Roman Catholic (Latin Rite) presence and a Jewish community. In mid-2005 legislation was introduced, which required all religious organizations and communities to register with the state authorities.

ISLAM

The Kazakhs were converted to Islam only in the early 19th century, and for many years elements of animist practices remained. Over the period 1985–90 the number of mosques in Kazakhstan increased from 25 to 60. By 1991 there were an estimated 230 Muslim religious communities functioning in Kazakhstan and an Islamic institute had been opened in Almaty. The Islamic revival intensified following Kazakhstan's independence from the USSR, and during 1991–94 some 4,000 mosques were reported to have been opened.

Religious Administration of Muslims of Kazakhstan (Kazakhstan musylmandary dini baskarmasy): 050000 Almaty; tel. (727) 230-63-65; fax (727) 297-94-23; e-mail susaev@bk.ru; internet www .muftyat.kz; Chair. Chief Mufti ABSATTAR B. Haji DERBISALI.

CHRISTIANITY

The Roman Catholic Church

The organization of the Roman Catholic Church in Kazakhstan comprises one archdiocese, two dioceses and one apostolic administration. There were an estimated 183,600 adherents at 31 December 2006.

Archbishop of the Archdiocese of the Most Holy Virgin Mary at Astana: Rt Rev. TOMASZ PETA, 010010 Astana, Tashenova 3, POB 622; tel. (7172) 37-29-35; fax (7172) 37-29-27; e-mail catholic_astana@mail.ru; internet www.catholic-kazakhstan.org.

The Russian Orthodox Church (Moscow Patriarchate)

Metropolitanate of Astana and Almaty: 050014 Almaty, mikroraion Dorozhnik 29; tel. (727) 298-94-15; e-mail office@orthodox.kz; internet www.orthodox.kz; f. 2003; three dioceses; Metropolitan MEFODII (NEMTSOV).

JUDAISM

Mitsva Association of Kazakhstan: Almaty; tel. (727) 273-5449; e-mail contact@mitsva.kz; internet www.mitsva.kz; f. 1992; unites Jewish communities from across Kazakhstan; Pres. ALEKSANDR BARON.

Rabbi of Almaty: Rabbi MENACHEM GERSHOVICH.

The Press

At July 2001 an estimated 950 newspaper and 342 periodical titles were published in Kazakhstan. In addition, 15 news agencies were operating in the country.

PRINCIPAL DAILY NEWSPAPERS

Almaty Asia Times: 050000 Almaty, Jandosova 60/412; tel. (727) 44-74-54; fax (727) 44-78-40.

Almaty Herald: 050000 Almaty, ul. Rozybakiyeva 37; tel. (727) 241-45-69; fax (727) 241-40-78; e-mail herald@nursat.kz; Editor-in-Chief OLESSYA IVANOVA.

Ekspress–K: 050044 Almaty, Abdullinykh 6; tel. (727) 259-60-00; fax (727) 259-60-39; e-mail daily@express-k.kz; internet www .express-k.kz; f. 1920; 5 a week; in Russian; Editor-in-Chief ADILKHAN NUSUPOV; circ. 19,500.

Kazakhstanskaya Pravda (Kazakhstani Truth): 050044 Almaty, Gogolya 39; tel. (727) 263-65-65; fax (727) 250-18-73; tel. (3172) 32-19-44; e-mail kpam@kaznet.kz; internet www.kazpravda.kz; f. 1920; 5 a week; publ. by the Govt; in Russian; Editor-in-Chief V. MIKHAILOV; circ. 34,115.

Khalyk Kenesi (Councils of the People): 010000 Astana; tel. (727) 233-10-85; f. 1990; 5 a week; publ. by Parliament; in Kazakh; Editor-in-Chief ZH. KENZHALIN.

Vechernii Almaty (Evening Almaty): 050016 Almaty, pr. Abylai-khana 2; tel. and fax (727) 279-28-90; e-mail vecherni_almaty@mail .ru; internet www.vechorka.kz; f. 1968; in Russian; Editor-in-Chief ELMIRA R. PASHINA.

Yegemen Kazakhstan (Sovereign Kazakhstan): 050044 Almaty, Gogolya 39; Astana; tel. and fax (727) 263-25-46; tel. (7172) 34-16-41; e-mail astegemen@nursat.kz; f. 1919; 6 a week; organ of the Govt; in Kazakh; Editor-in-Chief M. SERKHANOV; circ. 31,840.

OTHER PUBLICATIONS

Aktsionery (Shareholders): 050004 Almaty, Chaikovskogo 11; tel. (727) 232-96-09; fax (727) 239-98-95; f. 1990; in Russian; two a week; business, investment, Editor-in-Chief VIKTOR SHATSKY.

Ana Tili (Native Language): 050044 Almaty, pr. Dostyk 7; tel. (727) 233-22-21; fax (727) 233-34-73; f. 1990; weekly; in Kazakh; Editor-in-Chief ZH. BEISENBAY-ULY; circ. 11,073.

Ara-Shmel (Bumble-bee): 050044 Almaty, Gogolya 39; tel. (727) 263-59-46; f. 1956; monthly; satirical; in Kazakh and Russian; Editor-in-Chief S. ZHUMABEKOV; circ. 53,799.

Arai (Dawn): 050000 Almaty, Furmanova 53; tel. (727) 232-29-45; f. 1987; every two months; socio-political; Editor-in-Chief S. KUTTY-KADAMOV; circ. 7,500.

Atameken (Fatherland): 050010 Almaty, pr. Dostyk 85; tel. (727) 263-58-43; f. 1991; ecological; publ. by Ministry of Environmental Protection; circ. 25,063.

Aziya Kino (Asian Cinema): 050000 Almaty; tel. (727) 261-86-55; f. 1994; monthly; in Russian and Kazakh; Editor-in-Chief G. ABI-KEYEVA.

Baldyrgan (Sprout): 050044 Almaty, pr. Zhibek-zholy 50; tel. (727) 233-16-73; f. 1958; monthly; illustrated; for pre-school and first grades of school; in Kazakh; Editor-in-Chief T. MOLDAGALIYEV; circ. 150,000.

Business World: 010000 Astana, Pushkina 166; tel. and fax (7172) 75-19-34; e-mail areket-kz@hotmail.com; f. 1999; weekly; circ. 10,000.

Continent: 050000 Almaty, POB 271; tel. (727) 250-10-39; fax (727) 250-10-41; e-mail bzchyt@kaznet.kz; f. 1999; policy and society journal; Editor-in-Chief ANDREI KUKUSHKIN; circ. 10,000.

Delovaya Nedelya (Business Week): 050044 Almaty, pr. Zhibek-zholy 64; tel. (727) 250-62-72; fax (727) 273-91-48; e-mail rikki@ kazmail.asdc.kz; internet www.dn.kz; f. 1992; weekly; in Russian; Editor-in-Chief S. A. KORZHUMBAYEV; circ. 10,600.

Deutsche Allgemeine Zeitung: 050044 Almaty, pr. Zhibek-zholy 50/418; tel. (727) 273-42-69; fax (727) 273-92-91; e-mail daz@ok.kz; f. 1966; weekly; political, economic, cultural, social; in German; Editor-in-Chief IRINA ZIRENTSCHIKOWA; circ. 1,700.

Ekonomika i Zhizn (Economics and Life): 050000 Almaty; tel. (727) 263-96-86; f. 1926; monthly; publ. by the Govt; in Russian; Editor-in-Chief MURAT T. SARSENOV; circ. 4,800.

Ekspert Kazakhstan: 05000 Almaty, Furmanov 122; tel. (727) 295-28-32; fax (727) 295-28-33; e-mail expert@expertkazahstan.kz; internet www.expert.ru/printissues/kazakhstan/; f. 2003; weekly; business and economics; in Russian; Chief Editor ANDREI SKIRKA.

Globe: 050009 Almaty, pr. Abaya 155/13–14; tel. (727) 250-76-39; fax (727) 250-63-62; e-mail ipa@mailonline.kz; f. 1995; two a week; in English and Russian; Editor-in-Chief NURLAN ABLYAZOV; circ. 5,550.

Golos Kazakha/Kazakh Uni (Voice of a Kazakh): 050000 Almaty, Zenkov 75; tel. (727) 261-79-09; fax (727) 261-94-47; f. 1989; weekly; organ of the Federation of Trade Unions of Kazakhstan; in Russian and Kazakh.

Karavan (Caravan): 050000 Almaty, pl. Respubliki 13; tel. (727) 232-08-39; fax (727) 232-97-57; e-mail kaztag@caravan.kz; internet www.caravan.kz; f. 1991; weekly; in Russian; Editor-in-Chief ANDREI SHUKHOV; circ. 250,000.

Kazakh Adebiety (Kazakh Literature): 050000 Almaty, pr. Ablai-khana 105; tel. and fax (727) 269-54-62; f. 1934; weekly; organ of the Union of Writers of Kazakhstan; in Kazakh; Editor-in-Chief A. ZHAKSYBAYEV; circ. 7,874.

Kazakhstan: 050044 Almaty, pr. Zhibek-zholy 50; tel. (727) 233-13-56; f. 1992; weekly; economic reform; in English; Editor-in-Chief N. ORAZBEKOV.

Kazakhstan Aielderi (Women of Kazakhstan): 050044 Almaty, pr. Zhibek-zholy 50; tel. (727) 233-06-23; fax (727) 246-15-53; f. 1925; monthly; literary, artistic, social and political; in Kazakh; Editor-in-Chief ALTYNSHASH K. JAGANOVA; circ. 15,200.

Kazakstan Business: 050044 Almaty, pr. Zhibek-zholy 50; tel. (727) 233-42-56; f. 1991; weekly; in Russian; Editor-in-Chief B. SUKHARBEKOV.

Kazakstan Mektebi (Kazakh School): 050004 Almaty, pr. Ablai-khana 34; tel. (727) 239-76-65; f. 1925; monthly; in Kazakh; Editor-in-Chief S. ABISHEVA; circ. 10,000.

Kazakstan Mugalimi (Kazakh Teacher): 050010 Almaty, Jambula 25; tel. (727) 261-60-58; f. 1935; weekly; in Kazakh; Editor-in-Chief ZH. TEMIRBEKOV; circ. 6,673.

Kazakstan Zaman (Kazakh Time): 050002 Almaty, pr. Dostyk 106G; tel. (727) 265-07-39; e-mail kazakstanzaman@mail.ru; f. 1992; in Kazakh and Turkish; weekly; circ. 15,000; Gen. Dir ERSIN DEMIRCI.

Korye Ilbo (Korean News): 050044 Almaty, pr. Zhibek-zholy 50; tel. (727) 233-90-10; fax (727) 263-25-46; f. 1923; weekly; in Korean and Russian; Editor-in-Chief YAN WON SIK.

Kredo (Credo): 100029 Karaganda, Oktyabrskaya 25; e-mail credogazeta@topmail.kz; internet www.catholic-kazakhstan.org/Credo/index.htm; f. 1995; monthly; Roman Catholic; in Russian; Chief Editor N. MAMAYEV.

Medicina (Medicine): 050004 Almaty, pr. Ablai-khana 63; tel. (727) 273-48-01; fax (727) 273-16-90; e-mail zdrav_kz@nursat.kz; f. 2000; monthly; in Kazakh; Editor-in-Chief A. SH. SEYSENBAYEV; circ. 5,000.

Novoye Pokoleniye (New Generation): 050091 Almaty, ul. Bogenbai batyra 139/1–2; tel. (727) 261-31-06; fax (727) 250-95-46; e-mail np@host.kz; internet www.np.kz; f. 1998; weekly; in Russian; Editor-in-Chief SERGEI APARIN; circ. 95,000.

Oasis: 080000 Jambul obl., Taraz, ul. Lenina 31–34; tel. and fax (7262) 23-27-93; e-mail alex@zagribelny.jambyl.kz; organ of the Green Movement Socio-Ecological Centre; environmental matters; Editor-in-Chief ALEKSANDR ZAGRIBELNYI.

Panorama: 050013 Almaty, pl. Respubliki 15/647; tel. (727) 263-28-34; fax (727) 263-66-16; e-mail panorama@kazmail.asdc.kz; internet www.panorama.kz; f. 1992; weekly; in Russian; Editor-in-Chief LERA TSOY; circ. 18,500.

Parasat: 050000 Almaty, Aiteke bi 28; tel. (727) 293-94-71; fax (727) 293-94-74; f. 1958; monthly; socio-political, literary, illustrated; in Kazakh; Editor-in-Chief BAKKOZHA S. MUKAY; circ. 20,000.

Petroleum of Kazakhstan: 050091 Almaty, Nauryzbai batyr 58; tel. (727) 258-28-33; fax (727) 250-50-82; e-mail office@petroleumjournal.kz; internet www.petroleumjournal.kz; every two months; in Russian and English; Editor-in-Chief OLEG C. CHERVINSKY; circ. 2,000.

Prostor (Expanse): 050091 Almaty, pr. Abylai-khana 105; tel. (727) 272-61-87; e-mail info@prstr.samal.kz; internet prostor.samal.kz; f. 1933; monthly; literary and artistic; in Russian; Editor-in-Chief VALERII F. MIKHAILOV; circ. 1,800.

Respublika—Delovoye obozreniye (The Republic—Business Review): 050010 Almaty, Satpayeva 2/17; tel. and fax (727) 53-46-71; e-mail assandy@fromru.com; internet www.respublika.kz; weekly; in Russian; Editor-in-Chief IRINA PETRUSHOVA.

Russkii Yazyk i Literatura (Russian Language and Literature): 050091 Almaty, pr. Abylai-khana 34; tel. (727) 239-76-68; f. 1962; monthly; in Russian; Editor-in-Chief B. S. MUKANOV; circ. 17,465.

Sovety Kazakhstana (Councils of Kazakhstan): 050044 Almaty, pr. Zhibek-zholy 15; tel. (727) 234-92-19; f. 1990; weekly; publ. by Parliament; in Russian; Editor-in-Chief YU. GURSKII; circ. 30,000.

Turkistan: 050009 Almaty, ul. Abaya 143; tel. (727) 243-32-42; fax (727) 243-58-11; e-mail turkestan_gazeta@mail.ru; internet www.turkystan.kz; f. 1994; weekly; political; in Kazakh; Editor SH. A. PATTEYEV; circ. 10,000.

Uigur Avazi (Uigur Voice): 050044 Almaty, pr. Zhibek-zholy 50; tel. (727) 233-84-59; f. 1957; 2 a week; publ. by the Govt; socio-political; in Uigur; Editor-in-Chief I. AZAMATOV; circ. 9,000.

Ulan (Hey You!): 050044 Almaty, pr. Zhibek-zholy 50; tel. (727) 233-80-03; f. 1930; weekly; in Kazakh; Editor-in-Chief S. KALIYEV; circ. 183,014.

Vremya (Time): 050000 Almaty, pr. Raiymbeka 115; tel. and fax (727) 258-10-06; internet www.time.kz; f. 1999; weekly; in Russian; Editor-in-Chief IGOR MELTSER; circ. 250,000 (2004).

Zerde (Intellect): 050044 Almaty, pr. Zhibek-zholy 50; tel. (727) 233-83-81; f. 1960; monthly; popular, scientific, technical; in Kazakh; Editor-in-Chief E. RAUSHAN-ULY; circ. 68,600.

Zhas Alash (Young Generation): 050044 Almaty, Makatayeva 22; tel. (727) 230-60-90; fax (727) 230-24-69; internet www.zhasalash.kz; f. 1921; publ. by the Kazakhstan Youth Union; in Kazakh; Editor-in-Chief ZHUSIPBEK KORGASBEK; circ. 133,000.

NEWS AGENCIES

Khabar News Agency: see Broadcasting and Communications.

National Information Agency 'Kazinform': 010000 Astana, Beibitshilik 10; tel. and fax (7172) 32-75-67; e-mail product@inform.kz; internet www.inform.kz; f. 1997; 100% state-owned open jt-stock co; provides information on govt activities in Kazakhstan and abroad; Pres. ZHANAI S. OMAROV.

Publishers

Gylym (Science): 050010 Almaty, Pushkin 111–113; tel. (727) 291-18-77; fax (727) 261-88-45; f. 1946; books on natural sciences, humanities and scientific research journals; Dir S. G. BAIMENOV.

Kainar (Spring): 050009 Almaty, pr. Abaya 143; tel. (727) 242-27-96; e-mail kainar_baspasy@mail.ru; f. 1962; agriculture, history, culture, religion; Dir ORAZBEK S. SARSENBAYEV.

Kazakhskaya Entsiklopediya (Kazakh Encyclopedia): 050000 Almaty; tel. (727) 262-55-66; f. 1968; Editor-in-Chief R. N. NURGALIYEV.

Kazakhstan Publishing House: 050000 Almaty, pr. Abaya 143; tel. and fax (727) 242-29-29; f. 1920; political science, economics, medicine, general and social sciences; Dir E. KH. SYZDYKOV; Editors-in-Chief M. D. SITKO, M. A. RASHEV.

Mektep: 050009 Almaty, pr. Abaya 143; tel. (727) 242-26-24; fax (727) 277-85-44; e-mail mektep@mail.ru; internet www.mektep.kz; f. 1947; mainly literature for educational institutions; dictionaries, phrase books, children's textbooks, teaching materials, reference books; publishes books in Kazakh, Russian, Uigur and Uzbek; Gen. Dir E. SATYBALDIYEV; Editor-in-Chief SH. GUSAKOVA.

Oner (Art): 050000 Almaty, pr. Abaya 143; tel. (727) 242-08-88; f. 1980; Dir S. S. ORAZALINOV; Editor-in-Chief A. A. ASKAROV.

Zhazushy (Writer): 050000 Almaty, pr. Abaya 143; tel. (727) 242-28-49; f. 1934; literature, literary criticism, essays and poetry; Dir D. I. ISABEKOV; Editor-in-Chief A. T. SARAYEV.

Broadcasting and Communications

GOVERNMENT AGENCY

Republican Agency for Information and Communications: 010000 Astana, Ministry Bldg, Levoberezhiye, Ishim; tel. (7172) 74-01-35; fax (7172) 74-10-03; e-mail press@aic.gov.kz; internet www.aic.gov.kz; Chair. KUANYSHBEK B. YESEKEYEV.

TELECOMMUNICATIONS

Altel: 050000 Almaty, ul. Zhurgeneva 9; tel. (727) 230-16-30; fax (727) 230-01-43; e-mail info@altel.kz; internet www.altel.kz; f. 1994; provides mobile cellular communications in Kazakhstan (as Dalacom and PAThWORD).

GSM Kazakhstan: 050000 Almaty, Samal 2/100; tel. (727) 258-11-48; fax (727) 258-89-11; e-mail webmaster@kcell.kz; internet www.kcell.kz; f. 1998; 51% owned by Fintur Holdings (Finland/Turkey),

49% by Kazakhtelecom; provides mobile cellular telecommunications services (as K-Cell and Activ) in 180 settlements and along principal roads across Kazakhstan; 2m. subscribers (April 2005).

KaR-tel (K-Mobile): 050000 Almaty, Tole bi 55; tel. (727) 250-60-60; fax (727) 295-23-97; e-mail csales@kartel.kz; internet www.k-mobile .kz; f. 1999; 100% subsidiary of VympelKom-Bilain (Russia); provides mobile cellular telecommunications services (as K-Mobile, Excess and Beeline) in more than 100 settlements and along principal roads across Kazakhstan; Gen. Dir DMITRII KROMSKII; 1.6m. subscribers (mid-2005).

Kazakhtelekom: 050000 Almaty, pr. Abylai-khana 86; tel. (727) 262-05-41; fax (727) 263-93-95; internet www.itte.kz; f. 1994; national telecommunications corpn; 60% state-owned, 40% owned by Daewoo Corpn (Republic of Korea); Pres. SERIK BURKITBAYEV.

KazTransCom: 050012 Almaty, Baitursynov 46A; tel. (727) 270-13-10; fax (727) 270-13-18; e-mail ktc@kaztranscom.kz; jt-stock co; provides telecommunications services to the petroleum and natural gas sectors; won licence in 2004 to provide long-distance and international telephone calls country-wide, becoming Kazakhstan's second long-distance provider.

BROADCASTING

Private radio and television stations began operating in Kazakhstan in the 1990s. In mid-2001 there were an estimated 124 radio and television stations.

Kazakh State Television and Radio Broadcasting Corpn: 050013 Almaty, Zheltoksan 175A; tel. (727) 263-37-16; f. 1920; Pres. YERMEK TURSUNOV.

Radio

Kazakh Radio: 050013 Almaty, Zheltoksan 175A; tel. (727) 263-19-68; fax (727) 265-03-87; e-mail kazradio@astel.kz; internet www .radio.kz; f. 1921; broadcasts in Kazakh, Russian, Uigur, German and other minority languages; Gen. Dir TOREKHAN DANIYAR.

Radio 31: 050060 Almaty, Tazhibayevoi 155; tel. (727) 315-29-31; e-mail radio@31.kz; internet www.31.kz; f. 1994; news and music; Dir SABIT SULEIMENOV.

Television

Khabar News Agency: 050013 Almaty, pl. Respubliki 13; tel. (727) 263-83-69; fax (727) 250-63-45; e-mail naz@khabar.almaty.kz; internet www.khabar.kz; f. 1959; international broadcasts in Kazakh, Uigur, Russian and German; two television channels; Chair. of the Bd of Dirs MAULEN ASHIMBAYEV; Dir GULNAR IKSANOVA.

KTK (Kazakh Commercial Television): 050013 Almaty, pl. Respubliki 13; tel. (727) 263-44-28; fax (727) 250-66-25; e-mail ktkao@ kzaira.com; f. 1990; independent; Gen. Dir ANDREI SHUKHOV; Pres. SHOKAN LAUULIN.

NTK (Association of TV and Radio Broadcasters of Kazakhstan): 050013 Almaty, pl. Respubliki 13, 6th Floor; tel. (727) 270-01-83; fax (727) 270-01-85; e-mail kaztvradio@nursat.kz; f. 2000; privately owned; Pres. AIDAR ZHUMABAYEV.

Finance

(cap. = capital; res = reserves; dep. = deposits; m. = million; brs = branches; amounts in tenge, unless otherwise indicated)

BANKING

Central Bank

National Bank of Kazakhstan (NBK): 050040 Almaty, Koktem-3 21; tel. (727) 270-45-91; fax (727) 250-60-90; e-mail hq@nationalbank .kz; internet www.nationalbank.kz; f. 1990; cap. 20,000.0m., res 83,734.6m., dep. 2,325.4m. (Dec. 2006); Gov. ANVAR G. SAIDENOV; 19 brs.

Major Commercial Banks

Alliance Bank: 050000 Almaty, Kunayev 32; tel. (727) 258-40-40; fax (727) 259-67-87; e-mail info@alb.kz; internet www.alb.kz; f. 1999; cap. 96,380m., res 3,2987m., dep. 929,386m. (Dec. 2007); Chair. DAUREN KEREIBAYEV.

ATF Bank: 050000 Almaty, Furmanova 100; tel. (727) 250-30-40; fax (727) 250-19-95; e-mail info@atfbank.kz; internet www.atfbank.kz; f. 1995; present name adopted 2002; cap. 57,897.6m., res 576.0m., dep. 851,514.8m. (Dec. 2007); Chair. TIMUR ISSATAYEV; 10 brs.

Bank Centercredit: 050000 Almaty, Panfilov 98; tel. (727) 259-85-98; fax (727) 258-45-10; e-mail info@centercredit.kz; internet www .centercredit.kz; f. 1988; present name adopted 1996; cap. 36,298.0m., res 1,448.0m., dep. 760,334.0m. (Dec. 2007); Chair. of Bd BAKHYTBEK R. BAYSEITOV; 19 brs.

BTA Bank: 050051 Almaty, Samal 2, Zholdasbekov 97; tel. (727) 250-40-70; fax (727) 250-02-24; e-mail post@bta.kz; internet www .bta.kz; f. 1997 as Bank TuranAlem; name changed as above 2008; cap. 303,427.0m., res –646.0m., dep. 2,578,698.0m. (Dec. 2007); Chair. ROMAN SOLODCHENKO; 23 brs.

Caspian Bank (Bank Kaspiiskii): 050012 Almaty, Adi Sharipov 90; tel. (727) 250-18-00; fax (727) 250-95-96; e-mail office@bankcaspian .kz; internet www.bc.kz; 96% owned by Caspian Group (Netherlands); cap. 17,507.4m., res 2,200.1m., dep. 212,274.6m. (Dec. 2007); Chair. MIKHEIL LOMTADZE; 17 brs.

Demir Kazakhstan Bank: 050012 Almaty, Tole bi 83; tel. (727) 244-92-44; fax (727) 244-92-35; e-mail demirbank@demirbank.kz; internet www.demirbank.kz; f. 1997; cap. 1,000m., res 39.5m., dep. 11,263.0m. (Dec. 2006); Gen. Man. YAVUZ AHMET EROL; 3 brs.

Development Bank of Kazakhstan: 010000 Astana, pr. Respublika 32; tel. (7172) 58-02-60; fax (7172) 58-02-76; e-mail info@kdb .kz; internet www.kdb.kz; wholly state-owned; cap. 70,572.9m., res 8,424.8m., dep. 95,413.4m. (Dec. 2006); Pres. ZHANAT ZHAKANOV.

Eurasian Bank: 050002 Almaty, Kunayeva 56; tel. (727) 250-86-07; fax (727) 250-86-50; e-mail info@eurasian-bank.kz; internet www .eurasian-bank.kz; f. 1994; cap. 7,999.9m., res 702.3m., dep. 129,932.7m. (Dec. 2007); Chair. ZHOMART YERTAYEV; 18 brs.

Eurasian Development Bank: 050000 Almaty, Panfilov 98; tel. (727) 244-40-44; fax (727) 244-65-70; e-mail info@eabr.org; internet www.eabr.org; f. 2006; cap. US \$804.8m., res US \$4.9m., dep. US \$454.7m. (Dec. 2007); Chair. IGOR FINOGENOV.

Halyk Bank: 050046 Almaty, Rozybakiyeva 97; tel. (727) 259-00-00; fax (727) 259-02-71; e-mail halykbank@halykbank.kz; internet www .halykbank.kz; f. 1936 as br. of Savings Bank of USSR; fully privatized in Nov. 2001; cap. 65,531.0m., res 94,139.0m., dep. 1,410,618.0m. (Dec. 2007); Chair. GRIGORII MARCHENKO; 611 brs.

HSBC Bank Kazakhstan: 050010 Almaty, pr. Dostyk 43; tel. (727) 259-69-00; fax (727) 259-69-02; e-mail info@hsbc.kz; internet www .hsbc.kz; f. 1998; 100% owned by HSBC Bank PLC (United Kingdom); cap. 3,360.0m., res 514.2m., dep. 63,749.7m. (Dec. 2007); Chair. of Bd of Dirs DEREK P. LUNT.

KazInvestBank: 050051 Almaty, pr. Dostyk 176; tel. (727) 261-90-60; fax (727) 259-86-58; e-mail info@kib.kz; internet www.kib.kz; f. 1993; open jt-stock co; cap. 9,466.1m., res 99.7m., dep. 37,430.7m. (Dec. 2007); Chair. ADNAN ALLY AGHA; 3 brs.

Kazkommertsbank (KKB): 050060 Almaty, Gagarina 135; tel. (727) 258-53-01; fax (727) 258-51-61; e-mail mailbox@kkb.kz; internet www.kkb.kz; f. 1991; cap. 6,998.0m., res 299,669.0m., dep. 2,365,932.0m. (Dec. 2007); Chair. NURZHAN S. SUBKHANBERDIN; Man. Dir ANDREI I. TIMCHENKO; 23 brs.

Nurbank: 050010 Almaty, pr. Dostyk 38; tel. (727) 259-97-10; fax (727) 250-16-09; e-mail bank@nurbank.kz; internet www.nurbank .kz; f. 1992; cap. 25,036.2m., res 272.4m., dep. 159,432.9m. (Dec. 2007); Chair. NURMUKHAMED BEKTEMISSOV; 56 brs.

Temirbank: 050008 Almaty, pr. Abaya 68/74; tel. (727) 257-88-88; fax (727) 250-62-41; e-mail board@temirbank.kz; internet www .temirbank.kz; f. 1992; cap. 34,568.5m., res –107.1m., dep. 284,714.4m. (Dec. 2007); Chair. MURAT YULDASHEV; 15 brs.

Tsesnabank: 010000 Astana, Zhengis dangghyly 29; tel. (7172) 77-07-70; fax (7172) 77-01-95; e-mail info@tsb.kz; internet www.tsb.kz; f. 1992; cap. 13,500.0m., res 1,738.5m., dep. 123.355.8m. (Dec. 2007); Chair. YERKEGALI YEDENBAYEV; 9 brs.

Bankers' Organization

Bank Association of Kazakhstan: 010000 Almaty, Panfilova 98; tel. (727) 273-16-89; fax (727) 273-90-85; Pres. BAKHYTBEK BAISEITOV.

STOCK EXCHANGE

Kazakhstan Stock Exchange (KASE): 050000 Almaty, Aiteke bi 67; tel. (727) 272-98-98; fax (727) 272-09-25; e-mail info@kase.kz; internet www.kase.kz; f. 1993; Pres. and Chief Exec. AZAMAT M. JOLDASBEKOV.

INSURANCE

Almaty International Insurance Group: 050000 Almaty, Kabanbai batyr 112; tel. and fax (727) 250-12-31; internet www.aiig.escort .kz; f. 1994; Chair. SUREN AMBARTSUMIAN.

Centras Insurance: 050008 Almaty, Manas 32A; tel. (727) 259-77-55; fax (727) 259-77-66; e-mail insurance@centras.kz; internet www .cic.kz; f. 1997; non-life insurance and reinsurance; Chair. TALGAT USENOV.

Dynasty Life Insurance Co: 050000 Almaty, Seifullina 410; tel. (727) 250-73-95; e-mail dynasty@bta.nursat.kz; Chair. SERIK TEMIR-GALEYEV.

Industrial Insurance Group (IIG): 050046 Almaty, Nauryzbai Batyr 65–69; tel. (727) 250-96-95; fax (727) 250-96-98; e-mail iig@kaznet.kz; f. 1998; Pres. IVAN MIKHAILOV.

KazAgroPolits Insurance Co: 050000 Almaty, Nauryzbai Batyr 49–61; tel. (727) 232-13-24; fax (727) 232-13-26; e-mail kazagropolise@mail.banknet.kz; Chair. YERMEK USPANOV.

Kazakhinstrakh (Kazakh International Insurance Co): 050044 Almaty, pr. Zhibek-zholy 69; tel. (727) 233-73-49; fax (727) 250-74-37; e-mail kiscentr@nursat.kz; Chair. NURLAN MOLDAKHMETOV.

Kazkommerts-Polits Insurance Co: 050013 Almaty, Satpayeva 24; tel. (727) 258-48-08; fax (727) 292-73-97; e-mail info@kkp.kz; internet www.kkp.kz; f. 1996; non-life; Chair. MEIRAM B. SERGAZIN; Dir TALGAT K. USSENOV.

MSCA (Medical Systems of Central Asia) Interteach: 050000 Almaty, Kabanbai batyr 122A; tel. and fax (727) 258-23-32; e-mail interteach@kaznet.kaz; f. 1989; medical and travel insurance, health care, accident and employee liability insurance; 290 employees; 48 brs; Gen. Dir ERNST M. KURLEUTOV.

Trade and Industry

GOVERNMENT AGENCY

Republican Agency for the Regulation of Natural Monopolies: 010000 Astana, Bukeikhan 14; tel. (7172) 59-16-77; fax (7172) 21-54-73; e-mail info@arem.kz; internet www.regulator.kz; Chair. NURLAN SH. ALDABERGENOV.

CHAMBERS OF COMMERCE

Union of Chambers of Commerce and Industry of Kazakhstan: 050000 Almaty, Masanchi 26; tel. (727) 292-00-52; fax (727) 250-70-29; e-mail tpprkaz@online.ru; internet www.ccikaz.kz; f. 1959; Chair. ABLAI MYRZAKHMETOV.

Aktobe Oblast Chamber of Commerce and Industry: 030000 Aktobe, Zhubanova 289/1; tel. (7132) 51-02-26; e-mail akbtpp@mail.ru; Chair. ELENA A. RUDENKO.

Almaty City Chamber of Commerce and Industry: 050000 Almaty, Tole bi 45; tel. (727) 262-03-01; e-mail alcci@nursat.kz; internet www.atpp.marketcenter.ru; Chair. ZULFIYA K. AKHMETZHANOVA.

Astana City Chamber of Commerce and Industry: 010000 Astana, Auezov 66, POB 1966; tel. (7172) 32-38-33; e-mail akmcci@dan.kz; internet www.chamber.kz; Chair. TATYANA I. KONONOVA.

Jambul Oblast Chamber of Commerce and Industry: 080012 Jambul obl., Taraz, Karakhana 2; tel. (7262) 43-05-98; Chair. ADILKHAN ZHAPARBEKOV.

Karaganda Oblast Chamber of Commerce and Industry: 100000 Karaganda, bulv. Mira 31; tel. (7212) 30-06-84; fax (7212) 30-05-05; e-mail karcci@mail.ru; internet www.karcci.kz; f. 1959; Chair. of Presidium NESSIP SEITOVA.

Kostanai Oblast Chamber of Commerce and Industry: 110003 Kostanai, Taran 165; tel. (7142) 54-66-72; fax (7142) 54-44-03; e-mail ko_tpp@mail.kz; f. 1973; Chair. VALENTINA N. TRIBUSHNAYA.

Pavlodar Oblast Chamber of Commerce and Industry: 140002 Pavlodar, Toraigyrova 95/1; tel. (7182) 75-79-69; e-mail pav-cci@kaznet.kz; Chair. RAJHANGUL SATABAYEVA.

Southern Kazakhstan Oblast Chamber of Commerce and Industry: 160000 Southern Kazakhstan obl., Chimkent, Taukekhan 31; tel. (7252) 21-14-05; Chair. SYRLYBAJ ORDABEKOV.

EMPLOYERS' ORGANIZATIONS

Confederation of Employers of the Republic of Kazakhstan (KRRK): 050022 Almaty, pr. Abaya 42/44; tel. (727) 293-07-42; fax (727) 292-27-68; e-mail krrk@krrk.kz; internet www.krrk.kz; Pres. KADYR BAYIKENOV.

Kazakhstan Petroleum Association: 050010 Almaty, pr. Dostyk 43/517; tel. (727) 250-18-16; fax (727) 250-18-17; e-mail kpa@arna.kz; internet www.kpa.kz; f. 1998; Chair. NURZHAN KAMALOV; 61 mem. cos.

UTILITIES

Electricity

KEGOS—Kazakhstan Electricity Grid Operating Co (Elektr zhelilerin baskaru zhanindegi Kazakstan kompaniyasy): 050000 Almaty, ul. Kozybayeva 23; tel. (727) 271-93-59; internet www.kegoc.kz; f. 1997; technical electricity network operator; Pres. ALMASADAM M. SATKALIYEV.

Water

Almaty Vodocanal: 050057 Almaty, Zharokov 196; tel. (727) 274-84-02; fax (727) 274-98-41; e-mail vk.prm@itte.kz; internet www.almaty-vodokanal.kz; f. 1936; state-owned; responsible for water supply and sewerage in Almaty and surrounding villages; Gen. Dir VLADISLAV GALIYEV.

STATE HYDROCARBONS COMPANIES

KazMunaiGaz: 010000 Astana, pr.Kabanbai batyr 22; tel. (7172) 97-60-00; fax (7172) 97-60-01; e-mail info@kmg.kz; internet www.kmg.kz; f. 2002 by merger of KazakhOil and Transneftegas; national jt-stock co; subsidiaries include petroleum-transportation co KazTransOil, and gas-transportation co KazTransGas; Pres. KAIRGELDY KABYLDIN.

Munaigaz: 010000 Astana, Zheltoksan 7/1; tel. and fax (7172) 39-03-11; e-mail info@munaygas.com; internet www.munaygas.com; f. 2004; petroleum and gas prospecting and producing; Pres. YE. V. BELYAYEV.

MAJOR COMPANIES

Chemicals

Kazphosphate Chimkent: 160000 Southern Kazakhstan obl., Chimkent, Lengerskoye; tel. (7252) 44-53-54; fax (7252) 50-61-07; internet www.kazphosphate.kz; f. 1964; formerly Fosfor Production Association; production and sale of phosphorus and phosphorus products; Gen. Dir EMIL U. ZHOMARTBAYEV; 4,500 employees.

Khimprom-2030: 080000 Jambul obl., Taraz, Industrial Zone 26; tel. (7262) 34-21-80; fax (7262) 34-30-60; e-mail berrimor@rambler.ru; f. 1968; production and export of yellow phosphorus and its products; Pres. N. O. UALIYEV; 4,800 employees.

Kramds: 050000 Almaty, pr. Kabanbai batyra 164; tel. (727) 250-93-51; fax (727) 267-18-50; f. 1988; production of petroleum, and organic and inorganic chemicals; Pres. KANAT S. BAKBERGENOV; Man. Dir VALERII V. VRUBLEVSKII; 15,000 employees.

Nodfos: 080000 Jambul obl., Taraz; tel. (7262) 25-26-19; fax (7262) 25-35-05; f. 1979; jt-stock co; produces chemicals; Dir M. A. AKHMEDOV; 6,000 employees.

Polipropilen Co: 060005 Atyrau, Sevetnaya 1; tel. (7122) 29-40-00; fax (7122) 29-40-04; manufacturer of polypropylene products; Man. Dir VLADIMIR PASHKIN.

Metals

Alyumini Kazakhstan: 140012 Pavlodar; tel. and fax (7182) 46-49-86; f. 1996 by merger; Dir ALMAZ IBRAGIMOV.

Ispat Karmet Steel Plant: 101417 Karaganda obl., Temirtau, pr. Lenina 1; tel. (7213) 56-22-00; fax (7213) 55-46-27; e-mail general.karmet@ispat.com; f. 1995 by Ispat International (United Kingdom); joint-stock co; owns Karmet steelworks; production and export of pig-iron, manufacturer of hot and cold-rolled flat and long steel, tin, coke and chemicals; Man. ADIL VADOLIVALA; 28,600 employees.

Kazakhmys: 100600 Karaganda obl., Jezkazgan, Gogol 5; internet www.kazakhmys.kz; f. 1928; formerly Zhezkazkantsvetmet; owned by Samsung Deutschland (a subsidiary of Samsung, Rep. of Korea); producer of copper, zinc, gold, silver and electricity; Chair. of Bd VLADIMIR KIM; 65,000 employees.

Kazchrome TNC: 050002 Almaty, Kunayev 56; tel. (727) 260-26-64; fax (727) 250-78-59; f. 1995; production of ferrous metals and alloys, incl. chrome; 15,000 employees.

Petroleum and Natural Gas

Agip Kazakhstan North Caspian Operating Co (AgipKCO): 060002 Atyrau, Dossorskaya 5; tel. (7122) 25-50-91; fax (7122) 25-50-96; e-mail reception@agipkco.kz; internet www.agipkco.kz; fmrly Offshore Kazakhstan International Operating Co; present name adopted 2001; operates the Kashagan oilfield, on behalf of a seven-member consortium of international petroleum cos; subsidiary co of the ENI Group (Italy); Regional Dir ANDREA CHIURA.

Batystransgas: 090007 Western Kazakhstan obl., Oral, Esenzhanova 42/1; tel. (7112) 22-79-15; fax (7112) 24-76-24; f. 1995; joint-stock co; processing, storage and transport of natural gas; Pres. YESSET ASERBAYEV; 8,128 employees.

BP Kazakhstan: 050010 Almaty, Satpayev 29/6, Hyatt Regency Business Centre; tel. (727) 250-32-35; fax (7272) 250-32-40; owned by BP (United Kingdom); extracting and refining of petroleum, exploration and survey work; Dir ERZHAN BUZURBAYEV.

Karazhanbasmunai: 130000 Mangistau obl., Aktau, 15 Mikroraion 3; tel. (7292) 43-36-00; fax (7292) 43-50-62; e-mail kbm@kbm.kz; internet www.kbm.kz; jt-stock co; formerly Karazhanmunaigaz; production of petroleum and natural gas; Pres. HASHIM DHOJOHADIKUSUMO; 2,394 employees.

Kazakhgas State Holding Company: 090007 Western Kazakhstan obl., Oral, Poymennaya 2/4; tel. (7112) 22-79-15; fax (7112) 24-76-24; f. 1991; production, storage and transport of natural gas from Karachaganak; Pres. Dr ERSET AZERBAYEV; 16,000 employees.

Kazakhoil–Emba Joint Stock Company: 060002 Atyrau, Valikhanov 1; tel. (7122) 22-29-24; fax (7122) 25-41-27; f. 1911; production of petroleum and natural gas; fmrly Embamunaigas and Tengizmunaigas; Pres. MAKHAMBET BATYRBAYEV; 5,800 employees.

Kaznefteprodukt: 050000 Almaty; tel. (727) 262-43-50; fax (727) 262-30-79; f. 1993; wholesale trade in petroleum products and provision of services; Gen. Dir KALDYBAY U. USENOV.

KPO BV Astana: 050000 Almaty, Samal, Astana Tower Business Centre; tel. and fax (727) 258-08-09; e-mail skeeld@kpo.kz; internet www.kpo.kz; formerly BG Kazakhstan; owned by KPO BV; exploration and production of natural gas; Country Rep. DAVID D. SKEELS.

MangistauManaiGaz: 130000 Mangistau obl., Aktau, 6-oi Mikroraion 1; tel. (7292) 51-45-57; fax (7292) 43-39-19; f. 1963; jt-stock co; production of petroleum and natural gas; Gen. Dir V. MIROSHNIKOV; 24,000 employees.

PetroKazakhstan: 050009 Almaty, Karasai batyra 204; tel. (727) 258-18-48; fax (727) 258-18-60; e-mail info@petrokazakhstan.com; internet www.petrokazakhstan.com; 67% owned by China National Petroleum Corpn (CNPC), 33% by KazMunaiGaz; principal Kazakhstan subsidiaries: PetroKazakhstan Kumkol Resources (94%, fmrly Yuzhneftegaz), PetroKazakhstan Oil Products (97%, fmrly Chimkentnefteorgsyntez—Chimkent Petroleum Refinery), Turgai Petroleum (50%), Kazgermunai (50%); gas and petroleum production and sales; Pres. BERNARD F. ISAUTIER.

Shell Kazakhstan: 050000 Almaty, Abai 155/7–8; tel. (727) 250-63-58; fax (727) 250-93-04; internet www.shell.kz; extraction and refining of petroleum; subsidiary of Shell International Petroleum; Pres. MARTIN FERSTL; Gen. Dir D. SMETHURST.

Miscellaneous

Agrocentre-Astana: 010000 Astana, pr. Pobedy 104; tel. (7172) 31-49-03; fax (7172) 31-97-00; e-mail agrocenter@kepter.kz; f. 1997; production and distribution of agricultural products (grain, meat and milk); Gen. Dir VLADIMIR M. PETROV; 8,000 employees.

Astanatechnopark: 010000 Astana, Pushkin 166; tel. (7172) 32-88-25; fax (7172) 32-88-34; e-mail astanatechnopark@nursat.kz; f. 1942; 90% state-owned; fmrly Akmolaselmash JSC; production of agricultural machinery for soil conservation; Pres. BAURZHAN N. BAYMUKHANOV; Gen. Dir SERIK I MASSELOV; 180 employees.

Butya: 050010 Almaty, Bogenbai batyra 80; tel. (727) 250-06-00; fax (727) 250-70-83; import and export of grain and metal and petroleum products; construction.

Chimkent Industrial Amalgamation: 160008 Southern Kazakhstan obl., Chimkent, Abai 28; tel. (7252) 12-29-43; fax (7252) 23-88-40; f. 1942; state-owned co; specializes in the production of pressforging equipment; Pres. VLADIMIR D. PLYATSUK; 2,000 employees.

Electromontazh (ELMO): 050061 Almaty, Utegen batyr 7; tel. (727) 277-14-75; fax (727) 276-65-64; e-mail amyelmo@mail.ru; manufactures wiring products and provides wiring services; Dir VALERYI I. VOLOHOV.

Kazstroipolimer: 100000 Karaganda; tel. and fax (7212) 46-01-32; f. 1969; production of textiles, linoleum, foam, dyes, plastic consumer goods, crystal.

Kurylys Holding Co: 050000 Almaty, Zheltoksana 147 A; tel. (727) 233-01-72; fax (727) 233-10-84; e-mail nhc_ak@almatykurylys.kz; internet www.almatykurylys.kz; construction, reconstruction of dwellings and civil engineering; Pres. MUKHAMEDZHAN S. KARBAEV; 9,700 employees.

Merey Furniture Co: 050000 Almaty; jt-stock co; manufactures and exports furniture; Chair. NADJAT KADYROV; 1,500 employees.

Tagam: 050012 Almaty, Bogenbai batyra 148; tel. (727) 262-03-62; fax (727) 262-86-52; f. 1989; joint-stock co; production and sale of sugar and alcohol, sale of tobacco products; Pres. T. M. DNISHEV; 40 employees.

Tsesna-Astyk: 010000 Astana, Ugolnaya 24; tel. (7172) 31-01-69; fax (7172) 31-01-54; e-mail marketing@tsesnaastyk.kz; internet www.tsesnaastyk.kz; f. 1988; wheat, wheat products, mineral and metal exports, fertilizers; Chair. NIKOLAI I. MERSHERYAKO.

Ust-Kamenogorsk Capacitor Plant Joint-Stock Co: 070001 Eastern Kazakhstan obl., Ust-Kamenogorsk; tel. (7232) 26-02-91; fax (3232) 26-02-92; e-mail kvar@ukg.kz; internet www.ukkz.com; f. 1959; produces complete capacitor installations, coupling capacitors, water-cooled capacitors, etc.; Pres. VLADIMIR AKSENOV; 477 employees.

Ust-Kamenogorsk Titanium and Magnesium Combined Plant: 070017 Eastern Kazakhstan obl., Ust-Kamenogorsk; tel. (7232) 33-74-50; fax (7232) 33-66-00; f. 1965; Pres. BAGHDAD M. SCHAYAKHMETOV.

Zavod Plasticheskih Mass (Plastics Production Plant): 130000 Mangystau obl., Aktau, Industrial Zone; tel. (7292) 51-45-19; fax (7292) 33-12-10; e-mail stirene2@nursat.kz; internet www.polystirol.ru; f. 1980; fmrly Akpo; manufacturer of plastic products; Gen. Dir M. GERASIMOV; 1,500 employees.

TRADE UNIONS

Confederation of Free Trade Unions of Kazakhstan: f. 1991; fmrly Independent Trade Union Centre of Kazakhstan; 9 regional brs with 2,200 mems; Chair. SERGEI BELKIN.

Confederation of Free Trade Unions of Coal and Mining Industries: 050000 Almaty; Chair. V. GAIPOV.

Federation of Trade Unions of Kazakhstan: 010000 Astana, pr. Abaya 94; tel. (7172) 216-68-14; fax (7172) 21-68-35; e-mail fprkastana@nursat.kz; internet www.fprk.kz; 30 affiliated unions with 2,300,000 mems (2001); Chair. SIYAZBEK MUKASHEV.

Transport

RAILWAYS

In 2003 the total length of rail track in use was 13,601 km (3,661 km of which were electrified). The rail network is most concentrated in the north of the country, where it joins the rail lines of Russia. In mid-2003 Kazakhstan and Kyrgyzstan announced that a 100-km railway link was to be built between Almaty and lake Issyk-Kul in Kyrgyzstan. Construction work was expected to be completed by 2008. A main line runs from Chimkent south to Uzbekistan, and another between Druzhba, on the eastern border of Kazakhstan, and Alataw Shankou, in the People's Republic of China.

In the early 2000s construction was under way of the first line of a new underground railway (metro) in Almaty.

In December 2004 a new rail line was opened, linking Altynsarino in Kostanai Oblast and Khromtau in Western Kazakhstan, greatly reducing travel time between the northern and central parts of the country and the petroleum-producing regions in the west.

Kazakstan Temir Zholy (Kazakhstan Railways): 010011 Astana, Zhengis dangghyly 98; tel. (7172) 93-44-00; fax (7172) 32-82-30; e-mail temirzhol@railways.kz; internet www.railways.kz; f. 1991; Pres. YERLAN D. ATAMKULOV.

ROADS

In 2004 Kazakhstan's total road network was 90,018 km, including 23,055 km of main roads.

INLAND WATERWAYS

Kazakhstan has an inland waterway network extending over some 4,000 km. The main navigable river is the Irtysh, accounting for approximately 80% of cargo transported by river. The Kazakhstan River Fleet Industrial Association, comprising 11 water companies, administers river traffic.

Department of Water Transport (Ministry of Transport and Communications): 010000 Astana, pr. Abaya 49; tel. (7172) 32-03-58; fax (7172) 32-10-58; Dir JENYS M. KASYMBEK.

SHIPPING

A ferry port was inaugurated at Aktau, on the eastern shore of the Caspian Sea, in September 2001 as part of the Transport Corridor Europa—Caucasus—Asia (TRACECA) programme, with services operating to Azerbaijan, Iran and Russia; the port was capable of processing some 10m. tons of petroleum and up to 30m. tons of dry goods per year. At 31 December 2007 Kazakhstan's merchant fleet comprised 63 vessels, with a combined total displacement of 54,291 grt.

Aktau International Commercial Sea Port: 130000 Mangystau obl., Aktauskii akimat, Umirzak; tel. (7292) 51-45-49; fax (7292) 44-51-01; e-mail aktauport@aktauport.kz; internet www.portaktau.kz; f. 1963; Dir TALGAT B. ABYLGAZIN; 609 employees.

CIVIL AVIATION

There are 18 domestic airports and four airports with international services (at Almaty, Aktau, Astana and Atyrau). A new passenger terminal opened at Astana International Airport in 2005.

Department of Aviation (Ministry of Transport and Communications): 010000 Astana, pr. Abaya 49; tel. (7172) 32-63-16; fax (7172) 32-16-96; Dir S. BURANBAYEV.

Air Astana: 050000 Almaty, Biznes Tsentr Samal Tauers, ul. Zholdasbekova 97; tel. (7172) 58-41-35; fax (7172) 59-87-01; e-mail hr@air-astana.kz; internet www.air-astana.kz; f. 2001 jointly by the Government (51%) and BAE Systems (United Kingdom—49%); domestic and international flights; Pres. PETER FOSTER.

Tourism

Tourism is not widely developed in Kazakhstan. In 2006 there were 4.7m. tourist arrivals in Kazakhstan. In 2005 receipts from tourism (including passenger transport) amounted to US $809m.

Kazakhstan Tourist Association (KTA): 050022 Almaty, pr. Abaya 42/44/302; tel. (727) 292-53-31; fax (727) 292-48-53; e-mail kta@mail.kz; f. 1999.

Culture

NATIONAL ORGANIZATION

Ministry of Culture and Information: see The Government (Ministries).

CULTURAL HERITAGE

In 2003 there were 143 museums in Kazakhstan, which were attended by some 3.8m. people, and 3,462 libraries.

Central State Museum of Kazakhstan: 050000 Almaty, Mikroraion Samal-1, ul. Fermanova 44; e-mail csmrk@hotmail.kz; internet www.unesco.kz/heritagenet/kz/participant/museum/csmrk/rus/default.htm; f. 1931; 90,000 exhibits of history and natural history; Dir ALIMBAY NURSAN.

Kasteyev Kazakhstan State Museum of Arts: 050000 Almaty, Satpayeva 30A; tel. (727) 247-82-49; fax (727) 250-95-67; e-mail kazart@nursat.kz; internet www.art.nursat.kz; f. 1976; 20,000 exhibits; library of 50,000 vols; Kazakh art, folk art, Soviet and European art; Dir BAYTURSUN E. UMORBEKOV.

National Library of Kazakhstan: 050013 Almaty, Abai 14; tel. and fax (727) 267-28-83; e-mail org@nlrk.kz; internet www.nlrk.kz; f. 1910; over 5.5m. vols; library, science research centre; organizes international seminars; Dir MURAT M. AUEZOV.

SPORTING ORGANIZATIONS

Ministry of Tourism and Sport: see The Government (Ministries).

National Olympic Committee of the Republic of Kazakhstan: 050012 Almaty, Abai 48; tel. (727) 293-53-35; fax (727) 258-85-33; e-mail olymp@nursat.kz; f. 1990; Pres. TIMUR DOSSYMBETOV.

PERFORMING ARTS

In 2003 there were 48 theatres in Kazakhstan (including 24 drama theatres, three musical comedy theatres, three puppet theatres, and two opera and ballet theatres), with an annual attendance of 1.5m.

Almaty

Abai State Academic Opera and Ballet Theatre: 050000 Almaty, Kabanbai batyra 110; tel. (727) 272-79-34; fax (727) 262-27-42; e-mail gatob2002@mail.ru; f. 1933; Gen. Dir KUANISH URAZGALIYEV.

M. Auezov Kazakh Academic Drama Theatre: 050000 Almaty, Abai 103; tel. (727) 292-33-07; f. 1926; Dir T. ZHAMANKULOV.

DTA—Deutsches Theater Almaty (Republican Germany Drama Theatre): 050000 Almaty, ul. Satpayeva 64D; tel. (727) 246-97-13; e-mail deutschestheateralmaty@rambler.ru; internet www.theater-dta.com; f. 1980 in Temirtau (Karaganda obl.), established in Almaty in 1989; Dir TATYANA V. KALININA.

Kumhamyyarov State Uigur Musical Comedy Theatre: 050012 Almaty, Nauryzbai batyra 83; tel. (727) 261-18-17; f. 1934; Dir M. AKHMADIYEV.

M. Yu. Lermontov State Academic Russian Drama Theatre: 050000 Almaty, Abai 43; tel. (727) 267-31-31; internet www.tl.kz; f. 1933; Artistic Dir RUBEN S. ANDRIASYAN.

State Republican Korean Musical Comedy Theatre: 050012 Almaty, Papanin 70/71; tel. (727) 246-97-13; f. 1937; Dir G. S. KIM.

Astana

K. Baiseitova National Opera and Ballet Theatre: 010000 Astana, Akzhaik 10; tel. (7172) 39-27-60; fax (7172) 39-00-86; f. 2000; Dir TOLEUBEK N. ALPIYEV.

ASSOCIATIONS

Association of Kazakhstani Authors and Artists: 050000 Almaty, pr. Dostyk 85; tel. (727) 063-69-22; e-mail askar@anesmi.almaty.kz; Pres. ASKAR NURMANOV.

Uigur Association: 050012 Almaty, Nauryzbai batyra 83; Pres. KAKHARMAN KHOZAMBERDI.

Education

General education (primary and secondary) is compulsory, and is fully funded by the state. Primary education begins at seven years of age and lasts for four years, while secondary education, beginning at 11 years of age, lasts for a further seven years. In 1995/96 a total of 52.1% of pupils in general schools were taught in Russian, 44.8% in Kazakh, 2.3% in Uzbek, 0.7% in Uigur and 0.1% in Tajik. In 2005/06 there were 8,157 general schools. After completing general education, pupils may continue their studies at specialized secondary schools; there were 415 such schools in 2005/06. In 1995/96 some 24.2% of students at specialized schools were instructed in Kazakh; 203 subjects were taught, with the subject of market economics receiving particular attention.

In the early 1990s the number of university-level institutions was considerably increased, particularly with regard to private institutions. By 2005/06 there was a total of 181 higher schools (including universities), attended by 775,800 students. Ethnic Kazakhs formed a greater proportion (64% in 1995/96) of students in higher education than in general education, since many ethnic Russians chose to study at universities outside Kazakhstan. None the less, the majority of higher-education students (approximately 75% in 1997) were instructed in Russian. Government expenditure on education in 2001 was 105,024m. tenge (14.7% of total spending).

UNIVERSITIES

Al-Farabi Kazakh National University: 050038 Almaty, pr. Al-Farabi 71; tel. (727) 247-16-71; fax (727) 247-26-09; e-mail a.rector@kazsu.kz; internet www.kazsu.kz; f. 1934; languages of instruction: Russian and Kazakh; 14 faculties, seven research institutes; 2,000 teachers; 17,000 students; Rector Prof. T. A. KOZHAMKULOV.

Eastern Kazakhstan State University: 070000 Eastern Kazakhstan obl., Ust-Kamenogorsk, 30-oi Gvardeiskoi Divisii 34B; tel. (7232) 27-29-11; fax (3232) 40-64-07; e-mail vkgu@ukg.kz; f. 1952, current name since 1991; 7 institutes, 10,000 students, 700 lecturers; Rector Prof. ABDUMUTALIP ABZHAPPAROV.

L. N. Gumilev Eurasian University: 010008 Astana, Munaitpassov 5; tel. (7172) 35-39-09; fax (7172) 35-38-08; e-mail emu@emu.kz; internet www.enu.kz; f. 1996; 8 faculties; Rector Prof. SARSENGALI A. ABDYMANAPOV.

Karaganda Ye. A. Buketova State University: 100026 Karaganda, ul. Universitetskaya 28; tel. (7212) 74-49-50; e-mail root@kargu.krg.kz; internet www.ksu.kz; f. 1972; 15 faculties, 17,700 students, 1,600 teachers; library of 1.5m. volumes; Rector ERKIN K. KUBEYEV.

Kazakh K. I. Satbayev National Technical University: 050013 Almaty, Satbayev 22; tel. (727) 292-69-01; fax (327) 292-60-25; e-mail allnt@ntu.kz; internet www.ntu.kz; f. 1934 as Kazakh Polytechnic Institute, name changed as above 1996; Rector Prof. DOSYM K. SULEYEV.

Kostanai A. Baitursynov State University: 110000 Kostanai, ul. Baitursynova 47; tel. and fax (7142) 51-11-95; e-mail ksu47@topmail.kz; internet www.ksu.kst.kz; seven institutes and college of Kazakh State University; Rector KHUSAIN KH. VALIYEV.

Northern Kazakhstan N. Kozybayev State University: 150000 Northern Kazakhstan obl., Petropavlovsk, ul. Universitetskaya 18; tel. and fax (7152) 49-33-52; fax (7152) 49-33-42; e-mail mail@nkzu.edu; internet www.nkzu.edu; f. 1937; Rector UNDASYN B. ASHIMOV.

Pavlodar S. Toraigyrov State University: 140003 Pavlodar, Lomova 64; tel. (7182) 45-12-24; fax (7182) 45-11-10; e-mail pgu@psu.kz; internet www.psu.kz; f. 1960; 12 faculties, 348 teachers, 12,000 students; Rector FEDOR K. BOIKO.

Taraz M. Kh. Dulati State University: 080012 Jambul obl., Taraz, Suleimanov 7; tel. (7262) 45-42-20; fax (7262) 45-97-25; e-mail targu@nursat.kz; internet www.tarsu.kz; f. 1998; 646 teachers, 9,387 students; Rector Prof. ABDIMANAP Y. BEKTURGANOV.

Social Welfare

Reforms were introduced in the early 1990s with the aim of making the social-security system self-financing. Of the three new funds introduced, the Pension and Social Insurance Funds were entirely financed by employer and employee contributions. New pensions legislation enacted in 1996, and due to be fully implemented by 2002, gradually raised the retirement age from 60 to 63 years for men and from 55 to 58 years for women. In January 1998 a new pensions law came into effect introducing private pension funds. A State Employment Fund was established in 1991 financed by contributions, which in 1993 amounted to 2% of an employer's wage bill. In June 1997 the Government introduced a comprehensive reform of the system of public pensions provision, which involved the dissolution of the Pension Fund and the creation of a funded system from January 1998.

In 2006, according to official statistics, there were 7.8 hospital beds, and 3.9 physicians per 1,000 persons. In 2001 state budget expenditure for health care, social insurance and social security, together represented 34.8% of total budgetary spending.

NATIONAL AGENCIES

Ministry of Labour and Social Security: see The Government (Ministries).

Agency for Health Care: 010000 Astana, Moskovskaya 66; tel. (7172) 33-74-09.

Social Insurance Fund: 050003 Almaty, Zheltoksan 37–41; tel. (7272) 62-28-95; f. 1991; Dir MAKSUT S. NARIKBAYEV.

State Employment Fund: 050000 Almaty; f. 1991; Chair. SAYAT D. BEYSENOV.

HEALTH AND WELFARE ORGANIZATIONS

Caritas Kazakhstan: 100022 Karaganda, Chetskaya 65 A; tel. (7212) 72-36-57; fax (7212) 72-06-05; e-mail caritaskazakhstan@nursat.kz; f. 1998; Roman Catholic welfare org.; Pres. Bishop JAN PAVEL LENGA; Sec.-Gen. Fr JANUSCH PETER WOLLNIE.

Charity and Health Fund of Kazakhstan: 050010 Almaty, D. Kunayev 86; tel. (727) 262-41-62.

Kazakhstan Children's Fund: 050000 Almaty, Furmanova 162; tel. (727) 262-24-02; Chair. KOZHAKHMET B. BALAKHMETOV.

Kazakhstan Society of Disabled Women with Children: 050000 Almaty, Abai 42–44; tel. (727) 292-90-88; f. 1992; 5,000 mems; 14 regional groups; library; Chief BIBIGUL H. IMANGAZINA.

Red Crescent Society of Kazakhstan: 050010 Almaty, Kunayev 86; tel. (727) 291-62-91; fax (727) 291-81-72; e-mail kazrc2@yahoo.co.uk; f. 1937; Pres. ERKEBEK K. ARGYMBAYEV.

Voluntary Society of Invalids of Kazakhstan (DOUK): 050010 Almaty, Kunayev 122; tel. (727) 261-75-87; f. 1988; provides assistance and representation for the disabled; Chair. SAIDALIM N. TANEKEYEV.

Zhan Society for Support of Families with Disabled Children: 050000 Almaty, Orbit 2, Bldg 17A, No 36; tel. (727) 229-32-98.

The Environment

Kazakhstan developed severe environmental problems during the period of Soviet rule, mainly because of the considerable industrialization, but also because of ambitious agricultural projects in the region. The three main concerns of environmentalists, who led the first popular expressions of opposition to the Soviet regime during the 1980s, were: atmospheric and water pollution from industrial toxins and chemical fertilizers; the desiccation of the Aral Sea, owing to irrigation works; and nuclear testing. The shrinking of the Aral Sea, once the world's fourth largest freshwater lake, is one of the greatest ecological disasters world-wide. An International Fund for Saving the Aral Sea has been established, although little progress has been made. From late 1999 fears were expressed about the threat of anthrax spores, buried on Vozrozhdeniye Island, spreading to the mainland, owing to the decreasing water level. In October 2003 plans were reported for the construction of a large dam to restore the northern part of the Sea.

Nuclear testing, which used to be carried out at Semipalatinsk, in the north of the country, was a major focus for opposition to the former communist regime. The legacy of the nuclear industry remained of concern (in 1994 it was estimated that the tests at Semipalatinsk had affected the health of some 500,000 people in Kazakhstan). In July 2000 Kazakhstan's remaining nuclear-testing capabilities at Semipalatinsk were destroyed. However, in May radiation levels in the regions of Eastern and Western Kazakhstan were reported to be twice as high as those at Semipalatinsk, owing to uranium and beryllium production. In March of the same year the Mangyshlak nuclear reactor was decommissioned, with a US $1m. grant from the International Scientific and Technical Centre, based in Russia.

In February 2001 Kazakhstan began the implementation of a five-year, US $61m. rural water supply and sewage project jointly funded by the Asian Development Bank, the Islamic Development Bank and the Government. The World Bank was to provide more than US $300m. in 2003–05 for seven projects in water and forestry management, and environmental and rural development.

GOVERNMENT ORGANIZATIONS

Ministry of Environmental Protection: see The Government (Ministries); comprises the Committee on Environmental Protection; the Committee on Forestry, Fish and Hunting Economy; the Committee on Water Resources; and the Committee on Geological Protection.

International Fund for Saving the Aral Sea (IFAS): 050000 Almaty, Bogenbai batyra 124; tel. (727) 262-51-96; fax (727) 250-77-17; e-mail ifas-almaty@alnet.kz; internet www.ifas-almaty.kz; f. 1993 by the World Bank; finances programmes and projects concerned with the preservation of the Aral Sea and the rehabilitation of the surrounding environment; Exec. Dir ALMABEK NURUSHEV.

Kazekologiya Republican Scientific Production and Information Centre: 050000 Almaty, Panfilov 106A; tel. (727) 261-12-03; fax (727) 261-12-10; Gen. Dir AMANGELDY A. SKAKOV.

ACADEMIC INSTITUTE

National Academy of Sciences of Kazakhstan: 050021 Almaty, Shevchenko 28; tel. (727) 269-55-93; fax (727) 269-57-09; e-mail daukeev@academset.kz; f. 1947; several attached institutes involved in environmental research; 6 depts; Pres. SERIKBEK DAUKEYEV; Sec.-Gen. MURAT MUKHAMEDZHANOV.

NON-GOVERNMENTAL ORGANIZATIONS

ACCA: 050005 Almaty, S. Kovalevskaya 63/13; tel. (727) 241-29-91; e-mail kamilya@itte.kz; f. 1997; implements educational programmes, with the involvement of the local population, on resolving ecological and cultural problems, provides environmental consultancy service to local and international organizations; Exec. Dir KAMILYA SADYKOVA.

Aral-Asia-Kazakhstan International Public Committee: 050000 Almaty, Abai 7; tel. (3272) 33-14-94; Pres. MUHTAR SHAHANOV.

Ecofund of Kazakhstan: 050037 Almaty, Toslonko 31; tel. (727) 229-55-59; fax (727) 267-21-24; f. 1988; once one of largest environmental groups in Kazakhstan, subsequently split several times; Co-Chair. LEV I. KURLAPOV, VIKTOR ZONAV.

Ecology and Public Opinion (EKOM) (Ekologiya i Obshchestvennoye Mneniye): 140011 Pavlodar, Suvarov 12/131; tel. (7182) 72-67-75; f. 1987; Chair. NIKOLAI S. SAVUKHIN; Sec. VALERI P. GALENKO.

Fund in Support of Ecological Education: 050005 Almaty, S. Kovalevskaya 63/13; tel. (727) 241-29-91; fax (727) 263-66-34; f. 1991; environmental education and ecological library; Chair. ZHARAS ABU-ULY TAKENOV.

Green Movement Socio-Ecological Centre (GMC): 080006 Jambul obl., Taraz, Lunacharskii 42/2; tel. and fax (72622) 3-27-93; e-mail alex@zagribelny.jambyl.kz; f. 1990; opposition to manufacture of phosphorus fertilizers; publishes Oasis monthly newspaper, documentary films; Chair. ALEKSANDR ZAGRIBELNYI; Sec. LUBA RAUPOVA.

Green Salvation Ecological Society (Zelonoye Spaseniye): 050000 Almaty, Shagabutdinova 58/28; tel. (727) 234-17-60; fax (727) 253-62-56; e-mail grsalmati@mail.ru; internet www.greensalvation.org; f. 1990; provides environmental education and participates in developing environmental legislation; Chair. SERGEI G. KURATOV.

International Ecology Centre (Biosphere Club): 071300 Eastern Kazakhstan obl., Ridder, Mikroraion 3, 19/10; Chair. VLADIMIR P. KARAMANOV.

Kazakh Community for Nature Protection (Central Council): 050044 Almaty, pr. Zhibek-zholy 15; tel. (727) 261-65-16; Chair. KAMZA B. ZHUMABEKOV.

Nevada–Semipalatinsk International Anti-nuclear Movement (IAM): 050000 Almaty; tel. (727) 263-49-02; fax (727) 250-71-87; f. 1989; environmental group opposed to nuclear testing; developed and implemented the Programme for the Ecological, Economic and Spiritual Regeneration of regions where nuclear testing took place; Pres. S. O. OMAROVICH; Head of Exec. Cttee MIRZAHAN ERIMBETOV.

  Lop-Nor Semipalatinsk Ecological Committee: 050000 Almaty; tel. (727) 263-04-64; fax (727) 263-12-07; f. 1992; semi-autonomous dept of Semipalatinsk-Nevada Movement, campaigns against nuclear testing in neighbouring parts of China; Chair. AZAT M. AKIMBEK.

Defence

Kazakhstan was one of the four former Union Republics to become a nuclear power in succession to the USSR, but undertook to dismantle its nuclear facilities. Its remaining nuclear-testing capabilities at Semipalatinsk were destroyed in July 2000. In mid-1992 Kazakhstan signed a Collective Security Treaty with five other members of the Commonwealth of Independent States (CIS); in May 2001 it was announced that the signatory countries were to form a Collective Rapid Reaction Force to combat Islamist militancy in Central Asia. In April 2003 the Collective Security Treaty Organization (CSTO) was inaugurated as the successor to the CIS collective security system, comprising Armenia, Belarus, Kazakhstan, Kyrgyzstan, Russia and Tajikistan. Kazakhstan participates, with Russia and Azerbaijan in the operation of the Caspian Sea Flotilla, based at Astrakhan, Russia. Kazakhstan established a navy in 2003. In May 1994 Kazakhstan joined the North Atlantic Treaty Organization's (NATO) 'Partnership for Peace' programme of military co-operation. In August 1999 Kazakhstan became a member of the UN Conference on Disarmament. At the beginning of 2006 the length of military service was reduced from two years to one year, in conformity with proposals eventually to replace the existing conscription-based

armed forces with a professional, contract-based army. As assessed at November 2007, the country's total armed forces numbered some 49,000, with an army of 30,000, an air force of 12,000 and a navy of 3,000. There were also 31,500 paramilitary troops (including some 20,000 internal security troops, under the command of the Ministry of Internal Affairs) and some 9,000 border guards. The defence budget for 2007 was an estimated 142,000m. tenge.

Chairman of Joint Chiefs of Staff: Gen. MUKHTAR K. ALTYN-BAYEV.

Bibliography

Akiner, S. *The Formation of Kazakh Identity: from Tribe to Nation-State*. London, Royal Institute of International Affairs, 1995.

Alexandrov, M. *Uneasy Alliance: Relations between Russia and Kazakhstan in the Post-Soviet Era, 1992–1997*. Westport, CT, Greenwood, 1999.

Alichev-Himy, B. *Les Allemands des steppes: histoire d'une minorité de l'Empire russe à la CEI*. Bern, Peter Lang, 2005.

Bantekas, I. (Ed.) et al. *Oil and Gas Law in Kazakhstan: National and International Perspectives*. Deventer, Kluwer Law and Taxation Publishers, 2004.

Cohen, A. *Kazakhstan: Energy Cooperation with Russia: Oil, Gas and Beyond*. London, GMB Publishing Ltd, 2006.

Cummings, S. *Centre-Periphery Relations in Kazakhstan*. Washington, DC, Brookings Institution, 2000.

  Kazakhstan: Power and the Elite. London, I. B. Tauris, 2005.

Davé, B. *Kazakhstan: Ethnicity, Language and Power*. Abingdon, Routledge, 2006.

Demko, C. *The Russian Colonization of Kazakhstan, 1896–1916*. Bloomington, VA, Mouton, 1969.

Fergus, M. and Jandosova, J. (Eds) *Kazakhstan's Coming of Age*. London, Stacey International Publishers, 2004.

Frank, A. J. *Muslim Religious Institutions in Imperial Russia: the Islamic World of the Novouzensk District and the Kazakh Inner Horde, 1790–1910*. Boston, MA, Leiden, 2001.

Jha, M. *Ethnicity, Modernity and Nationalism in Central Asia: Nation Building Experiences in Kazakhstan*. New Delhi, Academic Excellence, 2007.

Kaser, M. *The Economies of Kazakhstan and Uzbekistan*. Washington, DC, Brookings Institution, 1997.

Kerven, C. (Ed.). *Prospects for Pastoralism in Kazakhstan and Turkmenistan: from State Farms to Private Flocks*. London, RoutledgeCurzon, 2003.

Kolst, P. *Nation-building and Ethnic Integration in Post-Soviet Societies: an Investigation of Latvia and Kazakhstan*. Boulder, CO, Westview Press, 1999.

Martin, V. *Law and Custom in the Steppe: the Kazakhs of the Middle Horde and Russian Colonialism in the Nineteenth Century*. Richmond (Surrey), Curzon, 2002.

Nathan, J. *Kazakhstan's New Economy: Post-Soviet, Central Asian Industries in a Global Era*. Scranton, PA, University of Scranton Press, 2006.

Nazarbayev, N. *The Kazakhstan Way*. London, Stacey International, 2008.

Nazpary, J. *Post-Soviet Chaos: Violence and Dispossession in Kazakhstan*. London, Pluto Press, 2002.

Nysanbayev, A. *Kazakhstan: Cultural Inheritance and Social Transformation*. Washington, DC, Council for Research in Values and Philosophy, 2004.

Olcott, M. B. *The Kazakhs*. 2nd edn. Stanford, CA, Hoover Institution Press, 1995.

  Kazakhstan: Unfulfilled Promise. Washington, DC, Carnegie Endowment for International Peace, 2002.

Qazag Sovet Enciklopedeyasi (10 vols). Almaty, Qazag Sovet Enciklopedeyasi, 1972–78.

Peck, R. *Economic Development in Kazakhstan: the Role of Large Enterprises and Foreign Investment (Central Asia Research Forum, SOAS Series)*. London, RoutledgeCurzon, 2003.

Schatz, E. *Modern Clan Politics: the Power of 'Blood' in Kazakhstan and Beyond*. Seattle, WA, University of Washington Press, 2004.

Also see the Select Bibliography.

KYRGYZSTAN

Geography

PHYSICAL FEATURES

The Kyrgyz Republic is a small, landlocked state situated in eastern Central Asia. Kazakhstan borders it to the north, Uzbekistan to the west, Tajikistan to the south-west and south, and the People's Republic of China to the south-east. The country's western border is pincer-shaped, with the Uzbekistan part of the Farg'ona (Fergana) basin abutting into Kyrgyzstan. The country covers an area of 199,900 sq km (77,182 sq miles).

The terrain is largely mountainous, dominated by the western reaches of the Tien Shan range in the north-east and the Pamir-Alay range in the south-west. The highest mountain is Jenish Chokusu (also known as Tomur Feng or, colloquially, by its Soviet and Russian, name of Pik Pobedy—Victory Peak, 7,439 m—24,406 ft), at the eastern tip of the country, on the border with China. Much of the mountain region is permanently covered with ice and snow, and there are many glaciers. The Farg'ona mountain range, running from the north-west across the country to the central-southern border region, separates the eastern and central mountain areas from the Farg'ona valley in the west and south-west. Other lowland areas include the Chui and Talas valleys near the northern border with Kazakhstan. The most important rivers are the Naryn (at 535 km in length—335 miles), which flows through the central regions and eventually joins the Syr Dar'ya, and the Chui (221 km), which forms part of the northern border with Kazakhstan, into the deserts of which it flows. In the north-east of the country is the world's second largest crater lake, the Issyk-Kul (with an area of 6,236 sq km).

CLIMATE

The country has an extreme, continental climate, although there are distinct variations between low-lying and high-altitude areas. In the valleys the mean temperature in July is 28°C (82°F), whereas in January it falls to an average of 18°C (0.5°F). Annual precipitation ranges from 180 mm (7 ins) in the eastern Tien Shan to 750 mm–1,000 mm in the Farg'ona mountains. In the settled valleys the annual average varies between 100 mm and 500 mm.

POPULATION

At the census of 1999, at which the total resident population was 4,822,938, 64.9% of the population were ethnic Kyrgyz,

13.8% Uzbek, 12.5% Russian, 1.1% Dungan and 1.1% Ukrainian. There were also small numbers of Uigurs, Tatars, Kazakhs, Tajiks, Turks, Germans and Koreans. Kyrgyz replaced Russian as the official language in September 1989, although the two languages were given equal status in May 2000. In April 2004 Kyrgyz was designated the state language, and Russian received the status of the country's official language. Kyrgyz is a member of the Southern Turkic group of languages and, since 1941, has been written in the Cyrillic script. (The Arabic script was in use until 1928, and a Latin script in 1928–41.) According to the census of 1999, 70% of the population were fluent in Kyrgyz, compared with 53% in 1989. The major religion is Islam, with ethnic Kyrgyz and Uzbeks traditionally being Sunni Muslims of the Hanafi school. Russians and Ukrainians are mostly adherents of Eastern Orthodox Christianity.

According to official estimates, the total population numbered 5,224,300 at the end of 2007; thus, the population density (persons per sq km) was 26.1. There is a relatively low level of urbanization, with 35.3% of the total population living in the major towns in 1999. Bishkek (known as Frunze in 1926–91), the capital, is situated in the Chui valley in the north of the country. Including the suburbs, it had a population of 837,000 at mid-2007, according to UN estimates. The only other town of significant size is Osh (208,520 at the 1999 census), in the Farg'ona valley, near the border with Uzbekistan. Important regional centres include Karakol, Jalal-Abad and Naryn.

Chronology

10th century: The Turkic ancestors of the Kyrgyz began to migrate from the upper reaches of the Yenisei (now in the Tyva region of the Russian Federation), towards the Tien Shan.

13th century: The rise of the Mongol Empire hastened the southwards migrations, although the ancestors of the Kyrgyz remained dominated by the Eastern Turkic tribes.

1685: The Kyrgyz, reckoned to have emerged as a distinct ethnic group within the previous 200 years, came to be ruled by the Oirot Mongols, against whom the Kyrgyz rulers waged a fierce struggle.

1758: The Manzhous (Manchus) defeated the Oirots and the Kyrgyz became nominal subjects of the Chinese emperors.

1863: The northern Kyrgyz acknowledged the sovereignty of the Russian tsar, thus providing the official date of the 'voluntary' incorporation of Kyrgyzstan into Russia.

1866: The Russians defeated the Khanate of Qoqand (Kokand), which had acquired suzerainty over the southern Kyrgyz earlier in the century.

1876: The Khanate of Qoqand was abolished and the territory formally incorporated into the Russian Empire; however, there were several Kyrgyz uprisings in the following decades.

1916: An attempt to impose labour and military service on the non-Russian peoples of the Empire occasioned a widespread revolt in Central Asia; the savage repression of the rebellion caused many Kyrgyz to emigrate to China.

25 October (New Style 7 November) 1917: The Bolsheviks, led by Lenin (Vladimir Ulyanov), staged a *coup d'état* and seized control of government in Petrograd (St Petersburg); the Russian Soviet Federative Socialist Republic (RSFSR or Russian Federation) was proclaimed.

30 April 1918: The Autonomous Soviet Socialist Republic (ASSR) of Turkestan (based in Tashkent, Uzbekistan) was proclaimed, as part of the Russian Federation; this included Kyrgyzstan, although Bolshevik control was not established here until 1919–20, because of fierce resistance to the Red Army from the 'Whites' and from local *basmachi* insurgents.

1923: The reform of the Arabic script helped the formation of a vernacular standard language.

14 October 1924: The Kara-Kyrgyz Autonomous Oblast (region) was created, as part of the Russian Federation (until the mid-1920s the Russians knew the Kyrgyz as the 'Kara-Kyrgyz', to differentiate them from the Kazakhs who were called 'Kyrgyz'). In the following year the oblast was renamed the Kyrgyz Autonomous Oblast, and the territory was upgraded to the status of an ASSR, still within the Russian Federation, in 1926. In that year the capital city, Bishkek, was renamed Frunze.

1927–28: The second programme of land reform (there had been some in 1921–22) continued with the aim of resettling the nomadic Kyrgyz; this policy, which had a disastrous effect on the herds and resources of the Kyrgyz, was carried out despite the protests of leading local communists ('the Thirty'), who were subsequently purged. The agricultural reforms and later collectivization revived the *basmachi* struggle.

1928: A Latin script replaced the Arabic.

5 December 1936: Under the second ('Stalin') Constitution of the USSR; Kyrgyzstan became a full Union Republic (Soviet Socialist Republic—SSR).

1941: A Cyrillic script replaced the Latin.

1953: A Soviet campaign against the epic poetry of Central Asia (such as the Kyrgyz saga *Manas*) provoked strong opposition in Kyrgyzstan.

1980: The Chairman of the Council of Ministers, Sultan Ibraimov, was murdered.

November 1985: Absamat Masaliyev was appointed as First Secretary of the Kyrgyz Communist Party (KCP).

September 1989: Kyrgyz replaced Russian as the official language.

February 1990: In elections to the republican Supreme Soviet (Supreme Council) most seats were won, unopposed, by KCP candidates; those opposition candidates who were elected were united in the Kyrgyzstan Democratic Movement (KDM).

April 1990: Masaliyev was elected to the post of Chairman of the Supreme Soviet, effectively becoming the republican executive Head of State.

4 June 1990: Eleven people were killed and 21 injured in local clashes in the Farg'ona (Fergana) valley region on the border between Kyrgyzstan and Uzbekistan; numerous other deaths followed.

5 June 1990: More than 300 people were killed when ethnic Kyrgyz attacked Uzbeks in the town of Uzgen, in the Osh region, and three-quarters of the town was destroyed by fire. The state of emergency was partially lifted in November.

30 October 1990: The Kyrgyz SSR was declared a sovereign state and renamed the Socialist Republic of Kyrgyzstan. This followed the election by the Supreme Soviet of a liberal academic, Askar Akayev, to the new post of executive President of the Republic.

15 December 1990: The country was renamed the Republic of Kyrgyzstan (the capital, Frunze, reverted to its pre-Soviet name of Bishkek in February 1991). In the same month Masaliyev resigned as Chairman of the Supreme Soviet (now the post of parliamentary speaker).

17 March 1991: In an all-Union referendum on the issue of the future state of the USSR, 87.7% of those eligible to vote approved the concept of a 'renewed federation'. The next month

Masaliyev was replaced as leader of the KCP by Jumgalbek Amanbayev.

31 August 1991: Following the failure of the Moscow (Russia—the Soviet capital) coup attempt and the banning of the KCP, the Supreme Soviet of Kyrgyzstan adopted a declaration of independence.

12 October 1991: Akayev was confirmed as President in direct elections, winning some 95% of the votes cast.

21 December 1991: At a meeting in Almaty, Kazakhstan, the leaders of 11 former Union Republics signed a protocol on the formation of the new Commonwealth of Independent States (CIS) and, thereby, the effective dissolution of the USSR.

11 February 1992: Tursunbek Chyngyshev was appointed Prime Minister of Kyrgyzstan; Akayev subordinated the Government to the presidency and reduced the number of ministries by one-half.

June 1992: The communists re-formed as the Party of Communists of Kyrgyzstan (PCK), led by Masaliyev and Amanbayev.

5 May 1993: The republican legislature, the Zhogorku Kenesh (Supreme Council), enacted and promulgated the new Constitution of the renamed Kyrgyz Republic.

10 May 1993: Kyrgyzstan introduced its own currency, the som; Kazakhstan and Uzbekistan immediately suspended trading relations and the latter introduced what amounted to economic sanctions for a short time.

13 December 1993: Although a parliamentary vote of confidence was inconclusive, President Akayev dismissed the Chyngyshev Government in the hope of securing political stability.

21 December 1993: Apas Jumagulov, who had been Chairman of the Council of Ministers in 1986–91, returned as premier, heading a Government that included members of the PCK.

30 January 1994: Some 96% of those who voted in a national referendum (with a rate of participation of 96%) supported the continued presidency of Akayev.

22 October 1994: The results of a referendum approved the introduction of a bicameral parliament, still known as the Zhogorku Kenesh, with a 70-seat El Okuldor Palatasy (People's Assembly—upper chamber) to represent regional interests at twice-yearly sessions, and a permanent 35-seat Myizam Chygaru Palatasy (Legislative Assembly—lower chamber) representing the whole country.

19 February 1995: A general election to the new Zhogorku Kenesh was contested by more than 1,000 candidates; 89 of the 105 seats were filled after a second round of voting (the first had been held on 5 February). Jumagulov was confirmed as premier in April.

24 December 1995: Akayev received 71.6% of the votes cast in the presidential election; the second-placed of the three candidates was Masaliyev, who had recently been reinstated as the leader of the KCP, with 24.4% of the votes cast.

10 February 1996: A referendum sanctioned enhanced powers for the presidency, prompting the resignation of the Government, to permit restructuring. A new Government, led by Jumagulov, was appointed in the following month.

24 March 1998: Jumagulov announced his retirement. He was replaced the next day by Kuvachbek Jumaliyev, the former head of the presidential administration, and a new Government was formed.

17 October 1998: Some 90% of those voting in a referendum approved a number of constitutional amendments proposed by President Akayev, including the legalization of private land ownership; an increase in the number of deputies in the

Myizam Chygaru Palatasy from 35 to 60; and restrictions on parliamentary immunity.

20 December 1998: Kyrgyzstan became the first CIS member state to join the World Trade Organization (WTO).

23 December 1998: President Akayev dissolved the Government, on the grounds that it had failed to address the country's economic problems. Five days later Jumabek Ibraimov was appointed Prime Minister, with extended powers, which gave him the right to appoint and dismiss ministers.

21 April 1999: Amangeldy Muraliyev, a former regional governor, was approved as the new Prime Minister, following the death of Ibraimov.

May 1999: A new electoral law was introduced, whereby 15 of the seats in the Myizam Chygaru Palatasy were, henceforth, to be allocated on a proportional basis for those parties that secured at least 5% of the votes. The following month legislation banning those political parties considered to threaten the country's stability was introduced.

12 March 2000: Following two rounds of parliamentary elections (the first had been held on 20 February), 73 of the 105 seats in the two legislative chambers were obtained by independent candidates. The largest party grouping represented was the Union of Democratic Forces, with 12 seats, followed by the KCP, with six.

25 May 2000: Parliament approved the use of Russian as a second official language. This was confirmed by a constitutional amendment adopted on 24 December 2001.

11 August 2000: Islamist rebels commenced a series of incursions into Kyrgyzstan from Tajikistan, leading to armed conflict with government forces. Although the Government stated that all rebel forces had left Kyrgyzstan by the end of October, renewed attacks on Kyrgyzstani territory were reported from mid-2001.

29 October 2000: Askar Akayev was re-elected President, with 74.5% of the votes cast, although international observers declared that the voting arrangements had violated international standards. Kurmanbek Bakiyev was appointed Prime Minister on 21 December, and a new cabinet was subsequently installed.

22 January 2001: Former Vice-President Feliks Kulov, the leader of the Dignity (Ar-Namys) Party, who had been accused of abusing his official position while serving as Minister of National Security in 1997–98, was sentenced to seven years' imprisonment. Supporters subsequently demonstrated in Bishkek, to demand his release from prison, but the Supreme Court upheld Kulov's sentence in July (although one charge of abuse of office was dismissed). Having been found guilty of embezzlement, Kulov was sentenced to an additional 10 years' imprisonment in May 2002, to be served simultaneously. The 10-year sentence was reduced by one-third in October.

25 September 2001: President Akayev announced that he would be prepared to open Kyrgyzstani airspace to US military aircraft for the aerial bombardment of Afghanistan, which hosted the Islamist fundamentalist, Osama bin Laden, who was held responsible for co-ordinating the suicide attacks of 11 September against targets in the USA. In late November the Government agreed to give the US-led coalition access to its military bases and, later, its main airport.

5 January 2002: Azimbek Beknazarov, an opposition deputy and the former Chairman of a parliamentary committee on court reforms and legality, was arrested, owing to allegations that he had misused his powers while investigating a murder case in 1995.

17–18 March 2002: During protests in Jalal-Abad against the detention of Beknazarov (which was widely believed to have been politically motivated), six people were reportedly killed and more than 60 injured, after members of the security forces clashed violently with demonstrators.

10 May 2002: The Myizam Chygaru Palatasy ratified the controversial Sino-Kyrgyzstani border treaty, signed in 1999, which ceded some 95,000 ha of territory to the People's Republic of China. The treaty was ratified by the El Okuldor Palatasy one week later, despite demands for its rescission; protesters claimed the agreement to be illegal, since Akayev had initially signed it without the consent of the legislature.

22 May 2002: Following a series of country-wide anti-Government protests, Bakiyev tendered his resignation as Prime Minister, prompting, under the terms of the Constitution, the resignation of the entire Government. The First Deputy Prime Minister, Nikolai Tanayev, was appointed as acting Prime Minister, and confirmed as Prime Minister eight days later. Meanwhile, on 28 May Akayev signed into law the Sino-Kyrgyzstani border treaty.

19 June 2002: Tanayev announced the formation of a new Government.

28 June 2002: A law approving an amnesty for those involved in the unrest of mid-March was passed by the Myizam Chygaru Palatasy. On the same day Beknazarov's one-year, suspended prison sentence, received one month earlier, was annulled.

2 February 2003: A referendum was held on proposed constitutional amendments, and the extension of President Akayev's term of office. Despite international concern about both the scheduling of the referendum and alleged procedural violations, 86.7% of the electorate reportedly participated, with 76.6% of voters approving the constitutional amendments, and 78.7% supporting President Akayev's remaining in office until 2005. One of the principal amendments provided for the reorganization of the Zhogorku Kenesh as a unicameral legislature from 2005.

28 April 2003: Representatives from Armenia, Belarus, Kazakhstan, Kyrgyzstan, Russia and Tajikistan formally inaugurated the successor to the Collective Security Treaty, a new regional defence organization known as the Collective Security Treaty Organization (CSTO).

23 October 2003: A Russian airbase opened in Kant, some 30 km from the US-led coalition's airbase at Manas.

2 April 2004: President Akayev signed legislation designating Kyrgyz as the state language; Russian remained the official language. Measures to promote the learning of Kyrgyz and encourage bilingualism were introduced.

27 February 2005: Elections took place to the Zhogorku Kenesh, in which only 31 candidates, mostly known supporters of President Akayev, secured representation in the 75-seat legislature. Monitors from the Organization for Security and Co-operation in Europe (OSCE) concluded that the elections had not fully complied with democratic standards, while opposition and independent observers asserted that large-scale electoral fraud had taken place. Demonstrations took place prior to the second round of elections.

13 March 2005: The second round of voting was conducted, as a result of which a further 37 candidates were reported to have been elected. However, according to preliminary results, only six opposition candidates had obtained representation in the new legislature. Large-scale protests against the conduct of the poll followed, as a result of which the Government lost control of the southern cities of Jalal-Abad and Osh.

22 March 2005: The Central Election Commission (CEC) declared the results of voting for 69 of the 75 seats to be valid; investigations into the conduct of voting in the remaining six districts were to continue. However, the Supreme Court ruled that the outgoing legislature should remain in place.

23 March 2005: President Akayev dismissed the Prosecutor-General, Myktybek Abdyldayev, and the Minister of Internal

Affairs, Bakirdin Subanbekov. Subanbekov's replacement, Keneshbek Dushebayev, asserted that he would be willing to use to force to end the protests if necessary. Meanwhile, demonstrations had spread to Bishkek.

24 March 2005: Akayev was reported to have fled the country and Tanayev resigned as Prime Minister, after protesters stormed the presidential palace and government buildings. The lower chamber of the legislature elected in 2000 named Kurmanbek Bakiyev acting Prime Minister (he automatically became acting President, in Akayev's absence). Demonstrators released Feliks Kulov from gaol on the same day.

25 March 2005: Bakiyev appointed several senior officials in the interim Government.

27–28 March 2005: The lower and upper chambers of the Zhogorku Kenesh dissolved themselves, following a ruling from the CEC terminating the powers of the bicameral legislature elected in 2000. On 28 March the new Zhogorku Kenesh confirmed Bakiyev in his position as interim Prime Minister.

4 April 2005: Akayev, speaking from Moscow, announced his resignation, which was accepted by the Zhogorku Kenesh on 11 April.

13 May 2005: Bakiyev reached an agreement with Feliks Kulov, according to which Kulov agreed not to contest the presidential election scheduled to take place on 10 July, in return for a guarantee from Bakiyev that he would be appointed Prime Minister should Bakiyev secure the presidency.

10 July 2005: Bakiyev was elected President, winning 88.7% of the votes cast in the presidential election, in which some 74.9% of the electorate reportedly took part. He was inaugurated on 14 August.

1 September 2005: The Zhogorku Kenesh confirmed Kulov's appointment as Prime Minister. A number of new ministers were appointed during September.

20 December 2005: A new Government was sworn in. Notably, Alikbek Jekshenkulov became Minister of Foreign Affairs and Marat Kaiypov became Minister of Justice.

27 February 2006: The Zhogorku Kenesh voted to accept the resignation of the Chairman, Omurbek Tekebayev. Tekebayev had resigned earlier in the month after criticizing President Bakiyev, who had accused deputies of exceeding their responsibilities and fomenting political instability. Marat Sultanov was elected as the new Chairman in early March.

2 May 2006: Bakiyev rejected offers of resignation from most of the members of his Government. On 28 April the Zhogorku Kenesh had been asked to put to a 'vote of confidence' the performance of each member of the Cabinet: only Kulov and two other ministers had secured the legislature's approval.

10 May 2006: Bakiyev announced a reshuffle of the Cabinet. Notably, Daniyar Usenov (an opponent of Kulov) was appointed to replace Kerimkulov as First Deputy Prime Minister.

14 July 2006: The Government announced that the USA had signed an agreement to pay Kyrgyzstan US $150m. to continue using the airbase at Manas airport from 2007. Previously, the USA had paid just $2.6m. to use the facility, but from early 2006 Kyrgyzstan had begun to urge the USA to accept a significant increase in rent.

8 November 2006: Following a week of mass protests by opposition supporters in Bishkek, the Zhogorku Kenesh approved a new Constitution, which was to transfer many presidential powers to an enlarged legislature. President Bakiyev signed the new Constitution into effect on the following day.

19 December 2006: Kulov tendered the resignation of his Government, with the stated aim of forcing early parliamentary elections.

15 January 2007: A new Constitution was signed into effect by President Bakiyev, following its approval by the Zhogorku Kenesh at the end of December. This Constitution replaced the document that had been approved by Bakiyev on 9 November 2006, and restored various powers to the President that had been transferred to the legislature.

25 January 2007: The Zhogorku Kenesh rejected a second attempt by Bakiyev to reappoint Kulov to the premiership.

29 January 2007: Bakiyev appointed Azimbek Isabekov as Prime Minister, with confirmation by the Zhogorku Kenesh, subsequently reorganizing the Government.

29 March 2007: Isabekov resigned from the premiership, after Bakiyev reversed his decision to remove five government ministers. He was replaced by Almazbek Atambayev, a parliamentary deputy and leader of the Social Democratic Party of Kyrgyzstan.

2 April 2007: A government reorganization included the removal of Daniyar Usenov from the post of First Deputy Prime Minister.

27 June 2007: Bakiyev signed into force legislation amending the criminal code, which (in accordance with constitutional provisions) notably included the abolition of the death penalty.

14 September 2007: The Constitutional Court ruled that the adoption of Constitutions in both November 2006 and January 2007 had been illegal, since the drafts had not been submitted to a national referendum. Bakiyev subsequently announced that a further new Constitution was to be proposed at a referendum on 21 October.

21 October 2007: The new, revised Constitution was endorsed by 76.1% of the votes cast (with a participation rate of 81.6%) at a national referendum; the single-constituency electoral system was changed to a proportional all-party list system, and the number of parliamentary seats was increased from 75 to 90. On the following day Bakiyev dissolved the Zhogorku Kenesh and announced that early legislative elections would take place later in the year.

24 October 2007: The Government submitted its resignation, remaining in office in an interim capacity.

29 November 2007: Bakiyev removed Atambayev from the premiership; on the same day he appointed Iskenderbek Aydaraliyev, hitherto Governor of Jalal-Abad Oblast, as First Deputy Prime Minister and also assigned him the role of acting Prime Minister.

16 December 2007: At the legislative elections, Bright Road won about 46.9% of the votes cast, securing 71 seats in the 90-member Zhogorku Kenesh, followed by the Social Democratic Party of Kyrgyzstan, with 5.1% of the votes and 11 seats, and the Communist Party of Kyrgyzstan, with 5.1% of the votes and eight seats. The Fatherland Socialist Party (Ata-Meken), despite securing 8.3% of votes overall, narrowly failed to qualify for representation, owing to a new electoral requirement that each party obtain at least 0.5% of the votes cast in each of the country's seven oblasts and two largest cities. Although the stipulation was criticized by OSCE observers, who stated that the conduct of the elections failed to meet democratic standards, the CEC upheld the election results.

25 December 2007: Igor Chudinov, hitherto the Minister of Industry, Energy and Fuel Resources, was appointed Prime Minister. A new Government, which retained the principal members of the former administration, was approved in the Zhogorku Kenesh on 27 December.

26 May 2008: The head of the pro-presidential faction in the Zhogorku Kenesh, Elmira Ibragimova, was appointed Deputy Prime Minister, succeeding Dosbol Nur uulu (who had been transferred to the post of State Secretary). On the same day Bakytbek Kalyev, hitherto the head of the State Border Guard Service, was appointed Minister of Defence, succeeding Ismail Isakov, who became Secretary of the National Security Council.

10 September 2008: On the recommendation of the Prime Minister, Bakiyev dismissed the Minister of Justice, Marat Kaiyypov, and the head of the Penal Department, following an investigation into a prison riot, in which two officers were killed, in August. A deputy prosecutor-general, Nurlan Tursunkulov, was appointed as the new Minister of Justice on 24 September.

25 September 2008: Shortly before local elections were due to take place, the Chairman of the CEC, Klara Kabilova, fled the country, subsequently accusing Maksim Bakiyev, the son of the President, of intimidation and threats against her as part of a government-orchestrated conspiracy to suppress the participation of opposition supporters in the elections.

5 October 2008: Local elections were held throughout the country. Observers from local non-governmental organizations alleged that numerous irregularities had enabled government candidates to win most seats in municipal councils, and contested the CEC's estimate of a participation rate of 61.6%. The new, acting CEC Chairman, Damir Lisovsky, denied widespread allegations of electoral fraud.

History

Prof. JOHN ANDERSON

EARLY HISTORY

The ancestors of the Kyrgyz, a people of mixed Turkic, Mongol and Kipchak descent, probably originated from the area around the upper reaches of the Yenisei, in what is now the Tyva region of Russia. Southwards migration, towards the Tien Shan mountain range, began in the 10th–11th centuries, by which time tribal groups in the area appear to have described themselves as Kyrgyz, although the designation only became common around the 15th century. At various times they were ruled by the Turkic and Chinese empires, before coming under the authority of the Khanate of Qoqand (Kokand) at the beginning of the 19th century. In the mid-19th century the Khans of Qoqand struggled to gain control of the territory now known as Kyrgyzstan. The mountainous terrain, which had defeated other would-be conquerors, proved particularly problematic and, for a brief period around 1870, the Khanate faced a systematic revolt led by Kurmanja-datka, the widow of a Kyrgyz tribal leader. The loose tribal structures and nomadic lifestyles of the Kyrgyz, however, did ensure them some degree of independence.

When Russia began to encroach on Central Asia in the mid-19th century, some Kyrgyz tribes sought its support for their resistance to the Khanate and when the latter was formally incorporated into the Russian Empire in 1876 the Kyrgyz effectively found themselves ruled from St Petersburg, the tsarist capital. Various revolts followed, of which the most significant was the 1916 rebellion, which spread across Central Asia when Russia sought to mobilize the local population to support its First World War campaign. The harsh suppression of that revolt caused many Kyrgyz to emigrate to China.

SOVIET KYRGYZSTAN

During 1917 revolutionary activity in the region was largely confined to the Russian settlers, although there were spontaneous rebellions by Kyrgyz groups seeking to take advantage of the collapse of tsarist authority. Despite the efforts of those Kyrgyz who joined *basmachi* groups of Muslim and nationalist resistance fighters, in 1918 the territory formally became part of a Turkestan Autonomous Soviet Socialist Republic (ASSR). This was, in turn, incorporated into the Russian Soviet Federative Socialist Republic (RSFSR—Russian Federation), although Soviet control over the territory was not clearly established until the early 1920s. The administrative territory of the Kyrgyz underwent various changes in the mid-1920s, first to the Kara-Kyrgyz Autonomous Oblast within the RSFSR in 1924 (the Russians used the term Kara-Kyrgyz for the Kyrgyz until the mid-1920s, to distinguish them from the Kazakhs, who were, at the time, known to the Russians as Kyrgyz), then to the Kyrgyz Autonomous Oblast in 1925 and the Kyrgyz ASSR in 1926; the status of full Union Republic (SSR) was finally achieved in December 1936.

During the Soviet period Kyrgyzstan shared many of the experiences of its Central Asian neighbours, with land reform, collectivization and the attempt to settle a largely nomadic population leading to thousands of deaths and the dramatic reduction of livestock levels. Those local communists who had sought to give socialism a nationalist content were purged during the 1930s, and some effort was made to rewrite the nation's past in ways that were not deemed threatening to Soviet rule. Although there is considerable evidence to suggest that traditional Kyrgyz culture and lifestyles survived during the communist period, especially in rural areas, throughout most of the post-Stalinist era the Kyrgyz SSR appeared to be among the most loyal of Soviet regions. This was, in part, owing to the First Secretary of the Kyrgyz Communist Party (KCP), Turdakan Usubaliyev, under whose guidance the republic's officials praised the Soviet leadership and promoted the use of the Russian language, while at the same time encouraging the further development of Kyrgyz-dominated patronage networks.

THE NATIONALIST MOVEMENT

In November 1985, soon after Mikhail Gorbachev was appointed to head the Communist Party of the Soviet Union (CPSU), Usubaliyev resigned and was replaced by Absamat Masaliyev, who immediately levelled charges of corruption and general misrule against his predecessor. Although Masaliyev resisted opening Kyrgyzstan to genuine political freedom, by 1989 signs of popular resistance were beginning to appear. Some elements of the media cautiously adopted a more critical tone towards the Government and a number of informal political groups emerged. A particular focus for dissent was the acute housing crisis; in 1989 homeless ethnic Kyrgyz began to seize vacant land around the capital, Frunze (Bishkek), and to build houses on it. Conflicts also developed in the southern Osh Duban (Oblast or region), where local Kyrgyz, supported by an organization known as Osh Aymaghi, took similar actions to acquire land for housing, in a region traditionally dominated by Uzbeks. Masaliyev and his colleagues chose to ignore the various reports from Osh suggesting that violence was imminent. In June 1990 serious intercommunal fighting broke out between Uzbeks and Kyrgyz, leaving several hundred dead and many more injured.

In February 1990 parliamentary elections were held, but these were largely manipulated by the Communist Party in order to prevent any real opposition emerging. In April Masaliyev was elected to the post of Chairman of the Supreme Soviet (Supreme Council—a post that he held until December); he sought to follow Gorbachev's example and create an executive presidency but, discredited by the violence in Osh, and under attack from a more vocal opposition group in parliament, which had united as the Kyrgyzstan Democratic Movement, Masaliyev failed to win election. Eventually, a compromise candidate, Askar Akayev, the President of the Kyrgyz Academy of Sciences and a liberal who had worked only briefly within the party apparatus, was elected to the presidency.

During the attempted coup in the USSR, in August 1991, Akayev was the first republican leader to denounce the conspirators and offer support to Boris Yeltsin, the President of the RSFSR. Within days Akayev announced his resignation from the CPSU and issued a decree prohibiting party involvement in state and military bodies. By the end of August the Kyrgyz Supreme Soviet had voted for independence from the USSR, a status eventually achieved with the de facto dissolution of the Union by the end of the year. In October Akayev reinforced his own position by seeking direct election to the presidency, albeit unopposed, and received 95% of the votes cast.

INDEPENDENT KYRGYZSTAN

Askar Akayev's early speeches as President of newly independent Kyrgyzstan placed much emphasis on the need to develop a liberal democracy, based upon a developed civil society and a market economy. This rhetorical commitment earned him considerable praise abroad, as well as financial aid from the IMF and some Western countries, but was met with less enthusiasm at home. None the less, the first year of independence witnessed the emergence of an embryonic civil society with a thriving press, which proved to be the most open and critical in Central Asia. Political parties also began to develop, although, as in much of the former USSR, many of these were ephemeral, subject to constant fragmentation and grouped around leaders prominent in specific regions of the country.

Amid continuous confrontation with the Uluk Kenesh (as the parliament was by this time known), the President sought the adoption of a new constitution, which would create a smaller and more professional parliament. The document eventually accepted on 5 May 1993 provided for a parliamentary form of government, but left the President with considerable authority, having the power to appoint the Prime Minister, initiate legislation and dissolve parliament. Although the Constitution established formal political rules, much of Kyrgyzstan's political life took place at a level beneath the institutional surface. Many politicians had their roots not in parties or legislative bodies, but in regionally based clan and tribal networks; in particular, there was a strong distinction between northern and southern groups. At the senior level this was apparent in the tensions between President Akayev, who came from the northern Chui Duban, and the former KCP First Secretary, Masaliyev, from the southern Osh Duban. This phenomenon also made it difficult for the central authorities to assert their influence in some parts of the country.

President Akayev also had to respond to the needs of the non-Kyrgyz population, especially the Slavs and Germans, who feared for their future in the new Kyrgyzstan. Although citizenship was open to all those resident on Kyrgyz territory at the time of independence, many felt that the rise of nationalist groups, the increasing use of national criteria in the selection of leading personnel, and the gradual imposition of language laws that might exclude Slavs from education and senior appointments rendered their position within Kyrgyzstan untenable. The name of the country was changed by the 1993 Constitution from the Republic of Kyrgyzstan to the less ethnically neutral Kyrgyz Republic. By the end of 1994 about 40% of Germans and nearly 20% of Russians who had been resident in Soviet Kyrgyzstan had left the country, many of them skilled professionals. Considerable efforts were made to persuade them to stay: the creation of a Slavic university in the capital Bishkek, in September 1993; the postponement of the implementation of the law establishing Kyrgyz as the state language, first from 1995 to 2000, and later to 2005; and, in early 1996, an agreement on the continued use of Russian as an official language in areas predominantly populated by Russian speakers. In May 2000 Russian was finally accorded the status of an official language, but, none the less, at the end of July President Akayev expressed concern at the increasing numbers of Slavs leaving Kyrgyzstan, and in 2001 some 25,000 left the country. In December 2001 a constitutional amendment was adopted, describing Russian as an official language in the republic. Despite these developments, however, following the

unrest of March 2005 and the subsequent period of lawlessness (see below), the number of ethnic Russians seeking to leave the country appeared to be increasing. According to the 1999 census, 65% of the population was ethnic Kyrgyz, compared with 52% in 1989.

In mid-1993 tensions were also present in the south, where some Uzbeks agitated openly for union with neighbouring Uzbekistan, although, in general, such efforts were confined to a minority and did not initially seem to have been encouraged by Uzbekistan's President, Islam Karimov. Members of the non-Kyrgyz population continued to fear exclusion from politics, and in July 1998 a group of Uzbek deputies and Russian activists in the southern Jalal-Abad region formed a new political party, with the principal aim of ensuring minority representation in the next parliamentary elections.

In addition to pressure from the nationalist constituency, President Akayev also experienced communist-led criticism of economic reforms, which were blamed for the deteriorating economic situation, and was accused of betraying Kyrgyz interests to foreign investors. A series of allegations of corruption culminated in a vote of no confidence in the Prime Minister, Tursunbek Chyngyshev, and his Government in the Uluk Kenesh in December 1993. Although the necessary two-thirds' majority was not obtained, President Akayev responded by dismissing the entire Government. He appointed Apas Jumagulov (who had been the last premier of Soviet Kyrgyzstan) Prime Minister, while bringing the leader of the KCP, Jumgalbek Amanbayev, into the Government, as a Deputy Prime Minister. Simultaneously, he arranged a referendum for 30 January 1994, in which 96% of those voting supported Akayev remaining in office until the end of his allotted term (scheduled, at that time, to expire in late 1996). Following the dissolution of parliament, a further referendum was held on 22 October 1994 to approve proposed constitutional amendments, including the transformation of the Zhogorku Kenesh into a bicameral parliament (with a 70-member El Okuldor Palatasy—People's Assembly—the upper chamber, to represent regional interests, and a 35-member lower chamber, the Myizam Chygaru Palatasy—Legislative Assembly—to represent the population as a whole).

A presidential election was scheduled for 24 December 1995. The election was contested by Akayev, Masaliyev (who had recently been reinstated as leader of the KCP), and Medetkan Sherimkulov. During the campaign the media strongly supported Akayev, and there were complaints about the harassment of opposition supporters in many areas. The results provided, as expected, a victory for Akayev, with 71.6% of the votes cast (the participation rate was 86.2%). Yet, in some areas, notably Masaliyev's home region of Osh, Akayev received as little as 50.0% of the votes cast, with Masaliyev taking 46.5% of votes; critics alleged that even this narrow majority was falsified. Akayev followed the election with a referendum on 10 February 1996, in which 94.3% of those participating voted in favour of constitutional amendments that greatly increased his formal powers. Even these enhanced powers did not guarantee implementation of his will, however. The Government resigned in late February, and in March Akayev reinstated Jumagulov as Prime Minister and appointed a new administration.

POLITICAL DEVELOPMENTS

Following the referendum of February 1996, President Akayev was accused of ending Kyrgyzstan's course towards democratization and sustained reform. Pressure on the media persisted throughout the late 1990s, as members of the élite became impatient with journalistic criticism, although attacks on newspapers were often justified by reference to their breach of the law. At the formal level of government, the period following the 1996 referendum witnessed considerable turnover in government ministries, as well as a continual rotation of regional leaders. In March 1998 the Prime Minister, Jumagulov, announced his retirement, and was replaced by a young 'technocrat', Kuvachbek Jumaliyev. The Government's main concerns were to maintain the process of macroeconomic stabilization, to combat corruption and to guarantee social stability. The need to improve living conditions and to provide an adequate social-welfare system was much debated, but, in practice, the Government found it extremely difficult to confront such fundamental structural problems. In December 1998, as a result of the financial crisis that affected Russia and other countries in that year, Jumaliyev was replaced as Prime Minister by Jumabek Ibraimov. However, Ibraimov died in April 1999, and was replaced by Amangeldy Muraliyev, the former Governor of Osh Duban.

Of growing political and social importance in the late 1990s was the issue of religion. From the state's perspective, the primary concern was the threat of Islamist fundamentalism. The advances of the Taliban, in Afghanistan, in the second half of the 1990s, and the discovery of alleged religious extremists (described as Wahhabis, followers of an austere interpretation of Islam originating in Saudi Arabia) in southern Kyrgyzstan and neighbouring Uzbekistan, increased these fears. In August 1999 a group of Islamist activists, believed to be members of the Islamic Movement of Uzbekistan (IMU), seized four Japanese geologists and several local officials in the southern Batken Duban. Following large-scale military intervention by Kyrgyzstani troops, with Uzbekistani military support, the situation was resolved in October, and in early 2000 the Kyrgyzstani authorities arrested and tried a number of alleged Islamists. However, in August there were further armed incursions into Batken Duban, and it took several months to repel the militants. Such incursions appeared likely to pose a persistent threat in future years, and the Kyrgyzstani authorities also suggested that a growing number of young people in the south were being attracted by the Islamist teachings of the transnational Hizb-ut-Tahrir al-Islami (Party of Islamic Liberation). Economic problems appeared to have created a marginal class of under-employed or unemployed young people, who found Islamist criticism of the socio-economic and political situation convincing, both in terms of analysis and as a guide to action, and the continuing failure of the state to meet the needs of many sections of the population helped to create a fertile recruiting ground for radical organizations. The suicide attacks on the US cities of New York and Washington, DC, on 11 September 2001, attributed to the extreme Islamist al-Qa'ida (Base) organization of Osama bin Laden, focused international attention on the potential threat posed by organizations such as the IMU, which had continued its armed incursions into Kyrgyzstan in mid-2001. Kyrgyzstan undertook joint exercises with US troops in February 2002, which aimed to facilitate attempts to counter insurgency in the country's mountainous regions. Since 2002 several hundred Hizb-ut-Tahrir activists have been arrested and tried in Kyrgyzstan, and the Minister of Internal Affairs claimed that this hitherto peaceful organization was on the verge of turning to violence. Indeed, during 2005 there were reports of major divisions emerging within the movement, as several leading figures argued that it should abandon its non-violent stance. In 2006 a prominent imam in Kyrgyzstan, an ethnic Uzbek, Rafiq Qori Kamoluddin (also known as Muhammadrafiq Kamalov), invited members of Hizb-ut-Tahrir to worship in his mosque so long as they did not try to proselytize. However, in early August Kamoluddin, together with two suspected members of the IMU, was shot dead in Osh in a counter-terrorism operation by the Kyrgyzstani and Uzbekistani national security services; they were reportedly connected with a border incursion in May and with the murder of eight police officers in Tajikistan. Kamoluddin, who had been targeted because of suspected links with the IMU, had always denied membership of Hizb-ut-Tahrir, but had asserted that he did not consider its members to be terrorists. Later police accounts suggested that he was not involved with radicalism but had been killed in an exchange of fire during the operation.

The other significant political matter confronting the country as it entered the 2000s was the question of elections and succession. Parliamentary elections were held on 20 February 2000, the preparations for which were characterized by substantial state efforts to eliminate opposition candidates from the poll. In the event, the Central Electoral Commission (CEC) reported that some 64% of the electorate participated in the election, and six parties obtained more than 5% of the votes cast and thus acquired representation for election by party lists. A second round of voting was held two weeks later, on 12 March.

As a result of the second round of voting, the KCP secured 27.7% of the votes cast, the pro-Government Union of Democratic Forces obtained 18.6%, the Women's Democratic Party of Kyrgyzstan obtained 12.7%, with the remaining parties receiving 8% or less. However, a prominent critic of the Government, Daniyar Usenov, was excluded from the poll, allegedly for returning a false statement of his income, and Feliks Kulov, a potential presidential challenger, was defeated, despite entering the second round with a substantial majority. This pattern of intimidation and exclusion was repeated in the presidential election of October 2000. Prior to the election, opposition candidates were subject to harassment, and particular controversy was aroused by an electoral rule that required candidates to appear before a linguistic commission to prove their ability to communicate in Kyrgyz. In consequence, Akayev's only effective challenger, Feliks Kulov, was barred from standing. At the election, held on 29 October, there were further irregularities, but according to official reports, some 75% of the population participated in the election, and Akayev was duly re-elected as President with 74.5% of the votes cast. His closest challenger was Omurbek Tekebayev, the leader of the Fatherland (Ata-Meken) Socialist Party, who obtained 13.9% of the votes. The first consequence of the election was a change in government, as Muraliyev was replaced as Prime Minister in late December by Kurmanbek Bakiyev, who subsequently introduced a number of new ministers to the cabinet. In January 2001 Kulov was sentenced to seven years' imprisonment, on charges of abuse of office (in May 2002 Kulov was sentenced to a further 10 years' imprisonment, to run concurrently, although an amnesty reduced the sentence by three years in October). In January 2002 the arrest and then trial of an opposition deputy and a former Chairman of a parliamentary committee on court reforms and legality, Azimbek Beknazarov, on charges of abuse of power, prompted protesters to demand his release and to denounce his detention as politically motivated. On 17–18 March large-scale protests took place in Jalal-Abad against the ongoing trial; six people died, following clashes with security forces. Although the trial was subsequently suspended and Beknazarov was temporarily released, the Government accused the opposition of instigating the riots in an attempt to stage a *coup d'état* and maintained that the security forces had acted in self-defence.

On 10 May 2002 the Myizam Chygaru Palatasy ratified the controversial Sino-Kyrgyzstani border treaty (see Foreign Affairs), prompting two weeks of anti-Government demonstrations, hunger strikes and acts of civil disobedience. Nevertheless, the border treaty was ratified by the El Okuldor Palatasy in mid-May, and subsequently signed into law by the President. Meanwhile, a state commission established to investigate the protests in Jalal-Abad issued a report, in which it criticized all levels of government and the law-enforcement bodies for not having recognized the instability of the political situation and the rising levels of popular discontent in the region during Beknazarov's trial. The commission also stated that the security forces' use of weapons to control the demonstrators had been illegal.

On 22 May 2002, as a result of increasing opposition, Prime Minister Bakiyev tendered his resignation; the entire Government duly resigned, in accordance with the Constitution. The Chief of the Presidential Administration also resigned, together with a senior prosecutor, and several senior police officers were dismissed. The First Deputy Prime Minister, Nikolai Tanayev, was subsequently appointed Prime Minister, and in early June a new Government was announced.

At a referendum, held on 2 February 2003, constitutional amendments providing for the introduction of a unicameral legislature were approved by 76.6% of votes, and the extension of the presidential term until 2005 was approved by more than 78.7%, although international bodies expressed doubts about some aspects of the referendum process. By 2004 Kyrgyzstani politics was increasingly dominated by the matter of succession, as Akayev's second term formally expired in 2005 and, in accordance with the Constitution, he was not permitted to serve a third. Many observers speculated that Akayev would seek to retain his position or perhaps rearrange the political order in order to make the post of Prime Minister dominant and then assume that office. However, while the succession question dominated the political agenda, several other controversies emerged during 2002–04. These included the discovery of illicit listening devices in the offices of several parliamentary deputies; a narrowly defeated vote of no confidence in Prime Minister Tanayev, following allegations of financial impropriety; and the adoption of a new language law. The latter required all candidates for political office to demonstrate proficiency in Kyrgyz, but this engendered resentment among members of the significant Uzbek and Russian populations, who felt that this might reduce their political representation yet further.

THE 'TULIP REVOLUTION'

In the event, speculation about the presidential succession was rendered redundant by the political revolution that took place in early 2005, initiated by the parliamentary elections held on 27 February, in which a reported 60% of the electorate took part. Despite allegations of considerable irregularities in the period preceding the elections and successful attempts by the authorities to prevent opposition figures from participating, the ballot proved inconclusive in 44 of the 75 constituencies, prompting a second round of voting to be held on 13 March. Further evidence of electoral manipulation and the promotion of Akayev's children as deputies and possible successors, as well as the suppression of pro-opposition media outlets, appeared to galvanize the opposition into disregarding their differences, with the aim of forcing the President's resignation. Meanwhile, for the first time the largely passive population began to give some support to protests against electoral fraud. The rate of participation by the electorate in the second round of voting was reported at some 55%. Preliminary election results gave opposition candidates just six of the 75 seats in the Zhogorku Kenesh.

From mid-March 2005 protest actions took place throughout the country, as demonstrators seized local administration buildings, blocked major roads and captured senior officials. By 21 March the opposition controlled the two southern cities of Osh and Jalal-Abad. Nevertheless, on 22 March the CEC declared that the results of voting for 69 constituencies were valid; investigations into the conduct of voting in the six remaining districts were to continue. The Supreme Court, however, revoked the mandate of the newly elected Zhogorku Kenesh and confirmed the continuing authority of the previous legislature. On the following day Akayev dismissed the Prosecutor-General as well as the Minister of Internal Affairs, Bakirdin Subanbekov, appointing as his replacement Keneshbek Dushebayev, who declared his willingness to use force to suppress the continuing demonstrations. On 24 March protesters gained access to the presidential palace and government buildings in the capital. Akayev, asserting that he remained Kyrgyzstan's Head of State, fled the country, and Tanayev resigned as Prime Minister. A provisional administration was created under Kurmanbek Bakiyev, who had served as Prime Minister in 2000–02, and who had led a nine-party opposition electoral bloc, the People's Movement of Kyrgyzstan, since late 2004. In Akayev's absence, Bakiyev automatically became acting President. On 27 March 2005 the CEC ruled that the majority of the results announced following the elections were valid, and both chambers of the Zhogorku Kenesh elected in 2000 consequently dissolved themselves, effectively confirming the legitimacy of the newly elected legislature. On 4 April 2005 Akayev signed a resignation agreement in Moscow, Russia, which was accepted by the Zhogorku Kenesh on 11 April. A presidential election was subsequently scheduled for 10 July.

The period following Akayev's resignation was characterized by a degree of disorder as politicians sought positions of influence, and for a short time it appeared likely that lawlessness might engulf the country. Several politicians and administrators were physically attacked and even murdered, and the police struggled to deal with looting in the days after Akayev fled the country. (According to an estimate by the Ministry of Internal Affairs, looting caused US $24m. of damage on the night of 24 March alone.)

Meanwhile, tensions emerged between acting President Bakiyev and Feliks Kulov, who had been liberated by protesters on 24 March 2005 and initially appeared likely to pose a serious challenge to Bakiyev in the presidential contest. Eventually, in mid-May a compromise arrangement was reached, according to which Kulov agreed not to stand as a candidate in the election, in return for a guarantee from Bakiyev that he would be appointed Prime Minister should Bakiyev be elected to the presidency. In the event, seven presidential candidates were registered (one of whom withdrew his candidacy), none of whom posed a serious threat to Bakiyev. This was, in part, because none (with the possible exception of the human rights ombudsman, Tursunbai Bakir-uulu) enjoyed national prominence, but also because the majority of media outlets tended to favour the acting President. At the presidential election on 10 July, which Bakiyev won with 88.7% of the votes cast, the Organization for Security and Co-operation in Europe (OSCE) reported some irregularities in the counting of votes and expressed reservations over the officially recorded rate of participation of 74.9%. Bakiyev was inaugurated on 14 August, and Kulov was officially confirmed as Prime Minister on 1 September.

Although the 'tulip revolution' promised much, there remained considerable debate as to what had led to the transferral of political power. For Akayev and for the Russian Government, the revolutions in Kyrgyzstan, Georgia and Ukraine were largely a product of external intervention, events engineered by foreign-funded non-governmental organizations (NGOs) and governments that wished to see alternative regimes established in the former Soviet territories. For others, the revolution in Kyrgyzstan was a genuine popular uprising, a spontaneous reaction to the failure of the Akayev regime to deliver either economically or politically, while using the privilege of office to enrich those close to the presidential family. Even less clear was what the instigators of the revolution planned to do once they had secured power, and whether they had a clear programme for change beyond the ousting of Akayev.

A NEW POLITICAL ORDER?

From September 2005 Kyrgyzstani politics were characterized by a high degree of instability as President Bakiyev struggled to impose his authority on a divided country. Moreover, on occasion Bakiyev utilized similar techniques to those that had led to criticism for his predecessor, such as the attempt to delegitimize opposition groups, or the promotion of his own relatives or allies to important state positions. Although Bakiyev came from the south of Kyrgyzstan, southerners felt that he had done little to promote the interests of their region, while some northerners resented being ruled by a southerner. Bakiyev was also criticized for having failed to reverse the results of the flawed 2005 parliamentary voting or to announce new elections. In early February 2006 the President made an unexpected appearance in the Zhogorku Kenesh and told deputies to desist from the pursuit of their own interests, accusing them of fomenting political instability and exceeding their responsibilities. The legislative Chairman, Omurbek Tekebayev, responded by severely criticizing the President, and subsequently resigned; he was replaced in the following month by Marat Sultanov, the preferred candidate of Bakiyev. (The Zhogorku Kenesh had initially rejected Tekebayev's resignation.) However, there remained tensions over the redrafting of the Constitution, as Bakiyev appeared less enthusiastic about the prospect of expanding parliamentary powers than had been the case when leading the 'tulip revolution'.

These tensions came to a head during the second half of 2006, as constitutional debate intensified. In September the head of the security services was forced to resign, after a parliamentary committee concluded that drugs found in the possession of Tekebayev during a visit to Poland had been placed in his baggage by officials at Bishkek airport. More important, however, was the shifting balance over the relative powers of the President and Zhogorku Kenesh, with Bakiyev continuing to renege on previous pledges to transfer more powers to the latter. By November a division of power appeared to be emerging as more than one-half of the deputies were boycotting parliamentary sessions; however, on 8 November deputies approved constitutional changes that empowered the Zhogorku Kenesh to form a government, with the party that secured the most seats having the right to nominate the Prime Minister. Bakiyev accepted reluctantly, perhaps recognizing the popular desire to avoid further confrontations and disorders.

Political peace proved short-lived, however, as in mid-December 2006 the Government of Prime Minister Feliks Kulov resigned and Kulov duly became an opposition leader, claiming that the President had failed to fulfil the promises of the 'tulip revolution'. Subsequently, in mid-January 2007 a new Constitution, which restored various powers to the President that had been transferred to the Zhogorku Kenesh by the previous document, was signed into effect by Bakiyev, having obtained the approval of the legislature at the end of the previous month. Azimbek Isabekov was appointed Prime Minister at the end of January; however, Isabekov only remained in the premiership until the end of March, when he resigned and was replaced by an opposition deputy and leader of the Social Democratic Party, Almazbek Atambayev. Although the opposition encouraged protests, it proved increasingly incapable of attracting large numbers of supporters or of maintaining its own unity, a fact President Bakiyev was able to exploit for his own ends by authorizing police raids on groups and newspapers that he claimed were encouraging violent unrest.

One of the more significant problems confronting the country following the overthrow of Akayev was public perception of an increase in criminality and corruption. Foreign investors complained that in the past they had only to deal with Akayev's associates, whereas there were now increasing uncertainties, and both government ministers and opposition leaders emphasized the influence of criminal elements on the new political order. Despite attempts to control high-level corruption, the Government simultaneously began work on reforming the legal system, a process that concluded in June 2007 with the enactment of amendments to the criminal code, which notably included the abolition of the death penalty.

An additional problem experienced by the Government was that of the ongoing ethnic tensions within Kyrgyzstan. Although Akayev's commitment to some degree of affirmative action for minority groups had helped to address concerns, there were increasing complaints from Uzbek community leaders that they experienced discrimination in the courts and in carrying out their business activities, although some officials countered that this resulted from the high degree of corruption in the southern parts of the country where most Uzbeks lived. By mid-2006 parts of the Uzbek community within Kyrgyzstan appeared to be acquiring a new militancy, with a major demonstration in Jalal-Abad repeating demands for greater political representation for ethnic Uzbeks in Kyrgyzstan and the recognition of Uzbek as an official language. The Government, anxious to demonstrate to Uzbekistan its ability to police its own territories, also continued to identify what it termed as 'religious extremism' as a serious issue, but campaigns against 'terrorism' often appeared to be conforming with the Uzbekistani strategy of treating indications of religious devotion as reflecting an association with radical groups. Meanwhile, some members of society, including at least one government member, were seeking to secure legal recognition for 'traditional' customs such as polygamy, a measure that critics claimed would encourage religious activists. Interreligious tensions were also present, as missionary-orientated Protestant groups continued to work with ethnic Kyrgyz.

In late 2007 further constitutional debate resulted in the presentation by Bakiyev of a new document, seemingly modelled on the Russian system under President Vladimir Putin. The new Constitution was adopted by 76.1% of the votes cast at a national referendum on 21 October. The amended electoral system created a larger legislature, to be elected under a proportional all-party list system, with representation requiring the achievement of a 5% threshold in every region of the country. In the subsequent legislative elections on 16 December, Bakiyev's newly created pro-presidential party, Ak Zhol (Bright Road), won 46.9% of the votes and 71 seats in the expanded, 90-member Zhogorku Kenesh. Under the new electoral requirements, the main opposition Fatherland Socia-

list Party (Ata-Meken), although obtaining 8.3% of the votes overall, failed to meet the threshold in every region and therefore was denied representation. Despite protests by OSCE observers and an appeal by Ata-Meken, the results were upheld by the CEC. The wider population appeared to have lost the will for further demonstrations or political engagement, leaving Bakiyev with a seemingly quiescent political order. However, elections to municipal councils on 5 October 2008 were again marred by allegations of fraud. Shortly before the elections, on 25 September, the Chairman of the CEC, Klara Kabilova, fled the country, accusing Maksim Bakiyev, the son of the President, of intimidation and threats against her as part of a government plan to suppress opposition participation in the elections. International observers, including those from the OSCE, had been denied permission to monitor the elections, on the grounds that their applications to the CEC had been submitted late. Observers from local NGOs alleged that numerous irregularities had enabled government candidates to win a majority of seats, citing procedural violations and coercive measures in Bishkek, and contested the CEC's estimate that participation by the electorate had reached 61.6%. The new, acting CEC Chairman, Damir Lisovsky, denied widespread allegations of electoral fraud.

FOREIGN AFFAIRS

In an attempt to strengthen its independence, Kyrgyzstan sought international partners from a variety of quarters, with economic relations being of primary concern. President Akayev sought support, in particular, from the IMF and the USA, with his early commitment to democracy and market reform attracting substantial aid and credits. This support continued into the late 1990s, and in 1998 Kyrgyzstan became the first member country of the Commonwealth of Independent States (CIS) to join the World Trade Organization (WTO).

At the same time Kyrgyzstan also aimed to establish links in the Middle East and Asia, and the People's Republic of China quickly became an important partner. Despite their very different approaches to politics, the Kyrgyzstani and Chinese Governments developed good relations, signing agreements on water and trade, and establishing a number of Free Economic Zones in the Kyrgyzstan. From early 1997, however, Kyrgyzstan expressed concerns about unrest on its borders with China, owing to activity by an organization known as For a Free Eastern Turkestan, which sought to create an Islamic state on the territory of China's Xinjiang Uygur (Uigur) Autonomous Region.

Kyrgyzstan also cultivated relations with its former Soviet neighbours, especially Kazakhstan and Uzbekistan. These connections were not without problems, in part because of the great disparity in size. Kyrgyzstan was highly dependent on both for energy, and sometimes had to suffer direct interference in its internal affairs by its larger neighbours, as when Uzbekistani security officials arrested opponents of the President of Uzbekistan, Islam Karimov, who were active in Kyrgyzstan. Relations worsened for a brief period in mid-1993, following Kyrgyzstan's decision to issue its own currency, rather than to continue with the vagaries of the rouble zone. Produced hastily and without consultation, this development prompted a temporary break in economic relations with Kazakhstan and Uzbekistan, and ended with an apology. By the end of 1994 good relations had been resumed, although tensions remained. When Uzbekistan demanded overdue payments for supplies of natural gas, Kyrgyzstan retaliated by suggesting that Uzbekistan pay for the free water supplies it received from Kyrgyzstan's reservoirs. Negotiations over the issue began in late 1997, but little progress was made. Tensions briefly increased again in 1999, when Uzbekistan criticized Kyrgyzstan's handling of the hostage crisis (see above), and Karimov made unfavourable remarks about Akayev. There were also reports that Uzbekistan had unilaterally taken control of parts of the republic's southern territory and established border positions within Kyrgyzstani territory. Tensions subsequently intensified when Uzbekistan created border posts and laid landmines in part of the contested territory, leading to the deaths of at least 10 Kyrgyzstani farmers, in addition to many injuries. In August it was announced that, following negotiations between the Kyrgyzstani and Uzbekistani Prime Ministers, a treaty was expected to be signed by both sides, delineating their common border. These tensions were exacerbated in mid-2005, when the Kyrgyzstani authorities refused to return many of the refugees fleeing Uzbekistan in the wake of violence in Andijon, Uzbekistan, which reportedly left hundreds dead (see the History of Uzbekistan). Although a few refugees were sent back to Uzbekistan, most were either given refuge in Kyrgyzstan or permitted to leave the country for other parts of the world. In response, Uzbekistan accused Kyrgyzstan of training Islamist militants and later in the year, following persistent Kyrgyzstani refusals to hand over refugees, Uzbekistan suspended shipments of natural gas to Kyrgyzstan and the Uzbekistani authorities continued to criticize Kyrgyzstan. Tension over this issue continued, as the Kyrgyzstani Government proved unable to prevent occasional rallies protesting against the Andijon events, yet by the end of 2006 there were unconfirmed reports of joint Uzbekistani-Kyrgyzstani security forces carrying out operations against alleged militants in southern Kyrgyzstan. These followed an improvement in relations after Bakiyev's visit to Uzbekistan in October, when visa requirements for those crossing the border were lifted and promises were made to create a new crossing point in the Farg'ona valley. However, despite formal cordiality, tensions continued, with local disputes over land, trade and, particularly in mid-2008, over water, with some Uzbeks in the border region of Batken claiming that Kyrgyz officials were denying them supplies to irrigate their land. Similar tensions have been reported on the Kyrgyz-Tajik border, presaging a future where conflict over water was likely to become an issue of increasing importance.

Equally, if not more, important was Kyrgyzstan's relationship with Russia. As the country's most significant trading partner it could not be ignored and, in light of the civil war in the 1990s in neighbouring Tajikistan, President Akayev recognized the need for some guarantor of his nation's security. However, this was a highly unbalanced relationship, with Kyrgyzstan also dependent on Russia for many manufactured goods. In early 1996, moreover, Kyrgyzstan was forced to cede to Russia shares in certain vital industries, in order to repay existing debts. In late March the continuing reliance on Russia was given further emphasis when Akayev joined the Presidents of Belarus, Kazakhstan and Russia in signing a formal treaty committing the countries to closer economic integration. Kyrgyzstan was able to offer some support to Russia in helping to mediate the conflict in Tajikistan. It was under the auspices of Kyrgyzstan that the Tajikistani Government and opposition leaders met in Bishkek in May 1997 and established some of the basic principles underlying the peace agreement concluded in June.

There was concern in Kyrgyzstan, however, at increased instances of drugs-trafficking across the border with Tajikistan, and in April 1997 the country signed an agreement with the People's Republic of China, Kazakhstan, Russia and Tajikistan (together constituting the Shanghai Five, now known as the Shanghai Co-operation Organization—SCO, and including Uzbekistan), aimed at improving joint border security. In August 2000 Kyrgyzstan and Russia signed a declaration on friendship, alliance and partnership. Despite all these signs of co-operation, however, the continued close ties with Russia had negative consequences, most notably following the economic crisis of late 1998, which caused the Kyrgyzstani currency to depreciate rapidly.

Thus, some tensions continued to persist between Kyrgyzstan and the other members of the Shanghai grouping, which some critics considered to be dominated by the People's Republic of China. There was criticism of the Government's perceived willingness to accept a Chinese agenda with regard to the Uigurs in return for that country's support against Islamist rebels, who staged repeated armed incursions into Kyrgyzstan. Tensions also surrounded the further delimitation of the Sino–Kyrgyzstani border, and some parliamentary deputies claimed that China had gained excessively from successive deals arranged during the 1990s. The ratification in May 2002 of a border treaty signed in 1999, which ceded almost 95,000 ha of disputed territory to China, prompted

widespread protests in Kyrgyzstan (see above). In mid-2001 the Presidents of the SCO's member countries signed the so-called Shanghai Convention on Combating Terrorism, Separatism and Extremism, under the auspices of which Kyrgyzstani forces participated in major anti-terrorist manoeuvres in August 2003, hosted by China and Kazakhstan. There was some concern that the post-Akayev authorities would seek to reopen the question of relations with China, but in practice, at least at the beginning of its term, the new Government focused primarily on domestic affairs.

Following the suicide attacks on the USA on 11 September 2001, President Akayev announced that he was prepared to allow US military aircraft to have access to Kyrgyz airspace for the aerial bombardment of al-Qa'ida militants and their Taliban hosts in Afghanistan. In late November the Government agreed to give the US-led coalition access to its military bases and, later, its main airport, and in December US aircraft launched attacks on Afghanistan from the former Soviet bomber base at Manas; a US military presence remained at the airbase in 2005. However, the stationing of US troops in the country led to political tensions, as some observers believed that Akayev's son-in-law had exploited his role in supplying the airbase, and others felt that Kyrgyzstan should not be involved in conflicts on the territory of other Islamic countries. Although many within Kyrgyzstan remained ambivalent about the US-led military action in Iraq that commenced in early 2003, and despite the presidential administration under Askar Akayev becoming increasingly irritated by international attacks on its human rights record, it remained, at least publicly, committed to good relations with the USA. None the less, at his first presidential news conference, in 2005, President Bakiyev suggested that the situation in Afghanistan was stabilizing and that the US military presence in Kyrgyzstan might not be required for much longer, although he later appeared to moderate this position. Bakiyev also followed Akayev's policy of using improved relations with the USA to strengthen ties with Russia. In late 2002 an agreement was signed permitting Russia to base its forces in Kyrgyzstan once again, and a Russian airbase at Kant (some 30 km from Manas) formally opened in October 2003 in the presence of Presidents Akayev and Vladimir Putin. In mid-2005 the Kyrgyzstani Government agreed to permit the Russian troop presence at the Kant base to be doubled, but the issue of stationing remained a source of tension, as competing pressures from the USA and Russia created something of a quandary for the Kyrgyzstani authorities. Although a Russian official visiting the republic in February 2006 proclaimed that Russia's base at Kant would be there indefinitely, Russia was keen to see the closure of the last remaining US base in Central Asia. In deference to Russia, Kyrgyzstan started to use a much more qualified tone about the future of the US presence at Manas airport, reportedly asking for the rent to be increased by around 100-fold (it was currently paying US $2.6m.). Further discussions in May failed to reach a full agreement, but there seemed to be no immediate pressure for the US troops to leave, and the Kyrgyzstani Government was reluctant to lose one of its most significant sources of income: the initial demand made by Bakiyev would represent nearly one-third of the state budget, although it was expected that Kyrgyzstan would almost certainly settle for less. Finally, in mid-July the USA signed an agreement to pay Kyrgyzstan $150m. for continued use of the airbase. None the less, relations with the USA have not been as smooth as in the past and there are some reports of a growing anti-Westernism in Kyrgyzstan, exacerbated by occasional incidents involving US servicemen around the Manas airbase and discomfort over allied involvement in the Middle East. In the south of the country, this may result from Islamist sympathies, and in the north from the continuing influence of the Russian media, but it also reflected an increasing perception that the Government did not always obtain the best arrangement for the country when negotiating with financial institutions or external investors.

CONCLUSION

At the end of 1991 Kyrgyzstan, under Akayev, seemed to have the best prospects of any former Soviet Central Asian country for the development of a market economy and a democratic polity. Although it lacked the huge potential energy resources of some of its neighbours, the political will to reform was much stronger. Seventeen years after independence, the future appeared less clear. The economy was relatively stable, although meeting the social consequences of economic reform had proved difficult, as government revenues were too low to promote adequate welfare provision. In political terms, the country was still more liberal than its neighbours, but full democratization remained distant. The ousting of Akayev and his replacement by Bakiyev provided the country with the opportunity to move in a more democratic direction, but there remained the threat that some of the problems encountered under the old system could re-emerge under the new. Indeed, soon after the change of regime, there were complaints that powerful politicians were promoting family members and associates to senior positions; that they were using their administrative positions to enrich themselves; and complaints of ongoing problems in the electoral process. Like Akayev in the early part of his tenure, Bakiyev enjoyed some support from both the USA and Russia, but whether this would be converted

into tangible results, particularly in promoting economic development, overcoming social deprivation and dealing with lawlessness, remained doubtful, especially since the recent period of unrest seemed to have undermined the gradual economic stabilization of the early part of the century as external and domestic investors remained wary of the political uncertainty. At the same time it had reduced the coherence of government, since ministerial and official turn-over, together with uncertainties about longer-term prospects, motivated too many officials to act principally in their own personal interests. Of greater concern might be the growing concentration of power heralded by the constitutional changes of late 2007, which appeared to follow Russia in reducing the pluralist element of the polity, although the President's fundamental pledge was that it would create a stability that would make the country more attractive to foreign investors. Russia remains Kyrgyzstan's principal external influence, but it is not clear whether Kyrgyzstan could take advantage of a renewed Russian security and economic investment without the risk of undermining its real independence.

Economy

Prof. JOHN ANDERSON

INTRODUCTION

Prior to independence, Kyrgyzstan remained one of the poorer Soviet republics, being heavily reliant on agriculture and dependent for many manufactured goods on other regions of the USSR. At the time of gaining independence in 1991, the country's gross national product (GNP) per head was around US $1,500, and it possessed a rapidly increasing rural population that encountered severe underemployment and an economy that relied heavily on transfers from central funds. Under Askar Akayev, elected President in October 1990, the country moved more rapidly to promote a market economy than did most of its neighbours. In May 1993 Kyrgyzstan was the first regional state to adopt its own currency, and by 1998 the rate of inflation had been reduced to 10.5%; it rose to 35.9% in 1999, before continuing to decline, to 4.3% in 2005, then increased in the following two years, reaching 5.6% in 2006 and some 10.2% in 2007. However, as in other member countries of the Commonwealth of Independent States (CIS), economic reform brought with it many problems, some of which originated from the technical difficulties associated with attempts to introduce a capitalist economic system in a country with little prior experience. Equally importantly, problems resulted from the social changes that followed reform and, in particular, the fact that although a small minority of the population appeared to have benefited, the vast majority struggled to survive in a new context, in which incomes declined dramatically and social welfare provision decreased.

ECONOMIC POLICY

From the outset, Akayev was committed to creating a market-dominated economy, in which private enterprise played a central role. Progress towards this objective began in early 1992, when most price controls were removed, although subsidies were maintained on a few essential goods and on utilities. Simultaneously, the Government implemented an austerity programme and declared its intention to privatize state industry. The principal problem confronting the country in the first two years of independence was the acceleration of inflation levels, from around 200% in 1991 to 900% in 1992. The situation was made worse by the fact that Kyrgyzstan was tied to the 'rouble zone' and subject to its high rates of inflation and to the impact of other countries, which were pursuing a variety of economic policies. In response to this, in May 1993 the Government decided to introduce a national currency, the som, although little thought was given to the likely consequences either for neighbouring states or for Kyrgyzstani businesses.

Following its introduction, Uzbekistan immediately suspended energy deliveries and demanded payment in US dollars, and suppliers in other CIS states refused to accept payment in soms. Yet, although inadequate preparations had been made for the currency's introduction, substantial financial support from the IMF helped to bring a degree of macroeconomic stability to the country and, in the long term, to reduce substantially inflation rates.

A second aspect of Kyrgyzstan's shift to the market economy was its privatization programme. In the initial phase, this entailed selling around one-third of state enterprises and two-thirds of housing stock within a two-year period. The process took various forms, such as selling to individuals, collective buyouts by the company's management and work-force, and the creation of joint-stock companies. In the first stage, the intention was to reduce state holdings in small enterprises and light industry, as well as in the services sector and in catering. The subsequent objective was to turn to larger industrial units, although certain sectors, including utilities, mineral resources, defence industries and transport, were initially destined to remain under state ownership. By the end of 1993 it was estimated that around 87% of industry was under private ownership, over 95% of services, and just under 60% of transport and construction. Among the industries sold during this period were tourist resorts, agricultural processing plants and some energy holdings, although the latter were broken up into their component parts. For all this, critics continued to note the failure of privatization to lead to a quantitative leap in productivity outside the gold sector. In early 1994 vouchers were issued to all citizens, which enabled them to buy shares in various categories of interest, and by the end of 1996 nearly two-thirds of state enterprises were privately owned. At the same time, plans were being developed for the privatization of heavy industry, and even some of those sectors that had previously been excluded, notably the energy and transportation sectors. In the new sales, foreign investors were to be allowed to buy majority shareholdings for the first time, although most potential investors proved to be wary of purchasing, when they knew so little about the Kyrgyzstani market or the real value of the businesses on offer. Despite a number of scandals, which involved the sale of state-owned enterprises at considerably less than their market value, by the end of 1999 at least 75% of former state enterprises were privately owned. However, most observers noted little change in business strategy, and not until the end of the decade did bankruptcy legislation begin to put pressure on the new owners to find ways of operating that were consonant with market principles.

Among the firms that were to be offered for tender in 1999–2000 were: the power company, Kyrgyzenergo; the gas provider, Kyrgyzgas; the telecommunications company, Kyrgyztelekom; and the national airline, Kyrgyzstan Airlines. In practice, however, the privatization of a number of enterprises proved to be politically sensitive, and members of the Zhogorku Kenesh (Supreme Council—the legislature) were especially reluctant to allow land and energy resources to be removed from state control. None the less, the Government announced a privatization plan for 2001–03 that resulted in a further 1,000 enterprises being transferred to private ownership, generating revenue of over 600m. soms. A further programme of privatization, planned for 2004–06, was to involve enterprises in the sectors of health care, tourism and culture, although this was disrupted somewhat by the removal of the Akayev administration (see History) and almost no privatization projects were realized in 2005. Political uncertainty has also created problems for privatization, especially as the Government has been investigating past sell-offs of state property associated with the Akayev family and thus making potential investors wary that their purchases might be too dependent upon political change. Nevertheless, during 2007 privatization appeared to have resumed, and in June the Zhogorku Kenesh approved the sale of two unfinished hydroelectric plants in the Naryn region, albeit motivated largely by the fact that the state could not afford to finish the projects. Further plans to privatize state electricity companies were announced in early 2008, including a decision to sell off the company that pipes hot water to the capital. Most of these companies had infrastructure in desperate need of investment and some predicted that the costs of these privatizations could lead to price increases of up to 30% for consumers, despite formal government commitments to provide cheap energy. Privatization was also facilitated by the adoption, in early 2008, of legislation that permitted the Government to authorize the sale of state assets without requiring the approval of the Zhogorku Kenesh.

One consequence of these developments was the need to develop a banking and financial system capable of handling the sort of transaction that was central to a market economy. The National Bank was formed shortly after independence, and given broad responsibility for monetary and exchange rate policy. It also adopted the strict monetary policy demanded by international financial institutions, thereby ensuring the continued approval of the IMF and other agencies. The National Bank also adopted a supervisory role in relation to the rest of the banking sector. A number of private banks were established in the mid-1990s, and by 1998 there were at least 20, although several struggled to survive the consequences of that year's economic crisis in the Far East and in Russia, and there were closures in 1999. From 1994 the central bank took a more active role in regulating the banking sector and it instituted a stricter regulatory framework. In practice, however, this only began to be effective from the beginning of 1997, when the National Bank started to require international accounting procedures to be adopted and to insist on minimum capital requirements. By 2005 there were some 18 commercial banks operating in Kyrgyzstan, of which two were state-owned and three were subsidiaries of banks in Turkey, Pakistan and the Republic of Korea (South Korea). In addition, there were a number of specialist banks, concentrated, for example, on the rural sector, although such banks tended to attract excessive numbers of unpaid loans. In 2003 the Zhogorku Kenesh enacted a new Law on Banks and Banking Activity, which strengthened the regulatory powers of the central bank to ensure good management, improve financial disclosure and control insider dealing. In the same year plans were announced to privatize a major public sector bank. Yet despite growing trust in the banks, the continued strength of the 'grey' (informal) economy, which some claim contributes as much as 40% of gross domestic product (GDP), means that many businessmen remain reluctant to put their capital in the formal banking system.

The creation of a functional stock exchange proved more difficult, as many Kyrgyzstani businessmen had little understanding of the role of capital and security markets. The

Kyrgyz Stock Exchange opened in the same month as that in which the som was issued, but during the first two years of operation the level of trading was very low. In 1997–98 the volume of trading on the stock market increased considerably, with its value rising from around 3m. soms in 1996 to 46m. soms in 1998, and the number of companies listed on the stock exchange rose to 50. The number of listed companies subsequently declined, although capitalization increased significantly, as the exchange sought to ensure that only major long-term businesses were listed. However, many informed observers noted a reluctance to 'float' companies, and only around 10% of those companies that possessed the capacity to enter the market were represented. For all this, the volume of activity within the stock exchange increased by over 20% in 2004 and nearly the same amount again in 2005.

AGRICULTURE

Agriculture was the mainstay of the Kyrgyzstani economy, and by 2007 it provided around 34% of GDP, according to preliminary official figures, and employed just under 40% of the population, according to ILO. The Kyrgyz are traditionally a nomadic people, and the enforced settlement encouraged first by Russian and then by Soviet rulers did not end the country's concentration on cattle-herding and related activities. The Kyrgyz farmers also produced a range of crops, including cereals, sugar beet, tobacco, silk, cotton, fruit and vegetables and, more controversially, wild cannabis and opium. Within this sector there was a degree of regional and ethnic differentiation. Ethnic Kyrgyz tended to focus on livestock, especially in the northern and eastern regions. The inhabitants of the south, however, where there were sizeable ethnic Uzbek minorities, were more inclined to settled agriculture, revolving around grain, fruit and vegetables. It was also the case that much agricultural produce was produced in private plots, which, even during the 1970s, were responsible for the production of about 50% of vegetables and 28% of meat.

Following independence, the agricultural sector experienced a series of crises, recording a major decline in output in the first half of the 1990s. According to the IMF, output fell by around 9% in 1990, by 19% in 1992, by 10% in 1993 and by 15% in 1994. Particularly notable was the decline in livestock production, as a shortage of fodder and the loss of some export markets led farmers to slaughter their cattle. During 2002–07 meat production registered a small annual increase in most years, but not averaging much above 0.5%, while the production of milk, cheese and eggs rose by around 3% in 2006 and 2007. Overall, official reports indicated that the general decline that characterized the agricultural sector in the 1990s had been halted, despite a contraction in 2005, which was thought likely to be temporary, and some slight improvements recorded in many types of production. The general trend also appeared to be towards private farms registering the highest increases, state farms recording modest increases and household production declining. Problems remained in the agricultural sector, as high levels of corruption and bureaucratic obstruction made it difficult to initiate private farming activity, but by the mid-2000s there were signs that these obstacles were becoming easier to overcome.

Official figures reported an increase in agricultural output of 15.2% in 1996 and of 12.3% in 1997, although there was a subsequent decline. From 2000 agricultural production increased, rising by 6.8% in 2001, by 3.3% in 2002, by just under 9% in 2003 and by 10% in 2004. According to the Asian Development Bank (ADB), agricultural production decreased by some 4.2% in 2005, largely because the weather delayed the harvest season, and as a consequence of a dispute between producers and buyers over the prices the former were being paid for their goods. In part, the earlier improvement resulted from the contribution of household plots to production, although a severe drought in 2000 reduced harvests of grain and other crops, and grain production fell again in 2005. Others attributed the apparent recovery to the Government's encouragement of private sector investment, despite land privatization remaining politically sensitive. In early 1994 a presidential decree gave individuals or legal entities the right to lease and cultivate plots for 49 years (subsequently extended to 99 years), and allowed the exchange or sale of leases to other Kyrgyzstani citizens. At the same time, the distribution of land-use shares contributed to the disintegration of many collective and state farms, and their replacement by agricultural co-operatives. In 2000 it was planned to end the recent moratorium on land sales, as a result of the inadequate regulation of such activity, and to eliminate various state monopolies in the agricultural sector, most notably that imposed on seed production. In February 2004 Akayev offered farmers further relief, by revoking a government decree that would have increased the level of land taxation two-fold. None the less, although by that time some 80%–90% of farming took place on leased land, the formal position on land ownership remained ambiguous, with urban dwellers and foreign companies denied the possibility of owning agricultural land, and disputes between official agencies, former collective-farm officials and those interested in acquiring control of agricultural land were widespread in 2005–06. The impact of these changes is hard to determine at present, and slight increases, of about 1.5%, in agricultural production in 2006 and 2007 indicate that dramatic improvements are unlikely in the short term.

MINING AND INDUSTRY

Industry arrived late in Kyrgyzstan, and on the eve of the Russian Bolshevik Revolution only around 1,500 people were employed in the industrial sector. The Second World War (1939–45) provided a stimulus to industrial development, as industries threatened by the German advances were shipped from western Russia to Central Asia, often accompanied by Slavic and European personnel. In Kyrgyzstan most were located in the northern regions, leading to the development of defence-related product and engineering works, with particular focus on the production of cars, machine tools, electrical equipment and torpedoes, which were tested in lake Issyk-Kul. The republic lacked, however, many of the energy resources available in neighbouring states, and although it possessed considerable mineral resources, many of these were located in relatively inaccessible and mountainous areas. Finally, Kyrgyzstan was involved in the processing of materials produced elsewhere in the USSR, notably furniture, textiles and footwear, as well as sugar, shipped from Cuba.

After independence, the single most important sector of the economy was mineral exploitation, and, in particular, the development of the Kumtor gold mine. With reserves estimated at over 500 metric tons and valued at almost US $7,000m., the field remained undeveloped by the Soviets, who were concerned by the inaccessibility of the site, which was located at an altitude of around 4,000 m (13,123 ft), and by the inadequacy of the transport infrastructure in the region. After 1991, however, the site proved attractive to foreign investors, and a consortium led by the Cameco Corporation (of Canada) quickly assembled proposals for the development of the field, with a later deal ensuring that the country would receive 70% of the profits. In January 1997 the first gold began to be produced by the mine, and 500,000 troy oz were extracted by the end of the first year of operation. Productivity continued to increase in subsequent years, reaching 20.0 tons in 1999, 22.0 tons in 2000 and 24.6 tons in 2001. Although the project created several hundred jobs in the republic, there was growing criticism of the working conditions of those involved, and a spillage of industrial cyanide at Barskoon, near lake Issyk-Kul, in May 1998, led to further criticism of safety standards. Another accident in July 2002, together with the need to work less ore-rich seams, led to a 27% decline in production in 2002, which seriously undermined industrial growth in the economy as a whole. Production increased in 2003, reaching 22.7 tons, and the Government embarked upon negotiations that would transfer full ownership of the mine to Cameco, in return for a greater share of the profits. However, there was a growing recognition that, although the operation could provide a partial basis for the reconstruction of the economy, its potential was limited by time constraints, as production was scheduled to decline from around 2004 (production was reported to be lower in that year), and to be exhausted by 2010. In 2005 production fell by 24%, which precipitated a decline of 18.3% in the contribution of the mining sector to

GDP, and a 0.6% decline in GDP, which was highly dependent upon gold. Production fell again in 2006, and then again in 2007 owing to a collapsed pit wall, but the discovery of a new seam at the end of that year and technical improvements were projected to lead to a revival of production in the following couple of years. The Government was keen to encourage the development of other gold sources, most notably the smaller Jeruy mine, which commenced operations in 2002, but was not expected to produce significant quantities until 2006–07. This may have been delayed further, however, after the Bakiyev administration annulled a contract issued to the Oxus Gold company (of the United Kingdom), claiming that the deal negotiated with them had not served Kyrgyzstani interests. Oxus Gold was replaced by an Austrian company, Global Gold, although Oxus contested this in the courts, and the tensions surrounding this issue were evident when an Oxus representative was the target of an assassination attempt in July 2006. However, in 2007 the Kyrgyzstani Government announced an agreement granting the state gold company 40% of the equity in the mine and requiring Global Gold to fund local infrastructure projects. Once commissioned, this mine is expected to have a life of around 11 years. Controversies over gold continued in 2007–08, as the Government announced its intention to renegotiate its arrangement with Cameco to acquire a greater share of the profits than its current 16%, at a time when international gold prices were rising.

Other projects that used foreign funding were created for the development of mineral resources, notably mercury, for which Kyrgyzstan was among the major sources in the former USSR. Foremost was the Khaidarakan Mercury Plant, the productivity of which increased to nearly 700,000 metric tons per year in the late 1990s, and most of the products of which were exported from the country. Another major source of income was the Kara-Balta Mining Plant, which produced uranium and molybdenum. Production of the latter was planned to increase from 450 tons to 700 tons in 2000—perhaps reaching 60% of capacity—and the same company also began to refine gold. Around 5% of Kyrgyzstan's energy resources were provided by coal in 2001, when production reached 475,000 tons. Production declined to 415,300 tons in 2003 owing to the stripping and restructuring of several mines, but recovered to 456,300 tons in 2004. However, there was a further decline in 2005, when only 331,600 tons of coal were produced. Problems also emerged during 2006 as coal became a subject of political dispute, when an entrepreneur associated with the controversial businessman Ryspek Akmatbayev seized the Beshary mine and threatened to withhold coal supplies from the city of Bishkek in the winter of 2005–06. (Akmatbayev was assassinated in mid-2006.) Despite these issues, the Government's objective was to increase production to a consistent annual amount of about 460,000 tons by 2010. Kyrgyzstan lacked significant petroleum and gas reserves, although deposits discovered at an oilfield in the west of the country in May 2001 were thought to be sufficient to meet its domestic energy requirements for a 20-year period. More importantly, however, Kyrgyzstan had potentially limitless supplies of water and, thus, the potential for the major development of hydroelectric energy, which by the early 2000s supplied over 90% of the country's energy needs. Under Soviet rule the region's energy supplies were integrated into a common system (see the essay on the politics of water in Central Asia in Part One—General Survey), but as neighbouring states began to increase their charges for energy supplies it was suggested that Kyrgyzstan should charge more for the water that originated in the republic.

Industrial production was more problematic, and most sectors experienced a dramatic decline after 1991. By the end of the 1990s industrial output was about 60% of its level at the time of the collapse of the USSR. In 1992 production was about 75% that of the previous year, and it continued to decline until 1995, at which point it was less than one-half the level it had been at the time of the Soviet collapse. In 1996 the National Statistical Committee reported an increase in production of around 10%, rising to nearly 50% in 1997, and for some time it appeared that the situation might stabilize. The Russian economic crisis of 1998, however, raised fears of a further decline, and output consequently decreased by 4.0% in 1999. The sector appeared to recover thereafter, and industrial GDP increased, in real terms, by 5.2% in 2001. If gold output were discounted, however, the figures suggested that there had, in fact, been a decline, and in 2002 the decline in gold production at the Kumtor mine led to a fall of 11.2% in industrial output, although light industry demonstrated marked growth in that year. In 2003 industrial production recovered somewhat, with output increasing by 2.5% and indications that growth might be becoming less dependent on gold production alone. There was a further increase in industrial production of 3.5% in 2004, and the non-gold increase of 4.2% in 2006 reinforced the impression that another sector of the economy was experiencing a slight but perceptible period of growth, albeit from a relatively low starting point. This was undermined by the collapse in gold production during 2005, and the figures for the first three months of the year suggested that, without some replacement for gold, industrial production would continue to decline in that year. According to the ADB, industrial GDP declined by 9.5% in 2005, and by 5.3% in 2006. In 2007 industrial production rose by 7.3% compared with the previous year and figures for the early months of 2008 suggested that this upward trend was continuing, although it was unclear how dependent this was on an improvement in gold production.

FOREIGN AID, TRADE AND INVESTMENT

From the beginning of Kyrgyzstan's experiment with economic reform, it was hoped that its commitment to the market economy would bring substantial rewards, in terms of both aid and investment. In the former, this hope was realized, to some extent, as the country received more aid per head than any other CIS member state. In addition, the country received substantial amounts of aid from the IMF and the World Bank. A series of loans and credits from the former organization served to bolster the introduction of a new currency in 1993, and to support economic reform. An Enhanced Structural Adjustment Facility (ESAF) from the IMF, of US $80m., was arranged in 1998, and in February 2000, following delays in policy implementation resulting from the financial crisis of 1998, the IMF approved the last part of this funding, under the Poverty Reduction and Growth Facility (PRGF—the successor to the ESAF). At the end of 2001 the IMF approved a new, three-year PRGF. Funds under this programme were made available to the republic at the end of 2005, and then again in May 2006, although the latter represented a very small amount of just under $2m. Institutions that provided additional support included the ADB, which provided resources to support agricultural reform and the improvement of transport infrastructure (and reportedly offered a further $120m. to Kyrgyzstan for 2009) and the European Bank for Reconstruction and Development (EBRD), which supported the National Bank in opening credit lines for small and medium-sized enterprises, contributed towards the upgrading of the electricity transmission networks, and helped to fund a variety of other commercial activities. The World Bank offered a total of five loans worth just under $100m. for use on projects relating to urban transport, irrigation, agricultural infrastructure, and the modernization of water supplies and sewage networks. In mid-2006 the World Bank made a further $15m. available for agricultural investment and, together with the Japanese Government, provided $24m. for improving irrigation networks. During 2007 the US Agency for International Development (USAID) also announced funding of around $20m. for projects involving health care, financial management and good governance.

Although Kyrgyzstan was relatively successful in generating financial aid, it found it harder to attract direct investment. To facilitate this, the Zhogorku Kenesh and the Government approved a series of measures simplifying foreign entry into the local market, sought to improve the legal and regulatory framework, and tried, without a great deal of success, to tackle the corruption that pervaded economic relationships in the region. In 1996 a new Civil Code was introduced in two stages, providing for the proper legal regulation of contracts and giving equal status to foreign and domestic companies.

By far the most successful internationally funded venture was the Kumtor gold mine, developed by Cameco, with support from Chase Manhattan Bank of the USA and the EBRD. In

consequence, Canada accounted for almost one-half of foreign direct investment (FDI) in the republic in the first half of the 1990s, and it was joined in later years by major investors from the People's Republic of China, Germany, Japan, Switzerland, Turkey and the USA. None the less, foreign investment in the country remained low, amounting to around US $383m. in 1993–98, about $42m. in 2000 and some $73m. in 2001. There were, however, overall rises in FDI in 2004 (when it increased by 19%, compared with the previous year), but the unsettled political climate in 2005 appeared to have prevented any major new investments, although several British, Austrian and German companies continued to express interest in various sections of the mining sector. Nevertheless, the National Statistical Agency reported a rise in investment of about $42m. during 2005, with much of the funding being allocated to small projects in the hotels and tourism sector (particularly mountain-based tourism), the financial sector and in household trading activities, such as car-repair groups. After 2002 the primary source of income arose from the basing of Western military forces in the country, which provided both direct income and opportunities to various Kyrgyzstani suppliers, although in 2006 FDI began to rise again, reaching $182m.

At least one-half of Kyrgyzstan's economic transactions remained with the countries of the former USSR, and Russia, in particular, acquired controlling shares in a number of Kyrgyzstani businesses, in particular in the sectors of tobacco and hydroelectric power, in lieu of the payment of debts. In 2006 Kyrgyzstan's major sources of imports were Russia and China. Exports to Germany, which had accounted for 28.7% of total exports in 2000, subsequently declined to negligible levels. In 2006 Switzerland was the main purchaser of Kyrgyzstani exports (accounting for 26.1%); other major purchasers included Kazakhstan, Russia, Afghanistan and China. Foreign trade increased by 12.8% in 2003 compared with 2002, and again in 2004, but fell in 2005, before rising in 2006 and 2007. More difficult to quantify were the informal relations developing in the region, for alongside recorded economic exchanges, the relatively permeable borders with other Central Asian states meant that agricultural goods, in particular, were sold in a burgeoning, but undocumented, private market. From late 1999 Uzbekistan moved to halt this trade, and for periods of time effectively closed its borders with Kyrgyzstan, leaving many Kyrgyzstani citizens unable to buy even basic foodstuffs. Even more difficult to evaluate were the economic activities of the numerous Chinese traders who regularly passed through Kyrgyzstan in order to sell their wares throughout the region. Russia appeared likely to remain the major investor, seeking to increase its strategic influence in the region through shrewd, if expensive, economic engagement. This became more evident in early 2008, when the Russian state-controlled company Gazprom announced a massive US $300m. venture to explore new fields and build pipeline infrastructure, and also indicated its willingness to buy a 75% stake in state gas company Kyrgyzgaz. In late 2008 Kyrgyzstan and Russia reached a co-operation agreement in the hydroelectric sector to assist the Kyrgyzstani Government to avoid an anticipated large-scale energy crisis that winter.

PROSPECTS

The consequences of the economic changes in Kyrgyzstan were mixed. An embryonic free market was created, albeit one with high levels of corruption, which inhibited foreign investment; indeed, the extent of corruption appears to be greater since the 'tulip revolution' of 2005. For the population as a whole the post-independence period was characterized by a growing divide between a small minority of those who gained from reform and the large mass of the population that saw its position worsen. Living standards declined, real incomes decreased by at least 50% and unemployment increased. The official unemployment rate was 8.1% in 2005, although many sources suggested that if the rising population, seasonal employment accompanying agricultural production and the frequent quasi-closures of industrial enterprises were taken into account, the real figure would be nearer 20%. In 2006 the official rate of unemployment increased slightly, to 8.3%. At the same time the social welfare infrastructure declined, as falling state revenues made it impossible for the state to ensure the lifelong provision of earlier years. Thus, by the end of 2001 free schooling had disappeared, and the availability of hospital beds declined dramatically by the end of the 1990s. Problems also arose in health care, from the inability of the authorities to maintain basic water and irrigation facilities, which contributed to poor hygiene and the spread of disease. All of this was made worse by the inflationary pressures of the early 1990s, which seriously affected those on fixed incomes, such as pensioners and the disabled. The human impact of this was hard to assess with any accuracy, as households developed a variety of coping strategies, and in rural areas they became increasingly adept at under-reporting produce to official agencies. Despite these developments of the post-Soviet period, official figures for 2003–05 suggested that 40% of the population was still living below the subsistence level, with some 13% said to be living in extreme poverty. The World Bank estimated that more than 60% of Kyrgyzstani citizens were living on less than US $2.15 per day in 2003. Although low rates of inflation and real wage growth (of around 12% in 2006) had improved the economic situation for some, this was only just beginning to have an impact on the poorest sections of the population by 2006, and one consequence was that rural youth were continuing to drift to the cities in search of work.

At the macroeconomic level, 1996–98 witnessed an expansion, albeit from a low base, with declining inflation and increased output. In 1997 GDP grew by 9.8%, and the rate of inflation fell to around 23%. The Russian financial crisis, however, caused progress to slow, and Kyrgyzstan remained highly dependent upon Russia in many sectors. Consequently, GDP growth was only 2.1% in 1998 and 3.6% in 1999. Inflation rose to 35.9% in 1999, and the prices of food and services increased by 41% and by more than 35%, respectively, in that year. There was some economic recovery thereafter, and annual inflation declined to 2.1% in 2002, before rising slightly, to 3.1% in 2003 and 4.1% in 2004. Annual inflation was recorded at 4.3% in 2005 and 5.6% in 2006. There was a concurrent slight increase in GDP, which rose by 5.4% in 2000 and by 5.3% in 2001, but it declined by some 0.5% overall in 2002, largely owing to the problems at the Kumtor mine. From 2003 increased gold production combined with general growth in most sectors, and GDP increased by 6.0% in 2003 and by 7.1% in 2004, but it fell again, by 0.2%, in 2005, in part owing to political instability,

but also to a large extent to declining gold production. In 2006 GDP rose by 2.7% and the Government's prediction of improved growth in 2007 proved justified, as it rose by 8.2%, and then by 6.1% in the first quarter of 2008.

Kyrgyzstan had made considerable progress in the transition from functioning as part of a centrally planned economy to operating as an independent, market-based state. By 2000 virtually all small and medium-sized enterprises had been privatized, and in 2001–03 over 150 companies, including some major state-owned concerns, were divested, although some economic disruption ensued following the 'tulip revolution'. Political instability continued, creating, together with declining gold production and despite rising gold prices, considerable uncertainty in the Kyrgyzstani economy. However, projections from some international financial institutions appeared to inject some confidence about the future, and there were signs of new investments coming to the country and a return to the path of economic growth. None the less, there was a perception that the new regime had struggled to contain criminality and corruption, thereby making many potential investors wary. More problematic in the long term, however, was the state budget's dependence upon three sources of income. The first was gold, reserves of which were becoming scarcer, despite the exploitation of new resources; the second was the US airbase at Manas airport, a lucrative source of income but one very much dependent upon political circumstances. Within the country there were those who objected to the USA using facilities within Kyrgyzstan to pursue its 'war on terror', while elements within the Russian authorities very much wanted to see this last US military base in Central Asia cease operations. While, Kyrgyzstan could not afford to lose the income associated with the US military presence, it was not inconceivable that in the future the political costs of hosting such troops could outweigh the economic benefits. Third, the growing Russian involvement in the economy might help to resolve short-term problems, but might also foster a return to economic dependence on Russia. The country also continued to struggle with a significant debt burden, although this fell from 109.0% of GNI in 2003 to 85.0% in 2005, before increasing slightly, to 85.6% in 2006, when the country's total debt stocks amounted to US $2,382m. With all of these problems and the high level of dependency on just two major sources of income, the Kyrgyzstani Government was still far from guaranteeing a prosperous future for all its citizens.

Statistical Survey

Source (unless otherwise stated): National Statistical Committee, 720033 Bishkek, Frunze 374; tel. (312) 22-63-63; fax (312) 22-07-59; e-mail zkudabaev@nsc.bishkek.su; internet www.stat.kg.

Area and Population

AREA, POPULATION AND DENSITY

Area (sq km)	199,900*
Population (census results)†	
12 January 1989	4,257,755
24 March 1999	
Males	2,380,465
Females	2,442,473
Total	4,822,938
Population (official estimates at 31 December)	
2005	5,138,700
2006	5,189,800
2007	5,224,300
Density (per sq km) at 31 December 2007	26.1

* 77,182 sq miles.

† The figures refer to *de jure* population. The *de facto* total was 4,290,442 at the 1989 census and 4,850,700 at the 1999 census.

PRINCIPAL ETHNIC GROUPS
(permanent inhabitants, 1999 census)

	Number	%
Kyrgyz	3,128,147	64.86
Uzbek	664,950	13.79
Russian	603,201	12.51
Dungan	51,766	1.07
Ukrainian	50,442	1.05
Others	324,432	6.73
Total	**4,822,938**	**100.00**

ADMINISTRATIVE DIVISIONS
(1999 census)

	Area (sq km)	Population	Density (per sq km)	Principal city
Oblasts (Regions) .				
Batken . . .	17,000	382,426	22.5	Batken
Chui . . .	20,200	770,811	38.2	Tokmok
Issyk-Kul . .	43,100	413,149	9.6	Karakol
Jalal-Abad . . .	33,700	869,259	25.8	Jalal-Abad
Naryn . . .	45,200	249,115	5.5	Naryn
Osh	29,200	1,175,998	40.3	Osh
Talas . . .	11,400	199,872	17.5	Talas
City				
Bishkek . . .	100	762,308	7,623.1	—
Total	199,900	4,822,938	24.1	

PRINCIPAL TOWNS
(population at census of March 1999)

Bishkek (capital)* .	750,327	Karakol† . . .	64,322
Osh . . .	208,520	Tokmok . . .	59,409
Jalal-Abad . . .	70,401	Kara-Balta . .	53,887

* Known as Frunze between 1926 and 1991.
† Formerly Przhevalsk.

Mid-2007 (incl. suburbs, UN estimate): Bishkek 837,000 (Source: UN, *World Urbanization Prospects: The 2007 Revision*).

BIRTHS, MARRIAGES AND DEATHS

	Registered live births		Registered marriages		Registered deaths	
	Number	Rate (per 1,000)	Number	Rate (per 1,000)	Number	Rate (per 1,000)
1997 . .	102,050	21.6	26,588	5.6	34,540	7.3
1998 . .	104,183	21.7	25,726	5.4	34,596	7.2
1999 . .	104,068	21.4	26,033	5.4	32,850	6.8
2000 . .	96,770	19.7	24,294	4.9	34,111	6.9
2001 . .	98,138	19.8	27,455	5.5	32,677	6.6
2002 . .	101,012	20.2	31,240	6.3	35,235	7.1
2003 . .	105,490	20.9	34,266	6.8	35,941	7.1
2004 . .	109,939	21.6	34,542	6.8	35,061	6.9

2005: Birth rate 21.4 per 1,000 persons; Death rate 7.2 per 1,000 persons.

2006: Birth rate 23.3 per 1,000 persons; Death rate 7.4 per 1,000 persons.

2007: Birth rate 23.5 per 1,000 persons; Death rate 7.3 per 1,000 persons.

Expectation of life (years at birth, official estimates): 67.8 (males 63.6; females 72.2) in 2007.

ECONOMICALLY ACTIVE POPULATION
(annual averages, '000 persons)

	2004	2005	2006
Agriculture, hunting and forestry	773.9	799.0	760.0
Fishing	0.7	0.6	0.2
Mining and quarrying	13.5	12.4	11.8
Manufacturing	153.4	163.9	177.9
Electricity, gas and water supply .	39.1	35.2	35.6
Construction	144.0	153.7	181.4
Wholesale and retail trade; repair of motor vehicles, motor cycles and personal and household goods	281.6	301.5	308.4
Hotels and restaurants . . .	44.5	49.0	49.0
Transport, storage and communications	112.9	115.7	120.2
Financial intermediation . . .	8.5	8.2	9.5

—continued	2004	2005	2006
Real estate, renting and business activities	38.4	34.1	36.5
Public administration and defence; compulsory social security . .	91.8	102.3	101.0
Education	161.8	161.8	152.9
Health and social work . . .	73.9	85.4	87.0
Other services	53.2	54.2	64.6
Total employed	1,991.2	2,077.1	2,096.1
Unemployed	185.7	183.5	188.9
Total labour force	2,176.9	2,260.6	2,285.0
Males	1,239.5	1,291.6	1,310.1
Females	937.4	969.0	974.9

Source: ILO.

Health and Welfare

KEY INDICATORS

Total fertility rate (children per woman, 2006) . . .	2.5
Under-5 mortality rate (per 1,000 live births, 2006) . . .	41
HIV/AIDS (% of persons aged 15–49, 2005)	0.1
Physicians (per 1,000 head, 2006)	2.4
Hospital beds (per 1,000 head, 2006)	5.1
Health expenditure (2005): US $ per head (PPP)	113
Health expenditure (2005): % of GDP	6.0
Health expenditure (2005): public (% of total)	39.5
Access to water (% of persons, 2004)	77
Access to sanitation (% of persons, 2004)	59
Human Development Index (2005): ranking	116
Human Development Index (2005): value	0.696

For sources and definitions, see explanatory note on p. vi.

Agriculture

PRINCIPAL CROPS
('000 metric tons)

	2004	2005	2006
Wheat	998.2	950.1	840.3
Rice (paddy)	18.3	17.1	18.7
Barley	233.4	213.5	204.0
Maize	452.9	437.3	438.0
Potatoes	1,362.5	1,141.5	1,254.9
Sugar beet	642.4	288.8	226.0
Sunflower seed	67.2	69.2	61.5*
Cabbages and other brassicas .	113.2	94.7	98.0†
Tomatoes	168.1	171.2	177.0†
Cucumbers and gherkins . . .	55.7	62.4	64.5†
Dry onions	117.1	110.0	113.5†
Garlic	25.0	24.2	25.0†
Carrots and turnips . . .	127.1	144.9	150.0†
Apples	124.5*	102.4*	130.0†
Apricots	15.4*	13.0*	16.5†
Peaches and nectarines* . . .	3.5	3.0	3.8†
Grapes	14.6	11.4	14.7
Watermelons	88.1	85.8	97.7
Cotton (lint)†	40.0	39.0	39.0
Cottonseed†	72.0	70.0	69.0
Tobacco (leaves)	13.0	13.4	13.7

* Unofficial figure(s).
† FAO estimate(s).

Aggregate production ('000 metric tons, may include official, semi-official or estimated data): Total cereals 1,708.9 in 2004, 1,621.6 in 2005, 1,499.0 in 2006; Total roots and tubers 1,362.5 in 2004, 1,141.5 in 2005, 1,254.9 in 2006; Total vegetables (incl. melons) 830.3 in 2004, 825.1 in 2005, 859.0 in 2006; Total fruits (excl. melons) 190.6 in 2004, 158.6 in 2005, 109.7 in 2006.

Source: FAO.

LIVESTOCK
('000 head at 1 January)

	2004	2005	2006
Horses	341	347	350*
Asses, mules or hinnies . . .	49	44	42*
Cattle	1,004	1,035	1,074
Pigs	83	83	78
Sheep	2,884	2,965	3,062†
Goats	770	808	814†
Chickens	3,949	4,121	4,300*
Turkeys	149	154	160

* FAO estimate.
† Unofficial figure.

Source: FAO.

LIVESTOCK PRODUCTS
('000 metric tons)

	2004	2005	2006
Cattle meat	94.6	90.9	91.2*
Sheep meat	37.7	39.2	39.4*
Goat meat	7.1	7.2	7.2*
Pig meat	25.2	18.7	18.8*
Horse meat	18.1	20.3	20.4*
Chicken meat	4.9	5.4	5.4*
Cows' milk	1,132.5	1,151.4	1,157.0*
Hen eggs	16.6	17.7	18.3*
Honey	1.3	1.3	1.4*
Wool: greasy	10.2	10.0	10.6

* FAO estimate.

Source: FAO.

Forestry

ROUNDWOOD REMOVALS
('000 cubic metres, excl. bark, unofficial figures)

	2002	2003	2004
Sawlogs, veneer logs and logs for sleepers	6	6	5
Other industrial wood	6	6	5
Fuel wood	25	25	18
Total	37	37	28

2005–06: Figures assumed to be unchanged from 2004 (FAO estimates).

Source: FAO.

SAWNWOOD PRODUCTION
('000 cubic metres, incl. railway sleepers)

	2002*	2003	2004
Coniferous (softwood)	2.0	8.0	6.3
Broadleaved (hardwood) . . .	4.0	7.2	15.7
Total	6.0	15.2	22.0

* FAO estimates.

2005–06: Figures assumed to be unchanged from 2004 (FAO estimates).

Source: FAO.

Fishing
(metric tons, live weight)

	2003	2004	2005*
Capture	14	7	7
Freshwater bream	1	2	2
Common carp	1	—	—
Silver carp	2	—	—
Other cyprinids	5	1	1
Pike-perch	1	2	2
Whitefishes	3	1	1
Aquaculture	12	20	20
Common carp	7	8	8
Grass carp	1	2	2
Silver carp	4	10	10
Total catch	26	27	27

* FAO estimates.

2006: Catch assumed to be unchanged from 2005 (FAO estimates).

Source: FAO.

Mining
('000 metric tons, unless otherwise indicated)

	2003	2004	2005
Coal	415.3	456.3	331.6
Crude petroleum	69.5	73.8	74.4
Natural gas (million cu metres) .	27.1	28.6	24.7

Coal ('000 metric tons): 321 in 2006; 353 in 2007 (Source: Asian Development Bank).

Gold (metric tons): 16.6 in 2005; 10.6 in 2006; 10.5 in 2007 (Source: Gold Fields Mineral Services, *Gold Survey 2008*).

Industry

SELECTED PRODUCTS
('000 metric tons, unless otherwise indicated)

	2003	2004	2005
Vegetable oil	10.7	12.3	15.2
Refined sugar	75.5	88.1	44.5
Vodka ('000 hectolitres) . . .	24.3	21.8	16.5
Beer ('000 hectolitres)	7.7	11.6	12.3
Cigarettes (million)	3,102.4	3,169.5	3,164.7
Textile fabrics ('000 sq metres) .	1,814.2	1,264.8	1,921.2
Footwear ('000 pairs)	237.8	245.7	220.5
Motor spirit (petrol)	25.0	19.7	14.0
Gas-diesel (distillate fuel) oil . .	21.9	26.3	31.4
Cement	757.3	870.1	975.1
Electric energy (million kWh) .	14,021.1	15,091.2	14,838.7

Electric energy (million kWh): 14,486 in 2006; 14,800 in 2007 (Source: Asian Development Bank).

Finance

CURRENCY AND EXCHANGE RATES

Monetary Units
100 tiyiyns = 1 som.

Sterling, Dollar and Euro Equivalents (30 May 2008)
£1 sterling = 71.617 soms;
US $1 = 36.289 soms;
€1 = 56.277 soms;
1,000 soms = £13.96 = $27.56 = €17.77.

Average Exchange Rate (soms per US $)
2005   41.012
2006   40.153
2007   37.316

Note: In May 1993 Kyrgyzstan introduced its own currency, the som, replacing the Russian (former Soviet) rouble at an exchange rate of 1 som = 200 roubles.

BUDGET
(million soms)*

Revenue†	2005	2006	2007
Taxation	16,361.4	19,981.2	26,544.8
Corporate income taxes . .	1,744.2	1,820.3	2,322.9
Personal income taxes . .	1,283.2	1,191.6	1,736.1
Value-added tax	7,088.6	9,150.6	10,701.6
Excise taxes	1,149.7	1,205.4	1,448.2
Taxes on international trade and transactions	1,664.0	2,803.3	3,789.5
Other current revenue . . .	3,567.9	4,696.0	7,195.3
Capital revenue	46.1	138.0	465.3
Total	19,975.4	24,815.2	34,205.4

Expenditure‡	2005	2006	2007
General public services . . .	3,039.6	3,358.4	5,154.8
Education	4,917.7	6,314.2	9,178.0
Health care	2,283.3	3,059.1	4,028.8
Social insurance and security .	2,858.1	3,610.6	3,816.9
Housing and public utilities . .	1,040.6	1,415.5	2,657.3
Cultural and religious activity .	606.9	813.0	1,239.9
Total (incl. others)	20,143.7	25,297.8	35,864.9

* Figures represent a consolidation of the budgetary transactions of the central Government and local governments. The operations of extra-budgetary accounts, including the Social Fund (formed in 1994 by an amalgamation of the Pension Fund, the Unemployment Fund and the Social Insurance Fund), are excluded.
† Excluding grants received (million soms): 392.6 in 2005; 266.1 in 2006; 1,789.5 in 2007.
‡ Including lending minus repayments.

Source: National Bank of the Kyrgyz Republic.

INTERNATIONAL RESERVES
(US $ million at 31 December)

	2005	2006	2007
Gold	42.6	52.8	69.5
IMF special drawing rights . .	5.3	33.3	13.8
Foreign exchange	564.5	731.1	1,093.4
Total	612.4	817.2	1,176.7

Source: IMF, *International Financial Statistics*.

MONEY SUPPLY
(million soms at 31 December)

	2004	2005	2006
Currency outside banks . .	11,109	13,065	19,410
Demand deposits at banking institutions	1,935	2,123	3,655
Total money	13,045	15,188	23,065

Source: IMF, *International Financial Statistics*.

COST OF LIVING
(Retail Price Index; base: previous year = 100)

	2005	2006	2007
Food and non-alcoholic drinks .	107.0	109.5	114.7
Fuel and light	108.5	107.3	113.2
Clothing and footwear . . .	101.1	101.1	102.9
All items (incl. others) . . .	104.3	105.6	110.2

NATIONAL ACCOUNTS
(million soms at current prices)

Expenditure on the Gross Domestic Product

	2005	2006	2007
Final household expenditure . .	85,305.1	108,253.1	141,335.7
Final general government expenditure	17,667.3	20,469.6	24,809.5
Gross fixed capital formation . .	16,357.3	26,666.9	35,717.5
Changes in stocks	208.5	867.9	1,076.0
Total domestic expenditure	119,538.2	156,257.5	202,938.7
Exports of goods and services . .	38,650.0	47,478.1	62,446.5
Less Imports of goods and services	57,289.0	89,935.5	125,614.5
Statistical discrepancy	—	—	−21.3
GDP in purchasers' values	100,899.2	113,800.1	139,749.4

Source: Asian Development Bank.

Gross Domestic Product by Economic Activity

	2005	2006	2007*
Agriculture, forestry and fishing .	28,739.4	32,638.2	40,552.9
Mining	556.4	488.7	548.7
Manufacturing	12,968.0	12,509.0	13,687.8
Electricity, gas and water supply	3,896.7	3,937.4	3,922.8
Construction	2,725.9	3,041.9	4,711.0
Trade, repair of motor vehicles, household appliances and articles of personal use . .	18,001.6	20,883.9	25,484.4
Hotels and restaurants . . .	1,350.6	1,549.0	1,870.6
Transport and communications .	6,617.7	6,887.2	10,181.7
Housing, social and personal services	1,197.9	1,531.4	1,860.4
Health care and social services . .	2,064.9	2,588.5	2,711.7
Education	3,854.4	4,561.6	5,409.8
Financial activities	2,250.8	2,986.4	605.7
Real estate, rent and rendering services	2,814.1	3,321.7	3,777.9
Government administration . .	4,659.8	5,053.9	5,474.7
Sub-total	91,698.2	101,978.8	120,800.1
Less Imputed bank service charge	1,735.2	2,380.7	—
GDP at basic prices	89,963.0	99,598.1	120,800.1
Taxes on products . . . } *Less* Subsidies on products . . }	10,936.2	14,202.0	18,949.3
GDP in purchasers' values . .	100,899.2	113,800.1	139,749.4

* Preliminary figures.

BALANCE OF PAYMENTS
(US $ million)

	2005	2006	2007
Exports of goods f.o.b.	686.8	810.8	1,151.8
Imports of goods f.o.b.	−1,105.5	−1,792.3	−2,627.1
Trade balance	−418.7	−981.5	−1,475.3
Exports of services, and other income received	272.1	416.1	566.6
Imports of services, and other income paid	−382.9	−530.7	−666.2
Balance on goods, services and income	−529.5	−1,096.1	−1,574.9
Current transfers received	538.2	766.1	1,062.0
Current transfers paid	−37.9	−50.0	−78.3
Current balance	−29.2	−380.0	−591.2
Capital account (net)	−20.5	−43.9	−75.5
Direct investment (net)	42.6	182.0	187.9
Portfolio investment (net)	2.3	−3.0	−3.0
Other investments (net)	−23.4	148.6	117.8
Net errors and omissions	57.4	279.9	663.4
Overall balance	29.1	183.7	299.3

Source: Asian Development Bank.

External Trade

PRINCIPAL COMMODITIES
(US $ million)

Imports c.i.f.	2005	2006	2007
Vegetable products	40.6	62.6	119.1
Prepared foodstuffs, beverages and tobacco	101.3	141.6	185.6
Mineral products	334.0	527.4	781.4
Products of chemical or allied industries	130.8	145.5	222.7
Plastics, rubber and articles thereof	60.1	85.2	104.8
Textiles and fabrics	36.6	50.9	47.9
Metals and articles thereof	66.5	104.9	177.7
Machinery, electrical equipment and parts	156.1	271.9	343.7
Vehicles and transport equipment	41.4	136.6	144.2
Total (incl. others)	1,101.3	1,718.2	2,417.0

Exports f.o.b.	2005	2006	2007
Vegetable products	19.9	36.6	80.3
Prepared foodstuffs, beverages and tobacco	37.2	28.9	37.3
Mineral products	96.8	177.8	330.0
Products of chemical or allied industries	13.5	14.4	24.4
Raw hides and skins, leather, fur, travel articles and bags	12.2	14.3	16.0
Textiles and fabrics	77.4	96.7	122.3
Natural and cultured pearls, precious and semi-precious stones, precious metals and products, and coins	236.2	212.6	228.5
Metals and articles thereof	23.2	27.0	52.9
Machinery, electrical equipment and parts	32.1	51.1	69.9
Vehicles and transport equipment	18.5	23.7	42.3
Total (incl. others)	672.0	794.2	1,134.2

Source: Asian Development Bank.

PRINCIPAL TRADING PARTNERS
(US $ million)

Imports c.i.f.	2005	2006
China, People's Republic	102.9	245.6
Germany	37.6	39.9
Kazakhstan	174.4	199.8
Korea, Republic	27.8	24.3
Netherlands	18.9	27.7
Russia	378.9	652.3
Turkey	33.4	39.5
Ukraine	40.1	41.9
USA	67.2	97.5
Uzbekistan	60.1	65.0
Total (incl. others)	1,111.6	1,710.5

Exports f.o.b.	2005	2006
Afghanistan	12.4	74.8
Canada	22.5	0.2
China, People's Republic	26.6	38.1
Kazakhstan	116.1	162.6
Russia	134.4	153.8
Switzerland	65.3	207.7
Tajikistan	22.9	23.9
Turkey	18.2	27.2
United Arab Emirates	173.1	8.9
Uzbekistan	17.1	27.9
Total (incl. others)	633.8	796.5

Note: Data reflect the IMF's direction of trade methodology and, as a result, the totals may not be equal to those presented for trade in commodities.

Source: Asian Development Bank.

Transport

RAILWAYS
(traffic)

	2002	2003	2004
Passenger-km (million)	43	50	45
Freight net ton-km (million)	395	562	715

ROAD TRAFFIC
(vehicles in use at 31 December)

	2001	2002	2003
Passenger cars	189,796	188,711	188,900
Motorcycles and mopeds	14,319	12,288	11,221

CIVIL AVIATION
(traffic on scheduled services)

	2002	2003	2004
Kilometres flown (million) . .	6	7	7
Passengers carried ('000) . . .	185	218	258
Passenger-km (million) . . .	342	411	459
Total ton-km (million)	39	43	46

Tourism

FOREIGN TOURIST ARRIVALS

Country of residence	2004	2005	2006
China, People's Republic . . .	11,822	15,747	18,681
Germany	9,724	9,128	9,148
Kazakhstan	236,712	150,904	479,119
Korea, Republic	3,127	3,850	4,667
Russia	36,540	32,001	83,438
Tajikistan	8,190	4,565	16,588
Turkey	9,032	9,362	9,981
USA	11,111	11,727	12,772
Uzbekistan	40,655	49,376	95,091
Total (incl. others)	398,078	315,290	765,850

Tourism receipts (US $ million, incl. passenger transport): 65 in 2003; 97 in 2004; 94 in 2005.

Source: World Tourism Organization.

Communications Media

	2002	2003	2004
Television receivers ('000 in use) . .	7	7	7
Telephones ('000 main lines in use) .	394.8	396.2	416.4
Mobile cellular telephones ('000			
subscribers)	53.1	138.3	263.4
Internet users ('000)	152	200	263
Personal computers ('000 in use) . .	65	75	87
Daily newspapers:			
number	1	2	2
average circulation	35,900	65,000	21,000
Non-daily newspapers:			
number	62	77	83
average circulation	319,100	376,600	427,800
Book production:			
titles	672	642	703
copies ('000)	1,056.6	1,885.0	1,600.3

Radio receivers ('000 in use): 520 in 1997 (Source: UNESCO, *Statistical Yearbook*).

Telephones ('000 main lines in use): 438.2 in 2005.

Mobile cellular telephones ('000 subscribers): 541.7 in 2005.

Personal computers ('000 in use): 100 in 2005.

Internet users ('000): 280.0 in 2005; 298.1 in 2006.

Broadband subscribers ('000): 2.5 in 2005.

Source: International Telecommunication Union.

Education

(2004/05)

	Institutions	Teachers	Students
Pre-primary	440	2,333	50,935
Primary	2,104	17,729	436,159
Secondary: general	n.a.	50,526	692,724
Secondary: vocational . . .	187	6,212	59,659
Higher (all institutions) . . .	49	13,337	218,273

Adult literacy rate (official estimate): 98.7% in 2006.

Directory

The Constitution

In September 2007 the Constitutional Court ruled that the adoption of two successive Constitutions in November 2006 and January 2007 had been illegal. It restored the Constitution proclaimed on 5 May 1993, which had been revised on numerous subsequent occasions. President Kurmanbek Bakiyev subsequently scheduled a referendum on the adoption of a new Constitution for 21 October 2007. The new Constitution, which was approved by 76.1% of votes cast at the national referendum, entered into effect on 23 October. The following is a summary of its main provisions.

GENERAL PROVISIONS

The Kyrgyz Republic is a sovereign, unitary, democratic republic founded on the principle of the rule of law. All state power originates from the people of Kyrgyzstan, who exercise this power through elections and referendums, and through the state bodies and bodies of local self-government, on the basis of the Constitution and laws. Matters of legislation and other issues pertaining to the state may be decided by the people by referendum. The President of the Republic, the deputies of the Zhogorku Kenesh (Supreme Council) and representatives of local administrative bodies are all elected directly by the people. Elections are held on the basis of universal, equal and direct suffrage by secret ballot. All citizens of 18 years and over are eligible to vote.

The territory of the Kyrgyz Republic is integral and inviolable. The state language is Kyrgyz, and Russian is used as an official language. The equality and free use of other languages by representatives of the national and ethnic groups that constitute the people of Kyrgyzstan are guaranteed. The rights and freedoms of citizens may not be restricted on account of ignorance of the state language. The adoption of a state religion is prohibited. Political parties may not be formed on a religious basis, and certain provisions provide for a separation of the activities of political parties from those of the organs of the State.

HUMAN RIGHTS AND CIVIL LIBERTIES

Human rights and freedoms are absolute and inalienable. All people are equal before the laws and courts of the Kyrgyz Republic.

The freedoms of movement, association, peaceful assembly, of place of residence within the territories of the Kyrgyz Republic, and of property ownership are guaranteed. The privacy of written and telephonic conversation is respected. The freedoms of religion and thought, speech and expression are guaranteed. Citizens of the Kyrgyz Republic are permitted to obtain citizenship of another state, subject to international agreements entered into by the Kyrgyz Republic.

THE PRESIDENT

The President of the Kyrgyz Republic is Head of State. The President is a symbol of the unity of the people and state power, a guarantor of the Constitution, human rights and civil liberties. The term of office is five years, and no more than two consecutive terms may be served. The President is directly elected by the people. Any citizen of the republic between the ages of 35 and 65, who has a command of the state language, and who has resided in the Republic for at least 15 years, is permitted to contest the presidency. Presidential candidates must be nominated by no less than 50,000 electors.

The President: appoints the Prime Minister and members of the Government; dismisses members of the Government either of his own accord or at the behest of the Prime Minister; appoints heads of local state administration in consultation with the Prime Minister and orders their dismissal; appoints other leading state posts; and appoints one-half of the members of the Central Commission for Elections and Referendums. With the agreement of the Zhogorku Kenesh, he appoints the Prosecutor-General, other senior judicial posts, the Chairman of the National Bank and the Chairman of the Central Commission for Elections and Referendums. The President: presents draft legislation to the Zhogorku Kenesh; signs legislation approved by the Zhogorku Kenesh or returns it for further scrutiny; signs international agreements; may call referendums on issues of state on his own initiative or in response to proposals presented by at least 300,000 electors and a majority of deputies in the Zhogorku Kenesh; and calls elections to the Zhogorku Kenesh and to local assemblies. The President declares a state of war.

The President may be removed from office only on the basis of a charge of high treason or relating to other grave crimes made by the Zhogorku Kenesh, as confirmed by the Prosecutor-General. Any ensuing demands for a vote of impeachment must be supported by no less than two-thirds of the total membership of the Zhogorku Kenesh. For the vote of impeachment to be approved it must be supported by no less than three-quarters of the total membership of the Zhogorku Kenesh; this vote must be held no more than three months after the vote to commence impeachment proceedings was taken. In the event of impeachment being approved, the executive duties of the President are assumed on an acting basis by the Chairman of the Zhogorku Kenesh; in the event that the Chairman of the Zhogorku Kenesh is unable to assume executive powers, they are transferred to the Prime Minister. Elections for a new President must be held no later than three months after the removal from office of the outgoing President.

ZHOGORKU KENESH

Supreme legislative power is vested in the Zhogorku Kenesh, which comprises one 90-member chamber. Deputies are elected for a term of five years on the basis of party lists. Any citizen of the Kyrgyz Republic aged 25 years or older, and enjoying full civil rights, may be elected to the Zhogorku Kenesh.

The Zhogorku Kenesh: adopts the Constitution; approves amendments and additions to the Constitution; enacts legislation; confirms the republican budget and supervises its execution; determines questions pertaining to the administrative and territorial structure of the republic; designates presidential elections; approves the governmental structure proposed by the Prime Minister; may approve a vote of no confidence in the Government or in individual members thereof; consents to the appointment of the Procurator-General, as nominated by the President; elects judges of the Constitutional court, judges of the Supreme Court and the Chairman of the National Bank, at the proposal of the President; and ratifies or abrogates international agreements. The Zhogorku Kenesh may be dissolved by resolution of no less than two-thirds of its deputies.

THE GOVERNMENT

The Government of the Kyrgyz Republic is the highest organ of executive power in Kyrgyzstan. A political party that receives more than 50% of the mandates in the Zhogorku Kenesh presents its candidate for the Prime Minister for presidential approval, no later than five days from the convening of a new Zhogorku Kenesh. In the event that the nominated candidate fails to obtain the approval of the Zhogorku Kenesh, the President may request a second political party to nominate a candidate as Prime Minister, and similarly from a third political party in the event that the second candidate is not approved. In the event that the third candidate for the premiership is rejected, the President shall form an interim Government pending fresh legislative elections. A vote of no confidence in the Government may be held if demanded by at least one-third of the membership of the Zhogorku Kenesh, except in the six-month period before a presidential election, when such a vote may not be held. The President is not obliged to dismiss the Government following a vote of no confidence, unless two such votes take place within a period of three months, in which case the President may either dismiss the Government and appoint a new administration or call fresh legislative elections. The President is obliged to dismiss an individual member of the Government subject to two votes of no confidence in a six-month period.

The Government: determines all questions of state administration, other than those ascribed by the Constitution to the competence of the President and the Zhogorku Kenesh; drafts the republican budget and submits it to the Zhogorku Kenesh for approval; co-ordinates budgetary, financial, fiscal and monetary policy; administers state property; takes measures to defend the country and state security; executes foreign policy; and strives to guarantee the rights and freedoms of the citizens and to protect property and social order.

The authorities, duties, organization and form of local territorial-administrative bodies are determined by law.

THE CENTRAL ORGANS OF STATE POWER

The central organs of state power of the Kyrgyz Republic comprise: the Office of the Prosecutor-General; the National Bank; the Central Commission for Elections and Referendums; the Audit Chamber; and the Akyikatchi (Ombudsman), which protects the observation of human rights and civil freedoms in the Republic.

JUDICIAL SYSTEM

The judicial system comprises the Constitutional Court, the Supreme Court and regional courts. Courts are independent and governed only by the Constitution and by law. Judges of all courts remain in office for as long as their behaviour is deemed to be irreproachable. Judges of the Constitutional Court and the Supreme Court are elected by the Zhogorku Kenesh, on the recommendation of the President. Judges of local courts are appointed by the President of the Republic at the proposal of the National Council for the Judiciary, for terms of five years. The Constitutional Court comprises seven judges. The Supreme Court is the highest organ of judicial power in the sphere of civil, criminal and administrative justice.

ON REFORM

The proposed introduction of amendments or additions to the existing Constitution, or the proposed adoption of a new Constitution, may be examined by the Zhogorku Kenesh in response to a request of the President or of a majority of deputies of the Zhogorku Kenesh, or in response to an initiative supported by no less than 300,000 electors. A law amending and supplementing the existing Constitution may be adopted by a majority of no less than two-thirds of the total membership of the Zhogorku Kenesh after the holding of no fewer than two readings with an interval of three months between readings. At the demand of the majority of the total membership of the Zhogorku Kenesh, a law amending and supplementing the present Constitution may be submitted to referendum.

The Government

HEAD OF STATE

President: Kurmanbek S. Bakiyev (elected 10 July 2005; inaugurated 14 August 2005).

GOVERNMENT
(September 2008)

Prime Minister: Igor V. Chudinov.

First Deputy Prime Minister: Iskenderbek R. Aydaraliyev.

Deputy Prime Minister: Elmira S. Ibragimova.

Minister of Foreign Affairs: Ednan O. Karabayev.

Minister of Defence: Bakytbek T. Kalyev.

Minister of Internal Affairs: Moldomusa T. Kongantiyev.

Minister of Justice: Nurlan Zh. Tursunkulov.

Minister of Finance: Tazhikan B. Kalimbetova.

Minister of Economic Development and Trade: Akylbek U. Zhaparov.

Minister of Agriculture, Water Resources and Processing Industry: Arstanbek I. Nogoyev.

Minister of Transport and Communications: Nurlan Ch. Sulaimanov.

Minister of Emergency Situations: Kamchibek K. Tashiyev.

Minister of Education and Science: Ishenkul S. Boljurova.

Minister of Health: Marat A. Mambetov.

Minister of Culture and Information: Sultan A. Rayev.

Minister of Labour and Social Welfare: Uktomkhan A. Abdullayeva.

Minister of Industry, Energy and Fuel Resources: Sapar E. Balkibekov.

Note: The Chairmen of the State Committees for National Security, Migration and Labour, for the Management of State Property, for Taxes and Collections, and for Customs are also members of the Government.

MINISTRIES

Office of the President: 720003 Bishkek, Dom Pravitelstva; tel. (312) 63-85-11; fax (312) 63-86-86; e-mail office@mail.gov.kg; internet www.president.kg.

Office of the Prime Minister: 720003 Bishkek, Dom Pravitelstva; tel. (312) 66-12-20; fax (312) 66-66-58; e-mail pmoffice@mail.gov.kg; internet www.government.gov.kg.

Ministry of Agriculture, Water Resources and Processing Industry: 720040 Bishkek, Kiyevskaya 96A; tel. (312) 62-14-27; fax (312) 62-36-32; e-mail agroprod@elcat.kg; internet www.agroprod.kg.

Ministry of Culture and Information: 720040 Bishkek, Pushkina 78; tel. (312) 62-12-00; internet www.minculture.gov.kg.

Ministry of Defence: 720001 Bishkek, Logvinenko 26; tel. (312) 66-38-28; fax (312) 66-16-02; e-mail ud@bishkek.gov.kg; internet www.mil.kg.

Ministry of Economic Development and Trade: 720002 Bishkek, pr. Chui 106; tel. (312) 66-38-00; fax (312) 66-34-98; e-mail mert_kg@mail.ru; internet www.mert.kg.

Ministry of Education and Science: 720040 Bishkek, Tynystanova 257; tel. (312) 62-36-33; fax (312) 62-36-22; e-mail monk@monk.bishkek.gov.kg; internet www.minedu.kg.

Ministry of Emergency Situations: 720055 Bishkek, Toktonaliyeva 2/1; tel. (312) 54-79-86; fax (312) 54-11-79; e-mail mecd@bishkek.gov.kg; internet www.mchs.in.kg.

Ministry of Finance: 720040 Bishkek, pr. Erkindik 58; tel. (312) 66-13-50; fax (312) 66-16-45; e-mail it@minfin.kg; internet www.minfin.kg.

Ministry of Foreign Affairs: 720040 Bishkek, bul. Erkindik 57; tel. (312) 62-05-45; fax (312) 66-05-01; e-mail gendep@mfa.gov.kg; internet www.mfa.kg.

Ministry of Health: 720040 Bishkek, Moskovskaya 148; tel. (312) 62-26-80; fax (312) 66-07-17; e-mail mz@med.kg; internet www.med.kg.

Ministry of Industry, Energy and Fuel Resources: 720055 Bishkek, Ahunbayeva 119; tel. (312) 56-18-22; fax (312) 56-20-28; internet www.mpe.gov.kg.

Ministry of Internal Affairs: 720040 Bishkek, Frunze 469; tel. (312) 66-24-50; fax (312) 68-20-44; e-mail mail@mvd.bishkek.gov.kg; internet www.mvd.kg.

Ministry of Justice: 720040 Bishkek, M. Gandi 32; tel. (312) 65-64-90; fax (312) 65-65-02; e-mail admin@minjust.gov.kg; internet www.minjust.gov.kg.

Ministry of Labour and Social Welfare: 720041 Bishkek, Tynystanova 215; tel. (312) 66-34-00; fax (312) 66-57-24; e-mail mlsp@mlsp.kg; internet www.mlsp.kg.

Ministry of Transport and Communications: 720017 Bishkek, Isanova 42; tel. (312) 61-04-72; fax (312) 66-47-81; e-mail mtk@mtk.gov.kg; internet www.mtk.gov.kg.

President

Presidential Election, 10 July 2005*

Candidates							Votes	%
Kurmanbek S. Bakiyev	.	.	.	.	.	.	1,776,156	88.72
Tursunbai Bakir-uulu	.	.	.	.	.	.	78,701	3.93
Akbaraly Y. Aitikeyev	.	.	.	.	.	.	72,604	3.63
Others	.	.	.	.	.	.	38,864	1.94
Total†	.	.	.	.	.	.	2,001,974	100.00

* Preliminary official results.
† Including 18,197 votes (0.91% of the total) 'against all candidates' and 17,452 invalid votes (0.87% of the total).

Legislature

Zhogorku Kenesh
(Supreme Council)

720053 Bishkek, ul. Abdymomunov 207; tel. (312) 61-16-04; fax (312) 62-50-12; e-mail zs@kenesh.gov.kg; internet www.kenesh.kg.

Chairman: AITIBAI TAGAYEV.

General Election, 16 December 2007*

Parties	% of votes†	Seats
Bright Road (Ak Zhol)	46.90	71
Social Democratic Party of Kyrgyzstan . .	5.12	11
Communist Party of Kyrgyzstan . .	5.05	8
Fatherland Socialist Party (Ata-Meken) . .	8.29	—
Others	34.64	—
Total	100.00	90

* Provisional final results.
† Parties were required to obtain at least 0.5% of votes cast in each of the country's six regions and two largest cities in order to be eligible for legislative representation.

Local Government

In March 1996 the heads of local administrations, who represent the main executive authority, were given extended powers. In April a resolution in the legislature made provision for the reorganization of regional councils into regional governments, with governors to be appointed locally. For the purposes of local government, Kyrgyzstan is divided into seven oblasts (regions) and the capital city, Bishkek. Each of the oblasts is further subdivided into raions (districts) and cities. Local elections took place in two rounds in December 2001. Partial local elections took place in December 2005. Further local elections were conducted on 5 October 2008.

CAPITAL CITY

Bishkek City Administration: 720000 Bishkek, pr. Chui 160; tel. (312) 61-11-66; fax (312) 66-06-21; e-mail meria@bishkek.gov.kg; internet www.e-bishkek.kg; Mayor NARIMAN TULEYEV.

OBLASTS

Batken Oblast Administration: 715100 Batken, ul. Sadykova 1; tel. (3622) 3-64-52; fax (3622) 3-60-17; e-mail ksjoldoshova@gmail.com; Gov. MARATBEK JUMABEKOV.

Chui Oblast Administration: 722200 Chui Oblast, Tokmok, ul. Lenina 385; tel. (3138) 6-22-10; fax (3138) 6-22-04; e-mail chuy@bishkek.gov.kg; internet www.chuy.in.kg; Gov. KUBANYCHBEK S. SYIDANOV.

Issyk-Kul Oblast Administration: 722360 Issyk-Kul Oblast, Karakol, ul. Yu. Abdrakhmanova 105; tel. (3922) 2-32-20; fax (3922) 2-22-27; e-mail karakol@bishkek.gov.kg; Gov. KYDYKBEK ISAYEV.

Jalal-Abad Oblast Administration: 715600 Jalal-Abad, ul. Erkindik 11; tel. (3722) 5-00-01; fax (3722) 5-51-96; e-mail djalal-abad@bishkek.gov.kg; Gov. KOSHBAI MASIROV.

Naryn Oblast Administration: 722600 Naryn, ul. Lenina 76; tel. (3522) 5-00-19; fax (3522) 5-08-78; e-mail naryn@bishkek.gov.kg; internet www.naryn.gov.kg; Gov. OMURBEK SUVANALIEV.

Osh Oblast Adminstration: 714018 Osh, ul. Lenina 221; tel. (3222) 5-55-40; fax (3222) 5-92-00; e-mail obladm@osh.gov.kg; internet www.osh.gov.kg; Gov. AALY A. KARASHEV.

Talas Oblast Administration: 722720 Talas, ul. Frunze 287; tel. (3422) 5-30-94; fax (3422) 5-29-53; e-mail talas@bishkek.gov.kg; Gov. BEISHENBEK BOLOTBEKOV.

Election Commission

Kyrgyz Respublikasynyn Shailoo Zhana Referendum Otkoruu Boyuncha Borborduk Komissiyasy (Central Commission for Elections and Referendums of the Kyrgyz Republic): 720040 Bishkek, ul. Razzakova 59; tel. (312) 62-68-25; fax (312) 66-58-60; e-mail cec@shailoo.gov.kg; internet www.shailoo.gov.kg; independent govt organ; one-half of the mems are appointed by the President of the Republic, and one-half by the Zhogorku Kenesh; Chair. DAMIR V. LISOVSKY (acting).

Political Organizations

At December 2007 50 political organizations were registered with the Central Election Commission. The following were among the most important operating in 2008.

Agrarian Party of Kyrgyzstan: 720000 Bishkek, Kiyevskaya 96; tel. (312) 66-28-72; f. 1993; campaigns for agrarian reform, and for the protection of the rights and interests of people working in agriculture; Leader ERKIN ALIYEV; c. 8,000 mems (1999).

Banner Party of National Revival (Asaba): 720000 Bishkek, pr. Chui 26; tel. (312) 43-04-45; fax (312) 28-53-64; f. 1990; re-registered 2001; nationalist, pro-democracy; mem. of the People's Movement of Kyrgyzstan electoral alliance; critical of the progress made by the administration of Kurmanbek Bakiyev in tackling issues such as crime and corruption; Co-Chair. AZIMBEK BEKNAZAROV, ROZA OTUN-BAYEVA.

Bright Road People's Party (Ak Zhol) (Ak Zhol Eldik Partiyasy): 720000 Bishkek, Toktogul 175/15; tel. (312) 62-82-45; internet www .akjolnarod.kg; f. Oct. 2007; supports administration of Pres. Bakiyev; Chair. ELMIRA S. IBRAIMOVA (acting).

Democratic Movement of Kyrgyzstan: 720000 Bishkek, Abdy-momunova 205; tel. (312) 27-14-95; f. 1990; registered as a political party in 1993, re-registered in 2000; campaigns for civil liberties, for democratic social and legal development; participated in 2005 leg-islative elections as mem. of People's Movement of Kyrgyzstan electoral bloc; Leader JYPAR JEKSHEYEV; Chair. of the Exec. Cttee EDILBEK SARYBAYEV; Chair. of the Political Council VIKTOR CHERNO-MORETS.

Dignity (Ar-Namys): 720033 Bishkek, Togolok Moldo 60 A; tel. (312) 32-52-89; e-mail ar-namys@mail.kg; internet www.ar-namys .org; f. 1999; pro-democracy; mem. of political bloc For a Worthy Future of Kyrgyzstan United Front, formed Feb. 2007; Chair. FELIKS KULOV; c. 11,000 mems.

Fatherland Socialist Party (Ata Meken) (Ata Meken Sotsialist-tik Partiyasy): 720040 Bishkek, Orozbekova 110A/2; tel. (312) 66-34-92; fax (312) 66-46-38; e-mail atameken@elcat.kg; internet www .atameken.kg; f. 1992; nationalist; supports state control of the economy; participated in 2005 legislative elections as mem. of For Fair Elections electoral bloc; mem. of political bloc People's Coalition of Democratic Forces, formed Jan. 2006 with declared aim of introducing parliamentary system of govt; Leader OMURBEK CH. TEKEBAYEV; more than 2,000 mems.

Forward, Kyrgyzstan (Alga, Kyrgyzstan): 720000 Bishkek, Moskovskaya 217; tel. (312) 65-13-57; f. 2003 by merger of the Manas El Party of Spiritual Revival, New Time, New Movement and the Party of Co-operators; merged with Birimdik in 2003, and with the Unity Party of Kyrgyzstan in 2004; fmrly supportive of regime of President Akayev; Chair. BOLOT BEGALIYEV; c. 7,000 mems (2004).

Free Kyrgyzstan Progressive-Democratic Party (ERK) (Erkin Kyrgyzstan): 720000 Bishkek, Abdymomunova 207; tel. (312) 22-49-57; fax (312) 22-60-35; f. 1991; social-democratic; participated in 2005 legislative elections as mem. of People's Movement of Kyrgyzstan electoral alliance; Chair. BAKIR UULU TURSUNBAI.

Justice (Adilet): 720000 Bishkek, Bokonbayev 109; tel. (312) 66-48-17; fax (312) 66-50-84; f. 1999; re-registered 2003; campaigns for economic reform, modernization and investment; Hon. Chair. CHIN-GIZ T AITMATOV; Co Chair. TOICHUDEK KAZYMOV, KUBANYCHBEK JUMALIYEV, ALTAI BORUBAYEV; c. 15,000 mems (2003).

Liberty (Erkindik): 720000 Bishkek; f. 2000; participated in 2005 legislative elections as mem. of People's Movement of Kyrgyzstan electoral bloc; Chair. TOPCHUBEK TURGUNALIYEV; c. 3,700 mems (June 2004).

New Kyrgyzstan (Jany Kyrgyzstan): 720000 Bishkek, Kiyevs-kaya 120; tel. (312) 21-19-61; fax (312) 21-65-04; f. 1994 as Agrarian Labour Party of Kyrgyzstan; re-registered 2001; participated in 2005 legislative elections as mem. of People's Movement of Kyrgyzstan electoral bloc; Chair. DOSBOL NUR UULU.

Party of Communists of Kyrgyzstan (KCP): 720001 Bishkek, pr. Chui 114/206; tel. (312) 62-49-99; fax (312) 67-02-55; e-mail anashparties@mail.ru; disbanded 1991, re-established 1992, re-registered 2007; successor to the Communist Party of Kyrgyz SSR; participated in 2005 legislative elections as mem. of People's Movement of Kyrgyzstan election bloc; Chair. ISKHAK MASALIYEV; 25,000 mems.

Republican Party of Kyrgyzstan (RPK): 720000 Bishkek, Isa-nova 8; tel. (312) 21-14-16; registered in 1999; advocates absolute freedom of speech, full equality of all citizens before the law and environmental protection; participated in 2005 legislative elections as mem. of People's Movement of Kyrgyzstan electoral alliance; Chair. GIYAZ TOKOMBAYEV.

Social Democratic Party of Kyrgyzstan: 720000 Bishkek, Alma-Atinskaya 4B/203; tel. (312) 43-15-07; f. 1993; mem. of political bloc People's Coalition of Democratic Forces, formed Jan. 2006 with declared aim of reforming Kyrgyzstan's constitution and introducing parliamentary system of govt; Chair. ALMAZBEK ATAMBAYEV.

Union of Democratic Forces: 720040 Bishkek, Abdumomunova 207; tel. (312) 66-19-10; fax (312) 62-50-27; e-mail smanbaeva@ kenesh.kg; f. 2005; registered Dec. 2005; seeks constitutional, judicial and economic reform in order to combat corruption, stimulate the economy and establish a strong state; advocates creation of parliamentary republic and introduction of parliamen-tary elections by party lists; mem. of political bloc People's Coalition

of Democratic Forces (led by party's leader), formed Jan. 2006 with declared aim of reforming Kyrgyzstan's constitution and introducing parliamentary system of govt; Leader KUBATBEK BAIBOLOV.

The following Islamist groups were banned by the Supreme Court in November 2003: **Hizb-ut-Tahrir al-Islami** (Party of Islamic Lib-eration), the **Islamic Party of Turkestan**, the **East Turkestan Islamic Party** (Sharq Turkestan Islam Partiyasy) and the **East Turkestan Liberation Organization** (Sharq azzat Turkestan).

Diplomatic Representation

EMBASSIES IN KYRGYZSTAN

Azerbaijan: 720040 Bishkek, Shurukova 41; tel. (312) 51-07-70; fax (312) 51-31-72; e-mail bishkek@mission.mfa.az; Ambassador ARIF AGHAYEV.

Belarus: 720040 Bishkek, Moskovskaya 210; tel. (312) 65-13-65; fax (312) 65-11-77; e-mail kyrgyzstan@belembassy.org; Ambassador VALERY A. BRYLYOV.

China, People's Republic: 720001 Bishkek, Toktogula 196; tel. (312) 61-08-58; fax (312) 66-30-14; e-mail chinaemb_kg@mfa.gov.cn; Ambassador ZHANG YANNIAN.

Germany: 720040 Bishkek, Razzakova 28; tel. (312) 90-50-00; fax (312) 66-66-30; e-mail info@bischkek.diplo.de; internet www .bischkek.diplo.de; Ambassador HOLGER GREN.

India: 720044 Bishkek, ul. Aeroportinskaya 15A; tel. (312) 54-92-14; fax (312) 54-32-45; e-mail indembas@infotel.kg; Ambassador JYOTI SWARUP PANDE.

Iran: 720026 Bishkek, Razzakova 36; tel. (312) 62-49-17; fax (312) 22-74-98; e-mail sefabish@amil.elcat.gg; Ambassador MUHAMMAD REZA SABOURI.

Japan: 720033 Bishkek, Frunze 503; tel. (312) 61-18-75; fax (312) 61-18-82; Ambassador TETSUO ITO.

Kazakhstan: 720040 Bishkek, pr. Mira 95 A; tel. (312) 66-21-01; fax (312) 69-20-94; e-mail kaz_emb@kazemb.elcat.kg; Ambassador BAKYT S. OSPANOV.

Pakistan: 720040 Bishkek, Serova Bayalinova 37; tel. (312) 62-17-11; fax (312) 66-15-50; e-mail parepbishkek@elcat.kg; Ambassador ALAM BROHI.

Russia: 720040 Bishkek, Razzakova 17; tel. (312) 62-47-38; fax (312) 62-18-23; e-mail rusemb@saimanet.kg; internet www.kyrgyz.mid .ru; Ambassador VALENTIN S. VLASOV.

Syria: 720000 Bishkek; Ambassador WAHIB FADEL.

Tajikistan: 720031 Bishkek, ul. Kara-Darinskaya 36; tel. (312) 51-23-43; fax (312) 51-14-64; e-mail tojsaforat@oxnot.kg; Ambassador MAKHMUD N. SOBIROV.

Turkey: 720040 Bishkek, Moskovskaya 89; tel. (312) 62-23-54; fax (312) 66-05-19; e-mail biskbe@infotel.kg; Ambassador FATMA SERPIL ALPMAN.

Ukraine: 720040 Bishkek, bulv. Akhunbayeva 201; tel. (312) 49-04-07; fax (312) 49-10-48; e-mail emb_kg@mfa.gov.ua; internet www .mfa.gov.ua/kirgizia; Ambassador VOLODYMYR V. SOLOVEY.

USA: 720016 Bishkek, pr. Mira 171; tel. (312) 55-12-41; fax (312) 55-12-64; internet bishkek.usembassy.gov; Ambassador TATIANA C. GFOELLER.

Uzbekistan: 720040 Bishkek, Tynistanova 213; tel. (312) 66-20-65; fax (312) 66-44-03; e-mail uzbembish@infotel.kg; Ambassador ZIYADULLA S. PULATKHOJAYEV.

Judicial System

Supreme Court: 720000 Bishkek, Orozbekova 37; tel. (312) 66-33-18; fax (312) 66-29-46; e-mail scourt@bishkek.gov.kg; Chair. JANYL ALIYEVA.

Constitutional Court: 720040 Bishkek, pr. Erkindik 39; tel. (312) 62-04-95; fax (312) 66-28-19; e-mail konsud@bishkek.gov.kg; Chair. SVETLANA SYDYKOVA.

Office of the Prosecutor-General: 720040 Bishkek; Prosecutor-General ELMURZA R. SATYBALDIYEV.

Religion

ISLAM

The majority of Kyrgyz are Sunni Muslims (Hanafi school), as are some other groups living in the republic, such as Uzbeks and Tajiks.

Chief Mufti of the Muslims of Kyrgyzstan: Haji MURATALY AJY JUMANOV, 720000 Bishkek.

International Islamic Centre of Kyrgyzstan: 714018 Osh; Pres. Haji SADYKZHAN KAMALUDDIN.

CHRISTIANITY
Roman Catholic Church

The Church is represented in Kyrgyzstan by an Apostolic Administration, established in March 2006. There were an estimated 500 adherents in the country at 31 December 2006.

Apostolic Administrator: Most Rev. NIKOLAUS MESSMER (Titular Bishop of Carmeiano), 720040 Bishkek, Muyukovskogo 25; tel. (312) 28-50-03; fax (312) 67-03-92; e-mail nikmessmer@hotmail.com; internet www.catholic-kyrgyzstan.org.

Russian Orthodox Church (Moscow Patriarchate)

The Russian Orthodox Church (Moscow Patriarchate) in Kyrgyzstan comes under the jurisdiction of the Eparchy of Tashkent and Central Asia, headed by the Metropolitan of Tashkent and Central Asia, VLADIMIR (IKIM), resident in Uzbekistan.

JUDAISM

At the 1989 census, around 6,000 Jews were enumerated as living within the Kyrgyz SSR, mostly in Bishkek. By 1993 around 3,000 Jews had emigrated from Kyrgyzstan, mostly to Israel, and out-migration continued subsequently.

Chief Rabbi: Rabbi ARIYE RAICHMAN, 720000 Bishkek, Sutombayev 193, Khabad Lyubavich Synagogue; tel. and fax (312) 68-19-66; e-mail arier@mail.ru.

The Press

In 2004 there were 83 non-daily newspapers, with an average circulation of 427,800 copies. Two daily newspapers were published in that year, with an average circulation of 21,000 copies.

PRINCIPAL NEWSPAPERS

Asaba (The Standard): 720000 Bishkek; tel. (312) 26-47-39; weekly; in Kyrgyz; supplement in Russian *Asaba-Bishkek*; Editors JUMABEK MEDERALIYEV (*Asaba*), BERMET BUKASHEVA (*Asaba-Bishkek*).

Belyi Parokhod (White Steamship): 720040 Bishkek, Ibraimova 24; tel. (312) 42-24-80; e-mail parohod@list.ru; internet www.parohod.kg; f. 1997; in Russian; independent.

Bishkek Observer: 720021 Bishkek, Frunze 429; tel. (312) 28-95-96; fax (312) 68-22-61; e-mail observer@elcat.kg; f. 2000; weekly; independent; in English; Editor AVTAR SINGH.

Bishkek Taims (Bishkek Times): 720040 Bishkek, Pushkina 70; tel. (312) 62-15-68; e-mail b-times@yandex.ru; internet www.presskg.com/bt; Editor-in-Chief NURALY KAPAROV.

Chui Baayni/Chuiskiye Izvestiya (Chui News): 720300 Bishkek, Ibraimova 24; tel. (312) 42-83-31; weekly; organ of Chui Oblast administration; Kyrgyz and Russian edns; Editor (Kyrgyz edn) KURMANBEK RAMATOV; Editor (Russian edn) A. BLINDINA.

Delo Nº... (Case Number...): 720000 Bishkek; tel. (312) 62-19-80; fax (312) 66-38-66; e-mail cactus@elcat.kg; internet delo.to.kg; f. 1991; weekly; in Russian; independent; politics, crime; Editor VIKTOR ZAPOLSKII; circ. 30,000.

Erkin Too (Free Mountain): 720040 Bishkek, Ibraimova 24; tel. (312) 42-03-15; fax (312) 42-22-42; f. 1991; 2 a week; organ of the Government; publishes laws, presidential, parliamentary and govt decrees, and other legal documents; Kyrgyz; Editor-in-Chief NURLAN SHAKIYEV; circ. 10,000.

Gazeta.kg: 720000 Bishkek; internet gazeta.kg; online only; in Russian and English; independent; politics and analysis of current affairs; culture; regional news; f. 2003.

Kyrgyz Madaniyaty (Kyrgyz Culture): 720301 Bishkek, Bokonbayeva 99; tel. (312) 26-14-58; f. 1967; weekly; organ of the Union of Writers; Editor NURALY KAPAROV; circ. 15,940.

Kyrgyz Rukhu: 720040 Bishkek, Abdymomunova 193; tel. and fax (312) 66-45-43; f. 1991; weekly; Kyrgyz; Editor-in-Chief BAKBYRBEK ALENOV; circ. c. 5,000.

Kyrgyz Tuusu (Flag of Kyrgyzstan): 720040 Bishkek, Abdymomunova 193; tel. (312) 62-20-18; fax (312) 62-20-25; e-mail tuusu@infotel.kg; internet www.tuusu.kg; f. 1924; fmrly *Sovettik Kyrgyzstan*; daily; organ of the Government; Kyrgyz; Editor-in-Chief ZHEDIGER I. SAALAYEV; circ. 17,000–20,000.

Limon (Lemon): 720040 Bishkek, Moskovskaya 189; tel. (312) 65-03-03; fax (312) 65-02-04; e-mail limon@akipress.org; internet www.limon.kg; f. 1994; in Russian; youth newspaper; independent; Editor-in-Chief VENERA JAMONA KULOVA.

MSN—Moya Stolitsa—Novosti (My Capital City—News): 720001 Bishkek, Turusbekova 47; tel. (312) 21-29-79; fax (312) 21-58-94; e-mail city@infotel.kg; internet www.msn.kg; f. 2001; independent; 3 a week; in Russian; Editor-in-Chief ALEXANDER KIM; circ. 5,000 (Tues. and Thurs.), 50,000 (Fri.).

Slovo Kyrgyzstana (Word of Kyrgyzstan): 720004 Bishkek, Abdymomunova 193; tel. (312) 66-60-88; fax (312) 66-59-28; e-mail slovo@infotel.kg; internet www.sk.kg; f. 1925; daily; organ of the Government; in Russian; Editor ALEKSANDR I. MALEVANY.

The Times of Central Asia: 720000 Bishkek, Abdrahmanova 175A/303–304; tel. (312) 66-17-37; fax (312) 66-42-95; e-mail edittimes@infotel.kg; internet www.timesca-europe.com; f. 1995; weekly; in English; also distributed in Kazakhstan, Turkmenistan and Uzbekistan, and internationally; Editor-in-Chief LYDIA SAVINA.

Vechernii Bishkek (Bishkek Evening News): 720021 Bishkek, Usenbayeva 2; tel. (312) 68-21-21; fax (312) 68-02-68; e-mail webmaster@vb.kg; internet www.vb.kg; f. 1974; daily; independent; in Russian; Editor-in-Chief GENNADII A. KUZMIN; circ. (Mon.–Thur.) 20,000, (Fri.) 50,000.

Zaman Kyrgyzstan (Herald of Kyrgyzstan): 720040 Bishkek, Ibraimova 24; tel. (312) 42-62-35; e-mail zamantur@elcat.kg; f. 1992; weekly; independent; in Kyrgyz, Turkish and English; Editor-in-Chief A. KUSH; circ. 15,000.

PRINCIPAL PERIODICALS

Monthly, unless otherwise indicated.

Aalam (Universe): 720000 Bishkek, Baitik Baatyra 73; tel. (312) 54-42-07; fax (312) 54-42-09; e-mail aalamga@hotmail.kg; f. 1991; independent; Kyrgyz; weekly; Editor-in-Chief ELNURA SHABDANBEKOVA; circ. 18,000.

Agym (Current): 720040 Bishkek, pr. Manasa 40; tel. (312) 66-56-70; fax (312) 66-55-48; e-mail agym@users.kyrnet.kg; internet presskg.com/agym; f. 1992; 2 a week; in Kyrgyz; political; Editor-in-Chief MELIS ESHIMKANOV.

AKIpress: 720010 Bishkek, Moskovskaya 189; tel. and fax (312) 61-18-23; fax (312) 65-02-02; e-mail admin@akipress.org; internet www.akipress.org; f. 1993; in Russian; independent; analysis of political and economic affairs; Editor-in-Chief SAMAGAN AITYMBETOV; circ. 1,000.

Kut Bilim (Good Knowledge): 720001 Bishkek, Tynystanova 257; tel. (312) 62-04-86; e-mail kutbilim@elcat.kg; internet kb.host.net.kg; f. 1953 as *Mugalimder Gazetasy*; current name adopted 1993; organ of the Ministry of Education and Science; weekly; in Kyrgyz; Editor-in-Chief KUBATBEK CHEKIROV; circ. 6,000.

Literaturnyi Kyrgyzstan (Literary Kyrgyzstan): 720301 Bishkek, Pushkina 70; tel. (312) 626-16-01; e-mail literary_kyrgyzstan@rambler.ru; internet www.lk.to.kg; f. 1955; journal of the Union of Writers; fiction, literary criticism, journalism; in Russian; Editor-in-Chief A. I. IVANOV; circ. 3,000.

Zdravookhraneniye Kyrgyzstana (Healthcare of Kyrgyzstan): 720005 Bishkek, Moskovskaya 148; tel. (312) 62-26-80; fax (312) 66-07-17; e-mail mz@med.kg; f. 1938; 4 a year; publ. by the Ministry of Health; health research; in Russian; Editor-in-Chief T. ABDRAIMOV; circ. 3,000 (2007).

NEWS AGENCY

Kabar Kyrgyz News Agency: 720011 Bishkek, Sovetskaya 175; tel. (312) 62-05-74; fax (312) 66-11-68; e-mail s1@kabar.gov.kg; internet www.kabar.kg; Dir OLEG RYABOV.

Publishers

Ilim (Science): 720071 Bishkek, pr. Chui 265A; tel. (312) 65-56-88; e-mail ilimph@mail.ru; f. 1954; state-owned; scientific and science fiction; Dir L. V. TARASOVA.

Kyrgyz-Russian Slavic University Publishing House (Izdatelstvo Kyrgyzsko-Rossiiskogo slavyanskogo universiteta): 720000 Bishkek, Kiyevskaya 44; tel. (312) 25-53-60; internet www.krsu.edu.kg/Rus/EduIzd.htm; f. 1995; academic works of university staff; textbooks; Dir LARISA V. TARASOVA.

Kyrgyzstan: 720000 Bishkek, Abdrakhmanova 170; tel. (312) 62-19-47; politics, science, economics, literature; Dir BERIK N. CHALAGYZOV.

Tsentr Gosudarstvennogo Yazyka i Kyrgyzskoi Entsiklopedii (Centre for the State Language and the Kyrgyz Encyclopedia): 720040 Bishkek, bul. Erkindik 56; tel. (312) 62-50-72; fax (312) 62-50-03; e-mail gocst.ensk@mail.ru; dictionaries and encyclopedias; Dir BAKTYGUL KALDYBAYEVA; Editor-in-Chief USEN A. ASANOV.

Broadcasting and Communications

National Communications Agency of the Kyrgyz Republic: 720005 Bishkek, Baytik Baatyra 7B; tel. (312) 54-41-03; fax (312) 54-41-05; internet www.nas.kg; f. 1997; Dir KUBAT S. KYDYRALIYEV.

TELECOMMUNICATIONS

BiMoKom: tel. (555) 50-00-00; fax (312) 90-52-40; internet www.megacom.kg; f. 2006; provides mobile cellular telecommunications services in Bishkek, Manas Airport, the shores of Lake Issyk-Kul and in Chui, Issyk-Kul, Osh, Dzalal-Abad, Naryn, Talas and Batken Oblasts under the Megacom brand name; Dir ANDREI G. SILICH; c. 600,000 subscribers (Jan. 2008).

Kyrgyztelekom: 720000 Bishkek, pr. Chui 96; tel. (312) 68-16-16; fax (312) 66-24-24; e-mail info@kt.kg; internet www.kt.kg; f. 1993, transformed into joint stock co in 1997; state telecommunications co; 77.84% state-owned; 51% scheduled for privatization; Chair. of the Bd of Dirs SALAIDIN A. AVAZOV; Mems of the Bd of Dirs MYKTARBEK JUMABAYEV, BURKAN JUMABAYEV, DUISHENBEK R. ABDYLDAYEV, MYR-BEK T. BATAKANOV.

Sky Mobile: 720011 Bishkek, pr. Chui 121; tel. (312) 58-79-15; fax (312) 90-09-16; e-mail office@bitel.kg; internet www.bitel.kg; f. 1997; provides mobile cellular telecommunications services under the Bitel and Mobi brand names; Dir-Gen. D. V. SHERSHNEV; over 1m. subscribers (Jan. 2008).

BROADCASTING

Radio and Television

State National Television and Radio Broadcasting Corpn: 720010 Bishkek, Molodoi Gvardii 59; tel. (312) 65-56-77; internet www.ktr.kg; Pres. MELIS ESHIMKANOV.

Kyrgyz Public Educational Radio and Television (Kyrgyzs-koye Obshchestvennoye Obrazovatelnoye Radio i Televideniye—KOORT): 720031 Bishkek, Ibraimova 24; tel. (312) 54-77-27; fax (312) 54-77-15; e-mail office@koort.kg; f. 1997; broadcasts in Kyrgyz and Russian; educational programmes and entertainment; Gen. Dir AZIMA ABDIMAMINOVA; 103 employees.

Radio

Radio Azattyk: 720000 Bishkek; tel. (312) 66-88-17; fax (312) 66-68-14; internet www.azattyk.org; Kyrgyz language news broadcasts by Radio Free Europe/Radio Liberty (USA—based in the Czech Republic); Dir TYNTCHTYKBEK TCHOROEV; Bureau Chief KUBAT OTORBAEV.

Kyrgyz Radio: 720010 Bishkek, Molodoi Gvardii 59; tel. (312) 65-79-36; fax (312) 65-10-64; internet www.ktr.kg; f. 1931; broadcasts in Kyrgyz, Russian, English, German, Ukrainian, Uzbek, Dungan and Uigur; subsidiary of State National Television and Radio Broad-casting Corpn; Dir BAIMA SUTENOVA.

Radio Television Pyramid: 720300 Bishkek, Jantosheva 70; tel. and fax (312) 51-00-15; e-mail pyramid@tom.kg; f. 1992; privately owned; broadcasts to Bishkek and neighbouring regions; Pres. MIRBEK OROZOV.

There are several other private radio stations operating in Kyrgyz-stan.

Television

Kyrgyz Television: 720300 Bishkek, Molodoi Gvardii 63; tel. (312) 25-79-36; fax (312) 25-79-30; internet www.ktr.kg; subsidiary of State National Television and Radio Broadcasting Corpn; Pres. KYYAS MOLDOKASYMOV.

TV Pyramid: 720005 Bishkek; tel. and fax (312) 41-01-31; e-mail pyramid@ss5-22.kyrnet.kg; f. 1991; privately owned; broadcasts to Bishkek and neighbouring regions; Pres. ADYLBEK T. BIINAZAROV.

Finance

(cap. = capital; res = reserves; m. = million; brs = branches; amounts in soms, unless otherwise indicated)

BANKING

Central Bank

National Bank of the Kyrgyz Republic (Kyrgyz Respublikasy-nyn Uluttuk Banky): 720040 Bishkek, Umetaliyeva 101; tel. (312) 66-90-08; fax (312) 61-04-56; e-mail mail@nbkr.kg; internet www.nbkr.kg; f. 1991, name changed in 1992, and as above in 1993; cap. 50.0m., res 1,069.1m., dep. 14,540.7m. (Dec. 2006); Chair. MARAT O. ALAPAYEV.

Other Banks

Amanbank: 720400 Bishkek, Tynystanova 249; tel. and fax (312) 62-20-77; fax (312) 90-04-97; e-mail bank@amanbank.kg; internet www.amanbank.kg; f. 1995; cap. 65m., res 8.6m., dep. 116.0m. (Aug. 2006); Chair. JOHN I. JAPARKULOV; 6 brs.

AsiaUniversalBank: 720001 Bishkek, Toktogula 187; tel. (312) 62-02-52; fax (312) 62-02-50; e-mail reception@aub.kg; internet www.aub.kg; f. 1997; present name adopted 2000; cap. 300.0m., res 296.4m., dep. 4,772.6m. (Dec. 2006); Chair. MIKHAIL NADEL; Chief Exec. NURDIN ABDRAZAKOV; 2 brs.

ATFBank-Kyrgyzstan: 720070 Bishkek, Jibek Jolu 493; tel. and fax (312) 67-04-71; e-mail bank@atfbank.kg; internet www.atfbank.kg; f. 1992; fmrly Energobank, present name adopted 2006; cap. 500.0m., res 1.5m., dep. 1,876.0m. (Dec. 2006); Pres. BAKIRDIN E. SARTKAZIYEV; 7 brs.

Bank Bakai: 720001 Bishkek, Isanov 77; tel. (312) 66-06-10; fax (312) 66-06-12; e-mail bank@bakai.kg; internet www.bakai.kg; f. 1998; cap. 100.0m., dep. 544.2m. (Aug. 2007); Chair. BAKYTA MUNDUZBAYEVA; Pres. MUHAMMAD IBRAGIMOV; 5 brs.

Demir Kyrgyz International Bank (DKIB): 720001 Bishkek, pr. Chui 245; tel. (312) 61-06-10; fax (312) 66-64-44; e-mail dkib@demirbank.kg; internet www.demirbank.kg; f. 1997; cap. 132.5m., res 0.0, dep. 124.3m. (Dec. 2006); Chair. ISMAIL HASAN AKCAKAYA-LIOGLU; Gen. Man. AHMET KAMIL PARMAKSIZ; 3 brs.

Ecobank: 720031 Bishkek, Geologicheskii per. 17; tel. (312) 54-35-82; fax (312) 54-35-80; e-mail office@ecobank.kg; internet www.ecobank.kg; f. 1996 as Bank Rossiiskii Kredit; name changed 1998; joint-stock commercial bank; cap. 78.0m., dep. 181.5m. (Oct. 2003); Chair. NURLANBEK A. SAGYNDYKOV; Deputy Chair. GALINA V. HOHLOVA, LARISA G. CHENGIZ; 5 brs.

Investment Export-Import Bank—Ineximbank: 720001 Bish-kek, Kalyk Akiyeva 57; tel. (312) 65-06-10; fax (312) 62-06-54; e-mail info@ineximbank.com; internet www.ineximbank.com; f. 1996; pres-ent name adopted 2001; cap. 480.0m., res 3.4m., dep. 2,894.2m. (Dec. 2006); Chair.of Bd MURAT KUNAKUNOV; 4 brs.

Kyrgyz Investment and Credit Bank: 720001 Bishkek, Ibrai-mova 115A, Dordoi Plaza Business Centre; tel. (312) 69-05-55; fax (312) 69-05-60; e-mail kicb@kicb.net; internet www.kicb.net; f. 2001; 21% owned by Aga Khan Fund for Economic Development, 18% by Habib Bank (Pakistan), 17% by Deutsche Investitions und Entwick-lungsgesellschaft GmbH (Germany), 17% by European Bank for Reconstruction and Development (United Kingdom), 17% by International Finance Corpn; cap. US $10m., res $8.1m., dep. $36.6m. (Aug. 2008); Chief Exec. KUANG YOUNG CHOI; 8 brs.

Kyrgyzstan Bank: 720001 Bishkek, Togolok Moldo 54A; tel. (312) 21-95-98; fax (312) 61-02-20; e-mail akb@bankkg.kg; internet www.bankkg.kg; f. 1001; cap. 100.9m., res 5.1m., dep. 1,582.0m. (Dec. 2006); Chair. ABIROV NURBEK; 29 brs.

Tolubay Bank: 720040 Bishkek, Umetaliyeva 105; tel. (312) 65-88-88; fax (312) 25-63-14; e-mail tolubay@infotel.kg; internet www.tolubaybank.kg; f. 1996; cap. 63.0m., res 12.5m., dep. 293.1m. (Dec. 2006); Chair. JENISHBEK S. BAIGUTTIYEV; 1 br.

COMMODITY EXCHANGE

Kyrgyzstan Commodity and Raw Materials Exchange: 720001 Bishkek, Belinskaya 40; tel. (312) 22-13-75; fax (312) 22-27-44; f. 1990; Gen. Dir TEMIR SARIYEV.

STOCK EXCHANGE

Kyrgyz Stock Exchange (Kyrgyz Fonduk Birzhasy/Kyrgyzskaya Fondovaya Birzha): 720010 Bishkek, Moskovskaya 172; tel. (312) 66-50-59; fax (312) 66-15-95; e-mail kse@kse.kg; internet www.kse.kg; Pres. ANDREI V. ZALEPO.

INSURANCE

At 1 July 2005 there were 12 private insurance companies operating in Kyrgyzstan, including two that were partly Russian-owned and three that were entirely British-owned. In late 2007 there were 15 insurance companies operating in the country.

Anglo-Kyrgyz Insurance Co: 720000 Bishkek, ul. Akhunbaeva 100; tel. (312) 54-90-23; fax (312) 54-90-49; e-mail anglokgz@elcat.kg.

ATN Polis: 720000 Bishkek, ul. Isanova 42/1; tel. (312) 93-79-37; fax (312) 90-32-52; e-mail info@atnpolis.kg; internet www.atnpolis.kg; f. 2001; life and non-life.

Insurance Group of Central Asia: 720000 Bishkek, Baitik Baa-tyra 191, Hyatt Hotel, room 103; tel. (312) 68-12-21.

Kyrgyzinstrakh: 720001 Bishkek, pr. Chui 219; tel. (312) 61-45-88; fax (312) 61-46-45; e-mail kinstrakh@infotel.kg; internet kyrgyzinstrakh.com.kg; f. 1996 by the Russian joint-stock insurance company Investstrakh and the Kyrgyz Government to insure foreign investors; brs in Karakol and Osh; insurance and reinsurance; Chair. of Bd E. M. SEIDAKHMETOVA.

Kyrgyzstan Insurance Co: 720000 Bishkek, ul. Moskovskaya 76B; tel. (312) 28-28-15; e-mail office@insurance.kg; internet www .insurance.kg; f. 1991; Dir MARIYA ADENOVA.

Trade and Industry

GOVERNMENT AGENCIES

National Institute of Standards and Metrology: 720040 Bishkek, Panfilova 197; tel. (312) 62-68-70; fax (312) 66-13-67; e-mail nism@nism.gov.kg; internet www.nism.gov.kg; f. 1927 as the Division of the Chamber of Measures and Weights; present name adopted 2005; certification, control and testing of products and services; standardization, metrology, accreditation; Dir PATIDIN ATAKHANOV.

State Agency for Geology and Mineral Resources: 720739 Bishkek, pr. Erkindik 2; tel. (312) 66-49-01; fax (312) 66-03-91; e-mail mail@geoagency.bishkek.gov.kg; internet www.kgs.bishkek .gov.kg; Chair. SHEISHENALY MURZAGAZIYEV.

State Committee for Management of State Property: 720017 Bishkek, Moskovskaya 151; tel. (312) 62-68-52; fax (312) 66-02-36; e-mail mail@spf.bishkek.gov.kg; internet www.spf.gov.kg; f. 1991; responsible for the privatization of state-owned enterprises and deals with bankruptcies; Chair. TURSUN O. TURDUMAMBETOV.

CHAMBER OF COMMERCE

Chamber of Commerce and Industry of the Kyrgyz Republic: 720001 Bishkek, Kiyevskaya 107; tel. (312) 21-05-65; fax (312) 21-05-75; e-mail cci-kr@totel.kg; internet www.ihk-kg.de; f. 1959; supports foreign economic relations and the development of small and medium-sized enterprises; Pres. BORIS V. PERFILIYEV.

TRADE ASSOCIATION

Kyrgyzvneshtorg: 720033 Bishkek, Abdymomunova 276; tel. (312) 21-39-78; fax (312) 66-08-36; e-mail kvt@infotel.kg; f. 1992; export-import org.; Gen. Dir KADYRBEK K. KALIYEV.

UTILITIES

Electricity

NES Kyrgyzstana (National Electric Grid of Kyrgyzstan) (NESK): 720070 Bishkek, pr. Jibek Zholu 326; tel. (312) 66-10-00; fax (312) 66-06-56; e-mail nesk@elcat.kg; internet www.energo.kz; f. 2001; comprises seven companies, including four regional distribution companies, Severeletro, Oshelektro, Zhalabadelektro, Vostoelektro; one heating company, Bishkekteploset; 80.5% state-owned, 13.2% by the Social Fund of the Kyrgyz Republic; reorganization and privatization pending in 2008; cap. 1,597.4m. som (June 2006); Gen. Dir AVTANDIL CH. SYDYKOV.

Gas

Kyrgyzgaz: 720661 Bishkek, Gorykogo 22; tel. (312) 53-45-10; fax (312) 53-00-33; e-mail admin@kg.elcat.kg; internet www.kyrgyzgaz .kg; state gas distributor; Chair. KENESHBAY T. MOLDOBAYEV; Dir-Gen. SALAMAT K. AYTIKEEV.

MAJOR COMPANIES

Electrical Goods

Issyk-Kul Electrical Engineering Plant: 722452 Issyk-Kul Oblast, Tonskii raion, pos. Kajysai; f. 1963; produces semiconductors and low voltage equipment; Gen. Dir DUSHENBAYEV DUSHENBAYEVICH ISHENTUR; 2,000 employees.

Dastan: 720005 Bishkek, Baitik Batyr 36; tel. (312) 54-45-97; fax (312) 54-45-96; e-mail tnkdastan@elcat.kg; internet www.tnkdastan .com; f. 1956; jt-stock co, transnational corpn; manufactures industrial electronic equipment, medical equipment and consumer goods; Pres. KANYBEK TABALDYEV; 1,500 employees.

Metals

Aidarkan Mercury Plant: 715213 Batken Oblast, Kadamzhaiskii raion, Aidarkan, ul. Kyrgyzstana 19A.

Kumtor Operating Co: 720300 Bishkek, Ibraimov 24; tel. (312) 42-22-82; fax (312) 54-08-50; f. 1992; development of Kumtor gold deposit, one of the largest in the world; wholly owned by Kumtor Gold Co., a subsidiary of Centerra Gold Inc. (Canada); Pres. ANDREW LOUIS; 1,500 employees.

Kyrgyzaltyn: 720040 Bishkek, Abdumamunov 195; tel. (312) 66-66-70; fax (312) 66-67-00; internet www.kyrgyzaltyn.kg; f. 1992; jt-stock co; mining and processing of rare and precious metals, incl. gold and antimony; Pres. KAMCHYBEK S. KUDAIBERGENOV.

Kadamjai Antimony Plant: 715211 Osh Oblast, Kadamjai, Zavodskaya 12; tel. (365) 53-60-36; fax (365) 53-61-12; e-mail kaf@infotel.kg; f. 1936; produces antimony concentrate; Gen. Dir YURIY K. DOSTOVALOV; 2,000 employees.

Kara-Balta Mining Processing Plant: 722130 Chui Oblast, Kara-Balta, Truda 1A; tel. (313) 37-21-89; fax (313) 62-06-84; f. 1952; ore refining, production of gold ingots, rolled aluminium, silver, uranium oxide; Pres. N. J. KOJOMATOV; 1,500 employees.

Textiles

Avgul: 720343 Bishkek, pr. Chui 147; tel. (312) 28-18-64; fax (312) 28-18-76; jt-stock co; manufacturers of woollen and semi-woollen clothing; Pres. SATAROV; 140 employees.

BAKAI: 722030 Chui Oblast, Kara-Balta, Otorbayeva 1; tel. (233) 2-13-46; fax (233) 2-37-72; produces sugar, spirits; Dir MUHAMED IBRAGIMOV.

Enterprise Developments International: 720033 Bishkek, Jibek Jolu 382A; tel. (312) 61-00-66; fax (312) 61-02-58; e-mail edi@elcat.kg; corporate development, licensing of new plastics technologies, engineering, hydropower and construction-sector investments management; CEO SEAN DALEY; 45 employees.

Ilbirs: 720393 Bishkek, Kiyevskaya 77; tel. (312) 21-26-35; fax (312) 22-07-91; f. 1992; jt-stock co; manufactures of cotton and woollen clothing; Gen. Dir D. A. TENTIYEV.

Jibek: 714003 Osh, Gagarina 108; tel. (322) 22-15-69; fax (322) 22-84-163; jt-stock co; produces silk fabric; Dir SHEPELEV BALERY EVGENEVICH.

Kasiet: 722213 Chui Oblast, Tokmak, Frunze 1; tel. (314) 61-00-66; fax (314) 61-02-58; e-mail office@kasiet.com; f. 1977; produces semi-woollen and pure wool yarn; CEO SEAN DALY; Gen. Dir JAINAK KASYMBEKOV.

Kyrgyz Worsted Woollens Factory: 720022 Bishkek, pr. Chui 4; tel. (312) 28-15-74; fax (312) 53-10-21; e-mail kamvol@elcat.kg; f. 1963; privately owned jt-stock co; produces and sells blankets and worsted, woollen and semi-woollen fabrics for garments; sales of US $1.37m. (2000); Pres. BULAT A. AKKAZIEV; 1,300 employees.

Textilshic: 714024 Osh, Kasymbekova 8A; tel. (3322) 23-03-34; fax (3322) 52-67-46; jt-stock co; produces fabric; Dir SATIBALDIYEV KAKHROMON.

Miscellaneous

Ak-Maral Trading: 720300 Bishkek, ul. Shabdan Batyra 6; tel. (312) 43-29-97; fax (312) 53-00-20; e-mail ak_maral@infotel.kg; f. 1993; produces cable and satellite television sets, home appliances, telecommunications apparatus, fluorescent lamps, textiles; lathe operator; owns hotel complex on lake Issyk-Kul; Chair. MARAT D. SHARSHEKEYEV; 450 employees.

Bishkek Agricultural Machinery Plant: 720008 Bishkek, Intergelpo 1; tel. (312) 25-31-50; fax (312) 24-48-10; manufactures agricultural machinery and equipment; Man. Dir MIKHAIL I. BARISHKURA.

Eridan Group: 720000 Bishkek, Orozbekov 133; tel. (312) 27-25-58; fax (312) 27-08-65; e-mail eridan1@elcat.kg; f. 1993; agriculture, banking, construction, freight forwarding, furniture, medical supplies and equipment, packaging, security, wood-processing; Pres. ELDIYAR T. USSENOV; 1,100 employees.

Kant Cement and Slate Combine: 722140 Chui Oblast, Kant, Promzona; tel. (232) 2-22-80; fax (232) 24-57-50; produces cement and slates; Dir ILYA BEZSMERTNYI.

Kyrgyzneftegaz: 715622 Jalal-Abad Oblast, Nookenskii raion, Kochkor-Ata, Lenin 44; tel. (312) 66-74-53; fax (312) 52-60-21; 85.2% state-owned; natural gas and petroleum co; Chair. of Bd KABYLZHAN A. TURGUNBAYEV.

Kyrgyz Petroleum Co: 715600 Jalal-Abad, ul. Promyshlennaya 202; tel. (372) 25-03-10; fax (372) 25-23-15; e-mail kpcadmin@infotel .kg; internet www.kpc.kg; f. 1996; jt venture between Kyrgyzneftegaz (50%) and Petrofac (United Kingdom—50%); petroleum extraction and refineries; Pres. ROBERT J. BROWN.

Kyrgyzavtomash Industrial Group: 720031 Bishkek, Matrosova 1; tel. (312) 43-91-13; jt-stock co; manufactures motor-vehicle parts, machine tools and metal forgings; Gen. Dir VLADIMIR I. CHUMAKOV; 2,750 employees.

Avtomash-Radiator: 720031 Bishkek, Matrosova 1; tel. (312) 43-91-13; fax (312) 53-00-09; e-mail radiator@mail.kg; f. 2001; produces automobile cooling radiators; Gen. Dir BAYAZITOV MARSEL.

Krygyzhaberdashery: 720661 Bishkek, Matrosova 5; tel. (312) 44-45-65; fax (312) 42-89-13; haberdashery products; Pres. ANARALI MATENOVICH SADIKOV.

Kyrgyzkilem—Kara-Balta Carpet Factory: 722030 Chui Oblast, Kara-Balta, P. Tolyatti 1; tel. (313) 32-36-61; fax (313) 32-00-47; f. 1983; produces carpets; 3,200 employees.

Mailuu-Suu Electric Lamp Plant: 715420 Jalal-Abad Oblast, Mailuu-Suu, Lenina 210; tel. (324) 42-11-50; fax (324) 42-12-90; e-mail msel@infotel.kg; internet www.msel.kg; f. 1964; jt-stock co; produces incandescent lamps; Dir NIKOLAI A. MELKER; 3,700 employees.

OKKO: 720015 Bishkek, Khvoinaya 64; tel. (312) 27-08-41; fax (312) 27-29-30; jt-stock co; manufactures leather accessories; Dir NIKOLAI GELNOV.

Tashkumyr Semiline Materials Plant: 715430 Jalal-Abad Oblast, Tashkumyr, Promzona 1; tel. (33542) 28-95-10; fax (33542) 62-04-40; produces semiline materials; Dir JUMAGULOV SAGYNBEK.

TRADE UNIONS

Kyrgyzstan Federation of Trade Unions: 720032 Bishkek, Chui 207; tel. (312) 21-49-30; fax (312) 21-76-87; affiliated with the General Confed. of Trade Unions; Chair. SAGYN BOZGUNBAYEV.

Transport

RAILWAYS

Kyrgyzstan's railway network consists of only one main line (340 km) in northern Kyrgyzstan, which connects the country, via Kazakhstan, with the railway system of Russia. Osh, Jalal-Abad and other towns in regions of Kyrgyzstan bordering Uzbekistan are linked to that country by short lengths of railway track. In 2001 the Governments of Kyrgyzstan and the People's Republic of China signed a memorandum on the construction of a rail link from Kashgar (China) to Bishkek. In 2003 Kyrgyzstan and Kazakhstan announced that a 100-km railway link was to be built between Issyk-Kul and Almaty, Kazakhstan, although by mid-2007 work had yet to commence.

Kyrgyz Railway Administration (Kyrgyz Temir Jolu): 720009 Bishkek, L. Tolstogo 83; tel. (312) 62-48-65; fax (312) 65-06-90; e-mail asoup@imfiko.bishkek.su; internet railway.aknet.kg; f. 1992; Pres. I. S. OMURKULOV.

ROADS

In 1999 Kyrgyzstan's road network totalled an estimated 18,500 km, including 140 km of motorway; in 1996 there were 3,200 km of main roads and 6,380 km of secondary roads. About 91% of roads were paved. Work on the third and final phase of a project to reconstruct the main Bishkek—Osh highway was completed in 2004.

CIVIL AVIATION

There are three international airports at Bishkek (Manas), Osh and Tamchy (in the Issyk-Kul region).

Air Kyrgyzstan (AK): 720040 Bishkek, pr. Manasa 12A; tel. (312) 61-02-47; fax (312) 61-02-35; e-mail company@air.kg; internet www.air.kg; f. 2006 by merger of Altyn Air and Kyrgyzstan Airlines; state-owned; charter passenger services.

Itek Air: Bishkek, pr. Chui 128/10; tel. (312) 66-46-79; e-mail itek@infotel.kg; internet www.itekair.kg; f. 1999; scheduled domestic flights and flights to the People's Republic of China, Iran and Russia.

Tourism

There was little tourism in Kyrgyzstan during the Soviet period. However, the Government hoped that the country's spectacular and largely unspoilt mountain scenery, as well as the great crater lake of Issyk-Kul, might attract foreign tourists and investment. In 2006 there were 765,850 tourist arrivals, compared with 398,078 in 2004. Tourism receipts (including passenger transport) amounted to US $94m. in 2005.

State Committee for Tourism, Sport and Youth Policy: 720033 Bishkek, Togolok Moldo 17; tel. (312) 62-24-99; fax (312) 21-28-45; e-mail gktsm@gks.gov.kg; Chair. TURUSBEK CH. MAMASHEV.

Culture

The Kyrgyz tradition is a nomadic one, and that influence is apparent in modern, urban expressions of Kyrgyz culture. Kyrgyz was not a written language until the period of Russian rule, but there was a rich oral canon, the most notable work being the epic poem *Manas*.

CULTURAL HERITAGE

G. Aitiyev Kyrgyz National Museum of Fine Arts: 720000 Bishkek, ul. Abdrahmanova 196; tel. (312) 66-16-23; fax (312) 62-05-48; e-mail knmii@mail.ru; internet www.knmii.lg.kg; f. 1935; 4,000 modern exhibits; Dir MAIRAM YUSUPOVA.

Archives Dept, attached to the Ministry of Culture and Information: 720040 Bishkek, ul. Toktogula 105; tel. (312) 62-48-89; fax (312) 66-33-68; e-mail gaskr@gks.gov.kg; Dir KALIPA OMURALIEVA.

National Library of the Kyrgyz Republic: 720040 Bishkek, Sovetskaya 208; tel. (312) 66-20-90; fax (312) 66-21-55; e-mail library@nlpub.bishkek.gov.kg; internet www.nlkr.gov.kg; f. 1934; re-named as above 1993; over 6m. vols; Dir ZHYLDYZ K. BAKASHOVA.

State Historical Museum of Kyrgyzstan: 720000 Bishkek, pl. Ala-Too; internet museumkg.narod.ru; f. 1925; fmrly Lenin Museum; 80,000 items; Dir N. M. SEITKAZIYEVA.

SPORTING ORGANIZATIONS

State Agency for Physical Training, Sport, Youth Policy and Protection of Children: 720033 Bishkek, Togolok Moldo 17; tel. (312) 62-24-99; fax (312) 66-15-95; e-mail gktsm@gks.gov.kg; Dir BEKTUR ASANOV.

National Olympic Committee of the Republic of Kyrgyzstan: 720001 Bishkek, pr. Chui 207; tel. (312) 98-63-62; fax (312) 62-23-74; e-mail sergeshov@yahoo.com; f. 1991; Pres. MURAT SARALINOV; Gen. Sec. KANAT M. AMANKULOV.

PERFORMING ARTS

Kyrgyz Academic Drama Theatre: 720000 Bishkek, ul. Abdumomunova 222; tel. (312) 21-69-12; f. 1927; Dir ALMAZ CH. SARYLYKBEKOV.

A. Maldybayev Kyrgyz National Academic Opera and Ballet Theatre: 720040 Bishkek, ul. Abdrakhmanova 167; tel. (312) 66-18-41; e-mail operaballetkg@rambler.ru; internet www.operaballet.lg.kg; Dir-Gen. TIMUR S. SALAMATOV.

Russian State Academic Drama Theatre: 720000 Bishkek, Dubovyi park, ul. Tynystanova 122; tel. (312) 62-15-71; f. 1935; Dir ANDREI PETUKHOV.

T. Satylganov Kyrgyz National Philharmonia: 720000 Bishkek, pr. Chui 253; tel. (312) 21-22-62.

A. Umuraliyev Bishkek City Drama Theatre: 720000 Bishkek, ul. Ogonbayeva 242; tel. (312) 66-54-24; internet www.bcdt.in.kg; f. 1993.

Education

Education is compulsory for nine years, comprising four years of primary education (between the ages of seven and 10), followed by five years of lower secondary school (ages 11 to 15). Pupils may then attend upper secondary schools (for two years), specialized secondary schools (two to four years) or technical and vocational schools (from 15 years of age). In 2005/06 total enrolment at primary schools included 85.9% of children in the relevant age group; enrolment at secondary schools included 80.5% of the school-age population. In 1993/94 some 63.6% of primary and secondary schools used Kyrgyz as the sole language of instruction, 23.4% Russian, 12.7% Uzbek and 0.3% Tajik. Russian, however, was the principal language of instruction in higher educational establishments. A decree signed in December 2001 abolished free schooling. In April 2001, as part of a policy to combat Islamist extremism, the Government banned religious education in state schools and decreed that specialist religious schools would require a licence. In 2004/05 there were 49 institutes of higher education in Kyrgyzstan, providing courses lasting between four and six years, and attended by 218,273 students. Government budgetary expenditure on education in 2007 was 9,178.0m. soms (representing 25.6% of total spending).

UNIVERSITIES

Bishkek Humanities University: 720044 Bishkek, pr. Tynchtyk 27; tel. and fax (312) 48-40-35; e-mail rectorat@bgupub.freenet.bishkek.su; internet bhu.freenet.kg; f. 1979; seven faculties; Rector Prof. ISHENGUL S. BOLJUROVA.

International University of Kyrgyzstan: 720001 Bishkek, pr. Chui 255; tel. (312) 21-83-35; fax (312) 21-96-15; e-mail webmaster@iuk.kg; internet www.iuk.kg; f. 1993; comprises Higher Schools of Economy and Business, of Diplomacy and International Law, of New Informational Technologies, of State and Public Administration, of Ecology and Biotechnology, of Public Health, Institutes of Foreign Languages, of Management, of Business and Tourism, of International Business, of Multimedia Training Means, the International Higher School of Medicine and the Kyrgyz-American, Kyrgyz-Indian and Kyrgyz-Russian Institutes of Distance Education; Pres. ASILBEK A. AYDARALIYEV.

Jalal-Abad University: 715600 Jalal-Abad, Lenina 57; tel. (3372) 73-22-06; fax (3372) 23-39-72; internet www.freenet.kg/jalal_abad/

jala_e.html; f. 1993; 5 faculties; 4,300 students; Pres. TURSUNBEK BEKBOLOTOV; Vice-Pres. NURMAT JAILOBAYEV.

Kyrgyz-Russian Slavic University: 720000 Bishkek, Kiyevskaya 44; tel. (312) 22-06-95; fax (312) 28-27-76; e-mail krsu@krsu.edu.kg; internet www.krsu.edu.kg; f. 1993; 6 faculties; Rector VLADIMIR NIFADIYEV.

Kyrgyz State National University: 720024 Bishkek, Frunze 537; tel. (312) 26-26-34; internet www.ksnu.it.kg; f. 1951; renamed as above in 1993; 12 faculties; 600 teachers; 22,000 students; Rector ASKAR CH. KAKEYEV.

Kyrgyz Technical University: 720044 Bishkek, pr. Mira 66; tel. (312) 54-51-25; fax (312) 54-51-62; e-mail root@ktu.bishkek.su; internet ktu.freenet.kg; f. 1954; renamed as above in 1992; 8 faculties; 2 research institutes; 530 teachers; 8,730 students; Pres. UTAN BRIMKULOV.

Kyrgyz-Turkish Manas University: 720042 Bishkek, Manasa 56; tel. (312) 54-19-41; fax (312) 54-19-35; e-mail webmaster@manas.kg; internet www.manas.kg; f. 1995; Rectors Prof. Dr UGUR ORAL, Prof. Dr SULEYMAN KAYIPOV.

Osh State University: 714000 Osh, Lenina 331; tel. (3222) 2-22-73; fax (3222) 5-75-58; e-mail idosu@rambler.ru; internet www.oshsu.kg; f. 1992; 18 faculties; 26,000 students; Rector MUKHTAR O. OROZBEKOV.

Social Welfare

Even before the dissolution of the USSR, reforms aimed to make the social security system self-financing, rather than being dependent upon transfers from the all-Union budget. In 1990 a Pension Fund and an Employment Fund were established in Kyrgyzstan, and they began operations in 1991. A social security (payroll) tax was paid directly into the Pension Fund (in 1991 the tax was 37% of the wage bill of enterprises and 26% for collectives and state farms, as well as a 1% tax on salaries and grants from the central Government). The Employment Fund was intended to provide for those affected by the expected increase in unemployment, and was also responsible for retraining, public works projects and job centres. Most of its revenue came from a 1% levy on enterprise wage bills. In 1994 the Pension Fund, the Employment Fund and the country's third extrabudgetary fund, the Social Insurance Fund, were consolidated into one Social Fund, as was a Medical Insurance Fund, established in 1997. In early 1998 778,010 people were in receipt of benefits from the Social Fund. A comprehensive reform of the pensions system was undertaken in 1998–2000, and the retirement age was to increase by three years by 2007, from 60 years for men and 55 years for women. At October 2002 the average monthly pension amounted to some 559 soms.

According to official figures, in 2003 40.8% of the population lived in conditions of poverty, with 9.4% living in extreme poverty, without access to adequate nutrition. In July 2005 the average monthly wage amounted to 2,573.2 soms. In 2006 there were 2.4 physicians and 5.1 hospital beds per 1,000 people. According to official figures, there were 988 non-state and 205 private medical establishments in 2001. Of total current budgetary expenditure in 2007, 4,028.8m. soms (11.2%) was for health, and 3,816.9m. soms (10.6%) for social insurance and security.

NATIONAL AGENCIES

Ministry of Health: see The Government (Ministries).

Ministry of Labour and Social Welfare: see The Government (Ministries).

Social Fund: 720300 Bishkek, pr. Chui 106; tel. (3312) 26-48-00; fax (3312) 26-55-37; f. 1994 by merger of the Pension Fund, Employment Fund and Social Insurance Fund; responsible for social protection, training and retraining of the unemployed, all social benefits; Chair. A. KYPCHAKBAYEVA.

HEALTH AND WELFARE ORGANIZATIONS

Mercy and Health Fund of Kyrgyzstan: 720040 Bishkek, pr. Erkindik 10; tel. (312) 26-26-70; fax (312) 26-26-55; provides medical assistance to those in need.

Red Crescent Society of Kyrgyzstan: 720040 Bishkek, pr. Erkindik 10; tel. (312) 62-48-57; fax (312) 66-21-81; e-mail redcross@elcat.kg; f. 1926; provides medical and social assistance to the elderly, assistance in emergencies and to refugees, youth activities; Chair. RAISA B. IBRAIMOVA.

The Environment

As a result of its low level of industrialization and its distance from the ecological problems of the Aral Sea, Kyrgyzstan was less affected than some of its neighbouring countries by environmental problems.

Nevertheless, the climate of the entire Central Asian region was affected by the climatic changes engendered by the desiccation of the Aral Sea. In January 1994, together with the other Central Asian states, Kyrgyzstan agreed to contribute to an international Aral Sea fund and that there should be a limit on the amount of water taken from the upper reaches of the Syr-Dar'ya (which has its sources in Kyrgyzstan) and the Amu-Dar'ya rivers. The issue of water resources prompted a number of agreements between Kyrgyzstan and its neighbours. Local environmentalists were mainly concerned with the protection of the country's extensive mountain environment and the large lake of Issyk-Kul; it was also hoped that both would attract tourist visitors. At the end of the 1990s there was concern that waste materials from Kyrgyzstan's mines, situated in areas susceptible to earthquakes and snow- and mud-slides, could cause environmental damage. The southern town of Mayluu Suu, bordering Uzbekistan, which had 23 radioactive waste sites, caused particular concern.

GOVERNMENT ORGANIZATIONS

Ministry of Emergency Situations: see The Government (Ministries).

State Agency for Geology and Mineral Resources: see Trade and Industry (Government Agencies).

State Agency for Environmental Protection and Forestry: 720001 Bishkek, ul. Toktogula 228, Abdymomunov 276; tel. (312) 61-00-16; fax (312) 61-13-96; e-mail envforest@elcat.kg; f. 2005; Dir ARSTANBEK A. DAVLETKELDIYEV.

State Agency for Hydrometeorology: 720017 Bishkek, Korembekova 1; tel. (312) 21-38-62; fax (312) 21-44-22; e-mail meteo@meteo.ktnet.kg; internet www.meteo.ktnet.kg; f. 1926; Gen. Dir MURATBEK BAKANOV.

ACADEMIC INSTITUTES

National Academy of Sciences of the Kyrgyz Republic: 720071 Bishkek, pr. Chui 265A; tel. (312) 61-00-93; fax (312) 24-36-07; e-mail interdep@aknet.kg; internet academ.aknet.kg; f. 1954; several attached institutes involved in environmental research; collaboration with foreign academies of science, research centres and universities; conferences; publications; Pres. JANYBEK JEENBAYEV.

Institute of Water Problems and Hydropower Engineering: 720033 Bishkek, Frunze 533; tel. (312) 21-45-72; e-mail mamatkanov@sdnp.kyrnet.kg; Dir DUISHEN MAMATKANOV.

Noosphere Organizational Bureau of the Open Scientific Association (OSA): 720000 Bishkek, Panfilova 237, kv. 303; tel. and fax (312) 22-51-76; e-mail sgi@imfiko.bishkek.su; development, organization and implementation of scientific, commercial and intergovernmental ecological development projects; Chair. VIKTOR ALEKSANDROVICH BOBROV.

NON-GOVERNMENTAL ORGANIZATIONS

Asian Ecological Group: 720033 Bishkek, Isanov 131; tel. (312) 61-04-11; e-mail azamat@sdnp.kyrnet.kg; Head AZAMAT HUDAIBERGENOV.

'Aleyne' Movement for Environmental Protection in Kyrgyzstan: 720071 Bishkek, POB 50; tel. (312) 66-26-09; e-mail emil@aleyne.bishkek.su; Chair. EMIL SHUKUROV.

BIOM Youth Ecological Movement: 720001 Bishkek, Abdymomunova 328, Kyrgyz State Scientific University, Faculty of Biology, Rm 105; tel. (312) 25-18-78; e-mail biom@infotel.kg; Head NATALIA KRAVZOVA.

Committee for the Defence of Lake Issyk-Kul: 720023 Bishkek, 10 Micro-rayon 32–31; tel. (312) 22-19-68; f. 1990; Pres. OMOR SULTANOV.

Consortium of Ecological NGOs: 720033 Bishkek, Isanov 131, Rm 403; tel. (312) 21-26-28; e-mail ecocons@cango.net.kg; Co-ordinator CHINARA SYDYKOVA.

Green Party of Kyrgyzstan: 720033 Bishkek, Togolok Moldo 60A/103; tel. (312) 62-81-50; fax (312) 66-38-34; e-mail greens.kg@mail.ru; Leader ERKIN K. BULEKBAYEV.

Independent Ecologists' Association: 720025 Bishkek, POB 702; tel. (312) 29-99-35; Head PAVEL GREBER.

International Science Centre: 720017 Bishkek, pr. Manas 22A; tel. and fax (312) 21-36-48; e-mail isc@freenet.kg; internet www.isc.freenet.kg; f. 1994; Dir AZAMAT TYNYBECOV.

Lop Nor-Kyrgyz Anti-Nuclear Movement: 720000 Bishkek; f. 1994; seeks the total banning of nuclear testing at Lop Nor (People's Republic of China) and other sites; Chair. A. K. KARIMOV.

Public Centre of Ecological Information: 720020 Bishkek, Suerkulova 6 A–11; tel. and fax (312) 42-60-26; e-mail pcei@usa.net; Dir STANISLAV ZOPOV.

Tabiyat (Kyrgyzstan Environmental Movement): 720044 Bishkek, pr. Manas 27; tel. and fax (312) 48-48-35; e-mail rectorat@bgurub .freenet.bishkek.su; f. 1994; Head TEMIRBEK CHODURAYEV.

Defence

Kyrgyzstan reorganized its armed forces in mid-1993, creating a General Staff in August. Military service is compulsory, and lasts for 18 months. As assessed at November 2007, Kyrgyzstan's total armed forces numbered 10,900, comprising an army of 8,500 and an air force of 2,400. There were also an estimated 9,500 paramilitary forces. In early 2008 the US Administration stationed some 1,000 forces at its base at Manas airport, while about 400 Russian troops were deployed at the Kant airbase (established by Russia in October 2003). The defence budget for 2007 allocated 1,460m. soms to defence.

Chief of the General Staff: Maj.-Gen. BORIS A. UGAI.

Bibliography

Abazov, R. *Historical Dictionary of Kyrgyzstan*. Lanham, MD, Scarecrow Press, 2004.

Akayev, A. *Kyrgyzstan: An Economy in Transition*. Canberra, Asia Pacific Press at the Australian National University, 2001.

Anderson, J. *Kyrgyzstan: Central Asia's Island of Democracy?* Reading, Harwood Academic Publishers, 1998.

'The Politics of Civil Society in Kyrgyzstan' in *RIIA Briefing*, No. 18, May 1999.

Azymbakiev, M. 'Kyrgyzstan-European Union: Facets of Cooperation' in *Central Asia and the Caucasus: Journal of Social and Political Studies*, Vol. 27, No. 3, 2004. Luleå, Central Asia and the Caucasus Centre for Social and Political Studies.

Earle, L., et al. *Community Development in Kazakhstan, Kyrgyzstan and Uzbekistan: Lessons Learnt from Recent Experience*. Occasional papers series, Oxford, Oxford University Press, 2004.

Elebaeva, A., 'Labor migration in Kyrgyzstan' in *Central Asia and the Caucasus: Journal of Social and Political Studies*, Vol. 27, No. 3, 2004. Luleå, Central Asia and the Caucasus Centre for Social and Political Studies.

Handayani, S. W. *The Kyrgyz Republic: A Gendered Transition, Soviet Legacies and New Risks*. Country gender assessment, Asian Development Bank, Manila, 2005.

Hetmanek, A. 'Kirgizstan and the Kirgiz', in *Handbook of Major Soviet Nationalities*. New York, Free Press, 1975.

Huskey, E. 'Kyrgyzstan: the Politics of Demographic and Economic Frustration', in *New States, New Politics: Building the Post-Soviet Nations*. Cambridge, Cambridge Univ. Press, 1997.

Korth, B. *Language Attitudes Towards Kyrgyz and Russian: Discourse, Education and Policy in Post-Soviet Kyrgyzstan*. New York, Peter Lang, 2005.

Kuehnast, K., and Dudwick, N. *Better a Hundred Friends Than a Hundred Rubles?: Social Networks in Transition—The Kyrgyz Republic*. World Bank Working Paper, Washington, DC, World Bank, 2004.

Marat, E. *The Tulip Revolution: Kyrgyzstan One Year After*. Washington, DC, The Jamestown Foundation, 2006.

Plater-Zyberk, H. *Kyrgyzstan: Focusing on Security*. Camberley, Conflict Studies Research Centre, 2003.

Kyrgyzstan after Akayev. Camberley, Conflict Studies Research Centre, 2005.

World Bank. *Enhancing the prospects for growth and trade of the Kyrgyz Republic*. Country Study, Washington, DC, World Bank, 2005.

See also the Select Bibliography.

MOLDOVA

Geography

PHYSICAL FEATURES

The Republic of Moldova is situated in south-eastern Europe. It includes only a small proportion of the historical territories of Moldova (Moldavia), most of which are in Romania, while others (southern Bessarabia and Northern Bucovina—Bukovyna) are in Ukraine. The country is bounded to the north, east and south by Ukraine. To the west there is a frontier with Romania. Moldova covers an area of 33,800 sq km (13,050 sq miles).

Moldova is a fertile plain with small areas of hill country in the centre and north of the country. The main rivers are the Nistru (Dniester or Dnestr), which flows through the eastern regions into the Black Sea, and the Prut (Prutul), which marks the western border with Romania. The Prut joins the Dunărea (Danube) at the southern tip of Moldova.

CLIMATE

The climate is very favourable for agriculture, with long, warm summers and relatively mild winters. Average temperatures in Chişinău (Kishinev) range from 21°C (70°F) in July to −4°C (24°F) in January.

POPULATION

At the census of 2004, at which the total population was 3,383,332, 75.8% of the population defined their ethnicity as Moldovan, 8.4% as Ukrainian, 5.9% as Russian, 4.4% as Gagauz, 2.2% as Romanian and 1.9% as Bulgarian. The ethnic Moldovans speak a dialect of Romanian, a Romance language, which replaced Russian as the official language in 1989. It is now mostly written in the Latin alphabet; in 1941 the Cyrillic script had been introduced and the language referred to as Moldovan. At the 2004 census 60% of the population claimed Moldovan as their mother tongue (and 16.5% claimed Romanian). Ethnic minorities continue to use their own languages; only some 12% of them are fluent in Romanian, whereas most speak Russian. The Gagauz speak a Turkic language, formerly written in the Cyrillic script, but more commonly found in a variant of the Latin script since the 1990s. During the late Soviet period less than 5% of the Gagauz claimed fluency in Moldovan, although more than 70% were fluent in Russian. Russian was declared to be their language of habitual usage by 16.0% at the 2004 census.

Most of the inhabitants of Moldova profess Christianity, the largest denomination being the Eastern Orthodox Church (93.3% in 2004). The Gagauz, despite their Turkish origins, are adherents of Orthodox Christianity. The Russian Orthodox Church (Moscow Patriarchate) has jurisdiction in Moldova, but there are Romanian and Turkish liturgies.

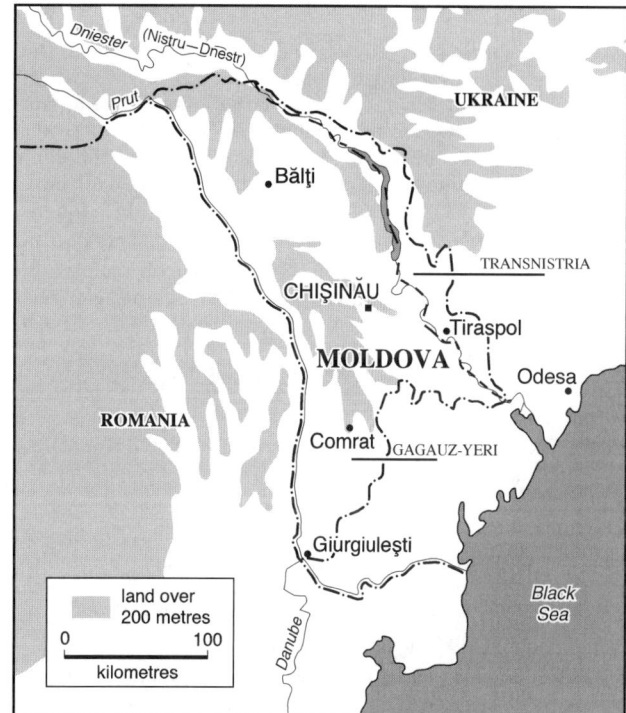

The total population at 1 January 2008 was an estimated 3,572,703. The population density at that time was 105.7 per sq km. (Both of these figures exclude Transnistria.) The capital is Chişinău, which is situated in the central region of the country. It had an estimated population of 663,100 at 1 January 2008. Other important centres are the northern town of Bălţi (with an estimated population of 143,200 in 2008) and Tiraspol (187,000 in January 1996), which is situated in Transnistria, where a majority of the population are ethnic Slavs, Russians or Ukrainians. The Gagauz mostly inhabit the southern districts, especially the region around the town of Comrat (Komrat). According to the preliminary results of a census carried out in the unrecognized 'Transnistrian Moldovan Republic' in November 2004, the overall population totalled some 555,000 (some 31.9% of the population declared themselves to be Moldovan, 30.3% Russian and 28.9% Ukrainian).

Chronology

106: Emperor Trajan made Dacia a province of the Roman Empire (by 118 Rome had secured its hegemony over an area including much of modern Moldova).

270: Rome abandoned Dacia to Visigothic invaders, the first of many incursions by peoples from the north and east.

c. 1359: According to tradition, a Transylvanian prince, Dragoş, became the first lord, or domn, of the region between the Carpathians and the Dnestr (a region that takes its name from the river Molda). Other independent principalities emerged at this time, on the borders of Hungarian territory—the dominant peoples of these Moldovan (Moldavian) and Wallachian lands were Orthodox Christians speaking a Latinate tongue.

1457: Ştefan III ('the Great') came to power in Moldova, ruling until his death in 1504; under Ştefan, Moldova reached the height of its political and military power, and gained control of the lands stretching from the Carpathians to the Dnestr (Nistru) and the Black Sea.

1512: Moldova became a dependency of the Turkish Ottoman Empire.

1612: The Ottomans regained control of Moldova from Sigismund III of Poland.

1711: Following periodic uprisings by local nobles (boieri), Moldova's autonomous status within the Ottoman Empire was revoked, and directly appointed Turkish administrators, Phanariots, were introduced; these Phanariots made Greek the official language and the Romanian Orthodox Church fell under Hellenic influence.

1768–74: The first Russian–Turkish war took place; the Ottomans were assisted by the Habsburg Empire in resisting a Russian attempt to occupy Moldova and Wallachia.

1806–12: In another Russian–Turkish conflict, Russian forces gained control of the lands between the Prut and the Dnestr rivers; the war was ended by the Treaty of Bucharest, under which Moldova was divided; the part west of the Prut remained in the Ottoman Empire, while the eastern territory of Bessarabia (between the Prut and the Dnestr, extending to the Black Sea) became an autonomous region within the Russian Empire.

1815: The annexation of Bessarabia by Tsar Alexander I (1801–25) was approved by the Congress of Vienna.

1828: Bessarabia's autonomy was abolished and it became an imperial district (oblast); the use of the Romanian language in public pronouncements was suspended.

1854: Russian was made the official language of Bessarabia.

1871: Bessarabia became a province (guberniya) of the Russian Empire, by which time western Moldova (Moldavia) and Wallachia had been united in a single Romanian state (the Ottomans recognized its independence in 1878).

1905: The first Romanian-language publications appeared in Bessarabia, during a revolutionary threat to tsarist authority.

1917: With the collapse of tsarist authority in the 1917 Revolutions, revolutionary committees of soldiers and peasants quickly established a parliament (Sfatul Ţării) in the Bessarabian capital, Chişinău (Kishinev), and declared a Bessarabian Democratic Moldovan Republic.

27 March 1918: The Sfatul Ţării, having declared Bessarabia's independence on 24 January, voted for union with Romania (to counter threats from Bolshevik, 'White' Russian and Ukrainian interests).

1 December 1918: The unification of Romania was declared, after Transylvania and Northern Bucovina had also voted to join the Romanian kingdom.

28 October 1920: The union of Bessarabia with Romania was recognized in the Treaty of Paris.

1924: A Moldovan Autonomous Oblast (the Moldavian Soviet Socialist Republic—ASSR—from later in the year) was established in Soviet Ukraine, in territory to the east of the Dnestr river; the USSR claimed that the Romanians, in occupying Bessarabia, had violated Moldova's right to self-rule.

23 August 1939: The Treaty of Non-Aggression (the Nazi-Soviet or Molotov-Ribbentrop Pact), which was signed by the USSR and Germany, included the 'Secret Protocols', sanctioning territorial gains for the USSR in Bessarabia.

28 June 1940: The Soviet Red Army entered Bessarabia.

2 August 1940: Bessarabia officially became part of the USSR; parts of annexed Moldova were united with the existing ASSR, and the resulting Moldovan Soviet Socialist Republic (SSR) was declared a Union Republic of the USSR; two Bessarabian counties on the Black Sea, one county in the north and more than one-half of the counties of the former Moldovan ASSR were apportioned to Ukraine.

1941–44: The introduction of a Cyrillic alphabet for the 'Moldovan' language was interrupted by the Romanian occupation of Bessarabia, following the German invasion of the USSR; the Romanians were expelled towards the end of the Second World War.

1950–52: Leonid Brezhnev (Soviet leader 1964–82) was First Secretary of the Communist Party of Moldova (CPM).

May 1989: The Popular Front of Moldova (PFM) was established; among its aims were the abolition of the use of the Cyrillic script and the return to a Latin one, and the acceptance of Romanian as the country's state language.

31 August 1989: The Moldovan Supreme Soviet adopted laws that returned Moldovan to the Latin script, made it the state language of the republic and recognized its unity with the Romanian language. After protests by the Slav population, Russian was to be retained as the language of inter-ethnic communication.

November 1989: Semion Kuzmich Grossu, First Secretary of the CPM since 1982, was replaced by the more reformist Petru Lucinschi, an ethnic Romanian, following rioting in Chişinău.

25 February 1990: Elections to the Moldovan Supreme Soviet (Supreme Council) were held; the PFM won the largest number of seats.

April 1990: The new Moldovan Supreme Soviet convened; Mircea Snegur, a CPM member supported by the PFM, was re-elected Chairman of the Supreme Soviet. The legislature later adopted a modified version of the Romanian tricolour as Moldova's national flag.

May 1990: Petr Paskar's Government resigned after losing a vote of no confidence; Mircea Druc was appointed Chairman of a Council of Ministers (Prime Minister) dominated by radical reformers; the new Government immediately undertook a series of political reforms, including revoking the CPM's constitutional monopoly of power.

23 June 1990: The Moldovan Supreme Soviet adopted a declaration of sovereignty, which asserted the supremacy of Moldova's Constitution and laws throughout the republic; the 1940 annexation of Bessarabia by the USSR was declared to have been illegal and, on the following day, thousands of Moldovans and Romanians assembled at the border in commemoration of the 50th anniversary of the occupation.

19 August 1990: Five districts (raione) in southern Moldova, largely populated by ethnic Gagauz, declared a separate 'Gagauz SSR' (Gagauz-Yeri).

2 September 1990: Slavs in the territory east of the Dnestr river (and in parts of the west-bank town of Tighina—Bender) proclaimed their secession from Moldova and the establishment of a 'Dnestr SSR' (Transnistria—Transdnestr).

September 1990: Snegur was elected by the Supreme Soviet to the newly instituted post of President of the Republic.

25 October 1990: Elections to a Gagauz-Yeri Supreme Soviet were held, despite the opposition of some 50,000 armed Moldovan nationalists, who were prevented from violence only by Soviet troops.

December 1990: Stepan Topol, hitherto Chairman of the regional Supreme Soviet, was elected to a newly created position, President of Gagauz-Yeri.

February 1991: The Moldovan Supreme Soviet resolved not to conduct the all-Union referendum on the future of the USSR, but to endorse proposals for a confederation of states without central control.

May 1991: Druc was replaced as Prime Minister by Valeriu Muravschi, having lost support in the legislature, which later renamed the state the Republic of Moldova; the Supreme Soviet was renamed Parlamentul (the Parliament).

27 August 1991: Following the attempted coup in the Russian and Soviet capital, Moscow, Moldova declared its independence from the USSR and the CPM was banned. Romania recognized Moldova's independence and diplomatic relations between the two countries were established.

8 December 1991: The first popular presidential election in Moldova took place; Snegur, the only candidate, received 98.2% of the votes cast.

21 December 1991: Moldova, as well as 10 other former Union Republics, signed the Almaty Declaration, by which was formed the Commonwealth of Independent States (CIS). In the same month armed conflict broke out in Transnistria between the Slavic 'Dnestr Guards' and government troops.

February 1992: The PFM re-formed as the Christian Democratic People's Front (CDPF).

June 1992: The CDPF-dominated Government resigned; Andrei Sangheli was appointed Prime Minister and, over the following two months, negotiated a new coalition administration. The pro-Romanian minority in Parlamentul (including the CDPF) remained able to prevent the enactment of basic or constitutional legislation (which required a two-thirds' majority).

21 July 1992: A peace agreement accorded Transnistria 'special status' within Moldova; Russian, Moldovan and Transnistrian peace-keeping forces were deployed in the region to monitor the cease-fire.

January 1993: Alexandru Moşanu was replaced as Chairman of Parlamentul by Lucinschi, the former First Secretary of the CPM and now leader of the Agrarian Democratic Party (ADP), which dominated the Government.

August 1993: Parlamentul failed to secure the necessary majority for ratification of the Almaty Declaration and to formalize the country's entry into the CIS. Nevertheless, President Snegur continued to sign CIS documents, including a treaty on economic union in September.

January 1994: The 'President' of Transnistria, Igor Smirnov, declared a state of emergency in the region, until 1 March, in an attempt to prevent the inhabitants of the region from participating in the forthcoming Moldovan general election.

27 February 1994: Multi-party elections to the new, 104-member, unicameral Parlamentul took place; the ADP emerged as the largest party (winning 43.2% of the votes cast and 56 seats), followed by the Slav-dominated former communists, the Socialist Party, in alliance with the Yedinstvo (Unity) movement (28 seats). The remaining 20 seats were shared between the Peasants' Party of Moldova-Congress of Intelligentsia alliance (with 11) and the CDPF alliance (with nine).

March 1994: In a national referendum on Moldova's statehood, more than 95% of those who voted were in favour of the country's continuing independence. Sangheli and Lucinschi were re-elected Prime Minister and Chairman of Parlamentul, respectively.

April 1994: Parlamentul finally ratified membership of the CIS by 76 votes to 18. Later in the month Sangheli appointed a new Council of Ministers, consisting solely of members of the ADP.

28 July 1994: Parlamentul adopted a new Constitution, which described Moldova as a sovereign, independent, unitary state. The official state language was described as 'Moldovan', although that was acknowledged to be identical to Romanian. The Constitution proclaimed the country's neutrality and provided for a 'special autonomous status' for Transnistria and Gagauz-Yeri; the exact terms of this status were to be determined at a later date.

December 1994: Parlamentul adopted legislation on the special status of Gagauz-Yeri: the region was to enjoy a considerable degree of autonomy; Gagauz was to be one of three official languages; and legislative power was to be vested in a regional assembly, the Halk Toplusu (Popular Assembly), while a directly elected Başkan was to hold a quasi-presidential position. This law entered into force in February 1995.

March–April 1995: Local elections in Transnistria confirmed the popularity of the Union of Patriotic Forces, which had led the self-proclaimed republic for the previous four years. In a referendum, some 91% of those who voted were against the agreed withdrawal from the region of the 14th Army (according to an agreement signed on 21 October 1994, troops of the 14th Army, under Russian jurisdiction, were originally to have been withdrawn from Moldova within three years). President Snegur declared both the elections and the referendum illegal.

June 1995: In response to the rejection by Parlamentul of his proposal to make Romanian (rather than Moldovan) the country's official language, Snegur resigned his membership of the ADP and established, in the following month, the Party of Revival and Conciliation (PRC), with the support of 11 rebel ADP deputies.

24 December 1995: A new bicameral legislature was elected in Transnistria. At the same time, two referendums were held in the region; 82.7% of the electorate endorsed a new Constitution, which proclaimed Transnistria's independence, while 89.7% voted for the region to become a member of the CIS as a sovereign state.

21 July 1996: Officials from the Moldovan and Transnistrian legislatures initialled a memorandum on the principles for a peace settlement, which envisaged Transnistria as having 'special status' within a Moldovan confederation; Snegur declared his opposition to the memorandum and announced that any decision on the issue should be postponed until after the presidential election.

17 November 1996: In the first round of the presidential election, Snegur received 38.7% of the votes cast, while his closest rival, the parliamentary speaker, Lucinschi, obtained 27.7%; the Party of Communists of the Republic of Moldova (PCRM—the former CPM) candidate, Vladimir Voronin, won 10.2% of the ballot.

December 1996: As no candidate in the presidential election had received more than one-half of the votes cast, the two leading candidates contested a second round of voting: Lucinschi obtained 54.1% of the ballot, defeating Snegur. Later in the month Smirnov was re-elected for a second term as President of Transnistria.

15 January 1997: Lucinschi was inaugurated as President of Moldova. His nomination of Ion Ciubuc, Chairman of the State Accounting Chamber, as Prime Minister was confirmed later in the month.

8 May 1997: A memorandum of understanding on the normalization of relations between Moldova and Transnistria was signed by Lucinschi and Smirnov in Moscow; the memorandum committed both sides to further negotiations on the status of the region; Russia and Ukraine were guarantors of the agreement.

10 November 1997: Ciubuc and Smirnov signed a document designed to foster economic and social co-operation between Moldova and Transnistria.

17 February 1998: At a meeting sponsored by the Organization for Security and Co-operation in Europe (OSCE), President Lucinschi and Smirnov signed protocols on economic co-operation in Tiraspol; following the meeting Lucinschi declared that Transnistria remained an integral part of Moldova, but Smirnov stressed the partnership of two equal states.

20 March 1998: At a meeting in Odesa, Ukraine, representatives of Moldova, Transnistria, Russia and Ukraine agreed a reduction in Moldovan and Transnistrian peace-keeping forces; Russian troops were to remain in Transnistria until a final political settlement had been reached.

22 March 1998: In a general election the PCRM won the largest number of seats (40) in the 104-seat Parlamentul, while the Democratic Convention of Moldova (CDM), an alliance that included the PRC and the CDPF, obtained 26 seats and the pro-Lucinschi Movement for a Democratic and Prosperous Moldova (MDPM) came third with 24 seats.

21 April 1998: The CDM, the MDPM and the Party of Democratic Forces agreed to form a parliamentary alliance, led by Snegur; the PCRM, therefore, was excluded from all major parliamentary and government posts. Two days later Dumitru Diacov of the MDPM was elected speaker of the legislature.

21 May 1998: Parlamentul approved a new Government, again led by Ciubuc, a member of the CDM; the cabinet included other members of the CDM and its parliamentary allies.

4 August 1998: Moldova and Ukraine agreed a border delineation so as to facilitate Moldova's construction of a petroleum terminal on the Danube; the two countries also agreed to draft a 10-year economic co-operation treaty.

1 February 1999: Prime Minister Ciubuc resigned, as, subsequently, did the parliamentary leader, Snegur, when his candidate for the premiership was rejected. Ion Sturza was confirmed as premier on 12 March.

23 May 1999: A referendum on increasing presidential powers was held. The Constitutional Court later deemed it to be valid (despite the rate of participation being below the stipulated threshold of 60%), but not binding.

May 1999: Following local elections in Moldova, both Transnistria and Gagauz-Yeri were designated autonomous entities.

10 November 1999: Ion Sturza's Government was dismissed following a vote of 'no confidence' by Parlamentul.

18–19 November 1999: At a summit meeting of the OSCE, held in İstanbul, Turkey, Russia agreed to withdraw its troops from Moldova by the end of 2002. However, this deadline was subsequently extended, initially by one year, and Russian troops remained stationed in Moldova in 2008.

20 December 1999: Parlamentul approved a new Government under Dumitru Braghiş, ending six weeks of political crisis, in which two previous nominees had failed to attract a sufficient number of votes.

March 2000: An agreement was signed between the Transnistrian Supreme Soviet and Parlamentul, to the effect that Transnistrian deputies would, henceforth, participate in the work of international parliamentary organizations as part of the Moldovan delegation.

22 June 2000: The Transnistrian Supreme Soviet was converted to a unicameral parliament, and reduced in number from 67 to 43 deputies.

21 July 2000: Parlamentul overturned a veto imposed by the President on a law that introduced parliamentary rule to Moldova, by permitting the legislature to elect the head of state; Lucinschi had favoured a national constitutional referendum on the issue. Meanwhile, the President of Transnistria, Igor Smirnov, dismissed his Government the next day, and introduced a form of presidential rule.

28 July 2000: Constitutional amendments transforming Moldova into a parliamentary state were enacted.

4 December 2000: The first election for the presidency to be held under new legislation took place, following the annulment of the ballot held three days previously, owing to procedural irregularities. The PCRM candidate, Voronin, was supported by 50 of the 101 parliamentary deputies, and his opponent, the Chairman of the Constitutional Court, Pavel Barbalat, received 35 votes. Neither candidate secured the level of support required to be elected (three-fifths of the votes). A second inconclusive round of voting took place two days later.

10 December 2000: Parliamentary elections were held in Transnistria. Of the 43 seats available, 25 were won by independent candidates.

21 December 2000: A further round of voting for the presidency, between Voronin and Barbalat, proved inconclusive after a number of centre-right deputies boycotted the parliamentary session. After consulting the Constitutional Court, Lucinschi dissolved Parlamentul, with effect from 12 January 2001, and scheduled parliamentary elections for 25 February.

25 February 2001: In the parliamentary elections, the PCRM won 71 of the 101 seats, the centrist Braghiş Alliance won 19 seats, and the People's Christian Democratic Party (PCDP—as the CDPF was known by this time) won 11 seats.

20 March 2001: The outgoing Government of Braghiş tendered its resignation. On the same day Eugenia Ostapciuc was elected Chairman of Parlamentul, obtaining 72 of the 98 votes cast.

4 April 2001: Another presidential election took place, at which Voronin was finally elected President, securing 71 of the 89 votes cast by legislative deputies. Braghiş received 15 votes; the 11 deputies of the PCDP abstained from voting.

19 April 2001: A new cabinet was approved, with Vasile Tarlev as Prime Minister.

27 July 2001: Moldova became a full member of the World Trade Organization.

9 December 2001: Smirnov was re-elected as President of Transnistria, receiving 82% of the votes cast.

9 January 2002: A demonstration, organized by the PCDP and attended by an estimated 3,000 people, took place in Chişinău, in protest at proposals to introduce the compulsory teaching of Russian language to the national curriculum. Daily protests, attended by up to 60,000 people, continued thereafter.

6 February 2002: The reformist Minister of Finance, Mihai Manole, resigned. His resignation, which followed that of the Deputy Prime Minister and Minister of the Economy, Andrei Cucu, prompted international concern that the loss of the only two non-PCRM members of the Council of Ministers would hinder the implementation of economic reforms.

26 February 2002: The continuing domestic crisis led to the dismissal of the Minister of Education, Ilie Vancea. The Minister of the Interior, Vasile Draganel, resigned the following day, amid reports that he had been unwilling to dispel protesters by force.

24 April 2002: The Parliamentary Assembly of the Council of Europe (PACE) adopted a resolution demanding that a moratorium be placed on the introduction of compulsory Russian language lessons in schools, and the cessation of the continuing anti-Government demonstrations. The PCDP agreed to end its protests five days later.

25 June 2002: Dumitru Croitor announced his resignation as Başkan of Gagauz-Yeri, following months of conflict with the region's legislature. On 20 October Gheorghe Tabunscic, who had held the post of Başkan in 1995–99, was elected to succeed him.

3 July 2002: Mediators from Russia, Ukraine and the OSCE submitted a new draft agreement (the 'Kyiv agreement'), under the terms of which Moldova would become a federal state, in which autonomous territories would maintain their own legislature and constitution; Smirnov permitted participation in negotiations on the proposals, but insisted that recognition of Transnistria's independence would be a fundamental prerequisite in negotiations.

27 February 2003: The countries of the European Union (EU) and the USA (and subsequently other countries), imposed travel restrictions on 17 Transnistrian officials, including Smirnov, considered to be 'primarily responsible for a lack of co-operation in promoting a political settlement'; in retaliation, in March the Transnistrian authorities declared 14 Moldovan officials *personae non gratae* in the region. Also in March the Transnistrian authorities sanctioned unconditionally the withdrawal of Russian military equipment from the region.

28 February 2003: After two days of negotiations, the Moldovan and Transnistrian authorities reached a preliminary agreement on proposals by Voronin for the joint drafting of a new constitution for a federal Moldovan state, which would be subject to approval by a nation-wide referendum by February 2004. However, no further progress was made towards organizing a plebiscite on the issue.

25 July 2003: Parlamentul approved a constitutional amendment, officially recognizing the autonomous status of Gagauz-Yeri and granting the Halk Toplusu the right to self-determination and the initiation of legislation. At legislative elections, held in the region in November and December, the PCRM and independent candidates each won almost one-half of the seats contested.

November 2003: The Russian President, Vladimir Putin, announced new proposals for a political settlement. Drafted by the deputy head of the presidential administration, Dmitrii Kozak, the plan envisaged the establishment of an 'asymmetrical federation', comprising Moldova and Transnistria, with unified defence, customs and finance systems. The leaders of both Transnistria and Moldova initially responded positively to the proposals, but Voronin withdrew his support in late November, following opposition protests and reservations expressed by the OSCE.

19 December 2003: Parlamentul approved legislation intended to promote the use of Russian as a language of inter-ethnic communication, although Moldovan was to remain the official language.

6 March 2005: The PCRM won 45.6% of the votes cast in legislative elections, and 56 seats. The new Democratic Moldova bloc, comprising the Democratic Party of Moldova, the Our Moldova Alliance and the Social Liberal Party, obtained 28.5% of the votes and 34 seats, while the PCDP secured 9.1% and 11 seats.

4 April 2005: Voronin was formally re-elected for a second presidential term by 75 of the 101 deputies in the legislature.

19 April 2005: A new Council of Ministers, again led by Tarlev, was approved by Parlamentul.

10 June 2005: The legislature approved a new plan for the settlement of the Transnistria conflict, proposed by Ukrainian President Viktor Yushchenko. The 18-month plan envisaged, *inter alia*, awarding 'special status' to Transnistria, as an autonomous entity within Moldova, followed by democratic elections to the Transnistrian legislature. The powers of both the central and autonomous government bodies were to be clearly delineated. The plan also provided for a Transnistrian constitution (to comply with the Moldovan Constitution) and symbols, and allowed Transnistria to participate in foreign-policy decisions affecting Transnistria's interests. Notably, the proposals made no mention of the withdrawal of Russian troops from Transnistria.

10 October 2005: Zinaida Grecianîi, hitherto Minister of Finance, was appointed First Deputy Prime Minister.

17 January 2006: Former Minister of Defence Valeriu Pasat was sentenced to 10 years' imprisonment, having been convicted of defrauding the state in 1997, when in office. There were allegations that the trial was politically motivated. (His sentence was reduced by five years in October.)

23 May 2006: The leaders of Georgia, Ukraine, Azerbaijan and Moldova met in Kyiv, Ukraine, to revive the regional GUAM organization, renaming it the Organization for Democracy and Economic Development—GUAM.

17 September 2006: The Transnistrian authorities held an internationally unrecognized referendum on the territory's independence and potential options for eventual integration, in which some 97% voted for a continued course of independence with the aim of unification with Russia, and some 95% voted against unification with Moldova.

3 December 2006: Elections for the post of Başkan of Gagauz-Yeri were held, with a second round of voting on 17 December. Mihail Formuzal, who was supported by the opposition, emerged victorious, with 56% of the votes.

10 December 2006: Smirnov was re-elected to a fourth term as President of Transnistra, securing 82.4% of votes cast.

12 March 2007: Viktor Neumoin, head of the Tiraspol branch of the Patriotic Party of Transnistria, was shot dead in Tiraspol.

3 June 2007: Local elections were conducted throughout Moldova; the rate of participation by the electorate was recorded at 52.3%. Overall, the PCRM secured 334 mayoralties, 465 seats in district and municipal councils, and 4,040 seats in city and village councils; the Our Moldova Alliance won 157 mayoralties, 220 seats in district and municipal councils, and 1,987 seats in city and village councils. The PCRM won 16 seats on Chişinău Municipal Council; however, Dorin Chritoacă of the Liberal Party, which had obtained 11 seats in the Council, was elected Mayor.

11 June 2007: Voronin dismissed the Minister of Defence, Valeriu Plesca, after a civilian was killed when journalists were permitted to participate in a military training exercise. (In July he was replaced by Vitalie Vrabie, hitherto Deputy Prime Minister and Minister of Local Public Administration.)

16 January 2008: Voronin appointed a prominent member of the PCRM, Victor Stepaniuc, as a Deputy Prime Minister.

16 March 2008: In Gagauz-Yeri, the first round of elections to the 35-member Halk Toplusu took place. After a second round on 30 March, a PCRM-led coalition, known as the Bloc for a Flourishing Gagauzia into a Renewed Moldova, held 17 seats, and a grouping of opposition candidates, the United Gagauzia Movement, eight seats.

19 March 2008: Tarlev submitted his resignation and that of his Government; Tarlev announced that he intended to leave political life. Grecianîi was subsequently nominated to succeed him, becoming the country's first female Prime Minister.

31 March 2008: A new Government formed by Grecianîi was approved by Parlamentul by 56 votes, with opposition deputies abstaining from voting; Igor Dodon, the Minister of Economy and Trade, succeeded Grecianîi as First Deputy Prime Minister.

10 April 2008: Parlamentul approved an amendment to the electoral code that increased the minimum required for parliamentary representation from 4% to 6% of votes cast.

11 April 2008: Voronin and Smirnov met, for the first time since 2001, in Tighina (Bender), Transnistria, with the aim of resuming talks on a political solution to the disputed status of the region. Following the meeting, Voronin announced that he and Smirnov had agreed to continue negotiations.

History

Dr STEVEN D. ROPER

EARLY HISTORY

Contemporary Moldova is a landlocked country located between Romania and Ukraine. According to the results of the 2004 census, Moldova's population by ethnicity was approximately 75.8% Moldovan, 8.4% Ukrainian, 5.9% Russian, 4.4% Gagauz and 1.9% Bulgarian. The country consists of 33 districts, two municipalities, the capital Chişinău (Kishinev) and Bălţi, and two semi-autonomous regions. It covers Bessarabia to the west and Transnistria (Transdnestria) to the east. The Prut river forms a natural border between Romania and Moldova, while the Nistru (Dnestr—Dniester) river, which rises in Ukraine, generally forms the border between Bessarabia and Transnistria. A Moldovan principality was first established during the mid-14th century. This principality covered areas in contemporary Moldova and Romania (in the region known as Moldavia). By the 1530s Moldova became a tributary state to the Ottoman Porte (Empire); although it was part of the Empire, local princes ruled the region.

By the 18th century the increasing power of Russia and Austria was challenging Ottoman pre-eminence in the region. In 1774 Russia was awarded the right to represent Moldova at the Ottoman Sultanate, and in 1775 Austria annexed Bucovina, the northern portion of Moldova. In 1792 the territory of present-day Transnistria was ceded by the Ottoman Turks to Russia. Following the Russo–Turkish war of 1806–12, the eastern area of Moldova, between the Prut and Dnestr rivers, became formally known as Bessarabia. An influx of Russians and other ethnic groups reduced the percentage of Moldovans in the population to less than one-half. Meanwhile, in 1859 the principalities of Western Moldova (eastern Romania to the Prut) and Wallachia (southern Romania) each elected Alexandru Ioan Cuza as Prince, thereby creating a de facto union. Following the Berlin Congress in 1878, the principalities achieved independence, and in 1881 they were recognized as the Kingdom of Romania.

The First World War (1914–18) and the Russian Revolution (1917) provided Bessarabia's pan-Romanian nationalists with an opportunity to press their claims for Romanian integration. On the request of the Bessarabian national assembly (Sfatul Ţării), Romanian troops entered Chişinău in January 1918 and, in the same month, the Sfatul Ţării voted to form an independent Moldovan Democratic Republic of Bessarabia. Two months later, on 27 March, the Sfatul Ţării voted to unite with Romania, and by the end of 1918 Bucovina and Transylvania had joined Bessarabia to form 'Greater Romania'. Prior to the Second World War (1939–45), Bessarabia was an integral part of Romania. Of all Romania's regions, Bessarabia had one of the lowest concentrations of ethnic Romanians. Therefore, during the inter-war period, the Romanian Government undertook linguistic and educational reform to increase Romanian language literacy rates and to promote Romanian culture. At the same time the Soviet authorities constructed (within the existing Ukrainian Soviet Socialist Republic—SSR) a competing political region, the Moldovan (Moldavian) Autonomous Soviet Socialist Republic (ASSR), on the 'left' (East) bank of the Nistru, in present-day Transnistria.

SOVIET MOLDOVA

In August 1939 Germany and the USSR signed the Molotov-Ribbentrop or Nazi-Soviet Pact (also known as the Treaty of Non-Aggression). The agreement included the 'Secret Protocols', which conceded the USSR's interest in Bessarabia. On 26 June 1940 the USSR issued an ultimatum to Romania, demanding the immediate cession of Bessarabia and Northern Bucovina, and by 3 July both territories were under Soviet control, as the Moldovan Soviet Socialist Republic (SSR). The SSR of Moldova was formed by joining Bessarabia with six counties that had formed part of the ASSR. Moldova inherited a large Russian-speaking community, and immigration, particularly of ethnic Russian industrial workers, caused the majority population of many cities to become heavily russified. Throughout the Soviet period, the leadership encouraged the creation of a distinct Moldovan nation. As part of the policy of russification, the alphabet for the dialect of Romanian spoken in Moldova was changed from Latin to Cyrillic, and the language referred to as Moldovan, while Russian once again became the language of inter-ethnic communication, higher education and public life.

As occurred elsewhere, reforms introduced by the Soviet leader Mikhail Gorbachev in the mid-1980s created conditions in which long-standing resentment against Soviet ethnic policies could be expressed. In 1987 Moldovan intellectuals organized informal discussion groups that focused on promoting the use of the Romanian language. Within a year these groups had become formally organized around the issue of linguistic and cultural freedom. By mid-1988 Moldovan intellectuals and the pro-Romanian opposition had formed the Democratic Movement in Support of Restructuring (later renamed the Popular Front—PF) to advocate democratization and redress for discriminatory practices imposed upon the majority population. The prospect of ethnic Moldovans gaining political power provoked an immediate response from Russian-speaking minorities. Many non-ethnic Moldovans supported the Internationalist Movement for Unity (Yedinstvo), a pro-Russian movement, for which the strongest base of support existed in Transnistria.

By 1989 the PF had become the leading Moldovan opposition force, proposing a strong Romanian and unionist agenda. In August the Moldovan Supreme Soviet (Supreme Council, parliament) proclaimed Moldovan (using the Latin alphabet) as the state language. Moldova's last Soviet-era parliament was elected in March 1990. Following the elections, the PF entered into a parliamentary coalition with several other parties, which together held over 66% of the seats. The parliament confirmed a Government composed almost entirely of ethnic Moldovans. The Supreme Soviet also re-elected Mircea Snegur as its Chairman and, subsequently, President of the Republic (he was popularly elected in 1991). During this period PF members of parliament and the Government of Prime Minister Mircea Druc pursued a pro-Romanian and pro-unionist agenda that alienated the Russian minority. In May the designation 'Soviet Socialist' was removed from the republic's name and the Supreme Soviet was renamed Parlamentul (the Parliament).

INDEPENDENT MOLDOVA

The early actions of the legislature and the Government had an immediate negative consequence. Ethnic minorities, including ethnic Russians, Ukrainians and Gagauz, felt that they were being marginalized by the pro-Romanian nationalists. On 27 August 1991 Moldova proclaimed its independence, which escalated demands for independence by Transnistria. The resulting civil conflict and the cease-fire agreement of mid-1992 marked the turning point in the political fortunes of the PF. The party was perceived as responsible for the war with Transnistria, and in August 1992 several PF members defected and formed an alliance to remove the party's leadership. In early 1993 the PF, re-formed as the Christian Democratic Popular Front (CDPF), was in total disarray. The party's voting strength in parliament was reduced to a mere 25 deputies (of a total of 380). The Prime Minister, Valeriu Muravschi, who had replaced Druc in May 1991, was, in turn, replaced by Andrei Sangheli in June 1992, and in January 1993 the Chairman of Parlamentul, Alexandru Mosanu, was replaced by Petru Lucinschi. However, these changes only increased tensions. The reformist communists and the less nationalistic forces, which comprised the core support for the Sangheli Government, dominated Parlamentul, and this led to a legislative impasse. Finally, Parlamentul was dissolved and new legislative elections were held in February 1994.

The result of these first, entirely post-communist elections marked a sharp reversal from the politics of the early transition period. Nationalist and pro-Romanian forces were rejected in favour of those supporting Moldovan independence and accommodation with ethnic minorities. The Agrarian Democratic Party (ADP) won 43% of the votes cast and received 56 of the 104 seats in Parlamentul. Another 28 seats were won by the socialist bloc, which received 22% of the votes. The pro-Romanian parties suffered a severe reverse. The PF, which two years earlier led the coalition Government, received only 7.5% of the votes cast and nine seats. Members of the ADP controlled all the leadership positions in Parlamentul, and Lucinschi was reappointed as Chairman. President Snegur joined the party in February 1994.

The ADP was a coalition of diverse ideological views and, although the party held a majority of seats, it later suffered several important defections. Several members of Parlamentul left the party in 1995, among them Snegur, who left in June. The parliamentary defections forced the ADP to rely increasingly on the socialists. By the time of the November 1996 presidential election, the ADP was losing its influence. In the first round of presidential election, none of the main three candidates were ADP members. In the 'run-off' election on 1 December, Lucinschi received 54% of the votes cast, defeating Snegur. Shortly thereafter, Prime Minister Sangheli resigned and was replaced by Ion Ciubuc. Lucinschi's victory did not create a major reorientation of Moldovan foreign or domestic policy; while he emphasized relations with other members of the Commonwealth of Independent States, Lucinschi continued the country's existing foreign policy with regard to Romania and Russia.

By the time of the parliamentary elections of March 1998 the party formations and alliances within Moldova had changed. Snegur's Party of Revival and Conciliation (PRC), merged with other rightist parties, including the Popular Front, to form the Democratic Convention of Moldova (CDM). In addition, the pro-Lucinschi Movement for a Democratic and Prosperous Moldova (MDPM) was established in February 1997. Economic issues dominated the election campaign, and because of the dissatisfaction that many Moldovans felt about the economy, the Party of Communists of the Republic of Moldova (PCRM) received 30% of the votes cast and approximately 40% of parliamentary seats. However, the remaining three parties in Parlamentul, the Party of Democratic Forces, the CDM and the MDPM, formed a parliamentary coalition called the Alliance for Democratic Reform (ADR), and confirmed Ciubuc as Prime Minister once again. In February 1999 tensions in the coalition prompted the resignation of Ciubuc, and in March Ion Sturza was confirmed as Prime Minister. His Government was considered much more pro-reform than the previous two Ciubuc Governments and enjoyed real popular support. Con-flict with Lucinschi and Parlamentul, perhaps because of Sturza's popularity, resulted in the Prime Minister's removal from office in November, and in the following month Dumitru Braghiş was confirmed as Sturza's replacement.

The discord between Sturza and Lucinschi formed part of a larger conflict between the legislature and the President. In May 1999 Lucinschi held a consultative referendum proposing constitutional changes to increase his presidential powers. However, Lucinschi lacked a parliamentary majority, and conflict with Parlamentul increased as, by mid-2000, the ADR had fragmented, and even the pro-presidential MDPM—which changed its name to the Democratic Party of Moldova (PDM) in April—began openly to criticize the President. In July Parlamentul approved a series of constitutional amendments, allowing the President to be elected and dismissed by the legislature; Lucinschi vetoed the proposed changes, but Parlamentul overturned his decision later in the month.

Although Parlamentul was united in its opposition to Lucinschi, the process of voting for a new president demonstrated significant differences between party factions. As a result of this inability to elect a president, Lucinschi was able to dissolve Parlamentul and announce an early general election in February 2001. In the legislative elections the PCRM received 50% of the votes cast and 71 seats (of a total of 101) in Parlamentul. The only other parties to obtain seats were the Braghiş Alliance (formed by Dumitru Braghiş) and the People's Christian Democratic Party (PCDP, the former CDPF), as fewer parties qualified for entry into the legislature following the increase of the electoral threshold to 6%. On 4 April 2001 Vladimir Voronin, the First Secretary of the PCRM, was finally elected to the presidency, securing 71 votes. Following his inauguration on 7 April, Voronin nominated Vasile Tarlev as Prime Minister.

The first real test of the political strength of the PCRM occurred during the local elections of May–June 2003, for mayors and county and city councils. Although the PCRM won more than 54% of the seats on the county and city councils and more than 40% of the mayoralties, it did not win the important mayoral election in the city of Chişinău. Moreover, for the first time, the electoral observation mission of the Organization for Security and Co-operation in Europe (OSCE) was critical of the state's interference in the local elections, in particular its manipulation of the state media. The electoral code was amended in 2002, with several significant changes: most importantly, the new system of legislative elections mandated significant thresholds for parties and blocs to secure representation in Parlamentul (for example, parties required 6% of the votes, blocs of two parties 9%, and blocs of more than two parties 12%). In the legislative elections held on 6 March 2005 only the PCRM, the Democratic Moldova bloc (which consisted of the Our Moldova Alliance, the Democratic Party of Moldova and the Social Liberal Party) and the PCDP passed the threshold. The PCRM won 46% of the votes cast (56 seats), the Democratic Moldova bloc received 28.5% (34 seats) and the PCDP obtained 9% (11 seats). On 4 April the newly elected Parlamentul held a presidential ballot, re-electing Voronin as President with 75 of the 101 votes available. Voronin subsequently reappointed Tarlev as Prime Minister.

However, after six years in power, the first significant indication of a decline in the PCRM's influence occurred during local elections held in June 2007. Although the PCRM had been very effective at the national level in elections throughout the 2000s, it had always struggled in local polls, particularly in Chişinău. While the PCRM received a plurality of seats on the county and city councils, and more than 36% of the mayoralties in the June 2007 elections, the overall share of the vote for the party declined by approximately 10%. In addition, a young Liberal Party candidate, Dorin Chirtoacă, easily defeated the PCRM candidate in the second round of the mayoral contest for Chişinău. Throughout 2007 and 2008 the Chişinău Municipal Council became a primary forum for the conflict between the PCRM and opposition parties. The central authorities used financial means to pressure the Mayor's office, and in June 2008 a questionable change in the leadership of the Municipal Council was orchestrated by forces loyal to the PCRM. Indeed, the PCRM's local election losses in Gagauz-Yeri and Chişinău, and the relative success of the opposition, have increased the likelihood that the legislative elections scheduled to take place in 2009 could prove a critical event in the country: as Parlamentul now elects the President, the elections may lead to a change in both executive and legislative power. In view of these possibilities, the PCRM's March 2008 party congress promoted the modernization of the party by elevating several new, younger members to the party's Central Committee. Subsequently, in March 2008 Prime Minister Tarlev was replaced by Zinaida Greceanîi. All of these changes, as well as the resumption of negotiations on the status of Transnistria, were viewed as a prelude to the 2009 legislative elections.

TRANSNISTRIA

Transnistria's ethnic composition is unlike that of the rest of Moldova. In Transnistria approximately 59% of the population are ethnic Ukrainians and Russians, and the region, excluding the city of Tighina (Bender) and a few villages, was never part of Romania. Therefore, pan-Romanian appeals by the PF in the early 1990s were especially resented in Transnistria. The Transnistrians refused to acknowledge the 1989 language law, and in early May 1990 the city governments of Tiraspol and Tighina refused to accept any of the measures passed by the Moldovan Supreme Soviet. Following the formation of the 'Transnistrian Moldovan SSR' in September 1990, relations with the separatists emerged as the dominant issue for the Moldovan Government.

After the declaration of Moldovan independence in August 1991, the future separatist leader' of Transnistria, Igor Smirnov, and other Transnistrian officials negotiated for the creation of a confederal government. During 1991 and 1992 several clashes occurred between the Moldovan military and Transnistrian paramilitary units. The latter greatly benefited from equipment and personnel provided by the Russian 14th Army, located in Tiraspol. As the Transnistrian separatists consolidated their position, nationalists inside the Moldovan legislature became increasingly militant. This brought intense pressure on President Snegur to undertake decisive action to resolve the conflict. In late March 1992 a state of emergency was declared and an effort was made to disarm units of the separatist militia by force. This attempt met with violent resistance, and by May the conflict had escalated into a full-scale civil war. The heaviest fighting occurred in the cities of Dubăsari and Tighina. There are various estimates of the number of casualties, but perhaps as many as 1,000 died during this period. The violence in Tighina compelled the Russian Government to intervene actively in the conflict. In July the Russian President, Boris Yeltsin, and Snegur signed a cease-fire agreement that established a Joint Control Committee to observe the military forces in the security zone and maintain order.

After July 1992 the relationship between the central Moldovan and Transnistrian authorities did not change fundamentally: there were periods of negotiation, followed by months of inactivity. In July 1996 a memorandum on the settlement of the conflict was endorsed by Moldovan and Transnistrian officials. The memorandum recognized Transnistria's right to maintain international contacts and to develop relations in the framework of a 'common state'. President Snegur refused to sign the memorandum, and it was hoped that Lucinschi's election would represent a turning point in the relationship. Many believed that his relations with the former Communist Party would enable him to resolve the conflict. However, after taking office, President Lucinschi did not achieve any significant progress in the negotiation process. Initially, he too refused to sign the memorandum, but finally, in May 1997, he and Smirnov signed the document in Moscow. From then there were a number of high-level meetings in Odesa and Kyiv, both in Ukraine, but the negotiating positions generally remained unchanged, and little substantive progress was made. Transnistria asserted that the concept of a common state should be defined as an equal partnership between two states, but the Moldovan Government rejected this definition, as did international bodies, including the Organization for Security and Co-operation in Europe (OSCE). According to a document signed at an OSCE summit, held in İstanbul,

Turkey, in November 1999, Russia was to withdraw its military presence from Transnistria in three stages, with all 'hardware' to be removed by the end of 2001 and troops by 2002. Although three convoys, carrying limited weaponry and non-combat material, were dispatched immediately, only one convoy left Transnistria in 2000, and the first destruction of equipment did not begin until July 2001. In late 2001 several more trains carrying material departed from Transnistria, and by the end of the year Russia claimed to have met its obligations under the agreement reached in 1999. Meanwhile, the Transnistrian leadership continued to oppose the planned withdrawal, and demanded some form of financial compensation. Following an agreement by Russia to cancel part of the US $100m. natural gas debt owed by Transnistria, Russia withdrew a substantial quantity of ammunition and weapons in the first half of 2003, but progress continued to be hampered by the Transnistrian authorities. In an attempt to ensure that the full evacuation of ammunition was completed by the end of the year, the USA eventually offered to provide financial aid to Transnistria. However, by 2008 Russia still had approximately 1,200 troops deployed in Transnistria.

Following the election of President Voronin in early 2001, there was a great deal of optimism that a conclusive status could be negotiated for Transnistria. The negotiations between Voronin and Smirnov were initially successful: in May Transnistria released the Romanian-Moldovan nationalist, Ilie Ilascu, from a Transnistrian jail, following his imprisonment on charges of terrorism in 1992. The release of Ilascu had been a long-standing demand of the Moldovan Government, and Voronin and Smirnov met on subsequent occasions to negotiate a wide range of issues. However, by late 2001 Voronin had concluded that Smirnov had no real interest in ending the status quo and, therefore, the negotiations produced no lasting agreement on resolving the conflict.

In July 2002 the first signs of possible progress in the negotiating process were finally discernible. Mediators from Russia, Ukraine and the OSCE submitted a new draft agreement to the Moldovan and Transnistrian sides, which constituted the most detailed and far-reaching proposals thus far. Fundamentally, the 'Kyiv agreement' (so-called owing to the location at which it was presented) envisioned the federalization of Moldova, with state-territorial formations (specifically Transnistria) exercising local power over a range of issues, subordinate to the Moldovan central administration. The proposals included plans for the creation of a bicameral parliament, the upper house of which would represent the territorial formations. Although the proposal was well received by President Voronin and leading members of the PCRM, opposition parties were very critical. There were concerns that the proposal did not specify the number of territorial formations to be created and that it failed to provide a mechanism for constitutional revision.

The Kyiv agreement continued to serve as a basis for discussion between Moldovan and Transnistrian officials throughout 2003. In February Voronin proposed that a new constitution be adopted, based on the federal principles of the Kyiv agreement. Voronin established a Joint Constitutional Commission (JCC), charged with drafting a new constitution (in collaboration with Transnistrian representatives), which was to be submitted to the population at a referendum and which, if passed, would result in new elections to all nationwide offices. Although the OSCE, the European Union (EU) and Western countries, such as the USA, were in favour of the federalization of the country, most opposition parties remained firmly opposed to both the principle of federalization and the Kyiv agreement. To the opposition, the proposed federalization of the country represented a 'Russian view' that would end the sovereign integrity of the country. However, international organizations, such as the OSCE, argued that federalization was the only basis for ending the long-standing conflict. The negotiations, however, made only limited progress. While Voronin was publicly committed to the principles laid out in the 2002 Kyiv proposal, he secretly entered into negotiations with Russia. The First Deputy Chairman of the Russian Presidential Administration, Dmitrii Kozak, was appointed by President Vladimir Putin to mediate between Moldova and Transnistria and produce a memorandum that would serve as the basis of a new constitution. For several months in mid-2003 Kozak was engaged in 'shuttle diplomacy' between the authorities in Moscow, Chişinău and Tiraspol. On 17 November Russia presented the OSCE and Ukraine with a final draft of what became known as 'the Kozak Memorandum'. The document provided for the establishment of an upper legislative chamber, a senate. One-half of the 26 members of the senate were to be elected within Transnistria and Gagauz-Yeri, in effect providing these regions, particularly Transnistria, with the ability to veto national legislation. Moldovan civil society and opposition groups, which generally regarded proposals for federalization as detrimental to their national interests, expressed concern that the Kozak Memorandum undermined the Moldovan state. The international community was equally concerned about the document, and there was an escalation of diplomatic activity centred on Chişinău following the announcement of the plan. Voronin realized that the Memorandum had only limited domestic or international support and declined to approve the document. From 2003–05 the failure to approve the Kozak document, together with the closure of Romanian-language schools in Transnistria, increased tensions and led to some sharp verbal exchanges.

In May 2005 a plan developed by Ukrainian President Viktor Yushchenko was announced publicly after a meeting in Ukraine. The Yushchenko Plan envisioned a three-stage settlement in which the Moldovan Parlamentul would approve a basic law on the status of Transnistria, followed by OSCE-organized elections in Transnistria, and the establishment of a Conciliation Committee to address specific elements of the Moldovan law. The Plan simply ignored many of the critical issues that had made the Kozak Memorandum unworkable. In June Parlamentul passed a declaration endorsing the Yushchenko Plan, and in the following month the parliament endorsed new legislation on the special status of Transnistria. The law was very brief and did not address issues related to the distribution of power and competencies between the central authorities and the autonomous regions. The Transnistrian head of state, Smirnov, indicated that the passage of the Moldovan law without consultation with the region eliminated the Yushchenko Plan as a viable option. Instead, the Transnistrian élite refer to the referendum on independence (from the State Union of Serbia and Montenegro) held in Montenegro and the final status talks on the territory of Kosovo (which declared independence from Serbia in 2008, having been a province within that country) as a model for the eventual status of Transnistria. As expected, there was an almost complete endorsement of the territory's course of independence and eventual unification with Russia in the unofficial referendum held on 17 September. In addition, in December 2006 Smirnov was again re-elected President, although the election marked a growing divide in Transnistria between the old guard and an emerging opposition led by individuals including the journalist Andrei Safonov, who was placed third in the election.

Relations with Russia deteriorated in 2006, seemingly as a result of events related to Transnistria (and possibly ever since the failure of the Kozak proposition). Following the imposition of a strict new customs regime along the border, with the co-operation of the Ukrainian authorities, in March 2006 the Russian authorities imposed a punitive ban on Moldovan wine imports (in effect until late 2007), as well as significantly raising the price of natural gas exports to Moldova. These economic pressures negated much of Moldova's pro-European rhetoric so that by 2007 the Government could claim very few concrete foreign policy successes with relation to the EU. While a Common EU Visa Application Centre was created in April 2007 (see below), the failure to restart the so-called '5 + 2' negotiating format (that is, Moldova, Transnistria, Russia, Ukraine, and the OSCE, together with the USA and the EU) prompted speculation that President Voronin had once again resumed bilateral talks with Russia. Indeed, in January 2008 Voronin met with President Putin to discuss Transnistria. Russia has exerted pressure on the Moldovan authorities to remain permanently neutral with respect to NATO in exchange for facilitating a settlement, while Voronin, who is from the area now controlled by Transnistria, has a personal interest in ending the conflict and a stated commitment to reunification of the state. With the 2009 legislative elections

less than a year away, Voronin held a telephone conversation with Smirnov, which later resulted in a direct meeting with him in Tighina in April 2008. These discussions, the first between the two in almost seven years, prompted speculation that Voronin would attempt to reach an agreement before his term of office ended in March 2009. After Russian President Dmitrii Medvedev met Voronin in late August 2008 and Smirnov in September, it was reported that the initiation of a new bilateral negotiating process mediated by Russia (thereby abandoning the '5 + 2' format) was under discussion.

GAGAUZ-YERI

The Gagauz constitute some 4.4% of the Moldovan population and are concentrated in the south. They are a Turkic language-speaking people of Orthodox Christian faith who originated in Bulgaria, and they have inhabited the same area of southern Moldova for centuries. The Gagauz were highly russified during the Soviet period and, even by the beginning of the 2000s, Russian remained their primary language of commerce and education. The Gagauz initially participated in the meetings of the PF, as they had formed an organization called the Gagauz Halki (Gagauz People), which co-operated with the Front. However, as the PF transformed from a reformist to a pan-Romanian organization, the Gagauz Halki demanded Gagauz independence. In August 1990 the Gagauz announced the formation of a republic with Comrat (Komrat) as the capital; national symbols were adopted and a local defence force was organized. Also during this time Gagauz and Transnistrians began to co-operate in several areas. However, the formation of a Gagauz state never achieved the same degree of development as it did in Transnistria. The industrial base, significant ethnic Russian population and the presence of the Russian 14th Army provided Transnistria with several advantages that the Gagauz never possessed.

In October 1990 the Gagauz conducted parliamentary elections to a 'Supreme Soviet'. As in Transnistria, Gagauz élites supported the August 1991 coup, and the Moldovan declaration of independence only hardened the Gagauz position. In December Stepan Topol, hitherto Chairman of the Gagauz Supreme Soviet, was elected 'President of Gagauz-Yeri'. (Topol held this post until the Gagauz Presidency was abolished, in 1995.) At the time, the Moldovan Government was unable to exercise authority over the area, and the region was essentially independent of Moldova. However, the Transnistrian civil war convinced the Moldovan leadership that moderation was the best approach to conflict resolution. This, combined with a change in the Moldovan leadership, made negotiations much easier. After the February 1994 parliamentary elections and the passage of the Constitution in July, the Moldovan Government entered into the final phase of negotiations with the Gagauz élite. The legislation creating Gagauz-Yeri recognized the territory as an autonomous territorial unit with a special status of self-determination. The Gagauz were to elect a Governor (Başkan) and a Halk Toplusu (Popular Assembly). Elections for the post of Başkan and for the Halk Toplusu were held in 1995, in 1999 and, separately for Başkan, in 2002. The Moldovan Government hoped that the special status of Gagauz-Yeri would serve as an example for Transnistria. However, paradoxically, many Transnistrians were unwilling to accept territorial autonomy, precisely because of the example of Gagauz-Yeri from 1995. Most Transnistrians and, indeed, almost all Gagauz, believed that Gagauz-Yeri did not enjoy a truly autonomous status within Moldova and, instead, considered there to have been a transfer of power away from Comrat to the Moldovan authorities in Chişinău. The Gagauz leadership began to make increasing demands for greater local autonomy towards the end of the 1990s, and Dumitru Croitor (Başkan from September 1999 until July 2002) campaigned for authority over local taxation, as well as the power to undertake territorial-administrative reorganization.

On 25 July 2003 Parlamentul approved a constitutional amendment, officially recognizing the autonomous status of Gagauz-Yeri and granting the Halk Toplusu the right to self-determination and the initiation of its own legislation. Legislative elections were held in the region at the end of the year, in which the PCRM and independent candidates each won almost one-half of the seats contested. However, the authoritarian approach of the PCRM and the central authorities impacted upon the party's popularity, which was reflected in elections to the post of Başkan, the first round of which was held on 3 December 2006. The candidate supported by the opposition, Mihail Formuzal, and the Mayor of Comrat, Nicolai Dudoglo, received the highest number of votes in the first round of voting, thus securing their places in a second round. The incumbent Başkan, Gheorghe Tabunscic, who was supported by the PCRM, failed to proceed to the second round, despite, according to OSCE reports, significant favour by the authorities and media bias towards him during the electoral campaign. Formuzal emerged victorious from the second poll, winning about 56% of votes cast. Relations between the Moldovan Government and Gagauz authorities remained strained throughout 2007 and 2008. Formuzal continued to make proposals that would allow Gagauz-Yeri greater flexibility in local matters, as well as provide more input in foreign policy issues (especially in terms of relations with Russia and Turkey). Conflict with the central Government in June 2008 also impeded the election of a new Chairman of the Halk Toplusu for a prolonged period; the PCRM-led coalition claimed that its candidate had won the office, and refused to recognize the election of an independent deputy (see Autonomous Territories).

EXTERNAL RELATIONS

Relations with Romania Since 1991

After Moldova proclaimed its independence, the Romanian Government adopted an ambivalent policy. On the one hand, Romania was the first country to recognize Moldova's independence; on the other, Romanian politicians articulated a policy of eventual reunification. The Romanian Government always maintained that reunification should be a Moldovan decision. In 1991 and 1992 President Snegur maintained a policy of 'one people, two states'. Throughout this period, Snegur resisted demands for reunification and, at the same time, the majority that had earlier supported the Popular Front had became a minority by 1994. The Moldovan public's zeal for reunification had clearly waned, and in March 1994 a non-binding referendum was held on the question of statehood. Some 95% of the electorate voted for the continuation of Moldovan statehood. This result was not surprising considering that, even in 1992, fewer than 15% of ethnic Moldovans had favoured reunification. In the mid-1990s Snegur changed his position somewhat, however. He attempted to change the Constitution and rename the state language as Romanian, while maintaining a pro-independence stance. During the 1996 presidential election, Snegur and his chief opponent, Lucinschi, both articulated a pro-independence position. Following Lucinschi's election, relations between the two countries generally remained cordial, if sometimes distant, although Romania's relationship with the EU caused tensions.

Many Moldovans feared that Romania's application for full EU membership might eventually force the country to impose stricter controls on its common border with Moldova. From mid-2001 Moldovans entering Romania were required to carry a passport (as opposed to a Moldovan identity card), although Romania agreed to provide financial assistance to Moldova to facilitate the issuing of passports.

Meanwhile, after the electoral victory of the PCRM in 2001, Moldovan–Romanian relations began to show severe strain. The Moldovan and Romanian Governments diverged on several issues, including proposals for the registration in Moldova of a pro-Romanian (Bessarabian Metropolitan) Orthodox Church—which eventually took place at the end of July 2002; the language to be used in the long-delayed bilateral friendship treaty; and the enrolment of Moldovan students in Romanian educational institutions. At mid-2003 relations had improved marginally and the legislature passed amendments allowing dual citizenship. The law came into effect in July, and more than 5,000 Moldovans had applied for Romanian citizenship by the following month. From 2004 Moldova demonstrated a greater openness towards Europe and the EU in its foreign policy, embracing a common outlook with Romania and resulting in a greater convergence of interests. In January 2005 the newly elected President of Romania, Traian Băsescu, visited Moldova and declared his support for the country's aspirations eventually to accede to the EU. Since 2005 relations between the two countries have vacillated between indifference and hostility. Certainly the issue of dual citizenship and Romania's formal accession to the EU on 1 January 2007 have complicated the relationship, with the Romanian authorities reporting that by February of that year more than 800,000 Moldovans had applied to Romania for citizenship. Relations between Romania and Moldova remained tense throughout 2007 and 2008. In October 2007 the EU Commissioner responsible for Multilingualism, Leonard Orban, a Romanian, ordered EU officials to avoid references to the 'Moldovan language', following a protest from Romania. In December Parlamentul passed legislation prohibiting public servants from holding dual citizenship, with the obvious target being Romanian nationals. Later that month two Romanian diplomats were expelled from Moldova, and throughout 2008 Romanian President Băsescu repeatedly stated that he had no intention of signing a formal treaty on delineation of borders with Moldova.

Relations with the EU and European States

In the 2000s there was a re-alignment in Moldovan foreign policy. As the borders of the EU and North Atlantic Treaty Organization (NATO) changed and extended eastwards in Europe, Moldovan foreign policy orientation moved further westwards. Moldova has increased diplomatic and economic links with the EU and its member states. This policy re-orientation from Russia towards the EU and Europe has been accompanied by a steady increase in public support for EU membership. While Moldovan foreign policy has become more aligned with Europe, economic considerations, especially concerning natural gas imports from Russia, have forced the country to balance competing needs and foreign policies. President Voronin has often spoken of the special relationship between Moldova and Russia, and while short-term factors such as the changes of regime in Georgia, Ukraine and Romania in the mid-2000s can partially explain the change in Moldovan foreign policy, there are more fundamental economic, demographic and sociological changes that account for the changing perspectives on domestic and foreign policy. As Moldovan identity has evolved over the past decade, there has been a noticeable shift in the cultural and the social affiliation of Moldovans.

Prior to the 2005 parliamentary elections, the Moldovan leadership intensified discussions with the EU concerning economic and political co-ordination. Before the elections, the EU and Moldovan Government announced the agreement of an EU-Moldova Action Plan, designed to facilitate the harmonization of Moldovan legislation with EU norms. The Action Plan was signed in February 2005 and extended over a three-year period. Its implementation was designed to encourage Moldova's further integration into a European economic space, as part of the EU's European Neighbourhood Policy.

Following the 2005 legislative elections, in which a PCRM majority was returned to Parlamentul, EU contacts with Moldova intensified. In March 2005 the EU Council appointed Jacobovits de Szeged as its special representative to deal with the Transnistria issue. In order to address the smuggling that occurs on the Transnistrian–Ukrainian border, as well as to encourage the legitimate collection of revenue, Moldova, Ukraine and the EU introduced a border-monitoring mission in October 2005. Initially, seven checkpoints were monitored, and EU customs officials and border guards worked with local officials to inspect shipments. Furthermore, the opening in April 2007 of a Common EU Visa Application Centre in Chişinău was intended to facilitate the visa application process for Moldovans wishing to enter EU member states. Although in 2008 the Moldovan Government continued to make progress in implementing the EU-Moldova Action Plan, several impediments to the integration process emerged in the period preceding the legislative elections in March 2009. Although a number of surveys indicated that the vast majority of Moldovans supported EU membership, the European Commission was not expected to issue a mandate for the initiation of negotiations on an Association Agreement with the EU prior to the elections.

Economy

Dr STEVEN D. ROPER

INTRODUCTION

By late 2008 the Moldovan economy had recovered from a Russian embargo on imports of wine (see below), as well as consecutive poor harvests. Economic growth remained strong, and the Moldovan currency had increased in value against both the US dollar and the common European currency, the euro. By 2008 the IMF predicted the rate of growth in gross domestic product (GDP) in Moldova to be among the highest in Europe. However, these positive economic indicators disguised several problems, including a resurgence in inflation, government indebtedness and an excessive reliance on remittances from workers abroad. Towards the end of the 2000s, Moldova's economy exhibited many of the same strengths and weaknesses as it did throughout the 1990s.

In the mid-1990s Moldova was regarded by international financial organizations such as the World Bank and the IMF as one of the success stories of the former USSR. Owing to its pursuit of a strict monetary policy, the Moldovan currency, the leu, was one of the most stable in the region. Although the country experienced 'hyperinflation' in the early 1990s, the Government was able to reduce annual inflation to 11.8% by 1997. However, in 1998 the collapse of the Russian economy and the loss of Moldova's markets contributed to a 6.5% decline in GDP. Although the Government attempted to enact economic reforms, the economy continued to decline throughout 1999 and, overall, GDP declined by 4.4% in that year. Between September 1998 and September 1999 the leu lost one-half of its value against the US dollar, and the annual rate of inflation increased from 4% in August 1998 to 50% by August 1999. The annual inflation rate for 1999 was 39.3%, which was the highest level recorded over the previous five years.

Although the economic picture was bleak, the Government of Prime Minister Ion Sturza (March–November 1999) undertook several reforms that eventually led to a stronger economy. These reforms were cautiously continued by his successor, Dumitru Braghiş (December 1999–March 2001), and GDP increased by some 1.9% in 2000, while the annual rate of inflation decreased to 31.3%. Despite significant political turmoil in 2001, the economy continued to improve. The rate of GDP growth in that year was a remarkable 6.1% and the rate of inflation continued to decline. By 2002 annual GDP growth had reached its highest recorded level since independence (7.2%) and the annual rate of consumer price inflation was 5.5%. In 2003 GDP continued to grow, by 6.3%, but the rate of inflation increased to 11.8% (far in excess of the government target of 8%). Moldova continued to amass substantial foreign debts, notably for energy supplies. By the end of 2003 total external debt was valued at US $1,700m. The Government remained capable of meeting its external debt obligations, but by 2003 the administration of Vasile Tarlev was unable to offer a reform package that met with the approval of the IMF, and consequently all sovereign lending by international institutions was suspended. Throughout 2004 and 2005 economic conditions did not change substantially: while GDP continued to be robust, inflation remained in double digits (13.1% in 2005). The security provided by remittances from abroad resulted in the failure of the authorities to address several important economic reforms. Finally, in May 2006 the country secured an IMF loan allowing for the resumption of negotiations over debt arrears owed to members of the so-called 'Paris Club' of donors. Debt restructuring was vital, as the trade deficit, a Russian embargo on Moldovan wine imports and a new higher natural gas tariff, in particular, were exerting pressure on the fragile economy. While imports of wine to Russia officially resumed in November 2007, high tariffs for natural gas and rising food prices posed serious problems for the Moldovan economy. Although GDP growth in 2007 and 2008 was among the highest in south-eastern Europe, government indebtedness and inflation (at 12.4% in 2007) remained a concern.

Trade and energy issues are important not only because of Moldova's dependence on Russian markets and energy imports, but also because of the status of the breakaway region known as Transnistria (Transdnestria), which is situated mostly on the 'left' (East) bank of the Nistru (Dnestr) river. Following civil conflict in May 1992 this area remained de facto independent from Moldova (see History). The Moldovan Government conducted negotiations with the Transnistrian leadership from 1992, but several political and economic issues separated the two sides. The inability to collect income (both corporate taxes as well as customs duties) from Transnistria had particularly severe consequences for the Moldovan state, because most light industries and energy facilities in the country were located in that region. Moreover, as the Moldovan Government attempted to negotiate a new, federalized constitution with Transnistria from 2003, one of the major issues of concern was whether the central Government or the local Transnistrian authorities would be responsible for the area's large debt. In addition, it remained unclear whether the Moldovan authorities would recognize the ongoing privatization, conducted by the Transnistrian authorities, of important industries.

In order to end the widespread smuggling of goods on the Transnistrian–Ukrainian border, as well as to provide much-needed income, Moldova, Ukraine and the European Union (EU) introduced a border-monitoring mission in October 2005. Initially, seven checkpoints were monitored, and EU customs officials and border guards worked with local officials to inspect shipments. Securing these checkpoints was an essential requirement if Moldova was to be included in the EU's Autonomous Trade Preference programme, as part of which the country could benefit from asymmetric trade preferences with the EU. At the same time, Moldova resumed the registration of Transnistrian enterprises. By May 2006 approximately 160 Transnistrian economic agents had registered with the Moldovan authorities. In negotiations between the two sides in mid-2008, the Transnistrian authorities recognized that they would be responsible for the large debt owed to Russia, while the Moldovan authorities stressed that previous privatization in Transnistria would be recognized by the central Government. Creating a common economic space between the sides remained a priority of the negotiations.

After the Party of Communists of the Republic of Moldova (PCRM) came to power in 2001, one of its principal economic promises was to reduce economic inequality and alleviate the social crisis that was particularly acute in the late 1990s. By the following year salary arrears to pensioners and other state employees had been paid. However, the lack of new opportunities and the closure of many state-owned enterprises caused the large-scale emigration of Moldovans to neighbouring countries. This illegal emigration was accompanied by the trafficking of women, as well as the 'brain-drain' of skilled workers that has affected many post-communist countries.

Perhaps as a result of privatization efforts, employment in industry decreased sharply in the 1990s. However, industrial employment was not reduced as significantly as that in the agricultural sector. Based on an internationally established definition of unemployment, the World Bank calculated that between 10% and 20% of the labour force was not working at any one time. According to the UN Development Programme (UNDP), at the end of the 1990s 240,000–250,000 individuals were unemployed. Even those who are employed have difficulty sustaining their existence. While the percentage of Moldovans living below the poverty line had improved slightly, to 75% by 2005, the country remained the poorest in Europe and emigration continued unabated. By the end of 2006, according to official statistics, the number of Moldovans working abroad totalled 335,000. The International Organization for Migration estimated the figure at more than 400,000 in 2007. According to a World Bank report, also released in 2007, Moldova (and Tajikistan) had the largest share of remittances as a percentage of GDP world-wide. Remittances accounted for more than 35% of GDP, and continued to increase in 2008.

ECONOMIC POLICY

Currency and Foreign Investment

The Moldovan leu was introduced in November 1993. Before that time the Russian rouble and a Moldovan coupon were the recognized currencies. Once the leu was issued, all Soviet and Russian money issued between 1961 and 1992, and all Moldovan coupons, had to be exchanged for the new currency by December 1993. There were many reasons why Moldova left the so-called 'rouble zone'. First, there was a shortage of roubles in Moldova because of the restrictive early monetary policy of the Central Bank of the Russian Federation. Second, Moldova did not want to be dependent on Russia for monetary policy, since this made it difficult for the Moldovan Government to implement its own domestic stabilization programme. Third, the leu was an obvious sign of sovereignty. For some observers, the naming of the leu was controversial. Romania's currency is also called the leu, and the Moldovan Government's decision to adopt the same name for its own currency was used by certain political parties and authorities in Transnistria as evidence that the national Government was seeking union with Romania.

The law on foreign investment was passed in April 1992. The Government realized that restructuring the economy would require foreign capital. Moreover, the privatization process required certain state-owned enterprises to be purchased with 'hard' (convertible) currency by foreign investors. The foreign investment law recognized various forms of investment: joint enterprise ownership, intellectual property, buildings and other areas of construction. However, initially foreign investors were not allowed to purchase land. In 1992 and 1993 many companies were reluctant to invest in Moldova, because they were concerned that the Transnistrian civil war would spread to other regions, particularly to Gagauz-Yeri, in the south. Therefore, during 1990–92 only 257 enterprises with foreign investment were registered. By 1998 annual foreign direct investment (FDI) had reached almost US $75m., and by 2000 annual foreign investment totalled $125m. In 2001 the privatization of various energy enterprises resulted in the highest level of annual FDI recorded, amounting to approximately $300m. However, in 2002 FDI declined markedly, to only $37m. This reflected concerns expressed by many companies over the worsening business environment in Moldova, particularly after the Spanish company Unión Eléctrica Fenosa (UEF), a strategic investor and owner of three power distribution networks in Moldova, experienced persistent difficulties in its relationship with organs of both central and local government. Unsurprisingly, in 2006 Moldova had the lowest amount of FDI per head in Europe. Although the percentage of FDI had increased throughout the 2000s, its absolute value was insignificant. By 2006 earnings from privatization and the sale of state property had reached nearly $13m. Owing to the more aggressive sale of shares in state-owned enterprises, FDI increased in 2007 and into 2008. However, this greater flow of FDI capital had the unintended consequence of further fuelling inflationary pressures.

Trade and International Organizations

The Moldovan economy has always been orientated towards agriculture, as this is where the country enjoys a comparative advantage over most of the other former Soviet republics. During the Soviet period Moldova was the sixth largest agricultural producer of the 15 union republics and the most productive in relative terms. Commerce with the member states of the CIS accounted for over 70% of Moldovan trade during the 1990s. From 2000 there was a reorientation towards Western markets (non-CIS exports accounted for 49% of export trade in 2005). However, Moldova created a growing trade deficit with the West. For example, in 1997 the Western trade deficit was US $343m., of which $340m. resulted from trade with the EU. Since then trade with the EU has become more active and balanced: in 2005 the EU accounted for 30% of Moldova's total exports in that year, which amounted to $1,104.6m., an increase of 10.8% compared with 2004. In 2005 imports totalled $2,296.1m., an increase of 30.0% compared with the previous year. A proportion of this demand for imports was provided by the high level of financial remittances entering the economy from Moldovans working abroad. Moldova's trade deficit continued to widen in 2006, when it totalled $1,591.5m., compared with $1,191.5m. in 2005. Much of this trade deficit was with Russia, owing not only to the increase in gas imports (the price was raised to $170 per 1,000 cu m), but also to the Russian ban on Moldovan wine imports (as well as some other agricultural produce), which came into effect in March 2006. Wine exports to Russia resumed in late 2007, but the ban and a lack of industrial output had a significant impact on Moldova's trade deficit, which increased to $2,316.0m., as well as on the nature of export relations. Trade with Romania continued to increase after that country's admission to the EU in January 2007, and it subsequently became Moldova's largest export market (owing to the Russian embargo on wine, which contributed to a 50% decline in the value of Moldovan exports to Russia). As a result of a decline in agricultural production, the strengthening of the local currency and rising inflation, the trade deficit with countries such as Russia and Ukraine continued to widen.

Following independence in 1991, economic policy was orientated towards securing Moldova's membership of international economic organizations. Within one year of proclaiming independence, Moldova became a member of the European Bank for Reconstruction and Development (EBRD). In July 1992 the USA granted Moldova most-favoured nation trade status, and in mid-August Moldova joined both the IMF and the World Bank. By 2000 the World Bank had granted Moldova credits worth over US $200m. However, in 1996 the World Bank encountered strong criticism from the Moldovan legislature, when, as part of the terms for the receipt of a Structural Adjustment Loan, the Government was required to increase tariffs for electricity, reduce the budgetary deficit and reform the pensions system. The World Bank and the IMF demanded an increase in the retirement age for men to 65 years (from 60 years) and for women to 60 years (from 55 years). The parliament refused to enact many of these measures, and the PCRM, in particular, protested against raising the retirement age. In 1999 the World Bank suspended the disbursement of further lending until concessions were finally enacted by the legislature in late 2000.

The first use of IMF resources in Moldova occurred in 1993, when the IMF granted a US $19m. credit to defray the cost of cereal imports, under its Compensatory and Contingency Financing Facility. In mid-September Moldova received a further loan of $32m., under the Fund's Systemic Transformation Facility, in order to assist the Government's reform programme. In 1995 the IMF's Executive Board described Moldova's performance under the three-year extended arrangement (1993–95) as highly satisfactory. The IMF was particularly pleased with the ability of the Moldovan Government to reduce inflation and maintain the strength of its currency. In May 1996 the IMF approved a $185m. Extended Fund Facility (EFF). However, after that time the IMF, like the World Bank, encountered opposition to its monetary policies from the parliament. In November 1997 the IMF refused to release the fourth tranche of the EFF, owing to continuing budgetary deficits and the refusal of the legislature to implement pension reform.

Following the general election of March 1998 IMF officials stated that there were grounds for optimism concerning Moldovan economic reform. However, in February 1999, less than one year after taking office, Prime Minister Ion

Ciubuc resigned his post; Sturza was confirmed as his successor in March. Sturza was generally regarded as being far more pro-Western and pro-reform than previous premiers. By August his Government had negotiated a new IMF loan and the release of a tranche of an earlier World Bank loan, but conflict with the then President, Petru Lucinschi, and with parliament prompted Sturza's removal from office in November. After two failed nominations, Braghiş was confirmed as Prime Minister in December. However, by this time Moldova's relationship with the international lending organizations had deteriorated significantly. The IMF had halted lending, and financing was only resumed after commitments from Sturza that the necessary reforms would occur. The removal of Sturza and the failure of parliament to privatize large state-owned enterprises, including those of the tobacco and wine sectors, compelled the IMF to suspend the disbursement of further lending. Credits were subsequently suspended until further concessions by the Government were made in late 2000, when the IMF approved a new, three-year loan. However, disbursement of the third tranche of this loan was also suspended, following the parliamentary elections of February 2001, as the new PCRM-dominated Government of Prime Minister Tarlev refused to abide by the previous IMF and World Bank agreements. Moldova desperately needed the continuing financial support of both organizations in order to repay its foreign debt. Subsequently, following repeated negotiations with the Tarlev Government, both the IMF and the World Bank began to resume limited financing to Moldova in mid-2002, although lending was suspended once again in 2003, leading to a financial moratorium from international creditors. By 2006 the IMF had resumed lending to Moldova (which signed a letter of intent for a Poverty Reduction and Growth Facility—PRGF). In mid-2001 Moldova joined both the World Trade Organization (WTO) and the EU's Stability Pact for South Eastern Europe. Following its accession to the WTO, Moldova substantially reduced the tariffs it levied on many imported goods.

The Budget

As in many former Soviet republics, Moldova's foreign debt continues to rise, placing severe pressure on the budget. By the second quarter of 2008 foreign debt was equivalent to about 75% of GDP, having increased by 30% during 2007 alone. Foreign indebtedness has been a continual problem for successive Governments since the mid-1990s. Budgetary deficits began to be generated in late 1992, and in 1994, as a percentage of GDP, the deficit reached 8.1%. In 1998 Moldova paid more than US $120m. towards debt-servicing, and by 2001 debt-servicing comprised almost 30% of the budget. In 2002 some 75% of the budget was devoted to debt-servicing. By 2002 President Vladimir Voronin, elected in April 2001, acknowledged that unless external debt was restructured, the country would have to default on its repayments. The Government was successful in renegotiating its Eurobonds, and urged the Paris Club of international creditors to renegotiate some $300m. of debt. As a consequence of the prospect of default, rating agencies downgraded the country's foreign liabilities and investment rating. As a result of the significant value of remittances to the country, the Government was able to finance budget expenditure without relying on external lending or defaulting on previous loans.

However, there are a number of reasons why foreign debt and the budgetary deficit have become such intractable problems in Moldova. First, the industrial sector, which, of all the economic sectors, had the greatest potential for generating capital, is inefficient, and, moreover, many of the most productive industries are located in Transnistria. Moldova's industrial sector is superior to its agricultural sector in its capacity for economic production. In fact, in the past, Moldovan industry was responsible for 60%–70% of the country's budgetary revenue. However, owing to the uncertain status of Transnistria, budgetary revenue from industry declined. In the early 2000s almost 25% of industrial production was located in Transnistria, and 87% of Moldova's electricity and all of its large electric machinery output came from that region. However, in 2000 industrial output finally registered an increase, of 2.8%, after years of decline, and in 2004 industrial output contributed approximately 23% of GDP, according to preliminary figures. However, by 2007 there was a significant decline in industrial output in various agro-industrial sectors (including alcoholic beverages and tobacco). Production in the first quarter of 2007 was almost 12% less than that recorded during the same period in 2006. Much of this decline was attributed to the Russian ban on Moldovan wine imports that was implemented in March 2006.

Although the industrial sector is an important source of revenue, the agricultural sector, and especially the agro-industrial sector, are important contributors to the budgetary deficit. Using Soviet-style accounting procedures, agriculture in the early 1990s accounted for 40% of net material product (NMP). An additional 20% (or one-half of the industrial sectoral share of NMP) came from the agro-industrial sector (mainly food-processing). While output from the agricultural sector diminished because of severe floods and droughts in 1993 and 1994 and an extremely harsh winter in 1997, if the figures are analyzed, the evidence indicates that the state collective farms were primarily responsible for the negative performance of agriculture. In 1993 the production level of private farms was almost twice that of 1989. One of the problems with the agro-industrial sector is that the food-processing plants are not located in proximity to the produce. For example, 65% of the agro-industrial capacity for fruits and vegetables is located in the south-east, whereas produce is located in the northern and central regions. This difficulty reflects a significant resource problem throughout the former Soviet republics. None the less, agriculture continues to be an important economic sector. In 2002 the sector accounted for 21% of GDP and for 75% of exports, despite the adverse effects of severe weather problems. The sector contributed some 19.1% of GDP and some 53.4% of exports in 2005. In 2007 agriculture provided 11.6% of GDP. Adverse effects on agricultural production as a result of poor harvests in 2006 and 2007 contributed to problems in this crucial sector.

AGRICULTURAL PRIVATIZATION

The political debate surrounding agricultural privatization was much more controversial in Moldova than that concerning industrial privatization (see below). This is not surprising given the relative political importance of the old-style Soviet farm system and the significance of the agricultural sector. The issue was also more politically sensitive because there was no overwhelming support for agricultural privatization. Although industrial privatization was supported by a large segment of Moldovan society, surveys conducted in 1994 found that only 51% of respondents believed that there should be a programme to allow citizens to become landowners. Owing to the sensitivity surrounding agricultural privatization, a very different approach was used to privatize state farms. Although there were two types of farm during the Soviet era (*sovkhozy* and *kolkhozy*), the actual difference between the farms was minimal. *Sovkhozy* were state farms, in which workers received a monthly wage, and *kolkhozy* were collective farms, in which assets were shared by the collective and members were paid according to the profits generated, together with a minimum living wage. However, the fixed component of income, for those working on a *kolkhoz*, was increased, at the expense of the variable component, so that the difference between the two kinds of farm became nominal. Agricultural assets could be privatized or converted into municipal property. Each year from 1 April, the mayor's office decided which land plots would be transferred to landowners. National patrimonial bonds (see below) could not be used to acquire land; however, employees of collective farms or enterprises residing in rural areas, and veterans of the Second World War or the Transnistrian civil war, could obtain free land. Article 82 of the Land Code entitled all citizens living in a rural area to receive a plot of land near their home; individuals in urban areas could also obtain land plots under certain circumstances. Land privatization involved two components: small-scale privatization, that is the privatization of land near home (domestic land), and large-scale privatization of land for production purposes.

In 1993 the land to be privatized for production purposes was assessed at 1.9m. hectares (ha), or 63% of the total, while 1.1m. ha remained under state control. Once individuals received land from the state, they had two options. They could continue in either type of farm system and use their share of land within the farm as a shareholder, or they could use their plot of land as a private farm (in essence leaving the farm system). One of the problems with leaving the *kolkhozy* was that most fixed assets (such as tractors and trucks) were not physically divided, so those who left the collective farm would no longer have access to these assets. Moreover, owing to the structure of these agro-industrial farms, the incentive structure typical of a Soviet *kolkhoz* remained largely in place.

One of the critical issues surrounding land privatization was the accurate definition of land boundaries. In 1997 the World Bank proposed a US $16m. loan to provide for the first national public register of land for fiscal purposes; however, parliament rejected the draft legislation. Finally, in February 1998 the legislature passed a law that established a system for the registration of property and rights, and this assisted in accelerating the process of land privatization. The programme, known as *pamint*, began in late October and completed its first phase in October 2000; approximately 1m. individuals received land titles under the programme. By 2004 some 71.4% of agricultural land was privately owned, and in 2003 the private sector accounted for some 99% of production.

INDUSTRIAL PRIVATIZATION

The privatization programme in Moldova borrowed heavily from the Czech, Romanian and Russian experiences but was, none the less, uniquely Moldovan. The programme had two major objectives. First, the Government hoped to maximize revenue from the sale of state-owned enterprises, the proceeds of which were distributed to the local and the national government at a ratio of 20:80. Second, the Government wanted privatization to spread ownership widely throughout society. The privatization programme took place in two stages: initially, there was privatization based on national patrimonial bonds and privatization for cash, or indexed savings only. This stage was scheduled to take place between 1993 and 1994, and the second stage was to be conducted in 1995–96 (however, many important state-owned enterprises had yet to be privatized by the early 2000s). Privatization was accomplished through two types of auction. Small and medium-sized state-owned enterprises were sold at regional, open auctions for enterprises valued up to 100,000 lei. These auctions involved enterprises sold almost exclusively for national patrimonial bonds. The second type of auction involved subscriptions for shares. These were national auctions for enterprises valued at over 100,000 lei that took two weeks to complete. The Government had wanted all auctions to be open, but it became clear that this would be impractical for medium-sized and large enterprises and the subscription-for-shares model was adopted instead.

The distribution of national patrimonial bonds began in September 1993 and lasted until mid-September 1995. Bonds were distributed to all citizens born before 15 September 1993, along with a number of coupons, each of which had a different face value. This was unlike the system adopted in the Czech Republic, Romania and Russia, where every bond had the same value. Each Moldovan received a bond based on the number of years worked (including military service, post-graduate studies, higher- and trade-schools, and periods of disability). As a result, pensioners as a group had as much purchasing power as the rest of the population. Those who had never worked, and children, were granted a minimum of five working-years' worth of coupons. The bond itself was not tradeable; shares could only be traded once invested. However, the bond could be transferred without proxy to immediate family members. The stocks purchased with the bond could be sold to both Moldovans and foreigners, and the bond could be used to purchase shares in state commercial enterprises or housing units. Despite the fact that over 90% of Moldovans had received their national patrimonial bonds by 1994, there were problems with the distribution system. The initial problem with the privatization programme was the structure of the bond itself. The fact

that the coupons had arbitrary denominations unrelated to share price increased the number of transactions and made the system unnecessarily complex.

The fact that the bonds were not tradeable was another problem. The international auditors found that this normally resulted in delays before vouchers could be used to buy shares, resulting in frustration on the part of the population. However, the Government felt that freely tradeable vouchers might create a parallel, uncontrolled currency with inflationary consequences. The Government also believed that the poorest members of society would be the first to sell their bonds, depriving those that ultimately needed them most from enjoying ownership rights.

During 1993–94 citizens received 3,646,000 bonds, worth 1,900m. monetary units. The objective at this stage of the process was to privatize 1,500 small, medium-sized and large-scale state-owned enterprises. At 1 February 1994 265 small, and 372 medium-sized and large-scale, enterprises had been privatized. However, most officials did not regard the first stage of privatization as successful; the number of enterprises privatized was far less than had been anticipated, and the process was much slower than expected. In addition, illegal or so-called 'spontaneous' privatization began to occur. In September 1994 the Government announced that the 1993–94 programme target had not been realized.

By the second stage of privatization, the programme had gathered pace. There were 61,400 economic entities registered for privatization at 1 January 1995. As privatization based on national patrimonial bonds did not immediately contribute to the strength of an individual enterprise or the economy, it was felt that many enterprises needed an influx of capital. Therefore, this second stage was based on cash or indexed savings (which, in essence, replaced the bonds after 15 September 1995). The 1995–96 privatization law stated that the objective was to begin mass privatization, in exchange for cash, upon completion of the national patrimonial bond phase. In addition, with effect from 1 January 1995, the value of state-owned enterprises was raised from 100,000 to 200,000 lei for open auctions, and to over 200,000 lei for share subscription auctions. This confirmed the criticism made by individuals that the Government had increased the starting-bid price and supported the claim that the bonds had been devalued.

In 1997 the Ministry of Privatization announced that 77m. lei of state property had been privatized. However, after 85 auctions offering 636 assets, only 90 objects had been privatized. The Russian economic crisis in 1998 further slowed the pace of privatization. None the less, in 1999 approximately 360 enterprises were privatized, for a total of US $34m., although most of the country's strategic companies remained under state control. The rate of privatization increased in 2000–01. In 2000 three of the country's five energy grids were sold to UEF of Spain, for $26m. However, owing to disputes between UEF and the municipal administration of Chişinău, the former was discouraged from purchasing the remaining energy grids (prompting it to consider international arbitration). Moreover, some of the companies that had been privatized were subject to renationalization. For example, the Government sold 49% of its interest in Air Moldova, the national airline company, to a German consortium in mid-2000, only to announce plans for the possible repossession of the shares in 2002. In general, privatization results in 2003–05 were relatively insignificant. While several small companies and two wineries were privatized, the Government proved unable to privatize several larger state enterprises, notably Moldtelecom and two electricity distribution companies. By mid-2006 these same companies had been excluded from the privatization programme submitted to the parliament for approval.

PROSPECTS

By late 2008 Moldova registered one of the highest GDP rates in south-eastern Europe, the IMF projecting GDP growth of 6%–8% for that year. However, this growth further fuelled inflation, which was recorded at 12.4% in 2007. Inflationary pressures, combined with a growing trade deficit and foreign debt, left the country in a vulnerable economic situation. One of the concerns for the monetary authorities remained the country's reliance on remittances. Since 2005 increases in the percentage of remittances had been increasing by between 20% and 40% annually. In 2007 workers transferred over US $1,2000m. in remittances through Moldovan banks (a significant increase compared with 2006). However, these capital flows into the country failed to alleviate the foreign debt problems and further fuelled inflationary pressures.

In 2004 foreign debt represented 76% of GDP, and Moldova's trade deficit widened to US $783m. In the following year foreign debt had risen to in excess of $1,000m. (approximately the same level as in 2000), and the country was spending almost as much money to service the debt as it was on primary education. Without an IMF agreement, Moldova could not negotiate with official creditors via the Paris Club. Therefore, in early 2006 Moldova reached an agreement with the IMF for a new loan. The loan, of $118m., was approved by the IMF in May, allowing the country to resume debt-restructuring negotiations with Paris Club members. However, Moldova took out further loans in 2006, and gross foreign debt increased by over $400m. to reach $2,000m. by the end of that year.

Moldova's resumption of IMF financing was part of a wider policy of closer engagement with Western states and institutions. In February 2005 an EU-Moldova Action Plan was signed, which stipulated a number of requirements necessary before the country could negotiate EU associate membership. While Moldova lagged behind in fulfilling its commitments as part of this plan, there was, none the less, a reorientation towards European markets. Moldovan exports to the EU in 2006 increased by almost 14%, with a significant increase in the volume of trade with EU member states such as Romania and Poland. This trend continued in 2007, with EU countries remaining the major export market for Moldova. However, following the slowing of the world's economy and the strengthening of the leu, there were troubling indications that the trade deficit would only continue to increase. Although GDP levels remained robust, the significant monetary difficulties that the country confronted in 2008 could undermine economic growth.

Statistical Survey

Principal sources (unless otherwise indicated): State Department for Statistics and Sociology, 2028 Chişinău, şos. Hînceşti 53D; tel. (22) 73-37-74; fax (22) 22-61-46; e-mail dass@statistica.md; internet www.statistica.md.

Note: Most of the figures from 1993 onwards exclude the Transnistria (Pridnestrovie) region, which remained outside central government control.

Area and Population

AREA, POPULATION AND DENSITY

Area (sq km)	33,800*
Population (census results)†	
12 January 1989	4,335,360
5–12 October 2004 (preliminary)	
Males	1,632,519
Females	1,755,552
Total	3,388,071
Population (official estimates at 1 January)‡	
2006	3,589,936
2007	3,581,110
2008	3,572,703
Density (per sq km) at January 2008‡	105.7

* 13,050 sq miles.

† Figures refer to the *de jure* population. The *de facto* total at the 1989 census was 4,337,592 (males 2,058,160, females 2,279,432).

‡ Excluding Transnistria.

POPULATION BY ETHNIC GROUP*
(permanent inhabitants, 2004 census)

	Number	%
Moldovan	2,564,849	75.8
Ukrainian	282,406	8.4
Russian	201,218	5.9
Gagauz	147,500	4.4
Romanian	73,276	2.2
Bulgarian	65,662	1.9
Others and unknown	48,421	1.4
Total	**3,383,332**	**100.0**

* According to official declaration of nationality.

ADMINISTRATIVE DIVISIONS
('000, population estimates at 1 January 2008)

Districts (raione)

Anenii Noi . . .	83.1		Nisporeni . . .	67.4
Basarabeasca . .	29.5		Ocniţa	56.8
Briceni	76.6		Orhei	125.9
Cahul	123.8		Rezina . . .	53.2
Cantemir . . .	63.4		Rîşcani	71.3
Călăraşi . . .	79.6		Sîngerei	93.9
Căuşeni . . .	92.9		Soroca	101.5
Cimişlia . . .	62.9		Străşeni . . .	91.5
Criuleni . . .	72.2		Şoldăneşti . . .	44.1
Donduşeni . .	46.4		Ştefan Vodă . .	72.5
Drochia . . .	91.5		Taraclia	44.6
Dubăsari . . .	35.2		Teleneşti . . .	74.9
Edineţ	83.9		Ungheni . . .	117.2
Făleşti	93.6		*Municipalities*	
Floreşti . . .	91.5		Bălţi	148.1
Glodeni . . .	62.9		Chişinău . . .	785.1
			Autonomous	
Hînceşti . . .	123.5		*Territory*	
Ialoveni . . .	98.0		Gagauz-Yeri . .	159.7
Leova	53.9		**Total**	**3,572.7**

Population of Transnistria (Pridnestrovie) (estimated figure obtained as residual from total country population estimates at 1 January 2003): 601,088.

PRINCIPAL TOWNS
(estimated population at 1 January 1996)

Chişinău (capital) .	655,000	Tighina (Bender) .	128,000
Tiraspol	187,000	Râbnita (Rybnitsa) .	62,900
Bălţi	153,500		

2008 (1 January, estimates): Chişinău 663,100; Bălţi 143,200.

BIRTHS, MARRIAGES AND DEATHS

	Registered live births		Registered marriages		Registered deaths	
	Number	Rate (per 1,000)	Number	Rate (per 1,000)	Number	Rate (per 1,000)
2000*	36,939	8.7	21,684	5.1	41,224	9.7
2001	36,448	10.0	21,200†	5.8	40,100†	11.0
2002	35,705	9.9	21,700†	6.0	41,900†	11.6
2003	36,471	10.1	n.a.	6.9	43,079	11.9
2004	38,272	11.3	n.a.	7.0	41,700†	12.3
2005	37,695	10.5	27,187	7.6	44,689	12.4
2006	37,587	10.5	27,128	7.6	43,137	12.0
2007	37,973	10.6	29,213	8.2	43,050	12.0

* Numbers exclude, but rates include, Transnistria.
† Rounded figures.

Sources: partly UN, *Population and Vital Statistics Report*.

Expectation of life (years at birth, WHO estimates): 68.0 (males 63.8; females 72.1) in 2006 (Source: WHO, *World Health Statistics*).

ECONOMICALLY ACTIVE POPULATION
('000 persons aged 15 years and over)

	2004	2005	2006
Agriculture, hunting and forestry	531.9	534.0	421.6
Fishing	1.0	1.5	0.8
Mining and quarrying	0.8	1.8	3.4
Manufacturing	135.4	131.8	134.5
Electricity, gas and water supply	25.6	25.8	23.5
Construction	52.0	51.6	67.3
Wholesale and retail trade; repair of motor vehicles, motorcycles and personal and household goods	159.6	159.9	174.1
Hotels and restaurants	19.1	23.0	21.8
Transport, storage and communications	73.4	71.0	65.3
Financial intermediation	13.6	13.4	15.0
Real estate, renting and business activities	28.9	28.7	31.0
Public administration and defence; compulsory social security	64.1	61.5	71.9
Education	107.9	108.2	120.4
Health and social work	68.7	60.4	61.3
Other community, social and personal service activities	30.3	32.1	36.5
Private households with employed persons	3.3	3.3	4.7
Extra-territorial organizations and bodies	0.4	0.5	1.1
Total employed	1,316.0	1,318.7	1,257.3
Unemployed	116.5	103.7	99.9
Total labour force	1,432.5	1,422.3	1,357.2
Males	701.6	689.5	690.3
Females	731.0	732.9	666.9

Source: ILO.

Health and Welfare

KEY INDICATORS

Total fertility rate (children per woman, 2006)	1.4
Under-5 mortality rate (per 1,000 live births, 2006)	19
HIV/AIDS (% of persons aged 15–49, 2005)	1.1
Physicians (per 1,000 head, 2006)	2.7
Hospital beds (per 1,000 head, 2006)	6.3
Health expenditure (2005): US $ per head (PPP)	170
Health expenditure (2005): % of GDP	7.5
Health expenditure (2005): public (% of total)	55.5
Access to water (% of persons, 2004)	92
Human Development Index (2005): ranking	111
Human Development Index (2005): value	0.708

For sources and definitions, see explanatory note on p. vi.

Agriculture

PRINCIPAL CROPS
('000 metric tons)

	2004	2005	2006
Wheat	861.0	1,056.7	691.4
Barley	268.3	212.0	200.1
Maize	1,794.5	1,492.0	1,322.2
Potatoes	317.7	378.2	377.0
Sugar beet	911.3	991.2	1,177.3
Dry beans	20.3	27.4	26.6
Dry peas	28.9	33.9	33.8
Sunflower seed	335.2	331.1	379.9
Cabbages and other brassicas	40.9	53.2	64.9
Tomatoes	74.2	84.6	104.4
Cucumbers and gherkins	21.3	28.0	38.1
Chillies and green peppers	20.5	32.1	46.0
Aubergines (Eggplants)	4.8	7.2	8.6
Dry onions	42.3	52.3	54.4
Carrots and turnips	15.6	19.3	2.4
Watermelons	54.8	36.8	89.0
Apples	310.1	278.4	202.8
Plums and sloes	55.6	41.4	75.9
Grapes	685.6	518.5	466.1
Tobacco (leaves)	7.9	6.7	4.9

Aggregate production ('000 metric tons, may include official, semi-official or estimated data): Total cereals 2,942.5 in 2004, 2,771.7 in 2005, 2,222.4 in 2006; Total roots and tubers 317.7 in 2004, 378.2 in 2005, 377.0 in 2006; Total vegetables (incl. melons) 372.4 in 2004, 438.1 in 2005, 567.7 in 2006; Total fruits (excl. melons) 1,098.0 in 2004, 891.9 in 2005, 783.7 in 2006.

Source: FAO.

LIVESTOCK
('000 head at 1 January)

	2004	2005	2006
Horses	77.4	72.5	69.1
Cattle	372.8	330.6	310.5
Pigs	445.9	398.0	460.7
Sheep	817.1	822.8	818.3
Goats	120.9	119.4	119.4
Chickens	15,755*	17,522*	22,100

* FAO estimate.

Source: FAO.

LIVESTOCK PRODUCTS
('000 metric tons)

	2004	2005	2006
Cattle meat	16.0	15.6	15.0
Sheep meat	2.6	2.4	2.3
Pig meat	41.3	39.7	48.0
Chicken meat	24.4	28.0	30.9
Cows' milk	604.0	627.1	595.3
Sheep's milk	17.7	21.1	19.9
Goats' milk	6.0	10.4	12.3
Hen eggs	23.4	26.7	26.8
Honey	2.1	2.4	2.7
Wool: greasy	2.0	2.1	2.1*

* FAO estimate.

Source: FAO.

Forestry

ROUNDWOOD REMOVALS
('000 cubic metres, excl. bark)

	1999	2000	2001
Sawlogs, veneer logs and logs for sleepers	3	5	3
Other industrial wood	9	24	24*
Fuel wood	36	30	30*
Total	48	59	57

* FAO estimate.

2002–06: Annual production as in 2001 (FAO estimates).

Source: FAO.

SAWNWOOD PRODUCTION
('000 cubic metres, incl. railway sleepers)

	1998	1999	2000
Coniferous (softwood)	25	—	—
Broadleaved (hardwood) . . .	5	6	5
Total	30	6	5

2001–06: Annual production as in 2000 (FAO estimates).

Source: FAO.

Fishing

(metric tons, live weight)

	2004	2005	2006
Capture	487	531	612
Common carp	128	160	239
Crucian carp	152	170	186
Aquaculture	4,470	4,470*	4,470*
Common carp	1,660	1,660*	1,660*
Grass carp (White amur) . .	21	21*	20*
Silver carp	2,780	2,780*	2,780*
Total catch	4,957	5,001*	5,082*

* FAO estimate.

Source: FAO.

Mining

('000 metric tons)

	2003	2004	2005
Gypsum	116.1	102.5	110.0
Peat*	475	475	475
Sand and gravel*	300.0	300.0	300.0

* Estimated production.

Source: US Geological Survey.

Industry

SELECTED PRODUCTS
('000 metric tons, unless otherwise indicated)

	2002	2003	2004
Vegetable oil	51.7	72.8	85.3
Flour	151.4	116.7	45.3
Raw sugar	165.5*	107.1	112.0
Wine ('000 hectolitres)† . .	1,480	1,900	3,060
Mineral water ('000 hectolitres) .	535	n.a.	n.a.
Soft drinks ('000 hectolitres)† . .	420	600	550
Cigarettes (million)	6,310	7,126	7,300
Carpets ('000 sq m)	2,444	3,537	4,467
Footwear ('000 pairs, excl. rubber)	1,925	2,738	2,877
Cement	279.0	255.4	439.7
Washing machines ('000 units) .	40.1	47.7	53.8
Television receivers ('000 units) .	7.6	10.3	0.5
Electric energy (million kWh) .	1,180	1,046	1,022

* Including production in Transnistria.
† Rounded figures.

Finance

CURRENCY AND EXCHANGE RATES

Monetary Units
    100 bani (singular: ban) = 1 Moldovan leu (plural: lei).

Sterling, Dollar and Euro Equivalents (30 April 2008)
    £1 sterling = 20.397 lei;
    US $1 = 10.371 lei;
    €1 = 16.116 lei;
    1,000 Moldovan lei = £49.03= $96.42 = €62.05.

Average Exchange Rate (Moldovan lei per US$)
    2005   12.600
    2006   13.131
    2007   12.140

Note: The Moldovan leu was introduced (except in Transnistria) on 29 November 1993, replacing the Moldovan rouble at a rate of 1 leu = 1,000 roubles. The Moldovan rouble had been introduced in June 1992, as a temporary coupon currency, and was initially at par with the Russian (formerly Soviet) rouble.

STATE BUDGET
(million lei)*

Revenue†	2006	2007	2008‡
Tax revenue	14,889	18,154	20,020
Taxes on profits	1,079	1,388	418
Taxes on personal incomes .	1,128	1,329	1,294
Value-added tax	6,194	7,587	8,885
Excises	1,071	1,392	1,501
Taxes on international trade .	828	899	1,050
Social Fund contributions . .	3,691	4,350	5,257
Health Fund contributions .	558	841	1,175
Other taxes	342	368	441
Non-tax revenue	1,154	1,627	1,450
Total	16,044	19,781	21,470

Expenditure§	2006	2007	2008‡
Current expenditure	14,312	18,448	20,126
Wages	4,123	4,875	5,517
Goods and services	3,703	4,779	5,357
Health insurance fund . .	1,485	1,895	2,646
Interest payments	455	635	692
Transfers	6,032	8,159	8,510
Other current expenditure . .	—	—	50
Capital expenditure	3,488	3,965	4,387
Total	17,800	22,413	24,513

* Figures refer to a consolidation of the operations of central (republican) and local governments, including the Social Fund.
† Excluding grants received (million lei): 315 in 2006; 919 in 2007; 1,175 in 2007 (preliminary).
‡ Preliminary.
§ Excluding net lending (million lei): –61 in 2006; –60 in 2007; –66 in 2008 (preliminary).

Source: IMF, *Republic of Moldova: 2007 Article IV Consultation and Third Review Under the Three-Year Arrangement Under the Poverty Reduction and Growth Facility - Staff Report; Staff Supplement; Public Information Notice and Press Release on the Executive Board Discussion; and Statement by the Executive Director for the Republic of Moldova* (April 2008).

INTERNATIONAL RESERVES
(US $ million at 31 December)

	2005	2006	2007
IMF special drawing rights . .	0.01	0.19	0.15
Reserve position in IMF . . .	0.01	0.01	0.01
Foreign exchange	597.43	775.28	1,333.53
Total (excl. gold)	597.45	775.48	1,333.68

Source: IMF, *International Financial Statistics*.

MONEY SUPPLY
(million lei at 31 December)

	2005	2006	2007
Currency outside banks . .	4,571.22	5,145.81	6,664.94
Demand deposits at commercial banks	2,760.86	3,122.03	4,258.52
Total money (incl. others) . .	7333.21	8,268.34	10,923.61

Source: IMF, *International Financial Statistics*.

COST OF LIVING
(Consumer Price Index; base: 2000 = 100)

	2005	2006	2007
Food	168.0	183.4	203.4
All items (incl. others) . . .	162.7	183.5	206.2

Source: ILO.

NATIONAL ACCOUNTS
(million lei at current prices, excl. Transnistria)

Expenditure on the Gross Domestic Product

	2005	2006	2007
Government final consumption expenditure	6,674.3	9,612.2	11,277.6
Private final consumption expenditure	34,694.1	41,360.3	48,826.2
Changes in inventories . . .	2,348.5	1,964.6	2,604.1
Gross fixed capital formation . .	9,257.9	12,691.5	17,763.9
Total domestic expenditure .	52,974.8	65,628.6	80,471.8
Exports of goods and services . .	19,264.1	20,254.0	24,176.0
Less Imports of goods and services	34,587.1	41,128.2	51,294.1
GDP in market prices . . .	37,651.9	44,754.4	53,353.7

Gross Domestic Product by Economic Activity

	2005	2006	2007
Agriculture, hunting, forestry and fishing	6,174.9	6,488.8	5,303.7
Industry	7,192.8	8,357.3	10,467.7
Construction	1,257.0	1,776.5	2,575.3
Services	19,005.1	23,609.1	30,037.3
Wholesale and retail trade, and repairs of vehicles and personal and household goods	3,928.6	5,144.8	6,389.4
Transport, storage and communications	4,603.9	5,288.7	6,456.0
Sub-total	32,372.8	38,454.4	45,808.7
Less Financial intermediation services indirectly measured .	756.9	1,116.5	1,503.0
Gross value added in basic prices	31,615.9	37,338.7	44,305.6
Taxes, *less* subsidies, on products and imports	6,036.0	7,415.6	9,048.1
GDP in market prices . . .	37,651.9	44,754.4	53,353.7

Source: National Bank of Moldova.

BALANCE OF PAYMENTS
(US $ million)

	2005	2006	2007
Exports of goods f.o.b.	1,104.6	1,053.0	1,360.7
Imports of goods f.o.b.	–2,296.1	–2,644.4	–3,676.7
Trade balance	–1,191.5	–1,591.5	–2,316.0
Exports of services	398.9	488.6	646.1
Imports of services	–419.7	–484.4	–626.5
Balance on goods and services	–1,212.2	–1,587.2	–2,296.4
Other income received . . .	539.3	605.8	710.0
Other income paid	–129.0	–205.2	–286.6
Balance on goods, services and income	–802.0	–1,186.6	–1,873.0
Current transfers received . .	596.8	854.9	1,206.6
Current transfers paid . . .	–43.2	–60.0	–80.5
Current balance	–248.4	–391.6	–746.9
Capital account (net)	–16.9	–22.8	–8.0
Direct investment abroad . . .	0.2	0.7	–12.0
Direct investment from abroad .	197.4	241.9	459.3
Portfolio investment assets . .	–1.2	–0.2	–0.1
Portfolio investment liabilities .	–5.8	–4.6	–4.5
Financial derivatives assets . .	–1.7	–0.1	–0.5
Financial derivatives liabilities .	0.1	0.3	0.1
Other investment assets . . .	–77.9	–73.2	55.4
Other investment liabilities . .	91.4	153.3	452.8
Net errors and omissions . . .	178.0	105.2	166.5
Overall balance	115.2	8.9	362.2

Source: IMF, *International Financial Statistics*.

External Trade

PRINCIPAL COMMODITIES
(US $ million)

Imports c.i.f.	2005	2006	2007
Vegetable products	65.0	72.8	150.4
Foodstuffs, beverages and tobacco	147.5	179.8	237.9
Mineral products	504.7	663.7	788.4
Mineral fuels, mineral oils and related materials	484.9	649.7	774.8
Chemicals and related products	232.3	223.3	317.7
Plastics, rubber and articles thereof	139.7	168.5	225.0
Plastics	114.2	137.1	178.4
Raw hides, skins, leather and articles thereof	69.6	22.8	27.5
Pulp of wood, paper and paperboard and articles thereof	82.3	75.5	101.4
Textiles and textile articles .	179.9	206.5	249.8
Articles of stone, plaster, cement, ceramic or glass .	67.3	79.9	102.2
Base metals and articles of base metals	160.6	219.4	336.7
Machinery and mechanical appliances	313.0	379.8	544.6
Vehicles and associated transport equipment . . .	130.3	162.4	286.2
Total (incl. others)	2,292.3	2,693.2	3,689.9

Exports f.o.b.	2005	2006	2007
Live animals and animal products	17.2	16.2	13.6
Vegetable products	131.9	136.5	162.9
Edible fruit	61.0	64.6	92.9
Animal or vegetable fats . .	37.8	34.9	55.3
Foodstuffs, beverages and tobacco	396.0	276.4	276.0
Preparations of vegetables or fruits	46.5	42.7	79.5
Mineral products	20.1	27.4	57.1
Raw hides, skins and leather .	71.6	23.6	29.1
Textiles and textile articles .	193.9	228.3	276.3
Articles of apparel and clothing accessories, not knitted . . .	71.9	78.5	96.2
Base metals and articles of base metals	48.7	75.8	110.5
Machinery and mechanical appliances	46.2	53.1	90.7
Total (incl. others)	1,091.3	1,051.6	1,341.8

PRINCIPAL TRADING PARTNERS
(US $ million)

Imports c.i.f.	2005	2006	2007
Belarus	84.3	74.6	118.7
Belgium	30.1	37.0	37.6
Bulgaria	29.0	35.1	50.4
China, People's Repub. . . .	73.9	116.9	202.9
Czech Republic	18.2	32.6	38.2
France	64.4	62.7	94.8
Germany	191.1	214.1	319.4
Hungary	33.8	33.0	46.4
Italy	152.0	196.3	269.3
Kazakhstan	66.8	5.7	11.4
Netherlands	31.0	19.4	41.3
Poland	65.1	73.4	89.1
Romania	257.3	346.0	449.1
Russia	267.8	417.0	498.6
Turkey	93.0	113.8	166.8
Ukraine	479.7	516.5	687.0
USA	40.8	35.9	46.8
Total (incl. others)	2,292.3	2,693.2	3,689.9

Exports f.o.b.	2005	2006	2007
Austria	11.7	13.1	30.8
Belarus	71.2	74.0	82.0
Belgium	14.6	14.1	11.2
France	16.5	23.9	24.8
Germany	47.4	51.9	86.3
Hungary	14.7	14.6	5.1
Italy	133.4	116.9	140.2
Kazakhstan	17.3	24.2	45.5
Poland	25.3	39.2	48.3
Romania	111.7	155.6	211.2
Russia	347.5	182.0	232.7
Slovakia	15.1	22.7	8.9
Turkey	24.7	28.5	32.1
Ukraine	99.9	128.8	167.9
USA	37.5	16.2	15.2
Total (incl. others)	1,091.3	1,051.6	1,341.8

Transport

RAILWAYS
(traffic, incl. Transnistria)

	2002	2003	2004
Passenger journeys (million) . .	5.1	5.3	5.1
Passenger-km (million) . . .	355	352	346
Freight transported (million metric tons)	12.6	14.7	13.3
Freight ton-km (million) . . .	2,748	3,019	3,006

ROAD TRAFFIC
(motor vehicles in use)

	1997	1998	1999
Passenger cars	205,973	222,769	232,278
Buses and coaches	11,169	12,917	13,582
Lorries and vans	56,924	57,404	52,430

2004 (motor vehicles in use): Passenger cars 274,472; Buses and coaches 19,741; Lorries and vans 73,855; Motorcycles and mopeds 15,700.

Source: IRF, *World Road Statistics*.

INLAND WATERWAYS
(traffic, '000 metric tons)

	2002	2003	2004
Freight transported	107.5	120.0	119.7

CIVIL AVIATION
(traffic)

	2002	2003	2004
Passengers carried ('000) . .	240	250	310
Passenger-km (million) . . .	324	304	365
Freight transported ('000 metric tons)	0.9	0.75	0.72
Freight ton-km (million) . . .	1.3	0.9	1.0

Tourism

FOREIGN VISITOR ARRIVALS
(incl. excursionists)

Country of origin	2004	2005	2006
Belarus	1,072	1,161	580
Bulgaria	471	448	295
Germany	632	703	673
Italy	1,019	1,141	663
Netherlands	223	268	199
Poland	428	443	262
Romania	2,350	3,496	2,787
Russia	3,952	3,294	1,353
Turkey	3,521	3,038	3,038
Ukraine	3,173	3,406	1,472
United Kingdom	3,054	365	291
USA	2,494	3,088	4,534
Total (incl. others)	26,045	25,073	14,240

Receipts from tourism (US $ million, incl. passenger transport): 112 in 2004; 138 in 2005; 145 in 2006.

Source: World Tourism Organization.

Communications Media

	2004	2005	2006
Telephones ('000 main lines in use)	863.4	929.4	1,018.1
Mobile cellular telephones ('000 subscribers)	787.0	1,089.8	1,358.2
Personal computers ('000 in use)	112	112	n.a.
Internet users ('000)	406.0	550.0	727.7
Broadband subscribers ('000) . .	2.4	10.4	21.8

Television receivers ('000 in use): 1,300 in 2000.

Radio receivers ('000 in use): 3,220 in 1997.

Book production (including pamphlets): 921 titles (2,779,000 copies) in 1996.

Facsimile machines ('000 in use): 716 in 1999.

Daily newspapers: 4 (average circulation 261,000) in 1996.

Non-daily newspapers: 206 (estimated average circulation 1,350,000) in 1996.

Other periodicals: 76 (average circulation 196,000) in 1994.

Sources: UNESCO, *Statistical Yearbook*; International Telecommunication Union.

Education

(2005/06 unless otherwise indicated)

	Institutions	Teachers	Students
Primary	104	40,877	13,954
Secondary: general .	1,454		505,073
Secondary: vocational . .	78	2,200*	25,005
Higher: colleges .	51	1,898*	27,060
Higher: universities .	35	5,909*	126,132

* 2004/05.

Adult literacy rate (UNESCO estimates): 99.2% (males 99.6%; females 98.9%) in 2007 (Source: UNESCO Institute for Statistics).

Directory

The Constitution

The Constitution of the Republic of Moldova, summarized below, was adopted by the Moldovan Parliament on 28 July 1994 and entered into force on 27 August. In 2000 amendments to the Constitution were enacted, which transformed Moldova into a parliamentary republic. The Constitution was further amended, to recognize the autonomous status of Gagauz-Yeri (Gagauzia) in July 2003.

GENERAL PRINCIPLES

The Republic of Moldova is a sovereign, independent, unitary and indivisible state. The rule of law, the dignity, rights and freedoms of the people, and the development of human personality, justice and political pluralism are guaranteed. The Constitution, the supreme law, upholds democracy and political pluralism, the separation and co-operation of the legislative, executive and judicial powers, respect for international law and treaties, fundamental principles regarding property, free economic initiative and the right to national identity. The national language of the republic is Moldovan and its writing is based on the Latin alphabet, although the right to use other languages spoken within the country is acknowledged.

FUNDAMENTAL RIGHTS, FREEDOMS AND DUTIES

All citizens are equal before the law and are presumed innocent until proven guilty.

The State guarantees the right to life and to the freedoms of movement, conscience, expression, assembly and political association, and the enfranchisement of Moldovan citizens aged over 18 years. Moldovan citizens have the right of access to information and education, of health security, of establishing and joining a trade union, of working and of striking. Obligations of the citizenry include the payment of taxes and the defence of the motherland.

PARLAMENTUL

Parlamentul (The Parliament) is the sole legislative authority of Moldova, comprising 101 members, who are directly elected for a four-year term. The Chairman of Parlamentul is elected by members. Parlamentul's basic powers include: the enactment of laws, the calling of referendums, the approval of state policy, the approval or suspension of international treaties, the election of state officials and the declaration of the states of national emergency, martial law and war.

THE PRESIDENT OF THE REPUBLIC

The President of the Republic is the Head of State and is elected by the legislature for a four-year term. A candidate must be at least 40 years of age, a Moldovan citizen and a speaker of the official language. The candidate must be in good health and must submit the written support of a minimum of 15 parliamentarians. A decision on the holding of a presidential election is taken by parliamentary resolution, and the election must be held no fewer than 45 days before the expiry of the outgoing President's term of office. To be elected President, a candidate must obtain the support of three-fifths of the parliamentary quorum. If necessary, further ballots must then be conducted, contested by the two candidates who received the most votes. The candidate who receives more votes becomes President. The post of President may be held by the same person for not more than two consecutive terms.

The President's main responsibilities include the promulgation of laws, the issue of decrees, the scheduling of referendums, the conclusion of international treaties and the dissolution of Parlamentul. The President is allowed to participate in parliamentary proceedings. The President, after consultation with the parliamentary majority, is responsible for nominating a Prime Minister-designate and a Government. The President may preside over government meetings and may consult the Government on matters of special importance and urgency. On proposals submitted by the Prime Minister, the President may revoke or renominate members of the Government in cases of vacancies or the reallocation of portfolios. The President is Commander-in-Chief of the armed forces.

If the President has committed a criminal or constitutional offence, the votes of two-thirds of the members of Parlamentul are required to remove the President from office; the removal must be confirmed by the Supreme Court of Justice, for a criminal offence, or by a national referendum, for a constitutional offence.

THE COUNCIL OF MINISTERS

The principal organ of executive government is the Council of Ministers, which supervises state policy and public administration of the country. The Council of Ministers is headed by a Prime Minister, who co-ordinates the activities of the Government. The Council of Ministers must resign if Parlamentul votes in favour of a motion of 'no confidence' in the Council.

LOCAL ADMINISTRATION

For administrative purposes, the Republic of Moldova is divided into districts, towns and villages. At village and town level, elected local councils and mayors operate as autonomous administrative authorities. At district level, an elected council co-ordinates the activities of village and town councils.

The area on the left bank of the Dniester (Dnestr or Nistru) river, as well as certain other places in the south of the republic (i.e. Gagauz-Yeri) may be granted special autonomous status, according to special statutory provisions of organic law.

JUDICIAL AUTHORITY

Every citizen has the right to free access to justice. Justice shall be administered by the Supreme Court of Justice, the Court of Appeal, tribunals and courts of law. Judges sitting in the courts of law and the Supreme Court of Justice are appointed by the President following proposals by the Higher Magistrates' Council. They are elected for a five-year term, and subsequently for a 10-year term, after which their term of office expires on reaching the age limit. The Higher Magistrates' Council is composed of 11 magistrates, who are appointed for a five-year term. It is responsible for the appointment, transfer and promotion of judges, as well as disciplinary action against them.

The Prosecutor-General, who is appointed by Parlamentul, exercises control over the enactment of law, as well as defending the legal order and the rights and freedoms of citizens.

THE CONSTITUTIONAL COURT

The Constitutional Court is the sole authority of constitutional judicature in Moldova. It is composed of six judges, who are appointed for a six-year term. The Constitutional Court's powers include: the enforcement of constitutionality in laws, decrees and governmental decisions, as well as international treaties endorsed by the Republic; the confirmation of the results of elections and referendums; the explanation and clarification of the Constitution; and decisions over matters of the constitutionality of parties. The decisions of the Constitutional Court are final and are not subject to appeal.

CONSTITUTIONAL REVISIONS

A revision of the Constitution may be initiated by one of the following: a petition signed by at least 200,000 citizens from at least one-half of the country's districts and municipalities; no less than one-third of the members of Parlamentul; the President of the Republic; the Government. Provisions regarding the sovereignty, independence, unity and neutrality of the State may be revised only by referendum.

The Government

HEAD OF STATE

President: VLADIMIR VORONIN (indirectly elected 4 April 2001; indirectly re-elected 4 April 2005).

COUNCIL OF MINISTERS
(September 2008)

Prime Minister: ZINAIDA GRECIANÎI.

First Deputy Prime Minister and Minister of the Economy and Trade: IGOR DODON.

Deputy Prime Minister: VICTOR STEPANIUC.

Deputy Prime Minister and Minister of Foreign Affairs and European Integration: ANDREI STRĂTAN.

Minister of Local Public Administration: VALENTIN GUZNAC.

Minister of Agriculture and the Food Industry: ANATOLIE GORODENCO.

Minister of Finance: MARIANA DURLESTEANU.

Minister of Information Development: PAVEL BUCEATCHI.

Minister of Transport and Road Management: VASILE URSU.

Minister of Construction and Territorial Development: VLADIMIR BALDOVICI.

Minister of Ecology and Natural Resources: VIOLETA IVANOV.

Minister of Education and Youth: LARISA SAVGA.

Minister of Health: LARISA CATRINICI.

Minister of Social Protection, the Family and Children: GALINA BALMOS.

Minister of Culture and Tourism: ARTUR COZMA.

Minister of Justice: VITALIE PÎRLOG.

Minister of Internal Affairs: VALENTIN MEJINSCHI.

Minister of Defence: VITALIE VRABIE.

Minister of Reintegration: VASILE ŞOVA.

Note: the President of the Moldovan Academy of Sciences, GHEORGHE DUCA, and the Başkan (Governor) of the Autonomous Territory of Gagauz-Yeri (Gagauzia) are also members of the Government. MIHAIL FORMUZAL was elected to the latter position in December 2006.

MINISTRIES

Office of the President: 2073 Chişinău, bd. Ştefan cel Mare 154; tel. (22) 23-47-93; e-mail president@prm.md; internet www .president.md.

Office of the Council of Ministers: 2033 Chişinău, Piaţa Marii Adunări Naţionale 1; tel. (22) 25-01-04; fax (22) 24-26-96; e-mail anteprim@moldova.md; internet www.gov.md.

Ministry of Agriculture and the Food Industry: 2012 Chişinău, bd. Ştefan cel Mare 162; tel. (22) 23-34-27; fax (22) 23-23-68; e-mail adm_maia@moldova.md; internet www.maia.gov.md.

Ministry of Construction and Territorial Development: Chişinău.

Ministry of Culture and Tourism: 2033 Chişinău, Piaţa Marii Adunări Naţionale 1, Of. 326; tel. (22) 22-76-20; fax (22) 23-23-88; e-mail culture@turism.md; internet www.turism.md.

Ministry of Defence: 2021 Chişinău, şos. Hînceşti 84; tel. (22) 25-22-22; fax (22) 23-26-31; e-mail ministru@army.md; internet www .army.md.

Ministry of Ecology and Natural Resources: 2005 Chişinău, str. Cosmonauţilor 9; tel. and fax (22) 21-45-33; e-mail cima@moldova .md; internet www.cim.moldova.md.

Ministry of the Economy and Trade: 2033 Chişinău, Piaţa Marii Adunări Naţionale 1; tel. (22) 23-74-48; fax (22) 23-40-64; e-mail mineconcom@mec.gov.md; internet www.mec.gov.md.

Ministry of Education and Youth: 2033 Chişinău, Piaţa Marii Adunări Naţionale 1; tel. (22) 23-33-48; fax (22) 23-35-15; e-mail consilier@edu.md; internet www.edu.md.

Ministry of Finance: 2005 Chişinău, str. Cosmonauţilor 7; tel. (22) 23-35-75; fax (22) 22-13-07; e-mail protocol@minfin.moldova.md; internet www.minfin.md.

Ministry of Foreign Affairs and European Integration: 2012 Chişinău, str. 31 August 80; tel. (22) 57-82-07; fax (22) 23-23-02; e-mail secdep@mfa.md; internet www.mfa.md.

Ministry of Health: 2009 Chişinău, str. Vasile Alecsandri 2; tel. (22) 72-99-07; fax (22) 73-87-81; e-mail cancelaria@mednet.md; internet www.ms.md.

Ministry of Information Development: Chişinău, str. Puşkin 42; tel. (22) 22-91-23; fax (22) 22-80-20; internet www.mdi.gov.md.

Ministry of Internal Affairs: 2012 Chişinău, bd. Ştefan cel Mare 75; tel. (22) 22-45-47; fax (22) 22-27-43; e-mail mai@mai.md; internet www.mai.md.

Ministry of Justice: 2012 Chişinău, str. 31 August 1989 82; tel. (22) 23-47-95; fax (22) 23-47-97; e-mail secretariat@justice.gov.md; internet www.justice.gov.md.

Ministry of Local Public Administration: 2033 Chişinău, Piaţa Marii Adunări Naţionale 1; tel. (22) 20-01-70; fax (22) 23-89-22; e-mail info@mapl.gov.md; internet www.mapl.gov.md.

Ministry of Reintegration: Chişinău, str. A. Mateevici 109/1; tel. (22) 25-01-46; fax (22) 25-08-72; e-mail reintegrarea@moldova.md; internet www.reintegrarea.gov.md.

Ministry of Social Protection, the Family and Children: 2009 Chişinău, str. Vasile Alecsandri 1; tel. (22) 28-07-92; fax (22) 73-75-72; e-mail secretariat@mpsfc.gov.md; internet www.mpsfc.gov.md.

Ministry of Transport and Road Management: 2012 Chişinău, bd. Ştefan cel Mare 134; tel. (22) 25-11-17; fax (22) 54-65-64; e-mail secretary@mci.gov.md; internet mci.gov.md.

President

The President of the Republic is elected by parliamentary deputies, and is required to receive the support of at least 61 of the 101 members of Parlamentul. VLADIMIR VORONIN was re-elected President on 4 April 2005, receiving 75 votes. His sole opponent, GHEORGHE DUCA, obtained one vote.

Legislature

Parlamentul
(Parliament)

2073 Chişinău, bd. Ştefan cel Mare 105; tel. (22) 23-33-52; fax (22) 23-30-12; e-mail info@parlament.md; internet www.parlament.md.

Chairman: MARIAN LUPU.

General Election, 6 March 2005

Parties and alliances	Votes	%	Seats
Party of Communists of the Republic of Moldova	716,336	45.98	56
Democratic Moldova*	444,377	28.53	34
People's Christian Democratic Party	141,341	9.07	11
Other parties, alliances and independents	255,774	16.42	—
Total	1,557,828	100.00	101

* An electoral bloc, comprising: the Democratic Party of Moldova; the Our Moldova Alliance; and the Social Liberal Party.

Local Government

In January 2003 the Government approved legislation introducing an administrative structure to Moldova similar to that in existence during the late Soviet period. As a result, the republic comprised 33 districts (raione) and two municipalities, Chişinău and Bălţi. (Gagauz-Yeri and Transnistria retained their autonomous status, see below.) In March 2003 legislation was passed by Parliament confirming the direct election of mayors, and abolishing the position of prefect. Local elections were held on 25 May and 8 June. The 1994 Constitution provided for the granting of special autonomous status to the regions of Gagauz-Yeri (Gagauzia) and Transnistria; such status was duly conferred, by a constitutional amendment, to Gagauz-Yeri in 2003, while Transnistria remained outside central government control—see Autonomous Territories. Local elections were conducted on 3 June 2007, with second rounds of voting following on 17 June. Overall, the Party of Communists of the Republic of Moldova secured 334 mayoralties, 465 seats in district and municipal councils, and 4,040 seats in city and village councils, while the Our Moldova Alliance won 157 mayoralties, 220 seats in district and municipal councils, and 1,987 seats in city and village councils.

Bălţi Municipal Council: 3100 Bălţi, str. Independentii 1; tel. (231) 2-31-81; fax (231) 2-23-48; internet www.balti.md; f. 1421; Mayor VASILE PANCIUC.

Chişinău Municipal Council: 2012 Chişinău, bd. Ştefan cel Mare 83; tel. (22) 22-10-02; fax (22) 22-12-89; e-mail primaria@pmc.md; internet www.chisinau.md; f. 1436; Mayor DORIN CHIRTOACĂ.

Election Commission

Comisia Electorală Centrală a Republicii Moldova (Central Electoral Commission of the Republic of Moldova): Chişinău, str. Vasile Alecsandri 119; tel. (22) 25-14-51; fax (22) 25-14-50; e-mail cec@molddata.md; internet www.cec.md; Pres. EUGENIU ŞTIRBU.

Political Organizations

In March 2007 27 political parties were registered with the Ministry of Justice; the following were among the most important.

Agrarian Party of Moldova (APM) (Partidul Agrar din Moldova): Chişinău, str. Teatrului 15; tel. (22) 22-22-74; fax (22) 22-60-50; f. 1991 by moderates from both the Popular Front of Moldova and the Communist Party of Moldova; supports economic and agricultural reform; Chair. ANATOL POPUŞOI.

Centrist Union of Moldova (Uniunea Centristă din Moldova): Chişinău, str. Tricolorului 35; tel. (22) 21-13-26; fax (22) 22-46-71; f. 2000; Chair. MIHAI PETRACHE.

Democratic Party of Moldova (PDM) (Partidul Democrat din Moldova): 2001 Chişinău, str. Tighina 32; tel. (22) 27-82-29; fax (22) 27-82-30; e-mail secretariat@pdm.md; internet www.pdm.md; f. 1997; centrist; fmrly Movement for a Democratic and Prosperous Moldova, name changed in April 2000; contested 2005 legislative elections as mem. of the Democratic Moldova bloc; merged with Social Liberal Party in Feb. 2008; Chair. DUMITRU DIACOV.

Equal Rights (Ravnopravie) Socio-political Movement (RSPMR) (Mişcarea social-politică Ravnopravie'): Chişinău, str. Sarmisegetuza 90/2/201; tel. (22) 27-12-71; f. 1998; Chair. VALERIU CLIMENCO.

Liberal Party (Partidul Liberal): Chişinău, str. Bucureşti 87; tel. (22) 23-26-89; fax (22) 22-80-97; e-mail liberal@pl.md; internet www .pl.md; f. 1993 as Party of Reform; renamed as above 2005; Chair. MIHAI GIMPU; 12,000 mems.

National Liberal Party (Partidul Naţional Liberal): Chişinău, str. Puşkin 62 A; tel. (22) 54-85-27; fax (22) 54-85-28; e-mail vitlaia@ch .moldpac.md; f. 2006 in split from Our Moldova Alliance; Pres. VITALIA PAVLICENCO.

Our Moldova Alliance (AMN) (Alianţa 'Moldova Noastră'): 2012 Chişinău, str. M. Eminescu 68 A; tel. (22) 26-00-07; fax (22) 21-13-94; e-mail alianta@amn.md; internet www.amn.md; f. 2003 by merger of the Alliance of Independents of Moldova, the Liberal Party (which left the Alliance in Dec. 2006), the Social Democratic Alliance of Moldova and the Popular Democratic Party of Moldova; supports Moldova's integration into Europe, a market economy and inter-ethnic harmony; contested 2005 legislative elections as mem. of the Democratic Moldova bloc; Chair. SERAFIM URECHEAN; c. 100,000 mems (2007).

Party of Communists of the Republic of Moldova (PCRM) (Partidul Comuniştilor din Republica Moldova): 2012 Chişinău, str. N. Iorga 11; tel. (22) 23-46-14; fax (22) 23-36-73; e-mail info@pcrm .md; internet www.pcrm.md; fmrly the Communist Party of Moldova (banned Aug. 1991); revived as above April 1994; Chair. VLADIMIR VORONIN.

People's Christian Democratic Party (PPCD) (Partidul Popular Creştin Democrat): 2009 Chişinău, str. N. Iorga 5; tel. (22) 28-25-34; fax (22) 23-86-66; e-mail echipa@ppcd.md; internet www.ppcd.md; f. 1989 as the People's Front of Moldova, renamed 1992, and as above 1999; advocates Moldova's entry into the EU and NATO; Chair. IURIE ROŞCA.

Republican Party of Moldova (PRM) (Partidul Republican din Moldova): Chişinău, str. Cuza-Voda 35/2, ap. 21; tel. and fax (22) 76-94-22; e-mail acurteanma@yahoo.com; f. 1999; Chair. ION CURTEAN.

Social Democratic Party (PSD) (Partidul Social Democrat): 2005 Chişinău, str. Petru Rareş 33/1; tel. (22) 29-64-67; fax (22) 29-03-09; e-mail info@psdm.md; internet www.psdm.md/ro; f. 1990; merged with Party of Social Democracy in Dec. 2007; Leader DUMITRU BRAGHIŞ; Sec.-Gen. EDUARD MUŞUC.

Socialist Party of Moldova (Partidul Socialist din Moldova): Chişinău, str. V. Alecsandri 35 A; tel. (22) 73-12-96; f. 1992; successor to the former Communist Party of Moldova; favours socialist economic and social policies, defends the rights of Russian and other minorities and advocates continued CIS membership; contested 2005 legislative election as mem. of the Fatherland-Motherland (Patria-Rodina) electoral bloc; Pres. VICTOR MOREV.

Parties and organizations in Transnistria include: **Renewal** (Obnovleniye), led by YEVGENII SHEVCHUK; **Transnistrian Communist Party (PKP)** (Pridnestrovskaya Kommunisticheskaya Partiya), led by OLEG KHORZHAN; **Patriotic Party of Transnistria (PPP)** (Patrioticheskaya Partiya Pridnestroviya), led by OLEG SMIRNOV; and **Republic** (Respublica), led by YURII SUKHOV.

Parties and organizations in Gagauz-Yeri include: **Fatherland** (Vatan), led by ANDREI CHESHMEJI; **Gagauz People** (Gagauz Halky), led by KONSTANTIN TAUSHANDJI; and **People's Republican Party**, (Respublika Halk Partiyası), led by, *inter alia*, MIHAIL FORMUZAL.

Diplomatic Representation

EMBASSIES IN MOLDOVA

Austria: 2009 Chişinău, Mateevici 23B; tel. (22) 73-93-70; fax (22) 72-14-11; e-mail chisinau@ada.gv.at.

Azerbaijan: 2012 Chişinău, str. Kogelnichanu 64; tel. (22) 23-22-77; fax (22) 22-75-58; e-mail chisinau@mission.mfa.gov.az; Ambassador ISFENDIYAR VAHABZADEH.

Belarus: 2012 Chişinău, str. Mateevici 35; tel. (22) 23-83-02; fax (22) 23-83-00; e-mail moldova@belembassy.org; internet www .belembassy.org/moldova; Ambassador VASILIY A. SAKOVICH.

Bulgaria: 2012 Chişinău, str. Bucureşti 92; tel. (22) 23-79-83; fax (22) 23-79-78; e-mail ambasada-bulgara@meganet.md; internet www.mfa.bg/kishinev; Ambassador NIKOLAI ILIYEV.

China, People's Republic: 2004 Chişinău, str. Mitropolit Dosoftei 124; tel. (22) 24-85-51; fax (22) 29-59-60; e-mail chinaembassy@mtc .md; internet md.chineseembassy.org; Ambassador SHI LONG-ZHUANG.

Czech Republic: 2005 Chişinău, str. Moara Roşie 23; tel. (22) 29-65-04; fax (22) 29-64-37; e-mail chisinau@embassy.mzv.cz; internet www.mzv.cz/chisinau; Ambassador PETR KYPR.

France: Chişinău, str. Vlaicu Pîrcălab 6; tel. (22) 20-04-00; fax (22) 20-04-01; e-mail amb-fr@cni.md; internet www.ambafrance.md; Ambassador PIERRE ANDRIEU.

Germany: 2012 Chişinău, str. Maria Cibotari 35; tel. (22) 20-06-00; fax (22) 23-46-80; e-mail info@chisinau.diplo.de; internet www .chisinau.diplo.de; Ambassador NIKOLAUS VON DER WENGE GRAF LAMBSDORFF.

Hungary: 2004 Chişinău, bd. Ştefan cel Mare 131; tel. (22) 22-34-04; fax (22) 22-45-13; e-mail hu.emb@cni.md; Ambassador MIHÁLY BAYER.

Lithuania: 2001 Chişinău, str. I. Valilenco 24/1; tel. (22) 54-31-94; fax (22) 23-42-87; e-mail amb.md@urm.lt; Ambassador VYTAUTAS ŽALYS.

Poland: 2019 Chişinău, str. Grenoble 126; tel. (22) 28-59-50; fax (22) 28-90-00; e-mail polemb@mtc.md; internet www.kiszyniow.polemb .net; Ambassador KRZYSZTOF SUPROWICZ.

Romania: Chişinău, str. Bucureşti 66/1; tel. (22) 21-30-37; fax (22) 22-81-29; e-mail ambrom@moldnet.md; internet chisinau.mae.ro; Ambassador FILIP TEODORESCU.

Russia: 2004 Chişinău, bd. Ştefan cel Mare 153; tel. (22) 23-49-43; fax (22) 23-51-07; e-mail domino@mtc.md; internet www.moldova .mid.ru; Ambassador VALERII I. KUZMIN.

Turkey: Chişinău, str. Valeriau Cupcea 60; tel. (22) 50-91-00; fax (22) 22-55-28; e-mail tremb@moldova.md; Ambassador FATMA FIRAT TOPÇUOĞLU.

Ukraine: 2008 Chişinău, bd. Vasile Lupu 17; tel. (22) 58-21-51; fax (22) 58-51-08; e-mail emb_md@mfa.gov.ua; internet www.mfa.gov .ua/moldova; Ambassador SERHIY I. PYROZHKOV.

United Kingdom: 2012 Chişinău, str. N. Iorga 18; tel. (22) 22-59-02; fax (22) 25-18-59; e-mail enquiries.chisinau@fco.gov.uk; internet ukinmoldova.fco.gov.uk/en; Ambassador JOHN BEYER.

USA: 2009 Chişinău, str. Mateevici 103; tel. (22) 40-83-00; fax (22) 23-30-44; e-mail irchisinau@state.gov; internet moldova .usembassy.gov; Ambassador ASIF CHAUDHRY.

Judicial System

Supreme Court of the Republic of Moldova (Curtea Supremă de Justiţie a Republicii Moldova): 2009 Chişinău, str. M. Kogălniceanu 70; tel. and fax (22) 22-15-47; internet www.scjustice.md; Pres. ION MURUIANU.

Constitutional Court of the Republic of Moldova (Curtea Constitutionala a Republicii Moldova): 2004 Chişinău, str. A. Lapuş-neanu 28; tel. (22) 25-37-08; fax (22) 25-37-46; e-mail curtea@ constcourt.md; internet www.constcourt.md; f. 1994; Chair. DUMI-TRU PULBERE.

Prosecutor-General: VALERIU GURBULEA, 2005 Chişinău, str. Mitropolit Bănulescu-Bodoni 26; tel. (22) 22-50-75; fax (22) 21-20-32; internet www.procuratura.md.

Religion

The majority of the inhabitants of Moldova profess Christianity, the largest denomination being the Eastern Orthodox Church. The Gagauz, of Turkic descent, are also adherents of Orthodox Christianity.

CHRISTIANITY

Eastern Orthodox Church

In December 1992 the Patriarch of Moscow and All Russia issued a decree altering the status of the Eparchy of Chişinău and Moldova to that of a Metropolitan See. In 2002 the Government permitted the registration of an Autonomous Metropolitate of Bessarabia. The recognition of the church, an exarchate of the Romanian Orthodox Church, was confirmed by the Supreme Court in late 2004. In late 2007 the Romanian Orthodox Church announced that three dioceses in Moldova, which had been abolished in 1944 following the Soviet occupation of the territory, were to be reactivated.

Metropolitanate of Bessarabia, Archbishop of Chişinău: 2004 Chişinău, str. 31 August 161; e-mail gbadea2006@yahoo.com; internet www.mitropoliabasarabiei.ro; Metropolitan of Bessarabia PETRU (PĂDURARU).

Russian Orthodox Church (Moscow Patriarchate): 2004 Chişinău, str. Bucureşti 119; tel. (22) 23-78-78; e-mail sec@mitropolia .md; internet www.mitropolia.md; 1,520 parishes (2004); Metropolitan of Chişinău and all-Moldova VLADIMIR (KANTARYAN).

Roman Catholic Church

In October 2001 the diocese of Chişinău, covering the whole country, was established. At 31 December 2006 there were an estimated 20,000 Roman Catholics in Moldova.

Bishop of Chişinău: Rt Rev. ANTON COŞA, 2012 Chişinău, str. Mitropolit Dosoftei 85; tel. (22) 22-34-70; fax (22) 22-52-10; e-mail episcopia@starnet.md.

The Press

The publications listed below are in Moldovan, except where otherwise indicated.

PRINCIPAL NEWSPAPERS

Accente Libere: Chişinău, str. Renasterii 22/1, bir. 48; tel. (22) 23-86-28; e-mail accente@rambler.ru; weekly; Editor-in-Chief SERGIU AFANASIU.

Dnestrovskaya Pravda (Dnestr Truth): Tiraspol, str. 25 October 101; tel. and fax (533) 9-46-86; f. 1941; 3 a week; in Russian; Editor TATYANA M. RUDENKO; circ. 7,000.

Ekonomicheskoye Obozreniye (Economic Review): Chişinău, bd. Ştefan cel Mare 180; tel. (22) 24-69-52; fax (22) 24-69-50; e-mail red@ logos.press.md; internet logos.press.md; f. 1990; weekly; in Russian; Editor-in-Chief SERGEI MIŞIN.

Glasul Naţiunii (The Voice of the Nation): Chişinău, str. 31 August 15; tel. and fax (22) 54-31-37; e-mail glasul_natiunii@hotmail.com; 4 a month; Editors VASILE NĂSTASE, EMANUELA JORGA.

GP Flux: Chişinău, str. Corobceanu 17; tel. (22) 23-22-14; fax (22) 24-75-29; e-mail secretar@flux.press.md; internet flux.press.md; daily; Editor-in-Chief IGOR BURCIU.

Jurnal de Chişinău: 2012 Chişinău, str. Puşkin 22/444; tel. (22) 23-40-41; fax (22) 23-42-30; e-mail cotidian@jurnal.md; internet www .jurnal.md; f. 1999; daily; Editor-in-Chief RODICA MAHU; circ. 13,400.

Kishinevskii Obozrevatel (Chişinău Correspondent): Chişinău, bd. Ştefan cel Mare 162/604/7; tel. (22) 21-02-34; fax (22) 21-02-64; e-mail oboz@molodvacc.md; weekly; in Russian; Editor-in-Chief IRINA ASTAKHOVA.

Kishinevskiye Novosti (Chişinău News): Chişinău, str. Puşkin 22; tel. (22) 23-39-18; fax (22) 23-42-40; e-mail kn@kn.md; internet www .kn.md; weekly; in Russian; Editor-in-Chief MAIA FILILOVNA IONKO.

Kommersant Moldovy (Businessman of Moldova): 2012 Chişinău, str. Puşkin 22/601; tel. (22) 23-36-94; fax (22) 23-33-31; e-mail info@ commert.press.md; internet www.km.press.md; weekly; in Russian; also known as *Kommersant Plus*; Editor-in-Chief ARTEM VARENIŢA.

Komsomolskaya Pravda—v Moldove (Young Communist League Truth—in Moldova): Chişinău, str. Vlaicu Pîrcălab 45; tel. (22) 22-96-62; fax (22) 22-12-74; e-mail ser@kp.md; internet www.kp.md; daily; owned by Komsomolskaya Pravda (Basarabia), a subsidiary of Komsomolskaya Pravda (Russia); in Russian; Editor-in-Chief SERGEI CIURICOV.

Moldavskiye Vedomosti (Moldovan Gazette): 2012 Chişinău, str. Bănulescu-Bodoni 21; tel. and fax (22) 23-86-18; e-mail editor@mv .net.md; internet vedomosti.md; f. 1995; weekly; in Russian; Editor-in-Chief DMITRII A. CIUBASENKO; circ. 5,100 (2004).

Moldova Suverană (Sovereign Moldova): 2012 Chişinău, str. Puşkin 22, 3rd Floor; tel. (22) 23-35-38; fax (22) 23-31-96; e-mail cotidian@moldova-suverana.md; internet www.moldova-suverana .md; f. 1924; daily; fmrly organ of the Govt; Editor ION BERLINSCHI; circ. 105,000.

Nezavisimaya Moldova (Independent Moldova): 2012 Chişinău, str. Puşkin 22, 303; tel. (22) 23-36-05; fax (22) 23-31-41; e-mail admin@nm.mldnet.com; internet www.nm.md; f. 1991; daily; fmrly organ of the Govt; Editor IURII TISCENCO; circ. 60,692.

Tinerimya Moldovei/Molodezh Moldovy (Youth of Moldova): Chişinău; f. 1928; 3 a week; editions in Romanian (circ. 12,212) and Russian (circ. 4,274); Editor V. BOTNARU.

Trudovoi Tiraspol (Working Tiraspol): Tiraspol, str. 25 October 101; tel. (533) 3-04-12; f. 1989; in Russian; Editor DIMA KONDRATO-VICH.

Viață Satului (Life of the Village): 2612 Chişinău, str. Puşkin 22, Casa presei, 4th Floor; tel. (22) 23-03-68; f. 1945; weekly; govt publ; Editor V. S. SPINEY.

Vremya (Time): 2068 Chişinău, str. Alecu Russo 1, 166; tel. (22) 44-09-41; fax (22) 44-73-33; e-mail nata@vremea.md; internet www .vremea.net; f. 1999; daily; in Russian; Editor NATALIA UZUN.

PRINCIPAL PERIODICALS

Basarabia (Bessarabia): 2004 Chişinău, str. 31 August 98, 401; tel. (22) 21-05-13; e-mail libr@mnc.md; f. 1931; fmrly *Nistru*; monthly; journal of the Union of Writers of Moldova; fiction; Editor-in-Chief D. MATKOVSKY.

Chipăruş (Peppercorn): 2612 Chişinău, str. Puşkin 22; tel. (22) 23-38-16; f. 1958; fortnightly; satirical; Editor-in-Chief ION VIKOL.

Democratia (Democracy): 2012 Chişinău, str. Puşkin 22, 516–518; tel. (22) 24-32-53; fax (22) 24-35-85; e-mail democratia@cfem.md; internet www.democratia.cfem.md; f. 2001; weekly; political; Editor-in-Chief CORNEL CIUREA.

Femeia Moldovei (Moldovan Woman): 2470 Chişinău, str. 28 June 45; tel. (22) 23-31-64; f. 1951; monthly; popular, for women.

Lanterna Magică (Magic Lantern): Chişinău, str. Puşkin 24, 49; tel. (22) 74-86-43; fax (22) 23-23-88; e-mail lung_ro@yahoo.com; internet www.iatp.md/lanternamagica; f. 1990; publ. by the Ministry of Culture and Tourism; 6 a year; art, culture.

Literatură şi Artă: 2009 Chişinău, str. Sfatul Ţării 2; tel. (22) 23-82-12; fax (22) 23-82-17; e-mail literatura@moldnet.md; f. 1954; weekly; organ of the Union of Writers of Moldova; literary; Editor NICOLAE DABIJA.

Moldova si Lumea (Moldova and the World): 2012 Chişinău, str. Puşkin 22, 510; tel. (22) 23-75-81; fax (22) 23-40-32; f. 1991; monthly; state-owned; international socio-political review; Editor BORIS STRA-TULAT.

Noi (Us): Chişinău; tel. (22) 23-31-91; f. 1930; fmrly Scînteia Leninista (Leninist Sparks); monthly; fiction; for 12-to-18 year-olds; Man. VALERIU VOLONTIR; circ. 5,000.

Politica: 2033 Chişinău, bd. Ştefan cel Mare 105; tel. (22) 23-74-03; fax (22) 23-32-10; e-mail vppm@cni.md; f. 1991; monthly; political issues.

Săptămína (The Week): Chişinău, str. 31 August 107; tel. (22) 22-44-61; fax (22) 21-37-07; e-mail saptamin@mom.mldnet.com; internet www.net.md/saptamina; weekly magazine; Editor-in-Chief VIOREL MIHAIL.

Sud-Est Cultural (South-East Cultural). Chişinău, str. 31 August 78; tel. (22) 23-21-03; fax (22) 76-55-80; e-mail vtazlauanu@dnt.md; internet www.sud-est.md; f. 2004; quarterly; art, culture; Editor-in-Chief VALENTINA TAZLAUANU.

Timpul de Dimineaţa (The Morning Times): Chişinău, str. Mitro-politul Dosoftei 95; tel. (22) 29-40-45; fax (22) 29-24-28; e-mail timpul@mdl.net; internet www.timpul.md; weekly; independent; Editor-in-Chief CONSTANTIN TANASE.

NEWS AGENCIES

AP Flux Press Agency: Chişinău, str. Corobceanu 17; tel. (22) 24-92-72; fax (22) 24-91-51; e-mail flux@cni.md; internet flux.press.md; f. 1995; Dir NADINE GOGU.

BASA-press—Moldovan Information and Advertising Agency: 2012 Chişinău, str. Vasile Alecsandri 72; tel. and fax (22) 22-03-90; e-mail basa@basa.md; internet www.basa.md; f. 1992; independent; co-operates with Mediafax News Agency (Romania); Gen. Dir VALERIU RENITA.

DECA Press Agency: Bălţi, str. M. Viteazul 18, 3rd Floor; tel. (231) 60-744; fax (231) 61-385; e-mail info@deca.md; internet www .deca-press.net; f. 1996; local news; non-profit; Dir VITALIE CAZACU.

InfoMarket.MD (Denimax Grup): Chişinău; tel. (22) 27-76-26; e-mail redactor@infomarket.md; internet www.infomarket.md; on-line business news; Editor ALECSANDRU BURDEINII.

Infotag News Agency: 2014 Chişinău, str. Kogâlniceanu 76; tel. (22) 23-49-30; fax (22) 23-49-33; e-mail office@infotag.md; internet www.infotag.md; f. 1993; leading private news agency; Dir ALEXAN-DRU TANAS.

Interlic News Agency: 2012 Chişinău, str. M. Cibotari 37, bir. 306; tel. and fax (22) 25-16-49; fax (22) 23-20-67; e-mail info@interlic.md; internet www.interlic.md; f. 1995; independent; Dir IVAN SVEAT-CENKO.

Olvia-Press: 3300 Tiraspol, str. Pravda 31; tel. (3022) 8-24-97; fax (3022) 8-20-04; e-mail olvia@idknet.com; internet www.olvia.idknet .com; f. 1992; sole press agency of the 'Transnistrian Moldovan

Republic'; reports political, economic and cultural developments in the region; Editor-in-Chief OLEG A. YELKOV.

Reporter.md: 2012 Chişinău, str. V. Alecsandri 90/1; tel. (22) 81-57-46; fax (22) 21-15-35; e-mail info@reporter.md; internet www .reporter.md; f. 2000 as an online journal; began operating as an independent news agency from 2002.

State Information Agency—Moldpres: 2012 Chişinău, str. Puşkin 22; tel. (22) 23-34-28; fax (22) 23-26-98; e-mail inform@ moldpres.md; internet www.moldpres.md; f. 1940 as ATEM, reorganized 1990 and 1994; Dir VALERIU RENITA.

PRESS ASSOCIATIONS

Association of Independent Press (API): 2012 Chişinău, str. Bucuresti 77; tel. and fax (22) 22-09-96; e-mail api@api.md; internet www.api.md; f. 1997; Pres. ION MITITELU; Exec. Dir PETRU MACOVEI.

Independent Journalism Centre (IJC): 2012 Chişinău, str. Sciusev 53; tel. (22) 21-36-52; fax (22) 22-66-81; e-mail editor@ijc .md; internet www.ijc.md; f. 1994; non-governmental org.

Publishers

Editura Cartea Moldovei: 2004 Chişinău, bd. Ştefan cel Mare 180; tel. (22) 24-65-10; fax (22) 24-64-11; f. 1977; fiction, non-fiction, poetry, art books; Dir DUMITRU FURDUI; Editor-in-Chief RAISA SUVEICA.

Editura Hyperion: 2004 Chişinău, bd. Ştefan cel Mare 180; tel. (22) 24-40-22; f. 1976; fiction, literature, arts; Dir VALERIU MATEI.

Editura Lumina (Light): 2004 Chişinău, bd. Ştefan cel Mare 180; tel. (22) 24-63-95; f. 1966; educational textbooks; Dir VICTOR STRATAN; Editor-in-Chief ANATOL MALEV.

Editura Ştiinţa (Science): 2028 Chişinău, str. Academiei 3; tel. (22) 73-96-16; fax (22) 73-96-27; e-mail prini@stiinta.asm.md; f. 1959; textbooks, encyclopedias, dictionaries, children's books and fiction in various languages; Dir GHEORGHE PRINI.

Broadcasting and Communications

TELECOMMUNICATIONS

Regulatory Authority

National Regulatory Agency in Electronic Communications and Information Technology (ANRCETI) (Agenţia Naţională pentru Reglementare în Comunicaţii Electronice şi Tehnologia Informatiei). 2012 Chişinău, bd. Ştefan cel Mare 134; tel. (22) 25-13-17; fax (22) 22-28-85; internet www.anrceti.md; f. 2000; Dir SERGIU SITNIC.

Service Providers

Eventis: Chişinău, str. Ghioceilor 1; tel. (22) 30-05-67; fax (22) 71-95-85; internet www.eventismobile.md; f. 2007; 51% owned by Eventis Telecom Holdings (Cyprus); mobile cellular telecommunications; Man. Dir IURIE CEBAN.

Moldcell: 2060 Chişinău, str. Belgrad 3; tel. (22) 20-62-06; fax (22) 20-62-07; e-mail moldcell@moldcell.md; internet www.moldcell.md; f. 1999; mobile telecommunications; owned by Fintur Holdings b.v. (Netherlands).

Moldtelecom: 2001 Chişinău, bd. Ştefan cel Mare 10; tel. (22) 57-01-01; fax (22) 57-01-11; e-mail office@moldtelecom.md; internet www .moldtelecom.md; f. 1993; telephone communication and internet service provider; scheduled for partial privatization; Gen. Dir STELA SCOLA.

Orange Moldova: 2071 Chişinău, str. Alba-Iulia 75; tel. (22) 57-50-10; e-mail orange@orange.md; internet www.orange.md; f. 1998 as Voxtel SA; present name adopted 2007; mobile cellular telecommunications; 56.7% owned by France Telecom Mobiles (France), 33.4% by MMT-BIS; Dir.-Gen. BRUNO DUTOIT.

Unité: 2001 Chişinău, bd. Ştefan cel Mare 10; tel. (22); e-mail marketing@unite.md; internet www.unite.md; f. 2007; mobile cellular communications; 100% owned by Moldtelecom.

BROADCASTING

Regulatory Authorities

National Radio Frequencies Centre (Centrul National pentru Frecvente Radio): 2021 Chişinău, str. Drumul Viilor 28/2; tel. (22) 73-53-64; fax (22) 73-39-41; e-mail cnfr@cnfr.md; internet www.mdi.gov .md/main_gis_md; f. 1993; responsible for frequency allocations and monitoring, certification of post and communications equipment and services; Gen. Dir TEODOR CICLICCI.

Radio and Television Co-ordinating Council (Consiliul Coordonator al Audiovizualului): 2012 Chişinău, str. Mihai Eminescu 28; tel. (22) 27-74-70; fax (22) 27-74-71; e-mail office@cca.md; internet www.cca.md; f. 1995; state owned; regulatory and licensing body; Pres. GHEORGHE ION GORINCIOI.

Radio

State Radio and Television Company of Moldova (Teleradio) (Televiziunea de Stat a Republicii Moldova): 2028 Chişinău, str. Miorița 1; tel. (22) 72-10-77; fax (22) 72-33-52; e-mail info@trm.md; internet www.trm.md; f. 1994; Pres. VALENTIN TODERCAN; Exec. Dir (Radio) SERGIU PATOC.

 Radio Moldova: 2028 Chişinău, str. Miorița 1; tel. and fax (22) 72-33-47; e-mail directorzodio@tzm.md; f. 1930; broadcasts in Romanian, Russian, Ukrainian, Gagauz and Yiddish; Exec. Dir GHEORGHIŞENCO VEACESLAV.

Television

State Radio and Television Company of Moldova (Teleradio) (Televiziunea de Stat a Republicii Moldova): 2028 Chişinău, str. Miorița 1; tel. (22) 72-10-77; fax (22) 72-33-52; e-mail info@trm.md; internet www.trm.md; f. 1994; Pres. VALENTIN TODERCAN; Exec. Dir (TV) ADELA RAILEANU.

Finance

(cap. = capital; res = reserves; dep. = deposits; m. = million; brs = branches; amounts in Moldovan lei, unless otherwise stated)

BANKING

The National Bank of Moldova, established in 1991, is independent of the Government (but responsible to Parlamentul) and has the power to regulate monetary policy and the financial system. At February 2006 there were 16 commercial banks in operation.

Central Bank

National Bank of Moldova (Banca Națională a Moldovei): 2006 Chişinău, bd. Renaşterii 7; tel. (22) 40-90-06; fax (22) 22-05-91; e-mail official@bnm.org; internet www.bnm.org; f. 1991; cap. 288.9m., res 711.1m., dep. 3,639.4m. (Dec. 2006); Gov. LEONID TALMACI.

Commercial Banks

Banca de Economii a Moldovei: 2012 Chişinău, str. Columna 115; tel. (22) 21-80-05; fax (22) 21-80-06; e-mail bem@bem.md; internet www.bem.md; f. 1992; cap. 614.5m., res 99.6m., dep. 2,280.7m. (Dec. 2007); Pres. GRIGORE GACIKEVICI; 37 brs.

Banca de Finanțe şi Comerț (FinComBank SA—Finance and Trade Bank JSC): 2012 Chişinău, str. Puşkin 26; tel. (22) 22-74-35; fax (22) 23-73-08; e-mail fincom@fincombank.com; internet www.fincombank.com; f. 1993; cap 179.7m., dep. 854.7m., total assets 1,229.8m. (June 2007); Chair. VICTOR KHVOROSTOVSKY; 13 brs.

Banca Socială: 2005 Chişinău, str. Bănulescu-Bodoni 61; tel. (22) 22-14-94; fax (22) 22-42-30; e-mail office@socbank.md; internet www.socbank.md; f. 1991; jt-stock commercial bank; cap. 57.6m., res 27.5m., dep. 1,005.6m. (Dec. 2005); Pres. VLADIMIR SUETNOV; Chair. VALENTIN CUNEV; 20 brs.

Energbank: 2012 Chişinău, str. Vasile Alecsandri 78; tel. (22) 54-43-77; fax (22) 27-98-55; e-mail office@energbank.com; internet www.energbank.com; f. 1997; cap. 80.0m., dep. 681m., total assets 1,237m. (June 2008); Chair. IURII VASILACHI; 68 brs.

EuroCreditBank: 2001 Chişinău, str. Ismail 33; tel. (22) 50-01-01; fax (22) 54-88-27; e-mail info@ecb.md; internet www.telebank.md; f. 1992; jt-stock co; commercial investment bank; cap. 108.0m., res 8.4m. (March 2007), dep. 64.0m. (June 2008); Pres. AURELIU CINCILEI; 3 brs.

Eximbank: 2004 Chişinău, bd. Ştefan cel Mare şi Sfânt 6; tel. (22) 30-11-02; fax (22) 60-16-11; e-mail info@eximbank.com; internet www.eximbank.com; f. 1994; Gen. Dir MARCEL CHIRCĂ.

Investprivatbank: 2001 Chişinău, str. Şciusev 34; tel. (22) 26-78-03; fax (22) 54-05-10; e-mail ipb@ipb.md; internet www.ipb.md; f. 1994; cap. 123m., res 25m., dep. 1,294m. (Aug. 2008); Chair. IVAN CHIRPALOV; 20 brs.

Mobiasbanca: 2012 Chişinău, bd. Ştefan cel Mare şi Sfânt 81A; tel. and fax (22) 54-19-74; e-mail office@mobiasbanca.md; internet www.mobiasbanca.md; f. 1990; 67.9% owned by Société Générale (France); acquired Bancoop in 2001; commercial bank; cap. 100.0m., res 10.7m., dep. 1,948.1m. (Sept. 2008); Chair. of Bd JEAN-FRANÇOIS MYARD; 11 brs.

Moldindconbank (Moldovan Bank for Industry and Construction): 2012 Chişinău, str. Armeneasca 38; tel. (22) 57-67-82; fax (22) 27-91-95; e-mail info@moldinconbank.com; internet www.moldindconbank

.com; f. 1991; jt-stock commercial bank; cap. 29.4m., res 4.8m., dep. 1,863.1m. (Dec. 2006); Chair. of Bd VALERIAN MIRZAC; 21 brs.

Moldova Agroindbank: 2006 Chişinău, str. Cosmonauților 9; tel. (22) 21-28-28; fax (22) 22-80-58; e-mail aib@maib.md; internet www.maib.md; f. 1991; joint-stock commercial bank; cap. 207.5m., res 31.0m., dep. 3,901.8m. (Dec. 2006); Chair. of Bd VICTOR MICULEȚ; Chair. NATALIA VRABIE; 45 brs.

Unibank: 2012 Chişinău, str. Mitropolit G. Bănulescu-Bodoni 45; tel. (22) 25-38-01; fax (22) 22-05-30; e-mail welcome@unibank.md; internet www.unibank.md; f. 1993; jt-stock commercial bank; cap. 186.1m., res 24.6m., dep. 232.2m. (Jan. 2008); Pres. DUMITRU TUGULSCHI; 5 brs.

Universalbank: 2004 Chişinău, bd. Ştefan cel Mare 180; tel. (22) 26-97-00; fax (22) 26-96-99; e-mail stataru@mail.universalbank.md; internet www.universalbank.md; f. 1994; cap. 86.8m., res 10.0m., dep. 91.5m. (Aug. 2008); Chair. of Bd OKSANA DEMIDEVSCHI; 7 brs.

Victoriabank: 2004 Chişinău, str. 31 August 1989 141; tel. (22) 57-61-00; fax (22) 23-45-33; e-mail office@vb.md; internet www.victoriabank.md; f. 1990; cap. 702.4m., res 170.8m., dep. 2,970.7m. (Aug. 2008); Pres. NATALIA POLITOV-CANGAS; 55 brs.

STOCK EXCHANGE

Moldovan Stock Exchange (Bursa de Valori a Moldovei SA): 2001 Chişinău, bd. Ştefan cel Mare 73; tel. (22) 27-75-94; fax (22) 27-73-56; e-mail dodu@moldse.md; internet www.moldse.md; f. 1994; Chair. Dr CORNELIU DODU.

INSURANCE

In April 2007 there were 32 insurance companies operating in Moldova.

State Inspectorate for the Supervision of Insurance and Non-state Pension Funds (Inspectoratul de Stat pentru Supravegherea Asigurarilor si Fondurilor Nestatale de Pensii—ISSA): 2001 Chişinău, bd. Ştefan cel Mare si Sfânt 124; tel. (22) 27-86-53; e-mail issa@tmg.md; internet www.issa.md; f. 1996; Dir ALEXANDRU MUNTEANU.

Asito: 2005 Chişinău, str. Bănulescu-Bodoni 57/1; tel. (22) 22-62-12; fax (22) 22-11-79; e-mail asito@qbe-asito.com; internet www.qbe-asito.com; f. 1991; 48.3% owned by Moldova Investment Group (United Kingdom); fmrly QBE Asito; Gen. Man. EUGEN SHLOPAK.

Donaris Group: 2012 Chişinău, str. Columna 72; tel. (22) 22-82-33; fax (22) 27-83-94; e-mail office@donaris.md; internet www.donaris .md; life and non-life, insurance and reinsurance.

Moldasig: 2009 Chişinău, str. M. Eminescu 2; tel. (22) 23-81-61; fax (22) 23-83-46; e-mail moldasig@dnt.md; internet www.moldasig.md; f. 2002; 51% owned by Banca de Economii SA, 25% owned by Calea Ferată din Moldova, 24% owned by Poşta Moldovei; 25% market share in Moldova in 2006; Gen. Dir VITALI I. BODYA.

Moldcargo: 2012 Chişinău, str. V. Alecsandri 97; tel. (22) 24-55-67; fax (22) 23-36-70; e-mail office@moldcargo.md; internet www.moldcargo.md; f. 1999; life and non-life; Pres. VLADIMIR FLOREA.

Victoria Asigurari: Chişinău; tel. (22) 22-83-53; fax (22) 22-83-52; e-mail office@victoria-asiguari.md; Dir.-Gen. OCTAVIAN LUNGU.

Trade and Industry

GOVERNMENT AGENCIES

State Department for Privatization (Departamentul Privatizarii al Republicii Moldova): 2012 Chişinău, str. Puşkin 26; tel. (22) 23-43-50; fax (22) 23-43-36; e-mail dep.priv@moldtelecom.md; Dir-Gen. ALEKSANDR BANNICOV.

Moldovan Investment and Export Promotion Organization (MEPO) (Organizația de Atragere a Investițiilor şi Promovare a Exportului din Moldova): 2009 Chişinău, str. Mateevici 65; tel. (22) 27-36-54; fax (22) 22-43-10; e-mail office@miepo.md; internet www.miepo.md; f. 1999; assists enterprises in increasing exports and improving business environment; Dir.-Gen. LILIA RUSSU.

CHAMBER OF COMMERCE

Chamber of Commerce and Industry of the Republic of Moldova (Camera de Comerț şi Industrie a Republicii Moldova): 2012 Chişinău, str. M. Eminescu 28; tel. (22) 22-15-52; fax (22) 24-14-53; e-mail inform@chamber.md; internet www.chamber.md; f. 1969; Chair. GHEORGHE CUCU.

UTILITIES

Regulatory Authority

National Energy Regulatory Agency (ANRE): 2012 Chişinău, str. Columna 90; tel. (22) 54-13-84; fax (22) 22-46-98; e-mail anre@

anre.md; internet www.anre.md; f. 1997; autonomous public institution; Dir ANATOL BURLACOB; Gen. Dir NICOLAE TRIBOI.

Electricity

The sector comprises one transmission company, five distribution companies and four power generation plants.

MoldElectrica IS: 2012 Chişinău, str. V. Alecsandri 78; tel. (22) 22-22-70; fax (22) 25-31-42; e-mail disp@moldelectrica.md; internet www.moldelectrica.md; f. 2000 to assume the transmission and distribution functions of Moldtranselectro; Dir MARC RÎMIŞ.

Red Union Fenosa: 2024 Chişinău, str. A. Doga 4; tel. (22) 43-16-55; fax (22) 43-16-75; e-mail info@ufmoldova.com; internet www .ufmoldova.com; privatized in 2000; wholly owned by Unión Eléctrica Fenosa (Spain); distribution co supplying electricity to Chişinău; Pres. RADU SILVIA.

Gas

MoldovaGaz SA: 2005 Chişinău, str. Albişoara 38; tel. (22) 57-80-02; fax (22) 22-00-02; f. 1999; national gas pipeline and distribution networks; comprises 2 transmission companies and 18 distribution companies; 64% owned by Gazprom (Russia), 35% owned by Govt of Moldova; Gen. Dir GHENADIE ABAŞCHIN (acting).

MAJOR COMPANIES

Electrical Products

Alfa Production Association: 2071 Chişinău, str. Alba Yuliya 75; tel. (22) 75-37-18; fax (22) 74-15-20; e-mail ctc_alfa@mdl.net; f. 1995; household appliances and repairs.

Bender Mechanical Engineering Factory: 2100 Tighina, Bend-erskogo vosstaniya 5; tel. (552) 2-68-43; fax (552) 2-24-73; f. 1972; specialized electronic aviation equipment.

Chişinău Refrigerator Plant: 2036 Chişinău, str. Mesterul Manole 9; tel. (22) 47-34-34; fax (22) 47-16-17; f. 1964; mfrs of refrigerators and freezers; Dir VYACHESLAV S. USATLI; 1,000 employees.

Compecs Factory: Chişinău; tel. (22) 33-36-34; fax (22) 33-36-76; f. 1986; computers, radio-electronic equipment, electronic components, washing machines.

Elcas-Market SRL: 2005 Chişinău, str. P. Rareş 77; tel. (22) 22-00-30; fax (22) 22-04-19; f. 1998; construction materials and home appliances.

Electroapparatura Plant: 3200 Tighina, str. Tiraspol 3; tel. (552) 2-78-40; fax (552) 2-41-17; e-mail elektroapparatura@bendery.md; internet www.elektroapparatura.bendery.md; f. 1959; electrical equipment for cranes, manual drilling machines; 142 employees.

Elektromash SP CJSC: 3300 Tiraspol, str. Sakrieru 1; tel. (533) 7-84-08; fax (533) 7-84-80; e-mail elmash@ao-electromash.ru; internet www.ao-electromash.ru; f. 1959; electric motors, diesel generators, transformers, synchronized electric motors; Gen. Dir FELIX S. KREICHMAN.

Moldovahidromash SA: 2023 Chişinău, str. Mesterul Manole 7; tel. (22) 47-37-68; fax (22) 47-40-69; e-mail mold@hidromas.mldnet .com; internet www.moldhidromash.nm.ru; f. 1953; centrifugal leakproof electric pumps of various types; Chair. MIKHAIL VLAS; 700 employees.

Raut SA: 3101 Bălţi, str. Decebal 13; tel. (231) 2-30-90; fax (231) 2-71-30; e-mail raut99@beltsy.md; internet www.beltsy.md/reut; f. 1944; underwater sonar navigation and research equipment, household appliances, telephones, umbrellas, thermal cabinets; cap. 49.3m. lei, sales 21.5m. lei (2006); Gen. Dir KIABURU EVGENII.

Revel Computers SRL: 2004 Chişinău, bd. Ştefan cel Mare 202, et. 1; tel. (22) 22-13-52; fax (22) 22-23-47; e-mail all@revel-moldova.com; internet www.revel-moldova.com; f. 1994; network equipment, installation and services; Pres. and Dir ALECSANDRU KOPANSKIY.

Semnal Joint-Stock Venture: 2032 Chişinău, str. Zelinschi 11; tel. (22) 52-80-65; fax (22) 55-30-87; radios, home computers, consumer goods.

Sigma SA: 2038 Chişinău, bd. Decebal 99; tel. and fax (22) 76-57-82; e-mail schiotmash@hotbox.ru; f. 1963; plastic casting, radio receivers, power metres; Dir ANDREI NITSOU.

Tiraspol Electrical Equipment Plant Joint-Stock Co: 3300 Tiraspol, str. Ilyin 33; tel. (533) 9-43-59; fax (533) 9-51-87; e-mail info@tez.md; internet www.tez.md; f. 1958; development and manufacturing of automatic switches up to 63 amps; Dir V. NAMASHKO.

Pharmaceuticals

Farmaco SA: 2023 Chişinău, str. Vadul-lui-Voda 2; tel. (22) 47-33-50; fax (22) 47-20-74; e-mail farmaco@ch.moldpac.md; f. 1929; produces pharmaceutical goods; Chief Exec. DORIN UNGUREANU; 400 employees.

Textiles

Floare-Carpet SA: 2062 Chişinău, str. Grădina Botanică 15; tel. (22) 55-80-57; fax (22) 52-20-00; e-mail mk@floare-carpet.md; internet www.floare-carpet.md; f. 1978; mfr of carpets; Gen. Man NICOLAE RABI; 850 employees.

Ionel SA: 2001 Chişinău, str. Bulgară 47; tel. (22) 57-88-11; fax (22) 57-88-00; e-mail partners@ionel.moldnet.md; internet www.ionel-sa .com; f. 1945; woollen and cotton clothing; Gen. Dir AGLAYA OSTROVSKAYA; 2,500 employees.

Pielart SA: 2069 Chişinău, str. Calea Ieşilor 10; tel. (22) 22-13-23; fax (22) 74-03-64; e-mail pielart@dnt.md; internet www.pielart.md; f. 1957; artificial leather, rubber and thermoelastoplastic articles for the textiles, footwear and food industries; Gen. Dir A. BOTNARI.

Vestra: 3200 Tighina, str. Lazo 16; tel. (552) 2-05-03; fax (552) 2-33-60; e-mail secretary@vestra.bendery.md; f. 1944; manufactures clothing for women and children; Man. Dir TAMARA IVANOVA POLOZ; 1,083 employees.

Miscellaneous

Agromashina SA: 2023 Chişinău, str. Uzinelor 21; tel. (22) 47-12-16; fax (22) 47-22-00; f. 1949; machines for cultivation, sowing and processing, for use in horticulture, viniculture, arboriculture and fruit-growing; Gen. Dir STEPAN V. NANI; 150 employees.

Alimentarmash SA: 2044 Chişinău, str. Mesterul Manole 12; tel. (22) 47-43-20; fax (22) 47-13-36; e-mail almash@mdl.net; internet www.almash.net.md; f. 1945; industrial equipment for use in the food-processing industry; scheduled for privatization; Dir-Gen. BEREGOI VICTOR VASILIEVICH; 271 employees (2003).

Chişinău Glass Factory: 2023 Chişinău, str. Transnistria 20; tel. (22) 47-39-06; fax (22) 47-39-26; e-mail moldova@glassf.midnet.com; f. 1970; mfr of glass containers (bottles, jars); sales US $20m. (2000); Dir. A.M. LUŢENCO; 1,140 employees.

Floarea-Soarelui Joint Stock Co: 3101 Bălţi, str. 31 August 6; tel. (231) 22-280; fax (231) 25-414; e-mail florea@beltsy.md; f. 1922; produces sunflower and soya oil and associated products, incl. butter and soap; Pres. VASILIY KIRTOKA; Gen. Dir EMIL BUTU; 611 employees.

Gloden Sugar Refinery: 4900 Glodeni, str. Ştefan cel Mare 48; tel. (249) 2-33-83; fax (249) 2-45-90; f. 1977; processing of sugar beet and raw sugar; sales US $10m. (2001); 850 employees.

Hidropompa SA: 2001 Chişinău, bd. Gagarin 2; tel. (22) 27-02-69; fax (22) 27-03-56; e-mail ovs@hidropompa.company.md; f. 1984; production of submersible pumps; Dir IVAN IVANOVICH MARTYA.

Kirov Litmash Plant: 3300 Tiraspol, str. Sacrieru 2 v; tel. (533) 9-43-61; fax (533) 9-40-97; e-mail info@litmash.com; internet www .litmash.com; f. 1924; injection-moulding machines and equipment; sales US $1.7m. (2000); Gen. Dir STANISLAVSKII VLADIMIR; 600 employees.

Mobila-Grup: 2001 Chişinău, bd. Ştefan cel Mare 69/1; tel. (22) 27-81-01; fax (22) 27-80-52; e-mail info@mobilagrup.md; f. 1992; financing industrial gp; manufactures furniture and paper products; sales US $4.9m. (1999); Pres. NICOLAE DORIN; Gen. Dir PETRU TISHACOV; 2,056 employees.

Moldagrotehnica SA: 3100 Bălţi, str. Industrială 4; tel. (231) 2-01-02; fax (231) 4-61-68; e-mail agroteh@moldagrotehnica.md; internet www.moldagrotehnica.md; f. 1944; agricultural equipment; Dir PETRU T. FRUNZA; 456 employees.

Moldavizolit SATI: 3300 Tiraspol, str. Şevçenko 90; tel. (533) 3-42-28; fax (533) 3-51-33; e-mail moldavizolit@tirastel.md; f. 1960; foil-clad paper-based laminate, insulation plastics; 1,410 employees.

Molddata IS: 2012 Chişinău, str. Armeneasca 37/1; tel. and fax (22) 27-45-15; e-mail info@molddataa.md; internet www.molddata.md; f. 1993; state-owned; service provider, software, registration of domain names, computer technology and training.

Moldimpex: 2018 Chişinău, str. Botanicheskaia 15; tel. (22) 55-70-36; foreign-trade org.; Gen. Dir V. D. VOLODIN.

Moldova Steel Works: 5500 Rîbnita, str. Industrialnaya 1; tel. (555) 3-26-92; fax (555) 4-23-10; e-mail mark@aommz.com; internet www.aommz.com; f. 1985; steel bars and steel wire rods; Gen. Dir ANDREY A. YUDIN.

Moldavcable Plant: 3200 Tighina, str. Industrialnaya 10; tel. (552) 24-337; fax (552) 21-529; e-mail yunis@moldavcable.com; internet www.moldavcable.com; f. 1958; production of enamelled, magnet and lighting wires and power cables; sales US $18m. (2003); Gen. Dir YUNIS T. RAGIMOV; 1,000 employees.

Natur Bravo Joint Stock Co SA: 2004 Chişinău, str. Lapuşneanu 16; tel. (22) 23-29-42; fax (22) 23-39-89; e-mail naturbravo@tmg.md; f. 2002; export of apple juice concentrates, canned fruits and vegetables, tomato paste and jams; sales €10m. (2004); Chair. VLADIMIR ANTOSII.

Pribor Plant: 3215 Tighina, str. 28 Iunie 1; tel. (552) 2-84-63; fax (552) 2-11-76; f. 1971; technological equipment and tools; 600 employees.

Rif-Acvaaparat Research Institute Joint-Stock Company: 3121 Bălți, str. Decebal 9; tel. (231) 21-147; fax (231) 26-441; e-mail rifacva@beltsy.md; f. 1957; navigation equipment for river- and sea-vessels, sonar equipment; Dir Vladimir Bogorad; 179 employees.

Terminal: construction of Danube petroleum terminal in Giurgiulesti; Tirex-petrol owns 41%, Technovax (Greece) 39% and the EBRD 20%.

Tirex-Petrol SA: 2012 Chișinău, str. Columna 90; tel. (22) 23-30-78; fax (22) 24-05-09; f. 1940; joint-stock co; Mabanaft (Germany) won the tender for 82% of state shares in July 2000; a consortium of Romanian companies were also allocated shares in exchange for debt-cancellation; Pres. M. Ciornii.

Topaz Plant: 2004 Chișinău, pl. Dm. Cantemir 1; tel. (22) 50-81-04; fax (22) 74-17-20; e-mail topaz@mtc.md; internet www.topaz.md; f. 1978; injection and press moulds for plastic items, circuit boards and non-standard metal constructions; Gen. Man. Valeriu Butsanu; 650 employees.

Tractor Factory Production Association: 2004 Chișinău, pl. Cantemir 170; tel. (22) 63-29-33; fax (22) 22-24-73; f. 1961; caterpillar tractors, stone-cutting machines, heating equipment.

Vibroapparat: 2001 Chișinău, bd. Gagarin 10; tel. (22) 26-95-15; fax (22) 26-02-83; gas equipment and optics.

Zorile SA: 2069 Chișinău, str. Calea Iesilor 8; tel. (22) 75-86-33; fax (22) 74-08-42; e-mail zorile@starnet.md; f. 1945; manufacturing and sale of footwear; Gen. Dir T. Iacovlenco; 1,400 employees.

TRADE UNIONS

Confederation of Trade Unions of the Republic of Moldova (Confederația Sindecatelor din Republica Moldova): 2012 Chișinău, str. 31 August 129; tel. (22) 23-76-74; fax (22) 23-76-98; e-mail cfsind@cni.md; f. 1990; Pres. Petru Chiriac.

Transport

RAILWAYS

Plans for the reconstruction and upgrading to European gauge of the rail link connecting Chișinău with Iași, Romania, were announced in mid-2002 and resumed in 2005.

Calea Ferată din Moldova: 2012 Chișinău, str. Vlaicu Pîrcălab 48; tel. (22) 25-44-08; fax (22) 22-13-80; internet www.railway.md; f. 1992; total network 1,075 km; Dir.-Gen. Miron Gagauz.

ROADS

In 2000 Moldova's network of roads totalled 12,691 km (86.1% of which was hard-surfaced), including 3,328 km of main roads.

INLAND WATERWAYS

In 1997 the total length of navigable waterways in Moldova was 424 km. The main river ports are located within the separatist territory of Transnistria, at Tighina (Bendery), Râbnița.

CIVIL AVIATION

The refurbishment of Chișinău International Airport was completed in 2000. Moldova has four civilian airports, in Chișinău, Tiraspol, Bălți and Mărculești.

Civil Aviation Administration (Administrația de stat a Aviației Civile): 2026 Chișinău, Aeroportul Chișinău; tel. (22) 52-40-64; fax (22) 52-91-18; e-mail info@caa.md; internet www.caa.md; f. 1993; Dir.-Gen. Valentin Vizant.

Air Moldova (Compania Aeriana Moldova): 2026 Chișinău, bd. Dacia 80/2, Aeroportul Chișinău; tel. (22) 52-55-02; fax (22) 52-60-09; e-mail info@airmoldova.md; internet www.airmoldova.md; f. 1993; wholly state-owned; scheduled and charter passenger and cargo flights to destinations in Europe and the CIS; Dir.-Gen. Vasile Botnari.

Moldavian Airlines: 2026 Chișinău, Aeroportul Chișinău; tel. (22) 52-93-56; fax (22) 52-50-64; e-mail sales@mdv.md; internet www.mdv.md; f. 1994; scheduled flights to Budapest (Hungary) and to Timisoara (Romania); also charter passenger and cargo flights; Pres. and Chief Exec. Nicolae Petrov.

Tourism

There were 14,240 tourist arrivals in 2006; receipts from tourism (including passenger transport) totalled US $145m. in that year.

Department of Tourism Development: 2004 Chișinău, bd. Ștefan cel Mare și Sfânt 180, bir. 901; tel. (22) 21-07-74; fax (22) 23-26-26; e-mail dept@turism.md; internet www.turism.md.

Culture

NATIONAL ORGANIZATION

Ministry of Culture and Tourism: see The Government (Ministries).

CULTURAL HERITAGE

Institute of Ethnography and Folklore: 2012 Chișinău, bd. Ștefan cel Mare 1; tel. (22) 26-45-14; f. 1991; attached to the Academy of Sciences of Moldova; Dir N. A. Demcenco.

National Art Museum of Moldova (Muzeul Național de Arta al Moldovei): 2012 Chișinău, str. 31 August 1989 115; tel. (22) 24-12-30; e-mail art.museum@mail.md; f. 1939; over 36,000 exhibits; incorporates National Museum of Plastic Arts; Dir Tudor Zbarnea.

National Archive of the Republic of Moldova (Arhiva Națională a Republicii Moldova): 2028 Chișinău, str. Gh. Asachi 67B; tel. and fax (22) 72-20-57; e-mail arhiva.nationala@moldova.md.

National Library of the Republic of Moldova: 2012 Chișinău, str. 31 August 1989 78A; tel. (22) 24-04-43; fax (22) 22-14-75; e-mail biblioteca@bnrm.md; internet www.bnrm.md; f. 1832; 3.0m. vols; Dir Alexe A. Rău.

National Museum of Ethnography and Natural History: 2009 Chișinău, str. M. Kogalniceanu 82; tel. (22) 24-40-02; fax (22) 23-88-48; e-mail ursu@etno.museum.dnt.md; f. 1989; 135,000 exhibits; Dir Mihai Ursu.

National Museum of the History of Moldova: 2012 Chișinău, str. 31 August 1989 121A; tel. (22) 24-43-25; fax (22) 24-36-77; e-mail museum@mnc.md; f. 1983; 190,000 exhibits; Dir Nicolae Raileanu.

National Museum of the Plastic Arts (Muzeul Național de Arte Plastice): 2012 Chișinău, str. 31 August 1989 115; tel. (22) 24-53-32; fax (22) 24-13-12; f. 1939.

SPORTING ORGANIZATIONS

Federation of Sport and Tourism of the Republic of Moldova: Chișinău; tel. (22) 44-51-81; e-mail ftsmd@narod.ru; internet www.ftsmd.narod.ru; Pres. Ivan D. Zabunov.

Moldovan Olympic Committee: 2012 Chișinău, str. Pușkin 11; tel. (22) 22-31-83; fax (22) 22-88-21; e-mail president@olympic.md; internet www.olympic.md; f. 1991; Pres. Nicolae Juravschi.

PERFORMING ARTS

Vasile Alecsandri National Theatre: 3121 Bălți, Piața Vasile Alecsandri 1; tel. (231) 2-00-05; f. 1990; Gen. Dir Anatol Recila.

A. Cehov Russian Drama Theatre: 2012 Chișinău, str. Vlaicu Pîrcâlab 75; tel. and fax (22) 22-33-62; f. 1934 in Tiraspol, transferred to Chișinău 1940; plays and concerts; Dir Vladimir Yuza.

Eugene Ionesco Theatre: 2012 Chișinău, str. Sfatul Tarii 18; tel. (22) 23-36-71; fax (22) 23-38-33; e-mail teatrul.ionesco@starnet.md; internet www.tei.md; f. 1991; organizes biennale International Theatre Festival; Artistic Dir Petru Vutcărău.

M. Eminescu National Theatre: 2012 Chișinău, bd. Ștefan cel Mare 79; tel. (22) 22-64-27; fax (22) 22-27-93; e-mail tnme@eminescu.md; internet www.eminescu.md; Dir-Gen. Ion Grosu.

Licurici Puppet Theatre (Teatrul republican de papusi 'Licurici'): 2012 Chișinău, str. Bucuresti 68; tel. (22) 24-47-25; fax (22) 24-30-46; e-mail director@licurici.md; internet www.licurici.md; f. 1945; Artistic Dir Titus Jucov.

Moldova National Philharmonic (Filarmonică Națională 'Serghei Lunchevici'): 2012 Chișinău, str. Metropolit Varlaam 78; tel. (22) 22-61-91; fax (22) 22-82-93; e-mail simphony@moldovacc.md; f. 1940; Gen. Man. Svetlana Bivol; Art. Dir Marian Stircea.

National Theatre of Opera and Ballet (Teatrul Național de Operă și Balet RM): 2012 Chișinău, bd. Ștefan cel Mare 152; tel. (22) 24-51-04; e-mail info@nationalopera.md; internet www.nationalopera.md.

ASSOCIATIONS

Nistru (Dniester) Writers' Union (Uniunea Scriitorilor Nistru/Dnestr): f. 2003; publishes *Nistru* in Moldovan and Russian; Chair. Nikolai Savostin.

PEN Centre of Moldova: 2068 Chișinău, bd. Ștefan cel Mare 134, POB 231; tel. (22) 44-35-40; e-mail contrafort@moldnet.md; f. 1991; Pres. Vitalie Ciobanu; 25 mems.

Theatrical Union of Moldova (Uniunea Teatrala din Moldova): 2012 Chişinău, str. A. Puşkin 24; tel. (22) 22-41-38; fax (22) 21-20-98; e-mail unitem@mail.ru; f. 1958.

Union of Cineasts of Moldova (Uniunea Cineaştilor din Moldova): Chişinău, str. Alexandru cel Bun 18; tel. (22) 54-52-12; fax (22) 54-11-46; f. 1962.

Union of Composers and Musicologists of Moldova (Uniunea Compozitorilor şi Muzicologilor din Moldova): 2004 Chişinău, str. 31 August 1989 153; tel. (22) 23-53-48; fax (22) 23-49-22; e-mail moldcomposers@mail.md; f. 1940.

Union of Musicians of Moldova (Uniunea Muzicienilor din Moldova): 2012 Chişinău, str. A. Puşkin 24/19/20; tel. (22) 24-34-43; fax (22) 21-23-90; f. 1991.

Union of Plastic Artists of Moldova (Uniunea Artistilor Plastici din Moldova): 2009 Chişinău, str. A. Mateevici 50; tel. (22) 24-50-24; fax (22) 22-75-04; f. 1903.

Union of Writers of Moldova (Uniunea Scriitorilor din Moldova): 2004 Chişinău, str. 31 August 1989, 98; tel. (22) 23-71-18; f. 1920.

Education

Until the late 1980s the system of education was an integral part of the Soviet system, with most education in the Russian language. In 1990 and 1991 there were extensive changes to the education system, with Romanian literature and history added to the curriculum. Many Russian-language schools were closed in the early 1990s. Primary education begins at seven years of age and lasts for four years. Secondary education, beginning at 11, lasts for a maximum of seven years, comprising a first cycle of five years and a second of two years. In 2005/06 total enrolment at primary schools included 87.8% (males 87.8%, females 87.7%) of children in the relevant age-group, while the comparable figure for secondary schools was 81.3% (males 79.7%, females 83.1%). In that year 74.9% of those enrolled in primary and secondary schools were taught in Moldovan and 20.4% in Russian. In the same year 544,032 students were enrolled at Moldova's 104 primary and 1,532 secondary (1,454 general; 78 vocational) schools, while 153,192 students were enrolled at one of the 86 higher education institutions. In 2004 general government expenditure on education amounted to 1,689m. lei (equivalent to 15.1% of GDP).

UNIVERSITIES

Alecu Russo State University of Bălţi: 3121 Bălţi, str. Puşkin 38; tel. (231) 2-30-66; fax (231) 2-30-39; e-mail rectorat@usb.md; internet www.usb.md; f. 1945; 8 faculties; 410 teachers; 10,300 students; Rector EUGENIU PLOHOTNIUC.

Moldova State University: 2009 Chişinău, str. A. Mateevici 60; tel. (22) 57-74-01; fax (22) 24-42-48; e-mail gaugash@usm.md; internet www.usm.md; languages of instruction: Romanian and Russian; f. 1946; 13 faculties; 1,164 teachers; 16,200 students; Rector GHEORGHE CIOCANU.

N. Testemiţeanu State Medical and Pharmaceutical University: 2004 Chişinău, bd. Ştefan cel Mare şi Sfânt 165; tel. (22) 24-34-08; fax (22) 24-34-44; e-mail rector@usmf.md; internet www.usmf.md; f. 1945; 5 faculties; 1,000 teachers; 5,500 students; Vice Rector NICOLAE EŞANU.

State University of Tiraspol: 2069 Chişinău, str. G. Iablocichin 5; tel. (22) 75-49-24; e-mail scs_ust@moldova.cc; f. 1930; moved from Tiraspol to present location in 1992, due to civil unrest; 3,140 students; Rector MITROFAN CIOBAN.

Technical University of Moldova: 2004 Chişinău, bd. Ştefan cel Mare 168; tel. (22) 24-92-05; fax (22) 24-90-28; e-mail amariei@mail .utm.md; internet www.utm.md; languages of instruction: Moldovan and Russian; f. 1964; 9 faculties; 750 teachers; 17,000 students; Rector Dr S. ION BOSTAN.

Social Welfare

The health and social security systems provided a comprehensive service. In 1991 a Social Fund was established in order to dispense a system of social benefits, including family benefits and allowances, pensions and social insurance. Social security provided allowances for families, especially those with low incomes, pensioners and invalids. Women aged 55 who have worked for at least 20 years, and men who are 60 and who have worked for at least 25 years, were eligible for a pension. In January 2005 an estimated 620,700 people were in receipt of pensions, 73.5% of these were old-age pensioners. Social Fund outlay accounted for 2,769m. lei, 24.8% of total government expenditure in 2004.

In 2006 there were 63 hospital beds and 27 doctors per 10,000 persons. In 2008 general government expenditure on the Health Fund was 2,646m. lei (10.8% of total expenditure).

GOVERNMENT AGENCIES

Ministry of Health: see The Government (Ministries).

Ministry of Social Protection, the Family and Children: see The Government (Ministries).

National Office of Social Insurance (Casa Nationala de Asigurari Sociale a Republicii Moldova): 2028 Chişinău, str. Gh. Tudor 3; tel. (22) 72-57-97; fax (22) 73-51-81; e-mail natalia.vlas@cnas.gov.md; internet www.cnas.md; f. 2001; comprises Dept of the State Social Insurance Budget, Dept of Pensions and Allowances and Dept of Medical Examinations; statement and payment of pensions and allowances; registration and collection of contributions to social insurance; Pres. MARIA BORTA.

HEALTH AND WELFARE ORGANIZATIONS

Caritas Moldova: 2004 Chişinău, Str. Sf. Andrei 7; tel. (22) 29-31-56; fax (22) 29-31-49; e-mail secretariat@caritas.md; internet www .caritas.md; Roman Catholic welfare org.; Pres. Fr ALFRED WEISS; Sec.-Gen. OTILIA SIRBU.

Charity Centre for Refugees: tel. (22) 74-57-51; fax (22) 74-57-98; e-mail ccr@mdl.net; f. 1999; with the support of the United Nations High Commission for Refugees.

Clipa Siderala Charitable Children's Foundation: 2068 Chişinău, str. Dimo 17/4; tel. (22) 43-04-30; fax (22) 43-30-00; e-mail info@clipa.md; internet www.clipa.md; f. 1996; support and integration of orphans; Pres. SALAVAT JDANOV.

Moldovan Charity and Health Fund: 2012 Chişinău, str. Vasile Alecsandri 1; tel. (22) 72-96-89; fax (22) 73-53-22; f. 1988; provides social, moral, medical and material assistance for pensioners, invalids, families with many children and other needy people; Pres. ION P. CUZUIOC.

National Society of Invalids: 2009 Chişinău, str. Hînceşti 1; tel. (22) 73-57-31; fax (22) 73-57-51; Pres. VASILE NECULCE.

Organization of the Red Cross in Moldova: 277028 Chişinău, str. Asachi 67A; tel. (22) 72-96-44; fax (22) 72-97-00; e-mail moldredcross@mdtc.md; f. 1924; Pres. LARISA N. BYRCA.

The Environment

GOVERNMENT ORGANIZATIONS

Ministry of Ecology and Natural Resources: see The Government (Ministries).

Environment Protection Information Centre (Centrul Informaţional de Mediu): 2005 Chişinău, str. Cosmonautilor 9, etaj 6, cam. 602; tel. and fax (22) 21-45-33; e-mail cim@moldova.md; internet www.cim.moldova.md; f. 2001; created with the support of the Danish Environment Protection Agency.

AS Moldsilva (State Agency for Silviculture): 2001 Chişinău, str. Ştefan cel Mare 124; tel. (22) 27-23-06; fax (22) 27-73-45; e-mail msilva@mtc.md; internet moldsilva.gov.md; manages national forests; Dir ANATOLIE POPUŞOI.

ACADEMIC INSTITUTES

Academy of Sciences of Moldova: 2001 Chişinău, bd. Ştefan cel Mare 1; tel. (22) 27-14-78; fax (22) 54-28-23; e-mail consiliu@asm.md; internet www.asm.md; f. 1946; Pres. GHEORGHE DUCA; attached institutes incl.:

> **Commission on Nature Conservation:** 2612 Chişinău, bd. Ştefan cel Mare 1; tel. (22) 26-14-78; fax (22) 22-33-48; e-mail presidiu@academy.moldova.su; attached to the Presidium of the Academy; Chair. S. I. TOMA.

> **Institute of Botany:** 2002 Chişinău, str. Pădurii 18, Botanical Garden; tel. (22) 55-04-43; fax (22) 52-38-98; e-mail grbot@moldova .md; f. 1950; over 10,000 species of plant; Dir Dr ALECSANDRU TELEUTA.

> **Institute of Ecology and Geography:** 2028 Chişinău, str. Academiei 1; tel. and fax (22) 73-98-38; e-mail const@asm.md; Exec. Dir TATIANA CONSTANTINOV.

> **Republic of Moldova Committee on the UNESCO 'Man and the Biosphere' Programme:** 2002 Chişinău, str. Pădurii 18, Botanical Gardens (Institute); tel. (22) 24-75-93; e-mail unesco@ moldova.md; works to create a world network of biosphere reserves; attached to the Presidium of the Academy; Chair. Prof. ION TODERAS.

> **Research Institute for Plant Protection and Agricultural Ecology:** 2060 Chişinău, bd. Dacia 58; tel. (22) 77-04-66; fax (22) 77-96-41; e-mail slipbp@cc.acad.md; f. 1969; Dir LEONID VOLOSCIUC.

NON-GOVERNMENTAL ORGANIZATIONS

BIOTICA Ecological Society: 2068, Chişinău, str. Nicolae Dimo 17/4, of. 22; tel. and fax (22) 24-32-74; e-mail biotica@biotica-moldova .org; internet www.biotica-moldova.org; f. 1993; environmental law, biodiversity conservation and environmental education, development of civil society; Bd ALECSEI ANDREEV, PIOTR GORBUNENKO, ILYA TROMBITSKY.

Ecological Movement of Moldova (EMM) (Mişcarea Ecologistă din Moldova): 2004 Chişinău, str. Serghei Lazo 13; tel. (22) 23-71-57; fax (22) 23-24-08; e-mail mem@mem.md; internet www.mem.md; f. 1990; nat. green movement; environmental education and legislation development; mem. of the World Conservation Union for Nature; founded Natura newspaper; Pres. ALECU RENIŢA; 17 brs.

Ecosfera (Asociatia de Informare si Educatie Ecologica): 2028 Chişinău, str. Schinoasa Deal 78/4; tel. (22) 32-30-42; fax (22) 22-27-71; e-mail ecosfera@mail.md; internet ecosfera.ournet.md; f. 1997; produces electronic magazine; also includes the Young Ecologists' Club; Contact CORNELIU MARZA.

Eco-Tiras (International Environmental Association of River Keepers): 2012 Chişinău, str. Teatrala 11A; tel. (22) 55-09-53; fax (22) 22-56-15; e-mail ecotiras@mtc.md; internet www.eco-tiras.org; f. 1999; regd Nistru (Dniester) River transboundary basin asscn of NGOs involved in the promotion of integrated management of the river basin and inter-state water co-operation; active also in the promotion of environmental security, public participation and conflict resolution; 50 mems; Exec. Dir ILYA TROMBITSKY.

Grupul Fauna: 2004 Chişinău, POB 409; tel. (22) 57-78-09; e-mail gfauna@excite.com; f. 1994; research, conservation and education in biodiversity; non-profit ecological org.; Pres. SERGIU ANDREEV.

Moldovan Society of Animal Protection: Chişinău, str. Serghei Lazo 17/6; tel. (22) 24-75-99; environmental education, co-operates with government agencies and NGOs with interests in animal welfare and the environment; Pres. Prof. P. I. NESTEROV.

Regional Environmental Centre—Moldova (REC-Moldova): 2005 Chişinău, str. Bănulescu-Bodoni 57/1, bir. 107; tel. (22) 23-86-85; fax (22) 23-86-86; e-mail info@rec.md; internet www.rec.md; f. 1998; independent, international, non-commercial, non-political org.; Chair. ARCADIE CAPCELEA.

SalvaEco: 2032 Chişinău, str. Vasile Lupu 33; tel. (22) 58-20-40; fax (22) 22-77-71; e-mail salvaeco@salvaeco.org; internet www.salvaeco .org; f. 1999; independent, non-profit ecological org.; Pres. NICU ARHIP.

Defence

Following independence from the USSR (declared in August 1991), the Moldovan Government initiated the creation of national armed forces. As assessed at November 2007, these numbered 6,750, including an army of 5,150 (including conscripts) and an air force of 850. There are paramilitary forces attached to the Ministry of the Interior, numbering 3,279. Following a military reform plan, launched in 2002, the length of compulsory military service was reduced from 18 to 12 months (graduates of higher education were to serve only three months). In 2003 proposals were announced to convert Moldova's only military airbase, in Mărculeşti, into a civilian airport.

Under an agreement concluded by the Moldovan and Russian Governments in late 1994, the former Soviet 14th Army (under Russian jurisdiction) was to have been withdrawn from the separatist Transnistria region within three years, but in March 1998 it was agreed that Russian forces would remain in Transnistria until a political settlement for the region was reached. Despite subsequent agreements providing for a withdrawal, Russian troops, numbering some 1,200, remained in Transnistria in 2008. In early 1994 Moldova joined NATO's 'Partnership for Peace' programme of military co-operation. According to an Individual Partnership Action Plan agreed with that organization in 2006, Moldova was to have transformed its armed forces to NATO standards by 2010 (albeit that the country's constitution guarantees a neutral status). In 2007 the budget allocated 194m. lei to defence.

Chief of General Staff and Commander of the National Army: Brig.-Gen. ION COROPCEAN.

AUTONOMOUS TERRITORIES

The territory of Transnistria (Transdniestr, Pridnestrovie), which is dominated by ethnic Russians and Ukrainians, does not acknowledge the authority of the central Moldovan Government, while Gagauz-Yeri (Gaugazia), dominated by ethnic Gagauz (Turkic Orthodox Christians), has autonomous status.

AUTONOMOUS TERRITORY OF GAGAUZ-YERI

Following the dissolution of the USSR, five districts (not all of which were contiguous) in southern Moldova dominated by the Gagauz (Turkic Christians) declared a 'Gagauz Soviet Socialist Republic' ('Gagauz-Yeri' or 'Gagauzia'), based in Comrat (Komrat), and the central Moldovan authorities lost de facto control over the region. Parliamentary elections to a 'Supreme Soviet' were conducted in October 2000. In December Stepan Topol, hitherto Chairman of the regional 'Supreme Soviet', was elected to a newly created position, President of Gagauz-Yeri, remaining in this position until the abolition of the presidency in 1995. The separatist authorities, like those in Transnistria, were sympathetic to the restoration of the USSR, and supported the attempted *putsch* by conservative communists in Moscow, the Russian and Soviet capital, in August 1991. However, following the outbreak of civil war in Transnistria, and the subsequent election of a less nationalist Government in Moldova, the Gagauz authorities demonstrated greater willingness to seek a compromise concerning the status of the region than those in Transnistria. (It should be noted, however, that Russian troops, who were widely regarded to be broadly supportive of the separatists, were based in Transnistria, whereas the Gagauz separatists lacked any overt support from any external source.) The new Moldovan Constitution, adopted in July 1994, provided for a 'special autonomous status' for Gagauz-Yeri, as for Transnistria, and negotiations duly commenced on the details of this status. Agreement was quickly reached between the Government and the Gagauz authorities, and in December the Moldovan Parliament adopted legislation on the 'special status of Gagauz-Yeri'. The regions of southern Moldova populated by the Gagauz were to enjoy broad self-administrative powers, and Gagauz was to be one of three official languages (together with Moldovan and Russian). Legislative power was to be vested in a regional assembly, the Halk Toplusu (Popular Assembly) and a directly elected Başkan (Governor) was to hold a quasi-presidential position. The law on the status of Gagauz-Yeri entered into force in February 1995, and in the following month a referendum was held in the region to determine which settlements would form part of the region. Elections to the 35-seat Halk Toplusu took place in late May–early June. Elections held concurrently, to the post of Başkan, were won by Gheorghe Tabunscic, the First Secretary of the Comrat branch of the Party of Communists of the Republic of Moldova (PCRM). Under the new Constitution, Tabunscic, as Gagauz leader, became a member of the Council of Ministers. At the first session of the assembly the self-proclaimed 'Gagauz Republic' was declared defunct. Following local elections in Moldova in late May 1999, Gagauz-Yeri, like Transnistria, was designated an autonomous entity. Elections to the Halk Toplusu and to the post of Başkan were held in late August. Following a second round of voting in early September, Dumitru Croitor was elected as Başkan, with 61.5% of the votes cast.

In February 2002 the Halk Toplusu approved a vote of no confidence in Croitor, and scheduled a referendum in the hope of securing his dismissal. However, as the confidence vote had been passed without the required majority, it was declared to be unconstitutional by supporters of Croitor. On 24 February, the date on which the referendum was scheduled to have taken place, the regional security forces reportedly seized the offices of the regional Election Commission, declaring its mandate to have expired and the plebiscite to be illegal. President Voronin subsequently visited the region and demanded the resignations of both Croitor and the Chairman of the Halk Toplusu. Croitor finally resigned at the end of June. At a second round of voting on 11 October, Tabunscic secured the highest proportion of the votes cast and regained the position of Başkan; a new Government was subsequently approved. (Croitor had been prohibited from contesting the elections, owing to a legal technicality.) On 25 July 2003 the Moldovan Paramentul officially recognized the autonomous status of Gagauz-Yeri through an amendment to the national Constitution, which awarded the Halk Toplusu the right to self-determination and to propose its own legislation. At legislative elections, which were held in the region in November and December, the PCRM and independent candidates each won almost one-half of the seats contested. An election to the post of Başkan was held on 3 December 2006. The two candidates to obtain the most votes—Mayor of Comrat Nicolai Dudoglo and opposition candidate Mihail Formuzal—contested a second round on 17 December. Formuzal emerged victorious from this second round of voting, securing 56% of the votes, despite claims by the Organization for Security and Co-operation in Europe (OSCE) of significant bias during the election campaign on the part of the ruling party, local and central authorities, and the state-funded media.

The political groupings that had contested the election in December 2006 were realigned prior to elections to the Halk Toplusu in March 2008: the PCRM formed the Bloc for a Flourishing Gagauzia into a Renewed Moldova (BFRGM), comprising party and affiliated independent candidates; and supporters of Formuzal were grouped together in the United Gagauzia Movement (UGM). A number of independent candidates were affiliated to Dudoglo, who hoped to be elected as parliamentary Chairman in exchange for alignment with one of the two main alliances. After two rounds of voting, on 16 and 30 March, the BFRGM obtained 14 seats, the UGM eight seats, supporters of Dudoglo six seats and the Democratic Party of Moldova two seats. (Of the remaining six unaffiliated independent candidates, four subsequently joined the BFRGM, increasing its strength to 17 deputies.) However, neither of the two main groupings accepted the compromise arrangement proposed by Dudoglo; an attempt to elect a Chairman at the end of April resulted in failure, with none of the three candidates receiving a majority vote. Following a continued impasse, Formuzal addressed the Halk Toplusu, urging the formation of a broader coalition. On 12 July the BFRGM candidate, Demian Cărăşeni, was elected Chairman, but the result was later revoked after a number of ballots were pronounced invalid. An independent deputy and prominent journalist, Ana Harlamenco, was subsequently elected Chairman; however, the BFRGM refused to recognize the legality of her election and staged a parliamentary boycott in protest. On 31 July Harlamenco was re-elected unanimously by the 30 deputies present, with Cărăşeni and a UGM member becoming Vice-Chairmen under a compromise agreement. On 22 September the Halk Toplusu narrowly approved a resolution that announced the formal recognition of the separatist regions of Abkhazia and South Ossetia as independent from Georgia, following Russian recognition of those territories as independent states, and declaring support for Russia's military action in Georgia in August (see the chapter on Georgia).

Başkan of Gagauz-Yeri: Mihail Formuzal, 3800 Comrat, str. Lenin 194; tel. (298) 2-46-36; fax (298) 2-22-22; e-mail contact@gagauzia.md; internet www.gagauzia.md.

Chairman of the Halk Toplusu (Popular Assembly): Ana Harlamenco, 3800 Comrat.

'TRANSNISTRIAN MOLDOVAN REPUBLIC'

The self-styled 'Transnistrian Moldovan Republic' (formerly 'Transnistrian Moldovan Soviet Socialist Republic') was proclaimed in 1991 (see below). The territory comprises the entire eastern region of Moldova, including all territories on the east ('left') bank of the Nistru (Dniester) river, and also certain districts of the city of Tighina (Bender) on the west bank. The entire eastern boundary of the territory borders Ukraine. The local administration consists of five raione (districts).

In September 1990 the region of Moldova on the east ('left') bank of the Nistru (Dniester) river, Transnistria, which was dominated by ethnic Russians and Ukrainians, proclaimed its secession from the Moldovian SSR. (The secessionist region also included a small amount of territory on the west bank of the Nistru in Tighina—Bender.) In the following year separatists announced the establishment of a 'Transnistrian Moldovan Soviet Socialist Republic', based in Tiraspol. The separatists were dominated by conservative communist elements, who were largely opposed to the dissolution of the USSR. Armed conflict broke out in December 1991, as the leadership of the self-proclaimed republic, opposed to the Moldovan Government's objective of reunification with Romania, launched a campaign to gain control of Transnistria (with the ultimate aim of unity with the Russian Federation). More than six months of military conflict ensued. The Moldovan Government claimed that the east-bank forces were actively supported by the Russian Government, while the Moldovans were, in turn, accused of receiving military and other assistance from Romania. The situation was complicated by the presence of the former Soviet (now Russian) 14th Army, which was still stationed in Transnistria. Peace negotiations were held at regular intervals, with the participation of Moldova, Russia, Ukraine and Romania; however, none of the agreed cease-fires was observed. By June 1992 some 700 people were believed to have been killed in the conflict, with a further estimated 50,000 people forced to take refuge in neighbouring Ukraine. On 21 July, however, a peace agreement was finally negotiated by Presidents Snegur of Moldova and Yeltsin of Russia, whereby Transnistria was accorded 'special status' within Moldova (the terms of which were to be formulated later). In late July Russian, Moldovan and Transnistrian peace-keeping troops were deployed in the region to monitor the cease-fire. However, Moldova's relations with Russia remained strained.

Transnistria continued to demand full statehood, and in January 1994 the Moldovan Government accepted proposals by the Conference on (later Organization for) Security and Co-operation in Europe (CSCE—later OSCE) for greater autonomy for Transnistria, including economic independence, within a Moldovan confederation. The Transnistrian leadership expressed its approval of the proposals, and the result of the Moldovan parliamentary elections of the following month, which eliminated the possibility of Moldova's future unification with Romania, further enhanced the prospects for peace in the region. In April President Snegur and the Transnistrian leader, Igor Smirnov, pledged their commitment to holding negotiations for a peaceful resolution of the conflict, based on the CSCE recommendations.

In July 1994, following the adoption of the new Moldovan Constitution, which provided for a 'special autonomous status' for Transnistria, negotiations duly commenced on the details of the region's future status within Moldova. Progress was obstructed, in particular, by disagreement over the future of the 15,000-strong 14th Army, since the Transnistrian leadership demanded the continued presence of the Army in the region as a guarantor of security. In October, however, the Moldovan and Russian Governments reached an agreement, under which Russia was to withdraw the 14th Army within a period of three years, whereupon Transnistria's negotiated 'special autonomous status' would take effect. A referendum (declared illegal by President Snegur) was held in Transnistria in March 1995, in which some 91% of participants voted against the withdrawal of the 14th Army. In June, however, the withdrawal of the weapons and ammunition of the 14th Army began. In December a new bicameral legislature was elected in Transnistria, and two further referendums were held: 82.7% of the electorate endorsed a new constitution proclaiming the region's independence, while 89.7% voted for Transnistria to join the Commonwealth of Independent States (CIS) as a sovereign state. In February 1996, however, the CIS ruled out admittance for Transnistria on such terms.

In July 1996 the executive and legislative authorities of Moldova and Transnistria initialled a memorandum, drafted with the aid of Russian, Ukrainian and OSCE mediators, on normalizing relations; this was viewed as an important stage towards defining the 'special status' of Transnistria within a future Moldovan confederation. However, Snegur subsequently declared his opposition to the memorandum, claiming that it effectively formalized Moldova's 'disintegration into two states', and announced that any decision on the issue should be postponed until after the forthcoming presidential

election. Following his election as Moldova's new President in December, Petru Lucinschi announced his intention to sign the memorandum. In that month Igor Smirnov was re-elected 'President' of Transnistria, with more than 70% of the votes cast.

Meanwhile, the withdrawal of contingents of the 14th Army continued, and by early 1997 its strength had reportedly been reduced to some 5,000–6,000 men. None the less, the withdrawal agreement, although signed by the respective Governments, still awaited ratification by the Russian State Duma, the lower legislative chamber. In April it was announced that substantial progress had been achieved in the negotiations concerning the status of Transnistria. A new article was added to the memorandum initialled in mid-1996, stating that the two sides would develop relations within the framework of one state, the borders of which would correspond to those of the former Moldovan (Moldavian) SSR. The memorandum was signed in Moscow, in May, by Lucinschi and Smirnov, with Russia and Ukraine acting as guarantors of the document. It was agreed to resume negotiations on the defining of Transnistria's 'special status', and commissions were constituted for that purpose. Representatives of the two sides, meeting in Moscow in October, reached agreement on a number of 'confidence-building measures', and an agreement was signed in Odesa, Ukraine, by Lucinschi, Smirnov, Russian premier Viktor Chernomyrdin and President Leonid Kuchma of Ukraine on 20 March 1998. A reduction in Moldovan and Transnistrian peace-keeping forces was envisaged, while Russian troops were to remain in Transnistria until a final political settlement could be reached.

The success of Snegur's Democratic Convention of Moldova (CDM) at the March 1998 legislative elections raised concerns among the Transnistrian leadership regarding the future of relations with the Moldovan Government. In June, however, the Russian and Moldovan delegations to the joint commission monitoring the Odesa Accords agreed proposals for the composition of peace-keeping forces in the Transnistrian security zone. In August the joint monitoring commission approved the deployment of Ukrainian peace-keeping forces in the security zone: at this time, there were some 700 troops each from Moldova, Transnistria and Russia. Meanwhile, Moldova's peace-keeping troops were gradually reduced in number (to about 500), and Moldova continued to urge Russia to accelerate the withdrawal of its troops and weaponry from the area. From late May 1999, following local elections in Moldova (in which the region refused to participate), Transnistria was designated an autonomous entity. In July Lucinschi met Smirnov, along with Russian premier Sergei Stepashin and an OSCE representative, in Kyiv, Ukraine. Although the negotiations concluded with the signature of a joint declaration on the normalization of relations between Moldova and Transnistria, Smirnov declared that differences remained. At an OSCE summit in İstanbul, Turkey, in November, Russia agreed to withdraw from Transnistria in three stages, with all hardware to be removed by the end of 2001, and all troops by the end of 2002.

In June 2000 the 'Transnistrian Supreme Soviet' was converted to a reduced, unicameral legislature. Smirnov introduced a form of presidential rule in the following month, and a new cabinet was installed to act as a consultative body. Legislative elections were held in December. Following his election in April 2001, the new Moldovan President, Vladimir Vorodin, declared the pursuit of a final political settlement for Transnistria to be a priority but, although a number of bilateral agreements were signed in Tiraspol in May, no substantive progress was made. In June the OSCE welcomed the Moldovan Government's announcement that it was to reduce the strength of its peace-keeping forces in the security zone. A deterioration in Transnistria's relations with the Moldovan Government came about in September, however, following the Government's introduction of new customs procedures, in accordance with World Trade Organization specifications. The withholding of new customs seals from the Transnistrian authorities, thereby preventing the region from conducting its own external economic activities, led to claims that the Moldovan Government was attempting to impose an 'economic blockade' on the region, and the curtailment of negotiations. On 9 December Igor Smirnov was re-elected as 'President' of Transnistria, receiving almost 82% of the votes cast; the election result was recognized by neither the Moldovan Government nor the international community. A new Transnistrian Government was appointed in February 2002. Meanwhile, the agreed withdrawal of Russian military hardware from the region was subject to delays, and in December 2002 the OSCE amended the deadline agreed in 1999 for the removal of Russian forces from Moldova, extending it for a further year, until 31 December 2003. Nonetheless, Russia indicated that some troops might remain, with a possible mandate for maintaining peace and stability in the event of agreement on reunification.

In July 2002 mediators from Russia, Ukraine and the OSCE submitted a new draft agreement (the 'Kyiv agreement'), according to which Moldova would become a 'federal state, in which the autonomous territories would maintain their own legislature and constitution. Smirnov agreed that his regime would participate in talks on the draft, but insisted that recognition of Transnistria's 'independence' was a fundamental prerequisite. On 28 February 2003 the Moldovan Government and the Transnistrian authorities reached preliminary agreement on proposals by President Voronin for the joint drafting of a new constitution, which would be subject to approval by referendum by February 2004. However, no further progress was made towards organizing a plebiscite on the issue. In November 2003 the Russian President, Vladimir Putin, announced new proposals for a political settlement. Drafted by the First Deputy Head of the presidential administration, Dmitrii Kozak, the plan envisaged the establishment of an 'asymmetrical federation' comprising Moldova and Transnistria, with unified defence, customs and finance systems. The leaders of both Transnistria and Moldova initially responded positively to the proposals, but Voronin withdrew his support in late November, following opposition protests and reservations expressed by the OSCE. (Notably, the proposals provided for the creation of an upper legislative chamber for Moldova, Senatul—the Senate—one-half of the members of which would represent Transnistria and Gagauz-Yeri.) The 'Kozak memorandum' had also attracted criticism from some observers, who considered it to serve Russian interests. In February 2004 the Moldovan and Transnistrian sides submitted new proposals for Moldova's federalization to OSCE mediators. However, the Transnistrian authorities considered the new proposals to offer the region insufficient autonomy, and representatives of the Moldovan Government criticized the draft for its failure to clarify the issue of the continued presence of Russian troops and military equipment in Transnistria. Earlier in the month the Russian Minister of Defence had indicated that, despite the agreements on troop withdrawal reached in 1999 and 2002, Russia intended to maintain troops in the region, in response to the increasing numbers of US troops based in eastern Europe. In July 2004 the Transnistrian authorities ordered the closure of an orphanage and several schools that used the Latin-script form of the Moldovan language, claiming that the institutions lacked the requisite registration; these measures resulted in the Moldovan authorities blockading railway lines into Transnistria, and issuing economic sanctions against the region, to protest against the closures. Further school closures took place following the beginning of the new school year in September. The European Union (EU), the USA and other international parties condemned the closure of the schools as an infringement of human rights, adding a further 10 Transnistrian officials to a list of those prohibited from travelling to their countries. A case was submitted to the European Court of Human Rights.

In December 2001 at a meeting of the OSCE, held in Sofia, Bulgaria, the Russian delegation obstructed the adoption of a final statement containing a reference to Russian commitments to withdraw troops and ammunition from Moldova and Georgia (first made in 1999, see above). Similarly, Russian representatives refused to sign the Moldovan-drafted Declaration of Stability and Security for the Republic of Moldova, which proposed the inclusion of the EU and the USA in talks for the resolution of the Transnistrian conflict and acknowledged the failure of the existing five-party panel. In January 2005 Moldova banned foreign diplomats and representatives from visiting Transnistria, although the decision was rescinded the following month in order to allow for the free movement of international election monitors. In response the Russian Duma approved a resolution in March, recommending certain punitive sanctions against Moldova. In April President Viktor Yushchenko of Ukraine presented a plan for the resolution of the Transnistrian problem (which became known as the Yushchenko Plan or the Kyiv Plan) during a summit in Chişinău; the plan appeared to be well received by all parties. The plan envisaged, *inter alia*, awarding 'special status' to Transnistria, as an autonomous entity within the Republic of Moldova. The plan provided for a Transnistrian Constitution (to comply with the Moldovan Constitution) and Transnistrian symbols, and would permit Transnistria to participate in foreign policy decisions affecting its own interests. In June the Moldovan parliament endorsed the Yushchenko Plan, while noting in a special resolution that it did not provide for the withdrawal of Russian troops or the establishments of border control along the Transnistrian section of the border with Ukraine.

Following amendments to the legislation concerning citizenship adopted by the Ukrainian legislature in July 2005, many residents of Transnistria of Ukrainian ethnicity were expected to pursue citizenship. At the end of July the Moldovan authorities ceased the trade sanctions against Transnistrian companies that had been implemented the preceding year. On 27 September 2005 all five negotiating parties agreed to invite the EU and the USA (but not Romania) to participate as observers in the process, as suggested in the Yushchenko plan. Legislative elections (unrecognized by the Moldovan Government or the international community) were held in the region

on 11 December. Notably the reformist, pro-western Obnovleniye (Renewal) bloc won the largest number of mandates in the Supreme Soviet.

In November 2005 the EU launched a Border Assistance Mission to help secure the Transnistrian–Ukrainian border, following appeals from Presidents Voronin and Yushchenko. As part of the same initiative, at the end of December the Prime Ministers of Moldova and Ukraine signed a joint declaration on external trade, whereby Ukraine agreed not to recognize Transnistria's customs regime and to deal only in goods processed through the Moldovan customs system, in an attempt to combat smuggling. The new measures came into force in March 2006. In response, the Transnistrian authorities, which interpreted the new regulations as an economic blockade, withdrew from the internationally mediated negotiations and, in May, rescinded a 1993 resolution on the creation of a Moldovan confederation. The Transnistrian authorities subsequently introduced legislation banning all foreign-financed non-governmental organizations, and Smirnov appealed to Russia to dispatch more troops to the region. (In February Russia had reportedly confirmed that it did not intend to complete the withdrawal of its troops from Transnistria before a final settlement on the region's status had been reached.) In June Smirnov declared that the region planned to form joint peace-keeping forces with the Georgian separatist regions of Abkhazia and South Ossetia, following a meeting between the heads of these regions. In the same month the Supreme Council voted unanimously to schedule a referendum on independence or possible integration with either Russia or Moldova for 17 September. The Moldovan and international authorities declared that it would hold no legal force. In the event, some 97% of votes cast were in favour of independence and eventual unification with Russia, and some 95% of votes were cast against unification with Moldova.

In 'presidential' elections held on 10 December 2006, Smirnov was re-elected for a fourth five-year term, securing 82.4% of the votes, although, as previously, the result was recognized by neither the Moldovan Government nor the international community. Nadezhda Bondarenko, the candidate of the opposition Transnistrian Communist Party (PKP), was placed second, with just 8.1% of the vote. Voter participation was reported to be 65.4%.

Unrest became apparent in the region in July and August 2006 when incendiary devices exploded on a minibus (killing eight passengers and injuring 20 others), and a trolley bus in Tiraspol (killing two and injuring a further 10). On 11 March 2007 the Transnistrian authorities had detained five members of the PKP, including its leader, Oleg Khorzhan, while handing out leaflets and urging passers-by to attend an unauthorized anti-Smirnov rally outside the offices of the 'President', planned for 13 March. On the eve of the rally Viktor Neumoin, the head of the Tiraspol branch of the Patriotic Party of Transnistria (PPP) and a close associate of the PPP's leader, Oleg Smirnov (son of Igor), was shot dead outside his Tiraspol apartment. It was not clear whether Neumoin's killing was in any way connected to the detention of the PKP members, who were released on 14 March.

In April 2007 Russia announced proposals for a new settlement plan regarding Transnistria. The proposals demanded parallel, but separate, legislative elections in Moldova and Transnistria, to be held by November of that year; 18 or 19 of the 101 seats in the legislature would be reserved for Transnistrian deputies, while a first deputy prime minister, as well as deputy ministers in each of the ministries, would be reserved for Transnistrian representatives. The plan would also require the Moldovan Government to pledge its continuing adherence to its existing position of permanent neutrality; to allow only Russian troops to be deployed in Transnistria; and to refrain from acceding to the North Atlantic Treaty Organization (NATO); in turn, Russia would withdraw its troops within two years. On 11 April 2008 President Voronin and Smirnov met, for the first time since 2001, in Tighina (Bender), Transnistria, with the aim of resuming talks on a political solution to the disputed status of the region. Following the meeting, Voronin announced that he and Smirnov had agreed to continue negotiations, amid speculation that Voronin hoped to reach an agreement before his term of office ended in March 2009. The Russian President, Dmitrii Medvedev, met Voronin in late August 2008 and Smirnov in September, and it was subsequently reported that the initiation of a new bilateral negotiating process under the aegis of Russia (which would therefore necessitate the '5 plus 2' format to be abandoned) was under discussion. The Transnistrian authorities were also expected to seek the support of pro-Russia leaders in Gagauz-Yeri to exert pressure on the Moldovan Government. Later in September, however, it was reported that Smirnov had decided to delay further negotiations, after the Russian Minister of Foreign Affairs made a statement emphasizing that Russia's decision to recognize the independence of the separatist Georgian regions of South Ossetia and Abkhazia could not be regarded as setting a precedent for developments in Transnistria.

President of the 'Transnistrian Moldovan Republic': Igor N. Smirnov, 3300 Tiraspol, ul. 25 Oktyabrya 45; tel. (30) 30-70-78; e-mail president@presidentpmr.org; internet presidentpmr.org.

President of the 'Transnistrian Moldovan Supreme Soviet': Yevgenii V. Shevchuk, Tiraspol; tel. (373) 53-39-44-49; e-mail sec@vspmr.org; internet www.vspmr.org.

Bibliography

Argunsah, M., and Gungor, H. *The Gagauz*. London, Caucasus World, 2001.

Brezianu, A. *Historical Dictionary of the Republic of Moldova*. Lanham, MD, Scarecrow Press, 2000.

Bruchis, M. *The Republic of Moldova: from the Collapse of the Soviet Empire to the Restoration of the Russian Empire*. Boulder, CO, East European Monographs, 1996.

Ciorănescu, G. *Bessarabia. Disputed Land between East and West*. Bucharest, Editura Fundaţei Culturale Romane, 1993.

Ciscel, M. *The Language of the Moldovans: Romania, Russia, and Identity in an Ex-Soviet Republic*. Lanham, MD, Lexington Books, 2007.

Dima, N. *From Moldavia to Moldova: the Soviet–Romanian Territorial Dispute*. Boulder, CO, East European Monographs, 1991.

Moldova and the Transdnestr Republic. New York, Columbia University Press, 2001.

Dyer, D. L. (Ed.). *Studies in Moldovan: The History, Culture, Language and Contemporary Politics of the People of Moldova*. Boulder, CO, East European Monographs, 1996.

Hill, R. J. *Soviet Political Élites: the Case of Tiraspol*. London, Martin Robertson, 1977.

Ionescu, D. *From SSMR to the Republic of Moldova*. Chişinău, Museum, 2002.

King, C. *Post-Soviet Moldova: a Borderland In Transition*. Iaşi, Center for Romanian Studies, 1997.

The Moldovans: Romania, Russia, and the Politics of Culture. Stanford, CA, Hoover Institute Press, 1999.

Kolstø, P. (Ed.). *National Integration and Violent Conflict in Post Soviet Societies: the Cases of Estonia and Moldova*. Lanham, MD, Rowman and Littlefield, 2002.

Lewis, A. (Ed.). *The EU and Moldova: on a Fault-line of Europe*. London, Federal Trust, 2004.

Manoliu-Manea, M. (Ed.). *The Tragic Plight of a Border Area: Bessarabia and Bucovina*. Humboldt, CA, Humboldt State University Press, 1983.

Mitrasca, M. *Moldova: a Romanian Province*. New York, Algora Publishing, 2002.

Ruzé, A. *La Moldova entre la Roumanie et la Russie: De Pierre le Grand à Boris Eltsine*, Collection Pays de l'Est. Paris, L'Harmattan, 1997.

See also the Select Bibliography.

THE RUSSIAN FEDERATION

Geography

PHYSICAL FEATURES

The Russian Federation is bounded to the west by Norway (in the far north-west), Finland, Estonia and Latvia. Belarus and Ukraine lie to the south-west of European Russia, the southern borders of which are with the South Caucasus states of Georgia and Azerbaijan, and with Kazakhstan. There is a short coastline in the north-west, near St Petersburg (Sankt-Peterburg—the old tsarist capital, Petrograd 1914–24, Leningrad 1924–91), where the country has access to the Baltic Sea via the Gulf of Finland. In the south, towards the Caucasus, European Russia has a coastline on the Black Sea and the Sea of Azov in the south-west, and with the Caspian Sea to the east. Beyond the Ural Mountains, the Siberian and Far Eastern regions have southern frontiers with Kazakhstan, the People's Republic of China, Mongolia and, in the south-east, there is a short frontier with the Democratic People's Republic of Korea (North Korea). The eastern coastline is on the Sea of Japan, the Sea of Okhotsk, the Pacific Ocean and the Barents Sea. The northern coastline is on the Arctic Ocean. In the west, the region around Kaliningrad (formerly Königsberg in East Prussia), on the Baltic Sea, became part of the Russian Federation in 1945. It is separated from the rest of Russia by Lithuania and Belarus. It borders Poland to the south, Lithuania to the north and east and has a coastline on the Baltic Sea. Russia covers a total area of 17,075,400 sq km (6,592,850 sq miles), making it by far the largest country in the world.

The territory includes a wide variety of physical features. European Russia (traditionally meaning that part of Russia to the west of the Urals) and western Siberia form a vast plain, interrupted only by occasional outbreaks of hill country and wide river valleys. In the south, between the Black and Caspian Seas, the territory is more undulating, until it reaches the foothills of the Caucasus (Kavkaz) mountain range in the far south. The Ural Mountains provide only a symbolic barrier between Siberia and European Russia, their mean altitude being just 500 m (1,640 ft). Beyond them the Western Siberian Plain extends for some 2,000 km, before reaching the Central Siberian Plateau and high mountain ranges on the southern border with Mongolia. The territory of eastern Siberia and the Far East is dominated by several mountain ranges (notably the Verkhoyansk, Cherskii and Anadyr mountains), which extend offshore in a series of islands and peninsulas. The Kamchatka Peninsula, which extends 1,200 km south to the northernmost of the Kurile (Kuril) Islands, has 100 active volcanoes, the highest being Klyuchevskaya Sopka, at an altitude of 4,800 m. Only the basins of the Amur and Ussuri rivers in the south of the Far Eastern region can support any significant population. The northern regions of both Asian and European Russia are inhospitable areas, much of the territory being covered by permafrost.

CLIMATE

The climate of Russia is extremely varied. The central regions experience the climatic conditions characteristic of central and eastern Europe, although in a more extreme form. There are wide temperature differences between summer and winter, and there is considerable snow in winter. The average temperature in Moscow in July is 19°C (66°F); the average for January is −9°C (15°F). Average annual precipitation in the capital is 575 mm. Further south the climate is more temperate, especially along the Black Sea coastline. Average temperatures in Rostov-on-Don (Rostov-na-Donu) range from −5.3°C (22.5°F) in January to 23.5°C (74.3°F) in July. In the northern areas of Russia and in much of Siberia the climate is severe, with Arctic winters and short, hot summers. Only the northern fringe is under the polar ice-cap; the zone of permafrost is, however, extensive. Average temperatures in the

southern Siberian town of Irkutsk range from −20.8°C (−5.4°F) in January to 17.9°C (64.2°F) in July. Average annual rainfall is 458 mm, most of which falls in the summer months. In Verkhoyansk, in the far north of Siberia, the average January temperature is −46.8°C (−52.2°F). The Far Eastern region combines the extreme temperatures of Siberia with monsoon-type conditions common elsewhere in Asia, although they are not so pronounced, owing to the protection of mountain ranges on the Pacific coast. The mean temperature in January in the eastern port of Vladivostok is −14°C (7°F); in August the average is 21°C (70°F).

POPULATION

At the 1989 census, Russians formed the largest ethnic group in the Federation, accounting for 81.5% of the population, although by 2002 this had fallen to 79.8%. (However, it should be noted that these figures are not directly comparable, because of the different methodologies used to collate data on ethnicity in the two censuses: in 1989 ethnicity was recorded on the basis of the official declaration of nationality recorded in Soviet internal passports, whereas in 2002 ethnicity was recorded on the basis of self-identification.) Other important ethnic groups included Tatars (3.8% in 2002), Ukrainians (2.0%), Bashkirs (1.2%) and Chuvash (1.1%). There were also significant communities of Chechens, Armenians, Mordovians, Avars, Belarusians, Kazakhs, Udmurts, Azeris, Mari and Germans. There were more than 200 ethnic groups in total. Religious adherence was equally varied, with many religions closely connected with particular ethnic groups. Christianity was the major religion, mostly adhered to by ethnic Russians and other Slavs. The Russian Orthodox Church (Moscow Patriarchate) was the largest grouping. Christianity as a whole was adhered to by about 59% of the population, with the next largest religion being Islam, at about 10%; a large part of the population (31%) claimed to have no religious adherence. The main concentrations of Muslims were among Volga Tatars, Chuvash and Bashkirs, and the peoples of the North Caucasus, including the Chechens, Ingush, Kabardins and the peoples of Dagestan. Buddhism was the main religion of the Buryats, the Tyvans and the Kalmyks. The large pre-1917 Jewish population was depleted by war and emigration, but some 229,938 citizens described their 'nationality' (ethnicity) as Jewish (including Mountain Jews, and smaller numbers of Georgian Jews and Central Asian Jews) at the 2002 census.

The official language is Russian, but a large number of other languages are in daily use. The majority of the population lives in European Russia, the population of Siberia and the Far East being only 18.3% of the total in 2008, according to official estimates. In 2002 some 73.3% of the population lived in urban areas, although there were substantial regional differences. Thus, more than four-fifths of the inhabitants of the North-Western Federal Okrug (district—based in St Petersburg) and the Urals Federal Okrug (based in Yekaterinburg) resided in cities, towns and urban settlements, compared with fewer than three-fifths of the population of the Southern Federal Okrug (based in Rostov-on-Don and including, among other territories, the North Caucasus region).

The total population of Russia at the census of October 2002 was 145,166,731, and the population density was 8.5 per sq km. By January 2008, according to official estimates, the population had declined to 142,008,838, and the population density to 8.3 per sq km. The capital of Russia is Moscow, which had an estimated population of 10,425,100 at January 2006, according to official estimates. The second city is St Petersburg, with a population of 4,571,200. Other important regional centres are Novosibirsk (1,397,200), Yekaterinburg (1,308,400), Nizhnii Novgorod (1,283,600), Samara (1,143,300), Omsk (1,138,800),

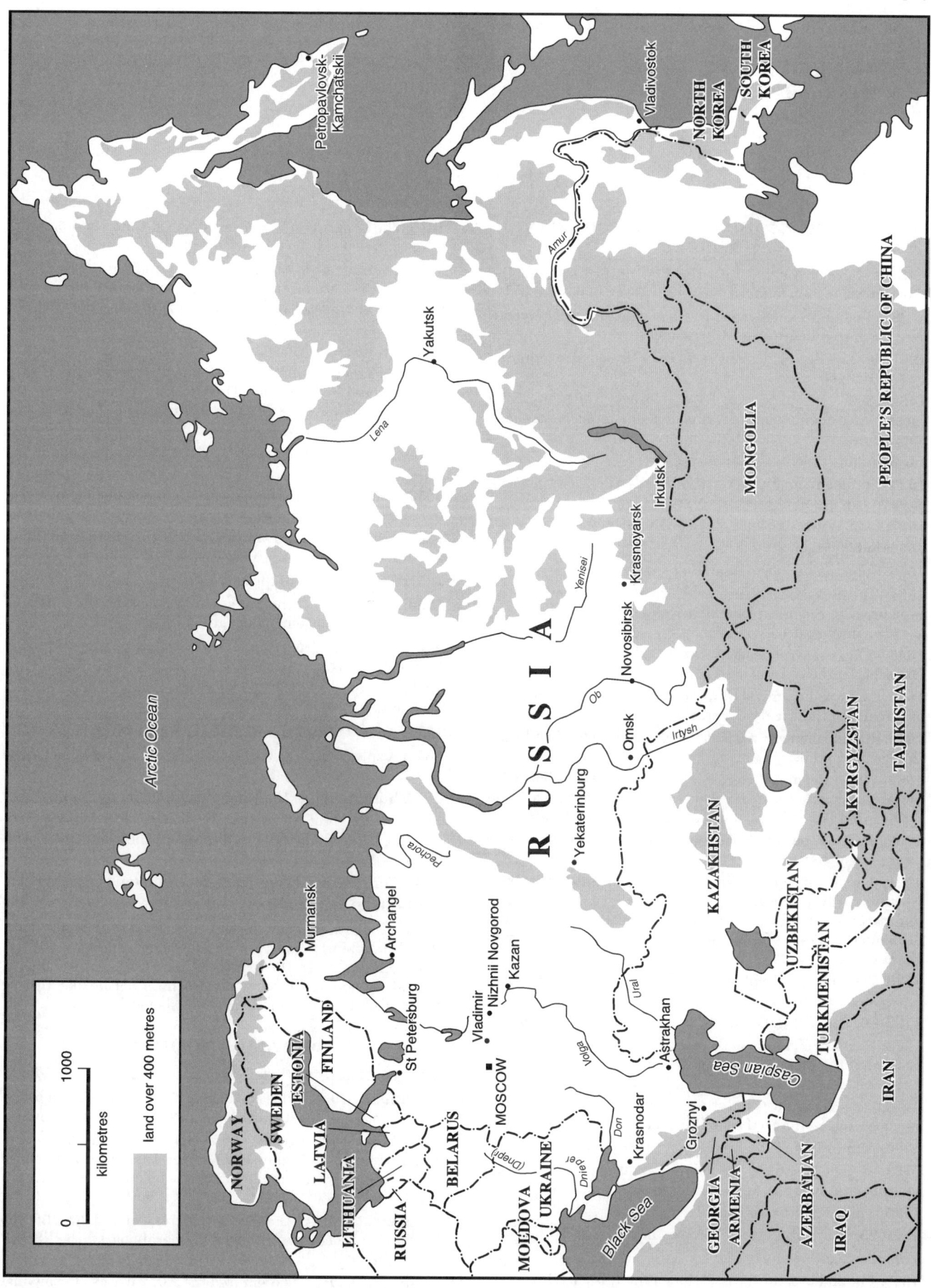

Kazan (1,112,700), Chelyabinsk (1,093,000), Rostov-on-Don (1,054,800) and Ufa (1,029,600).

Many ethnic Russians lived beyond the borders of the Russian Federation, in the other countries of the former USSR. They formed significant minorities in the countries of Estonia, Latvia, Belarus, Ukraine, Kazakhstan and Uzbekistan. Large Russian communities were also present in Moldova and, following significant migration by Russians of Jewish extraction in the late 20th century, in Germany, Israel and the USA.

Chronology

KYIVAN RUS, MUSCOVY AND THE RUSSIAN EMPIRE

c. 878: Kyivan (Kievan) Rus, the first unified state of the Eastern Slavs, was founded, with Kyiv (Kiev) as its capital.

c. 988: Vladimir (Volodymyr) I—'the Great', ruler of Kyivan Rus, converted to Orthodox Christianity.

1237–40: The Rus principalities were invaded and conquered by the Mongol Tatars.

1462–1505: Reign of Ivan III of Muscovy (Moscow), who consolidated the independent Rus domains into a centralized state.

1480: Renunciation of Tatar suzerainty.

1533–84: Reign of Ivan IV—'the Terrible', who began the eastern expansion of Russian territory.

1547: Ivan IV was crowned 'Tsar of Muscovy and all Russia'.

1552: Subjugation of the Khanate of Kazan.

1556: Subjugation of the Khanate of Astrakhan.

1581: The Russian adventurer, Yermak Timofeyev, led an expedition to Siberia, pioneering Russian expansion beyond the Ural Mountains.

1645: A Russian settlement was established on the Sea of Okhotsk, on the coast of eastern Asia.

1654: Eastern and central Ukraine came under Muscovite rule as a result of the Treaty of Pereyaslavl.

1679: Russian pioneers reached the Kamchatka Peninsula and the Pacific Ocean.

1682–1725: Reign of Peter (Petr) I—'the Great', who established Russia as a European Power, expanded its Empire, and modernized the civil and military institutions of the state.

1703: St Petersburg was founded at the mouth of the River Neva, in north-west Russia.

1721: The Treaty of Nystad with Sweden ended the Great Northern War and brought Estonia and Livonia (now Latvia and parts of Estonia) under Russian rule. Peter I, who was declared the 'Tsar of all the Russias', proclaimed the Russian Empire.

1728: The Treaty of Kyakhta with China secured the Russian annexation of Transbaikal.

1762–96: Reign of Catherine (Yekaterina) II—'the Great'.

1772: Parts of Belarus were incorporated into the Russian Empire at the First Partition of Poland.

1774: As a result of the Treaty of Kuçuk Kainavci with the Turks, the Black Sea port of Azov was annexed and Russia became protector of Orthodox Christians in the Balkans.

1783: Annexation of the Khanate of Crimea.

1793: Second Partition of Poland; acquisition of western Ukraine and Belarus.

1795: Third Partition of Poland.

1801–25: Reign of Alexander (Aleksandr) I.

1801: Annexation of Georgia.

1809: Finland became a possession of the Russian Crown.

1812: Bessarabia (now mostly in the Republic of Moldova) was acquired from the Turks. Napoleon I of France invaded Russia.

1815: The Congress of Vienna established 'Congress Poland' as a Russian dependency (annexed 1831).

1825: On the death of Alexander I, a group of young officers, the 'Decembrists', attempted to seize power; the attempted *coup d'état* was suppressed by troops loyal to the new Tsar, Nicholas (Nikolai) I.

1825–55: Reign of Nicholas I.

1853–56: The Crimean War was fought, in which the United Kingdom and France aided Turkey against Russia, after the latter had invaded the Ottoman tributaries of Moldavia and Wallachia; the War was concluded by the Congress of Paris.

1855–81: Reign of Alexander II, who introduced economic and legal reforms.

1859: The conquest of the Caucasus was completed, following the surrender of rebel forces.

1860: Acquisition of provinces on the Sea of Japan from China and the establishment of Vladivostok.

1861: Emancipation of the serfs.

1864: Final defeat of the Circassian peoples and the confirmation of Russian hegemony in the Caucasus.

1867: The North American territory of Alaska was sold to the USA for US $7m.

1868: Subjugation of the Khanates of Samarqand and Bukhara (Buxoro).

1873: Annexation of the Khanate of Khiva (Xiva).

1875: Acquisition of Sakhalin from Japan in exchange for the Kurile Islands.

1876: Subjugation of the Khanate of Kokand (Qoqand).

1881–94: Reign of Alexander III, who acceded following the assassination of his father and re-established autocratic principles of government.

1891: Construction of the Trans-Siberian Railway was begun.

1894–1917: Reign of Nicholas II, the last Tsar.

1898: The All-Russian Social Democratic Labour Party (RSDLP), a Marxist party, held a founding congress in Minsk (now in Belarus). In 1903, at the Second Congress in London, United Kingdom, the party divided into 'Bolsheviks' (led by Lenin—Vladimir Ulyanov) and 'Mensheviks'.

WAR AND REVOLUTION

1904–05: Russia was defeated in the Russo–Japanese War.

22 January 1905: Some 150 demonstrators were killed by the Tsar's troops, in what came to be known as 'Bloody Sunday'.

17 October 1905: Strikes and demonstrations in the capital, St Petersburg, and other cities forced the Tsar to introduce limited political reforms, including the holding of elections to a Duma (parliament).

January 1912: At the Sixth Congress of the RSDLP the Bolsheviks formally established a separate party, the RSDLP (Bolsheviks).

1 August 1914: Russia entered the First World War against Austria-Hungary, Germany and the Ottoman Empire (the Central Powers).

2 March (New Style 15 March) 1917: Abdication of Tsar Nicholas II after demonstrations and strikes in Petrograd (as St Petersburg had been renamed in 1914); a Provisional Government, led by Prince Lvov, took power.

9 July (22 July) 1917: In response to widespread public disorder, Prince Lvov resigned; he was replaced as Prime Minister by Aleksandr Kerenskii, a moderate socialist.

25 October (7 November) 1917: The Bolsheviks, led by Lenin, staged a *coup d'état* and overthrew Kerenskii's Provisional Government; the Russian Soviet Federative Socialist Republic (RSFSR or Russian Federation) was proclaimed.

6 January (19 January) 1918: The Constituent Assembly, which had been elected in November 1917, was dissolved on Lenin's orders. A civil war between the Bolshevik Red Army and various anti-Communist leaders (the 'Whites'), who received support from German and from Entente or Allied forces, was by now under way and lasted until 1921.

14 February (1 February) 1918: Adoption of the Gregorian Calendar by the Russian civil authorities.

3 March 1918: Treaty of Brest-Litovsk: the Bolsheviks ceded large areas of western territory to Germany, including the Baltic regions, and recognized the independence of Finland and Ukraine. Belarus, Georgia, Armenia and Azerbaijan subsequently proclaimed their independence.

6–8 March 1918: The RSDLP (Bolsheviks) was renamed the Russian Communist Party (Bolsheviks)—RCP (B).

9 March 1918: The capital of Russia was moved from Petrograd (renamed Leningrad in 1924) to Moscow.

10 July 1918: The first Constitution of the RSFSR was adopted by the Fifth All-Russian Congress of Soviets.

18 July 1918: Tsar Nicholas II and his family were murdered in Yekaterinburg (Sverdlovsk, 1924–91) by Bolshevik troops.

11 November 1918: The Allied Armistice with Germany (which was denied its gains at Brest-Litovsk) ended the First World War.

March 1921: As the civil war ended, the harsh policy of 'War Communism' was replaced by the New Economic Policy (NEP), which allowed peasants and traders some economic freedom.

18 March 1921: A rebellion by Russian sailors in the island garrison of Kronstadt (near St Petersburg) was suppressed by the Red Army. Signature of the Treaty of Rīga between Russia, Ukraine and Poland, which formally concluded the Soviet–Polish War of 1919–20, with territorial gains for Poland.

3 April 1922: Stalin (Iosif Dzhugashvili) was elected General Secretary of the RCP (B).

18 April 1922: The Soviet-German Treaty of Rapallo was signed, which established diplomatic relations between the two powers.

THE UNION OF SOVIET SOCIALIST REPUBLICS

30 December 1922: The Union of Soviet Socialist Republics (USSR) was formed by the RSFSR, the Transcaucasian (South Caucasus) Soviet Federative Socialist Republic (TSFSR), the Ukrainian SSR (Soviet Socialist Republic), the Belarusian SSR, and the Central Asian states of the Khorezm (Xorazm) People's Socialist Republic and the People's Soviet Republic of Bukhara.

6 July 1923: Promulgation of the first Constitution of the USSR (the Constitution was ratified by the Second All-Union Congress of Soviets in January 1924).

21 January 1924: Death of Lenin.

October 1927: Expulsion of Trotskii (Lev Bronstein) and other opponents of Stalin from the Communist Party.

1928: The NEP was abandoned; beginning of the First Five-Year Plan and forced collectivization of agriculture, which resulted in widespread famine, particularly in Ukraine.

November 1933: Recognition of the USSR by the USA.

18 September 1934: The USSR was admitted to the League of Nations.

1 December 1934: Sergei Kirov, a leading member of the Political Bureau (Politburo) of the Communist Party, was shot and killed in Leningrad; following the shooting, Stalin initiated a new campaign of repression.

26 September 1936: Nikolai Yezhov was appointed head of the security police, the People's Commissariat for Internal Affairs (NKVD); a series of mass arrests and executions, which came to be known as the 'Great Purge, began.

25 November 1936: The anti-Comintern (Third Communist International—established in 1919) Pact was signed between imperial Japan and Nazi Germany.

5 December 1936: The second Constitution of the USSR (the 'Stalin' Constitution) was adopted; two new Union Republics (the Kyrgyz and Kazakh SSRs) were created, and the TSFSR was dissolved into the Georgian, Armenian and Azerbaijani SSRs. The decade was also dominated by a number of ruthless political purges.

March 1938: Nikolai Bukharin, Aleksei Rykov and other prominent Bolsheviks were sentenced to death at the Moscow 'Show' Trials.

23 August 1939: Signing of the Treaty of Non-Aggression with Germany (the Nazi-Soviet Pact), including the 'Secret Protocols', which sanctioned territorial gains for the USSR in eastern Poland, Estonia, Latvia and Bessarabia.

17 September 1939: Soviet forces invaded eastern Poland.

28 September 1939: The Treaty on Friendship and Existing Borders was signed by Germany and the USSR, by which the two powers agreed that the USSR should annex Lithuania.

30 November 1939: The USSR invaded Finland.

14 December 1939: The USSR was expelled from the League of Nations.

June 1940: The Baltic states (Estonia, Latvia and Lithuania) and Bessarabia were annexed by the USSR.

22 June 1941: Germany invaded the USSR.

2 February 1943: German forces surrendered at Stalingrad (now Volgograd), marking the first reverse for the German Army.

1944: In a consolidation of domestic authority, Stalin ordered a number of mass deportations of populations from the North Caucasus and Crimea. Tannu-Tuva (Tyva), a Russian protectorate from 1914, was formally incorporated into the USSR (as part of the RSFSR).

8 May 1945: German forces surrendered to the USSR in Berlin, and Germany subsequently capitulated; most of Eastern and Central Europe had come under Soviet control.

26 June 1945: The USSR, the USA, the United Kingdom, China and 46 other countries, including the Belarusian and Ukrainian SSRs, signed the Charter of the United Nations (UN).

8 August 1945: The USSR declared war on Japan and occupied Sakhalin and the Kurile Islands.

25 January 1949: The Council for Mutual Economic Assistance (CMEA or Comecon) was established, as an economic alliance between the USSR and its Eastern European allies.

14 July 1949: The USSR exploded its first atomic bomb.

5 March 1953: Death of Stalin; he was replaced by a collective leadership, which included Georgii Malenkov and Nikita Khrushchev.

September 1953: Khrushchev was elected First Secretary of the Central Committee of the Communist Party of the Soviet Union (CPSU).

1954: The Soviet authorities transferred control of the Black Sea peninsula of Crimea from Russia to Ukraine.

14 May 1955: The Warsaw Treaty of Friendship, Co-operation and Mutual Assistance was signed by Albania, Bulgaria, Czechoslovakia, the German Democratic Republic (GDR—East Germany), Hungary, Poland, Romania and the USSR. The Treaty established a military alliance between these countries, known as the Warsaw Treaty Organization (or the Warsaw Pact).

14–25 February 1956: At the 20th Party Congress, Khrushchev denounced Stalin in the 'secret speech'.

26 August 1956: The first Soviet inter-continental ballistic missile (ICBM) was launched.

4 November 1956: Soviet forces invaded Hungary to overthrow Imre Nagy's reformist Government.

June 1957: Malenkov, Vyacheslav Molotov and Lazar Kaganovich (the so-called 'Anti-Party' group) were expelled from the CPSU leadership after attempting to depose Khrushchev.

March 1958: Khrushchev consolidated his position in the leadership by being elected Chairman of the Council of Ministers (premier), while retaining the office of CPSU First Secretary.

October 1961: Stalin's body was removed from its place of honour in the mausoleum in Red Square, in Moscow.

18–28 October 1962: The discovery of Soviet nuclear missiles in Cuba by the USA led to the 'Cuban Missile Crisis'; tension eased when Khrushchev announced the withdrawal of the missiles, following a US blockade of the island.

5 August 1963: The USSR signed the Partial Nuclear Test Ban Treaty.

13–14 October 1964: Khrushchev was deposed from the leadership of the CPSU and the USSR, and replaced as First Secretary by Leonid Brezhnev and as premier by Aleksei Kosygin.

20–21 August 1968: Soviet and other Warsaw Pact forces invaded Czechoslovakia to overthrow the reformist Government of Alexander Dubček.

May 1972: The US President, Richard Nixon, visited Moscow, thus marking a relaxation in US-Soviet relations, a process which came to be known as *détente*.

16 June 1977: Brezhnev became Chairman of the Presidium of the Supreme Soviet (Supreme Council), the titular head of state.

7 October 1977: The third Constitution of the USSR was adopted.

24 December 1979: Soviet forces invaded Afghanistan (troops were withdrawn between July 1986 and February 1989).

10 November 1982: Death of Brezhnev; Yurii Andropov, former head of the Committee for State Security (KGB), succeeded him as party leader.

9 February 1984: Death of Andropov; Konstantin Chernenko succeeded him as General Secretary.

THE GORBACHEV ERA AND THE END OF THE USSR

10 March 1985: Death of Chernenko; he was succeeded as General Secretary by Mikhail Gorbachev.

2 July 1985: Andrei Gromyko was replaced as Minister of Foreign Affairs by Eduard Shevardnadze; Gromyko became Chairman of the Presidium of the Supreme Soviet.

24 February–6 March 1986: At the 27th Congress of the CPSU, Gorbachev proposed radical economic and political reforms and 'new thinking' in foreign policy; emergence of the policy of glasnost (openness).

26 April 1986: An explosion occurred at a nuclear reactor in Chernobyl (Chornobyl), Ukraine, which resulted in discharges of radioactive material.

January 1987: At a meeting of the CPSU Central Committee, Gorbachev proposed plans for the restructuring of the economy and some democratization of local government and the CPSU (perestroika).

21 October 1987: Boris Yeltsin, the First Secretary of the Moscow City Party Committee in 1985, resigned from the Politburo.

8 December 1987: In Washington, DC, USA, Gorbachev and President Ronald Reagan signed a treaty to eliminate all intermediate-range nuclear forces in Europe.

1 October 1988: Andrei Gromyko resigned as Chairman of the Presidium of the Supreme Soviet, to be replaced by Gorbachev.

1 December 1988: The all-Union Supreme Soviet approved constitutional amendments creating a new legislative system, consisting of the Congress of People's Deputies and a full-time Supreme Soviet (a number of wide-ranging reforms, including partly free elections, had been agreed by the Party earlier in the year).

6 December 1988: In a speech at the UN, Gorbachev announced troop withdrawals from Eastern Europe.

25 March 1989: Multi-party elections to the newly established legislature, the Congress of People's Deputies took place.

25 May 1989: The Congress of People's Deputies convened for the first time; Gorbachev was elected to the new post of Chairman of the USSR Supreme Soviet (executive President).

27 May 1989: Congress elected an all-Union Supreme Soviet, which would act as a full-time legislature, in which only a few reformers managed to secure seats.

6 December 1989: After issuing declarations of political and economic sovereignty in May, the Supreme Soviet of Lithuania abolished the Communist Party's constitutional right to power, thus establishing the first multi-party system in the USSR. Lithuanian independence was declared on 11 March 1990.

4 February 1990: Some 150,000 people joined a pro-reform march in the centre of Moscow. Three days later the CPSU Central Committee approved draft proposals to abolish Article 6 of the Constitution, which had guaranteed the CPSU's monopoly of power.

4 March 1990: Elections took place to the local and republican soviets of the Russian Federation; reformists made substantial gains in the larger cities, notably Moscow and Leningrad.

15 March 1990: The all-Union legislature approved the establishment of the post of President of the USSR and elected Mikhail Gorbachev to that office.

29 May 1990: Boris Yeltsin was elected as Chairman of the Supreme Soviet of the Russian Federation. On 12 June Congress adopted a declaration of Russian sovereignty.

16 July 1990: The Supreme Soviet of Ukraine declared Ukraine to be a sovereign state, with the right to maintain its own armed forces. In the following month Turkmenistan and Tajikistan made similar declarations.

3 September 1990: Boris Yeltsin announced a 500-day programme of economic reform to the Supreme Soviet of the Russian Federation.

October 1990: Legislation allowing the existence of other political parties, apart from the CPSU, was adopted by the all-Union Supreme Soviet. It also approved a reform programme designed to establish a market economy. In Georgia pro-independence parties won an overall majority in the Supreme Soviet. Kazakhstan and Kyrgyzstan declared their sovereignty.

December 1990: Eduard Shevardnadze resigned as Minister of Foreign Affairs, claiming that the USSR was moving towards dictatorship. Congress subsequently granted Gorbachev extended presidential powers. Gennadii Yanayev was eventually endorsed as Vice-President.

13 January 1991: Thirteen people died when Soviet troops occupied radio and broadcasting buildings in Vilnius, Lithuania. One week later four people died in Rīga, Latvia, when Soviet troops occupied government buildings.

22 February 1991: Some 400,000 people demonstrated in Moscow, in support of Boris Yeltsin, who had demanded Gorbachev's resignation.

17 March 1991: In an all-Union referendum on the issue of the future of the USSR, some 75% of participants approved Gorbachev's concept of a 'renewed federation' (several republics did not participate).

12 June 1991: Yeltsin was elected President of the Russian Federation in direct elections, with Aleksandr Rutskoi as Vice-President; residents of Leningrad voted to change the city's name back to St Petersburg.

1 July 1991: The USSR and the other member countries of the Warsaw Pact signed a protocol, formalizing the dissolution of the alliance.

31 July 1991: The USSR and the USA signed the first Strategic Arms' Reduction Treaty (START 1).

18–21 August 1991: With Gorbachev placed under house arrest in his summer residence in Crimea, Ukraine, a hardline communist 'State Committee for the State of Emergency' (SCSE), under Vice-President Yanayev, attempted to seize power in a *coup d'état*. Thousands of people demonstrated against the coup in St Petersburg and in Moscow. Yeltsin demanded the restoration of Gorbachev to power and, amid increasing institutional opposition, the coup collapsed and Gorbachev was reinstated. Estonia declared independence on 20 August and Latvia on the next day.

23 August 1991: Gorbachev replaced supporters of the coup attempt, in the Council of Ministers and in the KGB. Yeltsin suspended the activities of the Russian Communist Party (RCP) and the publication of six CPSU newspapers (the RCP was formally banned in November).

24 August 1991: Gorbachev resigned as General Secretary of the CPSU, nationalized the party's property, demanded the dissolution of the Central Committee and banned party cells in the Armed Forces, the KGB and the police. The Supreme Soviet of Ukraine adopted a declaration of independence, pending approval by referendum on 1 December (90% of the participating voters were to approve the decision).

25 August 1991: Gorbachev established an interim government. The Supreme Soviet of Belarus adopted a declaration of independence. Later that month the Supreme Soviets of Moldova, Azerbaijan, Uzbekistan and Kyrgyzstan also adopted declarations of independence.

6 September 1991: The newly formed State Council, which comprised the supreme officials of the Union Republics, recognized the independence of Estonia, Latvia and Lithuania.

9 September 1991: The Supreme Soviet of Tajikistan adopted a declaration of independence. Two weeks later, following a referendum, Armenia also declared its independence.

27 September 1991: Ivan Silayev, the reformist leader of the interim Government in Russia, became Soviet Prime Minister.

5 October 1991: The USSR was officially admitted as an associate member of the IMF.

18 October 1991: A treaty, which established an Economic Community between its signatories, was signed by representatives of the Russian Federation and Armenia, Belarus, Kazakhstan, Kyrgyzstan, Tajikistan, Turkmenistan and Uzbekistan; four other republics had earlier agreed to some form of economic co-operation.

21 October 1991: The first session of the newly established all-Union Supreme Soviet was attended by delegates of the Russia and six other republics.

27 October 1991: Following a referendum, Turkmenistan declared its independence. An election was held in the Checheno-Ingush Autonomous Republic to the presidency of the self-proclaimed 'Chechen Republic' (Chechnya) and was won by Gen. Dzhokhar Dudayev.

November 1991: President Yeltsin announced the formation of a new Russian Government, with himself as Chairman (Prime Minister).

8 December 1991: The leaders of the Russian Federation, Belarus and Ukraine, meeting at Belovezhskaya Pushcha, Belarus, agreed to form a Commonwealth of Independent States (CIS) to replace the USSR.

16 December 1991: Kazakhstan declared its independence, following a decision by it and the four other Central Asian republics to join the CIS.

21 December 1991: At a meeting in Almaty, the leaders of 11 former Union Republics of the USSR signed a protocol on the formation of the new CIS. Georgia did not sign, but sent observers to the meeting.

25 December 1991: Mikhail Gorbachev formally resigned as President of the USSR, thereby confirming the effective dissolution of the Union.

30 December 1991: The 11 members of the CIS agreed, in Minsk, Belarus, to establish a joint command for armed forces (this arrangement was formally ended in 1993); use of nuclear weapons was to be under the control of the Russian Federation's President, after consultation with other Commonwealth leaders and the agreement of the presidents of Belarus, Kazakhstan and Ukraine.

POST-SOVIET RUSSIA

2 January 1992: A radical economic reform programme was introduced.

31 March 1992: The leaders of the Russian administrative regions and the mayors of Moscow and St Petersburg signed the Russian Federation Treaty; representatives from the 'Chechen Republic' and Tatarstan did not participate.

15 May 1992: At a meeting of the CIS Heads of State in Tashkent, Uzbekistan, a Five-Year Collective Security Agreement was signed by Armenia, Kazakhstan, Russia, Tajikistan, Turkmenistan and Uzbekistan.

June 1992: Ingushetiya (which had hitherto formed part of a Checheno-Ingush ASSR) was recognized as a federal republic separate from Chechnya.

1 October 1992: The Government's voucher privatization programme was initiated.

9 December 1992: The Congress rejected Yeltsin's nomination of a supporter of radical economic reform, Yegor Gaidar, as Prime Minister (Gaidar had been serving as premier, in an acting capacity, since mid-June); Yeltsin subsequently appointed Viktor Chernomyrdin to the post.

3 January 1993: President Yeltsin and the US President, George Bush, signed START 2, which envisaged a reduction in the strategic nuclear weapons of both powers. It was ratified by the Russian legislature on 14 April 2000, and signed into law on 4 May.

11 March 1993: Congress granted itself the right to suspend any presidential decrees that contravened the Constitution, pending a ruling by the Constitutional Court.

20 March 1993: Following the rejection by Congress of his proposal to hold a referendum on the issue of the respective powers of the presidency and the legislature, Yeltsin announced his intention to rule Russia by decree until such a referendum could take place.

25 April 1993: In a referendum organized by President Yeltsin, in order to resolve the increasing conflict between the executive and the legislature, 57.4% of the electorate endorsed the President and 70.6% voted in favour of early parliamentary elections.

21 September 1993: Yeltsin issued a decree 'On Gradual Constitutional Reform' (Decree 1,400), which suspended the powers of the legislature with immediate effect and scheduled elections to a new bicameral legislature. An emergency session of the Supreme Soviet appointed Rutskoi acting President, although the Constitutional Court ruled against this.

24 September 1993: At a meeting of the CIS Council of Heads of State, in Moscow, an agreement was reached on a framework for economic union, including the gradual removal of tariffs and a currency union; nine states signed the agreement.

28 September 1993: An unarmed police officer was killed in disturbances in the centre of Moscow, as a crowd of several thousand supporters of Ruslan Khasbulatov (the parliamentary Chairman and one of Yeltsin's leading opponents) and Rutskoi attempted to break through the police cordon around the White House.

3 October 1993: Negotiations between the Government and parliament broke down. A state of emergency was declared in Moscow after a group of anti-Yeltsin demonstrators stormed the office of the Mayor of Moscow and the Ostankino television building. Rutskoi was formally dismissed.

4 October 1993: The White House was shelled by government forces and severely damaged by fire, and over 140 people were killed. Later that day Khasbulatov and Rutskoi surrendered and the perpetrators of the violence were arrested.

12 December 1993: A proposed new Constitution was approved by 58.4% of participating voters in a referendum. On the same day elections to the new Federalnoye Sobraniye (Federal Assembly—comprising an upper chamber, the Sovet Federatsii—Federation Council and a lower chamber, the Gosudarstvennaya Duma—State Duma or Duma) were held, producing an unexpected number of votes in the polling to the latter (22.8% of the total) for Vladimir Zhirinovskii's nationalist Liberal Democratic Party of Russia (LPDR) and for the Communist Party (12.4%).

February 1994: The Duma granted an amnesty to the members of the SCSE of the 1991 coup attempt and to the organizers of the parliamentary resistance of September–October 1993.

22 June 1994: Russia became a signatory to the 'Partnership for Peace' co-operation programme drawn up by the North Atlantic Treaty Organization (NATO). A broader accord with NATO also came into effect.

30 July 1994: Against a background of armed raids by rebel Chechens, Yeltsin declared his support for an 'Interim Council' in Chechnya. The Council, headed by Umar Avturkhanov, had proclaimed itself the rightful Government of Chechnya, in opposition to the administration of President Dudayev, which, within two weeks, ordered mobilization in Chechnya.

11 December 1994: Following the collapse of peace negotiations, Yeltsin ordered the invasion of Chechnya by some 40,000 ground troops. In the following month, after a bitterly fought resistance, Dudayev fled Groznyi, the capital of Chechnya, and established his headquarters outside the city.

March 1995: The Russian Government installed a 'Government of National Revival' in Chechnya, chaired by Salambek Khadzhiyev; this existed alongside the Interim Council, by this time largely discredited, but was replaced in November by a new Government, under Doku Zavgayev.

14 June 1995: The militant Chechen leader, Shamil Basayev, took over 1,000 people hostage in a hospital in Budennovsk (Stavropol Krai). After a few days, to secure the release of the captives, the Prime Minister, Chernomyrdin, intervened in the negotiations and agreed to resume peace talks with the Chechen rebels. More than 100 people died during the hostage-taking, and, particularly, during the operations to end the siege.

21 June 1995: A vote of 'no confidence' in the Government was overwhelmingly approved by the Duma.

12 July 1995: An impeachment motion against the President was defeated, largely owing to the fact that Yeltsin was hospitalized at the time, having suffered a heart attack.

30 July 1995: A military accord was signed on the gradual disarmament of the Chechen rebels, in return for the partial withdrawal of federal troops from Chechnya; it remained in effect until October.

17 December 1995: In elections to the Duma, in which an estimated 64.4% of eligible voters participated, the Communist Party of the Russian Federation (CPRF) achieved the greatest success, winning 22.7% of the votes cast; the LDPR won 11.2% of the votes, Our Home is Russia (an electoral bloc headed by Viktor Chernomyrdin) 10.1% and Yabloko (headed by the liberal, Grigorii Yavlinskii) 6.9%.

9 January 1996: Chechen rebels, led by Salman Raduyev, held some 2,000 civilians captive in the town of Kizlyar, Dagestan. Some hostages were later released, while others were taken in convoy to the nearby village of Pervomaiskoye. The village was bombarded for several days by federal air and ground troops, resulting in the release of the captives at the expense of many casualties.

25 January 1996: Russia was admitted to the Council of Europe.

2 April 1996: The Russian President signed a treaty with President Alyaksandr Lukashenka of Belarus establishing a 'Community of Sovereign Republics'. The treaty envisaged closer integration, with a view to the eventual creation of a confederation.

21 April 1996: Dudayev was killed in a Russian missile attack. He was succeeded by his erstwhile deputy, Zemlikhan Yandarbiyev.

27 May 1996: A cease-fire agreement, to take effect from 1 June, was concluded between Yeltsin and Yandarbiyev.

16 June 1996: Eleven candidates contested the presidential election; Yeltsin secured the greatest number of votes (35%), followed by the leader of the CPRF, Gennadii Zyuganov (32%); Lt-Gen. (retd) Aleksandr Lebed won an unexpectedly high level of support, with 15% of the votes cast, and was later appointed as Secretary of the National Security Council.

3 July 1996: Amid increasing speculation about his health, Boris Yeltsin won the second round of voting in the presidential election, with 53.8% of the votes cast. Yeltsin was inaugurated as President on 9 August.

31 August 1996: Following a successful attack by Chechen forces on Groznyi, Lebed negotiated a cease-fire agreement (the Khasavyurt Accords) with the rebel chief of staff, Col Khalid 'Aslan' Maskhadov; the basic principles of the agreement included postponing a solution to the issue of Chechen sovereignty until 2001. Despite the peace deal, Lebed was dismissed in mid-October.

1 January 1997: Maskhadov was elected as President of Chechnya (which subsequently renamed itself 'the Chechen Republic of Ichkeriya'), defeating Basayev.

2 April 1997: A Treaty of Union was signed by the Presidents of Russia and Belarus; the following month a Charter of the Union of Belarus and Russia was concluded, committing the two countries to closer integration.

27 May 1997: At a NATO summit meeting in Paris, France, a Founding Act on Mutual Relations, Co-operation and Security between NATO and the Russian Federation was signed, which *inter alia* enhanced Russia's consultative rights with the Alliance.

28 May 1997: The Russian–Ukrainian dispute over ownership of the Soviet Black Sea Fleet was resolved: a few days later a Treaty on Friendship, Co-operation and Partnership was signed by the Presidents of the two countries.

November 1997: During a visit by President Yeltsin to the People's Republic of China, it was agreed to end a long-running border dispute and allow for the implementation of a 1991 accord demarcating the entire 4,300-km frontier.

1 December 1997: A Partnership and Co-operation Agreement reached between Russia and the European Union (EU) in 1994 took effect.

27 March 1998: Following the dismissal of Chernomyrdin and his Government a few days before, Sergei Kiriyenko, hitherto Minister of Fuel and Energy, was nominated as premier; a new Government was gradually appointed over the following month. Kiriyenko was confirmed as premier by the Duma on 24 April, his nomination having been rejected twice earlier in the month.

17 July 1998: Following the approval, four days earlier, of an IMF loan of US $22,600m., the Duma rejected two of the main tax proposals in the government programme of emergency fiscal measures demanded by the Fund.

17 August 1998: Following an escalating financial crisis, and in a complete reversal of its monetary policies, the Government announced a series of emergency measures, which included the effective devaluation of the rouble.

21 August 1998: The Duma reconvened for an extraordinary plenary session to debate the financial and economic crisis in Russia; a resolution was passed urging the voluntary resignation of President Yeltsin. Two days later President Yeltsin dismissed the Government and reappointed Chernomyrdin premier.

11 September 1998: Following the Duma's second rejection of Chernomyrdin's nomination as Prime Minister, the foreign minister, Yevgenii Primakov, was confirmed as premier by the Duma. On the same day Viktor Gerashchenko was reappointed as Chairman of the Central Bank, following the resignation of Sergei Dubinin.

5 November 1998: The Constitutional Court ruled that Boris Yeltsin was ineligible to seek a third presidential term in 2000.

24 March 1999: Russia condemned NATO air-strikes against Yugoslav targets, initiated in response to the repression of ethnic Albanians in the Serbian province of Kosovo, and suspended relations with the Alliance.

12 May 1999: Yeltsin dismissed Primakov, and appointed Sergei Stepashin, hitherto First Deputy Prime Minister and Minister of the Interior, as acting premier; he was approved by the Duma one week later.

15 May 1999: An attempt by the Duma to impeach the President failed to muster sufficient votes in favour of the motion.

7 August 1999: Armed Chechen guerrillas invaded neighbouring Dagestan and seized control of two villages. Federal troops retaliated and claimed, by the end of the month, to have quelled the rebel action.

9 August 1999: Stepashin was dismissed by Yeltsin, and replaced as premier by Vladimir Putin, hitherto the Secretary of the Security Council and head of the Federal Security Service (FSB), one of the successor bodies to the KGB.

9 and 13 September 1999: Two bomb attacks, which targeted apartment blocks in Moscow, killing almost 200 people, were attributed by the federal authorities to Chechen rebels. In August a bomb explosion at a Moscow shopping centre had injured more than 30 people, and further bombings in southern Russia, against both civilian and military targets, took place in mid-September.

23 September 1999: Russia initiated major air-strikes against Chechnya, officially in retaliation for the bombings, and as part of a declared 'anti-terrorism' campaign.

6 December 1999: Following the full-scale invasion of Chechnya at the beginning of November, Russian forces warned residents of the capital, Groznyi, to evacuate the city by 11 December, resulting in strong international disapproval. A ground offensive against the city subsequently commenced.

8 December 1999: The signature of the Union Treaty of Russia and Belarus took place in Moscow. The Treaty entered into force on 26 January 2000, following its ratification by the Russian executive.

19 December 1999: At elections to the Duma, the CPRF secured the most seats, winning 113. Unity, formed by 31 leaders of Russia's regions, took 72 seats, and the Fatherland-All Russia bloc obtained 67 seats. The pro-market Union of Rightist Forces (URF) obtained 29 seats, Yabloko took 21 and the Zhirinovskii bloc (contesting the election in place of the LDPR) won 17. Some 62% of the electorate participated.

31 December 1999: Boris Yeltsin unexpectedly resigned as President. Putin assumed the role in an acting capacity.

14 January 2000: A new national security concept was published, which lowered the threshold for the use of nuclear weapons, in an attempt to contain the threat from the West's perceived attempts to achieve global domination.

THE PUTIN PRESIDENCY

26 March 2000: Putin achieved a clear victory in the first round of the presidential election, with 52.9% of the votes cast. Gennadii Zyuganov was the second-placed candidate, with 29.2% of the votes cast.

6 April 2000: The Parliamentary Assembly of the Council of Europe voted to suspend Russia's membership unless progress was made to end human rights abuses in Chechnya.

5 May 2000: Putin decreed that, henceforth, Chechnya was to come under direct federal, rather than direct presidential, rule. Maskhadov was no longer to be recognized as President of the Republic, and on 19 June a new administrative leader for Chechnya, Akhmad haji Kadyrov, was inaugurated.

7 May 2000: Putin was inaugurated as President of the Russian Federation. He subsequently relinquished the post of premier and formed a new Government headed by the former First Deputy Chairman, Mikhail Kasyanov.

13 May 2000: The President issued a decree dividing Russia's 89 constituent regions and republics between seven federal okrugs (districts). Each district was to come under the control of a presidential envoy, who was to oversee local regions' compliance with federal legislation. Of the new presidential envoys, five were senior officers of the security services or the military.

31 May 2000: Three pieces of legislation, proposed by Putin to extend the powers of the President and curtail those of the regional governors, were passed by the Duma. The first proposed that regional governors should lose their seats in the Sovet Federatsii, and be replaced by representatives elected from regional legislatures; following its ratification by the Sovet Federatsii in July, all existing Council members were to be replaced by the beginning of 2002. The second bill accorded the President the right to dismiss regional governors, and the third allowed governors to remove from office elected officials who were subordinate to them.

September 2000: The General Staff issued an order specifying a reduction of some 350,000 in the strength of the Russian armed forces; the reductions were expected to take place in 2001–03. On 9 November the Security Council voted to reduce the overall strength of the armed forces by 600,000 (approximately one-fifth of the 2000 level) by 2005.

20 September 2000: The Minister for the Press, Broadcasting and Mass Media, Mikhail Lesin, admitted that he had approved a document stating that criminal charges against Vladimir Gusinskii, the Chairman of the Mediya-MOST holding company, would be dropped in return for the sale of Gusinskii's media interests to the partially state-owned gas monopoly, Gazprom.

10 October 2000: President Putin and the Presidents of Belarus, Kazakhstan, Kyrgyzstan and Tajikistan signed a treaty creating a new customs union, to be known as the Eurasian Economic Community.

30 November 2000: The Presidents of Russia and Belarus signed an agreement on the introduction of a common currency unit for the two countries by 2008.

13 December 2000: Following the issuance of a federal arrest warrant on charges of fraud, Gusinskii, who had lost control of Mediya-MOST in the previous month, was arrested in Spain. Spain refused to extradite Gusinskii to Russia, however, and he travelled to Israel (where he held dual citizenship) in April 2001, purportedly to complicate conditions for his extradition. Another 'oligarch', the former Executive Secretary of the CIS, Boris Berezovskii, had entered self-imposed exile, after corruption charges were brought against him in November.

22 January 2001: Putin signed a decree transferring control of operations in Chechnya from the defence ministry to the FSB.

7 March 2001: The Duma approved the introduction of a new national anthem, which combined the tune of the former Soviet Anthem, abandoned in 1990, with new words, written by the composer of the original lyrics, Sergei Mikhalkov.

28 March 2001: Putin announced a ministerial reshuffle, in which, notably, Sergei Ivanov was appointed as Minister of Defence.

12 July 2001: New conditions for the registration of political parties were introduced, which were intended to facilitate the consolidation of national parties.

October 2001: Following the commencement of US-led military action against targets of the Taliban regime, and the al-Qa'ida militant Islamist organization, in Afghanistan, on 7 October, Russia provided military intelligence, and allowed the coalition access to its airspace. Russia also increased logistical and military support to the anti-Taliban forces of the United Islamic Front for the Salvation of Afghanistan (the 'Northern Alliance').

1 December 2001: The founding congress of the Unity and Fatherland-United Russia party (later United Russia—UR), uniting two hitherto separate centrist movements, Fatherland-All Russia and Unity, took place.

16 January 2002: A new session of the Sovet Federatsii opened; for the first time, the Council comprised the full-time appointees of both regional governors and the chairmen of regional legislative assemblies.

3 April 2002: The Duma voted to revoke seven of the nine committee chairmanships held by the CPRF, leading that party to assume a more aggressively oppositional role than had hitherto been the case.

25 April 2002: The rebel Arab Islamist leader, al-Khattab, who had led a faction in the war in Chechnya, was killed.

9 May 2002: During Victory Day processions in Kaspiisk, Dagestan, 45 people were killed and more than 130 others injured as the result of a bomb attack attributed to Chechen militants.

24 May 2002: President Putin and the US President, George W. Bush, signed an agreement, in accordance with which Russia and the USA were each to reduce their stocks of strategic nuclear warheads by more than one-half over a period of 10 years. This development followed an announcement by the USA in late 2001 that it was to withdraw from the Anti-Ballistic Missile (ABM) Treaty, signed between the USA and the USSR in 1972, with effect from June 2002. On 13 June Russia withdrew from the START 2 Treaty, which had been superseded by the new nuclear arms reduction agreement.

28 May 2002: The new NATO-Russia Council, which made Russia a full partner of NATO in discussions on a number of issues, including counter-terrorism, non-proliferation and emergency planning, was inaugurated at a NATO conference in Rome, Italy.

25 July 2002: President Putin approved legislation permitting the sale and purchase of agricultural land; however, the sale of farmland to foreign purchasers or to foreign-controlled enterprises remained prohibited. The law came into effect in January 2003.

19 August 2002: In the single largest loss of life since the resumption of military operations in Chechnya in 1999, some 118 federal troops were killed when rebels shot down a military helicopter.

23 October 2002: Some 50 heavily armed Chechen rebels took more than 700 people hostage in a Moscow theatre, demanding the immediate withdrawal of federal troops from Chechnya. On 26 October élite Russian troops stormed the theatre, killing the rebels in an operation that also resulted in the deaths of some 129 hostages, according to official figures. It rapidly emerged that the vast majority of these deaths had resulted from the use of an incapacitating gas by the federal troops.

5 November 2002: The Russian authorities requested the extradition of Berezovskii from the United Kingdom (where he had taken up residence), but he was granted political asylum in September 2003.

27 December 2002: At least 83 people died, and more than 150 others were injured, when suicide bombers detonated bombs in two vehicles stationed outside the headquarters of the Chechen republican Government in Groznyi.

11 March 2003: Several presidential decrees provided for a reorganization of the federal security agencies, as a result of which the powers of the FSB were expanded.

23 March 2003: A referendum was held in Chechnya on the draft republican constitution, which described the region as an integral part of the Russian Federation. According to the official results, some 88.4% of the electorate participated in the plebiscite, of whom 96.0% voted in favour. Two further questions, on the method of electing the president and the parliament of the republic, were also overwhelmingly approved.

28 April 2003: Representatives from Armenia, Belarus, Kazakhstan, Kyrgyzstan, Russia and Tajikistan formally inaugurated the successor to the Collective Security Treaty, a new regional defence organization known as the Collective Security Treaty Organization (CSTO).

12 May 2003: At least 59 people were killed when suicide bombers attacked offices of the Chechen Government in Znamenskoye, in the north of the republic. Two days later another suicide bombing in Chechnya, at a religious festival attended by Kadyrov, resulted in at least 14 deaths.

16 June 2003: Vladimir Yakovlev, hitherto Governor of St Petersburg, was appointed to the federal Government as a Deputy Chairman, with particular responsibility for housing and utilities.

18 June 2003: A vote of 'no confidence' in the Government, presented to the Duma by the CPRF and the liberal Yabloko factions, was defeated.

22 June 2003: The national independent television channel, TVS, was forced to cease operations, ostensibly for financial reasons.

6 July 2003: Fifteen people were killed as a result of a suicide bombing, attributed to Chechen militants, at a music festival outside Moscow.

21 August 2003: Gusinskii was arrested in Greece, on an international arrest warrant issued in 2001, following his return from Israel. He was released on bail later in the month and ordered to remain in Greece (on 14 October a Greek court rejected Russia's request for his extradition).

1 September 2003: The overall command for military operations in Chechnya was transferred from the FSB to the Ministry of Internal Affairs. Moreover, the Minister of Internal Affairs, Boris Gryzlov, stated that such operations were no longer regarded as having an 'anti-terrorist' character, but were rather, henceforth, to form part of an 'operation to protect law and constitutional order'.

5 October 2003: Kadyrov was elected President of Chechnya, with 88% of the votes cast, according to official figures. However, many observers were critical of the conduct of voting, noting that several of Kadyrov's principal rivals had withdrawn, or been obliged to withdraw, their candidacies.

26 October 2003: Mikhail Khodorkovskii, the Chief Executive of Yukos Oil Co, and a prominent supporter of the pro-market URF and the liberal Yabloko party, was arrested and detained, reportedly following his failure to attend a court hearing at which various charges of fraudulent practice by the company were being investigated. Khodorkovskii, who was the third senior executive of the company to be arrested since July, was subsequently charged with tax evasion and fraud.

7 December 2003: Duma elections were dominated by UR, which won 222 of the 450 seats. The CPRF secured 53 seats, the LDPR 38, and the newly formed Motherland electoral bloc received 37. Yabloko and the URF failed to obtain the 5% of votes necessary to obtain representation on the basis of federal party lists, and their legislative representation was much reduced, to only four and three seats, respectively. Turn-out was relatively low, at 55.75%.

9 December 2003: Six people were killed when a bomb exploded in Moscow, outside a hotel located close to the Kremlin; the intended target was thought to have been the Duma building. Four days earlier a bomb attack had targeted a passenger train in Stavropol Krai, killing some 45 people and injuring about 170.

6 February 2004: An explosion on the Moscow metro attributed to Chechen militants killed at least 39 people.

24 February 2004: Putin dismissed the Government of Mikhail Kasyanov. Mikhail Fradkov, former representative to the EU, was subsequently appointed Chairman of the new Government, in which the number of ministries was reduced from 30 to 17. Among the new appointments, Sergei Lavrov, hitherto Permanent Representative to the UN, was appointed as Minister of Foreign Affairs, succeeding Igor Ivanov.

14 March 2004: Vladimir Putin was overwhelmingly re-elected as President, receiving 71.3% of votes cast. His closest rival, Nikolai Kharitonov of the CPRF, received 13.7%. A total of 64.4% of registered voters participated in the election. Notably, both the CPRF and LDPR declined to nominate

leading members of their parties as candidates, in both cases presenting relatively obscure figures.

9 May 2004: Chechen President Akhmad haji Kadyrov was killed in a bombing in Groznyi.

21–22 June 2004: A series of raids on Ministry of Internal Affairs targets in Ingushetiya, variously attributed to Chechen, Ingush and international militants, left 97 people dead.

24 August 2004: Two passenger planes, both flying from Moscow's Domodedovo airport, crashed, killing all 89 people on board. Both crashes were attributed to suicide bombers.

29 August 2004: The presidential election in Chechnya was won by Maj-Gen. Alu Alkhanov, who was perceived to be the favoured candidate of the federal authorities. Council of Europe observers described the elections as undemocratic.

31 August 2004: An explosion outside a Moscow Metro station, reportedly caused by a suicide bomber, killed 10 people.

1 September 2004: Armed militants occupied a school in Beslan, North Osetiya—Alaniya, on the first day of the school year, taking up to 1,500 parents, teachers and children hostage. After two days of largely fruitless negotiations, on 3 September members of the special forces stormed the school. More than 330 hostages, including at least 150 children, were killed during the course of the siege, according to official figures.

13 September 2004: Putin announced plans for political reform, including the appointment by the federal President of regional governors and the introduction of a system of fully proportional representation for Duma elections.

13 October 2004: The Duma voted in favour of overturning a law that had hitherto prevented members of the Government holding membership of political parties.

12 December 2004: Putin signed legislation providing for the appointment of regional governors, subject to the approval of regional legislatures.

19 December 2004: The main petroleum-producing subsidiary of Yukos, Yuganskneftegaz, was sold at auction, in order that the company pay tax demands issued against it by the Government. Yuganskneftegaz was acquired by a previously unknown company, Baikalfinansgrup, which in turn, was acquired by the state-controlled company Rosneft shortly after the auction.

22 December 2004: Putin approved legislation increasing the minimum membership of a political party to 50,000 in order for it to be registered and to participate in elections.

9 February 2005: A vote of 'no confidence' in the Government was overwhelmingly defeated in the Duma; the vote had been initiated by the CPRF and Motherland factions in response to widespread protests nation-wide at the recent monetization of various state benefits granted to pensioners and certain other groups of citizens.

8 March 2005: The Russian military announced that Maskhadov had been killed during a special operation in the settlement of Tolstoi-Yurt, north of the Chechen capital Groznyi; Maskhadov was succeeded as leader of the rebel 'State Defence Committee' by Abdul-Khalim Sadulayev.

31 May 2005: Khodorkovskii was sentenced to nine years' imprisonment, having been found guilty on six charges, including tax evasion and embezzlement; two other former Yukos executives also received custodial sentences. Khodorkovskii announced that he would appeal against the verdict, and stated that he intended to establish a foundation to promote Russian culture whilst in gaol.

26 August 2005: It was reported that Sadulayev had appointed a new rebel Chechen 'Government', following his implementation of personnel changes to representations of the separatists internationally; the 'Government' was notable for its inclusion of Basayev as 'First Deputy Prime Minister'; Basayev had been distanced from the rebel authorities following the theatre siege in Moscow in late 2002.

13 October 2005: Some 100 militants staged a series of co-ordinated attacks against government, police, and commercial buildings across Nalchik, the capital of the Kabardino-Balkar Republic, in the North Caucasus. According to official figures, at least 130 people were killed in the ensuing clashes, including more than 90 militants. Basayev claimed responsibility for the organization of the attacks, although it was unclear whether the principal insurgents were associated with a local Islamist group, Yarmuk, with a broader 'Caucasus Front' associated with Basayev and Sadulayev, or with both groups.

14 November 2005: President Putin implemented a minor governmental reorganization. Dmitrii Medvedev, hitherto Head of the Presidential Administration, was appointed as First Deputy Chairman of the Government; he was to retain his position as Chairman of the Board of Directors of Gazprom. Sergei Ivanov, the Minister of Defence, was additionally appointed as a Deputy Chairman of the Government.

27 November 2005: UR secured an absolute majority of seats in elections to a new bicameral legislature in Chechnya.

27 December 2005: Andrei Illarionov, a principal economic adviser to the President, resigned, expressing strong disapproval of recent political and economic policies in Russia, including, notably, the Yukos affair, and stating that he no longer regarded Russia as a 'free country'.

17 January 2006: It was announced that President Putin had signed into law controversial new legislation that, *inter alia*, permitted the authorities to close non-governmental organizations deemed to infringe Russia's sovereignty, unity or cultural heritage.

4 March 2006: The Chechen legislature unanimously approved the nomination of Ramzan Kadyrov (the son of the assassinated President of the Republic) as premier, confirming the position he had held de facto following the hospitalization of his predecessor, Sergei Abramov, in November 2005.

17 June 2006: Sadulayev was killed in an operation by special forces in Chechnya. He was succeeded as leader of the separatist Chechen rebels by Doku Umarov, a militant Islamist believed to be closely associated with Basayev.

19 June 2006: President Putin nominated the Minister of Justice, Yurii Chaika, to serve as Prosecutor-General; he was succeeded as Minister of Justice on 23 June by Vladimir Ustinov, who had been dismissed as Prosecutor-General at his own request earlier in the month.

10 July 2006: Basayev was killed, reportedly by federal special forces, in an explosion in Ingushetiya.

3 October 2006: Russia closed all transport, postal and banking communications with Georgia. This measure followed the detention, in late September, of four Russian military officers in Georgia, on charges of spying. In subsequent weeks large numbers of Georgian citizens residing illegally in Russia were deported. (Earlier in the year Russia had banned the import of Georgian wines and mineral water, purportedly on hygiene grounds.)

7 October 2006: A journalist of the independent newspaper *Novaya Gazeta*, Anna Politkovskaya, who was a leading critic of the Russian military campaigns in Chechnya and of the official Chechen leadership, was shot dead at her apartment building in Moscow. (Preliminary hearings into the trial of three suspects, of whom two were Chechen nationals, in connection with her killing began in October 2008.)

28 October 2006: A new party, A Just Russia (AJR), regarded as broadly supportive of the federal authorities, was established by the merger of Motherland, the Russian Party of Life and Russian Pensioners' Party. (The People's Party of the Russian Federation joined the organization in April 2007.)

23 November 2006: Aleksandr Litvinenko, a former officer in the FSB and exile to the United Kingdom, died in a London hospital as a result of poisoning with the radioactive isotope Polonium-210, having issued a statement accusing Putin of responsibility for his sickness. Russia's subsequent refusal to accede to a request by the British Government for the extradition of the principal suspect, Andrei Lugovoi, exacerbated relations between the two countries.

15 February 2007: Putin reorganized the Government, appointing Sergei Ivanov to the office of First Deputy Chairman (thereby granting him equal formal status to Medvedev). Anatolii Serdyukov, hitherto the head of the Federal Tax Service, succeeded Ivanov as Minister of Defence. Putin also appointed the President of the Chechen Republic, Maj.-Gen. Alu Alkhanov, to the post of deputy justice minister in the federal Government, enabling the Prime Minister of Chechnya, Ramzan Kadyrov, to become acting President of the Republic.

2 March 2007: Putin's nomination of Kadyrov as President of Chechnya was confirmed by the republican legislature.

27 March 2007: Vladimir Churov was elected Chairman of the Central Electoral Commission, succeeding Aleksandr Veshnyakov (who had served in the post since 1999).

14 September 2007: Following the resignation of Fradkov and his Government, the Duma approved Putin's nomination of Viktor Zubkov, hitherto head of the Federal Financial Monitoring Service, as Chairman.

25 September 2007: Putin announced a government reorganization; three ministers were replaced, while the Minister of Finance, Aleksei Kudrin, also became a Deputy Chairman.

1 October 2007: Putin announced, in a statement made at UR's party congress, that he would head the party's list of candidates in the forthcoming legislative elections on 2 December and that he considered a proposal by delegates that he, eventually, become Chairman of the Government to be 'wholly realistic'.

16 October 2007: Putin visited the Iranian capital, Tehran, to attend a summit meeting of the five Caspian state leaders. The declaration adopted by the parties at the end of the summit postponed settlement of territorial issues, but asserted that they would not allow their territories to be used by other states for the purposes of a military attack.

14 September 2007: Following the resignation of Fradkov and his Government, the Duma approved Putin's nomination of Viktor Zubkov, hitherto head of the Federal Financial Monitoring Service, as Chairman. Later that month Putin announced a government reorganization; three new ministers were appointed, including Elvira Nabiullina, who received the economic development and trade portfolio, while the Minister of Finance, Aleksei Kudrin, also became a Deputy Chairman.

2 December 2007: At the elections to the Duma, UR won a substantial majority, winning 64.3% of the votes cast, according to official results, and secured 315 seats; the CPRF received 11.6% of votes and 57 seats, the LDPR 8.1% and 40 seats, and AJR 7.7% and 38 seats. Voter turn-out was 63.7% of the electorate. Reports emerged that students and public sector workers had been placed under considerable pressure by the authorities to vote in favour of UR. The Russian Government dismissed a subsequent joint statement by the OSCE and the Council of Europe that the conduct of the elections had failed to meet international standards for democracy, following widespread allegations of media bias in favour of UR and voting irregularities. (A report by CIS observers upheld the organization of the elections.)

10 December 2007: Putin announced his support for the nomination by UR and three other parties of Medvedev as a candidate in the forthcoming presidential election. Putin subsequently indicated approval of a proposal made by Medvedev that he serve as premier in the event that Medvedev be elected to the presidency.

2 March 2008: Medvedev (following his endorsement by Putin) was overwhelmingly elected to the presidency, with some 70.3% of votes cast, according to final official results; Zyuganov of the CPRF received 17.7% of votes, and Zhirinovskii of the LDPR about 9.4% of votes. Official voter turn-out was estimated at about 69.8%. Observers from the Parliamentary Assembly of the Council of Europe acknowledged popular support for Medvedev, but reported that aspects of the electoral campaign had failed to meet democratic principles. Elections were also conducted to a number of regional legislatures.

THE MEDVEDEV PRESIDENCY

7 May 2008: Medvedev was inaugurated as President; Putin, on relinquishing the presidency, became Chairman of UR.

8 May 2008: The Duma approved Medvedev's nomination of Putin as Chairman of the Government by an overwhelming majority.

12 May 2008: Putin announced a government reorganization, in which an additional three ministries were created. Zubkov became First Deputy Chairman, and was to assume particular responsibility for the agricultural sector, while a senior presidential aide, Igor Shuvalov, was also accorded the post of First Deputy Chairman. Igor Sechin, the Chairman of Rosneft and hitherto deputy head of the presidential administration, was appointed to the Government as Deputy Chairman and was to supervise industrial development programmes. Ivanov remained in the new administration as a Deputy Chairman; other principal ministers, including Kudrin and Lavrov, retained their posts.

31 July 2008: President Medvedev announced a new, extensive programme to suppress corruption by state officials; anti-corruption legislation was to be submitted to the Duma later in the year.

8 August 2008: Following an offensive by Georgia against the Russian-supported separatist region of South Ossetia, Russia launched an intensive counter-attack, dispatching large numbers of troops through the Roki tunnel to South Ossetia, where they engaged in hostilities with Georgian forces at Tskhinvali; the Russian Government stated that it sought to protect its citizens and peace-keeping troops present in the region, and alleged that Georgia sought to commit 'genocide' against the South Ossetian population. (Many South Ossetians had been issued with Russian passports by the separatist authorities since the mid-2000s.) Russian aircraft commenced bombardment of Georgian targets beyond the separatist territory, including the port of Poti and the military base at Senaki. Russian forces rapidly gained control of Tskhinvali, expelling the Georgian troops, and also advanced into the other separatist region of Abkhazia.

12 August 2008: President Medvedev ordered an end to Russia's military operation in Georgia, claiming that its aims had been achieved. Georgia and Russia agreed to a peace plan, mediated by French President Nicolas Sarkozy (on behalf of the EU), providing for an immediate cease-fire, the provision of humanitarian assistance, and the withdrawal of Russian troops to pre-conflict positions.

19 August 2008: After Russia failed to implement fully the withdrawal of troops as stipulated, NATO foreign ministers decided to suspend meetings of the NATO-Russia Council until Russia was considered to have observed the terms of the peace plan. Two days later Russia announced its suspension of military co-operation with NATO.

26 August 2008: President Medvedev endorsed a resolution, which had been approved in both chambers of the Russian legislature, officially recognizing South Ossetia and Abkhazia as independent sovereign states. Georgia, the USA and EU condemned the decision. By September Nicaragua was the only other state to have recognized the two regions as independent states.

29 August 2008: Georgia formally suspended diplomatic relations with Russia, in protest at the continued Russian occupation of South Ossetia and Abkhazia, and security zones around the two regions.

8 September 2008: Following further negotiations with an EU delegation led by President Sarkozy in Moscow, Russia agreed on additional measures for the implementation of the August cease-fire plan, principally the withdrawal of all remaining forces from Georgian territory (apart from South Ossetia and Abkhazia) within 10 days of the deployment of EU monitors (scheduled for 1 October).

17 September 2008: Russia signed friendship and co-operation treaties with the leaders of South Ossetia and Abkhazia, pledging to support the two regions militarily; the treaties also formalized economic co-operation between Russia and the regions.

10 October 2008: Following the deployment of EU monitors in Georgia as scheduled, the withdrawal of the remaining Russian troops from areas adjacent to South Ossetia and Abkhazia was verified. However, the Georgian Government claimed that Russia continued to be in violation of the cease-fire agreement until it reduced the number of troops it deployed within South Ossetia and Abkhazia to pre-conflict levels and also withdrew from areas previously held by Georgian forces. (Russia had announced its intention to maintain a total of 7,600 troops within the two separatist regions.)

14 October 2008: Dmitrii Kozak, hitherto Minister of Regional Development, was appointed as a Deputy Chairman of the Government.

15 October 2008: Direct negotiations between Russia and Georgia, convened in Geneva, Switzerland, under the aegis of the UN, EU and OSCE, were abandoned, after the Russian delegation rejected Georgia's refusal to grant equal status participation to the representatives of South Ossetia and Abkhazia. (Further consultations were provisionally scheduled for November.)

History

Based on an earlier essay by ANGUS ROXBURGH

Revised for this edition by Dr KENNETH WILSON

EARLY HISTORY

The Russians are Eastern Slavs, inhabitants of the huge Eurasian land mass, which is a territory with no great natural frontiers. This fact has made the Russians throughout history both vulnerable to invaders and themselves inclined to migration and expansion. Their first state was established towards the end of the ninth century, around Kyiv (Kiev—now in Ukraine). Kievan Rus (forerunner not only of the 'Great' Russians, but also of the Belarusians or 'White Russians' and the Ukrainians or 'Little Russians') was a slave-holding society, which was officially Christianized in 988. The state did not exist for long, however. Much of its population, tired of constant enemy attacks from the south and west, gradually migrated to the north and east. By the late 12th century the early Russians were scattered over a large area in what is now western Russia, Belarus and Ukraine. Their territory was fragmented among a large number of (usually warring) principalities, the most powerful centred on the town of Vladimir.

The disintegration of the Russian nation was halted, ironically, by outsiders. In 1237 ferocious invaders from the east, the Mongol Tatars, led by Batu (a descendant of Chinghiz or Genghis Khan), crossed the River Volga and imposed almost 250 years of subjugation on the Russian people. Mongol rule established in Russia a social, political, administrative and military system quite unlike that of Western Europe. It was based on the unquestioning submission of all individuals to the group and to the absolute power of the ultimate ruler, the Khan. Russia's feuding princes all became vassals of the Golden Horde, as the Khan and his entourage were known. One of the smallest principalities, Muscovy (based in the town of Moscow—Moskva), rose to prominence, largely as a reward for its devotion to the Khan and its position as chief tax-collector for the Golden Horde.

From the late 14th century the Mongol empire began to disintegrate into smaller khanates. In 1480 a new Russian state finally emerged, when the Muscovite prince, Ivan III, proclaimed complete independence from the Tatars. Moreover, with the fall of Constantinople (İstanbul) to the Turks in 1453, Moscow could lay claim to being the 'Third Rome', the capital of the most pre-eminent Orthodox Christian state. The new state retained many features of the Mongol system, including the supremacy of the state over the individual and the principle of universal compulsory service to the state. The Russian historian, Nikolai Berdyayev, described Muscovite Russia as a 'Christianized Tatar kingdom'. Ivan IV ('the Terrible') was the first of many a Russian Tsar (Caesar or Emperor) to use his unquestioned rights as supreme ruler to establish a despotic regime in which terror was, effectively, an instrument of state policy. His *oprichniki*, a secret police force, were used to suppress dissent, whether real or imagined, in barbaric fashion. Ivan IV annexed the Mongol Khanates of Kazan and Astrakhan to Moscow and began to colonize the middle and upper reaches of the Volga. This led to a mass migration of peasants to these more fertile areas. It was under Ivan's rule that the Cossack leader, Yermak Timofeyev, began Russia's expansion eastwards beyond the Ural Mountains into Siberia, where villages, forts and trading posts were soon established. For the first time the Russian Empire extended into two continents. In 1645, under the first Tsar of the Romanov dynasty, Muscovite rule reached the Sea of Okhotsk, and the port town of Okhotsk was founded.

Over subsequent centuries Russia's development was marked by almost continuous expansionism and by arguments over whether to follow a 'Western', European model of civilization, or to create a peculiarly Russian one. Peter (Petr) I ('the Great') combined despotic methods with a determination to modernize Russia and establish it as a great European power. To symbolize this, in 1712 he moved the capital from Moscow to a newly built city on the Baltic coast, St Petersburg (Sankt-Peterburg), which he called his 'window on the West'. Under Catherine (Yekaterina) II ('the Great') the Russian Empire was expanded south to the Black Sea and west into Poland. The Tsars Alexander (Aleksandr) I (1801–25), Nicholas (Nikolai) I (1825–55) and Alexander II (1855–81) extended the Russian frontiers into the Caucasus and parts of Central Asia. In 1885 the Turkmen became the last of the Muslim peoples of Central Asia to be incorporated into the Empire. During this period new territories were also claimed in the Far East, reaching Vladivostok in 1860. Politically, 19th-century Russia alternated between reactionary Tsars, such as Nicholas I, and enlightened ones, such as Alexander II (whose most famous act was the emancipation of the serfs in 1861). European liberal and revolutionary ideas constantly threatened the political order and the last Tsar, Nicholas II, was obliged to introduce elements of parliamentary democracy, with the establishment of a legislative assembly, the Duma, in 1906.

In 1917 the pressures of defeats in the First World War and growing economic and social chaos in the country at large brought two revolutions. The first, which occurred in March, overthrew the Tsar and established a Provisional Government, which, however, soon found itself sharing power with new workers' councils (soviets). The second, the Bolshevik Revolution, on 7 November (25 October under the old-style calendar, which remained in use by the civil authorities until 1918), brought the communists, under Vladimir Ulyanov (Lenin), to power in the capital (renamed Petrograd in 1914) and, after three years of civil war, throughout most of the territory of the Russian Empire.

SOVIET RUSSIA

In the new Union of Soviet Socialist Republics (USSR—established in 1922), Russia (the Russian Soviet Federative Socialist Republic—RSFSR) became just one of (eventually) 15 national republics. In 1918 Moscow again became the capital city of Russia and, subsequently, of the USSR. Under Stalin (Iosif Dzhugashvili, 1924–53), especially after a surge of Russian nationalism during the Second World War, into which the USSR entered in 1941, the accepted dogma was that the Soviet nations would not merely 'come together' (a process referred to as *sblizheniye*), but eventually 'merge' (*sliyaniye*—which most understood to mean the subjugation of the other nations by the Russian people). Even after Stalin, Russians remained the *de facto* colonial masters, their Empire simply renamed the USSR. Many of the characteristics of pre-Soviet Russia came to dominate the political culture of the USSR. The communist regime was highly centralized. It encouraged and relied upon traditions of collectivism in the population. The three basic principles of tsarism (orthodoxy, autocracy and nationality—*pravoslaviye*, *samoderzhaviye* and *narodnost*) were transmuted into the communist doctrines of Marxism-Leninism, Communist Party dictatorship and the idealization of the People (*Narod*). Russia ensured the loyalty of non-Russian parts of the Soviet empire by the appointment of Russian second secretaries in all republican Communist Party organizations, by establishing Russian as the language of the Soviet state and by making the republics' economies dependent on each other as well as on the all-Union Government in Moscow. Russian migration to the other republics was encouraged. Additionally, the RSFSR lacked the republican institutions granted to the other national republics in the USSR, thereby encouraging the assimilation of Russian national identity to that of the entire Union. Until Mikhail Gorbachev's policy of glasnost (openness) in the late 1980s, the colonized Soviet nations rarely protested in public, although the suppression of certain non-Russian nationalities caused bitter resentment throughout the Soviet period and became a major focus of political protest from the late 1980s.

Soviet rule transformed Russia from a largely peasant, illiterate society into an industrialized, urbanized and educated one, but this was achieved at the cost of untold human suffering. Tens of millions of people lost their lives in a series of man-made disasters: the civil war of 1918–21; the enforced collectivization of agriculture and resultant famines in the early 1930s; Stalin's purges from 1936; and the Second World War. For most of the 74 years of communist rule, political freedoms were stifled and dissidents were incarcerated in labour camps. Even during Nikita Khrushchev's 'thaw' (when he was First Secretary of the Communist Party of the Soviet Union—CPSU, 1953–64), as part of which he denounced Stalin's 'cult of personality', the one-party state remained intact.

Under Leonid Brezhnev, who served as First Secretary of the CPSU's Central Committee from 1964 until his death in 1982, the USSR developed into a military 'superpower', competing with the USA to build up supplies of nuclear armaments, a policy that placed a serious strain on the economy. The Soviet authorities sponsored governments sympathetic to communism and 'national liberation movements' throughout the world, and its forces invaded Afghanistan in 1979, in an attempt to establish and uphold a client regime. Domestically, political dissent was not tolerated, and the centrally run economy entered what was later termed a 'period of stagnation', unable to meet the requirements of the populace.

PERESTROIKA AND THE END OF THE USSR

Between 1985 and 1991 Mikhail Gorbachev, as CPSU leader and later President of the USSR, introduced far-reaching economic and political reforms known as perestroika (reconstruction), which were initially intended to improve, and later to transform, the Soviet system. The economic reforms ended the state monopoly on legal economic activity and introduced elements of the market into the Soviet economy; they failed, however, to invigorate the economy which continued to decline. Gorbachev also introduced glasnost, an unprecedented commitment to 'openness' or freedom of speech, which was intended to rally public support behind his reforms. Political reform became increasingly radical, culminating in the introduction of competitive elections and the ending of the CPSU's monopoly on political life. Gorbachev also transformed the USSR's foreign policy. Arms control agreements were negotiated with the USA, Soviet troops were withdrawn from Afghanistan, and Eastern Bloc nations were allowed to determine their own internal affairs. International tensions were greatly eased and the Cold War ultimately ended.

Throughout his years in power, Gorbachev had to steer a course between hardline communist leaders, who opposed his reforms, and radicals such as Boris Yeltsin, who demanded faster change. Soviet politics became increasingly polarized along this axis as perestroika progressed. The defining issue of the late Gorbachev era was the 'nationalities question' as several of the Union Republics (especially the Baltic states—Estonia, Latvia and Lithuania) used the opportunities provided by glasnost and competitive elections to fight for greater autonomy, and even independence, from the all-Union Government. Russia was a latecomer to the 'national movement'; from mid-1990 its newly elected parliament (a 1,068-member Congress of People's Deputies, which elected a standing parliament, or Supreme Soviet, of 274 members, both then chaired by Boris Yeltsin) began to oppose 'Soviet' centralism and demand greater financial autonomy. These rights were inscribed in a Declaration of Sovereignty approved by the RSFSR Congress of People's Deputies (then a minor body compared with the USSR Congress elected one year earlier) on 12 June 1990. One year later Yeltsin became Russia's first directly elected executive President, with 57.3% of the votes cast and, from then on, Russia's political power matched, or even outweighed, that of the Soviet central authorities. Unlike Gorbachev, who had never experienced a popular election, Yeltsin had a real mandate for reform. When it became clear that the centralized 15-republic USSR could not be preserved without resort to repression on a massive scale Gorbachev negotiated a new Union Treaty, which devolved much more power to the nine republics that chose to participate.

However, the signing of the Treaty, scheduled for 20 August 1991, was pre-empted by an attempted *coup d'état*, led by conservative communists determined to maintain the old Union. Their plan, though, was poorly organized and opposition to it, led bravely by Yeltsin, was strong. The coup, launched to preserve the Union, hastened its demise for when Gorbachev returned to Moscow, having been briefly held under house arrest in Crimea, Yeltsin led an invigorated crusade against both central Soviet power and communist rule. On 23 August he suspended the activities of the Russian Communist Party (which had been active within the RSFSR). One day later Gorbachev resigned as General Secretary of the CPSU, demanded that the Central Committee disband itself and nationalized the Party's assets and property. In the following months the Russian Supreme Soviet adopted numerous decrees that removed the all-Union Government's control over key economic and financial apparatus.

On 7–8 December 1991 the leaders of the RSFSR and the Ukrainian and Belarusian Soviet Socialist Republics met at Belovezhskaya Pushcha, Belarus, and signed a treaty, according to which the USSR ceased to exist and was replaced by a new Commonwealth of Independent States (CIS). With the exception of the three Baltic states, all of the former Soviet republics eventually joined the CIS. On 25 December 1991 Gorbachev resigned, marking the end of the USSR. As Gorbachev left office the state he had sought to preserve no longer existed and the economy he wanted to improve was in chaos. The process, however, had been managed with comparatively little bloodshed, the Cold War was over and Russia was freer than it had ever been before. Above the Kremlin, the red Soviet flag was replaced by the white, blue and red tricolour of Russia (which was formally renamed the Russian Federation on the same day). President Yeltsin was the first leader of a Russian state for centuries to rule over such a truncated territory. The population of the Russian Federation was less than 150m., compared with the 290m. of the USSR. It remained, however, in terms of area, the largest country in the world.

YELTSIN'S RUSSIA

President Yeltsin had two principal aims as Russia emerged as a new state. First, to transform the country into a genuine democracy, something it had never been. Second, to abandon the centrally planned economy in favour of a capitalist one, based on a free market and private ownership. A far-reaching economic reform programme, termed 'shock therapy', was introduced from January 1992, initially under the guidance of a radical economist, Yegor Gaidar. It comprised two phases: the liberalization of prices; and the privatization of state industries. The immediate effect, for most people, was a dramatic decline in living standards and, in many cases, extreme poverty. In April Western nations announced a US $24,000m. aid package, intended to bolster the reforms and alleviate poverty. The reforms were fiercely opposed by a loose 'red-brown' coalition of communists and nationalists, who accused the Government of humiliating Russia by losing its empire; abandoning 25m. ethnic Russians to live in countries of what was now termed the 'near abroad'; and 'betraying' ordinary citizens by promising them prosperity, yet turning them into paupers. Under the influence of this coalition, the Congress of People's Deputies and the Supreme Soviet obliged Yeltsin to moderate his policies. In December the seventh Congress refused to endorse Gaidar as Chairman of the Government (prime minister) and forced Yeltsin to nominate a centrist figure, Viktor Chernomyrdin, whose premiership signalled a deceleration of the reform process.

In March 1993 the eighth Congress of People's Deputies stripped the President of his emergency powers (granted to him in April 1992) to introduce reforms by decree. On 20 March 1993 Yeltsin introduced emergency rule, effectively bypassing parliament. One week later an emergency session of the Congress attempted to impeach Yeltsin for violating the Constitution, but narrowly failed to achieve the required two-thirds majority. None the less, a national vote of confidence in Yeltsin was arranged. The referendum, held on 25 April, included four questions: on confidence in Yeltsin as President; on support for his economic reforms; and on whether to hold early presidential and parliamentary elections. The result confounded the President's enemies. Not only did he win 57.4% in the personal vote of confidence, but a majority even endorsed his economic policies. The voters also narrowly rejected an early presidential election while favouring an early parliamentary poll.

In the event, the referendum did little to resolve the impasse and in September 1993 the power struggle between the parliament and the President turned into serious confrontation. On 21 September, in defiance of the Constitution, Yeltsin dissolved parliament and announced that elections would be held to a new, bicameral legislature, the Federalnoye Sobraniye (Federal Assembly). The Supreme Soviet responded by summoning an emergency session of the Congress of People's Deputies. About 180 parliamentary deputies barricaded themselves inside the parliament building, known as the White House. Yeltsin had power supplies to the building suspended, and surrounded it with barbed wire and riot police. On 3–4 October armed hostilities occurred between supporters of the defiant deputies and the army and interior ministry troops. On 3 October the Ostankino television tower was attacked by anti-Yeltsin demonstrators. The following day the army bombarded the White House and overcame the resistance. Some 146 people were reported to have died in the conflict, and around 1,000 were purportedly injured. The organizers of the resistance, among them the Chairman of the Supreme Soviet, Ruslan Khasbulatov, and the Russian Vice-President, Aleksandr Rutskoi, were arrested, and later imprisoned.

Having suppressed the rebellion, Yeltsin moved ahead with a new constitution, which provided for an exceptionally strong presidency with few legislative checks on its power. On 10 November 1993 a Constitutional Convention agreed upon a text that was put to a nation-wide referendum on 12 December. Some 54.8% of registered voters in Russia participated in the plebiscite (although there were reports that the turn-out had been artificially inflated to ensure that the minimum of 50% was met); of those that participated, 58.4% voted in favour of the Constitution. Anticipating the outcome of the referendum, elections were held on the same day to the Federalnoye Sobraniye—the legislature established by the new Constitution. The Sobraniye was to consist of a lower chamber, the Gosudarstvennaya Duma (State Duma or Duma, comprising 450 deputies), and an upper chamber, the Sovet Federatsii (Federation Council, comprising two deputies for each of the constituent units of the Russian Federation). In the Duma 225 deputies were elected in single-member constituencies—a majoritarian (first-past-the-post) system—and the remaining 225 seats were contested by proportional representation on the basis of party lists.

Results in the proportional voting amounted to a serious indictment of Yeltsin's policies (and, possibly, of his violent attack on the White House): only 15.5% voted for Russia's Choice, a coalition of radical reformers led by Yegor Gaidar. By contrast, the Liberal Democratic Party of Russia (LDPR), an anti-Western, nationalist party led by Vladimir Zhirinovskii, won an unexpectedly large proportion of the votes cast (some 22.9%). Overall, Russia's Choice obtained 70 seats, the LDPR 64, the relegalized Communist Party of the Russian Federation (CPRF) 48 and its ally, the Agrarian Party of Russia (APR), 33 seats. The new Duma was an essentially conservative body, although its powers were highly restricted by the new Constitution.

THE NEW CONSTITUTIONAL ORDER, 1994–99

Yeltsin responded to the December 1993 election result by replacing some of his more reformist ministers. As premier, Chernomyrdin appointed conservative, Soviet-era managers to key positions. The champions of 'shock therapy', including Gaidar, resigned. Only Yeltsin's Chairman of the State Committee for Property Management, Anatolii Chubais, who was appointed as first deputy premier, kept the reformers' hopes alive.

Chernomyrdin found himself caught between his own conservative instincts and the need for reform, driven both by Yeltsin and by Russia's need to satisfy the demands of the IMF and Western governments, in order to continue to receive economic aid. The impetus for reform was never completely lost, and measures to establish improved financial discipline were established in late 1994. A second stage of privatization was initiated in 1995 and the IMF was sufficiently convinced of the Government's intentions to release, in stages, a loan of US $6,800m.

As Yeltsin struggled to accommodate his critics, however, he lost many of his original, pro-democracy supporters. Russia's Choice effectively moved into opposition, and in early 1995 a new pro-Government 'party of power', Our Home is Russia (OHR), was founded by Chernomyrdin. This was a centrist grouping, more compatible with the President's new political stance. Meanwhile, evidence of Yeltsin's physical decline (he suffered two heart attacks during 1995) and increasing signs of his weakness for alcohol resulted in doubts concerning the President's capacity for office.

Confirmation of Yeltsin's shift to the political centre ground came in December 1994, with Russia's military intervention in the self-styled 'Chechen Republic of Ichkeriya' (Chechnya), designed to put an end to the southern region's three-year bid for independence. This had been proclaimed in October 1991, after the election of Gen. Dzhokhar Dudayev to the republican presidency. The most vociferous opponents of the war were Yeltsin's erstwhile liberal supporters: Gaidar led anti-war rallies, and Sergei Kovalev, a fellow democrat, and the President's human rights commissioner, devoted himself to publicizing Russian human rights abuses against the civilian population in Chechnya. Thus, the Chechen war became one of Russia's most acute political issues.

Elections on 17 December 1995 to a new Duma, with a mandate of four years, demonstrated an impressive revival for the CPRF, which became the largest party, winning 22.3% of the popular vote and 157 out of 450 seats. Another 30 directly elected single-member seats went to the allied APR and other left-wing groupings. Disillusionment with the Government had been heightened by the state's inability to pay wages and pensions to millions of people. Zhirinovskii's LDPR came second on the list vote, with 11.2% of the votes cast and 51 seats overall. Only 10.1% of the votes cast were won by OHR, but, owing to its success in directly elected constituencies, it represented the second largest grouping in the Duma, with 55 seats. Yeltsin's Government was, thus, isolated in parliament, and it became clear that if the CPRF followed its victory with similar success in the June 1996 presidential election, it would be able to effect a significant change in Russia's policies.

Yeltsin's opinion poll ratings in early 1996 were so low that he apparently came close to cancelling the presidential election. In the run up to the ballot Yeltsin adopted a number of populist policies, which often involved lavish public spending commitments. His campaign was also the first to make full use of the state media and a huge election budget (supplied by the so-called 'oligarchs'—powerful business tycoons or plutocrats—and far in excess of the legal maximum) to support his case and discredit his opponents, largely by playing on fears of a communist return to power. In the presidential election of 16 June 1996 Yeltsin secured 35.3% of the votes cast and Gennadii Zyuganov (of the CPRF) attracted 32.0%. As neither had obtained the required overall majority, a second round of voting was scheduled for 3 July. In the interim period Yeltsin formed an alliance with the third-placed candidate, Gen. (retd) Aleksandr Lebed, whom Yeltsin appointed as Secretary of the Security Council. Lebed had obtained 14.5% of the votes cast, largely owing to his outspoken criticism of Russia's crime and corruption problems and of the war in Chechnya. Yeltsin's obvious absence from public life during the last week of June gave rise to renewed concern over the state of his health. Nevertheless, on 3 July he won 53.8% of the votes cast, becoming independent Russia's first directly elected Head of State.

By the time of Yeltsin's inauguration on 9 August 1996 the President had already moderated some of his more populist positions of the previous months and had dismissed the most anti-democratic members of his administration. Moreover, some reformists, among them Chubais, reappeared in office. Lebed, a plain-speaking populist, negotiated an end to the conflict in Chechnya, which was increasingly proving unwinnable for the federal Government. It was agreed that the federal troops would withdraw, and the question of Chechnya's ultimate status would be deferred for five years. In December the troops pulled out, and in January 1997 the Chechen military commander, Khalid 'Aslan' Maskhadov, was elected President of the republic. The war had cost tens of thousands of lives and left Chechnya in ruins, but heading for *de facto* independence.

Lebed was removed from office in October 1996, following his public criticism of President Yeltsin. Shortly after his dismissal, a prominent business executive, Boris Berezovskii, was appointed Deputy Secretary of the Security Council. His political influence with Chernomyrdin and Yeltsin grew rapidly, making him the first of a group of oligarchs who came to shape Russian politics in the latter part of the 1990s. Berezovskii bought a major stake in the former state-owned television channel, ORT, and several newspapers. Using a variety of what were often considered dubious business practices, a number of oligarchs, including the head of Oneksimbank, Vladimir Potanin (who became Deputy Chairman of the Government), and the banking and industrial magnates Mikhail Khodorkovskii and Roman Abramovich, built up massive fortunes, much of it contained in foreign bank accounts. Between them, the oligarchs controlled much of the country's natural resources, including its petroleum and gas reserves, which were sold off in the mid-1990s, and they came to exercise great influence over the Government, the economy and the media.

The oligarchs were only the most visible part of a huge clandestine and, often, criminal system that gained a hold over the Russian economy. Many businesses paid as much to 'mafia' (*mafiya*) gangs for 'protection' (*krysha*—literally meaning 'a roof') as they did to the tax authorities. Organized crime, along with complex and ever-changing taxation rules, served as a deterrent to all but the most audacious foreign companies contemplating investing in the new Russia.

President Yeltsin, his health so weakened that he had to undergo major heart bypass surgery in November 1996, appeared for several months to have little control over events, and retreated further and further from public life. At the beginning of 1998 Yeltsin returned to his duties with more vigour and embarked on the first of two years of constant government reshuffles, intended, apparently, not only to improve the economy, but also to identify a possible successor. In March the President's unexpected dismissal of Chernomyrdin and the entire Government was widely interpreted as an attempt to reassert his authority. Chernomyrdin was replaced by a relatively unknown figure, the Minister of Fuel and Energy, Sergei Kiriyenko, who was immediately presented with the threat of economic collapse in Russia, largely owing to the combined effects of a decline in world petroleum prices and the Asian financial crisis. Kiriyenko introduced austerity measures designed to reduce government spending by around 25%, and in July Western governments responded by granting a total of US $22,600m. in aid, on condition that certain political requirements were met.

This failed to quell a widespread lack of confidence in the Russian currency, however, and on 17 August 1998, despite assurances by President Yeltsin to the contrary, the rouble was effectively devalued, precipitating a major financial crisis. The market was paralyzed by liquidity shortages, share prices plunged and Russia defaulted on its foreign loans. Six days later Yeltsin dismissed Kiriyenko and reinstated Chernomyrdin as acting premier. Far from being perceived as a reliable figure who would bring about economic stability, however, Chernomyrdin was held largely responsible for the crisis, and his appointment was twice rejected by the Duma. A compromise candidate, Yevgenii Primakov, hitherto the Minister of Foreign Affairs, and a former foreign intelligence chief, was finally endorsed as Chairman of the Government in September.

The following year saw some improvement in the performance of the Russian economy owing to three factors: Primakov's steady leadership; a sharp increase in the world price for petroleum (Russia's prime export); and the devaluation of the rouble, which encouraged domestic production by making imports more expensive. None the less, in May 1999 Primakov, too, was abruptly dismissed by Yeltsin. His successor, Sergei

Stepashin, hitherto the Minister of Internal Affairs, remained in office for less than three months. In August Yeltsin dismissed Stepashin and appointed the relatively unknown head of the Federal Security Service (FSB), Vladimir Putin, to the post. The move shocked everyone, but was evidently linked to Yeltsin's quest for a successor: nominating Putin, Yeltsin declared that he eventually wanted Putin to take over from him as President.

Putin was aided in this ambition by a surge of Chechen rebel activity, which he brutally suppressed with the enthusiastic approval of most Russians. Chechnya had effectively been independent since 1997, but even sympathetic Russians were horrified by what had happened there: elements of *Shari'a* (Islamic religious law) had been introduced, and hostage-taking as well as, on occasion, the murder of foreign aid workers, journalists and others had led the republic to become widely regarded as a hub of terrorism and organized crime. In August 1999 a group of Islamist militants based in Chechnya invaded the neighbouring republic of Dagestan; Putin responded vigorously and had them driven out. Moreover, in late August and September more than 300 people were killed in a series of mysterious bomb explosions in Moscow (where two entire apartment blocks were destroyed), in Dagestan and in Volgodonsk, in Rostov Oblast, southern Russia, all of which Putin attributed to Chechen militant groups. The attacks provided the pretext for Putin to launch renewed military operations—termed an 'anti-terrorist operation'—on 23 September, to bring the separatist republic back under the jurisdiction of the Russian Federation.

Despite the brutality of the campaign (civilian casualties were high and human rights violations reportedly widespread) the conflict, unlike the previous one, proved popular among Russians, and Putin's opinion poll ratings soared. The Duma election of 19 December 1999 was essentially a dress rehearsal for the presidential election, scheduled for June 2000. A new party, Unity, was formed by the Kremlin to act as a support base for Putin and establish him as the most likely candidate to succeed Yeltsin. Unity's main rivals were the CPRF and Fatherland-All Russia (FAR), an alliance of regional governors led by the Mayor of Moscow, Yurii Luzhkov, and the former premier, Yevgenii Primakov. The campaign was again characterized by biased media coverage designed to discredit Unity's rivals, particularly FAR. The CPRF won the most seats (113) but Unity's success in winning 73 seats established Putin as the clear favourite to replace Yeltsin, and FAR, which had 68 seats, expediently decided to co-operate with Putin and Unity.

Putin was by this time well placed to stand for the presidency, but no one could have anticipated how soon that would happen. On 31 December 1999, unpredictable to the last, Yeltsin suddenly made a televised announcement of his resignation; Putin was to become acting President forthwith, pending an election, which was to be brought forward from July 2000 to 26 March. Yeltsin had come to power as Russia's leading democratic politician. The Russia he left behind, however, was only semi-democratic. Many freedoms remained and there had certainly been no return to totalitarianism, but state manipulation of elections had become standard practice and many democratic institutions were weak. The economy was still in a lamentable state and the 'system' was an ugly hybrid of communist leftovers, capitalist excesses and organized crime. Moreover, the uncertainties and hardships had brought about an unprecedented demographic crisis: from 1992 Russia's population began to decline by some 400,000 per year, reaching around 146m. at the end of the 1990s. The way Yeltsin left office—handing power to a personally selected successor, whose first act was to sign a decree giving Yeltsin and his associates immunity from prosecution—also undermined his democratic legacy. Nevertheless, Yeltsin was likely to be remembered as the man who dragged Russia into a new era.

THE PUTIN PRESIDENCY

Vladimir Putin had spent almost his entire career in the Committee for State Security (KGB) and one of its post-Soviet successor organizations, the FSB. In 1990 he returned to

Russia from what was then the German Democratic Republic (GDR or East Germany), where he had been working as a foreign agent, and became deputy to the reformist Mayor of St Petersburg, Anatolii Sobchak, before moving to Moscow to work in the Kremlin administration. In 1998 President Yeltsin appointed Putin as head of the FSB.

Given that few Russians had heard of Putin only one year earlier and given that he had shown no ambition to become a political leader, his popularity by late 1999 was astounding. It was a result not only of his apparent determination to resolve the Chechen question, but also of the image he cultivated of strength and directness. He spoke of restoring Russia's status as a world power and of rebuilding a strong state. Putin secured victory in the first round of the presidential election on 26 March 2000. He won by a comfortable margin, with the assistance of favourable media coverage, garnering 52.9% of the votes cast, while his nearest rival, Zyuganov, attracted just 29%. His election slogan was 'Dictatorship of the Law', appealing to the longing of many Russians for a strong hand to re-establish the rule of law and to combat crime.

Serious concerns were raised, however, by what was widely regarded as a concerted attempt to impose control on the critical mass media, in particular those companies owned by Vladimir Gusinskii's Mediya-MOST group and those associated with Berezovskii, following Putin's election as President. In April 2001 the only independent national television station, NTV, was taken over by the state-controlled natural gas monopoly, Gazprom, and its senior journalists were dismissed. This was followed by the editorial take-over of Gusinskii's other outlets—the influential daily newspaper *Segodnya* (Today) and the weekly news magazine *Itogi* (Results)—both of which had, hitherto, been fiercely independent and critical of the Government. These measures were considered to be a demonstration of Putin's stated determination to limit the powers of the oligarchs. Ultimately, both Gusinskii and Berezovskii (whose financial assistance had contributed to Putin's election victory) left the country after warrants were issued for their arrest on corruption charges. However, media sources that represented a vocal source of opposition to government policies encountered further pressure, which resulted in, *inter alia*, the closure in 2002, purportedly on financial grounds, of the television station TV6, to which many of the former journalists of NTV had transferred. Its successor, TVS, was, in turn, compelled to cease broadcasting in June 2003 and was replaced by a sports channel. The loss of Russia's last privately owned national television network, again officially because of financial and management difficulties, was regarded by many as a reverse for press diversity. All the remaining national stations were, to a greater or lesser degree, pro-Government in their coverage.

Politically, Putin attempted to tackle the centrifugal forces that had undermined central government authority under Yeltsin. In mid-2000 Putin announced the establishment of seven federal districts (okrugs), each headed by a presidential representative (five of whom had been recruited from the military and security services), whose task was to co-ordinate federal and regional laws and restore a measure of central control. The governors of the Federation's 89 regions lost their ex officio seats in the Sovet Federatsii, and had their power further reduced by the reallocation of tax revenues, which awarded a larger proportion to the centre and less to the regions. A major overhaul of the judicial system was initiated, and new criminal and administrative law codes came into effect at the beginning of July 2002. These codes envisaged the introduction of trials by jury (provided for by the 1993 Constitution, but never fully implemented); removed some powers from prosecutors, including the authority to order arrests; and strengthened the independence of judges. It was hoped that corruption would be reduced by changing the system used for selecting judges, by raising their salaries and by ending their lifetime tenure. Human rights observers, though, claimed that corruption and political interference remained unchecked.

The issue of restoring peace and federal order in Chechnya appeared certain to remain a long-term problem, however, as federal forces struggled to impose their control over a largely hostile population, while under constant attack from rebel fighters. Meanwhile, bomb attacks, primarily in southern regions and in Moscow, which were attributed to Chechen militants and which had occurred intermittently since the late 1990s, became more widespread and devastating, with the increasing use of suicide attacks in the early 2000s. Putin, in particular, became progressively more outspoken about the purported links of Chechen rebels with international Islamist militant groups, frequently seeking to portray the military operations in Chechnya as part of the US-led international 'war on terror'.

However, despite ongoing insecurity in the republic, the Government insisted that it sought a political settlement in Chechnya. On 23 March 2003 a referendum was held in Chechnya, with three questions: on the introduction of a new constitution for the republic; and on the eventual holding of elections to the republican presidency and legislature. With participation in the plebiscite at almost 90%, and with a positive response in excess of 95% reported to each of the three questions, the Government expressed satisfaction with the outcome of its policies in the republic. Such high figures, however, were interpreted by many as clear evidence of falsification, and international observers cast doubt on the referendum's legitimacy and value. Meanwhile, alleged human rights violations by Russian troops and attacks by Chechen rebels continued. In one of the most audacious attacks, in October 2002 a group of heavily armed militants held some 800 people hostage in a theatre in Moscow. After three days élite special forces stormed the theatre, killing all 41 rebels; some 129 theatre-goers also died, according to official figures, the vast majority apparently from exposure to an incapacitating gas used by the special forces. Suicide bombers destroyed the republican government headquarters in the Chechen capital, Groznyi, in December 2002. On 5 October 2003 Akhmad haji Kadyrov, a former rebel leader and mufti, who had been appointed to head the republican administration by Putin in mid-2000, won the presidential election held in the republic by a substantial majority, although several candidates regarded as his principal rivals had withdrawn from the contest. His election failed to end the violence. In February 2004 at least 39 people were killed in a bomb attack on the Moscow Metro, attributed to Chechen militants. Three months later Kadyrov himself was assassinated in a bomb explosion at an open-air Second World War commemoration in Groznyi. In September television viewers in Russia and across the world watched in horror when an armed group seized up to 1,500 people, including hundreds of children, at a school in Beslan, North Osetiya—Alaniya, in the North Caucasus. The incident ended with the loss of 331 lives, according to official figures. One of the most militant Chechen rebels, Shamil Basayev, claimed responsibility for the organization of the hostage-taking. Although further bombings attributed to separatist, or Islamist, militants continued, the Government hailed the killing of Basayev in a 'special operation' in July 2006 as a major success. None the less, Chechnya remained a serious problem for President Putin, with increasing indications during the mid-2000s that Islamist extremism was becoming a growing factor in promoting instability in other Russian republics within and near the North Caucasus.

Meanwhile, the economy, under the guidance of premiers Mikhail Kasyanov (2000–04) and Mikhail Fradkov (2004–07), made steady progress. A fixed, uniform rate of personal income tax (of 13%) was introduced in January 2001, with the aim of bolstering the state's finances by reducing tax evasion. Robust economic growth was recorded in 1999–2007, averaging 6.5% per year, helped, in particular, by rising world petroleum prices and the 1998 devaluation of the rouble. With the CPRF increasingly marginalized in the Duma, largely as a result of enhanced co-operation between the two centrist, pro-presidential factions, FAR and Unity, and their subsequent merger, in 2001, to form United Russia (UR), the Government was able to pass market-oriented economic reforms. A new Labour Code, introduced in February 2002, gave formal recognition to private employment, and a reformed Land Code, approved by the Duma in September 2001, permitted the sale and purchase of urban plots of land for the first time since the 1920s. In June 2002 these provisions were extended to include agricultural land, finally ending the era of collectivization—although foreign ownership of farmland remained proscribed.

In the same month, with around 70% of the economy estimated to be in the private sector, the European Union (EU) and the US Department of Commerce officially designated Russia a 'market economy'. More and more ordinary Russians were exposed to the rigours of the market in 2003, as a result of reforms in utilities and housing, which encouraged local authorities to reduce subsidies for domestic power, heating and building maintenance. Changes to the state benefits system, including the replacement of free or subsidized public transport for pensioners with cash payments, caused the first mass protests for a decade in January 2005, followed by a confidence vote in the Duma, which the Government easily survived.

The business climate, however, was severely affected by legal measures taken, apparently with President Putin's approval, against the private sector petroleum concern Yukos and its Chief Executive, Mikhail Khodorkovskii. In July 2003 one of the company's principal shareholders, Platon Lebedev, was arrested on charges of embezzlement, and in October Khodorkovskii himself was seized in a dawn raid, before being put on trial in June 2004, accused of fraud and tax evasion. Yukos was one of the country's biggest companies, and the moves were widely interpreted as part of Putin's promised crackdown on oligarchs. The President had allegedly concluded a deal with the oligarchs, whereby they would be permitted to maintain their business interests in Russia as long as they did not seek to intervene in politics. However, Khodorkovskii openly funded opposition political parties (seemingly including the CPRF, as well as the pro-market Union of Rightist Forces and the liberal Yabloko) and lobbied against changes to the petroleum industry's tax regime. In May 2005 Khodorkovskii and Lebedev were each found guilty on six charges, including tax evasion and embezzlement, and sentenced to nine years in prison. Even while the trial was in progress, Yukos was ordered to pay US $3,400m. in tax arrears, and the authorities seized the assets of its main production unit, Yuganskneftegaz, in order to pay the debt. Yuganskneftegaz was then, indirectly, sold to the state-owned concern Rosneft, effectively renationalizing a major part of Russia's petroleum industry. The imprisonment of Khodorkovskii was widely considered to have been politically motivated, while the partial renationalization of Yukos was regarded by many as an attempt by the state to seize control of Russia's energy resources.

By the end of his first term as President, Putin commanded huge popular support, which turned into overwhelming election victories. In the Duma election on 7 December 2003 UR, which was openly supportive of President Putin, won 37.6% of the votes, well ahead of the CPRF (12.6%) and the LDPR (11.5%). Motherland, a new 'patriotic' electoral bloc with close ties to the ruling authorities, won 9.0% of votes cast, but Yabloko and the Union of Rightist Forces failed to muster the 5% of votes necessary to obtain seats in the Duma on the basis of party lists, and their representation was much reduced. Overall, UR won 223 of the Duma's 450 seats; however, its representation in the Duma subsequently grew to around 300 as independent candidates and representatives of small parties joined the grouping. This gave the Kremlin a loyal majority in the Duma, effectively turning the legislature into an extension of the presidential administration. Putin's victory in the presidential election, due on 14 March 2004, was so assured that no other major party put up its leader as a candidate, and Putin went on to win even more convincingly than four years earlier, securing 71.3% of votes cast. He did not even campaign actively, refusing to participate in televised debates with other candidates, but demonstrated his power by reshuffling his Government two weeks before polling day, bringing in a little-known official, Mikhail Fradkov, as his new Chairman of the Government. Fradkov had previously served as head of the federal tax police service and as Russia's ambassador to the EU, and was regarded as a premier likely to do the President's bidding. Neither election was deemed by international observers to have been fair. In particular, the state-controlled media were heavily biased in Putin and UR's favour. The arrest of Khodorkovskii also helped create a strong anti-oligarch atmosphere prior to the Duma elections, which damaged opposition parties with financial links to Yukos and

other big businesses. An alternative count conducted by opposition parties also suggested that Yabloko and the Union of Rightist forces had, contrary to the official results, received enough votes to cross the 5% threshold; the suggestion was that electoral fraud had denied these parties party-list representation in the Duma.

It remained true, none the less, that the President was extremely popular. As he began his second term, most Russians appeared to believe that Putin was slowly rescuing Russia from the drift of the Yeltsin years, restoring order and improving the economy. Opposition came mainly from Western-orientated *intelligentsiya* circles, who criticized Putin's authoritarian tendencies and the President's reliance on the so-called *siloviki*, politicians and advisers whose background was in the security services. They pointed to Putin's response to the Beslan crisis—particularly a decision to abolish the direct election of regional governors in favour of presidential appointments—as proof of his desire to centralize and concentrate power in his own hands. Other policy changes implemented by Putin during his second term of office attracted strong disapproval from foreign governments and from former allies, such as Andrei Illarionov, who resigned as the chief economic adviser to the President in December 2005, having criticized what he described as 'the emergence of a corporatist model of the state'. Particular targets of censure included legislation on non-governmental organizations (NGOs), approved in 2006, which human rights activists claimed could be used to curtail their activities, and changes in electoral legislation that included the abolition of single-member constituencies in elections to the Duma and an increase, to 7%, of the threshold required for parties to obtain legislative representation. More generally, there were concerns about the decline in democratic freedoms, with the political system that had emerged under Putin often described by analysts, both domestically and internationally, as a 'managed democracy', in which many of the freedoms regarded as essential to Western democracies had been circumscribed, despite outward appearances of democratic practice. The assassination in Moscow of the outspoken political journalist Anna Politkovskaya in October 2006 highlighted the dangers of investigating highly controversial topics in Russia, such as corruption and human rights violations. In April 2007 peaceful protests by the coalition of opposition groups, Another Russia, were violently dispersed by the police, an action that confirmed for many the regime's intolerance of any organized dissent.

Internationally, President Putin was widely regarded as determined to reintegrate Russia into the world's political and economic system, but few—including his own advisers—expected the apparently radical reversal of Russian foreign policy that followed the September 2001 suicide attacks against the USA. Putin immediately declared Russia's support for the US-led 'anti-terrorist' coalition formed in the aftermath of the attacks, and offered logistical support and intelligence to the USA when military operations against Afghanistan (the Taliban regime of which was harbouring al-Qa'ida militants) commenced in October. Putin gave tacit approval to the stationing of US and allied troops at former Soviet bases in Central Asia and, in mid-2002, to the dispatch of US military instructors to Georgia. The rapprochement with the USA went further. Putin abandoned his opposition to plans by the US President, George W. Bush, to abrogate the 1972 Anti-Ballistic Missile (ABM) Treaty, in order to develop a space-based anti-missile shield. Putin also appeared to override widespread domestic objections to the eastward expansion of the North Atlantic Treaty Organization (NATO), and in late May he signed an historic treaty in Rome, Italy, which established a new NATO-Russia Council in place of the more limited Permanent Joint Council that had been established in 1997, and awarded Russia equal influence with the 19 full members of NATO on a range of issues such as counter-terrorism, peace-keeping and arms control. There were limits, however, to Putin's acquiescence to US foreign policy. In January 2002 Bush controversially identified Iran, Iraq and the Democratic People's Republic of Korea (North Korea) as forming an 'axis of evil', said to sponsor terrorism and to be involved in the development and proliferation of weapons of mass destruction. Despite this, Russia continued to assist Iran with the construction of a nuclear power plant, and played host to the North Korean leader, Kim Jong Il. Russia opposed the military action taken by a coalition led by the USA and the United Kingdom against Iraq from early 2003, which removed from power the Iraqi President, Saddam Hussain. Russia sided with several European states, notably France and Germany, in calling for UN weapons inspectors to be given longer to search for Iraq's alleged stockpiles of prohibited weaponry, and refused to back military action unless it was explicitly justified by a new UN Security Council resolution. Russia's approach to the crisis appeared to reflect Putin's unease over increasing US domination of world affairs, as well as his need to retain the support of the public at home, the vast majority of whom were opposed to the conflict.

Putin's second term was marked by increasing assertiveness internationally. Wary about the enlargement of the EU in 2004, to include eight formerly communist states of Central and Eastern Europe, among them the three Baltic states of Estonia, Latvia and Lithuania (which had been incorporated into the USSR during the Second World War, and the first two of which had significant ethnic Russian populations), the Russian authorities became more active in defending the rights of ethnic Russians and Russian speakers in these states, many of whom did not hold citizenship of the country in which they resided. In particular, Putin resolutely rejected demands that Russia acknowledge that the USSR had 'occupied' the Baltic states during the Second World War. Indeed, in Putin's second term Russia adopted a more aggressive stance towards a number of its neighbours. Putin openly supported the candidacy of Viktor Yanukovych in the Ukrainian presidential election of late 2004, even after a court had ruled that the result of the initial second round of polling, held on 21 November, and in which Yanukovych had been declared the victor, was fraudulent (see the History of Ukraine). Further controversy arose in January 2006 when Gazprom cut gas supplies to Ukraine during a period of sub-zero temperatures, which consequently disrupted supplies to other Central and Western European states. Although this action was taken because of a failure to resolve a pricing dispute, many observers interpreted it as Russia seeking to 'punish' Ukraine for the 'orange revolution', which had brought a pro-Western administration, led by President Viktor Yushchenko, to power after repeat elections on 26 December 2004. Relations with Georgia, already strained by Russian support for separatists in Abkhazia and South Ossetia and Georgia's desire to join NATO, also deteriorated. In January 2006 unexplained explosions inside Russia damaged gas pipelines and an electricity cable, leaving Georgia, briefly, with severe energy shortages. Then, in October 2006 Georgia arrested four Russian army officers on charges of espionage. Russia responded, even after the officers had been released and deported, by recalling its ambassador, cutting travel links, imposing economic sanctions and deporting hundreds of ethnic Georgians from Russia. In January 2007 a dispute over the price of oil erupted between Russia and Belarus (a recipient of heavily subsidized Russian oil and gas), and further escalated when Russia stopped pumping oil into the pipeline network that crosses Belarus and delivers around 12.5% of the EU's oil needs. Supplies to Germany, Poland and other countries were effectively suspended. The matter was resolved after a few days, when Belarus acceded to Russia's pricing terms. Many observers interpreted these developments as a move by the Russian Government to re-establish a sphere of influence in the 'near abroad' (the territory of the former USSR), with energy supplies as a key foreign policy lever. More widely, such disputes increased concerns about Russia's perceived reliability as an energy supplier to the West.

The announcement in early 2007 that the USA planned to develop an anti-ballistic missile shield in Europe, potentially utilizing bases in Poland and the Czech Republic, resulted in a further deterioration in relations with the West. The USA stated that the shield was not aimed against Russia but was intended to protect the USA and Europe from the threat of long-range missiles from countries such as Iran and North Korea; Russia insisted that the plan was a threat to its national security. President Putin publicly voiced his displeasure with the missile shield proposal at the Munich Conference on Security Policy in February. Putin stated that this would cause

an 'inevitable' arms race and emphasised that neither of the countries presented as a threat possessed long-range missiles. Putin was also sharply critical of US policy more generally, claiming that the US Administration had overstepped its national borders 'in every way' and that the 'almost uncontained' use of military force was plunging the world into 'an abyss of permanent conflict'. This speech, delivered to an audience containing US Secretary of Defense Robert Gates and several US Congressmen, prompted talk by international observers of a 'new Cold War'. A meeting between Presidents Bush and Putin in July, in the Bush family estate in Kennebunkport, Maine, USA, was intended to soothe relations but failed to resolve any of the substantive issues.

Relations with the United Kingdom were seriously damaged by the murder of Aleksandr Litvinenko, a British citizen, in London in November 2006. Litvinenko, a former Russian security agent and critic of President Putin, died after being poisoned with the radioactive isotope Polonium-210. In a statement shortly before his death in hospital, Litvinenko blamed Putin for his poisoning, an accusation that the Russian authorities dismissed as 'absurd'. In May 2007 the British Crown Prosecution Service announced its intention to prosecute Andrei Lugovoi, an ex-FSB officer, for the murder. Russia refused the British Government's request to extradite Lugovoi, on the grounds that the Russian Constitution prohibits the extradition of its citizens. Consequently, the United Kingdom expelled four diplomats from the Russian embassy in London; Russia retaliated by expelling four British diplomats from Moscow.

There could be little doubt that Russia was increasingly determined to advance its interests more forcefully. In part, though, this assertive foreign policy seemed an attempt to bolster domestic support for Putin's administration prior to legislative and presidential elections by appealing to national pride.

Speculation concerning Putin's intentions mounted as his second term as President entered its closing stages. The President had repeatedly averred that he would stand down at the end of his second term, as required by the Constitution, but hinted, enigmatically, that he would not leave the political scene altogether, fuelling speculation that he would remain an important figure in some capacity. His administration, moreover, seemed determined to ensure the election of a handpicked successor, with First Deputy Chairmen Sergei Ivanov and Dmitrii Medvedev, both close associates of Putin, generally seen as the frontrunners. It was anticipated that one or the other would be installed as premier in advance of the forthcoming elections. It was a surprise, then, when Putin accepted the resignation of Fradkov and his Government on 12 September and nominated the little-known Viktor Zubkov, a longterm associate and hitherto head of the Federal Financial Monitoring Service, as Chairman of the Government. On 25 September Putin announced a government reshuffle in which only three ministers were replaced; the incumbent Minister of Finance, Aleksei Kudrin, also became a Deputy Chairman. Putin clarified his intentions when he announced, in a statement made at UR's eighth party congress in early October, that he would head that party's list of candidates in the forthcoming parliamentary elections and asserted that his becoming prime minister in the future was 'an entirely realistic proposition'.

The Duma elections on 2 December 2007 was held under new rules: all of the chamber's 450 seats were to be allocated by proportional representation on the basis of party lists and parties had to win 7% of the vote to secure parliamentary representation. UR maximized its association with Putin by claiming that the election was effectively a referendum in support of the President and by running on a manifesto called 'Putin's Plan'. Predictably, UR won an overwhelming victory, securing 315 seats with 64.3% of votes cast in elections that were criticized domestically and internationally for having failed to meet democratic standards. The CPRF came a distant second, with 11.6% of the votes and 57 seats. The LDPR took 40 seats with 8.1% of votes cast. The socialist A Just Russia (AJR—established in 2006 by a merger of Motherland, the Russian Party of Life and the Russian Pensioners' Party), contesting its first Duma elections, won 38 seats with 7.7% of votes cast. Overall, the result further strengthened the executive's command of the legislature. Most obviously, UR maintained the two-thirds majority required to initiate changes to the Constitution. A Just Russia, moreover, is widely believed to be a Kremlin invention and was openly supportive of Putin. The LDPR too, in spite of its nationalist appeal, has been consistently loyal to the executive. Of the four parties represented in the Duma, only the CPRF is an opposition force.

A few days later, on 10 December 2007, UR, AJR and two minor political parties nominated Medvedev as their presidential candidate. Putin stated that he 'completely and fully' supported this proposal, thereby naming Medvedev as his preferred successor. On the following day Medvedev made it clear that if he won the presidential election, he would invite Putin to head the Government. These manoeuvres virtually guaranteed that Medvedev would win and that Putin would become prime minister. Medvedev was duly elected on 2 March 2008, with a resounding 70.2% of votes cast, in a contest that was widely regarded as unfair. CPRF leader Gennadii Zyuganov came a poor second with 17.7%, followed by the head of the LDPR Vladimir Zhirinovskii, with 9.4%, and the leader of the Democratic Party of Russia, Andrei Bogdanov, with 1.3%. Putin confirmed his intention to become Chairman of the Government at UR's ninth party congress on 15 April; he simultaneously accepted an invitation to lead that party (despite not being a member thereof), a move that was generally seen as strengthening his future premiership.

In spring 2008 as Putin's second term of office neared its end, Russia's foreign policy was far less concessionary than it had been under Yeltsin or Gorbachev; foreign relations, however, were also increasingly strained. Russia's international assertiveness played well at home but whether this would actually advance Russia's national interests in the longer term remained to be seen. Putin had also presided over a period of economic stability and prosperity. Economic growth was high and Russia was attracting foreign investment from major Western corporations. The country had paid back all its debts to the 'Paris Club' of official creditors and used its petroleum and gas revenues to build up a substantial 'stabilization fund'. This economic resurgence, however, was largely due to record-high energy prices, the distribution of wealth was still extremely unequal, and inflation in excess of 10% was causing concern. Domestically, Putin remained, with the assistance of media management by the presidential administration, immensely popular. The main criticism of Putin as his presidency ended concerned the extent to which democracy in Russia had been eroded. In some crucial ways Russia was less free under Putin than it had been in the late Soviet era. The media under Gorbachev was far freer, and the legislature a far more serious check on the executive, than at the end of Putin presidency. Elections that were decisively manipulated by the authorities had become the norm. Putin's exit from the presidency was in keeping with this: by stepping down at the end of his second term he observed the terms of the Constitution, but by installing himself as Chairman of the Government with a hand-picked successor as President there was little doubt that he had violated its democratic spirit.

THE MEDVEDEV PRESIDENCY

On 7 May 2008 Medvedev was sworn in as Russia's third President. He immediately nominated Putin to become prime minister, a move that was approved by the Duma on 8 May by 392 votes to 56 (only the CPRF voted against). Little was known about the political leanings of Russia's new President, who had never held elective office before. A law lecturer by profession, Medvedev had first begun working for Putin in the early 1990s when they were both involved in politics in St Petersburg. In 1999 Medvedev was brought to Moscow by Putin and subsequently held a number of senior administration positions. He was appointed deputy head of the presidential administration in December 1999 and headed Putin's presidential election campaign in the following year. In 2003 he was promoted to head of the presidential administration and in 2005 became First Deputy Chairman of the Government. He also served as Chairman of Gazprom, Russia's gas monopoly from 2000 (with a short time as Deputy Chairman in

2001–02), a position he still held on his election as President. Medvedev had never served in the security services and had displayed some liberalizing inclinations in speeches prior to his election, emphasizing in particular the importance of the rule of law. Some observers, consequently, believed that Medvedev's instincts were more democratic than those of Putin. Others doubted this, noting that Medvedev owed his entire political career to Putin and had explicitly pledged to continue the path set by his predecessor.

It also was not clear how the Putin-Medvedev relationship, or 'tandem' as it became known, would work. The new President stated that he would co-operate effectively with his prime minister in the interests of stability, although some observers believed that the arrangement was unsustainable and ill-suited to a country accustomed to a single dominant leader. Certainly few believed that this constituted a genuine handover of power from Putin to Medvedev, and some even speculated that Medvedev would be little more than a figurehead president. Putin, in view of his personal popularity and leadership of UR, was undoubtedly a stronger premier than any of those that had preceded him. In the first weeks of Medvedev's presidency Putin appeared the dominant figure. On 12 May 2008 Putin's Government was announced at a meeting with Medvedev. Most key ministers were reappointed and several important figures from the presidential administration were given posts in the new Government. At this meeting Putin spoke first—a breach of presidential protocol—and sat in the seat traditionally used by the President. Putin also remained active in foreign affairs undertaking a 'presidential-style' visit to France in June and attending the opening ceremony of the Olympic Games in Beijing, the People's Republic of China, in August.

Medvedev had campaigned on an economically liberal programme aimed at stability and growth, which focused on the 'four I's': institutions, infrastructure, innovation and investment. Specific objectives within these areas included removing administrative barriers and reducing taxes to encourage investment and innovation. Other aims involved tackling tax evasion and increasing levels of home ownership. Medvedev was also sharply critical of what he called 'legal nihilism' in Russia and pledged to combat corruption. One of the first decrees Medvedev issued in office was aimed at reducing excessive administrative interference in business activities. This was followed by the creation of a high level anti-corruption council, headed by Medvedev, charged with producing a national anti-corruption plan. The plan, published in early August 2008, outlined a number of measures aimed at preventing and punishing corruption, which were to be set out in legislation later in the year. Whether this legislation would produce tangible results remained to be seen. Many observers even doubted the sincerity of the campaign, citing alleged state interference in a dispute concerning the petroleum company TNK-BP (established in 2003 by the merger of two Russian companies with the Russian interests of BP of the United Kingdom), which some interpreted as an attempt to establish Russian, or even state, control over the company by forcing BP out of the joint venture.

Medvedev's first major foreign policy engagement was the EU-Russia summit meeting, held in the Siberian town of Khanty-Mansiisk on 26–27 June 2008. Russian and European officials commended the summit, at which the sides agreed to begin long-delayed negotiations on a new Partnership and Cooperation Agreement, as a success. European leaders refused to compare Medvedev to Putin but spoke warmly of the new President and praised the constructive atmosphere of the summit. Both sides, however, warned that the ensuing negotiations would be difficult. Medvedev also made a positive impression at his first meeting of the Group of Eight leading industrial nations (G8) in Toyako, Japan, in early July, when President Bush described Medvedev as 'a smart guy' who understands the issues very well, and means what he says. However, there was no change on the major issues: Russia remained opposed to US plans to place missile shield installations in Europe and to US support for Georgia and Ukraine in their drive to join NATO. Medvedev also met with British Prime Minister Gordon Brown for the first time, but again there was no progress on issues such as the United Kingdom's demand that Russia extradite Lugovoi, the main suspect in the murder of Litvinenko. It seemed that foreign policy under Medvedev was little changed, even if the language he employed was less confrontational. On 11 July Russia (along with the People's Republic of China) vetoed a US-backed attempt to impose sanctions on Zimbabwe in response to President Robert Mugabe's rigging of presidential elections. Russia maintained that the sanctions constituted interference in internal affairs and as such violated the UN's charter.

Russia's relations with Georgia, long tense, ignited in August 2008. Following a series of clashes between separatists and Georgian forces in South Ossetia, the Georgian military launched a military assault on 7 August in an attempt to regain control of the breakaway region that has enjoyed de facto independence from Georgia since 1992. Medvedev declared that Russia was constitutionally obliged to intervene to defend its peace-keeping troops and other Russian citizens (Russian passports had been widely distributed among residents of South Ossetia since the early 2000s). The Russian 58th army was sent into South Ossetia and quickly took control of the regional capital Tskhinvali. Russian forces also mobilized in Abkhazia, another breakaway region in Georgia, and drove Georgian forces out of those districts of Abkhazia that they controlled. Russian aircraft and troops moved beyond the borders of South Ossetia and Abkhazia and engaged targets inside Georgia proper. On 12 August President Medvedev halted military operations, stating that the objective of safeguarding Russian citizens and peace-keeping troops had been achieved. The international community, which had criticized Russia's response as disproportionate, sought to mediate a peace agreement. On 16 August Georgia and Russia signed an EU-brokered deal, which called for both sides to end military actions and return their forces to pre-conflict positions. It was several days, however, before Russian troops began to pull back and when they did they remained on Georgian territory in 'buffer zones' around the territories of South Ossetia and Abkhazia, and the Black Sea port of Poti. The West and Georgia denounced this as a blatant violation of the peace agreement; the Russian Government claimed it was covered by a provision allowing temporary 'additional security measures'. On 26 August Russia formally recognized the independence of South Ossetia and Abkhazia, a move that was widely condemned by western countries. After further EU-led talks in Moscow, President Medvedev agreed to pull Russian troops out of Georgia, following the deployment of some 200 EU monitors in South Ossetia, ahead of international talks to be held in Geneva on 15 October. Russian forces, however, remained in Abkhazia and South Ossetia, and Medvedev maintained that Russia's recognition of the disputed territories was 'irrevocable'. On 17 September Russia signed friendship and co-operation treaties with the separatist leaders in South Ossetia and Abkhazia, pledging to support the two regions militarily; the treaties also formalized economic co-operation between Russia and the regions.

The conflict in Georgia extinguished any hopes that the West's relations with Russia would improve under Medvedev. Russia had scored a convincing military victory, which was popular domestically and exposed the limits of western influence in the post-Soviet space. Russia's actions, however, seriously damaged relations with the West and alarmed many of Russia's neighbours. The conflict also seemed to make membership of NATO for Georgia more likely, rather than less. It also damaged business confidence: in the month following the war the Russian stock market fell by 30% and an estimated US $20,000m. left the country. Russia's tactical military success, then, seemed likely to become an economic and strategic failure.

The war with Georgia was the first crisis faced by Russia's new ruling 'tandem'. Both Medvedev and Putin played prominent roles and maintained the same tough stance, claiming that Russia's actions were a justified response to Georgian aggression. More generally, there was little evidence of any serious tension between the President and the premier. Nor was there any sign of radically different policies under Medvedev. Moves to combat corruption had been set in motion but his presidency could not be considered truly liberal until state interference in business genuinely ceased, state-owned television was opened up to alternative voices and steps were taken to promote free and fair political competition. The overall impression, in the early months of the 'tandem' was that Medvedev and Putin were, as promised, working together to ensure continuity and stability.

Economy

Prof. PHILIP HANSON

INTRODUCTION

Since the last years of communism the Russian economy has experienced nine years of steep decline followed by ten years of rapid growth. Production fell precipitously from 1989 to 1998, before reviving strongly from 1999 onwards. The decline in economic activity in Russia during the 1990s was one of the most dramatic economic collapses ever experienced by a large country. The Russian Federal Service of State Statistics series for gross domestic product (GDP) at constant prices showed a decline in 1989–98 of about 45%. This collapse in output in the 1990s was, in reality, somewhat less dramatic than the official data reported. Nevertheless, output and income certainly declined, while the attempt to change the Russian economic system from centrally administered socialism to market capitalism was implemented in a confused and confusing fashion.

It was important politically that the true decline in the population's economic welfare during the decade was less than the GDP figures implied. First, state-enterprise managers had previously overstated their output in order to qualify for plan-fulfilment bonuses. This incentive to exaggerate output figures disappeared with the abandonment of central planning. Second, some of the output actually produced before the changes was an unwanted side-effect of the planning system, the loss of which caused no reduction in welfare. Third, some of the loss of output was a loss of military production, which made no contribution to consumption or the growth of capital stock.

Fourth, there was a far greater decline in investment than in consumption; although potentially damaging for future prosperity, this entailed no immediate loss to the population. Fifth, the movement of prices towards market equilibrium levels meant a reduction in shortages and, therefore, in time spent queuing—a welfare gain not reflected in output figures. Finally, the private sector's output was inadequately reported in the official statistics and was more dynamic than that of the state sector. The new, private firms were increasing output rapidly, albeit from very low levels. Other important, long-established private sector activities, such as household production of food (which was extensive among the urban as well as the rural population), had always been important and under-reported; such production declined only slightly, or even increased.

For these reasons, the decline in officially measured output suggested a more desperate situation than actually prevailed. Substantial numbers of people who started their own businesses, or were employed in the private sector, or who had other new opportunities created by the changes, actually benefited. At the same time, however, economic conditions became more uncertain for everyone, and some sections of the population, particularly large families with low incomes, experienced a significant deterioration in their standard of living. Moreover, many of Russia's 'entrepreneurs' were members of criminal gangs, which operated an illegal ('black') market with a level of violence hitherto unknown in Russian cities.

In any event, Russian society somehow coped with drastic and disturbing economic change until the financial crisis of August 1998, after which the economy began a recovery that lasted into 2007. In 1999–2007 annual GDP growth averaged 7.0%. By 2004, when GDP growth of 7.1% was recorded, the upturn in economic activity could no longer be discounted as merely a brief respite in an inexorable decline. Indeed, there was considerable debate among economic commentators about the character of this growth, in particular as to whether its rapid rate meant that it should be more accurately described as merely a recovery, utilizing hitherto large, underutilized capacity, or as sustainable, investment-driven growth.

At the same time, there was a slowdown after mid-2004 in the petroleum industry, where growth in the volume of output slowed from 9%–10% per year to just over 2%. This was connected with a major shift in Russian state policy: a marked lurch towards more state intervention in the economy and to the imposition of a higher tax burden on the industry. This shift was signalled most visibly by the state's 'attack' on the private sector Yukos petroleum company (see below), although the Yukos affair was not the only sign of change. The state expanded its ownership of businesses in the petroleum, metals and engineering sectors, and large claims for tax arrears were made against a number of large companies, in addition to Yukos. In 2006–07 the state, in the form of the state-controlled gas giant, Gazprom, purchased controlling stakes in the Sakhalin Energy project and, provisionally, in the East Siberian Kovykta gas field. These purchases were from Royal Dutch Shell (plus Mitsui and Mitsubishi) and the BP joint venture, TNK-BP, respectively. They were preceded by administrative pressures from the state on the incumbent foreign companies. The doctrine of 'sovereign democracy', proclaimed by Vladislav Surkov, from 2004 the Deputy Chief of Staff, and from 2008 the First Deputy Chief of Staff of the Presidential Administration, was linked with tighter restrictions on the role of foreign companies in so-called 'strategic' sectors of industry.

After a long delay, while some radically different drafts were debated within the Government, a law on foreign investors' participation in strategic industries came into effect on 7 May 2008. This covered a list of 42 industries, plus oil, gas and metals extraction from fields deemed to be of 'strategic' size, in which foreign investment was to be restricted or prohibited. Outside natural resources, most of the industries covered were more or less defence-related. However, publishing and broadcasting for large audiences were also included.

The restrictions were complex. In strategic industries outside the natural resource sector a foreign investor would not be allowed to acquire a stake greater than 50% (25% if the foreign investor were a state entity) except by special exemption. In oil and gas fields above a certain size (70m. tons of oil deposits or 50,000m. cu m of gas) the normal limits were set much lower: 10% for a private foreign investor and 5% for a foreign state-controlled company. For most of the metals listed, the limit was zero. How this legislation would work in practice remained to be seen.

Meanwhile, foreign bank lending to Russian companies was growing strongly, and in 2005–07 inward foreign direct investment (FDI) rose substantially. The indications were that foreign confidence in the Russian economy, which had suffered in 2004 as a result of the Yukos affair, was recovering in 2005–08.

While the recovery in production after 1998 could be partly attributed to government policies, other factors proved more significant. The recovery began as an unintended consequence of the forced devaluation of the rouble in mid-1998. Russian society was more resistant to radical economic reform than those of the former communist states of Central Europe or the Baltic states of Estonia, Latvia and Lithuania. One consequence in the 1990s was that Russian policy-makers struggled to implement coherent transformation measures, such as the liberalization of markets, the implementation of monetary and fiscal austerity and privatization.

By 1998 Russia's economic system had been radically altered, but many problems remained. Around 70% of output was attributable to the private sector; however, privatized companies had been mainly sold to 'insiders', FDI remained limited and informal state intervention continued to be pervasive. Moreover, the banks and stock markets were underdeveloped and, although inflation had been reduced, the public finances were consistently in deficit. It was these failures of fiscal policy that were significant factors in creating the financial crisis of 1998. Additionally, the Government effectively maintained a large and thinly disguised subsidy to most sectors of the economy, and in particular manufacturing, by ensuring that the domestic prices of petroleum products and fuels were kept artificially low. In consequence, overall, competition did not operate freely in either product or capital markets.

Thus, for much of the 1990s the real economy was not adjusting successfully to the financial pressures of monetary stabilization. Loss-making state and privatized enterprises remained open even when the prospect of their recovery was minimal. They did this, in part, by simply not paying employees, suppliers and taxes and, in part, by using barter deals and money surrogates to 'settle' some of their debts. Two main groups of immediate losers emerged from this state of affairs: workers with wage arrears; and the public provision of health, education and other services, which were under pressure from chronic budget problems, as well as the adverse consequences of the widespread non-payment of wages in these sectors.

In 1997–98 Russia's precarious 'virtual' economy began to feel the effects of the financial crisis in Asia. The IMF had persuaded the Russian Government to open debt markets (chiefly for treasury bills) to foreign investors. With problems in other emerging markets, these investors began to pay more attention to the fragile state of Russian public finances, and to fear a rouble devaluation.

The Russian financial crisis of August 1998 forced an unintended major devaluation of the rouble, which declined dramatically in value against the US dollar; prior to the crisis, from mid-1995, the rouble exchange rate had been maintained in a 'corridor', which shifted downwards only slowly. Many feared that the major devaluation would trigger a resurgence of the high levels of inflation that had characterized the economy in the early 1990s. In fact, the devaluation served to benefit the manufacturing sector, while enhanced fiscal discipline kept inflation moderate. Previously unable to compete with imported food, clothing and engineering goods, Russian producers suddenly found that their foreign competitors had been priced out of the Russian market.

The revival of production was startling. In 1999 the economy received further encouragement from an increase in world petroleum prices, leading to official GDP growth of 10.0% in 2000. Although the rate of growth declined to 5.1% in 2001—a rate that President Vladimir Putin described as inadequate—it appeared that the economy was not lapsing into stagnation. Although growth might not have meant catching up with the developed world as rapidly as an ambitious leader would have liked, there were, none the less, indications that the economy was moving in the right direction. Kick-started by devaluation, the recovery was thereafter propelled chiefly by rising petroleum and natural gas prices. These did not directly account for the growth of output, which was, after all, a growth in real (constant-price) production; it was, however, largely the indirect result of rising export prices for hydrocarbons and metals. These brought rapidly growing revenue streams into the country even though a good deal of the proceeds was placed off shore. Swelling company profits, government revenues and personal incomes supported a strong growth in domestic demand.

As economic performance improved, so at first did the implementation of economic reforms. Between 2000, when he took office, and 2003 President Putin and his Government displayed a determination to advance reform, aided by a more compliant parliament than those with which President Boris Yeltsin's Governments had contended in the 1990s. Legislation that sought to simplify the tax system and reduce the official tax burden on companies and individuals (while simultaneously intended to reduce the high rate of tax evasion) was approved in 2001–03. This led to the introduction of a uniform tax rate (of 13%) on all personal incomes above a certain threshold, a reduction in profit tax from 35% to 24%, a reduction in value-added tax (VAT) to 18% with effect from January 2004, and a reduction in social (payroll) tax from January 2005. Another innovation was the introduction, in 2001–02, of laws that, for the first time in more than 70 years, permitted the sale and purchase of land. Bankruptcy law was revised, after earlier legislation had been exploited to obtain assets at artificially low prices. The difficult process of reforming the monopoly in electricity was embarked upon, and radical reform of the judicial system was initiated.

Other reforms started in this period were in public administration and in small-business regulation (an attempt, which met with some success, to reduce the burden of regulation on small firms), while long-standing efforts to reduce housing subsidies and strengthen the regulation of commercial banking continued, though with mixed results. Reform of the state pension system meant that in 2004 part of the work-force began (to a very limited extent, initially) to accumulate pension entitlement that would, in part, be funded by their own contributions—with the eventual, very long-term prospect of a transition to a fully funded pension system.

Privatization continued. The bulk of production assets had already passed into private hands, but in mid-2004 the state still owned 9,000 so-called 'unitary state enterprises' and had stakes in about 4,000 partially privatized joint-stock companies. Policy-makers aimed to sell off much of this state property, but it was a slow process.

At least until mid-2003 the signals that the Russian business community was receiving from the Russian state were encouraging, and boosted business confidence. Thereafter, the Russian state began to assert greater direct, ad hoc control of particular economic activities, thereby bringing about an overall change in expectations. This turn towards statism is reviewed below.

Even after 2003, however, one major development went against the general tendency towards recentralization and increased state control: the reform of the electricity industry. In 2006–08 the long-delayed privatization of electricity generation got under way. By July 2008 almost all generating assets had been sold off; the former state monopoly electricity company, Unified Energy System of Russia (RAO EES Rossii), had been liquidated, and only transmission, hydroelectric and nuclear power plants remained in state ownership, under successor state companies. Russian electricity had been, in regulators' jargon, 'unbundled'.

A tendency towards ad hoc state intervention became apparent from mid-2003, and reform legislation slowed, as people who shared Putin's security services background began to replace liberals in the presidential administration. Economic liberals, including the former Minister of the Economy, Yevgenii Yasin, and President Putin's own economic adviser, Andrei Illarionov, stressed the urgency of further reform, arguing that economic growth could be sustained at an annual rate of around 8% if the burden of the state on the economy were systematically reduced. In particular, the liberals had sought: the reduction of government taxation and spending from around 37% of GDP to around 30%; a rapid limiting of government regulation of business; the diminution of the remaining state stakes in enterprises; a reduction in housing subsidies; the reform of the military and the state bureaucracy; and the break-up of the state monopoly of natural gas and of petroleum pipelines. However, during 2003–05 it became clear that Putin and most of those now close to him in the presidential administration were deeply attached to the notion of ultimate central control, in the sense that they would allow no major concentration of economic and social power to operate independently of the wishes of the leadership.

This fundamental mindset was dramatically illustrated by the state's attack on the leading Russian private sector petroleum company, Yukos, and its core shareholder and Chief Executive, Mikhail Khodorkovskii. Khodorkovskii and his associates were accused of personal tax evasion and of embezzlement and fraud. Yukos was additionally presented with bills for tax allegedly underpaid in 2000 and 2001, and its assets were frozen by court order. In December 2004 the main production subsidiary of Yukos, Yuganskneftegaz, was in effect renationalized in compensation for alleged underpayment of taxes, as a consequence of its, indirect, acquisition

by the state-controlled petroleum company Rosneft. In May 2005 Khodorkovskii and an associate, Platon Lebedev, were each sentenced to nine years' imprisonment on charges of fraud, tax evasion and embezzlement (several other associates had prudently emigrated). In September 2006, after an appeal, Yukos was finally declared bankrupt. In 2007 its remaining assets were auctioned off, mostly to Rosneft and mostly at just above the reserve price.

Thus, the leading private petroleum company, which had been established by admittedly irregular methods in the 1990s, when the legislative environment was incomplete and confused, but which from 2000 had exhibited far greater transparency and legality in its corporate governance, was effectively destroyed. This set back confidence, particularly in the petroleum sector, where investment declined and output and export volume growth—until recently very rapid—slowed dramatically.

The attack on Yukos was not seen by Russian observers as a simple matter of law enforcement; it was understood from the outset to be political, given Khodorkovskii's funding for opposition political parties and his own apparent political ambitions. Similar charges could have been brought against many other people and companies, particularly given the circumstances in which privatizations were conducted in the mid-1990s. In the view of many, most, if not all, of the charges brought against the Yukos executives would not have stood up to serious legal scrutiny in truly independent courts.

The attack underlined the fact that property rights in Russia remained insecure and the Russian state still declined to be bound, in its dealings with its subjects, by an independent judicial system. Thus, economic policy under Putin turned from liberal to selectively statist from mid-2003. There seemed little doubt that Putin understood the advantages of private enterprise and free markets, and that many of his policies were designed to promote them, and also to reduce corruption and make public administration more effective. At the same time, the actions of the leadership revealed an unwillingness to limit state power. These two elements in policy could not easily coexist. In December 2005 Andrei Illarionov resigned from his post as presidential economic adviser, declaring that Russia was becoming not only economically illiberal, but politically autocratic as well.

Some recovery of confidence took place from late 2006. In mid-2007 a survey conducted by the international professional services company Ernst and Young asked 809 international business leaders to name the country most attractive for investment. Russia, previously low in the ranks, on this occasion was placed fifth, having been nominated by 12% of respondents. It appeared that both Russian and foreign investors were coming to believe they understood a new set of informal 'rules of the game', and were willing to invest accordingly in a large, growing and relatively underdeveloped market.

The ending of capital controls in mid-2006 helped. Estimated capital flight, which had been designed partly to evade those controls, fell. In 2005, 2006 and 2007 the net flow of privately controlled capital was increasingly positive—that is, more private capital flowed into Russia than flowed out. For a decade and a half before then, the net flow had been negative.

GROSS DOMESTIC PRODUCT

In addition to the statistical problems already noted in the post-communist period, the reporting system that existed was generally rather weak. The figures that are quoted here must, therefore, be treated with some caution.

At current prices, GDP amounted to 32,987,400m. roubles in 2007, according to official preliminary estimates. Official statistics are somewhat misleading (although not deliberately so) about the shares of different sectors in the supply side of GDP: in reality, industry accounts for about 40% of the total, agriculture for 5% or so, and retail and wholesale distribution for about 15%. On the demand side, household consumption in 2007 accounted for about 48% of the aggregate demand for Russian output, government consumption of goods and services for around 18%, fixed investment for about 21% and net exports (that is, exports less imports) of goods and services for

8.7%, with the remainder of about 5% being mostly accounted for by the change in stocks of goods. The change in fixed investment has been particularly striking. In real terms, gross fixed investment declined particularly steeply, by about 76%, in 1991–98. The subsequent recovery of investment was, therefore, from a dangerously low level; none the less, for sustained rapid economic growth, it was widely agreed that the share of fixed investment in GDP needed substantially to exceed its recent average of around 18%. The increase recorded in 2007, to 21%, appeared to be a step in the right direction.

From the late 1990s the estimated share of the private sector in GDP was 70%. The changes in economic policy from 2003 reduced that share to around 65% in 2005.

AGRICULTURE

In 1991, when the USSR disintegrated, the Russian Federation inherited an agricultural sector that was particularly dysfunctional. It contained about 26,000 Soviet state and collective farms, plus several million family plots, the size and livestock holdings of which had been severely restricted. Some 11m. people were employed on the big farms, an average of more than 400 per farm. There was little doubt that efficient large farms would employ far fewer people than were working on Russian state and collective farms.

The Russian Government's policy, announced in December 1991, was to require all state and collective farms to hold meetings of their employees in early 1992, at which decisions would be taken on the future form of organization of the farm. In this way, the most radical and politically provocative option, namely, enforcing the disbanding of these 'socialized' farms, was avoided. By the end of the year more than three-quarters of the farms had taken their decision and been re-registered. About one-third of these, some 7,000 farms, had opted to retain their previous status as a collective or state farm. Another 9,000 had elected to be registered as companies and 1,700 as farm co-operatives. In practice, very little changed in the organization of these farms during the 1990s.

A hard-fought struggle ensued between reformers and traditionalists over the crucial question of property rights in land. Land in agricultural use tended to be treated in legislation as a category separate from other land, such as urban real estate, and was an area of particular contention. In the Russian Constitution of December 1993, President Yeltsin managed to have an article inserted that made individual ownership of land a basic right of Russian citizens. To give legislative effect to the intention behind this, however, additional laws and regulations were needed, concerning such matters as the acquisition of private plots of land from existing farms and the sale and purchase of land. These proposals were contested successfully in the Russian parliament over the following eight years. A reform to the land code, approved by the Duma in September 2001, finally permitted the sale and purchase of urban real estate across the Federation. In June 2002 similar legislation was passed approving the sale of agricultural land, although restrictions on foreign ownership remained in place.

In early 1993 there were 184,000 peasant farms, occupying some 3%–4% of Russian farmland. Thereafter, many private farming ventures were abandoned, as financial circumstances in the sector continued to worsen. Nevertheless, the scale of the new private sector continued, on balance, to increase, albeit slowly. At the same time, the long-established household subsidiary plots were being increased in size, and various pre-existing 'kitchen garden' (*ogorod*) associations in urban areas were also being encouraged. By 1997 these two sources of private food production occupied only around 10% of farmland, but, according to official statistics, accounted for 91% of the country's production of potatoes, 76% of green vegetables, 55% of meat and 67% of milk. By 1998 the private sector accounted for almost 60% of farm output. This combination of private farming and horticulture was devoted mainly to subsistence production for the extended families of the households that worked the plots of land in question. In the late 1990s private agricultural businesses also began to develop under the guise of groups of nominally separate household plots, apparently so as to avoid taxation. In 2000–03 some large Russian businesses began to buy farmland, prior to the implementation of the new land code.

In the short term, the administrative problems encountered by the private farms and household plots were less important than the deteriorating terms of trade that confronted the sector. It could be roughly estimated that in 1989–97 farm prices rose so much less than non-farm prices that the terms of trade between the farm sector and the rest of the economy declined by about 72%. Thus, agricultural workers saw their ability to buy both consumer goods and farm inputs of machinery, fertilizers, fuel, etc., decline sharply. This led to a fall in industrial inputs, with a negative impact on farm output, and a growth in farm debt. State subsidies to the agricultural sector did little to offset this. In 1992 farm subsidies totalled 3.6% of GDP. From 1995 policy-makers made a concerted effort to resist the traditional pressure for budgetary subsidies for the farms at sowing and harvesting seasons (much of the money went missing), and by 2001 explicit farm subsidies from the federal budget were equivalent to only 0.5% of GDP. Some support continued from regional and local budgets, but not enough to counter the decline in federal subsidies.

By 2005–08, despite the sale of farmland having been legal since 2002, the structure of the sector was still reminiscent of the Soviet period. About 25,000 corporate farms, averaging 2,600 ha in size, were mostly inefficient and often loss-making, while a larger number of much smaller independent farms contributed a small but rising share of farm output, estimated at about 6% in 2006. More than one-half of all output came from no less than 16m. private plots, each of which averaged only 0.43 ha. In July 2005 new legislation was put in place that strengthened the security of property rights in land, but commentators were not convinced that this would make a big difference to the structure of the sector.

None the less, a category of large agribusinesses, often holdings run by food-industry concerns, began to emerge. It is estimated that in 2003–05 the 300 largest agro-holdings produced about 25% of all farm output and 75% of farm profits. The range between weak and strong farms was very large, and a process of concentration was under way. This concentration was also regional, with one-half of all farm output coming from just 15 out of the more than 80 Russian regions.

The level of farm subsidies was, for a time, one of the main areas of contention in negotiations on Russia's bid to join the World Trade Organization (WTO). It is now accepted that Russia may increase farm subsidies somewhat from their very low level. It is probably in infrastructure development (chiefly roads) and in credit and equipment-leasing schemes that help is needed.

Despite all the difficulties of farm-sector development, officially recorded agricultural output declined no more severely in 1989–98 than industrial production or GDP as a whole—by about 45%. The reduction in agricultural output was concentrated in the livestock sector. The decline in many households' purchasing power produced a shift in the composition of retail food sales, with greater emphasis on bread and potatoes, and less on meat and milk. When the economy began to grow again after 1998, so did farm production. Measured at 2000 prices, agricultural output rose at an average annual rate of 3.1% between 1998 and 2004, and 2.8% in 2003–06.

In general, the farming sector in Russia was full of anomalies. By 2005 a market in farmland had still to develop, even though the legislative basis was in place. The sector had been impoverished by the relative movement of agricultural and non-agricultural prices. Subsidies were disappearing. At the same time, farm output had proved to be relatively resilient and, in practice, the private production and distribution of food had grown in importance.

INDUSTRY

Industrial output declined, officially, by about one-half between 1989 and 1998. Within that total, electricity generation decreased by only 23% (surprisingly, given the general recorded decline in economic activity); the fuel sector (petroleum, natural gas and coal) by just over one-third; and the chemicals sector, steel and non-ferrous metals by about three-fifths. After 1995 recorded output in the fuel sector remained relatively stable. Steel and non-ferrous metals production, increasingly linked to exports, stabilized and, in 1997 and 1999, slightly increased. The largest declines were in light industry (footwear, clothing and textiles), which had been particularly affected by heightened competition from imports, and in the engineering sector. Light-industrial output in 1998 was only around one-eighth of its 1989 level. By 1998 engineering production had declined by more than 70%, but showed signs of recovery in 1999.

Those output declines, combined with substantial changes in relative producer prices for different branches of industry, produced a significant change in the composition of industrial output by branch. In particular, the relative importance of the fuel and energy sub-sector, plus steel and non-ferrous metals, rose substantially. When Russian critics of the changes spoke of a 'deindustrialization' of Russia, they referred to both the lesser role of industry, as a whole, in the economy and the reduced importance of manufacturing, especially processing, as distinct from extractive industry. The decline in engineering output was particularly emphasized. The underlying problem was that much Russian manufacturing was uncompetitive. At least some of its output was 'value subtracting'—i.e. was unable to be sold as finished output on competitive markets for as substantial a sum as could be made by selling the materials and energy used during the manufacturing process. This pattern changed somewhat during the post-1998 recovery, as branches of industry hitherto in decline began to revive.

Even the more resilient branches of industry experienced difficulties in the 1990s. Crude petroleum output in 1999, amounting to about 6.8m. barrels per day (b/d), was little more than one-half of its highest level in 1987. Thereafter, the leading private Russian petroleum companies restructured, invested, introduced improved technology and rapidly increased total production, which reached almost 10m. b/d in 2007. Meanwhile, investment in the exploration and proving-up of new reserves remained low, so the ratio of reserves to production fell slightly. In late 2007 and the first half of 2008 oil production first levelled off and then declined slightly.

The state's attack on Yukos (see above) and subsequent harassment of foreign oil and gas companies increased uncertainty in the sector. This coincided with the increase in taxation in 2003–04 of petroleum company profits and subsequent increases in the excise duties on petroleum exports. These changes were an attempt to tap natural-resource rents for the state and to equalize private rates of return between the petroleum industry and manufacturing. The shift of tax burden towards the petroleum industry was conducted in the cause of diversification of the economy, and had been encouraged by the World Bank. However, the combined effect of the treatment of Yukos and of higher taxes on the development of this recently buoyant sector depressed petroleum-industry investment. A combination of influences slowed production growth in the sector dramatically after 2003: reduced trust in property rights following the Yukos affair; higher taxation of the industry; and export pipeline 'bottlenecks' restricting exports. The politicians, seeing the problem and more open to industry lobbying now that more of the oil industry was state-owned, took steps to undo some of the damage. From the beginning of 2007, tax breaks were introduced for companies involved in the development of new petroleum fields in eastern Siberia and operating highly depleted fields. Further tax concessions were made in 2008. None the less, the state, in one way or another, had contrived to damage its leading export industry.

Natural gas output, which had risen continuously in the late Soviet period, albeit at an increasingly slow rate, declined slightly after 1991, and then fluctuated. Gazprom, a state-controlled company, was a near-monopolist. It accounted for nearly 90% of output in 2006 and had total control of Russia's long-distance gas pipelines, gas storage and exports outside the Commonwealth of Independent States (CIS). The absence of competition in the sector had the effect of blunting incentives to raise efficiency. Output grew much more slowly than in the petroleum industry, despite high world prices and a weakening of non-Russian sources of natural gas supply to the European market. Labour productivity in the industry decreased between 1997 and 2003, whereas in 26 out of 30 industrial

branches it grew. By mid-2006 serious structural reform in the gas industry had been abandoned. Instead, Gazprom expanded by acquisitions. It acquired, in October 2005, 75.7% of Sibneft, a previously private petroleum company. In 2006 it acquired a controlling stake in Sakhalin Energy, and in 2007 it negotiated the acquisition of a majority stake in the Kovykta gas field, although final settlement of this deal remained unresolved in mid-2008. In 2006 legislation was adopted that entrenched Gazprom's monopoly over gas exports. Domestic gas prices were regularly raised, but this remained a political decision, and most gas continued to be sold domestically at regulated prices. In 2008 the regulated price was still far below the prices for gas exported to world markets.

Other branches of industry, broadly speaking, grew strongly after 1998. Growth was led by those natural-resource based industries that were strongly export-orientated and mostly privately owned: petroleum, metals and timber. In 2001–04 petroleum, natural gas, non-ferrous metals and forest products accounted for 70% of industrial growth. However, moderate growth was also recorded in several branches of industry orientated towards the domestic market.

In 1991–98 most industrial enterprises underwent privatization and also experienced a steep decline in demand. They shed labour, but less rapidly than output fell. After the rouble devaluation of 1998 some more systematic restructuring began, as output increased and previously underutilized capacity began to be brought back into use. Some restructuring in manufacturing occurred as a result of foreign direct investment (FDI). This had strong, positive effects on labour productivity, particularly in industries like tobacco and brewing, which attracted comparatively large amounts of foreign capital. In the context of booming world markets, Russian private-sector petroleum companies, led by Yukos, restructured and streamlined themselves largely of their own accord, although they also bought in advanced foreign technology through international oil services companies. In manufacturing there may have been some gains as a result of acquisitions by the leading Russian business groups.

These groups, often originating from a banking operation, but latterly based, with rare exceptions, around a petroleum or metals company, began to acquire downstream manufacturing assets and, quite often, other manufacturing facilities not technologically related to their core business. According to a Russian study published in 2003, by 2001 the 10 leading private integrated business groups accounted for 35.6% of all industrial output and 13.7% of all production. This degree of concentration of industrial control was slightly greater than in the Republic of Korea (South Korea), with its dominant *chaebol* (conglomerate) groups, and significantly greater than in Japan, Germany or the USA. These findings inspired a good deal of critical debate. However, on the one hand it was by no means certain that the high degree of concentration would endure for long—a trend seemed to be under way for leading groups to divest themselves of non-core activities—while, on the other hand, it was not obvious that other means existed to facilitate the flow of finance for investment from the natural-resource-exporting industries to other parts of the economy.

Although its market capitalization reached the respectable level of 40% of GDP in late 2005—and later rose above 100%—the stock market remained extremely illiquid, with little trading except in a small group of shares. Turnover in 2005 was equivalent to 29% of GDP, or well below market capitalization. It was therefore not an effective source of finance for new investment. From 2002 Russian companies began to raise money quite extensively abroad, by borrowing from Western banks, by corporate bond issues and, latterly, by share issues on foreign stock exchanges. Russian banks themselves were only beginning to act, as yet on only a modest scale, as intermediaries between savers and borrowers. Russian firms increasingly raised money on foreign stock exchanges with initial public offerings (IPOs) of shares. The London Stock Exchange (United Kingdom) was the favoured platform for these floatations. In July 2006 Rosneft raised US $10,400m. in an IPO in London in which it issued shares equivalent to 14.8% of its equity. This was controversial, but, from the Russian state's point of view, successful. Rosneft had acquired major assets from Yukos in a legally dubious fashion but had, none the less, been able to list its shares on a major Western stock market and raise an exceptionally large amount of capital there. The Rosneft IPO brought the total raised by Russian IPOs on the London markets to about $17,000m. since December 2004.

The worldwide sharp contraction in credit markets of 2007–08 tended to raise the cost of foreign finance for Russian firms and generally to lead international investors to behave more warily. The number of Russian company IPOs declined, and corporate borrowing abroad decreased somewhat. None the less, leading Russian companies, especially in oil and gas, were able to raise money on international markets fairly readily, albeit at some increase in cost. They were helped by two considerations. First, Russia's extremely robust fiscal, balance of payments and reserves position kept the country's sovereign credit rating high (indeed, the credit rating agency Moody's raised its rating of Russia from Baa2 to Baa1 in July 2008), and this tended to ease the way for Russian corporate borrowing. Second, Russian exporters of oil, gas and metals could borrow against the security of their future exports, the prices of which remained historically high, and which, in some cases, were continuing to climb. Thus, Rosneft was able to raise almost US $3,000m. in a syndicated loan in mid-2008, for a five-year term at Libor (London inter-bank offered rate) plus 1.25%; analysts considered this to be a favourable deal under the prevailing circumstances. However, the RTS (Russian Trading System) stock market in Moscow was affected severely by the international economic downturn in 2008, losing more than one-half of its value during June–October of that year, with trading being suspended on several occasions as a result of intense share-price volatility. Moreover, substantial capital outflow from Russia was reported in the aftermath of the military conflict between Russia and Georgia in August (see History).

Growth in the industrial sector in 1999–2008 was broadly based. Doubts centred on the extent to which this industrial expansion was dependent on a favourable exchange rate and on the capacity of Russian industry to develop internationally competitive products beyond the short list of petroleum, natural gas, steel, aluminium and some forest products. As the rouble appreciated in real terms—that is, taking account of inflation—against the US dollar and the euro, the initial competitive advantage achieved by rouble devaluation was eroded. By mid-2006 the rouble was worth rather more, in real terms, against the euro and dollar than it had been on the eve of the 1998 financial crisis, and Russian producers appeared to have no significant competitive advantages outside the natural-resource sector. A Bank of Finland study in 2007 found strong evidence that domestic producers, though still increasing their output quite strongly in absolute terms, were losing market share to imports of manufactures.

In 2007–08 the Russian leadership embarked on a policy of establishing state-controlled holding companies that would steer developments in high-technology industries and thus, they hoped, promote the diversification of the economy. These holding companies were in aerospace, shipbuilding, nanotechnology and in an agglomeration of mainly defence-related lines of business called the Rostekhnologii (Russian Technologies) State Corporation. These new holding companies were controversial. Liberal critics saw them as both excessively controlled by senior officials and potentially corrupt, and as unlikely to produce a rapid and general upgrading of the technological level of Russian industry.

FOREIGN TRADE AND PAYMENTS

From the 1990s until 2005 Russia was in the curious position, for an economy of its level of development, of transferring more resources to the rest of the world than it had been absorbing from other countries. This is curious because Russia is a middle-income country with possibilities over the long term of catching up with, or at any rate of greatly reducing its present lag behind, the most advanced economies. Countries in such a position gain from importing more goods and services than they export and covering the financial gap in their current accounts with a net inflow of foreign capital—preferably long-

term and in the form of inward FDI—which can be expected to boost productivity. Russia was failing to obtain this benefit.

However, there were signs from 2005 onwards that the situation was changing. Inward foreign investment, including direct investment, rose quite strongly. Capital flight fell in 2006 when capital convertibility of the rouble was introduced. Private capital flows into the country exceeded flows out for the first time in 2005, and this was repeated in 2006 and 2007.

At the same time Russian external finances remained very robust. Foreign reserves at the end of 2007, at about US $465,000m., were twice annual imports. Merchandise exports in 2007 were nearly $354,401m., with about 62% of the total comprising petroleum, petroleum products and natural gas. Adding metals to this sum would bring Russia's dependence on natural resources up to about four-fifths of its exports. Merchandise imports were $223,486m., so the trade surplus was still huge—equivalent to about 10% of GDP. In recent years two-fifths of imports have comprised machinery and equipment, including cars, and around one-sixth to one-fifth food imports. Arms exports declined sharply in 1992, but from the late 1990s considerable official efforts were made to reorganize and promote the Russian arms export trade, and by the mid-2000s Russia was the fourth largest exporter of arms, measured by value of sales. Russia's arms exports in 2007 were estimated at about $7,000m.

The figures for total merchandise trade imply a rather trade-dependent economy. If 2007 GDP is measured in US dollars at the annual average exchange rate, merchandise exports were equivalent to 27.5% of GDP and imports were equivalent to 17.3% of GDP. Both exports and imports had risen rapidly since 1999. On the export side, the rise in dollar totals was heavily assisted by rising petroleum prices. On the import side, growth was mostly a matter of volume growth resulting from increasing domestic demand. However, the dollar totals were also increased latterly by the appreciation of the euro (in which a substantial part of Russian imports was invoiced by the mid-2000s) against the dollar. Rather more than one-half of Russia's trade was conducted with Europe. Other former Soviet republics in the CIS now play only a modest role in Russian trade: less than one-fifth if imports and exports are taken together. For reasons primarily of geography, the USA is a minor partner, accounting for less than 5% of Russian merchandise trade.

Net interest and dividend payments abroad, plus a negative balance in services, meant that the overall current account surplus was considerably smaller than the merchandise trade surplus, but, at US $76,163m. in 2007, it remained sizeable, being equivalent to just under 6% of GDP. This current account surplus showed up in an increase over the year of $148,928m. in the national gold and foreign-exchange reserves, but the new and growing net inflow of capital also contributed. Capital flows were a mixture of large and fluctuating capital flight, growing outward FDI and large and increasing inflows of foreign bank lending and direct investment from abroad, the latter amounting to $54,294m. in 2007. The growth of inward FDI was a welcome development. Some of it was attributable to Russian-controlled offshore funds acquiring assets in Russia, while some of it comprised funds controlled by non-residents. At the same time, the strong inflow of corporate borrowing and the continuing large capital outflow tell a rather more ambiguous story: a large part of the Russian business community, evidently, still felt safer putting substantial assets off-shore; and the foreign borrowing by Russian companies would, in a downturn, be problematic in ways that FDI would not—credit lines could be terminated and debt-servicing would become more difficult.

One encouraging sign was the development of a number of leading Russian companies into multinationals. This process became particularly marked in 2006–08. In 2006 Russian steel, nickel and aluminium companies, in particular, made major acquisitions around the world, including in Africa and in the USA. By 2008 RUSAL was the world's second largest aluminium producer. In mid-2007 Norilsk Nickel acquired the Canadian company LionOre, which has nickel and gold mines in South Africa, Botswana and Australia. These new Russian multinationals were in the natural resource sector, where Russia's competitive strength lay. Similar development on the part of oil and gas companies was less striking—reflecting perhaps the effects of increased state control. Gazprom continued to develop downstream distribution assets in Europe. LUKoil—still privately owned but by all accounts well connected to the Kremlin, added a chain of petrol stations in Europe to those it already owned in the USA.

Government external debt was not only being serviced, but there was little new borrowing, with the effect that total sovereign external debt was being reduced. This public debt was also being paid off ahead of time, saving future interest costs and helping to curb the inflationary effect of what would otherwise have been even larger inflows of foreign funds into Russia. At the end of 2007 Russia's sovereign external debt amounted to US $44,000m., a mere 3% of GDP. The end result was that the Russian Government was no longer dependent on the external support of the IMF or other creditors.

Russian companies, despite all the weaknesses of the Russian business environment, were able to borrow on fairly good terms in the West, and continued to do so, raising $90,800m. in 2007 (excluding borrowing by Russian banks). Foreign borrowing by Russian companies slowed markedly in the first half of 2008, as the credit crisis affected international markets; but borrowing remained quite high by the standards of a few years earlier. As the Russian state was becoming markedly less dependent on foreign finance, Russian companies were becoming markedly more so. One development that blurred this distinction was that amongst the companies borrowing a significant amount were state-controlled Russian firms and banks. By the beginning of 2008 Russian companies owed the outside world almost 10 times as much as the Russian state did.

One very large direct investment deal had challenged the established pattern of FDI in Russia—the agreement, worth some US $6,150m., finalized by BP (formerly British Petroleum—of the United Kingdom) with the Tyumen Oil Company (TNK) and Sidanco in June 2003, to form a joint venture, NewCo, which was to trade as TNK-BP. The new company would control current output of about 1m. b/d of petroleum, as well as substantial reserves of both petroleum and natural gas in Russia. This deal alone was equivalent to almost three times the previous annual rate of FDI in Russia, and was the first instance of a major Western energy company acquiring a major stake in Russian petroleum production. By 2005 it appeared that TNK-BP was a Western investment in Russia of a kind that would not be repeated for several years. In 2007 TNK-BP lost control of the giant Kovykta gas field, which had constituted an important part of its portfolio. Administrative pressure opened the way for Gazprom to buy a controlling stake. In general, foreign energy companies were ceasing to expect to operate in Russia in any significant field except as minority partners. This position seemed to be entrenched by a new law, effective in May 2008, on foreign investment in 'strategic' industries (see above).

The issue of 'strategic' resources and measures, allegedly intended to preserve Russian 'sovereignty' by limiting the scope of FDI, was treated in a way that suggested a lack of clear vision and conclusive decision-making on the part of the Russian leadership. It remains to be seen how the new law on FDI in strategic industries will be implemented in practice.

Pressures for the liberalization of foreign trade and investment came from international organizations. In 2000–08 Russia was in intensive negotiations over accession to the WTO. By the end of 2006 almost all WTO members engaged in bilateral negotiations over Russia joining the Organization had reached provisional agreements with the Russian authorities. The late-2006 agreement with the USA was an important breakthrough. However, a great deal of detail remained to be negotiated, mainly in a multilateral framework. Here Russia's apparent dilatoriness in clarifying its regulations, such as on phytosanitary controls on farm products, appeared to be a source of further delay. Russia also did not help its cause by imposing export duties on unprocessed wood (roundwood) in 2007, upsetting the Nordic timber industry in particular.

The immediate trading benefits of WTO membership for Russia would not be substantial. As a petroleum and gas exporter, Russia relies heavily for its export earnings on products that are in any case subject to only very minimal trade barriers, if any. By contrast, for metals (in the export of

which Russia encounters extensive 'anti-dumping' measures from importing nations) and for economic diversification in the longer term, WTO membership would usefully improve the country's ability to bargain over trade barriers with its main partners. WTO membership should also allow more foreign competition within Russia, particularly in financial services. This should, in the long run, assist the overall development of the economy. Perhaps more than anything else, the symbolic value of WTO membership was what mattered to Russian politicians. Membership would imply that Russia was a full participant in the trading world; remaining non-members of WTO are relatively few and include several so-called 'pariah' states.

The rouble exchange rate stabilized in 2003–08, after more than 10 years of turbulence and (mainly) decline against Western currencies. From mid-1992 to mid-1995 the rouble's exchange rate against the US dollar declined steeply. None the less, the rouble appreciated in real terms against the dollar. As domestic inflation slowed, the Russian monetary authorities sought to control the decline of the rouble and keep it in conformity with relative inflation rates—in other words, to keep the real exchange rate approximately constant. To this end, the rouble 'corridor' ensured that the exchange rate remained within a periodically adjusted band, varying from around 4.40 roubles to the dollar in mid-1995 to 6.10 roubles to the dollar in August 1998, prior to the abolition of this arrangement and the rapid decline of the exchange rate, to around 24 roubles to the dollar, in the immediate aftermath of the financial crisis. Subsequently, a more gradual decline ensued, with the effect that in 2002 an average exchange rate of 31.35 roubles to the dollar was recorded. Thereafter, the rouble tended to strengthen against the US dollar while weakening against the euro. In mid-2007 the rate was slightly less than 26 roubles to the dollar, and by mid-2008 the rate was less than 24 roubles to the dollar.

In 2005–07 one major issue in trade policy captured a great deal of attention: Russia's allegedly political manipulation of its oil and gas supplies to 'punish' countries that had in some way displeased it. Cuts in gas supplies to Ukraine at the beginning of 2006 briefly affected supplies (transported through that country) to several Western European states. A somewhat similar, brief disruption occurred in oil supplies through Belarus in January 2007. In July 2008 oil supplies to the Czech Republic were cut soon after the Czech Government had agreed to host US radar systems as part of the controversial US anti-ballistic-missile defence system in Central Europe.

Critics alleged that the cuts in 2006 were intended to punish Ukraine for its perceived political shift away from Russia following the so-called 'orange revolution' that resulted in Viktor Yushchenko being elected as President in December 2004. Although different factors no doubt influenced the interruption of oil supplies through Belarus, it was again possible to argue that political conflicts were its cause, and this is also true of the interruption in supplies to the Czech Republic in 2008. These critics concluded that Russia could not be relied upon as an energy supplier. The Russian political leaders maintained that, on the contrary, the brief cuts in supplies had been the result of a breakdown in negotiations over increases in the gas prices charged to Ukraine and Belarus, and of technical problems in the Czech case. As such, the first two interruptions in supply could be regarded as the fault of the Ukrainian and Belarusian, rather than the Russian, authorities, as the price of energy supplies to these, and other CIS states, had been kept artificially low and, in effect, subsidized by Russia. The EU purchased between one-third and one-quarter of its gas supplies from Russia in the mid-2000s, and that share was expected to rise.

Despite increasing demands for a unified EU energy policy that would include diversification of sources of supply, there was no indication by mid-2008 that EU member states were capable of co-ordinating in order to reduce, or at least limit, their dependence on Russia. Their energy relationships with Russia varied greatly, so a common approach was hard to secure. Meanwhile, doubts grew, not so much about Russian deliberate manipulation of European energy supplies, but about Russia's capacity to meet the rising demand for gas both in Europe and in Russia itself. Gazprom continued to make deals whereby it planned to corner much of Central Asian gas production for resale at much higher prices to Europe. In 2008 Russia moved energetically in attempts to secure additional gas supplies from Azerbaijan, the post-Soviet states of Central Asia, Libya and Iran, apparently both to meet its own export commitments to Europe and to deter other CIS suppliers from embarking on pipeline projects with European support that would bypass or exclude Russia.

BUDGET AND FINANCES

Austere fiscal and monetary policies are the banal but unavoidable prescription for dealing with a rise in consumer prices. In 1991–94 Russian policy-makers failed to follow this rule. This failure in stabilization, although neither complete nor irredeemable, was of the greatest significance. The control of inflation is desirable in all circumstances. When a government and a whole population are trying to make the transition from a centrally administered to a market economy, however, it is vital.

In 1991–95 Russia avoided 'hyperinflation', but the rate of growth of consumer prices remained high. The immediate causes of this, themselves closely related, were a large budgetary deficit and an excessive expansion of credit. The struggle to reduce inflation to manageable proportions was the most controversial issue of the transition, reflecting a history of state financial support for all sanctioned economic activities. Once it became clear to members of the Soviet-era élite that they had a good chance of profiting from privatization and from freer links with the outside world, the removal of a state 'safety net' for their economic ventures came to be seen as the greatest threat posed by the reformers.

A 'reform team' remained in place in successive governments in 1991–98, but with frequent changes of personnel. These reformers fought tenaciously to contain government spending and reduce the rate of growth of the money supply. 'Post-reform' Governments in 1998–99, led by Yevgenii Primakov and Sergei Stepashin, did not, in the event, reverse the policies of the reformers. When Vladimir Putin became acting President at the end of 1999 and, after the March 2000 election, President, reform policies were strengthened. The reform process in general ground to a halt in 2003–04 (see above). None the less, financial stabilization was maintained and annual inflation rates were gradually reduced in 2004–06 to less than 10%, largely as a result of maintaining tight controls on public spending. Meanwhile, recovering economic activity and high and mostly rising petroleum prices led, simultaneously, to an increase in government revenue. One result was federal budgetary surpluses in 2000–06, equivalent to 7.7% of GDP in 2005 and 7.3% in 2006, which enabled the Government to set aside funds for the repayment of the principal of its foreign debts as, or even before, they became due.

Macroeconomic control slackened in 2007 as parliamentary and presidential elections loomed. The budget remained in surplus but it was a reduced surplus at a time of steeply rising revenues. Public expenditure was increased, in current prices, by more than a third. Not surprisingly, inflation revived, consumer prices rising by 11.9% between December 2006 and December 2007. The Finance Ministry fought hard to reassert control in the 2008 budget and plans for budgets in 2009–11, but inflation continued to surge in early 2008, running at about 15% year-on-year. The Central Bank of Russia was attempting to move at this time towards inflation-targeting, with a reduced priority for holding down the exchange rate of the rouble, but it faced an uphill struggle.

From the beginning of 2004 a budgetary stabilization fund was established. The idea was to provide some insulation for the public finances from fluctuations in petroleum prices. But the fund also served the purpose of neutralizing petro-dollar inflows—that is to say, withdrawing a large part of the inflows from circulation and thus reducing the potentially inflationary growth of the money supply. Protection of the budget against oil-price declines was important because revenue from oil and gas was contributing between one-third and one-half of the revenue of the federal budget. By 2006 revenue from all taxes on petroleum, petroleum products and gas, including taxes on the profits of firms in the hydrocarbons sector, provided around 50% of federal budget income. The price of a barrel of Urals petroleum, which had been as little as US \$12 in 1998, averaged \$27 in 2003, increasing to more than \$34 in 2004, to \$50 in 2005 and to \$61 in 2006. In 2007 it averaged \$69, and in early 2008 more than \$100.

The stabilization fund was initially to draw revenue from petroleum sold at prices in excess of US \$20 per barrel, hold it in readily tradable foreign-government securities, which would be used and be available to support government spending commitments (such as interest on foreign debt) in the event of petroleum prices falling to low levels. At the end of 2006 the fund was worth some \$89,100m. From early 2008 it was split into two funds: a Reserve Fund to support the budget if needed; and a National Prosperity Fund for longer-term investment. The latter is a sovereign wealth fund, able to invest in somewhat riskier, higher-yield assets than is the Reserve Fund.

Unsurprisingly, many politicians presented proposals for spending the resources of the stabilization fund, as well as gold and foreign-currency reserves, including projects to increase public sector pay, improve the road network and increase state support for scientific research and development. The Ministry of Finance, supported by President Putin, firmly resisted any such proposals, arguing that their main effect would be to accelerate inflation. It was only in 2007 that this vigilance was relaxed (see above), contrary to the wishes of the Ministry of Finance and with the predicted results. In 2007 the Government introduced three-year budgeting. This meant that the main components of the federal budget would be set for a period of three years, rather than just one year at a time. After the setbacks of 2007, the Ministry of Finance pushed hard to plan budgets so that there would be a 'non-oil-and-gas' balance (a modest deficit), to be plugged by strictly limited transfers from hydrocarbons revenue.

Another important issue was that of monetary and exchange-rate policy, as balance of payments surpluses tended to strengthen the rouble against other currencies, but it was feared that Russian industry could not cope with too rapid a real appreciation of the rouble (see above). Thus, the Central Bank bought US dollars and euros and built up the reserves of foreign currency in order to slow the real appreciation of the rouble. However, the purchase of foreign currency was done by issuing roubles, raising the rouble money supply. That, in turn, threatened to create inflationary pressure. The monetary authorities were in no position to reduce the liquidity of the banking system by selling government securities, because the emission of government securities had been left at very low levels after the 1998 crisis and the re-creation of a market for them would take a long time. The monetary authorities were therefore obliged to maintain a difficult balance between constraining the appreciation of the exchange rate and constraining inflation. In maintaining this balance, the Central Bank was helped by the economic recovery and the growing confidence in the Russian currency. Continuing growth meant that demand for the rouble was rising strongly, partly offsetting the inflationary effects of the large increases in the supply of the currency.

Inflation, as measured by the consumer price index (CPI), finally dipped below the 10% mark in 2006, falling to 9.0% if measured December-to-December. It had been 10.9% in 2005, 11.7% in 2004, 12.0% in 2003 and 15.1% in 2002, so the deceleration of inflation was only gradual. None the less, a prudent fiscal stance, maintained under a great deal of political pressure to increase spending faster, was being rewarded. Another influence was a process that was unfamiliar to established market economies. Rapid growth in economic activity and growing business confidence had increased the demand for money from very low levels relative to GDP. This growth of monetization helped to offset the rapid growth in money supply that resulted from the inflow of 'petrodollars' (income from petroleum exports), reducing its inflationary effect. The fiscal relaxation of 2007 pushed consumer price inflation in that year back up to 11.9%. A return to fiscal prudence was required. Part of the problem was the worldwide one of knock-on effects from rises in the prices of oil and foodstuffs. However, rapid money-wage growth and low unemployment suggested that the Russian economy was also in danger of 'overheating', independently of those influences.

Altogether, the stabilization process had proved to be extremely difficult. The rise in inward foreign investment created another source of growth in the money supply, and one that the stabilization or reserve fund was not designed to mitigate.

PROSPECTS

By mid-2008 the Russian economy had been growing for 10 years. Market-friendly reforms of taxation, business regulation, property laws and much more had been undertaken. The Russian business community had been showing signs of a major shift from 'asset-stripping' to ensuring the longer-term growth of its enterprises. All of these factors were encouraging for the future, while a simple extrapolation of recent rates of change would present a reasonably positive overview, indicating the likelihood that, although Russia's economy would remain far behind those of Western Europe and North America, it would grow somewhat faster, with manageable inflation, strong reserves and a very low burden of public debt. In such circumstances, most Russian citizens could expect their material circumstances to improve steadily, if not dramatically.

These prospects were not, however, secure, being vulnerable to an international downturn in growth and any consequent sharp fall in the petroleum price. Moreover, the basis of Russia's recent economic successes had the effect of transforming the country into a quasi-'petro-state', which did not necessarily provide a sound basis for sustained or balanced economic growth over a long period. At the same time, many of the basic institutions of a well-functioning market economy remained underdeveloped. Further reforms remained necessary in many areas, including banking, accounting, public administration and the legal system, in order to ensure that the progress achieved in recent years would be repeated and extended. Additionally, recently established smaller firms, a source of dynamism in any economy, appeared to be chronically underdeveloped in Russia, accounting for only around 20% of employment in 2000–04, compared with 40%–60% in much of Central and Western Europe. This lagging development appeared to be connected with the particularly oppressive character of local bureaucracy in Russia, where licensing and certification processes are cumbersome and commonly corrupt. Although Putin and his Government attempted to resolve these problems through various 'debureaucratization' measures, and there was some evidence of a reduction in the regulatory burden, it remained unclear just how much direct impact these measures were making.

Underlying these phenomena were the dominance of informal networking and the casual interpretation of formal rules. Few formal institutions—from shareholders' meetings to tax payment and contract enforcement—worked according to the official rules. Accordingly, the cost of doing business outside a small circle of known partners was high. It was argued that

much the same could be said of several highly successful economies, such as the People's Republic of China and South Korea. International business perceptions of the degree of corruption, investigated by the German-based non-governmental organization, Transparency International, and others, suggested, however, that the problem might be greater in Russia than in many Asian economies. If, as World Bank economists argued, the key requirement for Russia is rapid investment growth, this assessment was not encouraging. Should it indeed be the case that Russia has what some economic historians call 'poor institutional quality', the historical evidence suggests that this is not something that readily changes, even over extended periods of time. For all these reasons, many economists, both Russian and Western, doubted that Russia could, in the foreseeable future, exhibit sustained growth at above the average for the industrialized member countries of OECD.

Several developments suggested a slowdown was likely in 2008–12. The population had been falling for several years, but it was only after 2007 that the working-age population began to decline. That decline will continue in the medium term. Spare production capacity left unused through the 1990s depression was generally agreed to have become more or less fully used once more, while new investment, though growing fast, may not be enough to keep capacity rising rapidly. Russian manufacturing, as distinct from the natural-resource-based oil, gas and metals industries, lacked competitiveness and showed signs of continuing to do so as the rouble strengthened in real terms. In 2003–08 a new concern had become apparent: that Putin and his administration (and from spring 2008 the successor administration of Dmitrii Medvedev) were setting limits on the process of liberalization. This became extremely clear in the development of the Yukos affair, although that was not the only source of this unease. There were also administrative pressures exerted against some other Russian firms, and also against Shell and its partners in Sakhalin, against TNK-BP in East Siberia and against the Moscow office of the international accountancy and auditing firm PricewaterhouseCoopers, in relation to the latter company's initial defence of its audits of Yukos. These Western (or in the case of TNK-BP, partly Western) firms all backed down and complied with the demands of the Russian authorities. All of this seemed to be a reaffirmation of the Russian tradition of state authority unconstrained by law: another form of the predominance of informal over formal rules.

How long these negative effects would last remained to be seen. From a long-term point of view, the limits to growth imposed by weak institutions and deteriorating macroeconomic conditions were of concern. Many analysts were forecasting average annual GDP growth of around 5%–6% in 2009–15, somewhat less than could be achieved in a country with Russia's long-term potential and resources but with stronger institutions.

Statistical Survey

Source (unless otherwise indicated): Federal Service of State Statistics103450 Moscow, ul. Myasnitskaya 39; tel. (495) 207-49-02; fax (495) 207-40-87; e-mail stat@gks.ru; internet www.gks.ru.

Area and Population

AREA, POPULATION AND DENSITY

Area (sq km)	17,075,400*
Population (census results)	
12 January 1989	147,021,869
9–16 October 2002	
Males	67,605,133
Females	77,561,598
Total	145,166,731
Population (official estimates at 1 January)	
2006	142,753,551
2007	142,220,968
2008	142,008,838
Density (per sq km) at 1 January 2008	8.3

* 6,592,850 sq miles.

POPULATION BY ETHNIC GROUP
(census of 9–16 October 2002)

	’000	%
Russian[1]	115,889.1	79.83
Tatar[2]	5,554.6	3.83
Ukrainian	2,943.0	2.03
Bashkir	1,673.4	1.15
Chuvash	1,637.1	1.13
Chechen[3]	1,360.2	0.94
Armenian	1,130.5	0.78
Mordovian[4]	843.4	0.58
Avar[5]	814.5	0.56
Belarusian	808.0	0.56

—continued	’000	%
Kazakh	654.0	0.45
Udmurt	636.9	0.44
Azeri	621.8	0.43
Mari[6]	604.3	0.42
German	597.2	0.41
Kabardin	520.1	0.36
Osetiyan[7]	514.9	0.35
Dargin[8]	510.2	0.35
Others[9]	7,853.5	5.41
Total	145,166.7	100.00

[1] Including Cossacks (140,028) and Pomors (6,571).
[2] Including Astrakhan Tatars (2,003), Kryashens (Christian Tatars, 24,668) and Siberian Tatars (9,611), but excluding Crimean Tatars (4,131).
[3] Including Chechen-akkintsy (218).
[4] Including Erzya-Mordovians (84,407) and Moksha-Mordovians (49,624).
[5] Including Akhvakhtsy (6,376), Andiitsy (21,808), Archintsy (89), Bagulaly (40), Bezhtintsy (6,198), Botlikhtsy (16), Chamalaly (12), Didoitsy (15,256), Ginukhtsy (531), Godoberintsy (39), Gunzibtsy (998), Karatintsy (6,052), Khvarshiny (128) and Tindaly (44).
[6] Including Lugovo-Vostochnye Mari (56,119) and Mountain Mari (18,515).
[7] Including Digor-Osetiyans (607) and Irontsy-Osetiyans (97).
[8] Including Kaitagtsy (5) and Kubachintsy (88).
[9] Including 1,460,751 respondents (1.01% of the total) who did not state their nationality or ethnic group.

ADMINISTRATIVE DIVISIONS
(1 January 2008, official estimates, except where otherwise stated)

Federal territory	Area (’000 sq km)	Population	Density (per sq km)	Capital (with population, ’000)[1]
Central Federal Okrug	650.7	37,150,741	57.1	Moscow
Moscow City	1.0	10,470,318	10,470.3	Moscow (10,425.1)
Belgorod Oblast	27.1	1,519,137	56.1	Belgorod (344.2)
Bryansk Oblast	34.9	1,308,479	37.5	Bryansk (420.0)
Ivanovo Oblast	21.8	1,079,605	49.5	Ivanovo (413.1)
Kaluga Oblast	29.9	1,005,648	33.6	Kaluga (329.1)
Kostroma Oblast	60.1	697,043	11.6	Kostroma (274.5)
Kursk Oblast	29.8	1,162,475	39.0	Kursk (405.5)
Lipetsk Oblast	24.1	1,168,814	48.5	Lipetsk (502.8)
Moscow Oblast	46.0	6,672,773	145.1	Moscow[2]
Orel Oblast	24.7	821,934	33.3	Orel (326.0)
Ryazan Oblast	39.6	1,164,530	29.4	Ryazan (513.3)
Smolensk Oblast	49.8	983,227	19.7	Smolensk (317.9)
Tambov Oblast	34.3	1,106,035	32.2	Tambov (284.5)
Tula Oblast	25.7	1,566,295	60.9	Tula (509.0)
Tver Oblast	84.1	1,379,542	16.4	Tver (405.6)
Vladimir Oblast	29.0	1,449,475	50.0	Vladimir (340.7)
Voronezh Oblast	52.4	2,280,406	43.5	Voronezh (846.3)
Yaroslavl Oblast	36.4	1,315,005	36.1	Yaroslavl (603.7)
North-Western Federal Okrug . .	1,677.9	13,501,038	8.0	St Petersburg
St Petersburg City	0.6	4,568,047	7,613.4	St Petersburg (4,571.2)
Republic of Kareliya	172.4	690,653	4.0	Petrozavodsk (265.1)
Republic of Komi	415.9	968,164	2.3	Syktyvkar (229.3)
Archangel Oblast	587.4	1,271,877	2.2	Archangel (349.8)
Nenets Autonomous Okrug	176.7	42,019	0.2	Naryn-Mar (19.1)
Kaliningrad Oblast	15.1	937,404	62.1	Kaliningrad (423.7)
Leningrad Oblast	85.3	1,633,350	19.1	St Petersburg[2]
Murmansk Oblast	144.9	850,929	5.9	Murmansk (321.0)
Novgorod Oblast	55.3	652,437	11.8	Velikii Novgorod (217.7)
Pskov Oblast	55.3	705,289	12.8	Pskov (197.1)
Vologda Oblast	145.7	1,222,888	8.4	Vologda (287.0)

Federal territory—*continued*	Area ('000 sq km)	Population	Density (per sq km)	Capital (with population, '000)[1]
Southern Federal Okrug	589.2	22,835,216	38.8	Rostov-on-Don
Republic of Adygeya	7.6	441,176	58.0	Maikop (156.8)
Chechen (Nokchi) Republic[3] . . .	n.a.	1,209,040	n.a.	Groznyi (218.2)
Republic of Dagestan	50.3	2,687,822	53.4	Makhachkala (466.3)
Republic of Ingushetiya[3] . . .	n.a.	499,502	n.a.	Magas (0.3)
Kabardino-Balkar Republic	12.5	891,338	71.3	Nalchik (271.4)
Republic of Kalmykiya	75.9	285,541	3.8	Elista (103.0)
Karachai-Cherkess Republic	14.1	427,418	30.3	Cherkessk (116.9)
Republic of North Osetiya—Alaniya .	8.0	702,456	87.8	Vladikavkaz (314.1)
Krasnodar Krai	76.0	5,121,799	67.4	Krasnodar (710.4)
Stavropol Krai	66.5	2,705,067	40.7	Stavropol (358.4)
Astrakhan Oblast	44.1	1,000,874	22.7	Astrakhan (499.0)
Rostov Oblast	100.8	4,254,421	42.2	Rostov-on-Don (1,054.8)
Volgograd Oblast	113.9	2,608,762	22.9	Volgograd (991.7)
Volga Federal Okrug	1,038.0	30,241,581	29.1	Nizhnii Novgorod
Republic of Bashkortostan	143.6	4,052,731	28.2	Ufa (1,029.6)
Chuvash Republic	18.3	1,282,567	70.1	Cheboksary (442.4)
Republic of Marii-El	23.2	703,220	30.3	Yoshkar-Ola (251.4)
Republic of Mordoviya	26.2	840,391	32.1	Saransk (297.1)
Republic of Tatarstan	68.0	3,762,809	55.3	Kazan (1,112.7)
Udmurt Republic	42.1	1,532,736	36.4	Izhevsk (619.5)
Perm Krai[4]	160.6	2,718,227	16.9	Perm (993.3)
Kirov Oblast	120.8	1,413,257	11.7	Kirov (448.5)
Nizhnii Novgorod Oblast	76.9	3,359,816	43.7	Nizhnii Novgorod (1,283.6)
Orenburg Oblast	124.0	2,119,003	17.7	Orenburg (533.9)
Penza Oblast	43.2	1,388,021	32.1	Penza (510.0)
Samara Oblast	53.6	3,172,787	59.2	Samara (1,143.3)
Saratov Oblast	100.2	2,583,808	25.8	Saratov (850.1)
Ulyanovsk Oblast	37.3	1,312,208	35.2	Ulyanovsk (617.2)
Urals Federal Okrug	1,788.9	12,240,382	6.8	Yekaterinburg
Chelyabinsk Oblast	87.9	3,510,990	39.9	Chelyabinsk (1,093.0)
Kurgan Oblast	71.0	960,410	13.5	Kurgan (330.0)
Sverdlovsk Oblast	194.8	4,395,617	22.6	Yekaterinburg (1,308.4)
Tyumen Oblast	1,435.2	3,373,365	2.4	Tyumen (542.5)
Khanty-Mansii Autonomous Okrug— Yugra	523.1	1,505,248	2.9	Khanty-Mansiisk (59.6)
Yamalo-Nenets Autonomous Okrug .	750.3	542,732	0.7	Salekhard (39.4)
Siberian Federal Okrug	5,114.8	19,553,461	3.8	Novosibirsk
Altai Republic	92.6	207,122	2.2	Gorno-Altaisk (53.1)
Republic of Buryatiya	351.3	959,892	2.7	Ulan-Ude (347.8)
Republic of Khakasiya	61.9	537,230	8.7	Abakan (164.0)
Republic of Tyva	170.5	311,619	1.8	Kyzyl (109.1)
Altai Krai	169.1	2,508,478	14.8	Barnaul (604.2)
Krasnoyarsk Krai[5]	2,339.7	2,890,350	1.2	Krasnoyarsk (920.9)
Chita Oblast[6]	431.5	1,118,931	2.6	Chita (306.2)
Aga-Buryat Autonomous Okrug[6] .	19.0	76,383	4.0	Aginskoye (13.1)
Irkutsk Oblast[7]	767.9	2,507,676	3.3	Irkutsk (571.8)
Kemerovo Oblast	95.5	2,823,539	29.6	Kemerovo (520.1)
Novosibirsk Oblast	178.2	2,635,642	14.8	Novosibirsk (1,397.0)
Omsk Oblast	139.7	2,017,997	14.4	Omsk (1,138.8)
Tomsk Oblast	316.9	1,034,985	3.3	Tomsk (489.9)
Far Eastern Federal Okrug . . .	6,215.9	6,486,419	1.0	Khabarovsk
Republic of Sakha (Yakutiya) . . .	3,103.2	951,436	0.3	Yakutsk (239.2)
Kamchatka Krai[8]	472.3	345,669	0.7	Petropavlovsk-Kamchatskii (195.2)
Khabarovsk Krai	788.6	1,403,712	1.8	Khabarovsk (578.1)
Maritime (Primorskii) Krai	165.9	1,995,828	12.0	Vladivostok (583.7)
Amur Oblast	363.7	869,617	2.4	Blagoveshchensk (212.2)
Magadan Oblast	461.4	165,820	0.4	Magadan (100.0)
Sakhalin Oblast	87.1	518,539	6.0	Yuzhno-Sakhalinsk (173.4)
Jewish Autonomous Oblast	36.0	185,535	5.2	Birobidzhan (75.2)
Chukot Autonomous Okrug	737.7	50,263	0.1	Anadyr (11.2)
Russian Federation	17,075.4	142,008,838	8.3	Moscow

[1] Official estimates at 1 January 2006.

[2] Although Moscow and St Petersburg are the administrative centres of Moscow and Leningrad Oblasts, respectively, the cities themselves do not form part of the oblasts.

[3] Before 1992 the territories of the Chechen (Nokchi) Republic and the Republic of Ingushetiya were combined in the Checheno-Ingush Autonomous Republic (area 19,300 sq km).

[4] Perm Krai was formed on 1 December 2005 by the merger of Perm Oblast and the Komi-Permyak Autonomous Okrug.

[5] Krasnoyarsk Krai was formally merged with the Evenk and Taimyr (Dolgano-Nenets) Autonomous Okrugs with effect from 1 January 2007.

[6] Chita Oblast and the Aga-Buryat Autonomous Okrug merged to form Transbaikal Krai on 1 March 2008.

[7] Irkutsk Oblast was formally merged with the Ust-Orda Buryat Autonomous Okrug with effect from 1 January 2008.

[8] Kamchatka Krai was formed on 1 July 2007 by the merger of Kamchatka Oblast and the Koryak Autonomous Okrug.

PRINCIPAL TOWNS
(1 January 2006, official estimates)

Moskva (Moscow, the capital) . .	10,425,100	Tula	509,000
Sankt-Peterburg (St Petersburg)* . .	4,571,200	Naberezhnye Chelnyi . .	507,200
Novosibirsk . . .	1,397,200	Lipetsk . . .	502,800
Yekaterinburg* .	1,308,400	Astrakhan . . .	499,000
Nizhnii Novgorod* .	1,283,600	Tomsk . . .	489,900
Samara* . . .	1,143,300	Makhachkala . .	466,300
Omsk	1,138,800	Kirov* . . .	448,500
Kazan	1,112,700	Cheboksary . . .	442,400
Chelyabinsk . .	1,093,000	Kaliningrad . .	423,700
Rostov-na-Donu (Rostov-on-Don) .	1,054,800	Bryansk	420,000
Ufa	1,029,600	Magnitogorsk . .	413,200
Perm	993,300	Ivanovo	413,100
Volgograd . . .	991,700	Tver*	405,600
Krasnoyarsk . .	920,900	Kursk	405,500
Saratov	850,100	Nizhnii Tagil . .	379,700
Voronezh . . .	846,300	Stavropol . . .	358,300
Krasnodar . . .	710,400	Arkhangelsk (Archangel) . .	349,800
Tolyatti	704,900	Ulan-Ude . . .	347,800
Izhevsk* . . .	619,500	Belgorod . . .	344,200
Ulyanovsk* . . .	617,200	Vladimir . . .	340,700
Barnaul	604,200	Kurgan	330,000
Yaroslavl . . .	603,700	Sochi	329,500
Vladivostok . . .	583,700	Kaluga	329,100
Khabarovsk . .	578,100	Orel	326,000
Irkutsk	571,800	Murmansk . . .	321,000
Novokuznetsk . .	562,400	Smolensk . . .	317,900
Tyumen . . .	542,500	Vladikavkaz* . .	314,100
Orenburg . . .	533,900	Volzhskii . . .	308,500
Kemerovo . . .	520,100	Cherepovets . .	308,400
Ryazan	513,300	Chita	306,200
Penza	510,000		

* Some towns that were renamed during the Soviet period have reverted to their former names: St Petersburg (Leningrad); Nizhnii Novgorod (Gorkii); Yekaterinburg (Sverdlovsk); Samara (Kuibyshev); Izhevsk (Ustinov); Naberezhnye Chelny (Brezhnev); Tver (Kalinin); Vladikavkaz (Ordzhonikidze). The towns of Ulyanovsk and Kirov, which retained their Soviet-era names in the mid-2000s, are sometimes unofficially referred to by their pre-Soviet designations, of Simbirsk and Vyatka, respectively.

Note: Figures are rounded.

Mid-2007 ('000, incl. suburbs, UN estimates): Moskva (Moscow, the capital) 10,452; Sankt-Peterburg (St Petersburg) 4,553; Novosibirsk 1,389; Yekaterinburg 1,313; Nizhnii Novgorod 1,278 (Source: UN, *World Urbanization Prospects: The 2007 Revision*).

BIRTHS, MARRIAGES AND DEATHS

	Registered live births		Registered marriages		Registered deaths	
	Number	Rate (per 1,000)	Number	Rate (per 1,000)	Number	Rate (per 1,000)
1999 . .	1,214,689	8.3	911,162	6.2	2,144,316	14.7
2000 . .	1,266,800	8.7	897,327	6.2	2,225,332	15.3
2001 . .	1,311,604	9.0	1,001,589	6.9	2,254,856	15.6
2002 . .	1,396,967	9.7	1,019,762	7.1	2,332,272	16.2
2003 . .	1,477,301	10.2	1,091,778	7.6	2,365,826	16.4
2004 . .	1,502,477	10.4	979,667	6.8	2,295,402	16.0
2005 . .	1,457,376	10.2	1,066,366	7.5	2,303,935	16.1
2006* . .	1,476,600	10.4	1,113,600	7.8	2,166,700	15.2
2007* . .	1,602,400	11.3	1,262,600	8.9	2,080,100	14.7

* Numbers are rounded to the nearest 100.

Expectation of life (years at birth, WHO estimates): 66.4 (males 60.0; females 73.2) in 2006 (Source: WHO, *World Health Statistics*).

IMMIGRATION AND EMIGRATION

	2005	2006	2007
Immigrants	177,230	186,380	286,879
Emigrants	69,798	54,061	47,012

ECONOMICALLY ACTIVE POPULATION
(sample surveys, '000 persons aged 15 to 72 years, at November, excl. Chechen Republic)

	2004	2005	2006
Agriculture, hunting and forestry	6,627	6,769	6,685
Fishing	205	166	176
Mining and quarrying	1,212	1,236	1,196
Manufacturing	12,674	12,534	12,470
Electricity, gas and water supply .	2,001	1,959	2,063
Construction	4,127	4,575	4,460
Wholesale and retail trade; repair of motor vehicles and motorcycles and personal and household goods	10,131	10,383	10,594
Restaurants and hotels . .	1,223	1,297	1,392
Transport, storage and communications	6,261	6,249	6,212
Financial intermediation . . .	918	962	1,060
Real estate, renting and business activities	4,119	4,039	4,146
Public administration and defence; compulsory social security . .	4,702	4,815	4,875
Education	6,142	6,204	6,196
Health and social work . . .	4,833	4,701	4,894
Other community, social and personal service activities . .	2,100	2,247	2,389
Private households with employed persons	—	26	21
Extra-territorial organizations and bodies	1	4	4
Total employed	67,275	68,169	68,834
Males	34,181	34,549	34,685
Females	33,094	33,620	34,149
Unemployed	5,675	5,263	5,312
Total labour force	72,950	73,432	74,146

Source: ILO.

Health and Welfare

KEY INDICATORS

Total fertility rate (children per woman, 2006)	1.3
Under-5 mortality rate (per 1,000 live births, 2006) . . .	13
HIV/AIDS (% of persons aged 15–49, 2005)	1.1
Physicians (per 1,000 head, 2006)	4.3
Hospital beds (per 1,000 head, 2006)	9.7
Health expenditure (2005): US $ per head (PPP)	561
Health expenditure (2005): % of GDP	5.2
Health expenditure (2005): public (% of total)	62.0
Access to water (% of persons, 2004)	97
Access to sanitation (% of persons, 2004)	87
Human Development Index (2005): ranking	67
Human Development Index (2005): value	0.802

For sources and definitions, see explanatory note on p. vi.

Agriculture

PRINCIPAL CROPS
('000 metric tons)

	2004	2005	2006
Wheat	45,412.7	47,697.5	45,006.3
Rice (paddy)	471.1	574.6	686.4
Barley	17,179.7	15,791.4	18,153.6
Maize	3,515.7	3,210.8	3,668.6
Rye	2,871.9	3,628.4	2,965.1
Oats	4,954.8	4,564.5	4,880.3
Millet	1,117.2	455.9	600.4
Buckwheat	649.6	605.6	865.5
Potatoes	35,914.2	37,279.8	38,572.6
Sugar beet	21,848.3	21,420.1	30,861.2
Dry peas	1,242.5	1,126.8	1,157.6
Soybeans (Soya beans) . . .	555.3	688.7	806.6
Sunflower seed	4,800.7	6,440.9	6,752.9
Rapeseed	275.9	302.7	522.2
Cabbages and other brassicas .	4,067.7	4,051.1	4,073.2
Tomatoes	2,017.9	2,295.9	2,414.9
Cucumbers and gherkins . . .	1,321.9	1,414.0	1,423.2
Dry onions	1,673.4	1,758.7	1,788.8
Garlic	236.2	257.3	255.9
Carrots and turnips	1,762.0	1,793.3	1,918.4
Watermelons	920.4	964.6	985.5
Apples	2,047*	1,800*	1,609†
Sweet cherries	100*	93*	47†
Sour (Morello) cherries . . .	225*	230†	111†
Plums and sloes	178*	169*	98†
Strawberries	207*	221*	235†
Raspberries	170*	175*	n.a.
Currants	396*	432*	435†
Grapes	318.3	333.3	243.5

* Unofficial figure.
† FAO estimate.

Aggregate production ('000 metric tons, may include official, semi-official or estimated data): Total cereals 76,231.4 in 2004, 76,563.6 in 2005, 76,866.1 in 2006; Total roots and tubers 35,914.2 in 2004, 37,279.8 in 2005; 38,572.6 in 2006; Total primary oilcrops 2,214.3 in 2004, 2,923.4 in 2005, 3,148.3 in 2006; Total pulses 1,887.4 in 2004, 1,645.1 in 2005, 1,763.5 in 2006; Total vegetables (incl. melons) 14,808.7 in 2004; 16,126.1 in 2005; 16,629.2 in 2006; Total fruits (excl. melons) 3,949.7 in 2004, 3,731.1 in 2005, 2,978.8 in 2006.

Source: FAO.

LIVESTOCK
('000 head at 1 January)

	2004	2005	2006
Horses	1,499	1,409	1,319
Cattle	24,935	22,988	21,474
Pigs	15,980	13,413	13,455
Sheep	14,669	15,494	16,074
Goats	2,361	2,277	2,138
Chickens	328,338	328,707	342,866
Turkeys	9,823	8,518	9,429
Geese and guinea fowls . . .	500	500	500

Source: FAO.

LIVESTOCK PRODUCTS
('000 metric tons)

	2004	2005	2006
Cattle meat	1,951.2	1,793.4	1,704.9
Sheep meat	125.4	134.4	135.4
Pig meat	1,643.4	1,520.1	1,641.5
Chicken meat	1,152.2	1,345.7	1,580.2
Cows' milk	31,904.2	30,892.6	31,186.2
Goats' milk	268.2	253.7	249.1
Hen eggs	1,991.5	2,049.9	2,100.0
Honey	52.7	52.1	55.3
Wool: greasy	47.1	48.0	49.3

Source: FAO.

Forestry

ROUNDWOOD REMOVALS
('000 cubic metres, excl. bark)

	2004	2005	2006
Sawlogs, veneer logs and logs for sleepers	67,900	70,400	73,800
Pulpwood	48,000	53,500	56,000
Other industrial wood	14,700	14,100	14,800
Fuel wood	47,800	47,000	46,000
Total	178,400	185,000	190,600

Source: FAO.

SAWNWOOD PRODUCTION
('000 cubic metres, incl. railway sleepers)

	2004	2005	2006
Coniferous (softwood)	18,770	19,770	19,800
Broadleaved (hardwood)	2,585	2,730	2,700
Total	21,355	22,500	22,500

Source: FAO.

Fishing

('000 metric tons, live weight)

	2004	2005	2006
Capture	2,941.5	3,197.6	3,284.1
Pink (humpback) salmon . .	114.8	202.3	202.3
Atlantic cod	205.0	203.7	207.5
Alaska (Walleye) pollock . .	849.6	961.7	1,021.7
Blue whiting (Poutassou) . .	346.8	332.2	329.4
Atlantic herring	123.3	140.1	131.1
Pacific herring	194.4	205.4	222.3
Aquaculture	109.8	114.8	105.5
Total catch	3,051.3	3,312.3	3,389.7

Note: Figures exclude seaweeds and other aquatic plants ('000 metric tons): 58.2 (capture 58.0, aquaculture 0.2) in 2004; 50.5 (capture 50.3, aquaculture 0.2) in 2005; 61.4 (capture 60.6, aquaculture 0.8) in 2006. Also excluded are aquatic mammals, recorded by number rather than weight. The number of whales caught was: 139 in 2004; 131 in 2005; 139 in 2006. The number of seals (incl. walrus) caught was: 14,855 in 2004; 28,379 in 2005; 23,176 in 2006.

Source: FAO.

Mining

('000 metric tons, unless otherwise indicated)

	2003	2004	2005
Iron ore: gross weight	91,760	96,980	96,764
Copper ore*†	675	675	700
Nickel ore*†	260	261	266
Bauxite	5,442	6,000*	6,400*
Lead ore*†	24.0	23.0	36.0
Zinc ore*†	159	179	180
Tin (metric tons)*†	2,000	2,500	3,000
Manganese ore*†	23	23	23
Chromium ore	116.5	320.2	772.0
Tungsten concentrates (metric tons)*†	5,450	5,500	600
Molybdenum (metric tons)*	2,900	2,900	2,900
Cobalt ore (metric tons)*†	4,800	4,700	5,000
Mercury (metric tons)*	50	50	50
Silver (metric tons)*†	700	1,277	1,350
Uranium concentrate (metric tons)*†	3,150	3,200	3,430
Gold (metric tons)*†	170.1	163.1	169.3
Platinum (metric tons)*	28	28	30
Palladium (metric tons)*	97	97	97
Kaolin (concentrate)*	45	45	45
Magnesite*	1,200	1,200	1,200
Phosphate rock (Apatite)*‡	4,121	4,120	4,200
Potash*§	4,740	5,000	5,000
Native sulphur*	50	50	50
Fluorspar (concentrate)	170	226	246
Barite (Barytes)*	78	63	63
Salt (unrefined)*	2,800	2,800	2,800
Diamonds: gems ('000 metric carats):			
gem*	20,000	21,400	23,000
industrial*	13,000	14,200	15,000
Gypsum (crude)*	1,750	2,077	2,200
Asbestos	878	923	925*
Mica*	100	100	100
Talc*	100	100	100
Feldspar*	45	45	45
Peat (horticulture and fuel use)	1,000	1,500	1,500

* Estimated production.
† Figures refer to the metal content of ores.
‡ Figures refer to the phosphoric acid content. The data exclude sedimentary rock (estimates, '000 metric tons): 300 per year in 2002–05.
§ Figures refer to the potassium oxide content.

Source: US Geological Survey.

Crude petroleum (incl. gas condensate, '000 metric tons): 379,563 in 2002; 421,341 in 2003; 459,318 in 2004; 470,175 in 2005.

Natural gas (million cu m): 595,106 in 2002; 620,234 in 2003; 632,623 in 2004; 640,801 in 2005.

Coal ('000 metric tons): 255,754 in 2002; 276,664 in 2003; 281,744 in 2004; 298,500 in 2005.

Industry

SELECTED PRODUCTS

('000 metric tons, unless otherwise indicated)

	2005	2006	2007
Flour	10,356	10,364	10,095
Granulated sugar	5,600	5,833	6,069
Cotton fabrics (million sq metres)	2,225	2,222	2,143
Woollen fabrics (million sq metres)	30.3	29.0	28.5
Linen fabrics (million sq metres)	122	124	101
Footwear, excl. rubber footwear ('000 pairs)	47,200	57,300	50,800
Plywood ('000 cubic metres)	2,556	2,615	2,763
Particle board ('000 cubic metres)	3,750	3,880	4,020
Newsprint	1,753	1,716	2,087
Cardboard	3,125	3,396	3,496
Paper	4,001	4,038	4,063
Sulphuric acid	9,452	9,379	9,652
Soda ash (sodium carbonate)	2,582	2,938	2,940
Mineral fertilizers	16,625	16,207	17,655
Synthetic ammonia	12,473	12,954	13,005

—continued	2005	2006	2007
Gasoline	32.0	34.4	35.1
Rubber tyres ('000)	41,436	40,413	43,214
Rubber footwear ('000 pairs)	16,100	17,400	22,100
Cement	48,500	54,700	59,900
Pig-iron	49,175	52,362	51,523
Steel	66,262	70,816	72,389
Steel pipes	6,695	7,898	8,706
Rolled metal products	54,661	58,215	59,635
Tractors (number)	8,600	10,900	13,500
Refrigerators and freezers ('000)	2,777	2,995	3,573
Domestic washing machines ('000)	1,582	2,016	2,708
Televisions ('000)	6,278	4,601	6,154
Electric vacuum cleaners ('000)	890	584	626
Passenger motor cars ('000)	1,069	1,178	1,290
Electric energy (million kWh)	953,000	996,000	1,016,000

Finance

CURRENCY AND EXCHANGE RATES

Monetary Units
100 kopeks = 1 Russian rubl (ruble or rouble).

Sterling, Dollar and Euro Equivalents (30 May 2008)
£1 sterling = 46.848 roubles;
US $1 = 23.738 roubles;
€1 = 36.814 roubles;
1,000 roubles = £21.35 = $42.13 = €27.16.

Average Exchange Rate (roubles per US dollar)
2005   28.2844
2006   27.1910
2007   25.5808

Note: On 1 January 1998 a new rouble, equivalent to 1,000 of the former units, was introduced. Figures in this Survey are expressed in terms of new roubles, unless otherwise indicated.

FEDERAL BUDGET

(million roubles)

Revenue	2003	2004	2005
Tax revenue	1,892,363.7	2,071,384.5	3,151,745.6
Taxes on corporate profit and capital gains	179,550.5	164,587.4	259,003.3
Taxes on goods and services	1,178,971.2	1,088,389.6	791,822.6
Value-added tax	946,218.5	988,389.6	713,226.9
Excise duties	227,708.8	94,357.7	78,595.7
Natural gas	133,112.1	20,000.0	—
Taxes on the use of natural resources	183,129.5	279,381.1	483,035.6
Taxes on international trade and transactions	335,975.5	532,538.2	919,093.8
Customs duties on imports	150,355.9	180,613.5	249,762.0
Customs duties on exports	185,619.6	351,924.7	618,207.0
Non-tax revenue	145,721.8	219,194.4	174,295.5
Income from state property and activities	83,158.8	165,612.1	73,004.0
Special budgetary funds	14,066.3	14,061.5	—
Contribution of unified social tax to federal budget	365,640.0	438,210.0	—
Total	2,417,791.8	2,742,850.4	3,326,041.1

Expenditure	2003	2004	2005
State administration	66,506.9	76,967.2	123,353.1
Judicial system	25,481.9	33,250.8	36,769.0
National defence	219,884.6	255,390.2	531,139.2
Public order and state security .	190,080.1	250,025.3	398,889.5
Education	97,672.0	117,791.9	155,338.0
Health and sport	39,344.8	47,097.8	85,672.2
Social security and welfare . .	150,685.0	161,193.5	167,360.9
Servicing of government debt . .	277,510.1	287,570.6	244,150.4
Federal transfers	714,600.2	813,969.8	954,545.2
Total (incl. others)	2,123,424.9	2,400,751.2	3,047,929.3

2005 ('000 million roubles, budget execution excl. deficit financing): *Revenue:* Tax revenue 3,188.2 (Value-added tax 1,472.2, Profit tax 377.6, Excise taxes 107.2, Social Tax (ST) revenues 267.5, Other 963.6); Non-tax revenue 1,936.9 (Customs duties 1,622.8, Other non-tax revenues 314.1); Total 5,125.1. *Expenditure:* Debt service 208.4 (Domestic 53.4, Foreign 154.9); Non-interest expenditure 3,303.8 (State administration 290.9, Defence, law and order 1,031.2, Social and cultural sphere 475.9, National economy 260.1, Financial aid to regions 486.7, Transfers to extrabudgetary accounts 758.9); Total 3,512.2.

2006 ('000 million roubles, budget execution excl. deficit financing): *Revenue:* Tax revenue 3,569.7 (Value-added tax 1,510.9, Profit tax 509.9, Excise taxes 110.5, Social Tax (ST) revenues 315.8, Other 1,122.6); Non-tax revenue 2,532.2 (Customs duties 2,306.3, Other non-tax revenues 225.9); Total (incl. others) 6,278.9. *Expenditure:* General government 533.1 (Debt service 172.8); National defence and national security and militia 1,232.0; National economy 345.0 (Fuel and electric power 7.5; Agriculture and fishing 26.1; Transport 132.2; Communication and informatics 6.1); Housing and communal utilities 52.7; Social and cultural activities 616.4; Transfers to non-budget funds 914.3; Total (incl. others) 4,284.8.

2007 ('000 million roubles, budget execution excl. deficit financing, provisional): *Revenue:* Tax revenue 4,604.1 (Value-added tax 2,261.5, Profit tax 641.3, Excise taxes 135.0, Social Tax (ST) revenues 405.0, Other 1,161.3); Non-tax revenue 2,735.0 (Customs duties 2,408.3, Other non-tax revenues 326.7); Total (incl. others) 7,779.1. *Expenditure:* General government 812.1 (Debt service 143.1); National defence and national security and militia 1,498.9; National economy 692.6 (Fuel and electric power 8.3; Agriculture and fishing 27.8; Transport 172.6; Communication and informatics 14.1; Other 409.0); Housing and communal utilities 294.9; Social and cultural activities 776.1; Transfers to non-budget funds 1,043.9; Total (incl. others) 5,983.0.

Source: Ministry of Finance, Moscow.

INTERNATIONAL RESERVES
(US $ million at 31 December)

	2005	2006	2007
Gold (national valuation) . .	6,349.0	8,164.4	12,011.9
IMF special drawing rights . .	5.6	7.1	0.8
Reserve position in IMF . .	195.9	283.3	373.9
Foreign exchange	175,689.9	295,277.1	464,004.3
Total	182,240.4	303,731.9	476,390.9

Source: IMF, *International Financial Statistics.*

MONEY SUPPLY
('000 million roubles at 31 December)

	2005	2006	2007
Currency outside banks . .	2,009.2	2,785.2	3,702.2
Demand deposits at banks . .	1,805.7	2,754.4	3,825.9
Total money (incl. others) . .	3,858.5	5,598.4	7,582.1

Source: IMF, *International Financial Statistics.*

COST OF LIVING
(Consumer Price Index; base: previous year = 100)

	2005	2006	2007
Food and beverages	109.6	108.7	115.6
Other consumer goods . . .	106.4	106.0	106.3
Services	121.0	113.9	113.3
All items	110.9	109.0	111.9

NATIONAL ACCOUNTS
('000 million roubles at current prices)

Expenditure on the Gross Domestic Product

	2005	2006	2007
Final consumption expenditure .	14,318.9	17,616.0	21,810.9
Households	10,590.0	12,880.9	15,815.5
Non-profit institutions serving households	138.2	159.0	175.0
General government . . .	3,590.7	4,576.1	5,820.4
Gross capital formation . . .	4,338.7	5,736.8	8,102.0
Gross fixed capital formation . Acquisitions, less disposals, of valuables	3,836.9	4,968.4	6,951.1
Changes in inventories . .	501.8	768.4	1,150.9
Total domestic expenditure .	18,657.6	23,352.8	29,912.9
Exports of goods and services .	7,607.3	9,079.3	10,057.2
Less Imports of goods and services	4,648.3	5,656.8	7,186.7
Sub-total	21,616.6	26,775.3	32,783.4
Statistical discrepancy* . .	8.8	104.5	204.0
GDP in market prices . .	21,625.4	26,879.8	32,987.4

* Referring to the difference between the sum of the expenditure components and official estimates of GDP, compiled from the production approach.

Gross Domestic Product by Economic Activity

	2005	2006	2007
Agriculture, hunting and forestry .	962.4	1,096.1	1,275.9
Fishing	65.5	68.3	72.8
Mining and quarrying . . .	2,084.9	2,556.8	2,952.8
Manufacturing	3,521.0	4,185.6	5,387.4
Electricity, gas and water supply .	632.5	754.8	886.2
Construction	1,012.0	1,211.4	1,671.0
Wholesale and retail trade; repair of motor vehicles, motorcycles and personal and household goods	3,649.4	4,761.9	5,840.9
Hotels and restaurants . . .	170.6	199.4	256.9
Transport, storage and communication	1,925.1	2,282.2	2,669.6
Financial intermediation . .	759.0	1,050.1	1,347.9
Real estate, renting and business activities	1,848.2	2,344.8	2,936.9
Public administration and defence; compulsory social security . .	959.1	1,189.2	1,495.4
Education	494.1	621.8	790.1
Health and social work . . .	500.3	770.2	968.8
Other community, social and personal services	326.0	428.4	548.3
Sub-total	18,976.4	23,521.0	29,100.9
Less Financial intermediation services indirectly measured .	442.9	578.6	772.3
Gross value added in basic prices	18,533.3	22,942.5	28,328.6
Taxes, *less* subsidies, on products .	3 092.1	3,937.3	4,658.7
GDP in market prices . . .	21 625.4	26 879.8	32,987.4

BALANCE OF PAYMENTS
(US $ million)

	2005	2006	2007
Exports of goods f.o.b.	243,798	303,550	355,465
Imports of goods f.o.b.	−125,434	−164,281	−223,421
Trade balance	118,364	139,269	132,043
Exports of services	24,970	31,102	39,347
Imports of services	−38,865	−44,839	−59,182
Balance on goods and services	104,470	125,533	112,209
Other income received	17,382	29,504	46,798
Other income paid	−36,371	−59,133	−77,191
Balance on goods, services and income	85,481	95,904	81,816
Current transfers received . .	4,490	6,403	8,423
Current transfers paid	−5,528	−7,940	−11,929
Current balance	84,443	94,367	78,309
Capital account (net)	−12,764	191	−10,224

—continued	2005	2006	2007
Direct investment abroad . .	−12,767	−23,151	−45,652
Direct investment from abroad .	12,886	32,387	52,475
Portfolio investment assets .	−10,666	6,248	−7,039
Portfolio investment liabilities .	−828	9,124	12,729
Financial derivatives assets . .	858	1,242	2,762
Financial derivatives liabilities .	−1,091	−1,342	−2,430
Other investment assets . . .	−32,623	−49,408	−55,161
Other investment liabilities . .	45,846	30,340	136,798
Net errors and omissions . . .	−8,326	7,468	−13,640
Overall balance	64,968	107,466	148,929

Source: IMF, *International Financial Statistics*.

External Trade

PRINCIPAL COMMODITIES
(US $ '000 million)

Imports	2005	2006	2007
Foodstuffs and agricultural raw materials (excl. textiles) . .	17.4	21.6	27.6
Mineral products	3.0	3.3	4.7
Chemical products and rubber .	16.3	21.8	27.5
Leather, fur, and articles thereof .	0.3	0.4	0.7
Wood, pulp and paper products .	3.3	4.0	5.3
Textiles, textile articles and footwear	3.6	5.5	8.6
Metals, precious stones, and articles thereof . .	7.6	10.6	16.4
Machinery, vehicles and transport equipment	43.4	65.7	102.0
Other	3.7	4.8	7.1
Total	98.7	137.5	199.7

Exports	2005	2006	2007
Foodstuffs and agricultural raw materials (excl. textiles) . .	4.5	5.5	9.1
Mineral products	156.0	199.0	228.0
Chemical products and rubber .	14.4	16.8	20.8
Leather, fur, and articles thereof .	0.3	0.4	0.3
Wood, pulp and paper products .	8.3	9.5	12.3
Textiles, textile articles and footwear	1.0	1.0	0.9
Metals, precious stones, and articles thereof . . .	40.6	48.9	56.9
Machinery, vehicles and transport equipment	13.5	17.4	19.7
Other	2.5	3.1	4.4
Total	241.5	301.2	352.5

PRINCIPAL TRADING PARTNERS
(US $ million)

Imports	2005	2006	2007
Austria	1,211	1,845	2,458
Belarus	5,716	6,845	8,887
Belgium	1,476	2,178	3,185
Brazil	2,346	2,987	4,108
China, People's Republic . . .	7,265	12,910	24,401
Czech Republic	989	1,530	2,451
Denmark	921	1,347	1,595
Finland	3,100	4,003	5,023
France	3,673	5,863	7,759
Germany	13,272	18,464	26,572
Hungary	1,100	1,868	2,602
India	784	968	1,310
Italy	4,416	5,726	8,535
Japan	5,834	7,787	12,712
Kazakhstan	3,225	3,840	4,613
Korea, Republic	4,005	6,781	8,836

Imports—continued	2005	2006	2007
Netherlands	1,941	2,685	3,853
Poland	2,747	3,410	4,629
Spain	1,227	1,952	3,197
Sweden	1,861	2,145	3,123
Turkey	1,738	2,753	4,180
Ukraine	7,819	9,238	13,323
United Kingdom	2,776	3,674	5,642
Uzbekistan	904	1,292	1,451
USA	4,563	6,405	9,425
Total (incl. others)	98,707	137,807	199,708

Exports	2005	2006	2007
Austria	2,353	3,353	2,737
Belarus	10,118	13,099	17,187
Belgium	2,464	2,694	2,810
China, People's Republic . . .	13,048	15,758	15,893
Cyprus	5,095	4,515	4,838
Czech Republic	3,817	4,665	4,655
Finland	7,651	9,192	10,722
France	6,111	7,675	8,674
Germany	19,736	24,498	26,290
Greece	1,930	2,752	2,613
Hungary	5,004	6,245	6,092
India	2,314	2,925	4,012
Israel	1,538	1,544	2,031
Italy	19,053	25,090	27,518
Japan	3,740	4,457	7,383
Kazakhstan	6,524	8,967	11,963
Korea, Republic	2,359	2,735	6,150
Netherlands	24,614	35,884	42,786
Poland	8,623	11,481	13,298
Romania	3,041	3,272	3,211
Slovakia	3,190	4,587	5,151
Spain	2,823	3,343	4,318
Sweden	2,320	2,198	3,001
Switzerland	10,774	12,167	14,201
Taiwan	1,438	930	895
Turkey	10,841	14,290	18,332
Ukraine	12,402	14,983	16,323
United Kingdom	8,280	10,396	11,024
USA	6,323	8,638	8,048
Total (incl. others)	241,473	301,244	352,473

Transport

RAILWAYS
(traffic)

	2005	2006	2007
Paying passengers ('000 journeys).	1,339,000	1,347,000	1,278,000
Freight carried ('000 metric tons) .	1,273,000	1,312,000	1,344,000
Passenger-km (million) . . .	172,200	177,800	174,100
Freight ton-km (million) . . .	1,858,000	1,951,000	2,090,000

ROAD TRAFFIC
(motor vehicles in use)

	1998	1999	2000
Passenger cars	18,819,600	19,717,800	20,353,000
Buses and coaches	627,500	633,200	640,100
Lorries and vans	4,260,000	4,387,800	4,400,600
Motorcycles and mopeds . . .	7,165,900	6,328,600	n.a.

Source: IRF, *World Road Statistics*.

SHIPPING

Merchant Fleet
(registered at 31 December)

	2005	2006	2007
Number of vessels	3,722	3,656	3,481
Total displacement ('000 grt) . .	8,334.5	8,046.0	7,587.3

Source: Lloyd's Register-Fairplay, *World Fleet Statistics*.

International Sea-borne Freight Traffic
('000 metric tons, rounded data)

	2004	2005	2006
Goods loaded	8,200	9,100	7,700
Goods unloaded	1,100	700	400

Note: Annual data extrapolated from monthly averages.

Source: UN, *Monthly Bulletin of Statistics*.

CIVIL AVIATION
(traffic on scheduled services)

	2001	2002	2003
Kilometres flown (million) . .	568	653	602
Passengers carried ('000) . . .	20,301	20,892	22,723
Passenger-km (million) . . .	48,321	49,890	53,894
Total ton-km (million) . . .	5,292	5,580	6,018

Source: UN, *Statistical Yearbook*.

Tourism

FOREIGN VISITOR ARRIVALS
('000, incl. excursionists)

Country of origin	2004	2005	2006
Armenia	377.3	386.5	390.5
Azerbaijan	823.5	824.6	935.5
China, People's Republic . . .	813.1	798.7	765.3
Estonia	521.1	510.3	438.2
Finland	1,092.3	1,115.5	1,078.2
Georgia	320.8	229.0	125.9
Germany	567.2	550.8	553.7
Kazakhstan	2,761.5	2,453.2	2,598.6
Kyrgyzstan	306.6	293.6	409.0
Latvia	371.1	709.3	380.7
Lithuania	949.6	1,251.5	980.5
Moldova	804.9	837.1	925.9
Poland	1,128.5	1,195.9	1,149.0
Tajikistan	456.4	466.5	600.8
Ukraine	6,683.2	6,416.9	6,447.0
USA	308.3	280.9	351.3
Uzbekistan	677.0	660.6	958.9
Total (incl. others)	22,064.2	22,200.6	22,486.0

Receipts from tourism (US $ million, incl. passenger transport): 7,262 in 2004; 7,806 in 2005; 9,720 in 2006.

Source: World Tourism Organization.

Communications Media

	2003	2004	2005
Telephones ('000 main lines in use)	36,993	39,616	40,100
Mobile cellular telephones ('000 subscribers)	36,500	74,420	120,000
Personal computers ('000 in use) .	15,364	15,000	17,400
Internet users ('000) . . .	10,000	18,500	21,800
Broadband subscribers ('000) . .	343.0	675.0	1,589.0

2006: Internet users ('000) 25,689.

Source: International Telecommunication Union.

Television receivers ('000 in use): 79,000 in 2000.

Radio receivers ('000 in use): 61,500 in 1997.

Facsimile machines (number in use): 52,900 in 1998.

Book production (including pamphlets): 36,237 titles in 1996 (421,387,000 copies).

Daily newspapers: 285 in 1996 (average circulation 15,517,000 copies); 333 in 2000.

Non-daily newspapers: 4,596 in 1996 (average circulation 98,558,000 copies); 10,188 in 2000.

Other periodicals: 2,751 in 1996 (average circulation 387,832,000 copies).

Sources: UNESCO, *Statistical Yearbook*; and UN, *Statistical Yearbook*.

Education

(2006/07, except where otherwise specified)

	Institutions	Students*	Teachers
Pre-primary	46,200	4,713,000	610,828†
Primary and general secondary .	61,042	14,798,000	1,537,000*
Vocational secondary	2,847	2,514,000	136,400
Higher	1,090	7,310,000	387,300*‡

* Rounded figure(s).
† 2004/05.
‡ 2005/06.

Adult literacy rate (UNESCO estimates): 99.5% (males 99.7%; females 99.4%) in 2007 (Source: UNNESCO Institute for Statistics).

Directory

The Constitution

The current Constitution of the Russian Federation came into force on 12 December 1993, following its approval by a majority of participants in a nation-wide plebiscite. It replaced the Constitution originally adopted on 12 April 1978, but amended many times after 1990.

THE PRINCIPLES OF THE CONSTITUTIONAL SYSTEM

The Russian Federation (Russia) is a democratic, federative, law-based state with a republican form of government. Its multi-ethnic people bear its sovereignty and are the sole source of authority. State power is divided between the legislative, executive and judicial branches, which are independent of one another. Ideological pluralism and a multi-party political system are recognized. The state is secular.

HUMAN AND CIVIL RIGHTS AND FREEDOMS

Basic human rights and freedoms of the Russian citizen are guaranteed regardless of sex, race, ethnicity or religion. The rights to life and to freedom and personal inviolability are guaranteed. The principles of freedom of movement, freedom of expression and freedom of conscience are upheld. Censorship is prohibited. Citizens are guaranteed the right to vote in and to contest state and local elections and to participate in referendums. Individuals shall have equal access to state employment, and may establish trade unions and public associations. The State is committed to the protection of motherhood and childhood and the granting of social security, state pensions and social benefits. Each person has the right to housing. Health care and education are free of charge. Basic general education is compulsory. Citizens are guaranteed the right to receive qualified legal assistance. Payment of statutory taxes and levies is obligatory, as is military service.

THE ORGANIZATION OF THE FEDERATION

The federal subjects (territorial units) of the Federation are named. Russian is declared the state language, but all peoples of the Federation are guaranteed the right to preserve their native tongue. The state flag, emblem and anthem of the Federation are established by constitutional law. The separate roles of the authority of the Federation, as distinct from that of the joint authority of the Federation and the federal subjects, are defined. The powers of the federal executive bodies and the executive bodies of the members of the Federation are defined.

THE PRESIDENT OF THE RUSSIAN FEDERATION

The powers and responsibilities of the Head of State, the President of the Russian Federation, are defined. The President, who must be aged at least 35 years, and have been resident in Russia for at least 10 years, is elected to office for a term of four years by universal, direct suffrage, for no more than two consecutive terms. The President appoints the Chairman of the Government (Prime Minister) of the Russian Federation, with the approval of the Gosudarstvennaya Duma (State Duma), and may dismiss the Government. The President is entitled to chair sessions of the Government. The President's responsibilities include scheduling referendums and elections to the Gosudarstvennaya Duma, dissolving the Gosudarstvennaya Duma, submitting legislative proposals to the Gosudarstvennaya Duma, promulgating federal laws and nominating candidates, subject to approval by the Federalnoye Sobraniye, to the posts of Chairman of the Central Bank, judges of the Constitutional Court, the Supreme Court and the Supreme Arbitration Court, and of Prosecutor-General. The President forms and heads the Security Council, the status of which is determined by federal law. The President is responsible for the foreign policy of the Russian Federation. The President is Commander-in-Chief of the Armed Forces and may introduce martial law or a state of emergency under certain conditions.

If the President is unable to carry out the presidential duties, these will be assumed by the Chairman of the Government. The acting President, however, will not possess the full powers of the President, such as the right to dissolve the Gosudarstvennaya Duma or to order a referendum. The President may only be removed from office by the Sovet Federatsii (Federation Council) on the grounds of a serious accusation by the Gosudarstvennaya Duma.

THE FEDERALNOYE SOBRANIYE

The Federalnoye Sobraniye (Federal Assembly) is the highest representative and legislative body in the Russian Federation. It comprises two chambers: the Sovet Federatsii (upper chamber) and the Gosudarstvennaya Duma (lower chamber). The Sovet Federatsii comprises two representatives from each member of the Russian Federation, one appointed by its legislative and one by its executive body. The Gosudarstvennaya Duma is composed of 450 deputies, elected for a term of four years. The deputies of the Russian Federation must be over 21 years of age and may not hold government office or any other paid job.

Both chambers of the Federalnoye Sobraniye elect their Chairman and Deputy Chairmen. The powers of the Sovet Federatsii include the approval of the President's decrees on martial law and a state of emergency, the scheduling of presidential elections and the impeachment of the President. The Gosudarstvennaya Duma has the power to approve the President's nominee to the office of Chairman of the Government. Both chambers of the Federalnoye Sobraniye adopt resolutions by a majority vote of the total number of members. All federal and federal constitutional laws are adopted by the Gosudarstvennaya Duma and submitted for approval first to the Sovet Federatsii and then to the President. If the Sovet Federatsii or the President reject proposed legislation it is submitted for repeat consideration to one or both chambers of the Federalnoye Sobraniye.

The Gosudarstvennaya Duma may be dissolved by the President if it adopts two successive votes of 'no confidence' in the Government. If the Gosudarstvennaya Duma rejects three candidates to the office of Chairman, the President will appoint the Chairman, dissolve the Gosudarstvennaya Duma and order new elections. However, it may not be dissolved during a period of martial law or a state of emergency or in the case of charges being lodged against the President. A newly elected Gosudarstvennaya Duma should be convened no later than four months after dissolution of the previous parliament.

THE GOVERNMENT OF THE RUSSIAN FEDERATION

The executive authority of the Russian Federation is vested in the Government, which comprises the Chairman, the Deputy Chairmen and federal ministers. The Chairman is appointed by the President and his nomination approved by the Gosudarstvennaya Duma. The Government submits the federal budget to the Gosudarstvennaya Duma and supervises its execution, guarantees the implementation of a uniform state policy, conducts foreign policy, ensures the country's defence and security.

Regulations for the activity of the Government are determined by a federal constitutional law. The Government adopts resolutions and directives, which may be vetoed by the President. The Government must submit its resignation to a newly elected President of the Russian Federation, which the President may accept or reject. A vote of 'no confidence' in the Government may be adopted by the Gosudarstvennaya Duma. The President can reject this decision or demand the Government's resignation. If the Gosudarstvennaya Duma adopts a second vote of 'no confidence' within three months, the President will announce the Government's resignation or dissolve the Gosudarstvennaya Duma.

JUDICIAL POWER

Justice is administered by means of constitutional, civil, administrative and criminal judicial proceedings. Judges in the Russian Federation must be aged 25 or over, have a higher legal education and have a record of work in the legal profession of no less than five years. Judges are independent, irremovable and inviolable. Proceedings in judicial courts are open. No criminal case shall be considered in the absence of a defendant. Judicial proceedings may be conducted with the participation of a jury.

The Constitutional Court comprises 19 judges. The Court decides cases regarding the compliance of federal laws and enactments, the constitutions, statutes, laws and other enactments of the federal subjects, state treaties and international treaties that have not yet come into force. The Constitutional Court settles disputes about competence among state bodies. Enactments or provisions thereof that have been judged unconstitutional by the Court are invalid. At the request of the Sovet Federatsii, the Court will pronounce its judgment on bringing an accusation against the President of the Russian Federation.

The Supreme Court is the highest judicial authority on civil, criminal, administrative and other cases within the jurisdiction of the common plea courts. The Supreme Arbitration Court is the highest authority in settling economic and other disputes within the jurisdiction of the courts of arbitration.

The judges of the three higher courts are appointed by the Federation Council on the recommendation of the President. Judges of other federal courts are appointed by the President.

The Prosecutor's Office is a single centralized system. The Prosecutor-General is appointed and dismissed by the Sovet Federatsii on the recommendation of the President. All other prosecutors are appointed by the Prosecutor-General.

LOCAL SELF-GOVERNMENT

The exercise of local self-government is provided for through referendums, elections and through elected and other bodies. The responsibilities of local self-government bodies include: independently managing municipal property; forming, approving and executing the local budget; establishing local taxes and levies; and maintaining law and order.

CONSTITUTIONAL AMENDMENTS AND REVISION OF THE CONSTITUTION

No provision contained in Chapters One (on The Principles of the Constitutional System), Two (on Human and Civil Rights and Freedoms) and Nine (on Constitutional Amendments and Revision of the Constitution) may be reviewed by the Federalnoye Sobraniye, while amendments to the remaining Chapters may be passed in accordance with the procedure for a federal constitutional law. If a proposal for a review of the provisions of Chapters One, Two and Nine wins a three-fifths' majority in both chambers, a Constitutional Assembly will be convened.

CONCLUDING AND TRANSITIONAL PROVISIONS

Should the provisions of a federal treaty contravene those of the Constitution, the constitutional provisions will apply. All laws and other legal acts enforced before the Constitution came into effect will remain valid unless they fail to comply with the Constitution.

The Government

HEAD OF STATE

President of the Russian Federation: DMITRII A. MEDVEDEV (elected 2 March 2008; inaugurated 7 May).

THE GOVERNMENT
(October 2008)

Chairman: VLADIMIR V. PUTIN.

First Deputy Chairman: VIKTOR A. ZUBKOV.

First Deputy Chairman: IGOR I. SHUVALOV.

Deputy Chairman: ALEKSANDR D. ZHUKOV.

Deputy Chairman: SERGEI B. IVANOV.

Deputy Chairman: DMITRII N. KOZAK.

Deputy Chairman, Minister of Finance: ALEKSEI L. KUDRIN.

Deputy Chairman: IGOR I. SECHIN.

Deputy Chairman, Head of the Government Staff: SERGEI S. SOBYANIN.

Minister of Agriculture: ALEKSEI V. GORDEYEV.

Minister of Civil Defence, Emergencies and Clean-up Operations: Col-Gen. SERGEI K. SHOIGU.

Minister of Communications and the Mass Media: IGOR O. SHCHEGOLEV.

Minister of Culture: ALEKSANDR A. AVDEYEV.

Minister of Defence: ANATOLII E. SERDYUKOV.

Minister of Economic Development: ELVIRA S. NABIULLINA.

Minister of Education and Science: ANDREI A. FURSENKO.

Minister of Energy: SERGEI I. SHMATKO.

Minister of Foreign Affairs: SERGEI V. LAVROV.

Minister of Health and Social Development: TATYANA A. GOLIKOVA.

Minister of Industry and Trade: VIKTOR B. KHRISTENKO.

Minister of Internal Affairs: Col-Gen. RASHID G. NURGALIYEV.

Minister of Justice: ALEKSANDR V. KONOVALOV.

Minister of Natural Resources and Ecology: YURII P. TRUTNEV.

Minister of Regional Development: VIKTOR F. BASAGRIN.

Minister of Sport, Tourism and Youth Policy: VITALII L. MUTKO.

Minister of Transport: IGOR YE. LEVITIN.

MINISTRIES

Office of the President: 103132 Moscow, Staraya pl. 4; tel. (495) 925-35-81; fax (495) 206-07-66; e-mail president@gov.ru; internet www.kremlin.ru.

Office of the Government: 103274 Moscow, Krasnopresnenskaya nab. 2; tel. (495) 205-57-35; fax (495) 205-42-19; internet www.government.ru.

Ministry of Agriculture: 107139 Moscow, Orlikov per. 1/11; tel. (495) 607-83-62; fax (495) 607-80-80; e-mail info@mcx.ru; internet www.mcx.ru.

Ministry of Civil Defence, Emergencies and Clean-up Operations: 109012 Moscow, Teatralnyi proyezd 3; tel. (495) 626-35-00; fax (495) 623-57-45; e-mail info@mchs.gov.ru; internet www.mchs.gov.ru.

Ministry of Communications and the Mass Media: 125375 Moscow, ul. Tverskaya 7; tel. (495) 771-81-00; fax (495) 771-87-18; internet www.minsvyaz.ru.

Ministry of Culture: 125009 Moscow, M. Gnezdnikovskii per. 7/6; tel. (495) 629-67-93; e-mail info@mkrf.ru; internet www.mkrf.ru.

Ministry of Defence: 105175 Moscow, ul. Myasnitskaya 37; tel. and fax (495) 696-71-71; internet www.mil.ru.

Ministry of Economic Development: 125993 Moscow, ul. 1-ya Tverskaya-Yamskaya 1/3; tel. (495) 694-03-53; fax (495) 251-69-65; e-mail presscenter@economy.gov.ru; internet www.economy.gov.ru.

Ministry of Education and Science: 103905 Moscow, ul. Tverskaya 11; tel. (495) 629-70-63; fax (495) 629-08-91; internet www.mon.gov.ru.

Ministry of Energy: 109074 Moscow, ul. Kitaigorodskii proyezd 7; e-mail esipova@mte.gov.ru; internet minenergo.com.

Ministry of Finance: 109097 Moscow, ul. Ilinka 9; tel. (495) 987-91-01; fax (495) 925-08-89; internet www.minfin.ru.

Ministry of Foreign Affairs: 119200 Moscow, Smolenskaya-Sennaya pl. 32/34; tel. (495) 244-16-06; fax (495) 230-21-30; e-mail ministry@mid.ru; internet www.mid.ru.

Ministry of Health and Social Development: 127994 Moscow, Rakhmanovskii per. 3/25; tel. (495) 927-28-48; fax (495) 928-58-15; internet www.mzsrrf.ru.

Ministry of Industry and Trade: 109074 Moscow, Kitaigorodskii proyezd 7; tel. (495) 710-55-00; fax (495) 710-57-22; e-mail info@mte.gov.ru; internet www.minprom.gov.ru.

Ministry of Internal Affairs: 119049 Moscow, ul. Zhitnaya 16; tel. (495) 239-05-54; fax (495) 293-59-98; e-mail mvd12@mvdrf.ru; internet www.mvd.ru.

Ministry of Justice: 119991 Moscow, ul. Zhitnaya 14; tel. (495) 955-59-99; fax (495) 916-29-03; internet www.minjust.ru.

Ministry of Natural Resources and Ecology: 123995 Moscow, ul. B. Gruzinskaya 4/6; tel. (495) 254-48-00; fax (495) 254-43-10; e-mail admin@mnr.gov.ru; internet www.mnr.gov.ru.

Ministry of Regional Development: 127994 Moscow, ul. Sadovaya-Samotechnaya 10/23/1; tel. (495) 980-25-47; fax (495) 699-38-41; e-mail info@minregion.ru; internet www.minregion.ru.

Ministry of Sport, Tourism and Youth Policy: 103274 Moscow, Krasnopresnenskaya nab. 2; tel. (495) 605-58-09; fax (495) 605-58-18; e-mail minsportturism@mail.ru; internet www.minstm.gov.ru.

Ministry of Transport: 109012 Moscow, ul. Rozhdestvenka 1/1; tel. (495) 626-10-00; e-mail info@mintrans.ru; internet www.mintrans.ru.

President

Presidential Election, 2 March 2008

Candidates	Votes	%
Dmitrii A. Medvedev (United Russia) .	52,530,712	70.28
Gennadii A. Zyuganov (Communist Party of the Russian Federation) .	13,243,550	17.72
Vladimir V. Zhirinovskii (Liberal Democratic Party of Russia) . . .	6,988,510	9.36
Andrei V. Bogdanov (Independent) .	968,344	1.30
Total*	74,746,649	100.00

* Including 1,005,533 invalid votes, equivalent to 1.34% of the total.

Legislature

The Federalnoye Sobraniye (Federal Assembly) is a bicameral legislative body, comprising the Sovet Federatsii (Federation Council) and the Gosudarstvennaya Duma (State Duma).

Sovet Federatsii
(Federation Council)

103426 Moscow, ul. B. Dmitrovka 26; tel. (495) 692-11-50; fax (495) 692-43-05; e-mail post_sf@gov.ru; internet www.council.gov.ru.

The Sovet Federatsii is the upper chamber of the Federalnoye Sobraniye. It comprises two deputies appointed from each of the constituent members (federal territorial units) of the Russian Federation, representing the legislative and executive branches of power in each republic and region.

Chairman: SERGEI M. MIRONOV.

Gosudarstvennaya Duma
(State Duma)

103265 Moscow, Okhotnyi ryad 1; tel. (495) 692-80-00; fax (495) 203-42-58; e-mail stateduma@duma.ru; internet www.duma.ru.

Chairman: BORIS V. GRYZLOV.

General Election, 2 December 2007

Parties and blocs	Votes	%	Seats
United Russia	44,714,241	64.30	315
Communist Party of the Russian Federation	8,046,886	11.57	57
Liberal Democratic Party of Russia	5,660,823	8.14	40
A Just Russia: Motherland/Pensioners/Life . . .	5,383,639	7.74	38
Agrarian Party of Russia . .	1,600,234	2.30	—
Yabloko	1,108,985	1.59	—
Civic Force	733,604	1.05	—
Union of Rightist Forces . .	669,444	0.96	—
Patriots of Russia . . .	615,417	0.89	—
Party of Social Justice . . .	154,083	0.22	—
Democratic Party of Russia . .	89,780	0.13	—
Invalid votes	759,929	1.09	
Total	69,537,065	100.00	450

Local Government

For much of the 1990s and the first half of the 2000s the Russian Federation comprised 89 federal territorial units (subjects—for details, see section on the Members of the Russian Federation, see p. 377). The basic divisions of local government are republics, oblasts (regions), krais (provinces), autonomous okrugs (districts), cities, raions (boroughs), and municipal and village authorities. The Federation Treaty, which was signed on 31 March 1992, provided for a Russian Federation comprising 20 republics, one autonomous oblast and six krais. There were 10 autonomous okrugs, which remained under the jurisdiction of the oblast or krai within which they were situated. A further republic, Ingushetiya, was created in June 1992. Two cities, Moscow and St Petersburg, subsequently assumed the status of federal cities. In May 2000 a presidential decree grouped the administrative entities into seven federal districts. Several territorial mergers took place between December 2005 and March 2008, following which the number of federal territories stood at 83, comprising 21 republics, nine krais (provinces), 46 oblasts, two cities of federal status, one autonomous oblast and four autonomous okrugs.

In 2001 President Vladimir Putin established a commission to investigate the possibility of reform to the sub-federal organs of local government, which at that time comprised numerous levels of administration. Subsequent legislation, approved in 2003, provided for only three types of local institutions—settlements, municipal counties and city districts—each of which would have clearly defined responsibilities. The legislation was initially due to take effect from January 2006, but in late 2005 a 'transitional period' of three years was announced, as a result of which the full implementation of the reforms would not be obligatory until January 2009. None the less, by late 2005 around 11,000 new municipalities had been established. At mid-2006 there were 12,215 municipalities in Russia, including 625 cities. Of the municipalities, 12,045 had elected bodies, and 4,519 an elected mayor.

Election Commission

Central Electoral Commission of the Russian Federation (Tsentralnaya izbiratelnaya komissiya Rossiiskoi Federatsii): 109012 Moscow, B. Cherkassii per. 9; tel. (495) 606-79-57; e-mail info@cikrf.ru; internet www.cikrf.ru; Chair. VLADIMIR CHUROV.

Political Organizations

Legislation approved by President Vladimir Putin in July 2001 required each political party to have at least 10,000 members, including no fewer than 100 members in at least 50 of the 89 subjects of the Russian Federation, in order to register and to function legally. The elections to the Gosudarstvennaya Duma (State Duma), held on 7 December 2003, were contested by 27 electoral associations (parties) and five electoral blocs. In December 2004 President Putin signed into law a series of amendments to the legislation of 2001, notably increasing the minimum membership required for registration of a political party to 50,000, with the additional requirement that at least 500 members of the party must be resident in more than one-half of the subjects (territorial units) of the Federation, with at least 250 members in each of the remaining regions. Parties previously registered under the original legislation were obliged to meet the new membership requirements by 1 January 2006. In July 2005 new legislation increased the threshold for parties to obtain representation in the Gosudarstvennaya Duma from 5% to 7%, while single-mandate constituencies (which hitherto provided one-half of deputies) were to be abolished. Based on the requirements of the amended legislation, only 11 parties were officially registered to contest elections to the Gosudarstvennaya Duma in December 2007.

Agrarian Party of Russia (APR) (Agrarnaya partiya Rossii): 107045 Moscow, per. B. Golovin 20/1; tel. (495) 607-99-51; fax (495) 607-99-01; e-mail press@agroparty.ru; internet www .agroparty.ru; f. 1993; left-wing, supports the agricultural sector; absorption into United Russia announced Sept. 2008; Chair. VLADIMIR N. PLOTNIKOV; 163,317 mems (2008).

Civic Force (Grazhdanskaya sila): 101000 Moscow, ul. Myasnitskaya 16; tel. (495) 229-32-09; fax (495) 777-27-62; e-mail fps@gr-sila .ru; internet www.gr-sila.ru; f. 2004 by fmr mems of the Union of Rightist Forces (q.v.); fmrly Free Russia (Svobodnaya Rossiya); name changed as above 2007; Leader MIKHAIL YU. BARSHCHEVSKII.

Communist Party of the Russian Federation (CPRF) (Kommunisticheskaya partiya Rossiiskoi Federatsii—KPRF): 103051 Moscow, per. M. Sukharevskii 3/1; tel. (495) 628-04-90; fax (495) 292-90-50; e-mail kprf2005@yandex.ru; internet www.kprf.ru; f. 1993; claims succession to the Russian Communist Party, which was banned in 1991; Chair. of Central Committee GENNADII A. ZYUGANOV; 184,181 mems (2006).

Democratic Party of Russia (Demokraticheskaya partiya Rossiya): 127287 Moscow, ul. Poltavskaya 18; tel. (495) 611-30-11; fax (495) 611-56-70; internet www.democrats.ru; f. 1990; liberal-conservative; Chair., Central Committee ANDREI V. BOGDANOV; Chair., Exec. Committee VYACHESLAV N. SMIRNOV; 82,183 mems (2006).

A Just Russia (AJR) (Spravedlivaya Rossiya): 107031 Moscow, ul. B. Dmitrovka 32/1; tel. (495) 650-38-80; e-mail nfo@spravedlivo.ru; internet www.spravedlivo.ru; f. 2006 by merger of Motherland, Russian Party of Life and Russian Pensioners' Party; absorbed People's Party of the Russian Federation in Apr. 2007; statist, patriotic party; Chair. SERGEI M. MIRONOV.

Liberal Democratic Party of Russia (LDPR) (Liberalno-demokraticheskaya partiya Rossii): 103045 Moscow, Lukov per. 9; tel. (495) 692-11-95; fax (495) 692-92-42; e-mail pressldpr@rambler .ru; internet www.ldpr.ru; f. 1988; nationalist; generally supportive of Pres. Putin; Chair. VLADIMIR V. ZHIRINOVSKII; 168,000 mems (2008).

Patriots of Russia (Patrioty Rossii): 119121 Moscow, Smolenskii bulv. 11/2; tel. (495) 692-15-50; fax (495) 692-15-50; e-mail partia-korn@rambler.ru; internet www.patriot-rus.ru; f. 2002; fmrly Russian Party of Labour; Leader GENNADII YU. SEMIGIN.

Union of Rightist Forces (URF) (Soyuz pravykh sil—SPS): 109544 Moscow, ul. M. Andronyevskaya 15; tel. (495) 232-04-06; e-mail edit@sps.ru; internet www.sps.ru; f. 1999 as alliance of nine movements, which merged to form one party in 2001; pro-market, economically liberal; dissolution of party announced Sept. 2008; Chair. of Federal Political Council LEONID GOIZMAN (acting).

United Russia (UR) (Yedinaya Rossiya): 129110 Moscow, Pereyaslavskii per. 4; tel. (495) 786-82-89; fax (495) 975-30-78; e-mail centrpr@edinros.ru; internet www.er.ru; f. 2001 as Unity and Fatherland—United Russia, on the basis of Unity (f. 1999, incorporating Our Home is Russia), Fatherland (f. 1999, and led by Mayor of Moscow YURII LUZHKOV) and the All Russia grouping of regional governors; pragmatic centrist grouping that promotes moderate economic reforms and a strong state; Chair. VLADIMIR V. PUTIN; Chair of Supreme Council BORIS V. GRYZLOV; 659,654 mems (2006).

Yabloko Russian United Democratic Party (Rossiiskaya obyedinennaya demokraticheskaya partiya 'Yabloko'): 119034 Moscow, per. M. Levshinskii 7/3; tel. (495) 201-43-79; fax (495) 292-34-50; e-mail admin@yabloko.ru; internet www.yabloko.ru; f. 1993 on the basis of the Yavlinskii-Boldyrev-Lukin electoral bloc; present name adopted 2008; democratic, politically and socially liberal; Chair. SERGEI S. MITROKHIN; 60,440 mems (2006).

Diplomatic Representation

EMBASSIES IN RUSSIA

Afghanistan: 121069 Moscow, ul. Povarskaya 42; tel. (495) 290-16-80; fax (495) 290-01-46; e-mail safarat_moscow@yahoo.com; Ambassador ZALMAI AZIZ.

Albania: 119049 Moscow, ul. Mytnaya 3/8; tel. (495) 230-77-32; fax (495) 230-76-35; e-mail embassy.moscow@mfa.gov.al; Chargé d'affaires a.i. HALIT FURRIKU.

Algeria: 103051 Moscow, Krapivinskii per. 1A; tel. (495) 937-46-00; fax (495) 937-46-25; e-mail algamb@ntl.ru; internet www .algerianembassy.ru; Ambassador AMAR ABBA.

Angola: 119590 Moscow, ul. U. Palme 6; tel. (495) 939-95-18; fax (495) 956-18-80; e-mail angomosc@col.ru; Ambassador SAMUEL TITO ARMANDO.

Argentina: 119017 Moscow, ul. B. Ordynka 72; tel. (495) 502-10-20; fax (495) 502-10-21; e-mail efrus@co.ru; Ambassador LEOPOLDO BRAVO.

Armenia: 101990 Moscow, Armyanskii per. 2; tel. (495) 924-32-43; fax (495) 924-45-35; e-mail info@armen.ru; internet www .armenianembassy.ru; Ambassador ARMEN B. SMBATIAN.

Australia: 109028 Moscow, Podkolokolii per. 10A/2; tel. (495) 956-60-70; fax (495) 956-61-70; e-mail austembmos@dfat.gov.au; internet www.russia.embassy.gov.au; Ambassador MARGARET TWOMEY.

Austria: 119034 Moscow, Starokonyushennyi per. 1; tel. (495) 502-95-12; fax (495) 937-42-69; e-mail moskau-ob@bmeia.gv.at; internet www.aussenministerium.at/moskau; Ambassador Dr MARTIN VUKOVICH.

Azerbaijan: 125009 Moscow, Leontyevskii per. 16; tel. (495) 629-43-32; fax (495) 202-50-72; e-mail azerirus@cnt.ru; internet www .azembassy.msk.ru; Ambassador POLAD BÜLBÜLOĞLU.

Bahrain: 109017 Moscow, ul. B. Ordynka 18/1; tel. (495) 953-00-22; fax (495) 953-74-74; e-mail moscowbah@yahoo.com; Ambassador ABDULHAMEED ALI HASAN ALI.

Bangladesh: 119121 Moscow, Zemledelcheskii per. 6; tel. (495) 246-78-04; fax (495) 248-31-85; e-mail moscow.bangla@com2com.ru; internet www.bangladeshembassy.ru; Ambassador AMIR HUSSAIN SIKDER.

Belarus: 101990 Moscow, ul. Maroseika 17/6; tel. (495) 777-66-44; fax (495) 777-66-33; e-mail mail@embassybel.ru; internet www.embassybel.ru; Ambassador VASIL DALHALYOV.

Belgium: 121069 Moscow, ul. M. Molchanovka 7; tel. (495) 780-03-31; fax (495) 780-03-32; e-mail moscow@diplobel.org; internet www.diplomatie.be/moscow; Ambassador VINCENT MERTENS DE WILMARS.

Benin: 127006 Moscow, Uspenskii per. 7; tel. (495) 299-23-60; fax (495) 200-02-26; e-mail ambabeninmoscou@hotmail.com; Ambassador VISSINTO AYI D'ALMEIDA.

Bolivia: 115191 Moscow, ul. Serpukhovskii Val 8/135–137; tel. (495) 954-06-30; fax (495) 958-07-55; e-mail embolrus@online.ru; internet www.emborus.com; Ambassador SERGIO SÁNCHEZ BALLIVIÁN.

Bosnia and Herzegovina: 119590 Moscow, ul. Mosfilmovskaya 50/1/484; tel. (499) 147-64-88; fax (499) 147-64-89; e-mail embassybih@mail.cnt.ru; Ambassador ENVER HALILOVIĆ.

Brazil: 121069 Moscow, ul. B. Nikitskaya 54; tel. (495) 363-03-66; fax (495) 363-03-67; e-mail brasrus@brasemb.ru; internet www.brasemb.ru; Ambassador CARLOS AUGUSTO REGO SANTOS-NEVES.

Brunei: 121059 Moscow, Berezhkovskaya nab. 2, Radisson-Slavyanskaya Hotel, kom. 440–441; tel. (495) 941-82-16; fax (495) 941-82-14; e-mail moscow.russia@mfa.gov.bn; Ambassador JANIN BIN ERIH.

Bulgaria: 119590 Moscow, ul. Mosfilmovskaya 66; tel. (495) 143-67-00; fax (495) 232-33-02; e-mail bulemrus@bolgaria.ru; internet www.bolgaria.ru; Ambassador PLAMEN I. GROZDANOV.

Burundi: 119049 Moscow, Kaluzhskaya pl. 1/226–227; tel. (495) 230-25-64; fax (495) 230-20-09; e-mail bdiam@mail.cnt.ru; Ambassador RENOVAT NDAYIRUKIYE.

Cambodia: 121002 Moscow, Starokonyushennyi per. 16; tel. (495) 637-47-36; fax (495) 956-65-73; e-mail cambemoscow@stream.ru; Ambassador KHIEU THAVIKA.

Cameroon: 121069 Moscow, ul. Povarskaya 40, POB 136; tel. (495) 290-65-49; fax (495) 290-61-16; Ambassador ANDRÉ NGONGANG OUANDJI.

Canada: 119002 Moscow, Starokonyushennyi per. 23; tel. (495) 925-60-00; fax (495) 925-60-25; e-mail mosco@international.gc.ca; internet www.dfait-maeci.gc.ca/missions/russia-russie/menu.asp; Ambassador RALPH JAMES LYSYSHYN.

Central African Republic: 117571 Moscow, ul. 26-i Bakinskikh Kommissarov 9/124–125; tel. (495) 434-45-20; fax (495) 933-28-99; Ambassador CLAUDE BERNARD BELOUM.

Chad: 117393 Moscow, ul. A. Pilyugina 14/3/895–896; tel. (495) 936-17-63; fax (495) 936-11-01; Ambassador DJIBRINE ABDOUL.

Chile: 119002 Moscow, Denezhnii per. 7/1; tel. (495) 241-01-45; fax (495) 241-68-67; e-mail echileru@col.ru; internet www.embachilerusia.ru; Ambassador CESAR AUGUSTO PARRA MUÑOZ.

China, People's Republic: 117330 Moscow, ul. Druzhby 6; tel. (495) 956-11-68; fax (495) 956-11-69; e-mail chiemb@microdin.ru; internet ru.china-embassy.org; Ambassador LIU GUCHANG.

Colombia: 119121 Moscow, ul. Burdenko 20/2; tel. (495) 248-30-42; fax (495) 248-30-25; e-mail emoscu@cancilleria.gov.co; Ambassador DIEGO JOSÉ TÓBON ECHEVERRI.

Congo, Democratic Republic: 117556 Moscow, Simferopolskii bulv. 7A/49-50; tel. and fax (495) 113-83-48; e-mail rdcambamoscou@yahoo.fr; Ambassador RAPHAËL MUTOMBO TSHITAMBWE.

Congo, Republic: 119034 Moscow, Kropotinskii per. 12; tel. (495) 236-33-68; fax (495) 236-41-16; Ambassador JEAN-PIERRE LOUYÉBO.

Costa Rica: 121615 Moscow, Rublevskoye shosse 26/1/23; tel. (495) 415-40-14; fax (495) 415-40-42; e-mail conscr@rol.ru; internet www.geocities.com/posolstvo.kosta_rika; Chargé d'affaires a.i. PAUL CHRISTIAN CHEN WENDORF.

Côte d'Ivoire: 119034 Moscow, Korobeinikov per. 14/9; tel. (495) 637-24-00; fax (495) 637-21-57; e-mail ambacimow@hotmail.com; internet ambaci-russie.org; Ambassador GNAGNO PHILIBERT FAGNIDI.

Croatia: 119034 Moscow, Korobeinikov per. 16/10; tel. (495) 637-38-68; fax (495) 637-46-24; e-mail croemb.russia@mvpei.hr; internet ru.mvp.hr; Ambassador BOŽO KOVAČEVIĆ.

Cuba: 119017 Moscow, ul. B. Ordynka 66; tel. and fax (495) 933-79-57; e-mail embsecret@ecurusia.ru; Ambassador JORGE MARTÍ MARTÍNEZ.

Cyprus: 121069 Moscow, ul. Povarskaya 9; tel. (495) 744-29-44; fax (495) 744-29-45; e-mail moscowembassy@mfa.gov.cy; internet www.mfa.gov.cy/embassymoscow; Ambassador LEONIDAS PANTELIDES.

Czech Republic: 123056 Moscow, ul. Yu. Fuchika 12/14; tel. (495) 251-05-44; fax (045) 250-15-23; e-mail moscow@embassy.mzv.cz; internet www.mfa.cz/moscow; Ambassador MIROSLAV KOSTELKA.

Denmark: 119034 Moscow, Prechistenskii per. 9; tel. (495) 642-68-00; fax (495) 775-01-91; e-mail mowamb@um.dk; internet www.ambmoskva.um.dk; Ambassador PER CARLSEN.

Ecuador: 103064 Moscow, Gorokhovskii per. 12; tel. (499) 261-55-27; fax (499) 267-70-79; e-mail embajada@ecuaemb.ru; internet www.ecuaemb.ru; Ambassador PATRICIO CHÁVEZ.

Egypt: 119034 Moscow, Kropotkinskii per. 12; tel. (495) 246-02-34; fax (495) 246-10-64; e-mail egyemb_moscow@yahoo.com; Ambassador EZZAT SAAD AS-SAYED AL-BURAEY.

Equatorial Guinea: 119017 Moscow, Pogorelskii per. 7/1; tel. (495) 953-27-66; Ambassador FAUSTO ABESO FUMA.

Eritrea: 129090 Moscow, ul. Meshchanskaya 17; tel. (495) 631-06-20; fax (495) 631-37-67; Ambassador TEKLAY MINASSIE ASGEDOM.

Estonia: 125009 Moscow, M. Kislovskii per. 5; tel. (495) 737-36-40; fax (495) 737-36-46; e-mail embassy.moskva@estemb.ru; internet www.estemb.ru; Ambassador SIIMU TIIK.

Ethiopia: 129041 Moscow, Orlovo-Davydovski per. 6; tel. (495) 680-16-16; fax (495) 680-66-08; e-mail eth-emb@col.ru; Ambassador Dr TEKETEL FORSIDO.

Finland: 119034 Moscow, Kropotkinskii per. 15/17; tel. (495) 787-41-74; fax (495) 247-33-80; e-mail sanomat.mos@formin.fi; internet www.finland.org.ru; Ambassador MATTI ANTTONEN.

France: 119049 Moscow, ul. B. Yakimanka 45; tel. (495) 937-15-00; fax (495) 937-14-46; e-mail amba@ambafrance.ru; internet www.ambafrance.ru; Ambassador STANISLAS LEFEBVRE DE LABOULAYE.

Gabon: 119002 Moscow, Denezhnyi per. 16; tel. (495) 241-00-80; fax (495) 244-06-94; Ambassador PAUL BIÉ EYENÉ.

Germany: 119285 Moscow, ul. Mosfilmovskaya 56; tel. (495) 937-95-00; fax (495) 938-23-54; e-mail germanmo@aha.ru; internet www.moskau.diplo.de; Ambassador Dr WALTER SCHMID.

Ghana: 121069 Moscow, Skatertnyi per. 14; tel. (495) 202-18-71; fax (495) 202-18-89; e-mail embghmos@astelit.ru; Ambassador Air Vice-Marshall EDWARD A. MANTEY.

Greece: 103009 Moscow, Leontiyevskii per. 4; tel. (495) 290-14-46; fax (495) 771-65-10; e-mail gremb.mow@mfa.gr; internet www.hellas.ru; Ambassador ILIAS KLIS.

Guatemala: 119049 Moscow, ul. Korovii Val 7/98; tel. (495) 238-22-14; fax (495) 238-14-46; e-mail embrusia@minex.gob.gt; Ambassador LARS HENRIK PIRA PÉREZ.

Guinea: 119034 Moscow, Pomerantsev per. 6; tel. (495) 201-36-01; fax (502) 220-21-38; Ambassador Lt-Col AMARA BANGOURA.

Guinea-Bissau: 117556 Moscow, Simferopolskii bulv. 7A/183; tel. and fax (495) 317-95-82; Ambassador ROGERIO ARAUJO ADOLPHO HERBERT.

Holy See: 127055 Moscow, Vadkovskii per. 7/37; tel. (495) 726-59-30; fax (495) 726-59-32; e-mail nuntius@cityline.ru; Apostolic Nuncio Most Rev. ANTONIO MENNINI (Titular Archbishop of Ferentium).

Hungary: 119590 Moscow, ul. Mosfilmovskaya 62; tel. (495) 796-93-70; fax (495) 796-93-80; e-mail mow.missions@kum.hu; internet www.mfa.gov.hu/emb/moscow; Ambassador ÁRPÁD SZÉKELY.

Iceland: 121069 Moscow, Khlebnyi per. 28; tel. (495) 956-76-04; fax (495) 956-76-12; e-mail mo.mow@mfa.is; internet www.iceland.org/ru; Ambassador BENEDIKT ÁSGEIRSSON.

India: 101000 Moscow, ul. Vorontsovo Pole 6/8; tel. (495) 783-75-35; fax (495) 975-23-37; e-mail india@online.ru; internet www.indianembassy.ru; Ambassador PRABHAT SHUKLA.

Indonesia: 109017 Moscow, ul. Novokuznetskaya 12; tel. (495) 951-95-50; fax (495) 230-64-31; e-mail kbrimos@online.ru; internet www.kbrimoskow.org; Ambassador (vacant).

Iran: 117292 Moscow, Pokrovskii bulv. 7; tel. (495) 917-72-82; fax (495) 230-28-97; Ambassador MAHMOUD REZA SADJADI.

Iraq: 119121 Moscow, ul. Pogodinskaya 12; tel. (495) 246-55-07; fax (495) 230-29-22; e-mail mosemb@iraqmofamail.net; Ambassador Dr ABDUL-KARIM HASHIM.

Ireland: 129010 Moscow, Grokholskii per. 5; tel. (495) 937-59-11; fax (495) 680-06-23; e-mail moscowembassy@dfa.ie; internet www.embassyofireland.ru; Ambassador JUSTIN HARMAN.

Israel: 115095 Moscow, ul. B. Ordynka 56; tel. (495) 660-27-00; fax (495) 660-27-68; e-mail info@moscow.mfa.gov.il; internet moscow.mfa.gov.il; Ambassador ANNA AZARI.

Italy: 121002 Moscow, Denezhnyi per. 5; tel. (495) 796-96-91; fax (495) 253-92-89; e-mail embitaly.mosca@esteri.it; internet www.ambmosca.esteri.it; Ambassador VITTORIO CLAUDIO SURDO.

Japan: 129090 Moscow, Grokholskii per. 27; tel. (495) 229-25-50; fax (495) 229-25-55; e-mail embjapan@mail.cnt.ru; internet www.ru.emb-japan.go.jp; Ambassador YASUO SAITO.

Jordan: 123001 Moscow, Mamonovskii per. 3; tel. (495) 699-12-42; fax (495) 699-43-54; e-mail emjordan@umail.ru; Ambassador ABDELILAH MUHAMMAD ALI AL-KURDI.

Kazakhstan: 101000 Moscow, Chistoprudnyi bulv. 3A; tel. (495) 927-17-01; fax (495) 608-15-49; e-mail kazembassy@kazembassy.ru; internet www.kazembassy.ru; Ambassador NURTAI A. ABYKAYEV.

Kenya: 119034 Moscow, Lopukhinskii per. 5; tel. (495) 637-21-86; fax (495) 637-54-63; e-mail kenemb@kenemb.ru; internet www.kenemb.ru; Ambassador Dr SOSPETER MAGITA MACHAGE.

Korea, Democratic People's Republic: 107140 Moscow, ul. Mosfilmovskaya 72; tel. (499) 143-62-49; fax (499) 143-63-12; Ambassador KIM YONG JAE.

Korea, Republic: 131000 Moscow, ul. Plyushchikha 56/1; tel. (495) 783-27-27; fax (495) 783-27-77; e-mail info@koreaemb.ru; internet rus-moscow.mofat.go.kr; Ambassador KIM JAE-SUP.

Kuwait: 119285 Moscow, ul. Mosfilmovskaya 44A; tel. (499) 147-00-40; fax (495) 956-60-32; Ambassador SULEIMAN IBRAHIM AL-MORJAN.

Kyrgyzstan: 119017 Moscow, ul. B. Ordynka 64; tel. (495) 237-48-82; fax (495) 951-60-62; e-mail embassy@embas-kyrg.msk.ru; Ambassador RAIMKUL A. ATTAKUROV.

Laos: 121069 Moscow, ul. Kachalova 18; tel. (495) 203-14-54; fax (495) 203-01-58; e-mail thingsavanh_ph@yahoo.com; Ambassador THONGSAVANH PHOMVIHANE.

Latvia: 105062 Moscow, ul. Chaplygina 3; tel. (495) 232-97-60; fax (495) 232-97-50; e-mail embassy.russia@am.gov.lv; internet www.am.gov.lv/lv/moscow; Ambassador ANDRIS TEIKMANIS.

Lebanon: 103051 Moscow, ul. Sadovaya-Samotechnaya 14; tel. (495) 200-00-22; fax (495) 200-32-22; Ambassador Dr ASSEM JABER.

Libya: 131940 Moscow, ul. Mosfilmovskaya 38; tel. (495) 143-03-54; fax (495) 938-21-62; Ambassador ABDUL-ADIM KHIMALI.

Lithuania: 121069 Moscow, Borisoglebskii per. 10; tel. (495) 785-86-05; fax (495) 785-86-00; internet ru.mfa.lt; Ambassador RIMANTAS ŠIDLAUSKAS.

Luxembourg: 119034 Moscow, Khrushchevskii per. 3; tel. (495) 203-53-81; e-mail moscou.amb@mae.etat.lu; Ambassador CARLO KRIEGER.

Macedonia, former Yugoslav republic: 117292 Moscow, ul. D. Ulyanova 16/2/8/509–510; tel. (495) 124-33-57; fax (495) 982-36-34; e-mail mkambmos@mail.tascom.ru; Ambassador ZLATKO LEČEVSKI.

Madagascar: 119034 Moscow, Kursovoi per. 5; tel. (495) 290-02-32; fax (495) 202-34-53; e-mail info@ambamadagascar.ru; internet www.ambamadagascar.ru; Ambassador ELOI MAXIME DOVO.

Malaysia: 119192 Moscow, ul. Mosfilmovskaya 50; tel. (499) 147-15-14; fax (495) 937-96-02; e-mail malmoscow@kln.gov.my; Ambassador Dato' MUHAMMAD KHALIS ALI HASSAN.

Mali: 113184 Moscow, ul. Novokuznetskaya 11; tel. (495) 951-06-55; fax (495) 230-28-89; e-mail amaliru@mail.ru; Ambassador Gen. BRÉHIMA SIRÉ TRAORÉ.

Malta: 119049 Moscow, ul. Korovii Val 7/219; tel. (495) 237-19-39; fax (495) 237-21-58; e-mail maltaembassy.moscow@gov.mt; Ambassador Dr MARIO COSTA.

Mauritania: 119049 Moscow, ul. B. Ordynka 66; tel. (495) 237-37-92; fax (495) 237-28-61; e-mail m_embassy@oss.ru; Ambassador MUHAMMAD MAHMOUD OULD DAHI.

Mexico: 119034 Moscow, B. Levshinskii per. 4; tel. (495) 969-28-79; fax (495) 969-28-77; e-mail info@embamex.ru; Ambassador ALFREDO ROGERIO PÉREZ BRAVO.

Moldova: 107031 Moscow, ul. Kuznetskii most 18; tel. (495) 924-53-53; fax (495) 924-95-90; e-mail moscova@mfa.md; internet www.moldembassy.ru; Ambassador VASILE STURZA.

Mongolia: 121069 Moscow, Borisoglebskii per. 11; tel. (495) 690-67-92; fax (495) 291-46-36; e-mail mongolia@online.ru; internet www.mongoliaembassy.ru; Ambassador LUVSANDANDARYN KHANGAI.

Montenegro: 119049 Moscow, ul. Mytnaya 3; tel. (499) 230-18-65; fax (499) 230-18-86; e-mail ambasadacg@ya.ru; Ambassador SLOBODAN BACKOVIĆ.

Morocco: 121069 Moscow, bulv. B. Nikitskaya 51; tel. (495) 291-17-62; fax (495) 291-16-42; e-mail sifmamos@df.ru; Ambassador NOUREDDINE SEFIANI.

Mozambique: 129090 Moscow, ul. Gilyarovskogo 8/25; tel. (495) 684-40-07; fax (495) 684-36-54; e-mail embamocru@hotmail.com; Ambassador BERNARDO MARCELINO CHERINDA.

Myanmar: 119049 Moscow, ul. Korovii Val 7/135; tel. (495) 230-24-26; fax (495) 730-96-46; e-mail mofa.aung@mptmail.net.mm; Ambassador U TIN SOE.

Namibia: 113096 Moscow, 2-i Kazachii per. 7; tel. (495) 230-32-75; fax (495) 230-22-74; e-mail namembrf@online.ru; Ambassador Dr SAMUEL K. MBAMBO.

Nepal: 119121 Moscow, 2-i Neopalimovskii per. 14/7; tel. (495) 244-02-15; fax (495) 244-00-00; e-mail nepalemb@mtu-net.ru; internet www.nepalembassyrus.org; Ambassador SURYA KIRAN GURUNG.

Netherlands: 125009 Moscow, Kalashnyi per. 6; tel. (495) 797-29-00; fax (495) 797-29-04; e-mail mos@minbuza.nl; internet www.netherlands-embassy.ru; Ambassador JAN-PAUL DIRKSE.

New Zealand: 121069 Moscow, ul. Povarskaya 44; tel. (495) 956-35-79; fax (495) 956-35-83; e-mail nzembmos@umail.ru; internet www.nzembassy.com/home.cfm?c=42; Ambassador CHRISTOPHER J. ELDER.

Nigeria: 121069 Moscow, ul. M. Nikitskaya 13; tel. (495) 290-37-83; fax (495) 956-28-25; e-mail ngrmosco@online.ru; Ambassador Air Cdre (retd) DAN SULEIMAN.

Norway: 131940 Moscow, ul. Povarskaya 7; tel. (495) 933-14-10; fax (495) 933-14-11; e-mail emb.moscow@mfa.no; internet www.norvegia.ru; Ambassador ØYVIND NORDSLETTEN.

Oman: 109180 Moscow, Staromonetnii per. 14/1; tel. (495) 230-15-87; fax (495) 230-15-44; e-mail embomn-mos@rambler.ru; Ambassador ABDULLAH BIN ZAHER AL-HUSSNI.

Pakistan: 123001 Moscow, ul. Sadovaya-Kudrinskaya 17; tel. (495) 254-97-91; fax (495) 956-90-97; e-mail parepmoscow@yahoo.com; internet www.pakistanembassy.ru; Ambassador KHALID KHATTAK.

Panama: 119590 Moscow, ul. Mosfilmovskaya 50/1; tel. (495) 956-07-29; fax (495) 956-07-30; e-mail empanrus@aha.ru; Ambassador (vacant).

Peru: 121002 Moscow, Smolenskii bulv. 22/14/15; tel. (495) 248-27-66; fax (495) 230-20-00; e-mail leprumoscu@mtu-net.ru; Ambassador Dr HUMBERTO UMERES ALVARES.

Philippines: 121099 Moscow, Karmanitskii per. 6; tel. (495) 241-05-63; fax (495) 241-26-30; e-mail moscowpe@utsmail.ru; internet www.phil-embassy.ru; Ambassador ERNESTO V. LLAMAS.

Poland: 123557 Moscow, ul. Klimashkina 4; tel. (495) 231-15-00; fax (495) 231-15-15; e-mail embassy@polandemb.ru; internet www.moskwa.polemb.net; Ambassador JERZY BAHR.

Portugal: 129010 Moscow, Botanicheskii per. 1; tel. (495) 981-34-10; fax (495) 981-34-16; e-mail embptrus@moscovo.dgaccp.pt; Ambassador MANUEL MARCELO MONTIERO CURTO.

Qatar: 117049 Moscow, ul. Korovii Val 7/196–198; tel. (495) 980-69-18; fax (495) 980-69-17; e-mail moscow@mofa.gov.qa; Ambassador SAAD MUHAMMAD SAAD AL-KOBAISI.

Romania: 119590 Moscow, ul. Mosfilmovskaya 64; tel. (499) 143-04-24; fax (499) 143-04-49; e-mail ambasada@orc.ru; internet moscova.mae.ro; Ambassador CONSTANTIN MIHAIL GRIGORIE.

Saudi Arabia: 119121 Moscow, 3-i Neopalimovskii per. 3; tel. (495) 245-23-10; fax (495) 246-94-71; e-mail saudimoscow@yahoo.com; internet www.mofa.gov.sa/detail.asp?InServiceID=238; Chargé d'affaires a.i. GAZI SHERBINI.

Senegal: 119049 Moscow, ul. Korovii Val 7/193–194; tel. (495) 230-20-72; fax (495) 230-20-63; Ambassador Maj.-Gen. MOUNTAGA DIALLO.

Serbia: 119285 Moscow, ul. Mosfilmovskaya 46; tel. (499) 147-41-06; fax (499) 147-41-04; e-mail ambasada@co.ru; Ambassador STANIMIR VUKIĆEVIĆ.

Sierra Leone: 121615 Moscow, Rublevskoye shosse 26/1/58–59; tel. (495) 415-41-24; fax (495) 415-29-85; Chargé d'affaires IBRAHIM VANDI KONDOH.

Singapore: 121099 Moscow, per. Kamennoi Slobody 5; tel. (495) 241-39-13; fax (495) 241-78-95; e-mail singemb_mow@sgmfa.gov.sg; internet www.mfa.gov.sg/moscow; Ambassador MICHAEL TAY CHEOW ANN.

Slovakia: 123056 Moscow, ul. Yu. Fuchika 17/19; tel. (495) 250-10-70; fax (495) 250-15-91; e-mail embassy@moskva.mfa.sk; internet www.moscow.mfa.sk; Ambassador Dr AUGUSTÍN ČISÁR.

Slovenia: 127006 Moscow, ul. M. Dmitrovka 14/1; tel. (503) 737-63-55; fax (495) 694-15-68; e-mail vmo@gov.si; internet moskva.veleposlanistvo.si; Ambassador ANDREJ BENEDEJČIČ.

Somalia: 117556 Moscow, Simferopolskii bulv. 7A /145; tel. and fax (495) 317-06-22; e-mail somemb@nabad.org; Chargé d'affaires a.i. MOHAMED MOHAMED HANDULLE.

South Africa: 123001 Moscow, Granatnyi per. 1/9; tel. (495) 540-11-77; fax (495) 540-11-78; e-mail moscow.ambassador@foreign.gov.za; internet saembassy.ru; Ambassador Dr B. W. J. BHEKI LANGA.

Spain: 121069 Moscow, ul. B. Nikitskaya 50/8; tel. (495) 690-30-02; fax (495) 291-91-71; e-mail embespru@correo.maec.es; internet www.maec.es/embajadas/moscu; Ambassador JUAN ANTONIO MARCH PUJOL.

Sri Lanka: 129090 Moscow, ul. Shchepkina 24; tel. (495) 688-16-20; fax (495) 688-17-57; e-mail lankaemb@com2com.ru; Ambassador U. WEERATUNGA.

Sudan: 127006 Moscow, Uspenskii per. 4A; tel. (495) 299-54-61; fax (495) 299-33-42; e-mail sudmos@cityline.ru; Ambassador CHOL DENG ALAK.

Sweden: 119590 Moscow, ul. Mosfilmovskaya 60; tel. (495) 937-92-00; fax (495) 937-92-02; e-mail moscow.sweinfo@foreign.ministry.se; internet www.swedenabroad.com/moscow; Ambassador TOMAS BERTELMAN.

Switzerland: 101000 Moscow, per. Ogorodnoi Slobody 2/5; tel. (495) 258-38-30; fax (495) 621-21-83; e-mail mos.vertretung@eda.admin .ch; internet www.eda.admin.ch/moscow; Ambassador ERWIN H. HOFER.

Syria: 119034 Moscow, Mansurovskii per. 4; tel. (495) 203-15-21; fax (495) 956-31-91; Ambassador WAHIB AL-FADEL.

Tajikistan: 103001 Moscow, Granatnyi per. 13; tel. (495) 290-38-46; fax (495) 291-89-98; e-mail embassy_moscow@tajikistan.ru; internet www.tajikistan.ru; Ambassador ABDULMAJID S. DOSTIYEV.

Tanzania: 109017 Moscow, ul. Pyatnitskaya 33; tel. (495) 953-82-21; fax (495) 956-61-30; e-mail tzmos@wm.west.call.com; Ambassador PATRICK SEGEJA CHOKALA.

Thailand: 129090 Moscow, ul. B. Spasskaya 9; tel. (495) 608-08-17; fax (495) 290-96-59; e-mail thaiemb@nnt.ru; internet www .thaiembassymoscow.com; Ambassador SUPHOT DHIRAKAOSAL.

Tunisia: 113105 Moscow, ul. M. Nikitskaya 28/1; tel. (495) 291-28-58; fax (495) 291-75-88; Ambassador MUHAMMAD BELLAGI.

Turkey: 119121 Moscow, 7-i Rostovskii per. 12; tel. (495) 956-55-95; fax (495) 956-55-97; e-mail turemb@co.ru; Ambassador KURTULUŞ TAŞKENT.

Turkmenistan: 119019 Moscow, Filippovskii per. 22; tel. (495) 291-66-36; fax (495) 291-09-35; Ambassador KHALNAZAR A. AGAKHANOV.

Ukraine: 103009 Moscow, Leontiyevskii per. 18; tel. (495) 629-35-42; fax (495) 629-46-81; e-mail emb_ru@mfa.gov.ua; internet www .mfa.gov.ua/russia; Ambassador KOSTYANTYN I. HRYSHCHENKO.

United Arab Emirates: 101000 Moscow, ul. U. Palme 4; tel. (499) 147-00-66; fax (495) 234-40-70; e-mail uae@col.ru; Ambassador MUHAMMAD ALI AL-OSAIMI.

United Kingdom: 121099 Moscow, Smolenskaya nab. 10; tel. (495) 956-72-00; fax (495) 956-72-01; e-mail moscow@britishembassy.ru; internet www.britaininrussia.ru; Ambassador ANNE PRINGLE.

USA: 121099 Moscow, B. Devyatinskii per. 8; tel. (495) 728-50-00; fax (495) 728-50-90; e-mail pamoscow@pd.state.gov; internet moscow .usembassy.gov; Ambassador JOHN BEYRLE.

Uruguay: 119049 Moscow, ul. Mytnaya 3; tel. (495) 143-04-01; fax (495) 938-20-45; e-mail ururus@mrree.gub.uy; internet www .uruguay.org.ru; Ambassador JORGE ALBERTO MEYER LONG.

Uzbekistan: 109017 Moscow, Pogorelskii per. 12; tel. (495) 230-00-76; fax (495) 238-89-18; e-mail info@uzembassy.ru; internet www .uzembassy.ru; Ambassador BAKHTIYOR A. ISLAMOV.

Venezuela: 115127 Moscow, B. Karetnyi per. 13/15; tel. (495) 699-40-42; fax (495) 956-61-08; e-mail info@embaven.ru; internet www .embaven.ru; Ambassador Dr ALEXIS RAFAEL NAVARRO ROJAS.

Viet Nam: 119021 Moscow, ul. B. Pirogovskaya 13; tel. (495) 245-09-25; fax (495) 246-31-21; e-mail dsqvn@com2com.ru; Ambassador NYUGEN VAN NGANG.

Yemen: 119121 Moscow, 2-i Neopalimovskii per. 6; tel. (495) 246-15-40; fax (495) 230-23-05; Ambassador ABDULWAHAB MUHAMMAD ALI AL-RAWHANI.

Zambia: 129041 Moscow, pr. Mira 52A; tel. (495) 688-50-01; fax (495) 975-20-56; Ambassador Rev. Dr PETER L. CHINTALA.

Zimbabwe: 119121 Moscow, per. Serpov 6; tel. (495) 248-43-67; fax (495) 230-24-97; e-mail zimbabwe@rinet.ru; Ambassador Brig. (retd) AGRIPPAH MUTAMBARA.

Judicial System

In January 1995 the first section of a new code of civil law came into effect. It included new rules on commercial and financial operations, and on ownership issues. The second part of the code was published in January 1996. The Constitutional Court rules on the conformity of government policies, federal laws, international treaties and presidential enactments with the Constitution. Following its suspension in October 1993, the Court was reinstated, with a new membership of 19 judges, in April 1995. The Supreme Arbitration Court rules on disputes between commercial bodies. The Supreme Court oversees all criminal and civil law, and is the final court of appeal from lower courts. A system of Justices of the Peace, to deal with certain civil cases, and with criminal cases punishable by a maximum of two years' imprisonment, was established in 1998. In December 2001

President Putin approved several reforms to the judicial system, including the introduction of trials by jury across the Russian Federation, and procedures to guarantee the independence of judges. The majority of Russia's administrative regions introduced jury trials, in many cases only for the most serious crimes, during 2003.

Constitutional Court of the Russian Federation (Konstitutsionnyi Sud Rossiiskoi Federatsii): 190000 St Petersburg, pl. Dekabristov 1; tel. (812) 404-33-11; e-mail ksrf@krsf.ru; internet www.ksrf .ru; f. 1991; Chair. VALERII D. ZORKIN; Sec.-Gen. YELENA V. KRAVCHENKO.

Office of the Prosecutor-General: 125993 Moscow, ul. B. Dmitrovka 15A; tel. (495) 692-26-82; fax (495) 292-88-48; internet www.genproc.gov.ru; Prosecutor-General YURII YA. CHAIKA.

Supreme Arbitration Court of the Russian Federation (Vysshii Arbitrazhnyi Sud Rossiiskoi Federatsii): 101000 Moscow, M. Kharitonevskii per. 12; tel. (495) 208-11-19; fax (495) 208-11-62; internet www.arbitr.ru; f. 1993; Chair. ANTON A. IVANOV.

Supreme Court of the Russian Federation (Verkhovnyi Sud Rossiiskoi Federatsii): 103289 Moscow, ul. Ilinka 7/3; tel. (495) 924-23-47; fax (495) 202-71-18; e-mail gastello@ilinka.supcourt.ru; internet www.supcourt.ru; Chair. VYACHESLAV M. LEBEDEV.

Religion

The majority of the population of the Russian Federation are adherents of Christianity, but there are significant Islamic, Buddhist and Jewish minorities.

In 1997 legislation restricted the operation of religious groups to those that were to prove that they had been established in Russia for a minimum of 15 years. Russian Orthodoxy, Islam, Buddhism and Judaism, together with some other Christian denominations, were deemed to comply with the legislation. Religious organizations failing to satisfy this requirement were, henceforth, obliged to register annually for 15 years, before being permitted to publish literature, hold public services or invite foreign preachers into Russia. Moreover, foreign religious groups were additionally obliged to affiliate themselves to Russian organizations.

CHRISTIANITY

The Russian Orthodox Church (Moscow Patriarchate)

The Russian Orthodox Church (Moscow Patriarchate) is the dominant religious organization in the Russian Federation, with an estimated 75m. adherents. In 2004 there were 12,638 parishes operating under the auspices of the Patriarchate in Russia.

Moscow Patriarchate: 115191 Moscow, Danilov Monastery, ul. Danilovskii Val 22; tel. (495) 954-04-54; fax (495) 633-72-81; e-mail cs@mospatr.ru; internet www.mospat.ru; Patriarch of Moscow and all Rus ALEKSEI II RIDIGER.

The Roman Catholic Church

At 31 December 2006 there were an estimated 774,900 Roman Catholics in the Russian Federation. In 1991 administrative structures of the Roman Catholic Church in Russia were restored. The organization of the Church in Russian comprises one archdiocese, three dioceses, one apostolic prefecture, and an apostolic exarchate for adherents of the Byzantine Rite.

Conference of Catholic Bishops of the Russian Federation

101031 Moscow, ul. Petrovka 19/5/35; tel. and fax (495) 923-16-97; e-mail ostastop@glasnet.ru; internet www.catholic.ru.

f. 1999; Pres. Most. Rev. JOSEPH WERTH (Bishop of the Diocese of the Transfiguration at Novosibirsk).

Archbishop of the Archdiocese of the Mother of God at Moscow: Most Rev. PAOLO PEZZI, 107078 Moscow, POB 116, ul. N. Basmannaya 16/31; tel. and fax (499) 261-67-14; e-mail cathmos@dol .ru.

Protestant Churches

Russian Church of Christians of the Evangelical Faith: 123363 Moscow, ul. Fabritsiusa 31A; tel. (495) 493-57-88; internet hve.ru; f. 1907, re-established 1990; fmrly known as Union of Christians of the Evangelical Faith-Pentecostalists in Russia; 1,600 parishes and more than 300,000 adherents in 2005; Elder NAZAR P. RESHCHIKOVETS.

Russian Union of Evangelical Christians-Baptists: 117015 Moscow, Varshavskoye shosse 29/2; tel. (495) 958-13-36; fax (495) 975-23-67; e-mail bapt.un@g23.relcom.ru; internet baptist.org.ru; affiliated to the Euro-Asiatic Federation of Evangelical Christians-Baptists; Exec. Sec. YURII APATOV.

Other Christian Churches

Armenian Apostolic Church: 123022 Moscow, ul. S. Makeyeva 10; tel. (495) 255-50-19.

Russian Orthodox Old Belief (Old Ritual) Church (Russkaya Pravoslavnaya Staroobryadcheskaya Tserkov): 109052 Moscow, ul. Rogozhskii pos. 1в/3; tel. (495) 361-51-92; e-mail expers2rpsc.ru; internet www.rpsc.ru; f. 1666 by separation from the Moscow Patriarchate; some 300 groups registered in 2005; divided into two main branches: the *popovtsi* (which have priests) and the *bespopovtsi* (which reject the notion of ordained priests and the use of all sacraments, other than that of baptism). Both branches are further divided into various groupings. The largest group of *popovtsi* are those of the Belokrinitskii Concord, under the Archbishop of Novozybkov, Moscow and All Rus, KORNILII (TITOV); c. 250 parishes, seven bishops in Russia, Ukraine and Moldova; a further significant group of *popovtsi* Old Believers are those of the Beglopopovtsyi Concord.

Russian Autonomous Orthodox Church: 125212 Moscow, Church of the New Martyrs and Confessors of Russia, Golovinskoye shosse 13 A; tel. (495) 152-50-76; formally established in 1990 as the Free Russian Orthodox Church; re-registered in 1998 under above name following opposition by local, 'catacomb' priests to moves of reconciliation between the Russian Orthodox Church Abroad and the Moscow Patriarchate; 100 parishes in 2001; First Hierarch Metropolitan of Suzdal and Vladimir VALENTIN (RUSANTSOV).

ISLAM

Most Muslims in the Russian Federation are adherents of the Sunni sect. Islam is the predominant religion among many peoples of the North Caucasus, such as the Chechens, the Ingush and many smaller groups, and also in the Central Volga region, among them the Tatars, Chuvash and Bashkirs.

Central Muslim Spiritual Board for Russia and European Countries of the CIS: 450057 Bashkortostan, Ufa, ul. Tukaya 50; tel. (3472) 50-80-86; f. 1789; 27 regional branches in the Russian Federation, and one branch in Ukraine; Chair. (vacant).

Council of Muftis of Russia: 129090 Moscow, per. Vypolzov 7; tel. and fax (495) 681-49-04; e-mail mufty@muslim.ru; internet www .muslim.ru; Chair. Mufti Sheikh RAVIL KHAZRAT GAINUTDIN.

JUDAISM

At the beginning of the 20th century approximately one-half of the world's Jews lived in the Russian Empire. Although many Jews emigrated from the USSR in the 1970s and 1980s, there is still a significant Jewish population (230,000 in late 2002, according to the official results of the census, although some estimates were considerably higher) in the Russian Federation.

Congress of Jewish Religious Communities and Organizations of Russia: 101000 Moscow, B. Spasoglinishevskii per. 10, Moscow Choral Synagogue; tel. (495) 917-95-92; fax (495) 740-12-18; e-mail keroor@mail.ru; f. 1996; co-ordinates activities of 120 Jewish communities throughout Russia; Chief Rabbi ADOLF SHAYEVICH; Dir ZINOVY KOGAN.

Federation of the Jewish Communities of Russia: 121099 Moscow, ul. Novyi Arbat 36/9/2; tel. (495) 290-75-18; fax (495) 290-86-49; e-mail office@fjc.ru; internet www.fjc.ru; unites 179 communities in Russia; affiliated to Federation of the Jewish Communities of the CIS and the Baltic States; Chief Rabbi of Russia, Chair. of Rabbinical Alliance of Russia and the CIS BEREL LAZAR.

Russian Jewish Congress: 101000 Moscow, B. Spasoglinishchevskii per. 9/1/936; tel. (495) 780-61-00; fax (495) 780-60-90; e-mail rjc@ rjc.ru; internet www.rjc.ru; Pres. VYACHESLAV KANTOR.

BUDDHISM

Buddhism (established as an official religion in Russia in 1741) is most widespread in the Republic of Buryatiya, where the Traditional Buddhist Sangkha of Russia has its seat, the Republics of Kalmykiya and Tyva, in Transbaikal Krai (formerly Chita Oblast) and in Irkutsk Oblast.

Buddhist Traditional Sangkha of Russia (Buddiiskaya Traditsionnaya Sangkha Rossii): 670000 Buryatiya, Ulan-Ude, Ivolginskii datsan; e-mail buddhism@buryatia.ru; internet buddhism.buryatia .ru; Head Pandito Khambo Lama DAMBA AYUSHEYEV.

The Press

In 2004 there were 46,000 officially registered printed media, including some 26,000 newspapers. However, the number of titles in circulation was only around one-half of the total. The total print run of Russian newspapers in that year was 8,500m. copies, and that of magazines was around 600m. copies. At that time *Moskovskii Komsomolets*, with a circulation of 2.2m., was the best-selling daily,

while the weekly, *Argumenty i Fakty*, which had a circulation of 2.9m. in 2007, was the best-selling newspaper overall.

Federal Agency for the Press and the Mass Media (Federalnoye Agentstvo po pechati i massovym kommunikatsiyam): 127994 Moscow, Strastnoi bulv. 5; tel. (495) 650-39-86; e-mail sekretarr@fapmc .ru; internet www.fapmc.ru; f. 2004; Chair. MIKHAIL V. SESLAVINSKII.

PRINCIPAL NEWSPAPERS
Moscow

Argumenty i Fakty (Arguments and Facts): 101000 Moscow, ul. Myasnitskaya 42; tel. (495) 923-35-41; fax (495) 925-61-82; e-mail n-boris@aif.ru; internet www.aif.ru; f. 1978; weekly; Editor-in-Chief NIKOLAI ZYATKOV; circ. 2.9m. (2007).

Gazeta (Newspaper): 123242 Moscow, ul. Zoologicheskaya 4; tel. (495) 787-39-99; fax (495) 787-39-98; e-mail info@gzt.ru; internet www.gzt.ru; f. 2001; Editor-in-Chief PETR YE. FADEYEV; circ. 726,000 (2005).

Gazeta.ru: 117152 Moscow, Zagorodnoye shosse 1/1; tel. (495) 785-09-76; internet www.gazeta.ru; online only; has no asscn with the newspaper *Gazeta* ; Editor-in-Chief ALEKSANDR PISAREV.

Grani.ru: Moscow; tel. (495) 363-36-08; e-mail info@grani.ru; internet grani.ru; f. 2000; online only; Dir-Gen. YULIYA BEREZOVSKAYA; Editor-in-Chief VLADIMIR KORSUNSKII.

Gudok (The Horn): 105066 Moscow, ul. Staraya Basmannaya 38/2/3; tel. (495) 262-26-53; fax (495) 262-45-74; e-mail welcome@gudok .ru; internet www.gudok.ru; f. 1917 as newspaper of railway workers; daily; Editor-in-Chief IGOR T. YANIN; circ. 214,000 (2007).

Izvestiya (News): 127994 Moscow, ul. Tverskaya 18/1, POB 4; tel. (495) 209-05-81; fax (495) 933-64-62; e-mail info1@izvestia.ru; internet www.izvestia.ru; f. 1917; 50.19% owned by Gazprom Mediya, 49.81% by Prof-Mediya; Editor-in-Chief VLADIMIR MAMONTOV; circ. 130,000 (2007).

Kommersant (Businessman): 125080 Moscow, ul. Vrubelya 4/1; tel. (499) 943-97-71; fax (499) 943-97-28; e-mail kommersant@ kommersant.ru; internet www.kommersant.com; f. 1989; daily; Editor ANDREI VASILYEV; circ. 119,322 (2007).

Komsomolskaya Pravda (Young Communist League Truth): 103287 Moscow, Staryi Petrovsko-Razumovskii proyezd 1/23/1; tel. (495) 257-51-39; fax (495) 200-22-93; e-mail kp@kp.ru; internet www .kp.ru; f. 1925; fmrly organ of the Lenin Young Communist League (Komsomol); independent; weekly supplements *KP-Tolstushka* (KP-Fat volume), *KP-Ponedelnik* (KP-Monday); managed by Prof-Mediya; Chair. OLEG RUDNOV; Editor VLADIMIR SUNGORKIN; circ. 700,000.

Krasnaya Zvezda (Red Star): 123007 Moscow, Khoroshevskoye shosse 38; tel. (495) 941-21-58; fax (495) 941-40-66; e-mail redstar@ mail.cnt.ru; internet www.redstar.ru; f. 1924; organ of the Ministry of Defence; Editor N. N. YEFIMOV; circ. 80,000 (2000).

The Moscow News: 127018 Moscow, ul. Polkovaya 3/1; tel. (495) 234-32-23; fax (495) 232-62-29; internet www.mnweekly.ru; f. 1930; weekly; in English; democratic, liberal; Chief Editor ROBERT BRIDGE.

Moscow Times: 127018 Moscow, ul. Polkovaya 3/1; tel. (495) 234-32-23; fax (495) 232-65-29; e-mail moscowtimes.editors@imedia.ru; internet www.themoscowtimes.com; f. 1992; daily; in English; Publr MAXINE MATERS; Editor ANDREW MCCHESNEY.

Moskovskaya Pravda (The Moscow Truth): 123846 Moscow, ul. 1905 Goda 7, POB D-22; tel. (495) 259-82-33; fax (495) 259-63-60; e-mail newspaper@mospravda.ru; internet www.mospravda.ru; f. 1918; fmrly organ of the Moscow city committee of the CPSU and the Moscow City Council; 5 a week; independent; Editor SHOD S. MULADZHANOV; circ. 400,000 (2007).

Moskovskii Komsomolets (MK): 123995 Moscow, ul. 1905 Goda 7; tel. (495) 259-50-36; fax (495) 259-46-39; e-mail letters@mk.ru; internet www.mk.ru; f. 1919 as *Moskovskii Komsomolets* (The Moscow Young Communist); 6 a week; independent; circ. 800,000 in Moscow, 2.2m. nation-wide (2004); Editor-in-Chief PAVEL GUSEV.

Nezavisimaya Gazeta (NG) (Independent Newspaper): 101000 Moscow, ul. Myasnitskaya 13; tel. (495) 645-61-54; e-mail info@ng .ru; internet www.ng.ru; f. 1990; 5 a week; regular supplements include *NG-Nauka* (NG-Science), *NG-Regiony* (NG-Regions), *NG-Politekonomiya* (NG-Political Economy), *NG-Dipkuryer* (NG-Diplomatic Courier); Gen. Man. and Editor-in-Chief KONSTANTIN REMCHUKOV; circ. 53,000 (2005).

Novaya Gazeta (New Newspaper): 101000 Moscow, Potapovskii per. 3; tel. and fax (495) 623-68-88; e-mail pr@novayagazeta.ru; internet www.novayagazeta.ru; f. 1993; weekly; Editor DMITRII A. MURATOV.

Novye Izvestiya (New News): 107076 Moscow, ul. Elektrozavodskaya 33; tel. (495) 783-06-36; fax (495) 783-06-37; e-mail webmaster@ newizv.ru; internet www.newizv.ru; f. 2003 following the closure of the fmr *Novye Izvestiya* (f. 1997); daily; Editor-in-Chief VALERII YAKOV.

Parlamentskaya Gazeta (Parliamentary Newspaper): 125993 Moscow, ul. 1–ya Yamskogo Polya 28; tel. (495) 257-50-90; fax (495) 257-50-82; e-mail pg@pnp.ru; internet www.pnp.ru; f. 1998; 5 a week; organ of the Federanoye Sobraniye; Editor-in-Chief PETR A. KOTOV; circ. 50,000 (2005).

Polit.ru: 101000 Moscow, Krivokolennyi per. 10/6A; tel. (495) 624-80-09; e-mail edit@polit.ru; internet www.polit.ru; f. 1998; independent; online only; Editor-in-Chief ANDREI LEVKIN.

Pravda (Truth): 125867 Moscow, ul. Pravdy 24; tel. (499) 257-52-13; e-mail pravda2@cnt.ru; internet www.gazeta-pravda.ru; f. 1912; fmrly organ of the Cen. Cttee of the CPSU; independent; communist; Editor-in-Chief VALENTIN S. SHURCHANOV; circ. 100,300 (2007).

Pravda.ru: Moscow, ul. Staraya Basmannaya 16/2; tel. and fax (499) 261-48-85; e-mail home@pravda.ru; internet pravda.ru; f. 1999; online only, in Russian, English and Portuguese; has no asscn with the newspaper *Pravda*; Editor-in-Chief INNA S. NOVIKOVA.

Rossiiskaya Gazeta (Russian Newspaper): 125993 Moscow, ul. Pravdy 24, POB 40; tel. (495) 257-52-52; fax (495) 973-22-56; e-mail sekretar@rg.ru; internet www.rg.ru; f. 1990; organ of the Russian Govt; 6 a week; Gen. Man. ALEKSANDR N. GORBENKO; Editor-in-Chief VLADISLAV A. FRONIN; circ. 373,820 (2004).

Rossiiskiye Vesti (Russian News): 119034 Moscow, ul. Prechistenka 28; tel. (495) 933-06-47; fax (495) 201-51-02; e-mail mail@rosvesty.ru; internet www.rosvesty.ru; f. 1991; weekly; Editor-in-Chief ALEKSEI TITKOV.

Russkii Zhurnal (Russian Journal): 125009 Moscow, per. M. Gnezdnikovskii 9/8/3A; tel. and fax (495) 745-52-25; e-mail russ@russ.ru; internet www.russ.ru; f. 1997; online only; culture, politics, society; Editor-in-Chief and Publr GLEB PAVLOVSKII.

Selskaya Zhizn (Country Life): 125869 Moscow, ul. Pravdy 24, POB 137; tel. (495) 257-51-51; fax (495) 257-58-39; e-mail sg@sgazeta.ru; internet www.sgazeta.ru; f. 1918 as *Bednota* (Poverty), present name adopted in 1960; 2 a week; fmrly organ of the Cen. Cttee of the CPSU; independent; Editor-in-Chief and Gen. Man. SHAMUN M. KAGERMANOV; circ. 94,500.

Tribuna (Tribune): 125993 Moscow, ul. Pravdy 24, POB A-40; tel. (495) 257-59-13; fax (495) 973-20-02; e-mail tribuna@tribuna.ru; internet www.tribuna.ru; f. 1969; national industrial daily; Editor-in-Chief OLEG KUZIN.

Trud (Labour): 125993 Moscow, ul. Pravdy 24/5; tel. (495) 580-66-93; e-mail letter@trud.ru; internet www.trud.ru; f. 1921; 5 a week; Editor ALEKSANDR S. POTAPOV.

Vechernyaya Moskva (Evening Moscow): 123995 Moscow, ul. 1905 Goda 7, POB 5/22; tel. (495) 259-81-87; fax (495) 253-95-75; e-mail post@vm.ru; internet www.vm.ru; f. 1923; Chair. VLADIMIR V. ZUBKOV.

Vedomosti (Gazette): 125212 Moscow, ul. Vyborgskaya 16; tel. (495) 232-32-00; fax (495) 956-07-16; e-mail vedomosti@media.ru; internet www.vedomosti.ru; f. 1999; independent business newspaper, publ. jointly with the *Financial Times* (United Kingdom) and the *Wall Street Journal* (USA); Editor-in-Chief YELIZABETA OSETINSKAYA.

Vremya Novosti (News Time): 115326 Moscow, ul. Pyatnitskaya 25; tel. (495) 231-18-77; e-mail nter@vremya.ru; internet www.vremya.ru; f. 2000; Editor-in-Chief VLADIMIR S. GUREVICH.

Zhizn (Life): 125212 Moscow, ul. Vyborgskaya 16/1; tel. (495) 510-29-84; fax (495) 510-29-81; e-mail info@zhizn.ru; internet www.zhizn.ru; weekly; Editor-in-Chief RUSLAN SAGAYEV; circ. 2.2.m. within Russia (2007).

St Petersburg

Peterburgskii Chas Pik (Petersburg Rush Hour): 191040 St Petersburg, Nevskii pr. 81; tel. (812) 579-25-65; fax (812) 579-19-12; e-mail nabor@chaspik.spb.ru; internet www.chaspik.spb.ru; f. 1990; weekly; owned by Gazprom-Mediya; Editor-in-Chief LARISA AFONINA; circ. 30,000 (2005).

Novosti Peterburga (Petersburg News): 191084 St Petersburg, Mitrofanyevskoye shosse 29T; tel. (812) 334-27-21; e-mail pr@novosti.sp.ru; internet www.novostispb.ru; f. 1997; independent; Editor-in-Chief KIRILL METELEV.

Sankt-Peterburgskiye Vedomosti (St Petersburg Gazette): 191025 St Petersburg, ul. Marata 25; tel. (812) 325-31-00; fax (812) 764-48-40; e-mail post@spbvedomosti.ru; internet www.spbvedomosti.ru; f. 1991 as revival of 1728–1917 title; re-established 1991; Editor-in-Chief and Gen. Man. SERGEI A. SLOBODSKOI.

Smena (The Rising Generation): 191119 St Petersburg, ul. Marata 69; tel. (812) 315-04-76; fax (812) 315-03-53; e-mail info@smena.ru; internet www.smena.ru; f. 1919; 6 a week, controlled by Sistema Mass-Mediya; Editor-in-Chief LEONID DAVYDOV; circ. 80,000 (2002).

The St Petersburg Times: 190000 St Petersburg, Isaakevskaya pl. 4; tel. and fax (812) 325-60-80; e-mail letters@sptimesrussia.com; internet www.sptimes.ru; f. 1993; 2 a week; in English; independent; Editor TOBIN AUBER.

Vechernii Peterburg (Evening Petersburg): 191023 St Petersburg, ul. Fontanka 59; tel. (812) 311-88-75; fax (812) 314-31-05; e-mail gazeta@vspb.spb.ru; internet vppress.ru; f. 1917; Editor VLADIMIR G. GRONSKII.

PRINCIPAL PERIODICALS
Agriculture, Forestry, etc.

Ekologiya i Promlyshlennost Rossii (The Ecology and Industry of Russia): 119049 Moscow, Leninskii pr. 4; tel. (495) 913-80-94; fax (495) 647-23-08; e-mail ecip@online.ru; internet ecip.kalvis.ru; f. 1996; monthly; environmental protection; Editor-in-Chief Prof. Dr V. D. KALNER.

Ekonomika Selskokhozyaistvennykh i Pererabatyvayushchikh Predpriyatii (Economics of Agricultural and Processing Enterprises): 107996 Moscow, ul. Sadovaya-Spasskaya 18/423; tel. (495) 207-15-80; fax (495) 207-18-56; internet www.reason.ru/economy; f. 1926; monthly; publ. by Ministry of Agriculture; Editor S. K. DEVIN.

Lesnaya Promyshlennost (Forest Industry): 101934 Moscow, Arkhangelskii per. 1/234; tel. (495) 207-91-53; f. 1926; 3 a week; publ. by the state forest industrial company, Roslesprom; Editor V. G. ZAYEDINOV; circ. 250,000.

Veterinariya (Veterinary Science): 107996 Moscow, ul. Sadovaya-Spasskaya 18; tel. (495) 207-10-60; fax (495) 207-28-12; f. 1924; monthly; Editor V. A. GARKAVTSEV; circ. 4,860 (2000).

Zashchita i Karantin Rastenii (The Protection and Quarantine of Plants): 107996 Moscow, ul. Sadovaya-Spasskaya 18, GSB-6, B-78; tel. (495) 207-21-30; fax (495) 207-21-40; e-mail fitopress@ropnet.ru; internet www.z-i-k-r.ru; f. 1932; monthly; Editor YURII N. NEIPERT; circ. 4,500 (2007).

Zemledeliye (Farming): 127434 Moscow, POB 9; tel. and fax (495) 976-11-93; e-mail zemledelie@mtu-net.ru; internet www.jurzemledelie.ru; f. 1939; 8 a year; publ. by Ministry of Agriculture, Russian Academy of Agricultural Sciences, Russian Scientific Research Institute of Farming; Editor MARIANNA G. LOGVINOVA; circ. 2,500 (2005).

For Children

Koster (Campfire): 193024 St Petersburg, ul. Mytninskaya 1/20; tel. (812) 274-15-72; fax (812) 274-46-26; e-mail root@kostyor.spb.org; internet www.kostyor.ru; f. 1936; monthly; journal of the International Union of Children's Organizations (UPO-FCO); fiction, poetry, sport, reports and popular science; for ages 10–14 years; Editor-in-Chief N. B. KHARLAMPIYEV; circ. 7,500 (2000).

Murzilka: 127015 Moscow, ul. Novodmitrovskaya 5A; tel. and fax (495) 685-18-81; e-mail murzilka@dateline.ru; internet www.murzilka.org; f. 1924; monthly; illustrated; for first grades of school; Editor TATYANA ANDROSENKO; circ. 75,000 (2007).

Pionerskaya Pravda (Pioneers' Truth): 127994 Moscow, ul. Sushchevskaya 21; tel. and fax (495) 787-62-43; e-mail info@pionerka.ru; internet www.pionerka.ru; f. 1925; 4 a week; fmrly organ of the Union of Pioneer Organizations (Federation of Children's Organizations) of the USSR; Editor MIKHAIL N. BARANNIKOV.

Veselye Kartinki (Merry Pictures): 127015 Moscow, POB 60, ul. Pravdy 24/830; tel. (495) 411-31-28; fax (495) 257-32-01; e-mail info@merrypictures.ru; internet www.merrypictures.ru; f. 1956; monthly; humorous, illustrated; for pre-school and first grades; Editor MARINA DRUZHININAYA.

Yunyi Naturalist (Young Naturalist): 125015 Moscow, ul. Novodmitrovskaya 5A; tel. (495) 685-39-31; e-mail post@unnaturalist.ru; internet www.unnaturalist.ru; f. 1928; monthly; popular science for children of fourth–10th grades, who are interested in biology; Editor L. M. SAMSONOVA.

Yunyi Tekhnik (Young Technician): 125015 Moscow, ul. Novodmitrovskaya 5A; tel. (495) 285-44-80; e-mail yt@got.mmtel.ru; internet jt-arxiv.narod.ru; f. 1956; monthly; popular science for children and youth; Editor BORIS CHEREMISINOV.

Culture and Arts

Iskusstvo Kino (The Art of the Cinema): 125319 Moscow, ul. Usiyevicha 9; tel. (495) 151-56-51; fax (495) 151-02-72; e-mail filmfilm@mtu-net.ru; internet www.kinoart.ru/main.html; f. 1931; monthly; journal of the Russian Film-makers' Union; Editor DANIIL DONDUREI; circ. 5,000 (2004).

Knizhnoye Obozreniye (The Book Review): 129272 Moscow, ul. Sushchevskii Val 64; tel. (495) 681-62-66; fax (495) 681-51-45; internet www.knigoboz.ru; f. 1966; weekly; publ. of the Ministry of the Press, Broadcasting and Mass Media; summaries of newly published books; Editor-in-Chief ALEKSANDR F. GAVRILOV; circ. 10,500 (2003).

Kultura (Culture): 127055 Moscow, ul. Novoslobodskaya 73; tel. (495) 685-06-40; fax (496) 685-31-50; e-mail kultura@dol.ru; internet www.kulturagz.ru; f. 1929; controlled by Sistema Mass-Mediya; weekly; Editor-in-Chief YURII I. BELYAVSKII; circ. 30,000 (2008).

Literaturnaya Gazeta (Literary Newspaper): 109028 Moscow, Khokhlovskii per. 10/6; tel. and fax (499) 788-02-10; e-mail litgazeta@lgz.ru; internet www.lgz.ru; f. 1831; publ. restored 1929; weekly; literature, politics, society; controlled by Sistema Mass-Mediya; Editor-in-Chief YU. M. POLYAKOV.

Literaturnaya Rossiya (Literary Russia): 103051 Moscow, Tsvetnoi bulv. 32/3; tel. and fax (495) 694-50-10; e-mail litrossia@litrossia.ru; internet www.litrossia.ru; f. 1958; weekly; essays, verse, literary criticism; Editor VYACHESLAV OGRYZKO; circ. 19,650 (2007).

Oktyabr (October): 125040 Moscow, ul. Pravdy 11/13; tel. (495) 214-62-05; fax (495) 214-50-29; internet magazines.russ.ru/october/ f. 1924; monthly; independent literary journal; new fiction and essays by Russian and foreign writers; Editor-in-Chief IRINA N. BARMETOVA.

Sem Dnei (Seven Days): 125871 Moscow, Leningradskoye shosse 5A; tel. (495) 195-92-76; fax (495) 753-41-32; e-mail 7days@7days.ru; internet www.7days.ru; f. 1967; celebrity news and television listings magazine; Editor V. V. ORLOVA; circ. 937,000 (2000).

Znamya (Banner): 103001 Moscow, ul. B. Sadovaya 2/46; tel. (495) 299-52-38; e-mail info@znamlit.ru; internet magazines.russ.ru/znamia; f. 1931; monthly; independent; novels, poetry, essays; Editor-in-Chief SERGEI I. CHUPRININ; circ. 5,300 (2004).

Economics and Finance

Chelovek i Trud (Man and Labour): 105064 Moscow, Yakovoapostolskii per. 6/3; tel. and fax (495) 917-76-36; e-mail chelt@yandex.ru; internet www.chelt.ru; monthly; f. 1956 as *Sotsialisticheskii trud* (Socialist Labour); present name adopted 1992; employment issues, unemployment, social policy, pensions, personnel management etc.; Editor-in-Chief M. A. BARINOVA; circ. 10,000 (2005).

D': 125866 Moscow, Bumazhnyi proyezd 14/1; tel. (495) 609-64-98; fax (495) 228-00-78; e-mail shu@expert.ru; internet www.expert.ru/printissues/d; f. 2005; personal finance; Chief Editor TATYANA GUROVA; circ. 50,500 (2008).

Deloviye Lyudi (Business People): 123995 Moscow, ul. 1905 goda 7; tel. (495) 781-47-37; fax (495) 781-47-44; e-mail dl@mk.ru; internet www.dl.mk.ru; f. 1990; monthly; business, management and economics; Editor-in-Chief SERGEI I. ROGOZHKIN; circ. 50,000 (2007).

Dengi (Money): 125080 Moscow, ul. Vrubelya 4/1; tel. (499) 943-97-71; fax (499) 943-97-28; e-mail dengi@kommersant.ru; internet www.kommersant.ru/k-money; weekly; publ. by the Kommersant Publishing House; Chief Editor SERGEI YAKOVLEV.

Dengi i Kredit (Money and Credit): 107016 Moscow, ul. Neglinnaya 12; tel. (495) 771-99-87; fax (495) 771-99-93; e-mail ggv@cbr.ru; internet www.cbr.ru/publ/main.asp?Prtid=MoneyAndCredit; f. 1927; monthly; publ. by the Central Bank; all aspects of banking and money circulation; Chief Editor VLADIMIR S. PALEVICH; circ. 5,430 (2002).

Ekonomika i Zhizn (Economics and Life): 125319 Moscow, ul. Chernyakhovskogo 16; tel. and fax (495) 152-51-38; e-mail eg@ekonomika.ru; internet www.ekonomika.ru; f. 1918; weekly; fmrly *Ekonomicheskaya gazeta*; news and information about the economy and business; Editor TATYANA A. IVANOVA; circ. 150,000 (2005).

Ekspert (Expert): 127137 Moscow, ul. Pravdy 24, Novyi Gazetnyi kor., POB 33; tel. (495) 510-56-43; fax (495) 510-56-39; e-mail ask@expert.ru; internet www.expert.ru; weekly; business and economics; financial and share markets; policy and culture; regional edns: *Ekspert Severo-Zapad* (St Peterburg and North-Western Russia), *Ekspert Sibir* (Siberia), *Ekspert Ural* (Urals), *Ekspert Volga* (The Volga region), *Ekspert Yug* (Southern Russia); Editor-in-Chief VALERII FADEYEV.

Finans (Finance): 127238 Moscow, Lokomotivnyi proyezd 21A; tel. and fax (495) 788-53-10; e-mail inform@finansmag.ru; internet www.fr.ru; f. 2003; weekly; economics, business, finance, society; Editor-in-Chief OLEG ANISIMOV; circ. 48,700 (2007).

Finansy (Finances): 125009 Moscow, ul. Tverskaya 22B; tel. (495) 699-44-27; fax (495) 699-96-16; e-mail finance-journal@mail.ru; internet www.finance-journal.ru; f. 1926; monthly; theory and information on finances; compilation and execution of the state budget, insurance, lending, taxation etc.; Editor YU. M. ARTEMOV; circ. 10,000 (2004).

Kompaniya (The Firm): 109544 Moscow, ul. B. Andronyevskaya 17; tel. (495) 745-84-10; e-mail ko@idr.ru; internet www.ko.ru; f. 1997; weekly; politics, economics, finance; Editor-in-Chief ANDREI GRIGORYEV; circ. 78,000 (2007).

Mirovaya Ekonomika i Mezhdunarodniye Otnosheniya (World Economy and International Relations): 117859 Moscow, ul. Profsoyuznaya 23; tel. (495) 128-08-83; fax (495) 310-70-27; e-mail memojour@imemo.ru; internet www.imemo.ru; f. 1957; monthly; journal of the Institute of the World Economy and International

Relations of the Russian Academy of Sciences; theory and practice of socio-economic development, international policies, economic co-operation; Editor A. V. RYABOV.

Profil (Profile): 109544 Moscow, ul. B. Andronyevskaya 17; tel. (495) 745-94-01; e-mail web@idr.ru; internet www.profil.orc.ru; f. 1996; weekly; Editor-in-Chief MIKHAIL LEONTYEV; circ. 83,000 in Russia and 27,600 in Ukraine (2007).

Rossiiskii Ekonomicheskii Zhurnal (Russian Economic Journal): 109542 Moscow, Ryazanskii pr. 99; tel. and fax (495) 377-25-56; internet www.e-rej.ru; f. 1958; monthly; economics; Editor A. YU. MELENTEV; circ. 6,100 (2004).

Voprosy Ekonomiki (Questions of Economics): 117218 Moscow, Nakhimovskii pr. 32; tel. and fax (495) 124-52-28; e-mail mail@vopreco.ru; internet www.vopreco.ru; f. 1929; monthly; journal of the Institute of Economics of the Russian Academy of Sciences; theoretical problems of economic development, market relations, social aspects of transition to a market economy, international economics, etc.; Editor L. ABALKIN; circ. 6,000 (2008).

Education

Semya (The Family): 107996 Moscow, Orlikov per. 5; tel. (495) 975-05-29; fax (495) 975-00-76; e-mail mail@semya.ru; internet www.semya.ru; f. 1988; weekly; Editor-in-Chief SERGEI A. ABRAMOV; circ. 50,000 (2004).

Semya i Shkola (Family and School): 129278 Moscow, ul. P. Korchagina 7; tel. (495) 683-82-21; fax (495) 683-86-14; e-mail mag7a@narod.ru; internet www.mag7a.narod.ru; f. 1871; monthly; for parents and children; Editor-in-Chief P. I. GELAZONIYA; circ. 3,000 (2007).

Shkola i Proizvodstvo (School and Production): 127254 Moscow, ul. Sh. Rustaveli 10/3; tel. and fax (495) 219-83-80; e-mail sip@schoolpress.ru; internet www.schoolpress.ru/jornal/issues/sip/index.php; f. 1957; 8 a year; Chief Editor G. V. PICHUGINA; circ. 17,000 (2007).

Uchitelskaya Gazeta (Teachers' Gazette): 107045 Moscow, Ananyevskii per. 4/2/1; tel. (495) 928-82-53; fax (495) 928-82-53; e-mail ug@ug.ru; internet www.ug.ru; f. 1924; weekly; independent; Editor PETR POLOZHEVETS; circ. 95,000 (2007).

International Affairs

Ekho Planety (Echo of the Planet): 103860 Moscow, Tverskoi bulv. 10/12; tel. (495) 202-67-48; fax (495) 290-59-11; e-mail echotex@itar-tass.com; internet www.explan.ru; f. 1988; weekly; publ. by ITAR—TASS; international affairs, economic, social and cultural; Editor-in-Chief VALENTIN VASILETS.

Mezhdunarodnaya Zhizn (International Life): 105064 Moscow, Gorokhovskii per. 14; tel. (495) 265-37-81; fax (495) 265-37-71; e-mail inter_affairs@mid.ru; f. 1954; monthly; Russian and English; publ. by the Pressa Publishing House; foreign policy and diplomacy; Editor-in-Chief B. D. PYADYSHEV; circ. 70,000.

Novoye Vremya—The New Times: 125009 Moscow, Tverskoi bulv. 14/1; tel. (495) 648-07-60; fax (495) 648-07-61; e-mail info@newtimes.ru; internet www.newtimes.ru; f. 1943; weekly; foreign and Russian affairs; Editor-in-Chief IRENA LESNEVSKAYA.

Russkii Reporter (Russian Reporter): 125866 Moscow, Bumazhnyi proyezd 14/1; tel. (495) 609-66-74; e-mail reporter@expert.ru; internet www.expert.ru/printissues/russian_reporter; f. 2007; monthly; domestic and international affairs and culture; Chief Editor VITALII LEIBIN.

Language and Literature

Ex Libris-NG: 113935 Moscow, ul. Myasnitskaya 13; tel. (495) 928-48-50; fax (495) 975-23-46; e-mail ex@ng.ru; internet exlibris.ng.ru; weekly; literature; Editor-in-Chief IGOR ZOTOV.

Russkaya Literatura (Russian Literature): 199034 St Petersburg, nab. Makarova 4; tel. (812) 328-16-01; fax (812) 328-16-01; e-mail musliter@mail.ru; f. 1958; quarterly; journal of the Institute of Russian Literature of the Russian Academy of Sciences; development of Russian literature from its appearance up to the present day; Editor N. N. SKATOV; circ. 1,099 (2004).

Voprosy Literatury (Questions of Literature): 125009 Moscow, B. Gnezdnikovskii per. 10; tel. (495) 629-49-77; fax (495) 629-64-71; e-mail vopli@arion.ru; internet magazines.russ.ru/voplit; f. 1957; 6 a year; publ. by Foundation for Literary Criticism; theory and history of modern literature and aesthetics; Editor L. I. LAZAREV; circ. 2,500 (2007).

Leisure and Sport

Afisha (Poster): 103009 Moscow, per. B. Gnezdnikovski 7/28/1; tel. (495) 785-17-00; fax (495) 785-17-01; e-mail info@afisha.net; internet www.afisha.ru; f. 1999; every 2 weeks; listings and reviews of events;

3 edns, for Moscow, St Petersburg, and the rest of Russia; Chief Editor YURII SAPRYKIN.

Avtopilot (Autopilot): 123308 Moscow, Khoroshevskoye shosse 41; tel. (495) 493-91-44; fax (495) 493-91-64; e-mail autopilot@ kommersant.ru; internet autopilot.kommersant.ru; cars; publ. by the Kommersant Publishing House; Editor-in-Chief ALEKSANDR FEDOROV.

Bolshoi Gorod (Big City): 125009 Moscow, B. Gnezdnikovskii per 7/ 28/1; tel. (495) 785-17-00; fax (495) 785-17-01; e-mail info@bg.ru; internet www.bg.ru; f. 2001; every two weeks; Moscow and St Petersburg edns; culture, travel, technology; Chief Editors FILIPP DZYADKO (Moscow edn), YULIYA TARNAVSKAYA (St Petersburg edn).

Fizkultura i Sport (Exercise and Sport): 125130 Moscow, per. 6-i Novopodmoskovnii 3, POB 198; tel. (495) 786-60-62; fax (495) 786-61-39; e-mail fisemail@mtu-net.ru; internet www.fismag.ru; f. 1922; monthly; activities and development of Russian sports, health; Editor I. SOSNOVSKII.

Rossiiskaya Okhotnichya Gazeta (Russian Hunters' Magazine): 123995 Moscow, ul. 1905 Goda 7; tel. (495) 256-94-74; e-mail rog@mk .ru; internet www.mk.ru/blogs/idmk/ROG; weekly; hunting, shooting, fishing; Editor-in-Chief PAVEL GUSEV.

Sport Ekspress (Sport Express): 123056 Moscow, ul. Krasina 27/2; tel. (495) 254-47-87; fax (495) 733-93-08; e-mail sport@sport-express .ru; internet www.sport-express.ru; f. 1991; daily; sport; Editor-in-Chief VLADIMIR KUCHMII; circ. in Moscow and St Petersburg 190,000 (2004).

Sovetskii Sport (Soviet Sport): 103287 Moscow, Staryi Petrovsko-Razumovskii proyezd 1/23/1; tel. (495) 637-64-33; fax (495) 637-64-24; e-mail sport@sovsport.ru; internet www.sovsport.ru; f. 1924; weekly; Editor-in-Chief IGOR KOTS.

Za Rulem (Behind The Wheel): 103045 Moscow, per. Selivyerstov 10; tel. (495) 607-23-82; fax (495) 737-43-07; e-mail stas@zr.ru; internet www.zr.ru; f. 1928; monthly; cars and motorsport; Editor-in-Chief PETR S. MENSHIKH.

Politics and Military Affairs

Litsa (People): 121099 Moscow, Smolenskaya pl. 13/21, POB 99; tel. (495) 241-37-92; e-mail litsa@aha.ru; f. 1996; monthly; Editor-in-Chief ARTEM BOROVIK; circ. 100,000 (2002).

Na Dne (The Lower Depths): 195112 St Petersburg, Novocherkasskii pr. 37/1A; tel. (812) 528-04-14; fax (812) 310-52-09; f. 1994; current affairs; social issues; 2 a month.

Nezavisimoye Voyennoye Obozreniye (Independent Military Review): 101000 Moscow, ul. Myasnitskaya 13; tel. and fax (495) 925-88-29; internet nvo.ng.ru; f. 1995; Editor VADIM SOLOVYEV; circ. 20,140 (2004).

Rossiya v Globalnoi Politike/Russia in Global Affairs: 103873 Moscow, ul. Mokhovaya 11/3v; tel. (495) 980-73-53; fax (495) 937-76-11; e-mail info@globalaffairs.ru; internet www.globalaffairs.ru; f. 2002; co-founded by the Russian Union of Industrialists and Entrepreneurs, the Council for Foreign and Defence Politics and the newspaper *Izvestiya*, in collaboration with the US journal, *Foreign Affairs*; 6 a year (Russian); 4 a year (English); online edns in Czech and Polish; Chair. of Editorial Bd SERGEI A. KARAGANOV; Editor-in-Chief FEDOR A. LUKYANOV.

Rossiiskaya Federatsiya Segodnya (The Russian Federation Today): 103800 Moscow, ul. M. Dmitrovka 3/10; tel. (495) 933-54-79; fax (495) 933-54-74; e-mail rfs@russia-today.ru; internet www .russia-today.ru; f. 1994; journal of the Gosudarstvennaya Duma; Editor YURII A. KHRENOV.

Russia Profile: 119021 Moscow, Zubovskii bulv. 4; tel. (495) 981-64-86; fax (495) 201-30-71; e-mail info@russiaprofile.org; f. 1966; monthly; in English; publ. by Independent Media for RIA-Novosti in association with the International Relations and Security Network (Zurich, Switzerland) and the Center for Defense Information (Washington, DC, USA); Editor ANDREI ZOLOTOV, Jr.

Shchit i Mech (Shield and Sword): 127434 Moscow, Ivanovskii pr. 18; tel. (495) 976-66-44; fax (495) 619-80-90; e-mail gazeta@simech .ru; internet www.simech.ru; f. 1989; weekly; military, security, geopolitical concerns; publ. by the Ministry of Internal Affairs; Editor-in-Chief VALERII KULIK; circ. 50,000 (2004).

Sovershenno Sekretno (Top Secret): 121099 Moscow, Smolenskaya pl. 13/21, POB 255; tel. (495) 241-68-73; fax (495) 241-75-55; e-mail velekhov@topsecret.cnt.ru; internet sovsekretno.ru; f. 1989; monthly; Editor-in-Chief GALINA SIDOROVA.

Vlast (Power): 123308 Moscow, Khoroshevskoye shosse 41; tel. (499) 943-97-71; fax (499) 234-16-60; e-mail vlast@kommersant.ru; internet www.kommersant.ru/k-vlast; f. 1997; weekly; Chief Editor MAKSIM KOVALSKII.

Yezhenedelnyi Zhurnal (Weekly Magazine): 129110 Moscow, Pereyaslavskii per. 4; tel. (495) 785-82-50; fax (495) 785-82-51;

e-mail info@ej.ru; internet www.ej.ru; f. 2001; Editor-in-Chief SERGEI PARKHOMENKO.

Zavtra (Tomorrow): 119146 Moscow, Frunzenskaya nab. 18/60; tel. (495) 726-54-83; e-mail zavtra@zavtra.ru; internet www.zavtra.ru; extreme left, nationalist; Editor-in-Chief ALEKSANDR A. PROGANOV.

Popular, Fiction and General

Inostrannaya Literatura (Foreign Literature): 109017 Moscow, ul. Pyatnitskaya 41; tel. (495) 953-51-47; fax (495) 953-50-61; e-mail inolit@rinet.ru; internet magazines.russ.ru/inostran; f. 1891; monthly; independent; Russian translations of modern foreign authors and literary criticism; Editor-in-Chief ALEKSEI SLOVESNII.

Molotok (Little Hammer): 125080 Moscow, vul. Vrubelya 4; tel. (495) 209-11-32; fax (495) 200-40-55; e-mail molotok@unity .kommersant.ru; internet www.zabey.ru; f. 2000; weekly; popular culture.

Nash Sovremennik (Our Contemporary): 127994 Moscow, Tsvetnoi bulv. 32/2; tel. (495) 200-24-24; fax (495) 200-24-12; e-mail mail@ nash-sovremennik.ru; internet nash-sovremennik.ru; f. 1956; monthly; publ. by the Union of Writers of Russia; contemporary prose and 'patriotic polemics'; Editor STANISLAV KUNAYEV.

Novyi Krokodil (New Crocodile): 129090 Moscow, Potapovskii per. 3, POB 94; tel. (495) 956-37-17; e-mail crocodile@vf-m.ru; internet www.crocodile.su; f. 2005 to replace *Krokodil* (Crododile—founded 1922); monthly; satirical; Editor SERGEI MOSTOVSHCHIKOV.

Novyi Mir (New World): 103806 Moscow, M. Putinkovskii per. 1/2; tel. and fax (495) 200-08-29; e-mail nmir@aha.ru; internet magazines .russ.ru/novyi_mi; f. 1925; monthly; publ. by the Izvestiya (News) Publishing House; new fiction and essays; Editor ANDREI V. VASILEVSKII; circ.c. 8,000 (2005).

Ogonek (Beacon): 127055 Moscow, ul. Lesnaya 55/1–2; tel. (495) 660-94-47; fax (499) 973-14-30; e-mail ogoniok@ogoniokpress.ru; internet www.ogoniok.com; f. 1899; weekly; politics, popular science, economics, literature; Editor VIKTOR LOSHAK; circ. 69,000 (2007).

Politicheskii Klass (The Political Class): 119002 Moscow, per. Sivtsev Vrazhek 29/16/415; tel. (495) 241-43-67; e-mail info@ politklass.ru; internet politklass.ru; f. 2004; monthly; domestic and international affairs, philosophy and politics; Chief Editor V. T. TRETYAKOV.

Rodina (Motherland): 127025 Moscow, ul. Novyi Arbat 19; tel. (495) 203-75-98; fax (495) 203-47-45; e-mail istrodina@mail.ru; internet www.istrodina.com; f. 1989 as revival of 1879–1917 publication; monthly; publ. by Administration of the President of the Russian Federation and Government of the Russian Federation; popular historical; supplement *Istochnik* (Source), every two months, documents state archives; Chief Editor YURII BORISENOK; circ. 20,000 (2003).

Rodnaya Gazeta (Native Gazette): 125137 Moscow, ul. Pravdy 24/2; tel. (495) 789-44-00; fax (495) 789-44-01; e-mail info@rodgaz.ru; internet www.rodgaz.ru; f. 2003; weekly; politics, culture, nationalist, left-wing; Editor-in-Chief ALEKSANDR KOLODNYI.

Rossiiskii Kto Yest Kto (Russian Who's Who): 117335 Moscow, POB 81; tel. (495) 234-46-92; e-mail zhurnal@whoiswho.ru; internet www.whoiswho.ru; 2 a year; biographical and directory material; Editor-in-Chief SVYATOSLAV RYBAS; circ. 10,000.

Sobesednik (Interlocutor): 101484 Moscow, ul. Novoslobodskaya 73, POB 4; tel. (495) 685-56-65; fax (495) 973-20-54; e-mail info@ sobesednik.ru; internet www.sobesednik.ru; f. 1984; weekly; Editor-in-Chief YURII PILIPENKO.

SPID-Info: 125284 Moscow, POB 42; tel. (495) 255-02-99; fax (495) 252-09-20; e-mail mail@si.ru; internet www.s-info.ru; f. 1991; two a month; popular; Editor-in-Chief OLGA BELAN; Gen. Dir IGOR SAZONOV; circ. 850,000 (2008).

Versiya (Possibility): 121099 Moscow, Smolenskaya pl. 13/21, POB 255; tel. (495) 291-23-76; e-mail versia@topsecret.cnt.ru; internet www.versiasovsek.ru; f. 1998; weekly; Editor-in-Chief A. V. BOKSHITSKAYA.

Vokrug Sveta (Around the World): 125015 Moscow, ul. Argunovskaya 12/1/6A; tel. (495) 491-96-45; fax (495) 490-57-25; e-mail editor@ vokrugsveta.ru; internet www.vokrugsveta.ru; f. 1861; monthly; geographical, travel and adventure; illustrated; Chief Editor YELENA KNYAZEVA (acting).

Zvezda (Star): 191028 St Petersburg, ul. Mokhovaya 20; tel. (812) 272-71-38; fax (812) 273-52-56; e-mail mail@zvezdaspb.ru; internet zvezdaspb.ru; f. 1923; monthly; publ. by the Zvezda Publishing House; novels, short stories, poetry and literary criticism; Editors A. YU. ARYEV, YA. A. GORDIN.

Popular Scientific

Meditsinskaya Gazeta (Medical Gazette): 129090 Moscow, B. Sukharevskaya pl. 1/2; tel. (495) 608-86-95; fax (495) 208-69-80;

e-mail inform@mgzt.ru; internet www.mgzt.ru; f. 1938; 2 a week; professional international periodical; Editor ANDREI POLTORAK.

Nauka i Zhizn (Science and Life): 101990 Moscow, ul. Myasnitskaya 24; tel. (495) 624-18-35; fax (495) 200-22-59; e-mail mail@nkj.ru; internet www.nkj.ru; f. 1890, resumed 1934; monthly; recent developments in all branches of science and technology; Chief Editor I. K. LAGOVSKII; circ. 46,000 (2007).

PC Week: 109047 Moscow, ul. Marksistskaya 34/10; tel. (495) 974-22-60; fax (495) 974-22-63; e-mail editorial@pcweek.ru; internet www.pcweek.ru; f. 1995; 48 a year; Editor-in-Chief EDUARD PROYDAKOV.

Priroda (Nature): 117810 Moscow, Maronovskii per. 26; tel. (495) 238-24-56; fax (495) 238-26-33; f. 1912; monthly; publ. by the Nauka (Science) Publishing House; journal of the Presidium of the Academy of Sciences; natural sciences; Editor A. F. ANDREYEV.

Radio: 107045 Moscow, per. Seliverstov 10/1; tel. (495) 207-31-18; fax (495) 208-77-13; internet www.radio.ru; f. 1924; monthly; audio, video, communications, practical electronics, computers; Editor Y. I. KRYLOV.

Tekhnika-Molodezhi (Engineering—For Youth): 127051 Moscow, ul. Petrovka 26/3, POB 94; tel. (495) 625-17-41; fax (495) 628-34-79; e-mail post@tm-magazin.ru; internet www.tm-magazin.ru; f. 1933; monthly; engineering and science; Editor A. N. PEREVOZCHIKOV.

Vrach (Physician): 119991 Moscow, ul. Trubetskaya 8/2; tel. and fax (499) 766-07-57; e-mail rvrach@mmascience.ru; internet www.rusvrach.ru; f. 1990; monthly; medical, scientific and socio-political; illustrated; Editor-in-Chief I. N. DENISOV; circ. 3,700 (2004).

Zdorovye (Health): 127994 Moscow, Bumazhnyi proyezd 14/1; tel. (495) 250-58-28; fax (495) 257-32-51; e-mail zdorovie@zdr.ru; internet www.zdr.ru; f. 1955; monthly; Editor TATYANA YEFIMOVA; circ. 170,000 (2006).

The Press, Printing and Bibliography

Bibliografiya (Bibliography): 119019 Moscow, Kremlevskaya nab. 1/9; tel. (499) 766-00-85; e-mail bibliogr@bookchamber.ru; internet www.bookchamber.ru/international/bibliography_mag.html; f. 1929; 6 a year; theoretical, practical and historical aspects of bibliography; Editor K. M. SUKHORUKOV; circ. 2,300 (2005).

Poligrafist i Izdatel (Printer and Publisher): 119313 Moscow, Leninskii pr. 87/392-395; tel. (499) 134-78-43; fax (495) 288-94-44; e-mail mediarama@mediarama.ru; internet www.mediarama.ru/pp/pp.html; f. 1994; monthly; Editor A. I. OVSYANNIKOV; circ. 3,000 (2008).

Poligrafiya (Printing): 129272 Moscow, ul. Sushchevskii Val 64; tel. and fax (495) 681-74-81; e-mail polimag@aha.ru; internet www.polimag.ru; f. 1924; 6 a year; equipment and technology of the printing industry; Dir N. N. KONDRATIYEVA; circ. 5,000 (2007).

Zhurnalist (Journalist): 125190 Moscow, Chezniyahovskogo ul. 16; tel. (495) 152-88-71; e-mail jour-nal@yandex.ru; internet www.journalist-virt.ru; f. 1920; monthly; publ. by Ekonomicheskaya Gazeta Publishing House; Editor G. P. MALTSEV; circ. 10,150 (2007).

Religion

Bratskii Vestnik (Herald of the Brethren): 109028 Moscow, M. Vuzovskii per. 3; tel. (495) 917-96-26; internet moscowseminary.ru/bv/index.html; f. 1945; 6 a year; organ of the Russian Union of Evangelical Christians-Baptists; Chief Editor VITALII KULIKOV.

Istina i Zhizn (Truth and Life): 105264 Moscow, ul. 7-aya Parkovaya 26/1/303; tel. and fax (495) 786-35-89; e-mail istina@aha.ru; internet istina.religare.ru; f. 1990; inter-confessional magazine of Christian culture; monthly; Editor Fr ALEKSANDR KHMELNITSKII.

Mezhdunarodnaya Yevreyskaya Gazeta (International Jewish Newspaper): 107005 Moscow, Pleteshkovskii per. 3A; tel. and fax (495) 225-44-84; e-mail meg@spacenet.ru; internet www.jig.ru; f. 1989; weekly; Dir-Gen. YAKOV POLISCHUK; circ. 15,000 (2002).

NG-Religii (The Independent-Religions): 101000 Moscow, ul. Myasnitskaya 13; tel. (495) 923-42-40; fax (495) 921-58-47; e-mail ngr@ng.ru; internet religion.ng.ru; f. 1997; analysis of religious affairs and their domestic and global social and political implications; 2 a month; Editor-in-Chief MAKSIM SHEVCHENKO.

Tserkovnyi Vestnik (Church Herald): 119435 Moscow, ul. Pogodinskaya 20/2; tel. and fax (495) 246-01-65; e-mail info03@rop.ru; internet www.tserkov.info; f. 1989; 24 a year; organ of the Russian Orthodox Church (Moscow Patriarchate); Editor-in-Chief Very Rev. VLADIMIR SILOVYEV; circ. 30,000 (2005).

Yevreiskoye Slovo (The Jewish Word): 127018 Moscow, 2-i Vysheslavtsev per. 5A; tel. (495) 792-31-13; e-mail redaktor@e-slovo.ru; internet www.e-slovo.ru; f. 2000; Editor-in-Chief VLADIMIR DYNKIN.

Zhurnal Moskovskoi Patriarkhii (Journal of the Moscow Patriarchate): 119435 Moscow, ul. Pogodinskaya 20/2; tel. (495) 246-98-48; fax (495) 246-21-41; e-mail eugpol@rop.ru; internet www.jmp.ru;

f. 1934; monthly; official publication of the Russian Orthodox Church (Moscow Patriarchate); Editor Archpriest VLADIMIR (SILOVYEV).

Transport and Communication

Grazhdanskaya Aviatsiya (Civil Aviation): 125993 Moscow, Leningradskii pr. 37; tel. (495) 155-59-23; fax (495) 155-51-64; f. 1931; monthly; journal of the Union of Civil Aviation Workers; development of air transport; utilization of aviation in construction, agriculture and forestry; Editor A. M. TROSHIN.

Radiotekhnika (Radio Engineering): 103031 Moscow, Kuznetskii most 20/6/31; tel. (495) 921-48-37; fax (495) 925-92-41; e-mail iprzhr@online.ru; f. 1937; monthly; publ. by the Svyaz (Communication) Publishing House; journal of the A. S. Popov Scientific and Technical Society of Radio Engineering, Electronics and Electrical Communication; theoretical and technical problems of radio engineering; other publications include Advances in Radio Science, Radio Systems and Antennae; Editor YU. V. GULYAYEV.

Vestnik Svyazi (Herald of Communication): 101000 Moscow, Krivokolennyi per. 14/1; tel. (495) 625-42-57; fax (495) 621-27-97; e-mail vs@vestnik-sviazy.ru; internet www.vestnik-sviazy.ru; f. 1917; monthly; telecommunications; Editor E. B. KONSTANTINOV.

Women's Interest

Domovoi (House-Sprite): 113035 Moscow, ul. B. Ordynka 16; tel. (495) 675-52-48; e-mail dom@kommersant.ru; internet www.domovoy.ru; monthly; Chief Editor VALERIYA KUDRYAVTSEVA.

Elle: 115162 Moscow, ul. Shabolovka 31B; tel. (495) 891-39-10; e-mail achukovskaya@hfs.ru; internet www.elle.ru; f. 1996; monthly; fashion; Editor-in-Chief YELENA SOTNIKOVA.

Krestyanka (Peasant Woman): 127994 Moscow, Bumazhnyi proyezd 14; tel. (495) 257-39-39; fax (495) 257-39-63; e-mail mail@krestyanka.ru; internet www.krestyanka.ru; f. 1922; monthly; publ. by the Krestyanka Publishing House; popular; supplements *Khozyayushka* (Dear Hostess), *On i ona* (He and She), *Moda v dome* (Fashion at Home), *Samochuvstviye* (Health), *Nasha Usadba* (Our Garden), *Pyatnashki* (Game of Tag); Pres. and Editor-in-Chief ANASTASIYA V. KUPRIYANOVA; circ. 85,000 (2004).

Mir Zhenshchiny (Woman's World): 101999 Moscow, Glinishchevskii per. 6; tel. and fax (495) 209-95-33; f. 1945; monthly; fmrly *Zhenshchina* (Woman); in Russian, Chinese, English, French, German and Spanish; fmrly publ. by the Soviet Women's Committee and the General Confederation of Trade Unions; popular; illustrated; Editor-in-Chief V. I. FEDOTOVA.

Rabotnitsa (Working Woman): 101458 Moscow, Bumazhnyi proyezd 14; tel. (495) 257-36-49; fax (495) 956-90-94; e-mail webmaster@rabotnitsa.ru; internet www.rabotnitsa.ru; f. 1914; monthly; popular; Editor ZOYA P. KRYLOVA.

Youth

Rovesnik (Contemporary): 125015 Moscow, ul. Novodmitrovskaya 5A; tel. (495) 285-89-20; fax (495) 285-06-27; e-mail rovesnik@rovesnik.ru; internet www.rovesnik.ru/dom/rovesnik.asp; f. 1962; popular illustrated monthly of fiction, music, cinema, sport for 10–19 year olds; Editor I. A. CHERNYSHKOV; circ. 70,000 (2007).

Smena (The Rising Generation): 127994 Moscow, Bumazhnyi proyezd 19/2; tel. (495) 612-15-07; fax (495) 250-59-28; e-mail jurnal@smena-id.ru; internet www.smena-id.ru; f. 1924; monthly; popular illustrated, short stories, essays and problems of youth; Editor-in-Chief M. G. KIZILOV.

Yunost (Youth): 125047 Moscow, ul. Tverskaya-Yamskaya 8/1, POB 182; tel. and fax (495) 250-40-74; e-mail unost-contact@mail.ru; internet www.unost.org; f. 1955; monthly; novels, short stories, essays and poems by beginners; Editor TAMARA ANDREYEVA.

NEWS AGENCIES

ANP—Agentstvo novostei i prognozy (News and Forecasting Agency): 103009 Moscow, Kalashnyi per. 10/2; tel. (495) 782-33-71; fax (495) 153-57-45; e-mail aninons@online.ru; f. 2001 on basis of ANI News and Information Agency (f. 1991); Editor-in-Chief ALEKSEI SHCHAVELEV.

Interfax: 127006 Moscow, ul. 1-aya Tverskaya-Yamskaya 2; tel. (495) 250-98-40; fax (495) 250-97-27; e-mail info@interfax.ru; internet www.interfax.ru; f. 1989; independent information agency; Chief Exec. MIKHAIL KOMISSAR.

ITAR—TASS (Information Telegraphic Agency of Russia—Telegraphic Agency of the Sovereign Countries): 125993 Moscow, Tverskoi bulv. 10/12; tel. (495) 202-29-81; fax (495) 202-54-74; e-mail worldmarket@itar-tass.com; internet www.itar-tass.com; f. 1904 as St Petersburg Telegraph Agency, renamed as TASS (Telegraph Agency of the Soviet Union) in 1925; present name adopted 1992; state information agency; 74 bureaux in Russia and the states of the former USSR, 65 foreign bureaux outside the former USSR; Dir-Gen. VITALII N. IGNATENKO.

Prima Human Rights News Agency: 111399 Moscow, POB 5; tel. and fax (495) 455-30-11; e-mail prima@prima-news.ru; internet www.prima-news.ru; f. 2000; Editor-in-Chief ALEKSANDR PODRABI-NEK.

RIA—Novosti (Russian Information Agency—News): 103786 Moscow, Zubovskii bulv. 4; tel. (495) 201-82-09; fax (495) 201-45-45; e-mail marketing@rian.ru; internet www.rian.ru; f. 1961 as Agenstvo Pechati 'Novosti' (APN); present name adopted 1991; collaborates by arrangement with foreign press and publishing organizations in 110 countries; provider of Russian news features and photographs; Chair. SVETLANA MIRONYUK.

RosBalt Information Agency: 190000 St Petersburg, Konnogvardeiskii bulv. 7; tel. (812) 320-50-30; fax (812) 320-50-31; e-mail rosbalt@rosbalt.ru; internet www.rosbalt.ru; news coverage of European Russia and other countries in northern Europe; Chair. NATALIYA CHERKESOVA.

Rossiiskoye Informatsionnoye Agentstvo 'Oreanda' (RIA 'Oreanda'): 117342 Moscow, POB 21; tel. (495) 330-98-50; fax (495) 23-04-39; e-mail info@oreanda.ru; internet www.oreanda.ru; f. 1994.

Strana.Ru (Country-Russia): 119021 Moscow, Zubovskii bulv. 4, podyezd 8; tel. (495) 981-62-52; fax (495) 981-62-53; e-mail mail@strana.ru; internet www.strana.ru; f. 2000; news agency; central bureau in Moscow, regional bureaux in Groznyi (Chechen—Nokchi Republic) and in Kyiv, Ukraine; controlled by the All-Russian State Television and Radio Broadcasting Company (VGTRK); Editor-in-Chief YULIYA PANFILOVA.

PRESS ASSOCIATIONS

Russian Guild of Publishers of Periodical Press: 125047 Moscow, ul. Lesnaya 20/6-211; tel. and fax (495) 978-41-89.

Union of Journalists of Russia: 119021 Moscow, Zubovskii bulv. 4; tel. (495) 201-51-01; fax (495) 201-35-47; f. 1991; Sec.-Gen. IGOR YAKOVENKO.

Publishers

Ad Marginem-Ad Patres: Moscow; e-mail ad_marg@livejournal .com; internet ad-marg.livejournal.com; f. 1994; fiction, philosophy, artistic and literary criticism; Dir ALEKSANDR IVANOV.

Aleteiya (Aletheia): 193019 St Petersburg, pr. Obukhovskoi oborony 13; tel. (812) 567-22-39; e-mail aleteia@rol.ru; internet www .orthodoxia.org/aletheia; f. 1992; classics, ancient and medieval history, social sciences; Dir-Gen. I. A. SAVKIN.

AST: 129085 Moscow, Zvezdnyi bulv. 21; tel. (495) 215-01-01; fax (495) 215-51-10; e-mail astpub@aha.ru; internet www.ast.ru; original and translated fiction and non-fiction, children's and schoolbooks.

Avrora (Aurora): 191065 St Petersburg, Nevskii pr. 7/9; tel. (812) 312-37-53; fax (812) 312-54-60; e-mail aurora@mail.nevalink.ru; f. 1969; fine arts; Dir ZENOBIUS SPETCHINSKII.

Azbuka (Alphabet): 196105 St Petersburg, ul. Reshetnikova 15, POB 192; tel. (812) 327-04-55; fax (812) 327-01-60; e-mail post@ azbooka.spb.ru; internet www.azbooka.ru; literary fiction, including translations; f. 1995; Dir-Gen. MAKSIM I. KRYUTCHENKO.

Bolshaya Rossiiskaya Entsiklopediya (The Great Russian Encyclopedia): 109028 Moscow, Pokrovskii bulv. 8; tel. (495) 917-90-00; fax (495) 916-01-22; e-mail secretar@greatbook.ru; internet www .greatbook.ru; f. 1925; encyclopedias and reference; Dir-Gen. NIKOLAI S. ARTEMOV.

Detskaya Entsiklopediya (Children's Encyclopedia): 107042 Moscow, ul. Bakuninskaya 55; tel. (495) 269-52-76; f. 1933; science fiction, literature, poetry, biographical and historical novels.

Drofa: 127018 Moscow, ul. Sushchevskii Val 49; tel. (495) 795-05-50; fax (495) 795-05-44; e-mail info@drofa.ru; internet www.drofa.ru; f. 1991; school textbooks, children's fiction; Dir-Gen. ALEKSANDR F. KISELEV.

Ekonomika (Economy): 123955 Moscow, Berezhkovskaya nab. 6; tel. (499) 240-58-18; fax (499) 240-48-178; e-mail info@economizdat .ru; internet www.economizdat.ru; f. 1963; various aspects of economics, management and marketing; Dir YELIZABETA V. POLIYEVKTOVA.

Eksmo: 127299 Moscow, ul. K. Tsetkina 18/5; tel. and fax (495) 411-68-86; e-mail info@eksmo.ru; internet www.eksmo.ru; f. 1991; fiction; Gen. Dir OLEG YE. NOVIKOV.

Energoatomizdat (Atomic Energy Press): 113114 Moscow, Shluzovaya nab. 10; tel. (495) 925-99-93; f. 1981; different kinds of energy, nuclear science and technology; Dir A. P. ALESHKIN.

Finansy i Statistika (Finance and Statistics): 101000 Moscow, ul. Pokrovka 7; tel. (495) 625-47-08; fax (495) 625-09-57; e-mail mail@ finstat.ru; internet www.finstat.ru; f. 1924; education, economics, tourism, finance, statistics, banking, insurance, accounting, computer science; Dir Dr ALEVTINA N. ZVONOVA.

Forum: 101000 Moscow, Kolpachnyi per. 9A; tel. and fax (495) 625-52-43; e-mail mail@forum-books.ru; internet www.forum-books.ru; f. 2001; general and professional educational textbooks; Gen. Man. SVETLANA P. SILVANOVICH.

Galart: 125319 Moscow, ul. Chernyakhovskogo 4; tel. and fax (495) 151-25-02; e-mail galart@m9com.ru; internet www.galart-moscow .ru; f. 1969; fmrly Sovetskii Khudozhnik (Soviet Artist); art reproduction, art history and criticism; Gen. Dir A. D. SARABYANOV.

Gorodets: 109386 Moscow, ul. Krasnodonskaya 20/2; tel. and fax (495) 351-55-80; e-mail info@gorodets.com; internet www.gorodets .com; f. 1996; law, politics, international relations, economics.

INFRA-M: 127282 Moscow, ul. Polyarnara 31B; tel. and fax (495) 363-42-60; e-mail books@infra-m.ru; internet www.infra-m.ru; f. 1992; economics, law, computing, history, reference works, encyclopedias; Man. Dir VADIM D. SINYANSKII.

Izobrazitelnoye Iskusstvo (Fine Art): 129272 Moscow, ul. Sushchevskii Val 64; tel. (495) 681-65-48; fax (495) 681-41-11; e-mail iskusstvo@id.ru; reproductions of pictures, pictorial art, books on art, albums, calendars, postcards; Dir G. SH. YERITSYAN.

Khimiya (Chemistry): 107976 Moscow, ul. Strominka 21/2; tel. (495) 268-29-76; f. 1963; chemistry and the chemical industry; Dir BORIS S. KRASNOPEVTSEV.

Khudozhestvennaya Literatura (Fiction): 107078 Moscow, ul. Novobasmannaya 19; tel. (499) 261-88-65; fax (499) 261-83-00; fiction and works of literary criticism, history of literature, etc.; Dir A. N. PETROV; Editor-in-Chief V. S. MODESTOV.

Kolos (Ear of Corn): 107996 Moscow, ul. Sadovaya-Spasskaya 18/1; tel. (495) 207-19-45; fax (495) 207-28-70; internet www.koloc.ru; f. 1999; all agricultural production; Dir ANATOLII M. ULYANOV.

Kompozitor (Composer): 119034 Moscow, M. Levshinskii per. 7/2; tel. (495) 955-19-66; fax (495) 209-54-98; e-mail komp@kompubl.com; internet www.idk.su; f. 1957; music and music criticism; Dir GRIGORII A. VORONOV.

Meditsina (Medicine): 101838 Moscow, Petroverigskii per. 6/8; tel. (495) 924-87-85; fax (495) 928-60-03; e-mail meditsina@iname.com; internet www.medlit.ru; f. 1918; state-owned; imprint of Association for Medical Literature; books and journals on medicine and health; Dir A. M. STOCHIK.

Mezhdunarodnye Otnosheniya (International Relations): 107078 Moscow, ul. Sadovaya-Spasskaya 18/709; tel. (495) 207-67-93; fax (495) 200-22-04; e-mail info@inter-rel.ru; internet www .inter-rel.ru; f. 1957; international relations, economics and politics of foreign countries, foreign trade, international law, foreign language textbooks and dictionaries, translations and publications for the UN and other international organizations; Dir B. P. LIKHACHEV.

Molodaya Gvardiya (The Young Guard): 127994 Moscow, ul. Sushchevskaya 21; tel. (495) 972-05-46; fax (495) 972-05-82; e-mail dsel@gvardiya.ru; f. 1922; books, magazines; Gen. Dir V. F. YURKIN.

Moscow M. V. Lomonosov State University Press: 119899 Moscow, ul. Khokhlova 11; tel. (495) 939-33-23; fax (495) 203-66-71; e-mail kd_mgu@rambler.ru; internet www.msu.ru/depts/ MSUPubl2005; f. 1756; scientific, educational and reference, books and journals; Dir YURIY YU. PETRUNIN.

Muzyka (Music): 127051 Moscow, ul. Petrovka 26; tel. (495) 921-51-70; fax (495) 928-33-04; e-mail muz-sekretar@yandex.ru; f. 1861; sheet music, music scores and related literature; Dir MARK ZILBERQUIT.

Mysl (Thought): 117071 Moscow, Leninskii pr. 15; tel. (495) 955-04-58; f. 1963; science, popular science, philosophy, history, political science, geography; Dir YEVGENYI A. TIMOFEYEV.

Nauka (Science): 117997 Moscow, ul. Profsoyuznaya 90; tel. (495) 334-71-51; fax (495) 420-22-20; e-mail secret@naukaran.ru; internet www.naukaran.ru; f. 1923; publishing house of the Academy of Sciences; general and social science, mathematics, physics, chemistry, biology, earth sciences, oriental studies, books in foreign languages, university textbooks, scientific journals, translation, export, distribution, typesetting and printing services; Dir-Gen. V. VASILIYEV.

Nauka i Tekhnologiya (Science and Technology): 107076 Moscow, Stromynskii per. 4; tel. (495) 164-47-74; fax (495) 164-47-74; e-mail admin@nait.ru; internet www.nait.ru; f. 2000; journals on chemistry, electronics and telecommunications; Gen. Dir MAKSIM A. KOVALEVSKII.

Nedra Biznestsentr (Natural Resources Business Centre): 125047 Moscow, pl. Tverskoi Zastavy 3; tel. (495) 251-31-77; fax (495) 250-27-72; e-mail business@nedrainform.ru; internet www.nedrainform.ru;

f. 1964; geology, natural resources, mining and coal industry, petroleum and gas industry; Dir V. D. MENSHIKOV.

Nezavisimaya Gazeta ('Independent Newspaper' Publishing House): 101000 Moscow, ul. Myasnitskaya 13/10; tel. and fax (495) 981-61-53; e-mail ngbooks@ng.ru; internet www.ng.ru/izdatelstvo; f. 1991; books on history, literary essays, poetry, history of literature and of art, biography, dictionaries, encyclopaedias; Dir VIKTOR A. OBUKHOV.

Pedagogika Press (Pedagogy Press): 119034 Moscow, Smolenskii bulv. 4; tel. and fax (495) 246-59-69; f. 1969; scientific and popular books on pedagogics, didactics, psychology, developmental physiology; young people's encyclopaedia, dictionaries; Dir I. KOLESNIKOVA.

Pressa (The Press): 127137 Moscow, ul. Pravdy 24; tel. (499) 257-46-22; fax (499) 257-09-38; e-mail adm@media-pressa.ru; internet www.media-pressa.ru; f. 1934 as Pravda (Truth) Publishing House; booklets, newspapers and periodicals; Dir I. V. POLTAVTSEV.

Profizdat (Professional Publishers): 101000 Moscow, ul. Myasnitskaya 13/18; tel. (495) 924-57-40; fax (495) 975-23-29; e-mail profizdat@profizdat.ru; f. 1930; books and magazines; Gen. Dir VLADIMIR SOLOVYEV.

Progress (Progress): 119992 Moscow, Zubovskii bulv. 17; tel. (495) 246-90-32; fax (495) 230-24-03; e-mail progress@mcn.ru; f. 1931; translations of Russian language books into foreign languages and of foreign language books into Russian; political and scientific, fiction, literature for children and youth; encyclopedias; Dir-Gen. SARKIS V. OGANIAN.

Prosveshcheniye (Enlightenment): 127521 Moscow, 3-i proyezd Maryinoi roshchi 41; tel. (495) 789-30-40; fax (495) 789-30-41; e-mail prosv@prosv.ru; internet www.prosv.ru; f. 1930; school textbooks, dictionaries, atlases, reference and scientific books, educational materials; Dir ALEKSANDR M. KONDAKOV.

Raduga (Rainbow): 129090 Moscow, Grokholskii per. 32/2; tel. and fax (495) 680-12-39; e-mail radugarel@sumail.ru; internet www.raduga-publ.ru; f. 1982; translations of Russian fiction into foreign languages and of foreign authors into Russian; Gen. Dir KSENIYA ATAROVA.

Respublika (Republic): 125811 Moscow, Miusskaya pl. 7; tel. and fax (495) 656-09-70; e-mail respublik@dataforce.net; internet www.republik.ru; f. 1918; fmrly Politizdat (Political Publishing House); dictionaries, books on politics, human rights, philosophy, history, economics, religion, fiction, arts, reference; Dir VLADIMIR V. AKIMOV.

Rosmen (Rosman): 127018 Moscow, ul. Oktyabskaya 4/2; tel. (495) 933-70-70; fax (495) 933-71-36; e-mail rosman@rosman.ru; internet www.rosman.ru; children's literature, general, popular science; Dir-Gen. OLEG V. ZHIVYKH.

Rosspen Publishing House—Russian Political Encylopedia: 117393 Moscow, ul. Profsoyuznaya 82; tel. and fax (495) 334-81-62; e-mail rosspen@rosspen.com; internet www.rosspen.com; f. 1992; politics, history, other academic and reference publishing; Dir-Gen. A. K. SOROKIN.

Russkii Yazyk (Russian Language): 117303 Moscow, ul. M. Yushunski 1; tel. (495) 319-83-13; fax (495) 319-83-16; e-mail rlm@tpost.net; f. 2001; textbooks, reference, dictionaries; Dir ELIZABET BRATERSKAYA.

Shkola-Press (School-Press): 127254 Moscow, ul. Sh. Rustaveli 10/3; tel. and fax (495) 219-83-80; e-mail marketing@schoolpress.ru; internet www.schoolpress.ru; books on psychology, pedagogy, magazines.

Slovo (Word): 109147 Moscow, ul. Vorontsovskaya 41; tel. and fax (495) 911-61-33; internet www.slovo-online.ru; f. 1989; illustrated books on art, world literature in translation; Gen-Dir. NATALIYA AVETISYAN.

Stroyizdat (Construction Publishing House): 101442 Moscow, ul. Kalyayevskaya 23A; tel. (495) 251-69-67; f. 1932; building, architecture, environmental protection, fire protection and building materials; Dir V. A. KASATKIN.

Tekst (Text): 127299 Moscow, ul. Kosmonavta Volkova 7; tel. and fax (495) 150-0472; e-mail textpubl@yandex.ru; internet www.textpubl.ru; f. 1988; foreign poetry and prose fiction in translation, Russian poetry and prose, children's literature, social sciences, history, law; Dir OLGET M. Libkin.

Vagrius: 125993 Moscow, ul. Nikoloyamskaya 1; tel. (495) 221-61-80; fax (495) 510-56-10; e-mail vagrius@vagrius.com; internet www.vagrius.com; f. 1992; fiction, politics, history; Pres. and Dir-Gen. GLEB USPENSKII.

Ves Mir (The Whole World): 101000 Moscow, Kolpachnyi per. 9A; tel. (495) 623-68-39; fax (495) 625-42-69; e-mail info@vesmirbooks.ru; internet www.vesmirbooks.ru; f. 1994; university textbooks, scholarly works in social sciences and humanities; Dir Dr OLEG A. ZIMARIN.

Vysshaya Shkola (Higher School): 127994 Moscow, ul. Neglinnaya 29/14; tel. (495) 200-04-56; fax (495) 200-34-86; e-mail info_vshkola@mail.ru; internet www.vshkola.ru; f. 1939; textbooks for higher-education institutions; Dir MIKHAIL L. ZORIN.

Yuridicheskaya Literatura (Legal Literature): 121069 Moscow, ul. M. Nikitskaya 14; tel. (495) 203-83-84; fax (495) 291-98-83; internet www.jurizdat.ru; f. 1917; legal; official publishers of enactments of the Russian President and Govt; Dir IVAN A. BUNIN.

Znaniye (Knowledge): 101835 Moscow, proyezd Serova 4; tel. (495) 928-15-31; f. 1951; popular books and brochures on politics and science; Dir V. K. BELYAKOV.

Broadcasting and Communications
TELECOMMUNICATIONS

Golden Telecom: 115114 Moscow, Kozhevnicheskii proyezd 1; tel. (495) 797-93-00; fax (495) 797-93-32; e-mail publicrelations@gldn.net; internet www.goldentelecom.ru; f. 1994; operates mobile cellular telecommunications network in cities across the Russian Federation, and in Almaty (Kazakhstan) and Kyiv (Ukraine); Chief Exec. JEAN-PIERRE VANDROMME.

Megafon: 119435 Moscow, Savvinskaya nab. 15; tel. (495) 504-50-20; fax (495) 504-50-21; e-mail aklimov@megafon.ru; internet www.megafon.ru; f. 2002; operates mobile cellular communications networks across Russia; 6 regional cos; 15.6m. subscribers (March 2005); Gen. Dir SERGEI SOLDATENKOV.

Mobilnye TeleSistemi/Mobile TeleSystems (MTS): 109147 Moscow, ul. Marksistskaya 4; tel. (495) 766-01-77; e-mail info@mts.ru; internet www.mts.ru; f. 1993; provides mobile cellular telecommunications in 82 regions of Russia; majority-owned by Sistema Telecom; 35.1% owned by Deutsche Telekom (Germany); Pres. LEONID A. MELAMED; over 85m. subscribers (incl. subsidiary cos in Armenia, Belarus, Turkmenistan, Ukraine and Uzbekistan) (2008).

Moscow City Telephone Network (MGTS—Moskovskaya Gorodskaya Telefonnaya Set): 103051 Moscow, Petrovskii bulv. 12/3; tel. (495) 950-00-00; fax (495) 950-06-18; e-mail mgts@mgts.ru; internet www.mgts.ru; f. 1882; provides telecommunications services in Moscow City; Gen. Man. NIKOLAI A. MAKSIMENKA.

Petersburg Telephone Network (PTS—Peterburgsskaya Telefonnaya Set): 119186 St Petersburg, ul. B. Morskaya 24; tel. (812) 314-15-50; fax (812) 110-68-34; e-mail office@ptn.ru; internet www.ptn.ru; f. 1993; Dir IGOR N. SAMYLIN.

Rostelekom (Rostelecom): 125047 Moscow, ul.1-aya Tverskaya-Yamskaya 14; tel. (495) 787-28-49; fax (495) 972-82-83; e-mail info@rostelecom.ru; internet www.rt.ru; 50.7% owned by Svyazinvest; dominant long-distance and international telecommunications service provider; 7 regional cos based in St Petersburg, Samara, Novosibirsk, Yekaterinburg, Khabarovsk, Moscow and Rostov-on-Don; Dir DMITRII YEROKHIN.

Svyazinvest: 119121 Moscow, ul. Plyushchikha 55/2; tel. (495) 248-24-71; fax (495) 248-24-53; e-mail dms@svyazinvest.ru; internet www.sinvest.ru; f. 1995; 75% state-owned; holds controlling stakes in 7 'mega-regional' telecommunications operators, 1 international and domestic long–distance operator, and 2 local telecommunications cos, and non-controlling stakes in 2 city telecommunications cos; Chair. LEONID D. REIMAN.

VympelKom-Bilain (Vympelcom-Beeline): 127006 Moscow, ul. Krasnoproletarskaya 4; tel. (495) 725-07-00; fax (495) 991-79-03; e-mail info@beeline.ru; internet www.beeline.ru; operates mobile cellular telecommunications in 78 regions of Russia, and in Armenia, Georgia, Kazakhstan, Tajikistan, Ukraine and Uzbekistan; 26.6% owned by Telenor (Norway); Chief Exec. ALEKSANDR V. IZOSIMOV.

BROADCASTING
Pervyi Kanal (First Channel), operated by Public Russian Television (ORT), is received throughout Russia and many parts of the CIS. The All-Russian State Television Company (VGTRK) broadcasts Telekanal 'Rossiya', which reaches some 92% of the Russian population, and Telekanal 'Kultura' and Telekanal 'Sport'. In addition to the nation-wide television channels, there are local channels, and the NTV (Independent Television) channel (65% owned by the gas utility, Gazprom, in which the Government holds a majority stake) is broadcast in most of Russia. In the regions, part of Rossiya's programming is devoted to local affairs, with broadcasts in minority languages. A state-supported international English-language TV station, Russia Today, commenced broadcasts in 2006. In mid-2005 there were four nation-wide radio stations, as well as 11 urban radio networks and more than 200 regional stations. At that time Radio Rossiya had more listeners than any other state-run channel, but the commercial music station, Russkoye Radio, established in 1995, was the most popular station overall.

Association of Regional State Television and Radio Broadcasters: 113326 Moscow, ul. Pyatnitskaya 25/226; tel. and fax (495)

950-60-28; e-mail fstratyv@rzn.rosmail.com; Chair. of Bd ALEKSANDR N. LEVCHENKO.

Regulatory Authority

Russian Television and Radio Broadcasting Network: 113326 Moscow, ul. Pyatnitskaya 25; tel. (495) 233-66-03; fax (495) 233-28-93; f. 2001; Gen. Man. GENNADII I. SKLYAR.

Radio

All-Russian State Television and Radio Broadcasting Company (VGTRK): 125040 Moscow, ul. 5-aya Yamskogo Polya 19/21; tel. (495) 745-39-78; fax (495) 975-26-11; e-mail rtrinterdep@rfn.ru; internet www.tvradio.ru; f. 1991; broadcasts 'Rossiya', 'Kultura', 'Sport' and 'Planeta' television channels, 89 regional television and radio cos, and national radio stations 'Radio Rossiya', 'Radio Mayak' and 'Radio Nostalzhi'; Chair. OLEG DOBRODEYEV.

Radio Mayak (Radio Beacon): 113326 Moscow, ul. Pyatnitskaya 25; tel. (495) 950-67-67; fax (495) 959-42-04; e-mail inform@radiomayak.ru; internet www.radiomayak.ru; f. 1964; state-owned; Chair. IRINA A. GERASIMOVA.

Radio Nostalzhi (Radio Nostalgia): 113162 Moscow, ul. Shabolovka 37; tel. (495) 955-84-00; e-mail nostalgie@vimain.vitpc.com; f. 1993; Gen. Man. IRINA A. GERASIMOVA.

Radio Rossiya (Radio Russia): 125040 Moscow, ul. 5-aya Yamskogo Polya 19/21; tel. (495) 234-85-94; fax (495) 730-42-77; e-mail direction@radiorus.ru; internet www.radiorus.ru; f. 1990; broadcasts information, social, political, musical, literary and investigate progamming; Dir-Gen. ALEKSEI V. ABAKUMOV.

Ekho Moskvy (Moscow Echo): 119992 Moscow, ul. Novyi Arbat 11; tel. (495) 202-92-29; e-mail info@echo.msk.ru; internet www.echo.msk.ru; f. 1990; stations in Moscow, St Petersburg, Rostov-on-Don and Vologda; also broadcasts from Moscow to Chelyabinsk, Krasnoyarsk, Novosibirsk, Omsk, Perm, Saratov and Yekaterinburg; 66% owned by Gazprom-Mediya, 34% staff-owned; Gen. Man. YURII FEDUTINKOV.

Golos Rossii (The Voice of Russia): 115326 Moscow, ul. Pyatnitskaya 25; tel. (495) 950-63-31; fax (495) 951-20-17; e-mail voiceofrussia@ruvr.ru; internet www.vor.ru; fmrly Radio Moscow International; international broadcasts in 34 languages; Man. Dir ARMEN G. OGANESIAN.

Russkoye Radio (Russian Radio): 105064 Moscow, ul. Kazakova 16; tel. (495) 232-16-36; fax (495) 956-13-60; internet www.rusradio.ru; f. 1995; owned by Russkaya Mediyagruppa (Russian Media Group); nation-wide commercial music station; broadcasts to more than 700 towns in Russia, Ukraine, Kazakhstan, Moldova, Kyrgyzstan, the Baltic Republics and the USA; also *Russkoye Radio 2*, principally news and talk programming, broadcast to Moscow; Dir-Gen. SERGEI KOZHEVNIKOV.

Serebryanyi Dozhd (Silver Rain): 127083 Moscow, Petrovsko-Razumovskaya alleya 12A; tel. (495) 925-10-01; internet www.silver.ru; f. 1995; commercial station broadcasting information and entertainment programming; broadcasts to 98 cities in Russia and the 'near abroad'; Dir-Gen. DMITRII SAVITSKII.

Yevropa Plyus (Europa Plus): 127427 Moscow, ul. Akademika Koroleva 19; tel. (495) 217-82-57; fax (495) 956-35-08; e-mail main@europaplus.ru; internet www.europaplus.ru; FM station, broadcasting music, entertainment and information programmes to 500 cities; Pres. ZHORZH POLINSKI.

Television

All-Russian State Television and Radio Broadcasting Company (VGTRK): 125040 Moscow, ul. 5-aya Yamskogo Polya 19/21; tel. (495) 745-39-78; fax (495) 975-26-11; e-mail rtrinterdep@rfn.ru; f. 1991; broadcasts 'Rossiya' 'Kultura', 'Sport' and 'Planeta' television channels, 89 regional television and radio cos, and national radio stations 'Radio Rossiya', 'Radio Mayak' and 'Radio Nostalzhi'; Chair. OLEG DOBRODEYEV.

Telekanal 'Kultura' (Television Channel 'Culture'): 123995 Moscow, ul. M. Nikitskaya 24; e-mail kultura@tvkultura.ru; internet www.tvkultura.ru; f. 1997; Gen. Dir ALEKSANDR S. PONOMAREV.

Telekanal 'Rossiya' (Television Channel 'Russia'): 115162 Moscow, ul. Shabolovka 37; tel. (495) 924-63-74; fax (495) 234-87-71; e-mail info@rutv.ru; internet www.rutv.ru; fmrly RTR-TV; name changed as above in 2002; Dir-Gen. ALEKSANDR S. PONAMAREV.

Telekanal 'Sport' (Television Channel 'Sport'): 115162 Moscow, ul. Shabolovka 37; e-mail reception@sport.vgtek.com; internet sportbox.ru; f. 2003; Dir-Gen. VASILII KIKNADZE.

Telekanal 'Zvezda' (Television Channel 'Star'): 129110 Moscow, Suvorovskaya pl. 2; tel. (495) 631-58-83; internet www.tvzvezda.ru; f. 2005; Gen. Dir SERGEI V. SABUSHKIN.

NTV—Independent Television: 127427 Moscow, ul. Akademika Koroleva 12; tel. (495) 725-54-03; fax (495) 725-54-01; e-mail info@ntv.ru; internet www.ntv.ru; f. 1993; 65% owned by Gazprom-Mediya; also NTV World (NTV Mir), broadcasting to Russian communities in Israel, Europe and the USA; Dir-Gen. NIKOLAI YU. SENKEVICH.

Pervyi Kanal—First Channel (Channel One): 127427 Moscow, ul. Akademika Koroleva 12; tel. (495) 617-73-87; fax (495) 215-82-47; e-mail ort_int@ortv.ru; internet www.1tv.ru; f. 1995; fmrly ORT—Public Russian Television; name changed as above in 2002; 51% state-owned; 49% owned by private shareholders; Chair. MIKHAIL PYATKOVSKII; Dir-Gen. KONSTANTIN ERNST.

Ren-TV Network: 119843 Moscow, Zubovskii bulv. 17/510; tel. (495) 246-25-06; fax (495) 245-09-98; e-mail site@rentv.dol.ru; internet www.ren-tv.com; f. 1991; network of more than 100 television stations in the Russian Federation and 60 stations in republics of the CIS; Chair. LYUBOV SOVERSHAYEVA; Gen. Man. DMITRII A. LESNEVSKII.

STS—Network of Television Stations: 123298 Moscow, ul. 3-aya Khoroshevskaya 12; tel. (495) 797-41-73; fax (495) 797-41-01; e-mail www@ctc-tv.ru; internet www.ctc-tv.ru; f. 1996; owned by StoryFirst Communications (USA); broadcasts programmes of popular entertainment to 350 cities in Russia; Dir-Gen. ALEKSANDR YE. RODNYANSKII.

TNT—Territory of Our Viewers—TV Network: 127427 Moscow, ul. Akademika Koroleva 19; tel. (495) 217-81-88; fax (495) 748-14-90; e-mail info@tnt-tv.ru; internet www.tnt-tv.ru; f. 1997; cable television network broadcasting to 582 cities in Russia; Chief Exec. ALEKSANDR DYBAL; Dir-Gen. ROMAN PETRENKO.

TV-Tsentr (TVTs—TV-Centre): 113184 Moscow, ul. B. Tatarskaya 33/1; tel. (495) 959-39-87; fax (495) 959-39-66; e-mail info@tvc.ru; internet www.tvc.ru; f. 1997; broadcasting consortium for terrestrial cable and satellite television; receives funding from Govt of Moscow City; Pres. OLEG M. POPTSOV; Dir PAVEL V. KASPAROV.

Finance

(cap. = capital; res = reserves; dep. = deposits; m. = million; brs = branches; amounts in new roubles, unless otherwise stated)

BANKING

Central Bank

Bank Rossii—Central Bank of the Russian Federation: 107016 Moscow, ul. Neglinnaya 12; tel. (495) 771-91-00; fax (495) 621-64-65; e-mail webmaster@www.cbr.ru; internet www.cbr.ru; f. 1990; cap. 3,000m., res 303,732m., dep. 9,700,000m. (Jan. 2007); Chair. SERGEI M. IGNATIYEV; 79 brs.

Major Banks

Absolut Bank (Absolyut Bank): 127051 Moscow, Tsvetnoi bulv. 18; tel. (495) 995-10-01; fax (495) 995-10-22; e-mail info@absolutbank.ru; internet www.absolutbank.ru; 95% owned by KBC Bank NV (Belgium); f. 1993; cap. 1,714.6m., res 2,442.4m., dep. 56,896.5m. (Dec. 2006); Chair. of Management Bd NIKOLAI SIDOROV.

AK BARS Bank: 420066 Tatarstan, Kazan, ul. Dekabristov 1; tel. (843) 519-38-02; fax (843) 519-39-75; e-mail mail@akbars.ru; internet www.akbars.ru; f. 1993; cap. 25,244.0m., res 349.6m., dep. 109,497.3m. (Dec. 2007); Chair. of Bd ROBERT MINNEGALIYEV; 22 brs.

Alfa-Bank: 107078 Moscow, ul. Kalanchevskaya 27; tel. (495) 974-25-15; fax (495) 745-57-84; e-mail mail@alfabank.ru; internet www.alfabank.ru; f. 1990; cap. US $344.8m., res $26.0m., dep. $9,906.4m. (Dec. 2006); Chair. of Exec. Bd RUSHAN KHVESYUK; Pres. PETR AVEN.

Bank of Moscow (Bank Moskvy): 107996 Moscow, ul. Rozhdestvenka 8/15/3; tel. (495) 925-80-00; fax (495) 795-26-00; e-mail info@mmbank.ru; internet www.mmbank.ru; f. 1995 as Moscow Municipal Bank—Bank of Moscow; name changed as above 2004; 60% owned by Govt of Moscow City; cap. 14,786.8m., res 2,629.6m., dep. 348,161.8m. (Dec. 2006); Pres. and Chief Exec. ANDREI BORODIN; 117 brs.

Bank Petrocommerce (Bank Petrokommertz): 127051 Moscow, ul. Petrovka 24; tel. (495) 625-95-65; fax (495) 623-36-07; e-mail welcome@pkb.ru; internet www.pkb.ru; f. 1992; cap. 6,752.6m., res −17.6m., dep. 108,376.9m. (Dec. 2006); Pres. and Chair. of Bd VLADIMIR N. NIKITENKO.

Bank Rossiiskii Kredit (Russian Credit Bank): 119002 Moscow, Smolenskii bulv. 26/9; tel. (495) 967-34-43; fax (495) 247-39-39; e-mail info@roscredit.ru; internet www.roscredit.ru; f. 1990; cap. 7,520.9m., res 3,989.5m., dep. 2,871.7m. (Dec. 2005); Pres. ANDREI A. DREMIN; Chair. PAVEL I. LYSENKO.

Bank Sankt-Peterburg: 191167 St Petersburg, Nevskii pr. 178; tel. (812) 329-50-34; fax (812) 329-50-70; e-mail corel@bspb.ru; internet www.bspb.ru; f. 1990; cap. 3,564.3m., res 10,867.4m., dep. 103,418.6m. (Dec. 2007); Chair. ALEKSANDR SAVELIYEV.

Bank Soyuz: 127006 Moscow, ul. Dolgorukovskaya 34/1; tel. (495) 729-55-00; fax (495) 729-55-05; e-mail info@banksoyuz.ru; internet www.banksoyuz.ru; f. 1993; cap. 4,413.7m., res 91.6m., dep. 56,498.8m. (Dec. 2006); Chair. STUART M. LAWSON.

Bank Uralsib: 119048 Moscow, ul. Yefremova 8; tel. (495) 705-90-39; fax (495) 745-70-10; e-mail pr@nikoil.ru; internet www.uralsib.ru; f. 1993; cap. 32,606.7m., res 8,699.5m., dep. 248,666.5m. (Dec. 2006); Chair. NIKOLAI TSVETKOV.

Bank VTB 24: 101000 Moscow, ul. Myasnitskaya 35; tel. (495) 771-78-78; fax (495) 980-46-66; e-mail info@vtb24.ru; internet www.vtb24.ru; f. 1991; cap. 17,611.9., res 658.8m., dep. 127,105.8m. (Dec. 2006); CEO MIKHAIL M. ZADORNOV; 44 brs.

Bank VTB Severo-Zapad (Bank VTB North-West): 191014 St Petersburg, ul. Kovenskii 17/18; tel. (812) 329-84-51; fax (812) 310-61-73; e-mail lider@icbank.ru; internet www.vtb-sz.ru; f. 1870 as Volga-Kama Bank; fmrly Industry and Construction Bank; present name adopted 2007; cap. 1,932.7m., res 2,477.6m., dep. 112,948.0m. (Dec. 2006); Chair. VLADIMIR SKATIN; 54 brs.

Bank Zenit: 129110 Moscow, Bannyi per. 9; tel. (495) 937-07-37; fax (495) 777-57-06; e-mail info@zenit.ru; internet www.zenit.ru; f. 1994; 26% owned by Tatneft; cap. US $392.9m., res $60.8m., dep. $3,216.3m. (Dec. 2006); Chair. of Bd ALEKSEI A SOKOLOV; 4 brs.

Banque Société Générale Vostok (BSGV): 119180 Moscow, Yakimanskaya nab. 2; tel. (495) 783-00-00; fax (495) 720-67-49; internet www.bsgv.ru; f. 2003; 98.0% owned by Société Générale (France); cap. 1,138.0m., res 904.8m., dep. 44,467.8m. (Dec. 2006); Pres. and Dir-Gen. MARC-EMMANUEL VIVES.

BIN Bank: 121471 Moscow, ul. Grodnenskaya 5A; tel. (495) 755-50-60; fax (495) 440-09-75; e-mail binbank@binbank.ru; internet www.binbank.ru; f. 1993; cap. 4,959.1m., res 2,500.6m., dep. 49,790.2m. (Dec. 2006); Chair. of Bd SERGEI YE. YEGOROV; Pres. and Chief Exec. MIKHAIL O. SHISHKHANOV; 69 brs and sub-brs.

Gazprombank: 117420 Moscow, ul. Nametkina 16/1; tel. (495) 719-17-63; fax (495) 913-73-19; e-mail mailbox@gazprombank.ru; internet www.gazprombank.ru; f. 1990; 87.5% owned by Gazprom; cap. US $1,160.9m., res $1,824.3m., dep. $23,183.9m. (Dec. 2006); Chair. of Management Bd ANDREI I. AKIMOV; 32 brs.

Globeks Commercial Bank (GLOBEXBANK): 123242 Moscow, Novinskii bulv. 31; tel. (495) 785-22-22; fax (495) 795-13-08; e-mail post@globexbank.ru; internet www.globex-bank.com; f. 1992; cap. 10,084.4m., res 3,214.3m., dep. 56,801.1m. (Jan. 2008); Chair. ANDREI F. DUNAYEV; Pres. ANATOLII L. MOTYLEV; 6 brs.

Impexbank (Import-Export Bank): 125252 Moscow, ul. Novopeschanaya 20/10/1A; tel. and fax (495) 752-52-32; e-mail mail@impexbank.ru; internet www.impexbank.ru; f. 1993; cap. US $130.8m., res $35.4m. dep. $1,697.4m. (Dec. 2005); Chair. of Bd PAVEL I. LYSENKO; more than 400 brs in Moscow.

ING Bank (Eurasia): 127473 Moscow, ul. Krasnoproletarskaya 36; tel. (495) 755-54-00; fax (495) 755-54-99; e-mail russia@ingbank.com; internet www.ing.ru; f. 1993; 99% owned by ING Bank NV (Netherlands); cap. 2,024.7m., res 2,788.1m., dep. 43,464.3m. (Dec. 2006); Dir-Gen. HENDRICK WILLEM TEN BOSCH.

International Moscow Bank (Mezhdunarodnyi Moskovskii Bank): 119034 Moscow, Prechistenskaya nab. 9; tel. (495) 258-72-00; fax (495) 258-72-72; e-mail imbank@imbank.ru; internet www.imb.ru; f. 1989; 47.4% owned by Bayerische Hypo- und Vereinsbank AG (Germany), by Nordea Bank Finland, 20% by Banque Commerciale pour l'Europe du Nord—EUROBANK (France), 10.2% owned by European Bank for Reconstruction and Development—EBRD (UK); cap. US $348.2m., res $16.6m., dep. $8,205.0m. (Dec. 2006); Chair. of Bd of Dirs ERICH HAMPEL; 22 brs.

Khanty-Mansiiskii Bank: 628012 Tyumen obl., Khanty-Mansii AOk—Yugra, Khanty-Mansiisk, ul. Mira 38; tel. (34671) 302-10; fax (34671) 302-19; e-mail hmbank@khmb.ru; internet www.khmb.ru; f. 1992; cap. 5,787.3m., res 1,455.3m., dep. 60,521.5m. (Dec. 2006); Pres. DMITRII MIZGULIN; 16 brs.

MDM Bank (Moskovskiy Delovoy Mir—Moscow Business World): 115172 Moscow, Kotelnicheskaya nab. 33/1; tel. (495) 797-95-00; fax (495) 797-95-01; e-mail info@mdmbank.com; internet www.mdmbank.ru; f. 1993; cap. 1,794m., res 17,229m., dep. 273,999m. (Dec. 2007); Chief Exec. MICHEL PERKHIRIN; 98 brs and sub-brs.

Mezhdunarodnyi Promyshlennyi Bank (International Industrial Bank): 125009 Moscow, ul. B. Dmitrovka 23/1; tel. (495) 626-44-46; fax (495) 692-82-84; e-mail mail@iib.ru; internet www.iib.ru; f. 1992; cap. 25,000m., res 405.6m., dep. 60,299.3m. (Dec. 2006); Chair. ALEKSANDR V. GNUSAREV; 5 brs.

Moscow Bank for Reconstruction and Development (Moskovskii Bank Rekonstruktsii i Razvitiya): 119034 Moscow, Yeropkinskii per. 5; tel. and fax (495) 101-28-00; fax (495) 232-27-54; e-mail mbrd@mbrd.ru; internet www.mbrd.ru; 58.44% owned by Sistema; cap. 943.4m., res 3,650.4m., dep. 52,301.5m. (Dec. 2006); Chair. of Bd SERGEI YE. CHEREMIN.

Nomos-Bank: 109240 Moscow, ul. Verkhnyaya Radishchevskaya 3/1; tel. (495) 737-73-55; fax (495) 797-32-50; e-mail nmosmail@online.ru; internet www.nomos.ru; f. 1992; cap. 5,318.1m., res 3,696.8m., dep. 87,539.8m. (Dec. 2006); Pres. DMITRII SOKOLOV; 8 brs.

Promsvyazbank: 109052 Moscow, ul. Smirnovskaya 10/2–3/22; tel. (495) 727-10-20; fax (495) 727-10-21; e-mail postmaster@psbank.ru; internet www.psbank.ru; f. 1995; cap. 6,188.8m., res 5,679.8m., dep. 147,673.3m. (Dec. 2006); Chair. of Council DMITRII N. ANANIYEV; Pres. ALEKSANDR A. LEVKOVSKII; 100 brs.

Raiffeisenbank ZAO: 129090 Moscow, ul. Troitskaya 17/1; tel. (495) 721-99-00; fax (495) 721-99-01; e-mail info@raiffeisen.ru; internet www.raiffeisen.ru; f. 1996; owned by Raiffeisenbank (Austria); present name adopted 2007; cap. 13,439.3m., res 1,368.1m., dep. 166,355.6m. (Dec. 2006); Chair. of Man. Bd JOHANN JONACH; 7 brs and sub-brs.

Rosbank: 107078 Moscow, ul. M. Poryvayevoi 11, POB 208; tel. (495) 921-01-01; fax (495) 725-05-11; e-mail mailbox@rosbank.ru; internet www.rosbank.ru; f. 1993; 50% owned by Société Générale (France); cap. 9,270.9m., res 21,773.6m., dep. 356,105.8m. (Dec. 2007); Pres. and Chair. of Bd of Dirs ANDREI KLISHAS; Chief Exec. ALEKSANDR POPOV; 68 brs.

Russkii Standart Bank: 105066 Moscow, ul. Spartakovskaya 2/1/6; tel. (495) 748-15-19; fax (495) 797-84-04; e-mail nignatova@rs.ru; internet www.rs.ru; f. 1993; cap. 1,738.5m., res 809.7m., dep. 154,165.9m. (Dec. 2006); Chair. RUSTAM V. TARIKO; Chief Exec. DMITRII O. LEVIN.

Sberbank—Savings Bank of the Russian Federation: 117997 Moscow, ul. Vavilova 19; tel. (495) 957-58-62; fax (495) 957-57-31; e-mail sbrf@sbrf.ru; internet www.sbrf.ru; f. 1841 as a deposit-taking institution, reorganized as a joint-stock commercial bank in 1991; 60.6% owned by Bank Rossii—Central Bank of the Russian Federation; cap. 79,981m., res 25,360m., dep. 2,997,389m. (Dec. 2006); Chair. of Bd and Chief Exec. GERMAN O. GREF; 17 regional head offices, 823 brs and 19,307 sub-brs.

Sobinbank: 123022 Moscow, ul. Rochdelskaya 15/56; tel. (495) 725-25-25; fax (495) 937-99-23; e-mail mail@sobin.ru; internet www.sobinbank.ru; f. 1990; cap. 6,194.1m., res 1,144.2m., dep. 48,080.2m. (Dec. 2006); Chair. of Bd VLADIMIR RYKUNOV; 17 brs.

Svyaz-Bank (Interregional Bank for Settlements of the Telecommunications and Postal Services): 125375 Moscow, ul. Tverskaya 7; tel. (495) 771-32-60; fax (495) 771-32-76; e-mail MAV@sviaz-bank.ru; internet www.sviaz-bank.ru; f. 1991; cap. 5,745.8m., res −3.2m., dep. 56,230.2m. (Dec. 2006); Chair. of Bd of Dirs ANDREI KONOVAL.

TransKreditBank (TransCreditBank): 105066 Moscow, ul. N. Basmannaya 37A/1; tel. (495) 788-08-80; fax (495) 788-08-79; e-mail info@bnk.ru; internet www.tcb.ru; f. 1992; 75.0% owned by Russian Railways; cap. 3,373.6m., res 2,602.9m., dep. 72,011.2m. (Dec. 2006); Pres. SERGEI N. PUSHKIN.

URSA Bank: 630102 Novosibirsk, ul. Inskaya 54; tel. (3832) 27-75-99; fax (3832) 34-00-25; e-mail secret@ursabank.ru; internet www.ursabank.ru; f. 1990; present name adopted 2006; cap. 1,434.9m., res 11,501.5m., dep. 90,690.2m. (Dec. 2006); Chair. of Bd of Dirs IGOR KIM.

Vneshekonombank (Bank for Foreign Economic Affairs): 107996 Moscow, pr. Sakharova 9; tel. (495) 207-10-37; fax (495) 975-21-43; e-mail info@veb.ru; internet www.veb.ru; f. 1924; state-owned; dep. US $11,042m., total assets $12,429m. (Dec. 2006); Chair. VLADIMIR A. DMITRIYEV.

Vozrozhdeniye—V-Bank (Rebirth—Moscow Jt-Stock Commercial Bank Vozrozdeniye): 101999 Moscow, per. Luchnikov 7/4/1, POB 9; tel. (495) 777-08-88; fax (495) 620-19-99; e-mail vbank@co.voz.ru; internet www.vbank.ru; f. 1991; cap. US $293m., res $120m., dep. $2,687m. (Jul. 2007); Chair. of Supervisory Bd YURII M. MARINICHEV; Chair. of Managing Bd DMITRII L. ORLOV; 160 brs.

VTB Bank: 190000 St Petersburg, ul. B. Morskaya 29; tel. (812) 314-60-59; fax (812) 312-78-18; e-mail info@vtb.ru; internet www.vtb.ru; f. 1990; frmly Bank for Foreign Trade; present name adopted 2007; 77.5% owned by Govt of Russian Federation; cap. US $2,500m., res $2,360m., dep. $39,140m. (Dec. 2006); Chair. of Bd and Chief Exec. ANDREI L. KOSLIN.

Yevrofinans Mosnarbank (Evrofinance Mosnarbank): 121099 Moscow, ul. Novyi Arbat 29; tel. (495) 967-81-82; fax (495) 967-81-33; e-mail info@evrofinance.ru; internet www.evrofinance.ru; f. 1990; present name adopted 2003; cap. 3,510.3m., res 7,765.9m., dep. 44,321.2m. (Dec. 2006); Pres. and Chair. of Bd VLADIMIR STOLYARENKO.

Bankers' Association

Association of Russian Banks (Assostiatsiya Rossiiskikh Bankov): 121069 Moscow, Skatertnyi per. 20/1; tel. (495) 291-66-

30; fax (495) 291-66-66; e-mail arb@arb.ru; internet www.arb.ru; f. 1991; 755 mem. orgs, incl. 576 credit orgs (2007); Pres. Garegin A. Tosunyan.

INSURANCE

Agroinvest Insurance Co: 127422 Moscow, ul. Timiryazevskaya 26; tel. (495) 976-94-56; fax (495) 977-05-88; health, life and general insurance services; Pres. Yurii I. Mordvintsev.

AIG Russia: 103009 Moscow, ul. Tverskaya 16/2; tel. (495) 935-89-50; fax (495) 935-89-52; e-mail aig.russia@aig.com; internet www .aigrussia.ru; f. 1994; mem. of the American International Group Inc; personal and business property insurance, also marine, life, financial etc.; Pres. Gary Coleman.

Allianz Insurance Co: 127473 Moscow, 3-i Samotechnii per. 3; tel. (495) 937-69-96; fax (495) 937-69-80; e-mail allianz@allianz.ru; internet www.allianz.ru; engineering, professional liability, life, medical, property, marine and private; Man. Dir Michael Herge-sell.

Ingosstrakh Insurance Co: 115998 Moscow, ul. Pyatnitskaya 12/2; tel. (495) 232-32-11; fax (495) 959-45-18; e-mail ingos@ingos.ru; internet www.ingos.ru; f. 1947; undertakes all kinds of insurance and reinsurance; Chair. Nataliya A. Rayevskaya; Gen. Dir Yevgenii Tumanov.

Medstrakh—Medical Insurance Fund of the Russian Federation: 107076 Moscow, pl. Preobrazhenskaya 7A /1; tel. (495) 964-84-27; fax (495) 964-84-21; e-mail mz@mcramn.ru; internet www .medstrah.ru; f. 1991; health, life, property, travel, liability; also provides compulsory medical insurance; Pres. Petr Kuznetsov.

RESO-Garantiya Insurance Co: 125047 Moscow, ul. Gasheka 12/1; tel. (495) 730-30-00; fax (495) 956-25-85; e-mail reso@orc.ru; internet www.reso.ru; f. 1991; Dir-Gen. Dmitrii G. Rakovshchik.

Rosgosstrakh—Russian State Insurance Co: 127994 Moscow, ul. Novoslobodskaya 23; tel. (495) 781-24-00; fax (495) 978-27-64; e-mail admin@rgs.ru; internet www.gosstrah.ru; majority state-owned; 49% stake transferred to private ownership in 2001; undertakes domestic insurance; subsidiary cos in 80 federal subjects (territorial units) of the Russian Federation; Chair. Vladislav Reznik; Gen. Dir Ruben Vardanian.

ROSNO—Russian National Society Insurance Co: 115184 Moscow, Ozerkovskaya nab. 30; tel. (495) 232-33-33; fax (495) 232-00-14; e-mail info@rosno.ru; internet www.rosno.ru; f. 1992; 100 brs and 186 agencies; 47% owned by AFK Sistema; 45.3% owned by Allianz AG (Germany); CEO Leonid Melamed.

Russkiye Strakhovye Traditsii (Russian Traditions Insurance Co): 129366 Moscow, Raketnyi bulv. 13/2; tel. (495) 283-88-03; fax (495) 283-88-05; e-mail info@rustrad.ru; internet www.rustrad.ru; f. 1992; Pres. Ivan I. Davydov.

SOGAZ—Insurance Co of the Gas Industry: 117997 Moscow, ul. Nametkina 16; tel. (495) 782-09-17; fax (495) 432-90-05; e-mail sogaz@sogaz.ru; internet www.sogaz.ru; f. 1993; owned by gas industry interests; Chair. of Bd of Dirs Sergei A. Lukash.

Soglasiye (Agreement) Insurance Co: 109017 Moscow, M. Tolmachevskii per. 8–11/3; tel. and fax (495) 959-46-32; e-mail official@soglasie.ru; internet www.soglasie.ru; f. 1993 as Interros-Soglasiye; owned by Interros; Gen. Man. Igor Zhuk.

STOCK EXCHANGES

Moscow Stock Exchange (MSE) (Moskovskaya Fondovaya Birzha): 125047 Moscow, Miusskaya pl. 2/2; tel. (495) 771-35-80; fax (495) 250-17-34; e-mail mse@mse.ru; internet www.mse.ru; f. 1997; Pres. Roman N. Myltsev.

Siberian Stock Exchange: 630104 Novosibirsk, ul. Frunze 5, POB 233; tel. (3832) 21-60-67; fax (3832) 21-06-90; e-mail sibex@sibex.nsk .su; f. 1991; Pres. Aleksandr V. Novikov.

COMMODITY EXCHANGES

Asiatic Commodity Exchange: 670000 Buryatiya, Ulan-Ude, ul. Sovetskaya 23/37; tel. and fax (3012) 22-26-81; f. 1991; Chair. Andrei Firsov.

European-Asian Exchange (EAE): 101000 Moscow, ul. Myasnitskaya 26; tel. and fax (495) 787-58-93; e-mail info@eae.ru; internet www.eae.ru; f. 2000; Chair. of Council Tatyana S. Sokolova; Gen. Man. Aleksandr B. Yeremin.

Khabarovsk Commodity Exchange (KhCE): 680000 Khabarovsk; tel. and fax (4212) 33-65-60; f. 1991; Pres. Yevgenii V. Panasenko.

Komi Commodity Exchange (KoCE): 167610 Komi, Syktyvkar, Oktyabrskii pr. 16; tel. (8212) 22-32-86; fax (8212) 23-84-43; f. 1991; Pres. Petr S. Luchenkov.

Kuzbass Commodity and Raw Materials Exchange (KECME): 650090 Kemerovo, ul. Novgorodskaya 19; tel. (3842) 23-45-40; fax (3842) 23-49-56; f. 1991; Gen. Man. Fedor Masenkov.

Moscow Commodity Exchange (MCE): 129223 Moscow, pr. Mira, Russian Exhibition Centre, Pavilion 69 (4); tel. (495) 187-86-14; fax (495) 187-88-76; f. 1990; organization of exchange trading (cash, stock and futures market); Pres. and Chair. of Bd Yurii Milyukov.

Petrozavodsk Commodity Exchange (PCE): 185028 Kareliya, Petrozavodsk, ul. Krasnaya 31; tel. and fax (8142) 7-80-57; f. 1991; Gen. Man. Valerii Sakharov.

Russian Exchange (RE): 101000 Moscow, ul. Myasnitskaya 26; tel. (495) 787-84-34; fax (495) 262-57-57; e-mail ic@ci.re.ru; internet www.re.ru; f. 1990; Pres. Pavel Panov.

Russian Commodity Exchange of the Agro-Industrial Complex (RosAgroBirzha): 125080 Moscow, Volokolamskoye shosse 11; tel. (495) 209-52-25; f. 1990; Chair. of Exchange Cttee Aleksandr Vasiliyev.

St Petersburg Exchange: 199026 St Petersburg, Vasilyevskii Ostrov, 26-aya liniya 15; tel. (812) 322-44-11; fax (812) 322-73-90; e-mail spbex@spbex.ru; internet www.spbex.ru; f. 1991; Pres. and Chief Exec. Viktor V. Nikolayev.

Udmurt Commodity Universal Exchange (UCUE): 426075 Udmurt Rep., Izhevsk, ul. Soyuznaya 107; tel. (3412) 37-08-88; fax (3412) 37-16-57; e-mail iger@udmnet.ru; f. 1991; Pres. N. F. Lazarev.

Yekaterinburg Commodity Exchange (UCE): 620012 Sverdlovsk obl., Yekaterinburg, pr. Kosmonavtov 23; tel. (343) 234-43-01; fax (343) 251-53-64; f. 1991; Chair. of Exchange Cttee Konstantin Zhuzhlov.

Trade and Industry

GOVERNMENT AGENCY

Russian Federal Property Fund (Rossiiskii Fond Federalnogo Imushchestva): 119049 Moscow, Leninskii pr. 9; tel. (495) 236-71-15; fax (495) 956-27-80; e-mail rffi@dol.ru; internet www.fpf.ru; f. 1992 to ensure consistency in the privatization process and to implement privatization legislation; Chair. Yurii A. Petrov.

NATIONAL CHAMBER OF COMMERCE

Chamber of Commerce and Industry of the Russian Federation (Torgovo-Promyshlennaya Palata RF): 109012 Moscow, ul. Ilinka 6; tel. (495) 929-00-09; fax (495) 929-03-60; e-mail dios-inform@tpprf.ru; internet www.tpprf.ru; f. 1991; Pres. Yevgenii M Primakov.

REGIONAL CHAMBERS OF COMMERCE

In early 2002 there were a total of 148 regional chambers of commerce in the Russian Federation. The following are among the most important.

Astrakhan Chamber of Commerce: 414040 Astrakhan, ul. Zhelyabova 50; tel. (8512) 25-58-44; fax (8512) 28-14-42; e-mail cci@mail .astrakhan.ru; internet astrcci.astrakhan.ru; f. 1992; Pres. Aleksei D. Kantemirov.

Bashkortostan Chamber of Commerce: 450007 Bashkortostan, Ufa, ul. Vorovskogo 22; tel. (3472) 23-23-80; fax (3472) 51-70-79; e-mail office@tpprb.ru; internet www.tpprb.ru; f. 1990; Chair. Boris A. Bondarenko.

Central Siberian Chamber of Commerce: 660049 Krasnoyarsk, ul. Kirova 26; tel. (3912) 23-96-13; fax (3912) 23-96-83; e-mail cstp@ mail.ru; internet www.cstpp.ru; f. 1985; Chair. Valerii A. Kostin.

East Siberian Chamber of Commerce: 664003 Irkutsk, ul. Sukhe-Batora 16; tel. (3952) 33-50-60; fax (3952) 33-50-66; e-mail info@ccies.ru; internet www.ccies.ru; f. 1974; Pres. Konstantin S. Shavrin.

Far East Chamber of Commerce: 680670 Khabarovsk, ul. Sheronova 113; tel. (4210) 30-47-70; fax (4210) 30-54-58; e-mail dvtpp@ fecci.khv.ru; f. 1970; Pres. Mikhail V. Kruglikov.

Kaliningrad Chamber of Commerce and Industry: 236010 Kaliningrad, ul. Vatutina 20; tel. (4012) 95-68-01; fax (4012) 95-47-88; e-mail kaliningrad_cci@baltnet.ru; internet www .kaliningrad-cci.ru; f. 1990; Pres. Igor V. Tsarkov.

Kamchatka Chamber of Commerce: 683000 Kamchatka Krai, Petropavlovsk-Kamchatskii, ul. Leninskaya 38/208; tel. and fax (4152) 12-35-10; e-mail kamtpp@iks.ru; Pres. Alla V. Parkhomchuk.

Krasnodar Chamber of Commerce: 350063 Krasnodar, ul. Kommunarov 8; tel. and fax (861) 268-22-13; e-mail tppkk@tppkuban.ru; internet www.tppkuban.ru; f. 1969; Chair. Yurii N. Tkachenko.

Kuzbass Chamber of Commerce: 650099 Kemerovo, pr. Sovetskii 63/407; tel. and fax (3842) 58-77-64; e-mail ktpp@mail.kuzbass.net; internet city.info.kuzbass.net/ktpp; f. 1991; Pres. TATYANA O. IVLEVA.

Maritime (Primorskii) Krai Chamber of Commerce: 690600 Maritime Krai, Vladivostok, Okeanskii pr. 13A; tel. (4232) 26-96-30; fax (4232) 22-72-26; e-mail palata@online.vladivostok.ru; internet www.ptpp.ru; f. 1964; Pres. VLADIMIR B. BREZHNEV.

Moscow Chamber of Commerce: 117393 Moscow, ul. Akademika Pilyugina 22; tel. (495) 132-07-33; fax (495) 132-75-03; e-mail extern@mtpp.org; internet www.mtpp.org; f. 1991; Chair. YURII I. KOTOV; Pres. LEONID V. GOVOROV.

Nizhnii Novgorod Chamber of Commerce: 603005 Nizhnii Novgorod, pl. Oktyabrskaya 1; tel. (8312) 19-42-10; fax (8312) 19-40-09; e-mail tpp@rda.nnov.ru; internet www.tpp.nnov.ru; f. 1990; Pres. GENNADII M. KHODYRYEV.

Northern Chamber of Commerce and Industry: 183766 Murmansk, per. Rusanova 10; tel. (8152) 47-29-99; fax (8152) 47-39-78; e-mail ncci@online.ru; internet www.ncci.ru; f. 1990; Pres. ANATOLII M. GLUSHKOV.

Novosibirsk Chamber of Commerce: 630064 Novosibirsk, pr. K. Marksa 1; tel. and fax (383) 346-41-50; e-mail org@ntpp.ru; internet www.ntpp.ru; f. 1991; Chair. BORIS V. BRUSILOVSKII; 315 mems (2002).

Omsk Chamber of Commerce: 644007 Omsk, ul. Gertsena 51/53; tel. (3812) 25-43-50; fax (3812) 23-45-80; e-mail omtpp@omsknet.ru; internet www.omsktpp.ru; f. 1992; Pres. TATYANA A. KHOROSHAVINA.

Rostov Chamber of Commerce: 344022 Rostov-on-Don, ul. Pushkinskaya 176; tel. and fax (836) 264-45-47; e-mail tpp@rost.ru; internet www.tpp.tis.ru; f. 1992; Pres. NIKOLAI I. PRISYAZHNYUK.

Sakha (Yakutiya) Chamber of Commerce: 677000 Sakha (Yakutiya), Yakutsk, ul. Lenina 22/214; tel. (4112) 26-64-96; e-mail palata91@mail.ru; f. 1991; Chair. SERGEI G. BAKULIN.

Samara Chamber of Commerce: 443099 Samara, ul. A. Tolstogo 6; tel. (8462) 32-11-59; fax (8462) 70-48-96; e-mail ccisr@samara.ru; internet cci.samara.ru; f. 1988; Pres. BORIS V. ARDALIN.

Saratov Regional Chamber of Commerce and Industry: 410600 Saratov, ul. B. Kazachya 30; tel. (8452) 27-70-78; fax (8452) 27-70-82; e-mail srcci@sgtpp.ru; internet www.sgtpp.ru; f. 1986; Pres. MAKSIM A. FATEYEV.

Smolensk Chamber of Commerce: 214000 Smolensk, ul. Bakunina 10A; tel. and fax (481) 238-74-50; e-mail smolenskcci@keytown .com; internet www.smolcci.keytown.com; f. 1993; Pres. VLADIMIR P. ARKHIPENKOV.

South Urals Chamber of Commerce: 454080 Chelyabinsk, ul. S. Krivoi 56; tel. (351) 266-18-16; fax (351) 265-41-53; e-mail mail@ uralreg.ru; internet www.uralreg.ru; f. 1992; Pres. FEDOR L. DEGTYAREV; 550 mems (2007).

St Petersburg Chamber of Commerce: 191123 St Petersburg, ul. Chaikovskogo 46–48; tel. (812) 273-48-96; fax (812) 273-48-96; e-mail spbcci@spbcci.ru; internet www.spbcci.ru; f. 1921; Pres. VLADIMIR I. KATENEV.

Stavropol Chamber of Commerce and Industry: 355003 Stavropol, ul. Lenina 384; tel. (8652) 94-53-34; fax (8652) 34-05-10; e-mail stcci@statel.stavropol.ru; f. 1991; Pres. VITALII S. NABATNIKOV.

Tatarstan Republic Chamber of Commerce and Industry: 420111 Tatarstan, Kazan, ul. Pushkina 18; tel. (843) 264-62-07; fax (843) 264-09-66; e-mail tpprt@tpprt.ru; internet www.tpprt.ru; f. 1992; Gen. Dir SHAMIL R. AGEYEV; 1,200 mems (2007).

Ulyanovsk Chamber of Commerce: 432063 Ulyanovsk, ul. Engelsa 19; tel. (8422) 41-03-61; fax (8422) 41-02-31; e-mail info@ ultpp.ru; f. 1992; Pres. YEVGENII S. BALANDIN.

Urals Chamber of Commerce and Industry: 620027 Sverdlovsk obl., Yekaterinburg, ul. Vostochnaya 6; tel. (343) 353-04-49; fax (343) 353-58-63; e-mail ucci@ucci.ur.ru; internet ucci.ur.ru; f. 1959; Pres. YURII P. MATUSHKIN.

Volgograd Chamber of Commerce: 400005 Volgograd, ul. 7-aya Gvardeiskaya 2; tel. (8442) 93-61-35; fax (8442) 34-22-02; e-mail cci@ volgogradcci.ru; internet www.volgogradcci.ru; f. 1990; Pres. ALEKSANDR D. BELITSKII.

Vologda Chamber of Commerce and Industry: 160000 Vologda, ul. Lermontova 15; tel. and fax (8172) 72-46-87; e-mail grant@ vologda.ru; internet www.vologdatpp.ru; f. 1992; Pres. GALINA D. TELEGINA.

Voronezh Chamber of Commerce: 394030 Voronezh, 'Voronezhvnesh-servis', POB 63; tel. and fax (473) 252-49-38; e-mail mail@ oootpp.vm.ru; f. 1991; fmrly Central-Black Earth Chamber of Commerce and Industry; Pres. VYACHESLAV A. KONDRATYEV.

EMPLOYERS' ORGANIZATIONS

Co-ordinating Council of Employers' Unions of Russia (Koordinatsionnyi Sovet Obyedinenii Rabotodatelei Rossii—KSORR):

109017 Moscow, per. M. Tolmachevskii 8–11; tel. (495) 232-55-77; fax (495) 959-46-06; e-mail official@ksorr.ru; internet www.ksorr.ru; f. 1994; co-ordinates and represents employers in relations with government bodies and trade unions, and represents Russian employers in the ILO and the International Organization of Employers (IOE); Chair. OLEG V. YEREMEYEV; Gen. Dir SERGEI V. LUKONIN; unites 35 major employers' unions, including the following:

Agro-Industrial Union of Russia: 107139 Moscow, POB 139; tel. (495) 204-41-04; fax (495) 207-83-62; e-mail sva@gvs.aris.ru; Pres. VASILII A. STARODUBTSEV.

All-Russian Social Organization of Small and Medium-sized Businesses (OPORA Rossii) (Obshcherossiiskaya Obshchestvennaya Organizatsiya Malogo i Srednego Predprinimatelstva): 125047 Moscow, ul. 4-ya Tverskaya-Yamskaya 21/22/3; tel. (495) 775-81-11; fax (495) 775-81-91; internet www.opora.ru; f. 2002; Pres. SERGEI BORISOV.

Russian Union of Industrialists and Entrepreneurs (Employers) (RSPPR) (Rossiiskii Soyuz Promyshlennikov i Predprinimatelei): 103070 Moscow, Staraya pl. 10/4; tel. (495) 748-42-37; fax (495) 206-11-29; e-mail pr_dep@rspp.net; internet www.rspp.ru; f. 1991; Pres. ALEKSANDR SHOKHIN; Exec. Sec. NIKOLAI TONKOV.

UTILITIES

Electricity

Federal Energy Commission: 103074 Moscow, Kitaigorodskii proyezd 7; tel. (495) 220-40-15; fax (495) 206-81-08; e-mail fecrf@ orc.ru; regulatory authority for natural energy monopolies; sole responsibility for establishing tariff rates for energy, transportation, shipping, postal and telecommunications industries in the Russian Federation from Sept. 2001; Chair. ANDREI ZADERNYUK.

Irkutskenergo (Irkutsk Energy Co): 664000 Irkutsk, ul. Sukhe-Batora 3; tel. (3952) 21-73-00; fax (3952) 21-78-99; e-mail idkan@ irkutskenergo.ru; internet www.irkutskenergo.ru; f. 1954; generation and transmission of electrical and thermal energy; Dir-Gen. VLADIMIR V. KOLMOGOROV.

Mosenergo (Moscow Energy Co): 113035 Moscow, Raushskaya nab. 8; tel. (495) 957-35-30; fax (495) 957-34-70; e-mail press-centre@ mosenergo.ru; internet www.mosenergo.ru; f. 1887; 49% owned by Unified Energy System of Russia; power generator and distributor; Chair. YURII A. UDALTSOV.

Rosenergoatom (Russian Atomic Energy Concern): 119017 Moscow, ul. B. Ordynka 24/26; tel. (495) 239-24-22; fax (495) 239-46-03; e-mail npp@rosatom.ru; internet www.rosenergoatom.ru; f. 1992; electricity generating co, manages Russia's 10 nuclear reactors; Dir-Gen. SERGEI OBOZOV.

Sverdlovenergo (Sverdlovsk Energy Co): 620219 Sverdlovsk obl., Yekaterinburg, pr. Lenina 38; tel. (343) 259-13-99; fax (343) 259-12-22; e-mail post@energo.pssr.ru; internet www.po.pssr.ru; f. 1942; Chair. of Bd ALEKSANDR V. CHIKUNOV; Gen. Man. VLADIMIR V. KALSIN.

Uralenergo (Ural Energy): 454006 Chelyabinsk, ul. Rossiiskaya 17; tel. (3512) 67-59-54; fax (3512) 67-59-48; e-mail info@uralenergo .com; internet www.uralenergo.com; manages 22 joint-stock cos; oversees 55 thermal power stations and 6 hydroelectric stations; total installed capacity of over 28,500m. kW; Dir ALEKSANDR S. NEMTSEV.

Gas

Gazprom: 117997 Moscow, ul. Nametkina 16; tel. (495) 719-30-01; fax (495) 719-83-33; e-mail gazprom@gazprom.ru; internet www .gazprom.ru; f. 1989 from assets of Soviet Ministry of Oil and Gas; became independent joint-stock co in 1992, privatized in 1994; 51% state-owned; Chair. of Bd of Dirs VIKTOR A. ZUBKOV; Chair. of Management Bd and Deputy Chair. of Bd of Dirs ALEKSEI B. MILLER.

Mezhregiongaz (Inter-Regional Gas Co): 142770 Moscow obl., Leninskii raion, p/o Kommunarkap. Gazoprovod; tel. (495) 719-53-36; fax (495) 719-52-67; e-mail pr@mrg.gazprom.ru; internet www .mrg.ru; f. 1997; gas marketing co; subsidiary of Gazprom; brs in more than 60 federal subjects; Dir-Gen. KIRILL SELEZNEV.

Water

MosVodoKanal: 105005 Moscow, per. Pleteshkovskii 2; tel. (495) 763-34-9634; fax (495) 265-22-01; e-mail post@mosvodokanal.ru; internet www.mosvodokanal.ru; f. 1937; state-owned; provides water and sewerage services to Moscow and the surrounding region; Dir-Gen. STANISLAV KHRAMENKOV.

Vodokanal: 191015 St Petersburg, ul. Kavalergardskaya 42; tel. (812) 274-16-79; fax (812) 274-13-61; e-mail office@vodokanal.spb.ru; internet www.vodokanal.spb.ru; water and sewerage utility; Gen. Man. FELIKS V. KARMAZINOV.

MAJOR COMPANIES

Bearings

Desyatyi (10th) Bearings Plant (OAO 10–GPZ) (10–i podshipni-kovkyi zavod): 344091 Rostov-on-Don, ul. Peskova 1; tel. (863) 200-21-14; fax (863) 237-43-17; e-mail gpz-10@aaanet.ru; internet www.gpz-10.aaanet.ru; manufacture of machine tools, industrial trucks and tractors and anti-friction bearings; Gen. Dir BORIS M. AMBARTSUMOV; 3,000 employees.

European Bearing Corpn (EPK) (Yevropeyskaya podshipniko-vaya korporatsiya): 115088 Moscow, ul. Novoostapovskaya 5/14; tel. (495) 775-81-30; fax (495) 775-81-33; e-mail td@epkgroup.ru; internet www.ebcorp.ru; f. 2001; design, manufacture and sale of over 2,000 types of bearings; operates factories in Moscow, Volzhskii (Volgograd obl.), Samara, Saratov, and in Stepnogorsk (Kazakh-stan); Gen. Dir ALEKSANDR KOPETSKII; 14,421 employees (2008).

Roltom—Tomskii podshipnik (Tomsk Bearings) ZAO: 634006 Tomsk, Severnyi gorodok 9; tel. (3822) 65-02-68; fax (3822) 65-51-25; internet www.roltom.ru; produces all types of bearings; Dir VIKTOR N. KAZANTSEV; 1,300 employees (2005).

SPZ Group: 443009 Samara, ul. Kalinina 1; tel. (846) 995-36-02; fax (846) 995-00-03; e-mail spz@spzgroup.ru; internet www.spzgroup.ru; operates two factories in Samara; manufacture and export of single, double and four-row tapered and cylindrical roller bearings, bearing parts, forgings and cast parts; Chair. ALEKSANDR I. SHVIDAK; Dir-Gen. MIKHAIL I. MAZUROV; over 7,000 employees (2008).

Vologda Bearing Corpn ZAO (VBF) (Vologodskii podshipnikovyi zavod): 160028 Vologda, Okruzhnoye shosse 13; tel. (8172) 53-23-70; fax (8172) 51-07-79; e-mail okid@vbf.ru; internet www.vbf.ru; f. 1967; manufactures ball-bearings; Chair. ALEKSANDR I. ELPERIN; Gen. Dir ALEKSANDR A. MELNIKOV; 3,330 employees (2007).

Chemicals

Acron OAO (Akron): 173012 Velikii Novgorod, ul. Mochenkova 17; tel. (8162) 99-61-09; fax (8162) 73-19-40; e-mail root@acron.natm.ru; internet www.acron.ru; f. 1967; fmrly Azot JSC; produces mineral fertilizers, synthetic ammonia, methanol, formalin, glues and other chemical products; owns factories in Velikii Novgorod, Verkhnedne-provskii (Smolensk obl.) and People's Republic of China; Chair. of Bd IVAN N. ANTONOV; Chair. and Dir-Gen. VALERII A. IVANOV; 10,200 employees (2003).

Apatit OAO: 184257 Murmansk obl., Kirovsk, ul. Leningradskaya 1; tel. (81531) 1-25-91; e-mail a.alexandrov@apatit.com; production of apatite concentrate and nepheline concentrate; Dir-Gen. ALEKSEI GRIGORYEV; 15,000 employees.

Kaprolaktam OAO: 606003 Nizhnii Novgorod obl., Dzerzhinsk; tel. (8313) 27-56-05; fax (8313) 33-59-87; e-mail gup@capr.nnov.ru; f. 1939; produces caustic soda, mineral fertilizers, synthetic resins and plastics; Gen. Man. ILYA P. VASYANIN; 11,960 employees.

Middle Volga Chemical Plant—Samkhimprom (Srednevolzhs-kii zavod khimikatov): 446102 Samara obl., Chapayevsk, ul. Ordz-honikidze 1; tel. (84639) 2-40-21; fax (84639) 2-39-61; e-mail komc@mail.samtel.ru; f. 1912; manufactures chemical products; Dir SERGEI V. TROPANOV; 4,000 employees.

Nizhnekamsk Oil and Chemical Plant (Nizhnekamsknefte-khim) OAO: 423574 Tatarstan, Nizhnekamsk; tel. (8555) 37-53-81; fax (095) 255-38-21; e-mail nknh@nknh.ru; internet www.nknh.ru; f. 1967; manufactures chemical products; sales 56,468.1m. (2007); Chair. of Bd ALBERT K. SHIGABUTDINOV; Gen. Man. VLADIMIR M. BUSYGIN.

Russian Scientific Centre of Applied Chemistry (Rossiiskii nauchnyi tsentr 'Prikladnaya khimiya'): 197198 St Petersburg, pr. Dobrolyubova 14; tel. (812) 499-94-84; fax (812) 703-10-94; e-mail rscac@rscac.spb.ru; internet www.rscac.spb.ru; f. 1919; research and development of chemical products, etc.; Dir-Gen. ALEKSANDR A. SHAPOVALOV; 4,500 employees.

Coal

Gukovugol (Gukovo Coal) OAO: 347879 Rostov obl., Gukovo-9, ul. Komsomolskaya 31; tel. (86361) 3-36-46; fax (86361) 5-20-30; e-mail office@hq.gukov.ugol.ru; internet www.gukov.ugol.ru; coal production; exports to Bulgaria, Greece, Turkey, etc.; Dir-Gen. A. V. GALANTSEV.

Kuzbassrazrezugol (Kuzbass Open-Cast Coal Mines): 650054 Kemerovo, Pionerskii bulv. 4A; tel. (3842) 44-03-00; fax (3842) 44-06-58; e-mail office@kru.ru; internet www.kru.ru; f. 1964; coal-mining at 13 sites in Kemerovo Oblast; Dir VASILII V. YAKUTOV.

Kuzbassugol (Kuzbass Coal) OAO: 650002 Kemerovo, pr. Shakh-terov 14A; tel. (3842) 64-18-00; fax (3842) 64-22-89; e-mail company@kuzcoal.ru; f. 1999 on basis of fmr co Severokuzbassugol (Northern Kuzbass Coal); coal-mining; Dir-Gen. MAKSIM D. BASOV.

Rosugol—Rossiiskii ugol (Russian Coal) ZAO: 121910 Moscow, ul. Novyi Arbat 15/1; tel. (495) 202-03-90; e-mail zir@cnet.rosugol.ru;

internet www.rosugol.ru; f. 1994; state-owned coal co; Gen. Dir YURII MALYSHEV.

Tulaugol (Tula Coal) OAO IVTs: 300028 Tula, ul. 9 Maya 1; tel. (487) 235-23-24; fax (487) 254-59-81; e-mail root@coalnet.ru; internet tula.coalnet.ru; production of fuel; Dir-Gen. VLADIMIR YE. SAVCHEN-KOV; 37,605 employees.

Vostsibugol—East Siberian Coal Energy Co: 664047 Irkutsk, ul. Sukhe-Batora 4; tel. (3952) 79-10-42; fax (3952) 79-11-12; e-mail press@aovsu.ru; internet www.kvsu.ru; produces coal; Pres. VLADI-MIR P. SMAGIN.

Yuzhnyi Kuzbass (Southern Kuzbass) OAO: 652870 Kemerovo obl., Mezhdurechensk, ul. Yunosti 6A; tel. (38475) 2-40-93; fax (38475) 2-23-26; e-mail priem@kuz.rikt.ru; f. 1993; 93% owned by Mechel; coal-mining at four sites in Kemerovo Oblast; Gen. Dir V. A. BEKKER; 7,500 employees.

Electrical Goods

Astrakhan Progress Machine-Construction Factory OAO (Astrakhanskii mashinostroitelnyi zavod 'Progress'): 414056 Astra-khan, ul. Savushkina 61A; tel. (8512) 25-44-54; household appli-ances, computers, lighting equipment; Dir VIKTOR A. KARCHENKO; 1,240 employees (2002).

Elektropribor (Electrical Appliances) OAO: 428000 Chuvash Rep., Cheboksary, pr. I. Yakovleva 3; tel. (8352) 21-99-12; fax (8352) 21-25-62; e-mail comm@elpr.cbx.ru; internet www.elpribor.ru; f. 1960; produces electronic measuring instruments and micropro-cessor controllers; Dir-Gen. GENNADII V. MEDVEDEV; 1,400 employees.

Elektrovypryamitel (Electrical Rectifiers) OAO: 420001 Mor-doviya, Saransk, ul. Proletarskaya 126; tel. (8342) 47-18-31; fax (8342) 47-16-64; e-mail info@elvpr.ru; internet www.elvpr.ru; f. 1941; manufactures conversion equipment and semi-conductor devices; Chair. of Bd LEV A. ROZHKOV; Dir-Gen. VLADIMIR V. CHIBIRKIN; 4,500 employees.

ELORG (Elektronorgtekhnika) VAO: 121099 Moscow, Novinskii bulv. 11A/1; tel. (495) 205-38-76; fax (495) 205-39-01; research and development of original hi-tech products for application in micro-electronics, computer software, fire-fighting systems, heating ele-ments, etc.; legal protection of intellectual property for domestic and foreign markets; Dir-Gen. YURII V. TRIFONOV.

Kaskad (Cascade) Central Scientific Production Asscn (Tsen-tralnoye nauchno-proizvodstvennoye obyedineniye 'Kaskad'): 125047 Moscow, ul. 1–aya Brestskaya 35; tel. (499) 978-58-73; fax (499) 251-66-77; e-mail kaskad@kaskad.ru; internet www.kaskad.ru; f. 1997; non-profit organization; research, design, development and manufacture of electronic, telecommunications and cybernetic systems; union of 46 enterprises; Chair. of Bd ADOLF P. KAZNACHEYEV; Dir-Gen. VALENTIN TITOV; 40,000 employees.

Kvant Industrial Asscn (FGUP NII 'Kvant'): 125438 Moscow, 4–i Likhachevskii per. 15; tel. (495) 156-73-21; fax (495) 154-14-18; e-mail info@rdi-kvant.ru; internet www.rdi-kvant.ru; f. 1958; radio and satellite communications equipment for military purposes; 3,500 employees; Dir Dr V. V. KARATANOV.

Petrovsk Molot (Hammer) Electro-Mechanical Factory GUP (Molot, Petrovskii elektromekhanicheskii zavod): 412520 Saratov obl., Petrovsk, ul. Gogolya 40; tel. (84555) 3-37-01; fax (84555) 2-94-72; f. 1938; state-owned; auto-steering devices, 'Liliya' washing-machines; 6,000 employees; Dir VLADIMIR V. ZAKHAROV.

Schetmash (Calculating Machines) OAO: 305901 Kursk, ul. Republikanskaya 6; tel. and fax (471) 226-15-22; e-mail mail@schetmash.ru; internet www.schetmash.ru; f. 1948; production of personal computers, cash registers, printers, typewriters and other consumer goods; Dir-Gen. ALEKSEI B. FORTOV; 5,000 employees.

Ufa Svet (Light) Electric Lamp Factory OAO (UELZ–Svet) (Ufimskii elektrolampovyi zavod 'Svet'): 450029 Bashkortostan, Ufa, ul. Yubileinaya 1; tel. (3472) 42-52-13; fax (3472) 42-52-30; e-mail uelz@ufanet.ru; internet svet.ufanet.ru; produces electric light bulbs and lamps; Dir-Gen. TAISA S. KOSILOVA; 2,300 employees (2002).

Export and Import

AtomStroiEksport (Atomic Construction Export) ZAO (ASE): 115184 Moscow, ul. M. Ordynka 35/3; tel. (495) 737-90-37; fax (495) 232-37-25; e-mail post@atomstroyexport.ru; internet www.atomstroyexport.ru; f. 1998 by merger of Atomenergoeksport (Atomic Energy Export) and Zarubezhatomenergostroi (Foreign Atomic Energy Construction); export and import of equipment for nuclear-power generation and research; undertakes projects and services in the field of nuclear science and technology; Pres. SERGEI SHMATKO.

Aviaeksport (Aviation Export) VO: 127018 Moscow, ul. Obraz-tsova 21A; tel. (495) 737-31-50; fax (495) 737-31-11; e-mail info@aviaexport.com; internet www.aviaexport.ru; f. 1961; export sales and product support of aircraft, air navigational aids and other civil aviation equipment; Chair. of Bd M. P. MAIOROV; 1,300 employees.

Eksportkhleb (Bread Export) ZAO: 119002 Moscow, per. Sivtsev Vrazhek 25/9; tel. (495) 244-47-01; fax (495) 253-90-69; e-mail aza@khleb.tz.ru; f. 1923; transferred to private ownership 1991; grain production, trade, export and import of wheat, rye, barley, maize, oil seeds etc.; chartering, forwarding, transportation, insurance; Pres. ALEKSANDR N. BELIK.

Eksportles (Forestry Export) ZAO: 101986 Moscow, Archangelskii per. 1; tel. (495) 660-34-26; fax (495) 728-40-50; e-mail info@exportlesimport.ru; internet www.exportles.ru; f. 1926; exports and imports sawn and round timber, wooden articles, wood pulp, paper and cardboard; imports machines and equipment for timber enterprises, consumer goods and foodstuffs; sets up joint ventures, carries out import and export operations under compensation agreements, conducts market research and consulting services; Dir-Gen. ALEKSANDR I. KRYLOV; 200 employees.

Gammachim (Gammakhim): 107078 Moscow, POB 183; 125167 Moscow, 4–aya ul. 8–go Marta; tel. (495) 975-00-23; fax (495) 975-88-66; e-mail info@gammachim.net; internet www.gammachim.net; f. 1990 to replace Soyuzkhimeksport (Union of Chemical Exporters); exports and imports soaps, plant oils, animal fats, petroleum and chemical products; Pres. V. A. ROMANOV.

Litsenzintorg (Licenintorg—Licensed International Trade) GPVO: 115093 Moscow, ul. Podoliskoye shosse 8/5; tel. (495) 797-63-60; fax (495) 958-09-83; e-mail info@licenz.ru; internet www.licenz.ru; f. 1962; foreign economic and commercial activities; Chair. ALEKSANDR V. ZEMSKOV.

Mashinoimport (Machine Import) GPVO: 109017 Moscow, ul. B. Ordinka 40/37/1; tel. (495) 244-33-09; fax (495) 244-38-07; e-mail general@machin.ru; internet www.machim.ru; f. 1933; exports services associated with the construction of pipelines, coal mines, etc.; imports power engineering and pumps, compressors, hoisting and conveying equipment, extracting equipment for the petroleum and natural-gas industries, industrial fittings; Gen.-Dir OLGA M. VDOVICHENKO; 180 employees.

Novoeksport (New Export) GUP VO: 117393 Moscow, ul. Arkhitektora Vlasova 13; tel. (495) 128-09-54; fax (495) 128-16-12; e-mail novoexport@tsr.ru; imports and exports textile fibres, yarn, fabrics, petroleum products, raw materials, ferrous and non-ferrous metals and products, porcelainware; Chair. VLADIMIR A. KRUZHKOV; 30 employees.

Soyuzpromexport (Union of Industrial Exports) GPVO (Industrial Exports Union): 129090 Moscow, Vasnetsova per. 1; tel. (495) 244-19-73; fax (495) 631-64-50; e-mail spe@mail.cnt.ru; internet www.sojuzpromexport.ru; f. 1930; imports and exports coal and coal by-products, manganese, chrome and iron ore, asbestos and other mineral and semi-finished products; provides intermediary, legal and consultancy services to Russian and foreign partners; Chair. VALERII V. IGNATOV; 90 employees.

Soyuzpushnina OAO VO (Furs Union): 123557 Moscow, B. Tishinskii per. 38; tel. (495) 648-00-71; fax (495) 648-00-73; e-mail sojuzpushnina@sojuzpushnina.ru; internet www.sojuzpushnina.ru; f. 1996; opened to private ownership in 1999; exports and imports furs, bristles, animal hair, hides, skins and casings, oils, etc.; organizes international fur auctions in St Petersburg, concludes long-term agreements for deliveries of fur goods to foreign firms; Chair. V. M. IVANOV.

SoyuzVneshTrans OOO (SVT) (Internal Transit Union): 119019 Moscow, Gogolevskii bulv. 17; tel. (495) 637-37-95; fax (495) 913-63-53; e-mail svt@svt.ru; internet www.svt.ru; f. 1962; handles transport and forwarding of imports, exports and transit goods; Dir-Gen. DMITRII ANTONOV; 100 employees.

Sudoeksport (Maritime Export) GVP: 123242 Moscow, ul. Sadovaya-Kudrinskaya 11; tel. (499) 252-11-83; fax (499) 200-22-50; e-mail info@sudoexport.ru; internet www.sudoexport.ru; f. 1988; exports ships, ships' equipment and equipment for shipbuilding; repairs of ships and equipment; foreign-trade services; import of services and delivery of goods, etc.; Dir-Gen. YEVGENII A. GARNOV.

Sudoimport (Maritime Import) GVP: 127006 Moscow, Uspenskii per. 10; tel. (495) 699-02-14; fax (495) 755-57-17; e-mail sudoim@dol.ru; internet www.sudoimport.ru; f. 1954; exports and imports all kinds of ships, marine equipment and spare parts, licences and allied consultancy services; provides maintenance and repairs of ships and marine equipment; Dir-Gen. MIKHAIL R. MAKSIMENKO; 40 employees (2008).

Tekhsnabeksport (Technical Supplies and Export) OAO (TENEX): 119180 Moscow, Staromonetnyi per. 26; tel. (495) 239-26-83; fax (495) 230-26-38; e-mail tenex@online.ru; internet www.tenex.ru; f. 1963; export and import of isotopes, ionizing radiation sources; export of heat-producing elements for various types of atomic reactors, components and parts for nuclear-power stations, rare and rare-earth metals, nuclear physics equipment, laboratory and medical facilities; Dir-Gen. VLADIMIR A. SMIRNOV; 200 employees.

Traktoroexport (Tractor Export) OAO: 123100 Moscow, Shmitovskii pr. 3; tel. and fax (495) 660-02-54; e-mail trex-ltd@mostcom.ru; f. 1961; import and export, sales promotion, marketing, and aftersale service of tractors, commercial vehicles and agricultural and construction machinery; Gen. Dir IGOR K. TERENTIYEV.

Vneshintorg: 109147 Moscow, Marksistskaya ul. 5; tel. (495) 911-90-12; fax (495) 274-01-02; e-mail vit@col.ru; f. 1992 by merger of Vneshposyltorg and Vostokintorg; exports and imports foodstuffs, consumer goods and raw materials; participates in joint-venture operations and wholesale and retail trade; Gen. Dir NAZAR BELYAYEV; 320 employees.

Food, Beverages and Tobacco

Baltika Brewery OAO (Pivovarennaya kompaniya Baltika): 194292 St Petersburg, 6-oi Verkhnii per. 3; tel. (812) 329-91-38; fax (812) 329-78-78; e-mail post@baltika.ru; internet www.baltika.ru; f. 1990; beer and soft drinks; Pres. ANTON O. ARTEMYEV.

Donskoi Tabak (Don Tobacco) OAO: 344000 Rostov-on-Don, ul. Krasnoarmeiskaya 170; tel. (8632) 250-58-14; fax (863) 240-29-34; e-mail info@dontabak.ru; internet www.dontabak.ru; f. 1992; Chair. SERGEI SAPOTNITSKII; 1,346 employees.

Krasnyi Oktyabr (Red October) Moscow Confectionery Factory OAO (Moskovskaya konditerskaya fabrika 'Krasnyi Oktyabr'): 119072 Moscow, Bersenevskaya nab. 6; tel. (495) 230-07-33; fax (495) 230-03-66; internet www.konfetki.ru; f. 1867; affiliated to Obyedinennye konditery (United Confectioners) Holdings within the Guta-Gruppa; manufacture of confectionery; Chair. MIKHAIL YU. CHEBOTAREV; Pres. ANATOLII N. DAURSKII; 3,200 employees.

Murmansk Fish (Murmanrybprom) OAO: 183001 Murmansk, ul. Tralovaya 38; tel. (8152) 28-62-39; fax (8152) 47-67-25; manufacture and sale of fish and fish-food products; Dir-Gen. ALEKSEI I. KOLESOV.

Nestlé Food Rossiya OOO: 115054 Moscow, ul. Valovaya 1/1; tel. (495) 725-70-00; fax (495) 725-70-70; e-mail consumer.services@ru.nestle.com; internet www.nestle.ru; f. 1995; manufacture and distribution of confectionery, coffee and various foodstuffs; Dir JENNIFER GALENKAMP.

Obyedinennye Konditery (United Confectioners): 115184 Moscow, 2-i Novokuznetskii per. 13/15; tel. (495) 730-69-80; fax (495) 730-69-46; e-mail info@uniconf.ru; f. 2002; managing co for 20 confectionery factories across Russia, inc. Red October, Rot Front and Babayevskii; Gen. Dir SERGEI NOSENKO.

Prodintorg GUP VO: 103084 Moscow, ul. Myasnitskaya 47; tel. (495) 244-20-60; fax (495) 244-26-29; e-mail pit@ropnet.ru; f. 1952; exports and imports meat, sugar, milk powder, butter, tobacco and tobacco products, vegetable oil, other oils; equipment for food industry; Pres. LEONID V. TIKHOMIROV; 50 employees.

Rot-Front OAO: 115184 Moscow, 2-i Novokuznetskii per. 13/15; tel. (495) 951-84-78; fax (495) 953-91-63; e-mail info@rotfront.ru; internet www.rotfront.ru; f. 1826; production of confectionery, sweets and chocolate products; affilated to Obyedinennye konditery (United Confectioners) Holdings within the Gruppa-Guta; Gen. Dir VALERII I. PYSHNYAK; 2,500 employees.

Soyuzplodoimport (Union of Food Imports) FKP—SPI: 113191 Moscow, Gamsonovskii per. 2/2; tel. (495) 781-73-15; fax (495) 780-90-62; internet www.spimport.ru; state-owned; export and import of alcoholic and soft drinks, fresh and processed fruit and vegetables, teas, coffees and spices; Dir-Gen. VLADIMIR G. LOGINOV.

SPI Group: 103030 Moscow, ul. Dolgorukovskaya 34/2; tel. (495) 973-23-08; fax (495) 973-21-00; e-mail pr@spi.ru; internet www.spi-group.com; fmrly Soyuzplodimport; manufactures and exports vodka, wine, spirits; Dir-Gen. ANDREI SKURIKHIN.

Vimm-Bill-Dann Produkty Pitaniya (Wimm-Bill-Dann Food Products) OAO: 109028 Moscow, ul. Solyanka 13/2; tel. (495) 925-58-05; fax (495) 925-58-00; e-mail media@wbd.ru; internet www.wbd.ru; f. 1992; dairy products and fruit juices; 40 factories nation-wide, and in Ukraine and Kyrgyzstan; Chair. DAVID M. YAKOBASHVILI; Chief Exec. SERGEI A. PLASTININ.

Machinery and Precision Equipment

ALNAS OAO: 423461 Tatarstan, Almetyevsk; tel. (8553) 25-66-77; fax (8553) 39-34-90; e-mail alnas@alnas.ru; internet www.alnas.ru; f. 1993 on basis of Almetyevsk Electrical Submersible Pumps Plant; owned by ChTPZ group (Chelyabinsk Tube Factory); principal producer of electrical pumps for crude petroleum production and water extraction from artesian wells in Russia.

Donetsk Excavator (Donetskii Ekscavator) OAO: 346330 Rostov obl., Donetsk, pl. Lenina 30; tel. and fax (863) 203-70-55; e-mail marketing@donex.ru; internet www.donex.ru; f. 1968; produces excavators for use in construction and road-building, etc.; Chair. of Bd of Dirs KONSTANTIN V. KUZIN; Gen. Dir MIKHAIL YU. DAVYDOV; 1,300 employees (2004).

Energomashkorporatsiya (Energy Machines Corpn) OAO: 119034 Moscow, per. Butikovskii 14/5; tel. (495) 792-39-34; fax

(495) 792-39-49; e-mail corp@energomash.ru; internet www .energomash.ru; owns 9 cos producing machinery and precision equipment in Russia; Chair. of Bd ALEKSANDR YU. STEPANOV.

Gidromash (Hydraulic Machinery) NPO: 129626 Moscow, 2-aya Mytishchinskaya ul. 2; tel. (495) 687-35-55; fax (495) 687-35-89; e-mail info@gidromash.com.ru; internet www.npo-gidromash.ru; f. 1931; development and manufacture of pumps and other products; Dir-Gen. NATALYA M. KAZARYAN.

Kaliningrad Elektrosvarka (Electric Welding) OAO: 236034 Kaliningrad, ul. Dzerzhinskogo 136; tel. (4012) 49-57-31; fax (4012) 49-57-51; e-mail esva@kaliningrad.ru; manufactures electric welding equipment and ballast rheostats; Dir-Gen. STANISLAV G. SOKOLOV; 731 employees.

Kaluga Turbine Works OAO (KTZ) (Kaluzhskii turbinnyi zavod): 129090 Moscow, Protopovskii per. 25; tel. (495) 688-47-65; fax (495) 688-47-65; e-mail kaluga@power-m.ru; internet www.ktz.kaluga.ru; owned by Power Machines (q.v.); produces steam and geothermal turbines, turbo-generators, heat exchangers, separators and centrifuges; Dir YURII A. MAKSIMOV; 5,200 employees (2004).

Krasnyi Proletarii (Red Proletarian) OAO: 117342 Moscow, ul. Butlerova 17; tel. (495) 424-28-33; fax (495) 424-30-55; e-mail sergeev@aokp.ru; internet www.aokp.ru; f. 1857; privatized in 1992; manufactures lathes, and wood-working and brick-making machinery; Dir-Gen. YURII I. KIRILLOV; 955 employees.

Power Machines (Silovye mashiny): 129090 Moscow, Protopopovskii per. 25A; tel. (495) 725-27-63; fax (495) 725-27-42; e-mail mail@ power-m.ru; internet www.power-m.ru; f. 2000; manufactures and modernizes power-generating equipment for hydro-, thermal- and nuclear-power plants; owned by Interros; unites the following companies: Elektrosila (Electric Power); Energomasheksport (Energy Machinery Export Co); Leningradskii metallicheskii zavod (Leningrad Metal Plant); Kaluzhskii turbinnyi zavod (Kaluga Turbine Works—q.v.); NPO TsKTI im. I. I. Polzunova, Zavod turbinnykh lopatok (Turbine Blades Plant); Chair. of Bd ALEKSEI A. MORDASHOV; Dir-Gen. IGOR YU. KOSTIN.

Proletarskii Zavod (Proletarian Factory) OAO: 192029 St Petersburg, ul. Dudko 3; tel. (812) 600-12-80; fax (812) 567-37-33; e-mail info@proletarsky.ru; internet proletarsky.ru; f. 1826; manufacture of marine, power engineering and general engineering machinery; Dir-Gen. TATYANA V. LYUTIKOVA (acting); 4,000 employees (2005).

Pskov Electro-machine Construction Plant) OAO (PEMZ) (Pskovskii elektromashinostroitelnyi zavod): 180004 Pskov, Oktyabrskii pr. 27; tel. (8112) 70-06-90; fax (8112) 70-06-75; e-mail sales@pemz.ru; internet www.pemz.ru; f. 1895; manufactures DC generators, low-capacity electric motors, low-voltage units, outboard engines; Gen. Dir VASILII A. IGNATIYEV; 1,500 employees.

Sibagromash (Siberian Agricultural Machines) FPG: 658205 Altai Krai, Rubtsovsk, ul. Krasnaya 100; tel. (38557) 4-26-25; fax (38557) 2-30-00; e-mail altaiselmash@mail.ru; f. 1941; transferred to private ownership 1992; design and manufacture of all types of agricultural machinery and hand tools; Dir-Gen. VIKTOR K. TOLSTOV; 5,500 employees.

Sibenergomash (Siberia Energy Machines) OAO: 656037 Altai Krai, Barnaul, pr. Kalinina 26; tel. (3852) 77-85-40; fax (3852) 77-81-77; e-mail par@energomash.ru; internet www.sibenergomash.ru; f. 1942; subsidiary of Energomashkorporatsiya; forging and pressing machines, automatic machines and semi-automatic machine-tools; Dir-Gen. IVAN V. KONEV; 5,402 employees.

Taganrog Metallurgical Plant OAO (TagMet) (Taganrogskii metallurgicheskii zavod): 347928 Rostov obl., Taganrog, ul. Zavodskaya 1; tel. (8634) 32-42-01; e-mail general@tagmet.ru; internet www.tagmet.ru; f. 1896; 57% owned by Rinako-MDM; production of steel tubing, boring equipment; Chair. of Bd ANDREI YU. KAPLUNOV; Dir-Gen. NIKOLAI I. FARTUSHNYI.

Tulamashzavod—Tula Machine Plant OAO: 300002 Tula, ul. Mosina 2; tel. (487) 236-24-65; fax (487) 227-26-20; e-mail reclama@ tulamash.ru; internet www.tulamash.ru; f. 1939; manufactures equipment and machinery for mining and the petroleum and gas industry, motorcycles, laser tools, woodworking machinery and sewing machines; Dir-Gen. YEVGENII A. DRONOV; 1,500 employees.

Tyazhmash (Heavy Machinery) OAO: 446010 Samara obl., Syzran, ul. Gidroturbinnaya 13; tel. (8464) 37-22-81; fax (8464) 99-06-10; e-mail ztm-serv@tyazhmash.com; internet www.tyazhmash .com; f. 1941; heavy turbines and conveyor belts; equipment for hydroelectric power stations; Dir-Gen. SERGEI F. TRIFONOV.

United Machinery Plants OAO (OMZ) (Obyedinennye mashinostroitelnye zavody): 119021 Moscow, ul. T. Frunze 24; tel. (495) 662-10-40; fax (495) 662-10-41; e-mail mail@omzglobal.ru; internet www .omz.ru; undertakes research and development, and manufacture of heavy industrial engineering equipment; Chair. FARID M. KANTSEROV; Dir-Gen. VIKTOR G. DANILENKO.

Volgatsemmash (Volga Cement Machines) OAO: 445621 Samara obl., Tolyatti, ul. M. Gorkogo 96; tel. (8482) 29-53-31; fax (8482) 22-28-59; e-mail mail@zavod-vcm.ru; internet www .zavod-vcm.ru; f. 1956; manufactures equipment for building-materials and ore-mining industries, autoclaves, steel, iron and bronze castings, vessels and tanks for chemical industry, steel forgings and steel-machined forgings, welded metal-working; Dir-Gen. ANATOLII V. KOMIN; 6,000 employees.

Yaroslavl Electric-Machine Construction Plant (ELDIN) (Yaroslavskii Elektromashinostroitelnyi Zavod): 150040 Yaroslavl, pr. Oktyabrya 74; tel. (485) 278-00-00; fax (485) 278-00-01; e-mail info@eldin.ru; internet www.eldin.yaroslavl.ru; Dir-Gen. TURSUN A. AKHUNOV.

Metals

Evraz Group (Yevraz): 127006 Moscow, ul. Dolgorukovskaya 15/4–5; tel. (495) 234-46-31; fax (495) 234-46-30; e-mail info@evraz.com; internet www.evraz.com; f. 1999; fmrly YevrazKholding; owns steel plants, iron-ore and coal mines in Russia, and Nakhodka sea port, in addition to interests in Czech Republic, Italy, Ukraine and the USA; sales US $6,508.1m. (2005); Chair. ALEKSANDR V. FROLOV.

Kamensk-Uralskii Metallurgical Works OAO (KUMZ) (Kamensk-Uralskii metallurgicheskii zavod): 623405 Sverdlovsk obl., Kamensk-Uralskii, ul. Zavodskaya 5; tel. (3439) 39-53-00; fax (3439) 39-55-12; e-mail any@kumz.ru; internet www.kumz.ru; f. 1944; produces alloys and semi-finished and rolled product types from copper, bronze, brass, nickel and zinc; Man. Dir ALEXEI V. FILIPPOV.

Krasnoyarsk Metallurgical Plant (KraMZ) (Krasnoyarskii metallurgicheskii zavod): 660111 Krasnoyarsk, Prombaza; tel. (3912) 56-35-25; fax (3912) 65-67-89; e-mail secretary@kramz .rusal.ru; 41.7% state-owned, 28% owned by Russian Aluminium (RusAl); public joint-stock co; manufacture and sale of rolled, extruded, drawn and forged aluminium products; Dir-Gen. YURII I. VOLCHENKO; 4,500 employees.

MMK—Magnitogorsk Iron and Steel Works OAO (MMK) (Magnitogorskii metallurgicheskii kombinat): 455002 Chelyabinsk obl., Magnitogorsk, ul. Kirova 93; tel. (3519) 24-40-09; fax (3519) 24-73-09; e-mail azovtseva@mmk.ru; internet www.mmk.ru; f. 1932; sales US $4,635,000m. (2004); Chair. VIKTOR F. RASHNIKOV; 31,300 employees (2004).

Mechel OAO: 125993 Moscow, ul. Krasnoarmeiskaya 1; tel. (495) 221-88-88; fax (495) 221-88-00; e-mail alexander.tolkach@mechel .com; internet www.mechel.ru; f. 1943; iron and steel; Dir-Gen. I. V. ZYUZIN.

Metalloinvest: 125047 Moscow, ul. Lesnaya 3; tel. (495) 981-55-55; fax (495) 981-99-92; e-mail info@metinvest.ru; internet www .metinvest.ru; f. 1999; own various plants across Russia for production, export, erection, installation, commissioning, maintenance and servicing of full-range equipment for ferrous and non-ferrous metallurgy and steel-making; Founding Dir ALISHER B. USMANOV; Chair. of Bd ARDAVAN MOSHIRI; 5,600 employees.

Nizhnii Tagil Iron and Steel Plant OAO (NTMK) (Nizhnetagilskii metallurgicheskii kombinat): 622025 Sverdlovsk obl., Nizhnii Tagil, ul. Metallurgov 1; tel. (3435) 49-72-70; fax (3435) 49-06-94; e-mail post@ntmk.ru; internet www.ntmk.ru; f. 1940; owned by Evraz Group; mining; production of coke-chemical, refractory, blast, smelted-steel and rolled products; Man. Dir ALEKSEI V. KUSHNAREV; 27,000 employees.

Norilsk Nickel OAO GMK (Norilskii Nikel): 125993 Moscow, per. Voznesenskii 22; tel. (495) 787-82-94; fax (495) 786-83-94; e-mail erohin@nk.nornik.ru; internet www.nornik.ru; f. 1994; nickel and platinum-group metals; owned by Interros; subsidiary cos in Russia, and in Finland, Africa (Botswana and South Africa), Australia and the USA; sales US $7,030m. (2005); Dir-Gen. VLADIMIR STRZHALKOVSKII.

Novokuznetsk Metallurgical Plant OAO (Novokuznetskii metallurgicheskii kombinat—NKMK): 654010 Kemerovo obl., Novokuznetsk, pl. Pobedy 1; tel. (3843) 79-22-20; fax (3843) 79-58-58; e-mail pcn@nkmk.ru; internet www.nkmk.ru; f. 2003 on basis of Kuznetsk Metallurgical Plant; owned by Evraz Group; steel products, principally rails; Man. Dir ALEKSEI B. YURYEV.

Novolipetsk (New Lipetsk) Metallurgical Group OAO (Novolipetskii metallurgicheskii kombinat): 398040 Lipetsk, pl. Metallurgov 2; tel. (474) 244-40-06; fax (474) 244-11-11; e-mail info@nlmk.ru; internet www.nlmksteel.com; f. 1931; transferred to private ownership 1992; production of cast-iron, rolled stock, dynamo steel, transformer steel, etc.; Chair. of Bd VLADIMIR S. LISIN; Pres. ALEKSEI LAPSHIN; 35,291 employees.

Pervouralskii Tube Manufacturing Plant OAO (Pervouralskii novotrubnyi zavod): 623112 Sverdlovsk obl., Pervouralsk, ul. Torgovaya 1; tel. (34392) 7-77-77; fax (34392) 7-77-78; e-mail mail@pntz .com; internet www.pntz.com; f. 1934; owned by ChTPZ group

(Chelyabinsk Tube Factory); production of steel piping and steel cylinders; Chair. of Bd M. A. GRESKO; 22,000 employees.

RUSAL: 109240 Moscow, ul. Nikoloyamskaya 13/1; tel. (495) 720-51-70; fax (495) 720-51-71; e-mail press-center@rusal.ru; internet www.rusal.ru; f. 2000 by merger; producer of aluminium, with operations in Russia and internationally; Chair. OLEG V. DERIPASKA; Chief Exec. ALEKSANDR BULYGIN.

Severovostokzoloto (North-Eastern Gold) OAO: 685005 Magadan, ul. Proletarskaya 12; tel. (41322) 2-38-21; fax (41322) 2-38-65; e-mail postmaster@svz.magadan.su; production of gold, silver, tin and mining equipment; Gen. Dir ALEKSANDR V. POLYAKOV.

Severstal (Northern Steel) OAO: 162600 Vologda obl., Cherepovets, ul. Mira 30; tel. (8202) 53-09-09; fax (8202) 57-12-76; internet www.severstal.ru; f. 1951; Dir-Gen. ANATOLII N. KRUCHININ.

Severstal-Metiz (ChSPZ): 162600 Volodga obl., Cherepovets, ul. 50-letiya Oktyabrya 1/33; tel. (8202) 53-91-91; fax (8202) 53-85-20; e-mail press@chspz.ru; internet www.severstalmetiz.com; f. 1966; fmrly Cherepovets Steel-Rolling Plant; hardware, steel wire, wire nails, meshes, electrodes, fasteners, wire ropes, reinforcing steel, steel bars; Chair. of Bd VADIM A. SHVETSOV; Dir-Gen. OLGA V. NAUMOVA; 15,000 employees (2005).

Volgograd Krasnyi Oktyabr (Red October) Metallurgical Plant OAO (Volgogradskii metallurgicheskii zavod 'Krasnyi Oktyabr'): 400007 Volgograd, pr. Lenina 110; tel. (8442) 74-80-91; fax (8442) 74-89-99; e-mail ved@vmzko.ru; internet www.vmzko.ru; f. 1898; transferred to private ownership 1999; manufacture of grade steels, round rolled products, rolled wire, hexahedron, drilling hollow rolled sheets, ingots, cableware; Dir-Gen. SERGEI K. NOSOV; 15,000 employees.

VSMPO-AVISMA: 624760 Sverdlovsk obl., Verkhnyaya Salda, ul. Parkovaya 1; tel. (34345) 2-14-37; fax (34345) 2-47-36; internet www.vsmpo.ru; f. 2005 by merger; production of ingots and semi-finished products from titanium alloys, pressed products from aluminium alloys, etc.; entered into partnership with Boeing (USA) to manufacture aircraft parts from titanium; incorporated into Rostekhnologii (Russian Technologies) State Corpn in late 2007; Pres. VLADISLAV V. TETYUKHIN; Dir-Gen. YEVGENII V. ROMANOV.

Zapsib—West Siberian Metal Works OAO (Zapsib—Zapadno-Sibirskii metallurgicheskii kombinat): 654043 Kemerovo obl., Novokuznetsk; tel. (3843) 59-59-08; fax (3843) 59-43-43; internet www.zsmk.ru; f. 1964; owned by Evraz Group; manufacture and sale of pig iron and products in carbon and alloy steel; Gen. Dir RASHID F. NUGUMANOV; 35,000 employees.

Motor Vehicles and Components

Agromash-Holding: 125040 Moscow, ul. Verkhnyaya 34; tel. and fax (495) 580-70-10; e-mail amh-info@agromh.com; internet www.vgtz.com; owns 14 concerns producing industrial, agricultural, machine-construction and defence machinery and equipment, incl. Krasnoyarsk Combine Plant, Altai Motor Plant, Vladimir Motor-tractor Plant, Lipetsk Tractor Co and Volgograd Tractor Plant; Pres. NATALYA YU. PARTASOVA; Dir-Gen. YEVGENII L. ALEKSEYEV.

Altai Tractor Production Asscn (PO Altaiskii traktor): 658212 Altai Krai, Rubtsovsk, ul. Traktornaya 17; tel. (38557) 3-83-09; fax (38557) 3-32-96; e-mail www@alttrak.ru; internet www.alttrak.ru; f. 1942; design and production of tractors; Gen. Dir ARTUR A DERFLER.

Avtoeksport (Automobile Export) ZAO: 115998 Moscow, 2-oi Verkhnii Mikhailovskii pr. 9; tel. (495) 958-54-96; fax (495) 633-15-35; e-mail avtoex@dol.ru; internet www.avtoexport.ru; f. 1956; subsidiary of Avtotraktoroeksport; publicity and promotion of sales, engineering, marketing and after-sale servicing of motor vehicles and equipment; 4 subsidiary cos; Dir-Gen. BORIS D. BORISOV.

Avtoframos OAO: 109147 Moscow, ul. Vorontsovskaya 35; tel. (495) 775-48-08; fax (495) 775-40-05; e-mail fleet.sales-avtoframos@renault.com; internet www.renault.ru/ru/about/avtoframos/company; f. 1998; 94.1% owned by Renault (France), 5.9% by Moscow City Govt; manufactures Renault automobiles; also sole authorized importer of Renault automobiles to Russia; Dir-Gen. GUY BARA.

AvtoUAZ (Ulyanovsk Automobile Plant) OAO (UAZ) (Ulyanovskii avtomobilnyi zavod): 432008 Ulyanovsk, Moskovskoye shosse 8; tel. (8422) 40-97-55; fax (8422) 40-60-70; e-mail press@uaz.ru; internet www.uaz.ru; f. 1941; manufacture of enhanced cross-country capability vehicles; sales 12,623m. (2004); Man. Dir B. I. KUPERMAN.

AvtoVAZ (Volga Automobile Plant) OAO: 445024 Samara obl., Tolyatti, Yuzhnoye shosse 36; tel. (8482) 73-80-09; fax (8482) 73-71-71; e-mail press@vaz.ru; internet www.lada-auto.ru; f. 1966; manufactures the Lada brand of cars; in 2002 began to manufacture Chevrolet Niva automobiles and sports-utility vehicles as part of a jt venture with General Motors (USA); controlled by Rosoboroneksport since 2005; incorporated into Rostekhnologii (Russian Technologies) State Corpn in late 2007; Chair. of Bd SERGEI V. CHEMEZOV; Pres. BORIS I. ALESHIN.

Fuel Systems (Toplivnye sistemy) OAO: 192102 St Petersburg, ul. Samoilovoi 5; tel. (812) 766-44-05; fax (812) 766-63-13; e-mail Gogichashvili.COMM@topsys.spb.ru; internet www.topsys.spb.ru; f. 1999 as successor to the Leningrad Carburettor Plant (LenKarZ); design, development and manufacture of 'Pekar' and other carburettors, fuel injection components, fuel pumps, cooling system pumps for automobiles and light commercial vehicles; Dir TATYANA V. FILIPPOVA; 2,500 employees (2003).

Chelyabinsk Tractor Plant—Uraltrak (ChTZ) (Chelyabinskii traktornyi zavod 'Uraltrak'): 454007 Chelyabinsk, pr. Lenina 3; tel. (351) 717-17-60; fax (351) 772-95-83; e-mail tractor@chtz.chel.su; internet www.chtz-uraltrac.ru; f. 1933; caterpillar tractors; Gen. Dir VALERII M. PLATONOV; 35,000 employees.

ChETRA—Industrial Machinery Co (OAO 'ChETRA—Promyshlennye mashiny'): 428028 Chuvash Rep., Cheboksary, pr. Traktorostroitelei 101; tel. (8352) 63-36-30; e-mail marketing@chetra.ru; internet www.chetra.ru; f. 1974; transferred to private ownership 1993; production, maintenance and repair of heavy-duty crawler tractors and associated parts; manufacture of plastic and metal children's toys, garden accessories and tools; wood-working, etc.; Chair. of Bd NIKOLAI A. GROMOV; 14,500 employees.

GAZ Group (Gruppa GAZ): 603004 Nizhnii Novgorod, pr. Lenina 88; tel. (8312) 56-26-02; fax (8312) 53-88-89; e-mail general@atom.gaz.ru; internet www.gazgroup.ru; f. 2005; majority stake owned by Russian Machines Holding; owns several automobile factories, including the Gorky Automobile Plant, the Pavlovsky Automobile Plant, the Likinsky Automobile Plant, Avtodizel, the Ural Automobile Plant and the Tver Excavator Plant; manufactures trucks, cars, buses, spare parts, motor vehicles, excavators, components and consumer goods under various brand names including GAZ, PAZ, LiAZ, GAZel, Sobol, Valdai, Sadko, Volga, YaMZ, Ural and TvEks; also owns LDV automobile factory in Birmingham (United Kingdom); sales 152,800m. (2007); Pres. SERGEI G. ZANOZIN; Chair. of Bd LARS ERIK EBBE EBERKHARDSON.

Kaluga Factory of Auto-Electro Equipment—KZAE (OAO Kaluzhskii zavod avtoelektro oborudovaniya): 248017 Kaluga, ul. Azarovskaya 18; tel. and fax (484) 253-15-03; e-mail ovs@kzae.kaluga.ru; internet www.kzae.ru; f. 1941; design and manufacture of a wide range of electronic motors and control units for the automobile industry; Chair. of Bd ANATOLII N. FAYEROVICH; Gen. Dir ALEKSANDR G. VERYASOV (acting); 4,000 employees (2008).

KamAZ (Kama Automobile Plant) OAO: 423800 Tatarstan, Naberezhnye Chelny, pr. M. Dzhalilya 29; tel. and fax (8552) 37-19-08; e-mail pr@kamaz.net; internet www.kamaz.net; f. 1971; manufactures and distributes heavy trucks, diesel engines, spare parts and tools; Dir-Gen. SERGEI A. KOGOGIN.

I. A. Likhachev Automobile Plant OAO (AMO ZIL) (Avtomobilnyi zavod im. Likhacheva): 115280 Moscow, ul. Avtozavodskaya 23; tel. (495) 675-33-28; fax (495) 674-61-62; e-mail abulova.amozil@mail.ru; internet www.amo-zil.ru; f. 1916; manufactures ZIL trucks and spare parts, church bells; Gen. Dir KONSTANTIN V. LAPTEV.

Lipetsk Tractor Co (OAO Lipetskii traktor): 398000 Lipetsk, ul. Krasnozavodskaya 1; tel. (474) 273-14-59; fax (474) 273-23-46; e-mail ltz@lipetsk.ru; internet www.ltz.lipetsk.ru; f. 1944; manufactures tractors; Dir-Gen. ANDREI I. STOLPOVSKII; 9,500 employees.

Motordetal-Kostroma (OOO 'Motordetal-Kostroma'): 156001 Kostroma, ul. Moskovskaya 105; tel. (494) 262-84-05; fax (494) 262-84-30; e-mail info@motordetal.ru; internet www.motordetal.ru; f. 1967; manufactures pistons and other automobile spare parts; cap. 515.3m.; sales 1,872.6m. (2004); Dir-Gen. SERGEI V. KALASHNIK; 4,739 employees (2005).

Pavlovo Bus Co (OAO Pavlovskii avtobus): 606108 Nizhnii Novgorod obl., Pavlovo, ul. Suvorova 1; tel. (83171) 3-12-27; fax (83171) 6-03-18; e-mail bereg@paz.nnov.ru; internet www.paz.nnov.ru; f. 1932; manufactures buses; Dir-Gen. ANDREI V. VASILYEV; 9,000 employees.

SM Holding: 660021 Krasnoyarsk, ul. Bograda 109; tel. (3912) 77-91-10; fax (3912) 59-56-85; e-mail info@smh.ru; internet www.smh.ru; fmrly Krasselmash Production Technological Complex, subsequently renamed SibmashKholding; production of Yenisei combine harvesters, parts, and diesel motors; Pres. IGOR V. RAZDAIBEDA; 12,000 employees.

Staryi Oskol Automobile and Tractor Equipment Plant ZAO (SOATE) (Staroskolskii zavod avtotraktronogo oborudovaniya): 309507 Belgorod obl., Staryi Oskol, ul. Vatutina 54; tel. (472) 522-09-65; fax (472) 524-10-15; e-mail info@soate.ru; internet www.soate.com; f. 1959; parts for tractors, automobiles and household goods; Dir-Gen. YEVGENII A. ARZAMASTSEV; 3,500 employees.

Tyumen Automobile and Tractor Electrical Equipment ZAO (TATE) (Tyumenskii zavod avtotraktornogo elektrooborudovaniya ZAO): 625002 Tyumen, ul. Tsiolkovskogo 1; tel. (3452) 24-12-34; fax (3452) 24-15-32; e-mail marktate@sbtx.tmn.ru; produces coil distributors, plugs, electric stoves, electric immersion heaters; Plant Dir VLADISLAV P. ZAGVAZDIN; 2,500 employees.

Directory

Vladimir Motor-tractor Plant (VMTZ) (OAO Vladimirskii motoro-traktornyi zavod): 600000 Vladimir, ul. Traktornaya 43; tel. (49) 223-18-31; fax (492) 223-13-55; e-mail vmtz@vladtractor.ru; internet www.vladtractor.ru; f. 1945; design and manufacture of diesel air-cooled engines and tractors; Exec. Dir IGOR B. KALINICHENKO; 3,032 employees (July 2004).

Paper and Pulp

Archangelsk (Archangel) Pulp and Paper Mill OAO (ARKh-BUM) (Arkhangelskii tsellyulozno-bumazhnyi kombinat): 164900 Archangel obl., Novodvinsk, ul. Melnikova 1; tel. (81852) 6-31-23; fax (81852) 6-32-79; e-mail market@appm.ru; internet www.appm.ru; f. 1940; joint-stock co. since 1992; manufactures pulp and paper; annual capacity of 834,478 metric tons (2006); sales US \$385m. (2006); Chair. of Bd HEINZ ZINNER; Dir-Gen. VLADIMIR BELOGLAZOV; 6,421 employees (2006).

Ilim Group: 191025 St Petersburg, ul. Marata 17; tel. (812) 718-60-50; fax (812) 718-60-06; e-mail office@ilimgroup.ru; internet www.ilimgroup.ru; f. 1992; incorporated assets of Ilim Pulp Enterprises 2006; subsidiary units incl. Ilim-Zapad, Ilim-Vostok, Ilim Gofroupakovka, Fintrans and Ilim Eksim; Chair. of Bd ZAKHAR D. SMUSHKIN; Dir-Gen. PAUL HERBERT.

Segezha Pulp and Paper Mill OAO (Segezhskii TsBK) (Segezhskii tsellyulozno-bumazhnyi kombinat): 186420 Kareliya, Segezha, ul. Zavodskaya 1; tel. (81431) 3-40-00; fax (81431) 4-32-53; e-mail office@scbk.ru; internet www.scbk.ru; f. 1939; paper-sack, kraft-liner and kraft-paper manufacturer; pulp producer; Exec. Dir VLADIMIR I. YERMAKOV; 3,600 employees (2008).

Petroleum, Petrochemicals and Natural Gas

Astrakhangazprom OOO: 416154 Astrakhan obl., Krasnoyarsk raion, pos. Aksaraisk, ul. Babushkina 9; tel. (8512) 31-41-84; fax (8512) 39-11-33; e-mail adm@astrakhan.gazprom.ru; internet www.astrakhangazprom.ru; subsidiary of Gazprom; production of gasoline, liquefied gas and diesel oil; Dir-Gen. VITALII A. ZAKHAROV.

Gazprom neft OAO: 117647 Moscow, ul. Profsoyuznaya 125A; tel. (495) 777-31-52; fax (495) 777-31-51; e-mail Vyalkina.NV@gazprom-neft.ru; internet www.gazprom-neft.ru; f. 1995 as Sibneft; present name adopted 2006; petroleum co, 28 subsidiary production cos, incl. eight production cos, and one refining co; 75.7% owned by Gazprom from 2005; Chair. of Bd ALEKSEI B. MILLER; Dir-Gen. ALEKSANDR V. DYUKOV.

Komi Oil ZAO (KNK) (Komi neftyanaya kompaniya): 169400 Komi, Ukhta, ul. Oktyabrskaya 13; tel. (82147) 6-26-12; fax (82147) 6-18-08; f. 2000 by merger; exploration and development of petroleum and natural-gas fields and associated activities in the Republic of Komi and Archangel Oblast; Pres. VASILII V. DEVYATOV; 22,000 employees.

Lukoil OAO: 101000 Moscow, Sretenskii bulv. 11; tel. (495) 627-44-44; fax (495) 625-70-16; e-mail pr@lukoil.com; internet www.lukoil.com; extraction, refining and distribution of petroleum; f. 1991 by merger; five principal production subsidiary cos, four principal refining subsidiary cos, three principal national marketing and distribution subsidiary cos, 14 regional marketing and distribution subsidiary cos, two subsidiary cos conducting international operations (refining, marketing, distribution, exploration and production); 51% acquired by subsidiary of Gazprom, Gazprom neft OAO, in March 2007; Chair. of Bd VALERII I. GRAIFER; Pres. and Dir VAGIT YU. ALEKPEROV; 114,000 employees.

Rosneft Oil Co (OAO NK Neftyanaya kompaniya 'Rosneft'): 115035 Moscow, Sofiiskaya nab. 26/1; tel. (495) 777-44-22; fax (495) 777-44-44; e-mail postman@rosneft.ru; internet www.rosneft.ru; f. 1995; 100% state-owned; petroleum exploration and production; 40 subsidiary operations in the North Caucausus, Northern Russia, Sakhalin and Western Siberia; acquired fmr subsidiary of Yukos, Yugaskneftegaz in 2004 and other fmr assets of Yukos in May 2007; Chair. of Bd of Dirs IGOR I. SECHIN; Pres. SERGEI M. BOGDANCHIKOV; 69,880 employees.

SIBUR Kholding OAO: 117997 Moscow, ul. Krzhizhanovskogo 16; tel. and fax (495) 777-55-00; e-mail info@sibur.ru; internet www.sibur.ru; Chair. of Bd ALEKSANDR V. DYUKOV; Chair. of Management DMITRII V. KONOV.

Slavneft NGK: 125047 Moscow, 4–i Lesnoi per. 4; tel. (495) 787-82-06; fax (495) 777-73-17; e-mail slavneft@slavneft.ru; internet www.slavneft.ru; f. 1994; transferred to private ownership in 2002; 19 subsidiary cos, incl. six extraction cos, three refining cos; Chair. of Bd GERMAN B. KHAN; Pres. YURII YE. SUKHANOV.

Stroitransgaz OAO (Stroytransgaz): 117418 Moscow, ul. Novocheremushkinskaya 65; tel. (495) 332-90-73; fax (495) 332-79-66; e-mail smi@stroytransgaz.com; internet www.stroytransgaz.com; f. 1990; 25% owned by Gazprom; pipeline design and construction; involved in the 'Blue Stream' project for the transportation of petroleum from Russia to Turkey, under the Black Sea, and in construction of petroleum sector infrastructure internationally, incl.

in India and Saudi Arabia; Chair. of Bd ALEKSANDR KRASNENKOV; Pres. VIKTOR YA. LORENZ.

Surgutneftegaz (Surgut Oil and Gas) OAO (SNG): 628400 Tyumen obl., Khanty-Mansii AOk—Yugra, Surgut, ul. Kukuyevitskogo 1; tel. (3462) 42-61-33; fax (3462) 42-63-63; e-mail secret_b@surgutneftegas.ru; internet www.surgutneftegas.ru; f. 1993; petroleum and natural-gas production; Dir-Gen. VLADIMIR L. BOGDANOV; 84,500 employees.

Tatneft (Tatar Oil) OAO: 423400 Tatarstan, Almetyevsk, ul. Lenina 75; tel. (8533) 25-58-56; fax (8553) 25-68-65; e-mail tnr@tatneft.ru; internet www.tatneft.ru; f. 1950; transferred to private ownership 1990; petroleum survey and exploration; petroleum drilling; production and export; civil and industrial construction; manufacture of plastic coated metal pipes, cable and wire products and petroleum production equipment and tools; Chair. of Bd RUSTAM N. MINNIKHANOV (Prime Minister of the Republic of Tatarstan); Gen. Dir SHAFAGAT F. TAKHAUTDINOV; 65,489 employees.

TNK-BP: 119019 Moscow, ul. Arbat 1; tel. (495) 777-77-07; fax (495) 787-96-68; e-mail company@tnk-bp.ru; internet www.tnk-bp.ru; f. 2003 by merger of Sidanco, Tyumen Oil Co (TNK) and the Russian interests of BP (United Kingdom); 50% owned by Alfa-Group and Access/Renova, 50% owned by BP; 13 subsidiary cos involved in extraction, 5 subsidiary cos in refining, 11 subsidiary cos in marketing and distribution; Chair. MIKHAIL M. FRIDMAN; Exec. Dir GERMAN KHAN; 93,000 employees in Russia and Ukraine (2006).

Miscellaneous

Alrosa AK: 678170 Sakha (Yakutiya), Mirnyi, ul. Lenina 6; tel. (41136) 3-01-80; fax (41136) 3-04-51; e-mail info@alrosa.ru; internet www.alrosa.ru; f. 1957; joint stock co since 1992; 47.6% owned by the Federal State Property Fund, 32.0% by the Govt of the Republic of Sakha (Yakutiya), 8.0% by four district govts within Sakha (Yakutiya); 48 subsidiary or dependent cos; producer of rough diamonds, commercial diamond mining, manufacturing of polished diamonds, trade in rough and polished diamonds, development of diamondiferous deposits, construction, transportation; cap. 61,538.9m. roubles (Jan. 2005), sales US \$2,692.6m. (2007); Pres. SERGEI A. VYBORNOV.

Altaidizel—Altai Motor Plant (OAO PO Altaidizel—Altaiskii motornyi zavod): 656023 Altai Krai, Barnaul, pr. Kosmonavtov 8; tel. (3852) 77-37-86; fax (3852) 75-16-43; internet www.altdiesel.ru; f. 1992 on basis of Altai Motor Plant; owned by SM Holding; manufactures diesel engines, fuel pumps, etc.; Gen. Dir VLADIMIR M. ZAKHAROV; 3,800 employees.

Aviastar (AO Aviastar SP): 432072 Ulyanovsk, pr. Antonova 1; tel. (8422) 28-17-18; fax (8422) 21-00-39; internet www.aviastar-sp.ru; f. 1977; established as a joint stock co 1992; 75% plus 1 share owned by the Russian Govt, 25% less one share owned by Sirocco Aerospace International (Egypt); production and export of TU 204 and AN 124 aircraft; Chair. of Bd DENIS V. MANTUROV; Dir-Gen. VIKTOR V. MIKHAILOV; 35,000 employees.

Interros: 119180 Moscow, ul. B. Yakimanka 9; tel. (495) 785-63-63; fax (495) 785-63-64; e-mail info@interros.ru; internet www.interros.ru; holding co for energy, financial and media cos, including Norilsk Nickel (q.v.), Power Machinery (q.v.), Prof-Mediya and Rosbank (q.v.); Pres. VLADIMIR POTANIN; Dir-Gen. and Chair. ANDREI KLISHAS.

Kama-Volga Rubber Products Corpn—QUART (Kamsko-Volzhskoye AO rezinotekhniki—KVART): 420045 Tatarstan, Kazan, ul. Tekhnicheskaya 25; tel. (843) 278-48-91; fax (843) 237-75-62; e-mail kvart@bancorp.ru; internet kvart.knet.ru; f. 1942; transferred to private ownership 1992; manufactures rubber products; Dir-Gen. MUSLIM G. KHAIRETDINOV; 5,000 employees.

S. P. Korolev Energiya Space-Rocket Corpn (Raketno-kosmicheskaya korporatsiya 'Energiya' im. S. P. Koroleva): 141700 Moscow obl., Korolev, ul. Lenina 4A; tel. (495) 513-72-48; fax (495) 187-98-77; e-mail mail@rsre.ru; internet www.energia.ru; f. 1946; development and operation of manned space technology, special-purpose satellite complexes; development and production of non-space products based on space technologies, including prosthetic and orthopedic products, consumer goods, automatic ecological monitoring stations, power facilities; operates the Mir space station; involved, with Boeing (USA), Kvaerner (United Kingdom/Norway) and Pivdenne Yuzhnoye MK Yangel NPO (Ukraine), in the Sea Launch programme, which aims to launch communications satellites from the Pacific Ocean; cap. 1,100m. roubles, sales (2001) 3,400m. roubles; Pres. VITALII A. LOPOTA; 17,000 employees (incl. subsidary cos) in 2002.

Maritime Satellite Communications (Morsvyazsputnik) FGUP: 107564 Moscow, Krasnobogatyrskaya 2/2, POB 28; tel. (495) 967-18-50; fax (495) 967-18-34; e-mail root@marsat.glasnet.ru; internet www.marsat.ru; communications and navigational aids; Pres. VALERII A. BOGDANOV; 75 employees.

Moscow Rubin Co (OAO MTZ 'Rubin'): 121087 Moscow, Bagrationovskii proyezd 7/1; tel. (495) 737-92-92; fax (495) 730-00-40; e-mail info@rubin.ru; internet www.rubin.ru; construction of commercial and residential buildings; Dir-Gen. UPENDRA MAKHATO.

Rosoboroneksport (Russian Defence Export) Co: 119991 Moscow, Gogolevskii bulvar 21; tel. (495) 637-81-77; fax (495) 202-45-94; e-mail media@post.rusarm.ru; internet www.roe.ru; state-owned; export/import of defence-related and dual-use products, technologies and services; f. 2001 by merger of Rosvooruzheniye (Russian Weapons Co) and Promeksport (Industrial Export Co); sales US $5,300m. (2006); incorporated into Rostekhnologii (Russian Technologies) State Corpn in late 2007; Dir-Gen. ANATOLII P. ISAIKIN.

Rostekhnologii (Russian Technologies) State Corpn: 119992 Moscow, Gogolevskii bulv. 21; tel. (495) 291-81-77; fax (495) 202-45-94; internet www.rostechnologii.ru; f. 2007; state special exporter of machine products in the civilian and military spheres; subsidiary cos include AvtoVAZ (Volga Automobile Plant), Rosoboroneksport (Russian Defence Export) Co and VSMPO-AVISMA; Dir-Gen. SERGEI V. CHEMEZOV.

Selkhozpromeksport (Agro-Industrial Export) FGUP VVO: 115324 Moscow, Ovchinnikovskaya nab. 18/1; tel. (495) 950-16-92; fax (495) 921-93-64; e-mail agiro@4unet.ru; internet www.shpex.mpi.ru; f. 1964; assists in construction of hydrotechnical and irrigation facilities, storage plants and other agricultural projects; also involved in the fishing industry, petroleum extraction and the timber, microbiological and confectionary industries; Chair. VLADIMIR P. MORGUTOV; 120 employees.

Slava—Second Moscow Watch and Clock Factory OAO (Slava—Vtoroi moskovskii chasovoi zavod): 125040 Moscow, Leningradskii pr. 8; tel. and fax (495) 223-27-70; e-mail info@slava.ru; internet www.slava-moscow.ru; f. 1924; produces 'Slava' mechanical and electronic watches and clocks; Dir-Gen. N. A. ANANYEV; 10,000 employees.

Sukhoi Co (OAO Komaniya 'Sukhoi'): 125284 Moscow, ul. Polikarpova 23B, POB 604; tel. (495) 940-26-63; fax (495) 945-68-06; e-mail avpk@sukhoi.org; internet www.sukhoi.org; manufactures military and civilian aircraft; seven subsidiary cos; Gen. Dir MIKHAIL A. POGOSYAN; c. 31,000 employees (2008).

Tekhnopromeksport (Techno-Industry Export) OAO VO: 119019 Moscow, ul. Novyi Arbat 15/2; tel. (495) 950-15-23; fax (495) 953-33-73; e-mail inform@tpe.ru; internet www.tpe.ru; f. 1955; power equipment and materials; construction of power projects on a turn-key basis; mediatory and consultancy services on foreign economic activities in Russia and abroad; Dir-Gen. SERGEI V. MOLOZHAVYI; 250 employees.

Tekhnopromimport (Techno-Industry Import) VO: 125284 Moscow, 1–i Khoroshevskii proyezd 3A/2; tel. (495) 940-07-06; fax (495) 940-09-66; e-mail tpi-admin@mtu-net.ru; internet www.technopromimport.ru; f. 1930; assists in petroleum production; construction of industrial plants, pharmaceutical plants, hospitals, schools; Chair. V. V. ILIN; 70 employees.

Terekalmaz—Terek Diamond Tool Factory OAO (Terskii zavod almaznogo instrumenta 'Terekalmaz'): 361200 Kabardino-Balkar Rep., Terek, ul. Tatuyeva 1; tel. (86632) 4-36-90; fax (86632) 4-36-26; e-mail mail@terekalmaz.ru; internet www.terekalmaz.ru; f. 1961; produces diamond-boring tools, diamond drills, etc.; Gen. Dir ADALBI B. TLEUZHEV; 2,000 employees.

Tyazhpromeksport (Heavy Industry Export) VO: 113324 Moscow, Ovchinnikovskaya nab. 18/1; tel. (495) 950-16-10; fax (495) 230-22-03; e-mail tyazh@dol.ru; f. 1957; assists construction and extension of integrated iron and steel mining complexes and hardware plants; Chair. NIKOLAI V. ULYANOV; 171 employees.

Vneshstroiimport (External Construction Import) OAO: 125009 Moscow, Tverskoi bulv. 6; tel. (495) 200-32-04; fax (495) 291-35-60; e-mail info@sovstrim.ru; f. 1974; arranges joint construction projects with foreign and domestic firms; consultancy relating to engineering, construction and investment; Pres. VALERII A. AINBUND; Man. Dir BORIS YURIYEV; 150 employees (2003).

Vologda Timber-Industry Holding Co (OOO Kholdingovaya kompaniya vologodskiye lesopromyshlenniki): 160604 Vologda, ul. Blagoveshchenskaya 47; tel. and fax (8172) 72-88-14; e-mail mail@volwood.ru; internet www.volwood.ru; f. 1997; produces birch and coniferous sawn timber, plywood, etc.; Chair. of Bd ALEKSANDR N. CHUPKIN.

Yantar (Amber) Baltic Shipyard OAO (Pribaltiiskii sudostroitelnyi zavod 'Yantar'): 236005 Kaliningrad, Transportnyi tupik 10; tel. (4012) 47-22-43; fax (4012) 47-22-43; e-mail marketing@shipyard-yantar.ru; internet www.shipyard-yantar.ru; ship-building, ship repair, mechanical engineering; Dir-Gen. NIKOLAI F. VOLOV.

TRADE UNIONS

In 1990 several branch unions of the All-Union Central Council of Trade Unions (ACCTU) established the Federation of Independent Trade Unions of the Russian Federation (FITUR), which took control of part of the property and other assets of the ACCTU. The ACCTU was re-formed as the General Confederation of Trade Unions of the USSR, which was, in turn, renamed the General Confederation of Trade Unions—International Organization in 1992.

All-Russian Labour Confederation: 103031 Moscow, ul. Rozhdestvenka 5/7; tel. (495) 785-21-30; fax (495) 915-83-67; e-mail vktrussia@online.ru; internet www.trud.org/guide/VKT.htm; f. 1995; unites five national trade unions and 40 regional orgs with 1,270,900 mems; Pres. ALEKSANDR N. BUGAYEV.

General Confederation of Trade Unions (VKP): 119119 Moscow, Leninskii pr. 42; tel. (495) 938-01-12; fax (495) 938-15-29; e-mail inter@vkp.ru; internet www.vkp.ru; f. 1992 to replace General Confederation of Trade Unions of the USSR; co-ordinating body for trade unions in CIS member states; unites 10 national and 32 regional industrial orgs with 52m. mems; publishes *Profsoyuzy* (Trade Unions), weekly, *Vestnik profsoyuzov* (Herald of the Trade Unions), every two weeks, and *Inform-Contact*, in English and French, quarterly; Pres. MIKHAIL SHMAKOV; Sec.-Gen. VLADIMIR SCHERBAKOV.

Federation of Independent Trade Unions of Russia (FITUR) (Federatsiya Nezavisimykh Profsoyuzov Rossii—FNPR): 119119 Moscow, Leninskii pr. 42; tel. (495) 938-73-12; fax (495) 137-06-94; e-mail korneev@fnpr.ru; internet www.fnpr.ru; f. 1990; Pres. MIKHAIL V. SHMAKOV.

FITUR unites 48 national trade unions and 78 regional orgs (with c. 40m. mems), including the following:

All-Russian 'Electroprofsoyuz': 117119 Moscow, Leninskii pr. 42/3; tel. (495) 938-83-78; fax (495) 930-98-62; f. 1990; electrical workers; Pres. VALERII P. KUZICHEV.

Automobile and Farm Machinery Construction Industries Workers' Union: 117119 Moscow, Leninskii pr. 42/3; tel. (495) 938-76-13; fax (495) 938-86-15; Pres. YULII G. NOVIKOV.

Communication Workers' Union of Russia: 117119 Moscow, Leninskii pr. 42/3; tel. (495) 938-72-06; fax (495) 930-22-86; f. 1905; Pres. ANATOLII G. NAZEIKIN.

Construction and Building Materials Industry Workers' Union of the Russian Federation: 117119 Moscow, Leninskii pr. 42/1; tel. (495) 930-71-74; fax (495) 952-55-47; f. 1991; Pres. BORIS A. SOSHENKO.

Health Workers' Union of the Russian Federation: 117119 Moscow, Leninskii pr. 42/3; tel. (495) 938-84-43; fax (495) 938-81-34; e-mail ckprz@online.ru; f. 1990; Chair. MIKHAIL M. KUZMENKO.

Moscow Trade Unions Federation: 121205 Moscow, ul. Novyi Arbat 36/9; tel. (495) 290-82-62; fax (495) 202-92-70; e-mail main@mtuf.ru; f. 1990; largest regional branch of FITUR; Chair. MIKHAIL D. NAGAITSEV; 2.2m. mems.

Motor Transport and Road Workers' Union of Russia: 117218 Moscow, ul. Krzhizhanovskogo 20/30/5; tel. (495) 125-23-30; fax (495) 125-07-98; e-mail profavtodor@mtu.ru; f. 1990; Pres. VIKTOR I. MOKHNACHEV.

National Educational and Scientific Workers' Union of the Russian Federation: 117119 Moscow, Leninskii pr. 42/3; tel. (495) 938-87-77; fax (495) 930-68-15; f. 1990; Pres. VLADIMIR M. YAKOVLEV.

Oil, Gas and Construction Workers' Union: 119119 Moscow, Leninskii pr. 42/4; tel. (495) 930-69-74; fax (495) 930-11-24; e-mail rogwu@rogwu.ru; internet www.rogwu.ru; f. 1990; Pres. LEV A. MIRONOV.

Russian Chemical Industry Workers' Union: 117119 Moscow, Leninskii pr. 42/3; tel. (495) 930-69-93; fax (495) 938-21-55; e-mail rcwu@fnpr.ru; f. 1990; Pres. ALEKSANDR SITNOV (acting).

Russian Fishing Industry Workers' Union: 117119 Moscow, Leninskii pr. 42/3; tel. (495) 938-77-82; fax (495) 930-77-26; e-mail bfish@fnpr.ru; f. 1991; Pres. YURII V. SHALONIN.

Russian Independent Trade Union of Coal-industry Workers (Rosugleprof): 109004 Moscow, ul. Zemlyanoi Val 64/2; tel. (495) 915-28-52; fax (495) 915-30-77; Chair. IVAN I. MOKHNACHUK.

Russian Radio and Electronics Industry Workers Union: 109180 Moscow, 1-i Golutvinskii per. 3; tel. (495) 238-08-02; fax (495) 238-17-31; Pres. VALERII YE. MARKOV.

Russian Textiles and Light Industry Workers' Union: 117119 Moscow, Leninskii pr. 42/3; tel. (495) 938-78-24; fax (495) 938-84-05; f. 1990; Pres. TATYANA I. SOSNINA.

Russian Trade Union of Railwaymen and Transport Construction Workers (Rosprofzhel): 109029 Moscow, ul. Novorogozhskaya 29; tel. (495) 262-17-90; fax (495) 623-96-70; e-mail ckpintd@css-rzd.ru; Pres. NIKOLAI NIKIFOROV.

Shipbuilding Workers' Union: 117119 Moscow, Leninskii pr. 42/5; tel. (495) 938-88-72; fax (495) 938-84-74; Pres. VLADIMIR YE. MAKAVCHIK.

Timber Industry Workers' Union of the Russian Federation: 117119 Moscow, Leninskii pr. 42/1; tel. (495) 938-89-03; fax (495) 137-06-81; Pres. VALERII N. OCHEKUROV.

Union of Agro-industrial Workers of the Russian Federation: 119119 Moscow, Leninskii pr. 42/3; tel. (495) 938-77-35; fax (495) 938-82-63; e-mail info@profagro.ru; f. 1919; Pres. NATALIYA N. AGAPOVA; 2.3m. mems (2007).

Union of Engineering Workers of the Russian Federation: 127486 Moscow, ul. Deguninskaya 1/2; tel. (495) 487-3507; fax (495) 487-56-37; Pres. YURII S. SPICHENOK.

Union of Food Industry and Production Co-operative Workers of the Russian Federation: 117119 Moscow, Leninskii pr. 42/3; tel. (495) 938-75-03; fax (495) 930-10-56; Pres. VALERII K. ZHOVTERIK.

Independent Trade Unions

Federation of Air Traffic Controllers' Unions of Russia (FPAR): 125993 Moscow, Leningradskii pr. 37/472, POB 3; tel. (495) 155-57-01; fax (495) 155-59-17; e-mail postmaster@fatcurus.ru; internet www.fatcurus.ru; f. 1989; Pres. SERGEI A. KOVALEV.

Metallurgical Industry Workers' Union: Moscow, ul. Pushkinskaya 5/6; left the FITUR in 1992 to form independent organization; Pres. BORIS MISNIK.

Transport

RAILWAYS

At the end of 2006 the total length of railway track in use was 84,821 km, around one-half of which was electrified.

Russian Railways OAO (RZhD) (Rossiiskie zheleznyye dorogi): 107174 Moscow, ul. Novobasmannaya 2; tel. (495) 262-16-28; fax (495) 975-24-11; e-mail info@rzd.ru; internet www.rzd.ru; f. 2003; Pres. VLADIMIR YAKUNIN.

City Underground Railways

Moscow Metro: 129110 Moscow, pr. Mira 41/2; tel. (495) 622-10-01; fax (495) 631-37-44; e-mail info@mosmetro.ru; f. 1935; 12 lines (294 km) with 176 stations in 2007; Gen. Man. DMITRII V. GAYEV.

Nizhnii Novgorod Metro: 603002 Nizhnii Novgorod, pl. Revolutsii 7; tel. (8312) 44-17-60; fax (8312) 44-20-86; e-mail metro@sandy.ru; f. 1985; 15 km with 13 stations; Gen. Man. A. KUZMIN.

Novosibirsk Metro: 630099 Novosibirsk, ul. Serebrennikovskaya 34; tel. (3832) 90-81-10; fax (3832) 46-56-82; e-mail nsk@metro.snt .su; internet www.nsk.su/~metro; f. 1986; 2 lines (13.2 km) with 11 stations, and a further 6 km under construction; Gen. Man. V. I. DEMIN.

St Petersburg Metro: 190013 St Petersburg, Moskovskii pr. 28; tel. (812) 251-66-68; fax (812) 316-14-41; e-mail np@metro.spb.ru; internet www.metro.spb.ru; f. 1955; 4 lines (106 km) with 60 stations; Gen. Man. VLADIMIR A. GARYUGIN.

Short underground railways began to operate in Samara, Yekaterinburg and Kazan in 1987, 1991 and 2005, respectively. In 2008 the construction of underground railways was under way in Chelyabinsk, Krasnoyarsk and Omsk, and a light railway was scheduled to open in Sochi, prior to the holding of the Winter Olympics there in 2014.

ROADS

At the end of 2006 the total length of roads was 597,421 km, and 85.2% of roads were paved. In Siberia and the Far East there are few roads, and they are often impassable in winter, while the *rasputitsa*, or spring thaw, notoriously impedes rural road traffic, even in European Russia.

SHIPPING

The seaports of the Russian Federation provide access to the Pacific Ocean, in the east, the Baltic Sea and the Atlantic Ocean, in the west, and the Black Sea, in the south. Major eastern ports are at Vladivostok, Nakhodka, Vostochnyi, Magadan and Petropavlovsk. In the west St Petersburg and Kaliningrad provide access to the Baltic Sea, and the northern ports of Murmansk and Archangel (Arkhangelsk) have access to the Atlantic Ocean, via the Barents Sea. Novorossiisk and Sochi are the principal Russian ports on the Black Sea.

Principal Shipowning Companies

Baltic Shipping Co: 198035 St Petersburg, Mezhevoi kanal 5; tel. (812) 251-33-97; fax (812) 186-85-44; freight and passenger services; Chair. MIKHAIL A. ROMANOVSKII.

Baltic Transport Systems: 199106 St Petersburg, pl. Morskoi Slavy 1; tel. (812) 303-99-14; fax (812) 380-34-76; e-mail bts@baltics .ru; internet www.baltics.ru; f. 1994; freight and passenger services; Gen. Dir ALEKSEI E. SHUKLETSOV.

Far Eastern Shipping Co: 690019 Maritime (Primorskii) Krai, Vladivostok, ul. Aleutskaya 15; tel. (4232) 41-14-32; fax (4232) 52-15-51; e-mail 41401@41.fesco.ru; internet www.fesco.ru; f. 1880; Gen. Man. YEVGENII N. AMBROSOV.

Kamchatka Shipping Co: 683600 Kamchatka Krai, Petropavlovsk-Kamchatskii, ul. Radiosvyazi 65; tel. (41522) 2-82-21; fax (41522) 2-19-60; f. 1949; freight services; Pres. NIKOLAI M. ZABLOTSKII.

Murmansk Shipping Co: 183038 Murmansk, ul. Kominterna 15; tel. (8152) 48-10-48; fax (8152) 48-11-48; e-mail postmaster@msco.ru; f. 1939; shipping and icebreaking services; Gen. Dir VYACHESLAV RUKSHA.

Northern Shipping Co (NSC Arkhangelsk) (Severnoye morskoye parokhodstvo OAO—SMP): 163000 Archangel, nab. Severnoi Dviny 36; tel. (8182) 63-72-03; fax (8182) 63-71-95; e-mail nsosnina@ ansc.ru; internet www.ansc.ru; f. 1870; dry cargo shipping, liner services; Gen. Dir VIKTOR A. IZBITSKII.

Novorossiisk Shipping Co: 353900 Krasnodar Krai, Novorossiisk, ul. Svobody 1; tel. (8617) 25-31-26; fax (8617) 25-11-43; e-mail novoship@novoship.ru; internet www.novoship.ru; f. 1992; Chair. V. I. YAKUNIN.

Primorsk Shipping Corpn: 692900 Maritime (Primorskii) Krai, Nakhodka-4, Administrativnyi Gorodok; tel. (4236) 69-45-05; fax (4236) 69-45-75; e-mail psc@prisco.ru; internet www.prisco.ru; f. 1972, tanker shipowner; Dir-Gen. ALEKSANDR MIGUNOV.

Sakhalin Shipping Co: 694620 Sakhalin obl., Kholmsk, ul. Pobedy 16; tel. (42433) 6-62-07; fax (42433) 6-60-20; e-mail chief@sasco .sakhalin.ru; internet www.sasco.org; f. 1945; shipowners and managers, carriage of cargo and passengers; Pres. YAKUB ZH. ALEGEDPINOV.

Sovfrakht: 127944 Moscow, Rakhmanovskii per. 4, Morskoi Dom; tel. (495) 258-27-41; fax (495) 230-26-40; e-mail general@sovfracht .ru; internet www.sovfracht.ru; f. 1929; jt-stock co; chartering and broking of tanker, cargo and other ships; forwarding, booking and insurance agency; ship management; Dir-Gen. D. YU. PURIM; 120 employees (2003).

White Sea and Onega Shipping Co (Belomorsko-Onezhskoye parokhodstvo): 185005 Kareliya, Petrozavodsk, ul. Rigachina 7; tel. (8142) 71-12-01; fax (8142) 71-12-67; e-mail dir@bop.onego.ru; internet bop.onego.ru; f. 1940; cargo shipping, cargo-ship construction and repair; Gen. Dir STANISLAV ROZOLINSKII; Pres. ALEKSANDR LYALLYA.

CIVIL AVIATION

Until 1991 Aeroflot—Soviet Airlines was the only airline operating on domestic routes in the former USSR. In 1992–94 some 300 different independent airlines emerged on the basis of Aeroflot's former regional directorates. Several small private airlines were also established. In 2003 there were 451 airports in Russia.

Aeroflot-Don: 344009 Rostov-on-Don, pr. Sholokhova 272; tel. (863) 276-78-11; fax (863) 252-11-78; e-mail avia1@aeroflot-don.ru; internet www.aeroflot-don.ru; f. 1925; present name adopted 2000; 100% owned by Aeroflot—Russian Airlines; operates scheduled and chartered passenger and cargo flights to various domestic and international destinations (incl. Armenia, Austria, Egypt, Germany, Israel, Turkey, Ukraine, United Arab Emirates) from Rostov-on-Don, Moscow and Sochi, and betwen Moscow and Groznyi; Dir-Gen. MIKHAIL S. KRITSKII.

Aeroflot—Russian Airlines: 125167 Moscow, Leningradskii pr. 37/9; tel. and fax (495) 155-66-43; internet www.aeroflot.ru; f. 1923; 51% state-owned; operates flights to 108 destinations in 54 countries, and to 26 destinations in Russia; Gen. Dir VALERII M. OKULOV.

Domodedova Airlines: 142045 Moscow, Domodedova Airport; tel. (495) 504-03-00; fax (495) 787-86-18; e-mail ak_e3@tch.ru; internet www.akdal.ru; f. 1964; scheduled passenger flights to domestic and CIS destinations; chartered passenger and freight flights to domestic, CIS and international destinations; Gen. Dir ANDREI MASLOV.

Gazpromavia: 117997 Moscow, ul. Novocheremushkinskaya, 71/32; tel. (495) 719-18-32; fax (495) 719-11-85; e-mail gazpromavia@ gazprom.ru; internet www.gazpromavia.ru; f. 1995; Dir-Gen. ANDREI S. OVCHARENKO.

KD Avia: 238315 Kaliningrad obl., Guryevskii raion, Khrabrovo, Aeroport; tel. (401) 235-51-75; e-mail info@kdavia.ru; internet www .kdavia.ru; f. 1945; present name adopted 2005; international and domestic flights from Kaliningrad; Dir-Gen. VALERII MIKHAILOV.

Kuban Airlines (Kubanskiye Avialinii): 350026 Krasnodar, Krasnodar—Pashkovskaya Airport; tel. (861) 237-06-00; fax (861) 237-38-11; e-mail info@kuban-airlines.com; internet www.kuban-airlines .de; f. 1932; regional and international flights.

Pulkovo Airlines: 196210 St Petersburg, ul. Pilotov 18/4; tel. (812) 324-36-34; fax (812) 104-37-02; internet www.pulkovo.ru; operates regular, direct flights from St Petersburg to domestic and international destinations; Gen. Dir B. G. DEMCHENKO.

S7 Airlines (Siberia Airlines): 633115 Novosibirsk obl., gorod Ob-4; tel. (3832) 59-90-11; fax (3832) 59-90-64; e-mail pr@s7.ru; internet www.s7.ru; fmrly Sibir Airlines; scheduled and charter flights to domestic, CIS, Asian, European and Middle Eastern destinations; Gen. Dir VLADISLAV FILEV.

SkyExpress: 119027 Moscow, Vnukovo, ul. Tsentralnaya 2/2; tel. (495) 648-93-60; fax (495) 980-74-61; e-mail info@skyexpress.ru; internet www.skyexpress.ru; f. 2006; 'low cost' airline operating passenger flights between Moscow (Vnukovo) and Murmansk, Rostov-on-Don and Sochi (Krasnodar Krai); Chief Exec. MARINA BUKALOVA.

Transaero Airlines: 121099 Moscow, 2-i Smolenskii per. 3/4; tel. (495) 937-84-71; fax (495) 937-84-64; e-mail info@transaero.ru; internet www.transaero.ru; f. 1991; Russia's largest privately owned airline; operates scheduled and charter passenger services to the CIS, Europe, Asia and Central America; Chief Exec. OLGA PLESHAKOVA.

Ural Airlines (Uralskiye Aviyalinii): 620910 Sverdlovsk obl., Yekaterinburg, ul. Sputnikov 6; tel. (343) 226-81-26; fax (343) 226-82-49; e-mail margarita@uralairlines.ru; internet www.uralairlines.ru; f. 1993; flights from Yekaterinburg to domestic and international destinations; Gen. Dir SERGEI SKURATOV.

Vladivostok Avia: 692756 Maritime (Primorskii) Krai, Artem, ul. Portovaya 41, Vladivostok Airport; tel. (4232) 30-73-33; fax (4232) 30-73-43; e-mail office@vladavia.ru; internet www.vladavia.ru; f. 1994; freight and scheduled passenger services from Vladivostok and Moscow to domestic and international destinations; Gen. Dir VLADIMIR SAIBEL.

Tourism

In 2006 there were 22,486,043 tourist arrivals in Russia, and receipts from tourism totalled US $9,720.

Intourist: 129366 Moscow, pr. Mira 150; tel. (495) 956-42-07; fax (495) 730-19-57; e-mail info@intourist.ru; internet www.intourist.ru; f. 1929; brs throughout Russia and abroad; Pres. NIKOLAI KAKORA.

Culture

NATIONAL ORGANIZATIONS

Ministry of Culture: see The Government (Ministries).

Federal Agency for Culture and Cinema (Federalnoye agenstvo po kulture i kinematografii): 125009 Moscow, M. Gnezdnikovskii per. 7/6; tel. (495) 229-23-11; e-mail givc@givc.ru; internet www.roskultura.ru; f. ; Dir MIKHAIL YE. SHVYDKOI.

Russian Association for International Co-operation (Rossiiskaya assotsiatsiya mezhdunarodnogo sotrudnichestva—RAMS): 121009 Moscow, ul. Vozdvizhenka 14; tel. (495) 203-90-83; fax (495) 203-84-92; f. 1992; unites more than 80 societies of cultural relations with foreign countries; Pres. ELEONORA V. MITROFANOVA.

Russian Cultural Foundation (Rossiiskii fond kultury): 119019 Moscow, 6/7/1 Gogolevskii bulv.; tel. (495) 202-69-84; fax (495) 291-71-80; e-mail info@culture.ru; f. 1986 as Cultural Foundation of the USSR; encourages interest in, and study of, cultural heritage at Russian and abroad, especially architecture, literature, music and education; Pres. NIKITA S. MIKHALKOV; Dir-Gen. VALERII ZAITSEV.

CULTURAL HERITAGE

Moscow

Museum on Delegatskaya—All-Russian Museum of Decorative, Applied and Folk Art (Muzei na Delegatskoi—Vserossiiskii muzei dekorativno-prikladnogo i narodnogo iskusstva): 127473 Moscow, ul. Delegatskaya 3; tel. (495) 923-77-25; fax (495) 923-06-20; e-mail info@vmdpni.ru; internet www.vmdpni.ru; f. 1981; decorative art from the 16th to the late 20th centuries; Dir VLADIMIR A. GULYAYEV.

S. T. Morozov Folk-Art Museum (Narodnogo isskusstva muzei im. S. T. Morozova): 103009 Moscow, Leontyevskii per. 7; tel. (495) 290-21-14; e-mail rosizo@sovintel.ru; f. 1885; handicrafts connected with peasant life, applied arts, and experimental decorative applied art; about 800,000 exhibits; Dir G. A. YAKOVLEVA.

Central A. A. Bakhrushin State Theatrical Museum (Gosudarstvennyi tsentralnyi teatralnyi muzei im. A. A. Bakhrushina): 115054 Moscow, ul. Bakhrushina 31/12; tel. (495) 953-48-48; fax (495) 953-54-48; e-mail gctm@ncport.ru; internet projects.gertstein.org/bakhrushin/web/index.html; f. 1894; materials on history and theory of theatre, including archives of original MSS of Ostrovskii, Stanislavskii, etc.; 1.3m. exhibits; library of 120,000 vols; Dir Prof. BORIS LYUBIMOV.

Central M. I. Glinka State Museum of Musical Culture (Muzikalnoi kultury gosudarstvennyi tsentralnty muzei im. M. I. Glinki): 125047 Moscow, ul. Fadeyeva 4; tel. and fax (495) 739-62-26; e-mail mglinka@rol.ru; internet www.museum.ru/glinka; f. 1912; 800,000 items, including archives, manuscripts and memorabilia, musical instruments, records and tape recordings, etc.; Dir ANATOLII D. PANYUSHKIN.

Central S. V. Obraztsov State Puppet Theatre Museum (Muzei teatralnykh kukol muzei GATsTK im. S. V. Obraztsova): 103473 Moscow, ul. Sadovo-Samotechnaya 3; tel. and fax (495) 699-79-72; e-mail gactk@mail.ru; internet www.puppet.ru/museum; f. 1937; 3,500 puppets from 60 countries; library of 15,000 vols; Dir BORIS M. KIRKIN.

Central Andrei Rublev Museum of Ancient Russian Art and Culture (Drevnerusskoi kulturi i iskusstva tsentralnyi muzei im. Andreya Rubleva): 105120 Moscow, Andronyevskaya pl. 10; tel. (495) 678-14-89; fax (495) 678-50-55; e-mail rublevmu@aha.ru; internet www.museum.ru/M422; f. 1947; collection of Russian icons dating from 14th to 19th Centuries, located in former Spaso-Andronikov Monastery; library of 23,000 vols; Dir GENNADII V. POPOV.

Moscow Kremlin State Historic-Cultural Museum-Reserve (Gosudarstvennyi istoriko-kulturnyi muzei-zapovednik 'Moskovskii kreml'): 103073 Moscow, Kreml; tel. (495) 924-55-03; fax (495) 921-63-23; e-mail head@kremlin.museum.ru; internet www.kreml.ru; includes the Armoury (f. 1857; 100,000 items; weapons, arms and jewels from the 12th century to 1917) and the Kremlin Cathedrals (including Cathedral of the Assumption—f. 1479, icons of the 14th–17th centuries, throne of Ivan IV—'the Terrible'); Dir YELENA YU. GAGARINA.

Russian State Arts Library (Rossiiskaya gosudarstvennaya biblioteka po iskusstvu): 103031 Moscow, ul. B. Dmitrovka 8/1; tel. and fax (495) 692-06-53; e-mail bisk@liart.ru; internet www.liart.ru; f. 1922; over 2m. items (books, periodicals, press cuttings, engravings, sketches, postcards, photographs, posters); Dir ADA A. KOLGANOVA.

Russian State Library (Rossiiskaya gosudarstvennaya biblioteka): 121019 Moscow, ul. Vozdvizhenka. 3/5; tel. (495) 202-35-65; fax (495) 913-69-33; e-mail mbs@rsl.ru; internet www.rsl.ru; f. 1852 as the Rumyantsev Library, reorganized 1925; fmrly Lenin State Library of the USSR; 42.7m. books, periodicals and serials, newspapers in all 91 languages of the former USSR and 156 foreign languages, 480,600 manuscripts, 860 archival collections, etc.; Dir VIKTOR V. FEDOROV.

A. V. Shchusev State Scientific-Research Museum of Architecture (MUAR) (Gosudarstvennyi naucho-issledovatelskii muzei arkhitektury im. A. V. Shchuseva): 119019 Moscow, ul. Vozdvizhenka 5/25; tel. and fax (495) 291-21-09; e-mail schusev@muar.ru; internet www.muar.ru; f. 1934; exhibitions and research in the field of architectural history; over 70,000 sheets of architectural drawings and prints; over 500,000 negatives and 600,000 photographs of architectural monuments; architectural materials; painting, sculpture, furniture and clothing from the 16th to the 20th centuries; library of 50,000 vols; Dir DAVID A. SARKISYAN; Curator I. V. SEDOVA.

State Archives of the Russian Federation (Gosudarstvennyi arkhiv Rossiiskoi Federatsii): 119992 Moscow, ul. B. Pirogovskaya 17; fax (495) 245-12-87; e-mail garf@online.ru; internet garf.narod.ru; f. 1920; more than 5.6m. items; Dir SERGEI V. MIRONENKO.

State Historical Museum (Gosudarstvennyi istoricheskii muzei): 109012 Moscow, Krasnaya pl. 1/2; tel. (495) 692-56-60; fax (495) 692-62-67; e-mail shkurko@shm.ru; internet www.shm.ru; f. 1872; 4.5m. exhibits on Russian history; library of 100,000 vols, 29,000 manuscripts, collection of birch-bark writings; 3 br. museums; Dir-Gen. ALEKSANDR I. SHKURKO.

Novodevichii Convent Museum (Muzei 'Novodevichii monastyr'): 119435 Moscow, Novodevichii proyezd 1; tel. (495) 246-22-01; fax (495) 246-85-26; e-mail m337@mail.museum.ru; internet www.shm.ru/novodev.html; Russian fine and decorative art of the 16th and 17th centuries, situated in a late 17th-century convent including the Smolensk Cathedral (1624), converted into a museum in 1922; Dir IRINA G. BORISENKO.

State Literature Museum (Gosudarstvennyi literaturnyi muzei): 103051 Moscow, ul. Petrovka 28; tel. (495) 921-38-57; fax (495) 924-60-24; e-mail silvercentury@mtu-net.ru; internet www.museum-glm.ru; f. 1934; library of 400,000 vols; 450,000 works of art and prints; collections of manuscripts and materials on folklore; 12 br. museums; Gen. Dir NATALIYA V. SHAKHALOVA.

State Museum of Ceramics and the 18th Century Kuskovo Estate (Gosudarstvennyi muzei keramiki i usadba Kuskovo XVIII veka): 111402 Moscow, ul. Yunosti. 2; tel. (495) 370-01-50; fax (495)

918-65-40; e-mail kuskovo@kuskovo.ru; internet www.kuskovo.ru; large collection of Russian and foreign art, ceramics and glass, located in fmr country residence of the Counts Sheremetevo; Dir YELENA S. YERITSYAN.

State Museum of Oriental Art (Gosudarstvennyi muzei iskusstva narodov vostoka): 1190190 Moscow, Nikitskii bulv. 12A; tel. (495) 291-03-41; fax (495) 202-48-46; e-mail info@orientalart.ru; internet www.orientalart.ru; f. 1918; large collection of art of the Middle and Far East, and of the fmr Soviet Central Asian Republics and Transcaucasia, carpets, fabrics, ceramics; Dir-Gen. VLADIMIR A. NABATCHIKOV.

State A. S. Pushkin Museum of Fine Arts (Gosudarstvennyi muzei izobrazitelnykh iskusstv im. A. S. Pushkina): 121019 Moscow, ul. Volkhonka 12; tel. (495) 203-95-78; fax (495) 203-46-74; e-mail finearts@gmii.museum.ru; internet www.museum.ru/gmii; f. 1912; some 558,000 items of ancient Eastern, Graeco-Roman, Byzantine, European and American art; library of 200,000 vols; Dir IRINA A. ANTONOVA.

State L. N. Tolstoi Museum (Gosudarstvennyi muzei L. N. Tolstogo): 119034 Moscow, ul. Prechistenka 11; tel. (495) 202-21-90; fax (495) 202-93-38; e-mail tolstoy@comcor.ru; internet www .tolstoymuseum.ru; f. 1911; contains 300,000 manuscripts and archive material, incl. 170,000 sheets of Tolstoi's writings; library of 79,000 works by or about Lev Tolstoi; 100,000 newspaper cuttings, and more than 47,000 exhibits in the form of painting, sculpture, photographs, etc; Dir VITALII B. REMIZOV.

State Tretyakov Gallery (Gosudarstvennaya Tretyakovskaya Galereya): 109017 Moscow, Lavrushinskii per. 10; tel. (495) 230-77-88; fax (495) 231-10-51; e-mail tretyakov@tretyakov.ru; internet www.tretyakov.ru; f. 1856; collection of 40,000 Russian icons and works of Russian and Soviet painters, sculptors and graphic artists; 7 br. museums; Dir VALENTIN A. RODIONOV.

St Petersburg

All-Russian A.S. Pushkin Museum (Vserossiiskii muzei A. S. Pushkina): 191186 St Petersburg, nab. Moiki 12; tel. (812) 117-38-01; e-mail vmp@mail.admiral.ru; internet www.museumpushkin.ru; f. 1879; 200,000 exhibits illustrating the life and work of Pushkin and his epoch; Dir S. M. NEKRASOV; 4 brs in St Petersburg and 2 brs in Tsarskoye Selo (Leningrad oblast, fmrly Pushkin); Contact ANNA GRYAZNOVA.

Central Music Library, attached to the Mariinskii Theatre (Tsentralnaya muzykalnaya biblioteka Mariinskogo teatra): 191000 St Petersburg, ul. Zodchego Rossi 2; tel. (812) 312-35-73; fax (812) 314-17-44; e-mail cml@mariinsky.ru; contains one of the largest collections in the world of Russian music; Dir Prof. Dr MARIYA N. SHCHERBAKOVA.

F. M. Dostoyevskii Literary-Memorial Museum (Literaturno-memorialnyi muzei F. M. Dostoyevskogo): 191002 St Petersburg, Kuznechnyi per. 5/2; tel. (812) 571-40-31; fax (812) 712-00-03; e-mail info@md.spb.ru; internet www.md.spb.ru; f. 1971; fmr residence of author F. M. Dostoyevskii in 1878–81; manuscripts, documentary material; library of 23,000 vols; also includes a theatre; Dir NATALYA I. ASHIMBAYEVA.

Literary Museum of the Institute of Russian Literature—Pushkin House (Literaturnyi muzei instituta russkoi literatury—Pushkinskii dom): 199034 St Petersburg, nab. Makarova 4; tel. (812) 328-05-02; fax (812) 328-11-40; e-mail irliran@mail.ru; internet www .pushkinhouse.spb.ru; 95,000 exhibits and over 120,000 items of reference material on 18th–20th-century Russian classical literature; based on the material of the Pushkin Anniversary Exhibition of 1899; seven halls containing permanent exhibitions devoted to A. N. Radishchev, M. Yu. Lermontov, N. V. Gogol, F. M. Dostoevskii, I. S. Turgenev, and other Russian writers; Dir YURII M. PROZOROV (acting).

Peter the Great Museum of Anthropology and Ethnography (Kunstkamera) (Muzei antropologii i etnografii im. Petra Velikogo): 199034 St Petersburg, Universitetskaya nab. 3; tel. (812) 328-14-12; fax (812) 328-08-11; e-mail info@kunstkamera.ru; internet www.kunstkamera.ru; f. 1714; attached to Russian Acad. of Sciences; 900,000 items of ethnographical, archaeological and anthropological material on the native peoples of Africa, North and South America, Australasia, the Middle East, Central and Eastern Asia, Russia and Europe; Dir Prof. Dr YURII K. CHISTOV.

Peterhof (Petrodvorets) State Museum Reserve (Gosudarstvennyi muzei-zapovednik Petergof—Petrodvorets): 198516 St Petersburg, Peterhof, ul. Razvodnaya 2; tel. (812) 427-74-25; fax (812) 427-93-30; e-mail peterhofmuseum@mail.ru; internet www .peterhof.org; f. 1918; 18th–20th century architecture, paintings and landscape gardening, library of 21,000 vols; Dir VADIM V. ZNAMENOV.

Russian Ethnographical Museum (Rossiiskii etnograficheskii muzei): 191186 St Petersburg, ul. Inzhenernaya 4/1; tel. (812) 313-47-68; fax (812) 315-85-02; e-mail rme@peterlink.ru; internet www

.ethnomuseum.ru; f. 1992; 600,000 exhibits; 150,000 photographs; library of 112,000 vols; Dir VLADIMIR M. GRUSMAN.

St Petersburg State Museum of Theatre and Music (Sankt-Peterburgskii Gosudarstvennyi musei teatralnogo i muzykalnogo iskusstva): 191011 St Petersburg, pl. Ostrovskogo 6; tel. (812) 315-52-43; fax (812) 31477-46; e-mail theatre@museums.org.ru; internet www.theatremuseum.ru; f. 1918; over 440,000 exhibits depicting the history of Russian, Soviet and foreign theatre; collection of 3,000 musical instruments; library of 5,000 vols; 4 brs; Dir IRINA V. YEVSTIGNEYEVA.

State Anna Akhmatova Literary-Memorial Museum in Fountain House (Literaturno-memorialnyi muzei Anny Akhmatovoi v Fontannom Dome): 191014 St Petersburg, pr. Liteinyi 53; tel. (812) 272-22-11; fax (812) 272-20-34; e-mail nina_popova@mail.ru; internet www.akhmatova.spb.ru; f. 1989; former residence of the poet Anna Akhmatova in 1925–52; manuscripts and documentary material relating to the literary life of Leningrad under Stalin (Iosif V. Dzhugashvili) in 1924–53; 46,300 exhibits; Dir NINA I. POPOVA.

State Hermitage Museum (Gosudarstvennyi Ermitazh): 190000 St Petersburg, Dvortsovaya nab. 34; tel. (812) 110-34-20; e-mail chancery@hermitage.ru; internet www.hermitagemuseum.org; f. 1764 as a court museum, opened to the public in 1852; richest collection in the fmr USSR of the art of prehistoric, ancient Eastern, Graeco-Roman and medieval times; also has a large Western European collection; Dir MIKHAIL B. PETROVSKII.

State Russian Museum (Gosudarstvennyi Russkii Muzei): 191186 St Petersburg, ul. Inzhenernaya 2; tel. (812) 318-46-91; e-mail info@ rusmuseum.ru; internet www.rusmuseum.ru; f. 1895; over 400,000 exhibits of Russian and Soviet art, ranging from icons to the avant-garde; 5 brs; Dir VLADIMIR A. GUSEV.

Summer Garden (Letni sad) and Summer Palace-Museum of Peter I (Letnii sad i Letnii dvorets-muzei Petra I): 191041 St Petersburg, Letnii Sad, nab. Kutuzova 2; tel. (812) 312-77-15; fax (812) 312-96-66; e-mail m126@mail.museum.ru; f. 1934; 18th-century architecture and sculpture; Dir TATYANA D. KOZLOVA.

Other Regions

Mordovian Republic S. D. Erzi Museum of Fine Arts (Mordovskii respublikanskii muzei izobrazitelnykh iskusstv im. S. D. Erzi): 430000 Mordoviya, Saransk, ul. Kommunisticheskaya 61; tel. (8342) 47-56-38; fax (8342) 17-56-38; e-mail erzia@mail.ru; internet www.museum.ru/M1451; f. 1960; 8,977 exhibits; painting, sculpture, prints, decorative arts; library of 10,000 vols; Dir LYUDMILA N. NARBEKOVA.

National Museum of the Republic of Tatarstan (Natsionalnyi muzei Respubliki Tatarstana): 420111 Tatarstan, Kazan, ul. Kremlevskaya 2; tel. (8432) 92-71-62; fax (8432) 92-14-84; e-mail tatar_museum@mail.ru; internet www.tatar.museum.ru; f. 1895; fmrly State United Museum of the Republic of Tatarstan; history, archaeology, ethnography, natural resources and decorative applied art of Tatarstan, Russia and other countries; over 500,000 exhibits; library of 12,000 vols; 6 brs in Kazan; Dir-Gen. GENNADII S. MUKHANOV.

Novocherkassk Museum of the History of the Don Cossacks (Muzei istorii Donskogo kazachestva): 346430 Rostov obl., Novocherkassk, ul. Atamanskaya 38; tel. (86352) 4-80-59; e-mail museum@novoch.ru; internet www.doncossacks.ru; f. 1899; collections of porcelain and painting; library of 17,000 vols; Dir SVETLANA A. SEDINKO.

Perm-36 Memorial Centre of the History of Political Repressions—Museum of the GULag (Memorialnyi tsentr istorii politicheskii repressii 'Perm-36'—Muzei GULaga): 618225 Perm Krai, Chusovskoi raion, Kuchino; tel. (901) 954-19-26; fax (342) 236-36-62; e-mail director@gulagmuseum.ru; internet www.perm36.ru; f. 1992; museum on site of fmr corrective labour camp for political prisoners; seeks to record the abuses of the oppressions undertaken during the USSR, particularly during the Stalin and Brezhnev eras, the workings of the GULag (State Corrective Camps) system, and to provide a memorial to the victims thereof; Dir VIKTOR A. SHMYROV.

Sergiyev Posad State History and Art Museum-Reserve (Sergiyevo-Posadskii Gosudarstvennyi Istoricho-khudozhestvennyi Muzei-zapovednik): 141300 Moscow obl., Sergiyev Posad, pr. Krasnoi Armii 144; tel. and fax (9654) 4-13-58; e-mail sergiev@divo.ru; internet www.musobl.divo.ru; f. 1920; 120,000 items dealing with the development of Russian history and art from the 14th century to the present; located partly within 14th-century Trinity St Sergius monastery; library of 17,000 vols; Dir FELIKS KH. MAKOYEV.

S. Stalskii Literary Memorial Museum (Literaturno-memorialnyi dom muzei Suleimana Stalskogo): 368765 Dagestan, Suleiman-Stalskii raion, selo Ashaga-stalsk; tel. (87200) 7-53-85; e-mail m1802@museum.ru; internet www.museum.ru/M1802; f. 1950; exhibits on the history of the literature of the peoples of Dagestan, in fmr home (1934–37) of poet Suleiman Stalskii; library of 20,000 vols; Dir LIDIYA M. STALSKAYA.

State Artistic-Architectural Palace and Park Museum-Reserve of Pavlovsk (Gosudarstvennyi khudozhestvenno-arkhitekturnyi dvortsovo-parkovyi muzei-zapovednik Pavlovsk): 196621 St Petersburg, Pavlovsk, ul. Sadovaya 20; tel. (812) 470-21-55; fax (812) 465-11-04; e-mail pavlovsk@mail.ru; internet www.pavlovskart.spb.ru; f. 1918; many examples of Russian garden architecture; sculpture by 18th-century Italian and French masters; European paintings of the 16th–19th centuries; Russian portraits of the 18th century; Russian decorative art of the 18th and 19th centuries; furniture, porcelain, bronzes and textiles; library of 17,000 vols; Dir NIKOLAI S. TRETYAKOV.

State Artistic-Architectural Palace and Park Museum-Reserve of Tsarskoye Selo (Gosudarstvennyi muzei-zapovednik Tsarskoye Selo): 189690 Leningrad obl., Tsarskoye Selo, ul. Sadovaya 7; tel. (812) 466-66-69; fax (812) 465-21-96; e-mail tzar@cityline.spb.ru; internet www.tzar.ru; f. 1918; Russian garden architecture, sculpture by Italian and French masters of the 18th and 19th centuries, palace of Catherine (Yekaterina) II ('the Great'), collection of the costumes of the Imperial Family; library of 6,800 vols; Dir. IVAN P. SAUTOV.

State Central Museum of the Contemporary History of Russia (Gosudarstvennyi tsentralnyi muzei sovremennoi istorii Rossii): 125009 Moscow, ul. Tverskaya 21; tel. (495) 699-52-17; fax (495) 699-85-15; e-mail sovrhistory@mtu-net.ru; internet www.sovr.ru; f. 1917; fmrly Museum of the Revolution, present name adopted 1998; Dir Dr TAMARA SHUMNAYA.

State Museum of Palekh Art (Gosudarstvennyi muzei palekhskogo iskusstva): 155620 Ivanovo obl., Palekh, ul. Bakanova 50; tel. (493) 342-20-54; fax (493) 342-26-41; e-mail m1571@mail.museum.ru; internet www.museum.ru/M1571; more than 6,000 items of Palekh art, including more than 2,000 miniature varnished Palekh boxes, and also icons and manuscripts; Dir ALEVTINA G. STRAKHOVA.

State Union of the Museums of the Artistic Culture of the Russian North (Gosudarstvennoye muzeinoye obyedineniye 'Khudozhestvennaya kultura Russkogo Severa'): 163061 Archangel, pl. Lenina 2; tel. (818) 3-26-73; e-mail artmus@arh.ru; internet www.museum.ru/M1444; incorporates Archangel Oblast Museum of Fine Arts (f. 1737); 150,000 items featuring the history of the north-coast area of Russia, dating back to ancient times; library of 30,000 vols; Dir MAIYA V. MITKEVICH.

Yaroslavl State Historical, Architectural and Art Museum-Reserve (Yaroslavskii gosudarstvennyi istoriko-arkhitekturnyi muzei-zapovednik): 150000 Yaroslavl, pl. Bogoyavlenskaya pl. 25; tel. (485) 230-56-30; fax (485) 230-40-72; e-mail mp@yarmp.yar.ru; internet www.yarmp.yar.ru; f. 1865; over 280,000 exhibits on the history of the Russian people from ancient times to the present; library of 42,000 vols; Dir YELENA A. ANKUDINOVA.

Yasnaya Polyana—State Memorial and Natural Reserve-Museum and Estate of L. N. Tolstoi (Yasnaya Polyana—Gosudarstvennyi memorialnyi i prirodnyi zapovednik muzei-usadba L. N. Tolstogo): 301214 Tula obl., Shchekinskii raion, Yasnaya Polyana; tel. and fax (487) 238-67-10; e-mail yaspol@tula.net; internet www.yasnayapolyana.ru; f. 1921; former house and estate of the author Lev N. Tolstoi; literary museum, estate with park grounds and forest; Dir VLADIMIR I. TOLSTOI.

SPORTING ORGANIZATIONS

Federal Agency for Exercise and Sport (Rossport): 103064 Moscow, ul. Kazakova 18; tel. (495) 925-72-50; e-mail info@rossport.ru; internet www.goskomsport.ru; f. 2004 to replace State Committee for Exercise and Sport (Goskomsport); Chair. VYACHESLAV A. FETISOV.

'Rossiya' (Russia) Trade Unions' Physical Culture and Sports Society (Fizkulturno-sportivnoye obshchestvo profsoyuzov 'Rossiya'): 109004 Moscow, ul. Vorontsovskaya 6/1; tel. and fax (495) 911-73-37; f. 1991; principal organization for professional and amateur participants in sports in Russia; supported by Federation of Independent Trade Unions of the Russian Federation; owns 50,200 sporting establishments including 30,100 sports fields, 7,920 sports halls, 2,980 sports-health clubs, 1,795 ski centres, 1,190 shooting ranges, 1,046 stadiums, 798 swimming pools (Jan. 2005); owns 432 youth sports schools, employing more than 5,000 coaches and catering for some 220,000 children and youths; Pres. of Central Council GENNADII N. SHIBAYEV.

Russian Olympic Committee (Olimpiiskii komitet Rossii): 119270 Moscow, Luzhnetskaya nab. 8; tel. (495) 248-00-44; fax (495) 248-23-09; e-mail pr@olympic.ru; internet www.roc.ru; f. 1989; Pres. LEONID V. TYAGACHEV; Gen. Sec. LEONID A. MIROSHNICHENKO.

Russian Paralympic Committee (Paralimpiiskii komitet Rossii): 119270 Moscow, Luzhnetskaya nab. 8; tel. (495) 201-94-15; e-mail pkr@paralymp.ru; ieternet www.paralymp.ru; public, non-profit organization, associated with the All-Russian Society of Invalids (q.v.); Pres. VLADIMIR P. LUKIN.

PERFORMING ARTS

Helikon Opera State Musical Theatre (Gelikon Opera gosudarstvennyi muzykalnyi teatr): 125009 Moscow, ul. B. Nikitskaya 19; tel. (495) 291-85-70; fax (495) 291-13-23; e-mail viktoria_opera@mail.ru; internet www.helikon.ru; f. 1990; traditional and avant-garde productions of classical operas; temporarily relocated to ul. Novyi Arbat 11 in 2006 during restoration of historical theatre; Artistic Dir Prof. DMITRII BERTMAN; Man. Dir VIKTORIYA PAVLOVA.

International A. P. Chekhov Theatre Festival (Mezhdunarodnyi teatralnyi festival im. A. P. Chekhov): 103009 Moscow, Leontievskii per. 21/1; tel. (495) 929-70-27; fax (495) 742-09-33; e-mail olympic@cf.mos.ru; internet www.chekhovfest.ru; f. 1992; biennial; Dir-Gen. VALERII SHADRIN.

Lenkom Moscow State Theatre (Lenkom Moskovskii gosudarstvennyi teatr): 127006 Moscow, ul. M. Dmitrovka 6; tel. (495) 699-12-61; fax (495) 699-77-30; e-mail nimfa@lenkom.ru; internet www.lenkom.ru; f. 1927 as Moscow Young Workers' Theatre; Artistic Dir MARK A. ZAKHAROV.

Malyi Drama Theatre—Theatre de l'Europe (St Petersburg) (MDT) (Malyi dramaticheskii teatr—teatr yevropy): 191002 St Petersburg, ul. Rubinshteina 18; tel. (812) 713-20-28; fax (812) 713-20-39; e-mail levdodin@mdt.sp.ru; internet www.mdt-dodin.ru; Artistic Dir LEV A. DODIN.

Mariinskii Theatre: 190000 St Petersburg, Teatralnaya pl. 1; tel. (812) 114-12-11; fax (812) 314-17-44; e-mail post@mariinsky.ru; internet www.mariinsky.ru; f. 1860; fmrly Kirov Theatre; ballet, opera, orchestral music; also organizes the arts festival, *Stars of the White Nights (Zvezdy Belykh Nochei)* annually, usually in May–June, in and around St Petersburg, and annual *International Ballet Festival Mariinskii*, usually held in St Petersburg in March; Artistic Dir VALERII A. GERGIYEV.

Moscow A. P. Chekhov Art and Academic Theatre (MKhAT im. Chekhova) (Moskovskii khudozhestvennyi akademicheskii teatr im. A. P. Chekhova): 103009 Moscow, Kamergerskii per. 3; tel. (495) 229-67-48; fax (495) 975-21-96; e-mail mxat@theatre.ru; internet www.mxat.ru; f. 1897; Dir MARIYA YE. REVYAKINA; Artistic Dir OLEG P. TABAKOV.

Moscow V. Mayakovskii Academic Theatre (Moskovskii akademicheskii teatr im. Vl. Mayakovskogo): 103009 Moscow, ul. B. Nikitskaya 19; tel. (495) 290-27-25; e-mail mayak_teatr@mail.ru; internet www.mayakovsky.ru; f. 1922; Dir MIKHAIL P. ZAITSEV; Artistic Dir SERGEI N. ARTSIBASHEV.

Moscow Taganka Comedy and Drama Theatre (Moskovskii teatr dramy i komedii na Taganke): 109004 Moscow, ul. Zemlyanoi Val 76/21; tel. and fax (495) 915-11-48; e-mail taganka@krls.ru; internet www.taganka.org; f. 1964; Dir YURII LYUBIMOV.

Rudolph Nuriyev International Festival of Classical Ballet (Mezhdunarodnyi festival klassicheskogo baleta im. Rudolfa Nuriyeva): 420015 Tatarstan, Kazan, pl. Svobody, Tatar Musa Dzhalil Academic Theatre of Opera and Ballet; tel. (8432) 38-45-58; internet www.kazan-opera.oooportal.ru/nuriev19fest.shtml; f. 1987; held annually, in May.

Russian National Orchestra (RNO) (Rossiiskii natsionalnyi orkestr): 117335 Moscow, ul. Garibaldi 19; tel. (495) 504-07-81; e-mail info@mo.ru; internet www.rno.ru; f. 1990; Founder and Artistic Dir MIKHAIL PLETNEV; Dir SERGEI FROLOV.

Sovremennik (Contemporary) Moscow Theatre (Moskovskii teatr 'Sovremennik'): 101000 Moscow, Chistoprudnyi bulv. 19A; tel. (495) 921-17-90; fax (495) 921-66-29; e-mail theatre@sovremennik.ru; internet www.sovremennik.ru; f. 1956; Artistic Dir GALINA VOLCHEK.

State Academic Bolshoi Theatre (Gosudarstvennyi akademicheskii Bolshoi teatr): 103009 Moscow, Teatralnaya pl. 1; tel. (495) 292-08-18; fax (495) 292-33-67; e-mail pr@bolshoi.ru; internet www.bolshoi.ru; f. 1776; opera and ballet company; Dir-Gen. ANATOLII IKSANOV.

State Academic Malyi Drama Theatre (Moscow) (Gosudarstvennyi akademicheskii Malyi teatr): 103009 Moscow, Teatralnaya pl. 1/6; tel. (495) 925-98-68; fax (495) 921-03-50; e-mail theatre@maly.ru; internet www.maly.ru; f. 1824; Artistic Dir YURII M. SOLOMIN; Dir VIKTOR I. KORSHUNOV.

P. I. Tchaikovsky Moscow State Conservatoire (Moskovskaya Gosudarstvennaya Konservatoriya im. P. I. Chaikovskogo): 125009 Moscow, ul. B. Nikitskaya 13; tel. (495) 629-20-60; fax (495) 290-22-73; e-mail spravka@mosconsv.ru; internet www.mosconsv.ru; Rector TIGRAN A. ALIKHANOV.

Yugo-Zapandnyi (South-Western) Studio-Theatre: 117526 Moscow, pr. Vernadskogo 125; tel. (495) 433-11-91; internet www.teatr-uz.ru; f. 1977; Dir VALERII R. BELYAKOVICH.

ASSOCIATIONS

All-Russia Music Society (VMO) (Vserossiiskoye Muzykalnoye Obshchestvo): 103009 Moscow, M. Kislovskii per. 9; tel. (495) 290-40-54; fax (495) 290-56-49; f. 1859; promotes music throughout Russia, especially among young people; organizes competitions, festivals, etc.; supports music groups; Chair. ALEKSEI ZHIDKOV.

International Arts Fund (Mezhdunarodnyi khudozhestvennyi fond): 119034 Moscow, B. Levshinskii per. 8/1; tel. (495) 202-74-77; fax (495) 201-52-55; e-mail mail@artfund.ru; internet www.artfund .ru; f. 1992; 10 regional brs; Pres. ROMAN N. VASILYEV; Dir-Gen. LARISA A. KOMAROVA.

International Organization of Writers—Russian PEN Centre (Russkii PEN-Tsentr): 107031 Moscow, ul. Neglinnaya 18/1/2; tel. (495) 209-45-89; fax (495) 200-02-93; e-mail penrussian@dol.ru; internet www.penrussia.org; f. 1989; Pres. ANDREI BITOV; Gen. Sec. ALEKSANDR TKACHENKO; 276 mems (2005).

Russian Union of Composers (Soyuz· kompozitorov Rossii): 103878 Moscow, Bryusov per. 8/10/2; tel. and fax (495) 229-52-18; f. 1960; Chair. VLADISLAV I. KAZENIN; 1,450 mems.

Theatre Union of the Russian Federation (Soyuz teatralnykh deyatelei RF): 101000 Moscow, per. M. Kharitonyevskii 8/18; tel. (495) 937-75-53; fax (495) 230-22-58; e-mail stdrf@stdrf.ru; internet www.stdrf.ru; f. 1986; 76 regional orgs; library of 500,000 vols; Chair. ALEKSANDR A. KALYAGIN; 24,000 mems.

Union of Architects of Russia (Soyuz arkhitektorov Rossii): 123001 Moscow, Granatnyi per. 22; tel. (495) 291-55-78; fax (495) 202-81-01; e-mail sarrus@rambler.ru; internet www.uar.ru; f. 1932; Pres. YURII P. GNEDOVSKII; 12,000 mems.

Union of Artists of Russia (Soyuz khudozhnikov Rossii): 121019 Moscow, Gogolevskii bulv. 10/1; tel. (495) 290-68-70; Chair. VALENTIN M. SIDOROV.

Union of Film-makers of the Russian Federation (Soyuz kinematografistgov Rossiiskoi Federatsii): 123056 Moscow, ul. Vasilyevskaya 13; tel. (495) 251-53-70; internet www.unikino.ru; f. 1990; 51 regional brs; Chair. NIKITA S. MIKHALKOV.

Union of Writers of Russia (Soyuz pisatelei Rossii): 119087 Moscow, Komsomolskii pr. 13; tel. (495) 246-43-50; internet sp .voskres.ru; Chair. of Bd VALERII N. GANICHEV.

United Nations Educational, Scientific and Cultural Organization (UNESCO)—Moscow Office: 119034 Moscow, B. Levshinskii per. 15/28/2; tel. (495) 202-80-97; fax (495) 202-05-68; e-mail moscow@unesco.ru; internet www.unesco.ru; responsible for the work of UNESCO in Azerbaijan, Armenia, Belarus, Georgia, Moldova and the Russian Federation; Dir PHILIPPE QUÉAU.

Znaniye (Knowledge) Society of Russia (Obshchestvo ZNANIYE Rossii): 101990 Moscow, Novaya pl. 3/4; tel. (495) 921-90-58; fax (495) 925-42-49; e-mail znanie@znanie.org; internet www.znanie .org; f. 1947; independent public educational organization; implementation of educational, information, scientific and research programmes, participation in establishment of a system of lifelong (supplementary) general and vocational education; publishes quarterly journal, Novye Znaniye (New Knowledge); Pres. GURII I. MARCHUK; Chair. V. P. RYBALKO.

Education

Education is compulsory for nine years, to be undertaken between the ages of six and 15 years. State education is generally provided free of charge, although in 1992 some higher education establishments began charging tuition fees. Students of selected courses in higher education receive a small stipend from the state. Primary education usually begins at seven years of age and lasts for three years. Secondary education, beginning at 10 years of age, lasts for seven years, comprising a first cycle of five years and a second of two years. In 2005 the total enrolment at primary schools included an estimated 92.2% of children in the appropriate age-group. Secondary enrolment in that year was equivalent to 88.9% of children in the appropriate age-group.

The level of education in the Russian Federation is relatively high, and 7.1m. students were enrolled at institutes of higher education in 2005/06. Although Russian is the principal language used in educational establishments, a number of local languages are also in use. Consolidated budget expenditure on education in 2007 amounted to a 1,342,300m. roubles (representing 23.6% of total expenditure).

All educational institutions were state-owned under Soviet rule, but a wide range of independent schools and colleges commenced operations in the early 1990s. In 2000/01 there were some 635 independent schools and 358 independent higher education institutions. In the early 1990s there were extensive changes to the curriculum in all branches of the education system, including an end to the study of politically inspired subjects, a new approach to the

study of Soviet and Russian history, and the introduction of study of previously prohibited literary works.

UNIVERSITIES

Altai State University: 656099 Altai Krai, Barnaul, pr. Lenina 61; tel. (3852) 66-75-84; fax (3852) 66-76-26; e-mail rector@asu.ru; internet www.asu.ru; f. 1973; 15 faculties; 681 teachers; 15,000 students; Chancellor YURII KIRUSHIN.

Amur State University: 675027 Amur obl., Blagoveshchensk, Ignatevskoye shosse 21; tel. (4162) 35-06-87; fax (4162) 35-03-77; e-mail master@amursu.ru; internet www.amursu.ru; f. 1975; 9 faculties; 528 teachers; 5,315 students; Rector ANDREI D. PLUTENKO.

Bashkir State University: 450074 Bashkortostan, Ufa, ul. Frunze 32; tel. (3472) 22-63-70; fax (3472) 23-66-80; e-mail interdpt@bsu .bashedu.ru; internet www.bashedu.ru; f. 1909; 12 faculties; 825 teachers; 22,300 students; Rector MUKHAMET KH. KHARASOV.

Chechen State University: 364907 Chechen (Nokchi) Rep., Groznyi, ul. Sheripova 32; tel. (8712) 23-40-89; 11 faculties; 620 teachers; 10,000 students; Rector ADNAN D. KHAMZAYEV.

Chelyabinsk State University: 454021 Chelyabinsk, ul. Br. Kashirinykh 129; tel. (3512) 42-05-31; fax (3512) 42-09-25; e-mail odou@cgu.ru; internet www.csu.ru; f. 1976; 14 faculties; 578 teachers; 7,800 students (full time), 6,569 students (by correspondence); Rector Prof. VALENTIN D. BATUKHTIN.

Chuvash I. N. Ulyanov State University: 428015 Chuvash Rep., Cheboksary, Moskovskii pr. 15; tel. (8352) 62-61-89; fax (8352) 45-80-86; e-mail oper@chuvsu.ru; internet www.chuvsu.ru; f. 1967; 24 faculties; 1,458 teachers; 20,051 students; Rector Prof. Dr LEV P. KURAKOV.

Dagestan State University: 367025 Dagestan, Makhachkala, ul. Gadzhiyeva 43A; tel. (8722) 68-23-26; fax (8722) 67-06-33; e-mail dgu@dgu.ru; internet www.dgu.ru; f. 1931; 16 faculties; 1,000 teachers; 20,000 students; Rector Prof OMAR A. OMAROV.

Dubna State International University of Nature, Society and Man: 141980 Moscow obl., Dubna, ul. Universitetskaya 19; tel. (09621) 2-20-71; fax (09621) 2-24-64; e-mail rector@uni-dubna.ru; internet www.uni-dubna.ru; f. 1994; 17 faculties; Pres. V. G. KADY-SHEVSKII; Rector O. L. KUZNETSOV.

Far Eastern State University: 690600 Maritime Krai, Vladivostok, ul. Sukhanova 8; tel. (4232) 26-12-80; fax (4232) 25-72-00; e-mail office@dip.dvgu.ru; internet www.dvgu.ru; f. 1899; 27 faculties; 7 institutes; 1 college; 993 teachers; 16,000 students; Rector Prof. VLADIMIR I. KURILOV.

Irkutsk State University: 664003 Irkutsk, ul. K. Marksa 1; tel. (3952) 24-34-53; fax (3952) 24-22-38; e-mail rector@isu.ru; internet www.isu.ru; f. 1918; 13 faculties; 7 institutes; 853 teachers; 12,230 students; Rector Prof. ALEKSANDR I. SMIRNOV.

Ivanovo State University: 153025 Ivanovo, ul. Yermaka 39; tel. (493) 232-62-10; fax (493) 232-46-77; e-mail rector@ivanovo.ac.ru; internet www.ivanovo.ac.ru; f. 1974; 9 faculties; 9,500 students; Rector VLADIMIR N YEGOROV.

Kabardino-Balkar Kh. M. Berbekov State University: 360004 Kabardino-Balkar Rep., Nalchik, ul. Chernyshevskogo 173; tel. (8662) 42-52-54; fax (095) 337-99-55; e-mail bsk@kbsu.ru; internet www.kbsu.ru; f. 1932; 18 faculties, 6 colleges; 1,092 teachers, more than 20,000 students (2004); Rector Prof. BARASBI S. KARAMURZOV.

Kaliningrad State University: 236041 Kaliningrad, ul. A. Nevskogo 14; tel. (4012) 46-59-17; fax (4012) 46-58-13; e-mail rector@admin.albertina.ru; internet www.albertina.ru; f. 1967; 13 faculties; 610 teachers; 10,821 students; Rector Dr A. P. KLEMESHEV.

Kalmyk State University: 358000 Kalmykiya, Elista, ul. Pushkina 11; tel. (84722) 5-34-31; fax (84722) 5-37-29; e-mail uni@kalmsu.ru; internet kalmsu.ru; f. 1970; 8 faculties; 5,000 students; Rector GERMAN M. BORLIKOV.

Kazan State University: 420008 Tatarstan, Kazan, ul. Kremlevskaya 18; tel. (843) 292-69-77; fax (843) 292-44-48; e-mail public.mail@ ksu.ru; internet www.ksu.ru; f. 1804; 17 faculties; 3 research institutes; 1,200 teachers; 16,000 students (2007); Rector MYAKZYUM SALAKHOV.

Kemerovo State University: 650043 Kemerovo, Krasnaya ul. 6; tel. (3842) 23-12-26; fax (3842) 23-30-34; e-mail rector@kemsu.ru; internet www.kemsu.ru; f. 1974; 11 faculties; 780 teachers; 8,834 students; Rector YU. A. ZAKHAROV.

Krasnoyarsk State University: 660041 Krasnoyarsk, pr. Svobodnyi 79; tel. (3912) 44-82-13; fax (3912) 44-86-25; e-mail vip@krasu.ru; internet www.lan.krasu.ru; f. 1969; 719 teachers; 9,600 students; Rector Prof. A. S. PROVOROV.

Kuban State University: 350040 Krasnodar, ul. Stavropolskaya 149; tel. (861) 219-95-02; fax (861) 219-95-17; e-mail rector@kubsu .ru; internet www.kubsu.ru; f. 1924; 17 faculties; 12 research institutes; 1,500 teachers; 23,000 students; Rector V. A. BABESHKO.

Mari State University: 424001 Marii-El, Yoshkar-Ola, pl. Lenina 1; tel. (8362) 42-59-20; fax (8362) 45-45-81; e-mail postmaster@ marsu.ru; f. 1972; 9 faculties; 384 teachers; 4,055 students; Rector Dr V. I. MAKAROV.

Mordoviyan N. P. Ogarev State University: 430000 Mordoviya, Saransk, ul. Bolshevistskaya 68; tel. (8342) 24-72-42; fax (8342) 24-79-51; e-mail interdept@freemail.mrsu.ru; internet www.mrsu.ru; f. 1957; 13 faculties; 6 institutes; 1,500 teachers; 26,000 students; Rector Prof. NIKOLAI P. MAKARKIN.

Moscow M. V. Lomonosov State University (MGU): 111992 Moscow, Vorobyevy gory; tel. (495) 939-10-00; fax (495) 938-01-26; e-mail info@rector.msu.ru; internet www.msu.ru; f. 1755; 29 faculties; 15 institutes; 9,800 teachers; 40,000 students; Rector VIKTOR A. SADOVNICHII.

Nizhnii Novgorod N. I. Lobachevskii State University: 603950 Nizhnii Novgorod, pr. Gagarina 23; tel. (8312) 65-84-90; fax (8312) 65-85-92; e-mail rector@unn.ac.ru; internet www.unn.ac.ru; f. 1916; 18 faculties; 1,500 teachers; 31,000 students; Rector Prof. ROMAN G. STRONGIN.

North-Osetiyan K. L. Khetagurov State University: 362025 North Osetiya—Alaniya, Vladikavkaz, ul. Vatutina 46; tel. and fax (8672) 74-31-91; e-mail indep@nosu.ru; internet www.nosu.ru; f. 1969; 15 faculties; 700 teachers; 10,500 students; Chancellor AKHURBEK M. MAGOMETOV.

Novgorod Yarolslavl the Wise State University (NovSU): 173003 Velikii Novgorod, ul. B. St Peterburgskaya 41; tel. and fax (81622) 2-37-07; e-mail zelenin@novsu.ac.ru; internet www.novsu.ac .ru; f. 1993; 23 faculties; 1,050 lecturers; 22,000 students; Pres. ANATOLII L. GAVRIKOV.

Novosibirsk State University: 630090 Novosibirsk, ul. Pirogova 2; tel. (383) 330-32-44; fax (383) 330-32-55; e-mail rector@nsu.ru; internet www.nsu.ru; f. 1959; 13 faculties; 1,864 teachers; 6,360 students; Rector Prof. VLADIMIR A. SOBYANIN.

Omsk F. M. Dostoyevskii State University: 644077 Omsk, pr. Mira 55A; tel. (3812) 26-84-22; fax (3812) 28-55-81; e-mail gering@ omsu.omskreg.ru; internet www.omsu.ru; f. 1974; 13 faculties; 900 teachers; 13,000 students; Rector Dr GENNADII I. GERING.

Perm State University: 614600 Perm, ul. Bukireva 15; tel. (3422) 33-61-83; fax (3422) 33-39-83; e-mail info@psu.ru; internet www.psu .ru; f. 1916; 11 faculties; 4 attached research institutes; 756 teachers; 11,869 students; Rector VLADIMIR V. MALANIN.

Petrozavodsk State University: 185640 Kareliya, Petrozavodsk, pr. Lenina 33; tel. (8142) 78-51-40; fax (8142) 71-10-00; e-mail rector@mainpgu.karelia.ru; internet petrsu.karelia.ru; f. 1940; 13 faculties; 740 teachers; 14,800 students; Rector VIKTOR N. VASILYEV.

Russian Friendship of Peoples' University: 117198 Moscow, ul. Miklukho-Maklaya 6; tel. (495) 434-66-41; fax (495) 433-15-11; e-mail rector@rudn.ru; internet www.rudn.ru; f. 1960 as Patrice Lumumba Friendship of Peoples' University, to train students from Africa, Asia and Latin America; 10 faculties; 1,800 teachers; 18,000 students; Rector Prof. VLADIMIR M. FILIPPOV.

St Petersburg State University: 199034 St Petersburg, Universitetskaya nab. 7/9; tel. (812) 328-20-00; fax (812) 328-13-46; e-mail office@inform.pu.ru; internet www.spbu.ru; f. 1724; 19 faculties; 2,954 teachers; 22,680 students; Rector L. A. VERBITSKAYA.

Samara State University: 443011 Samara, ul. Ak. Pavlova 1; tel. (846) 278-09-08; fax (846) 334-54-17; e-mail ssuinter@ssu.samara.ru; internet www.ssu.samara.ru; f. 1969; 14 faculties; 800 teachers; 14,000 students (2006); Rector G. P. YAROVOI.

Saratov N. G. Chernyshevskii State University: 410012 Saratov, ul. Astrakhanskaya 83; tel. (8452) 24-16-46; fax (8452) 51-16-35; e-mail rector@sgu.ru; internet www.sgu.ru; f. 1909; 28 faculties; 6 br. institutes; Rector LEONID YU. KOSSOVICH.

Southern Federal University: 344006 Rostov-on-Don, ul. B. Sadovaya 105; tel. (863) 263-84-98; fax (863) 263-87-23; e-mail rectorat@mis.sfedu.ru; internet www.sfedu.ru; f. 2006; 15 faculties; 11 attached institutes; 8,563 teachers; 19,123 students; Rector Prof. Dr VLADISLAV. G. ZAKHAREVICH.

Southern Ural State University: 454080 Chelyabinsk, pr. Lenina 76; tel. (3512) 65-65-04; fax (3512) 34-74-08; e-mail lnv@susu.ac.ru; internet www.susu.ac.ru; f. 1943, fmrly Chelyabinsk State Technical University; 35 faculties; 13 brs; 8 regional campuses; 1,500 teachers; 53,000 students; Rector Dr GERMAN P. VYATKIN.

Syktyvkar State University: 167001 Komi, Syktyvkar, Oktyabrskii pr. 55; tel. and fax (8212) 43-68-20; e-mail rector@syktsu.ru; internet www.syktsu.ru; f. 1972; 15 faculties; 331 teachers; 6,140 students; Rector Dr VASILII N. ZADOROZHNII.

Tomsk State University: 634050 Tomsk, pr. Lenina 36; tel. (3822) 23-44-65; fax (3822) 41-55-85; e-mail rector@tsu.ru; internet www .tsu.ru; f. 1878; 18 faculties; 1,410 teachers; 14,000 students; Rector Prof. G. MAYER.

Tver State University: 170000 Tver, ul. Zhelyabova 33; tel. (482) 232-15-50; fax (482) 232-12-74; e-mail m000061@tversu.ru; internet university.tversu.ru; f. 1971; 15 faculties; Rector ALEKSEI N. KUDINOV.

Tyumen State University: 625003 Tyumen, ul. Semakova 10; tel. (3452) 46-19-30; fax (3452) 46-17-98; e-mail international@utmn.ru; internet www.utmn.ru; f. 1930; 10 faculties; 3 institutes; 26,000 students; Rector GENNADII F. KUTSEV.

Udmurt State University: 426034 Udmurt Rep., Izhevsk, ul. Universitetskaya 1; tel. (3412) 75-16-10; fax (3412) 75-56-69; e-mail inter@uni.udm.ru; internet www.uni.udm.ru; f. 1931; 14 faculties,. 7 institutes, 1 research centre; 959 teachers; 25,150 students (2007); Rector SEMEN D. BUNTOV.

Urals A. M. Gorkii State University: 620083 Sverdlovsk obl., Yekaterinburg, pr. Lenina 51; tel. (343) 255-74-20; fax (343) 255-59-64; e-mail vladimir.tretyakov@usu.ru; internet www.usu.ru; f. 1920; 12 faculties; 4 research institutes; 900 teachers; 12,400 students; Rector Prof. VLADIMIR E. TRETYAKOV.

Volgograd State University: 400062 Volgograd, pr. Universitetskii 100; tel. and fax (8442) 46-02-79; e-mail oms@volsu.ru; internet www.volsu.ru; f. 1980; 11 faculties; 568 teachers; 12,904 students (2005); Rector OLEG V. INSHAKOV.

Voronezh State University: 394006 Voronezh, pl. Universitetskaya 1; tel. (473) 220-75-22; fax (473) 220-87-55; e-mail office@main .vsu.ru; internet www.vsu.ru; f. 1918; 18 faculties; 5 research institutes, 8 museums, 1,300 teachers; 21,000 students; library of 3m. volumes (2002); Rector Prof. IVAN. I. BORISOV.

Yakut State University: 677000 Sakha (Yakutiya), Yakutsk, ul. Belinskogo 58; tel. (4112) 36-33-44; fax (4112) 36-14-53; e-mail oip@ sitc.ru; internet www.ysu.ru; f. 1956; languages of instruction: Russian and Yakut; 2 brs; 8 institutes; 9 faculties; 1,270 teachers; 20,000 students; Chancellor Prof. ANATOLII N. ALEKSEYEV.

Yaroslavl State University: 150000 Yaroslavl, ul. Sovetskaya 14; tel. (485) 272-51-38; fax (485) 279-77-46; e-mail depint@uniyar.ac.ru; internet www.uniyar.ac.ru; f. 1970; 9 faculties; 530 teachers; 6,500 students; Rector Prof. ALEKSANDR I. RUSAKOV.

Social Welfare

A basic social-security and health system exists in the Russian Federation. The Social Insurance Fund provides maternity benefit (which is payable for up to 18 weeks), payments for the loss of earnings owing to ill-health and, in certain instances, child allowance. Old-age pensions are provided from a Pension Fund (financed largely by employer contributions, but also including contributions from workers, and with a budgetary transfer to pay for family benefits). Women over the age of 55 years and men over the age of 60 are entitled to receive old-age pensions if they have worked for at least 20 years (women) or 25 years (men). A social pension, equivalent to two-thirds of the minimum pension, may be paid to citizens who have worked a maximum of five years less than the qualifying period. Disability benefits are also payable from the Pension Fund. A new pension system was introduced from the early 2000s, consisting of a basic state pension financed by the budget, a state pension based on contributions by employees and employers and private pension schemes. The monetization of certain benefits granted to old-age pensioners and certain other categories of citizens (e.g. war veterans), which took effect from early 2005, proved a major source of controversy.

Unemployment benefit was introduced in Russia in 1991, with the establishment of the Federal Employment Fund (financed by employer contributions and government funds), and is paid to those who have been without employment for a period of more than three months (for the first three months the previous employer is obliged to continue paying the former employee's salary). In 2005 federal budgetary expenditure on social security and welfare amounted to 167,360.9m. roubles (5.5% of the total).

A basic health service is provided for all citizens. All health care in the Russian Federation was previously financed by the state. In 1993, however, a health-insurance scheme, the Medical Insurance Fund, was introduced, funded by employers' contributions. In 2006 there were 4.3 physicians and 9.7 hospital beds per 1,000 head of population.

In 2005 federal budgetary expenditure on health care (including sport) was 85,672.2m. roubles (2.8% of the total). The difficulties experienced by the health-care system following the dissolution of the USSR were reflected by a serious deterioration in the health of the population. The reasons cited for this were unsatisfactory environmental conditions, a decline in immunity, a shortage of vitamins and medicine and insufficient inoculations. Average life expectancy for males had decreased from 64 years in 1990 to 58 years by 2003, although it had increased to 60.0 years by 2006, when female life expectancy was 73.2 years. By the early 2000s the spread of HIV/

AIDS had become a serious problem in Russia; in 2005 around 1.1% of the working-age population were infected. Widespread alcohol misuse was also a matter for concern.

GOVERNMENT AGENCIES

Presidential Council for the Development of Civil Society Institutions and the Protection of Human Rights (Sovet pri Prezidente Rossiiskoi Federatsii po sodeistviyu razvitiyu institutov grazhdanskogo obshchestva i pravam cheloveka): 103132 Moscow, Staraya pl. 4; tel. (495) 606-49-14; fax (495) 606-48-55; e-mail sovetpamfilova@yandex.ru; internet www.sovetpamfilova.ru; f. 2004 on basis of Presidential Commission for Human Rights (founded 1993); Chair. ELLA PAMFILOVA.

Ministry of Health and Social Development: see The Government (Ministries).

Commission for the Affairs of Women, the Family and Demography: 103132 Moscow, Ipatyevskii per. 4/10; tel. (495) 206-06-55; f. 1996; Chair. YEKATERINA F. LAKOVA.

Commission for the Rehabilitation of Victims of Political Repression: 103132 Moscow, Staraya pl. 4; tel. (495) 206-34-53; f. 1991; Chair. ALEKSANDR N. YAKOVLEV.

Federal Employment and Labour Service (Federalnaya sluzhba po trudu i zanyatosti): 109012 Moscow, Birzhevaya pl. 1/2; tel. (495) 298-87-14; e-mail pressa@rostrud.info; internet www.rostrud.info; Dir M. A. TOPILIN.

Federal Migration Service (FMS) (Federalnaya migratsionnaya sluzhba): 107078 Moscow, Boyarskii per. 4; tel. (495) 928-98-48; internet www.fmsrf.ru; Dir. KONSTANTIN O. ROMODANOVSKII.

Federal Scientific-Methodogical Centre for the Prevention of and Combat of AIDS (Federalnyi nauchno-metodicheskii tsentr po profilaktike i borbe so SPID): 111123 Moscow, ul. Novogireyevskaya 3A/11; tel. (495) 672-11-58; fax (495) 304-22-09; e-mail info@pcr.ru; internet www.pcr.ru; affiliated to the Central Scientific—Research Institute of Epidemiology of the Ministry of Health and Social Development; Head VADIM POKROVSKII.

Medstrakh—Medical Insurance Fund of the Russian Federation: see Insurance.

Pension Fund of the Russian Federation (Pensionnyi fond RF): 119991 Moscow, ul. Shabolovka 4; tel. (495) 230-92-95; fax (495) 959-97-87; f. 1991; financed by contributions from employers and employees; Chair. of Bd GENNADII BATANOV.

Social Insurance Fund of the Russian Federation (Fond sotsialnogo strakhovaniya RF): 107139 Moscow, per. Orlikov 3A; tel. (495) 970-37-26; e-mail mail@ca.fss.ru; internet www.fss.ru; f. 1991; financed by employers on behalf of their workers by means of tax inspectorate; administered by the federal Government; Chair. GALINA N. KARELOVA.

State Inspectorate of Non-State Pension Funds (Inspektsiya negosudarstvennykh pensionnykh fondov pri MTSR RF): 109074 Moscow, Slavyanskaya pl. 4/1; tel. and fax (495) 925-85-00; e-mail npfinsp@dol.ru; internet npfinsp2.narod.ru; supervises operations of private sector and non-state pension funds; Dir-Gen. VYACHESLAV V. BATAYEV.

HEALTH AND WELFARE ORGANIZATIONS

All-Russian Association of the Blind (Vserossiiskoye obshchestvo slepykh): 101012 Moscow, Novaya pl. 14; tel. (495) 923-61-60; fax (495) 923-91-49; e-mail oms@vos.org.ru; internet www.vos.org.ru; f. 1925; social rehabilitation, training of guide dogs, leisure and sports; Pres. ALEKSANDR YA. NEUMYVAKIN.

All-Russian Society of the Deaf (VOG) (Vserossiiskoye obshchestvo glukhikh): 123022 Moscow, ul. 1905 Goda 10A; tel. (495) 252-10-43; fax (495) 252-06-74; e-mail deaf_russia@mail.ru; internet www.vog.su; f. 1926; 150,000 mems; Pres. VALERII N. RUKHLEDEV.

All-Russian Society of Invalids (VOI) (Vserossiiskoye obshchestvo invalidov): 117415 Moscow, ul. Udaltsova 11; tel. (495) 935-00-12; fax (495) 936-13-00; e-mail id.voi@relcom.ru; f. 1988; non-profit, non-governmental organization; concerned with the protection of the rights and interests of disabled people and the integration of the disabled into Russian society; Chair. ALEKSANDR V. LOMAKHIN.

Baikal Foundation: 665718 Irkutsk obl., Bratsk, POB 52; fax (095) 292-65-11; founded to promote voluntary work in the Russian Federation; organizes work camps to increase international participation in community development projects.

Federal Caritas of Russia: 198005 St Petersburg, ul Krasnoarmeiskaya 11; tel. and fax (812) 317-81-27; e-mail caritas@caritas-russia.ru; internet www.caritas-russia.ru; Roman Catholic welfare org.; Pres. Bishop JOSEPH WERTH; Sec.-Gen. Fr ALEXANDRE PIETRZYK.

Caritas of Asian Russia: 630033 Novosibirsk, POB 38; tel. (3832) 55-11-56; fax (3832) 47-65-47; e-mail secretariat@caritas.sib.ru; f. 1991; Sec.-Gen. Sr ELISABETH JAKUBOWITZ.

Caritas of European Russia: 127434 Moscow, Dmitrovskoye shosse 5/1/136, POB 93; tel. (495) 956-05-85; fax (495) 976-24-38; e-mail secretary@caritas.ru; internet www.caritas.ru; Pres. Archbishop TADEUSZ KONDRUSIEWICZ.

For Human Rights (Za prava cheloveka): 103009 Moscow, M. Kislovskii per. 7/1/21; tel. (495) 291-62-33; fax (495) 202-22-24; e-mail info@zaprava.ru; internet zaprava.ru; f. 1997; 80 regional and local branches; Exec. Dir L. A. PONOMAREV.

Foundation for Help and Assistance to Women Victims of Stalinist Repressions (MARIYA): 101458 Moscow, Bumazhnyi proyezd 14; tel. (495) 257-32-30; fax (495) 956-90-94; f. 1990; provides support and assistance to women who suffered human-rights abuses under Stalin's (Iosif Dzhugashvili's) leadership of the USSR (1924–53); Pres. ZOYA KRYLOVA.

International Charity and Health Fund (Mezhdunarodnyi obshchestvennyi blagotvoritelnyi fond miloserdiya i zdorovya): 101990 Moscow, ul. Pokrovka 22; tel. (495) 917-79-05; fax (495) 916-23-22; f. 1988 as Soviet Charity and Health Fund, renamed 1992; provides humanitarian aid to the elderly, disabled and chronically ill; operates in the territories of the former USSR in the fields of medicine, health and social welfare; organizes conferences, programmes and training courses; provides grants to institutions and individuals; Chair. VLADIMIR MUDRAK.

Memorial Human Rights Centre: 103051 Russia, M. Karetnyi per. 12; tel. (495) 650-78-83; fax (495) 609-06-94; e-mail info@memo.ru; internet www.memo.ru; researches into and provides support for victims of Stalinist repression; campaigns for the observance of human rights; Chair. SERGEI A. KOVALYEV.

Russian Charity and Health Foundation (RFMZ) (Rossiiskii fond miloserdiya i zdorovya): 101971 Moscow, ul. Pokrovka 22; tel. (495) 916-18-88; fax (495) 975-22-45; e-mail ruschf@rambler.ru; f. 1989; brs in 78 regions; operates through scholarships and fellowships, conferences, international training courses and publications, humanitarian projects, health education; Pres. OLEG FILIPPOV.

Russian Children's Foundation (Rossiiskii Detskii Fond): 101990 Moscow, per. Armyanskii 11/2A; tel. (495) 625-82-00; fax (495) 624-24-90; e-mail madf@yandex.ru; fax www.detfond.org; Chair. ALBERT A. LIKHANOV.

Russian Foundation of Disabled Afghanistan War Veterans: 603011 Nizhnii Novgorod, ul. Magistratskaya 11, POB 66; tel. (8312) 33-03-72; fax (8312) 33-82-05.

Russian Red Cross (Rossiiskii Krasnyi Krest): 117036 Moscow, Cheremushinskii proyezd 5; tel. (495) 126-75-71; fax (495) 230-28-67; e-mail e-mail@redcross.ru; internet www.redcross.ru; f. 1867; Chair. TATYANA A. NIKOLAYENKO.

Union of the Committees of Soldiers' Mothers of Russia (Soyuz Komitetov Soldatskikh Materei Rossii—SKSMP): 101000 Moscow, Luchnikov per. 4/3/5; tel. (495) 928-25-06; fax (495) 206-89-58; internet ucsmr.ru; unites some 300 regional organizations; Sec. VALENTINA MELNIKOVA.

Voluntary Service of the Urals: 614000 Perm, ul. Siberskaya 8; tel. and fax (3422) 12-97-36; e-mail vsu@pi.cci.ru; f. 1995; voluntary youth work in spheres of culture, ecology, education, organizes international work camps; Chair. SERGEI BRITVIN.

Women's Union of Russia (Soyuz zhenshchin Rossii): 103832 Moscow, Glinishchevskii per. 6; tel. (495) 229-32-23; fax (495) 200-02-74; e-mail wur@newmail.ru; f. 1990; Chair. ALEVTINA V. FEDULOVA.

The Environment

Serious environmental problems developed in the Russian Federation during the Soviet period. Although there was a marked improvement during the 1990s in the ability of the Russian authorities to implement environmental legislation, there were an estimated 250,000 violations of such laws in 1997.

During the Soviet period weapons-grade material production sites were located in closed cities near Tomsk, Yekaterinburg and Krasnoyarsk. Prolonged nuclear testing at the testing-range in Semipalatinsk, Kazakhstan, caused substantial damage in the neighbouring Altai Krai. The accident at the Chernobyl (Chornobyl) nuclear power station in Ukraine in 1986 resulted in widespread contamination, in particular of the Bryansk, Orel and Tula Oblasts. In January 1996 the Russian Government adopted a programme of rehabilitation of the area affected by the disaster and agreed to pay some 11,700m. roubles in compensation to the victims; at that time an estimated 2.9m. people were living in contaminated areas. Accidents connected with outdated, Soviet-designed nuclear reactors continued to occur: in April 1993 an explosion at the closed city of Tomsk-7 in Siberia contaminated an area of 40 sq km; and in February 1996, at Dimitrovgrad on the River Volga, an accident involving one of seven nuclear reactors caused 1.2 metric tons of radioactive gas to be released into the atmosphere.

The issue of disposing of radioactive waste at sea, which the USSR had done for over 30 years, was also important at this time. In 1993 the Barents Council was created by the Governments of Russia, Finland, Norway and Sweden to formalize co-operation with regard to the widespread pollution of the Kola Peninsula (in Murmansk Oblast). The Peninsula was home to Russia's ageing Northern Fleet, and to 182 working nuclear reactors, 135 reactors no longer in operation and 15 waste storage sites on land and at sea. Of particular urgency was the safe disposal of the nuclear warheads and reactors contained in the Northern Fleet's nuclear storage ships and submarines.

In June 2002 the leaders of the Group of Seven (G7) industrialized nations agreed to provide some US \$20,000m. to Russia, over a 10-year period, to assist in the protection and decommissioning of existing nuclear materials and weaponry, partly owing to international fears that terrorist organizations might gain access to dangerous substances. Under the Chemical Weapons Convention, which Russia signed in 1993, the Government was obligated to destroy all of its Soviet chemical weapon stockpiles by 2012. By 2007 three chemical weapon destruction plants had been established, and a further four were under construction.

GOVERNMENT ORGANIZATIONS

Ministry of Natural Resources and Ecology: see The Government (Ministries).

Arctic and Antarctic Research Unit: 199397 St Petersburg, ul. Beringa 38; tel. (812) 352-00-96; fax (812) 352-26-88; f. 1920; research into ecology of the Arctic and Antarctic; responsible for the Russian Antarctic Expedition; Dir I. YE. FROLOV.

Federal Service for Ecological, Technological and Atomic Monitoring (Federalnaya sluzhba po ekologicheskomu, tekhnologicheskomu i atomnomu nadzoru—Rostekhnadzor): 109147 Moscow, ul. Taganskaya 34; tel. (495) 911-64-75; fax (495) 912-40-41; e-mail bla@gan.ru; internet www.gosnadzor.ru; f. 2004; Chair. KONSTANTIN B. PULIKOVSKII.

Federal Hydrometeorology and Environmental Monitoring Service of the Ministry of Natural Resources (Federalnaya sluzhba po nadzoru v sfere prirodopolzovaniya MPR): 123995 Moscow, ul. B. Gruzinskaya 4/6/242; tel. (495) 254-54-00; Dir SERGEI I. SAI.

Interdepartmental Commission for Ecological Security (Mezhvedomstvennaya komissiya po ekologicheskoi bezopastnosti): 103070 Moscow, Staraya pl. 6; f. 1993; commission of the Security Council; Chair. ALEKSEI V. YABLOKOV.

Institute of Global Climate and Ecology: 107258 Moscow, ul. Glebovskaya 20 B; tel. (495) 160-24-30; fax (495) 160-08-31; responsible to the Russian Federal Service for Hydrometeorology and Environmental Monitoring (q.v.) and the Russian Academy of Sciences (q.v.); Dir Prof. YURII A. IZRAEL.

International Science and Technology Centre (ISTC) (Mezhdunarodnyi nauchno-tekhnicheskii tsentr—MNTT): 115516 Moscow, ul. Luganskaya 9; tel. (495) 797-60-10; fax (495) 797-60-47; e-mail istcinfo@istc.ru; internet www.istc.ru; f. 1992 under an intergovernmental agreement between the Russian Federation, the European Union, Japan and the USA; carries out research in the fields of nuclear safety and environmental protection and utilizes the skills of former weapons scientists and engineers with a view to ensuring nuclear non-proliferation; Exec. Dir M. KRÖNING.

RUSSIAN ACADEMY OF SCIENCES

Russian Academy of Sciences: 119991 Moscow, Leninskii pr. 14; tel. (495) 954-29-05; fax (495) 954-33-20; e-mail uvs@presidium.ras.ru; internet www.ras.ru; f. 1724; renamed Academy of Sciences of the USSR 1925; original name reinstated 1991; 9 depts; Pres. YURII S. OSIPOV; a Commission on Questions of Ecology is attached to the Presidium of the Academy; the principal sections and institutes involved in environmental matters incl.:

All-Russia Research Institute for Nature Conservation: 113628 Moscow, ul. Znamenskoye Sadki; tel. (495) 423-03-22; fax (495) 423-23-22; f. 1981; research, general methodology, environmental protection strategy domestically and internationally; five departments; major repository of research material; Dir B. L. SAMOILOV.

Section of Chemical, Technological and Biological Sciences

Institute of the Ecology of the Volga River Basin: 445003 Samara obl., Tolyatti, ul. Komzina 10; tel. and fax (8482) 48-95-04; f. 1983; attached to the Dept of Biological Sciences; monitors the environment of the Volga; Dir Prof. G. S. ROZENBERG.

Institute of Soil Science and Photosynthesis: 142260 Moscow obl., Pushchino; tel. (495) 923-35-58; fax (0967) 79-05-32; attached to the Dept of Biochemistry, Biophysics and Physiological Chemistry; research incl. soil conservation and land reclamation; Dir V. I. KEFELYA.

I.D. Papanin Institute of the Biology of Inland Waters (IBIW RAS): 152742 Yaroslavl obl., Nekouzskii raion, pos. Borok; tel. and fax (485) 472-40-42; e-mail ibiw@mail.ru; internet www.ibiw.ru; scientific research, postgraduate education; publishes journal, Biology of Inland Waters, quarterly; Dir Dr ALEKSANDR I. KOPYLOV.

A. N. Severtsov Institute of Ecology and Evolution: 119071 Moscow, Leninskii pr. 33; tel. (495) 952-20-88; fax (495) 954-55-34; e-mail admin@sevin.ru; internet www.sevin.ru; f. 1934; attached to the Dept of Biological Sciences; research of general ecology, morphology, ecology and ethology of animals, animal evolution, problems of biodiversity and nature conservation; Dir D.S. PAVLOV.

Section of Earth Sciences

119991 Moscow, Leninskii pr. 32 A; tel. (495) 983-09-40; fax (495) 938-18-59; Dir Prof. YURII LEONOV.

Institute of Hydrology: 107078 Moscow, ul. Novaya Basmannaya 10, POB 231; tel. (495) 265-97-57; fax (495) 265-18-87; e-mail iwapr@iwapr.msk.su; f. 1968; complex evaluation of water resources; development of scientific substantiation for their rational use and protection; Dir M. G. KHUBLARYAN.

The Section of Earth Sciences also includes the Institute of Lake Conservation and the Scientific Council on Study of the Caspian Sea.

Section of Social Sciences

Centre for Environmental Legal Studies, Institute of State and Law: 119841 Moscow, ul. Znamenka 10; tel. (495) 291-38-27; fax (495) 291-85-74; e-mail isl_ran@rinet.ru; f. 1972; research into Russian, comparative and international environmental law; Dir Prof. MIKHAIL M. BRINCHUK.

Regional Divisions

Siberian Division: 630090 Novosibirsk, pr. Akademika Lavrenteva 17; tel. (3832) 30-05-67; fax (3832) 30-18-46; e-mail dobr@sbras.nsc.ru; internet www.sbras.nsc.ru; Chair. NIKOLAI L. DOBRETSOV; institutes involved in environmental matters incl.:

Chita Institute of Natural Resources: 672014 Transbaikal Krai, Chita, ul. Butina 16, POB 147; tel. (3022) 21-16-89; fax (3022) 21-25-82; e-mail root@cinr.chita.su; f. 1981; scientific research into the region's ecosystems; Dir Prof. ALEKSEI B. PTITSYN.

Limnological Institute: 664033 Irkutsk, ul. Ulan-Batorskaya 3, POB 4199; tel. (3952) 46-05-04; fax (3952) 46-69-33; e-mail info@lin.irk.ru; internet www.lin.irk.ru; studies the ecology of lakes; particularly concerned with the conservation programme in Lake Baikal; Dir Prof. MIKHAIL A. GRACHEV.

Institute of Water and Ecological Problems: 656099 Altai Krai, Barnaul, ul. Papanintsev 105; tel. (3852) 36-78-56; fax (3852) 24-03-96; e-mail iwep@iwep.secna.ru; f. 1987; research into water-resource use, land reclamation and environmental protection in Siberia; experimental and mathematical methods for analysis of hydrophysical, hydrochemical and other natural processes in the aquatic environment; environmental assessment of large-scale engineering projects; development of information- and modelling systems for specific research projects and management resources; decision support systems; Dir Prof. YURII I. VINOKUROV.

Far Eastern Division: 690950 Maritime Krai, Vladivostok, ul. Svetlanskaya 50; tel. (4232) 22-25-28; fax (4232) 22-87-50; e-mail sergienko@hq.febras.ru; internet www.febras.ru; f. 1932; Chair. VALENTIN I. SERGIYENKO; attached institutes incl.:

Institute of Biological Problems of the North: 685000 Magadan, ul. Portovaya 18; tel. and fax (4132) 63-44-63; e-mail office@ibpn.ru; e-mail www.ibpn.ru; f. 1972; Dir IGOR A. CHERESHNEV.

Institute of Water and Ecological Problems: 680063 Khabarovsk, ul. Kim Yu Chena 65; tel. (4212) 22-75-73; fax (4212) 32-57-55; e-mail ivep@ivep.khv.ru; f. 1968; research into Far Eastern ecosystems and their biodiversity and the sustainable use of natural resources; Dir B. A. VORONOV.

Urals Division: 620219 Sverdlovsk obl., Yekaterinburg, ul. Pervomaiskaya 91; tel. (343) 274-02-23; e-mail romanov@prm.uran.ru; internet www.uran.ru; Chair. V. A. CHERESHNEV; attached institutes incl.:

Institute of Industrial Ecology: 620219 Sverdlovsk obl., Yekaterinburg, ul. S. Kovalevskoi 20A; tel. and fax (343) 274-37-71; e-mail chukanov@ecko.uran.ru; f. 1992; environmental research; research into health, socio-economics, demographic consequences of environmental contamination, risk assessment and radioecology; Dir Prof. V. N. CHUKANOV.

Institute of Plant and Animal Ecology: 620144 Sverdlovsk obl., Yekaterinburg, ul. 8-go Marta 202; tel. (343) 260-82-55; fax

(343) 260-65-00; e-mail common@ipae.uran.ru; internet www.ipae
.uran.ru; f. 1944; environmental research; Dir V. N. BOLSHAKOV.

NON-GOVERNMENTAL ORGANIZATIONS

All-Russian Society for Nature Conservation (VOOP) (Vserossiiskoye obshchestvo okhrany prirody): 103012 Moscow, Bogoyavlenskii per. 3/3; tel. (495) 924-77-65; fax (495) 921-78-12; f. 1924; promotes environmental education and the implementation of environmental law; 34 regional brs; Dir-Gen. IVAN F. BARISHPOL.

Association for Environmental Education (AsEkO) (Assotsiatsiya 'Ekologicheskoye obrazovaniye'): 249039 Kaluga obl., Obninsk-9, POB 9081; e-mail web@online.ru; internet a-s-e-k-o.narod.ru; f. 1991; educational programmes and projects; initiation of environmental education at all levels and promotion of sustainable development; support for teachers; development of a network for information exchange; training seminars and conferences; produces regular journal and e-mail bulletin; Chair. VADIM KALININ.

Biodiversity Conservation Centre (Tsentr okhrany dikoi prirody): 117312 Moscow, ul. Vavilova 41/2; tel. and fax (495) 124-71-78; e-mail biodivers@biodiversity.ru; internet www.biodiversity.ru; f. 1992; Dir-Gen. ALEKSEI ZIMENKO; Sec. IRINA TRETYAKOVA.

Ekoline: 125047 Moscow, POB 7; tel. and fax (495) 978-90-61; e-mail office@ecoline.ru; internet www.ecoline.ru; f. 1995; environmental and sustainability management, environmental monitoring and assessment; Chief Expert SERGEI DAIMAN.

Ekozashchita!—Ecodefense!: 236000 Kaliningrad, POB 1477; tel. (4012) 43-72-86; fax (4012) 75-71-06; e-mail ecodefense@ecodefense.ru; internet www.ecodefense.ru; f. 1990; nation-wide environmental asscn; promotes environmental education, brs in Kaliningrad, Moscow and Voronezh.

Green World Environmental Association (Zelenyi Mir): 197371 St Petersburg, Komendantskii pr. 29/1/307; tel. and fax (812) 306-40-37; e-mail greenworld@spb.org.ru; internet www.greenworld.org.ru; f. 1988; applied research institute; Chair. OLEG BODROV.

Greenpeace Russia: 127994 Moscow, ul. N. Bashilovka 6, POB 4; tel. (495) 257-41-06; fax (495) 257-41-10; e-mail join@ru.greenpeace.org; internet www.greenpeace.org/russia_ru; f. 1992; national office of Greenpeace International; activities include a campaign for the protection of Lake Baikal; Exec. Dir SERGEI TSYPLENKOV.

Laboratory for Radiation Control: 650070 Kemerovo, Kemerovo State University, ul. Tukhachevskaya 33; tel. and fax (3842) 31-14-98; e-mail nl@irk.da.ru; f. 1994; concerned with control of radiation, environmental monitoring; Head of Laboratory NADEZHDA ALUKER.

Moscow Ecological Federation: 121019 Moscow, per. Bogoyavlenskii 3/3; tel. (495) 924-77-65; e-mail ecology-mef@narod.ru; internet ecology-mef.narod.ru; concerned with Moscow's ecological problems; provides environmental information; assists with urban development plans; Chair. TATYANA ZAKHARCHENKO.

Moscow Society of Naturalists (MOIP) (Moskovskoye obshchestvo ispytatelei prirody): 103009 Moscow, ul. B. Nikitskaya 6; tel. (495) 203-67-04; internet www.seminarium.narod.ru/moip/moip.htm; f. 1805; 2,500 mems; library of 522,000 vols; Chair. V. A. SADOVNICHII.

Russian Ecological Party—Greens (Rossiiskaya Ekologicheskaya Partiya—Zelenye): 103045 Moscow, Poslednyi per. 26; tel. (495) 231-31-29; fax (495) 737-54-29; e-mail info@greenparty.ru; internet www.greenparty.ru; f. 2002 on the basis of the Cedar Tree—Ecological Party of Russia (Ekologicheskaya partiya Rossii—Kedr); Chair. of the Presidium ANATOLII A. PANFILOV; 60,989 mems (2006).

Socio-Ecological Union International (SoES) (Sotsialno-ekologicheskii soyuz): 117312 Moscow, ul. Vavilova 41; tel. and fax (495) 124-79-34; e-mail soceco@seu.ru; internet www.seu.ru; f. 1987; co-ordinates 250 environmental committees, clubs and societies in all countries of the CIS, as well as Estonia, Norway and the USA; international co-operation; campaigns on issues of the environment, human rights, biodiversity protection, energy efficiency, nuclear energy and radioactive pollution; environmental education; Sec. N. I. ZABELIN.

Defence

In May 1992 the Russian Federation established its own armed forces, on the basis of former Soviet forces on the territory of the Russian Federation, and former Soviet forces outside its territory not subordinate to other former republics of the USSR. As assessed at November 2007, the total Russian active armed forces numbered an estimated 1,027,000, with an estimated 20,000,000 reserves. These included an estimated 80,000 permanent members of the Strategic Deterrent Forces, an estimated 395,000 in the army (including some 190,000 conscripts), 142,000 in the navy, and an estimated 160,000 in the air force (including an unspecified number of conscripts), following its merger with the air defence troops. There were a further 419,000 paramilitary troops. A presidential decree in March 2007 reduced the length of compulsory military service (for males over the age of 18 years) from two years to one, starting on 1 January 2008.

By late 2000 most member states of the Commonwealth of Independent States (CIS) had formed national armies. The formation of a joint CIS military force, which had initially won much support from the organization's members, became increasingly less popular. None the less, in April 2003 the Government announced that citizens of other CIS countries were to be eligible to serve in the Russian armed forces, for a period of up to three years, after which time they were to become eligible to apply for Russian citizenship. The budget for 2007 allocated 821,000m. roubles to defence.

Chief of the General Staff, First Deputy Minister of Defence: Gen. NIKOLAI YE. MAKAROV.

Chief of Staff of the Internal Troops: Col-Gen. MIKHAIL PANKOV.

Commander-in-Chief of the Army: Gen. VLADIMIR A. BOLDYREV.

Commander-in-Chief of the Navy: Adm. VLADIMIR S. VYSOTSKII.

Chief of Staff of the Air Force: Col-Gen. ALEKSANDR N. ZELIN.

MEMBERS OF THE RUSSIAN FEDERATION

For much of the 1990s and the first half of the 2000s the Russian Federation comprised 89 federal territorial units. The status of the federal subjects had begun to be regularized by the Federation Treaty of 31 March 1992, which had provided for a union of 20 republics (16 of which had been nominally Autonomous Soviet Socialist Republics—ASSRs under the old regime, and four of which were autonomous oblasts), six krais, 49 oblasts and one autonomous oblast. The 10 autonomous okrugs remained under the jurisdiction of the krai or oblast within which they were located (a situation that largely continued thereafter), but, as federal units, were raised to the same status as oblasts and krais. The former republic of Checheno-Ingushetiya was divided into two republics in June 1992, by the formal recognition of a republic of Ingushetiya. Moscow and St Petersburg subsequently assumed the status of cities of federal status. Following the formation of Perm Krai by the merger of Perm Oblast with the Komi-Permyak Autonomous Okrug (AOk), which took effect from 1 December 2005, the number of federal subjects was reduced to 88. The total number of territories was further reduced on 1 January 2007, to 86, and on 1 July 2007 to 85. The number of territories was further reduced, to 84 from 1 January 2008, following the merger of Irkutsk Oblast and the Ust-Orda Buryat AOk, and to 83 from 1 March of that year, following the creation of Transbaikal Krai by the merger of Chita Oblast and the Aga-Buryat AOk. The 83 territories comprised 21 republics, nine krais (provinces), 46 oblasts, two cities of federal status, one autonomous oblast and four autonomous okrugs. Republics, autonomous okrugs and the autonomous oblast are ethnically defined, while krais, oblasts and the cities of federal status are defined on territorial grounds. Under the terms of the 1992 treaties, republics were granted far wider-reaching powers than the other federal units, specifically over the use of natural resources and land. The republics, autonomous okrugs and the autonomous oblast are (sometimes nominally) ethnically defined, while krais and oblasts are defined on territorial grounds. One of Vladimir Putin's earliest actions after his election as federal President in March 2000 was to group the federal subjects into seven Federal Okrugs (districts). These seven Federal Okrugs are the Central Federal Okrug (based in the capital, Moscow), the North-Western Federal Okrug (St Petersburg), the Southern Federal Okrug (Rostov-on-Don), the Volga Federal Okrug (Nizhnii Novgorod), the Urals Federal Okrug (Yekaterinburg), the Siberian Federal Okrug (Novosibirsk) and the Far Eastern Federal Okrug (Khabarovsk). Additionally, the federal subjects are grouped into 11 economic areas, which, with the exception of that in the Far East, differ from the newer Federal Okrugs of the same name. These are the Central Economic Area, the Central Chernozem (Black Earth) Economic Area, the East Siberian Economic Area, the Far Eastern Economic Area, the North Caucasus Economic Area, the North-Western Economic Area, the Northern Economic Area, the Urals Economic Area, the Volga Economic Area, the Volga-Vyatka Economic Area and the West Siberian Economic Area.

The republics each have their own governments and ministries; in many cases there is also a republican president. Under the terms of the 1992 treaties, republics were granted far wider-reaching powers than the other federal units, specifically over the use of natural resources and land. The remaining federal units are governed by a local administration, the head or governor of which is the highest official in the territory, and a representative assembly. Governors are able to veto regional legislation, although their vetoes may be overridden by a two-thirds' parliamentary majority. The federal legislature, which created the post of governor in August 1991, intended that the official be elected by popular vote. The federal President, Boris Yeltsin, however, secured an agreement that the governors be appointed. In many regions conflict subsequently arose between the executive and legislative bodies, as the presidential appointees encountered much resistance from the communist-dominated assemblies. In those cases where a vote of 'no confidence' was passed in the governor, elections were permitted. (This occurred in eight territories in April 1993.) Following President Yeltsin's dissolution of the Russian legislature in September 1993, and parliament's violent resistance, it was announced that all heads of local administrations would, henceforth, be appointed and dismissed by presidential decree. However, this ruling was relaxed in December 1995, when gubernatorial elections were held in one krai and 11 oblasts. From the late 1990s elected governors became the norm across the Federation, as initial terms of office expired, and Vladimir Putin (who was elected as President in March 2000) made no use of presidential decrees to appoint or dismiss regional governors during his first term of office (2000–04). However, in September 2004 Putin announced proposed legislation, in accordance with which governors

of all federal subjects would henceforth be appointed by the federal authorities, subject to approval by regional legislatures; following the approval of this legislation in late December, the election of a Governor in the Nenets AOk, held in January–February 2005, represented the final such poll. From 2005 the appointment of governors became widespread, sometimes occurring when an incumbent regional leader's mandate expired, but also taking place when a leader requested an expression of confidence from the federal President.

As Russian President, before the disintegration of the USSR Yeltsin strongly advocated decentralization within the Russian Federation, and hence increasing political and economic diversity among the federal units. From 1995 the undertaking of bilateral treaties to delineate powers between federal Government and the regional authorities became increasingly commonplace. This resulted in the establishment, in March 1996, of the precise terms of the delimitation of jurisdiction and powers between federal and regional authorities. Any treaties on the delimitation of powers could not change the status of a federal unit, threaten the territorial integrity of the Russian Federation or violate the terms of the federal Constitution. Fears that the country was being transformed from a constitution-based to a treaty-based federation became more widespread as these power-sharing agreements were signed by a majority of federal subjects.

Attempts to regulate the subsequent peripheral–central tensions in the governance of Russia took a variety of forms, particularly after the election of Vladimir Putin to the presidency. In particular, the establishment of the Federal Okrugs, each of which was headed by a presidential appointee, was considered by many to be a device to ensure closer central supervision of regional activity. A series of presidential decrees in 2000–01 ruled that laws specific to certain regions were unconstitutional and must be amended. The republics, which had the greatest degree of autonomy to lose under the new arrangements, were most severely affected; by April 2002 some 28 of the 42 'power-sharing treaties' signed between the regional and federal authorities had been annulled, and many of those which remained had been amended, in order to bring regional legislation into conformity with the federal norm. In the mid-2000s, however, the negotiation of new power-sharing treaties between the federal authorities and two of the republics that had been most persistent in asserting their autonomy—the Chechen (Nokchi) Republic and the Republic of Tatarstan—were undertaken. In March 2007 the recently appointed President of the Chechen Republic, Ramzan Kadyrov, announced that he opposed the ratification of a new treaty delineating the separation of powers between the republican and federal authorities. In July of that year a bilateral treaty between the federal authorities and Tatarstan was approved by the Sovet Federatsii (Federation Council—the upper house of the federal parliament); a previous draft had been rejected earlier that year. A new body, the State Council of the Russian Federation, was created by presidential decree in September 2000, the members of which were the heads of the federal subjects. The organization's presidium was chaired by the Russian President, and was to be formed on a rotational basis every six months. Since the Russian Constitution remained unchanged, the State Council's functions were consultative, and participation in it was voluntary. According to its founding decree, the body was to advise the President mainly on issues concerning the relationship between the central administration and Russia's regions.

Presidential Representative to the Central Federal Okrug: Lt-Gen. GEORGII S. POLTAVCHENKO (appointed 18 May 2000), 103132 Moscow, Nikolskii per. 6; tel. (495) 206-12-76; e-mail malakhov_dm@ gov.ru.

Presidential Representative to the Far Eastern Federal Okrug: OLEG A. SAFONOV (appointed 30 October 2007), 680030 Khabarovsk, ul. Sheronova 22; tel. (4212) 31-39-78; fax (4212) 31-38-04; internet www.dfo.gov.ru.

Presidential Representative to the North-Western Federal Okrug: ILYA I. KLEBANOV (appointed 1 November 2003), 199004 St Petersburg, Vasilyevskii ostrov, 3-ya liniya 12; tel. (812) 323-07-74; fax (812) 323-75-87; internet www.szfo.ru.

Presidential Representative to the Siberian Federal Okrug: ANATOLII V. KVASHNIN (appointed 9 September 2004), 630091 Novosibirsk, ul. Derzhavina 18/120; tel. (3832) 20-17-56; fax (3832) 20-13-90; e-mail sibokrug@atlas-nsk.ru; internet www.sfo.nsk.su.

Presidential Representative to the Southern Federal Okrug: VLADIMIR V. USTINOV (appointed 12 May 2008), 344006 Rostov-on-Don, ul. B. Sadovaya 73; tel. (863) 249-99-43; fax (863) 249-99-47; e-mail pppufo@ufo.gov.ru; internet www.ufo.gov.ru.

Presidential Representative to the Urals Federal Okrug: Col-Gen. PETR M. LATYSHEV (appointed 18 May 2000), 620031 Sverdlovsk obl., Yekaterinburg, pl. Oktyabrskaya 3; tel. (343) 277-18-96; e-mail support@uralfo.ru; internet www.uralfo.ru.

Presidential Representative to the Volga Federal Okrug: GRIGORII A. RAPOTA (appointed 12 May 2008), 603082 Nizhnii Novgorod, Kreml, kor. 1; tel. (8312) 31-46-07; fax (8312) 31-47-51; internet www.pfo.ru.

Central Federal Okrug

Moscow City

Moscow (Moskva) is located in the west of European Russia, on the River Moskva, which crosses the city from the north-west to the south-east. It is connected to the Volga river system by the Moscow–Volga Canal. Moscow is included in the Central Federal Okrug and the Central Economic Area. The city's total area is 994 sq km (384 sq miles). Moscow is the largest city in the Russian Federation and had a total population of 10.4m. at January 2007, according to official estimates, and a population density of 10,505.7 per sq km. Zelenograd, formerly a separate city, is located in the north-west of the federal unit. In 2002 some 84.8% of Moscow city's population were ethnically Russian, 2.4% Ukrainian, 1.6% Tatar, 1.2% Armenian, 0.9% Azeri and 0.8% were Jewish. The city is included in the time zone GMT+3.

HISTORY

Moscow city was founded in about 1147. In 1325 it became the seat of the Eastern Orthodox Metropolitan of Rus (in 1589–1721 and after 1917 the Patriarch of Moscow and all Rus) and the steadily expanding Muscovite state became the foundation for the Russian Empire. The capital city was moved to St Petersburg in 1712. However, Moscow was restored as the Russian and Soviet capital in 1918. Following the invasion of the USSR by Nazi Germany in 1941, the Government was removed from the city (and relocated, principally, to Kuibyshev—now Samara) until 1943.

In the 1990s reformists enjoyed considerable support in the city. In June 1991 Gavriil Popov won the city's first mayoral elections. He resigned in June 1992, following a serious deterioration in the economic situation, and Yurii Luzhkov, head of the City Government, was appointed by federal President Boris Yeltsin in his place. In October 1993 a presidential decree suspended the powers of the City Soviet (Council); elections to a new 35-member Municipal Duma were held on 12 December.

In June 1996 Luzhkov was elected Mayor, with 89.9% of the votes cast. In June 1998 he signed a power-sharing treaty with the federal authorities. Luzhkov concluded a number of trade agreements with other regions, and in 1998 he established the nation-wide, centrist Fatherland movement. Following several bomb attacks in the city in 1999, which killed more than 200 people, the city authorities intensified their implementation of regulations on residence permits, despite this legislation having been deemed unconstitutional by the federal Constitutional and Supreme Courts.

Luzhkov was re-elected as Mayor, with 69.9% of votes cast, in December 1999. In elections to the Municipal Duma held in December 2001 Unity and Fatherland-United Russia (UF-UR—formed by the merger of Fatherland with another centrist group, Unity) secured the largest number of seats. Further attacks attributed to Chechen militants in the city in 2002–04 included an armed siege in a Moscow theatre in October 2002, as a result of which at least 129 hostages died, and the bombing of an underground train in February 2004, which killed at least 39 people.

Luzhkov was again re-elected as Mayor on 7 December 2003, receiving 74.8% of the votes cast. The rate of participation by the electorate was 57.4%. In elections to the Municipal Duma, held on 4 December 2005, United Russia (UR—as UF-UR was now known) won a sizeable majority, having received some 47.3% of votes cast. The Communist Party of the Russian Federation won 16.8%, while the liberal Yabloko party took 11.1% and the nationalist Liberal Democratic Party of Russia obtained 8.0%. Another nationalist party, Motherland, was banned from participating in the elections following a decision, upheld by the Supreme Court, that one of its television advertisements incited inter-ethnic strife. Furthermore, inter-ethnic tensions (notably between Slavs and various Caucasian groups) in the city were evident towards the end of 2006, when extreme nationalist demonstrators defied a ban imposed by Luzhkov on a march organized for 4 November, to coincide with the national holiday, People's Unity Day. In the 2000s there were also numerous racially motivated attacks in Moscow (as well as in certain other locations nation-wide, notably St Petersburg and Voronezh) by extreme nationalists, notably against African university students and market traders of Caucasian origin. In April 2007 the Municipal Duma adopted further restrictions on public demonstrations that placed severe limitations on the number of people permitted to attend such gatherings. Despite repeated bans imposed on an informal coalition of opposition groups, Another Russia, proscribing the staging of demonstrations, large rallies, nevertheless, proceeded in Moscow (and in other cities) in mid-April and were violently suppressed by special police units attached to the federal Ministry of the Interior, which temporarily detained some leaders of the opposition coalition. Although Luzhkov had stated that he would not seek to renew his mandate, on 27 June the Municipal Duma confirmed his nomination by Putin for a fifth term as Mayor (with 32 of the 35 deputies voting in favour). In late November special police suppressed a further unauthorized rally, staged by Another Russia, in Moscow, prior to elections to the State Duma (the lower chamber of the federal legislature) on 2 December; some 200 opposition protesters and two prominent opposition leaders were temporarily detained. According to preliminary results, UR secured about 54.2% of votes cast in Moscow, one of its poorest results in the Federation. In April 2008, amid rumours of his impending resignation to take a senior government position, Luzhkov urged that a process to merge Moscow City and Moscow Oblast into one territory be initiated.

ECONOMY

In 2004 the city of Moscow's gross regional product amounted to 2,759,100.9m. roubles, equivalent to 265,323.1 roubles per head. In 2006 the city accounted for 19% of the Russian Federation's gross domestic product (GDP). There are nine railway termini in the city and 11 electrified radial lines. The metro system included 12 lines and 194 stations and extended to 294 km at 2007; further extension of the network was underway. The entire public transport system carries more than 6.5m. passengers per day. Moscow's waterways connect with the Baltic, White, Caspian and Black Seas. There are also four airports in the city.

Moscow's industry consists primarily of mechanical engineering, metal-working, electricity production, production of chemicals and petrochemicals, petroleum-refining and food-processing. Industry employed around 27.0% of the city's working population in 2005 (in contrast to the 0.2% engaged in agriculture) and generated 533,336m. roubles in 2004, a figure surpassed in the Russian Federation only by the Khanty-Mansii Autonomous Okrug—AOk (and therefore Tyumen Oblast, which incorporates the AOk). The Moskvich Automobile Plant, in which the City Government held a controlling stake from 1998, is one of Moscow's principal companies. There are also significant defence sector industries in the city. In 2005 some 24.8% of the working population were engaged in trade and commerce, while 13.5% were employed in the construction sector. As the Russian capital, the city is the site of a large number of government offices, as well as being the centre for major business and financial companies. Tourism is another important service industry. In November 2005 the federal authorities announced that one of six special economic zones to be established across the Federation was to be located in the north-western Zelenograd district. This zone was to specialize in microelectronics.

In 2005 the economically active population of the city numbered 5,866,000, and the proportion of the labour force that was unemployed, at 0.8%, was the lowest in the Russian Federation. Those in employment earned, on average, 14,424.6 roubles per month, one of the highest rates in the Federation. The 2005 budget recorded a surplus of 19,517.6m. roubles. In 2005 international trade amounted to a value of US $84,142.2m. in exports and $37,175.7m. in imports, by far the highest level of any federal subject. Capital investment in the city represents around one-10th of that in Russia as a whole. Total foreign investment in the city amounted to $25,228.0m. in 2005. In that year some 7,112 enterprises and organizations involving foreign capital, representing some 44.1% of the total quantity of such enterprises in Russia, were situated in Moscow City and the surrounding Moscow Oblast. Of these, 962 were joint ventures with partners from Cyprus, 798 were joint ventures with partners from the People's Republic of China, 549 had German partners, 540 had partners from the USA, 470 from the United Kingdom and 229 from Belarus. At the end of 2005 there were 200,480 small businesses registered in the city, employing 1,757,400 people; slightly more than one-fifth of all small businesses registered in the Federation in that year were located in Moscow City.

DIRECTORY

Mayor and Prime Minister of the City Government: YURII M. LUZHKOV (appointed 6 June 1992, elected 16 June 1996, re-elected 19 December 1999, 7 December 2003; appointment confirmed 27 June 2007), 125032 Moscow, ul. Tverskaya 13; tel. (495) 777-77-77; fax (495) 232-18-74; e-mail mayor@mos.ru; internet www.mos.ru.

Chairman of the Municipal Duma: VLADIMIR M. PLATONOV, 127994 Moscow, ul. Petrovka 22; tel. (495) 957-03-30; fax (495) 921-92-02; e-mail spravka@duma.mos.ru; internet www.duma.mos.ru.

Belgorod Oblast

Belgorod Oblast is situated in the south-west of the Central Russian Highlands. It forms part of the Central Federal Okrug and the Central Chernozem Economic Area. The Oblast lies on the international border with Ukraine, with the Oblasts of Kursk to the north and Voronezh to the east. Its main rivers are the Severnii Donets, the Vorskla and the Oskol. The territory occupies 27,100 sq km (10,460 sq miles). At January 2007, according to official estimates, Belgorod Oblast had a total population of 1,513,620, giving a population density of 55.9 per sq km. Some 66.4% of the population inhabited urban areas. Some 92.9% of the Oblast's inhabitants were ethnic Russians and 3.8% were Ukrainians at the time of the 2002 census. The Oblast's administrative centre is at Belgorod, which had 344,200 inhabitants in January 2006. A further major city is Staryi Oskol (218,200). Belgorod Oblast is included in the time zone GMT+3.

HISTORY

Belgorod was established as a bishopric during the early days of Orthodox Christianity. The region was part of Lithuania until 1503, when it was annexed by the Muscovite state. The new city of Belgorod was founded in 1593. On 12 July 1943, north-east of the city, the Red Army defeated the Germans in the largest single tank battle in the Second World War, the most vital action in the wider Kursk offensive. Belgorod Oblast was formally established on 6 January 1954.

In October 1993 President Boris Yeltsin dismissed the region's Governor, Viktor Berestovoi, and arranged for elections to a new regional Duma to be held. The communists enjoyed a majority in this body, too, and there was constant conflict with the administration headed by Yeltsin's appointee, Yevgenii Savchenko, who, however, also enjoyed popular support. The Oblast was one of 12 areas in the Federation to be permitted gubernatorial elections in December 1995, when Savchenko was duly elected. He was re-elected in May 1999 and again in May 2003. In elections to the regional legislature, held on 16 October 2005, the pro-presidential United Russia won 53.0% of the votes cast. President Putin's nomination of Savchenko for a fifth term as Governor was formally approved by the regional Duma (with 20 of the 32 deputies voting in favour) on 16 June 2007. The local branch of the Communist Party of the Russian Federation, which had opposed the nomination, protested to the Presidential Representative in the Central Federal Okrug, and expressed support for the reintroduction of a system of direct election for regional governors.

ECONOMY

In 2004 Belgorod Oblast's gross regional product amounted to 113,181.1m. roubles, or 74,838.0 roubles per head. The main industrial centres in the territory are situated at Belgorod and Shebekino. At the end of 2005 there were 700 km of railway lines and 6,579 km of paved roads on the Oblast's territory.

Belgorod Oblast's principal crops are grain, sugar beet, sunflower seeds and essential-oil plants. Horticulture, animal husbandry and bee-keeping are also important. In 2005 agriculture engaged 18.0% of the labour force and generated 33,889m. roubles. The Oblast has substantial reserves of bauxite, iron ore and apatites. Its main industries are ore-mining (iron ores), the production of electricity, mechanical engineering, metal-working, chemicals, the manufacture of building materials and food-processing. Industry employed 29.3% of the work-force in 2005 and generated 120,778m. roubles in 2004.

The economically active population in Belgorod Oblast numbered 714,000 in 2005, when 6.0% of the region's labour force were unemployed. In the mid-2000s the region was reported to host the greatest quantity of labour migrants of any region in the Central Chernozem Economic Area, with migrants arriving in approximately equal numbers from other regions of Russia (particularly from the Far East and Siberia) and from abroad (notably Ukraine) in the first half of 2005. The average monthly salary in 2005 was 6,775.4 roubles, and there was a budgetary deficit of 1,053.2m. roubles. Export trade totalled US $1,412.4m. in that year, while import trade amounted to $1,919.7m. Foreign investment in the Oblast totalled $21.1m. in 2005. At the end of 2005 there were 8,567 small businesses registered in the Oblast, providing employment to 53,600 people.

DIRECTORY

Head of the Regional Administration (Governor): YEVGENII S. SAVCHENKO (appointed 18 December 1993, elected 17 December 1995, re-elected 30 May 1999 and 25 May 2003, appointment confirmed 16 June 2007), 308005 Belgorod, pl. Revolyutsii 4; tel. (472) 222-42-47; fax (472) 222-33-43; e-mail admin@regadm.bel.ru; internet www.belregion.ru.

Chairman of the Regional Duma: ANATOLII YA. ZELIKOV, 308005 Belgorod, pl. Revolyutsii 4; tel. (472) 232-24-37; fax (472) 227-65-88; e-mail duma@bel.ru; internet duma.bel.ru.

Chief Representative of Belgorod Oblast in the Russian Federation: ALEKSANDR G. MATSEPURO, 113152 Moscow, Zagorodnoye shosse 5/21; tel. (495) 952-59-30; fax (495) 952-28-36; e-mail moscow@bel.ru.

Head of Belgorod City Administration: VASILII N. POTRYASAYEV, 308800 Belgorod, ul. Lenina 38; tel. (472) 227-34-11; e-mail adm@belgorod.info; internet m207.bel.ru/goradm.

Bryansk Oblast

Bryansk Oblast is situated in the Central Russian Highlands and is in the Central Federal Okrug and the Central Economic Area. It has international borders to the west (Belarus) and south (Ukraine), and domestic borders with Kursk and Orel Oblasts to the east, Kaluga to the north-east and Smolensk to the north-west. Two villages, Sankovo and Medvezhye, which are surrounded by Belarusian territory, form an exclave that also constitutes part of the Oblast. Bryansk's main river is the Desna, a tributary of the Dnepr (Dnieper), and just under one-third of its area is forested. The Oblast occupies 34,900 sq km (13,480 sq miles) of territory. At January 2007, according to official estimates, the region had a total population of 1,317,589, giving a population density of 37.8 per sq km. Some 68.3% of the population inhabited urban areas. Some 96.3% of the population were ethnic Russians and 1.5% were Ukrainians at the time of the 2002 census. Bryansk, with a population of 420,000 at January 2006, according to official estimates, is the Oblast's administrative centre. Bryansk Oblast is included in the time zone GMT+3.

HISTORY

The city of Bryansk (first mentioned in 1146) was part of the independent principality of Novgorod-Seversk until 1356. It was an early Orthodox Christian bishopric. The Muscovite state acquired the city from Lithuania in the 16th century. In the early 17th century the city figured in the insurrections associated with the pretenders to the tsarist throne known as the 'false Dmitriis'. Generally, it was a loyal garrison town. Bryansk Oblast was founded on 5 July 1944.

Bryansk was one of eight federal territories permitted gubernatorial elections in December 1992. The incumbent (appointed in December 1991), Vladimir Barabanov, was defeated by the communist-backed candidate, Yurii Lodkin. During the constitutional crisis of September–October 1993 Lodkin was dismissed and the Soviet disbanded, and an oblast Duma formed. After a series of scandals involving successive, short-lived (and non-communist) Governors, Lodkin was elected Governor in December 1996. A power-sharing agreement was signed between the oblast and federal authorities in July 1997. Lodkin was re-elected as Governor in December 2000, although he obtained only 29% of the votes cast. Shortly before the gubernatorial election scheduled for December 2004, the oblast court prohibited Lodkin's candidacy, on the grounds that he had breached several campaign rules. Nikolai Denin, the candidate of the pro-presidential United Russia (UR), was elected as Governor following two rounds of voting. In elections to the regional Duma, held concurrently with the first round of gubernatorial polling, 14 of the 30 deputies elected were representatives of UR. Putin's nomination of Denin for a further gubernatorial term was confirmed by the regional Duma on 18 October 2007.

ECONOMY

Bryansk Oblast's gross regional product was 55,108,3m. roubles in 2004, equivalent to 40,705.5 roubles per head. Its main industrial centres are at Bryansk and Klintsy. At the end of 2005 there were 1,010 km of railway track on its territory, and 6,507 km of paved roads.

The Oblast's agriculture, which employed 13.7% of its work-force and generated 15,716m. roubles in 2005, consists mainly of grain, sugar beet and potato production, and animal husbandry. Around one-half of the territory's area is used for agricultural purposes. The Oblast's main industries are mechanical engineering, food-processing, electrical energy, the manufacture of building materials and timber-working. Industry employed 23.3% of the work-force in 2005 and generated 35,200m. roubles in 2004.

In 2005 the economically active population of Bryansk Oblast numbered 648,000, and 6.7% of the region's labour force were unemployed. The average monthly wage was 5,235.3 roubles. There was a regional government budgetary deficit of 652.0m. roubles in 2005. In that year international trade comprised US $260.4m. of exports and $676.6m. of imports, while foreign investment amounted to $17.7m. At the end of 2005 there were 3,220 small businesses registered in the region, providing employment to 33,700 people.

DIRECTORY

Head of the Regional Administration (Governor): NIKOLAI V. DENIN (elected 19 December 2004, appointment confirmed 18 October 2007), 241002 Bryansk, pr. Lenina 33; tel. (483) 266-26-11; fax (483) 241-38-95; e-mail gubernator@bryanskobl.ru; internet www .bryanskobl.ru.

Chairman of the Regional Duma: VLADIMIR I. GAIDUKOV, 241000 Bryansk, pl. K. Marksa 2; tel. (483) 243-36-91; fax (083) 274-31-95; e-mail main@duma.bryansk.ru; internet duma.bryansk.ru.

Chief Representative of Bryansk Oblast in the Russian Federation: ANDREI R. IVANOV, 127025 Moscow, ul. Novyi Arbat 19; tel. (495) 203-64-36.

Head of Bryansk City Administration (Mayor): IGOR I. ALEKHIN, 241002 Bryansk, pr. Lenina 35; tel. (483) 274-30-13; fax (483) 274-47-30; e-mail postmaster@comimm.bryansk.su; internet admin .debryansk.ru.

Ivanovo Oblast

Ivanovo Oblast is situated in the central part of the Eastern European Plain. It forms part of the Central Federal Okrug and the Central Economic Area. It is surrounded by the Oblasts of Kostroma (to the north), Nizhnii Novgorod (east), Vladimir (south) and Yaroslavl (north-west). Its main river is the Volga and one-half of its territory is forested. The Oblast covers a total area of 21,800 sq km (9,230 sq miles). At January 2007, according to official estimates, the Oblast's population numbered 1,087,886, giving a population density of 49.9 per sq km. At the time of the 2002 census 93.7% of the population were ethnic Russians and 0.9% were Ukrainians. Some 80.7% of the population inhabited urban areas in 2007. The Oblast's administrative centre, Ivanovo, had a population of 413,100. Ivanovo Oblast is included in the time zone GMT+3.

HISTORY

A village of Ivanovo was first mentioned in 1561. The city of Ivanovo (initially Ivanovo-Voznesensk) was founded in 1871. It was an important centre of anti-government activity during the strikes of 1883 and 1885 and in the 1905 Revolution. Ivanovo Oblast was founded on 20 July 1918.

Moderate candidates were successful in the gubernatorial and regional legislative elections held in 1996, when Vladislav Tikhomirov was elected as Governor. Following two rounds of polling in December 2000, the Communist Party of the Russian Federation (CPRF) candidate, Vladimir Tikhonov, was elected as Governor. In July 2004 Tikhonov was elected as leader of a breakaway, left-wing, faction of the CPRF, although attempts by the faction to form a separate party proved unsuccessful. On 22 November 2005 the regional legislature approved the nomination of Mikhail Men, hitherto Deputy Mayor of Moscow, as the new Governor; Men took up office on 27 December. Meanwhile, at regional legislative elections held on 4 December, the pro-presidential United Russia was the most successful party, winning 32.1% of the votes cast; the nationalist Liberal Democratic Party of Russia received 13.0%, while the CPRF and another nationalist party, Motherland, each obtained more than 10% of the votes cast. Concerns about the freedom of the press in Ivanovo, and in Russia more generally, were heightened in mid-2006, when Vladimir Rakhmankov, the editor of *Kursiv*, an online publication based in the region, was brought to trial on charges of insulting a public official, following his publication of an article that had satirized Putin's annual address to the federal legislature. Rakhmankov's trial began in September; he was fined 20,000 roubles in the following month.

ECONOMY

In 2004 Ivanovo Oblast's gross regional product totalled 43,303.2m. roubles, equivalent to 38,581.6 roubles per head. The region's main industrial centres are at Ivanovo, Shuya, Vichuga, Furmanov and Teikovo. There are well-developed rail, road and river transport networks in the region and the largest international airport in central Russia. At the end of 2005 there were 345 km of railways and 3,603 km of paved roads on the Oblast's territory.

Ivanovo Oblast was the historic centre of Russia's cotton-milling industry. Flax production was still an important agricultural activity in the region in the 2000s, as were grain and vegetable production and animal husbandry. However, agriculture employed just 7.3% of the work-force in 2005, when the sector generated 6,978m. roubles. The region's main industries are light manufacturing (especially textiles—73.3% of the total production of cloth in the Russian Federation in 2005 was attributable to industries in the Oblast), electrical energy, mechanical engineering and metal-working, food-processing and handicrafts (especially lacquerware). In 2005 some 29.8% of the working population were engaged in the sector, which generated 33,533m. roubles in 2004.

The territory's economically active population amounted to 575,000 in 2005, when 6.8% of the labour force were unemployed. The average monthly wage was 5,143.7 roubles in 2005. A report issued in 2006 by a state body found that Ivanovo Oblast was one of the 11 most impoverished federal subjects in Russia. In 2005 the budget recorded a surplus of 67.3m. roubles. External trade amounted to US $124.2m. in exports and $228.6m. in imports. Foreign investment amounted to just $0.9m. in 2005. At the end of 2005 there were 3,815 small businesses registered in the region, providing employment to 40,700 people.

DIRECTORY

Head of the Regional Administration (Governor): MIKHAIL A. MEN (appointment confirmed 22 November 2005, assumed office 27 December), 153002 Ivanovo, ul. Baturina 5; tel. (493) 241-77-05; fax (493) 241-92-31; e-mail aio@adminet.ivanovo.ru; internet ivadm .ivanovo.ru.

Chairman of the Legislative Assembly: ANDREI V. NAZAROV, 153000 Ivanovo, ul. Pushkina 9; tel. (493) 241-60-68; fax (093) 241-92-21; e-mail zsio@gov.ivanovo.ru.

Chief Representative of Ivanovo Oblast in the Russian Federation: ALEKSANDR D. KULIKOV, 127025 Moscow, ul. Novyi Arbat 19; tel. (495) 203-41-34; fax (495) 203-93-45.

Head of Ivanovo City Administration: ALEKSANDR G. FOMIN, 153000 Ivanovo, pl. Revolyutsii 6; tel. (493) 259-45-10; fax (493) 241-25-12; e-mail office@ivgoradm.ru; internet www.ivgoradm.ru.

Kaluga Oblast

Kaluga Oblast is situated in the central part of the Eastern European Plain. It forms part of the Central Federal Okrug and the Central Economic Area. Tula and Orel Oblasts lie to the south-east, Bryansk to the south-west, Moscow Oblast to the north-east and Smolensk to the north-west. It occupies 29,900 sq km (11,540 sq miles). At January 2007, according to official estimates, the Oblast's population totalled 1,008,968, giving a population density of 33.7 per sq km. At the time of the 2002 census 93.5% of the population were ethnic Russians and 2.2% were Ukrainians. Some 76.0% of the population inhabited urban areas in January 2007. In January 2006, the administrative centre, Kaluga, a river-port on the Oka river, had a population of 329,100, according to official estimates. Other major cities in the Oblast include Obninsk (105,400), the site of the world's first nuclear power station. Kaluga Oblast is included in the time zone GMT+3.

HISTORY

The city of Kaluga, first mentioned in the letters of a Lithuanian prince, Olgerd, in 1371, was founded as a Muscovite outpost. The region was the scene of an army mutiny in 1905 and was seized by Bolshevik troops at the end of 1917. Kaluga Oblast was founded on 5 July 1944.

Communist-affiliated managers of industrial and agricultural bodies dominated the new representative body, the Legislative Assembly, elected in March 1994. Valerii Sudarenkov, the Governor from November 1996, had previously been the Deputy Chairman of the Government (Prime Minister) of the Uzbek SSR (Uzbekistan). Sudarenkov did not stand for re-election in November 2000; his former deputy, Anatolii Artamonov, was elected to succeed him. Artamonov was re-elected for a second term on 14 March 2004, receiving 66.9% of votes cast. At elections to the regional Legislative Assembly, held on 14 November, the pro-presidential United Russia obtained a far greater share of support than any other party, with 41.0% of the votes cast. In July 2005 Artamonov announced his resignation, in order to seek a further term as an appointed Governor. Artamonov was duly nominated to serve a further term of office, which was confirmed by vote of the regional legislature on 26 July.

ECONOMY

In 2004 gross regional product in Kaluga Oblast totalled 64,787.9m. roubles, equivalent to 63,197.5 roubles per head. Apart from Kaluga, the region's main industrial centres are at Lyudinovo, Kirov and Maloyaroslavets. At the end of 2005 there were 872 km of railway track in the Oblast, and 3,648 km of paved roads.

Certain areas of the Oblast contain fertile black earth (*chernozem*). Agriculture employed 8.8% of the work-force and generated 12,129m. roubles in 2005. The Oblast's main industries are mechanical engineering, food-processing and timber and timber-processing. The industrial sector employed 31.2% of the working population in 2005 and generated 54,086m. roubles in 2004. In November 2007 the German automobile manufacturer Volkswagen opened a plant in Kaluga Oblast, to assemble automobiles of the VW Polo and Škoda brands. Some 66,000 vehicles were expected to be assembled at the plant during 2008.

The territory's economically active population totalled 547,000 in 2004, when 5.7% of the labour force were unemployed. The average monthly wage in Kaluga Oblast was 7,066.4 roubles in 2005. There was a budgetary deficit of 348.4m. roubles. In that year external trade comprised US \$168.4m. of exports and \$435.5m. of imports. Total foreign investment amounted to \$25.3m. in 2005. At the end of that year there were 5,862 small businesses registered in the region, providing employment to 59,700 people.

DIRECTORY

Head of the Regional Administration (Governor): ANATOLII D. ARTAMONOV (elected 12 November 2000, re-elected 14 March 2004, appointment confirmed 26 July 2005), 248600 Kaluga, pl. Staryi Torg 2; tel. (484) 256-23-57; fax (484) 253-13-09; e-mail admgub@adm .kaluga.ru; internet www.artamonovad.ru.

Chairman of the Legislative Assembly: PAVEL F. KAMENSKII, 248600 Kaluga, pl. Staryi Torg 2; tel. (484) 256-21-89; fax (484) 259-15-63; internet www.admoblkaluga.ru/New_SERVER/VLAST/ Zaksobr/default.htm.

Chief Representative of Kaluga Oblast in the Russian Federation: VLADIMIR V. POTEMKIN, 119002 Moscow, per. Glazovskii 8; tel. and fax (495) 241-66-36; e-mail kaluga@orc.ru.

Head of Kaluga City Administration: NIKOLAI LYUBIMOV, 248600 Kaluga, ul. Lenina 93; tel. (484) 256-26-46; fax (484) 224-41-78; e-mail pressa@kaluga-gov.ru; internet www.kaluga-gov.ru.

Kostroma Oblast

Kostroma Oblast is situated in the central part of the Eastern European Plain. It forms part of the Central Federal Okrug and the Central Economic Area. It is bordered by Vologda Oblast to the north, Kirov Oblast to the east, Nizhnii Novgorod and Ivanovo Oblasts to the south and Yaroslavl Oblast to the west. Its main rivers include the Volga, the Kostroma, the Unzha and the Vetluga. The total area of Kostroma Oblast is 60,100 sq km (23,200 sq miles), almost three-quarters of which is forested. At January 2007, according to official estimates, the region had a population of 702,209 and a population density of 11.7 per sq km. At the time of the 2002 census 95.6% of the population were ethnic Russians and 1.1% were Ukrainians. Some 68.3% of the population inhabited urban areas in 2007. The Oblast's administrative centre is Kostroma, a river-port situated on both banks of the Volga, which is a popular tourist resort of the 'Golden Ring' and had 274,500 inhabitants, according to official estimates in January 2006. Kostroma Oblast is included in the time zone GMT+3.

HISTORY

The city of Kostroma was founded in the 12th century and became the base of the Gudunov family, as well as, later, an important centre for the Romanovs (Mikhail Romanov was proclaimed tsar in the Ipatiyevskii Monastery here in 1613). The city became an industrial centre from the mid-18th century. Kostroma Oblast was formed on 13 August 1944. The region remained loyal to the communist *nomenklatura* in the 1990s—its oblast Soviet supported the federal parliament in its 1993 defiance of federal President Boris Yeltsin, and was replaced by a new representative body, the Duma, in 1994. The Communist Party of the Russian Federation (CPRF) was the predominant party in this body, and the CPRF candidate, Viktor Shershunov, was elected Governor in December 1996. Shershunov was re-elected to serve a further term of office in December 2000. In April 2005 federal President Vladimir Putin nominated Shershunov to serve a further term of office; this nomination was duly confirmed by vote of the regional Duma on 11 May. At elections to the regional Duma, held on 4 December 2005, the pro-presidential United Russia (UR) was the most successful grouping, obtaining 30.0% of all votes cast. The CPRF was placed second, with 17.5%, followed by the Agrarian Party of Russia (11.7%), Motherland (9.1%) and the nationalist Liberal Democratic Party of Russia (8.6%). Some 10.2% of all votes were cast 'against all candidates'. In September 2007 Shershunov was killed in an automobile collision. On 25 October the

regional Duma voted to confirm the appointment of Igor Slyunyayev of UR as Governor.

ECONOMY

In 2004 gross regional product in Kostroma Oblast amounted to 38,278.2m. roubles, or 53,048.0 roubles per head. The Oblast's main industrial centres are at Kostroma, Sharya, Galich and Manturovo. At the end of 2005 there were 640 km of railways in the Oblast and 3,743 km of paved roads. There were 985 km of navigable waterways in 1998.

Agriculture in Kostroma Oblast, which employed 10.8% of the work-force and generated 9,888m. roubles in 2005, consists mainly of the production of grain, flax (the region is one of Russia's major producers of linen) and vegetables, and animal husbandry. Electricity generation contributed 33.3% of total industrial production in 2004; around four-fifths of electrical energy produced in the region is exported. The other main industries in the region are light manufacturing, mechanical engineering, food- and timber-processing and handicrafts (especially jewellery). Some 26.8% of the Oblast's working population was engaged in industry in 2005, while the sector generated 29,211m. roubles in 2004.

The economically active population numbered 367,000 in 2005, when 4.8% of the labour force of the region were unemployed. The average wage in the Oblast was 5,974.6 roubles per month. There was a budgetary deficit of 689.0m. roubles. External trade comprised US \$196.0m. of exports and \$143.3m. of imports. Foreign investment totalled \$214.8m. in that year. At the end of 2005 there were 3,007 small businesses registered in the Oblast, providing employment to 21,600 people.

DIRECTORY

Head of the Regional Administration (Governor): IGOR SLYU-NYAYEV (appointment confirmed 25 October 2007), 156000 Kostroma, ul. Dzerzhinskogo 15; tel. (494) 231-34-72; fax (494) 231-33-95; internet kos-obl.kmtn.ru.

Chairman of the Regional Duma: ANDREI I. BYCHKOV, 156000 Kostroma, Sovetskaya pl. 2; tel. (494) 231-62-52; fax (494) 231-21-73; e-mail info@kosoblduma.ru; internet www.kosoblduma.ru.

Chief Representative of Kostroma Oblast in the Russian Federation: VASILII M. DUMA, 119019 Moscow, ul. Novyi Arbat 19/1811; tel. (495) 203-57-14; fax (495) 203-41-69.

Head of Kostroma City Administration: IRINA V. PEREVERZEVA, 156000 Kostroma, pl. Sovetskaya 1; tel. (494) 231-44-40; fax (494) 231-39-32.

Kursk Oblast

Kursk Oblast is situated within the Central Russian Highlands. It forms part of the Central Federal Okrug and the Central Chernozem Economic Area. An international boundary with Ukraine lies to the south-west, and there are borders with the Oblasts of Bryansk in the north-west, Orel and Lipetsk in the north, Voronezh in the east and Belgorod in the south. Its main river is the Seim. The Oblast occupies 29,800 sq km (11,500 sq miles). At January 2007, according to official estimates, the Oblast had a total population of 1,170,730, giving a population density of 39.3 per sq km. At the time of the 2002 census 95.9% of the population were ethnic Russians and 1.7% were Ukrainians. Some 63.1% of the population inhabited urban areas in January 2007. The Oblast's administrative centre is at Kursk, with 405,500 inhabitants in January 2006, according to official estimates. Kursk Oblast is included in the time zone GMT+3.

HISTORY

The city of Kursk was founded in 1032, destroyed by the Tatars in 1240 and fortified as a Muscovite outpost in the 16th century. The region was the scene of an army mutiny in 1905 and, in 1943, of a decisive battle against German forces. Kursk Oblast was formed on 13 July 1934.

The Communist Party of the Russian Federation (CPRF) dominated the regional Duma at elections in 1994, 1996 and 2001. The former federal Vice-President, Aleksandr Rutskoi, a noted opponent of liberal reforms, was elected Governor in October 1996. However, he was prevented from contesting the gubernatorial election of late 2000 owing to a legal technicality, and the CPRF candidate, Aleksandr Mikhailov, was elected as Governor, defeating the candidate most supportive of the federal Government, Viktor Surzhikov, a former Federal Security Service (FSB) general. (During the campaign Mikhailov had attracted some notoriety, after he made a series of anti-Semitic remarks.) In early 2005 Mikhailov resigned from the CPRF and announced his affiliation to the pro-presidential United

Russia (UR). Shortly afterwards, federal President Vladimir Putin nominated Mikhailov to serve a further term of office as Governor; this nomination was confirmed by vote of the regional Duma on 22 February. In June, following a substantial increase (of some 500%–600%) in prices charged for communal services in the Oblast, demonstrations, attended by several hundred people, demanding the resignation of Mikhailov were held in Kursk. In August the regional authorities imposed severe restrictions on public gatherings. At elections to the regional Duma, held on 12 March 2006, UR was the most successful grouping, receiving 37.4% of the votes cast. The CPRF was placed second, with 11.3%, while the Russian Party of Life (7.3%) was the only other party to obtain representation on the basis of party lists. Some 10.0% of all votes were 'against all candidates' overall, but the figure was in excess of 30% in the constituency in which Rutskoi's candidacy had been rejected by a court shortly before polling day.

ECONOMY

Kursk Oblast's gross regional product was 83,059.0m. roubles in 2004, equivalent to 68,826.2 roubles per head. Its main industrial centres are at Kursk and Zheleznogorsk. At the end of 2005 there were 1,061 km of railway lines and 6,206 km of paved roads on the Oblast's territory.

The region's agriculture, which employed 21.3% of the working population and generated 25,154m. roubles in 2005, consists mainly of sugar beet and grain production, horticulture and animal husbandry. The territory contains a major iron ore basin, the Kursk Magnetic Anomaly. Kursk Oblast's main industries are the production of electricity, production and enrichment of iron ores, mechanical engineering, chemicals and petrochemicals, ferrous metallurgy and food-processing. Some 23.3% of the work-force were engaged in industry in 2005; the sector generated 68,503m. roubles in 2004.

The economically active population in Kursk Oblast numbered 609,000 in 2005, when 7.1% of the labour force were unemployed. The average monthly wage in the region was 5,475.9 roubles in that year. There was a budgetary surplus of 418.7m. roubles. In 2005 external trade comprised US $344.0m. in imports and $256.1m in exports. Foreign investment in 2005 amounted to $4.9m. At the end of that year 4,288 small businesses were registered in the Oblast, providing employment to 35,700 people.

DIRECTORY

Head of the Regional Administration (Governor): ALEKSANDR N. MIKHAILOV (elected 5 November 2000, appointment confirmed 22 February 2005), 305002 Kursk, Krasnaya pl., Dom Sovetov; tel. (471) 222-62-62; fax (471) 256-65-73; e-mail glava@region.kursk.ru; internet www.rkursk.ru.

Chairman of the Regional Duma: ALEKSANDR A. KICHIGIN, 305001 Kursk, ul. S. Perovskoi 24; tel. (471) 254-86-54; fax (471) 254-86-50; e-mail oblduma@kursknet.ru; internet oblduma.kursknet.ru.

Chief Representative of Kursk Oblast in the Russian Federation: SERGEI M. KLUSHIN, 119019 Moscow, ul. Novyi Arbat 19/1506; tel. (495) 203-74-87; fax (495) 202-53-14.

Head of Kursk City Administration: VIKTOR P. SURZHIKOV, 305040 Kursk, ul. 50 let Oktyabrya 149; tel. (471) 255-47-01; fax (471) 222-43-16; e-mail gorod@kurskadmin.ru; internet www .kurskadmin.ru.

Lipetsk Oblast

Lipetsk Oblast is situated within the Central Russian Highlands, some 508 km (315 m) south-east of Moscow. It forms part of the Central Federal Okrug and the Central Chernozem Economic Area. It is bordered by Voronezh and Kursk to the south, Orel to the west, Tula to the north-west, Ryazan to the north and Tambov to the east. Its main rivers are the Don and the Voronezh. The Oblast occupies 24,100 sq km (9,300 sq miles). At January 2007, according to official estimates, the Oblast had a total population of 1,173,870, and a population density of 48.7 per sq km. At the 2002 census 95.8% of the population were ethnic Russians and 1.1% were Ukrainians. Some 63.8% of the Oblast's population inhabited urban areas at January 2007. Its administrative centre is at Lipetsk, with a population of 502,800 in January 2006, according to official estimates. The Oblast's second largest city is Yelets (with a population of 113,400). Lipetsk Oblast is included in the time zone GMT+3.

HISTORY

Lipetsk city was founded in the 13th century. In the late tsarist and Soviet periods the region became industrialized. Lipetsk Oblast was formed on 6 January 1954. In April 1993, when Lipetsk was permitted to hold a gubernatorial election, a left-wing candidate, Mikhail Narolin, was elected. In September 1993 both the oblast Soviet (Council) and Narolin denounced the Russian President's dissolution of the federal parliament. In April 1998 the Chairman of the regional legislature, Oleg Korolev, who was supported, primarily, by the Communist Party of the Russian Federation (CPRF), but also by the local branch of the liberal party Yabloko, was elected as Governor, with some 79.5% of the votes cast, conclusively defeating Narolin. Korolev, who was now the candidate supported by the federal Government, was re-elected on 14 April 2002, with 73% of the votes cast, after his principal rival withdrew his candidacy. On 28 May 2005 the regional legislature approved federal President Vladimir Putin's nomination of Korolev to serve a further term of office. At regional legislative elections, held on 8 October 2006, the pro-presidential United Russia obtained an absolute majority of votes (50.7%) cast, followed by the Russian Party of Life (with 11.7%), the Russian Pensioners' Party (11.2%) and the CPRF (10.7%); 4.9% of votes were cast 'against all candidates'.

ECONOMY

In 2004 Lipetsk Oblast's gross regional product totalled 143,456.7m. roubles, or 120,006.4 roubles per head. Its main industrial centres are at Lipetsk, Yelets, Dankov and Gryazi. At the end of 2005 there were 757 km of railway lines and 5,276 km of paved roads on the Oblast's territory.

The region's agriculture consists mainly of animal husbandry and the production of grain, sugar beet and sunflower seeds. In 2005 agriculture employed 13.0% of the work-force and generated 21,386m. roubles. The industrial sector employed 28.2% of the region's working population in 2005 and generated 185,748m. roubles in 2004. The Oblast's main industries are ferrous metallurgy (which comprised 70.6% of the region's total industrial output in 2004), mechanical engineering, metal-working and food-processing. Novolipetsk MetKom (New Lipetsk Metallurgical Group), based in the region, is one of the country's major industrial companies. The production of refrigerators increased markedly in Lipetsk Oblast during the first half of the 2000s, and by 2005 it was the leading producer of this product in the Federation. In November 2005 the federal authorities announced that one of six proposed special economic zones was to be located in the Oblast; a joint Italian-Russian project to manufacture household appliances was to be established in the zone, near Gryazi.

The economically active population totalled 585,000 in 2005, when 8.0% of the labour force were unemployed. Those in employment earned, on average, 6,929.4 roubles per month. In 2005 the regional budget recorded a deficit of some 2,597.5m. roubles. In that year exports amounted to US $2,795.1m. and imports were worth $535.8m. Foreign investment amounted to some $442.1m. in 2005. At the end of 2005 there were 5,314 small businesses registered in the Oblast, providing employment to 40,000 people.

DIRECTORY

Head of the Regional Administration (Governor): OLEG P. KOROLEV (elected 12 April 1998, re-elected 14 April 2002, appointment confirmed 28 May 2005), 398014 Lipetsk, Sobornaya pl. 1; tel. (474) 277-65-96; fax (474) 272-24-26; e-mail office@admlr.lipetsk.ru; internet www.admlr.lipetsk.ru.

Chairman of the Regional Council of Deputies: PAVEL I. PUTILIN, 398014 Lipetsk, Sobornaya pl. 1; tel. (474) 274-38-63; fax (474) 272-24-15; e-mail info@oblsovet.ru; internet www.oblsovet.ru.

Chief Representative of Lipetsk Oblast in the Russian Federation: PAVEL A. GUCHEK, 111024 Moscow, ul. Aviyamotornaya 49/1; tel. and fax (495) 918-03-90.

Head of Lipetsk City Administration (Mayor): MIKHAIL V. GULEVSKII, 398001 Lipetsk, ul. Sovetskaya 5; tel. (474) 277-65-24; fax (474) 274-44-30; internet www.lipetskcity.ru.

Moscow Oblast

Moscow Oblast is situated in the centre of the Eastern European Plain, forming part of the Central Federal Okrug and the Central Economic Area. Moscow is surrounded by seven other oblasts: Tver and Yaroslavl to the north, Vladimir and Ryazan to the east, Tula and Kaluga to the south-west and Smolensk to the west. Moscow City is enclosed by the Oblast. The main rivers are the Moskva and the Oka. The Oblast covers 46,000 sq km (17,761 sq miles). At January 2007, according to official estimates, the Oblast had a population of 6,645,672 and a population density of 144.5 per sq km. At the time of the 2002 census 91.0% of the population were ethnic Russians, 2.2% were Ukrainians and 0.8% were Tatars. Some 80.8% of the population inhabited urban areas in January 2007. The Oblast's administrative centre is Moscow. There are several cities with a population of over 125,000, including Balashikha (182,800 at January 2006, according to official estimates), Khimki (180,100), Podolsk (179,500), Korolev (172,800), Mytishchi (161,800), Lyubertsy (158,700), Kolomna (148,000), Elektrostal (146,200), Odintsovo (131,800) and Serpukhov (125,000). The populations of several of these cities (notably Balashikha and Khimki) expanded substantially during the 1990s and first half of the 2000s. Moscow Oblast is included in the time zone GMT+3.

HISTORY

The city of Moscow was established in the mid-12th century and became the centre of a burgeoning Muscovite state. The region, an important trade route between the Baltic and Black or Caspian Seas, became industrialized in the early 18th century, with the development of the textiles industry. The region and the city of Moscow were captured by the troops of Emperor Napoleon I of France in 1812, but the invaders were forced to retreat later that year. German invaders reached Moscow Oblast (which had been formed on 14 January 1929) in 1941, although by early 1942 the German forces had been driven from the region. Otherwise, the region has benefited from Moscow being the Soviet, and the Russian, capital since 1918.

Col-Gen. Boris Gromov, a former member of the State Duma and a Deputy Minister of Defence, was elected as Governor in January 2000. He was re-elected to the position on 7 December 2003, with 85.5% of the valid votes cast; the rate of participation by the electorate was 51.9%. At elections to the regional Duma, which took place on 11 March 2007, the pro-presidential United Russia attracted 49.5% of votes cast, the Communist Party of the Russian Federation obtained 18.6%, and A Just Russia 8.9%; four other parties contesting the poll narrowly failed to achieve the 7% minimum required for representation. Voter turn-out was only 29.8% of the electorate.

ECONOMY

In 2004 Moscow Oblast's gross regional product amounted to 548,642.3m. roubles, or 82,803.2 roubles per head. The main industrial centres are at Podolsk, Lyubertsy, Kolomna, Mytishchi, Odintsovo, Noginsk, Serpukhov, Orekhovo-Zuyevo and Shchelkovo. At the end of 2005 there were 2,699 km of railways and 16,810 km of paved roads in Moscow Oblast and Moscow City. In mid-2003 the regional Government announced proposals for the construction of the first toll motorway in Russia.

Moscow Oblast's agriculture, which employed 4.4% of the region's work-force and generated 47,551m. roubles in 2005, consists mainly of the production of vegetables and animal husbandry. The Oblast's industry, in which some 23.7% of the working population were engaged in 2005, mainly comprises heavy industry. The region's major industries are mechanical engineering, radio electronics, chemicals, light manufacturing, textiles, ferrous and non-ferrous metallurgy, metal-working, the manufacture of building materials, wood-working and handicrafts. The region's military-industrial complex is also important. Industrial output was worth 420,558m. roubles in 2004, one of the highest levels recorded in any federal subject. In November 2005 the federal authorities announced that one of six proposed special economic zones to be established was to be located in the Oblast, at Dubna. This zone was intended to specialize in the development of nuclear technology.

The economically active population of the Oblast was 3,581,000 in 2005, when 3.3% of the labour force were unemployed. The average monthly wage was 9,557.7 roubles. In the same year there was a budgetary deficit of 1,804.5m. roubles. In 2005 external trade comprised US $2,091.2m. in exports and $6,513.7m. in imports, while total foreign investment in Moscow Oblast amounted to $2,737.4m. At the end of 2005 there were 41,593 small businesses registered in the Oblast, providing employment to some 408,000 people.

DIRECTORY

Governor: BORIS V. GROMOV (elected 9 January 2000, re-elected 7 December 2003), 103070 Moscow, pl. Staraya 6; tel. (495) 623-24-13; fax (495) 628-98-12; e-mail amo@mosreg.ru; internet www.mosreg.ru.

Chairman of the Regional Duma: VIKTOR A. AKSKAKOV, 103070 Moscow, pl. Staraya 6; tel. (495) 924-81-53; fax (495) 925-17-46; internet www.mosoblduma.ru.

Chief Representative of Moscow Oblast in the Russian Federation: NIKOLAI P. CHURKIN, 103070 Moscow, pl. Staraya 6; tel. (495) 206-66-13.

Orel Oblast

Orel Oblast is situated in the central part of the Eastern European Plain, in the Central Russian Highlands. The Oblast forms part of the Central Federal Okrug and the Central Economic Area. It is surrounded by five other oblasts: Kursk (to the south), Bryansk (west), Kaluga (north-west), Tula (north-east) and Lipetsk (east). The Oblast's major river is the Oka. Orel Oblast covers some 24,700 sq km (9,530 sq miles). At January 2007, according to official estimates, the total population of the Oblast was 826,588 and the population density was 33.5 per sq km. At the time of the 2002 census 95.3% of the population were ethnic Russians and 1.3% were Ukrainians. Some 64.2% of the inhabitants of the region lived in urban areas in January 2007. The Oblast's administrative centre is at Orel, which had 326,000 inhabitants in January 2006, according to official estimates. Orel Oblast is included in the time zone GMT+3.

HISTORY

Orel was founded as a fortress in 1566. In the 1860s it served as a place of exile for Polish insurgents and was later a detention centre for prisoners on their way to exile in Siberia. Orel Oblast was formed on 27 September 1937. The region was permitted gubernatorial elections in April 1993, which were won by Yegor Stroyev (who was, additionally, the speaker of the Federation Council, the upper house of the federal parliament, in 1996–2001). A 50-seat regional Duma, elected in March 1994, was dominated by the Communist Party of the Russian Federation (CPRF). The CPRF candidate, Gennadii Zyuganov, who originated from the Oblast, obtained the greatest regional show of support in the presidential election of 1996. Stroyev was re-elected Governor, with more than 97% of the votes cast, in October 1997, and was elected to a further term of office, with 91.5% of the votes, in October 2001. In March 2003 Stroyev was elected to the Supreme Council of the pro-presidential United Russia (UR). On 23 April 2005 federal President Vladimir Putin's nomination of Stroyev to serve a further term of office was confirmed by the regional legislature.

In early 2007, prior to regional legislative elections, Stroyev demanded that CPRF candidates be disqualified in accordance with federal legislation, accusing party leaders of supporting a member who had allegedly attempted to incite extremist sentiments. At the elections to the regional Duma on 11 March, UR won 39.0% of votes cast, the CPRF 23.8% (the party's highest share in all contested regions), A Just Russia 12.6% and the nationalist Liberal Democratic Party of Russia 7.3%.

ECONOMY

Orel Oblast's gross regional product amounted to 51,588.4m. roubles in 2004, equivalent to 60,965.9 roubles per head. The principal industrial centres in the region are at Orel, Livny and Mtsensk. Orel lies on the Moscow–Simferopol (Crimea, Ukraine) highway and is an important railway junction. At the end of 2005 there were 596 km of railway track in the Oblast and 4,268 km of paved roads.

Orel Oblast is an important agricultural trade centre. In 2005 around 17.3% of the economically active population were engaged in agriculture. Agricultural production, which amounted to 16,588m. roubles in 2005, consists mainly of the cultivation of grain and sugar beet. There are some 17.5m. cu m of timber reserves in the Oblast and a major source of iron ore, at Novoyaltinskoye. However, this and reserves of other minerals in the region have generally not been exploited to their full potential. The industrial sector employed around 26.6% of the economically active population in 2005 and generated 26,806m. roubles in 2004. The Oblast's main industries are mechanical engineering, metal-working, the production of building materials and food-processing.

The region's economically active population numbered 425,000 in 2005, when 6.1% of the labour force were unemployed. Those in employment earned an average of 5,430.6 roubles per month. There was a budgetary deficit of 95.5m. roubles. In that year external trade amounted to a value of US $181.8m. in exports and $242.8m. in imports. Total foreign investment in Orel Oblast amounted to $19.7m. in 2005. At the end of that year 3,404 small businesses were registered in the Oblast, providing employment to 23,900 people.

DIRECTORY

Head of the Regional Administration (Governor): YEGOR S. STROYEV (elected 11 April 1993, re-elected 26 October 1997 and 29 October 2001, appointment confirmed 23 April 2005), 302021 Orel, pl. Lenina 1; tel. (486) 241-63-13; fax (486) 241-25-30; e-mail post@adm.orel.ru; internet www.adm.orel.ru.

Chairman of the Regional Council of People's Deputies: NIKOLAI A. VOLODIN, 302021 Orel, pl. Lenina 1; tel. (486) 241-58-53; fax (486) 241-60-22; e-mail ito@sovet.orn.ru.

Chief Representative of Orel Oblast in the Russian Federation: MARINA G. ROGACHEVA, 109240 Moscow, ul. Goncharnaya 12/3; tel. (495) 915-85-51; fax (495) 915-86-14.

Head of Orel City Administration (Mayor): ALEKSANDR A. KASYANOV, 302000 Orel, Proletarskaya gora 1; tel. (486) 243-33-12; fax (486) 243-37-35.

Ryazan Oblast

Ryazan Oblast is situated in the central part of the Eastern European Plain and forms part of the Central Federal Okrug and the Central Economic Area. The region neighbours the Oblasts of Moscow (to the north-west), Vladimir (north), Nizhnii Novgorod (north-east), Penza (south-east), Tambov and Lipetsk (south) and Tula (west). The Republic of Mordoviya lies to the east. The Oblast occupies 39,600 sq km (15,290 sq miles). At January 2007, according to official estimates, the population of Ryazan Oblast totalled 1,172,325, giving a population density of 29.6 per sq km. At the time of the 2002 census 94.6% of the population were ethnic Russians and 1.0% were Ukrainians. Some 70.0% of the population inhabited urban areas in January 2007. The Oblast's principal city is Ryazan, with a population of 513,300 in January 2006, according to official estimates. Ryazan Oblast is included in the time zone GMT+3.

HISTORY

Ryazan city was an early Orthodox Christian bishopric. The Oblast was formed on 26 September 1937. In the mid-1990s the Communist Party of the Russian Federation (CPRF) dominated the regional Duma. In October 1996 the incumbent Governor (appointed in January 1994), Gennadii Merkulov, was removed by the federal Government. Gubernatorial elections held in December were won by Vyacheslav Lyubimov, the candidate of the People's Patriotic Union of Russia (led by Gennadii Zyuganov, also the leader of the CPRF). Lyubimov was re-elected as Governor in December 2000. At gubernatorial elections held in March 2004, Lyubimov failed to qualify for the second round of voting. Instead, the former Commander-General of the Air Force (who had recently been elected to the State Duma as a member of the nationalist Motherland electoral bloc), Georgii Shpak, was elected Governor on 29 March, receiving 53.7% of the votes cast. In March 2005, prior to the holding of elections to the regional Duma, Shpak announced that he had left Motherland and joined the pro-presidential United Russia (UR) party. At these elections UR emerged as the most successful group, with about 22.2% of the votes cast. The CPRF was placed second, with 15.2%, followed by Motherland, with 13.0%. (The relatively poor performance of UR was, in part, attributable to a schism in the regional organization of the party in late 2004.) With Shpak's mandate due to expire, the presidential nomination of Oleg Kovalev, a UR deputy of the State Duma with no previous connections to the Oblast, to the office was approved unanimously by the regional legislature on 14 March 2008.

ECONOMY

In 2004 Ryazan Oblast's gross regional product amounted to 79,927.7m. roubles, or 66,525.4 roubles per head. The Oblast's industrial centres are at Ryazan, Skopin and Kasimov. At the end of 2005 there were 978 km of railways and 6,937 km of paved roads in the region.

The Oblast's warm, moist climate is conducive to agriculture, which consists mainly of production of grain, vegetables, fruit, potatoes and sugar beet, and animal husbandry, and employed 11.4% of the work-force in 2005. Total agricultural production amounted to a value of 16,483m. roubles in that year. There are substantial reserves of timber, brown coal and peat in the region. The Oblast's main industries are mechanical engineering, metal-working, the generation of electrical energy, petroleum processing, the production of building materials, light manufacturing and food-processing. In 2005 some 27.8% of the working population were engaged in industry, which generated a total of 57,257m. roubles in 2004.

The economically active population numbered 607,000 in 2005, when 5.3% of the labour force were unemployed. In that year those in employment earned, on average, 6,149.7 roubles per month. The regional budget recorded a deficit of 644.9m. roubles in 2005, when foreign investment in the region totalled US $7.5m. In 2005 external trade amounted to a value of $172.2m. in exports and $192.2m. in imports. At the end of that year 5,379 small businesses were registered in the Oblast, providing employment for 59,000 people.

Head of the Regional Administration (Governor): OLEG I. KOVALEV (appointment confirmed 14 March 2008, assumed office 12 April), 390000 Ryazan, ul. Lenina 30; tel. (491) 27-21-25; fax (491) 44-25-68; e-mail korn@adm1.ryazan.su; internet www.ryazanreg.ru.

Chairman of the Regional Duma: VLADIMIR K. SIDOROV, 390000 Ryazan, ul. Pochtovaya 50/57; tel. (491) 225-58-48; fax (491) 221-64-22; e-mail post@duma.ryazan.ru; internet www.duma.ryazan.net.

Chief Representative of Ryazan Oblast in the Russian Federation: ILEKSEI KHON, 119019 Moscow, ul. Novyi Arbat 19/2213; tel. (495) 203-61-78; fax (495) 203-61-85.

Head of Ryazan City Administration (Mayor): FEDOR I. PROVOTOROV, 390000 Ryazan, ul. Radishcheva 28; tel. (491) 221-73-74; fax (491) 224-05-70; e-mail glava@cityadmin.ryazan.ru; internet www.admrzn.ru.

Smolensk Oblast

Smolensk Oblast is situated in the central part of the Eastern European Plain on the upper reaches of the Dnepr (Dnieper). It forms part of the Central Federal Okrug and the Central Economic Area. An international boundary with Belarus lies to the south-west, while the Oblasts of Pskov and Tver lie to the north, Moscow to the north-east and Kaluga and Bryansk to the south-east. The Oblast covers 49,800 sq km (19,220 sq miles). At January 2007, according to official estimates, the population numbered 993,514, giving a population density of 20.0 per sq km. At the time of the 2002 census 93.4% of the population were ethnically Russian, 1.7% were Ukrainian and 1.5% were Belarusian. Some 71.4% of the region's inhabitants lived in urban areas in January 2007. The Oblast's administrative centre is at Smolensk, a river-port on the Dnepr, with 317,900 inhabitants in January 2006, according to official estimates. Smolensk Oblast is included in the time zone GMT+3.

HISTORY

Smolensk city was first documented in 863, as the chief settlement of the Krivichi, a Slavic tribe. It became an Orthodox Christian bishopric in 1128. It achieved prosperity during the 14th and 15th centuries as it was situated on one of the Hanseatic trade routes. Smolensk was the site of a major battle in 1812 between the Russian imperial army and the forces of Emperor Napoleon I of France. Smolensk Oblast was formed on 27 September 1937.

In the gubernatorial election of 1998, the CPRF candidate and Mayor of Smolensk, Aleksandr Prokhorov, defeated the incumbent, Anatolii Glushenkov. Support for the CPRF declined significantly in the regional legislative elections held in May 2002. In the same month Viktor Maslov, a general in the Federal Security Service, was elected as the new Governor, receiving 41.6% of the votes cast, narrowly defeating Prokhorov. Maslov's campaign had concentrated on concern about organized crime, which was subsequently heightened following the assassination of Vladimir Prokhorov, the First Deputy Governor, in early August. In June 2005 federal President Vladimir Putin nominated Maslov to serve a further term of office; this nomination was unanimously approved by the regional Duma on 24 June.

At an election to the Regional Duma held on 2 December 2007, the pro-presidential United Russia (UR) won 51.3%, the CPRF 17.9%, the nationalist Liberal Democratic Party of Russia 13.7% and A Just Russia 13.6% of votes. According to preliminary results, UR received 53.9% of votes cast in the concurrent elections to the State Duma, one of its poorest results in the country. On 24 December the Regional Duma, meeting at an extraordinary session, voted unanimously to confirm the appointment of the federal nominee, Sergei Antufeyev, a former Chairman of the Regional Duma, as Governor

ECONOMY

In 2004 Smolensk Oblast's gross regional product amounted to 57,340.2m. roubles, or 55,901.9 roubles per head. Its major industrial centres are at Smolensk, Safonovo and Vyazma. At the end of 2005 there were 1,109 km of railway lines and 8,901 km of paved roads in the Oblast.

Agriculture in Smolensk Oblast, which employed 11.5% of the work-force and generated 11,935m. roubles in 2005, mainly consists of animal husbandry, bee-keeping, and the production of flax, potatoes, fruit and vegetables, grain, sugar beet and sunflower seeds. The Oblast's main industries are mechanical engineering (in particular the production of automobiles), metal-working, chemicals and petrochemicals, food-processing and electrical energy production. In 2005 some 30.3% of the work-force were engaged in industry. Total industrial production in 2004 amounted to a value of 56,818m. roubles.

The region's economically active population numbered 535,000 in 2005, when 7.8% of the labour force were unemployed. The average monthly wage in the Oblast was 6,190.6 roubles. The 2005 budget recorded a surplus of 391.5m. roubles. The value of external trade in that year amounted to US $677.3m. in exports and $282.4m. in imports, while total foreign investment in the region amounted to $29.7m. At the end of 2005 there were 3,218 small businesses registered in the Oblast, providing employment to 26,800 people.

DIRECTORY

Head of the Regional Administration (Governor): SERGEI V. ANTUFYEV (appointment confirmed 24 December 2007), 214008 Smolensk, pl. Lenina 1; tel. (481) 238-66-11; fax (481) 223-68-51; e-mail maslov@admin.smolensk.ru; internet admin.smolensk.ru.

Chairman of the Regional Duma: ANATOLII I. MISHNEV, 214008 Smolensk, pl. Lenina 1; tel. (481) 238-67-00; fax (481) 238-71-85; e-mail duma@admin.smolensk.ru; internet parlament.smolensk.ru.

Chief Representative of Smolensk Oblast in the Russian Federation: VLADIMIR V. MALITIKOV, 123610 Moscow, Krasnopresnenskaya nab. 12/3; tel. (495) 221-23-36; fax (495) 221-23-34.

Head of Smolensk City Administration: VLADISLAV N. KHALETSKII, 214000 Smolensk, ul. Oktyabrskoi Revolyutsii 1/2; tel. (481) 238-11-81; e-mail smol@admin.smolensk.ru; internet www.admcity.smolensk.ru.

Tambov Oblast

Tambov Oblast is situated in the central Oka-Don plain. It forms part of the Central Federal Okrug and the Central Chernozem Economic Area. Penza and Saratov Oblasts lie to the east, Voronezh to the south, Lipetsk to the west and Ryazan to the north. Its major river is the Tsna. It occupies 34,300 sq km (13,240 sq miles). At January 2007, according to official estimates, its population was 1,117,119, and its population density 32.6 per sq km. At the time of the 2002 census 96.5% of the population were ethnically Russian and 0.9% were Ukrainian. Around 57.7% of the population inhabited urban areas in January 2007. The administrative centre is at Tambov, which had a population of 284,500 in January 2006, according to official estimates. Tambov Oblast is included in the time zone GMT+3.

HISTORY

Tambov city was founded in 1636 as a Muscovite fort. The region was the scene of an army mutiny during the anti-tsarist uprising of 1905, and came under Bolshevik control immediately after the October Revolution in 1917. Numerous peasant revolts against the Bolsheviks were brutally suppressed in the region in the early 1920s. Tambov Oblast was formed on 27 September 1937.

Having appointed Oleg Betin as Governor in March 1995, President Boris Yeltsin permitted a gubernatorial election in December of that year. Betin lost to the Communist Party of the Russian Federation (CPRF) candidate, Aleksandr Ryabov, and was instead appointed as presidential representative to the region. Betin was elected Governor in December 1999, with the support of two centrist movements, Fatherland and Unity, and was re-elected in December 2003. In mid-2005 Betin requested that federal President Vladimir Putin demonstrate his confidence in his leadership. Putin's subsequent nomination of Betin to serve a further term of office was unanimously approved by the regional Duma on 13 July. The pro-presidential United Russia (the successor organization to both Fatherland and Unity) obtained the largest share of the votes cast (40.5%) at elections to the regional Duma on 18 December. The second-placed party was the CPRF, with 20.0%, followed by the nationalist Liberal Democratic Party of Russia (with 9.7%). Some 6.6% of votes were cast 'against all candidates'.

ECONOMY

In 2004 Tambov Oblast's gross regional product amounted to 60,163.6m. roubles, equivalent to 52,232.7 roubles per head. The region's industrial centres are at Tambov, Michurinsk and Morshansk. At the end of 2005 there were 738 km of railway lines and 5,542 km of paved roads in the region.

The Oblast's agriculture, which employed some 23.7% of the workforce in 2005, consists mainly of the production of grain, sugar beet, sunflower seeds and potatoes. Total agricultural output was worth 19,851m. roubles in that year. The principal industries in the Oblast are mechanical engineering, metal-working, chemicals and petrochemicals, the production of electrical energy, light manufacturing

and food-processing. Industry employed 19.0% of the working population in 2005 and generated 25,563m. roubles in 2004.

The economically active population stood at 555,000 in 2005, when 8.5% of the labour force were unemployed. In 2005 the average monthly wage in the Oblast was just 5,008.5 roubles, although living costs in the region were relatively low. There was a budgetary deficit of 86.8m. roubles in 2005, when external trade amounted to US $50.7m. in exports and $70.7m. in imports. Both of these figures were markedly lower than those of any other federal subject in the Central Federal Okrug. In 2005 foreign investment in the Oblast amounted to $5.9m. At the end of 2005 some 3,391 small businesses were registered in the region, providing employment to 29,300 people.

DIRECTORY

Head of the Regional Administration (Governor): OLEG I. BETIN (elected December 1999, re-elected 7 December 2003, appointment confirmed 13 July 2005), 392000 Tambov, ul. Internatsionalnaya 14; tel. (475) 272-10-61; fax (475) 272-25-18; e-mail post@tambov.ru; internet www.tambov.ru.

Chairman of the Regional Duma: VLADIMIR N. KAREV, 392017 Tambov, ul. Internatsisionalnaya 14; tel. (475) 271-23-70; fax (475) 271-07-72; e-mail regduma@duma.tambov.gov.ru; internet www.regadm.tambov.ru/duma.

Chief Representative of Tambov Oblast in the Russian Federation: VALERII I. YEVDOKIMOV, 119019 Moscow, ul. Novyi Arbat 19/2325; tel. and fax (495) 203-83-39.

Head of Tambov City Administration (Mayor): MAKSIM YU. KOSENKOV, 392000 Tambov, ul. Kommunalnaya 6; tel. (475) 272-20-30; fax (475) 272-47-71; e-mail cvc_t@rambler.ru; internet www.cityadm.tambov.ru.

Tula Oblast

Tula Oblast is situated in the central part of the Eastern European Plain in the northern section of the Central Russian Highlands. It forms part of the Central Federal Okrug and the Central Economic Area and is bordered by the Oblasts of Ryazan to the east, Lipetsk to the south-east, Orel to the south-west, Kaluga to the north-west and Moscow to the north. The Oblast covers 25,700 sq km (9,920 sq miles). At January 2007, according to official estimates, it had a population of 1,580,531 and a population density of 61.5 per sq km. At the time of the 2002 census 95.2% of the population were ethnically Russian and 1.3% were Ukrainian. Some 80.0% of the Oblast's population inhabited urban areas in January 2007. The Oblast's administrative centre is at Tula, which had a population of 509,000 in January 2006, according to official estimates. Its second largest city is Novomoskovsk, with 127,800 inhabitants. Tula Oblast is included in the time zone GMT+3.

HISTORY

The city of Tula was founded in the 12th century. It became an important economic centre in 1712, with the construction of the Imperial Small Arms Factory. Tula Oblast was founded on 26 September 1937.

The Communist Party of the Russian Federation (CPRF) remained the most widely supported party in the Oblast throughout the 1990s. The Oblast had a prominent CPRF Governor, following the election of Vasilii Starodubtsev (who had been a participant in the attempted coup organized against the Soviet leader, Mikhail Gorbachev, in Moscow in August 1991) in March 1997. Starodubtsev was elected to a second term of office in April 2001; his opponent had refused to campaign in the second round of voting, following the withdrawal of the second-placed candidate in the first round, who had expressed dissatisfaction with the conduct of the electoral commission.

Some controversy was aroused by the decision that the votes of some 100,000 overseas Russian citizens resident in Israel would be assigned to Tula Oblast (where they comprised nearly one-quarter of registered voters) at the elections to the federal State Duma held in December 2003. In contrast to previous elections in the Oblast, the CPRF was overwhelmingly defeated by the pro-presidential United Russia.

On 30 March 2005 the regional Duma voted in favour of federal President Vladimir Putin's nomination of Vyacheslav Dudka, hitherto chief engineer at a state company, as Governor. Starodubtsev thereby became the second Governor to be removed from office as a result of the new system of gubernatorial appointments. In July 2007 a dispute in which one person was killed precipitated protests, led by members of an extremist nationalist organization, the Movement Against Illegal Immigration, against the ethnic Armenian community in the north-east of the Oblast.

ECONOMY

In 2004 Tula Oblast's gross regional product amounted to 88,000.4m. roubles, or 53,877.1 roubles per head. Its important industrial centres are at Tula, Novomoskovsk and Shchekino. At the end of 2005 there were 972 km of railway lines and 5,137 km of paved roads in the Oblast.

Around 73.7% of the Oblast's territory is used for agricultural purposes. Agriculture, which engaged 7.8% of the work-force and generated 18,329m. roubles in 2005, consists primarily of the production of grain, potatoes, fruit and vegetables, and sugar beet, as well as animal husbandry. The Oblast's main industries are mechanical engineering, metal-working, chemicals and petrochemicals, ferrous metallurgy, food-processing, the production of brown coal (lignite) and the generation of electricity. Industry employed 28.9% of the work-force in 2005 and generated 127,932m. roubles in 2004. Ferrous metallurgy, mechanical engineering and metal-working dominated exports in the region.

The economically active population in the Oblast numbered 805,000 in 2005, when 5.0% of the labour force were unemployed. The average monthly wage was 6,412.4 roubles. The 2005 budget recorded a surplus of 239.4m. roubles. In that year external trade comprised US $2,128.5m. of exports and $375.0m. of imports. Total foreign investment amounted to $235.6m. in 2005. At the end of that year 6,995 small businesses were registered in the Oblast, providing employment to 59,100 people.

DIRECTORY

Head of the Regional Administration (Governor): VYACHESLAV D. DUDKA (appointment confirmed 30 March 2005), 300600 Tula, pl. Lenina 2; tel. (487) 227-84-36; fax (487) 220-63-26; e-mail admin@region.tula.ru; internet www.admportal.tula.ru.

Chairman of the Regional Duma: OLEG V. TATARINOV, 300600 Tula, pl. Lenina 2; tel. (487) 220-50-24; fax (487) 236-47-66; e-mail oblduma@duma.tula.ru.

Chief Representative of Tula Oblast in the Russian Federation: ISMAIL I. BARATOV, 127006 Moscow, Veskovskii per. 2; tel. (495) 978-14-56; fax (495) 978-06-43.

Head of Tula City Duma, Head of the City: VLADIMIR MOGILNIKOV, Tula; tel. (487) 227-80-85.

Tver Oblast

Tver Oblast is situated in the central part of the Eastern European Plain. It forms part of the Central Federal Okrug and the Central Economic Area. Moscow and Smolensk Oblasts lie to the south, Pskov to the west, Novgorod and Vologda to the north and Yaroslavl to the east. The major rivers in the region are the Volga, which rises within its territory, the Mologa and the Tvertsa. The Oblast occupies 84,100 sq km (32,460 sq miles). At January 2007, according to official estimates, the Oblast had a total of 1,390,444 inhabitants, and a population density of 16.5 per sq km. At the time of the 2002 census 92.5% of the population were ethnically Russian, 1.5% were Ukrainian and 1.0% were Kareliyan. Some 73.8% of the population inhabited urban areas in January 2007. The administrative centre is at Tver (Kalinin, 1931–90), a river-port, with a population of 405,600 in January 2006, according to official estimates. Tver Oblast is included in the time zone GMT+3.

HISTORY

Tver was founded as a fort in 1135 and its princes rivalled those of Moscow in the 14th and 15th centuries. The Oblast was formed in January 1935. A new elected body, the Legislative Assembly, which was dominated by the Communist Party of the Russian Federation (CPRF), replaced the Oblast Soviet in 1994. In December 1995 Vladimir Platov of the CPRF defeated the incumbent, Vladimir Suslov, in a gubernatorial election. Platov, by then one of the founders of the Unity electoral bloc, was re-elected in January 2000. However, Platov failed to progress to a second round of voting at gubernatorial elections held in December 2003, in which Dmitrii Zelenin of United Russia (UR—as Unity had become) was victorious. In 2005 Platov was sentenced to five years' imprisonment for abuse of office, in connection with the misappropriation of oblast funds. At elections to the regional Legislative Assembly, held on 18 December 2005, UR received 33.2% of the votes cast, followed by the CPRF, with 14.7%. Three nationalist groups obtained representation in the Assembly: Motherland, People's Will and the Liberal Democratic Party of Russia. On 10 July 2007 the Legislative Assembly endorsed federal President Vladimir Putin's nomination of Zelenin for a second term as Governor. In November demonstrations in support of Putin were staged in the Oblast, prior to elections to the State Duma on 2 December; it was reported, however, that regional government officials had ordered local schools to inform students to attend rallies. In the same month an 'All Russia Council of Initiative Groups to Support Putin' was convened in Tver.

ECONOMY

In 2004 Tver Oblast's gross regional product amounted to 87,843.8m. roubles, equivalent to 61,230.9 roubles per head. Industry is the dominant branch of the Oblast's economy. The principal industrial centres are Tver, Vyshnii Volochek and Rzhev. In 2005 there were 1,830 km of railways and 15,055 km of paved roads in the Oblast. In 2006 Governor Zelenin announced that the region was prepared to accept some 7,300 ethnically Russian migrants from other countries of the Commonwealth of Independent States as part of a federal programme to encourage immigration, and that the region would offer significant financial benefits to migrants.

Around 2.4m. ha of the Oblast's territory is used for agricultural purposes. Agriculture in Tver Oblast, which employed 11.0% of the work-force and generated 12,169m. roubles in 2005, consists mainly of the production of vegetables, potatoes and flax and animal husbandry. The region's major industries are mechanical engineering, metal-working, electricity generation, food-processing and light manufacturing. Industry employed 26.7% of the work-force in 2005 and generated 67,323m. roubles in 2004.

The region's economically active population numbered 734,000 in 2005, when 5.9% of the labour force were unemployed. The average wage amounted to 6,486.3 roubles per month. The 2005 regional budget recorded a deficit of 315.2m. roubles. In that year external trade amounted to a value of US $123.2m. in exports and $207.1m. in imports. Total foreign investment in the Oblast amounted to $1.4m. in 2005. At the end of that year around 6,869 small businesses were registered in the Oblast, providing employment to 49,200 people.

DIRECTORY

Head of the Regional Administration (Governor): DMITRII V. ZELENIN (elected 21 December 2003, appointment confirmed 10 July 2007), 170000 Tver, ul. Sovetskaya 44; tel. (482) 235-37-77; fax (482) 242-55-08; e-mail tradm@tversa.ru; internet www.region.tver.ru.

Chairman of the Legislative Assembly: ANDREI N. YEPISHIN, 170100 Tver, ul. Sovetskaya 33; tel. (482) 232-10-11; fax (482) 234-10-15; e-mail zsto@zsto.ru; internet www.zsto.ru.

Chief Representative of Tver Oblast in the Russian Federation: (vacant), 103246 Moscow, ul. B. Dmitrovka 26; tel. (495) 926-65-19; fax (495) 292-14-85.

Head of Tver City Administration (Mayor): OLEG S. LEBEDEV, 170640 Tver, ul. Sovetskaya 11; tel. (482) 233-01-31; fax (482) 242-59-39; e-mail info@www.tver.ru; internet www.tver.ru.

Vladimir Oblast

Vladimir Oblast is situated in the central part of the Eastern European Plain. It forms part of the Central Federal Okrug and the Central Economic Area. It borders the Oblasts of Ryazan and Moscow to the south-west, Yaroslavl and Ivanovo to the north and Nizhnii Novgorod to the east. The Oblast's main rivers are the Oka and its tributary, the Klyazma. Over one-half of its territory is forested. It occupies 29,000 sq km (11,200 sq miles). At January 2007, according to official estimates, the region had a total population of 1,459,574, giving a population density of 50.3 per sq km. At the time of the 2002 census 94.7% of the population were ethnically Russian and 1.1% were Ukrainian. Some 77.7% of the population inhabited urban areas in January 2007. The Oblast's administrative centre is at Vladimir, which had a population of 340,700 at that time, according to official estimates. Other major cities are Kovrov (151,600) and Murom (122,100). Vladimir Oblast is included in the time zone GMT+3.

HISTORY

Founded in 1108 as a frontier fortress by Prince Vladimir Monomakh, after the disintegration of Kyivan Rus, Vladimir city was the seat of the principality of Vladimir-Suzdal and an early Orthodox Christian bishopric. Vladimir fell under the rule of Muscovy in 1364 and declined in importance from the 15th century, being supplanted by Moscow as the seat of the Russian Orthodox patriarch, although Vladimir was chosen for the coronations of several Muscovite princes. Vladimir Oblast was formed on 14 August 1944.

The Communist Party of the Russian Federation (CPRF) secured the election of Nikolai Vinogradov, former Chairman of the regional Legislative Assembly, to the post of Governor in late 1996. A new oblast flag was adopted in April 1999 that, notably, incorporated the

Soviet symbol of a hammer and sickle. Vinogradov was re-elected Governor in December 2000, with some 66% of the votes cast, defeating Yurii Glasov, who had held the post in 1991–96. In February 2005 federal President Vladimir Putin nominated Vinogradov to serve a further term of office; on 18 February the regional Legislative Assembly overwhelmingly approved this nomination. At elections to the regional legislature, held on 20 March, the pro-presidential United Russia obtained the greatest share of the votes cast, with 20.5%, ahead of the CPRF, with 20.3%. Some 17.9% of votes were cast 'against all candidates', a greater share of the vote than was received by any other party.

ECONOMY

Vladimir Oblast's gross regional product in 2004 totalled 74,749.6m. roubles, or 49,984.3 roubles per head. The Oblast's main industrial centres are at Vladimir, Kovrov, Murom, Aleksandrov, Kolchugino and Gus-Khrustalnyi. At the end of 2005 there were 922 km of railway track and 2,872 km of paved roads on its territory.

Agriculture in the region, which employed 7.4% of the work-force and generated 14,315m. roubles in 2005, consists mainly of animal husbandry, vegetable production and horticulture. Vladimir is rich in peat deposits and timber reserves, but relies on imports for around 70% of its energy supplies. The Oblast's main industries are mechanical engineering, metal-working, food-processing, the production of electrical energy, light manufacturing, chemicals, glass-making and handicrafts. Industry employed 34.2% of the work-force in 2005 and generated 77,206m. roubles in 2004.

Vladimir Oblast's economically active population numbered 809,000 in 2005, when 9.0% of the labour force were unemployed. The average monthly wage in the Oblast was 6,066.8 roubles. In 2005 there was a regional budgetary surplus of 409.5m. roubles. In that year external trade constituted US $236.6m. in exports and $300.1m. in imports; total foreign investment amounted to $205.9m. At the end of 2005 some 7,569 small businesses were registered in the Oblast, providing employment to 64,100 people.

DIRECTORY

Head of the Regional Administration (Governor): Nikolai V. Vinogradov (elected 8 December 1996, re-elected 10 December 2000, appointment confirmed 18 February 2005), 600000 Vladimir, pr. Oktyabrskii 21; tel. (492) 233-15-52; fax (492) 225-34-45; e-mail post@avo.ru; internet avo.ru.

Chairman of the Legislative Assembly: Anatolii V. Bobrov, 600000 Vladimir, Oktyabrskaya pr. 21; tel. (492) 232-66-53; fax (492) 223-08-06; e-mail zsvo@zsvo.ru; internet www.zsvo.ru.

Chief Representative of Vladimir Oblast in the Russian Federation: (vacant), 125009 Moscow, ul. Tverskaya 20/1; tel. (495) 299-66-49.

Head of Vladimir City Administration: Aleksandr P. Rybakov, 600000 Vladimir, ul. Gorkogo 36; tel. (492) 223-28-17; fax (492) 223-85-54; e-mail mayor@vladimir-city.ru; internet www.vladimir-city.ru.

Voronezh Oblast

Voronezh Oblast is situated in the centre of the Eastern European Plain on the middle reaches of the Volga. It forms part of the Central Federal Okrug and the Central Chernozem Economic Area. There is a short border with Ukraine in the south. Belgorod and Kursk lie to the west, Lipetsk and Tambov to the north, Saratov to the north-east, Volgograd to the east and Rostov to the south-east. The west of the territory is situated within the Central Russian Highlands and the east in the Oka-Don lowlands. Its main rivers are the Don, the Khoper and the Bityug. The Oblast occupies 52,400 sq km (20,230 sq miles). At January 2007, according to official estimates, the total population was 2,294,616, and the population density 43.8 per sq km. At the time of the 2002 census 94.1% of the population were ethnically Russian and 3.1% were Ukrainian. Some 62.8% of the population lived in urban areas in January 2007. The region's administrative centre is at Voronezh, which had a population of 846,300 in January 2006, according to official estimates. Voronezh Oblast is included in the time zone GMT+3.

HISTORY

Voronezh city was founded in 1586 as a fortress. Tsar Petr (Peter) 'the Great' founded the first units of what became the imperial Russian Navy in Voronezh in 1696. The centre of a fertile region, the city began to industrialize in the tsarist period. Voronezh Oblast was formed in June 1934.

In the immediate post-Soviet years the region was largely supportive of the Communist Party of the Russian Federation (CPRF). Ivan Shabonov, a member of that party, was elected Governor in December 1996. At the gubernatorial election held in December 2000 Shabonov was defeated by Vladimir Kulakov, a general in the Federal Security Service (FSB). At the regional legislative elections, held in March 2001, the level of CPRF representation was reduced from 23 seats to five. In elections to the State Duma in December 2003 the Oblast recorded the lowest level of support for the pro-presidential United Russia (UR) of any federal subject. At a gubernatorial election, held on 14 March 2004, Kulakov was re-elected, with 52.5% of votes cast. At elections to the regional Duma, held on 20 March 2005, UR obtained the largest share of the votes cast (29.1%); the nationalist Motherland party was placed second, with 21.0%. At the end of May 2007 a demonstration staged by an informal coalition of opposition groups, Another Russia, was officially authorized by the municipal authorities in Voronezh, although, in the event, its organization was disrupted and several leaders were temporarily detained.

ECONOMY

In 2004 Voronezh Oblast's gross regional product amounted to 116,975.9m. roubles, equivalent to 49,908.8 roubles per head. The important industrial centres in the Oblast are at Voronezh, Borisoglebsk and Rossosh. In 2005 the territory contained some 1,149 km of railway track and 9,168 km of paved roads. The road network includes sections of major routes, including the Moscow–Rostov and Moscow–Astrakhan highways. There were some 640 km of navigable waterways in 1998.

Around 90% of the Oblast's territory is used for agricultural purposes. In 2005 agriculture employed 16.8% of the work-force, and generated 32,394m. roubles. The Oblast's agriculture consists mainly of the production of grain, sugar beet, sunflower seeds, potatoes and vegetables. Animal husbandry is also important. The main industries are mechanical engineering, metal-working, chemicals and petrochemicals, the production of electricity, the manufacture of building materials and food-processing. In 2005 industry employed 23.0% of the work-force in 2005 and generated 76,631m. roubles in 2004.

The Oblast's economically active population numbered 1,136,000 in 2005, when 7.5% of the labour force were unemployed. In 2005 the Oblast's average monthly wage was 6,066.8 roubles. There was a budgetary deficit of 626.8m. roubles in 2005. In that year the value of external trade amounted to US $619.9m. in exports and $385.6m. in imports, while foreign investment amounted to $53.3m. At the end of 2005 some 14,962 small businesses were registered in the region, providing employment to 124,400 people.

DIRECTORY

Head of the Regional Administration (Governor): Vladimir G. Kulakov (elected 24 December 2000, re-elected 14 March 2004), 394018 Voronezh, pl. Lenina 1; tel. (473) 253-23-96; fax (473) 253-28-02; e-mail serzh@comch.ru; internet admin.vrn.ru.

Chairman of the Regional Duma: Vladimir I. Klyuchnikov, 394018 Voronezh, ul. Kirova 2; tel. and fax (473) 252-09-22; e-mail root@vrnoblduma.ru; internet www.vrnoblduma.ru.

Chief Representative of Voronezh Oblast in the Russian Federation: Aleksandr I. Firsov, 125047 Moscow, ul. 2-aya Tverskaya-Yamskaya 26; tel. and fax (495) 250-98-55.

Head of Voronezh City Administration (Mayor): Sergei M. Koliukh, 394067 Voronezh, ul. Plekhanovskaya 10; tel. (473) 255-34-20; fax (473) 255-47-16; e-mail admin@city.vrn.ru.

Yaroslavl Oblast

Yaroslavl Oblast is situated in the central part of the Eastern European Plain. It forms part of the Central Federal Okrug and the Central Economic Area. The region borders the Oblasts of Ivanovo to the south-east, Vladimir and Moscow to the south, Tver to the west, Vologda to the north and Kostroma to the east. There is a large reservoir at Rybinsk, formed in 1941, following the completion of a dam and a hydroelectric power plant nearby. The Volga river flows through the region. The Oblast covers 36,400 sq km (14,050 sq miles). At January 2007, according to official estimates, the Oblast's population was 1,320,140, and the population density 36.3 per sq km. In 2002 some 95.2% of the population were ethnically Russian and 1.0% were Ukrainian. Some 81.6% of the population inhabited urban areas in January 2007. The Oblast's administrative centre is at Yaroslavl, which had a population of 603,700 in January 2006, according to official estimates. The second largest city in the

Oblast is Rybinsk (214,900). Yaroslavl Oblast is included in the time zone GMT+3.

HISTORY

Yaroslavl city is reputed to be the oldest town on the River Volga, having been founded c. 1024. The region was acquired by the Muscovite state during the reign of Ivan III (1462–1505) and the city briefly served as the capital when Moscow was captured by Polish and Lithuanian invaders in 1610. The Oblast was formed in March 1936. In December 1995 federal President Boris Yeltsin permitted his appointed Governor, Anatolii Lisitsyn, to contest a direct election for the post, which Lisitsyn won. He was re-elected on 19 December 1999, and, with the support of the pro-presidential United Russia (UR), was re-elected on 7 December 2003. At elections to the regional Duma, held on 14 March 2004, UR was the most successful grouping, followed by the nationalist Motherland bloc. On 2 November 2006 the regional Duma approved the nomination of Lisitsyn for a further term as Governor. Lisitsyn was elected to the federal State Duma in December 2007, following which he announced the intention of resigning as Governor. Sergei Vakhurov, a former Chairman of the regional Duma and representative of the Oblast in the upper chamber of the federal legislature, the Federation Council, was appointed as Governor, initially in an acting capacity. His appointment was confirmed by vote of the regional Duma on 25 December. UR were again the most successful party at elections to the regional Duma held on 2 March 2008, when they obtained 50.0% of the votes cast. The Communist Party of the Russian Federation were placed second, with 14.6% and the nationalist Liberal Democratic Party of Russia third, with 12.6%

ECONOMY

In 2004 Yaroslavl Oblast's gross regional product amounted to 121,290.6m. roubles, equivalent to 90,191.2 roubles per head. The major industrial centres in the region are at Yaroslavl, Rybinsk and Pereslavl-Zalesskii. There are river-ports at Yaroslavl, Rybinsk and Uglich. In 2005 there were 654 km of railways and 6,207 km of paved roads in the region. The Oblast lies on the Moscow–Archangel highway.

Agricultural activity, which employed 8.4% of the work-force and generated 11,787m. roubles in 2005, consists primarily of the production of vegetables, fruit and flax and of animal husbandry. In 2005 industry employed 33.1% of the work-force while in 2004 production generated 93,810m. roubles. The main industries are mechanical engineering (particularly the manufacture of aircraft engines), chemicals and petrochemicals, petroleum-refining, peat production, the production of electricity and food-processing.

The Oblast's economically active population numbered 709,000 in 2005, when the region had an unemployment rate of 4.0%. The average monthly wage was 7,366.2 roubles. In 2005 there was a regional budgetary deficit of 398.3m. roubles, while external trade comprised US $355.3m. in exports and $198.7m. in imports, and total foreign investment in the region amounted to $77.1m. At the end of 2005 there were 9,454 small businesses registered in the Oblast, providing employment to 58,000 people.

DIRECTORY

Governor: SERGEI A. VAKHRUKOV (appointment confirmed 25 December 2007), 150000 Yaroslavl, pl. Sovetskaya 3; tel. (485) 272-81-28; fax (485) 232-84-14; internet www.adm.yar.ru.

Chairman of the Regional Duma: VIKTOR V. ROGOTSKII, 150000 Yaroslavl, pl. Sovetskaya 5; tel. (485) 272-89-35; fax (485) 272-76-45; e-mail dumpress@region.adm.yar.ru; internet www.adm.yar.ru/duma/index.asp.

Chief Representative of Yaroslavl Oblast in the Russian Federation: OLEG N. RASSADKIN, 119034 Moscow, Mansurovskii per. 15; tel. and fax (495) 201-24-86.

Head of Yaroslavl City Administration (Mayor): VIKTOR V. VOLONCHUNAS, 150000 Yaroslavl, ul. Andropova 6; tel. (485) 230-46-41; fax (485) 230-52-79; e-mail info@city.yar.ru; internet www.city.yar.ru.

North-Western Federal Okrug

St Petersburg City

St Petersburg (Sankt-Peterburg) is a seaport at the mouth of the River Neva, which drains into the easternmost part of the Gulf of Finland (part of the Baltic Sea). St Petersburg is included in the North-Western Federal Okrug and the North-Western Economic Area. The city's territory, including a total of 42 islands in the Neva delta, occupies an area of 570 sq km (220 sq miles), making it the smallest of Russia's federal subjects), of which its waterways comprise around 10%. There are more than 580 bridges in the city and surrounding area, including 22 drawbridges. At January 2007, according to official estimates, the population of the city was 4,571,184, with a population density of 7,618.7 per sq km. At the time of the 2002 census 84.7% of the population were ethnic Russians, 1.9% Ukrainians, 1.2% Belarusians, 0.8% Jews and 0.8% were Tatars. St Petersburg is included in the time zone GMT+3.

HISTORY

St Petersburg was founded by Tsar Peter (Petr) I ('the Great') in 1703, as a 'window on the West', and became the Russian capital in 1712. In 1914 the city was renamed Petrograd. Following the fall of the Tsar and the Bolshevik Revolution, in 1918 the Russian capital was moved back to Moscow. A revolt at the naval base of Kronstadt, west of mainland Petrograd, in March 1921 presented one of the most serious challenges to the nascent Bolshevik authorities, as the island had hitherto been renowned as a stronghold of support for the Bolsheviks; the rebels, who were protesting against the steady centralization of powers, were quashed by troops led by Trotskii (Lev Bronstein), and several thousand deaths resulted on both sides. In 1924 the city was renamed Leningrad. During the Second World War it was besieged by German troops between November 1941 and January 1944. In June 1991 a supporter of economic reform, Anatolii Sobchak, was elected as Governor, and in October the city name reverted to St Petersburg. In 1994–96 the future federal President, Vladimir Putin, was First Deputy Governor of the City Government. In May 1996 another liberal, the hitherto First Deputy Mayor, Vladimir Yakovlev, was elected as Mayor, defeating Sobchak.

In the mid-1990s the reformist Yabloko bloc was the dominant political force in the city, although the party went into opposition following the December 1998 municipal legislative elections. Yakovlev was re-elected as Mayor on 14 May 2000, obtaining 72.7% of the votes cast, having secured the support of the Communist Party of the Russian Federation (CPRF) and nationalist elements.

At the municipal legislative election held in December 2002 some 38 of the 50 incumbent deputies were re-elected to the Assembly; the rate of participation in the elections was only 29.4%. Some 31 of the 50 deputies in the new Assembly held no party allegiance. Yakovlev's political position appeared to have been weakened by the formation of an opposition majority in the new legislature and, in particular, by the appointment of a close ally of Putin (who was generally regarded as an opponent of Yakovlev) and a former ambassador, Valentina Matviyenko, as Presidential Representative to the North-Western Federal Okrug in mid-March. On 16 June 2003 Putin appointed Yakovlev as a Deputy Chairman of the federal Government; he was thereby obliged to resign as Mayor. In mid-June Matviyenko announced her candidacy for the forthcoming mayoral elections, which received the public endorsement of Putin to an unprecedented extent. In addition, Matviyenko was supported by the pro-presidential United Russia (UR), the pro-market Union of Rightist Forces, Yabloko and the CPRF, and she also received the backing of Yakovlev. In a 'run-off' election, held on 5 October, Matviyenko was elected Governor, receiving 63.2% of the votes cast, defeating Anna Markova, Yakovlev's former Deputy Governor. The rate of participation in both rounds was less than 30%. The decision, formally announced in December 2006, to transfer the headquarters of the federal Constitutional Court from Moscow to St Petersburg was perceived as a significant boost to the status of the city. On 7 December Putin nominated Matviyenko for a second term as Mayor; the Legislative Assembly endorsed this proposal on 22 December.

In early March 2007, shortly before the holding of municipal legislative elections, a mass rally was organized in St Petersburg by Another Russia, an informal coalition of groups opposing President Putin; some demonstrators demanded Matviyenko's resignation from office. Members of the Legislative Assembly subsequently protested at measures taken against demonstrators by special police units. At the elections to the Legislative Assembly on 11 March, UR won 37.4% of votes cast, while A Just Russia received 21.9%, the CPRF 16.0% and the nationalist Liberal Democratic Party of Russia 10.9% of votes. According to opposition representatives, the poll was marred with irregularities. In April a further large rally held by Another Russia was violently suppressed by special police forces. In May, after four members of a local extremist group were arrested in a security operation, the Federal Security Service announced that a planned assassination attempt against Matviyenko had been thwarted; three of the suspects were subsequently charged with terrorist activities. In September it was announced that Matviyenko (while not a party member) was to head the regional UR list of candidates in forthcoming elections to the State Duma (the lower chamber of the federal legislature) on 2 December. In November special police again dispersed an unauthorized opposition rally in St Petersburg, temporarily detaining some 300 protesters. At the State Duma elections, UR won about 50.3% of the votes cast in St Petersburg (one of its poorest results in the Federation).

ECONOMY

In 2004 St Petersburg's gross regional product amounted to 518,885.3m. roubles, or 112,506.7 roubles per head.

Industry in St Petersburg, which employed around 28.3% of the work-force in 2005 (compared with the 0.5% engaged in agriculture) and which generated 370,736m. in 2004, consists mainly of mechanical engineering, metal-working and food-processing. Other important areas are ferrous and non-ferrous metallurgy, electricity generation, manufacture of chemicals and petrochemicals, rubber production, light manufacturing, the manufacture of building materials, timber-processing and printing. There is also a significant defence sector industry. In mid-2006 construction work commenced on an automobile factory in the city by General Motors of the USA. This was to comprise the first such project in Russia that was not part of a joint venture with a Russian company; the production of sports-utility vehicles (four-wheel drive cars) at the plant was expected to begin in 2008. In mid-2007 the Japanese automobile manufacturer Nissan began construction of a factory in St Petersburg, which was forecast to produce around 50,000 vehicles per year by 2009. The city is also an important centre for service industries, such as tourism, financial services and leisure activities. In November 2005 the federal authorities announced that one of six special economic zones to be established across the Federation was to be located in St Petersburg; the zone was to specialize in the development of information technologies and analytical instruments.

The economically active population of St Petersburg amounted to 2,570,000 in 2005, when 2.2% of the work-force was unemployed, the second lowest rate in Russia, after Moscow City. In 2005 the average monthly wage in St Petersburg was 10,133.9 roubles, somewhat higher than the national average. The city budget in 2005 recorded a deficit of 612.3m. roubles. The city is an important centre of trade: in 2005 external trade comprised some US $4,918.2m. in exports and $10,054.0m. in imports. In 2005 foreign investment in St Petersburg amounted to $1,417.2m., which was equivalent to only 5.6% of the sum of foreign investment in Moscow City in that year. At the end of 2005 there were some 114,503 small businesses registered in the city, providing employment to 632,800 people.

DIRECTORY

Mayor (Governor and Premier of the City Government): VALENTINA I. MATVIYENKO (elected 5 October 2003, appointment confirmed 22 December 2006), 191060 St Petersburg, Smolnyi; tel. (812) 576-45-01; fax (812) 276-18-27; e-mail gubernator@gov.spb.ru; internet www.gov.spb.ru.

Chairman of the Legislative Assembly: VADIM A. TYULPANOV, 190107 St Petersburg, Isaakiyevskaya pl. 6; tel. (812) 570-39-31; fax (812) 319-90-01; e-mail vtulpanov@assembly.spb.ru; internet www.assembly.spb.ru.

Chief Representative of St Petersburg in the Russian Federation: VITALII M. AZAROV, 123001 Moscow, ul. Spiridonovka 20/1; tel. (495) 290-43-64; fax (495) 203-50-60.

Republic of Kareliya

The Republic of Kareliya is situated in the north-west of Russia, on the edge of the Eastern European Plain. The Republic forms part of the North-Western Federal Okrug and the Northern Economic Area. It is bordered by Finland to the west and by the oblasts of: Murmansk to the north and, beyond the White Sea, to the north-east; Archangel to the east; Vologda to the south-east; and Leningrad to the south. Kareliya contains some 83,000 km (51,540 miles) of waterways, including its major rivers, the Kem and the Vyg, and its numerous lakes (the Ladoga and the Onega being the largest and second largest lakes in Europe, respectively). A canal system 225 km long, the White Sea Canal, connects the Kareliyan port of Belomorsk to the St Petersburg. One-half of Kareliya's territory is forested and much of the coastal region is marshland. Kareliya occupies 172,400 sq km (66,560 sq miles). At January 2007, according to official estimates, the Republic had a total population of 693,150, and a population density of 4.0 per sq km. In 2002 some 76.6% of the population were ethnically Russian, 9.2% Kareliyan, 5.2% Belarusian, 2.7% Ukrainian and 2.0% Finnish. The dominant religion is Orthodox Christianity. The Kareliyan language consists of three dialects of Finnish—Livvi, Karjala and Lyydiki. In 1989, however, more than one-half of the ethnically Kareliyan population spoke Russian as their first language. Some 75.8% of the Republic's population inhabited urban areas in January 2007. The capital of Kareliya is at Petrozavodsk, with a population of 265,100 in 2006, according to official estimates. Kareliya is included in the time zone GMT+3.

HISTORY

Kareliya was an independent, Finnish-dominated state in medieval times. In the 16th century the area came under Swedish hegemony, before being annexed by Russia in 1721. A Kareliyan Labour Commune was formed on 8 June 1920 and became an autonomous republic within the Russian Federation (RSFSR, in the USSR) in July 1923. A Karelo-Finnish SSR (Union Republic), including territory annexed from Finland, was created in 1940. However, part of its territory was ceded to the RSFSR in 1946 and in 1956 Kareliya resumed the status of an ASSR subordinate to the RSFSR.

The Republic declared sovereignty on 9 August 1990. A republican Constitution was adopted in January 1994, and in April of that year elections took place to a bicameral Legislative Assembly. On 17 May 1998 Viktor Stepanov, the incumbent, was narrowly defeated in the second round of direct elections to the premiership (Head of the Republic) by the hitherto Mayor of Petrozavodsk, Sergei Katanandov. In March 2001 a number of reforms to the Republic's Constitution were approved. Notably, an executive presidency was to be established, and the legislature was to be reconstituted on a unicameral basis. Katanandov was elected to the reconstituted office of Head of the Republic on 28 April 2002. Non-partisan candidates were elected to a majority of seats in the concurrent legislative elections. On 3 March 2006 the republican Legislative Assembly unanimously approved Katanandov's nomination to a further term of office as Head of the Republic. On 30 August, in the eastern city of Kondopoga, two ethnic Russians died during clashes between Slavs and natives of the Caucasus. The ensuing tension in the Republic was exacerbated by the arrival in Petrozavodsk of numerous extreme Russian nationalists, who demanded that Chechens and Azeris be deported from Kareliya. (In November 2007 12 defendants, of whom six were ethnic Russians and six natives of the Caucasus, were convicted and were sentenced to three years' imprisonment each for involvement in the September 2006 rioting.) On 5 October federal President Vladimir Putin dismissed the republican interior minister and head of the security services. Pro-presidential parties dominated in the republican legislative elections held on 8 October: United Russia (UR) won 38.9% of the votes cast and the Russian Party of Life 16.3%. The Communist Party of the Russian Federation, with 12.8% of the votes cast, the Russian Pensioners' Party (RPP—12.1%) and the nationalist Liberal Democratic Party of Russia (8.9%) also obtained parliamentary representation.

In November 2006 the Legislative Assembly approved a motion by Katanandov in favour of the dissolution of the Petrozavodsk City Council for non-compliance with court decisions. Elections to the Council were consequently conducted on 11 March 2007; in contrast to the composition of the Legislative Assembly, A Just Russia (which incorporated the RPP) and the liberal Yabloko party together obtained a two-thirds' majority in the Council. In September Petrozavodsk City Council adopted a motion expressing 'no confidence' in Katanandov, on the grounds that he was responsible for corruption in the Republic, and voted for an appeal to President Putin to dismiss Katanandov and appoint a new Head of the Republic. (A regional court subsequently ruled against the decision, and ordered those deputies in favour of the motion to pay Katanandov damages.)

ECONOMY

The economy of Kareliya is largely based on its timber industry. In 2004 the Republic's gross regional product was 55,905.1m. roubles, equivalent to 79,198.3 roubles per head. Its major industrial centres include Petrozavodsk, Sortavala and Kem. In 2005 there were 2,226 km of railway lines and 6,648 km of paved roads in the Republic. Kareliya's main port is at Petrozavodsk.

Kareliya's agriculture employed 9.8% of the work-force in 2005 and generated 2,956m. roubles. The Republic ranks among the leading producers of rosin and turpentine in the Russian Federation. The Republic also has important mineral reserves. Industry engaged some 25.3% of the Republic's labour force in 2005 and generated 48,457m. roubles in 2004. Kareliya's main industries, apart from the processing of forestry products, are food-processing, ferrous metallurgy, the production of electrical energy, and the extraction of iron

ore and muscovite (mica). The Republic's major enterprise, the Segezha Pulp and Paper Mill, is one of the world's largest pulp and paper manufacturers. Although forestry and the processing of forestry products comprised 41.2% of the Republic's industrial production in 2004, forestry only accounted for 1.3% of employment in that year.

The economically active population totalled 380,000 in 2005, when 8.8% of the labour force were unemployed. The average monthly wage in the Republic was 8,730.3 roubles. The republican budget recorded a surplus of 280.7m. roubles in 2005. In that year exports from the Republic were worth US $997.5m., and the value of imports was $183.3m. Foreign investment in Kareliya in 2005 amounted to $74.5m. At the end of that year 4,628 small businesses were registered in the Republic, providing employment to 31,900 people.

DIRECTORY

Head of the Republic: Sergei L. Katanandov (elected 28 April 2002, appointment confirmed 3 March 2006), 185028 Kareliya, Petrozavodsk, pr. Lenina 19; tel. (8142) 79-93-00; fax (8142) 76-41-48; e-mail government@karelia.ru; internet www.gov.karelia.ru.

Prime Minister of the Republican Government: Pavel V. Chernov, 185028 Kareliya, Petrozavodsk, pr. Lenina 19; tel. (8142) 79-93-03; fax (8142) 76-41-48; e-mail government@karelia.ru; internet www.gov.karelia.ru.

Chairman of the Legislative Assembly: Nikolai I. Levin, 185610 Kareliya, Petrozavodsk, ul. Kuibysheva 5; tel. (8142) 78-02-95; fax (8142) 78-28-27; e-mail inbox@zsrk.onego.ru; internet www.karelia-zs.ru.

Chief Representative of the Republic of Kareliya in the Russian Federation: Anatolii A. Markov, 101000 Moscow, per. Armyanskii 9; tel. (495) 207-87-24; fax (495) 208-03-18; e-mail kareliap@rambler.ru.

Head of Petrozavodsk Autonomous Administration: Viktor N. Maslyakov, 185910 Kareliya, Petrozavodsk, pr. Lenina 2/501; tel. and fax (8142) 78-47-53; e-mail admcity@karelia.ru; internet www.petrozavodsk-mo.ru.

Republic of Komi

The Republic of Komi is situated in the north-east of European Russia. It forms part of the North-Western Federal Okrug and the Northern Economic Area. Mountains of the Northern, Circumpolar and Polar Urals occupy the eastern part of the Republic. Its major rivers are the Pechora, the Vychegda and the Mezen. Komi is bordered to the north and west by Archangel Oblast (including the Nenets Autonomous Okrug—AOk), and to the east by Tyumen Oblast (including the Khanty-Mansii AOk—Yugra and the Yamalo-Nenets AOk). To the south there are borders with Kirov Oblast, Perm Krai and Sverdlovsk Oblast. Some 90% of its territory is taiga (forested marshland), while the extreme north-east of the Republic lies within the Arctic tundra zone. The Republic occupies an area of 415,900 sq km (160,580 sq miles). At January 2007, according to official estimates, it had a population of 974,617, and a population density of 2.4 per sq km. At the time of the 2002 census 59.6% of the population were ethnically Russian, 25.2% Komi (including 1.2% who stated their ethnicity as Komi-Izhemets), 6.1% Ukrainian, 1.5% Tatars, 1.5% Belarusian and 0.9% German. The predominant religion in the region is Orthodox Christianity, although among the Komi this faith is combined with strong animist traditions. The language of the Komi population, spoken as a native tongue by some 74%, belongs to the Finnic branch of the Uralo-Altaic family. Some 75.7% of the population lived in urban areas in January 2007. Komi's capital is at Syktyvkar, which had a population of 229,300 in 2006, according to official estimates. The Republic's second largest city is Ukhta (103,300). The Republic of Komi is included in the time zone GMT+3.

HISTORY

The Komi (known historically as the Zyryans or the Permyaks) are descended from inhabitants of the river basins of the Volga, the Kama, the Pechora and the Vychegda. From the 12th century Russian settlers began to inhabit territory along the Vychegda, and later the Vym, rivers. The Vym subsequently acquired a strategic significance as the main route along which Russian colonists advanced to Siberia, and Ust-Sysolsk (now Syktyvkar), the territory's oldest city, was founded in 1586. The number of Slavs increased after the territory was annexed by Russia in 1478. The region soon acquired importance as the centre of mining and metallurgy, following the discovery of copper and silver ores. In 1697 petroleum was discovered in the territory; the first primitive refinery was built in the territory in 1745. The Komi exploited important trade routes between Archangel and Siberia, trading in fish, furs and game animals, while coal, timber, iron ore and paper became significant prior to the 1917 revolutions. The Komi Autonomous Oblast, established on 22 August 1921, became an ASSR in 1931.

The territory declared its sovereignty on 30 August 1990. A new republican Constitution was adopted on 17 February 1994, establishing a quasi-presidential premiership and a new legislature, the State Council. The Republic repudiated its declaration of sovereignty in September 2001, following a ruling by the federal Supreme Court that over one-half of the provision's declarations were in contravention of federal law. The republican presidential election, held on 16 December, was won by Vladimir Torlopov, hitherto Chairman of the republican legislature, who narrowly defeated the incumbent, Yurii Spiridonov. Torlopov received the support of the liberal Yabloko party, whereas Spiridonov's supporters included the pro-presidential Unity and Fatherland-United Russia (later United Russia—UR). In May 2002 a power-sharing treaty signed by the federal and republican authorities in March 1996 was annulled. A new State Council was elected in March 2003. In early December 2005 Putin nominated Torpolov to serve a further term of office as Head of the Republic; this nomination was approved unanimously by the republican legislature on 7 December. At elections to the State Council on 11 March 2007, UR secured 36.2% of votes cast, followed by the broadly pro-Government A Just Russia, with 15.5%, the Communist Party of the Russian Federation (14.3%), the nationalist Liberal Democratic Party of Russia (13.6%) and the Union of Rightist Forces (8.8%).

ECONOMY

The Republic of Komi is one of Russia's principal fuel- and energy-producing regions. Apart from a wealth of natural resources, it is strategically placed close to many of Russia's major industrial centres and has a well-developed transport network. In 2004 gross regional product in the Republic amounted to 141,163.9m. roubles, equivalent to some 141,012.6 roubles per head. Komi's major industrial centres are at Syktyvkar, Ukhta and Sosnogorsk. At the end of 2005 the Republic contained 1,671 km of railway lines and 5,510 km of paved roads.

Komi's agriculture, which employed just 8.5% of the work-force and generated 4,553m. roubles in 2005, consists principally of animal husbandry, especially reindeer-breeding. Ore-mining was developing from the mid-1990s: the Republic contained the country's largest reserves of bauxite, titanium, manganese and chromium ore, and also had significant reserves of petroleum and natural gas. Total industrial production, which was based on the production and processing of petroleum and natural gas, the production of coal and electrical energy, and the processing of forestry products, was worth 87,493m. roubles in 2004. In 2005 the sector employed 24.2% of the work-force. The Republic contains the Vorgashorskaya coal mine, the largest in Europe. In the mid-2000s a programme to relocate some 150,000 people from the far northern coal-mining cities of Vorkuta and Inta to the more hospitable southern regions of the Republic was under way. In 2005 the Republic produced 12.9m. metric tons of coal, making it the Federation's third-largest producer.

In 2005 the economically active population numbered 547,000, and 11.5% of the labour force were unemployed. In 2005 the average monthly wage in the Republic was relatively high, at 11,612.1 roubles. The budgetary surplus in that year amounted to 973.7m. roubles. In 2005 external trade comprised US $696.3m. in exports and $224.3m. in imports. Foreign investment in Komi was substantial in the late 1990s, and amounted to $159.8m. in 2005. In March 2002 the South African company Anglo-American purchased a majority stake in the Republic's leading paper manufacturer, Syktyvkar Forest Enterprise. At the end of 2005 there were 4,533 small businesses registered in the Republic, providing employment to 49,900 people.

DIRECTORY

Chairman of the Government (Head of the Republic): VLADIMIR A. TORLOPOV (elected 16 December 2001, appointment confirmed 7 December 2005), 167000 Komi, Syktyvkar, ul. Kommunicheskaya 9; tel. (8212) 28-51-05; fax (8212) 21-43-84; e-mail glava@rkomi .ru; internet www.rkomi.ru.

Chairman of the State Council: MARINA D. ISTIKHOVSKAYA, 167000 Komi, Syktyvkar, ul. Kommunisticheskaya 8; tel. (8212) 28-55-28; fax (8212) 24-44-90; e-mail gs@rkomi.ru; internet gs.rkomi.ru.

Chief Representative of the Republic of Komi in the Russian Federation: STEPAN V. IGNATOV, 123367 Moscow, Volokolamskoye shosse 62; tel. (495) 490-44-33; fax (495) 490-51-57.

Head of Syktyvkar City Administration: ROMAN V. ZENISHCHEV, 167000 Komi, Syktyvkar, ul. Babushkina 22; tel. (8212) 29-44-71; fax

(8212) 24-17-23; e-mail zenishev@syktyvkar.komi.com; internet www.syktyvkar.komi.com.

Archangel Oblast

Archangel Oblast is situated in the north of the Eastern European Plain. It lies on the White, Barents and Kara Seas (parts of the Arctic Ocean) and includes the northern archipelago of Franz-Josef Land (Zemlya Frantsa-Iosifa) and the Novaya Zemlya islands. The Oblast forms part of the North-Western Federal Okrug and the Northern Economic Area. In the north-east the Nenets Autonomous Okrug (AOk), a constituent part of the Oblast, runs eastwards along the coast to end in a short border with the Yamalo-Nenets AOk (within Tyumen Oblast). The Republic of Komi lies to the east of the Oblast. Kirov and Vologda Oblasts form the southern border and the Republic of Kareliya lies to the west. North-west, across the White Sea, lie the Kola Peninsula and Murmansk Oblast, while to the north there is access to the Barents Sea. The Oblast contains several large rivers (including the Onega, the Severnaya Dvina and the Pechora) and some 2,500 lakes. Some two-fifths of its entire area is forested and almost one-quarter classed as reindeer pasture. The Oblast occupies an area of 587,400 sq km (226,800 sq miles). It spans three climatic zones—arctic, sub-arctic and continental. At January 2007, according to official estimates, the Oblast's total population was 1,280,187 and its population density 2.2 per sq km. At the time of the 2002 census 94.2% of the population were ethnically Russian, 2.1% were Ukrainian and 0.8% were Belarusian. Some 73.2% of the population lived in urban areas in January 2007. Archangel Oblast's administrative centre is at Archangel (Arkhangelsk), which had 349,800 inhabitants in January 2006, according to official estimates. The Oblast's second city is Severodvinsk (with a population of 195,200). Archangel Oblast is included in the time zone GMT+3.

HISTORY

The city of Archangel was founded in the 16th century, to further Muscovite trade. It was the first Russian seaport and the country's main one until the building of St Petersburg in 1703. The port played a major role in the attack by the Entente fleet (British and French navies) against the Red Army in 1918, and was an important route for supplies from the Allied Powers during the Second World War. Archangel Oblast was founded on 23 September 1937.

On 13 October 1993 the Archangel Regional Soviet transferred its responsibilities to the regional administration. Communist candidates initially formed the largest single group elected to the regional Assembly of Deputies, although supporters of the federal Government and liberal reformists also enjoyed some support in the cities. In February 1996 the regional Governor appointed in September 1991, Pavel Balakshin, was dismissed, following the opening of a judicial enquiry into alleged corrupt practices. His successor, Anatolii Yefremov (appointed in March 1996), was confirmed as Governor by his popular election to the post in December 1997, and by his re-election in December 2000.

Yefremov contested a further term in the gubernatorial election on 14 March 2004. His perceived main rival, a federal parliamentary deputy, Vladimir Krupchak, had withdrawn his candidacy on 2 March, allegedly in response to pressure from the federal authorities. In the event, however, Yefremov was defeated in the 'run-off' election, held on 28 March, by dairy owner Nikolai Kiselev, who received 75.1% of the votes cast. In early July 2007 Kiselev requested that federal President Vladimir Putin renew his mandate as Governor. In August the Head of Archangel City Administration, Aleksandr Donskoi, was arrested, after a video, allegedly of Kiselev accepting a bribe, appeared on his personal internet site. (Donskoi, an outspoken opponent of the federal authorities, had announced his intention of contesting the federal presidential election scheduled for early 2008.) Four criminal cases had already been brought against Donskoi, and relations between he and the Governor (who denied any wrongdoing) were reported to have long been acrimonious. (Although there was widespread speculation regarding Kiselev's involvement in malpractice and his possible resignation, the Oblast's Prosecutor announced in August that the video was a fabrication.) In early September Donskoi received a one-year suspended custodial sentence and a fine of 75,000 roubles, after being convicted of forging his university certificate and engaging in illegal commercial activity; he claimed that the charges against him had been fabricated. However, in October the conviction against him was overturned, owing to procedural violations, and a new trial began in November. In early March 2008 Donskoi, who was described by human rights activists as a political prisoner, was released from detention; he announced his immediate withdrawal from political activity. Kiselev was not, in the event, nominated to serve for a further term as Governor, being succeeded by Ilya Mikhalchuk, who during 1988–2007 had been Mayor of Yakutsk, in the Republic of Sakha (Yakutiya), in the

Russian Far East. Mikhalchuk's nomination as Governor was approved by the Regional Assembly of Deputies on 19 March.

ECONOMY

All figures in this survey incorporate data for the Nenets AOk (q.v.), which is also treated separately. Archangel Oblast's gross regional product totalled 153,856.7m. roubles in 2004, equivalent to 117,337.4 roubles per head. The Oblast's main industrial centres are at Archangel, Severodvinsk, Novodvinsk and, in the south-east, Kotlas. At the end of 2005 there were 1,781 km of railways and 7,445 km of paved roads on the Oblast's territory. Its main ports are Archangel, Onega, Mezen and, in the Nenets AOk, Naryan-Mar.

The Oblast's agriculture, which employed just 9.5% of the labour force and generated 6,431m. roubles in 2005, consists mainly of potato and vegetable production, animal husbandry (livestock and reindeer) and hunting. The Oblast's industry, which employed 23.1% of the working population in 2005 and generated 108,698m. roubles in 2004, is based on timber and timber-processing and wood-working, (which together accounted for 31.7% of industrial production in 2004) and petroleum and natural gas (the fuel sector accounted for 30.6% of industrial production in that year). Other important areas of industry are the extraction of minerals (in particular, bauxite), electrical energy, mechanical engineering and metal-working, and the processing of fish products. Diamonds are also mined in the Oblast, although repeated licensing problems and legal disputes have inhibited the growth of the sector. In mid-2006 the state-owned atomic energy concern, Rosenergoatom, announced that it was to construct the first floating nuclear power station in the world in the region, in order to generate energy for particularly remote areas; the plant was expected to be completed in 2010 and to cost US $340m.

The Oblast's economically active population amounted to 698,000 in 2005, when 5.5% of the region's labour force were unemployed. The average monthly wage was 9,874.3m. roubles. In 2005 the Oblast recorded a budgetary surplus of 220.1m. roubles. External trade in that year comprised US $1,036.8m. in exports and $132.4m. in imports. Total foreign investment amounted to $643.3m. in 2005. At the end of that year there were 4,750 small businesses registered in the Oblast, providing employment to 31,500 people.

DIRECTORY

Head of the Regional Administration (Governor): ILYA F. MIKHALCHUK (nomination approved 19 March 2008), 163004 Archangel, pr. Troitskii 49; tel. (8182) 65-30-41; fax (8182) 64-85-97; internet www.dvinaland.ru.

Chairman of the Regional Assembly of Deputies: VITALII S. FORTYGIN, 163000 Archangel, pl. Lenina 1; tel. (8182) 21-56-46; fax (8182) 20-03-43; e-mail duma@dvinaland.ru; internet www.aosd.ru.

Chief Representative of Archangel Oblast in the Russian Federation: IGOR T. ZOLOYEV, 103006 Moscow, ul. M. Dmitrovka 3/10/222; tel. (495) 299-68-62; fax (495) 209-45-94; e-mail arxpred@rambler.ru.

Head of Archangel City Administration (Mayor): VIKTOR N. PAVLENKO, 163000 Archangel, pl. Lenina 5; tel. (8182) 65-27-44; fax (8182) 65-20-71; e-mail dios@arhcity.ru; internet www.arhcity.ru.

Kaliningrad Oblast

Kaliningrad Oblast forms the westernmost part of the Russian Federation, being an exclave separated from the rest of the country by Lithuania (which borders it to the north and east) and Belarus. Poland lies to the south. The Oblast falls within the North-Western Federal Okrug and is sometimes included in the North-Western Economic Area. The city of Kaliningrad is sited at the mouth of the River Pregolya, where it flows into the Vistula Lagoon, an inlet of the Baltic Sea. The other main river is the Neman. The Oblast occupies 15,100 sq km (5,830 sq miles), of which 13,300 sq km are dry land, the rest of its territory comprising the freshwater Curonian Lagoon, in the north-east, and the Vistula Lagoon. The coastline is 140 km (87 miles) long. At January 2007, according to official estimates, it had a total population of 937,353 and its population density was 62.1 per sq km. At the time of the 2002 census 82.4% of the population were ethnically Russian, 5.3% Belarusian, 4.9% Ukrainian, 1.5% Lithuanian, 0.9% Armenian and 0.9% German. Some 76.8% of the population inhabited urban areas in January 2007. The Oblast's administrative centre is at Kaliningrad, which had a population of 423,700 in 2006, according to official estimates. The Oblast is included in the time zone GMT+2.

HISTORY

The city of Kaliningrad was founded in 1255, as Königsberg, during German expansion eastwards. The chief city of East Prussia, it was the original royal capital of the Hohenzollerns (from 1871 the German emperors). After the Second World War it was annexed by the USSR and received its current name (1945). Most of the German population was deported and the city almost completely destroyed and rebuilt. On 7 April 1946 the region became an administrative-political unit of the Russian Federation.

In mid-1993 Kaliningrad Oblast requested the status of a republic, a petition refused by the federal authorities. On 15 October the regional Soviet was disbanded by the head of the regional Administration for failing to support the federal presidency's struggle against the federal parliament. A regional Duma was later formed. In January 1996 Yurii Matochkin was one of the first oblast governors to sign a power-sharing agreement with the federal Government. Leonid Gorbenko, an independent candidate, was elected Governor in October. In 1998 a proposal that the region be awarded the status of an autonomous Russian Baltic republic was submitted to the upper chamber of the federal legislature, the Federation Council. However, Gorbenko opposed plans for greater autonomy. In gubernatorial elections held in November 2000, Gorbenko was defeated by Adm. Vladimir Yegorov, the former Commander of the Baltic Fleet, who was elected largely on the basis of his anti-corruption campaign.

As the European Union (EU) prepared to admit several Eastern European countries, including neighbouring Lithuania and Poland, to take effect from May 2004, the status of Kaliningrad became an increasing source of contention; in particular, Russia initially objected to proposals that residents of Kaliningrad would require visas to travel to metropolitan Russia. In November 2002, at an EU-Russia summit meeting, held in Brussels, Belgium, Russia finally agreed to an EU proposal for simplified visa arrangements; the new regulations took effect from 1 July 2003.

In late August 2005 federal President Vladimir Putin nominated Georgii Boos, hitherto a Deputy Chairman of the State Duma, and a member of the pro-presidential United Russia (UR) to replace Yegorov as Governor. On 16 September the regional Duma voted to confirm Boos's nomination, which took effect from 19 November, following the expiry of Yegorov's term of office. At elections to the regional legislature, held on 12 March 2006, UR obtained 34.1% of the votes cast. The option to vote 'against all candidates' received more support than did any other party, accounting for 16.8% of the votes cast. The other parties to win seats on the basis of proportional representation were the Communist Party of the Russian Federation (with 15.1%), the Russian Pensioners' Party (8.9%), the nationalist Liberal Democratic Party of Russia (7.5%) and the Patriots of Russia (7.2%). In July 2007 the Russian Government indicated that it did not rule out the eventual deployment of missile bases in Kaliningrad Oblast, as part of its eventual response to plans by the USA to establish missile defence establishments in Poland and the Czech Republic.

ECONOMY

Kaliningrad Oblast is noted for containing more than 90% of the world's reserves of amber. Within Russia it also became noted for its reputedly flourishing parallel ('black') market, despite the establishment of a 'free trade zone' in the Oblast in 1991, with federal officials suggesting in 1999 that the region had become a major transshipment point for illegal drugs. Kaliningrad also suffers from a military and industrial legacy of severe pollution. In 2004 its official gross regional product totalled 65,580.5m. roubles, or 69,227.5 roubles per head. Its main industrial centres are at Kaliningrad, Gusev and Sovetsk. There are rail services to Lithuania and Poland, and there were 618 km of railways on the Oblast's territory at the end of 2004. In September 2006 a new rail ferry was inaugurated between Baltiisk, in the south-west of Kaliningrad Oblast, and Ust-Luga, in Leningrad Oblast, thereby facilitating direct transport between Kaliningrad and metropolitan Russia without the need to cross the territory of any other state. Although initially the twice-weekly service was to carry cargo only, it was anticipated that a passenger service would eventually be provided on the route. In 2004 Kaliningrad Oblast's road network consisted of 4,615 km of paved roads. Its main ports are at Kaliningrad and Baltiisk.

Kaliningrad Oblast's agricultural sector, which employed 9.4% of its work-force and generated 8,371m. roubles in 2005, consists mainly of animal husbandry, including fur-farming, and vegetable-growing and fishing. The Oblast has substantial reserves of petroleum (around 275m. metric tons), more than 2,500m. cu m in peat deposits and 50m. tons of coal. The industrial sector employed 22.4% of its working population in 2005 and generated 60,971m. roubles in 2004. The region's main industries are mechanical engineering and metal-working, the processing of fishing and forestry products, electrical energy, and the production and processing of amber. Petroleum is also extracted in the Oblast. Kaliningrad is by far the largest producer of television sets in the Federation, accounting for 3.8m. units, or 59.7% of Russia's total production in 2005. The industry has grown substantially since 2001, when just 144,500 sets were produced in the Oblast. A plant to construct German BMW automobiles for the Russian market opened in 1999. A special economic zone was established in the Oblast in 1996; in January 2006 federal President Vladimir Putin approved legislation extending the zone's regime for a further 25 years, although several of the taxation and tariff exemptions associated with the zone were to cease with effect from 2012 or 2018. The continuing strategic geopolitical situation of Kaliningrad Oblast meant that demilitarization proceeded at a much slower pace than it did elsewhere in the former USSR; in 1998 there were still around 200,000 members of military units in the Oblast. The coastal town of Svetlogorsk (formerly Rauschen) is an important tourist resort.

The economically active population numbered 519,000 in 2005, when some 6.6% of the labour force were unemployed, compared with 15.4% in 2000. The average monthly wage was 6,781.3 roubles in 2005. The 2005 regional budget recorded a deficit of 1,137.7m. roubles. In the mid-2000s the region experienced severe problems related to the prevalence of organized crime and ill health, with the rate of HIV infection a particular source of concern. Concern was also expressed at the additional expenses resulting from new requirements for documentation for the transit of goods between Kaliningrad and metropolitan Russia introduced in 2003 (see above); some reports suggested that transshipment costs for some goods had increased by as much as 25%. In 2005 export trade amounted to US $859.5m., and imports were worth $3,795.5m, while foreign investment amounted to $75.3m. At the end of 2005 there were 9,045 small businesses registered in the Oblast, providing employment to 105,000 people.

DIRECTORY

Head of the Regional Administration (Governor): GEORGII V. BOOS (appointment confirmed 16 September 2005, assumed office 19 November), 236007 Kaliningrad, ul. D. Donskogo 1; tel. (401) 259-90-01; fax (401) 246-35-54; e-mail first@gov.39.ru; internet www.gov .kaliningrad.ru.

Chairman of the Regional Duma: SERGEI V. BULYCHEV, 236000 Kaliningrad, ul. Kirova 17; tel. (401) 292-84-39; fax (401) 222-84-82; e-mail letters@duma.kaliningrad.org; internet duma.kaliningrad .org.

Chief Representative of Kaliningrad Oblast in the Russian Federation: YEVGENII I. IZOTOV, 123242 Moscow, ul. M. Krasnaya Presnya 7; tel. (495) 252-66-00; fax (495) 292-12-87; e-mail rngs@ online.ru.

Head of Kaliningrad City Administration (Mayor): YURII A. SAVENKO, 236040 Kaliningrad, pl. Pobedy 1; tel. (401) 292-31-22; fax (401) 221-16-77; e-mail cityhall@klgd.ru; internet www.klgd.ru.

Leningrad Oblast

Leningrad Oblast is situated in the north-west of the Eastern European Plain. It lies on the Gulf of Finland, an inlet of the Baltic Sea, and forms part of the North-Western Federal Okrug and the North-Western Economic Area. The Republic of Kareliya lies to the north, while the Oblast of Vologda lies to the east and those of Novgorod and Pskov are to the south. There is an international border with Estonia to the west and with Finland to the north-west. Two-thirds of the Oblast is forested. The Oblast occupies 85,300 sq km (32,935 sq miles). At January 2007, according to official estimates, its population was 1,637,737, giving a population density of 19.2 per sq km. At the time of the 2002 census 89.6% of the population were ethnic Russians, 2.5% Ukrainians and 1.6% Belarusians. The administrative centre is St Petersburg, which does not itself comprise part of the Oblast. Some 66.3% of the population of the Oblast inhabited urban areas in January 2007. The largest cities within the Oblast are Gatchina (with an estimated population of 88,800 in 2006) and Vyborg (78,500 in 2005). Leningrad Oblast is included in the time zone GMT+3.

HISTORY

The city of St Petersburg (known as Petrograd in 1914–24 and Leningrad until 1991) was built in 1703. Leningrad Oblast, which was formed on 1 August 1927, was heavily industrialized during the Soviet period, particularly during 1926–40. The region did not change its name when the city reverted to the name of St Petersburg in October 1991.

Gubernatorial elections, held in late 1996, were won by an independent candidate, Vladimir Gustov. Gustov resigned to take office in the federal Government in September 1998, and his replacement, Valerii Serdyukov, secured 30% of the votes cast in an election contested by 16 candidates on 5 September 1999. Serdyukov was re-elected Governor on 21 September 2003, receiving 56.8% of the votes cast; less than 30% of the electorate participated in the elections. At elections to the Regional Legislative Assembly on 11 March 2007, the pro-presidential United Russia (with a list headed by Serdyukov) won 35.2% of votes cast, while A Just Russia received 20.9%, the Communist Party of the Russian Federation 17.1%, and the nationalist Liberal Democratic Party of Russia 12.1% of the votes. On 9 July Serdyukov's federal presidential nomination for a third term as Governor was endorsed by the regional Legislative Assembly.

ECONOMY

Leningrad Oblast's gross regional product amounted to 174,297.9m. roubles in 2004, equivalent to 105,225.7 roubles per head. A new port opened at Primorsk in December 2001, as part of Russia's Baltic Pipeline System, to facilitate the transportation of petroleum. In 2005 it was announced that a further port under construction, at Ust-Luga, was eventually to form part of a special economic zone intended to attract foreign investment. A railway ferry service, which commenced in late 2005, provides a direct link between metropolitan Russia (at Ust-Luga) and the exclave of Kaliningrad. In 2005 Leningrad Oblast and St Petersburg City together contained 2,872 km of railway track and 10,679 km of paved roads.

The Oblast's agricultural sector employed 11.8% of the working population and generated 30,512m. roubles in 2005. The region's timber reserves are estimated to cover 6.1m. ha. Its major industries are the processing of forestry and agricultural products, petroleum-refining and the production of electrical energy. The industrial sector employed 28.4% of the Oblast's work-force in 2005 and generated 169,212m. roubles in 2004.

The economically active population numbered 899,000 in 2005, when 7.4% of the labour force were unemployed. The average monthly wage was 8,595.9 roubles in 2005. In that year the regional budget recorded a deficit of 28.3m. roubles. In 2005 external trade comprised US $6,048.7m. in exports and $3,187.1m. in imports. Foreign investment amounted to $351.2m. in that year. At the end of 2005 there were 11,740 small businesses registered in the Oblast, providing employment to 138,700 people.

DIRECTORY

Head of the Regional Administration (Governor): VALERII P. SERDYUKOV (elected 5 September 1999, re-elected 21 September 2003, appointment confirmed 9 July 2007), 191311 St Petersburg, Suvorovskii pr. 67; tel. (812) 274-42-42; fax (812) 274-67-33; e-mail guber@lenreg.ru; internet www.lenobl.ru.

Chairman of the Regional Legislative Assembly: IVAN F. KHABAROV, 191311 St Petersburg, Suvorovskii pr. 67; tel. (812) 274-68-73; fax (812) 274-85-39; e-mail mail@lenoblzaks.ru; internet www .lenoblzaks.ru.

Chief Representative of Leningrad Oblast in the Russian Federation: ALEKSEI I. AKULOV, 119019 Moscow, ul. Novyi Arbat 15/1/1601; tel. and fax (495) 291-44-54; e-mail plorf@mail.ru.

Murmansk Oblast

Murmansk Oblast occupies the Kola Peninsula, which borders the Barents Sea to the north and the White Sea to the south-east. It forms part of the North-Western Federal Okrug and the Northern Economic Area. The Oblast has international borders with Norway and Finland to the west, while Kareliya lies to the south. Much of its territory lies within the Arctic Circle. The Oblast covers 144,900 sq km (55,930 sq miles). The climate is severe and changeable, influenced by cold fronts from the Arctic and warm, moist weather from the Atlantic. At January 2007, according to official estimates, the population of the Oblast was 856,969, giving a population density of 5.9 per sq km. At the time of the 2002 census 85.2% of the population were ethnic Russians, 6.4% were Ukrainians, 2.3% were Belarusians and 0.9% were Tatars. Some 91.3% of the population inhabited urban areas in January 2007. Its administrative centre is at Murmansk, a major seaport, which had a population of 321,000 in 2006, according to official estimates. Murmansk Oblast is included in the time zone GMT+3.

HISTORY

The city of Romanov-on-Murman was founded in 1916. Following the Bolshevik Revolution of 1917 (after which the city was renamed Murmansk), the region was a centre of anti-communist resistance. Murmansk Oblast was formed on 28 May 1938.

Yurii Yevdokimov, a candidate favoured by the former Chairman of the National Security Council, Gen. (retd) Aleksandr Lebed, was elected in the Oblast's first direct poll to the governorship, held in November 1996. Yevdokimov was re-elected Governor in 2000 and in March 2004. Federal President Vladimir Putin's nomination of Yevdokimov for a fourth gubernatorial term was endorsed by the regional Duma on 14 February 2007. At elections to the regional Duma on 11 March, the pro-presidential United Russia (with a list headed by Yevdokimov) secured 42.9% of votes cast, while the Communist Party of the Russian Federation won 17.5%, A Just Russia 16.2% and the nationalist Liberal Democratic Party of Russia 12.6% of votes.

ECONOMY

In 2004 Murmansk Oblast's gross regional product was 118,165.0m. roubles, or 134,831.1 roubles per head. The Oblast's principal industrial centres are at Murmansk, Zapolyarnyi and Apatity. At the end of 2005 there were 870 km of railway track in the region and 2,474 km of paved roads. The port at Murmansk is Russia's sole all-weather Northern port, through which some 12m. metric tons of cargo pass every year, and is the base for the world's only nuclear ice breaker fleet, the Northern Fleet. There is an international airport at Murmansk.

The Oblast's agricultural sector, which employed just 3.3% of the work-force in 2005, consists mainly of fishing (the region typically produces around 45% of the country's fish supplies), animal husbandry (reindeer and other livestock) and vegetable production. In 2005 agricultural production generated a total of 1,610m. roubles. The territory is rich in natural resources, including phosphates, iron ore and rare and non-ferrous metals. In 1985 exploitation of the Shtokman gas condensate deposit, began on the continental shelf of the Barents Sea. Industry engaged 22.9% of the work-force in 2005 and generated 85,811m. roubles in 2004. The region is a major producer of apatites, nickel, copper and iron concentrates. In 1999 LUKoil, the domestic petroleum producer, signed an agreement that made Murmansk a base for exploration of the Barents Sea, in association with the state-controlled gas producer Gazprom. Despite the absence of any pipeline connection from Russia's principal petroleum and natural gas fields, the city is a major centre for the export of petroleum products, particularly to the USA. In the mid-2000s Gazprom was to construct a liquefying plant in Murmansk, so as to facilitate an increase in exports of liquefied natural gas.

In 2005 the region's economically active population numbered some 523,000. Unemployment declined from the late 1990s, from 21.1% of the labour force in 1998, to 8.8% in 2005. In that year the average monthly wage in the Oblast was some 12,509.6 roubles, one of the highest in the Federation, while the regional budget recorded a surplus of 551.9m. roubles In 2005 exports amounted to US $1,195.8m., and imports were worth $203.3m., while foreign investment totalled $29.4 m. At the end of 2005 there were 3,013 small businesses registered in the Oblast, providing employment to 30,600 people.

DIRECTORY

Head of the Regional Administration (Governor): YURII A. YEVDOKIMOV (elected November 1996, re-elected 26 March 2000 and 14 March 2004, appointment confirmed 14 February 2007), 183006 Murmansk, pr. Lenina 75; tel. (8152) 47-65-03; fax (8152) 47-65-40; e-mail evdokimov@murman.ru; internet gov.murman.ru.

Chairman of the Regional Duma: YEVGENII V. NIKORA, 183036 Murmansk, ul. S. Perovskoi 2; tel. (8152) 45-36-72; fax (8152) 45-97-79; e-mail murduma@com.mels.ru; internet duma.murman.ru.

Chief Representative of Murmansk Oblast in the Russian Federation: RENAT I. KARCHAA, 125009 Moscow, ul. B. Nikitskaya 12; tel. (495) 629-03-31; fax (495) 229-53-51.

Head of Murmansk City Administration (Mayor): MIKHAIL I. SAVCHENKO, 183006 Murmansk, pr. Lenina 75; tel. (8152) 45-81-60; fax (8152) 45-93-62.

Novgorod Oblast

Novgorod Oblast is situated in the north-west of the Eastern European Plain, some 500 km north-west of Moscow and 180 km south of St Petersburg. It forms part of the North-Western Federal Okrug and the North-Western Economic Area. Tver Oblast lies to the south-east, Pskov Oblast to the south-west and Leningrad and Vologda Oblasts to the north. The Oblast covers 55,300 sq km (21,350 sq miles). At January 2007, according to official estimates, the population of the Oblast was 657,595 and its population density was 11.9 per sq km. At the time of the 2002 census 93.9% of the population were ethnic Russians, 1.5% were Ukrainians and 0.8%

were Belarusians. Some 70.6% of the population lived in urban areas in January 2007. The region's administrative centre is at Velikii (Great) Novgorod (Novgorod), which had a population of 217,700 in January 2006, according to official estimates. Novgorod Oblast is located in the time zone GMT+3.

HISTORY

One of the oldest Russian cities, Novgorod remained a powerful principality after the dissolution of Kievan Rus. In 1478 Ivan III ('the Great'), prince of Muscovy and the first Tsar of All Russia, destroyed the Republic of Novgorod. The wealth and importance of the city, based on trade, declined after the foundation of St Petersburg in the early 18th century. Novgorod Oblast was formed on 5 July 1944.

In the mid-1990s the region displayed a relatively high level of support for reformists and centrists. The Oblast was permitted gubernatorial elections in December 1995, which were won by the pro-Yeltsin incumbent appointed in October 1991, Mikhail Prusak, the leader of the Democratic Party of Russia. Prusak was re-elected for a further term of office on 5 September 1999, with 90% of the votes cast. He combined demands for regional governors to be appointed rather than elected, and even for the end of direct elections to the federal presidency, with support for the purported (historical) 'Novgorod model' of federalism, property rights and subsidiarity. Prusak was re-elected Governor on 7 September 2003, receiving 78.7% of the votes cast. In 2005 Prusak became a member of the pro-presidential United Russia (UR). At the regional legislative election, held on 8 October 2006, UR received 43.8% of the votes cast, followed by the Communist Party of the Russian Federation, with 14.9%, A Free Russia (11.0%) and the nationalist Liberal Democratic Party of Russia (7.0%).

In August 2007 Prusak resigned as Governor, following public criticism of the high level of official corruption in the Oblast by the Presidential Representative in the North-Western Federal Okrug, Ilya Klebanov. On 7 August the regional Duma approved the presidential nomination of Sergei Mitin (a member of UR) as Governor.

ECONOMY

In 2004 Novgorod Oblast's gross regional product amounted to 47,071.3m. roubles, or 69,391.0 roubles per head. The Oblast's major industrial centres are at Velikii Novgorod and Staraya Russa (a resort town famous for its mineral and radon springs). The Moscow–St Petersburg road and rail routes pass through the region. In 2005 there were 1,144 km of railways and 8,791 km of paved roads in the Oblast.

The region's agriculture, which employed 11.1% of the work-force and generated 7,753m. roubles in 2005, consists mainly of flax production and animal husbandry. The region's major industries include mechanical engineering and metal-working, chemicals and petrochemicals, wood-working, the processing of forestry and agricultural products, and electricity production. Industry engaged 30.5% of the work-force in 2005 and generated 47,153m. roubles in 2004. Velikii Novgorod is an important international tourist destination.

The economically active population totalled 348,000 in 2005, when 5.8% of the labour force were unemployed. Those in employment earned an average wage of 6,940.8 roubles per month. In that year the regional budget recorded a surplus of 529.2m. roubles and the external trade of the Oblast comprised US $763.6m. in exports and $298.9m. in imports. In 2005 total foreign investment in the region amounted to some $279.1m. At the end of 2005 there were 2,502 small businesses registered in the Oblast, employing 37,600 people.

DIRECTORY

Head of the Regional Administration (Governor): SERGEI G. MITIN (appointment confirmed 7 August 2007), 173005 Novgorod obl., Velikii Novgorod, Sofiiskaya pl. 1; tel. (8162) 27-47-79; fax (8162) 13-13-30; e-mail infoserv@niac.natm.ru; internet region.adm.nov.ru.

Chairman of the Regional Duma: ANATOLII A. BOITSEV, 173005 Novgorod obl., Velikii Novgorod, Sofiiskaya pl. 1; tel. and fax (8162) 73-25-14; internet duma.niac.ru.

Chief Representative of Novgorod Oblast in the Russian Federation: VLADIMIR N. PODOPRIGORA, 127006 Moscow, ul. M. Dmitrovka 3/219–220; fax (495) 299-40-04.

Head of Velikii Novgorod City Administration (Mayor): YURII I. BOBRYSHEV, 173007 Novgorod obl., Velikii Novgorod, ul. B. Vasilyevskaya 4; tel. (8162) 77-25-40; fax (8162) 13-25-99; e-mail mayor@adm.nov.ru; internet www.adm.nov.ru.

Pskov Oblast

Pskov Oblast is situated on the Eastern European Plain. The Oblast forms part of the North-Western Federal Okrug and the North-Western Economic Area. It has international borders with Belarus to the south and Latvia and Estonia to the west. There are borders with the oblasts of: Smolensk in the south-east; Tver and Novgorod in the east; and Leningrad in the north-east. Around two-fifths of the Oblast's territory is forested. On its border with Estonia lie the Pskov (Pihkva) and Chudskoye (Peipsi) lakes. Pskov Oblast covers an area of 55,300 sq km (21,350 sq miles). At January 2007, according to official estimates, the population numbered 713,392 and the population density was 12.9 per sq km. At the time of the 2002 census 94.3% of the population were ethnic Russians, 1.6% were Ukrainians and 1.3% were Belarusians. Some 67.4% of inhabitants lived in urban areas in January 2007. The Oblast's administrative centre is at Pskov, which had a population of 197,100 in 2006, according to official estimates. The second largest city is Velikiye Luki (102,400). Pskov Oblast is included in the time zone GMT+3.

HISTORY

Pskov city was founded in 903, and in 1242 was the area in which Muscovite Prince Aleksandr Nevskii defeated an army of Teutonic Knights, who sought to expand eastwards. The Muscovite state finally acquired the region in 1510. The Oblast was created on 23 August 1944. Some territory to the south of Lake Pskov was transferred from Estonia to Pskov Oblast in 1945, remaining a cause for dispute between newly independent Estonia and Russia in the 1990s. In 1995 Estonia formally renounced any territorial claim, but it remained eager to secure Russian acknowledgement of the 1920 Treaty of Tartu (by which Estonia had been awarded the disputed territory), which would render the Soviet occupation of the Baltic republic illegal.

The Oblast was a bastion of support for the extreme nationalist policies of Vladimir Zhirinovskii's Liberal Democratic Party of Russia (LDPR) in the 1990s; a gubernatorial election was held on 21 October 1996, which was won by Yevgenii Mikhailov, a former deputy of the LDPR. Mikhailov was re-elected Governor in November 2000. In November 2004 a court in the Oblast ruled that Mikhailov (who was now supported by the pro-presidential United Russia—UR) was eligible to contest a further term as Governor, on the grounds that the Oblast's charter (which prohibited governors from serving more than two consecutive terms) did not conform with an earlier ruling of the federal Constitutional Court. Meanwhile, the federal Supreme Court annulled the candidacy in the gubernatorial elections of the Mayor of Pskov, Mikhail Khoronen (who had been widely regarded as Mikhailov's most credible competitor in the elections), after he had been found to have used his office as Mayor to promote his campaign. Following the first round of polling, held on 14 November, Mikhailov, with 29.7% of the votes cast, and a local business executive, Mikhail Kuznetsov (with 18.3%), progressed to a second round; 17.4% of the votes cast in the first round had been cast 'against all candidates'. In the 'run-off' poll, held on 5 December, Kuznetsov was elected Governor, receiving 49.2% of the votes cast, compared with the 41.7% won by Mikhailov. From November 2006 security forces took measures to disperse protests by extremist nationalist youth organizations outside the Estonian consulate in Pskov; the protesters had gathered in response to the relocation of a Soviet war memorial monument in the Estonian capital. At elections to the Regional Assembly of Deputies, held on 11 March 2007, UR won 45.4% of votes cast, while the Communist Party of the Russian Federation obtained 19.4%, A Just Russia 15.7% and the LDPR 8.4% of the votes cast.

ECONOMY

In 2004 Pskov Oblast's gross regional product amounted to 36,538.5m. roubles, equivalent to 49,233.8 roubles per head—by far the lowest figure in the North-Western Federal Okrug. The Oblast's principal industrial centres are at Pskov and Velikiye Luki. At the end of 2005 there were 1,092 km of railway track in the region and 9,951 km of paved roads. There is an international airport at Pskov.

Agricultural activity, which employed 16.1% of the work-force and generated 8,925m. roubles in 2005, consists mainly of animal husbandry and the production of flax. A major project to improve the agricultural infrastructure of the region was implemented in the mid-1990s. Fishing is an important source of income in the north of the territory. The region's major industries are the production of electricity, mechanical engineering and metal-working, and food-processing. Industry employed 23.9% of the working population in 2005 and generated 21,703m. roubles in 2004.

Pskov Oblast's economically active population numbered 372,000 in 2005, when 6.6% of the labour force were unemployed, compared with 5.6% in the previous year. Those in employment earned, on average, 5,734.5 roubles per month. There was a regional budgetary surplus of 6,454.1m. roubles in that year, when external trade amounted to a value of US $402.2m. in exports and $326.1m. in imports, while foreign investment in the region totalled $9.2m. At the end of 2005 some 3,769 small businesses were registered in the Oblast, providing employment to 35,000 people.

DIRECTORY

Head of the Regional Administration (Governor): MIKHAIL V. KUZNETSOV (elected 5 December 2004), 180001 Pskov, ul. Nekrasova 23; tel. (8122) 69-97-50; fax (8122) 16-03-90; e-mail glava@obladmin.pskov.ru; internet www.pskov.ru.

Chairman of the Regional Assembly of Deputies: BORIS G. POLOZOV, 180001 Pskov, ul. Nekrasova 23; tel. (8122) 16-24-44; fax (8122) 16-00-51; internet www.pskov.ru/ru/authority/obl_sobranie.

Chief Representative of Pskov Oblast in the Russian Federation: IGOR P. NOVOSELOV, 109013 Moscow, ul. Nikolskaya 10/2; tel. (495) 628-07-95; fax (495) 928-07-95.

Head of Pskov City Administration (Mayor): MIKHAIL YA. KHORONEN, 180000 Pskov, ul. Nekrasova 22; tel. (8122) 16-26-67; internet gorodpskov.ru.

Vologda Oblast

Vologda Oblast is situated in the north-west of the Eastern European Plain. It forms part of the North-Western Federal Okrug and the Northern Economic Area. It has a short border, in the north-west, with the Republic of Kareliya, which includes the southern tip of Lake Onega. Onega also forms the northern end of a border with Leningrad Oblast, which lies to the west of Vologda. Novgorod Oblast lies to the south-west and Tver, Yaroslavl and Kostroma Oblasts to the south. Kirov Oblast lies to the east and Archangel Oblast to the north. Vologda Oblast occupies 145,700 sq km (56,250 sq miles). At January 2007, according to official estimates, the Oblast's population totalled 1,227,778 and the population density was 8.54 per sq km. In 2002 some 96.6% of the population were ethnically Russian and 1.0% were Ukrainian. Some 68.4% of the total population inhabited urban areas in January 2007. The Oblast's administrative centre is at Vologda, which had a population of 287,000 in 2006, according to official estimates. The largest city in the Oblast is Cherepovets (308,400). Vologda Oblast is included in the time zone GMT+3.

HISTORY

The Vologda province was annexed by the state of Muscovy in the 14th century. Vologda Oblast was formed on 23 September 1937. In October 1991 the recently elected Russian President, Boris Yeltsin, appointed a new regional head of administration, Nikolai Podgornov. In mid-1993 Vologda Oblast declared itself a republic, but failed to be acknowledged as such by the federal authorities. In October the regional Soviet transferred its responsibilities to the regional administration and elections were later held to a Legislative Assembly. There was a high level of support for the nationalist Liberal Democratic Party of Russia (LDPR) for much of the 1990s. In June 1996 Boris Yeltsin dismissed Podgornov, who was subsequently arrested and imprisoned on charges of corruption. His successor, Vyacheslav Pozgalev, won 80% of the votes cast in a direct election in late 1996, and was re-elected for further terms of office on 19 December 1999 and 7 December 2003. In March 2003 Pozgalev was elected to the Supreme Council of the pro-presidential United Russia (UR). At elections to the Legislative Assembly, held on 11 March 2007, UR won 44.8% of votes cast, while A Just Russia won 16.9%, the Agrarian Party of Russia 13.1%, the LDPR 11.6% and the Communist Party of the Russian Federation 10.2% of the votes. On 21 June the Legislative Assembly approved federal President Vladimir Putin's nomination of Pozgalev for a fourth term as Governor.

ECONOMY

In 2004 Vologda Oblast's gross regional product amounted to 163,981.6m. roubles, or 131,131.3 roubles per head. The main industrial centres are at Vologda and Cherepovets. At the end of 2005 there were 769 km of railway track in use on its territory, as well as 11,353 km of paved roads. There are some 1,800 km of navigable waterways, including part of the Volga–Baltic route network.

Agriculture in Vologda Oblast, which employed 11.4% of the work-force and generated 16,833m. roubles in 2005, consists mainly of animal husbandry and production of flax and vegetables. Its main industries are ferrous metallurgy; the region produces around one-fifth of each of Russia's iron, rolled stock and steel, as well as significant quantities of textiles and chemicals, including, notably, mineral fertilizers. Industry engaged 31.3% of the region's working population in 2005 and generated 200,264m. roubles in 2004. Severstal, the largest privately owned steel manufacturer in Russia is one of the major employers in the Oblast. In 2005 the Oblast produced 10.8m. metric tons of steel, or 16.3% of total steel production in the Federation.

The Oblast's economically active population numbered 660,000 in 2005, when the rate of unemployment was 5.2%. Those in employment earned, on average, 8,827.9 roubles per month. In 2005 the regional budget recorded a deficit of 21.7m. roubles, and export trade comprised US $3,040.6m. in exports and $316.9m. in imports. Total foreign investment in the Oblast in that year amounted to $431.0m. At the end of 2005 some 4,794 small businesses were registered in the Oblast, providing employment to 62,000 people.

DIRECTORY

Governor: VYACHESLAV YE. POZGALEV (appointed 3 June 1996, elected 6 October 1996, re-elected 19 December 1999 and 7 December 2003, appointment confirmed 21 June 2007), 160035 Vologda, ul. Gertsena 2; tel. (8172) 72-07-64; fax (8172) 25-15-54; e-mail governor@vologda-oblast.ru; internet www.vologda-oblast.ru.

Chairman of the Legislative Assembly: NIKOLAI V. TIKHOMIROV, 160000 Vologda, ul. Pushkinskaya 25; tel. (8172) 72-02-60; fax (8172) 25-11-33; e-mail sobranie@zs.gos35.ru; internet www.zs.gos35.ru.

Chief Representative of Vologda Oblast in the Russian Federation: VLADIMIR S. SMIRNOV, 119034 Moscow, Starokonyushennyi per. 4/5; tel. (495) 201-58-58; fax (495) 201-55-24.

Head of Vologda City Administration (Mayor): YEVGENII B. SHULEPOV, 160000 Vologda, ul. Kamennyi most 4; tel. (8172) 72-00-42; fax (8172) 72-25-29; e-mail admgor@vologda-city.ru; internet www.vologda-city.ru.

Nenets Autonomous Okrug

The Nenets Autonomous Okrug (AOk) is part of Archangel Oblast and, hence, the North-Western Federal Okrug and the Northern Economic Area. It is situated in the north-east of European Russia, its coastline lying, from west to east, on the White, Barents and Kara Seas, parts of the Arctic Ocean. Most of the territory lies within the Arctic Circle. Archangel proper lies to the south-west, but most of the southern border is with the Republic of Komi. At its eastern extremity the district touches the Yamalo-Nenets AOk (part of Tyumen Oblast) and, stretching away to the north-east, the island of Novaya Zemlya, which forms a part of Archangel Oblast proper. The territory occupies 176,700 sq km (68,220 sq miles). At January 2007, according to official estimates, the population of the AOk was 41,960, giving a population density of 0.2 per sq km. At the time of the 2002 census 62.4% of the population were ethnically Russian, 18.7% Nenets, 10.9% Komi, 3.2% Ukrainian and 1.0% Belarusian. The language spoken by the Nenets belongs to the Samoyedic group of Uralian languages, which is part of the Uralo-Altaic linguistic group. Around 64.2% of the population inhabited urban areas in January 2007. The district capital is Naryan-Mar, which had a population of 19,100 in 2006, according to official estimates. The AOk is included in the time zone GMT+3.

HISTORY

The Nenets were traditionally concerned with herding and breeding reindeer. A Samoyedic people, they are believed to have broken away from other Finno-Ugrian groups in around 3000 BC and migrated east where, in about 200 BC, they began to mix with Turkic-Altaic people. By the early 17th century AD their territory had come entirely under the control of the Muscovite state.

The Nenets National Okrug was formed on 15 July 1929, becoming a nominally Autonomous Okrug in 1977. During the Soviet period, collectivization of the Nenets' economic activity, together with the exploitation of petroleum and natural gas (particularly from the 1960s) resulted in mass migration of ethnic Russians to the region.

In March 1994 the federal President, Boris Yeltsin, suspended a resolution by the district administration that had ordered a referendum on the reconstitution of the territory as the 'Nenets Republic'. A businessman, Vladimir Butov, was elected as head of the district administration in December 1996 and was re-elected in 2001. In June 2002 a warrant was issued for the arrest of Butov on charges of abuse of office. A further arrest warrant against Butov was issued in July 2003, after he had allegedly assaulted a police officer in St Petersburg. A prominent source of opposition to Butov was believed to be the petroleum company LUKoil, which objected to the preferential treatment granted in the AOk to the Nenets Oil Company (NNK), which Butov controlled. In January 2005 the federal Supreme Court ruled that Butov was not permitted to seek a further term in office at the forthcoming gubernatorial election. On 6 February Aleksei

Barinov, the former head of a subsidiary of LUKoil, was elected Governor, receiving 48.5% of votes cast, in the final such election in Russia prior to the introduction of a system of appointed regional leaders. Some 20% of votes were cast 'against all candidates', and the candidate of the pro-Government United Russia was placed only fourth in the first round of polling.

In May 2006 Sergei Mironov, the Chairman of the upper house of the federal parliament, the Federation Council, ordered the dismissal of one of the representatives of the Nenets AOk in the chamber, alongside three other senators, officially on the grounds that they were involved in commercial activities forbidden by law on account of their status. However, the district legislature rejected this demand. Later in the month all four senators dismissed by Mironov announced what was termed their 'voluntary resignation'. Meanwhile, the federal Office of the Prosecutor-General commenced an investigation into Barinov on charges of embezzlement and the misuse of budgetary funds. Two days after Barinov's arrest on 23 May, around 500 people were reported to have participated in a demonstration in Naryan-Mar in support of the Governor. Reports suggested that one cause of the dispute between the federal and district authorities was Barinov's insistence that Severnaya Neft, a local subsidiary of the state-controlled petroleum firm Rosneft, pay tax arrears of around US $33m. In June federal president Vladimir Putin suspended Barinov from office and appointed the Chief Federal Inspector for the AOk, Valerii Potapenko, as acting Governor. In mid-July a district court in Archangel ruled that Barinov should remain in custody, pending the outcome of the investigation into the charges against him. On 21 July Putin dismissed Barinov as Governor and nominated Potapenko as his successor; this nomination was approved by a unanimous vote of the district legislature on 7 August. In September 2007 the Archangel court imposed a three-year suspended sentence on Barinov for financial malpractice and abuse of office.

Meanwhile, in May 2007 the Governor of Archangel Oblast, Nikolai Kiselev, failed to sign a bilateral co-operation agreement with the authorities of the Nenets AOk; the agreement had been reached after lengthy negotiations in late 2006 in order to avert a transfer of powers from the Nenets AOk to Archangel. At elections to the State Duma on 2 December, UR won about 48.8% of votes cast in the AOk (with a turn-out of 52.5%); the Chairman of the Deputies' Assembly attributed this result (one of the lowest in the country) to continuing strong opposition within the AOk to a proposed merger with Archangel.

ECONOMY

In 2004 the Nenets AOk's gross regional product amounted to 42,354.0m. roubles. At the end of 2005 the AOk contained 183 km of railway track and 69 km of paved roads. The AOk's major ports are Naryan-Mar and Amderma.

The territory's agriculture, which in 2005 employed 10.4% of the work-force and produced goods to a value of 281m. roubles, consists mainly of reindeer-breeding (around two-thirds of its territory are reindeer pasture), fishing, hunting and fur farming. There are substantial reserves of petroleum, natural gas and gas condensate. In 1997 Exxon Arkhangelsk, an affiliate of Exxon of the USA (now ExxonMobil), purchased a 50% stake in the development of oilfields in Timan-Pechora, although it was forced to withdraw after problems with tender arrangements. Petroleum deposits in the region were developed only slowly, although a new sea terminal for petroleum transportation was opened at Varandei in 2000. The initial annual capacity of this terminal, which was constructed by LUKoil and which was to be served by its fleet of ice-breaking tankers, was over 1m. metric tons. Meanwhile, the US company ConocoPhillips announced its intention to invest US $500m. in a joint-venture in the region in association with the regional subsidiary of LUKoil, Naryanmarneftegaz. Other sectors of the district's industry included the processing of agricultural products and the generation of electricity. Industry employed 47.8% of the AOk's work-force in 2005 and produced output worth 33,749m. roubles in 2004.

The economically active population in the territory numbered 23,000 in 2005, when 11.4% of the labour force were unemployed. In 2005 the average monthly wage was some 23,016.8 roubles. The AOk government budget recorded a deficit of 1,722.5m. roubles in 2005. No figures were available for external trade in that year. In 2005 foreign investment totalled US $553.8m., compared with $39.4m in the previous year. At the end of 2005 there were 90 small businesses registered in the AOk, providing employment to around 800 people.

DIRECTORY

Head of the District Administration: VALERII N. POTAPENKO (appointment confirmed 7 August 2006), 164700 Archangel obl., Nenets AOk, Naryan-Mar, ul. Smidovicha 20; tel. (81853) 4-21-13;

fax (81853) 4-22-69; e-mail nenadm@inbox.ru; internet www
.adm-nao.ru.

Chairman of the Deputies' Assembly: Igor V. Koshin, 164700
Archangel obl., Nenets AOk, Naryan-Mar, ul. Smidovicha 20; tel.
(81853) 4-21-59; fax (81853) 4-20-11; e-mail pred@atnet.ru.

**Chief Representative of the Nenets Autonomous Okrug in
Archangel Oblast:** Sergei P. Kozlov, 163000 Archangel, ul. K.
Marksa 9; tel. (822) 20-78-89; fax (822) 20-78-90.

**Chief Representative of the Nenets Autonomous Okrug in the
Russian Federation:** Tatyana A. Malysheva, 119019 Moscow, ul.
Novyi Arbat 19/1120; tel. (495) 203-90-39; fax (495) 203-91-74; e-mail
neninter@atnet.ru.

Head of Naryan-Mar City Administration (Mayor): Yurii V.
Rodionovskii, 164700 Archangel obl., Nenets AOk, Naryan-Mar, ul.
Lenina 12; tel. (81853) 2-21-53; fax (495) 253-51-00; e-mail goradm@
atnet.ru; internet www.adm-nmar.ru.

Southern Federal Okrug

Republic of Adygeya

The Republic of Adygeya is situated in the foothills of the Greater Caucasus, a land-locked region in the basin of the Kuban river, surrounded by Krasnodar Krai. The Republic is in the Southern Federal Okrug and the North Caucasus Economic Area. The Republic is characterized by open grassland and fertile soil. The Republic covers 7,600 sq km (2,930 sq miles). At January 2007, according to official estimates, it had 441,199 inhabitants and a population density of 58.1 per sq km. At the time of the 2002 census 64.5% of the population were ethnically Russian, 24.2% were Adyge (Lower Circassian or Kiakh), 3.4% Armenian, 2.0% Ukrainian and 0.8% Kurdish. Almost all of the Adyge population speak the national tongue, Adyge (part of the Abkhazo-Adyge group of Caucasian languages), as their native language, although most also speak Russian. The dominant religion in Adygeya, owing to the preponderance of ethnic Russians, is Orthodox Christianity, but the traditional religion of the Adyges is Islam. Some 52.5% of the population of the Republic lived in urban areas in January 2007. The administrative centre of Adygeya is the only large city, Maikop, which had a total of 156,800 inhabitants in January 2006, according to official estimates. The Republic is included in the time zone GMT+3.

HISTORY

The Adyges were traditionally renowned for their unrivalled horsemanship and marksmanship. They emerged as a distinct Circassian ethnic group in the 13th century, when they inhabited much of the area between the Don river and the Caucasus, and the Black Sea and the Stavropol plateau. They were conquered by the Mongol Empire in the 13th century. In 1557 the Adyges entered into an alliance with the Russian Empire, as protection against the Tatar Khanate of Crimea and against Turkic groups such as the Karachai, the Kumyks and the Nogai, which had retreated into the Caucasus from the Mongol forces of Temujin (Chinghiz or Ghengis Khan). Russian settlers subsequently moved into the Don and Kuban regions, causing unrest among the Adyges and other Circassian peoples, many of whom supported the Ottoman Empire against Russia in the Crimean War of 1853–56. The Circassians were finally defeated by the Russians in 1864. Most were forced either to emigrate or to move to the plains that were under Russian control. A Kuban-Black Sea Soviet Republic was established in 1918, but the region was soon occupied by anti-communist forces ('Whites'). Eventually the Red Army prevailed. The Adyge Autonomous Oblast was established on 27 July 1922. From August 1922 until August 1928 it was known as the Adyge (Circassian) Autonomous Oblast. The Oblast was ruled from Stavropol until it was included in Krasnodar Krai, which was constituted in 1937.

From the mid-1980s the Adyge Khase Movement, which demanded the formation of a national legislative council for Adyges, was formed. Adygeya officially declared its sovereignty on 28 June 1991; an inter-parliamentary council was subsequently formed between Adygeya and the other Circassian federal subjects (Kabardino-Balkariya and Karachayevo-Cherkessiya). A Constitution, which formally provided for the recognition of Adygeya as a republic, separate from the surrounding Krai, was adopted on 10 March 1995, confirming a decision of the Supreme Soviet of the RSFSR of 3 June 1991. The new Constitution provided for the institution of a bicameral legislature, the Khase (State Council), comprising a Council of Representatives (the upper chamber) and a Council of the Republic.

In an election held on 13 January 2002 the republican President Aslan Dzharimov was conclusively defeated; he was succeeded by Khazrat Sovmen, the owner of a gold-mining co-operative, who was subsequently appointed to a senior position in the pro-presidential United Russia (UR). In 2003 the Khase approved constitutional changes providing for the reconstitution of the legislature on a unicameral basis with effect from the elections due to be held in 2006. Some 10,000 people took part in a demonstration in Maikop in April 2005 to protest against proposals to reunite Adygeya with Krasnodar Krai. The demands for territorial reunification were led within Adygeya by the Union of Slavs of Adygeya and by the republican branch of the Communist Party of the Russian Federation (CPRF). In mid-May Sovmen issued a decree dissolving the Khase, the first time that a regional governor or president had issued such a decree in post-Soviet Russia. Following a meeting between Sovmen and the Presidential Representative in the Southern Federal Okrug, Dmitrii Kozak, Sovmen annulled the decree.

In December 2005 a congress of the Union of Slavs of Adygeya adopted a resolution requesting that federal President Vladimir Putin consider the reabsorption of the Republic into Krasnodar Krai, and announced that it was to launch a petition in support of a merger. In January 2006, moreover, the Council of the Republic approved draft legislation that permitted the holding of a referendum on the dissolution of the Republic. These proposals were rejected, however, by the Council of Representatives in February. At the end of the month the leaders of Adygeya and Krasnodar Krai, meeting in Maikop, declared that no political merger of the two territories was planned. However, later in the year, various state administrative agencies in Adygeya were merged with those of Krasnodar Krai, while others were liquidated or renamed. At elections to the new unicameral Khase, held on 12 March 2006, UR was the most successful grouping, receiving 33.7% of the votes for those seats elected on the basis of proportional representation (and, in all, 30 of the 54 elective seats). The CPRF was placed second, with 14.9%, followed by the Industrial Party (the Unified Industrial Party of Russia, with the support of the Union of Slavs of Adygeya and various Cossack groups), which obtained 12.9% of the votes cast. The Agrarian Party of Russia also won election to the Khase on the basis of proportional representation, with 11.3%. Some 6.6% of votes were cast 'against all candidates', and the rate of participation in the elections was around 45%.

In early April 2006 reports that President Sovmen had announced his resignation at the second session of the new Khase prompted rallies in his support (and against any change to the status of Adygeya). Sovmen stated that the principal factor behind his offer to resign was the imposition of pressure on the republican authorities by Kozak, who was regarded as the principal proponent of the possible merger of the territory with Krasnodar. On 11 April Sovmen met the Chief of Staff of the office of the federal President, Sergei Sobyanin, and formally presented his written resignation. Consequently, Sovmen met federal President Putin in Moscow on 17 April, when he again tendered his formal resignation. However, Putin was reported to have refused the resignation, and requested that Sovmen remain in office until the end of his mandate, which was due to expire in early 2007. On 25 October 2006 the Khase voted to approve UR's nomination of Aslan Tkhakushinov (who had won only 2.1% of votes cast in the republican presidential election in 2002) as President of Adygeya. Despite a vociferous campaign waged by Sovmen for his re-election, Putin officially submitted Tkhakushinov's nomination on 6 December, and it was confirmed by the Khase on 13 December. Tkhakushinov was inaugurated as President on 13 January 2007, upon the expiry of Sovmen's mandate; he dismissed speculation that the reabsorption of Adygeya into Krasnodar Krai remained under discussion.

ECONOMY

In 2004 the gross regional product of Adygeya was 13,299.5m. roubles, or 29,897.3 roubles per head. In 2005 there were 160 km of railway track and 1,589 km of paved roads in Adygeya.

Agricultural production consists mainly of animal husbandry, grain, sunflowers, sugar beet, tobacco and vegetables, cucurbit (gourds and melons) cultivation and viniculture, and is one of Russia's principal centres for the production of grape wine. Agriculture employed 13.9% of the work-force and generated 4,372m. roubles in 2005. There is some extraction of natural gas. Food-processing typically accounts for almost one-half of industrial production. Timber-processing, mechanical engineering and metal-working are also significant. Adygeya lies along the route of the Blue Stream pipeline, completed in 2002, which delivers gas to Turkey, and planned petroleum pipelines from the South Caucasus and Dagestan to the Black Sea ports of Novorossiisk and Tuapse (both in Krasnodar Krai). In 2005 industry engaged 17.0% of the work-force and generated 5,761m. roubles in 2004.

In 2005 the economically active population numbered 202,000, and some 12.9% of the labour force were unemployed. The average monthly wage was 5,123.0 roubles. A report issued in 2006 by a state body found that Adygeya was one of the 11 most impoverished federal subjects in Russia. In 2005 there was a budgetary surplus of 72.0m. roubles. In that year external trade amounted to only US $3.1m. in exports and $7.6m. in imports. There was relatively little foreign investment in the Republic: in 2005 it amounted to just $1.6m. At the end of that year there were 2,164 small businesses registered in Adygeya, providing employment to 13,100 people.

DIRECTORY

President: ASLAN TKHAKUSHINOV (appointment confirmed 13 December 2006, assumed office 13 January 2007), 352700 Adygeya, Maikop, ul. Zhukovskogo 22; tel. (8772) 52-45-63; fax (8772) 52-27-17; internet adygea.kubic.ru.

Prime Minister: MURAT KUMPILOV, 352700 Adygeya, Maikop, ul. Pionerskaya 199; tel. (8772) 57-00-22; fax (8772) 52-27-17; e-mail premier@adygheya.ru.

Chairman of the State Council (Khase): ANATOLII S. IVANOV, 385000 Adygeya, Maikop, ul. Zhukovskogo 22; tel. (8772) 52-10-38; fax (8772) 57-11-94; e-mail info@gshra.ru; internet www.gshra.ru.

Chief Representative of the Republic of Adygeya in the Russian Federation: ALEKSANDR YE. SHINDER, 115184 Moscow, per. Staryi Tolmachevskii 6; tel. (495) 230-30-01; fax (495) 230-07-48.

Head of Maikop City Administration: MIKHAIL N. CHERNI-CHENKO, 352700 Adygeya, Maikop, ul. Krasnooktyabrskaya 21; tel. (8772) 52-27-61; fax (8772) 52-63-19; e-mail inform@admins.maykop.ru; internet www.admins.maykop.ru.

Chechen (Nokchi) Republic

The Chechen (Nokchi) Republic is located on the northern slopes of the Caucasus. It forms part of the Southern Federal Okrug and the North Caucasus Economic Area. To the east, the Republic abuts into Dagestan. Stavropol Krai lies to the north-west and North Osetiya—Alaniya and Ingushetiya lie to the west. There is an international boundary with Georgia to the south-west. The exact delimitation of much of the western boundary remained uncertain, awaiting final agreement between the Chechen and Ingush authorities on the division of the territory of the former Checheno-Ingush ASSR. The Republic comprises lowlands along the principal waterway, the River Terek, and around the capital, Groznyi, in the north; mixed fields, pastures and forests in the Chechen plain; and high mountains and glaciers in the south. The former Checheno-Ingush ASSR had an area of some 19,300 sq km (7,450 sq miles), most of which subsequently became the Chechen Republic. At January 2007, according to official estimates, the Republic had a population of 1,183,745. At the time of the 2002 census 93.5% of the population were ethnically Chechen, 3.7% were Russian and 0.8% Kumyk. The Chechens, who refer to themselves as Nokchi, are closely related to the Ingush (both of whom are known collectively as Vainakhs). They are Sunni Muslims, and their language is one of the Nakh dialects of the Caucasian linguistic family. Only 34.4% of the Republic's population lived in urban areas in January 2007. The capital of the Republic, Groznyi, was founded in 1818 and had a population of 218,200 in January 2006, according to official estimates, compared with a total of 405,000 in 1989. The Republic is included in the time zone GMT+3.

HISTORY

In the 18th century the Russian, Ottoman and Persian (Iranian) Empires fought for control of the Caucasus region. The Chechens violently resisted the Russian forces with the uprising of Sheikh Mansur in 1785 and throughout the Caucasian War of 1817–64. Chechnya was finally conquered by Russia in 1858 after the resistance led by Imam Shamil (an ethnic Avar) ended. In 1865 many Chechens were exiled to the Ottoman Empire. Subsequently, ethnic Russians began to settle in the lowlands, particularly after petroleum reserves were discovered around Groznyi in 1893. Upon the dissolution of the Mountain (Gorskaya) People's Republic in 1922, Chechen and Ingush Autonomous Oblasts were established; they merged in 1934 and became the Checheno-Ingush ASSR in 1936. This was dissolved in 1944, whereupon both peoples were deported en masse to Central Asia and Siberia. On 9 January 1957 the ASSR was reconstituted, but with limited provisions made for the restoration of property to the dispossessed.

During 1991 an All-National Congress of the Chechen People seized effective power in the Checheno-Ingush ASSR and agreed with Ingush leaders to divide the Republic into two units. Exact borders were to be decided by future negotiation, but by far the largest proportion of the territory was to constitute a Chechen Republic (Chechnya). Elections to the presidency of this new polity, which claimed independence from Russia, were held on 27 October, and were won by Gen. Dzhokhar Dudayev. In 1993 the territory refused to participate in the Russian general election and rejected the new federal Constitution. Against a background of armed raids by rebel Chechens, in July 1994 federal President Boris Yeltsin declared his support for an Interim Council, headed by Umar Avturkhanov, which had proclaimed itself the rightful Government of Chechnya, in opposition to the administration of Dudayev. By September armed conflict had broken out between the two groups. On 11 December Yeltsin ordered the invasion of Chechnya by some 40,000 ground troops. By January 1995 the federal forces had taken control of Groznyi. In an effort to end hostilities, Yeltsin signed an accord with the Chechen premier granting the Republic special status. In March the federal authorities installed a Government of National Revival in Chechnya, chaired by Salambek Khadzhiyev. In April more than 100 civilians were reported to have been killed by federal troops in a so-called 'cleansing' operation (*zachistka*) in the village of Samashki. In June the federal premier, Viktor Chernomyrdin, intervened in telephone negotiations to end a siege, in which more than 100 people

were killed, by militants associated with the rebel Chechen leader, Shamil Basayev, who had taken hostage around 1,000 people in a hospital in Budennovsk, Stavropol Krai. In November a new Chechen Government loyal to the federal authorities, headed by Doku Zavgayev, was appointed. A further substantial hostage-taking incident conducted by Chechen militants took place in Kizlyar, Dagestan, in January 1996, increasing demands across Russia for the Government to find a settlement to the Chechen conflict; other incidences of hostage-taking attributed to supporters of Chechen independence took place in Chechnya, in other regions of Russia and, less frequently, internationally during the late 1990s and early 2000s.

On 21 April 1996 Dudayev was killed in a Russian missile attack; he was succeeded by Zelimkhan Yandarbiyev, who concluded a cease-fire agreement with Yeltsin on 27 May. The truce, which took effect from 1 June, ended following Yeltsin's re-election as President in July. In August rebel forces led a successful assault on Groznyi, prompting the negotiation of a cease-fire by Lt-Gen. Aleksandr Lebed, the recently appointed Secretary of the Security Council. An agreement, the Khasavyurt Accords, was signed in Dagestan on 31 August. The proposed peace settlement incorporated a moratorium on discussion of Chechnya's status for five years. An agreement on the withdrawal of all federal troops by January 1997 was signed in November 1996, signalling the end of a war that had claimed up to 100,000 lives. A formal Treaty of Peace and Principles of Relations was signed on 12 May 1997 and ratified by the Chechen Parliament the following day.

Meanwhile, on 1 January 1997 a presidential election was held in the Republic (which subsequently renamed itself the Chechen Republic of Ichkeriya), at which Khalid (Aslan) Maskhadov, a former rebel chief of staff, obtained 64.8% of the votes cast, defeating Basayev. Basayev, none the less, served as Maskhadov's First Deputy Prime Minister for several months in 1997, being reappointed to that position for a period of six months in 1998. During 1998 two incidents drew attention to the continuing disorder in Chechnya: Valentin Vlasov, the representative of the federal President to the Republic, was kidnapped in May and held hostage for six months; later in the year four engineers from the United Kingdom and New Zealand were captured and killed. By the end of the year Groznyi was no longer secure for the Government and Maskhadov was mainly based on the outskirts of the city.

Meanwhile, in 1997 the republican authorities announced their intention to introduce Islamic *Shari'a* law, in contravention of the federal Constitution. Hostilities between armed groupings in Gudermes in July 1998 resulted in the outlawing of oppositionist Islamist groups purportedly associated with the austere Wahhabi sect. From August 1999 Islamist factions associated with Basayev launched a series of attacks into Dagestan, with the aim of protecting and extending the jurisdiction of a 'separate Islamic territory' proclaimed by rebels in Dagestan in the previous year. (The territory was returned to federal rule in mid-September.) A series of bomb explosions in August and September in Moscow, Dagestan and Volgodonsk (Rostov Oblast), officially attributed to Chechen separatists, killed almost 300 people, prompting the redeployment of federal armed forces in Chechnya from late September in what the recently appointed federal premier Vladimir Putin described as an 'anti-terrorist operation'. The federal authorities declined requests from Maskhadov for the negotiation of a settlement, stating that it recognized only the Moscow-based State Council of the Chechen Republic, which had been established by former members of the republican legislature.

In February 2000 federal forces took control of Groznyi and proceeded to destroy much of the city; many republican and federal administrative bodies were relocated to Gudermes. On 20 June Akhmad haji Kadyrov, a former senior mufti and previously an ally of Maskhadov, was inaugurated as the Head of the Republican Administration (directly responsible to the federal presidency, to which Putin had recently been elected). In October it was announced that all Chechen ministries and government departments were to be relocated from Gudermes to Groznyi, with effect from the following month.

In January 2001 Putin transferred control of military operations in Chechnya from the Ministry of Defence to the Federal Security Service (FSB), which was to strengthen its presence in the region. The majority of defence ministry troops in the region were to be withdrawn, leaving a 15,000-strong infantry division and 7,000 interior ministry troops. Stanislav Ilyasov, a former Governor of Stavropol Krai, was appointed as Chechen premier.

In late September 2001, encountering increasing international demands for a political solution to the Chechen conflict, Putin announced a 72-hour amnesty. However, the first official, direct negotiations to take place since 1999 were insufficient to result in any substantive agreement. Rebel activity increased markedly during the first half of 2002; although the political authority of Maskhadov, who remained in hiding, had dwindled, his military leadership of what was known as the State Defence Committee (to which Basayev was reportedly appointed, in a senior position, in July) became increasingly prominent as a focus for resistance to federal troops. In August federal forces experienced their single largest loss of life since the commencement of operations in 1999, when rebels shot down a military helicopter, killing 118 troops. In September Chechen rebels staged incursions into Ingushetiya, with intense fighting taking place near the village of Galashki.

On 23–26 October 2002 a so-called 'suicide battalion' of more than 40 heavily armed rebels held captive more than 800 people in a Moscow theatre, demanding the withdrawal of federal troops from Chechnya. The siege ended when élite federal forces stormed the theatre, having filled the building with an incapacitating gas. The rebels were killed and it subsequently emerged that at least 129 hostages had died, in almost all cases owing to the toxic effects of the gas. Although Maskhadov issued a statement condemning the rebels' use of terrorist methods, his deputy premier, Akhmed Zakayev, was arrested in Denmark on the orders of the federal Government. In early November Basayev announced that groups linked to him had perpetrated the hostage-taking in Moscow, and stated that Maskhadov had not known of the incident. Denmark formally rejected demands for Zakayev's extradition, and he took up residence in the United Kingdom, which granted him asylum in November 2003.

In November 2002 Ilyasov was appointed to the federal Government as Minister without Portfolio, with responsibility for the development of Chechnya. He was succeeded as republican premier by Capt. (retd) Mikhail Babich, who had previously held senior positions in the regional administrations of Ivanovo and Moscow Oblasts. However, Babich's premiership proved short-lived, and he resigned in January 2003. Anatolii Popov, hitherto the deputy chairman of the state commission for the reconstruction of Chechnya, was appointed in his stead in mid-February. Meanwhile, in late November 2002 Ilyasov announced that a referendum on a new republican constitution was to be held in March 2003. In December 2002 at least 83 people were killed, and more than 150 others injured, when suicide bombers detonated bombs in two vehicles stationed outside the headquarters of the republican Government in Groznyi. (Basayev subsequently claimed responsibility for the attack.)

The referendum on the draft constitution for Chechnya, describing the republic (which was henceforth to be known as the Chechen–Nokchi Republic) as both a sovereign entity, with its own citizenship, and an integral part of the Russian Federation, proceeded, as scheduled, on 23 March 2003, despite concerns that the instability of the Republic would prevent the poll from being free and fair. The draft Constitution also provided for the holding of fresh elections to a strengthened republican presidency and legislature. According to the official results, some 88.4% of the electorate participated in the plebiscite, of whom 96.0% supported the Constitution. Two further questions, on the method of electing the republican president and parliament, were supported by 95.4% and 96.1% of participants, respectively. However, independent observers challenged the results, reporting that the rate of participation by the electorate had been much lower than officially reported.

Political violence continued to dominate Chechen affairs. In April 2003 at least 22 people were killed in two separate incidents when their vehicles detonated landmines. In May at least 59 people were killed when suicide bombers attacked government offices in the northern city of Znamenskoye. Two days later another suicide bombing at a religious festival attended by Kadyrov resulted in at least 14 deaths, although Kadyrov escaped unhurt. On 21 June Kadyrov inaugurated an interim legislative body, the 42-member State Council, comprising appointees. In July Putin announced that a presidential election in Chechnya was to be held on 5 October.

From 1 September 2003 the control of military operations in Chechnya, which had previously been the domain of the FSB, was assumed by the federal Ministry of Internal Affairs; it was announced that such operations were no longer regarded as having an 'anti-terrorist' character but were, rather, to form part of an 'operation to protect law and constitutional order'. Meanwhile, campaigning for the presidential election commenced; however, the withdrawal of Aslanbek Aslakhanov, a representative of the Republic to the State Duma, the lower chamber of the federal legislature, and the debarring of business executive Malik Saidullayev effectively removed any major challenges to Kadyrov's candidacy. On 5 October Kadyrov was elected President, receiving 87.7% of votes cast, according to official figures. Participation in the poll was reported to be 82.6%. Kadyrov subsequently reappointed Popov as premier, although he was replaced on 16 March 2004 by Sergei Abramov, hitherto an official in the audit chamber of the Gosudarstvennaya Duma.

A raid into Dagestan in December 2003, in which border guards were killed and hostages taken, was attributed to Chechen militants. In February 2004 Yandarbiyev was killed by a car bomb in Qatar. Two Russian citizens, widely reputed to be secret service agents, were subsequently tried for the murder by a Qatari court; in June they were both sentenced to life imprisonment. However, they were returned to Russia to serve out their sentences in December, and in early 2005 it was reported that they were no longer being held in detention.

An explosion in Groznyi on 9 May 2004, at a commemoration to mark Victory Day, resulted in the deaths of several senior officials, including Kadyrov and Khusain Isayev, the head of the republican legislature. Abramov assumed presidential responsibilities in an acting capacity, pending elections, while Ramzan Kadyrov, the son of the assassinated President and the leader of the presidential security service (known unofficially as the *Kadyrovtsy* and reported to number some 3,000), which was widely believed to have been implicated in several unexplained 'disappearances', was appointed as First Deputy Prime Minister. Chechen militants were widely suspected of involvement in a series of raids on interior ministry targets in Ingushetiya, which took place in June. A presidential election was held on 29 August, when Maj.-Gen. Alu Alkhanov, an officer in the republican interior ministry troops, and the favoured candidate of the federal Government, was victorious, receiving some 73.5% of votes cast, according to official figures. The rate of participation was reported to be 85.2%. Council of Europe observers criticized the election as undemocratic. Suggestions that the political process had become more stable appeared to be inaccurate; there were several attacks by Chechen militants in Moscow, including the destruction by suicide bombers of two passenger planes that had departed from the city, as a result of which around 100 people were killed, in the days preceding and following Alkhanov's election. The taking of hostages at a school in Beslan, North Osetiya—Alaniya, in September, which was also attributed to Chechen elements, and as a result of which 331 people, including 186 children, were killed (according to official figures), further illustrated the destabilizing effect on the North Caucasus region of the unresolved status of Chechnya. Indeed, in 2004–06 there was a marked increase in militant activity, including bombings and assassinations of police and state officials, in several republics of the North Caucasus, including Dagestan, Ingushetiya, North Osetiya—Alaniya and the Kabardino-Balkar Republic. Meanwhile, following his inauguration, Alkhanov subsequently reappointed Abramov as Prime Minister of Chechnya, and in October Ramzan Kadyrov was made an adviser on security to the recently appointed Presidential Representative in the Southern Federal Okrug, Dmitrii Kozak, while retaining his existing positions within Chechnya. In April 2005 Alkhanov announced that he had joined the United Russia (UR) party, which was strongly supportive of the federal authorities.

Meanwhile, in February 2005 Maskhadov announced that he had ordered separatist fighters to observe a unilateral one-month cease-fire. On 8 March, however, he was killed during a special operation by FSB forces in the village of Tolstoi-Yurt, north of Groznyi, and was replaced as leader of the State Defence Committee (and, as such, 'President' of the 'Chechen Republic of Ichkeriya') by Abdul-Khalim Sadulayev; Sadulayev, like Maskhadov before him, announced his willingness to enter into negotiations with the federal authorities in order to restore peace to Chechnya, but stated that, in the absence of such negotiations, the use of force was legitimate. In early May a senior rebel commander, Doku Umarov, stated that Chechen militants would launch large-scale military operations in other regions of Russia before the end of the year; later in the month Sadulayev announced the appointment of new military commanders to what were described as various sectors of the 'Caucasus Front' (several of these commanders were killed during the following year). In late May Sadulayev issued a decree naming Umarov as 'Vice-president' of the rebel leadership and a statement to the effect that the expulsion of Russian forces from Chechnya would not constitute an end to the conflict, as the Chechens would be obligated to take vengeance against those he termed 'unbelievers' (i.e. non-Muslims) for their actions in Chechnya. In July at least 15 people were killed by a car bomb in Znamenskoye. In August Sadulayev dismissed the rebel Chechen 'parliament-in-exile' and a network of 'ambassadors', whom he collectively accused of financial malpractice and incompetence; he also appointed a new rebel 'Government' at the end of the month, to which Basayev was appointed as 'First Deputy Prime Minister', while Zakayev was appointed to represent the rebel authorities internationally. In September Basayev was interviewed by a US television station, and stated that he accepted his designation as a 'terrorist'. In October Basayev claimed responsibility for the organization, earlier in the month, of a co-ordinated series of attacks against law enforcement bodies in Nalchik, the Kabardino-Balkar Republic, in which at least 130 people were reported to have been killed.

Tensions between Chechens and the most numerous ethnic group in neighbouring Dagestan, the Avars, were also heightened on several occasions from the first half of 2005. This was the result of security forces associated with the Chechen authorities, particularly *Kadyrovtsy*, making incursions into Dagestan, apparently in response to Chechen rebels taking refuge in that Republic. Moreover, in June 11 villagers were abducted during a 'cleansing' operation in the eastern village of Borozdinovskaya. Some 400 people, principally ethnic Avars, subsequently fled to Dagestan and remained there for several weeks. The operation was condemned by both the Chechen and federal authorities, and Alkhanov subsequently dismissed the administrator of the district in which the village was located. A number of clashes in Chechnya were also reported between members of the *Kadyrovtsy* and federal forces.

On 27 November 2005 elections were held in the Republic to a new, bicameral legislature, comprising the 18-seat Council of the Republic (the upper chamber) and the 40-seat People's Assembly (the lower chamber). Voter turn-out was alleged to be around 60%, but international observers expressed doubt that the vote was free and fair. The majority of deputies in the new parliament (33 out of 58) were from UR, while the Communist Party of the Russian Federation, the pro-market Union of Rightist Forces and the Eurasian Union also obtained representation, as did 14 deputies with no party affiliation. Thus, the position of Kadyrov, a member of UR was consolidated; furthermore, Kadyrov at this time held the position of acting premier, following an injury to Abramov in a automobile accident earlier in the month. Members of UR were elected to chair both chambers in mid-December. Visiting the legislature at its opening session, President Putin made a speech referring to Russia as 'one of the pillars of the Islamic world'. Later in the month Putin appointed Sergei Ivanov, Deputy Chairman and Minister of Defence in the federal Government, to take charge of the reconstruction of Chechnya; it was also announced that the Chechen presidential security service (i.e. the *Kadyrovtsy*) was to be abolished and integrated into a restructured military command in the Republic. (This measure took effect from late April 2006.) In late December 2005, speaking at a press conference in Moscow, Alkhanov demanded a sharp reduction in the federal military presence in Chechnya, calling for increased powers to be granted to republican and local law enforcement agencies. He also stated that there had been a steep decline in the number of acts of terrorism committed in the Republic, from 113 in 2004 to 39 in 2005.

In February 2006 Sadulayev reorganized the separatist 'Government', notably dismissing Zakayev; it was reported that the reorganization was intended to strengthen the Islamic orientation of the rebel administration. (Zakayev was, however appointed as 'Minister of Foreign Affairs' in May.) Also in early February Kadyrov was nominated to head the republican branch of UR. On 28 February Abramov formally resigned as Prime Minister. On 4 March the People's Assembly unanimously approved the appointment of Kadyrov as his successor. Although this appointment effectively confirmed the distribution of power that had been in place in the Republic for several months, it was not without controversy. As acting Prime Minister, Kadyrov had spoken in favour of permitting men to marry up to four women (although this would be in clear breach of the family code, he stated that no change to legislation would be required for this to be permitted) and had expressed support for other policies associated with Islamism. Meanwhile, rebel forces intensified their operations in Chechnya, and a statement by the separatist authorities claimed that some 70 supporters of the official administration had been killed in fighting in late February–early March. Rebel sources reported that some 98 Russian military personnel had been killed or injured in clashes in the first week of May. In mid-June Akhmar-haji Gazikhanov, who had been elected as Chairman of the Council of the Republic in December 2005, was dismissed; he was replaced by Vakhit Mantsayev.

On 17 June 2006 Sadulayev was killed by special forces in Chechnya. He was succeeded as the separatist 'President' by Umarov, who, on 27 June, announced the appointment of Basayev as his deputy. On 10 July it was announced that Basayev had been killed by federal special forces in an explosion in Ingushetiya. Basayev's death was expected to weaken the rebels substantially, as he had repeatedly proven to be an efficient and ruthless military leader. On 15 July the director of the FSB, Nikolai Patrushev, demanded that Chechen rebels surrender their arms and enter into negotiations with the federal or official republican authorities. Alkhanov subsequently suggested that this effective amnesty be extended until 1 January 2007, and also proclaimed August 2006 as a 'month of reconciliation and agreement'. On 25 September the State Duma approved an amnesty by President Putin for all fighters in the North Caucasus, except for those associated with particularly severe crimes or acts of terrorism. The amnesty was to cover the period between 13 December 1999 and 14 January 2007.

In the mid-2000s there was increasing speculation that the federal authorities were seeking to reunite Chechnya and Ingushetiya in one federal subject. In December 2005, speaking as acting premier of Chechnya, Ramzan Kadyrov urged Chechnya's legislature to take steps to restore the Chechen polity's previous borders (i.e. those of the Checheno-Ingush ASSR). In March 2006 the Chairman of the People's Assembly, Dukvakha Abdurakhmanov, also expressed support for such a proposal. However, the Ingush authorities repeatedly ruled out the possibility of re-establishing a combined polity. Tensions between the two Republics were heightened in September 2006, when eight people were killed in an exchange of fire between Ingush traffic police and Chechen interior ministry troops at a border checkpoint. Several days after the clashes, Abdurakhmanov and the Chairman of the Ingush legislature, Makhmud Sakalov, issued a joint statement calling for calm; a similar statement was issued one day later by Kadyrov and the President of Ingushetiya, Murat Zyazikov. In the same month, at a meeting in Mozdok, North Osetiya—Alaniya, attended by Alkhanov, Kozak and Zyazikov, it was agreed that Chechen and North Osetiyan security forces should be free to apprehend suspected militants on the territory of Ingushetiya without intervention by that Republic's authorities.

On 31 October 2006, at a Congress of Chechen Peoples in Groznyi, Kadyrov was elected to the ceremonial position of Chairman of the Assembly of Chechen Peoples; there had been widespread speculation that Alkhanov would cede the republican presidency to Kadyrov following the latter's 30th birthday earlier that month, following which Kadyrov would be constitutionally eligible to serve as President. There were indications that the security situation in Chechnya was deteriorating towards the end of 2006: in early November seven interior ministry troops were killed by Chechen rebels in the Sharoi district; a member of the same unit had been killed following an explosion on the previous day. On 18 November Movladi Baisarov, a former ally of Kadyrov (and an FSB commander) who had become one of his most outspoken opponents, was shot dead in Moscow by Chechen security forces. In November the commander of the foreign insurgent fighters in Chechnya, the Jordanian Abu Hafs al-Urdani, who was suspected of having played a key role in the school siege in Beslan in 2004, was killed in Khasavyurt, Dagestan, by federal troops. (In December Amir Mukhannad was selected to replace al-Urdani.) In February 2007 it was reported that two Chechens had been arrested on suspicion of involvement in the killing of an investigative journalist, Anna Politkovskaya, who had been a leading critic of the Russian military campaigns in Chechnya and the official Chechen leadership, in Moscow in October 2006.

In early February 2007 Alkhanov officially denied rumours that his resignation from the republican presidency was imminent and, in a reference to Kadyrov, criticized 'the cult of personality and idealization of one person'. However, on 15 February federal President Putin announced that he had accepted Alkhanov's resignation and appointed him to the post of deputy justice minister in the federal Government, thereby enabling Kadyrov, as Prime Minister, to assume the office of republican President in an acting capacity. Putin's subsequent nomination of Kadyrov to the republican presidency was approved by 56 of the 58 deputies in the People's Assembly on 2 March. Following Kadyrov's inauguration on 5 April, he reorganized the Republican Government, appointing a relation and hitherto deputy premier, Odes Baisultanov, as Prime Minister; the nomination was approved by the People's Assembly on 10 April. Kadyrov identified as main priorities the reduction of unemployment, the reconstruction of housing and payment of post-conflict compensation owed to civilians. He emphasized his opposition to the signature of a power-sharing treaty between the Chechen Republic and the federal authorities, as had been mooted since 2004.

In March 2007 the Council of Europe issued a statement condemning the continued use of torture and unlawful detention of civilians by law enforcement agencies operating in Chechnya, including a regional subdivision of the federal interior ministry. Two rebel military commanders were killed in operations by federal special forces in March and April. In June four officers attached to the federal interior ministry were sentenced to terms of imprisonment for the killing of six Chechen civilians during an operation in January 2002. On 21 June 2007 the Chechen Constitutional Assembly approved amendments to the Constitution, proposed by Kadyrov to bring it into accordance with federal legislation, which included the replacement of the bicameral People's Assembly with a unicameral legislature, the abolition of direct elections to the republican presidency, and the extension of the presidential term from four to five years; it was announced that the changes would be submitted to a referendum in the Republic on 2 December (to coincide with elections to the State Duma).

In September 2007 the People's Assembly voted to initiate legal action against a federal opposition leader (and former international chess champion), Garri Kasparov, after he described Kadyrov as a 'bandit'. In October the federal authorities announced that nine suspects, including a former Chechen senior official and a senior FSB officer, had been charged with involvement in the killing of Politkovskaya. Also in October a federal military commander announced that the number of federal troops in Chechnya would not be reduced in the immediate future (although Kadyrov had expressed support for a gradual withdrawal). Later that month Umarov issued a statement proclaiming himself emir of a 'North Caucasus Islamic state'. In response, in early November the rebel Chechen 'parliament-in-exile' announced that Umarov's powers as 'President' of the 'Chechen Republic of Ichkeriya' had been formally removed. The rebel 'Minister of Foreign Affairs' based in London, United Kingdom, Zakayev, condemned Umarov's statement, and subsequently received the support of senior rebel commanders. Later in October the chairman of the 'parliament-in-exile' issued a decree appointing Zakayev as 'Prime Minister', although this appointment was not recognized by supporters of Umarov.

In October 2007, during the campaign for the elections to the State Duma, four rallies (of which the largest, attended by some 20,000, was in Groznyi) were staged in support of Putin serving a third presidential term. In the same month leaders of the local branches of political parties, meeting in Groznyi, adopted a joint statement of confidence in Kadyrov. The official rate of participation in the elections to the State Duma, of 99.5%, was claimed to be the highest in any federal subject (although some opposition sources stated that the turn-out had been as low as 10%); UR were reported to have received about 99.4% of votes cast. About 96.2% of the electorate participated in the concurrent referendum on constitutional amendments, which were approved by 96.9% of votes cast, according to official figures.

From early 2008 there were frequent reports of insurgent attacks and clashes between militants and local police units reporting to Kadyrov throughout the Republic. Prior to the Russian military action in Georgia in August of that year, the presence of large numbers of Chechen combatants in the Georgian separatist regions of Abkhazia and South Ossetia was reported. Several thousand Chechen militia (who were presumed to have the approval of Kadyrov) supported Russian troops in their successful counter-offensive against Georgian forces in both regions. However, there was concern that Russia's recognition of the independence of Abkhazia and South Ossetia might encourage separatist sentiment in the Republic.

Early elections to the People's Assembly were conducted on 12 October 2008. In September the seven political parties registered in the Republic had signed a joint declaration pledging their commitment to abide by democratic standards, while, in an effort to create an impression of transparency, the regional authorities had created a public committee, 'For Honest Elections', to monitor the poll. On 15 October the regional Election Commission confirmed the validity of the results; UR, with 88.4% of votes cast, had won 37 seats and A Just Russia: Motherland/Pensioners/Life (having obtained 9.20% of votes) four seats in the 41-member legislature.

In late September 2008 Ruslan Yamadayev, a military leader, businessman and politician, who, together with his brother, Sulim, and other members of his family, had been engaged in a fierce feud with Kadyrov, was shot dead in central Moscow. Kadyrov denied any involvement in Yamadayev's killing; two suspects were arrested by police in Moscow in mid-October. Meanwhile, the reconstruction of much of Groznyi following the conflict was marked in October by the opening of a substantial mosque, named after the late President of Chechnya Akhmad haji Kadyrov, after the completion of a US $20m. project.

ECONOMY

Prior to the outbreak of armed hostilities in the region in 1994, Groznyi was the principal industrial centre in Chechnya. At the end of 2005 there were 304 km of railways and 2,800 km of paved roads in the Republic.

Chechnya's agriculture consisted mainly of horticulture, production of grain and sugar beet, grape wine and animal husbandry. Measured agricultural output in 2005 amounted to 4,784m. roubles. The Republic's main industrial activities were production of petroleum and petrochemicals, petroleum-refining, power engineering, manufacture of machinery and the processing of forestry and agricultural products. Conflict in 1994–96, and again from 1999, seriously damaged the economic infrastructure and disrupted both agricultural and industrial activity. A significant asset that could be sabotaged by, or displaced because of violence was one of Russia's major petroleum pipelines that crossed Chechnya: in the event of stability, transit fees from Caspian hydrocarbons could be a major source of revenue for the Republic. Moreover, all three petroleum refineries in the Republic were destroyed during the 1994–96 conflict. (The Republic had previously been the principal producer of aviation fuel within Russia.) In mid-1999 the Chechen section of a petroleum pipeline from Baku (Bakı), Azerbaijan, to Novorossiisk (Krasnodar Krai), was closed, owing to the lack of security in the region. However, attempts were being made to restore industry in the Republic; a sugar refinery and a brickworks were in operation there in 2001, and several new businesses opened thereafter. The principal petroleum company operating in the Republic in the early 2000s was Grozneftegaz, which was 51% owned by the state-controlled Rosneft and 49% by the republican Government. Output of petroleum in 2005 was 2.2m. metric tons; although this was somewhat less than one-half the production recorded in the Checheno-Ingush ASSR in 1990, it none the less reflected a sustained upturn in output that had commenced in 2001. Although no geological surveys had been carried out in the region since the 1980s, the reserves of petroleum in Chechnya were reportedly estimated at 83.2m. tons in the mid-2000s. A new polypropylene fabric factory was constructed in Groznyi in 2002. In March 2006 the republican authorities reached an agreement with the State Development Bank of the People's Republic of China on the establishment of a system of financing investment in Chechnya. It was reported that the bank was initially to invest some US $100m. in the region, principally in the construction sector, although it was anticipated that future investment might occur in the fields of automobile manufacturing and petroleum.

In 2005 the economically active population numbered 450,000, compared with 363,000 in 2003. (This increase was partially attributable to the return of former refugees to the Republic, particularly from Ingushetiya.) In 2005 the rate of unemployment was 74.2%. The average monthly wage in 2005 (the most recent year for which data were available) was 6,715.9 roubles. In 2005 the republican budget recorded a surplus of 1,396.1m. roubles. In that year, imports to and exports from the Republic were negligible. The federal budget for 2003 allocated some 3,500m. roubles to the Republic, under a programme that aimed to promote economic and social recovery. A five-year US $63.3m. programme of reconstruction, announced in 2006 and funded by the federal authorities, was to place particular emphasis on educational establishments and the repair and construction of highways. In March 2007 the airport at Groznyi was reopened, restoring air connections to Moscow for the first time since 1994. At the end of 2005 there were 139 small businesses officially registered in Chechnya, providing employment to 1,500 people.

DIRECTORY

President and Head of the Administration: Ramzan A. Kadyrov (appointment confirmed 2 March 2007, inaugurated 5 April 2007), 364000 Chechen (Nokchi) Rep., Groznyi, ul. Garazhnaya 10a; tel. (8712) 22-24-80; e-mail info@chechnya.gov.ru; internet www.chechnya.gov.ru.

Chairman of the Republican Government (Prime Minister): Odes Baisultanov, 364000 Chechen (Nokchi) Rep., Groznyi, ul. Garazhnaya 10a; tel. (8712) 22-00-01.

Chairman of the Council of the Republic: Vakhit Zh. Mantsayev, 364000 Chechen (Nokchi) Rep., Groznyi, ul. Garazhnaya 10a.

Chairman of the People's Assembly: Dukvakha Abdurakhmanov, 364000 Chechen (Nokchi) Rep., Groznyi, ul. Garazhnaya 10a.

Chief Representative of the Chechen (Nokchi) Republic in the Russian Federation: Ziyad M. Sabsadi, 127025 Moscow, ul. Novyi Arbat 19/1804; tel. (495) 203-63-47; fax (495) 203-63-52.

Head of Groznyi City Administration (Mayor): Muslim Khuchiyev, 364000 Chechen (Nokchi) Rep., Groznyi; tel. (8712) 22-01-42.

Republic of Dagestan

The Republic of Dagestan is situated in the North Caucasus on the Caspian Sea. Dagestan forms part of the Southern Federal Okrug and the North Caucasus Economic Area. It has international borders with Azerbaijan to the south and Georgia to the south-west. The Chechen (Nokchi) Republic and Stavropol Krai lie to the west and Kalmykiya to the north. Its largest rivers are the Terek and the Sulak. It occupies 50,300 sq km (19,420 sq miles). Its Caspian Sea coastline, to the east, is 530 km long. The north of the Republic is flat, while in the south are the foothills and peaks of the Greater Caucasus. The Republic's lowest-lying area is the Caspian lowlands, at 28 m (92 feet) below sea level, while its highest peak is over 4,000 m (13,120 feet) high. The climate in its mountainous areas is continental and dry, while in coastal areas it is subtropical, with strong winds. At January 2007, according to official estimates, Dagestan had a population of 2,658,630, and a population density of 52.9 per sq km. At the time of the 2002 census 29.4% of the population described themselves as ethnically Avar (including 0.8% of the total population who described themselves as Andiyets), 16.5% as Dargin, 14.2% as Kumyk, 13.1% as Lezgin, 5.4% as Lak, 4.7% as ethnically Russian, 4.3% as Azeri, 4.3% as Tabasaran, 3.4% as Chechen, 1.5% as Nogai, 0.9% as Rutul and 0.9% as Agul. Only 42.6% of the Republic's population inhabited urban areas in January 2007. Dagestan's capital is at Makhachkala, which had 466,300 inhabitants in January 2006, according to official estimates. The city lies on the Caspian Sea and is the Republic's main port. Other major cities are Khasavyurt (124,000) and Derbent (104,800). The Republic of Dagestan is included in the time zone GMT+3.

HISTORY

Dagestan formally came under Russian rule in 1723, when the various Muslim khanates on its territory were annexed from Persia (Iran). The Dagestani peoples conducted a series of rebellions against the Russian Tsar, including the Murid Uprising of 1828–59, before Russian control could be established. A Dagestan ASSR was established on 20 January 1920.

The Republic of Dagestan acceded to the Federation Treaty in March 1992 and officially declared its sovereignty in May 1993. The Republic voted against the new federal Constitution in December and adopted a new republican Constitution on 26 July 1994. On 21 March 1996 the powers of the republican State Council, the supreme executive body, which comprised a representative of each of the 14 largest ethnic groups in the Republic, were prolonged by a further two years. When this extra term had elapsed, the republican legislature convened as a Constituent Assembly and, on 26 June 1998, confirmed Magomedali Magomedov, an ethnic Dargin, as the Chairman of the State Council, a position he had held since the inauguration of the Council, on 26 July 1994. Parliamentary elections for a new People's Assembly were held on 7 March 1999, concurrently with a referendum to decide whether to institute an executive presidency in Dagestan; the proposal was rejected for a third time. Constitutional changes, approved in March 1998, permitted Magomedov to serve a further term and removed the ethnicity requirements for senior republican positions.

Concern was expressed at a growth in support for Islamist groups in Dagestan from the late 1990s. In 1997 militants seized two villages in Buinaksk district, where they established 'a separate Islamic territory'. In May a group of 200–300 fighters belonging to the Union of Russian Muslims, a political party represented in the republican parliament, occupied a government building in Makhachkala; simultaneously, 2,000 demonstrators gathered in the main city square to demand the resignation of the republican Government. There was also reported to be evidence of close ties between militant Islamist groups in Dagestan and those operating abroad and/or internationally. In 1996–97 Ayman al-Zawahiri, the leader of Egyptian Islamic Jihad and a close ally of the Saudi-born leader of the Islamist al-Qa'ida (Base) organization, Osama bin Laden, was imprisoned for six months in Dagestan, having been found guilty of entering Russia illegally.

Chechen militants, aided by local militant Islamists, invaded Dagestan on 2 August 1999 and again on 5 September; fighting ceased on 16 September, when federal troops additionally regained control over the villages that had been controlled by the rebels. In late September, following the recommencement of military operations in Chechnya, an explosion in Buinaksk, outside accommodation used by federal troops, killed about 60 people. Subsequently a number of explosions in Dagestan were attributed to supporters of Chechen separatism, including a bombing on 9 May 2002 in Kaspiisk, in which 45 people were killed.

On 25 June 2002 the Constituent Assembly voted by an overwhelming majority for Magomedov to be permitted to serve a third term as Chairman of the State Council. In March 2003 Magomedov was duly re-elected to that post. On 10 July a new republican Constitution, which implemented wide-ranging reforms to the structure of government, was approved; it came into effect later in the month. Notably, a directly elected presidency was to be established, to replace the State Council, with effect from the expiry of the latter's mandate in 2006. Meanwhile, it was reported that at least eight deputies of the republican legislature had been assassinated in Dagestan in 1992–2003. In December 2003 a group of militants entered Dagestan from Chechnya, killing a unit of border guards and fleeing with several hostages. A state of emergency was declared and élite troops were dispatched to the region. Although the armed group fled after releasing the hostages, at the end of the month it was reported that the majority of the militants had been killed and the remainder taken prisoner.

Instability in the Republic heightened markedly in the mid-2000s, with political opposition to Magomedov's administration increasingly being voiced by a so-called 'Northern Alliance' formed in 2003 that included a number of prominent politicians in Khasavyurt, but which was also reportedly supported by elements close to the First Deputy Prime Minister (and subsequent Prime Minister) of Chechnya, Ramzan Kadyrov. The ethnic Nogai community, principally resident in the north of the Republic, also became a focus of opposition to the authorities. Assassinations and attempted assassinations of law enforcement officers and regional government officials in Dagestan continued in 2004–06 (according to the republican Ministry of the Interior, there were an estimated 68 militant attacks in Dagestan in the first half of 2005; at least 28 police officers were reported to have been killed during the same period). In May 2005 the republican Minister of the Interior, Zagir Arukhov, was assassinated, in a bombing apparently co-ordinated by the Islamist Shari'a Jamaat group. In July the leader of Shari'a Jamaat, Rasul Makshapirov, was killed by republican security forces. Tensions were also raised on several occasions in 2005 by incursions into Dagestan, particularly the Khasavyurt region, by security forces associated with the Chechen authorities, most notably those answerable to Ramzan Kadyrov, seemingly without the agreement or prior knowledge of the Dagestani authorities and allegedly in response to Chechen rebels taking refuge in the region. Relations with Chechnya were further strained after 11 villagers were abducted during a 'cleansing' operation in Borozdinovskaya, Chechnya, in June. Some 400 people, principally ethnic Avars, subsequently fled to Dagestan and remained there, living in tents, for several weeks. In late July a new exodus of villagers to Dagestan was reported, and in early August clashes broke out between Avars and ethnic Chechens from neighbouring villages near Khasavyurt.

Clashes between Islamist insurgents and security forces continued into late 2005 and 2006, although there were fewer attacks perpetrated by militants than in previous years. In separate incidents in October 2005 law enforcement agencies in Dagestan killed three rebel leaders. In November police officers in the Levashi district discovered five large explosive devices at a house reportedly owned by a member of Shari'a Jamaat. Meanwhile, Shari'a Jamaat launched a media offensive against both the republican Government and Dagestan's 'official' Muslim clergy, whom, it declared, it now regarded as a legitimate target of attack. In January 2006 the police killed three militants during a raid on a residence in Khasavyurt. Two more Islamist rebels were killed by the police during a raid in Kaspiisk in February, and two Nogai militants were killed by the police in the north of Dagestan later in the month.

In mid-February 2006 Magomedov announced his resignation as Chairman of the State Council on the grounds of old age. On 20 February the People's Assembly approved the candidacy of Mukhu Aliyev, hitherto the legislative speaker, for the newly created post of President of the Republic. On the same day Aliyev was succeeded as Chairman of the People's Assembly by Magomedsalam Magomedov, the son of the outgoing Chairman of the State Council. Aliyev appointed a new Government in March; although a new Prime Minister, Shamil Zainalov, was named, the majority of ministerial positions remained unchanged from the outgoing administration.

In March 2006 around 20 people were injured as clashes broke out between the inhabitants of two neighbouring villages in a dispute concerning the allocation of land previously belonging to a collective farm. A senior member of Shari'a Jamaat was shot dead by interior ministry troops in mid-April; three other rebels and two police officers were killed in clashes later in the month. At the end of April one demonstrator was shot dead by the police during a rally, reportedly attended by several hundred villagers, to demand the dismissal of an allegedly corrupt local administrator, who had recently become the subject of a criminal investigation. In mid-May two armed militants were killed during a police raid on a residence in the northern town of Kizilyurt. Aliyev criticized the conduct of the raid (in which one police officer was killed and some 20 apartments damaged) as excessively disruptive. Also in mid-May, rebels claimed to have killed 13 police officers and soldiers during fighting in Buinaksk. Later in the month two militants were killed by the police in Khasavyurt, and a further two in Buinaksk. Following the deaths of another two militants during a police raid in Buinaksk in July, the recently appointed federal Prosecutor-General, Yurii Chaika, appointed Igor Tkachev as Dagestan's republican prosecutor; his appointment was regarded as part of an effort to make greater administrative efforts against Islamist militancy in the region. At the end of July one rebel and two police officers were killed during clashes near Khasavyurt. The apparent abduction of some 70 young male citizens of Khasavyurt over a two-year period precipitated a series of public protests in late 2006. Many of the protesters believed that the so-called *Kadyrovtsy* troops associated with the Chechen leader (and, from early 2006, premier), Ramzan Kadyrov, had been responsible for the kidnappings.

In January 2007 the Dagestan Election Commission annulled the registration of the Communist Party of the Russian Federation (CPRF) and Union of Rightist Forces (URF) prior to March legislative elections, on the grounds that they had failed to comply with a regional electoral regulation that parties submit separate candidate lists for each of the Republic's 53 raions (districts). (The CPRF subsequently succeeded in reversing the annulment.) The forthcoming elections exacerbated ethnic tension in the Republic between Avars (comprising about 30% of the population of Dagestan), Dargins, and other minority groups, since all the Avar candidates were reportedly on the list of the pro-presidential United Russia (UR) and were consequently expected to dominate the legislature. In February the Chairman of the local branch of Patriots of Russia was severely injured in an attack in the capital. Also in February Shari'a Jamaat staged unsuccessful assassination attempts against the Republic's Minister of Interior and deputy police chief, in which four aides were killed, and local militants attacked a convoy of federal troops in the district of Buinaksk. In early March two people were killed in an exchange of fire between supporters of UR and Union of Rightist Forces in the Dakhadayev raion (district). Following the elections to the People's Assembly on 11 March, the Election Commission announced that UR had won 63.7% of the votes, securing 47 of the 72 seats; the broadly pro-Government A Just Russia received 10.7% of the votes and eight seats, the Agrarian Party of Russia 9.1% of votes and seven seats, the CPRF 7.2% of votes and five seats, and Patriots of Russia 7.1% of votes and five seats. A new Chairman of the People's Assembly, Magomed Suleimanov, a member of the Dargin ethnic group, was elected in early April.

In July 2007 Shari'a Jamaat claimed responsibility for the killing of a senior Islamic cleric (the 11th such killing recorded in nine years). In September President Putin issued a decree appointing a new head of the Dagestan administration of the FSB, shortly after Aliyev had replaced the secretary of the Republic's Security Council, who had been perceived widely as having proved unable to prevent the series of killings of senior officials. (Despite continued attacks on federal military personnel, Aliyev claimed that the security situation in the Republic had improved significantly.) Later in September Rappani Khalilov, who had been appointed leader of the Dagestan Front by Chechen rebel commander Doku Umarov in 2006, was killed in a special operation by federal and republican interior ministry troops. Shari'a Jamaat claimed responsibility for two subsequent killings of interior ministry officials in retaliation for Khalilov's death. At the end of October federal police, in co-operation with local officials, arrested a group operating an illegal armaments factory. In November Farid Babayev, who was to head the regional candidate list of the liberal Yabloko Russian Democratic Party in forthcoming elections to the State Duma, was shot at his residence in Makhachkala and subsequently died in hospital. He had complained several days earlier that Yabloko had been deprived of broadcasting time to which it was entitled prior to the elections, and that, in violation of the relevant legislation, a weekly newspaper had failed to publish the party's election programme. Later in November about 500 people demonstrated in Makhachkala, in protest at the arrest on the previous day of Nukh Nukhov of the URF, who was accused of clashing with police during a municipal election earlier in the year; he was sentenced to two months' detention prior to trial, and his election as mayor was annulled. Around 92% of the electorate were reported to have participated in the elections to the State Duma held on 2 December, considerably higher than the national average. According to the official results, UR received some 89% and the CPRF 8% of votes cast. The CPRF subsequently claimed that mass falsification of the elections had been perpetrated and submitted formal protests against the results.

Rebel attacks and clashes between militants and security forces increased in frequency. Despite continued security operations against militant fundamentalists, by mid-2008 it appeared that the insurgents were continuing to increase in strength and to expand the territory in which they were able to operate, and also succeeded in assassinating high-ranking police officers. On 25 September 2008 the People's Assembly voted in favour of amending the republican Constitution to increase the executive powers of the President of the Republic, granting him the additional authority to form and head the Government.

ECONOMY

In 2004 gross regional product in Dagestan amounted to 76,082.8m. roubles, or 29,129.3 roubles per head. The economic situation in the Republic was severely affected by the wars in Chechnya. The Republic's major industrial centres are at Makhachkala, Derbent, Kaspiisk and Khasavyurt. In 2005 there were 516 km of railways and 7,553 km of paved roads in the Republic. There are fishing and trading ports in Makhachkala, which is a major junction for trading routes by rail, land and sea. The major railway line between Rostov-on-Don and Baku (Bakı), Azerbaijan, runs across the territory, as does the Caucasus highway. There is an airport 15 km from Makhachkala.

Owing to its mountainous terrain, Dagestan's economy is largely based on animal husbandry, particularly sheep-breeding. Its agriculture also consists of grain production, viniculture, horticulture and fishing. The agricultural sector generated 25,925m. roubles and employed around 20.5% of the Republic's work-force in 2005. Dagestan's main industries are petroleum and natural gas production, electricity generation, mechanical engineering, metal-working and food-processing. Industry engaged 11.0% of the work-force in 2005 and generated 10,766m. roubles in 2004.

Dagestan's economically active population comprised 1,175,000 inhabitants in 2005, when 22.3% of the Republic's labour force were unemployed, a rate considerably in excess of the federal average. The average monthly wage was 3,659.8 roubles, the lowest recorded in the Federation. There was a budgetary deficit of 473.6m. roubles in 2005. External trade amounted to US $123.9m. in exports and $140.9m. in imports in the same year. Foreign investment in the territory was minimal. At the end of 2005 there were 4,897 small businesses registered in Dagestan, providing employment to 41,400 people.

DIRECTORY

President (Head of the Republic): MUKHU G. ALIYEV (appointment confirmed 20 February 2006), 367005 Dagestan, Makhachkala, pl. Lenina 1; tel. (8722) 67-30-59; fax (8722) 67-30-60.

Chairman of the Cabinet of Ministers (Head of Government): SHAMIL M. ZAINALOV, 367005 Dagestan, Makhachkala, pl. Lenina; tel. (8722) 67-20-17; internet www.e-dag.ru.

Chairman of the People's Assembly: MAGOMED SULEIMANOV, 367005 Dagestan, Makhachkala, pl. Lenina; tel. (8722) 67-30-55; fax (8722) 67-30-66.

Chief Representative of the Republic of Dagestan in the Russian Federation: YURII A. LEVITSKII, 105062 Moscow, ul. Pokrovka 28, POB 116; tel. (495) 916-15-36; fax (495) 928-41-12.

Head of Makhachkala City Administration: SAID D. AMIROV, 367012 Dagestan, Makhachkala, pl. Lenina 2; tel. (8722) 67-21-09; e-mail z999@km.ru; internet www.makhachkala.dgu.ru.

Republic of Ingushetiya

The Republic of Ingushetiya is situated on the northern slopes of the Greater Caucasus, in the centre of the Northern Caucasus mountain ridge. It forms part of the Southern Federal Okrug and the North Caucasus Economic Area. The Chechen (Nokchi) Republic lies to the east and north (although the border has not been exactly determined) and North Osetiya—Alaniya to the west. (The boundary between these two Republics was partially disputed.) In the southern mountains there is an international border with Georgia. The Terek and the Assa are the territory's main rivers. The Republic is extremely mountainous, with some peaks over 3,000 m high. The Republic occupies about 3,600 sq km (1,400 sq miles). At January 2007, according to official estimates, the population of the Republic was 492,669. At the time of the 2002 census 77.3% of the population were ethnically Ingush, 20.4% were Chechen and 1.2% were ethnically Russian. The Ingush are a Muslim people closely related to the Chechens (collectively they are known as Vainakhs). They are indigenous to the Caucasus Mountains and have been known historically as Galgai, Lamur, Mountaineers and Kist. Like the Chechen language, their native tongue is a dialect of the Nakh group of the Caucasian language family. Only 42.9% of the population lived in urban areas in January 2007. Ingushetiya's administrative centre is at Magas, a new city, opened officially in 1998, which was named after the medieval Alanic capital believed to have been situated thereabouts. Initially the city consisted solely of a gold-domed presidential palace and government buildings, and by January 2006 its population was only about 300, according to official estimates. The former capital of Nazran remained the largest city in the Republic, with a population of 130,200 at that time. The Republic of Ingushetiya is included in the time zone GMT+3.

HISTORY

The Ingush are descended from the western Nakh people, whose different reaction to Russian colonization of the Caucasus region in the 1860s distinguished them from their eastern counterparts (subsequently known as the Chechens). The Chechens resisted the invaders violently and were driven into the mountains, while the Ingush reacted more passively and settled on the plains. The Ingush suffered severely under Soviet rule. In 1920 their territory was temporarily integrated into the Mountain (Gorskaya) People's Republic, but became the Ingush Autonomous Oblast on 7 July 1924. In 1934 the region was merged into a Checheno-Ingush Autonomous Oblast, which was upgraded to the status of an ASSR in 1936. Many Ingush intellectuals became victims of purges and the Ingush literary language was banned. In February 1944 the entire Ingush population (74,000, according to the 1939 census) was deported to Soviet Central Asia, and the territory was subsequently handed over to the Osetiyans, although the Ingush were permitted to return following their rehabilitation in 1957.

With the ascendancy in the Checheno-Ingush ASSR of the All-National Congress of the Chechen People in 1991, a de facto separation between Chechen and Ingush territories was achieved. In June 1992 the federal Supreme Soviet recognized Ingushetiya as a separate republic, although the borders between the two new units were not delineated. In addition, Ingushetiya claimed the eastern regions of North Osetiya and part of the North Osetiyan capital, Vladikavkaz (which had been shared until the 1930s). Prigorodnyi raion (district), with a majority of Ingush inhabitants, was at the centre of the dispute. (The federal Law on the Rehabilitation of Repressed Peoples, approved in April 1991, established the right for deported peoples to repossess their territory.) Armed hostilities between informal militias based in the two Republics ensued for six days in October 1992, with the Osetiyan militias receiving some support from federal security forces, and tens of thousands of Ingush were reported to have fled North Osetiya. Some 500 people were reported to have been killed during the fighting, and no peace agreement was signed between the two Republics until 1994.

On 27 February 1994, alongside simultaneous parliamentary and presidential elections in the Republic, 97% of the electorate voted in favour of a draft republican constitution, which took immediate effect. At the republican presidential election, held in March 1998, Ruslan Aushev (who had headed the Republic since November 1992) was re-elected. His popular mandate emboldened him to seek to amend republican laws to conform more closely to what he termed 'national traditions', and which incorporated aspects of *Shari'a* Islamic law. Following a declaration by federal President Boris Yeltsin that a planned referendum, which sought, to pardon those charged with crimes such as revenge killings, was unconstitutional, in February 1999 Aushev signed a power-sharing agreement with the federal Government. In July Aushev issued a decree permitting men up to four wives, in breach of the Russian Federation's family code.

The population of Ingushetiya remained generally supportive of the federal authorities, and in the federal presidential election of 26 March 2000 awarded Vladimir Putin a larger proportion of the votes cast (85.4%) than in any federal subject. The successful implementation of a settlement between Ingushetiya and North Osetiya, signed in March 2001, according to which the Ingush could return to their former homes in Prigorodnyi and Vladikavkaz, was inhibited by logistical difficulties and protests. In December 2001 Aushev resigned as President. Murat Zyazikov, a general in the Federal Security Service (FSB), was elected in his stead in April 2002. In September some 70 people were killed near the village of Galashki as Chechen rebels, who were reported to have entered the territory from the Pankisi Gorge in Georgia, clashed with federal forces. In October Ingushetiya and North Osetiya signed an Agreement on the Development of Co-operation and Good Neighbourly Relations, which committed both sides to adopting measures to resolve their remaining differences. In September 2003 an explosive device, assembled outside the residence of Zyazikov, was detected and successfully disabled. Later in the month three people were killed and another 31 injured when a truck bomb was detonated by two suicide bombers outside the offices of the FSB in Magas. At the end of September further clashes between several hundred Chechen rebels and troops and police broke out near Galashki, in which at least 17 deaths were reported.

In the March 2004 elections to the federal presidency, Ingushetiya again recorded the highest proportion of support of any federal subject for Putin: 98.2%, according to the Central Election Commission. In April Zyazikov was briefly hospitalized following an apparent attempt on his life by a suicide bomber. In June the final camp in Ingushetiya for persons displaced by the war in Chechnya was closed, despite widespread concern that the refugees were being forced to return to Chechnya against their will. (In 1999–2000 the camps had accommodated some 200,000 persons.) Meanwhile, according to human rights organizations, there were more than 40 instances of kidnapping in the Republic in the first half of 2004. On 21–22 June a series of raids, led by the militant Islamist Chechen rebel, Shamil Basayev, took place on interior ministry targets in the Republic, in which more than 90 people were killed. By early 2006 more than 20 people had received custodial sentences for their involvement in the attacks. In June 2005 Zyazikov resigned, in order to seek a demonstration of confidence from Putin; Putin duly nominated Zyazikov for a further term of office; this was endorsed by the republican legislature on 14 June. In September Putin proposed a revision to the 1991 Law on the Rehabilitation of Repressed Peoples that would prevent the restoration of the internal borders between the Republics of the North Caucasus that existed prior to 1944, and thus impede the return of Prigorodnyi to Ingushetiya. During the second half of the year attacks against security officials, and against the homes of police officers became increasingly frequent, and in December military aircraft and heavy artillery attacked those southern regions of the Republic in which rebel bases were believed to be located.

In February 2006 Magomed Chakhkiyev, a deputy in the People's Assembly and the co-ordinator of a federal programme to encourage ethnic Russians who had left the North Caucasus since 1991 to return, was abducted in Nazran by an Islamist group. Chakhkiyev, who was the father-in-law of both Zyazikov and the republican Prosecutor-General, was released in April. In the same month two militants and one police officer were killed in a gun battle in Nazran. In May a car bomb exploded in Nazran, killing seven people, including the republican First Deputy Minister of the Interior. In early June an assassination attempt was committed against the republican health minister, while the residence of the republican Minister of the Interior also came under attack. In the same month two officers of the FSB were shot dead in Nazran; a police commander (along with his brother, bodyguard and his three children) was shot dead later in the month. Several branches of the security services subsequently launched a large-scale operation near Nazran, killing several rebels and destroying a militant base. The republican interior minister survived an assassination attempt in August.

The announcement in February 2006, by the Presidential Representative in the Southern Federal Okrug, Dmitrii Kozak, of a revised plan for the resolution of the Ingush–North Osetiyan dispute was received with considerable hostility in Ingushetiya and was formally rejected by vote of the republican legislature. Notably, Kozak proposed that new settlements should be constructed elsewhere in North Osetiya for the purpose of rehousing those Ingush displaced from Prigorodnyi. In March it was reported that the Osetiyan authorities were forcibly resettling Ingush refugees in a newly

constructed settlement, where amenities were poor and where there were to be only limited opportunities for employment. These measures were regarded as unacceptable by the Ingush authorities, who presented their own proposals for a resolution of the conflict in late June, under which Prigorodnyi would revert to Ingush control.

In the mid-2000s there was increasing speculation that the federal authorities were seeking to reunify the territories of Chechnya and Ingushetiya. In December 2005, notably, the acting premier of Chechnya, Ramzan Kadyrov, urged Chechnya's legislature to take steps to restore the Chechen polity's former borders (i.e. those of the former Checheno-Ingush ASSR). However, the Ingush authorities repeatedly ruled out the possibility of re-establishing a combined polity. Tensions between the two Republics were heightened in September 2006, when a gun battle occurred at a Checheno-Ingush border checkpoint between Ingush traffic police and members of the Chechen interior ministry special forces, in which eight people were killed. Several days after the clashes, the chairman of the lower legislative chamber in Chechnya and the Chairman of the Ingush legislature issued a joint statement calling for calm; a similar statement issued one day later by Zyazikov and Kadyrov (by then the President of Chechnya) insisted that the clashes had not resulted from inter-ethnic hatred. Later in the month it was agreed by several senior federal officials, meeting with republican leaders, that special forces from both Chechnya and North Osetiya should be permitted to operate in Ingushetiya in order to apprehend militants without being subject to any hindrance by the Ingush authorities.

In March 2007 the Republic's Prosecutor-General, Makhmud-Ali Kalimatov, resigned from office, reportedly in protest at Zyazikov's failure to address high-level corruption, to solve a series of murder cases, and to investigate the abductions of young Ingush by police and security forces, and to reverse an economic decline. A civil society organization, Justice and Dignity, in April urged the population of Ingushetiya to stage co-ordinated protests and to launch legal action to oust Zyazikov.

In early July 2007 the Chairman of the Republican branch of the pro-presidential United Russia (UR), Mukharbek Aushev, tendered his resignation, thereby allowing Zyazikov, who had joined UR in the previous month, to be elected. (An earlier vote for the party chairmanship, in which Aushev received 90 votes and Zyazikov only 40, had been annulled by UR's General Council). Also in July Vakha Vedzizhev, an Islamic cleric and unofficial adviser to Zyazikov, was killed by militants, while on the same day an unsuccessful attack was attempted against the republican presidential motorcade. The federal Minister of the Interior subsequently announced a special security operation in Ingushetiya, dispatching reinforcements to the Republic. Nevertheless, killings of officials from the republican Prosecutor's Office, Ministry of the Interior and the police, and attacks against federal military personnel persisted, particularly in Nazran, while there were reports of summary arrests and killings of suspected militants by security forces.

From mid-2007 inter-ethnic tensions in Ingushetiya intensified, following a series of attacks upon, and the killing of, a number of ethnic Russians resident in the region. In September, additionally, three members of a Roma family were killed near Sunzha. In late September responsibility for the killing of an FSB officer, who had been dispatched to the region to investigate the abduction of Ingush in Prigorodnyi, was claimed by a local Islamist group known as the Ingushetiya Jamaat. The Ingush authorities stated that the series of killings had been perpetrated by a group of young militants connected with the transnational extreme Islamist al-Qa'ida (Base) organization, members of which were alleged to be based in the Republic while planning a major attack elsewhere in Russia.

In early October 2007 the federal Minister of the Interior announced that 2,500 additional troops deployed in Ingushetiya since August had been withdrawn, while the State Duma rejected a proposal to declare a state of emergency in the Republic. Later in October it was announced that a security operation initiated in early September to prevent further killings of civilians was to continue at least until December. In late November federal interior ministry special forces violently dispersed an unauthorized demonstration, staged in Nazran in protest at Zyazikov's administration; some 100 protesters were arrested. Despite reports of a widely observed boycott of elections to the State Duma on 2 December, the Republic's authorities claimed that voter turn-out was about 98.4% of the electorate, and that UR had received 98.7% of votes cast. In January 2008 an opposition demonstration was violently suppressed by police forces, which reportedly continued measures against suspected militants, killing two people; a number of protesters were detained, including two leaders who were charged with organizing mass unrest. UR obtained some 74.1% of the votes cast at elections to the People's Assembly, held on 2 March. The nationalist Liberal Democratic Party of Russia were placed second, with 11.1%, followed by A Just Russia, with 7.4%, and the Communist Party of the Russian Federation, with 7.3%. On 12 March President Zyazikov dismissed the Government of Prime Minister Ibragim Malsagov and other district officials. On 14 March Kharun Dzeitov (a former republican deputy premier and energy sector executive) was appointed Prime

Minister, and a new administration was formed. Several days later it was announced that Zyazikov had been removed from the leadership of the regional branch of UR.

Also in March 2008 the federal Supreme Court rejected a case submitted by the Ingush authorities for the closure of a pro-opposition news website, *ingushetiya.ru* (the internet address of which was almost identical to that of the official website of the republican authorities), which had increasingly focused on criticism of Zyazikov's administration and had also sought to collate evidence of electoral malpractice in Ingushetiya at the 2007 elections. In early July 2008 opposition leaders presented a petition to the federal authorities as part of a campaign organized by *ingushetiya.ru* to remove Zyazikov from the republican presidency and reinstate Aushev. In that month attacks against local police and FSB officers became almost daily occurrences, and in early August rebel militia entered Nazran and attacked private residences belonging to Dzeitov and a local imam. At the end of August the owner of *ingushetiya.ru*, Magomed Yevloyev, who had accused Zyazikov of waging 'civil war against the Ingush people', was shot and killed, after being detained by police at an airport on his return from Moscow. Official reports stated that his death had been accidental; local and international human rights organizations demanded a full investigation into the circumstances of his killing. In early October a suicide bomb attack narrowly failed to kill the republican Minister of the Interior, whom elements of the opposition held responsible for Yevloyev's death.

ECONOMY

In 2004 the gross regional product of Ingushetiya totalled 6,022.2m. roubles, or 12,582.9 roubles per head, the lowest figure recorded in any federal subject (no figures were available for Chechnya). In 2005 there were 39 km of railways and 866 km of paved roads in the Republic.

By the early 2000s the role of agriculture in Ingushetiya's economy had considerably declined (the sector employed 4.1% of the Republic's work-force in 2005, compared with 28.5% in 1995), its primary activity being cattle-breeding. In 2005 the sector generated 2,318m. roubles. Ingushetiya's industry, which employed 6.3% of the working population in 2005 and generated 948m. roubles in 2004 (one of the lowest levels of industrial output among the federal subjects), consists of electricity production, petroleum-refining and food-processing. The major petroleum company, LUKoil, was a participant in the construction of the Caspian pipeline running through the territory. From the mid-1990s the services sector had also made a contribution to the economy, with the local economy receiving substantial benefits from registration fees paid by companies operating in the so-called 'offshore' zone that was in operation in 1994–97. At that time, the resources of this zone accounted for some 70% of the Republic's capital investments, but it was terminated following criticism by the IMF.

In 2005 the economically active population of Ingushetiya numbered 196,000, when 64.9% of the Republic's labour force were unemployed—by far the highest level of any federal subject, excluding Chechnya—compared with 34.9% in 2001. In 2005 the average monthly wage in the Republic was 5,448.9 roubles. A report issued in 2006 by a state body found that Ingushetiya was one of the 11 most impoverished federal subjects in Russia, and the Republic remained heavily dependent on federal transfers. In 2005 the Republic recorded a budget deficit of 93.5m. roubles. In the same year the value of the Republic's foreign trade amounted to US $497.5m. in exports and $21.0m. in imports. Foreign investment in the Republic was minimal. At the end of 2005 there were 478 small businesses registered in Ingushetiya, providing employment to around 1,800 people.

DIRECTORY

President: MURAT M. ZYAZIKOV (elected 28 April 2002, appointment confirmed 14 June 2005), 366720 Ingushetiya, Magas, Dom Pravitelstva; tel. and fax (8734) 55-11-55; e-mail murad@ingushetia.ru; internet ingushetia.ru.

Chairman of the Government (Prime Minister): KHARUN M. DZEITOV, 366720 Ingushetiya, Magas, Dom Pravitelstva; tel. (8734) 55-11-05.

Chairman of the People's Assembly: MAKHMUD S. SAKALOV, 366720 Ingushetiya, Magas, pr. I. Zyazikova 16; tel. (8734) 55-17-35; e-mail parlament@ingushetia.ru; internet www.parlamentri.ru.

Chief Representative of the Republic of Ingushetiya in the Russian Federation: KHAMZAT M. BELKHAROYEV, 109044 Moscow, ul. Vorontsovskaya 22/2; tel. (495) 912-93-09; fax (495) 912-92-75.

Head of Magas City Administration: VAKHA U. MERZHOYEV; tel. (8734) 55-12-33.

Kabardino-Balkar Republic

The Kabardino-Balkar Republic is situated on the northern slopes of the Greater Caucasus and on the Kabardin Flatlands. It forms part of the Southern Federal Okrug and the North Caucasus Economic Area. North Osetiya—Alaniya (Ossetia) lies to the east and there is an international border with Georgia in the south-west. Stavropol lies to the north, with the Karachai-Cherkess Republic to the west. The Republic's major rivers are the Terek and the Baksan. The Republic occupies 12,500 sq km (4,800 sq miles), of which one-half is mountainous. The highest peak in Europe, twin-peaked Elbrus, at a height of 5,642 m (18,517 feet), is situated in the Republic. At January 2007, according to official estimates, the population of the Republic was 891,299 and the population density 71.3 per sq km. At the time of the 2002 census 55.3% of the population were Kabardin, 25.1% were ethnically Russian, 11.6% were Balkar, 1.1% Osetiyan, 1.0% Turkish and 0.8% Ukrainian. Both the Kabardins and the Balkars are Sunni Muslims. The Kabardins' native language belongs to the Abkhazo-Adyge group of Caucasian languages. The Balkars speak a language closely related to Karachai, part of the Kipchak group of the Turkic branch of the Uralo-Altaic family. Both peoples almost exclusively speak their native tongue as a first language, but many are fluent in the official language, Russian. Some 58.5% of the population lived in urban areas in January 2007. The capital of the Republic is at Nalchik, which had a population of 271,400 in January 2006, according to official estimates. The Kabardino-Balkar Republic is included in the time zone GMT+3.

HISTORY

The Turkic Kabardins, a Muslim people of the North Caucasus, are believed to be descended from the Adyges. They settled on the banks of the Terek river, mixed with the local Alan people, and became a distinct ethnic group in the 15th century. They were converted to Islam by the Khanate of Crimea in the early 16th century, but in 1561 appealed to Tsar Ivan IV for protection against Tatar rule. The Ottoman Turks and the Persians (Iranians) also had interests in the region, and in 1739 Kabardiya was established as a neutral state between the Ottoman and Russian Empires. In 1774, however, the region once again became Russian territory under the terms of the Treaty of Kuçuk Kainavci. Although the Kabardins were not openly hostile to the Russian authorities, in the 1860s many of them migrated to the Ottoman Empire. The Balkars were pastoral nomads until the mid-18th century, when they were forced to retreat further into the Northern Caucasus Mountains, where they settled as farmers and livestock breeders. They were converted to Islam by Crimean Tatars, although their faith retained strong elements of their animist traditions. Balkariya came under Russian control in 1827, when it was dominated by the Kabardins. Many ethnic Russians migrated to the region during the 19th century. In 1921 autonomous Balkar and Kabardin Okrugs were created within the Mountain (Gorskaya) People's Republic. In January 1922 the two former Okrugs (which had been reconstituted as Autonomous Oblasts) were merged into a Kabardino-Balkar Autonomous Okrug (which became an ASSR on 5 December 1936), although the process of integrating the two polities was achieved in defiance of widespread hostility from both peoples. In 1944 the Balkars were deported to Kazakhstan and Central Asia, in response to their alleged collaboration with German forces during the Second World War, and the territory thereby became the Kabardin ASSR. After the rehabilitation of the Balkars in 1956, in the following year the Republic reverted to its previous name.

Thus, although greatly outnumbered by Kabardins and Russians, the Balkars had developed a strong sense of ethnic identity. In 1991 they joined the Assembly of Turkic Peoples and on 18 November 1996 the first congress of the State Council of the Balkar People declared the formation of a 'Republic of Balkariya' within the Russian Federation; this declaration, which had little support among the Balkar population, was rescinded later in the month. Meanwhile, the Kabardino-Balkar Republic declared its sovereignty on 31 December 1991, and signed a bilateral treaty with the federal authorities during 1995. Valerii Kokov was elected as President in January 1992 and elected to a second term of office in January 1997.

A new republican Constitution was adopted in July 2001, which prevented the Republic from existing independently of the Russian Federation. In August it was reported that an attempt to stage a coup in the Republic, and in the neighbouring Karachai-Cherkess Republic, had been prevented, and that the alleged leaders of the plot had been arrested. On 13 January 2002 Kokov was elected to serve a third term as republican President, receiving 87.2% of the votes cast. Republican legislative elections to a new, unicameral, legislature (replacing its bicameral predecessor) took place on 7 December 2003, concurrently with elections to the Gosudarstvennaya Duma (State Duma).

From mid-2004 increasing concern was expressed at an apparent rise in support for militant Islamist groups in the Republic, in particularly among the Balkar population. Militant Islamists associated with the Yarmuk Jamaat group, aligned with the Chechen rebel leader, Shamil Basayev, claimed responsibility for an attack, in December, on the offices of the Federal Anti-Narcotics Service in Nalchik, in which four people were killed; a significant quantity of weapons and ammunition was also stolen in the attack. Members of Yarmuk had also been implicated in the killing of two police officers in August, when eight militants had reportedly escaped capture by up to 400 heavily armed members of the security forces. The leader of Yarmuk, Muslim Atayev, was shot dead in Nalchik in January 2005, while his presumed successor, Rusam Bekanov, was also killed in a gun-battle in April. Meanwhile, the abolition of the separate administrative status of a number of ethnically Balkar villages, and their absorption into Nalchik city, in February 2005 was a further source of discontent. In August the Nalchik authorities prohibited public rallies in the city, following the killing of a total of six police officers on two occasions over the previous month.

On 16 September 2005 Kokov submitted his resignation, on grounds of ill health. (He died in the following month.) On 28 September the republican legislature approved federal President Vladimir Putin's nominee, a former State Duma deputy, Arsen Kanokov, as President. On 13 October some 100 militants staged a series of co-ordinated attacks against government, police, and commercial buildings across Nalchik. In the fighting that ensued between rebels and members of the security forces some 130 people were killed, including 93 militants and 12 civilians, according to official reports. Basayev subsequently claimed responsibility for the organization of the attacks. The bodies of many of those killed were buried in unmarked graves by the authorities, in accordance with federal anti-terrorist legislation, a measure that gave rise to demonstrations by relatives of the dead, who also appealed to the European Court of Human Rights. Several hundred people were detained on suspicion of involvement in the raids later in the month; by late November 43 people had been charged.

In addition to adopting measures intended to improve the Republic's economy, Kanokov pledged in the weeks following the attacks to reopen all unofficial mosques closed during Kokov's administration, and announced other attempts to reach out to disaffected citizens. The apparent disappearance of a leading Islamic scholar in the Republic, Ruslan Nakhushev, in November 2005, who had not been seen after leaving the republican headquarters of the Federal Security Service, where he had been summoned in connection with the recent violence, was regarded as representing a significant reverse to these proposals.

In March 2006 Putin issued a decree dismissing the republican Minister of the Interior, Lt-Gen. Khachim Shogenov, whose removal from office had been sought by various human rights groups; Shogenov was, none the less, appointed as a special adviser to Kanokov. (However, Kanokov subsequently described the use of force by the interior ministry troops in late 2005 as having been indiscriminate.) Later in the month the republican Supreme Court ordered the dissolution of the State Council of the Balkar People. In early April an attempt to assassinate a Balkar leader opposed to separatism, Gen. (retd) Supyan Beppayev, who was also the chairman of a republican presidential commission on the rehabilitation of repressed peoples, was condemned by Kanokov. In late April two militants were killed in a gun battle with the security forces in Nalchik. In mid-June Kanokov announced a three-year programme intended to enforce respect for human rights by the organs of local and republican government. The appointment by Kanokov of a new Prime Minister, Andrei Yarin, was confirmed by the legislature on 22 June. Yarin had previously held various administrative posts in Chechnya, Ryazan Oblast and the office of the Presidential Representative in the Southern Federal Okrug.

In June 2007 two suspected Islamist militants (one of whom had been detained for several years at the US military camp in Guantánamo Bay, Cuba) were killed in a special security operation. In July the Council of Elders of the Balkar People organized a protest gathering in Nalchik to oppose policies of the Kabardino-Balkar authorities, which it regarded as discriminatory against the Balkar ethnic group, including the failure to amend the Republic's laws on administrative-territorial administration to allow Balkar-populated districts a greater degree of self-government; Kanokov subsequently criticized the unauthorized meeting. In November 2007 the republican prosecutor's office suspended the activities of the Council of Elders of the Balkar People (established in 2006), in accordance with federal legislation on extremist organizations. Also in November six people were killed in an explosion on a bus travelling from Nalchik to North Osetiya. Voter turn-out in the Republic in the elections to the State Duma on 2 December was reported at 96.7%, with the pro-presidential United Russia winning some 96.1% of votes cast, according to official figures. In April 2008 the trial began in Nalchik of 58 suspects charged with participating in the attacks on police and security facilities in the city in late 2005. Increasing incidences of attacks against Balkar activists were reported. In early October Kanokov for the first time met Balkar representatives to discuss their complaints of discrimination. Nevertheless, the Council of

Elders of the Balkar People was shortly afterwards refused permission to conduct its annual congress in a public building in Nalchik.

ECONOMY

Gross regional product in the Kabardino-Balkar Republic amounted to 32,064.8m. roubles in 2004, equivalent to 35,709.2 roubles per head. The Republic's main industrial centres are at Nalchik, Tyrnauz and Prokhladnyi. In 2005 there were 133 km of railways and 2,978 km of roads in the Republic. Prokhladnyi is an important junction on the North Caucasus Railway. There is an international airport at Nalchik, from which there are regular flights to the Middle East, as well as to other cities within the Russian Federation.

The Republic's main agricultural activities are the production of grain, fruit and vegetables, and animal husbandry. In 2005 agriculture engaged 17.3% of the work-force and generated 14,705m. roubles. The Republic is rich in minerals, with reserves of petroleum, natural gas, gold, iron ore, garnet, talc and barytes. The industrial sector, which employed 20.8% of the work-force in 2005 and generated 10,451m. roubles in 2004, chiefly comprises mechanical engineering, metal-working, non-ferrous metallurgy, food-processing, the production of electricity, and the production and processing of tungsten-molybdenum ores.

In 2005 the economically active population numbered 386,000, when 23.4% of the labour force were unemployed. The average monthly wage was 4,653.3 roubles. In 2005 there was a budgetary deficit of 331.6m. roubles. External trade amounted to US $47.4m. in exports and $12.1m. in imports in 2005. Foreign investment in the Republic was minimal. At the end of 2005 there were 2,339 small businesses registered in the Republic, providing employment to 18,500 people.

DIRECTORY

President: Arsen B. Kanokov (appointment confirmed 28 September 2005), 360028 Kabardino-Balkar Rep., Nalchik, pr. Lenina 27; tel. (8662) 40-41-42; fax (8662) 47-61-74; internet www.prezident-kbr.ru.

Prime Minister: Andrei V. Yarin, 360028 Kabardino-Balkar Rep., Nalchik, pr. Lenina 27; tel. (8662) 40-29-70; fax (8662) 47-61-83.

Chairman of Parliament: Ilyas B. Bechelov, 360028 Kabardino-Balkar Rep., Nalchik, pr. Lenina 55; tel. (8662) 47-13-65; fax (8662) 47-27-13.

Chief Representative of the Kabardino-Balkar Republic in the Russian Federation: Mukhamed M. Shogenov, 109004 Moscow, ul. B. Kommunisticheskaya 4; tel. (495) 911-18-52; fax (495) 912-40-53.

Head of Nalchik City Administration: Khazretali Berdov, 360000 Kabardino-Balkar Rep., Nalchik, ul. Sovetskaya 70; tel. (8662) 22-20-04.

Republic of Kalmykiya

The Republic of Kalmykiya is situated in the north-western part of the Caspian Sea lowlands. It forms part of the Southern Federal Okrug and the Volga Economic Area. The south-eastern part of the Republic lies on the Caspian Sea. It borders Dagestan in the south and Stavropol Krai in the south-west, while Rostov, Volgograd and Astrakhan Oblasts lie to the west, north-west and north-east, respectively. The Republic occupies 75,900 sq km (29,300 sq miles), one-half of which is desert. At January 2007, according to official estimates, it had a population of 287,199 and a population density of 3.8 per sq km. At the time of the 2002 census 53.3% of the population were Kalmyk, 33.6% ethnically Russian, 2.5% Dargin, 2.0% Chechen, 1.7% Kazakh, 1.1% Turkish, 0.9% Ukrainian and 0.8% were Avar. Uniquely for Europe, the dominant religion among the Kalmyks is Lamaism (Tibetan Buddhism). Some 90% of the indigenous population speak the Kalmyk language, which is from the Mongol division of the Uralo-Altaic family. Only 44.2% of the Republic's population lived in urban areas in January 2007. The republican capital is Elista, which had 103,000 inhabitants in January 2006, according to official estimates. Kalmykiya is included in the time zone GMT+3.

HISTORY

The Kalmyks (also known as the Kalmuks, Kalmucks and Khalmgs) originated in Eastern Turkestan (Dzungaria or Sungaria, mostly in the People's Republic of China) and were a semi-nomadic Mongol-speaking people. Displaced by the Han Chinese, some 100,000 Oirots (Kalmyks) migrated westwards, in 1608 reaching the Volga basin, which had been under Russian control since 1556. The region became the Kalmyk Khanate, until its dissolution in 1771. By this time many Kalmyks had been slaughtered during a mass migration back eastwards in an attempt to rejoin their Oirot kinsmen. Those that remained were dispersed: some settled along the Ural, Terek and Kuma rivers, some were moved to Siberia, while others became Don Cossacks. Many ethnic Russians and Germans settled in Kalmykiya during the 18th century. A Kalmyk Autonomous Oblast was established on 4 November 1920. Its status was upgraded to that of an ASSR in 1935. In 1943 the Republic was dissolved as retribution for the Kalmyks' alleged collaboration with German forces in the Second World War. The Kalmyks were deported to Central Asia, where they lived until the reconstitution of a Kalmyk Autonomous Oblast in 1957, which regained the status of an ASSR in the following year. In the late 1990s a territorial dispute between Kalmykiya and Astrakhan resurfaced, with Kalmykiya claiming a particularly fertile area known as the Black Lands that it had possessed prior to 1943.

The Republic adopted a declaration of sovereignty on 18 October 1990 and was known as the Republic of Kalmykiya-Khalmg Tangch in 1992–96. In April 1993 a business executive, Kirsan Ilyumzhinov, was elected as republican President. A new Constitution, which provided for a presidential term of seven years, was adopted on 5 April 1994.

In October 1995 Ilyumzhinov was the sole candidate in the presidential election, in contravention of federal legislation. Ilyumzhinov was re-elected President in 2002, receiving around 57% of the votes cast in a 'run-off' election. In January 2003 Ilyumzhinov dismissed the Prime Minister since 1999, Aleksandr Dorzhdeyev, and assumed the responsibilities of the premier. Republican legislative elections took place on 7 December 2003, concurrently with federal legislative elections. Suspicion that the vote-counting in the federal elections had been influenced in favour of a candidate supported by Ilyumzhinov prompted protests by opposition groups outside the President's office in Elista. Later in December Ilyumzhinov announced the appointment of a premier, Anatolii Kozachko. Further anti-Ilyumzhinov demonstrations took place in Elista in February and September 2004; on the latter occasion 11 demonstrators were hospitalized, when a demonstration was violently dispersed. In November the Tibetan Buddhist leader, the Dalai Lama (Tenzin Gyatso), visited the Republic, as he had done in 1992, a measure that on both occasions precipitated criticism from the authorities of the People's Republic of China. (The Russian authorities refused to grant the Dalai Lama a visa in advance of a further proposed visit to the region in 2006.)

In October 2005 Ilyumzhinov requested an expression of confidence in his administration from federal President Vladimir Putin. Putin's nomination of Ilyumzhinov for a further term was confirmed by the republican legislature on 24 October.

On 6 December 2007 Ilyumzhinov dismissed Kozachko as republican premier and appointed Vladimir Sengleyev, hitherto Deputy Prime Minister and Minister of the Economy, to head a new administration. At an emergency session later in December, the republican legislature (by 14 of 26 deputies) voted to dissolve itself and to conduct early elections; an amended voting system was also approved. At the elections to the People's Khural, held on 2 March 2008, the pro-Government United Russia (UR) obtained a narrow majority of the votes cast (54.6% of the total votes cast to those seats elected on the basis of party lists). The Communist Party of the Russian Federation were placed second, with 22.6%, and the Agrarian Party of Russia (which merged with UR later in the year) third, with 7.7%.

ECONOMY

In 2004 Kalmykiya's gross regional product amounted to 11,347.4m. roubles, or 39,094.6 roubles per head. Kalmykiya is primarily an agricultural territory. In the 1990s much of its agricultural land suffered from desertification, a consequence of its over-exploitation by the Soviet authorities during the 1950s. Kalmykiya's major industrial centres are at Elista and Kaspiiskii. At the end of 2005 there were 165 km of railway lines and 2,882 km of paved roads in the Republic. The Republic is intersected by the Astrakhan–Kizlyar (Dagestan) railway line. The Republic has serious problems with its water supply, with a deficit of fresh water affecting almost all regions.

Although agricultural output declined sharply, in real terms, throughout much of the 1990s, in 2005 the sector employed 21.2% of the work-force, and generated 4,179m. roubles. In that year only in the Ust-Orda Buryat AOk (subsequently absorbed into Irkutsk Oblast) was a higher proportion of the work-force engaged in agriculture. Kalmykiya's agriculture consists mainly of animal husbandry. Industry, which engaged 9.9% of the working population in 2005 and generated 2,191m. roubles in 2004, consists mainly of electricity production, the manufacture of building materials, and the production of petroleum and natural gas. The Republic has major hydrocarbons reserves, which, however, remain largely unexploited, and Kalmykiya remains a net importer of energy.

The economically active population in the Republic amounted to 145,000 in 2005, when 18.0% of the Republic's labour force were unemployed. The average monthly wage was 4,495.0 roubles. A report issued in 2006 by a state body found that Kalmykiya was one of the 11 most impoverished federal subjects in Russia. There was a budgetary deficit of 548.1m. roubles in 2005, when external trade comprised US $148.6m. in exports and $75.1m. in imports. Foreign investment in the Republic was minimal. At the end of 2005 some 276 small businesses were registered in the Republic, providing employment to 2,600 people.

DIRECTORY

President: KIRSAN N. ILYUMZHINOV (elected 11 April 1993, re-elected unopposed 15 October 1995, re-elected 27 October 2002, appointment confirmed 24 October 2005), 358000 Kalmykiya, Elista, pl. Lenina, Dom Pravitelstva; tel. (84722) 3-30-88; fax (84722) 3-38-57; e-mail ki@kalm.ru; internet www.glava.kalm.ru.

Chairman of the Government (Prime Minister): VLADIMIR B. SENGLEYEV, 358000 Kalmykiya, Elista, pl. Lenina, Dom Pravitelstva; tel. (84722) 6-13-88; fax (84722) 6-28-80; e-mail kalmykia@data.ru; internet gov.kalmportal.ru.

Chairman of the People's Khural (Parliament): IGOR V. KICHIKOV, 358000 Kalmykiya, Elista, pl. Lenina, Dom Pravitelstva; tel. (84722) 5-27-35; fax (84722) 5-03-02.

Chief Representative of the Republic of Kalmykiya in the Russian Federation: ALEKSEI M. ORLOV, 121170 Moscow, ul. Poklonnaya 12/2; tel. (495) 249-87-47; fax (495) 249-87-41; e-mail kalmykia@data.ru; internet www.kalmykiaembassy.ru.

Head of Elista City Administration (Mayor): ALEKSANDR YERMOSHENKO (acting), 358000 Kalmykiya, Elista, ul. Lenina 249; tel. (84722) 5-23-14; fax (84722) 5-42-56; e-mail pressaelista@yandex.ru; internet www.gorod-elista.ru.

Karachai-Cherkess Republic

The Karachai-Cherkess Republic is situated on the northern slopes of the Greater Caucasus. It forms part of the Southern Federal Okrug and the North Caucasus Economic Area. There are borders with Krasnodar to the north-west, Stavropol to the north-east and the Kabardino-Balkar Republic to the east. There is an international boundary with Georgia (mainly Abkhazia) to the south. Its major river is the Kuban. The Republic occupies 14,100 sq km (5,440 sq miles). At January 2007, according to official estimates, it had a population of 428,706 and a population density of 30.4 per sq km. At the time of the 2002 census 38.5% of the population were Karachai, 33.6% ethnically Russian, 11.3% Cherkess, 7.4% Abazin, 3.4% Nogai, 0.8% Osetiyan and 0.8% Ukrainian. Both the Karachai and the Cherkess are Sunni Muslims of the Hanafi school. The Cherkess speak a language close to Kabardin, from the Abkhazo-Adyge group of Caucasian languages, while the Karachais' native tongue, from the Kipchak group, is the same as that of the Balkars. Only 44.0% of the Republic's population inhabited urban areas in January 2007. The capital city, Cherkessk, had a population of 116,900 in January 2006, according to official estimates. The Karachai-Cherkess Republic is included in the time zone GMT+3.

HISTORY

The Karachai, a transhumant group descended from Kipchak tribes, were driven into the highlands of the North Caucasus by Mongol tribes in the 13th century. Their territory was annexed by the Russian Empire in 1828 and they continued to resist Russian rule throughout the 19th century. In the 1860s and 1870s many Karachai migrated to the Ottoman Empire to escape oppression by the tsarist regime, as did many Cherkess, a Circassian people descended from the Adyges who inhabited the region between the lower Don and Kuban rivers. They had come under Russian control in the 1550s, having sought protection from the Crimean Tatars and some Turkic tribes, including the Karachai. Relations between the Cherkess and Russia deteriorated as many Russians began to settle in Cherkess territory. Following the Treaty of Adrianople in 1829, by which the Ottomans abandoned their claim to the Caucasus region, a series of rebellions by the Circassians and reprisals by the Russian authorities occurred. In 1864 Russia completed its conquest of the region and many Cherkess fled.

The Cherkess Autonomous Oblast was established in 1928 and was subsequently merged with the Karachai Autonomous Oblast to form the Karachai-Cherkess Autonomous Oblast, which was subordinate to the territory governed from Stavropol (q.v.). Following the deportation of the Karachai to Central Asia in late 1943, the region was renamed the Cherkess Autonomous Oblast, until the Karachai were rehabilitated and permitted to return in 1957. In February 1992, after the dissolution of the USSR, the President of the Russian Federation, Boris Yeltsin, presented draft legislation to the federal legislature that provided for the formation of a Karachai Republic within the Federation. However, a referendum held in the Oblast in March 1992 demonstrated widespread opposition to the sub-division of the territory, which was itself separated from Stavropol Krai and upgraded to the status of a Republic in the same month.

In 1995 the Republic signed a power-sharing treaty with the federal authorities. The Republic's first presidential election, in 1999, provoked violence and ethnic unrest, when a second round of voting, in May, reversed the positions achieved by the 'run-off' candidates, Stanislav Derev, an ethnic Cherkess (who secured 40% of the votes in the first round and 12% in the second), and Gen. Vladimir Semonov, an ethnic Karachai and a former Commander-in-Chief of the Russian Ground Troops (who secured 18% of the votes in the first round and 85% in the second). Semonov was confirmed as the winning candidate in August and sworn in on 14 September; Semonov's failure to implement a campaign promise to appoint a Cherkess as Chairman of the Government precipitated further protests throughout 1999 and 2000. (The leader of the region in 1979–99, Vladimir Khubiyev, was also Karachai.)

Following two rounds of voting in August 2003 (in the first round of which all five candidates were Karachai), Mustafa Batdyyev, hitherto director of the republican bank, was elected President, narrowly defeating Semonov. Further unrest occured in late 2004. In October Ansar Tipuyev, a deputy chairman of the Government, who in his previous post of first deputy interior minister had taken an uncompromising stance against militant Islamists, was assassinated in Cherkessk. The killing, in early November, of seven shareholders (all of whom were Karachai) in a cement company controlled by Ali Kaitov, Batdyyev's former son-in-law, following a meeting at Kaitov's home, resulted in organized demonstrations against the republican authorities. Some 400 people protested outside the presidential offices and demanded Batdyyev's resignation, ransacking the building and occupying it for two days. Kaitov and 15 other men were subsequently arrested on charges related to the killings, and the resignation of the republican prosecutor later in the month, was regarded as a significant concession to the wishes of the demonstrators.

In May 2005 six Islamist militants were killed by security forces in Cherkessk. In June some 200 members of the Abazin population in the Republic broke into the republican parliamentary building in order to protest at recent changes to the structures of local government, which, it was claimed, discriminated against the ethnic group. In July the changes that had prompted the recent protests were suspended. The creation of a new Abazin district, comprising five villages, was approved by referendum on 25 December; the district was expected to come into existence in January 2009. During 2005 and 2006 similar demands by members of the Nogai ethnic group for their own autonomous district were supported by the republican President, and a referendum on the establishment of such a district, in which some 94% of participants voted in favour, was held concurrently with elections to the republican legislature on 8 October 2006. The republican legislature approved the creation of the district on 15 December.

Meanwhile, in January 2006 an explosion destroyed a section of the electricity-transmission line in the Republic that served as one of the major conduits for energy supply from Russia to Georgia. (Two other bomb attacks on the same day damaged two pipelines in the Republic of North Osetiya—Alaniya that supplied natural gas to Georgia.) Although the perpetrators of these bombings remained unknown, the President of Georgia, Mikheil Saakashvili, accused the Russian authorities of having sabotaged energy supplies to Georgia in an attempt to undermine the country's independence. In late April republican interior ministry forces, operating in collaboration with federal security officers, killed four alleged Islamist militants and arrested a fifth. In late December two militants were killed and a further two arrested in Cherkessk. On the same day sentence was passed on the 16 men accused of committing murder in October 2004: Kaitov was sentenced to 17 years' imprisonment, two defendants received life sentences, while the remaining sentences ranged from 16 years to eight-and-one-half years. A subsequent appeal by the 16 convicted men was rejected by the federal Supreme Court in October 2007.

Shortly before elections to the State Duma in December 2007, the republican legislature urged voters to demonstrate support for the United Russia (UR) party that was supportive of federal President Vladimir Putin. A concurrent ballot was scheduled to select a district administration head and local council in the newly established Abazin district. Voter turn-out in the elections to the State Duma on 2 December was about 92.4%, with UR winning some 92.9% of votes cast, according to official figures.

On 5 September 2007 a local insurgent leader, Rustam Ionov (also known as Abu-Bakr), was killed as he attempted to escape into neighbouring Georgia. In early 2008, following a number of operations in the south-west of the Republic and the elimination of Ionov's

group, the federal director of the FSB, Nikolai Patrushev, announced that the principal local Islamist militia, the Karachayevo Jamaat, had been liquidated. Nevertheless, three police patrol officers were killed in an attack attributed to militants in the southern city of Karachayevsk in July 2008.

In August 2008, shortly before the expiry of the mandate of Batdyyev as republican President, the 66 deputies present (of a total of 73) at a session of the People's Assembly voted unanimously to confirm the nomination of Boris Ebzeyev as his successor. Ebzeyev, a Karachai, who had hitherto served as a judge at the federal Constitutional Court, announced that the combat of corruption was to be among his priorities. He assumed office in early September, appointing a new Prime Minister later in the month.

ECONOMY

In 2004 gross regional product in the Karachai-Cherkess Republic totalled 14,467.8m. roubles, or 33,218.3 roubles per head. The Republic's major industrial centres are at Cherkessk and Karachayevsk. In 2005 it contained 51 km of railway track and 1,895 km of paved roads, including the Stavropol–Sukhumi (Abkhazia, Georgia) highway.

Agriculture employed some 17.6% of the working population and generated 7,273m. roubles in 2005. The principal crops include grain, sunflower seeds, sugar beet and vegetables, while animal husbandry is also significant. The Republic's main industries are petrochemicals, chemicals, mechanical engineering and metal-working, although the manufacture of building materials, food-processing and coal production are also important. Industry employed 19.0% of the work-force in 2005 and generated 7,345m. roubles in 2004.

In 2005 the economically active population of the Republic numbered 205,000, and 13.6% of the Republic's labour force were unemployed. The average monthly wage was 4,710.1 roubles. In 2005 the republican budget recorded a deficit of 27.5m. roubles. International trade was minimal, amounting to US $17.3m. in exports, and $12.7m. in imports in 2005, and foreign investment in the Republic was also extremely limited. At the end of 2005 there were 1,654 small businesses registered in the Republic, providing employment to 10,000 people.

DIRECTORY

President and Head of the Republic: Boris S. Ebzeyev (appointment confirmed 5 August 2008, assumed office 4 September), 357100 Karachai-Cherkess Rep., Cherkessk, ul. Krasnoarmeiskaya 54; tel. (87822) 5-40-11; fax (87822) 5-29-80; e-mail info@kchr.info; internet www.kchr.info.

Chairman of the Government: Vladimir G. Kaishev, 357100 Karachai-Cherkess Rep., Cherkess, ul. Krasnoarmeiskaya 54; tel. (87822) 5-40-08; fax (87822) 5-40-20; e-mail info@kchr.info; internet www.kchr.info/government/index.php?section=premier.

Chairman of the People's Assembly: Sergei A. Smorodin, 357100 Karachai-Cherkess Rep., Cherkess, ul. Krasnoarmeiskaya 54; e-mail info@kchr.info; internet www.kchr.info/parlament/index .php?section=speeker.

Chief Representative of the Republic of the Karachai-Cherkess Republic in the Russian Federation: Emma M. Kardanova, 119333 Moscow, ul. D. Ulyanova 4/2/2; tel. (495) 137-65-40.

Head of Cherkessk City Administration (Mayor): Petr V. Korotchenko, 357100 Karachai-Cherkess Rep., Cherkessk, pr. Lenina 54a; tel. (87822) 5-37-23; fax (87822) 5-78-43.

Republic of North Osetiya— Alaniya

The Republic of North Osetiya—Alaniya, is situated on the northern slopes of the Greater Caucasus and forms part of the Southern Federal Okrug and the North Caucasus Economic Area. Of the other federal subjects, the Kabardino-Balkar Republic lies to the west, Stavropol Krai to the north, and the Chechen (Nokchi) Republic and Ingushetiya to the east. There is an international boundary with Georgia (South Ossetia) in the south. Its major river is the Terek. In the north of the Republic are the steppelands of the Mozdok and Osetiyan Plains, while further south in the foothills are mixed pasture and beech forest (about one-fifth of the territory of the Republic is forested). Narrow river valleys lie in the southernmost, mountainous region. The territory of North Osetiya covers 8,000 sq km (3,090 sq miles). At January 2007, according to official estimates, it had a population of 701,444 and a population density of 87.7 per sq km. At the time of the 2002 census 62.7% of the population were Osetiyan, 23.2% ethnically Russian, 3.0% Ingush,

2.4% Armenian, 1.8% Kumyk and 1.5% Georgian. Around one-quarter of Russians resident in the Republic were thought to have left North Osetiya between 1989 and 1999, largely owing to the decline of the military-industrial complex in the Republic, which had been their major employer. The Osetiyans speak an Indo-European language of the Persian (Iranian) group. Some 64.6% of the Republic's population inhabited urban areas in January 2007. The capital, Vladikavkaz, situated in the east of the Republic, had a population of 314,100 in January 2006, according to official estimates. The Republic is included in the time zone GMT+3.

HISTORY

The Osetiyans (Ossetins, Oselty) are descended from the Alans, a tribe of the Samartian people. The Alans were driven into the foothills of the Caucasus by the Huns in the fourth century and their descendants (Ossetes) were forced further into the mountains by Tatar and Mongol invaders. Although the Osetiyans had been converted to Orthodox Christianity in the 12th and 13th centuries by the Georgians, a sub-group, the Digors, adopted Islam from the Kabardins in the 17th and 18th centuries. Perpetual conflict with the Kabardins forced the Osetiyans to seek the protection of the Russian Empire, and their territory was eventually ceded to Russia by the Ottoman Turks at the Treaty of Kuçuk Kainavci in 1774 and confirmed by the Treaty of Iaşi in 1792. (Transcaucasian Osetiya, or South Ossetia, subsequently became part of Georgia.) The Russians fostered good relations with the Osetiyans, as they represented the principal Christian group among the Muslim peoples of the North Caucasus. Furthermore, both ends of the strategic Darial pass were situated in the region. The completion of the Georgian Military Road in 1799 facilitated the Russian conquest of Georgia in 1801.

After the Bolshevik Revolution, and having briefly been part of the Mountain (Gorskaya) People's Autonomous Republic, North Osetiya was established as an Autonomous Oblast on 7 July 1924, and as an ASSR in 1936. The Osetiyans were rewarded for their loyalty to the Soviet Government during the Second World War: in 1944 their territory was expanded by the inclusion of former Ingush territories to the east and of part of Stavropol Krai to the north. Furthermore, for 10 years the capital, renamed Ordzhonikidze in 1932, was known as Dzaudzhikau, the Osetiyan form of Vladikavkaz. The Digors, however, were deported to Central Asia in 1944.

The Republic declared sovereignty in mid-1990. From 1991 there was considerable debate about some form of unification with South Ossetia (which had, however, been deprived of its autonomous status and merged with adjoining regions by the Georgian Supreme Soviet in December 1990). This resulted in armed hostilities between the South Ossetians and Georgian troops, during which thousands of refugees fled to North Osetiya. Meanwhile, the Republic's administration refused to recognize claims by the Ingush to the territory they were deprived of in 1944 (the Prigorodnyi raion—district), which led to the onset of violence between informal militia groups from Ingushetiya and North Osetiya (with the latter obtaining some support from federal troops) in October 1992 and the imposition of a state of emergency in the affected areas. Around 500 people were killed in six days of fighting, and tens of thousands of Ingush were reported to have fled North Osetiya. Despite a peace settlement in 1994, the region remained unstable. (In late 1999 there were approximately 37,000 registered refugees from the armed hostilities in South Osetia in the Republic, while at that time about 35,000 Ingush were still displaced from the Prigorodnyi raion, most of whom were living in Ingushetiya.) Under the terms of its Constitution, adopted on 7 December 1994, the Republic's name was amended to North Osetiya—Alaniya. A power-sharing agreement was signed with the federal authorities in 1995.

The territory was a redoubt of the Communist Party of the Russian Federation during the late 1990s. In January 1998 Aleksandr Dzasokhov, a former member of the Communist Party of the Soviet Union Politburo, was elected as republican President, with 75% of the votes cast.

Instability in North Osetiya, as elsewhere in the North Caucasus, increased from 1999, as insurgency became increasingly widespread. A bomb exploded in Vladikavkaz in March, killing 42. In March 2001 three simultaneous explosions in the republic killed over 20. On 27 January 2002 Dzasokhov was re-elected as President. In September the power-sharing agreement of 1995 was dissolved, and in October North Osetiya and Ingushetiya signed an Agreement on the Development of Co-operation and Good Neighbourly Relations, which committed both sides to adopting measures to resolve remaining differences. Following republican legislative elections held in May–June 2003, supporters of the pro-presidential United Russia (UR) were reported to have a working majority in the chamber. In early June a suicide bomber detonated explosives close to a bus carrying federal air-force personnel near Mozdok (a principal base for federal troops fighting in Chechnya), killing 17 people. On 1 August more than 50 people were killed, and at least 100 others injured, following a suicide bombing outside a military hospital at Mozdok.

On 1 September 2004, the first day of the school year, some 32 armed militants seized control of a school in the city of Beslan, taking at least 1,100 pupils, parents and teachers hostage. Federal special forces officers stormed the school on 3 September, following a series of explosions. Official figures claimed that some 331 hostages were killed, including 186 children, although some independent estimates placed the number of fatalities at closer to 600. The siege was characterized by conflicting information and uncertainty regarding the number of hostages, the number of casualties, the cause of the storming of the school and the number and ethnicity of the hostage takers. Their demands were variously reported as the withdrawal of Russian troops from Chechnya and the release of militants captured in raids in Ingushetiya in mid-June. Accusations of deliberate obfuscation and incompetence were levied at the regional and federal authorities; the chief of the regional Federal Security Service (FSB) and interior minister both resigned and, after some 3,500 gathered in Vladikavkaz on 8 September to demand the resignation of President Dzasokhov, the entire republican Government of Mikhail Shatalov was dismissed. Alan Boradzov was appointed Chairman of the Government on 10 September.

Following continuing demands for his resignation from the relatives of those killed in Beslan, Dzasokhov resigned as President on 31 May 2005. The nomination by federal President Vladimir Putin of Taimuraz Mamsurov, hitherto Chairman of the republican legislature, as Head of the Republic—the title of President no longer being used—was approved by voting in that body on 7 June. Aleksandr Merkulov (hitherto First Deputy Chairman of the republican Government), was approved as premier by the republican legislature several days later. (Dzasokhov was subsequently appointed as one of the Republic's two representatives to the upper chamber of the federal legislature.) Meanwhile, in May 2005 the trial of Nurpasha Kulayev, a Chechen militant who was reported to be the sole survivor of the instigators of the hostage-taking at Beslan, commenced in Vladikavaz; in May 2006 Kulayev was found guilty of terrorist activity and of participating in hostage-taking and murder and sentenced to life imprisonment. Kulayev announced that he was to appeal against the verdict.

In mid-January 2006 a series of explosions caused significant damage to two natural gas pipelines in the Republic, severely disrupting energy supplies to Georgia. Although the perpetrators of these bombings remained unknown, the President of Georgia, Mikheil Saakashvili, accused the Russian authorities of having sabotaged energy supplies to Georgia in an attempt to undermine the country's independence. In early February the simultaneous detonation of bombs in three casinos in Vladikavkaz resulted in the deaths of two people and the injury of around 20 others; responsibility for the blasts was claimed by a militant Islamist group. On the day after the explosions the republican authorities ordered the closure of all gambling establishments in North Osetiya—Alaniya.

The announcement, in February 2006, by the Presidential Representative in the Southern Federal Okrug, Dmitrii Kozak, of a revised plan for the resolution of the Prigorodnyi dispute precipitated considerable controversy; Kozak proposed that the region should remain under Osetiyan control and that new settlements should be constructed elsewhere in North Osetiya for the purpose of rehousing those Ingush displaced from the region. In March it was reported that the Osetiyan authorities were forcibly resettling Ingush refugees in a newly constructed settlement, where amenities were poor and where there were to be only limited opportunities for employment. These measures were regarded as unacceptable by the Ingush authorities, which presented a set of counter-proposals, under which Prigorodnyi would revert to Ingushetiyan control. On 29 August Mamsurov dismissed the republican Government, expressing dissatisfaction with its performance. However, the new administration appointed in early September was substantially unchanged from the outgoing Government, although Merkulov was replaced as premier by Nikolai Khlyntsov.

In May 2007 the leader of a group of Ingush displaced persons met with representatives of the federal presidency in Moscow, in an effort to secure permission to return to their homes in Prigorodnyi; the delegation staged a temporary hunger strike in protest at the unresolved situation. In July the disappearance of a further two Ingush from the Prigorodnyi region prompted a local protest by residents of the village of Chermen, who appealed to the UN and Council of Europe to intervene in order to end a series of abductions; it was reported that 17 Ingush and Chechens had disappeared in two years. There were unconfirmed reports that an organized group in North Osetiya was responsible for the abduction of Ingush, apparently in retaliation for the taking of hostages at a school in Beslan in September 2004.

Acting on an appeal by the Prosecutor-General's Office, the Supreme Court of the Republic of North Osetiya in early May 2007 overturned a ruling by a Vladikavkaz district court that would have allowed criminal charges to be brought against police and emergency situations ministry personnel, in connection with the deaths of large numbers of hostages during the storming of the Beslan school in September 2004; the district court had ruled illegal the refusal by the Prosecutor-General's Office to bring charges against the officials in question, and also against senior members of the administration. At the end of May relatives of those killed in Beslan (who had formed the Beslan Mothers Committee) declared that they would appeal against the acquittal by the district court of three police officers charged with dereliction of duty. In September representatives of the Beslan Mothers Committee, meeting with Kozak and the federal State Duma Speaker, reiterated demands that an independent investigation into the siege be undertaken.

Elections to the 70-member republican Parliament (comprising 35 deputies elected in single-mandate constituencies and 35 on the basis of party lists), and to local councils were conducted concurrently with polls to the State Duma on 2 December 2007. According to preliminary results for the elections to the Republican Parliament, UR secured 60.7%, the Communist Party of the Russian Federation 14.3%, and A Just Russia 8.9% of votes cast.

The increase of tensions between Georgian government troops and those of the secessionist (and Russian-backed) 'Republic of South Ossetia', in Georgia, in mid-2008, and which escalated into a conflict between Russia and Georgia for several days in August, prompted a mass evacuation of civilians to North Osetiya; refugees were estimated to number some 14,000 at the height of the conflict, necessitating the delivery of emergency assistance by the federal authorities. After the Russian forces gained control of South Ossetia, its internationally unrecognized 'President', Eduard Kokoyev, repeated pledges to seek unification of the territory with North Osetiya—Alaniya, although this stance was officially rejected by the Russian federal leadership.

ECONOMY

In 2004 the gross regional product of North Osetiya—Alaniya totalled 25,324.0m. roubles, equivalent to 35,885.4 roubles per head. Its major industrial centres are at Vladikavkaz, Mozdok and Beslan. In 2005 the Republic contained 144 km of railway track. There were 2,288 km of paved roads, including one of the two principal road routes from Russia to the South Caucasus, the Transcaucasian Highway. There is an international airport at Vladikavkaz.

Agriculture in North Osetiya, which employed 14.4% of the labour force and generated 8,331m. roubles in 2005, consists mainly of vegetable and grain production, horticulture, viniculture and animal husbandry. The Republic is one of the principal vodka-producing territories within the Russian Federation. Industry employed 23.5% of the work-force in 2005 and generated 14,373m. roubles in 2004. The Republic's main industries are radio-electronics, non-ferrous metallurgy and food-processing. There are also five hydroelectric power stations, with an average capacity of around 80 MWh.

Despite political instability in the Republic and an economic downturn in several of the territories neighbouring North Osetiya, the economic situation within the Republic generally improved in the first half of the 2000s. By 2005 the rate of unemployment, which had reached 28.5% in 2000, had declined to 11.4%. In that year the economically active population totalled 330,000. Those in employment earned an average wage of 4,722.3 roubles per month in 2005. The republican budget recorded a deficit of 406.4m. roubles in 2005. In that year external trade comprised US $63.5m. in exports and $51.4m. in imports. In 2005 foreign investment was negligible. At the end of that year there were 1,915 small businesses registered in the Republic, providing employment to 13,800 people.

DIRECTORY

Head of the Republic: TAIMURAZ D. MAMSUROV (appointment confirmed 7 June 2005), 362038 North Osetiya—Alaniya, Vladikavkaz, pl. Svobody 1, Dom Pravitelstva; tel. (8672) 53-35-24; fax (8672) 74-92-48.

Chairman of the Government: NIKOLAI A. KHLYNTSOV, 362038 North Osetiya—Alaniya, Vladikavkaz, pl. Svobody 1, Dom Pravitelstva; tel. (8672) 53-35-56; fax (8672) 75-87-30; internet alania .osetia.ru.

Chairman of the Parliament: LARISA B. KHABITSOVA, 362038 North Osetiya—Alaniya, Vladikavkaz, pl. Svobody 1, Parlament; tel. (8672) 53-81-01; fax (8672) 53-93-46; e-mail parliament@rno-a .ru; internet parliament.rno-a.ru.

Chief Representative of the Republic of North Osetiya— Alaniya in the Russian Federation: VLADIMIR Z. GUGKAYEV, 109028 Moscow, per. Durasovskii 1/9; tel. (495) 916-21-47; fax (495) 916-25-22.

Head of Vladikavkaz City Administration (Mayor): KAZBEK KH. PAGIYEV, 362040 North Osetiya—Alaniya, Vladikavkaz, pl. Shtyba 1; tel. (8672) 75-12-27; fax (8672) 55-34-72; internet vladikavkaz.osetia .ru.

Krasnodar Krai

Krasnodar Krai, often known as the Kuban, is situated in the south of European Russia, in the north-western region of the Greater Caucasus and in the Kuban-Azov lowlands. The Krai forms part of the Southern Federal Okrug and the North Caucasus Economic Area. It has a short international border with Georgia (Abkhazia) in the south, while the Karachai-Cherkess Republic and Stavropol Krai lie to the east and Rostov Oblast to the north-east. The Krai's territory encloses the Republic of Adygeya. The Krai lies on the Black Sea in the south-west and on the Sea of Azov in the north-west. The narrow Kerch Strait, in places only 10 km (six miles) wide, separates the western tip of the province from Crimea (Ukraine). Its major river is the Kuban. The Krai covers 76,000 sq km (29,340 sq miles). At January 2007, according to official estimates, the territory had a population of 5,101,081, and thus a population density of 67.1 per sq km. At the time of the 2002 census 86.6% of the population were ethnically Russian, 5.4% Armenian and 2.6% Ukrainian. Some 52.6% of the population lived in urban areas in January 2007. Krasnodar, the Krai's administrative centre, had a population of 710,400 in January 2006, according to official estimates. Other important cities included the resort town of Sochi (329,500), Novorossiisk (230,700) and Armavir (190,700). Krasnodar Krai is included in the time zone GMT+3.

HISTORY

Krasnodar city (known as Yekaterinodar until 1920) was founded as a military base in 1793, during the campaign of Catherine (Yekaterina) II 'the Great' to win control of the Black Sea region for the Russian Empire, which was eventually achieved in 1796. Dominated by the 'Whites' in the civil wars that followed the collapse of the tsarist regime, the Krai, which then included the territory that now forms the Republic of Adygeya (which held the status of a nominally autonomous Oblast), was formed on 13 September 1937. In post-Soviet Russia the area became a stronghold of the Communist Party of the Russian Federation (CPRF). In September 1993 the Krai Soviet condemned President Boris Yeltsin's dissolution of the federal legislature. In October the Soviet refused to dissolve itself, but announced that elections would be held to a new 32-member legislature in March 1994, although this poll was subsequently postponed. The CPRF maintained a leading role in the new Legislative Assembly.

During 1996 attempts by the incumbent Governor, Nikolai Yegorov, to postpone the gubernatorial election scheduled for December failed and Nikolai Kondratenko, a communist and the former Chairman of the Krai Soviet, was elected Governor by a large majority. Kondratenko attracted national notoriety for his incitement of hostility towards minority groups, particularly Jews and Armenians, while a voluntary Cossack militia in the region, established in the late 1990s, was also accused of persecuting members of ethnic minorities. Following a gubernatorial election, held on 3 December 2000, Kondratenko was replaced as Governor by Aleksandr Tkachev, who obtained 82% of the votes cast. Kondratenko did not stand as a candidate in the election, citing ill health. (However, in advance of elections to the federal State Duma in December 2003, the CPRF chose Kondratenko as its second-placed candidate on its federal party list.) Tkachev also became noted for his chauvinist remarks, on occasion urging various groups of non-ethnic Russians to leave the region (to which there had been substantial migration—principally of ethnic Russians—from the North Caucasus for much of the 1990s). At the provincial legislative election, held on 24 November 2000, Kondratenko's Fatherland movement won 32 of the 50 seats. Tkachev was re-elected as Governor on 14 March 2004, receiving 84% of the votes cast.

From the late 1990s the presence of some 21,000 Meshketians in the Krai was exploited by the Fatherland movement. The Meshketians, the majority of whom were stateless, had been exiled to the region from Georgia under Stalin (Iosif Dzhugashvili—Soviet leader 1924–53), or had sought refuge in the Krai following the outbreak of inter-ethnic violence in the Fergana valley (in Kyrgyzstan, Tajikistan and Uzbekistan) in 1989. In 2002 the Krai restricted the granting of permanent residency permits to migrants, and limited access to housing and education for those without permanent residency. In October the US mission to the Organization for Security and Co-operation in Europe (OSCE) issued a statement criticizing the treatment of Meshketians by the provincial authorities and urging the federal authorities to ensure that full civil rights were granted to them. By mid-2004 almost 5,000 Meshketians had received Russian citizenship. A large proportion of the remainder, however, accepted an offer to emigrate to the USA. In November 2005 it was reported that more that 5,000 Meshketians had resettled in the USA, with a further 4,400 preparing to leave Krasnodar Krai for that country. In the same month a law was passed by the State Duma (the lower chamber of the federal legislature) allowing Cossacks to serve in special units in the military and to work with police and border control authorities.

Meanwhile, in September 2003 work commenced to construct a causeway across the Kerch Strait, which separates Crimea, in Ukraine, from the Taman peninsula, between the Black Sea and the Sea of Azov. The regional authorities stated that the causeway was required to protect part of the Krai from environmental erosion; however, Ukraine argued that the causeway would encroach on its territory and dispatched border troops to the nearby island of Tuzla, of which it claimed ownership. In October, following talks between the leaders of the Russian and Ukrainian Governments, Russia agreed to halt work on the causeway's construction, provided that Ukraine withdrew its troops from Tuzla. On 24 December the Presidents of the two countries signed an agreement recognizing the status of the Sea of Azov and the Kerch Strait as inland waters of both Russia and Ukraine, granting freedom of navigation to vessels of both countries in those waters (but excluding the military vessels of other countries without invitation) and pledging to co-operate in clearly defining the border between the two states in the area. However, despite prolonged negotiations, no final agreement was reached on defining the border in the Kerch Strait region, while the final status of the Sea of Azov also remained to be determined.

In the mid-2000s there was much speculation that the Republic of Adygeya would be abolished and reabsorbed into the Krai; despite official denials that this was government policy, including a statement by federal President Vladimir Putin to that end in December 2006, various state agencies of the two entities were merged during the course of that year. In April 2007 Tkachev requested that Putin reconfirm his mandate; the Legislative Assembly approved his nomination for a third term (with 59 of 60 votes in favour) on 23 April. In May Tkachev and the President of Adygeya, Aslan Tkhakushinov, signed a friendship and co-operation agreement between the two territories.

In September 2007 the Legislative Assembly voted to dissolve itself and to schedule elections to be held concurrently with those to the State Duma, on 2 December. Tkachev headed the United Russia (UR) list in both the federal and regional legislative elections; according to preliminary results for the Legislative Assembly, UR won 67.1%, the CPRF 15.0% and A Just Russia 9.4% of votes cast.

ECONOMY

In 2004 gross regional product in Krasnodar Krai amounted to 325,811.2m. roubles, or 63,843.8 roubles per head. Krasnodar is one of the Krai's main industrial centres, as are Armavir, Novorossiisk and Kropotkin. Novorossiisk is one of the largest seaports in Russia, while Tuapse, Yeisk and Temryuk are also important seaports. In 2005 the Krai contained 2,088 km of railway track and 10,239 km of paved roads.

The Krai's principal crops are grain, sugar beet, rice, tobacco, essential-oil plants, tea and hemp. Horticulture, viniculture and animal husbandry are also important. In 2005 agricultural output was worth 101,771m. roubles, a far greater agricultural sum than that of any federal subject, while 17.3% of the work-force were engaged in agriculture. There are important reserves of petroleum and natural gas in Krasnodar Krai, and petroleum is refined in the territory. In 2003 the Krai administration, in association with two major petroleum sector companies, Rosneft and LUKoil, formed a new company, Priavozneft, with a view to facilitating the eventual greater exploitation of the natural resources of the Sea of Azov region. (However, exploitation of such resources would necessitate the conclusion of a border agreement with Ukraine favourable to Russia—see above.) The Krai's main industries are food-processing, electricity generation, fuel extraction, mechanical engineering and metal-working, and building materials. Industry employed 20.8% of the work-force in 2005 and generated 134,121m. roubles in 2004. The tourism sector is also important: the region's climate, scenery and mineral and mud springs attracted around 6m. visitors annually in the mid-1990s, when some 400,000 people were employed in tourism. The Krai contains the resort towns of Sochi, Anapa, Tuapse and Adler. In July 2007 it was announced that the 2014 Winter Olympic Games, due to be held in February of that year, had been awarded to Sochi. Substantial construction and infrastructural projects were to be undertaken in the region in order to facilitate the hosting of the games. The transportation and refinery of Caspian Sea hydrocarbons reserves has brought economic benefits to the region. Major petroleum pipelines from Baku (Bakı), Azerbaijan, and Tengiz, Kazakhstan, which opened in 1997 and 2001, respectively, terminate at Novorossiisk.

In 2005 the economically active population numbered 2,422,000, and 7.5% of the labour force were unemployed. The average monthly wage was 6,462.3 roubles. In 2005 there was a budgetary surplus of 1,525.7m. roubles. International trade in that year comprised US $1,424.0m of exports and $1,409.2m. of imports. Foreign investment amounted to $463.9m. in 2005. At the end of that year 35,513 small businesses were registered in the Krai, providing employment to 267,100 people.

DIRECTORY

Head of the Provincial Administration: ALEKSANDR N. TKACHEV (elected 3 December 2000, re-elected 14 March 2004, appointment confirmed 23 April 2007), 350014 Krasnodar, ul. Krasnaya 35; tel. (861) 262-57-16; fax (861) 268-35-42; e-mail registry@kuban.ru; internet admkrai.kuban.ru.

Chairman of the Legislative Assembly: VLADIMIR A. BEKETOV, 350014 Krasnodar, ul. Krasnaya 3; tel. (861) 268-50-07; fax (861) 268-37-41; internet www.kubzsk.ru.

Chief Representative of Krasnodar Krai in the Russian Federation: DMITRII L. MIKHEYEV, 119180 Moscow, per. 2-i Kazachii 6; tel. and fax (495) 238-20-28.

Head of Krasnodar City Administration (Mayor): VLADIMIR L. YEVLANOV, 350000 Krasnodar, ul. Krasnaya 122; tel. (861) 255-43-48; fax (861) 255-01-56; e-mail post@krd.ru; internet www.krd.ru.

Stavropol Krai

Stavropol Krai is situated in the central Caucasus region and extends from the Caspian lowlands in the east to the foothills of the Greater Caucasus Mountains in the south-west. It is part of the Southern Federal Okrug and the North Caucasus Economic Area. It borders Krasnodar Krai to the west, Rostov Oblast, Kalmykiya in the north and north-east and Dagestan to the east. There are borders to the south with (from east to west) the Chechen (Nokchi) Republic, North Osetiya—Alaniya, the Kabardino-Balkar Republic and the Karachai-Cherkess Republic. Much of the territory is steppe. Its total area is 66,500 sq km (25,670 sq miles). At January 2007, according to official estimates, the population numbered 2,701,215 and the population density 40.6 per sq km. At the time of the 2002 census 81.6% of the population were ethnically Russian, 5.5% Armenian, 1.7% Ukrainian, 1.5% Dargin, 1.2% Greek and 0.8% Nogai. Some 56.5% of the population lived in urban areas in January 2007. The Krai's administrative centre is at Stavropol, which had a population of 358,400 in January 2006, according to official estimates. Other major cities are Pyatigorsk (139,500), Nevinnomyssk (130,000) and Kislovodsk (128,700). Stavropol Krai is included in the time zone GMT+3.

HISTORY

Stavropol city was founded in 1777 as part of the consolidation of Russian rule in the Caucasus. The territory was created on 13 February 1924, although it was originally known as the South-Eastern Oblast (when it also incorporated territories of Krasnodar Krai) and, subsequently, North Caucasus Krai. It was named Ordzhonikidze Krai in 1937–43, before adopting its current title. The former Karachai-Cherkess Autonomous Oblast formed part of the Krai until its reconstitution as the Karachai-Cherkess Republic upon the adoption of the 1992 Federation Treaty.

In March 1994 elections were held to a new representative body, the Provincial State Duma. In June 1995 the town of Budennovsk, in the east of the Krai, was the scene of a large-scale hostage-taking operation at a hospital by rebel Chechen forces led by Shamil Basayev; over 1,000 civilians were seized, and more than 100 people were killed during the siege. In the gubernatorial elections of November 1996 the Communist Party of the Russian Federation candidate, Aleksandr Chernogorov, defeated the government-supported incumbent. Chernogorov was re-elected for a further term as Governor in December 2000. In June 2002 the provincial legislature approved legislation, which, in contravention of federal requirements, sought to place restrictions on the number of immigrants permitted to settle in specific regions of the Krai. There was a series of bomb attacks in the Krai during 2000–03, which official sources attributed to Chechen separatists, and in which more than 75 people died. These included a bomb attack on a train near the town of Yessentuki, in the south of the Krai, in December 2003, which killed at least 45 people and injured about 170.

In September 2005 Chernogorov sought an expression of confidence from federal President Vladimir Putin (which would thereby result in his being appointed to a further term of office), three months before the expiry of his mandate. During a subsequent radio broadcast Putin stated that Chernogorov's reappointment would be conditional on the resolution of a particular local issue, namely the restoration of water supplies to a village; on the same day the Governor allocated 80m. roubles for the required repairs. He was duly nominated for a third term, and on 31 October the Krai's legislature approved his appointment. In February 2006 some 300 special forces troops launched operations in the eastern village of Tukui-Mekteb against ethnic Nogai militants believed to be associated with the Islamist Shelkovskii Jamaat group, who were alleged to have been planning a bomb attack against an unidentified target.

According to official reports, eight militants and at least seven law enforcement officials were killed in the ensuing clashes.

In February 2007 the leader of a local Terek Cossack group was shot and severely injured in the town of Novoaleksandrovsk, reportedly precipitating attacks against immigrants from Armenia and Georgia. At elections to the Provincial State Duma on 11 March, the broadly pro-Government A Just Russia (AJR), led by the Mayor of Stavropol, Dmitrii Kuzmin, secured 37.6% of votes cast, while the pro-presidential United Russia (UR) won 23.9%; the Communist Party of the Russian Federation received 14.1%, the nationalist Liberal Democratic Party of Russia 11.8% and the Union of Rightist Forces 7.7% of the votes. After its failure to become the leading party in the regional legislature (in contrast to the results of the elections to 13 other regional legislative organs held concurrently) the federal leadership of UR voted to revoke Chernogorov's membership of the party. In June, following the killing of two students, ethnic Russian nationalists staged an unauthorized protest in Stavropol to demand the expulsion of ethnic Chechens from the Krai and the resignation of Chernogorov; special police forces clashed with demonstrators. A suspect originating from the Karachai-Cherkess Republic was subsequently arrested in connection with the killings. Prior to elections to the State Duma on 2 December, a number of incidents of malpractice, including offers of financial incentives to voters, were reported in the Krai during the campaign.

In April 2008 Chernogorov tendered his resignation as Governor, citing personal reasons. (However, his replacement had been widely expected, following UR's defeat by AJR in the regional legislative elections in March 2007.)

ECONOMY

In 2004 Stavropol Krai's gross regional product was 132,820.8m. roubles, or 48,792.5 roubles per head. Its main industrial centres are at Stavropol, Nevinnomyssk and Budennovsk. In 2005 there were 922 km of railway lines and 7,561 km of paved roads in Stavropol Krai.

The Krai contains extremely fertile soil. Agriculture, which employed 17.5% of the work-force and generated 45,393m. roubles in 2005, consists mainly of grain, sunflower seeds, sugar beet and vegetables. Horticulture, viniculture, bee-keeping and animal husbandry are also important. The Krai's main industries are food-processing, mechanical engineering, production of building materials, chemicals and petrochemicals and the production of natural gas, petroleum, non-ferrous metal ores and coal, and electrical energy. Industry employed 20.5% of the labour force in 2005 and generated 62,978m. roubles in 2004.

The economically active population of Stavropol Krai numbered 1,290,000 in 2005, when 7.0% of the region's labour force were unemployed. The average monthly wage was 5,416.3 roubles. In 2005 there was a budgetary deficit of 291.0m. roubles. In that year the value of exports from the Krai amounted to US $641.2m., and imports were worth $177.1m. Foreign investment in the territory amounted to $61.0m. At the end of 2005 there were some 12,633 small businesses registered in the Krai, providing employment to 108,700 people.

DIRECTORY

Head of the Provincial Administration (Governor): VALERII V. GAYEVSKII (appointment confirmed 23 May 2008), 355025 Stavropol, pl. Lenina 1; tel. (8652) 35-22-52; fax (8652) 35-03-30; e-mail adminf@stv.runnet.ru; internet gubernator.stavkray.ru.

Chairman of the Provincial State Duma: YURII A. GONTAR, 355025 Stavropol, pl. Lenina 1; tel. (8652) 34-82-55; fax (8652) 35-14-55; internet www.dumask.ru.

Chief Representative of Stavropol Krai in the Russian Federation: ANATOLII L. KOLIYEV, 119034 Moscow, ul. Prichistenka 40/2/1; tel. (495) 708-33-66; fax (495) 203-55-39.

Head of Stavropol City Administration (Mayor): DMITRII S. KUZMIN, 355000 Stavropol, pr. K. Marksa 96; tel. (8652) 29-62-63; fax (8652) 26-28-23; e-mail goradm@stv.runnet.ru; internet www.stavropol.stavkray.ru.

Astrakhan Oblast

Astrakhan Oblast is situated in the Caspian lowlands and forms part of the Southern Federal Okrug and the Volga Economic Area. Lying between the Russian federal subject of Kalmykiya to the south and Kazakhstan to the east, Astrakhan is a long, relatively thin territory, which flanks the River Volga as it flows out of Volgograd Oblast in the north-west towards the Caspian Sea to the south-east, via a delta at Astrakhan. The delta is one of the largest in the world and occupies more than 24,000 sq km (9,260 sq miles) of the Caspian lowlands. The Oblast has some 200 km (over 120 miles) of coastline and occupies 44,100 sq km (17,000 sq miles). At January 2007, according to official estimates, its population was 994,127 and its population density 22.5 per sq km. At the time of the 2002 census 69.7% of the population were ethnically Russian, 14.2% Kazakh, 7.0% Tatar, 1.3% Ukrainian, 1.0% Chechen and 0.8% Azeri. Some 66.0% of the population lived in urban areas in January 2007. The Oblast's administrative centre is at Astrakhan (formerly Khadzhi-Tarkhan), which had a population of 499,000 in January 2006, according to official estimates. The city lies at 22 m (72 feet) below sea level and is protected from the waters of the Volga delta by 75 km of dykes. Astrakhan Oblast is included in the time zone GMT+3.

HISTORY

The Khanate of Astrakhan, which was formed in 1446, following the dissolution of the Golden Horde, was conquered by the Russians in 1556. The region subsequently became an important centre for trading in timber, grain, fish and petroleum. Astrakhan Oblast was founded on 27 December 1943. (The region had briefly formed part of the Kazakh SSR in the early 1920s.)

There was considerable hardship in the region following the dissolution of the USSR and the economic reforms of the early 1990s. Dissatisfaction was indicated by the continued pre-eminence of the Communist Party of the Russian Federation (CPRF) in the Oblast and also by the emergence of new Islamic groupings, although, in contrast with the situation in several regions of Russia in the North Caucasus, these groupings did not seek to enter into armed hostilities with the state authorities. The Governor, Anatolii Guzhvin, initially a federal appointee, retained his post at elections in 1997 and was re-elected for a further term of office in December 2000, receiving 81% of the votes cast. Elections to the regional legislature, the Representative Assembly, were held on 28 October 2001; in the following month the Assembly voted to rename itself the State Duma. On 17 August 2004 Guzhvin died, having suffered a heart attack. On 5 December Aleksandr Zhilkin, hitherto First Deputy Governor, was elected Governor, with the support of the pro-presidential United Russia (UR), receiving 65.3% of the votes cast in an election contested by seven candidates. The rate of participation in the election was 48.5%. The decision of the oblast authorities, in late 2005, to order the demolition of a mosque (the construction of which was ongoing) in Astrakhan, apparently on the grounds that it was located too close to an electric power line, was a cause of considerable controversy. The campaign for the demolition was reported to have commenced following a visit to the city by the federal President, Vladimir Putin, when he was purported to have made a comment critical of the location of the proposed place of worship. Although several deadlines, issued by the city government, for the demolition of the structure passed without incident, in September 2006 the federal Supreme Court rejected an appeal by members of the Astrakhan Islamic community against the proposed demolition; the latter was to seek a ruling on the case at the European Court of Human Rights, based in Strasbourg, France. In elections to the regional legislature, held on 8 October, UR received 38.7% of the votes cast, the nationalist Motherland party 16.1%, the CPRF 13.6% and the Russian Pensioners' Party 9.6%. Some 6.0% of the votes were cast 'against all candidates'. In December the Prosecutor's Office initiated criminal proceedings against six members of a local militant Islamist organization, who were suspected of planning an attack in the Oblast. At elections to the State Duma held on 2 December 2007, at which turn-out was 62.4%, UR won 58.0% of votes cast in the Oblast, somewhat lower than the national share of the vote attributed to the party.

ECONOMY

Astrakhan Oblast's gross regional product was 62,567.6m. roubles in 2004, equivalent to 62,584.2 roubles per head. The Oblast's main industrial centres are at Astrakhan and Akhtubinsk. In 2005 there were 602 km of railways and 2,641 km of paved roads on the Oblast's territory. In October 2003 Russia's first container terminal on the Caspian Sea opened at the port of Olya, as part of work towards the construction of a 6,500 km north–south transport corridor to connect India with northern Europe, via Iran and Russia. The rise in the level of the Caspian Sea (by some 2.6 m between the late 1970s and the late 1990s) and the resulting erosion of the Volga delta caused serious environmental problems in the region, which were exacerbated by water pollution and the consequent death of a significant proportion of fish reserves.

The Oblast remains a major producer of vegetables and cucurbits (gourds and melons). Grain production and animal husbandry are also important. Agriculture engaged 14.4% of the work-force and generated 8,333m. roubles in 2005. The Oblast is rich in natural resources, including gas and gas condensate, sulphur, petroleum and salt. Its main industries are the production of petroleum and natural gas, food-processing (particularly fish products), mechanical engineering, ship-building and electricity production. It was anticipated that the extraction of petroleum and natural gas would improve the economic fortunes of the region from the mid-2000s. Industry employed 21.3% of the labour force in 2005 and generated 31,182m. roubles in 2004. Regional trade was also important to the economy of Astrakhan. The Lakor freight company established important shipping links with Iran, and in early 2000 announced plans to develop a trade route with India. Astrakhan's exports to Iran mainly comprised paper, metals, timber, mechanical equipment, fertilizers and chemical products.

Astrakhan Oblast's economically active population numbered 494,000 in 2005, when 12.0% of the region's labour force were unemployed. The average monthly wage was 6,884.2 roubles. In 2005 there was a budgetary deficit of 736.9m. roubles. In that year export trade totalled US $247.1m., and the value of imports amounted to $150.4m, while foreign investment in the territory in 2005 amounted to $32.3m. At the end of that year some 3,936 small businesses were registered in the Oblast, providing employment to 45,500 people.

DIRECTORY

Head of the Regional Administration (Governor): ALEKSANDR A. ZHILKIN (elected 5 December 2004), 414000 Astrakhan, ul. Sovetskaya 14–15; tel. (8512) 22-85-19; fax (8512) 22-95-14; e-mail ves@astrakhan.ru; internet www.jilkin.ru.

Chairman of the Regional Government (Vice-Governor and Prime Minister): KONSTANTIN A. MARKELOV, 414000 Astrakhan, ul. Sovetskaya 14–15; tel. (8512) 22-85-19; fax (8512) 22-95-14; e-mail adm@astranet.ru; internet www.astrobl.ru.

Chairman of the State Duma of Astrakhan Oblast: ALEKSANDR B. KLYKANOV, 414000 Astrakhan, ul. Volodarskogo 15; tel. (8512) 22-96-44; fax (8512) 22-22-48; e-mail gdao@astranet.ru; internet duma.astranet.ru.

Chief Representative of Astrakhan Oblast in the Russian Federation: ANATOLII A. VOLODIN, 129090 Moscow, pr. Mira 3/1; tel. and fax (495) 207-95-78.

Head of Astrakhan City Administration (Mayor): SERGEI A. BOZHENKOV, 414000 Astrakhan, ul. Chernyshevskogo 6; tel. (8512) 22-55-88; fax (8512) 24-71-76; e-mail admin@astrgorod.ru; internet www.astrgorod.ru.

Rostov Oblast

Rostov Oblast is situated in the south of the Eastern European Plain, in the Southern Federal Okrug and the North Caucasus Economic Area. It lies on the Taganrog Gulf of the Sea of Azov. It borders Krasnodar and Stavropol Krais in the south, Kalmykiya in the south and east, Volgograd in the north-east and Voronezh in the north-west. There is an international border with Ukraine to the west. Its major rivers are the Don and the Severnyi Donets. The Volga–Don Canal runs through the region. The Oblast covers 100,800 sq km (38,910 sq miles). At January 2007, according to official estimates, there were 4,275,978 inhabitants and a population density of 42.4 per sq km. At the time of the 2002 census 89.3% of the population were ethnically Russian (including 2.0% of the total that defined their ethnic identity as Cossack), 2.7% Ukrainian and 2.5% Armenian. Some 66.8% of the region's inhabitants resided in urban areas in January 2007. The administrative centre is at Rostov-on-Don (Rostov-na-Donu), which had a population of 1,054,800 in January 2006, according to official estimates. Other major cities are Taganrog (with a population of 268,600), Shakhty (247,700), Novocherkassk (179,500), Volgodonsk (170,800), Novoshakhtinsk (115,300) and Bataisk (104,000). Rostov Oblast is included in the time zone GMT+3.

HISTORY

The city of Rostov-on-Don was established as a Cossack outpost in 1796. It became an important grain-exporting centre in the 19th century, and increased in economic importance after the completion of the Volga–Don Canal. Rostov Oblast was formed in September 1937. The region became heavily industrialized after 1946 and, therefore, considerably increased in population.

In the mid-1990s the liberal Yabloko party enjoyed its highest level of support outside the two federal cities and Kamchatka Oblast (now Kamchatka Krai) in Rostov. The regional Government signed a power-sharing treaty with the federal authorities in June 1996. The incumbent Governor (appointed in October 1991), Vladimir Chub, was elected to that post in September 1996. He was re-elected on 23 September 2001, as the candidate of the pro-presidential Unity bloc (which later became United Russia—UR), receiving 78.1% of the votes cast. On 29 March 2003, one day before regional legislative elections were held, Chub was elected to the Supreme Council of UR.

In the regional elections, supporters of UR were successful in 39 (of a total of 45) districts, although it was reported that many of these candidates had, in fact, concealed their party allegiance. Commentators observed that regional media legislation had resulted in severe restrictions being placed on coverage of candidates' campaigns.

In mid-2004 considerable social tension was reported in Rostov Oblast as workers from several sectors, particularly coal miners, staged strikes and protests. The main source of complaint was non-payment of back wages: reports estimated the total wage arrears for the Oblast at 500m. roubles. In June 2005 Chub submitted his resignation as Governor to federal President Vladimir Putin, in order to seek confirmation that he would be nominated for a further term of office. Putin duly nominated Chub, and his reappointment was confirmed by the regional legislature on 14 June.

In late June 2005 a private aeroplane carrying Garri Kasparov, a former world chess champion and, as leader of the United Civil Front (UCF), a prominent opponent of President Putin, was refused permission to land at the airports at both Rostov and Taganrog. The subsequent cancellation of a proposed press conference in a state-owned building in Rostov, at which Kasparov had intended to promote the opposition Committee 2008 grouping, was similarly attributed to the reluctance of the regional authorities to permit the expression of viewpoints hostile to the federal Government. Meanwhile, it was announced that mounted Cossack patrols, comprising volunteers, were to be established in rural areas across the Oblast in order to assist the law enforcement agencies. (Similar patrols in neighbouring regions had been accused of harassing members of minority ethnic groups.) In November the lower chamber of the federal parliament approved legislation that set out the legal and organizational foundations for such units. In the same month, the UCF regional co-ordinator, Roman Motunov, was attacked in Rostov. In the mid-2000s Rostov Oblast obtained some notoriety as a base of support for extremist Russian nationalist organizations, with inter-ethnic clashes and incidences of violence against members of minority groups being frequently reported. In May 2006, moreover, around 10 members of the prohibited extreme nationalist National Bolshevik Party seized the Rostov office of the state savings bank, Sberbank, to protest against various aspects of Russian economic policy, and threatened to set fire to the building, before being overpowered and arrested. Following this incident the Presidential Representative in the Southern Federal Okrug, Dmitrii Kozak, criticized the regional and local authorities in Rostov for their inability to maintain order.

Elections were held to the regional Legislative Assembly on 2 March 2008. Of the 50 deputies elected (25 from single-member constituencies, 25 on the basis of party lists), 45 were members of UR; the remaining five were members of the Communist Party of the Russian Federation.

ECONOMY

In 2004 Rostov Oblast's gross regional product amounted to 224,024.3m. roubles, or 51,500.2 roubles per head. The Oblast's main industrial centres are at Rostov-on-Don, Taganrog, Novocherkassk, Shakhty, Novoshakhtinsk and Volgodonsk. In 2005 there were 1,846 km of railways and 4,889 km of paved roads in the Oblast. Its ports are both river-ports, at Rostov-on-Don and Ust-Donetskii.

The Oblast is one of the major grain-producing regions in Russia, with agricultural land comprising some 85% of its territory. Agriculture employed 14.4% of the work-force and generated 62,312m. roubles in 2005. The production of sunflower seeds, coriander, mustard, vegetables and cucurbits (gourds and melons) is also important, as are viniculture and horticulture. Industry engaged 22.6% of the Oblast's work-force in 2005 and generated 164,395m. roubles in 2004. The Oblast is situated in the eastern Donbass coal-mining region. Some 6.4m. metric tons of coal were mined in the Oblast in 2004, when it was the ninth-largest producer of coal of any federal subject. It is also rich in natural gas. Its other principal industries are food-processing, ferrous metallurgy, electricity generation, metal-working and mechanical engineering (Rostov-on-Don contained some 50 machine-building plants). The largest industrial concern in the oblast is the Taganrog Metallurgical Plant (TagMet).

The economically active population numbered 2,126,000 in 2005, when 8.6% of the labour force were unemployed, compared with 12.3% in 2003. Those in employment earned an average monthly wage of 5,944.7 roubles. The 2005 regional budget recorded a surplus of 759.6m. roubles. In that year external trade amounted to US $1,818.4m. in exports and $2,044.7m. in imports; total foreign investment in the region amounted to $412.0m. At the end of 2005 there were some 29,099 small businesses registered in the Oblast, providing employment to 185,300 people.

DIRECTORY

Head of the Regional Administration (Governor): VLADIMIR F. CHUB (appointed 8 October 1991, elected 29 September 1996, re-elected 23 September 2001, appointment confirmed 14 June 2005), 344050 Rostov-on-Don, ul. Sotsialisticheskaya 112; tel. (863) 244-18-10; fax (863) 244-15-59; e-mail rra@donpac.ru; internet www.donland.ru.

Chairman of the Legislative Assembly: VIKTOR YE. DERYABKIN, 344050 Rostov-on-Don, ul. Sotsialisticheskaya 112; tel. (863) 240-14-47; fax (863) 240-55-82; e-mail zsrnd@donpac.ru; internet www.zsro.ru.

Chief Representative of Rostov Oblast in the Russian Federation: VIKTOR P. VODOLATSKII, 115184 Moscow, ul. B. Ovchinnikovskii 26/4; tel. (495) 953-90-01; fax (495) 953-89-80; e-mail info@rostovregion.ru; internet www.rostovregion.ru.

Head of Rostov-on-Don City Administration (Mayor): MIKHAIL A. CHERNYSHEV, 344002 Rostov-on-Don, ul. B. Sadovaya 47; tel. (863) 244-15-05; fax (863) 266-62-62; e-mail meria@rostov-gorod.ru; internet www.rostov-gorod.ru.

Volgograd Oblast

Volgograd Oblast is situated in the south-east of the Eastern European Plain. It forms part of the Southern Federal Okrug and the Volga Economic Area. The Oblast has an international border with Kazakhstan to its east. Astrakhan and Kalmykiya lie to the south-east, Rostov to the south-west, Voronezh to the north-west and Saratov to the north. The Oblast's main rivers are the Volga and the Don. Its terrain varies from fertile black earth (*chernozem*) to semi-desert. The region occupies 113,900 sq km (43,980 sq miles). At January 2007 the Oblast had an estimated 2,619,955 inhabitants and a population density of 23.0 per sq km. At the time of the 2002 census 88.9% of the population were ethnically Russian (including 0.8% that described themselves as Cossacks), 2.1% Ukrainian, 1.7% Kazakh, 1.1% Tatar and 1.0% Armenian. Some 75.3% of the population lived in urban areas in January 2007. The Oblast's administrative centre is at Volgograd, which had a population of 991,700 in January 2006, according to official estimates. Other major cities include Volzhskii (308,500) and Kamyshin (121,800). Volgograd Oblast is included in the time zone GMT+3.

HISTORY

The city of Volgograd (known as Tsaritsyn until 1925 and Stalingrad in 1925–61) was founded in the 16th century, at the point where the River Volga flows nearest to the Don (the two river systems were later connected by a canal at this point). The Oblast was formed on 10 January 1934. In 1942–43 the city was the scene of a decisive battle between Soviet and Nazi German forces.

The Communist Party of the Russian Federation (CPRF) held the largest grouping of deputies in the new Oblast Duma, following elections held in 1994. The December 1996 gubernatorial election

was won by Nikolai Maksyuta, the CPRF candidate. Maksyuta was re-elected in December 2000 and December 2004. In May 2007 Roman Grebennikov of the CPRF, hitherto the Chairman of the regional Duma, was elected Head of Volgograd City Administration (Mayor), with 32.5% of votes cast, defeating the candidates of the pro-presidential United Russia and broadly pro-Government A Just Russia.

ECONOMY

In 2004 Volgograd Oblast's gross regional product amounted to 161,688.2m. roubles, or 60,690.9 roubles per head. Its main industrial centres are at Volgograd, Volzhskii and Kamyshin. In 2005 there were 1,617 km of railways and 8,941 km of paved roads.

The region's principal agricultural products are grain, sunflower seeds, vegetables and cucurbits (gourds and melons). Horticulture, bee-keeping and animal husbandry are also important. In 2005 agriculture engaged 16.4% of the work-force and generated 33,735m. roubles. The Oblast's mineral reserves include petroleum, natural gas and phosphorites. The main industries in the Oblast are petroleum-refining, chemicals and petrochemicals, mechanical engineering, metal-working, ferrous metallurgy, the production of electricity, food-processing and the production of petroleum and natural gas. Industry employed 26.7% of the working population in 2005 and generated 128,505m. roubles in 2004.

The economically active population of the Oblast numbered 1,319,000 in 2005, when 6.8% of the labour force were unemployed. The average monthly wage was 6,160.0 roubles in 2005. In that year there was a budgetary deficit of some 482.1m. roubles. In that year external trade constituted US $2,081.8m. in exports and $545.8m. in imports; total foreign investment amounted to $16.4m. At the end of 2005 some 14,323 small businesses were registered in the Oblast, providing employment to 104,300 people.

DIRECTORY

Head of the Regional Administration (Governor): NIKOLAI K. MAKSYUTA (elected 29 December 1996, re-elected 24 December 2000 and 26 December 2004), 400098 Volgograd, pr. Lenina 9; tel. (8442) 30-70-00; fax (8442) 30-73-24; e-mail glava@volganet.ru; internet www.volganet.ru.

Chairman of the Regional Duma: VITALII V. LIKHACHEV, 400098 Volgograd, pr. Lenina 9; tel. (8442) 30-78-44; fax (8422) 36-44-03; internet www.volgoduma.ru.

Chief Representative of Volgograd Oblast in the Russian Federation: TATYANA YE. TRUBITSYNA, 119121 Moscow, Smolenskaya-Sennaya pl. 27–29/1/6; tel. and fax (495) 241-52-02.

Head of Volgograd City Administration (Mayor): ROMAN G. GREBENNIKOV, 400131 Volgograd, ul. Volodarskogo 5; tel. (8442) 33-16-82; fax (8442) 38-54-66; e-mail kancelyaria@volgadmin.ru; internet www.volgadmin.ru.

Volga Federal Okrug

Republic of Bashkortostan

The Republic of Bashkortostan is situated on the slopes of the Southern Urals. It forms part of the Volga Federal Okrug and the Urals Economic Area. There are borders with Perm Krai to the north, the Udmurt Republic in the north-west, Tatarstan in the west, and with the oblasts of Orenburg in the south-west and south, Chelyabinsk in the east and Sverdlovsk to the north. The north of the Republic is forested, while the southern part is steppe. The Republic occupies 143,600 sq km (55,440 sq miles). At January 2007, according to official estimates, Bashkortostan had a total population of 4,050,989 and a population density of 28.2 per sq km. At the time of the 2002 census 36.3% of the population were ethnically Russian, 29.8% Bashkir, 24.1% Tatar, 2.9% Chuvash, 2.6% Mari and 1.3% Ukrainian. (According to the 1989 census, which recorded ethnicity on the basis of official declaration of nationality, rather than self-definition, Tatars outnumbered Bashkirs in the Republic, representing 28% and 22% of the population, respectively.) Bashkir, spoken by the majority of ethnic Bashkirs, is a Kipchak language closely related to that spoken by the Tatars, and has two distinct dialects: Kuvakan, spoken in the north of the Republic; and Yurmatin, current in the south. The majority of Bashkirs and Tatars are Sunni Muslims of the Hanafi school, although some Bashkirs, the Nagaibak, are Orthodox Christians. Some 59.6% of the Republic's population inhabited urban areas in January 2007. The Republic's administrative centre is at Ufa, which had a population of 1,029,600 in January 2006, according to official estimates. Its other major cities include Sterlitamak (265,500), Salavat (157,000), Neftekamsk (118,300) and Oktyabrskii (107,800). Bashkortostan is included in the time zone GMT+5.

HISTORY

The Bashkirs were thought to have originated as a distinct ethnic group during the 16th century, out of the Tatar, Mongol, Volga, Bulgar, Oguz, Pecheneg and Kipchak peoples. The territory was annexed by Russia in 1557, during the reign of Ivan IV ('the Terrible'), and many Bashkirs subsequently lost their land and were forced into servitude. Rebellions against Russian control, most notably that led by Salavat Yulai in 1773, were unsuccessful, and the identity and survival of the Bashkir community came under increasing threat. A large migration of ethnic Russians to the region in the late 19th century resulted in their outnumbering the Bashkir population. A Bashkir ASSR was formed on 23 March 1919.

The Bashkir Autonomous Republic declared its sovereignty on 11 October 1990. On 12 December 1993, when Murtaza Rakhimov (hitherto President of the republican Supreme Soviet) was elected to the new post of President, a republican majority voted against acceptance of the new federal Constitution. On 24 December the republican Supreme Soviet adopted a new Constitution, which stated that its own laws had supremacy over federal laws. The name of Bashkortostan was adopted and a bicameral legislature, the Kurultai, established. Further autonomy was granted under treaties signed in 1994 and in 1995. The administration of the Republic remained highly centralized, with the executive additionally retaining extensive controls over the petroleum sector. Rakhimov was re-elected as President in June 1998. In the federal legislative elections of December 1999, the candidates of Rakhimov's favoured grouping, Fatherland-All Russia (FAR), were successful in the Republic; prior to the election, Rakhimov was rebuked by the federal premier Vladimir Putin for blocking the transmission of two television channels opposed to the grouping. Commentators also observed the absence of any opposition press in Bashkortostan and the removal from electoral lists of most of Rakhimov's opponents, owing to alleged electoral violations.

In May 2000 Putin, now the federal President, ordered that Bashkortostan's Constitution be altered to conform with Russia's basic law. A new Constitution was introduced in November. In January 2001 a provision in the new document that republican legislation should take precedence over federal law was rescinded. In June 2002, however, the federal Supreme Court ruled that some 37 articles of Bashkortostan's Constitution still failed to comply with federal law.

On 3 December 2002 a further new republican Constitution was adopted, which transferred several powers from the Prime Minister to the President and referred to the 'statehood' of the Republic, but not its 'sovereignty', the term used in the previous documents. None the less, the text was widely regarded as broadly conforming with federal laws, and the power-sharing treaties signed between the republican and federal authorities were annulled.

At elections to the new, unicameral Kurultai, held on 16 March 2003, the successor to FAR, Unity and Fatherland-United Russia (later United Russia—UR) obtained control of 91 of the 120 seats. In the first round of the republican presidential election, held on 7 December, no candidate received an absolute majority of the votes cast. Rakhimov (who received 42.6% of the votes cast) and the second-placed candidate, who had been initially favoured by the federal authorities, Sergei Veremeyenko (with 23.0%), duly proceeded to a second round of voting on 21 December. Prior to the 'run-off' election, Veremeyenko announced that he had ceased campaigning, although his name remained on the ballot. This effective lack of opposition, now combined with public support from Putin, enabled Rakhimov to secure re-election to a third term, with some 78.0% of the votes cast. Putin's change of position was seen partly as the result of Rakhimov's highly effective campaigning on behalf of UR in the federal legislative elections, also held on 7 December.

Some controversy arose nationally following an incident in the city of Blagoveshchensk, north-east of Ufa, in December 2004, in which police officers were reported to have seized up to 1,000 men over a period of five days and beaten a number of them severely, apparently in revenge for an attack against a police patrol. In March 2005 some 20,000 people were reported to have participated in a demonstration in Ufa organized by the republican branches of eight political parties, including the Communist Party of the Russian Federation, the Liberal Democratic Party of Russia, Motherland and Yabloko, against human rights abuses in Bashkortostan. The demonstrators demanded Rakhimov's resignation and the payment of compensation to those beaten. In May, following further protests, it was announced that at least nine police officers were to be charged with exceeding their authority or abuse of office, although the case made only slow progress. Meanwhile, in August the Supreme Court of Bashkortostan sentenced nine members of the proscribed militant Islamist group, Hizb-ut-Tahrir al-Islami (Party of Islamic Liberation), to custodial sentences, representing the first use of federal anti-extremist legislation approved in 2003. In September the first police officer to be convicted in connection with the police abuse scandal of December 2004 was given a three-year suspended sentence. In the same month the Kurultai made an official appeal to Putin to restore the power-sharing treaties between the republican and the federal authorities that had been annulled in 2002. On 10 October 2006 the Kurultai voted to approve Putin's nomination of Rakhimov to a further term of office. The pro-Government United Russia secured an overwhelming victory in elections to the Kurultai, held on 2 March 2008, winning 85.8% of the votes cast. The Communist Party of the Russian Federation were placed second, with 7.2%.

In April 2008 Rafael Baidavletov tendered his resignation as Prime Minister, after he was appointed to the Federation Council. It was reported that President Rakhimov had engineered Baidavletov's replacement with the intention of ensuring that power was inherited by his son, Ural, after his own retirement. The hitherto republican Minister of Property Relations, Rail Sarbayev, a close associate of Ural Rakhimov, was appointed Prime Minister. In June Rakhimov removed the presidential Chief of Staff, who was subsequently charged with corruption (although criminal proceedings against him were reported to have been abandoned). In October the Republic's Minister of the Interior was also removed.

ECONOMY

Bashkortostan's economy is dominated by its fuel and energy and agro-industrial complexes. The Republic is one of Russia's key petroleum-producing areas and the centre of its petroleum-refining industry. It produced 11.1m. metric tons of petroleum in 2005. The quantity of petroleum produced and refined in the Republic declined significantly during the 1990s. In 2004 the territory's gross regional product amounted to 336,930.8m. roubles, or 82,468.7 roubles per head. Amid concerns that the federal Government was seeking to gain increased control over the natural resources of the Republic, at the expense of the republican authorities, republican President Rakhimov announced, in mid-2002, that several of the republican petroleum companies were to be transferred to private ownership. (Subsequently, Rakhimov's son, Ural, obtained control of significant energy assets in the Republic.) However, in an apparent attempt to gain support from the federal authorities in late 2003, Rakhimov ceded management of the Republic's largest petrochemical plant, Salavatnefteorgsintez, to the state-controlled corporation, Gazprom, which announced proposals to privatize the plant in 2008. Bashkortostan's major industrial centres are at Ufa, Sterlitamak, Salavat and Ishimbai. At the end of 2005 there were 1,457 km of railways on its territory, and 22,263 km of paved roads. There is an international airport at Ufa.

Bashkortostan's agriculture employed 15.3% of the work-force and generated 62,789m. roubles in 2005. The main agricultural activities are animal husbandry, bee-keeping, and grain and vegetable production. As well as its petroleum resources, Bashkortostan contains deposits of natural gas, brown coal (lignite), iron ore, copper, gold, zinc, aluminium, chromium, salt, manganese, gypsum and limestone. The Republic's other industries include mechanical engineering, metal-working, electricity generation, and chemicals and pet-rochemicals. Industry employed 26.0% of the Republic's working population in 2005 and generated 358,657m. roubles in 2004.

In 2005 the economically active population of the Republic numbered 2,019,000, and 7.1% of the labour force were unemployed. The average monthly wage was 6,612.0 roubles. There was a budgetary surplus of 4,475.4m. roubles in 2005, when the Republic's external trade comprised US $6,456.6m. in exports and $484.4m. in imports. In 2005 foreign investment in the Republic amounted to $242.7m. At the end of 2005 some 19,340 small businesses were registered in the Republic, providing employment to 229,700 people.

DIRECTORY

President: MURTAZA G. RAKHIMOV (elected 12 December 1993, re-elected 14 June 1998 and 21 December 2003, appointment confirmed 10 October 2006), 450101 Bashkortostan, Ufa, ul. Tukayeva 46; tel. (3472) 50-27-24; fax (3472) 50-02-81; e-mail web@presidentrb.ru; internet www.bashkortostan.ru.

Prime Minister: RAIL S. SARBAYEV, 450101 Bashkortostan, Ufa, ul. Tukayeva 46, Dom Respubliki; tel. (3472) 50-58-64; fax (3472) 50-46-78; e-mail letters@bashkortostan.ru.

Chairman of the State Assembly (Kurultai): KONSTANTIN B. TOLKACHEV, 450000 Bashkortostan, Ufa, ul. Frunze 46; tel. (3472) 50-19-04; fax (3472) 50-08-86; e-mail kurultai@rb.ru.

Chief Representative of the Republic of Bashkortostan in the Russian Federation: ALBERT M. KHARISOV, 105066 Moscow, ul. Dobroslobodskaya 6/2; tel. (495) 642-91-05; fax (495) 621-47-14; e-mail pprb-la@mail.ru; internet www.bashpred.ru.

Head of Ufa City Administration (Mayor): PAVEL R. KACHKAYEV, 450098 Bashkortostan, Ufa, pr. Oktyabrya 120; tel. (3472) 79-05-79; fax (3472) 33-18-73; e-mail ufacity@ufacity.info; internet www .ufacity.info.

Chuvash Republic

The Chuvash Republic is situated in the north-west of European Russia. It forms part of the Volga Federal Okrug and the Volga-Vyatka Economic Area. The Republic lies on the Eastern European Plain, on the middle reaches of the Volga. Ulyanovsk neighbours it to the south, Mordoviya to the south-west, Nizhnii Novgorod to the west and Marii-El and Tatarstan to the north and the east, respectively. The Republic's major rivers are the Volga and the Sura, and one-third of its territory is covered by forest. It occupies 18,300 sq km (7,070 sq miles). At January 2007, according to official estimates, the Republic had a total population of 1,286,239 and a population density of 70.3 per sq km. At the time of the 2002 census 67.7% of the population were ethnically Chuvash, 26.5% Russian, 2.8% Tatar and 1.2% Mordovian. An estimated 76.5% of the ethnically Chuvash population speak Chuvash, which has its origins in the Bulgar group of the Western Hunnic group of Turkic languages, as a first language. The dominant religions in the Republic are Islam and Orthodox Christianity. Some 57.3% of the population lived in urban areas in January 2007. The Republic's capital is at Cheboksary (Shupash-kar), which had a population of 442,400 in January 2006, according to official estimates. Its other major town is Novocheboksarsk (125,500). The Republic is included in the time zone GMT+3.

HISTORY

The Chuvash, traditionally a semi-nomadic people, were conquered by the Mongol-Tatars in the 13th century. Their territory subsequently became part of the dominion of the Golden Horde and many were converted to Islam. From the late 1430s the Chuvash were ruled by the Kazan Khanate. In 1551 the region became a part of the Russian Empire. Despite intense Christianization and 'russification' on the part of the Russian state, the Chuvash acquired their own national and cultural identity, which had Suvar-Bulgar and Finno-Ugric components, by the end of the 15th century. The Chuvash capital was founded at Cheboksary in 1551, at the site of a settlement first mentioned in Russian chronicles in 1469. The construction of other towns and forts, intended to encourage migration into the area, followed. After 1917 the Chuvash people made vociferous demands for autonomy to the Soviet Government. A Chuvash Autonomous Oblast was established in June 1920, which was upgraded to the status of an ASSR on 21 April 1925.

Chuvash nationalism re-emerged in the early 1990s: the Chuvash ASSR declared its sovereignty on 27 October 1990 and adopted the name of the Chuvash (Chavash) Republic in March 1992. In December 1993 the Republic voted against acceptance of the federal Constitution. In that month Nikolai Fedorov, a supporter of economic reform and former Minister of Justice in the federal Government,

was elected republican President. In May 1996 the republican Government signed a treaty with federal President Boris Yeltsin on the delimitation of powers between their respective authorities. Fedorov was elected to a further term of office on 28 December 1997, receiving 56.5% of the votes cast. In October 2001, following the resignation of the incumbent Chairman of the republican Council of Ministers (Prime Minister), Fedorov appointed himself to the position, announcing that combining the roles of republican president and premier would increase the Government's accountability. On 16 December Fedorov was re-elected as Governor, with 41% of the votes. Immediately following his re-election, Fedorov announced that he was to rescind his position as Prime Minister. In August 2005 federal President Vladimir Putin nominated Fedorov to serve a further term of office; this nomination was approved by the republican legislature on 29 August. The pro-presidential United Russia secured a comfortable victory in elections to the State Council, held on 8 October 2006, winning 51.9% of the votes cast, compared to the 19.5% acquired by its nearest rival, the Communist Party of the Russian Federation. The nationalist Liberal Democratic Party of Russia also obtained representation, with 8.9%.

ECONOMY

In 2004 the Republic's gross regional product amounted to 61,971.6m. roubles, equivalent to 47,591.9 roubles per head. The major industrial centres are at Cheboksary, Novocheboksarsk and Kanash. At the end of 2005 there were 397 km of railways and 4,746 km of paved roads in the Republic.

Agriculture, which employed 13.5% of the work-force and generated 14,821m. roubles in 2005, consists mainly of animal husbandry and of grain, potato and hop production. The Republic contains deposits of peat, sand, limestone and dolomite. Its main industries are mechanical engineering, metal-working, electricity generation, production of chemicals and petrochemicals, light industry and food-processing. The industrial sector employed 29.0% of the working population in 2005 and generated 50,482m. roubles in 2004.

The economically active population in the Chuvash Republic amounted to 662,000 in 2005; 11.4% of the Republic's labour force were unemployed, while the average monthly wage in the territory was 5,073.1 roubles. In 2005 there was a budgetary deficit of 678.4m. roubles, while exports from the Republic amounted to US $188.4m., and imports to the Republic to $92.8m. Foreign investment in 2005 amounted to $15.6m. At the end of that year 5,965 small businesses were registered in the Republic, providing employment to 68,200 people.

DIRECTORY

President: NIKOLAI V. FEDOROV (elected 12 December 1993, re-elected 28 December 1997 and 16 December 2001, appointment confirmed 29 August 2005), 428004 Chuvash Rep., Cheboksary, pl. Respubliki 1, Dom Pravitelstva; tel. (8352) 39-33-01; fax (8352) 62-17-99; e-mail president@cap.ru; internet www.cap.ru.

Chairman of the Cabinet of Ministers (Prime Minister): SERGEI A. GAPLIKOV, 428004 Chuvash Rep., Cheboksary, pl. Respubliki 1; tel. (8352) 62-01-76; fax (8352) 62-01-46; e-mail km@cap.ru; internet gov.cap.ru/main.asp?govid=17.

Chairman of the State Council (Parliament): MIKHAIL A. MIKHAILOVSKII, 428004 Chuvash Rep., Cheboksary, pl. Respubliki 1; tel. (8352) 62-22-72; fax (8352) 62-23-15; e-mail gs@cap.ru; internet www.gs.chuvashia.com.

Chief Representative of the Chuvash Republic in the Russian Federation: GENNADII S. FEDOROV, 109017 Moscow, ul. B. Ordynka 46/1; tel. and fax (495) 953-21-59; e-mail polprcheb@cap.ru; internet gov.cap.ru/main.asp?govid=100.

Head of Cheboksary City Administration (Mayor): NIKOLAI I. YEMELYANOV, 428000 Chuvash Rep., Cheboksary, ul. K. Marksa 36; tel. (8352) 62-35-76; fax (8352) 62-40-50; e-mail gcheb@cap.ru; internet www.gcheb.cap.ru.

Republic of Marii-El

The Republic of Marii-El is situated in the east of the Eastern European Plain in the middle reaches of the River Volga. It forms part of the Volga Federal Okrug and the Volga-Vyatka Economic Area. Tatarstan and the Chuvash Republic neighbour it to the south-east and to the south, respectively. Nizhnii Novgorod lies to the west and Kirov to the north and north-east. Marii-El occupies 23,200 sq km (9,000 sq miles). At January 2007, according to official estimates, the population of the Republic was 706,680, and the population density 30.5 per sq km. At the time of the 2002 census 47.5% of the population were ethnically Russian and 42.9% were

Mari (Cheremiss), including Lugovo-Vostochnye Mari (7.2% of the total population) and Mountain Mari (2.4%); 6.0% of the population were Tatar; and 1.0% were Chuvash. Orthodox Christianity is the predominant religion in Marii-El, although many Mari adhere to aspects of their traditional animistic religion. Their native language belongs to the Finnic branch of the Uralo-Altaic family. Some 63.2% of the population inhabited urban areas in January 2007. The capital of the Republic is at Yoshkar-Ola, with a population of 251,400 in January 2006, according to official estimates. Marii-El is included in the time zone GMT+3.

HISTORY

The Mari emerged as a distinct ethnic group in the sixth century. In the eighth century they came under the influence of the Khazar empire, but from the mid-ninth to the mid-12th century they were ruled by the Volga Bulgars. In the 1230s Mari territory was conquered by the Mongol Tatars and remained under the control of the Kazan khanate until its annexation by Russia in 1552. Nationalist feeling on the part of the Mari did not become evident until the 1870s, when a religious movement, the Kugu Sorta (Great Candle), attacked the authority of the Orthodox Church in the region. A Mari Autonomous Oblast was established in 1920. On 5 December 1936 the territory became the Mari ASSR.

The Republic declared its sovereignty on 22 October 1990. A presidential election was held on 14 December 1991. In December 1993 elections were held to a new 300-seat parliament, the State Assembly, which was dominated by the Communist Party of the Russian Federation (CPRF). The new legislature adopted a republican Constitution in June 1995 that designated the territory as the Republic of Marii-El. A power-sharing agreement between the republic and federal authorities was signed in May 1998. At parliamentary elections held in the Republic in October 2000, CPRF and other left-wing candidates secured the highest proportion of the votes cast. At the gubernatorial election in December, the incumbent, Vyacheslav Kislitsyn, was defeated by Leonid Markelov, of the nationalist Liberal Democratic Party of Russia. He was re-elected to a further term of office on 19 December 2004, receiving 56.9% of the votes cast. Markelov's candidacy was supported by, among others, the republican branch of the pro-presidential United Russia party. The rate of participation in the election was 63.6%.

In the mid-2000s increasing concern was expressed, in Marii-El and by members of other Finno-Ugric peoples both within and outwith Russia, at the apparently systematic marginalization of the cultural and political expression and organization of ethnic Mari groups in the Republic, while the use of the Mari language in education and broadcasting was increasingly subject to restrictions. In July 2005 a prominent Finno-Ugric scholar and vocal opponent of Markelov, Yurii Anduganov (who had ceased to reside in the Republic, apparently as a result of political pressures against him), died in a road accident, in circumstances that remained unexplained. Moreover, two prominent Mari leaders were assaulted in the Republic during the first half of 2005.

ECONOMY

In 2004 the Republic's gross regional product amounted to 30,338.4m. roubles, equivalent to 42,172.9 roubles per head. Its major industrial centres are at Yoshkar-Ola and Volzhsk. At the end of 2005 there were 181 km of railway lines and 3,308 km of paved roads on the Republic's territory.

Marii-El's agriculture, which in 2005 employed 14.9% of the workforce and generated 11,612m. roubles, consists mainly of animal husbandry and the production of flax, vegetables, potatoes and grain. The Republic's main industries are mechanical engineering, metalworking, electricity production and the processing of forestry and food products. Industry employed 23.8% of the work-force in 2005 and generated 22,892m. roubles in 2004.

In 2005 the economically active population in the Republic numbered 381,000, and 9.9% of the labour force were unemployed; the average monthly wage was 4,938.2 roubles, substantially lower than the average wage in the Federation or in most neighbouring regions. In 2005 there was a budgetary deficit of 9.0m. roubles. In that year external trade comprised US $54.0m. in exports and $31.1m. in imports. Foreign investment in Marii-El was minimal, amounting to $5.2m. in 2005. At the end of that year 4,465 small businesses were registered in the Republic, providing employment to 31,900 people.

DIRECTORY

President and Head of the Government: LEONID I. MARKELOV (elected 17 December 2000, re-elected 19 December 2004), 424001 Marii-El, Yoshkar-Ola, Leninskii pr. 29; tel. (8362) 64-15-25; fax (8362) 64-19-21; e-mail president@gov.mari.ru; internet gov.mari .ru.

Chairman of the State Assembly: YURII A. MINAKOV, 424001 Marii-Ola, Leninskii pr. 29; tel. (8362) 64-14-17; fax (8362) 64-14-11; e-mail info@parliament.mari.ru; internet parlament.mari.ru.

Chief Representative of the Republic of Marii-El in the Russian Federation: SERGEI V. SEMKIN, 119019 Moscow, ul. Novyi Arbat 21/1827; tel. and fax (495) 291-48-34.

Head of Yoshkar-Ola City Administration (Mayor): OLEG P. VOINOV, 424001 Marii-El, Yoshkar-Ola, Leninskii pr. 27; tel. (8362) 41-44-89; fax (8362) 63-03-71; internet capital.mari-el.ru.

Republic of Mordoviya

The Republic of Mordoviya is situated in the Eastern European Plain, in the Volga river basin. The north-west of the Republic occupies a section of the Oka-Don plain and the south-east lies in the Volga Highlands. The region forms part of the Volga Federal Okrug and the Volga-Vyatka Economic Area. The Chuvash Republic lies to the north-east, with the Oblasts of Ulyanovsk to the east, Penza to the south, Ryazan to the west and Nizhnii Novgorod to the north. The major rivers are the Moksha, the Sura and the Insar. Mordoviya occupies 26,200 sq km (10,110 sq miles). At January 2007, according to official estimates, the Republic had a population of 847,645 and a population density of 32.4 per sq km. At the time of the 2002 census 60.8% of the population were ethnic Russians, 31.9% were Mordovians (including 8.9% of the total population who described themselves as Erzya-Mordovians and 5.3% who described themselves as Moksha-Mordovians) and 5.2% were Tatars. The majority of Mordovians inhabited the agricultural regions of the west and north-east. The dominant religion is Orthodox Christianity. The native tongue of the Mordovians belongs to the Finnic group of the Uralo-Altaic family. Some 59.4% of the Republic's population inhabited urban areas in January 2007. Mordoviya's capital is at Saransk, which had a population of 297,100 in January 2006, according to official estimates. The Republic is included in the time zone GMT+3.

HISTORY

The Mordovians first appear in historical records of the sixth century, when they inhabited the area between the Oka and the middle Volga rivers. In the late 12th and early 13th centuries a feudal society began to form in Mordoviya. One of its most famous fiefdoms was that headed by Prince Purgas. The Mordovians came under the control of the Mongols and Tatars between the 13th and the 15th centuries and, at the fall of the Khanate of Kazan in 1552, were voluntarily incorporated into the Russian state. Many thousands of Mordovians fled Russian rule in the late 16th and early 17th centuries to settle in the Ural Mountains and in southern Siberia, while those that remained were outnumbered by ethnic Russian settlers. The region was predominantly agricultural until the completion of the Moscow–Kazan railway in the 1890s, when it became more commercial and its industry developed.

Although Mordovians had become increasingly assimilated into Russian life from the late 19th century, a Mordovian Autonomous Okrug was created in 1928, which was upgraded to an Autonomous Oblast in 1930 and to an ASSR in 1934. It declared its sovereignty on 8 December 1990 and was renamed the Republic of Mordoviya in January 1994. A Constitution was adopted on 21 September 1995, establishing an executive presidency and a legislative State Assembly. Nikolai Merkushkin, Chairman of the republican legislature since January and a former head of the Republican Komsomol (V. I. Lenin Young Communist League), became President. In February 1998 Merkushkin was elected President, with 96.6% of the votes cast, after all opponents other than the director of a local pasta factory, who had frequently announced his support for Merkushkin's policies, had been disqualified. On 16 February 2003 Merkushkin was re-elected to a further term of office, receiving 87.3% of the votes cast in an election contested by five candidates; 83.2% of the electorate voted. Merkushkin was subsequently appointed to the Supreme Council of the pro-presidential United Russia (UR); the party performed strongly in Mordoviya at elections to the federal State Duma on 7 December, held concurrently with elections to the republican State Assembly. In November 2005, some three years ahead of the expiry of his term of office, Merkushkin was nominated by federal President Vladimir Putin to serve a further term; on 10 November this appointment was confirmed by the republican parliament. On 19 September 2007 the State Assembly adopted a resolution in favour of dissolving itself and moving elections forward, from March 2008 to 2 December 2007, to coincide with elections to the State Duma. UR secured 90.4% of votes cast to the State Assembly and, at the concurrent elections to the State Duma, won 93.4% of votes cast in the Republic, according to official results.

ECONOMY

In 2004 the gross regional product of Mordoviya was 52,265.1m. roubles, or 59,980.6 roubles per head. The territory's major industrial centres are at Saransk and Ruzayevka. At the end of 2005 there were 546 km of railway lines and 4,461 km of paved roads on the Republic's territory.

The principal crops in Mordoviya are grain, sugar beet, potatoes and vegetables. Animal husbandry (especially cattle) and bee-keeping are also important. Agriculture employed 18.0% of the working population and generated 15,999m. roubles in 2005. Industry employed 28.3% of the labour force in 2005 and generated 36,884m. roubles in 2004. The main industries are mechanical engineering and metal-working. There is also some production of electricity, production of chemicals and petrochemicals, and food-processing. Mordoviya is the centre of the Russian lighting equipment industry.

In 2005 the economically active population was 434,000, and 7.0% of the labour force were unemployed. The average monthly wage in the Republic was 5,060.7 roubles in that year. In 2005 there was a budgetary deficit of some 449.3m. roubles. External trade amounted to US $58.6m. in exports and $86.1m. in imports. In 2005 foreign investment in the Republic amounted to $43.4m. At the end of that year 2,476 small businesses were registered in the Republic, providing employment to 28,100 people.

DIRECTORY

President: Nikolai I. Merkushkin (assumed office 22 September 1995, elected 15 February 1998, re-elected 16 February 2003, appointment confirmed 10 November 2005), 430002 Mordoviya, Saransk, ul. Sovetskaya 35; tel. (8342) 47-54-71; fax (8342) 47-45-26; e-mail radm@whrm.moris.ru; internet www.e-mordovia.ru.

Chairman of the Government (Prime Minister): Vladimir D. Volkov, 430002 Mordoviya, Saransk, ul. Sovetskaya 35; tel. (8342) 32-74-69; fax (8342) 47-36-28; e-mail pred@whrm.moris.ru; internet www.e-mordovia.ru/main/gossobranie/index.php.

Chairman of the State Assembly: Valerii A. Kechkin, 430002 Mordoviya, Saransk, ul. Sovetskaya 26; tel. (8342) 32-79-50; fax (8342) 47-04-95; e-mail gsprot@whrm.moris.ru.

Chief Representative of the Republic of Mordoviya in the Russian Federation: Viktor I. Chindyaskin, 127018 Moscow, ul. Obraztsova 29; tel. (495) 602-67-44; fax (495) 218-01-42.

Head of Saransk City Administration: Vladimir F. Sushkov, 430000 Mordoviya, Saransk, ul. Sovetskaya 30; tel. (8342) 47-68-36; fax (8342) 47-67-70; e-mail saransk@moris.ru.

Republic of Tatarstan

The Republic of Tatarstan is situated in the east of European Russia and forms part of the Volga Federal Okrug and the Volga Economic Area. Bashkortostan lies to the east, the Udmurt Republic to the north, Marii-El to the north-west, and the Chuvash Republic to the west. Ulyanovsk, Samara and Orenburg Oblasts lie to the south and Kirov is to the north. The Republic's major rivers are the Volga and the Kama. Tatarstan occupies 68,000 sq km (26,250 sq miles). At January 2007 it had an estimated population of 3,760,534 and a population density of 55.3 per sq km. In 2002 some 52.9% of the population were Tatars, 39.5% ethnic Russians and 3.3% were Chuvash. Although figures on ethnicity in the 2002 census are not directly comparable with those in previous censuses, they suggested an increase of around one-10th in the proportion of the population accounted for by Tatars since 1989, and a similar decline in the proportion of Russians. Some 74.6% of the Republic's population inhabited urban areas in January 2007. Tatarstan's capital is Kazan, which lies on the River Volga and had a population of 1,112,700 in January 2006, according to official estimates. Other major cities include Naberezhnye Chelny (formerly Brezhnev—with a population of 507,200), Nizhnekamsk (226,900) and Almetyevsk (141,700). The Republic is included in the time zone GMT+3.

HISTORY

After the dissolution of the Mongol Empire the region became the Khanate of Kazan, the territory of the Golden Horde. The city of Kazan was founded in 1005. Kazan was conquered by Russian troops, led by Tsar Ivan IV ('the Terrible') in 1552. Some of the Muslim Tatars succumbed to Russian pressures to convert to Orthodox Christianity, becoming known as Kryashens, but most did not. A modernist school of thought in Islam, Jadidism, originated among the Volga Tatars in the 19th century. A Tatar ASSR was established on 27 May 1920.

On 31 August 1990 the Chairman of the republican Supreme Soviet, Mintimer Shaimiyev, declared Tatarstan a sovereign republic. In 1991 Shaimiyev was elected as republican President. Apart from secessionist Chechnya, Tatarstan was the only Republic to reject the Federation Treaty of the following year, adopting its own Constitution on 6 November 1992, which provided for a presidential republic with a bicameral legislature, the State Council. In February 1994 Shaimiyev won concessions from the federal Government by signing a treaty that ceded extensive powers to Tatarstan, including full ownership rights over its petroleum reserves and industrial companies, the right to retain most of its tax revenue and the right to pursue its own foreign-trade policy. This was the first agreement of its kind in the Federation and, despite significant contradictions and weaknesses, it became a model for other federal subjects seeking to determine their relations with the federal centre.

In a republican presidential election, held on 24 March 1996, Shaimiyev was re-elected unopposed, in breach of federal legislation. During 1999 Shaimiyev was among those regional governors most active in the creation of the All Russia political bloc. Shaimiyev was elected to a further term of office in March 2001, when he obtained some 80% of the votes cast, becoming the first Governor of any federal subject in the Russian Federation to be elected three times to that post.

As the administration of federal President Vladimir Putin, from mid-2000, sought to harmonize federal legislation with that of the constituent units of the Russian Federation, Tatarstan became one of the principal regions in which the republican authorities demonstrated sustained resistance to these measures. In May 2001 the federal Supreme Court declared that some 42 articles of the Republic's Constitution were at variance with federal law (a ruling by the republican Supreme Court confirmed these findings in October). The text of a new Constitution was approved by the republican State Council in February 2002 and took effect from 19 April. However, in June the office of the federal Prosecutor-General demanded that several articles of the Constitution be amended, notably those that preserved the notion of Tatar citizenship and that referred to the 'limited' and 'residual' sovereignty of the Republic. In September the State Council rejected any notion that the constitutional text was in breach of federal law. Meanwhile, tensions between the federal and republican authorities were further heightened by federal legislation, approved in November 2002, that demanded that all state languages of federal subjects be written in Cyrillic on official documents—the republican authorities had, in September 1999, begun to implement a programme to reintroduce the Latin script (previously used in the 1920s–30s) for the Tatar language. In mid-2003 the power-sharing treaty signed in 1994 was annulled. In February 2004 the State Council appealed to the federal Constitutional Court to review the law on Cyrillic-based alphabets, but this appeal was rejected in November; this ruling was upheld by the federal Supreme Court in the following month.

In March 2005, following the introduction of a system of presidential appointment for regional governors and presidents, and the amendment of the republican Constitution to that end, Shaimiyev (who was by now regarded as an important ally of Putin) requested that Putin nominate him to serve a further term as President of Tatarstan. Shaimiyev was duly nominated, and his appointment to a further five-year term of office was confirmed by the republican State Council on 25 March. On 28 October the republican legislature approved a new draft power-sharing treaty with the federal authorities, which would be, upon its eventual implementation, the first such agreement to take effect for several years; although the proposed new treaty attributed less autonomy to the Republic than that of 1994–2003, the document none the less provided for certain economic and cultural concessions not granted to other federal subjects, including tax exemptions on natural resources, the right of the local language (i.e. Tatar) to be declared the official language of the Republic and the inclusion of an insert in Tatar in federal passports of those resident in the Republic. In November 2006 Putin submitted the draft treaty, already signed by himself and Shaimiyev, to the federal legislature for approval. (Some analysts believed that the emergence of a several radical groups in Tatarstan, both nationalist and Islamist, and a recent wave of bombings, attributed to militants, in the Republic may have been a factor in Putin's signing of the treaty, which would serve to strengthen Shaimiyev's position as republican leader.) On 9 February 2007 the lower chamber of the federal legislature, the State Duma, approved the power-sharing treaty. However, the treaty remained subject to significant opposition, and on 21 February it was rejected by the upper federal legislative chamber, the Federation Council, on the grounds that it contravened the federal Constitution. A revised version of the treaty was ratified by both chambers of the federal legislature in July. In September a former aide to Shaimiyev appealed to the federal Supreme Court to annul the endorsement of the treaty, on the grounds that a requirement that the President of Tatarstan speak both Russian and Tatar was in contravention of both the federal and republican Constitutions. In mid-2008 Shaimiyev reiterated his support for the restoration of a system of gubernatorial elections, rather than the selection of heads of regions by federal presidential nomination.

ECONOMY

In 2004 the Republic's gross regional product totalled 410,905.9m. roubles, or 108,972.5 roubles per head. The territory is one of the most developed economic regions of the Russian Federation and has vast agricultural and industrial potential. Its main industrial centres are Kazan, Naberezhnye Chelny, Zelenodolsk, Nizhnekamsk and Almetyevsk. Kazan is the most important port on the Volga and a junction in the national rail, road and air transport systems. An important petroleum export pipeline to Europe starts in Almetyevsk. At the end of 2005 there were 866 km of railway lines and 13,478 km of paved roads on the Republic's territory.

Agriculture, which employed 10.2% of the work-force and generated 66,071m. roubles in 2005 (the third-highest output of any federal subject), consists mainly of grain production, animal husbandry, horticulture and bee-keeping. The Republic has significant reserves of hydrocarbons reserves. Industry accounted for 31.1% of employment in 2005 and generated 369,810m. roubles in 2004. Kazan, Zelenodolsk and Vasilyevo are centres for light industry, the manufacture of petrochemicals and building materials, and mechanical engineering. The automobile and petroleum industries are major employers in the region. The petrochemicals company Kazanorgsintez is the largest polyethylene producer in Russia. Output of petroleum in the region in 2005 amounted to 30.7m. metric tons, a figure surpassed among federal subjects only by the Khanty-Mansii and Yamalo-Nenets AOks in Tyumen Oblast. Industries connected with the extraction, processing and use of petroleum typically represent around 40% of the Republic's total industrial production. In the mid-1990s the US automobile company, General Motors, signed a contract to manufacture automobiles at the plant, in the city of Yelabuga, which later became the centre of a zone offering special tax incentives. In 2005 some 30,400 automobiles were manufactured in the Republic. In November 2005 the federal authorities announced that one of six special economic zones to be established across the Federation was to be located in Tatarstan; the zone, near Yelabuga, was to be dedicated to the production of automobile components and high-technology petroleum sector products.

The economically active population in the Republic amounted to 1,879,000 in 2005, when 6.7% of the labour force were unemployed. The average monthly wage was 7,067.8 roubles in 2005. The 2005 budget recorded a deficit of some 565m. roubles. The value of exports amounted to US $8,960.1m. in 2005, and imports to $563.6m. Foreign investment in the Republic amounted to $432.6m. in 2005. At the end of that year some 18,642 small businesses were registered in the Republic, providing employment to 146,500 people.

DIRECTORY

President: Mintimer Sh. Shaimiyev (elected 12 June 1991, re-elected unopposed 24 March 1996, re-elected 25 March 2001, appointment confirmed 25 March 2005), 420014 Tatarstan, Kazan, Kreml; tel. (843) 292-74-66; fax (843) 291-78-66; e-mail secretariat@tatar.ru; internet president.tatar.ru.

Prime Minister: Rustam N. Minnikhanov, 420060 Tatarstan, Kazan, pl. Svobody 1; tel. (843) 264-77-02; fax (843) 264-32-64; e-mail enter@kabmin.tatarstan.ru; internet prav.tatar.ru.

Chairman of the State Council: Farid Kh. Mukhametshin, 420060 Tatarstan, Kazan, pl. Svobody 1; tel. (843) 267-63-00; fax (843) 267-64-89; e-mail gossov@gossov.tatarstan.ru; internet www.gossov.tatarstan.ru.

Chief Representative of the Republic of Tatarstan in the Russian Federation: Nazif M. Mirikhanov, 107813 Moscow, per. 3-i Kotelnicheskii 13/15/1; tel. (495) 915-58-02; fax (495) 915-06-10; e-mail adm@msk.tatarstan.ru.

Head of Kazan City Executive: Marat F. Zagidullov, 420014 Tatarstan, Kazan, ul. Kremlevskaya 1; tel. (843) 299-18-18; fax (843) 299-16-61; e-mail kanc@kazan.gov.tatarstan.ru; internet www.kazan.org.ru.

Udmurt Republic

The Udmurt Republic occupies part of the Upper Kama Highlands. It forms part of the Volga Federal Okrug and the Urals Economic Area. Tatarstan lies to the south, Bashkortostan to the south-east, Perm Krai to the east and Kirov Oblast to the north and west. Its major river is the Kama. About one-half of its territory is forested. The Republic covers 42,100 sq km (16,250 sq miles). At January 2007, according to official estimates, the Republic had a population of

1,537,858 and a population density of 36.5 per sq km. At the time of the 2002 census 60.1% of the population were ethnically Russian, 29.3% were Udmurt and 7.0% were Tatar. The dominant religion in the Republic is Orthodox Christianity. In 1989 some 70% of Udmurts spoke their native tongue, from the Permian group of the Finnic branch of the Uralo-Altaic family, as their first language. Some 69.2% of the population inhabited urban areas in January 2006. The capital of the Udmurt Republic is at Izhevsk (formerly Ustinov), which had a population of 619,500 in January 2006, according to official estimates. The Republic is included in the time zone GMT+4.

HISTORY

The first appearance of the Votyaks (the former name for Udmurts) as a distinct ethnic group occurred in the sixth century. The territories inhabited by Votyaks were conquered by the Khazars in the eighth century, although Khazar influence gave way to that of the Volga Bulgars in the mid-ninth century. In the 13th century the Mongol Tatars occupied the region, but were gradually displaced by the Russians from the mid-15th century. By 1558 all Votyaks were under Russian rule. A Votyak Autonomous Oblast was established on 4 November 1920. On 1 January 1932 it was renamed the Udmurt Autonomous Oblast, which became an ASSR on 28 December 1934.

The Republic declared sovereignty on 21 September 1990, although a new republican Constitution was not adopted until 7 December 1994. The Chairman of the legislature, the State Council, remained head of the Republic, and a premier chaired the Government. Measures to introduce a presidential system of republican government were endorsed by a referendum held on 26 March 2000 and in June the Udmurt State Council adopted a number of draft laws transferring the Republic to presidential rule. Aleksandr Volkov, hitherto the parliamentary speaker, was elected President on 15 October. Volkov was re-elected on 14 March 2004, with 54.3% of the votes cast in an election contested by nine candidates. Some 67.3% of the electorate participated in the elections.

At elections to the State Duma on 2 December 2007, the pro-presidential United Russia (UR) secured 60.6% of votes, with a turn-out of 61.3% of the electorate. The Mayor of Glazov subsequently tendered his resignation, after UR received only 41% of votes cast in that town. Concurrent elections were conducted to the State Council; UR won some 56.0% of votes cast, while the Communist Party of the Russian Federation obtained 13.3%, A Just Russia 12.9% and the nationalist Liberal Democratic Party of Russia 9.0%.

ECONOMY

In 2004 the Republic's gross regional product amounted to 107,251.9m. roubles, equivalent to 68,905.4 roubles per head. The Udmurt Republic possesses significant hydrocarbons reserves and is an important arms-producing region. Its major industrial centres are at Izhevsk, Sarapul and Glazov. Its main river-ports are at Sarapul and Kambarka. At the end of 2005 there were 768 km of railway track and 5,937 km of paved roads on its territory. In 1998 there were 178 km of navigable waterways. Twelve major gas pipelines and two petroleum pipelines pass through the Republic.

In 2005 agriculture, which consisted mainly of animal husbandry and grain and potato production, employed 11.7% of the work-force and generated 18,656m. roubles. Industry employed 31.6% of the labour force in 2005 and generated 100,070m. roubles in 2004. The main industries, apart from the manufacture of weapons, are mechanical engineering, metal-working, metallurgy, food-processing, petroleum production and the production of peat. There are substantial reserves of coal and of petroleum. In 2005 some 45,600 automobiles were produced in the Republic, a figure exceeded among federal subjects only by Samara Oblast. In early 2006 Sinopec, a company controlled by the state authorities of the People's Republic of China, purchased a 49% stake in the formerly republican-owned petroleum company Udmurtneft from the British-Russian consortium TNK-BP, representing the first instance of Chinese involvement in the Russian energy sector. (The remaining 51% of Udmurtneft was acquired by the Russian state-controlled firm Rosneft at the same time.) From the 1990s the disposal of chemical weapons on the territory of the Republic proved to be a serious social and ecological problem—the Republic was thought to contain around one-quarter of Russia's entire arsenal of such weapons; a new plant for the destruction of chemical weapons was inaugurated in the Udmurt Republic in 2006, the second such facility in the Russian Federation.

In 2005 the economically active population amounted to 821,000, and 7.8% of the labour force were unemployed; the average monthly wage was 6,373.3 roubles. The republican budget recorded a deficit of 231.2m. roubles in 2005, when foreign investment in the Republic amounted to US $79.1m., compared to $7.1m. in 2004. Export trade in 2005 comprised $412.7m. in exports, and $211.2m. in imports. The principal exports are metallurgical products, engines and machinery, and rifles. At the end of 2005 some 8,239 small businesses were registered in the Republic, providing employment to 31,700 people.

DIRECTORY

President: ALEKSANDR A. VOLKOV (elected 15 October 2000, re-elected 14 March 2004), 426074 Udmurt Rep., Izhevsk, pl. 50 let Oktyabrya 15; tel. and fax (3412) 49-70-10; e-mail president@udmurt .ru; internet www.udmurt.ru/ru/president.

Chairman of the Government: YURII S. PITKEYVICH, 426007 Udmurt Rep., Izhevsk, ul. Pushkinskaya 214; tel. (3412) 25-50-89; fax (3412) 25-50-17; e-mail premier@udmurt.ru; internet www .udmurt.ru.

Chairman of the State Council (Legislature): IGOR N. SEMENOV, 426074 Udmurt Rep., Izhevsk, ul. 50 let Oktyabrya 15; tel. (3412) 75-34-98; fax (3412) 75-20-58; e-mail gossovet@gossovet.ru; internet www.udmgossovet.ru.

Chief Representative of the Udmurt Republic in the Russian Federation: ANDREI V. SAKOVICH, 119019 Moscow, ul. Novyi Arbat 19; tel. (495) 203-53-52; fax (495) 203-91-47.

Head of Izhevsk City Administration (Mayor): VIKTOR V. BALA-KIN, 426070 Udmurt Rep., Izhevsk, ul. Pushkinskaya 276; tel. (3412) 22-45-90; fax (3412) 43-91-53; e-mail org@izh.ru; internet www.izh .ru.

Perm Krai

Perm Krai (formed in 2005 by the merger of Perm Oblast and the Komi-Permyak Autonomous Okrug, the latter of which was located in the north-western part of the territory) is situated on the western slopes of the Central and Northern Urals and the eastern edge of the Eastern European Plain. It forms part of the Volga Federal Okrug and the Urals Economic Area. The Republic of Komi lies to the north, Kirov Oblast and the Udmurt Republic lie to the west, Bashkortostan to the south and Sverdlovsk Oblast to the east. The major rivers are the Kama, the Chusovaya and the Kosva. The Kamsk reservoir lies in the centre of the region. The Krai occupies 160,600 sq km (61,990 sq miles). At January 2007, according to official estimates, the region's total population was 2,730,892, giving a population density of 17.0 per sq km. At the time of the 2002 census 85.2% of the population were ethnically Russian, 4.8% Tatar, 3.7% Komi-Permyak, 0.9% Udmurt and 0.9% were Ukrainian. Some 74.9% of the population inhabited urban areas in January 2007. The Krai's administrative centre is at Perm, which had a population of 993,300 in January 2006, according to official estimates. Other major cities include Berezniki (with a population of 168,300). Perm Krai is included in the time zone GMT+5.

HISTORY

Perm city was founded in 1723, with the construction of a copper foundry. Industrial development was such that by the latter part of the 20th century the city extended for some 80 km along the banks of the Kama. Perm Oblast was formed on 3 October 1938. Perm city was called Molotov in 1940–57 and entry was forbidden to foreigners until 1989.

In December 1993 there were regional elections for a new parliament, the Legislative Assembly. In May 1996 the regional administrations of both Perm Oblast and the Komi-Permyak AOk (located in the north-west of the Oblast) signed separate power-sharing treaties with the federal President, Boris Yeltsin. In December the Governor of Perm Oblast appointed earlier that year, Gennadii Igumnov, retained his post in direct elections, and pro-reform candidates loyal to Igumnov were successful in securing an absolute majority of seats in elections to the regional legislature in December 1997. Following the gubernatorial election held in December 2000, Igumnov was replaced by Yurii Trutnev, hitherto the Mayor of Perm. Elections to a new Legislative Assembly were held in December 2001.

In July 2002 Trutnev announced that measures to merge Perm Oblast and the Komi-Permyak AOk would be initiated in the near future. In February 2003 the legislative bodies of both territories voted in favour of a merger, and in March the Governors of the two regions met federal President Vladimir Putin, who expressed support for the proposal. On 7 December a referendum was held to seek approval for the merger. More than 80% of the participating electorate in both territories supported the unification to form a new federal subject, to be known as Perm Krai. On 26 March 2004, following the acceptance of the measures by the federal legislature, Putin signed legislation approving the formation of the Krai, which came into existence on 1 December 2005. He also confirmed Oleg Chirkunov as acting Governor of Perm Oblast. (Chirkunov had been nominated by the outgoing Governor, Yurii Trutnev, following the latter's appointment as the Minister of National Resources in the federal Government in March 2004.) Chirkunov's nomination as Governor of Perm Krai was confirmed by the legislatures of the two territories on 10 October 2005. Elections were held to the new

Legislative Assembly of Perm Krai on 3 December 2006, in which the pro-presidential United Russia (UR) was the most successful grouping, receiving 34.6% of the votes cast. However, UR failed to secure a majority of deputies in the legislature, obtaining 29 of the 60 elective seats. The economically liberal Union of Rightist Forces recorded its most successful result in any regional election since the party's foundation, with 16.4% of the votes cast, followed by the nationalist Liberal Democratic Party of Russia (13.8%), the Russian Pensioners' Party (11.7%) and the Communist Party of the Russian Federation (8.6%).

ECONOMY

In 2004 the gross regional product of Perm Oblast (including the Komi-Permyak AOk) amounted to 267,976.1m. roubles, or 96,379.7 roubles per head. Perm Krai's industrial centres are at Perm, Berezniki, Chusovoi and Krasnokamsk. At the end of 2005 there were 1,494 km of railways and 10,820 km of paved roads on the Oblast's territory.

Agriculture in the territory, which in 2005 employed 9.4% of the working population and generated 19,814m. roubles, consists mainly of grain and vegetable production, bee-keeping and animal husbandry. Industry engaged 32.8% of the working population in 2005 and generated 248,117m. roubles in 2004. The main industries are coal, petroleum, natural gas, potash and salt production, mechanical engineering, chemicals and petrochemicals, petroleum-refining and electricity generation. There is also a significant defence sector.

The economically active population numbered 1,419,000 in 2005, when 7.0% of the labour force were unemployed. The average wage amounted to 7,748.9 roubles per month in 2005. The economic situation in the former Komi-Permyak AOk was far harsher than in the region as a whole, and the territory was one of the most underdeveloped and deprived regions of European Russia. In 2005 the unified territory recorded a budgetary surplus of some 986.3m. roubles, while external trade amounted to a value of US $2,978.6m. in exports and $320.1m. in imports. Foreign investment in 2005 amounted to $201.1m. At the end of that year 10,640 small businesses were registered in Perm Krai, providing employment for 89,400 people.

DIRECTORY

Governor: OLEG A. CHIRKUNOV (assumed office 1 December 2005), 614006 Perm, ul. Kuibysheva 14; tel. (342) 217-70-72; fax (342) 236-09-52; e-mail webmaster@perm.ru; internet www.perm.ru.

Chairman of the Provincial Government: NIKOLAI YU. BUKHVA-LOV, 614006 Perm, ul. Kuibysheva 14; tel. (342) 217-71-70; internet www.perm.ru/power/vlastpermobl/?document=1269.

Chairman of the Legislative Assembly: NIKOLAI A. DEVYATKIN, 614006 Perm, ul. Lenina 51; tel. (342) 217-75-55; fax (342) 235-12-57; e-mail parliament@perm.ru; internet www.parliament.perm.ru.

Chief Representative of Perm Krai in the Russian Federation: ALEKSANDR A. POTEKHIN, 103006 Moscow, ul. M. Dmitrovka 3/10/205; tel. (495) 299-48-36; fax (495) 209-08-97.

Head of Perm City, Chairman of Perm City Duma: IGOR N. SHUBIN, 614000 Perm, ul. Lenina 15; tel. (342) 212-11-41; fax (342) 212-74-57; e-mail info@perm.permregion.ru; internet shubin.perm .ru.

Kirov Oblast

Kirov Oblast is situated in the east of the Eastern European Plain. It forms part of the Volga Federal Okrug and the Volga-Vyatka Economic Area. It is bordered by Archangel and Komi Oblasts to the north, Perm Krai and the Udmurt Republic to the east, Tatarstan and Marii-El to the south, and Nizhnii Novgorod, Kostroma and Vologda Oblasts to the west. Its main rivers are the Kama and the Vyatka. The Oblast occupies 120,800 sq km (46,640 sq miles). At January 2007, according to official estimates, the Oblast's population numbered 1,426,917 and the population density was 11.8 per sq km. At the time of the 2002 census 90.8% of the population were ethnically Russian, 2.9% Tatar, 2.6% Mari, 1.2% Udmurt and 0.8% Ukrainian. Some 71.7% of the population inhabited urban areas in January 2007. The Oblast's administrative centre is at Kirov, a river-port, which had 448,500 inhabitants in January 2006, according to official estimates. The territory is included in the time zone GMT+3.

HISTORY

The city of Khlynov was founded in 1181 as an outpost of Novgorod, and came under Muscovite rule in 1489. The city was renamed

Vyatka in 1781, and Kirov in 1934, when Kirov Oblast was formed. In September 1993 a draft constitution for the region was prepared, which referred to the Oblast as Vyatka Krai, although the federal authorities refused to acknowledge the area's redesignation.

Vladimir Sergeyenkov, the Communist Party of the Russian Federation (CPRF) candidate, was elected as Governor in October 1996, and was re-elected in March 2000. In December 2003 Nikolai Shaklein, an ally of the Presidential Representative to the Volga Federal Okrug Sergei Kiriyenko, was elected as Governor. At elections to the regional Legislative Assembly held on 12 March 2006 the pro-presidential United Russia (UR) was the most popular party, with 28.5% of the votes cast. The other parties to obtain legislative representation were the CPRF, with 15.1%, the nationalist Liberal Democratic Party of Russia, with 14.6%, the Russian Pensioners' Party, with 12.4%, and the Agrarian Party of Russia, with 7.8%. Some 8.0% of votes were cast 'against all candidates'. At elections to the State Duma on 2 December 2007, UR received 55.4% of votes cast in the Oblast (with a turn-out of 71.1%), one of its poorest results in the Federation.

ECONOMY

In 2004 the Oblast's gross regional product stood at 73,677.6m. roubles, equivalent to 50,109.9 roubles per head. Its main industrial centres are at Kirov and Slobodskoi. At the end of 2005 there were 1,100 km of railway track in the region and 9,094 km of paved roads. Owing to the high density of rivers in the region its soil is high in mineral salts, reducing its fertility.

The Oblast's agriculture, which employed 14.1% of the working population and generated 19,564m. roubles in 2005, consists mainly of animal husbandry and the production of grain, flax and vegetables. The Oblast has significant deposits of peat and phosphorites. Its main industries are mechanical engineering, the production of electrical energy, metal-working, chemicals and petrochemicals and the processing of agricultural and forestry products. Industry employed 25.9% of the work-force in 2005 and generated 56,694m. roubles in 2004.

The economically active population numbered 797,000 in 2005, when 7.1% of the Oblast's labour force were unemployed. The average monthly wage was 5,695.8 roubles in 2005. In that year the Oblast recorded a budgetary deficit of 811.1m. roubles. External trade comprised US $389.8m. in exports and $47.1m. in imports. In 2005 foreign investment amounted to $7.9m. At the end of that year around 5,969 small businesses were registered in the Oblast, providing employment to 61,600 people.

DIRECTORY

Head of the Regional Administration (Governor): NIKOLAI I. SHAKLEIN (elected 21 December 2003), 610019 Kirov, ul. K. Libknekhta 69; tel. (8332) 62-95-64; fax (8332) 62-89-58; e-mail region@ ako.kirov.ru; internet ako.kirov.ru.

Chairman of the Legislative Assembly: VLADIMIR A. VASILYEV, 610019 Kirov, ul. K. Libknekhta 69; tel. (8332) 62-48-00; fax (8332) 38-17-50; e-mail ozs@ako.kirov.ru; internet www.zsko.ru.

Chief Representative of Kirov Oblast in the Russian Federation: ALEKSANDR L. ZIMENKOV, 121248 Moscow, Kutuzovskii pr. 12/7; tel. (495) 243-23-51; fax (495) 243-23-36; e-mail kirov-pred@sovintel .ru; internet www.ako.kirov.ru/power/executive/representation.

Head of Kirov City Administration (Mayor): GENNADII I. PLEKHOV, 610000 Kirov, ul. Vorovskogo 39; tel. (8332) 62-89-40; fax (8332) 67-69-91; e-mail inbox@admkirov.ru; internet www.admkirov .ru.

Nizhnii Novgorod Oblast

Nizhnii Novgorod Oblast is situated on the middle reaches of the Volga river. It forms part of the Volga Federal Okrug and the Volga-Vyatka Economic Area. Mordoviia and Ryazan lie to the south, Vladimir and Ivanovo to the west, Kostroma to the north-west, Kirov to the north-east and Marii-El and the Chuvash Republic to the east. Its major rivers are the Volga, the Oka, the Sura and the Vetluga. The terrain in the north of the Oblast is mainly low lying, with numerous forests and extensive swampland. The southern part is characterized by fertile black soil (*chernozem*). The Oblast occupies a total area of 76,900 sq km (29,690 sq miles). At January 2007, according to official estimates, the Oblast had a population of 3,381,328 and a population density of 44.0 per sq km. At the time of the 2002 census 95.0% of the population were ethnically Russian and 1.4% were Tatar. Some 78.6% of the Oblast's inhabitants resided in urban areas in January 2007. Its administrative centre is at Nizhnii Novgorod, which lies at the confluence of the Volga and Oka rivers. The city is Russia's fifth largest, with a population of 1,283,600 in January 2006, according to

official estimates. Other major cities include Dzerzhinsk (formerly Chernorech—with a population of 252,500) and Arzamas (106,800). The territory is included in the time zone GMT+3.

HISTORY

Nizhnii Novgorod city was founded in 1221 on the borders of the Russian principalities. With the decline of Tatar power the city was absorbed by the Muscovite state. Industrialization took place in the late tsarist period. In 1905 mass unrest occurred in the region, which in late 1917 was one of the first areas of Russia to be seized by the Bolsheviks. Nizhnii Novgorod Oblast was formed on 14 January 1929. In 1932–90 the city and region were named Gorkii, and for much of the time the city was 'closed', owing to the importance of the defence industry.

In 1991 the Russian President, Boris Yeltsin, appointed a leading local reformer, Boris Nemtsov, as regional Governor. Nemtsov instituted a wide-ranging programme of economic reform, which was widely praised by liberals and by the federal Government. Nemtsov secured popular election in December 1995, and was a prominent advocate of democratization and decentralization in the Federation. In June 1996 Nemtsov signed a treaty on the delimitation of powers with the federal Government, giving the Oblast greater budgetary independence. In April 1997 Nemtsov was appointed to the federal Government; gubernatorial elections were subsequently held, in which the pro-presidential candidate, Ivan Sklyarov (hitherto Mayor of Nizhnii Novgorod), defeated Gennadii Khodyrev, who was supported both by the Communist Party of the Russian Federation (CPRF) and the nationalist Liberal Democratic Party of Russia (LDPR). The Oblast's economic situation subsequently deteriorated somewhat, and the federal Government withheld funds for the continuing conversion of the Oblast's defence industry. In July 2001 Khodyrev, by this time a CPRF deputy in the State Duma (Gosudarstvennaya Duma—the lower chamber of the federal legislature), was elected Governor, obtaining almost 60% of the votes cast in the second round of polling. Following his election, Khodyrev suspended his membership of the CPRF. (By late 2003 he was associated with the pro-presidential United Russia—UR.) In September 2001 the regional legislature voted in favour of a proposal made by Khodyrev that he act both as Governor and as Prime Minister of the Oblast. Elections to the regional Legislative Assembly in March 2002 resulted in the formation of a centre-right majority in the new chamber, with UR becoming the single largest party grouping. In the following month the power-sharing treaty agreed in 1996 was annulled. In March 2005, in association with the recently introduced system whereby regional governors were to be appointed, Khodyrev was reported to have asked federal President Vladimir Putin for an expression of his confidence (which would have therefore resulted in Khodyrev's nomination for a further term as Governor). However, despite legislation requiring that such a request be responded to within the period of one week, no response was forthcoming until July, shortly before the expiry of Khodyrev's mandate. In the event Putin selected the hitherto Deputy Mayor of Moscow, Valerii Shantsev, as his nominee; this appointment was confirmed by vote of the regional legislature on 8 August. At elections to the assembly, held on 12 March 2006, UR was again the most popular grouping, receiving 43.9% of the votes cast, ahead of the CPRF (17.8%) and the Russian Pensioners' Party (17.2%). Some 7.3% of votes were cast 'against all candidates'. In March 2007 security forces dispersed an unauthorized protest organized by Another Russia, an informal coalition of groups opposing President Putin, in Nizhnii Novgorod; a smaller rally took place in April.

ECONOMY

In 2004 the Oblast's gross regional product amounted to 264,625.8m. roubles, or 76,430.2 roubles per head. Its principal industrial centres are at Nizhnii Novgorod, Dzerzhinsk and Arzamas. Nizhnii Novgorod contains a major river-port, from which it is possible to reach the Baltic, Black, White and Caspian Seas. At the end of 2005 there were 13,494 km of paved roads and 1,214 km of railway track in the region. Since 1985 an underground railway system has operated in the city and in 1994 an international airport was opened.

Agriculture, which employed 7.1% of the working population and generated 28,552m. roubles in 2005, consists mainly of animal husbandry and the production of grain, sugar beet, flax and onions and other vegetables. The sector was subject to extensive privatization and restructuring in the 1990s. It is the Oblast's industry that dominates the regional economy, however; the sector employed 34.5% of the labour force in 2005 and generated 235,625m. roubles in 2004. The principal industries of the Oblast include mechanical engineering and metal-working, ferrous metallurgy, chemicals, petrochemicals and the processing of agricultural and forestry products. During the Soviet period the region was developed as a major military-industrial centre, with the defence sector accounting for around three-quarters of the regional economy. The Gorkii Automobile Plant (RusAvtoGAZ) is also a significant employer. In the 1990s the Oblast was among those territories of the Federation that dealt most successfully with the transition from military to civilian industry.

The economically active population numbered 1,801,000 in 2005, when 6.0% of the labour force were unemployed and the average monthly wage was 5,695.8 roubles. The regional budget in that year recorded a deficit of 12.6m. roubles. In 2005 the external trade of the Oblast amounted to US $1,672.8m. in exports and $1,010.9m. in imports. In 2005 foreign investment in the region totalled $102.8m. At the end of that year some 20,714 small businesses were registered in the Oblast, providing employment to 283,000 people.

DIRECTORY

Head of the Regional Administration (Governor and Prime Minister): VALERII P. SHANTSEV (appointment confirmed 8 August 2005), 603082 Nizhnii Novgorod, Kreml, kor. 1; tel. (831) 419-90-12; fax (831) 439-00-48; e-mail official@kreml.nnov.ru; internet www.government.nnov.ru.

Chairman of the Legislative Assembly: YEVGENII B. LYULIN, 603082 Nizhnii Novgorod, Kreml, kor. 2; tel. (831) 439-05-38; fax (831) 439-06-29; e-mail nnovg@duma.gov.ru; internet www.zsno.ru.

Chief Representation of Nizhnii Novgorod Oblast in the Russian Federation: VIKTOR A. GULYASHKO, 127006 Moscow, Nastasyinskii per. 5/3; tel. and fax (495) 956-92-48.

Head of Nizhnii Novgorod City Administration (Mayor): VADIM YE. BULAVINOV, 603082 Nizhnii Novgorod, Kreml, kor. 5; tel. (831) 439-15-06; fax (831) 439-13-02; e-mail ann@admgor.nnov.ru; internet www.admgor.nnov.ru.

Orenburg Oblast

Orenburg Oblast is situated in the foothills of the Southern Urals. It forms part of the Volga Federal Okrug and the Urals Economic Area. An international border with Kazakhstan lies to the south and east, and there are borders with Samara Oblast to the west, Bashkortostan and Chelyabinsk to the north and a short border with Tatarstan in the north-west. The region occupies 124,000 sq km (47,860 sq miles). At January 2007, according to official estimates, the population of the Oblast was 2,125,503 and the population density 17.1 per sq km. At the time of the 2002 census 73.9% of the population were ethnically Russian, 7.6% Tatar, 5.8% Kazakh, 3.5% Ukrainian, 2.4% Bashkir, 2.4% Mordovian, 0.8% German and 0.8% were Chuvash. Some 57.4% of the population lived in urban areas in January 2007. The Oblast's administrative centre is at Orenburg, which had 533,900 inhabitants in January 2006, according to official estimates. Other major cities are Orsk (247,000) and Novotroitsk (103,900). Orenburg is included in the time zone GMT+5.

HISTORY

The city of Orenburg originated as a fortress in 1743. During the revolutionary period Orenburg was a headquarters of 'White' forces and possession of it was fiercely contested with the Bolsheviks. The city was also a centre of Kazakh (then known to the Russians as Kyrgyz) nationalists and was the capital of the Kyrgyz ASSR in 1920–25. The region was then separated from the renamed Kazakh ASSR. Orenburg Oblast was formed on 7 December 1934.

Gubernatorial elections in December 1995 were won by the incumbent appointed in October 1991, Vladimir Yelagin. A power-sharing treaty was agreed between the regional and federal authorities in 1996. (The treaty was annulled in 2002.) Yelagin was defeated in the gubernatorial elections of December 1999 by Aleksei Chernyshev, who was elected to a further term in December 2002. In June 2005 Chernyshev resigned, in order to request that federal President Vladimir Putin confirm him in office. Putin duly nominated Chernyshev, and his reappointment was confirmed by the Legislative Assembly on 15 June. The pro-presidential United Russia was the most successful grouping at elections to the regional legislature held on 12 March 2006, obtaining 40.4% of the votes cast. The Communist Party of the Russian Federation was placed second, with 16.6%, followed by the nationalist Liberal Democratic Party of Russia (8.3%). Some 8.7% of votes were cast 'against all candidates'.

ECONOMY

Orenburg Oblast's gross regional product was 175,899.2m. roubles in 2004, or 81,567.9 roubles per head. At the end of 2005 there were 1,655 km of railways and 13,240 km of paved roads on the Oblast's territory. Its principal industrial centres are at Orenburg, Orsk and Novotroisk. There is a high level of atmospheric pollution in the region, while the intensive exploitation of petroleum and gas deposits have caused serious damage to arable land.

Agriculture, which employed 20.3% of the work-force and generated 31,430m. roubles in 2005, consists mainly of grain, vegetable and sunflower production and animal husbandry. The Oblast's major industries are ferrous and non-ferrous metallurgy, mechanical engineering, metal-working, natural gas production, electrical energy and the production of petroleum, ores, asbestos and salt. In 2005 production of petroleum in the Oblast amounted to 17.5m. metric tons, a figure exceeded among federal subjects only by Tatarstan and the two AOks (Khanty-Mansii and Yamalo-Nenets) within Tyumen Oblast. In that year production of natural gas amounted to 21,037m. cu m, an amount exceeded in the Federation only by the two AOks within Tyumen Oblast. Industry engaged 24.8% of the working population in 2005 and generated a total of 153,208m. roubles in 2004.

The economically active population numbered 1,058,000 in 2005, when 9.4% of the labour force were unemployed. The regional average monthly wage was 6,163.5 roubles. The regional budget for 2005 recorded a deficit of 424.5m. roubles. In 2005 external trade comprised US $2,099.5m. in exports and $796.1m. in imports. Total foreign investment in the region in that year amounted to $112.6m. At the end of 2005 some 8,401 small businesses were registered in the Oblast, providing employment to 103,200 people.

DIRECTORY

Head of the Regional Administration (Governor): ALEKSEI A. CHERNYSHEV (elected 26 December 1999, re-elected 7 December 2003, appointment confirmed 15 June 2005), 460015 Orenburg, Dom Sovetov; tel. (3532) 77-96-00; fax (3532) 77-38-02; e-mail office@gov.orb.ru; internet www.orb.ru.

Chairman of the Legislative Assembly: DMITRII V. KULAGIN, 460015 Orenburg, Dom Sovetov; tel. (3532) 77-33-20; fax (3532) 77-42-12; e-mail speaker@gov.orb.ru; internet www.parlament.orb.ru.

Chief Representative of Orenburg Oblast in the Russian Federation: VYACHESLAV S. RYABOV, 127025 Moscow, ul. Novyi Arbat 19/2014; tel. (495) 203-85-32; fax (495) 203-59-76.

Head of Orenburg City Administration (Mayor): YURII N. MISHCHERYAKOV, 461300 Orenburg, ul. Sovetskaya 60; tel. (3532) 98-70-10; fax (3532) 77-60-58; e-mail glava@admin.orenburg.ru; internet www.admin.orenburg.ru.

Penza Oblast

Penza Oblast is situated in the Volga Highlands. It forms part of the Volga Federal Okrug and the Volga Economic Area and borders Mordoviya to the north, Ulyanovsk to the east, Saratov to the south, Tambov to the south-west and Ryazan to the north-west. The Oblast covers 43,200 sq km (16,750 sq miles). At January 2007, according to official estimates, the population of the Oblast was 1,395,981 and the population density 32.3 per sq km. At the time of the 2002 census 86.4% of the population were ethnically Russian, 6.0% Tatar, 4.9% Mordovian and 0.9% were Ukrainian. Some 66.1% of the population inhabited urban areas in January 2007. The Oblast's administrative centre, Penza, had a population of 510,000 in January 2006, according to official estimates. The territory is included in the time zone GMT+3.

HISTORY

The city of Penza was founded in 1663 as an outpost on the south-eastern border of the Russian Empire. The region was captured by Bolshevik forces in late 1917 and remained under the control of the Red Army throughout the period of civil war. Penza Oblast was formed on 4 February 1939.

In April 1993 the Communist candidate, Anatolii Kovlyagin, defeated the pro-Government incumbent appointed in 1991, Aleksandr Kondratyev, in elections to head the regional administration. On 12 April 1998 Vasilii Bochkarev, an independent regarded as a technocrat, was elected as Governor. He was re-elected on 14 April 2002, with the support of the pro-presidential Unity and Fatherland-United Russia (later known simply as United Russia—UR). The adoption, in 2002, of a new oblast flag, depicting an image based upon a Russian Orthodox icon, resulted in protests in the region; concern was expressed that the design could breach the separation of religion and state guaranteed by the federal Constitution. In May 2005 Bochkarev resigned, in order to seek nomination by federal President Vladimir Putin to a further term of office. Putin duly nominated Bochkarev and his reappointment was confirmed by the regional Legislative Assembly on 14 May. At elections to the Legislative Assembly, held concurrently with elections to the State Duma on 2 December 2007, UR secured 67.6% of votes cast, while the Communist Party of the Russian Federation won 15.9% and A Just Russia 7.0%.

ECONOMY

In 2004 Penza's gross regional product was 62,654.4m. roubles, or 43,834.6 roubles per head. The Oblast's principal industrial centres are at Penza and Kuznetsk. Several major railway routes pass through the Oblast; at the end of 2005 there were 828 km of railway track and 6,693 km of paved roads in the region, including several major highways.

Around three-quarters of the agricultural land in the Oblast consists of fertile black earth (*chernozem*). Agriculture, which employed 18.4% of the work-force and generated 15,988m. roubles in 2005, consists mainly of the production of grain and vegetables and animal husbandry. In late 2003 a British company secured a lease on 1,000 ha of land in the Oblast, becoming the first foreign business to purchase a lease on agricultural land in Russia. The Oblast's main industries are mechanical engineering, the processing of timber and agricultural products, chemicals and petrochemicals and light manufacturing. Industry employed some 27.0% of the working population in 2005 and generated 36,516m. roubles in 2004.

The economically active population in Penza Oblast numbered 715,000 in 2005, when 6.5% of the labour force were unemployed. Those in employment earned an average of 5,206.8 roubles per month. The 2005 regional budget recorded a surplus of 83,121m. roubles. The external trade of the Oblast was relatively low, amounting to US $66.8m. in exports and $78.0m. in imports in 2005. Foreign investment in the Oblast in that year amounted to just $3.9m. At the end of 2005 some 8,247 small businesses were registered in the Oblast, providing employment to 77,900 people.

DIRECTORY

Governor: VASILII K. BOCHKAREV (elected 12 April 1998, re-elected 14 April 2002, appointment confirmed 14 May 2005), 440025 Penza, ul. Moskovskaya 75; tel. (8412) 56-11-94; fax (8412) 55-04-11; e-mail pravobl@sura.ru; internet www.penza.ru.

Chairman of the Regional Government: VYACHESLAV A. SATIN, 440025 Penza, ul. Moskovskaya 75; tel. (8412) 56-46-80; internet www.penza.ru/authority/ex_power_01/list.

Chairman of the Regional Legislative Assembly: VIKTOR A. CHERUSHOV, 440025 Penza, ul. Moskovskaya 75; tel. (8412) 55-30-70; fax (8412) 55-25-95; e-mail zsobl@sura.ru.

Chief Representative of Penza Oblast in the Russian Federation: ALEKSANDR A. RODIONOV, 127025 Moscow, ul. Novyi Arbat 19/1914; tel. (495) 203-10-75; fax (495) 203-48-93.

Head of Penza City Administration: ROMAN B. CHERNOV, 440064 Penza, pl. Marshala Zhukova 4, Gorodskaya Duma; tel. (8412) 68-52-67; internet www.penza-gorod.ru.

Samara Oblast

Samara Oblast is situated in the south-east of the Eastern European Plain on the middle reaches of the Volga river. It forms part of the Volga Federal Okrug and the Volga Economic Area. Its southernmost tip lies on the border with Kazakhstan. Saratov lies to the south-west, Ulyanovsk to the west, Tatarstan to the north and Orenburg to the east. The Volga snakes through the west of the territory. The region occupies 53,600 sq km (20,690 sq miles). Owing to its proximity to the Kazakhstan desert, the far south of the Oblast is prone to drought. At January 2007, according to official estimates, the region had a total population of 3,178,577 and a population density of 59.3 per sq km. At the time of the 2002 census 83.6% of the population were ethnically Russian, 3.9% Tatar, 3.1% Chuvash, 2.7% Mordovian and 1.9% Ukrainian. Some 80.4% of the population inhabited urban areas in January 2007. The administrative centre is at Samara, which had 1,143,300 inhabitants in January 2006, according to official estimates. The region's second city is Tolyatti (704,900), and other major cities include Syzran (181,500) and Novokuibyshevsk (111,800). The Oblast is included in the time zone GMT+4.

HISTORY

Samara was founded in 1586 as a fortress. It became rich from the Volga grain trade and further increased in prosperity after the construction of the railways in the late 19th century. A Middle Volga Oblast was formed on 14 May 1928. In 1929 it was upgraded to the status of a krai, which was renamed Kuibyshev Krai in 1935 (Samara city was similarly renamed). On 5 December 1936 the Krai reverted to oblast status. Kuibyshev was the headquarters of the Soviet

Government between 1941 and 1943, when Moscow was threatened by the German invasion. Both the city and oblast assumed their current name in 1991.

The local legislature defied President Boris Yeltsin in the constitutional crisis of 1993, and was dissolved in October and replaced by a regional Duma. The head of the regional administration, Konstantin Titov, who had been appointed to that position by Yeltsin in August 1991 was regarded as a strong proponent of economic reform. On 1 December 1996 Titov was elected Governor. Titov sought to protect the relative autonomy of governors and strongly urged the regional Duma to approve legislation on land ownership, which was achieved in June 1998. Titov contested the presidency of the Russian Federation at the elections of March 2000. However, his performance, even in Samara Oblast, where he obtained only 20% of the votes cast and was placed third, was disappointing. Consequently, he resigned from the post of Governor in April, but stood as a candidate for re-election in July in an attempt to confirm his legitimacy; he was re-elected with 53% of the votes cast. In November 2001 Titov, who had hitherto led a small social-democratic party, was elected as co-chairman of the recently formed Social Democratic Party of Russia, alongside the former executive President of the USSR, Mikhail Gorbachev, although both co-chairmen resigned from their positions in 2004. In April 2005 Putin nominated Titov to serve for a further term as Governor; this nomination was confirmed by the regional Duma on 26 April. In November Titov announced his membership of the pro-presidential United Russia (UR).

At elections to the regional Duma on 11 March 2007, UR won 33.5% of votes cast, followed by the Communist Party of the Russian Federation (19.0%), the broadly pro-Government A Just Russia (15.1%), the Liberal Democratic Party of Russia (11.6%), the Union of Rightist Forces (8.1%), and the Greens—Russian Ecological Party (7.6%). A protest rally was organized by Another Russia, an informal coalition of groups opposing President Putin, to coincide with a summit of EU and Russian leaders, to take place at a resort 200 km from Samara in May. Following Titov's resignation, on 27 August, as Governor, which had been reportedly tendered under pressure from the federal authorities, Putin nominated Vladimir Artyakov, hitherto head of the locally based vehicle manufacturer AvtoVAZ, as his successor; the appointment was confirmed by the regional Duma on 29 August. In November (prior to elections to the federal State Duma on 2 December) the local edition of an independent newspaper was closed and criminal proceedings initiated against its editor, reportedly on charges of assisting in the organization of the May protest rally.

ECONOMY

In 2004 Samara Oblast's gross regional product amounted to 349,047.9m. roubles, or 108,756.4 roubles per head. The Oblast's major industrial centres are at Samara, Tolyatti and Syzran. At the end of 2005 there were 1,368 km of railways and 7,649 km of paved roads in the region.

Agriculture in the Oblast, which employed 6.2% of the working population and generated 26,557m. roubles in 2005, consists mainly of the production of grain, sugar beet and sunflower seeds, and of animal husbandry and bee-keeping. There are some reserves of petroleum and natural gas in the Oblast. Samara Oblast is one of Russia's principal industrial regions. Industry employed 32.5% of the work-force in 2005 and generated 394,852m. roubles in 2004. Its main industries are mechanical engineering, metal-working, the production and refining of petroleum, food-processing, and chemicals and petrochemicals. The Oblast's principal company is AvtoVAZ (Volga Automobile Plant), manufacturer of the Lada automobile. In 2002, as part of a joint venture with the US corporation General Motors, AvtoVAZ also began to manufacture Chevrolet Niva automobiles and sports-utility (four-wheel drive) vehicles. In 2005 some 796,200 automobiles, equivalent to 74.5% of all automobiles manufactured in Russia, were produced in Samara Oblast. Some controversy arose in late 2005 when AvtoVAZ was acquired by the state-controlled arms export monopoly, Rosoboroneksport. (Both companies were absorbed into the state-controlled Russian Technologies Corporation in late 2007.)

The economically active population of Samara Oblast numbered 1,728,000 in 2005, when 5.3% of the labour force were unemployed—one of the lowest rates of unemployment in the Federation. Those in employment earned an average monthly wage of 7,764.9 roubles, the highest average wage among the territories of the Volga Federal Okrug in that year. In 2005 the regional budget recorded a surplus of 2,667.0m. roubles. By 1998 some 300 foreign companies, including some of the world's largest, such as Coca-Cola and General Motors of the USA and Nestlé of Switzerland, had invested in the region, attracted by its technologically advanced industrial base and well educated, urbanized labour force. In 2005 the external trade of the region amounted to some US $6,259.9m. in exports and $1,026.9m. in imports, one of the highest levels of trade of any federal subject. In 2005 total foreign investment in the region amounted to $922.6m.— around 42.5% of all foreign investment in the Volga Federal Okrug in that year. At the end of 2005 some 28,940 small businesses were registered in the Oblast, providing employment to 222,100 people.

DIRECTORY

Governor: VLADIMIR V. ARTYAKOV (appointment confirmed 29 August 2007), 443006 Samara, ul. Molodogvardeiskaya 210; tel. (846) 332-22-68; fax (846) 332-13-40; e-mail governor@samara.ru; internet www.adm.samara.ru.

Chairman of the Regional Duma: VIKTOR F. SAZANOV, 443110 Samara, ul. Molodogvardeiskaya 187; tel. (846) 332-75-06; fax (846) 342-38-08; e-mail samgd@duma.sam-reg.ru; internet www.samgd.ru.

Chief Representative of Samara Oblast in the Russian Federation: ALEKSANDR P. BARANOVSKII, 103030 Moscow, per. Veskovskii 2; tel. (495) 973-19-95; fax (495) 973-05-54; e-mail tradoc@samarapostpred.ru.

Head of Samara City District Administration (Mayor): VIKTOR A. TARKHOV, 443010 Samara, ul. Kuibysheva 137; tel. (846) 332-20-68; fax (846) 333-67-41; e-mail city@samadm.ru; internet city.samara.ru.

Saratov Oblast

Saratov Oblast is situated in the south-east of the Eastern European Plain. It forms part of the Volga Federal Okrug and the Volga Economic Area. Saratov Oblast has an international border with Kazakhstan (to the south-east), and shares borders with the Oblasts of Volgograd (to the south), Voronezh and Tambov (west), and Penza, Ulyanovsk and Samara (north). Its main river is the Volga. Those regions of the Oblast on the west bank of the Volga are mountainous, those to the east are low-lying. The region occupies 100,200 sq km (38,680 sq miles). At January 2007, according to official estimates, Saratov Oblast had 2,595,315 inhabitants and a population density of 25.9 per sq km. At the time of the 2002 census 85.9% of the population were ethnically Russian, 2.9% Kazakh, 2.5% Ukrainian, 2.2% Tatar and 0.9% were Armenian. Some 73.9% of the Oblast's population inhabited urban areas in January 2007. Its administrative centre is at Saratov, a major river-port on the Volga, with a population of 850,100 in January 2006, according to official estimates. Other major cities include Balakovo (199,200) and Engels (formerly Pokrovsk—194,800). The region is included in the time zone GMT+3.

HISTORY

Saratov was founded in 1590 as a fortress, to protect against nomad raids on the Volga trade route. In the mid-18th century the area was colonized by some 30,000 settlers, mainly from the Hesse and Palatinate regions of present-day Germany. Strategically placed on the Trans-Siberian Railway, Saratov city was seized by Bolshevik forces in late 1917 and remained under communist control, despite attacks by the 'White' forces under Adm. Aleksandr Kolchak in 1918–19. The Autonomous Commune of Volga German Workers was established in the region in 1918 and renamed the Volga German ASSR in 1924. (The ASSR had its capital at Pokrovsk—renamed Engels in 1931—on the opposite bank of the Volga from Saratov city.) Saratov Oblast was formed in 1936, having been part of a Saratov Krai from 1934. The region became heavily industrialized in the Soviet period, before the Second World War. In 1941 the Volga German ASSR was abolished and its inhabitants deported to Siberia, Central Asia and the North Caucasus. In 1972 they were permitted to return to the region, although from the mid-1980s many German-Russians were allowed to emigrate to Germany, and at the 2002 census only 0.5% of the Oblast's population described their ethnicity as German.

In September 1996 Dmitrii Ayatskov, who had been appointed as head of the regional administration in April, was elected as Governor, receiving 81.4% of the popular vote. Ayatskov carried out extensive reform to the region's agro-industrial sector, which culminated, in November 1997, in the passing in the Oblast of the first law in Russia to provide for the purchase and sale of agricultural land. The law greatly diminished the power base of communists and nationalists in the region, as well as generating a significant income for the regional economy. (A series of bilateral trade agreements signed with the Mayor of Moscow, Yurii Luzhkov, in August 1996, also had beneficial effects for Saratov Oblast.) Ayatskov was re-elected for a further term in March 2000, amid accusations of electoral manipulation, which removed all other serious candidates from the contest, and of press censorship.

In May 2004 the federal Government filed corruption charges against Ayatskov. These related to the alleged misuse of 70m. roubles (US $2.4m.) in budgetary funds, which had apparently been used to

pay import duties on behalf of a state-owned company. The charges were subsequently dropped. In 2005 Ayatskov became the first incumbent Governor not to be reappointed under recently introduced arrangements whereby regional governors would be subject to presidential appointment, rather than direct election; on 3 March 2005 the regional Duma approved Putin's nomination of Pavel Ipatov, the former director of a nuclear power station; Ipatov took office on 5 April, following the expiry of Ayatskov's term as Governor. (The appointment of Ayatskov as Ambassador to Belarus, announced later in the year, was subsequently withdrawn after he made a speech that included several controversial remarks about Russian-Belarusian relations.) In September 2007 journalists in the Oblast appealed to the President to intervene in a legal case involving a local newspaper's publication of a montage featuring Putin's image, and complained of a repressive campaign launched against the media by the pro-presidential United Russia (UR). At elections to the regional Duma held concurrently with those to the federal State Duma on 2 December, UR won 60.8% of votes cast, while the Communist Party of the Russian Federation received 14.2% and a Just Russia 13.5%. In February 2008 the Oblast's Prosecutor, who had investigated the charges of alleged corruption against Ayatskov and other cases involving former public officials, was shot dead.

ECONOMY

In 2004 Saratov Oblast's gross regional product totalled 153,301.9m. roubles, equivalent to 58,187.0 roubles per head. The region's major industrial centres are at Saratov, Engels and Balakovo. At the end of 2005 there were 2,297 km of railways and 10,469 km of paved roads on the Oblast's territory. The river port at Saratov is an important transshipment point on routes between Moscow and Central Asia, Siberia and southern Russia. The major Soviet and Russian arsenal for chemical weapons was located in the Oblast, although in January 1996 it was announced that chemical weapons stored locally were to be destroyed, in accordance with international agreements. A new processing plant to facilitate this commenced operations at Gornyi in late 2002.

The Oblast's agriculture, which employed some 13.6% of the working population and generated 36,950m. roubles in 2005, consists primarily of the production of grain (the Oblast is one of Russia's major producers of wheat) and sunflower seeds. Animal husbandry is also significant. The Oblast's main industries are mechanical engineering and metal-working, the production of electricity, petroleum-refining, chemicals and petrochemicals, food-processing and the production of petroleum and natural gas. Significant quantities of cement and mineral fertilizer are also produced in the Oblast. Industry employed 22.7% of the work-force in 2005 and generated 102,379m. roubles in 2004.

The region's economically active population numbered 1,334,000 in 2005, when 9.1% of the labour force were unemployed. The average wage in the Oblast was 5,439.3 roubles per month. The regional budget for 2005 recorded a deficit of 1,147.5m. roubles. In that year the value of external trade amounted to US $1,681.4m. in exports and $453.6m. in imports, while foreign investment amounted to only $3.6m. At the end of 2005 some 12,737 small businesses were registered in the Oblast, providing employment to 85,700 people.

DIRECTORY

Head of the Regional Administration (Governor): PAVEL L. IPATOV (appointment confirmed 3 March 2005), 410042 Saratov, ul. Moskovskaya 72; tel. (8452) 27-20-86; fax (8452) 72-52-54; e-mail governor@saratov.gov.ru; internet www.saratov.gov.ru.

Chairman of the Regional Duma: PAVEL V. BOLSHEDANOV, 410031 Saratov, ul. Radishcheva 24A; tel. (8452) 27-99-80; fax (8452) 27-53-31; e-mail post@srd.ru; internet www.srd.ru.

Chief Representative of Saratov Oblast in the Russian Federation: SERGEI V. KHRISTOLYUBOV, 109028 Moscow, per. Podkopayevskii 7/3; tel. and fax (495) 917-05-19.

Head of Saratov City Administration (Mayor): VYACHESLAV L. SOMOV, 410031 Saratov, ul. Pervomaiskaya 78; tel. (8452) 23-77-78; fax (8452) 27-84-44; e-mail mayor@admsaratov.ru; internet www.saratovmer.ru.

Ulyanovsk Oblast

Ulyanovsk Oblast is situated in the Volga Highlands. It forms part of the Volga Federal Okrug and the Volga Economic Area. Mordoviya, the Chuvash Republic and Tatarstan lie to the north-west and to the north. There are also borders with Samara in the south-east, Saratov in the south and Penza in the south-west. The region's major river is the Volga. The region occupies 37,300 sq km (14,400 sq miles). At January 2007, according to official estimates, the total population of the Oblast was 1,321,710, and the population density was 35.4 per sq km. At the time of the 2002 census 72.8% of the population were ethnically Russian, 12.2% Tatar, 8.0% Chuvash, 3.6% Mordovian and 1.1% were Ukrainian. Some 73.1% of the population inhabited urban areas in January 2007. The administrative centre at Ulyanovsk had a population of 617,200 in January 2006, according to official estimates. The other major city in the region is Dimitrovgrad (128,000). The Oblast is included in the time zone GMT+3.

HISTORY

Simbirsk city was founded in 1648. Lenin (Vladimir Ulyanov) was born there in 1870, and it was his home until 1887. The city was renamed Ulyanovsk, on the basis of Lenin's family name, following his death in 1924. Ulyanovsk Oblast, which was formed on 19 January 1943, was regarded as part of the 'red belt' of communist support in post-Soviet Russia. It refused to revert to its pre-Soviet name, and in December 1996 the Communist Party of the Russian Federation-backed candidate, Yurii Goryachev (who had been appointed to the position in 1992), won the election to the governorship of the Oblast.

Goryachev banned local privatization and collective farm reforms, imposed restrictions on imports and exports, and subsidized bread prices until early 1997. Goryachev was defeated in the gubernatorial election held in December 2000, and replaced by Lt-Gen. Vladimir Shamanov, who was regarded as an ally of the federal authorities. In October 2004 the pro-presidential United Russia (UR) announced that it would not support Shamanov's candidacy at the forthcoming gubernatorial election; the duration of his governorship had been characterized by ongoing difficulties in the housing and utilities sectors. UR instead announced its support for another candidate, Sergei Morozov, hitherto Mayor of Dmitrovgrad. At the first round of voting, held on 5 December, Morozov received 27.8% of the votes cast and was to progress to a 'run off' against a local dairy farmer, Sergei Gerasimov, who had garnered 20.9% of the ballot. However, Gerasimov's candidacy was subsequently disqualified by the oblast electoral commission, following allegations of electoral malpractice, and the second round was instead contested by the third-placed candidate, Margarita Barzhanova, a State Duma deputy of UR and an ally of Morozov (who had received 14.6% of the votes cast), instead contested the second round. On 26 December Morozov was elected Governor, with 52.8% of the votes cast. The option to vote 'against all candidates' received 25.2% of the votes cast, while Barzhanova obtained 20.6%. The voter turn-out in the second round of polling was only 38.8%. Morozov resigned in early 2006 in order to seek nomination to a new term of office from federal President Vladimir Putin, and thereby to strengthen his position. Putin's nomination of Morozov as Governor was approved by the regional legislature on 28 March. At elections to the Legislative Assembly, held on 2 March 2008, UR obtained 66.4% of the votes cast, ahead of the Communist Party of the Russian Federation, with 16.0%, A Just Russia, with 7.8%, and the nationalist Liberal Democratic Party of Russia, with 7.4%

ECONOMY

In 2004 Ulyanovsk Oblast's gross regional product amounted to 68,089.8m. roubles, or 50,154.9 roubles per head. The Oblast's major industrial centres are at Ulyanovsk and Melekess. At the end of 2005 there were 714 km of railway lines and 4,844 km of paved roads on the Oblast's territory.

Around 1.5m. ha of its territory is used for agricultural purposes, of which over four-fifths is arable land. Agriculture in the region, which employed some 12.4% of the working population and generated 12,498m. roubles in 2005, consists primarily of animal husbandry and the production of grain, sunflower seeds and sugar beet. The Oblast's main industries are mechanical engineering (which accounted for over 56% of industrial output in 2002), food-processing and electrical energy. Industry employed 30.3% of the working population in 2005 and generated 53,988m. roubles in 2004. The region's major companies include the UAZ automobile plant and the Aviastar aeroplane manufacturer. In late 2002 Aviastar signed a contract, apparently worth US $335m., to construct 25 TU-204-120 jets, following the acquisition of a 25% stake (less one share) in the firm by the Egyptian concern Sirocco Aerospace International; Sirocco expressed the intention of further developing the capacities of the Aviastar plant.

The economically active population numbered 695,000 in 2005, when 7.7% of the labour force were unemployed. Those in employment earned an average of 5,343.8 roubles per month. There was a budgetary surplus of 668.1m. roubles in 2005, when external trade constituted US $194.0m. in exports and $68.4m. in imports; total foreign investment in the Oblast amounted to $0.2m in that year, compared with $48.0m. in 2004. At the end of 2005 some 5,820 small businesses were registered in the Oblast, providing employment to 53,600 people.

DIRECTORY

Governor and Chairman of the Regional Government: Sergei I. Morozov (elected 26 December 2004, appointment confirmed 28 March 2006), 432063 Ulyanovsk, pl. Lenina 1; tel. (8422) 41-27-60; fax (8422) 41-48-12; e-mail mail@ulgov.ru; internet www.ulgov.ru.

Chairman of the Legislative Assembly: Boris I. Zotov, 432970 Ulyanovsk, ul. Radishcheva 1; tel. (8422) 41-20-74; internet www.zsuo.region73.ru.

Chief Representative of Ulyanovsk Oblast in the Russian Federation: Aleksandr F. Kotelevskii, 119002 Moscow, per. Denezhnyi 12; tel. (495) 241-31-42; fax (495) 241-38-99.

Head of Ulyanovsk City Administration (Mayor): Sergei N. Yermakov, 432700 Ulyanovsk, ul. Kuznetsova 7; tel. and fax (8422) 41-45-08; e-mail meria@mv.ru; internet www.ulmeria.ru.

Urals Federal Okrug

Chelyabinsk Oblast

Chelyabinsk Oblast is situated in the Southern Urals, with much of the region lying on the eastern slopes of the Southern Ural Mountains. It forms part of the Urals Federal Okrug and the Urals Economic Area. Orenburg Oblast lies to the south, the Republic of Bashkortostan to the west, Sverdlovsk Oblast to the north and Kurgan Oblast to the east. There is an international border with Kazakhstan in the south-east. The major rivers in the Oblast are the Ural and the Miass. It has over 1,000 lakes, the largest of which are the Uvildy and the Turgoyak. The Oblast covers an area of 87,900 sq km (34,940 sq miles). At January 2007, according to official estimates, Chelyabinsk Oblast had a population of 3,516,355, giving a population density of 40.0 per sq km. At the time of the 2002 census 82.3% of the population were ethnically Russian, 5.7% Tatar, 4.6% Bashkir, 2.1% Ukrainian, 1.0% Kazakh and 0.8% were German. Some 81.4% of the population inhabited urban areas in January 2007. The Oblast's administrative centre is at Chelyabinsk, a city with a population of 1,093,000 in January 2006. Other major cities are Magnitogorsk (413,200), Zlatoust (190,300), Miass (154,500) and Kopeisk (137,800). Chelyabinsk Oblast is included in the time zone GMT+5.

HISTORY

Chelyabinsk city was established as a Russian frontier post in 1736, but was deep within Russian territory by the 19th century. The Oblast was created on 17 January 1934. The region was heavily industrialized during the Soviet period and remained dominated by communist cadres following the disintegration of the USSR.

Following the attempted coup by conservative communists in August 1991, the head of Chelyabinsk oblast administration, Petr Sumin, who had expressed sympathy for the rebels, was dismissed, and replaced by Vadim Solovyev. Sumin subsequently became the Chairman of the oblast legislature, which in January 1993 announced its intention of holding elections for a regional governor. Solovyev announced that he would challenge this decision at the oblast court, and on 25 March the federal Supreme Court overturned the ruling of the oblast legislature, prohibiting the holding of gubernatorial elections in Chelyabinsk. None the less, at elections held in the Oblast on 11 April, Sumin obtained some 60% of votes cast (although the rate of participation was low, at around 30% of the electorate), and won a second round of polling, held on 25 April. The federal President, Boris Yeltsin, expressed support for Solovyev; however, the federal Constitutional Court subsequently declared that the elections had been unlawful. Yeltsin re-established his authority in late 1993 and required the election of a Duma during 1994. Both in this body, and in the local results of the general election of 1995, pro-Yeltsin and reformist forces obtained significant levels of support. In the gubernatorial election of late 1996, however, Sumin was returned to power. Sumin's pro-communist movement also won an absolute majority of seats in the regional legislature at elections held in December 1997. Sumin was re-elected Governor in December 2000. In April 2005 federal President Vladimir Putin nominated Sumin to serve a further term of office; this nomination was confirmed by the regional legislature on 18 April. In elections to the regional Legislative Assembly held on 25 December 2005, United Russia secured an absolute majority (52.0%) of the votes cast; the Communist Party of the Russian Federation was placed second, with 12.6%, while two nationalist groups, the Liberal Democratic Party of Russia and Motherland, also secured representation by obtaining more than 5% of the votes cast. Some 10.4% of votes were cast 'against all candidates'. In October 2007 the regional Legislative Assembly adopted a resolution urging Putin to serve a third presidential term, following the expiry of his mandate in the following year, despite the federal Constitution restricting the President to two consecutive mandates.

ECONOMY

In 2004 the gross regional product of the Oblast amounted to 304,326.0m. roubles, equivalent to 85,425.6 roubles per head. The region's major industrial centres are at Chelyabinsk, Magnitogorsk, Miass and Zlatoust. At the end of 2005 there were 1,796 km of railway track in the Oblast and 8,968 km of paved roads.

The Oblast's agriculture, which employed just 7.6% of the working population in 2005, and generated 35,651m. roubles, consists mainly of animal husbandry, horticulture and the production of grain. Chelyabinsk Oblast is one of the most polluted in the Federation; in particular, high rates of disease and environmental despoilation resulted from the Kyshtym nuclear accident of 1957, in the north of the region, when up to three times the levels of radiation emitted at the Chornobyl (Chernobyl) disaster in Ukraine in 1986 were released

into the surrounding area. In 2001–04 several dozen million cu m of liquid radioactive waste were released into the Techa river from the Mayak nuclear fuel reprocessing plant. Chelyabinsk Oblast became one of the most industrialized territories of the Russian Federation, following the reconstruction of plants moved there from further west during the Second World War. In 2005 industry employed some 35.0% of the economically active population, while generating 383,742m. roubles in 2004. The Oblast's main industries are ferrous metallurgy (which accounted for a total of 65.0% of industrial output in 2004), non-ferrous metallurgy, ore-mining, mechanical engineering, metal-working, and fuel and energy production. Although steel output in the Oblast declined by almost one-third between 1990 and 2004 (even taking into account a sustained recovery from 1999), it remained the dominant steel-producing region of Russia, producing 17.5m. metric tons in 2005, representing 26.4% of the federation's total output. In the north-west, the 'closed' city of Ozersk is a major plutonium-processing and -storage site, while in the west are located centres for weapons manufacturing and space technology.

The economically active population numbered 1,816,000 in 2005, when 5.4% of the labour force were unemployed. Those in employment earned an average wage of 7,462.7 roubles per month. The 2005 regional budget recorded a surplus of some 6,714.4m. roubles. Export trade amounted to US $4,909.1m. in 2005, when imports were worth $1,547.2m. Attempts to attract foreign investment in the Oblast from the mid-1990s were largely successful: foreign capital amounted to $832.9m. in 2005. At the end of that year some 19,095 small businesses were registered in the Oblast, providing employment to 153,400 people.

DIRECTORY

Governor: Petr I. Sumin (elected 22 December 1996, re-elected 24 December 2000, appointment confirmed 18 April 2005), 454089 Chelyabinsk, ul. Tsvillinga 27; tel. (351) 263-92-41; fax (351) 263-12-83; e-mail gubernator@chel.surnet.ru; internet www.gubernator74.ru.

Chairman of the Legislative Assembly: Vladimir V. Myakush. 454009 Chelyabinsk, ul. Kirova 114; tel. (351) 239-25-05; fax (351) 263-63-79; e-mail zscr@chel.surnet.ru.

Chief Representative of Chelyabinsk Oblast in the Russian Federation: Valerii A. Shubin, 127422 Moscow, Dmitrovskii pr. 4A; tel. (495) 210-88-59; fax (495) 977-08-35.

Head of Chelyabinsk City Administration: Mikhail V. Yurevich, 454113 Chelyabinsk, pl. Revolyutsii 2; tel. (351) 263-34-60; fax (351) 263-38-05; internet www.cheladmin.ru.

Kurgan Oblast

Kurgan Oblast is situated in the south of the Western Siberian Plain. It forms part of the Urals Federal District and the Urals Economic Area. Chelyabinsk Oblast lies to the west, Sverdlovsk Oblast to the north and Tyumen Oblast to the north-east. There is an international border with Kazakhstan to the south. The main rivers flowing through Kurgan Oblast are the Tobol and the Iset and there are more than 2,500 lakes in the south-east of the region. The Oblast occupies 71,000 sq km (27,400 sq miles) and had a total population of 969,304 at January 2007, according to official estimates, and a population density of 13.7 per sq km. At the time of the 2002 census 91.5% of the population were ethnically Russian, 2.0% Tatar, 1.5% Bashkir, 1.5% Kazakh and 1.1% were Ukrainian. Some 56.6% of the population inhabited urban areas in January 2007. The administrative centre is at Kurgan, which had a population of 330,000 in January 2006, according to official estimates. Kurgan Oblast is included in the time zone GMT+5.

HISTORY

The city of Kurgan was founded as a tax-exempt settlement in 1553, on the edge of Russian territory. Kurgan Oblast was formed on 6 February 1943. The Communist Party of the Russian Federation (CPRF) was the largest party in the regional Duma elected on 12 December 1993, and remained the most popular party in the Oblast at elections to the State Duma in 1995. The CPRF candidate, Oleg Bogomolov, hitherto speaker of the regional Duma, was elected Governor in late 1996, running unopposed in the second round of the election after his opponent stood down. Bogomolov was re-elected in December 2000. On 19 December 2004 Bogomolov, with the support of the pro-presidential United Russia (UR), was again re-elected Governor, securing 49.2% of the votes cast, compared with 40.1% obtained by his rival, Yevgenii Sobakin. (The candidacy of a business executive, Sergei Kapchuk, who had been regarded as one of Bogomolov's principal challengers in the election, had been disallowed by the oblast court several days before the first round of voting on 28 November.) UR was the most successful party in elections to the regional Duma, which were held concurrently with the second round of the gubernatorial election.

ECONOMY

In 2004 the gross regional product of Kurgan Oblast amounted to 44,857.9m. roubles, equivalent to 44,946.4 roubles per head, the lowest figure in the Urals Federal Okrug. The Oblast's main industrial centres are at Kurgan, a river-port in the south-east of the region, and Shadrinsk, on the Iset. At the end of 2005 there were 746 km of railways and 6,570 km of paved roads on the Oblast's territory. The Trans-Siberian Railway passes through the Oblast, as do several major petroleum and natural gas pipelines.

The Oblast's important agricultural sector employed 17.5% of the work-force in 2005 and consists mainly of grain production and animal husbandry. Total agricultural production in the region was worth 12,028m. roubles in 2005. Kurgan Oblast's main industries are mechanical engineering, metal-working, electricity production and food-processing. The industrial sector employed 21.2% of the working population in 2005 and generated 27,763m. roubles in 2004.

The economically active population numbered 491,000 in 2005. The rate of unemployment was 11.3% in 2005, the highest level recorded in any federal subject in the Urals Federal Okrug in that year. Those in employment earned, on average, 5,691.5 roubles per month, significantly less than the federal average. There was a budgetary surplus of 243.9m. roubles in 2005, when foreign investment totalled US $4.9m. In 2005 exports amounted to a value of $182.1m., while imports totalled $158.3m. The economic situation of the region deteriorated markedly from the late 1990s, and in mid-2002 it was reported that up to 60% of the Oblast's budget comprised transfers from the federal Government. The relatively weak economic situation of the region, particularly compared with that of its neighbours, encouraged speculation that the Oblast would be merged with one or more of the surrounding territories, although by early 2008 no definite proposals to that end had been announced. At the end of 2005 some 3,586 small businesses were registered in the Oblast, providing employment to 29,000 people.

DIRECTORY

Head of the Regional Administration (Governor): OLEG A. BOGOMOLOV (elected 8 December 1996, re-elected 10 December 2000 and 19 December 2004), 640024 Kurgan, ul. Gogolya 56; tel. (3522) 57-83-48; fax (3522) 41-71-32; e-mail kurgan@kurganobl.ru; internet www.kurganobl.ru.

Chairman of the Regional Duma: MARAT N. ISLAMOV, 640024 Kurgan, ul. Gogolya 56; tel. (3522) 41-74-77; fax (3522) 41-88-91; e-mail mail@oblduma.kurgan.ru; internet www.oblduma.kurgan.ru.

Chief Representative of Kurgan Oblast in the Russian Federation: SERGEI N. YAGOVITIN, 103006 Moscow, ul. M. Dmitrovka 3/10/313; tel. and fax (495) 200-39-78.

Head of Kurgan City Administration (Mayor): ANATOLII F. YELCHANINOV, 640000 Kurgan, pl. Lenina; tel. (3522) 6-22-25; fax (3522) 41-70-40; e-mail inform@munic.kurgan.ru; internet www.kurgan-city.ru.

Sverdlovsk Oblast

Sverdlovsk Oblast is situated on the eastern, and partly on the western, slopes of the Central and Northern Urals and in the Western Siberian Plain. It forms part of the Urals Federal Okrug and the Urals Economic Area. Tyumen Oblast lies to the east (with its constituent Khanty-Mansii AOk to the north-east); there is a short border with the Republic of Komi in the north-west and Perm Krai lies to the west. To the south are Bashkortostan, Chelyabinsk and Kurgan. The region's major rivers are those of the Ob and Kama basins. The west of the region is mountainous, while much of the eastern part is taiga (forested marshland). The Oblast covers an area of 194,800 sq km (75,190 sq miles). At January 2007, according to official estimates, the population totalled 4,399,738 and the population density was 22.6 per sq km. At the time of the 2002 census 89.2% of the population were ethnically Russian, 3.7% Tatar, 1.2% Ukrainian and 0.8% were Bashkir. Some 83.2% of the region's inhabitants lived in urban areas in January 2007. The Oblast's administrative centre is at Yekaterinburg, which had a population of 1,308,400 in January 2006, according to official estimates. Other major cities are Nizhnii Tagil (379,700), Kamensk-Uralskii (182,500) and Pervouralsk (132,900). The territory is included in the time zone GMT+5.

HISTORY

Yekaterinburg city was founded in 1821 as a military stronghold and trading centre. Like the Oblast (formed on 17 January 1934) it was named Sverdlovsk in 1924 but, unlike the Oblast, reverted to the name of Yekaterinburg in 1991. The city was infamous as the location where the last Tsar, Nicholas II, and his family were assassinated in 1918. The region became a major industrial centre after the Second World War.

Following the disintegration of the USSR, Sverdlovsk Oblast was among the most forthright in demanding the devolution of powers from the centre. In October 1993 the Regional Soviet and the head of the regional administration, Eduard Rossel, proclaimed a 'Ural Republic'. The self-styled Republic was dissolved by presidential decree, however, and Rossel was dismissed on 9 November and replaced by Aleksei Strakhov. In August 1995 Rossel was reinstated as Governor, having won a direct election to head the regional administration.

In January 1996 Rossel signed a power-sharing treaty with the federal authorities, the first such accord to be signed with a federal territory that did not have republican status. In April elections were held to the oblast bicameral Legislative Assembly, comprising the 28-member regional Duma, the lower chamber, and the 21-member House of Representatives, the upper chamber. Less than one-third of the electorate participated, but 35% voted for Rossel's Transformation of the Urals bloc, which had also obtained greater support than any other party in the region at elections to the federal legislature in December 1995. However, although in 1998 the Transformation bloc won just 9.3% of the votes to the regional legislature and claimed just two seats in the regional Duma (where it had previously held a majority), Rossel was re-elected as Governor in September 1999.

It was suggested that the Urals Federal Okrug, formed in mid-2000 by President Vladimir Putin, incorporated several regions traditionally regarded as part of Siberia (notably Tyumen Oblast), while excluding other regions that were included in the Urals Economic Area, so as to inhibit any revival of an appeal for a 'Ural Republic'. In September Rossel was re-elected as Governor. Rossel subsequently adopted a less oppositional stance towards the federal authorities, becoming a senior member of the pro-presidential United Russia (UR). In late 2003 Rossel instigated a proposal to merge Sverdlovsk Oblast with Chelyabinsk and Kurgan Oblasts; this, however, met with opposition from both territorial administrations and in April 2004 the Governor retracted his proposal. Rossel continued to express support for radical reforms to the administrative structure of the Russian Federation, declaring in mid-2005 that the ethnically defined Republics should be abolished and replaced by entities defined in purely territorial terms, so as to ensure equal rights for citizens of all ethnic groups and to lessen the possibility of the Federation disintegrating. On 21 November the regional legislature voted unanimously to confirm Rossel's appointment to a further term of office, following his nomination by Putin four days earlier. Elections were held to the regional Duma on 8 October 2006, at which UR were the most successful party, receiving 40.5% of the votes cast, while the Russian Pensioners' Party—RPP (18.8%), the Russian Party of Life—RPL (11.5%) and the Communist Party of the Russian Federation (CPRF—7.3%) also obtained representation. In April 2007 a demonstration by trade unions, supported by the regional branches of the CPRF and the liberal Yabloko party, was staged in Yekaterinburg to demand an increase in pensions. The popularity of UR had increased somewhat by the elections to the Regional Duma held on 2 March 2008; the party obtained 58.4% of the votes cast to those seats elected on the basis of party lists, ahead of the nationalist Liberal Democratic Party of Russia, which obtained 16.1%, and the CPRF, with 12.2%. Notably, A Just Russia (formed by a merger of the RPP, the RPL and Motherland) obtained only 6.2% of the votes cast, thereby failing to obtain representation.

ECONOMY

Sverdlovsk Oblast is a leading territory of the Russian Federation in terms of industry. In 2004 the territory's gross regional product amounted to 366,610.2m. roubles, equivalent to 82,604.0 roubles per head. Its most important industrial centres are at Yekaterinburg, Nizhnii Tagil, Pervouralsk and Serov. At the end of 2005 there were 3,535 km of railway lines and 10,874 km of paved roads on the Oblast's territory. There is an international airport, Koltsovo, outside Yekaterinburg.

The Oblast's agriculture, which employed just 5.9% of its workforce in 2005, consists mainly of animal husbandry and grain production. In 2006 Governor Rossel announced that unused pasture land in the Oblast was to be offered to Chinese guest workers who sought to cultivate it. Total agricultural output in 2005 was worth 32,029m. roubles. There is some extraction of gold and platinum in the Oblast. Its main industries are ferrous and non-ferrous metallurgy, the production of electrical energy, mechanical engineering, food-processing, and the production of copper and other ores, bauxite, asbestos, petroleum, peat and coal. There is also a significant defence sector. Industry employed some 33.3% of the working population in 2005 and generated 407,649m. roubles in 2004. In mid-2006 the titanium producer based in the Oblast, VSMPO-AVISMA, Russia's largest (which became part of the Russian Technologies Corporation formed in late 2007), entered into a joint venture with the US aircraft manufacturer Boeing to produce aircraft parts.

Sverdlovsk's economically active population numbered 2,367,000 in 2005, when 6.7% of the labour force were unemployed. The average monthly wage in the region was 8,675.9 roubles. The 2005 regional budget showed a deficit of 2,848.6m. roubles, and total foreign investment in that year was US $1,093.8m.; international trade amounted to some $5,991.3m. in exports and $1,574.4m. in imports. At the end of 2005 there were 29,149 small businesses, employing 232,900 people, registered in the Oblast.

DIRECTORY

Chairman of the Administration (Governor): EDUARD E. ROSSEL (elected 20 August 1995, re-elected 12 September 1999 and 21 September 2003, appointment confirmed 21 November 2005), 620031 Sverdlovsk obl., Yekaterinburg, pl. Oktyabrskaya 1; tel. (343) 217-87-17; fax (343) 378-18-30; e-mail press@midural.ru; internet www.rossel.ru.

Chairman of the Regional Government: ALEKSEI P. VOROBYEV, 620031 Sverdlovsk obl., Yekaterinburg, pl. Oktyabrskaya 1; tel. (343) 371-79-20; fax (343) 377-17-00; e-mail webmaster@midural.ru; internet www.midural.ru.

Chairman of the Regional Duma of the Legislative Assembly: NIKOLAI A. VORONIN, 620031 Sverdlovsk obl., Yekaterinburg, pl. Oktyabrskaya 1; tel. (343) 378-91-08; fax (343) 371-80-48; e-mail webmaster@duma.midural.ru; internet www.duma.midural.ru.

Chairman of the House of Representatives of the Legislative Assembly: NIKOLAI A. VORININ, 620031 Sverdlovsk obl., Yekaterinburg, pl. Oktyabrskaya 1; tel. (343) 378-91-08; fax (343) 371-80-48; e-mail duma@midural.ru; internet www.duma.midural.ru.

Chief Representative of Sverdlovsk Oblast in the Russian Federation: VLADIMIR S. MELENTYEV, 119957 Moscow, ul. Nezhinskaya 14/5; tel. and fax (495) 441-11-80.

Head of Yekaterinburg City Administration (Mayor): ARKADII M. CHERNETSKII, 620014 Sverdlovsk obl., Yekaterinburg, pl. Lenina 24A; tel. (343) 355-29-90; fax (343) 271-79-26; e-mail glava@sov.ekburg.ru; internet www.ekburg.ru.

Tyumen Oblast

Tyumen Oblast is situated in the Western Siberian Plain, extending from the Kara Sea in the north to the border with Kazakhstan in the south. It forms part of the Urals Federal Okrug and the Western Siberian Economic Area. Much of its territory comprises the Khanty-Mansii—Yugra and Yamalo-Nenets Autonomous Okrugs (AOks). To the west (going south to north) lie Kurgan and Sverdlovsk Oblasts, the Republic of Komi and the Nenets AOk—part of Archangel Oblast; to the east lie Omsk and Tomsk Oblasts and Krasnoyarsk Krai. The region has numerous rivers, its major ones being the Ob and the Irtysh. Much of its territory is taiga (forested marshland). The Oblast occupies 1,435,200 sq km (554,130 sq miles). In January 2007, according to official estimates, the population was 3,345,127 and the population density was only 2.3 per sq km. At the time of the 2002 census 71.6% of the population were ethnically Russian, 7.4% Tatar, 6.5% Ukrainian, 1.4% Bashkir, 1.3% Azeri, 1.1% Belarusian, 0.9% Chuvash, 0.9% Nenets, 0.8% German and 0.8% were Khant. Some 79.2% of the Oblast's inhabitants lived in urban areas in January 2007. The Oblast's administrative centre is at Tyumen, which had a population of 542,500 in January 2006, according to official estimates. There are several large cities within the Khanty-Mansii AOk—Yugra (q.v.) Another major city within that section of the Oblast not included in either of the AOks is Tobolsk, with a population of 106,000. The territory is included in the time zone GMT+5.

HISTORY

Tyumen city was founded in 1585 on the site of a Tatar settlement, and subsequently became an important centre for trade with the Chinese Empire. Tyumen Oblast was formed on 14 August 1944.

On 21 October 1993 the Oblast Soviet repealed its earlier condemnation of government action against the federal parliament but refused to disband itself. Eventually a new assembly, the regional Duma, which remained communist-led, was elected.

From the mid-1990s the exact nature of the relationship between Tyumen Oblast and the two AOks, which wished to retain a greater share of the income from their wealth of natural resources, became a source of intra-élite contention, despite the establishment of a co-ordinating administrative council between the three entities in 1995. In 1997 the two AOks had boycotted the oblast gubernatorial election, while a subsequent Constitutional Court ruling failed to clarify the status of the autonomies in relation to the Oblast. In 1998 Sergei Korepanov, the former Chairman of the Yamalo-Nenets legislature, was elected Chairman of the Tyumen Oblast Duma. At the gubernatorial election, held in January 2001, Sergei Sobyanin, a former speaker in the Khanty-Mansii legislature and the First Deputy Presidential Representative in the Urals Federal Okrug, defeated the incumbent Governor, Leonid Roketskii.

Sobyanin initially stated his opposition to any absorption of the two AOks into Tyumen Oblast. None the less, in February 2004 a meeting was held between Sobyanin and the Governor of the Yamalo-Nenets AOk, Yurii Neyelov, and protocols of intention relating to an eventual merger of the three entities were signed. However, in July representatives of the three administrations signed a power-sharing agreement, subsequently ratified by the three regional legislatures, which would have the effect of delaying any such unification until after the end of 2010. In January 2005 Sobyanin resigned as Governor, requesting a declaration of confidence from federal President Vladimir Putin. Putin subsequently nominated Sobyanin for a further term as Governor, which was approved by the regional Duma on 17 February, when Sobyanin became the second regional leader to assume office under the new procedure. On 14 November Sobyanin was appointed head of the federal presidential administration; he was replaced as Governor by the hitherto Mayor of Tyumen, Vladimir Yakushev, whose appointment was confirmed by the regional Duma on 24 November. At elections to the regional Duma on 11 March 2007, the pro-presidential United Russia secured an overwhelming victory, with 65.9% of votes cast; the nationalist Liberal Democratic Party of Russia won 10.8%, A Just Russia 8.7% and the Communist Party of the Russian Federation 8.4%.

ECONOMY

All figures in this survey include data for the two AOks, which are also treated separately. Tyumen Oblast was considered to have great economic potential, owing to its vast hydrocarbons and timber reserves (mainly located in the Khanty-Mansii—Yugra and Yamalo-Nenets AOks). In 2004 its gross regional product amounted to 1,898,156.1m. roubles, equivalent to 575,411.2 roubles per head (by far the highest figure in the Russian Federation). Its main industrial centres are at Tyumen, Tobolsk, Surgut, Nizhnevartovsk (the last two in the Khanty-Mansii AOk—Yugra) and Nadym (Yamalo-Nenets AOk). At the end of 2005 there were 2,451 km of railway lines and 10,880 km of paved roads on the Oblast's territory.

The Oblast's agriculture, which employed just 5.3% of its work-force in 2004 and generated 26,428m. roubles, consists mainly of animal husbandry (livestock- and reindeer-breeding and fur-farming), and the production of grain, potatoes and vegetables. Industry employed some 38.2% of the Oblast's working population in 2005 and generated a total of 1,245,872m. roubles in 2004, by far the highest level of any federal subject (The overwhelming majority of this output was produced within the Khanty-Mansii AOk—Yugra). In the late 1990s the Oblast's reserves of petroleum, natural gas and peat were estimated at 60%, 90% and 36%, respectively, of Russia's total supply. TNK-BP, formed in 2003 by the merger of the Tyumen Oil Company (TNK) with Sidanco and the Russian interests of BP (of the United Kingdom—formerly British Petroleum) is among the largest petroleum companies in Russia. Overall petroleum output in the region totalled 320.2m. metric tons in 2005, when output of natural gas amounted to 585,311m. cu m. The Oblast's other major industry is the production of electrical energy; in 2005 the Oblast's output amounted to 78,100m. kWh, of which 66,400m. kWh was produced within the Khanty-Mansii AOk—Yugra.

The economically active population totalled 1,824,000 in 2005, when 6.7% of the work-force were unemployed. The average monthly wage was 26,428 roubles in 2005, among the highest in the Federation. The regional budget for 2005 recorded a surplus of some 36,041.5m. roubles. In 2005 the external trade of the Oblast comprised US $30,529.m. in exports and $693.2m. of imports. Total foreign investment in the Oblast (which, like the Oblast's export trade, was particularly concentrated within the Khanty-Mansii AOk—Yugra) amounted to some $3,433.2m. in that year. At the end of 2005 some 14,466 small businesses, employing 151,800 people, were registered in the Oblast.

DIRECTORY

Governor: VLADIMIR V. YAKUSHEV (appointment confirmed 24 November 2005), 625004 Tyumen, ul. Volodarskogo 45; tel. (3452) 46-35-36; fax (3452) 46-55-42; e-mail kancelaria@mail.ru; internet admtyumen.ru.

Chairman of the Regional Duma: SERGEI YE. KOREPANOV, 625018 Tyumen, ul. Respubliki 52; tel. (3452) 45-50-81; e-mail inbox@ duma72.ru; internet www.duma72.ru.

Chief Representative of Tyumen Oblast in the Russian Federation: ALEKSANDR N. LOTOREV, 119017 Moscow, ul. Pyatnitskaya 47/2; e-mail pr_tumen@insar.ru; tel. and fax (495) 953-06-22.

Head of Tyumen City Administration: YEVGENII V. KUIVASHEV, 625036 Tyumen, ul. Pervomaiskaya 20; tel. (3452) 46-42-72; fax (3452) 24-33-64; e-mail glava@tyumen-city.ru; internet www .tyumen-city.ru.

Khanty-Mansii Autonomous Okrug—Yugra

The Khanty-Mansii Autonomous Okrug (AOk)—Yugra is situated in the Western Siberian Plain and the Ob-Irtysh river basin. The district forms part of the Urals Federal Okrug and the Western Siberian Economic Area, and lies within the territory of Tyumen Oblast. The other autonomous okrug within Tyumen Oblast, the Yamalo-Nenets AOk, lies to the north, while to the south of the district's centre lies the 'core' area of Tyumen Oblast. The Republic of Komi is to the west and Sverdlovsk to the south-west; to the south-east lies Tomsk and to the east Krasnoyarsk Krai. The district has numerous lakes, and much of its territory is Arctic tundra (frozen steppe) and taiga (forested marshland). The AOk occupies a total of 523,100 sq km (201,970 sq miles). At January 2007, according to official estimates, the AOk had a total of 1,488,297 inhabitants, giving a population density of 2.8 per sq km. Ethnic Khants and Mansi are greatly outnumbered by ethnic Russians in the district: at the time of the 2002 census some 66.1% of the population were ethnically Russian, 8.6% were Ukrainian, 7.5% Tatar, 2.5% Bashkir, 1.8% Azeri, 1.4% Belarusian, 1.2% Khant, 1.1% Chuvash, 0.8% Moldovan and only 0.7% Mansi. The Khanty and the Mansii languages are grouped together as an Ob-Ugrian sub-division of the Ugrian division of the Finno-Ugrian group. Some 91.2% of the population lived in urban areas in January 2007. The AOk's administrative centre is at the town of Khanty-Mansiisk, which had 59,600 inhabitants in January 2006, according to official estimates. Other major, and larger, cities in the Okrug include Surgut (290,600), Nizhnevartovsk (240,800) and Nefteyugansk (113,000). The Khanty-Mansii AOk—Yugra is included in the time zone GMT+5.

HISTORY

The Khanty-Mansii region, known as Yugra in the 11th–15th centuries, came under Russian control in the late 16th and early 17th centuries, as Russian fur traders established themselves in western Siberia. Attempts were made to assimilate the Khants and Mansi into Russian culture, and many were forcibly converted to Orthodox Christianity. The modern territory was created in December 1930, as the East Vogul (Ostyako-Vogulskii) National Autonomous Okrug. The territory became the Khanty-Mansii Autonomous Okrug in 1943, the name Yugra being appended to its designation in 2003.

From about the time of the Second World War the district became heavily industrialized, causing widespread damage to fish catches and reindeer pastures. In 1996 the okrug authorities appealed to the Constitutional Court against Tyumen Oblast's attempt to legislate for the control of district petroleum and natural gas reserves, and a protracted dispute ensued. As in the neighbouring Yamalo-Nenets AOk, the exact nature of the constitutional relationship between the Khanty-Mansii AOk and Tyumen Oblast remained obscure.

Aleksandr Filipenko, the head of the district administration appointed in December 1991, was returned to power in the gubernatorial election held in late 1996. He was re-elected, with 91% of the votes cast, in March 2000. Legislative elections were held on 14 January 2001; the district legislature, notably, incorporated a four-member Assembly of Representatives of Native Small Peoples of the North, with a particular remit to settle disputes over land use. Filipenko was more resistant than his counterpart in the Yamalo-Nenets AOk to the idea of a union with Tyumen Oblast: he believed that as the wealthiest of the three entities, Khanty-Mansii AOk, would gain little from a such a merger, and also warned of its potential threat to the rights of the territory's indigenous population. A power-sharing treaty, signed by representatives of the three entities in July 2004 and subsequently ratified by the three regional legislatures, delayed any possible unification until after the end of 2010. In February 2005 federal President Vladimir Putin nominated Filipenko to serve a further term of office; this nomination was approved by a unanimous vote of the district Duma on 24 February. At elections to the district Duma, held on 12 March 2006, the pro-presidential United Russia obtained an absolute majority (54.6%) of votes cast; the option to vote 'against all candidates', with 11.8% of the votes cast, obtained greater support than any other party, although the nationalist Liberal Democratic Party of Russia (with 10.5%), the Communist Party of the Russian Federation (9.2%) and the Russian Pensioners' Party (9.1%) also obtained legislative representation.

ECONOMY

The district economy is based on industry, particularly on the extraction and refining of petroleum. In 2004 the territory's gross regional product amounted to 1,276,184.3m. roubles. The AOk's main industrial centre is at the petroleum-producing town of Surgut. Its major river-port is at Nizhnevartovsk. At the end of 2005 there were 1,073 km of railway track and 2,197 km of paved roads; the extent of paved roads in the AOk increased by more than two-fold in 1995–2004.

Agriculture in the AOk, which employed just 1.1% of the work-force in 2004 and generated 2,972m. roubles in 2005, consists mainly of vegetable production and fishing, reindeer-breeding, fur-farming, hunting and vegetable production. In 2005 industry employed 43.8% of the work-force and generated 906,554m. roubles. The extraction of petroleum and natural gas and the production of electricity are the principal areas of industrial activity. The most significant producers of petroleum in the region were Surgutneftegaz (SNG), LUKoil-Western Siberia and Yuganskneftegaz, a subsidiary of Yukos Oil Co until late 2004, when, following a controversial auction and subsequent resale, it became a subsidiary of the state-controlled firm, Rosneft. Yukos assisted in the construction of housing and leisure facilities and in the operation of educational establishments during the early 2000s. Overall petroleum output in the region totalled 268.0m. metric tons in 2005, equivalent to 57.0% of the entire petroleum production in the Russian Federation in that year. In 2005 the AOk's production of electrical energy amounted to 66,400m. kWh, and output of natural gas amounted to 27,513m. cu m.

The economically active population of the district numbered 850,000 in 2005, when 7.8% of the labour force were unemployed. The average monthly wage was some 22,828.5 roubles. In 2005 the local budget recorded a deficit of some 586.8m. roubles. There was considerable foreign investment in the district from the late 1990s, and it totalled some US $3,433.2m. in 2005. The external trade of the AOk constitutes a substantial proportion of that attributed to Tyumen Oblast as a whole; in 2005 the external trade of the AOk comprised $11,615.3m of exports and $433.9m of imports, amounting to 38.6% of the total trade of the Oblast in that year. At the end of 2005 some 5,663 small businesses, which provided employment to 54,100 people, were registered in the AOk.

DIRECTORY

Governor, Chairman of the Government: ALEKSANDR V. FILIPENKO (appointed 18 December 1991, elected 27 October 1996, re-elected 26 March 2000, appointment confirmed 24 February 2005), 628006 Tyumen obl., Khanty-Mansii AOk, Khanty-Mansiisk, ul. Mira 5; tel. (34671) 3-20-95; fax (34671) 3-34-60; e-mail kominf@ admhmao.ru; internet www.hmao.wsnet.ru.

Chairman of the District Duma: VASILII S. SONDYKOV, 628007 Tyumen obl., Khanty-Mansii AOk, Khanty-Mansiisk, ul. Mira 5; tel. (34671) 9-28-29; fax (34671) 3-16-84; e-mail dumahmao@hmansy .wsnet.ru; internet www.hmao.wsnet.ru/power/duma/index.htm.

Chief Representative of the Khanty-Mansii Autonomous Okrug—Yugra in Tyumen Oblast: NIKOLAI M. DOBRYNIN, 626002 Tyumen, ul. Komsomolskaya 37; tel. (3452) 46-67-79; fax (3452) 46-00-91; e-mail hmaoda@tmn.ru.

Chief Representative of the Khanty-Mansii Autonomous Okrug—Yugra in the Russian Federation: VLADIMIR A. KHARITON, 119002 Moscow, Starokonyushennyi per. 10/10/2; tel. (495) 982-04-00; fax (495) 982-04-04; e-mail ugra_msk@dial.cnt.ru.

Head of Khanty-Mansiisk City Administration (Mayor): ANDREI G. BUKARINOV, 626200 Tyumen obl., Khanty-Mansii AOk, Khanty-Mansiisk, ul. Dzerzhinskogo 6; tel. (34671) 5-23-01; fax (34671) 3-21-74; e-mail adm@admhmansy.ru; internet www .admhmansy.ru.

Yamalo-Nenets Autonomous Okrug

The Yamalo-Nenets Autonomous Okrug (AOk) is situated on the Western Siberian Plain on the lower reaches of the Ob river. It forms part of Tyumen Oblast and, therefore, the Urals Federal Okrug and the Western Siberian Economic Area. The territory lies on the Asian side of the Ural Mountains and has a deeply indented northern coastline; the western section, the Yamal Peninsula, being separated from the eastern section by the Gulf of Ob. The rest of Tyumen Oblast, including the Khanty-Mansii AOk—Yugra, lies to the south. To the west lie the Nenets AOk (within Archangel Oblast) and the Republic of Komi, and to the east Krasnoyarsk Krai. The territory of the AOk occupies 750,300 sq km (289,690 sq miles). At January 2007, according to official estimates, it had a total population of 538,575 inhabitants and a population density of 0.7 per sq km. At the time of the 2002 census 58.8% of the population were ethnically Russian, 13.0% Ukrainian, 5.5% Tatar, 5.2% Nenets, 1.8% Belarusian, 1.7% Khant, 1.6% Azeri, 1.6% Bashkir, 1.2% Komi and 1.1% were Moldovan. Some 85.0% of the population inhabited urban areas in January 2007. The district administrative centre is at Salekhard, which had a population of 39,400 in January 2006, according to official estimates. The largest cities in the AOk were Novyi Urengoi (112,500) and the 'closed' city of Noyarbsk (108,500). The Yamalo-Nenets AOk is included in the time zone GMT+5.

HISTORY

The Nenets were traditionally a nomadic people, who were totally dominated by Russia from the early 17th century. The Yamalo-Nenets AOk was formed within Tyumen Oblast on 10 December 1930. Environmental concerns provoked protests in the 1980s and 1990s, and prompted the local authorities (comprising an administration and, from 1994, an elected Duma) to seek greater control over natural resources and their exploitation. The main dispute was with the central Tyumen Oblast authorities (more pro-communist than the AOk's own), and the AOk's rejection of oblast legislation on petroleum and natural gas exploitation first reached the Constitutional Court during 1996.

The economic importance of the fuel industry in the Yamalo-Nenets AOk was reflected in its political situation. Viktor Chernomyrdin, the former Chairman of the federal Government, was elected to the State Duma (the lower chamber of the federal legislature) as a representative of the Yamalo-Nenets AOk in 1998, and he retained his seat until his appointment as Ambassador to Ukraine in May 2001. At the gubernatorial election of 26 March 2000 the incumbent, Yurii Neyelov, who was regarded as sympathetic to the interests of the domestic gas monopoly Gazprom (the largest employer in the AOk, of which Chernomyrdin had previously served as head), was re-elected, securing some 90% of the votes cast. In early 2004 Neyelov, who had initially expressed opposition to such a measure, participated in several meetings with Sergei Sobyanin, Governor of Tyumen Oblast, to discuss proposals for the formal merger of the Oblast with its two constituent AOks. However, a power-sharing treaty, signed by representatives of the three entities in July and subsequently ratified by the three regional legislatures, delayed any possible unification until after the end of 2010. In early March 2005 federal President Vladimir Putin nominated Neyelov to serve for a further term as Governor; this nomination was confirmed by a unanimous vote of the District State Duma on 11 March. United Russia achieved an overwhelming victory in elections to the district legislature held on 27 March, obtaining some 60.2% of the votes cast; the option to vote 'against all candidates' received a greater share of votes cast (14.2%) than any other party. The nationalist Liberal Democratic Party of Russia, which had obtained some 15% of votes cast at the previous elections to the district legislature, had not been permitted to contest the elections, as a result of irregularities in registration documents for the party's proposed candidates.

In May 2006 Sergei Mironov, the Chairman of the upper house of the federal parliament, the Sovet Federatsii (Federation Council), and an ally of Putin, ordered the dismissal of one of the two representatives of the AOk in the chamber, together with three other senators, officially on the grounds that they were involved in commercial activities prohibited on account of their status. Whereas two of the four federal subjects concerned by this request refused to comply with Mironov's decision, the Yamalo-Nenets legislature sanctioned the dismissal of its representative and approved the nomination of a new senator selected by Mironov.

ECONOMY

In 2004 the territory's gross regional product amounted to 420,933.0m. roubles. At the end of 2005 there were 496 km of railway track and 1,050 km of paved roads (in 1990 there had been only 59 km of paved roads in the territory). The major industrial centres include Noyabrsk, Novyi Urengoi and Urengoi.

Agriculture, which employed just 2.1% of the work-force in 2005 and generated 504m. roubles, consists mainly of fishing, reindeer-breeding (reindeer pasture occupies just under one-third of its territory), fur-farming and the hunting of fur-bearing animals. The AOk's main industries are the extraction of natural gas and, to a lesser extent, of petroleum and the production of electricity. In 2005 the industrial sector employed 52.5% of the work-force and generated some 297,814m. roubles in 2004. The Yamal-Europe natural gas pipeline, of which the state-controlled Gazprom is the major shareholder, connects the gas fields of the territory with Frankfurt-an-der-Oder on the German–Polish border. Output of natural gas amounted to 557,776m. cu m in 2005, when 50.8m. metric tons of petroleum were extracted in the AOk. In October 2007 it was announced that a new deposit holding an estimated 90m. tons of crude oil, of which 30m. tons were considered recoverable, had been discovered in the territory.

The economically active population numbered 312,000 in 2004, when 7.1% of the labour force were unemployed. These statistics, like the high average monthly wage of 27,534.1 roubles (the highest in the Russian Federation) in 2005, have more in common with those of the Khanty-Mansii AOk than with those of those parts of Tyumen Oblast outwith the AOks. In 2005 the district government budget recorded a surplus of some 12,424.1m. roubles. The Yamalo-Nenets AOk has been successful in attracting foreign investment, receiving US $64.9m. in 2005. The external trade of the Yamalo-Nenets AOk is, however, substantially smaller than that of the Khanty-Mansii AOk; in 2005 exports amounted to US $532.2m. and imports to $130.3m. At the end of 2005 some 1,798 small businesses, which employed 20,500 people, were registered in the AOk.

DIRECTORY

Governor: YURII V. NEYELOV (appointed 4 August 1994, elected 13 October 1996, re-elected 26 March 2000, appointment confirmed 11 March 2005), 626608 Tyumen obl., Yamalo-Nenets AOk, Salekhard, ul. Respubliki 72; tel. (04922) 4-40-02; fax (34922) 4-52-89; e-mail yanao@salekhard.ru; internet adm.yanao.ru.

Chairman of the District State Duma: SERGEI N. KHARYUCHI, 629008 Tyumen obl., Yamalo-Nenets AOk, Salekhard, ul. Respublika 72; tel. (34922) 4-14-29; fax (34922) 4-20-23; e-mail gdyanao@salekhard.ru; internet www.gdyanao.ru.

Chief Representative of Yamalo-Nenets Autonomous Okrug in Tyumen Oblast: FUAT G. SAIFITDINOV, 625048 Tyumen, ul. Kholodilnaya 136/1; tel. (3422) 27-32-11; fax (3422) 40-24-80.

Chief Representative of Yamalo-Nenets Autonomous Okrug in the Russian Federation: NIKOLAI A. BORODULIN, 101000 Moscow, per. Arkhangelskii 15/3; tel. (495) 624-67-89; fax (495) 625-83-38.

Head of Salekhard City Administration: ALEKSANDR M. SPIRIN, 629008 Tyumen obl., Yamalo-Nenets AOk, Salekhard, ul. Respubliki 72; tel. (34922) 4-50-67; fax (34922) 4-01-82; e-mail stadnik@salekhard.org; internet www.salekhard.org.

Siberian Federal Okrug

Altai Republic

The Altai Republic is situated in the Altai Mountains, in the basin of the Ob river. The Republic forms part of the Siberian Federal Okrug and the Western Siberian Economic Area. It has international borders with Kazakhstan in the south-west, a short border with the People's Republic of China to the south and with Mongolia to the south-east. Kemerovo lies to the north, Khakasiya and Tyva to the north-east, and Altai Krai to the north-west. The Republic includes the highest peak in Siberia, Belukha, at 4,506 m (14,783 feet), and about one-quarter of its territory is forested. It contains one of Russia's major national parks, the Altai State National Park, covering an area of some 9,000 sq km (3,475 sq miles). The Republic occupies 92,600 sq km (35,753 sq miles). At January 2007, according to official estimates, the Republic had a population of 205,387 and a population density of 2.2 per sq km. At the time of the 2002 census, 57.4% of the population were ethnically Russian, 30.6% Altai, 6.0% Kazakh, 1.2% Telengit and 0.8% Tubalar. The Altai people can be divided into two distinct groups: the Northern Altai, or Chernnevye Tatars, consisting of the Tubalar, the Chelkan or Leberdin and the Kumandin; and the Southern Altai, comprising the Altai Kizhi, the Telengit, the Telesy and the Teleut. The language spoken by both groups is from the Turkish branch of the Uralo-Altaic family: that of the Northern Altai is from the Old Uigur group, while the language of the Southern Altai is close to the Kyrgyz language and is part of the Kipchak group. In 1989 over 84% of Altai spoke one or other language as their native tongue, and some 62% of the Altai population were fluent in Russian. Although the traditional religion of the Altai was animist or Lamaist, many were converted to Christianity, so the dominant religion in the Republic is Russian Orthodoxy. Only 26.1% of the population resided in urban areas in January 2007. The Republic's administrative centre is at Gorno-Altaisk (known as Ulala until 1932, then as Oirot-Tura until 1948), which had a population of 53,100 in 2006, according to official estimates. The Republic is included in the time zone GMT+6.

HISTORY

From the 11th century the Altai peoples inhabited Dzungaria (Sungaria—now mainly in the north-west of the People's Republic of China). The region was under Mongol control until 1389, when it was conquered by the Tatar forces of Timur or Tamerlane ('the Great'); it subsequently became a Kalmyk confederation. In the first half of the 18th century many Altai moved westwards, invading Kazakh territory and progressing almost as far as the Urals. In 1758, however, most of Dzungaria was incorporated into Xinjiang (Sinkiang), a province of the Chinese Empire. China embarked on a war aimed at exterminating the Altai peoples. Only a few thousand survived, finding refuge in the Altai Mountains or in Russian territory. In the 19th century Russia began to assert its control over the region, which was finally annexed in 1866. In the early 1900s Burkhanism or Ak Jang (White Faith), a nationalist religious movement, emerged. The movement was led by Oirot Khan, who claimed to be a descendant of Chinghiz (Genghis) Khan and promised to liberate the Altai from Russian control. However, in February 1918 it was a secular nationalist leader, V. I. Anuchin, who convened a Constituent Congress of the High Altai and demanded the establishment of an Oirot Republic—to include the Altai, the Khakass and the Tyvans. In partial recognition of such demands, in July 1922 the Soviet Government established an Oirot Autonomous Oblast as part of an Altai Krai (province). In 1948 the Oblast was renamed the Gorno-Altai (Mountainous Altai) Autonomous Oblast, in an effort to suppress nationalist sentiment.

In the late 1980s nationalism re-emerged in the region, which became the Altai Republic, separate from Altai Krai, at the signing of the Russian Federation Treaty in March 1992, having adopted a declaration of sovereignty on 25 October 1990. A resolution adopted on 14 October 1993 provided for the establishment of the El Kurultai (State Assembly) as the highest body of power in the Republic. A reform of the republican Government, implemented in August 1997, introduced the position of Head of the Republic, Chairman of the Government; this position was assumed by Vladilen Volkov, who had become Chairman of the El Kurultai in February of that year. In December 1997 Semen Zubakin was elected as Chairman of the Government in direct elections. The Republic was one of only four subjects of the Russian Federation to award the communist candidate, Gennadii Zyuganov, a higher proportion of the votes than Vladimir Putin in the presidential election of 2000. In February 2001 several amendments to the republican Constitution were approved by the El Kurultai, in order to bring them into conformity with federal legislation.

In a second round of polling to the post of Head of the Republic, held on 20 January 2002, Mikhail Lapshin, the leader of the Agrarian Party of Russia (APR), decisively defeated Zubakin. Lapshin received the support of the pro-presidential Unity and Fatherland-United Russia party (later known simply as United Russia—UR) in the second round, in addition to that of the Communist Party of the Russian Federation (CPRF). Legislative elections were held in the Republic in December. In October 2005 it was announced that Lapshin would not be nominated to serve again following the expiry of his term in January 2006, apparently in consequence of the Republic's poor economic performance. On 22 December the El Kurultai overwhelmingly voted in favour of the gubernatorial candidate proposed by federal President Putin, Aleksandr Berdnikov, a former republican Minister of Internal Affairs. Berdnikov assumed office on 20 January 2006. At elections to the El Kurultai, held on 12 March, UR obtained 27.2% of the votes cast, followed by Motherland, with 10.5%, and the APR, with 10.4%. The other parties to obtain legislative representation were the CPRF (9.0%), the Russian Party of Life (8.8%) and the nationalist Liberal Democratic Party of Russia (8.3%). Some 6.1% of votes were cast 'against all candidates'. On 31 October some 5,000 demonstrators protested against the proposed reunification of the Republic with Altai Krai; Berdnikov subsequently announced that no such merger would occur until 2008 at the earliest. At elections to the State Duma on 2 December 2007, UR secured about 54.7% of votes cast in the Altai Republic (one of the party's poorest results in the Federation).

ECONOMY

The Altai Republic is predominantly an agricultural region. Its gross regional product amounted to 9,122.0m. roubles in 2004, or 44,814.3 roubles per head. The main industrial centre in the Republic is at its capital, Gorno-Altaisk. At the end of 2005 the Republic contained 2,851 km of paved roads. There are no railways or airports. In March 1996 the Russian Government allocated some 1,800m. old roubles to alleviate the effects in the Republic of the nuclear tests conducted at Semey (Semipalatinsk), Kazakhstan, in 1949–62. However, in the early 2000s further concern was expressed about the negative effect of frequent rocket launches from the Baikonur Cosmodrome (located within Kazakhstan, but administered by Russia) on both the health of the residents of the Altai Republic and the surrounding environment.

Agriculture in the Republic, which employed 18.1% of the working population and generated 3,163m. roubles in 2005, consists mainly of livestock-breeding (largely horses, deer, sheep and goats). The export of the antlers of Siberian maral and sika deer, primarily to South-East Asia, is an important source of convertible currency to the Republic. The Republic's mountainous terrain often prevents the easy extraction or transport of minerals, but there are important reserves of manganese, iron, silver, lead and wolfram (tungsten), as well as timber. Stone, lime, salt, sandstone, gold, mercury and non-ferrous metals are also produced. There are also food-processing and construction materials industries. Industry employed just 13.0% of the working population in 2005 and generated 1,102m. roubles in 2004.

In 2005 the economically active population of the Republic numbered 94,000, and 10.0% of the labour force were unemployed. The average monthly wage was the relatively low figure of 5,736.1 roubles in 2005. There was a budgetary deficit of 202.0m. roubles in 2005. In that year external trade comprised US $32.0m. in exports and $102.3m. in imports. There was a very low level of foreign investment in the Republic. At the end of 2005 some 968 small businesses were registered in the Republic, providing employment to 7,600 people.

DIRECTORY

Head of the Republic, Chairman of the Government: ALEKSANDR V. BERDNIKOV (appointment confirmed 22 December 2005), 659700 Altai Rep., Gorno-Altaisk, ul. Kirova 16; tel. (38822) 2-26-30; e-mail altai-republic@altai-republic.com; internet www.altai-republic.com.

Chairman of the El Kurultai (State Assembly): IVAN I. BELEKOV, 649000 Altai Rep., Gorno-Altaisk, ul. Erkemena Palkina 1; tel. (38822) 2-26-18; fax (38822) 9-51-65; e-mail tvr@altek.gorny.ru; internet kurultai.altai-republic.ru.

Chief Representative of the Altai Republic in the Russian Federation: NADEZHDA CH. MANZYROVA, 103006 Moscow, ul. M. Dmitrovka 3/10; tel. and fax (495) 299-50-87.

Head of Gorno-Altaisk City Administration: VIKTOR A. OBLOGIN, 659700 Altai Rep., Gorno-Altaisk, pr. Kommunisticheskii 18; tel. (38822) 2-23-40; fax (38822) 2-25-59.

Republic of Buryatiya

The Republic of Buryatiya is situated in the Eastern Sayan Mountains of southern Siberia and forms part of the Siberian Federal Okrug and the Eastern Siberian Economic Area. It lies mainly to the east of Lake Baikal, although it also extends westwards along the international boundary with Mongolia in the south, to create a short border with the Russian federal subject of Tyva in the extreme west. Irkutsk Oblast lies to the north and west, and Transbaikal Krai to the east. Buryatiya's rivers mainly drain into Lake Baikal, the largest being the Selenga, the Barguzin and the Upper Angara, but some, such as the Vitim, flow northwards into the Siberian plains. Lake Baikal possesses over 80% of Russia's surface freshwater resources and 20% of the world's total, and is the oldest and deepest lake in the world. Intensive industrialization along its shores threatened Baikal's environment, and only from the 1990s were serious efforts made to safeguard the lake. Some 70% of Buryatiya's territory, and its valleys are open steppe. The Republic covers 351,300 sq km (135,640 sq miles). The winter is protracted but sees little snow, with the average temperature in January falling to –27.1°C; the average temperature in July is 16.0°C. At January 2007, according to official estimates, Buryatiya had a population of 959,985 and a population density of 2.7 per sq km. At the time of the 2002 census 67.8% of the population were ethnically Russian, 27.8% Buryat, 1.0% Ukrainian and 0.8% Tatar. The industrialized areas of the Republic are mainly inhabited by ethnic Russians. The Buryats are a native Siberian people of Mongol descent. The Buryats' native tongue is a Mongol dialect. Some Buryats are Orthodox Christians, but others practise Lamaism (Tibetan Buddhism), which has been syncretized with the region's traditional animistic shamanism. The Pandito Hambo Lama, a Buddhist spiritual leader, resides in Buryatiya's capital, Ulan-Ude, the only large city in the Republic, which had a population of 347,800 in January 2006, according to official estimates. Some 55.2% of the Republic's population inhabited urban areas in January 2007. The Republic is included in the time zone GMT+8.

HISTORY

Buryatiya was regarded as strategically important from the earliest years of the Muscovite Russian state, as it lay on the Mongol border. Russian influence reached the region in the 17th century and Transbaikal was formally incorporated into the Russian Empire by the Treaties of Nerchinsk and Kyakhta in 1689 and 1728, respectively. The latter agreement ended a dispute over the territory between the Russian and the Chinese Manzhou (Manchu) Empires. Many ethnic Russians subsequently settled in the region, often inhabiting land confiscated from the Buryats, many of whom were 'russified'. However, there was a resurgence of nationalist feeling in the 19th century; Jamtsarano, a prominent nationalist, led a movement that recognized the affinity of Buryat culture to that of the Mongols, most of whom were ruled from China, following a series of congresses in 1905 demanding Buryat self-government and the use of the Buryat language in schools. Russia's fears about the Buryats' growing allegiance to its eastern neighbour were allayed, however, after a formal treaty signed with Japan in 1912 recognized Outer Mongolia (later the Mongolian People's Republic) as a Russian sphere of influence.

With the dissolution of the Far Eastern Republic, a Buryat-Mongol ASSR was established on 30 May 1923. In the early 1930s, following Stalin's (Iosif Dzhugashvili's) policy of collectivization, many Buryats fled the country or were found guilty of treason and executed. In 1937 the eastern section of the Republic was transferred to Chita Oblast (now Transbaikal Krai) and a westerly region to Irkutsk Oblast. Furthermore, the Buryat language's Mongolian script was replaced with a Cyrillic one. In 1958 the Buryat-Mongol ASSR was renamed the Buryat ASSR, amid suspicions of increasing co-operation between Mongolia and the People's Republic of China. The territory declared its sovereignty on 10 October 1990 and was renamed the Republic of Buryatiya in 1992.

In March 1994 the republican Supreme Soviet (legislature) adopted a Constitution. The hitherto Chairman of the Supreme Soviet, Leonid Potapov, became the Republic's first President, following elections on 30 June, and the legislature was redesignated the People's Khural. A treaty on the division of powers was signed with the federal Government in 1995. Potapov was re-elected as President in June 1998. In October 2000 the People's Khural approved several amendments to Buryatiya's Constitution, but rejected others required by federal legislation, including the abolition of the stipulation that presidential candidates know both state languages, Russian and Buryat. In early 2002 Potapov resigned from the Communist Party of the Russian Federation (CPRF), and in April he oversaw the rescission of the declaration of sovereignty issued in 1990. In June 2002 Potapov was again re-elected as President, having obtained the support of the pro-presidential Unity and Fatherland-United Russia (later known as United Russia—UR). In the period preceding the election three of the four independent

radio stations in Ulan-Ude had their operations suspended by the republican State Communications Inspectorate. In June 2007 the People's Khural voted to approve President Putin's nomination of Vyacheslav Nagovitsyn, hitherto Deputy Governor of Tomsk Oblast, as Potapov's successor.

ECONOMY

In 2004 Buryatiya's gross regional product amounted to 64,826.6m. roubles, equivalent to 66,714.2 roubles per head. Its major industrial centre is at Ulan-Ude, which is situated on the Trans-Siberian Railway. At the end of 2005 there were 1,227 km of railways on Buryatiya's territory, and 3,825 km of paved roads.

The Republic's agriculture, which employed around 12.4% of the work-force and generated 9,103m. roubles in 2005, consists mainly of animal husbandry (livestock and the breeding of animals for fur) and the production of grain, vegetables and potatoes. Buryatiya is rich in mineral resources, including gold, uranium, coal, wolfram (tungsten), molybdenum, brown coal, graphite and apatites. In 1996 its gold reserves were estimated at 3.2m. troy oz (almost 100 metric tons). In early 2006 the Government announced that a new uranium field in the Republic was to be opened up to exploitation. Apart from ore-mining and the extraction of minerals, the main industries are mechanical engineering, metal-working, food-processing, timber production and wood-working. The Republic is also a major producer of electrical energy. The industrial sector employed 18.7% of the Republic's work-force in 2005 and generated 29,319m. roubles in 2004. The services sector with the most potential is tourism, owing to the attractions of Lake Baikal.

Buryatiya's economically active population numbered 453,000 in 2005, when 12.0% of the Republic's labour force were unemployed. The average monthly wage in the Republic was 7,650.5 roubles. A report issued in 2006 by a state body found that the Republic was one of the 11 most impoverished federal subjects in Russia. In 2005 there was a budgetary deficit of 278.6m. roubles. Foreign trade in that year comprised US $220.1m. in exports and $41.9m. in imports. It was hoped that Buryatiya's economy might be buoyed by the construction of the Angarsk–Nakhodka petroleum pipeline through its territory; in mid-2004 it was reported that the borders of the Republic's national park had been adjusted to accommodate the project, and in April 2006, in order to protect the environmental conditions around Lake Baikal, federal President Vladimir Putin decreed that the pipeline should pass no closer than 40 km from the littoral of the lake. Foreign investment in Buryatiya amounted to $49.6m. in 2005. At the end of that year 3,206 small businesses were registered in the Republic, providing employment to 24,600 people.

DIRECTORY

President and Chairman of the Government: Vyacheslav V. Nagovitsyn (appointment confirmed 15 June 2007), 670001 Buryatiya, Ulan-Ude, ul. Sukhe-Batora 9; tel. (3012) 21-51-86; fax (3012) 21-28-22; e-mail hural@icm.buryatia.ru; internet president.buryatia.ru.

Chairman of the People's Khural: Aleksandr G. Lubsanov, 670001 Buryatiya, Ulan-Ude, ul. Sukhe-Batora 9; tel. (3012) 21-31-57; fax (3012) 21-49-61; e-mail kontup01@icm.buryatia.ru; internet chairman.buryatia.ru.

Chief Representative of the Republic of Buryatiya in the Russian Federation: Bair G. Balzhirov, 107078 Moscow, ul. Myasnitskaya 43/2; tel. (495) 625-95-00; fax (495) 623-60-46.

Head of Ulan-Ude City Administration (Mayor): Gennadii A. Aidayev, 670000 Buryatiya, Ulan-Ude, ul. Lenina 54; tel. (3012) 21-57-05; fax (3012) 26-32-44.

Republic of Khakasiya

The Republic of Khakasiya is situated in the western area of the Minusinsk hollow, on the left bank of the River Yenisei, which flows northwards towards, ultimately, the Arctic Ocean. It lies on the eastern slopes of the Kuznetsk Alatau and the northern slopes of the Western Sayan Mountains. It comprises part of the Siberian Federal Okrug and the Eastern Siberian Economic Area. Tyva lies to the south-east and the Altai Republic to the south-west. Kemerovo lies to the west, and Krasnoyarsk Krai to the north and east. Khakasiya occupies 61,900 sq km (23,900 sq miles). At January 2007, according to official estimates, the Republic had a population of 536,609 and a population density of 8.7 per sq km. At the time of the 2002 census 80.3% of the population were ethnically Russian, 12.0% Khakass, 1.7% German and 1.5% were Ukrainian. In 1989 over 76% of the Khakass spoke the national language—primarily derived from the Uigur group of Eastern Hunnic languages of the Turkic family—as their native tongue. Some 71.1% of the population lived in urban areas in January 2007. Khakasiya's capital is at Abakan, which had 164,000 inhabitants in January 2006, according to official estimates. The Republic is included in the time zone GMT+7.

HISTORY

The Khakass or Khakasiyans were traditionally known as the Minusinsk (Minusa), the Turki, the Yenisei Tatars or the Abakan Tatars. They were semi-nomadic hunters, fishermen and livestock-breeders. Khakasiya was a powerful state in Siberia, owing to its trading links with Central Asia and the Chinese Empire. Russian settlers began to arrive in the region in the 17th century and their presence was perceived as valuable protection against Mongol invasion. The annexation of Khakass territory by the Russians was eventually completed during the reign of Peter (Petr) I 'the Great', with the construction of a fort on the River Abakan. The Russians subsequently imposed heavy taxes, seized the best land and imposed Orthodox Christianity on the Khakass. After the construction of the Trans-Siberian Railway in the 1890s the Khakass were heavily outnumbered. Following the Bolshevik Revolution a Khakass national uezd (district) was established in 1923, becoming an okrug in 1925, and the Khakass Autonomous Oblast on 20 October 1930, within Krasnoyarsk Krai. In 1992 it was upgraded to the status of a Republic under the terms of the Federation Treaty, having declared its sovereignty on 3 July 1991. On 25 May 1995 the Republic adopted its Constitution.

Aleksei Lebed, an independent candidate and younger brother of the politician and former general, Aleksandr Lebed (who was Governor of Krasnoyarsk Krai from May 1998 until his death in 2002), was directly elected as Chairman of the Government (Head of the Republic) of Khakasiya, in December 1996, having served as the Republic's representative in the State Duma, the lower chamber of the federal parliament, since the previous year. Lebed was elected to a second term of office in December 2000. In early 2004 the republican authorities were involved in a dispute with the electricity monopoly Unified Energy System of Russia (RAO EES Rossii), which owned a majority share in the Sayano-Shushenskaya hydroelectric plant, situated on the border with Krasnoyarsk Krai. When Aleksei Lebed's application to have extended a deal that had hitherto offered Khakasiya preferential rates for electricity was rejected by RAO EES Rossii, he applied to have the plant renationalized. The Republic eventually won its case on appeal in March 2004, but in June Lebed agreed to drop all demands for the renationalization of the installation in return for RAO EES Rossii abandoning plans to re-register the plant in Krasnoyarsk Krai. Lebed was re-elected on 26 December 2004, receiving 59.2% of the votes cast. In concurrent elections to the republican legislature the pro-presidential United Russia was the most successful grouping, closely followed by the regional Khakasiya bloc. The rate of participation in both elections was around 30%.

In May 2006 Sergei Mironov, the Chairman of the upper house of the federal parliament, the Federation Council, and an ally of federal President Vladimir Putin, ordered the dismissal of one of the two representatives of Khakasiya in the chamber, alongside three other senators, officially on the grounds that they were involved in commercial activities forbidden by law on account of their status. However, the Supreme Council in Khakasiya (in common with the district legislature of the Nenets AOk) refused to recall its representative from Moscow. Later in the month all four senators dismissed by Mironov announced what was termed their 'voluntary resignation'. One apparent consequence of the Khakasiyan authorities' failure to comply with the wishes of the federal authorities was the commencement by the federal Ministry of Internal Affairs of an investigation into the alleged misuse of budgetary funds by the republican Government. In late July Lebed was charged with abuse of office, and other senior officials in Khakasiya were issued with similar charges; a court case commenced in September. In November, moreover, Lebed was ordered to pay 500 roubles in compensation by an Abakan court to a member of the republican legislature whose reputation he was deemed to have harmed.

ECONOMY

Khakasiya's gross regional product amounted to 33,962.5m. roubles in 2004, or 62,682.8 roubles per head. Khakasiya's major industrial centres are at Abakan, Sorsk, Sayanogorsk and Chernogorsk. At the end of 2005 there were 667 km of railway lines and 2,630 km of paved roads in the Republic.

The Republic's agriculture, which employed around 9.2% of the working population and generated 4,093m. roubles in 2005, consists mainly of animal husbandry and potato and vegetable production. The Republic's main industries are ore-mining and non-ferrous metallurgy. Electricity generation is also important; the Sayano-Shushenskaya plant is the fourth largest hydroelectric power station in the world, producing around 245,000m. kWh per year. The territory is also renowned for its handicrafts (wood-carving and embroidery). There are significant reserves of coal and iron ore. Other mineral reserves included molybdenum, lead, zinc, barytes,

aluminium and clay. There was also the potential for extraction of petroleum and natural gas. Industry employed 24.6% of the workforce in 2005 and generated 26,541m. roubles in 2004.

The Republic's economically active population numbered 278,000 in 2005, when 8.9% of the labour force were unemployed. The average monthly wage was 7,770.8 roubles. The republican budget for 2005 recorded a surplus of 140.2m. roubles. In 2005 external trade comprised US $741.3m. in exports and $324.4m. in imports. Foreign investment in Khakasiya was less substantial, however, amounting to only $3.5m. in 2005. At the end of that year 2,140 small businesses were registered in the Republic, providing employment to 27,700 people.

DIRECTORY

Chairman of the Government: ALEKSEI I. LEBED (elected 22 December 1996, re-elected 24 December 2000 and 26 December 2004), 655019 Khakasiya, Abakan, pr. Lenina 67; tel. (3902) 29-91-02; fax (3902) 22-50-91; e-mail pressa@khakasnet.ru; internet www.rhlider.ru.

Chairman of the Supreme Council: VLADIMIR N. SHTYGASHEV, 655019 Khakasiya, Abakan, pr. Lenina 67; tel. (3902) 22-53-35; e-mail info@vskhakasia.ru; internet vskhakasia.ru.

Chief Representative of the Republic of Khakasiya in the Russian Federation: MONYA M. BERGMAN, 127025 Moscow, ul. Novyi Arbat 19/1820; tel. (495) 203-83-41; fax (495) 203-83-45.

Head of Abakan City Administration: NIKOLAI G. BULAKIN, 655000 Khakasiya, Abakan, ul. Shchetinkina 10A/6, POB 6; tel. (3902) 26-37-91; fax (3902) 26-31-91; internet meria.abakan.ru.

Republic of Tyva

The Republic of Tyva is situated in the south of eastern Siberia in the Sayan Mountains. It forms part of the Siberian Federal Okrug and the Eastern Siberian Economic Area. Tyva has an international border with Mongolia to the south and east. The Altai Republic lies to the west, Khakasiya to the north-west and Krasnoyarsk Krai to the north. Irkutsk Oblast lies to the north-east and Buryatiya forms part of the eastern border. Tyva's major river is the Yenisei, which rises in the Eastern Sayan range. The territory of the Republic consists of a series of high mountain valleys. The Republic has more than 12,000 rivers and 8,400 freshwater lakes. Tyva occupies 170,500 sq km (65,830 sq miles). At January 2007, according to official estimates, Tyva had a population of 309,439 and a population density of only 1.8 per sq km. At the time of the 2002 census 77.0% of the population were Tyvan (Tuvinians), including 1.5% of the total population who categorized themselves as Tuvan-Todzhin, and 20.1% were ethnically Russian. Lamaism (Tibetan Buddhism) is the predominant religion in the Republic. The Tyvan language belongs to the Old Uigur group of the Turkic branch of the Uralo-Altaic linguistic family. Some 51.4% of the population lived in urban areas in January 2007. The capital of Tyva is at Kyzyl, which had a population of 109,100 in January 2006, according to official estimates. The Republic is included in the time zone GMT+7.

HISTORY

The Tyvans (known at various times as Soyons, Soyots and Uriankhais) emerged as an identifiable ethnic group in the early 18th century. The territory of what is now Tyva was occupied in turn between the sixth and the ninth centuries by the Turkish Khanate, the Chinese, the Uigurs and the Yenisei Kyrgyz. The Mongols controlled the region from 1207 to 1368. In the second half of the 17th century the Dzungarians (Sungarians) seized the area from the Altyn Khans. In 1758 the Manzhous (Manchus) annexed Dzungaria and the territory thus became part of the Chinese Empire. Russian influence dates from the Treaty of Beijing (Peking) of 1860, after which trade links were developed and a number of Russians settled there. One year after the Chinese Revolution of 1911 Tyva declared its independence. In 1914, however, Russia established a protectorate over the territory, which then became the Tannu-Tuva People's Republic. This was a nominally independent state until October 1944, when it was incorporated into the USSR as the Tuvinian Autonomous Oblast. It became an ASSR on 10 October 1961, within the Russian Federation.

The Republic declared sovereignty on 11 December 1990 and renamed itself the Republic of Tuva in August 1991. On 21 October 1993 the republican Supreme Soviet resolved that the Republic's name was Tyva (as opposed to the russified Tuva) and adopted a new Constitution. The Constitution provided for a legislature, the Supreme Khural, and a supreme constitutional body, the Grand Khural. The new parliament was elected on 12 December, when the new republican Constitution was approved by 62.2% of votes cast.

Only 32.7%, however, voted in favour of the Russian Constitution. In 2000 the Grand Khural was obliged to make 26 amendments to the republican Constitution, in order to comply with the federal Constitution. A new Constitution, which removed Tyva's rights to self-determination and to secede from the Federation, was approved by referendum in May 2001. In March 2002 various amendments to the Constitution were approved, in order to bring it more closely into compliance with federal norms. The Supreme Khural was renamed the Grand Khural and was reconstituted as a bicameral legislature, comprising an upper chamber, the 130-member Chamber of Representatives, and a lower chamber, the 32-member Legislative Chamber. On 17 March the incumbent President (previously elected in 1992 and 1997), Sherig-ool Oorzhak, was elected to serve a third term of office, receiving 53% of the votes cast. Elections to the bicameral legislature were held on 2 June 2002.

Further elections to the Grand Khural took place on 8 October 2006. The pro-presidential United Russia (UR) secured 46.4% of the votes cast, while the Russian Party of Life, the only other party to obtain seats on the basis of proportional representation, received 32.3%. Investigations into electoral irregularities alleged by the Russian Party of Life commenced, but were delayed in mid-November when 10 UR deputies withdrew from the outgoing legislature, leaving it without a quorum; consequently, the inauguration of the new Grand Khural was delayed. Results were annulled in four constituencies, in all of which candidates of the Russian Party of Life (RPL) had won; ballots were repeated on 11 March 2007. The chairman of the republican election commission announced that the results of the repeat vote had been annulled in three constituencies where the RPL candidates had again been placed first, and validated the outcome only in one constituency where a candidate from the pro-presidential UR won. Five members of the Tyva branch of the RPL declared a hunger strike in protest at the decision, and the party (which subsequently merged into A Just Russia) boycotted the Grand Khural. The republican Prosecutor initiated a criminal case into the alleged falsification of the outcome of the elections. On 6 April, shortly before the expiry of Oorzhak's mandate, the Grand Khural approved federal President Vladimir Putin's nomination of Sholban Kara-Ool of UR as Governor.

ECONOMY

Tyva's economy is largely agriculture-based and is relatively underdeveloped. In 2004 its gross regional product stood at 9,767.2m. roubles, or 31,809.3 roubles per head. The Republic's main industrial centres are at Kyzyl and Ak-Dovurak. At the end of 2005 there were 2,046 km of paved roads in the Republic. There are no railways in Tyva.

Tyva's agriculture, which employed 9.5% of the work-force and generated 2,460m. roubles in 2005, consists mainly of animal husbandry, although forestry and hunting are also important. Gold extraction was developed from the mid-1990s; in 1996 it amounted to almost one metric ton. Tyva's main industries were ore-mining (asbestos, coal, cobalt and mercury), production of electricity, food-processing and non-ferrous metallurgy. Industry employed 11.9% of the working population in 2005 and generated 1,897m. roubles in 2004.

The economically active population of Tyva totalled 133,000 in 2005, when 21.8% of the labour force were unemployed—the highest rate of unemployment of any territory outwith the Southern Federal Okrug. In 2005 the average monthly wage in the Republic was 6,814.4 roubles, somewhat lower than the national average. A report issued in 2006 by a state body found that the Republic was one of the 11 most impoverished federal subjects in Russia. The 2005 budget recorded a surplus of 116.9m. roubles. Foreign investment in the Republic was negligible. External trade was also minimal, amounting to just US $3.0m. in exports and $4.0m. in imports in 2005. At the end of that year 800 small businesses were registered in the Republic, providing employment to around 3,800 people.

DIRECTORY

Chairman of the Government: SHOLBAN V. KARA-OOL (appointment confirmed 6 April 2007), 667000 Tyva, Kyzyl, ul. Chulduma 18; tel. (39422) 1-12-77; fax (39422) 3-74-59; e-mail tuva@tuva.ru; internet gov.tuva.ru.

President of the Chamber of Representatives of the Grand Khural: MONGUSH KHONUK-OOL, 667000 Tyva, Kyzyl, ul. Lenina 32; tel. (39422) 1-31-79; fax (39422) 3-33-71; e-mail parlament@tuva.ru.

President of the Legislative Chamber of the Grand Khural: VASILII M. OYUN, 667000 Tyva, Kyzyl, ul. Lenina 32; tel. (39422) 3-74-78; fax (39422) 1-16-32; e-mail parlament@tuva.ru; internet gov.tuva.ru/gosvo/velhur.htm.

Chief Representative of the Republic of Tyva in the Russian Federation: ORLAN O. CHOLBENEI, 119049 Moscow, ul. Donskaya 8/2; tel. (495) 236-48-01; fax (495) 236-45-53.

Head of Kyzyl City Administration (Mayor): DMITRII K. DONGAK, 667000 Tyva, Kyzyl, ul. Lenina 32; tel. (39422) 1-00-34.

Altai Krai

Most of Altai Krai lies within the Western Siberian Plain. Part of the Siberian Federal Okrug and the Western Siberian Economic Area, it has an international boundary to the south with Kazakhstan. Novosibirsk lies to the north, Kemerovo to the north-east and the Altai Republic to the south-east. Its major river is the Ob. There are many thousands of lakes, about one-half of which are fresh water. About one-third of its total area is forested. In the east of the Krai are mountains, in the west steppe. The Krai occupies 169,100 sq km (65,290 sq miles). At January 2007, according to official estimates, it had a total population of 2,523,308 and a population density of 14.9 per sq km. At the time of the 2002 census 92.0% of the population were ethnically Russian, 3.0% German, 2.0% Ukrainian and only 0.1% were Altai. Some 53.6% of the population lived in urban areas in January 2007. The Krai's administrative centre is at Barnaul, which had a population of 604,200 in January 2006, according to official estimates. Other major cities are Biisk (225,300) and Rubtsovsk (158,600). Altai Krai is included in the time zone GMT+6.

HISTORY

The territory of Altai Krai was annexed by Russia in 1738 (for more on the Altais, see the Republic of Altai). The region was heavily industrialized during the Soviet period. Altai Krai was formed on 28 September 1937, at which time it included the territory of what is now the Altai Republic. This territory, then known as the Gorno-Altai (Mountainous Altai) Autonomous Oblast, declared its sovereignty in 1990 and its secession from the Krai was formally recognized in 1992.

On 13 March 1994, in accordance with a federal presidential decree of October 1993, a new provincial legislature, the Legislative Assembly, was elected to replace the provincial Soviet. The new legislature comprised a lower chamber of 25 deputies and an upper chamber of 72 deputies. The Chairman of the provincial Council of People's Deputies (the lower chamber), Aleksandr Surikov, a communist, defeated the incumbent Governor, Lev Korshunov, in the gubernatorial election of November 1996. Surikov retained his post in the election of 26 March 2000, obtaining 77% of the votes cast. Later that year legislation was approved reforming the provincial legislature on a unicameral basis. In the gubernatorial election of 2004 Surikov was unexpectedly defeated in a second round of voting on 4 April by the marketing director for a local coal company, Mikhail Yevdokhimov, who was regarded as a populist. Surikov won 46.3% of votes cast, compared with Yevdokhimov's 49.5%. Surikov, who had allied himself with the pro-presidential United Russia (UR) and still had the support of local communists, had generally been perceived as a competent economic manager of the region and had been widely expected to obtain re-election. The victory of Yevdokhimov was regarded as indicating widespread dissatisfaction at the consequences of the ambitious privatization programme implemented in the region in the early 1990s. However, Yevdokhimov failed to bring about an improvement in the economic situation in the Krai. In March 2005 the leaders of the provincial branches of 21 political organizations, including UR, the Communist Party of the Russian Federation—CPRF, the Agrarian Party of Russia and the pro-market Union of Rightist Forces, urged federal President Vladimir Putin to dismiss Yevdokhimov. Later in March a similar petition was filed by a majority of the municipal agencies in the Krai, and at the end of the month the provincial legislature overwhelmingly approved a vote of 'no confidence' in the Governor. A further vote of 'no confidence' in Yevdokhimov was approved, again by an overwhelming majority, at the end of April, although the Governor stated that he would not resign. On 7 August Yevdokhimov was killed as a result of an automobile accident in the Krai. Following Yevdokhimov's death, Putin nominated Aleksandr Karlin, a former deputy Minister of Justice in the federal Government and hitherto Chairman of the presidential administration's Civil Service Directorate (who was also native to the Krai), as Governor; this nomination was confirmed by vote of the provincial legislature on 25 August.

In October 2005 protests were staged in the capital of the Altai Republic against proposals for its eventual reunification with Altai Krai. Although plans for a merger were subsequently suspended, in September 2007, at a formal ceremony in Barnaul to mark the 70th anniversary of the formation of Altai Krai, the Head of the Altai Republic, Aleksandr Berdnikov, declared his support for the reunification.

UR were the most successful party at elections to the provincial Legislative Assembly, held on 2 March 2008, obtaining 53.4% of the votes cast. The CPRF were placed second, with 19.6%, ahead of the nationalist Liberal Democratic Party of Russia, with 16.5%, and A Just Russia: Motherland/Pensioners/Life, with 7.7%

ECONOMY

Altai Krai's gross regional product totalled 111,817.6m. roubles in 2004, equivalent to 43,432.7 roubles per head. Its main industrial centres are at Barnaul, Biisk, Rubtsovsk and Novoaltaisk. There are major river-ports at Barnaul and Biisk. The Krai contained 1,584 km of railway lines at the end of 2005, and 14,508 km of paved roads. In 1998 there were some 1,000 km of navigable waterways in the territory. There are five airports, including an international airport at Barnaul, with a service to Düsseldorf, Germany. The Krai is bisected by the main natural gas pipeline from Tyumen to Barnaul.

The Krai's principal crops are grain, flax, sunflowers and sugar beet. Animal husbandry, including fur-farming and bee-keeping, is also important. In 2005 agriculture engaged 17.6% of the work-force and generated 41,946m. roubles. Altai Krai contains substantial mineral resources, including salt, iron ore, soda and precious stones, most of which are not industrially exploited. Its main industries are mechanical engineering (including tractor-manufacturing), food-processing (the Krai's agro-industrial complex is one of the largest in the country), metal-working, electricity production, and chemicals and petrochemicals. In addition, Barnaul contains one of the largest textiles enterprises in Russia, producing cotton fibre and yarn for cloth. Industry employed 21.0% of the work-force in 2005 and generated 80,079m. roubles in 2004.

In 2005 the economically active population of Altai Krai totalled 1,296,000, and 9.0% of the Krai's labour force were unemployed. The average monthly wage was just 4,913.8 roubles in 2005, substantially lower than the federal average. Living costs are, however, low in the region. In 2005 the provincial budget recorded a deficit of 1,096.5m. roubles. External trade in that year amounted to a value of US $744.1m. in exports and $206.6m. in imports. Foreign investment in the territory totalled only $1.6m in 2004. At the end of that year 13,671 small businesses were registered in the Krai, providing employment to 109,500 people.

DIRECTORY

Head of the Provincial Administration (Governor): ALEKSANDR B. KARLIN (appointment confirmed 25 August 2005), 656035 Altai Krai, Barnaul, pr. Lenina 59; tel. (3852) 35-69-35; fax (3852) 36-38-63; e-mail glava@alregn.ru; internet www.altairegion22.ru.

Chairman of the Legislative Assembly: IVAN I. LOOR, 656035 Altai Krai, Barnaul, pr. Lenina 59; tel. (3852) 35-69-38; fax (3852) 36-35-27; e-mail ps@alregn.ru; internet www.altsovet.ru.

Chief Representative of Altai Krai in the Russian Federation: ALEKSANDR S. POMENOV, 109017 Moscow, per. B. Tolmachevskii 5/9; tel. (495) 953-36-83; fax (495) 953-01-84; e-mail altay.pred@mail.ru.

Head of Barnaul City Administration: VLADIMIR N. KOLGANOV, 656099 Altai Krai, Barnaul, pr. Lenina 18; tel. (3852) 39-33-39; e-mail info@barnaul.org; internet www.barnaul.org.

Krasnoyarsk Krai

Krasnoyarsk Krai occupies the central part of Siberia and extends from the Arctic Ocean coast in the north to the Western Sayan Mountains in the south. The Krai, which fully absorbed the former Evenk and Taimyr (Dolgano-Nenets) Autonomous Okrugs (AOks), which were located in the centre and north of the territory, respectively, in January 2007, forms part of the Siberian Federal Okrug and the Eastern Siberian Economic Area. It is bordered by Sakha (Yakutiya) and Irkutsk to the east and by Tyva to the south. To the west lie Khakasiya, Kemerovo and Tomsk, as well as the Khanty-Mansii—Yugra and Yamalo-Nenets AOks within Tyumen Oblast. Its major river is the Yenisei, one of the longest in Russia, measuring 4,102 km (2,549 miles). Most of its area is covered by taiga (forested marshland). The Krai covers a total area of 2,339,700 sq km (903,358 sq miles), the second largest federal unit in Russia. Krasnoyarsk Krai measures almost 3,000 km from south to north. The Krai lies within three climatic zones—arctic, sub-arctic and continental. At January 2007, according to official estimates, it had a total population of 2,893,748 and a population density of 1.2 per sq km. At the time of the 2002 census 88.9% of the population were ethnically Russian, 2.3% Ukrainian, 1.5% Tatar and 1.2% were German. Some 75.4% of the population inhabited urban areas in January 2007. The Krai's administrative centre is at Krasnoyarsk, which had a population of 920,900 in January 2006, according to official estimates. Other major cities include Norilsk (213,200), Achinsk (112,700) and Kansk (101,600). The territory is included in the time zone GMT+7.

HISTORY

The city of Krasnoyarsk was founded in 1628 by Cossack forces as an ostrog (military transit camp) during the period of Russian expansion across Siberia (1582–1639). The region gained importance after the discovery of gold, and with the construction of the Trans-Siberian Railway. The Krai was formed on 7 December 1934. During the Soviet era the region was closed to foreigners, owing to its nuclear-reactor and defence establishments.

A gubernatorial election in December 1992 was won by Valerii Zubov, a supporter of federal President Boris Yeltsin, and elections to a new parliament, the Legislative Assembly, were held on 6 March 1994. In June 1997 Zubov signed the first of a number of agreements with Evenk AOk, which declared the AOk to be a constituent part of Krasnoyarsk Krai and obliged its residents to participate in all the territory's elections. In October the two entities, with the Taimyr (Dolgano-Nenets) AOk, signed a power-sharing agreement with the federal authorities. In the mid-1990s Zubov's regime proved to be increasingly ineffectual, and a poor record on paying wage arrears contributed to the victory in the gubernatorial election, held on 17 May 1998, of Gen. (retd) Aleksandr Lebed, the former secretary of the National Security Council. Lebed died in a helicopter crash on 28 April 2002. A gubernatorial election, held on 8 September, and contested by 14 candidates, proved inconclusive; the Chairman of the provincial legislature, Aleksandr Uss, whose campaign was supported by the aluminium company RusAl, received 27.6% of the votes cast, closely followed by the Governor of the Taimyr AOk and the former General Director of Norilsk Nickel, Aleksandr Khlopanin, with 25.2%; these two candidates proceeded to a second round. In the 'run-off' election, held on 22 September, Khlopanin was the first-placed candidate, winning 48.1% of the votes cast, while Uss received 41.8% of votes. However, the Krai's electoral commission annulled the results of the election, citing irregularities in the conduct of Khlopanin's campaign. On 1 October a court in Krasnoyarsk overturned the decision of the commission, and two days later federal President Vladimir Putin appointed Khlopanin to serve as acting Governor; on the following day the central electoral commission confirmed Khlopanin as Governor, and he was inaugurated shortly afterwards. The Supreme Court confirmed the validity of the election results in November. In March 2003 Khlopanin was elected to the Supreme Council of the pro-presidential Unity and Fatherland-United Russia party (later known as United Russia—UR). Following his inauguration as Governor of Krasnoyarsk Krai, Khlopanin resigned as Governor of the Taimyr AOk. Khlopanin's victory appeared to heighten speculation that Krasnoyarsk Krai and the two AOks contained therein would eventually merge to form a single unit. (A proposed referendum on such a merger had been cancelled in 2002, following the death of Lebed.) A Council of Governors and a council of the legislative assemblies of the three entities were subsequently established. In referendums on the merger of the three polities, held on 17 April 2005, the unification was approved by a clear majority of votes in all three territories. In August President Putin submitted draft legislation providing for the merger, which confirmed that the reunified territory would continue to be known as Krasnoyarsk Krai, to the federal State Duma. Both chambers of the federal legislature had approved legislation by early October. The merger took effect on 1 January 2007.

Elections to a new 52-member Legislative Assembly of the unified territory were conducted on 15 April 2007; UR won 42% of the votes, securing a total of 29 seats, followed by the Communist Party of the Russian Federation (CPRF, with 20% of the votes), A Just Russia (12%), the nationalist Liberal Democratic Party of Russia (11%) and the pro-market Union of Rightist Forces (7%). A local CPRF official condemned allegations by Sergei Mironov, the leader of A Just Russia and Chairman of the upper house of the federal parliament, that the CPRF had obtained more votes than A Just Russia as a result of criminal connections. In May the new Legislative Assembly proposed to President Putin that Khlopanin, whose mandate was due to expire later in 2007, be appointed for a further term; it approved the nomination on 4 June.

ECONOMY

All figures in this survey incorporate data for the former Evenk and Taimyr (Dolgano-Nenets) Autonomous Okrugs. Krasnoyarsk Krai is potentially one of Russia's richest regions, containing vast timber reserves and deposits of minerals, gold and petroleum, although, particularly since the late 1990s, it has experienced serious economic problems, many of them typical of northern regions. All of the figures included in this survey include figures for the two former autonomous okrugs. In 2004 the Krai's gross regional product amounted to 380,403.5m. roubles, equivalent to 129,668.5 roubles per head. The Krai's major industrial centres are at Krasnoyarsk, Norilsk, Achinsk, Kansk and Minusinsk. In 2005 there were 2,066 km of railway track and 13,005 km of paved roads on the Krai's territory.

The principal crops are grain, potatoes and vegetables. Animal husbandry and bee-keeping are also important. The agricultural sector employed 9.1% of the working population and generated 30,052m. roubles in 2005. The Krai's main industries are non-ferrous metallurgy (which accounted for 68.9% of total industrial output in 2004), electricity production (in which it is one of the dominant federal subjects) and ore-mining (particularly of bauxite). Industry employed 24.9% of the work-force in 2005 and generated 310,107m. roubles in 2004. The Krai contains the world's second largest aluminium smelter, Krasnoyarsk Aluminium, which forms part of the Krasnoyarsk Metallurgical Plant (KraMZ). In 2005 output of coal amounted to 36.6m. metric tons, equivalent to 12.3% of the coal mined in the Russian Federation in that year, while production of electrical energy amounted to 52,400m. kWh.

In 2005 the territory's economically active population totalled 1,564,000, and 9.0% of the labour force were unemployed. The average monthly wage in the Krai was 10,502.4 roubles, somewhat in excess of the national average, while the average wages paid in both of the AOks at that time was substantially higher still, reflecting both the presence of the highly paid energy sector and the very low population density in those regions. In 2005 the krai budget recorded a deficit of some 4,755.6m. roubles. In that year export trade amounted to US $6,539.7m., and imports to $645.7m. Foreign investment totalled $660.7m. in 2005. At the end of that year 9,819 small businesses were registered in the Krai, providing employment to 90,500 people.

DIRECTORY

Head of the Provincial Administration (Governor): ALEKSANDR G. KHLOPANIN (elected 22 September 2002, appointment confirmed 4 June 2007), 660009 Krasnoyarsk, pr. Mira 110; tel. (3912) 49-30-40; fax (3912) 22-11-78; e-mail public@krskstate.ru; internet www.krskstate.ru.

Chairman of the Provincial Legislative Assembly: ALEKSANDR V. USS, 660009 Krasnoyarsk, pr. Mira 110; tel. (3912) 49-30-26; fax (3912) 22-22-24; e-mail dyure@sobranie.info; internet www.sobranie.info.

Chief Representative of Krasnoyarsk Krai in the Russian Federation: ANATOLII V. TIKHONOV, 107031 Moscow, Zvonarskii per. 9; tel. (495) 517-90-86; fax (495) 284-82-41.

Head of Krasnoyarsk City Administration: PETR I. PIMASHKOV, 660049 Krasnoyarsk, ul. K. Marksa 93; tel. (3912) 22-22-31; fax (3912) 22-25-12; e-mail webmaster@admkrsk.ru; internet www.admkrsk.ru.

Transbaikal Krai

Transbaikal Krai (formed in March 2008 by the merger of Chita Oblast and the Aga-Buryat Autonomous Okrug) is situated in Transbaikal, and forms part of the Siberian Federal Okrug and the Eastern Siberian Economic Area. Buryatiya lies to the west, Irkutsk to the north and Sakha (Yakutiya) and Amur to the east. To the south there are international borders with the People's Republic of China and Mongolia. The western part of the region is situated in the Yablonovii Khrebet mountain range. The Oblast covers 431,500 sq km (166,600 sq miles). At January 2007, according to official estimates, the population of the region was 1,122,104 and the population density 2.6 per sq km. At the census of 2002 some 89.8% of the population were ethnically Russian, 6.1% Buryat and 1.0% were Ukrainian. Some 63.4% of the region's inhabitants lived in urban areas in January 2007. The Krai's administrative centre is at Chita, which had a population of 306,200 in January 2006, according to official estimates. The territory is included in the time zone GMT+9.

HISTORY

The city of Chita was established by the Cossacks in 1653, at the confluence of the Chita and Ingoda rivers. Chita was pronounced the capital of the independent, pro-Bolshevik Far Eastern Republic upon its establishment in April 1920. It united the regions of Irkutsk, Transbaikal, Amur and the Pacific coast, but merged with Soviet Russia in November 1922. Chita Oblast was founded on 26 September 1937.

A new regional Duma was elected in 1994. The Communist Party of the Russian Federation and the nationalist Liberal Democratic Party of Russia were the most popular parties in the mid- and late 1990s. In a gubernatorial election held on 29 October 2000 the incumbent, Ravil Genialutin (who had been elected in October 1996, having been appointed as Governor by federal President Boris Yeltsin earlier that year), was re-elected. In July 2003 one of the Oblast's vice-governors, Aleksandr Shapnevskii, was murdered, in what was suspected of being a contract killing. Genialutin won a third term on 14 March

2004 with a comfortable majority in an election contested by three candidates.

Widespread speculation, during the mid-2000s, that the unification of Chita Oblast with the Aga-Buryat AOk was under consideration was confirmed by the announcement, in September 2006, that referendums on the proposed amalgamation were to be held in March 2007. On 11 March 2007 the merger was approved in a referendum by 90.3% of votes cast in Chita Oblast (with a voter turn-out of 80.4% of the electorate) and 94.0% of votes in the Aga-Buryat AOk (with an 89.9% turn-out); legislation to that end was endorsed by both chambers of the federal legislature in early July and approved by President Vladimir Putin on 23 July. The new territory, known as Transbaikal Krai, officially came into existence on 1 March 2008, when Geniatulin assumed the office of its first Governor. Elections to the newly formed Legislative Assembly of the unified territory were held on 12 October, at which the pro-Government United Russia were the most successful party, winning 54.8% of the votes cast on the basis of party lists. The Communist Party of the Russian Federation were placed second, with 13.4%, ahead of the Liberal Democratic Party of Russia, with 10.8%, and a Just Russia, with 9.3%.

ECONOMY

All figures in this survey incorporate data for the former Aga-Buryat AOk. Chita Oblast's gross regional product amounted to 63,528.7m. roubles in 2004, equivalent to 55,736.8 roubles per head. The region's main industrial centres are at Chita, Nerchinsk and Darasun. In 2005 there were some 2,399 km of railway track in the territory, including sections of the Trans-Siberian and the Baikal–Amur Railways, and 10,196 km of paved roads. In 1998 there were 1,000 km of navigable waterways. The Chita–Khabarovsk highway (forming part of a direct route between Moscow and Vladivostok) opened in September 2003.

Chita Oblast's agriculture, which employed some 12.9% of its working population and generated 8,963m. roubles in 2005, consists mainly of animal husbandry (livestock- and reindeer-breeding) and the hunting of animals for fur. The region's major industries are non-ferrous metallurgy, electrical energy, fuel extraction (including uranium), food-processing and ore-mining. Industry employed some 16.2% of the work-force in 2005 and generated 18,973m. roubles in 2004. Coal-mining in the Oblast is centred around the Vostochnaya mine; gold- and tin-mining are based at Sherlovaya Govra; and lead and zinc-ore mines are situated at Hapcheranga. In 1992 it was revealed that thorium and uranium had been mined until the mid-1970s at locations just outside Balei. The resulting high levels of radiation had serious consequences among the town's population, with abnormally high incidences of miscarriages and congenital defects in children. The regional Government lacked sufficient funds to relocate Balei's inhabitants and reduce radiation in the area. In 1997, however, the Australian mining company, Armada Gold, announced that it planned to seal the abandoned mines and exploit the nearby gold deposits. In 2006 the federal authorities announced that uranium production was to be expanded at existing mines in the Krasnokamensk area of the Oblast. A 'Chinese market' in Chita city reflects the importance of the People's Republic of China as a major trading partner of the Oblast, in particular as a source of imports.

The territory had an economically active population of 543,000 in 2005, when 11.1% of the labour force were unemployed; the average monthly wage was 8,152.7 roubles. In 2005 the regional budget showed a deficit of 328.2m. roubles. In that year the Oblast's exports amounted to US $157.9m., and imports to $163.9m. Foreign investment in the Oblast amounted to some $28.8m. in 2005. At the end of that year 2,602 small businesses were registered in Chita Oblast, providing employment to 21,000 people.

DIRECTORY

Head of the Regional Administration (Governor): RAVIL F. GENIATULIN (assumed office 1 March 2008), 672021 Transbaikal Krai, Chita, ul. Chaikovskogo 8; tel. (3022) 23-34-93; fax (3022) 35-74-89; e-mail pressadm@mail.ru; internet obladm.chita.ru.

Chairman of the Legislative Assembly: ANATOLII P. ROMANOV, 672021 Transbaikal Krai, Chita, ul. Chaikovskogo 8; tel. (3022) 23-58-59; e-mail info@oblduma.chita.ru; internet oblduma.chita.ru.

Chief Representative of Transbaikal Krai in the Russian Federation: VIKTOR M. STOLYAROV, 127025 Moscow, ul. Novyi Arbat 19/2001; tel. (495) 203-33-28; fax (495) 203-45-39.

Head of Chita City Administration (Mayor): ANATOLII D. MIKHALEV, 672090 Transbaikal Krai, Chita, ul. Butina 39; tel. (3022) 23-24-07; fax (3022) 32-06-85; e-mail info@admin.chita.ru.

Irkutsk Oblast

Irkutsk Oblast is situated in eastern Siberia in the south-east of the Central Siberian Plateau. The Oblast forms part of the Siberian Federal Okrug and the Eastern Siberian Economic Area. The Republic of Sakha (Yakutiya) lies to the north-east, Krasnoyarsk Krai to the north-west and Tyva to the south-west. Most of the long south-eastern border is with Buryatiya and, in the east, with Transbaikal Krai. The former Ust-Orda Buryat Autonomous Okrug (AOk), which was absorbed fully into the Oblast in 2008, was located in the south of the region. Lake Baikal (which forms part of the border with Buryatiya) is the deepest in the world, possessing over 80% of Russia's, and 20% of the world's, surface freshwater resources. The Oblast's main rivers include the Angara (the only river to drain Lake Baikal), the Nizhnyaya Tunguska and the Lena. More than four-fifths of the region's territory is covered with forest (mainly coniferous). The Oblast covers 767,900 sq km (296,500 sq miles). At January 2007, according to official estimates, the Oblast's total population was 2,513,808, giving a population density of 3.3 per sq km. In 2002 some 89.9% of the population were ethnically Russian, 3.1% Buryat, 2.1% Ukrainian and 1.2% were Tatar. Some 79.0% of the total population lived in urban areas in January 2007. The administrative centre is at Irkutsk, which had a population of 571,800 in January 2007, according to official estimates. Other major cities in the region include Bratsk (254,900) and Angarsk (245,700). Irkutsk Oblast is included in the time zone GMT+8.

HISTORY

The city of Irkutsk was founded as a military transit camp in 1661, at the confluence of the Irkut and Angara rivers, 66 km to the west of Baikal. Irkutsk became one of the largest economic centres of eastern Siberia. After the collapse of the Russian Empire, the region was part of the pro-Bolshevik Far Eastern Republic based in Chita, which was established in April 1920 and merged with Soviet Russia in November 1922. The Buryat-Mongol ASSR, created in 1923, was restructured by Stalin (Iosif Dzhugashvili) in September 1937 (see the Republic of Buryatiya). The Ust-Orda Buryat AOk, which represented the four western-most counties of the ASSR, was established within Irkutsk Oblast.

In late 1993 the executive branch of government secured the dissolution of the Regional Soviet, and in 1994 a Legislative Assembly was elected in its place. In May 1996 the regional and federal authorities signed a power-sharing agreement. Following the resignation of the Governor, Yurii Nozhikov, the Government-supported candidate, Boris Govorin, was elected as his successor, on 27 July 1997. At the gubernatorial election held in August 2001, Govorin was re-elected for a further term of office with 47.5% of votes cast; however, the relatively high proportion of votes awarded to the Communist Party of the Russian Federation candidate, Sergei Levchenko, who received 45.4%, appeared to reflect increasing dissatisfaction with the economic situation in the region. In August 2005, shortly before the expiry of Govorin's term of office, federal President Vladimir Putin nominated Aleksandr Tishanin, previously the head of the East Siberian Railway, as Govorin's successor; Tishanin's nomination was approved by the regional legislature on 26 August.

During the early 2000s proposals to unite the Ust-Orda Buryat AOk and Irkutsk Oblast appeared to gain the supported of the authorities in both territories. Referendums held in both polities on 16 April 2006 overwhelmingly approved the merger; in those areas of the Oblast outwith the AOk, 89.8% voted to approve the union. The degree of support for the merger was even higher in the AOk, at some 97.8%. Following its approval by both chambers of the federal parliament, in December 2006 Putin signed a constitutional law providing for the merger of the territories. In February 2007 Tishanin was appointed to the governorship of the Ust-Orda Buryat AOk concurrently with Irkutsk Oblast, thereby becoming the first governor to lead two federal subjects concurrently. The new unified territory, which continued to be known as Irkutsk Oblast, officially entered into existence on 1 January 2008, with Tishanin serving as Governor, in an acting capacity until 15 April, when he was succeeded, also in an acting capacity, by Igor Yesipovskii. At elections to the legislature of the unified territory, held on 12 October, the pro-Government United Russia won the largest proportion of the votes cast on the basis of party lists (49.5%), followed by the nationalist Liberal Democratic Party of Russia (15.1%), the Communist Party of the Russian Federation (13.3%) and A Just Russia: Motherland/Pensioners/Life (8.1%). The nomination of a new governor was expected to be approved at the first session of the new legislative assembly, scheduled for 24 October.

ECONOMY

All figures in this survey incorporate data for the former Ust-Orda Buryat Autonomous Okrug. Irkutsk Oblast is one of the most economically developed regions in Russia, largely owing to its significant fuel, energy and water resources, minerals and timber, and its location on the Trans-Siberian Railway. In 2004 the Oblast's gross regional product totalled 209,690.7m. roubles, or 82,131.7 roubles per head. The region's main industrial centres are at Irkutsk, Bratsk, Ust-Ilimsk and Angarsk. The Oblast, which is traversed by the Trans-Siberian and the Far Eastern (Baikal–Amur) Railways, contained 2,478 km of railway track at the end of 2005, when there were 12,341 km of paved roads in the region. The Oblast has two international airports, at Irkutsk and Bratsk, from which there are direct and connecting flights to Japan, the People's Republic of China, the Republic of Korea (South Korea), Mongolia and the USA. In the late 1990s approximately one-10th of the region's freight was transported by river—there are two major river-ports on the Lena river, at Kirensk and Osetrovo (Ust-Kut). These are used to transport freight to Sakha (Yakutiya) and the northern seaport of Tiksi.

Agriculture, which employed 10.4% of the Oblast's work-force and generated 22,575m. roubles in 2005, consists mainly of animal husbandry (fur animal-, reindeer- and livestock-breeding), hunting and fishing and grain and potato production. The region contains huge energy reserves, including the Kovytkinskoye gas field and the Angarsk petroleum field. Despite a non-binding agreement, signed in 2003 and backed by the petroleum company Yukos, which envisaged building a pipeline from the Angarsk field to Daqing in China, in February 2004 the federal Government decided in favour of the construction by the state-controlled company Transneft of a 3,900-km pipeline linking Angarsk with the Pacific coast, to facilitate the export of petroleum to Japan. The first stage of the pipeline commenced operations in late 2005. Industry engaged some 22.2% of the work-force in 2005 and generated some 173,796m. roubles in 2004. The main industries are non-ferrous metallurgy, the processing of forestry products, mining (coal, iron ore, gold, muscovite or mica, gypsum, talc and salt), mechanical engineering, metal-working and electricity generation (in which field the Oblast is among Russia's leading producers). Production of electrical energy amounted to 56,700m. kWh in 2005.

The economically active population in Irkutsk Oblast totalled 1,308,000 in 2005, when 10.0% of the labour force were unemployed. For those in employment, the average wage amounted to 9,125.3 roubles per month. In 2005 there was a budgetary deficit of 1,615.9m. roubles. In that year the value of exports from the Oblast amounted to some US $3,301.1m., while imports were worth $836.2m. Foreign investment in the territory amounted to some $217.1m. in 2005. At the end of that year 9,175 small businesses were registered in the Oblast, providing employment to 76,800 people.

DIRECTORY

Governor: Igor E. Yesipovkskii (acting), 664047 Irkutsk, ul. Lenina 1 A; tel. (3952) 20-00-15; fax (3952) 24-33-40; e-mail mail@admirk.ru; internet www.govirk.ru.

Chairman of the Legislative Assembly: Viktor K. Kruglov, 664047 Irkutsk, ul. Lenina 1 A; tel. (3952) 24-17-60; fax (3952) 20-00-27; e-mail adm@duma.irkutsk.ru; internet irk.gov.ru.

Chief Representative of Irkutsk Oblast in the Russian Federation: Tatyana I. Ryutina, 109028 Moscow, per. Durasovskii 3/2; tel. (495) 916-17-08; fax (495) 915-70-58.

Head of Irkutsk City Administration (Mayor): Vladimir V. Yakubovskii, 664000 Irkutsk, ul. Lenina 14; tel. (3952) 20-12-07; fax (3952) 24-30-27; e-mail deu@goradm.irkutsk.ru; internet www1.irkutsk.ru.

Kemerovo Oblast

Kemerovo Oblast, known as the Kuzbass, is situated in southern central Russia and forms part of the Siberian Federal Okrug and the Western Siberian Economic Area. Krasnoyarsk Krai and Khakasiya lie to the east, Tomsk to the north, Novosibirsk to the west and Altai Krai and the Republic of Altai to the south-west. The region lies in the Kuznetsk basin, the area surrounding its main river, the Tom. The territory of the Oblast occupies 95,500 sq km (36,870 sq miles). At January 2007, according to official estimates, the total population numbered 2,826,295 and the population density was 29.6 per sq km. At the time of the 2002 census 91.9% of the population were ethnically Russian, 1.8% Tatar, 1.3% Ukrainian and 1.2% were German. Some 85.0% of the population inhabited urban areas in January 2007. The region's administrative centre is at Kemerovo, which had a population of 520,100 in January 2006, according to official estimates. The largest city in the region is Novokuznetsk (with a population of 562,400), and other major cities include Prokopevsk (216,700), Leninsk-Kuznetskii (107,800), Mezhdurechensk (103,700) and Kiselevsk (103,600). Kemerovo Oblast is included in the time zone GMT+7.

HISTORY

Kemerovo was founded in 1918 (as Shcheglovsk) and became the administrative centre of the Oblast upon its formation on 26 January 1943. The city is at the centre of Russia's principal coal-mining area. In July 1997 the Governor appointed in August 1991, Mikhail Kislyuk, was dismissed by federal President Boris Yeltsin, as the result of a dispute over unpaid pensions arrears. Kislyuk had earned criticism, as had the federal authorities, for refusing to schedule elections to a new regional Duma to replace the bicameral Regional Assembly that had been elected in March 1994 and suspended in 1995.

In the December 1995 elections to the federal State Duma, the Communist Party of the Russian Federation (CPRF) won 48% of the regional votes cast, its second highest share of the vote recorded in any constituent unit of the Federation. Much of this support was secured because of the popular leadership of Aman-Geldy Tuleyev, speaker of the suspended local assembly. Tuleyev contested the federal presidency in 1991, 1996 and 2000, and spent 11 months in 1996–97 as the Minister for Co-operation with Members of the Commonwealth of Independent States. Having been appointed Governor by Yeltsin in July 1997, Tuleyev's position was confirmed by an overwhelming victory in popular elections to the post in October, when he received 94.6% of the votes cast.

In mid-1998 Tuleyev's administration signed a framework agreement with the federal Government on the delimitation of powers, which was accompanied by 10 accords aimed at strengthening the economy of the region. Despite an economic decline, which had resulted in widespread industrial action by coal miners, who blockaded a section of the Trans-Siberian Railway, Tuleyev was widely considered to be Russia's most popular regional leader. When he contested the presidency of the Russian Federation in March 2000, Tuleyev received 51.6% of the votes cast in Kemerovo Oblast, more than two times the number of votes cast there for the victor, Vladimir Putin. In January 2001 Tuleyev announced his resignation, thus bringing forward the gubernatorial election to April of that year, several months earlier than previously scheduled. In the election, held on 22 April, Tuleyev received 93.5% of the votes cast. In March 2003 Tuleyev was appointed to the Supreme Council of the pro-presidential Unity and Fatherland-United Russia party (later simply known as United Russia—UR). Supporters of Tuleyev, comprising the oblast organizations of UR and the People's Party of the Russian Federation, united in the 'I Serve the Kuzbass!' electoral bloc, won an overwhelming majority in oblast legislative and municipal elections held on 20 April 2003; the bloc obtained 34 seats in the 35-member legislature, and obtained control of 11 of 12 municipalities where elections were held. In January 2004 Tuleyev encouraged the CPRF to support President Putin in his campaign for re-election to the presidency in March. In April 2005 Putin nominated Tuleyev, who remained extremely popular in the Oblast, to serve a further term of office; this nomination was confirmed by a unanimous vote in the regional legislature on 20 April. At elections to the Regional Council of People's Deputies, held on 12 October 2008, UR won some 84.8% of the votes cast on the basis of party lists, becoming the only party to cross the 7% threshold required to obtain representation.

ECONOMY

The economy of Kemerovo Oblast is based on industry. It is rich in mineral resources and contains the Kuzbass basin, one of the major coal reserves of the world. In 2004 Kemerovo's gross regional product amounted to 254,606.6m. roubles, equivalent to 88,912.8 roubles per head. The Oblast's main industrial centres are at Kemerovo, Novokuznetsk, Prokopevsk, Kiselevsk and Leninsk-Kuznetskii. At the end of 2005 the region had 1,685 km of railway track and 5,809 km of paved roads on its territory.

Kemerovo Oblast's agriculture, which employed just 4.1% of the work-force in 2005, consists mainly of potato and grain production, animal husbandry and bee-keeping. The value of agricultural output in 2005 was 17,811m. roubles. In the mid-1990s reserves of coal to a depth of 1,800 m (5,900 feet) were estimated at 733,400m. metric tons. In the same period deposits of iron ore were estimated at 5,250m. tons. In 2005 output of coal amounted to 164.3m. metric tons, equivalent to 55.1% of the coal mined in the Russian Federation in that year, and intensive mining has resulted in severe environmental degradation. Production of complex ores, ferrous metallurgy and electricity generation are also important industries in the region. Production of steel amounted to 8.5m. metric tons in 2005, representing 12.8% of the Russian Federation's total output in that year. The industrial sector as a whole employed 32.3% of the working population in 2005 and generated 291,093m. roubles in 2004.

The economically active population numbered 1,486,000 in 2005, when 8.6% of the labour force were unemployed. The average monthly wage was 8,653.6 roubles. The 2005 regional budget recorded a deficit of some 447.6m. roubles. In that year export trade comprised US $4,966.2m. in exports and $689.3m. in imports. Total foreign investment in the Oblast amounted to $547.6m. in 2005. At the end of that year 13,934 small businesses were registered in the Oblast, providing employment to 108,500 people.

DIRECTORY

Head of the Regional Administration (Governor): AMAN-GELDY M. TULEYEV (appointed 1 July 1997, elected 19 October 1997, re-elected 22 April 2001, appointment confirmed 20 April 2005), 650099 Kemerovo, pr. Sovetskii 62; tel. (3842) 36-43-33; fax (3842) 58-31-56; e-mail postmaster@ako.ru; internet www.ako.ru.

Chairman of the Regional Council of People's Deputies: GENNADII T. DYUDYAYEV, 650099 Kemerovo, pr. Sovetskii 58; tel. (3842) 58-41-42; fax (3842) 58-54-51; internet www.sovet.kem.ru.

Chief Representative of Kemerovo Oblast in the Russian Federation: NATALYA V. KHAPII, 113184 Moscow, ul. B. Tatarskaya 5/14/9; tel. and fax (495) 953-54-89.

Head of Kemerovo City Administration (Mayor): VLADIMIR V. MIKHAILOV, 650099 Kemerovo, pr. Sovetskii 54; tel. (3842) 36-46-10; fax (3842) 58-18-91; e-mail adm-kemerovo@ako.ru; internet kemerovo.ru.

Novosibirsk Oblast

Novosibirsk Oblast is situated in the south-east of the Western Siberian Plain, at the Ob-Irtysh confluence. The Oblast forms part of the Siberian Federal Okrug and the Western Siberian Economic Area. There is an international border with Kazakhstan in the south-west. Altai Krai borders to the south, as do the Oblasts of Omsk to the west, Tomsk to the north and Kemerovo to the east. The region's major rivers are the Ob and the Om. It occupies a total area of 178,200 sq km (68,800 sq miles). At January 2007, according to official estimates, the Oblast had a population of 2,640,656 and a population density of 14.8 per sq km. At the time of the 2002 census 93.0% of the population were ethnically Russian, 1.8% German, 1.3% Ukrainian and 1.0% were Tatar. Some 75.2% of the population inhabited urban areas in January 2007. More than one-half of the region's inhabitants live in its administrative centre, Novosibirsk, which had a population of 1,397,000 in January 2006, according to official estimates. The Oblast is included in the time zone GMT+6.

HISTORY

The city of Novosibirsk (known as Novonikolayevsk until 1925) was founded in 1893, during the construction of the Trans-Siberian Railway. It became prosperous through its proximity to the Kuznetsk coal basin (in Kemerovo Oblast). The Oblast, which was formed on 28 September 1937, became a major centre of industry during and after the Second World War.

In October 1993 the federal President, Boris Yeltsin, dismissed the head of the regional administration appointed in 1991, Vitalii Mukha, and appointed Ivan Indinok in his place. In 1994 elections were held to a new representative body, which was dominated by the Communist Party of the Russian Federation (CPRF). President Yeltsin permitted the Oblast a gubernatorial election in December 1995, as a result of which Mukha was returned to office as the CPRF candidate. In January 2000 another politician regarded as a statist, Viktor Tolokonskii, a former Mayor of Novosibirsk, was elected Governor following two rounds of voting. Tolokonskii was re-elected in December 2003, securing 58.3% of the votes cast. In September 2005 Tolokonskii joined the pro-presidential United Russia (UR). In elections to the Regional Council of Deputies, held on 11 December 2005, UR was the most successful party, obtaining 33.1% of the votes cast. The CPRF was placed second, with 21.7%, ahead of the Agrarian Party of Russia, with 13.4%, and the nationalist Liberal Democratic Party of Russia, with 9.7%. Some 8.8% of votes were cast 'against all candidates'. On 12 July 2007 federal President Vladimir Putin's nomination of Tolokonskii for a third gubernatorial term was confirmed by the Regional Council of Deputies.

ECONOMY

In 2004 Novosibirsk Oblast's gross regional product stood at 254,606.6m. roubles, or 74,985.5 roubles per head. Novosibirsk has a port on the Ob river, and is the region's principal industrial centre. At the end of 2005 there were 1,529 km of railways and 9,924 km of paved roads in the Oblast. There are 12 airports in the region, including Tolmachevo, an international airport.

The Oblast's agriculture employed 11.4% of its working population and generated 31,932m. roubles in 2005. It consists mainly of the production of grain, vegetables, potatoes and flax, animal husbandry and bee-keeping. In 2005 the Oblast was the first of seven federal subjects in which cases of avian influenza were reported, resulting in the slaughter of large numbers of poultry. Industry employed 21.9% of the labour force in 2005 and generated 105,168m. roubles in 2004. Extraction industries involved the production of coal, petroleum, natural gas, peat, marble, limestone and clay. Manufacturing industry includes non-ferrous metallurgy, mechanical engineering, metal-working, electricity generation and food-processing.

The economically active population totalled 1,371,000 in 2005, when 7.8% of the labour force were unemployed. The average monthly wage was 7,264.3 roubles. The 2005 regional budget recorded a deficit of some 1,061.6m. roubles. In 2005 the Oblast's external trade comprised US \$954.0m. in exports and \$606.8m. in imports. In the same year foreign investment totalled \$71.7m. At the end of 2005 some 25,510 small businesses were registered in the Oblast, providing employment to 126,200 people.

DIRECTORY

Head of the Regional Administration (Governor): VIKTOR A. TOLOKONSKII (elected 9 January 2000, re-elected 7 December 2003, appointment confirmed 12 July 2007), 630011 Novosibirsk, Krasnyi pr. 18; tel. (3832) 23-29-95; fax (3832) 23-57-00; e-mail pochta@obladm.nso.ru; internet www3.adm.nso.ru.

Chairman of the Regional Council of Deputies: ALEKSEI A. BESPALIKOV, 630011 Novosibirsk, ul. Kirova 3; tel. (3832) 23-09-36; fax (3832) 23-23-78; e-mail info@sovet-nso.ru; internet www.sovet-nso.ru.

Chief Representative of Novosibirsk Oblast in the Russian Federation: VADIM B. FILATOV, 101000 Moscow, ul. Myasnitskaya 35/522; tel. (495) 204-13-00.

Head of Novosibirsk City Administration (Mayor): VLADIMIR F. GORODETSKII, 630099 Novosibirsk, Krasnyi pr. 34; tel. (3832) 22-49-32; fax (3832) 22-08-58; e-mail cic@admnsk.ru; internet www.novo-sibirsk.ru.

Omsk Oblast

Omsk Oblast is situated in the south of the Western Siberian Plain on the middle reaches of the Irtysh river. Kazakhstan lies to the south. Tyumen lies to the north-west and Tomsk and Novosibirsk to the east. Omsk forms part of the Siberian Federal Okrug and the Western Siberian Economic Area. The major rivers are the Irtysh, the Ishim, the Om and the Tara. The Oblast covers some 139,700 sq km (53,920 sq miles). At January 2007, according to official estimates, the region had a population of 2,025,626 and a population density of 14.5 per sq km. At the time of the 2002 census 83.5% of the population were ethnically Russian, 3.9% Kazakh, 3.7% Ukrainian, 3.7% German and 2.3% were Tatar. Some 69.2% of the population lived in urban areas in January 2007. The administrative centre is at Omsk, the only large city in the Oblast, which lies at the confluence of the Om and Irtysh rivers and had a population of 1,138,800 in January 2006, according to official estimates. The region is included in the time zone GMT+6.

HISTORY

The city of Omsk was founded as a fortress in 1716. In 1918 it became the seat of Adm. Aleksandr Kolchak's 'all-Russian Government'. Omsk fell to the Bolsheviks in 1919 and Kolchak 'abdicated' in January 1920. Omsk Oblast was formed on 7 December 1934.

In the 1990s the region was generally supportive of the Communist Party of the Russian Federation (CPRF). The regional Governor, Leonid Polezhayev, although a supporter of the federal state President, Boris Yeltsin, was well respected locally and was elected to that position in December 1995, having been appointed in November 1991. In May 1996 the regional and federal administrations signed a treaty on the delimitation of powers. Polezhayev was re-elected in September 1999, defeating the regional leader of the CPRF. Nevertheless, Omsk was one of only four regions in which the CPRF candidate, Gennadii Zyuganov, received a larger proportion of the votes cast than Vladimir Putin in the federal presidential election of March 2000. The Oblast abolished its power-sharing treaty with the federal Government in mid-2001. At elections to the regional Legislative Assembly on 24 March 2002 supporters of Polezhayev, including, notably, members of the Unity and Fatherland-United Russia party (later simply known as United Russia—UR), obtained control of the Assembly. Polezhayev was re-elected Governor on 7 September 2003, receiving 57% of the votes cast.

At elections to the regional Legislative Assembly on 11 March 2007, the pro-presidential UR secured a significant victory, with 55.6% of votes cast, while the CPRF won 22.4% of votes; a further five

political parties contesting the poll failed to secure the minimum 7% of the votes required for parliamentary representation. On 24 May President Putin's nomination of Polezhayev as Governor was confirmed by the regional Legislative Assembly (with the approval of 37 of the 43 deputies attending the session). Following elections to the State Duma on 2 December, Polezhayev announced that he would take measures against Omsk City Administration, in response to a voter turn-out in the city that was considerably lower than that recorded in rural areas of the Oblast.

ECONOMY

In 2004 Omsk Oblast's gross regional product amounted to 209,211.0m. roubles, equivalent to 101,926.2 roubles per head. Omsk is one of the highest-ranking cities in Russia in terms of industrial output. The region lies on the Trans-Siberian Railway and is a major transport junction. At the end of 2005 it contained 752 km of railway track and 8,000 km of paved roads. In 1998 there were some 1,250 km of navigable waterways on the Oblast's territory and some 580 km of pipeline, carrying petroleum and petroleum products. There are three airports; an international terminal was opened at Omsk airport in 1997, and the airport was undergoing further modernization and reconstruction in the mid-2000s.

The Oblast's soil is the fertile black earth (*chernozem*) characteristic of the region. Its agriculture, which generated a total of 35,513m. roubles in 2005 and employed some 15.1% of the work-force, consists mainly of animal husbandry (including fur-farming) and hunting and the production of grain. The region's mineral reserves include clay, peat and lime. There are also deposits of petroleum and natural gas. Industry employed 22.6% of the work-force in 2005 and generated 70,376m. roubles in 2004. The Oblast's main industries are electricity generation, fuel, chemical and petrochemical production, mechanical engineering, petroleum-refining and food-processing. There is a petroleum refinery at Omsk, operated by Sibneft. The region's exports primarily comprise chemical, petrochemical and petroleum products. The defence sector is also significant to the economy of the region.

The economically active population numbered 1,038,000 in 2005, when 8.6% of the region's labour force were unemployed. The average wage in the Oblast was 7,124.3 roubles per month. The 2005 regional budget recorded a deficit of some 61.2m. roubles. In that year external trade comprised US \$7,170.9m. in exports and \$289.8m. in imports. In 2005 foreign investment in the region totalled some \$5,145.8m. At the end of that year 14,435 small businesses were registered in the Oblast, providing employment to 90,200 people.

DIRECTORY

Head of the Regional Administration (Governor): LEONID K. POLEZHAYEV (appointed 11 November 1991, elected 17 December 1995, re-elected September 1999 and 7 September 2003, appointment confirmed 24 May 2007), 644002 Omsk, ul. Krasnyi Put 1; tel. and fax (3812) 24-47-45; e-mail guptr@omskportal.ru; internet www.omskportal.ru.

Chairman of the Regional Legislative Assembly: VLADIMIR A. VARNAVSKII, 640002 Omsk, ul. Krasnyi Put 1; tel. (3812) 24-23-33; fax (3812) 23-24-66; e-mail root@topos.omsk.ru; internet www.omsk-parlament.ru.

Chief Representative of Omsk Oblast in the Russian Federation: BORIS S. TSYBA, 107078 Moscow, per. B. Kozlovskii 14/15/1; tel. and fax (495) 621-65-54.

Head of Omsk City Administration (Mayor): VIKTOR F. SHREIDER, 644099 Omsk, ul. Gagarina 34; tel. (3812) 24-30-33; fax (3812) 24-49-34; e-mail media@grad.omsk.ru; internet www.omsk.ru.

Tomsk Oblast

Tomsk Oblast is situated in the south-east of the Western Siberian Plain. It forms part of the Siberian Federal Okrug and the Western Siberian Economic Area. Kemerovo and Novosibirsk lie to the south, Omsk to the south-west, the Khanty-Mansii AOk—Yugra (part of Tyumen Oblast) to the north-west and Krasnoyarsk Krai to the east. The major rivers are the Ob, the Tom, the Chulym, the Ket and the Vasyugan. The largest lake is the Mirnoye. Almost all the Oblast's territory is taiga (forested marshland). It occupies 316,900 sq km (122,320 sq miles). At January 2007, according to official estimates, the oblast's population was 1,033,102, and the population density 3.3 per sq km. In 2002 some 90.8% of the population were ethnically Russian, 1.9% Tatar, 1.6% Ukrainian and 1.3% were German. Some 68.6% of the population inhabited urban areas in January 2007. The administrative centre of the Oblast is at Tomsk, which had a population of 489,900 in January 2006, according to official estimates. The other major city in the region is Seversk (formerly Tomsk-7, with 108,100 inhabitants). Tomsk Oblast is included in the time zone GMT+7.

HISTORY

Tomsk city was founded as a fortress in 1604. It was a major trading centre until the 1890s, when the construction of the Trans-Siberian Railway promoted other centres. Tomsk Oblast was formed on 13 August 1944.

In 1993 the Regional Soviet was initially critical of President Boris Yeltsin's dissolution of the federal parliament. It was thus disbanded, and replaced by a regional State Duma. In a gubernatorial election held in December 1995, the pro-Yeltsin incumbent appointed in October 1991, Viktor Kress, won the popular mandate. Kress was re-elected in September 1999 and in September 2003.

In March 2007 President Vladimir Putin nominated Kress (by now allied with the pro-presidential United Russia—UR) for a fifth gubernatorial term. At the elections to the regional State Duma on 11 March, UR won 46.8% of votes cast; the Communist Party of the Russian Federation received 13.4% of the votes, the nationalist Liberal Democratic Party of Russia 12.9%, A Just Russia 7.9% and the pro-market Union of Rightist Forces 7.8%. The new legislature endorsed the nomination of Kress as Governor on 10 March.

ECONOMY

In 2004 the gross regional product of Tomsk Oblast amounted to 146,968.1m. roubles, equivalent to 141,499.0 roubles per head. The major industrial centres are at Tomsk, Kolpashevo and Asino. In 2005 there were 346 km of railways and 3,244 km of paved roads in the Oblast. In late 2006 the authorities of the Oblast and of the Khanty-Mansii AOk—Yugra signed an agreement providing for a construction of a road bridge to link the two regions.

The Oblast's agricultural sector, which generated 9,547m. roubles and employed 8.7% of the work-force in 2005, consists mainly of animal husbandry and the production of grain, vegetables and potatoes. Around 1.4m. ha (3.4m. acres) of the Oblast's territory was used for agricultural purposes, of which one-half was arable land. The Oblast has substantial reserves of coal, as well as of petroleum and natural gas. Its other main industries are mechanical engineering, metal-working, chemicals and petrochemicals, non-ferrous metallurgy and electricity generation. Industry employed 27.1% of the working population in 2005 and generated 94,570m. roubles in 2004. In November 2005 the federal authorities announced that one of six special economic zones to be established across the Federation, a technological research centre, was to be located in the Oblast.

The economically active population of the Oblast numbered 522,000 in 2005, when 10.5% of the work-force were unemployed. The average monthly wage was 9,609.9 roubles. There was a budgetary deficit of 83.9m. roubles in 2005. In 2005 the value of external trade amounted to US $1,112.9m. in exports and $54.8m. in imports. In that year total foreign investment amounted to $64.1m. At the end of 2005 some 7,651 small businesses were registered in the Oblast, providing employment to 60,900 people.

DIRECTORY

Head of the Regional Administration (Governor): VIKTOR M. KRESS (appointed 20 October 1991, elected 17 December 1995, re-elected 5 September 1999 and 21 September 2003, appointment confirmed 10 March 2007), 634050 Tomsk, pl. Lenina 6; tel. (3822) 51-05-05; fax (3822) 51-03-23; e-mail khalin@trecom.tomsk.ru; internet www.tomsk.gov.ru.

Chairman of the Regional State Duma: BORIS A. MALTSEV, 634050 Tomsk, pl. Lenina 6; tel. (3822) 51-04-24; fax (3822) 51-06-02; e-mail duma@tomsk.gov.ru; internet duma.tomsk.ru.

Chief Representative of Tomsk Oblast in the Russian Federation: ALEKSANDR N. CHEREVKO, 103006 Moscow, ul. M. Dmitrovka 3/10; tel. and fax (495) 200-39-80; e-mail tomskadm@chat.ru.

Head of Tomsk City Administration (Mayor): NIKOLAI NIKOLAI-CHUK (acting), 634050 Tomsk, pr. Lenina 73; tel. (3822) 52-68-90; fax (3822) 52-68-60; e-mail admin@admin.tomsk.ru.

Far Eastern Federal Okrug

Republic of Sakha (Yakutiya)

The Republic of Sakha (Yakutiya) is situated in eastern Siberia on the Laptev and Eastern Siberian Seas. Two-fifths of the Republic's territory lies within the Arctic Circle. It forms part of the Far Eastern Federal Okrug and the Far Eastern Economic Area. To the west it borders Krasnoyarsk Krai. Irkutsk Oblast and Transbaikal Krai lie to the south-west, Amur Oblast to the south, Khabarovsk Krai and Magadan Oblast to the south-east, and the Chukot AOk to the north-east. The main river is the Lena, which drains into the Laptev Sea at a large swampy delta. Apart from the Central Yakut Plain, the region's territory is mountainous and four-fifths is taiga (forested marshland). Sakha is the largest federal unit in Russia, occupying an area of 3,103,200 sq km (1,198,150 sq miles), making it larger than Kazakhstan, itself the second largest country, after Russia, in Europe or the former USSR. The north of the Republic lies within the arctic zone whereas the south has a more temperate climate. The average temperature in January is as low as $-35.6°C$, and the average temperature in July is around $13.3°C$. At January 2007, according to official estimates, the Republic had a population of 949,972 and a population density of 0.3 per sq km. At the time of the 2002 census 45.5% of the population were Yakut, 41.2% ethnically Russian, 3.6% Ukrainian, 1.9% Evenk, 1.2% Even, 1.1% Tatar and 0.8% Buryat. In the late 1990s and early 2000s there was a continuous outflow of population from the Republic, particularly of ethnic Russians, who had accounted for an absolute majority (50.3%) of the Republic's population at the 1989 census. (Yakuts accounted for 33.4% of the population at that time.) Orthodox Christianity is the dominant religion in the region. The Yakuts' native tongue, spoken as a first language by over 93% of the indigenous population, is part of the North-Eastern branch of the Turkic family, although it is considerably influenced by Mongolian. Some 64.5% of the population inhabited urban areas in January 2007. The capital is Yakutsk, with a population of 239,200 at January 2006, according to official estimates. The Republic spans three time zones: GMT+9 (Yakutsk), GMT+10 (Verkhoyansk) and GMT+11 (Cherskii).

HISTORY

The Yakuts (Iakuts), also known as the Sakha, were historically known as the Tungus, Jekos and the Urangkhai Sakha. They are believed to be descended from peoples from the Lake Baikal area, Turkish tribes from the steppe and the Altai Mountains, and indigenous Siberian peoples, including the Evenks. They were traditionally a semi-nomadic people, with those in the north of the region occupied with hunting, fishing and reindeer-breeding, while those in the south were pastoralists who bred horses and cattle and were also skilled blacksmiths. Their territory, briefly united by the toion (chief), Tygyn, came under Russian rule in the 1620s and a fur tax was introduced. This led to violent opposition between 1634 and 1642, although all rebellions were crushed. Increasing numbers of Russians began to settle in the region, as the result of the completion of a mail route to the Far East, the construction of camps for political opponents to the tsars and the discovery of gold in 1846. The territory became commercialized after the construction of the Trans-Siberian Railway in the 1880s and 1890s and the development of commercial shipping on the River Lena. The territory was designated as an ASSR in 1922. Collectivization and the purges of the 1930s greatly reduced the Yakut population, and the region was rapidly industrialized, largely involving the extraction of gold, coal and timber.

Nationalist feeling re-emerged during the late 1980s. Cultural, ecological and economic concerns led to the proclamation of a 'Yakut-Sakha SSR' (i.e. a Union Republic) on 27 April 1990, although this effective declaration of independence from Russia went unrecognized. On 15 August 1991 the republican Supreme Soviet demanded republican control over local reserves of gold, diamonds, timber, coal, petroleum and tin. On 22 December elections for an executive presidency were won by the hitherto Chairman of the republican Supreme Soviet, Mikhail Nikolayev. The territory was renamed the Republic of Sakha (Yakutiya) in March 1992 and a new Constitution was promulgated on 27 April. On 12 October 1993 the Supreme Soviet dissolved itself and scheduled elections to a 60-seat bicameral legislature for 12 December. On 26 January 1994 the new parliament named itself the State Assembly (Il Tumen); it comprised an upper Chamber of the Republic and a lower Chamber of Representatives. Native languages were designated official in certain areas and attempts to protect traditional lifestyles even involved the restoration of land. Thus, a Even-Bytantai okrug (district) was established in the mid-1990s.

In December 1996 Nikolayev was re-elected President. He continued his efforts to win greater autonomy from the federal centre. A power-sharing agreement signed in June 1995 was followed, in March 1998, by a framework agreement on co-operation between the republican and federal authorities in the mining and energy sectors.

In December 2001 Nikolayev withdrew his candidacy from the forthcoming gubernatorial election, and urged voters to transfer their support to Vyacheslav Shtyrov, the head of the local diamond-producing joint-stock company, Alrosa (Almazy Rossii-Sakha), who was the candidate of the pro-presidential Unity and Fatherland-United Russia party (later known simply as United Russia—UR). Shtyrov was elected, following a second round of voting on 13 January 2002, when he received 59% of the votes cast. The election was characterized by widespread allegations of malpractice.

In 2002 controversy ensued with regard to discrepancies between the republican and federal Constitutions; in March the republican legislature approved amendments to 11 articles of Sakha's Constitution. Elections to the new, unicameral, 70-member State Assembly (Il Tumen) provided for by the revised Constitution were held on 29 December; some 14 employees of Alrosa and its subsidiaries were among the deputies elected. Federal President Vladimir Putin's nomination of Shtyrov to a second presidential term was endorsed by the republican legislature on 7 December 2006. At elections to the Il Tumen held on 2 March 2008 UR obtained 51.8% of the votes cast to those seats elected on the basis of party lists, ahead of the Communist Party of the Russian Federation, with 16.0%, A Just Russia: Motherland/Pensioners/Life, with 14.9% and the Agrarian Party of Russia (which merged with UR later in the year), with 8.5%

ECONOMY

The Republic's gross regional product in 2004 was 164,245.7m. roubles, equivalent to 172,923.5 roubles per head. The Republic's major industrial centres are at Yakutsk, Mirnyi, Neryungri and Lensk. Its main seaport is at Tiksi. At the end of 2004 there were 165 km (103 miles) of railways in the Republic. In October 2003 the republican Government announced its intention to complete the rail link between Yakutsk and the Baikal–Amur main line, in order to lessen dependency on the River Lena's decreasing water levels. Work on the rail link had commenced in 1985, but stopped after the dissolution of the USSR. In December 2005 there were 7,566 km of paved roads in Sakha.

Sakha's agriculture, which engaged 8.7% of the working population and generated 12,175m. roubles in 2005 consists mainly of animal husbandry (livestock- and reindeer-breeding), hunting and fishing. Grain and vegetable production tends to be on a small scale. Industry employed 24.7% of the Republic's working population in 2005 and generated 133,439m. roubles in 2004: the main industries are non-ferrous metallurgy (which accounted for 63.9% of industrial output in 2004), mining (for gold, diamonds, tin, muscovite or mica, antimony and coal), the production of electricity and natural gas production. In early 2006 the Government announced that a new uranium field in the south of the Republic, at Elkonskii Gorst, was to be opened up to exploitation. In 1997 Alrosa signed the first of a series of trade accords with the South African diamond producer, De Beers. In the first half of the 2000s Alrosa acquired majority stakes in several petroleum and natural-gas assets in the Republic. In early 2006 it was agreed by Alrosa's board of directors that the federal Government (which owned 37% of the company) would increase its holding to a majority stake (50% plus one share) in the company, although it was anticipated that the Governments of Sakha and of several municipalities within the Republic would continue to own 40% of the share equity. In August 2007 the Finnish Wärtsilä Corpn was awarded a contract to provide equipment for a power station in Olekminsk, in the south-west of the Republic, that would provide electricity for the Eastern Siberia—Pacific Ocean Pipeline (ESPO).

The economically active population of the Republic amounted to 483,000 in 2005, when 8.9% of the labour force were unemployed. The average monthly wage was 13,436.9 roubles in 2005. In 2005 the republican budget recorded a deficit of some 12,760.4m. roubles. In the same year external trade amounted to US $2,139.6m. of exports and $70.2m. of imports. Foreign investment in Sakha amounted to $669.0m. in 2005. At the end of that year there were around 2,577 small businesses registered in the Republic and providing employment to 22,400 people.

DIRECTORY

President: VYACHESLAV A. SHTYROV (elected 13 January 2002, appointment confirmed 7 December 2006), 677000 Sakha (Yakutiya), Yakutsk, ul. Kirova 11; tel. (4112) 43-50-50; fax (4112) 43-55-57; e-mail info@gov.sakha.ru; internet www.sakha.gov.ru.

Chairman of the Government: YEGOR A. BORISOV, 677000 Sakha (Yakutiya), Yakutsk, ul. Kirova 11; tel. (4112) 43-53-88; fax (4112) 24-06-07; e-mail gs@iltumen.sakha.ru; internet www.sakha.gov.ru/main.asp?c=11.

Chairman of the State Assembly (Il Tumen): VITALII N. BASY-GYSOV, 677022 Sakha (Yakutiya), Yakutsk, ul. Yaroslavskogo 24/1; tel. (4112) 43-51-94; fax (4112) 43-53-33; e-mail gs@iltumen.sakha.ru; internet il-tumen.sakha.ru.

Chief Representative of the Republic of Sakha (Yakutiya) in the Russian Federation: ALEKSANDR A. PAKHOMOV, 107078 Moscow, Myasnitskii pr. 3/26; tel. (495) 925-52-81; fax (495) 928-42-21; e-mail postpred@sakha.msk.ru.

Head of Yakutsk City Administration (Mayor): YURII V. ZABO-LEV, 677000 Sakha (Yakutiya), Yakutsk, pr. Lenina 15; tel. (4112) 42-30-20; fax (4112) 42-48-80; e-mail yakutsk@sakha.ru; internet www.yakutsk-city.ru.

Kamchatka Krai

Kamchatka Krai occupies the Kamchatka Peninsula and forms part of the Far Eastern Federal Okrug and the Far Eastern Economic Area. The Peninsula, some 1,600 km (1,000 miles) in length and 130 km in width, separates the Sea of Okhotsk, in the west, from the Bering Sea, in the east. The Oblast also includes Karaganskii Island and the Commander Islands and the southernmost part of the Chukotka Peninsula. There are land borders with the Chukot Autonomous Okrug (AOk) to the north and Magadan Oblast to the west. This northern part of the Oblast formerly comprised the Koryak AOk. The region is dominated by the Sredinnyi Khrebet mountain range, which is bounded to the west by a broad, poorly drained coastal plain, and to the east by the Kamchatka river valley. Two-thirds of its area is mountainous (including the highest point in the Russian Far East, Mt Klyuchevskaya, at 4,685 m—15,961 feet) and it contains many hot springs. Kamchatka Krai covers an area of 472,300 sq km (182,350 sq miles). There is a high annual rate of precipitation in the region, sometimes as much as 2,000 mm, and temperatures vary considerably according to region. The average temperature for January is −16.4°C, while that for July is 13.0°C. At January 2007, according to official estimates, the total population of the region was 347,123 and the population density was 0.7 per sq km. At the time of the 2002 census 80.9% of the population were ethnically Russian, 5.8% Ukrainian, 2.0% Koryak, 1.0% Tatar and 1.0% were Belarusian. Some 79.6% of the region's population inhabited urban areas in January 2007. The Oblast's administrative centre is at Petropavlovsk-Kamchatskii, in the south-east, which was inhabited by 195,200 people at January 2006, according to official estimates. Kamchatka Krai is included in the time zone GMT+12.

HISTORY

The Kamchatka Peninsula was annexed by Russia during the 18th century. Petropavlovsk came under Russian control in 1743. After the Soviet Revolution Kamchatka was part of the short-lived Far Eastern Republic. Kamchatka Oblast was formed on 20 October 1923, but constituted part of Khabarovsk Krai until 23 January 1956.

Following the dissolution of the USSR in 1991, Kamchatka tended to be supportive of the federal Government. In the general election of December 1995, however, the most successful party was the liberal Yabloko, which obtained 20% of the votes cast in the Oblast (a higher proportion than the reformists obtained in the major cities). However, as the Oblast continued to suffer from economic and social hardship, support for the Communist Party of the Russian Federation (CPRF) experienced a resurgence. At the gubernatorial election held in December 2000, the CPRF candidate, Mikhail Mashkovtsev, was elected Governor. In March 2004 criminal proceedings were initiated against Mashkovtsev on charges of having misused budgetary funds. None the less, on 19 December, following two rounds of polling, Mashkovtsev was elected to a second term as Governor. (The third-placed candidate in the first round, Oleg Kozhemyako, whose candidacy had been supported by the Presidential Representative in the Far Eastern Federal Okrug, Konstantin Pulikovskii, was appointed as Governor of the Koryak AOk, in the northern part of Kamchatka Oblast, in March 2005.) In June 2005 all charges against Mashkovtsev were dismissed. Meanwhile, in April 2005 the legislatures of both territories voted to approve a request to federal President Vladimir Putin that a process to merge Kamchatka Oblast with the Koryak AOk be commenced. In May the two regional Governors signed a protocol, announcing that referendums on the act of unification would be held in both territories on 23 October. In the referendum on unification, held as scheduled, 84.9% of votes cast in the Oblast (with 52.2% of the electorate participating) were in favour of the proposal. The merger was approved by the lower chamber of the federal legislature, the Gosudarstvennaya Duma (State Duma), in June 2006 and signed into constitutional law by President Putin on 12 July; the new territory was to be known as Kamchatka Krai.

On 23 May 2007 Mashkovtsev resigned as Governor, and President Putin appointed Aleksei Kuzmitskii (hitherto Mashkovtsev's deputy) his interim replacement. Putin's official nomination of Kuzmitskii as Governor of Kamchatka Krai was approved by the Kamchatka Oblast legislature on 30 May, and by the Koryak AOk legislature on 1 June. Kamchatka Krai was formally constituted on 1 July, and elections to the new provincial legislature were scheduled to take place on 2 December (coinciding with elections to the State Duma). At the provincial elections, the pro-presidential United Russia won 62.9%, the nationalist Liberal Democratic Party of Russia 12.9%, the CPRF 11.4%, and Patriots of Russia 7.4%.

ECONOMY

All figures in this survey pertain to the former Kamchatka Oblast, including the Koryak Autonomous Okrug (AOk). The waters around Kamchatka (the Sea of Okhotsk, the Bering Sea and the Pacific Ocean) being extremely rich in marine life, fishing, especially for crabs, is the dominant sector of the region's economy. The region's fish stocks comprise around one-half of Russia's total. In 2004 Kamchatka Oblast's gross regional product amounted to 33,217.2m. roubles, or 93,984.9 roubles per head. Petropavlovsk is one of two main industrial centres and ports in the territory, the other being Ust-Kamchatsk. There is an international airport, Yelizovo, situated 30 km from Petropavlovsk-Kamchatskii. In 2005 there were 1,440 km of paved roads in the Oblast. There are no railways.

Apart from fishing, agriculture in the territory consists principally of vegetable production. Animal husbandry (livestock, reindeer, mostly in the north, and fur animals) and hunting. In 2005 some 12.6% of the working population were employed in agriculture, while agricultural output amounted to 3,236m. roubles. There are deposits of gold, silver, natural gas, sulphur and other minerals in the Oblast, which were in the process of development in the mid-2000s. The industrial sector, which employed 17.8% of the work-force in 2005 and generated 27,160m. roubles in 2004, is based on the processing of agricultural products, non-ferrous metallurgy and coal and electricity production. The first geothermal energy plant in Russia, at Mutnovo, commenced operations in 2002; the plant was expected to produce around one-quarter of the Oblast's energy requirements. In mid-2005 the Minister of Defence, Sergei Ivanov, announced plans to develop military facilities in the Oblast.

The economically active population of Kamchatka Oblast numbered 209,000 in 2005, when 9.5% of the labour force were unemployed. Those in employment earned an average of 15,477.1 roubles per month. There was a budgetary deficit of 887.2m. roubles in 2005, when international trade amounted to US $149.2m. in exports and $40.6m. in imports. Foreign investment in the Oblast amounted to $28.1m. in 2005. At the end of that year some 2,038 small businesses were registered in the Oblast, employing 15,800 people.

DIRECTORY

Governor: ALEKSEI A. KUZMITSKII (assumed office 1 July 2007), 683040 Kamchatka Krai, Petropavlovsk-Kamchatskii, pl. Lenina 1; tel. (4152) 11-27-61; fax (4152) 11-26-95; e-mail kra@svyaz.kamchatka.su; internet www.ako.kamchatka.ru.

Chairman of the Council of People's Deputies: NIKOLAI YA. TOKOMANTSEV, 683040 Kamchatka Krai, Petropavlovsk-Kamchatskii, pl. Lenina 1; tel. (4152) 42-56-06; fax (4152) 11-26-95; e-mail sndko@sovet.kamchatka.ru; internet www.sovet.kamchatka.ru.

Chief Representative of Kamchatka Krai in the Russian Federation: DMITRII YU. LATYSHEV, 119002 Moscow, Denezhnyi per. 12/16; tel. (495) 241-03-13; fax (495) 241-35-46.

Head of Petropavlovsk-Kamchatskii City District Administration (Mayor): VLADISLAV V. SKVORTSOV, 683000 Kamchatka Krai, Petropavlovsk-Kamchatskii, ul. Leninskaya 14; tel. (4152) 41-21-00; fax (4152) 41-25-58; e-mail citiadm@svyaz.kamchatka.su; internet petropavlovsk.kamchatka.ru.

Khabarovsk Krai

Khabarovsk Krai is situated in the Far East, on the Sea of Okhotsk. The region forms part of the Far Eastern Federal Okrug and the Far Eastern Economic Area. Maritime Krai lies to the south, the Jewish Autonomous Oblast to the south-west, Amur Oblast to the west, the Republic of Sakha (Yakutiya) to the north-west and Magadan Oblast lies to the north-east. The island of Sakhalin (Sakhalin Oblast) lies off shore to the east, across the Tatar Strait. There is a short international border with the People's Republic of China in the south-west. Khabarovsk's main river is the Amur (Heilong Jiang). More than one-half of the Krai's total area of 788,600 sq km (304,400 sq miles) is forested and almost three-quarters comprises mountains or plateaux. The territory, one of the largest in the Federation, has a 2,500-km coastline. The climate is monsoon-like in character, with hot, humid summers. Annual average precipitation in mountain areas can be as much as 1,000 mm (40 inches), while in the north it averages 500 mm. At January 2007, according to official estimates, the population of Khabarovsk Krai was 1,405,452 and the population density 1.8 per sq km. At the time of the 2002 census 89.8% of the population were ethnic Russians, 3.4% Ukrainian, 0.8% Nanaits and 0.8% Tatar. Some 80.6% of the population lived in urban areas in January 2007. The administrative centre is at Khabarovsk, which had a population of 578,100, at January 2006, according to official estimates. The Krai's second largest city is Komsomolsk-on-Amur (Komsomolsk-na-Amure), with a population of 273,300. Khabarovsk Krai is included in the time zone GMT+10.

HISTORY

Khabarovsk city was established as a military outpost in 1858. The region prospered significantly with the construction of the Trans-Siberian Railway, which reached Khabarovsk in 1905. The Krai was formally created on 20 September 1938, and until 1947 included Sakhalin island (now part of Sakhalin Oblast). The province was industrialized in 1946–80. The Jewish Autonomous Oblast, located in the south-east and based around the city of Birobidzhan, constituted part of the Krai until March 1991.

Elections to a new, provincial legislature, the Legislative Duma, were held in March 1994. In April 1996 the federal President, Boris Yeltsin, and the head of the provincial administration appointed in October 1991, Viktor Ishayev, signed an agreement on the division of powers between the provincial and federal governments. Ishayev was elected Governor in December 1996 and re-elected on 10 December 2000. Legislative elections were held on 9 December 2001. Ishayev, who was elected to the Supreme Council of the pro-presidential Unity and Fatherland-United Russia (later simply United Russia—UR) in March 2003, was re-elected to a further gubernatorial mandate in December 2004, receiving 85.3% of the votes cast. A border dispute in the territory between Russia and the People's Republic of China was resolved in June 2005, when federal President Vladimir Putin ratified a treaty previously approved by the legislatures of the two countries, as a result of which around 340 sq km of territory was to be transferred to Chinese control. In elections to the provincial Legislative Duma, held on 11 December 2005, UR obtained 41.0% of the votes cast. The Communist Party of the Russian Federation was placed second, with 15.5%, ahead of the nationalist Liberal Democratic Party of Russia, with 11.6%, and another nationalist group, Motherland, with 10.6%. Some 12.5% of votes were cast 'against all candidates'.

In early April 2007 one of the largest of several demonstrations staged nation-wide, in support of an increase in pensions and supported by local trade unions, was held in Khabarovsk. On 9 July the provincial Legislative Duma approved President Putin's nomination of Ishayev to a further gubernatorial term.

ECONOMY

The Krai's principal land use is forestry. In 2004 its gross regional product totalled 135,039.0m. roubles, or 94,854.8 roubles per head. Its main industrial centres are at Khabarovsk, Komsomolsk-on-Amur, Sovetskaya Gavan and Nikolayevsk-on-Amur. Its principal ports are Vanino (near Sovetskaya Gavan), Okhotsk and Nikolayevsk-on-Amur. It is traversed by two major railways, the Trans-Siberian and the Far Eastern (Baikal–Amur). At the end of 2005 there were 2,099 km of railway lines and 4,844 km of paved roads in the territory. The Chita (Transbaikal Krai)–Khabarovsk highway (forming part of a direct route between Moscow and Vladivostok) opened in September 2003. A ferry service runs between the Krai and Sakhalin Oblast, and there are extensive national and international air services from the Krai.

Agriculture, which employed 7.6% of the working population in 2005 and generated 9,085m. roubles, consists mainly of the production of grain, soybeans, vegetables and fruit, animal husbandry (including reindeer-breeding) and hunting. The Krai's main industries are mechanical engineering, electricity production, metalworking, non-ferrous and ferrous metallurgy, food-processing, the processing of forestry products, extraction of coal, ores and non-ferrous metals, shipbuilding (including oil rigs) and petroleum-refining. Industry engaged 24.0% of the work-force in 2005 and generated 93,060m. roubles in 2004.

Khabarovsk Krai's economically active population numbered 761,000 in 2005, when 5.7% of the labour force were unemployed. The average monthly wage was 11,335.6 roubles. In 2005 the provincial budget recorded a deficit of some 2,070.7m. roubles. In the 1990s the territory began to develop its trade links with 'Pacific Rim' nations apart from Japan (with which it had a long trading history), such as Canada, the People's Republic of China, the Republic of Korea (South Korea), Australia, Singapore and the USA. Its exports largely consisted of raw materials (timber, petro-

leum products, fish and metals). External trade amounted to a value of some US $2,808.6m. in exports and $562.7m. in imports in 2005. In that year total foreign investment amounted to $245.5m. At the end of 2005 some 7,416 small businesses were registered in the Krai, providing employment to 84,900 people.

DIRECTORY

Head of the Provincial Administration (Governor and Chairman of the Provincial Government): VIKTOR I. ISHAYEV (appointed 24 October 1991, elected 8 December 1996, re-elected 10 December 2000 and 19 December 2004, appointment confirmed 9 July 2007), 680000 Khabarovsk, ul. K. Marksa 56; tel. (4212) 32-55-40; fax (4212) 32-87-56; e-mail svi@adm.khv.ru; internet www.adm .khv.ru.

Chairman of the Provincial Legislative Duma: YURII I. ONO-PRIYENKO, 680002 Khabarovsk, ul. Muravyeva-Amurskogo 19; tel. (4212) 32-52-19; fax (4212) 32-44-57; e-mail duma@duma.khv.ru; internet www.duma.khv.ru.

Chief Representative of Khabarovsk Krai in the Russian Federation: VALERII F. BELYAYEV (acting), 119019 Moscow, ul. Novyi Arbat 19/2029; tel. (495) 203-41-28; fax (495) 203-83-25; e-mail khab .rep@g23.relcom.ru.

Head of Khabarovsk City Administration (Mayor): ALEKSANDR N. SOKOLOV, 680000 Khabarovsk, ul. K. Marksa 66; tel. and fax (4212) 31-53-46; e-mail root@mayor.kht.ru; internet www.khabarovsk.kht .ru.

Maritime (Primorskii) Krai

Maritime (Primorskii) Krai, also known as Primorye, is situated in the extreme south-east of Russia, on the Sea of Japan. The province is part of the Far Eastern Federal Okrug and the Far Eastern Economic Area. Khabarovsk Krai lies to the north. There is an international border with the People's Republic of China to the west and a short border with the Democratic People's Republic of Korea (North Korea) in the south-west. The province's major river is the Ussuri. The territory occupies 165,900 sq km (64,060 sq miles), more than two-thirds of which is forested. At January 2007, according to official estimates, the population of the territory was 2,005,917 and the population density was 12.1 per sq km. At the time of the 2002 census 89.9% of the population were ethnically Russian, 4.5% Ukrainian and 0.9% were Korean. Some 75.4% of the population lived in urban areas in January 2007. Maritime Krai's administrative centre is at Vladivostok, which had 583,700 inhabitants at January 2006, according to official estimates. Other major cities are Nakhodka (171,700), Ussuriisk (formerly Voroshilov—154,800) and Artem (102,300). Maritime Krai is included in the time zone GMT+10.

HISTORY

The territories of the Maritime Krai were recognized as Chinese possessions by Russia in the Treaty of Nerchinsk in 1687. They became part of the Russian Empire in 1860, being ceded by China under the terms of the Treaty of Beijing (Peking), and the port of Vladivostok was founded. After the collapse of the Russian Empire, the territory was part of the pro-Bolshevik Far Eastern Republic until its reintegration into Russia under Soviet rule in 1922. Maritime Krai was created on 20 October 1938.

The territory failed to obtain recognition as a republic in mid-1993. In 28 October 1993 the provincial Soviet (Council) was disbanded. Elections for a Governor, scheduled for October 1994, were cancelled by presidential decree, after alleged improprieties during the campaign of the incumbent, Yevgenii Nazdratenko. Nazdratenko was elected, however, in December 1995, with 76% of the votes cast, and was re-elected by a similar majority in December 1999. An ongoing energy crisis, owing to non-payment of bills, finally forced the resignation of Nazdratenko (officially on health grounds) in February 2001. Sergei Darkin, a local businessman, was elected Governor in June following two rounds of voting, with 40% of the votes cast. Viktor Cherepkov, the former Mayor of Vladivostok, who had taken second place in the first round, was barred from standing as a candidate in the second round by the provincial court, which cited irregularities in his campaign. Cherepkov encouraged his supporters to vote against all candidates in the 'run-off' election, and 33.7% of those who voted (only 36.0% of the electorate) did so. In January 2005 Darkin resigned, in order to request that federal President Vladimir Putin demonstrate his confidence in his leadership, becoming the first regional leader to take such a step following the abolition of elections for regional governors. Putin duly nominated Darkin to serve a further term of office, and his appointment was confirmed by a vote of the provincial Legislative Assembly on 4 February. The Presidential Representative in the Far Eastern Federal Okrug appointed in late 2005, Kamil Iskhakov, criticized the tolerance shown by the provincial authorities towards corruption and organized crime when he visited Maritime Krai in early 2006.

In May 2006 Sergei Mironov, the Chairman of the upper house of the federal parliament, the Federation Council, ordered the dismissal of one of the representatives of Maritime Krai in the chamber, together with three other senators, officially on the grounds that they were involved in commercial activities forbidden by law on account of their status. Whereas two of the four federal subjects affected by this request refused to comply with Mironov's wishes, the Maritime Krai legislature accepted the measure at a second vote and approved Mironov's nomination of a new senator. On 8 October, in elections to the regional legislature, the pro-presidential United Russia (UR) dominated proceedings, winning 48.3% of the votes cast; the Communist Party of the Russian Federation was its nearest rival, with 12.1%. The Russian Pensioners' Party, with 9.1%, and Freedom and People-Power (led by Cherepkov), with 8.7%, also obtained representation. Concern about the alleged connections between politicians and organized crime in the territory were heightened when, later in October, the UR candidate in the mayoral election in the eastern city of Dalnegorsk, Dmitrii Fotyanov, was shot dead in the city. In February 2007 the mayor of Vladivostok, Vladimir Nikolayev, was suspended on charges of abuse of office and misappropriation of funds. At elections to the State Duma, conducted on 2 December, UR secured about 54.9% of votes cast in Maritime Krai, one of the party's poorest results in the Federation.

ECONOMY

Maritime Krai's gross regional product totalled 147,233.7m. roubles in 2004, equivalent to 72,047.7 roubles per head. Its major industrial centres are at Vladivostok, the terminus of the Trans-Siberian Railway, Ussuriisk, Nakhodka and Dalnegorsk. The Krai's most important ports are at Vladivostok, Nakhodka and Vostochnyi (Vrangel). Vessels based in these ports comprise around four-fifths of maritime transport services in the Far East. The construction of a new port at Perevoznaya, near Nakhodka, was underway in 2005, and the first stage of the pipeline, which would link the oilfield with the Trans-Siberian Railway, commenced operations towards the end of that year. Maritime Krai has rail links with Khabarovsk Krai and, hence, other regions, as well as international transport links with North Korea. At the end of 2005 there were 1,553 km of railway lines and 7,094 km of paved roads in the Krai.

The Krai's agricultural sector, which employed 9.6% of the labour force and generated 10,764m. roubles in 2005, consists mainly of grain, vegetable and soybean production, animal husbandry (including fur-farming), bee-keeping and fishing. The Krai contains substantial reserves of coal and timber. The hydroelectric energy potential of the region's rivers is estimated at 25,000m. kWh. Its main industries are food processing (which accounted for 33.3% of industrial production in 2004), fuel and electrical energy production, ore-mining, the processing of forestry products and mechanical engineering and ship repairs. Industry employed 21.3% of the work-force in 2005 and generated 64,223m. roubles in 2004. The territory is well placed, in terms of its proximity to the Pacific nations, for international trade, although the perception of widespread corruption and political mismanagement has restrained its development. A new railway crossing into the People's Republic of China at Makhalino-Hunchun opened in 1998. The construction of a cross-border trade and economic centre commenced in early 2003.

The economically active population of Maritime Krai numbered 1,079,000 in 2005, when 8.0% of the labour force were unemployed. The average monthly wage was 8,925.7 roubles in 2005. In 2005 there was a budgetary surplus of 448.0m. roubles. External trade in that year amounted to US $1,047.0m. in exports and $2,211.2m. in imports. Foreign investment totalled $30.4m. in 2005. At the end of that year there were 17,860 small businesses registered in the Krai, employing 103,500 people.

DIRECTORY

Head of the Provincial Administration (Governor): SERGEI M. DARKIN (elected 17 June 2001, appointment confirmed 4 February 2005), 690110 Maritime Krai, Vladivostok, ul. Svetlanskaya 22; tel. (4232) 22-38-00; fax (4232) 22-17-69; e-mail gubernator@primorsky .ru; internet www.primorsky.ru.

Chairman of the Legislative Assembly: VIKTOR V. GORCHAKOV, 690110 Maritime Krai, 690110 Vladivostok, ul. Svetlanskaya 22; tel. (4232) 20-55-11; fax (4232) 26-90-23; e-mail chairman@zspk.gov.ru; internet www.zspk.gov.ru.

Chief Representative of Maritime (Primorskii) Krai in the Russian Federation: ALEKSEI V. BESPALOV, 123100 Moscow, 1-i Krasnogvardeiskii proyezd 9; tel. (495) 255-82-13; fax (495) 292-14-83.

Head of the Vladivostok City Administration (Mayor): IGOR S. PUSHKAREV, 690950 Maritime Krai, Vladivostok, Okeanskii pr. 20;

tel. (4232) 22-98-00; fax (4232) 22-31-29; e-mail guestbook@vlc.ru; internet www.vlc.ru.

Amur Oblast

Amur Oblast is situated in the south-east of the Russian Federation. It forms part of the Far Eastern Federal Okrug and the Far Eastern Economic Area. Khabarovsk Krai lies to the east, the Jewish Autonomous Oblast lies to the south-east, Transbaikal Krai to the west and the Republic of Sakha (Yakutiya) to the north. Southwards it has an international border with the People's Republic of China. The Oblast's main river is the Amur (Heilong Jiang), which forms the international border with China. A little under three-quarters of the Oblast's territory is forested. Its total area occupies 363,700 sq km (140,430 sq miles). At January 2007, according to official estimates, the territory's inhabitants numbered 874,613 and the population density was 2.4 per sq km. At the time of the 2002 census 92.0% of the population were ethnically Russian, 3.5% Ukrainian and 0.9% were Belarusian. Some 65.6% of the population lived in urban areas in January 2007. The Oblast's administrative centre is at Blagoveshchensk, which had a population of 212,200 at January 2006, according to official estimates. Amur Oblast is included in the time zone GMT+9.

HISTORY

The Amur region was first discovered by European Russians in 1639 and came under Russian control in the late 1850s. Part of the pro-Bolshevik Far Eastern Republic (based in Chita) until its reintegration into Russia in 1922, Amur Oblast was formed on 20 October 1932.

In the first year of post-Soviet Russian independence, the federal President, Boris Yeltsin, called for a gubernatorial election to be held in the region in December 1992. However, his appointed head of the administration, Albert Krivchenko, was defeated by Aleksandr Surat. In July 1993 Amur Oblast declared itself a republic, a measure that was not recognized by the federal authorities. Surat was subsequently dismissed and the regional Soviet dissolved. In January 1996 the oblast administration brought action against the regional Assembly for adopting a Charter, referred to as a republican constitution, some of the clauses of which ran counter to federal laws and presidential decrees. In elections to the new legislature, held in March, candidates of the Communist Party of the Russian Federation (CPRF) won up to 40% of the votes cast. In June President Yeltsin dismissed the regional Governor appointed in December 1994, Vladimir Dyachenko, and appointed Yurii Lyashko in his place. A gubernatorial election was held on 22 September 1996. The CPRF candidate, Anatolii Belonogov, narrowly defeated Lyashko (with 41.0%), but the results were subsequently annulled because of alleged irregularities. Belonogov succeeded in securing a clear majority in the repeat election held in March 1997. In a gubernatorial election held in two rounds in March–April 2001 Belonogov was defeated by Leonid Korotkov. In February 2005 federal President Vladimir Putin nominated Korotkov to serve a further term of office; his appointment was confirmed by a unanimous vote of the regional legislature on 24 February. At elections to the oblast legislature, held on 27 March, an alliance of the statist Russian Party of Life and the liberal, pro-market Yabloko, known as 'We Support the Development of Amur', was the most successful bloc or party, obtaining 17.7% of the votes cast, compared with the 16.3% won by the pro-presidential United Russia (UR). However, the legislative Chairman elected following the polling, Oleg Turkov, transferred his allegiance from the alliance to UR several weeks later.

On 10 May 2007 President Putin signed a decree dismissing Korotkov as Governor, after he had been formally charged with abuse of office for having increased electricity tariffs to cover losses incurred by a local football club. Korotkov thereby became the first regional Governor appointed by Putin to be removed from office. Later in May Putin nominated Nikolai Kolesov, hitherto a deputy in the Republic of Tatarstan legislature and little known in Amur Oblast, as Governor; the oblast legislature approved the appointment on 1 June.

ECONOMY

Amur Oblast's gross regional product (GRP) was 66,152.4m. roubles in 2004, equivalent to 74,241.6 roubles per head. Its main industrial centres are at Blagoveshchensk, Belogorsk, Zeya and Svobodnyi. At the end of 2005 there were 7,276 km of paved roads in the Oblast. There were 2,934 km of railway track, including sections of two major railways, the Trans-Siberian and the Far Eastern (Baikal–Amur). There are five river-ports, at Blagoveshchensk, Svobodnensk, Poyarkovsk, Amursk and Zeisk. There is an international airport at Blagoveshchensk.

Agriculture in Amur Oblast, which employed 10.4% of the workforce in 2005, consists mainly of grain and vegetable production, animal husbandry (including the breeding of reindeer and animals for fur) and bee-keeping. The soil in the south of the region is particularly fertile. In 2005 agricultural output amounted to 9,815m. roubles. The region is rich in mineral resources, but by the end of the 1990s it was estimated that only around 5% of these resources were being exploited. None the less, the mining sector produced around 15% of GRP in the late 1990s. At this time around 10–12 metric tons of gold were extracted annually, making the Oblast the third largest producer of gold in Russia. The eventual liberalization of the artisanal sector could be expected to increase the output of gold appreciably. Other raw material deposits in the Oblast include bituminous coal, lignite (brown coal) and kaolin. There are also substantial reserves of iron, titanium and silver ores. Coalmining is important, as are mechanical engineering, electricity generation, electro-technical industry and the processing of agricultural and forestry products. Industry engaged 21.2% of the workforce in 2005 and generated 23,640m. roubles in 2004. The region contains the Amur Shipbuilding Plant and produces nuclear-powered submarines. There is a hydroelectric power plant at Zeya, with a reservoir of 2,400 sq km. Two units of another power station, at Bureya, commenced operations in 2003; a third unit opened in November 2004.

Amur's economically active population numbered 424,000 in 2005, when 10.3% of the region's labour force were unemployed. Those in employment earned, on average, 9,391.8 roubles per month in 2005. There was a budgetary surplus of 371.6m. roubles in 2005. In that year export trade amounted to a value of US $164.7m., and import trade totalled $114.0m. The Oblast's main trading partners include the People's Republic of China, Japan and the Democratic People's Republic of Korea (North Korea). Foreign investment totalled $95.3m. in 2005. At the end of that year there were some 2,777 small businesses registered in the Oblast, employing 23,100 people.

DIRECTORY

Head of the Regional Administration: Nikolai A. Kolesov (appointment confirmed 1 June 2007), 675023 Amur obl., Blagoveshchensk, ul. Lenina 135; tel. (4162) 44-03-22; fax (4162) 44-62-01; e-mail governor@amurobl.ru; internet www.amurobl.ru.

Chairman of the Regional Council of People's Deputies: Oleg A. Turkov, 675023 Amur obl., Blagoveshchensk, ul. Lenina 135; tel. (4162) 42-38-53; fax (4162) 42-38-54; e-mail svl@snd.amur.ru; internet www.sndamur.ru.

Chief Representative of Amur Oblast in the Russian Federation: Sergei A. Lavrikov, 127006 Moscow, ul. M. Dmitrovka 3/606; tel. (495) 299-46-08; fax (495) 299-42-02.

Head of Blagoveshchensk City Administration (Mayor): Aleksandr A. Migulya, 675023 Amur obl., Blagoveshchensk, ul. Lenina 133; tel. (4162) 52-68-25; internet www.admblag.ru.

Magadan Oblast

Magadan Oblast is situated in the north-east of Russia and forms part of the Far Eastern Federal Okrug and the Far Eastern Economic Area. To the north-east lies the Chukot Autonomous Okrug (AOk), and there is a border to the east with Kamchatka Krai. Magadan has a coastline on the Sea of Okhotsk in the south-east. Khabarovsk Krai lies to the south-west of the region and Sakha (Yakutiya) to the north-west. Its main river is the Kolyma, which flows northwards and drains into the Arctic Ocean by way of Sakha. A considerable proportion of the territory of the region is mountainous, whereas the south is dominated by larch forests and coastal marshland. Much of the Oblast is tundra or forest-tundra. The Oblast occupies a total area of 461,400 sq km (178,150 sq miles). The climate in the region is severe, with winters lasting from six to over seven months. The average temperature in January is –29.4°C, while that in July is 14.4°C. At January 2007, according to official estimates, the Oblast had a total population of 168,530. It is one of the more sparsely populated regions of Russia, with a population density of just 0.4 per sq km. At the time of the 2002 census 80.2% of the population were ethnically Russian, 9.9% Ukrainian, 1.4% Even, 1.2% Belarusian and 1.1% were Tatar. Some 94.5% of the population inhabited urban areas in January 2007. The Oblast's administrative centre is at the only large city, Magadan, which had a population of 100,000 at January 2006, according to official estimates. Magadan Oblast is included in the time zone GMT+11.

HISTORY

Russians first reached the Magadan region in the mid-17th century. Following the Soviet Revolution Magadan was part of the Far Eastern Republic, which in 1922 was reintegrated into Russia. The region held many penal establishments of the GULag (State Corrective Camps) system established during the regime of Stalin (Iosif Dzhugashvili, 1924–53). Magadan Oblast was formed on 3 December 1953, although it then included the Chukot national district. The successful rejection of Magadan's jurisdiction over the Chukot AOk (as it had by then become) in 1992 significantly reduced Magadan's territory.

Deteriorating social conditions contributed to local feeling of disaffection with the federal authorities in the 1990s, which was exemplified by high levels of support for the nationalist Liberal Democratic Party of Russia in the region. The gubernatorial election of 3 November 1996 was won by a gold mine proprietor, Valentin Tsvetkov, who was backed by the Communist-dominated People's Patriotic Union of Russia. Tsvetkov was re-elected Governor in November 2000; however, in October 2002 he was killed in Moscow, in an apparent contract killing. Following the first round of the gubernatorial election, held on 2 February 2003 and contested by 12 candidates, Nikolai Dudov, formerly First Vice-Governor, who received 26.0% of the votes cast, and Nikolai Karpenko, the Mayor of Magadan, with 37.6%, proceeded to a second round, held on 16 February. In this poll Dudov, who was supported by the pro-presidential Unity and Fatherland-United Russia party (later simply known as United Russia—UR), obtained 50.4% of the votes cast, thereby being elected Governor. In elections to the regional legislature, held on 22 May 2005, UR received the largest share of votes cast (around 29%); notably, Our Home Is Kolyma—an alliance of the liberal, reformist and pro-Western parties, the Democratic Party of Russia, the Union of Rightist Forces and Yabloko—was prohibited from participating in the elections, in accordance with electoral legislation, after eight of the bloc's 24 candidates withdrew their candidacies. Allegations persisted that various administrative resources had been used to encourage these candidates to withdraw, as a result of which the bloc was disqualified from contesting the election. At elections to the federal State Duma, conducted on 2 December 2007, UR won 55.2% of votes cast in the Oblast, one of its poorest results in the Federation. On 4 February 2008 the Regional Duma unanimously approved the nomination of Dudov for a further five-year term of office.

ECONOMY

Magadan Oblast is Russia's principal gold-producing region. In 2004 its gross regional product amounted to 23,670.5m. roubles, equivalent to 134,101.6 roubles per head. The Oblast's main industrial centres are at Magadan and Susuman. Magadan and Nagayevo are its most important ports. There are no railways in the territory, but there were 2,212 km of paved roads at the end of 2005. There is an international airport at Magadan.

The region's primary economic activities are fishing, animal husbandry and hunting. These and other agricultural activities, which employed only 3.8% of the region's work-force, generated just 697m. roubles in 2005. Ore-mining is important: apart from gold, the region contains considerable reserves of silver, tin and wolfram (tungsten). It is also rich in peat and timber. In early 1998 the regional Government hired a prospecting company to explore offshore petroleum deposits in the Sea of Okhotsk, in a zone thought to hold around 5,000m. metric tons of petroleum and natural gas. The Kolyma river is an important source of hydroelectric energy. In the late 2000s preliminary work began on the construction of a new hydroelectric plant at Ust-Srednekanskaya. In 1997 the Pan American Silver Corporation of Canada purchased a 70% stake in local company Dukat, to reopen a defunct silver mine in the Oblast, which contained an estimated 477m. troy oz of silver and 1m. troy oz of gold. However, licensing and other bureaucratic obstacles delayed operations. Other industry includes non-ferrous metallurgy (which accounted for 64.7% of total industrial output in 2004), food-processing, electricity generation, mechanical engineering and metalworking. Industry engaged 26.1% of the work-force in 2005 and generated 19,776m. roubles in 2004.

The economically active population of the Oblast numbered 102,000 in 2005, when 7.0% of the labour force were unemployed. The average monthly wage was some 14,672.6 roubles in 2005. In 2005 the regional budget recorded a deficit of 50.6m. roubles. In 2005 external trade comprised US $19.9m. of exports and $80.4m. of imports. Foreign investment in the Oblast amounted to just $2.9m. in that year. At the end of 2005 there were some 1,585 small businesses registered in the Oblast, employing 16,700 people.

DIRECTORY

Governor: Nikolai N. Dudov (elected 16 February 2003, appointment confirmed 4 February 2008), 685000 Magadan, ul. Gorkogo 6;

tel. (4132) 62-31-34; fax (4132) 69-78-07; e-mail amo@regadm
.magadan.ru; internet www.magadan.ru.

Chairman of the Regional Duma: ALEKSANDR P. ALEKSANDROV,
685000 Magadan, ul. Gorkogo 8 A; tel. (4132) 62-55-50; fax (4132) 62-
55-12; internet www.magoblduma.ru.

**Chief Representative of Magadan Oblast in the Russian
Federation:** YURII L. GUTIN, 119019 Moscow, ul. Novyi Arbat 19/
2023; tel. (495) 203-92-82.

Head of Magadan City Administration (Mayor): VLADIMIR P.
PECHENYI, 685000 Magadan, pl. Gorkogo 1; tel. (4132) 62-50-47; fax
(4132) 62-55-48; e-mail admin@cityadm.magadan.ru; internet www
.magadangorod.ru.

Sakhalin Oblast

Sakhalin Oblast comprises the island of Sakhalin and the Kurile
(Kuril) Islands in the Pacific Ocean. It forms part of the Far Eastern
Federal Okrug and the Far Eastern Economic Area. The island of
Sakhalin lies off the coast of Khabarovsk Krai, separated from the
mainland by the Tatar Strait. The Kurile Islands (annexed by the
USSR in 1945, but claimed by Japan), an archipelago of some 56
islands extending from the Kamchatka Peninsula in the north-east
to Hokkaido Island (Japan) in the south-west, lie to the east.
Sakhalin Island is 942 km (just over 580 miles) in length and contains
two parallel mountain ranges running north to south and separated
by a central valley. The highest peaks on the island, both belonging to
the eastern range of mountains, are Lopatin (1,609 m or 5,281 feet)
and Nevelskogo (1,397 m). The north-west coast of the island is
marshland, and much of its area is forested. The Kurile Islands are
actively volcanic and contain many hot springs. There are some
60,000 rivers on Sakhalin Island, the major ones being the Poronai
and the Tym (330 km), both of which are frozen during the winter
months. The Kurile Islands contain around 4,000 rivers and streams
and the largest waterfall in the Russian Federation, Ilya Muromets.
Sakhalin Oblast covers a total area of 87,100 sq km (33,620 sq miles).
At January 2007, according to official estimates, the Oblast's population was 521,206 and the population density 6.0 per sq km. At the
time of the 2002 census 84.3% of the population were ethnically
Russian, 5.4% Korean, 4.0% Ukrainian, 1.2% Tatar and 1.0% were
Belarusian. The population of the Oblast declined during the 1990s,
largely reflecting migration from the region as a result of the decline
of its industrial base. Some 77.9% of the region's population resided
in urban areas in January 2007. The Oblast's administrative centre
is at Yuzhno-Sakhalinsk, which had 173,400 inhabitants at January
2006, according to official estimates. Sakhalin Oblast is included in
the time zone GMT+12.

HISTORY

Sakhalin was originally inhabited by the indigenous Gilyak people.
The island was conquered by the Japanese in the late 18th century,
but Russia established a military base at Korsakov in 1853. Joint
control of the island followed until 1875, when it was granted to
Russia in exchange for the Kurile Islands. Karafuto, the southern
part of the island, was captured by Japan during the Russo–Japanese
War (1904–05), but the entire island was ceded to the USSR in 1945.
The Kurile Islands were divided between Japan and Russia in the
18th century and ruled jointly until 1875. The USSR occupied the
islands in 1945 and assumed full control in 1947. After the disintegration of the USSR in 1991, the southern Kuriles remained a
disputed territory. Sakhalin Oblast had been formed on 20 October
1932 as part of Khabarovsk Krai. It became a separate administrative unit in 1947, when the island was united with the Kuriles.
Having previously been a place of exile for political opponents to the
tsars, the region contained several penal institutions of the GULag
(State Corrective Camps) system established during the regime of
Stalin—Iosif Dzhugashvili (1924–53)—and remained closed to foreigners until 1990.

On 16 October 1993 the head of the regional administration
disbanded the oblast Soviet; a Regional Duma was elected in its
place. In May 1995 a major earthquake destroyed the northern
settlement of Neftegorsk, killing an estimated 2,000 people. In May
1996 the federal President Boris Yeltsin signed a power-sharing
treaty with the regional Government. The gubernatorial elections of
October 1996 and October 2000 were won by the incumbent, Igor
Farkhutdinov. In December 1998 the Oblast authorities signed an
economic co-operation accord with the Japanese province of Hokkaido, and a further agreement was signed in January 2000, despite
the continuing dispute over the sovereignty of four of the Southern
Kuriles (known as the 'Northern Territory' to Japan) between Russia
and Japan.

On 20 August 2003 Farkhutdinov and several senior oblast
officials were killed in a helicopter crash. The first round of voting

in a gubernatorial election was held on 7 December (concurrently
with elections to the federal State Duma). The acting Governor, Ivan
Malakhov, and the Mayor of Yuzhno-Sakhalinsk, Fedor Sidorenko,
proceeded to a second round on 21 December, in which Malakhov
emerged as the victor, with around 53% of the votes cast. Malakhov
joined the pro-presidential United Russia party in January 2005. In
August 2006, as an indication that Russia had ruled out any
immediate resolution to the territorial dispute, the federal Government announced a strategy for improving social and economic
conditions on the disputed islands, with a view to doubling their
population over a 10-year period. In mid-August Russian security
troops killed one Japanese fisherman and detained three others who
had allegedly been fishing illegally in Russian waters; the captain of
the Japanese vessel subsequently received a fine for intrusion into
Russian waters and poaching. The revocation, in the following
month, of an environmental permit associated with the Sakhalin-2
natural gas project, and the subsequent enforced reduction of the
stake held in the project by Japanese companies (see Economy,
below), was a further cause of heightened tensions between Russia
and Japan.

On 7 August 2007 federal President Vladimir Putin accepted the
resignation of Malakhov, having criticized him publicly for the
Sakhalin authorities' alleged mishandling of relief measures following three earthquakes in the region earlier that month. On the
following day the regional Duma approved Putin's nomination of
Aleksandr Khoroshavin, a former Mayor of Okha, as Governor.
Following his confirmation in the post, Khoroshavin announced
that his first priority would be to reconstruct Nevelsk and provide
housing for some 2,000 people left homeless following the earthquakes.

The pro-Government United Russia was the most successful party
at elections to the Regional Duma, held on 12 October 2008, obtaining
55.2% of the votes cast on the basis of party lists. The Communist
Party of the Russian Federation was placed second, with 23.1%,
ahead of the Liberal Democratic Party of Russia, with 9.9% and A
Just Russia: Motherland/Pensioners/Life, with 8.5%.

ECONOMY

In 2004 Sakhalin Oblast's gross regional product amounted to
88,339.9m. roubles, or some 165,048.5 roubles per head. The Oblast's
principal industrial centres are at Yuzhno-Sakhalinsk, Kholmsk and
Okha (the administrative centre of the petroleum-producing region).
At the end of 2005 there were 805 km of railways and 762 km of paved
roads in the Oblast. The Oblast's ports are Kholmsk (from where a
ferry links Sakhalin Island with Vanino, Khabarovsk Krai) and
Korsakov. An airport at Yuzhno-Sakhalinsk serves flights to Moscow, Khabarovsk, Vladivostok, Petropavlovsk-Kamchatskii and
Novosibirsk, and international services to Alaska (USA), the Republic of Korea and Japan.

Agriculture in the region is minimal, owing to unfavourable
climatic conditions. The sector employed 8.2% of the working population and generated 4,091m. roubles in 2005, and consists mainly of
potato and vegetable production and animal husbandry (largely
comprising reindeer-breeding and fur-farming). Annual catches of
fish and other marine life amount to around 400,000 metric tons–
500,000 metric tons. Fishing and fish-processing is the major traditional industry. The industrial sector employed some 24.5% of the
region's work-force in 2005 and generated 41,152m. roubles in 2004.
Food-processing accounted for 28.6% of industrial output in 2004.
There is some extraction of coal and, increasingly, petroleum and
natural gas in, and to the north of, Sakhalin Island. Some petroleum
is piped for refining to a plant in Komsomolsk-on-Amur (Khabarovsk
Krai), although from 1994 the Oblast had its own refinery, with a
capacity of some 200,000 tons per year.

By the end of the 1990s four major consortiums had been formed to
exploit the natural resources of the region. Sakhalin-1, a project to
produce petroleum on the continental shelf of Sakhalin Island,
comprises ExxonMobil of the USA (30%), Japan's Sodeco consortium
(30%), Rosneft (of which Sakhalinmorneftegaz is a local subsidiary,
20%) and India's Oil and Natural Gas Corporation (20%). Sakhalin-2,
two fields containing an estimated 1,000m. barrels of petroleum and
408,000m. cu m of natural gas, was initiated by Sakhalin Energy
Investment, comprising Royal Dutch/Shell (Netherlands/United
Kingdom), which held a 55% share, and Mitsui and Mitsubishi (of
Japan), with 45%. Sakhalin-2 was the single largest foreign direct
investment project to be recorded in Russia, worth some
US $10,000m., and was to include the world's largest liquefied
natural gas (LNG) plant. Sakhalin-3, backed by a consortium of
Mobil (now ExxonMobil), Texaco (now Chevron—of the USA) and the
state-owned Russian company Rosneft, was seeking to develop what
was potentially the largest field on the Sakhalin shelf, containing an
estimated 320m. metric tons of recoverable reserves. In January
2004 the federal authorities annulled the tender to develop Sakhalin-
3 won in 1993, while in 2005 it was announced that the project
constituted one of the strategically important deposits of natural
resources in which non-Russian companies were henceforth to be

prohibited from participating. Moreover, in September 2006, the federal Government announced that it had revoked an environmental permit associated with the Sakhalin-2 project. There was, however, widespread speculation that the decision was principally motivated by political, rather than environmental, concerns. In December the Russian state-controlled monopoly Gazprom acquired a 50%-plus-one-share stake in the project, thereby reducing Royal Dutch/Shell's share to 27.5% and those of Mitsui and Mitsubishi to 12.5% and 10.0%, respectively. Meanwhile, in mid-2002 it was announced that Rosneft was to undertake the development of a further project, Sakhalin-5, in association with BP (United Kingdom—the Russian interests of which subsequently were merged into TNK-BP).

Sakhalin Oblast's economically active population totalled 309,000 in 2005, when 7.6% of the labour force were unemployed and when the average monthly wage in the region amounted to 15,242.6 roubles. The 2005 regional budget recorded a deficit of 0.6m. roubles. In the same year exports from the Oblast were valued at US $1,062.4m. and imports to the Oblast were worth $2,486.9m.; total foreign investment in the region amounted to some $4,861.6m. in 2005 (some 81.9% of all foreign investment in the Far Eastern Federal Okrug, or 9.1% of all foreign investment in the Russian Federation in that year). At the end of 2005 some 3,286 small businesses were registered in the Oblast, employing 28,800 people.

DIRECTORY

Governor: ALEKSANDR V. KHOROSHAVIN (appointment confirmed 9 August 2007), 693011 Sakhalin obl., Yuzhno-Sakhalinsk, Kommunisticheskii pr. 39; tel. (4242) 46-91-05; fax (4242) 48-08-31; e-mail ad_app@sakhalin.ru; internet www.adm.sakhalin.ru.

Chairman of the Regional Duma: VLADIMIR I. YEFREMOV, 693000 Sakhalin obl., Yuzhno-Sakhalinsk, ul. Chekhova 37; tel. (4242) 42-14-89; fax (4242) 72-15-46; e-mail duma@duma.sakhalin.ru; internet www.duma.sakhalin.ru.

Chief Representative of Sakhalin Oblast in the Russian Federation: ARKADII I. PINCHEVSKII, 119019 Moscow, ul. Novyi Arbat 19/1132; tel. (495) 203-79-09; fax (495) 203-84-56; e-mail prsakh2001@mail.ru.

Head of Yuzhno-Sakhalinsk City Administration (Mayor): ANDREI I. LOBKIN, 693023 Sakhalin obl., Yuzhno-Sakhalinsk, ul. Lenina 173; tel. (4242) 72-25-11; fax (4242) 23-00-06; e-mail ys_mayor@sctel.ru; internet yuzhno.sakh.ru.

Jewish Autonomous Oblast

The Jewish Autonomous Oblast (AOb) is part of the Amur river basin, and is included in Russia's Far Eastern Federal Okrug and Far Eastern Economic Area. It is situated to the south-west of Khabarovsk Krai, on the international border with the People's Republic of China. There is a border with Amur Oblast in the north-west. The Amur (Heilong Jiang) and the Tungusk are the region's major rivers. It occupies 36,000 sq km (13,900 sq miles). At January 2007, according to official estimates, the Jewish AOb had a population of 185,645 and a population density of 5.2 per sq km. At the time of the 2002 census 89.9% of the population were ethnically Russian and 4.4% Ukrainian. Just 1.2% described their ethnicity as Jewish; in the early 1950s Jews were believed to have constituted around one-quarter of the population of the region, and at the 1989 census 4.2% of the population of the AOb were Jewish according to 'official declaration of nationality' (ethnicity). The subsequent decline was believed to be largely attributable to emigration, particularly to Israel. Some 66.1% of the population inhabited urban areas in January 2007. The regional capital is at Birobidzhan, which had a population of 75,200 at January 2006, according to official estimates. The Jewish Autonomous Oblast is included in the time zone GMT+10.

HISTORY

The majority of Russian Jews came under Russian control following the Partitions of Poland in 1772–95. In Imperial Russia, between 1835 and 1917, Jews were required to receive special permission to live outside the 'Pale of Settlement' in the south-west of the Empire, which constituted territories largely in present-day Belarus, Lithuania, Poland and Ukraine, and were subject to widespread discrimination in the regions that they did inhabit. Attempts by the Soviet authorities in the 1920s to create nominally Jewish regions in Ukraine and Crimea were largely unsuccessful, in part because of hostility from the local population in these regions, although some nominally Jewish administrative sub-districts existed in southern Ukraine prior to the Nazi German invasion of the USSR in 1941. The Soviet regime established a national Jewish district at Birobidzhan in 1928, but it never became the centre of Soviet (or Russian) Jewry,

largely because of its remote location and the absence of any prior Jewish settlement there. The district received the status of an Autonomous Oblast in May 1934 and formed part of Khabarovsk Krai until 25 March 1991.

In the early post-Soviet period the region remained a redoubt of communist support. In October 1993 the Regional Soviet announced that it would not disband itself. Subsequently, however, the council was replaced by a new body, the Legislative Assembly, elections to which confirmed Communist Party domination. A gubernatorial election, held on 20 October 1996, was won by the incumbent, Nikolai Volkov; he was re-elected with 57% of the votes cast on 26 March 2000. On 25 February 2005 the Legislative Assembly unanimously approved federal President Vladimir Putin's nomination of Volkov to a further term as Governor. In elections to the Legislative Assembly, held on 8 October 2006, the pro-presidential United Russia received 55.3%, the Communist Party of the Russian Federation 18.5% and the Russian Pensioners' Party 9.9% of votes cast.

ECONOMY

In 2004 the Jewish AOb's gross regional product stood at 11,485.2m. roubles, equivalent to 60,685.9 roubles per head. Birobidzhan is the region's main industrial centre. At the end of 2005 there were 513 km of railway track, including a section of the Trans-Siberian Railway, and 1,533 km of paved roads in the region. In 2000 the opening of a bridge across the Amur river provided improved road and rail links with the city of Khabarovsk and the People's Republic of China. There were around 600 km of navigable waterways in the AOb in 1998.

Agriculture, which employed 12.7% of the region's work-force and generated a total of 3,064m. roubles in 2005, consists mainly of grain, soybean, vegetable and potato production, and animal husbandry. From the late 1990s the oblast authorities encouraged Chinese farmers to undertake agricultural activity in the region; greater diversity of crops, as well as an improvement in productivity, resulting in part from a higher level of farming technology, were reported as a result. There are major deposits of coal, peat, iron ore, manganese, tin, gold, graphite, magnesite and zeolite, although they are largely unexploited. The main industries are mechanical engineering and metal-working, the manufacture of building materials, the production of electricity, wood-working and light manufacturing. Industry employed 19.8% of the Jewish AOb's work-force in 2005 and generated 2,512m. roubles in 2004.

In 2005 the Jewish AOb's economically active population numbered 91,000. Although more than one-quarter of the labour force were unemployed in 1997, by 2005 the unemployment rate had declined to 7.9%. In 2005 the average monthly wage in the region was 8,190.2 roubles—the lowest figure of any federal subject in the Far Eastern Federal Okrug. The 2005 budget recorded a deficit of 6.4m. roubles. In that year external trade amounted to just US $8.4m. in exports and $9.1m. in imports. In 2005 foreign investment amounted to $1.9m.; four of the five foreign- or jointly owned enterprises operating in the territory in 2004 had Chinese partners. At the end of 2005 some 613 small businesses were registered in the region, employing 7,900 people.

DIRECTORY

Head of the Regional Administration (Governor and Chairman of the Government): NIKOLAI M. VOLKOV (appointed 14 December 1991, elected 20 October 1996, re-elected 26 March 2000, appointment confirmed 25 February 2005), 679016 Jewish AOb, Birobidzhan, pr. 60-letiya SSSR 18; tel. (42622) 6-02-42; fax (42622) 4-07-25; e-mail gov@eao.ru; internet www.eao.ru.

Chairman of the Legislative Assembly: ANATOLII F. TIKHOMIROV, 679016 Jewish AOb, Birobidzhan, pr. 60-letiya SSSR 18; tel. (42622) 6-04-72; e-mail press-zs@eao.ru; internet www.eao.ru/?p=zakon.

Representation of the Jewish Autonomous Oblast in the Russian Federation: Moscow.

Head of Birobidzhan City Administration: ALEKSANDR A. VINNIKOV, Jewish AOb, 679016 Birobidzhan, ul. Lenina 29; tel. (42622) 6-91-92; fax (42622) 4-04-93; e-mail goriao@on-line.jar.ru; internet www.eao.ru/?p=746.

Chukot Autonomous Okrug

The Chukot Autonomous Okrug (AOk) is situated mostly on the Chukotka Peninsula and forms part of the Far Eastern Federal Okrug and the Far Eastern Economic Area. It is the easternmost part of Russia and faces the Eastern Siberian Sea (Arctic Ocean) to the north and the Bering Sea to the south; the Anadyr Gulf, part of the Bering Sea, cuts into the territory from the south-east. The USA (Alaska) lies eastwards across the Bering Straits. The western end of the district borders the Republic of Sakha (Yakutiya) to the west, and Magadan Oblast to the south. Also to the south lies Kamchatka Krai. The district's major river is the Anadyr. The Chukot AOk occupies an area of 737,700 sq km (284,830 sq miles), of which approximately one-half lies within the Arctic Circle. Its climate is severe; the average temperature in January is −29.2°C, and in July it is 9.4°C. At January 2007, according to official estimates, it had a total of 50,484 inhabitants and a population density of 0.1 per sq km. At the time of the 2002 census 51.9% of the population were ethnically Russian, 23.5% Chukchi, 9.2% Ukrainian, 2.9% Eskimo (Inuit), 1.8% Chuvanets, 1.0% Tatar and 1.0% were Belarusian. Around 80,000 people left the AOk between 1991 and 2002. The Chukchi (who call themselves the Lyg Oravetlyan, and are also known as the Luoravetlan, Chukcha and Chukot) speak the Chukotic language as their native tongue, which belongs to the Paleo-Asiatic linguistic family. Traditionally they were divided into nomadic and semi-nomadic reindeer herders (the Chavchu or Chavchuven), and coastal dwellers (known as the An Kalyn). Some 66.5% of the territory's population inhabited urban areas in January 2007. The district's administrative centre is at Anadyr, which had a population of 11,200 at January 2006, according to official estimates, compared with 17,000 in 1989. The Chukot AOk is included in the time zone GMT+12.

HISTORY

Russian settlers first arrived in the territories inhabited by Chukchi tribes in the mid-17th century. Commercial traders, fur trappers and hunters subsequently established contact with the Chukchi, many of whom were forcibly converted to Orthodox Christianity and enserfed. A Chukot national okrug was created within Magadan Oblast by the Soviet Government on 10 December 1930, as part of its policy to incorporate the peoples of the north of Russia into the social, political and economic body of the USSR. (It acquired nominally autonomous status in 1980.) Simultaneously, collectivization was introduced into the district, while industrialization resulted both in an extensive migration of ethnic Russians to the area and a drastic reduction of the territory available to the Chukchi for herding reindeer. Many abandoned their traditional way of life to work in industry.

In March 1990 the Chukchi participated in the creation of the Association of the Peoples of the North. They also campaigned for the ratification of two international conventions, which would affirm their right to the ownership and possession of the lands they traditionally inhabited. In February 1991 the legislature of the Chukot AOk seceded from Magadan Oblast and declared the territory to be an autonomous republic. This measure failed to be recognized by the federal Government, although the district was acknowledged as a constituent member of the Russian Federation by the Treaty of March 1992 and, subsequently, as free from the jurisdiction of Magadan Oblast.

At the gubernatorial election held in December 2000, the incumbent Governor, Aleksandr Nazarov, withdrew his candidacy. Roman Abramovich, a prominent 'oligarch' (politically influential businessman), was elected in his place, receiving 91% of the votes cast. Abramovich was generally regarded as a popular Governor in the district, owing largely to improvements to public services and utilities implemented following his election. Meanwhile, Abramovich sought to cultivate closer ties between the region and the nearby US state of Alaska. The first Alaska-Chukotka summit was held in Nome, Alaska, in mid-2001 to that end; it was intended that this summit would henceforth be an annual occurrence. Following the 2002 summit, Abramovich and the Governor of Alaska, Tony Knowles, signed a document that provided for the eventual establishment of regular air services between Nome and Anadyr and for the promotion of co-operation in a number of sectors.

In early 2004 the Audit Chamber of the State Duma conducted an audit of the finances of the AOk. The findings, promulgated in May, declared the district to be insolvent, with debts of 9,300m. roubles at the beginning of 2004, compared with revenues of only 3,900m. roubles in 2003. The Chamber also launched an investigation into possible fraud and misuse of public funds committed by Abramovich in connection with the sale of the Maiskoye gold mine. The Chairman of the Audit Chamber, former federal premier Sergei Stepashin, called on Abramovich to resign as Governor, while some commentators suggested the investigations were politically motivated. How-

ever, although Abramovich divested much of his financial and business interests in Russia, taking up residence in the United Kingdom, in September 2005, despite earlier indications to the contrary, it was reported that he had agreed to serve a second term; following his nomination by federal President Vladimir Putin, the appointment was confirmed by the district Duma on 21 October. In December 2006 Abramovich announced he intended to submit his resignation as Governor to Putin. On 3 July 2008 the federal President Dmitrii Medvedev, who had recently assumed office, signed a decree accepting Abramovich's resignation. The nomination of his hitherto deputy, Roman Kopin, to the gubernatorial office was confirmed by the District Duma on 13 July. At a poll to fill three vacant seats in the District Duma on 12 October Abramovich was elected to the legislature with a reported 97% of votes cast; there was speculation that he would be offered the post of its Chairman.

ECONOMY

In 2004 the Chukot AOk's gross regional product amounted to 15,124.5m. roubles, equivalent to 296,215.7 roubles per head. Although relatively high, this level of regional wealth was highly dependent on federal transfers. At the end of 2005 the territory had 591 km of paved roads and a relatively undeveloped infrastructure. Anadyr is one of the district's major ports, the others being Pevek, Providenya, Egvekinot and Beringovskii.

The AOk's agricultural sector, which employed 10.0% of the workforce and generated 294m. roubles in 2005, consists mainly of fishing, animal husbandry (especially reindeer-breeding) and hunting. The region contains reserves of coal and brown coal (lignite), petroleum and natural gas, as well as gold, tin, wolfram (tungsten), copper and other minerals. It is self-sufficient in energy, containing two coal-mines, six producers of electricity and one nuclear power station. Its main industries are electricity generation (which accounted for 53.1% of industrial output in 2004), ore-mining, non-ferrous metallurgy and food-processing. Industry employed some 45.0% of the district's working population in 2005 and generated 5,452m. roubles in 2004.

The AOk's economically active population numbered 32,000 in 2005. The rate of unemployment has been relatively low; in 2005 only 4.4% of the labour force were unemployed. Those in employment earned an average of 23,314.4 roubles per month, well above the national average and the highest of any federal subject in the Far Eastern Federal Okrug, although this was counterbalanced by some of the highest living costs in the Federation; in December 2005 a minimum 'consumer basket' of goods and services in the Chukot AOk was the most expensive of that in any federal subject, costing over two times the federal average, and around 60% higher than the average for the Far Eastern Federal Okrug. The 2005 district government budget recorded a deficit of some 918.9m. roubles. The external trade of the district, which had previously been relatively minimal increased substantially in 2005. In that year exports amounted to US $1,524.3m. and imports to $71.3m.; almost all of this trade was with countries outside the Commonwealth of Independent States. Foreign investment in the district, however, remained negligible. At the end of 2005 there were around 286 small businesses registered in the AOk, employing 2,500 people.

DIRECTORY

Head of the District Administration (Governor): ROMAN V. KOPIN (appointment confirmed 13 July 2008, assumed office 24 July 2008), 689000 Chukot AOk, Anadyr, ul. Beringa 20; tel. (42722) 2-90-00; fax (42722) 2-29-19; internet www.chukotka.org.

Chairman of the District Duma: VASILII N. NAZARENKO, 689000 Chukot AOk, Anadyr, ul. Otke 29; tel. (42722) 2-93-50; fax (42722) 2-93-51; e-mail duma@anadyr.ru; internet dumachao.anadyr.ru.

Chief Representative of the Chukot Autonomous Okrug in the Russian Federation: ALEKSANDR V. MOSKALENKO, 119034 Moscow, M. Kursovoi per. 4; tel. (495) 502-97-30; fax (495) 925-82-27.

Head of Anadyr City Administration: ANDREI G. SHCHEGOLKOV, 689000 Chukot AOk, Anadyr, ul. Lenina 45; tel. (42722) 2-21-02; fax (42722) 2-22-16; internet adm.anadyr.ru.

Bibliography

Aldis, A., and McDermott, R. (Eds). *Russian Military Reform, 1992–2002*. London, Frank Cass, 2003.

Andrews, C. M., and Mitrokhin, V. *The Sword and the Shield: The Mitrokhin Archive and the Secret History of the KGB*. New York, Basic Books, 1999.

Applebaum, A. *Gulag: A History*. London, Allen Lane, 2003.

Babchenko, A. *How Free is the Russian Media?* Abingdon, Routledge, 2008.

Baev, P. *Russian Energy Policy and Military Power: Putin's Quest for Greatness*. Abingdon, Routledge, 2008

Baker, P., and Glasser, S. *Kremlin Rising: Vladimir Putin's Russia and the End of Revolution*. New York, Simon & Schuster, 2005.

Barany, Z. *Democratic Breakdown and the Decline of the Russian Military*. Princeton, Princeton University Press, 2007.

Bellamy, C. *Absolute War: Soviet Russia in the Second World War: a Modern History*. London, Macmillan, 2007.

Berlin, I. *The Soviet Mind: Russian Culture Under Communism*. Washington, DC, Brookings Institution Press, 2004.

Blanch, L. *The Sabres of Paradise: Conquest and Vengeance in the Caucasus*. London, I. B. Tauris, 2004.

Boobbyer, P. *The Stalin Era*. London, Routledge, 2000.

Bradshaw, M. *New Economic Geography of Russia*. Abingdon, Routledge Curzon, 2008.

Braithwaite, R. *Moscow 1941: A City and Its People at War*. London, Profile, 2007.

Carrère d'Encausse, H. *The Russian Syndrome: One Thousand Years of Political Murder*. Hadleigh, Holmes & Meier, 1994.

Cheterian, V. *War and Peace in the Caucasus: Russia's Troubled Frontier*. London, C. Hurst and Co, 2008.

Clarke, S. *The Development of Capitalism in Russia*. Abingdon, Routledge, 2006.

Colton, T. J., and Holmes, S. (Eds). *The State After Communism: Governance in the New Russia*. Lanham, MD, Rowman & Littlefield, 2006.

Conquest, R. *The Great Terror: A Reassessment*. London, Pimlico, 1992.

De Madariaga, I. *Ivan the Terrible*. New Haven, CT, Yale University Press, 2005.

Duncan, P. S. *Russian Messianism: Third Rome, Revolution, Communism and After*. London, Routledge, 2000.

Dunlop, J. B. *Russia Confronts Chechnya: Roots of a Separatist Conflict*. Cambridge, Cambridge University Press, 1998.

Felshtinsky, Y. and Pribylovsky V. *The Age of Assassins: the Rise and Rise of Vladimir Putin*. London, Gibson Square, 2008.

Figes, O. *A People's Tragedy: The Russian Revolution 1891–1924*. London, Jonathan Cape, 1996.

The Whisperers: Private Life in Stalin's Russia. London, Allen Lane, 2007.

Fitzpatrick, S. *The Russian Revolution*, 2nd edn. Oxford, Oxford University Press, 1994.

Gaddy, C. G., and Ickes, B. W. *Russia's Virtual Economy*. Washington, DC, Brookings Institution Press, 2002.

Gall, C., and de Waal, T. *Chechnya: Calamity in the Caucasus*. New York, New York University Press, 1998.

Gnevko, V. A. *Innovative Development of Russian Regions: Challenges and Goals*. Washington, DC, American University, 2007.

Goldman, M, I. *Petrostate: Putin, Power, and the New Russia*. New York, New York University Press, 2008.

Hale, H. E. *Why Not Parties in Russia? Democracy, Federalism and the State*. Cambridge, Cambridge University Press, 2005.

Hardt, J. P. (Ed.). *Russia's Uncertain Economic Future*. Armonk, NY, M. E. Sharpe, 2002.

Herspring, D. R. (Ed.). *Putin's Russia: Past Imperfect, Future Uncertain*, 2nd edn. Lanham, MD, Rowman & Littlefield, 2004.

Hosking, G. *Russia: People and Empire 1552–1917*. HarperCollins, London, 1997.

Russia and the Russians. Harmondsworth, Penguin, 2001.

Hughes, L. *Peter the Great: A Biography*. New Haven, CT, Yale University Press, 2002.

Ivanov, I. *The New Russian Diplomacy*. Washington, DC, Brookings Institution Press, 2002.

Kahn, J. *Federalism, Democratization and the Rule of Law in Russia*. Oxford, Oxford University Press, 2002.

Khasbulatov, R. *The Struggle for Russia: Power and Change in the Democratic Revolution*. London, Routledge, 1993.

Kirschenbaum, L. *The Legacy of the Siege of Leningrad, 1941-1995*. Cambridge, Cambridge University Press, 2006.

Klein, L. R., and Pomer, M. (Eds). *The New Russia: Transition Gone Awry*. Palo Alto, CA, Stanford University Press, 2002.

Konitzer, A. *Voting for Russia's Governors: Regional Elections and Accountability Under Yeltsin and Putin*. Woodrow Wilson Center Press Series. Baltimore, MD, Johns Hopkins University Press, 2006.

Krickus, R. J. *The Kaliningrad Question*. Lanham, MD, Rowman & Littlefield, 2002.

Kuchins, A. (Ed.). *Russia After the Fall*. Washington, DC, Carnegie Endowment for International Peace, 2002.

Liebich, A. *From the Other Shore: Russian Social Democracy after 1921*. Cambridge, MA, Harvard University Press, 1997.

Lieven, A. *Chechnya: Tombstone of Russian Power*. New Haven, CT, Yale University Press, 1998.

Litvinenko, A. *Allegations: Selected Works by Alexander Litvinenko*. Berkshire, Aquilion Ltd, 2007.

Lucas, E. *The New Cold War: the Future of Russia and the Threat to the West*, New York, Palgrave Macmillan, 2008.

Lynch, D. *Russian Peacekeeping Strategies towards the CIS*. London, Macmillan, 1999.

McCauley, M. *Who's Who in Russia since 1900*. London, Routledge, 1997.

McFaul, M. *Russia's Unfinished Revolution: Political Change from Gorbachev to Putin*. Ithaca, NY, Cornell University Press, 2001.

March, L. *The Communist Party in Post-Soviet Russia*. Manchester, Manchester University Press, 2002.

Mickiewicz, E. P. *Television, Power, and the Public in Russia*. Cambridge, Cambridge University Press, 2008.

Mostashari, F. *On the Religious Frontier: Tsarist Russia and Islam in the Caucasus*. London, I. B. Tauris, 2005.

Murray, J. *The Russian Press from Brezhnev to Yeltsin*. Cheltenham, Edward Elgar Publishing, 1994.

Neumann, I. B. *Russia and the Idea of Europe: A Study in Identity and International Relations*. London, Routledge, 1994.

Ostrovski, D. *Muscovy and the Mongols: Cross-cultural Influences on the Steppe Frontier, 1304–1589*. Cambridge, Cambridge University Press, 1998.

Pilkington, H. *Migration, Displacement and Identity in Post-Soviet Russia*. London, Routledge, 1998.

Pipes, R. *A Concise History of the Russian Revolution*. London, Harvill, 1995.

Russia Under the Old Regime. London, Penguin, 1995.

Russian Conservatism and Its Critics: A Study in Political Culture. New Haven, CT, Yale University Press, 2007.

Pitcher, H. *Witnesses of the Russian Revolution*. London, John Murray, 1994.

Politkovskaya, A. *A Dirty War: A Russian Reporter in Chechnya*. London, Harvill, 2001.

A Small Corner of Hell: Dispatches from Chechnya. Chicago, IL, University of Chicago Press, 2007.

A Russian Diary: A Journalist's Final Account of Life, Corruption, and Death in Putin's Russia. London, Random House, 2007.

Pravda, A. (Ed.). *Leading Russia: Putin in Perspective*. Oxford, Oxford University Press, 2005.

Ra'anan, U. (Ed.). *Flawed Succession: Russia's Power Transfer Crises*. Lanham, MD, Lexington Books, 2006.

Reddaway, P., and Orttung, R. W. (Eds). *The Dynamics of Russian Politics: Putin's Reform of Federal-Regional Relations*. Vol 1, Lanham, MD, Rowman & Littlefield, 2004

Reese, R. R. *The Soviet Military Experience*. London, Routledge, 1999.

Roberts, G. *The Soviet Union in World Politics*. London, Routledge, 1998.

Robinson, N. (Ed.). *Institutions and Political Change in Russia*. Basingstoke, Macmillan, 2000.

Rose, R., and Munro, N. *Elections without Order: Russia's Challenge to Vladimir Putin*. Cambridge, Cambridge University Press, 2002.

Ross, C. *Urban Politics and Democratisation in Russia*. Abingdon, Routledge, 2006.

Rumer, E. B. *Russian Foreign Policy Beyond Putin*. Abingdon, Routledge/International Institute for Strategic Studies, 2007.

Russell, J. *Chechnya—Russia's 'War on Terror'*. Abingdon, Routledge, 2007.

Sakwa, R. *Putin: Russia's Choice*. London, Routledge, 2004.

Russian Politics and Society, 4th edn. Abingdon, Routledge, 2008.

Seely, R. *The Russo-Chechen Conflict 1800–2000*. London, Frank Cass, 2001.

Service, R. A. *A History of Twentieth-Century Russia*. Cambridge, MA, Harvard University Press, 1997.

Russia: Experiment With a People: From 1991 to the Present. London, Macmillan, 2002.

Sixsmith, M. *The Litvinenko File: The Life and Death of a Russian Spy*. London, St Martin's Press, 2007.

Smith, S. *Allah's Mountains: The Battle for Chechnya*, 2nd edn. New York, Tauris Parke, 2005.

Steen, A., and Gelman, V. (Eds) *Elites and Democratic Development in Russia*. London, Routledge, 2003.

Szászdi, L. F. *Russian Civil-Military Relations and the Origins of the Second Chechen War*. Lanham, MD, University Press of America, 2008.

Talbott, S. *The Russia Hand: A Memoir of Presidential Diplomacy*. New York, Random House, 2002.

Taylor, B. D. *Politics and the Russian Army: Civil-Military Relations, 1689–2000*. Cambridge, Cambridge University Press, 2003.

Thornton, J. (Ed.). *Russia's Far East: A Region at Risk*. Seattle, WA, University of Washington Press, 2002.

Tishkov, V. *Chechnya: Life in a War-torn Society*. Berkeley, CA, University of California Press, 2004.

Trenin, D. *The End of Eurasia: Russia on the Border between Geopolitics and Globalization*. Washington, DC, Carnegie Endowment for International Peace, 2002.

Varese, F. *The Russian Mafia: Private Protection in a New Market Economy*. Oxford, Oxford University Press, 2001.

Volkov, V. *Violent Entrepreneurs: The Use of Force in the Making of Russian Capitalism*. Ithaca, NY, Cornell University Press, 2002.

Weiler, J. *Human Rights in Russia: A Darker Side of Reform*. Boulder, CO, Lynne Reinner, 2004.

Wood, A. *Stalin and Stalinism*, 2nd edn. London, Routledge, 1990.

The Origins of the Russian Revolution, 2nd edn. London, Routledge, 1993.

Chechnya: The Case for Independence. London, Verso, 2007.

Yakovlev, A. N. *A Century of Violence in Soviet Russia*. New Haven, CT, Yale University Press, 2002.

Also see the Select Bibliography.

TAJIKISTAN

Geography

PHYSICAL FEATURES

The Republic of Tajikistan is situated in the south-east of Central Asia. To the north and west it is bounded by Uzbekistan, and to the north-east by Kyrgyzstan. Its eastern boundary is with the People's Republic of China, while to the south lies Afghanistan. Its territory includes the nominally autonomous viloyat (oblast or region) of Kuhistoni Badakhshon (of which the capital is Khorog), in the east of the country. Tajikistan covers an area of 143,100 sq km (55,251 sq miles).

The terrain is almost entirely mountainous, with more than one-half of the country above 3,000 m. The main agricultural areas are in the lower-lying regions of the south-west (Khatlon Viloyat) and the north-west. The latter region, Soghd (formerly Leninabad) Viloyat, north of mountains that separate it from the rest of the country and surrounding the city of Khujand (Khodzhent—formerly Leninabad), is part of the prosperous Farg'ona (Fergana) basin. The major mountain ranges are the western Tien Shan in the north, the southern Tien Shan in the central region and the Pamirs in the south-east. The highest mountain of Tajikistan, and of the former USSR, Peak Ismail Samani (formerly Peak Communism—7,495 m), is situated in the northern Pamirs. There is a dense river network, which is extensively used to provide hydroelectric power. The major rivers are the upper reaches of the Syr Dar'ya and of the Amu Dar'ya, which forms the southern border with Afghanistan, as the Pyanj. The Zeravshan river flows through the centre of the country. Most settlement is in the valleys of the south-west and the northern areas around Khujand.

CLIMATE

The climate varies considerably according to altitude. The average temperature in January in Khujand (lowland) is −0.9°C (30.4°F); in July the average is 27.4°C (81.3°F). In the southern lowlands the temperature variation is somewhat more extreme. Precipitation is low in the valleys, ranging from 150 mm–250 mm per year. In mountain areas winter temperatures can fall below −45°C (−51°F); the average January temperature in Murgab, in the mountains of south-east Kuhistoni Badakhshon, for example, is −19.6°C (−3.3°F). Levels of rainfall are very low in mountain regions and seldom exceed 60 mm–80 mm per year. Snow and ice, however, can make many parts of the country inaccessible for many months of the year.

POPULATION

In 1992–93, as a result of the civil conflict, many were killed (estimates range from 20,000 to 50,000 or more) and some

600,000 were reckoned to have become refugees. At the census of January 2000 the population numbered 6,127,493. According to official estimates, at mid-2007 the population was 7,130,000, thus the population density was 49.8 per sq km. The largest ethnic group is the Tajiks (79.9% of the population at the 2000 census), followed by Uzbeks (15.3%), Russians (1.1%), Kyrgyz (1.1%), Lakaits (0.8%), Turkmens (0.3%) and Tatars (0.3%). Other ethnic minorities included Kongrats, Arabs, Ukrainians, Germans and Koreans. In 1989 Tajik replaced Russian as the official language of the republic. Tajik belongs to the south-western Iranian group of languages and is closely related to Farsi (Persian). From 1940 the Cyrillic script has been used.

The major religion is Islam. Most Tajiks and Uzbeks follow the Sunni tradition, but the Pamiris are mostly Isma'ilis, members of a Shi'ite sect. There are also representatives of the Russian Orthodox Church and a small minority of Protestant Christian groups. There is a small Jewish community.

The capital is Dushanbe (Stalinabad 1929–61), which is situated in the west of the country, and had a population of 553,000 in mid-2007, including the suburbs, according to UN estimates. Khujand, to the north, is Tajikistan's second largest city (with a population of 147,400 in January 2002). Important regional centres are the towns of Qurgonteppa (Kurgan-Tyube) and Kulob (Kulyab), in Khatlon Viloyat to the south of Dushanbe. In 2005 only 26.4% of the population lived in urban areas, according to official data.

Chronology

7th century: The Arabs, the latest non-Iranian (Persian) invaders of the area, conquered and converted to Islam the peoples of the great 'Silk Road' cities (notably Samarqand and Buxoro—Bukhara), anciently the provinces of Sogdiana and Bactria.

8th century: The Persic, islamicized urban dwellers began to be identifiable as a distinct Tajik people, distinguished from their Turkic neighbours.

16th century: The Turkic Uzbek people were established as the rulers of the previously Tajik cities and were overlords of the Tajik clans of modern Tajikistan; a variety of khanates,

notably those based in the cities of Bukhara, Samarqand and Kokand, struggled for control in the following centuries.

1868: The Emirate of Bukhara became a Russian protectorate and ceded some of what is northern Tajikistan to the Russian Empire, but retained the central and southern regions.

1876: The Khanate of Qoqand, conquered by the Russians in 1866, was abolished and parts of northern Tajikistan and the Eastern Pamir were incorporated into the Russian Empire.

1895: Russia acquired the Western Pamir, after it and the United Kingdom defined their spheres of influence in Afghanistan.

November 1917: Khujand (later renamed Leninabad until 1991) fell to the Bolsheviks, mainly helped by soviets of Slavs, but there were also Tajik groups such as the Union of Muslim Workers; most of the rest of north and east Tajikistan was under Bolshevik control by the end of the next year.

September 1920: The Emir of Bukhara was driven from his city by the Bolsheviks, but his supporters retained control of much of the south and centre of modern Tajikistan for another two years, with the help of fierce *basmachi* resistance, some of which lasted until the 1930s.

15 March 1925: A Tajik Autonomous Soviet Socialist Republic (ASSR) was formed, with its capital at Dushanbe (called Stalinabad 1929–61), by uniting parts of the old Turkestan ASSR and eastern territories of the Bukhara People's Soviet Republic.

1927: It was decided to replace the Arabic script with a Latin alphabet for the Tajik language.

16 October 1929: The Tajik ASSR, now including the territory of Khujand, became a full Union Republic and no longer part of the Uzbek Soviet Socialist Republic (SSR).

1940: A Cyrillic script replaced the Latin one.

1978: Amid increasing Islamic influence, there were reports of anti-Russian riots in Tajikistan.

1985: The former republican premier, Rakhmon Nabiyev, was replaced as leader of the Communist Party of Tajikistan (CPT) by Kakhar Makkhamov, who criticized his predecessor and acknowledged the economic problems of Tajikistan.

1989: Increasing nationalism was evidenced by a law making Tajik the state language and by ethnic clashes.

11 February 1990: Nationalist violence in Dushanbe led to 22 deaths.

March 1990: Elections to the Supreme Soviet (Supreme Council) produced an overwhelmingly communist legislature; voting took place under a state of emergency prompted by rioting the previous month, after which the leadership became less tolerant of dissent.

19 March 1990: The Deputy Chairman of the Council of Ministers and the Minister of Culture were dismissed for their alleged role in an attempt to overthrow the Government in February.

25 August 1990: The Tajik Supreme Soviet proclaimed the Republic's independence, suspended all USSR legislation that contravened Tajikistan's sovereign rights, and asserted the Republic's right to secede from the USSR.

November 1990: Makkhamov was elected to the new post of President of the Republic by the Supreme Soviet, opposed only by Nabiyev.

17 March 1991: In an all-Union referendum on the future of the USSR, 90% of the participating electorate favoured a 'renewed federation'.

31 August 1991: Mass demonstrations forced the resignation of President Makkhamov, who had failed to condemn the abortive coup in Moscow, the Russian and Soviet capital. Demonstrations continued into the following month, organized by the opposition: the nationalist Rastokhez (Rebirth) movement; the secular, Westernized Democratic Party of Tajikistan (DPT); and the Islamic Renaissance Party (IRP).

9 September 1991: The Supreme Soviet declared the independence of the renamed Republic of Tajikistan.

22 September 1991: Conceding the demands of the continuing demonstrations, the Chairman of the Supreme Council and acting Head of State, Kadriddin Aslonov, banned the CPT and nationalized its assets. The next day the Supreme Council rescinded his decree, declared a state of emergency and replaced Aslonov with Nabiyev.

2 October 1991: The Supreme Council reimposed the ban on the CPT (known as the Socialist Party, September 1991–February 1992), after Nabiyev had conceded to key opposition demands some days previously. The IRP was legalized and the state of emergency ended.

24 November 1991: Nabiyev (who had resigned as Head of State on 6 October to contest the presidential election) won 57% of the votes cast, compared with 30% for his main rival, the opposition-backed liberal Davlat Khudonazarov.

21 December 1991: Tajikistan and 10 other former Soviet republics declared the foundation of the Commonwealth of Independent States (CIS), thereby finally dissolving the USSR.

March 1992: Opposition demonstrations were provoked by President Nabiyev's dismissal of prominent sympathizers of the opposition, the Islamic and democratic elements of which were co-ordinated into a united front largely through the efforts of the Chief *Qazi*, Haji Akbar Turajonzoda.

3 May 1992: Pro-communist counter-demonstrators engaged in the first armed conflicts with the opposition supporters; this marked the start of the civil war.

6 May 1992: Nabiyev and the opposition agreed a new Government of National Reconciliation including eight opposition ministers. Peace was secured in Dushanbe, but there was fighting in the south as pro-communist forces based in Kulob (Kulyab) formed militias to harass the opposition.

7 September 1992: Dispossessed, captured and threatened by demonstrators supporting the Islamic-democratic parties, President Nabiyev resigned and his powers were assumed by the legislative Chairman, Akbarsho Iskandarov. The latter supported the continuing coalition Government, but the premier, Akbar Mirzoyev, resigned and was replaced by a Khujand communist, Abdumalik Abdullojonov.

25 October 1992: Safarli Kenjayev, leader of a southern militia, was expelled from Dushanbe, having attempted to proclaim himself head of state. He then placed the city under siege.

10 November 1992: With civil war still raging, and having agreed to a session of the Supreme Council, Iskandarov and the Government resigned.

27 November 1992: Having convened in Khujand, the Supreme Council instituted a communist reaction by abolishing the presidency and appointing a Kulyabi, Emomali Rakhmonov, as its Chairman (Head of State) and dismissing all opposition figures from the Government.

10 December 1992: The pro-communist Kulyabi militias seized control of the capital; there were allegations of widespread atrocities against supporters of the Islamic-democratic opposition, most of the leaders of which fled into exile or to the eastern mountains.

22 January 1993: A collective security treaty signed by Tajikistan, Kazakhstan, Kyrgyzstan, Russia and Uzbekistan marked the end of formal CIS neutrality in the civil war.

21 June 1993: The Supreme Court banned four political parties, including the IRP and the DPT, having found the organizations guilty of illegally establishing militias, fomenting civil conflict and murdering or abducting legislators.

23 May 1993: A bilateral treaty between Tajikistan and Russia re-emphasized the latter's concern for the former's southern borders, now that the armed Tajikistani opposition had fled to Afghanistan (estimates for the number of civil-war dead ranged between 20,000 and 100,000, and the number of refugees was put at more than 800,000).

July 1993: Russia's concerns at Tajikistani opposition incursions increased after a number of its border troops were killed; both Tajikistan and Afghanistan complained to the UN about border violations.

December 1993: Abdullojonov resigned as Prime Minister and was replaced by Abdujalil Samadov.

5–8 January 1994: Tajikistan's introduction of the new Russian rouble effectively formalized its economic subjection to Russia.

18 September 1994: Government and rebel negotiators agreed to a temporary cease-fire. The cease-fire was eventually implemented in late October (and extended several times), although it was only observed sporadically.

6 November 1994: Rakhmonov won the country's first direct presidential election, securing 58% of the votes cast, defeating Abdullojonov. A simultaneous plebiscite approved the new Constitution. In the following month Jamshed Karimov became Chairman of the Council of Ministers.

26 February 1995: A majority of pro-Rakhmonov candidates was elected to a new legislature, the Supreme Assembly; despite reports that they had sought legalization, the IRP and the DPT did not contest the elections, to which the Organization for Security and Co-operation in Europe (OSCE) refused to send observers.

10 May 1995: Tajikistan introduced its own currency, the rouble. Later in the month President Rakhmonov met Sayed Abdullo Nuri, the leader of the IRP, in Kabul, Afghanistan (they met again in July in Tehran, Iran), although at subsequent negotiations the opposition refused to extend the cease-fire (this was eventually agreed for a further six months in August).

June 1995: The DPT leader, Shodman Yusuf, was criticized for accommodation with the Government and declared deposed; a more intransigent faction elected Jumaboy Niyazov as its leader, and he participated in the armed opposition's negotiations with the Government. The Yusuf faction had been permitted to register as the DPT with the Ministry of Justice by 1996.

September 1995: Some 300 people were reported to have been killed in fighting in Kurgan-Tyube.

21 January 1996: The Chief Mufti of Tajikistan, Fatkhullo Sharifzoda, was assassinated by unidentified killers; a strong supporter of the Government, his death was blamed on the IRP, which denied responsibility.

27 January 1996: Makhmoud Khudoberdiyev, the leader of one of the anti-Government military brigades involved in the September disturbances, took control of Kurgan-Tyube, claiming loyalty to the President, but alleging government corruption. Likewise, the previous day, in Tursan-Zade, another military commander, Ibodullo Boitmatov, began a revolt, to demand the resignation of senior government figures.

7 February 1996: Under pressure from Khudoberdiyev and Boitmatov, and following the dismissal of three senior government officials, Karimov resigned as premier; Yakhyo Azimov was appointed to be the new Chairman of the Council of Ministers.

19 July 1996: A five-month cease-fire agreement between government and opposition negotiators, mediated by the UN, was signed in Aşgabat, Turkmenistan, although with little discernible effect on the fighting.

23 December 1996: At a meeting in Moscow, President Rakhmonov and Sayed Abdullo Nuri agreed to form a National Reconciliation Council (NRC), to be headed by a representative of the United Tajik Opposition (UTO).

February 1997: At peace talks held in Iran, under UN auspices, it was agreed that the NRC would have 26 seats, divided equally between the Government and the UTO.

30 April 1997: President Rakhmonov was wounded when a grenade was thrown at his motorcade in Khujand; the UTO denied any involvement in the assassination attempt.

27 June 1997: The five-year civil war was formally ended when the provisions of the December 1996 peace agreement were confirmed by the General Agreement on Peace and National Accord in Tajikistan, signed in Moscow.

7–10 July 1997: Nuri was elected Chairman of the NRC at its inaugural session; an amnesty was granted whereby UTO fighters would be permitted to return to Tajikistan.

August 1997: The new Chief Mufti of Tajikistan, Amonullo Nematzoda, was kidnapped by Rizvon Sadirov, the brother of a rebel captured by government troops in March; the Mufti was freed when the Government decided to release several of Sadirov's supporters, although he himself was later killed by government forces.

12 March 1998: Six people, including the brother of Abdullojonov, were sentenced to death for their part in the attempted assassination of President Rakhmonov.

18 April 1998: President Rakhmonov was elected Chairman of the People's Democratic Party of Tajikistan (PDPT).

26 October 1998: At a meeting of the NRC, Nuri announced that Rakhmonov had agreed to grant the UTO a further 19 senior government positions.

4–7 November 1998: Fighting took place around Khujand, in what was considered to be the most violent uprising since the signature of the peace accord. Forces loyal to Makhmoud Khudoberdiyev seized the police and security headquarters and a nearby airport. Up to 300 people were killed. Criminal proceedings were initiated against the alleged instigators, who included Khudoberdiyev, former Prime Minister Abdulmalik Abdullojonov, his brother and former Mayor of Khujand, Abdughani Abdullojonov, and former Vice-President Narzullo Dustov.

17 June 1999: Following the UTO's withdrawal from the NRC late the previous month, President Rakhmonov and Nuri met and agreed a series of deadlines for the resolution of the differences that had prompted the UTO to threaten to suspend its participation in the NRC.

3 August 1999: The UTO announced that the integration of its fighters into the regular armed forces had been completed; in response, President Rakhmonov revoked a ban on opposition parties and their media, in force since 1993, in accordance with the agreement made in June.

26 September 1999: A national referendum took place on 27 proposed amendments to the 1994 Constitution, including the formation of a bicameral legislature, the Majlisi Oli, the extension of the presidential term of office from five years to seven, and the right to form religion-based political parties. Some 92% of the electorate were believed to have participated in the referendum, of whom 72% voted in favour of the amendments.

October 1999: Around 1,000 anti-Government rebels entered Tajikistan from Uzbekistan, straining relations between the two countries; however, many had left by November, following mediation by the UTO.

18 October 1999: The UTO again suspended its participation in the NRC, alleging that the Government was not acknowledging its demands.

6 November 1999: Rakhmonov won 97% of the votes cast in a presidential election contested by one other candidate; the participation rate was reportedly 99%. The OSCE refused to send observers to monitor the election, owing to widespread allegations of malpractice.

3 December 1999: The DPT was re-registered.

20 December 1999: A new cabinet was installed, headed by Akil Akilov.

27 February 2000: Elections were held to the new lower chamber of parliament, the Majlisi Namoyandagon (Assembly of Representatives); the PDPT was reported to have won 64.5% of the votes cast and to have secured 45 of the 63 seats available. The CPT took some 20.6% of the votes (13 seats), and the IRP (now restyled the Islamic Rebirth Party) 7.5% (two seats). Both the OSCE and opposition parties claimed that there had been electoral malpractice. A further round of voting took place on 12 March.

23 March 2000: Indirect elections to the Majlisi Milliy (National Assembly) took place for the first time. (Of the 33 members, eight are appointed by the President of the Republic.) A government reorganization had already taken place earlier in the month. The NRC was dissolved, having witnessed the elections, thereby fulfilling the final condition of the 1997 peace agreement.

15 May 2000: The mandate of the UN Mission of Observers in Tajikistan (UNMOT), approved in December 1994, expired.

30 October 2000: The Government introduced a new currency, the somoni, to replace the Tajik rouble.

18 April 2001: The Supreme Court imposed long prison sentences on three people for their role in the attempted coup of 1998.

2 May 2001: The IRP claimed that some of its members had been persecuted on the pretext of belonging to a banned movement seeking the restoration of an international Islamic Caliphate, Hizb-ut-Tahrir, and had been falsely accused of illegally storing weapons.

8 September 2001: The Minister of Culture, Abdurakhim Rakhimov, was assassinated.

16 September 2001: Russian troops along the Tajik–Afghan border were put on high alert in anticipation of US-led military strikes against Afghanistan.

8 October 2001: The Ministry of Foreign Affairs issued a statement in support of the US-led aerial bombardment of Afghanistan.

12 December 2001: It was reported that a court in Khujand had convicted 10 men on charges of treason, terrorism and sedition, relating to the November 1998 insurrection, and sentenced them to between eight and 25 years' imprisonment.

20 February 2002: Tajikistan joined the North Atlantic Treaty Organization (NATO)'s 'Partnership for Peace' programme of military co-operation.

12 March 2002: The Agreement on Public Accord in Tajikistan, signed in March 1996 by pro-Government political parties and non-governmental organizations to demonstrate support for the peace process, was extended indefinitely; the accord was signed by a representative of the IRP for the first time.

17 May 2002: Tajikistan and the People's Republic of China signed a border agreement, according to which Tajikistan ceded 1,000 sq km of disputed territory to China.

11 June 2002: Abdulaziz Khamidov, the former governor of Soghd Viloyat (region) was convicted of embezzlement and involvement in the 1996 assassination attempt on Rakhmonov, and sentenced to 15 years' imprisonment.

9 September 2002: The first independent radio station began broadcasting in Dushanbe.

January 2003: President Rakhmonov implemented a wide-ranging reshuffle of the Council of Ministers, state agencies, local government, state-owned joint-stock companies and the judiciary.

28 April 2003: Representatives from Armenia, Belarus, Kazakhstan, Kyrgyzstan, Russia and Tajikistan formally inaugurated the successor to the Collective Security Treaty, a new regional defence organization known as the Collective Security Treaty Organization.

22 June 2003: Some 96% of the electorate took part in a referendum on proposed amendments to the Constitution, which were approved by 93% of the voters. The amendments provided, *inter alia*, for the extension of judges' terms of office from five to 10 years, the removal of references to religious parties from the Constitution, and the abolition of the right to both free health care and higher education. Significantly, approval of the proposals would also enable President Rakhmonov to stand for two further terms of office when his term expired in 2006.

6 October 2003: It was reported that the Deputy Chairman of the IRP, Shamsiddin Shamsiddinov, was to be charged with a number of criminal activities, including treason. He was sentenced to 16 years' imprisonment in January 2004.

January 2004: Rakhmonov effected a number of high-level government changes. Among the appointments made, Khairinisso Mavlonova replaced Nigina Sharopova as Deputy Chairman of the Council of Ministers, and Jurabek Nurmakhmadov was appointed as Minister of Energy, in place of Abdullo Yorov.

25 May 2004: Tajikistan and the People's Republic of China officially opened the Kulma passage between the two countries.

16 October 2004: Following a meeting with Rakhmonov in Sochi (Russia) in June, President Vladimir Putin of Russia visited Tajikistan, where the two Presidents agreed that Russia would station 5,000 troops at a permanent base in Tajikistan and would retain rights over the use of the Nurek space-monitoring station. Russia, in return, was to cancel nearly US $300m. of Tajikistan's debt, and provide further investment in Tajikistani industry.

27 February and 13 March 2005: Two rounds of elections to the Majlisi Namoyandagon were held, contested by six political parties. The PDPT secured a total of 52 of the 63 seats available (receiving 74% of the votes cast nation-wide on the basis of party lists). The CPT won four seats (with 13% of the nation-wide vote), and the IRP two (8%); nominally independent candidates secured five seats. Some 92.6% of the electorate reportedly participated in the elections, which, according to the OSCE, as well as opposition parties, were marred by malpractice. The newly elected Majlisi Namoyandagon held its first session on 17 March 2005.

24 March 2005: Elections for the 25 indirectly elected seats in the Majlisi Milliy took place; the eight presidential nominees were announced the following day. The first session of the new chamber convened on 15 April.

1 September 2005: Russia completed the transfer (commenced in December 2004) of the Tajik–Afghan border to Tajikistan's jurisdiction.

5 October 2005: The Chairman of the DPT, Makhmadruzi Iskandarov, was sentenced to 23 years' imprisonment for banditry, terrorism and embezzlement.

9 August 2006: Nuri, the leader of the IRP, died; he was succeeded by his deputy, Muhiddin Kabiri.

11 August 2006: Lt-Gen. Gaffor Mirzoyev, the former commander of the presidential guard, was sentenced to life imprisonment, having been found guilty of charges of terrorism and plotting to overthrow the Government.

6 November 2006: President Rakhmonov secured re-election to a third seven-year term in office, with 79.3% of the ballot; Rakhmonov's closest rival, Olimjon Boboyev (Party of Economic Reforms), attracted just 6.2% of the votes. Turn-out was reported at over 90% of the registered electorate, prompting allegations that voting figures had been artificially inflated.

26 January 2008: President Rakhmonov implemented a government reorganization, and there were widespread personnel changes in many state institutions, including the

National Bank, organs of local government and a number of state committees.

20 March 2007: President Rakhmonov announced that he had abandoned the Russian-style '-ov' suffix from his surname and that henceforth he was to be known by the Tajik form of his name, Rakhmon, and decreed that Tajik babies be traditionally named. He also abolished certain school holidays and traditions associated with the Soviet period.

6 October 2007: Tajikistan assumed the rotational chairmanship of the Eurasian Economic Community (EURASEC) at a meeting in Dushanbe.

14 November 2007: It was reported that the central government office in Dushanbe had been damaged in a bomb explo-

sion, in which one civilian had been killed; the perpetrators of the attack remained unknown.

4 April 2008: The Chairman of the National Bank announced that Tajikistan would repay US \$47.7m. to the IMF, after the Fund discovered that it had been supplied with false financial information in order to obtain credits.

22 September 2008: The Tajikistan authorities announced criminal proceedings against a prominent opposition journalist and leader of popular movement Vatandor, Dodojon Atovulloyev, on charges of public incitement to violence and inciting the President.

History

Dr JOHN ANDERSON

Revised for this edition by Dr MATTEO FUMAGALLI

EARLY HISTORY

The territories of Sogdiana and Bactria, which covered what is now Tajikistan and parts of modern Uzbekistan, were part of the Persian Empire until their conquest by Alexander II ('the Great') of Macedon in the fourth century BC. In subsequent centuries the region was dominated by various nomadic confederations, until coming under Arab control at the end of the seventh century AD. Under the caliphate, the western Iranian branch of the Persian (Iranian) language came to dominate, and within one century there had emerged a distinctive urban-based ethnic group known as the Tajiks. The Tajik cities of Samarkand and Bukhara were great centres of Muslim art and learning, although by the 16th century the Turkic-speaking Uzbeks had gained political dominance over the region. From this period onwards Tajik groupings were subordinate to Uzbek rule, exchanging it for that of the Russian tsars in the late 19th century.

SOVIET TAJIKISTAN

In 1918 the Bolsheviks formally incorporated northern Tajikistan into the Turkestan Autonomous Soviet Socialist Republic (ASSR) within the Russian Federation, but it took until 1921 to establish real control over the region. Moreover, in the south-eastern parts of Tajikistan the imposition of Soviet rule proved much harder, for here were to be found some of the most militant strongholds of the *basmachi*, local guerrilla fighters, who resisted the efforts of the Red Army until the mid-1920s. Many of them later fled to Afghanistan. The administrative fate of Tajikistan became entangled with conflicts among Central Asian élites, with the dominant influence of Bukharan revolutionaries leading to the initial formation of a new Tajik ASSR within the Uzbek Soviet Socialist Republic (SSR) in 1925. Four years later the region of Khujand (Khodzhent) of Uzbekistan was added to the ASSR, which then acquired its own status as an SSR as well as that of full Union Republic of the USSR. Even so, this left the historically Tajik cities of Samarkand and Bukhara outside the republic, as well as a substantial Tajik population in Afghanistan. Conversely, the western parts of the new republic, as well as the old Khujand region, had substantial Uzbek minorities.

Soviet rule initially brought little change to the rural areas of Tajikistan, but from the late 1920s the collectivization of agriculture severely disrupted the traditional activity of cattle-breeding, while those described as representatives of the old order were subject to repression. In the cities the small indigenous élite that had opted for co-operation with the Bolsheviks was removed, and ethnic Russians were given many of the main positions.

After the Second World War some changes were made. In the economic sphere this entailed the dramatic increase in the cultivation of cotton in the southern areas. To provide labour for this expansion, the period from the 1940s to the mid-1960s witnessed a series of population resettlements, often forced, as whole villages were shifted from the north and east of the republic to the southern Kulob (Kulyab) and Qurghonteppa (Kurgan-Tyube, or Kurgan Teppe) regions. This created tensions between the new, dislocated settlers, many from the Garm raion (district), to the north-east of Dushanbe, who often found themselves in areas with few amenities, and older residents, many of them Uzbeks, who resented the influx of immigrants from the north. The other change that was to have consequences for the future was the Soviet regime's changing personnel policy. After the Second World War some effort was made to increase the number of ethnic Tajiks in the local communist administration, but in practice this meant that the Tajikistani leadership came to be dominated by representatives of the northern Leninabad Viloyat (region, as Khujand Viloyat had been renamed), a development that fostered resentment in other parts of the country. Whether the appointment of local cadres served to reinforce Soviet control, however, was less clear. There were frequent complaints that, under indigenous élites, central directives were all too often ignored or distorted, especially those that sought to eliminate past cultural traditions. Nowhere was this clearer than in the religious sphere, when the mass closure of mosques under the leadership of Stalin (Iosif Dzhugashvili, 1924–53) in the USSR left the officially registered number of mosques in the republic at less than 20. By the time of Leonid Brezhnev's tenure as Soviet leader (1964–82), however, it was well known that every village and district had a functioning place of worship, while thousands of self-appointed imams, often perpetuating a family tradition, operated with the acquiescence of local officials. In the early 1980s, following the Soviet invasion of Afghanistan at the end of 1979, there were repeated reports of growing Islamist sentiment, possibly exaggerated by the state, and also of occasional manifestations of anti-Russian feeling.

This growing independence was threatened by the accession in 1985, as Soviet leader, of Mikhail Gorbachev, who sought to bring Central Asia under much closer central control. The First Secretary of the Communist Party of Tajikistan (CPT), Rakhmon Nabiyev, was accused of corruption and nepotism and replaced by Qahhor Mahkhamov. Towards the end of the 1980s there was also some relaxation of censorship, which permitted greater discussion of the cultural heritage of the nation, in particular of its Iranian and Islamic connections. This led to the creation of the cultural organization Rastokhez (Rebirth). Rastokhez took the lead in agitating for the language law enacted at the end of 1989. This established Tajik as the primary medium of communication in state and educational establishments in the republic. In March 1990 strictly controlled elections to the republican legislature, the Supreme Soviet (Supreme Council), produced a parliamentary body in which 94% of the deputies were communists. Following the example of other Union Republics, Tajikistan declared its sovereignty in August 1990, and towards the end of the year parliament elected Mahkhamov as the republic's first executive President. During the August 1991 coup attempt in Moscow, the Russian and Soviet capital, Tajikistan's leadership effectively supported the plotters, and, with the failure of the *putsch*, Mahkhamov was forced to resign as President. On 9 September the Supreme Soviet declared the independence of Tajikistan, and two weeks later, against a background of demonstrations in the major cities, the acting Head of State, the Chairman of the parliament, Kadriddin Aslonov, formally banned the CPT. Aslonov had not, however, reckoned with the communist-controlled Supreme Soviet, which sought to relegalize the Party and succeeded in replacing him with Nabiyev, who served as the acting President until elections could be held on 24 November. Nabiyev won 57% of the votes cast, compared with the 30% won by the film-maker Davlat Khudonazarov, the candidate supported by the opposition. Although there was some evidence of electoral fraud, Nabiyev took office in early December, and it was under his presidency that Tajikistan acceded to the Commonwealth of Independent States (CIS) on 21 December and became independent at the end of the year.

INDEPENDENT TAJIKISTAN

Civil War

Independence failed to bring an end to conflict in Tajikistan. By early 1992 the united opposition, which mobilized Islamists, nationalists and democrats, was able seriously to challenge Nabiyev's regime, bringing thousands of demonstrators on to the streets of the capital. In response, the Government organized counter-rallies, bringing a considerable number of demonstrators from the southern Kulob region to the capital and then issuing them with armaments. In early September the opposition forced the resignation of Nabiyev and effectively took power at the centre. Some attempt was made to conciliate the old establishment, with the interim Head of State (Chairman of the Supreme Soviet), Akbarsho Iskandarov, recruiting the northerner Abdumalik Abdullojonov as Prime Minister (Chairman of the Council of Ministers), but the country rapidly disintegrated into a state of civil war.

The centre of resistance to the new regime came from the Kulob region, where there soon appeared a series of armed militias, the most powerful being that associated with a former criminal, Sanjak Safarov. While such forces quickly established a brutal ascendancy in the south, another armed group, led by a former parliamentary speaker, Safarali Kenjayev, attempted an attack on the capital in October 1992. Thereafter, along with other militias, Kenjayev's troops maintained a blockade of Dushanbe. By the end of the year the Government had collapsed and the old order appeared to have been restored, albeit with the balance of power resting firmly with the armed Kulyabis (Kulobis) of the south rather than with the traditional cadres of the northern Leninabad province (Viloyat).

Although some of the coalition Government remained, notably the Prime Minister, Abdullojonov, its leading supporters fled abroad before the end of the year. Haji Akbar Turajonzoda, the influential *qazi* (supreme religious judge) of Tajikistan, who, while sympathetic to the opposition, had sought to exercise a moderating influence during the struggles of the previous year, also went into exile. Some figures identified with the Islamist-democratic opposition chose to remain, but many disappeared during the period of terror that followed. Armed groups ranged around the south and centre of Tajikistan, looting and in many cases killing people whose passports revealed them to be from the 'wrong' parts of the country—that is those associated with the opposition.

Explaining the Conflict

The Tajikistan that acquired independence was one in which any sense of national unity was weak, in which the state lacked the capacity to create a sense of common belonging or to resolve conflict, and in which most people identified themselves more strongly with their region or family network than with the new nation state. As a result, in the conflict that broke out in 1992, apparent ideological differences overlaid regional distinctions, while opposition challenges to the regime could, in part, be explained in terms of regional resentments at previous exclusion from power. This was evident in the emergence of political parties in the country.

Leninabad Viloyat, which was renamed Soghd Viloyat in 2000, was traditionally the richest and most powerful region. In the capital, Dushanbe, were the more critical intellectuals who formed Rastokhez. Further south were the Viloyats of Kulob and Qurgonteppa, which were merged to form a new administrative unit, Khatlon Viloyat, in December 1992. Economically poor, dependent largely upon the production of cotton, these regions quickly divided during the civil war. Viloyati Kulob provided the armed units that were to be decisive during the events of 1992 and the legacy of which was to prove disastrous for the country thereafter. Qurgonteppa Viloyat was more fragmented: the resettled people tended to support the Islamist-democratic opposition, while the substantial Uzbek population of the region feared that these often impoverished settlers might prove the basis of a religious fundamentalist threat. In addition, some Tajiks in the region, notably those around the town of Hissar, traditionally enjoyed a role in the communist administration prior to independence and thus tended to support the old regime. To the east of the capital the opposition remained strong, with the Garm raion providing many of the supporters of the Islamic Rebirth Party (IRP). Further east still, in the Kuhistoni Badakhshon (Gornyi Badakhshan) Autonomous Viloyat, the small population of Pamiri mountaineers, followers of the Isma'ili tradition in Shi'ism, felt some degree of hostility towards the old regime, but many remained wary of the increasingly Islamist- and Sunni-dominated opposition.

Although regionalism played a vital role in the conflict, there were ideological tensions at work. The old regime may have used the fundamentalist threat for its own purposes, but there were clearly some among the opposition coalition who favoured giving a greater role to Islam in public life. Prior to the civil war *Qazi* Turajonzoda had repeatedly stressed that years of secularization had rendered all thought of an Islamic state impossible for the foreseeable future. Thus, he, along with the IRP, spoke of the need for the creation of a non-confessional state, but one in which Islam was allowed the freedom to reassert its influence. Within the ranks of the IRP not all shared this moderation, and one of the ironies of the civil war was that, as a consequence of the brutal suppression of opposition that followed the triumph of the Kulyabi militias in late 1992, many opposition activists were forced into exile in Afghanistan, where they were increasingly radicalized by their contacts with local *mujahidin*. (Turajonzoda himself sought exile in Iran.)

RESTORING POLITICAL ORDER

In November 1992 the 'rump' Supreme Council, purged of Islamic, democratic and nationalist elements, elected Emomali Rakhmonov, a Kulyabi, as its Chairman and Head of State, and formally abolished the presidency. Under Rakhmonov the new regime began to assert its authority, beginning with the detention of those opposition supporters who remained and continuing with an effort to gain control of those areas of the country still dominated by opponents of the regime. Within the regime tensions quickly emerged between the Khujand and Kulob élites, the former resentful of the loss of political dominance and the continued instability encouraged by the presence of numerous armed militia groups. The priority for the Khujand *nomenklatura* was to bring an end to the war, so that their traditionally wealthy region could begin the task of economic reconstruction. To this end they tended to be more conciliatory in negotiations with the opposition than the newly dominant Kulyabis. During early 1994 the Rakhmonov administration attempted to legitimize its position further by introducing a draft constitution, which included a proposal to restore the state presidency. On 6 November the people of

Tajikistan went to the polls, where they endorsed the new Constitution and selected a new President. The opposition outside the country had urged a boycott of voting, arguing that without a free press or adequate guarantees of human rights the election would be meaningless. In the event, however, there were two candidates: Rakhmonov and Abdullojonov. Official results reported the rate of participation by voters to be in excess of 90% of the registered electorate, of whom 58.3% voted for Rakhmonov.

A general election followed on 26 February 1995. Once again, all genuine opposition parties were excluded from the contest, although in the approach to the election Abdullojonov's Party of Popular Unity and Accord (PPUA) was granted registration, as were several other parties that favoured the old ruling élite, if not the Kulyabi-dominated Government itself. As during the presidential election, considerable evidence of abuse was reported and Abdullojonov was himself disallowed registration as a candidate. After two rounds of voting a Supreme Assembly of 181 deputies was formed, most coming from the old economic and state apparatus, although about one-quarter had been commanders in the various armed militias that had ensured Kulyabi successes at the end of 1992 and beginning of 1993. Although Rakhmonov tried to ensure some degree of regional representation in the selection of deputy parliamentary speakers, this could not hide the continued dominance of Tajikistan by the representatives of one region, nor could it hope to provide legitimacy in the absence of all genuine opposition.

FOREIGN INVOLVEMENT AND THE SEARCH FOR PEACE

The development of the conflict in Tajikistan from 1992 caused increasing alarm among the country's neighbours, with Uzbekistan's President, Islam Karimov, expressing particular concern. With his own Islamist troubles in the Farg'ona (Fergana) valley area, Karimov feared that unrest might traverse the region and unseat his and other regimes that had not fundamentally changed with independence. For that reason he joined other Central Asian states in seeking to encourage Russia, at the time focusing most of its energies on relations with the West, to take more positive action to prevent the spread of instability. In mid-1992 it became clear that some elements in the Russian 201st Motorized Rifle Division present in Tajikistan had been supplying arms to the Kulyabi militias and often choosing to ignore their atrocities. Towards the end of that year the CIS took the decision to create a peace-keeping force based upon this Division, and at the beginning of 1993 Kazakhstan, Kyrgyzstan, Russia and Uzbekistan formally committed themselves to the defence of Tajikistan's southern borders. Regional leaders feared that the chaos that had engulfed Afghanistan, stemming in large part from the lack of a sense of national unity, might gradually extend into Tajikistan and dissolve the country.

During late 1993 the Russian Minister of Foreign Affairs, Andrei Kozyrev, and other Russian diplomats engaged in intensive 'shuttle' diplomacy in the region, in an effort to find ways of bringing the warring sides together. Successive rounds of regional talks culminated in a meeting in Moscow in December 1996, at which Rakhmonov and Said Abdullo Nuri, the leader of the IRP, agreed to form a National Reconciliation Council (NRC). Serious progress on the details of a settlement was not made until a meeting in Bishkek, Kyrgyzstan, in May 1997, and two further sessions in Moscow in June. Following the last summit, a General Agreement on Peace and National Accord in Tajikistan was signed on 27 June. The accord envisaged: the legalization of the opposition political parties; the creation of the NRC (of which Nuri was elected Chairman in July); the granting of 30% of government posts to the opposition; the holding of elections before the end of 1998; the exchange of prisoners; and the integration of opposition forces into the national army.

UNEASY PEACE AND POLITICAL RECONSTRUCTION

The peace accord appeared to be in jeopardy, however, as rival factions within Tajikistan's armed forces fought for supremacy in the streets of Dushanbe. In January 1998 the delegation of the collection of opposition groups, the United Tajik Opposition (UTO), refused to attend NRC meetings, in protest at the slow pace at which the Government was implementing the peace agreement. In February, however, the government portfolios of labour and employment, the economy and foreign economic relations, and land reclamation and water resources, were formally allocated to UTO members; further appointments followed. Later that month, moreover, Turajonzoda, the deputy leader of the UTO and former *Qazi* of Tajikistan, who had made his return from exile conditional upon his appointment as a deputy premier, was appointed First Deputy Prime Minister with responsibility for relations with members of the CIS. In May, however, the legislature adopted a law banning all religious parties from operating in the country. This contravened the terms of the peace agreement and President Rakhmonov was subsequently obliged to veto the proposed legislation.

Although all opposition forces on Tajikistani territory were said to have sworn allegiance to the Government, many practical problems remained in disarming groups that remained sceptical about the deal. A series of uprisings during 1996–98 (in February 1996, August 1997, October 1997 and November 1998) in the northern Leninabad (Soghd) province caused a new wave of instability. The Tajikistani authorities accused Uzbekistan of fomenting the unrest, and alleged that two former prominent Tajikistani officials—former Prime Minister Abdullojonov and ex-army commander Mahmud Khudoyberdie—had also been involved. Successive amnesties brought most opposition members into conformity, however, with many units integrated (albeit uneasily) into the national army during 1999.

The issue of political parties remained more problematic, as did the constitutional definition of the republic as a secular state, although this was resolved by amendments to the Constitution approved in a referendum in September 1999. These amendments also provided for the election of a new, two-chamber parliament, the Majlisi Oli, and the extension of the presidential term of office to seven years. None the less, problems continued prior to the presidential election, scheduled for 6 November, as the Central Electoral Commission barred three of the challengers to President Rakhmonov, and then at the last moment gave the IRP candidate, Davlat Usmon (Usmonov), permission to stand; Usmon, however, refused to campaign under such conditions. According to official results, almost 97% of those who participated in the polls had voted in favour of Rakhmonov. The incumbent had notably been supported by Turajonzoda, who claimed that the IRP had lost its sense of political direction. Turn-out was reported at 99% of the registered electorate.

Following the election, preparations were begun for parliamentary elections, scheduled for February–March 2000. In December 1999 six parties were formally registered for the election to the lower chamber of parliament, the Majlisi Namoyandagon (Assembly of Representatives), including President Rakhmonov's People's Democratic Party of Tajikistan (PDPT), the CPT, the IRP, Adolatkoh and the Socialist Party of Tajikistan. Campaigning was beset by violence: beatings, kidnappings and murders targeting the political community culminated in the assassination of the Deputy Minister of Security 11 days before the first round of elections, which was held on 27 February 2000. Official election results recorded a participation rate of just over 87%, with 64.5% of the votes secured by the PDPT, 20.6% by the CPT and 7.5% by the IRP, although most observers considered the electoral process to be flawed. The other three parties failed to secure representation under the list system. In the single-member constituencies deputies were elected in 28 of a total of 41 constituencies; the remaining 13 seats were filled in 'run-off' elections on 12 March. Indirect elections to the upper chamber of parliament, the Majlisi Milliy (National Assembly), followed on 23 March. At the end of the month the NRC was dissolved, in accordance with the fulfilment of its mandate.

THE NEW POLITICAL ORDER

The holding of elections in 2000 formally ended the transition period envisaged by the 1997 peace agreement, but only partially resolved the divisions within Tajikistani society. Elements on both sides remained distrustful of their new political allies, and in reality power remained concentrated among a select group of senior officials of the executive. Violence also remained a problem, as armed groups continued to maintain de facto control over some parts of the country. Several assassinations of officials, including that of the administrator of Garm raion in June 2000 and of the First Deputy Minister of Interior Affairs in April 2001, exemplified the persistence of a culture of violence. In March 2002 a public accord agreement, signed in 1996 by pro-Government political parties and non-governmental organizations (NGOs) to express support for the peace process, and renewed in 1999, was extended indefinitely; the accord was signed by a representative of the IRP for the first time.

In 2003 political debate focused on the question of constitutional reform, after Rakhmonov's Government proposed a series of amendments to the existing text. The proposals provided for the abolition of free higher and vocational education and health care, and for judges to serve a 10-year, rather than a five-year, term. More controversial was a proposal to remove references to religious parties from the Constitution, which the main opposition party, the IRP, feared might lead to a ban on its activities. However, at the centre of the debate was a proposal to remove the restriction on the number of terms that the President might remain in office, which could enable Rakhmonov to serve for a further 14 years following the presidential election scheduled to take place in 2006 (see below). For several months the opposition political parties vehemently opposed the proposed changes, and some urged their members to boycott the referendum, scheduled to take place on 22 June 2003. However, the IRP eventually announced that, although it considered the amendments to be unnecessary, it would not strongly oppose the referendum, for fear of undermining the relative stability emerging in the country. Ultimately, the Government claimed that the rate of participation by the electorate was 96%, and that some 93% of votes had approved the proposals, although no international observers monitored the voting, and some commentators suggested than many voters had little real understanding of the referendum's purpose.

During the second half of 2003 the Government appeared increasingly to be placing pressure on potential opponents within its own coalition. Several IRP officials were dismissed, and Shamsuddin Shamsuddinov, the Deputy Chairman of the IRP, and a number of his colleagues were indicted for various alleged crimes, including murder, illegal border-crossing, treason and polygamy. Pressure on opponents continued in the first half of 2004 as senior opposition figures sought to create a new bloc to contest the parliamentary elections due to be held in February 2005. Although amendments to the electoral code approved in June 2004 appeared to have rendered the electoral process more transparent, the opposition and international observers still expressed concerns about inadequate safeguards over the balloting process. There were also concerns that the Government might not permit free press coverage in advance of the elections, as several newspapers were placed under pressure by the authorities following the publication of reports on alleged government corruption or tensions within the coalition. Furthermore, three opposition newspapers were effectively forced out of business in mid-2004 when the Government closed their printing house, ostensibly as a result of tax irregularities.

The elections to the Majlisi Namoyandagon, held in two rounds in February and March 2005, were characterized by increased government control, during both the campaign period and the ballot itself. Only five political parties were permitted to register candidates, and all opposition parties experienced problems with registration. Although the Government's PDPT fielded a substantial number of candidates in both the constituency and party-list sections, the opposition IRP was able to register only 15 list candidates and 20 constituency candidates for the 63 seats. The Democratic Party of Tajikistan (DPT), whose Chairman, Makhmadruzi Iskan-

darov, had been detained in Moscow in December 2004, accused of corruption and involvement in an attack on the Tajikabad region's Ministry of Internal Affairs and prosecutor's offices, was not permitted to register any candidates. Following a very partisan campaign, the governing PDPT took 52 seats, the CPT four and the IRP just two. The remaining seats went to nominal independents, but most of these were closely linked to the central or regional authorities. Almost immediately, the opposition challenged the results, supported by the Organization for Security and Co-operation in Europe, which declared the electoral process to have been flawed. Opposition members initially seemed reluctant to push their protests too far, perhaps wary of resurrecting civil strife, although events in neighbouring Kyrgyzstan during March, in which popular demonstrations effectively led to the overthrow of the Government (see the chapter on Kyrgyzstan), may have encouraged those who wanted to intensify their protests. For its part, the Government implemented measures to suppress foreign-based NGOs, perhaps mindful of their alleged role in upheavals in other former Soviet countries, and further repress the opposition. Several members of the IRP and other parties were imprisoned on charges of hooliganism or embezzlement, which were widely believed to be politically motivated, while the media encountered yet further pressures. Despite this, by mid-2005 the danger of a popular uprising appeared to have faded.

With a presidential election due in November 2006, the administration maintained the pressure on alternative voices, closing down the remaining opposition newspaper by the end of 2005 and continuing to imprison independent editors on nominally criminal charges. Repression was also directed against any potential political opponents, including Iskandarov, who was arrested in Dushanbe in April 2005, having apparently been kidnapped in Moscow, after the Russian authorities released him owing to lack of evidence and refused a request by Tajikistan for his extradition. In October the Supreme Court sentenced him to 23 years' imprisonment for banditry, terrorism and embezzlement, although critics claimed that his only crime was opposing the regime. Other potential opposition leaders faced vilification in the press in 2005–06, a leading activist of the IRP was allegedly murdered while in custody in May 2006, and formerly powerful figures within the regime, including the former commander of the presidential guard, Lt-Gen. Ghaffor Mirzoyev, underwent closed trials that prevented them from giving evidence of official corruption. Following his conviction on charges of terrorism and plotting to overthrow the Government, Mirzoyev was sentenced to life imprisonment in August.

Presidential elections were held according to schedule on 6 November 2006. Rakhmonov secured re-election for a third seven-year term, attracting 79.3% of the vote. His victory was partially attributable to the weak, divided and often harassed nature of the opposition, but the President remained a genuinely popular figure with the public in his own right. Rakhmonov's share of the vote was low by Central Asian standards and it has been suggested that this may have been artificially orchestrated to create a facade of contestation. The primary cause of suspicion was the reported rate of voter participation (over 90%), which was highly unlikely in a country where more than 1m. people (approximately one in six) work abroad. Rakhmonov was, in any case, virtually unchallenged; the IRP decided not to field a candidate, while the opposition DPT and the Social Democratic Party of Tajikistan boycotted the elections insisting that the polls would inevitably be beset by harassment and fraud and consequently would remain neither free nor fair. Of those candidates that did contest the election, Olimjon Boboyev (Party of Economic Reforms) won 6.7% of the vote; Abdukhalim Gafforov (Socialist Party) gained 2.8% and Ismoil Talbakov (CPT) 5.1%. Isolated protests against the elections were reported in some areas of the country, but none of these posed a challenge similar to those that led to the overthrow of the Government in Kyrgyzstan and other post-Soviet countries. Meanwhile, in August 2006 Nuri, one of the dominant figures of Tajikistani politics as leader of the IRP, died after a long period of illness. He was replaced by his deputy, Muhiddin Kabiri, who faced the daunting challenge of regrouping and redefining the party.

SECURITY ISSUES

Drugs-smuggling was a significant problem in Tajikistan in the late 1990s and 2000s, involving government officials, regional figures, as well as Islamist militants. Indeed, in August 2002 the former Deputy Minister of Defence, Col Nikolai Kim, was sentenced to 13 years' imprisonment for participating in drugs-trafficking and embezzlement while in office in 1998. Organized crime also remained a problem: in October 2002 a senior police official was sentenced to 25 years' imprisonment on charges of murder, fraud and extortion. Drugs-smuggling from Afghanistan via Tajikistan persisted, and the infiltration of large quantities of illegal narcotics from Tajikistan into Uzbekistan also continued. With an estimated three-quarters of the world's opium production originating in Afghanistan, it was hardly surprising to see Tajikistan emerging as a major transit point. Equally, given the endemic poverty of the country, where some sources put the average monthly income at around US $10, it was no surprise to find that many Tajikistani peasants were willing to work as drugs-couriers. In consequence, by 2005 many international organizations suggested that dealing with social welfare was as important as police enforcement in trying to curb the drugs trade. Several shoot-outs occurred on the Afghan border during April and May 2006, as drugs-smugglers proved willing to engage in gunfights with officials, and international observers reported that the regional trade in narcotics was growing.

In the early 2000s the problem of insecurity in Tajikistan was exacerbated by the presence of guerrillas from the Islamic Movement of Uzbekistan (IMU). During the Tajikistani civil war, members of the IMU fought alongside UTO militants, but after 1997 relations between the two sides became strained. Representatives of the UTO in the Tajikistani Government were reluctant to upset relations with Uzbekistan by supporting the IMU; at the same time, however, many members of the IRP were sympathetic to its Islamist agenda. In mid-2000 UTO members within the Government attempted to persuade the Uzbek militants to leave Tajikistan, but following IMU incursions into Kyrgyzstan the Tajikistani authorities often failed to prevent militants from crossing into their territory. This, in turn, caused a further deterioration in relations between Uzbekistan and Kyrgyzstan, as the two countries raised concerns about renewed IMU incursions into their countries. Uzbekistan's decision to place landmines along the Tajikistani–Uzbekistani border to prevent IMU infiltration provoked an angry response from the Tajikistani Government. The death of the IMU leader, Jumaboy Khojiyev (Juma Namangoniy), in the US-led military action in Afghanistan that commenced in October 2001, was expected to reduce the threat of the resurgence of radical Islamism in Tajikistan; however, the IMU remained active. Reports in mid-2002 claimed that members of the IMU were attempting to cross the Tajikistani–Afghan border to regroup in eastern Tajikistan. In response to pressure from other Central Asian states, the Tajikistani authorities deported several hundred alleged members of the IMU to Afghanistan in July. In September the Chairman of the Kyrgyz National Security Service reported that a new umbrella grouping—the Islamic Movement of Central Asia—had emerged, incorporating the IMU, Islamist militants from Tajikistan and the separatist Chechen Republic (in Russia), and Uyghur (Uighur) separatists from the Xinjiang Uyghur Autonomous Region of the People's Republic of China, although there was little evidence of any substantial activity on the part of the group in subsequent years.

Regional authorities also expressed concern about the growing influence of the banned transnational, fundamentalist organization Hizb-ut-Tahrir al-Islami (Party of Islamic Liberation), which, in the Central Asian region, was believed to have developed substantial membership in Uzbekistan. The organization, commonly known as Hizb-ut-Tahrir, was committed to creating an Islamic caliphate in Central Asia, and was attracting growing numbers of young people in the Farg'ona valley, which is shared by Kyrgyzstan, Tajikistan and Uzbekistan. In May 2001 the IRP claimed that a number of its members in the northern Soghd Viloyat had been falsely accused of belonging to Hizb-ut-Tahrir and of illegally storing weapons. There were reports that support for Hizb-ut-Tahrir was increasing in 2002–03, and between January 2003 and mid-2004 there were more than 120 arrests of alleged Hizb-ut-Tahrir activists and a series of trials, in which members were sentenced to terms of imprisonment ranging from three to 18 years. In mid-2004 several IRP spokesmen publicly denounced the activities of Hizb-ut-Tahrir, perhaps in an effort to portray themselves as moderate statesmen prior to the parliamentary elections in early 2005. In July 2005 the prosecutor's office reported that 209 Hizb-ut-Tahrir activists had been convicted since 2000, and at the end of 2005 officials claimed that 99 activists had been arrested during that year, with several sentenced to lengthy prison terms. In mid-2006 a prominent IRP activist, Dodojon Yakubov, claimed that, as a foreign organization, Hizb-ut-Tahrir had no right to operate in Tajikistan, and that its radicalism had no resonance among Tajik Muslims. However, the organization continued to trouble the authorities. In September 2006 three officials were assaulted in Isfara, a town in Soghd Viloyat. Militant members of IMU were blamed for the accident and 13 alleged members of the group were arrested soon after. By mid-2007 the activity of radical organizations (including Hizb-ut Tahrir, which advocates change through non-violent means) was reported to be increasing, with periodic arrests continuing throughout the 2000s, also due to the IRP's increasing unpopularity.

The situation in neighbouring Afghanistan has long threatened the stability of Tajikistan. The success of the de facto ruling Taliban regime from 1996 in reducing the influence of the Tajikistani-based opposition United Islamic Front for the Salvation of Afghanistan (commonly known as the United Front, or Northern Alliance) in the late 1990s threatened to destabilize the situation in Tajikistan. Some tens of thousands of refugees fled to the Tajikistani–Afghan border as a result of the civil war in Afghanistan. In November 2000 10,000 Afghan refugees were stranded on marshy islands on the Pyanj river at the border. The UN urged Tajikistan to accept the refugees; however, in early 2001, and on several occasions thereafter, President Rakhmonov announced that Tajikistan would not accept the displaced persons, alleging that armed militants were among the group of refugees. The number of refugees at the border increased to almost 15,000 as heavy fighting in northern Afghanistan continued.

The refugee situation, and the threat to Tajikistan's internal security as well as to regional stability, became much more critical in the latter part of 2001, as US-led forces launched retaliatory attacks against the Saudi-born Islamist militant Osama bin Laden and his Taliban hosts in Afghanistan. Bin Laden's al-Qa'ida organization, with which the IMU was alleged to be associated, was held responsible by the USA for perpetrating large-scale suicide attacks on New York and Washington, DC, on 11 September. Shortly after the attacks on the USA, the Russian troops stationed along the Tajikistani–Afghan border, numbering some 10,000, were put on high alert. Tajikistan continued to deny entry to refugees, again citing the presence of armed militants and also the strain placed on food supplies by the persistence of severe drought. The United Front's military successes from November, and the subsequent collapse of the Taliban regime (which, in fact, had not obtained control of those Afghan regions bordering Tajikistan), reduced pressure on Tajikistan to allow Afghan refugees to enter the country. Repatriation of Afghan refugees stranded on the Tajikistani–Afghan border took place in April 2002, and in less than two weeks nearly 9,000 displaced people had returned to northern Afghanistan. In the aftermath of violence in Andijon, Uzbekistan, in May 2005 (see the chapter on Uzbekistan), a small number of Uzbekistani refugees fled to Tajikistan, although the majority sought refuge in Kyrgyzstan. In 2006–07 covert operations in Tajikistani territory were conducted by Uzbekistani authorities seeking to arrest individuals allegedly involved in the Andijon events, and were an ongoing source of aggravation between Uzbekistan and Tajikistan. Border tensions between the two countries also resurfaced, and an Uzbekistani border guard was reported to have been shot dead by a Tajikistani counterpart in November 2006.

Relations with Russia have been subject to periods of tension since the attacks of 11 September 2001 against the USA. Russia initially opposed plans to station US troops on Tajikistani territory. However, in early November it was confirmed that Tajikistan had permitted US and North Atlantic

Treaty Organization troops to utilize three of its airbases, while the USA, for its part, lifted the embargo on the sale of military equipment to Tajikistan imposed in 1993. Despite a visit to Tajikistan by President Vladimir Putin of Russia in April 2003, the developing relationship between Tajikistan and the USA engendered tensions between the Tajikistani and Russian authorities. Notably, Russia placed greater restrictions on Tajikistani migrant workers employed in Russia, whose remittances brought in around US $250m. per year to the Tajikistani economy. In response, in March 2004 Tajikistan decided not to renew its border treaty with Russia, which permitted Russian troops to protect the Tajikistani–Afghan border, and, moreover, refused to permit Russia to open a permanent military base in the country for its troops. None the less, in early 2004 tensions appeared to ease, helped by the deportation to Tajikistan from Moscow of Yakub Salimov, a former Tajikistani politician wanted for fomenting rebellion. In June Putin and Rakhmonov met in Sochi, in southern Russia, and unexpectedly announced a series of bilateral proposals including the cancellation of part of Tajikistan's debt to Russia, the maintenance of Russian border guards until 2006 and the continuation of Russian rights over use of the Nurek space surveillance station. Putin visited Tajikistan in October 2004, and it was agreed that Russia would station 5,000 troops at a permanent base in Tajikistan and would continue to lease the Nurek site. In return, Russia agreed to cancel nearly $300m. of Tajikistani bilateral debt, and pledged further investment in the aluminium and other industrial sectors. This growing rapprochement continued in 2006, as Russia pledged to play a greater role in developing Tajikistan's energy sector and to increase investment in the hydroelectric sector, and the two countries participated in joint exercises aimed at preventing incursions by Islamist groups. Russian–Tajikistani tensions again resurfaced in early 2008 over the status and conditions of the large number of Tajik migrants to Russia (estimated at some 1.5m), with the Tajikistani authorities demanding that Russia exerted closer control over the abuses to which the legal and (mostly) illegal migrants were often subjected. In view of the importance of the remittances to the Tajikistani economy, Russia appeared to use the issue as a way of retaining some leverage over the country.

Tajikistan is a participant in the Shanghai Co-operation Organization (SCO—comprising the People's Republic of China, Kazakhstan, Kyrgyzstan, Russia, Tajikistan and Uzbekistan), and was a signatory of the 2001 Shanghai Convention on Combating Terrorism, Separatism and Extremism. In August 2003 Kazakhstan and China hosted anti-terrorist manoeuvres involving troops from the SCO countries. China also appeared likely to further its economic ties with Tajikistan, following the opening of a road linking Khorog (Kuhistoni Badakhshon) with Kashgar (China) in May 2004, although substantial work was needed to improve the quality of this connection. Within the SCO, Tajikistan has tended to support Russia on key issues, although it has kept largely silent in debates over the possible expansion of the Organization and, like other regional powers, may be wary of attempts to include Iran for fear that the latter's tensions with the USA over nuclear energy may draw it into external conflicts. At the same time, this has not prevented the conclusion of a growing series of co-operation agreements between Tajikistan and Iran, with the latter providing support for hydroelectric projects and citing the two countries' common heritage to emphasize the need for close ties. More surprising, perhaps, has been the developing connection with India, which has leased an airbase at Ayni, some 80 km south of Dushanbe and also used by the Russians, to station several Indian fighter bombers there. In August 2007 Tajikistan took part for the first time in joint military exercises within the SCO framework; held in Russia's Ural Mountains, these were the first such exercises to involve all six SCO members.

INSTABILITY ON THE RISE

National, albeit flawed, elections reinstated President Rakhmonov in November 2006, and legislative elections were scheduled to take place in 2010. During a large part of the 2000s Tajikistan appeared to experience overall stability. UN peace-keeping forces had left, following the expiry of their mandate. Tajikistani border guards have replaced Russian troops at the Afghan border.

The collapse of the Taliban regime in Afghanistan in late 2001, and the subsequent holding of a direct presidential election in that country in 2004, followed by legislative elections in 2005, had reduced regional tensions to a certain extent. The level of contestation in the 2006 presidential election has been widely disputed by international observers (with some parties not even fielding a candidate), but was relatively high by Central Asian standards. After the establishment of an interim administration in Afghanistan following the Taliban's collapse, Rakhmonov took advantage of the new peace by dismissing around 15% of the commanders of the border control forces. Nevertheless, for various reasons, Afghanistan remained one of the factors most likely to destabilize Tajikistan. The drugs trade, for example, contributed a large proportion of Tajikistan's illegal economy; weapons continued to be illegally imported from Afghanistan; and the threat of fundamentalist Islamism persisted, despite global efforts to combat terrorism (see Economy). International aid agencies agreed that the most effective way to combat drugs-trafficking was to increase humanitarian assistance to border communities.

Despite some positive indications, however, levels of violence remained unacceptably high and political assassinations, although decreasing, continued to be a reality. Tensions remained within the Government, and more active members of the Islamist opposition retained only a fairly loose commitment to supporting the regime.

Fears that flawed legislative elections in early 2005, together with events in neighbouring Kyrgyzstan, might lead to further civil conflict, have not been realized. President Rakhmonov (who in early 2007 decreed that the Russian name-endings '-ev' and '-ov' should be abandoned, thus renaming himself Rakhmon, allegedly to reflect a more authentic Persian heritage) has proved more than capable of repressing political opponents, whether secular or religious.

The period 2007–08 was marked by growing instability in Tajikistan. Explosions across the country in late 2007 demonstrated that some of the stability the Government claims to have brought since the end of the war might be only at a surface level. Inter-élite struggles came to the fore in May 2008, when Hassan Sadulloyev, President Rakhmonov's brother-in-law, was reportedly shot by the President's son, Rustam Rakhmon. Sadulloyev, who later died of his wounds, was head of Orienbank, the country's most profitable bank, and linked to a number of other important businesses. Despite being one of the most influential figures in the country, Sadulloyev's downfall originated from a dispute with Rakhmon's daughter, Tahima, over the control of a number of Tajikistan's economic assets.

For the first time since the end of the civil war, Rakhmon's popularity (as a guarantor of the peace agreements, and the population's restraint out of fear that political conflict may lead to further violence) seems to have eroded. Popular frustration and discontent have been on the rise, primarily due to the Government's inability to deal with the fuel and food crisis that left the population exposed to a particularly harsh winter in 2007–08, while facing sharply rising gas, electricity and food prices. Rampant corruption within and outside the Government (who failed to dismiss a regional chief of an anti-corruption agency) contributed to the unpopularity of the administration.

CONCLUSION

Over the past year Tajikistan has experienced the highest level of instability since the end of the civil war. Tensions originate in both intra-élite struggles, with occasional challenges from discontented elements of the regime or from regional power groupings against the President, and from rising popular discontent. The population's frustration with the apparent inability of the Government effectively to address economic problems and hardship also contributed to making the country increasingly unstable. It is unlikely, however, that either will put President Rakhmon's position in danger. As a result of constant pressure on the opposition and civil society, no leader was in a position to effectively mount a challenge to the current administration.

In order to improve internal stability, a programme of democratization and economic reform is essential. The Government has thus far strengthened its powers at the expense of the legislature, and opposition parties have not been awarded the same rights as the ruling party. Pressure on the opposition and foreign funded NGOs continues, as does the curtailment of religious freedom. It is widely agreed that the international community's renewed interest in the region was an insufficient incentive for the Tajikistani Government to implement much-needed changes to prevent political and economic collapse and social unrest; rather, international financial and technical aid

was required to assist public sector reform and to support poverty reduction programmes.

While the country has made some advancements in the areas of security and economic development, further progress is required to build upon existing achievements. There also remains a pressing need for the enactment of significant and lasting political reform, including, *inter alia*, the adoption and full implementation of measures to combat both the criminalization of political life and the institutional weaknesses of Tajikistan. Although guerilla activity has been contained since the end of the civil war, the failure effectively to neutralize criminal groups and the reluctance of regional figures to accept central authority has cast a long shadow on the country's political and economic systems.

Economy

Dr JOHN ANDERSON

Revised for this edition by Dr MATTEO FUMAGALLI

INTRODUCTION

Prior to independence Tajikistan was the poorest of the USSR's Union Republics, constituting 0.6% of the territory and 1.8% of the population at the beginning of 1991. With a rapidly growing population in the rural areas, by the time Mikhail Gorbachev came to power as Soviet leader in 1985 the republic was already experiencing grave problems of land shortages, and unemployment or underemployment was becoming a major, if not fully acknowledged, problem. Moreover, despite a degree of self-sufficiency in agricultural produce, some 44% of Tajikistan's republican state budget was provided by transfers from all-Union funds.

Tajikistan was not only seriously affected by the dissolution of the USSR, but also by its own rapid descent into civil conflict. The events of 1992 and their aftermath had a devastating impact on the country, with the destruction of much of the economic and social infrastructure in the south. According to UN estimates, more than 50,000 people were killed and many more wounded; some 55,000 children were orphaned; 2,000 or more businesses collapsed; 180 bridges and 1,800 km of roads were destroyed; harvesting was disrupted for several years; and as many as 800,000 refugees were created. Alongside those displaced by the fighting, the early 1990s saw the emigration of nearly 400,000 Russian-speakers, many highly skilled professionals, who felt threatened by the rise of violence and the possible 'Islamicization' of daily life. All of these factors contributed to a dramatic 29% decline in economic output in 1992, which continued, albeit at a slower pace, through the next five years. The signing of the General Agreement on Peace and National Accord in June 1997 enabled the Government to place more emphasis on Tajikistan's economy. However, the country encountered many problems in its search for economic well-being, and, despite positive growth in gross domestic product (GDP) from 1999, reaching 10.6% in 2004 before slipping to 6.7% in 2005, Tajikistan remained among the poorest of the successor states. GDP growth increased by 7.8% in 2007, but the rate was expected to decline moderately, to an average of 4.8%, during 2008–09.

ECONOMIC POLICY

The collapse of the USSR left Tajikistan with considerable economic problems, even before the outbreak of civil war. At the end of 1991 subsidies from the all-Union Government came to an end, although Russian petroleum was still sold to the country at below world market prices. The immediate consequence was a huge deficit on the state budget. Exacerbated by internal conflict, at the end of 1992 this had reached the equivalent of 30% of GDP, improving thereafter to 25% in 1993 and, officially, to 6% in 1994. The 1996 budget envisaged a deficit of 5.4% of GDP, but the Government had reduced the deficit to just over 3% by 1999 and to about 0.6% in 2000,

although it increased to just under 1% in 2002. In 2007 the state budget registered a small surplus of 1% of GDP, due to higher than expected tax revenues, low economic growth and high inflation. Apart from the loss of the Soviet subsidy, further difficulties were created as a result of corruption, tax avoidance and under-reporting of production by many enterprises, problems common to most of the economies of the Commonwealth of Independent States (CIS). The situation was not helped by the fact that in 1992–94, for instance, the Government had been forced to spend up to 50% of its revenue on military and security needs. Moreover, there was considerable unwillingness among international investors to become involved with such an unstable country.

In this situation Tajikistan was forced into almost total reliance on Russia, and during the mid-1990s was effectively managed from Moscow. From January 1994 the country became part of the new 'rouble zone' and was obliged to accept all the conditions that went with this, including control of monetary policy, foreign reserves and government expenditure being placed with the Central Bank of the Russian Federation. Increasingly, however, this became untenable, as Russia refused to allow sufficient quantities of roubles to reach the country, and in early 1995 the Government of Tajikistan started to discuss the introduction of a national currency.

The continuation of the civil war deterred most international financial organizations from aiding Tajikistan, although the introduction of the Tajikistani rouble in May 1995 was accompanied by a number of measures designed to attract IMF support. As elsewhere in the CIS, the currency initially declined dramatically in value against the US dollar, but the accompanying strict monetary policy appeared to be reducing the rate of decline by the beginning of 1996. At the same time the annual rate of inflation, which had been brought down from over 2,000% in 1993 to 341% in 1994, appeared to have been adversely affected by the introduction of the new currency, accompanied as it was by the freeing of many prices: the annual rate was some 635% in 1995.

During and after the negotiation of the peace agreement, however, the IMF, the World Bank and other major financial institutions proved more willing to become involved in the reconstruction of Tajikistan. In 1996 the IMF offered a stand-by arrangement to support government reform plans, followed by the World Bank's offer of substantial credits for restructuring. Following a visit by World Bank experts in June 1998, it was agreed to allocate a US $5m. loan to Tajikistan for the reform of its health care system, badly damaged by the violence of previous years. This, in turn, formed part of a $50m. credit to assist with structural adjustment programmes, involving mass privatization and reform of the financial sector, and to pay pension arrears.

In March 1998 Kazakhstan, Kyrgyzstan and Uzbekistan agreed to admit Tajikistan into the Central Asian Economic Union (superseded by the Central Asian Co-operation Organization in March 2002). In April 1998 the country was admitted to the CIS Customs Union (already comprising Belarus, Kazakhstan, Kyrgyzstan and Russia), although it was not entirely clear that either of these arrangements made a serious contribution to Tajikistan's economic recovery. Indeed, closeness to Russia was to have negative consequences that year, when the Russian economic crisis in August had a severe impact on Tajikistan's faltering recovery.

From 1999 increasing political stability permitted further support from international agencies. In July the IMF approved a further US $40m. loan to help the country strengthen its balance of payments and improve the prospects for economic growth. In announcing this, the Fund's directors commended the efforts of the Government in bringing inflation under control (the rate had declined dramatically, to 2.7% in 1998, although by 2007 it had increased substantially, to 13.1%) and in maintaining some degree of macroeconomic stability in difficult times. At the same time they expressed the hope that privatization would be developed further and that some of the basic problems created by a partially non-cash economy would be addressed in the coming years. In October 2000 the IMF approved further funds, worth some $51m., in support of the Government's efforts to structure the economy. In April 2001, however, the Fund urged the Tajikistani Government to introduce more measures to strengthen revenue-collection mechanisms and undertake further structural reforms. In July the IMF approved a further $8m. loan. By mid-2001 the European Bank for Reconstruction and Development (EBRD) had contributed more than €15m. to various infrastructure projects, including the upgrading of Dushanbe airport and the modernization of telecommunications. The EBRD was also encouraging private-sector activities, opening credit lines for the establishment of a bottled-water plant in Istravshan and a food-packaging plant in the Khujand region. Meanwhile, the USA pledged a total of $125m. in investment and aid to Tajikistan in 2002, and the country was also to benefit from a new initiative, endorsed by the IMF, the World Bank, the Asian Development Bank (ADB) and the EBRD in April, which aimed to reduce poverty and external debt, and stimulate growth in seven CIS states. Further support was promised during a World Bank Tajikistan Consultative Group meeting held in Dushanbe during May 2003, with around $99m. promised over a three-year period, although some of this funding was dependent on further reform of governance procedures and adequate guarantees for proper implementation in the country. Those attending the meeting placed particular emphasis on community-based initiatives and combating corruption. In July 2004 the IMF reported that Tajikistan's performance under a Poverty Reduction and Growth Facility (PRGF) arrangement, initially agreed in December 2002, had been satisfactory, that poverty had declined, inflation had decreased markedly, and that growth remained robust. In consequence, it approved the disbursement of a further $14.5m to support the PRGF. Following a relatively positive assessment of Tajikistan's achievements, in September 2005 the IMF authorized a further disbursement of some $14.3m. In 2006 the Tajikistani authorities announced their intention to replace the PRGF with a policy support instrument (PSI)—a mechanism used by the IMF in other low-income countries, which was intended to reduce the need for financial assistance. However, in March 2008 the IMF demanded that Tajikistan repay some $47m. in IMF loans as a penalty for having provided incorrect data about the country's economic situation (it had inflated its official international reserves from $115m. to $450m.). In April the Chairman of the National Bank announced that Tajikistan would repay the amount.

In mid-2006 the ADB announced a project to ensure that the poorest sections of society would continue to benefit from education. Equally important, despite having no impact on the lives of the impoverished Tajiks, was the World Bank's decision in June 2006 to help the Government create a better system for collecting, collating and publishing statistics on economic developments in a country where accurate data, and thus real evidence on progress, are often difficult to find. In 2006 the ADB also provided US $12m. of credit to help the country in its efforts to tackle the large cotton farmers' debt.

The international financial institutions were eager to promote the sale of state companies to private investors—a process that accelerated after the introduction of a privatization programme in 1998. Previously, the state had registered some 9,500 enterprises, of which approximately two-thirds had been sold by mid-2001. In early 2000 an auction organized by the State Property Committee resulted in the sale of more than 1,000 enterprises, mostly in the catering, agricultural and consumer services sector. By the end of 2000 the vast majority of small businesses had been privatized. Larger organizations, however, were overvalued and were thus proving harder to divest; by November 2001 359 of fewer than 1,500 medium-sized and large state-owned enterprises had been privatized. In 2000 all of the state cotton-processing plants were privatized, thereby allowing an element of competition in the important cotton sector. During 2002–03 there were few further initiatives in the area of privatization, and at the end of 2002 the IMF suggested insufficient effort was being made by the Government to promote the sale of state properties. In 2003 there were plans to transfer most cultural and health care facilities to private management or ownership, to be followed by the state railways company and coal mines in 2004. However, by mid-2007 only small elements of this ambitious plan had been implemented, and international agencies remained critical of the slow pace of privatization. While the role of international financial institutions remained important, loans and investments by individual countries were increasing annually, particularly in the energy sector (see below).

A major shift in policy was the introduction in October 2000 of a new currency, the somoni, to replace the Tajikistani rouble. Although there was some depreciation in the first two months after its introduction, the currency had stabilized by early 2001. After some small depreciations in the following years (5% in 2005, and about 6% in 2006), the somoni began to appreciate against the Russian rouble and the euro, with negative effects on the country's competitiveness.

AGRICULTURE

Agriculture was traditionally the principal sector of Tajikistan's economy, providing 45% of employment and more than 40% of net material product (NMP) prior to independence. In 2007 agriculture contributed 22.4% of GDP (compared with 36% in 1991) and engaged about 69.8% of the total employed labour force.

The major crop after the Second World War was cotton, over one-half of which was grown in the southern Kulob and Khatlon regions. The pressure to produce cotton had various consequences during the late Soviet era, with Communist Party leaders compelled to produce ever greater quantities and eventually resorting to misreporting actual production figures to satisfy central planners. Among the numerous negative outcomes for the region were that often unwilling settlers were brought in from the central and northern parts of the republic, children were forced to miss lengthy periods of schooling to help bring in the harvest, and water resources were depleted.

Cotton sowing and harvesting were severely affected by the violence that swept across the southern regions in 1992. Reliable statistics were hard to obtain, but reported annual production of seed (unginned) cotton declined from some 840,000 metric tons at the beginning of the 1990s to 515,000 tons during the civil war. Production continued to decline in the mid-1990s, reaching 317,707 tons in 1996. Nevertheless, in the late 1990s cotton still provided about one-fifth of total export earnings, and output rose to 383,721 tons in 1998. Official sources recorded a harvest of 313,000 tons in 1999, 335,000 tons in 2000 and 453,000 tons in 2001. Other agricultural products included silk, grains, fruit, vegetables and livestock. Some of these escaped the ravages of civil war, with the World Bank registering a high level of fruit production in 1992. Although fruit production was much reduced after that time, it remained steady throughout the 1990s. During the civil war there were also reported declines in the number of sheep and cattle, as those impoverished by war were forced to sell or consume their animals, thus preventing the reproduction of herds. Any gains that were achieved in the late 1990s were, however, reversed by a serious drought in 2000, which nearly halved grain production and meant that the country could only fulfil about one-quarter of its domestic needs. The continuing drought adversely affected agricultural output in 2001. Despite the devastating effects of torrential rains and floods, cotton production registered growth in each year in the period 2002–04, reaching 557,000 tons in 2004. A good cotton harvest and rising world prices for the commodity meant that agricultural production increased by 9.6% in 2003. This achievement was reduced in 2005, when bad weather conditions helped to reduce the cotton crop by some 20%, to 448,000 tons. A further decline of 8.9% was reported in 2006, largely owing to confusion and corruption surrounding the privatization of farms, bureaucratic interference, and the fact that many agricultural workers were choosing to work for higher wages in other parts of the former USSR. Production was expected to decline further, to 419,000 tons in 2007 and 400,000 tons in 2008. Given the small amount of arable land (6%) and inclement weather, crop vulnerability continues to plague Tajikistan (the grain harvest declined by 20% in 2006, compared with the previous year), forcing the authorities to import much of the country's wheat from Kazakhstan, Uzbekistan and Russia.

In the mid-1990s the administration of President Emomali Rakhmonov (Rakhmon), recognizing that the agricultural sector was the most fundamental part of the economy, sought to introduce a degree of reform. There was much rhetoric about the complete privatization of land by the end of the 20th century, and plans for agricultural privatization were announced in the first half of 1996, although there was much resistance to the notion of private land-ownership. In July 1998 the Government adopted a resolution on the establishment of a centre for the support of farm privatization. In practice, reform measures were slow to take hold, with the state retaining control of both machinery and fertilizer production as well as purchasing, and with local collective farms often unwilling to lease out good-quality land. By 2002 there still existed only a limited legal basis for the private ownership of land, although in many cases leased agricultural plots became the property of those who worked them, in all but name. Although the Government proved reluctant to opt for the full privatization of land, it made some efforts to reduce the burdens on those farming it, and in June 2005 substantially reduced the amount of land tax paid by farmers. It is also worth noting the considerable regional variations within the country, with the climate of lawlessness in the southern regions enabling powerful individuals simply to acquire large plots of land for themselves. In the impoverished Kuhistoni Badakhshon (Gornyi Badakhshan) Autonomous Viloyat in the east of the country, traditionally the home of the Isma'ili community, however, the Aga Khan Foundation for Economic Development has provided considerable financial support for the creation of peasant co-operatives and offered practical advice on methods of achieving success in such ventures. In 2002 Tajikistan received US $20m. from the International Development Association (IDA—part of the World Bank Group) towards a Farm Privatization Support Project. In 2003 a further $2.3m. was provided by FAO to deal with the social consequences of recent droughts. In particular, this money was aimed at projects to secure food for families in badly affected areas, to combat the expected outbreak of Moroccan locust infestation in 2003 and to control the spread of brucellosis amongst livestock. International agencies have also been concerned to ensure that the new generation of farmers are aware of the problems of poor use of land. In June 2004 the World Bank put together a package of credits worth just under $20m. that was intended to encourage both increased agricultural productivity and the sustainable use of land resources, and in July 2005 it approved a $13m. grant to improve irrigation efficiency in the Farg'ona (Fergana) valley region.

The peace process allowed international organizations to become involved in the reform of Tajikistan's agricultural sector. In 1996 and 1997 the World Bank committed funds to an agricultural recovery programme, although renewed

outbreaks of violence sometimes resulted in these and other international loans being diverted to defence needs. Nevertheless, in many parts of the south the regular cycles of sowing and harvesting were renewed, and from 1998 there was some hope that output of agricultural products would begin to increase. The restructuring of the food production sector, however, took longer than expected. Meat and dairy production declined, although the Director of the Government's Corporation for Food and Processing Industries claimed that output had risen in 1998 compared with previous years. Diversification of the agricultural sector was as important as ever in the 2000s, in order to reduce Tajikistan's dependence on cotton and aluminium.

The other major growth area was the illegal drugs trade, with the more remote parts of the country producing their own opium crops and trafficking becoming a major business. The armed opposition exploited the trade to raise money for weaponry, and some made this profitable business their prime occupation. Some of the pro-Government militias were also alleged to be involved in the drugs business. Thus, although the Government was formally committed to combating the trade, enforcement of anti-drugs laws was made problematic by the fact that too many groups had a vested interest in circumventing official policies. During a visit to the UN headquarters in New York, USA, in June 1998, President Rakhmonov stated that the drugs trade presented a major threat to Tajikistan's stability and was an obstacle in attempts to create a sense of statehood. The problem persisted in the early 2000s, and was compounded by the resumption of opium poppy cultivation by farmers in Afghanistan following the collapse of the Taliban regime in late 2001. Despite attempts by the Afghan authorities to eradicate opium cultivation, reports in August 2002 suggested that production had reached a level close to that experienced in the late 1990s, before the Taliban banned cultivation, while it was evident that the problem of drugs-trafficking through Tajikistan remained far from being resolved; indeed, the situation appeared to deteriorate further. Tajikistani officials reported that during 2003 nearly twice as much heroin was confiscated as in the previous year and, despite a US $2.4m. grant from US drug enforcement agencies, the problem continued to worsen during 2005–06 as a result of widespread poverty in Tajikistan and the fact that many officials at all levels were implicated in the trade. Although over 60 metric tons of narcotics have been seized by Tajikistani authorities since 1997 (about 5 tons a year), this represents barely 5%–10% of what is widely believed to have been transported through the country. Furthermore, there were growing concerns about the increase of intravenous drugs use, which was resulting in a concomitant increase in the incidence of HIV/AIDS within the republic (up to 60,000 persons are expected to be living with HIV by 2010, an increase of 1,200% from 2004).

The population (7.1m. in 2007) has been able to cope with the post-Soviet economic hardship, and the destruction subsequently wrought by the civil war, largely because of the remittances sent by the ever-growing number of Tajikistani citizens employed abroad, primarily in Russia. Official unemployment is low (2.6% in 2007), but this neglects both underemployment and the fact that salaries are so low that a considerable segment of the population still lives below the official poverty line (50% in 2007). Thus, at US $1,200m. in 2006 and $2,000m. in 2007, the contribution of remittances to GDP (at least 30% of the total in 2007, according to official estimates), and to the economic life of the country in general, is absolutely essential.

MINING, ENERGY AND INDUSTRY

Tajikistan has considerable mineral deposits, including gold, iron, lead, tin, mercury and coal, but extracting many of these has been problematic, given the mountainous terrain of much of the country. Production of gold increased in 1998, however, owing to greater foreign investment in the sector. The mountains proved advantageous in providing a river system, although the exploitation of this huge resource has remained problematic. By the time of the dissolution of the USSR a huge hydroelectric power (HEP) system, built up over previous decades, met nearly 80% of the republic's electricity needs and made Tajikistan the second largest producer of hydroelectric energy in the former USSR, after Russia. This system, closely guarded by Russian troops, emerged more or less unscathed from the civil war. Production of electricity amounted to 16,491m. kWh in 2004, 17,086m. kWh in 2005 and 17,152m. kWh in 2006. However, this represents only 5% of Tajikistan's production potential (estimated at 300,000m. kWh). In addition, Tajikistan has problems providing its citizens with clean water, with an estimated one-sixth of the water in Dushanbe remaining untreated, while poor water supplies throughout the country have led to outbreaks of cholera and typhoid. Tajikistan is dependent on imports for other energy sources, notably natural gas and petroleum. It has traditionally relied on imports from neighbouring Uzbekistan, although supplies have often been abruptly cut off by that country for political reasons (Uzbekistan views Tajikistan as a weak link in the 'war on terror', and often accuses the Tajikistani authorities of harbouring militants). Uzbekistan's decision to increase gas prices by 50% in 2008 did little to alleviate bilateral tensions.

Meanwhile, in May 2003 the Russian firm Gazprom signed a deal to develop Tajikistan's natural gas fields. Despite the country's extensive hydroelectric potential, Tajikistan has remained energy-deficient. However, construction of the Sangtuda power station (Sangtuda-1), commissioned at the end of the Gorbachev era, has resumed with Russian and Iranian financing. According to official sources, about one-half of the first plant had been constructed by mid-2006, with Russian investment in the project estimated at some US $1,000m., and it was hoped that production would begin, as planned, in 2009. A subsequent controversy between the Tajikistani Government and the Russian company expected to conduct the project caused considerable delays. Similarly, the construction of the Rogun hydroelectricity plant has been suspended, after a disagreement between the Tajikistani authorities and Russian Aluminium (RUSAL). If completed, the Sangtuda power station alone could comfortably meet all of Tajikistan's electricity needs, leaving a surplus that could be exported; other plants, still in the planning stage, will further bolster the energy sector. In 2006 the Presidents of Tajikistan and the People's Republic of China announced Chinese investment in two power transmission projects worth $281m. and $59m., respectively. Even Kazakhstan and Iran showed considerable interest in developing the country's hydroelectric sector, with the former seeking to construct a power line connecting Khujand in northern Tajikistan with Shymkent in southern Kazakhstan, and Iran (like Russia) building a power plant at Sangtuda (Sangtuda-2). A contentious issue in this respect is that the infrastructure is built along an east–west axis, effectively hindering the country's export potential towards its energy-needy southern neighbours (Afghanistan and Pakistan)

The industrial sector (including construction) remains relatively small, engaging 8.8% of the country's employed labour force and contributing 27.4% of GDP in 2007. Producing some 450,000 metric tons in 1991, production declined steadily after independence to stabilize at 237,000 tons in 1994 and 1995, when the plant was estimated to be producing at about 40% of full capacity, before decreasing to 198,300 tons in 1996. Aluminium provided 59% of export earnings in 1995, but also utilizes around 40% of the water supply, leading to persistent shortages for domestic users as well as other industrial sectors. However, the industry was not integrated into the national economy, being very dependent on input imports and with little value added to the product locally. Like the cotton sector, this was a feature of its development as part of the Soviet economic system, these two industries being based in Tajikistan to take advantage of its extensive water resources (for the aluminium industry this meant abundant energy). Despite the conclusion of the civil war, previous levels of aluminium production were not sustained, with production of unwrought aluminium slowing to 196,300 tons in 1998; aluminium provided almost 40% of export earnings in that year. Aluminium production gradually recovered, reaching 289,000 tons in 2001 and 308,000 tons in 2002, and aluminium accounted for 53.9% of total export earnings in 2002. Consequently, aluminium appeared likely to remain the country's

primary export commodity, and its position was strengthened by the October 2004 decision of Russia's largest aluminium company, RUSAL, to invest substantially in Tajikistani companies as well as Tajikistan's hydroelectric programme, with some estimates suggesting a total investment by the company of some US $1,600m. over a seven-year period. In 2005 aluminium production rose by 10%, to 375,000 tons, earning the republic around $560m. in exports; production was forecast to have reached a record high of 420,000 tons in 2006, before declining slightly, to 412,000 tons in 2007 and an estimated 411,000 tons in 2008.

Following the end of the civil conflict, geological explorations were resumed and various joint ventures with European companies in the mining sector were agreed. Indian companies have become involved in the extraction of silver, British companies in the mining of gold, and Uzbekistani groups in coal-mining. In 1996 industrial output decreased by an estimated 19.8%, but in 1997 it declined by only 2.5%. Some growth was anticipated for 1998, before the Russian economic crisis in August of that year caused expectations to be revised downwards. Despite all the signs of stabilization, in 1999 industrial output in Tajikistan still remained at around one-third of the figure for 1989. In 2000 the country finally reported a substantial 10.3% increase in industrial production, and further increases were recorded in subsequent years, with growth of 10.2% in 2003, although this was mainly the result of the rise in aluminium output, and industrial growth declined to around 8% in 2004. In 2006 output rose by 6.2%, largely owing to record production at the Tursunzade aluminium plant, to the west of the capital.

Other industries established in Tajikistan included engineering (mostly targeted towards the production of agricultural machinery), textiles and food-processing, which was concentrated largely on fruit, natural oils and tobacco. Much of the latter has in recent years been traded with Pakistan and China, rather than exported to the former USSR as before 1991. Industrial production outwith the Soghd region was badly affected by the civil war, with the destruction of factories, the obstruction of transport networks and the diversion of many workers from production. At the beginning of 1994 the State Statistical Agency produced a report on economic developments for the year, with a published version expressing optimism and a further account, marked 'not for publication', expressing considerable disquiet at Tajikistan's economic progress. The latter report showed that in the final quarter of 1994 production was down by 44%, compared with the corresponding period in 1993. In addition, it noted that the construction of social infrastructure, including hospitals and schools, had ceased. In 1995 the Government published a five-year plan to create a market-based economy by the end of the decade, on the basis of massive privatization in the agricultural and industrial sector, and the gradual freeing of all prices, although these proposals were hindered by the continuation of hostilities until 1997.

Industrial production declined by some 54.4% in 1990–94, owing to the civil conflict. This decline, and the collapse of the transport and construction sectors, was largely responsible for total GDP declining to only 46% of its 1991 level, in real terms, by 1995. In 1996 real GDP decreased by 4.4%. In 1997, however, there was an increase in GDP of 1.7%. In part because of the impact of the Russian crisis of 1998, Tajikistan's economic recovery during 1999 was less pronounced than had been hoped, at some 3.7%. In 2000 overall GDP was officially stated to have expanded by 8.3% compared with the previous year. This upward trend continued, with growth reaching 10.2% in 2001, 9.5% in 2002, 10.1% in 2003 and 10.6% in 2004, before slowing in 2005, to 6.7%. It recorded a moderate increase, to 7.0%, in 2006, but the rate of growth was expected to slow slightly, to 4.8%, during 2008–09.

PROSPECTS

By 2006 Tajikistan was still confronted with serious economic problems, caused mainly by political and civil conflict. There were, however, some indications that economic performance was improving. According to official statistics, real GDP increased each year between 1998 and 2004. Debt remained a major problem, being equivalent to some 108% and 65% of GDP in 2000 and 2003, respectively, although this had declined to some 30% of GDP by 2007. It was, nevertheless, expected to rise again, to 52.4% of GDP, in 2008, owing to the impact of high international commodity prices. The growth recorded in the late 1990s and early 2000s, moreover, reflected only marginal improvements for a weakened economy, and many within the country still endured harsh economic conditions. Political violence and crime remained prevalent in the south, the social infrastructure failed to meet the needs of the country's poorest citizens and, in real terms, unemployment was rising, officially reaching its highest level of 3.1% in May 1998, before declining to an average of 2.1% in 2005 (although the actual rate of unemployment, believed to be around 30% in 1999, was considerably greater than official figures showed). In 2001 an estimated 200,000 people left Tajikistan to seek work abroad, and by the late 2000s about 1.5m. Tajiks were working outside the country. Although this development had negative consequences for family life and reproduction, in 2005 it also produced some US $600m. in workers' remittances (some 13% of GDP), which was expected to increase to $1,200m. in 2006. These remittances were beginning to contribute to some growth in the light industry and service sectors. However, in practice, measuring the extent of poverty and unemployment was difficult, as many families adopted a series of coping strategies that generated income and welfare in ways that could not readily be tabulated or measured. According to the World Bank, poverty affected 50% of the population at the end of 2007, compared with more than 70% in 2002. The country's external debt amounted to just under $1,220m. in March 2008 (equivalent to 27% of GDP), although this was expected to increase due to the signing of several loan agreements using Chinese credit of $154m. A deficit on the balance of trade expanded significantly in the second half of 2000s due to rising energy and food prices. Tajikistan's trade deficit amounted to $557.2m. at mid-2008.

The poor economic situation was especially pronounced in the southern regions of the country, where violence continued to disturb everyday life, as opposed to the traditionally richer northern province around Khujand, which had experienced less disruption or destruction of economic assets. Here local élites seemed to have some degree of commitment to economic reform, albeit one which did not challenge their vested interests, and traditional trading habits were re-emerging in the form of a small, enterprising business class. In Dushanbe the city authorities were able to implement an initial privatization programme from 1998, which helped to develop the capital's entrepreneurial sector, but in the country as a whole privatization had only affected a minority of the larger enterprises. Nationally there were a few signs of a fragile recovery: foreign direct investment reached US $30m. in 2000, but declined dramatically to $8.1m. in 2001, before rising to $21m. in 2002, $45m. in 2005 and $197m. in the first half of 2006. The gradual, if halting, emergence of peace and a stabilization of the economic situation have encouraged a few foreign companies to invest in Tajikistan; the single largest investment was offered by the Bermuda-based Nelson Gold Corporation. Moreover, in May 2001 a UN-sponsored meeting of six donor countries and eight international organizations pledged some $430m. over the following two years.

Although political security and stability remained an elusive goal, the Government's objectives from 2007 were: to accelerate the pace of privatization in order to enhance economic stability; to sustain economic growth; to continue reform of the banking sector; to improve revenue collection; and to ensure a more predictable environment in an effort to encourage both domestic and external investment. Rakhmonov introduced a Poverty Reduction Strategy Paper (PRSP) in June 2002 in an attempt to address Tajikistan's socio-economic problems, and by the end of 2005 the IMF was expressing satisfaction that this was beginning to have a tangible impact on the general population. A second PRSP, covering 2007–09, was finalized in June 2006. In the aftermath of the US-led military campaign against neighbouring Afghanistan from October 2001, aid organizations and individual countries pledged financial and technical assistance to help Tajikistan to reform and develop its economy. Overall, the Government had some cause for optimism. Political opposition was neutered and President Rakhmonov had secured re-election in November 2006, albeit through a fundamentally flawed electoral process. Although national income had still not caught up with its 1991 level, the economy had stabilized and was beginning to show consistent signs of growth. None the less, the problems confronting the population of Tajikistan remained huge, with poverty, banditry in some parts of the country, and ongoing health problems that were largely attributable to decaying water systems and poor social welfare provision, exacerbated by persistent flooding in certain regions. In such circumstances it was not always clear that the statistical improvements reported by the Government from the late 1990s were having any significant impact on everyday life. Continued improvements would depend upon the commitment of the Government to structural reform and diversification, stability in world prices for core products such as aluminium and cotton, and continued political stability within the country and the region as a whole. The Government also had to resolve potential difficulties in its relationship with Russia. Investment from abroad was essential to the country's economic well-being, but came with the cost of a renewal of dependency on Russia.

In recent years the country has reported robust growth, primarily owing to increased cotton, gold and aluminium export levels. The Government has also pledged to undertake serious reforms in a number of areas, particularly poverty reduction, land reform and public administration. Attempts to curb corruption and combat drugs-trafficking have also been introduced, with varying success. However, notwithstanding positive macroeconomic results, the country still remains over-reliant on aid, credit and remittances from abroad.

Statistical Survey

Source (unless otherwise indicated): State Committee for Statistics, 734001 Dushanbe, Kuchai Boxtar 17; tel. (372) 23-25-53; fax (372) 21-43-75; e-mail stat@tojikiston.com; internet www.stat.tj.

Area and Population

AREA, POPULATION AND DENSITY

Area (sq km)	143,100*
Population (census results)†	
12 January 1989	5,092,603
20 January 2000	
Males	3,069,100
Females	3,058,393
Total	6,127,493
Population (estimates at mid-year)‡	
2005	6,850,000
2006	6,990,000
2007§	7,130,000
Density (per sq km) at mid-2007	49.8

* 55,251 sq miles.
† Figures refer to *de jure* population. The *de facto* total at the 1989 census was 5,108,576.
‡ Source: Asian Development Bank.
§ Provisional.

POPULATION BY ETHNIC GROUP
(2000 census)

	Number ('000 persons)	%
Tajik	4,898.4	79.9
Uzbek	936.7	15.3
Russian	68.2	1.1
Kyrgyz	65.5	1.1
Others	158.7	2.6
Total	6,127.5	100.0

ADMINISTRATIVE DIVISIONS
(1 January 2006, official estimates)

	Area (sq km)	Population	Density (per sq km)	Capital city
Viloyats				
Khatlon	24,800	2,519,600	101.6	Qurgonteppa
Soghd	25,400	2,095,700	82.5	Khujand
Autonomous Viloyat				
Kuhistoni				
Badakhshon . .	64,200	220,400	3.4	Khorog
Capital City				
Dushanbe . . .	100	660,900	6,609.0	—
Regions of				
Republican				
Subordination * .	28,600	1,567,200	54.8	—
Total	143,100	7,063,800	49.4	

* The Regions of Republican Subordination comprise 3 cities (Gissar; Kofarnikhon; Rogun) and 10 raions or districts (Faizabad; Garm; Gissar; Darban; Jirgital; Lenin; Shakhrinav; Tajikabad; Tavildara; and Varzov) in central Tajikistan where there is no higher tier of local government.

PRINCIPAL TOWNS
(population at 1 January 2002)

Dushanbe (capital) .	575,900	Kanibadam . . .	45,100
Khujand* . . .	147,400	Kofarnihon‡ . .	45,100
Kulob	79,500	Tursunzade . . .	38,100
Qurgonteppa . .	61,200	Isfara	37,300
Istravshan† . . .	51,700	Panjakent . . .	33,200

* Known as Leninabad between 1936 and 1992.
† Also known as Urateppa (Ura-Tyube).
‡ Formerly Ordzhonikidzeabad.

Mid-2007 (incl. suburbs, UN estimate): Dushanbe 553,000 (Source: UN, *World Urbanization Prospects: The 2007 Revision*).

BIRTHS, MARRIAGES AND DEATHS*

	Registered live births		Registered marriages		Registered deaths	
	Number	Rate (per 1,000)	Number	Rate (per 1,000)	Number	Rate (per 1,000)
1999 . .	180,888	29.8	22,536	3.9	25,384	4.2
2000 . .	167,246	27.0	26,257	4.2	29,387	4.7
2001 . .	171,623	27.2	28,827	4.6	32,015	5.1
2002 . .	175,600	27.3	32,299	5.0	31,100	4.8
2003 . .	177,900	27.1	39,102	6.0	33,200	5.0
2004 . .	179,600	26.8	47,320	7.1	29,700	4.4
2005 . .	180,800	26.4	52,352	7.6	31,500	4.6
2006 . .	186,500	26.7	57,278	8.2	32,000	4.6

* From 2002 onwards, figures for registered births and deaths are rounded to the nearest 100.

Expectation of life (years at birth, WHO estimates): 64.4 (males 62.6; females 66.3) in 2006 (Source: WHO, *World Health Statistics*).

IMMIGRATION AND EMIGRATION

	2004	2005	2006
Immigrants	15,244	17,962	19,646
Emigrants	24,663	27,311	30,554

ECONOMICALLY ACTIVE POPULATION
(annual averages, '000 persons)

	2004	2005	2006
Activities of the material sphere .	1,750	1,770	1,790
Agriculture*	1,391	1,424	1,432
Industry†	118	121	118
Construction	68	62	64
Trade and catering‡	109	101	110
Transport and communications .	64	62	66
Activities of the non-material			
sphere	338	342	341
Housing and municipal services	28	33	33
Health care, social security,			
physical culture and sports .	80	72	74
Education, culture and arts .	183	186	186
Science, research and			
development	4	4	4
Government and finance . .	29	31	34
Other non-material	14	16	10
Statistical discrepancy	—	—	6
Total employed	2,088	2,112	2,137
Unemployed	42	42	48
Total labour force	2,132	2,154	2,185

* Including forestry.
† Comprising manufacturing (except printing and publishing), mining and quarrying, electricity, gas, water, logging and fishing.
‡ Including material and technical supply.

Health and Welfare

KEY INDICATORS

Total fertility rate (children per woman, 2006)	3.5
Under-5 mortality rate (per 1,000 live births, 2006) . . .	68
HIV/AIDS (% of persons aged 15–49, 2005)	0.1
Physicians (per 1,000 head, 2006)	2.0
Hospital beds (per 1,000 head, 2006)	6.1
Health expenditure (2005): US $ per head (PPP) . . .	67
Health expenditure (2005): % of GDP	5.0
Health expenditure (2005): public (% of total)	22.8
Human Development Index (2005): ranking	122
Human Development Index (2005): value	0.673

For sources and definitions, see explanatory note on p. vi.

Agriculture

PRINCIPAL CROPS

('000 metric tons)

	2004	2005	2006
Wheat	631	618	625*
Rice (paddy)	51	62	49
Barley	63	64	65
Maize	113	156	139
Potatoes	527	555	574
Cabbages and other brassicas .	44†	47*	50*
Tomatoes	199†	209†	221*
Dry onions	180†	188†	199*
Carrots	111†	117†	124*
Watermelons	150	170	218
Apples	85†	85*	115*
Apricots	25†	28*	42*
Peaches and nectarines . .	20†	21*	32*
Grapes	93	91	108
Cotton (lint)	172†	151	145*
Tobacco (leaves)	3	2	2*

* FAO estimate.
† Unofficial figure.

Aggregate production ('000 metric tons, may include official, semi-official or estimated data): Total cereals 860 in 2004, 903 in 2005, 880 in 2006; Total roots and tubers 527 in 2004, 555 in 2005, 574 in 2006; Total vegetables (incl. melons) 832 in 2004, 888 in 2005, 978 in 2006; Total fruits (excl. melons) 238 in 2004, 239 in 2005, 302 in 2006.

Source: FAO.

LIVESTOCK

('000 head at 1 January)

	2004	2005	2006
Horses	74	77	75
Asses, mules or hinnies . .	147	156	160*
Cattle	1,219	1,303	1,372
Camels*	40	40	42
Sheep	1,672	1,782	1,894
Goats	920	1,040	1,160
Poultry	1,887	2,296	2,451

* FAO estimate(s).
Source: FAO.

LIVESTOCK PRODUCTS

('000 metric tons)

	2004	2005	2006
Cattle meat	21.8	24.3	25.3
Sheep meat	21.1	26.9	27.6
Chicken meat	0.2	0.2	0.6
Cows' milk	450.4	488.0	494.0
Goats' milk	39.8	45.0	50.9*
Cheese*	11.2	n.a.	n.a.
Wool: greasy	3.9	4.4	4.0*

* FAO estimate(s).

Source: FAO.

Fishing

(metric tons, live weight)

	2002	2003	2004
Capture	181	158	184
Freshwater bream	25	24	28
Common carp	51	52	45
Crucial carp	17	11	8
Silver carp	16	12	14
Sichel	4	2	10
Asp	5	3	9
Other cyprinids	27	23	32
Wels (Som) catfish . . .	12	9	18
Pike-perch	24	22	20
Aquaculture	143	167	26
Common carp	17	47	12
Grass carp (White amur) . .	29	30	3
Silver carp	95	88	7
Total catch	324	325	210

2005–06: Production assumed to be unchanged from 2004 (FAO estimates).
Source: FAO.

Mining

(metric tons, unless otherwise indicated)

	2003	2004	2005
Coal	46,500	88,30000	94,900
Crude petroleum	17,700	18,900	21,600
Natural gas (million cu m) . .	32.8	35.6	29.3
Lead concentrate*†	800	800	800
Antimony ore*†	1,800	2,000	2,000
Mercury*†	30	30	30
Silver (kilograms)†	5,000	5,000	5,000
Gold (kilograms)*†	2,700	3,000	3,000
Gypsum (crude)*	50,100	57,200	8,300

* Estimated production.
† Figures refer to the metal content of ores and concentrates.

Source: US Geological Survey.

2006 ('000 metric tons, unless otherwise indicated): Coal 105; Crude petroleum 24; Natural gas (million cu m) 20 (Source: Asian Development Bank).

2007 ('000 metric tons, unless otherwise indicated): Coal 165; Crude petroleum 26; Natural gas (million cu m) 17 (Source: Asian Development Bank).

Industry

SELECTED PRODUCTS
('000 metric tons, unless otherwise indicated)

	2000	2001	2002
Cottonseed oil (refined)* . . .	23	26	31
Wheat flour	307	315	304
Ethyl alcohol ('000 hectolitres) .	23	25	18
Wine ('000 hectolitres) . . .	39	56	63
Beer ('000 hectolitres)	4	8	9
Soft drinks ('000 hectolitres) . .	58	127	134
Cigarettes (million)	667	1,155	585
Wool yarn (pure and mixed) . .	0.5	0.6	0.7
Cotton yarn (pure and mixed) .	15.0	14.9	8.5
Woven cotton fabrics (million sq metres)	11	14	20
Woven silk fabrics ('000 sq metres)	253	248	136
Footwear, excl. rubber ('000 pairs)	110	100	84
Caustic soda (Sodium hydroxide) .	4	3	3
Clay building bricks (million) . .	30	24	29
Cement	55	69	89
Aluminium (unwrought): primary‡	269.2	289.0	307.6
Electric energy (million kWh)† .	14,247	14,382	15,302

2003 ('000 metric tons, unless otherwise indicated): Cottonseed oil (refined) 34*; Wheat flour 399†; Cement 166; Electric energy (million kWh) 16,509; Aluminium (unwrought): primary 319.4‡.

2004 ('000 metric tons, unless otherwise indicated): Wheat flour 458†; Cement 194†; Electric energy (million kWh) 16,491: Aluminium (unwrought): primary 358.1‡.

2005 ('000 metric tons, unless otherwise indicated): Cement 253; Electric energy (million kWh) 17,090; Aluminium (unwrought): primary 379.6‡; Wheat flour 459†.

2006 ('000 metric tons, unless otherwise indicated): Cement 282†; Electric energy (million kWh) 16,935; Wheat flour 457†.

2007 ('000 metric tons, unless otherwise indicated): Cement 313†; Electric energy (million kWh) 17,494; Wheat flour 470†.
* Unofficial figure(s) from FAO.
† Source: Asian Development Bank.
‡ Source: US Geological Survey.

Source (unless otherwise indicated): UN, *Industrial Commodity Statistics Yearbook*.

Finance

CURRENCY AND EXCHANGE RATES

Monetary Units
100 diram = 1 somoni.

Sterling, Dollar and Euro Equivalents (30 May 2008)
£1 sterling = 6.771 somoni;
US $1 = 3.431 somoni;
€1 = 5.321 somoni;
100 somoni = £14.77 = $29.15 = €18.79.

Average Exchange Rate (somoni per US $)
2005   3.1166
2006   3.2984
2007   3.4406

Note: The Tajikistani rouble was introduced in May 1995, replacing the Russian (formerly Soviet) rouble at the rate of 1 Tajikistani rouble = 100 Russian roubles. A new currency, the somoni (equivalent to 1,000 Tajikistani roubles), was introduced in October 2000.

BUDGET
(million somoni)*

Revenue†	2004	2005‡	2006§
Tax revenue	934	1,169	1,374
Income and profit tax . . .	105	142	156
Payroll taxes	120	146	172
Property taxes	34	51	66
Internal taxes on goods and services	482	625	728
International trade and operations tax	185	205	252
Non-tax revenue	129	143	154
Total	1,063	1,312	1,528

Expenditure‖	2004	2005‡	2006§
General administrative services .	117	157	185
Protection services	134	194	239
Social services	438	664	805
Education	161	250	336
Health	62	91	106
Social security and welfare .	153	228	238
Other	61	95	125
Economic services	119	148	167
Interest payments	43	56	57
Other purposes	211	144	156
External financing of public investment programme (PIP) .	189	284	336
Total	1,250	1,648	1,944

* Figures refer to the consolidated operations of the State Budget, comprising the budgets of the central (republican) Government and local authorities, and the Social Security Fund.
† Excluding grants received (million somoni): 41 in 2004; 38 in 2005 (preliminary); 38 in 2006 (budget proposal).
‡ Preliminary figures.
§ Budget proposals.
‖ Including lending minus repayments (million somoni): 3 in 2004; 2 in 2005 (preliminary); 2 in 2006 (budget proposal).

Source: IMF, *Republic of Tajikistan: Sixth Review Under the Poverty Reduction and Growth Facility—Staff Report; Staff Statement; Press Release on the Executive Board Discussion; and Statement by the Executive Director for the Republic of Tajikistan* (January 2006).

2007 (million somoni): Total revenue 3,659.5 (excl. grants 36.4); Total expenditure 3,467.3 (excl. net lending 7.8) (Source: Asian Development Bank).

INTERNATIONAL RESERVES
(US $ million at 31 December)

	2004	2005	2006
Gold (national valuation) . . .	14.6	20.7	28.7
IMF special drawing rights . .	1.3	5.4	3.5
Foreign exchange	156.2	162.8	171.6
Total	172.1	188.9	203.8

2007 (US $ million at 31 December): Gold (national valuation) 44.8; IMF special drawing rights 3.6.
Source: IMF, *International Financial Statistics*.

MONEY SUPPLY
(million somoni at 31 December)

	2004	2005	2006
Currency outside banks . . .	175.4	155.3	166.4
Demand deposits	64.4	84.8	146.2
Total money (incl. others) . .	241.1	241.0	314.2

Source: IMF, *International Financial Statistics*.

COST OF LIVING
(Consumer Price Index; base: previous year = 100)

	2005	2006	2007
Food	108.3	113.9	125.5
Non-food	102.7	105.3	107.5
All items	107.1	112.5	119.7

Source: Asian Development Bank.

NATIONAL ACCOUNTS
(million somoni at current prices)

Expenditure on the Gross Domestic Product

	2004	2005	2006
Final consumption expenditure.	5,292.8	6,899.4	8,773.8
Households			
Non-profit institutions serving households	4,566.0	5,847.1	7,502.1
General government	726.8	1,052.3	1,271.7
Gross capital formation	752.6	839.4	1,490.5
Gross fixed capital formation	640.0	801.3	1,445.3
Acquisitions, less disposals, of valuables	112.6	38.1	45.2
Changes in inventories			
Total domestic expenditure	6,045.4	7,738.8	10,264.3
Exports of goods and services	3,624.3	3,910.7	5,429.0
Less Imports of goods and services	4,293.1	5,245.0	7,748.0
Sub-total	5,376.6	6,404.5	7,945.3
Statistical discrepancy*	790.7	802.1	1,390.0
GDP in market prices	6,167.2	7,206.6	9,335.2

* Referring to the difference between the sum of the expenditure components and official estimates of GDP, compiled from the production approach.

Gross Domestic Product by Economic Activity

	2005	2006	2007
Agriculture	1,526.7	2,001.7	2,525.9
Mining, manufacturing and electricity, gas and water	1,645.1	1,987.0	1,966.9
Construction	327.1	567.5	1,115.6
Transport and communications	533.3	673.1	646.4
Trade	1,191.1	1,592.8	2,529.3
Others, including public administration and finance	1,152.1	1,453.5	2,475.9
GDP at factor cost	6,357.4	8,275.6	11,260.0
Indirect taxes, less subsidies	831.2	1,059.6	1,519.7
GDP in purchasers' values	7,206.6	9,335.2	12,779.7

Source: Asian Development Bank.

BALANCE OF PAYMENTS
(US $ million)

	2004	2005	2006
Exports of goods f.o.b.	1,096.9	1,108.1	1,511.8
Imports of goods c.i.f.	−1,232.4	−1,430.9	−1,954.6
Trade balance	−135.5	−322.8	−442.8
Exports of services	122.9	146.3	134.2
Imports of services	−212.5	−251.5	−394.5
Balance on goods and services	−225.1	−428.0	−703.1
Other income received	1.7	9.6	12.4
Other income paid	−59.2	−50.4	−76.4
Balance on goods, services and income	−282.7	−468.8	−767.0
Current transfers received	348.4	599.9	1,146.0
Current transfers paid	−122.8	−150.0	−400.4
Current balance	−57.0	−18.9	−21.4
Direct investment (net)	272.0	54.5	338.6
Portfolio investment (net)	5.3	—	n.a.
Other investment assets	−28.4	−71.3	−301.9
Other investment liabilities	−155.5	118.3	239.2
Net errors and omissions	−32.5	−76.3	−264.7
Overall balance	3.9	6.3	−10.1

Source: IMF, *International Financial Statistics.*

External Trade

PRINCIPAL COMMODITIES
(US $ million, excl. alumina and aluminium)

Imports c.i.f.*	2004	2005	2006
Natural gas	28	27	35
Petroleum products	107	126	191
Electricity	65	58	67
Grain and flour	48	76	77
Total (incl. others)	1,191	1,330	1,725

Exports f.o.b.†	2004	2005	2006
Cotton fibre	162	144	129
Electricity	58	53	49
Total (incl. others)	915	909	1,399

* These figures do not include separate data for imports of alumina, one of Tajikistan's principal import goods. The most recent data available were for 2001, when imports of alumina accounted for US $184m. of $688m. in total imports (c.i.f.).

† These figures do not include separate data for exports of aluminium, Tajikistan's principal export item. The most recent data available were for 2001, when imports of aluminium accounted for US $397m. of $909m. in total exports (f.o.b.).

2007 (US $ million): Total imports 2,547; Total exports 1,468 (Source: Asian Development Bank).

PRINCIPAL TRADING PARTNERS
(US $ million)

Imports	2005	2006	2007
Azerbaijan	114.9	138.2	164.9
China, People's Rep.	92.5	148.9	493.8
Italy	51.7	61.5	14.2
Kazakhstan	168.3	186.7	222.9
Russia	256.5	423.7	503.5
Turkey	21.9	36.5	129.4
Turkmenistan	53.8	60.3	71.9
Ukraine	82.0	64.3	76.8
USA	11.7	12.0	58.0
Uzbekistan	152.9	176.4	210.5
Total (incl. others)	1,330.0	1,725.3	2,384.6

Exports	2005	2006	2007
Iran	36.7	76.1	99.1
Italy	15.6	16.5	99.4
Kazakhstan	19.7	27.8	33.2
Latvia	44.2	35.1	0.8
Netherlands	423.4	569.4	26.0
Norway	—	—	152.4
Russia	82.8	65.4	85.8
Switzerland	27.0	24.5	27.1
Turkey	143.4	442.8	130.3
Uzbekistan	66.5	67.4	80.5
Total (incl. others)	908.7	1,398.9	979.0

Note: Data reflect the IMF's direction of trade methodology and, as a result, the totals may not be equal to those presented for trade in commodities.

Source: Asian Development Bank.

Transport

RAILWAYS

	2003	2004	2005
Passengers (million journeys) .	0.5	0.7	0.7
Freight carried ('000 metric tons) .	11,720.5	12,268.3	12,114.2

Passenger-km (million): 32 in 2001.

Freight ton-km (million): 1,248 in 2001.

CIVIL AVIATION
(traffic on scheduled services)

	2003	2004	2005
Passengers carried ('000) . . .	400	600	500
Freight carried ('000 metric tons) .	3.8	4.1	3.7

Kilometres flown (million): 4 in 1999.

Passenger-km (million): 229 in 1999.

Freight ton-km (million): 23 in 1999.

Source: partly UN, *Statistical Yearbook*.

Communications Media

	2004	2005	2006
Telephones ('000 main lines in use)	245.2	280.2	280.2
Mobile cellular telephones ('000 subscribers)	240.0	265.0	265.0
Internet users ('000)	5.0	19.5	19.5

Television receivers ('000 in use): 2,000 in 2000.

Facsimile machines (number in use): 2,100 in 1999.

Books published (titles): 150 in 1997.

Books published (copies): 997,000 in 1996.

Daily newspapers (estimates): 2 titles and 120,000 copies (average circulation) in 1996.

Non-daily newspapers: 73 titles and 153,000 copies (average circulation) in 1996.

Other periodicals: 11 titles and 130,000 copies (average circulation) in 1996.

Radio receivers ('000 in use): 850 in 1997.

Sources: UNESCO, *Statistical Yearbook*; International Telecommunication Union.

Education

(2006/07, unless otherwise indicated)

	Students ('000)		
	Males	Females	Total
Pre-primary	32,800	28,400	61,200
Primary			
Secondary:			
Lower	n.a.	n.a.	1,672,800*
Upper			
Vocational	13,800	18,600	32,400
Professional technical†	17,955	7,013	24,968
Higher (incl. universities)	106,100	40,100	146,200

* Figures exclude 18,700 pupils at evening classes (including those conducted by correspondence).
† 2005/06 data.

Institutions (2006/07, unless otherwise indicated): Pre-primary 485; Primary 670; Secondary—Lower 826; Secondary—Upper 2,282; Secondary—Vocational 52; Professional Technical 71 (2005/06); Higher (incl. universities) 34. Figures exclude 11 schools for pupils with mental or physical disabilities and 41 evening schools.

Teachers (2006/07, unless otherwise stated): Pre-primary 6,615 (1996/97); Primary *and* Secondary—Lower, Upper *and* Vocational 99,900; Professional Technical n.a.; Higher (incl. universities) 6,100 (2001/02).

Directory

The Constitution

Tajikistan's Constitution entered into force on 6 November 1994, when it was approved by a majority of voters in a nation-wide plebiscite. It replaced the previous Soviet republican Constitution, adopted in 1978. The following is a summary of its main provisions (including amendments approved by referendum on 26 September 1999 and 22 June 2003).

PRINCIPLES OF THE CONSTITUTIONAL SYSTEM

The Republic of Tajikistan is a sovereign, democratic, law-governed, secular and unitary state. The state language is Tajik, but Russian is accorded the status of a language of communication between nationalities.

Recognition, observance and protection of human and civil rights and freedoms is the obligation of the State. The people of Tajikistan are the expression of sovereignty and the sole source of power of the State, which they express through their elected representatives.

Tajikistan consists of Kuhistoni Badakhshon Autonomous Viloyat (Region), viloyats, towns, districts, settlements and villages. The territory of the State is indivisible and inviolable. Agitation and actions aimed at disunity of the State are prohibited.

No ideology, including religious ideology, may be granted the status of a state ideology.

The Constitution of Tajikistan has supreme legal authority and its norms have direct application. Laws and other legal acts which run counter to the Constitution have no legal validity. The State, its bodies and officials are bound to observe the provisions of the Constitution.

Tajikistan will implement a peaceful policy, respecting the sovereignty and independence of other states of the world, and will determine foreign relations on the basis of international norms. Agitation for war is prohibited.

The economy of Tajikistan is based on various forms of ownership. The State guarantees freedom of economic activity, entrepreneurship, equality of rights and the protection of all forms of ownership, including private ownership. Land and natural resources are under state ownership.

FUNDAMENTAL DUTIES OF INDIVIDUALS AND CITIZENS

The freedoms and rights of individuals are protected by the Constitution, the laws of the republic and international documents to which Tajikistan is a signatory. The State guarantees the rights and freedoms of every person, regardless of nationality, race, sex, language, religious beliefs, political persuasion, social status, knowledge and property. Men and women have the same rights. Every person has the right to life. No one may be subjected to torture, punishment or inhuman treatment. No one may be arrested, kept in custody or exiled without a legal basis, and no one is adjudged guilty of a crime except by the sentence of a court in accordance with the law. Every person has the right freely to choose their place of residence, to leave the republic and return to it. Every person has the right to profess any religion, individually or with others, or not to profess any, and to take part in religious ceremonies. Every citizen has the right to take part in political life and state administration; to elect and be elected from the age of 18; to join and leave political parties, trade unions and other associations; to take part in meetings, rallies or demonstrations. Every person is guaranteed freedom of speech. State censorship is prohibited.

Every person has the right: to ownership and inheritance; to work; to housing; to social security in old age, or in the event of sickness or disability. Basic general education is compulsory.

A state of emergency is declared as a temporary measure to ensure the security of citizens and of the State in the instance of a direct threat to the freedom of citizens, the State's independence, its territorial integrity, or natural disasters. The period of a state of emergency is up to three months; it can be prolonged by the President of the Republic.

MAJLISI OLI (SUPREME ASSEMBLY)

The Majlisi Oli (Supreme Assembly) is the highest representative and legislative body of the republic. It is a bicameral legislative body, comprising a 63-member lower chamber, the Majlisi Namoyandagon (Assembly of Representatives), and an upper chamber, the Majlisi Milliy (National Assembly). The members of the Majlisi Namoyandagon are elected for a five-year term, 22 by proportional representation and 41 in single-mandate constituencies. Twenty-five members of the Majlisi Milliy are indirectly elected for a term of five years by regional deputies. Eight members of the chamber are appointed by the President of the Republic. Additionally, former Heads of State of the Republic of Tajikistan are entitled to a seat in the chamber.

The powers of the Majlisi Oli include: enactment and amendment of laws, and their annulment; interpretation of the Constitution and laws; determination of the basic direction of domestic and foreign policy; ratification of presidential decrees on the appointment and dismissal of the Chairman of the National Bank, the Chairman and members of the Constitutional Court, the Supreme Court and the Supreme Economic Court; ratification of the state budget; determining and altering the structure of administrative territorial units; ratification and annulment of international treaties; ratification of presidential decrees on a state of war and a state of emergency.

Laws are adopted by a majority of the legislative deputies. If the President does not agree with the law, he may return it to the Majlisi Oli. If the legislature once again approves the law, with at least a two-thirds' majority, the President must sign it.

THE PRESIDENT OF THE REPUBLIC

The President of the Republic is the Head of State and the head of the executive. The President is elected by the citizens of Tajikistan on the basis of universal, direct and equal suffrage for a seven-year term. Any citizen who knows the state language and has lived on the territory of Tajikistan for the preceding 10 years may be nominated to the post of President of the Republic.

The President has the authority: to represent Tajikistan inside the country and in international relations; to establish or abolish ministries with the approval of the Majlisi Oli; to appoint or dismiss the Prime Minister and other members of the Council of Ministers and to propose them for approval to the Majlisi Oli; to appoint and dismiss chairmen of regions, towns and districts, and propose new appointments for approval to the relevant assemblies of people's deputies; to appoint and dismiss members of the Constitutional Court, the Supreme Court and the Supreme Economic Court (with the approval of the Majlisi Oli); to appoint and dismiss judges of lower courts; to sign laws; to lead the implementation of foreign policy and sign international treaties; to appoint diplomatic representatives abroad; to be Commander-in-Chief of the armed forces of Tajikistan; to declare a state of war or a state of emergency (with the approval of the Majlisi Oli).

In the event of the President's death, resignation, removal from office or inability to perform his duties, the duties of the President will be carried out by the Chairman of the Majlisi Oli until further

presidential elections can be held. New elections must be held within three months of these circumstances. The President may be removed from office in the case of his committing a crime, by the decision of at least two-thirds of deputies of the Majlisi Oli, taking into account the decisions of the Constitutional Court.

THE COUNCIL OF MINISTERS

The Council of Ministers consists of the President as Chairman, the Prime Minister, the First Deputy Prime Minister, Deputy Prime Ministers, Ministers and Chairmen of State Committees. The Council of Ministers is responsible for implementation of laws and decrees of the Majlisi Oli and decrees and orders of the President. The Council of Ministers leaves office when a new President is elected.

LOCAL GOVERNMENT

The local representative authority in regions, towns and districts is the assembly of people's deputies. Assemblies are elected for a five-year term. Local executive government is the responsibility of the President's representative: the chairman of the assembly of people's deputies, who is proposed by the President and approved by the relevant assembly. The Majlisi Oli may dissolve local representative bodies, if their actions do not conform to the Constitution and the law.

KUHISTONI BADAKHSHON AUTONOMOUS VILOYAT

Kuhistoni Badakhshon Autonomous Viloyat is an integral and indivisible part of Tajikistan, the territory of which cannot be changed without the consent of the regional assembly.

JUDICIARY

The judiciary is independent and protects the rights and freedoms of the individual, the interests of the State, organizations and institutions, and legality and justice. Judicial power is implemented by the Constitutional Court, the Supreme Court, the Supreme Economic Court, the Military Court, the Court of Kuhistoni Badakhshon Autonomous Viloyat, and courts of viloyats, the city of Dushanbe, towns and districts. The term of judges is 10 years. The creation of emergency courts is not permitted.

Judges are independent and are subordinate only to the Constitution and the law. Interference in their activity is not permitted.

THE OFFICE OF THE PROCURATOR-GENERAL

The Procurator-General and procurators subordinate to him ensure the control and observance of laws within the framework of their authority in the territory of Tajikistan. The Procurator-General is responsible to the Majlisi Oli and the President, and is elected for a five-year term.

PROCEDURES FOR INTRODUCING AMENDMENTS TO THE CONSTITUTION

Amendments and addenda to the Constitution are made by means of a referendum. A referendum takes place with the support of at least two-thirds of the people's deputies. The President, or at least one-third of the people's deputies, may submit amendments and addenda to the Constitution. The form of public administration, the territorial integrity and the democratic, law-governed and secular nature of the State are irrevocable.

The Government

HEAD OF STATE

President: EMOMALI RAKHMON (elected by popular vote 6 November 1994; re-elected 6 November 1999 and 6 November 2006).

COUNCIL OF MINISTERS
(September 2008)

Chairman of the Government: EMOMALI RAKHMON.

Prime Minister: AKIL AKILOV.

First Deputy Prime Minister: ASADULLO GHULOMOV.

Deputy Prime Minister: RUQIYA QURBONOVA.

Deputy Prime Minister: MURODALI ALIMARDON.

Minister of Justice: BAKHTIYOR KHUDOYOROV.

Minister of Agriculture: QOSIM QOSIMOV.

Minister of Internal Affairs: MAHMADNAZAR SOLEHOV.

Minister of Foreign Affairs: HAMROKHON ZARIFI.

Minister of Education: ABDUJABBOR RAHMONOV.

Minister of Land Reclamation and Water Resources: SAIDI YOKUBZOD.

Minister of Labour and Social Welfare: SHUKURJON ZUHUROV.

Minister of Finance: SAFARALI NAJMIDDINOV.

Minister of Defence: Maj.-Gen. SHERALI KHAYRULLOYEV.

Minister of Transport and Communications: ABDURAHIM ASHUR.

Minister of Economic Development and Trade: GHULOMJON BOBOZODA.

Minister of Health: NUSRATULLO SALIMOV.

Minister of Culture: MIRZOSHOHRUKH ASRORI.

Minister of Energy and Industry: SHERALI GUL.

Note: The Chairmen of the State Committees for National Security, Statistics, and Investment and the Management of State Property are also members of the Council of Ministers.

MINISTRIES

Office of the President: 734023 Dushanbe, Xiyoboni Rudaki 80; tel. (372) 21-04-18; fax (372) 21-18-37; e-mail mail@president.tj; internet www.president.tj.

Secretariat of the Prime Minister: 734023 Dushanbe, Xiyoboni Rudaki 80; tel. (372) 21-18-71; fax (372) 21-51-10.

Ministry of Agriculture: 734025 Dushanbe, Xiyoboni Rudaki 14; tel. (372) 21-15-96; fax (372) 21-57-94.

Ministry of Culture: 734025 Dushanbe, Xiyoboni Rudaki 34; tel. (372) 21-03-05; fax (372) 21-47-01.

Ministry of Defence: 734025 Dushanbe, Kuchai Bokhtar 59; tel. (372) 23-18-97; fax (372) 23-19-37.

Ministry of Economic Development and Trade: 734002 Dushanbe, Kuchai Bokhtar 37; tel. (372) 27-34-34; fax (372) 21-04-04; e-mail sharipov_jamshed@hotmail.com; internet www.met.tj.

Ministry of Education: 734025 Dushanbe, Kuchai Chexov 13A; tel. (372) 21-46-05; fax (372) 21-70-41.

Ministry of Energy and Industry: 734025 Dushanbe, Kuchai Boxtar 10; tel. (37) 221-50-64; fax (37) 227-90-10; e-mail energo@rs.tj; internet www.minenergo.tj.

Ministry of Finance: 734067 Dushanbe, Nazarov 64/14; tel. (37) 881-25-79; e-mail nii_finance@mail.tj; internet www.minfin.tj.

Ministry of Foreign Affairs: 734051 Dushanbe, Xiyoboni Rudaki 42; tel. (372) 21-18-08; fax (372) 21-02-59; e-mail dushanbe@mfaumo.td.silk.org; internet www.mid.tj.

Ministry of Health: 734025 Dushanbe, Kuchai Shevchenko 69; tel. (372) 21-30-64; fax (372) 21-48-71.

Ministry of Internal Affairs: 734025 Dushanbe, Kuchai Texron 29; tel. (372) 21-17-40; fax (372) 21-26-05.

Ministry of Justice: 734025 Dushanbe, pr. Rudaki 25; tel. (372) 21-44-05; fax (372) 21-80-66.

Ministry of Labour and Social Welfare: 734028 Dushanbe, Kuchai A. Navoi 52; tel. (372) 36-18-37; fax (372) 36-24-15.

Ministry of Land Reclamation and Water Resources: 734001 Dushanbe, Xiyoboni Rudaki 78; tel. (372) 35-35-66.

Ministry of Transport and Communications: 734025 Dushanbe, Xiyoboni Rudaki 57; tel. (37) 221-22-84; fax (37) 221-29-53; e-mail info@mincom.tj; internet www.mincom.tj.

President

Presidential Election, 6 November 2006, provisional results

Candidates	%
Emomali Rakhmonov* (People's Democratic Party of Tajikistan)	79.3
Olimjon Boboyev (Party of Economic Reforms) . . .	6.2
Amirkul Karakulov (Agrarian Party of Tajikistan) . .	5.3
Ismoil Talbakov (Communist Party of Tajikistan) . .	5.1
Abdukhalim Gafforov (Socialist Party of Tajikistan) .	2.8
Total†	100.0

* Known as Emomali Rakhmon from 2007.
† Including invalid votes, equivalent to 1.3% of the total.

Legislature

Constitutional amendments approved by a referendum in September 1999 provided for the establishment of a bicameral legislative body, the Majlisi Oli (Supreme Assembly), comprising a 63-member lower chamber, the Majlisi Namoyandagon (Assembly of Representatives), and an upper chamber, the Majlisi Milliy (National Assembly), which has a minimum of 33 members.

Majlisi Milliy
(National Assembly)

734051 Dushanbe, Xiyoboni Rudaki 42; tel. (372) 23-19-33; fax (372) 21-51-10; e-mail mejparl@parliament.tojikiston.com.

President: MAKHMADSAID UBAYDULLOYEV.

The Majlisi Milliy has a minimum of 33 members, of whom 25 (five from each of the five administrative regions of Tajikistan) are indirectly elected for a term of five years by regional deputies. Eight members of the chamber, who also serve for a term of five years, are appointed by the President of the Republic. All former Presidents of Tajikistan are also entitled to a seat in the Majlisi Milliy. Elections to the Majlisi Milliy were held on 24 March 2005, and the eight presidential nominees were announced on 25 March. The new chamber convened on 15 April.

Majlisi Namoyandagon
(Assembly of Representatives)

734051 Dushanbe, Xiyoboni Rudaki 42; tel. (372) 21-23-66; fax (372) 21-92-81; e-mail mejparl@parliament.tojikiston.com.

President: SAIDULLO KHAIRULLAYEV.

Elections, 27 February and 13 March 2005*

Parties	%†	A‡	B‡	Total
People's Democratic Party of Tajikistan (PDPT)	74	17	35	52
Communist Party of Tajikistan (CPT)	13	3	1	4
Islamic Rebirth Party of Tajikistan (IRP)	8	2	—	2
Independents	—	—	5	5
Total (incl. others)	100	22	41	63

* Final provisional results.
† Percentage refers to the share of the vote cast for seats awarded on the basis of party lists.
‡ Of the 63 seats in the Majlisi Namoyandagon, 22 (A) are awarded according to proportional representation on the basis of party lists, and 41 (B) are elected in single-mandate constituencies.

Local Government

From February 1991 Tajikistan had a three-tier system of local government, when the highest level of local government consisted of one Autonomous Viloyat (region), three Viloyats and the capital city of Dushanbe. In December 1992 the two Viloyats to the south of Dushanbe, Qurgonteppa (Kurgan-Tyube or Kurgan Teppe) and Kulob (Kulyab), were merged into a single Viloyat, Khatlon, which occupies the south-west of Tajikistan. Soghd (formerly Leninabad) Viloyat lies in the north-west, while the Kuhistoni Badakhshon Autonomous Viloyat (see Autonomous Territory) consists of the eastern part of the country. The second tier of local government comprises 62 raions (districts) and 22 towns. Four of the raions—all in Dushanbe—have the status of municipal raions. Ten raions and three towns of the central belt of territory were not united in a viloyat, being directly subordinate to the national authorities. The third tier of local government comprises 47 poseloks (settlements) and 354 kishlaks (villages).

Dushanbe City Administration (Khukumat): 734000 Dushanbe, Xiyoboni Rudaki 48; tel. (372) 21-27-04; Mayor MAKHMADSAID UBAYDULLOYEV.

Khatlon Viloyat Administration (Khukumat): 735140 Khatlon Viloyat, Qurgonteppa, Kuchai Gogol 2; tel. (37744) 2-23-33; f. 1992 by union of Qurgonteppa and Kulob Oblasts; Gov. GHAYBULLO AFZALOV.

Soghd Viloyat Administration (Khukumat): 735700 Soghd Viloyat, Khujand, Kuchai Dzerzhinski 45; tel. (3422) 4-02-44; fax (3422) 6-77-55; Gov. ABDUKAKHIR NAZIROV.

Note: the authorities of the following raions and cities are directly answerable to the republican authorities, not being included in any first-tier unit of local Government. *Cities:* Gissar; Kofarnikhon; Rogun, *Raions:* Faizabad; Garm; Gissar; Darban; Jirgital; Lenin; Shakhrinav; Tajikabad; Tavildara; and Varzov.

Election Commission

Central Commission for Elections and Referenda: 734051 Dushanbe, Xiyoboni Rudaki 42; tel. (372) 21-13-75; comprises Chair., Sec. and 13 mems, elected by the Majlisi Namoyandagon at the proposal of the President of the Republic; Chair. MIRZOALI BOLTUYEV; Sec. VERA NAIMOVA.

Political Organizations

In September 2006 there were eight registered parties in Tajikistan.

Agrarian Party of Tajikistan (Agrarnaya partiya Tadzhikistana): 734000 Dushanbe; f. 2005; supports creation of a civil society and aims to protect the interests of the agricultural sector and its workers; Chair. AMIRKUL KARAKULOV; 1,300 mems (2005).

Communist Party of Tajikistan (CPT) (Kommunisticheskaya partiya Tadzhikistana): 734002 Dushanbe, Kuchai F. Niyazi 37; tel. (372) 221-14-54; e-mail talbhakov_555@mail.ru; internet www.kpt .freenet.tj; f. 1924; sole registered party until 1991; Chair. SHODI D. SHABDOLOV; Sec. of Central Cttee ISMOIL TALBAKOV; 60,000 mems (Jan. 2005).

Democratic Party of Tajikistan (DPT) (Khizbi demokrati Tochikiston): 734000 Dushanbe, Kuchai Pushkin 64; tel. (372) 21-77-87; internet www.democrat-tj.org; f. 1990; banned in 1993; permitted to re-register 1996 and 1999; secular nationalist and pro-Western; Chair. SAIDJAFAR ISMONOV (acting) (Chair. of Vatan—Fatherland faction registered by the Ministry of Justice in Sept. 2006); Chair. (of unregistered faction) RAHMATULLO VALIEV; c. 4,500 mems (Jan. 2005).

Islamic Rebirth Party of Tajikistan (IRP): 734000 Dushanbe, pos. Kalinina, Kuchai Tukhagul 55; tel. (372) 27-25-30; fax (372) 27-53-93; f. 1990 by split from the All-Union Islamic Renaissance Party of the USSR; leadership fmrly based in Tehran, Iran; registered in 1991; banned 1993–99; Chair. MUHIDDIN KABIRI; 20,000 mems (Jan. 2005).

Justice (Adolatkoh): 734000 Dushanbe, Kuchai S. Nosirov 41; tel. (372) 24-90-55; f. and regd 1996; campaigns for the establishment of social justice and construction of a state based on the rule of law; registration revoked 2001; Leader ABDURAKHMON KARIMOV.

Party of Economic Reforms (Partiya ekonomicheskikh reform): 734000 Dushanbe; f. 2005; supports establishment of a market economy on the basis of democratic principles; aims to reduce poverty, undertake privatization and increase foreign investment; Chair. OLIMJON BOBOYEV; c. 1,000 mems (2005).

Party of Popular Unity and Accord (PPUA): 734000 Dushanbe; f. 1994; represents interests of northern Tajikistan; banned 1998; Leader ABDUMALIK ABDULLOJONOV.

People's Democratic Party of Tajikistan (PDPT) (Xizbi Xalkii Demokratii Tojikston): 734000 Dushanbe, Xiyoboni Rudaki 107; tel. (372) 21-63-21; e-mail ndpt1994@yahoo.com; internet www.hhdt.tj; f. 1994; campaigns for a united and secular state; Chair. EMOMALI SH. RAKHMON; First Dep. Chair. DAVLATALI DAVLATZODA; 100,000 mems (2008).

Social Democratic Party of Tajikistan (SDPT/KhSDT): 734000 Dushanbe, Xiyoboni Rudaki 81/49; tel. (372) 23-47-40; internet www .hsdt-tj.org; f. 1998; regd 2003; fmrly Justice and Progress of Tajikistan; Chair. RAKHMATULLO KH. ZOYIROV; 5,000 mems (Dec. 2004).

Socialist Party of Tajikistan: 734000 Dushanbe, Xiyoboni Rudaki 137; tel. (372) 34-77-11 (officially registered faction led by A. Gafforov); tel. (372) 27-39-59 (unregistered faction led by M. Narziyev); f. 1996; split into two factions in 2003, only one of which was registered by the Ministry of Justice; Chairmen ABDUKHALIM GAFFOROV (Chair. of faction registered by the Ministry of Justice), MIRKHUSEYN NARZIYEV (Chair. of unregistered faction); 15,000 mems (2003).

Union and Development Party (Xizb-i Ittihod va Taraqqiyot—Taraqqiyot): 734000 Dushanbe; f. 2000; unregistered; fmrly a faction of the Democratic Party of Tajikistan; Chair. SULTON KUVVATOV; 3,000 mems (2001).

Unity Party (Hizb-i-Vahdat): 734000 Dushanbe; f. 2001; unregistered.

The transnational militant Islamist **Hizb-ut-Tahrir al-Islami** (Party of Islamic Liberation—Hizb-ut-Tahrir) was believed to be operative in Tajikistan. As in neighbouring states, the organization was banned in Tajikistan, and a number of people have received gaol sentences for their alleged membership of the group, despite its stated intention of using only peaceful means of pursuing its goals, notably the restoration of a caliphate.

Diplomatic Representation

EMBASSIES IN TAJIKISTAN

Afghanistan: 734000 Dushanbe, Kuchai Pushkin 34; tel. (372) 221-67-35; fax (372) 251-00-96; e-mail afghanemintj@yahoo.com; Ambassador SAYED MUHAMMAD KHAIRKHOH.

China, People's Republic: 734002 Dushanbe, Xiyoboni Rudaki 143; tel. (372) 224-20-07; fax (372) 251-00-24; e-mail chinaembassy@ tajnet.com; internet tj.china-embassy.org; Ambassador ZUO XUE-LIANG.

France: 734025 Dushanbe, Kuchai Rakhimi 17; tel. (372) 21-78-55; fax (372) 51-00-82; e-mail ambassade.douchanbe@diplomatie.gouv .fr; Ambassador OLIVIER MAITLAND PELEN.

Germany: 734017 Dushanbe, Kuchai Varzov 16; tel. (372) 221-21-89; fax (372) 224-03-90; e-mail info@dusc.diplo.de; internet www .duschanbe.diplo.de; Ambassador RAINER MÜLLER.

India: 734000 Dushanbe, Kuchai Buxoro 45; tel. (372) 221-64-02; fax (372) 251-00-45; e-mail hocdushanbe@tojikiston.com; Ambassador AMAR SINHA.

Iran: 734000 Dushanbe, Kuchai Boxtar 18; tel. (372) 221-00-74; fax (372) 251-00-89; e-mail iranembassy.tj@gmail.com; internet www .iranembassy-tj.com; Ambassador ALIASGHAR SHERDOOST.

Japan: 734000 Dushanbe, Kuchai X. Nazarov 80A; tel. (372) 21-39-70; fax (44) 600-54-78; e-mail embjpn@embjpn.tojikiston.com; Ambassador YUICHI KUSUMOTO.

Kazakhstan: 734000 Dushanbe, Kuchai Xuseinzoda 31/1; tel. (372) 221-11-08; fax (372) 251-01-08; e-mail dipmiskz7@tajnet.com; Ambassador ABUTALIL I. AKHMETOV.

Kyrgyzstan: 734000 Dushanbe, Kuchai Said—Nusur 56; tel. and fax (372) 224-26-11; e-mail info@kgembassy.tj; internet www .kgembassy.tj; Ambassador TURATBEK E. JUNUSHALIYEV.

Pakistan: 734000 Dushanbe, Kuchai Dostoyevski 1–3, POB 55; tel. (372) 24-68-39; fax (372) 21-17-29; e-mail pareptaj@rs.tj; Ambassador KHALID USMAN QAISER.

Russia: 734000 Dushanbe, Kuchai Abu Ali ibni Sino 29/31; tel. (372) 235-70-65; fax (372) 235-88-06; e-mail rambtadjik@rambler.ru; internet www.rusemb.tj; Ambassador RAMAZAN G. ABDULATIPOV.

Turkey: 734019 Dushanbe, Xiyoboni Rudaki 17/2; tel. (372) 21-22-08; fax (372) 51-00-12; e-mail turemdus@tajik.net; Ambassador AKIF AYHAN.

Turkmenistan: 734000 Dushanbe, Kuchai Chexov 22; tel. and fax (372) 221-68-84; e-mail embturkm@tjinter.com; Ambassador AKHMED KURBANOV.

United Kingdom: 734002 Dushanbe, Kuchai M. Tursunzoda 65; tel. (372) 224-22-21; fax (372) 227-17-26; e-mail dushanbe.reception@ fco.gov.uk; internet ukintajikistan.fco.gov.uk; Ambassador GRAEME LOTEN.

USA: 734019 Dushanbe, Xiyoboni I. Somoni 109A; tel. (372) 229-20-00; fax (372) 229-20-50; e-mail usembassydushanbe@state.gov; internet dushanbe.usembassy.gov; Ambassador TRACEY ANN JACOBSON.

Uzbekistan: 734003 Dushanbe, Kuchai L. Sherali 15; tel. (372) 21-21-84; fax (372) 24-90-77; e-mail ruzintaj@rambler.ru; internet www .uzembassy-tadjik.mfa.uz; Ambassador SHOQOSIM I. SHOISLOMOV.

Judicial System

Chairman of the Constitutional Court: IZBILLO KHOJAYEV, 734025 Dushanbe, Kuchai Boxtar 48; tel. (372) 21-61-96.

Chairman of the Supreme Court: NASRATULLO ABDULLOYEV, 734000 Dushanbe, Xiyoboni N. Karabayev 1; tel. (372) 73-40-18.

Procurator-General: BOBOJON BOBOKHONOV, 734000 Dushanbe, Kuchai Abu Ali ibni Sino 126; tel. (372) 35-19-72.

Higher Economic Court: 734000 Dushanbe, Kuchai F. Niyazi 37; tel. (372) 21-15-58; f. 1995; Chair. AMIRKHOJA GOIBNAZAROV.

Religion

ISLAM

The majority of Tajiks are adherents of Islam and are mainly Sunnis (Hanafi school). Many of the Pamiri peoples, however, are Isma'ilis (followers of the Aga Khan), a Shi'ite sect. Under the Soviet regime the Muslims of Tajikistan were subject to the Muslim Board of Central Asia and a muftiate, both of which were based in Tashkent, Uzbekistan. The senior Muslim cleric in Tajikistan was the *qazi* (supreme judge). In 1992 the incumbent *qazi* fled to Afghanistan, and in 1993 the Government appointed an independent *mufti* (expert in Islamic law). The Tajikistani Government, however, abolished the post of *mufti* in 1996, following the murder of the incumbent, and established a Council of Islamic Scholars (or *ulema*), as the highest Islamic religious authority in the country.

Council of Islamic Scholars (Ulema): 734000 Dushanbe; Chair. QARI AMANULLOH NEMATZADE.

CHRISTIANITY

Most of the minority Christian population is Slav, the main denomination being the Russian Orthodox Church. There are some Protestant and other groups, notably a Baptist Church in Dushanbe.

Roman Catholic Church

The Church is represented in Tajikistan by a Mission, established in September 1997. There were an estimated 300 adherents at 31 December 2006.

Superior: Rev. CARLOS AVILA, 734006 Dushanbe, Xiyoboni Titova 21/10; tel. (372) 21-21-90; fax (372) 23-26-77; e-mail carlosavila@ive.org; internet tajikistan.ive.org.

The Russian Orthodox Church (Moscow Patriarchate)

The Church in Tajikistan comes under the jurisdiction of the Eparchy of Tashkent and Central Asia, based in Uzbekistan and headed by the Metropolitan of Tashkent and Central Asia, VLADIMIR (IKIM).

JUDAISM

In the mid-2000s there were an estimated 350 Jews in Dushanbe. In 2003 the Government announced that it intended to demolish the only synagogue remaining in Tajikistan, purportedly in order to construct state buildings. Dismantlement of the synagogue began in February 2006. However, following international protests, in late March the Government reversed its decision and announced that the Jewish community was to be permitted to reconstruct the synagogue, which by that time had been partially destroyed, at their own expense.

Leader of the Dushanbe Synagogue: VALERII DAVYDOV, 734001 Dushanbe, Kuchai N. Xikmata 26; tel. (372) 21-76-58.

The Press

In 2000 there were four national newspapers. In 1996 two daily newspapers and 73 non-daily newspapers were published in Tajikistan. There were also 11 periodicals published in that year.

PRINCIPAL NEWSPAPERS

Adabiyet va sanat (Literature and Art): 734001 Dushanbe, Kuchai I. Somoni 8; tel. (372) 24-57-39; f. 1959; weekly; organ of Union of Writers of Tajikistan and Ministry of Culture; in Tajik; Editor GULNAZAR KELDI; circ. 4,000.

Adolat (Justice): 731000 Dushanbe; in Tajik; organ of the Democratic Party of Tajikistan; publication suspended by Ministry of Culture in Sept. 2006, and again in Oct. 2006; Editor-in-Chief RAJAB MIRZO; circ. 1,000 (2006).

Biznes i Politika (Business and Politics): 734025 Dushanbe, Kuchai M. Tursunzoda 30; tel. (372) 23-52-50; e-mail b_p@rambler.ru; f. 1992; weekly; in Russian; Editor-in-Chief U. RAHMON; circ. 10,000.

Charxi gardun (Wheel of Fortune): 734018 Dushanbe, Xiyoboni S. Sherozi 16; tel. (372) 33-56-72; e-mail gazeta@tojikiston.com; f. 1996; weekly; in Tajik; Editor-in-Chief KHABIBULLO YEROV.

Daijest press (Press Digest): 734018 Dushanbe, Xiyoboni S. Sherozi 16; tel. (372) 33-25-03; e-mail gazeta@tojikiston.com; f. 1994; weekly; in Russian; overview of world press; economics; popular culture; Editor-in-Chief MARKHABO ZUNUNOVA.

Djavononi Tochikiston (Youth of Tajikistan): 734000 Dushanbe, Kuchai F. Niyazi 32; tel. (372) 23-38-01; f. 1930; weekly; organ of the Union of Youth of Tajikistan; in Tajik; Editor DAVLAT NAZRIYEV; circ. 3,000.

Ittixod (Unity): 734000 Dushanbe, Xiyoboni Rudaki 137; tel. (372) 34-77-11; organ of the Socialist Party of Tajikistan.

Jumhuriyat (Republic): 734018 Dushanbe, Xiyoboni S. Sherozi 16; tel. (372) 33-08-11; e-mail jumhuriyat@tojikiston.com; f. 1925; 3 a week; organ of the Govt and presidential administration; in Tajik; Editor-in-Chief KAMOL ABDURAHIMOV; circ. 8,000.

Kurer Tadzhikistana (Tajikistan Courier): 734018 Dushanbe, Xiyoboni S. Sherozi 16; tel. (372) 33-08-15; e-mail ttemirov@td.silk.org; weekly; independent; in Russian; Editor KH. YUSIPOV; circ. 40,000.

Millat (Nation): 734000 Dushanbe; f. 2005; in Tajik; independent; Editor ADOLAT UMAROVOI.

Minbari Xalk (People's Tribune): 734018 Dushanbe, Xiyoboni S. Sherozi 16; tel. (372) 33-72-10; organ of the People's Democratic Party of Tajikistan; Editor MANSUR SAIFIDDINOV.

Najot (Salvation): 734000 Dushanbe, Kuchai Toktogul 55; tel. (372) 31-47-38; weekly; organ of the Islamic Rebirth Party of Tajikistan; Editor-in-Chief SIDUMAR KHUSAINI.

Narodnaya Gazeta (People's Newspaper): 734018 Dushanbe, Xiyoboni S. Sherozi 16; tel. (372) 33-08-30; e-mail narodnaja2004@mail.ru; f. 1929; fmrly Kommunist Tadzhikistana (Tajik Communist); weekly; organ of the Govt; in Russian; Editor VLADIMIR VOROBIYEV; circ. 3,000.

Nerui Sukhan (Power of the Word): 734018 Dushanbe, Xiyoboni S. Sherozi 16; f. 2003; weekly; Editor-in-Chief MUKHTOR BOKIZODA.

Nidoi ranchbar (Call of the Workers): 734018 Dushanbe, Xiyoboni S. Sherozi 16; tel. (372) 33-38-50; f. 1992; weekly; organ of the Communist Party of Tajikistan; in Tajik; Editor-in-Chief KHABIBULLO YOROV; circ. 6,000.

Odamu olam (Person and World): 734000 Dushanbe; weekly; in Tajik; independent; socio-political; Editor-in-Chief MIRAHMAD AMIRSHO.

Oila: 734018 Dushanbe, Xiyoboni S. Sherozi 16; tel. (372) 33-32-51; weekly; independent; Editor-in-Chief FIRUZA SATTORI.

Omuzgor (Teacher): 734000 Dushanbe, Kuchai Aini 45; tel. (372) 21-63-36; f. 1932; weekly; organ of the Ministry of Education; in Tajik; Editor-in-Chief SAMIULLO SAIFULLOYEV; circ. 3,000.

Ruzi Nav (New Day): 734018 Dushanbe, Xiyoboni S. Sherozi 16; tel. (372) 33-14-40; f. 2003; weekly; independent; politics and government; Chief Editor RAJABI MIRZO.

Sadoi mardum (The Voice of the People): 734018 Dushanbe, Xiyoboni S. Sherozi 16; tel. (372) 22-42-47; f. 1991; 3 a week; organ of the legislature; in Tajik; Editor MURADULLO SHERALIYEV; circ. 8,000.

Tojikiston (Tajikistan): 734018 Dushanbe, Xiyoboni S. Sherozi 16; tel. (372) 34-94-11; e-mail nt@tajnet.com; f. 1938; weekly; social and political; in Tajik; Editor-in-Chief SHARIF KHAMDAMPUR; circ. (annual) 9,000.

Tojikiston ovozi/Golos Tadzhikistana (Voice of Tajikistan): 734018 Dushanbe, Xiyoboni S. Sherozi 16; tel. (372) 33-06-08; f. 1992; weekly; organ of the Central Committee of the Communist Party of Tajikistan; in Tajik and Russian; Editors SULAYMAN ERMATOV, INOM MUSOYEV; circ. 24,700.

Tribun.tj: 731000 Dushanbe, Xiyoboni Rudaki 107; tel. (372) 21-05-45; fax (372) 24-27-59; e-mail tribun.tj@mail.ru; internet www.tribun.tj; f. 2005; daily; online only; in Russian; organ of the People's Democratic Party of Tajikistan.

Vechernii Dushanbe (Dunshanbe Evening News): 734018 Dushanbe, Xiyoboni S. Sherozi 16; tel. (372) 33-08-15; fax (372) 33-30-25; e-mail anush@tajnet.com; f. 1968; weekly; social and political; in Russian; Editor-in-Chief SAIDALI SIDDIKOV.

Xalk ovozi (Voice of the People): 734018 Dushanbe, Xiyoboni S. Sherozi 16; tel. (372) 33-05-04; f. 1929; 3 a week; organ of the President; in Uzbek; Editor I. MUKHSINOV; circ. 8,600.

Zindagi (Life): 734000 Dushanbe; f. 2004; weekly; in Tajik; independent; politics; Editor-in-Chief KHURSHED ATOVULLO.

PRINCIPAL PERIODICALS

Monthly, unless otherwise indicated.

Adab: 734025 Dushanbe, Kuchai Chexov 13; tel. (372) 23-49-36; organ of the Ministry of Education; in Tajik; Editor SH. SHOKIRZODA; circ. (annual) 24,000.

Avitsenna: 734018 Dushanbe, Xiyoboni S. Sherozi 16; tel. (372) 34-34-44; weekly; in Russian; medicine, health, sport; Editor-in-Chief RUSTAM TURSUNOV.

Bunyod-i Adab (Culture Fund): 734000 Dushanbe; f. 1996 to foster cultural links among the country's Persian-speaking peoples; weekly; Editor ASKAR KHAKIM.

Djashma (Spring): 734018 Dushanbe, Xiyoboni S. Sherozi 16; tel. (372) 33-08-48; f. 1986; journal of the Ministry of Culture; for children; Editor KAMOL NASRULLO; circ. (annual) 10,000.

Farxang (Culture): 734003 Dushanbe, Xiyoboni Rudaki 124; tel. (372) 24-02-39; f. 1991; journal of the Culture Fund and Ministry of Culture; in Tajik; Editor-in-Chief J. AKOBIR; circ. 15,000.

Firuza: 734018 Dushanbe, Xiyoboni S. Sherozi 16; tel. (372) 33-89-10; f. 1932; organ of the Ministry of Culture; social and literary journal for women; Editor ZULFIYA ATOI; circ. (annual) 29,400.

Ilm va khayot (Science and Life): 734025 Dushanbe, Xiyoboni Rudaki 34; tel. (372) 27-48-61; f. 1989; organ of the Academy of Sciences; popular science; Editor T. BOIBOBO; circ. (annual) 12,000.

Istikbol: 734018 Dushanbe, Xiyoboni S. Sherozi 16; tel. (372) 33-14-52; f. 1952; organ of the Ministry of Culture; in Tajik; Chief Editor L. KENJAYEVA; circ. (annual) 10,000.

Marifat: 734024 Dushanbe, Kuchai Aini 45; tel. (372) 23-42-84; organ of the Ministry of Education; in Tajik; Editor O. BOZOROV; circ. (annual) 40,000.

Pamir: 734001 Dushanbe, Kuchai I. Somoni 8; tel. (372) 24-56-56; f. 1949; journal of the Union of Writers of Tajikistan; fiction; in Russian; Editor-in-Chief BORIS PSHENICHNYI.

Sadoi shark (Voice of the East): 734001 Dushanbe, Kuchai I. Somoni 8; tel. (372) 24-56-79; f. 1927; journal of the Union of Writers of Tajikistan; fiction; in Tajik; Editor URUN KUKHZOD; circ. 1,600.

NEWS AGENCIES

Asia-Plus TV-Radio Company: 734002 Dushanbe, Kuchai Boxtar 35/1, 8th Floor; tel. (372) 23-59-95; fax (372) 23-01-07; e-mail manager@asiaplus.tj; internet www.asiaplus.tj; f. 2002; independent; reports in Tajik and Russian; Gen. Dir UMED BABAKHANOV.

Avesta News Agency: 734025 Dushanbe, Xiyoboni Rudaki 21A; e-mail zafar@avesta.tj; internet www.avesta.tj; Dir ZAFAR ABDUL-LAYEV.

Khovar (East): 737025 Dushanbe, Xiyoboni Rudaki 40; tel. (372) 23-23-83; fax (372) 21-21-37; e-mail khovar@tojikiston.com; internet www.khovar.tj; f. 1925; govt information agency; Dir ZAFAR SAIDOV.

Mizon: 734000 Dushanbe; independent information agency; Dir ASATULLO VALIYOV.

Varorud: 735700 Soghd Viloyat, Khujand, Kuchai Ferdovsi 123; tel. and fax (342) 24-09-33; e-mail varorud@varorud.org; internet www.varorud.org; f. 2000; independent; Dir ILKHOM JAMOLOV.

PRESS ASSOCIATIONS

Internews Network—Tajikistan: 734025 Dushanbe, Kuchai Ak. Rajabov 7/1/4; tel. (372) 21-99-33; fax (372) 21-99-34; e-mail chuck@internews.tj; internet www.internews.tj; f. 1995; non-governmental org.; provides support and funding to media organizations, and in the training of journalists; Country Dir CHARLES RICE.

National Association of Independent Mass Media: 734025 Dushanbe, Kuchai Kuchai Xuseinzoda 34; tel. (372) 21-37-11; e-mail nansmit@tojikiston.com; internet www.nansmit.org; f. 1999; Chair. NURIDDIN KARSHIBOYEV.

Publishers

Adib (Writer): 734000 Dushanbe, Xiyoboni Rudaki 37; tel. (372) 23-08-92; fax (372) 23-37-94; state-owned; Tajik and Russian; fiction, incl. poetry, and non-fiction, incl. books on Tajikistani and Central Asian culture.

Donish (Knowledge): 734000 Dushanbe, Xiyoboni Akademiya Nauk 33; state-owned; Russian and Tajik; non-fiction, incl. geography, literature, history, and art; associated with the Academy of Sciences.

Irfon (Light of Knowledge) Publishing House: 734018 Dushanbe, Kuchai N. Karabayev 17; tel. (372) 33-39-06; f. 1925; politics, social sciences, economics, agriculture, medicine and technology; Dir J. SHARIFOV; Editor-in-Chief A. OLIMOV.

Maorif va Farxang (Education and Culture) Publishing House: 734018 Dushanbe, Kuchai N. Karabayev 17; tel. and fax (372) 33-93-97; e-mail najmidin@netrt.org; f. 1958; educational, academic; Gen. Dir NAJMIDDIN ZAYNIDDINOV.

Sarredaksiyai Ilmii Entsiklopediyai Millii Tajik (Tajik National Scientific Encyclopaedia) Publishing House: 731000 Dushanbe, Kuchai Aini 126; tel. (372) 25-81-55; e-mail encyclopedia@yahoo.com; f. 1969; Editor-in-Chief A. QURBONOV.

Sharki Ozod Publishing House: 734018 Dushanbe, Xiyoboni S. Sherozi 16; tel. (372) 34-94-11; e-mail tadjikis@tajnet.com; state-owned; Dir MANZURHON DODOHONOV.

Surushan Publishing House: 734025 Dushanbe, Xiyoboni Rudaki 37; tel. and fax (372) 21-54-62; e-mail surushan@net.org; f. 1997; literary fiction, educational; Dir NURIDDIN ZAYNIDDINOV.

Broadcasting and Communications

TELECOMMUNICATIONS

Babilon-Mobil (Babilon-M): 734001 Dushanbe, Kuchai I. Somoni 5; tel. (372) 24-20-21; e-mail babilon-m@tojikiston.com; internet www.babilon-m.com; f. 2002; mobile cellular telecommunications.

Beeline TJ: Dushanbe; e-mail pr@beeline.tj; internet www.beeline.tj; fmrly Tacom; 60% owned by VympelKom-Bilain (Russia); mobile cellular telecommunications services; f. 2006.

Indigo Somonkom: Khujand; internet www.somoncom.com; f. 2000; provides mobile cellular telecommunications in northern regions, particularly Soghd Viloyat; 130,000 subscribers (2006).

Indigo Tajikistan: 734000 Dushanbe, Kuchai M. Tursunzoda 23; tel. (372) 23-21-21; fax (372) 23-21-23; e-mail sales@indigo.tajnet.com; internet www.indigo.tj; f. 2001; mobile cellular telecommunications.

MLT (Mobile Lines of Tajikistan): 734025 Dushanbe, Xiyoboni Rudaki 57; tel. (372) 21-42-24; internet www.mlt.tj; f. 2001; fmrly TT Mobile; mobile cellular telecommunications.

Tajiktelecom: 734025 Dushanbe, Xiyoboni Rudaki 57A; tel. (372) 21-31-78; fax (372) 23-21-19; e-mail ttelecom@rs.tj; internet www.tajiktelecom.tj; f. 1996; national telecommunications operator; Dir-Gen. GULMAHMAD KAYUMOV.

BROADCASTING

In December 2001 there were some 20 independent television stations.

Regulatory Authority

State Committee for Broadcasting: 734000 Dushanbe; Chair. A. K. RAKHMONOV.

Radio

State TV-Radio Broadcasting Co of Tajikistan: 734025 Dushanbe, Kuchai Chapayev 31; tel. (372) 27-75-27; fax (372) 21-34-95; e-mail soro@ctvrtj.td.silk.org; Chair. ABDODZHABBOR RAKHMONOV.

Asia-Plus Radio: 734000 Dushanbe, Kuchai Boxtar 35/1, 8th Floor; tel. (372) 23-59-95; fax (371) 23-01-07; e-mail radio@asiaplus.tajik.net; f. 2002; country's first independent radio station; broadcasts 19 hours per day in Russian and Tajik; Dir UMED BABAKHANOV.

Tajik Radio: 734025 Dushanbe, Kuchai Chapayev 31; tel. (372) 27-65-69; broadcasts in Russian, Tajik and Uzbek.

Tiroz: 735700 Soghd Viloyat, Khujand, Mikroraion 27; tel. (342) 25-66-89; e-mail trrktiroz@sugdien.com; internet www.tiroz.sugdien.com; Dir KHURSHED ULMASOV.

Television

State TV-Radio Broadcasting Co of Tajikistan: 734025 Dushanbe, Kuchai Chapayev 31; tel. (372) 27-75-27; fax (372) 21-34-95; e-mail soro@ctvrtj.td.silk.org; Chair. ABDODZHABBOR RAKHMONOV.

Poitaxt: 734013 Dushanbe, Kuchai Azizbekov 20; tel. (372) 23-26-29; independent; Dir RAKHMON OSTONOV.

Tajik Television (TTV): 734013 Dushanbe, Kuchai Behzod 7; tel. (372) 22-43-57.

Finance

(cap. = capital; res = reserves; dep. = deposits; brs = branches; m. = million; amounts in somoni, unless otherwise stated)

BANKING

Central Bank

National Bank of the Republic of Tajikistan (Bonki Millii Tochikiston): 734025 Dushanbe, Xiyoboni Rudaki 23/2; tel. (372) 21-26-28; fax (372) 51-00-68; e-mail info@natbank.tajnet.com; internet www.nbt.tj; f. 1991; cap. 0.8m., res 25.4m., dep. 604.8m. (Oct. 2003); Chair. SHARIF RAHIMZODA.

State Savings Bank

Amonatbonk: 734018 Dushanbe, Kuchai Loxuti 24; tel. (372) 221-70-81; fax (372) 223-14-16; e-mail info@amonatbonk.tj; internet www.amonatbonk.tj; f. 1991; fmrly br. of USSR Sberbank; licensed by presidential decree and not subject to the same controls as the commercial and trading banks; Chair. of Bd MAXMADAMIN B. MAXMADAMINOV; 58 brs, 480 sub-brs.

Other Banks

In June 2005 President Rakhmonov announced the removal of all restrictions on the activities of foreign banks in Tajikistan. There were reported to be 16 commercial banks in operation in Tajikistan in early 2005, including the following:

Agroinvestbank: 734018 Dushanbe, Xiyoboni S. Sherozi 21; tel. (372) 233-21-14; fax (372) 236-51-66; e-mail pressa@agroinvestbank.tj; internet www.agroinvestbank.tj; f. 1992; fmrly Agroprombank; cap. US $22.4m., res $5.7m., dep. $118.6m. (Dec. 2007); Chair. NIYOZMUROD M. SAIDMURODOV; 62 brs.

Orienbank: 734001 Dushanbe, Xiyoboni Rudaki 95/1; tel. (372) 21-09-20; fax (372) 21-18-77; e-mail info@orienbank.com; internet www.orienbank.com; f. 1922; cap. 60m., res 25m., dep. 216m. (Aug. 2008); commercial bank; Chair. of Bd HASAN ASADULLOZODA; Chair. of Bank Council SHERMALIK MALIKOV; 32 brs.

Tajbank: 734064 Dushanbe, Kuchai I. Somoni 59/1; tel. (372) 27-46-54.

Tajprombank (Tajik Joint-Stock Bank for Reconstruction and Development): 734025 Dushanbe, Kuchai X. Dexlavi 12/3; tel.

(372) 21-27-20; e-mail tpb@tjinter.com; cap. US $1m., res $3m., dep. $4m.; Chair. DZHAMSHED ZIYAYEV; 8 brs.

Tojiksodirotbank (Bank for Foreign Economic Affairs of the Republic of Tajikistan): 734012 Dushanbe, Kuchai X. Dexlavi 4; tel. (372) 21-59-52; fax (372) 21-47-38; e-mail sham@sodirotbonk .com; fmrly br. of USSR Vneshekonombank; underwent restructuring in 1999; Chair. I. L. LALBEKOV; 6 brs.

COMMODITY EXCHANGES

Tajik Republican Commodity Exchange (NAVRUZ): 734001 Dushanbe, Kuchai Orjonikidze 37; tel. (372) 23-48-74; fax (372) 27-03-91; f. 1991; Chair. SULEYMAN CHULEBAYEV.

Vostok-Mercury Torgovyi Dom: 734000 Dushanbe; tel. and fax (372) 24-60-61; f. 1991; trades in a wide range of goods.

INSURANCE

Muin Insurance Co: 734025 Dushanbe, Kuchai Sh. Rustaveli 16/1; tel. (372) 21-32-80; fax (372) 21-72-09; e-mail ic_muin@mail.ru; f. 1992; Dir-Gen. SHARIFJON ISHAKOV.

Orien Insurance: 734001 Dushanbe, Xiyoboni Rudaki 100; tel. and fax (372) 21-12-30; e-mail info@orieninsurance.tj; internet www .orieninsurance.tj; f. 2004; life and non-life; Dir ISKANDAR KH. SHARIPOV.

Tojiksurguta State Insurance Co: 734025 Dushanbe, Kuchai Chexov 4A; tel. (372) 21-75-07.

Trud Insurance Co: 734000 Dushanbe, Kuchai Bekzod 70; tel. (372) 227-24-24; fax (372) 221-72-21; e-mail info@trud.tj; internet www.trud.tj; f. 2004; life and non-life.

Trade and Industry

GOVERNMENT AGENCIES

Presidential Agency for the Combat of Corruption and Economic Crime: 734000 Dushanbe.

Presidential Agency for Control of Narcotics: 734018 Dushanbe, Kuchai Karabayev 52; tel. (372) 34-81-30; fax (372) 34-81-29; e-mail dca@tojikiston.com; internet www.akn.tj; f. 1999; documents and curbs regional drugs-trafficking; receives financial and technical assistance from the UN Office on Drugs and Crime; Dir Lt-Gen. RUSTAM NAZAROV.

CHAMBER OF COMMERCE

Chamber of Commerce and Industry of the Republic of Tajikistan: 734012 Dushanbe, Kuchai Valamatzade 21; tel. (372) 21-52-84; fax (372) 21-14-80; e-mail chamber@tpp.tj; internet www .tpp.tj; f. 1960; brs in Khujant, Qurgonteppa, Khorog, and Chamber of Services in Dushanbe; Chair. SHARIF S. SAIDOV.

INDUSTRIAL ASSOCIATION

Tajikvneshtorg (Tajik External Trade) Industrial Asscn: 734035 Dushanbe, Xiyoboni Rudaki 25, POB 48; tel. (372) 23-29-03; fax (372) 22-81-20; f. 1988; co-ordinates trade with foreign countries in a wide range of goods; Pres. ABDURAKHMON MUKHTASHOV.

EMPLOYERS' ORGANIZATION

National Asscn of Small and Medium-Sized Businesses of Tajikistan: 734000 Dushanbe, Kuchai Bofanda 9; tel. (372) 27-79-78; fax (372) 21-17-26; f. 1993 with govt support; independent org.; Chair. MATLJUBA ULJABAEVA.

UTILITIES

Electricity

Barqi Tojik (Tajik Electricity): 734000 Dushanbe, Kuchai I. Somoni 64; tel. (372) 35-86-68; fax (372) 35-86-92; e-mail barkitojik@tajnet .com; Chair. BAHROM SIROJEV.

Pamir Energy Co (PamirEnergy): 736100 Kuhistoni Badakhshon, Khorog; e-mail daler.jumaev@pamirenergy.com; f. 2002; jt venture between Governments of Tajikistan and Switzerland, the Aga Khan Fund for Economic Development, the International Finance Corpn and the International Development Association to provide electricity to Kuhistoni Badakhshon; Gen. Dir DALER JUMAYEV.

Gas

Dushanbegaz: 734000 Dushanbe; tel. (372) 27-89-28; supplies gas to Dushanbe City.

Soghdgaz: 735700 Soghd Viloyat, Khujand, 20 Kvartal; tel. (342) 22-53-95; fax (342) 24-35-16; supplies gas to Soghd Viloyat.

Tojikgaz: 734012 Dushanbe, Xiyoboni Rudaki 6; tel. (372) 21-66-68; fax (372) 21-28-16; state-controlled gas utility co.; Dir FATXIDDIN MUXSIDDINOV.

MAJOR COMPANIES

Aluminium Works of Tajikistan (TADAZ): 735014 Tursunzade; tel. and fax (372) 21-06-47; e-mail tadaz@mail.ru; f. 1975; state-owned; aluminium producer; capacity of 400,120 metric tons per year; also producer of aluminium profiles, rolled metal, aluminium discs for car wheels, kitchen utensils; total sales US $434.9m. (2003); Dir ABDUKADIR ERMATOV; over 12,698 employees (2004).

Aprelevka: 735750 Soghd Viloyat, Kairakkum, pos. Kansai, Kuchai Gorki 43; tel. (3443) 7-18-00; fax (3443) 7-18-47; e-mail gulfint@ axionet.com; Tajikistan holds 51% of shares and Gulf International Minerals of Canada holds 49%; gold-mining at nine deposits; Pres. ALASTAIR RALSTON-SAUL.

Carpets of Kairakkum: 735750 Soghd Viloyat, Kairakkum, Kuchai Kovrovschikov 1; tel. (34) 432-36-01; fax (34) 226-07-93; e-mail kolinho@sugdien.com; f. 1960, privatized in 1992; produces half-woollen, woollen and cotton yarn, carpets, synthetic floor coverings; charter cap. US $1.84m.; Gen. Dir BAKHODUR AZIMOV; 3,000 employees.

Khima Textiles Corpn: 734003 Dushanbe, Kuchai Pavlov 21; tel. and fax (372) 24-81-36; f. 1996; operates cotton-processing plants at Gissar, Yavan; Chair. I. I. KHAYEYEV.

Kolkhozabad Cotton Mill: 735200 Khatlon Viloyat, Kolkhoza-badskii raion, PGT Isayev, Kuchai Zheleznodorozhnaya 36; tel. (3247) 4-38-02; fax (3774) 42-36-64; f. 1966; produces cotton; Gen. Dir SABZOV KHAIDAR.

Korxonai Mebelsozi: 734012 Dushanbe, Kuchai K. Mann 130; tel. (372) 21-75-05; manufactures domestic, school and office furniture.

Naftrason: 734025 Dushanbe, Kuchai Xuseinzoda 14; tel. (372) 21-59-37; fax (372) 21-34-83; e-mail naftrason@rs.tj; f. 1999; jt-stock co; petroleum products; Chair. NAZMULLIN M. MIRZOYEV.

Somonien: 734025 Dushanbe, Xiyoboni Rudaki 83; tel. (372) 23-29-03; fax (372) 21-81-20; e-mail siic_somonien@mail.ru; f. 1988; import, export and foreign trade, assists in the development of foreign trading activities, organizes exhibitions, tourism; Chair. ABDURAX-MAN MUXTASHOV; 73 employees.

Tajik Azot: 735147 Khatlon Viloyat, Sarband, Industrial Zone; tel. (3222) 2-35-84; fax (372) 21-82-81; e-mail tjazot@khatlon.com; f. 1964; producer of nitrogenous and other fertilizers and associated products at Vakhsh Fertilizer Plant.

Vostokredmet: 735730 Soghd Viloyat, Chkalovsk, Kuchai Oplan-chuk 12; tel. (3451) 5-92-45; fax (3451) 5-09-45; e-mail vostokredmet@e-mail.ru; refining of gold and silver, manufacture of items from ferrous metals; Dir ZAFAR RAZYKOV.

Zeravshan Co (ZGC): 735512 Soghd Viloyat, Panjakent raion, pos. Soghdiana; tel. (3475) 8-34-75; fax (3475) 5-35-64; e-mail avocetmining@avocet.co.uk; internet www.avocet.co.uk; f. 1996; 75%-owned by Avocet Mining (United Kingdom); mining of gold and silver; Gen. Man. JAY LAYMAN.

TRADE UNIONS

Federation of Trade Unions: 734012 Dushanbe, Xiyoboni Rudaki 20; tel. (372) 23-17-79; fax (372) 23-25-06; f. 1926; present name adopted 1992; Chair. MURODALI S. SALIKHOV; 1.3m. mems.

Transport

RAILWAYS

There are few railways in Tajikistan. In 1999 the total length of the rail network was 482 km. Lines link the major centres of the country with the railway network of Uzbekistan, connecting Khujand to the Farg'ona (Fergana) valley lines, and the cotton-growing centre of Qurgonteppa to Termiz. A new line, between the town of Isfara, in Soghd Viloyat, and Xavast, in Uzbekistan, was opened in 1995 and in 1997 a passenger route between Dushanbe and Volgograd, Russia, was inaugurated. The first section of a new line between Qurgonteppa and Kulob, in the south-west of Tajikistan, was inaugurated in 1998. In October 2002 a route from Kulob to Astrakhan, Russia, was opened. The predominantly mountainous terrain makes the construction of a more extensive network unlikely.

Tajik Railways: 734012 Dushanbe, Kuchai Nazarshoyev 35; tel. (372) 21-88-54; fax (372) 21-83-34; e-mail belugin@railway.td.silk .glas.apc.org; Pres. AMONULLO KH. KHUKUMOV.

ROADS

In mid-2002 Tajikistan's road network totalled an estimated 30,000 km, including 13,747 km of highways. The principal highway links the northern city of Khujand, across the Anzob Pass (3,372 m), with the capital, Dushanbe, continuing to Khorog (Kuhistoni Badakhshon), before wending through the Pamir Mountains, to the east and north, to Osh, Kyrgyzstan, across the Akbaytal Pass (4,655 m). This arterial route exhibits problems common to much of the country's land transport: winter weather is likely to cause the road to be closed by snow for up to eight months of the year. In 2000 Tajikistan and the Asian Development Bank signed a memorandum of understanding for the rehabilitation of the road linking Dushanbe to the south-western cities of Qurgonteppa and Kulob. In the same year a road linking eastern Tajikistan with the People's Republic of China was completed, giving Tajikistan access to the Karakorum highway, which connects China and Pakistan.

CIVIL AVIATION

The main international airport is at Dushanbe, and there is also a major airport at Khujand. The country is linked to cities in Russia and other former Soviet republics, and to a growing number of destinations in Europe and Asia.

TajikAir: 734006 Dushanbe, Kuchai Titova 32/1; tel. (372) 21-21-45; fax (372) 21-86-85; e-mail tt_gart@tajnet.com; internet www.tajikair .tj; state-owned; operates flights to destinations in Afghanistan, the People's Republic of China (Xinjiang Uygur autonomous region), Germany, India, Iran, Kazakhstan, Kyrgyzstan, Pakistan, Russia, Turkey and the United Arab Emirates; Dir VALERII S. SHARIPOV.

Tourism

There was little tourism in Tajikistan even before the 1992–97 civil war. There is some spectacular mountain scenery, hitherto mainly visited by climbers, and, particularly in the Farg'ona (Fergana) valley, in the north of the country, there are sites of historical interest, notably the city of Khujand.

State Committee for Youth, Sports and Tourism: 734000 Dushanbe; f. 2006.

Tajikistan Republican Council of Tourism and Excursions: 734008 Dushanbe, Xiyoboni Rudaki 20; tel. (372) 27-27-51; fax (372) 51-01-40; f. 1960; Chair. MADZHID SOBIROV.

Sayoh State Unitary Tourism Company: 734025 Dushanbe, Kuchai Pushkin 14; tel. (372) 23-14-01; fax (372) 21-71-84; e-mail gafarov@cada.tajik.net; internet www.tajiktour.tajnet.com; Chair. KASIM GAFAROV.

Culture

Tajikistan has a rich cultural heritage. A 14-m statue of a sleeping Buddha, dating from the fifth century, was uncovered by archaeologists in 1966. The region's largest ancient Buddha statue was placed on display in August 2001 in the newly opened Museum of National Antiquities. The museum also houses a fifth-century statue of the Hindu god Shiva, which is believed to be the largest artefact illustrating the spread of Hinduism into the northern part of Central Asia.

NATIONAL ORGANIZATION

Ministry of Culture: see The Government (Ministries).

CULTURAL HERITAGE

S. Aini Republican Museum: 734000 Dushanbe, Kuchai X. Xakimadze 1; tel. (372) 23-15-44; Dir SANGIN XAFIZOV.

K. Bekhtov Republican United Historical and Fine Arts Museum: 734000 Dushanbe, Kuchai Aini 31; tel. (372) 21-60-36; museum and art gallery; 55,000 items; library of over 17,000 vols; Dir GULCHEXRA NUMONOVA.

Ethnographic Museum: 734000 Dushanbe, Kuchai I. Somoni 14; tel. (372) 21-07-64; Dir ZEBO KAVRAKOVA.

Firdousi National Library: 734025 Dushanbe, Xiyoboni Rudaki 36; tel. (372) 27-47-26; e-mail toshew@yandex.ru; f. 1933; 3.1m. vols; Dir SH. TOSHEV.

Museum of Antiquities of Tajikistan: 734000 Dushanbe; includes ancient Islamic, Buddhist, Zoroastrian and Hindu artefacts; Dir SAIDMURAD BABAMULLOYEV.

Shahidi Museum of Musical Culture: 734000 Dushanbe, Kuchai Loiq Sherali 108; tel. (372) 24-23-42; e-mail munira_shahidi@yahoo .com; internet www.shahidifoundation.org; f. 1992; Dir MUNIRA SHAHIDI.

SPORTING ORGANIZATIONS

State Committee for Youth, Sports and Tourism: see Tourism.

National Olympic Committee of the Republic of Tajikistan: 734025 Dushanbe, Kuchai Aini 24, POB 2; tel. (372) 21-75-51; fax (372) 51-00-73; e-mail noc@tajik.net; f. 1992; Pres. GAFAR MIRSOYEV; Sec.-Gen. SHIRINDZHON MAMADSAFOYEV.

PERFORMING ARTS

S. Aini Tajik Academic Opera and Ballet Theatre: 734000 Dushanbe, Xiyoboni Rudaki 28; tel. (372) 21-80-47; f. 1940; Dir NARIMAN QARIMOV.

Akhorun State Experimental Studio Theatre For A Young Audience: 734000 Dushanbe; tel. (372) 27-09-68; f. 1988; Dir FARRUKH QOSIMOV.

Dushanbe Puppet Theatre: 734000 Dushanbe, Kuchai Shotemur 54/1; tel. (372) 21-66-97; f. 1985; Dir RUSTAM AKHMADOV.

A. Lohuti Tajik Academic Drama Theatre: 734000 Dushanbe, Xiyoboni Rudaki 86; tel. (372) 21-78-43; f. 1929; Dir ISO ABDURASHI-DOV.

Lola State Dance Ensemble: 734000 Dushanbe, Kuchai Aini 31; tel. (372) 21-12-13; f. 1965; Dir RADIF YAFAYEV.

V. Mayakovskii State Russian Drama Theatre: 734000 Dushanbe, Xiyoboni Rudaki 76; tel. (372) 21-31-32; e-mail teatrmayaktj@ mail.ru; f. 1937; Dir SUXROB MIRZOYEV.

ASSOCIATION

Union of Artists: 734000 Dushanbe, Xiyoboni Rudaki 89; tel. (372) 24-35-03; e-mail lozasurika@yahoo.com; Chair. SUXROB KURBONOV.

Education

Education is controlled by the Ministry of Education and was, under the Soviet system, fully funded by the state at all levels. Education is officially compulsory for nine years, to be undertaken between seven and 17 years of age. Primary education begins at seven years of age and lasts for four years. Secondary education, beginning at the age of 11, lasts for as much as seven years, comprising a first cycle of five years and a second of two years. In 2005/06 total enrolment at primary schools included 97.3% of the relevant age-group (males 99.4%; females 95.0%). In that year total enrolment at secondary schools included 80.4% of the relevant age-group (males 87.1%; females 73.5%).

The majority of pupils received their education in Tajik (66.0% of pupils in general day schools in 1988). Following the adoption of Tajik as the state language, greater emphasis was placed in the curriculum on Tajik language and literature, including classical Persian literature. In May 2003 President Emomali Rakhmonov announced that the compulsory teaching of Russian was to be reintroduced to schools from September of that year.

Constitutional amendments approved by referendum in June 2003 were to provide for the withdrawal of guarantees of free higher education. In 2006/07 there were 146,200 students enrolled at 34 institutes of higher education. Agreement on the establishment of a joint Russian-Tajik Slavonic University in Dushanbe was reached in 1997. In 2000 the Presidents of Kazakhstan, Kyrgyzstan and Tajikistan co-signed a charter of foundation for a new University of Central Asia, which was to be established in Khorog (in Kuhistoni Badakhshon Autonomous Viloyat) and administered by the Aga Khan Development Network, based in Geneva, Switzerland. Budgetary expenditure on education by all levels of government was forecast at 336m. somoni (17.3% of total anticipated government budgetary expenditure) in 2006.

UNIVERSITIES

Khujand B Gafurov State University: 735700 Soghd Viloyat, Khujand, Kuchai B. Mavlonbekov 1; tel. (34) 226-75-18; fax (34) 224-08-15; e-mail hgu-rector@sugdien.com; f. 1932 as Khujand Pedagogical Institute; current name since 1991; 15 faculties; 1 pedagogical college; languages of instruction: Tajik, Russian, Uzbek, English; Rector NOSIRJON SALIMOV.

Russian-Tajik Slavonic University: 734032 Dushanbe, Kuchai M. Tursunzoda 30; tel. (3772) 2-35-50; fax (3772) 21-05-79; f. 1996; Rector ABDUDZHABOR S. SATTOROV.

Tajik State Agricultural University: 734017 Dushanbe, Xiyoboni Rudaki 146; tel. (372) 24-72-07; f. 1931; languages of instruction: Tajik and Russian; 482 teachers; 6,960 students; Rector Prof. YU. S. NAZYROV.

Tajik State Medical University: 734003 Dushanbe, Xiyoboni Rudaki 139; f. 1996; fmrly Tajik Abu-Ali Ibn-Cina State Medical Institute; languages of instruction: Tajik and Russian.

Tajik State National University: 734025 Dushanbe, Xiyoboni Rudaki 17; tel. (372) 22-77-11; fax (372) 21-48-84; e-mail tgnu@mail .ru; internet www.tsnu.tojikiston.com; f. 1948 (present status 1997);

languages of instruction: Tajik and Russian; 12 faculties; 1,228 teachers; 13,060 students; Rector Prof. X. S. SAFIYEV.

Social Welfare

Under the Soviet system there was a fully state-funded health and social welfare system, largely dependent upon transfers from the all-Union budget. There were reforms aimed at making the social security system self-financing to a greater degree, notably with the help of employee and employer contributions. At the beginning of 1992 an Employment Fund was established and the Pension Fund and Fund for Social Expenditure (social insurance) were reformed. Even before the problems of the civil war their operations were expected to produce a deficit, and tax avoidance problems had increased significantly by the mid-1990s. In theory, social guarantees consisted of five elements: family allowances (including student grants and compensation for reductions in the bread price subsidy); Pension Fund provision for old age, disability or social reasons; Employment Fund assistance in training, labour placement and unemployment benefits; social insurance payments for sick pay, remedial health care services and maternity allowances; and price subsidies. Tajikistan also received a high level of international humanitarian assistance. In 1996 a Social Protection Fund was established to address the problem of pension arrears; the fund was abolished in late 2006, with relevant responsibilities being transferred to the Ministry of Labour and Social Welfare. In May 1998 new benefits were introduced for students, pensioners and disabled people to enable them to meet rising living costs.

The civil war of 1992–93 produced some 600,000 refugees, both internally and in neighbouring countries. Kuhistoni Badakhshon was largely isolated from supplies from November 1992 until August 1993. By the beginning of 1996 many refugees had been able to return to their homes and the confirmation in June 1997 of the peace agreement of December 1996 provided some stability in the country. Between July 1997 and January 1998 the last groups of refugees returned from camps in northern Afghanistan. In 2006 there were an estimated 2.0 physicians and 6.1 hospital beds per 1,000 inhabitants. Projected budgetary expenditure for 2006 on health (106m. somoni) and social security and welfare (238m. somoni) amounted to 17.7% of total anticipated budgetary expenditure. With effect from 1 April 2006 the maximum pension in Tajikistan amounted to 180 somoni per month.

NATIONAL AGENCIES

Ministry of Health: see The Government (Ministries).

Ministry of Labour and Social Welfare: see The Government (Ministries); assumed many responsibilities of fmr Social Protection Fund in Dec. 2006.

HEALTH AND WELFARE ORGANIZATIONS

Caritas Tajikistan: 734012 Dushanbe, Kuchai Titov 10, proyezd 21; tel. (37) 226-38-50; e-mail Caritas.TJ@ive.org; Pres. Fr CARLOS AVILA; Sec.-Gen. JUAN CARLOS SACK.

Red Crescent Society of Tajikistan (RCST): 734017 Dushanbe, Kuchai O. Xayom 120; tel. (772) 24-48-28; fax (772) 24-53-78; e-mail rcstj@yahoo.com; Pres. Dr JURA INOMZODA.

Society for the Blind: 734000 Dushanbe, Kuchai Karamov 205; tel. (372) 37-32-31; Chair. TURABEK DAVLATOV.

Society for the Deaf: 734000 Dushanbe, Kuchai Xuvaidulloyev 270; tel. (372) 36-71-21; Chair. GALINA MALISHEVA.

Society of Invalids: 734000 Dushanbe, Kuchai Telman 4; tel. (372) 21-38-37; f. 1989; Chair. XAKIM XAKNAZAROV.

The Environment

Tajikistan was less affected than other former Soviet Central Asian countries by the consequences of over-irrigation, but not completely immune, and there was some concern at intensive fertilizer use in the southern cotton-growing regions. The country was important as a water source for Turkmenistan, in particular. There was anxiety about the effect on the extensive glaciers of the Pamir mountains of wind-borne pesticides and other chemicals from the Aral region, and concern regarding the reduction of the water level of the Aral Sea basin, owing to over-utilization.

GOVERNMENT ORGANIZATION

Ministry of Land Improvement and Water Resources: see The Government (Ministries).

ACADEMIC INSTITUTES

Academy of Sciences of the Republic of Tajikistan: 734025 Dushanbe, Xiyoboni Rudaki 33; tel. (372) 221-50-83; fax (372) 221-49-11; e-mail ilolovm@gmail.com; internet www.ant.tj; f. 1951; Pres. MAMADSHO I. ILOLOV; institutes incl.:

Institute of Water, Hydro-energy and Ecology Issues: 734002 Dushanbe, Kuchai Parvin 12; tel. (37) 224-52-31; f. 2002; Dir INOM SH. NORMATOV.

NON-GOVERNMENTAL ORGANIZATIONS

Dushanbe Environmental Movement: 734000 Dushanbe; e-mail isarata@glas.apc.org; deals with ecotourism and environmental monitoring; Contact MIKHAIL TYUTIN.

Pamir Ecocentre: 736002 Kuhistoni Badakhshon, Khorog, Kuchai Michurin 1, Pamir Biological Institute; tel. (35220) 41-82; e-mail pamir@eco.khorugh.tajik.net; internet www.pbi.narod.ru; f. 1994; conducts environmental education programmes for youth and works to protect the environment of the Pamir region; 2 brs.

Scientific Education Centre for Tajik Ecologists: 734000 Dushanbe, Kuchai Chexov 13; tel. (372) 21-59-86.

Tajikistan Socio-Ecological Union: 734043 Dushanbe, Kuchai Mayakovski 46/2/34; tel. (372) 36-86-29; Chair. MUAZAMA A. BURXANOVA; Sec. HAMID A. ATAXANOV.

Defence

Following the dissolution of the USSR in December 1991, Tajikistan became a member of the Commonwealth of Independent States (CIS, see p. 694) and its Collective Security Treaty. In April 2003 the Collective Security Treaty Organization was inaugurated as the successor to the CIS collective security system, with the participation of Armenia, Belarus, Kazakhstan, Kyrgyzstan, Russia and Tajikistan. A Ministry of Defence was established in September 1992; in December it was announced that Tajikistan's national armed forces were to be formed on the basis of the Tajik People's Front and other paramilitary units supporting the Government. Integration of United Tajik Opposition force members into the Tajikistani armed forces took place from 1998. Military service lasts for 24 months (12 months for those with higher-education degrees). As assessed at November 2007, the armed forces numbered 8,800, comprising an army of 7,300 and an air force of 1,500. Some 7,500 paramilitary border guards were attached to the Ministry of Internal Affairs. There were plans to form an Air Force squadron. The budget for 2007 allocated an estimated 300m. somoni to defence. Tajikistan became a member of the North Atlantic Treaty Organization's 'Partnership for Peace' (see p. 715) programme of military co-operation in February 2002.

Chief of General Staff: RAMIL NODIROV.

Commander of the Air Force: RAXMONALI D. SAFARALIYEV.

AUTONOMOUS TERRITORY

Tajikistan includes one nominally autonomous territory, Kuhistoni Badakhshon Autonomous Viloyat.

KUHISTONI BADAKHSHON AUTONOMOUS VILOYAT

Kuhistoni Badakhshon (Mountainous Badakhshon, or, in Russian, Gornyi Badakhshan) Autonomous Viloyat is situated in the southeast of Tajikistan, constituting the entire eastern part of the country. The territory is dominated by the Pamir mountain range, and includes the highest mountain in the former USSR, Peak Ismail Samani (formerly Communism Peak—7,495 m). Its chief town is Khorog, in the west of the territory, near the border with Afghanistan (there are also international borders with the People's Republic of China in the east and Kyrgyzstan in the north). The population in 2000 was 206,000, of which some 28,000 lived in Khorog. By January 2006 the population of the region was estimated to have increased to 220,400, but the region remained sparsely populated, with a population density of only 3.4 per sq km. In 1993 an estimated 80,000 refugees from other parts of Tajikistan arrived in the region. The local administration consists of seven raions (districts).

Kuhistoni Badakhshon is dominated by the Pamiri people, distinct from the Tajiks in both language and religion (many are Isma'ilis and spoke one of six eastern Iranian languages only distantly related to Tajik). The territory was only acquired by the Russian Empire at the very end of the 19th century and was long an area of disputed sovereignty. Under Soviet rule it gained a special administrative status, becoming an Autonomous Oblast in 1925, but remained one of the poorest regions in the USSR. During the late 1980s a separatist movement, Lale Badakhshon, emerged, which allied itself with the Islamist and democratic opposition to the communist establishment of Tajikistan. In 1993, however, severely affected by the civil war and with the main road from Dushanbe to Khorog closed until August, the local administration pledged its loyalty to the Tajikistani state and appealed for urgent food and medical aid. Although this ended most conflict in the region, its borders remained vulnerable to penetration by opposition forces, and its territory, both because of the nature of its terrain and the sympathies of its inhabitants, remained a redoubt of rebels during the mid-1990s. The region remained economically impoverished in the mid-2000s, being dependent to a large extent on budgetary transfers from the national Government, although proposals, agreed by the Presidents of Kazakhstan, Kyrgyzstan and Tajikistan in 2000 to establish a campus of a proposed University of Central Asia in Khorog, which was to be administered by the Aga Khan Development Network (based in Switzerland), would, it was hoped, provide a focus for the regeneration of the region. Other campuses of the university were under construction in Tekeli, Kazakhstan, and in Naryn, Kyrgyzstan. In 2006 the university's first operational academic programme was launched—the School of Professional and Continuing Education—which offered university-based non-degree educational courses, providing vocational and professional training.

Chairman of Kuhistoni Badakhshon Autonomous Viloyat Administration (Khukumat): ALIMAMAD NIYOZMAMADOV, 736000 Kuhistoni Badakhshon, Khorog, ul. Lenina 47; tel. (352) 20-32-59; internet www.president.tj/guzorishho_vmkb.htm.

Representation of Kuhistoni Badakhshon Autonomous Viloyat to the Government of Tajikistan: 734000 Dushanbe, pr. Rudaki 48; tel. (372) 27-85-97.

Bibliography

Abdullaev, K., and Akbarzadeh, S. *Historical Dictionary of Tajikistan.* Lanham, MD, Rowman & Littlefield, 2002.

Akiner, S. *Islamic People of the Soviet Union: An Historical and Statistical Handbook*, 2nd edn. London and New York, Kegan Paul International, 1987.

Tajikistan. Washington, DC, Brookings Institution Press, 1998.

Tajikistan: Disintegration or Reconciliation? London, Royal Institute of International Affairs, 2002.

Anderson, J. *The International Politics of Central Asia.* Manchester, Manchester University Press, 1997.

Atkin, M. *The Subtlest Battle: Islam in Soviet Tajikistan.* Philadelphia Paper, Philadelphia, PA, Foreign Policy Research Institute, 1989.

Bergne, P. *The Birth of Tajikistan: National Identity and the Origins of the Republic.* London, I. B. Tauris, 2007.

Bliss, F. *Social and Economic Change in the Pamirs (Gorno-Badakhshan, Tajikistan).* Abingdon, Routledge, 2005.

Butler, W. (Ed. and Translator). *Tadzhikistan Legal Texts: The Foundations of Civic Accord and a Market Economy.* Boston, MA, Kluwer Law International, 1999.

Curtin, M. *Environmental Profile of Tajikistan.* Manila, Asian Development Bank, 2001.

De Martino, L. *Tajikistan at a Crossroad: The Politics of Decentralization.* Geneva, CIMERA Publications, 2004.

Djalili, M.-R., Grare, F., and Akiner, S. (Eds). *Tajikistan: The Trials of Independence.* Richmond, Curzon, 1998.

Falkingham, J. *Women and Gender Relations in Tajikistan.* Manila, Asian Development Bank, 2001.

Harris, C. *Control and Subversion: Gender Relations in Tajikistan.* London, Pluto Press, 2004.

Muslim Youth: Tensions and Transitions in Tajikistan. Boulder, CO, Westview Press, 2006.

Jawad, N., and Tadjbakhsh, S. *Tajikistan: A Forgotten Civil War.* London, Minority Rights Group, 1995.

Jonson, L. *The Tajik War: A Challenge to Russian Policy.* London, Royal Institute of International Affairs, 1998.

Tajikistan in the New Central Asia: Geopolitics, Great Power Rivalry and Radical Islam. London, I. B. Tauris, 2006.

Lynch, D. *Russian Peacekeeping Strategies in the CIS: The Cases of Moldova, Georgia and Tajikistan.* Basingstoke, Macmillan, 2000.

Mishra, N. N. *Ethnicity and Islam Revivalism in Tajikistan and Uzbekistan.* New Delhi, National Book Trust, 2007.

Nourzhanov, K. *Tajikistan: The History of an Ethnic State.* London, C. Hurst and Co, 2002.

Plater-Zyberk, H. *Tajikistan: Waiting For a Storm?* Camberley, Conflict Studies Research Centre, 2004.

Rubin, B. 'Russian Hegemony and State Breakdown in the Periphery: Causes and Consequences of the Civil War in Tajikistan', in Rubin, B., and Snyder, J. (Eds), *Post-Soviet Political Order: Conflict and State Building.* London, Routledge, 1998.

Saavalainen, T. *Republic of Tajikistan.* Washington, DC, IMF, 2001.

Also see the Select Bibliography.

TURKMENISTAN

Geography

PHYSICAL FEATURES

Turkmenistan is situated in the south-west of Central Asia. It is bordered to the north by Uzbekistan, to the north-west by Kazakhstan and to the west by the Caspian Sea. To the south lies Iran and, to the south-east, Afghanistan. The country has an area of 488,100 sq km (188,456 sq miles).

The Kara-Kum (Black Sand) desert, one of the largest sand deserts in the world, covers more than four-fifths of Turkmenistan, occupying the entire central region. There are mountainous areas along the southern and north-western borders, including the Kopet-Dag range, along the frontier with Afghanistan, which is prone to earthquakes. The main river is the Amu Dar'ya (Oxus), which flows through the eastern regions of the country and used to empty into the Aral Sea. The Kara-Kum Canal, which was begun in 1954, carries water from the Amu Dar'ya to the arid central and western regions of Turkmenistan, where there are no significant natural waterways. However, the existence of this Canal is one of the main factors contributing to the desiccation of the Aral Sea, as the Amu Dar'ya dries up before reaching it. The other major rivers are the Murgab, which flows south into Afghanistan, and the Tejen, which also flows south and forms part of the border with Iran.

CLIMATE

The climate is severely continental, with extremely hot summers and cold winters. The average temperature in January is −4°C (25°F), but winter temperatures can fall as low as −33°C (−27°F). In summer, temperatures often reach 50°C (122°F) in the south-east Kara-Kum; the average temperature in July is 28°C (82°F). Precipitation is slight throughout much of the region. Average annual rainfall ranges from only 80 mm in the north-west to about 300 mm per year in mountainous regions.

POPULATION

The largest ethnic group is the Turkmen (77.0% of the population, according to the census of January 1995). Minority groups included Uzbeks (9.2%), Russians (6.7%) and Kazakhs (2.0%). Among the Turkmen there remains a strong sense of tribal loyalty, reinforced by dialect. The largest tribes are the Tekke in central Turkmenistan, the Ersary in the south-east and the Yomud in the west of the country. Other Turkmen tribes live in Iran. In 1990 Turkmen was declared the official language of the republic. Russian is also used, but in 1989 only some 25% of Turkmen claimed fluency in Russian. Turkmen is a member of the Southern Turkic group of languages; in 1927 the traditional Arabic script was replaced by a Latin script, which was,

in turn, replaced by a Cyrillic script in 1938. In 1993 it was announced that the republic would gradually change to a Latin-based Turkish script. Most of the population are Sunni Muslims. Islam in Turkmenistan traditionally featured elements of Sufi mysticism and shamanism, and pilgrimages to local religious sites were reported to be common.

There are large discrepancies between official and external estimates of the total population. According to the National Institute of State Statistics and Information, the total estimated population at 1 April 2006 was 6,800,200. However, according to UN estimates, the population numbered 5,031,000 at mid-2008, giving a population density of 10.3 per sq km. In 2002, according to official estimates, 46% of the population was urban, although most non-Turkmen live in urban areas. The capital, Aşgabat, is in the south of the country, near the border with Iran. As with the country as a whole, estimates of population of the city varied considerably. According to UN estimates, and including suburbs, the capital had a population of 744,000 in mid-2007, whereas official estimates in 2002 placed the population of the city at 743,000. Türkmenabat (formerly Charjew), situated on the Amu Dar'ya, is the second largest city (its population was estimated at 203,000 in 1999). Other important centres include Daşoguz (165,000 in 1999), Mari (123,000), Balkanabat (formerly Nebit-Dag—119,000) and the Caspian port of Türkmenbaşi (formerly Krasnovodsk—70,000).

Chronology

552–659: Turkic tribes moved west and settled in the area of modern Turkmenistan.

644–61: Southern areas of modern Turkmenistan, including Mari, were conquered for Islam under Caliphs 'Uthman and 'Ali.

661–750: Central and eastern areas of Turkmenistan were taken by Muslims during the Ummayad dynasty.

10th century: Turkic Oguz tribes, ancestors of the Turkmen, migrated to Turkmenistan.

1038–1194: Southern and eastern areas of Turkmenistan formed part of the territory of the Seljuq Turkic dynasty.

1219–25: Mongol forces under Temujin (Chinghiz or Genghis Khan) attacked Khwarezm, formerly a territory owing allegiance to the Abbasid caliphate, conquering the Empire of the Khwarezm Shah.

1251–65: Hulagu, a grandson of Chinghiz Khan, established the Empire of the Il-Khans, which included all but the extreme north-west of modern Turkmenistan.

1353: The Il-Khans were replaced by a local Turkmen dynasty who established *beyliks*, administrative areas ruled by *beys* (princes).

1370–80: A Turkmen emir from Transoxania, in modern Uzbekistan, Timur (Tamerlane), founded the second Mongol

Empire, which included the territories of the Turkmen. Timur's empire disintegrated rapidly after his death in 1405, and control of Transoxania passed to the Uzbek tribes.

17th century: Southern areas of Turkmenistan, including Mari, were dominated by the Safavid dynasty of Persia (Iran).

1868–73: The Uzbek-ruled khanates of Bukhara and Khiva, which had disputed Persia for control of Turkmen territories for more than a century, were made protectorates of the Russian Empire. The Russians also gained control of western areas of Turkmenistan adjacent to the Caspian Sea.

1881: After a four-year campaign by the Russians against the tribes of central Turkmenistan, an estimated 14,500 Turkmen were killed at the battle of Gök Tepe (near Aşgabat).

1884: Persia ceded control of the territories near Mari, which became the southernmost part of the Russian Empire.

1895: The United Kingdom and Russia established the southern boundary of modern Turkmenistan, when they demarcated the British and Russian 'spheres of influence'.

1917: Following an unsuccessful Bolshevik attempt to gain power, an anti-Bolshevik Russian Provisional Government of Transcaspia and a Turkmen Congress were established.

30 April 1918: The Turkestan Autonomous Soviet Socialist Republic, including Transcaspia, was proclaimed after Bolshevik forces had occupied Aşgabat.

July 1918: Turkmen nationalists, with limited support from the British, overthrew the Bolshevik regime and created an independent state based in Aşgabat.

1920: Following the British withdrawal from the area, Aşgabat was captured by the Red Army and the Turkmen leader, Muhammad Qurban Junaid Khan, joined the *basmachi* resistance (which continued into the mid-1930s).

27 October 1924: The Turkmen Soviet Socialist Republic (SSR) was established, becoming a Union Republic of the USSR the following May.

1927: The traditional Turkmen Arabic script was replaced by a Latin script.

1929: An agricultural collectivization programme was begun, under which nomadic tribes were forced to settle in collective farms.

c. 1937: The execution of Nederbai Aitakov, 'nationalist' Chairman of the Turkmen Supreme Soviet (Supreme Council), was the most notable example of the persecution of Turkmen intellectuals, politicians and even communist officials, which was prevalent during the 1930s.

1938: The Latin alphabet introduced in 1927 was replaced by a Cyrillic script.

1954: Construction work began on the Kara-Kum Canal, which conveys water from the Amu Dar'ya river (the Oxus of ancient times) on the eastern border of Turkmenistan, to irrigate dry central and western areas of the country; the Canal is a principal cause of the desiccation of the Aral Sea.

1958: Sukhan Babayev, First Secretary of the Communist Party of Turkmenistan (CPT), proposed an increase in the number of ethnic Turkmen in positions of importance; subsequently Babayev and a large number of his political colleagues were dismissed from office.

1985: Saparmyrat Niyazov became First Secretary of the CPT.

September 1989: Turkmen intellectuals formed Unity (Agzybirlik), a 'popular-front' organization concerned with cultural, economic and environmental issues; the movement was banned in January 1990.

7 January 1990: Only the CPT and other approved organizations were allowed to participate in elections to the Supreme Soviet and local councils; consequently, the CPT obtained the majority of seats. Niyazov was later elected Chairman of the new Supreme Soviet.

May 1990: Turkmenistan declared Turkmen to be the official language of the Republic.

22 August 1990: The Turkmen Supreme Soviet adopted a declaration of sovereignty, which asserted Turkmenistan's right to secede from the USSR.

27 October 1990: Niyazov was unopposed in direct elections for the first executive President of the Republic, receiving 98.3% of the votes cast.

17 March 1991: An all-Union referendum was held on a new Union treaty; 95.7% of the participating electorate in Turkmenistan approved the 'renewal' of the USSR.

18–21 August 1991: There was little official reaction to the attempted conservative coup in the USSR; however, several leaders of opposition groups that denounced the *putsch* were arrested.

27 October 1991: The Supreme Council declared the country independent, the day after 94.1% of voters opted for independence in a national referendum on the issue.

December 1991: The CPT became known as the Democratic Party of Turkmenistan (DPT), under the chairmanship of Niyazov.

21 December 1991: Turkmenistan and 10 other former Union Republics signed the Almaty Declaration establishing the Commonwealth of Independent States (CIS), effectively dissolving the USSR.

18 May 1992: A new Constitution was adopted, increasing the powers of the President of the Republic, who became, conjointly, Chairman of the Government (Prime Minister) and Supreme Commander-in-Chief of the Armed Forces; the Constitution also established the Khalk Maslakhaty (People's Council) as a supervisory national assembly, while a new legislature, the Majlis, was to be formed.

21 June 1992: Niyazov was re-elected unopposed as President, receiving 99.5% of the votes cast.

July 1992: Abdy Kuliyev resigned as Minister of Foreign Affairs, allegedly over Niyazov's growing authoritarianism. Kuliyev subsequently established an opposition grouping based in Moscow, Russia.

November 1992: Elections for the 50 regional representatives to the Khalk Maslakhaty were held (the first session of the Council took place in mid-December).

January 1993: Electricity, gas and water supplies were made free to all citizens of Turkmenistan.

October 1993: The Khalk Maslakhaty conferred the title of Türkmenbaşi (Leader of the Turkmen) on President Niyazov.

1 November 1993: Turkmenistan introduced its own currency, the manat.

23 December 1993: President Niyazov and the Russian President, Boris Yeltsin, signed an agreement, unique in the former Soviet countries, granting ethnic Russians in Turkmenistan dual nationality with the Russian Federation.

15 January 1994: In a referendum proposed by the DPT, 99.9% of the electorate voted to exempt President Niyazov from having to seek re-election in 1997, ostensibly in order to allow the completion of economic reform.

11 December 1994: Elections to the 50-member Majlis were held, with the participation of 99.8% of the electorate; 49 of the deputies were elected unopposed. The Majlis convened later in the month.

12 July 1995: Demonstrations took place in Aşgabat and Mari, in criticism of Niyazov's leadership and of continuing economic hardship.

12 December 1995: The UN General Assembly recognized Turkmenistan's neutral status.

5 April 1998: Elections to the Khalk Maslakhaty were held, with the participation of 99.5% of the electorate.

12 December 1999: Legislative elections were held to the 50-seat Majlis, with an official participation rate of 98.9%. The DPT was the only party represented.

27 December 1999: The Khalk Maslakhaty voted to abolish the death penalty; Turkmenistan thereby became the first Central Asian state to do so. On the following day the new Majlis approved an amendment to the Constitution, permitting Niyazov to remain President indefinitely. In February 2001, however, Niyazov announced his intention to resign by 2010.

7 September 2000: Turkmenistan became a member of the Asian Development Bank (ADB).

24 September 2001: President Niyazov was reported to have given his consent to the use of Turkmenistan's ground and air transport corridors in order to deliver humanitarian aid to Afghanistan in the event of US-led air-strikes against that country's Taliban regime and targets associated with the Islamist fundamentalist Osama bin Laden.

19 October 2001: The Khalk Maslakhaty adopted Niyazov's national code of spiritual conduct, the *Ruhnama*.

1 November 2001: A former Minister of Foreign Affairs, Boris Shikhmuradov, who had fled to Moscow in October, publicly declared his opposition to President Niyazov. The Turkmenistani authorities subsequently filed a number of criminal charges against Shikhmuradov, amid reports that he was intending to instigate a coup.

4 January 2002: Shikhmuradov, who remained in exile, established the opposition People's Democratic Movement of Turkmenistan, and publicly urged Niyazov to resign from office.

14 March 2002: In response to increasing opposition activity, Niyazov began a large-scale purge of high-ranking officials from the security and intelligence agencies. Prominent dismissals included that of the Minister of Defence, Gurbandurdy Begenjev, and the head of the Committee for National Security (KNB), Mukhammed Nazarov. In May Begenjev was sentenced to 10 years' imprisonment, and in June Nazarov received a 20-year prison sentence, having been convicted of crimes including corruption, murder and drugs-trafficking.

30 May 2002: The Presidents of Turkmenistan, Pakistan and Afghanistan signed a memorandum of understanding to carry out a feasibility study on the construction of a proposed gas pipeline from Turkmenistan to Pakistan, via Afghanistan (suspended since August 1998). A framework agreement on the construction of the 1,680-km pipeline was signed on 27 December.

June 2002: The two opposition movements in exile, the People's Democratic Movement of Turkmenistan and the United Democratic Opposition of Turkmenistan (ODOT—led by Kuliyev), agreed to work together to promote democracy and the rule of law in Turkmenistan.

September 2002: A Ministry of National Security was created to replace the KNB; Niyazov subsequently devolved greater power to his personal security administration, the Presidential Guard.

25 November 2002: An assassination attempt was widely reported to have been made against the presidential motorcade in Aşgabat. At an emergency cabinet meeting, President Niyazov accused Shikhmuradov and Nurmukhammed Khanamov, founder of the Republican Party of Turkmenistan (RPT), of orchestrating a *coup d'état*.

30 December 2002: Following a one-day trial, Shikhmuradov was sentenced to 25 years' imprisonment (later increased to a life sentence by the Majlis). In all, more than 50 people received sentences for their involvement in the assassination attempt of November. At the end of December the Uzbekistani ambassador to Turkmenistan was expelled, amid accusations that the Government of Uzbekistan had supported the attempted coup, and given Shikhmuradov sanctuary in the Uzbekistani embassy in Aşgabat.

6 April 2003: Elections to the Khalk Maslakhaty and 5,535 local councils took place, with a reported participation rate of 89.3%.

15 August 2003: Constitutional amendments were approved, elevating the Khalk Maslakhaty to the status of 'permanently functioning supreme representative body of popular authority', and requiring it to remain in continuous session. Niyazov announced his intention to leave office before 2010. The constitutional changes also forbade citizens of Turkmenistan from holding dual citizenship, thereby effectively revoking the agreement on dual nationality reached with Russia in December 1993.

September 2003: Turkmen opposition leaders in exile, meeting in Prague, Czech Republic, announced the formation of the Union of Democratic Forces of Turkmenistan (UDFT), comprising Kuliyev's ODOT, the RPT, and two other groupings.

November 2003: New legislation restricting the activities of religious groups, by criminalizing any confession not registered with the Ministry of Justice, was approved. At that time the only state-registered faiths were Sunni Islam and Russian Orthodox Christianity, although new, more flexible provisions for registration were issued by Niyazov in March 2004, and unauthorized religious activity was made an administrative, rather than criminal, offence.

18 November 2004: The UN General Assembly adopted a second resolution expressing grave concern at human rights violations in Turkmenistan (the first had been adopted in November 2003). Russia abstained from voting, and Uzbekistan voted against the resolution.

19 November 2004: President Niyazov and President Islam Karimov of Uzbekistan signed three bilateral agreements at their first presidential summit meeting for over four years, held in Buxoro (Bukhara), Uzbekistan. In mid-December they celebrated the demarcation of their mutual border, and a new Uzbekistani ambassador to Turkmenistan was appointed in January 2005.

19 December 2004: Elections to the Majlis were held. Only representatives of the DPT took part in the poll, which no international observers were invited to monitor. A reported 76.9% of the registered electorate participated in the ballot, and a second round of voting was conducted in seven districts on 9 January 2005.

26 February 2005: President Niyazov ordered the closure of all hospitals outside Aşgabat, and of all rural libraries (asserting that, since the rural population was largely illiterate, it made little use of the existing facilities).

7 April 2005: Niyazov announced that a multi-candidate presidential election was to be conducted in 2009, following elections to appoint district governors in 2006, regional governors in 2007 and parliamentary deputies in 2008.

26 August 2005: Turkmenistan's decision to withdraw from the CIS, while remaining an associate member, was announced at a summit of the organization.

24 October 2005: The Khalk Maslakhaty amended the Constitution to provide for the direct election of district, city and regional councils. Elections to 40-member district and city councils were scheduled to be held in December 2006, followed by elections to 80-member regional councils in December 2007.

The right to appoint regional, district and city hakims (governors) was transferred from the President to the respective councils. At the same time it was decided to postpone discussion of the possibility of holding a presidential election until 2009.

3 April 2006: Turkmenistan and the People's Republic of China signed an agreement to construct a natural gas pipeline; China was to purchase 30,000m. cu m of Turkmenistani gas per year for 30 years from 2009.

3 December 2006: Elections were held to the 40-member district and city councils, with 6,142 candidates contesting 2,640 seats; it was announced that about 97% of the electorate had voted.

21 December 2006: President Niyazov died, having suffered a heart attack. The Chairman of the Majlis, Ovezgeldy Atayev, who, under the terms of the Constitution, should have assumed the role of acting President, was removed from his post shortly after Niyazov's death, and subsequently charged with criminal activity. The State Security Council appointed the Deputy Chairman and Minister of Health and the Medical Industry, Gurbanguly Berdymuhamedov, to act as President, pending an election.

11 February 2007: Six candidates contested the presidential election; Berdymuhamedov won by an overwhelming majority, receiving 89.2% of the votes cast. The authorities claimed that some 98.6% of the electorate participated.

14 February 2007: Berdymuhamedov was inaugurated as President. A number of government ministers and other senior state officials were subsequently replaced, including several ministers who had previously served under Niyazov. Among the principal appointments were those of Rashid Meredov as Deputy Chairman and Minister of Foreign Affairs, Maj.-Gen. Agageldy Mamatgeldiyev as Minister of Defence and Murad Karryev as Minister of Justice.

9 December 2007: Elections were held to councils in each of the country's regions.

1 January 2008: Foreign-exchange points were permitted to open, with two fixed rates of exchange: the state exchange rate was fixed at $1 = 6,250 manats, and the commercial rate was fixed at $1 = 19,800 manats, effectively eliminating the unofficial exchange rate.

18 April 2008: A commission was established to draw up proposed amendments to the Constitution.

1 May 2008: A unified, 'floating' exchange rate was introduced, at an initial rate of $1 = 14,250 manats. A redenominated currency was to come into circulation from the beginning of 2009. The following day Berdymuhamedov ordered the Neutrality Arch, which featured a large, revolving, gold-plated statue of Niyazov, and occupied a prominent position in central Aşgabat, to be relocated to the outskirts of the city.

10 June 2008: The Presidents of Turkmenistan and Azerbaijan, meeting in St Petersburg, Russia, reached agreement on the reopening of the Turkmenistani embassy in Baku, closed since 2001, and agreed to establish an intergovernmental commission on bilateral co-operation.

1 July 2008: Legislation restoring the traditional names of the months of the year and the days of the week came into force, following a decree by Berdymuhamedov in April.

21 July 2008: A new, draft Constitution was published.

12 September 2008: The state media reported that violent clashes had taken place in a suburb of Aşgabat between members of criminal groups associated with the illegal drugs trade and police officers.

26 September 2008: An extraordinary session of the Khalk Maslakhaty took place. The new Constitution was approved, providing, *inter alia*, for the dissolution of the Khalk Maslakhaty; its powers were to be divided between the President and the Majlis, which would henceforth comprise 125 deputies.

History

ANNETTE BOHR

EARLY HISTORY

Although there are various theories about their origin, the Turkmen are widely believed to have descended from the Oguz tribes that migrated from the Altai region north of Mongolia in the latter part of the 10th century. The Turkmen founded the Seljuq dynasty, which had its capital at Mari, and the empire of which encapsulated most of the eastern lands of the Islamic world. The largely nomadic Turkmen tribes did not form a national state, and overlordship was divided between the Persian (Iranian) Empire, the Khivan Khanate and the Bukharan Emirate. Over the centuries the Turkmen developed a formidable reputation as caravan raiders and brigands, who were notorious for abducting Persians and, later, Russians and selling them into slavery in the markets of Khiva (Xiva) and Bukhara (Buxoro).

The region comprising modern Turkmenistan was the last Central Asian territory to be brought under the control of tsarist Russia. The battle for the fortress of Gök Tepe in 1881, at which Russian troops mined and stormed the Turkmen citadel, killing some 14,500 defenders, broke the stubborn Turkmen resistance and decided the fate of the rest of Transcaspia. When tsarist annexation of the Turkmen region was completed in 1884–85, the tribe represented the highest form of political and economic power. A treaty signed in 1895 by the United Kingdom and the Russian Empire, which established an international boundary, and divided the region into British and Russian 'spheres of influence', left significant numbers of Turkmen outside the borders of what is now Turkmenistan.

The Turkmen eventually came under Bolshevik rule following the revolutions of 1917 and the ensuing civil wars. In the first years of Soviet rule Central Asia was divided along national lines, according to Stalin's (Iosif Dzhugashvili) four criteria: unity of economy, culture, territory and language. As a result, an autonomous Turkmen region was created in 1921, followed by the establishment of the Turkmen SSR on 27 October 1924. In the same year the Soviet Turkmen language, which was constructed from the dialects of the Yomud and Tekke tribes, was decreed the official language of the new Union Republic.

SOVIET TURKMENISTAN

The consolidation of Soviet power in the Turkmen region did not occur without a struggle. Turkmen participated in the *basmachi* guerrilla revolt, which swept Central Asia following the Bolshevik Revolution. Led by Muhammad Qurban Junaid Khan, Turkmen tribes successfully captured Khiva in 1918 and established their leader in power. A Red Army detachment drove him into the desert early in 1920, where he and his followers joined the *basmachi* resistance. The collectivization drive begun in Central Asia in 1929 forced many Turkmen, Kazakh and Kyrgyz nomads to settle and join collective farms. This trauma added impetus to the resistance, and Turkmen fighters waged war in the area of Krasnovodsk (now officially known as Türkmenbaşi) and the Kara-Kum desert throughout the early 1930s, until 1936.

A nascent Turkmen intelligentsia was also generally, but peacefully, opposed to Soviet rule. A Provisional Turkmen

Congress was established in Aşgabat following the 1917 Bolshevik Revolution. The Congress joined with the 'Whites' (anti-Bolshevik forces) in the latter half of 1918, to form the Government of the Transcaspian Region. This Government, with some British assistance, managed to resist the Bolsheviks for just over one year before succumbing to Soviet rule. It was between 1930 and 1935, however, that the Turkmen intelligentsia was most vocal in its demands for greater political autonomy. The Soviet authorities began purging Turkmen intellectuals on a large scale in 1934, soon widening the purges to include Turkmen government leaders. By 1937–38, when Nederbai Aitakov, the Chairman of the Supreme Soviet of the Turkmen SSR, was executed, the last of a generation of Turkmen nationalists had perished.

In 1928 the Soviet authorities began the implementation of an anti-religious policy, with the aim of completely eliminating Islam among the Turkmen. This campaign was perhaps the harshest of the anti-Islamic offensives simultaneously begun in all the republics of Central Asia. Of the approximately 500 mosques that were functioning in Turkmen territory in 1917, only four were still operational in 1979. As in the rest of Central Asia, all Islamic courts of law, *waqf* holdings (religious endowments that formed the basis of clerical economic power) and Muslim primary and secondary schools were liquidated in Turkmenistan by the end of the 1920s. During the Second World War the Soviet leadership temporarily suspended the persecution of Islam, in order to secure greater support for the war effort. An all-Union, official Muslim organization was established in 1942, consisting of four spiritual directorates (Turkmenistan was under the jurisdiction of the Muslim Board of Central Asia and Kazakhstan, based in Tashkent, Uzbekistan). After the War, discrimination against religion was resumed, although the official Islamic establishment remained. Distrust of official Islam among Soviet Muslims and the paucity of officially recognized mosques and clerics, however, forced Islam to establish itself covertly, enabling it to thrive in the post-War period, and especially in the later decades of the 20th century.

Despite two changes in alphabet (the Arabic script was replaced by a Latin script in 1927, and the Latin by a Cyrillic script in 1938), the strongly developed compulsory school system established in the 1920s, together with the mass campaigns against adult illiteracy, caused literacy rates to improve dramatically. According to official statistics, the literacy rate in Turkmenistan rose from 2.3% of the adult population to 99% between 1926 and 1970 (although this apparently included a large number of people only able to sign their names and spell a few words).

Tsarist Russia had made little attempt at the industrialization of Turkmenistan and it was not until the first years of Soviet rule that this began. Although in the 1920s the central authorities invested sizeable sums in the establishment of industrial enterprises in Turkmenistan and sent a large number of skilled Slavic workers to facilitate the process, industrial development began to decline as early as the 1930s, as the republic became increasingly orientated towards agriculture. At the time of the collapse of the USSR, the industrial enterprises established in Turkmenistan in the 1920s accounted for virtually all light industry in the republic. In the 1990s most heavy industry was directed towards the exploitation of Turkmenistan's large petroleum and natural gas deposits, with the exception of the Kara-Bogaz chemical works.

The Nationalist Movement

In the mid-1980s, when the twin policies of glasnost (openness) and perestroika (restructuring) were introduced, Turkmenistan was among the very poorest of the Soviet republics in terms of income per head, and it had the USSR's highest rate of infant mortality, as well as its lowest rate of life expectancy. Encouraged by glasnost, members of the intelligentsia and politicians alike began to describe their republic's relationship with the all-Union authorities based in Moscow, the Russian and Soviet capital, as, in essence, colonialist. In support of their argument, they cited an investment policy aimed at the export of massive amounts of raw cotton and natural gas from their republic, at artificially low prices, while neglecting the devel-

opment of industry. Concomitantly, a variety of cultural and ecological grievances surfaced, including demands for a reassessment of Turkmen history, the removal of Russian toponyms, the rehabilitation of disgraced Turkmen writers and a halt to environmental damage. In line with the other Soviet republics, in May 1990 Turkmen was made the state language of the republic, and both Russian and Turkmen were declared 'languages of inter-ethnic communication'. The Constitution adopted in 1992 failed to grant Russian any special status, however, either as a joint state language or as the language of inter-ethnic communication.

Opposition movements, which appeared in Turkmenistan in 1989, played only a limited role before the Government's policy of systematic harassment drove their most active members into exile. Turkmenistan's first and most significant popular movement, Unity (Agzybirlik), the programme of which focused on national revival, organized its first major demonstration on 14 January 1990 at Gök Tepe, the site of the historic last stand of Turkmen resistance to Russian rule. Despite official warnings, nearly 10,000 people gathered to commemorate those who had died in the famous battle. On the following day the Turkmenistani authorities banned the opposition movement, although it persisted with its founding congress a matter of weeks later.

Turkmenistan's leadership was silent during the attempted conservative coup of August 1991, publicly condemning the actions of the hardline communists in Moscow only once it had become clear that their 'State Committee for the State of Emergency' was doomed to failure. As the republics of the USSR began declaring their independence in rapid succession following the failure of the August coup attempt, Turkmenistan's leadership decided to put the question of self-rule to a national referendum, which was held in October 1991. Although the population of the Turkmen SSR had voted overwhelmingly in favour of preserving a federation (95.7% of all votes cast) in an all-Union referendum held only seven months before, 94.1% of the electorate cast their votes for independence. Thus, on 27 October 1991—exactly 67 years after the creation of the Turkmen SSR—the independent Republic of Turkmenistan was declared. At its 25th Congress in December, the Communist Party of Turkmenistan was renamed the Democratic Party of Turkmenistan (DPT). The leader of the party since December 1985, its First Secretary, Saparmyrat Niyazov, was confirmed in the post of Chairman, and the old communist power structure remained essentially intact. On 21 December, in the capital of Kazakhstan, Turkmenistan became a signatory of the Almaty Declaration, whereby the country became a founder member of the Commonwealth of Independent States (CIS).

INDEPENDENT TURKMENISTAN

The Niyazov Era

On 18 May 1992 Turkmenistan's parliament adopted a new Constitution, making it the first Central Asian state to enact such a document after the dissolution of the USSR. A direct presidential election was held on 21 June, under the new Constitution, although Niyazov had been popularly elected to the presidency by direct ballot only 20 months previously, in October 1990. According to official results, in 1992 the rate of participation by the electorate was 99.8%, with 99.5% of all votes cast in favour of Niyazov. In January 1994 a nation-wide referendum prolonged Niyazov's presidential mandate until 2002, exempting him from another popular election in 1997, as required by the Constitution. Following months of speculation on the introduction of a 'life presidency', at the end of December 1999 the republican legislature, the Majlis, taking up the recommendation of the Khalk Maslakhaty (People's Council—see below), approved amendments to the Constitution, which removed the maximum two-term provision, and thereby enabled Niyazov to remain as President for an unlimited period. Turkmenistan, therefore, became the first CIS country formally to abandon regularly scheduled presidential elections.

An unusual creation of Niyazov during the reorganization of political structures in May and June 1992 was the Yaqşular Maslakhaty (Council of Elders), which was proclaimed to be based on national tradition and which brought together nominated elders from all regions of Turkmenistan under the chairmanship of the President. The most original governing body created by President Niyazov, however, was the Khalk Maslakhaty. A pseudo-representative organ, it was intended to recall the Turkmen 'national tradition' of holding tribal assemblies to solve society's most pressing problems. According to a constitutional amendment and a constitutional law on the Khalk Maslakhaty, which were passed by that body on 15 August 2003, the Khalk Maslakhaty was elevated to the status of a 'permanently functioning supreme representative body of popular authority'. Whereas, before August 2003, the law dictated that the Khalk Maslakhaty convene at least once a year, the new law required the Khalk Maslakhaty to remain in continuous session. The 2,507-member body comprised: the President; the Majlis deputies; the Chairman of the Supreme Court; the Prosecutor-General; the members of the Council of Ministers; the hakims (governors) of the five velayats (regions) and of the city of Aşgabat; people's representatives elected from each district; the chairpersons of officially recognized parties; the Youth Association, trade unions, and the Women's Union (members of the All-national Galkynyş National Revival Movement of Turkmenistan); the chairpersons of public organizations; representatives of the Yaqsular Maslakhaty; the hakims of cities and etraps (districts); and the heads of the municipal councils (archins) of the towns and villages that were the administrative centres of the districts.

The August 2003 law ascribed to the Khalk Maslakhaty a number of legislative powers, including the adoption of constitutional laws, thereby displacing the Majlis as the country's leading legislative body. In reality, both the Khalk Maslakhaty and the Majlis simply served to validate officially the President's policies. At the same time as the status of the Khalk Maslakhaty was formally upgraded, Niyazov was unanimously elected as Chairman of the body, with a lifetime tenure.

The first parliamentary elections in independent Turkmenistan took place in December 1994, when 49 candidates stood unopposed for seats in the 50-member unicameral legislature, the Majlis (two candidates contested the remaining seat). Parliamentary elections were held again in December 1999, with a declared participation rate of 98.9% of the country's electorate. However, although 104 candidates stood for the 50 parliamentary seats, nearly all of them were members of Niyazov's ruling DPT and served the state in some official capacity. As with previous elections, the country's third parliamentary elections, which were held on 19 December 2004, were widely regarded as a ceremonial exercise. As in the past, the Turkmenistani authorities did not invite international observers (including observers from other CIS countries) to monitor the parliamentary elections, asserting that national officials were capable of monitoring the event without external help.

In October 2005 the Khalk Maslakhaty amended the Constitution to provide for the holding of direct elections to district, city, and regional councils from 2006–07. At that time executive power in Turkmenistan's five velayats and in the city of Aşgabat was vested in the hakims, who were appointed by the President to execute his instructions. Even at more diffuse levels of local administration, the President also appointed the executive heads of the cities and districts (şakher hakims and etrap hakims, respectively), ostensibly based upon the recommendations of the respective velayat hakims. In December 2006 elections were held to the largely ceremonial 40-member district and city people's councils (halk maslakhaty) for the first time in the post-Soviet era, with 6,142 candidates vying for 2,640 seats. Officials claimed that the creation of district, city and regional people's councils was intended to devolve governmental powers and responsibilities from the centre, in large part by allowing local governors to be elected by the councils, by a simple majority vote, rather than appointed by the President, as was the practice hitherto. However, as was reported by local media in December 2006, the President approved the nominations for governors that had been put forth by the councils, thereby greatly diminishing any decentralizing effect. Elections to 80-member regional councils were scheduled for December 2007.

Regarding representative organs in the villages and towns, the 1992 Constitution provided for the replacement of the local soviets by municipal councils (gengeşes), the members of which were directly elected for five-year terms. The 625 gengeşes were administered by archins, who were elected from among their respective memberships. On 23 July 2006 some 5,320 deputies were elected to local gengeşes from a field of 12,200 contenders. Despite multiple candidacies and the use of transparent ballot boxes for the first time in Turkmenistan, there was minimal pre-election campaigning and all candidates still represented Niyazov's DPT.

Authoritarianism and the 'Cult of Personality'

Throughout the duration of President Niyazov's rule, freedom of speech was severely restricted and official control of the mass media was complete. Censorship was carried out through the Committee for the Preservation of State Secrets, created in February 1991, which was responsible for registering and approving all national and regional newspapers and journals in Turkmenistan, while the four state television channels and the three state radio stations functioned as mouthpieces for government propaganda. In July 2002 the Government halted the import of Russian newspapers and magazines, and banned cable television (which provided access to Russian channels), thereby eliminating two of the very few sources of alternative information. In July 2004 the Turkmenistani authorities blocked transmission of Russia's Radio Mayak, which was highly popular in Turkmenistan and acted as one of the last independent media sources in the country, aside from a few foreign broadcasts on shortwave radio aimed at Turkmenistani listeners. In April 2005 the import and circulation of all foreign print media, including those produced in neighbouring countries, was prohibited. Satellite dishes were tolerated, but were prohibitively expensive for the majority of the population, particularly outside the capital of Aşgabat. Access to the internet was controlled by the country's sole internet service provider, Türkmentelekom, which blocked websites critical of government policy.

There were no political parties or movements officially registered in the country other than Niyazov's DPT and the pro-Government National Revival Movement. The opposition was divided into two primary groups, both of which were operating in exile: the United Democratic Opposition of Turkmenistan (ODOT—the 'old' opposition), led by former Minister of Foreign Affairs Abdy Kuliyev; and the People's Democratic Movement of Turkmenistan (PDMT—the 'oligarchic' opposition), led by Boris Shikhmuradov, who had served as Foreign Minister from 1993 to 2000 and was the main architect of Niyazov's policy of 'permanent neutrality'. Kuliyev, who joined the opposition-in-exile in 1992, criticized Shikhmuradov for having played a leading role in establishing Turkmenistan as a closed and corrupt state and for relentlessly persecuting the opposition during his long tenure as Deputy Chairman and Minister of Foreign Affairs. The new phase of repression following the failed coup of 25 November 2002 (see below) provided an impetus to President Niyazov's opponents to attempt to reconcile their differences and join forces. On 29 September 2003, following a two-day meeting in Prague, Czech Republic, several prominent members of Turkmenistan's opposition parties and movements, all of which were operating in exile, issued a communiqué announcing their decision to unite as the Union of Democratic Forces of Turkmenistan (UDFT). The UDFT consisted of four main groups: the Republican Party of Turkmenistan, the Fatherland (Watan) Social Political Movement, the ODOT and the Revival Social Political Movement. However, the UDFT did not manage to become an active organization. Despite the issuing of another joint statement by the Republican Party and Watan in May 2006, appealing for citizens of Turkmenistan to unite and resist Niyazov's regime, the opposition-in-exile remained small, weak, poor and prone to internal division.

The appointment of officials in Niyazov's regime was based on their complete loyalty and subservience to the President rather than on a system of merit. Niyazov regularly purged the upper and middle echelons of his Government as a means of diminishing the power bases of political élites and, hence, their potential ability to become his rivals (the official reason given for cadre reshuffling, however, was generally corruption, or simply 'failing in one's duties'). From 2000 Niyazov's reshuffling of ministers and other senior-level officials greatly accelerated in both intensity and scope, possibly reflecting an increasing inability to trust his officials as well as a growing sense of vulnerability. By mid-2005 nearly 60 deputy prime ministers had been dismissed in the 14-year history of independent Turkmenistan, only five of whom continued to hold civil service positions. The remainder were either imprisoned, in exile, unemployed or under house arrest.

Following independence, the leadership of Turkmenistan sanctioned the revival of Muslim practices, while simultaneously striving to keep religion within official structures. Niyazov consequently endorsed the construction of mosques, the teaching of basic Islamic principles in state schools, the refurbishment of holy places and the restoration of Islamic holidays. However, despite adopting limited measures to promote Islam, at the same time the Government required all religious communities to obtain legal registration and banned all religious parties. In April 1994 a council for religious affairs, the Genges, was created within the presidential apparatus 'to ensure the observance of the law'. In July 2000 a long-serving official in the Genges acknowledged that the organization controlled the selection, promotion and dismissal of all clergy in Turkmenistan. In 1997 the Turkmenistani leadership initiated the repression of Islamic activity by closing many of the mosques that had been opened only a few years earlier (mostly in Mari Velayat), closing virtually all institutions of Islamic learning, halting the importation of foreign religious literature and tightening restrictions on the legal registration of religious communities, which effectively denied minority confessions the right to gather publicly, proselytize and disseminate religious materials. Violators were subject to penalties under the administrative code. Before 2004 the only confessions that had managed to register successfully were Sunni Islam and Russian Orthodox Christianity, although they were still subject to extremely tight government controls. In March 2004 President Niyazov issued a decree pledging to register all religious groups, regardless of confession or number. As a result, a small number of minority religious groups managed to achieve registration in 2004–05. However, despite minimal progress, many minority religious communities remained unregistered. More importantly, registration did not bring the promised benefits, as registered and unregistered groups alike continued to experience police raids, detentions, fines and other forms of harassment, throwing into question the very purpose of the registration process.

In addition to incorporating elements of populism and despotism, President Niyazov's rule engendered a lavish 'cult of personality'. The honorary title of Türkmenbaşi (Turkmenbashy), meaning Leader of the Turkmen, was officially conferred on Niyazov in October 1993. In May of that year the Yaqşular Maslakhaty decided to erect monuments to the President in all cities and densely populated areas of the country. By 2005 Niyazov's name or his title of Türkmenbaşi (or his nickname, 'Serdar', meaning 'Supreme Chieftain') had been given to at least two cities, several districts and villages, the Kara-Kum Canal, the country's main airport, the Academy of Agricultural Sciences, a military institute, a police academy, sanatoriums, a multitude of schools, farms, mosques, avenues, streets and squares, as well as a cologne, a brand of vodka and the country's highest mountain peak. His portrait was ubiquitous throughout the state. After Niyazov changed his hair colour from grey to black in 1999, a large work-force was reported to have spent weeks incorporating this change into the thousands of presidential portraits and posters throughout the country. Additionally, a 70-m arch commemorating the country's neutrality was completed in 1999 in the centre of the capital, topped by a gold-plated, winged 12-m statue of President Niyazov, which revolved in conjunction with the sun's movements. Study of his multi-volumed writings was introduced as a mandatory subject in all educational establishments (see Nation-Building, below). Newspapers, radio and television referred daily to the former Communist Party First Secretary as the 'great thinker and politician of the 20th century', as 'the creator of Turkmenistan' and even, on occasion, as a prophet. All of the country's television stations

carried a golden logotype of the President's profile in the upper right-hand corner of the screen. Niyazov's cult of personality was officially extended to include his deceased parents, who were posthumously awarded the highest state titles of 'Hero of Turkmenistan' and 'National Mother and Heroine of Turkmenistan', respectively. In May 2001 the Humanitarian Association of World Turkmen awarded Niyazov the title 'Beik' ('the Great'), thereby amending his official title to 'President Saparmyrat Türkmenbaşi the Great'.

The November 2002 Coup Attempt

According to official reports, on 25 November 2002 President Niyazov's motorcade was fired upon in Aşgabat, as he was travelling to his office. The Turkmenistani authorities immediately publicized the attack as a failed assassination and coup attempt, co-ordinated by Turkmen oppositionists-in-exile with the aid of foreign mercenaries. At the end of December it was revealed that Niyazov's most renowned political rival, Shikhmuradov, had clandestinely returned to Turkmenistan from abroad prior to the attack, reportedly in order to organize a series of anti-Government actions inside the country. On 25 December Shikhmuradov was arrested in Aşgabat. In a statement claimed to be written by Shikhmuradov, which was dated 24 December and published on the website of his opposition group two days later, he announced plans to surrender to the authorities voluntarily in order to save his relatives from torture and to prevent further arrests. He warned that he could not take responsibility for any statements made after his arrest. Shikhmuradov subsequently made a televised confession, in which he referred to Niyazov as a 'gift given to the people from on high', named his allies in the putative assassination attempt and expressed his deep contrition. Human rights groups and opponents of Niyazov likened the confessions to the Stalinist 'show trials' of the 1930s, asserting that Shikhmuradov made his statement while subjected to torture and under the influence of psychotropic drugs.

Although many of the details of these events remained unclear, available evidence indicated that Shikhmuradov and his associates attempted forcibly to remove Niyazov from power, although with no intention to assassinate him. In the event, information about the planned operation had been disclosed to members of Niyazov's security agencies beforehand, enabling them to stage a counter-operation and subsequently present the coup attempt as a carefully planned plot to assassinate the President. Niyazov managed to use the attempted coup to his advantage by seizing the opportunity to incarcerate some of his major opponents and to implement a series of new measures that curbed civil liberties further still. The armed attack led to a new phase of repression, resulting in the arrests of at least 200 people with purported connections to the opposition, of whom approximately 60 were ultimately convicted for their alleged role in the coup attempt. Three of the four opposition leaders accused of co-ordinating the attack were given the maximum sentence of 25 years' imprisonment (two of them were convicted *in absentia*). However, following demands by the Khalk Maslakhaty for death sentences, Niyazov proposed that a new maximum penalty of life imprisonment, with no possibility of pardon, amnesty or parole, be introduced for the crime of treason, which was very broadly defined as any crime against the State or the President.

The Dismantling of the Social Sector

During the latter years of Niyazov's rule significant reductions in pensions, frequent redundancies, the introduction of fees for medical services, the accumulation of wage arrears owed to government employees and the use of military conscripts as a source of free labour all indicated that the state was having difficulty funding its huge social sector, despite official reports of record foreign trade surpluses. Although President Niyazov sought to place responsibility for budget shortfalls on his subordinates by accusing them of mass embezzlement, a more likely explanation was the continued diversion by Niyazov of ever larger sums from gas, petroleum and cotton revenues into a special presidential fund, held in foreign bank accounts. This foreign-exchange reserve fund, which did not form part of the state budget and was under Niyazov's personal control, was estimated to be worth at least 60% of the country's gross domestic product, with export revenues providing its main source of inflow. A significant portion of this fund was used to subsidize prestige construction projects commissioned by the President. By late 2006 more than US $3,000m. had been spent since independence on such projects, including a palace of congress and arts, two stadiums, a national museum, luxury hotels, a horse-racing centre, a national theatre of music and drama, a new library and exhibition centre, a children's attraction park, dozens of monuments, Central Asia's largest mosque and Central Asia's largest Olympic-standard, indoor watersports complex. In May 2006 work was completed on a $21.5m. palace made of ice in Aşgabat, despite the fact that temperatures regularly exceeded 40°C. Furthermore, Niyazov undertook the construction of a huge artificial lake in the Kara-Kum desert, with a planned capacity of two times that of Central Asia's entire reservoirs.

Budget shortfalls resulting from the diversion of export revenues by Niyazov's Government hastened the systematic dismantling of important areas of the social sector. From 2000 Niyazov's regime implemented several major reverses to the education system, with the consequence that scientific activity was severely curtailed and the majority of children in Turkmenistan no longer had adequate access to education. In many rural schools, it was estimated that one-half of classroom time was allocated to the study of Niyazov's quasi-spiritual guide, the *Ruhnama* (Book of the Soul), and other writings devoted to furthering his personality cult. In addition, students were required to demonstrate knowledge of the *Ruhnama* in order to be admitted to higher educational establishments. More than 12,000 teachers were made redundant in accordance with a 2000 presidential decree, including those with degrees from foreign universities, which were no longer recognized. The number of student places in institutes of higher education was reduced by nearly 75%, and the length of time spent in primary and secondary education was reduced (a circumstance that complicated the entry of Turkmenistani students into foreign universities). Only those who had completed two years of work experience after leaving school were allowed to enter higher education, and higher education courses were reduced to just two years. All correspondence and evening courses were liquidated. The dismantling of the education system placed in doubt the ability of the next generation of Turkmenistanis to compete successfully in the global market.

In addition to the education sector, health care services were systematically undermined. In March 2004 some 15,000 health workers (including doctors, nurses, midwives and medical attendants) were dismissed. In addition, the 'reforms' implemented in that month introduced fees for specialist services that had previously been free of charge, making treatment unaffordable for many patients. In February 2005 President Niyazov ordered the closure of all hospitals outside Aşgabat. Under Niyazov's proposals, citizens in the country's regions were to visit diagnostic centres, which required payment for services, to obtain prescriptions and general advice, while those in need of hospitalization or specialist care were to be compelled to travel to the capital. By late 2006 all rural district hospitals were reported to have closed, although hospitals in district centres continued to operate. While these hospitals offered some specialist care, many Turkmenistanis had to travel long distances to regional centres to receive both emergency and specialist medical treatment.

Nation-Building

As in other post-Soviet republics, the leadership of Turkmenistan embarked on an extensive process of nation-building in an effort to consolidate the citizenry around a single, national idea and imbue it with patriotic feeling. Hence, President Niyazov introduced an oath of loyalty to the homeland, recited on public occasions, and appearing on the mastheads of the country's newspapers. The glorification of Niyazov as the father of the nation was a major component of the larger nation-building project, and was exemplified by slogans, such as 'Nation, Homeland, Türkmenbaşi', prominently displayed throughout the country. Niyazov also sought to revive national customs by creating more than 15 new holidays from 1991, many of which paid homage to an object or tradition closely associated with Turkmen culture, such as Turkmen Carpet Day or Turkmen Melon Day.

From 2000 President Niyazov embarked on a fresh period of nation-building or 'Turkmenization', particularly in the spheres of education, culture and mass media. In October he ordered the destruction of thousands of new history textbooks for 'perverting our glorious past', by purportedly failing to stress sufficiently the Turkmen people's indigenousness and by including descriptions of positive advancements made under Russian and Soviet rule. Universities were encouraged to reject applicants with non-Turkmen surnames, and foreign qualifications were not recognized in Turkmenistan. All schools were required to adopt Turkmen as the main language of instruction. In April 2001 Niyazov announced the closure of Turkmenistan's only opera and ballet theatre, on the grounds that its repertoire was not 'in conformity with the national mentality'. A national music and drama theatre replaced the opera and ballet theatre, with the aim of increasing the prominence of the works of contemporary Turkmen authors. In the same month three new state television and radio channels were created to broadcast programmes 'with a national flavour'. In August 2002 Niyazov instructed the Khalk Maslakhaty to redesignate the months of the year and days of the week with Turkmen names, such as 'Türkmenbaşi', 'Ruhnama' and 'Gurbansoltan Eje' (the latter in honour of the President's mother). Senior state officials were compelled to demonstrate ethnic purity by tracing their Turkmen ancestry back several generations. Niyazov's Government also accorded a de facto higher status to its titular population, the ethnic Turkmen, and legitimized the adoption of policies and practices that promoted their specific interests.

The cornerstone of Niyazov's Turkmenization campaign was the creation and publication of the *Ruhnama*, a final version of the first volume of which was published in October 2001 to coincide with the country's 10th anniversary of independence. A second volume of the *Ruhnama*, which government officials described as 'the second book of the Turkmen spiritual and moral constitution', was published in September 2004. The purported task of the *Ruhnama* was to record definitively the sources and history of the consolidation of the Turkmen nation, and to depict its fundamental traits and traditions, as well as to provide moral directives to the Turkmen people on how 'to live today and in the future'. The two volumes, ostensibly written by Niyazov, were accorded the de facto status of a holy book. Imams were required to display the *Ruhnama* in mosques and to quote from it in sermons, and Niyazov regularly urged his country's citizens to study and memorize passages of the *Ruhnama*. In addition to fluency in Turkmen, knowledge of the *Ruhnama* was made a requirement for university entrance and for work in the public sector, which remained the main source of employment.

Independent Turkmenistan was still, in some respects, more of a tribal confederation than a modern nation. In fact, tribal loyalties were stronger there than in any other Muslim area of the CIS. There were some 30 tribes, comprising more than 5,000 clans. The largest tribes were the Tekke in south-central Turkmenistan, the Ersary near the region of the Turkmenistan–Afghanistan border, the Yomud in western and northeastern Turkmenistan and the Saryks in the southernmost corner of the country, below Mari. Although the tribes steadily lost their economic power from the early Soviet period, tribal loyalties continued to exercise an influence on the Turkmen and were reinforced by rules of endogamy and the persistence of dialects. Virtually all Turkmen had at least a minimal knowledge of their own tribal affiliation, which remained a relatively reliable indicator of birthplace. The exit of the Russian *nomenklatura* (beneficiaries of Soviet patronage) following the collapse of the USSR led to a gradual resurgence of traditionally minded regional élites vying for their economic interests, which, in turn, prompted Niyazov to rely increasingly on a policy of 'divide and rule' with regard to tribal and regional politics. While a sense of national unity and identity was ostensibly being promoted at a higher level, less important hakims tended to be members of the tribe that was dominant in their respective velayat, while a disproportionate number of influential positions in central government tended to go to members of Niyazov's own tribe, the Ahal-Tekke. Niyazov continued to demonstrate a strong preference for his home-town of Kipchak, close to Aşgabat, which had received an inordinate share of investment capital and was the site of a number of ostentatious monuments, including Central Asia's largest mosque, which can accommodate up to 20,000 visitors.

TURKMENISTAN AFTER NIYAZOV

Niyazov's Death and the Transfer of Power

On 21 December 2006 Niyazov, aged 66, died of cardiac failure, bringing to a close a long and critical chapter in the history of independent Turkmenistan. Appointed as first secretary of the Central Committee of the Communist Party of the Turkmen SSR on 21 December 1985, Niyazov had ruled Turkmenistan for exactly 21 years. Contrary to expectations, a smoothly orchestrated succession was carried out when an extraordinary session of the State Security Council and the Cabinet of Ministers appointed the 49-year-old Deputy Chairman of the Government and Minister of Health and the Medical Industry, Gurbanguly Berdymuhamedov, as acting Head of State within hours of the announcement of Niyazov's death. An effective constitutional coup was executed by the political élite in power at the time of Niyazov's death in order to secure the placement in power of the candidate of their choice: while the Constitution clearly stated that the parliamentary Chairman was to assume the presidency in an acting capacity until a new leader was elected, the incumbent Chairman of the Majlis, Ovezgeldy Atayev, was removed on the same day and charged with criminal activity by the Office of the Prosecutor-General.

Five days later, on 26 December 2006, an emergency session of the Khalk Maslakhaty approved the laws and constitutional amendments formalizing the arrangements for a smooth transfer of power, thereby ensuring stability in the short term. The Law on Presidential Elections was passed (this law had not been adopted under Niyazov owing to his 'life presidency'), and a presidential election was scheduled for 11 February 2007. The Constitution was amended to allow the interim Head of State to stand in the election and to designate the Chairman of the Government (Prime Minister, or a Deputy Chairman, in the event that the President and premier were the same person) as acting head of state if the President were unable to execute his duties. The latter constitutional amendment sought to legitimize the appointment of Berdymuhamedov as interim President, a role that expressly belonged to the Chairman of the Majlis under the unrevised Constitution. In a relatively swift procedure that did not reveal any latent power struggles, two candidates for the presidency were nominated from each of the country's five regions and the city of Aşgabat, although only six ultimately received the requisite number of votes (two-thirds of the membership of the Khalk Maslakhaty) to be permitted to contest the election. Aside from Berdymuhamedov, all the candidates were lesser known bureaucrats lacking political weight. In a scenario reminiscent of Niyazov's rule, only Berdymuhamedov received the unanimous support of the Khalk Maslakhaty, an excellent indicator that his victory in the February 2007 election was a foregone conclusion.

The Central Electoral Commission claimed that the rate of participation by voters in the presidential election was 98.6%, of which Berdymuhamedov received 89.2% of the votes cast. Although multi-candidate, the election could not be deemed free and fair, given that media coverage was state-controlled, all six candidates were from the same political party, the DPT, and the opposition-in-exile was barred from participation. In the immediate aftermath of President Niyazov's death, leading members of Turkmenistan's opposition had publicly announced their intention to agree on a single candidate to contest the forthcoming presidential election. Meeting in the Ukrainian capital, Kyiv, on 25 December 2006, the opposition-in-exile nominated a former deputy prime minister and Chairman of the Central Bank of Turkmenistan, Khudaiberdy Orazov, as their presidential candidate. In the event, Turkmenistani security agencies warned that opposition leaders would be arrested on arrival at any airport in the country should they attempt to return. Despite these impediments, the campaign meetings preceding the presidential election offered the Turkmenistani electorate the chance to express opinions regarding the country's most pressing problems, albeit in a limited fashion, which was an opportunity they had not been afforded since the years of perestroika.

Following the example of his predecessor, Berdymuhamedov kept the post of Prime Minister for himself when awarding posts in his new Government. The 20th convocation of the Khalk Maslakhaty on 30 March 2007 unanimously elected President Berdymuhamedov as that body's Chairman. In August, in a vote with no opposing candidates, Berdymuhamedov was elected as the leader of the DPT, which remained the country's only authorized political party, and he was also named the leader of the Galkynyş Revival Movement. Thus, by August, in similar fashion to his predecessor, Berdymuhamedov held the posts of President of the Republic, Chairman of the Khalk Maslakhaty, Chairman of the Government (Prime Minister), Chairman of the Yaqşular Maslakhaty, head of the Council for Religious Affairs (Gengeş), Supreme Commander-in-Chief of the National Armed Forces and Chairman of both the DPT and Galkynyş.

The Berdymuhamedov Presidency

Despite predictions that Niyazov's sudden death would lead to internal power struggles and possible chaos given the absence of an heir apparent, the transfer of power to Berdymuhamedov—who had survived innumerable purges since his appointment as health minister in 1997—was swift and orderly, indicating that a succession strategy had been worked out by Niyazov's inner circle in advance. The power brokers behind the agreement to appoint Berdymuhamedov as Niyazov's successor were most likely leading figures in the security agencies, who formed the most influential political force in the country at the time of Niyazov's death. First and foremost among them was Akmurad Rejepov, head of the President's personal militia and the only senior official who had managed to retain his place in Niyazov's inner circle throughout Niyazov's presidency. A career agent of the Committee for State Security (KGB) in Soviet times, Rejepov had provided personal security to Niyazov with unswerving loyalty since 1986, becoming head of the Presidential Guard in 1991.

Having very rapidly consolidated power, within a few months President Berdymuhamedov was secure enough in his new post to begin reshaping his cabinet. In April 2007 he dismissed the Minister of Internal Affairs, appointed under Niyazov, following harsh criticism of the interior ministry's performance. Perhaps the surest indication that Berdymuhamedov had successfully created his own power network was the removal in May of 'grey cardinal' Akmurad Rejepov as the chief of presidential security. By removing Rejepov, who was indelibly linked to the former regime, Berdymuhamedov gained the ability to act with greater autonomy, particularly when appointing leading figures in the 'power ministries'. In July Rejepov was sentenced to 20 years' imprisonment on charges of corruption and abuse of office. The purges continued apace in 2007–08, as Berdymuhamedov removed several senior officials, including two Supreme Court Chairmen, the Minister of Petroleum, Natural Gas and Mineral Resources, two Ministers for Culture and Media, the Prosecutor-General and the Minister of National Security. In the style of Niyazov, who was well known for the rapid appointment and removal of officials at all levels of government, the new President appeared to be repeating his predecessor's pattern of berating and summarily dismissing senior officials in publicized meetings in order to prevent the formation of alternative power centres.

Initial measures evident in the gradual phasing out of Niyazov's extensive personality cult included the replacement in June 2007 of the golden logotype of Niyazov's profile from television screens with the profile of the new President, although only during news broadcasts. Berdymuhamedov also removed the title 'Türkmenbaşi' from the state oath in favour of the term 'President', and limited significantly usage of the national oath. The dismantling of Niyazov's personality cult received a considerable impetus in the first few months of 2008 as Niyazov's portraits were steadily removed from government and public buildings and dozens of his monuments were dismantled in towns and villages. In May it was announced that the Neutrality Arch—a hallmark of Niyazov's rule featuring a revolving, gold-plated figure of Turkmenistan's first President at the top—was to be removed from the centre of Aşgabat to the city's outskirts. Although portraits of the new President appeared throughout the country, they were confined to the inside of buildings. The slow process of phasing out Niyazov's quasi-spiritual guidebook for the nation, the *Ruhnama*, was also begun in 2008. Billboards containing excerpts from the book began to be removed, recitals of the *Ruhnama* on radio and television were gradually reduced, and *Ruhnama* propaganda centres in towns and villages stood empty. From September 2008 the new Government abolished the study of the *Ruhnama* as a separate, compulsory subject in universities, although it remained part of the academic programme. As a replacement for the dual cults of Niyazov and the *Ruhnama*, in January President Berdymuhamedov had announced that 'a New Era of Revival' was to serve as the new national ideology. In the event, the only visible tenets of this ideology were a chain of planned, grandiose construction projects intended 'to serve as man-made symbols for the 'New Era of Revival,' including a US $70m. monument to the Turkmenistani Constitution, a sports complex, a cultural and entertainment centre, a five-star hotel, an international airport, and a $168m. building for the oil and gas industry. The Berdymuhamedov Government also announced that it would undertake a plan worth $4,000m. to develop the country's rural infrastructure and grant urban status to certain large villages with populations over 8,000. Despite the substantial funding officially allocated to the project, the leadership faced a number of daunting obstacles in its implementation, not least the absence of running water, working sewerage systems, electricity and even gas in many rural areas.

Turkmenistan's media organizations continued to uphold the ideological line of the state, which maintained its control over all forms of state-run mass media, comprising 23 newspapers and 17 journals, the four state television channels and four state radio stations. There was a single information agency, which had a monopoly on the information provided to Turkmenistan's mass media. Foreign journalists were rarely allowed to enter the country, and domestic journalists working for foreign news organizations continued to experience official harassment. Apart from the programmes of the Turkmen Service of Radio Liberty and the German Deutsche Welle in Russian, which were specifically targeted at Turkmenistani listeners, satellite television—in widespread use throughout Aşgabat as well as in other cities—provided the chief source of alternative information in Turkmenistan. However, in December 2007 the Government announced that increasing numbers of satellite antennae were ruining the appearance of Aşgabat's landscape, and in 2008 work commenced on the replacement of private satellite aerials on the walls and roofs of residential buildings in the capital city with 'single powerful dishes', for which the authorities reserved the right to determine the package of available channels. Although foreign printed matter remained generally inaccessible, selected print publications from abroad became available in 2008 after President Berdymuhamedov lifted the ban on the importation and circulation of foreign print media that had been introduced in 2005 by Niyazov. Inexpensive Chinese-made receivers were reported to have inundated the Turkmenistani market as people sought news about developments in their country, and mobile cellular telephones become more accessible than the internet for the average citizen. At September 2008 the Russian-owned company Mobile TeleSystems (MTS), which provided mobile telephony services in more than 20 Turkmenistani cities, reported more than 500,000 subscribers in Turkmenistan, which represented an increase of some 250% compared with 2007 figures.

Despite the President's pledge to make 'both the internet and all other advanced communication technologies available for every citizen of Turkmenistan', in mid-2008 only embassies, international organizations, large foreign firms, a few non-governmental organizations (NGOs) and a very small number of private citizens in the country's major cities had unhindered access to the internet. Although a few state-run internet cafes in Aşgabat and regional capitals had been established, they were reported to be virtually empty of users owing to high charges and poor technical quality. A more affordable option was the internet centres sponsored by some Western embassies and international organizations in Aşgabat and other regional centres, which offered free internet access to the general public. Access to internet websites critical of official government policy still tended to be blocked by the authorities, although several major foreign news sites, such as the British Broadcasting Corporation (BBC) or Cable News Network (CNN), were accessible, representing a distinct change from the Niyazov era. In a potentially important development, in June 2008 Russia's MTS introduced wireless internet in Turkmenistan, which offered the possibility of a significant expansion of internet access throughout the country and signalled the end to the monopoly on the internet that had been held by the state-run Türkmentelecom for much of the period since independence.

While much of the legacy of Turkmenistan's first President remained firmly in place, at the same time the new Government rapidly embarked on a number of significant reforms, most of which were intended to reverse some of Niyazov's most egregious socioeconomic policies. On 1 July 2007 a new social security law entered into force, granting state pensions to some 100,000 retirees, which effectively overturned legislation adopted by Niyazov shortly before his death. The new law also provided support to, among others, veterans of World War II, new mothers and disabled people. However, the most far-reaching and substantive reforms undertaken by the Berdymuhamedov leadership in 2007–08 concerned education. Shortly after coming to power, the Government implemented measures to rejuvenate Turkmenistan's decaying educational system, which were welcomed, both domestically and internationally. In March 2007 a presidential decree restored the 10th year of compulsory education and extended the period of higher education from two to five years with effect from September. Secondary school pupils were no longer required to complete two years of practical work experience before applying to universities, foreign degrees were once again given recognition and the university admission system was reported to have been made fairer. Physical education, the social sciences, art and foreign languages were restored to the national curriculum, the workload of teachers was reduced and limits were placed on classroom size. More than 20,000 teachers, many of whom had been dismissed under Niyazov, returned to work in 2007. However, although teachers were granted a 40% wage increase in theory, in practice the money was reportedly either not paid, or was negated by a reduction in working hours. In June Berdymuhamedov announced the re-opening of the defunct Academy of Sciences, which, before its closure in 1993, had acted as the mainstay of the scientific and academic community. He also decreed the establishment of a new presidential Higher Council on Science and Technology to co-ordinate the state's scientific and academic policy, and ordered the introduction of post-graduate and doctoral studies in certain higher educational establishments and scientific organizations. In June 2008 the Minister for Education reported that universities would increase their intake by 10% in order to generate more professional and specialist workers, thereby helping to reverse the reduction in the number of qualified professionals that had resulted from the Niyazov years.

Another meaningful reform enacted by the new Turkmenistani leadership in 2007 was the easing of internal travel restrictions, which meant a reduction in the number of roadside document checks and inspections between cities. Significantly, in July the President signed a decree abolishing the requirement to obtain a special permit in order to travel to the country's sensitive border regions. Not all of the reforms introduced by the new leadership were popular: in February 2008 Berdymuhamedov severely undermined the populist measures put in place by Niyazov, decreeing that prices for petrol would rise significantly, although motorists were to be provided with the first 120 litres per month free of charge. Increases in petrol prices had a seriously adverse impact on transport and food prices. Water and electricity remained free of charge, although, as was the case during the Niyazov era, the quotas set for free electricity were relatively small and water shortages persisted throughout the country.

Other reforms introduced in the first two years of Berdymuhamedov's presidency were of a more superficial nature. In a clear effort to promote Turkmenistan's image internationally before the President's trip to the USA, scheduled for September 2007, in August the Government pardoned 11 political prisoners held at the Ovan-Depe high-security prison, some of whom were convicted in connection with the 2002 coup attempt against Niyazov. The prisoners reportedly were required to admit their guilt in the presence of relatives before being released. The most well known among the prisoners was Nasrullah ibn Ibadullah, who had served as Turkmenistan's chief religious leader in 1996–2003 before being sentenced in 2004 to 22 years' imprisonment on charges of treason. Upon his release, Ibadullah thanked the President and accepted a post as adviser at the President's State Council for Religious Affairs, thus remaining under the close supervision of administration officials. In subsequent amnesties throughout 2007–08, none of the country's many known prisoners of conscience was released.

In January 2008 the Government reversed the ban on opera and circus performances announced by Niyazov seven years previously. Similarly, the old Gregorian calendar names for the months of the year and days of the week, which had been re-designated with Turkmen names by Niyazov in 2002, were restored from the beginning of July 2008.

A new Constitution was formally adopted in September 2008, which introduced a number of chiefly cosmetic reforms. After approving the new Constitution, Turkmenistan's highest representative body, the Khalk Maslakhaty, dissolved itself, delegating its powers to an expanded 125-member Majlis. In so doing, the Government reverted to having only one legislative body rather than two, although real power was still vested in the executive branch and the country continued to be run primarily by presidential decree and instruction. Strengthening executive power still further, the President was granted the power to appoint directly the country's governors at all levels, although Niyazov had changed the system to allow for local gubernatorial elections only a year before his death.

The closed nature of society under the new Turkmenistani leadership was emphasized by an unexpectedly fierce two-day battle that broke out in a northern suburb of Aşgabat in September 2008. Official reports provided little information, which served to increase speculation in foreign media sources. State-run media stated that armed criminal groups involved in the illegal drugs trade had clashed with police, leading to an unspecified number of casualties, although some Western news services and Russian media asserted that the violence was instigated by Islamist extremists. One opposition website speculated that the violence was the result of infighting between different clans within Turkmenistan's security services, while another claimed that radical oppositionists took forceful action in order to restore the constitutional system in Turkmenistan. Observers noted that reports of violent clashes in normally tranquil Aşgabat, whatever their cause, served to demonstrate the lack of information available regarding the state of Turkmenistan's internal security and potential sources of instability.

FOREIGN RELATIONS

Central to Turkmenistan's foreign policy under President Niyazov was the doctrine of 'permanent neutrality', a concept that was endorsed by the UN in December 1995 and subsequently enshrined in the country's Constitution. To mark the significance of the event, which was hailed in the country as 'the single greatest achievement of the independence period', President Niyazov declared 12 December a national holiday (Neutrality Day) and renamed the country's largest Russian-language newspaper *Neitralnyi Turkmenistan* (Neutral Turkmenistan). The primary tenets of permanent neutrality proclaimed Turkmenistan's official policy of non-interference and opposition to membership of any 'strongly affiliated' international organizations or military alliances. This included participation in CIS or other peace-keeping forces, which, it was thought, could lead to an infringement of its sovereignty. Although Niyazov regularly reaffirmed Turkmenistan's official policy of neutrality, he continued to lead his country down a path that more closely resembled isolationism. Turkmenistan refused to sign more than one-half of all agreements endorsed

by the majority of the other CIS member states, including those on collective security and the creation of an inter-state bank. Turkmenistan also declined to join either the Eurasian Economic Community (EURASEC—formerly the CIS Customs Union, comprising Belarus, Kazakhstan, Kyrgyzstan, Russia, Tajikistan and Uzbekistan), or the Central Asian Co-operation Organization (CACO—formerly the Central Asian Union, and later the Central Asian Economic Union, comprising Kazakhstan, Kyrgyzstan, Russia, Tajikistan and Uzbekistan). (CACO and EURASEC merged in 2006.) Turkmenistan also remained the only Central Asian state outside the Shanghai Co-operation Organization (SCO—comprising the People's Republic of China, Kazakhstan, Kyrgyzstan, Russia, Tajikistan and Uzbekistan)—formerly the Shanghai Forum—the primary function of which was to co-ordinate collective measures to counter terrorism and other threats to regional stability.

Following the change in government, President Berdymuhamedov vowed to end his country's 'self-imposed isolation' in an official address to the UN General Assembly in New York, USA, in September 2007, but also pledged to continue his predecessor's policy of neutrality. The first months of Berdymuhamedov's presidency were characterized by intensive diplomatic activity, including state visits to Saudi Arabia, Russia, Kazakhstan, Iran and China in an effort to forge personal relationships with the leaders of neighbouring states, to secure greater international legitimacy and to attract the economic investment necessary to take Turkmenistan's energy resources to world markets. None the less, there were indications that Turkmenistan's engagement with the international community would remain limited: in August 2007 Turkmenistan was present at a summit of the SCO for the first time, yet did not ask to be admitted as a member or even as an official observer of the organization, even using the occasion to emphasize Turkmenistan's neutral status. Similarly, although Berdymuhamedov travelled to Russia in June to participate in an informal CIS summit held in St Petersburg, pledging that Turkmenistan would take an active part in CIS meetings, he confirmed Turkmenistan's status as an associate, rather than a full, member of that organization. In June Berdymuhamedov declared that, while he welcomed closer economic and business co-operation with the USA, he would like ties with that country to remain 'apolitical', presumably in order to avoid any confrontation or unsolicited advice with regard to issues of human rights or democracy.

In the late 2000s Turkmenistan's closest foreign partner remained Russia, upon which it relied for much of its foreign trade, the export of its natural gas, and its main transport and communications networks. One of the most important post-independence developments was the agreement reached with Russia in December 1991 to allow Turkmenistan to export a limited amount of natural gas to European markets through Russian pipelines, in exchange for convertible ('hard') currency calculated at world prices. Consequently, the Russian decision of November 1993 severely to restrict Turkmenistan's access to its pipeline network deprived the latter state of an outlet to hard-currency markets and forced it to redirect sales of its main commodity to impoverished, unreliable clients, namely Ukraine, which proved unable to pay its debts to Turkmenistan. In March 1997 Turkmenistan halted all its exports through the Russian pipeline network, citing unfavourable conditions imposed by the Russian gas monopoly, Gazprom. In December 1999, however, despite earlier demands for higher prices, Turkmenistan came to an agreement with Gazprom to resume deliveries of gas, with 40% of the payments in hard currency and 60% in food and commodities. As a result, gas exports to Russia grew sharply during the first half of 2000, accounting for more than three-quarters of Turkmenistan's total gas exports and greatly boosting that state's economic indicators. From October 2000 Russia purchased relatively small amounts of Turkmenistani gas on an annual or semi-annual basis, albeit at Turkmenistan's higher asking price.

In April 2003 President Niyazov signed an agreement with President Vladimir Putin of Russia, under the terms of which Russia's purchases of Turkmenistani gas were to increase from 5,000m.–6,000m. cu m in 2004 to 10,000m. cu m in 2006, rising to 60,000m.–70,000m. cu m in 2007 and to 70,000m.–80,000m. cu m from 2009. Although significant, the agreement was not a contract, but rather a statement of non-binding intent. A long-term gas deal with Turkmenistan was vital to Russia in order to enable it to make its own gas available for export to the West at world-market rates and to postpone the development of high-cost Arctic and Siberian gas projects. Of near equal significance to the long-term agreement was a pledge by Russia to modernize Turkmenistan's transport infrastructure, insofar as the promised volumes of gas would require major investment in pipelines. The agreement envisaged the reconstruction of the Central Asia-Centre gas transport system, which could carry only 45,000m. cu m annually, as well as the expansion of an existing pipeline running along the Caspian coast.

Under the 2003 agreement, Gazprom's purchase price for Turkmenistani gas was to be renegotiated in 2007. However, in January 2005 Turkmenistani officials suspended gas deliveries to Russia after it refused to agree to a price increase, from US $44 per 1,000 cu m to $58 per 1,000 cu m. This impasse was resolved in mid-April, when officials from both countries agreed to maintain the contracted price, but abandon the partial barter system. Henceforth, gas supplies were to be fully paid for in cash. In order to strengthen Russia's near-monopoly on Turkmenistani gas exports, Russia signed a contract for the delivery of 30,000m. cu m of Turkmenistani gas in the first half of 2006—compared with the previously agreed amount of 10,000m. cu m for the whole year—at a slightly increased price of $65 per 1,000 cu m. However, the two states soon clashed again when, in June 2006, Turkmenistan threatened to halt supplies to Russia after Gazprom refused to agree to a higher price of $100 per 1,000 cu m of gas for deliveries in the final quarter of 2006 and 2007. Following months of difficult negotiations, in September Russia agreed to the substantial price increase, which was to cover an additional 12,000m. cu m of gas deliveries in 2006 and 50,000m. cu m per year in 2007–09. The acquiescence of Russia to Niyazov's demands demonstrated the importance of Turkmenistani gas imports to that country's economy. Realizing that it must raise purchase prices still further in order to retain its hold on the Turkmenistani market when confronted with increasing international competition, Gazprom raised the price paid for Turkmenistani gas from $100 per 1,000 cu m to $130 per 1,000 cu m for the first half of 2008, and to $150 per 1,000 cu m for the second half of the year. In July 2008 Gazprom signed an enormously beneficial agreement with the Turkmenistani Government promising to pay unspecified, world market prices for gas imports from 2009. Projected purchase prices for Turkmenistani gas in 2009 were some $225–$295 per 1,000 cu m.

In the post-independence period Turkmenistan's relations with Iran came to play an increasingly important role in its foreign policy. Given that Turkmenistan shares its longest border with Iran, which is also Turkmenistan's natural choice as a gas export route, a good relationship with its southern neighbour remains vital. In May 1996 a new railway, joining the Turkmenistani city of Tejen to the northern Iranian city of Mashad, was inaugurated, giving land-locked Central Asian states access to the Persian (Arabian) Gulf and incorporating the region into the greater railway system that linked Asia from Turkey to the People's Republic of China. Most importantly, in December 1997 President Niyazov and Iran's new President Muhammad Khatami officially opened the 200-km gas pipeline (built primarily with Iranian financing) linking the Korpeje field in western Turkmenistan with the industrial town of Kord Kuy in northern Iran. Until the opening of the Turkmenistan–Iran pipeline, Turkmenistan's sole gas export route had been controlled by Russia. The amounts of gas delivered to Iran were relatively small (approximately 8,000m. cu m per year in 2006–08, compared with 5,800m. cu m in 2005). In theory, Turkmenistan could export gas to Turkey via this southern route; in practice, however, Iran has no real interest in re-exporting Turkmenistani gas to Turkey, given its own huge reserves located in its southern regions. As part of its campaign to establish world-market rates for its hydrocarbons exports, on 31 December 2007 Turkmenistan halted gas exports via the Korpeje–Kord Kuy pipeline to Iran, thereby forcing Iran to halt its own exports of gas to Turkey. In a demonstration of Turkmenistan's increasing economic power

as an energy-producing nation, the Turkmenistani leadership was able to present Iran with an ultimatum: either accept a higher purchase price or face cuts, thereby provoking claims from Iran's leadership that Turkmenistan's behaviour towards its neighbour was 'immoral'. After months of stalled negotiations, in April 2008 Iran agreed to a nearly 100% increase in the price of gas imports, from $75 per 1,000 cu m to $140 per 1,000 cu m from 1 July. It was anticipated that Iran would have to further increase its purchase price in 2009 in order to approximate the prices paid by Turkmenistan's other customers.

Turkmenistan has occasionally supported Iran in the bitter dispute for control over the Caspian Sea's petroleum and gas resources, the division of the waters of which has not been formally clarified and has prompted rivalry between the littoral states (see also the essay on the Politics of Energy in the Caspian Sea Region). Turkmenistan also supported Iran in that state's conflict with Azerbaijan over the latter's exploration of oilfields claimed by both countries. This was an expected development, given that Turkmenistan itself remained locked in a dispute with Azerbaijan over the ownership of the Serdar (Kyapaz) field in the mid-Caspian, as well as portions of the Azeri and Çıraǧ fields (known as Khazar and Osman, respectively, in Turkmenistan). Turkmenistan's position on the legal status of the Caspian Sea has been ambiguous and subject to change over the years, shifting from an anti-division stance to one advocating the division of the seabed, waters and airspace into national sectors. Since 2001 Turkmenistan has supported the idea of 'divided sea floor, common surface waters' in line with Kazakhstan, Russia and Azerbaijan, although it also shared the Iranian view that national zones should be relatively large, thereby restricting Russian maritime traffic. However, while accepting the modified median line principle in general, Turkmenistan's interpretation of the median line was wholly unacceptable to Azerbaijan, as it incorporated inside its own sector disputed petroleum and gas deposits. In May 2003 officials from Azerbaijan, Kazakhstan and Russia signed an agreement demarcating their respective sectors of the Caspian seabed, under which Kazakhstan received a 29% share and Russia and Azerbaijan each received a 19% share. Turkmenistan's dispute with Azerbaijan over ownership of several petroleum and gasfields prevented it from joining the Azerbaijan-Kazakhstan-Russia agreement.

Immediately following the change of leadership in early 2007, Azerbaijani President İlham Aliyev made several overtures to the new President of Turkmenistan, with the aim of renewing relations and developing an active dialogue on energy transport projects in the Caspian. In June the two Presidents met at a summit of the CIS in St Petersburg, where they agreed to reopen Turkmenistan's embassy in Baku (Bakı, the Azerbaijani capital), which had been closed by Niyazov in 2001. In May 2008 President Berdymuhamedov made the first official visit to Azerbaijan by a Turkmenistani head of state in more than a decade, signalling a willingness to commence a new era of co-operation between the two states. The ongoing question of finding an enduring solution to the unresolved dispute over the status of the Caspian seabed was all the more topical in light of Niyazov's death and the potential for improvement in Turkmenistani-Azerbaijani bilateral relations, which, if realized, could have the effect of isolating Iran and forcing that state to reconsider its uncompromising stance. President Aliyev declared a willingness jointly to exploit the disputed Kyapaz/Serdar oilfield on a parity basis, although emphasized that the issue was tightly linked to producing an agreement on the status of the Caspian.

Perhaps more than with any of its other neighbours, Turkmenistan's relations with Kazakhstan were fundamentally reinvigorated in the aftermath of Niyazov's death. This development was not surprising, given that Turkmenistan holds strategic importance for Kazakhstan in two vital areas: as the holder of huge gas resources that require transit through Kazakhstani territory, and as a potential ally in Caspian Sea issues. The President of Kazakhstan, Nursultan Nazarbayev, and Berdymuhamedov met six times in the first nine months of 2007 alone, as the new Turkmenistani President sought to emulate his Kazakhstani counterpart's ability to formulate a successful 'multi-vector' foreign policy. While Kazakhstan already transported gas from Turkmenistan to

Russia for export to Gazprom's European customers, there were at least two possible routes under discussion—the Turkmenistan–China pipeline and the trans-Caspian pipeline (see below)—that would serve to facilitate the export of both countries' energy resources. From the point of view of Turkmenistan, the potential addition of Kazakhstan's gas reserves increased the feasibility of both projects. In May Turkmenistan and Kazakhstan agreed to build a new railway and highway connecting Russia, Kazakhstan, Turkmenistan and, possibly, Iran in order to expand trade routes through to Europe via Russia as well as to the Persian (Arabian) Gulf.

The leaders of Turkmenistan and Uzbekistan signed an agreement on the delimitation of their mutual border in September 2000, yet tensions between them increased as visa regimes were put in place and border controls became stricter. Tensions between the two states were also fuelled by disputes over shared resources and by reports of discrimination against Turkmenistan's sizeable ethnic Uzbek minority. Relations between Turkmenistan and Uzbekistan reached an unprecedented low following accusations that Uzbekistan had been complicit in the armed attack on President Niyazov in November 2002. Claiming that Uzbekistan had given shelter to Shikhmuradov at its embassy in Aşgabat, the Turkmenistani authorities declared Uzbekistan's ambassador *persona non grata* and expelled him from the country at the end of December. In the aftermath of the incident, both countries amassed troops on their respective sides of the common border. Following years of tense relations, Uzbekistan's President Islam Karimov held an important meeting with President Niyazov in Buxoro (Bukhara), Uzbekistan, in November 2004 (the Turkmenistani President's first visit to a foreign country in two years). The official agenda included the rational use of water resources and the development of the Kokdumalak oilfield, which is exploited by Uzbekistan, although located primarily in Turkmenistan. The Presidents signed a friendship treaty and two agreements on the simplification of travel for residents of border areas and for service personnel employed at facilities located in border regions. In recognition of the improvement in relations, Uzbekistan appointed a new ambassador to Turkmenistan in January 2005, after the post had been vacant for more than two years. Recognizing the need to revive co-operation with Uzbekistan, particularly in the areas of transport, trade, water protection and border management, President Berdymuhamedov scheduled a meeting with President Karimov for October 2007. Although the two countries had not reached agreement on the joint use of water from the Amu Dar'ya River or the sharing of resources at Kokdumalak, relations continued to improve in 2008. As Turkmenistan sought to create a new export route to the People's Republic of China, as well as to expand existing ones to Russia, Uzbekistan's importance as a transit state for Turkmenistani gas exports to both China and Russia continued to grow.

In Afghanistan, Turkmenistan had cultivated cordial political and trade relations with the Taliban regime in the post-independence period, in contrast to Russia and the other Central Asian states. Given that Islam remained relatively unpoliticized in Turkmenistan, President Niyazov did not view the Taliban as a threat, which, it was alleged, allowed Niyazov's regime to engage in systematic drugs-smuggling and to forge ties with poppy-producers in Afghanistan. Turkmenistan opened consulates in the Afghan cities of Herat and Mazar-i-Sharif, which were reported to operate as a cover for secret drug deals concluded by Niyazov's regime and the Taliban, the money from which was allegedly 'laundered' in the United Arab Emirates. Turkmenistan was also alleged to have given the leader of the Islamic Movement of Uzbekistan (IMU), Jumaboy Khojiyev (Juma Namangoniy), and some Taliban fighters permission to transit its territory. Following the large-scale suicide attacks on the USA on 11 September 2001, Turkmenistan succeeded in maintaining its neutral stance with regard to the ensuing conflict in Afghanistan. Citing the country's neutral status, which Niyazov repeatedly described as inviolate, Turkmenistan was the only Central Asian state that did not offer either its air-space or airfields to US aircraft for military operations in Afghanistan, or allow foreign troops on its soil (with the exception of a small group of US military personnel who refuelled cargo planes carrying aid to Afghani-stan). However, Turkmenistan served as the principal conduit for humanitarian assistance to Afghanistan during the US-led airstrikes against al-Qa'ida and Taliban targets in Afghanistan from early October, granting extensive ground and air transport 'corridors', and providing the International Security Assistance Force and international relief agencies with landing facilities and secure storage sites for supplies. Although unconfirmed by the Turkmenistani authorities, in May 2008 it was reported that the number of North Atlantic Treaty Organization (NATO) supply planes landing at a Turkmenistani military airbase on their way to Afghanistan had increased following talks between the Turkmenistani Government and NATO in April.

Pipeline Proposals

In order to diversify the client base for its natural gas and break Russia's near-monopoly on export routes, from the mid-1990s Turkmenistan pursued a number of different projects for the construction of pipelines to carry its gas to foreign markets, all of which were beset by serious obstacles (with the exception of the Korpeje–Kord Kuy connection described above). The proposed construction of a 1,500-km gas pipeline from Turkmenistan to Pakistan via Afghanistan, an initiative led by the US company Unocal, was suspended indefinitely in 1998, owing to fighting in Afghanistan. The Niyazov Government regarded Afghanistan as a natural 'bridge' between Turkmenistan and the vast markets of the Indian subcontinent. Consequent to the collapse of the Taliban regime in Afghanistan in late 2001, the Turkmenistani Government's primary interest was in reviving the trans-Afghanistan pipeline project, which would link Turkmenistan's Dauletabad field with Pakistan's gas transport network at Multan, with a possible extension to India. On 27 December 2002 the Presidents of Turkmenistan and Afghanistan and the Prime Minister of Pakistan signed a framework agreement on the construction of the trans-Afghanistan pipeline. In April 2003 Afghanistan, Pakistan and Turkmenistan formally invited India to participate in the project both as an investor and as a major purchaser of gas, although that state expressed concern that political tensions with Pakistan could jeopardize its ability to receive gas deliveries. However, in May 2006 the Indian Government reversed its earlier decision and approved India's participation in the trans-Afghanistan pipeline project. Despite a positive assessment by the Asian Development Bank in 2005, serious questions remained regarding virtually all aspects of the pipeline. The results of an audit of the Dauletabad field carried out by a US exploration firm in 2005 were classified by the Turkmenistani Government, leaving considerable uncertainty over the actual reserves needed to fill the pipeline. Moreover, major gas and petroleum companies were unwilling to commit themselves to financing the pipeline until concerns about regional stability were allayed.

Regarding a Western route to export its hydrocarbons resources, during the first years of independence Turkmenistan hoped for the planned construction of a pipeline through Iran to Turkey and, ultimately, to Europe. Although a route through Iran was the most direct and cost-effective way to deliver gas to Turkey, the USA's objections to Iran's inclusion in the pipeline scheme had concomitant repercussions for financing the project. As an alternative route, the US Administration strongly promoted the construction of a 2,000-km trans-Caspian pipeline (TCP), which would transport gas across the Caspian Sea to Azerbaijan and then to Europe via Georgia and Turkey. Turkish and US representatives reported in Aşgabat in July 1998 that both countries had agreed to support the project by providing guarantees to investors and offering large government credits. Prospects for the pipeline began to unravel in February 2000, however, when Azerbaijan laid claim to one-half of the pipeline's capacity, after finding a large gas deposit in its Caspian offshore field, much closer to Turkish markets. President Niyazov, in turn, insisted that Azerbaijan's demand would make Turkmenistan's own export plans unprofitable, leaving it with high construction costs and little return. In June the consortium of the US-based Bechtel Corporation and General Electric Capital Services, which had been formed to build the TCP, ended its operations in Aşgabat, after the Turkmenistani leadership failed to respond to a final offer for the project. As Russia's near-monopoly on Turkmenistani gas supplies intensified, in January 2006 US and Turkish officials conferred with Niyazov in an attempt to revive the idea of a trans-Caspian project as an alternative route to supply gas to Turkey and Europe. In the event, in September Niyazov declared that Russia and China were priority customers for gas, while casting grave doubts on the prospects for the proposed trans-Caspian and trans-Afghanistan pipelines. The TCP project's prospects were bolstered somewhat following Niyazov's death, when, in August 2007, the US Trade and Development Agency and the State Oil Company of Azerbaijan signed a US $1,500m. grant agreement for the purpose of working out the technical and economic basis for the pipeline, as well as for a project to transport Kazakh oil under the Caspian Sea to Azerbaijan. However, a number of major obstacles rendered the construction of the TCP in the near future unlikely, including Russian opposition to the project, sources of financing, competing pipeline projects and the unresolved status of the Caspian Sea. Not least, the Georgian crisis of August 2008 (see the chapter on Georgia) emphasized the political risk surrounding both completed and planned energy export routes via the Caspian for producer and consumer states alike. None the less, the new co-operation with Azerbaijan improved prospects for an ultimate resolution of the disputes over maritime boundaries and the three mid-Caspian hydrocarbons fields, which could, in turn, facilitate the joining of Turkmenistani offshore fields to the existing Azerbaijani infrastructure by means of a subsea tieback, thereby enabling the oil and gas produced to be carried by the Baku–Tbilisi (Georgia)–Ceyhan (Turkey) and Baku–Tbilisi–Erzerum (Turkey) pipelines to Europe. In April 2008 Turkmenistan agreed to provide 10,000m. cu m of gas per year to the European Union (EU) from 2009, although it remained unclear how that volume of gas, if available, would be transported.

Four years after a pledge by Russia to help modernize Turkmenistan's gas transport infrastructure, in May 2007 the Presidents of Kazakhstan, Uzbekistan and Turkmenistan signed a declaration of intent to upgrade and expand existing gas transport pipelines to Russia and to build a pipeline along the Caspian Sea coast to carry Turkmenistani gas to Europe via Russia. The project, as outlined, consisted of three components. First, the existing Central Asia-Centre-3 pipeline linking the western part of Turkmenistan along the Caspian coast was to be restored to its Soviet-era annual capacity of 10,000m. cu m by 2010, drawing on onshore Turkmenistani gas. Second, a parallel coastal pipeline was to be built by 2016–18 to carry another 20,000m. cu m annually, drawing on offshore fields on Turkmenistan's seabed that Russian companies planned to develop. Third, a plan was announced (which had been signed by Uzbekistani President Karimov in advance of the meeting) to increase the annual capacity of the Central Asia-Centre system (branches 1, 2 and 4, running through Turkmenistan, Uzbekistan and Kazakhstan to Russia) from 50,000m. cu m–60,000m. cu m to the Soviet-era level of 90,000m. cu m by 2010, and further to increase capacity thereafter in line with gas production. Insofar as it routed Turkmenistan's future gas production to Russia, the decision to upgrade and expand the Caspian pipeline was widely regarded both as a victory for Russia in its attempts to block energy-supply routes outside Russia's control, and simultaneously as a reverse for Western and Azerbaijani hopes for the construction of the trans-Caspian pipeline, despite statements by President Berdymuhamedov that there were sufficient gas reserves in Turkmenistan to fill a number of pipelines. Although the four participant countries pledged to sign intergovernmental agreements by September 2007, in the event, the signing was postponed owing to a failure by the Russian side to prepare the requisite technical and economic reports underlying the project. By mid-2008 a final agreement to commence construction of the pipeline had still not been signed by the participant states.

Although plans for a pipeline from Turkmenistan to the People's Republic of China were under consideration from 2000, they received a considerable impetus in April 2006 when President Niyazov visited Chinese President Hu Jintao in order to sign a number of documents, including a framework agreement for the annual delivery to China of 30,000m. cu m of

Turkmenistani gas for a 30-year period. Deliveries were scheduled to commence in 2009, by which time a proposed 4,000-km pipeline was expected to have been completed. The description of the pipeline project to China suggested that it was not based on proven reserves, given the stipulation that Turkmenistan would 'guarantee' supplies from other gas fields in the country should the fields designated to fill the pipeline (on the right bank of the Amu Dar'ya River) not yield sufficient volumes. In the event, the China National Petroleum Company succeeded in winning the first, and by late 2008 the only, onshore production-sharing agreement awarded to a foreign company by the Turkmenistani Government. In July 2007 Turkmenistani and Chinese government agencies signed further agreements on gas field development and gas sale-and-purchase. The adoption by the Chinese of an integrated approach to exploration, production, transport and marketing greatly enhanced the feasibility of the project, and the formal launch of the construction of the Turkmenistan–China gas pipeline took place in August 2007. Work on the pipeline was progressing rapidly, but first deliveries were expected only at the end of 2009, although even that date appeared highly optimistic. During a visit to Aşgabat in August 2008 President Berdymuhamedov awarded Chinese President Hu Jintao with Turkmenistan's highest honour, the 'Great First President Saparmyrat Türkmenbaşi Turkmenistani State Award'. Additionally, the two Presidents agreed to increase Chinese gas purchases from 30,000m. cu m per year to 40,000m. cu m per year, despite the lack of official audit results.

CONCLUSION

As President Berdymuhamedov ended the second year of his presidency, he had done little to reform the structure of government created by Niyazov, although he had adopted measures to reverse some of his predecessor's most destructive and isolationist policies in order to attract international support and improve the country's economic prospects. Since any far-reaching liberalization of society or the political system could pave the way for the regime's ultimate downfall, the post-Niyazov leadership chose to implement reforms in a limited and incremental fashion, while curtailing any attempts to create political pluralism. In 2008 Turkmenistan under Berdymuhamedov retained many of the distinguishing features of the Niyazov era, including the frequent purging of senior officials, complete control of the state-run mass media and severe restrictions on civil liberties. There was no revival of civil society under the new President, some religious communities continued to experience various forms of harassment and the vast majority of political prisoners remained incarcerated. Significantly, the state budget process continued to lack transparency and, like his predecessor, Berdymuhamedov persisted in using state revenue to fund a number of grandiose construction projects, such as the transformation of the Caspian Sea town of Türkmenbaşi into a free economic zone and world-class resort—complete with an artificial river, a yacht club and an oceanographic centre—at the cost of US $1,000m.

None the less, important reforms undertaken by the new regime to restore the beleaguered social sector—and the educational system, in particular—indicated a clear, albeit partial, break with the former regime. Considerable progress was made in 2008 in gradually weakening the dual cults of former President Niyazov and his quasi-spiritual guide, the *Ruhnama*. Less significant reforms included the restoration of the circus, the opera and the old Gregorian names for the months of the year and the days of the week, and the abolition of the pseudo-representative, national-level Khalk Maslakhaty.

With regard to foreign relations, the new President made considerable efforts to engage with the international community and to forge personal relationships with the leaders of neighbouring states, both to overcome the Niyazov era's legacy of isolation and economic stagnation and to attract foreign investment. Turkmenistan required some US $3,000m.–$4,000m. in near-term investment to reach the 2008 natural gas production target of 82,000m. cu m (compared with 73,000m. in 2007), and much greater sums were required if

Turkmenistan was to meet its target of increasing annual gas output to 120,000m. cu m by 2010. Berdymuhamedov repeatedly stated that his country supported the construction of a number of natural gas pipeline export routes, including routes to Russia, Afghanistan, Pakistan, China, and across the Caspian Sea, and also affirmed that his country had sufficient reserves to fill them. In October 2008 the long-awaited results of a preliminary, independent audit of Turkmenistan's major oil and gas reserves carried out by a British consultancy firm indicated that the South Yoloten-Osman gas deposits in the southeast of the country contained enough gas to make it the world's fourth or fifth richest gas deposit in the world, potentially doubling Turkmenistan's export potential in the medium to long term. The audit results were expected to lead to increased competition for Turkmenistan's uncommitted and undeveloped gas fields among Russia, Europe, China and East and South Asia, and in the process to re-focus attention on pipeline projects that bypassed Russia.

Economy

Prof. MICHAEL KASER

with subsequent revisions

INTRODUCTION

Since independence in 1991 the performance of Turkmenistan's economy laboured under the capricious dictatorship of President Saparmyrat Niyazov until his death in December 2006. The Deputy Chairman of the Government and Minister of Health and the Medical Industry, Gurbanguly Berdymuhamedov, was subsequently elected President in February 2007 (see History). The economy's viability was (and remains) supported by exports of petroleum, natural gas and cotton, three natural resources for which world prices were unusually high for most of that period, and living standards were sufficient to restrain popular revolt on purely economic grounds. The distribution of utilities to households without charge and subsidies for many consumer goods might have offset among citizens the irrational use of public resources—the closure of hospitals and schools while munificent monuments were built under Niyazov—but without democratic elections and a free media such an equation could hardly have been tested.

The economy as much as the polity entered the 21st century with much the same profile that they entered the 20th, although both had undergone remarkable change since the country entered the 19th century. The caesura was occupation by tsarist Russia in 1868-84 imposing an autocracy and fostering an export economy on the territories that today compose the Republic of Turkmenistan: a railway rapidly linked its Caspian port of Krasnovodsk (now Türkmenbaşi—with a later rail ferry across from Baku—Bakı, now in Azerbaijan) to Poltoratsk (now the capital, Aşgabat) and beyond, stimulating sales to Russia of cotton and petroleum. An economic imperative lay behind the incorporation of the Turkmen territories into the tsarist empire, as had been the case one decade earlier for what is now Uzbekistan: the blockade of the Confederate south by the Unionist north during the American Civil War (1861–66) deprived Russia of cotton to supply the textile mills of Ivanovo (to the east of Moscow), then a burgeoning part, after Urals metallurgy, of the second phase of Russia's industrial revolution. The desired raw-materials base within Russia's frontiers was swiftly secured by extensive cotton plantations; by the end of the century petroleum extraction supplemented that of Baku, where oil fields had been exploited from the 1870s. An industrial survey of 1898–99 indicated that cotton-ginning contributed 53% of production in the Transcaspian Oblast (region—an area slightly larger than present-day Turkmenistan—see below), flour-milling 33%, carpet-making 2%, and petroleum-refining just 1%; building materials, silk and wine made only minor contributions. Petroleum extraction had become significant by the outbreak of the First World War (with output of 138,000 metric tons in 1913), but all industrial production sharply declined as a consequence of the 1917 Revolutions and the Bolshevik struggle to control Central Asia. In 1928, at the beginning of Stalin's (Iosif Dzhugashvili's) First Five-Year Plan, petroleum-refining still contributed less than 1% of industrial output, with textiles (52%), food and beverages (32%) and engineering (11%) the largest sectors. By the end of the Stalinist era the petroleum industry had moved up to second place (21%), although textiles remained the largest sector (31%), with food and beverages down to 12%; engineering's share had increased to 14%, and that of chemicals, which had contributed 0.4% in 1928, increased to 3% by 1950. Soviet strategy for the economy was reflected in the state coat of arms. When the Turkmen SSR joined the USSR in 1925 (having been formed in 1924 as the successor to the Turkestan Autonomous Republic, proclaimed in 1918) the arms portrayed cotton, grapes, a Turkmen rug, a camel, a tractor and a silk worm; under the 'Stalin Constitution' of 1936, the latter three were replaced by an oil-rig and a factory building. Cotton fibre, petroleum, gas, rugs, karakul (Persian lambswool) and wine were sold to the rest of the USSR, and by the time of the dissolution of the USSR in 1991 Turkmenistan exhibited the highest exports per head in the Union: 98% went to other Soviet republics, and the potential for cross-border trade with Afghanistan and Iran was (for political reasons) ignored.

An urban economy in southern Turkmenistan can be traced as far back as 2300 BC from remains that have been found at Annau, south of Aşgabat, showing evidence of livestock-raising, irrigated farming, and the making of ceramics, bronze tools and gold jewellery; a stone seal, with lettering that has yet to be deciphered, indicates literacy. With the addition of horse-breeding and carpet-weaving, such was the structure of the economy in the ensuing millennia. The Parthian Empire, ruled from Nyssa, close to present-day Aşgabat, developed the export of pottery and weaponry and opened a trade route from the Roman and Persian Empires to China via Xorazm (Khorezm), Buxoro (Bukhara) and Samarqand. This line of the Great Silk Road fostered both economic and scientific development (with the astronomer and geologist Al-Biruni and the physician Ibn Sina—Avicenna), until the destructive Mongol invasions and the diversion of trade between Europe and South and East Asia to the maritime route around the Cape of Good Hope.

Thus, the tsarist armies of the second half of the 19th century incorporated into the empire a simple economy of farmers, pastoralists, artisans and traders. Designated the Transcaspian Oblast, it formed a territory 14% larger than the 488,100 sq km of the present Republic, and had a population of 372,193 at the 1897 census. Economic development was rapid, as reflected in the growth of the population, which was also swelled by immigration, to 914,600 in 1924 (even on the smaller area), although 90% of inhabitants were still rural. This paradox arose because export products were extracted in remote desert locations (petroleum) or were village-based: the cultivation of cotton (and also its ginning), karakul, silk and grapes, and the weaving of silk and cotton rugs and kelims. The base for urban industrialization was laid by electrification, predominantly from oil-fired generators, although a hydro-electric station had been built on the Murgab River in the Hindu Kush Mountains before the Revolution. To develop the Turkmen SSR, larger thermoelectric plants were constructed (at Kum-Dag, Cheleken and Nebit-Dag—now Balkanabat). Although more hydrostations were established on the Murgab, by the 1950s 95% of electricity was from thermal firing. The extraction of minerals, notably sulphates from the Kara-Bogaz

Gol, a large inlet of the Caspian Sea, and ozokerite from the Cheleken Peninsula, added to petroleum as input for the chemicals industry, of which the superphosphate and oxygen plants of Charjew (now Türkmenabat) formed the centre. Charjew became a major railway junction, with lines to the south to Mari and the Iranian frontier at Kushka, to the east to Daşoguz and beyond to the Kazakh network, and to the west to Buxoro and the Uzbek network. A link to Iran was completed in 1996 from Tejen (Tedzhen, on the Aşgabat–Mari line) to Mashad. The railways and parallel roads formed a corridor through the land under agriculture (only 2.6% of the total territory by 1950, 3.2% by 1996) and left the majority desert territory (substantial areas of which were designated and protected as nature reserves) to rough tracks. At the end of the Soviet period Turkmenistan had the lowest ratio of hard-surfaced roads to area (37 km per 1,000 sq km) of any of the 15 Union Republics. A significant addition to irrigable agricultural land was effected by the building in the 1950s of the Kara-Kum Canal, linking the Amu Dar'ya and Murgab rivers and extending beyond Aşgabat to Kazandzhik, at the foot of the western end of the Kopet Dag Mountains: the irrigated area is 1.7m. ha of a total 1.8m. ha of arable land. During Soviet times the exclusive use of Turkmenistani hydrocarbons within the USSR required a pipeline system in that direction, but later (1997) a gas pipeline, financed by Iran, took natural gas from the Korpeje field in western Turkmenistan to Kord Kuy in northern Iran.

Industrialization brought urbanization: by the end of the Soviet period, the rural share of the population of the Turkmen SSR was down to 55% (the lowest level in any of the Union Republics in Central Asia, other than Kazakhstan). However, it also signalled the typically Soviet 'extensive' form of development, for the rate of expansion of the work-force and of capital had exceeded the rate of economic growth. In 1970–90, within the material sector of the economy (Soviet statistical practice followed a Marxist separation of material product plus closely allied services from the rest of the services sector, a narrower production set than would be counted in gross domestic product—GDP), Turkmenistan was the only Union Republic to show negative labour productivity; in capital productivity, for which all Union Republics showed negative values, the decline in Turkmenistan was the largest. The consequences were felt when at the end of 1991 the country was opened to competition and confronted with severe production declines throughout its former Soviet export markets. By 1997 GDP was only equivalent to 61% of the level recorded in 1989, while industrial output was only 63% of the 1989 level. Turkmenistan did not, however, suffer the greatest decline in GDP or industrial output of all of the post-Soviet states, despite low world prices for cotton and petroleum in the later 1990s, and by 2002 industry had recovered to exceed the level recorded in 1989. According to the European Bank for Reconstruction and Development (EBRD), GDP in 2007 was 98% higher than the 1989 level. None the less, according to the United Nations Development Programme's (UNDP) *Human Development Report 2007/08*, by the end of 2007 Turkmenistan had not regained the level of per head GDP achieved in 1988. The recovery after 1997 owed more to higher prices for cotton, petroleum and natural gas than to any transition from central planning to a market system, as the Turkmenistani economy remained substantially unreformed. Although some small-scale state enterprises had been privatized and comprehensive price controls abandoned, widespread use of state subsidies and directives to enterprises inhibited the formation of a competitive market economy. A Strategy for Turkmenistan approved by the EBRD in June 2006 stated that, owing to the country's 'continued failure to take any measures which would indicate a willingness to make progress towards multi-party democracy, pluralistic society and a market-based economy', the bank would continue to suspend funding to the public sector and provide funding to the private sector only on condition that such investments would not be state-controlled and that government officials would not be able personally to benefit from them. At mid-2008 the EBRD considered that, despite a number of reforms announced by President Berdymuhamedov, there had been no significant change to the situation in the country. The economy continued to be largely dominated by the state-owned sector and the investment climate remained difficult. However, a gradual unification of the exchange rate was initiated from the beginning of 2008, effectively neutralizing the 'black' (unofficial) market. Moreover, changes to the legislation on foreign investment allowed foreigners to establish and fully own companies, as well as to buy property and rent land for long-term use. Under President Niyazov, the Government's engagement with international organizations had been reduced to formalities. Despite its suitability for membership of the UN Industrial Development Organization (UNIDO), Turkmenistan remained outside that agency; neither the World Bank nor the IMF operated lending programmes in Turkmenistan, and they have not publicly reported on the country since 1999 and 2000, respectively. The Interstate Statistical Committee of the Commonwealth of Independent States (CIS) has not received data from Turkmenistan since 1999. However, following a newly expressed willingness to engage with the World Bank and a request from the Government under President Berdymuhamedov, the Bank announced a Small Grants Programme in Turkmenistan in 2008. The programme was to focus on civic engagement, in line with the World Bank's social development agenda.

AGRICULTURE

The relative poverty of Turkmenistani peasants at the time of the Soviet delimitation of Central Asia in 1924 was a factor in the choice of republican status separate from Uzbekistan. Although Georgii Chicherin, Soviet Commissar for Foreign Affairs from 1923 to 1930, warned the Politburo in May 1924 that 'the Uzbek commercial bourgeoisie hope to get rid of poor areas and create a large cotton-producing region, which would provide them with commercial opportunities', Stalin and local Bolshevik leaders in Buxoro and Samarqand needed cotton merchants and rich farmers (daikhans) as allies in dismantling the long-autonomous Muslim states (khanates) of Buxoro and Khiva. Although cotton played a crucial role as the First Five-Year Plan brought the USSR nearer to autarky (whereas 40% of the cotton consumed in the USSR was imported in 1927/28, only 2.6% was imported in 1933), the daikhans were expropriated by the nationalization of wholesale trade and farm collectivization in the early 1930s. Collectivization of the cotton plantations was substantially complete by 1933, but was imposed with somewhat less draconian measures than elsewhere in the USSR. Thus, in 1933 around 34% of the collective farms were of the simplest category, 'associations for the mutual working of land', compared with 2% across the USSR, and the area under industrial crops was to remain constant. The expulsion of the better-off peasantry was proportionally less, and the driving of nomadic pastoralists into collectives did not quite degenerate into the mass murder that it became in Kazakhstan. That said, the compulsory replacement of food crops by cotton in the early 1930s was inadequately compensated for by grain imports, while the cotton crop was prioritized; by 1976–89 the annual output of cotton in Turkmenistan averaged 1,185,000 metric tons, although there were substantial annual variations. The wider area under cotton cultivation required much investment in irrigation, to which the completion of the Kara-Kum Canal in 1960 notably added; water abstraction from the Amu Dar'ya stabilized in the 1990s at 21.7 cu km. While it was unusually poor in 1996 (437,000 tons) and 1997 (635,000 tons), the raw cotton harvest regained the levels recorded during the Soviet period after independence, averaging 1,157,000 tons in 1999–2001. However, just as President Niyazov proclaimed annual targets of 2m. tons, output declined to 490,000 tons in 2002, mainly because salinity had reduced both the sown area and yields, before recovering to 714,000 tons in 2003 and 950,000 tons in 2007. Harvesting is very labour intensive, and compulsion has been required to bring in urban workers and secondary and university students.

When imports of grain were seriously disrupted by the dissolution of the USSR and of its central planning, the Government launched a programme for self-sufficiency in the crop, whereby farmers extended the area under grains, although bringing in marginal land led to a decline in average yields. The small wheat crop pre-independence (88,000 metric tons in 1985 and 134,000 tons in 1990) was rapidly increased, reaching 1.7m. tons in 2000 and 2.8m. tons in 2005. Both cotton and wheat remained under the Soviet 'state-order' system (which was soon reimposed for sugar beet), under which government agencies purchased specified quantities at far below world-market prices and farmers were set specific ploughing and sowing tasks with dates for fulfilment. The agencies also provided seed, fertilizer and technical advice at subsidized rates, which only partly offset the low procurement prices. In July 2006 President Niyazov reported that over 3m. tons of wheat had been harvested, but the country still experienced severe wheat shortages, revealing that the Soviet-era practice of exaggerated reporting remained. Independent sources reported that the actual harvest in 2006 was no greater than 800,000 tons. Having demanded truthful reporting of agricultural production and raised the state prices for wheat and cotton in 2007, President Berdymuhamedov declared that the state would no longer order more wheat than was necessary to meet domestic demand, whereas state orders for cotton would continue to increase. In 2007 the wheat harvest was slightly over 1m. tons, while domestic demand was estimated at 1.6m. tons. In July 2008 Berdymuhamedov reported that enough wheat had been harvested to meet domestic demand, although no official figures were released. Of other grains, irrigated land was enlarged for rice paddy (47,000 tons in 1990, 135,000 tons in 2006), and the production of potatoes has greatly increased (35,000 tons in 1990, 175,000 tons in 2006), while the maize crop has been almost eliminated (falling from 159,000 tons in 1990 to 10,000 tons in 2001, before recovering to 50,000 tons in 2006). Sugar beet has been increasingly cultivated under the state order (from just 35,240 tons in 1992 to 294,532 tons in 2005, declining to some 235,000 tons in 2006). Grape-growing and therefore wine production has increased (180,000 tons and 24,000 tons, respectively, in 2006). The sparse grazing-land supported some 2.1m. cattle and 16.6m. head of sheep and goats in 2006, according to FAO (including the 'Persian lamb', which provides the valuable export item karakul). Despite recommendations by the IMF in 2000 to phase out subsidization of traditional agriculture in favour of suitable niche produce and to institute 'credible property rights', President Niyazov intervened in 2003 to postpone the enactment of land privatization, which was to have been undertaken over a five- to 10-year period.

INDUSTRY AND MINING

Turkmenistan has the second largest proven gas reserves of the states of the former USSR (2,670,000m. cu m at the end of 2007), behind Russia (44,650,000m. cu m), as well as reserves of petroleum and petroleum condensates (100m. metric tons at the end of 2007). The country can therefore rely on export earnings for the foreseeable future, provided that there remain markets willing to pay for the cost of lengthy overland transportation. In the late 1980s Turkmenistan was the world's fourth largest gas producer. It was annually producing 90,000m. cu m of natural gas, of which some 80,000m. cu m was exported to the rest of the USSR, along with some 5m. tons of petroleum and petroleum condensates. Petroleum has hardly been used in electricity production, and since independence nearly 100% of electricity in Turkmenistan has been produced using natural gas (in 2002 658m. kWh were exported from 10,700m. kWh produced, and in 2006 1,646m. kWh from 13,300m. kWh, compared with exports of 4,400m. kWh from production of 13,051m. kWh in 1985). Extraction of both hydrocarbons decreased during the 1990s, but whereas output of petroleum subsequently increased to levels higher than those recorded in the Soviet period (9.0m. tons in 2002 and 9.8m. tons in 2007, compared with 5.7m.tons in 1990), production of gas, although increasing from its lowest figure (12,400 m. cu m in 1998), has remained more modest (67,400m. cu m in 2007, compared with 81,900m. cu m in 1990). More petroleum products were expected to be available for export in the late 2000s, following the proposed increase in capacity (from 2m. tons to up to 8m. tons) of the Seyidi refinery. By the mid-2000s electricity generation remained substantially lower than that recorded in the late Soviet period, reflecting both lower demand and the obsolescence of facilities. Electricity production

declined from 13,183m. kWh in 1992, the first year of independence, to 8,860m. kWh in 1999. From 2000 it increased steadily, having finally recovered to the level recorded in 1992 by 2006. As a result of an ambitious reconstruction plan, total capacity was envisaged to increase from 2,400 MW in 1995 to 5,935 MW in 2010. In 2007 there were eight power stations in Turkmenistan, with a total capacity of 3,300 MW. Coal reserves, estimated at 800m. tons in the Tuarkyrskoye deposit in the north-west, are not yet exploited. In October 2002 a prohibition on the privatization of energy enterprises was extended for 15 years.

Pipelines are essential for the export of the land-locked country's principal natural resource, hydrocarbons. Apart from a short line to Iran, the domestic gas network remains linked only to former Soviet states, although extensions to other countries were both under construction and projected. Russia's large state-controlled gas supplier, Gazprom, which controls the major pipeline linking Turkmenistan with Western markets, exercised its monopoly power until 2007. It first suspended Turkmenistan's access to Western European markets in 1993—thus effectively dealing with its competitor and limiting Turkmenistani gas sales to Armenia, Georgia and Ukraine, all of which defaulted on payments. In 1997 gas sales through the Gazprom pipeline were halted as the result of a dispute over transit payments. The improvement in Russian-Turkmenistani relations during 1999 resulted in the resumption of gas sales to Ukraine in that year. Following the election of President Vladimir Putin in Russia in 2000 and changes to Gazprom's senior management, direct gas sales to Russia resumed with the signature of a 25-year agreement in 2003. Under the agreement, Turkmenistani gas deliveries to Russia were to increase to 80,000m.–90,000m. cu m annually from 2009. However, supplies to both Russia and (via that country) to Ukraine were abruptly halted on 1 January 2005, in the absence of agreement on a new price. Supplies subsequently recommenced, when a price increase, from US $44 to $58 per 1,000 cu m of gas, was first agreed, for supplying 36m. cu m to Ukraine and 10m. cu m to Russia in 2005. The price later reverted to $44 per 1,000 cu m of gas, after effectively dispensing with a 50% barter payment provision that had existed for years in the gas industry. Ukraine's continual failure to meet its obligations on timely payments for gas supplies and the existence of third party beneficiaries from the gas trade eventually led to a further gas supply disruption and a price increase, to $65 per 1,000 cu m of gas, in late December 2005. In September 2006, following a threat by Turkmenistan to suspend supplies to Russia, the latter agreed to increase the price paid for Turkmenistani gas to $100 per 1,000 cu m from the last quarter of 2006 until the end of 2009. Russia received 42,000m. cu m of gas in 2006 and negotiated to receive 50,000m. cu m per year in 2007–09, thus effectively leaving no free capacity in the pipeline for transportation of gas to Ukraine. No new direct agreement on gas sales was made between Turkmenistan and Ukraine following the expiry of the earlier agreement for 2002–06. Increased international demand for Turkmenistani gas and the potential threat to Russia's control of the bulk of Turkmen gas exports posed by various gas pipeline projects actively supported by the European Union (EU), the USA and other countries following the death of President Niyazov led Russia to yield to subsequent demands by Turkmenistan for increased gas prices. Thus, in November 2007 a new price, of $130 per 1,000 cu m, was agreed for the first six months of 2008, and a price of $150 per 1,000 cu m was agreed for the second six months of the year. It was also agreed that the price paid for gas supplies from 1 January 2009 would be determined by market principles. Projected purchase prices were some $225–$295 per 1,000 cu m, although some reports indicated that Turkmenistan might receive as much as $400–$450 per 1,000 cu m for its gas supplies.

By 2008 a number of gas pipeline projects were under discussion or had already been agreed. The Asian Development Bank (ADB) funded a feasibility study for the proposed trans-Afghanistan pipeline, which was to carry Turkmenistani gas to Pakistan and on to India. In February 2006 Pakistan and Turkmenistan signed a memorandum of understanding, according to which Turkmenistan agreed to supply Pakistan with some 90.6m. cu m of gas per day for 30 years. The Indian

Government approved India's participation in the project in May. However, by mid-2008 the respective parties were still discussing pricing and other details of the agreement, and Afghanistan, India and Pakistan had yet to see independent verification of gas reserves at Turkmenistan's Dauletabad field. Meanwhile, in April 2006 Turkmenistan and the People's Republic of China signed an agreement to construct a natural gas pipeline; China was to purchase 30,000m. cu m of Turkmenistani gas each year for 30 years from 2009. During a state visit to China in July 2007 President Berdymuhamedov addressed the Chinese Government's concerns regarding Turkmenistan's ability to supply sufficient gas to fill the proposed Turkmenistan–China pipeline, and construction of the pipeline officially commenced in August. In December 2007 Turkmenistan, Russia and Kazakhstan signed an intergovernmental agreement on the construction of a new Caspian shore gas pipeline with a capacity of 30,000m. cu m per year and the upgrade of an old Caspian shore pipeline, Central Asia–Centre 3, with a capacity of 10,000m. cu m of gas per year. In July 2008 Turkmenistan announced that it started the implementation of the project work on the pipeline segment that would lie in its territory. In April 2008 Turkmenistan also agreed to supply 10,000m. cu m of gas to the EU annually, beginning from 2009. The EU was actively lobbying for the construction of the planned Nabucco pipeline, which would take Turkmenistan gas via Turkey to Western Europe. The USA continued to express support for the trans-Caspian gas pipeline that was first proposed in the 1990s. In 2000 disagreements arose between Turkmenistan and Azerbaijan over the allocation of quotas in the future pipeline, and disputed fields in the Caspian. Following the election of President Berdymuhamedov in 2007, relations between Turkmenistan and Azerbaijan improved and discussion of the trans-Caspian pipeline began to re-emerge.

While exports of fuels and energy continue, it is the Turkmenistani Government's industrial strategy to augment domestic value-added. Thus, cotton fibre exports declined between 1995 and 2002, whereas those of cotton yarn and cotton textiles increased dramatically. A higher price for cotton in 2003 pushed exports of fibre up to US $138.6m., but they declined to $94.7m. in 2005. Exports of petroleum and petroleum products increased more than 13-fold between 1995 and 2005 (to $1,854m.), whereas exports of natural gas increased more than two-fold (to $2,208.7m. in 2005). These results reflected the purchase on a 'turn-key' basis of textile mills, the modernization of the petroleum refinery at Türkmenbaşi, and the building of a smaller refinery at Atamurat in the Lebap Velayat (region). The extraction of sulphates from the Bay of Kara-Bogaz Gol and elsewhere furnished the basis for expanding the domestic supply of fertilizers. The manufacture of cotton and silk rugs and clothing and flour-milling expanded in the years after independence, although, reflecting the greater investment in imported equipment rather than in construction work, the output recorded by the cement industry was only 697,000 metric tons in 2005, compared with 1,085,000 tons in 1990.

New investment in manufacturing increased its contribution to GDP from 5.5% in 1993 to 22.0% in 2004, while that of the extractive and building industries declined from 58.5% to 18.7%, because the services sector, little developed in the Soviet period, expanded more rapidly, contributing 39.3% of GDP in 2004, compared with 16.5% in 1993. However, productivity in industry was relatively high, as indicated by the fact that it accounted for just 14.5% of total employment in 2005. Agriculture remained the dominant occupation (employing 42.6% of the total in 2004) and is likely to remain so as the country's population is expected to increase, according to UN estimates, to 5.2m. by 2010 (compared with 3.8m. in 1990 and 5.0m. in 2008).

CAPITAL INVESTMENT

The investment undertaken from the mid-1990s placed substantial demands on the construction sector, which increased in parallel with economic activity as a whole; the share of GDP generated by construction changed little (6.0% in 1995, compared with 4.5% in 2006, according to the ADB). However, the

long-term income generated by projects implemented during this period remained uncertain. The same concern regarding income generation applies to some of the construction projects launched under President Berdymuhamedov in 2007–08. Investment in hydrocarbons, usually by multinational petroleum companies, patently produces export returns, and the capital's luxury hotels might, like the stud farm and horse racing establishment for Akhal-Teke horses (one of the world's hardiest breeds), attract some income. However, that is scarcely true of the lavish presidential palaces and monuments, and the two vast mosques built by the French company Bouygues on the site of the Battle of Gök Tepe and in President Niyazov's home village of Kipchak. In April 2003, however, President Niyazov declared that no more mosques should be built, as the country 'already had sufficient'. There are also projects for which the economic return is either uncertain or very long term. These include the Turkmen Lake (Türkmen Koli) scheme (established by presidential decree in July 2002 and expected to cost US $8,000m. by its completion in 2020), an artificial reservoir of 2,092 sq km in the Kara-Kum desert, fed by the Amu Dar'ya. The objective is to guarantee water supply for irrigation irrespective of annual variations in water flow, which depends on the meltwater of glaciers and snow in the Pamir and Hindu Kush mountains, and on the release thereof by Afghanistan and Tajikistan, the head-water states. A constant supply of water would support plans for irrigating 4,000 sq km of marginal land to achieve self-sufficiency in food production and further expand cotton exports, and would stabilize the underground water level. Set against these possible gains is the fact that the new land could rapidly become salinated (as is much land in Daşoguz Velayat) as irrigation lifts the salt level of the soil, and that the off-take of water from the Amu Dar'ya will accelerate the desiccation of the Aral Sea, the water volume of which declined by 75% in 40 years. The prospective loss of the Aral Sea, once the world's fourth largest freshwater lake (and now the 10th largest), suggests that evaporation in so large and shallow a reservoir as the proposed Turkmen Lake could exceed the net water inflow. With a large share of GDP taken in government consumption (12.7%), private consumption represented only 54.9% in 2006 (net exports absorbed the rest). The EBRD reported that, based on 2006 data, the country ranked among 27 transition economies as having the lowest share of GDP generated by the private sector (25% in 2006, equal with Belarus). The investment that did generate growth was predominantly from abroad, almost all foreign direct investment (FDI), since the state-owned economy offered no scope for portfolio investment. The inflow of FDI as a share of GDP (6.4% in 2007) was just above the average for a transition economy, and higher than for the other petroleum producers (4.9% in Kazakhstan, 1.2% in Uzbekistan, 0.8% in Russia, and –16.6% in Azerbaijan). Most FDI in Turkmenistan has gone towards hydrocarbons production. During 1989–2007 the aggregate inflow amounted to US $3,928m., equivalent to $604 per head, higher than for the hydrocarbon-rich states of Russia ($199 per head) and Azerbaijan ($451 per head), but far below that for Kazakhstan ($2,329 per head).

TRANSPORT AND COMMUNICATIONS

The paucity of railways and roads, the sedentary nature of farming and the poverty of the population (with 58% living in poverty, according to World Bank estimates) are demonstrated by the modest contribution of transport and communications to GDP—6.9% in 2006. There were 2,523 km of railways in 2007 and 19,500 km of hard-surfaced roads in 1999, while private automobile ownership and household telephone connections were both relatively low. In the mid-2000s the highways linking Aşgabat with Türkmenbaşi and Türkmenabat were being upgraded. A new railroad from Aşgabat across the Kara-Kum desert to Daşoguz was also built and inaugurated in 2006. The rehabilitation of the road linking Atamurat, in the extreme east of Turkmenistan, with Imamnazar in Afghanistan was the only project in the country being supported by an international economic agency, the ADB. Motor transport was the most utilized form of public transport in 2005, accounting for 12,902m. passenger-km out of a total of 16,287m. passenger-km; railways and air transport provided 1,326m. and 1,913m. passenger-km, respectively. Pipelines dominated the freight pattern, carrying 28,373m. metric ton-km out of a total 44,570m. ton-km, followed by railways with 9,668m. ton-km and roads with 6,366m. ton-km. As throughout the CIS, save in the three Slavic states, the use of postal services declined dramatically in the 1990s. In Turkmenistan the decline continued until 2000, the year when only 1m. letters and parcels were posted, and since then the use of postal services has gradually increased to 1.7m. in 2005. However, this was still significantly below the 1991 level, when 55m. letters and 827,000 parcels were dispatched.

THE ECONOMIC SYSTEM

The classic methodology of Soviet planning employed money essentially as a reporting instrument, with both wholesale and retail prices set administratively, so that time series reflected changes in physical quantities as specified in quarterly, annual and quinquennial plans. Independent Turkmenistan abandoned such prescriptive planning, although it retained a predilection for indicative plans to delineate its long-term economic strategies. The scant privatization that was undertaken—24,000 small producers and suppliers of services were transferred to their operatives and all collective farms were converted to farmers' associations—was formal, and the new entities remained subject to control in much the same way as state-owned enterprises. However, the economic system, as elsewhere in the USSR, had already adopted some use of the price mechanism even before the glasnost (openness) of the Mikhail Gorbachev period (1985–91), when financial institutions suited to a market economy became widespread. The key date for the adoption of a money-orientated system was the removal of most price controls in January 1992. Supply rigidity (devolving from the abandonment of state contracts between enterprises to new controllers who often exercised local monopoly power), unfamiliarity with market practice, lack of confidence in the Soviet (and subsequently Russian) rouble, which continued in circulation, and unrestrained monetarization of the fiscal deficit quickly induced hyperinflation. Turkmenistan underwent the most serious inflation of any Central Asian post-Soviet state: in 1993–95 annual inflation percentage increases were in four digits (3,102% in 1993) and did not decline to less than 100% per year until 1997. The separation in 1993 of CIS currencies from the rouble began a slow moderation of price rises, but not before the new currency, the manat, had depreciated from an average of US $1 = 19.50 manats in 1994 to an average of $1 = 4,143 manats in 1997. Stabilization of the manat, at $1 = 5,200 manats in April 1998, temporarily unified the official and the unofficial exchange rates, and extensive subsidization restrained inflation, which increased by only 17% that year. The unofficial exchange rate soon diverged from the official rate, reaching $1 = 25,000 manats in 2002. A presidential decree of March 2004 (when the unofficial rate was $1 = 22,000 manats), entitled 'Strategy for the Political, Economic and Cultural Development of Turkmenistan to 2020', required the maintenance of the nominal exchange rate at $1 = 5,200 manats until at least 2010. This meant that the nominal rate became more and more unrealistic: inflation depreciated the unofficial exchange rate by an annual average of 10% during 2004–06. In 2006 the unofficial exchange rate was $1 = 24,000 manats. However, the situation changed in 2008. On 1 January 2008, after a 10-year suspension, foreign-exchange bureaux opened and two exchange rates were fixed: the state exchange rate was fixed at $1 = 6,250 manats for financing various state programmes, and the commercial rate was fixed at $1 = 19,800 manats for the general population, thereby virtually eradicating the unofficial market. On 1 May the Central Bank of Turkmenistan introduced a unified 'floating' exchange rate at $1 = 14,250 manats. A redenominated currency was to come into circulation from the beginning of 2009.

Just as Stalin fostered 'hurrah planning' (the promulgation of exaggerated economic achievements), so the National Institute of State Statistics and Information on Turkmenistan is required to publish figures that international observers have cause to doubt. The GDP reported for 2007 was officially 20%

higher than the previous year, which, in turn, was reported as 20% higher than 2005. The IMF estimated increments of 11.5% and 11.4%, respectively, to be more realistic, pointing out that GDP growth was largely the result of increased gas and oil prices, with hydrocarbons extraction increasing by just 6.8%.

Subsidization is pervasive, although President Berdymuhamedov decreased state subsidies for petrol in 2008, causing prices for bus, rail and domestic route air transportation to increase as much as 20-fold. Imported consumer goods are sold at subsidized prices, and a range of domestically produced goods (gas, water, electricity and salt) are distributed free of charge to households. Nine-10ths of the subsidies for those free supplies to households are paid from off-budget funds, but even the one-10th settled from the budget accounts for 10% of the central budget. Some import-substitutes, such as state joint ventures in cotton and silk textiles, are operating on negative value-added. The substantial export sector can be added to these inflationary pressures, since it generates domestic purchasing power, much of which is spent on non-traded goods and services. In theory, such pressure is restrained by a tight monetary policy, based on a balanced central budget and close state control over banks. In October 2002 a presidential decree required all commercial banks (except the state-owned Türkmenvnesheconombank—State Bank for Foreign Economic Affairs of Turkmenistan) to close correspondent accounts in foreign banks and to deal in foreign currency only through the Central Bank of Turkmenistan, which came under the President's personal control in 1999. Most lending was supplied by state-owned banks, and 95% of all loans in 2003 went to state-owned enterprises. The status of off-budget accounts has not been revealed, but from 2003 there were many signs that public funds were insufficient for expenditure, and the state resorted to borrowing from abroad and to domestic money creation. While civil service salaries were doubled every February in 2001–05 (but were often paid in arrears), dramatic job cuts were applied to the education and health care sectors in order to reduce expenditure. Officially, there was no unemployment in Turkmenistan. However, independent international sources estimated it at 70% in 2006. The many exceptions for state-owned enterprises and the paucity of a private sector suggested a declining tax base.

THE SOCIAL ECONOMY

While expenditure on objectives favoured by the late Niyazov was largely focused on conspicuous construction projects, as mentioned above, finance for education and health services was reduced markedly, with potentially serious long-term effects on economic growth and on society. The reduction in the length of general education, from 10 to nine years, and the dismissal of more than 12,000 teachers from 2002, was compounded in 2004 by the curtailment of health services, including the dismissal of 15,000 medical workers (in the mid-1990s there had been 69,000 schoolteachers and 113,000 doctors and nurses). Not only were the professional qualifications of the lost staff no longer productively deployed, but the content of the services provided by the remainder deteriorated. Thus, in education a high proportion of teaching hours were occupied by the study of Turkmenistan's neutrality and President Niyazov's quasi-spiritual text, the *Ruhnama* (see History), at the expense of mainstream subjects and physical training. The conversion of the national script from Cyrillic to Latin from the early 1990s was inadequately underwritten by textbook supply. In 2004 it was reported that only 20% of the required textbooks were available in secondary schools, although 10,000 copies of *Source of Wisdom*, an anthology of President Niyazov's poems, had been donated to school libraries. University enrolment declined from 42,000 in 1990 to 23,000 in 1998, putting the ratio to population aged 19–24 years at 3%, well below the 31% average for transition countries, and subsequently decreased further, to 15,000 in 2004, according to the UN Children's Fund (UNICEF). The constraint of entry to degree courses and the reduction of course lengths to two years (following two years of 'work experience') seriously reduced the formation of human capital. Although in the mid-2000s enrolment in higher education was only about one-10th of the level at independence in 1991, school-leavers were forced to apply to

Turkmenistani institutes because, by a Ministry of Education decree of June 2003, degrees obtained outside Turkmenistan after 1993 were no longer recognized, and those holding such qualifications were dismissed from state employment with effect from 1 June 2004. The reduction in health care services in March 2004 was followed by the closure of all hospitals outside Aşgabat in May 2005 and the instruction to physicians that infectious diseases should no longer be reported. Salt and other impurities in the water supply, especially in the northern province of Daşoguz, increased the incidence of hepatitis A and B and kidney stones. Although it was experiencing a serious problem with HIV/AIDS, the Government declined to join a regional AIDS Control Project launched by UNAIDS in May 2005. In conditions of widespread poverty (with 31% of the population consuming less than one-half the national mean in 2003), a significant decline in health standards was inevitable, especially among the malnourished (11% of children under the age of five). In early 2006 President Niyazov cancelled retirement pensions to one-third of the country's pensioners and reduced social security allowances.

In 2007 the new President, Gurbanguly Berdymuhamedov, reinstated retirement pensions. He also announced reforms in education and health care, including: the reopening of the Academy of Sciences (disbanded by President Niyazov in the 1990s); a return to the 10-year secondary and five-year higher education system; the reintroduction of physical education and foreign languages on the curriculum; sending Turkmenistani youths to study abroad (thus recognizing foreign diplomas); the reopening of rural hospitals; and an increase in employment levels and salaries in educational institutions. In 2007, for the first time since 2003, university enrolment increased by about 4,000 students. In the 2007/08 academic year some 13,800 students were studying at the country's 18 higher education institutions. The intake of students to higher education institutions in the academic year 2008/09 was to total some 4,940 students. The Government also intended to send some 2,200 students to study abroad in that academic year, representing almost a 10-fold increase from the 2007/08 state quota of 240 students. Some new areas of study (such as the Chinese, Italian, Korean and Spanish languages, world financial markets, insurance, international law, international relations and diplomacy, international economic relations, international journalism, agrochemistry and soil science, plant protection, land reclamation mechanization, animal husbandry, and industrial engineering) were to be introduced at institutions of higher education from 2008/09. Nevertheless, Turkmenistani young people who wished to study abroad continued to encounter bureaucratic obstacles. President Niyazov's works remained part of the school curriculum, albeit to a lesser extent than had previously been the case. Moreover, an examination on knowledge of the *Ruhnama* remained a compulsory requirement for entry to any higher education institution in Turkmenistan.

FOREIGN TRADE AND PAYMENTS

State economic regulation of the external sector in the mid-2000s was as intensive as it had been under Soviet planning. Every foreign trade deal had to be individually approved by the Council of Ministers: in April 2004, for example, President Niyazov deducted two months' salary from the Minister of Trade and Foreign Economic Relations for having exported metal without such authorization. Energy products accounted for four-fifths of exports and one-third of GDP and were likely to retain their dominance, given Russia's willingness to buy all the gas that Turkmenistan could deliver to its pipelines. The pre-eminence of a single product group has short- and long-term risks: price volatility and the exhaustion of recoverable deposits, respectively. A solution to both would be for the exporting state to channel part of its hydrocarbons revenue into a fund, some of which could be expended for current needs when the price of hydrocarbons is low, and the rest of which could be invested, preferably abroad, to secure a permanent income. In 2001 the World Bank advised the Turkmenistani authorities to establish such a fund under autonomous control, similar to those that were later successfully arranged by the IMF for Azerbaijan and Kazakhstan. Instead, President Niyazov established under his personal control a Foreign Exchange

Reserve Fund, which received one-half of convertible-currency revenue from gas exports and 30% of those from petroleum and cotton exports. By the mid-2000s the Fund was believed to finance the purchases of materials and professional services for prestige projects and to service the unreported, but certainly substantial, foreign debts.

The Foreign Exchange Reserve Fund and the magnitude of the external debt were only two of a large number of economic aggregates and indicators that were not made public by Turkmenistan, which, as noted above, had ceased reporting to the CIS Interstate Statistical Committee in 1999. The ADB, the World Bank and the EBRD publish estimates of Turkmenistan's balance of trade. In 2008 the EBRD reported that Turkmenistan's actual balance of trade recorded a surplus of US $4,598m. (exports $7,156m., imports $2,558m. in 2006). Net FDI amounted to $731m., and the known external debt of some $805m. was covered by the country's gross international reserves (excluding gold) of $7,477m. Service on that debt was equivalent to 3.9% of exports of goods and services, and the reserves covered 13 months of imports of goods and services. These, and the ratio of that external debt to GDP (7.9%), reflected more favourable external conditions, compared with those experienced by most other transition economies, including stable ones. This, however, was largely the result of continued higher world energy prices and the higher prices for gas agreed with Russia (see above).

Under President Niyazov, the Turkmenistani Government had minimized its relationships with international agencies, which had been deterred from further engagement by the adverse political and economic climate. The World Bank had given Turkmenistan three loans, as well as policy advice during transition, and observed in 2005 that 'unfortunately, there is little to show in terms of results', stating that it was 'unable to engage more actively with Turkmenistan in light of the country's failure to report its external debt, a violation of the Bank's negative pledge clause, and the fact that Turkmenistan has not yet met minimum public resource-management standards'. The International Finance Corporation (part of the World Bank Group) had tried for three years to implement a single private sector project without success. Turkmenistan became a member of the ADB in 2000, but by early 2008 had still to receive its ADB country programme funding, owing to ongoing consultations between the ADB and the Government. At that time the total funding approved by the ADB for four technical assistance projects in Turkmenistan had amounted to a modest US $715,000. Turkmenistan was the sole former Soviet republic to have neither applied for nor gained membership of the World Trade Organization. It did not join the Central Asian Co-operation Organization (superseded by the Eurasian Economic Community in January 2006), but remained a member of the Economic Co-operation Organization, with the remaining states of Central Asia, as well as Azerbaijan, Afghanistan, Iran, Pakistan and Turkey. The EBRD published a revised Strategy for Turkmenistan in June 2006 and, like the World Bank, made explicit proposals for structural change. The Organization for Security and Co-operation in Europe (OSCE), the central concern of which is the protection of human rights, maintained contact, running conferences and training programmes in the country and sending its Chairman-in-Office to Aşgabat from 2003 in the course of annual visits to all Central Asian states. Relations with the OSCE were strained, as the Turkmenistani authorities refused to extend diplomatic accreditation to the head of the OSCE mission in Aşgabat, Paraschiva Badescu, in 2004 and accused a staff member of plotting against the Government in June 2006. However, during 2007–08 the new President and Government of Turkmenistan showed signs of increased willingness to co-operate more closely with the international community. Thus, the World Bank, along with a few other international financial institutions, was consulted on the issue of the unification of the currency exchange rates in Turkmenistan. In December 2007 the World Bank announced a small grants programme for the country. In May 2008 the IMF undertook its first country consultation since November 1999. The number of state visits and exchanges of government delegations to and from Turkmenistan increased significantly, with a major focus on energy issues.

Statistical Survey

Principal sources (unless otherwise stated): IMF, *Turkmenistan, Economic Review, Turkmenistan—Recent Economic Developments* (December 1999); World Bank, *Statistical Handbook: States of the Former USSR.*

Area and Population

AREA, POPULATION AND DENSITY

Area (sq km)	488,100*
Population (census results)	
12 January 1989	3,533,925
10 January 1995	
Males	2,225,331
Females	2,257,920
Total	4,483,251
Population (UN estimates at mid-year)†	
2006	4,899,000
2007	4,965,000
2008	5,031,000
Density (per sq km) at mid-2008	10.3

* 188,456 sq miles.

† Source: UN, *World Population Prospects: The 2006 Revision*; these estimates are substantially lower than those produced by the state statistics institute (see below).

Population (official estimate): 6,800,200 at 1 April 2006 (Source: National Institute of State Statistics and Information).

POPULATION BY ETHNIC GROUP
(official estimates at 1 January 1993)

	Number	%
Turkmen	3,118,000	73.3
Russian	419,000	9.8
Uzbek	382,000	9.0
Kazakh	87,000	2.0
Others	248,000	5.8
Total	**4,254,000**	**100.0**

Ethnic groups (percentage of total, at census of 1995): Turkmen 77.0; Uzbek 9.2; Russian 6.7; Kazakh 2.0; Others 5.1 (Source: US Embassy in Turkmenistan).

PRINCIPAL TOWNS
(estimated population at 1 January 1999)

Aşgabat (capital) .	605,000	Türkmenbaşi‡ . .		70,000
Türkmenabat* . .	203,000	Bayramaly . . .		60,000
Daşoguz	165,000	Tejen		54,000
Mari	123,000	Serdar§		51,000
Balkanabat† . .	119,000			

* Formerly Charjew (Chardzhou).

† Formerly Nebit-Dag.

‡ Formerly Krasnovodsk.

§ Formerly Gyzylarbat (Kizyl-Arvat).

1 July 2002 (official estimate): Aşgabat 743,000.

Mid-2007 (incl. suburbs, UN estimate): Aşgabat 744,000 (Source: UN, *World Urbanization Prospects: The 2007 Revision*).

BIRTHS, MARRIAGES AND DEATHS

	Registered live births		Registered marriages		Registered deaths	
	Number	Rate (per 1,000)	Number	Rate (per 1,000)	Number	Rate (per 1,000)
1987 . .	126,787	37.2	31,484	9.2	26,802	7.9
1988 . .	125,887	36.0	33,008	9.4	27,317	7.8
1989 . .	124,992	34.9	34,890	9.8	27,609	7.7

Registered deaths: 25,755 (death rate 7.0 per 1,000) in 1990; 27,403 (7.3 per 1,000) in 1991; 27,509 (6.8 per 1,000) in 1992; 31,171 (7.2 per 1,000) in 1993; 32,067 (7.3 per 1,000) in 1994.

1998 (provisional): Live births 98,461 (birth rate 20.3 per 1,000); Marriages 26,361 (marriage rate 5.4 per 1,000); Deaths 29,628 (death rate 6.1 per 1,000).

Source: UN, *Demographic Yearbook.*

Births (annual averages, UN estimates): Birth rate (per 1,000): 32.5 in 1990–95; 24.5 in 1995–2000; 22.9 in 2000–05 (Source: UN, *World Population Prospects: The 2006 Revision*).

Deaths (annual averages, UN estimates): Death rate (per 1,000): 8.4 in 1990–95; 8.0 in 1995–2000; 8.3 in 2000–05 (Source: UN, *World Population Prospects: The 2006 Revision*).

2002: Birth rate 22.2 per 1,000; death rate 6.4 per 1,000 (Source: UN, *Statistical Yearbook for Asia and the Pacific*).

Expectation of life (years at birth, WHO estimates): 63.1 (males 59.6; females 66.7) in 2006 (Source: WHO, *World Health Statistics*).

EMPLOYMENT
('000 persons at 31 December)

	1996	1997	1998*
Agriculture	769.8	778.8	890.5
Forestry	2.5	2.9	1.9
Industry†	172.0	188.1	226.8
Construction	136.2	122.8	108.2
Trade and catering	91.8	101.2	115.8
Transport and communications .	77.7	77.9	90.7
Information-computing services .	1.3	1.0	1.2
Housing and municipal services .	50.2	46.8	48.3
Health care and social security .	97.4	100.4	89.2
Education, culture and arts . .	183.8	185.9	190.5
Science, research and development	9.2	6.9	5.2
General administration . . .	24.7	25.3	28.8
Finance and insurance . . .	8.7	9.6	12.6
Other activities	41.5	28.3	29.0
Total	**1,666.8**	**1,675.9**	**1,838.7**

* Provisional.

† Comprising manufacturing (except printing and publishing), mining and quarrying, electricity, gas, water, logging and fishing.

2004 ('000 persons at 31 December, estimates): Employed 2,110 (Agriculture 1,017, Industry 291, Other 802); Unemployed 62; Total labour force (incl. those not registered) 2,389 (Source: Asian Development Bank, *Key Indicators of Developing Asian and Pacific Countries*).

Mid-2005 ('000 persons, estimates): Agriculture, etc. 716,000; Total (incl. others) 2,276,000 (Source: FAO).

Health and Welfare

KEY INDICATORS

Total fertility rate (children per woman, 2006)	2.6
Under-5 mortality rate (per 1,000 live births, 2006) . . .	51
HIV/AIDS (% of persons aged 15–49, 2005)	<0.1
Physicians (per 1,000 head, 2006)	2.5
Hospital beds (per 1,000 head, 2006)	4.3
Health expenditure (2005): US $ per head (PPP)	308
Health expenditure (2005): % of GDP	4.8
Health expenditure (2005): public (% of total)	66.7
Access to water (% of persons, 2004)	71
Access to sanitation (% of persons, 2004)	62
Human Development Index (2005): ranking	109
Human Development Index (2005): value	0.713

For sources and definitions, see explanatory note on p. vi.

Agriculture

PRINCIPAL CROPS
('000 metric tons)

	2004	2005	2006*
Wheat	2,600	2,834†	3,260
Rice (paddy)	110	120†	135
Barley	60	65†	78
Potatoes	149*	151*	175
Sugar beet*	274	295	235
Cottonseed*	660	660	460
Cabbages	50*	56†	58
Tomatoes	250*	278†	282
Dry onions	85*	94†	96
Carrots	53*	58†	60
Watermelons*	250	253	250
Grapes*	180	170	180
Apples	35*	35*	43
Cotton (lint)*	330	330	230

* FAO estimate(s).
† Unofficial figure.

Aggregate production ('000 metric tons, may include official, semi-official or estimated data): Total cereals 2,785 in 2004; 3,035 in 2005; 3,489 in 2006; Total roots and tubers 160 in 2004; 160 in 2005; 175 in 2006; Total vegetables (incl. melons) 725 in 2004; 780 in 2005; 815 in 2006; Total fruits (excl. melons) 279 in 2004; 269 in 2005; 287 in 2006.

Source: FAO.

LIVESTOCK
('000 head at 1 January)

	2004	2005	2006
Horses*	16	16	17
Asses, mules or hinnies* . . .	25	25	26
Camels*	40	40	41
Cattle	2,000	2,025	2,065†
Pigs	30	30*	29*
Sheep†	13,150	14,267	15,694
Goats†	750	822	904
Chickens†	7,000	7,000	7,500
Turkeys*	200	200	200

* FAO estimate(s).
† Unofficial figure(s).
Source: FAO.

LIVESTOCK PRODUCTS
('000 metric tons, FAO estimates)

	2004	2005	2006
Cattle meat	100	100	102
Sheep meat	95	90	93
Goat meat	7	7	7
Chicken meat	14	12	14
Cows' milk	1,400	1,140	1,197
Hen eggs	35	35	37
Honey	10	10	9
Wool: greasy	20	20	20

Source: FAO.

Fishing

(metric tons, live weight)

	2003	2004	2005*
Capture	14,543	14,992	15,000
Azov sea sprat	14,276	14,674	14,680
Aquaculture	24	16	16
Total catch	14,567	15,008	15,016

* FAO estimates.
2006: Catch assumed to be unchanged from 2005 (FAO estimates).
Source: FAO.

Mining

('000 metric tons, unless otherwise indicated)

	2003	2004	2005
Crude petroleum*	10,000	10,100	9,500
Natural gas (million cu metres)* .	55,100	54,600	58,800
Bentonite†	50	50	50
Salt (unrefined)†	215	215	215
Gypsum (crude)†	100	100	100

* Source: BP, *Statistical Review of World Energy*.
† Estimates from US Geological Survey.

2006 ('000 metric tons, unless otherwise indicated): Crude petroleum 9,200; Natural gas (million cu metres) 62,200 (Source: BP, *Statistical Review of World Energy*).

2007 ('000 metric tons, unless otherwise indicated): Crude petroleum 9,800; Natural gas (million cu metres) 67,400 (Source: BP, *Statistical Review of World Energy*).

Industry

SELECTED PRODUCTS
('000 metric tons, unless otherwise indicated)

	2000	2001	2002
Cottonseed oil	48	45	26
Wheat flour	544	579	400
Woven cotton fabrics (million sq metres)	34	61	78
Woven silk fabrics ('000 sq metres)	216	115	283
Blankets	14	7	10
Knotted wool carpets and rugs ('000 sq metres)	1,040	1,434	1,475
Footwear, excl. rubber ('000 pairs)	478	444	253
Nitric acid (100%)	192	151	212
Ammonia (nitrogen content) . .	117	99	130
Nitrogenous fertilizers (a)* . .	89	72	103
Phosphate fertilizers (b)*† . .	11	11	17
Soap	3.0	2.5	1.6
Motor spirit (petrol)	1,132	1,283	1,292
Gas-diesel (distillate fuel) oil . .	2,247	2,547	2,360
Residual fuel oils	1,536	1,586	1,640
Clay building bricks (million) . .	309	269	279
Quicklime	17	17	15
Cement	420	448	486
Electric energy (million kWh) .	9,845	10,825	11,200

* Production in terms of (a) nitrogen or (b) phosphoric acid.
† Official figures.

Source: mainly UN, *Industrial Commodity Statistics Yearbook*.

Woven woollen fabrics (million sq metres): 2.8 in 1996; 3.2 in 1997; 2.5 in 1998 (Source: UN, *Industrial Commodity Statistics Yearbook*).

Ethyl alcohol ('000 hectolitres): 2 in 1997; 1 in 1998; 1 in 1999 (Source: UN, *Industrial Commodity Statistics Yearbook*).

2003 ('000 metric tons, unless otherwise indicated, estimates): Wheat flour 503; Nitrogenous fertilizers 96; Gas-diesel (distillate fuel) oil 1,750; Cement 239; Electric energy (million kWh) 10,800 (Source: Asian Development Bank, *Key Indicators of Developing Asian and Pacific Countries*).

Finance

CURRENCY AND EXCHANGE RATES

Monetary Units
  100 tenge = 1 Turkmen manat.

Sterling, Dollar and Euro Equivalents (30 April 2008)
  £1 sterling = 10,227.4 manats;
  US $1 = 5,200.0 manats;
  €1 = 8,080.8 manats;
  10,000 Turkmenistani manats = £0.98 = $1.92 = €1.24.

Note: The Turkmenistani manat was introduced on 1 November 1993, replacing the Russian (formerly Soviet) rouble at a rate of 1 manat = 500 roubles. Following the introduction of the Turkmenistani manat, a multiple exchange rate system was established. The foregoing information refers to the official rate of exchange. This rate was maintained at US $1 = 4,165 manats between May 1997 and April 1998. It was adjusted to $1 = 5,200 manats in April 1998. In addition to the official rate, there was a commercial bank rate of exchange until this market was closed in December 1998. There is also a 'parallel' market rate, which averaged $1 = 6,493 manats in 1998 and reached $1 = 14,200 manats at mid-1999.

BUDGET
('000 million manats)

Revenue*	1997	1998	1999†
State budget	2,067.3	1,867.5	2,382.3
Personal income tax . . .	108.3	157.4	224.9
Profit tax	579.6	412.0	422.0
Value-added tax	797.9	714.9	946.3
Natural resources tax . . .	231.2	43.1	201.1
Excise tax	92.4	221.3	377.8
Other receipts*	257.9	318.8	210.1
Pension and Social Security Fund	471.0	711.0	832.5
Medical Insurance Fund . . .	32.7	8.2	0.0
Repayments on rescheduled gas debt	246.6	474.1	478.3
Total	**2,817.6**	**3,060.8**	**3,693.1**

Expenditure	1997	1998	1999‡
National economy	843.9	461.1	623.3
Agriculture	632.5	331.4	223.2
Transport and communications	121.1	63.4	190.0
Other	90.3	66.3	210.1
Socio-cultural services† . . .	975.7	1,850.0	1,907.9
Education	435.3	919.2	1,048.7
Health	443.1	493.8	550.6
Communal services . . .	9.1	337.9	188.6
Culture, recreation and other purposes	88.2	99.1	120.0
Defence§	440.2	435.8	582.0
Pension and Social Security Fund	387.8	511.5	605.9
Interest payments	72.1	11.1	18.0
Public administration and other purposes	94.3	153.4	157.2
Total	**2,814.0**	**3,422.8**	**3,894.3**

* Including grants received and road fund revenues.
† Approved budget.
‡ Excluding expenditure of the Pension and Social Security Fund.
§ Variable coverage, owing to changes in classification.

1997 ('000 million manats, revised figures): Revenue 2,761.5; Expenditure 2,781.8 (Source: Asian Development Bank).

1998 ('000 million manats, revised figures): Revenue 3,077.5; Expenditure 3,440.3 (Source: Asian Development Bank).

1999 ('000 million manats, revised figures): Revenue 3,895.4; Expenditure 3,890.3 (Source: Asian Development Bank).

2000 ('000 million manats): Revenue 6,034.1 (Tax revenue 5,909.0); Expenditure 6,121.0 (Current expenditure 5,831.0, Capital expenditure 290.0) (Source: Asian Development Bank).

2001 ('000 million manats): Revenue 7,824.0 (Tax revenue 7,783.0); Expenditure 7,605.0 (Current expenditure 7,223.0, Capital expenditure 382.0) (Source: Asian Development Bank).

2002 ('000 million manats): Revenue 8,243.1 (Current revenue 8,243.1, incl. Tax revenue 7,827.0); Expenditure 8,166.0 (Current expenditure 7,684.0, Capital expenditure 482.0) (Source: Asian Development Bank).

2003 ('000 million manats): Revenue 10,716.0 (Current revenue 10,716.0, incl. Tax revenue 10,222.0); Expenditure 11,497.0 (Current expenditure 10,811.0, Capital expenditure 686.0) (Source: Asian Development Bank).

2004 ('000 million manats): Revenue 14,262.4 (Current revenue 14,262.0, incl. Tax revenue 13,454.0); Expenditure 13,188.0 (Current expenditure 13,188.0, Capital expenditure 754.0) (Source: Asian Development Bank).

2005 ('000 million manats): Revenue 18,285.0 (Current revenue 18,285.0, incl. Tax revenue 17,629.0); Expenditure 17,565.0 (Current expenditure 16,703, Capital expenditure 862) (Source: Asian Development Bank).

2006 ('000 million manats): Revenue 22,474 (Current revenue 22,474, incl. Tax revenue 21,085); Expenditure 16,631 (Current expenditure 15,665, Capital expenditure 966) (Source: Asian Development Bank).

INTERNATIONAL RESERVES
(US $ million at 31 December)

	2003	2004	2005
Total	2,673.0	2,714.0	3,600.0

Source: Asian Development Bank, *Key Indicators of Developing Asian and Pacific Countries.*

MONEY SUPPLY
('000 million manats at 31 December)

	1996	1997	1998
Currency in circulation . . .	270.2	407.7	1,040.2
Demand deposits at banks . .	130.0	423.4	259.8

Total money ('000 million manats at 31 December): 2,552 in 1999; 4,965 in 2000; 5,792 in 2001; 5,877 in 2002; 8,280 in 2003; 9,393 in 2004; 11,948 in 2005; 14,063 in 2006; 18,602 in 2007 (Source: Asian Development Bank).

COST OF LIVING
(Consumer Price Index; base: 2000 = 100)

	2005	2006	2007
All items	150.3	166.1	181.0

* Preliminary.

Source: Asian Development Bank.

NATIONAL ACCOUNTS
('000 million manats at current prices)

Expenditure on the Gross Domestic Product

	2004	2005	2006
Final consumption expenditure .	47,899.4	46,450.9	67,003.3
Households			
Non-profit institutions serving households	39,605.2	36,103.7	54,385.4
General government . . .	8,294.2	10,347.2	12,617.9
Gross capital formation . . .	15,061.0	17,904.7	23,707.3
Total domestic expenditure .	62,960.4	64,355.6	90,710.6
Exports of goods and services .	40,241.8	50,856.9	62,772.4
Less Imports of goods and services	38,857.8	37,365.8	54,462.0
GDP in market prices . .	64,344.4	77,846.7	99,020.9

Gross Domestic Product by Economic Activity

	2004	2005	2006
Agriculture	12,086.4	15,267.3	18,984.0
Mining and quarrying . . .			
Manufacturing	22,148.3	26,857.9	34,238.6
Electricity, gas and water . .			
Construction	2,593.5	3,667.2	4,230.6
Trade	2,850.3	3,263.0	4,214.1
Transport and communications . .	4,220.7	5,040.7	6,450.1
Finance			
Public administration . . .	16,798.2	19,506.9	25,325.8
Other activities			
GDP at factor cost	60,697.4	73,603.0	93,443.2
Indirect taxes, less subsidies . .	3,647.1	4,243.7	5,577.6
GDP in purchasers' values . .	64,344.4	77,846.7	99,020.9

Source: Asian Development Bank.

BALANCE OF PAYMENTS
(US $ million)

	1996	1997	1998
Exports of goods f.o.b.	1,692.0	774.0	614.1
Imports of goods f.o.b.	−1,388.3	−1,005.0	−1,137.1
Trade balance	303.7	−230.9	−523.0
Services (net)	−323.4	−402.5	−471.0
Balance on goods and services	−19.7	−633.5	−994.0
Other income (net)	16.7	84.8	32.6
Balance on goods, services and income	−3.0	−548.7	−961.4
Current transfers (net) . . .	4.8	−31.2	26.9
Current account	1.8	−579.9	−934.5
Direct investment	108.1	102.4	64.1
Trade credit (net)	60.8	−266.5	56.5
Other (net)	−211.6	1,035.9	749.7
Net errors and omissions . . .	46.4	−71.4	33.9
Overall balance	5.4	220.6	−30.3

Current balance (US $ million): 84 in 2004; 616 in 2005; 1,295 in 2006 (Source: Asian Development Bank, *Key Indicators of Developing Asian and Pacific Countries*).

External Trade

PRINCIPAL COMMODITIES
(US $ million)

Imports c.i.f.	2001	2002	2003
Food and live animals	129.4	114.3	130.3
Beverages and tobacco . . .	56.8	70.1	67.4
Mineral fuels, lubricants, etc. .	39.1	25.7	17.7
Chemicals	178.6	210.8	271.2
Basic manufactures	448.7	394.2	487.7
Machinery and transport equipment	1,204.7	857.6	1,125.6
Miscellaneous manufactured articles	128.1	112.7	165.2
Total (incl. others)	2,348.8	2,119.4	2,450.0*

Exports f.o.b.	2001	2002	2003
Food and live animals	4.7	3.4	2.9
Beverages and tobacco . . .	—	0.6	0.3
Mineral fuels, lubricants, etc. .	123.7	83.8	152.4
Chemicals	7.0	28.4	55.0
Basic manufactures	141.6	150.6	169.6
Machinery and transport equipment	14.5	17.1	16.9
Miscellaneous manufactured articles	52.8	74.1	80.8
Total (incl. others)	2,620.2	2,855.6	3,320.0*

* Estimate.

2004 (US $ million): Total imports 3,148.4; Total exports 3,853.9.

2005 (US $ million): Total imports 2,947.0; Total exports 4,944.1.

2006 (US $ million): Total imports 2,557.7; Total exports 7,155.5.

2007 (US $ million): Total imports 3,716.8; Total exports 8,932.9.

Source: Asian Development Bank.

PRINCIPAL TRADING PARTNERS
(US $ million)

Imports	2005	2006	2007
Azerbaijan	300.9	10.5	12.5
China, People's Repub. . . .	99.5	178.7	344.0
France	97.0	95.5	55.9
Germany	146.3	215.4	238.2
Iran	167.8	211.0	240.2
Russia	246.5	251.7	285.4
Turkey	198.7	309.5	372.9
Ukraine	205.9	254.4	303.7
United Arab Emirates . . .	343.3	431.5	491.3
USA	260.9	124.1	203.2
Total (incl. others)	2,703.3	2,781.2	3,427.9

Exports	2005	2006	2007
Afghanistan	110.7	136.8	163.3
Armenia	103.2	127.6	152.2
Azerbaijan	220.9	335.5	400.4
Hungary	103.2	127.6	152.2
Iran	841.1	1,038.3	1,351.7
Italy	201.1	221.0	197.4
Turkey	145.9	172.9	360.8
Ukraine	2,434.6	3,009.0	3,591.5
United Arab Emirates . . .	157.7	194.6	253.3
USA	132.5	73.6	213.0
Total (incl. others)	5,698.7	6,343.5	7,646.8

Note: Data reflect the IMF's direction of trade methodology, and, as a result, the totals may not be equal to those presented for trade in commodities.

Source: Asian Development Bank.

Transport

RAILWAYS
(traffic)

	1996	1997	1999*
Passenger journeys (million) . .	7.8	6.4	3.1
Passenger-km (million) . .	2,104	958	701
Freight transported (million metric tons)	15.9	18.5	17.2
Freight ton-km (million) . . .	6,779	7,445	7,337

* Data for 1998 were not available.

Source: *Railway Directory*.

SHIPPING

Merchant Fleet
(registered at 31 December)

	2005	2006	2007
Number of vessels	45	53	53
Total displacement ('000 grt) . .	48.5	53.4	51.9

Source: Lloyd's Register-Fairplay, *World Fleet Statistics*.

CIVIL AVIATION
(estimated traffic on scheduled services)

	2001	2002	2003
Kilometres flown (million) . .	22	22	22
Passengers carried ('000) . . .	1,407	1,407	1,412
Passenger-kilometres (million) .	1,608	1,608	1,538
Total ton-kilometres (million) .	156	156	150

Source: UN, *Statistical Yearbook*.

Tourism

FOREIGN VISITOR ARRIVALS*

Country of nationality	2003	2004	2005
France	298	636	683
Germany	466	1,191	1,028
Iran	5,623	9,341	7,173
Japan	269	770	428
Netherlands	84	324	453
Russia	115	318	13
USA	181	343	332
Total (incl. others)	8,214	14,799	11,611

* Arrivals of non-resident tourists at national borders.

Tourism receipts (US $ million): 66 in 1996; 74 in 1997; 192 in 1998.

Source: World Tourism Organization.

Communications Media

	2004	2005	2006
Telephones ('000 main lines in use)	376.1	398.1	398.1
Mobile cellular telephones ('000 subscribers)	50.1	105.0	105.0
Internet users ('000)	36	48	65

Television receivers ('000 in use): 880 in 2001.

Book production (including pamphlets): 450 titles (5,493,000 copies) in 1994.

Radio receivers ('000 in use): 1,225 in 1997.

Personal computers ('000 in use): 2 in 1999.

Sources: International Telecommunication Union; UNESCO, *Statistical Yearbook*.

Education

1990/91: 76,000 students at higher schools (Source: UNESCO, *Statistical Yearbook*).

Institutions (2005): Secondary schools 1,704; Secondary specialized schools 15; Higher schools (incl. universities) 16 (Source: Permanent Mission of Turkmenistan to the United Nations).

Students enrolled at universities (2003): 14,859 (Source: UNICEF).

Adult literacy rate (UNESCO estimates): 99.5% (males 99.7%; females 99.3%) in 2007 (Source: UNESCO Institute for Statistics).

Directory

The Constitution

A new Constitution was adopted on 18 May 1992, and significantly revised on 26 September 2008. The Constitution was organized into eight sections (detailing: fundamentals of the constitutional system; fundamental human and civil rights, freedoms and duties; the system of state governmental bodies; local self-government; the electoral system and provisions for referendums; judicial authority; the Office of the Prosecutor-General; and final provisions), and included the following among its main provisions:

The President of the Republic is directly elected by universal adult suffrage for a five-year term. A President may hold office for a maximum of two terms. The President is not only Head of State, but also Chairman of the Government (Prime Minister in the Council of Ministers) and Supreme Commander-in-Chief of the National Armed Forces. The President must ratify all parliamentary legislation and in certain circumstances may legislate by decree. The President appoints the Council of Ministers. Supreme legislative power resides with the Majlis, a unicameral parliament that is directly elected for a five-year term. Sovereignty, however, is vested in the people of Turkmenistan.

The Constitution, which defines Turkmenistan as a democratic state, also guarantees the independence of the judiciary and the basic human rights of the individual. The age of majority is 18 years (parliamentary deputies must be aged at least 21). Minority ethnic groups are granted equality under the law, although Turkmen is the only official language. A central tenet of Turkmenistan's foreign policy is that of 'permanent neutrality'.

Constitutional amendments approved on 26 September 2008 abolished the 2,057-member Khalk Maslakhaty (People's Council), dividing its powers between the President and the Majlis. (In August 2003 constitutional amendments had elevated the Khalk Maslakhaty to the status of 'permanently functioning supreme representative body of popular authority', and effectively displaced the Majlis as the country's leading legislative body.) The amendments restored responsibility for the appointment of local officials (which had been devolved to regional authorities in 2005) to the President, who was also to be responsible for appointing the country's electoral commission. The Majlis, which was to be expanded from 65 to 125 members after legislative elections due to take place in December 2008, was to have the authority to amend the Constitution, and to bring a vote of censure against the President.

The Government

HEAD OF STATE

President of the Republic: GURBANGULY BERDYMUHAMEDOV (elected 11 February 2007; inaugurated 14 February 2007).

COUNCIL OF MINISTERS
(September 2008)

Chairman of the Government: GURBANGULY BERDYMUHAMEDOV.

Deputy Chairman, responsible for Construction: DERIYAGELDI ORAZOV.

Deputy Chairman, responsible for Petroleum and Natural Gas: TACHBERDY TAGIYEV.

Deputy Chairman, responsible for Transport and Communications: NAZARGULY SHAGULYYEV.

Deputy Chairman, responsible for Economic Affairs: KHOJAMYRAT GELDYMYRADOV.

Deputy Chairman and Minister of Foreign Affairs: RASHID MEREDOV.

Deputy Chairman, responsible for Education, Science, Health, Culture, Sport, the Mass Media and Social Organizations: HYDYR SAPARLIYEV.

Deputy Chairman, responsible for the Textile Industry, Trade and the Chamber of Commerce and Industry: HOJAMUHAMMET MUHAMMEDOV.

Deputy Chairmen: MAISA YAZMUHAMMEDOV, MYRATGELDY AKMAMMEDOV.

Minister of National Security: CHARYMYRAT AMANOV.

Minister of Defence: Maj.-Gen. AGAGELDY MAMATGELDIYEV.

Minister of Justice: MURAD KARRYEV.

Minister of Internal Affairs: ORAZGELDY AMANMYRADOV.

Minister of Finance: ANNAMUHAMMET GOCHIYEV.

Minister of Social Security: GURBANGELDY KAKALIYEV.

Minister of Construction: SHAMUHAMMET DURDYLYYEV.

Minister of Culture, Television and Radio: GULMYRAT MEREDOV.

Minister of Energy and Industry: GURBANNUR ANNAVELIYEV.

Minister of Railways: ORAZBERDY HUDAIBERDIEV.

Minister of Communications: RESULBERDY KHOZHAGURBANOV.

Minister of Road Transport and Highways: GURBANMYRAT HANGULIYEV.

Minister of the Petroleum Industry and Mineral Resources: (vacant).

Minister of Trade and Foreign Economic Relations: NOKERGULY ATAGULYEV.

Minister of the Textile Industry: HOJAMYRAT METEKOV.

Minister of Health and the Medical Industry: ATA SERDAROV.

Minister of Education: MUHAMMETGELDY ANNAAMANOV.

Minister of Water Resources: ANNAGELDI YAZMYRADOV.

Minister of Agriculture: ESENMYRAT ORAZGELDIYEV.

Minister of the Economy and Development: BYASHIMMYRAT HOJAMAMMEDOV.

Minister of Environmental Protection: MAGTYMGULY AKMURADOV.

Note: The Chairmen of the three state concerns Türkmennebit (Turkmenneft—Turkmen Oil), Türkmengaz (Turkmengaz—Turkmen Gas) and Türkmenhaky (Turkmenkover—Turkmen Carpets) have the status of State Ministers.

MINISTRIES

Office of the President and the Council of Ministers: 744000 Aşgabat, Presidential Palace; tel. (12) 35-45-34; fax (12) 35-51-12; internet www.turkmenistan.gov.tm.

Ministry of Agriculture: 744000 Aşgabat, ul. Azad 63; tel. (12) 35-66-91; fax (12) 35-01-18; e-mail minselhoz@online.tm.

Ministry of Communications: 744000 Aşgabat, ul. Gurungan 40; tel. (12) 35-21-52; fax (12) 35-05-95; e-mail mincom@telecom.tm.

Ministry of Construction: 744000 Aşgabat, ul. 2049; tel. (12) 51-23-59.

Ministry of Culture, Television and Radio: 744000 Aşgabat, ul. Pushkin 14; tel. (12) 35-30-61; fax (12) 35-35-60.

Ministry of Defence: 744000 Aşgabat, ul. Galkynyş 4; tel. (12) 35-22-59.

Ministry of the Economy and Development: Aşgabat.

Ministry of Education: 744000 Aşgabat, ul. Gurungan 2; tel. (12) 35-58-03; fax (12) 39-88-11.

Ministry of Energy and Industry: 744000 Aşgabat, ul. 2008 6; tel. (12) 35-38-70; fax (12) 39-06-82.

Ministry of Environmental Protection: 744000 Aşgabat, ul. 2035 102; tel. (12) 35-43-17; fax (12) 51-16-13; e-mail ministr@nature-tm.org.

Ministry of Finance: 744000 Aşgabat, ul. 2008 4; tel. (12) 51-05-63; fax (12) 51-18-23.

Ministry of Foreign Affairs: 744000 Aşgabat, pr. Magtymguly 83; tel. (12) 26-62-11; fax (12) 35-42-41; e-mail mfatm@online.tm.

Ministry of Health and the Medical Industry: 744000 Aşgabat, pr. Magtymguly 90; tel. (12) 35-60-47; fax (12) 35-50-32.

Ministry of Internal Affairs: 744000 Aşgabat, pr. Magtymguly 85; tel. (12) 35-59-23.

Ministry of Justice: 744000 Aşgabat, ul. 2022 86; tel. (12) 38-04-11.

Ministry of National Security: 744000 Aşgabat, pr. Magtymguly 91; fax (12) 51-07-55.

Ministry of the Petroleum Industry and Mineral Resources: 744000 Aşgabat, ul. Gurungan 28; tel. (12) 39-38-27; fax (12) 39-38-21; e-mail ministryoilgas@online.tm.

Ministry of Railways: 744000 Aşgabat, ul. S. Türkmenbaşi 9.

Ministry of Road Transport and Highways: 744000 Aşgabat, ul. 1916 141; tel. (12) 35-02-36; fax (12) 35-18-43; e-mail tcentr@online.tm.

Ministry of Social Security: 744007 Aşgabat, ul. 2003 3; tel. (12) 25-30-03.

Ministry of the Textile Industry: 744000 Aşgabat, ul. Annadurdiyeva 52; tel. (12) 51-03-03.

Ministry of Trade and Foreign Economic Relations: 744000 Aşgabat, ul. Gurungan 1; tel. (12) 35-10-47; fax (12) 35-73-24; e-mail mtfer@online.tm.

Ministry of Water Resources: 744000 Aşgabat, ul. 2005 1; tel. (12) 39-06-15; fax (12) 39-85-39.

President

Following the death of President Gen. SAPARMYRAT NIYAZOV on 21 December 2006, the hitherto Deputy Chairman and Minister of Health and the Medical Industry, GURBANGULY BERDYMUHAMEDOV, assumed the presidency in an acting capacity, before being elected President in an election held on 11 February 2007. BERDYMUHAMEDOV was elected by 89.2% of votes cast, with a participation rate of some 98.6% of registered voters, according to official results; he was inaugurated on 14 February.

Legislature

Majlis
(Assembly)

744000 Aşgabat, ul. Bitarap Türkmenistan 17; tel. (12) 35-31-25; fax (12) 35-31-47.

Chairman: AKJA NURBERDIYEVA.

The 65-member Majlis is directly elected for a term of five years. Elections to the Majlis were held on 19 December 2004, officially with the participation of 76.88% of the registered electorate. A second round of voting took place in seven districts on 9 January 2005, where candidates had failed to obtain an absolute majority of votes. All contestants were believed to be members of the ruling party, the Democratic Party of Turkmenistan.

Local Government

Turkmenistan is divided into five velayats (oblasts or regions) for administrative purposes. A lower tier of local government further subdivides the country into 50 etraps (raions or districts). The President appoints the heads of the local administrations—hakims (governors) in the velayats and, at the next level, the şakher hakims and etrap hakims in the cities and districts, respectively. (Although the capital city, Aşgabat, forms part of Ahal Velayat, the hakim of the city enjoys similar privileges to the hakims of the velayats.) Each village or town has an elected soviet or council of elders (gengeşes) with five-year terms, presided over by an archin, who is chosen by the council from among its own number. Local government elections took place in April 1998 and April 2003. A constitutional amendment approved in October 2005 provided for regional, district and city councils to be directly elected. Elections to 40-member district and city councils were conducted in December 2006, and were followed by elections to 80-member regional councils on 9 December 2007. The right to appoint regional, district and city hakims was to be transferred from the President to the respective councils.

CAPITAL CITY

Aşgabat City Administration: 744000 Aşgabat; Hakim AZAT BILISHOV.

VELAYATS

Ahal Velayat Administration: 744000 Ahal Velayat, pos. Anau; tel. (12) 41-93-53; Hakim MAMMETNIYAZ NURMAMMEDOV.

Balkan Velayat Administration: 745100 Balkan Velayat, Balkanabat, Kvartal 149, kor. 6; tel. (12) 39-16-54; Hakim ORAZMYRAT NYAZLY.

Daşoguz Velayat Administration: 746300 Daşoguz, ul. Abadanchylyk 9/10; tel. (22) 5-31-95; Hakim SAPARMURAT ASHYROV.

Lebap Velayat Administration: 746000 Lebap Velayat, Türkmenabat, pr. S. Niyazov 46; tel. (22) 2-36-25; Hakim CHARYARGULY ODEBERDIYEV.

Mari Velayat Administration: 745400 Mari, ul. Moilanepes 41; tel. (22) 6-06-01; Hakim KAKAGELDY GURBANOV.

Election Commission

Central Commission for Elections and Referendums: Aşgabat; comprises a chairman, two vice-chairmen, a secretary and 12 mems, all appointed by the President of the Republic; Chair. MURAT KARIYEV; Sec. JEREN TAIMOVA.

Political Organizations

Democratic Party of Turkmenistan: 744014 Aşgabat, ul. Gurungan 28; tel. (12) 25-12-12; name changed from Communist Party of

Turkmenistan in 1991; Chair. GURBANGULY BERDYMUHAMEDOV; Sec. ONJIK MUSAYEV.

Unity (Agzybirlik): 744000 Aşgabat; e-mail agzybirlik@hotmail.com; internet hem.lidnet.se/~agzybirlik/; f. 1989; popular front organization; denied official registration except from Oct. 1991 to Jan. 1992; Leader NURBERDY NURMAMEDOV.

Turkmenistan is effectively a one-party state, with the Democratic Party of Turkmenistan (led by the President of the Republic) dominant in all areas of government. The President of the Republic is also the leader of the **National Revival Movement of Turkmenistan (Galknyş)**. There are, however, several unregistered opposition groups, such as **Unity (Agzybirlik)**. A **Social Democratic Party** was reportedly established in Aşgabat in August 1996, upon the merger of several small unofficial groups.

Other opposition elements are based in other republics of the Commonwealth of Independent States, in particular Russia. A leading opposition figure in exile is a former Minister of Foreign Affairs, ABDY KULIYEV, whose **United Democratic Opposition of Turkmenistan (ODOT)** is based in Moscow, Russia, while the **Movement for Democratic Reform**, founded in 1996, is based in Sweden. The **Fatherland (Watan)** movement is also based in Sweden (e-mail info@watan.ru; internet watan.ru) and comprises Turkmen and other Central Asian oppositionists. In January 2002 a former Minister of Foreign Affairs, BORIS SHIKHMURADOV, established the opposition **People's Democratic Movement of Turkmenistan** (PDMT; internet gundogar.org); however, he was imprisoned in December, having been convicted of orchestrating the attempted assassination of President Saparmyrat Nizayov in November. Another opposition leader accused of conspiring with Shikhmuradov was NURMUKHAMMED KHANAMOV, founder of the **Republican Party of Turkmenistan** (RPT; internet tmrepublican.org; Co-Chair. NURMUKHAMMET HANAMOV, SAPAR YKLYMOV).

Opposition leaders met in Prague, Czech Republic, in September 2003 and announced the formation of the **Union of Democratic Forces of Turkmenistan (UDFT)**, comprising four main groups: the RPT; Fatherland; the ODOT; and the **Revival Social Political Movement**.

Diplomatic Representation

EMBASSIES IN TURKMENISTAN

Afghanistan: 744000 Aşgabat, Gerogly 14; tel. (12) 39-58-21; fax (12) 39-58-20; Ambassador ABDUL KARIM KHADAM.

Armenia: 744000 Aşgabat, Gerogly 14; tel. (12) 35-44-18; fax (12) 39-55-38; e-mail eat@online.tm; Ambassador VLADIMIR BADALIAN.

Azerbaijan: 744000 Aşgabat, ul. 2062, Bldg 44; tel. (12) 36-46-08; fax (12) 36-46-10; e-mail azsefir_ashg@online.tm; internet www.azembassyashg.com; Ambassador ELKHAN BAKHADUR OĞLU GUSEYINOV.

Belarus: 744000 Aşgabat, ul. Esgerler 35; tel. (12) 36-46-88; fax (12) 36-46-91; e-mail turkmenistan@belembassy.org; Ambassador YURIY H. MALUMOV.

China, People's Republic: 744036 Aşgabat, Berzengi raion, ul. Archabil, Hotel 'Kuwwat'; tel. (12) 48-81-31; fax (12) 48-18-13; e-mail chemb@online.tm; Ambassador U. HUNBIN.

France: 744000 Aşgabat, ul. Esgerler 35; tel. (12) 36-35-50; fax (12) 36-36-40; e-mail cad.achgabat-amba@diplomatie.gouv.fr; Ambassador CHRISTIAN LECHERVY.

Georgia: 744000 Aşgabat, ul. Azadi 139A; tel. (12) 34-48-38; fax (12) 34-32-48; e-mail georgia@online.tm; internet www.turkmenistan.mfa.gov.ge; Ambassador ALEKSI PETRIASHVILI.

Germany: 744000 Aşgabat, ul. Hydyr Derzhazhev, Hotel 'Ak Altin'; tel. (12) 36-35-15; fax (12) 36-35-22; e-mail grembtkm@online.tm; Ambassador RAYNOR MOREL.

Holy See: 744000 Aşgabat, Merkezi Poçta, POB 98; tel. (12) 39-11-40; fax (12) 35-36-83; e-mail aszomi@online.tm; internet www.catholic-turkmenistan.org; Apostolic Nuncio ANTONIO LUCIBELLO (Titular Archbishop of Thurio) (resident in Ankara, Turkey).

India: 744000 Aşgabat, ul. Yu. Emre 2/1, Imperial International Business Centre; tel. (12) 45-81-52; fax (12) 45-61-56; e-mail indembhoc@online.tm; Ambassador Prof. RAM PAL KAUSHIK.

Iran: 744000 Aşgabat, ul. 2072 3; tel. (12) 35-02-37; fax (12) 35-05-65; e-mail isroiref@online.tm; Ambassador MOHAMMAD REZA FORQANI.

Israel: Aşgabat; Ambassador EHUD GOL.

Kazakhstan: 744036 Aşgabat, ul. Garaşizlik 11/13; tel. (12) 48-04-68; fax (12) 48-04-76; e-mail embkaz@online.tm; Ambassador ASKHAT OAZBAY.

Korea, Democratic People's Republic: Aşgabat; Ambassador KIM YON CHJE.

Korea, Republic: Aşgabat; Ambassador KIM CHONG YUL.

Kyrgyzstan: 744000 Aşgabat, ul. Gerogly 85; tel. and fax (12) 35-55-06; e-mail kg@online.tm; internet kyrgtm.by.ru; Ambassador BOR-UBEK ASHIROV.

Libya: 744000 Aşgabat, ul. Azad 17A; tel. (12) 35-49-17; fax (12) 39-35-26; Chargé d'affaires a.i. RAGAB BEN KHAMADI.

Pakistan: 744000 Aşgabat, ul. Garaşizlik 4/1; tel. (12) 48-21-28; fax (12) 48-21-30; e-mail parepashgabat@online.tm; Ambassador SAID AKBAR AFRIDI.

Poland: 744005 Aşgabat, ul. Azadi 17A; tel. (12) 27-40-35; fax (12) 27-31-22; e-mail ambasada.aszchabad@gmail.com; internet www.aszchabad.polemb.net; Ambassador MACIEJ LANG.

Romania: 744000 Aşgabat, ul. Kusayeva 107; tel. (12) 34-76-55; fax (12) 34-76-20; e-mail ambromas@online.tm; Chargé d'affaires a.i. CIOCAN LAURENŢIU.

Russia: 744005 Aşgabat, pr. S. Türkmenbaşi 11; tel. (12) 35-39-57; fax (12) 39-84-66; e-mail emb-rus@online.tm; internet www.mid.turkmenistan.ru; Ambassador IGOR A. BLATOV.

Saudi Arabia: 744000 Aşgabat, ul. Yu. Emre 2/1, Imperial International Business Centre; tel. (12) 45-49-63; fax (12) 45-49-70; e-mail tmemb@mofa.gov.sa; Ambassador ABD AL-AZIZ IBRAHIM AL-GHADEER.

Switzerland: 744000 Aşgabat; Ambassador ALAN GIDETTI.

Tajikistan: 744000 Aşgabat, ul. Gurungan 19; tel. (12) 35-56-96; fax (12) 39-31-74; e-mail tadjemb_tm@mail.ru; Ambassador KOZIDAVLAT KOIMDODOV.

Thailand: 744000 Aşgabat; Ambassador KANYA CHAIMAN.

Turkey: 744007 Aşgabat, ul. Gerogly 9; tel. (12) 35-41-18; fax (12) 39-19-14; e-mail askabat.be@mfa.gov.tr; Ambassador HAKKI AKIL.

Ukraine: 744001 Aşgabat, ul. Azadi 49; tel. (12) 39-13-73; fax (12) 39-10-28; e-mail emb_tm@mfa.gov.ua; internet www.mfa.gov.ua/turkmenistan; Ambassador VIKTOR A. MAYKO.

United Arab Emirates: 744000 Aşgabat, Khalifa Centre, pr. S. Türkmenbaşi 124; tel. (12) 45-69-15; fax (12) 45-69-16; Ambassador HASSAN ABDULLAH AL-ADHAB.

United Kingdom: 744001 Aşgabat, Four Points Ak Altin Hotel, 3rd Floor, Office Bldg; tel. (12) 36-34-62; fax (12) 36-34-65; e-mail beasb@online.tm; internet www.britishembassy.gov.uk/turkmenistan; Ambassador PETER BUTCHER.

USA: 744000 Aşgabat, ul. Pushkin 9; tel. (12) 35-00-45; fax (12) 39-26-14; e-mail irc-ashgabat@iatp.edu.tm; internet turkmenistan.usembassy.gov; Chargé d'affaires a.i. SYLVIA REED CURRAN.

Uzbekistan: 744006 Aşgabat, ul. Gerogly 50A; tel. (12) 33-10-55; fax (12) 34-23-37; Ambassador ALISHER K. KODIROV.

Judicial System

Chairman of the Supreme Court: YARANMURAT YAZMYRADOV.

Prosecutor-General: CHARY HOJAMYRADOV, 744000 Aşgabat, ul. Seidi; fax (12) 35-44-82.

Religion

The majority of the population are adherents of Islam. In June 1991 the Supreme Soviet of the Turkmen SSR adopted a Law on Freedom of Conscience and Religious Organizations. In April 1994 a council (gengeş) for religious affairs was established, within the office of the President; it was chaired by the qazi (supreme Islamic judge) of Turkmenistan, with the head of the Orthodox Church in Turkmenistan serving as Deputy Chairman. In November 2003 new legislation, replacing that of 1991, was approved, restricting the activities of religious groups, although registration requirements for religious communities were made more flexible by a presidential decree, issued in early 2004. Further legislation, approved in March of that year, reduced the membership threshold required for a group to register from 500 to five. Prior to these amendments, only Sunni Muslim and Russian Orthodox Christian groups had been permitted to register. By mid-2004 groups of Seventh-day Adventist and Baptist Christians, Hare Krishnas and Baha'is had also registered.

ISLAM

Turkmen are traditionally Sunni Muslims, but with elements of Sufism. Islam was severely persecuted by the Soviet regime from the late 1920s. Until July 1989 Aşgabat was the only Central Asian capital without a functioning mosque. The Muslims of Turkmenistan are officially under the jurisdiction of the Muslim Board of Central Asia, based in Tashkent, Uzbekistan, but, in practice, the Government permits little external influence in religious affairs. The Board is represented in Turkmenistan by a qazi, who is responsible for appointing Muslim clerics in all rural areas.

Qazi of Turkmenistan: ROVSHEN ALLABERDIYEV.

CHRISTIANITY

The Russian Orthodox Church (Moscow Patriarchate)

The Church in Turkmenistan comes under the jurisdiction of the Eparchy of Tashkent and Central Asia, headed by the Metropolitan of Tashkent and Central Asia, VLADIMIR (IKIM), based in Uzbekistan.

Roman Catholic Church

The Church is represented in Turkmenistan by a Mission, established in September 1997. There were an estimated 80 adherents at 31 December 2007.

Superior: Fr ANDRZEJ MADEJ, 744000 Aşgabat, ul. Gerogly 20A, POB 98; tel. (12) 39-11-40; fax (12) 35-36-83; e-mail amadej@oblaci.pl.

The Press

At 2008 23 newspapers and 17 periodicals were published in Turkmenistan. All publications listed below are in Turkmen, except where otherwise stated.

PRINCIPAL NEWSPAPERS

Adalat (Justice): 744005 Aşgabat, ul. 2033 1/4; tel. (12) 39-79-04; weekly; Editor-in-Chief DOVLET H. GURBANGELDIYEV; circ. 42,575.

Aşgabat/Ashkhabad: 744004 Aşgabat, ul. Galkynyş 20; tel. (12) 22-33-04; f. 1960; 3 a week; journal of the Union of Writers of Turkmenistan; popular; in Turkmen and Russian; Editor-in-Chief SAPARMYRAT GARAKHANOV; Deputy Editor-in-Chief ORAZ AKGAYEV; circ. 6,832.

Beyik Türkmenbaşiyn Nesli (Generation of Türkmenbaşi the Great): 744064 Aşgabat, ul. Galkynyş 20; tel. (12) 39-17-64; f. 1922; 3 a week; for young people; Editor ANNAGUL NARLIEVA; circ. 21,591.

Dogry ÿol (True Path): 744000 Aşgabat; internet www.dogryyol.com; in Russian; news of Turkmenistan and Central Asia; online only; pro-opposition.

Edebiyat we sungat (Literature and Art): 744004 Aşgabat, ul. Galkynyş 20; tel. (12) 35-30-34; f. 1958; weekly; Editor ANNAMYRAT POLADOV; circ. 19,111.

Esger (Soldier): 744004 Aşgabat, ul. 2038 29; tel. (12) 35-68-09; f. 1993; weekly; organ of the Council of Ministers; military newspaper; Editor-in-Chief AGAMYRAT GELDYEV; circ. 40,200.

Galkynyş (Revival): 744604 Aşgabat, ul. Galkynyş 20; tel. (12) 22-34-23; weekly; Editor-in-Chief KHUDAIBERDI DIVANGULIYEV; circ. 44,586.

Habarlar: 744004 Aşgabat, ul. Galkynyş 20; tel. (12) 46-84-70; weekly; in Russian and Turkmen; television and radio; business; advertisements; Editor-in-Chief R. BALABAN; circ. 3,596.

Mugallymlar gazeti (Teachers' Newspaper): 744004 Aşgabat, ul. G. Kuliyev 20; tel. (12) 35-09-66; f. 1952; 3 a week; organ of the Ministry of Education; Editor REJEPNUR GURBANNAZAROV; circ. 75,226.

Neitralnyi Turkmenistan (Neutral Turkmenistan): 744004 Aşgabat, ul. Galkynyş 20; tel. and fax (12) 39-42-76; e-mail nt@online.tm; internet www.tmpress.gov.tm; f. 1924; 6 a week; organ of the Majlis and the Council of Ministers; in Russian; Editor-in-Chief BEKDURDY AMANSARIYEV; circ. 30,091.

Novosti Turkmenistana (Turkmenistan News): 744000 Aşgabat, ul. Bitarap Turkmenistan 24A; tel. (12) 39-12-21; fax (12) 51-02-34; f. 1994; weekly; in Russian, English and Turkmen; publ. by Dowlet Khabarlar Gullugy news agency; circ. 500.

Syyasy sokhbetdeş (Political Symposium): 744604 Aşgabat, ul. Galkynyş 20; tel. (12) 25-10-84; f. 1992; weekly; organ of the Democratic Party of Turkmenistan; Editor AKBIBI YUSUPOVA; circ. 14,500.

Turkmenistan: Zolotoi Vek (Turkmenistan: The Golden Age): 744000 Aşgabat; internet www.turkmenistan.gov.tm; online only; in Russian; publ. by Democratic Union of Journalists of Turkmenistan.

Türkmening yupekyoli (Turkmen Railwayman): 744007 Aşgabat, ul. Chary Nurymov 3; tel. (12) 35-06-52; f. 1936; weekly; organ of the Turkmenistan State Railways; covers transport and communications; Editor BAYRAM SAHEDOV; circ. 7,000.

Türkmenistan: 744004 Aşgabat, ul. Galkynyş 20; tel. (12) 39-14-55; f. 1920; 6 a week; organ of the Council of Ministers and the Majlis; Editor-in-Chief JEREN TAIMOVA; circ. 25,591.

Watan (Fatherland): 744604 Aşgabat, ul. Galkynyş 20; tel. (12) 22-34-56; f. 1925; 3 a week; Editor-in-Chief AMANMUHAMMET REPOW; circ. 25,419.

PRINCIPAL PERIODICALS

Monthly, unless otherwise indicated.

Diller duniesi (World of Languages): 744014 Aşgabat, ul. O. Kuliyeva 22; tel. (12) 29-15-41; f. 1972; 6 a year; publ. by the Ministry of Education; in Russian and Turkmen.

Diyar: 744604 Aşgabat, ul. Galkynyş 20; tel. (12) 35-53-97; f. 1992; foreign policy and international relations; publ. by the President of the Republic and the Council of Ministers; Editor-in-Chief ASHIR-BERDY GURBANOV; circ. 12,881.

Finansovye vesti (Financial News): 744004 Aşgabat, ul. Galkynyş 20; tel. (12) 29-42-76; f. 1994; in Russian, English and Turkmen; publ. by the Ministry of Finance.

Garagum (Kara-Kum): 744005 Aşgabat, ul. Galkynyş 20; tel. (12) 35-11-15; f. 1928; literary; Editor SAPAR ORAYEV; circ. 2,546.

Guneş (The Sun): 744000 Aşgabat, ul. Galkynyş 20; tel. (12) 22-33-05; for children; Editor-in-Chief SHADURDY CHARYGYLLYEV; circ. 44,696.

Gurbansoltan Eje: 744604 Aşgabat, ul. Galkynyş 20; tel. (12) 22-33-09; f. 1931; fmrly *Ovadan* (Beautiful); for women; Editor AKBIBI YUSUBOVA; circ. 56,626.

Izvestiya Akademii Nauk Turkmenistana (Academy of Sciences of Turkmenistan News): 744000 Aşgabat, ul. Azad 59; f. 1946; 6 a year; in Russian and Turkmen.

Politicheskii sobesednik (Political Colloquium): 744604 Aşgabat, ul. Galkynyş 20; tel. (12) 25-10-84; f. 1937; in Russian; publ. by the Democratic Party of Turkmenistan; circ. 2,300.

Saglyk (Health): 744000 Aşgabat, ul. Kerbabayeva 39/57; tel. (12) 39-16-21; f. 1990; 6 a year; publ. by the Ministry of Health and the Medical Industry; Editor-in-Chief BAYRAMAMMED TACHMAMEDOV; circ. 35,071.

Türkmen dili khem edebiyati (Turkmen Language and Literature): 744000 Aşgabat; tel. (12) 41-88-03; f. 1991; 6 a year; publ. by the Ministry of Education.

Türkmen dunyasi: 744004 Aşgabat, ul. Azad 20; tel. (12) 47-81-18; organ of the Humanitarian Association of World Turkmen; Editor-in-Chief ANNABERDY AGABAYEV; circ. 11,956.

Türkmen medeniyeti (Turkmen Culture): 744007 Aşgabat, ul. O. Kuliyeva 21; tel. (12) 25-37-22; f. 1993; 2 a year; publ. by the Ministry of Culture, Television and Radio; Editor GELDYMYRAT NURMUKHAM-MEDOV.

Türkmen sporty/Sport Turkmenistana (Turkmen Sport): 744004 Aşgabat, ul. Galkynyş 20; tel. (12) 22-33-72; weekly; in Turkmen and Russian; Editor-in-Chief VIKTOR MIHAYLOV; circ. 2,500.

Türkmenistanyn Lukmancykygy: 744004 Aşgabat, ul. A. Gulmammedov 4A; tel. (12) 35-25-40; every two months; healthcare policy; Editor-in-Chief O. SERDAROV.

Türkmenistanyn oba khozhalygy (Agriculture of Turkmenistan): 744000 Aşgabat, ul. Azad 63; tel. (12) 35-19-38; f. 1929; Editor BYASHIM TALLYKOV; circ. 3,500.

Türkmenistanyng Mejlisining Maglumatlary (Bulletin of the Majlis of Turkmenistan): 744000 Aşgabat, ul. Garaşizlik 110; tel. (12) 35-50-39; fax (12) 35-31-47; e-mail mejlis@online.tm; f. 1960; 4 a year; in Russian and Turkmen.

Vozrozhdeniye (Rebirth): 744604 Aşgabat, ul. Galkynyş 20; tel. (12) 35-10-84; in Russian; political; Editor-in-Chief H. DIVANGULYEV; circ. 1,500.

NEWS AGENCY

Türkmen Dowlet Khabarlar Gullugy (Turkmen State News Service): 744000 Aşgabat, ul. Bitarap Turkmenistan 24A; tel. (12) 39-12-21; fax (12) 51-02-34; e-mail tpress@online.tm; f. 1967; Dir JEREN TAIMOVA.

Publishers

Magaryf Publishing House: 744000 Aşgabat; Dir N. ATAYEV.

Turkmenistan State Publishing Service: 744000 Aşgabat, ul. Galkynyş 20; tel. (12) 46-90-13; f. 1965; politics, science and fiction; Chair. ANNANUR CHARYYAROV.

Ylym Publishing House: 744000 Aşgabat, ul. Azad 59; tel. (12) 29-04-84; f. 1952; desert development, science; Dir N. I. FAIZULAYEVA.

Broadcasting and Communications

TELECOMMUNICATIONS

MTS Turkmenistan: Aşgabat, ul. 2038 56; tel. (12) 42-52-05; internet www.mts.tm; provides over 85% of mobile cellular telecommunications services in Turkmenistan; majority owned by Mobile TeleSystems (Russia); wireless internet services introduced in 2008; Pres. LEONID MELAMED.

Türkmentelekom: 744000 Aşgabat, ul. Asudalyk 36; tel. (12) 51-12-77; fax (12) 51-02-40; e-mail admin@telecom.tm; internet www .telecom.tm; f. 1993; Dir-Gen. ANNALY CH. BERDINOBATOV.

BROADCASTING

Turkmen State Information Agency (Türkmen Dovlet Habarlary): 744004 Aşgabat, ul. Gurungan; tel. (12) 39-12-21; fax (12) 51-02-34; e-mail tpress@online.tm; Head JEREN TAIMOVA.

Radio

Turkmen National Radio Co: 744000 Aşgabat, ul. Navoi 5; tel. (12) 39-25-20; Chair. MURAD ORAZOV.

Char Tarapdan (From All Sides): tel. (12) 39-86-72; Dir BERDI-MYRAT ABDYYEV.

Miras (Heritage): tel. (12) 35-68-50; Dir GURBANDURDY REJEPOV.

Watan (Fatherland): tel. (12) 51-12-96; Dir NURBERDI DADEBAYEV.

Television

Turkmen National Television Co: 744000 Aşgabat, ul. Navoi 5; tel. (12) 39-25-20; Chair. MURAD ORAZOV.

Altyn Asyr (Golden Age): tel. (12) 39-85-06; Dir SHADURDY ALOVOV (acting).

Miras (Heritage): tel. (12) 35-20-43; Dir BYAGUL CH. NURMURA-DOVA.

Türkmenistan: tel. (12) 35-00-86; Dir MURAD A. ORAZOV.

Yaşlyk (Youth): tel. (12) 35-00-86; Dir (vacant).

Finance

(cap. = capital; res = reserves; dep. = deposits; m. = million; brs = branches; amounts in Turkmen manats)

BANKING

In late 2002 there were 12 commercial banks operating in Turkmenistan. The state retains substantial interests and involvement in banking.

Central Bank

Central Bank of Turkmenistan: 744000 Aşgabat, ul. Bitarap Türkmenistan; tel. (12) 38-10-27; fax (12) 51-08-12; e-mail merkez3@online.tm; f. 1991; central monetary authority, issuing bank and supervisory authority; Chair. GUVANCH B. GEOKLENOV; 5 brs.

Other Banks

Daihanbank: 744000 Aşgabat, ul. 2067 60; tel. and fax (12) 41-98-68; e-mail daybank@online.tm; f. 1989 as independent bank, Agroprombank, reorganized 1999; specializes in agricultural sector; Chair. of Bd TUMAR MAMMEDOV; 70 brs.

Garagum International Joint-Stock Bank: 744000 Aşgabat, ul. O. Kuliyeva 3; tel. (12) 35-22-01; fax (12) 35-38-54; f. 1993 as International Bank for Reconstruction, Development and Support of Entrepreneurship, name changed 2000; Chair. BEKMAMED SOL-TANMEMEDOV.

Garaşyslyk Bank: 744000 Aşgabat, ul. Gerogly 30A; tel. (12) 35-48-75; fax (12) 39-01-24; e-mail garash@cbtm.net; f. 1999 following merger of Gas Bank and Aşgabat Bank; cap. US $5m. (Oct. 2003); Chair. (vacant); 5 brs.

Kreditbank: 744000 Aşgabat, pr. Magtymguly; tel. (12) 35-02-22; fax (12) 35-03-09; e-mail kreditbank@online.tm; f. 1995; fmrly Rossiiskii Kredit; Chair. BATYR BAYRIYEV.

President Bank: 744000 Aşgabat, ul. Gurungan 22; tel. (12) 35-79-43; fax (12) 51-08-12; e-mail presidentbank@cbtm.net; f. 2000; cap. US $60m.; Exec. Dir (vacant).

Savings Bank of Turkmenistan (Sberbank): 744000 Aşgabat, pr. Magtymguly 86; tel. (12) 35-46-71; fax (12) 35-40-04; f. 1923, reorganized 1989; wholly state-owned; Chair. BEGENCH BAYMUKHA-MEDOV; 120 brs.

Senagatbank: 744013 Aşgabat, pr. S. Türkmenbaşi 42; tel. (12) 45-31-33; fax (12) 45-44-09; e-mail senagat@online.tm; f. 1989; cap. 31,200m., res 1,394m., dep. 32,547m. (Feb. 2005); Chair. EYEBERDI ATAYEV; 5 brs.

Turkmen Turkish Commercial Bank: 744000 Aşgabat, pr. Magtumguly 111/2, POB 15; tel. (12) 51-14-07; fax (12) 51-11-23; e-mail ttcb@online.tm; f. 1993, with 50% Turkish ownership; cap. 26,000.0m., res 2,220.8m., dep. 34,463.5m. (Dec. 2005); Chair. BATIR SAHATOV.

Türkmenbank—State Commercial Bank 'Türkmenistan': 744000 Aşgabat, ul. Gurungan 10A; tel. (12) 51-07-21; fax (12) 39-

67-35; e-mail turkmenbank@ctbm.net; f. 1992; Chair. ATAMYRAT ATALYKOV.

Türkmenbaşi Bank: 744000 Aşgabat, ul. Annadurdiyeva 54; tel. (12) 51-24-50; fax (12) 51-11-11; e-mail mail@investbank.org; f. 1992 as Investbank, renamed in 2000; Chair. AMANMURAT PAJAYEV; 23 brs.

Türkmenvnesheconombank—State Bank for Foreign Economic Affairs of Turkmenistan: 744000 Aşgabat, ul. Garaşizlik 32; tel. (12) 40-60-40; fax (12) 40-65-63; e-mail tveb@online.tm; f. 1992 as independent bank, from Soviet Vneshekonombank; wholly state-owned; cap. 344,064m., dep. 4,599,973m., total assets 5,059,082m. (Dec. 2006); Chair. RAHIMBERDI JEPBAROV (acting); 5 brs.

COMMODITY EXCHANGE

State Commodity and Raw Materials Exchange of Turkmenistan: 744000 Aşgabat, pr. Magtymguly 111; tel. (12) 35-43-21; fax (12) 51-03-04; e-mail info@exchange.gov.tm; internet www.exchange .gov.tm; f. 1994; Chair. YAGMYRGELDY MYRATLYEV.

Trade and Industry

GOVERNMENT AGENCIES

National Institute of State Statistics and Information on Turkmenistan (Türkmenmillihasabat): 744000 Aşgabat, ul. 2033 72; tel. (12) 39-42-65; fax (12) 35-43-79; e-mail staff@natstat.gov.tm; f. 1997; Dir KAKAMYRAT MOMMADOV.

State Agency for Foreign Investment (SAFI): 744000 Aşgabat, ul. Azad 53; tel. and fax (12) 35-04-16; e-mail saffi@online.tm; f. 1996; monitors and regulates all foreign investment in Turkmenistan; registers foreign cos in Turkmenistan; Dir (vacant).

DEVELOPMENT ORGANIZATION

Small and Medium Enterprise Development Agency (SMEDA): 744000 Aşgabat, ul. 2015 8; tel. (12) 34-42-59; fax (12) 34-51-49; e-mail smeda@cat.glasnet.ru; jt venture between Turkmen Govt and the European Union (EU); Dir SERDAR BABAYEV.

CHAMBER OF COMMERCE

Chamber of Commerce and Industry of Turkmenistan: 744000 Aşgabat, ul. 2037 17; tel. (12) 35-64-03; fax (12) 35-13-52; e-mail mission@online.tm; f. 1959; Chair. ARSLAN F. NEPESOV.

INDUSTRIAL AND TRADE ASSOCIATION

Union of Manufacturers and Entrepreneurs: Aşgabat, ul. Ostrovskogo 26; tel. (12) 34-66-69; Chair. ALEXANDER DADEYEV.

UTILITIES

Electricity

Kuvvat Turkmen State Energy Technology Corpn: 744000 Aşgabat, ul. 2008 6; tel. (12) 35-68-04; fax (12) 39-06-82; e-mail kuvvat@online.tm; state electrical power generation co and agency; Chair. YUSUP DAVYDOV.

STATE HYDROCARBONS COMPANIES

Türkmenbaşi Oil Refinery: 745000 Balkan Velayat, Türkmenbaşi, POB 5; tel. (00222) 7-45-45; fax (00222) 7-45-44; production and refining of petroleum; sales of petroleum and liquefied natural gas; Dir (vacant).

Türkmengaz: 744036 Aşgabat, ul. 1939 56; tel. (12) 40-32-00; fax (12) 40-32-54; e-mail annam@online.tm; f. 1996; govt agency responsible for natural gas operations, incl. development of system of extraction, processing of gas and gas concentrate and gas transportation and sale; Chair. BAYMYRAT HOJAMUHAMMEDOV.

Türkmengeologiya: 744000 Aşgabat, ul. 2023 7/32; tel. (12) 35-13-46; fax (12) 35-50-15; govt agency responsible for natural gas and petroleum exploration; Chair. SAPARGELDI JUMAYEV.

Türkmenneft: 745100 Balkan Velayat, Balkanabat, pr. Magtymguly 49; tel. (00243) 2-19-45; govt agency responsible for petroleum operations and production; Chair. KARYAGDY TASHLIYEV; Gen. Dir KHAKIM IMAMOV.

Türkmenneftegazstroi: 744036 Aşgabat, ul. Arçabil 56; tel. (12) 40-35-01; fax (12) 40-35-01; e-mail tngg@online.tm; govt agency for construction projects in the hydrocarbons sector; Chair. GURBANBERDY ORAZMURADOV.

MAJOR COMPANIES

China National Petroleum Co (CNPC) International Turkmenistan: Aşgabat; tel. (12) 39-44-29; fax (12) 48-87-16; e-mail cnpcoffice_tm@cnpc.com.cn; internet www.cnpc.com.cn; involved in

the construction of the Turkmenistan–People's Republic of China gas pipeline project; Gen. Dir LIU GUMSYUN.

Energokhimmaşexport: 744000 Aşgabat, ul. 2008 4; tel. and fax (12) 39-58-36; e-mail ecme@online.tm; f. 1995; main trading dealer for Kuvvat, Türkmenkhimsenagat and Türkmenmaşingurlyşik; exports products from the above companies and imports food, consumer goods and raw materials; 55 employees.

Kaakhka Cotton Ginning Plant: 745340 Aşgabat, pos. Kaakhka, Poltoratskogo; tel. (12) 2-13-45; produces cotton and cotton fabrics; Gen. Dir M. ESENOV; 900 employees.

Türkmenhaly (Turkmen Carpets): 744000 Aşgabat, pr. 2033 95; tel. (12) 35-39-44; fax (12) 35-43-11; e-mail turkmenhali@online.tm; internet www.turkmenhali.gov.tm; state joint-stock co; produces and distributes hand-made, pure wool carpets; Chair. MINEVER BELLIYEV.

Türkmenintorg Foreign Trade Organization: 744000 Aşgabat, ul. 2035 92; tel. (12) 29-75-87; fax (12) 29-87-74; f. 1989; develops foreign trade in Turkmenistan by provision of consultancy services for foreign cos; currency transactions; marketing, tourism and organization of exhibitions; exports fibre, cotton seeds, fertilizers and carpets; Gen. Dir SAYED G. BEGIYEV; 60 employees.

Türkmenkhimsenagat: Balkan; state-owned chemical production co; supervises the Karabogazsulphate, Balkanabat Iodine Production Plant and Cheleken Chemical Plant enterprises.

Türkmenmaşingurlyşik: state machine-building production co.

Türkmenmebel (Turkmen Furniture Production Society): 744021 Aşgabat, ul. 2015; tel. and fax (12) 33-00-31; state-owned.

Türkmenpagta: 744000 Aşgabat, ul. Andalib 102; tel. (12) 32-46-01; state-owned cotton corpn; Head AMANMUKHAMMET MUKHADOV.

Türkmenprod (Turkmen Food Co): 744000 Aşgabat; f. 1994; state-owned; Dir NEDIRMAMMET ALOVOV.

Wool Primary Processing Factory: 745400 Mari; wool-processing.

TRADE UNIONS

Federation of Trade Unions of Turkmenistan: 744000 Aşgabat, pr. S. Türkmenbaşi 13; tel. (12) 35-62-08; fax (12) 35-21-30; Chair. ENEBAY G. ATAYEVA.

Committee of Trade Unions of Ahal Velayat: 744000 Ahal Velayat, pos. Anau, Gyaver etrap; tel. 41-39-19; Dir A. TAGANOV.

Committee of Trade Unions of Daşoguz Velayat: 746311 Daşoguz Velayat, Niyazovsk, S. Türkmenbaşi shayoly 8; Dir SH. IGAMOV.

Transport

RAILWAYS

The main rail line in the country runs from Türkmenbaşi (formerly Krasnovodsk), on the Caspian Sea, in the west, via Aşgabat and Mari, to Türkmenabat (formerly Charjew) in the east. From Türkmenabat one line runs further east, to the other Central Asian countries of the former USSR, while another runs north-west, via Uzbekistan and Kazakhstan, to join the Russian rail network. In 2007 the total length of rail track in use in Turkmenistan was 2,523 km. A 203-km rail link from Türkmenabat to Atamarut was opened in 1999. In 1996 a rail link was established with Iran (on the route Tejen–Serakhs–Mashhad), thus providing the possibility of rail travel and transportation between Turkmenistan and İstanbul, Turkey, as well as giving access to the Persian (Arabian) Gulf. A 540-km railway line, running south–north across the country from Aşgabat to Daşoguz, via Garagum, was completed in early 2006.

Turkmenistan State Railways (Türkmendemorjollari): 744007 Aşgabat, pr. S. Türkmenbaşi 7; tel. (12) 35-55-45; fax (12) 51-06-32; f. 1992; Pres. B. P. REDJEPOV.

ROADS

In 1999 there was an estimated total of 24,000 km of roads, of which some 19,500 km were hard-surfaced. In early 2008 construction was under way on a principal road of 1,200 km, which was to link Türkmenbaşi with the eastern town of Farap.

SHIPPING

Shipping services link Türkmenbaşi (formerly Krasnovodsk) with Baku (Bakı, Azerbaijan), Makhachkala (Dagestan, Russia) and the major Iranian ports on the Caspian Sea. The Amu Dar'ya river is an important inland waterway. From 2000 Türkmenbaşi port was undergoing an extensive process of modernization.

Shipowning Companies

Neftec: 745100 Balkan Velayat, Türkmenbaşi; tel. (2) 765-81; fax (2) 766-89.

Turkmen Maritime Steamship Co: 745100 Balkan Velayat, Türkmenbaşi, ul. Shagadama 8; tel. (2) 767-34.

Turkmen Shipping Co: 745100 Balkan Velayat, Türkmenbaşi, ul. Shagadama 8; tel. (2) 972-67; fax (2) 767-85.

Türkmenderyayollary: 746000 Lebap Velayat, Türkmenabat, ul. Gyamichiler 8; tel. (2) 223-12; fax (2) 23-46-88; f. 1992 as Turkmen River Shipping Co; renamed as above in 1998.

Türkmennefteflot: 745100 Balkan Velayat, Türkmenbaşi, POB 6; tel. (2) 762-62.

CIVIL AVIATION

Turkmenistan's international airport is at Aşgabat. In December 2007 it was announced that the National Civil Aviation Authority of Turkmenistan (Türkmenhovayollary) was to sign an agreement with the Turkish company Polimeks on the construction of an airport in Türkmenbaşi, at a cost of €125m.

National Civil Aviation Authority of Turkmenistan (Türkmenhovayollary): 744000 Aşgabat, ul. 2007 3A; tel. (12) 35-10-52; fax (12) 35-44-02; e-mail aviahead@online.tm; f. 1992; Dir-Gen. MERDAN AYAZOV.

Turkmenistan Airlines: 744000 Aşgabat, ul. Magtymguly 80; tel. (12) 35-10-52; fax (12) 35-44-02; f. 1992; domestic and international scheduled and charter passenger flights, incl. services to Europe, Central and South-East Asia, and the Middle East; three divisions: Ahal Air Co, Khazar Air Co and Lebap Air Co; Head GURBANYAZ TIRKISHOV.

Tourism

Although the tourism sector in Turkmenistan remains relatively undeveloped, owing, in part, to the vast expanse of the Kara-Kum desert (some 80% of the country's total area), the Government has made efforts to improve the standard of visitor accommodation (there are a number of new luxury hotels in Aşgabat) and to improve the capacity and efficiency of the capital's international airport. The scenic Kopet Dagh mountains, the Caspian Sea coast, the archaeological sites and mountain caves of Kugitang, and the hot subterranean mineral lake at Kov-Ata are among the country's natural attractions, while the ancient cities of Mari and Nisa—former capitals of the Seljuk and Parthian empires, respectively—are of considerable historical interest. In addition, Kunya-Urgench is an important site of Muslim pilgrimage. In 2005, according to the World Tourism Organization, there were 11,611 visitors from abroad; receipts from tourism totalled US $192m. in 1998.

State Committee for Tourism and Sport: 744000 Aşgabat, ul. Pushkin 17; tel. (12) 35-47-77; fax (12) 39-67-40; e-mail turkmentan@online.tm; internet www.tourism-sport.gov.tm; founded on the basis of the State Tourist Corpn Turkmensyyakhat; f. 2000; Chair. BYASHIM KERIMOV.

Culture

The Turkmen were, by tradition, a nomadic people. Their language was standardized into a national tongue in the Soviet period, based on the dialects of the Tekke and Yomud tribes. The traditional Arabic script was replaced by a Latin one in 1927 and a Cyrillic one in 1938, but, more importantly, under Soviet rule widespread literacy was achieved. This preserved the literary tradition of the Turkmen and, potentially, made it available to the mass of the population, despite the destruction of their traditional nomadic culture and normal means of transmission. National works were, however, subject to prohibitions by the Soviet authorities, and it was only with independence that, for example, the religious poems of the 18th century Sufi, Magtymguly, or the national epic of the Oguz Turkmen, *The Book of Gorkut Ata*, could properly be rehabilitated. Traditional Islamic culture also enjoyed cautious official encouragement in the 1990s, notably with the construction of many new mosques, in particular the memorial mosque at Gök Tepe, which commemorated the great battle of the Turkmen resistance in 1881. In 1993 the Turkmen Government announced that the country would return to a Latin-based script; from 1996 all schools were required to teach the new script. The first volume of the *Ruhnama* (Book of the Soul), a quasi-spiritual text apparently written by President Niyazov, was published in 2001, and the second volume in 2004. Proof of knowledge of the *Ruhnama* is reportedly a requirement for entry to various professions, and all mosques are required by law to keep a copy of the book. In February 2005 President Niyazov ordered the closure of the majority of the country's libraries.

NATIONAL ORGANIZATIONS

Ministry of Culture, Television and Radio: see The Government (Ministries).

Directorate for the Protection of Historical and Cultural Monuments and for National Exploration and Restoration: 744000 Aşgabat.

Institute of Culture: 744000 Aşgabat, ul. 2033 4; tel. (12) 47-39-44; Dir GURBANDURDY GURBANOV.

CULTURAL HERITAGE

National Library of Turkmenistan: 744000 Aşgabat, pl. 2001; tel. (12) 25-32-54; f. 1895; 5.5m. vols; Dir S. A. KURBANOV.

National Museum of Turkmenistan: 744000 Aşgabat, Novofiryuzinskoe 30; tel. (12) 51-90-20; fax (12) 51-90-22; e-mail vip@online.tm; f. 1998 by merger of the National Museum of History and Ethnography, the State Museum of History and the Turkmen State Museum of Fine Art; eight exhibition halls; Dir OVEZMUHAMMED MAMETNUROV.

Turkmenistan National Commission for UNESCO: 744000 Aşgabat, ul. Gurungan; tel. and fax (12) 35-53-67; e-mail poladov@tm.synapse.tm; Sec.-Gen. Dr K. POLADOV.

SPORTING ORGANIZATIONS

Athletics Federation of Turkmenistan: 744000 Aşgabat, POB 201; tel. (12) 36-23-86; e-mail amateur@online.tm; f. 1992; Pres. DURDY B. DURDYYEV; Gen. Sec. KURBAN M. KAJAROV.

National Institute of Tourism and Sport: 744001 Aşgabat, ul. 2038 15A; tel. (12) 36-25-40; fax (12) 36-24-56; f. 1981; activities include the provision of training in 15 types of sport, catering and tourism; Rector AŞIR MOMMADOV.

National Olympic Committee of Turkmenistan: 744000 Aşgabat, ul. Belinskii 32; tel. (12) 36-13-09; fax (12) 51-04-84; e-mail noctkm@online.tm; f. 1990; Chair. President of the Republic.

School of Higher Sporting Achievement of Turkmenistan: 744000 Aşgabat, ul. Industrialnaya 2A; tel. (12) 32-24-21; f. 1966; training for the Olympic games in eight sports; Dir TEIMUR A. FARZIYEV.

State Committee for Tourism and Sport: see section on Tourism.

PERFORMING ARTS

In April 2001 President Niyazov ordered a ban on performances of both opera and ballet, claiming these arts to be 'alien' to Turkmen culture. The ban was lifted in January 2008 by the Government of Niyazov's successor, President Gurbanguly Berdymuhamedov.

A. Arslan National Theatre for a Young Audience: 744000 Aşgabat, pr. 2033 115; tel. (12) 35-49-74; Dir ORAZGELDY A. AYDOGDIYEV.

Jan State Drama Theatre: 744000 Aşgabat; tel. (12) 35-10-76.

Magtymguly National Music and Drama Theatre: 744000 Aşgabat; Dir. HYMAMMET TSANGULYYEW.

Mollanepes Turkmen State Academic Drama Theatre: 744000 Aşgabat, ul. 2035 79; tel. (12) 35-69-58; Dir MAMMETVELIYEV TACHMAMMET.

Pushkin State Russian Drama Theatre: 744000 Aşgabat; Dir YUSUP BEKIYEV.

Turkmen National Conservatoire: 744000 Aşgabat, ul. Pushkin 22; tel. (12) 35-52-19.

Education

In September 2005 it was reported that all former Russian-language schools had adopted Turkmen as the main language of instruction, although one class with instruction in Russian was to be maintained in each school. In 2004 there was also one Turkish university and 14 Turkish schools. In 1990 the total enrolment at higher schools was equivalent to 21.8% of the relevant age-group. In 1995 34.4% of 15–18-year-olds were enrolled in general secondary education; in 1997 7.9% of those aged between 15 and 18 years were enrolled in technical and vocational schools. In 1997 21.0% of children aged between three and six years were enrolled in kindergartens. In that year 83.1% of children aged between seven and 15 years were enrolled in basic education. The 1999 budget allocated 26.9% of total expenditure (1,048,700m. manats) to education. Former President Saparmyrat Niyazov's quasi-spiritual code, the *Ruhnama* (Book of the Soul), formed a compulsory part of school curriculums.

From the second half of the 1990s reform of the education system left many children without access to free education; free education at Turkmenistan's 16 universities was reportedly abolished from 2003. Only those who had completed two years' relevant work experience after leaving school were permitted to enrol at institutes of higher education. In 2004 a presidential decree invalidating all higher-education degrees received abroad came into effect; all teachers with such degrees were to be dismissed. Between 2002 and 2005 more than 12,000 teachers were removed from their posts. In March 2007 the new President, Gurbanguly Berdymuhamedov, increased the period of compulsory primary and secondary education from nine to 10 years and extended the period of higher education from two to five years (effective from the beginning of the 2007/08 school year). Students were no longer required to complete two years of practical work experience before applying to universities, and foreign degrees were given recognition. In February 2007 it was also announced that internet access was to be introduced to all Turkmenistani schools. In June President Berdymuhamedov announced that the Turkmenistan Academy of Sciences, which had been closed in 1993, was to reopen. Some 13,800 students were enrolled at the country's 18 institutions of higher education in 2007/08. Passing an examination on knowledge of the *Ruhnama* remained a compulsory requirement for entry to higher-education institutions in Turkmenistan.

UNIVERSITY

Magtymguly Turkmen State University: 744005 Aşgabat, pr. S. Türkmenbaşi 31; tel. and fax (12) 35-11-59; e-mail math3@online.tm; internet www.tacistm.org/tempus/tgu.htm; f. 1931 as Aşgabat Pedagogical Institute, reorganized in 1950 as A. M. Gorkii State University; 11 faculties; 544 teachers; 11,000 students; languages of instruction: Turkmen and Russian; Rector Prof. KALAYEV RED-JEPMURAD CHARYEVICH.

Social Welfare

A basic, state-funded health system was introduced under Soviet rule, but the system was of low quality, and underfunded. In 2006 there were 2.5 physicians and 4.3 hospital beds for every 1,000 people (compared with 7.4 hospital beds for every 1,000 people in 1997). The high levels of disease in Turkmenistan (among adults, as well as children) were attributed to poor overall medical and sanitary conditions, and the critical state of the environment. In 2006 the average life expectancy at birth was 59.6 years for males and 66.7 years for females. In that year the rate of infant mortality was 51 per 1,000 live births.

In 1991 and the early years of independence the Government of Turkmenistan introduced extensive social protection measures (mostly the responsibility of a Pension Fund), which were relatively more generous than in other former Soviet states. New legislation on pensions and state allowances came into force in 1998. In 1999 some 397,000 people received pensions or allowances from the Pension and Social Security Fund (of these, 284,000 received an old-age pension of 98,000 manats per month). The basic retirement age is 62 years for men and 57 years for women. The minimum pension is equivalent to 40% of the minimum wage. The Pension and Social Security Fund also distributed allowances to low-income families and to families with children, as well as allocating death, disability and veterans benefits.

From the early 1990s electricity, gas and water were made free for all citizens, although in 1996 some charges were introduced for domestic electricity users. Consumer products such as flour, bread, rice, cotton oil and sugar were provided at highly subsidized prices, while salt was available free of charge. The 1999 budget allocated an estimated 14.1% of total spending (550,600m. Turkmen manats) to the health services and 15.6% of spending (605,900m. manats) to the Pension and Social Security Fund (and the Geological Fund). In March 2004 some 15,000 health workers were dismissed and fees were introduced for specialist services that had hitherto been free of charge. In May 2005 hospitals outside the capital were closed, after President Saparmyrat Niyazov declared them to be unnecessary, particularly given the shortage of doctors. Patients were instead required to visit diagnostic centres, requiring payment, while those in need of hospitalization or specialist care had to travel to Aşgabat. Also in May 2005 the Government declined to join a regional AIDS Control Project launched by UNAIDS. In early 2006 President Niyazov cancelled retirement pensions to approximately one-third of the country's pensioners and reduced social security allowances. In 2007 the new President, Gurbanguly Berdymuhamedov, reinstated retirement pensions, and announced the reopening of rural hospitals. In September 2008 Berdymuhamedov signed a decree authorizing increases of 10% to pensions, wages and state allowances in 2009.

Ministry of Health and the Medical Industry: see The Government (Ministries).

Ministry of Social Security: see The Government (Ministries).

HEALTH AND WELFARE ORGANIZATIONS

Central Sports Club of the Disabled of Turkmenistan: 744020 Aşgabat, ul. 2078 49; tel. (12) 34-05-38; fax (12)340538; e-mail fsc@ ashgabat.cpart.org; f. 1992; rehabilitation of the disabled; Chair. CHARY OVEZOV.

Children's Fund of Turkmenistan: 744000 Aşgabat, ul. 2014 9/2; tel. (12) 39-61-79; fax (12) 39-25-04; Chair. MATGELDYEV ATAMURAT.

Red Crescent Society of Turkmenistan: 744000 Aşgabat, ul. 2022 48A; tel. (12) 35-17-50; fax (12) 39-55-12; e-mail nrcst@online .tm; Pres. ZUKHRA ELLIEVA.

The Environment

Turkmenistan has experienced severe ecological problems as a result of the desiccation of the lower reaches of the Amu Dar'ya, the main source of water for Turkmenistan, and of the Aral Sea, which had lost 66% of its original surface area by 1990. From the dehydrated seabed of the Aral Sea large amounts of salted dust and sand are blown on to fertile areas in northern Turkmenistan, and eastern Turkmenistan suffers from high deposition rates of pesticide-contaminated dust. Excessive use of chemical pesticides and herbicides in cotton-growing areas has also caused severe problems. The chemicals enter the soil and the water supply and, since only 13% of the population was provided with piped water at the end of the 1980s, most water for domestic use was drawn directly from polluted water channels. In January 1994 Turkmenistan and the four other Central Asian countries agreed to take co-ordinated action against a further deterioration of the Aral Sea ecology and to attempt to reverse some of the damage. Thus, Turkmenistan and Uzbekistan agreed to guarantee a certain minimum level of water reaching the Aral Sea (conditions permitting). On the Caspian Sea, the problem was completely different: in the 1990s there was an increase in the level of the Sea, which caused severe flooding on the Caspian littoral. The Caspian Sea also suffered from 'run-off' phosphate pollution. In 2002 work began on a 2,092 sq km artificial reservoir, Lake Turkmen (Turkmen Koli), in the middle of the Kara-Kum desert; the reservoir, the completion of which was scheduled for 2020, was considered likely to exacerbate environmental problems and further deplete waters from the Amu Dar'ya, from which it was to feed.

GOVERNMENT ORGANIZATIONS

Ministry of Environmental Protection: see The Government (Ministries).

Ministry of Water Resources: see The Government (Ministries).

ACADEMIC INSTITUTES

Academy of Sciences of Turkmenistan: 744000 Aşgabat, ul. Bitarap Türkmenistan 15; tel. (12) 25-44-74; fax (12) 25-53-67; Pres. AGA M. KHODJAMAMEDOV; institutes incl.:

> **Commission on Nature Conservation:** 744000 Aşgabat, Gogolya 15; attached to the Presidium of the Academy of Sciences; Chair. A. O. TASHILIYEV.

> **Institute of Deserts, Flora and Fauna:** 744000 Aşgabat, ul. Bitarap Türkmenistan 15; tel. (12) 39-54-27; fax (12) 35-37-16; e-mail desert@online.tm; f. 1962; programmes incl. research into desert resources and arid environment problems; incl. International Centre for Research and Training in the Problems of Desertification; publ. journal *Problems of Desert Development* (4 a year); Dir Dr PALTAMET ESENOV.

> **Scientific Consultative Ecological Centre (EKOTSENTR):** 744000 Aşgabat, ul. Gurungan 15.

NON-GOVERNMENTAL ORGANIZATIONS

Catena Ecology Club: 744000 Aşgabat, pr. S. Türkmenbaşi 27; tel. (12) 39-85-95; e-mail timchik@nature-tm.org; f. 1994; Chair. ANDREI ARANBAYEV.

Daşoguz Ecological Guardians: 746301 Daşoguz, Mikroraion Ts-1, 8/23; tel. and fax (12) 566-83-51; e-mail azato@rol.ru; f. 1992 as Daşoguz Ecology Club; liquidated by court order 2003; refounded as non-registered environmental org.; education, public ecological monitoring and control, recycling and protection of biodiversity; Co-Chair. EVGENIYA ZATOKA, ANDREI ZATOKA.

Ecology Fund of Turkmenistan: 744000 Aşgabat, ul. Gurungan 15; tel. (12) 29-42-33; Dir A. BABAYEV.

Turkmenistan Society for the Conservation of Nature: 744000 Aşgabat, ul. 2084 62; tel. (12) 29-77-27; Dir A. K. RUSTAMOV.

Defence

The National Armed Forces of Turkmenistan began to be formed in mid-1992, based on former Soviet forces that had been based in the territory of the republic. By agreement with Russia, these forces were initially under joint Turkmen and Russian command. As assessed at November 2007, the estimated strength of the armed forces was 22,000, consisting of an army of 18,500, an air force of 3,000 and a navy (largely coastguard units) of 500. Military service is for a period of 24 months. In 1993–98 Russia and Kazakhstan co-operated with Turkmenistan in the operation of the Caspian Sea Flotilla, another former Soviet force, which was based at Astrakhan, Russia. In September 1993 the country's first military institute opened (for-merly a department of Magtymguly University), and in December of that year Turkmenistan agreed that Russian troops should be stationed on its southern borders. In May 1994 Turkmenistan became the first Central Asian republic of the former USSR to join NATO's 'Partnership for Peace' programme. Turkmenistan's policy of neutrality was recognized by the UN General Assembly in December 1995. Defence expenditure in 2006 was an estimated US $183m.

Bibliography

Abazov, R. *Historical Dictionary of Turkmenistan*. Lanham, MD, Scarecrow Press, 2005.

Amnesty International. *Turkmenistan: The Clampdown on Dissent and Religious Freedom Continues*. London, International Secretar-iat, 2005.

Anceschi, Luca. *Turkmenistan's Foreign Policy: Positive Neutrality and the Consolidation of the Turkmen Regime*. New York, Routledge, 2008.

Blackwell, C. *Tradition and Society in Turkmenistan: Gender, Oral Culture and Song*. London, RoutledgeCurzon, 2001.

Butler, W. E. (Ed. and Translator). *Turkmenistan Civil Code of Saparmurat Turkmenbashi*. The Hague, Kluwer Law International, 1999.

Edgar, A. L. *Tribal Nation: The Making of Soviet Turkmenistan*. Princeton, NJ, Princeton University Press, 2004.

Fenot, A., and Gintrac, C. *Achgabat: une capitale ostentatoire: urbanisme et autocratie au Turkmenistan*. Paris, L'Harmattan, 2006.

Gleason, G. *Turkmenistan-Russian Energy Relations*. London, Glo-bal Market Briefings, 2006.

Kerven, C. (Ed.). *Prospects for Pastoralism in Kazakhstan and Turkmenistan: From State Farms to Private Flocks*. London, Rou-tledgeCurzon, 2003.

Pastor, G., and Van Rooden, R. 'Turkmenistan—the Burden of Current Agricultural Policies' in *IMF Working Paper 00/98*, June 2000.

Rechel, B. *Human Rights and Health in Turkmenistan: Policy Brief*. London, London School of Hygiene and Tropical Medicine, 2005.

Saat, J. H. *Turkmenistan: People! Motherland! Leader?* Camberley, Conflict Studies Research Centre, 2005.

Saray, M. *The Turkmen in the Age of Imperialism: A Study of the Turkmen People and their Incorporation into the Russian Empire*. Ankara, Turkish Historical Society Printing House, 1989.

Sasakawa Peace Foundation. *Economic Reform in Turkmenistan: Issues and Challenges*. Tokyo, Sasakawa Peace Foundation, 2000.

Turkmenistan Research Group. *Executive Report on Strategies in Turkmenistan, 2000 Edition (Strategic Planning Series)*. San Diego, CA, Icon Group International, 2000.

Also see the Select Bibliography.

UKRAINE

Geography

PHYSICAL FEATURES

Ukraine is situated in Eastern Europe. It is bordered by Poland and Slovakia to the west and by Hungary, Romania and Moldova (principally the separatist region of Transnistria—Pridnestrovie) to the south-west. In the western part of the country, the northern border is with Belarus, while in eastern Ukraine the northern and eastern borders are with Russia. To the south lie the Black Sea and the Sea of Azov. Ukraine covers an area of 603,700 sq km (233,090 sq miles) and is the largest country entirely within Europe. Its territory includes the peninsula of Crimea (most of which comprises an Autonomous Republic) in the south of the country, almost entirely surrounded by the Sea of Azov, to the east, and by the Black Sea to the south, west and north-west.

The relief consists of a steppe lowland, bordered by uplands to the west and south-west, and by the Crimean mountains in the south, on the Crimean Peninsula. The main rivers are the Dnipro (Dniepr—Dnieper), which drains the central regions of the country and flows into the Black Sea, and the Dniestr (Dniester), which flows through western Ukraine and Moldova before also entering the Black Sea, near Odesa (Odessa). In the south, to the south-west of Odesa, Ukraine has a short border on the Danube (Dunay) delta.

CLIMATE

The climate is temperate, especially in the south. The north and north-west share many of the continental climatic features of Poland and Belarus, but the Black Sea coast is noted for its mild winters. Droughts are not infrequent in southern areas. Average temperatures in Kyiv range from −6.1°C (21°F) in January to 20.4°C (69°F) in July. Average annual rainfall in Kyiv is 615 mm (24 ins).

POPULATION

The total population at the census of 5 December 2001 was 48,457,102. According to official estimates, at 1 July 2008 the population was 46,221,981, giving a population density of 76.6 per sq km. Of permanent inhabitants recorded at the 2001 census, Ukrainians formed the largest ethnic group, comprising 78.1% of the total population, while 17.3% were Russians. There were also significant minorities of Belarusians and Moldovans. Ukraine's traditional Polish, Jewish and German minorities were all considerably reduced after the Second World War. The permanent resident population of Crimean Tatars was enumerated at 248,200; the vast majority of this mostly Muslim people, deported from Crimea in 1944, had returned to the peninsula (principally from Uzbekistan) after 1989. The increase in the proportion of the population that described itself as Ukrainian following independence from the USSR (from 72.7% of the total in 1989), and concomitant

decline in the proportion of the population describing itself as Russian (from 22.1% in 1989), was believed to reflect, in large part, the fluidity of identity between Ukrainian and Russian populations, particularly in eastern and southern regions of Ukraine, as well as changing political circumstances, rather than any significant migration into or out of the country. The official state language is Ukrainian, an Eastern Slavonic language written in the Cyrillic script, although Russian has official status in Crimea. Many Ukrainians and other minorities are Russian-speaking, while a dialect combining elements of Russian and Ukrainian, known as *surzhyk*, is also widely spoken. Most of the population are adherents of Christianity, with the major ecclesiastical organizations being the Ukrainian Orthodox Church (both the Kyiv Patriarchate and the Moscow Patriarchate), the Ukrainian Autocephalous Orthodox Church and the Roman Catholic Church (mostly 'Greek' Catholics or 'Uniates', who observe Byzantine Rites). There are also a number of Protestant churches and small communities of Jews and Muslims (the latter comprising principally Tatars and Crimean Tatars).

The capital is Kyiv (Kiev), which had a population of 2,611,000 in 2001. It is situated in the north of the country, on the Dnipro river. Other important towns include Kharkiv (population 1,470,000 in 2001), Dnipropetrovsk (1,065,000), the port of Odesa (1,029,000), Donetsk (1,016,000), Zaporizhzhia (815,000) and Lviv (733,000). The capital of the Autonomous Republic of Crimea is Simferopol (estimated population 344,000 in 2001), and another important town on the peninsula is the port of Sevastopol (which does not form part of the Autonomous Republic), with a population of 342,000 in 2001.

Chronology

c. 878: The Eastern Slavs founded the state of Kyivan (Kievan) Rus, with Kyiv (Kiev) as its capital.

c. 988: Kyivan Rus officially converted to Orthodox Christianity, following the baptism of its ruler, Volodymyr (Vladimir) I ('the Great').

1237–40: As a result of internecine feuds over succession, the defenceless Kyivan state was captured by invading Mongol Tatars, and Kyiv burned to the ground.

1475: Establishment of the Crimean Khanate of the Tatars.

1596: By the Union of Brest a number of Orthodox bishops, mainly in what is modern western Ukraine and Belarus, acknowledged the primacy of the Roman Catholic spiritual leader, the Pope, to form what became known as the Greek Catholic or 'Uniate' Church.

1648: Bohdan Khmelnytsky led a rebellion by Ukrainian Cossacks against their Polish overlords, which resulted in the formation of a Cossack state in eastern Ukraine, with its base near Zaporizhzhya.

1654: Eastern Ukraine came under Muscovite (Russian) rule by the terms of the Treaty of Pereyaslav.

1667: Ukraine was divided between the Polish-Lithuanian Commonwealth (which gained the western region) and the Russian Empire (which gained Ukrainian territory east of the Dnipro—Dnieper).

1709: Ivan Mazepa, Hetman (ruler) of the Ukrainian Cossack state, supported Charles XII of Sweden in his invasion of Ukraine, having previously pledged allegiance to Russia; the Russian army defeated the Swedes, and the Cossack state was incorporated into the Russian Empire.

1783: The Crimean Khanate was acquired by Russia.

1793: At the Second Partition of Poland the regions of Halychyna (Galicia) and Bukovyna (Bukovina) were acquired by the Habsburgs (who had acquired Transcarpathia—Carpatho-Ruthenia in the 11th century), while the rest of Western Ukraine came under Russian rule.

1839: The Greek Catholic Church was suppressed in Russian-controlled Ukraine.

1861: Emancipation of the serfs throughout the Russian Empire.

1876: The use of the Ukrainian language was banned in the tsarist territories, in reinforcement of a decree of 1863.

1917: Following the collapse of the Russian Empire, Ukrainian nationalists formed a Central Rada (council or soviet) in Kyiv.

9 January 1918: The Rada proclaimed a Ukrainian People's Republic (UPR).

9 February 1918: The Central Powers (Germany and Austria-Hungary) recognized the independence of the UPR in a peace treaty.

April 1918: Following the signing of the Treaty of Brest-Litovsk in March, under which the Bolshevik Russian authorities ceded Ukraine to Germany, the Government of the UPR was replaced by a pro-German administration, headed by Hetman Pavlo Skoropadsky.

December 1918: Following the defeat of Germany, Skoropadsky was deposed and a liberal Government, the Directorate, was established in Ukraine.

January 1919: The UPR was united with the Western Ukrainian People's Republic (formed in Halychyna and Bukovyna after the collapse of the Habsburg Monarchy the previous year).

December 1920: A Ukrainian Soviet Socialist Republic (SSR), with its capital in Kharkiv (Kharkov), was proclaimed in eastern Ukraine, following the occupation of the area by the Soviet Red Army; later that month (20 December) the Republic signed a Treaty of Alliance with the Bolshevik administration in Russia.

18 March 1921: The Soviet–Polish War was formally ended by the signing of the Treaty of Rīga; the Treaty provided for the division of Western Ukraine according to the provisions of earlier international agreements between Poland (which gained Volhynia and Halychyna), Czechoslovakia (Transcarpathia) and Romania (Bukovyna—Romania had also acquired the previously Russian territory of Bessarabia).

30 December 1922: At the 10th All-Russian (first All-Union) Congress of Soviets, the Union of Soviet Socialist Republics (USSR) was proclaimed; the Ukrainian SSR was a founding member.

1928: The New Economic Policy (NEP), in effect since 1921 and under which Ukraine had thrived, was abandoned by the All-Union Government; it was replaced by a system of forced collectivization of agriculture.

1932–33: The Great Famine (also known as the Holodomor—'Famine-Genocide'), the direct result of Stalin's (Iosif V. Dzhugashvili) policy of collectivization, resulted in the deaths of an estimated 5m.–7m. Ukrainians.

1936–38: Large numbers of the Ukrainian cultural and political élite suffered in what came to be known as the 'Great Purge', a series of mass arrests and executions by the Soviet security police, the NKVD (People's Commissariat for Internal Affairs).

June 1941: The German army invaded Ukraine, as part of 'Operation Barbarossa'. Later in the year, in Lviv, the Organization of Ukrainian Nationalists (OUN—founded in 1929 in Halychyna) declared the establishment of an independent Ukrainian entity.

1942: The Ukrainian Insurgent Army was established by the OUN; the partisans continued to carry out attacks against the Communist Government into the early 1950s.

9 May 1945: The Second World War ended in Europe; Ukraine had suffered considerable damage during the conflict, and some 6m. inhabitants were estimated to have died. The hitherto Czechoslovak region of Transcarpathia subsequently became part of the Ukrainian SSR; southern Bessarabia (a Romanian territory between the World Wars) became part of Ukraine; and some of the territories on the left (east) bank of the Dniester (Dniestr), taken to form a Moldovan (Moldavian) autonomous region in 1924, were regained. Northern Bukovyna had become part of the Ukrainian SSR in 1944.

26 June 1945: The Ukrainian SSR was one of 50 signatories of the Charter of the United Nations.

1954: The Soviet authorities transferred control of the Black Sea peninsula of Crimea from Russia to Ukraine. Crimea's Tatar population had been deported to Central Asia by Stalin in 1944.

1963: Petro Shelest became First Secretary of the Communist Party of Ukraine (CPU); during his time in office a nationalist intellectual movement developed, and many independent (*samvydav—samizdat*) publications were produced.

1972: Shelest was replaced as CPU leader by the more conservative Vladimir Shcherbytsky, who instigated widespread repression of dissidents.

26 April 1986: A serious explosion took place at the Chornobyl (Chernobyl) nuclear power station in northern Ukraine; large quantities of radioactive material were discharged, but information concerning the accident was suppressed.

September 1989: The Ukrainian People's Movement for Restructuring (Rukh) held its founding conference. On 28 September Vladimir Shcherbytsky resigned, following his failure to control the opposition movements and the miners' unrest in the Donbas (Donbass) region; Volodymyr Ivashko replaced Shcherbytsky as First Secretary.

December 1989: Soviet leader Mikhail Gorbachev granted official recognition to the Ukrainian Greek Catholic Church, after a meeting with Pope John Paul II.

4 March 1990: Elections were held to the Ukrainian legislature, the Verkhovna Rada (Supreme Council or Supreme Soviet); Rukh, participating as a member of the Democratic Bloc electoral coalition, won 108 of a total of 450 seats.

June 1990: Ivashko was elected Chairman of the Verkhovna Rada and subsequently resigned as First Secretary of the CPU.

16 July 1990: The Verkhovna Rada adopted a declaration of sovereignty, which asserted the right of Ukraine to possess its own military forces and proclaimed the supremacy of republican law on its territory. In the same month Ivashko was appointed Deputy General Secretary of the Communist Party of the Soviet Union (CPSU). One week later Leonid Kravchuk, formerly Second Secretary of the CPU, was elected Chairman of the Verkhovna Rada.

17 October 1990: Vitaliy Masol, Chairman of the Council of Ministers (Prime Minister), resigned, following two weeks of protests by students. Vitold Fokin was elected to replace him the following month.

20 January 1991: In a referendum, the inhabitants of Crimea voted to restore to the region the status of an autonomous republic.

17 March 1991: In an all-Union referendum on the issue of the future status of the USSR, 70.5% of Ukrainian participants approved Gorbachev's concept of a 'renewed federation'; an additional question on Ukrainian sovereignty secured the support of 80.2% of the electorate; a third question on outright independence, which was held only in parts of western Ukraine, was supported by 88.4% of voters.

24 August 1991: Following an attempted *coup d'état* in Moscow (the Russian and Soviet capital), the Verkhovna Rada adopted a declaration of Ukrainian independence, by 346 votes to one, pending approval by referendum on 1 December. The following week the CPU was proscribed (although it was permitted to re-form in June 1993, and the prohibition was formally rescinded in October 1994).

1 December 1991: Presidential elections were held simultaneously with a referendum on Ukraine's declaration of independence, in which 90.3% of participants voted in favour; Leonid Kravchuk was elected to the new post of executive President of the Republic, with 61.3% of the votes cast.

8 December 1991: At a meeting in Belarus, the leaders of Ukraine, Belarus and Russia agreed to form a Commonwealth of Independent States (CIS) to replace the USSR. On 21 December a protocol on the formation of the CIS was signed by the leaders of 11 former Soviet republics, meeting in Kazakhstan. Four days later Gorbachev resigned as President of the USSR, confirming the dissolution of the Union.

5 May 1992: The Crimean parliament, the Supreme Council, voted to declare independence from Ukraine. The resolution was annulled the following week by the Verkhovna Rada and rescinded by the Crimean parliament, following threats of an economic blockade and direct rule from Kyiv. The following month, however, Ukraine granted Crimea (except for the city of Sevastopol) a significant degree of autonomy.

30 September 1992: Fokin's Government resigned, having been defeated in a vote of no confidence, as the economic situation deteriorated rapidly.

13 October 1992: Leonid Kuchma was approved as Prime Minister by the Verkhovna Rada; several proponents of radical economic reform were appointed to the new Government.

13 November 1992: The Soviet currency ceased to be legal tender in Ukraine; it was replaced by a new currency, known as the karbovanets (also the Ukrainian name of the Soviet rouble), or coupon (kupon), intended as a transitional stage to the introduction of a new currency.

21 November 1992: The Verkhovna Rada granted Kuchma emergency powers to rule by decree for a period of six months, in order to implement economic reforms.

September 1993: Kuchma resigned for the third time in four months, in protest at continued parliamentary opposition to his economic programme. The premier's resignation was accepted by the Verkhovna Rada two weeks later, which simultaneously passed a vote of no confidence in the entire Council of Ministers. Later in the month President Kravchuk assumed direct leadership of the Government, having appointed Yufym Zvyahylsky as acting premier.

25 October 1993: Ukraine agreed with the USA that it would dismantle its ex-Soviet nuclear warheads, in return for US economic aid. Three months later the USA promised further aid and security guarantees in a nuclear-disarmament agreement with Ukraine and Russia, whereby Ukraine would transfer its remaining warheads to Russia. This process was completed in June 1996.

30 January 1994: The final round of voting in the first Crimean presidential elections was held; a Russian nationalist, Yurii Meshkov, secured 72.9% of the votes cast.

8 February 1994: Ukraine became a signatory to the 'Partnership for Peace' programme of military co-operation of the North Atlantic Treaty Organization (NATO).

27 March 1994: Elections were held to the Verkhovna Rada and the Crimean Supreme Council.

April 1994: Following a second round of voting in elections to the Verkhovna Rada, the CPU won the largest number of seats (86), with its allies, the Peasants' Party of Ukraine and the Socialist Party of Ukraine (SPU), obtaining a further 32 seats; Rukh secured 20 seats. A total of 112 seats remained unfilled; subsequent rounds of voting gradually reduced this number.

May 1994: Oleksandr Moroz, the leader of the SPU, was elected Chairman of the Verkhovna Rada. The Crimean Supreme Council voted overwhelmingly to restore the region's Constitution of May 1992, a move that was denounced by the all-Ukrainian Government.

June 1994: Vitaliy Masol, Prime Minister in 1987–90, was reappointed to the post.

10 July 1994: Following two rounds of voting, the former premier, Leonid Kuchma, was elected President, securing 52.1% of the votes cast, defeating the incumbent, Kravchuk.

16 November 1994: The Treaty on the Non-Proliferation of Nuclear Weapons was ratified by the Verkhovna Rada, thus enabling the implementation of the first Strategic Arms Reduction Treaty (START 1), the protocols to which had been signed in May 1992.

1 March 1995: Masol resigned as Prime Minister; he was replaced by Yevhen Marchuk.

17 March 1995: The Verkhovna Rada voted to abolish the Crimean Constitution of May 1992 and the republic's presidency. The following month President Kuchma imposed direct rule in Crimea, which remained in force until 28 August.

3 July 1995: President Kuchma appointed a new Government under Marchuk, in which the reformist Viktor Pynzenyk's jurisdiction over economic reform was effectively removed; Pynzenyk resigned in April 1997, following further obstruction to economic reforms.

9 November 1995: Ukraine was admitted to the Council of Europe.

27 May 1996: Marchuk was dismissed; he was succeeded by Pavlo Lazarenko, whose appointment was confirmed by parliament in July. A new Cabinet of Ministers was subsequently formed.

28 June 1996: After prolonged debate, the Verkhovna Rada adopted a new national Constitution.

2 September 1996: A new currency, the hryvnya, was introduced.

28 May 1997: An agreement on the division of the Soviet Black Sea Fleet, control over which had been disputed with Russia since 1992, and on the status of the naval base at Sevastopol was signed by President Boris Yeltsin of Russia and President Kuchma. Three days later, in a Treaty of Friendship, Co-operation and Partnership, Russia recognized for the first time the sovereignty of Ukraine.

16 July 1997: Following the removal from office of Lazarenko by President Kuchma, Valeriy Pustovoytenko was approved by the legislature as Prime Minister.

19 March 1998: Criminal proceedings were initiated against Lazarenko on charges of embezzlement. He was subsequently charged with money laundering in Switzerland. He sought asylum in the USA, but was detained in that country in February 1999 and indicted on similar charges. In June 2000 Lazarenko was convicted *in absentia* by a Swiss court, which imposed an 18-month suspended prison sentence, and confiscated some US $6.6m. from his Swiss bank accounts.

29 March 1998: At elections to the Verkhovna Rada, eight parties obtained the 4% of the votes necessary for legislative representation on the basis of proportional representation, in accordance with recently approved electoral legislation. The CPU secured 123 seats; of the 225 seats elected on a majoritarian basis, 136 were won by independent candidates. In elections to the Crimean Supreme Council, held concurrently at the demand of the Verkhovna Rada, the CPU secured 40 of the 100 seats, to become the largest faction.

7 July 1998: The Verkhovna Rada elected Oleksandr Tkachenko of the Peasants' Party as its Chairman.

12 January 1999: A new Crimean Constitution came into effect.

14 November 1999: Leonid Kuchma won the second round of the presidential elections, with 57.7% of the votes cast, defeating the CPU candidate, Petro Symonenko; Kuchma was inaugurated as President on 30 November.

22 December 1999: The nomination as Prime Minister of Viktor Yushchenko, hitherto the Chairman of the National Bank of Ukraine, was endorsed by the legislature, following the earlier rejection of the incumbent Prime Minister, Valeriy Pustovoytenko. A new Cabinet of Ministers was subsequently appointed.

January 2000: A new parliamentary majority faction, formed by deputies from centre-right parties and independents, led by Kravchuk, petitioned for the removal from office of the Verkhovna Rada Chairman, Oleksandr Tkachenko, and his deputy. The majority faction subsequently voted unanimously to remove the two men from office. In February Ivan Plyushch was elected legislative Chairman.

16 April 2000: Some 81% of the electorate participated in a referendum on constitutional change; four measures (on the dissolution of the Verkhovna Rada for non-approval of the budget within three months of its submission; a reduction in the corpus of deputies from 450 to 300; the limiting of deputies' immunity; and the introduction of a bicameral legislature) were overwhelmingly approved. These reforms were not, in the event, implemented, however.

28 November 2000: Following the discovery earlier in the same month of a body believed to be that of journalist Heorhiy Gongadze, SPU leader Oleksandr Moroz announced that he had taken possession of recordings in which a voice purported to be that of President Kuchma was heard ordering the killing of Gongadze. Controversy surrounded the authenticity of the recordings, and President Kuchma strongly denied the allegations.

19 January 2001: President Kuchma dismissed the Deputy Prime Minister, responsible for Energy Issues, Yuliya Tymoshenko, amid allegations of the illegal smuggling of Russian gas and of tax evasion.

February 2001: Following the release of further audio recordings, in which President Kuchma was purportedly heard to order electoral fraud in the presidential election of 1999, and the bribery of energy officials, demonstrations against Kuchma gathered strength, and opposition leaders formed a 'National Salvation Forum', in which Tymoshenko played a leading role, with the aim of unseating the President.

26 March 2001: President Kuchma dismissed Minister of Internal Affairs Yuriy Kravchenko (who had also been implicated in the recently released audio recordings). On the following day Tymoshenko was released from prison, after having been detained in February.

26 April 2001: Prime Minister Yushchenko lost a vote of no confidence in the Verkhovna Rada, and was thereby removed from office.

29 May 2001: Anatoliy Kinakh, the Chairman of the Party of Industrialists and Entrepreneurs of Ukraine, assumed the post of Prime Minister, having been nominated by President Kuchma.

March 2002: Further audio recordings were released, in which Kuchma was purported to discuss the sale of an anti-aircraft radar system to Iraq, in breach of UN sanctions. During the following months demonstrations against the President again gathered force, and the allegations served to discredit Kuchma internationally.

31 March 2002: At elections to the Verkhovna Rada, Yushchenko's Our Ukraine bloc won the largest number of seats of any grouping, with 112 of the 450 elective seats. The pro-Kuchma For A United Ukraine (FUU) bloc received 101 seats, while the CPU obtained only 66 seats, compared with the 123 held in the outgoing legislature, in which it had been the largest party. Representatives of seven other parties, and 93 independent candidates, were also elected. At concurrent elections to the Crimean Supreme Council, the Kunitsyn Team (associated with FUU) was the most successful bloc, obtaining 39 of the 100 seats, defeating the CPU (contesting the elections as the Grach bloc), which secured 28. Sergei Kunitsyn, the eponymous leader of his bloc, was elected as Prime Minister of Crimea in the following month.

28 May 2002: Volodomyr Lytvyn, formerly head of the presidential administration, and the Chairman of FUU, was elected Chairman of the Verkhovna Rada.

October 2002: In mid-October a senior judge in Kyiv, Yuriy Vasylenko, opened a criminal investigation into President Kuchma, who was charged with violating 11 articles of the criminal code. In late October the Supreme Court rejected an appeal declaring the case illegal. In early November an ally of Kuchma, Vasyl Malyarenko, was elected as the new Chairman of the Supreme Court, and in late December the Court ruled that the investigation into Kuchma had, indeed, been opened illegally.

16 November 2002: The hitherto Governor of Donetsk Oblast, Viktor Yanukovych, was appointed as Prime Minister, following the dismissal of Kinakh. A new Government was appointed later in the month.

April 2003: Yanukovych was elected as Chairman of the Party of the Regions (PR), and Mykola Azarov, First Deputy Prime Minister and Minister of Finance, became Chairman of the party's Political Council.

September 2003: A new draft of constitutional amendments, known as the Medvedchuk-Symonenko draft, was presented to the Verkhovna Rada by pro-presidential factions, following the failure of previous proposals to gain support. Proposed changes included the election of the President by the legislature from 2006, instead of by direct popular election, and elections to the Verkhovna Rada by a system of proportional representation with effect from 2007.

31 October 2003: The Our Ukraine bloc was prevented from holding a convention in Donetsk by large-scale demonstrations in the city, which accused Yushchenko of promoting Nazi ideology.

3 February 2004: The Verkhovna Rada voted to amend the Medvedchuk-Symonenko draft on constitutional reform by removing the proposals regarding the election of the President by the legislature.

8 April 2004: Despite further amendments and protracted debate, the Verkhovna Rada narrowly failed to approve the Medvedchuk-Symonenko constitutional reform proposals.

14 April 2004: Yanukovych was named as the pro-Kuchma bloc's candidate for the 2004 presidential elections, the first round of which was scheduled for 31 October.

3 June 2004: Lazarenko was convicted of 29 charges of money laundering, fraud and extortion by a federal court in San Francisco, California, USA; 15 of these charges were overturned on appeal in May 2005; Lazarenko was sentenced in August 2006 to nine years' imprisonment and was fined US $10m.

10 September 2004: As campaigning for the presidential election was under way, the principal opposition candidate, Yushchenko, was admitted to a hospital in Vienna, Austria, with an illness, characterized, *inter alia*, by severe facial scarring, that was subsequently confirmed to be the result of dioxin poisoning; reports suggested that Yushchenko had fallen ill following a meeting with senior officials of the Security Service of Ukraine. At least one further apparent assassination attempt against Yushchenko was reported during the presidential campaign.

22 September 2004: Kuchma announced that he had accepted the resignation of Marchuk as Minister of Defence, apparently in response to concerns that security at a plant for the recycling of ammunition was insufficient. He was replaced by Oleksandr Kuzmuk, who had previously resigned from the position in October 2001.

31 October 2004: The first round of voting in the presidential election took place, contested by 24 candidates; official results were not announced by the Central Electoral Commission until 10 days later, the final day on which the results could be declared constitutionally. As had been widely anticipated, Yushchenko, with 39.91% of the votes cast, and Yanukovych, with 39.27%, were to progress to a second round of polling. Moroz was placed third, with 5.82%, and Symonenko fourth, with 4.98%.

November 2004: The second round of presidential voting was held on 21 November, as scheduled. When preliminary results from the Central Electoral Commission declared Yanukovych to have won, hundreds of thousands of protesters rallied in Kyiv and other cities alleging large-scale electoral fraud and claiming victory for Yushchenko (who had been shown to be the winning candidate in apparently reputable exit polls). What were termed the final results of the second round of voting were released by the Central Electoral Commission on 24 November; these results attributed 49.5% of the votes cast to Yanukovych, compared with the 46.6% attributed to Yushchenko. On that day President Vladimir Putin of Russia congratulated Yanukovych for his victory (Putin had visited Ukraine before both of the previous rounds of voting, expressing support for Yanukovych on both occasions), but the USA, European Union, Council of Europe and Organization for Security and Co-operation in Europe all refused to accept the officially declared results. Despite severe climatic conditions, protests against alleged electoral fraud, and in support of Yushchenko, continued in Kyiv, with demonstrators establishing tent camps, demanding non-recognition of the officially declared election result; several government buildings in Kyiv were also occupied by demonstrators, who adopted the colour orange as an identifying symbol. (The protests were therefore widely referred to as part of the 'orange revolution'.) By the end of the month a significant number of state officials, including, notably, members of the law-enforcement agencies, had declared their support for Yushchenko.

3 December 2004: The Supreme Court annulled the results of the second round of the presidential election and ordered that the run-off poll between Yanukovych and Yushchenko be re-run.

8 December 2004: In an attempt to resolve the political crisis, a compromise package of constitutional amendments and electoral reforms was approved by the Verkhovna Rada and signed into law by President Kuchma, following a series of meetings between Kuchma, Yanukovych and Yushchenko, with international mediation. The constitutional amendments significantly reduced the powers of the presidency in favour of the prime minister and the legislature, especially with regard to the appointment of government ministers. (These measures were to take effect either from September 2005 or following the legislative elections scheduled for March 2006, depending on whether other reforms to local government had been implemented; in the event, the latter date prevailed.) Changes to the electoral system included a reduction in absentee voting (which had been regarded as a major factor in facilitating electoral fraud hitherto) and the abolition of single-mandate constituencies in the Verkhovna Rada. The new run-off poll was scheduled for 26 December.

26 December 2004: Yushchenko was elected as President, obtaining 51.99% of the votes cast, compared with the 44.2% awarded to Yanukovych, according to official results formally published on 10 January 2005. (Preliminary results issued in late December had shown Yushchenko as the winner by a similar margin.) A clear geographical divide in the voting was evident, with western and central regions, including Kyiv, voting overwhelmingly for Yushchenko, while Yanukovych had obtained a clear margin of victory in most eastern and southern regions, including Crimea.

23 January 2005: Yushchenko was inaugurated as President; this ceremony had been delayed following the launch of several appeals to the Supreme Court against the election result by Yanukovych; his final appeal had been rejected on 20 January.

4 February 2005: Yushchenko's nomination of Tymoshenko (who had been a prominent, charismatic leader of demonstrations during the 'orange revolution') as Prime Minister was approved by the Verkhovna Rada. The composition of an entirely new Cabinet of Ministers was subsequently announced. Notably, Kinakh was appointed as First Deputy Prime Minister. Anatolii Matviyenko, an ally of Tymoshenko, became Prime Minister of Crimea.

4 March 2005: Former Minister of Internal Affairs Yuriy Kravchenko was found dead, reportedly as the result of suicide, shortly before he had been due to be questioned at the office of the Prosecutor-General on matters relating to the disappearance and murder of Gongadze in 2000.

8 September 2005: Yushchenko dismissed the Government of Tymoshenko, expressing concern that the administration had been unable to work as a coherent team, and following allegations of rivalry between Tymoshenko and the Chairman of the National Security and Defence Council, Petro Poroshenko. This measure followed the resignation, over a period of several days, of several senior government and state officials amid allegations of corruption.

22 September 2005: The Verkhovna Rada approved the appointment of Yuriy Yekhanurov, a former Minister of the Economy and First Deputy Prime Minister, as premier; the PR faction agreed to support Yekhanurov's nomination, following the agreement of an accord between Yushchenko and Yanukovych. An earlier attempt, on 20 September, to obtain approval for Yekhanurov's candidacy had narrowly been defeated, when deputies of the Yuliya Tymoshenko bloc (YuTB) refused to support the nomination. Yekhanurov subsequently formed a new administration. Meanwhile, on 23 September, Anatolii Burdyugov, an ally of Yushchenko, was approved as Prime Minister of Crimea, following the resignation of Matviyenko on 20 September.

1 January 2006: Considerable hardship was experienced across Ukraine, which was then subject to sub-zero temperatures, as the Russian state-controlled company Gazprom suspended natural gas supplies to Ukraine, following the failure of the administration to negotiate new terms for its supply. Supplies were restored on 4 January, following agreement on new terms of supply less favourable to Ukraine.

10 January 2006: A vote of no confidence in the Yekhanurov administration, which had been brought in response to the agreement on natural gas supplies reached earlier in the month, was approved in the Verkhovna Rada by 250 votes to 50 votes against. Although such a vote should, theoretically, have resulted in the Government's removal from office, the constitutional position at this time was obscure (the transfer of many of the powers of appointment from the President to the Prime Minister and the Chairman of the Verkhovna Rada having taken effect on 1 January), and, in the absence of a functioning Constitutional Court, President Yushchenko requested that the Yekhanurov administration remain in office until after the forthcoming legislative elections.

26 March 2006: Elections to the Verkhovna Rada, for the first time being held on the basis of full proportional representation (with a 3% threshold), were contested by some 45 parties and blocs. Yanukovych's PR became the largest party in the new legislature, with 32.1% of the total votes, receiving 186 seats. The YuTB was placed second, with 22.3% and 129 seats, while the Our Ukraine bloc won only 14.0% and 81 seats. Two other groupings—the SPU, with 5.7% (33 seats), and the CPU, with 3.7% (21 seats)—secured legislative representation. The results of the elections demonstrated a renewed regional division in political allegiances, while the failure of any party or bloc to obtain a majority of legislative seats necessitated the formation of a coalition government. In concurrent elections to the Crimean Supreme Council (the results of which were not announced until mid-April, following the conclusion of an investigation into alleged electoral fraud), the For Yanukovych bloc (principally comprising the PR) obtained 44 of the 100 elective seats to become the largest grouping therein. Anatolii Gritsenko of the PR was elected as the new Crimean legislative Chairman.

2 June 2006: The Crimean Supreme Council approved the formation of a new coalition Government for the Autonomous Republic, chaired by Viktor Plakida, a former energy sector executive.

11 June 2006: Some 200 US reserve troops began to leave Feodosiya, Crimea, having been prevented from taking part in planned NATO exercises (which were also to have involved participants from the defence forces of 11 other countries) by protests seemingly instigated by local Russian nationalists opposed to Ukraine's emerging relationship with NATO. (It had emerged by this time that the exercises would, in any case, have breached the Ukrainian Constitution, as they had not been approved by the Verkhovna Rada.)

22 June 2006: Following prolonged negotiations, the three factions in the Verkhovna Rada that had supported the 'orange revolution' (the YuTB, Our Ukraine and the SPU) announced the establishment of a 'coalition of democratic forces' with an absolute majority of legislative seats. However, before such a coalition could approve the formation of a new administration, in early July the SPU withdrew from the coalition agreement and instead allied itself with the PR and the CPU as part of a so-called 'anti-crisis coalition', which would control a small parliamentary majority. However, Yushchenko refused to accept the nomination of Yanukovych as premier by the new coalition, which he claimed had been formed unconstitutionally, and threatened to suspend the legislature and call new elections.

4 August 2006: The Verkhovna Rada endorsed the appointment of Yanukovych as Prime Minister and also approved the formation of a new Government, comprising members of the PR, Our Ukraine, the SPU and the CPU. Notably, this Government was the first in post-Soviet Ukraine to include representatives of the CPU. Moreover, although the Government included four members of Our Ukraine (in addition to several non-party allies of Yushchenko), the bloc did not enter into a coalition agreement with the other parties represented in the administration. The formation of the administration followed the signature, on 3 August, by the leaders of four of the five parliamentary factions, of a document presented by Yushchenko, the 'Universal of National Unity', which outlined policy agreements in a number of important areas. The faction that refused to sign the document, the YuTB, thus became the focus of opposition within the Verkhovna Rada.

14 September 2006: Prime Minister Yanukovych declared that Ukraine was not ready to enter into a Membership Action Plan (MAP) with NATO, a statement that was criticized by both President Yushchenko and the Minister of Defence, Anatoliy Hrytsenko, and which, moreover, appeared to breach the constitutional provision for foreign policy decisions to be the remit of the President. Later in the month further controversy arose when Yanukovych refused to endorse several presidential decrees (the prime-ministerial signature of which had hitherto been regarded as a formality) and demanded the dismissal of several regional governors allied to Yushchenko.

4 October 2006: Our Ukraine announced that it was to go into opposition, and that the four ministers belonging to the bloc were to be withdrawn from the Government. However, the resignations of the ministers (formally announced in mid-October) had not been officially accepted by the President or Prime Minister by the end of the month.

1 December 2006: The Verkhovna Rada voted in favour of the dismissal of the Minister of Foreign Affairs, Borys Tarasyuk, and the Minister of Internal Affairs, Yuriy Lutsenko, although it was unclear whether it held the constitutional authority to dismiss Tarasyuk, as the appointment of the Minister of Foreign Affairs continued to be a presidential prerogative. (Tarasyuk finally resigned from the Government at the end of January 2007, after his dismissal was upheld by the appeals court in Kyiv, and after he had been prevented from attending meetings of the Council of Ministers.)

20 March 2007: The Verkhovna Rada rejected Yushchenko's nominated candidate to the post of Minister of Foreign Affairs; on the following day the legislature approved the appointment of Arseniy Yatsenyuk to that position, together with several other ministerial appointments. Later in the month a group of deputies hitherto loyal to Yushchenko announced that they would defect to the PR faction in the Verkhovna Rada, although such a defection appeared to be in breach of the revised Constitution.

2 April 2007: Yushchenko issued a decree dissolving the Verkhovna Rada and scheduling pre-term legislative elections for 27 May. Yanukovych initially refused to accept the presidential decree and asked the Constitutional Court to rule on the constitutionality of Yushchenko's dissolution of parliament, and the Verkhovna Rada continued to convene.

5 June 2007: Yushchenko issued a further decree rescheduling legislative elections (which had already been rescheduled once) for 30 September, under a compromise arrangement, reached on 27 May, between Yushchenko, Yanukovych and the Chairman of the Verkhovna Rada.

30 September 2007: According to official results of the legislative elections, released by the Central Electoral Commission in mid-October, Yanukovych's PR won 34.4% of the votes and 175 seats, the YuTB 30.7% and 156 seats, the reconstituted Our Ukraine-People's Self-defence bloc 14.2% and 72 seats, the CPU 5.4% and 27 seats, and the Lytvyn bloc 4.0% and 20 seats. Tymoshenko and the leader of the Our Ukraine-People's Self-defence bloc subsequently announced their intention to sign a coalition agreement, which would allow the two groupings a narrow parliamentary majority.

23 November 2007: Yanukovych formally relinquished the premiership at the first session of the Verkhovna Rada, continuing in office in an interim capacity.

29 November 2007: At a further session of the Verkhovna Rada, it was announced that a coalition with a narrow parliamentary majority had been formed, following an agreement reached in October between the YuTB and the Our Ukraine-People's Self-defence bloc after protracted inter-party negotiations.

18 December 2007: Tymoshenko's nomination as Prime Minister was finally approved by 226 votes in the Verkhovna Rada. Her Government comprised 12 representatives of the YuTB and 11 of the Our Ukraine-People's Self-defence bloc; the Minister of Foreign Affairs, Volodymyr Ohryzko, who, together with the Minister of Defence, had been nominated by the President in accordance with the Constitution, was non-partisan.

15 January 2008: The Ukraine Government, in a letter to the NATO Secretary-General, formally requested a MAP, which was regarded as preparatory to membership. Ukraine's aspirations to NATO membership were strongly contested by opposition parties, notably the PR and the CPU, which staged protests in the Verkhovna Rada.

5 February 2008: The World Trade Organization approved Ukraine's accession application (submitted in 1993). After ratification by Ukraine in April, its full membership became effective on 16 May.

1 April 2008: US President George W. Bush made an official visit to Ukraine, thereby demonstrating support for the Government's aspiration of NATO membership shortly before a NATO summit meeting. Anti-NATO demonstrations ensued in various regions of Ukraine. Ukraine (and Georgia) were not offered a MAP at the NATO summit meeting, which was convened in Bucharest, Romania, on 2–4 April; however, the Alliance made clear that it welcomed a closer relationship with both countries and would consider offering Ukraine a MAP in the future.

6 June 2008: The coalition of the YuTB and the Our Ukraine-People's Self-defence bloc lost its narrow parliamentary majority, after a deputy from each faction resigned.

11 July 2008: A parliamentary motion expressing no confidence in Tymoshenko's Government was defeated.

1 September 2008: PR parliamentary faction leader Raisa Bohatyryova, who had been appointed National Security and Defence Council Secretary in December 2007, was expelled from the party, after refusing to endorse Yanukovych's support for the declared independence of the separatist regions of South Ossetia and Abkhazia from Georgia.

2 September 2008: Yushchenko announced the withdrawal of the Our Ukraine-People's Self-defence bloc from the ruling coalition, after the YuTB supported the PR in a parliamentary motion approving legislation that strengthened the executive powers of the Government, while reducing those of the President.

16 September 2008: The Chairman of the Verkhovna Rada officially declared that the government coalition had failed; if no new coalition was formed within 30 days, the President was required, under the Constitution, to schedule new elections.

29 September 2008: Following Russia's military action in Georgia in early August, Yushchenko met US President Bush in Washington, DC, USA, to discuss Ukraine's aspirations for NATO membership.

8 October 2008: Yushchenko officially dissolved the Verkhovna Rada and announced that further legislative elections would take place on 7 December, although it appeared that the scheduling of polls was to be subject to a constitutional challenge from allies of Tymoshenko.

History

Dr TARAS KUZIO

EARLY HISTORY

Between the ninth and 13th centuries Ukraine was known as Kyivan (Kievan) Rus, with its capital at Kyiv (Kiev), a state that extended into what is now Belarus and parts of European Russia. In 988 its ruler, Volodymyr (Vladimir) I 'the Great' (980–1015), introduced Christianity into his realm from Byzantium. In 1240 Kyivan Rus disintegrated, after being attacked and occupied by Mongol Tatars. The successor state of Galicia-Volhynia existed in what is now western Ukraine, during the 13th and 14th centuries. The Galician-Volhynian kingdom was initially incorporated into the Lithuanian state, which, at the height of its power, stretched from the Baltic to the Black Sea, and, after the creation of the Polish-Lithuanian Commonwealth in 1569, the bulk of Ukrainian lands came under Polish rule.

However, in the 16th century a national revival began in Ukraine ('the borderlands'), led by Orthodox Cossacks, who opposed Catholic Polish rule on ethnic, social and religious grounds. Attempts by the Polish authorities to weaken the Ukrainian Orthodox Church led, in 1596, to the creation of the Ukrainian Catholic ('Uniate' or 'Greek') Church, a body that owed its allegiance to the Vatican, but maintained the Orthodox rite. In 1648 a large-scale Ukrainian Cossack rebellion assumed authority over most of the Ukrainian lands and removed Polish control. However, during 1648–54 the creation of a Ukrainian Cossack 'Hetmanate', or quasi-state, left the area vulnerable to military attacks from its neighbours. The

Ukrainian Cossack leader, Bohdan Khmelnytsky, attempted to overcome this problem, proposing the transformation of the Polish-Lithuanian Commonwealth through the addition of a third equal partner, Ukraine. Poland's rejection of the proposal led Khmelnytsky to search for allies in Muscovy (Russia), with whom he signed the Treaty of Pereyaslav in 1654. This Treaty, the subject of bitter controversy from then on, was believed by Ukraine to represent the creation of a confederation between two equal states, although for Russia it signified Ukraine's submission to its rule. Promises of Ukrainian autonomy within the Treaty were not honoured, and the Ukrainian Cossacks launched two rebellions, in 1659 at Konotop, and in 1709 at Poltava, but they failed to secure their autonomous status within the expanding Russian Empire.

By the late 18th century the Ukrainian autonomous Cossack Hetmanate had been abolished by Yekaterina (Catherine) II 'the Great' and the region was fully integrated into the Empire as separate provinces. The 'Uniate' Church was forbidden in 1839, and the Ukrainian language was banned from education, the media and the arts by two decrees in 1863 and 1876. Industrialization and urbanization in eastern and southern Ukraine brought many migrant workers from the Russian regions of the Empire, and the emerging urban centres increasingly became Russian in culture and language. Meanwhile, with the Partitions of Poland in 1793–95, the western Ukrainian lands of Galicia, Transcarpathia (Carpatho-Ruthenia) and Bukovyna came under Austrian and Hungarian rule. Unlike the tsarist regime in eastern Ukraine, the Austrian-Hungarian Empire permitted the growth of cultural, educational and political life for its Ukrainian subjects. The Eastern-rite Catholic Church was allowed to flourish, thereby becoming identified with Ukrainian national aspirations, since it differentiated Ukrainians from Latin-rite Catholic Poles and Orthodox Russians. Western Ukrainians also established an active civil society, co-operative movement and media outlets. By the eve of the First World War in 1914, therefore, national consciousness was far more developed in western than in eastern Ukraine.

The collapse of the Russian Empire in 1917 led to demands from Ukrainians organized in a central Rada (Council or Soviet) for the Empire to be transformed into a loose federation. The Provisional Government in Petrograd (as St Petersburg had been renamed) refused to accept these moderate proposals, but was itself overthrown by the Bolsheviks in November 1917. Three months later, on 22 January 1918, the Ukrainian People's Republic (UPR) declared independence and was embroiled in military conflict with both the Bolsheviks and the 'White' supporters of the deposed Russian Provisional Government until 1920. In November 1918 the Austrian-Hungarian Empire also collapsed, after the end of the First World War, leading to the declaration of a Western Ukrainian People's Republic (WUPR), centred upon Lviv, which united with the UPR in January of the following year. The WUPR was immediately involved in a bitter military conflict with the Poles for control over Galicia, and was finally defeated by 1919. In March 1921 the Treaty of Rīga divided Ukraine between Soviet Russia and Poland. The former created the Ukrainian Soviet Socialist Republic (SSR), a constituent member of the Union of Soviet Socialist Republics (USSR), with its capital city in Kharkiv (Kharkov), subsequently moved to Kyiv in 1934. Polish promises to grant autonomy to its large minorities (accounting for one-third of its population) were never honoured, and from 1929 integral nationalist radicals in the Organization of Ukrainian Nationalists (OUN) began a militant campaign against the Polish state.

SOVIET UKRAINE

Under Soviet rule, Ukraine experienced three periods of liberalization, followed by the reimposition of conservativism. In the 1920s, 1960s and the second half of the 1980s liberalization of the Soviet political system led to a reassertion of national communist tendencies in Ukraine, coupled with demands for greater autonomy. The 1920s were the high period of national communism, with a cultural renaissance and widespread indigenization, in an effort to broaden the ethnic base of the Communist Party of Ukraine (CPU) to include more

ethnic Ukrainians. Ukrainian communist leaders foresaw that industrialization and urbanization would lead to an influx of peasants to urban centres, the infrastructure (such as education and the media) of which would be in the Ukrainian language, and that the modernization of the republic would, therefore, be accompanied by nation-building. After consolidating his power, by the late 1920s Stalin (Iosif Dzhugashvili) perceived this as a threat to Soviet rule in Ukraine, believing that nation-building and nationalist sentiment would simply lead to political demands for greater autonomy or even independence. By 1933–34 Stalin had halted nationalist progress, engineered a famine that killed an estimated 5m.–7m. Ukrainians, purged the republic's élites and disbanded the Ukrainian Autocephalous Orthodox Church, which had been established during the period of the UPR as a focus of national identity.

Between 1939 and 1945, during the Second World War, the western Ukrainian lands of Galicia (currently the oblasts or regions of Lviv, Ivano-Frankivsk and Ternopil), Volhynia (Rivne and Volyn oblasts), Bukovyna (Chernivtsi oblast), southern Bessarabia (part of Odesa oblast) and Transcarpathia were incorporated into Ukraine from Poland, Romania and Czechoslovakia (now the Czech and Slovak Republics), bringing into the Ukrainian SSR the majority of ethnic Ukrainians in Eastern Europe (the ethnically non-Ukrainian Crimean region was added in 1954). The OUN, which had led an armed campaign against Polish rule in the inter-war period, turned its attention upon the Soviet regime. In early 1942 the OUN created the 100,000-strong, partisan Ukrainian Insurgent Army (UPA), which fought the Germans until 1943 and the Soviet authorities from 1944 until the early 1950s, primarily in western Ukraine. At the same time, millions of Ukrainians were drafted into the Soviet army to fight against Germany. Widespread support for the OUN and UPA reflected the high degree of national consciousness that existed in western Ukraine, as the result of its more liberal treatment under Habsburg rule from the late 18th century until 1918. Its incorporation into Soviet Ukraine reinforced this national consciousness, because ethnic Ukrainians became dominant in urban centres after having replaced ethnic Poles, who were deported to Poland, and Jews, who were executed by the National Socialist (Nazi) German Workers' Party during the War.

The 1960s again witnessed a period of liberalization prior to the consolidation of power by Soviet leader Leonid Brezhnev. In Ukraine, the leader of the CPU in 1963–72, Petro Shelest, supported moderate attempts to develop national interests and co-operated with the cultural intelligentsia, even ordering a report by Ivan Dziuba, entitled *Internationalism or Russification?*, which was later published in the West, and which lambasted Soviet nationalities policy for its assimilationist strategies concerning Ukrainians. The thaw ended in 1971, and Shelest was replaced in 1972 by Vladimir Shcherbytsky, who led Soviet Ukraine until late 1989 and was instrumental in introducing a widespread campaign of Russification. In 1972 Ukraine's large dissident movement was crushed by arrests, including those of leading cultural figures, such as Dziuba. None the less, the Shcherbytsky era witnessed the growth of a variety of dissident movements. Ukrainian political prisoners in the Soviet GULag (State Corrective Camps System) became the largest proportionately of all Soviet nationalities.

THE NATIONALIST MOVEMENT

Although the Soviet leader, Mikhail Gorbachev, launched his policies of perestroika (reconstruction) and glasnost (openness) in 1985, Shcherbytsky, who remained in power in Ukraine until September 1989, prevented the republic from fully participating in the new era of liberalization. From April 1986 the regime in Ukraine increasingly came under criticism from opposition civic groups, following an explosion at the Chornobyl (Chernobyl) nuclear power plant, located north of Kyiv, which caused widespread discharges of radioactive material and was initially hidden by the authorities. In 1987–88 the Soviet GULag was emptied of prisoners of conscience, and these activists returned to their respective republics to take up the process of democratization that they had championed since the 1960s. In Ukraine, released dissidents re-founded the Ukrainian Helsinki Group (now renamed the Ukrainian Helsinki Union), which allied itself with the cultural intelligentsia to launch the Ukrainian People's Movement for Restructuring (Rukh). The CPU prevented Rukh from holding its founding congress until September 1989, the same month that Shcherbytsky resigned as communist leader. He died shortly afterwards.

The authorities continued to stifle public initiatives in support of Gorbachev's policies, preventing Rukh from nominating candidates in the USSR's first relatively free elections to the republican parliament in March 1990. Nevertheless, civic groups allied to Rukh obtained one-quarter of the seats in the new Verkhovna Rada (Supreme Soviet or Supreme Council—parliament), which gradually rose to one-third with defections from the CPU. The Verkhovna Rada provided Rukh with a public platform from which to criticize the CPU and its opposition to the Gorbachev reformist programme. After the departure of Shcherbytsky, the CPU remained under conservative control, first under Volodymyr Ivashko (September 1989–July 1990) and then under Stanislav Hurenko (July 1990–August 1991). Between July 1990 and December 1991 the chairmanship of the legislature was held by Leonid Kravchuk, who also held a high-ranking position in the CPU, until it was banned by the Verkhovna Rada for supporting the attempted coup in Moscow, the Soviet and Russian capital, in August 1991 (see below).

Under Kravchuk's leadership, parliament increasingly began to show signs of supporting state sovereignty, and on 16 July 1990 it overwhelmingly adopted a radical Declaration of Ukrainian Sovereignty, which stressed the pre-eminence of Ukrainian over Soviet legislation in all areas, including economic and security policy. This laid the foundations for legislation adopted during the following year, which increased Ukraine's sovereignty at the expense of the central Soviet authorities. During this same period the conservative, so-called 'Group of 239' communist deputies in the Verkhovna Rada increasingly diverged into two camps. One group, termed 'imperial communists' and led by Hurenko, supported only token Ukrainian sovereignty. The second faction was more pragmatic and willing to co-operate with moderates in Rukh (represented in the Verkhovna Rada by the Democratic Bloc of deputies). This group, led by Kravchuk, increasingly came to be termed 'national' or 'sovereign communists' because they supported a high degree of Ukrainian sovereignty within a USSR transformed into a confederation of states. In March 1991 the national communists added a second question, supporting sovereignty, to the Soviet referendum devised by Gorbachev on a 'renewed federation'. The second question was endorsed by 80.2% of those who participated in the referendum, compared with the 70.5% that voted in favour of the Gorbachev-imposed question. Moreover, an additional question in certain western regions, which asked voters if they supported a fully independent Ukraine, secured the support of 88.4% of those voting.

The declining influence of the CPU and the growing authority of the Verkhovna Rada enabled Ukraine to prolong the discussions initiated by Gorbachev on the replacement of the 1922 Union Treaty with a modernized version. However, any attempt at transforming the USSR into a looser entity was anathema to uncompromising members of the Communist Party of the Soviet Union, including the CPU. On 19 August 1991 conservative communists launched a coup in Moscow, which collapsed after only three days. The response of all of the Soviet republics, apart from Russia, to the failure of the coup was to declare independence from the USSR; on 24 August the Ukrainian legislature voted by 346 votes to one to secede from the Union, and six days later it banned the CPU. The vote was supported not only by the Democratic Bloc and national communists, but also by the Hurenko wing of the former CPU, through fear of the anti-communist revolution then taking place in Moscow under the President of the Supreme Soviet of the Russian Federation, Boris Yeltsin.

On 1 December 1991 the declaration of independence was put to a national referendum. It was endorsed by 90.3% of the participants; since the CPU had been banned, no political forces agitated against a 'yes' vote. On the same day Ukraine

held its first presidential election, which Kravchuk, the only candidate from the former communist 'old guard', won with 61.3% of the votes cast, compared with the 23.3% achieved by the second-placed candidate, Vyacheslav Chornovil, a formerly imprisoned dissident and leader of Rukh. On 8 December Kravchuk and the leaders of Belarus and Russia announced the annulment of the 1922 Union Treaty and declared, thereby, that the USSR had ceased to exist; the replacement of the USSR with a less binding Commonwealth of Independent States (CIS) was announced. Although the leaders of all three hitherto Soviet republics represented agreed on the need to dissolve the Union and to remove its non-elected President, Gorbachev (who resigned on 25 December), Russia and Ukraine, in particular, continued to disagree fundamentally on the nature of the CIS.

INDEPENDENT UKRAINE

In December 1991 Ivan Plyushch replaced Kravchuk as legislative Chairman, following the latter's election to the presidency, and both presided over a Ukraine that increasingly sank into political and economic stagnation. The election of Kravchuk reflected the inability of nationalist and democratic leaders to obtain majority support from the population, particularly in the Russian-speaking east and south. Kravchuk allied himself with some 'national democrats', although Rukh, under Chornovil, stood in 'constructive opposition' to him. Kravchuk promoted a centrist path of consensus politics that placed greater emphasis upon stability than reform, and he adopted economic and political policies that would not disturb those of his allies among the former Soviet Ukrainian élite who had joined the national communist camp. Fresh elections in 1992 could have brought in a reformist legislature at a time when the CPU was still prohibited. Moreover, no economic reform programme was launched until October 1994 (after Kravchuk had left office), and the President appointed only conservative prime ministers to head the Government. The constitutional process persisted through numerous different drafts and, again, was only resolved after Kravchuk had left office, in 1996. In October 1993 a new CPU was registered, which became Ukraine's largest political party. Miners' strikes and regional discontent in eastern Ukraine by the second half of 1993 led the Verkhovna Rada to schedule early presidential elections for the following year, before the expiry of the five-year term to which Kravchuk had been elected.

THE KUCHMA PRESIDENCY

The two principal candidates in the presidential election of 26 June 1994 were the incumbent Kravchuk and the former Prime Minister and director of a missile factory in Dnipropetrovsk, Leonid Kuchma, whose Government had been responsible for implementing a brief programme of economic reform in 1992–93. Following an inconclusive first round of voting, a second round was held on 10 July, in which Kuchma won 52.1% of the votes cast. Legislative elections were held in March 1994, March 1998 and March 2002. The legislative elections of 1994 were held using a majoritarian (first-past-the-post) system, whereas in 1998 and 2002 a mixed system was used, whereby one-half of deputies were elected on a majority basis, and the other one-half by a proportional system of voting. Although 30 blocs contested the 1998 elections, only eight managed to exceed the 4% necessary to secure seats in the Verkhovna Rada. Despite the severity of the socio-economic crisis experienced by Ukraine during the 1990s, in both 1994 and 1998 left-wing parties were unable to obtain more than 40% of the votes cast in elections to the Verkhovna Rada. The CPU remained the largest legislative faction, with between 80 and 120 seats, of a total of 450, in both the 1994–98 and 1998–2002 parliaments. However, the left-wing allies of the CPU, comprising representatives of the Socialist Party of Ukraine (SPU), the Peasants' Party and the Progressive Socialist Party of Ukraine (PSPU), were unable to unite and, therefore, never succeeded in commanding a majority of votes. Therefore, these groups were unable to dominate parliament, although the Chairmen (speakers) of the legislature were usually members of left-wing parties, as exemplified by Oleksandr Moroz, the leader of the SPU, who held this position in 1994–98 and again from 2006, and by Oleksandr Tkachenko, a member of the Peasants' Party, who was Chairman from March 1998 until January 2000. This domination of the parliamentary leadership by left-wing politicians led to conflict with President Kuchma and helped to stall an already faltering reform programme.

The election of Kuchma as President in July 1994 shifted the political balance towards eastern Ukraine, which had largely remained passive in the drive to independence prior to 1991, primarily owing to the region's closer ethnic and cultural associations with Russia, and consequent lesser sense of Ukrainian national identity. A relatively radical programme of economic reform was introduced at Kuchma's behest in October 1994, which brought support from international financial organizations. The programme was, however, plagued by a lack of political will, conflict with a legislature in which the leadership was dominated by the left, and prime ministers who were either weak on reform or corrupt, or both. By 1996–97 the reform programme had stalled and Pavlo Lazarenko (Prime Minister in July 1996–July 1997) was accused of widespread corruption; he became the second Prime Minister of independent Ukraine to flee the country, seeking asylum in the USA, so as to hinder investigations into allegations of corruption (Yufym Zvyahylsky had fled Ukraine for Israel in 1994 when confronted with similar charges). In June 2000 Lazarenko, then in custody in the USA, was convicted, *in absentia*, of money-laundering by a court in Switzerland, and given an 18-month suspended prison sentence. A further trial of Lazarenko, who had issued statements implicating other leading Ukrainian politicians, including Kuchma, in various allegedly fraudulent actions, opened in San Francisco, California, USA, in 2004. In 2006 the Californian court sentenced Lazarenko to nine years' imprisonment and fined him US $10m., following his conviction on charges of extortion, fraud and money laundering, having previously absolved his then business ally, Yuliya Tymoshenko, of involvement in this corruption. Meanwhile, in early 2002 prosecutors in Ukraine charged Lazarenko, *in absentia*, with ordering the murders of two parliamentary deputies (Yevhen Shcherban and Vadyn Hetman) in 1996 and 1998.

An economic reform programme was only restored after Kuchma's election for a second term as President in November 1999, and the subsequent formation of a reformist majority in parliament. In January 2000 the non-left majority in parliament voted the leftist Tkachenko out of office and replaced him with Ivan Plyushch, previously Chairman under Kravchuk, in what was termed a 'Ukrainian velvet revolution'. In addition, the leadership of all of the parliamentary committees was assumed by members of the non-leftist majority. Three leftist factions within the Verkhovna Rada (Community—Hromada, the PSPU and the Peasants' Party) disintegrated as members defected, and they were disbanded when their numbers declined to below 14, the minimum number permitted to register a faction. Thereafter, only two leftist factions remained, opposed to the reformist majority—the CPU- and SPU-dominated blocs. Six years of parliamentary–presidential conflict abated when, in early 2000, the reformist majority in parliament outlined its support for President Kuchma and the reform programme of recently appointed Prime Minister Viktor Yushchenko (previously Governor of the National Bank of Ukraine—NBU, and, in contrast to many other members of the Ukrainian political élite, a well-respected figure internationally and noted reformist). The failure of the CPU leader, Petro Symonenko, to defeat Kuchma in the second round of the 1999 presidential election, and the left wing's loss to the reformist majority of an institutional platform in the legislature, signified that the faction was in a defensive position for the first time in many years.

Kuchma had greater success in political, rather than economic, reform. The President had made the adoption of a new Constitution a priority after coming to power. A temporary constitutional agreement was reached between Kuchma and the majority of the Verkhovna Rada in June 1995, which granted the President temporary, predominately economic, additional powers. This preliminary agreement was used as the basis for the adoption of Ukraine's first post-Soviet Constitution, which was finally adopted in June 1996, after Kuchma threatened to put to a referendum his preferred draft,

largely modelled on the Russian presidential Constitution of December 1993. Although the introduction of this Constitution represented a significant stage in the 'de-Sovietization' of Ukraine, the adopted 'semi-presidential' text was in many ways a compromise, which failed to resolve outstanding questions and unsettled tensions in areas such as the division of responsibilities between government, president and legislature. In April 2000 a referendum called by President Kuchma sought to make significant amendments to the Constitution, by effectively increasing the powers of the President with regard to the legislature. Although all four questions—on the dissolution of the Verkhovna Rada should deputies fail to approve the state budget within three months of its submission; the reduction of the number of deputies from 450 to 300; the establishment of a bicameral legislature; and the placing of limitations on the immunity enjoyed by deputies—were approved by the 81% of the electorate that participated, it remained uncertain as to when, or whether, the newly approved proposals would be adopted. Moreover, the Constitution was regularly flouted in several key areas—human rights, the rule of law, socio-economic policies and media freedom. The referendum results were never adopted due to international criticism and the onset of what came to be known as the 'Kuchmagate' scandal later that year in November (see below). The scandal and the subsequent vote of no confidence in the Yushchenko Government in April 2001 destroyed the centrist-national democratic alliance that had instituted the 'velvet revolution'.

THE 'KUCHMAGATE' SCANDAL

The most important domestic event of 2000–01 was what became known as the 'Kuchmagate' scandal. On 28 November 2000 the SPU leader, Oleksandr Moroz, disclosed tape recordings alleged to have been made illicitly in Kuchma's office by a former presidential bodyguard, Maj. Mykola Melnychenko, who had subsequently fled abroad (he was granted asylum in the USA in April 2001). Some of the hundreds of hours of recordings, made during 1999–2000, were gradually released over the course of several years. Although the authenticity of the tapes remains a controversial issue, the information contained in them was highly damaging, because it appeared to reveal evidence of high-level corruption, misuse of power, election and referendum fraud, and hostility towards the critical media. A particular source of opprobrium was the manner in which the tapes linked Kuchma to the disappearance in September 2000 of an oppositionist journalist, Heorhiy Gongadze, whose beheaded body was found near Kyiv two months later. These disclosures discredited Kuchma both domestically and internationally, and his credibility was further weakened when additional recordings were released in early 2002 (the authenticity of which was officially recognized by the US authorities), in which Kuchma allegedly discussed the sale of advanced 'Kolchuga' radar equipment to Iraq, in defiance of UN sanctions.

In May 2001, following an official investigation, Gongadze's death was officially attributed to a criminal attack, with no political motives. Increasing anti-Government sentiment over the Gongadze affair, in addition to the other revelations of executive malpractice, led to the dismissal of both the Chairman of the Security Service, Leonid Derkach, and the Minister of Internal Affairs, Yuriy Kravchenko. (In March 2005 Kravchenko was found dead, having seemingly committed suicide on the same day that he was due to testify at the investigation into Gongadze's killing.) International criticism of Kuchma resulted in a cooling of Ukraine's relations with the West, and a consequent improvement in relations with Russia (see below). Kuchma initially claimed that the tapes were forgeries, but subsequently claimed the tapes to have been created from misleadingly edited recordings of innocent conversations. Domestically, the discovery of the recordings led to the appearance of Ukraine's largest opposition movement since the collapse of the USSR, which coalesced into the Kyiv-based 'Ukraine Without Kuchma' and Lviv-based 'For Truth' civic movements, while high-ranking political leaders established what became known as the National Salvation Forum. At its height, in 2001–02, the anti-Kuchma movement mobilized

20,000–50,000 demonstrators on the streets of Kyiv, although, notably, the CPU, still Ukraine's largest political party, refused to join the anti-Kuchma opposition. However, by May 2001 Kuchma's position again appeared to be secure, owing to public apathy and the continued support for the President of the pro-oligarch parties and parliamentary factions, as well as the neutrality of the CPU. After the dismissal of the Yushchenko Government in April 2001, following a vote of 'no confidence' by the Verkhovna Rada, a long-standing Kuchma loyalist, Anatoliy Kinakh, Chairman of the Union of Industrialists and Entrepreneurs (later the Party of Industrialists and Entrepreneurs of Ukraine—PIEU), was appointed Prime Minister.

THE 2002 LEGISLATIVE ELECTIONS

For the first time in independent Ukraine, in the run up to parliamentary elections scheduled for 31 March 2002, the authorities faced a credible and popular non-communist opposition challenger in Yushchenko. The election campaign was fought between three main groupings. First, the CPU continued to reject both reform and Ukrainian statehood, and in the event appeared increasingly out of touch with the Ukrainian electorate, receiving 20.0% of the votes cast for the one-half of the seats elected on a basis of proportional representation, and obtaining 66 of the 450 legislative seats overall, compared with the 123 it had obtained in 1998. A significant section of the CPU's supporters, pensioners, had literally died out, and the party also lost votes because of its failure to present a coherent oppositionist stance to Kuchma, which was now being presented, albeit from a different ideological perspective, by other groupings. Moreover, from 2000, for the first time since independence, Ukraine was experiencing positive economic growth, meaning that wage and pension arrears were being paid, which had frequently not been the case hitherto. The CPU could capitalize far less on socio-economic hardship to obtain popular support.

The second major grouping to contest the elections consisted of pro-Kuchma oligarchs, in two main factions, which sought to preserve the status quo and such stability as is provided by an authoritarian, corporatist state, a system that could be further entrenched to resemble the most authoritarian CIS states. The largest of these two factions—For A United Ukraine (FUU), led by Volodymyr Lytvyn—served as a 'party of power' in the elections, and grouped five major parties on a pro-presidential platform, including Prime Minister Kinakh's PIEU, the Party of the Regions (PR), the People's Democratic Party and Labour Ukraine. None the less, despite support for FUU by the executive, the grouping performed poorly in the election, receiving only 11.8% of the votes on the proportional list. However, the party's success in majoritarian constituencies was sufficient to make it the second largest grouping in the new parliament, with 101 seats. The second pro-oligarch group, the Social-Democratic Party of Ukraine (United) (SDPU—U), led by Viktor Medvedchuk, obtained 6.3% of the votes on the proportional list and received 24 deputies.

The third grouping in the elections were those anti-Kuchma groups that had become radicalized, to varying degrees, and from different standpoints, as a result of the 'Kuchmagate' scandal, among them the SPU and the Yuliya Tymoshenko bloc (YuTB), which united Tymoshenko's own Fatherland party and a number of smaller, principally nationalist and liberal, groupings. Although Yushchenko's Our Ukraine grouping sought not to portray itself as an anti-Kuchma bloc as such, it may be included alongside the SPU (which was more opposed to economic reform) and the YuTB in this category because of the common support of the three blocs for increased democratization and the revival of Ukraine's national identity, and their shared opposition to the authoritarian policies favoured by the oligarchs. While the SPU and the YuTB received a total of 14.1% of the proportional votes cast, and won 45 seats between them, Our Ukraine won the largest share of the votes of any bloc (23.6%) in the proportional lists, although, as a result of its lesser success in majoritarian constituencies, it received only 112 seats. Although the presidential election of 1999 had appeared to indicate that regional divisions in party support had reduced, such divisions reappeared at the 2002

legislative elections, when the western and central regions expressed greater support for the oppositionist Our Ukraine, the YuTB and the SPU, while eastern and southern regions largely supported pro-oligarch parties and the CPU.

In the aftermath of the 2002 elections, and in an attempt to gain advantage in advance of the presidential election scheduled to be held in late 2004, the executive successfully obtained control of all significant state institutions. Lytvyn, a close ally of Kuchma and hitherto Chairman of the Presidential Administration, was elected Chairman of the Verkhovna Rada, and his two Deputy Chairmen were also chosen from among those parties supportive of the President. There then began an intensive campaign to organize a parliamentary majority supportive of Kuchma. Intense pressure was applied upon opposition deputies, and some 30 eventually switched allegiance to the pro-Kuchma grouping, which had thereby obtained an absolute, but narrow, majority in the Verkhovna Rada by the end of 2002, despite the emergence of various factions from within those deputies elected as members of FUU. In November 2002 Kinakh was replaced as Prime Minister by the hitherto Governor of Donetsk Oblast, Viktor Yanukovych, Kuchma's preferred candidate. In his previous position, which he had held since 1997, Yanukovych had developed a close association with Ukraine's wealthiest oligarch, Rinat Akhmetov, and also enjoyed other important business connections. It appeared that Yanukovych's appointment was intended, at least in part, as a 'reward' for helping to ensure that Our Ukraine had obtained less than 4% of votes cast in the region (the only other administrative regions in which Yushchenko's bloc had obtained such a low level of support were the neighbouring Luhansk Oblast and in Sevastopol city). Donetsk Oblast was the only region where FUU were placed first in the proportional list in the 2002 legislative elections, with 36.8% of the votes cast, in large part as a result of the effective domination of political life in the region by the PR, a constituent member of FUU. In the last two years of Kuchma's rule, the PR became the second largest parliamentary faction after Yushchenko's Our Ukraine, putting into third place the CPU.

PROPOSALS FOR CONSTITUTIONAL REFORM

Kuchma presented further proposals for constitutional changes to the Verkhovna Rada in draft form in March 2003. The major difference between Kuchma's 2000 and 2003–04 constitutional reform proposals was in direction; in the former, Ukraine would have moved towards a strengthened presidential system, whereas in the latter the intention was to move towards a parliamentary system by taking power from the executive that Kuchma feared Yushchenko could secure at the 2004 election.

The pro-presidential majority in the Verkhovna Rada proved incapable of mustering the 300 votes (two-thirds of all deputies) required for the approval of constitutional changes without the support of other groups. After failing to obtain the support of the Our Ukraine and YuTB factions, the pro-presidential majority turned to the left-wing factions, who had long preferred a parliamentary to a presidential system. The combined factions of the CPU and SPU amounted to 80 deputies, which, together with the pro-presidential majority's 230 deputies, could (narrowly) gather the required quorum of votes to agree constitutional amendments. The left-wing factions only agreed to support the proposed reforms if the law on parliamentary elections was amended to provide for a system of fully proportional voting, under which the opposition parties had performed more strongly in the 1998 and 2002 elections. The law on parliamentary elections was thereby changed to a fully proportional system with a 3% threshold, compared with the 4% threshold in force at the 1998 and 2002 elections. However, in April 2004 the Verkhovna Rada failed to approve the proposed constitutional reforms by the necessary majority, primarily because some centrists had defected to the opposition. Furthermore, attempts to change the Constitution in an election year were widely condemned by Western governments and by the Venice Commission, the legal advisory board of the Council of Europe.

PREPARATIONS FOR THE 2004 PRESIDENTIAL ELECTION

After the failure of the attempts to implement constitutional changes in early 2004, the centrist groupings loyal to President Kuchma nominated Prime Minister Yanukovych as their candidate for the forthcoming presidential election. The election campaign, which was eventually joined by a total of 24 candidates, officially began in July. The election, scheduled for 31 October, was expected mainly to be a contest between Yanukovych as the candidate of the incumbent authorities and Yushchenko as the candidate of the opposition. The election proved to be the most fraudulent since Ukraine had attained independence, and the abuse of state and government resources in support of Yanukovych's candidacy was widespread. The state-owned media failed to provide free and balanced coverage, persistently presenting Yushchenko as an extremist nationalist who would prioritize the interests of the USA, not least as a result of his marriage to an American-Ukrainian. Russian advisers (so-called 'political technologists') worked on many of the political manoeuvres used against Yushchenko during the campaign prior to the presidential election. These were co-ordinated by an 'unofficial' election campaign team led by First Deputy Prime Minister Andriy Kluyev, separate from the 'official' campaign for Yanukovych, which was managed by Serhiy Tihipko, leader of the Labour Ukraine party and hitherto Chairman of the NBU. The unofficial campaign worked closely with Russian advisers and the presidential administration of Ukraine. Russian President Vladimir Putin visited Ukraine prior to the first round of voting, and again before the (subsequently annulled) second round, openly expressing support for Yanukovych on both occasions. The election campaign also witnessed acts of violence committed against Yushchenko. Most notably, in early September he became seriously ill, seemingly following a meal with senior officials of the Security Service of Ukraine, travelling to a private clinic in Vienna, Austria, on two occasions that month for treatment. As a result of this illness, Yushchenko's face was badly disfigured, while his enforced confinement for medical treatment had effectively cost him a month away from the election campaign. By December Western medical experts had concluded that Yushchenko had been poisoned, principally with dioxins. This was not the only attempt to attack or assassinate Yushchenko. Two Russian citizens were arrested in mid-November in Kyiv, having been found with explosives in their car. It appeared that they had intended to blow up Yushchenko's election campaign headquarters; both were sentenced to prison terms in June 2006. The first round of the election, held on 31 October 2004, was inconclusive, as no candidate obtained more than the one-half of the votes required for a definitive result. Final results were only released by the Central Electoral Commission (CEC) 10 days after polling, on the last day on which the results could constitutionally be released. These results showed that Yushchenko had obtained 39.9% of the votes cast, compared with the 39.3% attributed to Yanukovych. A further source of suspicion about the legitimacy of the results, in addition to the delay that had elapsed before their announcement, was raised by the closeness of the published result, as apparently reliable exit polls had given Yushchenko a far greater lead over Yanukovych. Moroz was officially placed third, with only 5.8% of the votes cast, ahead of Symonenko (with 5.0%), the first time that the SPU's presidential candidate had outperformed that of the CPU. Many hitherto CPU voters, who were concentrated in the eastern Russian-speaking regions, had defected to Yanukovych, seemingly out of hostility to the perception that Yushchenko was a Ukrainian nationalist.

In the three weeks between the first and second rounds of polling, Ukraine's political forces aligned themselves with either of the two remaining candidates. Two presidential candidates who had failed to proceed to the second round, Moroz and Kinakh, declared their support for Yushchenko. Tymoshenko, who had agreed not to stand as a candidate, backed Yushchenko throughout the election campaign. Meanwhile, the only unsuccessful presidential candidate to declare her support for Yanukovych was Nataliya Vitrenko, the leader of the marginal and extreme left PSPU. The CPU, notably, officially refused to support the candidacy of either Yushchenko or Yanukovych. This refusal represented a major handicap for Yanukovych, who had hoped to receive the endorsement of the CPU. Most CPU voters none the less backed Yanukovych in the 2004 elections (and continued to support the PR in the 2006 and 2007 elections).

THE 'ORANGE REVOLUTION' AND THE YUSHCHENKO PRESIDENCY

Exit polls, conducted at the second round of voting on 21 November 2004, showed that Yushchenko had obtained significantly more votes (as many as 15%–20% of the total) than had Yanukovych. Nevertheless, the official election results presented a very different picture, attributing to Yanukovych, with 49.5% of the votes cast, a slim 2.85% margin of victory over Yushchenko. This falsification of the election result, coupled with evidence of even greater electoral fraud having been committed in the second round than had been the case in the first round, produced what became known as the 'orange revolution', after the colour adopted as a symbol by the pro-Yushchenko protesters. In the first few days after the second round of voting, supporters of Yushchenko from Kyiv and elsewhere in Ukraine established tents throughout the centre of the capital, notably in Maidan Nezalezhnosti (Independence Square) and along the city's principal street, Khreshchatyk, occupying several state and government buildings. As large numbers of demonstrators gathered and set up camp in central Kyiv, Yushchenko and Tymoshenko mobilized Ukrainians to protest against electoral fraud. The radical opposition, including the student and youth group Enough! (Pora!), was swelled by millions of Ukrainians, many of whom had previously not taken any active interest in politics. One in five Ukrainians participated in the 'orange revolution', with the highest numbers coming from western Ukraine and Kyiv. It was this large-scale mobilization that turned popular opinion in favour of Yushchenko. The authorities would have only been able to remove millions of protesters by force, a step that Kuchma proved reluctant to take. After first underestimating the willingness of Ukrainians to participate in mass protests, the authorities then effectively ignored these protests in as much as they were able, hoping that the extremely cold weather would serve to bring about an end to the demonstrations; however, the protests continued peacefully for 17 days.

On 24 November 2004 the CEC officially declared Yanukovych to have been elected as President, in response to which President Putin of Russia publicly congratulated Yanukovych. However, on the same day the USA, European Union (EU), Council of Europe and the Organization for Security and Co-operation in Europe all refused to accept the officially declared results. This served to embolden the protesters and, moreover, gave confidence to officials who had contemplated defecting to the opposition. Indeed, on 25 November an increasing number of officials, including members of several law-enforcement agencies, such as the police, military and intelligence services, declared their support for Yushchenko. Several television stations, which had hitherto broadcast partisan coverage of the election in support of Yanukovych, also began to adopt a more balanced approach. The authorities could not go ahead with the planned inauguration of Yanukovych, following an order of the Supreme Court that the official results be suspended while it investigated allegations of electoral fraud. On 27 November the Verkhovna Rada voted not to recognize the official result because of widespread election fraud and also approved a vote of no confidence in the Government. The pro-Yushchenko crowds used non-violent methods in order not to give the authorities an excuse to launch repressive measures. Nevertheless, Yanukovych lobbied for President Kuchma to initiate a state of emergency, in order that protesters be removed from central Kyiv and government buildings be unblocked. After the holding of an emergency session of the National Security and Defence Council, on 28 November, a decision was made to dispatch police special forces against demonstrators. However, roads leading into central Kyiv were blocked by taxis, and the military warned the Ministry of Internal Affairs that, if necessary, it would defend the protesters by force. The only attempt by the authorities to use violence had failed.

On 3 December 2004 the Supreme Court overturned the decision of the CEC to declare Yanukovych elected President. The Supreme Court called for the second round of polling to be repeated within a period of three weeks. A series of 'round table' meetings supported by the Presidents of Poland and Lithuania and by the EU, attended by Kuchma, Yanukovych and Yushchenko, were convened in order to establish a resolution of the crisis. These moderators assisted Yushchenko, Yanukovych and Kuchma to reach a negotiated settlement whereby a repeat 'run-off' poll would be held on 26 December. Another aspect of the agreement, confirmed by voting in the Verkhovna Rada, was that the electoral law would be amended in order to eliminate the possibilities of electoral fraud. The compromise agreed also included provision for a constitutional reform that would transform Ukraine, with effect from early 2006, from a presidential-parliamentary to a parliamentary-presidential republic, in which many powers of the President would be transferred to the Prime Minister and Verkhovna Rada (in effect implementing the constitutional reforms proposed by Kuchma two years earlier but which had failed to receive parliamentary support in April 2004). In the re-run election, Yushchenko obtained 51.99% of the votes cast, compared with the 44.2% awarded to Yanukovych; the votes demonstrated a clear geographical divergence between supporters of the two candidates, with Yushchenko being first-placed in western-central Ukraine and in Kyiv, whereas Yanukovych had obtained majorities in most eastern and southern regions, including Crimea. Yanukovych disputed the results of the polling in courts, and initially refused to concede defeat, forcing the postponement of Yushchenko's inauguration as President until 23 January 2005.

On 4 February 2005 the Verkhovna Rada voted to approve Yushchenko's nomination of Tymoshenko, a charismatic figure who had played a leading role in the protests during the 'orange revolution', as Prime Minister. Kinakh was appointed First Deputy Prime Minister, while the SPU obtained three ministerial posts and the chairmanship of the State Property Fund. The broadness of Yushchenko's coalition proved to be both an asset and a liability. Its positive aspect was that a broad political coalition could command widespread public support for its stated policies of uprooting corruption and expanding democratic reforms and the rule of law. Such a broad coalition could also effectively ward off opposition from the CPU (which was, in any case, of declining influence), and from those former pro-Kuchma centrists that had not defected to support Yushchenko. Yanukovych, meanwhile, announced his intention of leading a 'harsh opposition' to the Government. The negative aspect of the governing coalition was that it was inevitably divided between political forces who supported a greater degree of state intervention in the economy and supporters of free market policies. The significance of these divisions was to become increasingly apparent in subsequent months as debate ensued over several key issues, including economic reform, reprivatizations, energy price controls, and the adoption of legislation for Ukraine's bid for membership of the World Trade Organization (WTO).

The former allies of Kuchma emerged from their defeat in the 2004 election in a demoralized condition, not least as a result of allegations (still largely unconfirmed) that certain prominent figures may have been involved in corruption, abuse of office, election fraud, the murder of Gongadze and the poisoning of Yushchenko. By late 2005 it appeared that two of the three oligarch 'clans' were in terminal decline. The Dnipropetrovsk clan divided during the course of 2004 into groups that supported either Yanukovych or Yushchenko. Its political 'front', the Labour Ukraine party, became a marginal political force, particularly after the resignation of Tihipko from its leadership in April 2005, and it later merged with the PR. The Kyiv clan was never popular in its home base and therefore had established a base in Transcarpathia, which was effectively removed in mid-2005 when the former Governor of the Transcarpathian Oblast, Ivan Rizak, was arrested on charges of corruption and electoral fraud. The Kyiv clan's political 'front', the SDPU—U, had also become marginalized and failed to enter the Verkhovna Rada in 2006 and did not contest the 2007

pre-term elections. The only clan representing regional oligarch interests that emerged from the 2004 election retaining its dominant position was that based in Donetsk and associated with Yanukovych's PR, which became the largest party in the parliaments elected in 2006 and 2007. Indeed, the PR, together with the CPU, represented the main components of the opposition to the Yushchenko presidency.

DISMISSAL OF PRIME MINISTER TYMOSHENKO

Despite expectations that the pro-Yushchenko coalition would stay united at least until the 2006 legislative elections, ideological and personal tensions between those elements supportive of free market reforms, closer to President Yushchenko, and those more in favour of social market policies, closer to Prime Minister Tymoshenko, increased markedly in the first half of 2005. Indeed, it was suggested in some quarters that the tensions between these two factions (which were heightened by apparent rivalry between Tymoshenko and the Chairman of the National Security and Defence Council, Petro Poroshenko) had effectively created a paralysis in some areas of policy-making, and had contributed, moreover, to a marked slowdown in economic growth. On 8 September, following the resignation, over a period of several days, of several senior government and state officials amid allegations of corruption and tolerance of corruption by the President, Yushchenko dismissed Tymoshenko's Government. Yushchenko nominated Yuriy Yekhanurov, a former Chairman of the State Property Fund, Minister of the Economy and First Deputy Prime Minister (and whom Yushchenko had appointed as Governor of Dnipropetrovsk Oblast earlier in the year), as acting Prime Minister, and charged him with forming a new Government, pending approval of his appointment by the Verkhovna Rada. Yekhanurov was regarded as a technocrat and a close ally of Yushchenko, as well as leader of Yushchenko's People's Union-Our Ukraine party. However, Tymoshenko, who considered her dismissal 'unjust', declared that she would not support the appointment of Yekhanurov, and would instead go into opposition, in the belief that her bloc would perform sufficiently strongly at the 2006 legislative elections for her to be re-appointed as Prime Minister, following the implementation of the constitutional reforms amending the balance of powers away from the President towards the Prime Minister and a parliamentary coalition. Consequently, and in part as a result of the deputies of the YuTB voting against the nomination of Yekhanurov, his appointment narrowly failed to obtain legislative approval on 20 September. However, following a meeting between Yushchenko and Yanukovych, and the signing of an accord between the two, the deputies of the PR agreed to support Yekhanurov's appointment, and he was duly confirmed as Prime Minister following a vote in the Verkhovna Rada on 22 September. A new Government had been formed by mid-October, and Kinakh was appointed as Chairman of the National Security and Defence Council, replacing Poroshenko. There was widespread speculation that Yekhanurov's Government would effectively serve as an interim administration, which would be replaced following the legislative elections of March 2006. This largely proved to be the case, despite the Government's defeat in a vote of no confidence in the Verkhovna Rada on 10 January 2006, following a dispute with Russia over energy prices, as a result of which Russia temporarily halted natural gas supplies to Ukraine, also disrupting supplies to several countries in Western and Central Europe. Although such a vote should, theoretically, have resulted in the Government's removal from office, the constitutional position at this time was obscure (the transfer of many of the powers of appointment from the President to the Prime Minister and the Chairman of the Verkhovna Rada agreed in late 2004 had taken effect on 1 January 2006), and, in the absence of a functioning Constitutional Court, President Yushchenko requested that the Yekhanurov administration remain in office until after the forthcoming legislative elections.

President Yushchenko's position was weakened not only by his relative inaction in the months after assuming the presidency, but also by three specific policy decisions that he implemented. First, his dismissal of the Tymoshenko Government, six months before legislative elections, had the effect of dividing the supporters of the 'orange revolution'. One specific and particularly serious consequence of this division was that popularity ratings for Yanukovych's PR increased from an average of around 15%–20% for much of 2005, according to various opinion polls, to reach 32% in the March 2006 legislative elections. Second, the 10-point memorandum signed with Yanukovych, shortly after the dismissal of Tymoshenko's Government, incorporated proposals (including an amnesty for all those involved in electoral fraud at the annulled second round of presidential voting in 2004, and an extension of the immunity from prosecution enjoyed by legislative deputies to members of regional and local councils) that appeared to contradict promises made during Yushchenko's 2004 election campaign and during the 'orange revolution'. The perception that President Yushchenko was retreating from the values of the revolution was further reinforced by the increasingly close relationship between Prime Minister Yekhanurov and what he termed the 'national bourgeoisie' (i.e. the oligarchs). Third, Yushchenko's signature, in early January 2006, of an agreement with Russia on natural gas supplies reinforced divisions among supporters of the 'orange revolution' and heightened public perceptions that the President lacked strategic policy-making abilities and was beholden to corrupt business interests, particularly in the energy sector.

THE 2006 LEGISLATIVE ELECTIONS AND THE RETURN OF YANUKOVYCH

The supporters of the 'orange revolution' continued to demonstrate a weak grasp of strategy both in the campaign leading up to the March 2006 legislative elections (the first to be held on a fully proportional basis) and during the subsequent negotiations to form a governing coalition. An informal understanding between the two principal elements of the supporters of the revolution—Our Ukraine and the YuTB—had been reached that the nomination of the new Prime Minister would fall to whichever of the two parties obtained the greater support in the elections, which took place on 26 March. In the event, the election results came as something of a shock to Our Ukraine, which had expected to be the better placed of the two blocs prior to the elections. However, it received only 14.0% of the votes overall, compared with the 23.6% it had obtained in 2002, securing 81 of the 450 seats in the new legislature. Meanwhile, the YuTB, which had won only 7.3% of the votes cast in 2002, increased its share of the vote to 22.3%, taking 129 seats. Meanwhile, the only major centrist (former pro-Kuchma) political party to be represented in the new Verkhovna Rada was the PR, which obtained 32.1% of the votes cast and 186 seats, more than any other grouping. The only other parties to obtain legislative representation were the SPU, with 5.7% of the votes cast and 33 deputies, and the CPU, with 3.7% and 21 deputies.

The Verkhovna Rada elected in March 2006 was therefore polarized. Two antagonistic political forces, the PR and the YuTB, constituted the largest factions in parliament, holding a total of 315 of the 450 seats. This polarization was evident most strongly in policies concerning several extremely contentious issues, including Ukraine's relationship with the North Atlantic Treaty Organization (NATO), dealing with abuses of office committed during Kuchma's presidency and the status of the Russian language.

After prolonged negotiations between the various elements of Our Ukraine, the YuTB and the SPU, in late June 2006 it initially appeared that a reunited 'orange' coalition had been created, in which Tymoshenko would be appointed as Prime Minister, with Poroshenko as parliamentary Chairman. However, before any such administration could be formed, the SPU, which had wished to see its leader, Moroz, as Chairman of the Verkhovna Rada, withdrew from the agreement. Instead, on 6 July, an 'anti-crisis coalition' was formed, composed of the PR, CPU and SPU, which would collectively hold a small parliamentary majority, with 240 of the 450 legislative seats. Before a government could be formed, however, this was replaced, at the end of the month, following further drawn-out negotiations, by a so-called national unity coalition, marked by the signing by Yushchenko and the leaders of

four of the five parliamentary factions of a document, the Universal of National Unity, which defined certain domestic and foreign policy priorities. The YuTB was the sole parliamentary faction that refused to sign the Universal, instead announcing its intention of remaining in opposition, while the CPU signed the document despite stating that it had reservations with regard to certain key aspects of the treaty. Yushchenko had introduced the Universal as a means of seeking to resolve the political impasse that had arisen following four months of coalition negotiations and to avoid the creation of a coalition that excluded his allies in the Our Ukraine bloc. Consequently, the compromise agreed by President Yushchenko was to submit Yanukovych's candidacy only after the latter had endorsed the Universal, which effectively provided for a continuation of the President's domestic and foreign policies, including the maintenance of Ukrainian as the sole official language, the rejection of federalism, and the eventual integration of Ukraine (following referendums) into NATO and the EU. These policies, if implemented as agreed, would demonstrate that the Prime Minister and President shared common strategic priorities for Ukraine's future development and, in particular, that the country remained committed to integration with the transatlantic community of democratic nations. On 4 August the Verkhovna Rada endorsed the appointment of Yanukovych as Prime Minister and also approved the formation of a new Government, comprising members of the PR, Our Ukraine, the SPU and the CPU. Notably, this Government was the first in post-Soviet Ukraine to include representatives of the CPU, despite the marked decline in support for the party; moreover, although four ministers in the new Government were members of parties associated with Our Ukraine (and other principal positions were held by non-party allies of Yushchenko), the bloc, in contrast to the other groupings represented in the new administration, did not formally enter into the coalition agreement.

While the holding of the round-table negotiations between opposing political forces that led to the signature of the Universal appeared to constitute a form of democratic progress in Ukraine, given that such talks had been repeatedly ruled out during Kuchma's presidency (and were, moreover, unimaginable in Russia or most other states of the CIS), the long-term prospects for political stability remained unclear. Although the PR had formally agreed to compromise on various key policy areas, clear tensions emerged between Yushchenko as President and Yanukovych as Prime Minister, partly as a result of uncertainties about the amended constitutional balance of power between the two offices. Further political instability seemed likely as a result of the decision of Our Ukraine, in October 2006, to withdraw its members from the Government and formally enter into opposition. The ruling coalition and Government reverted back to the so-called 'anti-crisis coalition' of the CPU, SPU and PR, while the two principal 'orange' forces, Our Ukraine and the YuTB, remained in opposition, in which position they subsequently, in February 2007, re-established an alliance.

Relations between the 'orange' groups and President Yushchenko on the one hand and Prime Minister Yanukovych on the other hand steadily deteriorated. The ensuing crisis was exacerbated by a lack of clarity concerning the division of responsibilities between the two offices, and between the executive and legislature, provided for by the constitutional amendments approved at the time of the 'orange revolution' and that had taken effect earlier in 2006.

President Yushchenko complained that the Prime Minister was constantly attempting to encroach on to his responsibilities and powers, which under the revised Constitution were to include the responsibility for the appointment of the foreign and defence ministers, the Security Service Chairman and the Prosecutor-General. However, notably, in December 2006 Yanukovych's coalition in the Verkhovna Rada illegally voted to dismiss Borys Tarasyuk as Minister of Foreign Affairs. The Government went on to halt funding to the Ministry of Foreign Affairs and took measures to prohibit Tarasyuk from attending cabinet meetings. (Tarasyuk subsequently resigned.) The governing coalition also attempted to remove from office regional governors (whose appointment remained a presidential prerogative), while new legislation, approved in January

2007, sought to attribute greater powers to the Prime Minister and the Verkhovna Rada. Furthermore, and despite the revised Constitution prohibiting deputies from changing their factional allegiance after they had been elected, the parliamentary coalition sought to increase its size to a constitutional majority of 300, as had occurred following the 2002 elections when the pro-Kuchma majority had offered inducements to members of liberal parties and trade unionists to defect from the Our Ukraine faction. With a constitutional majority in place, Prime Minister Yanukovych would have been in a position to overrule presidential vetoes of parliamentary legislation and government policies, thereby rendering them ineffective. One defector from Our Ukraine (who had previously been an ally of Kuchma), Kinakh, was appointed as Minister of the Economy. This strategy gave President Yushchenko his strongest legal argument that the ongoing transfer of deputies' allegiance was effectively altering the outcome of the 2006 elections.

The President was also subject to growing opposition from the Ministry of Internal Affairs. In March 2007 police officers searched the residence of former internal affairs Minister Yuriy Lutsenko, apparently in response to allegations that illicit armaments were located there, and various members of the People's Self-defence political movement that Lutsenko headed (and which was allied to Yushchenko) were arrested. As had reportedly occurred at the time of the 2004 elections, weapons and explosives had apparently been placed in order to incriminate these opponents of the Yanukovych Government as alleged 'terrorists'. On 28 March 2007, moreover, the contract killing of Maksym Kurochkin, head of the pro-Yanukovych 'Russian Club' during the 2004 elections, contributed to a widely held perception that Ukraine was returning to the criminality of the Kuchma era. (Kurochkin had prominent political and business ties to the regime of former president Kuchma, together with links to organized crime.)

THE PRE-TERM 2007 LEGISLATIVE ELECTIONS AND NEW VERKHOVNA RADA

On 2 April 2007 President Yushchenko issued a decree dissolving the Verkhovna Rada, thereby intensifying the political and constitutional crisis. After two postponements, pre-term elections were rescheduled for 30 September, following a compromise agreement, reached on 27 May, between Yushchenko, Yanukovych and other political leaders, which provided for the formation of a 'grand coalition' following the elections. Yushchenko, a highly cautious politician, had previously ruled out the dissolution of parliament, and until March only the YuTB had supported a call for early elections, which were officially not due until March 2011. In July 2007 the Our Ukraine bloc was reconstituted as the Our Ukraine-People's Self-defence bloc; Lutsenko was to head the coalition's list of candidates in the forthcoming elections. Ukraine's regional divide again prevented overwhelming victories for either of the blocs in the pre-term elections on 30 September. According to official results, released by the CEC in mid-October, Yanukovych's PR won 34.4% of the votes and 175 seats, the YuTB 30.7% and 156 seats, the Our Ukraine-People's Self-defence bloc 14.2% and 72 seats, the CPU 5.4% and 27 seats, and the Lytvyn bloc (led by former FUU leader and parliamentary Chairman Volodymyr Lytvyn) 4.0% and 20 seats. The SPU, with 2.9% of the votes, narrowly failed to secure the minimum for parliamentary representation, for the first time in its history. Tymoshenko and Lutsenko subsequently signed a coalition agreement in November that allowed the two groupings a narrow parliamentary majority of 228 (the minimum requirement for which was 226). The Verkhovna Rada, in a second attempt, approved the appointment of Tymoshenko to the office of Prime Minister on 18 December; ministerial portfolios were to be divided equally between the two blocs in a new Government.

It became clear that Yushchenko, as he had been following the 2006 elections, was weary of Tymoshenko in the position of Prime Minister. Several days after her nomination, he appointed PR parliamentary faction leader, Raisa Bohatyryova, as secretary of the National Security and Defence Council (NSDC), seeking, it was widely supposed, to provide

a counterbalance to Tymoshenko. Her unexpected appointment was opposed by the PR presidium and caused division within the party (from which Bohatyryova was later expelled). The NSDC, comprising senior personnel, and strongly critical of the Tymoshenko Government, was expected become an alternative power base to that within the Verkhovna Rada. Meanwhile, the PR staged blockades of parliamentary sessions in January–March 2008 in protest at Ukraine's aim of joining NATO, also demonstrating the ineffectiveness of the ruling coalition's narrow majority. The PR's boycott obstructed parliamentary procedures and the adoption of significant legislation, such as the budget and the government programme. Yushchenko and his secretariat adopted a harshly critical stance towards the Government that was evident in the form of demands, ultimatums and obstruction of its decisions. Regional Governors were prevented by the presidential secretariat from attending government meetings where they were invited to present reports on the economic situation in their regions.

With the division between Yushchenko and Tymoshenko continuing to dominate Ukrainian politics, the governing coalition never functioned as a unified body. Its narrow majority was reduced to 227, when one Our Ukraine-People's Self-defence member, Ivan Plyushch, the NSDC Secretary in 2006–07, refused to sign the coalition accord. This was followed by further defections in February and May 2008, principally from the Our Ukraine-People's Self-defence bloc by supporters of an alternative broad coalition. including that of the head of the presidential secretariat, Viktor Baloha. With the failure of the Our Ukraine-People's Self-defence bloc to merge its nine parties into a pro-presidential organization, it slowly began to disintegrate, the most prominent of its component groups being the People's Self-defence bloc led by Lutsenko, now Minister of Internal Affairs and allied to Tymoshenko. Baloha became affiliated with a pro-presidential party, United Centre, which emerged in March 2008. The main purpose of United Centre, which was chaired by a strong opponent of Tymoshenko, Ihor Kril, was to support Yushchenko's re-election for a second term (thereby demonstrating Yushchenko's disillusionment with the Our Ukraine-People's Self-defence bloc).

The Our Ukraine-People's Self-defence bloc, with popularity ratings of under 10% and internal divisions into pro-Tymoshenko and pro-Yushchenko wings, continued to disintegrate. The decline of Our Ukraine-People's Self-defence was evident in elections to Kyiv City Administration and mayoralty on 25 May 2008, when it failed to achieve the 3% threshold to obtain election. Within the Verkhovna Rada, there were insufficient deputies of the Our Ukraine-People's Self-defence bloc to permit the withdrawal of the bloc from the 'orange' coalition to create a coalition with the PR. Consequently, the only alternative to the continuation of the existing coalition would be pre-term elections, which could be expected to result in an increase in representation of the PR and YuTB, while the Our Ukraine-People's Self-defence bloc was unlikely to remain as a coherent force, with some deputies expected to join Tymoshenko and others to align with United Centre. It was thus anticipated that pre-term elections would strengthen Tymoshenko's position prior to the presidential election due to be held in January 2010, with polls predicting that she would win by defeating Yanukovych in the second round.

Constitutional reform was again the critical factor, as it had been prior to the 2004 elections. Majority opinion accepts that the 2006 constitutional reforms were agreed hastily during negotiations in December 2004, and consequently contained many discrepancies and ambiguities over the division of power between the President and Prime Minister, particularly in regard to the conduct of economic policy. The Tymoshenko Government became acutely aware of these discrepancies that, together with Yushchenko's unconstitutional intervention into economic policy, have prevented it from undertaking meaningful reform. The result has been a shift in the YuTB position towards support for parliamentarism away from that of being a strong supporter of presidentialism (as demonstrated in having been the only electoral faction to have voted against the proposed reforms in December 2004).

On 2 September 2008 the ruling coalition disintegrated, after the Our Ukraine-People's Self-defence bloc withdrew in protest at the YuTB having voted with the PR in support of legislation that would reduce further the powers of the President. The YuTB and the PR have stated their intention of pressing for further constitutional reforms that would transform Ukraine further into a parliamentary republic. The YuTB's tactical voting was also in protest at accusations of 'treason' made by the President against Tymoshenko in August, following the military conflict between Russia and Georgia. Yushchenko had claimed that Tymoshenko had reached a clandestine agreement with Russia to support her in the 2010 election.

Despite further negotiations on reforming the 'orange' coalition, the main parliamentary parties failed to agree on a new coalition within 30 days (as stipulated in the Constitution). Although the YuTB had reached agreement with the centrist Lytvyn bloc to create an expanded 'orange' coalition, only 34 (of the 72) Our Ukraine-People's Self-defence deputies supported the proposed new coalition. On 8 October 2008 Yushchenko officially dissolved the Verkhovna Rada and announced that pre-term legislative elections would take place on 7 December; he accused Tymoshenko of having destroyed the government coalition through personal ambition. The head of the YuTB's parliamentary faction strongly criticized Yushchenko's announcement, protesting that he had acted unconstitutionally, and the presidential decree disbanding the Verkhovna Rada was subsequently challenged by the YuTB in the Constitutional Court, on the grounds that a parliament elected in pre-term elections could not be disbanded within one year. Critical to the legal appeal was whether the year should be calculated from the date of the previous elections (30 September 2007), or from the date that the new Verkhovna Rada began to operate with a constitutional majority (25 November). It was also possible that the elections might be delayed for financial and technical reasons, since the Tymoshenko Government refused to provide budgetary funds for the CEC to organize the poll. Following the elections, a new 'orange' coalition was unlikely, due to the continued acrimonious relations between Yushchenko and Tymoshenko. The remaining possibility was that Tymoshenko could win sufficient votes, with the support of smaller blocs, to create a pro-Tymoshenko coalition, which would retain her as Prime Minister. Alternatively, there could be a broad coalition between pro-presidential forces and the PR.

OLIGARCHS UNDER YUSHCHENKO

Four years of political instability in Ukraine did not damage the ability of Ukraine's oligarchs to increase their capitalization during Yushchenko's presidency. Although the 'orange revolution' was in part an anti-oligarch mass protest, no oligarchs have had their assets confiscated through reprivatization (other than in the case of the Kryvorizhstal steel plant), been imprisoned or forced to flee the country (as has been the case in Russia) and there has been little progress in the separation of business and politics.

The worth of Ukraine's wealthiest oligarch, Rinat Akhmetov, President of the System Capital Management group, was assessed at mid-2008 at more than US $31,000m., reportedly making him the richest man in Europe and Eurasia. The total financial worth of the wealthiest 50 Ukrainians is $112,700m., or the equivalent of two annual Ukrainian state budgets. Oligarchs can be found in most political factions, including that of the SPU that was represented in the legislature of 2006–07, although the greatest concentration of wealth (estimated at $35,400m.) was found within the PR. The wealth of Ukraine's 50 richest oligarchs was equivalent to 85% of the country's gross domestic product (compared with an equivalent of 35% in Russia), reflecting a higher degree of state capture by Ukraine's oligarchs. Viktor Pinchuk (head of Interpipe Corporation), who is married to a daughter of former President Kuchma, and Igor Kolomoysky (of Pryvat Group) are Ukraine's second and third wealthiest citizens, but with wealth at $8,800m. and $6,550m. respectively. Three other oligarchs associated with the Pryvat group are ranked third, fourth and sixth, controlling a combined sum of $17,700m.

Akhmetov was elected as a PR parliamentary deputy in both 2006 and 2007, after having fled to Monaco in 2005 owing to fears of being subject to criminal charges ordered by the Tymoshenko Government. Other oligarchs, such as Pinchuk, fulfilled their promise of separating business and politics by not contesting elections to the Verkhovna Rada. Kolomoysky, although never himself an election candidate, was aligned with Yushchenko and funded the 2006 and 2007 electoral campaigns of Our Ukraine. Other oligarchs have also supported the 'orange' coalition. Petro Poroshenko (with US $1,120m., the 22nd wealthiest citizen of Ukraine) has been an ally of Yushchenko since 2001 when Our Ukraine was formed and Channel 5, that Poroshenko owns, was one of only two television stations that gave coverage to the 2004 Yushchenko election campaign. (Poroshenko was appointed as head of the NSDC in 2005, in which position he was regarded as a principal rival of Prime Minister Tymoshenko.) Kyiv Mayor Leonid Chernovetsky (with $750m., 28th wealthiest) supported Yushchenko in the 2004 elections and has remained an ally.

The former head of the 2004 Yanukovych campaign, Serhiy Tihipko (with wealth of US $1,640m., 17th wealthiest), who, like Pinchuk, left politics after the 'orange revolution', has returned as head of the Tymoshenko Government's Council on Investors. Another Pinchuk protégé, Valeriy Khoroshkovskyi (with wealth of $1,550m., 18th wealthiest), is head of the State Customs Service. The joint heads of the Industrial Union of Donbas, Serhiy Taruta and Vitaliy Haydyuk (each having wealth of $2,370m., and in 11th and 12th places respectively) were aligned with the Tymoshenko Government. Konstantyn Zhevago ($5,200m., and in fifth place), the first and only Ukrainian businessman to float shares on the London Stock Exchange (United Kingdom) for his Ferrexpo company operating in Ukraine, was a YuTB parliamentary deputy.

FOREIGN RELATIONS

Ukraine and Russia emerged from the USSR with vastly different ideas as to how the CIS should be perceived: as a 'civilized divorce', or a loose confederation of sovereign states with joint armed forces, dominated by Russia, respectively. Security was a key factor in the early stages of the Ukrainian state, and all non-nuclear military assets and personnel were transferred to Ukrainian state control by early 1992. Ukraine failed, however, to gain control of the Black Sea Fleet located largely in Sevastopol, Crimea, and it was not until 1997 that the issue of a 20-year basing agreement for a reduced fleet was finally resolved. The nuclear question also proved to be problematic, as Ukraine had inherited the world's third largest nuclear force. By May 1992 all tactical nuclear weapons had been removed from Ukrainian soil, but Ukraine continued to demand that it receive security guarantees and financial compensation for the strategic nuclear weapons located on its territory. Negotiations continued until 1994, when the Verkhovna Rada ratified the first Strategic Arms Reduction Treaty (START 1) in February and the Nuclear Non-Proliferation Treaty in November. This change in Ukraine's position only occurred after most Western governments abandoned their 'russocentric' policies towards the former USSR and began to take a greater interest in Ukraine's security. The Trilateral Agreement of January 1994, between Ukraine, Russia and the USA, paved the way for the granting in December of security assurances (but not guarantees) by the world's five declared nuclear powers. The last strategic nuclear weapons left Ukraine in June 1996.

By the beginning of the 2000s Ukraine's foreign policy was defined as 'multi-vector'. This 'multi-vectorism' was oriented towards a number of strategic partners—Russia and the other countries of the CIS in the East, and the member countries of NATO, notably the USA and Poland (which was admitted to NATO in 1999 and to the EU in 2004), and of the EU in the West. The relative importance of these strategic partners depended on domestic and international events. At the height of the scandal surrounding President Kuchma in 2000–01, for example, when relations with the West deteriorated, Kuchma turned to his only international ally, Russia. Relations with the West cooled further in 2002, as a result of allegations that

Ukraine had sold military equipment illicitly, and in breach of UN sanctions, to Iraq; an investigation into these allegations by representatives of the United Kingdom and the USA was undertaken in October 2002. At more settled times, however, Ukraine's 'multi-vectorism' was orientated, politically and in strategic terms, to the West, while its Eastern orientation was economic and cultural in nature. A significant proportion of Ukraine's élite continued to harbour a strong mistrust of Russia's intentions towards Ukraine and the CIS as a whole. Ukraine, therefore, regarded NATO, and the USA in particular, as the guarantor of its independence and territorial integrity. At the same time, as the de facto 'second republic' of the USSR, and with broad cultural similarities and family links with Russia, Ukraine preferred to deal with the CIS economically, because this allowed short-term, rapid gain for oligarchs, as well as the non-transparent economic, trade and financial practices that were the norm in the majority of CIS countries. An orientation exclusively westwards would require Ukraine's élite to support a transparent, non-corrupt reform programme that would integrate it into 'Europe' (hence the opposition of Kuchma and the oligarchs to Yushchenko's programme of reform). Instead, through 'multi-vectorism', the Ukrainian élite could reap the benefits of political and strategic ties with the West and economic and cultural links with the East.

Russian-Ukrainian relations remained strained throughout the 1990s, until, in May 1997, Presidents Yeltsin and Kuchma signed the long-delayed interstate treaty recognizing the Russia–Ukraine border (a November 1990 Russian-Ukrainian treaty had only recognized their borders within the USSR and the CIS), although they remain undemarcated, in the absence of political will in Russia to give this separation physical form. This was followed by a 10-year economic co-operation agreement in February 1998. Fears over Russian territorial demands were exacerbated by the fact that both chambers of the Russian legislature laid claim to Crimea and the city of Sevastopol on a number of occasions in 1992–96. The interstate treaty was ratified by both houses of the Russian legislature by February 1999, while the Ukrainian legislature ratified the 20-year agreement on the stationing of the Black Sea Fleet and the introduction of a new Crimean Constitution. Thus, by the time of the presidential election of October–November 1999, relations with Russia had been normalized and did not feature in the campaign, unlike during the election of 1994, when Kuchma had accused Kravchuk of weakening links with Russia. Nevertheless, it took Kuchma his entire first term in office to bring about this normalization in Russian-Ukrainian relations.

Both Kravchuk and Kuchma restricted Ukraine's involvement in the CIS to that of a participant (rather than that of an active member) and to purely economic questions, preferring bilateral to multilateral ties (indeed, in December 1991, it was Ukraine's reluctance to continue a close union with Russia that was instrumental in the formation of the CIS to replace the USSR). Ukraine refused to ratify the CIS Charter (which it regarded as sanctioning the establishment of CIS supranational institutions), while supporting the initiative to establish charters for the Black Sea Economic Co-operation Agreement and GUAM (see below). Under Kuchma, particularly during his second term in office, Ukraine became less antagonistic towards the CIS, and gradually increased its co-operation, through, for example, membership of the CIS Air Defence Agreement (it held associate membership from 1995) and Inter-Parliamentary Assembly (from 1999), and the establishment of an anti-terrorist centre (from 2000). In January 2001 Ukraine and Russia signed their first large-scale military co-operation agreement. Nevertheless, Ukraine remained frustrated from 1994 by Russia's continued unwillingness to support a CIS free trade zone and in early 2002 finally decided to become an Observer of the Russian-dominated Eurasian Economic Community (EURASEC). Joining EURASEC also reflected, in part, Ukraine's frustration at being repeatedly rejected by the EU in its attempts to sign an association agreement. In January 2003 Kuchma was elected head of the CIS Council of Heads of State, the first time a non-Russian had ever held the position. (Kuchma was, however, replaced by Russian President Vladimir Putin in the following year.) In

September Kuchma, together with the leaders of Belarus, Kazakhstan and Russia, announced that a CIS Single Economic Space was to be created, confirming proposals that had been outlined earlier in the year. Within Ukraine—to a much greater extent than among the other countries concerned—this move generated contradictory claims as to whether the eventual introduction of such a zone would, or would not, contravene Ukraine's stated objective of seeking EU membership. Ukraine's support for a CIS Single Economic Space remained limited to only the first stage, a free trade zone. Russia always resisted giving Ukraine trade preferences without Ukraine also joining a customs and monetary union. The failure of Belarus and Russia to create a monetary union showed up the empty nature of many of the agreements signed in the CIS and showed up the economic protectionism many CIS states practised. The Single Economic Space has been marginalized under Yushchenko.

In 1997 Ukraine initiated the creation of the GUAM (Georgia-Ukraine-Azerbaijan-Moldova) regional grouping within the CIS, as a security framework and counterweight to Russian attempts at reintegration, and to capitalize on the export of energy from Azerbaijan. (Uzbekistan later acceded to the organization, and it became known as GUUAM, although it left the organization in 2005, which thereafter reverted to the designation GUAM.) In 2001 a meeting of GUUAM decided that it was to be structured into a regional organization, with a permanent office in Yalta, Crimea, and a charter. From 2000, as Ukraine re-orientated its foreign policy from East to West, the importance of GUUAM waned. None the less, in November 2002 the Verkhovna Rada ratified an agreement on the creation of a GUUAM free trade area. GUAM also sought to expand co-operation on energy by transporting Azerbaijani oil through Georgia and Ukraine to the EU.

Ukraine continues to be frustrated in its attempts to integrate westwards. Among its few successes were its membership of the Council of Europe in 1995 and the Central European Initiative in 1996; the Partnership and Co-operation Agreement signed with the EU in May 1994 did not enter into force until March 1998. At the EU summit meeting held in Helsinki, Finland, in December 1999, a strategic policy document was signed with Ukraine, but it was not included in the 'slow-track' group of future EU members. This was a disappointment to the Ukrainian leadership, which introduced programmes on integration with the EU in June 1998 and July 2000, and which had always sought to join the Union. The enlargement of the EU to Ukraine's western border in May 2004, with the accession of Hungary, Poland and Slovakia, therefore represents the eastern border of 'Europe' and, thereby, signifies a dividing line in Europe similar to that imposed at the Yalta Summit in 1945 by the leaders of the United Kingdom, the USSR and the USA. The EU did not alter its stance following the 'orange revolution', and at every subsequent annual EU summit, declined to consider Ukraine as a future member.

Ukraine's relationship with NATO was more accommodating than that with the EU, and from 1994 Ukraine was the most active member among the CIS states of NATO's 'Partnership for Peace' programme. This was coupled with growing bilateral security ties with key Western countries, such as the United Kingdom and the USA. Wary of harming relations with Russia, Ukraine did not initially pursue NATO membership but, instead, undertook a policy of co-operation that sought to obscure the differences between membership and non-membership, signing a Charter on Distinctive Partnership in July 1997 and adopting an all-embracing three-year government programme of co-operation in November 1998, which was extended until 2004 in January 2001. Ukraine supported the enlargement of NATO, which it did not consider to pose a threat to its security, as did Russia and Belarus. Moreover, the highest governing body of NATO, the North Atlantic Council, held a meeting in Ukraine, its first in a non-NATO country, in early March 2000, shortly before a Russian presidential election, in order to demonstrate its continued support for Ukrainian independence.

Following the 'Kuchmagate' scandal, which was revealed in November 2000, President Kuchma was increasingly isolated in the West, and undertook few diplomatic visits abroad. Moreover, in the aftermath of the September 2001 terrorist attacks, the USA shifted its priorities in the region from Ukraine to Russia, which was considered an important strategic ally in the US-led 'anti-terrorism' coalition forged to combat radical Islamist groups. Moreover, the acquiescence of the Russian authorities would be required in order to allow proposed large-scale enlargement of NATO to take place. These twin factors, and Kuchma's enforced reorientation towards Russia after the 'Kuchmagate' scandal unfolded, presented Ukrainian foreign policy with new dilemmas. In order not to be sidelined further, in May 2002, as the establishment of a NATO-Russia Council was announced, Ukraine publicly stated for the first time that it would seek eventual membership of NATO. This was confirmed by a presidential decree issued in July, during a visit to Kyiv by the NATO Secretary-General, Lord George Robertson. However, as a result of the so-called 'Kolchuga scandal' (in which Kuchma was implicated, according to tape recordings apparently released by his former bodyguard, in the transfer of military radar equipment to Iraq in defiance of UN sanctions), it was made clear that Kuchma's presence was not desired at the NATO summit, although he attended none the less, only to be rebuffed by leaders of the more influential NATO countries. Moreover, a meeting of the NATO-Ukraine Committee was downgraded to take place at the level of ministers of foreign affairs or their equivalents. Despite an apparent improvement in relations with NATO in 2003–04, which resulted from the dispatch of a chemical-weapons response unit to Kuwait, in March 2003, in advance of the US-led military action to remove the regime of Saddam Hussein in neighbouring Iraq, and the approval by the Verkhovna Rada, in June, of the dispatch of some 1,800 Ukrainian troops to Iraq as part of a multinational peace-keeping force, it became apparent that Ukraine would not be invited to enter the Membership Action Plan (MAP) process until after Kuchma's departure from office. Although Ukraine has been an active participant in UN peace-keeping programmes in Kosovo (which declared independence from Serbia in 2008), and in Sierra Leone, by the early 2000s the credibility of the Ukrainian military had been strained internationally, following a number of incidents in 2000–02 (notably the accidental shooting down of a passenger aircraft en route from Israel to Russia in October 2001).

The election of Yushchenko as President in December 2004 changed Ukrainian foreign policy more in terms of substance than in actual policies. Yushchenko, like Kuchma, supported Ukrainian membership of the WTO, EU and NATO. The major difference between them lies in the apparent willingness of Yushchenko to support domestic reform and anti-corruption policies that would underpin Ukraine's drive for integration into Euro-Atlantic structures. Under Kuchma, there had been a growing contradiction between domestic policies that tended toward authoritarianism and tolerated corruption and foreign policies that sought to increase Ukraine's integration with transatlantic structures. The major breakthrough in Ukraine's foreign policy has been with the USA and NATO, rather than with the EU. Although Yushchenko fulfilled his pledge to withdraw Ukrainian troops from Iraq in late 2005, he has successfully revived Ukraine's relations with the USA. In February and April 2005 Yushchenko met US President George W. Bush in NATO headquarters in Brussels, Belgium, and Washington, DC, USA, respectively. The Bush Administration has strongly backed the spread of democracy that the so-called 'colour revolutions' in Georgia (November 2003), Ukraine (November–December 2004) and Kyrgyzstan (March 2005) were believed to have brought to CIS countries following a similar revolution in Serbia in 2000. Ukraine's relations with NATO expanded in May 2005 to an Intensified Dialogue on Membership. This level of relationship precedes that of being invited to submit a MAP. Ukraine had been expected to seek, and the USA had been regarded as likely to support, Ukraine's accession to the MAP process at the November 2006 NATO summit in Rīga, Latvia, but this did not materialize following the failure to form a renewed 'orange' Government after the legislative elections of March and the return of Yanukovych as Prime Minister. Prime Minister Yanukovych explicitly stated that Ukraine was not seeking to enter the MAP process during a meeting at NATO headquarters in September, a statement that was criticized by both President Yushchenko and the

Minister of Defence, Anatoliy Hrytsenko. Ukraine lobbied intensively for entry into the MAP process at the NATO summit meeting, convened in Bucharest, Romania, in April 2008. President Yushchenko, Prime Minister Tymoshenko and parliamentary Chairman Arseniy Yatsenyuk signed an open letter in January 2008, requesting consideration of this question in Bucharest. President Bush visited Ukraine prior to the NATO summit to give his support for Ukraine's NATO membership. NATO failed to offer Ukraine and Georgia a MAP, but, as a compromise, stated that they would become future members, an unusual step for NATO to take as a MAP prepares candidates for the process of achieving membership. Five factors adversely affected Ukraine's application to receive a MAP in Bucharest. First, political instability in Ukraine (as in 2006) gave grounds for sceptics inside NATO to point to the lack of unity in the pro-reform camp. Second, there was low domestic support (of about 25% nation-wide) for NATO membership, with support particularly low in the PR heartland of eastern Ukraine. Third, by 2008 Bush was ineffectual, not least as he was in his final year in presidential office. Fourth, Western European sceptics were led by Germany, which for the first time adopted an independent position rather than following the stance of the USA. Fifth, the influence of Russia was significant, owing to the energy links of major EU members, such as Germany and Italy, with Russia and a desire to improve relations with Russia after the election of Dmitrii Medvedev as President in March.

In 2005–07 the Verkhovna Rada adopted the legislation necessary for the country's accession to membership of the WTO. Of particular importance was legislation prohibiting the production and distribution of 'pirate' compact discs, of which the country had been a major producer. Ukraine missed the opportunity to join the WTO in 2005 and 2006 but joined it in May 2008, before Russia. Following the 'orange revolution', the EU has been far more reserved than has NATO with regard to considering the eventual membership of Ukraine. In February 2005 Ukraine and the EU signed a three-year Action Plan that did not make any provisions for membership. Moreover, the rejection of the proposed EU constitutional treaty at referendums in France and the Netherlands in mid-2005, and of its successor Lisbon Treaty by Ireland in June 2008 appeared to reflect a political crisis in the EU and lack of popular support for the Union's enlargement. In 2007–08 Ukraine completed a 10-year Partnership and Co-operation Agreement (PCA) with the EU. The PCA was replaced by an Enhanced Agreement that would, however, offer greater co-operation than the European Neighbourhood Policy but would not include a provision for future membership. The EU had expressed its willingness to enter into a Deep Free Trade Agreement with Ukraine after the country was admitted to the WTO, but was not expected to offer any further preferential arrangements to Ukraine. Ukraine was also to sign a visa-free regime with the EU.

Relations with Russia were, inevitably, difficult after Putin had publicly supported, and Russian advisers had taken an active part in, Yanukovych's unsuccessful campaign for the Ukrainian presidency in late 2004. Moreover, United Russia, the country's effective 'party of power' led by Putin, had signed a co-operation agreement with Yanukovych's PR in 2005, thereby effectively giving it Russia's support in the 2006 and 2007 legislative elections. Yanukovych's appointment as Prime Minister in August 2006 strengthened relations between the two states, especially over opposition to NATO enlargement into the CIS and co-operation on energy issues. Russian-Ukrainian relations have revolved around five contentious issues: first, Russia's continued opposition to the series of 'colour revolutions' in several CIS states, which Russia regarded as US-backed attempts at removing Russia from its 'sphere of influence'; second, Ukraine's level of participation in the CIS declined even further than that under Kuchma; third, Ukraine's refusal to extend the 20-year lease for the Black Sea Fleet in Crimea after 2017 became a contentious issue owing to concern that Russia would not withdraw, a threat that led to the Government preparing legislation requiring it to do so; fourth, Russia's adamant opposition to the possibility of Ukraine (or Georgia, the only other CIS state that seeks to join) eventually joining NATO, which led Russia to reopen the territorial issue of Russia abrogating the 1997 treaty if Ukraine continued the process towards NATO membership; and fifth, the reform of Ukraine's energy relationship with Russia that would entail 'market prices' and discontinuation of the use of corrupt intermediaries. In Kuchma's last year in office, the Russian state-controlled Gazprom had agreed to provide Ukraine with a highly subsidized price of US $50 per 1,000 cu m of gas (at a time when Western Europe was paying $240). Russia dramatically increased the price of gas sold to Ukraine to that charged to Western European states for 2006, resulting in a crisis in January of that year when Gazprom suspended exports of natural gas to Europe in retaliation for Ukraine's refusal to pay the new price. Gazprom resumed supplies after severe criticism from Western governments and the EU, and Ukraine and Russia agreed to a new contract providing for a purchase price of $95 per 1,000 cu m that would increase to $150 in 2007 and $180 in 2008. By 2011–12 Ukraine was expected to be paying the same price for gas as the remainder of Europe. Russia exported 80% of its gas through Ukraine, a figure that was expected to decline to 60% after the Russian-German Baltic pipeline was constructed. Russia has always sought to take control of the gas pipeline system, but this has always been opposed by the Ukrainian authorities. Russia has maintained energy leverage over Ukraine because it has never developed a coherent energy policy towards Russia. In 2008 Tymoshenko and Yushchenko publicly quarrelled ahead of negotiations with Russia over the continued use of the RosUkrEnergo intermediary. Continued high-level corruption in the energy sector and a lack of transparency has continued under Yushchenko.

CRIMEA

Crimea's autonomous status within the Russian Federation was abolished in 1945, following the mass deportation of the Crimean Tatars to Soviet Central Asia in the previous year, and the region was transferred to Ukraine in 1954, after nine years as a Russian oblast (region). As the only region within Ukraine with a majority of ethnic Russians and a Black Sea Fleet base, the Ukrainian authorities have always sought not to inflame ethnic relations that could lead to conflict with Russia. In January 1991 the Ukrainian authorities acquiesced in the elevation of the status of the region (excluding Sevastopol city) to that of an autonomous republic within Ukraine, which obtained the support of 93% of participants in a referendum. In May 1992 a potentially serious clash occurred between the Ukrainian authorities and Crimea when the legislature of the latter declared independence, in a tactical attempt to obtain a greater degree of autonomy and economic sovereignty.

Further difficulties occurred in 1994–95 when Russian nationalist Yurii Meshkov resoundingly defeated the Ukrainian authorities' preferred choice, Nikolai Bagrov, the Chairman of the Crimean Supreme Council, in the Crimean presidential election. Meshkov wrongly calculated that Kuchma would favour a greater degree of rapprochement with Russia and that he would win substantial support from that country, which was reluctant to be seen to be promoting separatism in Ukraine when it was itself defending its territorial integrity against separatists in Chechnya. Support for Meshkov's Russian nationalism and separatism dramatically declined throughout 1994, as the Ukrainian authorities applied economic and political sanctions against Crimea. In March 1995 the Crimean presidency was abolished, and Russian nationalists were replaced by Bagrov's pro-Ukrainian loyalists in the local parliamentary and government leaderships. Relations between Crimea and the Ukrainian authorities settled down after the Crimean legislative elections of March 1998, which completely removed Russian nationalists from positions of influence within the peninsula. The local Communist Party took the largest number of seats in the Crimean Supreme Council, and its leader, Leonid Grach, became legislative Chairman. Meanwhile, the pro-Kuchma People's Democratic Party of Ukraine took control of the Government. Both parties remained committed to maintaining Crimea within Ukraine, a factor that helped Crimea to

adopt a Constitution in October 1998, which was ratified by the Verkhovna Rada two months later.

The adoption of the Crimean Constitution in late 1998 finalized the question of Crimea's autonomous status within Ukraine and ended any speculation that it might eventually return to Russian jurisdiction. Nevertheless, the estimated 270,000 Tatars living in Crimea continued to represent a potential ethnic problem, owing to radical elements among them that opposed any autonomous status for the region that did not define Crimea as a Tatar homeland. The 2001 Ukrainian census showed that the ethnic balance in Crimea was changing. While Russians were emigrating from the region, the number of Tatars returning from those regions of ex-Soviet Central Asia to which they had been exiled in 1944 was growing. The proportion of Russians had declined from 65% to 58% since the 1989 Soviet census.

In March 2002 elections were held to the Crimean legislature, concurrently with those to the Verkhovna Rada. In a similar manner to elections to the national parliament, the CPU, contesting the elections to the Crimean Supreme Council as the Grach bloc, saw its representation reduced from 40 of 100 seats to 28, while the pro-presidential bloc, contesting the elections as the Kunitsyn Team, became the largest faction in the Crimean Supreme Council, with 39 seats, and, having been able to form a 67-seat majority faction in association with independent deputies and those of other parties, took control of its leading positions. However, in elections to the Verkhovna Rada, the CPU remained the most popular party in the peninsula. Notably, for the first time, Crimean Tatar deputies were elected to the Verkhovna Rada, within Yushchenko's Our Ukraine bloc. Russian nationalists only successfully captured votes in the Crimean city of Sevastopol. Crimea, like much of eastern and southern Ukraine, voted overwhelmingly for Yanukovych in the 2004 elections. Following the election, many pro-Kuchma deputies in the Crimean parliament initially defected to Yushchenko. These defectors, coupled with the Crimean Tatar deputies, thereby obtained a slim parliamentary majority, which was assisted by the decline in support of, first, Russian nationalists and, second, the Communist Party in Crimea. This pro-Yushchenko majority was removed by the victory of the PR in the Crimean 2006 and 2007 elections.

The 2006 legislative elections in Crimea followed similar trends to those to the Verkhovna Rada. In the elections to the Crimean Supreme Council the For Yanukovych bloc, a coalition dominated by the PR, secured 44 of the 100 seats, while the pro-Russian Union party and the Kunitsyn bloc each obtained 10 seats, followed by the CPU, with nine. A new coalition Crimean Government, headed by Viktor Plakida, took office in June. Political forces and personalities from the Kuchma regime that had lost the 2004 elections re-grouped in the Crimean Supreme Council after the 2006 elections, when pro-Russian groups reinforced their domination. The 2007 pre-term elections to the Verkhovna Rada gave similar results in Crimea as those of the previous year. Winning 54%, the PR obtained a narrow majority of the votes cast on the peninsula, reinforced by the nearly 10% of votes received by two leftist forces, the CPU and the PSPU. 'Orange' forces obtained only a combined 13% of the vote. The vote for the Our Ukraine bloc was partially obtained from those Crimean Tatar voters (around 15% of the Republic's population) who have traditionally voted for pro-Ukrainian parties, including Our Ukraine and its predecessor, Rukh. Prominent leaders of the Crimean Tatar Mejlis (Assembly) have traditionally been included on the lists of Rukh and Our Ukraine in elections to the Verkhovna Rada. A large proportion of Crimean Tatars were able to vote for the first time in the 2002 elections, as around 90% of those resident in Crimea had obtained Ukrainian citizenship, whereas at the time of the 1998 elections many retained the citizenship of their former place of residence, Uzbekistan. In the 2002 elections, seven Tatars were elected to the Crimean Supreme Council, an increase of one on the 1998–2002 Crimean Supreme Council. However, this was still less than the 14 seats the Tatars had been proportionately allocated in the 1994–98 Crimean Supreme Council, before these reserved seats were abolished.

In the 2004 presidential election, Yushchenko obtained 15.4% support in the Autonomous Republic of Crimea; around two-thirds of these votes were estimated to have been attributable to Tatar voters, without the support of which Yushchenko would only have received around the level of support (4.2%) that he obtained in Yanukovych's eastern Ukrainian heartland of Donetsk Oblast.

Crimean Tatars placed high hopes in the election of Yushchenko after years of neglect during Kuchma's decade in office. By 2007 these high hopes remained unfulfilled and violence continued to simmer in Crimea between Russophone Slavs and Tatars. The homes of Tatar activists have been bombed, Tatar journalists have been murdered and Tatars have been sentenced to lengthy prison sentences for acts of civil disobedience. The most serious violence erupted over the re-use or misuse of historic Tatar sites by Russophone Slavs. Clashes between the two groups have occurred in response to attempts to build apartments and business dwellings on ancient Tatar sites, such as the former imperial seat of the Tatar Khans in Bakhcharai and an old Muslim cemetery used as a market. Tatars have also undertaken acts of civil disobedience to bring attention to their plight, particularly over social issues such as the lack of land allocated to them by the local authorities and changes to the criminal code giving severe punishments for illegal seizures of land.

The growing presence of Russian Cossacks has stoked inter-ethnic conflict. Although a small proportion of the Cossacks are from Donetsk, the majority are from regions of Russia that adjoin the North Caucasus, a region plagued by inter-ethnic violence since the 1990s. Some of the Russian Cossacks come from extreme Russian nationalist groups, which have multiplied in Russia and have been accused of inciting or conducting racist attacks. Russian Cossacks are allied with two local structures: the Russian Orthodox Church—Moscow Patriarchate (officially registered as the 'Ukrainian Orthodox Church' but coming under the jurisdiction of the Russian Orthodox Patriarch) and extreme Russian nationalist groups and the Communist Party. One of the most active Russian nationalists is Sergei Tsekov, the leader of the non-governmental organization the Russian Community of Crimea, and the head of the Russian Bloc political association. Russian Cossacks swear an oath of allegiance to the Russian Orthodox Church (Moscow Patriarchate), which aggressively supports its dominance of Crimea by seeking to block the construction of Tatar mosques and churches of the Ukrainian Autocephalous Orthodox Church.

Russian Cossacks and nationalists have also incited exaggerated fears of a growth of Islamic fundamentalism among Crimean Tatars and exaggerated fears of Russophones losing their land and property and of being themselves deported after the Tatars succeed in their alleged aim of creating a separate Islamic Crimean republic. Although Tatars have practised a moderate form of Islam, Saudi Arabian missionaries have been seeking converts among younger, disaffected Tatars for the stricter form of Islam sometimes referred to as Wahhabism. However, Crimea's senior Muslim cleric, Mufti Aje Nurali Ablaiyev, remained confident that Wahhabism would not become firmly established among Crimean Tatars.

The Tatars have several unfulfilled demands relating to various aspects of their position in Crimean society and their status in the local economy. Although 75% of Tatars live in rural areas, they only possess around one-half of the land allocated to Russophones. Prior to their deportation in 1944, Tatars accounted for 70% of the population along the southern coast of Crimea, an area that today they are effectively barred from living in because of its high value to tourism and developers. Tatars migrating to Crimea find that their former homes (or those of their family) are occupied by Russian settlers, prompting demands for restitution. (Between the 1989 Soviet and 2002 Ukrainian censuses, the Tatar population in Crimea increased more than six-fold; by 2007 there were an estimated 243,000 Crimean Tatars in the region, while a further 150,000 remained in Uzbekistan.) Moreover, the authorities have failed to allocate sufficient resources for returning Tatars to build new housing, resulting in the growth of shanty towns. Additionally, a significant proportion of the Crimean Tatar population are effectively forced to work in the 'shadow' economy, thereby exposing themselves to the risk of violence from organized crime groups who control operations at many

markets in the region: although, in 2001, Tatars accounted for 12.1% of the population of Crimea, it was estimated that they only comprised around 4% of the official working population. Apart from these economic concerns, Crimean Tatars also have various cultural demands, including the construction of mosques (the number of which amounted to only 160 in the mid-2000s, compared to 1,700 at the time of the 1944 deportation, or around 21,000 prior to the absorption of Crimea into the Russian Empire in the late 18th century). Additionally, the limited provision of Tatar-language schooling (which was sufficient to serve only around 14% of Crimean Tatar children in the mid-2000s) has led to accusations of continued enforced russification similar to that experienced during the Soviet period.

The Tatars also have three legal demands: first, that they be recognized as an indigenous national group in Crimea, not as a national minority; second, that their 1944 deportation be recognized as an act of genocide; and third, that legislation be adopted to provide for the formal rehabilitation of the Crimean Tatars. Tatar groups also demand the restoration of guaranteed representation in the Crimean Supreme Council, as had existed in 1994–98. The law on elections, revised in early 2004, provides for full proportional elections to local councils and the Crimean Supreme Council.

Crimea became a centre for the opposition to the 'orange' coalition in 2005–06, led by the PR and its extreme left-wing and Russian nationalist allies. Anti-US and anti-NATO demonstrations in Crimea were successful in blocking the holding of NATO military exercises, held under the auspices of the 'Partnership for Peace' programme, in mid-2006. These exercises had been routinely held on an annual basis in Crimea and Odesa from 1997. The background to these Crimean protests were two-fold: first, the anti-NATO and anti-US campaign adopted by some parties in the 2004 Ukrainian presidential elections; and second, Russian attempts to block Ukraine's path towards NATO membership, which the Russian leadership feared was likely to take place rapidly following Yushchenko's election. Russia has also sought to use the Crimean protests to pressure Ukraine to extend the lease of bays at Sevastopol port to the Black Sea Fleet beyond the 20-year period provided for by a 1997 treaty. Ukraine has refused to consider an extension and has prepared legislation requiring Russia to withdraw in 2017, while there has also been speculation that the charge for using the base may be increased. Russia reopened the territorial question with Ukraine in May 2008 during a visit by the Mayor of Moscow, Yurii Luzhkov, to Crimea. The lower chamber of the Russian legislature, the State Duma, voted a month later to link Russia's continued acceptance of the 1997 treaty that recognized the border between Russia and Ukraine with Ukraine's relationship to NATO, threatening to annul the treaty in the event that Ukraine joined a MAP. There was concern that Russia would threaten to not remove the Fleet in 2017 and to reopen a territorial conflict, in an attempt to halt Ukraine's membership of NATO.

CONCLUSION

Between 1991 and 1994 a combination of conservative strategies that sought to maintain the status quo domestically, and a foreign policy that sought to establish its presence internationally while dealing with Russia's inability to come to terms with its independence, left many wondering if the Ukrainian state would survive either at all, or within its Soviet-era borders. Separatism grew in Crimea and eastern Ukraine, and Western governments feared that the Ukrainian state was heading for a meltdown and possibly civil war. Under President Kuchma, the Ukrainian state consolidated itself from 1994, and these fears were largely allayed. Key aspects of this process included the granting of security assurances to Ukraine by the five declared nuclear powers in 1994; membership of the Council of Europe in 1995; the adoption of a post-Soviet Constitution and the introduction of a new currency, the hryvnya, in 1996; the signature of an inter-state treaty with Russia and a Charter with NATO, and a 20-year Black Sea Fleet agreement in 1997; and the adoption of the Crimean Constitution and ratification of the Ukrainian-Russian treaty by Russia in 1998–99. Moreover, it was thought that the re-election of Kuchma in November 1999, the creation of a reformist majority in the Verkhovna Rada and the appointment of Ukraine's first reformist Prime Minister (Yushchenko) might herald a new and decisive stage in Ukraine's state- and nation-building programme. The dismissal of Prime Minister Yushchenko in April 2001, however, returned Ukraine to its traditional strategy of balancing domestic and foreign interests through gradual reform and a 'multi-vector' foreign policy. During Kuchma's second term in office Ukraine's independence was no longer threatened, as it had been in 1993–94. The 2002 elections demonstrated that the principal potential domestic threat to independence, the CPU, was no longer Ukraine's most popular political grouping, and that non-communist groups had become the main source of opposition to the executive. Support for the CPU continued to decline from 20.0% of votes in the 2002 legislative elections to 5.4% in the 2007 elections. Following the collapse of the 'orange' coalition in September 2005, relations between those elements supporting Yushchenko and those supporting Tymoshenko failed to recover until February 2007, with Tymoshenko effectively becoming the principal focus of opposition to the administration, particularly after the formation of a Government headed by Yanukovych in August 2006. Ukraine's 'orange' parties re-established their alliance in February 2007 and created a coalition following the 2007 pre-term elections that returned Tymoshenko as Prime Minister. The new governing coalition remained divided and unstable, finally dissolving in September 2008 (see above).

Besides declining support for the CPU, the growth of support for Ukrainian independence was also assisted by economic recovery and a high growth rate, although this slowed somewhat during 2005, in comparison with the previous five years. Nevertheless, the main question that remained unresolved was that of deciding what was to be built in independent Ukraine. The 2004 election had been a choice between Ukraine moving towards consolidated oligarchic authoritarianism (Yanukovych) or towards consolidated democracy (Yushchenko). Yushchenko's election brought expectations that Ukraine would experience several years of democratic reform, even if implemented hesitantly and inconsistently. However, despite the optimism associated with his election, Yushchenko had largely failed the task of undoing the preceding 13 years of corruption and stagnation under Kravchuk and Kuchma. Moreover, the changes in the constitutional balance of power between the President and Prime Minister, following reforms that took effect in 2006, did not usher in political stability. Ukraine's internal convulsions and crises since the 'orange revolution', whether under 'orange' or Yanukovych-led Governments, have distracted it from domestic reform and external integration into transatlantic structures. Relations with the West have improved, and Ukraine is closer to the EU and NATO than it was under Kuchma, but membership of both organizations still eludes it. Meanwhile, relations with Russia remain poor and are likely to continue to deteriorate as Ukraine slowly becomes aligned to the West.

Economy

Dr TARAS KUZIO

Between independence in late 1991 and the 'orange revolution' in late 2004, Ukrainian Governments can be divided into four groups. The first group—comprising the Governments led by Vitold Fokin (October 1990–September 1992), and by Prime Minister Leonid Kuchma (October 1992–September 1993)—did not succeed in establishing a coherent programme of transition from a command administration to a market economy. The second group—the Governments led by Yufym Zvyahylsky (September 1993–June 1994), Vitaliy Masol (June 1994–March 1995), Anatoliy Kinakh (May 2001–October 2002) and Viktor Yanukovych (November 2002–December 2004)—are best understood as short-term, interim administrations. Under the Constitution that was approved in 1996 and remained substantially unchanged until January 2005, the Government came under the authority of the President. By mid-2003 it had become apparent that one of the principal purposes of the Yanukovych administration, which took office as part of the consolidation of power by allies of President Kuchma several months after the 2002 legislative elections, was to provide Yanukovych with a means to launch himself as a presidential candidate, and as Kuchma's chosen successor, at the election scheduled to be held in October 2004. The third group—the Governments of Yevhen Marchuk (June 1995–May 1996), Pavlo Lazarenko (July 1996–July 1997) and Valeriy Pustovoytenko (July 1997–December 1999)—were headed by representatives of the former Soviet Ukrainian *nomenklatura*, who preferred to ensure a 'state-regulated' transition and evolutionary economic reform. In particular, it was during the period that Ukraine was governed by Lazarenko and Pustovoytenko that the country sank into deeper economic and political stagnation, accompanied by the rise of an increasingly powerful group of wealthy and frequently corrupt business executives, widely referred to in Ukraine, as in the equivalent situation in Russia, as 'oligarchs'. The fourth and final group of Governments experienced by Ukraine in its first decade of independence were those that implemented relatively radical reform—the administration that immediately followed Kuchma's election as President in 1994–95, and the Government headed by Viktor Yushchenko

in December 1999–April 2001. Since the 'orange revolution' the country has been ruled by four Governments: on the one hand, three formed of parties that supported and led the orange revolution—those headed by Yuliya Tymoshenko (February–September 2005), Yuriy Yekhanurov (September 2005–August 2006) and Tymoshenko again (December 2007–); and on the other hand, one headed, again, by Yanukovych (August 2006–September 2007). The fourth Government since the 'orange revolution' began under Tymoshenko in December 2007, supported by a fragile 'orange' coalition. Both Tymoshenko Governments have been beset by continual disputes and antagonism between the Prime Minister and the President. This led to a short eight-month Government in 2005, and again resulted in the dissolution of the ruling coalition in September 2008 (see History).

ECONOMIC UNCERTAINTY UNDER THE FOKIN GOVERNMENT (1990–92)

Throughout the first year of Ukrainian independence the Government continued to be largely staffed by personnel from the Soviet era, and retained the same institutional structure. Prime Minister Fokin came to office while the USSR was intact, in October 1990, amid a crumbling economy and in the aftermath of widespread student protests and demands for greater national sovereignty, all of which had combined to bring down the Government of Vitaliy Masol. Committees on prices and production abounded, and the Ministry of Finance lacked the central importance that an equivalent ministry would have had in a market economy. There was, as yet, no procedure for establishing a centralized budget and no possibility of the Ministry disciplining either the spending of other departments or the populist parliament that had been elected in March 1990. The newly created National Bank of Ukraine did not, as yet, possess the classic levers of monetary control, such as a system of credit control and fiscal discipline.

A major factor propelling Ukraine to independence in 1990–91 was the view that the republic would benefit economically outside the USSR. When nationalists listed Ukraine's potential economic strengths at the time of independence, they tended to enumerate raw materials and Ukraine's historical role as the 'breadbasket of Europe'. This ignored the fact that most of Ukraine's productive capacity dated from the period of reconstruction after the Second World War (1939–45), and that its human and capital resources had no experience of competing in world markets. In addition, Ukraine's economy was a heavy and inefficient consumer of cheap Russian energy. When Russia increased energy prices to world levels in 1992–93, Ukraine's economy was severely affected, worsening a slump that had already begun throughout the USSR in the late 1980s.

The limited reforms initiated in 1990–91 by the Fokin Government were primarily crisis measures designed to secure Ukrainian control over the newly independent country's economy, rather than to introduce a market economy, following the slump in the Soviet economy after 1989. Prior to independence, as much as 95% of economic activity in Ukraine had been controlled by the central Soviet authorities in Moscow, the Soviet and Russian capital. The most important feature of the 'Fokin plan' approved by the Ukrainian Verkhovna Rada (Supreme Council, parliament) in late 1990 was the introduction of a protectionist system of the payment of Ukrainian salaries with coupons. These then had to be used for the purchase of those consumer goods deemed to be vulnerable to purchase by foreign (primarily Russian) consumers.

In June 1991 the Ukrainian parliament adopted a series of resolutions that established a National Bank, which was to introduce a national currency; claimed control over all Union enterprises on Ukrainian territory; and asserted the sole right of the republican Government to levy taxes within Ukraine. However, such declarations were not given practical effect until after the declaration of independence on 24 August 1991. The Verkhovna Rada had, rather optimistically in the context of Ukraine's international isolation, approved a 'Law Concerning Foreign Economic Activity' in April 1991 and a 'Law Concerning (Foreign) Investment Activity' in September, but, unsurprisingly, no deluge of foreign investment ensued. In January 1992 a presidential decree established UkrExIm-Bank—State Export-Import Bank of Ukraine—thus gaining control of the foreign-currency earnings that hitherto went to Russian institutions. (However, draconian rates of taxation in both Ukraine and Russia meant that most former Soviet enterprises preferred to keep their earnings outside either country or in the large 'shadow' or unofficial economies.)

In February 1992 a 'Law on the Limitation of Monopoly and the Promotion of Competition' provided another key prerequisite to the implementation of a free-market economy, although it worked through the limitation of profit margins. A presidential decree issued in January of that year limited the maximum profit margin permitted to most companies to only 25%–40%. Finally, in early 1992 a number of privatization laws were approved, for the most part authored by Volodymyr Lanovyi, then Minister for Privatization and Economic Reform, who was promoted in March 1992 to Deputy Prime Minister. Lanovyi argued that the Ukrainian economy was too weak, and still too interdependent with the other economies of the former USSR, for any rapid establishment of greater economic autonomy to be feasible. In contrast to the economic nationalists (who drew their strength from 'sovereign communists', such as President Leonid Kravchuk, and national-democratic parties, such as the Ukrainian People's Movement for Restructuring—Rukh), Lanovyi argued that a strong national economy would be best built by the reform of basic economic relations, so as to create domestically generated wealth.

On 10 January 1992, following the liberalization of prices eight days earlier in Russia, Ukraine introduced a system of reusable coupons (kupony), to operate as a makeshift currency in tandem with the former Soviet currency. Above all, the introduction of the kupon should be understood in the context of Ukraine's long-standing desire to introduce its own convertible currency, to be known as the hryvnya (which was introduced in 1996). Ukraine regarded the establishment of its own national currency as one of the necessary attributes of state-building. However, Ukraine would only be ready to introduce its own currency once it had gained control of

purchasing power and the budgetary deficit, had limited the supply of credits to enterprises, and had implemented structural changes so as to permit the establishment and growth of a market economy. These factors were not in evidence until September 1996 when the hryvnya was successfully introduced by National Bank Chairman Viktor Yushchenko.

The state budgetary process also remained chaotic. The former Soviet political system had given way to institutional pluralism and a consequent lack of discipline in the process of budget formation and finance. The Verkhovna Rada, in particular, was prone to voting for expenditure first and then considering how to fund it at a later date. Moreover, Minister of Defence Konstyantin Morozov stated that, during the first year of Ukrainian independence, no military budget had been set. As late as 2003, the Ministry of Defence had never undertaken an inventory of assets, particularly those inherited from the former USSR. Although a National Bank existed, the Ukrainian authorities had failed to create an institutional power-base capable of pushing for wholesale reform of the monetary system and acting as a future guardian of a sound currency. The Ministry of Finance had a staff of only 400; there was no tradition of economic forecasting (without which setting and implementing a realistic budget is impossible), and skilled economists were few and far between.

In early 1992 the Verkhovna Rada passed three key laws (one each on the privatization of large and small enterprises, and a 'Law on Privatization Vouchers'). None the less, mass privatization did not begin in Ukraine until almost three years later, in January 1995, after Kuchma's election as President in July 1994. According to the laws approved in 1992, the sale of all Ukrainian enterprises was to begin in the second half of that year, with certain notable exceptions: those that were 'the property of organs of state power'; those that were of national historical or cultural importance; educational and scientific institutions financed from the state budget; those involved in the preparation and manufacture of narcotics, arms, explosives and radioactive substances; nuclear power stations; and other items of state property necessary for the carrying out of state functions. The 'Law On Privatization Vouchers' envisaged that they could be index-linked, if inflation threatened to destroy their value, but could not be exchanged or sold between private citizens.

Ukraine had not adopted the ambitious privatization drive that Russia had adopted earlier, and there was little evidence that President Kravchuk regarded it as a national priority. At the same time, individual directors, the former *nomenklatura*, regional governors and various government bureaucrats had begun quietly to take over state enterprises semi-legally, often transforming them into leased companies. This procedure became known, by a pun on the word 'privatization' and the Ukrainian word for 'to grab', as *prykhvatyzatsiya* ('grabatization').

Kravchuk's relations with the reformer Lanovyi were always poor. Kravchuk was ideologically closer to Oleksandr Yemelianov, head of the economic section of the advisory State Duma (State Council) and a former member of the Ukrainian State Planning Agency (Gosplan/Derzhplan). As former 'sovereign communists', their enthusiasm for market reform was only tactical, finding it easier to make common cause with the nationalist opposition (Rukh) than with the liberal reformers in the New Ukraine political bloc, as they shared the formers desire to give priority to state-building measures. Consequently, the rival economic programme presented by Yemelianov to a closed session of parliament in late March 1992 differed from Lanovyi's by envisaging a rapid departure from the rouble zone, and by advocating protectionist and retaliatory measures against Russia, in response to measures introduced by Russian Prime Minister Yegor Gaidar in January, including price liberalization and measures towards charging world prices for Russian goods. The main aim of the programme was once again to finalize Ukrainian control over the nation's economy, rather than to establish a market economy. On the basis of radical reformer Lanovyi's alternative economic-reform programme, however, Ukraine was admitted to the IMF in March. Lanovyi's dismissal in July reflected Kravchuk's dislike for market economic reform.

The Kravchuk-Yemelianov plan was a dismal failure, leading the economy into further, accentuated, decline. At the end of September 1992 Kravchuk announced Ukraine's withdrawal from the rouble zone. He also outlined plans for the development of market relations, acceleration of privatization and de-monopolization, strengthening economic independence, and liberalization of foreign economic activities, at the same time as enhancing state control over the economy. Kravchuk's economic policies proved to be confused and contradictory.

'HYPERINFLATION' UNDER PRIME MINISTER KUCHMA (1992–93)

Although the Kuchma Government, which took office in October 1992, was initially welcomed as a more reformist alternative to the Fokin administration, analysis of Kuchma's 11 months in office will show that he had little clear vision at that time of what he wanted to accomplish. At different times during his tenure as Prime Minister, Kuchma advocated 'shock therapy', along the lines of that adopted in Poland, and at other times the 'Chinese model' of economic reform. Of the two, President Kravchuk undoubtedly favoured something closer to the latter—a state-directed transition to a social-market economy that would preserve social stability and introduce reforms without the authorities losing control over the transition.

The Kuchma Government failed to launch privatization, which would have to wait until he became President one year later. During 1993 gross domestic product (GDP) was 86.3% of its 1992 level, and average monthly wages steadily declined. Inflationary pressures increased, leading to hyperinflation in September–December, at an average monthly rate of 175%. The Government was plagued by a lack of consensus on reform, and by late 1993 was wholly dominated by representatives of the so-called 'red directors' (former members of the communist élite, in particular managers of industrial enterprises, who continued to support an interventionist role for the state in economic affairs), who were primarily interested in 'grabatization'. The resignation of Deputy Prime Minister Viktor Pynzenyk, the last proponent of economic reform within the Government, in August 1993 strengthened the hand of those demanding economic union with Russia as a means of avoiding the need to implement economic reforms. After Kuchma's resignation as Prime Minister, in September, he was elected to the posts of Chairman of the Union of Industrialists and Entrepreneurs of Ukraine (UIEU) and co-Chairman of the Inter-Regional Bloc of Reforms (MRBR), a newly established social democratic/liberal electoral bloc based in the predominantly Russian-speaking and industrialized eastern and southern regions of Ukraine. Kuchma became the presidential candidate of these two organizations (UIEU and MRBR) in the 1994 elections. Lanovyi and Pynzenyk maintained close relations with Yushchenko and have continued to participate in Ukrainian politics.

Although Kuchma was granted wide-ranging powers during his tenure as Prime Minister, particularly with regard to the economy, he never fully utilized them, and no radical reforms were forthcoming. Instead, the population became poorer, inflation increased to an unprecedented extent, taxes rose dramatically (including the introduction of excise taxes), enterprise indebtedness grew, and the value of the kupon karbovanets declined dramatically against the US dollar. Moreover, the Government's unbalanced foreign economic and currency policy generated a large outflow of money and capital from Ukraine to offshore areas, including Cyprus and the British Virgin Islands.

The June 1993 strikes by 400,000 miners and industrial workers, primarily in the Donetsk region of eastern Ukraine, were the first indication that the domestic stability that independent Ukraine had enjoyed was over. The strikers had also added political demands, such as local autonomy and a referendum on public confidence in the President and the Verkhovna Rada, to their economic demands. Not only had President Kravchuk lost his support in eastern Ukraine, which had ensured his victory in the December 1991 presidential election, but the strikers and local leadership also questioned his ability to manage the economy. The regional élite sought

greater power within Ukraine, after a period in which they perceived the demands of Ukrainian-speaking and more rural western Ukraine as holding undue influence over the Kravchuk leadership through his alliance with Rukh. Moreover, bitterness resulted from the fact that, during the Soviet era, Ukraine's ruling élites had traditionally been recruited from the eastern and Russian-speaking Donetsk and Dnipropetrovsk regions. Indeed, from the mid-1990s this pattern appeared to be recurring under Kuchma's presidency.

'CARETAKER' GOVERNMENTS UNDER ZVYAHYLSKY AND MASOL (1993–94)

In October 1993 Yufym Zvyahylsky, a former coal mine manager and Mayor of Donetsk, assumed the role of acting Prime Minister in a 'caretaker' Government, which remained dominated by representatives from the Donetsk region associated with the Labour Ukraine party and the UIEU. In June 1994 Zvyahylsky resigned as Ukraine's acting Prime Minister, and soon afterwards fled to Israel, seemingly in order to escape an investigation into charges of corruption issued against him. Zvyahylsky claimed credit for having stabilized the economy after the hyperinflation of 1993 and, although the financial measures that Zvyahylsky's Government had used were sharply criticized by the so-called industrial lobby, the programme of stabilization implemented in October 1994–April 1995, after the election of Kuchma as President, was to some extent dependent upon, and benefited from, the policies implemented under Zvyahylsky.

In mid-June 1994, on the eve of the presidential elections, Vitaliy Masol was confirmed as Ukraine's new Prime Minister, returning to the post that he had held for several months in 1990, before hunger strikes initiated by student protesters forced him out of office. Masol's appointment represented an unsuccessful attempt by Kravchuk to secure Kuchma's left-wing support in eastern Ukraine during the June–July 1994 presidential election. However, although he remained in office after Kravchuk had lost the presidency to Kuchma, Masol's Government served essentially as an interim administration.

In October 1994 President Kuchma announced a programme of radical economic reform, stating that private ownership was to be the catalyst for economic growth and development. As proved to be the case when a further programme of radical economic reform was supported by the Government, in 1999–2001 under Prime Minister Viktor Yushchenko, the reform programme of 1994–95 was supported by both 'national democrats' and by former 'sovereign communists'. The programme aimed rapidly to achieve stabilization in a country that had experienced a decline in living standards of 80% since 1991, and which had high levels of 'hidden' unemployment. In 1992–93 GDP declined at an average annual rate of 15.5%, and in 1994 the rate of decline accelerated further, reaching 22.9%, although in subsequent years the rate of GDP decline began to slow. Masol resigned in March 1995, following disagreements over IMF policy requirements; none the less, the initiation of Ukraine's first post-Soviet economic reform package, along with the country's decision to relinquish its nuclear weapons, resulted, in April, in the release of the first instalment of IMF funding, which, in this instance, went some way towards covering the large budgetary deficit.

'CORRECTED REFORM' UNDER MARCHUK (1995–96)

President Kuchma's task of encouraging the legislature to accept his reform programme was greatly aided by the resignation of the Masol Government, following a parliamentary vote of no confidence; thereafter, Kuchma was able to preside over a Government more sympathetic to policies of reform. Nevertheless, parliamentary opposition to the IMF conditions in the 1995 budget continued to grow, and was not confined solely to the parliamentary left who controlled the leadership positions in parliament from 1994–99. The 1995 budget envisaged a reduction in the monthly rate of inflation by 1%–2%, and measures implemented to ensure this included the abolition of agricultural and industrial credits, the introduction of a strict incomes policy and increases in utility prices to households. Moreover, subsidies to the coal industry were replaced by inter-industry transfers. In a further measure to accelerate reform and achieve fiscal stabilization, a presidential decree offered shares in restructured joint-stock companies on the Kyiv stock exchange. Up to 30% of these shares would be for sale to individual and corporate investors, the proceeds of which would finance the establishment of new voucher-auction centres, as well as a national electronic stock exchange. Ukraine also planned to reduce the budgetary deficit in 1995 by some 8%, through the issuance of bonds.

The programme of reform outlined in October 1994 by President Kuchma largely followed the prescriptions of international financial institutions, in particular the IMF. However, by early 1995 these prescriptions were not only being ignored, but were being denounced openly by the Ukrainian leadership, which now returned to the rhetoric of the Kravchuk era, announcing support for a state-regulated transition to a social-market economy. Ukraine's experiment with radical economic reform had proved to be short-lived, lasting somewhat less than one year and amounting to support for stabilization, but not subsequent structural reform. Ukraine's political leaders, most of whom had been trained in the USSR, found it difficult to allow fully free market economic reform, while many commentators observed that the process of transition had been structured to favour the political élite financially.

In his annual address to parliament on 4 April 1995, Kuchma criticized those supporting a 'blind monetarist policy'. Economic reform, he declared, should be 'state-regulated' and provide a social 'safety net'. An immediate casualty of this amendment to Ukraine's economic-reform programme was the radical reformer and former Deputy Prime Minister, responsible for Economic Reform, Pynzenyk. Kuchma initially did not include Pynzenyk in the new Government created after the June 1995 Constitutional Agreement (which preceded the adoption of the post-Soviet Constitution in July 1996). However, in October, at the time of a visit by IMF officials to Ukraine to negotiate the next instalment of lending, worth a total of US $1,500m., Pynzenyk was brought back into the Government in an apparent attempt to gain support from international financial institutions.

In June 1995 Kuchma announced a significant amendment to economic policy. Henceforth, the IMF-approved inflation target was to be replaced by a higher, 'corrected' monthly target of 4%–5%. The Government appointed in June 1995, led by Yevhen Marchuk, sought to implement a structural reorganization of the economy, to provide substantial support for domestic producers and to improve living standards and social welfare. However, as it turned out, the Government failed in all of these areas. The Government had failed to create the conditions for sustained economic progress, and targets for privatization were not met. There was, moreover, little public support for a programme of radical economic reform. It appeared, therefore, that the reforms introduced in the October 1994 programme merely reflected the post-election euphoria of an administration that sought to distance itself from its predecessors, and which sought the acceptance of international financial institutions and Western governments in return for nuclear disarmament.

Although Kuchma had announced his opposition to 'blindly copying the West's economic model', and despite the 'corrections' that had been made to the reform programme during 1995, the President continued to insist that Ukraine had not abandoned economic reform once again. The introduction of the new currency, the hryvnya (which had been printed as early as 1992, in Canada), had been long anticipated. In May 1995 the Chairman of the National Bank of Ukraine, Viktor Yushchenko, indicated that a number of factors, among them the stabilization of the karbovanets (which fluctuated against the US dollar in 1995–96, but did not decline markedly in value), a sharp decline in inflation, control of the budgetary deficit and currency emission, as well as large international credits, finally provided an opportunity to introduce the hryvnya. In August 1995 the National Bank of Ukraine announced that it was to be introduced at the beginning of September 1996, at a rate of 100,000 karbovanets to one hryvnya.

STAGNATION UNDER LAZARENKO AND PUSTOVOYTENKO (1996–99)

In reality, Ukraine would not possess a serious reform programme until Yushchenko was appointed as Prime Minister in December 1999. In particular, the resignation, in April 1997, of Pynzenyk from the position of Deputy Prime Minister, responsible for Economic Reform, for the second time, represented a serious challenge to the implementation of economic reforms. Indeed, the period of so-called 'correction' that lasted from 1995–99, rather than being a period of reform and progress, brought Ukraine close to bankruptcy and, to a much greater extent than in the preceding years, led to the creation of a corrupt class of 'oligarchs' (politically influential business executives). Critics of the Marchuk Government pointed to its perilous political balancing act between 'corrected' and 'state-led' economic reform and industrialist lobbies. Kuchma blamed the Government of Pavlo Lazarenko (July 1996–July 1997) for its poor performance, growing wage arrears and the lack of a budget for 1997 (the absence of which delayed further Western assistance), yet Governments were constitutionally answerable to the authority of the President. Meanwhile, Kuchma blamed the leftist-controlled Verkhovna Rada for failing to adopt legislation to overcome the economic crisis and support economic reforms. However, in appointing Lazarenko as Prime Minister, the President had known that he was appointing only a cautious reformer, whose governance would not instil greater momentum to the reform process. Lazarenko's three-year programme for economic recovery was supported by the left because it backed economic protectionist measures for Ukrainian industry (particularly directed against Russia) while omitting contentious issues relating to land privatization and agricultural reform. This programme, above all, reflected Lazarenko's willingness to amend his policies so as to obtain the support of the left, while doing little to dispel suspicions about his true commitment to a market economy. Lazarenko's government policies prepared the groundwork for Hromada (Community), the party he led, to align itself with the Socialist Party of Ukraine (SPU) in the 1998 elections and subsequently elected parliament.

Rumours of Lazarenko's impending dismissal surrounded the Prime Minister throughout his year-long Government. Lazarenko encountered accusations of permitting wage arrears to reach some US $2,300m. and of inhibiting expedited reform. Kuchma also complained, in his state of the nation speech, of enterprise directors who paid neither salaries nor taxes, as well as widespread corruption. However, the Lazarenko Government, and that led by Valeriy Pustovoytenko, which succeeded it from July 1997, were increasingly dominated by business executives who had little interest in radical economic reform or in the systematic implementation or introduction of anti-corruption measures. Lazarenko granted privileges to the state-controlled Russian energy grid, Unified Energy Systems, whose operations in Ukraine were led by Tymoshenko, which thus became a de facto monopoly importer of Russian gas into Ukraine.

Corruption, including that linked to Lazarenko himself, would have been impossible to undertake without the involvement of other high-ranking state officials, and, at best, a lack of acknowledgement by Kuchma. Lazarenko was permitted to leave Ukraine in February 1999, ostensibly for reasons of ill health, and eventually requested political asylum in the USA. His trial on charges of money laundering (the processing of illegally obtained funds into legitimate holdings) took place in San Francisco, California, USA, in 2003–04. In 2006 the Californian court sentenced Lazarenko to nine years' imprisonment and fined him US $10m., following his conviction on charges of extortion, fraud and money laundering. Lazarenko, along with two other senior Ukrainian officials convicted in Germany, are the only senior Ukrainian officials who have been charged for abuse of their office in the 1990s.

The appointment of Pustovoytenko as Prime Minister in 1997 signalled an end to political rivalry between the Prime Minister and the President, although the economy continued to stagnate, and corruption became increasingly prevalent. Pustovoytenko headed the pro-presidential People's Democratic Party of Ukraine, Kuchma's 'party of power' in the

March 1998 parliamentary elections. Reforms also proved difficult to implement following the election of Oleksandr Tkachenko, of the radical-leftist Peasants' Party, as parliamentary Chairman in July 1998, a position he retained until his removal from office in January 2000.

In May 1998 the Pustovoytenko Government outlined a new economic programme for 1999–2005, which took into account the successes of the 1994 IMF-approved programme. The new programme envisaged a reduction in the budgetary deficit and increased subsidies to industry. However, the initial implementation of the programme failed to stimulate economic growth, although the annual rate of decline in GDP decreased markedly, and was just 0.2% in 1999. In 1998–99 privatization primarily benefited oligarchs, rather than the Ukrainian economy. In particular, Viktor Pinchuk—Kuchma's son-in-law—had become the leading steel magnate of Ukraine, owning five major steelworks as part of his company, Interpipe. Meanwhile, Hryhoriy Surkis and Viktor Medvedchuk, the leader of the Social Democratic Party of Ukraine (United, SDPU—U), had, between them, taken control of a majority of regional electricity distribution companies. In November 1998 the Government, with the backing of Kuchma, rejected IMF prescriptions and resorted to Soviet-style economic policies, such as increasing support to industrial producers and proposing plans to curtail the independence of the National Bank. The reaction of international financial institutions and the European Union (EU) was to 'freeze' financial assistance to Ukraine, in consequence of which the financial situation of the country further deteriorated throughout 1999. When Yushchenko became Prime Minister in December 1999, following Kuchma's re-election as President for a second term the previous month, Ukraine was on the verge of bankruptcy.

REFORMER YUSHCHENKO PRESIDES OVER GROWTH (1999–2001)

Yushchenko claimed that when he was appointed as Prime Minister in December 1999 Ukraine was on the verge of default and that the new Government had inherited US $2,000m. in wage arrears. Ukraine was ranked 87th out of 90 countries on the annual corruption perception index (CPI) issued by the German-based non-governmental organization Transparency International. The Heritage Foundation's index of economic freedom in 2001 ranked Ukraine 133rd of 161 countries, and the US-based, pro-free market CATO Institute's 'Economic Freedom in the World' index also ranked Ukraine poorly. All of these findings reflected the consequences of slow and inconsistent reform that had been thus far applied in post-Soviet Ukraine during the 1990s: when Kuchma changed governments on an annual basis and Yushchenko was Chairman of the National Bank.

Yushchenko's Government, with Tymoshenko as Deputy Prime Minister in charge of energy, presided over Ukraine's only major experience in the 1990s of economic reform, with the exception of the short-lived programme of stabilization in 1994–95. The Government reduced corruption that had taken place through rent-seeking, liberalized supplies, curtailed 250 'hidden' state subsidies to favoured businessmen and, by reducing the excessive state regulation of the economy, finally created the circumstances in which the macroeconomic stabilization achieved in 1994–96 could generate positive growth, for the first time since Ukrainian independence. GDP increased by 5.9% in 2000, and by 9.1% in 2001. Barter trade, which had become widespread in many areas of the Ukrainian economy in the 1990s, was curtailed in the notoriously corrupt energy sector. It was estimated that, as a result of anti-corruption measures implemented under Yushchenko and Tymoshenko, some US $4,000m., equivalent to 13% of GDP, which otherwise would illicitly have benefited the oligarchs, was recovered by the state, most of which went to settle wage and pension arrears. A new land code, which permitted the eventual private ownership of land, was also approved by parliament in 2001, a year after the leftist leadership was replaced by centrists in what became known as the 'velvet revolution'. The reduction in taxation and state regulation helped encourage private small and medium-sized enterprises. As had earlier been the case with reformers Lanovyi and

Pynzenyk, Yushchenko was useful to Kuchma in encouraging the impression in the West that economic reform was still official policy in Ukraine. This, in turn, was persuasive in effecting the resumption of lending by international financial institutions to Ukraine in December 2000, when the IMF announced the release of funding worth up to $246m.

The major oligarchic groups based in Kyiv (Medvedchuk and Surkis's SDPU—U, and Oleksandr Volkov and Ihor Bakay's Democratic Union) and in Dnipropetrovsk (Pinchuk and Andrei Derkach's Labour Ukraine) were financially damaged by the reforms implemented by the Yushchenko Government. The alliance of centre-right reformers and oligarchic centrists that had controlled the Verkhovna Rada since early 2000 began to disintegrate after the 'Kuchmagate' crisis of November 2000 (see History), and as a result of increasing hostility on the part of the oligarchs to Yushchenko's reforms. Tymoshenko was the first pro-reform minister to be removed from office in February 2001, prior to her arrest on questionable charges of corruption stemming from her chairmanship of United Energy Systems in the mid-1990s. Following the removal of the Yushchenko Government by means of a parliamentary vote of no confidence two months later, supported primarily by communists and oligarchic centrists supportive of Kuchma, it appeared that the positive consequences of the economic reforms implemented in 2000–01 might prove to be both short-lived and limited in scope.

THE 'CARETAKER' ADMINISTRATIONS OF KINAKH AND YANUKOVYCH (2001–04)

Anatoliy Kinakh was a Kuchma loyalist who, like Pustovoytenko and Kuchma himself, had served as Chairman of the UIEU, the body Kuchma had used as a launching pad to achieve power in 1994. Kinakh's relative neutrality, unconnected as he was to any major grouping of oligarchs, facilitated Kuchma's continuation of 'divide and rule' tactics among the oligarchs, so as to prevent any one faction from dominating the economy. Kinakh's candidacy was backed by centrist oligarchs, the SPU, Communist Party of Ukraine (CPU) and independent parliamentary deputies, largely because of the fear that any viable alternative would have been far worse. Many ministers in Yushchenko's outgoing Government were, in fact, reappointed to the Kinakh Government, with the notable exception of Tymoshenko, who had become increasingly identified (particularly through her involvement with the National Salvation Forum) as an articulate leader of the anti-Kuchma opposition. Given that Kinakh effectively led a 'caretaker' Government in 2001–02, it appeared unlikely that any major economic reforms, or, conversely, any significant reversion to a more state-driven system, would be implemented under his leadership. Moreover, the appointment of further Kuchma loyalists, following legislative elections in March 2002, to significant positions in the state and legislative apparatus—notably the selection of Volodymyr Lytvyn as legislative Chairman, and of Medvedchuk as head of the presidential administration— meant that the policies of inertia and intermittent reform, and the tolerance of high-level corruption that characterized the Kuchma presidency, appeared likely to continue until the 2004 presidential election (see History).

The dismissal of Kinakh, and his replacement by the hitherto Governor of Donetsk Oblast, Viktor Yanukovych, in November 2002, appeared principally to reflect the political interests of Kuchma: there had been no other evident reason to remove the Kinakh administration from office, as it had not had sufficient time to prove its competence or, conversely, its lack thereof. The appointment of a new Government, however, did appear to result in the formation of a more coherent pro-presidential parliamentary majority, which thereby could be expected further to accentuate the policy trends that had already become evident under Kinakh. Meanwhile, the return to positive growth, recorded from 2000, also appeared set to continue in the early 2000s, despite the heightening political crisis that affected the country, with GDP growth of 4.8% being recorded in 2002, markedly less than in the two previous years. Despite the fact that GDP, industrial and agricultural production, and monetary income were all significantly less, in real terms, than had been the case in 1991, the return to growth might have served to inhibit demands, at least in the short term, for either more sustained or coherent reform or for a 'reinstallation' of Soviet-style policies. Indeed, an ambitious programme of privatization, which was intended to include eight strategic industries, such as coal-mining, was launched in 2003. Some aspects of this privatization programme were controversial as they took place on the eve of the 2004 presidential election and blocked foreign participants. In particular, the privatization of the Kryvorizhstal steel factory in 2004 was widely condemned by the opposition and by the IMF as having allegedly been managed in such a way so as to ensure its purchase by insider oligarchs Pinchuk and Rinat Akhmetov (the latter of whom was a close ally of Yanukovych). Meanwhile, by 2003 the privatization of agricultural land was estimated to have created some 6.5m. land-owning farmers, although a significant proportion of the agricultural sector still remained under state or collective ownership.

In May 2003 the Verkhovna Rada approved a uniform income-tax rate of 13% (based on a model that had apparently brought satisfactory results in Russia), to take effect from January 2004, rising to 15% in 2007, with the primary stated intention being to increase the proportion of economic activity taking place outside the parallel 'shadow' economy. (At the time that this measure was approved, income tax bands of 10%, 15%, 20%, 30% and 40% existed, with those who earned more than US $320 per month being placed in the uppermost band.)

Although the authorities sought to use Ukraine's high growth rate to win the presidential election scheduled for 31 October 2004, polls showed that voters did not believe that the overall economic situation and their living standards were improving greatly. The authorities felt frustration that their message of supporting a continuation of the existing regime because they had brought substantial economic growth was not getting through to voters. The Yanukovych Government therefore attempted to 'bribe' voters by increasing pensions, state salaries and student stipends. This was successful in encouraging the defection of pensioners from the candidate of the CPU, Petro Symonenko, to Yanukovych, even if, in the event, and after prolonged protests against electoral fraud that became known as the 'orange revolution' (see History), Yushchenko defeated Yanukovych in a re-run second round of polling on 26 December 2004.

THE YULIYA TYMOSHENKO GOVERNMENT (2005)

Following the appointment by the newly inaugurated President Yushchenko of Yuliya Tymoshenko as Prime Minister, in February 2005, the ruling coalition was divided between those who supported state intervention in the economy and those who were committed free-market liberals; this division inevitably led to clashes over economic policy. The supporters of greater state intervention in the economy were grouped around the SPU, which controlled three cabinet positions (holding responsibility for agriculture, education and internal affairs) and the State Property Fund. The Yuliya Tymoshenko bloc (YuTB) also included some supporters of state economic intervention. The supporters of free-market economics within the governing coalition were grouped around the People's Union-Our Ukraine party, which was the closest of the groups to President Yushchenko.

In an attempt to counterbalance the policies favoured by Tymoshenko, Yushchenko appointed his close ally Petro Poroshenko, a prominent oligarch and reputedly the wealthiest member of Our Ukraine, to the position of Secretary of the National Security and Defence Council. After Yushchenko's more direct intervention in Government policy in May 2005 (see below), following the Government's failed attempts to introduce price controls, and the holding of a 'mini-Davos' World Economic Forum in Kyiv in June, the Government tended to be more supportive of free-market policies. In order to ensure parliament adopted legislation required for Ukraine to be considered for membership of the World Trade Organization (WTO), Tymoshenko strongly supported Yushchenko; among members of the governing coalition, only the SPU joined with the former pro-Kuchma camp, now the opposition, in voting against WTO-required legislation, although the

legislation remained controversial, with some draft laws failing to gain legislative approval at the first attempt.

The divisions in the ruling coalition had an impact upon three sets of policies. The first area of policy affected was the degree of intervention in the market. In mid-2005 Ukraine suffered a fuel shortage, following the Government's decision to limit increases in the retail prices of fuel so as to minimize the impact on consumers of a sharp increase in the price charged to Ukraine for petroleum by its principal, Russian, suppliers. Both Yushchenko and Kinakh criticized the Government's handling of the crisis, in particular the departure from market principles. Indeed, Yushchenko reportedly suggested in a meeting with executives of Russian energy companies that Tymoshenko should tender her resignation, while the EU cited the imposition of price controls as justification for refusing to grant Ukraine the status of a market economy. Meanwhile, in an attempt to decrease the retail prices of meat and sugar and increase the availability of these products, the Tymoshenko Government attempted to increase imports and decrease custom duties. However, the Verkhovna Rada defeated each of these proposals, and, in fact, voted to decrease the quantity of sugar imports permitted into Ukraine. Prices immediately rose dramatically, as a result of which several parliamentary deputies with interests in the sugar industry benefited. Although, in this instance, it was ultimately the Verkhovna Rada that was responsible for this state of affairs, the Tymoshenko Government's interventionist policies failed to solve the problems of supply and pricing, only leading to further increases in price and decreases in supply.

The second policy area subject to dispute within the orange coalition was the extent to which the reprivatization of formerly state-owned companies that had been transferred to private ownership (often at lower prices than their market value, or in a corrupt manner) during the 1990s and early 2000s should be pursued. Whereas Tymoshenko and the head of the State Property Fund, Valentyna Semenyuk of the SPU, expressed support for investigating privatizations undertaken since 1992, with a view to future reprivatization, Yushchenko and Kinakh suggested that an absolute maximum of 30–40 privatizations should be subject to scrutiny. Moreover, while the SPU or the YuTB sought the maintenance of state controls over 'strategic' enterprises in the event that they were privatized, those close to Yushchenko supported either reprivatizing them on the basis of a new process of transparent tendering, or by asking their current owners to pay the market price. Although the Government did not, in fact, take any steps towards implementing a programme of mass reprivatization, and had, moreover, emphasized that current owners would be given the right to pay a legally determined price-differential to retain ownership of companies deemed to have been sold at below their market value, with disputes to be resolved judicially, Tymoshenko's failure to clarify the extent of the proposed reprivatization programme left her policies open to interpretation. This issue was largely dealt with in the 'mini-Davos' summit when Yushchenko and Tymoshenko agreed not to draw up a list of companies to be reprivatized. Instead, privatization problems would be dealt with by the State Property Fund and by the courts. The Kryvorizhstal steel works was taken back into state ownership, however, and was re-tendered in October 2005, when it was acquired by Mittal Steel (of the Netherlands—now ArcelorMittal) for the sum of US $4,800m., compared with the $800m. that was received when it was sold to oligarchs Akhmetov and Pinchuk in June 2004.

The third area in which there was a policy divide within the Tymoshenko administration concerned control over the National Bank and the associated ability of the authorities to increase pensions, salaries and stipends. Prior to the orange revolution this had been ensured by the appointment, in December 2002, of Serhiy Tihipko, a close ally of Kuchma, as Chairman of the Bank; Tihipko also managed Yanukovych's campaign in the first and subsequently annulled second round of presidential voting in 2004. The significant increase in pensions, salaries and stipends implemented towards the end of Yanukovych's premiership had a marked impact upon the economic performance and policy of the subsequent Tymoshenko-led Government. The doubling of pension rates in September 2004 had the effect of increasing total pension costs to some 16% of GDP, one of the highest ratios in the world. (Most Western European countries have public pension ratios equivalent to 6%–10% of GDP.)

Yushchenko's presidency could not reverse these fiscal policies without compromising its public support. The new administration was effectively obliged to abide by decisions made during the election campaign by the Yanukovych Government, so as not to risk losing support ahead of the parliamentary elections scheduled for March 2006. Indeed, Tymoshenko's Government further increased pension payments, to a monthly minimum of the equivalent of US $66. State salaries were also increased by 57%, and a new lump sum payment was introduced to encourage families to have children in an attempt to halt Ukraine's demographic crisis. Additionally, the monthly minimum wage was to be increased to reach the level of pensions with effect from September 2005. Total state revenues were set to rise to the equivalent of 40% of GDP, which would result in a budgetary deficit equivalent to 4% of GDP for 2005. This continuation of socially sensitive fiscal policies also resulted in inflation increasing in 2005. However, this could be offset by receipts to the budget growing by 26% as a result of anti-corruption measures by closing Free Economic Zones and halting the flow of contraband by improving customs controls. In the first four months of 2005, largely as a result of such measures, customs duties collected increased by 50%.

Two major economic disappointments occurred in the first year of Yushchenko's presidency. First, growth declined to only 2.6% in 2005, compared with 12.0% in 2004. Members of Tymoshenko's Government suggested that the rate of growth in 2004 had been overstated by the Yanukovych administration. There were other important factors that led to the lower GDP growth rate in 2005, including a downturn in demand for Ukraine's most important export, steel, and a drop in world steel prices, creating unfavourable external conditions and sluggish investment activity, despite high levels of domestic consumption. Metals, energy and chemicals account for two-thirds of Ukrainian exports, and these industries, being energy intensive, are sensitive to increases in energy and transportation costs. However, one important aspect of the Ukrainian economy that did change as a result of the orange revolution was that important industrial sectors were no longer 'managed' and assisted by 'insider' government forces.

Second, while more optimistic about Ukraine than had been the case prior to the orange revolution, potential and actual foreign investors remained cautious. Between 1991–2004 Ukraine attracted only US $8,353m. of foreign investment, equivalent to 14% of GDP in 2004. Despite acrimonious debate between the Yushchenko and Tymoshenko camps over possible reprivatizations; this debate, when placed alongside the uncertain nature of property rights in Ukraine, made some foreign investors wary. None the less, retail trade increased by 23% in 2005. Moreover, at $7,300m., foreign direct investment (FDI) was the highest in any year since Ukraine achieved independence. Ukraine's foreign investment in 2005 totalled nearly the entire amount it had received in 1992–2004. Of this total amount, $4,800m. was accounted for by the successful reprivatization of Kryvorizhstal and $1,000m. by the purchase of Aval Bank, one of the largest banks in the country, by Raiffeisen International Bank AG of Austria (which renamed it Raiffeisenbank Aval).

The Governments of Tymoshenko and Yekhanurov (the latter taking office following Tymoshenko's dismissal in September 2005) were the first in Ukraine to implement measures that could realistically result in Ukraine being granted membership of the WTO in 2007 or 2008. As such, both administrations can take credit for the EU and the USA granting Ukraine the status of a market economy, in December 2005 and February 2006, respectively. By spring 2007 all the required legislation for WTO membership had been adopted by the Verkhovna Rada. A particularly significant legislative act that was adopted dealt with the protection of intellectual property rights, as Ukraine had long been a principal manufacturer of 'pirate' audio compact discs. Notably, the CPU, Yanukovych's Party of the Regions (PR) and the SDPU—U, which had been closely allied to senior members of the Kuchma administration,

opposed the law when they were in opposition to the two orange Governments in 2005-06.

A total of 26 laws would have to be eventually adopted by Ukraine in order for it to accede to WTO membership. Yushchenko and the Tymoshenko Government supported Ukraine's application for membership of the WTO because they were convinced that it would result in annual GDP growth increasing by an additional 1.9%, annual exports increasing by some US $300m. and the opening of new markets to Ukrainian goods, as well as the establishment of a free trade zone between Ukraine and the EU. Conversely, parliamentary opposition to WTO membership argued that it would lead to price rises and the collapse of Ukraine's agriculture, automobile and metallurgical industries, although there were a variety of approaches among those opposed to expedited accession to the WTO. At one extreme, the CPU opposed Ukrainian membership of the WTO under all circumstances, while the SPU supported the phased implementation of measures that would permit the country to accede to membership in the longer term; conversely, those centrists previously close to Kuchma and now in opposition supported Ukraine's eventual accession to the WTO, in tandem with that of Russia. Attempts to obtain approval of all legislation by the Verkhovna Rada in 2005 were hampered by the lack of leadership on the part of Yushchenko and by the lack of unity in the governing coalition; this was particularly evident in the SPU, nominally a part of the coalition, joining the CPU, the PR and the SDPU—U in opposing the adoption of WTO-required legislation. The USA had restored benefits for Ukraine under its Generalized System of Preferences (GSP), which had been suspended in August 2001, and also 'graduated' Ukraine from the restrictions on trade associated with the Jackson-Vanik Amendment, which had been introduced by the USA in 1975 to tie trade benefits with the right to emigrate from non-market economies.

Transparency International's 2004 CPI, drawn up in the last year of Kuchma's presidency, placed Ukraine in joint 122nd position out of 146 countries listed, with a level of perceived corruption similar to Bolivia, Guatemala, Kazakhstan, Kyrgyzstan, Niger and Sudan. Such high levels of perceived corruption (considerably higher than those found in Russia in the same year), and an unwillingness to allow foreign participation in major privatizations (such as that of Kryvorizhstal in 2004), continued to dissuade large volumes of foreign investment from entering the Ukrainian market. Besides corruption, higher foreign investment was also dissuaded by an unstable and unpredictable legal environment, over-regulation and a complicated tax system. The Yushchenko coalition that came to power in 2005 promised to deal with corruption in a tough manner. Towards this end, it placed two long-time critics of corruption under Kuchma, the SPU's Yuriy Lutsenko and the YuTB's Oleksandr Turchynov, as heads of the Ministry of Internal Affairs and the Security Service of Ukraine (SBU), respectively. However, although the perception that the Government was engaged in combating corruption proved to be extremely popular with the electorate, it was unclear how much progress had been made in that regard by September 2005, when Tymoshenko was dismissed as Prime Minister. (Moreover, Turchynov alleged that certain investigations by the SBU, into the energy sector, for example, had been closed at Yushchenko's direct instruction or that of his senior advisers, such as Oleksandr Tretyakov.) The 2005 CPI appeared to indicate the perception, at least, that corruption was becoming slightly less widespread in Ukraine: in that year the country was placed joint 107th out of 159 countries listed, with a level of perceived corruption similar to Belarus, Eritrea, Honduras, Kazakhstan, Nicaragua, the Palestinian territories, Viet Nam, Zambia and Zimbabwe. Although this continued to reflect high levels of perceived corruption, this was notably the first year, according to the index, in which Ukraine was perceived as less corrupt than Russia. Fewer business firms indicated that corruption was a problem that affected them doing business. In 2005 an anti-smuggling campaign increased the volume of customs duties collected and reduced levels of cross-border smuggling. In November 2005 a National Programme on Combating Corruption was initiated by President Yushchenko. One priority was to reduce the size of the 'shadow' economy that reportedly accounted for

50% of GDP produced in Ukraine during the Kuchma era. By 2006 Ukraine's shadow economy had declined to around 27% of GDP.

Proceeds to the state budget from the state-owned petroleum and natural gas production and distribution company Naftohaz Ukrainy increased three-fold following the appointment of a new Chairman of the Board in March 2005; an investigation into the suspected misappropriation of some US $1,200m. by the company in 2003–04 was undertaken but was never completed, while it was reported that some $1,000m. of state and private funds had been transferred out of Ukraine during the last two months of 2004, as it became increasingly apparent that Yushchenko was likely to become President. It was evident that business corruption, electoral fraud and the pragmatic, centrist politics of the pro-oligarch parties that had been so prominent from the second half of the 1990s were intimately intertwined; in 2005 more than 100 investigations had been opened into alleged fraud within the Ministry of Transport; it also emerged that the Ministry had been a principal channel of illicit funding for Yanukovych's election campaign, and the hitherto Minister of Transport, Heorhiy Kirpa, died in mysterious circumstances (officially attributed to suicide) in December 2004 shortly after the re-run of the second round of the presidential election. Ihor Bakay, the former head of the Directorate for State Affairs and a former Chief Executive Officer of Naftogaz Ukrainy, was suspected of having been involved in the theft of some $1,000m. from the state. Bakay fled to Moscow in late 2004. An investigation of state enterprises found that some $2,000m. was unaccounted for in 2004, with a significant proportion of these funds believed to have financed Yanukovych's election campaign. The difficulty of prosecuting state officials became evident after Yushchenko's election. By late 2007 no senior official had been prosecuted, with criminal charges being blocked by a combination of a prosecutor's office that was, for several months in 2005, and again from 2007, headed by a former Kuchma loyalist, Svyatoslav Piskun, a parliament that was obstructive, an interior minister that was indecisive and a President that was reluctant to take forceful action.

THE 'CARETAKER' YEKHANUROV ADMINISTRATION (2005–06)

Economic policy would change as a result of the dismissal, by President Yushchenko, of Tymoshenko's Government in September 2005, by which time it had become apparent that the tensions and differences in outlook between the different factions of the orange coalition made continued co-operation untenable. The new Government was headed by an ally of Yushchenko, Yuriy Yekhanurov, who was regarded as a technocrat. As Chairman of the State Property Fund, Yekhanurov had overseen the privatization programme implemented in the mid-1990s. Yushchenko wished to see in place a Prime Minister who would not challenge him politically and would focus exclusively on government issues (Yushchenko had political and personal conflicts with both Tymoshenko and Yanukovych). Although there was little doubt that Yekhanurov was a competent technocrat, thus fulfilling Yushchenko's requirements for Prime Minister, his lack of expertise in politics was a significant factor in the poor result achieved by Yushchenko's Our Ukraine bloc at the March 2006 parliamentary elections.

Following the September 2005 crisis, Tymoshenko, with the loyalty of 129 out of 450 parliamentary deputies, positioned herself as an opponent of Yushchenko's and Yekhanurov's more accommodating and moderate policies. The YuTB faction in the Verkhovna Rada voted against Yekhanurov's nomination as Prime Minister, against the adoption of the 2006 budget and in favour of the January 2006 vote of no confidence in the Government that had been brought in response to a new deal for the supply of natural gas from Russia (see below). The YuTB adamantly opposed the renunciation by Russia of the agreement on the supply of natural gas to Ukraine reached in 2003–04, demanding that Yushchenko defend the agreement before the Arbitration Institute of the Stockholm Chamber of Commerce in Sweden. This agreement had provided for the supply of gas to Ukraine at a rate of US $50 per 1,000 cu m and was to

remain valid until 2009. When an appendix to the 2003 contract had been signed in July 2004, it was intended that this measure would serve to reinforce Russia's support for Yanukovych in the forthcoming election, but, following his defeat by Yushchenko, Russia announced that the previously agreed terms were no longer acceptable. The new gas agreement, signed on 4 January 2006, was denounced by Tymoshenko, the CPU and the PR, who together supported a vote of no confidence in the Yekhanurov Government. Tymoshenko described the gas agreement as a 'betrayal of national interests' and pledged that she would withdraw Ukraine from the arrangements in the event of her returning to the premiership. The YuTB also remained the only Ukrainian political force that consistently opposed the presence of the non-transparent intermediary RosUkrEnergo in the supply of Central Asian gas through Russia to Ukraine, as provided for by the new agreement. RosUkrEnergo replaced another Russian-Ukrainian intermediary company, Eural Trans Gas, that had operated in 2002–04.

The Yekhanurov Government ended policies that had made its predecessor unpopular, such as demands for reprivatization. Moreover, the fact that the candidacy of Yekhanurov had been rejected by the legislature in the first instance resulted in a rapprochement between Yushchenko and Yanukovych, with the signing of a 10-point memorandum between the two leaders. One month after Yekhanurov became Prime Minister, he ended all speculation on reprivatization by calling a meeting of Ukraine's oligarchs—whom he described positively as 'Ukraine's national bourgeoisie', in an attempt to mend relations between the Government and Ukraine's most prominent businessmen. Yushchenko called a second such meeting in July 2007.

THE YANUKOVYCH GOVERNMENT (2006–07)

The political instability that was evident in Ukraine during 2006, particularly following the inconclusive legislative elections held in March, as a result of which the country effectively lacked a coherent government for several months, further delayed economic reforms and, indeed, the implementation or development of any coherent economic policies. The economic policies that the Yanukovych-led so-called 'anti-crisis coalition' (ACC) administration that took office in August would favour remained unclear, as the administration (which itself was demonstrating instability within several weeks of being appointed) contained representatives of a wide array of political forces, including, notably, for the first time in independent Ukraine, the CPU. Although the PR dominated the ACC by virtue of its size, it had to take into account the demands of its two left allies to preserve its hold on power. The ACC therefore lacked ideological unity, and its three forces were brought together more out of opposition to the orange camp. A document, the Universal of National Unity, was signed by the three members of the anti-crisis coalition (PR, SPU and CPU) and Our Ukraine in August 2006, following a round-table meeting initiated by the President. The YuTB did not participate. The Universal included several policies concerning economic affairs, including provision for the state protection of property rights, the development of business and creation of a middle class, the promotion of competition in the provision of utility services, and the maintenance of economic growth at an annual rate of at least 5%. Our Ukraine subsequently refused to join the anti-crisis coalition, following the appointment of Yanukovych as their candidate for Prime Minister and the inclusion of the CPU. Continuing disputes between anti-crisis coalition members eventually led to the inception of rival, 'orange' and 'grand' coalitions, neither of which reached fruition. In October 2006 Our Ukraine refused to join the anti-crisis coalition and the economic agenda of the Universal of National Unity was unable to progress. Later, in February 2007, Our Ukraine signed an agreement of co-operation with the YuTB (see history). After Our Ukraine went into opposition, relations between the President and the Prime Minister continued to deteriorate culminating in the April–May 2007 constitutional crisis when Yushchenko disbanded parliament and called early elections (see History).

The performance of the Ukrainian economy was not adversely affected by the political turmoil that afflicted Ukraine during much of 2006–07. Economic growth for 2006 was estimated at a robust 7%, while average prices of shares listed on the Ukrainian stock market rose by 32%, making it one of the best performing markets in the world.

The ACC administration had three fault lines. First, the left-wing caucus controlled five key ministries. The SPU controlled the Transport and Communications, Interior, Science and Education Ministries, and the CPU controlled the Agriculture and Industrial Policy ministries. Although not a cabinet position, the SPU also controlled the State Property Fund. Second, while in office, Kuchma had ensured that no centrist party realized complete control of the Government apparatus. The PR, the only party affiliated with Kuchma and his policies that received a substantial share of votes at the 2006 election, is dominated by business interests associated with the eastern Donetsk region, and it was widely perceived that the party favoured these regional interests, and business interests, above those of Ukraine, or its population more broadly. In December 2006 a Council on Investors (CI) was created, attached to the Yanukovych Government, replacing the Council on Entrepreneurs (CE) that had existed for a decade. The CE had supported the small and medium-sized businesses, while the CI was primarily interested in promoting the interests of oligarchs and big businesses. Third, the ACC purged pro-orange ministers from government positions by bringing back discredited senior level members of the Kuchma regime who were assigned roles within the PR. The ACC adopted legislation, such as the law on the Cabinet of Ministers, that usurped the President's powers under the revised 2006 Constitution. Ideological amorphousness made the Yanukovych-led Government adopt populist policies and lack any overall strategy, and no formal programme was adopted publicly.

Although each of the three constituent parties that went on to form the ACC had supported the motion of no confidence in January 2006 in protest at the amendments made to the gas deal with Russia, once the coalition had been formed, it still agreed to uphold the terms of the deal as well as use of the firm RosUkrEnergo.

The question of the renationalization (and subsequent reprivatization) of industries deemed to have been sold on disputed terms under the Kuchma regime divided the orange coalition in 2005 with Yushchenko and Our Ukraine opposed and the YuTB in favour of limited reprivatization. The subsequent ACC administration ruled out a policy of reprivatization in favour of 'peace agreements' between the Government and the oligarchs. The proposed privatization of the telecommunications company Ukrtelekom, the Odesa Port fertilizer producer, and 12 electricity distribution firms was expected to yield US $2,100m. of revenue in 2007, compared to $55m. received from privatizations in 2006. However, reports indicated that this sum was not attained.

Article three of the 2007 state budget (adopted in December 2006) stipulated that firms operating with a state-ownership stake of more than 50%—including joint ventures and those subject to Joint Activity Agreements (JAA)—must sell their monthly output to a holding company to be later specified by the Government. In January 2007 Naftogas Ukrainy was granted distribution rights to this output; this company was also granted monopoly rights to the purchase and resale of gas from Ukraine's JAAs.

This policy was designed to control the price of gas for the population on a larger scale than had been achieved via the temporary restrictions on oil price increases introduced in 2005. The difference between the historic selling price of gas in Ukraine to industrial-end users at market prices of US $4.88 per 1,000 cu m and the fixed government price of US $1.63 is over 300%. The capped price did not cover the costs of exploration, development and production and led to lower production and investment. Consequently, many Western companies opted to halt all sales of gas.

Price capping also reduced the incentive for foreign investors to come to Ukraine at a time when only 28% of Ukraine's gas demand was met by domestic production. Furthermore, the capping of gas prices by the Government directly contradicted several items of Ukrainian legislation. Government policies were making it difficult for Western energy companies to enter the Ukrainian market. Substantial foreign investment could potentially diversify Ukraine's energy sector, thereby reducing the country's dependency on Russian gas imports. However, observers noted that a proportion of the political and business community wished to maintain the existing arrangements, as they were receiving large rents from the existing energy relationship with Russia. Corruption in the energy sector therefore overrides Ukraine's national interest and the country's national security. The main problem is the continued control of natural resources by oligarchic groups hostile to Western investors, with the two groups that benefit from these arrangements being RosUkrEnergo and local oligarchs. Consequently, foreign investors are deterred from involvement in the Ukrainian market.

Energy price capping and bans on grain exports appeared to contradict the wider economic objectives of the Yanukovych Government, which included accession to the WTO and the EU (with whom the Government wished to establish a free trade zone). The price control mechanism also threatened to discredit the Government's interest in attracting foreign investment as well as its desire for energy security and independence. Indeed, these regulative measures were widely perceived to form part of a populist agenda, to even a greater extent than that evident in the actions of the Tymoshenko Government in 2005.

According to official figures, Ukraine lost around US $12,900m. in capital outflows during 2004–06, although this was considered to be an underestimate by some outside sources. In addition, per head annual incomes remain low at $2,345, although real per head disposable incomes might be considerably higher if adjusted to include wages derived from the shadow economy. Indeed, real household disposable incomes grew by nearly 20% in 2006, which facilitated an increase in consumption.

TYMOSHENKO'S RETURN TO GOVERNMENT
(2007–08)

Despite an ongoing political crisis during the period of the second Tymoshenko Government, the country's economic growth continued unabated, while FDI has also continued to flow in relatively large amounts. Three main factors could change these positive economic trends: first, high inflation, approaching an annual rate of 30%, caused by a variety of factors; second, continuing increases in energy prices; and third, a world-wide downturn in economic activity that could lead to slower growth. The Government was prevented from adopting necessary legislation in the legislature by the PR (the revised and final 2008 budget was not approved until the middle of the year) and by a President who has attempted to undermine the Government personally, through the presidential secretariat or the National Security and Defence Council.

The Tymoshenko Government has focused on transparency, privatization and attracting FDI. In January 2008 she held a meeting with 250 foreign investors that featured presentations by government ministers followed by responses from the European Business Association and the European Bank for Reconstruction and Development (which held its annual meeting in Kyiv in May 2008). The meeting followed the publication, by the YuTB in September 2007, of a 'Contract with Investors', which outlined the platform of the bloc (then in opposition) to encourage domestic and foreign direct investment. In Kyiv and in Brussels, Belgium, Tymoshenko outlined a programme known as the 'Tymoshenko Transparency Initiative' and other procedures intended to improve Ukraine's struggle against corruption. She offered to co-operate with the EU on European energy security. The 'Contract with Investors' outlined key areas of emphasis for a future Tymoshenko government: policy reforms to improve the legal framework for foreign investors; the implementation of fiscal and administrative policies that would support foreign and domestic investment; creation of a comprehensive energy programme; a transparent privatization programme; and the advancement of trade opportunities through the Deep Free Trade Agreement with the EU and following Ukrainian membership of the WTO, which took effect later in 2008.

Economic growth continued to be high in the first part of 2008 but would undoubtedly be affected by world-wide trends later in the year. Annual real GDP growth since 2000 has averaged over 7%, making Ukraine one of the best performing transition countries, with 2005 the only year in which growth of less than 3% was recorded. A consumer boom fuelled Ukraine's high economic growth, with car purchases growing by 40%–50% per annum, expansion in the sectors of tourism and construction, and very substantial increases in property prices, particularly in Kyiv. The increasing availability, in the mid-2000s, of easy credit at low interest rates has helped to fuel this boom, as has high social spending since each government since the 'orange revolution' outbid its predecessor in social populism. However, real GDP growth and a massive increase in purchasing power have also made Ukraine's economy grow at record rates. Real wages have increased at 30%–50% per annum, which, while adding to the consumer boom, has also contributed to rapid inflation. Average salaries in Kyiv of US $600 per month were close to those in the capital cities of some Central-Eastern European countries within the EU. With Ukraine's shadow economy still flourishing, real disposable income remained higher than the average salary figures.

Inflation continued to be a major source of concern and, based on trends in early 2008, might rise to 30% per annum, although the Tymoshenko Government anticipated that the year-end rate of inflation would be around one-half that level. High inflation has been fuelled by the most heavily criticized government policy, that of repaying Soviet-era bank savings either confiscated by Russia after the collapse of the USSR or lost in the subsequent ensuing hyperinflation. The first tranche of the repayments was made in January 2008, a pledge that the YuTB fulfilled from its 2007 election programme. Other sources of inflation include growing energy prices, high food prices, and an exchange rate that pegged the hryvyna too high against the US dollar. Permitting the hryvyna to float rather than floating it within a controlled corridor would reduce the level of inflation imported into Ukraine from an overvalued dollar. Both Yanukovych Governments (of 2002–04 and 2006–07) recorded the highest inflation rates of that period. In 2004 and 2007 the annual rates of inflation were 12.3% and 16.6%, respectively. In comparison, the inflation rates under the first two orange Governments in 2005 (Tymoshenko) and 2006 (Yekhanurov) were 10.3% and 11.6%, respectively. Both Yanukovych Governments supported widespread price controls in the energy sector and grain export quotas. The energy price controls damaged foreign investors and forced some Western companies to withdraw from the Ukrainian market.

In 2005 Western and domestic observers criticized Prime Minister Tymoshenko's stated support for reprivatization (that is, the taking back into state control companies that had been privatized at below their market worth during the Kuchma era, prior to transferring them to new private owners) over privatization, notwithstanding the Government's facilitation of what was effectively Ukraine's first transparent privatization (itself a reprivatization), that of Ukraine's largest steel plant, Kryvorizhstal, to the Netherlands-based Mittal Steel, which brought in US $4,800m. to the budget. When initially privatized in July 2004, foreign interests were blocked from competing and Kryvorizhstal was sold to two Ukrainian oligarchs allied to President Kuchma for $800m. The second Tymoshenko Government announced an ambitious programme of privatization but its implementation was thwarted by dissent between the 'orange' coalition parties. In 2008 the Government planned to privatize 400 assets in 2008, with a portion of the anticipated proceeds of 8,600m. hryvnyas to go to cover the repayment of Soviet-era bank savings. However, President Yushchenko blocked the privatization programme, using national security arguments as outlined in a March decree that defined the energy, military-industrial complex, transportation and residential services as 'strategic' sectors and unavailable for privatization. In July Yushchenko issued a decree halting privatization of the Port of Odesa, despite having previously agreed to its proposed privatization as part of a programme drawn up by the 2007 Yanukovych Government. Corruption in the State Property Fund was being protected by senior officials, who felt threatened by the change

in the leadership of the Fund demanded by the Tymoshenko Government, while President Yushchenko's obstruction of elements of the privatization programme formed part of an overall strategy of undermining the Government and thereby providing a pretext for replacing the 'orange' coalition with a 'grand coalition' led by a technocratic Prime Minister. Furthermore, Yushchenko was aware of the popularity of the Government's plan to repay Soviet bank savings and viewed this as an effort to increase Tymoshenko's popularity prior to the presidential election scheduled to be held in January 2010 in which she was expected to be a candidate.

Trade turnover between the EU and Ukraine amounts to more than US $40,000m. annually, making it Ukraine's largest trading partner. However, in 2007 Russia remained Ukraine's largest market for exports (25.7%) and source of imports (27.8%), with the latter heavily dominated by energy. The price paid by Ukraine for Russian gas increased from $50 per 1,000 cu m in 2004 to $180 in 2008. Russia's threat to double the price in 2009 was unlikely to be realized, although Ukraine was expected to move to world prices. Russia still relies on Ukrainian pipelines to export 80% of its gas, so that any price increase could be partly offset by increased transit charges and increased storage charges of Russian gas designated for Europe, which are stored in western Ukraine. Ukraine's accession to the WTO in May 2008 meant that it could block Russia's entry to the Organization in the event that it used energy for political purposes. A comprehensive Barrier to Investment survey was to be incorporated into the Ukrainian Government's programmes, with an Action Plan to provide a timetable for implementation. The Government established a Council of Foreign and Domestic Advisers, consisting of businessmen, policy makers, and consultants, to work on improving Ukraine's investment climate. The Government cancelled a major foreign investment contract with the Texas (USA)-based Vanco in May 2008, a move that was heavily censured by the President because of the negative signal it conveyed to foreign investors. Vanco signed a contract in October 2007 with the outgoing Yanukovych Government to explore Ukraine's Black Sea shelf, after geological research indicated that it was likely to hold large reserves of oil and gas. One major factor in the Tymoshenko Government's cancellation of the contract was the presence of a company owned by the PR deputy and oligarch Rinat Akhmetov as one of Vanco's four investing co-partners. The Government also pointed out that the fact that ownership of two companies (one Austrian and one Russian) involved in the deal was undisclosed meant that the contract was not transparent. While Ukraine attracted little foreign investment during the 1990s, Tymoshenko made considerable progress in that area while Prime Minister in 2005, particularly with regard to the sale of Kryvorizhstal. The largest sources of foreign direct investment are Germany (25.4%), Austria (7.9%), the United Kingdom (7.6%), the Netherlands (7.5%) and the USA (6.1%). Two offshore zones, Cyprus (14.4%) and the British Virgin Islands (3.9%), are also large foreign investors. Russia's investment amounts to only 4.8%, at seventh place, but this could be undervalued as some of the foreign investment from offshore zones could be Russian capital.

CONCLUSION

Despite political instability and a three-fold increase in gas prices since 2004, Ukraine's economy continued to grow at a respectable rate in the period to 2008. Higher rates of growth have been recorded for Ukraine than for most other countries in the region, and in Central and South-Eastern Europe. During 2000–05 GDP increased, in real terms, at an annual average rate of 7.4%. In 2006 the economy grew by 6.5%, and the World Bank estimated GDP growth of 7.6% in 2007. The burgeoning export sector was responsible for much of the growth during 2000–04, while rising consumption drove the economy during 2005–06. However, substantial investment would be required to sustain these sectors in the future. Ukraine's GDP could be set to increase following WTO membership and a free trade agreement with the EU. Ukraine's foreign investment is still low when compared to the levels recorded in many countries of Central and Eastern

Europe, but is increasing from the low base during the Kuchma era. Foreign investment in 2005 (during the Tymoshenko Government) was 10% higher than in 2004. The ratio of public debt to GDP declined from 24.8% in 2004 to less than 19% in 2005. The contribution of Ukraine's shadow economy to overall GDP also declined to approximately 27% in 2006. Rising energy prices have forced restructuring in Ukrainian industry, and firms have substi-

tuted the use of natural gas towards more efficient technology, including the use of pulverized coal that requires no inputs of gas (Ukraine has the ninth largest coal deposits in the world). None the less, Ukraine remains one of the top five world consumers of gas, and although corruption continues to impede the management of relations with its main supplier, Russia, Ukraine is better able to absorb the effects of price increases than are many other post-Soviet states.

Statistical Survey

Principal source (unless otherwise stated): State Committee for Statistics, 01023 Kyiv, vul. Sh. Rustaveli 3; tel. (44) 226-20-21; fax (44) 235-37-39; e-mail info@ukrstat.gov.ua; internet www.ukrstat.gov.ua.

Area and Population

AREA, POPULATION AND DENSITY

Area (sq km)	603,700*
Population (census results)	
12 January 1989	51,706,742
5 December 2001	
Males	22,441,344
Females	26,015,758
Total	48,457,102
Population (official estimates at 1 July)	
2006	46,756,618
2007	46,490,819
2008	46,221,981
Density (per sq km) at 1 July 2008	76.6

* 233,090 sq miles.

POPULATION BY ETHNIC GROUP
(permanent inhabitants, census of 5 December 2001)

	'000	%
Ukrainian	37,541.7	78.13
Russian	8,334.1	17.34
Belarusian	275.8	0.57
Moldovan	258.6	0.54
Crimean Tatar	248.2	0.52
Others	1,393.9	2.90
Total	**48,052.3**	**100.00**

ADMINISTRATIVE DIVISIONS

	Area ('000 sq km)	Population (at 1 July 2008)*	Density (per sq km)
Regions			
Cherkasy	20.9	1,309,825	62.7
Chernihiv	31.9	1,128,277	35.4
Chernivtsi	8.1	903,431	11.2
Dnipropetrovsk	31.9	3,383,816	106.1
Donetsk	26.5	4,516,627	170.4
Ivano-Frankivsk	13.9	1,381,265	99.4
Kharkiv	31.4	2,784,042	88.7
Kherson	28.5	1,102,991	38.7
Khmelnytsky	20.6	1,345,454	65.3
Kirovohrad	24.6	1,033,289	42.0
Kyiv	28.1	1,732,082	61.6
Luhansk	26.7	2,342,720	87.7
Lviv	21.8	2,553,567	117.1
Mykolayiv	24.6	1,198,776	48.7
Odesa	33.3	2,391,190	71.8
Poltava	28.8	1,517,797	52.7
Rivne	20.1	1,150,790	57.3
Sumy	23.8	1,190,002	50.0
Ternopil	13.8	1,095,612	79.4
Transcarpathia	12.8	1,241,939	97.0
Vinnytsia	26.5	1,665,179	62.8
Volyn	20.2	1,035,935	51.3
Zaporizhzhya	27.2	1,825,744	67.1
Zhytomyr	29.9	1,299,401	43.5

—*continued*	Area ('000 sq km)	Population (at 1 July 2008)*	Density (per sq km)
Cities			
Kyiv	0.8	2,745,006	3,431.3
Sevastopol	0.9	379,379	421.5
Autonomous Republic			
Crimea	26.1	1,967,845	75.4
Total	603.7	46,221,981	76.6

* Official estimates.

PRINCIPAL TOWNS
(population at census of 5 December 2001, rounded figures)

Kyiv (Kiev, capital)	2,611,000	Poltava	318,000
Kharkiv	1,470,000	Chernihiv	305,000
Dnipropetrovsk	1,065,000	Cherkasy	295,000
Odesa	1,029,000	Sumy	293,000
Donetsk	1,016,000	Horlivka	292,000
Zaporizhzhya	815,000	Zhytomyr	284,000
Lviv	733,000	Dniprodzerzhynsk	256,000
Kryvyi Rih	669,000	Khmelnytsky	254,000
Mykolayiv	514,000	Kirovohrad	254,000
Mariupol*	492,000	Rivne	249,000
Luhansk†	463,000	Chernivtsi	241,000
Makiyivka	390,000	Kremenchuk	234,000
Vinnytsia	357,000	Ternopil	228,000
Simferopol	344,000	Ivano-Frankivsk	218,000
Sevastopol	342,000	Lutsk	209,000
Kherson	328,000	Bila Tserkva	200,000

* Known as Zhdanov from 1948 to 1989.
† Known as Voroshylovhrad from 1935 to 1958 and from 1970 to 1989.

BIRTHS, MARRIAGES AND DEATHS*

	Registered live births		Registered marriages		Registered deaths	
	Number	Rate (per 1,000)	Number	Rate (per 1,000)	Number	Rate (per 1,000)
2000	385,126	7.8	274,523	5.5	758,082	15.3
2001	376,479	7.8	309,602	6.4	745,953	15.4
2002	390,687	8.1	317,228	6.6	754,911	15.7
2003	408,591	8.5	370,966	7.8	765,408	16.0
2004	427,259	9.0	278,230	5.9	761,263	16.0
2005	426,085	9.0	332,138	7.1	781,964	16.6
2006	460,368	9.8	354,959	7.6	758,093	16.2
2007	472,657	10.2	416,427	9.0	762,877	16.4

* Rates for 1997–2000 are based on unrevised population estimates.

Expectation of life (years at birth, WHO estimates): 67.2 (males 61.5; females 73.1) in 2006 (Source: WHO, *World Health Statistics*).

IMMIGRATION AND EMIGRATION

	2005	2006	2007
Immigrants	39,580	44,227	46,507
Emigrants	34,997	29,982	29,669

ECONOMICALLY ACTIVE POPULATION
(annual averages, '000 persons aged 15–70 years)

	2004	2005	2006
Agriculture, hunting, forestry and fishing	3,998.3	4,005.5	3,649.1
Mining and quarrying; manufacturing; electricity, gas and water supply	4,077.1	4,072.4	4,036.9
Construction	907.5	941.5	987.1
Wholesale and retail trade; repair of motor vehicles, motorcycles and personal and household goods; hotels and restaurants	3,971.2	4,175.2	4,406.9
Transport, storage and communications	1,374.9	1,400.5	1,428.8
Financial intermediation	216.1	247.9	286.0
Real estate, renting and business activities	919.9	966.6	1,041.9
Public administration and defence; compulsory social security	1,050.2	1,028.9	1,033.7
Education	1,648.7	1,668.2	1,690.5
Health and social work	1,348.9	1,356.6	1,356.7
Other community, social and personal service activities; private households with employed persons; extra-territorial organizations and bodies	782.9	816.7	812.8
Total employed	20,295.7	20,680.0	20,730.4
Total unemployed	1,906.7	1,600.8	1,515.0
Total labour force	22,202.4	22,280.8	22,245.4

Source: ILO.

Health and Welfare

KEY INDICATORS

Total fertility rate (children per woman, 2006)	1.2
Under-5 mortality rate (per 1,000 live births, 2006)	24
HIV/AIDS (% of persons aged 15–49, 2005)	1.4
Physicians (per 1,000 head, 2006)	3.1
Hospital beds (per 1,000 head, 2006)	8.7
Health expenditure (2005): US $ per head (PPP)	488
Health expenditure (2005): % of GDP	7.0
Health expenditure (2005): public (% of total)	52.8
Access to water (% of persons, 2004)	96
Access to sanitation (% of persons, 2004)	96
Human Development Index (2005): ranking	76
Human Development Index (2005): value	0.788

For sources and definitions, see explanatory note on p. vi.

Agriculture

PRINCIPAL CROPS
('000 metric tons)

	2004	2005	2006
Wheat	17,520.2	18,699.2	13,947.3
Barley	11,084.4	8,975.1	11,341.2
Maize	8,866.8	7,166.6	6,425.6
Rye	1,592.5	1,054.2	583.6
Oats	1,007.0	790.7	690.2
Millet	458.8	140.6	123.5
Buckwheat	293.6	274.7	229.2
Potatoes	20,754.8	19,462.4	19,467.1
Sugar beet	16,600.4	15,467.8	22,420.7
Dry peas	636.3	616.0	652.7
Sunflower seed	3,050.1	4,706.1	5,324.3
Cabbages	1,544.5	1,475.4	1,490.6
Tomatoes	1,145.7	1,471.8	1,751.0
Pumpkins, squash and gourds	1,023.2	585.4	553.8
Cucumbers and gherkins	712.5	687.9	890.4
Chillies and green peppers	128.2	131.5	145.2
Dry onions	721.7	751.1	868.7

—*continued*	2004	2005	2006
Garlic	130.7	145.6	145.6
Carrots	674.9	645.3	719.5
Watermelons	307.1	256.4	562.8
Apples	716.9	719.8	536.5
Pears	151.7	177.3	81.4
Apricots	99.3	94.2	28.0
Sweet cherries	85.3	100.2	48.9
Sour (Morello) cherries	178.5	181.8	95.6
Plums	173.3	165.9	127.1
Grapes	374.0	442.6	300.9

Aggregate production ('000 metric tons, may include official, semi-official or estimated data): Total cereals 40,997 in 2004, 37,258 in 2005, 33,511 in 2006; Total roots and tubers 20,755 in 2004, 19,462 in 2005, 19,467 in 2006; Total vegetables (incl. melons) 6,964 in 2004, 7,295 in 2005, 8,750 in 2006; Total fruits (excl. melons) 1,934 in 2004, 2,056 in 2005, 1,319 in 2006.

Source: FAO.

LIVESTOCK
('000 head at 1 January)

	2004	2005	2006
Horses	637	591	555
Cattle	7,712	6,903	6,514
Pigs	7,322	6,466	7,053
Sheep	893	875	872
Goats	893	894	758
Chickens	122,100	131,976	142,600

Source: FAO.

LIVESTOCK PRODUCTS
('000 metric tons)

	2004	2005	2006
Cattle meat	618.0	561.8	567.5
Pig meat	558.8	493.7	526.0
Chicken meat	375.5	496.6	589.1
Cows' milk	13,390.1	13,423.8	13,017.1
Sheep's milk	30.4	24.1	22.9
Goats' milk	289.0	266.5	247.0
Poultry eggs	683.7	756.3	828.4
Hen eggs	677.4	748.1	815.6
Honey	57.9	71.5	75.6

Source: FAO.

Forestry

ROUNDWOOD REMOVALS
('000 cubic metres, excl. bark)

	2004	2005	2006
Sawlogs, veneer logs and logs for sleepers	4,571	4,632	4,888
Pulpwood	954	953	1,000
Other industrial wood*	941	876	865
Fuel wood*	8,396	8,146	8,494
Total	14,862	14,606	15,247

* Unofficial figures.
Source: FAO.

SAWNWOOD PRODUCTION
('000 cubic metres, incl. railway sleepers)

	2004	2005	2006*
Coniferous (softwood)	1,670	1,743	1,581
Broadleaved (hardwood)	722	673	611
Total	2,392	2,416	2,192

* Unofficial figures.
Source: FAO.

Fishing

('000 metric tons, live weight)

	2004	2005	2006
Capture	202.7	244.9	238.7
Azov sea sprat	8.5	14.6	11.7
Southern hake	1.0	n.a.	830
Blue grenadier	6.3	n.a.	7.5
Gobies	12.4	11.7	9.9
Snoek	7.4	n.a.	9.2
Sardinellas	3.8	5.0	12.9
European pilchard (sardine) .	28.1	38.0	51.5
European sprat	30.9	35.7	21.3
European anchovy . . .	9.4	6.9	7.0
Greenback horse mackerel . .	22.6	n.a.	20.6
Other jack and horse mackerels.	3.6	0.8	4.4
Other mackerels	5.5	0.5	6.6
Antarctic krill	12.3	22.4	15.2
Wellington flying squid . .	20.1	n.a.	12.9
Aquaculture	26.2*	28.7	4.0
Common carp	14.8	16.2	0.1
Silver carp	7.0*	7.5	2.4
Total catch	229.0*	273.7	242.8

* FAO estimate.

Source: FAO.

Mining

('000 metric tons, unless otherwise indicated)

	2003	2004	2005
Hard (incl. coking) coal . .	63,866	62,100	58,000
Brown coal (incl. lignite) . . .	950*	3,000	3,000
Crude petroleum	3,975	4,179	4,269
Natural gas (million cu m) . .	19,460	19,000	19,300
Iron ore: gross weight . . .	62,497.6	65,540.0	68,569.6
Manganese ore*†	880	810	770
Ilmenite concentrate . . .	421	370	370
Rutile concentrate . . .	60	60	60
Zirconium concentrates* . .	35.0	35.0	35.0
Uranium concentrate (metric tons)†	800	800	800
Bentonite*	300	300	300
Kaolin	225	225	225
Potash salts (crude)*‡ . . .	60	50	65
Native sulphur*	142	136	135
Salt (unrefined)*	2,757	3,339	3,400
Graphite (metric tons)* . . .	7,500	7,500	7,500
Peat*	1,000	1,000	1,000

* Estimated production.

† Figures refer to the metal content of ores and concentrates.

‡ Figures refer to potassium oxide content.

Source: US Geological Survey.

Industry

SELECTED PRODUCTS

('000 metric tons, unless otherwise indicated)

	2001	2002	2003
Margarine	167	170	123
Flour	2,686	2,724	2,540
Raw sugar*	1,947	1,621	2,486
Ethyl alcohol ('000 hectolitres) .	2,643	2,840	2,546
Wine ('000 hectolitres) . . .	1,425	2,081	2,045
Beer ('000 hectolitres) . . .	13,059	15,000	17,012
Cigarettes (million)	69,731	81,088	96,776
Wool yarn: pure and mixed . .	3.7	3.5	3.0
Cotton yarn: pure and mixed . .	11.0	10.7	8.7
Flax yarn	1.3	0.8	0.2
Woven cotton fabrics (million sq metres)	46	57	27

—continued	2001	2002	2003
Woven woollen fabrics (million sq metres)	7.4	7.0	6.5
Linen fabrics (million sq metres) .	5.7	4.1	0.3
Footwear, excl. rubber ('000 pairs)	15,155	15,016	15,939
Hydrochloric acid	66.8	60.5	76.9
Sulphuric acid	1,040	935	1,131
Nitric acid	6	4	436
Phosphoric acid	30.9	18.5	31.3
Caustic soda (Sodium hydroxide) .	134	133	160
Soda ash (Sodium carbonate) . .	651	679	656
Nitrogenous fertilizers (a)†	2,153	2,311	2,473
Phosphatic fertilizers (b)† . . .	61	28	38
Potassic fertilizers (c)†	20	8	14
Rubber tyres ('000)‡	6,862	6,244	6,107
Rubber footwear ('000 pairs) . .	2,527	2,665	3,588
Clay building bricks (million) . .	1,382	1,462	1,563
Quicklime	4,367	4,456	4,962
Cement	5,786	4,456	4,962
Pig-iron	26,379	27,633	29,529
Crude steel: for castings . . .	500	872	1,514
Crude steel: ingots	33,523	34,543	37,524
Tractors (number)§	3,640	2,980	4,531
Household refrigerators ('000) .	509	583	340
Household washing machines ('000)	166	232	251
Radio receivers ('000) . . .	26	33	21
Television receivers ('000) . . .	148	159	415
Passenger motor cars ('000) . .	26	44	102
Buses and motor coaches (number)	2,474	2,102	2,655
Lorries (number)	6,747	2,343	1,265
Bicycles ('000)‖	109	245	281
Electric energy ('000 million kWh)	173	174	180

* Production from home-grown sugar beet.

† Production of fertilizers is in terms of (a) nitrogen; (b) phosphoric acid; or (c) potassium oxide.

‡ Tyres for road motor vehicles.

§ Tractors of 10 horse-power and over, excluding industrial tractors and road tractors for tractor-trailer combinations.

‖ Excluding children's bicycles.

Source: UN, *Industrial Commodity Statistics Yearbook*.

Raw sugar ('000 metric tons): 2,147 in 2004; 2,139 in 2005; 2,592 in 2006.

Sulphuric acid ('000 metric tons): 1,425 in 2004; 1,606 in 2005; 1,493 in 2006.

Caustic soda (Sodium hydroxide) ('000 metric tons): 210 in 2004; 209 in 2005; 183 in 2006.

Nitrogenous fertilizers (nitrogen content, '000 metric tons): 2,407 in 2004; 2,633 in 2005; 2,566 in 2006.

Rubber tyres ('000): 7,940 in 2004; 7,531 in 2005; 7,093 in 2006.

Cement ('000 metric tons): 10,600 in 2004; 12,200 in 2005; 13,700 in 2006.

Pig-iron ('000 metric tons): 31,000 in 2004; 30,700 in 2005; 32,900 in 2006.

Tractors (number): 5,806 in 2004; 5,543 in 2005; 3,703 in 2006.

Household refrigerators ('000): 581 in 2004; 711 in 2005; 731 in 2006.

Household washing machines ('000): 345 in 2004; 322 in 2005.

Television receivers ('000): 443 in 2004; 651 in 2005; 431 in 2006.

Passenger motor cars ('000): 174 in 2004; 192 in 2005; 267 in 2006.

Buses and motor coaches (number): 2,598 in 2004; 4,655 in 2005; 7,660 in 2006.

Electric energy ('000 million kWh): 182 in 2004; 186 in 2005; 193 in 2006.

Finance

CURRENCY AND EXCHANGE RATES

Monetary Units
100 kopiykas = 1 hryvnya.

Sterling, Dollar and Euro Equivalents (30 May 2008)
£1 sterling = 9.571 hryvnyas;
US $1 = 4.850 hryvnyas;
€1 = 7.521 hryvnyas;
100 hryvnyas = £10.45 = $20.62 = €13.30.

Average Exchange Rate (hryvnyas per US $)
2005   5.1247
2006   5.0500
2007   5.0500

Note: Following the dissolution of the USSR in December 1991, Russia and several other former Soviet republics retained the rouble (known as the karbovanets—KRB in Ukraine) as their monetary unit. In November 1992 this currency ceased to be legal tender in Ukraine, and was replaced (initially at par) by a currency coupon, also known as the karbovanets, or kupon, for a transitional period. Following the introduction of the transitional currency, Ukraine operated a system of multiple exchange rates, but in October 1994 the official and auction rates were merged. The unified exchange rate at 31 December 1995 was US $1 = 179,400 KRB. On 2 September 1996 Ukraine introduced a new currency, the hryvnya, at a rate of 100,000 KRB per hryvnya (1.750 hryvnyas per $).

GOVERNMENT FINANCE
(general government transactions, million hryvnyas)

Summary of Balances

	2004	2005	2006
Revenue	127,509	183,407	234,374
Less Expense	130,946	183,071	230,772
Net operating balance . . .	−3,437	336	3,602
Less Net acquisition of non-financial assets	8,331	6,225	9,113
Net lending/borrowing . . .	−11,768	−5,889	−5,511

Revenue

	2004	2005	2006
Taxes	63,614	98,351	126,414
Taxes on income, profits and capital gains	30,539	42,328	50,448
Taxes on goods and services .	25,444	46,592	65,713
Social contributions	40,912	55,460	70,413
Grants	428	199	163
Other revenue	22,555	29,397	37,385
Total	127,509	183,407	234,374

Expense/Outlays

Expense by economic type	2004	2005	2006
Compensation of employees . .	33,511	43,729	56,470
Use of goods and services . . .	20,627	29,667	36,874
Interest	3,147	3,462	3,702
Subsidies	8,215	10,268	17,622
Grants	218	194	140
Social benefits	53,590	85,437	102,817
Other expense	11,640	10,315	13,148
Total	130,946	183,071	230,772

Outlays by functions of government*	2004	2005	2006
General public services . . .	12,116	14,798	19,899
Defence	5,111	5,066	5,547
Public order and safety . . .	7,855	10,210	12,701
Economic affairs	21,520	20,864	27,344
Environmental protection . . .	889	890	1,541
Housing and community amenities	3,008	4,630	8,696
Health	13,313	16,805	20,954
Recreation, culture and religion .	2,802	3,586	4,501
Education	17,999	26,374	33,274
Social protection	57,205	88,891	108,645
Total	141,818	192,112	243,102

* Including net acquisition of non-financial assets.

Source: IMF, *Government Finance Statistics Yearbook*.

INTERNATIONAL RESERVES
(US $ million at 31 December)

	2005	2006	2007
Gold (national valuation) . . .	402.5	513.5	693.1
IMF special drawing rights . .	1.0	1.5	2.8
Foreign exchange	18,987.0	21,843.2	31,783.2
Total	19,390.5	22,358.2	32,479.1

Source: IMF, *International Financial Statistics*.

MONEY SUPPLY
(million hryvnyas at 31 December)

	2005	2006	2007
Currency outside banks . . .	60,231.4	74,983.6	111,118.7
Demand deposits at banks . .	38,243.0	48,110.0	70,165.8
Total money (incl. others) . .	98,572.6	123,275.6	181,665.2

Source: IMF, *International Financial Statistics*.

COST OF LIVING
(Consumer Price Index; base: previous year = 100)

	2005	2006	2007
Food and beverages	110.7	103.5	122.9
Other consumer goods	104.0	102.5	106.0
Services	115.8	149.4	112.0
All goods and services . . .	110.3	111.6	116.6

NATIONAL ACCOUNTS
(million hryvnyas at current prices)
National Income and Product

	2004	2005	2006
Compensation of employees . .	157,450	216,600	268,631
Net operating surplus and mixed income	105,924	118,230	143,771
Domestic primary incomes .	263,374	334,830	412,402
Consumption of fixed capital . .	46,576	50,545	58,265
Gross domestic product (GDP) at factor cost	309,950	385,375	470,667
Taxes on production and imports .	40,018	62,777	82,377
Less Subsidies	4,855	6,700	8,891
GDP in market prices . . .	345,113	441,452	544,153
Primary incomes received from abroad	2,040	3,822	6,684
Less Primary incomes paid abroad	5,467	8,863	15,378
Gross national income (GNI) .	341,686	436,411	535,459
Less Consumption of fixed capital .	46,576	50,545	58,265
Net national income	295,110	385,866	477,194
Current taxes and transfers from abroad	14,481	16,185	18,245
Less Current transfers paid abroad	803	1,358	1,818
Net national disposable income	308,788	400,696	493,621

Expenditure on the Gross Domestic Product

	2005	2006	2007
Final consumption expenditure .	337,879	424,906	560,618
Households	252,624	319,383	422,837
Non-profit institutions serving households	4,727	5,173	5,843
General government . . .	80,528	100,350	131,938
Gross capital formation . . .	99,876	134,740	192,101
Gross fixed capital formation .	96,965	133,874	195,179
Changes in inventories . . .	2,736	655	-3,394
Acquisitions, less disposals, of valuables	175	211	316
Total domestic expenditure .	437,755	559,646	752,719
Exports of goods and services . .	227,252	253,707	323,205
Less Imports of goods and services	223,555	269,200	362,979
GDP in market prices . . .	441,452	544,153	712,945

Gross Domestic Product by Economic Activity

	2004	2005	2006
Agriculture, hunting, forestry and fishing	37,258	40,542	41,006
Mining and quarrying	12,518	17,939	22,064
Manufacturing	64,124	86,863	109,416
Electricity, gas and water supply .	12,423	15,169	18,610
Construction	14,463	16,370	21,168
Wholesale and retail trade; repair of motor vehicles, motorcycles and personal goods	41,057	56,041	68,573
Transport, storage and communication	42,694	47,435	56,053
Education	16,252	20,882	26,243
Health and social work . . .	10,952	13,965	17,722
Other economic activities . . .	66,580	80,797	106,277
Sub-total	318,321	396,003	487,132
Less Financial intermediation services indirectly measured .	5,275	7,402	13,009
Gross value added in basic prices	313,046	388,601	474,123
Taxes on products	33,122	54,183	71,618
Less Subsidies on products . .	1,055	1,332	1,588
GDP in market prices . . .	345,113	441,452	544,153

BALANCE OF PAYMENTS
(US $ million)

	2005	2006	2007
Exports of goods f.o.b.	35,024	38,949	49,840
Imports of goods f.o.b.	-36,159	-44,143	-60,412
Trade balance	-1,135	-5,194	-10,572
Exports of services	9,354	11,290	14,158
Imports of services	-7,548	-9,164	-11,461
Balance on goods and services	671	-3,068	-7,875
Other income received	758	1,332	2,188
Other income paid	-1,743	-3,054	-4,315
Balance on goods, services and income	-314	-4,790	-10,002
Current transfers received . .	3,111	3,533	4,591
Current transfers paid	-266	-360	-516
Current balance	2,531	-1,617	-5,927
Capital account (net)	-65	3	3
Direct investment abroad . . .	-275	133	-673
Direct investment from abroad .	7,808	5,604	9,891
Portfolio investment assets . .	—	-3	-29
Portfolio investment liabilities .	2,757	3,586	5,782
Other investment assets . . .	-7,936	-15,424	-22,192
Other investment liabilities . .	5,749	10,189	22,994
Net errors and omissions . . .	156	-62	-444
Overall balance	10,725	2,409	9,405

Source: IMF, *International Financial Statistics*.

External Trade

PRINCIPAL COMMODITIES
(distribution by Harmonized System, US $ million)

Imports f.o.b.	2005	2006	2007
Vegetable products	525.5	671.7	860.5
Prepared food, beverages, spirits, tobacco	1,454.9	1,654.7	2,090.9
Mineral products	11,567.8	13,506.2	17,280.4
Mineral fuels, oils, waxes and bituminous substances . . .	10,661.9	12,711.6	15,984.2
Coal	714.3	760.6	1,251.0
Crude petroleum	4,600.5	4,403.6	4,553.5
Natural gas	3,946.0	4,769.4	6,572.6
Chemicals and related products	3,097.0	3,888.6	5,316.5
Plastics, rubbers, and articles thereof	1,937.8	2,527.7	3,412.9
Plastic and articles thereof . .	1,497.3	1,988.7	2,693.5
Wood pulp, paper, paperboard, scrap and waste paper and articles thereof	1,003.9	1,173.3	1,523.0
Paper and paperboard, articles of paper pulp	866.5	1,014.2	1,317.8
Textiles and textile articles .	1,406.2	1,365.5	1,487.0
Base metals and articles thereof	2,468.7	3,327.3	4,742.7
Iron and steel	1,151.1	1,468.9	2,240.1
Machinery and mechanical appliances, electrical equipment and appliances, parts and accessories . .	6,340.0	7,873.4	10,571.7
Machinery and mechanical appliances, computers, etc. . .	4,050.2	5,191.4	7,436.6
Electrical machinery, equipment and parts, etc.	2,289.9	2,682.0	3,135.1
Vehicles, aircraft, vessels and associated transportation equipment	3,219.5	5,147.1	8,216.6
Vehicles other than railway or tramway rolling stock . . .	3,022.9	4,898.3	7,770.8
Total (incl. others)	36,136.3	45,034.5	60,669.9

Exports f.o.b.	2005	2006	2007
Vegetable products	1,694.8	1,951.1	1,726.4
Cereals	1,383.1	1,354.2	763.7
Prepared food, beverages, spirits, tobacco	1,290.8	1,394.4	2,056.2
Mineral products . . .	4,705.4	3,871.8	4,275.2
Ores, slag and ash . . .	1,045.2	912.3	1,105.0
Mineral fuels, oils, waxes and bituminous substances . .	3,343.0	2,553.5	2,630.1
Chemicals and related products	2,988.3	3,387.3	4,047.2
Textiles, textile articles, etc. .	914.0	915.3	990.3
Base metals and articles thereof	14,085.5	16,420.1	20,787.3
Iron and steel	11,451.2	13,051.2	16,743.8
Articles of iron and steel . .	1,848.3	2,361.6	2,912.5
Machinery and mechanical appliances, electrical equipment and appliances, parts and accessories . .	2,838.7	3,330.5	4,976.6
Machinery and mechanical appliances, computers, etc. . .	1,922.0	2,051.5	2,738.3
Electrical machinery, equipment and parts, etc.	916.7	1,279.0	2,238.2
Vehicles, aircraft, vessels and associated transportation equipment	1,648.0	2,081.1	3,304.7
Railway or tramway locomotives, rolling stock, track fixtures and fittings, signals, etc.	964.2	1,067.0	1,840.2
Total (incl. others)	34,284.4	38,367.7	49,248.1

PRINCIPAL TRADING PARTNERS
(US $ million)

Imports f.o.b.	2005	2006	2007
Austria	458.4	547.2	799.2
Belarus	939.8	1,255.2	1,444.8
Brazil	312.5	279.8	430.9
China, People's Republic . .	1,810.4	2,310.2	3,307.1
Czech Republic	594.0	825.1	1,154.6
Finland	351.1	391.8	544.6
France (incl. Monaco) . . .	798.9	989.8	1,330.0
Germany	3,384.0	4,267.6	5,830.0
Hungary	647.7	802.2	1,240.9
Italy	1,030.2	1,465.2	1,789.3
Japan	548.2	848.6	1,406.6
Kazakhstan	186.4	965.7	1,591.8
Korea, Republic	648.5	935.4	1,564.9
Netherlands	464.1	640.4	881.0
Poland	1,406.0	2,109.2	2,920.5
Russia	12,842.5	13,787.2	16,837.6
Sweden	547.4	565.0	610.3
Switzerland	252.5	283.2	429.8
Turkey	607.7	769.1	972.1
Turkmenistan	2,678.1	3,492.0	4,266.6
United Kingdom	502.7	620.6	886.4
USA	710.0	879.1	1,397.3
Total (incl. others)	36,136.3	45,034.5	60,669.9

Exports f.o.b.	2005	2006	2007
Algeria	617.2	466.7	440.0
Belarus	891.1	1,222.7	1,561.4
Bulgaria	543.0	595.7	554.0
China, People's Republic . .	711.1	544.7	431.7
Cyprus	217.0	251.8	174.5
Czech Republic . . .	376.9	341.6	429.0
Egypt	798.8	748.4	880.0
Estonia	125.1	123.4	218.2
Germany	1,285.2	1,283.8	1,644.5
Hungary	688.8	946.1	1,235.1
India	736.9	850.1	744.1
Iran	576.9	318.3	509.5
Italy	1,892.6	2,500.4	2,675.2
Kazakhstan	667.1	828.0	1,433.7
Korea, Republic	202.2	88.6	177.2
Latvia	311.4	286.1	258.6

Exports f.o.b.—*continued*	2005	2006	2007
Lithuania	209.3	278.3	363.3
Moldova	678.6	671.2	911.3
Netherlands	515.3	710.7	765.7
Poland	1,010.4	1,344.5	1,636.9
Romania	488.8	625.9	628.6
Russia	7,490.1	8,650.7	12,668.3
Saudi Arabia	386.5	537.0	523.5
Singapore	489.6	211.5	353.4
Slovakia	507.7	549.6	645.2
Spain	573.5	445.1	557.4
Switzerland	395.8	112.1	96.5
Syria	672.1	602.2	846.9
Turkey	2,026.7	2,390.0	3,650.0
United Arab Emirates . . .	345.2	392.6	612.2
United Kingdom	358.2	388.2	324.9
USA	956.5	1,201.7	1,058.1
Total (incl. others)	34,228.4	38,367.7	49,248.1

Transport

RAILWAYS
(traffic)

	2005	2006	2007
Passengers carried ('000 journeys)	444,700	448,800	447,400
Freight carried ('000 metric tons) .	448,700	476,800	512,500
Passenger-km (million) . . .	52,400	53,400	53,400
Freight ton-km (million) . . .	223,400	240,600	262,800

ROAD TRAFFIC
(motor vehicles in use)

	1998	1999	2000
Passenger cars	4,877,787	5,210,774	5,250,129
Motorcycles and mopeds . . .	2,609,201	2,432,787	2,251,505

2004: Passenger cars 5,445,830; Buses 175,945; Lorries and vans 917,427; Motorcycles 1,145,407.

Source: IRF, *World Road Statistics*.

INLAND WATERWAYS

	2005	2006	2007
Passengers carried ('000 journeys)	13,600	12,900	9,500
Freight carried ('000 metric tons) .	21,400	23,000	24,300
Passenger-km (million) . . .	100	100	200
Freight ton-km (million) . . .	15,900	18,600	18,000

SHIPPING

Merchant Fleet
(registered at 31 December)

	2005	2006	2007
Number of vessels	658	655	655
Total displacement ('000 grt) . .	1,154.0	1,136.5	1,144.6

Source: Lloyd's Register-Fairplay, *World Fleet Statistics*.

International Sea-borne Freight Traffic
('000 metric tons, incl. transit departures)

	2002	2003	2004
Goods loaded	62,196	55,704	65,424
Goods unloaded	6,648	7,860	11,400

Source: UN, *Monthly Bulletin of Statistics*.

CIVIL AVIATION
(traffic on scheduled services)

	2001	2002	2003
Kilometres flown (million) . .	30	32	38
Passengers carried ('000) . . .	986	1,120	1,476
Passenger-kilometres (million) .	1,418	1,578	2,351
Total ton-kilometres (million) .	149	156	231

Source: UN, *Statistical Yearbook*.

Tourism

TOURIST ARRIVALS

Country of residence	2004	2005	2006
Belarus	1,768,081	1,841,783	2,126,839
Hungary	2,011,315	1,957,708	1,158,771
Moldova	2,898,375	2,780,880	3,055,833
Poland	1,793,213	3,489,033	3,977,938
Romania	97,872	161,948	348,157
Russia	5,994,823	6,043,829	6,423,850
Slovakia	162,921	321,977	505,480
Total (incl. others)	15,629,213	17,630,760	18,900,263

Receipts from tourism (US $ million, incl. passenger transport): 2,931 in 2004; 3,542 in 2005; 4,018 in 2006.

Source: World Tourism Organization.

2007 ('000 arrivals): Belarus 2,919; Hungary 1,252; Moldova 3,999; Poland 4,430; Romania 1,010; Russia 7,258; Slovakia 665; Total (incl. others) 23,122.

Communications Media

	2004	2005	2006
Book production (titles) . . .	14,790	15,720	15,867
Newspapers (titles)	3,014	2,974	2,918
Magazines and other periodicals (titles)	2,385	2,182	2,301
Telephones ('000 main lines in use)	12,142.0	11,666.6	12,341.0
Mobile cellular telephones ('000 subscribers)	13,735.0	29,999.9	49,076.2
Personal computers ('000 in use) .	1,327	1,810	n.a.
Internet users ('000)	3,750	4,560	5,545

Radio receivers ('000 in use): 45,050 in 1997.

Television receivers ('000 in use): 23,000 in 2000.

Facsimile machines (number in use): 42,161 in 2000.

Sources: mainly UNESCO, *Statistical Yearbook*; International Telecommunication Union.

Education

(2007/08, unless otherwise indicated)

	Institutions	Teachers	Students
Pre-primary	15,300*	191,500†	1,137,000
Primary *and* General secondary .	21,200	531,000	4,857,000
Specialized secondary: vocational	1,022	285,100	454,400
Higher	904	121,300†	2,813,800

* Including some 1,400 with activities suspended.
† 1993/94 figure.

Adult literacy rate (UNESCO estimates): 99.7% (males 99.8%; females 99.6%) in 2007 (Source: UNESCO Institute for Statistics).

Directory

Constitution

The Constitution of Ukraine, summarized below, was adopted at the Fifth Session of the Verkhovna Rada on 28 June 1996. It replaced the Soviet-era Constitution (Fundamental Law), originally approved on 12 April 1978, but amended several times after Ukraine gained independence in 1991, and entered into force the day of its adoption. On 8 December 2004, following the disputed (and subsequently annulled) second round of voting in the presidential election, the Verkhovna Rada approved a number of constitutional amendments, principally concerned with transferring a number of presidential powers, including the appointment of the majority of ministerial posts, to the Prime Minister and to the Verkhovna Rada. These amendments, which were signed into law on the same day by the outgoing President, took effect from 1 January 2006, excepting those pertaining to the Verkhovna Rada or Prime Minister, which entered into force in May 2006, following the assembly of a legislature after the general election held in March.

FUNDAMENTAL PRINCIPLES

Ukraine is a sovereign and independent, unitary and law-based state, in which power is exercised directly by the people through the bodies of state power and local self-government. The life, honour, dignity and health of the individual are recognized as the highest social value. The Constitution is the highest legal authority; the power of the State is divided between the legislative, the executive and the judicial branches. The state language is Ukrainian. The use and protection of Russian and other languages of national minorities, and the development of minorities' ethnic and cultural traditions is guaranteed. The State ensures protection of all forms of ownership rights and management, as well as the social orientation of the economy. The state symbols of Ukraine, its flag, coat of arms and anthem, are established.

THE RIGHTS, FREEDOMS AND DUTIES OF CITIZENS

The rights and freedoms of individuals are declared to be unalienable and inviolable regardless of race, sex, political or religious affiliation, wealth, social origin or other characteristics. Fundamental rights, such as the freedoms of speech and association and the right to private property, are guaranteed. Citizens have the right to engage in political activity and to own private property. All individuals are entitled to work and to join professional unions to protect their employment rights. The Constitution commits the State to the provision of health care, housing, social security and education. All citizens have the right to legal assistance. Obligations of the citizenry include military service and taxes. The age of enfranchisement for Ukrainian citizens is 18 years. Elections to organs of state authority are declared to be free and conducted on the basis of universal, equal and direct suffrage by secret ballot.

THE VERKHOVNA RADA

The Verkhovna Rada (Supreme Council) is the sole organ of legislative authority in Ukraine. It consists of 450 members, elected for a four-year term on the basis of proportional representation. The constitutional reforms approved in late 2004 prohibit deputies from leaving the party or bloc for whom they have been elected during the term of their elective mandate. Only Ukrainian citizens aged over 21 years, who have resided in Ukraine for the five previous years are eligible for election to parliament. The Verkhovna Rada is a permanently acting body, which elects its own Chairman and Deputy Chairmen.

The most important functions of the legislature include: the enactment of laws; the approval of the state budget and other state programmes; the scheduling of presidential elections; the removal (impeachment) of the President; the appointment of the Prime Minister; the declaration of war or conclusion of peace; the foreign deployment of troops; and consenting to international treaty obligations within the time limit prescribed by law. Within 15 days of a law adopted by the Verkhovna Rada being received by the President, the President shall officially promulgate it or return it for repeat consideration by parliament. If, during such consideration, the legislature readopts the law by a two-thirds' majority, the President is obliged to sign it and officially promulgate it within 10 days. The

President of Ukraine may terminate the authority of the Verkhovna Rada if, within 30 days of a single, regular session, a plenary session cannot be convened, except within the last six months of the President's term of office.

THE PRESIDENT

The President of Ukraine is the Head of State, and is guarantor of state sovereignty and the territorial integrity of Ukraine. The President is directly elected for a period of five years. A presidential candidate must be aged over 35 years and a resident of the country for the 10 years prior to the election. The President may hold office for no more than two consecutive terms.

The President's main responsibilities include: the scheduling of elections and of referendums on constitutional amendments; the conclusion of international treaties; and the promulgation of laws. The President appoints certain senior members of the Cabinet of Ministers; the constitutional reforms agreed in late 2004 transferred responsibility for the appointment of the majority of Ministers to the Prime Minister.

The President is the Supreme Commander of the Armed Forces of Ukraine and chairs the National Security and Defence Council. The President may be removed from office by the Verkhovna Rada by impeachment, for reasons of state treason or another crime. The decision to remove the President must be approved by at least a three-quarters' majority in the Verkhovna Rada. In the event of the termination of the authority of the President, the Prime Minister executes the duties of the President until the election and entry into office of a new President.

THE CABINET OF MINISTERS

The principal organ of executive government is the Cabinet of Ministers, which is responsible before the President and accountable to the Verkhovna Rada. The Cabinet supervises the implementation of state policy and the state budget and the maintenance of law and order. The Cabinet of Ministers is headed by the Prime Minister. The duties of the Prime Minister include the submission of proposals to the President on the creation, reorganization and liquidation of ministries and other central bodies of executive authority. The Cabinet of Ministers must resign when a new President is elected, or in the event of the adoption of a vote of no confidence by the Verkhovna Rada.

JUDICIAL POWER

Justice in Ukraine is administered by the Constitutional Court and by courts of general jurisdiction. The Supreme Court of Ukraine is the highest judicial organ of general jurisdiction. Judges hold their position permanently, except for justices of the Constitutional Court and first judicial appointments, which are made by the President for a five-year term. Other judges, with the exception of justices of the Constitutional Court, are elected by the Verkhovna Rada. Judges must be at least 25 years of age, have a higher legal education and at least three years' work experience in the field of law, and have resided in Ukraine for no fewer than 10 years. The Procuracy of Ukraine is headed by the General Procurator, who is appointed with the consent of parliament and dismissed by the President. The term of office of the General Procurator is five years.

A Superior Justice Council, responsible for the submission of proposals regarding the appointment or dismissal of judges, functions in Ukraine. The Council consists of 20 members. The Chairman of the Supreme Court of Ukraine, the Minister of Justice, and the General Procurator are ex officio members of the Superior Justice Council.

LOCAL SELF-GOVERNMENT

The administrative and territorial division of Ukraine consists of the Autonomous Republic of Crimea, 24 provinces (oblasts), the cities of Kyiv and Sevastopol (which possess special status), districts (raions), cities, settlements and villages. Local self-government is the right of territorial communities. The principal organs of territorial communities are the district and provincial councils, which, with their chairmen, are directly elected for a term of four years. The chairmen of district and provincial councils are elected by the relevant council and head their executive structure. Provincial and district councils monitor the implementation of programmes of socio-economic and cultural development of the relevant provinces and districts, and adopt and monitor the implementation of district and provincial budgets, which are derived from the state budget.

THE AUTONOMOUS REPUBLIC OF CRIMEA

The Autonomous Republic of Crimea (which comprises the peninsula of Crimea, excluding the city of Sevastopol) is an inseparable, integral part of Ukraine. It has its own Constitution, which is adopted by the Supreme Council of the Autonomous Republic of Crimea (the representative organ of Crimea) and approved by the Verkhovna Rada. Legislation adopted by the Autonomous Republic's Supreme Council and the decisions of its Council of Ministers must not contravene the Constitution and laws of Ukraine. The Chairman of the Council of Ministers is appointed and dismissed by the Supreme Council of the Autonomous Republic of Crimea with the consent of the President of Ukraine. Justice in Crimea is administered by courts belonging to the single court system of Ukraine. An Office of the Representative of the President of Ukraine functions in Crimea.

The jurisdiction of the Autonomous Republic of Crimea includes: organizing and conducting local referendums; implementing the republican budget on the basis of the state policy of Ukraine; ensuring the function and development of the state and national languages and cultures; participating in the development and fulfilment of programmes for the return of deported peoples.

THE CONSTITUTIONAL COURT

The Constitutional Court consists of 18 justices, six of whom are appointed by the President, six by the Verkhovna Rada and six by the Assembly of Judges of Ukraine. Candidates must be citizens of Ukraine, who are at least 40 years of age and have resided in Ukraine for the previous 20 years. Justices of the Constitutional Court serve a term of nine years, with no right to reappointment. A Chairman is elected by a secret ballot of the members for a single three-year term.

The Constitutional Court provides binding interpretations of the Constitution. It rules on the constitutionality of: parliamentary legislation; acts of the President and the Cabinet of Ministers; the official interpretation of the Constitution of Ukraine; international agreements; and the impeachment of the President of Ukraine.

CONSTITUTIONAL AMENDMENTS AND THE ADOPTION OF A NEW CONSTITUTION

A draft law on amending the Constitution may be presented to the Verkhovna Rada by the President or at least one-third of the constitutional composition of the parliament. A draft law on amending the Constitution, which has been given preliminary approval by a majority of the constitutional composition of the Verkhovna Rada, is considered adopted if it receives the support of at least a two-thirds' parliamentary majority. In the case of its approval, it is confirmed by a nation-wide referendum designated by the President.

The Government

HEAD OF STATE

President: VIKTOR A. YUSHCHENKO (elected 26 December 2004; inaugurated 23 January 2005).

CABINET OF MINISTERS

(September 2008)

Prime Minister: YULIYA V. TYMOSHENKO.

First Deputy Prime Minister: OLEKSANDR V. TURCHYNOV.

Deputy Prime Minister: IVAN V. VASYUNYK.

Deputy Prime Minister: HRYHORIY M. NEMYRYA.

Minister of Education and Science: IVAN O. VAKARCHUK.

Minister of Transport and Communications: YOSYP V. VINSKY.

Minister of Culture and Tourism: VASYL V. VOVKUN.

Minister of the Economy: BOHDAN M. DANYLYSHYN.

Minister of Labour and Social Policy: LYUDMYLA L. DENISOVA.

Minister of Defence: YURIY I. YEKHANUROV.

Minister of the Protection of Health: VASYL M. KNYAZEVYCH.

Minister of Regional Development and Construction: VASYL S. KUYBIDA.

Minister of Housing and Communal Services: OLEKSIY YU. KUCHERENKO.

Minister of Internal Affairs: YURIY V. LUTSENKO.

Minister of Agrarian Policy: YURIY F. MELNYK.

Minister of Industrial Policy: VOLODYMYR S. NOVYTSKY.

Minister of Justice: MYKOLA V. ONISHCHUK.

Minister of Foreign Affairs: VOLODYMYR S. OHRYZKO.

Minister of the Family, Youth and Sports: YURIY O. PAVLENKO.

Minister of Finance: VIKTOR M. PYNZENYK.

Minister of the Coal Industry: VIKTOR I. POLTAVETS.

Minister of Fuel and Energy: YURIY V. PRODAN.

Minister of the Protection of the Environment: HEORHIY H. FILIPCHUK.

Minister for Emergency Situations and the Protection of the Population from the Consequences of the Chornobyl Catastrophe: VOLODYMYR M. SHANDRA.

Minister of the Cabinet of Ministers: PETRO M. KRUPKO.

MINISTRIES

Office of the President: 01220 Kyiv, vul. Bankova 11; tel. (44) 255-73-33; fax (44) 293-61-61; e-mail president@adm.gov.ua; internet www.president.gov.ua.

Office of the Cabinet of Ministers: 01008 Kyiv, vul. M. Hrushevskoho 12/2; tel. and fax (44) 254-05-84; e-mail web@kmu.gov.ua; internet www.kmu.gov.ua.

Ministry of Agrarian Policy: 01008 Kyiv, vul. Hrushevskoho 12/2; tel. (44) 278-71-18; fax (44) 229-87-56; e-mail ministr@minapk.kiev.ua; internet www.minagro.gov.ua.

Ministry of the Coal Industry: 01601 Kyiv, vul. Khmelnytskoho 4; tel. (44) 594-62-27; fax (44) 206-37-19; e-mail DSher@mvp.gov.ua; internet www.mvp.gov.ua.

Ministry of Culture and Tourism: 01601 Kyiv, vul. Ivana Franka 19; tel. (44) 226-26-45; fax (44) 235-32-57; e-mail ministr@mincult.gov.ua; internet www.mincult.gov.ua.

Ministry of Defence: 03168 Kyiv, Povitroflotskyi pr. 6; tel. (44) 226-26-56; fax (44) 226-20-15; e-mail pressmou@pressmou.kiev.ua; internet www.mil.gov.ua.

Ministry of the Economy: 01008 Kyiv, vul. M. Hrushevskoho 12/2; tel. (44) 253-93-94; fax (44) 226-31-81; e-mail meconomy@me.gov.ua; internet www.me.gov.ua.

Ministry of Education and Science: 01601 Kyiv, bulv. T. Shevchenka 16; tel. (44) 226-26-61; fax (44) 274-10-49; e-mail press@mon.gov.ua; internet www.mon.gov.ua.

Ministry of Emergency Situations and the Protection of the Population from the Consequences of the Chornobyl Catastrophe: 01030 Kyiv, vul. O. Honchara 55A; tel. (44) 247-31-44; e-mail main@mns.gov.ua; internet www.mns.gov.ua.

Ministry of the Family, Youth and Sport: 01019 Kyiv, vul. Esplanadna 42; tel. (44) 289-12-64; fax (44) 289-12-94; e-mail correspond@mms.gov.ua; internet www.kmu.gov.ua/sport/control.

Ministry of Finance: 01008 Kyiv, vul. M. Hrushevskoho 12/2; tel. (44) 253-62-56; fax (44) 253-82-43; e-mail infomf@minfin.gov.ua; internet www.minfin.gov.ua.

Ministry of Foreign Affairs: 01018 Kyiv, pl. Mykhailivska 1; tel. (44) 238-15-06; fax (44) 226-31-69; internet www.mfa.gov.ua.

Ministry of Fuel and Energy: 01601 Kyiv, vul. Khreshchatik 30; tel. (44) 206-38-00; fax (44) 462-05-61; e-mail kanc@mintop.energy.gov.ua; internet mpe.kmu.gov.ua.

Ministry of Housing and Communal Services: 03150 Kyiv, vul. Dymytrova 24; tel. (44) 287-23-84; fax (44) 289-01-66; e-mail minjkg@ukr.net; internet www.minjkg.gov.ua.

Ministry of Industrial Policy: 03035 Kyiv, vul. Surikova 3; tel. (44) 246-32-20; fax (44) 245-47-78; e-mail minister@industry.gov.ua; internet industry.kmu.gov.ua.

Ministry of Internal Affairs: 01024 Kyiv, vul. Ak. Bohomoltsya 10; tel. (44) 256-03-33; fax (44) 256-16-33; e-mail mail@centrmia.gov.ua; internet mvs.gov.ua.

Ministry of Justice: 01001 Kyiv, vul. Horodetskoho 13; tel. and fax (44) 228-37-23; e-mail themis@minjust.gov.ua; internet www.minjust.gov.ua.

Ministry of Labour and Social Policy: 01023 Kyiv, vul. Esplanadna 8/10; tel. (44) 226-24-45; fax (44) 289-00-98; e-mail info@mlsp.gov.ua; internet www.mlsp.gov.ua.

Ministry of the Protection of the Environment: 03035 Kyiv, vul. Uritskoho 35; tel. (44) 228-06-44; fax (44) 229-83-83; internet www.menr.gov.ua.

Ministry of the Protection of Health: 01021 Kyiv, vul. M. Hrushevskoho 7; tel. and fax (44) 253-00-56; internet www.moz.gov.ua.

Ministry of Regional Development and Construction: 01205 Kyiv, vul. V. Zhytomyrska 9; tel. (44) 226-22-08; fax (44) 226-20-97; e-mail mrb@minregionbud.gov.ua; internet www.minregionbud.gov.ua.

Ministry of Transport and Communications: 01135 Kyiv, pr. Peremohy 14; tel. (44) 226-22-04; fax (44) 216-72-06; e-mail portal@mtu.gov.ua; internet www.mintrans.gov.ua.

President

Presidential Election, First Ballot, 31 October 2004

Candidates	Votes	%
Viktor A. Yushchenko (Independent)	11,188,675	39.91
Viktor F. Yanukovych (Party of the Regions)	11,008,731	39.27
Oleksandr O. Moroz (Socialist Party of Ukraine)	1,632,098	5.82
Petro M. Symonenko (Communist Party of Ukraine)	1,396,135	4.98
Nataliya M. Vitrenko (Progressive Socialist Party of Ukraine)	429,794	1.53
Others	988,363	3.53
Against all candidates	556,962	1.99
Total*	28,035,184	100.00

* Including 834,426 invalid votes (2.98% of the total).

Second Ballot, 26 December 2004*

Candidates	Votes	%
Viktor A. Yushchenko (Independent)	15,115,712	51.99
Viktor F. Yanukovych (Party of the Regions)	12,848,528	44.20
Against all candidates	682,239	2.35
Total†	29,068,971	100.00

* The results of an initial second round of voting, conducted on 21 November 2004, in which the Central Electoral Commission had declared Yanukovych the winner, were annulled by the Supreme Court.

† Including 422,492 invalid votes (1.45% of the total).

Legislature

Verkhovna Rada
(Supreme Council)

01008 Kyiv, vul. M. Hrushevskoho 5; tel. (44) 255-21-15; fax (44) 253-32-17; e-mail umz@rada.gov.ua; internet www.rada.gov.ua.

Chairman: ARSENIY P. YATSENYUK.

General Election, 30 September 2007

Parties and blocs	Votes	%	Seats
Party of the Regions	8,013,895	34.37	175
Yuliya Tymoshenko bloc*	7,162,193	30.71	156
Our Ukraine-People's Self-defence bloc†	3,301,282	14.15	72
Communist Party of Ukraine	1,257,291	5.39	27
Lytvyn bloc‡	924,538	3.96	20
Socialist Party of Ukraine	668,234	2.86	—
Progressive Socialist Party of Ukraine	309,008	1.32	—
Others	661,928	2.78	—
Total§	23,315,257	100.00	450

* Electoral bloc comprising Fatherland, the Reforms and Order Party and the Ukrainian Social Democratic Party.

† Electoral bloc comprising nine parties, including Our Ukraine People's Union, the 'Enough!' Civic Party, the People's Movement of Ukraine-Rukh, the Synod Ukrainian Republican Party and the Ukrainian People's Party.

‡ Electoral bloc comprising the People's Party and the Labour Party of Ukraine.

§ The total number of votes cast was 23,315,257, including 379,703 invalid votes (representing 1.73% of the total), and 637,185 votes 'against all lists' (2.73% of the total).

Local Government

Ukraine is divided for administrative purposes into 24 oblasts (regions), two metropolitan areas (Kyiv and Sevastopol) and one Autonomous Republic (Crimea, see p. 568). Each oblast is governed by a directly elected council (rada) and a governor appointed by the President. The 1996 Constitution also guarantees local self-government to districts (raions), cities, settlements and villages.

METROPOLITAN AREAS

Kyiv City Administration: 01044 Kyiv, vul. Kreshchatyk 36; tel. (44) 221-28-01; fax (44) 235-63-48; e-mail kmda012@012.kyiv-city.gov.ua; internet www.kmv.gov.ua; Mayor LEONID M. CHERNOVETSKY.

Sevastopol City Administration: 99011 Sevastopol, ul. Lenina 2; tel. (692) 54-47-73; fax (692) 54-20-53; e-mail sgga@stel.sebastopol .ua; internet www.sev.gov.ua; Mayor SERGEI V. KUNITSYN.

OBLASTS

Cherkasy Oblast Administration: 18001 Cherkasy, bulv. Shevchenka 185; tel. (472) 47-33-33; fax (472) 54-04-70; e-mail cancelar@ oda.ck.ua; internet www.oda.ck.ua; Gov. OLEKSANDR V. CHEREVKO.

Chernihiv Oblast Administration: 14000 Chernihiv, vul. Shevchenka 7; tel. and fax (462) 67-50-71; e-mail post@regadm.cn.ua; internet cg.gov.ua; Gov. VOLODYMYR M. KHOMENKO.

Chernivtsi Oblast Administration: 58010 Chernivtsi, vul. Hrushevskoho 1; tel. (372) 51-30-10; fax (372) 55-37-76; e-mail oda@oda.cv.ua; internet www.oda.cv.ua; Gov. VOLODYMYR I. KULISH.

Dnipropetrovsk Oblast Administration: 49004 Dnipropetrovsk, pr. Kirova 1; tel. (562) 742-83-84; fax (562) 742-89-54; e-mail info@ adm.dp.ua; internet www.adm.dp.ua; Gov. VIKTOR V. BONDAR.

Donetsk Oblast Administration: 83105 Donetsk, bulv. Pushkina 34; tel. (622) 35-03-89; fax (622) 92-13-62; e-mail info@oda.dn.ua; internet www.donoda.gov.ua; Gov. VOLODYMYR I. LOHVYNENKO.

Ivano-Frankivsk Oblast Administration: 76004 Ivano-Frankivsk, vul. Hrushevskoho 21; tel. (3422) 22-291; fax (3422) 25-048; e-mail oda@mail.gov.if.ua; internet www.gov.if.ua; Gov. MYKOLA PALIYCHUK.

Kharkiv Oblast Administration: 61200 Kharkiv, vul. Sumska 64; tel. (57) 700-21-05; fax (57) 700-22-01; e-mail obladm@kharkivoda .gov.ua; internet www.kharkivoda.gov.ua; Gov. ARSEN B. AVAKOV.

Kherson Oblast Administration: 73000 Kherson, pl. Svobody 1; tel. (552) 32-11-00; fax (552) 26-36-02; e-mail vd-komp@oda.kherson .ua; internet www.oda.kherson.ua; Gov. BORYS V. SILENKOV.

Khmelnytsky Oblast Administration: 29005 Khmelnytsky, Maidan Nezalezhnosti, Budynok Rad; tel. (382) 76-50-25; fax (382) 76-51-72; e-mail regadm@infocom.km.ua; internet adm.km.ua; Gov. IVAN K. HAVCHUK.

Kirovohrad Oblast Administration: 25022 Kirovohrad, pl. Kirova 1; tel. (522) 24-16-52; fax (522) 22-35-66; e-mail public@kr-admin .gov.ua; internet www.kr-admin.gov.ua; Gov. VASYL K. MOTSNY.

Kyiv Oblast Administration: 01196 Kyiv, pl. L. Ukrainky 1; tel. (44) 286-82-30; fax (44) 286-15-10; e-mail ver@kra.kiev.ua; internet www.kyiv-obl.gov.ua; Gov. VIRA I. ULYANCHENKO.

Luhansk Oblast Administration: 91016 Luhansk, pl. Heroyiv Velykoyi Vitchyznyanoyi Viiny 3; tel. (642) 58-58-88; fax (642) 55-14-54; e-mail gubernator@loga.gov.ua; internet www.loga.gov.ua; Gov. OLEKSANDR M. ANTIPOV.

Lviv Oblast Administration: 79008 Lviv, vul. Vynnychenka 18; tel. (32) 261-28-70; fax (32) 261-23-25; e-mail admin@oda.lviv.ua; internet www.loda.gov.ua; Gov. MYKOLA I. KMIT.

Mykolayiv Oblast Administration: 54009 Mykolayiv, vul. Admiralska 22; tel. (512) 35-40-51; fax (512) 35-12-36; e-mail cancelar@oga .mk.ua; internet www.mykolayiv-oda.gov.ua; Gov. OLEKSIY M. HARKUSHA.

Odesa Oblast Administration: 65032 Odesa, pr. Shevchenka 4; tel. (48) 718-93-00; fax (482) 34-29-71; e-mail int_dep@odessa.gov.ua; internet oda.odessa.gov.ua; Gov. MYKOLA D. SERDYUK.

Poltava Oblast Administration: 36014 Poltava, vul. Zhovtenva 45; tel. (532) 56-02-90; fax (532) 56-53-14; e-mail oda@obladmin .poltava.ua; internet www.obladmin.poltava.ua; Gov. VALERIY M. ASADCHEV.

Rivne Oblast Administration: 33000 Rivne, Maidan Prosvity 1; tel. (362) 69-51-65; fax (362) 26-08-35; e-mail roda@rv.gov.ua; internet www.rv.gov.ua; Gov. VIKTOR I. MATCHUK.

Sumy Oblast Administration: 40030 Sumy, pl. Nezalezhnosti 2; tel. (542) 28-03-27; fax (542) 60-77-60; e-mail mail@state-gov.sumy .ua; internet www.state-gov.sumy.ua; Gov. MYKOLA I. LAVYRK (acting).

Ternopil Oblast Administration: 46021 Ternopil, vul. M. Hrushevskoho 8; tel. (352) 57-02-88; fax (352) 25-19-59; e-mail oda@te.gov.ua; internet www.oda.te.gov.ua; Gov. YURIY V. CHYZHMAR.

Transcarpathian (Zakarpatska) Oblast Administration: 88008 Transcarpathian obl., Uzhhorod, pl. Narodna 4; tel. (312) 61-34-19; fax (312) 61-33-56; e-mail admin@carpathia.gov.ua; internet www.carpathia.gov.ua; Gov. OLEH O. HAVASHI.

Vinnytsya Oblast Administration: 21100 Vinnytsya, vul. Soborna 70; tel. (432) 32-20-35; fax (432) 32-75-40; e-mail vinoda@ in.vn.ua; internet www.vin.gov.ua; Gov. OLEKSANDR H. DOMBROVSKY.

Volyn Oblast State Administration: 43027 Volyn obl., Lutsk, pl. Kyivska 9; tel. (332) 77-81-01; fax (332) 72-93-22; e-mail post@ obladmin.lutsk.ua; internet www.voladm.gov.ua; Gov. MYKOLA YA. ROMANYUK.

Zaporizhzhya Oblast Administration: 69107 Zaporizhzhya, pr. Lenina 164; tel. (612) 33-11-91; fax (61) 224-61-23; e-mail adm@zoda .gov.ua; internet www.zoda.gov.ua; Gov. OLEKSANDR V. STARUKH.

Zhytomyr Oblast Administration: 10014 Zhytomyr, Koroleva pl. 1; tel. (412) 41-34-90; fax (412) 47-50-00; internet www .zhitomir-region.gov.ua; Gov. YURIY V. ZABELA.

Election Commission

Central Electoral Commission of Ukraine (CEC) (Tsentralna vyborcha Komisiya Ukrainy): 01196 Kyiv, pl. L. Ukrainky 1; tel. (44) 286-84-62; e-mail post@cvk.gov.ua; internet www.cvk.gov.ua; Head VOLODYMYR SHAPOVAL.

Political Organizations

Since the 1990s Ukrainian politics has been characterized by frequent changes of formation and allegiance within and between various factions or blocs. At 2 October 2008 there were 153 political parties registered in Ukraine, of which the following were the most important:

Communist Party of Ukraine (CPU) (Komunistychna Partiya Ukrainy): 04070 Kyiv, vul. Borysohlibska 7; tel. (44) 425-54-87; e-mail press@kpu.net.ua; internet www.kpu.net.ua; banned 1991–93; advocates state control of economy and confederation with Russia; Sec. of Cen. Cttee PETRO M. SYMONENKO.

'Enough!' Civic Party (Hromadyanska Partiya 'Pora!'): 01025 Kyiv, vul. Desyatynna 1/3; tel. (44) 594-20-20; e-mail info@pora .org.ua; internet www.pora.gov.ua; f. 2005 on the basis of the 'Yellow Pora' civil organization; supports expansion of democratic freedoms and greater integration with the West; contested 2006 legislative elections as mem. of the Enough!-Party of Reforms and Order civic bloc and 2007 legislative elections as mem. of the Our Ukraine-People's Self-defence bloc; Chair. of Political Council VLADYSLAV V. KASKIV.

Fatherland (Batkivshchyna): 01133 Kyiv, bulv. Lesi Ukrainky 26/916, POB 81; tel. (44) 286-65-42; fax (44) 285-69-07; e-mail sector@ byti.org.ua; internet www.tymoshenko.com.ua; f. 1999; merged with Conservative Republican Party in 2002, and with Yabluko party in 2004; nationalist, populist, supportive of socially-orientated economics; contested 2006 and 2007 legislative elections as mem. of Yuliya Tymoshenko bloc; Chair. YULIYA V. TYMOSHENKO; 275,000 mems (2005).

Green Party of Ukraine (Partiya Zelenykh Ukrainy): 01030 Kyiv, vul. Chapayeva 2/16; tel. and fax (44) 278-26-63; e-mail sekretariat@ greenparty.ua; internet www.greenparty.ua; f. 1990; Pres. VOLODYMYR O. KOSTERIN.

Our Ukraine People's Union (Our Ukraine) (Narodnyi Soyuz 'Nasha Ukraina') (Nasha Ukraina): 04070 Kyiv, vul. Borychiv Tik 22A; tel. (44) 206-60-97; e-mail tak@ua.org.ua; internet www.razom .org.ua; f. 2005 as People's Union Our Ukraine to support administration of Pres. Yushchenko; present name adopted 2007; contested 2006 legislative elections as mem. of the Our Ukraine bloc and 2007 legislative elections as mem. of Our Ukraine-People's Self-defence bloc; Hon. Pres. VIKTOR A. YUSHCHENKO; Chair. of Council VYACHESLAV A. KYRYLENKO; 7,789 mems (Apr. 2005).

Party of the Regions (PR) (Partiya Rehioniv): 01053 Kyiv, vul. Kudryavska 3/5; tel. (44) 254-29-20; fax (44) 254-33-70; e-mail partreg@ln.ua; internet www.partyofregions.org.ua; f. 1997 as the Workers' Solidarity Party of Regional Rebirth of Ukraine; present name adopted 2001; Chair. VIKTOR F. YANUKOVYCH.

People's Movement of Ukraine-Rukh (PMU-R) (Narodnyi Rukh Ukrainy): 01034 Kyiv, vul. O. Honchara 33; tel. (44) 246-47-67; fax (44) 531-30-42; e-mail org@nru.org.ua; internet www.nru.org.ua; f. 1989 as popular movement (Ukrainian People's Movement for Restructuring); registered as political party in 1993; contested 2006 legislative elections as mem. of Our Ukraine bloc and 2007 legislative elections as mem. of Our Ukraine-People's Self-defence bloc; national democratic party; Chair. BORYS I. TARASYUK.

People's Party (Narodna Partiya): 01034 Kyiv, vul. Reitarska 6 A; tel. (44) 270-61-86; fax (44) 270-65-91; e-mail info@narodna.org.ua; internet narodna.org.ua; f. 1996 as Agrarian Party of Ukraine; renamed People's Agrarian Party of Ukraine in 2004; present name adopted 2005; contested 2006 legislative elections as mem. of Lytvyn's People's bloc and 2007 legislative elections as mem. of Lytvyn bloc; centrist; Leader VOLODYMYR M. LYTVYN.

Progressive Socialist Party of Ukraine (Prohresyvna Sotsialistychna Partiya Ukrainy): 01011 Kyiv, vul. P. Mirnoho 27/51; tel. (44) 254-18-40; fax (44) 278-54-91; e-mail pspu@svitonline.com; internet www.vitrenko.org; f. 1996 by members of the Socialist Party of Ukraine; contested 2006 legislative elections as mem. of the Nataliya

Vitrenko People's Opposition bloc; favours extension of Belarus-Russia Union to incorporate Ukraine; opposed to Ukraine seeking membership of NATO; Chair. NATALIYA M. VITRENKO.

Reforms and Order Party (Partiya 'Reformy i poryadok'): 01021 Kyiv, vul. Institutska 28; tel. (44) 536-91-26; fax (44) 536-91-27; e-mail ref_ord@i.com.ua; internet www.prp.org.ua; f. 1997 as Reforms and Order Party; changed name to Our Ukraine in mid-2004; in July 2005 the Ministry of Justice ruled that the party had acted unlawfully in adopting the name 'Our Ukraine', and the party reverted to its original name; contested 2006 legislative elections as part of the Enough!-Party of Reforms and Order civic bloc and 2007 legislative elections as part of the Yuliya Tymoshenko bloc; Chair. VIKTOR M. PYNZENYK.

Socialist Party of Ukraine (SPU) (Sotsialistychna Partiya Ukrainy): 02100 Kyiv, vul. Bazhova 12; tel. and fax (44) 573-58-97; e-mail pr@spu.in.ua; internet www.spu.in.ua; f. 1991; formed as partial successor to the CPU; advocates democratic socialism; Leader and First Sec. OLEKSANDR O. MOROZ.

Ukrainian People's Party (UPP) (Ukrainska Narodna Partiya): 01601 Kyiv, vul. Pushkinska 28A; tel. (44) 234-59-17; fax (44) 234-05-68; e-mail office@unp-ua.org; internet www.unp-ua.org; f. 1999 as breakaway faction of People's Movement of Ukraine-Rukh by fmr leader Vyacheslav Chornovil; fmrly Ukrainian People's Movement-Rukh; present name adopted 2003; contested 2006 legislative elections as mem. of Kostenko and Plyushch's Ukrainian People's bloc and 2007 legislative elections as mem. of Our Ukraine-People's Self-defence bloc; Chair. YURIY I. KOSTENKO.

Ukrainian Social Democratic Party (Ukrainska Sotsial-demokratychna Partiya): 03150 Kyiv, vul. Antonovycha 154; tel. (44) 286-49-90; fax (44) 254-47-13; internet www.usdp.kiev.ua; f. 1998; contested 2007 legislative elections as mem. of the Yuliya Tymoshenko bloc; Leader YEVHEN V. KORNIYCHUK.

United Centre (Yedyny Tsentr): 04070 Kyiv, vul. Yaroslavska 56A; tel. (44) 207-44-76; fax (44) 207-44-75; e-mail info@edc.org.ua; internet www.edc.org.ua; f. 1999; supportive of Pres. Yushchenko; Chair. IHOR I. KRIL.

Diplomatic Representation

EMBASSIES IN UKRAINE

Afghanistan: 01037 Kyiv, pr. Chervonozoryanyi 42; tel. and fax (44) 245-81-04; e-mail sm_kh2003@yahoo.com; Ambassador MOHAMMED ASIF DILAWAR.

Algeria: 01001 Kyiv, vul. B. Khmelnytskoho 64; tel. (44) 216-70-79; fax (44) 216-70-08; e-mail ambkv@ksv.net.ua; Ambassador MOKADDEM BAFDAL.

Argentina: 01901 Kyiv, vul. Ivana Franka 36, POB 217; tel. (44) 490-25-16; fax (44) 238-69-22; e-mail eucra@mrecic.gov.ar; Ambassador OLGA LILA ROLDÁN VÁZQUEZ.

Armenia: 01901 Kyiv, vul. Volodymyrska 45; tel. (44) 224-90-05; fax (44) 235-05-00; e-mail despanut@visti.com; Ambassador ARMEN KHACHATRIAN.

Austria: 01030 Kyiv, vul. Ivana Franka 33; tel. (44) 288-09-43; fax (44) 230-23-52; e-mail kiew-ob@bmeia.gv.at; internet www.aussenministerium.at/kiew; Ambassador JOSEF MARKUS WUKETICH.

Azerbaijan: 04050 Kyiv, vul. Hlubochytska 24; tel. (44) 484-69-39; fax (44) 484-69-46; e-mail embass@faust.kiev.ua; internet www.azembassy.org.ua; Ambassador TALYAT MUSEIB OĞLU ALIYEV.

Belarus: 01030 Kyiv, vul. M. Kotsyubynskogo 3; tel. (44) 537-52-00; fax (44) 537-52-13; e-mail inbox@belembassy.org.ua; internet www.belembassy.org.ua; Ambassador VALENTYN V. VELICHKO.

Belgium: 01030 Kyiv, vul. Leontovicha 4; tel. (44) 238-26-00; fax (44) 238-26-01; e-mail kiev@diplobel.org; internet www.diplomatie.be/kiev; Ambassador MARC VINCK.

Brazil: 01010 Kyiv, vul. Suvorova 14/12, POB 471; tel. (44) 280-63-01; fax (44) 280-95-68; e-mail kievbrem@brasil.kiev.ua; internet brasil.kiev.ua; Ambassador RENATO LUIZ RODRIGUES MARQUES.

Bulgaria: 01023 Kyiv, vul. Hospitalna 1; tel. (44) 246-72-37; fax (44) 235-51-19; e-mail embuln@i.kiev.ua; internet www.mfa.bg/kyiv; Ambassador DIMITAR VLADIMIROV.

Canada: 01901 Kyiv, vul. Yaroslaviv Val 31; tel. (44) 590-31-00; fax (44) 590-31-57; e-mail kyiv@international.gc.ca; internet www.kyiv.gc.ca; Ambassador G. DANIEL CARON.

China, People's Republic: 01901 Kyiv, vul. M. Hrushevskoho 32; tel. (44) 253-31-54; fax (44) 253-73-71; internet ua.china-embassy.org; Ambassador ZHOU LI.

Croatia: 01091 Kyiv, vul. Artema 51/50; tel. (44) 486-58-62; fax (44) 484-69-43; e-mail croemb.ukraine@mvpei.hr; internet ua.mvp.hr; Ambassador ŽELJKO KIRINČIĆ.

Cuba: 01901 Kyiv, prov. Bekhterevskyi 5; tel. (44) 486-57-43; fax (44) 486-19-07; e-mail embacuba@naverex.kiev.ua; Ambassador JULIO GARMENDÍA PEÑA.

Czech Republic: 01901 Kyiv, vul. Yaroslaviv Val 34A; tel. (44) 272-04-31; fax (44) 272-62-04; e-mail kiev@embassy.mzv.cz; internet www.mzv.cz/kiev; Ambassador JAROSLAV BAŠTA.

Denmark: 01901 Kyiv, vul. B. Khmelnytskoho 56; tel. (44) 200-12-60; fax (44) 200-12-81; e-mail ievamb@um.dk; Ambassador UFFE ANDERSSON BALSLEV.

Egypt: 01901 Kyiv, vul. Observatorna 19; tel. (44) 212-13-27; fax (44) 216-94-28; e-mail eg.emb_kiev@mfa.gov.eg; internet www.mfa.gov.eg/Missions/ukraine/kiev/embassy/en-GB/default; Ambassador YOUSSEF MOUSTAFA ZADA.

Estonia: 01901 Kyiv, vul. Volodymyrska 61/11–37; tel. (44) 590-07-80; fax (44) 590-07-81; e-mail embassy.kiev@mfa.ee; internet www.estemb.kiev.ua; Ambassador JAAN HEIN.

Finland: 01901 Kyiv, vul. Striletska 14; tel. (44) 278-70-49; fax (44) 278-20-32; e-mail sanomat.kio@formin.fi; internet www.finland.org.ua; Ambassador CHRISTER MICHELSSON.

France: 01034 Kyiv, vul. Reitarska 39; tel. (44) 590-36-00; fax (44) 590-36-24; e-mail pressefr@carrier.kiev.ua; internet www.ambafrance-ua.org; Ambassador JEAN-PAUL VEZIANT.

Georgia: 04119 Kyiv, vul. Melnikov 83D; tel. (44) 451-43-53; fax (44) 451-43-56; e-mail kiev@georgia.com.ua; Ambassador MERAB ANTADZE.

Germany: 01901 Kyiv, vul. B. Khmelnytskoho 25; tel. (44) 247-68-00; fax (44) 247-68-18; e-mail kanzlei@german-embassy.kiev.ua; internet kiew.diplo.de; Ambassador Dr HANS-JÜRGEN HEIMSOETH.

Greece: 01901 Kyiv, vul. Panfilovtsev 10; tel. (44) 254-54-71; fax (44) 254-39-98; e-mail greece@kiev.relc.com; internet www.greece.kiev.ua; Ambassador CHARALAMBOS DIMITRIOU.

Holy See: 01901 Kyiv, vul. Turhenyevska 40; tel. (44) 482-35-57; fax (44) 482-35-53; e-mail nuntius@visti.com; internet www.nuntiatura.kiev.ua; Apostolic Nuncio Most Rev. IVAN JURKOVIČ (Titular Archbishop of Corbavia).

Hungary: 01034 Kyiv, vul. Reitarska 33; tel. (44) 230-80-00; fax (44) 272-20-90; e-mail kev.missions@kum.hu; internet www.mfa.gov.hu/emb/kiev; Ambassador ANDRÁS BÁRSONY.

India: 01901 Kyiv, vul. Teryokhina 4; tel. (44) 468-66-61; fax (44) 468-66-19; e-mail india@public.ua.net; internet www.indianembassy.org.ua; Ambassador DEBABRATA SAHA.

Indonesia: 04107 Kyiv, vul. Nahirna 27B; tel. (44) 206-54-46; fax (44) 206-54-40; e-mail kbri@indo.ru.kiev.ua; internet www.kbri.kiev.ua; Ambassador ALBERTUS EMANUEL ALEXANDER LATURIUW.

Iran: 01901 Kyiv, vul. Kruhlouniversytetska 12; tel. (44) 229-44-63; fax (44) 229-32-55; Ambassador SEYYED MUSSA KAZEMI.

Israel: 01901 Kyiv, bulv. L. Ukrainky 34; tel. (44) 586-15-00; fax (44) 586-15-55; e-mail info@kiev.mfa.gov.il; internet ukraine.mfa.gov.il; Ambassador ZINA KALAY-KLEITMAN.

Italy: 01901 Kyiv, vul. Yaroslaviv Val 32B; tel. (44) 230-31-00; fax (44) 230-31-03; e-mail ambasciata.kiev@esteri.it; internet www.ambkiev.esteri.it; Ambassador PETRO GIOVANNI DONNICI.

Japan: 01901 Kyiv, Muzeiniy prov. 4; tel. (44) 490-55-00; fax (44) 490-55-02; e-mail jpembua7f@sovamua.com; internet www.ua.emb-japan.go.jp; Ambassador MUTSUO MABUCHI.

Kazakhstan: 01901 Kyiv, vul. Melnykova 26; tel. (44) 489-18-58; fax (44) 483-11-98; e-mail post@kazakh.kiev.ua; internet www.kazembassy.com.ua; Ambassador AMANGELDY ZH. ZHUMABAYEV.

Korea, Republic: 01034 Kyiv, vul. Volodymyrska 43; tel. (44) 246-37-59; fax (44) 246-37-57; e-mail korea@koremb.kiev.ua; internet ukr.mofat.go.kr; Ambassador HUR SEUNG-CHUL.

Kuwait: 04210 Kyiv, vul. Obolonska nab. 19; tel. (44) 391-51-60; fax (44) 391-51-64; e-mail kuwait_embassy@ukr.net; Ambassador HAMOOD YOUSSEF AL-ROUDHAN.

Kyrgyzstan: 01901 Kyiv, vul. Artema 51/50; tel. (44) 482-08-89; fax (44) 482-13-97; e-mail embassy.kg.kiev@silvercom.net; Ambassador ERKIN B. MAMKULOV.

Latvia: 01010 Kyiv, vul. I. Mazepy 6B; tel. (44) 490-70-30; fax (44) 490-70-35; e-mail embassy.ukraine@mfa.gov.lv; internet www.latemb.kiev.ua; Ambassador ATIS SJANITS.

Libya: 04050 Kyiv, vul. Ovrutska 6; tel. (44) 238-60-70; fax (44) 238-60-68; Chargé d'affaires FURJANI ABD AS-SALAM.

Lithuania: 01901 Kyiv, vul. Buslivska 21; tel. (44) 254-09-20; fax (44) 254-09-28; e-mail amb.ua@urm.lt; internet ua.mfa.lt; Ambassador ALGIRDAS KUMŽA.

Macedonia, former Yugoslav republic: 03150 Kyiv, vul. I. Fedorova 12; tel. (44) 238-66-16; fax (44) 238-66-17; e-mail embmac@carrier.kiev.ua; Ambassador ILIJA ISAJLOVSKI.

Malaysia: 1042 Kyiv, vul. Rayevskoho 4; tel. (44) 390-95-43; fax (44) 390-95-45; e-mail malkiev@kln.gov.my; internet www.kln.gov.my/perwakilan/kiev; Ambassador Dato ABDULLAH SANI OMAR.

Moldova: 01010 Kyiv, vul. I. Mazepy 8; tel. (44) 290-77-21; fax (44) 290-77-22; e-mail kiev@mfa.md; Ambassador SERGIU STATI.

Morocco: 03680 Kyiv, pr. Fedorov 12; tel. (44) 284-33-26; fax (44) 568-58-84; e-mail morocco@voilacable.com; Ambassador ABDELJALIL SAUBRY.

Netherlands: 01901 Kyiv, Kontraktova pl. 7; tel. (44) 490-82-00; fax (44) 490-82-09; e-mail kie@minbuza.nl; internet www .netherlands-embassy.com.ua; Ambassador RON KELLER.

Nigeria: 01015 Kyiv, bulv. Panfiliovtsiv 36; tel. (44) 254-58-50; fax (44) 254-53-71; Ambassador IGNATIUS HEKAYRE AJURU.

Norway: 01901 Kyiv, vul. Striletska 15; tel. (44) 590-04-70; fax (44) 234-06-55; e-mail emb.kiev@mfa.no; internet www.norway.com.ua; Ambassador OLAV BERSTAD.

Pakistan: 01015 Kyiv, pr. Panfilovtsiv 7; tel. (44) 280-25-77; fax (44) 254-45-30; e-mail parepkyiv@mail.kar.net; Ambassador GHAZANFAR ALI KHAN.

Poland: 01034 Kyiv, vul. Yaroslaviv Val 12; tel. (44) 230-07-00; fax (44) 270-63-36; e-mail ambasada@polska.com.ua; internet www .kijow.polemb.net; Ambassador JACEK KLUCZKOWSKI.

Portugal: 01901 Kyiv, vul. I. Fedorova 12/2; tel. (44) 287-58-61; fax (44) 230-26-25; e-mail geral@embport.kiev.ua; Ambassador JOSÉ MANUEL DA ENCARNAÇÃO PESSANHA VIEGAS.

Romania: 01030 Kyiv, vul. M. Kotsyubynskoho 8; tel. (44) 234-00-40; fax (44) 235-20-25; e-mail romania@adamant.net; internet kiev .mae.ro; Ambassador TRAIAN LAURENŢIU HRISTEA.

Russia: 03049 Kyiv, Povitroflotskyi pr. 27; tel. (44) 244-09-63; fax (44) 246-34-69; e-mail embrus@public.icyb.kiev.ua; internet www .embrus.org.ua; Ambassador VIKTOR S. CHERNOMYRDIN.

Serbia: 04070 Kyiv, vul. Voloska 4; tel. (44) 425-60-60; fax (44) 425-60-47; e-mail ambars@optima.com.ua; Ambassador GORAN ALEKSIĆ.

Slovakia: 01901 Kyiv, vul. Yaroslaviv Val 34; tel. (44) 212-03-10; fax (44) 272-32-71; e-mail embassy@kiev.mfa.sk; internet www.slovakia .kiev.ua; Ambassador URBAN RUSNÁK.

Slovenia: 01030 Kyiv, vul. B. Khmelnytskoho 48; tel. (44) 585-23-31; fax 585-23-43; e-mail vki@gov.si; internet kijev.veleposlanistvo.si; Ambassador PRIMOŽ ŠELIGO.

South Africa: 01004 Kyiv, vul. V. Vasylkivska 9/2, POB 7; tel. (44) 287-71-72; fax (44) 287-72-06; e-mail kiev.admin@foreign.gov.za; Ambassador ANDRIES VENTER.

Spain: 01901 Kyiv, vul. Zhoriva 46; tel. (44) 391-30-24; fax (44) 492-73-27; e-mail emb.kiev@maec.es; Ambassador LUIS JAVIER GIL CATALINA.

Sweden: 01901 Kyiv, vul. Ivana Franka 34/33; tel. (44) 494-42-70; fax (44) 494-42-71; e-mail ambassaden.kiev@foreign.ministry.se; internet www.swedenabroad.com/kiev; Ambassador JOHN-CHRISTER ÅHLANDER.

Switzerland: 01015 Kyiv, vul. Kozyatynska 12, POB 114; tel. (44) 281-61-28; fax (44) 280-14-48; e-mail kie.vertretung@eda.admin.ch; internet www.eda.admin.ch/kiev; Ambassador GEORG ZUBLER.

Syria: 04050 Kyiv, vul. Biloruska 5; tel. (44) 489-55-51; fax (44) 483-97-88; e-mail syrian-emb@ukr.net; Chargé d'affaires a.i. SULEIMAN ABUDIAB.

Turkey: 01901 Kyiv, vul. Arsenalna 18; tel. (44) 281-07-51; fax (44) 285-64-23; e-mail kievbe@binet.com.ua; Ambassador ALI BILGE CANKOREL.

Turkmenistan: 01901 Kyiv, vul. Pushkinska 6; tel. (44) 229-34-49; fax (44) 229-30-34; e-mail ambturkm@ukrpack.net; Ambassador ARSLAN S. NEPESOV.

United Kingdom: 01025 Kyiv, vul. Desyatynna 9; tel. (44) 490-36-60; fax (44) 490-36-62; e-mail ukembinf@sovamua.com; internet www.britishembassy.gov/ukraine; Ambassador ROBERT LEIGH TURNER.

USA: 01901 Kyiv, vul. Yu. Kotsyubynskoho 10; tel. (44) 490-40-00; fax (44) 490-40-85; e-mail press@usembassy.kiev.ua; internet kiev .usembassy.gov; Ambassador WILLIAM B. TAYLOR, Jr.

Uzbekistan: 01901 Kyiv, vul. Volodymyrska 16; tel. (44) 501-50-00; fax 501-50-01; e-mail embassy@uzbekistan.org.ua; internet www .uzbekistan.org.ua; Ambassador ILHOM Y. HAYDAROV.

Viet Nam: 01011 Kyiv, vul. Leskova 5; tel. (44) 254-45-89; fax (44) 294-80-87; e-mail dsq@dsqvn.kiev.ua; Ambassador NGUYEN VAN THANEM.

Judicial System

Constitutional Court of Ukraine (Konstytutsiyniy sud Ukraini): 01033 Kyiv, vul. Zhylianska 14; tel. (44) 289-05-53; fax (44) 287-20-01; e-mail idep@ccu.gov.ua; internet www.ccu.gov.ua; f. 1996; Chair. ANDRIY A. STRYZHAK.

Supreme Court (Verkhovnyi sud Ukraini): 01024 Kyiv, vul. P. Orlyka 4; tel. (44) 253-63-08; internet www.scourt.gov.ua; Chair. VASYL V. OPONENKO; Chair. of Civil Chamber ANDRIY V. HNATENKO; Chair. of Criminal Chamber MYKOLA YE. KOROTKEVYCH; Chair. of Economic Chamber VALENTYN P. BARBARA; Chair. of Administrative Chamber VIKTOR V. KRYVENKO; Chair. of Military Judicial Commission OLEKSANDR F. VOLKOV.

Supreme Economic Court (Vyshyi hospodarskyi sud Ukraini): 01011 Kyiv, vul. Kopylenka 6; tel. (44) 536-05-00; fax (44) 536-18-18; e-mail kantselariya@vasu.arbitr.gov.ua; internet www.arbitr.gov .ua; f. 1991; Chair. SERHIY F. DEMCHENKO.

Office of the Prosecutor-General: 01011 Kyiv, vul. Riznytska 13/15; tel. (44) 226-20-27; fax (44) 280-28-51; e-mail ilrd@gp.gov.ua; internet www.gp.gov.ua; Prosecutor-General OLEKSANDR L. MEDVEDKO.

Religion

State Department for Ethnic and Religious Affairs (Derzhavnyi departament u spravakh nationalnostei ta religii): 01025 Kyiv, vul. Volodymyrska 9; tel. (44) 278-17-18; e-mail mail@scnm.gov.ua; internet www.scnm.gov.ua; Chair. OLEKSANDR N. SAHAN.

CHRISTIANITY

The Eastern Orthodox Church

Eastern Orthodoxy is the principal religious affiliation in Ukraine. Until 1990 all legally constituted Orthodox church communities in Ukraine were part of the Ukrainian Exarchate of the Russian Orthodox Church (Moscow Patriarchate). In that year the Russian Orthodox Church in Ukraine was renamed the Ukrainian Orthodox Church (UOC), partly to counter the growing influence of the previously prohibited Ukrainian Autocephalous Orthodox Church (UAOC). A new ecclesiastical organization was formed in June 1992, when Filaret (Denisenko), the former Metropolitan of Kyiv, united with a faction of the UAOC to form the Kyiv Patriarchate. In July 1995 Filaret was elected as Patriarch, prompting some senior clergy to leave the church and join the UAOC. In the late 2000s the UOC (Moscow Patriarchate) remained the largest church organization in Ukraine.

Ukrainian Autocephalous Orthodox Church: 01001 Kyiv, vul. Tryokhsvyatytelska 8A; e-mail uapc-ptr@uapc-ptr.kiev.ua; internet www.uaoc.kiev.ua; f. 1921; forcibly incorporated into the Russian Orthodox Church (Moscow Patriarchate) in 1930; continued to operate clandestinely; formally revived in 1990; 1,178 parishes in 2008; Administrator Archbishop IHOR (ISICHENKO).

Ukrainian Orthodox Church (Kyiv Patriarchate): 01004 Kyiv, vul. Pushkinska 36; tel. (44) 234-10-96; fax (44) 234-30-55; e-mail patb@ukrpack.net; internet www.cerkva.info; f. 1992 by factions of the Ukrainian Orthodox Church (Moscow Patriarchate) and Ukrainian Autocephalous Orthodox Church; 4,500 parishes in 2008; 'Patriarch of Kyiv and all Rus-Ukraine' FILARET (DENISENKO).

Ukrainian Orthodox Church (Moscow Patriarchate): 01015 Kyiv, vul. I. Mazepy 25/49; tel. (44) 255-12-04; fax (44) 254-53-01; e-mail mitropolia@svitonline.com; internet www.pravoslavye.org .ua; exarchate of the Russian Orthodox Church (Moscow Patriarchate); 11,233 parishes in 2008; Metropolitan of Kyiv and All-Ukraine VLADIMIR (SABODAN).

Russian Orthodox Old Belief (Old Ritual) Church (Russkaya Pravoslavnaya Staroobryadcheskaya Tserkov): 49017 Dnipropetrovsk, pr. K. Marksa 60/8; tel. (44) 52-17-75; internet www .staroobryad.narod.ru; f. 1652 by separation from the Moscow Patriarchate; divided into two main branches: the *popovtsi* (which have priests) and the *bezpopovtsi* (which reject the notion of ordained priests and the use of all sacraments, other than that of baptism). Both branches are further divided into various groupings. The largest group of *popovtsi* are those of the Belokrinitskii Concord; 56 parishes of the Belokrinitskii Concord in Ukraine in 2008, and 10 parishes of *bezpopovtsi* at that time; Bishop of Kyiv and all Ukraine SAVVAYIYE.

The Roman Catholic Church

Most Catholics in Ukraine are adherents of the Byzantine rites observed by the so-called 'Greek' Catholic Church, which is based principally in western Ukraine and Transcarpathia. Some controversy arose, in August 2005, when the seat of the head of the Byzantine-rite Church was relocated from Lviv to the Ukrainian capital, Kyiv. In 2008 there were 3,681 parishes of the Byzantine rites in Ukraine, 895 parishes of the Latin rite and 24 parishes of the Armenian rite. Ukraine comprises one archbishopric-major (of the Byzantine rite), three archdioceses (including one each for Catholics of the Latin, Byzantine and Armenian rites), one exarchate, and 15 dioceses (of which one is directly responsible to the Holy See). At 31 December 2006 there were an estimated 4,723,456 adherents (excluding adherents of the Armenian rite, for whom figures were not available), equivalent to some 8.6% of the population. Of that number, around 83% followed the Byzantine rites.

Bishops' Conference: Bishops' Conference of Ukraine, 79008 Lviv, pl. Katedralna 1; tel. (32) 276-94-15; fax (32) 296-61-14; f. 1992; Pres. Cardinal MARIAN JAWORSKI (Metropolitan Archbishop of Lviv).

Byzantine Ukrainian Rite

Archbishop-Major of Kyiv and Halych: Cardinal LUBOMYR HUSAR, 01000 Kyiv, vul. Riznytska 11 B/28–29; tel. and fax (44) 254-56-10; e-mail arkyrparh-kv@voliacable.com; internet www.ugcc .org.ua; head of Ukrainian Greek Catholic Church; established in 1596 by the Union of Brest; forcibly integrated into the Russian Orthodox Church (Moscow Patriarchate) in 1946, but continued to function in an 'underground' capacity; relegalized in 1989; in 2005 the seat of the head of the Church was relocated from Lviv, in western Ukraine, to Kyiv.

Archbishop of Lviv: Most Rev. IHOR VOZNIAK, 79000 Lviv, pl. Sv. Yura 5; tel. and fax (32) 272-25-24; e-mail cerkvalviv@ugcc.org.ua.

Latin Rite

Archbishop of Lviv: Cardinal MARIAN JAWORSKI, 79008 Lviv, ul. Vynnitsenka 32; tel. (32) 240-37-47; fax (32) 240-37-48; e-mail rku@ lviv.farlep.net; internet www.rkc.lviv.ua.

Armenian Rite

Archbishop of Lviv: (vacant).

Protestant Churches
There were 8,417 Protestant communities registered in Ukraine in 2008.

All-Ukrainian Union of Associations of Evangelical Christians-Baptists: 01004 Kyiv, vul. L. Tolstoho 3B; tel. (44) 234-82-41; fax (44) 234-16-76; e-mail union@baptist.kiev.ua; 2,487 parishes in 2008, 134,757 adherents in 2006; affiliated to the Euro-Asiatic Federation of the Union of Evangelical Christians-Baptists; Pres. VYACHESLAV V. NESTERUK.

All-Ukrainian Union of Christians of the Evangelical Faith—Pentecostalists: 01033 Kyiv, vul. Karyerna 44; 1,433 parishes in 2008.

Embassy of the Blessed Kingdom of God for All Nations (Posolstvo Blagoslovennoho Tsarstva Bozhyeho dlya Vsekh Narodov Mira): 02152 Kyiv, vul. Tychchyny 18, Legkoatletletichesky manezh; tel. (44) 553-15-38; e-mail mail@godembassy.org; internet www .godembassy.org; f. 1994 as Word of Faith (Slovo Very); Pastor SUNDAY ADELAJA; 25,000 mems (2005).

Ukrainian Lutheran Church: 01004 Kyiv, vul. V. Vasylkivska 14/ 15; tel. (44) 235-77-21; fax (44) 234-08-00; e-mail vhorpynchuk@ yahoo.com; internet www.ukrlc.org; 40 parishes in 2008; Leader of Church Bishop Dr VYACHESLAV HORPYNCHUK.

ISLAM
In 2008 there were 512 Islamic communities officially registered in Ukraine, of which 341 were members of the Religious Administration of Muslims of Crimea. An Islamic University was established in Donetsk in 1998.

All-Ukrainian Association of Muslim Social Organizations (Arraid): 04119 Kyiv, vul. Dekhtyarivska 25A; tel. (44) 490-99-00; fax (44) 490-99-22; e-mail office@arraid.org; internet www.arraid .org; f. 1997; brs in Dnipropetrovsk, Donetsk, Kharkiv, Luhansk, Lviv, Odesa, Simferopol, Vinnytsya and Zaporizhzhya; publishes periodical *Arraid (Pioneer)* in Arabic and Russian and educational material in Russian, Tatar and Ukrainian; undertakes charitable and educational work; Chair. ISMAIL KADI.

Religious Administration of Muslims of Crimea: 95000 Crimea, Simferopol, Kebir Çami Mosque; 341 communities in 2008; Mufti AJE NURALI ABLAIYEV.

Religious Administration of Muslims of Ukraine: 04071 Kyiv, vul. Lukyanovska; tel. (44) 465-18-77; fax (44) 456-17-70; e-mail islam@i.kiev.ua; internet www.islamyat.org; f. 1992; 68 communities in 2008; Mufti Sheikh AHMED TAMIM.

JUDAISM
In 2001 there were 103,600 Jews in Ukraine (according to census results), despite high levels of emigration from the 1970s. From 1989 there was a considerable revival in the activities of Jewish communities. In 2005 there were 263 Jewish religious communities registered in Ukraine (of which 106 were members of the Chabad-Lubavitch sect), compared with 12 synagogues in 1989.

All-Ukrainian Jewish Congress: 01023 Kyiv, vul. Mechnykova 14/1; tel. (44) 235-71-20; fax (44) 235-10-67; e-mail vek@i.kiev.ua; internet www.jewish.kiev.ua; f. 1997; affiliated to the Federation of Jewish Communities of the CIS and the Baltic states; unites 183 communities; Chief Rabbi of Ukraine AZRIEL CHAIKIN.

Jewish Confederation of Ukraine: 04071 Kyiv, vul. Shekavystka 29; tel. (44) 463-70-75; fax (44) 463-70-88; e-mail eku@jewukr.org; internet www.jewukr.org; f. 1999; Chief Rabbi of Kyiv and All Ukraine YAAKOV DOV BLEICH.

The Press

In 2006 there were a total of 2,918 newspapers and 2,301 periodicals published in Ukraine. In addition to newspapers published in Ukraine, several newspapers and magazines published in Russia have a large circulation in Ukraine.

The publications listed below are in Ukrainian, except where otherwise stated.

PRINCIPAL NEWSPAPERS

Demokratychna Ukraina (Democratic Ukraine): 03047 Kyiv, pr. Peremohy 50; tel. (44) 454-88-30; fax (44) 456-91-21; e-mail du@uct .ua; internet www.dua.com.ua; f. 1918; fmrly *Radyanska Ukraina* (Soviet Ukraine); 4 a week; Editor VITALIY ADAMENKO; circ. 62,400 (2005).

Den (The Day): 04212 Kyiv, vul. Marshala Tymoshenka 2L; tel. (44) 414-40-66; fax (44) 414-49-20; e-mail master@day.kiev.ua; internet www.day.kiev.ua; f. 1998; in Ukrainian and Russian; 5 a week; publ. by the Presa Ukrainy (Press of Ukraine) Publishing House; Editor-in-Chief LARYSA IVSHYNA.

Fakty i Kommentarii (Facts and Commentaries): 04116 Kyiv, vul. V. Vasylevskoy 27–29; tel. (44) 244-57-81; fax (44) 246-85-50; e-mail info@facts.kiev.ua; internet www.facts.kiev.ua; daily; politics, economics, sport, law, culture; in Russian.

Gazeta po-Kiyevski (Kyiv Newspaper): 04080 Kyiv, vul. Frunze 104A; tel. (44) 205-43-85; e-mail tsn@pk.kiev.ua; internet pk.kiev.ua; in Russian; six a week; Chief Editor SERGEI TIKHII.

Holos Ukrainy/Golos Ukrainy (Voice of Ukraine): 03047 Kyiv, vul. Nesterova 4; tel. (44) 441-88-11; fax (44) 224-72-54; e-mail mail@ golos.com.ua; f. 1991; organ of the Verkhovna Rada; in Ukrainian and Russian; 5 a week; Editor SERHIY M. PRAVDENKO; circ. 150,000 (2002).

Kiyevskiye Vedomosti (Kyiv Gazette): 04086 Kyiv, vul. Olzhycha 29; tel. (44) 238-28-07; internet www.kv.com.ua; f. 1992; national daily; in Russian; also weekly edition (Fridays), in Ukrainian, *Kyivski Vidomosti*; Dir-Gen. VLADIMIR P. DERIKIT; Editor-in-Chief NIKOLAI V. ZAKREVSKII.

Kommersant-Ukraina (Businessman-Ukraine): Kyiv; internet www.kommersant.ua; f. 2005; owned by Kommersant Publishing House (Russia); in Russian; Dir-Gen. KAZBEK BEKTURSUNOV; Editor-in-Chief ANDREI VALILYEV.

Kyiv Post: 02140 Kyiv, pr. Bazhava 14A; tel. and fax (44) 496-45-63; e-mail editor@kyivpost.com; internet www.kyivpost.com; f. 1995; weekly; in English; Publr JED SUNDEN; Chief Editor STEFAN LADANAY; circ. 22,000 (2007).

Literaturna Ukraina (Literary Ukraine): 01061 Kyiv, bulv. L. Ukrainky 20; tel. (44) 286-36-39; e-mail lit_ukraine@ukr.net; f. 1927; weekly; organ of Union of Writers of Ukraine; Editor PETRO PEREBYJNIS; circ. 7,150 (2007).

Molod Ukrainy (The Youth of Ukraine): 03047 Kyiv, pr. Peremohy 50; tel. (44) 454-83-83; fax (44) 235-31-52; e-mail mu@pressa.com.ua; f. 1925; 3 a week; Editor-in-Chief V. I. NIKIPYELOV; circ. 24,000 (2007).

Pravda Ukrainy (The Truth of Ukraine): 03047 Kyiv, pr. Peremohy 50; tel. (44) 441-85-34; f. 1938; 5 a week; in Russian; Editor-in-Chief OLHA PRONINA; circ. 40,000.

Robitnycha Hazeta/Rabochaya Gazeta (Workers' Gazette): 03047 Kyiv, pr. Peremohy 50; tel. (44) 441-83-33; fax (44) 446-68-85; f. 1957; 5 a week; publ. by the Cabinet of Ministers and Inter-regional Association of Manufacturers; Ukrainian and Russian edns; Editor-in-Chief IVAN G. LITVIN.

Silski Visti (Rural News): 03047 Kyiv, pr. Peremohy 50; tel. (44) 441-86-32; fax (44) 446-93-71; e-mail ssk@silvist.kiev.ua; internet www.silskivisti.kiev.ua; f. 1920; 3 a week; Chief Editor V. D. HRUZIN.

Ukraina Moloda (Ukraine The Young): 03047 Kyiv, pr. Peremohy 50; tel. and fax (44) 454-83-92; e-mail politika@umoloda.kiev.ua; internet www.umoloda.kiev.ua; f. 1991; 5 a week; independent; Editor MYKHAYLO DOROSHENKO; circ. 131,657 (2008).

Ukrainska Pravda (Ukrainian Truth): Kyiv; e-mail ukrpravda@ gmail.com; internet www.pravda.com.ua; online only; in English, Russian and Ukrainian; Editor-in-Chief OLENA PRYTULA.

Ukrainske Slovo (The Ukrainian Word): 01010 Kyiv, vul. I. Mazepy 6; tel. (44) 280-70-59; fax (44) 280-62-65; e-mail info@ukrslovo.gu.ua; internet www.ukrslovo.com.ua; f. 1933; weekly; nationalist; Editor-in-Chief VOLODYMYR HAPTAR.

Uryadoviy Kuryer (Official Courier): 01008 Kyiv, vul. Sadova 1; tel. (44) 253-12-95; fax (44) 253-39-50; e-mail letter@ukcc.com.ua; internet www.ukcc.com.ua; f. 1990; 5 a week; organ of the Cabinet of Ministers; Editor-in-Chief ALLA KOVTUR; circ. 83,000 (2008).

Vechirniy Kyiv (Evening Kyiv): 04136 Kyiv, vul. Marshala Hrechka 13; tel. (44) 434-61-09; fax (44) 443-96-09; e-mail office@vechirka.kiev.ua; internet www.vechirka.kiev.ua; f. 1906; 5 a week; Editor-in-Chief OLEKSANDR BALABKO; circ. 45,000 (2005).

Vlada i Polityka/Vlast i Politika (Power and Politics): 01042 Kyiv, vul. P. Lumumby 4v/200; tel. (44) 201-01-28; fax (44) 201-01-29; e-mail vip@vipnews.com.ua; internet www.vipnews.com.ua; f. 2001; weekly; in Ukrainian and Russian; Dir-Gen. ANDRIY V. NAKONECH-NYI; Editor-in-Chief YURIY L. UZDEMYR; circ. 22,000 (2002).

Za Vilnu Ukrainu (For a Free Ukraine): 79000 Lviv, vul. Voronoho 3; tel. (32) 297-92-49; fax (32) 272-95-27; e-mail zwuky@mail.lviv.ua; f. 1990; 5 a week; independent; Editor-in-Chief MYKHAYLO SIRKIV; circ. 30,058 (2001).

PRINCIPAL PERIODICALS

Avto-Tsentr (Autocentre): 03047 Kyiv, pr. Peremohy 50, POB 2; tel. (44) 206-56-01; fax (44) 458-44-04; e-mail info@autocentre.ua; internet www.autocentre.ua; f. 1997; weekly; motoring; in Russian; Editor-in-Chief SERGEI TARNAVSKII; circ. 200,000.

Barvinok (Periwinkle): 04119 Kyiv, vul. Dekhtyarivska 38–44; tel. (44) 213-99-13; fax (44) 211-04-36; e-mail barvinok@kievweb.com.ua; f. 1928; fortnightly; illustrated popular fiction for school-age children; in Ukrainian; Editor VASYL VORONOVYCH; circ. 40,000.

Berezil: 61002 Kharkiv, vul. Chernyshevskoho 59; tel. (57) 700-32-23; fax (57) 700-54-37; f. 1956; fmrly Prapor; monthly; journal of Union of Writers of Ukraine; fiction and socio-political articles; Editor-in-Chief VOLODYMYR NAUMENKO; circ. 5,000.

Delovaya Stolitsya (Capital City Business): 01135 Kyiv, vul. Pavlovska 29; tel. (44) 502-02-21; fax (44) 502-02-27; e-mail dsnews@dsnews.ua; internet www.dsnews.ua; f. 2001; weekly; in Russian; Editor-in-Chief INNA KOVTUN; circ. 67,500 (2008).

Delovaya Ukraina (Business Ukraine): 01133 Kyiv, vul. Kutuzova 18/7/2; tel. and fax (44) 201-03-90; e-mail delukr@email.kiev.ua; internet www.delukr.kiev.ua; f. 1992; 2 a week; business issues; in Ukrainian and Russian; Editor ALLAL KOVTUM.

Dnipro (The Dnieper): 04119 Kyiv, vul. Dekhtyarivska 38–44; tel. (44) 446-11-42; f. 1927; 2 a month; novels, short stories, essays, poetry, social and political topics; Editor MYKOLA LUKIV.

Donbas/Donbass: 83055 Donetsk, vul. Artema 80 A; tel. (622) 93-82-26; f. 1923; monthly; journal of Union of Writers of Ukraine; fiction; in Ukrainian and Russian; circ. 20,000 (1991).

Dzerkalo Tyzhnya/Zerkalo Nedyeli (Mirror of the Week): 03680 Kyiv, vul. Tverska 6; tel. (44) 536-02-44; fax (44) 269-74-52; e-mail info@mirror.kiev.ua; internet www.zerkalo-nedeli.com; weekly; politics, economics, the arts; Ukrainian and Russian edns; also English edition (online only); Editor-in-Chief VLADIMIR MOSTOVOI; circ. 30,000 (Russian edn), 12,000 (Ukrainian edn).

Dzvin (Bell): 79005 Lviv, vul. Kn. Romana 6; tel. (32) 272-36-20; f. 1940; monthly; journal of Union of Writers of Ukraine; fiction; Editor ROMAN FEDORIV; circ. 152,500.

Interesna Hazeta (Interesting Newspaper): 03047 Kyiv, pr. Peremohy 50; tel. (44) 441-82-59; e-mail postmail@avkpress.kiev.ua; 2 a month; general; circ. 700,000.

Kompanyon (Companion): 01103 Kyiv, vul. Kykbydze 39; tel. (44) 494-25-01; fax (44) 494-25-05; e-mail komp@companion.ua; internet www.companion.ua; f. 1996; weekly; in Russian; economics, politics, business; Editor-in-Chief A. POHORELOV; circ. 25,000 (2004).

Kyiv: 01025 Kyiv, vul. Desyatinna 11; tel. (44) 229-02-80; f. 1983; monthly; journal of the Union of Writers of Ukraine and the Kyiv Writers' Organization; fiction; Editor-in-Chief PETRO M. PEREBYJNIS.

Malyatko (Child): 04119 Kyiv, vul. Dekhtyarivska 38–44; tel. and fax (44) 483-98-91; e-mail malyatko_1@online.com.ua; f. 1960; monthly; illustrated; for pre-school children; Editor-in-Chief ZINAIDA LESHENKO; circ. 35,780 (2005).

Nataly: 02156 Kyiv, vul. Kyoto 25; tel. (44) 519-34-33; fax (44) 518-77-90; internet www.nataly.com.ua; monthly; women's interest; Editor-in-Chief ZHANNA LAVROVA; circ. 679,115 (2002).

Natsionalna Bezpeka i Oborona (National Security and Defence): 01034 Kyiv, vul. Volodymyrska 46, Olekander Razumkov Ukrainian Centre for Economic and Political Studies; tel. (44) 201-11-98; fax (44) 201-11-99; e-mail info@uceps.com.ua; internet www.uceps.com.ua; f. 2000; monthly; politics, economics, international relations; in Ukrainian and English; Pres. ANATOLIY GRYTSENKO.

Obrazotvorche Mistetstvo (Fine Arts): 04055 Kyiv, vul. Artema 1–5; tel. (44) 272-02-86; fax (44) 272-14-54; e-mail spilka@nbi.com .ua; f. 1933; 4 a year; publ. by the National Union of Artists of Ukraine; Editor-in-Chief OLEKSANDR FEDORUK; circ. 1,500 (2007).

Perets (Pepper): 03047 Kyiv, pr. Peremohy 50; tel. (44) 454-82-14; fax (44) 234-35-82; e-mail prudnyk@bigmir.net; f. 1922; monthly; publ. by the Presa Ukrainy Publishing House; satirical; Editor MYKHAYLO PRUDNYK; circ. 15,000 (2007).

Politychna Dumka/Politicheskaya Mysl/Political Thought: 01030 Kyiv, vul. Leontovycha 5; tel. and fax (44) 235-02-29; e-mail politdumka@bigmir.net; internet www.politdumka.kiev.ua; f. 1993; current affairs and political analysis; Ukrainian, Russian and English edns; Editor-in-Chief VOLODOMYR POLOKHALO.

Polityka i Chas/Politics and the Times: 02160 Kyiv, pr. Vozyed-nanya 15–17; tel. and fax (44) 550-31-44; e-mail times@uct.kiev.ua; f. 1994 to replace *Pid praporam Lenina* (Under the Banner of Lenin); monthly; organ of the Ministry of Foreign Affairs; international relations and foreign affairs; in Ukrainian (monthly) and English (quarterly); Editor-in-Chief LEONID BAIDAK; circ. 6,000 (2003).

Ukraina (Ukraine): 03047 Kyiv, pr. Peremohy 50; tel. and fax (44) 454-88-31; internet ukraina-magazine.com.ua; f. 1907; monthly; social, political and cultural life in Ukraine; illustrated; Editor-in-Chief IHOR PARYMSKY; circ. 40,000 (2007).

Ukraina Business (Ukraine Business): 01004 Kyiv, vul. Push-kinska 20/24; tel. and fax (44) 224-25-55; f. 1990; weekly; Editor-in-Chief YURIY VASYLCHUK.

Ukrainskiy Teatr (Ukrainian Theatre): Kyiv; tel. (44) 228-24-74; f. 1936; 6 a year; journal of the Ministry of Art and Culture, and the Union of Theatrical Workers of Ukraine; Editor-in-Chief YURIY BOHDASHEVSKIY; circ. 4,100.

Vitchyzna (Fatherland): 01021 Kyiv, vul. M. Hrushevskoho 34; tel. (44) 253-28-51; f. 1933; 6 a year; Ukrainian prose and poetry; Editor OLEKSANDR HLUSHKO; circ. 50,100.

Vsesvit (The Whole World): 01021 Kyiv, vul. M. Hrushevskoho 34/1; tel. (44) 253-13-18; fax (44) 253-06-13; e-mail myk@vsesvit-review .kiev.ua; internet www.vsesvit-journal.com; f. 1925; monthly; foreign fiction, literary criticism and reviews of foreign literature and art; Exec. Editor OLEH MYKYTENKO; circ. 2,000–3,000 (2007).

Yeva (Eve): 04050 Kyiv, vul. Melnykova 12A/8; tel. (44) 568-59-53; fax (44) 568-58-96; e-mail info@evamag.com; f. 1998; 6 a year; fashion, design; Editor-in-Chief IRYNA B. DANYLEVSKA; circ. 10,000 (2002).

Zhinka (Woman): 03047 Kyiv, pr. Peremohy 50; tel. and fax (44) 446-90-34; e-mail zhinka@cki.ipri.kiev.ua; f. 1920; monthly; publ. by Presa Ukrainy Publishing House; social and political subjects; fiction; for women; Editor LIDIYA MAZUR; circ. 250,000.

NEWS AGENCIES

Interfax-Ukraina (Interfax-Ukraine): 01034 Kyiv, vul. Reitarska 8/5 A; tel. (44) 464-04-65; fax (44) 464-05-69; e-mail news@interfax .kiev.ua; internet www.interfax.kiev.ua; f. 1992; Dir OLEKSANDR MARTYNENKO.

Respublika Ukrainian Independent Information Agency (UNIAR): 02005 Kyiv, vul. Mechnykova 14/1; tel. (44) 246-46-34; e-mail naboka@uniar.kiev.ua; internet www.uniar.com.ua; independent press agency; Dir S. NABOKA.

Ukrainian Independent Information and News Agency (UNIAN): 01001 Kyiv, vul. Khreshchatyk 4; tel. (44) 279-33-53; fax (44) 461-91-11; e-mail info@unian.net; internet www.unian.net; f. 1993; press agency and monitoring service; selected services are provided in Ukrainian, Russian and English; Gen. Dir OLEH I. NALIVAIKO; Editor-in-Chief OLEKSANDR A. KHARCHENKO.

Ukrainski Novyni Informatsyonnoye Ahentstvo (Ukrainian News Information Agency): 01033 Kyiv, vul. Volodymyrska 61/11/41; tel. (44) 494-31-60; fax (44) 494-31-67; e-mail office@ukranews .com; internet www.ukranews.com; f. 1993; economic and political news; in Ukrainian, Russian and English.

UkrInform–Ukrainian National Information Agency: 01001 Kyiv, vul. B. Khmelnytskoho 8/16B; tel. (44) 279-81-52; fax (44) 279-86-65; e-mail office@ukrinform.com; internet news.ukrinform.com .ua; f. 1918; Dir-Gen. VIKTOR CHAMARA.

Publishers

In 1996 there were 6,460 book titles (including pamphlets and brochures) published in Ukraine (total circulation 50.9m.). By 2006 the number of book titles published in Ukraine had increased to 15,867.

Budivelnik (Builder): 04053 Kyiv, vul. Observatorna 25; tel. (44) 212-10-90; f. 1947; books on building and architecture; in Ukrainian and Russian; Dir S. N. BALATSKII.

Dnipro (The Dnieper): 01034 Kyiv, vul. Volodymyrska 42; tel. (44) 224-31-82; e-mail dnipro-pbl@svitonline.com; internet www .dnipro-publ.kiev.ua; f. 1919; classics, fiction, art and popular editions; in Ukrainian and Russian; Dir TARAS I. SERGIYCHUK.

Donbas/Donbass: 83002 Donetsk, vul. B. Khmelnytskoho 102; tel. (622) 93-25-84; fiction and criticism; in Ukrainian and Russian; Dir B. F. KRAVCHENKO.

Folio: Kharkiv; tel. and fax (572) 47-61-25; e-mail foliosp@kharkov .ukrpack.net; internet folio.com.ua; f. 1992; classic and contemporary fiction in Russian, Ukrainian and French; Gen. Man. ALEKSANDR V. KRASOVITSKII.

Kamenyar (Stonecrusher): 79000 Lviv, vul. Pidvalna 3; tel. and fax (32) 272-19-49; e-mail vyd_kamenyar@mail.lviv.ua; fiction and criticism; in Ukrainian; Dir DMYTRO I. SAPIGA.

Karpaty (The Carpathians): 88000 Transcarpathian obl., Uzhhorod, Radyanska pl. 3; tel. (312) 23-25-13; fiction and criticism; in Ukrainian and Russian; Dir V. I. DANKANICH.

Konsum: 61057 Kharkiv, POB 9123; tel. (572) 17-01-19; fax (572) 23-76-75; e-mail book@konsum.kharkov.ua; internet konsum.kharkov .ua; politics, economics, human rights, legal and medical books.

Lybid (Swan): 01001 Kyiv, vul. Pushkinska 32; tel. (44) 228-10-93; fax (44) 229-11-71; e-mail info@lybid.org.ua; internet www.lybid.org .ua; f. 1835; University of Kyiv press; Dir OLENA A. BOIKO.

Medytsyna Svitu (Medicines of the World): 79071 Lviv, vul. Kulparkivska 131; tel. (32) 263-34-65; fax (32) 261-34-65; e-mail msvitu@mail.lviv.ua; internet www.msvitu.lviv.ua; f. 1996; medical journals and books, history, art and religion; Dirs VOLODYMYR PAVLIUK, ZINOVIY MATCHAK.

Molod (Youth): 04119 Kyiv, vul. Dekhtyarivska 38–44; tel. (44) 213-11-60; fax (44) 213-11-92; in Ukrainian; Dir O. I. POLONSKA.

Muzichna Ukraina (Musical Ukraine): 01034 Kyiv, vul. Pushkinska 32; tel. (44) 225-63-56; fax (44) 224-63-00; f. 1966; books on music; in Ukrainian; Dir N. P. LINNIK; Editor-in-Chief B. R. VERESHCHAGIN.

Mystetstvo: 01034 Kyiv, vul. Zolotovoritska 11; tel. (44) 235-53-92; fax (44) 279-05-64; e-mail mystetstvo@ukr.net; f. 1932; fine art criticism, theatre and screen art, tourism, Ukrainian culture; in Ukrainian, Russian, English, French and German; Dir NINA PRYBEHA.

Naukova Dumka (Scientific Thought): 01601 Kyiv, vul. Tereshchenkivska 3; tel. (44) 234-40-68; fax (44) 234-70-60; e-mail ndumka@i.kiev.ua; internet www.ndumka.kiev.ua; f. 1922; scientific books and periodicals in all branches of science; research monographs; Ukrainian literature; dictionaries and reference books; in Ukrainian, Russian and English; Dir I. R. ALEKSEYENKO.

Osvita (Education): 04053 Kyiv, vul. Yu. Kotsyubynski 5; tel. and fax (44) 486-54-44; e-mail osvita@kv.ukrtel.net; internet www .osvitapublish.com.ua; f. 1920; state-owned; educational books for schools of all levels; Dir-Gen. IRAYIDA PODOLYUK.

Prapor (Flag): 61002 Kharkiv, vul. Chubarya 11; tel. (572) 47-72-52; fax (572) 43-07-21; fmrly Berezil; general; in Ukrainian and Russian; Dir V. S. LEBETS.

Prosvita (Enlightenment): 01032 Kyiv, bulv. Shevchenka 46; tel. (44) 234-15-86; fax (44) 234-95-23; internet www.prosvita.kiev.ua; f. 1990; textbooks for all levels of education from pre-school to higher education.

Rino (Beacon): 65111 Odesa, pr. Dobrovolskoho 118/264; tel. (482) 54-21-98; e-mail rino@farlep.net; fiction and criticism; in Ukrainian and Russian; Dir DMYTRO BUKHANENKO.

Rodovid: 01001 Kyiv, POB 548; tel. and fax (44) 220-48-29; e-mail rodovid@ln.ua; internet www.rodovid.net; history, ethnography, poetry, cultural history.

Sich (Camp): 49070 Dnipropetrovsk, pr. K. Marksa 60; tel. (562) 45-22-01; fax (562) 45-44-04; f. 1964; fiction, juvenile, socio-political, criticism; in Ukrainian, English, German, French and Russian; Dir V. A. SIROTA; Editor-in-Chief V. V. LEVCHENKO.

Tavria: 95000 Crimea, Simferopol, vul. Gorkogo 5; tel. (652) 27-45-66; fax (652) 27-65-74; e-mail ingvi@ukr.net; fiction, criticism, folklore and geography; in Ukrainian, Russian and Crimean Tatar; Dir Y. IVANICHENKO.

Tekhnika (Technology): Kyiv; tel. (44) 228-22-43; f. 1930; industry and transport books, popular science, posters and booklets; in Ukrainian and Russian; Dir M. G. PISARENKO.

Tsentr Yevropy (The Centre of Europe): 79000 Lviv, vul. Kostyushko 18/317; tel. (32) 272-35-66; fax (32) 272-76-71; e-mail centrevr@is.lviv.ua; f. 1994; books relating to the history and culture of Halychyna (Galicia); Dir SERHIY E. FRUKHT.

Ukraina: 01054 Kyiv, vul. Hoholivska 7н; tel. (44) 216-36-02; fax (44) 216-97-35; e-mail ua@alfacom.net; internet www.ua.alfacom .net; f. 1922; humanities, science, reference and literary works; Dir MYKOLA V. STETYUHA; Editor-in-Chief OLEKSANDR P. KOSYUK.

Ukrainska Ensyklopedia (Ukrainian Encyclopedia): 01030 Kyiv, vul. B. Khmelnytskoho 51; tel. (44) 224-80-85; encyclopedias, dictionaries and reference books; Dir A. V. KUDRITSKIY.

Ukrainskiy Pysmennyk (Ukrainian Writer): 01054 Kyiv, vul. O. Honshara 52; tel. (44) 486-25-92; e-mail ukps@ln.ua; f. 1933; publishing house of the National Union of Writers of Ukraine; fiction; in Ukrainian; Dir A. O. SAVCHUK.

Urozhai (Harvest): 03035 Kyiv, vul. Uritskoho 45; tel. (44) 220-16-26; f. 1925; books and journals about agriculture; Dir V. G. PRIKHODKO.

Veselka (Rainbow): 04050 Kyiv, vul. Melnikova 63; tel. (44) 483-95-01; fax (44) 483-33-59; e-mail veskiev@iptelecom.net.ua; internet www.veselka-ua.com; f. 1934; books for pre-school and school-age children; in Ukrainian and foreign languages; Dir YAREMA HOYAN.

Vyscha Shkola (High School): 01054 Kyiv, vul. Hoholivska 7; tel. and fax (44) 216-33-05; f. 1968; educational, scientific, reference, etc.; Dir V. P. KHOVKHUN; Editor-in-Chief V. V. PIVEN.

Zdorovya (Health): Kyiv; tel. (44) 216-89-08; books on medicine, physical fitness and sport; in Ukrainian; Dir A. P. RODZIYEVSKIY.

Znannya (Knowledge): 01034 Kyiv, vul. Striletska 28; tel. (44) 234-80-43; fax (44) 238-82-65; e-mail znannia@society.kiev.ua; internet www.znannia.com.ua; f. 1948; general non-fiction; Dir VOLODOMYR KARASOV.

Broadcasting and Communications

TELECOMMUNICATIONS

Regulatory Authority

State Committee for Communication and Information: 01001 Kyiv, vul. Khreshchatyk 22; tel. (44) 228-15-00; fax (44) 228-61-41; e-mail mailbox@stc.gov.ua; internet www.stc.gov.ua; Chair. IHOR V. KRAVETS.

Major Service Providers

Astelit: 03110 Kyiv, vul. Solomyanska 11 A; tel. (44) 233-31-31; internet www.life.com.ua; f. 2005; 51% owned by TurkCell (Turkey); provides mobile cellular telecommunications services under the brand name 'Life'.

Golden Telecom GSM: 01021 Kyiv, vul. Khreshchatyk 19 A; tel. (44) 490-00-90; fax (44) 490-00-70; e-mail info@goldentele.com; internet www.goldentele.com; mobile cellular telephone services; Gen. Man. YURIY BEZBORODIV.

KyivStar GSM: Kyiv, vul. I. Mazepy 24; tel. (44) 466-04-66; internet www.kyivstar.net; f. 1997; 54.2% owned by Telenor (Norway); provides mobile cellular telecommunications services under the brand names 'Ace & Base' and 'Djuice' in major cities and other regions across Ukraine; Pres. IHOR LITOVCHENKO; 15.1m. subscribers (May 2006).

MTS Ukraina: 01015 Kyiv, vul. Leiptsizka 15; fax (44) 230-02-56; e-mail slavik@umc.com.ua; internet www.umc.com.ua; f. 1991; fmrly Ukrainian Mobile Communications; present name adopted 2007; 100% owned by MTS (Russia); Gen. Man. ANDRIY DUBOVSKOV.

UkrTelecom: 01030 Kyiv, bulv. Shevchenka 18; tel. (44) 226-25-41; fax (44) 234-39-57; e-mail ukrtelecom@ukrtelecom.net; internet www.ukrtelecom.ua; f. 1993; national fixed telecommunications network operator; provides national and international telecommunications services; Chair. of Bd HEORHIY B. DZEKON.

BROADCASTING

Regulatory Authorities

National Council of Ukraine for Television and Radio Broadcasting: 01025 Kyiv, vul. Desyatynna 14; tel. (44) 278-68-32; fax (44) 228-75-75; e-mail shevch@ukr.net; internet www.nrada.gov.ua; f. 1994; monitoring and supervisory functions; issues broadcasting licences; Chair. VITALIY F. SHEVCHENKO.

State Committee for Television and Radio Broadcasting (Derzhavnyi komitet telebachennya i radiomovlennya Ukrainy): 01001 Kyiv, vul. Khreshchatyk 26/206; tel. (44) 239-63-89; internet comin.kmu.gov.ua; responsibilities include the supervision of 27 state-controlled television and radio companies; Chair. EDUARD PRUTNIK.

Radio

Hromadske (Community) Radio: 01025 Kyiv, vul. Volodymyrska 61/11/50; tel. (44) 494-40-14; information, news and discussion programmes.

National Radio Co of Ukraine-Ukrainian Radio (Natsionalna Radiokompaniya Ukrainy-Ukrainske Radio): 01001 Kyiv, vul. Khreshchatyk 26; tel. (44) 279-33-79; fax (44) 279-34-77; e-mail krutouz@nrcu.gov.ua; internet www.nrcu.gov.ua; state-owned; domestic broadcasts; also international broadcasts in English, German, Romanian and Ukrainian; Pres. VIKTOR I. NABRUSKO.

Several independent radio stations broadcast to the major cities of Ukraine.

Television

Ukrainian State Television and Radio Co (Derzhavna Teleradiomovna Kompaniya Ukrainy): 01001 Kyiv, vul. Khreshchatyk 26; tel. (44) 481-43-86; Chair. VITALIY DOKALENKO.

1+1: 01001 Kyiv, vul. Khreshchatyk 7/11; tel. and fax (44) 490-01-01; e-mail contact@1plus1.tv; internet www.1plus1.tv; f. 1995; independent; broadcasts for 24 hours daily to 95% of Ukrainian population; Chair. of Bd of Dirs OLEKSANDR YU. RODNYANSKY.

5 Kanal: 04176 Kyiv, vul. Elektrykiv 26; tel. (44) 239-16-86; internet 5.ua; terrestrial broadcasts to 14 cities, and cable and satellite broadcasts; 24-hour news broadcasts; Dir-Gen. IVAN ADAMCHUK.

Inter: 01601 Kyiv, vul. Dmitriyevska 30; tel. and fax (44) 490-67-65; e-mail pr@inter.ua; internet www.inter.kiev.ua; f. 1996.

Novy Kanal (New Channel): 04107 Kyiv, vul. Nahorna 24/1; tel. (44) 238-80-28; fax (44) 238-80-20; e-mail post@novy.tv; internet www .novy.tv; f. 1998; broadcasts in Ukrainian and Russian; Chair. OLEKSANDR M. TKACHENKO.

STB: 03113 Kyiv, vul. Shevtsova 1; tel. (44) 501-98-99; e-mail y@stb .ua; internet stb.ua; Chair. of Bd VOLODYMYR BORODYANSKY.

Finance

(cap. = capital; res = reserves; dep. = deposits; brs = branches; m. = million; amounts in hryvnyas, unless otherwise indicated)

In June 2004 there were 158 banks registered in Ukraine, of which two were state-owned, and 18 were majority or wholly foreign-owned. Some 127 of the banks had assets worth less than US $150m., and the largest 25 banks accounted for 72.3% of the total banking assets.

BANKING

Central Bank

National Bank of Ukraine (Natsionalny Bank Ukrainy): 01601 Kyiv, vul. Institutska 9; tel. (44) 253-38-22; fax (44) 230-20-33; e-mail postmaster@bank.gov.ua; internet www.bank.gov.ua; f. 1991; cap. 10m., res 5,872m., dep. 36,480m. (Dec. 2006); Gov. VOLODYMYR S. STELMAKH.

Other State Banks

Republican Bank of Crimea: 95000 Crimea, Simferopol, ul. Gorkogo; tel. (652) 51-09-46; e-mail webmaster@rbc.crimea.ua.

UkrExImBank—State Export-Import Bank of Ukraine: 03150 Kyiv, vul. Horkoho 127; tel. (44) 247-80-70; fax (44) 247-80-82; e-mail bank@eximb.com; internet www.eximb.com; f. 1992; fmrly br. of USSR Vneshekonombank (External Trade Bank); cap. 1,631.6m., res 0.0m., dep. 15,833.2m., (Dec. 2006); Chair. of Bd VIKTOR V. KAPUSTIN; 30 brs.

Commercial Banks

Aktyv-Bank (Active-Bank): 03127 Kyiv, vul. Borysohlibska 3; tel. (44) 258-26-10; fax (44) 258-26-12; e-mail bank@abank.com.ua; internet www.abank.com.ua; f. 2002; cap. 312.8m., dep. 1,133.5m., total assets 1,480.0m. (Dec. 2006); Chair. of Managing Bd OLEKSANDR YEGOROV.

Alfa-Bank (Ukraine): 01025 Kyiv, vul. Desyatinna 4/6; tel. (44) 490-46-00; fax (44) 490-46-01; e-mail mail@alfabank.kiev.ua; internet www.alfabank.com.ua; f. 1993; cap. US $272.6m., res $25.0m., dep. $1,552.2m. (Dec. 2007); Chair. ANDRIY VOLKOV.

Brokbiznesbank: 03057 Kyiv, pr. Peremohy 41; tel. (44) 206-29-83; fax (44) 459-67-80; e-mail bank@bankbb.com; internet www.bankbb .com; f. 1991; dep. US $766m., total assets $1,540m. (Jun. 2007); Chair. of Council MYKOLA STRILA; Chair. of Bd SERHIY P. MISHTA; 235 brs.

Calyon Bank Ukraine: 01034 Kyiv, vul. Volodymyrska 23A; tel. (44) 490-14-01; fax (44) 490-14-02; e-mail ukr-general@ua.calyon .com; internet www.calyon.kiev.ua; f. 1993; 100% owned by Crédit Agricole (France); cap. 172m., res 96m., dep. 1,800m. (Dec. 2007); Pres. and Dir-Gen. JACQUES MOUNIER.

Credit Europe Bank (Kredyt Yevropa Bank): 01601 Kyiv, vul. Mechnikova 2, Parus Biznis-Tsentr; tel. (44) 390-67-33; fax (44) 499-40-35; e-mail sahan.aydin@crediteurope.com.ua; internet www .crediteurope.com.ua; f. 2006 as Finansbank; present name adopted 2007; 99.9% owned by Credit Europe Bank NV (Netherlands); cap. 329.1m., res −0.2m., dep. 1,230.9m. (Dec. 2007); Chair. of Managing Bd C. METE ALTIN.

Donghorbank: 83086 Donetsk, vul. Artema 38; tel. (62) 332-73-03; fax (62) 332-73-24; e-mail pr_financing@dongorbank.com; internet www.dongorbank.com; f. 1992; cap. 228.7m., res 45.9m., dep. 2,301.4m. (Dec. 2006); Head of Management Bd VLADIMIR POPOVICH.

Finance and Credit Bank (Bank 'Financy ta Kredyt'): 04050 Kyiv, vul. Artema 60; tel. (44) 490-68-70; fax (44) 238-24-65; e-mail common@fc.kiev.ua; internet www.fc.kiev.ua; f. 1990; cap. 675.1m., dep. 6,111.7m., total assets 7,297.8m. (Dec. 2006); Chair. VLADIMIR H. KHLYVNYUK; 11 brs.

First Ukrainian International Bank/Pershyi Ukrainskyi Mizhnarodnyi Bank (FUIB): 83001 Donetsk, vul. Universitetska 2A; tel. (623) 32-45-03; fax (623) 32-47-00; e-mail corrbnk@fuib.com; internet www.fuib.com; f. 1991; cap. US $325.8m., res $78.8m., dep. $1,212.5m. (Dec. 2007); Chair. of Bd ALEKSANDRA G. VOROPAEVA.

Forum Bank (Bank Forum): 02100 Kyiv, bulv. Verkhovnoi Rady 7; tel. (44) 552-05-55; fax (44) 554-70-90; e-mail market@forum.com.ua; internet www.forum.com.ua; f. 1994; cap. 639.7m., res 40.3m., dep. 5,879.2m. (Dec. 2006); Chair. YAROSLAV V. KOLESNYK; 30 brs.

Indeks Bank: 01004 Kyiv, vul. Pushkinska 42/4; tel. (44) 581-07-76; fax (44) 581-07-76; e-mail liudmyla.leonova@indexbank.ua; internet www.indexbank.ua; f. 1993; 99.98% owned by Crédit Agricole (France); cap. 200.0m., res 37.4m., dep. 2,273.1m. (Dec. 2006); Chief Exec. and Chair. of Bd IGOR FRANTSKEVYCH.

Khreshchatyk Bank: 01001 Kyiv, vul. Khreshchatyk 8A; tel. and fax (44) 230-72-28; e-mail bank@xbank.com.ua; internet www .xcitybank.com.ua; f. 1993; present name adopted 1998; 23.7% owned by Kyiv City Administration; cap. US $109.0m., res $6.0m., dep. $890.1m. (Dec. 2007); Chair. of Bd DMYTRO M. GRYDZHYK; 160 brs.

Kredobank: 79026 Lviv, vul. Sakharova 78; tel. (32) 297-23-20; fax (32) 297-08-37; e-mail office@kredobank.com.ua; internet www .kredobank.com.ua; f. 1990; present name adopted 2006; 98.2% owned by PKO Bank Polski SA (Poland); cap. 273.4m., dep. 2,379.6m. (Jul. 2007); res 0.0m. (Dec. 2005); Pres. STEPAN I. KUBIV.

Kredytprombank: 01014 Kyiv, bulv. Druzhby Narodiv 38; tel. (44) 490-27-79; fax (44) 490-72-28; e-mail kpb@kreditprombank.com; internet www.kreditprombank.com; f. 1997; cap. 677.2m., res 62.0m., dep. 6,182.4m. (Dec. 2006); Chair. of Bd LYUDMILA V. RASPUTNA.

Nadra Bank: 04053 Kyiv, vul. Artema 15; tel. (44) 459-37-00; fax (44) 288-00-22; e-mail pr@nadrabank.kiev.ua; internet www.nadra .com.ua; f. 1993; cap. US $83.6m., res $144.6m., dep. $1,758.7m. (Dec. 2006); Pres. and Chair. of Bd IGOR V. GILENKO; 691 brs and sub-brs.

OTP Bank: 01033 Kyiv, vul. Zhylyanska 43; tel. (44) 490-05-00; fax (44) 490-05-01; e-mail infobox.rbu@rbu-kiev.raiffeisen.at; internet www.rbua.com; f. 1998; present name adopted 2006; 100% owned by OTP Bank plc (Romania); cap. 540.0m., res 2.7m., dep. 10,009.3m. (Dec. 2006); Chair. of Bd DMITRI ZINKOV.

Pivdennyi Bank (Southern Bank): 65059 Odesa, vul. Krasnova 6/1; tel. (482) 30-70-37; fax (482) 30-70-82; e-mail lds@pivdenny.odessa .ua; internet www.bank.com.ua; f. 1993; cap. 563.9m., res 99.6m., dep. 7,770.2m. (Dec. 2007); Chair. of Bd VADYM V. MOROKHOVSKIY; 16 brs.

PrivatBank: 49094 Dnipropetrovsk, nab. Peremohy 50; tel. (562) 39-05-11; fax (56) 778-54-74; e-mail privatbank@pbank.dp.ua; internet www.privatbank.ua; cap. 2,335.3m., res 448.8m., dep. 28,902.3m. (Dec. 2006); Chair. of Bd ALEKSANDR V. DUBILET; 51 brs.

ProCredit Bank Ukraine (ProKredyt Bank Ukraine): 03115 Kyiv, pr. Peremohy 107A; tel. (44) 590-10-00; fax (44) 590-10-01; e-mail procreditbank@procreditbank.com.ua; internet www.procreditbank .com.ua; f. 2000; present name adopted 2003; 60% owned by ProCredit Holding AG (Germany), 20% by Western NIS Enterprise Fund (Germany), 20% by European Bank for Reconstruction and Development (United Kingdom); cap. US $29.7m., res $0.2m., dep. $213.8m. (Dec. 2006); Gen. Man. DIRK HABOECK.

Prominvestbank (Industrial-Investment Bank): 01001 Kyiv, prov. Shevchenka 12; tel. (44) 201-51-20; fax (44) 201-50-44; e-mail bank@ pib.com.ua; internet www.pib.com.ua; f. 1922 as Stroibank, name changed 1992; cap. 200.2m., res 25.3m., dep. 15,767.4m. (Dec. 2006); Chair. VOLODYMYR P. MATVYENKO; 600 brs.

Raiffeisenbank Aval: 01011 Kyiv, vul. Leskova 9; tel. (44) 490-88-01; fax (44) 490-87-55; e-mail info@aval.ua; internet www.aval.ua; f. 1992 as Aval Bank; present name adopted 2006 following acquisition by Raiffeisen International Bank AG (Austria); cap. US $430.8m., res $125.3m., dep. $4,670.2m. (Dec. 2006); Pres. VOLODYMYR I. LAVRENCHUK; 1,400 brs and sub-brs.

Rodovid Bank: 04070 Kyiv, vul. P. Sahaidachniy 17; tel. (44) 255-86-47; fax (44) 255-86-54; e-mail info@rodovidbank.com; internet www.rodovidbank.com; f. 1990; present name adopted 2004; cap. 350.0m., res 77.6m., dep. 3,138.3m. (Dec. 2006); Chair. of Bd DENIS V. GORBUNENKO; 2 brs.

Sberbank Rossii (Ukraine): 01034 Kyiv, vul. Volodymyrska 46; tel. (44) 247-43-00; fax (44) 247-45-45; e-mail nrb@nrb-ukraine.com; internet www.nrb-ukraine.com; f. 2001; fmrly Bank NRB, present name adopted 2008; 100% owned by Sberbank—Savings Bank of the Russian Federation; cap. 75.6m., res 116.9m., dep. 1,522.9m. (Dec. 2007); Chair. of Bd VLADISLAV KRAVETS.

Swedbank: 01032 Kyiv, vul. Kominterna 30; tel. (44) 481-48-93; fax (44) 481-48-85; e-mail office@swedbank.ua; internet www.swedbank .ua; f. 1991; cap. US $147.2m., res $33.6m., dep. $1,750.0m. (Dec. 2007); Chair. of Bd SERHIY TIHIPKO.

Ukrgazbank: 01004 Kyiv, vul. Chervonoarmiyska 39; tel. (44) 594-11-63; fax (44) 239-28-44; e-mail office@ukrgasbank.com; internet www.ukrgasbank.com; f. 1993; cap. 512.8m., res 339.8m., dep. 8,903.1m. (Dec. 2007); Chair. VADYM P. LYASHKO.

Ukrprombank (Ukrainsky Promyslovy Bank): 01133 Kyiv, bulv. L. Ukrainky 26; tel. (44) 537-47-00; fax (44) 295-17-00; e-mail secretary@ukrprombank.kiev.ua; internet www .ukrprombank.com.ua; f. 1989; cap. 842.0m., res 12.9m., dep. 5,562.6m. (Dec. 2006); Chair. OLEKSANDR SOLTUS.

UkrSibbank: 04070 Kyiv, vul. Andriyevksa 2/12; tel. (44) 230-48-88; fax (44) 230-48-98; e-mail office@ukrsibbank.com; internet www .ukrsibbank.com; f. 1990; commercial and investment banking, non-banking financial services; 51% owned by BNP Paribas SA (France); cap. 3,518.7m., res 5.3m., dep. 29,527.3m. (Dec. 2007); Chair. of Bd OLEKSANDR ADARYCH; 1,000 brs and sub-brs.

UkrSotsBank—Bank for Social Development: 03150 Kyiv, vul. Kovpaka 29; tel. (44) 230-32-24; fax (44) 230-32-23; e-mail info@ ukrsotsbank.com; internet www.usb.com.ua; f. 1990; cap. 496.7m., res 387.6m., dep. 10,960m. (Dec. 2006); Chair. of Supervisory Council IHOR YUSHKO; Chair. of Bd BORIS TIMONKIN; over 500 brs.

VA Bank-Vseukrainsky Aktsionerny Bank (All-Ukrainian Share Bank): 04119 Kyiv, vul. Zoolohichna 5; tel. (44) 481-33-47; fax (44) 481-33-49; e-mail fi@vab.ua; internet www.vab.ua; f. 1992; cap. 128.6m., dep. 757.2m., total assets 1,345.0m. (Dec. 2007); Pres. SERHIY MAKSIMOV; Chair. PETR RASOCHA; 25 brs.

VTB Bank: 01601 Kyiv, vul. Hoholevskaya 24; tel. (44) 486-04-90; e-mail post@mriya.com; internet www.vtb.com; f. 1992; cap. 163.6m., res −0.6m., dep. 2,232.4m. (Dec. 2006); Chair. of Bd VADIM PUSHKAROV; 20 brs.

Savings Bank

State Savings Bank of Ukraine—Oschadbank (Derzhavnyi Oshchadnyi Bank Ukrainy): 01023 Kyiv, vul. Hospitalna 12 G; tel. (44) 247-85-69; fax (44) 247-85-68; internet www.oschadnybank.com; f. 1991; cap. 878.5m., res 484.7m., dep. 7,400m. (2006); Chair. ANATOLIY GULEY; 6,300 brs.

Banking Association

Association of Ukrainian Banks (Asotsiatsiya Ukrainskykh Bankiv): 02002 Kyiv, vul. M. Raskova 15/703; tel. (44) 516-87-75; fax (44) 516-87-76; e-mail aub@carrier.kiev.ua; internet www.aub .com.ua; fmrly Commercial Bank Asscn; Pres. OLEKSANDR SUGO-NIAKO.

COMMODITY EXCHANGES

Carpathian Commodity Exchange: 78200 Ivano-Frankivsk obl., Kolomiya, vul. Vahylevycha 1, POB 210; tel. and fax (343) 32-19-61; f. 1996; Gen. Man. IVAN P. VATUTIN.

Crimea Universal Exchange: 95050 Crimea, Simferopol, vul. L. Chaikinoy 1/421; tel. (652) 22-04-32; fax (652) 22-12-73; f. 1923 as Simferopol Commodity Exchange; present name adopted 1991; Pres. NATALIYA S. SYUMAK.

Dnipro (Pridniprovska) Commodity Exchange: 49094 Dnipro-petrovsk, vul. Nab. Peremohy 15A; tel. (562) 35-77-45; fax (56) 744-27-16; e-mail ptb@pce.dp.ua; originally founded 1908 as Katerino-slav Commodity Exchange; re-established with present name in 1991; brs in Dniprodzerzhynsk, Kryvyi Rih, Marhanets, Pavlohrad and Synelnykove; Gen. Man. VADYM F. KAMEKO.

Donetsk Commodity Exchange: 83086 Donetsk, vul. Pershotrav-nevska 12; tel. (62) 338-10-93; fax (62) 335-92-91; e-mail oltradex@ pub.dn.ua; f. 1991; Gen. Man. PETRO O. VYSHNEVSKYI.

Kharkiv Commodity Exchange: 61003 Kharkiv, vul. Universy-tetska 5; tel. (572) 12-33-21; fax (572) 12-74-95; e-mail ss@htb .kharkov.ua; f. 1993; Pres. IHOR V. ZOTOV.

Kyiv Universal Exchange: 01103 Kyiv, Zaliznychne shose 57; tel. (44) 295-11-29; fax (44) 295-44-36; e-mail nva@iptelecom.net.ua; internet www.kue.kiev.ua; f. 1990; Pres. KONSTANTIN LAPUSHEN.

Odesa Commodity Exchange: 65114 Odesa, vul. Lyustdorfska doroha 140A; tel. (482) 61-89-92; fax (482) 47-72-84; e-mail yuri@oce .odessa.ua; f. 1796; re-established 1990; Gen. Man. MYKOLA O. NIKOLISHEN.

Ukrainian Universal Commodity Exchange: 03680 Kyiv, pr. Akadmika Hlushkova 1/6; tel. (44) 251-94–90; fax (44) 251-95-40; e-mail birga@uutb.kiev.ua; internet www.uutb.com.ua; f. 1991; Pres. OLEKSANDR M. BORKOVSKYI.

Zaporizhzhya Commodity Exchange 'Hileya': 69037 Zaporizh-zhya, vul. 40 rokiv Radyanskoyi Ukrainy 41; tel. (612) 33-32-73; fax (612) 34-76-62; f. 1991; re-established 1996; Gen. Man. ANTON A. KHULAKHSIZ.

INSURANCE

In March 2004 there were 360 insurance companies operating in Ukraine, of which the following were among the most important:

State Insurance Companies

Crimean Insurance Co: 99011 Sevastopol, vul. Butakov 4; tel. (692) 55-30-28; fax (692) 54-23-00; e-mail ksk@ksk.in.ua; internet www.ksk.in.ua; f. 1993; Dir ISABELLA BILDER.

DASK UkrinMedStrakh: 01601 Kyiv, vul. O. Honshara 65; tel. (44) 216-30-21; fax (44) 216-96-92; e-mail ukrmed@ukrpack.com; f. 1999; provides compulsory medical insurance to foreigners and stateless persons temporarily resident in Ukraine.

Oranta Insurance Co: 01015 Kyiv, vul. Sichnevogo Povstannya 34B; tel. (44) 537-58-00; fax (44) 537-58-83; e-mail oranta@oranta.ua; internet www.oranta.ua; f. 1921; Chair. of Bd OLEG SPILKA.

Commercial Insurance Companies

AIG Ukraine: 01004 Kyiv, vul. Shovkovychna 42–44; tel. (44) 490-65-50; fax (44) 490-65-48; e-mail reception@aig.com.ua; internet www.aig.com.ua; f. 2000; affiliated to American International Group (USA); Gen. Man. IHOR KOVALENKO.

AKB Garant Insurance Co: 03062 Kyiv, pr. Peremohy 67; tel. (44) 459-52-00; fax (44) 459-52-07; e-mail akb@garant.kiev.ua; internet www.garant.kiev.ua; f. 1994; general insurance services; Gen. Man. OLEKSANDR I. DYACHENKO.

Alcona Insurance Co: 03150 Kyiv, vul. Chervonoarmiyska 102; tel. and fax (44) 247-44-77; e-mail hdi@hdi.kiev.ua; internet www.hdi .kiev.ua; f. 1992; insurance and reinsurance.

Aska Insurance Co: 03186 Kyiv, vul. Antonova 5; tel. (44) 241-11-67; e-mail office@aska.com.ua; internet www.aska.com.ua; life and non-life insurance; Chair. HALINA N. TRETYAKOVA; Gen. Man. A. SOSYS.

Dask Insurance Co: 49000 Dnipropetrovsk, vul. K. Libknekhta 4D; tel. (562) 32-09-75; fax (562) 32-09-81; e-mail dask@dask.dp.ua; internet www.dask.com.ua; f. 1993; affiliated to Dask Insurance Group; Dir IRINA MURASCHKO.

Disco Insurance Co: 49000 Dnipropetrovsk, vul. K. Libknekhta 4D; tel. (562) 32-09-78; fax (562) 32-09-81; e-mail disco@disco.dp.ua; internet www.disco.dp.ua; f. 1992; affiliated to Dask Insurance Group.

ECCO Insurance Co: 01034 Kyiv, vul. Prorizna 4/23; tel. (44) 228-10-82; e-mail insurance@ecco-alpha.kiev.ua; internet www .ecco-insurance.at; f. 1991; affiliated to ECCO (Austria); life and non-life insurance.

EnergoPolis Insurance Co: 03049 Kyiv, vul. Bohdanivska 10; tel. (44) 244-02-36; fax (44) 244-05-94; e-mail office@enpolis.com.ua; internet www.enpolis.com.ua; Chair. of Bd and Dir-Gen. VIKTOR MYKOLAYCHUK.

Galinstrakh Insurance Co: 79012 Lviv, vul. Ak. Sakharova 34; tel. (32) 275-70-30; fax (32) 297-10-40; e-mail gis@is.lviv.ua; internet www.gis.com.ua; f. 1991; general insurance services; Chair. of Bd STEPHAN SOVINSKIY.

Ingo—Ukraina Insurance Co: 01054 Kyiv, vul. Vorovskogo 33; tel. (44) 490-27-44; fax (44) 490-27-48; e-mail office@ingo.com.ua; internet www.ingo.com.ua; f. 1994; fmrly Ostra-Kyiv Insurance Co; re-insurance, medical, travel, property and cargo insurance; Chair. of Bd IHOR N. HORDYENKO.

Inter-Policy Insurance Co: 01033 Kyiv, vul. Volodymyrska 69; tel. (44) 287-70-96; fax (44) 289-74-45; e-mail office@inter-policy.com; f. 1993.

Kyiv Insurance Co: 04053 Kyiv, vul. Yu. Kotsubynskoho 20; tel. (44) 461-92-41; fax (44) 461-92-43; e-mail info@kic.kiev.ua; internet www.kic.kiev.ua; f. 1998.

Ostra Insurance Co: 65026 Odesa, vul. Pushkinska 13; tel. (482) 22-38-87; fax (482) 24-18-37; e-mail main@ostra.com.ua; internet www.ostra.com.ua; f. 1990; non-life; Chair. KHYRACH MAHDYEV.

QBE Ukraina Insurance: 01033 Kyiv, vul. Saksahanskoho 36D; tel. (44) 537-53-90; fax (44) 537-53-99; e-mail insurance@qbe-ukraine .com; internet www.qbe-ukraine.com; f. 1998; affiliate of QBE Insurance (New Zealand).

Skide Insurance Co: 04050 Kyiv, vul. Hlybochytska 72; tel. (44) 417-40-04; fax (44) 228-40-33; e-mail skide@iptelecom.net.ua; f. 1991; Pres. VOLODYMYR BESARAB.

Skide-West Insurance Co: 04053 Kyiv, vul. Artema 40; tel. (44) 238-62-38; fax (44) 246-96-25; e-mail mail@skide-west.com; internet www.skide-west.com; f. 1993; cap. US $389.1m. (2004); Pres. ANDRIY PERETYAZHKO; 37 brs and rep. offices.

Sun Life Ukraine: 01032 Kyiv, vul. Starovokzalna 17; tel. (44) 235-20-02; fax (44) 235-89-17; e-mail office@sunlife.com.ua; internet www.sunlife.com.ua; f. 1993; life; Pres. ROSTYSLAV B. TALSKYI.

UkrGazPromPolis Insurance Co: 01034 Kyiv, vul. O. Honshara 41; tel. (44) 235-25-00; e-mail office@ugpp.com.ua; internet www .ugpp.com.ua; f. 1996; jointly owned by UkrGazProm, UkrGazProm-Bank and KyivTransGaz; Pres. KONSTANTYN O. YEFYMENKO.

Insurance Association

League of Insurance Organizations of Ukraine: 02660 Kyiv, vul. M. Roskovoyi 11; tel. and fax (44) 516-82-30; internet www .uainsur.com; f. 1992; non-profit asscn of insurance cos; Pres. ALEKSANDR FILONYUK.

Trade and Industry

GOVERNMENT AGENCY

State Property Fund of Ukraine (Fond Derzhavnoho Maina Ukrainy): 01133 Kyiv, vul. Kutuzova 18/9; tel. (44) 200-33-33; fax (44) 286-79-85; e-mail marketing@spfu.kiev.ua; internet www.spfu .gov.ua; Head ANDRIY PORTNOV (acting).

NATIONAL CHAMBER OF COMMERCE

Ukrainian Chamber of Commerce and Industry (Torgovo-Promyslova Palata Ukrainy/Torgovo-Promyshlennaya Palata Ukrainy): 01601 Kyiv, vul. V. Zhytomyrska 33; tel. (44) 272-29-11; fax (44) 212-33-53; e-mail ucci@ucci.org.ua; internet www.ucci.org .ua; f. 1972; Chair. SERHIY P. SKRYPCHENKO; 27 regional brs with a total of c. 7,500 mems.

REGIONAL CHAMBERS OF COMMERCE

Chambers of Commerce are located in every administrative region of Ukraine, including the following:

Chamber of Commerce and Industry of Crimea: 95013 Crimea, Simferopol, ul. Sevastopolskaya 45; tel. (652) 24-86-38; fax (652) 49-33-45; e-mail cci@cci.crimea.ua; internet www.cci.crimea.ua; f. 1974; sub-brs in Armyansk, Dzhankoi, Feodosiya, Kerch, Yalta and Yevpatoriya; Pres. NEONILA M. GRACHEVA.

Dnipropetrovsk Chamber of Commerce: 49044 Dnipropetrovsk, vul. Shevchenka 4; tel. (562) 36-22-58; fax (562) 36-22-59; e-mail miv@dcci.dp.ua; internet www.dcci.dp.ua; brs at Kryvyi Rih and Dniprodzerzhynsk; Pres. VYTALIY H. ZHMURENKO.

Donetsk Chamber of Commerce: 83007 Donetsk, pr. Kyivsky 87; tel. (62) 387-80-00; fax (62) 387-80-01; e-mail dttp@dttp.donetsk.ua; internet www.cci.donbass.com; f. 1964; brs at Artemovsk, Horlivka, Kramatorsk, Makiyivka and Mariupol; Pres. GENNADII D. CHIZHIKOV.

Kharkiv Chamber of Commerce: 61037 Kharkiv, pr. Moskovsky 122; tel. (57) 714-96-90; fax (57) 738-64-79; e-mail info@kcci.kharkov .ua; internet www.kcci.kharkov.ua; Pres. VIKTOR I. LOBODA.

Kyiv Chamber of Commerce and Industry: 01504 Kyiv-54, vul. B. Khmelnytskoho 55; tel. (44) 246-83-01; fax (44) 246-99-66; e-mail info@kiev-chamber.org.ua; internet www.kiev-chamber.org.ua; Pres. MYKOLA V. ZASULSKIY.

Lviv Chamber of Commerce and Industry: 79011 Lviv, Stryiskiy park 14; tel. and fax (32) 276-46-11; e-mail lcci@cci.com.ua; internet www.lcci.com.ua; f. 1850; Pres. DMYTRO D. AFTANAS.

Odesa Chamber of Commerce and Industry: 65125 Odesa, vul. Bazarna 47; tel. (48) 38-04-82; fax (482) 49-63-07; e-mail orcci@orcci .odessa.ua; internet www.orcci.odessa.ua; f. 1924; brs at Illichivsk, Izmayil and Reni; Pres. SERHIY SHUVALOV.

Sevastopol Chamber of Commerce and Industry: 99011 Sevastopol, ul. B. Morskaya 34; tel. (692) 54-35-36; fax (692) 54-06-44; e-mail members@stpp.org.ua; internet www.stpp.org.ua; f. 1963; Pres. LYUDMILA I. VISHNYA.

Transcarpathian (Zakarpatska) Chamber of Commerce and Industry: 88015 Transcarpathian obl., Uzhhorod, vul. Hrushevskoho 62; tel. (312) 66-22-14; fax (312) 66-44-77; e-mail tpp@tpp .uzhgorod.ua; internet www.tpp.uzhgorod.ua; br. at Mukachevo; Pres. OTTO O. KOVCHAR.

Zaporizhzhya Chamber of Commerce: 69000 Zaporizhzhya, bulv. Tsentralnyi 4; tel. (612) 13-50-24; fax (612) 33-11-72; e-mail cci@cci.zp.ua; brs at Berdyansk and Melitopol; Pres. VOLODOMYR I. SHAMYLOV.

EMPLOYERS' ORGANIZATION

Congress of Business Circles of Ukraine: 01061 Kyiv, vul. Prorizna 15; tel. (44) 228-64-81; fax (44) 229-52-84; Pres. VALERIY G. BABICH.

UTILITIES

Regulatory Bodies

National Electricity Regulatory Commission of Ukraine: 03057 Kyiv, vul. Smolenska 19; tel. (44) 241-90-01; fax (44) 241-90-47; e-mail box@nerc.gov.ua; f. 1994; promotion of competition and protection of consumer interests; Chair. YURIY PRODAN.

State Committee for Nuclear Regulation (Derzhanvnyi komitet yadernoho rehulyuvannya Ukrainy): 01011 Kyiv, vul. Arsenalna 9/11; tel. (44) 254-33-47; fax (44) 254-33-11; e-mail pr@hq.snrc.gov.ua; internet www.snrc.gov.ua; Chair. OLENA A. MYKOLAICHUK.

Electricity

EnergoAtom: 01032 Kyiv, vul. Vetrova 3; tel. (44) 281-48-83; e-mail pr@nae.atom.gov.ua; internet www.energoatom.kiev.ua; f. 1996; responsible for scientific and technical policy within the nuclear power industry; manages all five nuclear power producing installations in Ukraine; Pres. ANDRIY L. DERKACH.

Kyivenergo: 01001 Kyiv, pl. Ivana Franka 5; tel. (44) 201-58-67; fax (44) 239-47-06; e-mail pubrel@kievenergo.com.ua; internet www .kievenergo.com.ua; power generation and distribution; Chair. SERHIY M. TITENKO.

Zakhidenergo (West Energy): 79011 Lviv, vul. Sventitskoho 2; tel. (32) 279-89-41; fax (32) 278-90-59; e-mail z_vtv@rdc.west.energy.gov .ua; f. 1995; power generation; Pres. and Gen. Dir VOLODYMYR PAVLYUK.

Gas

Naftogaz Ukrainy (Oil and Gas of Ukraine): 01001 Kyiv, vul. B. Khmelnytskoho 6в; tel. (44) 461-25-37; fax (44) 220-15-26; e-mail ngu@naftogaz.net; internet www.naftogaz.com; f. 1998; state-owned; production and distribution of gas and petroleum; storage of gas; gas- and condensate-processing; Chair. of Bd OLEH DUBYNA.

UkrGazEnergo: Kyiv; f. 2006; 50% owned by RosUkrEnergo (itself 50% owned by Gazprom, Russia), 50% owned by Naftogaz Ukrainy; exclusive provider of natural gas to industrial concerns; Co-Chair. ALEKSANDR RYAZANOV, IHOR VORONIN.

MAJOR COMPANIES

Chemicals

Cherkasy Nitrogen Production Asscn (VAT Azot): 18014 Cherkasy, vul. Pershotravnevska 72; tel. (472) 39-29-26; fax (472) 64-03-36; e-mail marketing@azot.cherkassy.net; internet www.azot .cherkassy.net; f. 1965; production of nitrogenous and phosphate fertilizers, ammonia, resins and consumer goods; Gen. Man. V. P. BYELYI; 6,285 employees (2001).

Darnitsa Pharmaceutical Co (Farmatsevticheskaya firma Darnytsa): 02093 Kyiv, vul. Borysopolska 13; tel. (44) 566-68-78; fax (44) 568-32-10; e-mail webmaster@darnitsa.kiev.ua; internet darnitsa .ua; f. 1954; jt-stock co; manufacture of chemicals, medicines and pharmaceuticals; sales US $40.0m. (2000); Pres. and Gen. Dir VOLODYMYR A. ZAHORIY; 800 employees (2005).

Lukor Karpatnaftokhim: 77305 Ivano-Frankivsk obl., Kalush; tel. (3472) 5-30-21; fax (3472) 5-19-48; e-mail mail@knh.com.ua; internet www.lukor.com.ua; f. 1867 as Oriana, present name adopted 2000; subsidiary of Lukoil (Russia); produces vinyl chloride, synthetic resins, caustic soda, and polyethylene; Dir-Gen. SERGEI V. CHMYKHALOV; 6,500 employees.

Slavyansk Soda Plant (Slavyansky sodovyi zavod OAO): 84104 Donetsk obl., Slavyansk, vul. Chubarya 91; tel. (6262) 3-43-49; fax (6262) 2-99-04; f. 1896; jt-stock co; production of various chemical products, including detergents, fire extinguishing powders, soda products, etc.; Pres. EDUARD E. KRECH; 4,000 employees (2001).

Sumykhimprom—Sumy Chemical Industrial Group: 40012 Sumy, vul. Kharkivska 10; tel. (542) 33-85-13; fax (542) 21-42-14; e-mail info@alphachemical.sumy.ua; internet www.sumykhimprom .com.ua; f. 1954; manufacture and distribution of chemicals, fertilizers, pigments, coagulants (water purifiers) and consumer products; Chair. YEVHEN V. LAPYN; 5,960 employees (2008).

Zaporozhabraziv—Zaporizhzhya Abrasive Factory (Zaporozhabraziv—Zaporozhskii abrazivnyi kombinat OAO): 69084 Zaporizhzhya, vul. Dmitrova 44; tel. (612) 61-63-09; fax (612) 65-09-14; e-mail abrasive@abrasive.zp.ua; internet www.abrasive.zp.ua; f. 1939; jt-stock co; manufacture of chemicals and abrasive tools, carbides etc.; Chair. of Bd ANATOLIY V. BEREZA; 3,000 employees (2002).

Electrical Goods

Element-Preobrazovatel OOO (Element-Transformer Co): 69069 Zaporizhzhya, Dnipropetrovske shose 9; tel. and fax (612) 52-71-48; e-mail office@element.zp.ua; internet www.element.zp.ua; f. 1967;

fmrly Preobrazovatel Zaporizhzhya Plant; present name adopted 1998; manufacture of power semi-conductor devices, modules and chips, power-conversion equipment, electrical appliances and power electric drives; Dir ANATOLIY I. SOLODOVNYK; 1,800 employees (2005).

HELZ Ukrelektromash—Kharkhiv Ukrainian Electrical Machinery (Khelz—Ukrelektromash—Kharkovskii elektrotekhnicheskii zavod 'Elektromash' OAO): 61050 Kharkiv, vul. Iskrinska 37; tel. (57) 732-45-50; fax (57) 732-79-19; e-mail office@helz.ua; internet www.helz.ua; jt-stock co; f. 1932; present name adopted 2002; produces electric motors, centrifugal pumps and electrical household appliances; Dir IHOR A. CHERNEHA; 900 employees (2007).

Mayak Kyiv Plant: 04073 Kyiv, pr. Chervonykh Kozakiv 8; tel. (44) 464-49-42; fax (44) 410-26-67; f. 1924; present name adopted 1963; manufacture of audio equipment; Dir NIKOLAI I. PIVEN; 1,310 employees (2001).

Yuzhelektromash: 74900 Kherson obl., Nova Kakhovka, vul. Pershotravnevska 35; tel. (5549) 4-34-18; fax (5549) 7-02-20; e-mail td_uemz2002@mail.ru; f. 1952; development and manufacture of electric motors and generators; Gen. Dir NIKOLAI N. IVANOV; 2,500 employees (2005).

Zaporozhtransformator (ZTR): 69600 Zaporizhzhya, Dniprope-trovske shose 3; tel. (61) 270-39-00; fax (61) 270-32-32; e-mail office@ztr.zp.ua; internet www.ztr.ua; f. 1947; manufactures transformers, high-voltage equipment and consumer goods; Dir IHOR S. KLEINER; 5,600 employees.

Food and Beverages

Obolon ZAT: 04655 Kyiv, vul. Bohatyrska 3; tel. (44) 414-84-10; fax (44) 412-76-03; e-mail general@obolon.kiev.ua; internet www.obolon.ua; f. 1974; produces beer and soft drinks; Gen. Man. OLEKSANDR D. PUCHOK.

Ukrainian Sugar Concern: 01001 Kyiv, vul. B. Hrinchenko 1; tel. (44) 228-11-37; fax (44) 229-65-83; f. 1913; operates sugar factories and refineries; Chair. of Bd HRIHORIY D. ZAHORODNYI; Gen. Man. MYKOLA M. YARCHUK; 210,000 employees (2001).

Machinery

Atek ZAO: 03062 Kyiv, pr. Peremohy 83/2; tel. and fax (44) 443-74-36; internet 1356.ukrindustrial.com; f. 1898; manufacture of excavators, loaders and components, hydraulic loaders and cylinders; Dir VASILIY M. MELNYCHUK; 4,000 employees (2001).

Chervona Zirka Plant: 25006 Kirovohrad, vul. Medvedeva 1; tel. (522) 35-61-03; fax (522) 22-88-66; internet www.chervonazirka.com; f. 1874; fmrly Krasnaya Zvezda Plant; present name adopted 2003; production of farm machinery; Chair. and Gen. Dir SERHIY H. KALAPA; 2,700 employees.

Kyiv Machine-Tool Building Plant: 01062 Kyiv, pr. Peremohy 67; tel. (44) 442-83-24; fax (44) 449-97-46; e-mail vercon@alfacom.net; production of automatic lathes and other machinery; Pres. VALENTIN DROZDENKO; 2,000 employees.

NKMZ—New Kramatorsk Machine-Construction Plant (Novo-Kramatorskii mashinostroitelnyi zavod ZAO): 84305 Donetsk obl., Kramatorsk; tel. (6264) 3-70-80; fax (6264) 7-22-49; e-mail ztm@nkmz.donetsk.ua; internet www.nkmz.donetsk.ua; f. 1934; manufactures pressing and forging equipment, rolling mill and smelting machinery, excavators and other industrial machinery; Pres. HEORHIY M. SKUDAR; Chair. and Dir-Gen. HENNADIY S. SUKOV.

Yasinovataya Machine-Construction Plant (Yasinovatskii mashinostroitelnyi zavod OAO—YMZ): 86000 Donetsk obl., Yasino-vataya, vul. Artema 31; tel. (62) 340-57-67; fax (62) 340-57-65; e-mail info@jscymz.com; internet www.jscymz.com; f. 1947; manufactures tunnelling machines and related equipment; Gen. Dir VIKTOR I. TRUBCHANIN; 4,000 employees.

Metals

Alchevsk Iron and Steel Works (AMK) (OAO Alchevskii metal-lurgicheskii kombinat): 94202 Luhansk obl., Alchevsk, vul. Shmidta 4; tel. (6442) 9-33-01; fax (6442) 9-33-76; e-mail abrosimov@amk.lg.ua; internet www.amk.lg.ua; f. 1896; jt-stock co; Dir TARAS H. SHEVCHENKO.

ArcelorMittal Kryvyi Rih VAT (Krivorozhskii gosudarstvennyi metallurgicheskii kombinat Krivorozhstal): 50095 Dnipropetrovsk obl., Kryvyi Rih, vul. Ordzhonikidze 1; tel. (564) 78-30-09; fax (564) 71-01-01; e-mail kmkpressa@kdgmk.com.ua; internet www.mittalsteel.com.ua; 93% owned by Mittal Steel (Netherlands); fmrly Kryvorizhstal; renamed Mittal Steel Krvyvi Rih in 2006; present name adopted 2008; Chief Exec. JEAN-ROBERT JOUET.

AzovStal Iron and Steel Works (Metalurhiynyi kombinat 'Azovstal'): 87500 Donetsk obl., Mariupol, vul. Leporskoho 1; tel. and fax (629) 52-70-00; e-mail oao@azovstal.com.ua; internet www.azovstal.com.ua; f. 1933; owned by Metinvest Holding; iron and steel works; Gen. Dir DMYTRO A. LIVSHITS; 25,827 employees (2001).

Dnipro Dzerzhinskiy Iron and Steel Integrated Works (Dne-provskii metallurgicheskii kombinat im. F. E. Dzerzhinskogo): 51902 Dnipropetrovsk obl., Dniprodzherzhinsk, vul. Kirova 18; tel. (569) 53-15-50; fax (569) 53-16-36; e-mail dmkd@unimetal.dp.ua; internet www.dmkd.dp.ua; f. 1889; manufacture of objects in carbon steel; Dir OLEG V. DUBINA; 20,500 employees (2001).

Dnipro Petrovskiy Iron and Steel Works (Dnepropetrovskii metallurgicheskii zavod im. Petrovskogo OAO): 49064 Dniprope-trovsk, vul. Mayakovskoho 31; tel. (562) 59-43-09; fax (562) 32-31-02; e-mail office@dmz-perovka.dp.ua; internet dmz-petrovka.dp.ua; production of pig-iron and steel products, manufacture of carbon-steel, seamless, round and rectangular section tubes; Gen. Dir YURIY D. DEYATKIN.

Interpipe: 49600 Dnipropetrovsk, vul. Pysarzhevskoho 1A; tel. (562) 47-69-69; fax (562) 70-20-01; e-mail office@bipe.dp.ua; internet www.interpipegroup.dp.ua; f. 1990; production of steel pipes; import and export of various metal products; also owns subsidiaries in Belarus, Germany, Kazakhstan, Russia and Uzbekistan; Pres. VIKTOR M. PINCHUK; Gen. Man. MYKHAYLO M. SHCHEHOLEVSKIY.

Khartsyzsk Tube Works (Khartsyzskii trubnyi zavod OAO): 86703 Donetsk obl., Khartsyzsk, vul. Patona 9; tel. (6257) 7-03-01; fax (6257) 4-55-45; e-mail marketing@ukrpipe.com.ua; internet www.ukrpipe.com.ua; f. 1988; owned by Metinvest Group; production of steel pipes; Dir-Gen. ANDRIY V. SHISHATSKIY; 7,500 employees.

Makiyivka Iron and Steel Combine (Makeyevskii metallurgi-cheskii kombinat ZAO—MMZ): 86101 Donetsk obl., Makiyivka, vul. Metalurhiyna 47; tel. and fax (6232) 9-20-31; e-mail mmk@tr.dn.ua; internet makmet.com.ua; f. 1899; production of iron products; 60.86% state-owned, 27.95% by employees; Dir-Gen. ENVER O. TSKITISHVILI; 13,800 employees (2001).

Mariupol Ilyich Iron and Steel Works (Mariupolskii metallur-gicheskii kombinat im. Illicha—MMK im. Illicha—OAO): 87504 Donetsk obl., Mariupol, vul. Levchenko 1; tel. (62) 332-23-05; fax (62) 953-00-04; e-mail kma@ilyich.donetsk.ua; internet www.ilyich.com.ua; f. 1996; production of carbon steel products; Pres. and Dir-Gen. VOLODYMYR S. BOYKO; 30,000 employees (2001).

Nikopol Ferro-alloy Plant (Nikopolskyi zavod Ferosplaviv—NZF): 49012 Dnipropetrovsk obl., Nikopol, vul. Gazety 'Pravda' 300; tel. (56662) 1-82-36.

Zaporizhstal (Zaporozhsyal)—Zaporizhzhya Integrated Iron and Steel Works: 69008 Zaporizhzhya, Pivdenne shose 72; tel. (61) 218-33-01; fax (61) 213-18-58; e-mail zstal@zaporizhstal.com; internet www.zaporizhstal.com; f. 1933; jt-stock co; produces and exports metal products for the automotive, tractor, railway, construction and mechanical engineering industries; Chair. and Dir-Gen. VITALIY A. SATSKIY; 20,000 employees (2006).

Mining and Mining Equipment

Azovmash—Azov Machines (Azovmash OAO): 87535 Donetsk obl., Mariupol, pl. Mashinostroitelei 1; tel. and fax (629) 53-09-96; e-mail ves@azovmash.com.ua; internet www.azovmash.com.ua; f. 1936; jt-stock co; research, development and manufacture of open-cast mining equipment, metallurgical equipment, cast and forged metal stock, and consumer goods; sales US $38.5m. (1999); Pres. OLEKSANDR V. SAVCHUK; Gen. Dir VOLODYMYR I. TELYTSYA.

Chornomornaftogaz—Black Sea Oil and Gas: 95000 Crimea, Simferopol, pr. Kirova 52; tel. (652) 52-34-00; fax (652) 51-11-51; e-mail office@gas.crimea.ua; internet www.blackseagas.com; f. 1979; jt-stock co; major producer of petroleum and natural gas from fields in the Black Sea and the Sea of Azov; Chair. IGOR FRANCHUK.

Dongormash—Donetsk Mining Machinery OAO: 83005 Donetsk, vul. I. Tkachenko 189; tel. (62) 341-95-09; fax (622) 66-22-09; e-mail admin@dongormash.donetsk.ua; f. 1889; subsidiary of Ukruglemash; research, design and production of mining equipment; Gen. Dir VLADISLAV V. YERYEMENKO; 2,200 employees (2001).

Druzhkivka Machine Construction Plant (Druzhkovskii mashi-nostroitelnyi zavod OAO—DMZ): 84205 Donetsk obl., Druzhkivka, vul. Lenina 7; tel. (6267) 4-34-04; fax (6267) 3-09-68; e-mail reklama-dmz@yandex.ru; f. 1893; subsidiary of Ukruglemash; production of mining equipment and electrical machinery; Gen. Dir SERGEI V. NOVOSELOV; 10,900 employees.

Kamyanka Machine Construction Plant (Kamenskii mashinos-trotelnyi zavod OAO): 20800 Cherkasy obl., Kamyanka, vul. Lenina 40; tel. (4732) 6-14-55; fax (4732) 6-11-91; e-mail kammash@kammash.ck.ua; internet www.kammash.com; f. 1936; manufactures industrial pumps, winding machinery, lifting equipment and trucks; Chair. VOLODYMYR I. HETSKO; 730 employees (2001).

Marhanets Manganese Plant (MGOK) (Marganetskii gorno-obogatitelnyi kombinat OAO): 53400 Dnipropetrovsk obl., Marha-nets, vul. Radyanska 62; tel. (5665) 2-22-02; fax (5665) 2-30-31; e-mail postmaster@mgok.dp.ua; internet 3002.ukrindustrial.com; f. 1885; produces manganese using underground mining methods; Dir-Gen. VALENTIN N. NADZOROV; 6,442 employees.

Ukrtatnafta—Ukrainian-Tatar Petroleum Co (Ukrtatnafta AOZT): 39609 Poltava obl., Kremenchuk, vul. Svyshtovska 3; tel. (536) 76-84-14; fax (536) 76-80-20; e-mail pobox@ukrtatnafta.com; internet www.ukrtatnafta.com; f. 1995; petroleum and gas exploration and development, production and sale of petroleum and gas, production and sale of petroleum products; 43.1% owned by State Property Fund of Ukraine, 28.8% by State Property Committee of the Republic of Tatarstan (Russian Federation); Chair. PAVEL V. OVCHARENKO.

Ukruglemash—Ukrainian Coal Mining Machinery TPK: 83000 Donetsk, vul. Artema 97; tel. (62) 381-53-00; fax (62) 381-53-53; e-mail uum@uum.dn.ua; f. 2000; controls six factories manufacturing mining equipment, including Druzhkivka Machine Construction Plant and Donetsgormash; Dir-Gen. SERGEI V. PAVLENKO; 16,000 employees (2006).

Motor Vehicles and Components

AvtoKrAZ—Kremenchuk Automobile Co: 39631 Poltava obl., Kremenchuk, vul. Kyivska 62; tel. (536) 76-62-00; fax (536) 76-62-08; e-mail autokraz@autokraz.s-net.net.ua; internet www.autokraz.com.ua; holding co controlling eight subsidiary cos manufacturing heavy trucks, automobiles and other machinery and equipment; Gen. Man. SERHIY V. SAZONOV; 20,000 employees.

AvtoZAZ—Zaporizhzhya Automobile Plant (ZAZ): 69600 Zaporizhzhya, pr. Lenina 8; tel. (612) 13-83-03; fax (612) 13-87-49; e-mail press@systems.zp.ua; internet www.avtozaz.com; f. 1863; 50% owned by Hirsch et Compagnie (Switzerland); produces automobiles, engines and tools; Chair. NIKOLAI YEVDOKIMENKO; 20,000 employees.

Elektromash: 73000 Kherson, pr. Ushakova 57; tel. (552) 22-62-68; fax (552) 24-21-25; e-mail contact@electromash.com.ua; internet www.electromash.com.ua; f. 2002 on basis of Kherson Electromechanical Engineering Plant (f. 1930); jt-stock co; manufactures starter motors and alternators for automobile, tractor and motorcycle engines, thermostats for automobile cooling systems, etc.; Dir ZAKHAR I. GORLOVSKIY; Chair. SERGEI V. KOROVIN; 1,371 employees.

Kharkiv Ordzhonykdze Tractor Plant (KhTZ) (Kharkovskii traktornyi zavom im. Ordzhonikidze OAO): 61007 Kharkiv, pr. Moskovsky 275; tel. (57) 758-09-73; fax (572) 94-17-60; e-mail td@tdxtz.com.ua; internet www.xtz.ua; f. 1931; production of tractors; Dir ANDREI A. KOVAL.

Rosava ZAO: 09108 Kyiv obl., Bila Tserkva, vul. Levanevskoho 91; tel. (4463) 5-54-39; fax (4463) 7-41-56; e-mail tyres@rosava.ua; internet www.rosava.ua; manufactures tyres for automobiles, trucks, etc.; f. 1964; restructured 1998; Chair. of Bd (acting) and Dir-Gen. ANDRIY I. KOLOMIYCHENKO; 6,000 employees (2003).

Vinnytsya Tractor-Unit Plant (Vinnitskii zavod traktornykh agregatov OAO—VETA): 21001 Vinnytsya, pr. Kotsyubynskoho 4; tel. and fax (432) 55-13-01; e-mail sales@vzta.com.ua; internet www.vzta.com.ua; jt-stock co; specializes in the production of hydraulic gear pumps and cylinders, and high-pressure hoses; Chair. OLEKSANDR F. PODDUBNYAK; 1,500 employees (2006).

Miscellaneous

O. K. Antonov Aeronautical Scientific and Technical Complex (ANTK Antonov): 03062 Kyiv, vul. Tupoleva 1; tel. (44) 441-31-49; fax (44) 442-41-44; e-mail info@antonov.com; internet www.antonov.com; f. 1946; designs, modifies, and engineers prototype and existing aircraft, trains air crew, and operates charter freight flights; Dir VOLODOMYR M. KAREL.

Dnipropetrovsk Air Aggregates Plant—Raketa (Dnepropetrovskii agregatnyi zavod OAO): 49052 Dnipropetrovsk, vul. Shchepkina 53; tel. (562) 37-28-05; fax (562) 42-22-10; e-mail aodaz@a-teleport.com; internet www.aodaz.com.ua; f. 1926; jt-stock co; manufacture and sale of hydraulics, centrifugal pumps and vacuum cleaners; Dir YEVGENIY V. MOROZENKO; 3,500 employees.

Kherson Shipbuilding Plant (Khersonskii sudostroitelnyi zavod OAO): 73019 Kherson, Karantinyi ostrov 1; tel. (552) 27-49-22; fax (552) 27-01-51; f. 1951; constructs ships, tankers, and related facilities; Gen. Dir VASILIY V. FEDIN.

Kyiv State Aviation Plant: 03062 Kyiv, pr. Peremohy 100/1; tel. (44) 443-72-45; fax (44) 442-43-85; e-mail avtant@carrier.kiev.ua; f. 1920; manufacture of aircraft, aircraft parts and equipment; Gen. Dir VASYL PELYKH; 5,300 employees (2002).

Ukrimpeks—Ukrainian Import and Export Co: 04053 Kyiv, vul. Artema 26; tel. (44) 486-19-26; fax (44) 486-21-74; e-mail info@ukrimpex.com.ua; internet www.ukrimpex.com.ua; f. 1987; jt-stock co; foreign-trade org.; import, export of various goods; consulting, marketing; development of new productive systems; Chair. STANISLAV I. SOKOLENKO.

Ukrspetseksport—Ukrainian Special Export Co: 04119 Kyiv, vul. Degtyarivksa 36; tel. (44) 269-20-06; fax (44) 269-10-01; e-mail aira@ukrspetsexport.com; internet www.ukrspetsexport.com; export and import of military and special-purpose goods and services; Dir-Gen. SERHIY BONDARCHUK.

Yuzhnoye Design Office (Yuzhnoye Konstruktornoye Byuro): 49008 Dnipropetrovsk, vul. Kryvorozhska 3; tel. (56) 770-15-65; fax (56) 770-01-25; e-mail info@yuzhnoye.com; internet www.yuzhnoye.com; f. 1954; space-rocket systems, missiles, launch vehicles, spacecraft, solid and liquid rocket motors; participant in several international programmes including Sea Launch (USA, Russia, Ukraine and Norway), Land Launch (Ukraine, Russia and USA), Alcantara-Cyclone (Ukraine, Brazil),Dnepr (Ukraine, Russia) and Vega (European Union); Dir-Gen. STANISLAV N. KONYUKHOV.

TRADE UNION FEDERATIONS

Confederation of Free Trade Unions of Ukraine (CFTUU) (Konfederatsiya Vilnykh Profspilok Ukrainy—KVPU): 03150 Kyiv, vul. V. Vasylkivska 54; tel. (44) 287-33-38; fax (44) 287-72-83; e-mail info@kvpu.org.ua; internet www.kvpu.org.ua; f. 1997; independent; Chair. MYKHAYLO YA. VOLYNETS.

Federation of Trade Unions of Ukraine (FTUU): 01012 Kyiv, Maidan Nezalezhnosti 2; tel. (44) 278-87-88; fax (44) 278-87-98; e-mail fpsu@fpsu.org.ua; internet www.fpsu.org.ua; f. 1990; fmr Ukrainian branch of General Confederation of Trade Unions of the USSR; affiliation of 46 trade union brs; Chair. IGOR LUTSYSHYN (acting).

Transport

RAILWAYS

In 2002 there were 22,078 km of railway track in use, of which more than 9,000 km were electrified. Lines link most towns and cities in the country, and with various major cities in other European countries.

State Railway Transport Administration—Ukrzaliznytsia: 03680 Kyiv, vul. Tverska 5; tel. (44) 223-00-10; fax (44) 258-80-11; e-mail ci@uz.gov.ua; internet www.uz.gov.ua; Dir-Gen. VASYL MELNIEHUK.

Ukrreftrans: 03049 Kyiv, vul. Furmanova 1/7; tel. (44) 245-47-22; e-mail sekretar@interntrans.com.ua; internet www.intertrans.com.ua; state-owned freight transportation service.

Dnipropetrovsk Metro: 49038 Dnipropetrovsk, vul. Kurchatova 8; tel. (562) 42-37-68; fax (56) 778-65-33; e-mail metrodp@ukr.net; internet gorod.dp.ua/metro; f. 1995; one line with six stations; total length 8 km; total planned network of 74 km.

Kharkiv Metro: 61012 Kharkiv, vul. Engelsa 29; tel. (572) 12-59-83; fax (572) 23-21-41; e-mail metro@tender.kharkov.com; internet www.metro.kharkov.ua; f. 1975; three lines with 26 stations; total length 34 km; Gen. Man. LEONID A. ISAYEV.

Kyiv Metro: 03055 Kyiv, pr. Peremohy 35; tel. (44) 238-44-21; fax (44) 238-44-46; e-mail nto@metro.kiev.ua; internet www.metro.kiev.ua; f. 1960; three lines with 42 stations; Dir MYKOLA M. SHAVLOVSKIY.

ROADS

At 31 December 2002 there were 169,678 km of roads, of which 96.8% were paved.

INLAND WATERWAYS

The Dnipro (Dniepr—Dnieper) River, which links Kyiv, Cherkasy, Dnipropetrovsk and Zaporizhzhya with the Black Sea, is the most important route for river freight.

SHIPPING

The main ports are Yalta and Yevpatoriya in Crimea, and Odesa. In addition to long-distance international shipping lines, there are services to the Russian ports of Novorossiisk and Sochi, and Batumi and Sukhumi in Georgia. Although many passenger routes on the Black Sea ceased to operate in the 1990s, there are regular passenger services from Odesa to Haifa (Israel) and Istanbul (Turkey), and, in the summer months, between Odesa and Crimea. At December 2007 Ukraine's merchant fleet (655 vessels) had a total displacement of 1.1m. grt.

Port Authority

Odesa Commercial Sea Port: 65026 Odesa, pl. Mytna 1; tel. (48) 729-35-55; fax (48) 729-36-27; e-mail welcome@port.odessa.ua; internet www.port.odessa.ua; f. 1794; state-owned; cargo handling and storage, marine passenger terminal services; Gen. Man. MYKOLA P. PAVLYUK.

Shipping Companies

Azov Shipping Co: 87510 Donetsk obl., Mariupol, pr. Admirala Lunina 89; tel. (629) 31-15-00; fax (629) 31-12-25; e-mail admin@c2smtp.azsco.anet.donetsk.ua; f. 1871; Pres. SERHIY V. PRUSIKOV.

State Black Sea Shipping Co: 65026 Odesa, vul. Lanzheronovska 1; tel. (482) 25-21-60; fax (482) 60-57-33; Pres. BORIS SCHERBAK.

Ukrainian Danube Shipping Co: 68600 Odesa obl., Izmayil, vul. Chervonaflotska 28; tel. (4841) 2-55-50; fax (4841) 2-53-55; e-mail udp_t@udp.izmail.uptel.net; f. 1944; cargo and passenger services; Pres. PETR S. SUVOROV.

Ukrainian Shipping Co (UkrShip): 65014 Odesa, vul. Marazlyevska 8; tel. (48) 734-73-50; fax (48) 777-07-00; e-mail admin@ukrship.odessa.ua; f. 1996; Pres. A. SAVITSKIY.

Ukrrechflot Co: 04071 Kyiv, Nizhny val. 51; tel. (44) 416-88-79; fax (44) 417-86-82; jt-stock co; Pres. NIKOLAY A. SLAVOV.

Yugreftransflot: 99014 Crimea, Sevastopol, ul. Rybakov 5; tel. (692) 41-25-41; fax (692) 42-39-19; e-mail jsc@urtf.com; jt-stock co; Chair. VOLODYMYR ANDREYEV.

CIVIL AVIATION

The principal international airport is at Boryspil (Kyiv), but several other airports, including those at Dnipropetrovsk and Odesa, also service international flights.

AeroSvit Airlines: 01032 Kyiv, bulv. Shevchenko 58A; tel. (44) 246-50-70; fax (44) 246-50-46; e-mail av@aswt.kiev.ua; internet www.aerosvit.com; f. 1994; operates scheduled and charter passenger services to domestic and international destinations; Chief Exec. and Dir-Gen. GRYGORIY GURTOVOY.

ARP 410: 03151 Kyiv, Vozdukhoflotsky pr. 94; tel. (44) 246-26-64; fax (44) 243-40-33; e-mail arp410-cs@svitonline.com; f. 1999; domestic passenger and international cargo flights; Dir-Gen. ANATOLIY P. KUDRIN.

Donbassaero Airlines (Donbass-Vostochnye Aviyalinii Ukrainy—Donbassaero): 83021 Donetsk, Donetsk International Airport; tel. (62) 388-51-03; fax (62) 332-00-55; e-mail info@donbass.aero; internet www.donbass.aero; f. 1933 as Donetsk State Airline; present name adopted 2003; passenger and cargo flights between Donetsk and domestic and international destinations; Dir-Gen. ALEKSANDR HRECHKO.

Khors Air Company: 01133 Kyiv, vul. L. Ukrainki 34; tel. (44) 294-94-11; fax (44) 573-86-72; e-mail aircargo@khors.com.ua; internet www.khors.com.ua; f. 1990; operates international, regional and domestic cargo and passenger services; Gen. Dir ANATOLIY VYSOCHANSKIY.

Ukraine International Airlines (Mizhnarodni Avialinyi Ukraini): 01054 Kyiv, ul. B. Khmelnytskogo 63A; tel. (44) 461-56-56; fax (44) 230-88-66; e-mail uia@ps.kiev.ua; internet www.ukraine-international.com; f. 1992; 61.6% state-owned, 22.5% owned jointly by SAir (Switzerland) and Austrian Airlines (Austria); operates domestic services, and international services to European and Middle Eastern destinations from Kyiv, Dnipropetrovsk, Kharkiv, Lviv, Odesa and Simferopol; Pres. VITALIY M. POTEMSKIY.

Tourism

The Black Sea coast of Ukraine has several popular resorts, including Odesa and Yalta. The Crimean peninsula is a popular tourist centre in both summer and winter, owing to its temperate climate. Kyiv, Lviv and Odesa have important historical attractions, and there are many archaeological monuments on the Black Sea coast, including the remains of ancient Greek and Ottoman settlements. However, the tourist industry remains relatively undeveloped. There were 23.1m. foreign tourist arrivals in Ukraine in 2007; receipts from tourism (including passenger transport) totalled US $4,018m. in 2006.

Ministry of Culture and Tourism: see The Government (Ministries).

Ministry of Health Resorts and Tourism of the Autonomous Republic of Crimea: 95005 Crimea, Simferopol, pr. Kirova 13; tel. (652) 54-46-68; fax (652) 25-94-38; e-mail tourism_crimea@ukr.net; internet www.tourism.crimea.ua; Minister VLADIMIR A. SOVOLYEV.

State Tourism Administration of Ukraine (Derzhavna turystychna administratsiya Ukrainy): 01034 Kyiv, vul. Yaroslaviv val 36; tel. (44) 272-42-15; fax (44) 272-42-77; e-mail info@tourism.gov.ua; internet www.tourism.gov.ua; f. 1999; Chair. VALERIY I. TSYBUKH.

Culture

NATIONAL ORGANIZATION

Ministry of Culture and Tourism: see The Government (Ministries).

CULTURAL HERITAGE

Bohdan and Varvara Khanenko Museum of Arts: 01004 Kyiv, vul. Tereshchenkivska 15–17; tel. (44) 235-02-25; fax (44) 235-02-06; e-mail khanenkomuseum@ukr.net; f. 1919; 25,300 items; Western European, Oriental and Ancient art; Dir VIRA I. VINOHRADOVA.

Kamyanets-Podilskyi National Historical and Architectural Reserve: 32300 Khmelnytsky obl., Kamyanets-Podilskyi, vul. Ivano-Predtechinska 2; tel. and fax (3849) 2-37-84; archaeological collection of 115,000 objects, including artefacts of the Roman and Russian empires, icons, sculptures, fortress of the 12th–18th centuries, art gallery; Dir L. P. STANISLAVSKA.

Kyiv Holy Dormition Monastery of the Caves (Svyato-Uspenska Kiyevo-Pecherska Lavra): 01015 Kyiv, vul. I. Mazepy 21; tel. (44) 254-22-57; fax (44) 290-46-48; e-mail lavra@lavra.kiev.ua; internet www.lavra.kiev.ua; large collection of icons; operated as a 'state historical-cultural museum-reserve' during Soviet period, returned to ecclesiastical usage from 1988; Gov. PAVEL (Bishop of Vyshhorod).

Kyiv Lesya Ukrainka State Literature Museum: 01032 Kyiv, vul. Saksahanskoho 97; tel. (44) 220-57-52; f. 1962; fmr residence of family of poet Lesya Ukrainka; exhibits on the life of the Ukrainian poets and artists of the 19th and early 20th centuries; library of 5,000 vols; Dir IRINA L. VEREMEYEVA.

Kyiv Museum of Russian Art: 01004 Kyiv, vul. Tereschenkivska 9; tel. (44) 451-40-27; fax (44) 451-40-27; e-mail museumru@ukr.net; f. 1922; 12,000 exhibits; library of 19,000 vols; Dir YURIY YAKULENKO.

Kyiv Museum of Ukrainian Folk and Decorative Art: 01015 Kyiv, vul. I. Mazepy 21; tel. (44) 254-36-42; e-mail musukrndm@kv.ukrtel.net; f. 1954; more than 54,000 exhibits from 15th century onwards; library of 6,500 vols; Dir ADRIANA VYALETS.

Kyiv Taras Shevchenko National University Maksymovych Academic Library: 01601 Kyiv, vul. Volodymyrska 58; tel. and fax (44) 235-70-98; e-mail info@libcc.univ.kiev.ua; internet www.library.univ.kiev.ua; f. 1834; 3.5m. vols; Dir V. G. NESTERENKO.

Lviv Historical Museum (Lvivskyi Istorychnyi Muzey): 79008 Lviv, pl. Rynok 4/6/24; tel. (32) 274-33-04; e-mail lhm@mail.lviv.ua; f. 1893; 330,000 exhibits; 4 brs; Dir BOHDAN CHAIKOVSKYI.

Museum of Theatrical, Musical and Cinematographic Art of Ukraine (Muzey teatralnoho, muzychnoho i kinomystetstva Ukrainy): 01015 Kyiv, vul. I. Mazepy 21/24; tel. and fax (44) 280-51-31; e-mail tmf-museum@ukr.net; internet tmf-museum.iatp.org.ua; f. 1923; more than 250,000 exhibits; library of 30,000 vols; Dir L. N. MATAT.

National Art Museum of Ukraine: 01001 Kyiv, vul. M. Hrushevskoho 6; tel. (44) 228-13-57; fax (44) 228-74-54; e-mail namu@i.com.ua; f. 1899; 30,000 items, including painting, sculpture, engraving, and wood-carvings dating from the Middle Ages; Dir A. I. MELNIK.

National Museum of the History of Ukraine: 01025 Kyiv, vul. Volodymyrska 2; tel. (44) 278-65-45; fax (44) 278-43-23; e-mail nmu@ukr.net; f. 1899; history, archaeology, religion, ethnography, numismatics; 2 brs; 600,000 exhibits; Dir SERHIY CHAIKOVSKYI.

National Taras Shevchenko Museum: 01004 Kyiv, bulv. T. Shevchenko 12; tel. (44) 234-25-23; fax (44) 246-54-91; e-mail m-shevchenka@ukr.net; f. 1940; exhibits on the life and work of the 19th-century Ukrainian national poet and political writer, Taras Shevchenko (1814–1861) and his contemporaries; Dir SERHIY HALCHENKO.

Odesa Archaeological Museum: 65026 Odesa, vul. Lanzheronovska 4; tel. (48) 722-01-71; e-mail arhaeology@farlep.net; internet www.arhaeology.odessa.ua; f. 1825; more than 160,000 items, including items from ancient Greece, Egypt and Italy; library of 29,000 vols; Dir I. V. BRUJAKO.

St Sophia of Kyiv National Architectural Conservation Area: 01034 Kyiv, vul. Volodymyrska 24; tel. (44) 278-26-20; fax (44) 278-67-06; e-mail stsophia@i.com.ua; internet www.sophia.org.ua; comprises 11th-century St Sophia cathedral, frescoes, mosaics, paintings, applied decorative arts, architectural monuments; Dir-Gen. NELYA M. KUKOVALSKA.

State Committee for Archives: 03110 Kyiv, vul. Solomyanska 24; tel. (44) 275-27-77; fax (44) 275-36-55; e-mail mail@archives.gov.ua; internet www.archives.gov.ua; Chair. OLHA P. GINZBURG.

State History Library: 01015 Kyiv, vul. I. Mazepy 21/24; tel. (44) 290-46-17; e-mail shlu@shlu.freenet.kiev.ua; f. 1939; Dir OLENA VINOHRADOVA.

State Parliamentary Library of Ukraine: 01001 Kyiv, vul. M. Hrushevskoho 1; tel. and fax (44) 228-85-12; e-mail nplu@nplu .kiev.ua; internet www.nplu.kiev.ua; f. 1866; 4.0m. vols; Dir ANATOLIY P. KORNIYENKO.

SPORTING ORGANIZATION

National Olympic Committee of Ukraine: 01601 Kyiv, vul. Esplanadna 42; tel. and fax (44) 246-62-33; e-mail info@noc-ukr .org; internet www.noc-ukr.org; Pres. SERHIY N. BUBKA; Sec.-Gen. VOLODYMYR V. GERASHCHENKO.

PERFORMING ARTS

Kharkiv N. V. Lysenko State Academic Opera and Ballet Theatre (KhATOB): 61057 Kharkiv, vul. Sumska 25; tel. (572) 47-72-16; fax (572) 47-80-64; e-mail th@vl.kharkov.ua; f. 1920; Dir HEORHIY SELIKHOV.

Lviv S. Krushelnytskyi State Academic Theatre of Opera and Ballet: 79000 Lviv, pr. Svobody; tel. (32) 272-85-62; internet www .lvivopera.org; f. 1900; Dir TADEI O. EDER; Artistic Dir MYRON YUSYPOVYCH.

National Ivan-Franko Academic Drama Theatre: 01001 Kyiv, pl. Ivana Franka 3; tel. (44) 229-58-51; fax (44) 229-59-51; e-mail nadift@gu.kiev.ua; internet www.franko-theatre.kiev.ua; f. 1920; Gen. Dir MYKHAYLO V. ZAKHAREVICH; Artistic Dir BOHDAN S. STUPKA.

National Lesya Ukrainka Academic Russian Drama Theatre: 01001 Kyiv, vul. B. Khmelnytskoho 5; tel. (44) 235-42-50; fax (44) 235-42-50; e-mail kievrusdram@mail.ru; f. 1926; Gen. and Artistic Dir MYKHAYLO REZNIKOVICH.

National Odesa Philharmonic Orchestra: 65026 Odesa, vul. I. Bunina 15; tel. (482) 25-01-89; e-mail info@odessaphilharmonic .org; internet www.odessaphilharmonic.org; f. 1937; Musical Dir HOBART EARLE.

National Philharmonia of Ukraine: 01001 Kyiv, 2 Volodymyrs-kyi uzviz; tel. (44) 279-62-51; fax (44) 278-03-30; e-mail filarmonia@g .com.ua; internet www.filarmonia.com.ua; f. 1863; symphony and chamber orchestras, chamber and folk ensembles, instrumental and vocal soloists; Gen. Dir DMYTRO I. OSTAPENKO; Artistic Dir. VOLODYMYR A. LUKASHEV.

National Taras Shevchenko Academic Opera and Ballet Theatre: 01034 Kyiv, vul. Volodymrska 50; tel. (44) 224-71-65; Dir PETR CHUPRYN.

Odesa State Academic Opera and Ballet Theatre: 65026 Odesa, prov. Chaikovskoho 1; e-mail opera-ballet@tm.odessa.ua; internet www.opera-ballet.tm.odessa.ua; f. 1810; Dir VASILIY NABROTSKIY.

Education

The reversal of the 'Russification' of the education system during the Soviet period was one of the principal demands of the opposition movements that emerged in the late 1980s. After Ukrainian was adopted as the state language, in 1990 policies were adopted to ensure that all pupils were granted the opportunity of tuition in Ukrainian. In the early 1990s there were significant changes to the curriculum, with more emphasis on Ukrainian history and litera-ture. Some religious and private educational institutions were established, including a private university, the Mohyla Academy—National University of Kyiv, which had been one of Europe's leading educational establishments before 1917.

In 2007/08 there were 15,300 pre-primary educational establish-ments in Ukraine (although 1,400 of these had their operations suspended), which provided for 1,137,000 students. In that year a total of 4,857,000 students attended 21,200 primary and general secondary institutions. There were approximately 531,000 teachers of primary and general secondary education. An additional 454,400 students attended 1,022 vocational secondary educational institu-tions, at which 285,100 teachers were employed. In 2005/06 some 90% of children in the relevant age-group were enrolled in primary education, while enrolment at secondary level included 84% of children in the relevant age-group. In 2007/08 there were 2,813,800 students enrolled in higher education. Government expen-diture on education in 2006 was 33,274m. hryvnyas (13.7% of total budgetary expenditure).

UNIVERSITIES

Chernivtsi National University: 58012 Chernivtsi, vul. Kotsyu-binskoho 2; tel. (3722) 2-62-35; fax (372) 25-38-36; e-mail rectro@ chnu.cv.ua; internet www.chnu.cv.ua; f. 1875; language of instruc-tion: Ukrainian; 13 faculties; 786 teachers; 7,421 full-time students, 6,682 part-time; Pres. M. V. TKACH.

Dnipropetrovsk State University: 49050 Dnipropetrovsk, Gagarinskii pr. 72; tel. (56) 373-67-90; fax (56) 776-58-33; e-mail admin@dsu.dp.ua; internet www.dsu.dp.ua; f. 1918; languages of

instruction: Ukrainian and Russian; 17 faculties; 1,267 teachers; 13,349 students; Pres. Prof. M. V. POLYAKOV.

Donetsk National University: 83055 Donetsk, vul. Universy-tetska 24; tel. (62) 337-19-45; fax (62) 345-21-76; e-mail postmaster@dongu.donetsk.ua; internet www.donnu.edu.ua; f. 1965; languages of instruction: Ukrainian and Russian; 12 faculties; 815 teachers; 17,300 students; Rector VOLODYMYR P. SHEVCHENKO.

Kharhiv V. N. Karazin National University: 61077 Kharkiv, pl. Svobody 4; tel. (57) 705-12-47; fax (57) 705-12-48; e-mail postmaster@ univer.kharkov.ua; internet www.univer.kharkov.ua; f. 1804; lan-guages of instruction: Russian and Ukrainian; 18 faculties; 4 research institutes; 2,000 teachers; 12,000 students; Rector V. S. BAKIROV.

Kyiv T. Shevchenko National University: 01033 Kyiv, vul. Volodmymyrska 64; tel. (44) 234-12-88; fax (44) 220-83-91; e-mail office@univ.kiev.ua; internet www.univ.kiev.ua; f. 1834; 21 faculties and academic institutes; 3 research institutes; 2,000 teachers; 20,000 students; Rector Prof. VIKTOR V. SKOPENKO.

Lviv Ivan-Franko National University: 79000 Lviv, vul. Uni-versytetska 1; tel. (32) 274-12-62; fax (32) 272-28-01; e-mail dirlu@ franko.lviv.ua; internet www.franko.lviv.ua; language of instruc-tion: Ukrainian; f. 1661; 16 faculties; 1,161 teachers; 22,000 students; Rector Prof. IVAN VAKARCHUK.

Mohyla Academy—National University of Kyiv: 04070 Kyiv, vul. Skovorody 2; tel. (44) 425-45-15; fax (44) 463-67-83; e-mail pr@ ukma.kiev.ua; internet www.ukma.kiev.ua; f. 1615; abolished 1817; re-founded 1991; acquired status of national university in 1994; languages of instruction: Ukrainian and English; 6 faculties; 550 teachers; 3,024 students; Pres. VYACHESLAV BRYUKHOVETSKIY.

Odesa I. I. Mechnikov National University: 65082 Odesa, vul. Dvoryanska 2; tel. (48) 723-52-54; fax (48) 723-35-15; e-mail oguint@ paco.net; internet www.onu.edu.ua; f. 1865; languages of instruc-tion: Russian, Ukrainian and English; 11 faculties; 6 educational institutes; 6 educational centres; 3,500 teachers; 20,000 students; Rector Prof. Dr VALENTIN A. SMYNTYNA.

Taurida National University: 95007 Crimea, Simferopol, ul. Yaltinskaya 4; tel. (652) 51-64-98; fax (652) 51-71-35; e-mail rector@tnu.crimea.ua; internet www.ccssu.crimea.ua; f. 1918; lan-guage of instruction: Russian; 17 faculties; 1,000 teachers; 17,000 students; Rector NIKOLAI V. BAGROV.

Uzhhorod State University: 88000 Transcarpathian obl., Uzh-horod, vul. Pidhirna 46; tel. and fax (3122) 3-33-41; e-mail admin@ univ.uzhgorod.ua; internet www.univ.uzhgorod.ua; f. 1945; lan-guage of instruction: Ukrainian; 14 faculties; 10,000 students; Rector VOLODYMYR YU. SLYVKA.

Zaporizhzhya State University: 69063 Zaporizhzhya, vul. Zhu-kovskoho 66; tel. and fax (612) 64-45-46; e-mail rektor@zsu.zp.ua; internet www.zsu.edu.ua; f. 1985; languages of instruction: Ukrai-nian and Russian; 14 faculties; 524 teachers; 9,200 students; Rector Prof. VALERIY SAVIN.

Social Welfare

Until independence in 1991, the Soviet state-funded system of social welfare was in existence in Ukraine. In 1991 three extra-budgetary funds were created: the Pension Fund, the Social Insurance Fund and the Employment Fund, which were intended to administer most of Ukraine's social-security benefits. The Social Insurance Fund is administered by the trade unions and finances health clinics at workplaces, sick leave, and benefits, such as maternity leave and child-birth allowances. The Employment Fund provides unemploy-ment insurance payments to workers for up to one year. A fourth fund, the Chornobyl Fund, was later established, providing a variety of benefits, including social payments, to victims of the Chornobyl nuclear accident of 1986. Family benefits, which are means-tested, are also paid by the state. There is a monthly minimum wage, which was equivalent to US $66 in late 2005.

In 2006 the average life expectancy at birth was 61.5 years for men and 73.1 years for women; the rate of mortality for under-fives was 24 per 1,000 live births. In that year there were 3.1 physicians and 8.7 hospital beds for every 1,000 people. The compulsory retirement age in Ukraine is 55 years for women and 60 years for men. Three forms of pensions have existed in Ukraine since reforms were implemented in the late 1990s: a labour pension, comprising contributions from employees' salaries; welfare pensions, paid from the central and local government budgets; and a supplementary pension, paid from private pension funds. In 2005 expenditure on health care amounted to US $488 per head of population (equivalent to 7.0% of GDP); 52.8% of this expenditure was in the public sector. In 2003 expenditure on social security and welfare totalled 40,715m. hryvnyas (41.2% of budgetary expenditure). However, prior to the presidential election in late 2004 the Government of Prime Minister Viktor Yanukovych increased the rate of state pensions two-fold, as a result of which state expenditure on pensions was to increase to approximately 16% of GDP, one of the highest levels in the world. The rate of state pensions was increased further in 2005, to a monthly minimum of US \$66.

Ministry of the Protection of Health: see The Government (Ministries).

Ministry of Labour and Social Policy: see The Government (Ministries).

Caritas Spes Ukraine—Caritas of the Roman Catholic Church in Ukraine: 01001 Kyiv, vul. Kostyolna 17; tel. (44) 228-19-37; fax (44) 228-17-84; e-mail caritas-spes@catholic.kiev.ua; internet www.caritas-spes.org.ua; Roman Catholic welfare org.; Pres. Fr VICTOR SIMON.

Caritas Ukraine—Caritas of the Greek Catholic Church in Ukraine: 04071 Kyiv, vul. Kostiantynivska 22/17; tel. (44) 467-60-80; fax (44) 416-63-75; e-mail caritas@caritas-ua.org; internet www.caritas-ua.org; Pres. ANDRIJ WASKOWYZ; Sec.-Gen. ANATOLIY KOZAK.

Chornobyl Fund: 04053 Kyiv, pl. Lvivska 8.

Employment Fund: 04053 Kyiv, vul. Kudryavska 26–28; f. 1991.

Pension Fund of Ukraine: 01014 Kyiv, vul. Bastionna 9; tel. (44) 294-89-33; fax (44) 294-73-37; e-mail pf-it@gu.kiev.ua; internet www.pfu.gov.ua; f. 1990; Chair. of Bd BORIS ZAYCHUK.

Social Insurance Fund: 04053 Kyiv, vul. Kudryavska 26–28; f. 1991.

The Environment

An explosion at the Chornobyl (Chernobyl) nuclear power station in April 1986 resulted in serious contamination of many areas in Ukraine (an estimated 40,000 sq km of territory), as well as areas in many other European countries. The incident, particularly the secrecy surrounding it and the subsequent decontamination operation, led to the formation of several environmental campaigning and political organizations. A report published in 2005 by the Chornobyl Forum, an organization established by the Governments of Belarus, Russia and Ukraine and several international organizations, stated that up to 4,000 deaths, caused by cancer, cardiovascular and neurological diseases, could eventually result from the Chornobyl accident. More than 600,000 people were believed to have received high levels of exposure. In 1998 cracks in the protective cover of the defective reactor were found; measures were swiftly taken to prevent leakage of radioactive material. The last functioning reactor at Chornobyl was finally shut down in December 2000, after the European Bank for Reconstruction and Development (EBRD) agreed to provide funds for the construction of new reactors. The other area of environmental concern was the heavily industrialized Donbas region. The country also participated in efforts to control pollution in the Black Sea.

GOVERNMENT ORGANIZATIONS

Ministry of Emergency Situations and the Protection of the Population from the Consequences of the Chornobyl Catastrophe: see The Government (Ministries).

Ministry of the Protection of the Environment: see The Government (Ministries).

Ukrainian Scientific Research Institute for Ecological Problems (USRIEP): 61166 Kharkov, vul. Bakulina 6; tel. and fax (57) 702-15-92; e-mail kovalenko@niiep.kharkov.ua; internet www.niiep.kharkov.ua; f. 1971; environmental protection, water resource management and treatment, environmental legislation and regulations; Dir HRIHORIY KOVALENKO.

ACADEMIC INSTITUTES

National Academy of Sciences of Ukraine: 01601 Kyiv, vul. Volodymyrska 54; tel. (44) 225-22-39; fax (44) 224-32-43; e-mail prez@nas.gov.ua; internet www.nas.gov.ua; f. 1918; Pres. B. E. PATON.

Attached institutes incl.:

Institute of General Energy: 04070 Kyiv, vul. Pokrovska 11; tel. and fax (44) 417-01-42; e-mail common@general-energy.gov.ua; f. 1997; publishes journal *The Problems of General Energy* (2–4 issues per year); Dir of Scientific Activity MICHAEL KULIK.

Ukrainian State Steppe Reservation: 87172 Donetsk obl., Telmanov raion, Samsonove; tel. (6279) 27-325; associated with the Institute of Biology; has some environmental responsibilities; Dir ANATOLIY P. HENOV.

NON-GOVERNMENTAL ORGANIZATIONS

Ecological Information Centre (EITs): 83000 Donetsk, bulv. Pushkina 13; tel. and fax (62) 335-43-09; e-mail webmaster@infoeco.dn.ua; f. 2001.

EcoPravo-Kharkiv: 61002 Kharkiv, POB 10479; tel. and fax (57) 719-10-21; e-mail eco@ecopravo.kharkov.ua; internet www.ecopravo.kharkov.ua; f. 1993; environmental law, legal assistance to citizens and non-governmental organizations, development and promotion of environmental legislation in Ukraine; Dir Prof. OLEKSIY M. SHUMYLO.

Green Party of Ukraine: see Political Organizations.

Interecocentre: 01601 Kyiv, vul. Tereschenkivska 2/69; tel. (44) 235-73-74; fax (44) 235-70-62; e-mail intereco@post.com.ua; internet www.geocities.com/interecocentre; f. 1994; seeks to monitor and protect the environment; Dir LEONID PROTSENKO.

Ukrainian Chornobyl Union: c/o 01655 Kyiv, pl. Lvivska 8; f. 1991; represents victims of the Chornobyl disaster; 420,000 mems; Pres. YURIY ANDREYEV.

Zeleniy Svit (Green World—Ukrainian Environmental Association): 01070 Kyiv, Kontraktova pl. 4; tel. (44) 417-02-83; fax (44) 417-43-83; e-mail zsfoe@melp.dp.ua; f. 1988; ecological asscn of various Ukrainian groups; affiliated to the Ukrainian Peace Council's campaign against nuclear power; Chair. YURIY SAMOYLENKO.

Defence

In December 1991 an independent Ukrainian military was established. As assessed at November 2007, there were an estimated 129,925 active personnel in the Ukrainian Armed Forces (excluding the Black Sea Fleet), including 70,753 ground forces, an air force of 45,240 and a navy of an estimated 13,932. There were also paramilitary forces, comprising some 45,000 in the Border Guard, 39,900 serving under the Ministry of Internal Affairs, 14,000 serving in the Coast Guard, and some 9,500 civil defence troops answerable to the Ministry of Emergency Situations and the Protection of the Population from the Consequences of the Chornobyl Catastrophe. There were, additionally, some 1m. reserves. Military service is compulsory for males over 18 years of age, for a period of 18 months in the ground forces and air forces, and two years in the navy. Legislation approved in March 2005 provided for the reduction by six months of the terms of conscription to the ground forces and the navy.

In 1993–94 a programme of nuclear disarmament was agreed with the USA and Russia, involving the dismantling of ex-Soviet nuclear warheads and, finally, the surrender of the remaining warheads. The transfer of strategic nuclear weapons to Russia for dismantling was funded by the USA and completed in mid-1996. Later that year Ukraine began a programme of destruction or conversion to civilian use of its missile silos. In November 1994 the Verkhovna Rada ratified the Treaty on the Non-Proliferation of Nuclear Weapons, which enabled the implementation of the first Strategic Arms Reduction Treaty (START 1), ratified in February 1994. On 31 May 1997 Ukraine and Russia signed an agreement on the division of the Soviet Black Sea Fleet, on the terms of its deployment and on the status of its base, Sevastopol. Defence spending in 2007 was budgeted at 9,100m. hryvnyas.

Chief of the General Staff: Lt-Gen. SERHIY O. KYRYCHENKO.

Commander-in-Chief of the Air Defence: Col-Gen. IVAN S. RUSNAK.

Commander-in-Chief of the Land Forces: Lt-Gen. IVAN YU. SVYDA.

Commander-in-Chief of the Navy: Vice-Adm. IHUR Y. TENYUKH.

AUTONOMOUS REPUBLIC

Despite being described by its 1996 Constitution as a unitary state, Ukraine includes one Autonomous Republic, in Crimea (which, prior to 1954, had formed part of the Russian Federation). The largest city on the Crimean peninsula, Sevastopol, is not incorporated into this Republic, and comprises a separate administrative unit.

AUTONOMOUS REPUBLIC OF CRIMEA

The Autonomous Republic of Crimea is bounded to the south and west by the Black Sea and is separated from mainland Ukraine—Kherson Oblast (to the north) by the Perekop Isthmus and from the Taman Peninsula (in Krasnodar Krai of the Russian Federation, to the east) by the Kerch Strait. The republic covers a total area of 26,100 sq km, a large proportion of which is dry steppeland. It is rich in minerals. The peninsula is divided into 14 administrative districts and 16 cities. The peninsula's main cities are Simferopol, the capital, Sevastopol (which does not, however, form part of the Autonomous Republic) and Kerch. The towns of the south coast, particularly Yalta, are popular tourist resorts. The population of the Republic at the census of 5 December 2001, according to rounded figures, was 2,033,700, with an additional 379,500 resident in Sevastopol. At 1 July 2008 the population of the Republic was estimated at 1,967,845, with an additional 379,379 resident in Sevastopol; the population density of the peninsula at that time was, therefore, 86.9 per sq km, or 75.4 per sq km within the Republic proper. In January 2001 62.6% of the Republic's population inhabited urban areas, a proportion that has remained approximately constant since the early 1960s. According to the census of January 1989, 82.6% of the population of Crimea (including Sevastopol) regarded Russian as their native language, compared with 13.7% who described Ukrainian in this way. (Notably, only 52.6% of those who defined their ethnicity as Ukrainian stated that Ukrainian was their native language.) At that time, an estimated 26% of the population of Crimea were ethnically Ukrainian and 67% Russian; by January 2001 the estimated figures were 58% Russian and 24% Ukrainian. Crimea's Tatar population was deported to Central Asia by Stalin (Iosif Dzhugashvili) in May 1944; some 100,000, about one-half of the population, died during the deportations. After Stalin's death in 1953 the Tatars were allowed to resettle in Central Asia (principally in Uzbekistan), but were not permitted to return to Crimea. After 1989, however, approximately 280,000 Tatars returned to the region and, by 2001, constituted some 12% of the population of the peninsula.

The Crimean peninsula was originally colonized by the ancient Greeks in the seventh century BC and subsequently invaded by the Goths (AD 250), the Huns (373), the Khazars (eighth century), the Eastern Roman, or 'Byzantine', Greeks (1016), the Kipchaks (1050), the Mongol Tatars (13th century) and the Ottoman Turks (late 15th century). An independent Crimean Khanate was founded by the Tatars in northern and central Crimea in 1475, and survived until the late 18th century, when the Russian Empire made repeated incursions into the peninsula. The Khanate was finally annexed in 1783. The Russians were defeated in the Crimean War (1854–55) by the Western Powers (France, the Kingdom of Sardinia and the United Kingdom) and the Ottoman Turks. Crimea formed part of the short-lived republic of Taurida (Tavria—established in 1918), until 18 October 1921, when the Crimean Autonomous Soviet Socialist Republic (ASSR) was created, within the Russian Soviet Federative Socialist Republic (RSFSR).

The Crimean ASSR was abolished on 30 June 1945, following the deportation of the Tatars, and the peninsula became merely an oblast (region) within the RSFSR. However, purportedly to mark the 300th anniversary of the de facto union of Ukraine and Russia in 1654, on 19 February 1954 Crimea was transferred to the control of the Ukrainian Soviet Socialist Republic (Ukrainian SSR). Following a referendum held on the peninsula on 20 January 1991, Crimea claimed the status of an Autonomous Republic. In February 1992, following the dissolution of the USSR, the Crimean Supreme Council (legislature) voted to transform the region into the self-styled 'Republic of Crimea'. The Ukrainian authorities subsequently offered the region greater powers of self-government, but on 5 May the Crimean Supreme Council declared independence from Ukraine. The decision was annulled by the all-Ukrainian Verkhovna Rada (legislature) the following week; however, in June the Ukrainian authorities recognized Crimea as an Autonomous Republic. On 16 January 1994 elections were held to the new presidency of the Crimea, won by Yurii Meshkov, a Russian nationalist and leader of the Republican Party of Crimea.

Elections to the republican legislature of Crimea, held on 27 March 1994, likewise demonstrated a large degree of popular support for pro-Russian parties. Meanwhile, in a concurrently held referendum, 70% of participants responded in favour of greater autonomy from Ukraine. In May the new Crimean Supreme Council voted to restore the May 1992 Constitution, which effectively represented a declaration of the Republic's independence. Compromise with the Ukrainian central authorities was later reached.

The main political concern in Crimea during 1994 was the struggle between the Meshkov presidency and the republican parliament, although both factions remained advocates of increased autonomy. In September the two sides agreed to draft a new basic law. On 17 March 1995 the Verkhovna Rada voted to abolish the May 1992 Crimean Constitution and the post of President of Crimea. Two weeks later the national President, Leonid Kuchma, in an effort to avert a political crisis, assumed direct control of the administration of Crimea and ordered the restoration of Anatolii Franchuk (who had been dismissed by the Crimean Supreme Council one week earlier) as republican premier. Direct presidential administration over the region ended on 28 August 1995.

Ukrainian control over the peninsula was consolidated in mid-1995, when the results of local elections demonstrated a significant decrease in support for pro-Russian parties. The new Crimean Supreme Council elected Yevhen Suprunyuk, thought to be more conciliatory towards the national Government, as its Chairman. In October 1995 the Crimean parliament adopted a new Constitution, which was not recognized by the national authorities until April 1996, when significant amendments were suggested. A fifth draft of this Constitution was approved by the Crimean parliament in October 1998. The Constitution stated that Crimea had the status of an Autonomous Republic, without sovereignty, and was a part of Ukraine. (Meanwhile, the Constitution of Ukraine, finally adopted on 28 June 1996, described Ukraine as a unitary state, recognizing the Autonomous Republic of Crimea as an integral part of that state.)

In October 1996 Suprunyuk resigned and was replaced by Vasyl Kiselev. In January 1997 the Crimean Supreme Council approved a motion of no confidence in the Council of Ministers, led by Arkadii Demydenko since January 1996. The following month, contrary to Ukrainian law, the parliament approved legislation whereby the Government was, in the future, to be appointed by the Crimean Supreme Council, rather than by the Ukrainian President. In April the parliament duly appointed Anatolii Franchuk as the new head of the Council of Ministers, a resolution suspended by President Kuchma. However, following a second vote of no confidence in Demydenko, President Kuchma consented to Franchuk's appointment.

In March 1998 elections to the Crimean Supreme Council were held simultaneously with the elections to the national Verkhovna Rada. Of the registered electorate, 63.8% participated in the elections. The Communist Party of Ukraine (CPU) obtained 40 of the 100 seats in the Crimean Supreme Council, by far the largest number gained by a single party. Independent candidates secured 44 seats. Leonid Grach, the leader of the CPU in Crimea, was elected Chairman on 14 May. The Organization for Security and Co-operation in Europe (OSCE) estimated that about one-half of the Tatars resident in Crimea in 1998 did not have Ukrainian citizenship and were, therefore, ineligible to vote (in October of that year the process of naturalization of Tatars was simplified). On 27 May 1998 a new Council of Ministers was appointed, with the centrist Sergei Kunitsyn, an ally of President Kuchma, as premier. On 12 January 1999 a new Crimean Constitution came into effect, establishing relations between the authorities in Kyiv and Simferopol and granting Crimea the right to draft a budget and manage its own property. In February the first Crimean Tatars received Ukrainian citizenship under the new, simplified criteria. This was believed to have increased the proportion of those Crimean Tatars resident on the peninsula holding Ukrainian citizenship to some 90% prior to the holding of legislative elections in March 2002. None the less, in May 2000 some 20,000 Crimean Tatars held a demonstration in Simferopol to demand greater political autonomy.

A political impasse developed from the second half of 2000, apparently as a result of political rivalry between Kunitsyn and Grach, and as a result of alleged corruption within the Crimean

Government. In September five ministers and two deputy prime ministers, all of whom were members of the CPU, resigned from the cabinet; Kunitsyn nominated new ministers in their place in December. In July 2001 the Supreme Council dismissed Kunitsyn from the premiership for the third time, appointing Deputy Prime Minister Lentun Bezaziyev as acting premier. Although Kuchma had refused to recognize two previous dismissals, on this occasion the removal of Kunitsyn was accepted, and Kuchma expressed support for the new premier elected by the Crimean Supreme Council, Valerii Gorbatov of the Labour Ukraine party. A new Crimean Government was appointed in mid-September; however, continuing tensions between the Government and the parliament resulted in 11 of the 30 ministerial posts remaining vacant in late November.

As campaigning for the concurrent elections to the Verkhovna Rada and the Crimean Supreme Council, to be held on 31 March 2002, got under way, controversy was provoked at the end of February by the invalidation of Grach's candidacy for a seat in the Supreme Council on technical grounds. Shortly after Grach's disqualification, some 30 candidates opposed to Grach were also disqualified, and Grach reportedly threatened to demand a referendum supporting the reversion of Crimea to Russian rule; additionally, supporters of Grach pitched tents in the centre of Simferopol in order to demand that he be permitted to contest the elections. Following the rejection of Grach's appeal by the Crimean Court of Appeal, the case was referred to the Ukrainian Supreme Court, but was not heard until after the elections, in April. Meanwhile, despite his disqualification, Grach's name appeared on ballot papers, and he was re-elected to the Supreme Council in defiance of the Crimean Appeal Court's decision. The elections to the Crimean Supreme Council demonstrated a sizeable shift in support away from the CPU, towards centrists close to Kunitsyn, who, contesting the elections as the Kunitsyn Team, won 39 of 100 seats and, subsequently, were able to organize a majority faction in the legislature. The CPU and their allies, contesting the elections as the Grach bloc, won 28 seats; three other parties gained representation, and 29 independent candidates were elected. In late April the Ukrainian Supreme Court approved Grach's appeal, thereby serving to legitimize his status as a deputy. However, Grach was unsuccessful in his campaign for re-election as speaker of the legislature, being resoundingly defeated by a former deputy speaker, Boris Deich, at the opening session in late April. The new parliament also voted for the dismissal of Gorbatov and the reappointment of Kunitsyn as Prime Minister, and reformists loyal to Kunitsyn were successful in establishing a majority in the legislature, which eventually became known as the 'Stability' bloc, comprising some 86 of 100 deputies. None the less, in the concurrent elections to the Verkhovna Rada, the CPU remained the most popular party on the peninsula. Notably, for the first time, Crimean Tatar deputies were elected to the Verkhovna Rada, within the Our Ukraine bloc. Russian nationalists only successfully attracted votes in the Crimean city of Sevastopol.

On 24 June 2004 the Verkhovna Rada adopted legislation 'On the restoration of rights to persons deported on grounds of ethnicity'. Under this law, the state guaranteed any returning deportees and their children equal rights with Ukrainian citizens, favourable conditions for resettlement (including provision of land, housing and work) and provision of education. However, on 19 July President Kuchma vetoed the law, citing legal objections to various terms in the document and apparent incompatibilities with Ukraine's Constitution and Family and Land Codes.

The continuing tension in Crimean society was reflected in the allegiances displayed in the presidential elections of late 2004, when the peninsula's Russophone majority strongly supported the candidacy of Viktor Yanukovych, while the Crimean Tatar minority were reported to have voted principally for the victorious candidate, Viktor Yushchenko, hoping that the latter would act to address their grievances regarding land distribution and greater ethnic autonomy. In late April 2005 Kunitsyn resigned as Prime Minister of Crimea, following his appointment as an adviser to President Yushchenko; the Crimean Supreme Council voted to approve Yushchenko's nomination of Anatolii Matviyenko as his replacement. The appointment of Matviyenko was a cause of some controversy on the peninsula, both because he had never held any position of responsibility in Crimea and because of his affiliations with both Ukrainian nationalists and the Yuliya Tymoshenko bloc (YuTB), which did not enjoy significant support in the Republic. Matviyenko was subject to frequent criticism as Prime Minister, particularly for failing to resolve concerns about widespread corruption in Crimea or the issue of land allocation to returning Crimean Tatars, and his premiership proved short-lived. Following the dismissal of Tymoshenko as Prime Minister of Ukraine, in early September, the Crimean Supreme Council voted to dismiss the republican Government; Matviyenko duly resigned on 20 September. On 23 September the Crimean Supreme Council approved the appointment of Anatolii Burdyugov, the leader of the Crimean branch of Yushchenko's People's Union Our Ukraine party, as Crimean Prime Minister, and a new Government was formed at the end of the month. In late February 2006 the Crimean legislature voted to hold a referendum on the proposed

introduction of Russian as a state language within the peninsula; however, President Yushchenko stated that the referendum would be unconstitutional, and this ruling was subsequently confirmed by the Central Electoral Commission.

Elections to the Crimean Supreme Council, held concurrently with local elections and with those to the Verkhovna Rada on 26 March 2006, were marred by allegations of electoral fraud; moreover, one candidate was killed on polling day. The results of the elections were finally announced on 19 April. The For Yanukovych bloc (principally comprising the Party of the Regions—PR) obtained the largest proportion of the votes cast, with 32.6%; it was awarded 44 of the 100 seats in the Supreme Council. The second-placed party was the pro-Russian Union party, with 7.6% of the votes and 10 seats. The Kunitsyn bloc also secured 10 seats, while the CPU took nine, the People's Movement of Ukraine-Rukh and the YuTB each won eight, the Nataliya Vitrenko People's Opposition bloc obtained seven, and the 'Ne Tak' Opposition bloc (which comprised several centrist parties associated with allies of former President Kuchma, most notably the Social Democratic Party of Ukraine—United) took four. Anatolii Gritsenko of the PR was elected as the new legislative Chairman, a position he had previously held in 1997–98. On 2 June the Crimean Supreme Council approved the formation of a new coalition Government, chaired by Viktor Plakida.

In late May 2006 the proposed staging of military exercises off the coast of Crimea, under the aegis of the North Atlantic Treaty Organization (NATO) and with the participation of the defence forces of 12 countries, were a focus for protests in the port of Feodosiya, in the east of Crimea, principally by Russian nationalists opposed to Ukrainian involvement with NATO. It was also reported that the local branches of the CPU and the PR supported the protests. Although similar exercises had taken place in the region on an annual basis since 1997, on each occasion, in accordance with the national Constitution, they had required the specific approval of the Verkhovna Rada. As the outgoing Verkhovna Rada had failed to vote to approve the exercises on three occasions, and the prolonged coalition negotiations following the elections to that body on 26 March had prevented the new legislature from convening, it became apparent that the forthcoming exercises had no legal standing. In early June the Crimean Supreme Council was reported to have voted to approve a statement declaring the peninsula a 'NATO-free territory'. (Some reports suggested, however, that this vote had not been taken within a formal parliamentary session, and, in any case, the statement had no constitutional meaning.) On 11 June some 200 US reserve troops began to leave Crimea, having been prevented from undertaking the construction work for which they had been contracted, and the proposed exercises were abandoned. In mid-August clashes between around 300 Crimean Tatars and a similar number of Slavs took place in Bakhcharai, south of Simferopol; the clashes, which reportedly followed several weeks of tension after several Crimean Tatars had been attacked, apparently by market traders, were related to demands that a market be relocated from the site of a Crimean Tatar cemetery. It was subsequently agreed that the market would be relocated by mid-September, as it had apparently been operating without a licence, and an agreement to that effect was signed by Plakida, a Deputy Chairman of the Crimean Supreme Council, Mikhail Bakharev, and Crimean Tatar representatives, while the alleged attacks on Crimean Tatars near the market were to be investigated by the police. (In late June inter-ethnic tensions had also arisen in Feodosiya, following the erection of a monument to the Christian saint St Andrew on a site claimed as a Crimean Tatar burial ground. Following the dismantlement of the statue by a group of Crimean Tatars and its subsequent re-erection by a Russian Cossack militia, it was agreed that the monument would be moved to a new location.) In late December the Crimean branch of the CPU organized a 'people's referendum' on the peninsula (which was not, however, recognized as having any official status) on Ukraine's aspirations towards NATO membership. According to the results of the poll issued by the CPU, some 58% of eligible voters participated in the 'referendum', of whom almost 99% rejected the notion that Ukraine should accede to membership of NATO.

In May 2007 Yushchenko removed Viktor Shemchuk as permanent Representative of the President in Crimea, after he was temporarily reinstated as the Crimean prosecutor on the grounds of a ruling by a Simferopol district court. In June Yushchenko appointed Lt-Gen. Volodymyr Khomenko, who had hitherto headed the Ministry of Internal Affairs in Crimea, to succeed Shemchuk. Following the dissolution of the Verkhovna Rada and scheduling of pre-term elections for 30 September, it was announced in July that Kunitsyn was again to head the pro-presidential coalition, reconstituted as the Our Ukraine-People's Self-defence bloc, in Crimea. A number of electoral irregularities were reported in the Republic on 30 September; Yanukovych's PR secured some 61.0% of votes cast in the Republic, followed by the Our Ukraine-People's Self-defence bloc, with only 8.2%, the CPU, with 7.6%, and the YuTB, with 6.9%. Following the elections, a temporary ban on demonstrations was ended by the Crimean authorities; in October some 2,000 Crimean Tatars demonstrated in Simferopol to demand land for resettlement, and further protests were planned. In March 2008 Crimean Tatars again gathered outside the parliamentary building in Simferopol, accusing the authorities of corruption and failing to resolve the land issue.

In May 2008 the Ukrainian authorities prevented the Mayor of Moscow, Russia, Yurii Luzhkov, from entering the country, after he declared that Sevastopol had not formed part of the territory of Crimea formally transferred from Russian to Ukrainian control in 1954. In July Luzhkov announced that Moscow City was to contribute US $34m. of its own budget to promote the teaching of the Russian language and to support Russians in Crimea.

Russia's military operation in Georgia in early August 2008, staged with the stated aim of seeking to protect its citizens in South Ossetia, and recognition of the separatist regions of South Ossetia and Abkhazia on 26 August (see the chapter on Georgia), increased domestic and international fears of a similar conflict eventually breaking out in Crimea (particularly in view of Ukraine's aspirations towards eventual NATO membership). In early September the Ukrainian Government expressed concern that Russian passports had been issued to residents of Crimea (as had widely occurred among residents of those regions of South Ossetia outwith Georgian control in the 2000s), and accused Russia of encouraging instability. The Ukrainian authorities formally protested to the Russian con-

sulate in Sevastopol; however, the Representative of the President of Ukraine in Crimea, Leonid Zhunko, denied that a large-scale issuance of Russian passports had been conducted. On 17 September 2008 the Crimean Supreme Council approved an appeal to the Verkhovna Rada for the recognition of the independence of Abkhazia and South Ossetia, while pro-Russian groups demonstrated outside the parliamentary building in support of the separatist authorities in those territories. In early October the leader of the Crimean Tatar organization Milly Firqa appealed to the Russian Government to protect Crimea's ethnic minority population against the nationalism of the Ukrainian authorities, prompting condemnation from other local politicians and Tatar leaders.

Chairman of the Presidium of the Supreme Council: ANATOLII P. GRITSENKO, 95000 Crimea, Simferopol, ul. K. Marksa 18; tel. (6566) 54-42-55; e-mail webmaster@rada.crimea.ua; internet www.rada .crimea.ua.

Chairman of the Council of Ministers (Prime Minister): VIKTOR PLAKIDA, 95005 Crimea, Simferopol, ul. Kirova 13; tel. (6566) 54-42-55; e-mail letter@ark.gov.ua; internet www .crimea-portal.gov.ua.

Representative of the President of Ukraine in Crimea: LEONID ZHUNKO, 95005 Crimea, Simferopol, ul. Kirova 13; tel. (652) 27-67-50.

Bibliography

Åslund, A., and McFaul, M. (Eds). *Revolution in Orange: The Origins of Ukraine's Democratic Breakthrough*. Washington, DC, Carnegie Endowment for International Peace, 2006.

Bilaniuk, L. *Contested Tongues: Language Politics and Cultural Correction in Ukraine*. Ithaca, NY, Cornell University Press, 2005.

Conquest, R. *The Harvest of Sorrow: Soviet Collectivization and the Terror-Famine*. London, Hutchinson, 1986.

D'Anieri, P. *Economic Interdependence in Ukrainian—Russian Relations*. New York, New York State University Press, 1999.

D'Anieri, P., and Kuzio, T. (Eds). *State-Led Nation Building in Ukraine*. Westport, CT, Praeger, 2002.

Dean, M. *Collaboration in the Holocaust: Crimes of the Local Police in Belorussia and Ukraine, 1941–44*. Basingstoke, Palgrave Macmillan, 2003.

Dekel-Chan, J. L. *Farming the Red Land: Jewish Agricultural Colonization and Local Soviet Power, 1924-1941*. New Haven, CT, Yale University Press, 2005.

Drohobycky, M. (Ed.). *Crimea: Dynamics, Challenges and Prospects*. Lanham, MD, Rowman and Littlefield, 1995.

Gesin, M. *The Destruction of the Ukrainian Jewry During World War II*. Lewiston, NY, Edwin Mellen Press, 2006.

Hann, C., and Magosci, P. R. (Eds). *Galicia: A Multicultured Land*. Toronto, University of Toronto Press, 2005.

Harasymiw, B. *Post-Communist Ukraine*. Toronto, Canadian Institute of Ukrainian Studies, 2002.

Kubicek, P. *The History of Ukraine*. Westport, CT, Greenwood Press, 2008.

Kuzio, T. *Ukraine: State and Nation Building*. London, Routledge, 1998.

Ukraine: Perestroika to Independence, 2nd edn, London, Macmillan, 2000.

Democratic Revolution in Ukraine: from Kuchmagate to Orange Revolution. Abingdon, Routledge, 2007.

Legwold, R., and Wallander, C. (Eds). *Swords and Sustenance: The Economics of Security in Belarus and Ukraine*. Cambridge, MA, MIT Press, 2004.

Lieven, A. *Ukraine and Russia: A Fraternal Rivalry*. Washington, DC, US Institute of Peace, 1999.

Lutz, H., and Mollers, F. (Eds). *Ukraine on the Road to Europe*. Heidelberg, Physica, 2001.

Magosci, P. R. *A History of Ukraine*. Toronto, University of Toronto Press, 1996.

The Roots of Ukrainian Nationalism: Galicia as Ukraine's Piedmont. Toronto, University of Toronto Press, 2001.

Makolkin, A. *A History of Odessa, the Last Italian Black Sea Colony*. Lewiston, NY, Edwin Mellen Press, 2004.

Miller, A. I. *The Ukrainian Question: the Russian Empire and Nationalism in the Nineteenth Century*. New York, Central European University Press, 2003.

Plokhy, S. *The Cossacks and Religion in Early Modern Ukraine*. Oxford, Oxford University Press, 2002.

Puglisi, R. *Economic Elites and Russian–Ukraine Relations*. London, RoutledgeCurzon, 2003.

Richardson, T. *Kaleidoscopic Odessa: History and Place in Contemporary Ukraine*. Toronto, University of Toronto Press, 2008.

Sanders, D. *Security Cooperation between Russia and Ukraine in the Post-Soviet Era*. New York, Palgrave, 2002.

Sasse, G. *The Crimea Question: Identity, Transition, and Conflict*. Cambridge, MA, Harvard University Press, 2007.

Satzewich, V. *The Ukrainian Diaspora*. London, Routledge, 2002.

Shandor, V. *Carpatho-Ukraine in the 20th Century: A Political History*. Cambridge, MA, Harvard University Press, 1997.

Skirda, A. *Nestor Makhno: Anarchy's Cossack: The Struggle for Free Soviets in the Ukraine: 1917–1921*. Oakland, CA, AK Press, 2003.

Solchanyk, R. *Ukraine: From Chernobyl to Sovereignty*. London, Macmillan, 1992.

Stewart, S. *Explaining the Low Intensity of Ethnopolitical Conflict in Ukraine*. Münster, LIT Verlag, 2005.

Subtelny, O. *Ukraine: A History*. Toronto, University of Toronto Press, 1988.

Swain, A. *Re-Constructing the Post-Soviet Industrial Region: The Donbas in Transition*. Abingdon, Routledge, 2007.

Tymoshenko, Y. 'Containing Russia', in *Foreign Affairs*. Vol. 86, No 3. Washington, DC, May–June 2007.

Uehling, G. L. *Beyond Memory: The Crimean Tatars' Deportation and Return*. New York, Palgrave Macmillan, 2004.

Whitmore, S. *State Building in the Ukraine: The Ukrainian Parliament, 1990–2003*. London, RoutledgeCurzon, 2004.

Williams, B. G. *The Crimean Tatars: The Diaspora Experience and the Forging of a Nation*. Leiden, Brill, 2001.

Wilson, A. *Ukrainian Nationalism in the 1990s: A Minority Faith*. Cambridge, Cambridge University Press, 1997.

The Ukrainians: Unexpected Nation. 2nd edn, New Haven, CT, Yale University Press, 2002.

Ukraine's Orange Revolution. New Haven, CT, Yale University Press, 2006.

Wolchik, S. L., and Zviglyanich, V. (Eds). *Ukraine: The Search for a National Identity*. Lanham, MA, Rowman and Littlefield, 2000.

Wolczuk, K. *The Moulding of Ukraine: The Constitutional Politics of State Formation*. Budapest, Central European University Press, 2001.

Yekelchyk, S. *Ukraine: Birth of a Modern Nation*. Oxford, Oxford University Press, 2007.

Zabarko, B. (Ed.). *Holocaust in the Ukraine*. Portland, OR, Vallentine Mitchell, 2005.

Also see the Select Bibliography.

UZBEKISTAN

Geography

PHYSICAL FEATURES

The Republic of Uzbekistan is located in the heart of Central Asia. The country lies along a north-west to south-east axis, and its eastern extremity, the Farg'ona (Fergana) valley region, abuts into Kyrgyzstan to the east, with Tajikistan to the south, forming the south-eastern border of the country. Uzbekistan has a short border with Afghanistan in the south, near the town of Termez, and Turkmenistan lies to the south-west. The north-western end of the country consists of the nominally Sovereign Republic of Qoraqalpog'iston (Karakalpakstan), to the west of which is Kazakhstan, which also lies to the north, beyond the Aral Sea, and forms the entire north-eastern border of Uzbekistan. The country covers an area of 447,400 sq km (172,740 sq miles), of which 165,600 sq km constitutes Qoraqalpog'iston.

Much of the land is desert, including the south-western part of the Kyzyl-Kum or Red Sands desert, but the western reaches of the Tien Shan range extend into the south-east of the country. The two main rivers are the Amu Dar'ya (anciently the Oxus) and the Syr Dar'ya (Jaxartes), both of which rise in the mountainous regions of the Tien Shan and flow north-westwards, to drain into the Aral Sea. However, severe overuse of these water resources for irrigation (notably the Kara-Kum Canal in Turkmenistan) from the 1950s, caused a dramatic depletion of the waters reaching the Aral Sea. The consequent decline in its water level and the increase in the area of toxic desert (owing to the use of chemical fertilizers) had severe environmental implications for the whole region. The Amu Dar'ya is the worst affected of the two rivers and usually dries up far short of the Aral Sea, in the region of Nukus. It is the more southerly river and flows through Turkmenistan, parallel to the Uzbek border, before forming that border, until it reaches the oasis towns of Xorazm, where it enters Uzbekistani territory and heads towards the Aral Sea. The Syr Dar'ya waters the prosperous Farg'ona valley region, crosses the Khujand region of Tajikistan, and then cuts north across Uzbekistan before entering Kazakhstan.

CLIMATE

The climate is marked by extreme temperatures and low levels of precipitation. Summers are long and hot with average temperatures in July of 32°C (90°F); daytime temperatures often exceed 40°C (104°F). During the short winter there are frequent severe frosts, and temperatures can fall as low as −38°C (−36°F).

POPULATION

Uzbeks form the largest ethnic group in the country (80.0% of the total population in 1996, according to estimates from the Uzbekistani Ministry of Health; the remainder includes Russians (accounting for an estimated 5.5%), Tajiks (5.0%),

Kazakhs (3.0%) and Tatars (1.5%). Other ethnic groups include Kara-Kalpaks (representing 2.5% of the population in 1996), most of whom are resident in Qoraqalpog'iston, Koreans, Kyrgyz, Ukrainians, Turkmen and Turks. The population of Qoraqalpog'iston was an estimated 6.0% of the total population of Uzbekistan in 1996, although its area is 37% of the total of the country.

Islam is the predominant religion. Most Uzbeks are Sunni Muslims (Hanafi school), but there are small communities of Salafis or Wahhabis, whose influence was reported to be growing. There were Orthodox Christians among the Slavic communities. The Roman Catholic Church is also represented. The official language is Uzbek, a member of the Eastern Turkic language group. From the 1940s it was written in Cyrillic (replacing a Latin alphabet introduced in the late 1920s), but in 1993 it was decreed that the country would proceed with the transition to the official use of a Latin script. The language is closely related to modern Uigur. Minority communities continued to use their own languages, and Russian was still widely used in business and official circles, although in 1989 only 49% of Uzbeks claimed fluency in Russian.

According to UN estimates, the total population at mid-2008 was 27,769,000, and the population density was 62.1 persons per sq km. In 2003 it was estimated that 36.6% of the population lived in urban areas. The capital is Toshkent (Tashkent), with an estimated population of 2,184,000 (including suburbs) in 2007. Other important urban centres were the historic towns of Samarqand (with a population of 361,339 in 2001), Buxoro (Bukhara) (237,361), Qarshi (204,690) and Qoqand (197,450), the industrial Farg'ona valley towns of Namangan (391,297), Andijon (338,366) and Farg'ona itself (183,037), and Nukus (212,012), the capital of Qoraqalpog'iston.

Chronology

7th century: Arabs conquered and brought Islam to the ancient provinces of Sogdiana and Bactria, notably the 'Silk Road' trading cities of Samarqand (Marakanda) and Buxoro (Bukhara, Bactra or Bacharia, previously the Kushan capital).

13th century: Nomadic Mongols settled among the predominantly Turkic population of Central Asia.

1313–41: Reign of Uzbeg, a khan of the Golden Horde, after whom the Uzbeks were named.

1370–1405: Reign of Timur (Tamerlane), originally from Transoxania (in modern Uzbekistan); he established a second Mongol Empire, which disintegrated rapidly after his death.

16th century: Competing Uzbek khanates had established their dominance in the territory of modern Uzbekistan, especially those of Buxoro (Bukhara), Xiva (Khiva), Qo'qon (Qoqand) and Samarqand.

1866: The Khanate of Qoqand was conquered by Russia, which was expanding southwards. In the following year much of the area that is now Qoraqalpog'iston (Karakalpakstan) was annexed by Russia from the Khanate of Xiva.

1868: With the fall of Samarqand to the Russians, the Emirate of Buxoro surrendered and became a protectorate of the Russian Empire, following over a century of struggle by the Uzbek khanates with Persia; Samarqand and Tashkent (Toshkent) were ceded to Russia.

1873: The Khanate of Xiva, which controlled much of what is western Uzbekistan, became a protectorate of the Russian Empire.

1876: The Khanate of Qokand was abolished and its territory absorbed into the Russian Empire.

November 1917: The Bolsheviks gained control of areas of Uzbekistan.

30 April 1918: The Turkestan Autonomous Soviet Socialist Republic (ASSR) was formed, covering an area that included Uzbekistan; Soviet forces withdrew temporarily when confronted by the nationalist *basmachi* movement, supported by British and 'White' (anti-Bolshevik) forces.

September 1919: Soviet forces re-established control over much of Uzbek territory.

February 1920: Xiva fell to the Red Army and the Xorazm (Khorezm) People's Socialist Republic was proclaimed.

September 1920: The Emir of Buxoro fled as the city and most of his territory was conquered by the Red Army, although *basmachi* resistance continued in the east for some years. A People's Soviet Republic of Buxoro, also nominally independent, was declared.

December 1922: Buxoro and Xorazm were founding states of the Union of Soviet Socialist Republics (USSR).

27 October 1924: The Uzbek Soviet Socialist Republic (SSR) was established. It formally became a constituent Union Republic of the USSR in May 1925.

1929: The Tajik ASSR, formerly part of the Uzbek SSR, became a full Union Republic of the USSR; the Khujand (Xujand—Leninabad) area of the Uzbek SSR was also incorporated within the Tajik SSR.

1936: Qoraqalpog'iston (which included much of the territory of Xiva, to the north and east of the city), to the south-east of the Aral Sea, passed from the Russian Federation to the Uzbek SSR. Before 1930 Qoraqalpog'iston had formed part of the Kazakh ASSR (initially named the Kyrgyz ASSR) within the Russian Federation.

1940: The Uzbek Latin script imposed in the late 1920s (replacing an Arabic script) was changed to a Cyrillic script.

1943: The Muslim Board of Central Asia was founded in Tashkent as part of a new governmental religious policy; in the same decade two religious colleges and a small number of mosques were allowed to open in Uzbekistan.

1954–60: The 'Virgin Lands' scheme brought more land into agricultural use, particularly for cotton, but the accompanying irrigation works eventually caused the environmental catastrophe of the Aral Sea and its environs.

1983: A major fraud was revealed in the cotton industry, involving some 3,000m. roubles—it eventually led to the removal from office of the Communist Party of Uzbekistan (CPU) leader, Inamzhon Usmankhojayev (in January 1988), the Chairman of the Uzbek Supreme Soviet (Supreme Council), Akil Salimov, and the CPU leaders in Buxoro and Samarqand.

November 1988: A group of Uzbek intellectuals founded Unity (Birlik), the first significant opposition movement. In March 1989 Unity failed in its attempt to put forward a candidate in elections to the Congress of People's Deputies of the USSR, having previously been refused official registration.

June 1989: More than 100 people died in riots resulting from conflict between ethnic Uzbeks and members of the minority Meskhetian Turk community (who had been exiled there from the Caucasus during the Second World War) in the Farg'ona (Fergana) valley.

October 1989: Legislation was adopted, which made Uzbek (rather than Russian) the official state language.

February 1990: There were further outbreaks of inter-ethnic conflict in Uzbekistan, culminating in three deaths during confrontations between the police and demonstrators in Parkent, near Tashkent.

18 February 1990: Members of Unity were prevented from standing as candidates in elections to the Uzbek Supreme Soviet; in many constituencies CPU candidates were elected unopposed.

24 March 1990: Islam Karimov, First Secretary of the CPU since 1989, was elected to the new position of executive President of the Republic at the first session of the Supreme Soviet; Shakurulla Mirsaidov was elected Chairman of the Council of Ministers (Prime Minister).

4 June 1990: Eleven people were killed and 21 injured in clashes in the Farg'ona valley; numerous deaths followed.

20 June 1990: The Uzbek Supreme Soviet adopted a declaration on the republic's sovereignty within a renewed Soviet federation.

November 1990: The Council of Ministers was abolished and replaced by the Cabinet of Ministers under the leadership of the President of the Republic; the position of Prime Minister ceased to exist, and Mirsaidov was appointed to the new position of Vice-President.

April 1991: Uzbekistan and eight other Union Republics agreed to sign a new Union Treaty.

19–21 August 1991: President Karimov did not condemn the attempted conservative coup in Moscow until it became apparent that it had failed.

31 August 1991: The Supreme Soviet voted to declare the Uzbek SSR independent, and on the following day its name was changed to the Republic of Uzbekistan.

November 1991: Having previously voted to sever links with the Communist Party of the Soviet Union, the CPU reorganized itself as the People's Democratic Party of Uzbekistan (PDPU), under the continued leadership of Karimov.

21 December 1991: Although it had remained a supporter of a new federation, Uzbekistan agreed to join 10 other former Soviet republics in the capital of Kazakhstan to sign the Almaty Declaration, which established the Commonwealth of Independent States (CIS) and signalled the final dissolution of the USSR.

29 December 1991: Karimov was re-elected as President, receiving an estimated 86% of the votes cast in direct popular elections; on the same day 98.2% of voters supported independence in a referendum.

8 January 1992: The post of Vice-President was abolished and that of Prime Minister was restored; Abdulkhashim Mutalov was appointed to the latter position.

15 May 1992: Uzbekistan signed the Collective Security Treaty with five other CIS countries, in Tashkent.

8 December 1992: The Supreme Council adopted a new Constitution, which declared Uzbekistan to be a secular, democratic republic and made provision for an Oly Majlis (Supreme Assembly) to replace the Supreme Council as the highest legislative body, following elections scheduled for 1994. On the following day Unity, was banned for its allegedly subversive activities.

January 1993: Uzbekistan, the main regional supporter of the new regime in Tajikistan, signed a security agreement with that country, Russia, Kazakhstan and Kyrgyzstan to provide troops for the defence of Tajikistan's southern borders. Uzbekistani forces were also reported to have acted directly against Tajikistani rebels.

June 1993: Mirsaidov was found guilty of the misuse of state funds, but was pardoned by President Karimov.

6 August 1993: Uzbekistan agreed to contribute troops to the CIS peace-keeping force to be sent to Tajikistan.

September 1993: It was decreed that the Latin script should be used for the Uzbek language, rather than the Cyrillic script; however, the new alphabet was different from the common script agreed upon earlier in the year by representatives from the other Central Asian states.

1 October 1993: The Government used technical pretexts to prevent both Unity and Freedom (Erk), the opposition party established in 1990, from registering; consequently, both organizations were permanently banned.

15 November 1993: Uzbekistan introduced a new currency, the sum coupon, announcing that roubles would no longer be legal tender after December.

December 1993: A compulsory re-registration of the mass media excluded all independent publications.

25 December 1994: Despite indications from the President in May that the parliamentary elections could be freely contested by opposition parties, the PDPU and its ally, Progress of the Fatherland (PF), were the only parties to participate (a second round of voting took place in January 1995); of the 83 contested seats, the PDPU obtained 69 and the PF 14. The remaining deputies were nominated by local councils, but most were PDPU members, giving the party overall representation in the Oly Majlis of 193 seats.

February 1995: Following Karimov's declaration in the previous month that the Government would welcome more parliamentary blocs, the Justice (Adolat) Social Democratic Party of Uzbekistan (JSDPU) was registered; it was believed to command the support of 47 deputies. A further two pro-Government parties were permitted registration in June.

26 March 1995: A referendum approved the extension of President Karimov's term of office until 2000.

21 December 1995: Abdulkhashim Mutalov was dismissed as Prime Minister, being replaced by Otkir Sultanov, previously the Minister of Foreign Economic Relations.

21 June 1996: President Karimov officially resigned as Chairman of the PDPU.

December 1996: The Oly Majlis passed a law prohibiting the organization of political parties on a religious or ethnic basis.

November 1997: Radical Islamists, described by the State authorities as members of the Wahhabi sect, were accused of assassinating the deputy head of the local administration of Namangan region; hundreds of suspected Muslim activists were later arrested.

1 May 1998: A law limiting the activities of religious organizations was adopted.

5 June 1998: Following the imprisonment of four suspected Islamist militants in May, seven activists were imprisoned for attempting to destabilize the country and establish an Islamic state. More arrests of militants followed in July, and one member of an Islamist organization was sentenced to death after being found guilty of murder and involvement in the training of Islamist fighters in Afghanistan.

9 January 1999: Five Islamist activists were found guilty of attempting to depose the Government.

16 February 1999: A series of bomb attacks, attributed to militant Islamists, took place in Tashkent, reportedly killing 15 people and injuring many more. A number of people found guilty of involvement in the attacks received lengthy gaol sentences, and at the end of June six people were sentenced to death.

24 April 1999: A bilateral agreement was signed with Russia on security, following Uzbekistan's departure from the CIS Collective Security Treaty in the previous month. On the same date Uzbekistan acceded to membership of the GUAM (Georgia-Uzbekistan-Azerbaijan-Moldova) organization, which was thereby renamed GUUAM.

12 May 1999: The Government introduced legislation imposing harsher punishments on those affiliated to 'religious, extremist, separatist and fundamentalist organizations'.

19 December 1999: In a second round of voting to the Oly Majlis, the PDPU secured the largest representation of any single party in the legislature, with 48 seats. The pro-Karimov Self-Sacrificers' (Fidokorlar) National Democratic Party (FNDP), established in December 1998, came second, obtaining 34 seats.

9 January 2000: In a presidential election in which an estimated 95% of the registered electorate participated, Karimov was reported to have obtained 91.9% of the votes cast. He was inaugurated for a second, five-year term on 22 January.

14 September 2000: The remaining members of a group of Islamist rebels that had made a number of incursions into Uzbekistan from Tajikistan in August were reported to have been killed by government troops.

17 November 2000: Two leaders of the opposition Islamic Movement of Uzbekistan (IMU) were convicted of acts of terrorism and sentenced to death *in absentia* by the Supreme Court.

26 June 2001: Ten Islamist militants were reported to have received prison sentences for attempting to overthrow the Government.

19 September 2001: President Karimov confirmed his support for US-led air-strikes against Afghanistan, if it were proven that the suicide attacks of 11 September, on the US cities of New York and Washington, DC, were prepared in that state.

7 October 2001: Uzbekistan and the USA signed a co-operation agreement, whereby Uzbekistan agreed to make its airbases available for use in humanitarian and 'search-and-rescue' operations during the US-led aerial bombardment of Afghanistan. The two countries also pledged to improve bilateral relations in order to combat militant Islamist terrorism and ensure long-term regional stability.

27 January 2002: At a referendum, a reported 91.8% of participants voted in favour of a constitutional amendment, proposed by President Karimov, which would extend the presidential term of office from five to seven years. In a simultaneous vote, some 93.7% of votes endorsed a proposal to create a second parliamentary chamber representing Uzbekistan's regions.

30 January 2002: Four police officers were found guilty of the torture of suspected Islamist activists, and sentenced to 20 years' imprisonment.

4 March 2002: The Independent Human Rights Organization of Uzbekistan was registered by the Ministry of Justice.

4 April 2002: The Oly Majlis approved a resolution delaying the next presidential election by two years, until 2007.

9 September 2002: At a meeting in the Kazakh capital, Astana, the Presidents of Uzbekistan and Kazakhstan signed a treaty fully demarcating their joint border. An agreement was signed with Tajikistan in the following month, on the demarcation of more than 85% of the Uzbek–Tajik border.

12 December 2002: The Oly Majlis adopted legislation on the election of the new, bicameral legislature following the end of the existing legislative session in December 2004.

20 December 2002: Turkmenistan declared the Uzbek ambassador *persona non grata*, following accusations of Uzbekistan's complicity in an alleged attempt to assassinate the President of Turkmenistan, Saparmyrat Niyazov. Diplomatic relations were restored in January 2005.

24 April 2003: The Oly Majlis approved a number of constitutional amendments permitting the redistribution of authority within the Government, to come into effect from the next legislative elections. The prime minister, rather than the president, was to be head of government, and the composition of the government was to be approved by the legislature rather than the Office of the President.

1 September 2003: Uzbekistan became a member of the Islamic Development Bank.

15 October 2003: The sum was made fully convertible.

11 December 2003: The Oly Majlis confirmed the appointment by Karimov of Shavkat Mirziyoyev, who had substantial experience in the agricultural sector, as Prime Minister. The hitherto Prime Minister, Otkir Sultanov, became a Deputy Prime Minister, with responsibility for energy, petroleum and the chemicals sector.

28–30 March 2004: At least 19 people were killed in a series of bomb blasts, principally aimed against police targets, and including what was reportedly the first instance of a suicide bombing in the country, in Tashkent and Buxoro. A further 23 people (three rebels and 20 police officers) died in a gun battle that followed the attacks. In August 15 Islamist militants were found guilty of involvement in the attacks and sentenced to prison terms ranging from six to 18 years. A further 43 defendants were convicted in connection with the bombings in October 2004 and July 2005.

30 July 2004: At least three people were killed, and several others injured, following three suicide bomb attacks in Tashkent, outside the US and Israeli embassies, and outside the office of the Prosecutor-General.

26 December 2004 and 9 January 2005: Elections were held to the 120-seat Qoqunchilik palatasi Kengashi (Legislative Chamber), the lower chamber of the new, bicameral Oly Majlis. The largest representation (41 seats) was secured by the pro-Karimov Movement of Entrepreneurs and Businessmen—Liberal Democratic Party of Uzbekistan; four other pro-Government parties were also represented in the chamber. Obser-

vers from the Organization for Security and Co-operation in Europe (OSCE) criticized the Government's failure to register opposition groups and independent candidates.

27 January 2005: The inaugural session of the new, 100-member upper chamber of the legislature, the Senat (Senate), took place. The 16 presidential appointees had been announced on 14 January, and indirect elections of senators had taken place on 17–20 January.

5 May 2005: Uzbekistan announced its decision to withdraw from the GUUAM grouping, which thereby reverted to its original designation of GUAM.

12–14 May 2005: Government troops opened fire in the country's fourth largest city, Andijon, after demonstrators released prisoners from gaol and occupied administrative buildings. According to government sources, the troops killed some 187 people, including around 94 armed Islamist militants; however, according to some independent reports, as many as 1,000 people were killed. The violence prompted condemnation from the UN and the USA, and others members of the international community. The Government subsequently refused to allow an international investigation into the events.

26 August 2005: The Senat unanimously approved legislation demanding that the USA remove its troops from the Qarshi-Khanabad ('K-2') airbase within a six-month period.

20 September 2005: The trial of 15 alleged Islamist extremists (including three Kyrgyzstani citizens) accused of organizing the unrest in Andijon in May commenced in Tashkent. All of the accused men pleaded guilty to charges including murder and terrorism, amid concern from the international community and human rights organizations about the use of torture. They were found guilty in mid-November and sentenced to prison terms of between 14 and 20 years. By late December more than 150 people had been sentenced to terms of imprisonment for their involvement in the uprising.

3 October 2005: The European Union (EU) decided to impose sanctions on Uzbekistan (including a ban on travel to EU states by officials suspected of involvement in the shooting of civilians in Andijon, and an embargo on the export of weapons and other equipment that could be used for internal repression), owing to the Government's refusal to permit an international investigation into events at Andijon.

14 November 2005: Karimov and Russia's President, Vladimir Putin, signed a Treaty of Allied Relations. The two countries agreed, *inter alia*, to provide mutual support in the event that one of them came under attack. Legislation on the ratification of the treaty was enacted by Karimov in March 2006.

21 November 2005: The USA completed its departure from the Qarshi-Khanabad airbase.

25 January 2006: Uzbekistan became a member of the Eurasian Economic Community, which had been founded in 2000 by Belarus, Kazakhstan, Kyrgyzstan, Tajikistan and Russia.

9 March 2006: Legislation providing for Uzbekistan's withdrawal from the GUUAM grouping was enacted by President Karimov.

16 August 2006: Karimov signed a protocol on Uzbekistan's membership of the Collective Security Treaty Organization (CSTO—the successor to the CIS Collective Security Treaty, from which Uzbekistan had withdrawn in March 1999). Full accession to the CSTO was expected to be achieved by 2008.

13 November 2006: The EU voted to extend the embargo on the export of armaments to Uzbekistan, imposed in October 2005, for a further 12 months and travel restrictions on 12 senior officials for another six months. (The travel sanctions were again extended, in May 2007.)

18 September 2007: The Central Elections Commission announced that a presidential election was to take place on 23 December, following the expiry of Karimov's seven-year term in the previous January (in accordance with a constitutional stipulation that the election be held in December of the year in which the presidential term of office ended). The election campaign subsequently began on 21 September.

15 October 2007: EU foreign ministers, while extending the embargo on the export of armaments to Uzbekistan for a further year, adopted a decision to suspend for a period of six months the travel restrictions on senior officials, including the incumbent Minister of Defence, with the stated aim of encouraging the authorities to improve the human rights situation in the country; the suspension of the restrictions was subsequently further extended, despite continuing concerns about human rights violations in Uzbekistan.

23 December 2007: Karimov was re-elected, receiving some 88.1% of votes cast at the presidential election (the other three candidates that contested the election were all considered to be loyal to Karimov); the rate of voter participation was officially recorded at 90.6%. An observer mission from the Office for

Democratic Institutions and Human Rights of the OSCE stated that the poll had failed to meet democratic standards, while Karimov's election to a third consecutive term of office appeared to be in breach of the Uzbekistani Constitution. New appointments were made later in the month to the posts of Minister of Justice and Minister of Higher and Secondary Specialized Education, and the Minister of Finance, Rustam Azimov, was additionally appointed to the role of First Deputy Prime Minister, responsible for the Economic Sector and Foreign Economic Relations.

1 January 2008: A presidential decree, approved in 2005, entered into effect, prohibiting capital punishment.

23 January 2008: Dilorom Tashmuhamedova, who had contested the presidential election in the previous month as the candidate of the JSDPU, was elected as the Speaker of the lower legislative chamber, replacing Erkin Halilov, who had been removed for abuse of office.

17 September 2008: President Karimov dismissed Ruslan Mirzayev as Minister of Defence, he was succeeded, on the same day, by Qobul Berdiyev.

History

Dr NEIL MELVIN

Revised for this edition by Dr MATTEO FUMAGALLI

EARLY HISTORY

In the 20th century Uzbekistan emerged as home to the most powerful and populous political community in Central Asia. Historically, however, the territory of what is now the Republic of Uzbekistan has been the centre for a wide variety of civilizations, cultures and peoples. The earliest recorded inhabitants of the region were Persian-speakers, who settled in the valleys of the Syr Dar'ya (Jaxartes) and Amu Dar'ya (Oxus) rivers. Scythians, as well as Persian-speakers and smaller groups of nomads, largely populated the plains to the north of the Syr Dar'ya. In the fourth century BC Alexander II ('the Great') of Macedon passed through Central Asia on the way to conquer India.

In the seventh century AD Arabs gained control over important parts of the region, bringing with them Islam and the Arabic script, and adding new cultural patterns to the existing Persian and Turkic ones. In 1219 the Mongols invaded and took control of Central Asia. Later, as Mongol rule weakened, particularly after the reign of Timur or Tamerlane ('the Great'), who established Samarqand as the capital of a revived empire, the name Uzbek first emerged as an important political label. Early in the 16th century Transoxania (the area between the two great rivers of the Oxus and Jaxartes) came under the control of Uzbek tribes moving from the steppe regions of the north and led by Muhammad Shaybani Khan. The Sheibanid invasion accelerated the disintegration and fragmentation of the political arrangements of the Mongol era. The term Uzbek was, thereafter, associated with a number of dynasties claiming descent from Shaybani.

As the Uzbek tribes took control of Transoxania, their nomadic lifestyle gradually gave way to a sedentary existence. Many settled in the cities and towns of the region and began to mix with the local inhabitants, including other Turkic peoples and Persian-speakers (Tajiks). While retaining their tribal identification, the Uzbeks simultaneously associated themselves with other sedentary peoples under the general label of Sart. Elite level bilingualism became an important part of the region's identity, with the political life of the court conducted mainly in a Turkic language (Chagatai), while high culture was largely the province of a form of Persian (Farsi).

From the 17th century the previously united Uzbek kingdom began to fragment and was replaced by smaller, highly autonomous kingdoms or khanates. Initially, the two most powerful khanates were Buxoro (Bukhara) and Xiva (Khiva). From the 18th century, however, the Khanate of Qo'qon (Kokand), centred on the Farg'ona (Fergana) valley, began to rival the other two. The near constant state of conflict between the khanates assisted the Russian conquest of the region.

All three of the khanates fell to the Russian Empire in the latter half of the 19th century. In 1867 the Russian governorate-general of Turkestan was established, and as a result of Russian military advances it was steadily expanded to embrace all the former kingdoms. Russian conquest of the region brought important economic and cultural changes. Toshkent (Tashkent), previously a minor town, but which fell to Russia as early as 1865, became the capital of Russian Turkestan and the home of a sizeable ethnic Russian population. Russian language, technology and administration spread rapidly throughout the region. Significant changes in agriculture were also introduced, notably improved irrigation for cotton production. Russian conquest did little, however, to alter fundamentally the way of life for the peoples of the area.

SOVIET UZBEKISTAN

For much of the Russian Revolution and the civil war that followed, Turkestan was isolated from events in the rest of the former Russian Empire. The Bolsheviks first seized Tashkent in November 1917. The region, however, was subject to control by competing forces during the civil war period—the British, the 'Whites' (anti-Bolsheviks) and the nationalist *basmachi* guerrilla movement—and it was not until September 1919 that Soviet control was re-established. In 1920 Buxoro and Xiva became the capitals of nominally independent Soviet republics, the Buxoro and the Xorazm (Khorezm) People's Socialist Republics, which became founder members of the Union of Soviet Socialist Republics (USSR) at the end of 1922. Meanwhile, the *basmachi* movement continued to control some peripheral areas of Turkestan until 1922.

On 27 October 1924 the Uzbek Soviet Socialist Republic (SSR) was created, with the merger of most of the territories of the three former khanates of the region. A separate Turkmen

SSR was created at the same time. The Tajik Autonomous Soviet Socialist Republic (ASSR) formed part of the Uzbek SSR until 1929, when it was granted the status of a full Union Republic (and the region of Khujand—Xujand, later renamed Leninabad—was detached from the Uzbek SSR and awarded to the new Tajik SSR). Qoraqalpog'iston, or the Kara-Kalpak ASSR (hitherto part of the Russian Federation, as it was a region annexed by the tsars from Xiva in advance of the rest of the Khanate), was united with the Uzbek SSR in 1936.

The territorial delimitation of Central Asia in the 1920s and 1930s was conducted on broadly ethno-linguistic lines. Soviet policy-makers intended the Uzbek SSR to become the ethnic homeland for Uzbeks. In the census conducted in the region following the creation of the SSR, many small Turkic groups were categorized together with the Uzbeks, although larger minorities, such as Kazakhs, Kyrgyz and Tajiks, continued to enjoy a separate ethnic identity. The formation of the Uzbek SSR was accompanied by the creation of national symbols, most significantly a new popular literary language. Soviet policies in the area also aimed to increase the literacy rate (between 1926 and 1932 literacy rose from 3.8% to 52.5% of the population) and to improve the status of women. At the same time, Soviet anti-religious campaigns resulted in the closure of Muslim institutions (courts, schools and mosques) and the imprisonment or execution of many of the clergy. Numerous Muslim traditions and rites continued to be observed, especially in rural areas, and the anti-religious campaigns were partially mitigated by the establishment of an Islamic spiritual directorate (Tashkent was the seat of the Muslim Board of Central Asia) during the Second World War.

State-led industrialization formed a key element of the Soviet model of development in Uzbekistan. In the initial decades of Soviet rule, there was a steady growth of industrial infrastructure and an expansion of major urban centres, driven primarily by Slavic immigration. Economic growth continued, although at lower levels, after the Second World War, with the help of industry transferred from areas in the USSR threatened by Nazi German invasion. Most Uzbeks, however, continued to live a traditional rural way of life largely untouched by Soviet policies of modernization, except for the dramatic expansion of cotton production initiated by Stalin (Iosif Dzhugashvili).

In 1959 Sharaf Rashidov became First Secretary of the Communist Party of Uzbekistan (CPU) and stayed in office until shortly before his death in October 1983. In the 1960s and 1970s there was a strong emphasis on stability, and Rashidov and the Uzbek provincial party chiefs gained extensive powers. The end of the Rashidov era and the accession (in November 1982) of Yurii Andropov as General Secretary of the Soviet Communist Party marked the onset of important changes in Uzbekistan's political order.

THE NATIONALIST MOVEMENT

Under Andropov (who himself died in 1984), a far-reaching purge of the Uzbekistani political establishment began (1983–89), initiated by revelations of serious fraud in the cotton industry. Aimed at breaking the local networks of power, which had built up in the course of the previous 25 years, the central authorities' drive to 'de-Rashidovize' the republic also served to bring a new generation of Uzbekistani leaders to the fore. In June 1989 the bloody ethnic riots in the Farg'ona valley (principally aimed against Meskhetians, who had been exiled to the region from the Caucasus during the Second World War) altered the all-Union Government's policy towards the Uzbek SSR. The centrally directed purge of cadres was moderated, and Islam Karimov was appointed leader, replacing Rafik Nishanov.

Karimov began to rehabilitate the disgraced Rashidov and to consolidate his own position. In March 1990 the new republican Supreme Soviet (Supreme Council) elected Karimov President of the Uzbek SSR. A leading member of the Uzbek political élite, Shakurulla Mirsaidov, became Chairman of the Council of Ministers. In November 1990 Mirsaidov was appointed to the newly established post of Vice-President, as President Karimov assumed the chairmanship of the redesignated Cabinet of Ministers.

During the perestroika (restructuring) period, mainly associated with Mikhail Gorbachev (Soviet leader in 1985–91), a number of new political groups appeared in Uzbekistan. The desiccation of the Aral Sea and the general deterioration of the environment caused by over-irrigation of land for cotton production served to mobilize ecological groups. As nationalist movements developed in the USSR as a whole, the status of the Uzbek language became an important issue for Uzbekistan's first non-communist political movement, Unity (Birlik). Formed in 1988, Unity campaigned for a range of political and nationalist goals, but its candidates were denied registration in the February 1990 elections to the Uzbekistani Supreme Soviet. Later in 1990 the first formal opposition party, Freedom (Erk), was created. Despite the continued institutional pre-eminence of the CPU, there were a number of opportunities for potential discontent, if not opposition. Ethnic tension continued to rise in parts of Central Asia, and in June clashes between Uzbeks and Kyrgyz in the Osh region of the Kyrgyz SSR threatened the stability of the whole Farg'ona valley. A state of emergency was declared on the Uzbekistani side of the border, in Andijon Viloyat (region).

Although Uzbekistan was preparing to sign a new Union Treaty in mid-1991, a coup attempt on 19 August by conservative communists in Moscow, the Soviet and Russian capital, undermined the agreement. Karimov adopted a neutral position during the attempted coup, but, after it collapsed, on 31 August an extraordinary session of the Supreme Soviet declared the Uzbek SSR independent and renamed it the Republic of Uzbekistan.

INDEPENDENT UZBEKISTAN

In November 1991 the CPU was renamed the People's Democratic Party of Uzbekistan (PDPU). In December, following the demise of the USSR, Karimov was re-elected President, but this time by direct popular vote; he was reported to have received some 86% of the votes cast. The only other candidate, the leader of Freedom, Muhammad Salih (Solikh), received 12% of the votes. On the same day 98.2% of voters ratified independence in a referendum.

Achieving a popular mandate was merely part of a process of political consolidation for the new President. In January 1992 the post of Vice-President was abolished, and Karimov's main potential rival, Mirsaidov, was thereby removed from office (he was initially retained in the post of State Secretary, but soon resigned). Abdulkhasim Mutalov was appointed to the restored premiership. At the same time, in a move to assert central control over the regions, the appointed position of hokim, or regional governor, was established to head the local administrations. The Government also sought to promote the mahallah, or neighbourhood, as the basic element of local government.

The increasingly authoritarian tendency of Uzbekistan's leadership was officially justified by the activity of the opposition movement. A series of student demonstrations in 1992 and the civil war in neighbouring Tajikistan provided the pretext for the repression of all opposition organizations. Distrust of opposition and of independent religious groups combined in the banning of Islamist parties (see below). The growing political authoritarianism also served to stifle initial attempts at economic reform. The increasing power of the presidency was paralleled by greater repression of opposition groups. Leading dissidents were arrested, and on 9 December Unity was banned, the day after a new Constitution formalized the extensive powers of the President. Throughout 1992–93 a number of opposition leaders disappeared or were assaulted. Many fled into exile. In October 1993 Freedom was denied registration as a political party (by the end of the year both it and Unity were banned organizations), and in December all but the official media were denied registration.

In 1994–95 President Karimov continued to strengthen his position. In mid-1994 Mavlon Umurzakov, one of the President's state counsellors, was removed from office. In July a presidential decree dismissed the Mayor of Tashkent, Adkham Fazylbekov, who had been a close associate of Mirsaidov. The previous month, in Almaty, Kazakhstan, two dissidents, Murod Zhorayev and Erkin Ashurov, were seized and forcibly taken to Uzbekistan to stand trial along with five others. All seven were sentenced to prison by the Supreme Court in March 1995.

On 22 September 1994 the Supreme Council met for the final time. The old parliament was replaced by a smaller, unicameral legislative body, the Oly Majlis (Supreme Assembly), elections to which were conducted on 25 December. Of the 250 seats in parliament, 144 went to candidates nominated by regional councils (84 of these were hokims). Overall, the PDPU took 193 seats, and the remaining 57 deputies elected were considered to be government supporters, whether nominally independent or members of the only other party permitted registration, Watan Taraqqioti (Progress of the Fatherland). At its first session in February 1995 the new parliament unanimously voted to hold a national referendum to approve an extension of the President's term of office. On 26 March 99.6% of the eligible electorate were reported to have voted to extend President Karimov's term of office by three years, to 2000.

In the wake of the parliamentary elections, in February 1995 a new party, the Justice (Adolat) Social Democratic Party of Uzbekistan (JSDPU), was created and 47 deputies of the PDPU were drafted to provide it with a parliamentary membership. In June two more 'official' parties (organizations known for their pro-Government, non-combative character) were established: the National Revival (Milly Tiklanish) Democratic Party and the People's Unity (Xalq Birligi) Movement. The titles of two of those parties gave rise to accusations that the names of the unregistered opposition, the banned Islamist group—Justice—and Unity were deliberately being exploited. Direct pressure on the opposition continued and in August Rashid Bekjan, the brother of Salih, leader of Freedom, was sentenced to five years' imprisonment for involvement in the party's youth wing. In October the creation of the Opposition Co-ordinating Centre in Tashkent, led by Mirsaidov, was announced, which brought together the remnants of Freedom, Unity, Justice and Mirsaidov's own party; however, the Centre closed in March 1998. Many Uzbek dissidents continued to be active abroad, notably in Russia, Sweden, Turkey and the USA.

On 21 December 1995 the Oly Majlis dismissed Prime Minister Mutalov, a decision ostensibly prompted by economic difficulties, notably the decline in value of the national currency, the sum. In February 1996 Mutalov and another deputy premier were removed from the Cabinet. With Mutalov's dismissal, President Karimov had replaced most of the core of politicians who had helped him to power, including Mirsaidov, the former Minister of Justice, a former minister and ambassador to the USA, Babur Malikov, and the former Minister of Foreign Affairs, Said-Mukhtar Saidkasimov.

Following the consolidation of his position, in 1996 Karimov briefly promoted a limited pluralism in the country, in part designed to halt the outflow of Slav and Uzbek professionals, but also to placate international criticism. Despite the change in the official tone, international human rights organizations continued to criticize the actions of the Uzbekistani authorities. At the end of the 1990s all forms of media remained under strict government control, and opposition groups were highly restricted and subject to violent repression.

Following independence, the Government sponsored a revival of Islam, and by 1995 there were more than 20,000 active mosques. In May President Karimov signed a decree establishing an international Islamic studies centre in Tashkent, at the behest of the state-controlled Muslim Board. Non-official and political Islam, however, endured continued repression from 1992. The Islamic Renaissance Party of Uzbekistan and the Justice movement were both banned in 1992 and remained prohibited. Muslim clergy who deviated from officially endorsed 'moderate' Islam were arrested or removed from their positions. In May 1998 the Oly Majlis approved legislation that imposed new restrictions on religious groups. The law required all mosques and religious groups with more than 100 members to be registered and restricted the construction of mosques, the establishment of religious associations and the teaching of theology.

As more conventional, or established, Islam was placed firmly under the Government's control, a variety of groups,

the actions of which were particularly undesirable for the Karimov regime, sought to operate independently of the state. From the mid-1990s the Uzbekistani authorities identified the so-called 'Wahhabi' movement (essentially, any conservative or independent Muslim group) as a major threat to stability in the country and in Central Asia as a whole. President Karimov argued that radical Islamism was poised to penetrate Central Asia and that Wahhabi proselytism from Saudi Arabia (the home of the original Wahhabi sect) was the central threat, together with the Taliban of Afghanistan and the United Opposition in Tajikistan.

Particularly close supervision was exercised in the Farg'ona valley, the traditional centre for Islam in Central Asia. Muslim leaders and activists from Namangan were imprisoned on various charges. Andijon's main Jami Mosque was closed in 1995 after its chief cleric, Abdu Alil Mirzayev—accused by the Government of being a follower of the austere Wahhabi Islamic sect and of having engaged in anti-constitutional activities— disappeared while en route to Moscow. In December 1997, in Namangan, a group of masked men killed a highly placed local official. The central authorities responded to the murder by dispatching élite troops to the area. Eventually, the Government accused a group of supposed Islamist militants from Tajikistan of being responsible for the murder. The actions of the Government proved to represent the first stage of a sustained campaign against a range of religious and opposition groups, particularly in the Farg'ona region.

In the late 1990s Karimov sought to entice some of the moderate Islamic leaders to return to Uzbekistan, but achieved only modest success. The most prominent returnee was Mohammad Sodiq, a former mufti, who had spent seven years in exile. Sodiq disapproved of the violent tactics of the Islamist movement and worked with the government-sponsored network of officially controlled mosques. In February 1999 the official image of Uzbekistan as a centre of regional stability was challenged by a series of bomb explosions in Tashkent, which killed 15 people and injured at least a further 100. The Government blamed radical Islamists and the opposition for the blasts and responded by arresting hundreds of suspects, continuing a series of arrests that had begun in 1998. A number of trials were organized, and six of those found guilty were sentenced to death in June.

Despite efforts to eradicate militant Islamism, a series of cross-border attacks was undertaken by the Islamist Movement of Uzbekistan (IMU) in 1999–2001. The IMU, founded in 1999, was banned by the Uzbekistani Government, and its spiritual leader, Tohir Yoldoshev, and his field commander, Jumaboy Khojiyev (Juma Namangoniy), were sentenced to death *in absentia* in November 2000. Between mid- and late 1999, Khojiyev organized a series of incursions from bases in Tajikistan. Although unsuccessful militarily, the infiltrations challenged the Government's assertions about the lack of support for such organizations in Uzbekistan. While the IMU was poorly organized, it successfully recruited new members from disaffected groups within Uzbekistan. In June 2001 the IMU reportedly changed its name to the 'Islamic Party of Turkestan', indicating an expansion of the group's political aspirations. In August it was reported that Khojiyev had been appointed Deputy Commander-in-Chief of the Taliban military forces in Afghanistan. The militant Islamist movement was further strengthened by the reported appointment of the Saudi-born leader of the al-Qa'ida (Base) organization, Osama bin Laden, to the post of Commander-in-Chief of the Taliban forces.

Meanwhile, in December 1999 parliamentary elections were held. Five parties, all of which supported the President, and a number of nominally independent candidates contested the elections to the Oly Majlis. As part of the preparations for the elections, Karimov sanctioned the creation of a new political party, the Self-Sacrificers' (Fidokorlar) National Democratic Party. The leading figures of the party were established members of the existing élite, and it secured 34 seats in the legislature, behind the PDPU, with 48 seats. In April 2000 it was announced that Fidokorlar and Watan Taraqqioti were to merge. The new party had a total of 54 deputies, representing the second largest parliamentary faction.

On 9 January 2000 Karimov was re-elected as President. A number of international organizations, including the Organization for Security and Co-operation in Europe (OSCE), refused to send observers to monitor the election and were critical of the entire electoral process. The only alternative candidate was Abdulhafiz Jalolov, a leading member of the PDPU, who had previously worked in the Ideology Department of the CPU. Karimov secured 92% of the votes cast by 95% of the electorate. Jalolov obtained just 4% of the votes cast, and even admitted to having voted for Karimov. Although the President's position appeared secure, Karimov continued to suppress potential challengers by frequently purging rivals and removing regional governors from their posts.

The domestic political situation in Uzbekistan underwent a shift following the large-scale suicide attacks against targets in the USA on 11 September 2001 (attributed to al-Qa'ida), and the subsequent US-led military campaign against the Taliban and radical Islamist groups in Afghanistan. In mid-October a large number of IMU members were reported to be fighting alongside Taliban forces there. However, in the course of the campaign, the IMU (which the US Government had already identified as a terrorist threat) was largely destroyed and its leader, Khojiyev, was reportedly killed during fighting in Afghanistan.

On 27 January 2002 President Karimov initiated a referendum to endorse his proposal to create a second parliamentary chamber, to represent Uzbekistan's regions, a proposal that reportedly received the support of 93.7% of voters. In addition, the referendum was used to extend the presidential term of office from five to seven years, apparently with the support of 91.8% of participants. However, the legitimacy of the referendum was questioned by both the USA and human rights groups. In early April the Oly Majlis approved a resolution delaying the next presidential elections by two years, until 2007. The Oly Majlis also endorsed a resolution on the election of the new, bicameral legislature in December 2004.

Under pressure from the USA, the Uzbekistani authorities undertook a number of measures to liberalize the political system. At the end of January 2002 four police officers were found guilty of torturing suspected Islamist activists while held in custody, and given 20-year prison terms. In early March the Ministry of Justice finally registered the Independent Human Rights Organization of Uzbekistan, following a five-year struggle for official recognition. Although these changes were symbolically important, many thousands of opposition and Islamist figures remained in custody, and the Government continued its campaign of repression against Islamist organizations, such as the proscribed transnational Hizb-ut-Tahrir al-Islami (Hizb-ut-Tahrir, the Party of Islamic Liberation), which sought, apparently by non-violent means, to establish an international Islamic Caliphate. The secular opposition and media remained tightly monitored, and human rights violations by law enforcement bodies were widespread. Corruption and poor governance continued to characterize the political order, helping to promote further problems in the country, such as a largely anthropogenic drought in Qoraqalpog'iston in 2002.

The engagement of the USA in Uzbekistan, as a result of the US-led military action in Afghanistan that commenced in late 2001 (see Foreign Relations), was widely regarded as an opportunity for significant change. In Uzbekistan, the US presence was viewed as likely to increase the status of the country and to help to address its immediate security threats, particularly from radical Islamist groups based in Afghanistan. There was little sense that the US engagement would necessitate serious domestic reform; instead, the Uzbekistani authorities drew attention to a series of possible changes, including proposals to introduce a bicameral parliament in 2004 (see above) and to alter the Constitution to prevent the President being simultaneously the Head of Government (approved by the Oly Majlis in April 2003). Many observers, however, viewed these changes as cosmetic. Indeed, there was considerable evidence of increasing repression, particularly against Hizb-ut-Tahrir, which was identified by the Government as the main threat to the country following the apparent military defeat of the IMU. For the international community, the increased US presence in Uzbekistan was interpreted as an opportunity to advance reform in the country. After a request by the UN Secretary-General, accompanied by considerable international pressure, the UN Commissioner on Human Rights visited Uzbekistan in December 2002 to investigate allegations of torture; following his visit, the Commissioner concluded that torture in Uzbekistan was 'systemic'. In 2002–03 the USA and the European Union (EU) became more openly critical of the human rights situation in Uzbekistan. Heightened international scrutiny appeared to do little, however, to change the Government's repressive practices.

In May 2003 the European Bank for Reconstruction and Development (EBRD) held its annual meeting in Tashkent, at which the opposing views of Uzbekistan's prescribed future development came to the fore. The international community sought to use the meeting as a means to induce the authorities in Uzbekistan to launch a variety of political and economic reforms, but President Karimov sought, instead, to use the meeting to convey to his domestic audience international support for his chosen development path. Although the Government did appear to make a number of small concessions following the meeting, notably registering a non-governmental organization, the Good Deed (Ezgulik) Human Rights Society, and allowing the Unity movement to hold its first public congress since 1992, overall there was little evidence of progress. With growing signs of social unrest under Karimov's repressive political and economic policies, and a lack of willingness on the part of the Uzbekistani authorities to countenance the prospect of meaningful reform, Karimov appeared to be confronting a narrowing range of options, a situation that was compounded by the absence of any obvious successor.

In 2004 the Uzbekistani authorities continued to pursue highly restrictive economic and political policies. Increased controls were placed on borders by the authorities in an attempt to prevent cross-border trading and smuggling and, thereby, to retain control over economic activity in the country. Corruption continued to proliferate. The repression of Islam was further intensified, with women in Islamic forms of dress a particular target. At the same time, pressure on opposition organizations was increased. In order to enforce control and surveillance of the population, the institution of the mahallah (neighbourhood community) was reinforced and associated more closely with the security services. As a result of these policies, social unrest grew in the country. At the end of March a series of bombings and shootings across the country, principally against police targets, left up to 50 people dead and dozens more wounded. The bombings were followed by widespread arrests (a total of 85 by late July), and the trial of 15 suspects, whom the authorities alleged were militant Islamists who had received training in Pakistan, commenced in that month; in August all 15 were found guilty of involvement in the attacks and sentenced to prison terms ranging from six to 18 years. A further 43 defendants were convicted in connection with the bombings in October 2004 and July 2005. Fearing a repeat of Georgia's 'rose revolution' (the overthrow, in late 2003, of Georgia's leadership by a popular revolt), in April 2004 Uzbekistan refused to register the George Soros-funded Open Society Institute Assistance Foundation, leading to its expulsion from the country. (In Central Asia allegations circulated that the financier and philanthropist had provided support to the proponents of change of regime in Georgia.)

In July 2004 three suicide bombers targeted the Israeli and US embassies and the Office of the Prosecutor-General in Tashkent, leading to five deaths. The President attributed the attacks to Hizb-ut-Tahrir, which it alleged was working in collusion with other international militant Islamist organizations. Many regional and international observers suggested that the authorities' repressive measures were, in fact, fuelling a home-grown insurgency. Indications of continuing discontent within the country became evident in early November when irate market traders took to the streets in several cities to protest against new regulations.

Confronted with increasing domestic instability, President Karimov sought to demonstrate to outsiders that the country was pursuing an agenda of democratization. On 26 December 2004 and 9 January 2005 parliamentary elections were held in two rounds for the 120-seat lower chamber (Qoqunchilik palatasi Kengashi—Legislative Chamber) of the new, bicameral Oly Majlis, without opposition participation. (These were the first parliamentary elections to take place since approval of a two-chamber parliament in 2002.) The OSCE stated that the elections failed to meet its own and other international standards for democratic elections. The parties that secured the largest number of seats were the Movement of Entrepreneurs and Businessmen—Liberal Democratic Party of Uzbekistan (established in 2003 by allies of Karimov, later known simply as the Liberal Democratic Party of Uzbekistan—LDPU), with 41, and the PDPU, with 28 seats. The Self-Sacrificers' National Democratic Party secured 18 seats, the National Revival Democratic Party and the JSDPU won 11 and 10 seats, respectively. The remaining 12 seats were gained by independents. On 14 January President Karimov announced the appointment of 16 members of the new 100-member legislative upper chamber, the Senat (Senate); regional council members elected 84 senators on 17–20 January. The inaugural session of the Senat took place on 27 January.

Karimov also sought to consolidate his hold on power, through frequent government reshuffles and the further repression of his opponents. In late 2004 Ismail Jurabekov, who had held senior positions in the Uzbekistani Government for the previous two decades, and who was widely regarded as a leader of the powerful Samarqand clan and an influential figure in the Karimov regime, appeared to lose Karimov's favour, being dismissed from the position of presidential adviser. The authorities also launched a criminal investigation against him. In early 2005 the President implemented a government reorganization, notably dismissing Sodyq Safayev, the Minister of Foreign Affairs appointed in 2003, who was viewed as having strong ties with the USA. His successor, Elyor G'aniyev, who oversaw the swift reversal in foreign policy in 2004–05, was himself replaced, in July 2006, by Vladimir Norov, although G'aniyev remained in the Cabinet as Minister of Foreign Economic Relations, Investment and Trade. Meanwhile, Karimov also forced the Minister of Defence, Qodir G'ulomov, to leave his post in November 2005. The Minister of Internal Affairs, Zokirjon Almatov, the longest-serving minister in the administration and, like Jurabekov, a prominent member of the Samarqand clan, unexpectedly resigned in the following month, ostensibly for health reasons, but possibly due to his handling of the Andijon uprising (see below). He was replaced by Bahodir Matlyubov, hitherto Chairman of the State Customs Committee. In April 2006 Vyacheslav Golyshev, the Deputy Prime Minister, responsible for the Economic Sector and Foreign Economic Relations, and Minister of the Economy, was dismissed from the Cabinet and appointed as state adviser to the President on socio-economic policy; Rustam Qosimov, the Minister of Finance, succeeded Golyshev as Deputy Prime Minister, a position he had previously held for five years until July 2005, while Batir Xodjayev became Minister of the Economy.

In 2004–05 the Karimov administration became increasingly concerned about the series of popular uprisings, referred to as 'colour revolutions', in former Soviet Republics that had begun with Georgia in November 2003, followed by Ukraine (in November–December 2004) and Kyrgyzstan (in March–April 2005), all of which had led to the collapse of the incumbent regime. The President was determined that there should be no similar revolution in Uzbekistan, and the security services tightened their hold on the country. Despite these measures, however, Uzbekistan continued to experience unrest. At the beginning of April 2005 hundreds of farmers rioted in the Dustlik district of Jizzax Viloyat, following the disappearance of a local opposition political activist.

Speculation mounted that a political struggle was under way within the country to decide on President Karimov's successor. For many years, the struggle was focused on the two leading security officials: Rustam Inoyatov, the Chairman of Uzbekistan's National Security Service, and Zokirjon Almatov, Minister of Internal Affairs from independence until his resignation in December 2005 (see above), who controlled Uzbekistan's vast police force. Under Karimov, these agencies had emerged as the two most important institutions in the country. As Karimov's frequent reshuffles and purges continued, the circle of the ruling élite shrank further. Karimov's

eldest daughter, Gulnora Karimova, controlled major Uzbekistani businesses (notably in the petroleum, natural gas, telecommunications and entertainment sectors) and, perhaps more crucially, could rely on close ties with the Russian authorities owing to experience working in Uzbekistan's embassy in Moscow. (In early 2008 she was appointed as Uzbekistan's representative to the UN and international organizations in Geneva, Switzerland.)

In May 2005 Uzbekistan experienced its greatest domestic crisis since independence, when the city of Andijon in the Farg'ona Valley was seized by opposition forces. The Uzbekistani Government claimed that the uprising was initiated by armed Islamist militant groups, some of whom crossed from neighbouring Kyrgyzstan. According to this version of events, the militants attacked the local prison on the night between 12 and 13 May, killing guards and freeing prisoners, before advancing into the city and taking control of government buildings. However, human rights groups noted widespread popular support for the uprising, reflecting discontent with the country's arduous socio-economic conditions, which took place during a trial of local businessmen allegedly involved in Akramiya, an Islamist group that the authorities claimed was linked to Hizb-ut-Tahrir. With the demonstrators taking charge of the city, the Government ordered troops to retake the administrative buildings. According to official reports, 187 people were killed in the violence that ensued; unofficial sources, however, cited figures of up to 1,000 dead. Hundreds of refugees fled Uzbekistan to Kyrgyzstan. In mid-2005, despite Uzbekistani requests for extradition, 400 refugees were airlifted from Bishkek, the Kyrgyzstani capital, to third countries willing to accept them, including Romania, Canada, and the USA. Since late 2005, however, over 70 of those refugees were reported to have returned to Uzbekistan, either owing to official assurances that they would not be prosecuted or to increasing pressure exerted by the authorities on the refugees' families in Uzbekistan. Following the government assault on Andijon, there were further arrests of the leaders of civil society associations. By late December more than 150 people had been sentenced to terms of imprisonment for their involvement in the protests, although human rights organizations expressed concern about the conduct of the trials. The Uzbekistani Government rejected all attempts to initiate an independent international inquiry into the events in Andijon, and instead convened a group composed of representatives of states friendly to Uzbekistan to report on the uprising and subsequent massacre.

There was no indication in 2007 that the trend of authoritarianism was being reversed or contained, and the politically motivated harassment of journalists, human rights activists and opposition figures continued unabated. The most prominent cases were those of Umida Niyazova, a human rights activist linked to the organization Human Rights Watch (HRW); Gulbanor Turayeva, an activist from Andijon; and Isroil Kholdarov, a member of Freedom. Niyazova was arrested on her return from a training session at the OSCE Academy in Bishkek at Tashkent Airport and was charged with smuggling extremist material and contraband into the country, and with crossing the border illegally. In May she was sentenced to seven years' imprisonment, although, following international pressure, her sentence was suspended. None the less, Niyazova was obliged to undertake a humiliating public repentance and issue a denunciation of all the activities of HRW and of her colleagues. Kholdarov was sentenced to six years' imprisonment in February 2007 and Turayeva to seven years' for allegedly infringing the constitutional order and distributing extremist material. As in the case of Niyazova, she also had her sentence suspended following a public denunciation of previous statements on the Andijon events. Requests for independent investigations into the Andijon events continued to be rejected by Uzbekistani authorities. This, along with the Government's long-standing reluctance to introduce political reforms, improve the human rights situation or to refrain from placing relentless pressure on the opposition, led to a further straining of relations with the West. In October 2006 President Karimov removed the Hokim of Andijon Viloyat, Saydullo Begaliyev, referring to the deteriorating social and economic conditions of the local population, thereby appearing to acknowledge that the roots of the 2005 unrest may have had more to do with socio-economic grievances than support for Islamist militance. In November 2006 the Uzbekistani authorities allowed a number of EU experts to conduct a limited (and controlled) investigation in Andijon in an attempt to improve the country's image and relations with the West. Within the EU, Germany (which held the EU presidency in the first half of 2007) played a leading role in seeking to improve relations with the Uzbekistani Government.

The dominant political issue in 2007 was that of the presidential election. Although Karimov's seven-year term expired in early January, only on 18 September did the Central Elections Commission announce that a presidential election was to take place on 23 December, citing a constitutional stipulation that the election be held in December of the year in which the presidential term of office ended. The election campaign subsequently began on 21 September, and by mid-October five political parties had presented candidates, although no representative of any opposition group was expected to be permitted to participate in the election. By mid-October it was still unclear whether Karimov might be willing to have the Constitution amended to allow him to seek a further term of office, or whether he would effectively appoint a successor. Finally, the LDPU nominated him as their presidential candidate and in November Karimov accepted the nomination. The Constitution was not amended, and no debate followed about the fact that, in contesting a further term of office, Karimov would be breaching the constitutional limit of two consecutive mandates as President. According to the Central Election Commission, the rate of participation was 90.6% and President Karimov received 88.1% of the votes cast. The other candidates (Asliddin Rustamov of the PDPU; Dilorom Tashmuhamedova of the JSDPU; and Akmal Saidov, an independent) received 3.2%, 2.9%, and 2.9%, respectively. The run-up to the elections was marked (outside Uzbekistan, mainly) by speculation over the identity of Karimov's preferred successor, in the event that he decided not to continue in office. The possibility of a dynastic succession had not been excluded, and in view of the power enjoyed by Karimov's daughter, Gulnora Karimova, it remains possible that she might replace her father as President in the future. Although with Karimov's election to a further term of office, the question of succession has again been postponed for the immediate future, the eventual resolution of this matter is far from determined. Since power has been so fiercely concentrated among few people, it is possible that the succession could be intense, and possibly violent. Apart from Karimova, potential contenders for the post include Alisher Usmanov, a Moscow-based 'oligarch', the SNB (National Security Service) chief Rustam Inoyatov, and Prime Minister Shavkat Mirziyoyev. The lack of institutional mechanisms for managing succession and the increased centralization of power and resources in the hands of very few do not bode well for Uzbekistan's medium-term stability.

Various observers have pointed to a possible resurgence of the IMU in recent years, although this has thus far failed to materialize. After the reverse received in the winter of 2001 during the early phases of the US-led operations in Afghanistan, IMU militants fled the country and found refuge in the Waziristan region of Pakistan. There the movement has regrouped and has continued to attract and recruit Uzbeks from Uzbekistan. However, following clashes between IMU militants and local tribesmen in Pakistan, who increasingly reacted against the IMU's reported brutality, the IMU may be moving elsewhere. Regardless of the fate of the IMU itself, the emergence of various splinter movements in the country has been reported. One of these is the so-called Jihad Islamic Group, which might possibly have been responsible for the 2004 bombings in the capital and elsewhere. As of late 2008 no episode of religiously motivated unrest has occurred in the country for several years.

FOREIGN RELATIONS

The central priorities of independent Uzbekistan's foreign policy have been to ensure stability on its borders, to guarantee the state's sovereignty and independence, to promote regional security, and to avoid reliance on support from one great power only. As Uzbekistan is a landlocked country surrounded by other landlocked countries, relations with Tajikistan, Turkmenistan, Kyrgyzstan, Afghanistan and Kazakhstan, and with leading regional powers, primarily Russia, have dominated its foreign policy agenda.

Ethnic and religious issues were of particular significance in Uzbekistan's relations with other Central Asian states. Of growing importance were its relations with Afghanistan and Tajikistan. The emergence of powerful Islamist groups and the regional instability produced by conflict within these two countries caused considerable alarm in Uzbekistan. In the first years of independence, the civil war in Tajikistan posed the greatest challenge. The Uzbekistani Government was unsympathetic towards the coalition of Islamist and democratic opposition groups in that country in the early 1990s. The situation was considerably complicated by the presence of large numbers of ethnic Uzbeks in the northern Leninabad region of Tajikistan, around the city of Khujand. As fighting flared in 1992, leaders of the Uzbek community reportedly advocated unification with Uzbekistan. In late 1992 Uzbekistan's military became involved in the Tajikistani conflict, in support of the communist regime. In January 1993 Uzbekistan co-operated with Russia and Kazakhstan in the deployment of troops to secure the southern borders of Tajikistan. Relations with Tajikistan deteriorated in October 1997, however, when the Uzbekistani authorities were linked to an uprising in western Tajikistan. While becoming a guarantor of the peace process that emerged in Tajikistan in 1997, Uzbekistan remained critical of the inclusion of Islamist representatives in the new Government and advocated the interests of the Leninabad region. Relations were further damaged by the suspicion that Uzbekistan supported an armed rebellion in November 1998, when forces loyal to Col Mahmoud Khudoberdiyev, a Tajikistani army officer, tried unsuccessfully to raise the province of Leninabad (later renamed Soghd) against the Tajikistani Government.

The Uzbekistani Government's concerns regarding the conflict in Tajikistan were exacerbated by developments in Afghanistan in the second half of the 1990s. In the early 1990s Uzbekistan was broadly supportive of the regime in Kabul, the capital of Afghanistan, particularly as the militant Islamist Taliban militia grew more powerful. When the Taliban advanced and seized Kabul in late 1996, the Uzbekistani Government extended considerable political and military support to the leader of an ethnic Uzbek militia, Gen. Abdul Rashid Dostam, in northern Afghanistan, to ensure the creation of a 'buffer' zone between Uzbekistan and the fighting in Afghanistan. Defeat of Dostam's forces and the Taliban's advance to Uzbekistan's southern border prompted a reorientation in official policy, directed towards rebuilding stronger ties with Russia.

The conflicts in Tajikistan and Afghanistan provided the main impetus towards co-operation between Uzbekistan and its neighbours and with Russia. Uzbekistan joined the Commonwealth of Independent States (CIS) at its foundation on 21 December 1991. In August 1993 Uzbekistan agreed to form an economic union with Kazakhstan and Russia, but later introduced its own currency and left the 'rouble zone'. In July 1995 Russia and Uzbekistan agreed on a wide range of bilateral agreements to strengthen economic ties, but President Karimov's Government was increasingly concerned to prevent excessive Russian dominance of the region. During the first decade of independence the country built up strong, independent armed forces, and encouraged military co-operation with the USA.

Following independence, Uzbekistan also sought closer ties with its neighbours. In mid-January 1994 Uzbekistan agreed to establish an economic union with Kazakhstan and Kyrgyzstan. In July the Presidents of Kazakhstan, Kyrgyzstan and Uzbekistan met in Almaty and signed seven agreements designed to implement this economic partnership. They also committed themselves to the creation of a Central Asian Bank for Co-operation and Development and an International Council, with executive bodies to carry out its decisions. In February 1995 the three countries again resolved to provide greater institutional substance to their 'common economic space' agreement of 1994. In 1998 they were joined by Tajikistan, and the grouping was later renamed the Central Asian Economic Community.

Uzbekistan's co-operation with its neighbours was most successful in the area of water resources and security issues. Considering the calamitous effects of the ecological situation of the Aral Sea on the country, the first issue was of vital significance. In September 1995 the Presidents of Kazakhstan, Kyrgyzstan and Uzbekistan, and a delegation from Turkmenistan, signed the Nukus Declaration on saving the Aral Sea. Subsequently, tensions were generated by suggestions that Kyrgyzstan would introduce water-pricing policies (negotiations on the issue began in 1997), although this was in response to Uzbekistan's complaint over unpaid gas supply debts. Tension over water management resurfaced periodically during the 2000s. In 2008 Uzbekistan expressed discontent at the smaller than habitual flow of water from Kyrgyzstan's Toktogul reservoir, and had disputes with Kazakhstan (and the other neighbouring republics) over the quantity of water that that country is supposed to share with the other states of Central Asia (see also the Essay in Part One on the Politics of Water in Central Asia). Uzbekistan has also co-operated with its neighbours on security issues. In May 1996 it agreed, with Kazakhstan and Kyrgyzstan, on the formation of a common Central Asian peace-keeping force (the Central Asian Peace-keeping Battalion—CENTRASBAT) for use at the behest of the UN. However, although relations with Kazakhstan and Kyrgyzstan were generally good throughout the 1990s, relations with Turkmenistan were noticeably cool.

In 1999 and early 2000 tensions between Uzbekistan and its regional neighbours developed as a result of advances by Uzbekistan to demarcate unilaterally its borders, which, like many in the region, had not been clearly determined in the 1920s. In the Farg'ona valley, considerable tension was generated over border questions, particularly following an incursion into Kyrgyzstan from Tajikistan by the IMU in August 1999, to which Uzbekistan responded by bombing parts of the border area; rebels again invaded the country in August 2000. Uzbekistan and Kazakhstan established a joint boundary commission, but Uzbekistan twice sought unilaterally to demarcate the frontier in early 2000. In 2001 similar problems emerged with respect to the demarcation of the border with Kyrgyzstan. A memorandum signed by the leaders of Uzbekistan and Kyrgyzstan was quickly abandoned, owing to strong criticism. In mid-September it was reported that Uzbekistan had occupied Kyrgyzstani territory, without the consent of the Kyrgyzstani Government. In 2001–02 a dispute flared between Uzbekistan and Kazakhstan over a small piece of land along their border. Although the territory was controlled by Uzbekistan, following a border demarcation accord in 2000, the majority of the area's residents were ethnically Kazakh. In December 2001 residents of the disputed village of Bagys declared an Independent Kazakh Republic of Bagys, and elected a president and legislature. Uzbekistani security forces subsequently made a number of arrests, and in April 2002 it was reported that troops had barricaded Bagys and the village of Turkestanets, after virtual martial law had been established there. In September Uzbekistan and Kazakhstan signed a treaty fully demarcating their joint border, and a border agreement was signed between Uzbekistan and Tajikistan in the following month. There were also some signs of improved co-operation between the Central Asian states in 2002, with the transformation of the Central Asian Economic Community into the Central Asian Co-operation Organization, an institution with a broader remit. Despite this measure, however, ambitions for intensive regional co-operation remained elusive. Relations with Tajikistan have been characterized by mutual distrust, and the Tajikistani authorities have repeatedly accused Uzbekistan of meddling in its domestic affairs, especially during and in the immediate aftermath of the civil war, whereas Uzbekistan has justified its policies against Tajikistan on the grounds that this country could harbour terrorists engaged in attempts to destabilize Uzbekistan and the broader region. Relations with Kyrgyzstan have also gone through several waves of tension, most recently when the Kyrgyzstani authorities allowed the refugees fleeing the Andijon crackdown in May 2005 to remain within Kyrgyzstan. Only

in 2006, and very reluctantly, did Uzbekistan agreed to implement a visa-free regime between the two countries.

From the 1990s the threat posed by the IMU created difficulties in the relationship between Uzbekistan and other Central Asian nations. The IMU used bases in Afghanistan and Tajikistan to launch attacks on Uzbekistan, usually crossing Kyrgyzstani territory en route. The Uzbekistani Government placed a great deal of pressure on Tajikistan to expel the IMU from its territory; a similar request to the Taliban in Afghanistan was rejected. By mid-2001 the Uzbekistani, Kyrgyzstani and Russian Governments were co-ordinating efforts to combat IMU attacks. However, relations were adversely affected when Uzbekistani government forces laid landmines along the Uzbekistani–Kyrgyzstani border, in order to deter IMU incursions, inadvertently killing several Kyrgyzstani civilians. As a result, the Kyrgyzstani legislature refused to ratify an agreement with Uzbekistan on arms supplies. Despite the apparent removal of the IMU threat, and thereby one of the main justifications for the militarization of Uzbekistan's borders, the country's relations with its neighbours showed little sign of improvement. Uzbekistan continued to restrict border-crossings with Kyrgyzstan and Tajikistan, and relations with Kazakhstan deteriorated in June 2004 over the shooting of a Kazakhstani national by Uzbekistani border guards. Deaths and injuries in border regions, caused by Uzbekistani landmines, also prompted further tensions in relations with Kyrgyzstan and Tajikistan. In July 2004 the Uzbekistani authorities indicated that they were ready to consider demining activities. At the same time, the Uzbekistani-Kyrgyzstani Border Commission appeared to reach an impasse in its efforts to demarcate the border. In late 2002 bilateral relations with Turkmenistan were adversely affected following an assassination attempt against President Saparmyrat Niyazov of Turkmenistan in November. The Turkmenistani authorities accused Uzbekistan of sheltering the principal suspect in the attempted coup, in the Uzbekistani embassy in Turkmenistan. In late December the Uzbekistani ambassador to Turkmenistan was expelled. Eventually, however, in November 2004 Presidents Karimov and Niyazov met in Buxoro to re-establish ties, and an Uzbekistani ambassador was accredited to Turkmenistan in January 2005.

Through its involvement in the campaign against militant Islamists in Afghanistan, Uzbekistan's international relations initially underwent a significant shift. As part of the US-led military campaign in Afghanistan, US troops were deployed in south-western Uzbekistan (at the Qarshi-Khanabad military base, also known as 'K-2'), fostering a closer relationship with the USA than had previously existed. (In the late 1990s US-Uzbekistani relations had deteriorated, largely as a result of Uzbekistan's poor record on human rights and its failure to adopt sustained economic reforms.) Once it became clear, in late 2001, that the Taliban regime would not surrender Osama bin Laden, held principally responsible by the USA for perpetrating the suicide attacks on its territory, Karimov reiterated his support for retaliatory attacks on Afghanistan. In a co-operation agreement signed with the USA in early October, Uzbekistan confirmed that it would allow access to its airbases for the purpose of undertaking humanitarian or 'search-and-rescue' operations during the US-led aerial bombardment of strategic positions in Afghanistan. In late November Uzbekistan and the USA signed a number of agreements pledging to improve bilateral relations and to increase economic co-operation. The USA agreed to donate more than US $150m. in aid towards improving Uzbekistan's security and economic development. However, disagreement over Uzbekistan's pace of democratization remained. Further bilateral agreements on political, economic and military co-operation were signed in early 2002, and in March President Karimov received a warm welcome during a high-level visit to the USA. During the visit a Strategic Partnership Framework agreement was signed between the two countries, which marked the highest point in their bilateral relations.

Prior to 1999, Uzbekistan had sought to distance itself from Russia and to assume the leading regional role in Central Asia. Although Uzbekistan withdrew from the CIS Collective Security Treaty at the end of March 1999 and joined the GUAM (Georgia-Ukraine-Azerbaijan-Moldova) grouping in April, which was thereby renamed GUUAM, the increasing challenge from radical Islamists led to a rapprochement with Russia. On a visit to Tashkent, the Russian premier (later President), Vladimir Putin, praised Uzbekistan's treatment of minorities and indicated that it was Russia's 'strategic partner' in the fight against insurgency, banditry, religious extremism and drugs-trafficking in Central Asia. In May 2001 President Karimov agreed to exchange foodstuffs and natural gas for Russian weapons, which were required to combat Islamist insurgents. Following President Putin's declaration of support for the US-led military campaign in Afghanistan in 2001, and Uzbekistan's new strategic relationship with the USA, relations improved further. By 2005 GUUAM, which had almost ceased to operate in the early 2000s, appeared to have been reinvigorated, following the so-called 'orange revolution' in Ukraine (see the chapter on Ukraine) and indications that the USA supported the grouping. Fearing the prospect of a Western-supported revolution spreading to that country, Uzbekistan announced its intention to withdraw from the organization in May 2005; legislation providing for the withdrawal was enacted by President Karimov in March 2006 (the organization then reverted to its original designation of GUAM). In 2006–07 relations between Uzbekistan and Russia became increasingly closer, as testified by the fact that in January 2006 Uzbekistan joined the Eurasian Economic Community (founded in 2000 by Belarus, Kazakhstan, Kyrgyzstan, Tajikistan and Russia), and in August Karimov signed a protocol on Uzbekistan's membership of the Collective Security Treaty Organization, which had evolved from the CIS Collective Security Treaty into a more formal military-political organization focused on regional security in 2003. Legal procedures allowing for Uzbekistan's full accession to the Organization were expected to be completed by 2008.

Meanwhile, in 2004 growing international concerns about the human rights situation in Uzbekistan, and the lack of political and economic reforms, placed Uzbekistan's relationship with the US Administration of George W. Bush under pressure. In July the USA withdrew its aid programme, citing 'disappointment' with Uzbekistan's human rights practices, and US Secretary of State Colin Powell noted that Uzbekistan was not fulfilling the terms of the 2002 Strategic Partnership Framework agreement, which mandated 'substantial and continuing progress' on democratization. The cooling of Uzbekistan's relations with the USA was accompanied by a renewed effort to strengthen relations with Russia and the People's Republic of China.

In the late 1990s the growing importance of regional security, as a result of Islamist insurgency, prompted Uzbekistan to express a desire to join the so-called Shanghai Forum, subsequently known as the Shanghai Co-operation Organization (SCO—comprising the People's Republic of China, Russia, Kazakhstan, Kyrgyzstan and Tajikistan). The organization, which was originally concerned with the demilitarization of the border between China and its CIS neighbours, had broadened its focus to include combating international terrorism, separatism and religious extremism. Although Uzbekistan joined the SCO in June 2001, its new relationship with the USA initially raised the prospect that Uzbekistan might not become an active participant in the grouping, and Uzbekistan failed to send a representative to the Organization's ministerial meetings in early 2002. Nevertheless, President Karimov did attend the seventh summit meeting of the grouping in June. Furthermore, an SCO anti-terrorism centre was established in Tashkent in 2004. At a summit meeting of the SCO held in mid-June 2004 Uzbekistan and Russia signed a strategic co-operation pact. The agreement was regarded as part of an initiative by Russia to re-establish the strategic position in Central Asia that it had lost following the US-led intervention in Afghanistan. Uzbekistan's geo-political realignment was completed in November 2005 when the US military base was closed (see below) and Karimov and Russia's President Putin signed a Treaty of Allied Relations. Notably, under the treaty, the two countries agreed to provide mutual support in the event that one of them came under attack. In August 2007 Uzbekistan attended, with the status of an observer, the SCO joint military exercises (Peace Mission 2007) held in eastern Siberia (Russia) along with the armed forces of Russia, China, Tajikistan,

Kyrgyzstan and Kazakhstan. While joint exercises between Russia and China have been held before, the involvement of other countries in such a drill was unprecedented.

Relations with a range of other international powers were also developed following independence, including countries in Western Europe, in particular Germany. Western investment in Uzbekistan was regarded as politically, as well as economically, significant. In the second half of the 1990s the souring of relations with the IMF and other international financial institutions, Western criticism of Uzbekistan's internal policies of repression (most notably toward Islamic groups) and the Government's improving links with Russia obscured political relations with the West, although from 1995 trade with Western industrialized countries expanded. Asian countries, particularly the Republic of Korea (South Korea) and, more recently, Japan, also contributed important investments to Uzbekistan. Relations with Afghanistan markedly improved following military action by Western powers, including those stationed in Uzbekistan, from 2001, and the establishment of a new administration in Afghanistan. Uzbekistan's relations with Pakistan and Iran also improved in 2006.

Uzbekistan's relationship with the international community deteriorated in 2003–04 as a result of concerns about the country's human rights record and its failure to conduct significant domestic reform. Following a review of Uzbekistan's progress in the areas of democratization, human rights and economic liberalization, in April 2004 the EBRD decided to limit its lending to the country. Following the crushing of the demonstrations in Andijon in May 2005 the EBRD curtailed its operations in Uzbekistan (see Economy). Relations with Turkey and the countries of the Middle East were also of importance to Uzbekistan. Together with other Central Asian states, the country joined the Economic Co-operation Organization (ECO), originally founded by Iran, Pakistan and Turkey in 1985. Uzbekistan was, however, critical of attempts to develop a political role for the organization, and the limited economic resources available to ECO member countries curbed the role that they could play in Uzbekistan. Instead, the Government promoted the role of international bodies, such as the OSCE, which opened a Central Asian office in Tashkent in October 1995, and the UN, which was the principal international forum for the important war against the trafficking of illegal drugs in the region and played an important role in mediating the conflict in Tajikistan.

The events in Andijon of May 2005 had a considerable impact on Uzbekistan's international relations. The USA, supported by the EU and other international organizations, urged Uzbekistan to agree to an international investigation into the events. However, Uzbekistan refused, and instead sought support from Russia and China, and other regional allies. As tension with the USA increased over the events at Andijon and Uzbekistan's general record on democratization and human rights, Uzbekistan raised the issue of the withdrawal of US troops from the Qarshi-Khanabad military base. In July, after a summit meeting, the SCO, prompted by Russia and China, issued a statement demanding that deadlines be imposed on the use of military bases in Central Asia by the West for operations in Afghanistan. Following intensive discussions between Uzbekistan and the USA, on 29 July Uzbekistan renounced the agreement under which approximately 1,000 US military personnel had been permitted to use the Qarshi-Khanabad base. The USA vacated the base by November. Meanwhile, in October the EU imposed a number of sanctions on Uzbekistan, in response to the Government's refusal to permit an international inquiry into the suppression of the uprising at Andijon. Following the Andijon events, Uzbekistan's relations with the West deteriorated further. The EU introduced a number of measures against the country to indicate its disapproval of Uzbekistan's actions during the uprising and subsequently, including the refusal to hold an independent investigation. Several high-ranking Uzbekistani officials were prohibited from travelling to the EU, and an arms embargo was placed on the country. It was only from late 2006 that the EU, at the initiative of Germany (which, uniquely among Western states, maintained a military base in Uzbekistan, in the southern city of Termez, on the Afghan border), attempted to improve political relations with Uzbekistan.

Tashkent's relations with the USA, in contrast, remain marked by a mutual impasse with neither of the two sides knowing how to overcome the current deadlock. In 2008 it appeared that Uzbekistan's international relations were about to change, once again. Relations with Russia have gone through a period of considerable chill, marked by periodic disputes over issues of bilateral trade (Uzbekistani agricultural exports were suspended for some time in 2008 due to the presence of a pest in Uzbekistani cotton) and the conditions of the hundreds of thousands of Uzbekistani labour migrants in Russia. Following a series of high profile visits to the country by senior officials, in March 2008 the USA announced that its troops were to be granted conditional access (to be determined on a case-by-case basis) to the military facilities at Termiz, near the border with Afghanistan. Previously the base was exclusively used by German personnel associated with the North Atlantic Treaty Organization (NATO)-commanded International Security Assistance Force (ISAF) operations in Afghanistan. Relations with the EU have been mixed. While progress in human rights and political reform continues to stagnate in Uzbekistan, the European authorities have continued to ease the sanctions imposed on Uzbekistan in 2005, including the travel ban on senior Uzbekistani officials.

CONCLUSION

After 1991 the few democratic institutions in Uzbekistan were eliminated. At the same time, there was a steady concentration of power in the state presidency. From the mid-1990s Uzbekistan operated as a highly authoritarian country, based upon the almost unchecked authority of President Karimov. Repression was justified as the only means to avoid ethnic conflict and Islamist militancy, and necessary for binding together a young nation and state. Karimov ensured that there were no plausible internal challengers to his rule, by purging and marginalizing potential rivals. The small and divided secular opposition posed no threat. The only real alternative to the President was the Islamist movement, but this was not a coherent force within Uzbekistan, being divided between radicals and moderates. The emergence of Islamist militant groups based outside the country from 1999 posed a more serious challenge to the Uzbekistani regime, a threat that was amplified following the suicide attacks on the USA in September 2001. Following the suppression of the Afghanistan-based IMU and its Taliban hosts by the US-led coalition, there were few subsequent signs of serious political and economic liberal-

ization in Uzbekistan. The regime continued to rely upon repression of all dissent, the systematic practice of torture and the abuse of human rights. By 2004 there were growing indications that the authorities' reliance on coercion was failing to stem the rise of domestic opposition, particularly based on radical forms of Islam, and was in fact serving to strengthen opposition to the Karimov regime. In 2005 the Andijon uprising represented the latest episode of popular resistance and the first serious direct challenge to the authorities. The bloody suppression of the uprising served to draw attention to the growing instability in the country. As repression intensified further in the following years, the Government demonstrated that it had no sense of direction except for an instinct for self-preservation at all costs. With Karimov's re-election in December 2007 there is no sign that this will change in the foreseeable future.

In foreign policy, Karimov failed in his original objective of transforming Uzbekistan into the dominant regional power. Kazakhstan's growing oil wealth posed a particular challenge to Uzbekistan's ambitions to lead the region. With signs that the Uzbekistani economy was faltering, and with growing internal popular dissatisfaction and powerful external challenges, Uzbekistan, too, was forced to rely increasingly on military and political support from the USA and Russia. Relations with the West were damaged by Uzbekistan's very poor record on human rights and its resistance to political and economic liberalization, although the country's support for US-led military action in Afghanistan temporarily produced some improvement in both political and economic relations. Domestic and external pressures to liberalize the system and a pattern of regime change elsewhere in former Soviet territories ultimately led to the souring of Uzbekistan's relations with the West. Events in Andijon were not the root cause of this, but rather an illustration of the problematic and controversial nature of Uzbekistani-Western relations. However, the actions of the Uzbekistani military in Andijon appeared to represent a turning point in the country's relations with the West. Seventeen years after the collapse of the USSR, the stability and independence that Karimov had pursued since independence remained as elusive as ever, while it was only in 2008 that relations with the USA and the EU started to show signs of mild improvement. Uzbekistan maintains close ties with Russia and China, both of which are ruled by regimes less keen on questioning the manner in which the Uzbekistani authorities run the country's internal affairs.

Economy

Dr NEIL MELVIN

Revised for this edition by Dr MATTEO FUMAGALLI

INTRODUCTION

Historically, the primary economic activities of the regions that constitute contemporary Uzbekistan were agriculture, trade and the production of handicrafts (textiles, jewellery and low-grade domestic goods). During the Soviet era, Uzbekistan's economy underwent a series of fundamental changes, including an extensive reorganization of agriculture, an intensification of production (notably of cotton) and the introduction of new industries. Overall, however, Soviet economic policies left the country poorly prepared for independence. Uzbekistan has an extensive natural resource base, but Soviet planners did little to create indigenous industries capable of exploiting these resources. In the USSR, Uzbekistan functioned primarily as a supplier of raw materials that were processed elsewhere. As a result, official Soviet figures identified the Uzbek SSR as one of the poorer republics in the USSR, with only the Tajik SSR having a lower per-head consumption.

The main economic function of the region during the Soviet era was the production of cotton and other agricultural goods. The legacy of this policy was a set of chronic ecological

problems, a largely rural work-force and a highly unbalanced economy. The country's population, which remains the largest in Central Asia (an estimated 27.8m. in 2008), is settled around the major oasis settlements of the region (Tashkent, Samarqand, Buxoro—Bukhara and Xiva—Khiva) and the fertile region of the Farg'ona (Fergana) valley. During the 1980s annual population growth averaged 2.5%, but this declined to 1.8% in the 1990s and to 1.2% annually in 2001–08 (equivalent to an increase of some 370,000 per year), owing to large-scale emigration by Slavs, Germans, Greeks, Jews and Crimean Tatars, and to a declining birth rate. While the official unemployment rate is very low (0.8% in 2007, with forecasts of 0.8% and 1.1% for 2008 and 2009, respectively), unofficial estimates (by the UNDP) put unemployment at a much higher 6% in 2007. In 2005 some 10,196,000 persons were employed, with 29.1% in agriculture, 13.2% in industry and 57.7% in other sectors. There was also considerable underemployment, believed to be around 20%. Overall, about 26.2% of the population was reported to be living below the national poverty line in 2005. A major achievement of the Soviet period was an increase in the human capital of Uzbekistan. With an adult literacy rate of 97.2% in 1993 (which had increased to 99.3% by 2004), the educational level of the population was high. The Soviet regime established a comprehensive educational system, including institutions for higher education. The scientific potential of the country was concentrated in more than 350 establishments, and well-trained research personnel were engaged in work in a number of areas. The emigration of some of the most skilled members of society in the early years of independence and a decline in educational standards, however, damaged the country's scientific and research base. Official statistics from the Ministry of Labour and Social Security estimated the number of Uzbekistani migrants working abroad to be approximately 700,000 in the mid-2000s (although this appears to be a rather conservative estimate, with a figure closer to 1.5m. seeming more realistic), making migrants' remittances (estimated at some US $1,000m. in 2006) an essential contribution to household budgets.

Uzbekistan's infrastructure was poorly developed during the Soviet years. Although the railway and road networks were built as a connection to Russia and other republics of the USSR, most routes leading out of Uzbekistan required upgrading if trade and transit traffic were to increase. The European Union (EU) devoted considerable resources to improving east–west communications in the country. The telecommunications system, traditionally very poor, is undergoing upgrading, with the mobile telephony sector, which had 5.5m. subscribers at December 2007, undergoing rapid expansion.

ECONOMIC POLICY

The main characteristic of economic policy in independent Uzbekistan is the high degree of government direction, designed officially to moderate the social dislocation brought about by the introduction of market-orientated reforms, but in actual fact primarily intended to preserve political control. Initially, the Government's attitude to change served to produce a gradualist approach to economic and structural reform in Uzbekistan. The World Bank estimated that there was an average annual decline in real gross domestic product (GDP) of 4.4% in 1990–95, and of 15% between 1992 and 1994 alone. The sectors most affected were construction and industry (the latter declining by an average of 6.6% per year in 1990–95), which experienced severe problems with supply from other states of the former USSR. Although these figures were high, they fell below the average output decline in the rest of the former USSR. Most of the decline in real GDP was concentrated in 1992, when the IMF gave a figure of 11.0% for the contraction, with the rate slowing to 4.2% in 1994. The IMF conceded that the economic contraction in Uzbekistan was less severe than in other post-Soviet states, but argued that this was achieved despite, rather than as a result of, government policy.

Following independence, 'hyperinflation' quickly took hold of Uzbekistan's economy. At one point in 1992 the annual rate of inflation reached 2,700%. During that year the increase in consumer prices was 818.7%, rising to 1,114.5% in 1993 and 1,515.9% in 1994. In an attempt to bring monetary policy under government control and, thereby, reduce inflation, Uzbekistan left the Russian-dominated 'rouble zone' in November 1993 and introduced its own transitional national currency, the sum-coupon. In July 1994 the new national currency, the sum, was introduced. After its introduction, the Government gradually raised the official exchange rate of the sum against other currencies, so that the official rate was close to that of the 'black' (unofficial) market rate.

The economy's slow progress during the early years of independence led to attempts to accelerate and deepen the reform process. In January 1994 President Islam Karimov issued a decree that bolstered the power of the state to promote economic reform. An inter-ministerial committee on economic reform, entrepreneurship and foreign investment was established, and there was an expansion of the powers of the privatization committee to include aspects of private sector development. In addition, stock, real-estate and commodity exchanges were to be created, permission for persons to hold foreign-currency accounts was granted, import duties were

eliminated for one year and a state insurance company capable of guaranteeing foreign investments was established.

The introduction in 1994 of a comprehensive reform programme supported by the President had important consequences. By the end of 1995 inflation appeared to have declined to around 10% per month. The small amount of data available suggests that the Government was maintaining a restrictive monetary policy, in accordance with IMF demands. The Central Bank reduced interest rates as inflation fell, but ensured that rates remained positive in real terms. Official figures suggested that GDP declined by just 0.9% in 1995, with real industrial output rising by 0.2%.

Despite the changes of 1994, it was only in 1995 that a coherent set of stabilization measures appeared in Uzbekistan. A particular point of criticism was the mixed performance of structural reform. The IMF expressed concern at Uzbekistan's failure to restructure enterprises and the manner in which privatization was conducted. The IMF did, however, praise the widespread withdrawal of state subsidies. By mid-1994, however, many consumer subsidies for food, utilities, housing, transport and energy (many of which had been introduced in response to price liberalization in Russia) had been removed. However, the IMF was critical of the way in which Uzbekistani economic policy developed, questioning the independence of the Central Bank and urging the President to reduce 'administrative interventions' in the economy.

In 1995 the disastrous domestic cotton harvest and low world prices for the commodity led the Uzbekistani leadership to impose foreign-exchange controls and to begin to print money, thereby encouraging inflation. The actions of the Government led the IMF to suspend a US $185m. stand-by loan in mid-December 1996 on the grounds that Uzbekistan had missed its inflation targets. The imposition of tight state controls over currency transactions caused severe problems for foreign firms operating in Uzbekistan, and foreign investment slowed.

The problems associated with the crisis in state finances represented the end of the limited economic reforms. A strong critic of the more radical economic transitions attempted among the other former Soviet republics, President Karimov effectively suspended market reforms in late 1996, for fear of provoking unrest within the population and opposition among powerful interests in the élite. In 1997–2001 the Uzbekistani authorities failed to launch significant economic change in the country, as political issues and control over society increasingly became the central policy focus of the authorities. The Government was criticized by international financial organizations, including the European Bank for Reconstruction and Development (EBRD—headquartered in the United Kingdom), the IMF and the US Department of Commerce, for creating a difficult business environment.

Throughout 1998–2002 the economic situation steadily deteriorated, despite official figures that pointed to growth, with GDP increasing by an average annual rate of only 0.5% in that period, and GDP per head decreasing at an average annual rate of 1.3%. The decline in world prices for Uzbekistan's two main exports, cotton and gold, deprived the country of export revenue and produced severe demands on domestic liquidity. With foreign-currency reserves dangerously low, the national currency continued to lose value at both official and black-market rates and inflation fluctuated at around 25%. By 2001 the economic situation had failed to improve significantly, although strong growth in the Commonwealth of Independent States (CIS) as a whole for 1999–2000, as a result of recovery from the Russian financial crisis of 1998, assisted Uzbekistan. A severe drought led to another poor cotton harvest in 2000. It remained, therefore, imperative that the Government introduced economic reform. However, the Government showed little willingness to relax exchange-rate controls or to close bankrupt and uncompetitive industries. According to official estimates, GDP grew by 4.1% in 2001 and by 3.2% in 2002 (below the target of 5.0%).

The macroeconomic situation significantly changed from 2004 onwards. GDP growth had officially reached 7.0% in 2005 (4.0%, according to EBRD estimates), up from 4.2% in 1999 and down from 7.7% in 2004. The rate of growth reached some 9.5% in 2007, but was expected to moderate slightly to 8%–8.5% in 2008–09. This nevertheless continued to point to a robust macroeconomic performance due to rising investment and a solid export base (as a result of high global commodity prices). Uzbekistani authorities reported that the year-end rate of inflation for 2007 was 12.5%, with a rate of 15.5% forecast for 2008, and 13.5% for 2009. However, the inflation rate is widely believed to have been under-reported, and most international estimates (although not those of the Asian Development Bank) put the inflation rate at about 20% annually. In part, the general decline in the rate of inflation in the mid-2000s was the result of tight fiscal policy, but it was also likely that the official data considerably under-estimated the actual rate. The more recent rise is the result of the pre-electoral government spending of late 2007.

At the end of 2001 a new relationship between Uzbekistan and leading international financial institutions and powerful Western states, principally the USA, created expectations of a shift in economic policy. In the new environment of international goodwill towards Uzbekistan that resulted from that country's co-operation with the US-led 'war on terror', initiated after the suicide attacks on the USA in September 2001, Uzbekistan pledged to undertake economic reforms, and contacts were re-established with the IMF (see below). None the less, the Uzbekistani leadership remained extremely cautious about serious economic reform, and by 2004 the relationship with international economic institutions had again deteriorated owing to Uzbekistan's reluctance to introduce substantial reform. Following the massacre in the city of Andijon in May 2005 (see History), a number of international financial organizations withdrew from or severely curtailed their operations in Uzbekistan. Towards the end of the decade relations with some of the organizations, including the World Bank, the EBRD and the IMF, showed signs of improvement, and new contracts and loans were agreed with the Uzbekistani authorities (see International Finance and Investment, below).

ECONOMIC INSTITUTIONS

Uzbekistan inherited little from the Soviet period in terms of the institutional infrastructure necessary for a market economy. In response to the new demands of macro- and micro-economic management, there was an attempt to create appropriate new structures. However, given the tendency for state intervention in the economy, and the weakly marketized nature of the system, establishing new institutional arrangements was often difficult. Although some progress was made in constructing a reformed and independent financial and economic system, Uzbekistan continues to be characterized by weak institutions, high levels of corruption and extensive state interference.

The President and the Cabinet of Ministers are responsible for major economic decisions. The Ministry of Finance develops the state budget, exercises financial supervision of enterprises, manages all inter-governmental credit agreements and international financial institutions, and oversees foreign-currency loans to enterprises. The Ministry also oversees external debt-servicing and manages repayments. Although the Central Bank is supposedly subordinated only to parliament, in practice it is controlled by the Government. The ability of the Central Bank to make independent decisions has frequently been doubted, as has its ability to control the banking sector in the country. In 1994 a reform of the banking sector was begun. A two-tier system was established, consisting of the Central Bank and about 30 commercial banks. The main aim of the reform was to restrict the availability of credit to enterprises, a major source of inflation. The poor supervision of the commercial sector by the Central Bank frequently undermined this aim and the continuing access to cheap credit weakened the process of enterprise privatization. In March 2005 the Government closed the only viable private bank in the country.

The failure to foster independent economic institutions ensured that all aspects of the Uzbekistani economy remained subordinate to the priorities and directives of the President. The economy lacked autonomous centres for significant economic decision-making and mechanisms for investment driven by economic efficiency. Instead, even the commercial-banking sector was tied to the state system, and banks allocated credit to priority sectors as identified by the Government. Commer-

cial banks were also used to maintain the sum at artificially high values. All economic activity remained centred upon the state and key figures in the ruling élite. By the mid-2000s there were increasing indications that corruption and powerful vested interests had penetrated almost all aspects of economic policy making. As a result, even the previously semi-autonomous activities of small-scale cross-border and local market trading were used by state officials as a source of revenue. Pressure on market traders intensified in 2004–06, prompting uprisings in several markets against the local authorities. Equivalent to some 31% of GDP and engaging around 49% of the labour force, the informal sector remained an important source of production and employment in the mid-2000s.

PRIVATIZATION

The Government followed a process of gradual privatization with the Law On Denationalization and Privatization, enacted in November 1991, which provided the legal basis for the process. To support privatization, the State Committee for the Management of State Property and Privatization (known by its local acronym of GKI) was established in February 1992. In the first stage of privatization, the GKI undertook the disposal of housing, agriculture and the retail sector. In 1994–95 the second stage began, with more than 5,000 enterprises scheduled for privatization.

The pace of privatization accelerated in March 1994, when President Karimov announced that the state would no longer finance insolvent enterprises. At the end of 1994 the GKI estimated that there were 67,660 enterprises in Uzbekistan, of which 20,758 were state enterprises and 46,902 private. In February 1995 Karimov claimed that 100,000 firms, or 67% of state firms, had been privatized, and that most of the workforce operated in the private sector. In fact, privatization enjoyed only partial success, with most enterprises still under the influence of state or local government to significant degrees.

From the mid-1990s the privatization programme slowed considerably. In 1998 the Government planned to privatize 346 state-owned firms, but in May it announced the postponement of the privatization of the petroleum and gas sectors. Despite privatization, many insolvent firms continued to function, with state support. Critically, the state retained strategic stakes in most enterprises. In 1999 Uzbekistan's need for foreign exchange prompted the Government to develop a list of potential assets for sale. However, even where privatization was carried out, the results were often far from favourable for the new owners, and it proved difficult to attract foreign investors. In the first nine months of 2000 income from privatization totalled some 10,954m. sum, and by the end of the year 189 medium-sized and large enterprises had been privatized. In March 2001 the Government listed more than 600 state companies that remained to be sold. In subsequent years the Government continued to publicize its intention to undertake privatization (2,250 enterprises were identified for sale in 2005–06), although actual sales remained modest.

State control over credit facilities, exchange controls, price formation and the activities of various bureaucratic agencies (principally the tax inspectorate) ensured that even nominally private enterprises operated in a tightly state-defined framework. Shareholders have only minor influence over firms. A decree signed in 1998 allowed the Government to block strategic decisions made by majority foreign shareholders if it deemed them not to be in the national interest. Privatization was heavily influenced by contacts with the Government and frequently served as the basis for the construction of networks of political patronage. Associates of the Government and their families staffed the most profitable firms. After President Karimov opted for an autarkic form of economic development in the mid-1990s there was no significant privatization. Following the revived contacts with the international financial community in late 2001, the Government again pledged to accelerate privatization, although foreign investors remained extremely cautious about the general business environment. Overall, little progress has been made in this sense since the mid-1990s. Small businesses accounted for only 42% of the economy in 2006 with privatization revenues at about $23m. in the same year. In January 2007 the Government announced a form of land privatization, and in July of that year launched a renewed privatization initiative aiming at disposing of several inefficient state-owned assets, including the natural gas and petroleum corporation Uzbekneftegaz, the automobile manufacturer UzDaewoo and the telecommunications company Uzbektelecom, within the following four–five years, although the business environment of Uzbekistan was not considered favourable to either the domestic or foreign private sector due to heavy government interference.

FINANCES

In 1992 Uzbekistan had a fiscal deficit equivalent to 11% of GDP. The deficit narrowed to some 9% in 1993 and to 4.8% in 1994. In the early years of independence, the Government had problems controlling spending, because credit was made available to enterprises and the Government sought to maintain public expenditure in the social and cultural sectors. As Uzbekistan began to abide by IMF conditions, government spending appeared to have been brought under control. In May 1996 it was announced that Uzbekistan had posted a deficit-free budget for the first quarter of the year, but it registered a deficit thereafter. Uzbekistan's external debt was relatively small, as it did not inherit any obligations of the former USSR. However, the economic crisis that afflicted the economy from 1996 placed a significant strain on the debt situation in Uzbekistan. In 1994 Uzbekistan recorded a small trade surplus, and in 1995, according to the Ministry of Foreign Economic Relations, a surplus of around US $293m. was recorded. The heavy reliance on cotton exports (60% of the total in 1992, but later nearer 30%), however, meant that Uzbekistan's trade balance was dependent on world cotton markets.

From 1996 difficulties raising external credit, because of the failure to conclude an agreement with the IMF, led the Uzbekistani authorities to keep fiscal accounts close to balance by accumulating wage and pension arrears, forcing loans from local banks and retaining a tight grip on local enterprises and their exports. Given the poor state of government finances in the late 1990s, the trade situation became critical. The poor cotton harvest and the decline in world prices for cotton in 1995–99 caused acute problems in balancing trade flows.

The trade deficit was managed by a steadily depreciating national currency, which priced imports out of the local market. Given the problems with government finances, lack of international credit and poor trade figures, the Government was running a significant current account deficit on the balance of payments by the late 1990s. Some independent estimates placed the deficit at US $329.4m. in 1999, although official figures identified a current account surplus of $10.6m. From the early 2000s Uzbekistan started to register a trade surplus, which increased from $276m. in 2002 to $1,318m. in 2005, according to the ADB. The EBRD forecast a trade surplus of $1.4m for 2007. After recording current account deficits (peaking at $979m., equivalent to 7.0% of GDP, in 1996), the country registered growing surpluses in the following years: $1,215m. in 2004 and $1,949m.) in 2005, with the surplus reaching $2,933m. in 2006. A surplus equivalent to 25.5% of GDP ($4,615m.) was estimated in 2007, with a surplus equivalent to 22% of GDP forecast for 2008.

The Government appeared to have financed the current account deficit of the late 1990s and industrial investment with foreign debt. External debt, owed largely to bilateral lenders, rose steadily and peaked at US $5,006.9m. in 2004 (equivalent to 42% of gross national income—GNI), according to the ADB. Thanks to a favourable environment in terms of commodity prices, the country's external debt declined significantly to about 21% of GNI ($3,927m.) in 2007, but it was expected to increase slightly in 2008 and 2009 (to around $4,100m. and $4,300m., respectively). Despite the considerable potential for investment, Uzbekistan had one of the lowest levels of foreign direct investment (FDI) in the former communist bloc ($250m. in 2005). Cumulative net inflows of FDI in 2006 amounted to about $1,700m. (13% of GDP). The lack of convertibility of the sum was usually identified as the principal factor discouraging foreign companies from investing in the

country. The sum was made freely convertible from October 2003 (see below), but in January 2004 the Government ended the preferential tax regime for foreign-owned businesses, further deterring foreign investment. However, the expansion of the Russian economy led to increased Russian investment in Uzbekistan, and in April 2005 the Government announced new tax incentives for foreign investment in Uzbekistani enterprises. Evidence suggested that in 2004–05 the Government followed a tight fiscal and monetary policy designed to cut spending, bring down inflation and reduce the fiscal deficit. According to official estimates, the budget deficit was equivalent to 0.4% of GDP in 2004 and to 1.0% in 2005, followed by a small surplus in 2006. With presidential elections (see History section) scheduled to take place in December 2007, the Government embarked on a new spending programme which was expected to lead to a budget deficit in the same year. This led to a rise in social benefits, wages and pensions of up to 25%. With the electoral period now over, the budget is forecast to revert to balance in 2008.

AGRICULTURE

Agriculture is fundamental to Uzbekistan's economy, and, although arid or semi-arid steppe constitutes 60% of the country, there are also a number of highly fertile regions, especially in the Farg'ona (Fergana) valley in the east of the country. The single most important crop in Uzbekistan is cotton, the country being the fourth largest producer and second largest exporter of seed cotton in the world. Uzbekistan is also the largest producer of silk and karakul pelts in the former USSR. Other important products include wheat, rice, jute, tobacco, fruit and vegetables. Despite the substantial contribution of agriculture to the economy (the agricultural sector, including forestry, accounted for 29.1% of GDP in 2005), Uzbekistan is not self-sufficient. A large proportion of foodstuffs are imported, including up to 66% of wheat requirements, 30% of meat, 25% of milk and 50% of potatoes.

The form of agriculture inherited from the Soviet era, with its reliance on the extensive use of land, water and chemicals (fertilizers and pesticides) was particularly damaging to the environment. Uzbekistan has an extensive but inefficient irrigation system to provide water for cotton production, and it is this system that has caused the problems of the Aral Sea and the overuse of water supplies. Irrigating the cotton monoculture depleted water resources in the region, leading to the desiccation of the Aral Sea, which was previously the world's fourth largest inland lake. By the late 1990s the lake was only one-quarter of its volume in 1960 and was predicted to disappear entirely early in the 21st century unless urgent measures were undertaken. The problem was compounded by salinity, industrial wastes, pesticides and fertilizers, which poisoned the remaining subsurface and surface waters, land and air in the region.

In an attempt to decrease environmental pollution and ameliorate the problems around the Aral Sea, a policy of shifting production to grain was introduced. This was also intended to reduce Uzbekistan's dependence on the import of foodstuffs and to help redress the balance of payments problem. After 1990 the area sown for grain increased from 1.0m. ha to reach a peak of 1.8m. ha in 1997. By 2002 the figure had fallen to 1.2m. ha. In 2002 the cereals harvest totalled some 5.5m. metric tons, according to the UN Food and Agriculture Organization (FAO), up from the annual average of 4.1m. tons over the previous four years. At the same time, the country continued to import grain, suggesting that official figures for production may have been over-estimated. In 2003 the Government claimed to have achieved self-sufficiency in grain, and began, for the first time, to export cereals. According to FAO, the harvest was 6.1m. tons in 2003, 5.9m. tons in 2004, 6.2m. tons in 2005, 5.6m. tons in 2006, and 6.3m. tons in 2007.

Cotton production remained of critical importance. The area devoted to cotton production was constant, at about 1.5m. ha. Production of seed (unginned) cotton declined steadily after reaching its highest level, of 5.4m. metric tons, in 1988. From 1995 the cotton crop consistently fell below target, causing severe problems for the whole economy. The poor harvests and shift of land from cotton to cereal production greatly damaged

Uzbekistan's ability to earn 'hard' currency. In 2001 the cotton harvest was 3.3m. metric tons, and this was followed by a further poor harvest, of 3.1m. tons, in 2002. In that year the Government introduced a limited liberalization of the state procurement system to ease pressure on farmers and encourage production. Prospects for the 2003 harvest were far better, with increased production under plastic sheeting expected to raise yields. However, production actually declined in 2003, to 2.8m. tons, before increasing to 3.5m. tons in 2004 and 3.7m. tons in 2005, only to decline again to 3.6m. tons in 2006. The Government placed increased emphasis on domestic processing of cotton fibres to raise value added, and aimed to process 50% of the crop domestically by 2008.

Following independence, an important change for agriculture was the abolition of state farms and their conversion to co-operative enterprises. Members of the new collectives did not have the right to sell their shares. Some private farms developed: in 1994 there were 10,408 and the area of land available for private farming by farm workers rose significantly (from 110,000 ha before 1991 to 630,000 ha in 1994). Land itself was not privatized, although agricultural land could be traded within the mahallah (local neighbourhood or commune), and land attached to an enterprise could be sold with it (leasehold). Despite the change in the formal structures of ownership, the state continued to dominate agricultural production and maintained a virtual monopoly over the purchase of important crops, notably cotton. In recent years there has, nevertheless, been a growing role for the private sector, in particular the household plot. Indeed, if they had access to investment and working capital, the farmers-entrepreneurs who account for the bulk of the country's fruit and vegetables production could penetrate export markets. Despite these changes, the difficult conditions for peasant farmers have led to social unrest in many rural areas.

MINING, ENERGY AND INDUSTRY

Uzbekistan has important natural reserves, and soon after independence the Government identified the development of mining and the processing of minerals and metals as a major priority. Metals production in Uzbekistan rose steadily from the mid-1990s, particularly in the gold sector. Uzbekistan has 30 gold deposits (2.1m. tons of proven reserves and 3.3m. tons of estimated total reserves). Gold production increased from 85,000 kg in 2000, to 90,000 kg in 2002 and to 93,000 kg in 2004, and was estimated at about 85,000 kg in 2007. Almost all of the gold produced is exported. In the mid-2000s high gold prices made an important contribution to the country's income of convertible currency. Other metals, such as copper, silver and non-ferrous metals, have also been produced in increasing amounts. The export of metals emerged as a critical element of Uzbekistani trade with the rest of the world, second only to cotton production.

Uzbekistan also has important reserves of hydrocarbons, and the Government pursued a policy of becoming self-sufficient in fuel with some success (in 2005 Uzbekistan had proven crude petroleum reserves of 600m. barrels). There were no significant imports of petroleum after 1995. The refining industry also performed well, raising production in the second half of the 1990s. Petroleum production, mostly concentrated in the western part of the country, along the Buxoro–Xiva axis, rose from 2.8m. metric tons in 1991 to 8.2m. tons in 1998, but had declined to 4.9m. tons (or 114,000 barrels per day) by 2007. Domestic prices remained low, reflecting the Government's policy of subsidizing the domestic economy. By 2010 annual production was planned to reach 9m. tons. Uzbekistan struggled, however, to develop high-grade refining. The practice of controlling energy prices created an important financial incentive to smuggle energy supplies to neighbouring countries.

Uzbekistan's proven natural gas reserves amounted to 1,740,000m. cu m at the end of 2007, in which year production of natural gas amounted to 58,500m. cu m, an increase of 5.6% on the previous year. However, if gas is to be exported in significant volumes, investment in infrastructure, including gas pipelines and refineries, will be required. Uzbekistan has also experienced serious difficulties in obtaining payment for

the gas exported to neighbouring states. Moreover, the economic difficulties in Uzbekistan have forced the Government to become increasingly assertive in demanding payment for gas from Kazakhstan, Kyrgyzstan and Tajikistan, and supplies to these countries have been reduced or suspended, owing to non-payment.

The petroleum and gas sector was attractive to some foreign investors. France and Japan agreed to provide US $200m. to finance the modernization of the Buxoro refinery undertaken by Technip of France. Unlike Kazakhstan, Uzbekistan did not plan to become a major exporter of petroleum, but rather to achieve self-sufficiency. Foreign investment was to finance the development of the Mingbulak and Kokdumalak fields as a way to lift total output. Overall, however, the petroleum and gas sector was controlled by the state-owned company, Uzbekneftegaz, and attracted very low levels of foreign direct investment. Stagnating production levels from the early 2000s prompted the Uzbekistani authorities to seek a closer involvement by Russian companies in domestic production in partnership with Uzbekneftegaz, notably for the development of the Kandym oil and gasfields. In 2004 significant foreign investment in the sector by Lukoil (worth US $1,000m.) and Gazprom (some $1,200m.), both of Russia, and the China National Petroleum Corporation ($600m.) was announced. Gazprom, in particular, has become increasingly involved in natural gas exploration and development in Uzbekistan and has, de facto, achieved a position of control over the hydrocarbons infrastructure in Central Asia. Gazprom announced plans to invest $99.1m. in exploration and surveying in 2007, as a part of a $260m. three-year project scheduled for completion in 2008. Gas exports to Russia have increased significantly from 7,000m. cu m in 2004 to 9,800m. cu m in 2006 and to an estimated 13,000m. cu m in 2007. Favourable deals with Russia over the sale of Uzbekistani gas have seen the price of gas exports increase to 'international prices' ($145 per 100 cu m) in 2008. Gas exports to Russia were forecast to increase by 45% in that year, following an increase of 65% in 2007.

Light industry predominates in the Uzbekistani economy. Despite the importance of cotton- and silk-growing, only a small percentage is processed domestically. Uzbekistan relies heavily on imports of textiles. The development of an indigenous textiles industry was given high priority in the 1990s. An important new departure for the domestic economy following independence was the production of small trucks and cars, and diesel-engine buses. A number of foreign firms established production facilities in Uzbekistan, and the country had ambitions to become a regional centre for the automotive industry. In 1995 Daimler-Benz of Germany expanded vehicle production in Uzbekistan, and in March 1996 Daewoo of the Republic of Korea (South Korea) opened a plant in Tashkent. Following the Asian financial crisis of 1998 Daewoo, experienced serious domestic financial difficulties, and the Uzbekistani Government was forced to support financially the UzDaewoo Auto plant, although at significantly lower levels of output, when Daewoo went bankrupt in 2000. In 2003 the automotive sector was reported to be performing poorly, with the UzDaewoo Auto plant operating at well below its annual capacity of 200,000 units. The automotive sector reported progress in 2004–06, with production reaching 140,080 units in 2006 (up 39% from previous year), and a significant export market to Russia. Automobile production increased 22% in 2007. In October 2007 Uzbekistan's O'zavtosanoat and the US-based General Motors (GM) signed a deal establishing a joint venture, GM Uzbekistan, to manufacture Chevrolet automobiles, with GM's initial stake of 25% due gradually to increase to 40%.

Limitations of infrastructure constrained tourism, which has considerable potential in the country because of its historical sites. The lack of an adequate infrastructure of transport, hotels and recreation facilities, however, meant that the sector's potential had yet to be fulfilled. Like almost all sectors of the Uzbekistani economy, success was dependent on foreign capital. The poor investment climate in the country, however, discouraged extensive developments in the tourism industry. In 2001 Uzbekistan had an estimated 344,900 foreign visitors, but numbers fell to 231,000 in 2003 and only mildly recovered in the following years, reaching 261,600 in 2004. Tourism receipts in 2003 totalled some US $48m., compared with $72m. in 2001. Overall, the period 2000–05 saw a decline of about 15% in terms of foreign visitors. A strict visa regime, customs and border procedures, lack of adequate infrastructure (as mentioned above), and episodic political unrest all contribute to reduce tourism arrivals and income.

INTERNATIONAL FINANCE AND INVESTMENT

A number of international firms have made sizeable investments in Uzbekistan. Daewoo originally invested nearly US $450m. in its car factories, while BAT Industries (based in the United Kingdom) began production of cigarettes at an existing factory and also constructed new manufacturing facilities. Other important Western firms were active in the mining, energy and telecommunications sectors. The announcement of significant Russian investment in Uzbekistan's hydrocarbons sector from 2004, in addition to investment amounting to some $600m. from the People's Republic of China, indicated an increasing economic reliance on these two countries. Relations with other East Asian countries have also flourished. Trade with South Korea has increased in recent years, with imports from that country valued at $471.6m. in 2005 and exports at $83.5m. It was hoped that a visit by the Japanese Prime Minister, Junichiro Koizumi, in August 2006 would lead to increased Japanese investment in Uzbekistan's energy and education sectors, which had already amounted to some $2,000m. since independence. Exports to Japan were valued at $113m. in 2005.

The activity of foreign firms is supported by financial assistance and guarantees provided by foreign governments. The large international organizations supply the final layer of assistance for market reforms and investment, providing finance for individual sectors of the economy and also for macroeconomic projects. In February 1995 the World Bank, the IMF, the Organisation for Economic Co-operation and Development (OECD) and the EBRD announced an international assistance programme to deliver more than US $900m. to Uzbekistan over the following two years ($300m. for balance of payments support, $45m. for technical assistance and $580m. for financing investments and export loans). Uzbekistan has also sought to attract other sources of international finance, and in September 1995 it became an official member of the ADB.

From 1996 the change of direction in economic policy undermined the international programmes of assistance. Foreign private investment, already very modest, was also reduced significantly. In early 1998 negotiations with the IMF failed to establish new stabilization measures. Negotiations foundered on Uzbekistan's refusal to reverse its anti-reformist path. In particular, the Government refused to make the sum convertible and, thereby, abandon the system of multiple exchange rates. The Government was also reluctant to commit itself to trade liberalization. Relations with the IMF were subsequently difficult, and the Fund published a number of reports critical of government economic policy, and which cast doubt on official statistics. Despite these problems, international institutions, such as the ADB, continued to lend money to Uzbekistan for infrastructure projects (Uzbekistan has received $974.9m. in loans and $34.1m. in technical assistance from the ADB since 1995), and export-guarantee agencies in Europe and the USA provided loan assistance for the purchase of imports.

At the beginning of 2000 the worsening domestic economic situation and a number of policy statements by President Karimov suggested that the Government was preparing to seek the re-establishment of the IMF stand-by arrangement loan that had previously been suspended. Negotiations, however, were inconclusive, and in April 2001 the IMF announced the permanent departure of its representative to Uzbekistan. This measure was interpreted as an implicit criticism of Uzbekistan's economic policies, which were viewed as ineffective, and even counter-productive.

Following Uzbekistan's support for the US-led 'war on terror' from late 2001, the country's relationship with international financial organizations was reviewed. After a pledge by the USA to secure US $100m. in loans and assistance to the country, a team from the IMF visited Uzbekistan in November 2001 and negotiated a Staff Monitored Programme, a crucial element of which was the Government's commitment to make the sum current-account convertible by 1 July 2002. In mid-July President Karimov promised US officials that Uzbekistan would sign an agreement with the IMF by the end of the year, in order to make the sum fully convertible. In 2001 Uzbekistan received assistance from the USA amounting to $161.8m., the highest amount recorded among the Central Asian states. Despite the commitment to reform expressed in 2001, reformist measures were not introduced in 2002 or the first half of 2003. In May 2003 the EBRD held its annual meeting in Tashkent, a location that was selected in an attempt to stimulate the long-delayed economic reform in Uzbekistan. Prior to the meeting, the Uzbekistani Government repeatedly intimated that it would reach agreement with the IMF on a stabilization programme. In fact, no agreement was achieved. Government restrictions on trade, the lack of significant reform in the agricultural sector and the failure to establish a single exchange rate were identified by observers as obstructing further IMF engagement. Finally, in mid-October Uzbekistan signed an agreement with the IMF confirming the sum's new status as a fully convertible currency. In April 2004 the EBRD decided to suspend lending to most of Uzbekistan's public sector projects, as a result of the poor human rights situation in the country and the Government's repeated failure to meet its promises regarding domestic economic reforms. In July 2005, following the violence in Andijon, the EBRD announced that it was to limit its operations in Uzbekistan to the private sector, and would not engage in any further public sector projects. In October, following repeated warnings, the 25 EU ministers of foreign affairs announced their decision to impose sanctions on Uzbekistan for its refusal to allow an independent investigation into the events in Andijon. The punitive measures included a reduction in aid to the country, the termination of a co-operation agreement and the imposition of an embargo on the import of arms. Sanctions were eased in late 2007. In June 2008 the World Bank announced a new Country Assistance Strategy for Uzbekistan, through which it would make funds available to finance the public and private sectors until 2011.

CONCLUSION

From 1991 Uzbekistan pursued sporadic economic reform and was reluctant to release data on the performance of the economy. Only in mid-1995 did Uzbekistan finally accede to the demands of the IMF structural adjustment programme. The economy as a whole, however, remained fragile and heavily dependent on agricultural production, in particular cotton. Although economic management and fiscal discipline improved, the state continued to intervene, particularly in areas such as the lucrative foreign-trade sector and the management of enterprises.

The new economic course embarked upon by the Government from 1996 changed significantly the nature of economic development in the country, as well as its prospects. Reform stalled, and many of the basic structural problems in the economy remained. Given the difficulties that the Government experienced with international financial institutions, raising international credit proved difficult.

Economic results were mixed, at best, by mid-2008. The Government claimed that the Uzbekistani economy was growing, achieving high levels of investment and modest levels of inflation, with a stable currency. Some international financial institutions, including the IMF, noted the country's strong macroeconomic performance. This could be attributed to the largely favourable international environment (high prices of the country's main commodity exports and increased net exports), as well as improved fiscal and monetary policy. However, most independent observers viewed these claims with scepticism and identified increasing economic difficulties and a failure to address the key structural impediments to economic progress. The country had experienced moderate growth in economic activity in recent years. Structural fiscal policy reforms had been introduced, while record cotton crops and high world prices for the country's natural resources had contributed to current account and trade surpluses. At the same time, the banking sector and the business environment constituted areas where progress was languishing. More crucially, it was difficult to find evidence that whatever progress the country had made in macroeconomic terms had led to a reduction in poverty and an improvement in the extremely low living standards experienced by large sections of the population.

The new environment in which Uzbekistan found itself from late 2001, as a result of its support for US-led efforts to combat global terrorism, presented an unexpected opportunity to undertake the significant economic reform that the Government had avoided during the previous decade. Despite considerable pressure from the international community to introduce reforms, the authorities in Tashkent remained reluctant to undertake serious change, and moreover, from around 2005, the Uzbekistani authorities became distanced increasingly from the USA and other Western states. Relations with international financial institutions became increasingly strained too. Concerns about the ways in which reform could undermine the political dominance of the leadership of the country, which had been established following independence on the basis of state patronage over the economy, appeared to be the principal obstacle to further economic progress. By 2008 high world prices for petroleum and natural gas were shielding the Uzbekistani economy from its generally poor domestic performance and helping to ease pressure on the national finances and increase exports. At the same time, the improvement of the state's economic position did little to ease the chronic poverty and corruption encountered by individuals. This failure to improve personal incomes prompted increasing socio-economic unrest.

Statistical Survey

Area and Population

AREA, POPULATION AND DENSITY

Area (sq km)	447,400*
Population (census results)†	
17 January 1979	15,389,307
12 January 1989	
Males	9,784,156
Females	10,025,921
Total	19,810,077
Population (UN estimates at mid-year)‡	
2006	26,981,000
2007	27,372,000
2008	27,769,000
Density (per sq km) at mid-2008 . . .	62.1

* 172,740 sq miles.

† Figures refer to *de jure* population. The *de facto* total at the 1989 census was 19,905,158.

‡ Source: UN, *World Population Prospects: The 2006 Revision*.

POPULATION BY ETHNIC GROUP
(1996, rounded estimates)

	%
Uzbek	80.0
Russian	5.5
Tajik	5.0
Kazakh	3.0
Kara-Kalpak	2.5
Tatar	1.5
Others	2.5
Total	100.0

Source: Ministry of Health, Tashkent.

ADMINISTRATIVE DIVISIONS
(1996, rounded figures, official estimates)

	Area (sq km)	Population	Density (per sq km)	Capital city (with population)
Sovereign Republic:				
Qoraqalpog'iston .	165,600	1,400,000	8.5	Nukus (236,700)
Viloyats				
Andijon . . .	4,200	1,899,000	452.1	Andijon (303,000)
Buxoro . . .	39,400	1,384,700	35.2	Buxoro (263,400)
Farg'ona . . .	6,800	2,597,000	381.9	Farg'ona (214,000)
Jizzax	20,500	910,500	44.4	Jizzax (127,200)
Namangan . .	7,900	1,862,000	235.7	Namangan (341,000)
Navoiy . . .	110,800	767,500	6.9	Navoiy (128,000)
Qashqadaryo . .	28,400	2,029,000	71.4	Qarshi (177,000)
Samarqand . .	16,400	2,322,000	141.6	Samarqand (366,000)
Sirdaryo . . .	5,100	648,100	127.1	Guliston (54,000)
Surxondaryo . .	20,800	1,676,000	80.6	Termiz (95,000)
Tashkent* . . .	15,300	4,450,000	290.9	Tashkent (2,100,000)
Xorazm . . .	6,300	1,200,000	190.5	Urgench (135,000)
Total	447,400	23,145,800	51.7	

* Including Tashkent City, which subsequently assumed a separate administrative status.

Source: Government of Uzbekistan.

PRINCIPAL TOWNS
(estimated population at 1 January 2001)

Toshkent (Tashkent, the capital) . .	2,137,218	Farg'ona . . .	183,037
Namangan . .	391,297	Margilan . . .	149,646
Samarqand . .	361,339	Chirchik . . .	141,742
Andijon . . .	338,366	Urgench . . .	138,609
Buxoro . . .	237,361	Navoiy	138,082
Nukus	212,012	Jizzax	131,512
Qarshi	204,690	Termiz	116,467
Qoqand . . .	197,450	Olmaliq	113,114

Source: UN, *Demographic Yearbook*.

Mid-2007 ('000, incl. suburbs, UN estimate): Toshkent (Tashkent) 2,184 (Source: UN, *World Urbanization Prospects: The 2007 Revision*).

BIRTHS, MARRIAGES AND DEATHS

	Registered live births		Registered marriages		Registered deaths	
	Number	Rate (per 1,000)	Number	Rate (per 1,000)	Number	Rate (per 1,000)
1994 . .	657,725	29.5	176,287	7.9	148,423	6.7
1995 . .	677,999	29.9	170,828	7.5	145,439	6.4
1996 . .	634,842	27.4	171,662	7.4	144,829	6.3
1997 . .	602,694	25.6	181,126	7.7	137,331	5.8
1999* . .	553,745	23.1	170,525	7.1	140,526	5.9
2000 . .	527,580	21.4	168,908	6.9	135,598	5.5
2001 . .	512,950	20.5	170,101	6.8	132,542	5.3

* Figures for 1998 are not available.

Source: UN, *Demographic Yearbook*.

Registered live births: 553,700 in 1998; 532,500 in 2002; 508,400 in 2003; 540,400 in 2004 (Source: UNDP Country Office and Center for Economic Research, Tashkent, *Uzbekistan in Figures*).

2005: Birth rate 20.9 per 1,000; Death rate 5.0 per 1,000 (Source: Ministry of Health, Tashkent).

Expectation of life (years at birth, WHO estimates): 67.8 (males 65.1; females 70.5) in 2006 (Source: WHO, *World Health Statistics*).

EMPLOYMENT
(annual averages, '000 persons)

	1998	1999	2000
Agriculture*	3,467	3,213	3,083
Industry†	1,114	1,124	1,145
Construction	573	640	676
Transport and communications .	362	370	382
Trade and catering‡	717	735	754
Other services	1,976	2,042	2,042
Housing, public utilities and personal services	235	240	246
Health care, social security, physical culture and sports . .	502	538	567
Education, culture and art . .	1,073	1,094	1,120
Banking and insurance . . .	50	48	51
General administration . . .	111	122	126
Information and computer services	5	—	—
Total (incl. others)	8,800	8,885	8,983

* Including forestry.

† Comprising manufacturing (except printing and publishing), mining and quarrying, electricity, gas, water, logging and fishing.

‡ Including material and technical supply.

Source: Centre for Economic Research, Tashkent, *Uzbek Economic Trends*.

2001 ('000 persons): Total employed 9,136 (Agriculture 3,062, Industry 1,160, Other 4,914) (Source: Asian Development Bank).

2002 ('000 persons): Total employed 9,333 (Agriculture 3,046, Industry 1,186, Other 5,101) (Source: Asian Development Bank).

2003 ('000 persons): Total employed 9,589 (Agriculture 3,063, Industry 1,223, Other 5,303) (Source: Asian Development Bank).

2004 ('000 persons): Total employed 9,911 (Agriculture 3,068, Industry 1,284, Other 5,559) (Source: Asian Development Bank).

2005 ('000 persons): Total employed 10,196 (Agriculture 2,970, Industry 1,348, Other 5,879) (Source: Asian Development Bank).

2006 ('000 persons): Total employed 10,467 (Source: Asian Development Bank).

2007 ('000 persons): Total employed 10,735 (Source: Asian Development Bank).

Unemployed ('000 persons registered): 38 in 2001; 35 in 2002; 32 in 2003; 35 in 2004; 28 in 2005; 26 in 2006; 23 in 2007 (Source: Asian Development Bank).

Health and Welfare

KEY INDICATORS

Total fertility rate (children per woman, 2006)	2.6
Under-5 mortality rate (per 1,000 live births, 2006) . . .	44
HIV/AIDS (% of persons aged 15–49, 2005)	0.2
Physicians (per 1,000 head, 2005)	2.7
Hospital beds (per 1,000 head, 2005)	5.2
Health expenditure (2005): US $ per head (PPP)	171
Health expenditure (2005): % of GDP	5.0
Health expenditure (2005): public (% of total)	47.7
Access to water (% of persons, 2004)	82
Access to sanitation (% of persons, 2004)	67
Human Development Index (2005): ranking	113
Human Development Index (2005): value	0.702

For sources and definitions, see explanatory note on p. vi.

Agriculture

PRINCIPAL CROPS
('000 metric tons)

	2004	2005	2006
Wheat	5,378	5,928	5,996
Rice (paddy)	181	166	220
Barley	108	109	73
Maize	156	164	194
Sorghum*	11	7	4
Potatoes	896	924	1,021
Dry broad beans*	5	4	4
Sunflower seed	11	10	9
Safflower seed	8	7	3
Sesame seed*	18	18	20
Cottonseed*	2,334	2,461	2,376
Cabbages and other brassicas .	274	287	369
Tomatoes	1,245	1,317	1,584
Cucumbers and gherkins .	184	200	259
Dry onions	539	546	591
Garlic	29	32	38
Carrots and turnips . . .	500	506	745
Watermelons	572	615	744
Apples	390*	402*	514
Pears	32*	41*	54
Apricots	162*	170*	236
Sweet cherries . . .	15*	17*	54
Peaches and nectarines . .	51*	56*	67
Plums and sloes . . .	65*	64*	57
Grapes	589	642	804
Tobacco (leaves)	19†	20*	20
Jute*	20	20	20
Cotton (lint)	1,150	1,250	1,171

* FAO estimate(s).

† Unofficial figure.

Aggregate production ('000 metric tons, may include official, semi-official or estimated data): Total cereals 5,860 in 2004, 6,531 in 2005, 6,511 in 2006; Total roots and tubers 896 in 2004, 924 in 2005, 1,021 in 2006; Total vegetables (incl. melons) 3,891 in 2004, 4,133 in 2005, 5,001 in 2006; Total fruits (excl. melons) 1,478 in 2004, 1,596 in 2005, 1,988 in 2006.

Source: FAO.

LIVESTOCK

('000 head at 1 January)

	2004	2005	2006
Horses	152	158	162
Asses, mules or hinnies . . .	269	289	293
Cattle	6,243	6,571	7,045
Camels	17	17	17
Pigs	87	87	93
Sheep	8,890	9,555	10,034
Goats	1,690	1,797	1,973
Chickens	18,833	20,540	24,188
Turkeys*	350	350	350
Rabbits and hares	76,800	92,000	101,400

* FAO estimates.

Source: FAO.

LIVESTOCK PRODUCTS

('000 metric tons)

	2004	2005	2006
Cattle meat	493.6	518.1	551.6
Sheep meat	69.6	73.6	83.6
Pig meat	13.8	16.0	18.1
Chicken meat	16.7	21.3	23.4
Cows' milk	4,211.9	4,447.2	4,821.4
Sheep's milk	31.7*	n.a.	n.a.
Goats' milk	68.4	107.5	34.2
Hen eggs	102.8	110.0†	116.5†
Other poultry eggs	1.6	3.2†	48.1†
Honey	1.9	2.1	2.0
Wool: greasy	18.6	20.1	21.4

* Unofficial figure.

† FAO estimate.

Source: FAO.

Fishing

(metric tons, live weight)

	2004	2005*	2006
Capture	1,230	2,000	3,400
Common carp	238	550	1,140
Crucian carp	191	190	188
Roach	234	230	223
Silver carp	106	140	180
Aquaculture	3,093	3,800	3,800
Common carp	574	700	266
Crucian carp	145	200	19
Grass carp (White amur) . .	249	300	190
Silver carp	1,189	2,400	3,268
Bighead carp	936	200	57
Total catch	4,323	5,800	7,200

* FAO estimates.

Source: FAO.

Mining

(metric tons, unless otherwise indicated)

	2003	2004	2005
Coal ('000 metric tons)* . . .	1,913	2,699	3,033
Crude petroleum ('000 metric tons)†	7,169	6,617	5,449
Natural gas ('000 million cu metres)	58	59	60
Copper ore‡§	80,000	95,000	100,000
Molybdenum ore‡§	500	500	500
Silver ore (kilograms)‡§ . . .	80,000	80,000	83,000
Gold (kilograms)‡§	90,000	93,000	90,000
Kaolin ('000 metic tons)§ . . .	5,500	5,500	5,500
Feldspar§	4,300	4,300	4,300
Uranium ore (metric tons)‡ . .	1,874	2,377	2,712

* Including lignite and brown coal.

† Including gas condensate.

‡ Figures refer to the metal content of ores.

§ Estimated production.

2006 ('000 metric tons): Crude petroleum 5,384.

2007 ('000 metric tons): Crude petroleum 4,937.

Sources: Asian Development Bank and US Geological Survey.

Industry

SELECTED PRODUCTS

('000 metric tons, unless otherwise indicated)

	1998	1999	2000
Beer ('000 hectolitres)	569	422	609
Cigarettes (million)	7,582	10,668	7,766
Wool yarn (pure and mixed) . .	2	3	3
Cotton yarn (pure and mixed) .	105	105	135
Woven cotton fabrics (million sq m)	314	333	360
Sulphuric acid	856	897	823
Nitrogenous fertilizers (a)* . .	755	707	717
Phosphate fertilizers (b)* . .	141	169	117
Motor spirit (petrol)	1,603	1,638	1,709
Gas-diesel (distillate fuel) oils .	2,227	2,220	1,900
Residual fuel oils	1,977	1,750	1,700
Lubricating oils	229	223	238
Cement	3,331	3,284	3,722
Domestic refrigerators ('000) . .	16	2	1
Domestic washing machines ('000)	5	—	—
Television receivers ('000) . . .	192	50	26
Electric energy (million kWh)† .	54,790	55,581	56,401

* Production in terms of (a) nitrogen; (b) phosphoric acid.

† Source: Asian Development Bank, *Key Indicators of Developing Asian and Pacific Countries*.

Source (unless otherwise indicated): UN, *Industrial Commodity Statistics Yearbook*.

2001: Cement ('000 metric tons) 3,722; Electric energy (million kWh) 47,961 (Source: Asian Development Bank).

2002: Cement ('000 metric tons) 3,927; Electric energy (million kWh) 49,398 (Source: Asian Development Bank).

2003: Cement ('000 metric tons) 4,062 (Source: Asian Development Bank).

2004: Cement ('000 metric tons) 4,805 (Source: Asian Development Bank).

2005: Cement ('000 metric tons) 5,058; Electric energy (million kWh) 47,706 (Source: Asian Development Bank).

2006: Cement ('000 metric tons) 5,583; Electric energy (million kWh) 49,300 (Source: Asian Development Bank).

2007: Cement ('000 metric tons) 6,043; Electric energy (million kWh) 48,950 (Source: Asian Development Bank).

Finance

CURRENCY AND EXCHANGE RATES

Monetary Units
100 teen = 1 sum.

Sterling, Dollar and Euro Equivalents (30 April 2008)
£1 sterling = 2,556.8 sum;
US $1 = 1,300.0 sum;
€1 = 2,020.2 sum;
10,000 sum = £3.91 = $7.69 = €4.95.

Average Exchange Rate (sum per US $)
2000   236.61
2001   423.31
2002   769.50

Note: Prior to the introduction of the sum (see below), Uzbekistan used a transitional currency, the sum-coupon. This had been introduced in November 1993 to circulate alongside (and initially at par with) the Russian (formerly Soviet) rouble. Following the dissolution of the USSR in December 1991, Russia and several other former Soviet republics retained the rouble as their monetary unit. The Russian rouble ceased to be legal tender in Uzbekistan from 15 April 1994.

On 1 July 1994 a permanent currency, the sum, was introduced to replace the sum-coupon at 1 sum per 1,000 coupons. The initial exchange rate was set at US $1 = 7.00 sum. Sum-coupons continued to circulate, but from 15 October 1994 the sum became the sole legal tender. On 15 October 2003 the sum became fully convertible.

CONSOLIDATED BUDGET
('000 million sum)

Revenue	2006	2007*	2008†
Tax revenue	4,365	5,870	6,791
Taxes on incomes and profits	1,293	1,758	2,002
Taxes on property	276	349	438
Taxes on goods and services	2,623	3,470	4,104
VAT	1,142	1,682	2,001
Excises	881	1,017	1,170
Customs duties	173	293	248
Other budget revenue	333	522	317
Social security contributions	1,253	1,761	2,650
Road fund and other extra-budgetary revenue	273	355	412
Education development tax	233	365	431
Grants	62	50	30
Total	**6,519**	**8,922**	**10,632**

Expenditure‡	2006	2007*	2008†
Socio-cultural expenditure	2,169	2,906	3,910
Social safety net	1,735	2,283	3,400
Low income support	366	397	620
Pension and employment fund	1,369	1,886	2,780
Pension fund	1,335	1,841	2,726
Employment fund	35	45	54
Economy	594	678	915
Public authorities and administration	124	176	243
Public investment	532	627	847
Interest expenditure	74	172	103
Other expenditure in the budget	879	1,138	1,078
Road fund	204	270	349
Extra-budgetary expenditure financed by grants	62	50	30
Statistical discrepancy	—	155	—
Total	**6,374**	**8,455**	**10,875**

* Preliminary.
† Projected.
‡ Excluding net lending ('000 million): 40 in 2006; 48 in 2007 (preliminary); −90 in 2008 (projected).

Source: IMF, *Republic of Uzbekistan: 2008 Article IV Consultation-Staff Report; Public Information Notice on the Executive Board Discussion; and Statement by the Executive Director for the Republic of Uzbekistan* (July 2008).

INTERNATIONAL RESERVES
(US $ million at 31 December)

	2002	2003	2004
Gold (national valuation)	505.8	558.0	418.5
IMF special drawing rights	1.1	0.1	0.0
Foreign exchange	709.8	1,101.2	1,728.0
Total	**1,215.0**	**1,659.3**	**2,146.5**

Total reserves (US $ million at 31 December): 2,895.0 in 2005; 4,604.0 in 2006.

Source: Asian Development Bank, *Key Indicators of Developing Asian and Pacific Countries*.

MONEY SUPPLY
(million sum at 31 December)

	2002	2003	2004
Currency outside banks	273,347	404,928	590,199
Demand deposits at deposit money banks	194,839	170,036	214,596
Total money	**468,186**	**574,964**	**804,795**

Source: Asian Development Bank, *Key Indicators of Developing Asian and Pacific Countries*.

COST OF LIVING
(Consumer Price Index; base: previous year = 100)

	2005	2006	2007
Food	106.7	103.9	103.3
Other goods	106.9	108.0	108.4
All items	**107.8**	**106.8**	**106.8**

Source: Asian Development Bank.

NATIONAL ACCOUNTS
('000 million sum at current prices)

Expenditure on the Gross Domestic Product

	2003	2004	2005
Final consumption expenditure	7,192.2	8,387.3	10,231.7
Households			
Non-profit institutions serving households	5,474.8	6,305.8	7,736.3
General government	1,717.4	2,081.5	2,495.4
Gross capital formation	2,042.8	2,913.1	3,499.5
Gross fixed capital formation	2,069.1	2,694.5	3,518.4
Acquisitions, less disposals, of valuables	−26.3	218.6	−18.9
Changes in inventories			
Total domestic expenditure	**9,235.0**	**11,300.4**	**13,731.2**
Exports of goods and services (net)	602.9	889.0	1,479.3
GDP in market prices	**9,837.8**	**12,189.5**	**15,210.4**

Gross Domestic Product by Economic Activity

	2005	2006	2007
Agriculture and forestry	3,802.6	5,003.0	6,116.4
Mining and quarrying			
Manufacturing	3,148.6	4,587.8	6,764.7
Electricity, gas and water			
Construction	745.3	1,058.7	1,550.2
Trade	1,399.4	1,972.1	2,649.5
Transport and communications	1,718.8	2,366.6	3,128.7
Finance			
Public administration	2,722.7	3,861.2	5,299.0
Other services			
GDP at factor cost	**13,537.4**	**18,849.4**	**25,508.5**
Indirect taxes			
Less Subsidies	1,673.1	1,909.9	2,677.7
GDP in purchasers' values	**15,210.4**	**20,759.3**	**28,186.2**

Source: Asian Development Bank.

BALANCE OF PAYMENTS
(US $ million)

	2005	2006	2007*
Exports of goods f.o.b.	4,757	5,615	8,026
Imports of goods f.o.b.	−3,310	−3,841	−5,730
Trade balance	1,446	1,774	2,296
Export of services	659	775	965
Import of services	−790	−828	−1,007
Balance on goods and services	1,315	1,721	2,254
Income (net)	−24	41	62
Current transfers (net) . . .	658	1,171	1,951
Current balance	1,949	2,933	4,267
Capital account (net) . . .	31	−116	−104
Foreign direct and portfolio investment (net)	88	195	739
Existing public and publicly-guaranteed debt (net) . . .	−241	−347	−213
Commercial non-guaranteed debt (net)	34	43	273
Foreign assets of commercial banks (net)	—	−290	−433
Other capital and statistical discrepancy	−1,093	−854	−2,430
Adjustment	—	—	56
Overall balance	768	1,564	2,155

* Preliminary.

Source: IMF, *Republic of Uzbekistan: 2008 Article IV Consultation-Staff Report; Public Information Notice on the Executive Board Discussion; and Statement by the Executive Director for the Republic of Uzbekistan* (July 2008).

External Trade

PRINCIPAL COMMODITIES
(US $ million)

Imports f.o.b.	1998	1999	2000
Chemicals and plastics . . .	407.2	363.0	399.5
Metals	303.6	245.4	253.5
Machinery and equipment . .	1,553.7	1,393.5	1,044.1
Food products	512.2	408.1	361.1
Energy products	16.3	66.6	112.7
Total (incl. others)	3,288.7	3,110.7	2,696.4

Exports f.o.b.	1998	1999	2000
Cotton fibre	1,361.0	883.7	897.1
Chemicals and plastics . . .	51.7	101.8	93.4
Metals	180.7	138.9	216.7
Machinery and equipment . .	146.6	103.2	111.8
Food products	111.9	206.7	176.4
Energy products	277.8	371.5	335.2
Total (incl. others)	3,528.2	3,235.8	3,264.7

Source: Center for Economic Research, Tashkent, *Uzbek Economic Trends*.

PRINCIPAL TRADING PARTNERS
(US $ million)

Imports	2005	2006	2007
China, People's Republic . . .	253.2	446.7	790.9
Germany	313.4	306.5	395.9
Italy	68.2	44.8	74.1
Kazakhstan	253.5	313.3	373.9
Korea, Republic	542.4	652.0	778.2
Russia	946.6	1,194.9	1,475.3
Tajikistan	73.2	74.2	88.5
Turkey	166.2	193.6	247.6
Ukraine	165.7	204.8	244.4
USA	80.9	59.3	97.6
Total (incl. others)	3,551.6	4,290.9	5,678.5

Exports	2005	2006	2007
Bangladesh	163.1	214.6	256.1
China, People's Republic . . .	410.0	514.4	333.5
Hungary	17.0	140.6	358.6
Japan	113.0	161.7	131.7
Kazakhstan	236.4	292.2	348.8
Poland	243.3	575.6	633.9
Russia	820.0	1,172.4	1,445.8
Tajikistan	139.0	160.3	191.4
Turkey	235.9	377.9	558.0
Ukraine	186.7	230.7	275.3
Total (incl. others)	3,467.5	4,944.3	5,912.5

Note: Data reflect the IMF's direction of trade methodology and, as a result, the totals may not be equal to those presented for trade in commodities.

Source: Asian Development Bank.

Transport

RAILWAYS
(traffic)

	2002	2003	2004
Passenger-km (million) . . .	2	2	2
Freight ton-km (million) . . .	18	19	18

Source: UN, *Statistical Yearbook*.

CIVIL AVIATION
(estimated traffic on scheduled services)

	2001	2002	2003
Kilometres flown (million) . .	57	39	40
Passengers carried ('000) . . .	2,256	1,451	1,466
Passenger-km (million) . . .	5,268	3,835	3,889
Total ton-km (million)	580	417	424

Source: UN, *Statistical Yearbook*.

Tourism

FOREIGN VISITOR ARRIVALS
('000, incl. excursionists)

Region of origin	2002	2003	2004
Africa	1.0	1.0	1.0
Americas	4.1	2.0	12.0
East Asia and the Pacific . . .	195.1	145.0	140.0
Europe	99.8	51.0	68.6
Middle East	23.5	24.0	30.0
South Asia	8.0	8.0	10.0
Total	331.5	231.0	261.6

Tourism receipts (US $ million, excl. passenger transport): 68 in 2002; 48 in 2003; 57 in 2004.

Source: World Tourism Organization.

Communications Media

	2003	2004	2005
Telephones ('000 main lines in use)	1,717.1	1,750.4	1,793.5
Mobile cellular telephones ('000			
subscribers)	320.8	544.1	720.0
Internet users ('000)	492.0	675.0	880.0
Broadband subscribers ('000) . .	2.8	5.5	8.3

Source: International Telecommunication Union.

2006: Internet users ('000) 1,700.0 (Source: International Telecommunication Union).

Book production: 1,003 titles and 30,914,000 copies in 1996 (Source: UNESCO, *Statistical Yearbook*).

Daily newspapers: 3 titles and 75,000 copies (average circulation) in 1996; 5 titles in 2004 (Sources: UNESCO, *Statistical Yearbook*; UNESCO Institute for Statistics).

Non-daily newspapers: 350 titles and 1,404,000 copies (average circulation) in 1996 (Source: UNESCO, *Statistical Yearbook*).

Other periodicals: 81 titles and 684,000 copies (average circulation) in 1996 (Source: UNESCO, *Statistical Yearbook*).

Radio receivers ('000 in use): 10,800 in 1997 (Source: UNESCO, *Statistical Yearbook*).

Television receivers ('000 in use): 7,000 in 2001 (Source: International Telecommunication Union).

Facsimile machines (number in use): 3,325 in 2001 (Source: International Telecommunication Union).

Education

(2006, unless otherwise indicated)

	Schools	Teachers	Students
Pre-primary	6,413	96,100*	562,200
Primary			1,905,693*
Secondary:	9,816†	463,100	
general			5,715,100
teacher training . .	n.a.	2,464‡	35,411‡
vocational	1,052	7,900*	214,500*
Higher	63§	18,400*	263,600§
Universities	20*	n.a.	131,100*

* 1994/95.
† Including 20 evening schools.
‡ 1993.
§ 2004.

Sources: UNESCO, *Statistical Yearbook* and Center for Economic Research, Tashkent.

Adult literacy rate (UNESCO estimates): 99.3% (males 99.6%; females 98.9%) in 2002 (Source: UN Development Programme, *Human Development Report*).

Directory

The Constitution

A new Constitution was adopted by the Supreme Council on 8 December 1992. It declares Uzbekistan to be a secular, democratic and presidential republic. Basic human rights are guaranteed. The principal features of the Constitution, as subsequently revised, are as follows:

THE OLY MAJLIS

The highest legislative body is the Oly Majlis (Supreme Assembly). The Oly Majlis comprises two chambers: the Qoqunchilik palatasi Kengashi (Legislative Chamber); and the Senat (Senate). The 120 deputies of the Qoqunchilik palatasi Kengashi are elected for a term of five years. Of the 100 members of the Senat, 84 members are indirectly elected by regional Council members, and 16 are appointed by the President of the Republic. The Oly Majlis may be dissolved by the President, with the agreement of the Constitutional Court. The Oly Majlis enacts legislation and constitutional legislation and elects its own officials, the judges of the higher courts and the Chairman of the State Committee for Environmental Protection. It confirms the President's appointments to ministerial office, the procuracy-general and the governorship of the Central Bank. It must ratify international treaties, changes to borders and presidential decrees on emergency situations. Legislation may be initiated by the deputies, by the President, by the higher courts, by the Procurator-General and by the Autonomous Republic of Qoraqalpog'iston.

PRESIDENT OF THE REPUBLIC

The President of the Republic, who is directly elected by the people for a seven-year term, is Head of State and holds supreme executive power. (The term of office was extended, with immediate effect, from five to seven years in April 2002.) An individual may be elected President for a maximum of two consecutive terms*. The President is required to form and supervise the Cabinet of Ministers, appointing the Prime Minister and Ministers, subject to confirmation by the Oly Majlis. The President also nominates the candidates for appointment to the higher courts and certain offices of state, subject to confirmation by the Oly Majlis. The President appoints the judges of the lower courts and the hokims (governors) of the regions. Legislation may be initiated, reviewed and returned to the Oly Majlis by the President, who must promulgate all laws. The President may dissolve the Oly Majlis. The President is also Commander-in-Chief of the Armed Forces and may declare a state of emergency or a state of war, subject to confirmation by the Oly Majlis within three days.

* Despite this constitutional restriction, ISLAM KARIMOV was elected to a third consecutive term of office in December 2007, his second term having formally ended in January of that year.

THE CABINET OF MINISTERS

The Cabinet of Ministers is the Government of the republic; it is subordinate to the President, who appoints its Prime Minister, Deputy Prime Ministers and Ministers, subject to the approval of the legislature. Local government is carried out by elected councils and appointed hokims, the latter having significant personal authority and responsibility.

JUDICATURE

The exercise of judicial power is independent of government. The higher courts, of which the judges are nominated by the President and confirmed by the Oly Majlis, consist of the Constitutional Court, the Supreme Court and the High Economic Court. There is also a Supreme Court of the Sovereign Republic of Qoraqalpog'iston. Lower courts, including economic courts, are based in the regions, districts and towns. The Procurator-General's office is responsible for supervising the observance of the law.

The Government

HEAD OF STATE

President of the Republic: ISLAM A. KARIMOV (elected by Supreme Soviet 24 March 1990; term of office extended by popular referendum 26 March 1995; re-elected 9 January 2000 and 23 December 2007; inaugurated 16 January 2008).

CABINET OF MINISTERS
(September 2008)

Prime Minister: SHAVKAT M. MIRZIYOYEV.

First Deputy Prime Minister, responsible for the Economic Sector and Foreign Economic Relations, and Minister of Finance: RUSTAM S. AZIMOV.

Deputy Prime Minister, responsible for the Construction Sector, Industry, Housing and Municipal Services and Transport: NODIRXON M. XANOV.

Deputy Prime Minister, responsible for Machine-construction, Metallurgy, Petroleum and Natural Gas, Geology, Elec-

trical Energy, Chemical Production, Standardization and Metrology and State Reserves: ERGASH R. SHOISMATOV.

Deputy Prime Minister, responsible for Information Systems and Telecommunications, Director-General of the Communications and Information Agency of Uzbekistan: ABDULLA N. ARIPOV.

Deputy Prime Minister: RUSTAM S. QOSIMOV.

Deputy Prime Minister, Chairman of the Committee of Women of Uzbekistan: FARIDA SH. AKBAROVA.

Minister of the Economy: BATIR A. XODJAYEV.

Minister of Foreign Economic Relations, Investment and Trade: ELYOR M. G'ANIYEV.

Minister of Labour and Social Protection: AKTAM A. XAITOV (acting).

Minister of Culture and Sports: RUSTAM J. QURBONOV.

Minister of Internal Affairs: BAHODIR A. MATLYUBOV.

Minister of Foreign Affairs: VLADIMIR I. NOROV.

Minister of Defence: QOBUL R. BERDIYEV.

Minister of National Education: G'AYRAT B. SHOUMAROV.

Minister of Higher and Secondary Specialized Education: AZIMJON P. PARPIEV.

Minister of Agriculture and Water Resources: SAYFIDDIN U. ISMOILOV.

Minister of Justice: RAVSHAN A. MUXITDINOV.

Minister of Health: FERUZ G. NAZIROV.

Minister of Emergency Situations: BAKHTIYOR SUBANOV.

Note: The Constitution provides for the Chairman of the Council of Ministers of the Republic of Qoraqalpog'iston to serve as an ex officio member of the Council of Ministers of the Republic of Uzbekistan. Since March 2006 this position has been held by BAXODIR YANGIBOYEV. The following are also members of the Cabinet of Ministers: the Chairman of the Central Bank and chairmen of state committees and agencies.

MINISTRIES

Office of the President: 100163 Tashkent, O'zbekiston shoh ko'ch. 43; tel. (71) 239-54-04; fax (71) 239-53-25; e-mail presidents_office@press-service.uz; internet www.press-service.uz.

Office of the Cabinet of Ministers: 100078 Tashkent, Mustaqillik maydoni 5; tel. (71) 239-82-95; fax (71) 239-84-63; internet www.gov.uz.

Ministry of Agriculture and Water Resources: 100004 Tashkent, A. Navoiy ko'ch. 4; tel. (71) 244-21-30; fax (71) 232-21-59; e-mail qshv@intal.uz; internet www.agro.uz.

Ministry of Culture and Sport: 100159 Tashkent, Mustaqillik maydoni 5; tel. (71) 239-46-11; fax (71) 239-45-52; e-mail madaniyat@sport.uz; internet www.madaniyat.sport.uz.

Ministry of Defence: 100000 Tashkent, Ak. Abdullaev ko'ch. 100; tel. (71) 269-82-43; fax (71) 269-82-28.

Ministry of the Economy: 100003 Tashkent, O'zbekiston shoh ko'ch. 45A; tel. (71) 232-63-20; fax (71) 232-63-72; e-mail mineconomy@mmes.gov.uz; internet www.mineconomy.uz.

Ministry for Emergency Situations: 100084 Tashkent, Yunusobodn tumani, Kichik xalka yo'li–4; tel. (71) 239-16-85; fax (71) 233-09-55; e-mail mes@st.uz; internet www.mchs.uz.

Ministry of Finance: 100008 Tashkent, Mustaqillik maydoni 5; tel. (71) 233-70-73; fax (71) 244-56-43; e-mail info@mf.uz; internet www.mf.uz.

Ministry of Foreign Affairs: 100029 Tashkent, O'zbekiston shoh ko'ch. 9; tel. (71) 233-64-75; fax (71) 239-15-17; e-mail rnews@mfa.uz; internet www.mfa.uz.

Ministry of Foreign Economic Relations, Investment and Trade: 100029 Tashkent, Shevchenko ko'ch. 1; tel. (71) 238-50-00; fax (71) 238-51-00; e-mail secretary@mfer.uz; internet www.mfer.uz.

Ministry of Health: 100011 Tashkent, A. Navoiy ko'ch. 12; tel. (71) 241-16-91; fax (71) 241-10-33; e-mail minzdrav@med.uz; internet www.minzdr.uz.

Ministry of Higher and Specialized Secondary Education: 100100 Tashkent, Bobur ko'ch. 53; tel. (71) 252-77-45; fax 252-77-83; e-mail oliy@uzsci.net; internet www.edu.uz.

Ministry of Internal Affairs: 100029 Tashkent, Yu. Rajaby ko'ch. 1; tel. (71) 239-73-36; fax (71) 233-89-34; internet www.mvd.uz.

Ministry of Justice: 100047 Tashkent, Sayilgoh ko'ch. 5; tel. (71) 233-13-05; fax (71) 233-51-76; e-mail info@minjust.gov.uz; internet www.minjust.uz.

Ministry of Labour and Social Security: 100100 Tashkent, A. Avloniy ko'ch. 20A; tel. (71) 239-41-21; fax (71) 239-41-12; e-mail mehnat@uzpak.uz; internet www.mintrud.uz.

Ministry of National Education: 100078 Tashkent, Mustaqillik maydoni 5; tel. (71) 239-13-10; fax (71) 239-19-34; e-mail info@uzedu.uz; internet www.uzedu.uz.

President

Presidential Election, 23 December 2007

Candidate	Votes	%
Islam Karimov (Liberal Democratic Party of Uzbekistan)	13,008,357	88.10
Asliddin Rustamov (People's Democratic Party of Uzbekistan)	468,064	3.17
Dilorom Tashmuhamedova (Justice Social Democratic Party of Uzbekistan)	434,111	2.94
Akmal Saidov (Independent)	420,815	2.85
Total*	14,765,444	100.00

* Including 434,097 invalid votes (2.94% of the total).

Legislature

The Oly Majlis (Supreme Assembly) is a bicameral legislative body, comprising the 100-member upper chamber, the Senat (Senate), and the 120-member lower chamber, the Qoqunchilik palatasi Kengashi (Legislative Chamber).

Qoqunchilik palatasi Kengashi
(Legislative Chamber)

100008 Tashkent, Xalqlar Do'stligi shoh ko'ch. 1; tel. (71) 239-87-07; fax (71) 239-41-51; internet www.parliament.gov.uz.

Speaker: DILOROM H. TASHMUHAMEDOVA.

General Election, 26 December 2004 and 9 January 2005

Parties, etc.	Seats
Movement of Entrepreneurs and Businessmen—Liberal Democratic Party of Uzbekistan	41
People's Democratic Party of Uzbekistan	28
Self-Sacrificers' National Democratic Party (Fidokorlar)	18
National Revival Democratic Party of Uzbekistan (Milliy Tiklanish)	11
Justice Social Democratic Party of Uzbekistan (Adolat)	10
Citizens' groups	12
Total	120

Senat
(Senate)

100029 Tashkent, Mustaqillik maydoni 6; tel. (71) 238-26-66; fax (71) 238-29-01; e-mail info@senat.uz; internet www.senat.gov.uz.

Of the 100 members of the chamber, 84 members are indirectly elected by regional Council members and 16 are appointed by the President of the Republic. The first presidential appointees to the Senat were announced on 14 January 2005, while the first indirect elections of senators were held on 17–20 January 2005. The inaugural session of the chamber convened on 27 January.

Speaker: ILGIZAR M. SOBIROV.

Local Government

Uzbekistan contains one Sovereign Republic (Qoraqalpog'iston), 12 viloyats (oblasts or regions), and one city (the capital, Tashkent). There were further local subdivisions, the basic unit being the mahallah, the neighbourhood or commune. From January 1992 the main figure in local government was the hokim (governor), who was appointed as the chief executive figure in the region by the President of the Republic. There is also a regional Council in each viloyat.

CITY

Toshkent (Tashkent) City Administration: 100060 Tashkent, Mirobod tumani, Movarounnaxr ko'ch. 3; tel. (71) 233-90-69; fax (71) 233-65-88; e-mail hokimiat@online.ru; internet www.tashkent.uz; Hokim ABDUQAHHOR H. TO'XTAEV.

VILOYATS

Andijon Viloyat Administration: 170120 Andijon, A. Fitrat ko'ch. 239; tel. (74) 22-25-82; fax (74) 22-19-32; e-mail andwork@uzpak.uz; internet www.andijan.uz; Hokim AHMAD T. USMONOV.

Buxoro Viloyat Administration: 200118 Buxoro, I. Mo'minov ko'ch. 1; tel. (365) 224-41-10; fax (365) 223-05-95; e-mail info@buxoro.uz; internet www.bv.uz; Hokim SAMOYDIN Q. XUSENOV.

Farg'ona Viloyat Administration: 150100 Farg'ona, A. Navoiy ko'ch. 13; tel. (73) 24-70-70; fax (73) 24-74-51; internet www.ferghana .uz; Hokim MATAMISAK B. GAFUROV.

Jizzax Viloyat Administration: 130100 Jizzax, Sh. Rashidov shoh ko'ch. 63; tel. (22) 6-39-54; fax (22) 6-64-84; e-mail jizvhok@rol.uz; Hokim UBAYDULLA YA. ALIQULOV.

Namangan Viloyat Administration: 160100 Namangan, A. Rahimov ko'ch. 57; tel. (69) 6-60-08; fax (69) 6-57-22; e-mail namangan1@ uzpak.uz; internet naman.uzpak.uz; Hokim IKROMHON X. NAJMIDDI-NOV.

Navoiy Viloyat Administration: 210103 Navoiy, Xalqlar Do'stligi ko'ch. 77A; tel. (79) 23-30-10; fax (79) 23-71-25; e-mail navoi@gov.uz; internet navoi.gov.uz; Hokim BAHRIDDIN M. RO'ZIYEV.

Qashqadaryo Viloyat Administration: 180100 Qashqadaryo viloyat, Qarshi, Mustaqillik maydoni 1; tel. (75) 221-12-88; fax (75) 221-13-40; e-mail kadr.qv@uzpak.uz; internet www.qashqadaryo .uz; Hokim NURIDDIN Z. ZAYNIYEV.

Samarqand Viloyat Administration: 140111 Samarqand, Ko'ksaroy ko'ch. 1; tel. (66) 35-03-42; Hokim O'KTAM I. BARNOYEV.

Sirdaryo Viloyat Administration: 120100 Sirdaryo viloyat, Guliston, Mustaqillik ko'ch. 60; tel. (67) 25-07-78; fax (67) 25-34-31; e-mail shokim@uzpak.uz; Hokim ABDURAHIM A. JALOLOV.

Surxondaryo Viloyat Administration: 190102 Surxondaryo viloyat, Termiz, At-Termiziy maydoni 1; tel. (76) 2-87-58; fax (76) 2-70-19; e-mail termez_hokim2@uzpak.uz; Hokim TUROBJON I. DJURAEV.

Toshkent (Tashkent) Viloyat Administration: 100060 Tashkent, Mirobod tumani, Movarounnaxr ko'ch. 17; tel. (71) 233-67-16; fax (71) 236-73-00; internet www.tashvil.gov.uz; Hokim MIRZA-MASHRAP KUCHCHIEV.

Xorazm Viloyat Administration: 220100 Xorazm viloyat, Urgench, Al-Xorazmiy ko'ch. 29; tel. (62) 24-31-81; fax (62) 26-44-15; Hokim OLLABERGAN X. OLLABERGANOV.

Election Commission

Central Election Commission (O'zbekiston Respublikasi Markaziy Saylov Kommissiyasi): 100000 Tashkent; tel. (71) 239-15-72; fax (71) 239-43-91; internet www.elections.uz; mems approved by the Oly Majlis; Chair. MIRZO-ULUG'BEK E. ABDUSALOMOV.

Political Organizations

Following Uzbekistan's independence (achieved in August 1991), the ruling People's Democratic Party of Uzbekistan (PDPU—the successor to the Communist Party of the Uzbek SSR) took increasingly repressive measures against opposition and Islamist parties. A new law on political parties was approved in 1996; among other provisions, the law prohibited the establishment of parties on a religious or ethnic basis and stipulated a minimum membership, per party, of 5,000 people (with stipulation that membership be distributed across the country's regions). From February 2004 the minimum membership requirement was increased to 20,000 people. Since independence a number of opposition elements have been based abroad, particularly in Russia.

Free Peasants' Party (Ozod Dehqonlar partiyasi—Ozod Dehqonlar): 100000 Tashkent; f. 2003; denied registration; Exec. Sec. of Political Council NIGORA HIDOYATOVA; Ideological Leader BABUR MALIKOV (in USA).

Freedom Democratic Party of Uzbekistan (O'zbekiston Erk Demokratik Partiyasi—Erk): 100055 Tashkent, Ipakchi ko'ch. 38; tel. (71) 220-65-30; e-mail erkparty@yahoo.com; f. 1990; banned in 1993; Chair. MUHAMMAD SALIH (based in Norway).

Islamic Renaissance Party: 100000 Tashkent; banned in 1991; advocates introduction of a political system based on the tenets of Islam; leader ABDULLAH UTAYEV 'disappeared' in 1992.

Justice Social Democratic Party of Uzbekistan ('Adolat' Sotsial Demokratik Partiyasi—Adolat): 100047 Tashkent, Musahanov ko'ch. 103; tel. (71) 233-26-75; f. 1995; advocates respect of human rights, improvement of social justice and consolidation of democratic reform; supports President Karimov; First Sec. TURG'UNPO'LAT O. DAMINOV; 50,000 mems (2003).

Liberal Democratic Party of Uzbekistan (O'zbekiston Liberal Demokratik Partiyasi—O'zlidep): 100015 Tashkent, Mirobod tumani, Nukus ko'ch. 73A; tel. (71) 233-28-46; e-mail uzlidep@intal .uz; f. 2003; supports President Karimov; Chair. MUHAMMADJON A. AHMADJONOV; 142,000 members (Dec. 2004).

National Revival Democratic Party of Uzbekistan (O'zbekiston Milliy Tiklanish Demokratik Partiyasi—Milliy Tiklanish): 100000 Tashkent, Navoiy ko'ch. 30; tel. (71) 244-81-28; f. 1995; supports President Karimov; Leader AZIZ KAYUMOV; Chair. of Central Council XURSHID N. DO'STMUHAMMEDOV; 50,000 mems (2003).

People's Democratic Party of Uzbekistan (O'zbekiston Xalq demokratik partiyasi): 100029 Tashkent, Mustaqillik maydoni 5/1; tel. (71) 239-83-11; fax (71) 233-59-34; f. 1991; successor of Communist Party of Uzbekistan; Leader ASLIDDIN A. RUSTAMOV; c. 580,000 mems (2003).

Self-Sacrificers' National Democratic Party (Fidokorlar Milliy Demokratik Partiyasi—Fidokorlar): 100000 Tashkent, Xalqlar Do's-tligi ko'ch. 1; tel. (71) 239-45-53; f. 2000; incorporates fmr Watan Taraqqioti (Progress of the Fatherland) party; supports President Karimov; First Sec. AXTAM S. TURSUNOV; 61,000 mems (2003).

Unity People's Movement Party ('Birlik' Xalq Harakati Partiyasi—Birlik): c/o Union of Writers of Uzbekistan, 100000 Tashkent, Neru ko'ch. 1; tel. (71) 233-63-74; e-mail webmaster@birlik.net; internet www.birlik.net; f. 1988; leading opposition group, banned in 1992; registered as a social movement; refused registration as a political party 2004; Chair. Prof. ABDURAKHIM PULAT; Sec.-Gen. VASILA INOYATOVA.

The militant Islamist group **Islamic Movement of Uzbekistan (IMU)** was founded in 1999. It was banned by the Uzbek Government in 1999 and its leaders sentenced to death *in absentia* in 2000. The IMU's activities were believed to have been seriously curtailed after the death of one its leaders during the US-led military campaign in Afghanistan that commenced in late 2001. The transnational militant Islamist **Hizb-ut-Tahrir al-Islami (Party of Islamic Liberation)** was believed to operate in Uzbekistan. In 2004 President Karimov accused the organization of instigating a series of suicide bomb attacks. As in neighbouring states, the organization was proscribed in Uzbekistan. A related organization, **Akramiya**, also banned, was founded in 1996 by AKRAM YULDOSHEV, who was given a 17-year gaol sentence in 1999 for alleged involvement in terrorist activity. Akramiya apparently regards violence as an appropriate means of pursuing its goals.

Diplomatic Representation

EMBASSIES IN UZBEKISTAN

Afghanistan: 100047 Tashkent, Gulomov ko'ch. 73; tel. (71) 234-84-58; fax (71) 234-84-65; e-mail afgemuz@mail.tps.uz; Ambassador FAROOQ BARAKI.

Algeria: 100000 Tashkent, Murtozaev ko'ch. 6; tel. (71) 234-17-74; fax (71) 220-62-75; Ambassador HASEN LASKRI.

Azerbaijan: 100000 Tashkent, Sharq Tongi ko'ch. 25; tel. (71) 273-61-67; fax (71) 273-26-58; e-mail sefir@tsk.sarkor.uz; Ambassador NAMIQ ABBASOV.

Bangladesh: 100015 Tashkent, 1-chi Kunaev ko'ch. 17; tel. (71) 252-26-92; fax (71) 220-67-11; e-mail bdoot.tas@online.ru; Ambassador A. B. M. ABDUS SALAM.

Belarus: 100047 Tashkent, Ya. G'ulomov ko'ch. 75; tel. (71) 220-72-54; fax (71) 220-72-53; e-mail uzbekistan@belembassy.org; internet www.uzbekistan.belembassy.org; Ambassador IGOR SOKOL.

Bulgaria: 100000 Tashkent, Rakatboshi ko'ch. 52; tel. (71) 258-48-88; fax (71) 252-39-52; e-mail misiyabg@bcc.com.uz; internet www .mfa.bg/tashkent; Chargé d'affaires STOYANKA G. RUSINOVA.

China, People's Republic: 100047 Tashkent, Ya. G'ulomov ko'ch. 79; tel. (71) 233-80-88; fax (71) 233-47-35; e-mail chinaemb@bcc.com .uz; internet uz.china-embassy.org; Ambassador YU HONGJUN.

Czech Republic: 100041 Tashkent, Mirzo-Ulugbek Tumani, Navnihol ko'ch. 6; tel. (71) 220-60-71; fax (71) 220-60-75; e-mail tashkent@embassy.mzv.cz; internet www.mzv.cz/tashkent; Ambassador ALEŠ FOJTÍK.

Egypt: 100115 Tashkent, Chilonzor ko'ch. 53A; tel. (71) 220-50-08; fax (71) 220-64-52; Ambassador NADIA IBRAHIM KFAFI.

France: 100041 Tashkent, Oxunboboev ko'ch. 25; tel. (71) 233-53-82; fax (71) 233-51-97; e-mail presse@ambafrance-uz.org; internet www .ambafrance-uz.org; Ambassador HUGUES PERNET.

Georgia: 100170 Tashkent, A. Muhitdinov ko'ch. 6; tel. (71) 262-62-43; fax (71) 262-91-39; e-mail gruzemb@geo-embassy.co.uz; Chargé d'affaires GIORGI CHKHEIDZE.

Germany: 100017 Tashkent, Sh. Rashidov ko'ch. 15, POB 4337; tel. (71) 220-84-40; fax (71) 220-66-93; e-mail info@taschkent.diplo.de; internet www.taschkent.diplo.de; Ambassador MATTHIAS MEYER.

India: 100000 Tashkent, Qarabulak ko'ch. 15–16; tel. (71) 240-09-83; fax (71) 240-09-99; e-mail indhoc@buzton.com; internet www.indembassy.uz; Ambassador SKAND RANJAN TAYAL.

Indonesia: 100000 Tashkent, Ya. G'ulomov ko'ch. 73; tel. (71) 232-02-36; fax (71) 220-65-40; e-mail tashkent@indonesia.embassy.uz; internet www.indonesia.embassy.uz; Ambassador SJAHRIL SABARUDIN.

Iran: 100007 Tashkent, Parkent ko'ch. 20; tel. (71) 268-69-68; fax (71) 220-67-61; e-mail iriemuz@hotmail.com; Ambassador MUHAMMAD KESHOVARZODA.

Israel: 100000 Tashkent, A. Kahhor ko'ch. 3; tel. (71) 240-75-00; fax (71) 240-75-55; e-mail info@tashkent.mfa.gov.il; internet tashkent.mfa.gov.il; Ambassador HILEL NEWMAN.

Italy: 100031 Tashkent, Yusuf Xos Hojib ko'ch. 40; tel. (71) 252-11-19; fax (71) 220-66-06; e-mail segreteria.tashkent@esteri.it; internet www.ambtashkent.esteri.it; Ambassador GIOVANNI RICCIULLI.

Japan: 100047 Tashkent, S. Azimov ko'ch., 1-tor 28; tel. (71) 220-80-60; fax (71) 220-80-77; internet www.uz.emb-japan.go.jp; Ambassador TSYTOMU HIRAOKA.

Jordan: 100000 Tashkent, Farhod ko'ch. 9; tel. (71) 274-24-79; fax (71) 220-66-44; e-mail jordanembuzb@mail.ru; Ambassador MUHAMMAD NOUR OTHMAN YOUSEF BALKAR.

Kazakhstan: 100015 Tashkent, Chekhov ko'ch. 23; tel. (71) 252-16-54; fax (71) 252-16-50; e-mail kazembassy@kaz.uz; Ambassador ASKAR I. MYRZAHMETOV.

Korea, Democratic People's Republic: 100000 Tashkent, Usmon Nosir ko'ch. 95A; tel. (71) 252-63-16; fax (71) 252-63-15; Ambassador RI TONG PHAL.

Korea, Republic: 100000 Tashkent, Afrosiab ko'ch. 7; tel. (71) 252-31-51; fax (71) 220-62-48; e-mail admin1@korea.anet.uz; internet uzb.mofat.go.kr; Ambassador KYUN JE-MIN.

Kuwait: 100000 Tashkent, Batumi ko'ch. 2; tel. (71) 220-58-88; fax (71) 220-84-96; Ambassador VALID AHMAD AL-KANDARI.

Kyrgyzstan: 100000 Tashkent, X. Samatov ko'ch. 30; tel. (71) 237-47-94; fax (71) 220-72-94; e-mail erkindik@sarkor.uz; Ambassador AZIZBEK M. MADMAROV.

Latvia: 100000 Tashkent, A. Lashkarbegi ko'ch. 16A; tel. (71) 237-22-15; fax (71) 220-70-36; e-mail embassy.uzbekistan@mfa.gov.lv; Ambassador IGORS APOKINS.

Malaysia: 100031 Tashkent, M. Yaqubov ko'ch. 28–30; tel. (71) 233-32-27; fax (71) 233-32-71; e-mail mwtskent@rol.uz; Ambassador ABDUL AZIZ BIN HARUN.

Pakistan: 100115 Tashkent, Kichik Halqa Yoli ko'ch. 15; tel. (71) 248-05-25; fax (71) 244-92-33; e-mail parepuzb@online.ru; Ambassador SAJJAD KAMRAN.

Poland: 100084 Tashkent, Firdavsiy ko'ch. 66; tel. (71) 220-86-50; fax (71) 220-86-51; e-mail ambasada@bcc.com.uz; internet www.taszkent.polemb.net; Chargé d'affaires a.i. JERZY STANKIEWICZ.

Romania: 100000 Tashkent, Rejametov ko'ch. 44A; tel. (71) 252-63-55; fax (71) 220-75-67; e-mail romanian_embassy@sarkor.uz; Ambassador CONSTANTIN ALEXA.

Russia: 100015 Tashkent, Nukus ko'ch. 83; tel. (71) 120-35-04; fax (71) 120-35-09; e-mail embassy@russia.uz; internet www.russia.uz; Ambassador FARIT M. MUKHAMETSHIN.

Saudi Arabia: 100000 Tashkent.

Slovakia: 100070 Tashkent, K. Beshyogoch ko'ch. 38; tel. (71) 220-68-52; fax (71) 220-68-51; e-mail slovakia@buzton.com; internet www.tashkent.mfa.sk; Ambassador JOSEF MAČISÁK.

Switzerland: 100070 Tashkent, U. Nosyr ko'ch., tupik 1/4; tel. (71) 220-67-38; fax (71) 220-62-59; e-mail tas.vertretung@eda.admin.ch; internet www.eda.admin.ch/tashkent; Ambassador Dr PETER BURKHARD.

Tajikistan: 100000 Tashkent, A. Kahhor ko'ch., 6-chi tor, 61; tel. (71) 254-99-66; fax (71) 254-89-69; e-mail tajembuz@yandex.ru; Ambassador BOBOKHON MAKHMADOV.

Turkey: 100000 Tashkent, Ya. G'ulomov ko'ch. 87; tel. (71) 233-03-00; fax (71) 213-03-33; e-mail turemb@bcc.com.uz; Ambassador RESHIT UMAN.

Turkmenistan: 100000 Tashkent, 1-chi Katta Mirobod ko'ch. 10; tel. (71) 220-52-78; fax (71) 220-52-81; Ambassador SOLTAN PIRMUHAMEDOV.

Ukraine: 100000 Tashkent, Ya. G'ulomov ko'ch. 68; tel. (71) 236-08-12; fax (71) 233-10-89; e-mail emb_uz@mfa.gov.ua; internet www.ukraine.uz; Ambassador VYACHESLAV V. POKHVALSKY.

United Kingdom: 100000 Tashkent, ul. Ya. G'ulomov ko'ch. 67; tel. (71) 220-15-00; fax (71) 220-15-20; e-mail brit@emb.uz; internet www.ukinuzbekistan.fco.gov.uk; Ambassador IAIN KELLY.

USA: 100093 Tashkent, Moyqorghon ko'ch. 3, Yunusobod District; tel. (71) 220-54-50; fax (71) 220-54-48; e-mail consulartashkent@state.gov; internet www.usembassy.uz; Ambassador RICHARD B. NORLAND.

Viet Nam: 100000 Tashkent, Sh. Rashidov ko'ch. 100; tel. (71) 234-03-93; fax (71) 220-62-65; e-mail dsqvntas@online.ru; Ambassador DO VAN DONG.

Judicial System

Supreme Court of the Republic of Uzbekistan
(O'zbekiston Respublikasi Oliy sud)

100000 Tashkent, A. Qodiriy ko'ch. 1; tel. and fax (71) 244-62-93; internet www.supcourt.gov.uz.

Chairman: FARUHA F. MUHITDINOVA.

Office of the Prosecutor-General: 100000 Tashkent, Ya. G'ulomov ko'ch. 66; tel. (71) 233-20-66; Prosecutor-Gen. RASHIDJON H. QODIROV.

Constitutional Court (Konstitutsiyaviy sud): 100000 Tashkent, Mustaqillik maydoni 6; tel. (71) 239-80-20; fax (71) 239-86-36; e-mail interconcourt@sarkor.uz; Chair. (vacant); Dep. Chair. BAKHTIYAR MIRBABAEV.

Supreme Economic Court (Oliy Xo'jalik Sudi): 100097 Tashkent, Cho'ponota ko'ch. 6; tel. (71) 267-36-18; fax (71) 273-84-78; e-mail economical-court@sarkor.uz; internet www.economical-court.uz; Chair. DILMURAD A. MIRZAKARIMOV.

Religion

The Constitution of 8 December 1992 stipulates that, while there is freedom of worship and expression, there may be no state religion or ideology. A new law on religion was adopted in May 1998, which severely restricted the activities of religious organizations.

The most widespread religion in Uzbekistan is Islam; the majority of ethnic Uzbeks are Sunni Muslims (Hanafi school), but the number of Salafi (often referred to, inaccurately, as Wahhabi) communities is increasing. At 1 October 2002 there were 1,965 Islamic organizations registered in Uzbekistan, including 11 educational institutions. Most ethnic Slavs in Uzbekistan are adherents of Orthodox Christianity: there were 36 Russian Orthodox organizations registered in Uzbekistan at 1 October 2002. At the end of 1993 there were some 32,000 Jews in Uzbekistan; many Jews have since emigrated to Israel.

State Committee for Religious Affairs: 100069 Tashkent, 18-chi Zarqaynar ko'ch., tupik 47A; tel. (71) 239-10-14; fax (71) 239-17-63; e-mail info@religions.uz; Chair. SHAAZIM SH. MINAVAROV.

ISLAM

Muslim Board of Central Asia: 100002 Tashkent, Zarkainar ko'ch. 103, Madrese 'Barakhan'; tel. (71) 240-39-33; fax (71) 240-08-31; f. 1943 as state body with 'official' spiritual jurisdiction over Muslims in the Kyrgyz, Tajik, Turkmen and Uzbek SSRs; Chair. USMON OLIMOV (Chief Mufti of Mowarounnahr—Central Asia).

CHRISTIANITY

Roman Catholic Church

The Church is represented in Uzbekistan by an Apostolic Administration, established in January 2005. There were an estimated 4,000 adherents at 31 December 2006.

Apostolic Administrator: Most Rev. JERZY MACULEWICZ, 100047 Tashkent, Musahanov ko'ch. 80/1; tel. (71) 233-70-25; fax (71) 233-70-35; e-mail adm.ap@agnuz.info.

Russian Orthodox Church (Moscow Patriarchate)

Eparchy of Tashkent and Central Asia (Moscow Patriarchate)—Orthodox Church of Central Asia: 100047 Tashkent, S. Azimov ko'ch. 22/3D; tel. (71) 233-33-21; fax (71) 236-79-39; e-mail church@albatros.uz; internet www.pravoslavie.uz; Metropolitan of Tashkent and Central Asia VLADIMIR (IKIM); has jurisdiction over Kyrgyzstan, Tajikistan and Uzbekistan.

JUDAISM

Chief Rabbi: Rabbi DAVID GUREVICH, 100100 Tashkent, Shohzhahon ko'ch. 30; tel. (71) 252-59-78; fax (71) 220-64-31; e-mail jewish@jewish.uz; internet www.jewish.uz.

The Press

The publications listed below are in Uzbek, unless otherwise stated.

REGULATORY AUTHORITY

Uzbek Agency for Press and Information: 100129 Tashkent, Navoiy ko'ch. 30; tel. (71) 233-65-03; fax (71) 233-66-45; e-mail info@ aci.uz; internet aci.uz; f. 2002; Gen. Dir ABDULLA N. ARIPOV.

PRINCIPAL NEWSPAPERS

Adolat (Justice): 100000 Tashkent, Matbuotchilar ko'ch. 32; tel. (71) 233-41-89; f. 1995; organ of the Justice Social Democratic Party of Uzbekistan (Adolat); Editor TOHTAMUROD TOSHEV; circ. 5,900.

Biznes-vestnik Vostoka (Business Bulletin of the East): 100000 Tashkent, Buxoro ko'ch. 26; tel. (71) 232-27-30; fax (71) 232-27-29; e-mail info@uzreport.com; f. 1991; 3 a week; in Russian and English; economic and financial news; Editor-in-Chief RALIF NIGMATULLIN (acting); circ. 10,000 (Russian), 1,000 (English).

Fidokor (Self-Sacrificer): 100000 Tashkent, Xalqlar Do'stligi ko'ch. 1; tel. (71) 239-45-53; weekly; organ of the Fidokorlar (Self-Sacrificers') National Democratic Party; Editor JALOLIDDIN SAFAYEV; circ. 32,000.

Hurriyat (Freedom): 100000 Tashkent; tel. (71) 244-25-06; fax (71) 244-36-16; e-mail amir@uzpac.uz; f. 1996; independent; circ. 5,000.

Inson va Qonun (Person and Law): 100047 Tashkent, Sayilgoh ko'ch. 5; internet www.minjust.uz/uz/group.scm?groupId=4146; weekly; organ of the Ministry of Justice; Editor-in-Chief SHODIQUL HAMROEV.

Ma'rifat (Enlightenment): 100000 Tashkent, Matbuotchilar ko'ch. 32; tel. (71) 233-50-55; e-mail mariat@ars-inform.uz; f. 1931; 2 a week; Editor KHALIM SAIDOV; circ. 33,000 (2006).

Menejer (Manager): 100000 Tashkent, Buyuk Turon ko'ch. 41; tel. (71) 236-58-85; f. 1997; weekly; in Russian and Uzbek; commercial information and advertising; Editor KHOTAM ABDURAIMOV; circ. 15,000.

Mulkdor (Property Owner): 100083 Tashkent, Buyuk Turon ko'ch. 41; tel. (71) 239-21-96; f. 1994; weekly; Editor-in-Chief MIRODIL ABDURAKHMANOV; circ. 10,000.

Novyi Vek (New Age): 100060 Tashkent, Movarounnaxr ko'ch. 19; tel. (71) 233-48-55; fax (71) 233-76-84; f. 1992; fmrly *Kommercheskii Vestnik* (Commerical Herald); in Russian; Editor VALERII NIYAZMATOV; circ. 22,000.

O'zbekiston Adabiyoti va San'ati (Literature and Art of Uzbekistan): 100000 Tashkent, Matbuotchilar ko'ch. 32; tel. (71) 233-52-91; f. 1956; weekly; organ of the Union of Writers of Uzbekistan; Editor AKHMAJON MELIBOYEV; circ. 10,300.

O'zbekiston ovozi/Golos Uzbekistana (Voice of Uzbekistan): 100000 Tashkent, Matbuotchilar ko'ch. 32; tel. (71) 236-55-15; fax (71) 233-65-45; e-mail info@uzbekistonovozi.uz; internet www.uzbekistonovozi.uz; f. 1918; Uzbek and Russian edns; organ of the People's Democratic Party of Uzbekistan; Editor-in-Chief SAFAR OSTONOV.

Postda/Na postu: 100029 Tashkent, Yu. Rajaby ko'ch. 1; f. 1930; in Uzbek and Russian; military; Editor Z. ATAYEV.

Pravda Vostoka (Truth of the East): 100000 Tashkent, Matbuotchilar ko'ch. 32; tel. (71) 233-56-33; fax (71) 233-70-98; e-mail pvbox@ mail.ru; internet www.pv.uz; f. 1917; 5 a week; in Russian; organ of the Cabinet of Ministers; Editor ABBASKHAN USMANOV; circ. 12,000 (2008).

Savdogar (Trader): 100000 Tashkent, Buyuk Turon ko'ch. 41; tel. (71) 233-34-55; f. 1992; Editor MUHAMMAD ORAZMETOV; circ. 17,000.

Soliq va Bojxona Xabarlari: 100011 Tashkent, Abaya ko'ch. 4; tel. (71) 244-02-01; e-mail normapress@mail.ru; f. 1994; weekly; Editor MIKHAIL PERPER; circ. 25,000.

Sport: 100000 Tashkent, O'zbekiston shoh ko'ch. 98 A; tel. (71) 244-07-52; f. 1932; Editor HAYDAR AKBAROV; circ. 8,490.

Toshkent Xakikati/Tashkentskaya Pravda (Tashkent Truth): 100000 Tashkent, Matbuotchilar ko'ch. 32; tel. (71) 233-64-95; fax (71) 233-58-85; internet www.th.uz; f. 1954; 2 a week; Uzbek and Russian edns; Editor FATKHIDDIN MUKHITDINOV; circ. 19,000 (Uzbek edn), 6,400 (Russian edn).

Turkiston (Turkestan): 100000 Tashkent, Matbuotchilar ko'ch. 32; tel. (71) 236-56-58; f. 1925 as *Yash Leninchy* (Young Leninist), renamed as above 1992; 2 a week; organ of the Kamolot Asscn of Youth of Uzbekistan; Editor GAFAR KHATOMOV; circ. 12,580.

Xalk Suzi/Narodnoye Slovo (People's Word): 100000 Tashkent, Matbuotchilar ko'ch. 32; tel. (71) 233-15-22; e-mail info@ narodnoeslovo.uz; internet www.narodnoeslovo.uz; f. 1991; Uzbek and Russian edns; 5 a week (Uzbek), weekly (Russian); organ of the Oly Majlis and the Cabinet of Ministers; Editor ABBASKHON USMANOV; circ. 41,580 (Uzbek edn), 12,750 (Russian edn).

Xamkor (Business Partner): 100077 Tashkent, Buyuk Ipak Yuli 75; tel. (71) 268-72-04; fax (71) 234-64-82; f. 1991; in Uzbek, Russian and English; Editor ISMAT HUSHEV; circ. 20,000.

PRINCIPAL PERIODICALS

Monthly, unless otherwise indicated.

Erk (Freedom): 100055 Tashkent, Ipakchi ko'ch. 38; tel. (71) 220-65-30; e-mail erkgazetasi@yahoo.com; internet www.erkgazetasi.org; organ of Freedom Democratic Party of Uzbekistan (Erk); f. 1991; four a year; Uzbek and Russian edns; circ. 5,300 (2007).

Fan va turmush (Science and Life): 100000 Tashkent, Ya. G'ulomov ko'ch. 70; tel. (71) 233-07-05; f. 1933; every 2 months; publ. by the Fan (Science) Publishing House; popular scientific; Editor MURAD SHARIF-KHOJAYEV; circ. 28,000.

Guliston: 100000 Tashkent, Buyuk Turon ko'ch. 41; tel. (71) 236-78-90; f. 1925; present name adopted 1967; every 2 months; socio-political, literary; Editor-in-Chief AZIM SUYUN; circ. 4,000.

Gulxan (Bonfire): 100000 Tashkent, Buyuk Turon ko'ch. 41; tel. (71) 236-78-85; f. 1929; illustrated juvenile fiction; Editor SAFAR BARNOYEV; circ. 26,000.

Guncha (Small Bud): 100000 Tashkent, Buyuk Turon ko'ch. 41; tel. (71) 236-78-80; f. 1958; illustrated; for pre-school-age children; Editor ERKIN MALIKOV; circ. 35,000.

Jahon Adabiyoti (World Literature): 100129 Tashkent, A. Navoiy ko'ch. 30; tel. (71) 244-41-60; fax (71) 244-41-61; f. 1997; Editor OZOD SHARAFIDDINOV; circ. 2,000.

Mushtum (Fist): 100000 Tashkent, Buyuk Turon ko'ch. 41; tel. (71) 233-99-72; internet www.mushtum.uz; f. 1923; fortnightly; satirical; Editor ASHURALI JURAYEV; circ. 10,650.

Obshchestvennye Nauki v Uzbekistane (Social Sciences in Uzbekistan): 100047 Tashkent, Ya. G'ulomov ko'ch. 70; tel. (71) 236-73-29; f. 1957; publ. by the Fan (Science) Publishing House of the Academy of Sciences of Uzbekistan; history, oriental studies, archaeology, economics, ethnology, etc.; in Russian and Uzbek; Editor A. MUKHAMEJANOV; circ. 500.

O'zbek Tili va Adabiyoti (Uzbek Language and Literature): 100000 Tashkent, Muminov ko'ch. 9; tel. (71) 262-42-47; f. 1958; every 2 months; publ. by the Fan (Science) Publishing House; journal of the Academy of Sciences of Uzbekistan; history and modern development of the Uzbek language, folklore, etc.; Editor AZIM KHAJIYEV; circ. 3,700.

Saodat (Happiness): 100083 Tashkent, Buyuk Turon ko'ch. 41; tel. (71) 233-68-10; f. 1925; 8 a year; women's popular; Editor OIDIN KHAJIYEVA; circ. 70,000.

Sharq Yulduzi/Zvezda Vostoka (Star of the East): 100000 Tashkent, Buyuk Turon ko'ch. 41; tel. (71) 233-09-18; f. 1932; journal of the Union of Writers of Uzbekistan; fiction; Uzbek and Russian edns; Editor (Uzbek edn) UTKUR KHASHIMOV; Editor (Russian edn) NIKOLAI KRASILNIKOV; circ. 10,000 (Uzbek edn), 3,000 (Russian edn).

Sikhat Salomatlik (Health): 100000 Tashkent, Parkent ko'ch. 51; tel. (71) 268-17-54; f. 1990; every 2 months; Editor DAMIN A. ASADOV; circ. 36,000.

Tafakkur (Contemplation): 100000 Tashkent, Movaraunnakhr ko'ch.; f. 1994; 4 a year; literary; organ of the (state-controlled) Republican Committee for Spirituality and Enlightenment; Editor-in-Chief ERKIN A'ZAM.

Tong Yulduzi (Morning Star): 100129 Tashkent, A. Navoiy ko'ch. 30; tel. (71) 244-62-34; e-mail ijod@uzpak.uz; internet www.tongyulduzi.uz; f. 1929; weekly; children's; Editor UMIDA ABDUAZIMOVA; circ. 60,000.

Yoshlik (Youth): 100000 Tashkent, Buyuk Turon ko'ch. 41; tel. (71) 233-09-18; f. 1932; literature and arts for young people; Editor SABIR UNAROV; circ. 10,000.

NEWS AGENCIES

Jahon (World) Information Agency: 100029 Tashkent, O'zbekiston shoh ko'ch. 9; tel. (71) 233-65-91; fax (71) 220-64-43; e-mail aajahon@mfa.uz; internet jahon.mfa.uz; information agency of Ministry of Foreign Affairs; Dir ABROR GULYAMOV.

Turkiston Press: 100047 Tashkent, Xorazm ko'ch. 51; tel. (71) 233-78-54; fax (71) 233-95-38; e-mail tpress@sarkor.uz; Dir-Gen. SAGDULA HAKIMOV.

Uzbekistan National News Agency (UzA): 100047 Tashkent, Musahanov ko'ch. 38; tel. (71) 233-16-22; fax (71) 233-24-45; internet www.uza.uz; Dir MAMATSKUL KHAZRATSKULOV.

Publishers

Uzbek Agency for Press and Information: 100129 Tashkent, A. Navoiy ko'ch. 30; tel. (71) 244-32-87; fax (71) 244-14-84; e-mail ozmaa@uzpak.uz; internet www.uzapi.gov.uz; f. 2002; mass media, press and information exchange; printing, publishing and distribution of periodicals; Gen. Dir BABUR ALIMOV.

Chulpon (Morning Star) Publishers: 100129 Tashkent, A. Navoiy ko'ch. 30; tel. (71) 239-13-75; fax (71) 244-20-52; e-mail chulpan@sarkor.uz; internet www.chulpon.uz; Dir R. ZAPAROV.

Fan (Science) Publishers: 100047 Tashkent, Ya. G'ulomov ko'ch. 70/102; tel. (71) 233-69-61; scientific books and journals; Dir N. T. KHATAMOV.

Gafur Gulom Publishing House: 100129 Tashkent, A. Navoiy ko'ch. 30; tel. (71) 244-22-53; fax (71) 241-35-47; f. 1957; fiction, the arts; books in Uzbek, Russian and English; Dir MIZROB M. BURONOV; Editor-in-Chief NAZIRA J. JURAYEVNA.

Mekhnat (Labour) Publishers: 100129 Tashkent, A. Navoiy ko'ch. 30; tel. (71) 244-22-27; f. 1985; Dir RUSTAM A. MIRZAYEV.

O'qituvchi (Teacher) Publishing-Printing and Creative House: 100129 Tashkent, A. Navoiy ko'ch. 30; tel. and fax (71) 244-26-89; f. 1936; literary textbooks, education manuals, popular science, juvenile; Dir R.O. MIRZAYEV.

O'zbekiston Milliy Entsiklopediyasi (Uzbekistan National Encyclopedias): 100129 Tashkent, A. Navoiy ko'ch. 30; tel. (71) 244-34-38; fax (71) 244-24-91; e-mail ume2@yandex.ru; internet www.ensiklopediya.uz; f. 1997; encyclopedias, dictionaries and reference books; Dir N. TUKHLIYEV.

O'zbekiston (Uzbekistan) Publishing and Printing Creative House: 100129 Tashkent, A. Navoiy ko'ch. 30; tel. (71) 244-34-01; fax (71) 244-38-10; e-mail aptpk@ars-inform.uz; f. 2004; politics, economics, law, history, art, illustrated, manuals and textbooks for schools and higher educational institutes; Dir ZAIR T. ISADJANOV; Editor-in-Chief SHOMUXITDIN SH. MANSUROV.

Yozuvchi (Writer) Publishers: 100129 Tashkent, A. Navoiy ko'ch. 30; tel. (71) 244-29-97; f. 1990; Dir M. U. TOICHIYEV.

Broadcasting and Communications

TELECOMMUNICATIONS

Communications and Information Agency of Uzbekistan (O'zbekistol Aloqa Va Axborotlashtirish Agentligi): 100011 Tashkent, A. Navoiy ko'ch. 28A; tel. (71) 233-65-03; fax (71) 239-87-82; e-mail info@aci.uz; internet www.aci.uz; Dir-Gen. ABDULLA N. ARIPOV.

Service Providers

Coscom: 100031 Tashkent, V. Vaxidov ko'ch. 118; tel. (71) 252-15-51; fax (71) 220-72-65; e-mail inform@coscom.uz; internet www.coscom.uz; f. 1996; Uzbekistani-US jt venture; mobile cellular telecommunications.

Unitel (Beeline): 100000 Tashkent, Buxoro ko'ch. 1; tel. (71) 233-33-30; fax (71) 232-12-22; internet www.beeline.uz; f. 1996; fmrly Daewoo Unitel; subsidiary of VympelKom-Bilain (Russia); mobile cellular telecommunications; more than 1m. subscribers (2007).

Uzbektelecom: 100000 Tashkent, Amir Temur ko'ch. 24; tel. (71) 233-42-59; fax (71) 236-01-88; e-mail uztelecom@intal.uz; internet www.uztelecom.uz; f. 2000; provides local, regional and international telecommunications services; partial privatization pending; Gen. Dir KH. A. MUKHITDINOV.

Uzdunrobita: 100000 Tashkent, Amir Temur ko'ch. 24; tel. (97) 130-01-01; fax (97) 130-01-05; e-mail office@uzdunrobita.com.uz; internet www.uzdunrobita.uz; f. 1991; mobile cellular telecommunications; 74% owned by Mobile Telesystems (Russia); Gen. Dir BEKHZOD AKHMEDOV.

BROADCASTING

State Television and Radio Broadcasting Company of Uzbekistan (UZTELERADIO): 100011 Tashkent, A. Navoiy ko'ch. 69; tel. (71) 233-81-06; fax (71) 244-16-60; e-mail uztele@tkt.uz; local broadcasts, as well as relays from Egypt, France, India, Japan, Russia and Turkey; Chair. ALISHER KHUJAYEV.

Television

Uzbekistan Television and Radio Company (Uzteleradio): 100011 Tashkent, A. Navoiy ko'ch. 69; tel. (71) 233-81-06; fax (71) 244-16-60; e-mail uztcint@hotmail.com; four local programmes as well as relays from Russia, Kazakhstan, Egypt, India and Turkey; Chair. ALISHER KHADJAYEV.

Kamalak Television: 100084 Tashkent, Amir Temur ko'ch. 109; tel. (71) 237-51-77; fax (71) 220-62-28; e-mail kam.tv@kamalak.co.uz; f. 1992; jt venture between State Television and Radio Broadcasting Company and a US company; satellite broadcasts; relays from

France, Germany, India, Russia, the United Kingdom and the USA; Gen. Dir PULAT UMAROV.

Finance

(cap. = capital; res = reserves; dep. = deposits; m. = million; amounts in Uzbek sum, unless otherwise stated; brs = branches)

BANKING

A reform of the banking sector was begun in 1994. A two-tier system was introduced, consisting of the Central Bank and about 30 commercial banks. An association of commercial banks was established in 1995 to co-ordinate the role of commercial banks in the national economy. At the end of 2002 there were reported to be 35 banks in Uzbekistan, of which 13 were under private ownership.

Central Bank

Central Bank of the Republic of Uzbekistan: 100001 Tashkent, O'zbekiston shoh ko'ch. 6; tel. (71) 212-61-94; fax (71) 233-00-44; e-mail webmaster@cbu.st.uz; internet www.cbu.uz; f. 1991; Chair. of Bd FAIZULLA M. MULLAJONOV.

State Commercial Bank

National Bank for Foreign Economic Activity of the Republic of Uzbekistan (NBU) (O'zbekiston Respublikasi Tashqi Iqtisodiy Faoliyat Milliy Banki): 100047 Tashkent, Oxunbabaev ko'ch. 23; tel. (71) 233-62-87; fax (71) 232-01-72; e-mail webmaster@central.nbu.com; internet eng.nbu.com; f. 1991; cap. 22,386m., res 434,316m., dep. 2,343,991m. (Dec. 2006); Chair. SAIDAKHMAT B. RAKHIMOV; 95 brs.

State Joint-Stock Commercial Banks

Asaka—Specialized State Joint-Stock Commercial Bank: 100015 Tashkent, Nukus ko'ch. 67; tel. (71) 120-81-11; fax (71) 120-86-91; e-mail contact@asakabank.com; internet www.asakabank.com; f. 1995; cap. US $150m., dep. $678.4m., total assets $1,000m. (Dec. 2007); 98.3% owned by Ministry of Finance; Chair. KAHRAMON T. ARIPOV; 27 brs.

Ipoteka Commercial Mortgage Bank: 100000 Tashkent, Pushkin ko'ch. 17; tel. (71) 233-11-22; fax (71) 232-13-23; e-mail info@ipotekabank.uz; internet www.ipotekabank.uz; f. 2005 by merger of UzJilSberBank and Zaminbank; cap. 15,814.6m., res 16,873.6m., dep. 378,338.7m. (Dec. 2006); Chair. of Bd ABDURASUL ABDULLAYEV; 38 brs.

Other Banks

Aloqabank: 100015 Tashkent, Tolstoy ko'ch. 1A; tel. (71) 252-78-74; fax (71) 252-78-03; e-mail alokauz@uzpak.uz; internet www.alokabank.uz; f. 1995; cap. 12,574.8m., dep. 21,190.2m., total assets 102,090.7m. (Dec. 2007); Chair. ABDULLA N. ARIPOV; 12 brs, 28 sub-brs (2007).

HamkorBank: 170111 Andijon, Babura ko'ch. 85; tel. and fax (74) 24-70-39; e-mail hamkorbank@mail.ru; internet www.hamkorbank.uz; f. 1991; Chair. IKRAM IBRAHIMOV; 15 brs.

Ipak Yuli Bank (Silk Road Bank): 100135 Tashkent, Farkod ko'ch. 12A; tel. (71) 220-00-09; fax (71) 220-38-86; e-mail info@ipakyulibank.com; internet www.ipakyulibank.com; f. 2000; Chair. of Bd ALISHER H. MUMINOV; Gen. Man. RUSTAMBEK R. RAHIMBEKOV.

O'zsanoatkurilishbank (Uzpromstroibank) (Uzbek Industrial Construction Bank): 100000 Tashkent, Shaxrisab ko'ch. 3; tel. (71) 233-24-88; fax (71) 232-06-14; e-mail cor_bank@uzpsb.com; internet www.uzpsb.com; f. 1922; cap. 23,843.7m., res 10,871.4m., dep. 485,679.6m. (Dec. 2005); Chair. KIYOMIDDIN K. RUSTAMOV; 47 brs, 79 sub-brs.

Paxta Bank (Pakhta Bank): 100096 Tashkent, Mukimi ko'ch. 43; tel. (71) 278-12-96; fax (71) 220-88-18; e-mail headoffice@pakhtabank.com; internet www.pakhtabank.com; f. 1995; cap. 65,625.0m., res 2,649.3m., dep. 468,049.0m. (Dec. 2007); Chair. ABDURAXMAT BOYMURATOV; 187 brs.

Savdogarbank: 100060 Tashkent, S. Barak ko'ch. 76; tel. (71) 254-19-91; fax (71) 256-56-71; internet www.savdogarbank.uz; Chair. MURSURMON N. NURMAMATOV.

Tadbirkor Bank: 100047 Tashkent, S. Azimov ko'ch. 52; tel. (71) 233-18-75; fax (71) 236-88-32; f. 2006; micro-credit bank; Chair. MUZAFFARBEK SABIROV.

Trustbank: 100038 Tashkent, A. Navoiy ko'ch. 7; tel. (71) 244-76-21; fax (71) 244-76-61; e-mail info@trustbank.uz; internet www.trustbank.uz; f. 1994; cap. 4,395.3m., res −103.2m., dep. 75,646.4m. (Dec. 2006); Chair. ILHOM F. SOLIYEV; 2 brs.

Turonbank: 100011 Tashkent, Abay 4A; tel. (71) 700-55-55; fax (71) 244-25-81; e-mail info@turonbank.uz; internet www.turonbank.uz;

f. 1990; cap. US $8m., res $1.7m., dep. $10.7m. (Jan. 2008); Chair. of Bd DANIYOR B. ARIFJANOV; 18 brs.

Uzbekistan-Turkish UT Bank: 100043 Tashkent, Xalqlar Do'stligi ko'ch. 15B; tel. (71) 273-83-25; fax (71) 220-63-62; e-mail utbank@utbk.com; internet www.utbk.com; f. 1993; 50% owned by Paxta Bank, 50% owned by Türkiye Cumhuriyeti Ziraat Bankası (Agricultural Bank of the Turkish Republic); cap. 2,608.8m., res 252.0m., dep. 17,037.0m. (Dec. 2006); Chair. AZIM TANGIRBERDIYEV.

INSURANCE

Ark Sug'urta: 100000 Tashkent, Pushkin ko'ch. 88; tel. (71) 240-03-69; fax (71) 267-70-28; e-mail info@arksugurta.uz; internet www.arksugurta.uz; f. 1991; life and non-life; Dir-Gen. ZAFAR O. TURSUNOV.

Ishonch: 100027 Tashkent, Xojaev ko'ch. 1 A; tel. and fax (71) 238-69-65; e-mail info@ishonch-iic.uz; internet www.ishonch-iic.uz; f. 1996; life and non-life; Dir-Gen. MIRSHAMSIDDIN M. XIKMATILLAEV.

Kalofat: 100000 Tashkent, Mustaqillik maydoni 5, 9th floor; tel. (71) 233-26-98; fax (71) 233-38-49; internet www.kalofatdask.uz; f. 1997; life and non-life; Dir-Gen. SHERALI B. IMAMOV.

O'zbekinvest (Uzbekinvest) National Export–Import Insurance Co: 100017 Tashkent, Suleimanov ko'ch. 49; tel. (71) 233-05-56; fax (71) 233-07-04; e-mail root@unic.gov.uz; internet www.unic.gov.uz; f. 1994, restructured 1997; jt venture with American International Group (AIG—USA); cap. US $60m.; Dir-Gen. SUNNAT A. UMAROV; Chief Exec. NODIR KALANDAROV.

Standard Insurance Group: 100015 Tashkent, Kunaev ko'ch. 25; tel. (71) 250-99-99; fax (71) 220-31-13; e-mail office@sig-insurance.uz; internet www.sig-insurance.uz; f. 2005; non-life; Dir-Gen. UMUD U. KAMILOV.

Temir Yo'llari Sug'urta: 100060 Tashkent, Shevchenko ko'ch. 7; tel. (71) 238-86-27; fax (71) 238-85-97; e-mail tys_KDilshod@mail.ru; internet www.tysugurta.sk.uz; f. 2002; non-life; Chair. of Bd YOKUBZHON MUHAMMEDOV; Dir-Gen. DILSHOD KADYROV.

COMMODITY EXCHANGE

Tashkent Republican Commodity and Raw Materials Exchange: 100003 Tashkent, O'zbekiston shoh ko'ch. 53; tel. (71) 239-83-77; fax (71) 239-83-92; Chair. of Bd NABIHON S. SAMATOV.

STOCK EXCHANGE

Tashkent Republican Stock Exchange (UZSE) (Respublika Fond Birjasi 'Toshkent'): 100047 Tashkent, Buxoro ko'ch. 10; tel. (71) 236-76-13; fax (71) 233-32-31; e-mail gairat@uzse.uz; internet www.uzse.uz; f. 1994; Chair. BAKHTIYOR I. KHUDOYAROV.

Trade and Industry

GOVERNMENT AGENCIES

Foreign Investment Agency: 100077 Tashkent, Buyuyk Ipak Yulli ko'ch. 75; tel. (71) 268-77-05; fax (71) 267-07-52; e-mail afi@mail.uznet.net; Gen. Dir SHAZIYATOV S. SHOAZIZ.

State Committee for De-monopolization and the Development of Competition (O'zbekiston Respublikasi Monopoliadan Chiqarish va Raqobatni Rivojlantirish Davlat Qo'mitasi): 100011 Tashkent, A. Navoiy ko'ch. 18A; tel. (71) 239-15-42; e-mail devonhona@antimon.uz; internet www.antimon.uz; Chair. BAIMUROD S. ULASHOV (acting).

State Committee for the Management of State Property and Support of Entrepreneurship (State Property Committee): 100003 Tashkent, O'zbekiston shoh ko'ch. 55; tel. (71) 239-44-46; fax (71) 239-14-84; e-mail ves@spc.gov.uz; internet www.spc.gov.uz; Chair. MAKHMUDJON A. ASKAROV.

CHAMBER OF COMMERCE

Chamber of Commerce and Industry of Uzbekistan (O'zbekiston Respublikasi Savdo-Sanoat Palatasi): 100047 Tashkent, Buxoro ko'ch. 6; tel. (71) 150-60-00; fax (71) 150-60-09; e-mail info@chamber.uz; internet www.chamber.uz; f. 1996 as Chamber of Commodity Producers and Entrepreneurs of Uzbekistan; re-established and renamed as above by presidential decree 2004; provides assistance, consultancy and support for businesses; Chair. ALISHER SHAIHOV.

STATE HYDROCARBONS COMPANY

Uzbekneftegaz (Uzbekistani Petroleum and Natural Gas Co): 100047 Tashkent, Akhunbabayev ko'ch. 21; tel. (71) 233-57-57; fax (71) 236-77-71; e-mail nhk@uzneftegaz.uz; internet www.uzneftegaz.uz; f. 1999; national petroleum and gas corpn; Chair. of Bd NURMUHAMMAD A. AHMETOV.

MAJOR COMPANIES

Cotton and Textiles

Andijon Joint-Stock Co: 170100 Andijon, Barbur ko'ch. 73; tel. (74) 222-13-53; fax (74) 222-13-52; e-mail aobabur@online.ru; cotton-processing company; possesses spinning, weaving, finishing and sewing plants; Chair. MUYDINOV KAHHOZBEK; 5,000 employees.

Buxoro (Bukhara) Cotton Industrial Group: 200122 Buxoro, Promyshlennaya 2; tel. (65) 223-06-21; fax (65) 222-65-86; e-mail bphbo@naytov.com; f. 1973; produces cotton cloth and yarns, imports equipment for the textile, knitwear and sewing industries; imports transport equipment; Chair. of Bd SHUKRULLO N. DAVIROV; 9,237 employees.

Tashselmash: 100048 Tashkent, Khamza ko'ch. 2; tel. (71) 236-72-27; fax (71) 236-72-78; manufactures cotton-picking machines.

Uzhlopkopromsbyt (Stock Asscn for Cotton-processing and Marketing): 100100 Tashkent, Nosir ko'ch. 8A; tel. (71) 256-12-60; fax (71) 256-02-31; produces cotton.

Uzmashprom: 100047 Tashkent, Nosir ko'ch. 53B; tel. and fax (71) 253-81-51; f. 1994; state-owned; produces machines, equipment and tools for the cotton and textile industries; Chair. T. K. SABIROV; 10,000 employees.

Furniture

Almalyk (Olmaliq) Furniture Works: 110100 Tashkent viloyat, Olmaliq, Izvestkovaya 14; tel. (71) 614-48-01; fax (71) 614-09-14; e-mail shark@mail.tps.uz; manufactures furniture; 1,000 employees.

Uzbek Furniture: 100011 Tashkent, Navoiy ko'ch. 18; tel. (71) 241-81-18; furniture for the home, offices, nurseries and schools.

Gases and Chemicals

Electrokhimprom: 111708 Tashkent viloyat, Chirchik, Tashkent ko'ch. 2; tel. (71) 719-32-00; fax (71) 715-12-97; f. 1940; produces mineral fertilizers, synthetic ammonium, nitric acid and liquefied gas; Dir-Gen. FATHULLA T. MIRZAYEV.

Muborak Gas Processing Plant: 180900 Qashqadaryo viloyat, Muborak; f. 1971; sulphur production, purification of exhaust gases, etc.; Dir NURITBIN ZAYNIYEV; 1,900 employees.

Uzneftegazkurilish: 100115 Tashkent, Mukimi ko'ch. 98; tel. (71) 253-65-01; fax (71) 253-53-77; f. 1999; construction for the petroleum and gas industry; Gen. Dir B. HAFIZOV.

Gold and Other Metals

Almalyk (Olmaliq) Mining and Metallurgical Complex: 110100 Tashkent viloyat, Olmaliq, Amir Timur ko'ch. 53; tel. (71) 220-20-09; fax (71) 220-20-33; e-mail info@agmk.uz; internet www.agmk.uz; f. 1949; processing of precious and non-ferrous metals; treats 12 chemical elements; Gen. Dir KUVANDYK S. SANAKULOV.

Amantaytau Goldfields: 100060 Tashkent, Mirabod ko'ch. 11; tel. (71) 256-06-10; fax (71) 220-64-35; f. 1993; joint venture between two state-owned Uzbekistani cos and a British co, Lonmin; gold mining near Zerafshan; started production 1996; Dir DAVID NEWTON.

Oxus Resources Corpn: 100031 Tashkent, Mirobod ko'ch. 20; tel. (71) 120-68-64; fax (71) 120-65-64; British co undertaking gold and base metal mining in Central Asia; Vice-Pres. VALERII AXANOV, ALEKSANDR POLIKASHIN.

Uzbtortzvetmet: 100000 Tashkent, Sh. Rustaveli ko'ch. 45; tel. (71) 258-80-01; fax (71) 255-34-07; aluminium plant, also processes copper scrap, brass, zinc and non-ferrous metals.

Zerafshan Gold Refinery: 200100 Buxoro; f. 1967; Dir VALERII NIKOLAYEVICH.

Motor Vehicles

GM Uzbekistan: Andijon Viloyat, Asaka; f. 2007; jt venture co 75% owned by O'zavtosanoat (q.v.) and 25% owned by General Motors (USA); fmrly UzDaewoo; produces Chevrolet automobiles; Dir-Gen. SHUKHRAT YUSUPOV.

O'zavtosanoat: 100000 Tashkent, Abdullayev ko'ch. 30; tel. (71) 267-92-45; fax (71) 267-71-69; e-mail info@uzavtosanoat.uz; internet www.uzavtosanoat.uz; f. 1994; car, lorry and bus production plants; Chair. of Bd ULUGBEG ROZUKULOV; 14,000 employees.

Tashkent Tractor Plant: 100142 Tashkent, Buyuk Ipak Yuli ko'ch. 434; tel. (71) 264-05-61; fax (71) 264-06-16; e-mail ttzth@ars.uz; f. 1942; produces tractors and trailers; became a govt corpn in 1996; Gen. Dir MAXAMADJON A. AXMEDJANOV; 7,000 employees.

Uzselkhozmash (Uzbek Agricultural Machinery) Holding Co (UzselkhozmashKholding): 100029 Tashkent, Mustaqillik maydoni 2; tel. (71) 239-48-06; fax (71) 239-49-09; f. 1996; 51% state-owned; produces tractors and agricultural machinery; cap.

7,818,749m. sum (2002); sales 42,552m. (2003); Chair. of Bd Prof. RAFIK D. MATCHANOV; 10,029 employees (2003).

Miscellaneous

British American Tobacco Uzbekistan (UzBAT AO): 100084 Tashkent, Nosirov ko'ch. 77; tel. (71) 220-55-55; fax (71) 220-62-12; e-mail cora@bat.uz; internet www.bat.com; f. 1995; manufacture and sale of tobacco products; Gen. Man. RENÉ IJSSELSTEIN.

Central Asia Trans State Joint-Stock Co: 100077 Tashkent, H. Abdullaeva ko'ch. 54A; tel. (71) 266-23-32; fax (71) 266-23-31; e-mail catrans@mail.ru; f. 1992 under the Ministry of Foreign Economic Relations; transports and forwards cargo within Central Asia; Chair. ABDUJALIL ABDUJABAROV; 550 employees.

GUKS (Main Board for Capital Construction): 100011 Tashkent, pr. Navoiy 2 A; tel. (71) 241-87-13; fax (71) 289-14-79; contractor to building companies; develops, designs, provides construction sites with equipment and carries out technical supervision and management.

Innovatsia State Joint-Stock Foreign Trade Co: 100077 Tashkent, Bujuk Ipak Yuli ko'ch. 75; tel. (71) 268-92-48; fax (71) 268-77-33; e-mail inovac@uzpak.uz; internet www.geocities.com/innovatsia; f. 1991; under the control of Agency of Foreign Economic Relations; export of chemical products, food products, tobacco, jewellery, textiles, and cotton and cotton products; tourist services; investment projects with Europe, Asia and the USA; Chair. of Bd SHAVKAT P. BARATOV.

Navoiy Mining and Metallurgy Combine (NMMC): 210102 Navoiy viloyat, Navoiy, Navoiy ko'ch. 27; tel. (79) 227-71-54; fax (79) 227-75-66; e-mail n_vasiukova@ngmk.uz; internet www.ngmk.uz; f. 1958; mines gold, extracts uranium; produces yarn and knitted goods, manufactures jewellery, produces marble slabs and tiles, manufactures lathes, and produces pipes; Gen. Dir NIKOLAI V. KUCHERSKIY.

Sovplastital: 100185 Tashkent, Xalqlar Do'stligi ko'ch. 29A; tel. (71) 276-53-33; fax (71) 220-64-01; e-mail spi@glb.net; internet www.sovplastitalonline.com; f. 1987; jt-stock co; manufactures plastic goods and handcrafted souvenirs, incl. coloured glass, porcelain and ceramics; Gen. Dir ALEKSANDR MELKUMOV; 600 employees (2007).

Sredazelektroapparat (Central Asia Electrical Apparatus) Co: 100005 Tashkent, Manjar ko'ch. 1; tel. (71) 291-29-04; fax (71) 293-09-32; engaged in the production of low-voltage equipment, incl. packet-type switches, cam switches, etc.; Gen. Dir ALIM ABDURAIMOVICH; 7,600 employees.

Tashkent Industrial Amalgamation: 100090 Tashkent, Barbur ko'ch. 73; tel. (71) 255-17-23; fax (71) 244-30-43; produces diamond and other grinding wheels, instruments of galvanic binder, etc.; Gen. Man. ANATOLII HEGAY; 1,100 employees.

Uzbek Refractory and Resistant Metals Integrated Plant: 111700 Tashkent viloyat, Chirchik, Khaydarov ko'ch. 1; tel. (71) 715-57-03; fax (71) 715-57-02; e-mail uzktzhm@chirkom.com; manufactures products from tungsten, molybdenum, rhenium and hard alloys; Gen. Dir FARHAD H. TASHMETOV; 2,000 employees.

Uzbekistan Metallurgical Plant: 100502 Tashkent viloyat, Bekabad; tel. (71) 910-24-23; f. 1944; manufactures carbon steel tubes and bars; Dir-Gen. A. M. ANOKHIN; 10,000 employees.

Uzbeklegprom (Uzbek Light Industry): 100100 Tashkent, Babur ko'ch. 45; tel. (71) 239-17-11; fax (71) 239-10-66; state asscn for the development of enterprises, mainly in the textile industry.

Uzmarkazimpex State Joint-Stock Co: 100077 Tashkent, Bujuk Ipak Yuli ko'ch. 75; tel. (71) 268-77-18; fax (71) 268-75-55; foreign-trading company; exports cotton, imports main food products, offers marketing and international trade services.

Uzmetcombinat (Uzbek Metal Plant): 110502 Tashkent viloyat, Bekabad; tel. (391) 62-24-23; fax (391) 62-25-73; manufactures steel products, including metal bars, angles, circular bars and welded pipes.

Uzplodovoschvinprom (State Co-operative Asscn for Fruit and Vegetable Growing and Viniculture): 100029 Tashkent, O'zbekiston shoh ko'ch. 41; tel. (71) 256-37-54; fax (71) 256-56-48; Chair. N. NASIROV.

Uzprommashimpeks (Uzbek Industrial Machinery Import) State Joint-Stock Co: 100077 Tashkent, Bujuk Ipak Yuli ko'ch. 75; tel. (71) 238-54-57; fax (71) 238-54-58; e-mail marketing@upm.uz; internet www.upm.uz; f. 1991; imports machine-building equipment, metallurgical equipment, chemical equipment; exports cotton fibre, cotton yarn, molybdenum, and other domestically produced goods; Chair. SHERZOD A. GUZAIROV; 106 employees.

Uzstroimaterialy (Uzbek Construction Materials): 100070 Tashkent, Mirakilov ko'ch. 68 A; tel. (71) 252-20-63; fax (71) 255-77-07; e-mail qursan@online.ru; f. 1989; produces more than 100 different building materials; cap. 2,622.2m. sum, sales 50,020m. sum (2002); Chair. ERKIN M. AKRAMOV.

TRADE UNIONS

Federation of Trade Unions of Uzbekistan: 100000 Tashkent; Chair. of Council KHULKAR JAMALOV.

Transport

RAILWAYS

Uzbekistan's railway network is connected to those of the neighbouring republics of Kazakhstan, Kyrgyzstan, Tajikistan and Turkmenistan, and to that of Russia. There were 3,645 km of track in 2007.

O'zbekiston Temir Yo'llari (Uzbekistan State Railway Co): 100060 Tashkent, T. Shevchenko ko'ch. 7; tel. (71) 238-80-00; fax (71) 233-45-49; e-mail uzrailway@uzpak.uz; internet www.uzrailway.uz; f. 1994; state-owned joint-stock co; Chair. of Bd ACHILBAY ZH. RAMATOV.

Toshkent metropoliteni (Tashkent Metro): 100027 Tashkent, O'zbekiston shoh ko'ch. 93A; tel. (71) 232-38-52; fax (71) 233-66-81; e-mail metro@sarkor.uz; f. 1977; three lines with total length of 36 km, and fourth line due to open by 2010; Chair. M. A. ODILOV.

ROADS

In 1999 the total length of the road network was estimated at 81,600 km, of which 87.3% was paved.

INLAND WATERWAYS

The extensive use of the waters of the Amu Dar'ya and Syr Dar'ya for irrigation lessened the flow of these rivers and caused the desiccation of the Aral Sea. This reduced a valuable transport asset. However, the Amu Dar'ya Steamship Co still operates important river traffic.

CIVIL AVIATION

There is an international airport at Tashkent. From 1996 the airports at Samarqand, Urgench and Buxoro were upgraded to stimulate tourism.

Uzbekistan Airways (Uzbekiston Havo Yollari): 100061 Tashkent, ul. Proletarskaya 41; tel. (71) 291-14-90; fax (71) 232-73-71; e-mail info@uzbekistan-airways.com; internet www.airways.uz; f. 1992; operates flights between Uzbekistan and destinations in Central Asia, South-East Asia, the USA, the Middle East and Europe; Dir-Gen. RAFIKOV GANIY; Gen. Dir VALERIY TYAN.

Tourism

Since independence, Uzbekistan has sought to promote tourism as an important source of revenue. The republic has more than 4,000 historical monuments, many of which are associated with the ancient 'Silk Route', particularly the cities of Samarqand (Timur—Tamerlane's capital), Xiva (Khiva) and Buxoro (Bukhara), as well as other historic sites. Infrastructural limitations, however, have constrained development. In 2004 Uzbekistan received an estimated 261,600 foreign visitors (including excursionists). In that year tourism receipts totalled some US $57m.

Uzbektourism: 100047 Tashkent, Xorazm ko'ch. 47; tel. (71) 233-54-14; fax (71) 233-80-68; f. 1992; Chair. ZAHID L. XAKIMOV.

Culture

Uzbekistan has a rich cultural heritage, particularly in the ancient cities of the 'Silk Road'. Islam, combined with Persian (largely Tajik), Turkic and Mongol (Uzbek) influences, provided a varied legacy. Samarqand, the capital and site of the mausoleum of the medieval khan Timur (Tamerlane), was revived as a pilgrimage site in the 1990s. The city is also the site of the Shah-e-Zinda shrine (formerly a museum), dedicated to the Prophet Muhammad's nephew, Kussam Ibn Abbas, who, according to tradition, evangelized the area for Islam. In 1996, in celebration of the 660th anniversary of Timur's birth, restoration work began on many of Samarqand's monuments, including Timur's mausoleum and the Bibi Khanym mosque, constructed during his khanate. In February of that year the ancient city of Buxoro (Bukhara) was listed by UNESCO as a World Heritage Site. Tashkent, long a centre of Russian influence in the territory, is the base for many cultural activities.

NATIONAL ORGANIZATIONS

Ministry of Culture and Sport: see The Government (Ministries).

CULTURAL HERITAGE

Buxoro State Architectural-Art Museum-Reserve: 200100 Buxoro, Siyavush ko'ch. 2; tel. (65) 4-13-49; internet ark.bukhara .uzsci.net; f. 1922; comprises nine museums containing a total of 68,000 exhibits; archaeology, numismatics, ethnography.

International Museum of Peace and Solidarity: 140100 Samarqand, POB 76; tel. and fax (66) 233-17-53; e-mail imps86@yahoo.com; internet peace.museum.com; f. 1986 by members of the Society for the Learning of Esperanto; aims to promote peace through diplomacy, culture and the arts; over 20,000 exhibits, incl. art, literature and memorabilia from over 100 countries; organizes various exhibitions and carries out educational activities; Dir ANATOLY I. IONESOV.

Kara-Kalpak Historical Museum: 230100 Qoraqalpog'iston, Nukus, Rakhmatov ko'ch. 3; contains material on the history of the Kara-Kalpak and Uzbek peoples.

T. Khanum Museum: 100000 Tashkent, T. Xanum ko'ch. 1/41; tel. (71) 267-86-90; e-mail tamarakhonim@mail.ru; internet mmt .freenet.uz; f. 1986; collection of national costumes from around the world; Dir MEKHRINISIO S. RAKHIMBAYEVA.

Museum of Applied Arts of Uzbekistan: 100031 Tashkent, Rohatboshi ko'ch. 15; tel. (71) 256-39-43; fax (71) 252-13-67; f. 1937; national handicrafts, incl. ceramics, embroidery, jewellery and wood-carving; Dir DUSTAYEV TURGUN.

Museum of Literature: 100011 Tashkent, A. Navoiy ko'ch. 69; tel. (71) 241-02-75; Dir N. S. KHASANOV.

A. Navoiy National Library of Uzbekistan: 100047 Tashkent, Xorazm ko'ch. 51; tel. (71) 239-16-58; fax (71) 233-09-08; e-mail navoi@tshtt.uz; internet www.natlib.uz; f. 1870; 10m. vols; Dir Dr ABSALOM UMAROV.

Samarqand State United Historic-Architectural and Art Museum-Preserve: 140100 Samarqand, Registan ko'ch. 1; tel. (66) 35-38-96; f. 1982; comprises nine museums in Samarqand city and viloyat containing more than 182,000 exhibits.

I. V. Savitskii State Museum of Art of the Republic of Qoraqalpog'iston: 230100 Qoraqalpog'iston, Nukus, Dustlik gazari 127; tel. (6122) 2-24-56; e-mail museum@online.ru; f. 1966; archaeology of ancient Xorazm, Kara-Kalpak folk art, modern art; library of 9,466 vols; Dir MARINIKA BABANAZAROVA.

State Museum of Art of the Republic of Uzbekistan: 100060 Tashkent, Mavaraunnakhr ko'ch. 16; tel. (71) 236-74-36; f. 1918; houses the private collection of Grand Duke Nikolai Romanov; Russian and Uzbek paintings, as well as Oriental and Western art; Dir K. A. ADYIMETOV.

State Museum of the History of Uzbekistan: 100029 Tashkent, Sh. Rashidov ko'ch. 3; tel. (71) 239-10-83; fax (71) 239-44-25; e-mail uzb.historymuseum@gmail.com; internet www.uzhistory.org; f. 1992 by merger of the Museum of the History of the People of Uzbekistan and the Lenin Central Museum; part of the Academy of Sciences; over 250,000 exhibits; Dir G. R. RASHIDOV.

U. Tansykbayev Museum: 100170 Tashkent, Cherdantsev ko'ch. 2; tel. (71) 262-62-30; f. 1981; paintings by late artist Ural Tansykbayev, renowned for his depictions of Uzbek landscapes; Dir SOLTAN I. TACHOYEV.

Xiva State Historic-Architectural Museum-Reserve: 220900 Xorazm viloyat, Xiva, Boltayev ko'ch. 41; tel. (6222) 5-31-69; f. 1969 on the basis of Xorazm History Museum and the Xiva Ichan-Kala Historic-Architectural Reserve; more than 35,000 exhibits.

SPORTING ORGANIZATIONS

National Olympic Committee of Uzbekistan: 100003 Tashkent, Almazar ko'ch. 15/1; tel. (71) 245-72-42; fax (71) 244-73-29; e-mail info@olympic.uz; internet www.olympic.uz; f. 1992; Pres. KURBANOV RUSTAM; Sec.-Gen. MALIK BABAYEV.

State Committee for Physical Education and Sport: 100027 Tashkent, Furkat ko'ch. 1; tel. (71) 245-16-18; fax (71) 239-41-87; Chair. KOMILJON YUSUPOV.

PERFORMING ARTS

M. Gorkii Russian Drama Theatre: 100000 Tashkent, Sayilgoh ko'ch. 28; tel. (71) 233-42-10; f. 1934.

A. Hidoyatov Uzbek Youth Drama Theatre (Abror Hidoyatov Nomidagi O'zbek Davlat Drama Teatri): 100000 Tashkent, Uighur ko'ch. 3; tel. (71) 234-19-94; fax (71) 244-34-44; e-mail center@sport .uz; internet www.teatr-hidoyatov.skm.uz; f. 1968; fmrly Yosh Gvardiya (Young Guard) Theatre; Dir AXROROV S. SAIDKARIMOVICH.

Ilkhom Theatre: 100000 Tashkent, Pahtakor ko'ch. 5, Kompleks 'Shodlik Palas', POB 5795; tel. (71) 241-22-41; fax (71) 244-04-03; e-mail ilkhom_theatre@mail.tps.uz; internet www.ilkhom.com; f. 1976; Dir-Gen. IGOR RATANOV.

Khamza Uzbek Drama Theatre: 100000 Tashkent, Navoiy shoh ko'ch. 34; tel. (71) 244-41-60.

Mukimi Musical Theatre: 100000 Tashkent, Almazar ko'ch. 187; tel. (71) 245-36-55.

A. Navoiy State Academic Bolshoi Theatre: 100000 Tashkent, A. Atatürk ko'ch. 28; tel. (71) 233-35-28; fax (71) 233-33-44.

O'zbeknavo (Uzbeknavo)—Uzbek State Variety Arts Association: 100000 Tashkent, Navoiy ko'ch. 2; tel. (71) 239-86-57; fax (71) 239-18-59; e-mail uznavo@uzpak.uz; internet www.uznavo.uz; f. 1996 as O'zbeknavo (Uzbeknavo)—Uzbek Touring Concert Association; present designation adopted 2001; promotes and funds wide range of performing arts, including traditional and folk music, in every region of Uzbekistan; Dir-Gen. BAHODIR A. ABDURAHIMOV.

Tashkent State Musical Comedy (Operetta) Theatre: 100000 Tashkent, Chilanzarskii raion, kv-l Ts., Cholon-ota ko'ch.; tel. (71) 277-86-11; e-mail teatr@tkt.uz; internet www.teatr-operetta.skm .uz; f. 1972; Dir MAHMUD M. MURATOV.

ASSOCIATION

National Association for International Cultural and Humanitarian Relations: 100003 Tashkent, T. Tula ko'ch. 1; tel. (71) 245-55-54; fax (71) 245-55-53; f. 1992 by merger of Society for Friendship and Cultural Relations with Foreign Countries and Vatan (Fatherland) Society for Cultural Relations with Uzbeks Abroad; promotes cultural and educational relations with other countries; Chair. NAIM YA. GAYBOV.

Education

Until the early 1990s education was based on the Soviet model, but some changes were introduced, including a greater emphasis on Uzbek history and literature. From 1993 a Latin script was introduced for the Uzbek language. In 2004/05 some 89.0% of pupils at day schools were educated in Uzbek, compared with 76.8% in 1988/89. Other languages used included Russian (4.5% in 2004/05, compared with 15.0% in 1988/89), Kara-Kalpak (2.2%), Kazakh (2.1%) and Tajik (1.7%). Primary education, beginning at seven years of age, lasts for four years. Secondary education, beginning at 11 years of age, lasts for seven years, comprising a first cycle of five years and a second cycle of two years. In 2006/07, according to UNESCO, gross enrolment at primary schools was equivalent to 95.5% of children in the relevant age-group. In 2002 the comparable ratio for secondary education in that year was 97% of males and 94% of females. In 2004 some 6.2m. pupils were enrolled in general secondary schools. Higher education was provided in 63 institutes in that year, with a total enrolment of 263,600 students. In 1993 private educational establishments were banned. In April 1999 the establishment of the Islamic University of Tashkent was agreed. The 2006 budget allocated 1,285,078.5m. sum (29.8% of total budgetary expenditure) to education.

UNIVERSITIES

Buxoro State University: 200118 Buxoro, M. Ikbol ko'ch. 11; tel. (65) 223-23-14; fax (65) 223-12-54; e-mail bukhsu-monitor@mail.ru; 361 teachers; 5,577 students.

Nukus State University: 230112 Qoraqalpog'iston, Nukus, Universitet ko'ch. 1; tel. (61) 223-23-72; f. 1979; 11 faculties; 7,000 students; Rector Prof. K. ATANIYAZOV.

Samarqand State University (Samarqand Davlat Universiteti): 140104 Samarqand, Universitet Xiyoboni 15; tel. (66) 235-16-02; e-mail support@samdu.uz; internet www.samdu.uz; f. 1927; 17 faculties; 800 teachers; 13,000 students; Rector Dr TEMIR SH. SHIRINOV.

Tashkent State University: 100095 Tashkent, Vozgorodok, Universitet ko'ch. 95; tel. (71) 246-02-24; f. 1920; 17 faculties; 1,480 teachers; 19,300 students; Rector Dr S. K. SIRAJINOV.

Social Welfare

The social welfare system comprises two funds, the Pension Fund (formerly the Social Insurance Fund) and the Employment Fund, as well as three additional forms of allowance, which are distributed to families on low incomes. Both the Pension Fund and the Employment Fund are administered by the Ministry of Labour and Social Protection and financed by payroll contributions. Benefits of the Pension Fund include survivors', old-age and disability pensions. The Employment Fund distributes unemployment benefits and administers employment training schemes.

Two new social security arrangements were introduced in 1994: allowances for low-income families; and compensation payments for a large part of the population. In 1996 there were three main forms of allowance: assistance was distributed to families on low incomes; allowances were paid to families with children under the age of 16 years; and aid was available to mothers with children under two years of age. At October 2005 the minimum monthly wage was some 9,400 sum; the minimum monthly pension was some 18,605 sum.

Health standards are relatively poor in the country, which is severely affected by environmental problems. Average life expectancy at birth, according to WHO estimates, was 63 years for males and 69 years for females in 2004. In 2005 there were 2.7 physicians and 5.2 hospital beds for every 1,000 inhabitants. The under-5 mortality rate was 44 per 1,000 live births in 2006. In 2006, according to provisional data, 494,675.1m. sum (or 11.5% of total budgetary expenditure) was allocated to health.

NATIONAL AGENCIES

Ministry of Health: see The Government (Ministries).

Ministry of Labour and Social Security: see The Government (Ministries).

HEALTH AND WELFARE ORGANIZATIONS

Caritas Uzbekistan: 100047 Tashkent, Musahanov ko'ch. 80/1; tel. (71) 214-64-26; e-mail caritas_uzbekistan@yahoo.com; Pres. Fr KRZYSZTOF KULKULKA; Sec.-Gen. Fr FRANCIS STOPKOWICZ.

Central Asian Free Exchange (CAFE): 100015 Tashkent, Minglar ko'ch. 10; tel. (71) 220-67-57; fax (71) 252-10-87; e-mail twessman@cafengo.org; internet www.cafengo.org; f. 1991; provides support and technical assistance to govt agencies working in social welfare development; Dir TODD WESSMAN.

Red Crescent Society of Uzbekistan: 100031 Tashkent, Yosuf Hos Hojib ko'ch. 30; tel. (71) 256-37-41; fax (71) 256-18-01; e-mail rcsuz@uzpak.uz; internet www.redcrescent.uz; Pres. OKTAMKHON T. VAKHIDOVA.

Uzbek Institute of Sanitation and Hygiene: 100000 Tashkent, Khamza ko'ch. 85.

The Environment

Environmental activism is not encouraged by the authorities. Although industrial pollution in Tashkent and the Farg'ona (Fergana) valley causes disquiet to local groups, the principal environmental concerns in Uzbekistan revolve around water resources and, in particular, the desiccation of the Aral Sea, to which the extensive use of the Syr Dar'ya and Amu Dar'ya rivers for irrigation purposes is a major contributing factor (see Economy). The Sea was once 69 m at its deepest, but in January 1997 it was measured at 37 m. Uzbekistan and other countries of the region again committed themselves to improving the situation by the Nukus Declaration of September 1995, following moves such as the guarantee of a certain level of water input to the Sea. In March 1996, at the meeting of the Inter-State Council on Aral Sea Problems, a new programme to restore the environment of the area was ordered to be drafted and submitted to the ecological commission of the Inter-State Council in July. Measures such as the improvement of irrigation channels, to prevent excessive loss of water, had already been taken. In October 2001 the USA agreed to provide funding of some US $6m. to enable the world's largest known site of buried anthrax, on the island of Vozrozhdeniye (a former location for biological testing, shared by Kazakhstan and Uzbekistan), to be destroyed. There were concerns not only that the continued desiccation of the Aral Sea might uncover live anthrax spores, but that militants might attempt to obtain the spores in order to perpetrate terrorist attacks.

GOVERNMENT ORGANIZATION

Ministry of Agriculture and Water Resources: see The Government (Ministries).

State Committee for Nature Protection (O'zbekiston Respublikasi Tabiatni muhofaza qilish davlat qo'mitasi): 100084 Tashkent, A. Timur ko'ch. 99; tel. (71) 239-11-71; fax (71) 235-79-20; e-mail envconf@uzsci.net; internet www.uznature.uz; Chair. BORY B. ALIKHANOV.

ACADEMIC INSTITUTES

Uzbekistan Academy of Sciences (UzAS): 100047 Tashkent, Ya. G'ulomov ko'ch. 70; tel. (71) 233-68-47; fax (71) 233-49-01; e-mail academy@uzsci.net; internet www.academy.uz; f. 1943; 47 attached research institutes, with more than 5,200 members of staff, involved in environmental research covering some 400 projects; Pres. Prof. SHAVKAT SAILKHOV.

Uzbekistan Academy of Sciences, Qoraqalpog'iston Branch: 230100 Qoraqalpog'iston, Nukus, Berdakh gazari 41; tel. (61) 227-72-29; fax (61) 224-06-04; e-mail udasa@uzpak.uz; f. 1959; scientific research; Chair. TURSUNBAI ESHANOV; Vice-Chair. NAGMET AIMBETOV.

> **Institute for Socio-economic Problems of the Aral Sea Region:** 230100 Qoraqalpog'iston, Nukus, Amir Temur ko'ch. 179 A; tel. (61) 224-22-09; fax (61) 217-72-28; e-mail udasa@uzpak.uz.

NON-GOVERNMENTAL ORGANIZATIONS

Aral Society: 100000 Tashkent, F. Khodjayev ko'ch. 28; tel. (71) 233-18-46; Dir AKMAL KARIMOV.

Aral SOS Society of the Republic of Qoraqalpog'iston: 230100 Qoraqalpog'iston, Nukus, Dustlik gazari 94A; tel. (61) 222-53-42; e-mail artik@silk.glas.apc.org; f. 1994; greening projects in rural areas, programmes for local development, UNDP water supply project, urban environmental rehabilitation; 30 mems.

Association for an Ecologically Clean Farg'ona: 150100 Farg'ona, Farg'ona ko'ch. 86; tel. and fax (732) 22-29-17; e-mail ekofergana@vodiy.uz; internet www.cango.net.kg/homepages/uz/CleanFergana; f. 1989; raises ecological awareness; Chief Officer IBRAGIMJON DOMULAJANOV; 200 mems.

ECOSAN (International Fund of Ecology and Health): 100000 Tashkent, Shahrisabz ko'ch. 1; tel. (71) 239-83-01; fax (71) 234-24-88; e-mail ecosan@uzpak.uz; f. 1992; increases ecological awareness, provides humanitarian aid, attracts foreign investment for realization of ecological projects; Chair. Prof. YUSUFJAN SH. SHADIMETOV.

> **Ecolog:** 100000 Tashkent, Nurlikhon ko'ch. 2; tel. and fax (71) 291-39-35; e-mail tashkent@glasnet.ru; f. 1987; asscn concerned with biodiversity and nature reserves, destruction of the Aral Sea, public health and ecological education; Chair. OLEG I. TSARUK; 50 mems.

> **ECOSAN Qoraqalpog'iston:** 230100 Qoraqalpog'iston, Nukus, Dustlik gazari 96; tel. (61) 217-32-14; f. 1993; Dir KHAYRULLA REIPNAZAROV; 17 mems.

> **Eremurus:** 100048 Tashkent, Botkin ko'ch. 7/47; tel. (71) 268-42-60; e-mail eremurus@hotbox.ru; f. 1982; promotes environmental awareness among the young; Chair. YELENA V. MELNIKOVA; 25 mems.

Green Wave: 140600 Samarqand viloyat, Ziadin, Istaklol ko'ch. 20; tel. (66) 403-10-67; e-mail ziadin@samarkand.uz; f. 1974; environmental protection and education; Dir BAXODIR HUDAIBERDIEV; 850 mems.

Lop-Nor Semipalatinsk Ecological Committee (Tashkent): 100000 Tashkent; tel. (71) 246-35-27; f. 1993 as br. of anti-nuclear group based in Kazakhstan; registered as Uigur social org.; Chair. ABDULJAN BARAYEV.

Union for the Defence of the Aral Sea and the Amu-Dar'ya: 230100 Qoraqalpog'iston, Nukus, Berdakh gazari 41; tel. (61) 224-29-50; fax (61) 224-06-16; e-mail info@udasa.org; internet www.udasa.org; f. 1989; activities incl. water management in the Aral Sea basin, and the collection of information pertaining to it, energy efficiency, and the publication of a newsletter, *Vdol' Amu* (*Along the Amu*); Chair. YUSUP SABIROVICH KAMALOV.

Defence

The establishment of Uzbekistani national armed forces was initiated in 1992. As assessed at November 2007, active armed forces numbered some 67,000, comprising an army of 50,000 and an air force of some 17,000. There were also paramilitary forces numbering up to 20,000 (comprising a 1,000-strong National Guard attached to the Ministry of Defence and up to 19,000 troops attached to the Ministry of Internal Affairs). Compulsory military service lasts for 12 months. The budget for 2006 allocated an estimated 103,000m. sum to defence. In July 1994 Uzbekistan joined the North Atlantic Treaty Organization's (NATO) 'Partnership for Peace' (see p. 715) programme of military co-operation. In April 1999 Uzbekistan withdrew its membership of the Collective Security Treaty of the Commonwealth of Independent States (CIS, see p. 694).

Joint Chief of Staff of the Armed Forces: Maj.-Gen. MAHMUDOV.

SOVEREIGN REPUBLIC

Uzbekistan includes one nominally Sovereign Republic, the Republic of Qoraqalpog'iston (formerly the Kara-Kalpak Autonomous Soviet Socialist Republic).

REPUBLIC OF QORAQALPOG'ISTON

The Republic of Qoraqalpog'iston is situated in western Uzbekistan and covers an area of 165,600 sq km (63,700 sq miles).

Qoraqalpog'iston is the main habitation of the Kara-Kalpak (Qaraqalpaq), a Turkic group, although at the time of the 1989 census they accounted for only 32.1% of the population of the Republic, being outnumbered by ethnic Uzbeks (32.1%). Some 27.0% of the population were ethnically Kazakh at that time. The capital is Nukus, on the Amu Dar'ya river, which had an estimated population of 212,012 in 2001. The territory is among the worst affected by the Aral Sea environmental problems, and was chosen as the site of a commitment to rehabilitation of the Sea by the states of Central Asia in September 1995 (the so-called Nukus Declaration).

Qoraqalpog'iston was ceded to the Russian Empire by the Khanate of Xiva (Khiva) in 1867. It thus formed part of the Bolshevik Russian Federation in the first years of Soviet rule, becoming an autonomous area within the Kazakh (initially known as the Kyrgyz) ASSR, itself part of the Russian Federation, from 1925. In 1930 the Republic was removed from the jurisdiction of the Kazakh ASSR, although it remained a constituent unit of the Russian Federation. On 5 December 1936 the Kara-Kalpak Autonomous Republic (Karakalpakstan) became an integral part of Uzbekistan. From 1938 to 1990 the most senior government position in the Autonomous Republic was the President of the Presidium of the republican Supreme Soviet (Supreme Council); in 1990–91 this position was replaced by that of the Chairman of the republican Supreme Soviet. In November 1991 Dauletbai Shamshetov, who had been Chairman of the Supreme Soviet since March of that year, was elected as the first, and, in the event, final, directly elected President of the Kara-Kalpak Autonomous Republic. On 14 February 1992, following the dissolution of the USSR, the Republic was reconstituted as the Republic of Qoraqalpog'iston (the Uzbek spelling of Karakalpakstan). In May of that year the President of Uzbekistan, Islam Karimov, dismissed Shamshetov as President of Qoraqalpog'iston and appointed his ally Ubbiniyaz Ashirbekov to that position.

The first elections to the Jo'qorg'i Kenges (Legislative Assembly) of the Republic—which replaced the Supreme Soviet—were held in June 1992; elections were subsequently held in July 1997 and May 2002. The Constitution of Uzbekistan, adopted in December 1992, abolished the position of the regional Presidency, but guaranteed the formal right of Qoraqalpog'iston to secede from Uzbekistan, subject to approval by referendum in Qoraqalpog'iston, and also granted official status to the Karakalpak language within the Republic. The most senior government position in Qoraqalpog'iston under this Constitution is that of the Chairman of the Council of Ministers, who is also an ex officio member of the Cabinet of Ministers of the Republic of Uzbekistan. Following the implementation of the new Constitution, the hitherto President, Ashirbekov, became Chairman of the Jo'qorg'i Kenges. In July 1997 Karimov, speaking at an extraordinary session of the Jo'qorg'i Kenges, dismissed Ashirbekov, criticizing his economic performance; he was replaced by Timur Kamalov, the hitherto First Deputy Minister of Agriculture and Water Resources in the Government of Uzbekistan. In May 2002 Kamalov resigned as legislative Chairman, being succeeded by Musa Erniyazov following a vote by the regional legislature. In March 2006 Tursinbai Tanipbergeov, who had held the position of Chairman of the Council of Ministers since October 2002, was replaced by Baxodir Yangiboyev, hitherto the Minister of Finance of Qoraqalpog'iston.

In the late 2000s increasing support for separatist movements, notably an organization known as the Free Qoraqalpog'iston National Revival Party, was reported, and up to 200,000 ethnic Kazakhs previously resident in the region were reported to have emigrated to Kazakhstan in the period following the disintegration of the USSR. The relative poverty of the region, and the severe environmental despoliation of large areas therein (associated particularly with the reduction in size of the Aral Sea) were regarded as being among the principal causes of discontent among those resident in the Republic.

Chairman of the Council of Ministers of the Republic of Qoraqalpog'iston: Baxodir Yangiboyev, 230102 Qoraqalpog'iston, Nukus, Dustlik Gazari 96; tel. (8361) 222-00-14; fax (8361) 222-26-46; e-mail info@sovminrk.gov.uz; internet sovminrk .gov.uz.

Chairman of the Jo'qorg'i Kenges (Legislative Assembly) of the Republic of Qoraqalpog'iston: Musa T. Erniyazov, 230102 Qoraqalpog'iston, Nukus, Dustlik Gazari 96.

Bibliography

Akbarzadeh, S. *Uzbekistan and the United States*. London, Zed Books, 2005.

Allworth, E. A. *The Modern Uzbeks: From the 14th Century to the Present: a Cultural History*. Stanford, CA, Hoover Institution Press, 1990.

Becker, S. *Russia's Protectorates in Central Asia: Bukhara and Khiva, 1865-1924*. London, RoutledgeCurzon, 2004.

Bohr, A. *Uzbekistan: Politics and Foreign Policy (Central Asian and Caucasian Prospects)*. London, Royal Institute of International Affairs, 1998.

Critchlow, J. *Nationalism in Uzbekistan: A Soviet Republic's Road to Sovereignty*. Boulder, CO, Westview Press, 1991.

Everett-Heath, T. (Ed.). *Central Asia: Aspects of Transition*. London, RoutledgeCurzon, 2003.

Human Rights Watch. *Creating Enemies of the State: Religious Persecution in Uzbekistan*. New York, Human Rights Watch, 2004.

Kalter, J. and Pavaloi, M. *Uzbekistan: Heirs to the Silk Road*. London, Thames and Hudson, 1997.

Kamp, M. *The New Woman in Uzbekistan: Islam, Modernity and Unveiling Under Communism*. Seattle, WA, University of Washington Press, 2006.

Kangas, R. D. *Uzbekistan in the Twentieth Century: Political Development and the Evolution of Power*. New York, St Martin's Press, 1994.

Kaser, M. *The Economies of Kazakhstan and Uzbekistan*. Former Soviet South Project, Washington, DC, Brookings Institution Press, 1997.

Lubin, N., Martin, K., and Rubin, B. R. *Calming the Ferghana Valley: Development and Dialogue in the Heart of Central Asia*. Washington, DC, Brookings Institution Press, 2000.

MacFadyen, D. *Russian Culture in Uzbekistan: One Language In The Middle of Nowhere*. Abingdon, Routledge, 2006.

Marozzi, J. *Tamerlane: Sword of Islam, Conqueror of the World*. London, HarperCollins, 2004.

Melvin, N. J. *Uzbekistan: Transition to Authoritarianism on the Silk Road (Post Communist States and Nations)*. London, Routledge, 2000.

Mishra, N. N. *Ethnicity and Islam Revivalism in Tajikistan and Uzbekistan*. New Delhi, National Book Trust, 2007.

Murray, C. *Murder in Samarkand: A British Ambassador's Defiance of Tyranny In The War on Terror*. Edinburgh, Mainstream, 2006.

Northrop, D. *Veiled Empire: Gender and Power in Stalinist Central Asia*. Cornell Univ. Press, 2004.

Rand, R. *Tamerlane's Children: Dispatches from Contemporary Uzbekistan*. Oxford, Oneworld Publications, 2006.

Sahadeo, J. *Russian Colonial Society in Tashkent: 1865-1923*. Bloomington, IN, Indiana University Press, 2006.

Thiébaud, Jean-Marie. *Personnages marquants d'Asie centrale, du Turkestan et de l'Ouzbekistan: dictionnaire biographique*. Paris, L'Harmattan, 2004.

Yalcin, R. *Rebirth of Uzbekistan: Politics, Economy and Society in the Post-Soviet Era*. London, Garnet Publishing, 2002.

Also see the Select Bibliography.

PART THREE

Who's Who of Eastern Europe, Russia and Central Asia

WHO'S WHO OF EASTERN EUROPE, RUSSIA AND CENTRAL ASIA

ABIYEV, Col-Gen. Safar Akhundbala oğlu: Azerbaijani politician and army officer; *Minister of Defence;* b. 27 June 1950, Baku. *Education:* Baku Troops Command Acad., Frunze Acad., Moscow. *Career:* served in Azerbaijani Army, attaining rank of Col-Gen.; currently Minister of Defence. *Address:* Ministry of Defence, 1139 Baku, Azarbaycan pr, Azerbaijan; tel. (12) 439-41-89; fax (12) 492-92-50.

ABRAMOVICH, Roman Arkadyevich: Russian business executive and fmr politician; b. 24 Aug. 1966, Saratov; m. 1st Olga Abramovich; m. 2nd Irina Malandina (divorced 2007); two s. three d. *Education:* Industrial Inst., Ukhta, Komi, Moscow Gubkin Inst. of Oil and Gas. *Career:* f. cos Super-technologia-Shishmarev, Elita, Petroltrans, GID, NPR 1992–95; Head, Moscow Office Runicom SA, Switzerland 1993–96; f. (with Boris Berezovskii) Jt Stock Co. P.K. Trust 1995; f. cos Mekong, Centurion-M, Agrofert, Multitrust, Oilimpex, Sibreal, Forneft, Servet, Branko, Vektor-A 1995–96; Founder and Dir-Gen. Runicom Ltd Gibraltar 1997–99; Dir Moscow br. Sibneft 1996–97, Dir Sibneft 1996–2005; acquired major interest in Evraz Group S.A. (steel and mining cos) 2006–; mem. State Duma 1998–2000; Gov. of Chukot Autonomous Okrug 2000–08 (resignation rejected by Pres. Putin 2007, accepted 2008), Head of Govt 2001–08; mem., Chukot Autonomous Okrug Duma, 2008–; Owner, Chelsea Football Club (UK) 2003–; Order of Honour 2006. *Address:* Evraz Group S.A., 127006 Moscow, ul. Dolgorukovskaya 15, Bldgs 4 and 5, Russia; tel. (495) 232-1370 (Evraz); fax (495) 232-1359 (Evraz); internet www.evraz.com.

AHMADJONOV, Muhammadjon A.: Uzbekistani politician; *Chairman, Liberal Democratic Party of Uzbekistan (O'zbekiston Liberal Demokratik Partiyasi);* b. 1955, Kuva, Farg'ona Viloyat; m.; three c. *Career:* mem. and Chair. Liberal Democratic Party of Uzbekistan (O'zbekiston Liberal Demokratik Partiyasi) 2004–. *Address:* Liberal Democratic Party of Uzbekistan (O'zbekiston Liberal Demokratik Partiyasi), 100015 Tashkent, Mirobod tumani, Nukus ko'ch. 73a, Uzbekistan; tel. (71) 133-28-46; e-mail uzlidep@intal.uz.

AKHMETOV, Danial Kenzhetayevich, BEng, BEcons; Kazakhstani politician; *Minister of Defence;* b. 15 June 1954, Pavlodar; m.; two c. *Education:* Pavlodar Industry Inst. *Career:* fmr racing cyclist; fmr Deputy Prime Minister and Minister of Industry, Energy, Transport and Communications; Akim (Gov.) Pavlodar Oblast 1995–97, 2001–03; Akim (Gov.) Northern Kazakhstan Oblast 1997–99; Deputy, then First Deputy Prime Minister, 1999–2001; Prime Minister of Kazakhstan 2003–07 (resgnd); Minister of Defence 2007–. *Address:* Ministry of Defence, 010000 Astana, Beibitshilik 51a, Kazakhstan; tel. (7172) 33-78-89; fax (7172) 33-78-89; internet www.mod.kz.

AKHMETOV, Rinat Leonidovych, BA; Ukrainian business executive; b. 21 Sept. 1966, Donetsk; m.; two c. *Education:* Donetsk State Univ. *Career:* f. Donetsk City Bank; Head, Donetsk Industrial Group (conglomerate of steel and mining cos); prin. shareholder, System Capital Man. (SCM) (holding co. with controlling shares in more than 90 cos); Pres. Shaktar Donetsk football club 1996–; Deputy, Verkhovna Rada (Supreme Council) 2006–; mem. Party of the Regions (PR) (Partiya Regioniv); Founder, Foundation for Effective Governance, Kyiv. *Address:* System Capital Management, 83001 Donetsk, vul. Postysheva 117; Verkhovna Rada (Supreme Council), 01008 Kyiv, vul. M. Hrushevskoho 5, Ukraine; tel. (44) 255-35-69 (Verkhovna Rada); fax (62) 334-99-08; e-mail Akhmetov.Rinat@rada.gov.ua; internet www.scm.com.ua; www.shakhtar.com.

AKILOV, Akil Gaibullayevich: Tajikistani politician and engineer; *Chairman, Council of Ministers (Prime Minister) and Minister of Construction;* b. 2 Feb. 1944, Leninabad (now Khujand); m.; three c. *Education:* Moscow Inst. of Construction and Eng. *Career:* various posts in construction orgs, Leninabad (now Sogdh) Viloyat 1960–76; worked for CP 1976–93; Minister of Construction of Tajikistan 1993–94; Deputy Prime Minister 1994–96; First Deputy Chair. Leninabad Viloyat 1996–99; Chair. Council of Ministers (Prime Minister) and Minister of Construction 1999–. *Address:* Secretariat of the Prime Minister, 734023 Dushanbe, Xiyoboni Rudaki 80, Tajikistan; tel. (372) 21-18-71; fax (372) 21-51-10.

ALEKPEROV, Vagit Yusufovich, DEcon; Russian-Azerbaijani business executive; *President and Director, Lukoil;* b. 1 Sept. 1950, Baku; m.; one s. *Education:* Azizbekov Inst. of Oil and Chem., Azerbaijan. *Career:* worked in oil industry in Azerbaijan and Western Siberia 1968–75; worked as engineer for Kasporneft, Surgntneftegaz.Bashneft cos 1975–84; Dir Kogalymneftegas (oil-extraction co.) 1984–90; Deputy, then First Deputy Minister of Oil and Gas Industry of USSR 1990–91; Chair. Bd Imperial Bank, Petrocommercial Bank; Founder, mem. Bd of Dirs and Pres. Lukoil 1993–, Chair. 1993–2000, currently Chair. Man. Cttee; Deputy Chair. Oil Exporters Union of Russia; Vice-Pres. Int. Oil Consortium; mem. Russian Acad. of Natural Sciences; awarded four orders and eight medals; winner of two Russian Govt prizes. *Publication:* Vertical Integrated Oil Companies in Russia. *Address:* Lukoil, Sretenskii bulv. 11, 101000 Moscow, Russia; tel. (495) 627-44-44; fax (495) 625-70-16; e-mail pr@lukoil.com; internet www.lukoil.com.

ALEKSEI II, His Holiness Patriarch, DCT; Russian ecclesiastic; *Patriarch of Moscow and All Russia;* b. (A. M. Ridiger), 23 Feb. 1929, Tallinn, Estonia. *Education:* Leningrad (now St Petersburg) Theological Acad. *Career:* ordained priest 1950; Vice-Bishop of Tallinn and Estonia 1961–64; mem. Cen. Cttee of WCC 1961–68; Vice-Chair. Dept of External Church Relations, Moscow Patriarchate 1961–64; mem. Holy Synod Comm. on Christian Unity and Inter-Church Relations; Archbishop 1964, Admin. Man. of Moscow Patriarchate 1964–86, Perm. mem. of Holy Synod 1964–, Chair. Teaching Cttee of Moscow Patriarchate 1965–86; Metropolitan of Tallinn and Estonia 1968–86; Metropolitan of Leningrad and Novgorod 1986–90; Patriarch of Moscow and All Russia 1990–; Chair. of Presidium Conf. of European Churches 1987–92; USSR People's Deputy 1989–91; mem. Russian Acad. of Educ.; Hon. mem. Moscow Acad. of Theology, St Petersburg Acad. of Theology; DTheol hc (Acad. of Theology, Debrecen, Hungary), (Acad. of Theology, Prague), (Gen. Seminary of Episcopal Church, USA) 1991, (St Vladimir's Theological Seminary, USA) 1991, (Alaska Pacific Univ., USA) 1993, (Tbilisi Theological Acad., Georgia) 1996; Hon. Prof. (Omsk State Univ.) 1993, (Moscow State Univ.) 1993; Dr hc (St Petersburg Univ.) 1994; Order of St Andrew the First-Called 1994, Order for Services to the Fatherland 1994. *Address:* Moscow Patriarchate, 115191 Moscow, Danilov Monastery, ul. Danilovskii Val 22, Russia; tel. (495) 954-24-39; fax (495) 633-72-81; e-mail es@mospatr.ru; internet www.mospat.ru.

ALIYEV, İlham Heydar oğlu: Azerbaijani business executive, politician and head of state; *President;* b. 24 Dec. 1961, Baku; one s. two d. *Education:* Moscow State Univ. of Int. Relations. *Career:* teacher, Moscow State Univ. of Int. Relations 1985–90; engaged in commercial activity in Moscow and İstanbul 1991–94; First Vice-Pres. State Oil Co. of the Azerbaijani Repub. (SOCAR) 1994–2003; mem. Parl.

1995–2003; Deputy Chair. Yeni Azerbaijan (New Azerbaijan Party) 1999–2001, First Deputy Chair. 2001–; Prime Minister of Azerbaijan Aug. 2003; Pres. of Azerbaijan Oct. 2003–; Pres. Nat. Olympic Cttee 1997–; Leader Del. to Council of Europe; Hon. Prof. L.N.Gumilev Eurasian Nat. Univ., Kazakhstan, Univ. of Nat. and World Economy, Bulgaria, Moscow State Univ. Order of Heydar Aliyev, of Sheikhulislam (Azerbaijan), Order of The Star of Romania, Order of King Abdul Aziz (Saudi Arabia), Order of Honour (Georgia), Grand Cross, Legion d'honneur, Grand Cross of Order of Merit (Poland); Dr hc (Lincoln Univ., USA, Moscow State Univ., Bilkent Univ., Turkey, Nat. Acad. of Taxes, Ukraine, Petroleum and Gas Univ. of Ploesti, Romania, Kyung Hee Univ., South Korea, Jordan Univ., Corvinus Univ., Hungary); PACE Medal 2004, Ihsan Dogramacı Prize for Int. Relations for Peace (Turkey). *Address:* Office of the President, 1066 Baku, İstiqlaliyet küç. 19, Azerbaijan; tel. (12) 492-17-26; fax (12) 492-35-43; e-mail office@apparat.gov.az; internet www.ilham-aliyev.com; www .president.az.

ALIYEV, Natiq: Azerbaijani oil industry executive and government official; *Minister of Industry and Energy. Career:* Pres., State Oil Co. of the Azerbaijani Repub. (SOCAR) 1993–2005; Minister of Industry and Energy 2005–. *Address:* Ministry of Energy and Industry, 1012 Baku, Hasanbek Zardabi küç. 88, Azerbaijan; tel. (12) 498-78-56; fax (12) 598-16-78; e-mail pressa@mie.gov.az; internet www.mie.gov.az.

AMANMYRADOV, Orazgeldy: Turkmenistani politician; *Minister of Internal Affairs;* b. 1970, Dostluk, Akhal Velayat. *Education:* Makhtumkuli Turkmen State Univ. *Career:* joined Ministry of Nat. Security 1995, held various positions; Vice Chancellor Mil. Acad. 2007; Minister of Internal Affairs 2007–. *Address:* Ministry of Internal Affairs, 744000 Aşgabat, pr. Magtymguly 85, Turkmenistan; tel. (12) 35-59-23.

ASADOV, Oktai S.: Azerbaijani engineer and politician; *Chairman, Milli Majlis;* b. 3 Jan. 1955, Shaharjik village, Gafan Dist; m.; two c. *Education:* Azerbaijan Chemistry Inst. *Career:* early position at Baku Air Conditioning Factory; Sr Engineer, Azerbaijan Special Installation and Construction Co. 1979–81; Sr Engineer Azerbaycantexqurashdirma 1981–83, Head of Dept No. 1 1983–89; CEO Santexqurash-dirma Industrial Union 1989–96; Pres. Absheron Regional Jt Stock Water Co. 1996–2004; Pres. Azersu Jt Stock Co. 2004–; mem. New Azerbaijan Party 1999–; Deputy, Milli Majlis (Nat. Ass.) 2000–, Chair. 2005–. *Address:* Milli Majlis (National Assembly), 1152 Baku, Parlament pr. 1, Azerbaijan; tel. (12) 439-97-50; fax (12) 493-49-43; e-mail azmm@meclis.gov.az; internet www.meclis.gov.az.

ATAMBAYEV, Almazbek Sharshenovich: Kyrgyzstani engineer and politician; b. 17 Sept. 1956, Alamudun, Chui Oblast. *Education:* Moscow Inst. of Man. *Career:* engineer with Kyrgyz SSR Ministry of Communications 1980–81; Sr Engineer with DU-4, Frunze (now Bishkek) 1981–83; held position in Presidium of Supreme Soviet, Kyrgyz SSR 1983–87; Deputy Chair. Exec. Cttee Pervomaisky Dist. Council of People's Deputies, Frunze 1987–89; Founder and Head, Forum (business firm) 1989; Deputy in Jogorku Kenesh (parl.) 1995–2000; Gen.-Dir Kyrgyzavtomash 1997–99; Chair. Social Democratic Party of Kyrgyzstan 1999–; Minister of Industry, Trade and Tourism 2005–06 (resgnd); Co-Chair. Opposition For Reforms movt 2006; apptd Prime Minister of Kyrgyzstan March–Nov. 2007; unsuccessful presidential cand. 2000; Dank Medal 1999. *Address:* Social Democratic Party of Kyrgyzstan, 720000 Bishkek, Alma-Atinskaya 4b/203, Kyrgyzstan; tel. (312) 43-15-07.

AZAROV, Mykola Yanovych, PhD; Ukrainian geologist, economist and politician; b. 17 Dec. 1947, Kaluga, Russia; m.; one s. *Education:* M. Lomonosov Moscow State Univ. *Career:* Lab. Man. and Head of Dept, Moscow Research Design Coal Inst. 1976–84; Deputy Dir Ukrainian State Research and Design Inst. of Mining Geology, Geomechanics and Mine Survey, Coal Ministry 1984–95; Chief of State Tax Admin 1996–2002; First Deputy Prime Minister and Minister of Finance 2002–05, 2006–07; Chair. Political Council, Party

of the Regions (Partiya Rehioniv) 2003–; Acting Prime Minister 2005; mem. Nat. Acad. of Sciences of Ukraine 1997–; Honored Economist of Ukraine 1997. *Publications:* author of numerous books and articles on geology and taxation. *Address:* Party of the Regions (Partiya Rehioniv), 01021 Kyiv, vul. Lypska 10, Ukraine; tel. (44) 254-29-20; fax (44) 254-33-70; e-mail partreg@ln.ua; internet www .partyofregions.org.ua.

AZIMOV, Rustam S., PhD; Uzbekistani economist and politician; *Deputy Prime Minister, responsible for the Economic Sector and Foreign Economic Relations and Minister of Finance;* b. 1958. *Education:* Tashkent Inst. of Agricultural Engineers. *Career:* Economist, Yulius Fuchik collective farm; Chief Economist of agricultural amalgamation in Djizak area; Chair. Nat. Bank for Foreign Econ. Activity 1991–98; mem. Oly Majlis (Supreme Ass.) 1994–; Minister of Finance 1998–2000, 2005–; Deputy Prime Minister and Minister of Macroeconomics and Statistics 2000–02; Deputy Prime Minister and Economy Minister 2002–05; Minister of Foreign Econ. Relations July–Nov. 2005; Deputy Prime Minister, responsible for the Econ. sector and Foreign Econ. Relations 2005–; Uzbekistan Del. to Asian Devt Bank; fmr lecturer in econs, Tashkent State Univ.; f. Ipak Yuli Bank. *Publications:* numerous articles on econs. *Address:* Ministry of Finance, 100008 Tashkent, Mustaqillik maydoni 5, Uzbekistan; tel. (71) 233-70-73; fax (71) 244-56-43; e-mail info@mf.uz; internet www.mf.uz.

BAGAPSH, Sergei Vasilyevich: Georgian (Abkhaz) politician; *'President of Republic of Abkhazia';* b. 1949, Sukhumi. *Education:* Georgian Inst. of Agronomy. *Career:* First Sec. of Abkhaz Komsomol 1980–82, Ochamchire Komsomol 1982–85; Perm. 'Rep. of Abkhaz' leadership in Moscow, Russian Fed. –1997; 'Prime Minister' of self-proclaimed 'Repub. of Abkhazia' 1997–2001; Gen.-Dir ChernoMorEnergo (BlackSeaEnergy) 2001–; 'Minister of Energy' 2001–04; jt cand. in Abkhaz presidential elections (for Amtsakhara and United Abkhazia opposition movts) 2004; 'Pres. of Repub. of Abkhazia' 2004–. *Address:* 'Office of the President', 6600 Abkhazia, Sukhumi, Georgia; tel. (122) 2-46-35; fax (122) 2-71-17; internet www.abkhaziagov.org.

BAKIYEV, Kurmanbek Saliyevich: Kyrgyzstani politician, engineer and head of state; *President;* b. 1 Aug. 1949, Masadan (now Teyyit), Suzdak Dist, Jalal-Abad; m. Tatyana Vasilyevna Bakiyeva; two s. *Education:* Kuibyshev (now Samara) Polytechnic Inst., Russia. *Career:* trained as electrical engineer 1972; served in Soviet Armed Forces 1974–86; electrical engineer Maslennikov Plant, Kuibyshev 1976–79; Sr Engineer, Head of VTs, then Deputy Chief Engineer, Jalal-Abad Electrical Factory 1979–85; Dir Profil Plant, Kok-Yangak 1985–90; First Sec. CP Kok-Yangak City Council 1990; Deputy Chair. W Jalal-Abad Council of People's Deputies 1991–92; Head of Toguz-Torou Regional Admin 1992–94; Deputy Chair. State Property Fund 1994–95; First Deputy Head, then Head W Jalal-Abad State Admin and Gov. of Jalal-Abad Duban 1995–97; Gov. of Chui Duban 1997–2000; Prime Minister of Kyrgyzstan 2000–02, Acting Prime Minister March–June 2005; mem. Zhogorku Kenesh (Parl.) 2003–05; Acting Pres. of Kyrgyzstan March–Aug. 2005, Pres. Aug. 2005–; Leader, People's Power Movt. *Address:* Office of the President, 720003 Bishkek, Dom Pravitelstva, Kyrgyzstan; tel. (312) 21-24-66; fax (312) 21-86-27; e-mail office@mail.gov.kg; internet www.president.kg.

BAKRADZE, Davit, MPA, CandPhys-MathSci; Georgian physicist and politician; *Chairman, Sakartvelos Parlamenti;* b. 1 July 1972, Tbilisi; m.; two c. *Education:* Georgian Tech. Univ., Georgian-American Inst. of Public Admin, Tbilisi State Univ., Diplomats' Training Course, Swiss Int. Relations Univ. Seminars (SIRUS), Geneva, Defence and Security Studies Course 'Leaders for the 21st Century', G. Marshall European Centre for Security Studies, Garmisch-Partenkirchen, Germany, Sr Course for Officers and Diplomats, NATO Defence Coll., Rome, Italy. *Career:* First Class State Counsellor; holds diplomatic rank of Chief Minister Counsellor; Deputy Head of Disarmament and Arms Control Div., Politico-Mil. Dept,

Ministry of Foreign Affairs 1996–98, Head of Disarmament and Arms Control Div. 1998–2000, Deputy Dir Politico-Mil. Dept 2000–02, Head, Service for Security Issues, Nat. Security Council of Georgia 2002–03, Dir Dept for Int. Security and Conflict Man. 2003–04, Dir Dept for Political Security 2004; mem. Parl. 2004–, Chair. Cttee on European Integration 2004–07, Standing Del. to European Parl., Co-Chair. EU-Georgia Parl. Co-operation Cttee, mem. numerous dels; State Minister on Conflict Resolution Issues 2007–08; Minister of Foreign Affairs Feb.–May 2008; Chair. Sakartvelos Parlamenti (Parl.) June 2008–; mem. United Nat. Movt (UNP) Party; Special Prize of Pres. of Georgia: Prize for Academic Excellence to the Best Student of Inst. of Public Admin 1996, NATO/EAPC Research Fellowship 1998, Special Gratification from Minister of Foreign Affairs No. 53/2: For Active Participation in Drawing up Adapted Agreements on the Conventional Forces in Europe at OSCE Istanbul Summit 2000, Special Gratification for Significant Professional Achievements in Drawing up Significant Agreements between the States, Pres. of Georgia 2000, Swiss Leadership Award in Int. Relations, Special Award of Grad. Inst. of Int. Studies, Geneva 2005. *Address:* Sakartvelos Parlamenti, 0118 Tbilisi, Rustaveli 8, Georgia; tel. (32) 93-61-70; fax (32) 99-93-86; e-mail hdstaff@parliament.ge; internet www.parliament.ge.

BALOHA, Viktor: Ukrainian politician; *Chief of the Presidential Secretariat;* b. 1963. *Career:* fmr commodities researcher; Chair. of Admin. Transcarpathian Oblast 1999–2001, Feb.–Sept. 2005; mem. Verkhovna Rada (Parl.) 2002–05, mem. Our Ukraine party; Mayor of Mukachevo 2004–06; Minister of Emergency Situations Aug.–Sept. 2006; Chief of the Presidential Secretariat Sept. 2006–. *Address:* Office of the President, 01021 Kyiv, vul. Shovkovichna 12, Ukraine; tel. (44) 226-20-77; fax (44) 293-61-61; e-mail president@adm.gov.ua; internet www.president.gov.ua.

BALUYEVSKII, Col-Gen. Yurii Nikolayevich: Russian army officer; *Chief of the General Staff, Russian Armed Forces;* b. 9 Jan. 1947, Trubavets, Drohobych Raion, Lviv Oblast, Ukrainian SSR. *Education:* Leningrad (now St Petersburg) Higher Mil. Command School of Gen. Army, M. Frunze Mil. Acad., Mil. Acad. of Gen. Staff. *Career:* infantry officer 1970–82; Sr Officer, Ooperator, and Head of Group Chief Operation Dept of Gen. Staff; First Deputy Commdr of Group, Russian Forces in Caucasus; Deputy Head Chief Operation Dept of Gen. Staff 1982–2001, First Deputy Chief of Gen. Staff 2001–04, Chief and First Deputy Minister of Defence 2004–; apptd to Security Council of Russian Fed. 2004; Order for Service to Motherland in Armed Forces, Order of Audacity; nine medals. *Address:* Ministry of Defence, 105175 Moscow, ul. Myasnitskaya 37, Russia; tel. (495) 293-38-54; fax (495) 296-84-36; internet www.mil.ru.

BARAMIDZE, Giorgi: Georgian politician; *Deputy Prime Minister and State Minister, responsible for Euro-Atlantic Integration;* b. 1968, Tbilisi; m. Eka Jafaridze; one d. *Education:* Polytechnic Inst. of Georgia, George C. Marshall Center for European Security Studies, Germany. *Career:* Founding mem. Green Party of Georgia 1990; commanded state centre responsible for the search for the missing and for freeing prisoners during war in Abkhazia 1992–93; Chair. Comm. for the Protection of Human Rights and Nat. Minorities 1992–94; mem. Parl. 1992–, Chair. Anti-Corruption Comm. 1996–98, Chair. Defence and Security Cttee 2000–03; Founding mem. Citizen's Union of Georgia 1995, Chair. Parl. Group 1996–98; Research Assoc., Georgetown Univ., Washington, DC 1998–99; Minister of Internal Affairs 2003–04, of Defence June–Dec. 2004; Deputy Prime Minister and State Minister, responsible for Euro-Atlantic Integration 2004–. *Address:* Office of the Deputy Prime Minister, State Minister, responsible for Euro-Atlantic Integration, 0105 Tbilisi, P. Ingorovka 7, Georgia; tel. (32) 93-28-67; fax (32) 93-27-22; internet www.eu-nato.gov.ge.

BAYMENOV, Alikhan Mukhamediyevich: Kazakhstani politician; *Chairman, Bright Road—Democratic Party of Kazakhstan;* b. 25 March 1959, Karaganda. *Career:* held numerous govt posts including Head, Presidential Admin 1998–99; Minister of Labour and Social Security 2000–01; Co-f. Democratic Choice of Kazakhstan party 2001; Co-founder and Chair. Bright Road—Democratic Party of Kazakhstan (Ak Zhol) 2002–; unsuccessful presidential cand. 2005. *Address:* Bright Road—Democratic Party of Kazakhstan (Ak Zhol), 010000 Astana, Imanov 18/7, Kazakhstan; tel. (7172) 22-10-66; fax (7172) 22-14-50; e-mail oral@kepter.kz; internet www.akzhol.kz.

BENDUKIDZE, Kakha Avtandilovich, BSc; Georgian business executive, government official and scientist; *Head, Chancellery of the Government;* b. 20 April 1956, Tbilisi. *Education:* Tbilisi State Univ., Lomonosov State Univ., Moscow, Russia. *Career:* Sr Lab. Asst and Scientific Research Asst, USSR Acad. of Sciences Inst. of Biochemistry and Physiology of Microorganisms 1981–85; Head, Molecular Genetics Lab., Scientific Research Inst. of Biotechnology 1985–92; f. Bioprocess Asscn 1988, Dir 1990–92; Chair. Bd of Dirs Promtorgbank (Industrial and Trade Bank) 1992–93; Chief Dir NIPEK (Nat. Oil Investment Corpn) 1993–95; co-f. Russian Business Round Table 1993; Chair. Uralmash-Izhora Group 1995–98, CEO 1998–2004; Prof., Higher School of Econs, Moscow 2002–; Minister of Econ. Devt June–Dec. 2004, State Minister, responsible for Econ. Reforms Dec. 2004–2007; Head, Chancellery of the Govt 2008–. *Address:* Chancellery of the Government, 0105 Tbilisi, P. Ingorovka 7, Georgia; tel. (32) 92-26-87; fax (32) 92-10-69; internet www.government.gov.ge.

BERDYMUKHAMMEDOV, Gurbanguly Myalikgulyyevich, PhD; Turkmenistani politician and head of state; *President and Prime Minister;* b. 1957, Babarab, Ahal Prov. *Education:* Turkmen State Medical Inst. *Career:* mem. Dentistry Faculty, Turkmen State Medical Inst. 1979–97, Assoc. Prof. and Dean 1995–97; Head of Dentistry Centre, Ministry of Health 1995–97; Minister of Health 1997–2001; Deputy Prime Minister 2001–06; acting Pres. (following death of Saparmurat Niyazov) 2006–07, Pres. and Prime Minister 2007–; Chair. Nat. Olympic Cttee 2007–. *Address:* Office of the President and the Council of Ministers, 744000 Aşgabat, Presidential Palace, Turkmenistan; tel. (12) 35-45-34; fax (12) 35-51-12; internet www.turkmenistan.gov.tm.

BEREZOVSKII, Boris Abramovich, DrMathSc; Russian mathematician, business executive and fmr politician; b. 23 Jan. 1946, Moscow; m.; one s. three d. *Education:* Moscow Inst. of Wood Tech., Moscow State Univ. *Career:* engineer, Research Inst. of Testing Machines, Equipment and Measurement Devices 1968–69; engineer, Hydrometeorological Research Cen. 1969; engineer, researcher, head of div. Inst. of Problems of Man. 1969–87; Corresp. mem. Russian Acad. of Sciences 1991; supervisor of introduction of automatization on Tolyatti Car Works (VAZ) 1973–91; Co-founder and Dir-Gen. LOGOVAZ Co. 1991–96, 1997–; Dir-Gen. All-Union Automobile Alliance (AVVA) 1993–96; Deputy Chair. Bd of Dirs Public Russian TV 1995–96; Deputy Sec., Security Council of Russian Fed. 1996–97; Exec. Sec., CIS 1998–99; elected to State Duma Dec. 1999, resgnd July 2000; f. Charity Foundation Triumph 1994; f. non-governmental Int. Foundation for Civil Liberties 2000; Co-f. Liberal Russia political party 2001, expelled from party after offering funding to CP of Russian Fed.; granted asylum in UK 2003. *Publications include:* over 100 scientific articles on applied math. and theory of man. *Address:* c/o International Foundation for Civil Liberties, 1230 Avenue of the Americas, 7th Floor, New York, NY 10020, USA; tel. (212) 397-2974.

BOHATYROVA, Raisa Vasylivna: Ukrainian gynaecologist and politician; *Chairman, National Security and Defence Council. Career:* fmr Minister of Health; mem. Verkhovna Rada (Parl.) 2002–, mem. Party of Regions, fmr Leader Parl. faction; Chair. Nat. Security and Defence Council 2008–. *Address:* National Security and Defence Council (RNBU), 01601 Kyiv, vul. Komandarma Kameneva 8, Ukraine; tel. (44) 255-05-36; fax (44) 255-05-36; e-mail public@rainbow.gov.ua; internet www.rainbow.gov.ua.

BORTNIKOV, Lt-Gen. Aleksander Vasilyevich: Russian government official; *Head, Federal Security Service (FSB);* b. 1951, Perm Oblast; m.; one s. *Education:* Leningrad Inst. for Railway Eng. *Career:* joined Leningrad KGB 1975, Deputy Head, Fed. Security Service (FSB) Directorate for St Petersburg and Leningrad Oblast in charge of counter-intelligence operations –2003, Head of Directorate 2003–04; Deputy Dir FSB and Head of Econ. Security Service 2004–08, Head of FSB 2008–; mem. Bd of Dirs Sovkomflot. *Address:* Federal Security Service (FSB), 103031 Moscow, Bolshaya Lubyanka, Building 1/3, Russia; tel. (495) 914-43-69; e-mail fsb@fsb.ru; internet www.fsb.ru.

BURJANADZE, Nino, JD, PhD; Georgian politician, lawyer and professor of international law; b. 16 July 1964, Kutaisi; m. Badri Bitsadze 1960; two c. *Education:* Akaki Tsereteli School, Kutaisi, Tbilisi State Univ., Moscow Lomonosov State Univ. *Career:* Prof. of Int. Relations and Int. Law, Tbilisi State Univ. 1991–; consultant to Ministry of Environmental Protection 1991–92, Parl. Cttee on Foreign Relations 1992–95; mem. Parl. 1995–, Deputy Chair. Cttee on Constitutional Legal Affairs and Rule of Law 1995–98, Chair. 1998–99, Chair. Cttee on Foreign Relations 2000–01, Speaker of Parl. of Georgia 2001–04, 2004–08; Rapporteur Gen. Cttee on Democracy, Human Rights and Humanitarian Issues, OSCE Parl. Ass. 1998–2000, Vice-Pres. OSCE Parl. Ass. 2000–; Pres. Parl. Ass. of Black Sea Econ. Co-operation 2001–02; fmr mem. Citizen's Union of Georgia, initiated efforts to organize opposition alliance of United Democrats, Nat. Movt and New Rights Party 2003; formed Burjanadze Democrats electoral bloc Aug. 2003; Interim Pres. of Georgia Nov. 2003–Jan. 2004; Chair. Perm. Parl. Del. to UK 1995–98; Co-Chair. EU–Georgian Parl. Co-operation Cttee 1999–2000; Pres. Black Sea Econ. Cooperation Parl. Ass. 2001–02; mem. Young Lawyers Asscn, Int. Justice Asscn, Int. Marine Justice Asscn, US Int. Justice Asscn; participant in numerous int. confs. *Publications include:* Legal Problems of International Organisations of a New Type; over 40 articles on issues related to int. law and int. relations. *Address:* Sakartvelos Parlamenti, 0118 Tblisi, Rustaveli 8, Georgia; tel. (32) 93-61-70; fax (32) 99-93-86; e-mail hdstaff@parliament.ge; internet www.parliament.ge.

CHAIKA, Yurii Yakovlevich: Russian lawyer and government official; *Prosecutor-General;* b. 1951, Nikolayevsk-on-Amur, Khabarovsk Krai; m.; two c. *Education:* Sverdlovsk Inst. of Law. *Career:* electrician at ship-building factory, Nikolayevsk-on-Amur 1970; joined Prosecutor's Office, Irkutsk Region 1976, held several positions including investigator, Deputy Regional Public Prosecutor, Taishetsk Transport Public Prosecutor, Head, Investigative Div. of East Siberian Transport Public Prosecutor's Office 1983–92, Public Prosecutor of Irkutsk Region 1992–95; instructor, Admin. Div., Irkutsk Regional CPSU Cttee 1984–92; First Deputy Prosecutor-Gen. of Russian Fed. 1995–99, Acting Prosecutor-Gen. 1999–2000; Minister of Justice 1999–2006; Prosecutor-Gen. of Russian Fed. 2006–; Hon. Lawyer of the Russian Fed., Hon. Officer, Prosecution Service of the Russian Fed.; Order of Merit for Country, IV Degree, Order of Honour. *Address:* Office of the Prosecutor-General, 125993 Moscow, ul. B. Dmitrovka 15a, Russia; tel. (495) 692-26-82; fax (495) 292-88-48; internet www.genproc.gov.ru.

CHUBAIS, Anatolii Borisovich, CEconSc; Russian economist, business executive and politician; *Chairman, Russian State Nanotechnology Corporation (Rosnanotech);* b. 16 June 1955, Borisov, Minsk Oblast, Belarusian SSR; m. 1st (divorced); one s. one d.; m. 2nd Mariya Chubais. *Education:* Leningrad Inst. of Tech. and Eng. *Career:* engineer and Asst to Chair. Leningrad (now St Petersburg) Inst. of Econs and Eng 1977–82, Asst Prof. 1982–90, Deputy, then First Deputy-Chair. of Leningrad Municipal Council Jan.–Nov. 1991; Minister of Russia and Chair. State Cttee for Man. of State Property 1991–98; Deputy Prime Minister and Chair. Co-ordination Council for Privatization 1992–94; First Deputy Prime Minister responsible for economy 1994–96; mem. State Duma (Parl.) 1993–95; Head of Pres. Admin 1996–97; First Deputy Prime Minister 1997–98, Minister of Finance March–

Nov. 1997; Russian Dir EBRD 1997–98; mem. Russian Security Council 1997–98; Head of Russian Fed. Interdepartmental Comm. on Co-operation with Int. Financial and Econ. Orgs and Group of Seven 1998; CEO Unified Energy Systems of Russia 1998–2001, CEO and Chair. Bd of Man. 2001–08; Chair. Russian State Nanotechnology Corpn. (Rosnanotech) 2008–; Co-Chair. Round Table of Russian and EU Producers 2000–; Pres. Electric Power Council of CIS 2000–; mem. Int. Advisory Bd JP Morgan Chase 2008–; mem. Man. Bd Russian Union of Mfrs and Entrepreneurs 2000–; mem. Govt Comm. on Co-operation with EU 2000–; joined Union of Rightist Forces 1999, Co-Chair. 2001–04 (resgnd); Best Minister of Finance Award (Euromoney magazine) 1997. *Address:* Russian State Nanotechnology Corporation (Rosnanotech), 117420 Moscow, ul. Nametkina 12a, Russia; tel. (495) 542-44-44; fax (495) 542-44-34; e-mail info@rusnano.com; internet www.rusnanotekh.ru; www.chubais.ru.

CHUDINOV, Igor Vitalyevich: Kyrgyzstani politician; *Prime Minister;* b. 21 Aug. 1961. *Education:* Kyrgyz State Univ., Int. Business School, Moscow, Russia. *Career:* held high-ranking positions in Komsomol; early career as computer programmer; worked in a variety of positions as business exec. 1991–2005; Dir-Gen. Kyrgyzgaz (state co. that procures gas supplies for Kyrgyzstan) 2005–07; Minister of Industry, Energy and Fuel Resources Feb.–Dec. 2007; Prime Minister Dec. 2007–; mem. Ak Zhol party. *Address:* Office of the Prime Minister, 720003 Bishkek, Dom Pravitelstvo, Kyrgyzstan; tel. (312) 66-12-20; fax (312) 66-66-58; e-mail pmoffice@mail.gov .kg; internet www.government.gov.kg.

DANYLYSHYN, Bohdan Myhaylovich, DEcon; Ukrainian economist, academic and government official; *Minister of the Economy;* b. 6 June 1965, Tserkivna, Dolyn dist, Ivano-Frankivsk Oblast. *Education:* Ternopol State Pedagogical Inst. *Career:* Prof. of Econs 2003–; fmr Head of Council on Productive Forces Research, Nat. Acad. of Sciences of Ukraine; Minister of the Economy 2007–; Corresp. mem. Nat. Acad. of Sciences of Ukraine 2004–; State Prize of Ukraine in of science and technology. *Publications include:* more than 150 scientific papers on regional policy, economics and exploration of nature resources. *Address:* Ministry of the Economy, 01008 Kyiv, vul. M. Hrushevskoho 12/2, Ukraine; tel. (44) 253-93-94; fax (44) 226-31-81; e-mail meconomy@me .gov.ua; internet www.me.gov.ua.

DERIPASKA, Oleg Vladimirovich: Russian business executive; *Chairman, RUSAL;* b. 2 Jan. 1968, Dzerzhinsk, Gorkii (now Nizhnii Novgorod) Oblast; m. Polina Yumashev; one s. *Education:* Moscow State Univ., Plekhanov Acad. of Nat. Econs. *Career:* Financial Dir Jt Stock Mil. Investment and Trade Co. 1990–92; Dir Gen. Rosaluminproduct 1992–93; Dir Krasnoyarskaluminproduct 1993; Dir-Gen. Aluminproduct 1993–94, Chief Financial Officer 1994–96; Dir Sayany Aluminium Plant 1996–2000; Pres. Sibizsky Aluminy Group 1997–2000; Chair., Russian Aluminium Corpn (RUSAL) 2000–06, mem. Bd of Dirs 2006–; Founder and Chair. Bd of Dirs Basic Element LLC (holding group for RUSAL), GAZ (automobile mfrs), Aviacor (aircraft mfrs), Ingosstrakh (insurance co.); Chair. Bd Russian Nat. Cttee of Int. Chamber of Commerce; mem. Entrepreneurship Council of Govt of Russian Fed.; mem. Business Advisory Council APEC 2007–; Vice-Pres. Russian Union of Businessmen and Entrepreneurs 1999–; Order of Friendship 1999. *Address:* RUSAL Corporate Headquarters, 109240 Moscow, ul. Nikoloyamskaya 13/1, Russia; tel. (495) 720-51-70; fax (495) 720-51-71; e-mail press-center@rusal.ru; internet www.rusal.com.

DODON, Igor, DEcon; Moldovan economist, academic and government official; *First Deputy Prime Minister and Minister of the Economy and Trade;* b. 18 Feb. 1975, Sadova, Straseni Dist; m.; one c. *Education:* Agrarian Univ. of Moldova, Acad. of Econ. Studies, Int. Inst. of Man. *Career:* worked at Moldovan Stock Exchange 1997–2005, positions included Sr Specialist in Clearing and Listing Depts, Man. of Electronic Systems of Negotiation, Dir of Marketing, Listing and Quotations Dept; Chair. Nat. Securities Depository 2001–05; Chair. Moldovan Commodity Exchange 2003–05;

Deputy Minister of Economy and Trade 2005–06, Minister of Economy and Trade 2006–08, First Deputy Prime Minister and Minister of Economy and Trade 2008–; fmr Prof., Acad. of Econ. Studies, Free Int. Univ. of Moldova, Int. Inst. of Man., State Univ. of Moldova. *Address:* Ministry of the Economy and Trade, 2033 Chişinău, Piaţa Marii Adunări Naţionale 1, Moldova; tel. (22) 23-74-48; fax (22) 23-40-64; e-mail mineconcom@mec.gov.md; internet www.mec.gov.md.

FORMUZAL, Mihail: Moldovan politician; *Başkan (Leader), Autonomous Territory of Gagauz-Yeri;* b. 7 Nov. 1959. *Career:* fmr Deputy Mayor, then Mayor of Ceadir-Lunga; Chair. People's Republican Party; Başkan, Autonomous Territory of Gagauz-Yeri 2007–. *Address:* Office of the Başkan of the Autonomous Territory of Gagauz-Yeri, 3800 Comrat, Moldova.

FRADKOV, Mikhail Yefimovich: Russian politician; *Director, Federal Foreign Intelligence Service;* b. 1 Sept. 1950, Kuibyshev (now Samara) Oblast; m. Yelena; two c. *Education:* Moscow Inst. of Machines and Tools, USSR Acad. of Foreign Trade. *Career:* on staff, office of Counsellor on econ. affairs USSR Embassy to India 1973–75; on staff Foreign Trade Agency Tyazhpromeksport, USSR State Cttee on Econ. Relations 1975–84; Deputy, First Deputy Dir of Dept USSR State Cttee on Econ. Relations 1985–91; Deputy Perm. Rep. of Russian Fed. to GATT 1991–92; Sr Adviser Perm. Mission of Russian Fed. to UN; Deputy, First Deputy Minister of External Econ. Relations 1993; Interim Acting Minister of External Econ. Relations 1997; Minister of External Econ. Relations and Trade 1997–98; Chair. Bd of Dirs Ingosstrakh 1998–99, Dir-Gen. 1999; Minister of Trade 1999–2000; First Deputy Sec. Security Council of Russia 2000–01; Head Fed. Service of Tax Police 2001–03; Plenipotentary Rep. to EU 2003–04; apptd Special Rep. of the Pres. of the Russian Fed. on the Devt of Relations with the EU June 2003; Chair. of the Govt (Prime Minister) of Russian Fed. 2004–07 (resgnd); Dir Fed. Foreign Intelligence Service (SVR) Russian Fed. 2007–. *Address:* Federal Foreign Intelligence Service, 101000 Moscow, Glavpochtamt, a/ya 958, Russia; tel. (499) 245-33-68; fax (499) 255-25-29; e-mail svr@gov.ru; internet svr.gov.ru.

GELDYMYRADOV, Khojamyrat: Turkmenistani politician; *Deputy Prime Minister, responsible for Economic Affairs.* *Career:* Deputy Minister of Economy and Finance 2005–07, Co-ordinator of Int. Tech. aid to Turkmenistan 2005–07, Deputy Prime Minister responsible for Econ. Affairs 2007–. *Address:* Ministry of Finance, 744000 Aşgabat, ul. 2008 4, Turkmenistan; tel. (12) 51-05-63; fax (12) 51-18-23.

GEVORGIAN, Armen: Armenian politician; *Deputy Prime Minister and Minister of Territorial Administration;* b. 8 July 1973, Yerevan; m.; two sons. *Education:* Orenburg State Pedagogical Inst., St Petersburg Inst. of State Service, Tventey Univ., Netherlands, St Petersburg Gertsen Russian Pedagogical Inst. *Career:* Asst to Prime Minister 1997–98; Asst to Pres. of Armenia and First Deputy Head of Admin.1998–2000, First Asst to Pres. 2000–06; Head of Pres.'s Admin. 2006–08; Sec., Nat. Security Council.2007–08; Deputy Prime Minister and Minister of Territorial Admin. 2008–; mem. CIS Econ.Council 2008–. *Address:* Ministry of Territorial Administration, 0010 Yerevan, Republic Sq., Government Bldg 2, Armenia; tel. (10) 51-13-02; fax (10) 51-13-31; e-mail mta@mta.gov.am; internet www.mta.gov.am.

GORBACHEV, Mikhail Sergeyevich: Russian organization official and politician; *Head, International Foundation for Socio-Economic and Political Studies;* b. 2 March 1931, Privolnoye, Krasnogvardeiskii Dist, Stavropol Krai; m. Raisa Titarenko 1953 (died 1999); one d. *Education:* Faculty of Law, Moscow State Univ. and Stavropol Agricultural Inst. *Career:* began work as machine operator 1946; joined CPSU 1952; Deputy Head, Dept of Propaganda, Stavropol Komsomol (V. I. Lenin Young Communist League) Territorial Cttee 1955–56, Second, then First Sec. 1958–62; First Sec., Stavropol Komsomol City Cttee 1956–58; del. to CPSU Congress 1961, 1971, 1976, 1981, 1986, 1990; Party Organizer, Stavropol Territorial Production Bd of Collective and State Farms 1962;

Head, Dept of Party Bodies of CPSU Territorial Cttee 1963–66; First Sec., Stavropol City Party Cttee 1966–68; Second Sec., Stavropol Territorial CPSU Cttee 1968–70, First Sec. 1970–78; mem. CPSU Cen. Cttee 1971–91, Sec. for Agric. 1978–85, alt. mem. Political Bureau CPSU, Cen. Cttee 1979–80, mem. 1980–91, Gen. Sec., CPSU Cen. Cttee 1985–91; Deputy Supreme Soviet of USSR 1970–89 (Chair. Foreign Affairs Comm. of Soviet Union 1984–85), mem. Presidium 1985–88, Chair. 1988–89, Supreme Soviet of RSFSR 1980–90, elected to Congress of People's Deputies of USSR 1989, Chair. 1989–90; Pres. of USSR 1990–91; Head, Int. Foundation for Socio-Economic and Political Studies (Gorbachev Foundation) 1992–; Head Int. Green Cross/Green Crescent 1993–; presidential candidate 1996; Co-founder and Co-Chair. Social Democratic Party of Russia 2000–04 (resgnd); syndicated columnist for numerous newspapers worldwide 1992–; Hon. Citizen of Berlin 1992, Freeman of Aberdeen 1993; Nobel Peace Prize 1990, Albert Schweitzer Leadership Award (jt recipient) 1992, Ronald Reagan Freedom Award 1992, Urania-Medaille (Berlin) 1996; Augsburg Peace Prize 2005; Order of Lenin (three times), Orders of Red Banner of Labour, Badge of Honour. *Recording:* Peter and the Wolf: Wolf Tracks (Grammy Award, Best Spoken Word Album for Children (jtly) 2004) 2003. *Publications:* A Time for Peace 1985, The Coming Century of Peace 1986, Speeches and Writings 1986–90, Peace Has No Alternative 1986, Moratorium 1986, Perestroika: New Thinking for Our Country and the World 1987, The August Coup (Its Cause and Results) 1991, December 1991: My Stand 1992, The Years of Hard Decisions 1993, Life and Reforms 1995. *Address:* International Foundation for Socio-Economic and Political Studies, 125167 Moscow, Leningradskii pr. 39/14, Russia; tel. (495) 945-74-01; fax (495) 945-74-01; e-mail gf@gorby.ru; internet www.gorby.ru.

GRECEANÎI, Zinaida, MA; Moldovan economist and politician; *Prime Minister;* b. 7 Feb. 1956; m.; two c. *Education:* Moldova State Univ. *Career:* various roles within finance and budget inspectorate 1974–91; Economist, then Prin. Economist, Dept of Int. Finance, Ministry of Finance 1995–97, various sr positions including Dir of World Bank Section 1997–2001; Vice-Minister of Finance 2001–02, Minister of Finance 2002–05; First Deputy Prime Minister 2006–08, Prime Minister 2008–; fmr Gov. for Moldova to IMF. *Address:* Government of Moldova, Piaţa Marii Adunări Naţionale 1, 2033 Chişinău, Moldova; tel. (22) 25-01-41; fax (22) 23-84-44; e-mail zinaida.greceanii@gov.md; internet www.gov.md.

GRYZLOV, Boris Vyacheslavovich, PhD; Russian engineer and politician; *Chairman, Gosudarstvennaya Duma (State Duma);* b. 15 Dec. 1950, Vladivostok; m. Ada; one s. one d. *Education:* Leningrad (now St Petersburg) Inst. of Electro-Tech. Communications. *Career:* radio engineer, Heavy Duty Radio Industry Scientific Research Inst. (Comintern), took part in devt of communications systems –1977; Head of construction, later Dept Dir, Electronpribor Production Co. 1977–96; Dir New Training Tech. Centre, Baltic State Tech. Univ. 1996–99; cand. in St Petersburg city elections; Pres. Interregional Business Co-operation Fund Devt of Regions 1999–; Chief of Staff for Viktor Zubkov 1999; Founder mem. Unity (Yedinstvo) Movt 1999–, Head of St Petersburg Regional Br. 1999, Chair. Unity Political Council 2000, Chair. United Russia (Yedinaya Rossiya) 2004–; mem. Gosudarstvennaya Duma (State Duma) 1999–2001, 2003–, Leader, Unity faction 2000–01, Chair. State Duma Dec. 2003–; Minister of Internal Affairs 2001–03; Chair. Inter-Parl. Ass., Eurasian Econ. Community (Eurasec IPA); Perm. mem., Security Council of Russian Fed. *Address:* Office of the Chairman, Gosudarstvennaya Duma, 103265 Moscow, Okhotnyi ryad 1, Russia; tel. (495) 292-83-10; fax (495) 292-94-64; e-mail stateduma@duma.ru; internet www.duma.ru; www.gryzlov.ru.

GURGENIDZE, Vladimer (Lado), MBA; Georgian/British banker and politician; *Prime Minister;* b. 7 Dec. 1970, Tbilisi; m. Larissa Gurgenidze; three c. *Education:* Tbilisi State Univ., Middlebury Coll., VT, USA, Goizueta School of Business of Emory Univ. *Career:* began his investment banking career with CEE corp. finance arm of MeesPierson; Dir ABN AMRO Corp. Finance in Russia and CIS 1997–98, served in various sr capacities at ABN AMRO Corp. Finance, London, including as a Dir and Head of Mergers and Acquisitions in the Emerging European Markets 1998–2000 and as a Man. Dir and Head of Tech. Corp. Finance 2001–03; Man. Dir and Regional Man. for Europe, Putnam Lovell NBF (boutique investment banking firm) 2003–04; CEO Bank of Georgia 2004–06, Chair. Supervisory Bd 2006–; Chair. Supervisory Bd Galt & Taggart Securities, Galt & Taggart Capital; mem. Supervisory Bd Georgian Stock Exchange; Prime Minister of Georgia 2007–. *Television:* hosted a reality TV show The Candidate on Rustavi 2 (Georgian version of Donald Trump's franchise The Apprentice) 2006. *Address:* Chancellery of the Government, P. Ingorovka 7, 0105 Tbilisi, Georgia; tel. (32) 92-22-43; fax (32) 92-10-69; e-mail primeminister@geo .gov.ge; internet www.government.gov.ge.

IGNATIYEV, Sergey Mikhailovich, Cand.Sci, PhD; Russian economist and central banker; *Chairman, Central Bank of the Russian Federation;* b. 10 Jan. 1948, Leningrad (now St Petersburg); m. *Education:* Moscow M. V. Lomonosov State Univ. *Career:* Sr Lecturer, Engels Leningrad Inst. of Soviet Trade 1978–88; Sr Lecturer and Assoc. Prof., Voznesenskii Leningrad Inst. of Finance and Econs 1988–91; Deputy Minister of Econs and Finance 1991–92, Deputy Minister of Finance 1992–94, Deputy Minister of Econs 1993–96, First Deputy Minister of Finance 1997–2002; Deputy Chair. Cen. Bank of the Russian Fed. 1992–93, Chair. 2002–; Econ. Adviser to Pres. 1996–97; Hon. Diploma, Russian Govt 1998; 850th Anniversary of Moscow Medal 1997; several govt awards. *Publications:* numerous articles and more than 20 research papers on econs. *Address:* Bank Rossii—Central Bank of the Russian Federation, 107016 Moscow, ul. Neglinnaya 12, Russia; tel. (495) 771-91-00; fax (495) 921-64-65; internet www.cbr.ru.

ISABEKOV, Azim Beishembayevich: Kyrgyzstani economist and politician; b. 4 April 1960, Arashan, Chui Oblast. *Education:* Kyrgyz State Univ. *Career:* Chief of Staff, Office of Gov. of Chui Oblast Kurmanbek Bakiyev 1997–2000; Head of Admin. Dept, Office of Prime Minister 2001–02; Dir State Fund for Econ. Devt 2002–04; Deputy Chief of Staff, Office of Pres. Kurmanbek Bakiyev 2005–06; Minister of Agric., Water Resources and Mfg Industry June–Dec. 2006; Prime Minister Jan.–March 2007. *Address:* c/o Office of the Prime Minister, Dom Pravitelstva, 720003 Bishkek, Kyrgyzstan.

IVANOV, Lt-Gen. Sergei Borisovich: Russian politician; *Deputy Chairman of the Government;* b. 31 Jan. 1953, Leningrad (now St Petersburg); m.; two s. *Education:* Leningrad State Univ., Yu V. Andropov Inst. at KGB. *Career:* various posts in KGB including missions abroad 1976–97; Deputy Dir Fed. Service of Security, 1998–2001; Head, Dept of Analysis, Prognosis and Strategic Planning 1998–99; Sec. Security Council of Russian Fed. 1999–2001; Minister of Defence 2001–07, Deputy Chair. of the Govt 2005–07, 2008–, First Deputy Chair. 2007–08; Order for Services to the Fatherland (2nd Class) 2003. *Address:* Office of the Government, Krasnopresnenskaya nab. 2, 103274 Moscow, Russian Federation; tel. (495) 205-57-35; fax (495) 205-42-19; internet www.government.ru.

KABIRI, Muhiddin: Tajikistani politician; *Chairman, Islamic Rebirth Party of Tajikistan;* b. (Muhiddin Tilloyevich Kabirov), 1966, Fayzobod dist.; m.; five c. *Education:* Tajik Nat. Univ., Sane Univ., Yemen, Diplomatic Acad., Moscow. *Career:* aide to Chair. Islamic Rebirth Party of Tajikistan 1997–2000, Deputy Chair. 2000–04, First Deputy Chair. 2004–06, Chair. 2006–; mem. Majlisi Namoyandagon 2005–, mem. Cttee on Science, Educ., Culture and Youth Police. *Address:* Islamic Rebirth Party of Tajikistan, 734000 Dushanbe, pos. Kalinina, Kuchai Tukhagul 55, Tajikistan; tel. (372) 27-25-30; fax (372) 27-53-93.

KADYROV, Ramzan Akhmadovich: Russian government official; *President, Chechen (Nokchi) Republic;* b. 5 Oct. 1976, Tsenteroi, Checheno-Ingush ASSR (now Chechen—Nokchi

Repub.); m.; seven c. *Career:* fmr Commdr of 'Kadyrovtsy' militia (Presidential security service); fmr Head of Security, Chechen (Nokchi) Repub.; First Deputy Chair. of Govt, Chechen (Nokchi) Repub. 2004–05, Acting Chair. of Govt 2005–06, Chair. of Govt 2006–07, Pres. 2007–; Chair. Ramzan boxing club, Terek Grozny football club; Hero of Russia Medal, Order of Courage, Order of Akhmad Kadyrov, Caucasus Service Medal, Defender of the Chechen Repub. Medal. *Address:* Office of the President, 364000 Chechen (Nokchi) Republic, Groznyi, ul. Garazhnaya 10a, Russian Federation; tel. (8712) 22-20-01; (8712) 22-20-09; fax (8712) 22-20-14; e-mail secretariat_chr@mail.ru; internet www.chechnya.gov .ru; www.ramzan-kadyrov.ru.

KALIMBETOVA, Tazhikan B.: Kyrgyzstani politician; *Minister of Finance;* b. 1964. *Career:* Deputy Minister of Finance –2007, also head financial intelligence service 2005–07, Minister of Finance 2007–, Chair. Iran-Kyrgyzstan Jt Econ. Comm.; Deputy Chair. EurAsian Group 2006–07; Chair. Social Fund 2007–. *Address:* Ministry of Finance, 720040 Bishkek, pr. Erkindik 58, Kyrgyzstan; tel. (312) 66-13-50; fax (312) 66-16-45; e-mail t.kalimbetova@mf.gov.kg; internet www.mf.gov.kg.

KARABAYEV, Ednan Oskonovich., PhD; Kyrgyzstani academic and government official; *Minister of Foreign Affairs;* b. 17 Jan. 1953, Talas. *Education:* Kyrgyz State Univ., Inst. of History of Kyrgyz SSR Acad. of Sciences. *Career:* early career as history teacher, Frunze (now Bishkek); Minister of Foreign Affairs 1992–93, 2007–; Head Int. Relations Dept, Kyrgyz-Russian Slavic Univ. 1994–2007, also fmr Dean; Advisor to Pres. 2000; Pres., UNA of Kyrgyzstan; mem. Cyril-Mefody Acad. of Slavic Enlightenment; Honored Worker of Educ. in Kyrgyz Republic. *Publications include:* more than 200 scientific and other articles and contribs to monographs. *Address:* Ministry of Foreign Affairs, 720040 Bishkek, bul. Erkindik 57, Kyrgyzstan; tel. (312) 62-05-45; fax (312) 66-05-01; e-mail gendep@mfa.gov.kg; internet www.mfa.kg.

KARIMOV, Islam Abduganiyevich, CandEconSc; Uzbekistani politician and head of state; *President;* b. 30 Jan. 1938, Samarqand; m. Tatyana Karimova; two d. *Education:* Cen. Asian Polytechnic Inst. and Tashkent Econs Inst. *Career:* mem. CPSU 1964–91; Engineer, then Leading Engineer-Constructor in Tashkent aviation construction factory 1960–66; Chief Specialist, Head of Dept, First Deputy Chair. State Planning Cttee 1966–83, Chair. 1986; Minister of Finance, Deputy Chair. of Council of Ministers, Uzbek SSR 1983–86; First Sec., Qashqadaryo Viloyat Party Cttee 1986–89; First Sec., Uzbek SSR CP Cen. Cttee 1989–91; USSR People's Deputy 1989–91; mem. Cen. Cttee CPSU and Politburo 1990–91; Pres. of Uzbek SSR 1990; Chair. People's Democratic Party of Uzbekistan 1991–96; Pres. of Uzbekistan 1991– (elected by Supreme Soviet 24 March 1990; term of office extended by popular referendum 27 March 1995; re-elected 9 Jan. 2000 and 23 Dec. 2007); concurrently Chair. Cabinet of Ministers; mem. Acad. of Sciences of Uzbekistan; Hon. Chair. Fund of Friendship of Cen. Asia and Kazakhstan; Hon. DEcon; Dr hc and from nine foreign univs and acads; Mustakillik (Independence) Award, Amir Temur Award, Borobudur Gold Medal, UNESCO 2006. *Publications:* Uzbekistan: Its Own Model of Renovation and Progress 1992, Uzbekistan—A State with a Great Future 1992, On the Priorities of the Economic Policy of Uzbekistan 1993, Uzbek Model of Deepening Economic Reforms 1995, Uzbekistan's Way of Restoration and Progress, To Complete the Noble Cause, Stability and Reforms 1996, Uzbekistan on the Threshold of the Twenty-First Century 1997, Uzbekistan Striving Towards the 21st Century 1999, The Spiritual Path of Renewal 2000. *Address:* Office of the President, 100163 Tashkent, O'zbekiston shox ko'ch. 43, Uzbekistan; tel. (71) 139-53-25; fax (71) 139-54-04; e-mail presidents_office@press -service.uz; internet www.press-service.uz.

KARIMOVA, Gulnora Islamovna: Uzbekistani business executive and diplomatist; *Permanent Representative, United Nations, Geneva;* b. 8 July 1972, Farg'ona; m. Mansur Maqsudi (divorced); one s. one d. *Education:* Tashkent State

Univ., Univ. of World Economy and Diplomacy, Tashkent, Univ. of Information and Tech., Tashkent, New York, Univ., Fashion Inst. of Tech., Harvard Grad. School of Arts and Sciences, USA. *Career:* early academic career at Univ. of World Economy and Diplomacy, Dept of Int. Studies, Tashkent; fmrly with Perm. Mission to UN, New York; returned to Uzbekistan and developed business interests in mobile cellular telephone operator and numerous industrial cos; consultant and adviser to Minister of Foreign Affairs; Minister-Counsellor, Embassy of Uzbekistan, Moscow 2003–08; Deputy Minister of Foreign Affairs, responsible for Cultural and Humanitarian Co-operation 2008; Perm. Rep. to UN and Int. Orgs, Geneva 2008–; Chair. Forum of Culture and Arts Foundation of Uzbekistan. *Publications:* Categories of Competitiveness of Countries with Transitional Economies: The Example of Uzbekistan 1998, Problems of Security in Central Asia: The Conditions, Tendency and Prospect of Development 2001. *Address:* Forum of Culture and Arts Foundation of Uzbekistan, 100057 Tashkent, O'zbekistan shoh ko'ch. 80, Uzbekistan; Permanent Representation of Uzbekistan, POB 50036, 21523 Geneva, Switzerland; tel. (71) 239-27-74; fax (71) 239-27-71; e-mail fonduz@mail.ru; internet www.fondforum.uz; www.googoosha.uz; www.guli.uz.

KASPAROV, Garry Kimovich: Russian-Armenian fmr chess player and political activist; *Leader, United Civil Front;* b. (Garry Weinstein), 13 April 1963, Baku; m. 1st Maria Arapova (divorced); one d.; m. 2nd Yulia Vovk 1996; one s. *Education:* Azerbaijan Pedagogical Inst. of Foreign Languages. *Career:* started playing chess in 1967; Azerbaijan Champion 1976; USSR Jr Champion 1976; Int. Master 1978, Int. Grandmaster 1980; World Jr Champion 1980; won USSR Championship 1981, subsequently replacing Anatolii Karpov at top of world ranking list; won match against Viktor Korchnoi, challenged Karpov for World Title in Moscow Sept. 1985, the match being adjourned due to the illness of both players; won rescheduled match to become the youngest-ever world champion in 1985; successfully defended his title against Karpov 1986, 1987, 1990; series of promotional matches in London Feb. 1987; won Times World Championship against Nigel Short 1993; stripped of title by World Chess Fed. 1993; winner Oscar Chess Prize 1982–83, 1985–89, World Chess Cup 1989; highest-ever chess rating of over 2800 1992–; f. Professional Chess Asscn (PCA) 1993; won PCA World Championship against V. Anand 1995, lost title against V. Kramnik 2000; won match against Deep Blue computer 1996, lost 1997; defeated in four-game match of rapid chess against Karpov, New York 2002; retd from professional chess 2005; Deputy Leader Democratic Party of Russia 1990–91; f. The Kasparov Foundation, Moscow; actively promotes use of chess in schools as an educational subject; f. Kasparov Int. Chess Acad.; Founder and Leader United Civil Front 2005–; Order of Red Banner of Labour. *Publications:* New World Chess Champion 1985, The Test of Time 1986, Child of Change (with Donald Trelford) 1987, London-Leningrad Championship Games 1987, Unlimited Challenge 1990, How Life Imitates Chess 2007. *Address:* 123610 Moscow, Krasnopresnenskaya nab. 12, Mezhdunarodnaya-2, Suite 1108; 121002 Moscow, Gagarinskii per. 26/12, Russia; tel. (095) 258-15-36; (095) 241-82-80; fax (095) 258-15-39; (095) 241-95-96; e-mail maiavia@dol.ru; internet www.rufront.ru.

KASYANOV, Mikhail Mikhailovich: Russian politician; *Leader, Russian People's Democratic Union;* b. 8 Dec. 1957, Solntsevo, Moscow Oblast. *Education:* Moscow Inst. of Automobile Transport. *Career:* held sr positions at RSFSR State Planning Comm., then Ministry of Econs 1981–90; Chief of Section for Foreign Econ. Relations, Russian State Cttee for Econs 1990–91; Head, Dept for Foreign Econ. Relations, Ministry of Finance 1991–93, Head, Dept of Overseas Credits 1993–95, Deputy Minister of Finance 1995–99, First Deputy Minister, then Minister 1999–2000; main negotiator with Western financial orgs on questions of Russian liabilities; Deputy Man. for Russian Fed., EBRD 1999; First Deputy Prime Minister Jan. 2000, Acting Chair. of Govt, then Chair. of Govt 2000–04; mem. Presidium of Russian Govt 1999–2004, Security Council 1999–2004; f. MK-Analytics (consultancy)

2005; currently Leader, Russian People's Democratic Union. *Address:* Russian People's Democratic Union (Rossiiskii narodno–demokraticheski soyuz), 117279 Moscow, ul. Profsoyuznaya 93, korp. 4, Russia; tel. (495) 429-61-70; fax (495) 429-63-10; e-mail newtypeparty@mail.ru; internet nardemsoyuz.ru; kasyanov.ru.

KAZULIN, Alyaksandr: Belarusian academic and politician; *Chairman, Assembly (Hramada)—Belarusian Social-Democratic Party;* b. 25 Nov. 1955, Minsk; m. Iryna Kazulina (died 2007); two c. *Education:* Belarusian State Univ. *Career:* mil. service in Soviet Navy as Marine 1974–76; Lecturer and Instructor, Youth Communist League (Komsomol), later Dean, Belarusian State Univ. 1980–88, Rector 1996–2003; Dept Chief, then First Deputy Minister, Educ. Ministry 1988–96; Minister of Educ. 1998–2001; f. People's Will political movt 2005; joined Belarusian Social-Democratic Party, March 2005, elected Chair. Assembly (Hramada)—Belarusian Social-Democratic Party following merger of parties in April 2005; sentenced to five-and-a-half years' imprisonment on charges of hooliganism July 2006. *Address:* Assembly (Hramada)—Belarusian Social-Democratic Party, 220035 Minsk, vul. Drozda 8/52, Belarus; tel. (17) 226-74-37; fax (17) 226-74-37; e-mail bsdggramada@tut.by; internet www.bsdp.org.

KEZERASHVILI, Davit: Georgian politician and government official; *Minister of Defence;* b. 22 Sept. 1978, Tbilisi; m.; two s. *Education:* Ivane Javakhishvili Tbilisi State Univ. *Career:* Sr Inspector, Penitentiary Dept, Ministry of Justice April–Sept. 2001; Head, Information and Analysis Div., Dept of Informatics, Ministry of Justice 2001–02; Asst to Chair. Tbilisi City Council 2002–04; Head, Finance Police, Ministry of Finance 2004–06; Minister of Defence 2006–. *Address:* Ministry of Defence, 0112 Tbilisi, Gen. Kvinitadze 20, Georgia; tel. (32) 91-19-63; fax (32) 91-06-45; e-mail pr@mod.gov.ge; internet www.mod.gov.ge.

KHAIRULLAYEV, Saidullo Khairullayevich: Tajikistani politician; *President, Majlisi Namoyandagon (Assembly of Representatives);* b. 10 Aug. 1945, Garm dist. *Education:* Tashkent Higher CPSU School, Tajik Inst. of Agric. *Career:* Engineer, Chief Engineer, then Head of Div. Garm irrigation system 1969–75; Chair. Exec. Cttee Garm Regional Soviet of People's Deputies 1975–77, Chair. Regional Soviet 1979–85; First Sec., Soviet region CP of Tajikistan 1985–88; Sec., Ktalon Regional CP Cttee 1988–90; Deputy Prime Minister of Tajikistan 1991–92; Minister of Environmental Protection, then Minister of Nature Protection 1992–94; Chair. Govt Cttee on Precious Metals 1994–95, Govt Cttee on Land Construction and Land Reform 1999–2000; Pres. Majlisi Namoyandagon 2000–; Merited Worker of Tajikistan, Order of Nishoni Fakhri. *Address:* Majlisi Oli, Majlisi Namoyandagon, 734051 Dushanbe, Xiyoboni Rudaki 42, Tajikistan; tel. (372) 21-23-66; fax (372) 21-92-81; e-mail mejparl@parliament.tojikiston.com.

KHAYRULLOYEV, Maj.-Gen. Sherali: Tajikistani government official and fmr army officer; *Minister of Defence;* b. 8 Nov. 1949, Dangarin Dist, Kulob Viloyat; m.; c. *Education:* Tajikistan State Univ. *Career:* conscripted to serve in USSR Ministry of Internal Affairs 1970, served in various positions including Platoon Commdr 1970–77, subsequently served in various Ministry depts; Deputy Internal Affairs Minister 1988–95; Minister of Defence 1995–. *Address:* Ministry of Defence, 734025 Dushanbe, Kuchai Bokhtar 59, Tajikistan; tel. (372) 23-18-97; fax (372) 23-19-37.

KHODORKOVSKII, Mikhail Borisovich: Russian business executive; b. 26 June 1963, Moscow; m. 1st Yelena Khodorkovskaya; one s.; m. 2nd Inna Khodorkovskaya; two s. one d. *Education:* Moscow Mendeleyev Inst. of Chemistry and Tech., G. V. Plekhanov Inst. of Nat. Economics. *Career:* Head, Centre of Interfield Research Programmes (NTTM), USSR State Cttee for Science and Tech. (now Menatep Asscn) 1986–93; Chair. Bd of Dirs Menatep Bank 1993–; Chair. Bd Commercial Innovation Bank of Scientific Progress 1989–90; Econ. Counsellor to Chair. of Russian Council of Ministers

1990–91; Deputy Minister of Fuel and Energy Industry 1991; Chair. Bd of Dirs Rosprom 1995–; Vice-Pres. YUKOS Asscn 1996, Chair. United Bd Rosprom-YUKOS Co. 1997–2000, Chair. Exec. Cttee OAO NK YUKOS, Man. Cttee YUKOS-Moscow 2000–03, CEO YUKOS –2003; owner, Moskovskiye Novosti newspaper 2003–; charged with fraud and tax evasion Oct. 2003, convicted May 2005 and sentenced to nine years in prison. *Address:* 105215 Moscow, a/ya 'Press-Tsentr', Russia. internet www.khodorkovsky.ru.

KHRISTENKO, Viktor Borisovich, BSc, DEcon; Russian politician; *Minister of Industry and Trade;* b. 28 Aug. 1957, Chelyabinsk; m. 2nd Tatyana Golikova; three c. *Education:* Chelyabinsk Polytechnical Inst. and Acad. of Nat. Economy. *Career:* sr teacher and lecturer, Faculty of the Econs of Machine Construction, Chelyabinsk Polytechnical Inst. 1979–90; Chair. Perm. Comm., First Deputy Chair. Econs Cttee, Chair. Property Man. Cttee, Chelyabink City Exec. Cttee 1990–91; Deputy Head Admin of Chelyabinsk Oblast 1991–94, First Deputy Head 1994–96; Plenipotentiary Rep. of the Pres. of the Russian Fed. in Chelyabinsk Oblast 1997; Deputy Minister of Finances, Russian Fed. June 1997, First Deputy Minister 1998; Deputy Chair. of Govt April–Sept. 1998, 2000, First Deputy Chair. 1999, 2000–04, Acting Chair. Feb. 2004; Minister of Industry and Energy (now Minister of Industry and Trade) 2004–; Special Presidential Envoy for Integration with CIS 2004–; mem. Presidium May–Aug. 1998; Chair. Comm. on Chechnya 2000, on Housing Policy 2001, on Reform of the Electrical Enery Sector 2001. *Address:* Ministry of Industry and Trade, 109074 Moscow, Kitaigorodskii proyezd 7, Russia; tel. (495) 710-55-00; fax (495) 710-57-22; e-mail info@mte.gov.ru; internet www.minprom.gov.ru.

KINAKH, Col Anatoliy Kyryllovych: Ukrainian politician; *Chairman, Party of Industrialists and Entrepreneurs;* b. 4 Aug. 1954, Bratuşani, Moldovan SSR; m. Marina Volodymyrivna Kinakh 1960; three d. *Education:* Leningrad (now St Petersburg) Vessel Construction Inst. *Career:* worked on vessel construction and in vessel repair plants in Tallinn and Nikolayev 1978–90; elected to Mykolayiv Oblast Parl. 1990; mem. Comm. on Econ. Reform and Nat. Econ. Man. 1990; Presidential Rep. in Mykolayiv Oblast, then Head of Mykolayiv Regional Admin. 1992–94; Head, Mykolayiv Regional Council of People's Deputies 1994–95; mem. Political Council People's Democratic Party of Ukraine, Deputy Chair. 1996; Deputy Prime Minister of Ukraine in charge of Industrial Policy 1995–96; Presidential Adviser on Industrial Policy, then Pres. Ukrainian Union of Businessmen 1996–97; First Deputy Head, Council of Int. Congress of Businessmen 1997–; mem. Higher Econ. Council at Ukrainian Presidency, Head of Co-ordination Council on Privatization of Industrial Enterprises of Strategic Importance 1997–; mem. Nat. Council of Ukraine on Quality Issues 1997–2001; Head, Verkhovna Rada Cttee on Industrial Policy 1998–2001; Chair. Nat. Cttee of Int. Trade Chamber 1998–2001; First Deputy Prime Minister of Ukraine Aug.–Dec. 1999, Jan.–Sept. 2005; Prime Minister of Ukraine 2001–02; mem. Parl. 2002–; presidential cand. 2004; Chair. Nat. Security and Defence Council 2005–06; Minister of the Economy 2007; currently Chair. Party of Industrialists and Entrepreneurs of Ukraine; mem. Acad. of Cybernetics. *Address:* Party of Industrialists and Entrepreneurs, 01203 Kyiv, vul. Sh. Rustaveli 11, Ukraine; tel. (44) 590-17-44; fax (44) 590-17-44; e-mail info@uspp.org.ua; internet www.pppu.info; www.kinakh.com.ua.

KOCHARIAN, Robert S.: Armenian politician and fmr head of state; b. 31 Aug. 1954, Xankandi (Stepanakert), Nagornyi Karabakh Autonomous Oblast; m. Bella L. Kocharian; two s. one d. *Education:* Yerevan Polytechnic Inst. *Career:* served in Soviet Army 1972–74; engineer and electrotechnician Electro-Technical plant, Stepanakert 1981–87; concurrently sec. factory CP Cttee 1987–89; co-founder Karabakh Movt 1988; Deputy to Armenian Supreme Council 1989–94; left CP 1989; after proclamation of 'Republic of Nagornyi Karabakh' in Azerbaijan 2 Sept. 1991 and Referendum 10 Dec. 1991 elected to Supreme Council 'Nagornyi Karabakh Repub.', Chair. State Cttee of Defence and Leader of Repub. 1992–94; apptd First Pres. of 'Nagornyi Karabakh Repub.' by Supreme

Council 1994–97; Prime Minister of Repub. of Armenia 1997–98, Pres. 1998–2008. *Address:* c/o Office of the President, 0077 Yerevan, Marshal Baghramian Ave. 26, Armenia.

KOKOYEV (KOKOITI), Eduard D.: Georgian politician; *'President of Republic of South Ossetia';* b. 31 Oct. 1964, Tskhinvali. *Career:* fmr mem. Russian nat. wrestling team; First Sec., Tskhinvali Br. of Komsomol 1989–92; business activities, Moscow 1992–2001; Rep. of 'Repub. of South Ossetia', Moscow 1997–99; 'Pres. of Republic of South Ossetia' 2001–. *Address:* 'Office of the President of the Republic of South Ossetia', 7300 Shida Kartli Mkhare, Tskhinvali, Georgia.

KONOVALOV, Aleksander Vladimirovich, PhD; Russian lawyer and government official; *Minister of Justice;* b. 19 June 1968, Leningrad. *Education:* Law Faculty, St Petersburg State Univ. *Career:* served in USSR Army 1986–88; joined St Petersburg Prosecutor's Office 1992, positions included Asst to Prosecutor of Vyborg Dist 1992, Investigator, Vyborg Dist Office 1992–94, Prosecutor, Fed. Security Law Enforcement Supervision Dept 1994–97, Deputy Prosecutor of Moskovsky Dist 1997–98, Prosecutor of Moskovsky Dist 1998–2001, First Deputy Prosecutor, St Petersburg 2001–05; Prosecutor, Repub. of Bashkortostan 2005; Presidential Envoy to Volga Fed. Dist 2005–08; Minister of Justice 2008–; fmr mem. Security Council of Russian Fed. *Address:* Ministry of Justice, 119991 Moscow, ul. Zhitnaya 14, Russia; tel. (495) 955-59-99; fax (495) 916-29-03; internet www.minjust.ru.

KOZAK, Dmitrii Nikolayevich: Russian lawyer and politician; *Deputy Chairman of the Government;* b. 7 Nov. 1958, Voroshylovhrad (now Kirovohrad) Oblast, Ukraine; m.; two s. *Education:* Vinnytsia Polytechnical Inst., Leningrad (now St Petersburg) State Univ. *Career:* Asst to Prosecutor of Leningrad; on staff, Asscn of Marine Trade Ports 1985–89; on staff, Exec. Cttee Leningrad City Council 1990–91; Head of Law Dept Office, St Petersburg 1991–94; Chair. Law Cttee Admin., St Petersburg; mem. Govt of St Petersburg, mem. Comm. on Human Rights 1994–96; apptd Deputy Gov. St Petersburg 1998, resgnd end of year; pvt. law practice 1998–99; Deputy Head of Admin. of Russian Pres. on Legal Problems May–Aug. 1999; First Deputy Head of Govt of Russian Fed. 1999, Head 1999–2000; Deputy Head Admin. of Russian Pres. 2000–03, First Deputy Head 2003–04; Head of Govt Admin. March–Sept. 2004; Presidential Rep. in the Southern Fed. Okrug 2004–07; Minister of Regional Devt 2007–08; Deputy Chairman of the Govt, 2008–. *Address:* Office of the Government, 103274 Moscow, Krasnopresnenskaya nab. 2 Russia; tel. (495) 205-57-35; fax (495) 205-42-19; internet www.government.ru.

KRAVCHUK, Leonid Makarovych, Cand. Econ. Sc; Ukrainian politician; b. 10 Jan. 1934, Velykyi Zhytyn (Poland, now in Rivne Oblast, Ukraine); m. Antonina Mikhailivna 1957; one s. *Education:* Kyiv State Univ. and Acad. of Social Sciences, Moscow. *Career:* teacher of Political Economy, Chernovitsky Tech. School; party work since 1960, on staff Ukrainian CP Cen. Cttee 1970–; Head, Propaganda Dept 1980–88, Ideology Dept 1988–89, Sec., Cen. Cttee, mem. Politburo 1990; Chair. Ukrainian Supreme Soviet 1990–91; Pres. of Ukraine 1991–94; C-in-C Armed Forces of Ukraine 1991–94; mem. Verkhovna Rada (Parl.) 1994–; f. Mutual Understanding Movt 1994; mem. Social Democratic Party; Head, All-Ukrainian Union of Democratic Forces Zlagoda 1999–; Chair. State Cttee for Admin. Reforms 1997–99; Protector Mohyla Acad. –Nat. Univ. of Kyiv 1991; Head, Trusteeship Council, Children and Youth Activity Cen. of Ukraine 1992; Hon. Pres. East European Asscn of Businessmen; Dr hc (La Salle Univ., Phila., USA) 1992. *Publications include:* State and Authorities: Experience of Administrative Reforms 2001, We Have What We Have 2002. *Address:* Verkhovna Rada, 01008 Kyiv, vul. M. Hrushevskoho 5, Ukraine; tel. (44) 255-21-15; fax (44) 253-32-17; e-mail umz@rada.gov.ua; internet www.rada.gov.ua.

KUCHMA, Leonid Maksimovych, CTechSc; Ukrainian politician and manager; b. 1938, Chatikine, Chernihiv Oblast; m.

Ludmyla Mykolayovna Kuchma; one d. *Education:* Dnipropetrovsk Nat. Univ. *Career:* mem. CPSU 1960–91; eng., constructor, Chief Constructor Research-Production Yuzmash eng. plant 1960–75, Sec., Party Cttee 1975–82, Deputy Dir-Gen. 1982–86, Dir-Gen. 1986–92; mem. Cen. Cttee CP Ukrainian SSR 1981–91; People's Deputy of Ukraine 1991–94; Prime Minister of Ukraine 1992–93 (resgnd); Chair. Ukrainian Union of Industrialists and Entrepreneurs 1993–94; Pres. of Ukraine 1994–2005; Lenin Prize 1981, State Prize 1993; Order of St Volodymyr (Gold) 1999. *Address:* Ukrainian Presidential Fund of Leonid Kuchma Charity Organisation, 01024 Kyiv, vul. P. Orlyka 1/15, Ukraine; tel. (44) 465-93-77; fax (44) 465-93-78; e-mail press@ldk-fund.org .ua; internet www.kuchma.org.ua.

KUDRIN, Aleksei Leonidovich, Cand Econ; Russian politician; *Deputy Chairman and Minister of Finance;* b. 12 Oct. 1960, Dobele, Latvian SSR; m. Irina; one d. *Education:* Leningrad (now St Petersburg) State Univ., Inst. of Econs USSR Acad. of Sciences. *Career:* on staff Inst. of Social-Econ. Problems Acad. of Sciences 1983–90; Deputy Chair. Cttee on Econ. Reform Leningrad City Exec. Bd 1990–91; Chair. Cttee on Finance St Petersburg Mayor's Office 1992–94; First Deputy Mayor of St Petersburg, Head Dept of Finance Mayor's Office, St Petersburg 1994–96; Deputy Head of Admin., Head Controlling Dept at Russian Presidency 1996–97; First Deputy Minister of Finance Russian Fed. 1997–99, concurrently Deputy Man. BRD 1997–99; First Deputy Chair. Unified Power Grids of Russia (state co.) 1999–2000; Deputy Chair. of the Govt 2000–04, 2007–, Minister of Finance 2000–. *Address:* Ministry of Finance, 109097 Moscow, ul. Ilyinka 9, Russia; tel. (495) 298-91-01; fax (495) 925-08-89; internet www.minfin.ru.

KULOV, Feliks Sharshenbayevich: Kyrgyzstani politician; *Chairman, Dignity (Ar-Namys);* b. 29 Oct. 1948, Frunze (now Bishkek). *Education:* Osh Univ. *Career:* began career with Ministry of Internal Affairs, held positions successively as Insp., Chief Insp., Head of Criminal Dept; apptd Vice-Chief, Internal Affairs Admin, Talas Duban 1978, later Vice-Minister of Internal Affairs, then Minister of Internal Affairs; resgnd party membership following coup attempt in Moscow 1991; Vice-Pres. of the Repub. 1992–93; investigated on charges of corruption 1993; resgnd following scandals surrounding Seabeco Affair 1993; Gov. of Chui Region 1993–97; Minister of Nat. Security 1997–98; Mayor of Bishkek 1998–99; Founding Chair. Dignity (Ar-Namys) Party 1999–; cand. in Parl. elections 2000; charged with abuse of office during term as Minister of Nat. Security and sent to closed mil. trial June 2000, acquitted by court Aug., sent to retrial Sept., sentenced to seven years imprisonment Jan. 2001; apptd Head of People's Congress (alliance among all opposition parties) Nov. 2001; sentenced to further 10 years' imprisonment on embezzlement charges May 2002, charges overturned 2005, temporarily in charge of armed forces and law enforcement April–July 2005; Prime Minister 2005–06 (resgnd); Co-founder and Chair. United Front For A Worthy Future For Kyrgyzstan Feb. 2007–. *Address:* Dignity (Ar-Namys), 720033 Bishkek, Togolok Moldo 60a, Kyrgyzstan; tel. (312) 32-52-89; e-mail ar-namys@mail.kg; internet www.ar-namys.org.

LAVROV, Sergei Viktorovich: Russian diplomatist and politician; *Minister of Foreign Affairs;* b. 21 March 1950, Moscow; m. Mariya Lavrova; one d. *Education:* Moscow State Inst. of Int. Relations. *Career:* has served in diplomatic service since 1972; attaché, USSR Embassy in Sri Lanka 1972–76, Sec., Dept of Int. Econ. Orgs, Ministry of Foreign Affairs 1976–81, Sec. and Counsellor, Perm. Mission of USSR to UN, New York 1981–88; Deputy Chair., then Chair. Dept of Int. Econ. Relations, Ministry of Foreign Affairs 1988–90; Dir Dept of Int. Orgs and Global Problems, Ministry of Foreign Affairs of Russia 1990–92, Deputy Minister 1992–94, Perm. Rep. to UN, New York 1994–2004, Minister of Foreign Affairs 2004–; Order of Honour 1996; Order of Service to the Nation 1997. *Address:* Ministry of Foreign Affairs, 119200 Moscow, Smolenskaya-Sennaya pl. 32/34, Russia; tel. (095) 244-16-06; fax (095) 230-21-30; e-mail ministry@mid.ru; internet www .mid.ru.

LEBEDEV, Col-Gen. Sergei Nikolayevich: Russian international organization official and fmr intelligence officer; *Executive Secretary, Commonwealth of Independent States;* b. 9 April 1948, Jizzax, Uzbek SSR; m. Vera Mikhailovna; two s. *Education:* Kyiv Polytechnic Inst., Diplomatic Acad. of USSR. *Career:* staff mem., Chernihiv br., Kyiv Polytechnic Inst. 1970; army service 1971–72; with state security bodies 1973–75, Foreign Intelligence Service 1975–78; Rep. of Foreign Intelligence Service to USA 1998–2000; Dir Fed. Foreign Intelligence Service, Russian Fed. 2000–07; Exec. Sec. CIS 2007–; numerous state awards. *Address:* Office of the Executive Secretary, Commonwealth of Independent States, 220000 Minsk, vul. Kirava 17, Belarus; tel. (17) 222-35-17; fax (17) 227-23-39; e-mail anna@cis.minsk.by; internet www.cis .minsk.by.

LUKASHENKA, Alyaksandr Rygorovich: Belarusian politician, economist and head of state; *President;* b. 30 Aug. 1954, Kopys; m. Halyna Rodionovna Lukashenko (estranged); two s. *Education:* Mogilev State Univ. and Belarus Agric. Acad. *Career:* served in Soviet Army 1975–77, 1980–82; Sec. Komsomol Cttee, Shklov, instructor Political Div. Komsomol Cttee W Border Dist 1975–77; Sec. Komsomol Cttee Mogilev City Food Dept; instructor regional Exec. Cttee 1977–80; Deputy Commdr of Co. 1980–82; Deputy Chair. Udarnik collective farm 1982–83; Deputy Dir Enterprise of Construction Materials 1983–85; Sec. CP Cttee Collective Farm of V. I. Lenin, Shklov Dist 1985–87; Dir Gorodets state farm 1987–94; elected Deputy of Supreme Council of Belarus SSR 1990–94; Chair. Parl. Comm. on Struggle against Corruption 1993–94; elected Pres. of Belarus 1994–; C-in-C Armed Forces of Belarus 1994–; Chair. Higher Council of Belarus and Russia Union 1997–; Chair. Supreme State Council of the Union State of Belarus and Russia 2000–; Hon. Academician of the Russian Acad. of Sciences 1995; Order of the Holy Cross of the Knights of the Holy Sepulchre 2000, Order of St Vladimir (First Class), Russian Orthodox Church 2007; M. Sholokhov Int. Award 1997. *Address:* Office of the President, 220016 Minsk, vul. K. Marksa 38, Dom Urada, Belarus; tel. (17) 222-35-03; fax (17) 222-30-20; e-mail press@president.gov.by; www.president.gov.by.

LUTSENKO, Yuriy Vitaliyovych: Ukrainian engineer and politician; *Minister of Internal Affairs;* b. 14 Dec. 1964, Rivne; m.; three s. *Education:* Lviv Polytechnical Inst. *Career:* mil. service in army 1984–86; Chief Constructor and Head, Technical Workshop, Gazotron, Rivne 1989–94; Deputy Head, Rivne Oblast Council of People's Deputies 1994–96; Head, Rivne Oblast Admin Econs Cttee 1996–97; Deputy Minister of Science and Tech. 1997–98; adviser to Prime Minister 1998–99; adviser to Leader of Socialist Party of Ukraine 1999–2002; Deputy, Verkhovna Rada (Parl.) 2002–; Minister of Internal Affairs 2005–06, 2007–; mem. Socialist Party of Ukraine, Sec., Political Council 1996, later held number of sr positions; mem. Construction, Transportation, Communal Services and Communications Cttee; active in Ukraine Without Kuchma! (UBK) campaign and 'orange revolution' of 2004. *Address:* Ministry of Internal Affairs, 01024 Kyiv, vul. Ak. Bohomoltsya 10, Ukraine; tel. (44) 256-03-33; fax (44) 256-16-33; e-mail mail@centrmia.gov.ua; internet mvs.gov.ua.

LUZHKOV, Yurii Mikhailovich: Russian politician; *Mayor of Moscow;* b. 21 Sept. 1936, Moscow; m. 1st; two s.; m. 2nd Yelena Baturina; two d. *Education:* Gubkin Inst. of Oil and Gas, Moscow. *Career:* researcher, Research Inst. of Plastic Materials 1958–64; Head of Div. Ministry of Chemical Industry 1964–87; First Deputy Chair. Exec. Cttee, Moscow City Council and Chair. Moscow Agric. Industry Dept 1987–90; Chair. Exec. Cttee, Moscow City Council 1990–91; Vice-Mayor of Moscow and Premier, Moscow City Govt 1991–92, Mayor and Head of City Govt 1992–, re-elected 1996, 1999, 2003, apptd 2007–; mem. Russian Council of Fed. 1996–2001; Founder and Co-Chair. Fatherland (Otechestvo) Movt 1998–2001, formed alliance with All Russia party in 1999, subsequently merged with pro-Putin Unity party to create Unity and Fatherland-United Russia party (UF-UR) 2001, later simply United Russia (Yedinaya Rossiya); Co-

Chair. Supreme Council, UF-UR; Chair. Int. Fund Assistance to Free Enterprise; Pres. Moscow Int. Business Asscn 2002–; Hon. Prof., Acad. of Labour and Social Relations; Lenin Order, Red Banner Order, Order in the Name of Russia 2004; Hon. DSc Lomonosov State Univ. Moscow; Golden Mask Prize for support of the arts. *Publications:* 72 Hours of Agony 1991, The Quietist Negotiations 1994, We Are Your Children, Moscow 1996. *Address:* Office of the Mayor and Prime Minister of the Government of Moscow City, 125032 Moscow, ul. Tverskaya 13, Russia; tel. (495) 777-77-77; fax (495) 234-32-97; e-mail mayor@mos.ru; internet www.mos.ru; www.luzhkov.ru.

LYTVYN, Volodymyr Mykhaylovych, DrHis; Ukrainian academic and politician; *Leader, People's Party (Narodna Partiya);* b. 28 April 1956, Sloboda, Zhytomyr Oblast; m. Tetyana Lytvyn; one s. one d. *Education:* Kyiv T. Shevchenko State (now Nat.) Univ. *Career:* researcher, Docent, Vice-Rector Kyiv State Univ. 1978–86; Head of Dept Ukrainian Ministry of Higher Educ. 1986–89; Lecturer, consultant, Asst to Sec., Cen. Cttee of Ukrainian Komsomol 1989–91; Docent and Prof., Kyiv State Univ. 1991–94; Adviser to Ukrainian Pres. 1994–2002, Deputy Head, Admin. to the Pres. 1995–96, Head Admin. 1999–2002; apptd to Nat. Security and Defence Council 1999; mem. Co-ordination Cttee on Problems of Foreign Policy 1996–; elected to Verkovna Rada (Parl.) 2002, Chair. 2002–06; currently Leader, People's Party (Narodna Partiya); Corresp. mem. Ukrainian Acad. of Sciences. *Publications include:* Political Arena of Ukraine 1995; over 200 articles on contemporary politics. *Address:* People's Party (Narodna Partiya), 01034 Kyiv, vul. Reitarska 6a, Ukraine; tel. (44) 270-61-86; fax (44) 270-65-91; e-mail info@narodna .org.ua; umz@rada.gov.ua; internet www.narodna.org.ua.

MAMMEDYAROV, Elmar Maharram oğlu, PhD; Azerbaijani diplomatist; *Minister of Foreign Affairs;* b. 2 July 1960, Baku; m.; two s. *Education:* Kyiv State Univ. School of Int. Relations and Int. Law, Ukrainian SSR, USSR Diplomatic Acad. *Career:* Second Sec. then First Sec., Ministry of Foreign Affairs 1982–88, Dir Div. of State Protocol 1991–92, First Sec. Perm. Mission to UN, New York 1992–95, Deputy Dir Dept of Int. Orgs 1995–98, Counselor, Embassy in Washington, DC 1998–2003; Amb. to Italy 2003–04; Minister of Foreign Affairs 2004–. *Address:* Ministry of Foreign Affairs, 1009 Baku, S. Qurbanov küç. 4, Azerbaijan; tel. (12) 596-90-00; fax (12) 498-84-80; e-mail press-service@mfa.gov.az; internet www.mfa.gov.az.

MARTYNOW, Syarhey M.: Belarusian politician and diplomatist; *Minister of Foreign Affairs;* b. 22 Feb. 1953; m.; two s. *Education:* Moscow State Inst. of Int. Econ. Relations, USSR. *Career:* with Dept of Int. Econ. Orgs, Ministry of Foreign Affairs, USSR 1975–80, Asst to Minister of Foreign Affairs 1980–88, Deputy Head Dept of Int. Orgs 1988–91; Deputy Perm. Rep. of Repub. of Belarus to UN, New York, 1991–92; Chargé d'Affaires, Washington, DC, 1992–93; Amb. to USA 1993–97; First Deputy Minister of Foreign Affairs 1997–2001; Amb. to Belgium, Head of Mission to European Communities and Head of Mission to NATO 2001–03; Minister of Foreign Affairs 2003–; Vice-Chair. First Cttee (Int. Security and Disarmament) of UN Gen. Ass. 1988–97; fmr Vice-Pres. Amendment Conf. of the State Parties to the (1963) Treaty Banning Nuclear Tests in the Atmosphere in Outer Space and Under Water; three-times Chair. Nuclear Disarmament Group of UN Disarmament Comm., several-times Vice-Chair. and Rapporteur UN Disarmament Comm., Chair. 1998; Pres. Conf. on Disarmament, Geneva 2000; mem. UN Cttee on Econ., Cultural and Social Rights, Geneva 2001–; mem. Minsk Int. Educational Centre. *Address:* Ministry of Foreign Affairs, 220030 Minsk, vul. Lenina 19, Belarus; tel. (17) 227-29-22; fax (17) 227-45-21; e-mail mail@mfabelar.gov.by; internet www .mfa.gov.by.

MASIMOV, Karim K., DEcon; Kazakhstani economist and politician; *Prime Minister;* b. 15 June 1965, Tselinograd (now Astana). *Education:* Beijing Linguistic Inst., Wuhan Univ., China and Kazakh State Acad. of Man. *Career:* began career as senior economist at Ministry of Labour; fmr senior specialist, Kazakh Ministry of Foreign Econ. Affairs, Urumqi,

China; fmr CEO, Kazakh Trading House, Hong Kong; Chair. Almaty Merchant Bank 1995–97, JSC Halyk Bank of Kazakhstan 1997–2000; Minister of Transport and Communications 2001–04; Chief Policy Adviser to Pres. Nazarbayev 2004–06; Deputy Prime Minister 2006–07; Minister of Economy and Budget Planning April–Oct. 2006; Prime Minister 2007–; Dr hc (Peoples' Friendship Univ., Russia) 2007. *Address:* Office of the Prime Minister, 010000 Astana, Beibitshilik 11, Kazakhstan; tel. (7172) 32-31-04; fax (7172) 32-40-89; internet www.government.kz.

MATLYUBOV, Lt-Gen. Bahodir Ahmedovich: Uzbekistani government official; *Minister of Internal Affairs;* b. 10 March 1952, Samarqand. *Education:* Samarqand State Univ. *Career:* held various positions at Samarqand Regional Internal Affairs Directorate 1978–94; Head, Buxoro Regional Internal Affairs Directorate 1994–97; held several sr positions in Ministry of Internal Affairs including Chair. State Cttee on Demonopolization and Competition and Business Support, Chair. State Customs Cttee 2004, First Deputy Minister of Internal Affairs 1997–2006, Minister of Internal Affairs 2006–; Shon-Saraf (Glory) Order (First and Second degree). *Address:* Ministry of Internal Affairs, 100029 Tashkent, Yu. Rajaby ko‘ch. 1, Uzbekistan; tel. (71) 139-73-36; fax (71) 133-89-34; internet www.mvd.uz.

MEDVEDEV, Dmitrii Anatolyevich, PhD; Russian business executive, government official and head of state; *President;* b. 14 Sept. 1965, Leningrad (now St Petersburg); m. Svetlana Medvedeva; one s. *Education:* Leningrad State Univ. *Career:* Asst Prof., Leningrad State Univ. 1990–99; Adviser to Chair. Leningrad City Council and Expert Consultant, Cttee for External Relations, St. Petersburg Mayor's Office 1990–95; Deputy Chief of Staff, Govt of Russian Fed. 1999–2000; Deputy Head, then First Deputy Head of the Presidential Admin 2000–03, Head 2003–05; mem. Bd of Dirs OAO Gazprom 2000–08, Chair. 2000–01, 2002–08, Deputy Chair. 2001–02; mem. Exec. Cttee on Int. Relations, St Petersburg Mayor's Office 1991–95; First Deputy Prime Minister 2005–08; Pres. 2008–; Order in the Name of Russia 2004. *Address:* Office of the President, 103132 Moscow, Staraya pl. 4; tel. (495) 925-35-81; fax (495) 206-07-66; e-mail president@ gov.ru; internet www.kremlin.ru.

MEREDOV, Rashid: Turkmenistani politician; *Deputy Chairman of the Government and Minister of Foreign Affairs;* b. 1960. *Career:* Deputy Dir Nat. Inst. for Democracy and Human Rights –1999, Dir 2001–05; apptd Speaker in Majlis (Nat. Ass.) 1999, Chair. –2001; Minister of Foreign Affairs 2001–, Deputy Chair. of the Govt 2003–. *Address:* Ministry of Foreign Affairs, 744000 Aşgabat, pr. Magtymguly 83, Turkmenistan; tel. (12) 26-62-11; fax (12) 35-42-41; e-mail mfatm@ online.tm.

MILINKEVICH, Alyaksandr, PhD; Belarusian politician; b. 25 July 1947, Grodno; m. (twice); two c. from first m. *Education:* Grodno Teacher Inst., USSR Acad. of Sciences, European Centre for Security Research, Garmisch-Partenkirchen, Fed. Repub. of Germany. *Career:* early career as teacher, Hrodna 1969–72; Jr Researcher, USSR Acad. of Sciences (Belarus) 1972–78; Assoc. Prof., Grodno State Univ. 1978–80, 1984–90; Head, Dept of Physics, Univ. of Setif, Algeria 1980–84; Deputy Chair. Hrodna Admin Exec. Cttee 1990–96; Leader, Ratusha (Town Hall) Org. 1996–2003; Pres. Grodna-93 football team; Founder and Head, Ratusha Resource Centre 1997 (closed by authorities 2003); headed presidential campaign of Syamyon Domash 2001; contested 2006 presidential election as cand. for coalition of United Democratic Forces; Founder Movt for Freedom (human rights group); European Parliament Sakharov Prize, 2006. *Address:* c/o United Civic Party (Abyadnanya Hramadzyanskaya Partya Belarusi), 220123 Minsk, vul. Khoruzhey 22, Belarus; tel. (17) 289-50-09; fax (17) 283-50-09; e-mail ucpb@ucpb.org; info@milinkevich.org; internet www.ucpb.org; en.milinkevich .org.

MILLER, Aleksei Borisovich, PhD; Russian business executive; *Deputy Chairman of the Board of Directors and Chair-*

man of the Management Committee, OAO Gazprom; b. 31 Jan. 1962, Leningrad (now St Petersburg); m.; one s. *Education:* N.A. Voznesenskii Leningrad Inst. of Finance and Econs. *Career:* engineer-economist, Gen. Planning Div., LenNII-Proekt – Leningrad Civil Construction Research and Design Inst.; researcher, Leningrad Inst. of Finance and Econs 1990–91; mem. Cttee on Foreign Econ. Relations, Office of the Mayor of St Petersburg 1991–96; Dir of Devt and Investments, Morskoy Port of St Petersburg Open Jt Stock Co. 1996–99; Dir-Gen. Balttiiskaya Truboprovodnaya Sistema (Baltic Pipeline System) 1999–2000; Deputy Minister of Energy 2000–01; Deputy Chair. Bd of Dirs and Chair. Man. Cttee OAO Gazprom 2001–; Medal for Outstanding Services to the Fatherland (2nd degree), Order for Services to Energy Co-operation (2nd degree), Hungary, St Mesrop Mashtots Order, Armenia, Dostyk Order (2nd degree) Kazakhstan, Sergei Radonezhskii Order of the Russian Orthodox Church, Patriarchal Merit Certificate. *Address:* OAO Gazprom, 117997 Moscow, ul. Nametkina 16, V-420, GSP-7, Russia; tel. (495) 719-30-01; fax (495) 719-83-33; e-mail gazprom@gazprom.ru; internet www.gazprom.ru.

MIRONOV, Sergei Mikhailovich, CandJur; Russian engineer and politician; *Chairman, Sovet Federatsii (Federation Council);* b. 14 Feb. 1953, Pushkin, Leningrad Oblast; m.; one s. one d. *Education:* Leningrad (now St Petersburg) Plekhanov Mining Inst., St Petersburg State Tech. Univ., North-Western Acad. of Civil Service, St Petersburg State Univ. *Career:* army service 1971–73; engineer, Rusgeophysica (production co.) 1978–86; Sr Geophysicist, USSR Ministry of Geology, Mongolia 1987–91; Exec. Dir Russian Trade Chamber 1991–93, Construction Corpn – Restoration of St Petersburg 1994–95; mem., First Deputy Chair. then Chair. Legis. Ass. of St Petersburg 1995–2000; Head, Political Council The Will of Petersburg (Volya Peterburga) regional political movt 2000–01; Rep. of St Petersburg Ass. to Fed. Council, June 2001, Chair. Fed. Council Dec. 2001–; Founder and Chair. Russian Leader Party of Life 2003, Chair. A Just Russia (Spravedlivaya Rossiya) (merger of Motherland, Russian Party of Life and Russian Pensioners' Party) 2006–; unsuccessful presidential cand. 2004. *Address:* Sovet Federatsii (Federation Council), 103426 Moscow, ul. B. Dmitrovka 26; A Just Russia (Spravedlivaya Rossiya), 107031 Moscow, ul. B. Dmitrovka 32/1, Russia; tel. (495) 203-90-74; (495) 650-38-80 (A Just Russia); fax (495) 203-46-17; e-mail VPParfenov@mironov.ru; info@spravedlivo.ru; internet www.council.gov .ru; www.spravedlivo.ru; www.mironov.ru; mironov.info.

MIRZIYOYEV, Shavkat Miromonovich: Uzbekistani politician; *Prime Minister;* b. 1957, Samarqand. *Education:* Tashkent Inst. of Irrigation, Eng and Agric. Mechanization. *Career:* Pro-rector Tashkent Inst. of Irrigation and Mechanization of Agric. –1996; Hokim (Gov.) Jizzax Viloyat 1996–2001, Samarqand Viloyat 2001–03; mem. Oly Majlis (Parl.) 1999–, Prime Minister 2003–. *Address:* Office of the Cabinet of Ministers, 100078 Tashkent, Mustaqillik maydoni 5, Uzbekistan; tel. (71) 139-82-95; fax (71) 139-84-63; internet www.gov.uz.

MOROZ, Oleksandr Oleksandrovych: Ukrainian politician; *Leader, Socialist Party of Ukraine;* b. 29 Feb. 1944, Buda, Kyiv Oblast; m. Valentina Andriyivna Moroz; two d. *Education:* Ukrainian Agric. Acad., Higher C.P. School. *Career:* trained as engineer in Kyiv; engineer and mechanic in state farm professional school, dist and regional enterprises of Selkhoztechnika 1965–76; sec. regional trade union, First Sec. Dist CP Cttee; Head of Agric. Div. Regional CP Cttee; co-f. Socialist party of Ukraine (SPU) 1991; People's Deputy of Ukrainian SSR, then mem. Verkhovna Rada (Parl.) 1994–, Chair. 1994–98, 2006–07; presidential cand. 1994, 1999, 2004. *Publications:* author and co-author of a number of legal projects including Code on Land: Where Are We Going?, Choice, Subjects for Meditation; several articles. *Address:* Socialist Party of Ukraine, 02100 Kyiv, vul. Bazhova 12, Ukraine; tel. (44) 573-58-97; e-mail pr@spu.in.ua; internet www.spu.in.ua.

MUHAMMEDOV, Hojamuhammet: Turkmenistani politician; *Deputy Chairman, responsible for the Textile Industry, Trade and the Chamber of Commerce and Industry;* b. 1966, Aşgabat. *Education:* Turkmen Inst. of Nat. Economy. *Career:* started career as forwarding agent, Turkmenengilazyksenagat Asscn, Ministry of Trade and Consumer Co-operation 1983, then worked as construction engineer, engineer of Supplies Dept of Turkmenhimsnabbyt, stock keeper, Dept of State Cttee for Logistics of Turkmenistan; Deputy Dir then Dir Harytimpeks Co., Ministry of Trade and Foreign Econ. Relations, then Dir Gulistan state trade center 1998–2005; Deputy Chair. State Commodity and Raw Materials Exchange 2005, Chair 2006; Chair. Supreme Supervisory Chamber of Turkmenistan July–Nov. 2007; Deputy Chairman of the Govt, responsible for the Textile Industry, Trade and the Chamber of Commerce and Industry Nov. 2007–. *Address:* Office of the President and the Council of Ministers, 744000 Aşgabat, Turkmenistan; tel. (12) 35-45-34; fax (12) 35-51-12; internet www.turkmenistan.gov.tm.

MUSIN, Aslan Yespulayevich: Kazakhstani government official; *Chairman, Majlis (Parliament);* b. 2 Jan. 1954. *Education:* Almaty Inst. of Econs. *Career:* fmr Akim (Gov.) Aktobe and Atyrau Oblasts; Minister of Econ. Affairs and Budget Planning 2006–07; Deputy Prime Minister Jan.–Sept. 2007; Chair. Majlis (Parl.) 2007–. *Address:* Office of the Chairman, 010000 Astana, Parliament House, Kazakhstan; tel. (7172) 15-30-19; fax (7172) 33-30-99; e-mail www@parlam .kz; internet www.parlam.kz.

MYNBAYEV, Sauat M., Cand. Econ.; Kazakhstani politician; *Minister of Energy and Mineral Resources;* b. 19 Nov. 1962, Taldy-Kurgan; m. Kaliyeva Zhanar Mynbayev; one s. one d. *Education:* Moscow State Univ. *Career:* teacher, Almaty Inst. of Nat. Economy, later Assoc. Prof. 1989–; Pres. Kazakhstan Exchange 1991–92; First Deputy Chair. and Dir Kazkommerts Bank 1992–95; Deputy Minister of Finance and Dir of Treasury 1995–98, Minister of Finance 1998–99; Deputy Head of Pres.'s Admin. 1999; Minister of Agric. 1999–2001; apptd Pres. Devt Bank of Kazakhstan 2001 Dir European Bank of Devt from Kazakhstan 2001; Deputy Prime Minister of Kazakhstan 2003–06; Minister of Industry and Trade 2004–06, of Energy and Mineral Resources 2007–. *Address:* Ministry of Energy and Mineral Resources, 010000 Astana, Beibitshilik 37, Kazakhstan; tel. (7172) 31-71-33; fax (7172) 31-71-64; e-mail ministr@minenergo.kegoc.kz; internet www .minenergo.kz.

NABIULLINA, Elvira Sakhipzadovna, PhD; Russian economist and government official; *Minister of Economic Development;* b. 29 Oct. 1963. *Education:* M.V.Lomonosov Moscow State Univ. *Career:* Chief Specialist, Russian Union of Industrialists and Businessmen on econ. policy 1992–94; Deputy Head, Dept of Econ. Reform 1994–96, Head of Dept 1996–97; Deputy Minister of the Economy 1997–98; Vice-Pres. Bd of Dirs Promtorgbank 1998–99; Exec. Dir Euroasian (rating service) 1999; First Deputy Minister of Econ. Devt and Trade 2000–07, Minister of Econ. Devt 2007–; Vice-Pres. Fund Centre of Strategic Devt 1999–2000, Pres. 2003–05, Head of Research Group 2005–07; Head of Advisory Council of Organizing Cttee on Preparation and Maintenance of Presidency of the Russian Fed. in G8 2005–06; fmr mem. Pres.'s Expert Council on Priority Nat. Projects and Demography; World Fellow, Yale Univ. 2007. *Address:* Ministry of Economic Development, 125993 Moscow, ul. 1-ya Tverskaya-Yamskaya 1/3, Russia; tel. (495) 200-03-47; e-mail presscenter@economy .gov.ru; internet www.economy.gov.ru.

NALBANDIAN, Edvard, Ph.D; Armenian diplomatist; *Minister of Foreign Affairs;* b. 1956; m.; one d. *Education:* Moscow State Inst. of Int. Relations, Inst of Oriental Studies, USSR Nat. Acad. of Sciences. *Career:* worked at USSR Embassy in Lebanon 1978–83; at USSR Ministry of Foreign Affairs, Moscow 1983–86; Counsellor of USSR Embassy (then Russian Fed. Embassy) in Egypt 1986–92; Chargé d'Affaires in Egypt 1992–93, Amb. to Egypt 1994–98 (also accred Morocco and Oman); Amb. to France 1999–2008 (also accred to Israel, the Vatican, to Andorra) 2004–08; Minister of Foreign Affairs

2008–; Special Rep. of the Pres.of Armenia to Int. Org. of Francophony 2006; Commdr, Légion d'honneur 2001, Grand Cross of St Gregory (Holy See) 2003; Award of Friendship of Nations (USSR) 1982, Mkhitar Gosh Medal 2001. *Address:* Ministry of Foreign Affairs, 0010 Yerevan, Republic Square, Government House 2, Armenia; tel. (10) 54-40-41; fax (10) 54-39-25; e-mail info@armeniaforeignministry.com; internet www.armeniaforeignministry.com.

NAZARBAYEV, Nursultan Abishevich, DSc; Kazakhstani politician and head of state; *President;* b. 6 July 1940, Chemolgan, Kaskelen Dist, Almaty Oblast; m. Sara Alplisovna Kounakayeva 1962; three d. *Education:* Higher Tech. Course at Karaganda Metallurgical Combine, Russian Acad. of Management and Higher Party School of Cen. Cttee CPSU. *Career:* mem. CPSU 1962–91; worked for Karaganda Metallurgical Plant 1960–64, 1965–69; Sec. Temirtau City Cttee of Kazakh CP 1969–84; Sec. party Cttee of Karaganda Metallurgical Combine 1973–77; Second, then First Sec. Karaganda Dist Cttee of Kazakh CP 1977–79; Sec. Cen. Cttee of Kazakh CP 1979–84; Chair. Council of Ministers of Kazakh SSR 1984–89; USSR People's Deputy 1989–91; First Sec. Cen. Cttee of Kazakh CP 1989–91, Socialist Party 1991–; Chair. Kazakh Supreme Soviet 1989–90; Exec. Pres. Kazakh SSR 1990–91; Pres. Repub. of Kazakhstan 1991–; Chair. World Kazakh Union 1992–; mem. Int. Eng Acad. 1993, Acad. of Social Sciences of the Russian Fed. 1994, Nat. Acad. of Sciences of the Repub. of Kazakhstan 1995; Hon. Citizen of Temirtau 1991, Duluth, USA 1991, Almaty 1995; Diploma of Freeman of Municipality of Bucharest 1998; Hon. Prof., Al-Farabi Kazakh State Nat. Univ., M.V. Lomonosov Moscow State Univ. 1996; Hon. mem. Belarusian Acad. of Sciences 1996, Nat. Acad. of Applied Sciences of Russia 1997; Order of the Red Banner of Labour; Badge of Honour 1972; Order of Saint Lord-and-Master Prince Daniil of Moscow, First Class 1996; Order of Yaroslav Mudryi (Ukraine) 1997; Order of Big Cross Holder with Ribbon (Italy) 1998; Order of Holy Apostole Andrei Pervosvannyi 1998; Ismoili Samoni Order (Tajikistan) 2000; Pi Order (Vatican) 2001; Dr hc (Kazakh Inst. of Man., Economy and Forecasting) 1995, (Bilkent Univ., Ankara) 1998; Capri Award (Italy) 1992, Rukhaniyat Man of the Year 1993, Gold Medal of Guild of Econ. Devt and Marketing of the City of Nurnberg (FRG) 1993, Award of Crans-Montana Int. Forum 1996, star No. Perseus RA 3h 23v Osd 40* 43 named after him 1997, Medal No. 1 of Al-Farabi Kazakh State Nat. Univ. 1998, Award for Int. Understanding, Indian Fund Unity International 1998, Award For Service to Turkish World 1998, Gold Medal and Diploma for Special Contrib. to Devt of CIS Aviation, Int. Aviation Comm. 1998, Peace Dove Prize, UNESCO Club of Dodecanese Islands (Greece) 1999, Man of the Century Award, Abylai Khan Int. Fund 2000, Grand Star of Respect for Merits (Austria) 2000. *Publications:* Steel Profile of Kazakhstan, With Neither the Right nor the Left, Strategy of Resource Saving and Market Transition, Strategy of Formation and Development of Kazakhstan as a Sovereign State, Market and Social-and-Economic Development, On the Threshold of the XXIst Century, Eurasian Union: Ideas, Practice, Prospects 1994–1997, In the Flood of History, The Epicenter of Peace, and others; numerous scientific articles and articles on econs. *Address:* Office of the President, 010000 Astana, Beibitshilik 11, Kazakhstan; tel. (7172) 32-13-99; fax (7172) 32-61-72; internet www.akorda.kz.

NAZARBAYEVA, Dariga Nursultanova, Dr rer. pol; Kazakhstani politician and media executive; b. 7 May 1963; m. Rakhat Aliyev (divorced 2007); two s. one d. *Education:* Moscow M. V. Lomonosov State Univ., S. M. Kirov State Univ., Russian Presidential Acad. of Public Service. *Career:* Vice-Pres. Khabar Broadcasting Agency 1994–95, Gen. Dir 1995–98, Pres. 1998–2001, Chair., Council of Dirs 2001–03; Founder and Chair. Mutual Help Republican Party (Asar, later Fatherland Republican Political Party, Otan' Respublikalyk Sayasi Partiyasy, following merger) 2003–06, Chair. Light of the Fatherland People's Democratic Party 2006–; Chair. Eurasian Media Forum; Leader, Congress of Journalists of Kazakhstan; Chair., Supervisory Bd of Int. Inst. for Modern Politics, Kazakhstan; mem. Bd Int. TV Acad., New York; Pres. Eurasian Centre for Strategic Studies, Russia; Vice-Pres. Eurasian TV Acad., Russia; Co-Chair. Eurasian TV Forum Organizing Cttee; Assoc. Mem., Int. Econ. Acad. Eurasia; Vice-Pres. Children's Charitable Fund Bobek 1992–94; mem. Nat. Comm. of Repub. of Kazakhstan for UNESCO; fmr Pres. Sports Gymnastics Fed. of Repub. of Kazakhstan. *Publications:* Democratization of Political Systems in the Commonwealth of Independent States 1997, The Eurasian Commonwealth 2000, From the Union Towards the Commonwealth (ed. and co-author) 2001, Ten Years of the Commonwealth of Independent States: Experience, Problems, Future Prospects (co-author) 2001. *Address:* Light of the Fatherland People's Democratic Party ('Nur Otan' Khalyktyk Demokratiyalyk Partiyasy), 050000 Almaty, Abylai khana 79, Kazakhstan; tel. (727) 279-78-00; fax (727) 279-40-66; e-mail partyotan@nursat.kz; internet www.ndp-nurotan.kz.

NOGHAIDELI, Zurab: Georgian business executive, academic and politician; b. 22 Oct. 1964, Kobuleti, Ajara; m. Nino Tsintsabadze; one s. *Education:* Moscow M. V. Lomonosov State Univ., USSR (now Russian Fed.). *Career:* Asst in the Inst. of Geography, Acad. of Sciences of Georgia, Batumi 1988–89; Guest Researcher in the Inst. of Geology, Acad. of Sciences of Estonia, Tallinn 1989–91; Sr Researcher and Head of Laboratory, Niko Berzenishvili Research Inst., Acad. of Sciences of Georgia, Batumi 1989–92; Exec. Sec. Georgia Greens 1992–93; mem. Parl. Chair. Cttee of Environment Protection and Natural Resources 1992–95, Chair. Cttee of Tax and Revenue 1999–2000; Co-ordinator Office of the Chair. 1995–99; Int. Sec., Citizens' Union of Georgia 1995–98; mem. Supreme Council, Adjara Autonomous Rep. 1996–98; Minister of Finance 2000–02, 2004–05; Prime Minister of Georgia 2005–07 (resgnd); bd mem. People's Bank of Georgia 2002–03; Pnr, Solidary Responsibilities Soc. Damenia, Varshalomidze, Noghaideli and Kavtaradze April–Nov. 2003; Chair. Kala Capital (investment co.) 2007–; Chair. Int. School of Econs Business Council, Tbilisi State Univ. 2008–. *Address:* Kala Capital, 4a, 1st drive, I. Chavchavadze, 0179 Tbilisi, Georgia; tel. (32) 91-92-22.

NOROV, Vladimir L., PhD; Uzbekistani diplomatist and government official; *Minister of Foreign Affairs;* b. 31 Aug. 1955, Buxoro; m.; three c. *Education:* Buxoro State Pedagogical Inst., Moscow Acad. of Internal Affairs. *Career:* school teacher 1976; mil. service 1976–77; worked in Dept of Internal Affairs, Buxoro 1978–88, Head of Criminal Investigation Dept 1990–93; consultant on admin. and legal issues, Pres.'s Office 1993–95, State Adviser for Foreign Relations 1996–98; Deputy Minister, Ministry of Foreign Affairs 1995–96, First Deputy Minister 2003–04, Minister of Foreign Affairs 2006–; Amb. to Germany 1998–2003 (also accred. to Switzerland and Poland 2002–03); Amb. to Belgium and Chief of Missions to EU and NATO, Brussels 2004–06. *Address:* Ministry of Foreign Affairs, 100029 Tashkent, O'zbekiston shoh ko'ch. 9, Uzbekistan; tel. (71) 233-64-75; fax (71) 239-15-17; e-mail letter@mfa.uz; internet www.mfa.uz.

NUR UULU, Dosbal, PhD; Kyrgyzstani politician; *Deputy Prime Minister;* b. 26 April 1948. *Education:* Kyrgyz State Univ. *Career:* Jr Research Asst, History Inst. of Kyrgyz SSR Acad. of Sciences 1972–81, Intern-Researcher 1981–83, Sr Research Asst 1983–89, doctorate degree study 1989–92, Head of Dept, History Inst. 1993–95; Deputy of Zhogorku Kenesh (Parl.) 1995–2000; Minister of Educ., Science and Youth Policy 2005–07; Deputy Prime Minister 2007–; Leader, New Kyrgyzstan (Jany Kyrgyzstan) party; fmr mem. Agrarian-Labor Party. *Address:* c/o Office of the Prime Minister, 720003 Bishkek, Dom Pravitelstva, Kyrgyzstan; tel. (312) 66-12-20; fax (312) 66-66-58; e-mail pmoffice@mail.gov.kg; internet www.government.gov.kg.

NURBERDIYEVA, Akja Tajiyevna: Turkmenistani politician; *Chairman, Majlis. Career:* mem. Majlis (Parl.), Vice-Chair. 2003–06, Acting Chair. 2006–07, Chair. 2007–. *Address:* Majlis, 744000 Aşgabat, ul. Bitarap Türkmenistan 17, Turkmenistan; tel. (12) 35-31-25; fax (12) 35-31-47.

NURGALIYEV, Col-Gen. Rashid Gumarovich, PhD; Russian politician and security officer; *Minister of Internal Affairs;* b. 8 Oct. 1956, Zhetygar, Kazakh SSR; m.; two c. *Education:* Kuusinen State Univ. *Career:* physics teacher, Nadvoitsy 1979–81; with KGB 1981–, Head of Anti-Terrorist Dept, Karelian Republican KGB 1991–95, Chief Inspector, Fed. Counterespionage Service 1995–98, Head, Office for Drug Trafficking Control, Dept of Econ. Security 1999–2000, Deputy Dir, Head of Inspectors Admin 2000–02; First Deputy Minister of Internal Affairs 2002–04, Head of Criminal Militia Service 2002–04, Minister of Internal Affairs 2004–. *Address:* Ministry of Internal Affairs, 119049 Moscow, ul. Zhitnaya 16, Russia; tel. (495) 239-69-71; fax (495) 293-59-98; e-mail mvd12@mvdrf.ru; internet www.mvd.ru.

OHANIAN, Col-Gen. Seyran: Armenian government official and fmr army officer; *Minister of Defence;* b. 1 July 1962, Shushi (Şuşa), Nagorno-Karabakh Autonomous Oblast, Azerbaijan SSR; m.; three s. *Education:* Baku Higher Jt Command Coll. *Career:* began mil. service serving as Platoon Commdr with USSR motorized rifle platoon, Germany 1987–88, Co. Commdr 1987–88; Co. Commdr, 366th motorized rifle regiment, Stepanakert 1988–89, Battalion Deputy Commdr 1989–90, Battalion Commdr 1990–92; Commander of 366th motorized rifle regiment; Chief of Staff of Self-Defence Forces, 'Repub. of Nagornyi-Karabakh' 1992–94, First Deputy Commdr of Defence Army 1994–98; Commdr 5th Army Corps of Armenia 1998–99; Minister of Defence, 'Repub. of Nagornyi-Karabakh' 1999–2000, Minister of Defence and Commdr of Defence Army 2000–07; Chief of Staff, Armenian Armed Forces 2007–08; Minister of Defence of Armenia 2008–; 70th Anniversary of USSR Armed Forces, For Perfect Service, For Excellency, Soviet Union Marshal Zhukov (all from USSR); Hero of Artsakh, Golden Eagle, Combat Cross 1st degree, For the Liberation of Shushi (Nagornyi-Karabakh); Combat Cross 1st degree, Tigranes the Great, For the Service to the Motherland, For Perfect Service 1st and 2nd Degrees, Drastamat Kanayan, Marshal Baghramyan, For the Strengthening of Co-operation, Maternal Gratitude, Coat of Arms. *Address:* Ministry of Defence, 0088 Yerevan, Proshian Settlement, G. Shaush St 60, Armenia; tel. (10) 28-72-03; fax (10) 28-26-30; e-mail press@mil.am; internet www.mil.am.

OHRYZKO, Volodymyr S., PhD; Ukrainian diplomatist; *Minister of Foreign Affairs;* b. 1 April 1956, Kyiv; m.; one s. two d. *Education:* Kyiv Taras Shevchenko Univ. *Career:* joined Ukrainian SSSR Ministry of Foreign Affairs 1978; Attaché, Press Dept 1978–80, Third Sec. 1980–81, 1983–85 (mil. service 1981–83), Second Sec. 1985–88; First Sec., Prin. Counselor's Dept 1988–91, Counselor June–July 1991; Counselor Political Analysis and Co-ordination Dept July 1991–March 1992; Counselor, Embassy in FRG 1992–93, 1994–96; Minister, Embassy in Vienna 1993–94; Head, Foreign Policy Dept and Head, Main Foreign Policy Dept of the Presidential Admin 1996–99; Chair. External Policy Dept 1996–99; Amb. to Austria and Perm. Rep. to Int. Orgs, Vienna 1999–2004; Amb.-at-Large, Dept of Euro-Atlantic Co-operation 2004–05; First Deputy Minister of Foreign Affairs 2005–07; Acting Minister of Foreign Affairs Jan.–March 2007, Minister of Foreign Affairs Dec. 2007–. *Address:* Ministry of Foreign Affairs, 01018 Kyiv, pl. Mykhailivska 1, Ukraine; tel. (44) 238-15-06; fax (44) 226-31-69; internet www.mfa.gov.ua.

OKRUASHVILI, Irakli: Georgian lawyer and politician; b. 6 Nov. 1973, Tskhinvali; m. Irina Gordeladze; one d. *Education:* Tbilisi State Univ. *Career:* leading specialist, Elections Cen. Comm. 1995; consultant, TACIS project, State Service Div. 1996; lawyer, Korzadze, Svanidze & Okruashvili, Okruashvili & Partners 1996–2000; Lecturer in Int. Trade Law, Tbilisi State Univ. 1997–2001; Deputy Minister of Justice 2000–01; mem. Tbilisi Sakrebulo (City Ass.) 2002–, Head of Revision Comm. Nov. 2002; Pres.'s plenipotentiary in Shida Kartli Mkhare Nov. 2003; Gen. Prosecutor Jan.–June 2004; Minister of Internal Affairs June–Dec. 2004, of Defence Dec. 2004–06, of Econ. Devt Nov. 2006; f. Movement for a United Georgia 2007; mem. Georgian Young Lawyers' Asscn, World Lawyers' Asscn, Lawyers' Int. Asscn; sentenced in absentia to 11 years

imprisonment on corruption charges March 2008; granted asylum in France April 2008.

OTUNBAYEVA, Roza Isakovna, CPhilSc; Kyrgyzstani diplomatist and politician; *Co-Chair, Banner (Asaba) Party of National Revival;* b. 23 Aug. 1950; m.; one s. one d. *Education:* Moscow State Univ. *Career:* sr teacher, Head of Chair Kyrgyz Univ. 1975–81; Second Sec. Regional CP Cttee in Frunze (now Bishkek), Sec. City CP Cttee 1979–86; Vice-Chair. Council of Ministers, Minister of Foreign Affairs of Kyrgyz SSR 1986–89; Exec. Sec. USSR Comm. on UNESCO 1989–90, Chair. 1990–91; Amb. of USSR to Malaysia 1991–92; Vice-Prime Minister and Minister of Foreign Affairs of Repub. of Kyrgyzstan Feb.–May 1992; Amb. of Kyrgyzstan to USA 1992–94 (also accred to Canada); Minister of Foreign Affairs 1994–97; Amb. to UK 1997–2002; apptd Deputy Special Rep. of UN Sec.-Gen. for Georgia (to regulate conflict between Georgia and Abkhazia) 2002; Chair. Ata-Jurt party 2004–06, key leader of Tulip Revolution that led to overthrow of Pres. Akayev 2005, Acting Minister of Foreign Affairs 2005; Co-Chair. Banner (Asaba) Party of Nat. Revival 2006–; mem. Advisory Bd (Moscow Br.), Carnegie Endowment for Int. Peace. *Address:* Banner (Asaba) Party of National Revival, 720000 Bishkek, pr. Chui 26, Kyrgyzstan; tel. (312) 43-04-45; fax (312) 28-53-64.

PATRUSHEV, Col-Gen. Nikolai Platonovich: Russian government security official; *Secretary of the Security Council;* b. 11 July 1951, Leningrad (now St Petersburg); m.; two s. *Education:* Leningrad Inst. of Vessel Construction. *Career:* on staff KGB, Kareliyan ASSR 1974; in Leningrad Oblast 1974–92; Minister of Security Republic of Kareliya 1992–94; Head Dept of Self-Security, Fed. Security Service 1994–98, Deputy Dir, then Head, Dept of Econs 1998–99, Dir 1999–; Head of Presidential Control Dept May–Aug. 1998; Deputy Head Admin. of Russian Presidency Aug.–Oct. 1998; Deputy Dir Fed. Security Service of Russia (FSB), Head of Econ. Security Dept 1998, First Deputy Dir April–Aug. 1999, Dir Aug. 1999–2008; Sec., Security Council 2008–. *Address:* Security Council, 103132 Moscow, Ipatyevskii per. 4/10, Russia; internet www.scrf.gov.ru.

PINCHUK, Viktor Mykhaylovych, PhD; Ukrainian business executive and politician; m. Lena Kuchma (d. of fmr Pres. of Ukraine, Leonid Kuchma). *Education:* Dnipropetrovsk Metallurgical Inst. *Career:* f. Interpipe Corpn (industrial conglomerate) 1990, Pres. 1997–98, fmr Chair. of Bd; owner of a wide range of businesses including Int. Commercial TV (first nat. commercial TV network in Ukraine), New Channel TV, STB TV channel, UkroBank, Fakty newspaper, Nizhnyodniprovsky Pipe Mill, Ukrainian News (news service) and other cos; mem. Verkhovna Rada (Supreme Council) 1998–2006; mem. Working Ukraine Party (Trudova Ukraina); f. Victor Pinchuk Foundation 2006. *Address:* c/o Interpipe Corporation, 49600 Dnipropetrovsk, vul. Pysarzhevskoho 1a, Ukraine; tel. (562) 47-69-69; fax (562) 70-20-01; e-mail press@pinchukfund.org; internet www.pinchukfund.org.

POPOV, Vadim Aleksandrovich: Belarusian politician; *Chairman, Palata Predstaviteley (House of Representatives);* b. 1940, Demidov, Smolensk Oblast, Russia; m.; two c. *Education:* Minsk Higher CPSU School, Belarus State Inst. of Agriculture Mechanisation. *Career:* army service 1961–64; Komsomol functionary 1964–71; Dir Sovkhoz Mogilev region 1972–76; party functionary, instructor, Head of Div. Mogilev Regional CP Cttee, First Sec. 1976–92; instructor Cen. Cttee CP of Belarus 1976–92; worked in agric. roles in complex of Mogilev region 1992–99; First Deputy Minister of Agric. and Food March–July 1999, Minister July–Nov. 2000; mem. Palata Predstaviteley (House of Reps), Nat. Ass. (Parl.) 2000–, Chair. 2000–04, 2007–; Deputy Prime Minister March–June 2001, Prime Minister June–Nov. 2001; Order, Labour Red Banner, three medals; Hon. Diploma Supreme Soviet Belarus SSR. *Address:* House of Representatives, 220010 Minsk, vul. Savetskaya 11, Belarus; tel. (17) 227-25-14; fax (17) 222-31-78; e-mail admin@gov.house.by; internet house.gov.by.

POROSHENKO, Petro Oleksiyovych: Ukrainian business executive and politician; *Chairman of the Executive Council, National Bank of Ukraine;* b. 26 Sept. 1965, Bolhrad, Odesa Oblast. *Education:* Taras Shevchenko Univ., Kyiv. *Career:* Deputy Dir-Gen. Respublika Asscn of Small Businesses and Businessmen 1990–91; Pres. Birzhovy Dim Ukraine 1991–93; Pres. and prin. shareholder PJSC Ukrprominvest 1993–98 (holding co. with control of Roshen confectionary, Mriya bank, Radomysh brewery, Leninsak Kuznia Works, Lutsk automobile plant, Cherkasy bus plant, Channel 5 (5 Kanal) TV station, now Hon. Pres.; mem. Verkhovna Rada (Parl.) 1998–, Chair. Sub-Cttee for Securities, Stock and Investment Markets 2000, Budget Cttee 2002–04, currently Chair. Finance and Banking Cttee; mem. United Social Democratic Party of Ukraine (SDPU) –2000, f. Solidarnist party 2000, then joined Party of Regions, then joined Our Ukraine party 2001; apptd mem. Pres.'s Coordinating Council for the Securities Market 1998; Deputy Man. Viktor Yushchenko's presidential campaign 2004; Sec., Nat. Security Council 2005; Chair. Exec. Council, Nat. Bank of Ukraine 2007–; State Prize of Ukraine, Merited Economist of Ukraine, Pylyp Orlyk Int. Prize. *Address:* National Bank of Ukraine (Natsionalny Bank Ukrainy), 01601 Kyiv, vul. Institutska 9, Ukraine; tel. (44) 253-38-22; fax (44) 230-20-33; e-mail postmaster@bank.gov .ua; press@poroshenko.com.ua; postmaster@bank.gov.ua; internet www.bank.gov.ua; www.poroshenko.com.ua.

PUTIN, Col Vladimir Vladimirovich, PhD; Russian politician and fmr head of state; *Chairman of the Government (Prime Minister);* b. 7 Oct. 1952, Leningrad (now St Petersburg); m. Lyudmila Putina 1983; two d. *Education:* Law Dept, Leningrad State Univ. *Career:* assigned to work on staff KGB USSR 1975–91, with First Chief Dept of KGB and in E Germany 1985–90; asst to Pro-Rector, Leningrad State Univ. 1990; adviser to Chair. of Leningrad City Exec. Cttee 1990–91; Chair. Cttee on Foreign Relations, St Petersburg City Council 1991–96, then also First Deputy Chair. St Petersburg City Govt (First Deputy Mayor) 1994–96; Deputy Head, Admin. of Russian Presidency, Property Man. Directorate 1996–98, then also Deputy Head, Exec. Office of Pres. (Presidential Admin) and Head, Cen. Supervision and Inspections Directorate 1997–98; First Deputy Head, Presidential Admin May–July 1998; Dir Fed. Security Service of Russian Fed. 1998–99; Sec. Security Council of Russia March–Aug. 1999; apptd Chair. of Govt (Prime Minister) Aug.–Dec. 1999, 2008–; Acting Pres. of Russian Fed. Dec. 1999–March 2000, Pres. March 2000–08; Chair. United Russia (UR) (Yedinaya Rossiya) party 2008–; Grand Cross Bundesverdienstkreuz (Germany) 2001, Grand Croix, Légion d'Honneur 2006, King Abdul Aziz Award, Saudi Arabia 2007, Order of Zayed (UAE) 2007; named Person of the Year by Time magazine 2007. *Address:* Office of the Chairman of the Government, 103274 Moscow, Krasnopresnenskaya nab. 2, Russia; tel. (495) 205-57-35; fax (495) 205-42-19; internet www.government.ru.

PYNZENYK, Viktor Mikhailovich, DEcon; Ukrainian politician and economist; *Minister of Finance;* b. 15 April 1954, Smologovitsa; m. Mariya Romanivna Pynzenyk; two d. one s. *Education:* Lviv State Univ. *Career:* Asst, then Docent, Sr Researcher, Prof., Chair. Lviv State Univ. 1975–92; mem. Vakhovna Rada (Parl.) 1991–2001; Deputy Chair. Bd on Problems of Econ. Policy 1992; Minister of Economy 1992–93, Deputy Prime Minister 1992–97; Pres. Foundation of Support to Reforms 1993; Chair. Council on Econ. Reforms 1994; Chair. Nat. Council on Statistics 1995; Head, State Comm. on Admin. Reform 1997–99; Head, Reforms and Order Party (Partiya 'Reformy i poryadok) 1998–; Minister of Finance 2005–06, 2007–; Dir Inst. of Reforms; Hon. Prof., Mohyla Acad.—Nat. Univ. of Kyiv 1996–. *Publications:* over 400 papers. *Address:* Ministry of Finance, 01008 Kyiv, vul. M. Hrushevskoho 12/2; Reforms and Order Party (Partiya 'Reformy i poryadok'), 01021 Kyiv, vul. Instytutska 28, Ukraine; tel. (44) 293-74-66 (Ministry); (44) 585-41-16; fax (44) 293-21-78 (Ministry); (44) 585-41-17; e-mail inform@ minfin.gov.ua; ref_ord@i.com.ua; internet www.minfin.gov .ua; www.prp.org.ua.

QAMBAR, İsa Yunis oğlu: Azerbaijani politician and historian; *Chairman, Müsavat (Equality Party);* b. 24 Feb. 1957, Baku; m. Dr. Aide Bagirova 1986; two s. *Education:* Baku State Univ. *Career:* researcher Azerbaijan Acad. of Sciences 1979–82, Inst. of Oriental Studies 1982–90; active participant in democratic movt in late 1980s, Head of organizational div. of Popular Front 1990–, Deputy Chair. 1990–91; mem. Supreme Soviet of Azerbaijan 1990–95, Chair. Milli Majlis (Parl.) and Acting Pres. of Azerbaijan 1992–93 (resgnd); Chair. Comm. on Foreign Affairs 1991–92; Chair. Müsavat (Equality Party) 1992–; Co-Founder and Chair. Democratic Congress 1999, 2001–03; joined United Opposition Alliance 2002; presidential cand. 2003. *Address:* Müsavat (Equality) Party (Müsavat Partiyası), 1025 Baku, Darnagül qasabasi 30/97, Azerbaijan; tel. (12) 448-23-82; (12) 461-15-00; fax (12) 448-23-84; (12) 498-31-66; e-mail info@musavat.org; isa.gambar@gmail.com; internet www.musavat.org; www .isagambar.az.

RAKHMON, Emomali, BEcons; Tajikistani politician and head of state; *President;* b. (Imamali Sharipovich Rakhmonov), 5 Oct. 1952, Dangar, Kulob Oblast; m.; nine c. *Education:* Lenin Tajikistan State Univ. *Career:* served in USSR army; early jobs as electrician, salesman, as trade union sec. and on various CP cttees; Dir Dangarin Sovkhoz (Soviet farm), Kulob Oblast 1982–92, Chair. Union Cttee 1976–88; Chair. Kulob Oblast Exec. Cttee 1992; Chair. Majlisi Oli (Supreme Ass.) 1992–94; Pres. of Tajikistan 1994–; World Peace Corps Acad. Gold Medal 2000. *Address:* Office of the President, 734023 Dushanbe, Xiyoboni Rudaki 80, Tajikistan; tel. (372) 21-04-18; fax (372) 21-18-37; e-mail mail@president .tj; internet www.president.tj.

RASIZADE, Artur Tahir oğlu: Azerbaijani politician and engineer; *Prime Minister;* b. 26 Feb. 1935, Ganca; m.; one d. *Education:* Azerbaijan Inst. of Industry. *Career:* engineer, Deputy Dir Azerbaijan Inst. of Oil Machine Construction 1957–73, Dir 1977–78; chief engineer Trust Soyuzneftemash 1973–77; Deputy Head Azerbaijan State Planning Cttee 1978–81; Head of Section Cen. Cttee of Azerbaijan CP 1981–86; First Deputy Prime Minister 1986–92; adviser Foundation of Econ. Reforms 1992–96; Asst to Pres. Heydar Aliyev Feb.–May 1996; First Deputy Prime Minister May–Nov. 1996; Prime Minister 1996–, demoted and apptd Deputy Prime Minister Aug. 2003 but resumed role as Prime Minister days later. *Address:* Office of the Prime Minister, 1066 Baku, Lermontov küç. 68, Azerbaijan; tel. (12) 492-66-23; fax (12) 492-91-79; e-mail nk@cabmin.gov.az; internet www.cabmin .gov.az.

SAAKASHVILI, Mikhail, LLM, SJD; Georgian politician, lawyer and head of state; *President;* b. 21 Dec. 1967, Tblisi; m. Sandra Roelofs; two s. *Education:* Faculty of Int. Relations, Kyiv State Univ., Ukraine, Columbia Univ. Law School, NY, USA, George Washington Univ., Washington, DC, USA, Int. Inst. of Human Rights, Strasbourg, France, Norwegian Inst. of Human Rights. *Career:* worked for Patterson, Belknap, Webb & Tyler (law firm), New York 1994; returned to Ukraine 1995; mem. Parl. (Union of Citizens of Georgia) 1995, Chair. Parl. Cttee responsible for creating new electoral system, ind. judiciary and non-political police force 1995–2000; Vice-Pres. Parl. Ass. of Council of Europe 2000; Minister for Justice 2000–01 (resgnd); resgnd from Union of Citizens of Georgia Party 2001; f. Nat. Movt opposition party 2001; elected Head, City Council of Tblisi 2002–03; Pres. of Georgia 2004–; named Man of the Year by panel of journalists and human rights activists 1997. *Address:* Office of the President, 0105 Tbilisi, P. Ingorovka 7, Georgia; tel. (32) 99-00-70; fax (32) 99-88-87; e-mail secretariat@admin.gov.ge; internet www.president .gov.ge.

SAHAKIAN, Bako: Azerbaijani government official; *President of the Republic of Nagornyi-Karabakh';* b. 30 Aug. 1960, Xankandi (Stepanakert); m.; two c. *Education:* Stepanakert High School, Artsakh State Univ. *Career:* served in Soviet Army 1978–80; metalworker and mechanical engineer, Stepanakert Mechanical Works 1981–83; worked on restoration of historical monuments 1983–87; worked for Stepanakert dist council 1987–90; various roles within 'Republic of Nagornyi-Karabakh' Self Defence Forces including Deputy Commdr of External Relations and Commdr of Headquarters 1990–97; Asst to Minister for Home Affairs and Nat. Security 1997–99; Minister for Home Affairs 1999–2001; Head, State Dept for Nat. Security 2001–07; 'Pres. of the Republic of Nagornyi-Karabakh' 2007–; Fighting Cross Order, Sparapet Vazgen Sargsian, Order of Peter the Great, Russia. *Address:* 'Office of the President of the Republic of Nagornyi-Karabakh', Xankandi, 20 February St 3, Nagornyi-Karabakh, Azerbaijan; tel. (1) 45-222; fax (1) 45-222; e-mail ps@president.nkr.am; internet www.president.nkr.am.

SALIH, Muhammad: Uzbekistani writer and politician; *Chairman, Freedom Democratic Party of Uzbekistan (Erk);* b. 20 Dec. 1949, Xorazm; m.; five c. *Education:* Tashkent State Univ., Moscow High Literary Inst. *Career:* military service in army 1968–70; worked as screenwriter in 1980s; wrote letter to Politbureau protesting political situation in Uzbekistan 1984; work published in Soviet newspapers 1985–86; elected Chair. Union of Writers of Uzbekistan 1988; co-f. Birlik (Unity People's Movt) 1988; f. Freedom Democratic Party of Uzbekistan (Erk) 1990, currently Chair.; Deputy, Oly Majlis (Supreme Ass.—Parl.) 1990–92 (resgnd); presidential candidate 1990; f. Democratic Forum 1992; refused offer of Deputy Prime Minister role in return for dissolution of Democratic Forum 1992, arrested and jailed for three days, and subsequently put under house arrest, left Uzbekistan to continue political activity abroad 1992; received sentence in absentia of 15 and a half years 1999; f. Nat. Salvation Cttee 2005; living in exile in Norway. *Publications:* The Golden Head of the Avenger (screenplay), more than 20 books. *Address:* c/o Freedom Democratic Party of Uzbekistan (O'zbekiston Erk Demokratik Partiyasi), 100055 Tashkent, Ipakchi ko'ch. 38, Uzbekistan; tel. (71) 120-65-30; e-mail erkparty@yahoo.com; internet www.muhammadsalih.info.

SANAKOYEV, Dimitri I.: Georgian government official; *President of the Provisional Administration of South Ossetia;* b. 10 May 1969, Java, S Ossetian Autonomous Oblast. *Career:* fought on Ossetian side during Georgian–Ossetian conflict 1991–92; Prime Minister and Minister of Defence of breakaway region of S Ossetia 2001; apptd Pres. of the Provisional Admin of S Ossetia by Georgian Pres. Mikhail Saakashvili 2007. *Address:* Office of the President, Provisional Administration of South Ossetia, 1427 Shida Kartli Mkhare, Gori Region, Kurta, Georgia. internet www.soa.ge.

SARKISSIAN, Serge: Armenian politician and head of state; *President;* b. 30 June 1954, Xankandi (Stepanakert, Nagornyi Karabakh Autonomous Oblast, Azerbaijan SSR); m. Rita Sarkissian 1983; two d. *Education:* Yerevan State Univ. *Career:* USSR army 1972–74; metal turner, Electrical Devices Factory, Yerevan 1975–79; Komsomol Sec., Head of Propaganda section City Cttee, Stepanakert 1979–88; Head of Self-Defence Cttee, Nagornyi Karabakh 1989–93; Deputy Supreme Council (Parl.) 1990–93, Minister of Defence 1993–95, 2000–07, of Nat. Security 1995–96, 1999, of Internal Affairs and Nat. Security 1996–99; Chief of Staff to Pres. 1999–2000; Sec. Council of Nat. Security 1999–2007; mem. Republican Party of Armenia (RPA) 2006–, Chair. Party Council 2006–07, Chair. RPA 2007–; Prime Minister 2007–08; Pres. of Armenia 2008–; Chair. Bd of Trustees, Yerevan State Univ.; Chair. Chess Federation of Armenia; Order of Marta-kan Khach, Kt of the Golden Eagle Order, Hero of Artsakh, Armenian Battle Cross, Tigran Mets. *Address:* Office of the President, 375077 Yerevan, Marshal Baghramian Street, Armenia; tel. (10) 52-02-04; fax (10) 52-15-51; e-mail frd@gov.am; internet www.president.am; www.serzhsargsyan.com.

SARKISSIAN, Tigran, PhD; Armenian politician and central banker; *Prime Minister;* b. 29 Jan. 1960, Kirovakan (now Vanadzor); m.; two s. and one d. *Education:* Voznesenskii Financial and Econ. Inst., Leningrad (now St Petersburg), USSR. *Career:* Chief of Dept for Foreign Econ. Relations, Scientific Research Inst. of Econ. Planning 1987–90; Chair. Republican Council of Young Specialists and Scientists

1988–93; mem. Supreme Council of the Repub. of Armenia and Chair. of Standing Comm. for Financial, Credit and Budget Affairs 1990–95; Dir of Scientific Research Inst. of Social Reforms 1995–98; Chair. Armenian Banks Asscn 1995–98; Chair. Cen. Bank of Armenia 1998–2008; Prime Minister 2008–. *Address:* Office of the Prime Minister, 0010 Yerevan, Republic Square 1, Government Bldg, Armenia; tel. (10) 52-03-60; fax (10) 15-10-35; internet www.gov.am/enversion/premier_2/primer_home.htm.

SECHIN, Igor Ivanovich: Russian politician and business executive; *Deputy Chairman of the Government;* b. 7 Sept. 1960, Leningrad (now St Petersburg); m.; one d. *Education:* Leningrad State Univ. *Career:* army service 1984–86; leading instructor, Exec. Cttee, Dept of Foreign Econ. Relations, Leningrad City Soviet 1988–91; Chief Expert, Asst to Head of Admin to First Vice-Mayor, Chair. Cttee on Foreign Relations, Office of Mayor of Leningrad 1991–96; Expert, Deputy Head of Div., Public Relations Dept, Dept of Foreign Affairs 1996–97; Head, Gen. Admin Dept, Advisor to Deputy Head then Head Chief Control Dept, Admin of the Russian Pres. 1998–99; Head, Secr. of First Deputy Chair., later Chair., Govt of Russian Fed. 1999–2000; Deputy Chief of Staff, Presidential Exec. Office 2000–08, Aide to the Pres. 2004–08; Deputy Chairman of the Govt, in charge of industry devt, nuclear power and environment 2008–; Chair. Rosneft Oil Co. 2004–. *Address:* Office of the Government, 103274 Moscow, Krasnopresnenskaya nab. 2, Russia; tel. (495) 205-57-35; fax (495) 205-42-19; internet www.government.ru.

SERDYUKOV, Anatolii Eduardovich: Russian politician; *Minister of Defence;* b. 8 Jan. 1962, Kholmskii village, Abin Dist., Krasnodar Krai. *Education:* Leningrad (now St Petersburg) Inst. of Soviet Trade and St Petersburg State Univ. *Career:* served in armed forces 1984–85; worked for furniture firm 1985–93, then Marketing Dir and Dir-Gen. St Petersburg furniture market 1993–2000; Deputy Head, Dist Inspectorate of Taxes, Ministry of Taxes and Dues 2000–01; Deputy Head then Head, St Petersburg Tax Authority 2001–04; Deputy Minister of Taxes and Dues Feb.–July 2004, Head Fed. Tax Service 2004–07; Minister of Defence 2007–. *Address:* Ministry of Defence, 105175 Moscow, ul. Myasnitskaya 37, Russia; tel. (495) 293-38-54; fax (495) 296-84-36; internet www.mil.ru.

SHAIMIYEV, Mintimer Sharipovich: Russian engineer and politician; *President, Republic of Tatarstan;* b. 20 Jan. 1937, Anyakovo, Aktanyshski Dist, Tatar ASSR; m. Sakina Shaimiyeva; two s. *Education:* Kazan Inst. of Agric. *Career:* Engineer, Chief Engineer Service and Repair Station, Mouslyumovski Dist, Tatar ASSR 1959–62; Man. Selkhoztekhnika Regional Asscn, Tatar ASSR 1962–67; Instructor, Deputy Chief of Agricultural Dept, Tatar Regional Cttee of CPSU, Tatar ASSR 1967–69; Minister of Land Improvement and Water Man., Tatar ASSR 1969–83; First Deputy Chair. Council of Ministers, Tatar ASSR 1983, Chair. 1985–89; Sec. Tatar Regional Cttee of CPSU 1983–85, First Sec. 1989–90; Chair. Supreme Soviet, Tatar ASSR 1990–91; Pres. of Tatarstan 1991–; f. All Russia political movt 1999, now part of United Russia (Yedinaya Rossiya); mem. Acad. of Tech. Sciences; Co-Chair., Higher Council, United Russia Party; Hon. mem. Presidium, Int. Parl. of World Confed. of Kts (under auspices of UN); Hon. mem. Int. Acad. of Informatization; Hon. Prof., Moscow State Inst. of Int. Relations; Order of Lenin 1966, Order of Red Banner of Labour 1971, Order of Oct. Revolution 1976, Order of Friendship of Peoples 1987, Order for Services to the Fatherland, Grade II 1997; Silver Avitsenna Medal, UNESCO 2001. *Address:* Office of the President, 420014 Tatarstan, Kazan, Kreml, Russia; tel. (843) 292-74-66; (843) 291-79-01; fax (843) 292-78-66; e-mail secretariat@tatar.ru; internet www.tatar.ru.

SHEVARDNADZE, Eduard: Georgian politician and fmr head of state; b. 25 Jan. 1928, Mamati, Larchkhuti, Transcaucasian SFSR (now in Georgia); m. Nanuli Tsagareishvili 1950 (died 2004); one s. one d. *Education:* Party School of the Cen. Cttee, CP of Georgia and Kutaisi Pedagogical Inst. *Career:* mem. CPSU 1948–91; Komsomol and party work 1946–56; Second Sec. 1956–57, First Sec., Komsomol in

Georgia 1957–61; First Sec., Mtskheti raion 1961–63, Pervo-maisky raion, Tbilisi, CP of Georgia 1963–64; First Deputy Minister 1964–65, Minister of Public Order (renamed Ministry of Internal Affairs 1968) 1965–72; First Sec., Tbilisi City Cttee of Cen. Cttee, CP of Georgia 1972; mem. Cen. Cttee, CP of Georgia 1958–64, 1966–91, mem. Politburo 1972–91, First Sec. 1972–85; mem. Cen. Cttee of CPSU 1976–91, Cand. mem. Politburo 1978–85, mem. 1985–90; Deputy to USSR Supreme Soviet 1978; mem. Political Consultative Council 1991; Minister of Foreign Affairs 1985–90, Nov.–Dec. 1991; Head of Soviet Foreign Policy Asscn 1991–92; mem. Presidential Council 1990–91; Founder mem. Bd Democratic Reform Movt 1991; Chair. Georgian State Council March–Oct. 1992; Chair. Parl. of Georgia and Head of State 1992–95, Pres. of Georgia 1995–2003 (resgnd); Hon. GCMG 2000; various decorations; Dr honoris causa numerous univs. *Publications:* My Choice 1991, The Future Belongs to Freedom 1991, The Great Silk Road 1999, Thoughts About The Past and Future 2006. *Address:* c/o Office of the President, 0134 Tbilisi, P. Ingorovka 7, Georgia.

SHIKHMURADOV, Boris Orazovich: Turkmenistani politician and diplomatist; b. 1949, Aşgabat; m. Tatyana Shikhmuradova; one s. *Education:* Moscow State Univ., Diplomatic Acad. *Career:* journalist, Press Agency Novosti and USSR Ministry of Foreign Affairs 1971–72; various positions in missions abroad, then on staff, USSR Ministry of Foreign Affairs 1983–86; worked in Embassies in Pakistan, India, missions to Turkey, Afghanistan, USA, China, Singapore; Deputy, then First Deputy Minister of Foreign Affairs of Turkmenistan May 1992; Deputy Chair. Cabinet of Ministers of Turkmenistan 1992; Minister of Foreign Affairs 1995–2000; Amb. to People's Repub. of China March–Nov. 2001; emigrated to Moscow 2001; est. opposition people's movt of Turkmenistan 2002; returned to Aşgabat Dec. 2002, arrested and sentenced to life imprisonment on charges of conspiracy to organize assassination of Pres. Niyazov.

SHOISMATOV, Ergash R.: Uzbekistani politician; *Deputy Prime Minister, responsible for Machine-construction, Metallurgy, Petroleum and Natural Gas, Geology, Electrical Energy, Chemical Production, Standardization and Metrology and State Reserves.* *Career:* apptd Minister of Power Eng. and Electrification 2000; Chair. Uzbekenergo (state energy co.) –2006; Deputy Prime Minister, responsible for Machine-construction, Metallurgy, Petroleum and Natural Gas, Geology, Electrical Energy, Chemical Production, Standardization and Metrology and State Reserves 2006–. *Address:* Office of the Cabinet of Ministers, 100078 Tashkent, Mustaqillik maydoni 5, Uzbekistan; tel. (71) 139-82-95; fax (71) 139-84-63; internet www.gov.uz.

SHUVALOV, Igor Ivanovich: Russian politician and lawyer; *First Deputy Chairman of the Government;* b. 4 Jan. 1967, Bilibino, Magadan Oblast, Russia; m.; one s. two d. *Education:* Moscow State Univ. *Career:* EKOS Research Inst., Moscow 1984–85; army service 1985–87; attaché Ministry of Foreign Affairs, Russian Fed. 1993; Sr legal adviser Stock co. (ALM) Consulting Moscow 1993–95; Dir Advocates' Bureau (ALM) 1995–97; Head Dept of State Cttee on Man. of State Property Russian Fed. 1997–98; Deputy Minister of State Property 1998; Chair. Russian Foundation of Fed. Property 1998–2000; Head of Govt Admin and Minister Without Portfolio 2000–2002, Deputy Head of Presidential Admin 2003–08; First Deputy Chair. of the Govt, in charge of external econ. relations and foreign trade, WTO negotiations and small business 2008–. *Address:* Office of the Government, 103274 Moscow, Krasnopresnenskaya nab. 2, Russia; tel. (495) 205-57-35; fax (495) 205-42-19; internet www .government.ru.

SIDORSKY, Syarhey Syarheyovich, DEngSci; Belarusian politician; *Prime Minister;* b. 13 March 1954, Gomel; m.; two d. *Education:* Belarus Inst. of Railway Transport Engineers. *Career:* worked as electrical fitter and electrician; foreman of assembly shop, head of lab., head of dept, Deputy Dir Gomel Radio Equipment Plant 1976–91, Dir 1991–92; Gen. Man. Gomel Scientific Production Asscn RATON 1992–98; Deputy

Chair. and First Deputy Chair. Gomel Oblast Admin 1998–2001; Deputy Prime Minister of Belarus 2001–02, First Deputy Prime Minister 2002–03, Acting Prime Minister July–Dec. 2003, Prime Minister Dec. 2003–; Academician, Int. Eng Acad.; Honoured Workman of Industry (Belarus). *Publications include:* more than 40 scientific publs and monographs. *Address:* Office of the Prime Minister, 220010 Minsk, vul. Savetskaya 11, Belarus; tel. (17) 222-69-05; fax (17) 222-66-65; e-mail timoshenko@government.by; internet www.government.by.

SMIRNOV, Igor Nikolayevich, DEconSc; Moldovan politician; *President, 'Transnistrian Moldovan Republic';* b. 23 Oct. 1941, Petropavlovsk-Kamchatskii, Russia; m.; two s. *Education:* Zaporizhzhya Machine Construction Inst., Ukrainian SSR. *Career:* mem. CPSU 1963–90; early career as engineer, chief engineer, chief of shop; Deputy Dir Novo-Kakhova Electromash plant, Ukrainian SSR; Dir Tiraspol Electromash plant 1987–1990, Moldovan SSR; Dir Tiraspol Jt Trade Union 1989–91, Chair. City Soviet and Tiraspol City Exec. Cttee 1990–91; Pres. Self-Declared 'Transnistrian Moldovan Repub.' (expelled from CPSU for separatism 1990) 1991–; People's Deputy of Moldova 1990–92; Academician of Ukrainian Economical-Cybernetics Acad.; mem. Int. Acad. of Informatization, Russian Acad. of Natural Sciences; Order of Republic 1995, Medal, Order of Prince Daniyl of Moscow 1998, Order of Sergei Radonejski 1999, Order for Benefit of Motherland, Russian Acad. of Sciences, Order of World Distributing Univ., Cross for Faith and Motherland (3rd Degree), Cross for Defence of 'Transnistrian Moldovan Repub.', Cross for Service to the Cossacks, Order of Lenin, Star of Hero, Order of Glory of Russia 2000, Order for Personal Courage 2001; Medal for Labour Prowess, Medal on 10th anniversary of 'Transnistrian Moldovan Repub.'. *Publications:* Human Beings, Science and Technical Progress in a Century of Information 2000, In Favour of the Republic 2000, To Live on Our Land (Sholohov Prize) 2004. *Address:* 'Office of the President of the Transnistrian Moldovan Republic', 3300 Tiraspol, ul. 25 Oktyabrya 45, Moldova; tel. (30) 30-70-78; e-mail president@presidentpmr.org; internet presidentpmr .org.

SOBYANIN, Sergei Semenovich, PhD; Russian politician; *Deputy Chairman of the Government;* b. 21 June 1958, Nyaksumvol, Khanty-Mansii Autonomous Okrug; m.; two d. *Education:* Kostroma State Inst. of Tech. *Career:* metalworker and then foreman at Chelyabinsk Pipe Plant 1980–82; Head of Admin. Dept Leninskii Dist Komsomol, Chelyabinsk 1982–84; party and admin. work in Khanty-Mansii Autonomous Okrug, Tyumen Region 1984–90; Head of State Tax Inspection Office, Kogalym in Khanty-Mansii Autonomous Okrug 1990–91; Mayor of Kogalym 1991–93; First Deputy Head Khanty-Mansii Autonomous Okrug 1993–94; Chair. Khanty-Mansii Autonomous Okrug Duma, mem. Fed. Council and Chair. Fed. Council Cttee on Constitutional Legislation and Judicial-Legal Matters 1994–2000; First Deputy to Presidential Plenipotentiary Envoy in Urals Fed. Dist 2000–01; Gov. of Tyumen Region 2001–05; Chief of Staff, Presidential Exec. Office 2005–08; Deputy Chairman of the Govt, in charge of co-ordinating Fed. Agencies 2008–; Chair. Bd of Dirs TVEL (state nuclear power co.) 2006–; Order of Merit, Medal For Services to the Fatherland, Second Degree, Ordre du Mérite Agricole (France) 2003; Russia's Man of the Year: Politician Prize 2003. *Address:* Office of the Government, 103274 Moscow, Krasnopresnenskaya nab. 2, Russia; tel. (495) 205-57-35; fax (495) 205-42-19; internet www.government.ru.

STRĂTAN, Andrei, DEcons; Moldovan government official; *Deputy Prime Minister and Minister of Foreign Affairs and European Integration;* b. 3 Sept. 1966, Chişinău; m.; two c. *Education:* Chişinău Polytechnic Inst., Moldova State Univ. *Career:* served in Soviet Customs Control Dept 1991–92, Repub. of Moldova Customs Dept 1992–2002, Head of Div. 1992–95, Deputy Dir-Gen. 1995–97, Prime Deputy Dir-Gen. 1997–99, Dir-Gen. 1999–2002; served on special missions with rank of Amb. including Head, Nat. Bureau of Stability Pact, Ministry of Foreign Affairs 2002–03; Deputy Prime Minister and Minister of Foreign Affairs 2003–04, Minister of

Foreign Affairs 2004, Deputy Prime Minister and Minister of Foreign Affairs and European Integration 2005–. *Address:* Ministry of Foreign Affairs, 2012 Chişinău, str. 31 August 80, Moldova; tel. (22) 57-82-07; fax (22) 23-23-02; e-mail secdep@ mfa.md; internet www.mfa.md.

SURKOV, Vladislav Yuryevich, MSc; Russian business executive and government official; *First Deputy Chief of Staff, Presidential Executive Office;* b. 21 Sept. 1964; m. Yuliya Vishnevskaya; one s. *Education:* International Univ. *Career:* army service 1983–85; Dir Metapress Agency (communications) 1990–92; Head of Advertising Dept Menatep Credit and Financial Enterprises Asscn (later Menatep Bank) 1992–94, Deputy Head of Client Services Dept 1992–94, Deputy Head of Public Relations Dept 1994–96, Vice-Pres. State Orgs Relations Dept 1996–97, mem. Bd of Dirs 1996–97; Deputy Head, Head of Public Relations Rosprom 1996–97; First Deputy Council Chair. Commercial Innovation Bank Alfa Bank 1996–97; First Deputy Dir-Gen., then Public Relations Dir Public Russian TV (ORT) 1998, First Sec., Supervisory Bd 1998–99; Aide to Chief of Staff, Presidential Exec. Office 1999, Deputy Chief of Staff, Presidential Exec. Office 1999–2008, Aide to Pres. 2004–08; First Deputy Chief of Staff, Presidential Exec. Office 2008–. *Address:* Office of the President, 103132 Moscow, Staraya pl. 4, Russia; tel. (495) 925-35-81; fax (495) 206-07-66; internet www.kremlin.ru.

SYMONENKO, Petro Mykolayovych: Ukrainian politician; *Secretary of Central Committee, Communist Party of Ukraine;* b. 1 Aug. 1952, Donetsk; m.; two s. *Education:* Donetsk State Polytechnical Inst. and Kyiv Inst. of Political Science and Social Admin. *Career:* joined Komsomol 1975; joined CP 1978, fmr Deputy Sec. Donetsk regional CP Cttee; Deputy Dir Ukrvuhlemash machine-building co. 1991–93; Sec., Cen. Cttee of CP of Ukraine 1993–; mem. Verkhovna Rada (Parl.) 1994–, Chair. CP Parl. faction; mem. Parl. Ass., Council of Europe 1997–; cand. in presidential election 1999. *Address:* Communist Party of Ukraine (Komunistychna Partiya Ukrainy), 04070 Kyiv, vul. Borysohlibska 7, Ukraine; tel. (44) 425-54-87; e-mail Symonenko.Petro@rada.gov.ua; press@kpu.net.ua; internet www.kpu.net.ua.

TAGAYEV, Aitibai: Kyrgyzstani economist and politician; *Chairman, Zhogorku Kenesh (Supreme Council);* b. 30 April 1958, Naukat dist., Osh; m.; three s. *Education:* Kyrgyz State Univ. *Career:* early career as bookkeeper; Deputy, Zhogorku Kenesh (Parl.) 2005–, Chair. 2008–; mem. Bright Road People's Party (Ak Zhol) 2007–. *Address:* Office of the Chairman, Zhogorku Kenesh, 720053 Bishkek, ul. Abdymomunov 207, Kyrgyzstan; tel. (312) 61-16-04; fax (312) 62-50-12; e-mail zs@kenesh.gov.kg; internet www.kenesh.kg.

TAGIYEV, Tachberdy: Turkmenistani engineer and politician; *Deputy Chairman of the Government, responsible for Petroleum and Natural Gas;* b. 1955, Etrek dist. *Education:* Turkmen Polytechnic Inst. *Career:* Minister of the Petroleum Industry and Mineral Resources 2002–03; Gov. Balkan Velayat 2003; Head of Turkmenbashi oil refinery 2006–07; Deputy Chairman of the Govt, responsible for Petroleum and Natural Gas 2007–, also Dir-Gen. Turkmengaz (state-run gas monopoly). *Address:* Office of the President and the Council of Ministers, 744000 Aşgabat, Turkmenistan; tel. (12) 35-45-34; fax (12) 35-51-12; internet www.turkmenistan.gov.tm.

TALBAKOV, Ismoil: Tajikistani economist and politician; *Secretary of Central Committee, Communist Party of Tajikistan;* m.; four c. *Education:* Tajik State Univ. *Career:* fmr officer in Soviet Army; mem. Majlisi Namoyandagon (Parl.); currently Sec., Cen. Cttee, CP of Tajikistan; unsuccessful cand. in presidential elections 2006. *Address:* Communist Party of Tajikistan, 734002 Dushanbe, Kuchai F. Niyazi 37, Tajikistan; tel. (372) 21-14-54; e-mail talbakov_555@mail.ru; internet www.kpt.freenet.tj.

TALIBOV, Vasif Yusif oğlu: Azerbaijani politician; *Chairman, Ali Majlis (Supreme Assembly) of the Autonomous Republic of Naxçivan;* b. 14 Jan. 1960, Aralig, Ilyich (now Şarur) Dist., Naxçivan ASSR, Azerbaijan SSR; m. Sevil

Sultanova; two s. one d. *Education:* Naxçivan State Pedagogical Inst., Baku State Univ. *Career:* began career with Sharur Dist Public Educ. Dept 1976; Cadre Inspector Naxçivan Knitted Goods Factory 1982; Sr Asst Ali Majlis (Supreme Ass.) of the Autonomous Repub. of Naxçivan 1991–94, First Deputy for Econ. Links 1994–95, Deputy (MP) 1995–, Chair. Ali Majlis 2005–; founder mem. New Azerbaijan Party (NAP), Chair. 1995–; mem. Co-ordinating Council, Congress of Azerbaijanis Worldwide 2001–. *Address:* Supreme Assembly of the Autonomous Republic of Naxçivan, 7000 Naxçivan, Azerbaijan; tel. (136) 44-01-01; fax (136) 44-01-01; e-mail ali-hasanov@mail.ru.

TARASYUK, Borys Ivanovych: Ukrainian politician and diplomatist; *Chairman, People's Movement of Ukraine-Rukh (Narodnyi Rukh Ukrainy);* b. 1 Jan. 1949, Dzerzhynsk, Zhytomyr Oblast; m.; one s. two d. *Education:* Kyiv State Univ. *Career:* attaché, Third, Second, First Sec., Ukrainian Ministry of Foreign Affairs 1975–81; Second, First Sec., Perm. Mission of Ukrainian SSR to UN, New York 1981–86; First Sec., Div. of Int. Orgs, Ukrainian Ministry of Foreign Affairs 1986–87; instructor, Div. of Foreign Relations, Ukrainian CP Cen. Cttee 1987–90; Head, Dept of Political Analysis and Planning, Ministry of Foreign Affairs 1991–92; Deputy, First Deputy Minister of Foreign Affairs, Head, Nat. Cttee on Disarmament Problems 1992–95; Amb. to Belgium (also accred to Netherlands, Luxembourg) 1995–98; Head, Mission to NATO, Brussels 1997–98; Minister of Foreign Affairs 1998–2000, 2005–07 (resgnd); mem. Nat. Security Defence Council; Chair. People's Movt of Ukraine-Rukh (Narodnyi Rukh Ukrainy) 2003–; mem. Bd of Dirs East-West Inst. 1993–2001; Chair. Cttee on European Integration 2002–; Dir Inst. of Social Studies and Int. Relations 2001–02; Founder and Dir Inst. of Euro-Atlantic Co-operation 2001–; Order of Merit 1996, 1999; Dr hc (Rivne Int. Econ. and Humanitarian Univ.) 2000, (Lviv Nat. Univ.) 2002, (Int. Personnel Acad.) 2002; State awards from Argentina, Brazil, France, Lithuania, Portugal, Sweden, Venezuela. *Address:* People's Movement of Ukraine-Rukh (Narodnyi Rukh Ukrainy), 01034 Kyiv, vul. O. Honchara 33, Ukraine; tel. (44) 246-47-67; fax (44) 531-30-42; e-mail org@nru.org.ua; internet www.nru.org .ua; www.ieac.org.ua.

TARLEV, Vasile Pavlovich, DTechSci; Moldovan business executive and politician; b. 9 Oct. 1963, Başcalia, Basarabeasca Dist; m.; three c. *Education:* Chişinău Polytechnical Inst. *Career:* worked as tractor driver; served in army of USSR 1981–83; Chief Mechanic, Bucuria confectionery factory, Chief Engineer Bucuria SA 1991–93, First Deputy Dir-Gen. 1993–95, Chair. Bd of Admin., Dir-Gen. 1995–2001; studied int. marketing and trade man. in USA; fmr mem. Supreme Econ. Council of Pres., Econ. Council of Govt; mem. Repub. Comm. on Collective Negotiations between Businessmen and Trade Unions 1998–99; mem. Party of Communists of the Repub. of Moldova; Prime Minister of Moldova 2001–08; fmr Chair. Nat. Asscn of Mfrs 1995–2001; mem. Council Int. Union of Mfrs, Int. Acad. of Sciences and Computing Systems 1998–; mem. Int. Acad. of Sciences and Informational Systems 1998; Order of Work Glory 1997; Businessman of the Year (six times) 1995–2000, Gold Medal for Efficient Man., Int. Acad. of Human Resources 2000, several medals for tech. inventions shown at int. exhbns 1997–. *Achievements include:* holds five patents on tech. inventions. *Publications:* more than 30 scientific publs. *Address:* Party of Communists of the Republic of Moldova, 2012 Chişinău, str. N. Iorga 11, Moldova; tel. (22) 23-46-14; fax (22) 23-36-73; e-mail info@pcrm.md; internet www.pcrm.md.

TASHMUHAMEDOVA, Dilorom Hafurjanovna, MD; Uzbekistani physician and politician; *Speaker, Qoqunchilik palatasi Kengashi (Legislative Chamber);* b. 1962, Tashkent Oblast; m. P. Tashmuhamedov; four c. *Education:* Tashkent State Medical Inst., Faculty of Intergovernmental Relations and External Econ. Relations, Acad. of State and Social Construction. *Career:* early career as teacher, Tashkent State Medical Inst.; f. Farmed (pharmaceuticals co.) 1994; Deputy Oly Majlis (Supreme Ass.) 2001–04, Deputy Qoqunchilik palatasi Kengashi (Legislative Chamber) 2004–, mem. Cttee for Int. Affairs and Interparliamentary Communication, Deputy Speaker 2007–08, Speaker 2008–; mem. Adolat (Justice) Social Democratic Party, First Sec., Political Council 2005–, also leader of parl. faction; unsuccessful cand. for Pres. of Uzbekistan 2007; Dustlik (Friendship) Order 2006. *Publications include:* series of academic works about medicine; numerous articles abou socio-political reform, the development of a multi-party system and of democratic institutions and the increasing involvement of women in social life. *Address:* Office of the Speaker, Qoqunchilik palatasi Kengashi, 100008 Tashkent, Xalqlar Do'stligi shoh ko'ch. 1, Uzbekistan; tel. (71) 139-87-07; fax (71) 139-41-51; internet www .parliament.gov.uz.

TAZHIN, Marat Muhanbetkaziyevich, PhD; Kazakhstani politician; *Minister of Foreign Affairs;* b. 8 April 1960, Aktubinsk. *Education:* Almaty Inst. of Nat. Economy and Kazakh State Univ. *Career:* began career as scientific researcher –1992; First Deputy Head, then Head of Internal Policy Dept, Deputy Chief of Presidential Apparatus, Head of Information and Analysis Center, Office of the Pres. 1992–94; State Adviser to Pres. 1994–95; Deputy Head, Admin of Pres. and Head, Analysis and Strategic Research Center 1995–99; Nat. Security Asst to Pres. 1999–2001, 2002, 2006–07; Sec., Security Council 1999–2001, Chair. 2001; First Deputy Chief, Admin of Pres. 2002–06; Minister of Foreign Affairs 2007–; Order of Kurmet, Order of Barys. *Address:* Ministry of Foreign Affairs, 010000 Astana, Tauelsizdik 31, Kazakhstan; tel. (3172) 72-05-18; fax (3172) 72-05-16; e-mail midrk@mid .kz; internet www.mfa.kz.

TKESHELASHVILI, Ekaterine (Eka), LLM; Georgian lawyer and government official; *Minister of Foreign Affairs;* b. 23 May 1977, Tbilisi; m.; four c. *Education:* Tbilisi State Univ., Univ. of Notre Dame, USA. *Career:* lawyer, Int. Cttee of Red Cross 1999–2000; intern, Appeals Office, Int. Tribunal of fmr Yugoslavia 2001–02; lawyer and Dir Institutional Reform and Non-governmental Sector, IRIS Georgia 2002–04; Deputy Minister of Justice 2004–05; Deputy Minister of Internal Affairs 2005–06; Chair. Tbilisi Court of Appeals 2006–07; Minister of Justice 2007; Gen. Prosecutor Jan.-May 2008; Minister of Foreign Affairs May 2008–. *Address:* Ministry of Foreign Affairs, 0108 Tbilisi, Sh. Chitadze 4, Georgia; tel. (32) 28-47-47; fax (32) 28-46-78; e-mail inform@mfa.gov.ge; internet www.mfa.gov.ge.

TOKAYEV, Kasym-Zhomart Kemelevich: Kazakhstani diplomatist and politician; *Chairman, Senat (Senate);* b. 17 May 1953, Almaty, Kazakhstan; m. Nadeyda Tokayeva (née Poznanskaya) 1983; one s. *Education:* Moscow Inst. of Int. Relations, Diplomatic Acad., USSR Ministry of Foreign Affairs, Inst. of the Chinese Language, Beijing. *Career:* with USSR Ministry of Foreign Affairs 1975; served at Embassy in Singapore 1975–79; Attaché, Third Sec. Ministry of Foreign Affairs 1979–83; Second Sec. of Dept 1984–85; Second, then First Sec., Embassy in Beijing 1985–91; attained rank of Amb. of Kazakhstan 1994; Deputy Minister, then First Deputy Minister of Foreign Affairs Repub. of Kazakhstan 1992–94; State Sec. and Minister 1994–99; Deputy Prime Minister March–Oct. 1999, Prime Minister of Kazakhstan 1999–2002; Minister of Foreign Affairs 2002–06; Chair. Senat 2007–; Parasat (Nat. Award) 1996, Astana Medal. *Publications:* How it was...Disturbance in Beijing 1993, United Nations: Half a Century of Serving for Peace 1995, Under the Banner of Independence 1997, Kazakhstani Foreign Policy in the context of Globalisation 2000, Diplomacy of the Republic of Kazakhstan 2001. *Address:* Office of the Chairman, Senat, 010000 Astana, pr. Abaya 33, Parliament House, Kazakhstan; tel. (7172) 15-33-76; fax (7172) 33-31-18; e-mail smimazh@ parlam.kz; internet www.parlam.kz.

TOROSSIAN, Tigran, PhD, DPolSci; Armenian engineer and politician; *Chairman, Azgayin Zhoghov (National Assembly);* b. 14 April 1956, Yerevan; m.; one d. *Education:* Yerevan Polytechnic Inst. *Career:* Engineer, then Leading Engineer, Yerevan Scientific Research Inst. of Math. Machines 1978–88, Subdivision Head, then Scientific Assoc. 1988–95; mem., Cen. Electoral Comm. 1996–98; Ed.-in-Chief, Republican Party

newspaper 1997–98; Deputy, Nat. Ass. (Republican Party of Armenia) 1999–, Vice-Chair. Nat. Ass. 1999–2006, Chair. 2006–, Chair. ad hoc Cttee on Constitutional Amendments 2001–03, ad hoc Cttee on Matters of Integration in European Structures 2003–; Head of Armenian Del., Parl. Ass. of Council of Europe, Vice-Chair. Parl. Ass. of the Council of Europe European Democrat Group 2004–; Vice-Chair. Cttee on the Honouring of Obligations and Commitments by Mem. States of Council of Europe 2006–; mem. Party Bd Republican Party of Armenia 1993–, Deputy Chair. 1998–2005, Deputy Chair. Republican Party of Armenia 2005–; Medal for Exceptional Services to Motherland 2006. *Achievements include:* holder of 10 eng patents. *Publications:* more than 30 scientific studies in math., one monograph and more than 20 scientific studies in political science and about 200 articles. *Address:* Azgayin Zhoghov (National Assembly), 0095 Yerevan, Marshal Baghramian St 19; Republican Party of Armenia (Haiastani Hanrapetakan Kusaktsutiun—HHK), 0010 Yerevan, Melik-Adamian St 2, Armenia; tel. (10) 58-82-25 (Government); (10) 58-00-31 (HHK); fax (10) 52-98-26 (Government); (10) 50-12-59 (HHK); e-mail toros@parliament .am; hhk@hhk.am; internet www.parliament.am; www.hhk .am.

TRUTNEV, Yurii Petrovich: Russian politician; *Minister of Natural Resources and Ecology;* b. 1 March 1956; m.; two s. *Education:* Perm Polytechnic Inst. *Career:* engineer, Perm Scientific Research Inst. of Oil 1978–81; instructor Regional Komsomol Cttee and Sport Cttee 1981–88; Pres. E.K.S Int. 1996, Dir 2000–; Deputy, Perm city Duma 1994–96, Chair. Cttee on Econ. Policy and Taxation; Mayor of Perm 1996–2000; Gov. of Perm Oblast 2000–04; Minister of Natural Resources and Ecology 2004–. *Address:* Ministry of Natural Resources, 123242 Moscow, ul. B. Gruzinskaya 4/6, Russia; tel. (495) 254-48-00; fax (495) 254-43-10; e-mail admin@mnr .gov.ru; internet www.mnr.gov.ru.

TURAJONZODA, Haji Akbar: Tajikistani ecclesiastic and politician; b. 16 Feb. 1954, Kafarnikhon; two s., four d. *Education:* Tashkent Islam Inst., Amman Univ., Jordan, Mir-e Arab School, Buxora. *Career:* teacher, Tashkent Islam Inst. 1987–88; Head of Office of Qaziate of Tajikistan 1988–90; apptd Chief Qazi of Tajikistan 1990, Qaziate position abolished 1993; elected mem. Supreme Soviet Tajik SSR 1990; participant in democratic movt against Islamic fundamentalists, forced to emigrate to Iran, in hiding 1993; First Deputy Chair. Islamic Renaissance Movt of Tajikistan 1993–99; headed United Tajik Opposition in negotiations with the Govt leading to peace settlement 1995–97; fmr First Deputy Chair. of Tajikistan; currently Senator in Majlisi Milliy (Nat. Ass.); Ismael Somoni Medal of Honour, World Islamic Centre Prize for Peace 1999. *Publication:* Between Water and Fire: The Peace Plan. *Address:* Majlisi Milliy (National Assembly), 734051 Dushanbe, Xiyoboni Rudaki 42, Tajikistan; tel. (372) 23-19-33; fax (372) 21-51-10; e-mail mejparl@parliament.tojikiston.com.

TURCHYNOV, Oleksandr Valentynovych, PhD; Ukrainian politician; *First Deputy Prime Minister;* b. 31 March 1964, Dnipropetrovsk; m.; one s. *Education:* Dnipropetrovsk Metallurgic Inst., Dept of Technology. *Career:* began career working at Kryvorizhstal complex then moved into Komsomol and CP apparatus; worked in Dnipropetrovsk regional admin; Co-founder and mem. All-Ukrainian Hromada Asscn 1993–99; apptd advisor on econ. issues to Prime Minister Leonid Kuchma 1993, then apptd Vice Pres. Ukrainian Union of Industrialist and Entrepreneurs; Dir Econ. Reforms Inst., Kyiv 1994–98, also head of Ukrainian Nat. Acad. of Science's Lab. of Shadow Econ. Research; mem. Parl. 1998–; joined Yuliya Tymoshenko's Fatherland (Batkivshchyna) party 1999; Chief of Security Service of Ukraine (SBU) 2004–05; Vice Chair. Yuliya Tymoshenko Bloc (BYuT) in charge of election campaign headquarters 2006–07; First Deputy Prime Minister 2007–; pastor of Baptist church, Kyiv. *Address:* Office of the Cabinet of Ministers, 01008 Kyiv, vul. M. Hrushevskoho 12/2, Ukraine; tel. (44) 254-05-84; fax (44) 254-05-84; e-mail web@kmu.gov.ua; internet www.kmu.gov .ua.

TUYAKBAI, Col-Gen. Zharmakhan Aitbaiuly, CandJur; Kazakhstani politician and jurist; *Leader, National Social-Democratic Party (Zhalpyulttyk Sotsial Demokratiyalyk Partiyasy);* b. 22 Nov. 1947; m. Bagilya Aptayeva; two s. one d. *Education:* Kirov Kazakh State Univ. *Career:* worked in prosecutors' bureau in S Kazakhstan until 1978; Deputy Prosecutor-Gen. Kazakh SSR 1981; prosecutor, Mangyshlak region, then Guryev region 1987–90; mem. Supreme Soviet, Repub. of Kazakhstan 1990; Prosecutor-Gen. Repub. of Kazakhstan 1990–95, Deputy Prosecutor-Gen., Chief Mil. Prosecutor 1997–99; Chair. State Investigation Comm. 1995–97; elected mem. Majlis (Parl.) Oct. 1999, Chair. Dec. 1999–2004; Leader, For a Just Kazakhstan Movement (Social Democrats) 2005–, Leader, Nat. Social Democratic Party, merged with Real Bright Road—Democratic Party of Kazakhstan (Naghyz Ak Zhol—Kazakstanyn Demokratiyalyk Partiyasy) 2007; unsuccessful presidential cand. 2005; Order of Barys 2001, Sodruzhestvo 2002. *Publications:* Development Prosecution in Kazakhstan in the period of reforms 1997; numerous articles. *Address:* National Social Democratic Party (Zhalpyulttyk Sotsial Demokratiyalyk Partiyasy), 050000 Almaty, Kabanbai batyr 58, Kazakhstan; tel. (727) 663-64-06; fax (727) 266-36-43; e-mail ocdp@mail.ru; internet www.osdp.kz.

TYMOSHENKO, Yuliya Volodymyrivna, CandEcon; Ukrainian business executive and politician; *Prime Minister;* b. 27 Nov. 1960, Dnipropetrovsk; m. Oleksandr Hennadyovych Tymoshenko; one d. *Education:* Dnipropetrovsk State Univ. *Career:* planning engineer, Dnipropetrovsk Machine-Construction Plant 1984–89; Commercial Dir Dnipropetrovsk Youth Centre Terminal 1989–91; Dir-Gen. Ukraine Benzine Corpn 1991–95; Pres. Union Unified Energy Systems of Ukraine (UES), First Deputy Chair. Bd of Dirs, Head Cttee on Budgetary Issues 1995–97; elected to Verkhovna Rada (parl.) 1996, joined political union Community (Hromada—with Pavlo Lazarenko), left Hromada to form and lead Fatherland (Batkivishchina) faction 1999; Deputy Prime Minister of Ukraine responsible for energy issues 1999–2001 (resgnd); joined opposition Nat. Salvation Forum 2001; arrested on charge of corruption March 2001, released due to pressure of opposition; led Yuliya Tymoshenko Bloc in 2002 and 2006 elections; Prime Minister of Ukraine Jan.–Sept. 2005, 2007–; Higher Order of Orthodox Church St Barbara Great Martyr 1997; ranked by Forbes magazine amongst 100 Most Powerful Women (third) 2005, (17th) 2008. *Publications:* about 50 papers on econs. *Address:* Office of the Cabinet of Ministers, 01008 Kyiv, vul. M. Hrushevskoho 12/2; Fatherland (Batkivshchyna), 01133 Kyiv, bulv. Lesi Ukrainky 26, POB 81, Ukraine; tel. (44) 293-21-71; (44) 286-65-42; fax (44) 293-20-93; (44) 285-69-07; e-mail web@kmu.gov.ua; sector@byti.org.ua; internet www.kmu.gov.ua; www.tymoshenko.com.ua.

UMAROV, Doku (Dokka): Russian/Chechen rebel leader; b. 13 April 1964, Kharsenoi, Shatoyskii Dist, Checheno-Ingush ASSR (now Chechen—Nokchi Repub.). *Career:* mem. Chechen separatist movt 1994–, field commdr southwestern front 2002–, 'Vice-Pres. Chechen Repub. of Ichkeriya' –2006, 'Pres.' 2006–07, proclaimed Caucasus Emirate and declared himself Emir 2007–; fmr Head of Chechen Security Council.

URECHEAN, Serafim, DEcon; Moldovan politician; *Chairman, Our Moldova Alliance;* b. 2 Feb. 1950, Larga, Briceni dist; m.; two c. *Education:* Chişinău Polytechnic Inst., Inst. of Political Studies, Leningrad (now St Petersburg), Russia. *Career:* Engineer, Briceni Construction Enterprise 1976–78; later Head of Dept for Industrial Devt; Second Sec., Briceni CP Cttee 1978–83; Chair. Anenii Noi CP Exec. Cttee 1985–87; Deputy Chair., First Deputy Chair., then Chair. Fed. of Ind. Trade Unions 1987–94; mem. Parl. 1990–94, 2005–, mem. Standing Bureau of Parl., Cttee for Social Policy, Healthcare and Family, Democratic Moldova electoral bloc; Mayor of Chişinău 1994–2005; Chair. Our Moldova Alliance 2003–; fmr mem. Fed. of Local and Regional Authorities; Corresp. mem. Inst. for Int. Affairs, Int. Acad. of Informatisation, Int. Acad. of Man.; Hon. mem. Int. Acad. of Eng.; Order of the Repub. (USSR), Medal for Public Order Protection (Moldova), St

Dumitru Order (2nd Class), Sergii Radonejsky Order (2nd Class), St Stanislav Order. *Address:* Our Moldova Alliance (Alianţa Moldova Noastră), 2012 Chişinău, str. M. Eminescu 68a, Moldova; tel. (22) 26-00-07; fax (22) 21-13-94; e-mail alianta@amn.md; internet www.amn.md.

USTINOV, Vladimir Vassilyevich: Russian lawyer and government official; *Presidential Representative in the Southern Federal Okrug;* b. 25 Feb. 1953, Nikolayevsk-on-Amur, Khabarovsk Krai, Russia; m.; one s. one d. *Education:* Kharkiv Inst. of Law, Ukrainian SSR. *Career:* prosecutor, Krasnodar Krai 1978–92, Sochi 1992–97; concurrently First Deputy Prosecutor Krasnodar Krai and Deputy Prosecutor-Gen. Russian Fed. 1997–2000; also Head, Dept Office of Prosecutor-Gen., N Caucasus 1998–99; Acting Prosecutor-Gen. Russian Fed. 1999–2000, Prosecutor-Gen. 2000–06; Minister of Justice 2006–08; Presidential Rep. in the Southern Fed. Okrug 2008–; Merited Jurist of Russian Fed. *Address:* Office of the Presidential Representative, 344006 Rostov-on-Don, ul. B. Sadovaya 73, Russia; tel. (863) 249-99-43; fax (863) 249-99-47; e-mail pppufo@ufo.gov.ru; internet www.ufo.gov.ru.

VORONIN, Vladimir Nikolayevich: Moldovan politician and head of state; *President;* b. 25 May 1941, Corjova, Chişinău Dist; m.; two c. *Education:* Tech. Coll., Chişinău, Union Inst. of the Alimentary Industry, Acad. of Social Sciences, Cen. CPSU Cttee, Acad. of Ministry of Internal Affairs. *Career:* bakery man., Criuleni 1961–66, Dubăsari 1966–71; fmr Deputy to Supreme Council, Moldovan SSR, First Sec., Party Cttee, Bender (Tighina) 1985–89, Minister of Internal Affairs, Moldovan SSR 1989–90; mem. Police Reserve, Russian Fed. 1989–93; Co-Pres. Organizational Cttee for Consolidation of CP 1993; revived CP Party of Moldova as Party of Communists of the Republic of Moldova 1994; presidential cand. (placed third) 1996; Deputy in Parl. Repub. of Moldova 1998; Pres. of Moldova 2001–. *Address:* Office of the President, 2073 Chişinău, bd Ştefan cel Mare 154, Moldova; tel. (22) 23-47-93; e-mail president@prm.md; internet www.president.md.

VRABIE, Vitalie: Moldovan politician; *Minister of Defence;* b. 2 Oct. 1964, Costuleni Village, Ungheni Dist; m.; two c. *Education:* Agricultural Inst., Chişinău, Acad. of Public Admin, Moscow. *Career:* began career as Sr Agronomist, Prut Farm; Dir JSV Garant-impex, Ungheni 1994–99; mem. Ungheni City Council 1995–99, fmr Dir Office of Chamber of Commerce and Industry; elected Mayor of Ungheni 1999, re-elected 2003; Chair. Asscn of Mayors and Local Communities 2003–06; fmr mem. Council of Europe Congress of Local and Regional Authorities, fmr Head Nat. Del.; Minister of Local Public Admin 2006–07; Minister of Defence 2007–. *Address:* Ministry of Defence, 2021 Chişinău, şos. Hînceşti 84, Moldova; tel. (22) 25-22-22; fax (22) 23-26-31; e-mail ministru@army.md; internet www.army.gov.md.

XODJAYEV, Batir Asadillaevich: Uzbekistani politician; *Minister of the Economy. Career:* fmr Prof., Univ. of World Economy and Diplomacy, Tashkent; Minister of the Economy 2006–. *Address:* Ministry of the Economy, 100003 Tashkent, O'zbekiston shox ko'ch. 45a, Uzbekistan; tel. (71) 132-63-20; fax (71) 132-63-72; e-mail mineconomy@mmes.gov.uz; internet www.mineconomy.uz.

YANGIBOYEV, Baxodir: Uzbekistani politician; *Chairman of the Council of Ministers of the Sovereign Republic of Qoraqalpog'iston. Career:* fmr Minister of Finance, Repub. of Qoraqalpog'iston, Chair. Council of Ministers 2006–, mem. Council of Ministers of Uzbekistan; fmr Gov. To'rtku'l Dist. *Address:* Office of the Chairman, Council of Ministers of the Republic of Qoraqalpog'iston, 230102 Qoraqalpog'iston, Nukus, Dustlik Gazari 96, Uzbekistan; tel. (361) 222-00-14; fax (361) 222-26-46; e-mail info@sovminrk.gov.uz; internet sovminrk.gov.uz.

YANUKOVYCH, Viktor Fedorovych, DEcon; Ukrainian politician; b. 9 July 1950, Yenakiyevo, Donetsk Oblast; m. Lyudmyla Oleksandrivna Yanukovych; two s. *Education:*

Donetsk Polytechnic Inst., Ukrainian Acad. of Foreign Trade. *Career:* worked in a variety of early jobs including welder, Yenakiyevo metal works 1969–70, fitter and mechanic in automobile factory 1972–76, dir of transport depot 1976–84; mem. CP of Soviet Union 1980–91; moved to Donetsk 1984, held exec. positions at transport cos; fmr Dir-Gen. of major production firms including Donbastransremont, Ukrvuhle-promtrans, Donetsk Oblast Motor Transport Territorial Production Asscn 1994–96; Deputy Gov., then First Deputy Gov. of Donetsk Oblast State Admin 1996–97, Gov. 1997–2002; Chair. Donetsk Oblast Council 1999–2001 (resgnd); Prime Minister of Ukraine 2002–04, 2006–07; presidential cand. 2004; Chair. Party of Regions (PR) 2003–; Prof., mem. Acad. of Econ. Sciences of Ukraine; mem. Presidium Nat. Acad. of Sciences of Ukraine; Orders of Ukraine 'For Merits' of three degrees; Merited Worker of Ukrainian Transport, and other decorations. *Address:* Party of the Regions (Partiya Regioniv), 01021 Kyiv, vul. Lypska 10, Ukraine; tel. (44) 254-29-20; fax (44) 254-33-70; e-mail partreg@ln.ua; internet www.partyofregions.org.ua.

YATSENYUK, Arseniy Petrovych, PhD; Ukrainian lawyer and politician; *Chairman, Verkhovna Rada (Parliament);* b. 22 May 1974, Chernivtsi; m.; two d. *Education:* Chernivtsi State Univ. and Kyiv Univ. of Trade and Econs. *Career:* Pres. Yurek Ltd (law firm), Chernivtsi 1992–97; consultant to credit dept, Aval Jt Stock Postal Pensions Bank, Kyiv 1998, Advisor to Chair. of Bd 1998–2001, Deputy Chair. of Bd Aug.–Sept. 2001; Minister of Economy, Autonomous Repub. of Crimea, Simferopol 2001–03; First Deputy Chair. Nat. Bank of Ukraine 2003–05; First Deputy Gov. Odesa Region Feb.–Sept. 2005; Minister of Economy 2005–06, of Foreign Affairs 2007; Deputy Head, Presidential Secr. 2006–07, Chair. Verkhovna Rada 2007–. *Address:* Office of the Chairman, Verkhovna Rada, 01008 Kyiv, vul. M. Hrushevskoho 5, Ukraine; tel. (44) 255-21-15; fax (44) 253-32-17; e-mail Yatseniuk.Arsenii@rada.gov.ua; internet www.rada.gov.ua.

YEKHANUROV, Yuriy Ivanovych: Ukrainian politician and economist; *Minister of Defence;* b. 23 Aug. 1948, Belkachi, Yakut ASSR (now the Republic of Sakha—Yakutiya) Russian Fed.; m. Olena Lvivna Yekhanurova; one s. *Education:* Kyiv Construction Tech. Coll.; Higher School of Econ. State Planning, Kyiv Inst. of Nat. Econs, Academic Research Econ. Inst. of State Planning. *Career:* master, then head of workshop, Chief Engineer, Dir, Kyivmiskbur Co. 1967–77, Head of Kyivmiskbudkomplekt Co. 1977–88; Head, Buddetal Co. 1977–88; Deputy Chief, Golovkyivmiskbud Co. 1988–91; elected to Kyiv City Rada (Council) 1990; Head of State Econ. Council, Cabinet of Ministers 1991–92; Deputy Head of Bd of Verkhovna Rada 1992; Deputy Head of Kyiv City Admin. 1992–93; Deputy Minister of the Economy 1993–94; Head of State Property Fund 1994–97; Minister of Economy Feb.–July 1997; Head of State Cttee on Entrepreneurship Devt 1997–98; mem. Verkhovna Rada (Parl.) 1998–, Deputy Head, Cttee on Econ. Policy, Man. Economy, Property and Investment 1998–99; First Deputy Prime Minister 1999–2001; Deputy Head of Presidential Admin 2001, 2004, re-elected mem. Verkhovna Rada for Our Ukraine bloc 2002, Head of Parl. Cttee on Industrial Policy and Entrepreneurship 2002; Deputy Head of Viktor Yushchenko's presidential campaign team 2004; Head of Cen. Exec. Cttee, Our Ukraine People's Union party March 2005; Gov. Dnipropetrovsk Oblast April–Sept. 2005; apptd acting Prime Minister Sept. 2005, Prime Minister Sept. 2005–06; Minister of Defence 2007–. *Publications:* more than 60 publs on econs. *Address:* Ministry of Defence, 03168 Kyiv, Povitroflotskyi pr. 6, Ukraine; tel. (44) 226-26-56; fax (44) 226-20-15; e-mail pressmou@pressmou.kiev.ua; internet www.mil.gov.ua.

YUSHCHENKO, Viktor Andriyovich, CandEconSc; Ukrainian economist, banker, politician and head of state; *President;* b. 23 Feb. 1954, Khoruzhivka, Sumy Oblast; m. Kateryna Mykhailivna Yushchenko; two s. three d. *Education:* Ternopil Inst. of Finance and Econ., Ukrainian Inst. of Econs and Agricultural Man. *Career:* economist, Br. Dir USSR State Bank, Ulianivskyi Dist, Sumy Oblast 1976–85, Deputy Dir of Agric. Credits, Ukrainian Br. of USSR State Bank

1985–87; Dept Dir Ukrainian Bank (fmrly Ukrainian Agro-Industrial Bank) 1987–91, First Deputy Chair. 1991–93; Gov. Nat. Bank of Ukraine 1993–99; Prime Minister of Ukraine 1999–2001; founder and Chair. Our Ukraine coalition 2002, mem. Parl. 2002–04; Pres. of Ukraine 2005–; mem. Ukrainian Acad. of Econ. Sciences, Acad. of Econ. and Cybernetics; Dr hc (Mohyla Acad.—National University of Kyiv), (Ostroh Acad.); Global Finance Award 1997, State Prize Laureate Science and Technology 1999, Chatham House Prize, UK 2005. *Publications:* over 250 articles and research papers in Ukrainian and int. journals. *Address:* Office of the President, 01220 Kyiv, vul. Bankova 11, Ukraine; tel. (44) 255-73-33; fax (44) 293-61-61; e-mail president@adm.gov.ua; viktor@yuschenko.com.ua; internet www.president.gov.ua; www.yuschenko.com.ua.

ZAKAYEV, Akhmed Khalidovich: Russian/Chechen rebel leader; b. 1959, Kazakhstan. *Career:* trained as an actor; field commdr, Chechen rebel movt 1994–96; fmr 'Minister for Culture', 'Chechen Repub. of Ichkeriya', 'Deputy Prime Minister and Special Overseas Envoy' 1997–2002; 'Minister for Foreign Affairs' 1997–2007; 'Prime Minister of Chechen Repub. of Ichkeriya' Nov. 2007–; currently living in exile in London, UK.

ZARIFI, Hamrokhon: Tajikistani diplomatist; *Minister of Foreign Affairs;* b. (Hamrokhon Zaripov), 25 Dec. 1948; m.; two c. *Education:* Kulob State Univ., Nat. Inst. of Modern Language, Pakistan, Korean Inst. for Econs and Trade. *Career:* Lecturer in Math., Kulob State Univ. 1971–74; Co-ordinator, Kulob Oblast Exec. Cttee 1974–84; held various posts in party org. and Tajikistan govt 1984–93; Deputy Chief Personnel Dept, Ministry of Foreign Affairs 1993–94, Chief of Dept 1994–96, Deputy Minister of Foreign Affairs 1995–97; Perm. Rep. to UN, Vienna 1996–2003, also Head of del. to OSCE, also Chargé d'Affaires, Embassy in Vienna 1996–97, Head of Mission to EEC 1997–2001, Amb. to Austria 1997–2003, to Switzerland 1998–2003, to Hungary 1999–2002, to USA 2003–06; Minister of Foreign Affairs 2006–. *Address:* Ministry of Foreign Affairs, 734051 Dushanbe, Xiyoboni Rudaki 42, Tajikistan; tel. (372) 21-18-08; fax (372) 21-02-59; e-mail dushanbe@mfaumo.td.silk.org; internet www.mid.tj.

ZAYCHANKA, Mikalay P.: Belarusian economist and politician; *Minister of the Economy;* b. 1948, Pogranichnyi, Maritime (Primorskii) Krai, Russia. *Education:* Belarusian Polytechnic Inst. *Career:* Engineer then Sr Engineer, Inst. of Machine Planning, Acad. of Sciences of Belarusian SSR; Sr Economist and Jr Scientific Colleague, Inst. of Econs, Acad. of Sciences of Belarusian SSR; Sr Scientific Colleague, responsible for methodology, Scientific Research Inst. of Gosplan (State Planning Cttee); First Deputy Minister of the Economy 1997–03, Minister of the Economy 2003–; Medal for Services to Labour. *Address:* Ministry of the Economy, 220050 Minsk, vul. Bersona 14, Belarus; tel. (17) 222-60-48; fax (17) 200-37-77; e-mail gen@plan.minsk.by; internet www.economy.gov.by.

ZHAKIYANOV, Galimzhan, PhD; Kazakhstani engineer and politician; b. 8 May 1963, Kurchumskii Dist, Eastern Kazakhstan Oblast; m.; two s. *Education:* Bauman Higher Inst., Moscow, Russia. *Career:* specialized in rocket and turbine eng; worked at Semipalatinsk Mil. Plant, Br. Head of Komsomol (CP Youth League), dismissed 1989; became leader of ind. youth movt; publr and ed. Sodeistviye (Assistance) newspaper 1989–91; Propr Semey coalmine 1990–94; Gov. of Semipalatinsk 1994–97; Chair. State Agency for Strategic Resources Control 1997; Akim (Gov.) of Pavlodar Oblast 1997–2001 (resgnd); Co-founder and Co-Chair. Democratic Choice of Kazakhstan (DCK) 2001; arrested on charges of abuse of power during tenure as Gov. April 2002, sentenced to seven-year prison term Aug. 2002, released on parole 2006.

ZHAMISHEV, Bolat Bidahmetovich, PhD; Kazakhstani banker and politician; *Minister of Finance. Education:* Kazakh Inst. of Agric. *Career:* First Vice-Minister of Finance 1999–2001, 2002–03; Vice-Minister of Internal Affairs 2001–02; Deputy Chair. Nat. Bank of Kazakhstan 2003–04; Chair. Agency for Regulation and Oversight of Financial Orgs

2004–06; Deputy Chair. Exec. Bd Russian-Kazakh Eurasian Devt Bank 2006–07; Minister of Finance 2007–. *Address:* Ministry of Finance, pl. Respubliki 60, 010000 Astana, Kazakhstan; tel. (7172) 28-00-65; fax (7172) 32-40-89; e-mail info@minfin.kz; internet www.minfin.kz.

ZHIRINOVSKII, Vladimir Volfovich, DPhil; Russian lawyer and politician; *Deputy Chairman, State Duma; Chairman, Liberal Democratic Party of Russia;* b. 25 April 1946, Almaty, Kazakh SSR; m. Galina Alexandrovna Zhirinovskaya; one s. *Education:* Inst. of Eastern languages (now Inst. of Asian and African Countries) and Faculty of Law, Moscow M. V. Lomonosov State Univ. (MGU). *Career:* officer, USSR Ministry of Defence, with Gen. Staff of Transcaucasian command 1970–72; with Int. Dept, Soviet Soc. of Friendship and Cultural Relations, Cttee for Peace 1973–75; with Office of Dean of Foreign Students, Higher School of Trade Union Movt 1975–77; legal consultant, Inyurcollegia 1977–83; Head of Legal Dept, Mir Publs 1983–90; f. Liberal-Democratic Party of Soviet Union (now of Russia—LDPR) 1989, Chair. 1990–, Chair. State Duma Parl. Group 1993–2000; mem. State Duma (Parl.) 1993–, Deputy Chair. 2000–; apptd head of Russian del. to NATO Parl. Ass. 2002; unsuccessful cand. in Russian Presidential elections 1991, 1996, 2000, 2008; attained rank of Col in Army Reserve 1995. *Publications:* The Last Leap South 1993, Political Landscape of Russia 1995, Economic Ideas of a Politician 1996, Geopolitics and the Russian Question 1997, The Zhirinovsky Phenomenon in Russia 1998 and more than 100 other books and publs. *Address:* Gosudarstvennaya Duma (State Duma), 103265 Moscow, Okhotnyi ryad 1; Liberal Democratic Party of Russia (Liberalno-demokraticheskaya partiya Rossii), 103045 Moscow, Lukov per. 9, Russia; tel. (495) 292-83-10 (Duma); (495) 692-11-95 (LDPR); fax (495) 292-94-64 (Duma); (495) 692-92-42 (LDPR); e-mail stateduma@duma.gov.ru; pressldpr@list.ru; internet www .duma.gov.ru; www.ldpr.ru.

ZHUKOV, Aleksandr Dmitreyevich: Russian politician and economist; *Deputy Chairman of the Government;* b. 1 June 1956; m. Yekaterina Zhukova; one s. *Education:* Moscow State Univ., Harvard Univ. *Career:* mem. All-Union Research Inst. of Systems Studies and State Cttee on Science and Tech. –1980; mem. Chief Currency Econ. Dept, USSR Ministry of Finance 1980–91; Vice-Pres. Avtotractorexport Co., Ministry of Foreign Trade 1991–93; mem. State Duma (Yabloko faction) 1993–97, 1999–2003, re-elected as ind. 2003–; Deputy Chair. Liberal Democratic Union of 12th Dec. 1994–96; Chair. Cttee on Budget, Taxes, Banks and Finance 1998–99, on Budget and Taxes 2000–; Deputy Chair. of Govt 2004–; mem. Russian Regions Faction 1996–; Pres. Russian Chess Fed. 2003–. *Address:* Office of the Government, 103274 Moscow, Krasnopresnenskaya nab. 2, Russia; tel. (495) 205-57-35; fax (495) 205-42-19; internet www.government.ru.

ZORKIN, Valerii Dmitrievich, LLD; Russian lawyer, academic and judge; *Chairman, Constitutional Court;* b. 18 Feb. 1943, Maritime (Primorskii) Krai; widower; one d. *Education:* Faculty of Law, Moscow State Univ. *Career:* Sr Lecturer in Law, Moscow State Univ. 1964–67, Asst Prof. 1967–79; Prof. of Constitutional Law and Theory of State, Law Acad. of the

USSR Ministry of Internal Affairs 1979–86, Prof. of Public Legal Disciplines 1986–; led group of experts on Constitutional Comm. 1990–91; Judge, Constitutional Court Oct. 1991, Chair. Nov. 1991–1993 (resgnd), re-elected 2003, 2006–. *Address:* Constitutional Court of the Russian Federation (Konstitutsionnyi Sud Rossiiskoi Federatsii), 190000 St Petersburg, pl. Dekabristov 1, Russia; tel. (812) 404-33-11; e-mail ksrf@ksrf.ru; internet www.ksrf.ru.

ZUBKOV, Viktor Alekseyevich, PhD; Russian government official and business executive; *First Deputy Chairman of the Government; Chairman of Board of Directors, OAO Gazprom;* b. 15 Sept. 1941, Arbat village, Kushvinskii Dist, Sverdlovsk Oblast; m.; one d. *Education:* Leningrad (now St Petersburg) Agricultural Inst. *Career:* began career in state farm network, Leningrad Oblast including Gen. Dir Pervomaiskoye Sovkhoz Union 1967–85; various roles within CP including First Sec. Priozersk Cttee and First Deputy Chair. Leningrad regional Cttee 1985–91; Deputy Chair. External Relations Cttee, St Petersburg City Council 1992–93; Deputy Chair. Fed. Tax Service and Head, State Tax Inspectorate, St Petersburg 1993–99; Deputy Minister for Tax 1999–2001; Deputy Minister of Finance 2001–04; Chair. Financial Monitoring Service, Ministry of Finance 2004–07; Chair. Govt of the Russian Fed. (Prime Minister) 2007–08, First Deputy Chair. of the Govt (First Deputy Prime Minister) 2008–; Chair. OAO Gazprom 2008–. *Address:* Office of the Chairman, Government of the Russian Federation, Krasnopresnenskaya nab. 2, 103274 Moscow; OAO Gazprom, ul. Nametkina 16, V-420, GSP-7, 117997 Moscow, Russia; tel. (495) 205-57-35; (495) 719-30-01; fax (495) 205-42-19; (495) 719-83-33; e-mail info@ government.ru;   gazprom@gazprom.ru;   internet   www .government.ru; www.gazprom.com.

ZYUGANOV, Gennadii Andreyevich, DPhil; Russian politician; *Chairman of the Central Committee, Communist Party of the Russian Federation;* b. 26 June 1944, Mymrino Village, Orel Oblast; m. Nadezhda Zyuganova. *Education:* Orel Pedagogical Inst., Acad. of Social Sciences of Cen. CPSU Cttee. *Career:* worked as secondary school teacher 1961–65; CP and trade union functionary 1967; First Sec., Dist, City, Regional Komsomol Cttees of Orel 1971–74, Sec., Second Sec., Head of Propaganda Div. Orel Regional CPSU Cttee 1974–83; Instructor and Head of Propaganda Div. Cen. CPSU Cttee 1983–89; Deputy Head of Ideology Div. Cen. CPSU Cttee 1989–90; mem. Politburo, Sec., Cen. Cttee of CP of Russian Fed. 1990, Chair. Cen. Cttee CP of Russian Fed. 1993–; Chair. Co-ordination Cttee of Patriotic Forces of Russia 1992–, Co-Chair. Duma of Russian Nat. Sobor 1992–; Co-Chair. Political Council of the Front of Nat. Salvation 1992–; mem. State Duma (Parl.) of Russia 1993–; CP Presidential cand. 1996, 2000, 2008. *Publications:* Russia and the Contemporary World 1995, Russia, My Homeland (The Ideology of State Patriotism) 1997. *Address:* Communist Party of the Russian Federation (Kommunistechiskaya partiya Rossiiskoi Federatsii—KPRF), 103051 Moscow, per. M. Sukharevskii 3/1, Russia; tel. (495) 628-04-90; fax (495) 292-90-50; e-mail kprf2005@yandex.ru; internet www.kprf .ru.

PART FOUR
Regional Information

REGIONAL ORGANIZATIONS

THE UNITED NATIONS

Address: United Nations, New York, NY 10017, USA.

Telephone: (212) 963-1234; **fax:** (212) 963-4879; **internet:** www.un .org.

The United Nations (UN) was founded on 24 October 1945. The organization, which has 192 member states, aims to maintain international peace and security and to develop international co-operation in addressing economic, social, cultural and humanitarian problems. The principal organs of the UN are the General Assembly, the Security Council, the Economic and Social Council, the International Court of Justice and the Secretariat. The General Assembly, which meets for three months each year, comprises representatives of all UN member states. The Security Council investigates disputes between member countries, and may recommend ways and means of peaceful settlement: it comprises five permanent members (the People's Republic of China, France, Russia, the United Kingdom and the USA) and 10 other members elected by the General Assembly for a two-year period. The Economic and Social Council comprises representatives of 54 member states, elected by the General Assembly for a three-year period: it promotes co-operation on economic, social, cultural and humanitarian matters, acting as a central policy-making body and co-ordinating the activities of the UN's specialized agencies. The International Court of Justice comprises 15 judges of different nationalities, elected for nine-year terms by the General Assembly and the Security Council: it adjudicates in legal disputes between UN member states.

Secretary-General: BAN KI-MOON (Republic of Korea) (2007–11).

MEMBER STATES IN EASTERN EUROPE, RUSSIA AND CENTRAL ASIA

(with assessments for percentage contributions to the UN budget for 2007–09, and year of admission)

Armenia	0.002	1992
Azerbaijan	0.005	1992
Belarus[1]	0.020	1945
Georgia	0.003	1992
Kazakhstan	0.029	1992
Kyrgyzstan	0.001	1992
Moldova	0.001	1992
Russia[2]	1.200	1945
Tajikistan	0.001	1992
Turkmenistan	0.006	1992
Ukraine[1]	0.045	1945
Uzbekistan	0.008	1992

[1] Until December 1991 both Belarus and Ukraine were integral parts of the USSR and not independent countries, but had separate UN membership.
[2] Russia assumed the USSR's seat in the General Assembly and its permanent seat on the Security Council in December 1991, following the USSR's dissolution.

Diplomatic Representation

PERMANENT MISSIONS TO THE UNITED NATIONS
(October 2008)

Armenia: 119 East 36th St, New York, NY 10016; tel. (212) 686-9079; fax (212) 686-3934; e-mail armenia@un.int; internet www.un .int/armenia; Permanent Representative ARMEN MARTIROSIAN.

Azerbaijan: 866 United Nations Plaza, Suite 560, New York, NY 10017; tel. (212) 371-2559; fax (212) 371-2784; e-mail azerbaijan@un .int; internet www.un.int/azerbaijan; Permanent Representative AGSHIN MEHDIYEV.

Belarus: 136 East 67th St, 4th Floor, New York, NY 10021; tel. (212) 535-3420; fax (212) 734-4810; e-mail belarus@un.int; internet www .un.int/belarus; Permanent Representative ANDREI DAPKIUNAS.

Georgia: 1 United Nations Plaza, 26th Floor, New York, NY 10021; tel. (212) 759-1949; fax (212) 759-1832; e-mail georgia@un.int; internet www.un.int/georgia; Permanent Representative IRAKLI ALASANIA.

Kazakhstan: 305 East St, 3rd Floor, New York, NY 10017; tel. (212) 230-1900; fax (212) 230-1172; e-mail kazakhstan@un.int; internet

www.un.int/kazakhstan; Permanent Representative BYRGANYM AITIMOVA.

Kyrgyzstan: 866 United Nations Plaza, Suite 477, New York, NY 10017; tel. (212) 486-4214; fax (212) 486-5259; e-mail kyrgyzstan@un .int; internet www.un.int/wcm/content/site/kyrgyzstan; Permanent Representative NURBEK JEENBAEV.

Moldova: 35 East 29th St, New York, NY 10016; tel. (212) 447-1867; fax (212) 447-4067; e-mail unmoldova@aol.com; internet www.un .int/moldova; Permanent Representative ALEXANDRU CUJBA.

Russia: 136 East 67th St, New York, NY 10021; tel. (212) 861-4900; fax (212) 628-0252; e-mail rusun@un.int; internet www.un.int/ russia; Permanent Representative VITALY CHURKIN.

Tajikistan: 216 East 49th St, 4th Floor, New York, NY 10017; tel. (212) 207-3315; fax (212) 207-3855; e-mail tajikistan@un.int; internet www.un.int/wcm/content/site/tajikistan; Permanent Representative SIRODJIDIN MUKHRIDINOVICH ASLOV.

Turkmenistan: 866 United Nations Plaza, Suite 424, New York, NY 10021; tel. (212) 486-8908; fax (212) 486-2521; e-mail turkmenistan@ un.int; internet www.un.int/wcm/content/site/turkmenistan; Permanent Representative Dr AKSOLTAN T. ATAEVA.

Ukraine: 220 East 51st St, New York, NY 10022; tel. (212) 759-7003; fax (212) 355-9455; e-mail uno_us@mfa.gov.ua; internet www.mfa .gov.ua/uno/en/news/top.htm; Permanent Representative YURIY A. SERGEEV.

Uzbekistan: 801 Second Ave, 20th Floor, New York, NY 10017; tel. (212) 486-4242; fax (212) 486-7998; e-mail uzbekistan@un.int; internet www.un.int/wcm/content/site/uzbekistan; Permanent Representative ALISHER VOHIDOV.

OBSERVERS

Asian-African Legal Consultative Organization: 404 East 66th St, Apt 12C, New York, NY 10021; tel. (212) 734-7608; e-mail aalco@ un.int; Permanent Representative K. BHAGWAT-SINGH (India).

International Committee of the Red Cross: 801 Second Ave, 18th Floor, New York, NY 10017; tel. (212) 599-6021; fax (212) 599-6009; e-mail log.nyc@icrc.org; Head of Delegation DOMINIQUE BUFF.

International Criminal Police Organization: One United Nations Plaza, Rm 2610, New York, NY 10017; tel. (917) 367-3463; fax (917) 367-3476; e-mail m.ragg@interpol.int; Special Representative (vacant).

International Organization for Migration: 122 East 42nd St, Suite 1610, New York, NY 10168; tel. (212) 681-7000; fax (212) 867-5887; e-mail unobserver@iom.int; Permanent Representative LUCA DALL'OGLIO.

IUCN (International Union for Conservation of Nature): 801 Second Avenue, Suite 405, New York, NY 10017; tel. (212) 286-1076; fax (212) 286-1079; e-mail iucn@un.int; Permanent Observer NARINDER KAKAR.

Organization of the Islamic Conference: 130 East 40th St, 5th Floor, New York, NY 10016; tel. (212) 883-0140; fax (212) 883-0143; e-mail oicny@un.int; internet www.oicun.org; Permanent Representative ABDUL WAHAB.

The Commonwealth of Independent States, the Council of Europe, the Economic Co-operation Organization, the Islamic Development Bank, the Organization for Democracy and Economic Development—GUAM, and the Organization for Security and Co-operation in Europe are among a number of intergovernmental organizations in the region that have a standing invitation to participate as Observers, but do not maintain permanent offices at the United Nations.

United Nations Information Centres/Services

Armenia: 375001 Yerevan, 2 Petros Adamyan St, 1st Floor; tel. (10) 560-212; fax (10) 561-406; e-mail dpi@un.am; internet www.un.am.

Azerbaijan: 1001 Baku, UN 50th Anniversary St 3; tel. (12) 498-98-88; fax (12) 498-32-35; e-mail dpi@un-az.org; internet azerbaijan .unic.org.

Belarus: 220050 Minsk, 17 Kirov St, 6th Floor; tel. (17) 227-48-76; fax (17) 226-03-40; e-mail dpi_unit.by@undp.org; internet www.un.by.

Georgia: 380079 Tbilisi, Eristavi St 9; tel. (32) 998558; fax (32) 250271; e-mail ketevan.ghioshvili@unic.org; internet georgia.unic.org.

Kazakhstan: 480091 Almaty, Tole bi 67; tel. (727) 269-53-27; fax (727) 258-26-45; e-mail registry.kz@undp.org; internet kazakhstan.unic.org.

Russia: 4/16 Glazovsky per., 119002 Moscow; tel. (495) 241-2894; fax (495) 230-2138; e-mail dpi-moscow@unic.ru; internet www.unic.ru.

Ukraine: 01021 Kyiv-21, Klovsky Uzviz, 1; tel. (44) 253-93-63; fax (44) 253-26-07; e-mail registry@un.org.ua; internet www.un.org.ua.

Uzbekistan: 700029 Tashkent, 4 Taras Shevchenko St; tel. (71) 133-09-77; fax (71) 120-34-50; e-mail registry.uz@undp.org; internet www.undp.uz.

Economic Commission for Europe—ECE

Address: Palais des Nations, 1211 Geneva 10, Switzerland.

Telephone: 229171234; **fax:** 229170505; **e-mail:** info.ece@unece.org; **internet:** www.unece.org.

The UN Economic Commission for Europe (ECE) was established in 1947 and was, with ECAFE (now ESCAP), the earliest of the five regional economic commissions set up by the UN Economic and Social Council (ECOSOC). The Commission promotes pan-European economic integration. It provides a regional forum for dialogue and co-operation on economic and sectoral issues for governments from European countries, as well as central Asian republics, the USA, Canada and Israel. It provides analysis, policy advice and assistance to governments, gives focus to UN global mandates on economic issues, and establishes norms, standards and conventions to facilitate international co-operation within and outside the region.

MEMBERS

Albania	Lithuania
Andorra	Luxembourg
Armenia	Macedonia, former Yugoslav
Austria	republic
Azerbaijan	Malta
Belarus	Moldova
Belgium	Monaco
Bosnia and Herzegovina	Montenegro
Bulgaria	Netherlands
Canada	Norway
Croatia	Poland
Cyprus	Portugal
Czech Republic	Romania
Denmark	Russia
Estonia	San Marino
Finland	Serbia
France	Slovakia
Georgia	Slovenia
Germany	Spain
Greece	Sweden
Hungary	Switzerland
Iceland	Tajikistan
Ireland	Turkey
Israel	Turkmenistan
Italy	Ukraine
Kazakhstan	United Kingdom
Kyrgyzstan	USA
Latvia	Uzbekistan
Liechtenstein	

Organization

(October 2008)

COMMISSION

The Commission, the highest decision-making body of the organization, holds annual formal sessions in Geneva to review the economic situation and decide on activities for the coming year. The 63rd session was to take place in April 2009. As well as taking strategic decisions the Commission provides a forum for senior-level dialogue on regional economic development policy.

EXECUTIVE COMMITTEE

The Executive Committee prepares the formal sessions of the Commission, implements the decisions of the Commission, and acts on behalf of the Commission between the sessions of that body. The Executive Committee also reviews and approves the programmes of work of the sectoral committees, which report at least once a year to the Executive Committee.

SECRETARIAT

The Secretariat services the meetings of the Commission and its sectoral committees and publishes periodic surveys and reviews, including a number of specialized statistical bulletins (see list of publications below). The Executive Secretary carries out secretarial functions for the executive bodies of several regional conventions and their protocols (see below).

Executive Secretary: MAREK BELKA (Poland) (until 31 October 2008).

SECTORAL COMMITTEES

Committee on Economic Co-operation and Integration;

Committee on Environmental Policy;

Committee on Housing and Land Management;

Committee on Inland Transport;

Committee on Sustainable Energy;

Committee on Timber;

Committee on Trade;

Conference of European Statisticians.

Activities

ECE's original purpose, when it was established by ECOSOC in 1947, was to give effective aid to the countries devastated by the Second World War. It was granted permanent status in 1951. During the 'cold war' period it served as the only major instrument of economic dialogue and co-operation linking the communist countries of central and eastern Europe with the countries of western Europe, and achieved the harmonization of a number of aspects of transport and trade, such as road signs, safety and anti-pollution standards for motor vehicles, standards for the transport of perishable or dangerous goods, and agreements on customs procedures. During the 1990s, when political changes in central and eastern Europe had allowed countries there to undergo transition from a centrally planned economy to a market economy, ECE adopted the role of assisting these countries, including the newly independent countries that had formerly been part of the USSR and Yugoslavia, and it extended its activities to the central Asian countries, which became members of both ECE and ESCAP.

The guiding principle of ECE activities is the promotion of sustainable economic growth among its member countries. To this end it provides a forum for communication among states; negotiates international legal instruments concerning trade, transport and the environment; and supplies statistics and economic and environmental analysis. The implications for ECE of the enlargement of the European Union (EU) and ongoing developments in member states with economies in transition, generated significant debate during the mid-2000s on the future direction of the Commission's work. The 59th session of ECE, convened in February 2004, commissioned a comprehensive, external evaluation on the state of ECE. The report, which was published in June 2005, included the following recommendations: more effective governance and management of the Commission, including restructuring work divisions and sub-programmes and identifying specialized areas of competence; raising the political profile of the Commission; co-ordinating the regional implementation of the UN Millennium Development Goals (MDGs); improving co-operation with other organizations, in particular a partnership with UNDP and with other regional commissions; and strengthening the participation of the private sector and non-governmental organizations in the Commission. Greater priority was to be given to the environment and transport, and to the specific problems affecting countries with economies in transition. The 61st session of ECE, convened in December 2005, adopted the resulting Work Plan on ECE Reform. The reform process, implemented in 2006, was to be reviewed by the Commission in 2009.

Economic Co-operation and Integration: The programme on Economic Co-operation and Integration, which is implemented by the Committee on Economic Co-operation and Integration and was established under the reform process approved in December 2005, has the following thematic focuses: strengthening the competitiveness of member states' economies by promoting the knowledge-based economy and innovation; facilitating the development of entrepreneurship and the emergence of new enterprises; facilitating effective regulatory policies and corporate governance, including those in the financial sector; promoting public-private partnerships for domestic and foreign investment; maintaining intellectual property rights; and other relevant aspects of international economic co-operation and integration. The Committee has created two teams of specialists, on innovation and competitiveness policies, and on intellectual property, who were to meet annually in support of work in these areas. The inaugural session of the Committee was convened in September 2006. During 2007 it focused on establishing networks of experts in other relevant fields, to allow dialogue and the exchange of information, with the particular aim of providing support for low-income countries undergoing economic transition. The second session of the Committee was held in December.

Environment: ECE aims to facilitate and promote co-operation among member governments in developing and implementing policies for environmental protection, the rational use of natural resources, and sustainable development. It supports the integration of environmental policy into sectoral policies, seeks solutions to environmental problems, particularly those of a transboundary nature, and assists in strengthening environmental management capabilities, particularly in countries in transition. A programme of Environmental Performance Reviews helps to improve the effectiveness of environmental management and policies in individual countries. The Committee on Environmental Policy brings governments together to formulate policy and provides a forum for the exchange of experience and good practices. It prepares the Environment for Europe (EfE) process (the focus of which is a ministerial-level conference normally held every four years: the 2007 meeting took place in Belgrade, Serbia, in October) and supports a Pan-European Programme on transport, health and the environment. ECE promotes the implementation of international agreements on the environment and assesses national policies and legislation. In addition, it has negotiated five conventions relating to the environment and serves as their secretariat: the Convention on Long-range Transboundary Air Pollution (which entered into force in 1983 and has been extended by eight protocols); the Convention on the Protection and Use of Transboundary Watercourses and International Lakes (Water Convention, entered into force in 1996, two protocols); the Convention on Environmental Impact Assessment in a Transboundary Context (Espoo Convention, entered into force in 1997, one protocol); the Convention on the Transboundary Effects of Industrial Accidents (entered into force in 2000, one protocol); and the Convention on Access to Information, Public Participation in Decision-making and Access to Justice in Environmental Matters (Aarhus Convention, entered into force in 2001, one protocol).

Forestry and Timber: ECE's Timber Committee works closely, through an integrated programme, with the European Forestry Commission of the FAO to promote sustainable forest management. It compiles data and analyses long-term trends and prospects for forestry and timber; keeps under review developments in the forest industries, including environmental and energy-related aspects; and publishes an annual market review of forest products. The Committee meets annually to review the programme, as well as to discuss policy and market trends and outlook. Assistance in the form of workshops and expert advice is provided to help countries that are undergoing economic transition to develop their forestry sectors. A special session of the Committee was convened in April 2008 to consider a draft strategic plan for the integrated programme of work on timber and forestry with FAO in the period 2008–13. It was to be considered for final approval at a joint meeting of the Committee and FAO Commission in October, held to coincide with events organized within the framework of a European Forest Week.

Housing, Land Management and Population: ECE's Committee on Housing and Land Management aims to improve housing conditions, spatial planning and land administration policies. In particular, it promotes the provision of adequate housing, both in the countries of eastern Europe that are undergoing socio-economic transition, and also in deprived neighbourhoods in western Europe. The Committee and its Working Party on Land Administration have prepared guidance on urban renewal, condominium management, housing finance, land administration and social housing. The

Committee organizes sub-regional workshops and seminars, and provides policy advice in the form of country profiles on the housing sector and land administration reviews, undertaken by experts. In early 2008 a Real Estate Market Advisory Group was established to support activities of the Working Party on Land Administration and to help to maintain a sustainable housing market. ECE's Generations and Gender Programme, begun in 2000, conducts research on population and demographic change. In November 2007 ECE organized a Conference on Ageing to discuss the implications of fertility rates that have fallen below replacement level. A further conference of experts and policy-makers, on the causes and consequences of demographic change, was held, in Geneva, Switzerland, in May 2008.

Statistics: The Conference of European Statisticians (CES) and ECE's Statistical Division have the task of co-ordinating international statistical activities in the region, by reviewing the most topical statistical areas, identifying gaps and duplication, and looking for issues not yet addressed. The CES plenary sessions and seminars offer a forum for senior statisticians, often leading to work in new areas and the preparation of new standards and recommendations. The CES and the Statistical Division work to develop methodology in compiling and disseminating economic, social and demographic statistics, for example in harmonizing methods of compiling the gross domestic product, national accounts and other economic indicators; measuring the distorting effect of globalization on national statistical systems; and finding sound methods of measuring sustainable development. The Division helps countries, especially those undergoing economic transition, to improve their statistical systems in accordance with the UN Fundamental Principles of Official Statistics, by advising on legislation and institutions and on how to ensure the independence and impartiality of official statistics. It maintains an on-line statistical database, allowing comparison of major economic and social indicators, and publishes guidelines on the editing of statistical data.

Sustainable Energy: ECE's Committee on Sustainable Energy provides a forum for intergovernmental dialogue, supports research by groups of experts, and provides technical assistance. Its chief concern is maintaining energy security, which is threatened by volatile petroleum prices and by disruptions in supply. It undertakes research on the classification and evaluation of energy reserves; improving energy efficiency so as to reduce dependence on imports and reduce greenhouse gas emissions; cleaner electricity production from coal and other fossil fuels; exploiting methane gas from coalmines; and the use of natural gas.

Trade: ECE's Committee on Trade received a new mandate following the reforms undertaken in 2006: it was to focus on the facilitation of international trade by means of simpler and better-integrated trade procedures, electronic business methods, common agricultural quality standards and the harmonization of technical regulations. The Committee was to continue working closely with other UN and non-UN organizations, and to provide a forum for dialogue between public and private sectors. The Committee was scheduled to hold a joint workshop with the Committee on Inland Transport in February 2009. The UN Centre for Trade Facilitation and Electronic Business (UN/CEFACT, established in 2002 as part of ECE) works to reduce delays and costs in international transactions by simplifying the necessary procedures. ECE's Working Party on Agricultural Quality Standards develops and updates commercial quality standards for fruit, vegetables and other agricultural products, in co-operation with OECD, and promotes the application of these standards through regional seminars and workshops. The Working Party on Regulatory Co-operation and Standardization Policies aims to harmonize diverse product regulations and standards, which can seriously impede trade, especially among the countries undergoing economic transition, for example when certificates accompanying goods are not recognized by the importing country. It has developed an international model for technical harmonization to assist countries wishing to standardize their rules on specific products or sectors. ECE's Advisory Group on Market Surveillance aims to combat the proliferation of counterfeit and pirated goods.

Transport: ECE aims to promote a coherent, efficient, safe and sustainable transport system through the development of international agreements, conventions, norms and standards relating to road, rail, inland water and combined transport. These international legal instruments, which are developed by intergovernmental specialized working parties with participation from transport equipment manufacturers and consumers and road users, include measures for improving vehicle safety and limiting vehicle emissions, simplifying border crossing procedures, improving road traffic safety, setting the conditions for developing coherent infrastructure networks, and providing for the safe transport of dangerous goods. One of the working groups, the World Forum for Harmonization of Vehicle Regulations, has global participation. In addition to these regulatory activities, ECE addresses transport trends and economics and compiles transport statistics; and it provides a forum for the exchange of technical and legal expertise. The Commission also assists eastern and south-eastern European countries and ECE member states from central Asia with the development of their transport systems and infrastructures. In 2005 a plan was elaborated, with ECE support, for investment in the Trans-European Motorway (TEM) and the Trans-European Railway (TER) projects, which were to develop the road and rail networks in 21 central, eastern and southeastern European countries. Another project, undertaken jointly with ESCAP, aims to develop Euro-Asian transport links. In February 2008 ECE established a Group of Experts on Hinterland Connections of Seaports, which was to study the effectiveness of existing container management and inland transport connections with seaports and compile a set of recommendations. In September the Transport Division organized a conference, held in Piraeus, Greece, addressing the need to develop hinterland connections. With the Europe Office of WHO, ECE administers a Transport, Health and Environment Pan-European Programme, in order to promote sustainable transport policies and systems.

SUB-REGIONAL PROGRAMME

Special Programme for the Economies of Central Asia (SPECA): initiated in 1998 as a joint programme of ECE and ESCAP, SPECA aims to strengthen sub-regional co-operation, by enabling the discussion of regional issues and offering technical assistance. Six Project Working Groups cover: transport and border crossing; water and energy; trade; information and communications technology for development; statistics; and gender and economy. The SPECA Economic Forum meets annually: in 2008 it was convened, in Moscow, Russia, in October, on the theme 'Investment Partnerships for Stronger Economic Co-operation and Integration in Central Asia'. In 2002 the SPECA Business Advisory Council was inaugurated to bring together business representatives from participating countries and from their major trading and economic partners. Participating countries: Afghanistan, Azerbaijan, Kazakhstan, Kyrgyzstan, Tajikistan, Turkmenistan and Uzbekistan.

ECE also provides technical assistance to the Southeast European Co-operative Initiative.

Finance

The allocation for ECE's regular budget in 2008 was US $28.3m.

Publications

UNECE Report (annually).
UNECE Weekly.
UNECE Compendium of Legal Instruments, Norms and Standards.
UNECE Countries in Figures.
Report of the Conference of European Statisticians (annually).
Trade Promotion Directory (annually).

For its different areas of activity ECE produces statistical bulletins, reports, performance reviews, country profiles, standards, agreements, recommendations, discussion papers, guidelines and manuals.

Economic and Social Commission for Asia and the Pacific—ESCAP

Address: United Nations Bldg, Rajadamnern Nok Ave, Bangkok 10200, Thailand.
Telephone: (2) 288-1234; **fax:** (2) 288-1000; **e-mail:** unisbkk.unescap@un.org; **internet:** www.unescap.org.

The Commission was founded in 1947, at first to assist in post-war reconstruction, and subsequently to encourage the economic and social development of Asia and the Far East; it was originally known as the Economic Commission for Asia and the Far East (ECAFE). The title ESCAP, which replaced ECAFE, was adopted after a reorganization in 1974. From 2002 ESCAP's administrative structures and programme activities underwent a process of intensive restructuring.

MEMBERS

Afghanistan	Korea, Democratic	Philippines
Armenia	People's Republic	Russia
Australia	Korea, Republic	Samoa
Azerbaijan	Kyrgyzstan	Singapore
Bangladesh	Laos	Solomon Islands
Bhutan	Malaysia	Sri Lanka
Brunei	The Maldives	Tajikistan
Cambodia	Marshall Islands	Thailand
China, People's	Micronesia,	Timor-Leste
Republic	Federated States	Tonga
Fiji	Mongolia	Turkey
France	Myanmar	Turkmenistan
Georgia	Nauru	Tuvalu
India	Nepal	United Kingdom
Indonesia	Netherlands	USA
Iran	New Zealand	Uzbekistan
Japan	Pakistan	Vanuatu
Kazakhstan	Palau	Viet Nam
Kiribati	Papua New Guinea	

ASSOCIATE MEMBERS

American Samoa	Hong Kong	Northern Mariana
Cook Islands	Macao	Islands
French Polynesia	New Caledonia	
Guam	Niue	

Organization
(October 2008)

COMMISSION

The main legislative organ of ESCAP is the Commission, which meets annually at ministerial level to examine the region's problems, to review progress, to establish priorities and to decide upon the recommendations of the Executive Secretary or the subsidiary bodies of the Commission. It reports to the UN Economic and Social Council (ECOSOC). Ministerial and intergovernmental conferences on specific issues may be held on an ad hoc basis with the approval of the Commission, although no more than one ministerial conference and five intergovernmental conferences may be held during one year.

COMMITTEES AND SPECIAL BODIES

The following Committees advise the Commission and help to oversee the work of the Secretariat. The Committees meet every two years, and their sub-committees meet in the intervening years.

Committee on Poverty Reduction: has sub-committees on Poverty Reduction Practices and Statistics.

Committee on Managing Globalization: has sub-committees on International Trade and Investment, Transport Infrastructure and Facilitation and Tourism, Environment and Sustainable Development, and Information, Communications and Space Technology.

Committee on Emerging Social Issues: has sub-committees on Socially Vulnerable Groups and Health and Development.

Special Body on Least Developed and Landlocked Developing Countries: meets every two years.

Special Body on Pacific Island Developing Countries: meets every two years.

In addition, an Advisory Committee of permanent representatives and other representatives designated by members of the Commission functions as an advisory body; it generally meets every month.

SECRETARIAT

The Secretariat operates under the guidance of the Commission and its subsidiary bodies. It consists of the Office of the Executive Secretary and two servicing divisions, covering administration and programme management, in addition to the following substantive divisions: Development of Pacific Island Countries and Territories; Environment and Sustainable Development; Information, Communication and Space Technology; Poverty and Development; Social Development (including Emerging Social Issues); Statistics; Trade and Investment; and Transport and Tourism. The Secretariat also includes a Least Developed Countries Co-ordination Unit, and the UN Information Service/Bangkok.

Executive Secretary: NOELEEN HEYZER (Singapore).

SUB-REGIONAL OFFICE

ESCAP Pacific Operations Centre (EPOC): Private Mail Bag, Suva, Fiji; tel. 3319669; fax 3319671; e-mail epoc@un.org; internet www.unescap.org/epoc; f. 1984, relocated to Fiji 2005; responsible for ESCAP's sub-programme on Development of Pacific Island Countries and Territories; assists Pacific island governments in forming and implementing national sustainable development strategies, particularly poverty reduction programmes that create access to services by socially vulnerable groups; conducts research, promotes regional co-operation and knowledge-sharing, and provides advisory services, training and pilot projects.

Activities

ESCAP acts as a UN regional centre, providing the only intergovernmental forum that includes the whole of Asia and the Pacific, and executing a wide range of development programmes through technical assistance, advisory services to governments, research, training and information. In 1992 ESCAP began to reorganize its programme activities and conference structures in order to reflect and serve the region's evolving development needs. The approach that was adopted focused on regional economic co-operation, poverty alleviation through economic growth and social development, and environmental and sustainable development. In May 2002, having considered the recommendations of an intergovernmental review meeting held in March, ESCAP determined to implement a further restructuring of its conference structures and thematic priorities. Three main thematic programmes were identified: poverty reduction (comprising sub-programmes on poverty and development, and on statistics), managing globalization (with sub-programmes on trade and investment, environment, and space technology); and emerging social issues (with sub-programmes on health and development, gender and development, and population and social integration). In May 2007 the Commission, convened in Almaty, Kazakhstan, commemorated the 60th anniversary of ESCAP and reaffirmed its central role in fostering regional and sub-regional co-operation.

Emerging Social Issues: ESCAP's Emerging Social Issues Division comprises three sections: Health and Development, Gender and Development, and Population and Social Integration. The Division's main objective is to assess and respond to regional trends and challenges in social policy and human resources development, with particular emphasis on the planning and delivery of social services and training programmes for disadvantaged groups, including the poor, youths, women, the disabled, and the elderly. It aims to strengthen the capacity of public and non-government institutions to address the problems of marginalized social groups and to foster partnerships between governments, the private sector, community organizations and all other involved bodies. The Health and Development section promotes health for all as a critical condition for economic growth and social stability: it supports the strengthening of human resources, adequate health financing, improved delivery of health services, access to affordable medicines, and health promotion. In 2008 ongoing projects included promotion of sustainable strategies for universal access to health care, particularly in the Greater Mekong sub-region; and strengthening life skills to reduce young people's vulnerability to HIV and AIDS and to substance abuse. The Gender and Development section promotes the advancement of women by helping to improve their access to education, economic resources, information and communication technologies and decision-making; it is also committed to combating violence against women, including trafficking. The Population and Social Integration section provides technical assistance to national population programmes, conducts research and assists the exchange of information; promotes the rights of people with disabilities; supports improvement of access to social services by poor people; and helps governments to form policies that take into account the increasing proportion of older people in the population. The Division implements global and regional mandates, such as the Programme of Action of the World Summit for Social Development and the Jakarta Plan of Action on Human Resources Development. The Biwako Millennium Framework for Action towards an Inclusive, Barrier-free and Rights-based Society for Persons with Disabilities in Asia and the Pacific was adopted by ESCAP as a regional guideline underpinning the Asian and Pacific Decade of Disabled Persons

(2003–12). In 1998 ESCAP initiated a programme of assistance in establishing a regional network of Social Development Management Information Systems (SOMIS). ESCAP collaborated with other agencies towards the adoption, in November 2001, of a Regional Platform on Sustainable Development for Asia and the Pacific. The Commission undertook regional preparations for the World Summit on Sustainable Development, which was held in Johannesburg, South Africa, in August–September 2002. In following up the summit ESCAP undertook to develop a bio-diversity park, which was officially inaugurated in Rawalpindi, Pakistan, in January 2005. The Commission also prepares specific publications relating to population and implements the Programme of Action of the International Conference on Population and Development. The Secretariat co-ordinates the Asia-Pacific Population Information Network (POPIN). The fifth Asia and Pacific Population Conference, sponsored by ESCAP, was held in Bangkok, Thailand, in December 2002. In September 2004 ESCAP convened a senior-level intergovernmental meeting on the regional review and implementation of the Beijing Platform for Action (Beijing + 10), relating to gender equality.

Environment and Sustainable Development: ESCAP is concerned to strengthen national capabilities to achieve environmentally sound and sustainable development by integrating economic concerns, such as the sustainable management of natural resources, into economic planning and policies. The Environment and Sustainable Development Division comprises sections on Energy Resources, Environment, and Sustainable Development and Water Resources. The Division was responsible for implementation of the Regional Action Programme for Environmentally Sound and Sustainable Development for the period 2001–05. Other activities have included the promotion of integrated water resources development and management, including water quality and conservation and a reduction in water-related natural disasters; strengthening the formulation of policies in the sustainable development of land and mineral resources; and the consideration of energy resource options, such as rural energy supply, energy conservation and the planning of power networks. Through the Division ESCAP prepares a report entitled State of the Environment in Asia and the Pacific which is published at five-yearly intervals, most recently in 2005. Following the massive earthquake and consequent devastating sea movements, or tsunamis, that occurred in late December 2004 in the Indian Ocean, ESCAP assisted other UN and international agencies with an initial emergency response and undertook early reviews of the impact of the event. In January 2005 the Executive Secretary appointed a Task Force on Tsunami Disaster Management to assist countries to address issues relating to natural disaster management, and to raise those issues at a regional level. The chairman of the Task Force was also appointed co-chair of an Inter-Agency Regional Task Force on Tsunami Relief and Rehabilitation that was established at a heads of agency meeting, convened by ESCAP later in that month, with particular responsibility to exchange information relating to rehabilitation and reconstruction in the aftermath of the tsunami disaster and to more general capacity-building on disaster preparedness. At the end of January a ministerial meeting, in Phuket, Thailand, approved the establishment of a regional tsunami early-warning system. ESCAP administers the voluntary, multi-donor Tsunami Regional Trust Fund which was inaugurated in late 2005 to support reconstruction and national and regional efforts to establish the early-warning system. ESCAP helped to organize a ministerial conference on environment and development, which was convened in Seoul, Republic of Korea, in March 2005. Representatives of the 52 countries attending the meeting adopted a Regional Implementation Plan for Sustainable Development in Asia and the Pacific (2006–10) and a Seoul Initiative on Environmentally Sustainable Economic Growth. The Division supports efforts to co-ordinate and monitor implementation of these initiatives. In particular, it received a mandate to work on issues related to climate change caused by global warming: it collates information, conducts regional seminars on adapting to climate change, and provides training in clean technology and guidance on reduction of harmful gas emissions. The inaugural meeting of the Asia-Pacific Regional Platform on Climate Change and Development was organized by ESCAP in March 2008. In April ESCAP organized the first Asia-Pacific Mayors' Forum on Environmentally Sustainable Urban Infrastructure Development, convened in Ulsan, Republic of Korea.

Information, Communication and Space Technology: ESCAP's Information, Communication and Space Technology Division comprises the following sections: Information and Communication Technology (ICT) Policy, ICT Applications, and Space Technology Applications. The Division aims to strengthen capacity for access to and the application of ICT and space technology, in order to maximize the benefits of globalization. It supports the development of cross-sectoral policies and strategies, and also supports regional co-operation aimed at sharing knowledge between advanced and developing economies and in areas such as cyber-crime and information security. In May 2005 the Commission approved the establishment, in the Republic of Korea, of the Asian and Pacific

Training Centre for ICT for Development (APCICT); APCICT was inaugurated in June 2006 (see below). In June 2005 the Division convened a senior-level meeting of experts to consider technical issues relating to disaster management and mitigation in Asia and the Pacific. The Division organized several conferences in preparation for the second phase of the World Summit on the Information Society (WSIS), which took place in November 2005, and co-ordinates regional activities aimed at achieving WSIS targets for the widespread use of ICT by 2015. During 2007 the Division organized projects and workshops in various countries of the region on the provision of ICT for rural communities, in particular for women entrepreneurs. It helps members to include space technology in their development planning, for example the use of satellites in meteorology, disaster prevention, remote sensing and distance learning. In August 2007 the Division hosted an international meeting on the use of space technology to combat avian influenza and other infectious diseases. A meeting of national policy-makers on disaster management was convened in March 2008 to discuss access to satellite information as a means of predicting and managing natural disasters.

Poverty and Development: The work of the Poverty and Development Division is undertaken by the following sections: Development Policy, Socio-economic Analysis and Poverty Reduction. The Division aims to increase the understanding of the economic and social development situation in the region, with particular attention given to the attainment of the UN Millennium Development Goals (MDGs), sustainable economic growth, poverty alleviation, the integration of environmental concerns into macroeconomic decisions and policy-making processes, and enhancing the position of the region's disadvantaged economies, including those Central Asian countries undergoing transition from a centrally-planned economy to a market economy. The Division is responsible for the provision of technical assistance, and the production of relevant documents and publications. The 63rd Commission, meeting in Almaty, Kazakhstan, in May 2007, endorsed a regional plan, developed by ESCAP, UNDP and the Asian Development Bank, to support poorer member countries to achieve the MDGs. Assistance was to be provided in the following areas: knowledge and capacity-building; expertise; resources; advocacy; and regional co-operation in delivering public goods (including infrastructure and energy security). The Commission also approved a resolution urging greater investment in health care in all member countries.

Statistics: ESCAP's Statistics Division provides training and advice in priority areas, including national accounts statistics, poverty indicators, gender statistics, population censuses and surveys, and the strengthening and management of statistical systems. It supports co-ordination throughout the region of the development, implementation and revision of selected international statistical standards, and, in particular, co-ordinates the International Comparison Programme (ICP) for Asia and the Pacific (part of a global ICP initiative). The Division disseminates comparable socio-economic statistics, with increased use of the electronic media, promotes the use of modern technology in the public sector and trains senior-level officials in the effective management of ICT. Training is provided by the Statistical Institute of Asia and the Pacific (see below).

Trade and Investment: ESCAP aims to help members to benefit from globalization by increasing global and regional flows of trade and investment. Its Trade and Investment Division provides technical assistance and advisory services. It aims to enhance institutional capacity-building; gives special emphasis to the needs of least-developed, land-locked and island developing countries, and to Central Asian countries that are in transition to a market economy, in accelerating their industrial and technological advancement, promoting their exports, and furthering their integration into the region's economy; supports the development of electronic commerce and other information technologies in the region; and promotes the intra-regional and inter-subregional exchange of trade, investment and technology through the strengthening of institutional support services such as regional information networks. The Division functions as the secretariat of the Asia-Pacific Trade Agreement (APTA), concluded in 1975 to promote regional trade through mutually agreed concessions by the participating states (in 2008 they comprised Bangladesh, the People's Republic of China, India, Laos and Sri Lanka). Since 2004 the Division has organized an annual Asia-Pacific Business Forum, involving representatives of governments, the private sector and civil society. It operates the Asia-Pacific Trade and Investment Agreements Database, the Trade and Transport Facilitation Online Database and an online Directory of Trade and Investment-Related Organizations, and publishes the Asia-Pacific Trade and Investment Review twice a year. The Division acts as the Secretariat of the Asia-Pacific Research and Training Network on Trade (ARTNeT), established in 2004, which aims to enhance the region's research capacity. ESCAP, with the World Trade Organization (WTO), implements a technical assistance programme, helping member states to implement WTO agreements and to participate in ongoing multilateral trade negotiations.

Transport and Tourism: ESCAP's Transport and Tourism Division aims to improve the regional movement of goods and people, and to strengthen the role of tourism in economic and social development. The Division has three sections: Transport Infrastructure, Transport Facilitation, and Transport Policy and Tourism. Its principal task is the implementation of the Asian Land Transport Infrastructure Development (ALTID) programme, initiated in 1992. ALTID projects include the development of the Trans-Asian Railway and of the Asian Highway road network. Other activities are aimed at improving the planning process in developing infrastructure facilities and services, in accordance with the Regional Action Programme (Phase II, 2002–06) of the New Delhi Action Plan on Infrastructure Development in Asia and the Pacific, which was adopted at a ministerial conference held in October 1996, and at enhancing private sector involvement in national infrastructure development through financing, management, operations and risk-sharing. The Division aims to reduce the adverse environmental impact of the provision of infrastructure facilities and to promote more equitable and easier access to social amenities. A Ministerial Conference on Infrastructure Development was organized by ESCAP in November 2001. An Intergovernmental Agreement on the Asian Highway Network (adopted in 2003, identifying some 141,000 km of roads in 32 countries) came into effect in July 2005. The first meeting of a working group on the highway, which was to convene twice a year, was held in December. By November 2007 about 10,000 km of the highway network had been upgraded to meet the minimum standards set by the Agreement, and in that month an Asian Highway Investment Forum was convened by ESCAP to finance the improvements still required on a further 12,000 km of the network. In November 2005 ESCAP organized an intergovernmental meeting to conclude a draft agreement on the establishment of a Trans-Asian Railway Network, comprising some 80,900 km of rail routes. The intergovernmental accord was adopted in April 2006 and signed by 18 member countries at a ministerial meeting held in Busan, Republic of Korea, in November (see below). In 2004 ESCAP and the UN Economic Commission for Europe (ECE) initiated a project for developing Euro-Asian transport linkages, aiming to identify and overcome the principal obstacles (physical and otherwise) along the main transport routes linking Asia and Europe. In November 2003 ESCAP approved a new initiative, the Asia-Pacific Network for Transport and Logistics Education and Research (ANTLER), to comprise education, training and research centres throughout the region. In November 2006 a Ministerial Conference on Transport was held in Busan, Republic of Korea. The Busan Declaration, adopted by the meeting, outlined a long-term development strategy for regional transport and identified investment priorities. The meeting also adopted a Ministerial Declaration on Road Safety which pledged to implement safety measures to save some 600,000 lives in the region in the period 2007–15. In April 2008 the ESCAP Commission determined to establish a Forum of Asian Ministers of Transport, to provide strategic guidance for the development of efficient, reliable and cost-effective transport services throughout the region.

ESCAP's tourism concerns include the development of human resources, improved policy planning for tourism development, greater investment in the industry, and minimizing the environmental impact of tourism. A Plan of Action for Sustainable Tourism in the Asia and Pacific Region (1999–2005) was adopted in April 1999, and a second phase of the Plan was to cover the period 2006–12. A Network of Asia-Pacific Education and Training Institutes in Tourism, established in 1997, comprised 211 institutes and organizations in 2008. Throughout all its activities the Division devotes particular attention to the needs and concerns of least-developed, land-locked and island developing nations, and economies in transition in the region.

CO-OPERATION WITH OTHER ORGANIZATIONS

ESCAP works with other UN agencies and non-UN international organizations, non-governmental organizations, academic institutions and the private sector; such co-operation includes joint planning of programmes, preparation of studies and reports, participating in meetings, and sharing information and technical expertise. In July 1993 a memorandum of understanding (MOU) was signed by ESCAP and the Asian Development Bank, outlining priority areas of co-operation between the two organizations. These were: regional and sub-regional co-operation; issues concerning the least-developed, land-locked and island developing member countries; poverty alleviation; women in development; population; human resource development; the environment and natural resource management; statistics and data bases; economic analysis; transport and communications; and industrial restructuring and privatization. The two organizations were to co-operate in organizing workshops, seminars and conferences, in implementing joint projects, and in exchanging information and data on a regular basis. A new MOU between the two organizations was signed in May 2004 with an emphasis on achieving poverty reduction throughout the region. In 2001 ESCAP, with the Bank and UNDP, established a regional partnership to promote the MDGs (see above); a joint regional report on implementation of the goals was prepared by the partnership and published in June 2005 prior to a global review, conducted at the UN General Assembly in September, and a further regional review was published in 2007. In May 2007 ESCAP endorsed a regional plan developed by the partnership with the aim of addressing regional challenges (in particular those faced by poorer countries) to the achievement of the MDGs. The UN Special Programme for the Economies of Central Asia (SPECA), begun in 1998, is implemented jointly by ESCAP and ECE: SPECA helps the participating countries to strengthen regional co-operation, particularly in the areas of water resources, energy and transport, and creates incentives for economic development and integration into the economies of Asia and Europe. In May 2007 ESCAP signed an MOU with ECE and the Eurasian Economic Community to strengthen co-operation in sustainable development, in support of the MDGs. In the following month ESCAP signed an MOU with the International Organization for Migration to provide for greater co-operation and co-ordination on international migration issues. In September 2008 ESCAP and the International Organization for Migration organized an Asia-Pacific high-level meeting on international migration and development.

REGIONAL INSTITUTIONS

Asian and Pacific Centre for Agricultural Engineering and Machinery (APCAEM): A-7/F, China International Science and Technology Convention Centre, 12 Yumin Rd, Chaoyang District, Beijing 100029, People's Republic of China; tel. (10) 8225-3581; fax (10) 8225-3584; e-mail info@unapcaem.org; internet www.unapcaem.org; f. 1977 as Regional Network for Agricultural Engineering and Machinery, elevated to regional centre in 2002; aims to reduce poverty by enhancing environmentally sustainable agriculture and food production, and applying 'green' and modern agro-technology for the well-being of producers and consumers; work programmes comprise agricultural engineering, food chain management, and agro-enterprise development and trade; undertakes research, training, technical assistance and the exchange of information. Active mems: Bangladesh, People's Republic of China, Democratic People's Republic of Korea, Fiji, India, Indonesia, Iran, Mongolia, Nepal, Pakistan, Philippines, Republic of Korea, Sri Lanka, Thailand, Viet Nam; Officer-in-Charge Dr AMITAVA MUKHERJEE (India); *APCAEM Policy Brief* (quarterly).

Asian and Pacific Centre for Transfer of Technology: APCTT Bldg, POB 4575, C-2 Qutab Institutional Area, New Delhi 110 016, India; tel. (11) 26966509; fax (11) 26856274; e-mail postmaster@apctt.org; internet www.apctt.org; f. 1977 to assist countries of the ESCAP region by strengthening their capacity to develop, transfer and adopt technologies relevant to the region, and to identify and promote regional technology development and transfer; operates Business Asia Network (www.business-asia.net) to promote technology-based co-operation, particularly between small and medium-sized enterprises; Dir Dr KRISHNAMURTHY RAMANATHAN; publs *Asia Pacific Tech Monitor*, *VATIS Updates on Biotechnology*, *Food Processing*, *Ozone Layer Protection*, *Non-Conventional Energy*, and *Waste Management* (each every 2 months).

Asian and Pacific Training Centre for ICT for Development (APCICT): Bonbudong, 3rd Floor Songdo Techno Park, 7-50 Songdodong, Yeonsu-gu, Incheon City, Republic of Korea; tel. 245-1700; fax 245-7712; e-mail info@unapcict.org; internet www.unapcict.org/; f. 2006 to provide training to ICT policy-makers and professionals, advisory services and analytical studies, to promote best practices in the field of ICT, and to contribute to narrowing the digital divide in the region; Dir HYUEN-SUK RHEE.

Centre for Alleviation of Poverty through Secondary Crops' Development in Asia and the Pacific (CAPSA): Jalan Merdeka 145, Bogor 16111, Indonesia; tel. (251) 343277; fax (251) 336290; e-mail capsa@uncapsa.org; internet www.uncapsa.org; f. 1981 as CGPRT Centre, current name adopted April 2004; initiates and promotes socio-economic and policy research, training, dissemination of information and advisory services to enhance the living conditions of rural poor populations reliant on secondary crop agriculture; Officer-in-Charge Dr KIOE SHENG YAP; publs *CAPSA Flash* (monthly), *Palawija News* (3 a year), working paper series, monograph series and statistical profiles.

Statistical Institute for Asia and the Pacific (SIAP): JETRO-IDE Building, 2–2 Wakaba 3-chome, Mihama-ku, Chiba-shi, Chiba 2618787, Japan; tel. (43) 2999782; fax (43) 2999780; e-mail staff@unsiap.or.jp; internet www.unsiap.or.jp; f. 1970 as Asian Statistical Institute, present name 1977; became a subsidiary body of ESCAP in 1995; trains government statisticians at the Institute and in various co-operating countries in Asia and the Pacific; prepares teaching materials, assists in the development of training on official statistics in national and sub-regional centres; Dir DAVAASUREN CHULTEM-JAMTS (Mongolia); *publ. SIAP Newsletter* (annually).

ASSOCIATED BODIES

ESCAP/WMO Typhoon Committee: Av. de 5 de Outubro, Coloane, Macao, People's Republic of China, SAR; tel. 88010531; fax 88010530; e-mail info@typhooncommittee.org; internet www.typhooncommittee.org; f. 1968; an intergovernmental body sponsored by ESCAP and the World Meteorological Organization for mitigation of typhoon damage; aims to establish efficient typhoon and flood warning systems through improved meteorological and telecommunication facilities; promotes disaster preparedness, trains personnel and co-ordinates research. The committee's programme is supported from national resources and also by UNDP and other international and bilateral assistance. Mems: Cambodia, People's Republic of China, Hong Kong, Japan, Democratic People's Republic of Korea, Republic of Korea, Laos, Macao, Malaysia, Philippines, Singapore, Thailand, USA, Viet Nam; Sec. OLAVO RASQUINHO.

WMO/ESCAP Panel on Tropical Cyclones: Technical Support Unit (TSU), c/o Pakistan Meteorological Dept, POB 1214, H-8/2, Islamabad, Pakistan; tel. (51) 9257314; fax (51) 4432588; e-mail tsupmd@hotmail.com; internet www.tsuptc-wmo.org; f. 1972 to mitigate damage caused by tropical cyclones in the Bay of Bengal and the Arabian Sea. Mems: Bangladesh, India, the Maldives, Myanmar, Oman, Pakistan, Sri Lanka, Thailand; TSU Co-ordinator Dr QAMAR-UZ-ZAMAN CHAUDHRY.

Finance

For the two-year period 2006–07 ESCAP's programme budget, an appropriation from the UN budget, was US $71.9m. The regular budget is supplemented annually by funds from various sources for technical assistance.

Publications

Annual Report.

Asia-Pacific Development Journal (2 a year).

Asia-Pacific in Figures (annually).

Asia-Pacific Population Journal (3 a year).

Asia-Pacific Trade and Investment Review (2 a year).

Bulletin on Asia-Pacific Perspectives (annually).

Economic and Social Survey of Asia and the Pacific (annually).

Environment and Sustainable Development News (quarterly).

ESCAP Energy News (2 a year).

ESCAP Human Resources Development Newsletter (2 a year).

ESCAP Population Data Sheet (annually).

ESCAP Tourism Review (annually).

Foreign Trade Statistics of Asia and the Pacific (every 2 years).

Key Economic Developments and Prospects in the Asia-Pacific Region (annually).

Population Headliners (several a year).

Poverty Alleviation Initiatives (quarterly).

Socio-Economic Policy Brief (several a year).

State of the Environment in Asia and the Pacific (every 5 years).

Statistical Indicators for Asia and the Pacific (quarterly).

Statistical Newsletter (quarterly).

Statistical Yearbook for Asia and the Pacific.

Technical Co-operation Yearbook.

Trade and Investment Information Bulletin (monthly).

Transport and Communications Bulletin for Asia and the Pacific (annually).

Water Resources Journal (annually).

Manuals; country and trade profiles; commodity prices; statistics; Atlas of Mineral Resources of the ESCAP Region (country by country).

United Nations Children's Fund—UNICEF

Address: 3 United Nations Plaza, New York, NY 10017, USA.
Telephone: (212) 326-7000; **fax:** (212) 887-7465; **e-mail:** info@unicef.org; **internet:** www.unicef.org.

UNICEF was established in 1946 by the UN General Assembly as the UN International Children's Emergency Fund, to meet the emergency needs of children in post-war Europe. In 1950 its mandate was expanded to respond to the needs of children in developing countries. In 1953 the General Assembly decided that UNICEF should become a permanent branch of the UN system, with an emphasis on programmes giving long-term benefits to children everywhere, particularly those in developing countries. In 1965 UNICEF was awarded the Nobel Peace Prize.

Organization

(October 2008)

EXECUTIVE BOARD

The Executive Board, as the governing body of UNICEF, comprises 36 member governments from all regions, elected in rotation for a three-year term by ECOSOC. The Board establishes policy, reviews programmes and approves expenditure. It reports to the General Assembly through ECOSOC.

SECRETARIAT

The Executive Director of UNICEF is appointed by the UN Secretary-General in consultation with the Executive Board. The administration of UNICEF and the appointment and direction of staff are the responsibility of the Executive Director, under policy directives laid down by the Executive Board, and under a broad authority delegated to the Executive Director by the Secretary-General. In 2007 there were more than 8,000 UNICEF staff positions, of which about 85% were in field offices.

Executive Director: ANN M. VENEMAN (USA).

UNICEF OFFICES

Regional Office for Central and Eastern Europe and the Commonwealth of Independent States: Palais des Nations, 1211 Geneva 10, Switzerland; tel. 229095111; fax 229095909; e-mail info@unicef.ch; internet www.unicef.org/ceecis.

UNICEF Innocenti Research Centre: Piazza SS. Annunziata 12, 50122 Florence, Italy; tel. (055) 20330; fax (055) 2033220; e-mail florence@unicef.org; internet www.unicef-irc.org; f. 1988.

UNICEF Supply Division: UNICEF Plads, Freeport 2100, Copenhagen, Denmark; tel. 35-27-35-27; fax 35-26-94-21; e-mail supply@unicef.org; internet www.unicef.org/supply.

NATIONAL COMMITTEES

UNICEF is supported by 37 National Committees, mostly in industrialized countries, whose volunteer members, numbering more than 100,000, raise money through various activities, including the sale of greetings cards. The Committees also undertake advocacy and awareness campaigns on a number of issues and provide an important link with the general public.

Activities

UNICEF is dedicated to the well-being of children, adolescents and women and works for the realization and protection of their rights within the frameworks of the Convention on the Rights of the Child, which was adopted by the UN General Assembly in 1989 and by 2008 was almost universally ratified, and of the Convention on the Elimination of All Forms of Discrimination Against Women, adopted by the UN General Assembly in 1979. Promoting the full implementation of the Conventions, UNICEF aims to ensure that children world-wide are given the best possible start in life and attain a good level of basic education, and that adolescents are given every opportunity to develop their capabilities and participate successfully in society. The Fund also continues to provide relief and rehabilitation assistance in emergencies. Through its extensive field network in some 156 developing countries and territories, UNICEF undertakes, in co-ordination with governments, local communities and other aid organizations, programmes in health, nutrition, education, water and sanitation, the environment, gender issues and development, and other fields of importance to children. Emphasis is placed on low-cost, community-based programmes. UNICEF programmes

are increasingly focused on supporting children and women during critical periods of their life, when intervention can make a lasting difference. UNICEF is actively involved in global-level partnerships for child protection, including the Inter-Agency Co-ordination Panel on Juvenile Justice; the Inter-Agency Working Group on Unaccompanied and Separated Children; the Donors' Working Group on Female Genital Mutilation/Cutting; the Better Care Network; the Study on Violence Against Children; the Inter-Agency Standing Committee (IASC) Task Force on Protection from Sexual Exploitation and Abuse in Humanitarian Crises; and the IASC Task Force on Mental Health and Psychological Support in Emergency Settings. In 2006 UNICEF allocated 11% of its total programme assistance towards policy advocacy and partnerships for children's rights.

Since 2005 young people from the Group of Eight (G8) nations (Canada, France, Germany, Italy, Japan, Russia, the United Kingdom and the USA) have participated in a Junior 8 (J8) summit, organized with support from UNICEF on the fringes of the annual G8 summit. The J8 summits address issues including education, energy, HIV/AIDS, and tolerance. The fourth J8 summit meeting took place in Chitose, Hokkaido, Japan, in July 2008.

The five principal themes of UNICEF's medium-term strategic plan for the period 2006–09 are: young child survival and development; basic education and gender equality, including the Fund's continued leadership of the UN Girls' Education Initiative (UNGEI); HIV/AIDS and children, including participation in the Joint UN Programme on HIV/AIDS (UNAIDS—see below); child protection from violence, exploitation and abuse; and policy advocacy and partnerships for children's rights. These priorities are guided by the relevant UN Millennium Development Goals (MDGs) adopted by world leaders in 2000, and by the 'A World Fit for Children' declaration and plan of action endorsed by the UN General Assembly Special Session on Children in 2002 (see below).

UNICEF served as the substantive secretariat for, and played a leading role in helping governments and other partners prepare for, the UN General Assembly Special Session on Children, which was held in May 2002 to assess the outcome of the World Summit for Children convened in 1990 (which had made commitments to reducing mortality rates for infants and children; reducing the maternal mortality rate; reducing severe malnutrition amongst children under five; ensuring universal access to safe drinking water and to sanitary means of excreta disposal; and ensuring universal access to basic education) and to determine a set of actions and objectives for the next 10 years. At the Session the General Assembly adopted a declaration entitled 'A World Fit for Children', reaffirming its commitment to the agenda of the 1990 summit, and outlining a plan of action that resolved to achieve as yet unmet World Summit goals by 2010 and to work towards the attainment by 2015 of 21 new goals and targets supporting the MDGs in the areas of education, health and the protection of children. The latter included: a reduction of mortality rates for infants and children under five by two-thirds; a reduction of maternal mortality rates by three-quarters; a reduction by one-third in the rate for severe malnutrition among children under the age of five; and enrolment in primary education by 90% of children. In December 2007 a special session of the UN General Assembly reviewed progress attained so far towards 'A World Fit for Children'. UNICEF's annual publication *The State of the World's Children* includes social and economic data relevant to the well-being of children. It was reported in this publication in 2007 that one of the most powerful constraints to realizing children's rights and achieving the MDGs was discrimination against women. In 1995 UNICEF developed its Multiple Indicator Cluster Survey (MICS) method of data collection, which was in the 2000s being used as a main tool in measuring progress towards the achievement of the UN MDGs.

In May 2001 UNICEF supported a conference of high-level representatives of European and Central Asian countries, convened under the auspices of the Governments of Bosnia and Herzegovina and Germany, in Berlin, Germany, to formulate a communal agenda concerning the welfare of children in the region over the coming decade.

In 2000 UNICEF launched a new initiative, the Global Movement for Children—comprising governments, private- and public-sector bodies, and individuals—which aimed to rally world-wide support to improve the lives of all children and adolescents. In April 2001 a 'Say Yes for Children' campaign was adopted by the Global Movement, identifying 10 critical actions required to further its objectives. These were: eliminating all forms of discrimination and exclusion; putting children first; ensuring a caring environment for every child; fighting HIV/AIDS; eradicating violence against and abuse and exploitation of children; listening to children's views; universal education; protecting children from war; safeguarding the earth for children; and combating poverty. UNICEF hosts the Child Survival Partnership, launched in 2003 by UNICEF, WHO, the World Bank and other partners to act as a forum for the promotion of co-ordinated action in support of efforts to reduce the level of child mortality in 42 targeted developing countries.

UNICEF, in co-operation with other UN agencies, promotes universal access to and completion of basic and good quality education. The Fund, with UNESCO, UNDP, UNFPA and the World Bank, co-sponsored the World Conference on Education for All, held in Thailand in March 1990, and undertook efforts to achieve the objectives formulated by the conference, which included the elimination of disparities in education between boys and girls. UNICEF participated in and fully supports the objectives and framework for action adopted by the World Education Forum in Dakar, Senegal, in April 2000. UNICEF supports education projects in sub-Saharan Africa, South Asia and countries in the Middle East, North Africa, and Latin America and the Caribbean, and leads and acts as the secretariat of the United Nations Girls' Education Initiative (UNGEI), which aims to increase the enrolment of girls in primary schools in more than 100 countries. In 2006 about 115m. school-age children world-wide, of whom more than one-half were girls, remained deprived of basic education. Some 21.3% of the Fund's programme assistance was allocated to basic education and gender equality in 2006.

UNICEF works to improve safe water supply, sanitation and hygiene, and thereby reduce the risk of diarrhoea and other water-borne diseases. In partnership with other organizations the Fund supports initiatives to make schools in more than 90 developing countries safer through school-based water, sanitation and hygiene programmes. UNICEF places great emphasis on increasing the testing and protection of drinking water at its source as well as in the home. In 2006 UNICEF and partners established the Global Task Force on Water and Sanitation with the aim of providing all children with access to safe water, and accelerating progress towards MDG targets on safe drinking water and basic sanitation.

UNICEF aims to break the cycle of poverty by advocating for the provision of increased development aid to developing countries, and aims to help poor countries obtain debt relief and to ensure access to basic social services. UNICEF is the leading agency in promoting the 20/20 initiative, which was endorsed at the World Summit for Social Development, held in Copenhagen, Denmark, in March 1995. The initiative encourages the governments of developing and donor countries to allocate at least 20% of their domestic budgets and official development aid respectively, to healthcare, primary education and low-cost safe water and sanitation.

UNICEF estimates that the births of some 50m. children annually are not officially registered, and promotes universal registration in order to prevent the abuse of children without proof of age and nationality, for example through trafficking, forced labour, early marriage and military recruitment. It estimates that some 218m. children were involved in exploitative labour (excluding domestic work) in 2004, and approximately 126m. children aged five–17 were believed to be engaged in hazardous work. It is estimated that, annually, around 1.2m. children world-wide are trafficked. The Fund, which vigorously opposes the exploitation of children as a violation of their basic human rights, works with ILO and other partners to promote an end to exploitative and hazardous child labour, and supports special projects to provide education, counselling and care in developing countries. UNICEF co-sponsored and actively participated in the Second Congress Against Commercial Sexual Exploitation of Children held in Yokohama, Japan, in December 2001. Some 10.2% of the Fund's direct programme assistance was allocated to the improved protection of children in 2006.

In 2006 UNICEF allocated 51% of its programme assistance to young child survival and development. The Fund estimated that around 9.7m. children under five years of age died in 2006 (compared with some 20m. and 13m. child mortalities in, respectively, 1960 and 1990), mainly in developing countries, and the majority from largely preventable causes. UNICEF has worked with WHO and other partners to increase global immunization coverage against the following six diseases: measles, poliomyelitis, tuberculosis, diphtheria, whooping cough and tetanus. In 2003 UNICEF, WHO, the World Bank and other partners established a new Child Survival Partnership, which acts as a forum for the promotion of co-ordinated action in support of efforts to save the children's lives in 42 targeted developing countries. In September 2005 UNICEF, WHO and other partners launched the Partnership for Maternal, Newborn and Child Health, formed to accelerate progress towards MDGs four and five, which aim to reduce child and maternal mortality respectively. In 2000 UNICEF, WHO, the World Bank and a number of public- and private-sector partners launched the Global Alliance for Vaccines and Immunization (GAVI, subsequently renamed the Gavi Alliance), which aims to protect children of all nationalities and socio-economic groups against vaccine-preventable diseases. GAVI's strategy includes improving access to sustainable immunization services, expanding the use of existing vaccines, accelerating the development and introduction of new vaccines and technologies and promoting immunization coverage as a focus of international development efforts.

The results of integrated approaches to child health, such as the Accelerated Child Survival and Development (ACSD) strategy and community-based Integrated Management of Childhood Illnesses (IMCI) programme, have demonstrated new potential to reduce child mortality. The ACSD strategy, implemented by UNICEF since 2002, is an intensive combination of life-saving interventions including the promotion of antenatal care, vaccination and breast-feeding, volunteer health-worker follow-up of newborns and the distribution of insecticide-treated mosquito nets. Focused in 97 high-mortality districts in 11 mainly West African countries, ACSD has reached around 16m. people, including 2.8m. children under the age of five.

In 2006 UNICEF issued a report entitled *Pneumonia: The Forgotten Killer of Children*, which identified pneumonia as the primary medical cause of all deaths of children under five years of age.

At the UN General Assembly Special Session on Children, in 2002, goals were set to reduce measles deaths by 50%. Expanded efforts by UNICEF, WHO and other partners led to a reduction in world-wide measles deaths by around 60% between 1999 and 2005.

UNICEF-assisted programmes for the control of diarrhoeal diseases promote the low-cost manufacture and distribution of prepackaged salts or home-made solutions. The use of 'oral rehydration therapy' has risen significantly in recent years, and is believed to prevent more than 1m. child deaths annually. During 1990–2000 diarrhoea-related deaths were reduced by one-half. UNICEF also promotes the need to improve sanitation and access to safe water supplies in developing nations in order to reduce the risk of diarrhoea and other water-borne diseases (see 20/20 initiative, above). To control acute respiratory infections, another leading cause of death in children under five in developing countries, UNICEF works with WHO in training health workers to diagnose and treat the associated diseases. Around 1m. children die from malaria every year, mainly in sub-Saharan Africa. In October 1998 UNICEF, together with WHO, UNDP and the World Bank, inaugurated a new global campaign, Roll Back Malaria, to fight the disease. UNICEF is actively engaged in developing innovative and effective ways to distribute highly-subsidized insecticide-treated mosquito nets at local level, thereby increasing the proportion of children and pregnant women who use them.

According to UNICEF estimates, around 25% of children under five years of age are underweight, while each year malnutrition contributes to about one-half of the child deaths in that age group and leaves millions of others with physical and mental disabilities. More than 2,000m. people world-wide (mainly women and children in developing countries) are estimated to be deficient in one or more essential vitamins and minerals, such as vitamin A, iodine and iron. UNICEF supports national efforts to reduce malnutrition, for example, fortifying staple foods with micronutrients, widening women's access to education, improving the nutritional status of pregnant women, improving household food security and basic health services, providing food supplies in emergencies, and promoting sound child-care and feeding practices. Since 1991 more than 19,000 hospitals in about 130 countries have been designated 'baby-friendly', having implemented a set of UNICEF and WHO recommendations entitled '10 steps to successful breast-feeding'. In 1996 UNICEF expressed its concern at the impact of international economic embargoes on child health, citing as an example the extensive levels of child malnutrition recorded in Iraq. UNICEF remains actively concerned at the levels of child malnutrition and accompanying diseases in Iraq and in the Democratic People's Republic of Korea, which has also suffered severe food shortages.

UNICEF estimates that more than 500,000 women die every year during pregnancy or childbirth, largely because of inadequate maternal healthcare. For every maternal death, approximately 30 further women suffer permanent injuries or chronic disabilities as a result of complications during pregnancy or childbirth. With its partners in the Safe Motherhood Initiative—UNFPA, WHO, the World Bank, the International Planned Parenthood Federation, the Population Council, and Family Care International—UNICEF promotes measures to reduce maternal mortality and morbidity, including improving access to quality reproductive health services, educating communities about safe motherhood and the rights of women, training midwives, and expanding access to family planning services. Under the Global Partnership for Maternal, Newborn and Child Health, UNICEF works with WHO, UNFPA and other partners in countries with high maternal mortality to improve maternal health and prevent maternal deaths. UNICEF and partners work with governments and policy-makers to ensure that emergency obstetric care is a priority in national health plans. In 200 UNICEF activities in this area included support for obstetric facilities and training in, and advocacy of, women's health issues such as avoiding child marriage, eliminating female genital mutilation/cutting (FGM/C), and preventing malaria and promoting the uptake of tetanus toxoid vaccinations and iron and folic acid supplements among pregnant women.

UNICEF is concerned at the danger posed by HIV/AIDS to the realization of children's rights and in 2006 allocated 5.5% of its programme expenditure to this area. At the end of 2007 it was estimated that 2.1m. children under the age of 15 were living with HIV/AIDS world-wide. During that year some 420,000 children under the age of 15 were estimated to have been newly infected with the HIV virus, while 290,000 died as a result of AIDS and AIDS-related illnesses. It is believed that more than 15m. children world-wide have lost one or both parents to AIDS since the start of the pandemic. UNICEF's priorities in this area include prevention of infection among young people (through, for example, support for education programmes and dissemination of information through the media), reduction in mother-to-child transmission, care and protection of orphans and other vulnerable children, and care and support for children, young people and parents living with HIV/AIDS. UNICEF works closely in this field with governments and co-operates with other UN agencies in the Joint UN Programme on HIV/AIDS (UNAIDS), which became operational on 1 January 1996. In July 2002 UNICEF, UNAIDS and WHO jointly produced a study entitled *Young People and HIV/AIDS: Opportunity in Crisis*, examining young people's sexual behaviour patterns and knowledge of HIV/AIDS. UNICEF advocates Life Skills-Based Education as a means of empowering young people to cope with challenging situations and encouraging them to adopt healthy patterns of behaviour. In July 2004 UNICEF and other partners produced a *Framework for the Protection, Care and Support of Orphans and Vulnerable Children Living in a World with HIV and AIDS*. In October 2005 UNICEF launched Unite for Children, Unite Against AIDS, a campaign that was to provide a platform for child-focused advocacy aimed at reversing the spread of HIV/AIDS amongst children, adolescents and young people; and to provide a child-focused framework for national programmes based on the following four pillars: the prevention of mother-to-child HIV transmission, improved provision of paediatric treatment, prevention of infection among adolescents and young people, and protection and support of children affected by HIV/AIDS. In January 2007 UNICEF issued *Children and AIDS: A stocktaking report* detailing the progress and challenges of the previous year.

UNICEF provides emergency relief assistance to children and young people affected by conflict, natural disasters and food crises. In situations of violence and social disintegration the Fund provides support in the areas of education, health, mine-awareness and psychosocial assistance, and helps to demobilize and rehabilitate child soldiers. In recent years several such operations have been undertaken, including in Afghanistan, Burundi, Democratic Republic of the Congo, Iraq, Liberia, the Palestinian territories, Sierra Leone, Somalia and Sudan. In December 2007 UNICEF appealed for some US $237.4m. through the UN Consolidated Inter-Agency Appeal Process to fund emergency assistance to children and women in emergencies in 2008. In 1999 UNICEF adopted a Peace and Security Agenda to help guide international efforts in this field. Emergency education assistance includes the provision of 'Edukits' in refugee camps and the reconstruction of school buildings. In the area of health the Fund co-operates with WHO to arrange 'days of tranquility' in order to facilitate the immunization of children in conflict zones. Psychosocial assistance activities include special programmes to support traumatized children and help unaccompanied children to be reunited with parents or extended families.

UNICEF has provided medical supplies, basic educational materials and other items to aid those displaced by the insecurity that has prevailed in the North Caucasus region since late 1999. UNICEF has condemned the killing of women and children there.

In 2006 UNICEF provided primary health care to some 2.1m. people in Darfur, Sudan, and worked with partners to supply camps with safe water and basic sanitation to the region. During that year UNICEF also conducted a 'Go to School' campaign in Darfur, and

1.2m. children were also immunized against polio and given vitamin A supplements.

In the mid-2000s UNICEF country offices prepared contingency plans for a possible future avian influenza pandemic among humans, with a particular focus on children, as part of the inter-agency response to the threat.

An estimated 250,000 children are involved in armed conflicts as soldiers, porters and forced labourers. UNICEF encourages ratification of the Optional Protocol to the Convention on the Rights of the Child on the involvement of children in armed conflict, which was adopted by the General Assembly in May 2000 and entered into force in February 2002, and bans the compulsory recruitment of combatants below the age of 18. The Fund also urges states to make unequivocal statements endorsing 18 as the minimum age of voluntary recruitment to the armed forces. It is estimated that land-mines kill and maim between 8,000 and 10,000 children every year. The Convention on the Prohibition of the Use, Stockpiling, Production and Transfer of Anti-Personnel Mines and on their Destruction was adopted in December 1997 and entered into force in March 1999. By July 2008 the Convention had been ratified by 156 countries. UNICEF is committed to campaigning for its universal ratification and full implementation, and also supports mine-awareness campaigns.

During 2005 the UN's Inter-Agency Standing Committee (IASC), concerned with co-ordinating the international response to humanitarian disasters, developed a concept of organizing agency assistance to IDPs through the institutionalization of a 'Cluster Approach', currently comprising 11 core areas of activity. UNICEF was designated the lead agency for the clusters on Education (jointly with Save The Children); Emergency Telecommunications (jointly with OCHA and WFP); Nutrition; Protection of IDPs in natural disaster situations and of non-IDP civilians in conflict situations (with UNHCR and OHCHR); and Water, Sanitation and Hygiene.

Finance

UNICEF is funded by voluntary contributions from governments and non-governmental and private-sector sources. UNICEF's income is divided into contributions for 'regular resources' (used for country programmes of co-operation approved by the Executive Board, programme support, and management and administration costs) and contributions for 'other resources' (for special purposes, including expanding the outreach of country programmes of co-operation and ensuring capacity to deliver critical assistance to women and children, for example during humanitarian crises). UNICEF's total income in 2007 was estimated at US $3,013m. and its total expenditure at $2,782m.

Publications

Progress for Children (in English, French and Spanish).

The State of the World's Children (annually, in Arabic, English, French, Russian and Spanish and about 30 other national languages).

UNICEF Annual Report (in English, French and Spanish).

UNICEF at a Glance (in English, French and Spanish).

Young People in Changing Societies (annually).

Reports and studies; series on children and women; nutrition; education; children's rights; children in wars and disasters; working children; water, sanitation and the environment; analyses of the situation of children and women in individual developing countries.

United Nations Development Programme—UNDP

Address: One United Nations Plaza, New York, NY 10017, USA.
Telephone: (212) 906-5295; **fax:** (212) 906-5364; **e-mail:** hq@undp.org; **internet:** www.undp.org.

The Programme was established in 1965 by the UN General Assembly. Its central mission is to help countries to eradicate poverty and achieve a sustainable level of human development, an approach to economic growth that encompasses individual well-being and choice, equitable distribution of the benefits of development, and conservation of the environment. UNDP advocates for a more inclusive global economy. UNDP is the focus of UN efforts to achieve the Millennium Development Goals.

Organization

(October 2008)

UNDP is responsible to the UN General Assembly, to which it reports through ECOSOC.

EXECUTIVE BOARD

The Executive Board is responsible for providing intergovernmental support to, and supervision of, the activities of UNDP and the UN Population Fund (UNFPA). It comprises 36 members: eight from

Africa, seven from Asia and the Pacific, four from eastern Europe, five from Latin America and the Caribbean and 12 from western Europe and other countries. Members serve a three-year term.

SECRETARIAT

Offices and divisions at the Secretariat include: an Operations Support Group; Offices of the United Nations Development Group, the Human Development Report, Development Studies, Audit and Performance Review, Evaluation, and Communications; and Bureaux for Crisis Prevention and Recovery, Resources and Strategic Partnerships, Development Policy, and Management. Five regional bureaux, all headed by an assistant administrator, cover: Africa; Asia and the Pacific; the Arab states; Latin America and the Caribbean; and Europe and the Commonwealth of Independent States.

Administrator: KEMAL DERVIŞ (Turkey).

Associate Administrator: AD MELKERT (Netherlands).

Assistant Administrator and Director, Regional Bureau for Europe and the CIS: KORI UDOVIČKI (Serbia).

COUNTRY OFFICES

In almost every country receiving UNDP assistance there is an office, headed by the UNDP Resident Representative, who usually also serves as UN Resident Co-ordinator, responsible for the co-ordination of all UN technical assistance and operational development activities, advising the Government on formulating the country programme, ensuring that field activities are undertaken, and acting as the leader of the UN team of experts working in the country. The offices function as the primary presence of the UN in most developing countries. In some countries the Resident Co-ordinator also acts as the UN Humanitarian Co-ordinator.

OFFICES OF UN RESIDENT CO-ORDINATORS IN EASTERN EUROPE, RUSSIA AND CENTRAL ASIA

Armenia: 0010 Yerevan, 14 Petros Adamyan St; tel. (10) 56-60-73; fax (10) 54-38-11; e-mail registry.am@undp.org; internet www.undp.am; Resident Co-ordinator CONSUELO VIDAL.

Azerbaijan: AZ 1001 Baku, UN 50th Anniversary St 3; tel. (12) 498-98-88; fax (12) 492-24-91; e-mail office@un-az.org; internet www.un-az.org/undp; Resident Co-ordinator BRUNO POUEZAT.

Belarus: 220050 Minsk, vul. Kirov 17, 6th Floor; tel. (17) 227-48-76; fax (17) 226-03-40; e-mail dpi_unit_by@undp.org; internet undp.by; Resident Co-ordinator ANTONIUS BROEK.

Georgia: 0179 Tbilisi, Eristavi 9, UN House; tel. (32) 25-11-26; fax (32) 25-02-71; e-mail registry.ge@undp.org; internet www.undp.org.ge; Resident Co-ordinator ROBERT DERWYN WATKINS.

Kazakhstan: 050000 Almaty, Tole bi 67; tel. (727) 258-26-43; fax (727) 258-26-45; e-mail registry.kz@undp.org; internet www.undp.kz; Resident Co-ordinator XU HAOLIANG.

Kyrgyzstan: 720040 Bishkek, pr. Chui 160; tel. (312) 61-12-11; fax (312) 61-12-17; e-mail registry.kg@undp.org; internet www.undp.kg; Resident Co-ordinator NEAL WALKER.

Moldova: 277012 Chişinău-2012, str. 31 August 131; tel. (22) 22-00-45; fax (22) 22-00-41; e-mail registry.md@undp.org; internet www.undp.md; Resident Co-ordinator KAARINA IMMONEN.

Russia: 119034 Moscow, ul. Ostozhenka 28; tel. (495) 787-21-00; fax (495) 787-21-01; e-mail office@undp.ru; internet www.undp.ru; Resident Humanitarian Co-ordinator MARCO BORSOTTI.

Tajikistan: 734024 Dushanbe, kuchai Aini 39; tel. (474) 41-06-41; fax (474) 41-06-46; e-mail registry.tj@undp.org; internet www.undp.tj; Resident Co-ordinator MICHAEL JONES.

Turkmenistan: 744000 Ashgabat, ul. Galkynysh 40; tel. (12) 42 52 50; fax (12) 42 53 17; e-mail registry.tm@undp.org; internet www.undptkm.org; Resident Co-ordinator RICHARD YOUNG.

Ukraine: 01021 Kyiv, Klovsky Uzviz 1; tel. (44) 253-93-63; fax (44) 253-26-07; e-mail registry.ua@undp.org; internet www.undp.org.ua; Resident Co-ordinator FRANCIS M. O'DONNELL.

Uzbekistan: 100029 Tashkent, ul. Taras Shevchenko 4, Rms 601–604; tel. (71) 120-34-50; fax (71) 120-34-85; e-mail registry.uz@undp.org; internet www.undp.uz; Resident Co-ordinator ERCAN MURAT.

Activities

UNDP provides advisory and support services to governments and UN teams with the aim of advancing sustainable human development and building national development capabilities. Assistance is mostly non-monetary, comprising the provision of experts' services, consultancies, equipment and training for local workers. Developing countries themselves contribute significantly to the total project

costs in terms of personnel, facilities, equipment and supplies. UNDP also supports programme countries in attracting aid and utilizing it efficiently. A network of nine Sub-regional Resource Facilities (SURFs) has been established to strengthen and co-ordinate UNDP's role as a global knowledge provider and channel for sharing knowledge and experience.

During the late 1990s UNDP undertook an extensive internal process of reform, 'UNDP 2001', which placed increased emphasis on its activities in the field and on performance and accountability. In 2001 UNDP established a series of Thematic Trust Funds to enable increased support of priority programme activities. In accordance with the more results-oriented approach developed under the 'UNDP 2001' process UNDP introduced a new Multi-Year Funding Framework (MYFF), which outlined the country-driven goals around which funding was to be mobilized, integrating programme objectives, resources, budget and outcomes. The MYFF was to provide the basis for the Administrator's Business Plans for the same duration and enables policy coherence in the implementation of programmes at country, regional and global levels. A Results-Oriented Annual Report (ROAR) was produced for the first time in 2000 from data compiled by country offices and regional programmes. In September 2000 the first ever Ministerial Meeting of ministers of development co-operation and foreign affairs and other senior officials from donor and programme countries, convened in New York, USA, endorsed UNDP's shift to a results-based orientation.

In accordance with the second phase of the MYFF, covering 2004–07, UNDP focused on the following five practice areas: democratic governance; poverty reduction; energy and the environment; crisis prevention and recovery; and combating HIV/AIDS. Other important 'cross-cutting' themes, to be incorporated throughout the programme areas, included gender equality and the empowerment of women, information and communication technologies, and human rights. UNDP's Strategic Plan for the period 2008–11 emphasized UNDP's 'overarching' contribution to achieving sustainable human development through capacity development strategies, to be integrated into all areas of activity. Other objectives identified by the Plan included strengthening national ownership of development projects and promoting and facilitating South-South co-operation.

From the mid-1990s UNDP assumed a more active and integrative role within the UN system-wide development framework. UNDP Resident Representatives—usually also serving as UN Resident Co-ordinators, with responsibility for managing inter-agency co-operation on sustainable human development initiatives at country level—were to play a focal role in implementing this approach. In order to promote its co-ordinating function UNDP allocated increased resources to training and skill-sharing programmes. In 1997 the UNDP Administrator was appointed to chair the UN Development Group (UNDG), which was established as part of a series of structural reform measures initiated by the UN Secretary-General, with the aim of strengthening collaboration between all UN funds, programmes and bodies concerned with development. The UNDG promotes coherent policy at country level through the system of UN Resident Co-ordinators (see above), the Common Country Assessment mechanism (CCA, a country-based process for evaluating national development situations), and the UN Development Assistance Framework (UNDAF, the foundation for planning and co-ordinating development operations at country level, based on the CCA). Within the framework of the Administrator's Business Plans for 2000–03 a new Bureau for Resources and Strategic Partnerships was established to build and strengthen working partnerships with other UN bodies, donor and programme countries, international financial institutions and development banks, civil society organizations and the private sector. The Bureau was also to serve UNDP's regional bureaux and country offices through the exchange of information and promotion of partnership strategies.

MILLENNIUM DEVELOPMENT GOALS

UNDP, through its leadership of the UNDG and management of the Resident Co-ordinator system, has a co-ordinating function as the focus of UN system-wide efforts to achieve the so-called Millennium Development Goals (MDGs), pledged by 189 governments attending a summit meeting of the UN General Assembly in September 2000. The objectives were to establish a defined agenda to reduce poverty and improve the quality of lives of millions of people and to serve as a framework for measuring development. There are eight MDGs, as follows, for which one or more specific targets have been identified:

i) to eradicate extreme poverty and hunger, with the aim of reducing by 50% the number of people with an income of less than US $1 a day and those suffering from hunger by 2015, and to achieve full and productive employment and decent work for all, including women and young people;

ii) to achieve universal primary education by 2015;

iii) to promote gender equality and empower women, in particular to eliminate gender disparities in primary and secondary education by 2005 and at all levels by 2015;

iv) to reduce child mortality, with a target reduction of two-thirds in the mortality rate among children under five by 2015;

v) to improve maternal health, specifically to reduce by 75% the numbers of women dying in childbirth and to achieve universal access to reproductive health by 2015;

vi) to combat HIV/AIDS, malaria and other diseases, with targets to have halted and begun to reverse the incidence of HIV/AIDS, malaria and other major diseases by 2015 and to achieve universal access to treatment for HIV/AIDS for all those who need it by 2010;

vii) to ensure environmental sustainability, including targets to integrate the principles of sustainable development into country policies and programmes, to reduce by 50% the number of people without access to safe drinking water by 2015, to achieve significant improvement in the lives of at least 100m. slum dwellers by 2020;

viii) to develop a global partnership for development, including efforts to deal with international debt, to address the needs of least developed countries and landlocked and small island developing states, to develop decent and productive youth employment, to provide access to affordable, essential drugs in developing countries, and to make available the benefits of new technologies.

UNDP plays a leading role in efforts to integrate the MDGs into all aspects of UN activities at country level and to ensure the MDGs are incorporated into national development strategies. The Programme supports efforts by countries, as well as regions and sub-regions, to report on progress towards achievement of the goals, and on specific social, economic and environmental indicators, through the formulation of MDG reports. These form the basis of a global report, issued annually by the UN Secretary-General since mid-2002. UNDP also works to raise awareness of the MDGs and to support advocacy efforts at all levels, for example through regional publicity campaigns, target-specific publications and support for the Millennium Campaign to generate support for the goals in developing and developed countries. UNDP provides administrative and technical support to the Millennium Project, an independent advisory body established by the UN Secretary-General in 2002 to develop a practical action plan to achieve the MDGs. Financial support of the Project is channelled through a Millennium Trust Fund, administered by UNDP. In January 2005 the Millennium Project presented its report, based on extensive research conducted by teams of experts, which included recommendations for the international system to support country level development efforts and identified a series of Quick Wins to bring conclusive benefit to millions of people in the short-term. International commitment to achieve the MDGs by 2015 was reiterated at a World Summit, convened in September. In November 2007 the UN, in partnership with two major US companies, launched an online MDG Monitor to track progress and to support organizations working to achieve the goals.

UNDP, ESCAP and the Asian Development Bank established a regional partnership in 2001 to promote the MDGs. In June 2005 the partnership published a joint regional report on the implementation of the goals. A regional road map developed by the partnership with the aim of addressing regional challenges to the achievement of the MDGs was endorsed by regional governments in May 2007. In July participants in the North and Central Asian Millennium Development Goal Forum, sponsored by UNDP, ESCAP and the Asian Development Bank, and convened in Bishkek, Kyrgyzstan, approved a specialized sub-regional action plan for promoting the MDGs. The Forum urged regional governments to redirect the proceeds of recent strong economic growth towards the development of the education and health care sectors. Participants also focused on monitoring regional water resources, establishing strong legal frameworks for the protection of children's rights, and the need for targeting social assistance to poor and marginalized groups.

DEMOCRATIC GOVERNANCE

UNDP supports national efforts to ensure efficient and accountable governance, to improve the quality of democratic processes, and to build effective relations between the state, the private sector and civil society, which are essential to achieving sustainable development. As in other practice areas, UNDP assistance includes policy advice and technical support, capacity-building of institutions and individuals, advocacy and public information and communication, the promotion and brokering of dialogue, and knowledge networking and sharing of good practices.

UNDP works to strengthen parliaments and other legislative bodies as institutions of democratic participation. It assists with constitutional reviews and reform, training of parliamentary staff, and capacity-building of political parties and civil organizations as part of this objective. UNDP undertakes missions to help prepare for and ensure the conduct of free and fair elections. Increasingly, UNDP is also focused on building the long-term capacity of electoral institutions and practices within a country, for example voter registration, election observation, the establishment of electoral commissions, and voter and civic education projects.

Within its justice sector programme UNDP undertakes a variety of projects to improve access to justice, in particular for the poor and disadvantaged, and to promote judicial independence, legal reform and understanding of the legal system. UNDP also works to promote access to information, the integration of human rights issues into activities concerned with sustainable human development, as well as support for the international human rights system.

Since 1997 UNDP has been mandated to assist developing countries to fight corruption and improve accountability, transparency and integrity (ATI). It has worked to establish national and international partnerships in support of its anti-corruption efforts and used its role as a broker of knowledge and experience to uphold ATI principles at all levels of public financial management and governance. UNDP publishes case studies of its anti-corruption efforts and assists governments to conduct self-assessments of their public financial management systems.

In March 2002 a UNDP Governance Centre was inaugurated in Oslo, Norway, to enhance the role of UNDP in support of democratic governance and to assist countries to implement democratic reforms in order to achieve the MDGs. The mandate for the work of the Centre during the period 2005–09 incorporated activities in the following areas: governance and poverty eradication; governance and conflict prevention; civil society, empowerment and governance; and learning and capacity development.

Within the democratic governance practice area UNDP supports more than 300 projects at international, country and city levels designed to improve conditions for the urban poor, in particular through improvement in urban governance. The Local Initiative Facility for Urban Environment (LIFE) undertakes small-scale projects in low-income communities, in collaboration with local authorities, the private sector and community-based groups, and promotes a participatory approach to local governance. UNDP also works closely with the UN Capital Development Fund to implement projects in support of decentralized governance, which it has recognized as a key element to achieving sustainable development goals.

UNDP aims to ensure that, rather than creating an ever-widening 'digital divide', ongoing rapid advancements in information technology are harnessed by poorer countries to accelerate progress in achieving sustainable human development. UNDP advises governments on technology policy, promotes digital entrepreneurship in programme countries and works with private sector partners to provide reliable and affordable communications networks. The Bureau for Development Policy operates the Information and Communication Technologies for Development Programme, which aims to promote sustainable human development through increased utilization of information and communications technologies globally. The Programme aims to establish technology access centres in developing countries. A Sustainable Development Networking Programme focuses on expanding internet connectivity in poorer countries through building national capacities and supporting local internet sites. UNDP has used mobile internet units to train people even in isolated rural areas. In 1999 UNDP, in collaboration with an international communications company, Cisco Systems, and other partners, launched NetAid, an internet-based forum (accessible at www.netaid.org) for mobilizing and co-ordinating fundraising and other activities aimed at alleviating poverty and promoting sustainable human development in the developing world. With Cisco Systems and other partners, UNDP has worked to establish academies of information technology to support training and capacity-building in developing countries. UNDP and the World Bank jointly host the secretariat of the Digital Opportunity Task Force, a partnership between industrialized and developing countries, business and non-governmental organizations that was established in 2000. UNDP is a partner in the Global Digital Technology Initiative, launched in 2002 to strengthen the role of information and communications technologies in achieving the development goals of developing countries. In January 2004 UNDP and Microsoft Corporation announced an agreement to develop jointly information and communication technology (ICT) projects aimed at assisting developing countries to achieve the MDGs.

POVERTY REDUCTION

UNDP's activities to facilitate poverty eradication include support for capacity-building programmes and initiatives to generate sustainable livelihoods, for example by improving access to credit, land and technologies, and the promotion of strategies to improve education and health provision for the poorest elements of populations (with a focus on women and girls). UNDP aims to help governments to reassess their development priorities and to design initiatives for sustainable human development. In 1996, following the World Summit for Social Development, which was held in Copenhagen, Denmark, in March 1995, UNDP launched the Poverty Strategies Initiative (PSI) to strengthen national capacities to assess and monitor the extent of poverty and to combat the problem. All PSI projects were to involve representatives of governments, the private sector, social organizations and research institutions in policy debate and formulation. Following the introduction, in 1999, by the World Bank and IMF of Poverty Reduction Strategy Papers (PRSPs), UNDP has tended to direct its efforts to helping governments draft these documents, and, since 2001, has focused on linking the papers to efforts to achieve and monitor progress towards the MDGs. In early 2004 UNDP inaugurated the International Poverty Centre, in Brasília, Brazil, which aimed to foster the capacity of countries to formulate and implement poverty reduction strategies and to encourage South-South co-operation in all relevant areas of research and decision-making. In particular, the Centre aimed to assist countries to meet Millennium goals and targets through the research and implementation of pro-poor growth policies and social protection and human development strategies, and the monitoring of poverty and inequality.

UNDP country offices support the formulation of national human development reports (NHDRs), which aim to facilitate activities such as policy-making, the allocation of resources and monitoring progress towards poverty eradication and sustainable development. In addition, the preparation of Advisory Notes and Country Co-operation Frameworks by UNDP officials helps to highlight country-specific aspects of poverty eradication and national strategic priorities. In January 1998 the Executive Board adopted eight guiding principles relating to sustainable human development that were to be implemented by all country offices, in order to ensure a focus to UNDP activities. Since 1990 UNDP has published an annual *Human Development Report*, incorporating a Human Development Index, which ranks countries in terms of human development, using three key indicators: life expectancy, adult literacy and basic income required for a decent standard of living. In 1997 a Human Poverty Index and a Gender-related Development Index, which assesses gender equality on the basis of life expectancy, education and income, were introduced into the Report for the first time. Also in 1997 a UNDP scheme to support private sector and community-based initiatives to generate employment opportunities, MicroStart, became operational.

UNDP is committed to ensuring that the process of economic and financial globalization, including national and global trade, debt and capital flow policies, incorporates human development concerns. It was actively concerned to ensure that the Doha Development Round of World Trade Organization (WTO) negotiations achieve an expansion of trade opportunities and economic growth to less developed countries. With the UN Conference on Trade and Development (UNCTAD), UNDP manages a Global Programme on Globalization, Liberalization and Sustainable Human Development, which aims to support greater integration of developing countries into the global economy. UNDP manages a Trust Fund for the Integrated Framework for trade-related technical assistance to least-developed countries, which was inaugurated in 1997 by UNDP, the IMF, the International Trade Centre, UNCTAD, the World Bank and the WTO, and is the lead agency for its capacity development component.

In June 2007 UNDP and the Organization of the Black Sea Economic Co-operation (BSEC) signed an agreement aimed at enhancing existing UNDP-BSEC co-operation under the Black Sea Trade and Investment Promotion Programme (BSTIP), with the aim of promoting regional economic development and advancing trade and investment linkages between the BSEC member economies, with a view to reducing poverty and improving political dialogue.

In 1996 UNDP initiated a process of collaboration between city authorities world-wide to promote implementation of the commitments made at the 1995 Copenhagen summit for social development and to help to combat aspects of poverty and other urban problems, such as poor housing, transport, the management of waste disposal, water supply and sanitation. The World Alliance of Cities Against Poverty was formally launched in October 1997, in the context of the International Decade for the Eradication of Poverty. The sixth global Forum of the Alliance (convened every two years) took place in March 2008.

UNDP sponsors the International Day for the Eradication of Poverty, held annually on 17 October.

ENVIRONMENT AND ENERGY

UNDP plays a role in developing the agenda for international co-operation on environmental and energy issues, focusing on the relationship between energy policies, environmental protection, poverty and development. UNDP promotes the development of national capacities and other strategies that support sustainable development practices, for example through the formulation and implementation of Poverty Reduction Strategies and National Strategies for Sustainable Development.

UNDP recognizes that desertification and land degradation is a major cause of rural poverty and promotes sustainable land management, drought preparedness and reform of land tenure as means of addressing the problem. It also aims to reduce poverty caused by land degradation through implementation of environmental conventions

at a national and international level. In 2002 UNDP inaugurated an Integrated Drylands Development Programme which aimed to ensure that the needs of people living in drylands are met and considered at a local and national level. The Drylands Development Centre implements the programme in 19 African, Arab and West Asian countries. UNDP is also concerned with sustainable management of forestries, fisheries and agriculture. Its Biodiversity Global Programme assists developing countries and communities to integrate issues relating to sustainable practices and biodiversity into national and global practices. Since 1992 UNDP has administered a Small Grants Programme, funded by the Global Environment Facility (GEF), to support community-based initiatives concerned with biodiversity conservation, prevention of land degradation and the elimination of persistent organic pollutants. The Equator Initiative was inaugurated in 2002 as a partnership between UNDP, representatives of governments, civil society and businesses, with the aim of reducing poverty in communities along the equatorial belt by fostering local partnerships, harnessing local knowledge and promoting conservation and sustainable practices.

UNDP promotes clean energy technologies (through the Clean Development Mechanism) and aims to extend access to sustainable energy services, including the introduction of renewable alternatives to conventional fuels, as well as access to investment financing for sustainable energy. In December 2005 UNDP launched an MDG Carbon Facility, which aimed to channel increased carbon financing to projects that contribute directly to achieving MDGs in developing countries. The first projects under the MDG Carbon Facility were inaugurated in February 2008, in Uzbekistan, the former Yugoslav republic of Macedonia, Yemen and Rwanda. UNDP supports other efforts to promote international co-operation in the management of chemicals. It was actively involved in the development of a Strategic Approach to International Chemicals Management which was adopted by representatives of 100 governments at an international conference convened in Dubai, UAE, in February 2006.

UNDP works to ensure the effective governance of freshwater and aquatic resources, and promotes co-operation in transboundary water management. It works closely with other agencies to promote safe sanitation, ocean and coastal management, and community water supplies. In 1996 UNDP, with the World Bank and the Swedish International Development Agency, established a Global Water Partnership to promote and implement water resources management. UNDP, with the GEF, supports an extensive range of projects which incorporate development and ecological requirements in the sustainable management of international waters. These include the Global Mercury Project, The Yellow Sea Large Marine Ecosystem project, the Dnipro Basin Environment Programme, and projects in the Gulf of Guinea, Lake Tanganyika, and the Red Sea and Gulf of Aden.

In September 2001 UNDP, with the World Bank, UNEP and GEF, approved a new fund, comprising resources of some US \$100m., in support of a strategic partnership to reduce nutrient emissions and toxic contamination of the Danube/Black Sea Basin. UNDP was to focus on legal and policy reform at national level, monitoring systems, the development of environmental indicators and promoting public participation.

CRISIS PREVENTION AND RECOVERY

UNDP collaborates with other UN agencies in countries in crisis and with special circumstances to promote relief and development efforts, in order to secure the foundations for sustainable human development and thereby increase national capabilities to prevent or mitigate future crises. In particular, UNDP is concerned to achieve reconciliation, reintegration and reconstruction in affected countries, as well as to support emergency interventions and management and delivery of programme aid. It aims to facilitate the transition from relief to longer-term recovery and rehabilitation. Special development initiatives in post-conflict countries include the demobilization of former combatants and destruction of illicit small armaments, rehabilitation of communities for the sustainable reintegration of returning populations and the restoration and strengthening of democratic institutions. UNDP is seeking to incorporate conflict prevention into its development strategies. UNDP has established a mine action unit within its Bureau for Crisis Prevention and Recovery in order to strengthen national and local demining capabilities including surveying, mapping and clearance of anti-personnel landmines. UNDP also works closely with UNICEF to raise mine awareness and implement risk reduction education programmes, and manages global partnership projects concerned with training, legislation and the socio-economic impact of anti-personnel devices.

UNDP is the focal point within the UN system for strengthening national capacities for natural disaster reduction (prevention, preparedness and mitigation relating to natural, environmental and technological hazards). UNDP's Bureau of Crisis Prevention and Recovery, in conjunction with the Office for the Co-ordination of Humanitarian Affairs and the secretariat of the International

Strategy for Disaster Reduction, oversees the system-wide Capacity for Disaster Reduction Initiative (CADRI), which was inaugurated in 2007, superseding the former United Nations Disaster Management Training Programme. In February 2004 UNDP introduced a Disaster Risk Index that enabled vulnerability and risk to be measured and compared between countries and demonstrated the correspondence between human development and death rates following natural disasters. UNDP was actively involved in preparations for the second World Conference on Disaster Reduction, which was held in Kobe, Japan, in January 2005. Following the Kobe Conference UNDP initiated a new Global Risk Identification Programme. During 2005 the Inter-Agency Standing Committee, concerned with co-ordinating the international response to humanitarian disasters, developed a concept of providing assistance through a 'cluster' approach, comprising core areas of activity. UNDP was designated the lead agency for the Early Reconstruction and Recovery cluster, linking the immediate needs following a disaster with medium- and long-term recovery efforts.

During 2004–07 UNDP implemented the Sustainable Reintegration and Recovery in the North Caucasus programme, which aimed to address development challenges in the region. In 2004 UNDP assumed responsibility for co-ordinating UN assistance to the areas of Belarus, Russia and Ukraine that had been affected by the nuclear accident at Chernobyl in 1986, and in April 2008 it presented an action plan for the regeneration of these areas. In mid-2007 UNDP initiated activities with four other UN agencies to assist some 135,000 people affected by drought in Moldova.

HIV/AIDS

UNDP regards the HIV/AIDS pandemic as a major challenge to development, and advocates for making HIV/AIDS a focus of national planning and national poverty reduction strategies; supports decentralized action against HIV/AIDS at community level; helps to strengthen national capacities at all levels to combat the disease; and aims to link support for prevention activities, education and treatment with broader development planning and responses. UNDP places a particular focus on combating the spread of HIV/AIDS through the promotion of women's rights. UNDP is a co-sponsor, jointly with WHO, the World Bank, UNICEF, UNESCO, UNODC, ILO, UNFPA, WFP and UNHCR, of the Joint UN Programme on HIV/AIDS (UNAIDS), which became operational on 1 January 1996. UNAIDS co-ordinates UNDP's HIV and Development Programme. Since 2003 UNDP has worked in partnership with the Global Fund to Fight HIV/AIDS, TB and Malaria, in particular to support the local principal recipient of grant financing and to help to manage fund projects.

UNDP administers a global programme concerned with intellectual property and access to HIV/AIDS drugs, to promote wider and cheaper access to antiretroviral drugs. In December 2005 the World Trade Organization agreed to amend the agreement on Trade-Related Aspects of Intellectual Property Rights (TRIPS) to allow countries without a pharmaceutical manufacturing capability to import generic copies of patented medicines.

In February 2004 UNDP issued a report entitled *Reversing the Epidemic: Facts and Policy Options* covering the extent of the HIV/AIDS epidemic in South-Eastern Europe, Eastern Europe and the CIS and addressing policy options for action to arrest its further spread.

Finance

UNDP and its various funds and programmes are financed by the voluntary contributions of members of the United Nations and the Programme's participating agencies, as well as through cost-sharing by recipient governments and third-party donors. In 2008–11 total voluntary contributions were projected at US $20,600m., of which $5,300m. constituted regular (core) resources, $5,000m. bilateral donor contributions, $5,500m. contributions from multilateral partners and $4,800m. cost-sharing by programme country governments.

Publications

Annual Report of the Administrator.

Choices (quarterly).

Human Development Report (annually).

Poverty Report (annually).

Results-Oriented Annual Report.

Associated Funds and Programmes

UNDP is the central funding, planning and co-ordinating body for technical co-operation within the UN system. A number of associated funds and programmes, financed separately by means of voluntary contributions, provide specific services through the UNDP network. UNDP manages a trust fund to promote economic and technical co-operation among developing countries.

GLOBAL ENVIRONMENT FACILITY (GEF)

The GEF, which is managed jointly by UNDP, the World Bank (which hosts its secretariat) and UNEP, began operations in 1991 and was restructured in 1994. Its aim is to support projects concerning climate change, the conservation of biological diversity, the protection of international waters, reducing the depletion of the ozone layer in the atmosphere, and (since October 2002) arresting land degradation and addressing the issue of persistent organic pollutants. The GEF acts as the financial mechanism for the Convention on Biological Diversity and the UN Framework Convention on Climate Change. UNDP is responsible for capacity-building, targeted research, pre-investment activities and technical assistance. UNDP also administers the Small Grants Programme of the GEF, which supports community-based activities by local non-governmental organizations, and the Country Dialogue Workshop Programme, which promotes dialogue on national priorities with regard to the GEF. In August 2006 some 32 donor countries pledged US $3,130m. for the fourth periodic replenishment of GEF funds (GEF-4), covering the period 2007–10. At February 2008 UNDP GEF-funded projects amounted to $7,470m. for 560 initiatives. An additional $479.7m. had been committed under the Small Grants Programme.

Chair. and CEO: MONIQUE BARBUT (France).

Executive Co-ordinator UNDP-GEF Unit: YANNICK GLEMAREC; 304 East 45th St, 9th Floor, New York, NY 10017, USA; fax (212) 906-6998; e-mail gefinfo@undp.org.

MONTREAL PROTOCOL

Through its Montreal Protocol Unit UNDP collaborates with public and private partners in developing countries to assist them in eliminating the use of ozone-depleting substances (ODS), in accordance with the Montreal Protocol to the Vienna Convention for the Protection of the Ozone Layer, through the design, monitoring and evaluation of ODS phase-out projects and programmes. In particular, UNDP provides technical assistance and training, national capacity-building and demonstration projects and technology transfer investment projects. By December 2006 the Executive Committee of the Montreal Protocol had approved grants for projects and activities that had resulted in the elimination of an estimated 158,737 metric tons of ODS production.

UNDP DRYLANDS DEVELOPMENT CENTRE (DDC)

The Centre, based in Nairobi, Kenya, was established in February 2002, superseding the former UN Office to Combat Desertification and Drought (UNSO). (UNSO had been established following the conclusion, in October 1994, of the UN Convention to Combat Desertification in Those Countries Experiencing Serious Drought and/or Desertification, Particularly in Africa; in turn, UNSO had replaced the former UN Sudano-Sahelian Office.) The DDC was to focus on the following areas: ensuring that national development planning takes account of the needs of dryland communities, particularly in poverty reduction strategies; helping countries to cope with the effects of climate variability, especially drought, and to prepare for future climate change; and addressing local issues affecting the utilization of resources.

Director: PHILIP DOBIE (United Kingdom); POB 30552, 00100 Nairobi, Kenya; tel. (20) 7624640; fax (20) 7624648; e-mail ddc@undp.org; internet www.undp.org/drylands.

UNITED NATIONS DEVELOPMENT FUND FOR WOMEN (UNIFEM)

UNIFEM is the UN's lead agency in addressing the issues relating to women in development and promoting the rights of women worldwide. The Fund provides direct financial and technical support to enable low-income women in developing countries to increase earnings, gain access to labour-saving technologies and otherwise improve the quality of their lives. It also funds activities that include women in decision-making related to mainstream development projects. UNIFEM has supported the preparation of national reports in 30 countries and used the priorities identified in these reports and in other regional initiatives to formulate a Women's Development Agenda for the 21st century. Through these efforts, UNIFEM played an active role in the preparation for the UN Fourth World Conference on Women, which was held in Beijing, People's Republic of China, in

September 1995. UNIFEM participated at a special session of the General Assembly convened in June 2000 to review the conference, entitled Women 2000: Gender Equality, Development and Peace for the 21st Century (Beijing + 5). In March 2001 UNIFEM, in collaboration with International Alert, launched a Millennium Peace Prize for Women. UNIFEM maintains that the empowerment of women is a key to combating the HIV/AIDS pandemic, in view of the fact that women and adolescent girls are often culturally, biologically and economically more vulnerable to infection and more likely to bear responsibility for caring for the sick. In March 2002 UNIFEM launched a three-year programme aimed at making the gender and human rights dimensions of the pandemic central to policy-making in 10 countries. A new online resource (www.genderandaid s.org) on the gender dimensions of HIV/AIDS was launched in February 2003. Following the massive earthquake and tsunami that struck parts of the Indian Ocean in late December 2004, UNIFEM undertook to promote the needs and rights of women and girls in all emergency relief and reconstruction efforts, in particular in Indonesia, Sri Lanka and Somalia, and supported capacity-building of grass-roots organizations. UNIFEM was a co-founder of WomenWatch (accessible online at www.un.org/women-watch), a UN system-wide resource for the advancement of gender equality. UNIFEM manages the UN's Trust Fund in Support of Actions to Eliminate Violence Against Women (established in 1996), which by early 2008 had awarded grants in excess of US \$19.0m. in support of more than 263 initiatives in around 115 countries. In November 2007 UNIFEM launched a year-long campaign, 'Say NO to Violence against Women', to raise awareness of the issue and generate world-wide support for efforts to end violence against women. Programme expenditure in 2006 totalled \$57.0m.

Director: INÉS ALBERDI (Spain); 304 East 45th St, 15th Floor, New York, NY 10017, USA; tel. (212) 906-6400; fax (212) 906-6705; e-mail unifem@undp.org; internet www.unifem.org.

UNITED NATIONS VOLUNTEERS (UNV)

The United Nations Volunteers is an important source of middle-level skills for the UN development system supplied at modest cost, particularly in the least-developed countries. Volunteers expand the scope of UNDP project activities by supplementing the work of international and host-country experts and by extending the influence of projects to local community levels. UNV also supports technical co-operation within and among the developing countries by encouraging volunteers from the countries themselves and by forming regional exchange teams comprising such volunteers. UNV is involved in areas such as peace-building, elections, human rights, humanitarian relief and community-based environmental programmes, in addition to development activities.

The UN International Short-term Advisory (UNISTAR) Programme, which is the private sector development arm of UNV, has increasingly focused its attention on countries in the process of economic transition. Since 1994 UNV has administered UNDP's Transfer of Knowledge Through Expatriate Nationals (TOKTEN) programme, which was initiated in 1977 to enable specialists and professionals from developing countries to contribute to development efforts in their countries of origin through short-term technical assignments. In March 2000 UNV established an Online Volunteering Service to connect development organizations and volunteers using the internet. As at November 2006 some 9,000 volunteers from 169 countries had been engaged in online collaborations.

At the end of April 2008 5,647 UNVs were serving in 123 countries. At that time the total number of people who had served under the initiative amounted to more than 35,000 in over 140 countries.

Executive Co-ordinator: FLAVIA PANSIERI (Italy); POB 260111, 53153 Bonn, Germany; tel. (228) 8152000; fax (228) 8152001; e-mail information@unvolunteers.org; internet www.unv.org.

United Nations Environment Programme—UNEP

Address: POB 30552, Nairobi 00100, Kenya.

Telephone: (20) 621234; **fax:** (20) 623927; **e-mail:** info@unep.org; **internet:** www.unep.org.

The United Nations Environment Programme was established in 1972 by the UN General Assembly, following recommendations of the 1972 UN Conference on the Human Environment, in Stockholm, Sweden, to encourage international co-operation in matters relating to the human environment.

Organization

(October 2008)

GOVERNING COUNCIL

The main functions of the Governing Council (which meets every two years in ordinary sessions, with special sessions taking place in the alternate years) are to promote international co-operation in the field of the environment and to provide general policy guidance for the direction and co-ordination of environmental programmes within the UN system. It comprises representatives of 58 states, elected by the UN General Assembly, for four-year terms, on a regional basis. The Global Ministerial Environment Forum (first convened in 2000) meets annually as part of the Governing Council's regular and special sessions. The Governing Council is assisted in its work by a Committee of Permanent Representatives.

SECRETARIAT

Offices and divisions at UNEP headquarters include the Offices of the Executive Director and Deputy Executive Director; the Secretariat for Governing Bodies; Offices for Evaluation and Oversight, Programme Co-ordination and Management, and Resource Mobilization; and divisions of communications and public information, early warning and assessment, policy development and law, policy implementation, technology and industry and economics, regional co-operation and representation, environmental conventions, and Global Environment Facility co-ordination.

Executive Director: ACHIM STEINER (Germany).

REGIONAL OFFICES

UNEP maintains six regional offices. These work to initiate and promote UNEP objectives and to ensure that all programme formulation and delivery meets the specific needs of countries and regions. They also provide a focal point for building national, sub-regional and regional partnership and enhancing local participation in UNEP initiatives. A co-ordination office has been established at headquarters to promote regional policy integration, to co-ordinate programme planning, and to provide necessary services to the regional offices.

Europe: 11–13 chemin des Anémones, 1219 Châtelaine, Geneva, Switzerland; tel. 229178279; fax 229178024; e-mail roe@unep.ch; internet www.unep.ch/roe.

UNEP Liaison Office in Moscow: 119034 Moscow, 28 Ostozhenka St, Russia; tel. (495) 787-21-56; fax (495) 787-77-63; e-mail gudyma .unep@undp.ru.

OTHER OFFICES

Convention on International Trade in Endangered Species of Wild Fauna and Flora (CITES): 15 chemin des Anémones, 1219 Châtelaine, Geneva, Switzerland; tel. 229178139; fax 227973417; e-mail info@cites.org; internet www.cites.org; Sec.-Gen. WILLEM WOUTER WIJNSTEKERS (Netherlands).

Global Programme of Action for the Protection of the Marine Environment from Land-based Activities: POB 16227, 2500 BE The Hague, Netherlands; tel. (70) 3114460; fax (70) 3456648; e-mail gpa@unep.nl; internet www.gpa.unep.org; Officer-in-Charge ANJAN DATTA (Bangladesh).

Secretariat of the Basel Convention: CP 356, 13–15 chemin des Anémones, 1219 Châtelaine, Geneva, Switzerland; tel. 229178218; fax 227973454; e-mail sbc@unep.ch; internet www.basel.int; Exec. Sec. KATHERINA KUMMER PEIRY.

Secretariat of the Multilateral Fund for the Implementation of the Montreal Protocol: 1800 McGill College Ave, 27th Floor, Montréal, QC, Canada H3A 3J6; tel. (514) 282-1122; fax (514) 282-0068; e-mail secretariat@unmfs.org; internet www.multilateralfund .org; Chief Officer MARIA NOLAN.

Secretariat of the UN Framework Convention on Climate Change: Haus Carstanjen, Martin-Luther-King-Str. 8, 53175 Bonn, Germany; tel. (228) 815-1000; fax (228) 815-1999; e-mail secretariat@ unfccc.int; internet www.unfccc.int; Exec. Sec. YVO DE BOER (Netherlands).

UNEP/CMS (Convention on the Conservation of Migratory Species of Wild Animals) Secretariat: Hermann-Ehlers-Str. 10, 53113 Bonn, Germany; tel. (228) 8152402; fax (228) 8152449; e-mail secretariat@cms.int; internet www.cms.int; Exec. Sec. ROBERT HEPWORTH.

UNEP Chemicals: International Environment House, 11–13 chemin des Anémones, 1219 Châtelaine, Geneva, Switzerland; tel. 229178192; fax 227973460; e-mail chemicals@unep.ch; internet www.chem.unep.ch; Head PER MENZONY BAKKEN (Norway).

UNEP Division of Technology, Industry and Economics: 15 rue de Milan, 75441 Paris, Cedex 09 France; tel. 1-44-37-14-50; fax 1-44-37-14-74; e-mail unep.tie@unep.fr; internet www.unep.fr; Dir SILVIE LEMMET (France).

UNEP International Environmental Technology Centre (IETC): 2–110 Ryokuchi koen, Tsurumi-ku, Osaka 538-0036, Japan; tel. (6) 6915-4581; fax (6) 6915-0304; e-mail ietc@unep.or.jp; internet www.unep.or.jp; Exec. Dir (vacant).

UNEP Ozone Secretariat: POB 30552, Nairobi, Kenya; tel. (20) 762-3850; fax (20) 762-4691; e-mail ozoneinfo@unep.org; internet ozone.unep.org; Exec. Sec. MARCO GONZÁLEZ (Costa Rica).

UNEP-SCBD (Convention on Biological Diversity—Secretariat): 413 St Jacques St, Office 800, Montréal, QC, Canada H2Y 1N9; tel. (514) 288-2220; fax (514) 288-6588; e-mail secretariat@cbd.int; internet www.cbd.int; Exec. Sec. AHMED DJOGHLAF (Algeria).

UNEP Secretariat for the UN Scientific Committee on the Effects of Atomic Radiation: Vienna International Centre, Wagramerstrasse 5, POB 500, 1400 Vienna, Austria; tel. (1) 26060-4330; fax (1) 26060-5902; e-mail malcolm.crick@unscear.org; internet www.unscear.org; Sec. Dr MALCOLM CRICK.

Activities

UNEP serves as a focal point for environmental action within the UN system. It aims to maintain a constant watch on the changing state of the environment; to analyse the trends; to assess the problems using a wide range of data and techniques; and to promote projects leading to environmentally sound development. It plays a catalytic and co-ordinating role within and beyond the UN system. Many UNEP projects are implemented in co-operation with other UN agencies, particularly UNDP, the World Bank group, FAO, UNESCO and WHO. About 45 intergovernmental organizations outside the UN system and 60 international non-governmental organizations have official observer status on UNEP's Governing Council, and, through the Environment Liaison Centre in Nairobi, UNEP is linked to more than 6,000 non-governmental bodies concerned with the environment. UNEP also sponsors international conferences, programmes, plans and agreements regarding all aspects of the environment.

In February 1997 the Governing Council, at its 19th session, adopted a ministerial declaration (the Nairobi Declaration) on UNEP's future role and mandate, which recognized the organization as the principal UN body working in the field of the environment and as the leading global environmental authority, setting and over-seeing the international environmental agenda. In June a special session of the UN General Assembly, referred to as 'Rio + 5', was convened to review the state of the environment and progress achieved in implementing the objectives of the UN Conference on Environment and Development (UNCED), held in Rio de Janeiro, Brazil, in June 1992. The meeting adopted a Programme for Further Implementation of Agenda 21 (a programme of activities to promote sustainable development, adopted by UNCED) in order to intensify efforts in areas such as energy, freshwater resources and technology transfer. The meeting confirmed UNEP's essential role in advancing the Programme and as a global authority promoting a coherent legal and political approach to the environmental challenges of sustainable development. An extensive process of restructuring and realignment of functions was subsequently initiated by UNEP, and a new organizational structure reflecting the decisions of the Nairobi Declaration was implemented during 1999. UNEP played a leading role in preparing for the World Summit on Sustainable Development (WSSD), held in August–September 2002 in Johannesburg, South Africa, to assess strategies for strengthening the implementation of Agenda 21. Governments participating in the conference adopted the Johannesburg Declaration and WSSD Plan of Implementation, in which they strongly reaffirmed commitment to the principles underlying Agenda 21 and also pledged support to all internationally-agreed development goals, including the UN Millennium Development Goals adopted by governments attending a summit meeting of the UN General Assembly in September 2000. Participating governments made concrete commitments to attaining several specific objectives in the areas of water, energy, health, agriculture and fisheries, and biodiversity. These included a reduction by one-half in the proportion of people world-wide lacking access to clean water or good sanitation by 2015, the restocking of depleted fisheries by 2015, a reduction in the ongoing loss in biodiversity by 2010, and the production and utilization of chemicals without causing harm to human beings and the environment by 2020. Participants determined to increase usage of renewable energy sources and to develop

integrated water resources management and water efficiency plans. A large number of partnerships between governments, private-sector interests and civil society groups were announced at the conference.

In May 2000 UNEP's first annual Global Ministerial Environment Forum (GMEF) was held in Malmö, Sweden, attended by environment ministers and other government delegates from more than 130 countries. Participants reviewed policy issues in the field of the environment and addressed issues such as the impact on the environment of population growth, the depletion of earth's natural resources, climate change and the need for fresh water supplies. The Forum issued the Malmö Declaration, which identified the effective implementation of international agreements on environmental matters at national level as the most pressing challenge for policy-makers. The Declaration emphasized the importance of mobilizing domestic and international resources and urged increased co-operation from civil society and the private sector in achieving sustainable development. The GMEF was subsequently convened annually.

ENVIRONMENTAL ASSESSMENT AND EARLY WARNING

The Nairobi Declaration resolved that the strengthening of UNEP's information, monitoring and assessment capabilities was a crucial element of the organization's restructuring, in order to help establish priorities for international, national and regional action, and to ensure the efficient and accurate dissemination of emerging environmental trends and emergencies.

In 1995 UNEP launched the Global Environment Outlook (GEO) process of environmental assessment. UNEP is assisted in its analysis of the state of the global environment by an extensive network of collaborating centres. The fourth umbrella report on the GEO assessment process (GEO-4) was issued in October 2007, identifying climate change, land degradation and loss of biodiversity as the world's greatest environmental challenges. The following regional and national GEO reports have been produced in recent years: Africa Environment Outlook (2002), Brazil Environment Outlook (2002), Caucasus Environment Outlook (2002), North America's Environment (2002), Latin America and the Caribbean Environment Outlook (2003), Andean Environment Outlook (2003), Pacific Environment Outlook (2005), Caribbean Environment Outlook (2005), Atlantic and Indian Oceans Environment Outlook (2005), and Africa Environment Outlook -2 (2006). UNEP is leading a major Global International Waters Assessment (GIWA) to consider all aspects of the world's water-related issues, in particular problems of shared transboundary waters, and of future sustainable management of water resources. UNEP is also a sponsoring agency of the Joint Group of Experts on the Scientific Aspects of Marine Environmental Pollution and contributes to the preparation of reports on the state of the marine environment and on the impact of land-based activities on that environment. In November 1995 UNEP published a Global Biodiversity Assessment, which was the first comprehensive study of biological resources throughout the world. The UNEP—World Conservation Monitoring Centre (UNEP—WCMC), established in June 2000 in Cambridge, United Kingdom, manages and interprets data concerning biodiversity and ecosystems, and makes the results available to governments and businesses. In 2007 the Centre undertook the 2010 Biodiversity Indicators Programme, with the aim of supporting decision-making by governments so as to reduce the threat of extinction facing vulnerable species. UNEP is a partner in the International Coral Reef Action Network—ICRAN, which was established in 2000 to manage and protect coral reefs world-wide. In June 2001 UNEP launched the Millennium Ecosystems Assessment, which was completed in March 2005. Other major assessments undertaken included GIWA (see above); the Assessment of Impact and Adaptation to Climate Change; the Solar and Wind Energy Resource Assessment; the Regionally-Based Assessment of Persistent Toxic Substances; the Land Degradation Assessment in Drylands; and the Global Methodology for Mapping Human Impacts on the Biosphere (GLOBIO) project.

UNEP's environmental information network includes the Global Resource Information Database (GRID), which converts collected data into information usable by decision-makers. The UNEP-INFO-TERRA programme facilitates the exchange of environmental information through an extensive network of national 'focal points'. By October 2008 177 countries were participating in the network. Through UNEP-INFOTERRA UNEP promotes public access to environmental information, as well as participation in environmental concerns. UNEP aims to establish in every developing region an Environment and Natural Resource Information Network (ENRIN) in order to make available technical advice and manage environmental information and data for improved decision-making and action-planning in countries most in need of assistance. UNEP aims to integrate its information resources in order to improve access to information and to promote its international exchange. This has been pursued through UNEPnet, an internet-based interactive environmental information- and data-sharing facility.

UNEP's information, monitoring and assessment structures also serve to enhance early-warning capabilities and to provide accurate information during an environmental emergency.

POLICY DEVELOPMENT AND LAW

UNEP aims to promote the development of policy tools and guidelines in order to achieve the sustainable management of the world environment. At a national level it assists governments to develop and implement appropriate environmental instruments and aims to co-ordinate policy initiatives. Training workshops in various aspects of environmental law and its applications are conducted. UNEP supports the development of new legal, economic and other policy instruments to improve the effectiveness of existing environmental agreements.

UNEP was instrumental in the drafting of a Convention on Biological Diversity (CBD) to preserve the immense variety of plant and animal species, in particular those threatened with extinction. The Convention entered into force at the end of 1993; by July 2008 189 states and the European Community were parties to the CBD. The CBD's Cartagena Protocol on Biosafety (so called as it had been addressed at an extraordinary session of parties to the CBD convened in Cartagena, Colombia, in February 1999) was adopted at a meeting of parties to the CBD held in Montréal, Canada, in January 2000, and entered into force in September 2003; by July 2008 the Protocol had been ratified by 146 states parties and the European Community. The Protocol regulates the transboundary movement and use of living modified organisms resulting from biotechnology in order to reduce any potential adverse effects on biodiversity and human health. It establishes an Advanced Informed Agreement procedure to govern the import of such organisms. In January 2002 UNEP launched a major project aimed at supporting developing countries with assessing the potential health and environmental risks and benefits of genetically modified (GM) crops, in preparation for the Protocol's entry into force. In February the parties to the CBD and other partners convened a conference, in Montréal, to address ways in which the traditional knowledge and practices of local communities could be preserved and used to conserve highly threatened species and ecosystems. The sixth conference of parties to the CBD, held in April 2002, adopted detailed voluntary guidelines concerning access to genetic resources and sharing the benefits attained from such resources with the countries and local communities where they originate; a global work programme on forests; and a set of guiding principles for combating alien invasive species. UNEP supports co-operation for biodiversity assessment and management in selected developing regions and for the development of strategies for the conservation and sustainable exploitation of individual threatened species (e.g. the Global Tiger Action Plan). It also provides assistance for the preparation of individual country studies and strategies to strengthen national biodiversity management and research. UNEP administers the Convention on International Trade in Endangered Species of Wild Flora and Fauna (CITES), which entered into force in 1975 and comprised 172 states parties at January 2008.

In October 1994 87 countries, meeting under UN auspices, signed a Convention to Combat Desertification (see UNDP Drylands Development Centre), which aimed to provide a legal framework to counter the degradation of arid regions. An estimated 75% of all drylands have suffered some land degradation, affecting approximately 1,000m. people in 110 countries. UNEP continues to support the implementation of the Convention, as part of its efforts to protect land resources. UNEP also aims to improve the assessment of dryland degradation and desertification in co-operation with governments and other international bodies, as well as identifying the causes of degradation and measures to overcome these.

UNEP is the lead UN agency for promoting environmentally sustainable water management. It regards the unsustainable use of water as the most urgent environmental and sustainable development issue, and estimates that two-thirds of the world's population will suffer chronic water shortages by 2025, owing to rising demand for drinking water as a result of growing populations, decreasing quality of water because of pollution, and increasing requirements of industries and agriculture. In 2000 UNEP adopted a new water policy and strategy, comprising assessment, management and co-ordination components. The Global International Waters Assessment (see above) is the primary framework for the assessment component. The management component includes the Global Programme of Action (GPA) for the Protection of the Marine Environment from Land-based Activities (adopted in November 1995), and UNEP's freshwater programme and regional seas programme. The GPA for the Protection of the Marine Environment for Land-based Activities focuses on the effects of activities such as pollution on freshwater resources, marine biodiversity and the coastal ecosystems of small-island developing states. UNEP aims to develop a similar global instrument to ensure the integrated management of freshwater resources. It promotes international co-operation in the management of river basins and coastal areas and for the development of tools and guidelines to achieve the sustainable management

of freshwater and coastal resources. In 2007 UNEP initiated a South-South Co-operation programme on technology and capacity-building for the management of water resources. UNEP provides scientific, technical and administrative support to facilitate the implementation and co-ordination of 14 regional seas conventions and 13 regional plans of action, and is developing a strategy to strengthen collaboration in their implementation. The new water policy and strategy emphasizes the need for improved co-ordination of existing activities. UNEP aims to play an enhanced role within relevant co-ordination mechanisms, such as the UN open-ended informal consultation process on oceans and the law of the sea.

In 1996 UNEP, in collaboration with FAO, began to work towards promoting and formulating a legally binding international convention on prior informed consent (PIC) for hazardous chemicals and pesticides in international trade, extending a voluntary PIC procedure of information exchange undertaken by more than 100 governments since 1991. The Convention was adopted at a conference held in Rotterdam, Netherlands, in September 1998, and entered into force in February 2004. It aims to reduce risks to human health and the environment by restricting the production, export and use of hazardous substances and enhancing information exchange procedures.

In conjunction with UN-Habitat, UNDP, the World Bank and other organizations and institutions, UNEP promotes environmental concerns in urban planning and management through the Sustainable Cities Programme, as well as regional workshops concerned with urban pollution and the impact of transportation systems. In 1994 UNEP inaugurated an International Environmental Technology Centre (IETC), with offices in Osaka and Shiga, Japan, in order to strengthen the capabilities of developing countries and countries with economies in transition to promote environmentally sound management of cities and freshwater reservoirs through technology co-operation and partnerships.

UNEP has played a key role in global efforts to combat risks to the ozone layer, resultant climatic changes and atmospheric pollution. UNEP worked in collaboration with the World Meteorological Organization to formulate the UN Framework Convention on Climate Change (UNFCCC), with the aim of reducing the emission of gases that have a warming effect on the atmosphere, and has remained an active participant in the ongoing process to review and enforce the implementation of the Convention and of its Kyoto Protocol. UNEP was the lead agency in formulating the 1987 Montreal Protocol to the Vienna Convention for the Protection of the Ozone Layer (1985), which provided for a 50% reduction in the production of chlorofluorocarbons (CFCs) by 2000. An amendment to the Protocol was adopted in 1990, which required complete cessation of the production of CFCs by 2000 in industrialized countries and by 2010 in developing countries. The Copenhagen Amendment, adopted in 1992, stipulated the phasing out of production of hydrochlorofluorocarbons (HCFCs) by 2030 in developed countries and by 2040 in developing nations. In 1997 the ninth Conference of the Parties (COP) to the Vienna Convention adopted a further amendment which aimed to introduce a licensing system for all controlled substances. The 11th COP, meeting in Beijing, People's Republic of China, in November–December 1999, adopted the Beijing Amendment, which imposed tighter controls on the import and export of HCFCs, and on the production and consumption of bromochloromethane (Halon-1011, an industrial solvent and fire extinguisher). The Beijing Amendment entered into force in December 2001. At the 19th COP (also the 20th anniversary meeting of the adoption of the Montreal Protocol), held in September 2007, states parties to the Vienna Convention agreed to advance the deadline for the elimination of HCFCs: production and consumption were to be frozen by 2013, and were to be phased out in developed countries by 2020 and in developing countries by 2030. A Multilateral Fund for the Implementation of the Montreal Protocol was established in June 1990 to promote the use of suitable technologies and the transfer of technologies to developing countries. UNEP, UNDP, the World Bank and UNIDO are the sponsors of the Fund, which by April 2008 had approved financing for about 5,700 projects and activities in 146 developing countries at a cost of around US $2,280m. Commitments of $400.4m. were made to the sixth replenishment of the Fund, covering the three-year period 2006–08. (The total budget for 2006–08 was $470.0m., the remainder deriving from the following sources: $59.6m. to be carried over from the 2003–05 triennium and $10m. to be provided from interest accruing.)

UNEP provides the secretariat for the Pan-European Biological and Landscape Diversity Strategy. UNEP also supports the preparation of an additional Protocol on Water and Health to the ECE Convention on Transboundary Waters, and a European Charter on Transport, Environment and Health.

POLICY IMPLEMENTATION

UNEP's Division of Environmental Policy Implementation incorporates two main functions: technical co-operation and response to environmental emergencies.

With the UN Office for the Co-ordination of Humanitarian Assistance (OCHA), UNEP has established a joint Environment Unit to mobilize and co-ordinate international assistance and expertise for countries facing environmental emergencies and natural disasters. In mid-1999 UNEP and UN-Habitat jointly established a Balkan Task Force (subsequently renamed UNEP Balkans Unit) to assess the environmental impact of NATO's aerial offensive against the then Federal Republic of Yugoslavia. In November 2000 the Unit led a field assessment to evaluate reports of environmental contamination by debris from NATO ammunition containing depleted uranium, concluding that there was no evidence of widespread contamination of the ground surface by depleted uranium, but that considerable scientific uncertainties remained, for example as to the safety of groundwater and the longer-term behaviour of depleted uranium in the environment, and recommending precautionary action. In 2007 UNEP's Post-Conflict Disaster Management Branch was established, replacing earlier initiatives, and in 2008 it was engaged in rehabilitation programmes in Afghanistan, Côte d'Ivoire, Lebanon, Nigeria and Sudan, while also focusing on the environmental effects of depleted uranium. Under its Environment, Conflict and Peace-building Programme, initiated in 2007, UNEP analyses the environmental causes of conflict, for example disputes over high-value commodities such as petroleum or diamonds, or over the control of scarce resources such as fertile land or water.

UNEP, together with UNDP and the World Bank, is an implementing agency of the Global Environment Facility (GEF), which was established in 1991 as a mechanism for international co-operation in projects concerned with biological diversity, climate change, international waters and depletion of the ozone layer. UNEP services the Scientific and Technical Advisory Panel, which provides expert advice on GEF programmes and operational strategies.

Through the GEF UNEP supports the Caspian Environment Programme (CEP, accessible at www.caspianenvironment.org), which was founded in 1995 by the Governments of Azerbaijan, Iran, Kazakhstan, Russia and Turkmenistan, following an environmental assessment conducted by UNEP, UNDP and the World Bank, and aims to reduce pollution in and to promote the sustainable management of the bioresources of the Caspian Sea. In November 2003 a Framework Convention for the Protection of the Marine Environment of the Caspian Sea (Tehran Convention), which had been negotiated under UNEP auspices, was signed by the five countries. The Convention aimed to support the activities of the CEP and strengthen co-ordinated efforts to ensure the sustainable use of the Sea's resources, and the protection and rehabilitation of its environment.

TECHNOLOGY, INDUSTRY AND ECONOMICS

The use of inappropriate industrial technologies and the widespread adoption of unsustainable production and consumption patterns have been identified as being inefficient in the use of renewable resources and wasteful, in particular in the use of energy and water. UNEP aims to encourage governments and the private sector to develop and adopt policies and practices that are cleaner and safer, make efficient use of natural resources, incorporate environmental costs, ensure the environmentally sound management of chemicals, and reduce pollution and risks to human health and the environment. In collaboration with other organizations and agencies UNEP works to define and formulate international guidelines and agreements to address these issues. UNEP also promotes the transfer of appropriate technologies and organizes conferences and training workshops to provide sustainable production practices. Relevant information is disseminated through the International Cleaner Production Information Clearing House. UNEP, together with UNIDO, has established 34 National Cleaner Production Centres to promote a preventive approach to industrial pollution control. In October 1998 UNEP adopted an International Declaration on Cleaner Production, with a commitment to implement cleaner and more sustainable production methods and to monitor results. In 1997 UNEP and the Coalition for Environmentally Responsible Economies initiated the Global Reporting Initiative, which, with participation by corporations, business associations and other organizations and stakeholders, develops guidelines for voluntary reporting by companies on their economic, environmental and social performance. In April 2002 UNEP launched the 'Life-Cycle Initiative', which aims to assist governments, businesses and other consumers with adopting environmentally sound policies and practice, in view of the upward trend in global consumption patterns. UNEP Finance Initiatives (FI) is a programme encouraging banks, insurance companies and other financial institutions to invest in an environmentally responsible way: an annual FI Global Roundtable meeting is held, together with regional meetings. In April 2007 UNEP hosted the first Business for Environment meeting, on corporate environmental responsibility, in Singapore, and in October UNEP's 24th annual consultative meeting with representatives of business and industry took place in Sao Paulo, Brazil. During 2007 UNEP's Programme on Sustainable Consumption and Production established an International Panel for Sustainable Resource Management (comprising experts whose initial subjects of study were to be the environmental risks of biofuels and of metal recycling), and initiated forums for businesses and non-governmental organizations in this field.

UNEP provides institutional servicing to the Basel Convention on the Control of Transboundary Movements of Hazardous Wastes and their Disposal, which was adopted in 1989 with the aim of preventing the disposal of wastes from industrialized countries in countries that have no processing facilities. In March 1994 the second meeting of parties to the Convention determined to ban the exportation of hazardous wastes between industrialized and developing countries. The third meeting of parties to the Convention, held in 1995, proposed that the ban should be incorporated into the Convention as an amendment. The resulting so-called Ban Amendment (prohibiting exports of hazardous wastes for final disposal and recycling from states and/or parties also belonging to OECD and, or, the European Union, and from Liechtenstein, to any other state party to the Convention) required ratification by three-quarters of the 62 signatory states present at the time of adoption before it could enter into effect; by July 2008 the Ban Amendment had been ratified by 63 parties. In 1998 the technical working group of the Convention agreed a new procedure for clarifying the classification and characterization of specific hazardous wastes. The fifth full meeting of parties to the Convention, held in December 1999, adopted the Basel Declaration outlining an agenda for the period 2000–10, with a particular focus on minimizing the production of hazardous wastes. At July 2008 the number of parties to the Convention totalled 170. In December 1999 132 states adopted a Protocol to the Convention to address issues relating to liability and compensation for damages from waste exports. The governments also agreed to establish a multilateral fund to finance immediate clean-up operations following any environmental accident.

The UNEP Chemicals branch was established to promote the sound management of hazardous substances, central to which has been the International Register of Potentially Toxic Chemicals (IRPTC). UNEP aims to facilitate access to data on chemicals and hazardous wastes, in order to assess and control health and environmental risks, by using the IRPTC as a clearing house facility of relevant information and by publishing information and technical reports on the impact of the use of chemicals.

The UNEP Chemicals office and the Russian Centre for International Projects (CIP) together run the CIP Project on Strengthening of National Chemicals Management in the CIS Countries. Pollutant Release and Transfer Registers (PRTRs), for collecting and disseminating data on toxic emissions, have been under development in Armenia, Azerbaijan, Belarus, Georgia, Kazakhstan, Moldova, the Russian Federation, Tajikistan, Ukraine and Uzbekistan.

UNEP's OzonAction Programme works to promote information exchange, training and technological awareness. Its objective is to strengthen the capacity of governments and industry in developing countries to undertake measures towards the cost-effective phasing-out of ozone-depleting substances. UNEP also encourages the development of alternative and renewable sources of energy. To achieve this, UNEP is supporting the establishment of a network of centres to research and exchange information of environmentally sound energy technology resources.

CONVENTIONS

UNEP aims to develop and promote international environmental legislation in order to pursue an integrated response to global environmental issues, to enhance collaboration among existing convention secretariats, and to co-ordinate support to implement the work programmes of international instruments.

UNEP has been an active participant in the formulation of several major conventions (see above). The Division of Environmental Conventions is mandated to assist the Division of Policy Development and Law in the formulation of new agreements or protocols to existing conventions. Following the successful adoption of the Rotterdam Convention in September 1998, UNEP played a leading role in formulating a multilateral agreement to reduce and ultimately eliminate the manufacture and use of Persistent Organic Pollutants (POPs), which are considered to be a major global environmental hazard. The agreement on POPs, concluded in December 2000 at a conference sponsored by UNEP in Johannesburg, South Africa, was adopted by 127 countries in May 2001 and entered into force in May 2004.

UNEP has been designated to provide secretariat functions to a number of global and regional environmental conventions (see above for list of offices). UNEP also organizes conferences, workshops and seminars at national and regional levels, and may extend advisory services or technical assistance to individual governments.

UNEP is the secretariat for the Pan-European Biological and Landscape Diversity Strategy. UNEP also supports the preparation of an additional Protocol on Water and Health to the ECE Convention on Transboundary Waters, and a European Charter on Transport, Environment and Health.

COMMUNICATIONS AND PUBLIC INFORMATION

UNEP's public education campaigns and outreach programmes promote community involvement in environmental issues. Further communication of environmental concerns is undertaken through the media, an information centre service and special promotional events, including World Environment Day, photography competitions, and the awarding of the Sasakawa Prize (to recognize distinguished service to the environment by individuals and groups) and of the Global 500 Award for Environmental Achievement. In 1996 UNEP initiated a Global Environment Citizenship Programme to promote acknowledgment of the environmental responsibilities of all sectors of society.

Finance

UNEP derives its finances from the regular budget of the United Nations and from voluntary contributions to the Environment Fund. A budget totalling US $152m. was approved by the Governing Council for 2008–09.

Publications

Annual Report.
APELL Newsletter (2 a year).
Cleaner Production Newsletter (2 a year).
Climate Change Bulletin (quarterly).
Connect (UNESCO-UNEP newsletter on environmental degradation, quarterly).
Earth Views (quarterly).
Environment Forum (quarterly).
Environmental Law Bulletin (2 a year).
Financial Services Initiative (2 a year).
GEF News (quarterly).
Global Water Review.
GPA Newsletter.
IETC Insight (3 a year).
Industry and Environment Review (quarterly).
Leave it to Us (children's magazine, 2 a year).
Managing Hazardous Waste (2 a year).
Our Planet (quarterly).
OzonAction Newsletter (quarterly).
Tierramerica (weekly).
Tourism Focus (2 a year).
UNEP Chemicals Newsletter (2 a year).
UNEP Update (monthly).
UNEP Year Book (annually).
World Atlas of Biodiversity.
World Atlas of Coral Reefs.
World Atlas of Desertification.
Studies, reports, legal texts, technical guidelines, etc.

United Nations High Commissioner for Refugees—UNHCR

Address: CP 2500, 1211 Geneva 2 dépôt, Switzerland.
Telephone: 227398111; **fax:** 227397312; **e-mail:** unhcr@unhcr.org; **internet:** www.unhcr.org.
The Office of the High Commissioner was established in 1951 to provide international protection for refugees and to seek durable solutions to their problems. In 1981 UNHCR was awarded the Nobel Peace Prize.

Organization

(October 2008)

HIGH COMMISSIONER

The High Commissioner is elected by the United Nations General Assembly on the nomination of the Secretary-General, and is responsible to the General Assembly and to the UN Economic and Social Council (ECOSOC).
High Commissioner: António Manuel de Oliveira Guterres (Portugal).
Deputy High Commissioner: L. Craig Johnstone (USA).

EXECUTIVE COMMITTEE

The Executive Committee of the High Commissioner's Programme (ExCom), established by ECOSOC, gives the High Commissioner policy directives in respect of material assistance programmes and advice in the field of international protection. In addition, it oversees UNHCR's general policies and use of funds. ExCom, which comprises representatives of 66 states, both members and non-members of the UN, meets once a year.

ADMINISTRATION

Headquarters include the Executive Office, comprising the offices of the High Commissioner, the Deputy High Commissioner and the Assistant High Commissioner. The Inspector General, the Director of the UNHCR liaison office in New York, and the Director of the Department of International Protection report directly to the High Commissioner. The other principal administrative units are the Division of Financial and Supply Management, the Division of Human Resources Management, the Division of External Relations, the Division of Information Systems and Telecommunications, the Division of International Protection Services, and the Department of Operations, which is responsible for the five regional bureaux covering Africa; Asia and the Pacific; Europe; the Americas and the Caribbean; and Central Asia, South-West Asia, North Africa and the Middle East; and also includes the Division of Operational Services and the Emergency and Security Service. At July 2006 there were 263 UNHCR offices in 116 countries world-wide. In 2008 UNHCR employed around 6,300 people (including short-term staff), of whom more than four-fifths were working in the field. In that year a Structural and Management Change Process was initiated, with the aim of reviewing and improving UNHCR's processes and structures.

Activities

The competence of the High Commissioner extends to any person who, owing to well-founded fear of being persecuted for reasons of race, religion, nationality or political opinion, is outside the country of his or her nationality and is unable or, owing to such fear or for reasons other than personal convenience, remains unwilling to accept the protection of that country; or who, not having a nationality and being outside the country of his or her former habitual residence, is unable or, owing to such fear or for reasons other than personal convenience, is unwilling to return to it. This competence may be extended, by resolutions of the UN General Assembly and decisions of ExCom, to cover certain other 'persons of concern', in addition to refugees meeting these criteria. Refugees who are assisted by other UN agencies, or who have the same rights or obligations as nationals of their country of residence, are outside the mandate of UNHCR.

In recent years there has been a significant shift in UNHCR's focus of activities. Increasingly UNHCR has been called upon to support people who have been displaced within their own country (i.e. with similar needs to those of refugees but who have not crossed an international border) or those threatened with displacement as a result of armed conflict. In addition, greater support has been given to refugees who have returned to their country of origin, to assist their reintegration, and UNHCR is working to enable local communities to support the returnees, frequently through the implementation of Quick Impact Projects (QIPs). In 2004 UNHCR led the formulation of a UN system-wide Strategic Plan for internally displaced persons (IDPs). During 2005 the UN's Inter-Agency Standing Committee (IASC), concerned with co-ordinating the international response to humanitarian disasters, developed a concept of organizing agency assistance to IDPs through the institutionalization of a 'Cluster Approach', currently comprising 11 core areas of activity. UNHCR is the lead agency for the clusters on Camp Coordination and Management (in conflict situations; IOM leads that cluster in natural disaster situations), Emergency Shelter, and (jointly with OHCHR and UNICEF) Protection.

In the mid-2000s UNHCR widened its scope from its mandate to protect and assist people fleeing persecution and violence in response to the enormous impact of two devastating natural disasters. Following the series of tidal waves (tsunamis), emanating from an earthquake in the Indian Ocean, that devastated coastal regions in 14 countries in South and South-East Asia and East Africa in December 2004, UNHCR requested emergency funding totalling US $77m. in support of a 12-month relief operation to provide shelter, non-food relief supplies and logistical support for survivors in Aceh, Indonesia (close to the epicentre of the earthquake), Sri Lanka and Somalia. This was part of a pan-UN inter-agency appeal for $1,100m. In October 2005 UNHCR provided an immediate response to support survivors of the South Asian earthquake that struck northern Pakistan and bordering areas of India and Afghanistan. In May 2008 UNHCR donated tents to provide shelter for some 55,000 people following a devastating earthquake in Sichuan province, People's Republic of China.

UNHCR has been increasingly concerned with the problem of statelessness, where people have no legal nationality, and promotes new accessions to the 1954 Convention Relating to the Status of Stateless Persons and the 1964 Convention on the Reduction of Statelessness. UNHCR maintains that a significant proportion of the global stateless population has not hitherto been systematically identified. In October 2006 ExCom urged member states to share with UNHCR data on stateless persons and on persons with undetermined nationality.

In July 2006 UNHCR issued a '10 Point Plan of Action on Refugee Protection and Mixed Migration' (*10 Point Plan*), a framework document detailing 10 principal areas in which UNHCR might make an impact in supporting member states with the development of comprehensive migration strategies. The 10 areas covered by the Plan were as follows: co-operation among key players; data collection and analysis; protection-sensitive entry systems; reception arrangements; mechanisms for profiling and referral; differentiated processes and procedures; solutions for refugees; addressing secondary movements; return of non-refugees and alternative migration options; and information strategy. A revised version of the *10 Point Plan* was published in January 2007. Addressing the annual meeting of ExCom in October 2007 the High Commissioner, while emphasizing that UNHCR was not mandated to manage migration, urged a concerted international effort to raise awareness and comprehension of the broad patterns (including the scale, complexity, and causes—such as poverty and the pursuit of improved living standards) of global displacement and migration. In order to fulfil UNHCR's mandate to support refugees and others in need of protection within ongoing mass movements of people, he urged better recognition of the mixed nature of many 21st century population flows, often comprising both economic migrants and refugees, asylum-seekers and victims of trafficking who required detection and support. It was also acknowledged that conflict and persecution—the traditional reasons for flight—were being increasingly compounded by factors such as environmental degradation and detrimental effects of climate change. A Dialogue on Protection Challenges, convened by the High Commissioner in December 2007, agreed that the *10 Point Plan* should be elaborated further. Regional activities based on the Plan have been focused on Central America, Western Africa, Eastern Africa and Southern Asia; and on countries along the Eastern and South-Eastern borders of European Union member states.

At December 2007 the total population of concern to UNHCR, based on provisional figures, amounted to 31.7m. At that time the refugee population world-wide totalled 9.7m. UNHCR was also concerned with some 730,640 recently returned refugees, 13.7m. IDPs, 2.1m. returned IDPs, 2.9m. stateless persons, 739,986 asylum-seekers, and 0.7m. others. UNHCR maintains an online statistical population database, accessible at www.unhcr.org/statistics/populationdatabase.

World Refugee Day, sponsored by UNHCR, is held annually on 20 June.

INTERNATIONAL PROTECTION

As laid down in the Statute of the Office, UNHCR's primary function is to extend international protection to refugees and its second function is to seek durable solutions to their problems. In the exercise of its mandate UNHCR seeks to ensure that refugees and asylum-seekers are protected against *refoulement* (forcible return), that they receive asylum, and that they are treated according to internationally recognized standards. UNHCR pursues these objectives by a variety of means that include promoting the conclusion and ratification by states of international conventions for the protection of refugees. UNHCR promotes the adoption of liberal practices of asylum by states, so that refugees and asylum-seekers are granted admission, at least on a temporary basis.

The most comprehensive instrument concerning refugees that has been elaborated at the international level is the 1951 United Nations Convention relating to the Status of Refugees. This Convention, the scope of which was extended by a Protocol adopted in 1967, defines the rights and duties of refugees and contains provisions dealing with a variety of matters which affect the day-to-day lives of refugees. The application of the Convention and its Protocol is supervised by UNHCR. Important provisions for the treatment of refugees are also contained in a number of instruments adopted at the regional level. These include the 1969 Convention Governing the Specific Aspects of Refugee Problems adopted by the Organization of African Unity (now the African Union—AU) member states in 1969, the European Agreement on the Abolition of Visas for Refugees, and the 1969 American Convention on Human Rights.

UNHCR has actively encouraged states to accede to the 1951 United Nations Refugee Convention and the 1967 Protocol: 147 states had acceded to either or both of these basic refugee instruments by July 2008. An increasing number of states have also adopted domestic legislation and/or administrative measures to implement the international instruments, particularly in the field of procedures for the determination of refugee status. UNHCR has sought to address the specific needs of refugee women and children, and has also attempted to deal with the problem of military attacks on refugee camps, by adopting and encouraging the acceptance of a set of principles to ensure the safety of refugees. In recent years it has formulated a strategy designed to address the fundamental causes of refugee flows. In 2001, in response to widespread concern about perceived high numbers of asylum-seekers and large-scale international economic migration and human trafficking, UNHCR initiated a series of Global Consultations on International Protection with the signatories to the 1951 Convention and 1967 Protocol, and other interested parties, with a view to strengthening both the application and scope of international refugee legislation. A consultation of 156 Governments, convened in Geneva, in December 2001, reaffirmed commitment to the central role played by the Convention and Protocol. The final consultation, held in May 2002, focused on durable solutions and the protection of refugee women and children. Subsequently, based on the findings of the Global Consultations process, UNHCR developed an Agenda on Protection with six main objectives: strengthening the implementation of the 1951 Convention and 1967 Protocol; the protection of refugees within broader migration movements; more equitable sharing of burdens and responsibilities and building of capacities to receive and protect refugees; addressing more effectively security-related concerns; increasing efforts to find durable solutions; and meeting the protection needs of refugee women and children. The Agenda was endorsed by ExCom in October 2002. In September of that year the High Commissioner for Refugees launched the *Convention Plus* initiative, which aimed to address contemporary global asylum issues by developing, on the basis of the Agenda on Protection, international agreements and measures to supplement the 1951 Convention and 1967 Protocol.

UNHCR is one of the 10 co-sponsors of UNAIDS.

ASSISTANCE ACTIVITIES

The first phase of an assistance operation uses UNHCR's capacity of emergency response. This enables UNHCR to address the immediate needs of refugees at short notice, for example, by employing specially trained emergency teams and maintaining stockpiles of basic equipment, medical aid and materials. A significant proportion of UNHCR expenditure is allocated to the next phase of an operation, providing 'care and maintenance' in stable refugee circumstances. This assistance can take various forms, including the provision of food, shelter, medical care and essential supplies. Also covered in many instances are basic services, including education and counselling.

As far as possible, assistance is geared towards the identification and implementation of durable solutions to refugee problems—this being the second statutory responsibility of UNHCR. Such solutions generally take one of three forms: voluntary repatriation, local integration or resettlement in another country. Where voluntary repatriation, increasingly the preferred solution, is feasible, the Office assists refugees to overcome obstacles preventing their return to their country of origin. This may be done through negotiations with governments involved, or by providing funds either for the physical movement of refugees or for the rehabilitation of returnees once back in their own country. UNHCR supports the implementation of the Guidance Note on Durable Solutions for Displaced Persons, adopted in 2004 by the UN Development Group.

When voluntary repatriation is not an option, efforts are made to assist refugees to integrate locally and to become self-supporting in their countries of asylum. This may be done either by granting loans to refugees, or by assisting them, through vocational training or in other ways, to learn a skill and to establish themselves in gainful occupations. One major form of assistance to help refugees re-establish themselves outside camps is the provision of housing. In cases where resettlement through emigration is the only viable solution to a refugee problem, UNHCR negotiates with governments in an endeavour to obtain suitable resettlement opportunities, to encourage liberalization of admission criteria and to draw up special immigration schemes. During 2006 an estimated 27,700 refugees (as well as 1,860 family reunification cases) were resettled under UNHCR auspices.

In the 1990s UNHCR consolidated efforts to integrate certain priorities into its programme planning and implementation, as a standard discipline in all phases of assistance. The considerations include awareness of specific problems confronting refugee women, the needs of refugee children, the environmental impact of refugee programmes and long-term development objectives. In an effort to improve the effectiveness of its programmes, UNHCR has initiated a process of delegating authority, as well as responsibility for operational budgets, to its regional and field representatives, increasing flexibility and accountability. A Policy Development and Evaluation Service reviews systematically UNHCR's operational effectiveness.

All UNHCR personnel are required to sign, and all interns, contracted staff and staff from partner organizations are required to acknowledge, a Code of Conduct, to which is appended the UN Secretary-General's bulletin on special measures for protection from sexual exploitation and sexual abuse. The post of Senior Adviser to the High Commissioner on Gender Issues, within the Executive Office, was established in 2004.

CENTRAL ASIA

In late 1992 people began to flee civil conflict in Tajikistan and to seek refuge in Afghanistan. During 1993 an emergency UNHCR operation established a reception camp to provide the 60,000 Tajik refugees with basic assistance, and began to move them away from the border area to safety. In December a tripartite agreement was concluded by UNHCR and the Tajik and Afghan Governments regarding the security of refugees returning to Tajikistan. UNHCR monitored the repatriation process and provided materials for the construction of almost 20,000 homes. The operation was concluded by the end of 1997. Nevertheless, at the end of 2000, there were still nearly 60,000 Tajik refugees remaining in other countries of the former USSR. In the early 2000s an initiative was implemented to integrate locally up to 10,000 Tajik refugees of Kyrgyz ethnic origin in Kyrgyzstan and 12,500 Tajik refugees of Turkmen origin in Turkmenistan; this process was facilitated by the conclusion in mid-2003 of a Kyrgyz-Tajik agreement on a simplified procedure for citizenship acquisition. From 1 July 2006 UNHCR terminated refugee status for exiled Tajiks, although the Office continued to support their voluntary repatriation. By the end of that year most of the former Tajik refugees in Kygyzstan and Turkmenistan had become naturalized citizens of those countries, as planned. From late 2001 about 9,000 Afghan refugees repatriated from Tajikistan under the auspices of UNHCR and the International Organization for Migration. During 2006 nearly 1,500 Afghan refugees were resettled from Tajikistan to third countries, leaving a remaining Afghan refugee poplation in that country of about 1,000 at 31 December. UNHCR expressed concern following the adoption by the Tajikistan authorities in May 2002 of refugee legislation that reportedly contravened the 1951 Convention relating to the Status of Refugees and its 1967 Protocol. In 2003 UNHCR agreed to participate in an European Union/UNDP Border Management Programme in Central Asia (BOMCA); BOMCA was ongoing in 2008. At the request of the Uzbekistan Government UNHCR closed its Uzbekistan office in April 2006.

EASTERN EUROPE

In June 2007, following the publication in June 2006 of its *10 Point Plan* for assisting member states with the management of refugee protection and mixed migration, UNHCR issued a '10 Point Plan of Action on Refugee Protection and Mixed Migration for Countries along the Eastern and South-Eastern Borders of European Union Member States', providing a framework for discussion between UNHCR and the Governments of Belarus, Moldova and Ukraine, and also clarifying UNHCR's operational relationship in that subregion with the International Organization for Migration and non-governmental organizations. During 2007 UNHCR undertook a study on the local integration of refugees in Belarus, Moldova and Ukraine, at the request of those countries' Governments.

In December 1992 UNHCR dispatched teams to establish offices in both Armenia and Azerbaijan to support more than 1m. people displaced from 1988 as a result of the war between the two countries, including some 360,000 ethnic Armenians who fled Azerbaijan for Armenia. A cease-fire agreement was signed between the two sides in May 1994, although violations of the accord were subsequently reported and relations between the two countries remained tense. The preliminary findings of a census of the ethnic Armenian Azerbaijani refugee population in Armenia conducted by the Armenian

Government in 2006, with the support of UNHCR, indicated that by that time many of the ethnic Armenian Azerbaijani refugees had either become naturalized Armenian citizens (this process having been facilitated by UNHCR-supported legislation introduced by the Armenian Government in 1995) or had resettled in third countries. Azerbaijan still supports a massive population of IDPs, totalling 686,586 at 31 December 2007. UNHCR's humanitarian activities have focused on improving shelter, in particular for the most vulnerable among the refugee population, and promoting economic self-sufficiency and stability. During 2006 UNHCR provided protection to some 1,900 Chechen refugees in Azerbaijan.

During 2003–07 more than 700 ethnically Armenian Iraqis sought protection in Armenia.

In Georgia, where almost 300,000 people left their homes as a result of civil conflict from 1991, UNHCR has attempted to encourage income-generating activities among the displaced population, to increase the Georgian Government's capacity to support those people and to assist the rehabilitation of people returning to their areas of origin. During 2006 UNHCR supported the Georgian Government in the preparation of a national IDP strategy, focusing on the right of IDPs to integrate locally without prejudicing their right eventually to return to their home communities. At 31 December 2007 there were 273,193 Georgian IDPs, affected by the ongoing conflicts in Abkhazia and South Ossetia. During August 2008 UNHCR provided humanitarian assistance, including the distribution of blankets, jerry-cans and kitchen sets, to people affected by a period of violent insecurity that escalated in July between Georgian and South Ossetian separatist forces, further intensifying in early August when Georgia launched a military offensive on the South Ossetian capital Tskhinvali, a stronghold of the separatists, and Russian forces responded by supporting the counter-attack and by crossing into Georgian territory. The heightened insecurity resulted in the temporary displacement of some 192,000 people: 127,000 within Georgia, 30,000 from South to North Ossetia (Russian Federation), and 35,000 inside North Ossetia. In the following month, once the conflict had abated, UNHCR teams began regular visits to assess the humanitarian situation in villages in the Georgia–South Ossetia buffer zone area north of the Georgian town of Gori. By October 2008 some 68,000 of those who had become displaced within Georgia in August were reported to have returned to their homes.

In late 1999 an estimated 7,000 refugees fleeing insecurity in Chechnya entered Georgia. UNHCR has delivered food to the Chechen refugees and the host families with whom the majority are staying, and has also assisted the refugees through shelter renovation, psychosocial support and the provision of child-care facilities and health and community development support, as well as monitoring refugee-host family relations. UNHCR planned to terminate during 2008 its food support programme to the Chechen refugees remaining in Georgia (numbering about 1,000 in 2007).

From 1994 UNHCR pursued a process to establish a comprehensive approach to the problems of refugees, returnees, IDPs and migrants in the Commonwealth of Independent States (CIS). A regional conference convened in Geneva, Switzerland, in May 1996, endorsed a framework of activities aimed at managing migratory flows and at developing institutional capacities to prevent mass population displacements. At that time it was estimated that more than 9m. former citizens of the USSR had relocated since its disintegration as a result of conflict, economic pressures and ecological disasters. The structures put in place by the 1996 CIS regional conference were terminated in October 2005. By 2008 all CIS member states excepting Uzbekistan had acceded to the 1951 Convention.

In March 1995 UNHCR initiated an assistance programme for people displaced as a result of conflict in the separatist republic of Chechnya (the Chechen Republic of Ichkeriya), the Russian Federation, as part of a UN inter-agency relief effort, in collaboration with the International Committee of the Red Cross (ICRC). UNHCR continued its activities in 1996, at the request of the Russian Government, at which time the displaced population within Chechnya and in the surrounding republics totalled 490,000. During 1997 UNHCR provided reintegration assistance to 25,000 people who returned to Chechnya, despite reports of sporadic violence. The security situation in the region deteriorated sharply in mid-1999, following a series of border clashes and incursions by Chechen separatist forces into the neighbouring republic of Dagestan. In September Russian military aircraft began an aerial offensive against suspected rebel targets in Chechnya, and at the end of the month ground troops moved into the republic. By November an estimated 225,000 Chechens had fled to neighbouring Ingushetiya. UNHCR dispatched food supplies to assist the IDPs and, from February 2000, periodically sent relief convoys into Chechnya, where there was still a substantial displaced population; the poor security situation, however, prevented other UNHCR deployment within Chechnya. During the first half of 2004 the Russian authorities closed the three tented refugee camps that had been operational in Ingushetiya at December 2003. Temporary lodging (consisting of rooms in accommodation centres or in private homes) was to be provided for those refugees who did not wish to return home. The Russian authorities implemented an information campaign to encourage Chechen refugees to return from Ingushetiya. UNHCR has conducted interviews of returnees to Chechnya from Ingushetiya in order to ensure that returns have been voluntary rather than enforced. It was estimated in September 2008 that around 18,500 Chechen refugees remained in Ingushetiya. At end-December 2006 there remained an estimated 57,349 IDPs within Chechnya.

CO-OPERATION WITH OTHER ORGANIZATIONS

UNHCR works closely with other UN agencies, intergovernmental organizations and non-governmental organizations (NGOs) to increase the scope and effectiveness of its operations. Within the UN system UNHCR co-operates, principally, with the World Food Programme in the distribution of food aid, UNICEF and the World Health Organization in the provision of family welfare and child immunization programmes, OCHA in the delivery of emergency humanitarian relief, UNDP in development-related activities and the preparation of guidelines for the continuum of emergency assistance to development programmes, and the Office of the UN High Commissioner for Human Rights. UNHCR also has close working relationships with the International Committee of the Red Cross and the International Organization for Migration. In 2007 UNHCR worked with 649 NGOs as 'implementing partners', enabling UNHCR to broaden the use of its resources while maintaining a co-ordinating role in the provision of assistance.

TRAINING

UNHCR organizes training programmes and workshops to enhance the capabilities of field workers and non-UNHCR staff, in the following areas: the identification and registration of refugees; people-orientated planning; resettlement procedures and policies; emergency response and management; security awareness; stress management; and the dissemination of information through the electronic media.

Finance

The United Nations' regular budget finances a proportion of UNHCR's administrative expenditure. The majority of UNHCR's programme expenditure (about 98%) is funded by voluntary contributions, mainly from governments. The Private Sector and Public Affairs Service aims to increase funding from non-governmental donor sources, for example by developing partnerships with foundations and corporations. Following approval of the Unified Annual Programme Budget any subsequently identified requirements are managed in the form of Supplementary Programmes, financed by separate appeals. The total Unified Annual Programme Budget for 2009 was projected at US $1,275.5m.

Publications

Global Trends (annually).

Refugees (quarterly, in English, French, German, Italian, Japanese and Spanish).

Refugee Resettlement: An International Handbook to Guide Reception and Integration.

Refugee Survey Quarterly.

Refworld (annually).

Sexual and Gender-based Violence Against Refugees, Returnees and Displaced Persons: Guidelines for Prevention and Response.

The State of the World's Refugees (every 2 years).

Statistical Yearbook (annually).

UNHCR Handbook for Emergencies.

Press releases, reports.

Statistics

PERSONS OF CONCERN TO UNHCR IN EASTERN EUROPE, RUSSIA AND CENTRAL ASIA
('000 persons, at 31 December 2007*)

Host country	Refugees	Asylum-seekers	Returned refugees	Others of concern†
Azerbaijan . .	2.4	0.1	0.0	689.1
Georgia . .	1.0	0.0	—	274.5
Kazakhstan . .	4.3	0.1	—	7.9
Kyrgyzstan . .	0.7	0.7	—	9.5
Russian Federation . .	1.7	3.1	0.3	244.6
Ukraine . . .	2.3	1.3	—	58.7

* Figures are provided mostly by governments, based on their own records and methods of estimation. Countries with fewer than 10,000 persons of concern to the UNHCR are not listed.

† Mainly internally displaced person (IDPs), recently returned IDPs, some 51,296 stateless persons in the Russian Federation, and some 58,704 stateless persons in Ukraine.

United Nations Peace-keeping

Address: Department of Peace-keeping Operations, Room S-3727-B, United Nations, New York, NY 10017, USA.

Telephone: (212) 963-8077; **fax:** (212) 963-9222; **internet:** www.un.org/Depts/dpko/.

United Nations peace-keeping operations have been conceived as instruments of conflict control. The UN has used these operations in various conflicts, with the consent of the parties involved, to maintain international peace and security, without prejudice to the positions or claims of parties, in order to facilitate the search for political settlements through peaceful means such as mediation and the good offices of the UN Secretary-General. Each operation is established with a specific mandate, which requires periodic review by the UN Security Council. In 1988 the United Nations Peace-keeping Forces were awarded the Nobel Peace Prize.

United Nations peace-keeping operations fall into two categories: peace-keeping forces and observer missions. Peace-keeping forces are composed of contingents of military and civilian personnel, made available by member states. These forces assist in preventing the recurrence of fighting, restoring and maintaining peace, and promoting a return to normal conditions. To this end, peace-keeping forces are authorized as necessary to undertake negotiations, persuasion, observation and fact-finding. They conduct patrols and interpose physically between the opposing parties. Peace-keeping forces are permitted to use their weapons only in self-defence.

Military observer missions are composed of officers (usually unarmed), who are made available, on the Secretary-General's request, by member states. A mission's function is to observe and report to the Secretary-General (who, in turn, informs the Security Council) on the maintenance of a cease-fire, to investigate violations and to do what it can to improve the situation. Peace-keeping forces and observer missions must at all times maintain complete impartiality and avoid any action that might affect the claims or positions of the parties.

The UN's peace-keeping forces and observer missions are financed in most cases by assessed contributions from member states of the organization. In recent years a significant expansion in the UN's peace-keeping activities has been accompanied by a perpetual financial crisis within the organization, as a result of the increased financial burden and some member states' delaying payment. At 31 May 2008 outstanding assessed contributions to the peace-keeping budget amounted to some US $1,800m.

By October 2008 the UN had deployed a total of 63 peace-keeping operations, of which 13 were authorized in the period 1948–88 and 50 since 1988. At 31 July 2008 119 countries were contributing some 87,957 uniformed personnel to the ongoing operations, of whom 74,076 were peace-keeping troops, 11,484 civilian police and 2,397 military observers.

UNITED NATIONS OBSERVER MISSION IN GEORGIA—UNOMIG

Address: Sukhumi, Georgia.

Special Representative of the UN Secretary-General and Head of Mission: JOHAN VERBEKE (Belgium).

Chief Military Observer: Maj.-Gen. NIAZ MUHAMMAD KHAN KHAT-
TAK (Pakistan).

UNOMIG was established in August 1993 to verify compliance with a
cease-fire agreement, signed in July between the Government of
Georgia and the Abkhazian separatist movement. The mission was
the UN's first undertaking in the former USSR. In October the UN
Secretary-General stated that a breakdown in the cease-fire agreement had invalidated UNOMIG's mandate. He proposed, however, to
maintain, for information purposes, the eight-strong UNOMIG team
in the city of Sukhumi, which had been seized by Abkhazian forces in
late September. In December the Security Council authorized the
deployment of additional military observers in response to the
signing of a memorandum of understanding by the conflicting parties
earlier that month. Further peace negotiations were conducted in
January–March 1994 under the authority of the UN Secretary-
General's Special Envoy. In May both sides signed an Agreement
on a Ceasefire and Separation of Forces. Consequently, in July, the
Security Council increased UNOMIG's authorized strength and
expanded the mission's mandate to incorporate the following tasks:
to monitor and verify the implementation of the agreement and to
investigate reported violations; to observe the operation of a new
Commonwealth of Independent States (CIS) peace-keeping force to
verify the accord; to verify that troops and heavy military equipment
remain outside the security zone and the restricted weapons zone; to
monitor the storage of the military equipment withdrawn from the
restricted zones; to monitor the withdrawal of Georgian troops from
the Kodori Gorge region to locations beyond the Abkhazian frontiers;
and to patrol regularly the Kodori Gorge. Peace negotiations were
pursued in 1995, despite periodic outbreaks of violence in Abkhazia.
In October 1996 the UN Security Council established a human rights
office as part of UNOMIG. In May 1997 the Security Council
endorsed a proposal of the UN Secretary-General to strengthen
the political element of UNOMIG in order to enable the mission to
assume a more active role in furthering a negotiated settlement. In
July direct discussions between representatives of the Georgian and
Abkhazian authorities, the first in more than two years, were held
under UN auspices. In December a new Abkhaz-Georgian Co-
ordinating Council was inaugurated. In early 1998 the security
situation in Abkhazia deteriorated. Following an outbreak of violence in May the conflicting parties signed a cease-fire accord, which
incorporated an agreement that UNOMIG and CIS forces would
continue to work to create a secure environment to allow for the
return of displaced persons to the Gali region of Abkhazia. In
addition, the UN Security Council urged both parties to establish
a protection unit to ensure the safety of UN military observers. In
December 2000, following a series of detentions and hostage-takings
of mission personnel in the Kodori Gorge during late 1999 and 2000,
UNOMIG suspended patrols of that area. Reviewing the operation in
January 2001 the UN Secretary-General expressed concern at the
recent recurrent abductions and urged the Abkhazian side to cease
imposing restrictions on the mission's freedom of movement. A
Programme of Action on confidence-building measures was concluded in March; however, the negotiation process was interrupted
from April, owing to increasing insecurity in the conflict zone and the
ongoing activities of illegal armed groups. In October a UNOMIG
helicopter was shot down in the Kodori Gorge, resulting in the deaths
of nine people. UNOMIG suspended its patrols of the area. Meetings
of the Abkhaz-Georgian Co-ordinating Council were suspended in
2001. In January 2002 a protocol was signed between the conflicting
parties providing for the withdrawal of Georgian troops from the
upper Kodori valley and the resumption of UN ground patrols.
Further discussion on implementation of the protocol resulted in
the first joint patrol being conducted in late March. In April a protocol
was concluded by both sides for a final withdrawal of Georgian troops
and the resumption of regular UNOMIG/CIS patrols. Renewed
diplomatic efforts to secure a political agreement on the future status
of Abkhazia initially focused on a paper of Basic Principles for the
Distribution of Competences between Tbilisi and Sukhumi, which
had been prepared by the Special Representative of the UN Secretary-General. The document was rejected as a basis for negotiations
by the Abkhazian leadership; however, discussions were held
between the leadership of the two sides to consider measures to
stabilize further the situation in the Kodori Gorge. Meeting in
Geneva, Switzerland, in February and July 2003 the UN Secretary-
General's so-called 'Group of Friends on Georgia', comprising France,
Germany, Russia, the United Kingdom and the USA, identified co-
operation in economic, political and security matters and the return
of refugees and internally displaced persons as being of key importance for the advancement of the peace process and therefore also
priority focus areas for UNOMIG. From November a new civilian
police component of UNOMIG became operational, although objections by certain Abkhaz groups prevented their deployment in the
Gali sector. UNOMIG's Engineering Section continued to undertake
small-scale reconstruction projects, in particular of roads and
bridges, in order to facilitate communications. In October 2003
UNOMIG and the CIS peace-keeping force signed a protocol entail-

ing closer co-operation in combating crime and improving security. In
May 2004 the Special Representative chaired a meeting with regard
to security guarantees, held in accordance with recommendations of
the UN Group of Friends on Georgia and with agreements reached at
a previous meeting convened in February. No further substantive
dialogue was held during the year, although in December the UN
hosted a high-level meeting of the Group of Friends which reviewed
the main challenges and determined to meet both sides in order to
consider the resumption of negotiations. Georgian and Abkhazian
representatives participated in a meeting of the Group of Friends
held in April 2005, and, in the following month, a meeting on security
issues that was organized by the Secretary-General's Special Representative and attended by representatives of the two sides and of
UNOMIG and the CIS peace-keeping mission, adopted a protocol
aimed at strengthening the implementation of the cease-fire agreement signed in May 1994 and other security commitments. In July
2005 UNOMIG hosted a high-level meeting on security aspects of the
proposed rehabilitation of the Sochi–Tbilisi railway. In August, at a
meeting chaired by the Special Representative, both sides renewed
their commitment to a peaceful settlement of the conflict and for a
safe return of all refugees and internally displaced persons. Efforts to
formulate joint documents on the non-use of force and the return of
all displaced persons were to be pursued through the good offices of
the Special Representative. In early 2006 UNOMIG, acting under its
humanitarian mandate, initiated a project with the European
Commission and UNDP to rehabilitate electricity, public health
facilities and agriculture in four districts. On 1 March the mission
inaugurated a free bus service connecting the Georgian and Abkhazian sides across the Inguri river bridge. During May meetings of the
Co-ordinating Council, inaugurated in 1997 and suspended in 2001,
were resumed.

Abkhaz–Georgian relations deteriorated in July 2006, following
the adoption by the Georgian legislature of a resolution urging the
suspension and withdrawal of the CIS peace-keeping mission from
Georgian territory. In late July a Georgian special military operation aimed at restoring law and order in the upper Kodori valley, in
contravention of the May 1994 cease-fire agreement, raised tensions
further. Consequently, UNOMIG established two temporary observation points to monitor movements in the upper Kodori valley area.
UNOMIG resumed patrolling the area in December 2006. In
October the UN Security Council adopted a resolution which urged
both sides to honour all previous agreements concluded regarding
non-violence and confidence-building measures and emphasized the
importance of effective co-operation between UNOMIG and the CIS
mission. In January 2007 UNOMIG increased its maritime patrols,
following allegations by the Abkhaz regime of provocative Georgian
activities in Abkhazian coastal waters. In early March UNOMIG
sent a fact-finding team to investigate an exchange of fire between
Abkhaz militia and Georgian security forces near the Inguri river
bridge, arising from an unofficial Georgian protest demonstration
against the staging in February and March by the Abkhaz regime of
local and parliamentary elections. (The polls were declared illegitimate by several international organizations, including the European Union—EU, NATO and the OSCE, and were not observed by
UNOMIG.) In mid-March the Georgian Government informed
UNOMIG that two villages in the upper Kodori valley had come
under aerial attack. Allegations by the Georgian Government of
Russian involvement were refuted by the Abkhaz and Russian
authorities. An UNOMIG-led quadripartite joint fact-finding group,
comprising UNOMIG, the CIS mission and representatives of the
Abkhaz and Georgian sides, was subsequently appointed to investigate the incident. At a meeting in late June of senior representatives of the Group of Friends and representatives of the Abkhaz and
Georgian sides, convened under UN auspices, in Bonn, Germany,
the two sides determined to advance their dialogue on security
matters and to co-operate in implementing humanitarian initiatives, including the European Commission/UNDP-sponsored
rehabilitation project initiated in 2006. In October 2007 UNOMIG
facilitated a meeting between the Georgian minister on conflict
resolution and the Abkhaz de facto minister for foreign affairs. The
two sides reached a preliminary understanding on convening meetings on security issues. The Georgian minister also agreed to release
seven Abkhaz prisoners, who had been detained during a armed
clash between both sides, outside of the conflict zone, in September.
The Group of Friends convened in February 2008 and secured
agreement by both sides that there was a need to pursue a dialogue
on security issues. In April UNOMIG initiated an investigation into
the crashing of a Georgian surveillance aircraft and concluded, in
May, that it had been shot down by the Russian air force. In early
July the UN Secretary-General condemned a series of bombings
within Abkhazia and near the cease-fire line on Georgian-controlled
territory and, noting an escalation of tensions, urged restraint by all
sides. During that month UNOMIG assisted Germany, as the Co-
ordinator of the Group of Friends, to advance a new settlement plan.
However, a meeting to discuss the plan, to be held in Berlin,
Germany, was postponed owing to an escalation of tensions within
Georgia and reports of violent clashes between Georgian govern-

ment troops and separatist forces in South Ossetia. In early August the conflict heightened when Russian forces and armoured vehicles countered attempts by Georgian troops to seize control of the Ossetian capital, Tskhinvali. UNOMIG (with no mandate in South Ossetia) withdrew patrols from the upper Kodori valley, at the request of the Abkhaz authorities, and reported a build-up of troops and artillery in the restricted weapons zone. At the end of that month Georgia declared the 1994 peace agreement to be null and void, following Russian recognition of Abkhazia and South Ossetia as independent states. On 1 September the Georgian authorities determined to terminate the CIS peace-keeping operation in Abkhazia. Under the provisions of a peace plan, formulated by France, holding the rotating presidency of the EU, UNOMIG was to maintain its existing role and mandate unless adjusted by the UN Security Council. In a report to the Council in early October, the UN Secretary-General acknowledged that the role of the mission may need to be adjusted given the post-conflict security environment but that it should remain as a mechanism of the international community to uphold peace in the region. From 1 October an EU monitoring mission was deployed to patrol the buffer zones close to the disputed territories. It aimed to ensure compliance with the EU peace plan and was to work closely with the UN and OSCE missions.

At 31 August 2008 UNOMIG comprised 126 military observers and 14 civilian police, and was supported by 267 international and local civilian personnel and by one UN Volunteer. The General Assembly budget appropriation to the Special Account for the mission amounted to US $36.1m. for the period 1 July 2008–30 June 2009.

World Food Programme—WFP

Address: Via Cesare Giulio Viola 68, Parco dei Medici, 00148 Rome, Italy.

Telephone: (06) 65131; **fax:** (06) 6513-2840; **e-mail:** wfpinfo@wfp.org; **internet:** www.wfp.org.

WFP, the principal food aid organization of the United Nations, became operational in 1963. It aims to alleviate acute hunger by providing emergency relief following natural or man-made humanitarian disasters, and supplies food aid to people in developing countries to eradicate chronic undernourishment, to support social development and to promote self-reliant communities.

Organization

(October 2008)

EXECUTIVE BOARD

The governing body of WFP is the Executive Board, comprising 36 members, 18 of whom are elected by the UN Economic and Social Council (ECOSOC) and 18 by the Council of the Food and Agriculture Organization (FAO). The Board meets four times each year at WFP headquarters.

SECRETARIAT

WFP's Executive Director is appointed jointly by the UN Secretary-General and the Director-General of FAO and is responsible for the management and administration of the Programme. In 2006 there were 10,587 staff members, of whom nearly 92% were working in the field. WFP administers some 87 country offices, in order to provide operational, financial and management support at a more local level, and maintains six regional bureaux, located in Bangkok, Thailand (for Asia), Cairo, Egypt (for the Middle East, Central Asia and Eastern Europe), Panama City, Panama (for Latin America and the Caribbean), Johannesburg, South Africa (for Southern Africa), Kampala, Uganda (for Central and Eastern Africa), and Dakar, Senegal (for West Africa).

Executive Director: JOSETTE SHEERAN (USA).

Activities

WFP is the only multilateral organization with a mandate to use food aid as a resource. It is the second largest source of assistance in the UN, after the World Bank group, in terms of actual transfers of resources, and the largest source of grant aid in the UN system. WFP handles more than one-third of the world's food aid. WFP is also the largest contributor to South–South trade within the UN system, through the purchase of food and services from developing countries. WFP's mission is to provide food aid to save lives in refugee and other emergency situations, to improve the nutrition and quality of life of vulnerable groups and to help to develop assets and promote the self-reliance of poor families and communities. WFP aims to focus its efforts on the world's poorest countries and to provide at least 90% of its total assistance to those designated as 'low-income food-deficit'. At the World Food Summit, held in November 1996, WFP endorsed the commitment to reduce by 50% the number of undernourished people, no later than 2015. During 2007 WFP food assistance benefited some 86.1m. people (including 53.6m. children) in 80 countries, of whom 23.8m. received aid through development projects, 15.3m. through emergency operations, and 47.0m. through Protracted Relief and Recovery Operations (PRROs). Total food deliveries in 2007 amounted to 3.3m. metric tons. WFP rations comprise basic food items (cereals, oil and pulses), and, where possible, additional complementary items (such as meat or fish, vegetables, fruit, fortified cereal blends, sugar and condiments).

WFP aims to address the causes of chronic malnourishment, which it identifies as poverty and lack of opportunity. It emphasizes the role played by women in combating hunger, and endeavours to address the specific nutritional needs of women, to increase their access to food and development resources, and to promote girls' education. It also focuses resources on supporting the food security of households and communities affected by HIV/AIDS and on promoting food security as a means of mitigating extreme poverty and vulnerability and thereby combating the spread and impact of HIV/AIDS. In February 2003 WFP and the Joint UN Programme on HIV/AIDS (UNAIDS) concluded an agreement to address jointly the relationship between HIV/AIDS, regional food shortages and chronic hunger, with a particular focus on Africa, South-East Asia and the Caribbean. In October of that year WFP became a co-sponsor of UNAIDS. WFP urges the development of new food aid strategies as a means of redressing global inequalities and thereby combating the threat of conflict and international terrorism.

WFP food donations must meet internationally-agreed standards applicable to trade in food products. In May 2003 WFP's Executive Board approved a policy on donations of genetically modified (GM) foods and other foods derived from biotechnology, determining that the Programme would continue to accept donations of GM/biotech food and that, when distributing it, relevant national standards would be respected.

WFP participated in the High-Level Conference on World Food Security and the Challenges of Climate Change and Bioenergy that was convened by FAO in June 2008 to address the impact of soaring levels of food and fuel prices in recent months. At that time WFP determined to allocate some US $1,200m. in extra-budgetary funds to alleviate hunger in 62 worst-affected countries. In mid-June WFP's Executive Board approved a four-year strategic plan that aimed to provide a new institutional framework to support vulnerable populations affected by the ongoing global food crisis and by possible future effects of global climate change. The plan emphasised prevention of hunger through early warning systems and analysis, local purchase of food, the use of focused cash and voucher programmes to ensure the accessibility to hungry people of already locally available food, and the maintenance of efficient and effective emergency response systems.

Since the 1990s WFP has developed a range of mechanisms to enhance its preparedness for emergency situations (such as conflict, drought and other natural disasters) and to improve its capacity for responding effectively to crises as they arise. A new programme of emergency response training was inaugurated in 2000, while security concerns for personnel was incorporated as a new element into all general planning and training activities. Through its Vulnerability Analysis and Mapping (VAM) project, WFP aims to identify potentially vulnerable groups by providing information on food security and the capacity of different groups for coping with shortages, and to enhance emergency contingency-planning and long-term assistance objectives. In 2008 VAM field units were operational in more than 50 countries.

Since 2003 WFP has been mandated to provide aviation transport services to the wider humanitarian community. The key elements of WFP's emergency response capacity are its strategic stores of food and logistics equipment, stand-by arrangements to enable the rapid deployment of personnel, communications and other essential equipment, and the Augmented Logistics Intervention Team for Emergencies (ALITE), which undertakes capacity assessments and contingency-planning. During 2000 WFP led efforts, undertaken with other UN humanitarian agencies, for the design and application of local UN Joint Logistics Centre facilities, which aimed to co-ordinate resources in an emergency situation. In 2001 a UN Humanitarian Response Depot was opened in Brindisi, Italy, under the direction of WFP experts, for the storage of essential rapid response equipment. In that year the Programme published a set of guidelines on contingency planning. During 2005 the UN's Inter-Agency Standing Committee (IASC), concerned with co-ordinating the international response to humanitarian disasters, developed a concept of organizing agency assistance to IDPs through the institutionalization of a 'Cluster Approach', currently comprising 11 core areas of activity. WFP was designated the lead agency for the clusters on Emergency Telecommunications (jointly with OCHA and UNICEF) and Logistics. During January 2008–June 2009 WFP was implementing a special operation to improve country-specific communications services in order to enhance country-level cluster capacities.

Through its development activities, WFP aims to alleviate poverty in developing countries by promoting self-reliant families and communities. Food is supplied, for example, as an incentive in development self-help schemes and as part-wages in labour-intensive projects of many kinds. In all its projects WFP aims to assist the most vulnerable groups and to ensure that beneficiaries have an adequate and balanced diet. Activities supported by the Programme include the settlement and resettlement of groups and communities; land reclamation and improvement; irrigation; the development of forestry and dairy farming; road construction; training of hospital staff; community development; and human resources development such as feeding expectant or nursing mothers and school children, and support for education, training and health programmes. No individual country is permitted to receive more than 10% of the Programme's available development resources. During 2001 WFP initiated a new Global School Feeding Campaign to strengthen international co-operation to expand educational opportunities for poor children and to improve the quality of the teaching environment. In 2003 WFP launched a *19-Cents-a-day* campaign to encourage donors to support its school feeding activities (19 US cents being the estimated cost of one school lunch). During 2007 school feeding projects benefited 19.3m. children.

Following a comprehensive evaluation of its activities, WFP is increasingly focused on linking its relief and development activities to provide a continuum between short-term relief and longer-term rehabilitation and development. In order to achieve this objective, WFP aims to integrate elements that strengthen disaster mitigation into development projects, including soil conservation, reafforestation, irrigation infrastructure, and transport construction and rehabilitation; and to promote capacity-building elements within relief operations, e.g. training, income-generating activities and environmental protection measures. In 1999 WFP adopted a new Food Aid and Development policy, which aims to use food assistance both to cover immediate requirements and to create conditions conducive to enhancing the long-term food security of vulnerable populations. During that year WFP began implementing PRROs, where the emphasis is on fostering stability, rehabilitation and long-term development for victims of natural disasters, displaced persons and refugees. PRROs are introduced no later than 18 months after the initial emergency operation and last no more than three years. When undertaken in collaboration with UNHCR and other international agencies, WFP has responsibility for mobilizing basic food commodities and for related transport, handling and storage costs. Some 31 new PRROs were approved in 2007.

In 2007 WFP operational expenditure in Europe and the CIS amounted to US $33.6m. (1% of total operational expenditure in that year).

WFP undertook a two-year PRRO to assist IDPs and other vulnerable people in Azerbaijan during July 2006–October 2008. A PRRO to provide transitional relief and recovery assistance to vulnerable populations in Armenia was being implemented during July 2007–December 2008. A transitional assistance and capacity-building PRRO aimed at supporting 212,000 beneficiaries in Georgia was being undertaken during January 2007–December 2008, and, during July 2007–June 2009, a PRRO was under way to provide transitional relief and recovery support to food-insecure households in Tajikistan (targeting 590,800 people).

Finance

The Programme is funded by voluntary contributions from donor countries, intergovernmental bodies such as the European Commission, and the private sector. Contributions are made in the form of commodities, finance and services (particularly shipping). Commitments to the International Emergency Food Reserve (IEFR), from which WFP provides the majority of its food supplies, and to the Immediate Response Account of the IEFR (IRA), are also made on a voluntary basis by donors. WFP's operational expenditures in 2007 amounted to some US $2,753m. Contributions by donors in that year totalled $2,705m.

Publications

Annual Report.
Food and Nutrition Handbook.
School Feeding Handbook.
World Hunger Series.

Food and Agriculture Organization of the United Nations—FAO

Address: Viale delle Terme di Caracalla, 00100 Rome, Italy.
Telephone: (06) 5705-1; **fax:** (06) 5705-3152; **e-mail:** fao-hq@fao.org; **internet:** www.fao.org.

FAO, the first specialized agency of the UN to be founded after the Second World War, aims to alleviate malnutrition and hunger, and serves as a co-ordinating agency for development programmes in the whole range of food and agriculture, including forestry and fisheries. It helps developing countries to promote educational and training facilities and to create appropriate institutions.

Organization

(October 2008)

CONFERENCE

The governing body is the FAO Conference of member nations. It meets every two years, formulates policy, determines the organization's programme and budget on a biennial basis, and elects new members. It also elects the Director-General of the Secretariat and the Independent Chairman of the Council. Regional conferences are also held each year.

COUNCIL

The FAO Council is composed of representatives of 49 member nations, elected by the Conference for rotating three-year terms. It is the interim governing body of FAO between sessions of the Conference. There are eight main Governing Committees of the Council: the Finance and Programme Committees, and the Committees on Commodity Problems, Fisheries, Agriculture, Forestry, World Food Security, and Constitutional and Legal Matters.

SECRETARIAT

There are some 3,600 FAO staff, of whom about one-half are based at headquarters. FAO maintains five regional offices (see below), nine sub-regional offices, five liaison offices (in Yokohama, Japan; Washington, DC, USA, liaison with North America; Geneva, Switzerland and New York, USA, with the UN; and Brussels, Belgium, with the European Union), and some 74 country offices. Work is undertaken by the following departments: Agriculture and Consumer Protection; Economic and Social Development; Fisheries and Aquaculture; Forestry; Human, Financial and Physical Resources; Knowledge and Communication; Natural Resource Management and Environment; and Technical Co-operation.

Director-General: Jacques Diouf (Senegal).

REGIONAL OFFICES

Europe and Central Asia: 1068 Budapest, Benczur u. 34, Hungary; tel. (1) 461-2000; fax (1) 351-7029; e-mail fao-seur@fao.org; internet www.fao.org/world/regional/reu; Regional Rep. Maria Kadlecikova.

Sub-regional Office for Central and Eastern Europe: 1068 Budapest, Benczur u. 34, Hungary; tel. (1) 461-2000; fax (1) 351-7029; e-mail fao-seur@fao.org; internet www.fao.org/regional/seur.

Sub-regional Office for Central Asia: Ivedik Cad. 55, 06170 Yenimahalle, Ankara, Turkey; tel. (312) 307-9517; fax (312) 307-1705; e-mail FAO-SEC@fao.org.

Activities

FAO aims to raise levels of nutrition and standards of living by improving the production and distribution of food and other commodities derived from farms, fisheries and forests. FAO's ultimate objective is the achievement of world food security, 'Food for All'. The organization provides technical information, advice and assistance by disseminating information; acting as a neutral forum for discussion of food and agricultural issues; advising governments on policy and planning; and developing capacity directly in the field.

In November 1996 FAO hosted the World Food Summit, which was held in Rome and was attended by heads of state and senior government representatives of 186 countries. Participants approved the Rome Declaration on World Food Security and the World Food Summit Plan of Action, with the aim of halving the number of people afflicted by undernutrition, at that time estimated to total 828m. world-wide, by no later than 2015. A review conference to assess progress in achieving the goals of the summit, entitled World Food Summit: Five Years Later, held in June 2002, reaffirmed commitment to this objective, which is also incorporated into the UN Millennium Development Goals (MDGs). During that month FAO announced the formulation of a global 'Anti-Hunger Programme', which aimed to promote investment in the agricultural sector and rural development, with a particular focus on small-scale farmers, and to enhance food access for those most in need, for example through the provision of school meals, schemes to feed pregnant and nursing mothers and food-for-work programmes. FAO hosts the UN System Network on Rural Development and Food Security, comprising some 20 UN bodies, which was established in 1997 as an interagency mechanism to follow-up the World Food Summits.

In November 1999 the FAO Conference approved a long-term Strategic Framework for the period 2000–15, which emphasized national and international co-operation in pursuing the goals of the 1996 World Food Summit. The Framework promoted interdisciplinarity and partnership, and defined three main global objectives: constant access by all people to sufficient, nutritionally adequate and safe food to ensure that levels of undernourishment were reduced by 50% by 2015 (see above); the continued contribution of sustainable agriculture and rural development to economic and social progress and well-being; and the conservation, improvement and sustainable use of natural resources. It identified five corporate strategies (each supported by several strategic objectives), covering the following areas: reducing food insecurity and rural poverty; ensuring enabling policy and regulatory frameworks for food, agriculture, fisheries and forestry; creating sustainable increases in the supply and availability of agricultural, fisheries and forestry products; conserving and enhancing sustainable use of the natural resource base; and generating knowledge. In October 2007 the report of an Independent External Evaluation into the role and functions of FAO recommended that the organization elaborate an immediate action plan for reform to ensure its continued efficiency and effectiveness.

In April 2008 the UN Secretary-General appointed FAO's Director-General as Vice-Chairman of a High Level Task Force (HLTF) on the Global Food Security Crisis, which aimed to address the impact of soaring levels of food and fuel prices in recent months and formulate a comprehensive framework for action.

World Food Day, commemorating the foundation of FAO, is held annually on 16 October.

AGRICULTURE AND CONSUMER PROTECTION

FAO's overall objective is to lead international efforts to counter hunger and to improve levels of nutrition. Within this context FAO is concerned to improve crop and grassland productivity and to develop sustainable agricultural systems to provide for enhanced food security and economic development. It provides member countries with technical advice for plant improvement, the application of plant biotechnology, the development of integrated production systems and rational grassland management. There are groups concerned with the main field cereal crops, i.e. rice, maize and wheat, which *inter alia* identify means of enhancing production, collect and analyse relevant data and promote collaboration between research institutions, government bodies and other farm management organizations. In 1985 and 1990 FAO's International Rice Commission endorsed the use of hybrid rice, which had been developed in the People's Republic of China, as a means of meeting growing demand for the crop, in particular in the Far East, and has subsequently assisted member countries to acquire the necessary technology and

training to develop hybrid rice production. In Africa FAO has collaborated with the West African Rice Development Association to promote and facilitate the use of new rice varieties and crop management practices. FAO is the lead agency for the International Year of the Potato (2008), which aims to highlight the importance of the potato in combating world hunger.

FAO is also concerned with the development and diversification of horticultural and industrial crops, for example oil seeds, fibres and medicinal plants. FAO collects and disseminates data regarding crop trials and new technologies. It has developed an information processing site, Ecocrop, to help farmers identify appropriate crops and environmental requirements. FAO works to protect and support the sustainable development of grasslands and pasture, which contribute to the livelihoods of an estimated 800m. people world-wide.

FAO's plant protection service incorporates a range of programmes concerned with the control of pests and the use of pesticides. In February 2001 FAO warned that some 30% of pesticides sold in developing countries did not meet internationally accepted quality standards. In November 2002 FAO adopted a revised International Code of Conduct on the Distribution and Use of Pesticides (first adopted in 1985) to reduce the inappropriate distribution and use of pesticides and other toxic compounds, particularly in developing countries. In September 1998 a new legally-binding treaty on trade in hazardous chemicals and pesticides was adopted at an international conference held in Rotterdam, Netherlands. The so-called Rotterdam Convention required that hazardous chemicals and pesticides banned or severely restricted in at least two countries should not be exported unless explicitly agreed by the importing country. It also identified certain pesticide formulations as too dangerous to be used by farmers in developing countries, and incorporated an obligation that countries halt national production of those hazardous compounds. The treaty entered into force in February 2004. FAO was co-operating with UNEP to provide an interim secretariat for the Convention. FAO has promoted the use of Integrated Pest Management (IPM) initiatives to encourage the use, at local level, of safer and more effective methods of pest control, such as biological control methods and natural predators.

FAO hosts the secretariat of the International Plant Protection Convention (first adopted in 1951, revised in 1997) which aims to prevent the spread of plant pests and to promote effective control measures. The secretariat helps to define phytosanitary standards, promote the exchange of information and extend technical assistance to contracting parties (169 at May 2008).

FAO is concerned with the conservation and sustainable use of plant and animal genetic resources. It works with regional and international associations to develop seed networks, to encourage the use of improved seed production systems, to elaborate quality control and certification mechanisms and to co-ordinate seed security activities, in particular in areas prone to natural or man-made disasters. FAO has developed a World Information and Early Warning System (WIEWS) to gather and disseminate information concerning plant genetic resources for food and agriculture and to undertake periodic assessments of the state of those resources. FAO is also developing, as part of the WIEWS, a Seed Information Service to extend information to member states on seeds, planting and new technologies. In June 1996 representatives of more than 150 governments convened in Leipzig, Germany, at an International Technical Conference organized by FAO to consider the use and conservation of plant genetic resources as an essential means of enhancing food security. The meeting adopted a Global Plan of Action, which included measures to strengthen the development of plant varieties and to promote the use and availability of local varieties and locally adapted crops to farmers, in particular following a natural disaster, war or civil conflict. In November 2001 the FAO Conference adopted the International Treaty on Plant Genetic Resources for Food and Agriculture, which was to provide a framework to ensure access to plant genetic resources and to related knowledge, technologies and funding. The Treaty entered into force in June 2004, having received the required number of ratifications, and the first meeting of the Treaty's Governing Body was convened in June 2006. At mid-2008 some 54 states had acceded to the Treaty.

FAO's Animal Production and Health Division is concerned with the control and management of major animal diseases, and, in recent years, with safeguarding humans from livestock diseases. Other programmes are concerned with the contribution of livestock to poverty alleviation, the efficient use of natural resources in livestock production, the management of animal genetic resources, promoting the exchange of information and mapping the distribution of livestock around the world. In 2001 FAO established a Pro-Poor Livestock Policy Initiative to support the formulation and implementation of livestock-related policies to improve the livelihood and nutrition of the world's rural poor, with an initial focus on the Andean region, the Horn of Africa, West Africa, South Asia and the Mekong.

The Emergency Prevention System for Transboundary Animal and Plant Pests and Diseases (EMPRES) was established in 1994 to strengthen FAO's activities in the prevention, early warning, control and, where possible, eradication of pests and highly contagious livestock diseases (which the system categorizes as epidemic diseases of strategic importance, such as rinderpest or foot-and-mouth; diseases requiring tactical attention at international or regional level, e.g. Rift Valley fever; and emerging diseases, e.g. bovine spongiform encephalopathy—BSE). EMPRES has a desert locust component, and has published guidelines on all aspects of desert locust monitoring. FAO has assumed responsibility for technical leadership and co-ordination of the Global Rinderpest Eradication Programme (GREP), which has the objective of eliminating the disease by 2010. In November 1997 FAO initiated a Programme Against African Trypanosomiasis, which aimed to counter the disease affecting cattle in almost one-third of Africa. In November 2004 FAO established a specialized Emergency Centre for Transboundary Animal Disease Operations (ECTAD) to enhance FAO's role in assisting member states to combat animal disease outbreaks and in co-ordinating international efforts to research, monitor and control transboundary disease crises. In May 2004 FAO and the World Organisation for Animal Health (OIE) signed an agreement to clarify their respective areas of competence and improve co-operation, in response to an increase in contagious transboundary animal diseases (such as foot-and-mouth disease and avian influenza, see below). The two bodies agreed to establish a global framework on the control of transboundary animal diseases, entailing improved international collaboration and circulation of information. In early 2006 the Global Early Warning and Response System for Major Animal Diseases, including Zoonoses (GLEWS), was established by FAO, OIE and the World Health Organization (WHO) to strengthen their joint capacity to detect, monitor and respond to animal disease threats.

In September 2004 FAO and WHO declared an ongoing epidemic in certain east Asian countries of the H5N1 strain of highly pathogenic avian influenza (HPAI) to be a 'crisis of global importance': the disease was spreading rapidly through bird populations and was also transmitting to human populations through contact with diseased birds (mainly poultry). In that month FAO published *Recommendations for the Prevention, Control and Eradication of Highly Pathogenic Avian Influenza in Asia*. In April 2005 FAO and OIE established an international network of laboratories and scientists (OFFLU) to exchange data and provide expert technical advise on avian influenza. In the following month FAO, with WHO and OIE, launched a global strategy for the progressive control of the disease. In November a conference on Avian Influenza and Human Pandemic Influenza, jointly organized by FAO, WHO and OIE and the World Bank, issued a plan of action identifying a number of responses, including: supporting the development of integrated national plans for H5N1 containment and human pandemic influenza preparedness and response; assisting countries with the aggressive control of H5N1 and with establishing a more detailed understanding of the role of wild birds in virus transmission; nominating rapid response teams of experts to support epidemiological field investigations; expanding national and regional capacity in surveillance, diagnosis, and alert and response systems; expanding the network of influenza laboratories; establishing multi-country networks for the control or prevention of animal transboundary diseases; expanding the global antiviral stockpile; strengthening veterinary infrastructures; and mapping a global strategy and work plan for co-ordinating antiviral and influenza vaccine research and development. In June 2006 FAO and OIE convened a scientific conference on the spread of H5N1 that advocated as a basis for H5N1 management early detection of the disease in wild birds, improved biosecurity and hygiene in the poultry trade, rapid response to disease outbreaks, and the establishment of a global tracking and monitoring facility involving participation by all relevant organizations, as well as by scientific centres, farmers' groupings, bird-watchers and hunters, and wildlife and wild bird habitat conservation bodies. The conference also urged investment in telemetry/satellite technology to improve tracking capabilities. International conference and pledging meetings on the disease have been convened in Beijing, People's Republic of China (PRC), in January 2006, Bamako, Mali, in December and in New Delhi, India, in December 2007. In January 2008 FAO warned that the virus remained a global threat with recent outbreaks confirmed in Bangladesh, Benin, PRC, Egypt, Germany, India, Indonesia, Iran, Israel, Myanmar, Poland, Russia, Ukraine, Turkey and Viet Nam. In August a new strain of HPAI not previously recorded in sub-Saharan Africa was detected in Nigeria.

In December 1992 FAO, with WHO, organized an International Conference on Nutrition, which approved a World Declaration on Nutrition and a Plan of Action, aimed at promoting efforts to combat malnutrition as a development priority. Since the conference, more than 100 countries have formulated national plans of action for nutrition, many of which were based on existing development plans such as comprehensive food security initiatives, national poverty alleviation programmes and action plans to attain the targets set by the World Summit for Children in September 1990. FAO promotes other efforts, at household and community level, to improve nutrition and food security, for example a programme to support home gardens. It aims to assist the identification of food insecure and vulnerable populations, both through its *State of Food Insecurity in the World* reports and taking a lead role in the development of Food Insecurity and Vulnerability Information and Mapping Systems (FIVIMS), a recommendation of the World Food Summit. In 1999 FAO signed a memorandum of understanding with UNAIDS on strengthening co-operation to combat the threat posed by the HIV/AIDS epidemic to food security, nutrition and rural livelihoods. FAO is committed to incorporating HIV/AIDS into food security and livelihood projects, to strengthening community care and to highlighting the importance of nutrition in the care of those living with HIV/AIDS.

FAO is committed to promoting food quality and safety in all different stages of food production and processing. It supports the development of integrated food control systems by member states, which incorporate aspects of food control management, inspection, risk analysis and quality assurance. The joint FAO/WHO Codex Alimentarius Commission, established in 1962, aims to protect the health of consumers, ensure fair trade practices and promote the co-ordination of food standards activities at an international level. In January 2001 a joint team of FAO and WHO experts issued a report concerning the allergenicity of foods derived from biotechnology (i.e. genetically modified—GM—foods). In July the Codex Alimentarius Commission agreed the first global principles for assessing the safety of GM foods, and approved a series of maximum levels of environmental contaminants in food. In June 2004 FAO published guidelines for assessing possible risks posed to plants by living modified organisms (LMOs). In July 2001 the Codex Alimentarius Commission adopted guidelines on organic livestock production, covering organic breeding methods, the elimination of growth hormones and certain chemicals in veterinary medicines, and the use of good quality organic feed with no meat or bone meal content. In January 2003 FAO organized a technical consultation on biological risk management in food and agriculture which recognized the need for a more integrated approach to so-called biosecurity, i.e. the prevention, control and management of risks to animal, human and plant life and health. FAO has subsequently developed a *Toolkit*, which was published in 2007, to help countries to develop and implement national biosecurity systems and to enhance biosecurity capacity. In October 2006 FAO inaugurated a new Crisis Management Centre (CMC) to co-ordinate the organization's response to outbreaks of H5N1 and other major emergencies related to animal or food health.

FAO aims to assist member states to enhance the efficiency, competitiveness and profitability of their agricultural and food enterprises. FAO extends assistance in training, capacity building and the formulation of agribusiness development strategies. It promotes the development of effective 'value chains' connecting primary producers with consumers and supports other linkages within the agribusiness industry. Similarly, FAO aims to strengthen marketing systems, links between producers and retailers and training in agricultural marketing and works to improve the regulatory framework for agricultural marketing. FAO promotes the use of new machinery and technologies to increase agricultural production and extends a range of services to support mechanization, including training, maintenance, testing and the promotion of labour saving technologies. Other programmes are focused on farm management, post-harvest management, food and non-food processing, rural finance, and rural infrastructure. FAO helps reduce immediate post-harvest losses, with the introduction of improved processing methods and storage systems. FAO participates in PhAction, a forum of 12 agencies that was established in 1999 to promote post-harvest research and the development of effective post-harvest services and infrastructure.

FAO's Joint Division with the International Atomic Energy Agency (IAEA) is concerned with the use of nuclear techniques in food and agriculture. It co-ordinates research projects, provides scientific and technical support to technical co-operation projects and administers training courses. A joint laboratory in Seibersdorf, Austria, is concerned with testing biotechnologies and in developing non-toxic fertilizers (especially those that are locally available) and improved strains of food crops (especially from indigenous varieties). In the area of animal production and health, the Joint Division has developed progesterone-measuring and disease diagnostic kits. Other sub-programmes of the Joint Division are concerned with soil and water, plant breeding and nutrition, insect pest control and food and environmental protection.

NATURAL RESOURCES MANAGEMENT AND ENVIRONMENT

FAO is committed to promoting the responsible and sustainable management of natural resources and other activities to protect the environment. FAO assists member states to mitigate the impact of climate change on agriculture, to adapt and enhance the resilience of agricultural systems to climate change, and to promote practices to reduce the emission of greenhouse gases from the agricultural sector. In recent years FAO has strengthened its work in the area of using natural biomass resources as fuel, both at grassroots level and industrial processing of cash crops. In 2006 FAO established the International Bioenergy Platform to serve as a focal point for research, data collection, capacity-building and strategy formulation by local, regional and international bodies concerned with bioenergy. FAO also serves as the secretariat for the Global Bioenergy Partnership, which was inaugurated in May 2006 to facilitate the collaboration between governments, international agencies and representatives of the private sector and civil society in the sustainable development of bioenergy. In June 2008 FAO hosted a High Level Conference on World Food Security and the Challenges of Climate Change and Bioenergy. The meeting adopted a Declaration on Food Security, urging the international donor community to increase its support to developing countries and countries with economies in transition. The Declaration also noted an urgent need to develop the agricultural sectors and expand food production in such countries and for increased investment in rural development, agriculture and agribusiness.

FAO aims to enhance the sustainability of land and water systems, and as a result to secure agricultural productivity, through the improved tenure, management, development and conservation of those natural resources. The organization promotes equitable access to land and water resources and supports integrated land and water management, including river basin management and improved irrigation systems. FAO has developed AQUASTAT as a global information system concerned with water and agricultural issues, comprising databases, country and regional profiles, surveys and maps.

Within the FAO's Natural Resources Management and Environment Department is a Research and Extension Division, which provides advisory and technical services to support national capacity-building, research, communication and education activities. It maintains several databases which support and facilitate the dissemination of information, for example relating to proven transferable technologies and biotechnologies in use in developing countries. The Division advises countries on communication strategies to strengthen agricultural and rural development, and has actively supported the use of rural radio. FAO is the UN lead agency of an initiative, 'Education for Rural People', which aims to improve the quality of and access to basic education for people living in rural areas and to raise awareness of the issue as an essential element of achieving the MDGs. The Research and Extension Division hosts the secretariat of the Global Forum on Agricultural Research, which was established in October 1996 as a collaboration of research centres, non-governmental and private sector organizations and development agencies. The Forum aims to strengthen research and promote knowledge partnerships concerned with the alleviation of poverty, the increase in food security and the sustainable use of natural resources. The Division also hosts the secretariat of the Science Council of the Consultative Group on International Agricultural Research (CGIAR), which, specifically, aims to enhance and promote the quality, relevance and impact of science within the network of CGIAR research centres and to mobilize global scientific expertise.

FISHERIES AND AQUACULTURE

FAO aims to facilitate and secure the long-term sustainable development of fisheries and aquaculture, in both inland and marine waters, and to promote its contribution to world food security. In March 1995 a ministerial meeting of fisheries adopted the Rome Consensus on World Fisheries, which identified a need for immediate action to eliminate overfishing and to rebuild and enhance depleting fish stocks. In November the FAO Conference adopted a Code of Conduct for Responsible Fishing, which incorporated many global fisheries and aquaculture issues (including fisheries resource conservation and development, fish catches, seafood and fish processing, commercialization, trade and research) to promote the sustainable development of the sector. In February 1999 the FAO Committee on Fisheries adopted new international measures, within the framework of the Code of Conduct, in order to reduce over-exploitation of the world's fish resources, as well as plans of action for the conservation and management of sharks and the reduction in the incidental catch of seabirds in longline fisheries. The voluntary measures were endorsed at a ministerial meeting, held in March and attended by representatives of some 126 countries, which issued a declaration to promote the implementation of the Code of Conduct and to achieve sustainable management of fisheries and aquaculture. In March 2001 FAO adopted an international plan of action to address the continuing problem of so-called illegal, unreported and unregulated fishing (IUU). In that year FAO estimated that about one-half of major marine fish stocks were fully exploited, one-quarter underexploited, at least 15% over-exploited, and 10% depleted or recovering from depletion. IUU was estimated to account for up to 30% of total catches in certain fisheries. In October FAO and the Icelandic Government jointly organized the Reykjavik Conference on Responsible Fisheries in the Marine Ecosystem, which adopted a declaration on pursuing responsible and sustainable fishing activities in the context of ecosystem-based fisheries management (EBFM). EBFM involves determining the boundaries of individual marine ecosystems, and maintaining or rebuilding the habitats and biodiversity of each of these so that all species will be supported at levels of maximum production. In March 2005 FAO's Committee of Fisheries adopted voluntary guidelines for the so-called eco-labelling and certification of fish and fish products, i.e. based on information regarding capture management and the sustainable use of resources.

FAO undertakes extensive monitoring, publishing every two years *The State of World Fisheries and Aquaculture*, and collates and maintains relevant databases. It formulates country and regional profiles and has developed a specific information network for the fisheries sector, GLOBEFISH, which gathers and disseminates information regarding market trends, tariffs and other industry issues. FAO aims to extend technical support to member states with regard to the management and conservation of aquatic resources, and other measures to improve the utilization and trade of products, including the reduction of post-harvest losses, preservation marketing and quality assurance. FAO promotes aquaculture (which contributes almost one-third of annual global fish landings) as a valuable source of animal protein and income-generating activity for rural communities. It has undertaken to develop an ecosystem approach to aquaculture (EAA) and works to integrate aquaculture with agricultural and irrigation systems. In February 2000 FAO and the Network of Aquaculture Centres in Asia and the Pacific (NACA) jointly convened a Conference on Aquaculture in the Third Millennium, which was held in Bangkok, Thailand, and attended by participants representing more than 200 governmental and non-governmental organizations. The Conference debated global trends in aquaculture and future policy measures to ensure the sustainable development of the sector. It adopted the Bangkok Declaration and Strategy for Aquaculture Beyond 2000.

FORESTRY

FAO is committed to the sustainable management of trees, forests and forestry resources. It aims to address the critical balance of ensuring the conservation of forests and forestry resources while maximising their potential to contribute to food security and social and economic development. FAO's Strategic Plan for Forestry was approved in March 1999; its main objectives were to maintain the environmental diversity of forests, to realize the economic potential of forests and trees within a sustainable framework, and to expand access to information on forestry. In March 2007 the Committee on Forestry requested that a consultative process be initiated to develop a new strategic plan, with the intention that it be presented for discussion at the next meeting of the Committee to be held in March 2009. Regional forestry commissions were to consider the strategy at their meetings to be convened throughout 2008.

FAO assists member countries to formulate, implement and monitor national forestry programmes, and encourages the participation of all stakeholders in developing plans for the sustainable management of tree and forest resources. FAO also helps to implement national assessments of those programmes and of other forestry activities. At a global level FAO undertakes surveillance of the state of the world's forests and publishes a report every two years. A separate Forest Resources Assessment is published every five years, the latest (for 2010) was initiated in March 2008. FAO is committed to collecting and disseminating accurate information and data on forests. It maintains the Forestry Information System (FORIS) to make relevant information and forest-related databases widely accessible.

FAO is a member of the Collaborative Partnership on Forests, which was established in April 2004 on the recommendation of the UN's Economic and Social Council. FAO organizes a World Forestry Congress, generally held every six years; the next was to be convened in Buenos Aires, Argentina, in October 2009.

ECONOMIC AND SOCIAL DEVELOPMENT

FAO provides a focal point for economic research and policy analysis relating to food security and sustainable development. It produces studies and reports on agricultural development, the impact of development programmes and projects, and the world food situation, as well as on commodity prices, trade and medium-term projections. It supports the development of methodologies and guidelines to improve research into food and agriculture and the integration of wider concepts, such as social welfare, environmental factors and nutrition, into research projects. In November 2004 the FAO Council adopted a set of voluntary Right to Food Guidelines, and established a dedicated administrative unit, that aimed to 'support the progressive realization of the right to adequate food in the context of national food security' by providing practical guidance to countries in support of their efforts to achieve the 1996 World Food Summit commitment and UN MDG relating to hunger reduction. FAO's Statistical Division assembles, analyses and disseminates statistical data on world food and agriculture and aims to ensure the consistency, broad coverage and quality of available data. The Division advises member countries on enhancing their statistical capabilities. It maintains FAOSTAT as a core database of statistical information relating to nutrition, fisheries, forestry, food production, land use, population etc. In 2004 FAO developed a new statistical framework to provide for the organization and integration of statistical data and metadata from sources within a particular country. CountrySTAT was piloted in Kenya, Kyrgyzstan and Ghana in 2005 and in 15 more developing countries in 2006/07. FAO's internet-based interactive World Agricultural Information Centre (WAICENT) offers access to agricultural publications, technical documentation, codes of conduct, data, statistics and multimedia resources. FAO compiles and co-ordinates an extensive range of international databases on agriculture, fisheries, forestry, food and statistics, the most important of these being AGRIS (the International Information System for the Agricultural Sciences and Technology) and CARIS (the Current Agricultural Research Information System). In June 2000 FAO organized a high-level Consultation on Agricultural Information Management (COAIM), which aimed to increase access to and use of agricultural information by policy-makers and others. The second COAIM was held in September 2002 and the third meeting was convened in June 2007.

FAO's Global Information and Early Warning System (GIEWS), which become operational in 1975, maintains a database on and monitors the crop and food outlook at global, regional, national and sub-national levels in order to detect emerging food supply difficulties and disasters and to ensure rapid intervention in countries experiencing food supply shortages. It publishes regular reports on the weather conditions and crop prospects in sub-Saharan Africa and in the Sahel region, issues special alerts which describe the situation in countries or sub-regions experiencing food difficulties, and recommends an appropriate international response. FAO has also supported the development and implementation of Food Insecurity and Vulnerability Information and Mapping Systems (FIVIMS) and hosts the secretariat of the inter-agency working group on development of the FIVIMS. In October 2007 FAO inaugurated an online Global Forum on Food Security and Nutrition, to contribute to the compilation and dissemination of information relating to food security and nutrition throughout the world. In August 2008 a regular report of the GIEWS identified 33 countries as being in crisis and requiring external assistance, of which 21 were in Africa, 11 in Asia and the Near East and one in Latin America and the Caribbean. All countries were identified as lacking the resources to deal with critical problems of food insecurity, including many severely affected by the high cost of food and fuel.

In September 2007 GIEWS issued a special report on the food production situation in Moldova.

TECHNICAL CO-OPERATION

The Technical Co-operation Department has responsibility for FAO's operational activities, including policy development assistance to member countries; the mobilization of resources; investment support; field operations; emergency operations and rehabilitation; and the Technical Co-operation Programme.

FAO provides policy advice to support the formulation, implementation and evaluation of agriculture, rural development and food security strategies in member countries. It administers a project to assist developing countries to strengthen their technical negotiating skills, in respect to agricultural trade issues. FAO also aims to co-ordinate and facilitate the mobilization of extrabudgetary funds from donors and governments for particular projects. It administers a range of trust funds, including a Trust Fund for Food Security and Food Safety, established in 2002 to generate resources for projects to combat hunger, and the Government Co-operative Programme. FAO's Investment Centre, established in 1964, aims to promote greater external investment in agriculture and rural development by assisting member countries to formulate effective and sustainable projects and programmes. The Centre collaborates with international financing institutions and bilateral donors in the preparation of projects, and administers cost-sharing arrangements, with, typically, FAO funding 40% of a project. The Centre is a co-chair (with the German government) of the Global Donor Platform for Rural Development, which was established in 2004, comprising multilateral, donor and international agencies, development banks and research institutions, to improve the co-ordination and effectiveness of rural development assistance.

FAO's Technical Co-operation Programme, which was inaugurated in 1976, provides technical expertise and funding for small-scale projects to address specific issues within a country's agriculture, fisheries or forestry sectors. An Associate Professional Officers programme co-ordinates the sponsorship and placement of young professionals to gain experience working in an aspect of rural or agricultural development.

In 1994 FAO initiated the Special Programme for Food Security (SPFS), designed to assist low-income countries with a food deficit to increase food production and productivity as rapidly as possible, primarily through the widespread adoption by farmers of improved production technologies, with emphasis on areas of high potential. Within the SPFS framework are national and regional food security initiatives, all of which aim towards the MDG objective of reducing the incidence of hunger by 50% by 2015. In 2007 the SPFS was operational in 102 countries, of which 82 were categorized as 'low-income food-deficit'. The Programme promotes South-South co-operation to improve food security and the exchange of knowledge and experience. By 2007 38 bilateral co-operation agreements were in force, for example, between Egypt and Cameroon, and Viet Nam and Benin.

FAO organizes an annual series of fund-raising events, 'TeleFood', some of which are broadcast on television and the internet, in order to raise public awareness of the problems of hunger and malnutrition. Since its inception in 1997 public donations to TeleFood have reached some US $20m., financing more than 2,500 'grass-roots' projects in 130 countries. The projects have provided tools, seeds and other essential supplies directly to small-scale farmers, and have been especially aimed at helping women.

The Technical Co-operation Division co-ordinates FAO's emergency operations, concerned with all aspects of disaster and risk prevention, mitigation, reduction and emergency relief and rehabilitation, with a particular emphasis on food security and rural populations. FAO works with governments to develop and implement disaster prevention policies and practices. It aims to strengthen the capacity of local institutions to manage and mitigate risk and provides technical assistance to improve access to land for displaced populations in countries following conflict or a natural disaster. Other disaster prevention and reduction efforts include dissemination of information from the various early-warning systems and support for adaptation to climate variability and change, for example by the use of drought-resistance crops or the adoption of conservation agriculture techniques. Following an emergency FAO works with governments and other development and humanitarian partners to assess the immediate and longer-term agriculture and food security needs of the affected population. It has developed an Integrated Food Security and Humanitarian Phase Classification Scheme to determine the appropriate response to a disaster situation. Emergency co-ordination units may be established to manage the local response to an emergency and to facilitate and co-ordinate the delivery of inter-agency assistance. In order to rehabilitate agricultural production following a natural or man-made disaster FAO provides emergency seed, tools, other materials and technical and training assistance. During 2005 the UN's Inter-Agency Standing Committee, concerned with co-ordinating the international response to humanitarian disasters, developed a concept of providing assistance through a 'cluster' approach, comprising core areas of activity. FAO was designated the lead agency for the Agriculture cluster. FAO also contributes the agricultural relief and rehabilitation component of the UN's Consolidated Appeals Process, which aims to co-ordinate and enhance the effectiveness of the international community's response to an emergency. In April 2004 FAO established a Special Fund for Emergency and Rehabilitation Activities to enable it to response promptly to a humanitarian crisis before making an emergency appeal for additional resources.

In 2008 FAO was implementing a programme to strengthen the production and marketing of high-value vegetable crops, under both open field and greenhouse cultivation, in the North Caucasus.

FAO Statutory Bodies
(based at the Rome headquarters, unless otherwise indicated)

Codex Alimentarius Commission (Joint FAO/WHO Food Standards Programme): e-mail codex@fao.org; internet www.codexalimentarius.net; f. 1962 to make proposals for the co-ordination of all international food standards work and to publish a code of international food standards; established Intergovernmental Task Force on Foods Derived from Biotechnology in 1999; Trust Fund to support participation by least-developed countries was inaugurated in 2003; there are numerous specialized Codex committees, e.g. for food labelling, hygiene and additives, pesticide residues, milk and milk products, and processed fruits and vegetables; 165 member states.

European Commission on Agriculture: f. 1949 to encourage and facilitate action and co-operation in technological agricultural problems among member states and between international organizations concerned with agricultural technology in Europe.

European Commission for the Control of Foot-and-Mouth Disease: internet www.fao.org/ag/againfo/commissions/en/eufmd/eufmd.html; f. 1953 to promote national and international action for the control of the disease in Europe and its final eradication.

European Forestry Commission: f. 1947 to advise on the formulation of forest policy and to review and co-ordinate its implementation on a regional level; to exchange information and to make recommendations; 27 member states.

European Inland Fisheries Advisory Commission: internet www.fao.org/fi/body/eifac/eifac.asp; f. 1957 to promote improvements in inland fisheries and to advise member governments and FAO on inland fishery matters; 34 member states.

International Poplar Commission: f. 1947 to study scientific, technical, social and economic aspects of poplar and willow cultivation; to promote the exchange of ideas and material between research workers, producers and users; to arrange joint research programmes, congresses, study tours; to make recommendations to the FAO Conference and to National Poplar Commissions.

Finance

FAO's Regular Programme, which is financed by contributions from member governments, covers the cost of FAO's Secretariat, its Technical Co-operation Programme (TCP) and part of the cost of several special action programmes. The budget for the two-year period 2008–09 totalled US $929.8m. Much of FAO's technical assistance programme is funded from extra-budgetary sources, predominantly by trust funds that come mainly from donor countries and international financing institutions.

Publications

Commodity Review and Outlook (annually).
Ethical Issues in Food and Agriculture.
FAO Statistical Yearbook (annually).
FAOSTAT Statistical Database (online).
Food Crops and Shortages (6 a year).
Food Outlook (5 a year).
Food Safety and Quality Update (monthly; electronic bulletin).
Forest Resources Assessment.
The State of Agricultural Commodity Markets (every 2 years).
The State of Food and Agriculture (annually).
The State of Food Insecurity in the World (annually).
The State of World Fisheries and Aquaculture (every 2 years).
The State of the World's Forests (every 2 years).
Unasylva (quarterly).
Yearbook of Fishery Statistics.
Yearbook of Forest Products.
Commodity reviews; studies, manuals. A complete catalogue of publications is available at www.fao.org/icatalog/inter-e.htm.

International Atomic Energy Agency—IAEA

Address: POB 100, Wagramerstrasse 5, 1400 Vienna, Austria.
Telephone: (1) 26000; **fax:** (1) 26007; **e-mail:** official.mail@iaea.org; **internet:** www.iaea.org.

The International Atomic Energy Agency (IAEA) is an intergovernmental organization, established in 1957 in accordance with a decision of the General Assembly of the United Nations. Although it is autonomous, the IAEA is administratively a member of the United Nations, and reports on its activities once a year to the UN General Assembly. Its main objectives are to enlarge the contribution of atomic energy to peace, health and prosperity throughout the world and to ensure, so far as it is able, that assistance provided by it or at its request or under its supervision or control is not used in such a way as to further any military purpose. The 2005 Nobel Peace Prize was awarded, in two equal parts, to the IAEA and to the Agency's Director-General.

Organization

(October 2008)

GENERAL CONFERENCE

The Conference, comprising representatives of all member states, convenes each year for general debate on the Agency's policy, budget and programme. It elects members to the Board of Governors, and approves the appointment of the Director-General; it admits new member states.

BOARD OF GOVERNORS

The Board of Governors consists of 35 member states elected by the General Conference. It is the principal policy-making body of the Agency and is responsible to the General Conference. Under its own authority, the Board approves all safeguards agreements, important projects and safety standards.

SECRETARIAT

The Secretariat, comprising 2,326 staff at 31 December 2007, is headed by the Director-General, who is assisted by six Deputy Directors-General. The Secretariat is divided into six departments: Technical Co-operation; Nuclear Energy; Nuclear Safety and Security; Nuclear Sciences and Applications; Safeguards; and Management. A Standing Advisory Group on Safeguards Implementation advises the Director-General on technical aspects of safeguards.

Director-General: Dr MOHAMED EL-BARADEI (Egypt).

Activities

In recent years the IAEA has implemented several reforms of its management structure and operations. The three pillars supporting the Agency's activities are: safety and security, science and technology (assisting research on and practical application of atomic energy for peaceful uses), and safeguards and verification (ensuring that special fissionable and other materials, services, equipment and information made available by the Agency or at its request or under its supervision are not used for any non-peaceful purpose).

TECHNICAL CO-OPERATION AND TRAINING

The IAEA provides assistance in the form of experts, training and equipment to technical co-operation projects and applications worldwide, with an emphasis on radiation protection and safety-related activities. Training is provided to scientists, and experts and lecturers are assigned to provide specialized help on specific nuclear applications. The IAEA supported the foundation in September 2003 of the World Nuclear University, comprising a world-wide network of institutions that aim to strengthen international co-operation in promoting the safe use of nuclear power in energy production, and in the application of nuclear science and technology in areas including sustainable agriculture and nutrition, medicine, fresh water resources management and environmental protection.

FOOD AND AGRICULTURE

In co-operation with FAO, the Agency conducts programmes of applied research on the use of radiation and isotopes in fields including: efficiency in the use of water and fertilizers; improvement of food crops by induced mutations; eradication or control of destructive insects by the introduction of sterilized insects (radiation-based Sterile Insect Technique); improvement of livestock nutrition and health; studies on improving efficacy and reducing residues of pesticides, and increasing utilization of agricultural wastes; and food preservation by irradiation. The programmes are implemented by the Joint FAO/IAEA Division of Nuclear Techniques in Food and Agriculture and by the FAO/IAEA Agriculture and Biotechnology Laboratory, based at IAEA's laboratory complex in Seibersdorf, Austria. A Training and Reference Centre for Food and Pesticide Control, based at Seibersdorf, supports the implementation of national legislation and trade agreements ensuring the quality and safety of food products in international trade.

LIFE SCIENCES

In co-operation with the World Health Organization (WHO), the IAEA promotes the use of nuclear techniques in medicine, biology and health-related environmental research, provides training, and conducts research on techniques for improving the accuracy of radiation dosimetry.

The IAEA/WHO Network of Secondary Standard Dosimetry Laboratories (SSDLs) comprises 81 laboratories in 62 member states.

The Agency's Dosimetry Laboratory in Seibersdorf performs dose inter-comparisons for both SSDLs and radiotherapy centres. The IAEA undertakes maintenance plans for nuclear laboratories; national programmes of quality control for nuclear medicine instruments; quality control of radioimmunoassay techniques; radiation sterilization of medical supplies; and improvement of cancer therapy.

PHYSICAL AND CHEMICAL SCIENCES

The Agency's programme in physical sciences includes industrial applications of isotopes and radiation technology; application of nuclear techniques to mineral exploration and exploitation; radio-pharmaceuticals; and hydrology, involving the use of isotope techniques for assessment of water resources. Nuclear data services are provided, and training is given for nuclear scientists from developing countries. The Physics, Chemistry and Instrumentation Laboratory at Seibersdorf supports the Agency's research in human health, industry, water resources and environment.

NUCLEAR POWER

At December 2006 there were 435 nuclear power plants in operation and 29 reactors under construction world-wide (of which 17 were located in developing countries). Nuclear power accounted for about 16% of total electrical energy generated during 2006. The IAEA helps developing member states to introduce nuclear-powered electricity-generating plants through assistance with planning, feasibility studies, surveys of manpower and infrastructure, and safety measures. The Agency also assesses life extension and decommissioning strategies for ageing nuclear power plants. It publishes books on numerous aspects of nuclear power, and provides training courses on safety in nuclear power plants and other topics. An energy data bank collects and disseminates information on nuclear technology, and a power-reactor information system monitors the technical performance of nuclear power plants. There is increasing interest in the use of nuclear reactors for seawater desalination and radiation hydrology techniques to provide potable water. In July 1992 the EC, Japan, Russia and the USA signed an agreement to co-operate in the engineering design of an International Thermonuclear Experimental Reactor (ITER). The project aimed to demonstrate the scientific and technological feasibility of fusion energy, with the aim of providing a source of clean, abundant energy in the 21st century. An Extension Agreement, signed in 1998, provided for the continuation of the project. Negotiations on the the Joint Implementation of ITER commenced in June 2001. The People's Republic of China and the Republic of Korea also participate in the process. In May 2001 the International Project on Innovative Nuclear Reactors and Fuel Cycles (INPRO) was inaugurated. INPRO, which has 28 members, aims to promote nuclear energy as a means of meeting future sustainable energy requirements and to facilitate the exchange of information by member states to advance innovations in nuclear technology. The IAEA is a permanent observer at the Generation IV International Forum (GIF), which was inaugurated in 2000 and aims to establish a number of international collaborative nuclear research and development agreements.

RADIOACTIVE WASTE MANAGEMENT

The Agency provides practical help to member states in the management of radioactive waste. The Waste Management Advisory Programme (WAMAP) was established in 1987, and undertakes advisory missions in member states. A code of practice to prevent the illegal dumping of radioactive waste was drafted in 1989, and another on the international transboundary movement of waste was drafted in 1990. A ban on the dumping of radioactive waste at sea came into effect in 1994, under the Convention on the Prevention of Marine Pollution by Dumping of Wastes and Other Matters. The IAEA was to determine radioactive levels, for purposes of the Convention, and provide assistance to countries for the safe disposal of radioactive wastes. A new category of radioactive waste—very low level waste (VLLW)—was introduced in the early 2000s in some countries. A VLLW repository, at Morvilliers, France, became fully operational in 2004. The Agency has issued modal regulations for the air, sea and land transportation of all radioactive materials.

In September 1997 the IAEA adopted a Joint Convention on the Safety of Spent Fuel Management and on the Safety of Radioactive Waste Management. The first internationally binding legal device to address such issues, the Convention was to ensure the safe storage and disposal of nuclear and radioactive waste, during both the construction and operation of a nuclear power plant, as well as following its closure. The Convention entered into force in June 2001, and had been ratified by 46 parties at March 2008.

NUCLEAR SAFETY

The IAEA's nuclear safety programme encourages international co-operation in the exchange of information, promoting implementation of its safety standards and providing advisory safety services. It includes the IAEA International Nuclear Event Scale (INES), which measures the severity of nuclear events, incidents and accidents; the Incident Reporting System; an emergency preparedness programme (which maintains an Emergency Response Centre, located in Vienna, Austria); operational safety review teams; the International Nuclear Safety Group (INSAG); the Radiation Protection Advisory Team; and a safety research co-ordination programme. The safety review teams provide member states with advice on achieving and maintaining a high level of safety in the operation of nuclear power plants, while research programmes establish risk criteria for the nuclear fuel cycle and identify cost-effective means to reduce risks in energy systems. A new version of the INES, issued in July 2008, incorporated revisions aimed at providing more detailed ratings of activities including human exposure to sources of radiation and the transportation of radioactive materials.

The nuclear safety programme promotes a global safety regime, which aims to ensure the protection of people and the environment from the effects of ionizing radiation and the minimization of the likelihood of potential nuclear accidents, etc. Through the Commission on Safety Standards (which has sub-committees on nuclear safety standards, radiation safety standards, transport safety standards and waste safety standards) the programme establishes IAEA safety standards and provides for their application. In September 2006 the IAEA published a new primary safety standard, the Fundamental Safety Principles, representing a unified philosophy of nuclear safety and protection that was to provide the conceptual basis for the Agency's entire safety standards agenda. The IAEA's Safety Glossary Terminology Used in Nuclear Safety and Radiation Protection is updated regularly.

The Convention on the Physical Protection of Nuclear Material was signed in 1980, which committed contracting states to ensuring the protection of nuclear material during transportation within their territory or on board their ships or aircraft. In July 2005 delegates from 89 states party adopted a number of amendments aimed at strengthening the Convention.

Following a serious accident at the Chornobyl (Chernobyl) nuclear power plant in Ukraine (then part of the USSR) in April 1986, two conventions were formulated by the IAEA and entered into force in October. The first, the Convention on Early Notification of a Nuclear Accident, commits parties to provide information about nuclear accidents with possible transboundary effects at the earliest opportunity (it had 102 parties by March 2008); and the second, the Convention on Assistance in the Case of a Nuclear Accident or Radiological Emergency, commits parties to endeavour to provide assistance in the event of a nuclear accident or radiological emergency (this had 100 parties by March 2008). During 1990 the IAEA organized an assessment of the consequences of the Chernobyl accident, undertaken by an international team of experts, who reported to an international conference on the effects of the accident, convened at the IAEA headquarters in Vienna in May 1991. In February 1993 INSAG published an updated report on the Chernobyl incident, which emphasized the role of design factors in the accident, and the need to implement safety measures in the RBMK-type reactor. In March 1994 an IAEA expert mission visited Chernobyl and reported continuing serious deficiencies in safety at the defunct reactor and the units remaining in operation. An international conference reviewing the radiological consequences of the accident, 10 years after the event, was held in April 1996, co-sponsored by the IAEA, WHO and the European Commission. The last of the Chernobyl plant's three operating units was officially closed in December 2000. During the 2000s the IAEA was offering a wide range of assistance with the decommissioning of Chernobyl.

In September 1999 the IAEA activated its Emergency Response Centre, following a serious incident at a fuel conversion facility in Tokaimura, Japan. The Centre was used to process information from the Japanese authorities and to ensure accurate reporting of the event. In October a three-member IAEA team of experts visited the site to undertake a preliminary investigation into the causes and consequences of the accident.

An International Convention on Nuclear Safety was adopted at an IAEA conference in June 1994. The Convention applies to land-based civil nuclear power plants: adherents commit themselves to fundamental principles of safety, and maintain legislative frameworks governing nuclear safety. The Convention entered into force in October 1996 and had been ratified by 61 states by March 2008.

In September 1997 more than 80 member states adopted a protocol to revise the 1963 Vienna Convention on Civil Liability for Nuclear Damage, fixing the minimum limit of liability for the operator of a nuclear reactor at 300m. Special Drawing Rights (SDRs, the accounting units of the IMF) in the event of an accident. The amended protocol also extended the length of time during which claims may be brought for loss of life or injury. It entered into force in October 2003. The International Expert Group on Nuclear Liability (INLEX) was established in the same year. A Convention on Supplementary Compensation for Nuclear Damage established a further compensatory fund to provide for the payment of damages following an accident; contributions to the Fund were to be calculated on the basis of the nuclear capacity of each member state. The Convention had three contracting states by March 2008.

In July 1996 the IAEA co-ordinated a study on the radiological situation at the Mururoa and Fangatauta atolls, following the French nuclear test programmes in the South Pacific. Results published in May 1998 concluded there was no radiological health risk and that neither remedial action nor continued environmental monitoring was necessary.

The IAEA is developing a training course on measurement methods and risk analysis relating to the presence of depleted uranium (which can be used in ammunition) in post-conflict areas. In November 2000 IAEA specialists participated in a fact-finding mission organized by UNEP in Kosovo and Metohija, which aimed to assess the environmental and health consequences of the use of depleted uranium in ammunition by NATO during its 1999 aerial offensive against the then Federal Republic of Yugoslavia. (A report on the situation was published by UNEP in March 2001.) In June 2003 the Agency published the results of an assessment undertaken in 2002 of the possible long-term radiological impact of depleted uranium residues, derived from the 1991 Gulf War, at several locations in Kuwait; it determined that the residues did not pose a health threat to local populations.

In May 2001 the IAEA convened an international conference to address the protection of nuclear material and radioactive sources from illegal trafficking. In September, in view of the perpetration of major terrorist attacks against targets in the USA during that month, the IAEA General Conference addressed the potential for nuclear-related terrorism. It adopted a resolution that emphasized the importance of the physical protection of nuclear material in preventing its illicit use or the sabotage of nuclear facilities and nuclear materials. Three main potential threats were identified: the acquisition by a terrorist group of a nuclear weapon; acquisition of nuclear material to construct a nuclear weapon or cause a radiological hazard; and violent acts against nuclear facilities to cause a radiological hazard. In March 2002 the Board of Governors approved in principle an action plan to improve global protection against acts of terrorism involving nuclear and other radioactive materials. The plan addressed the physical protection of nuclear materials and facilities; the detection of malicious activities involving radioactive materials; strengthening national control systems; the security of radioactive sources; evaluation of security and safety at nuclear facilities; emergency response to malicious acts or threats involving radioactive materials; ensuring adherence to international guidelines and agreements; and improvement of programme co-ordination and information management. It was estimated that the Agency's upgraded nuclear security activities would require significant additional annual funding. In March 2003 the IAEA organized an International Conference on Security of Radioactive Sources, held in Vienna. In April 2005 the UN General Assembly adopted the International Convention for the Suppression of Acts of Nuclear Terrorism. The Convention, which opened for signature in September of that year and entered into force in July 2007, established a definition of acts of nuclear terrorism and urged signatory states to co-operate in the prevention of terrorist attacks by sharing information and providing mutual assistance with criminal investigations and extradition proceedings. Under the provisions of the Convention it was required that any seized nuclear or radiological material should be held in accordance with IAEA safeguards. In 2006, a total of 149 incidents were reported by 95 states to the Illicit Trafficking Database (ITDB); this represented the highest number of incidents registered on the ITDB since 1993.

In June 2004 the Board of Governors approved an action plan on the decommissioning of nuclear facilities. In 2006 the IAEA provided decommissioning support in the form of technical co-operation projects to 12 member states.

DISSEMINATION OF INFORMATION

The International Nuclear Information System (INIS), which was established in 1970, provides a computerized indexing and abstracting service. Information on the peaceful uses of atomic energy is collected by member states and international organizations and sent to the IAEA for processing and dissemination (see list of publications below). The IAEA also co-operates with FAO in an information system for agriculture (AGRIS) and with the World Federation of Nuclear Medicine and Biology, and the non-profit Cochrane Collaboration, in maintaining an electronic database of best practice in nuclear medicine. The IAEA Nuclear Data Section provides cost-free data centre services and co-operates with other national and regional nuclear and atomic data centres in the systematic world-wide collection, compilation, dissemination and exchange of nuclear reaction data, nuclear structure and decay data, and atomic and molecular data for fusion.

SAFEGUARDS

The Treaty on the Non-Proliferation of Nuclear Weapons (known also as the Non-Proliferation Treaty or NPT), which entered into force in 1970, requires each 'non-nuclear-weapon state' (one which had not manufactured and exploded a nuclear weapon or other nuclear explosive device prior to 1 January 1967) which is a party to the Treaty to conclude a safeguards agreement with the IAEA. Under such an agreement, the state undertakes to accept IAEA safeguards on all nuclear material in all its peaceful nuclear activities for the purpose of verifying that such material is not diverted to nuclear weapons or other nuclear explosive devices. In May 1995 the Review and Extension Conference of parties to the NPT agreed to extend the NPT indefinitely, and reaffirmed support for the IAEA's role in verification and the transfer of peaceful nuclear technologies. At the next review conference, held in April–May 2000, the five 'nuclear-weapon states'— the PRC, France, Russia, the United Kingdom and the USA—issued a joint statement pledging their commitment to the ultimate goal of complete nuclear disarmament under effective international controls. A further review conference was convened in May 2005. By March 2008 185 non-nuclear-weapon states and the five nuclear-weapon states were parties to the Treaty. A number of non-nuclear-weapon states, however, had not complied, within the prescribed time-limit, with their obligations under the Treaty regarding the conclusion of the relevant safeguards agreement with the Agency.

The five nuclear-weapon states have concluded safeguards agreements with the Agency that permit the application of IAEA safeguards to all their nuclear activities, excluding those with 'direct national significance'. A Comprehensive Nuclear Test Ban Treaty (CTBT) was opened for signature in September 1996, having been adopted by the UN General Assembly. The Treaty was to enter into international law upon ratification by all 44 nations with known nuclear capabilities. A separate verification organization was to be established, based in Vienna. A Preparatory Commission for the treaty organization became operational in 1997. By March 2008 177 countries had signed the CTBT and 142 had ratified it, including 34 of the 44 states with known nuclear capabilities. However, the US Senate rejected ratification of the CTBT in October 1999.

Several regional nuclear weapons treaties require their member states to conclude comprehensive safeguards agreements with the IAEA, including the Treaty for the prohibition of Nuclear Weapons in Latin America (Tlatelolco Treaty, with 33 states party at March 2008); the South Pacific Nuclear-Free Zone Treaty (Rarotonga Treaty, 13 states party at March 2008); the Treaty in the South-East Asia Nuclear-Weapon Free Zone (Treaty of Bangkok, adopted in 1995, 10 states party at March 2008); and the African Nuclear-Weapon Free Zone Treaty (Pelindaba Treaty, adopted in 1996, with 24 states party at March 2008). In September 2006 experts from Kazakhstan, Kyrgyzstan, Tajikistan, Turkmenistan and Uzbekistan, adopted a treaty on establishing a Central Asian Nuclear Weapon Free Zone (CANWFZ); the treaty had been ratified by Kyrgyzstan and Uzbekistan at March 2008. At the end of 2006 a total of 237 IAEA safeguards agreements were in force with 162 states, covering 925 nuclear facilities. During that year the Agency conducted 2,142 inspections. Expenditure on the Safeguards Regular Budget for 2006 was US $92.0m., and extra-budgetary programme expenditure amounted to $8.4m. The IAEA maintains an imagery database of nuclear sites, and is installing digital surveillance systems (including unattended and remote monitoring capabilities) to replace obsolete analogue systems.

In June 1995 the Board of Governors approved measures to strengthen the safeguards system, including allowing inspection teams greater access to suspected nuclear sites and to information on nuclear activities in member states, reducing the notice time for inspections by removing visa requirements for inspectors and using environmental monitoring (i.e. soil, water and air samples) to test for signs of radioactivity. In April 1996 the IAEA initiated a programme to prevent and combat illicit trafficking of nuclear weapons, and in May 1998 the IAEA and the World Customs Organization signed a Memorandum of Understanding to enhance co-operation in the prevention of illicit nuclear trafficking. In May 1997 the Board of Governors adopted a model additional protocol approving measures to strengthen safeguards further, in order to ensure the compliance of non-nuclear-weapon states with IAEA commitments. The new protocol compelled member states to provide inspection teams with improved access to information concerning existing and planned nuclear activities, and to allow access to locations other than known nuclear sites within that country's territory. By December 2006 75 states had ratified additional protocols to their safeguards agreements.

IAEA's Safeguards Analytical Laboratory analyses nuclear fuel-cycle samples collected by IAEA safeguards inspectors. The Agency's Marine Environment Laboratory, in Monaco, studies radionuclides and other ocean pollutants.

In April 1992 the Democratic People's Republic of Korea (DPRK) ratified a safeguards agreement with the IAEA. In late 1992 and early 1993, however, the IAEA unsuccessfully requested access to two non-declared sites in the DPRK, where it was suspected that material capable of being used for the manufacture of nuclear weapons was stored. In March 1993 the DPRK announced its intention of withdrawing from the NPT: it suspended its withdrawal in June, but continued to refuse full access to its nuclear facilities for IAEA inspectors. In May 1994 the DPRK began to refuel an experimental nuclear power reactor at Yongbyon, but refused to allow the IAEA to analyse the spent fuel rods in order to ascertain whether plutonium had been obtained from the reactor for possible military use. In June the IAEA Board of Governors halted IAEA technical assistance to the DPRK (except medical assistance) because of continuous violation of the NPT safeguards agreements. In the same month the DPRK withdrew from the IAEA (though not from the NPT); however, it allowed IAEA inspectors to remain at the Yongbyon site to conduct safeguards activities. In October the Governments of the DPRK and the USA concluded an agreement whereby the former agreed to halt construction of two new nuclear reactors, on condition that it received international aid for the construction of two 'light water' reactors (which could not produce materials for the manufacture of nuclear weapons). The DPRK also agreed to allow IAEA inspections of all its nuclear sites, but only after the installation of one of the light water reactors had been completed (entailing a significant time lapse). In November IAEA inspectors visited the DPRK to initiate verification of the suspension of the country's nuclear programme, in accordance with the agreement concluded in the previous month. From 1995 the IAEA pursued technical discussions with the DPRK authorities as part of the Agency's efforts to achieve the full compliance of the DPRK with the IAEA safeguards agreement. By the end of 1999 the canning of spent fuel rods from the Yongbyon nuclear power reactor was completed. However, little overall progress had been achieved, owing to the obstruction of inspectors by the authorities in that country, including their refusal to provide samples for analysis. The IAEA was unable to verify the suspension of the nuclear programme and declared that the DPRK continued to be in non-compliance with its NPT safeguards agreement. In accordance with a decision of the General Conference in September 2001, IAEA inspectors subsequently resumed a continuous presence in the DPRK. The DPRK authorities permitted low-level inspections of the Yongbyon site by an IAEA technical team in January and May 2002. It was envisaged at that time that the new 'light water' reactors would become operational by 2008. However, in December 2002, following repeated requests by the IAEA that the DPRK verify the accuracy of reports that it was implementing an undeclared uranium enrichment programme, the DPRK authorities disabled IAEA safeguards surveillance equipment placed at three facilities in Yongbyon and took measures to restart reprocessing capabilities at the site, requesting the immediate withdrawal of the Agency's inspectors. (The inspectors were withdrawn at the end of the month.) In early January 2003 the IAEA Board of Governors adopted a resolution deploring the DPRK's non-co-operation and urging its immediate and full compliance with the Agency. Shortly afterwards, however, the DPRK announced its withdrawal from the NPT, while stating that it would limit its nuclear activities to peaceful purposes. In February the IAEA found the DPRK to be in further non-compliance with its safeguards agreement, and condemned the reported successful reactivation of the Yongbyon reactor. In August a series of six-party talks on the situation was launched, involving the DPRK, the PRC, Japan, the Republic of Korea, Russia and the USA, under the auspices of the PRC Government. In September 2004 the General Conference adopted a resolution that urged the DPRK to dismantle promptly and completely any nuclear weapons programme and to recognize the verification role of the Agency, while strongly encouraging the ongoing diplomatic efforts to achieve a peaceful outcome. In February 2005 the DPRK suspended its participation in the six-party talks, and asserted that it had developed nuclear weapons as a measure of self-defence. The talks resumed during July–September, when the six parties signed a joint statement, in which the DPRK determined to resume its adherence to the NPT and Agency safeguards, and consequently to halt its development of nuclear weapons; the USA and the Republic of Korea affirmed that no US nuclear weapons were deployed on the Korean Peninsula; the five other parties recognized the DPRK's right to use nuclear energy for peaceful purposes, and agreed to consider at a later date the provision of a light water reactor to that country; and all parties undertook to promote co-operation in security and economic affairs. A timetable for future progress was to be established at the next phase of the six-party talks, the first session of which convened briefly in early November; the DPRK, however, subsequently announced that it would only resume the talks pending the release by the USA of recently-frozen DPRK financial assets. In July 2006 the UN Security Council condemned a recent ballistic missile test by the DPRK, noting the potential of such missiles to be used for delivering nuclear, chemical or biological payloads, and urged the DPRK to return immediately to the six-party talks without precondition and work towards the implementation of the September 2005 joint statement. In early 2006 October the IAEA Director-General expressed serious concern in response to an announcement by the DPRK that it had conducted a nuclear test. In mid-October the Security Council adopted Resolution 1718, demanding that the DPRK suspend all

activities related to its ballistic missile programme, abandon all nuclear weapons and existing nuclear programmes, abandon all other existing weapons of mass destruction and ballistic missile programmes in a complete, verifiable and irreversible manner, and return to the six-party talks. The Council also imposed sanctions against the DPRK.

The six-party talks were resumed in February 2007, and resulted in an ad hoc agreement by all the participants that the DPRK would shut down and seal—for the purpose of eventual abandonment—the Yongbyon facility, and would invite back IAEA personnel to conduct all necessary monitoring and verifications; that the DPRK would discuss with the other parties a list of all its nuclear programmes; that the DPRK and the USA would enter into negotiations aimed at resolving pending bilateral issues and moving toward full diplomatic relations; that the USA would initiate the process of removing the designation of the DPRK as a state-sponsor of terrorism; that the DPRK and Japan would start negotiations aimed at normalizing their relations; and that the parties would agree to co-operate in security and economic affairs (as detailed under the September 2005 joint statement). In the latter regard, the parties agreed to the provision of emergency energy assistance to the DPRK. In mid-July 2007 an IAEA team visited the DPRK and verified the shutdown of the Yongbyon facility. Upon the resumption of the six-party talks in late September, the participants adopted an agreement wherein the DPRK resolved to disable permanently its nuclear facilities.

In June 2008 the IAEA Director-General asserted that, as long as the legal status of the DPRK's accession to the NPT remained unclear, the safeguards responsibilities of the Agency towards the DPRK were also uncertain. In August the DPRK authorities announced their intention to reactivate the Yongbyon facility in reaction to the refusal, hitherto, of the USA to remove the DPRK from its terrorism blacklist. In late September the IAEA reported that all Agency seals and surveillance equipment had been removed from Yongbyon, and that the DPRK authorities would no longer sanction visits by IAEA inspectors to the reprocessing facility. In mid-October, shortly after the US Government's removal of the DPRK from its terrorism blacklist, the DPRK authorities permitted the return of IAEA inspectors to Yongbyon.

In April 1991 the UN Security Council requested the IAEA to conduct investigations into Iraq's capacity to produce nuclear weapons, following the end of the war between Iraq and the UN-authorized, US-led multinational force. The IAEA was to work closely with a UN Special Commission of experts (UNSCOM), established by the Security Council, whose task was to inspect and dismantle Iraq's weapons of mass destruction (including chemical and biological weapons). In July the IAEA declared that Iraq had violated its safeguards agreement with the IAEA by not submitting nuclear material and relevant facilities in its uranium-enrichment programme to the Agency's inspection. This was the first time that a state party to the NPT had been condemned for concealing a programme of this nature. In October the sixth inspection team, composed of UNSCOM and representatives of the IAEA, was reported to have obtained conclusive documentary evidence that Iraq had a programme for developing nuclear weapons. By February 1994 all declared stocks of nuclear-weapons-grade material had been removed from Iraq. Subsequently, the IAEA pursued a programme of long-term surveillance of nuclear activity in Iraq, under a mandate issued by the UN Security Council. In September 1996 Iraq submitted to the IAEA a 'full, final and complete' declaration of its nuclear activities. However, in September–October 1997 the IAEA recommended that Iraq disclose further equipment, materials and information relating to its nuclear programme. In April 1998 IAEA technical experts were part of a special group that entered eight presidential sites in Iraq to collect baseline data, in accordance with a Memorandum of Understanding concluded between the UN Secretary-General and the Iraqi authorities in February. The accord aimed to ensure full Iraqi co-operation with UNSCOM and IAEA personnel. In August, however, Iraq suspended co-operation with UN inspectors, which prevented IAEA from implementing its programme of ongoing monitoring and verification (OMV) activities. Iraq's action was condemned by the IAEA General Conference in September. In October the IAEA reported that while there was no evidence of Iraq having produced nuclear weapons or having retained or obtained a capability for the production of nuclear weapons, the Agency was unable to guarantee that all items had been found. All IAEA inspectors were temporarily relocated from Iraq to Bahrain in November, in accordance with a decision to withdraw UNSCOM personnel owing to Iraq's failure to agree to resume co-operation. In March 2000 UNSCOM was replaced by a new arms inspection body, the UN Monitoring, Verification and Inspection Commission (UNMOVIC). Although the IAEA carried out inventory verifications of nuclear material in Iraq in January 2000, January 2001 and January 2002, pursuant to Iraq's NPT safeguards agreement, full inspection activities in conjunction with UNMOVIC remained suspended. In September 2002 the US President expressed concern that Iraq was challenging international security owing to its non-compliance with successive UN resolutions relating to the elimination of weapons of mass destruction. In November the UN Security Council adopted Resolution 1441 providing for an enhanced inspection mission and a detailed timetable according to which Iraq would have a final opportunity to comply with its disarmament obligations. Following Iraq's acceptance of the resolution, experts from the IAEA's so-called Iraq Nuclear Verification Office and UNMOVIC resumed inspections on 27 November, with Council authorization to have unrestricted access to all areas and the right to interview Iraqi scientists and weapons experts. In early December Iraq submitted a declaration of all aspects of its weapons programmes, as required under Resolution 1441. In January 2003 Dr Mohamed el-Baradei, the IAEA Director-General, requested an ongoing mandate for his inspectors to clarify the situation regarding nuclear weapons. In mid-March el-Baradei reported that no evidence had been found of nuclear weapons programme activities in Iraq, while also stating that the Agency had not had sufficient time to complete its investigations. Shortly before the initiation of unilateral military action against Iraq by US and allied forces on 19 March IAEA and UNMOVIC personnel were withdrawn from the country. Their field activities were suspended and, following the overthrow in April of the Saddam Hussain regime, responsibility for weapons inspections in Iraq were assumed by a US-led Iraq Survey Group. In late April el-Baradei emphasized the necessity of securing the sites of Iraq's declared nuclear materials from looting and damage. In June 2007 the UN Security Council, noting testimonials that all of Iraq's known weapons of mass destruction had deactivated and that the Iraqi Government had declared its support for international non-proliferation regimes, voted to terminate the mandates of the IAEA weapons inspectors in Iraq and of UNMOVIC.

In September 2003 the IAEA adopted a resolution demanding that the Iranian Government sign, ratify and fully implement an additional protocol to its safeguards agreement promptly and unconditionally. The Agency also urged Iran to suspend its uranium enrichment and reprocessing activities, pending satisfactory application of the provisions of the additional protocol. Iran issued a declaration of its nuclear activities in October, and, in December, signed an additional protocol and agreed to suspend uranium enrichment processing, as requested. The Agency dispatched inspectors to Iran from October to conduct an intensive verification process. In April 2004 the IAEA Director-General visited Iran and concluded an agreement on a joint action plan to address the outstanding issues of the verification process. Iran provided an initial declaration under the (as yet unratified) additional protocol in May. In June, however, the Director-General expressed his continued concern at the extent of Iranian co-operation with IAEA inspectors. In September the Board of Governors adopted a resolution in which it strongly regretted continuing enrichment-related and reprocessing activities by Iran and requested their immediate suspension. The Director-General announced in late November that the suspension had been verified. In August 2005 the Agency adopted a resolution condemning Iran for resuming uranium conversion. In the following month a further resolution was adopted by the Board of Governors, in support of a motion by the European Union, citing Iran's non-compliance with the NPT and demanding that Iran accelerate its co-operation with the Agency regarding the outstanding issues. In early February 2006 the Board of Governors adopted a resolution that recalled repeated failures by Iran to comply with its obligations under its NPT safeguards agreement, expressed serious concern at the nature of Iran's nuclear programme, and urged that, with a view to building confidence in the exclusively peaceful nature of the programme, Iran should suspend fully all activities related to uranium enrichment (reportedly resumed in January) and reprocessing; ratify and fully implement the additional protocol agreed in 2003; and implement transparency measures extending beyond its formal arrangements with the Agency. The resolution requested the IAEA Director-General to report the steps required of Iran to the UN Security Council and to inform the Security Council of all related IAEA documents and resolutions. In response, the Iranian authorities declared that they would suspend all legally non-binding measures imposed by the IAEA, including containment and surveillance measures provided for under the additional protocol, and that consequently all IAEA seals and cameras should be removed from Iranian sites by mid-February 2006. At the end of July the UN Security Council, having reviewed the relevant information provided by the IAEA Director-General, issued Resolution 1696, in which it demanded that Iran suspend all enrichment-related and reprocessing activities, including research and development, within a period of one month, and stipulated that non-compliance might result in the imposition on Iran of economic and diplomatic sanctions. The resolution requested that the IAEA Director-General submit to the Council at the end of August a report on Iran's response. The report, which was made public in mid-September, found that Iran had not suspended its enrichment-related activities and was still not in compliance with the provisions of the additional protocol. In December the Security Council imposed sanctions against Iran,

and in March 2007 the Council imposed a ban on the export of arms from that country.

In June 2007 the IAEA Director-General and the Iranian authorities agreed to develop within 60 days a plan on the modalities for resolving outstanding safeguards implementation issues; accordingly, in August, a work plan on this area (also detailing procedures and timelines) was finalized. At that time the IAEA declared that previous Agency concerns about plutonium reprocessing activities in Iran were now resolved, as its findings had verified earlier statements made by the Iranian authorities. At the end of that month the IAEA Director-General reported that Iran had not yet suspended its uranium enrichment activities. The IAEA Director-General visited Iran in January 2008 to discuss with the Iranian administration means of accelerating the implementation of safeguards and confidence-building measures. It was agreed that remaining verification issues that had been specified in the August 2007 workplan should be resolved by mid-February 2008. In February 2008 the IAEA Board of Governors reported that Iran was still pursuing its uranium enrichment activities, and that the Iranian Government needed to continue to build confidence about the scope and purported peaceful nature of its nuclear programme. Consequently, in the following month, the UN Security Council adopted a new resolution on Iran in which it professed concern for the proliferation risk presented by the Iranian nuclear programme and authorized inspections of any cargo to and from Iran suspected of transporting prohibited equipment; strengthened the monitoring of Iranian financial institutions; and added names to the existing list of individuals and companies subject to asset and travel restrictions.

In May 2008 the IAEA Director-General, at the request of the UN Security Council, circulated a report to both the Security Council and the IAEA Board of Governors on the *Implementation of the NPT Safeguards Agreement and Relevant Provisions of Security Council Resolutions 1737 (2006), 1747 (2007), and 1803 (2008) in the Islamic Republic of Iran*, which concluded that there remained several areas of serious concern, including an ongoing green salt project; high explosives testing; a missile re-entry vehicle project; some procurement activities of military-related institutions; outstanding substantive explanations regarding information with a possible military dimension; and Iran's continuing enrichment-related activities.

Following the announcement by Libya in mid-December 2003 that it would conclude an additional protocol to its safeguards agreement with the IAEA, the Agency worked closely with that country to verify the extent of its past undeclared and present nuclear materials and activities. The Libyan authorities signed an additional protocol in March 2004.

While assessing nuclear activities in Iran and Libya from late 2003 the Agency also undertook investigations into the supply routes and sources of the technology and materials used in their past undeclared nuclear programmes, demonstrating evidence of a complex black market. The Agency demanded full co-operation from the source countries involved.

In late 1997 the IAEA began inspections in the USA to verify the conversion for peaceful uses of nuclear material released from the military sector. In 1998 the United Kingdom announced that substantial quantities of nuclear material previously in its military programme would become available for verification under its voluntary offer safeguards agreement.

NUCLEAR FUEL CYCLE

The Agency promotes the exchange of information between member states on technical, safety, environmental, and economic aspects of nuclear fuel cycle technology, including uranium prospecting and the treatment and disposal of radioactive waste; it provides assistance to member states in the planning, implementation and operation of nuclear fuel cycle facilities and assists in the development of advanced nuclear fuel cycle technology. The Agency operates a number of databases and a simulation system related to the nuclear fuel cycle through its Integrated Nuclear Fuel Cycle Information System (iNFCIS). Every two years, in collaboration with OECD, the Agency prepares estimates of world uranium resources, demand and production.

Finance

The Agency is financed by regular and voluntary contributions from member states. Expenditure approved under the regular budget for 2008 amounted to some US $288.8m., and the target for voluntary contributions to finance the IAEA technical assistance and co-operation programme in that year was $80.0m.

Publications

Annual Report.
Atoms for Peace.
Fundamental Safety Principles.
IAEA Bulletin (quarterly).
IAEA Newsbriefs (every 2 months).
IAEA Safety Glossary Terminology Used in Nuclear Safety and Radiation Protection.
IAEA Yearbook.
INIS Atomindex (bibliography, 2 a month).
INIS Reference Series.
INSAG Series.

Legal Series.
Meetings on Atomic Energy (quarterly).
The Nuclear Fuel Cycle Information System: A Directory of Nuclear Fuel Cycle Facilities.
Nuclear Fusion (monthly).
Nuclear Safety Review (annually).
Nuclear Technology Review (annually).
Panel Proceedings Series.
Publications Catalogue (annually).
Safety Series.
Technical Directories.
Technical Reports Series.

International Bank for Reconstruction and Development— IBRD (World Bank)

Address: 1818 H St, NW, Washington, DC 20433, USA.

Telephone: (202) 473-1000; **fax:** (202) 477-6391; **e-mail:** pic@worldbank.org; **internet:** www.worldbank.org.

The IBRD was established in December 1945. Initially it was concerned with post-war reconstruction in Europe; since then its aim has been to assist the economic development of member nations by making loans where private capital is not available on reasonable terms to finance productive investments. Loans are made either directly to governments, or to private enterprises with the guarantee of their governments. The World Bank, as it is commonly known, comprises the IBRD and the International Development Association (IDA). The affiliated group of institutions, comprising the IBRD, the IDA, the International Finance Corporation (IFC), the Multilateral Investment Guarantee Agency (MIGA) and the International Centre for Settlement of Investment Disputes (ICSID, see below), is referred to as the World Bank Group.

Organization

(October 2008)

Officers and staff of the IBRD serve concurrently as officers and staff in the IDA. The World Bank has offices in New York, Brussels, Paris (for Europe), Frankfurt, London, Geneva and Tokyo, as well as in more than 100 countries of operation. Country Directors are located in some 30 country offices.

BOARD OF GOVERNORS

The Board of Governors consists of one Governor appointed by each member nation. Typically, a Governor is the country's finance minister, central bank governor, or a minister or an official of comparable rank. The Board normally meets once a year.

EXECUTIVE DIRECTORS

The general operations of the Bank are conducted by a Board of 24 Executive Directors. Five Directors are appointed by the five members having the largest number of shares of capital stock, and the rest are elected by the Governors representing the other members. The President of the Bank is Chairman of the Board.

PRINCIPAL OFFICERS

The principal officers of the Bank are the President of the Bank, three Managing Directors, three Senior Vice-Presidents and 24 Vice-Presidents.

President and Chairman of Executive Directors: ROBERT B. ZOELLICK (USA).

Vice-President, Europe and Central Asia: SHIGEO KATSU (Japan).

Activities

FINANCIAL OPERATIONS

IBRD capital is derived from members' subscriptions to capital shares, the calculation of which is based on their quotas in the IMF. At 30 June 2007 the total subscribed capital of the IBRD was US $189,801m., of which the paid-in portion was $11,486m. (6.1%); the remainder is subject to call if required. Most of the IBRD's lendable funds come from its borrowing, on commercial terms, in world capital markets, and also from its retained earnings and the flow of repayments on its loans. IBRD loans carry a variable interest rate, rather than a rate fixed at the time of borrowing.

IBRD loans usually have a 'grace period' of five years and are repayable over 15 years or fewer. Loans are made to governments, or must be guaranteed by the government concerned, and are normally made for projects likely to offer a commercially viable rate of return. In 1980 the World Bank introduced structural adjustment lending, which (instead of financing specific projects) supports programmes and changes necessary to modify the structure of an economy so that it can restore or maintain its growth and viability in its balance of payments over the medium-term.

The IBRD and IDA together made 301 new lending and investment commitments totalling US $24,695.8m. during the year ending 30 June 2007, compared with 279 (amounting to $23,641.2m.) in the previous year. During 2006/07 the IBRD alone approved commitments totalling $12,828.8m. (compared with $14,135.0m. in the previous year), of which $3,340.1m. (26%) was allocated to projects in Europe and Central Asia (including Turkey). Total disbursements by the IBRD in the year ending 30 June 2007 amounted to $11,055.0m.

The World Bank's primary objectives are the achievement of sustainable economic growth and the reduction of poverty in developing countries. In the context of stimulating economic growth the Bank promotes both private sector development and human resource development and has attempted to respond to the growing demands by developing countries for assistance in these areas. In March 1997 the Board of Executive Directors endorsed a 'Strategic Compact' to increase the effectiveness of the Bank in achieving its central objective of poverty reduction. The reforms included greater decentralization of decision-making, and investment in front-line operations, enhancing the administration of loans, and improving access to information and co-ordination of Bank activities through a knowledge management system comprising four thematic networks: the Human Development Network; the Environmentally and Socially Sustainable Development Network; the Finance, Private Sector and Infrastructure Development Network; and the Poverty Reduction and Economic Management Network. In 2000/01 the Bank adopted a new Strategic Framework which emphasized two essential approaches for Bank support: strengthening the investment climate and prospects for sustainable development in a country, and supporting investment in the poor. In September 2001 the Bank announced that it was to join the UN as a full partner in implementing the so-called Millennium Development Goals (MDGs), and was to make them central to its development agenda. The objectives, which were approved by governments attending a special session of the UN General Assembly in September 2000, represented a new international consensus to achieve determined poverty reduction targets. The Bank was closely involved in preparations for the International

Conference on Financing for Development, which was held in Monterrey, Mexico, in March 2002. The meeting adopted the Monterrey Consensus, which outlined measures to support national development efforts and to achieve the MDGs. During 2002/03 the Bank, with the IMF, undertook to develop a monitoring framework to review progress in the MDG agenda. The first *Global Monitoring Report* was issued by the Bank and IMF in April 2004. Other efforts to support a greater emphasis on development results were also undertaken by the Bank during 2003/04 as part of a new strategic action plan, and the Bank has continued closely to monitor its contribution to poverty reduction objectives.

The Bank's efforts to reduce poverty include the compilation of country-specific assessments and the formulation of country assistance strategies (CASs) to review and guide the Bank's country programmes. Since August 1998 the Bank has published CASs, with the approval of the government concerned. A new results-based CAS initiative was piloted in 2003/04. In 1998/99 the Bank's Executive Directors endorsed a Comprehensive Development Framework (CDF) to effect a new approach to development assistance based on partnerships and country responsibility, with an emphasis on the interdependence of the social, structural, human, governmental, economic and environmental elements of development. The Framework, which aimed to enhance the overall effectiveness of development assistance, was formulated after a series of consultative meetings organized by the Bank and attended by representatives of governments, donor agencies, financial institutions, non-governmental organizations, the private sector and academics.

In December 1999 the Bank introduced a new approach to implement the principles of the CDF, as part of its strategy to enhance the debt relief scheme for heavily indebted poor countries (HIPCs, see below). Applicant countries were requested to formulate, in consultation with external partners and other stakeholders, a results-oriented national strategy to reduce poverty, to be presented in the form of a Poverty Reduction Strategy Paper (PRSP). In cases where there might be some delay in issuing a full PRSP, it was permissible for a country to submit a less detailed 'interim' PRSP (I-PRSP) in order to secure the preliminary qualification for debt relief. The approach also requires the publication of annual progress reports. In 2001 the Bank introduced a new Poverty Reduction Support Credit to help low-income countries to implement the policy and institutional reforms outlined in their PRSP. The first credits were approved for Uganda and Viet Nam in May and June respectively. Increasingly, PRSPs have been considered by the international community to be the appropriate country-level framework to assess progress towards achieving the MDGs. A joint review of the poverty reduction strategy approach was undertaken by the Bank and IMF in 2004/05.

In September 1996 the World Bank/IMF Development Committee endorsed a joint initiative to assist HIPCs to reduce their debt burden to a sustainable level, in order to make more resources available for poverty reduction and economic growth. A new Trust Fund was established by the World Bank in November to finance the initiative. The Fund, consisting of an initial allocation of US $500m. from the IBRD surplus and other contributions from multilateral creditors, was to be administered by IDA. In early 1999 the World Bank and IMF initiated a comprehensive review of the HIPC initiative. In June the Group of Seven industrialized nations and Russia (known as the G8), meeting in Cologne, Germany, agreed to increase contributions to the HIPC Trust Fund and to cancel substantial amounts of outstanding debt, and proposed more flexible terms for eligibility. In September the Bank and IMF reached an agreement on an enhanced HIPC scheme, with further revenue to be generated through the revaluation of a percentage of IMF gold reserves. It was agreed that, in order to qualify for debt relief and additional concessional lending, countries were to formulate a PRSP, and should demonstrate prudent financial management in the implementation of the strategy for at least one year. Those countries still deemed to have an unsustainable level of debt at the pivotal 'decision point' of the process were to qualify for assistance. In the majority of cases a sustainable level of debt was targeted at 150% of the net present value (NPV) of the debt in relation to total annual exports (compared with 200%–250% under the original HIPC scheme). Other countries with a lower debt-to-export ratio were to be eligible for assistance under the initiative, providing that their export earnings were at least 30% of GDP (lowered from 40%) and government revenue at least 15% of GDP (reduced from 20%). In September 2005 the Bank and IMF endorsed a proposal of the G8 to cancel all debt owed by countries that had reached their completion point, under a new Multilateral Debt Relief Initiative. By October 2008 23 countries had reached completion point and a further 10 had reached decision point of the process.

During 2000/01 the World Bank strengthened its efforts to counter the problem of HIV and AIDS in developing countries. In November 2001 the Bank appointed its first Global HIV/AIDS Adviser. In 2002/03 the Bank identified the Europe and Central Asia region as having the world's fastest-growing HIV/AIDS epidemic in proportion to its population, and determined to make it a priority area for activity. During that year the Bank issued loans to Russia and Ukraine for HIV/AIDS programmes, extended an IDA grant to Moldova and continued work on a project in Belarus. With UNAIDS, the Bank has developed a Directory of Technical and Managerial Resources for HIV/AIDS Programmes in the region to help to improve access to technical advice. In March 2005 the Bank approved a five-year Central Asian AIDS Control Project, as a multi-country initiative to counter HIV/AIDS in Kazakhstan, Kyrgyzstan, Tajikistan, and Uzbekistan. The first Eastern European and Central Asian AIDS Conference was held in May 2006, in Moscow, Russia.

In March 2007 the Board of Executive Directors approved an action plan to develop further its Clean Energy for Development Investment Framework, which had been formulated in response to a request by the G8 heads of state, meeting in Gleneagles, United Kingdom, in July 2005. The action plan focused on efforts to improve access to clean energy, in particular in sub-Saharan Africa; to accelerate the transition to low carbon-emission development; and to support adaptation to climate change. During 2007 the Bank undertook to develop a strategic framework on climate change and development, which aimed to support the efforts of developing countries to adapt to climate change and to achieve low-carbon energy growth, while working to reduce poverty.

In addition to providing financial services, the Bank also undertakes analytical and advisory services, and supports learning and capacity-building, in particular through the World Bank Institute (see below), the Staff Exchange Programme and knowledge-sharing initiatives. The Bank has supported efforts, such as the Global Development Gateway, to disseminate information on development issues and programmes, and, since 1988, has organized the Annual Bank Conference on Development Economics (ABCDE) to provide a forum for the exchange and discussion of development-related ideas and research. In September 1995 the Bank initiated the Information for Development Programme (InfoDev) with the aim of fostering partnerships between governments, multilateral institutions and private-sector experts in order to promote reform and investment in developing countries through improved access to information technology.

TECHNICAL ASSISTANCE

The provision of technical assistance to member countries has become a major component of World Bank activities. The economic and sector work (ESW) undertaken by the Bank is the vehicle for considerable technical assistance and often forms the basis of CASs and other strategic or advisory reports. In addition, project loans and credits may include funds earmarked specifically for feasibility studies, resource surveys, management or planning advice, and training. The Economic Development Institute has become one of the most important of the Bank's activities in technical assistance. It provides training in national economic management and project analysis for government officials at the middle and upper levels of responsibility. It also runs overseas courses aiming to build up local training capability, and administers a graduate scholarship programme.

The Bank serves as an executing agency for projects financed by the UN Development Programme (UNDP). It also administers projects financed by various trust funds.

Technical assistance (usually reimbursable) is also extended to countries that do not need Bank financial support, e.g. for training and transfer of technology. The Bank encourages the use of local consultants to assist with projects and stimulate institutional capability.

The Project Preparation Facility (PPF) was established in 1975 to provide cash advances to prepare projects that may be financed by the Bank. In 1992 the Bank established an Institutional Development Fund (IDF), which became operational on 1 July; the purpose of the Fund was to provide rapid, small-scale financial assistance, to a maximum value of US $500,000, for capacity-building proposals. In 2002 the IDF was reoriented to focus on good governance, in particular financial accountability and system reforms.

ECONOMIC RESEARCH AND STUDIES

In the 1990s the World Bank's research, conducted by its own research staff, was increasingly concerned with providing information to reinforce the Bank's expanding advisory role to developing countries and to improve policy in the Bank's borrowing countries. The principal areas of current research focus on issues such as maintaining sustainable growth while protecting the environment and the poorest sectors of society, encouraging the development of the private sector, and reducing and decentralizing government activities.

The Bank chairs the Consultative Group on International Agricultural Research (CGIAR), which was founded in 1971 to raise financial support for international agricultural research work for improving crops and animal production in developing countries; it supports 15 research centres.

CO-OPERATION WITH OTHER ORGANIZATIONS

The World Bank co-operates with other international partners with the aim of improving the impact of development efforts. It collaborates with the IMF in implementing the HIPC scheme and the two agencies work closely to achieve a common approach to development initiatives. The Bank has established strong working relationships with many other UN bodies, in particular through a mutual commitment to poverty reduction objectives. In May 2000 the Bank signed a joint statement of co-operation with the OECD. The Bank holds regular consultations with other multilateral development banks and with the European Union with respect to development issues. The Bank-NGO Committee provides an annual forum for discussion with non-governmental organizations (NGOs). Strengthening co-operation with external partners was a fundamental element of the Comprehensive Development Framework, which was adopted in 1998/99 (see above). In 2001/02 a Partnership Approval and Tracking System was implemented to provide information on the Bank's regional and global partnerships.

In 1997 a Partnerships Group was established to strengthen the Bank's work with development institutions, representatives of civil society and the private sector. The Group established a new Development Grant Facility, which became operational in October, to support partnership initiatives and to co-ordinate all of the Bank's grant-making activities. Also in 1997 the Bank, in partnership with the IMF, UNCTAD, UNDP, the World Trade Organization (WTO) and International Trade Commission, established an Integrated Framework for Trade-related Assistance to Least Developed Countries, at the request of the WTO, to assist those countries to integrate into the global trading system and improve basic trading capabilities.

In June 1995 the World Bank joined other international donors (including regional development banks, other UN bodies, Canada, France, the Netherlands and the USA) in establishing a Consultative Group to Assist the Poorest (CGAP), which was to channel funds to the most needy through grass-roots agencies. An initial credit of approximately US $200m. was committed by the donors. The Bank manages the CGAP Secretariat, which is responsible for the administration of external funding and for the evaluation and approval of project financing. The CGAP provides technical assistance, training and strategic advice to microfinance institutions and other relevant bodies. As an implementing agency of the Global Environment Facility (GEF) the Bank assists countries to prepare and supervise GEF projects relating to biological diversity, climate change and other environmental protection measures. It is an example of a partnership in action which addresses a global agenda, complementing Bank country assistance activities. Other funds administered by the Bank include the Global Program to Eradicate Poliomyelitis, launched during the financial year 2002/03, the Least Developed Countries Fund for Climate Change, established in September 2002, an Education for All Fast-Track Initiative Catalytic Trust Fund, established in 2003/04, and a Carbon Finance Assistance Trust Fund, established in 2004/05. In 2006/07 the Bank established a Global Facility for Disaster Reduction and Recovery. In September 2007 the Bank's Executive Directors approved a Carbon Partnership Facility and a Forest Carbon Partnership Facility to support its climate change activities. In May 2008 the Bank inaugurated the Global Food Response Programme to provide financial support, with resources of some $1,200m., to help meet the immediate needs of countries affected by the escalating cost of food production and by food shortages. Grants and loans were to be allocated on the basis of rapid needs assessments, conducted by the Bank with the FAO, the WFP and IFAD. As part of the facility a Multi-Donor Trust Fund was to be established to facilitate co-ordination among donors and to leverage financial support for the rapid delivery of seeds and fertilizer to small-scale farmers. By September $152m. had been approved under the programme for 18 countries, including Kyrgyzstan, Moldova and Tajikistan.

The Bank has worked with FAO, WHO and the World Organisation of Animal Health (OIE) to develop strategies to monitor, contain and eradicate the spread of highly pathogenic avian influenza. In September 2005 the Bank organized a meeting of leading experts on the issue and in November it co-sponsored, with FAO, WHO and the OIE, an international partners conference, focusing on control of the disease and preparedness planning for any future related influenza pandemic in humans. In January 2006 the Bank's Board of Directors approved the establishment of a funding programme, with resources of up to US $500m., to assist countries to combat the disease. Later in that month the Bank co-sponsored, with the European Commission and the People's Republic of China, an International Ministerial Pledging Conference on Avian and Human Pandemic Influenza, convened in Beijing. Participants pledged some $1,900m. to fund disease control and pandemic preparedness activities at global, regional and country levels.

In December 1998 the World Bank convened a special donor conference to assist the countries most severely affected by the Russian economic crisis, which had led to the devaluation of that country's currency, the rouble, in August. The conference raised some US $200m. in additional balance-of-payments support for Armenia, Azerbaijan, Georgia, Kyrgyzstan, Moldova and Tajikistan. In 1997 a Partnerships Group was established to strengthen the Bank's work with development institutions, representatives of civil society and the private sector. The Group established a Development Grant Facility to support partnership initiatives in key areas of concern and to co-ordinate all of the Bank's grant-making activities. In April 2002 a CIS-7 initiative was launched by governments of the region, the World Bank, Asian Development Bank, European Bank for Reconstruction and Development and the IMF, together with several bilateral donors, in order to assist the participating countries (Armenia, Azerbaijan, Georgia, Kyrgyzstan, Moldova, Tajikistan and Uzbekistan) to implement poverty reduction strategies, through structural reform, knowledge and partnership support and improved regional co-operation. During 2003/04 the Bank completed Investment Climate Assessments in Kyrgyzstan, Moldova, Uzbekistan and Tajikistan, and, with the IMF, was undertaking a financial sector assessment programmes in Azerbaijan.

The Bank conducts co-financing and aid co-ordination projects with official aid agencies, export credit institutions, and commercial banks to leverage additional concessional funds for recipient countries. During the year ending 30 June 2007 130 Bank projects leveraged US $6,300m. in co-financing.

EVALUATION

The Independent Evaluation Group is an independent unit within the World Bank. It conducts Country Assistance Evaluations to assess the development effectiveness of a Bank country programme, and studies and publishes the results of projects after a loan has been fully disbursed, so as to identify problems and possible improvements in future activities. In addition, the department reviews the Bank's global programmes and produces the *Annual Review of Development Effectiveness*. In 1996 a Quality Assurance Group was established to monitor the effectiveness of the Bank's operations and performance.

In September 1993 the Bank established an independent Inspection Panel, consistent with the Bank's objective of improving project implementation and accountability. The Panel, which became operational in September 1994, was to conduct independent investigations and report on complaints from local people concerning the design, appraisal and implementation of development projects supported by the Bank. By mid-2008 the Panel had received 52 formal requests for inspection.

IBRD INSTITUTIONS

World Bank Institute (WBI): founded in March 1999 by merger of the Bank's Learning and Leadership Centre, previously responsible for internal staff training, and the Economic Development Institute (EDI), which had been established in 1955 to train government officials concerned with development programmes and policies. The new Institute aimed to emphasize the Bank's priority areas through the provision of training courses and seminars relating to poverty, crisis response, good governance and anti-corruption strategies. From 2004 the Institute was to place greater emphasis on individual country needs and on long-term institutional capacity-building. During 2006/07 WBI activities reached more than 75,000 participants world-wide. The Institute has continued to support a Global Knowledge Partnership, which was established in 1997 to promote alliances between governments, companies, other agencies and organizations committed to applying information and communication technologies for development purposes. Under the EDI a World Links for Development programme was also initiated to connect schools in developing countries with partner establishments in industrialized nations via the internet. In 1999 the WBI expanded its programmes through distance learning, a Global Development Network, and use of new technologies. A new initiative, Global Development Learning Network (GDLN), aimed to expand access to information and learning opportunities through the internet, videoconferences and organized exchanges. In 2007 there were some 120 GDLN centres, or affiliates. At that time formal partnership arrangements were in place between WBI and almost 200 learning centres and public, private and non-governmental organizations; a further 250 informal partnerships were also in place; Vice-Pres. RAKESH NANGIA (acting); publs *Annual Report, Development Outreach* (quarterly), other books, working papers, case studies.

International Centre for Settlement of Investment Disputes (ICSID): founded in 1966 under the Convention of the Settlement of Investment Disputes between States and Nationals of Other States. The Convention was designed to encourage the growth of private foreign investment for economic development, by creating the possibility, always subject to the consent of both parties, for a Contracting State and a foreign investor who is a national of another Contracting State to settle any legal dispute that might arise out of such an investment by conciliation and/or arbitration before an impartial, international forum. The governing body of the Centre is its Administrative Council, composed of one representative of each

Contracting State, all of whom have equal voting power. The President of the World Bank is (*ex officio*) the non-voting Chairman of the Administrative Council. By mid-2008 143 countries had signed and ratified the Convention to become ICSID Contracting States. At that time 268 cases had been registered with the Centre, of which 142 had been concluded and 126 were pending consideration; Sec.-Gen. NASSIB G. ZIADÉ (Chile/Lebanon) (acting).

Publications

Abstracts of Current Studies: The World Bank Research Program (annually).
African Development Indicators (annually).
Annual Report on Operations Evaluation.
Annual Report on Portfolio Performance.
Annual Review of Development Effectiveness.
Doing Business (annually).
EDI Annual Report.
Global Commodity Markets (quarterly).
Global Development Finance (annually).
Global Economic Prospects (annually).
ICSID Annual Report.
ICSID Review—Foreign Investment Law Journal (2 a year).
Joint BIS-IMF-OECD-World Bank Statistics on External Debt (quarterly).
New Products and Outreach (EDI, annually).
News from ICSID (2 a year).
Poverty Reduction and the World Bank (annually).
Poverty Reduction Strategies Newsletter (quarterly).

Research News (quarterly).
Staff Working Papers.
World Bank Annual Report.
World Bank Atlas (annually).
World Bank Economic Review (3 a year).
The World Bank and the Environment (annually).
World Bank Research Observer.
World Development Indicators (annually).
World Development Report (annually).

Statistics

IBRD LOANS APPROVED IN EASTERN EUROPE, RUSSIA AND CENTRAL ASIA, I JULY 2006–30 JUNE 2007
(US $ million)

Country		Purpose	Amount
Azerbaijan	. .	Real estate registration	30.0
		Water supply and sanitation	230.0
Kazakhstan	. .	Ust-Kamenogorsk environmental remediation	24.3
Russia	. . .	Judicial reform support	50.0
		Second state statistical system development adaptable programme loan	10.0
Ukraine	. . .	Second export development financial intermediary loan	154.5

Source: *World Bank Annual Report 2007.*

International Development Association—IDA

Address: 1818 H Street, NW, Washington, DC 20433, USA.
Telephone: (202) 473-1000; **fax:** (202) 477-6391; **internet:** www.worldbank.org/ida.

The International Development Association began operations in November 1960. Affiliated to the IBRD, IDA advances capital to the poorer developing member countries on more flexible terms than those offered by the IBRD.

Organization

(October 2008)

Officers and staff of the IBRD serve concurrently as officers and staff of IDA.
President and Chairman of Executive Directors: ROBERT B. ZOELLICK (USA).

Activities

IDA assistance is aimed at the poorer developing countries (i.e. those with an annual GNP per capita of less than US $1,065 were to qualify for assistance in 2007/08) in order to support their poverty reduction strategies. Under IDA lending conditions, credits can be extended to countries whose balance of payments could not sustain the burden of repayment required for IBRD loans. Terms are more favourable than those provided by the IBRD; credits are for a period of 35 or 40 years, with a 'grace period' of 10 years, and carry no interest charges. At mid-2007 80 countries were eligible for IDA assistance, including several small-island economies with a GNP per head greater than $1,065, but which would otherwise have little or no access to Bank funds, and 16 so-called 'blend borrowers' which are entitled to borrow from both the IDA and IBRD.

IDA's total development resources, consisting of members' subscriptions and supplementary resources (additional subscriptions and contributions), are replenished periodically by contributions from the more affluent member countries. An agreement to provide a substantial replenishment of funds, amounting to some US $34,000m. for the period 1 July 2005–30 June 2008, was con-

cluded in February 2005. New contributions pledged by 40 donor countries amounted to $20,700m. of the total replenishment. The agreement incorporated a renewed focus on stimulating economic growth in support of the Millennium Development Goals, with a strengthened monitoring and results-assessment agenda based on poverty reduction objectives. The replenishment programme also placed greater emphasis on the use of grants to address the needs of the poorest countries, in particular those most vulnerable to debt. Negotiations on the 15th replenishment of IDA funds (IDA15) commenced in March 2007, in Paris, France. Participants selected the following 'special themes' for further discussion: the role of IDA in global aid architecture; the effectiveness of IDA assistance at country level; and IDA's role in fragile states. In December an agreement was concluded to replenish IDA resources by some $41,600m., for the period 1 July 2008–30 June 2011, of which $25,100m. was pledged by 45 donor countries.

During the year ending 30 June 2007 IDA commitments amounted to US $11,867m. for 189 projects, compared with $9,506m. in the previous year. One-third of lending was for infrastructure projects. An increasing proportion of IDA lending, accounting for some 18% of total financing in 2006/07, is in the form of grants for the poorest or most vulnerable countries.

IDA administers a Trust Fund, which was established in November 1996 as part of a World Bank/IMF initiative to assist heavily indebted poor countries (HIPCs). In September 2005 the World Bank's Development Committee and the International Monetary and Financial Committee of the IMF endorsed a proposal of the Group of Eight (G8) industrialized countries to cancel the remaining multilateral debt owed by HIPCs that had reached their completion point under the scheme (see IBRD). In December IDA convened a meeting of donor countries to discuss funding to uphold its financial capability upon its contribution to the so-called Multilateral Debt Relief Initiative (MDRI). IDA's participation in the scheme was approved by the Board of Executive Directors in March 2006 and entered into effect on 1 July.

Publication

Annual Report.

Statistics

IDA CREDITS APPROVED IN EASTERN EUROPE, RUSSIA AND CENTRAL ASIA, 1 JULY 2006–30 JUNE 2007
(US $ million)

Country	Purpose	Amount
Armenia	Third social investment fund specific investment credit	25.0
	Third poverty reduction support operation development policy credit	28.0
	Second judicial reform specific investment credit	22.5
	Health system modernization	22.0
Azerbaijan	Real estate registration system	30.0
	Water supply and sanitation	230.0
Georgia	Second poverty reduction support operation development planning credit	20.0
	Education system realignment and strengthening programme	15.0
	East-West highway improvement	19.0
	Third poverty reduction support development policy credit	20.0
Kyrgyzstan	'Reducing technical barriers for entrepreneurship and trade' technical assistance grant	5.0
	Second village investment specific investment grant	15.0
	Second on-farm irrigation specific investment grant	16.0
Moldova	Poverty reduction support development planning credit	10.0
	Road sector investment and maintenance support	16.0
	Health services and social assistance	17.0
Tajikistan	Programmatic development policy grant	10.0
	Public sector reform technical assistance grant	5.0
	Dushanbe water supply specific investment credit/grant (additional financing)	3.5/1.5
	Cotton sector recovery	15.0
Uzbekistan	Basic education improvement and investment	15.0

Source: *World Bank Annual Report 2007.*

International Finance Corporation—IFC

Address: 2121 Pennsylvania Ave, NW, Washington, DC 20433, USA.
Telephone: (202) 473-3800; **fax:** (202) 974-4384; **e-mail:** information@ifc.org; **internet:** www.ifc.org.

IFC was founded in 1956 as a member of the World Bank Group to stimulate economic growth in developing countries by financing private-sector investments, mobilizing capital in international financial markets, and providing technical assistance and advice to governments and businesses.

Organization

(October 2008)

IFC is a separate legal entity in the World Bank Group. Executive Directors of the World Bank also serve as Directors of IFC. The President of the World Bank is *ex officio* Chairman of the IFC Board of Directors, which has appointed him President of IFC. Subject to his overall supervision, the day-to-day operations of IFC are conducted by its staff under the direction of the Executive Vice-President. In 2007 IFC initiated a process of revising and expanding its executive management. The senior management team was to include 10 Vice-Presidents responsible for regional and thematic groupings. At the end of June 2007 IFC had 3,134 staff members, of whom 51% were based in field offices.

PRINCIPAL OFFICERS

President: ROBERT B. ZOELLICK (USA).
Executive Vice-President: LARS THUNELL (Sweden).
Director, Tokyo Office: HIDEAKI SUZUKI (Japan).
Vice-President, Europe and Central Asia (and Global Financial Markets): JYRKI KOSKELO (Finland).
Director, Central and Eastern Europe Department: SNEZANA STOILJKOVIC.
Director, Southern Europe and Central Asia Department: SHABHAZ MAVADDAT.

OFFICES IN EASTERN EUROPE, RUSSIA AND CENTRAL ASIA

Armenia: 375010 Yerevan, V. Sargsyan St 9, Republic Sq.; tel. (10) 54-52-41; fax (10) 54-52-45; Country Rep. NERSES KARAMANUKYAN.
Azerbaijan: 1004 Baku, Icheri Sheher, Mirza Mansur St 91-95; tel. (12) 492-19-41; fax (12) 492-14-79; Country Officer ALIYA AZIMOVA.
Belarus: 220033 Minsk, pr. Partizanski 6 A, 3rd Floor; tel. (17) 219-78-11; fax (17) 222-74-40; Rep. CRAIG BELL.

Georgia: 0179 Tbilisi, Chavchavadze Ave 5A First Drive; tel. (32) 91-30-96; fax (32) 91-34-78; Country Rep. THEA GIGIBERIA.
Kazakhstan: 480100 Almaty, Kazybek bi 41, 4th Floor; tel. (727) 298-05-80; fax (727) 298-05-81; Regional Rep. and Country Man. GORTON M. DE MOND.
Kyrgyzstan: 720010 Bishkek, Moskovskaya 214; tel. (312) 61-06-50; fax (312) 61-03-56; Regional Rep. and Country Man. GORTON M. DE MOND.
Russia: 121069 Moscow, Bolshaia Molchanovka 36, Bldg 1; tel. (495) 411-75-55; fax (495) 411-75-56; Dir SNEZANA STOILJKOVIC.
Tajikistan: 734025 Dushanbe, ul. Shevchenko 91–10; tel. and fax (372) 21-07-56; fax (372) 51-00-42; Regional Rep.and Country Man. GORTON M. DE MOND.
Ukraine: 04070 Kyiv, Spaska 30A, Podil Plaza, block 2, 6th Floor; tel. (44) 490-64-00; fax (44) 490-64-20; Programme Officer ELENA VOLOSHINA.
Uzbekistan: 700048 Tashkent, Amir Temur 107B, 15th Floor; tel. (71) 138-59-28; fax (71) 138-59-27; Regional Rep. and Country Man. GORTON M. DE MOND.

Activities

IFC aims to promote economic development in developing member countries by assisting the growth of private enterprise and effective capital markets. It finances private sector projects, through loans, the purchase of equity, quasi-equity products, and risk management services, and assists governments to create conditions that stimulate the flow of domestic and foreign private savings and investment. IFC may provide finance for a project that is partly state-owned, provided that there is participation by the private sector and that the project is operated on a commercial basis. IFC also mobilizes additional resources from other financial institutions, in particular through syndicated loans, thus providing access to international capital markets. IFC provides a range of advisory services to help to improve the investment climate in developing countries and offers technical assistance to private enterprises and governments. Increasingly IFC is focused on extending assistance to 'frontier' markets, i.e. those designated by the World Bank as low-income or high-risk countries or regions. Other strategic priorities in 2006/07 included building long-term relationships with local companies; ensuring environmental and social sustainability; helping the private sector strengthen infrastructure, from ports and roads to schools and hospitals; and developing local financial markets. In November 2004 IFC announced the establishment of a Global Trade Finance Programme, with initial funding of some US $500m., which aimed to support small-scale importers and exporters in emerging markets, to facilitate South-South trade in goods and services, and to extend technical assistance and training to local financial institutions. (An additional $500m. was approved in January 2007.) By October 2008 some 200 banks were participating in the initiative.

To be eligible for financing projects must be profitable for investors, as well as financially and economically viable; must benefit the economy of the country concerned; and must comply with IFC's environmental and social guidelines. IFC aims to promote best corporate governance and management methods and sustainable business practices, and encourages partnerships between governments, non-governmental organizations and community groups. In 2001/02 IFC developed a Sustainability Framework to help to assess the longer-term economic, environmental and social impact of projects. The first Sustainability Review was published in mid-2002. In 2002/03 IFC assisted 10 international banks to draft a voluntary set of guidelines (the Equator Principles), based on IFC's environmental, social and safeguard monitoring policies, to be applied to their global project finance activities. A revised set of Equator Principles was released in July 2006. By mid-2008 60 financial institutions had signed up to the Equator Principles.

IFC's authorized capital is US $2,450m. At 30 June 2007 paid-in capital was $2,365m. The World Bank was originally the principal source of borrowed funds, but IFC also borrows from private capital markets. IFC's net income amounted to $2,618m. in 2006/07, compared with $1,278m. in the previous year.

In the year ending 30 June 2007 project financing approved by IFC amounted to US $9,995m. for 299 projects in 69 countries (compared with $8,275m. for 284 projects in the previous year). Of the total approved in 2006/07 $8,220m. was for IFC's own account, while $1,775m. was in the form of loan syndications and underwriting of securities issues and investment funds by more than 100 participant banks and institutional investors. Generally, IFC limits its financing to less than 25% of the total cost of a project, but may take up to a 35% stake in a venture (although never as a majority shareholder). Disbursements for IFC's account amounted to $5,841m. in 2006/07 (compared with $4,428m. in the previous year).

The dissolution of the USSR in 1991, and the transition to market economies there and in other Central and Eastern European countries, led to an increase in IFC activities in the region from the 1990s. In order to facilitate the privatization process in that region, the IFC has conducted several single-enterprise advisory assignments and has undertaken work to formulate models that can be easily replicated, notably for small-scale privatization and the privatization of agricultural land in Belarus, the Russian Federation and Ukraine. IFC has also been active in supporting and attracting foreign direct investment to exploit business opportunities in the region. IFC's Private Enterprise Partnership, established within the Central and Eastern Europe department in May 2000, provides technical assistance and works with donors, investors, local businesses and governments in the countries of the former Soviet Union to attract direct investment, to stimulate the growth of the private sector—including small and medium-sized enterprises—and to improve the business environment. In July 2005 the IFC Board of Directors agreed to extend the Partnership's mandate until 2011.

During 2006/07 IFC approved total financing of US $1,786m. for 67 projects in 15 countries in Europe and Central Asia (including Turkey), compared with $2,084m. for 80 projects in the previous

year. IFC has been actively involved in mobilizing financing for the development of an oilfield in Azerbaijan and the associated Baku–Tbilisi–Ceyhan pipeline project, as well as undertaking efforts to ensure that the projects meet required environmental and social standards. IFC has financed other schemes to improve energy efficiency in a range of projects throughout the region.

IFC's Private Sector Advisory Services (PSAS), jointly managed with the World Bank, advises governments and private enterprises on policy, transaction implementation and foreign direct investment. The Foreign Investment Advisory Service (FIAS), jointly operated and financed with the World Bank and MIGA, provides technical assistance and advice on promoting foreign investment and strengthening the country's investment framework at the request of governments. FIAS completed 83 projects in 2006/07, bringing a total of 760 projects since the Service was established in 1987. Under the Technical Assistance Trust Funds Program (TATF), established in 1988, IFC manages resources contributed by various governments and agencies to provide finance for feasibility studies, project identification studies and other types of technical assistance relating to project preparation. In 2004 a Grassroots Business Initiative was established, with external donor funding, to support businesses that provide economic opportunities for disadvantaged communities in Africa, Latin America, and South and Southeast Asia. Other areas covered by IFC's advisory services include carbon finance, cleaner technologies and sustainable investing.

In 2000 a Private Enterprise Partnership was established to serve countries of the former Soviet Union and Mongolia. It aimed to help develop financial markets in those countries, link smaller companies to major investors, improve corporate governance practices and regulations, and improve the regulatory environment for SMEs. Its mandate was extended in July 2005, for a period until July 2011, with an annual budget of US $6.07m. The Partnership administers programmes in the following areas: building agribusiness supply and distribution chains; attracting investment through improved corporate governance; improving the business enabling environment; building industrial supply chains and developing communities; building the leasing market for better access to finance; developing the market for sustainable energy finance; and building the capacity of lending institutions to improve access to affordable housing. IFC also administers a Central Asia Small Enterprise Fund and a Central Asia Micro and Small Enterprise Facility, established jointly with the European Bank for Reconstruction and Development in 2002/03.

Publications

Annual Report.
Doing Business (annually).
Emerging Stock Markets Factbook (annually).
Impact (quarterly).
Lessons of Experience (series).
Results on the Ground (series).
Review of Small Businesses (annually).
Sustainability Report (annually).
Discussion papers and technical documents.

Multilateral Investment Guarantee Agency—MIGA

Address: 1818 H Street, NW, Washington, DC 20433, USA.
Telephone: (202) 473-6163; **fax:** (202) 522-2630; **internet:** www .miga.org.

MIGA was founded in 1988 as an affiliate of the World Bank. Its mandate is to encourage the flow of foreign direct investment to, and among, developing member countries, through the provision of political risk insurance and investment marketing services to foreign investors and host governments, respectively.

Executive Vice-President: Izumi Kobayashi (Japan) (from Dec. 2008).

Activities

The convention establishing MIGA took effect in April 1988. Authorized capital was US $1,082m. In April 1998 the Board of Directors approved an increase in MIGA's capital base. A grant of $150m. was transferred from the IBRD as part of the package, while the capital increase (totalling $700m. callable capital and $150m. paid-in capital) was approved by MIGA's Council of Governors in April 1999. A three-year subscription period then commenced, covering the period April 1999–March 2002 (later extended to March 2003). At 30 June 2007 109 countries had subscribed $745.8m. of the new capital increase. At that time total subscriptions to the capital stock amounted to $1,885.6m., of which $359.7m. was paid-in.

MIGA guarantees eligible investments against losses resulting from non-commercial risks, under four main categories:

Organization

(October 2008)

MIGA is legally and financially separate from the World Bank. It is supervised by a Council of Governors (comprising one Governor and one Alternate of each member country) and an elected Board of Directors (of no less than 12 members).

President: Robert B. Zoellick (USA).

(i) transfer risk resulting from host government restrictions on currency conversion and transfer;

(ii) risk of loss resulting from legislative or administrative actions of the host government;

(iii) repudiation by the host government of contracts with investors in cases in which the investor has no access to a competent forum;

(iv) the risk of armed conflict and civil unrest.

Before guaranteeing any investment, MIGA must ensure that it is commercially viable, contributes to the development process and is not harmful to the environment. During the fiscal year 1998/99 MIGA and IFC appointed the first Compliance Advisor and Ombudsman to consider the concerns of local communities directly affected by MIGA- or IFC-sponsored projects. In February 1999 the Board of Directors approved an increase in the amount of political risk insurance available for each project, from US \$75m. to \$200m.

During the year ending 30 June 2007 MIGA issued 45 investment insurance contracts for 29 projects with a value of US \$1,400m. Since 1988 the total investment guarantees issued amounted to some \$17,400m., through 884 contracts in support of 556 projects.

MIGA works with local insurers, export credit agencies, development finance institutions and other organizations to promote insurance in a country, to ensure a level of consistency among insurers and to support capacity-building within the insurance industry. MIGA also offers investment marketing services to help to promote foreign investment in developing countries and in transitional economies, and to disseminate information on investment opportunities. In early 2007 MIGA's technical assistance services were amalgamated into the Foreign Advisory Investment Service (FIAS, see IFC), of which MIGA became a lead partner, along with IFC and the World Bank.

In October 1995 MIGA established a new network on investment opportunities, which connected investment promotion agencies (IPAs) throughout the world on an electronic information network. The so-called IPA*net* aimed to encourage further investments among developing countries, to provide access to comprehensive information on investment laws and conditions and to strengthen links between governmental, business and financial associations and investors. A new version of IPA*net* was launched in 1997 (and can

be accessed at www.ipanet.net). In June 1998 MIGA initiated a new internet-based facility, 'PrivatizationLink', to provide information on investment opportunities resulting from the privatization of industries in developing economies. In October 2000 a specialized facility within the service was established to facilitate investment in Russia (russia.privatizationlink.com). During 2000/01 an office was established in Paris, France, to promote and co-ordinate European investment in developing countries, in particular in Africa and Eastern Europe. In March 2002 MIGA opened a regional office, based in Johannesburg, South Africa. In September a new regional office was inaugurated in Singapore, in order to facilitate foreign investment in Asia.

In April 2002 MIGA launched a new service, 'FDIXchange', to provide potential investors, advisors and financial institutions with up-to-date market analysis and information on foreign direct investment opportunities in emerging economies (accessible at www.fdixchange.com). An FDIXchange Investor Information Development Programme was launched in January 2003. In January 2004 a new FDI Promotion Centre became available on the internet (www.fdi-promotion.com) to facilitate information exchange and knowledge-sharing among investment promotion professionals, in particular in developing countries. (A Serbian language version was launched in June 2005.) During 2003/04 MIGA established a new fund, the Invest-in-Development Facility, to enhance the role of foreign investment in attaining the Millennium Development Goals. In 2005/06 MIGA supported for the first time a project aimed at selling carbon credits gained by reducing greenhouse gas emissions; it provided US \$2m. in guarantee coverage to the El Salvador-based initiative. A new internet service, relating to political risk management and insurance, was launched during 2006/07 (www.pri-center.com).

Publications

Annual Report.

MIGA News (online newsletter; every 2 months).

Other guides, brochures and regional briefs.

International Fund for Agricultural Development—IFAD

Address: Via del Serafico 107, 00142 Rome, Italy.

Telephone: (06) 54591; **fax:** (06) 5043463; **e-mail:** ifad@ifad.org; **internet:** www.ifad.org.

IFAD was established in 1977, following a decision by the 1974 UN World Food Conference, with a mandate to combat hunger and eradicate poverty on a sustainable basis in the low-income, food-deficit regions of the world. Funding operations began in January 1978.

President and Chairman of Executive Board: LENNART BÅGE (Sweden).

Vice-President: KANAYO F. F. NWANZE (Nigeria).

Organization

(October 2008)

GOVERNING COUNCIL

Each member state is represented in the Governing Council (the Fund's highest authority) by a Governor and an Alternate. Sessions are held annually with special sessions as required. The Governing Council elects the President of the Fund (who also chairs the Executive Board) by a two-thirds majority for a four-year term. The President is eligible for re-election.

EXECUTIVE BOARD

Consists of 18 members and 18 alternates, elected by the Governing Council, who serve for three years. The Executive Board is responsible for the conduct and general operation of IFAD and approves loans and grants for projects; it holds three regular sessions each year. An independent Office of Evaluation reports directly to the Board.

The governance structure of the Fund is based on the classification of members. Membership of the Executive Board is distributed as follows: eight List A countries (i.e. industrialized donor countries), four List B (petroleum-exporting developing donor countries), and six List C (recipient developing countries), divided equally among the three Sub-List C categories (i.e. for Africa, Europe, Asia and the Pacific, and Latin America and the Caribbean).

Activities

IFAD provides financing primarily for projects designed to improve food production systems in developing member states and to strengthen related policies, services and institutions. In allocating resources IFAD is guided by: the need to increase food production in the poorest food-deficit countries; the potential for increasing food production in other developing countries; and the importance of improving the nutrition, health and education of the poorest people in developing countries, i.e. small-scale farmers, artisanal fishermen, nomadic pastoralists, indigenous populations, rural women, and the rural landless. All projects emphasize the participation of beneficiaries in development initiatives, both at the local and national level. Issues relating to gender and household food security are incorporated into all aspects of its activities. IFAD is committed to achieving the so-called Millennium Development Goals (MDGs), pledged by governments attending a special session of the UN General Assembly in September 2000, and, in particular, the objective to reduce by 50% the proportion of people living in extreme poverty by 2015. In 2001 the Fund introduced new measures to improve monitoring and impact evaluation, in particular to assess its contribution to achieving the MDGs.

In December 2006 the Executive Board adopted IFAD's Strategic Framework for 2007–10, in which it reiterated its commitment to enabling the rural poor to achieve household food security and to overcome their poverty. Accordingly, the Fund's efforts were to focus on ensuring that poor rural populations have improved and sustainable access to, and sufficiently developed skills to take advantage of: natural resources; better agricultural technologies and production services; a broad range of financial services; transparent competitive agricultural input and produce markets; opportunities for rural off-farm employment and enterprise development; and local and national policy and programming processes. Within this Framework the Fund has also formulated regional strategies for rural poverty reduction, based on a series of regional poverty assessments. In 2003 a new Policy Division was established under the External Affairs Department to co-ordinate policy work at the corporate level. A Policy Forum was launched in 2004, comprising IFAD senior management and staff. During 2007–09 IFAD was implementing a performance-enhancing Action Plan for Improving its Development Effectiveness.

IFAD is a leading repository in the world of knowledge, resources and expertise in the field of rural hunger and poverty alleviation. In 2001 it renewed its commitment to becoming a global knowledge institution for rural poverty-related issues. Through its technical assistance grants, IFAD aims to promote research and capacity-building in the agricultural sector, as well as the development of technologies to increase production and alleviate rural poverty. In recent years IFAD has been increasingly involved in promoting the use of communication technology to facilitate the exchange of information and experience among rural communities, specialized institutions and organizations, and IFAD-sponsored projects. Within the strategic context of knowledge management, IFAD has supported initiatives to establish regional electronic networks, such as Electronic Networking for Rural Asia/Pacific (ENRAP, currently in its third phase), and FIDAMERICA in Latin America and the Caribbean (established in 1995 and currently in its fourth phase), as well as to develop other lines of communication between organizations, local agents and the rural poor.

IFAD participated in the High-Level Conference on World Food Security and the Challenges of Climate Change and Bioenergy, convened by FAO in Rome, Italy, in June 2008. The meeting adopted a Declaration on Food Security, which noted an urgent need to develop the agricultural sectors and expand food production in developing countries and countries with economies in transition, and for increased investment in rural development, agriculture and agribusiness.

IFAD is empowered to make both loans and grants. Loans are available on highly concessionary, intermediate and ordinary terms. Highly concessionary loans carry no interest but have an annual service charge of 0.75% and a repayment period of 40 years, including a 10-year grace period. New Debt Sustainability Framework (DSF) grant financing was introduced in 2007 in place of highly concessional loans for heavily indebted poor countries (HIPCs). Intermediate term loans are subject to a variable interest charge, equivalent to 50% of the interest rate charged on World Bank loans, and are repaid over 20 years. Ordinary loans carry a variable interest charge equal to that charged by the World Bank, and are repaid over 15–18 years. In 2007 highly concessionary loans represented some 73% of total lending in that year, DSF grants 17.6%, intermediate loans 3.2%, and ordinary loans 6.2%. Research and technical assistance grants are awarded to projects focusing on research, training, and project preparation and development. In order to increase the impact of its lending resources on food production, the Fund seeks as much as possible to attract other external donors and beneficiary governments as cofinanciers of its projects. In 2007 external cofinancing accounted for some 33.5% of all project funding, while domestic contributions, i.e. from recipient governments and other local sources, accounted for 22%.

In October 2007 the HIPC Trust Fund, administered by the World Bank, transferred US $104.1m. to IFAD, representing the first instalment of about $282m. which was to offset the impact of IFAD's debt relief commitments to post-decision point HIPC countries on the Fund's available resources for the disbursement of loans and grants. At 31 December 2007 IFAD had fulfilled its debt relief requirements to all of the 30 HIPCs that had met their decision points at that time.

IFAD's development projects usually include a number of components, such as infrastructure (e.g. improvement of water supplies, small-scale irrigation and road construction); input supply (e.g. improved seeds, fertilizers and pesticides); institutional support (e.g. research, training and extension services); and producer incentives (e.g. pricing and marketing improvements). IFAD also attempts to enable the landless to acquire income-generating assets: by increasing the provision of credit for the rural poor, it seeks to free them from dependence on the capital market and to generate productive activities.

In addition to its regular efforts to identify projects and programmes, IFAD organizes special programming missions to certain selected countries to undertake a comprehensive review of the constraints affecting the rural poor, and to help countries to design strategies for the removal of these constraints. In general, projects based on the recommendations of these missions tend to focus on institutional improvements at the national and local level to direct inputs and services to small farmers and the landless rural poor. Monitoring and evaluation missions are also sent to check the progress of projects and to assess the impact of poverty reduction efforts.

The Fund supports projects that are concerned with environmental conservation, in an effort to alleviate poverty that results from the deterioration of natural resources. In addition, it extends environmental assessment grants to review the environmental consequences of projects under preparation. In October 1997 IFAD was appointed to administer the Global Mechanism of the Convention to Combat Desertification in those Countries Experiencing Drought and Desertification, particularly in Africa, which entered into force in December 1996. The Mechanism was envisaged as a means of mobilizing and channelling resources for implementation of the Convention. A series of collaborative institutional arrangements were to be concluded between IFAD, UNDP and the World Bank in order to facilitate the effective functioning of the Mechanism. IFAD is an executing agency of the Global Environmental Facility, specializing in the area of combating rural poverty and environmental degradation.

During 1998 the Executive Board endorsed a policy framework for the Fund's provision of assistance in post-conflict situations, with the aim of achieving a continuum from emergency relief to a secure basis from which to pursue sustainable development. In July 2001 IFAD and UNAIDS signed a memorandum of understanding on developing a co-operation agreement. A meeting of technical experts from IFAD, FAO, WFP and UNAIDS, held in December, addressed means of mitigating the impact of HIV/AIDS on food security and rural livelihoods in affected regions.

During the late 1990s IFAD established several partnerships within the agribusiness sector, with a view to improving performance at project level, broadening access to capital markets, and encouraging the advancement of new technologies. Since 1996 it has chaired the Support Group of the Global Forum on Agricultural Research (GFAR), which facilitates dialogue between research centres and institutions, farmers' organizations, non-governmental bodies, the private sector and donors. In October 2001 IFAD became a co-sponsor of the Consultative Group on International Agricultural Research (CGIAR). In 2006 IFAD reviewed the work of the International Alliance against Hunger, which was established in 2004 to enhance co-ordination among international agencies and non-governmental organizations concerned with agriculture and rural development, and national alliances against hunger.

Finance

In accordance with the Articles of Agreement establishing IFAD, the Governing Council periodically undertakes a review of the adequacy of resources available to the Fund and may request members to make additional contributions. The seventh replenishment of IFAD funds, covering the period 2007–09, amounted to US $720m. The provisional budget for administrative expenses for 2008 amounted to $74.1m., while some $5.5m. was budgeted in that year to the Fund's Office of Evaluation.

Publications

Annual Report.
IFAD Update (2 a year).
Rural Poverty Report.
Staff Working Papers (series).

Statistics

PROJECTS IN EASTERN EUROPE AND CENTRAL ASIA APPROVED IN 2007

Country	Purpose	Loan amount (SDR m.*)
Armenia	Farmer market access programme	7.9
Azerbaijan . . .	Rural development project for the North-west	10.9

* The average value of the SDR—Special Drawing Right—in 2007 was US $1.58025.

International Monetary Fund—IMF

Address: 700 19th St, NW, Washington, DC 20431, USA.
Telephone: (202) 623-7000; **fax:** (202) 623-4661; **e-mail:** publicaffairs@imf.org; **internet:** www.imf.org.

The IMF was established at the same time as the World Bank in December 1945, to promote international monetary co-operation, to facilitate the expansion and balanced growth of international trade and to promote stability in foreign exchange.

Organization
(October 2008)

Managing Director: DOMINIQUE STRAUSS-KAHN (France).

First Deputy Managing Director: JOHN LIPSKY (USA).

Deputy Managing Directors: TAKATOSHI KATO (Japan), MURILO PORTUGAL (Brazil).

Director, European Department: MAREK BELKA (Poland) (from 1 November 2008).

Director, Middle East and Central Asia Department: MASOOD AHMED (Pakistan) (designate).

BOARD OF GOVERNORS

The highest authority of the Fund is exercised by the Board of Governors, on which each member country is represented by a Governor and an Alternate Governor. The Board normally meets annually. The voting power of each country is related to its quota in the Fund. An International Monetary and Financial Committee (IMFC, formerly the Interim Committee) advises and reports to the Board on matters relating to the management and adaptation of the international monetary and financial system, sudden disturbances that might threaten the system and proposals to amend the Articles of Agreement.

BOARD OF EXECUTIVE DIRECTORS

The 24-member Board of Executive Directors is responsible for the day-to-day operations of the Fund. The USA, United Kingdom, Germany, France and Japan each appoint one Executive Director. There is also one Executive Director from the People's Republic of China, Russia and Saudi Arabia, while the remainder are elected by groups of the remaining countries.

REGIONAL REPRESENTATION

There is a network of regional offices and Resident Representatives in more than 90 member countries. In addition, special information and liaison offices are located in Tokyo, Japan (for Asia and the Pacific), in New York, USA (for the United Nations), and in Europe (Paris, France; Geneva, Switzerland; Belgium, Brussels; and Warsaw, Poland, for Central Europe and the Baltics).

Principal Office in Europe: 64–66 ave d'Iena, 75116 Paris, France; tel. 1-40-69-30-70; fax 1-47-23-40-89; Dir SALEH M. NSOULI.

Activities

The purposes of the IMF, as defined in the Articles of Agreement, are:

(i) To promote international monetary co-operation through a permanent institution which provides the machinery for consultation and collaboration on monetary problems;

(ii) To facilitate the expansion and balanced growth of international trade, and to contribute thereby to the promotion and maintenance of high levels of employment and real income and to the development of members' productive resources;

(iii) To promote exchange stability, to maintain orderly exchange arrangements among members, and to avoid competitive exchange depreciation;

(iv) To assist in the establishment of a multilateral system of payments in respect of current transactions between members and in the elimination of foreign exchange restrictions which hamper the growth of trade;

(v) To give confidence to members by making the general resources of the Fund temporarily available to them, under adequate safeguards, thus providing them with the opportunity to correct maladjustments in their balance of payments, without resorting to measures destructive of national or international prosperity;

(vi) In accordance with the above, to shorten the duration of and lessen the degree of disequilibrium in the international balances of payments of members.

In joining the Fund, each country agrees to co-operate with the above objectives. In accordance with its objective of facilitating the expansion of international trade, the IMF encourages its members to accept the obligations of Article VIII, Sections two, three and four, of the Articles of Agreement. Members that accept Article VIII undertake to refrain from imposing restrictions on the making of payments and transfers for current international transactions and from engaging in discriminatory currency arrangements or multiple currency practices without IMF approval. At the end of 2007 some 90% of members had accepted Article VIII status.

In 2000/01 the Fund established an International Capital Markets Department to improve its understanding of financial markets and a separate Consultative Group on capital markets to serve as a forum for regular dialogue between the Fund and representatives of the private sector. In mid-2006 the International Capital Markets Department was merged with the Monetary and Financial Systems Department to create the Monetary and Capital Markets Department, with the intention of strengthening surveillance of global financial transactions and monetary arrangements. In June 2008 the Managing Director presented a new Work Programme, comprising the following four immediate priorities for the Fund: to enable member countries to deal with the current crises of reduced economic growth and escalating food and fuel prices, including efforts by the Fund to strengthen surveillance activities; to review the Fund's lending instruments; to implement new organizational tools and working practices; and to advance further the Fund's governance agenda.

QUOTAS

Membership and Quotas in Eastern Europe, Russia and Central Asia
(SDR million*)

	October 2008
Armenia	92.0
Azerbaijan	160.9
Belarus	386.4
Georgia	150.3
Kazakhstan	365.7
Kyrgyzstan	88.8
Moldova	123.2
Russian Federation	5,945.4
Tajikistan	87.0
Turkmenistan	75.2
Ukraine	1,372.0
Uzbekistan	275.6

*The Special Drawing Right (SDR) was introduced in 1970 as a substitute for gold in international payments, and was intended eventually to become the principal reserve asset in the international monetary system. Its value (which was US $1.54635 at 1 October 2008, and averaged $1.58025 in 2007) is based on the currencies of the five largest exporting countries. Each member is assigned a quota related to its national income, monetary reserves, trade balance and other economic indicators; the quota approximately determines a member's voting power and the amount of foreign exchange it may purchase from the Fund. A member's subscription is equal to its quota. Quotas are reviewed at intervals of not more than five years, to take into account the state of the world economy and members' different rates of development. In January 1998 the Board of Governors approved an increase of some 45% of total IMF resources, bringing the total value of quotas to approximately SDR 212,000m. By January 1999 member states having at least 85% of total quotas (as at December 1997) had consented to the new subscriptions enabling the increase to enter into effect. The Thirteenth General Review was concluded in January 2008 without an increase in quotas. At October 2008 total quotas in the Fund amounted to SDR 217,372.7m.

RESOURCES

Members' subscriptions form the basic resource of the IMF. They are supplemented by borrowing. Under the General Arrangements to Borrow (GAB), established in 1962, the Group of Ten industrialized nations (G10—Belgium, Canada, France, Germany, Italy, Japan, the Netherlands, Sweden, the United Kingdom and the USA) and Switzerland (which became a member of the IMF in May 1992 but which had been a full participant in the GAB from April 1984) undertake to lend the Fund as much as SDR 17,000m. in their own currencies to assist in fulfilling the balance of payments requirements of any member of the group, or in response to requests to the Fund from countries with balance of payments problems that could threaten the stability of the international monetary system. In 1983 the Fund entered into an agreement with Saudi Arabia, in association with the GAB, making available SDR 1,500m., and other borrowing arrangements were completed in 1984 with the Bank for International Settlements, the Saudi Arabian Monetary Agency, Belgium and Japan, making available a further SDR 6,000m. In 1986 another borrowing arrangement with Japan made available SDR 3,000m. In May 1996 GAB participants concluded an agreement in principle to expand the resources available for borrowing to SDR 34,000m., by securing the support of 25 countries with the financial capacity to support the international monetary system. The so-called New Arrangements to Borrow (NAB) was approved by the Executive Board in January 1997. It was to enter into force, for an initial five-year period, as soon as the five largest potential creditors participating in NAB had approved the initiative and the total credit arrangement of participants endorsing the scheme had reached at least SDR 28,900m. While the GAB credit arrangement was to remain in effect, the NAB was expected to be the first facility to be activated in the event of the Fund's requiring supplementary resources. In July 1998 the GAB was activated for the first time in more than 20 years in order to provide funds of up to US $6,300m. in support of an IMF emergency assistance package for Russia (the first time the GAB had been used for a non-participant). The NAB became effective in November, and was used for the first time as part of an extensive programme of support for Brazil, which was adopted by the IMF in early December. (In March 1999, however, the activation was cancelled.) In November 2002 NAB participants approved Chile's Central Bank as the 26th participant.

FINANCIAL ASSISTANCE

The Fund makes resources available to eligible members on an essentially short-term and revolving basis to provide members with temporary assistance to contribute to the solution of their payments problems. Before making a purchase, a member must show that its balance of payments or reserve position makes the purchase necessary. Apart from this requirement, reserve tranche purchases (i.e. purchases that do not bring the Fund's holdings of the member's currency to a level above its quota) are permitted unconditionally. Exchange transactions within the Fund take the form of members' purchases (i.e. drawings) from the Fund of the currencies of other members for the equivalent amounts of their own currencies.

With further purchases, however, the Fund's policy of conditionality means that a recipient country must agree to adjust its economic policies, as stipulated by the IMF. All requests other than for use of the reserve tranche are examined by the Executive Board to determine whether the proposed use would be consistent with the Fund's policies, and a member must discuss its proposed adjustment programme (including fiscal, monetary, exchange and trade policies) with IMF staff. (New guidelines on conditionality, which, *inter alia*, aimed to promote national ownership of policy reforms and to introduce specific criteria for the implementation of conditions given different states' circumstances, were approved by the Executive Board in September 2002.) Purchases outside the reserve tranche are made in four credit tranches, each equivalent to 25% of the member's quota; a member must reverse the transaction by repurchasing its own currency (with SDRs or currencies specified by the Fund) within a specified time. A credit tranche purchase is usually made under a 'Stand-by Arrangement' with the Fund, or under the Extended Fund Facility. A Stand-by Arrangement is normally of one or two years' duration, and the amount is made available in instalments, subject to the member's observance of 'performance criteria'; repurchases must be made within three-and-a-quarter to five years. An Extended Arrangement is normally of three years' duration, and the member must submit detailed economic programmes and progress reports for each year; repurchases must be made within four-and-a-half to 10 years. A member whose payments imbalance is large in relation to its quota may make use of temporary facilities established by the Fund using borrowed resources, namely the 'enlarged access policy' established in 1981, which helps to finance Stand-by and Extended Arrangements for such a member, up to a limit of between 90% and 110% of the member's quota annually. Repurchases are made within three-and-a-half to seven years. In October 1994 the Executive Board approved a temporary increase in members' access to IMF resources, on the basis of a recommendation by the then Interim Committee. The annual access limit under IMF regular tranche drawings, Stand-by Arrangements and Extended Fund Facility credits was increased from 68% to 100% of a member's quota, with the cumulative access limit remaining at 300% of quota. The arrangements were extended, on a temporary basis, in November 1997.

In addition, special-purpose arrangements have been introduced, all of which are subject to the member's co-operation with the Fund to find an appropriate solution to its difficulties. The Compensatory Financing Facility (CCF) provides compensation to members whose export earnings are reduced as a result of circumstances beyond their control, or which are affected by excess costs of cereal imports. In December 1997 the Executive Board established a new Supplemental Reserve Facility (SRF) to provide short-term assistance to members experiencing exceptional balance of payments difficulties resulting from a sudden loss of market confidence. The SRF was activated immediately to provide SDR 9,950m. to the Republic of Korea, as part of a Stand-by Arrangement amounting to SDR 15,550m. (at that time the largest amount ever committed by the Fund). In July 1998 SDR 4,000m. was made available to Russia under the SRF and, in December, some SDR 9,100m. was extended to Brazil under the SRF as part of a new Stand-by Arrangement. In January 2001 some SDR 2,100m. in SRF resources were approved for Argentina as part of an SDR 5,187m. Stand-by Arrangement augmentation. (In January 2002 the Executive Board approved an extension of one year for Argentina's SRF repayments.) The SDR 22,821m. Stand-by credit approved for Brazil in September 2002 included some SDR 7,600m. committed under the SRF. In April 1999 an additional facility, the Contingent Credit Lines (CCL), was established to provide short-term financing on similar terms to the SRF in order to prevent more stable economies being affected by adverse international financial developments and to maintain investor confidence. No funds were ever committed under the CCL, however, and in November 2003 the Executive Board resolved to allow the facility to terminate, as scheduled, at the end of that month. The Board requested further consideration of other precautionary arrangements to limit the risk of financial crises. In April 2004 the Board approved a new initiative, the Trade Integration Mechanism, to support countries experiencing short-term balance of payments shortfalls as a result of multilateral trade liberalization. Bangladesh, in July, was the first country to obtain assistance in accordance with the Mechanism (in the form of an augmentation of an existing PRGF arrangement).

In April 1993 the Fund established the Systemic Transformation Facility (STF) to assist countries of the former USSR and other economies in transition. The STF was intended to be a temporary facility to enable member countries to draw on financial assistance for balance of payments difficulties resulting from severe disruption of their normal trade and payments arrangements. Access to the facility was limited to not more than 50% of a member's quota, and repayment terms were equal to those for the extended Fund facility. The expiry date for access to resources under this facility was extended by one year from 31 December 1994, to the end of 1995. During the STF's period of operation, purchases amounting to SDR 3,984m. were made by 20 countries, including Azerbaijan, Belarus and Uzbekistan.

In October 1995 the Interim Committee of the Board of Governors endorsed recent decisions of the Executive Board to strengthen IMF financial support to members requiring exceptional assistance. An Emergency Financing Mechanism was established to enable the IMF to respond swiftly to potential or actual financial crises, while additional funds were made available for short-term currency stabilization. (The Mechanism was activated for the first time in July 1997, in response to a request by the Philippines Government to reinforce the country's international reserves, and was subsequently used during that year to assist Thailand, Indonesia and the Republic of Korea, and, in July 1998, Russia.) Emergency assistance was also to be available to countries in a post-conflict situation, extending the existing arrangements for countries having been affected by natural disasters, to facilitate the rehabilitation of their economies and to improve their eligibility for further IMF concessionary arrangements. Assistance, typically, was to be limited to 25% of a member's quota, although up to 50% would be permitted in certain circumstances. In May 2001 the Executive Board decided to provide a subsidized loan rate for post-conflict emergency assistance for PRGF-eligible countries and an account was established to administer contributions from bilateral donors. In January 2005 the Executive Board decided to extend the subsidized rate for natural disasters. During 2006/07 the Fund approved assistance of SDR 50.8m. for Lebanon under the emergency post-conflict assistance facility.

In November 1999 the Fund's existing facility to provide balance of payments assistance on concessional terms to low-income member countries, the Enhanced Structural Adjustment Facility, was reformulated as the Poverty Reduction and Growth Facility, with greater emphasis on poverty reduction and sustainable development as key elements of growth-orientated economic strategies. Assistance under the PRGF (for which 77 countries were deemed eligible) was to be carefully matched to specific national requirements. Prior to drawing on the facility each recipient country was, in collaboration with representatives of civil society, non-governmental organizations and bilateral and multilateral institutions, to develop a national poverty reduction strategy, which was to be presented in a Poverty Reduction Strategy Paper (PRSP). PRGF loans carry an interest rate of 0.5% per year and are repayable over 10 years, with a five-and-a-half-year grace period; each eligible country is normally permitted to borrow up to 140% of its quota (in exceptional circumstances the maximum access can be raised to 185%). A PRGF Trust replaced the former ESAF Trust. In January 2006 a new Exogenous Shocks Facility was inaugurated to provide concessional assistance on the same terms as those of the PRGF for countries not eligible for funding under the PRGF.

During 2006/07 the IMF approved regular funding commitments for new arrangements amounting to SDR 237.4m. for two new Stand-by Arrangements, compared with a total of SDR 8,336m. in the previous year. Ten new PRGF arrangements, amounting to SDR 401.2m., were approved in 2006/07, together with the augmentation of two existing arrangements (SDR 36.8m.) and the reduction, by SDR 75m., of a further arrangement. During 2006/07 members' purchases from the general resources account amounted to SDR 2,329m., compared with SDR 2,156m. in the previous year. Outstanding IMF credit at 30 April 2007 totalled SDR 11,216m., compared with SDR 23,144m. in the previous year.

During the financial year 2006/07 a new PRGF arrangement, amounting to SDR 80.1m., was approved for Moldova, while an existing arrangement for that country was increased by SDR 30.8m.

The PRGF supports, through long-maturity loans and grants, IMF participation in an initiative to provide exceptional assistance to heavily indebted poor countries (HIPCs), in order to help them to achieve a sustainable level of debt management. In all 41 HIPCs were identified, of which 33 were in sub-Saharan Africa. Resources for the HIPC initiative are channelled through the PRGF Trust. In early 1999 the IMF and World Bank initiated a comprehensive review of the HIPC scheme, in order to consider modifications of the initiative and to strengthen the link between debt relief and poverty reduction. A consensus emerged among the financial institutions and leading industrialized nations to enhance the scheme, in order to make it available to more countries, and to accelerate the process of providing debt relief. In September the IMF Board of Governors expressed its commitment to undertaking an off-market transaction of a percentage of the Fund's gold reserves (i.e. a sale, at market prices, to central banks of member countries with repayment obligations to the Fund, which were then to be made in gold), as part of the funding arrangements of the enhanced HIPC scheme; this was undertaken during the period December 1999–April 2000. Under the enhanced initiative it was agreed that countries seeking debt relief should first formulate, and successfully implement for at least one year, a national poverty reduction strategy (see above). In May 2000 Uganda became the first country to qualify for full debt relief under the enhanced scheme. In September 2005 the IMF and World Bank endorsed a proposal of the Group of Eight (G8) nations to achieve the cancellation by the IMF, IDA and African Development Bank of 100% of debt claims on countries that had reached completion point under the HIPC initiative, in order to help them to achieve their Millennium Development Goals. The debt cancellation was to be undertaken within the framework of a Multilateral Debt Relief Initiative (MDRI). The IMF's Executive Board determined, additionally, to extend MDRI debt relief to all countries with an annual per capita of GDP $380, to be financed by IMF's own resources. Other financing was to be made from existing bilateral contributions to the PRGF Trust Subsidy Account. The initiative became effective in January 2006 once the final consent of the 43 contributors to the PRGF Trust Subsidy Account had been received. By September 2008 the IMF had committed some SDR 2,323.6m. under the HIPC initiative, of which SDR 1,713.0m. had been disbursed.

SURVEILLANCE

Under its Articles of Agreement, the Fund is mandated to oversee the effective functioning of the international monetary system. Accordingly, the Fund aims to exercise firm surveillance over the exchange rate policies of member states and to assess whether a country's economic situation and policies are consistent with the objectives of sustainable development and domestic and external stability. The Fund's main tools of surveillance are regular, bilateral consultations with member countries conducted in accordance with Article IV of the Articles of Agreement, which cover fiscal and monetary policies, balance of payments and external debt developments, as well as policies that affect the economic performance of a country, such as the labour market, social and environmental issues and good governance, and aspects of the country's capital accounts, and finance and banking sectors. In April 1997, in an effort to improve the value of surveillance by means of increased transparency, the Executive Board agreed to the voluntary issue of Press Information Notices (PINs) following each member's Article IV consultation with the Board, to those member countries wishing to make public the Fund's views. Other background papers providing information on and analysis of economic developments in individual countries continued to be made available. The Executive Board monitors global economic developments and discusses policy implications from a multilateral perspective, based partly on World Economic Outlook reports and Global Financial Stability Reports. In addition, the IMF studies the regional implications of global developments and policies pursued under regional fiscal arrangements. The Fund's medium-term strat-

egy, initiated in 2006, determined to strengthen its surveillance policies to reflect new challenges of globalization on international financial and macroeconomic stability. In June 2007 the Executive Board approved a Decision on Bilateral Surveillance to update and clarify principles for a member's exchange rate policies and to define best practice for the Fund's bilateral surveillance activities.

In April 1996 the IMF established the Special Data Dissemination Standard (SDDS), which was intended to improve access to reliable economic statistical information for member countries that have, or are seeking, access to international capital markets. In March 1999 the IMF undertook to strengthen the Standard by the introduction of a new reserves data template. By April 2007 64 countries had subscribed to the Standard. The financial crisis in Asia, which became apparent in mid-1997, focused attention on the importance of IMF surveillance of the economies and financial policies of member states and prompted the Fund further to enhance the effectiveness of its surveillance through the development of international standards in order to maintain fiscal transparency. In December 1997 the Executive Board approved a new General Data Dissemination System (GDDS), to encourage all member countries to improve the production and dissemination of core economic data. The operational phase of the GDDS commenced in May 2000. By September 2008 94 countries were participating in the GDDS. The Fund maintains a Dissemination Standards Bulletin Board (accessible at dsbb.imf.org), which aims to ensure that information on SDDS subscribing countries is widely available.

In April 1998 the then Interim Committee adopted a voluntary Code of Good Practices on Fiscal Transparency: Declaration of Principles, which aimed to increase the quality and promptness of official reports on economic indicators, and in September 1999 it adopted a Code of Good Practices on Transparency in Monetary and Financial Policies: Declaration of Principles. The IMF and World Bank jointly established a Financial Sector Assessment Programme (FSAP) in May 1999, initially as a pilot project, which aimed to promote greater global financial security through the preparation of confidential detailed evaluations of the financial sectors of individual countries. It remained under regular review by the Boards of Governors of the Fund and World Bank. During 2006/07 18 FSAP assessments were completed, of which six were updated assessments. As part of the FSAP Fund staff may conclude a Financial System Stability Assessment (FSSA), addressing issues relating to macroeconomic stability and the strength of a country's financial system. A separate component of the FSAP are Reports on the Observance of Standards and Codes (ROSCs), which are compiled after an assessment of a country's implementation and observance of internationally recognized financial standards. By March 2008 540 ROSCs had been published for 136 economies.

In March 2000 the IMF Executive Board adopted a strengthened framework to safeguard the use of IMF resources. All member countries making use of Fund resources were to be required to publish annual central bank statements audited in accordance with internationally accepted standards. It was also agreed that any instance of intentional misreporting of information by a member country should be made public. In the following month the Executive Board approved the establishment of an Independent Evaluation Office (IEO) to conduct objective evaluations of IMF policy and operations. The Office commenced activities in July 2001. In 2006/07 the Office concluded an evaluation on the IMF and Aid to Sub-Saharan Africa.

In April 2001 the Executive Board agreed on measures to enhance international efforts to counter money-laundering, in particular through the Fund's ongoing financial supervision activities and its programme of assessment of offshore financial centres (OFCs). In November the IMFC, in response to the terrorist attacks against targets in the USA, which had occurred in September, resolved, *inter alia*, to strengthen the Fund's focus on surveillance, and, in particular, to extend measures to counter money-laundering to include the funds of terrorist organizations. It determined to accelerate efforts to assess offshore centres and to provide technical support to enable poorer countries to meet international financial standards. In March 2004 the Board of Directors resolved that an anti-money laundering and countering the financing of terrorism (AML/CFT) component be introduced into regular OFC and FSAP assessments conducted by the Fund and the World Bank, following a pilot programme undertaken from November 2002 with the World Bank, the Financial Action Task Force and other regional supervisory bodies. The first phase of the OFC assessment programme was concluded in February 2005, at which time 41 of 44 contacted jurisdictions had been assessed and the reports published.

The IMF is a co-sponsor, with the World Bank, Asian Development Bank and European Bank for Reconstruction and Development of the CIS-7 Initiative, which was formally established in April 2002 to assist seven low-income countries in transition—Armenia, Azerbaijan, Georgia, Kyrgyzstan, Moldova, Tajikistan and Uzbekistan. The initiative evolved from a joint IMF-World Bank report, concerned with poverty reduction, economic growth, and debt sustainability in those countries, which was concerned at a conference held in

February. The initiative aimed to generate international awareness of the fiscal and economic situation in those countries and to promote capacity-building and structural reform in co-operation with the participating governments. A review of the initiative was published in April 2004.

TECHNICAL ASSISTANCE

Technical assistance is provided by special missions or resident representatives who advise members on every aspect of economic management, while more specialized assistance is provided by the IMF's various departments. In 2000/01 the IMFC determined that technical assistance should be central to the IMF's work in crisis prevention and management, in capacity-building for low-income countries, and in restoring macroeconomic stability in countries following a financial crisis. Technical assistance activities subsequently underwent a process of review and reorganization to align them more closely with IMF policy priorities and other initiatives.

The IMF Institute, which was established in 1964, trains officials from member countries in macroeconomic management, financial analysis and policy, balance of payments methodology and public finance. The IMF Institute also co-operates with other established regional training centres and institutes in order to refine its delivery of technical assistance and training services. The IMF is a co-sponsor, with UNDP and the Japan administered account, of the Joint Vienna Institute, which was opened in the Austrian capital in October 1992 and which trains officials from former centrally-planned economies in various aspects of economic management and public administration. In May 1998 an IMF—Singapore Regional Training Institute (an affiliate of the IMF Institute) was inaugurated, in collaboration with the Singaporean Government, in order to provide training for officials from the Asia-Pacific region. In January 1999 the IMF, in co-operation with the African Development Bank and the World Bank, announced the establishment of a Joint Africa Institute, in Abidjan, Côte d'Ivoire, which was to offer training to officials from African countries. Also in 1999 a joint Regional Training Programme, administered with the Arab Monetary Fund, was established in the United Arab Emirates. During 2000/01 the Institute established a new training programme with government officials in Liaoning Province, the People's Republic of China. A regional training centre for Latin America became operational in Brasilia, Brazil in 2001. In July 2006 the Joint India-IMF Training Programme was inaugurated in Pune, India.

Publications

Annual Report.
Balance of Payments Statistics Yearbook.
Civil Society Newsletter (quarterly).
Direction of Trade Statistics (quarterly and annually).
Emerging Markets Financing (quarterly).
Finance and Development (quarterly).
Financial Statements of the IMF (quarterly).
Global Financial Stability Report (2 a year).
Global Monitoring Report (annually, with the World Bank).
Government Finance Statistics Yearbook.
IMF Commodity Prices (monthly).
IMF Financial Activities (weekly, online).
IMF in Focus (annually).
IMF Research Bulletin (quarterly).
IMF Survey (monthly, and online).
International Financial Statistics (monthly and annually).
Joint BIS-IMF-OECD-World Bank Statistics on External Debt (quarterly).
Quarterly Report on the Assessments of Standards and Codes.
Staff Papers (quarterly).
World Economic Outlook (2 a year).
Other country reports, economic and financial surveys, occasional papers, pamphlets, books.

United Nations Educational, Scientific and Cultural Organization—UNESCO

Address: 7 place de Fontenoy, 75352 Paris 07 SP, France.
Telephone: 1-45-68-10-00; **fax:** 1-45-67-16-90; **e-mail:** bpi@unesco.org; **internet:** www.unesco.org.

UNESCO was established in 1946 'for the purpose of advancing, through the educational, scientific and cultural relations of the peoples of the world, the objectives of international peace and the common welfare of mankind'.

CO-OPERATING BODIES

In accordance with UNESCO's constitution, national Commissions have been set up in most member states. These help to integrate work within the member states and the work of UNESCO. Most member states also have their own permanent delegations to UNESCO. UNESCO aims to develop partnerships with cities and local authorities.

Organization

(October 2008)

GENERAL CONFERENCE

The supreme governing body of the Organization, the Conference meets in ordinary session once in two years and is composed of representatives of the member states. It determines policies, approves work programmes and budgets and elects members of the Executive Board.

EXECUTIVE BOARD

The Board, comprising 58 members, prepares the programme to be submitted to the Conference and supervises its execution; it meets two times a year.

SECRETARIAT

The organization is headed by a Director-General, appointed for a four-year term. There are Assistant Directors-General for the main thematic sectors, i.e education, natural sciences, social and human sciences, culture, and communication and information, as well as for the support sectors of external relations and co-operation and of administration.

Director-General: KOÏCHIRO MATSUURA (Japan).

FIELD CO-ORDINATION

UNESCO maintains a network of offices to support a more decentralized approach to its activities and enhance their implementation at field level. Cluster offices provide the main structure of the field co-ordination network. These cover a group of countries and help to co-ordinate between member states and with other UN and partner agencies operating in the area. In 2008 there were 27 cluster offices covering 143 states. In addition 21 national offices serve a single country, including those in post-conflict situations or economic transition and the nine most highly-populated countries. The regional bureaux (see below) provide specialized support at a national level.

UNESCO Office Moscow: 119034 Moscow, Bolshoi Levshinsky per15/28, bld 2, Russia; tel. (495) 637-28-75; fax (495) 956-36-66; e-mail moscow@unesco.ru; internet www.unesco.ru; also covers Armenia, Azerbaijan, Belarus, Georgia and Moldova; Dir DENDEV BADARCH.

REGIONAL BUREAUX

Regional Bureau for Science and Culture in Europe: Palazzo Zorzi, 4930 Castello, 30122 Venice, Italy; tel. (041) 260-1511; fax (041) 528-9995; e-mail veniceoffice@unesco.org; internet www.unesco.org/venice; Dir ENGELBERT RUOSS.

Activities

In the implementation of all its activities UNESCO aims to contribute to achieving the UN Millennium Development Goal (MDG) of halving levels of extreme poverty by 2015, as well as other MDGs concerned with education and sustainable development. UNESCO is the lead agency for the International Decade for a Culture of Peace and Non-violence for the Children of the World (2001–10). In November 2007 the General Conference approved a medium-term strategy to guide UNESCO during the period 2008–13. UNESCO's central mission as defined under the strategy was to contribute to building peace, the alleviation of poverty, sustainable development and intercultural dialogue through its core programme sectors (Education; Natural Sciences; Social and Human Sciences; Culture; and Communication and Information). The strategy identified five 'overarching objectives' for UNESCO in 2008–13, within this programme framework: Attaining quality education for all; Mobilizing scientific knowledge and science policy for sustainable development; Addressing emerging ethical challenges; Promoting cultural diversity and intercultural dialogue; and Building inclusive knowledge societies through information and communication.

EDUCATION

UNESCO recognizes education as an essential human right, and an overarching objective for 2008–13 was to attain quality education for all. Through its work programme UNESCO is committed to achieving the MDGs of eliminating gender disparity at all levels of education and attaining universal primary education in all countries by 2015. The focus of many of UNESCO's education initiatives are the nine most highly-populated developing countries (Bangladesh, Brazil, the People's Republic of China, Egypt, India, Indonesia, Mexico, Nigeria and Pakistan), known collectively as the E-9 ('Education-9') countries.

UNESCO leads and co-ordinates global efforts in support of 'Education for All' (EFA), which was adopted as a guiding principle of UNESCO's contribution to development following a world conference, convened in March 1990. In April 2000 several UN agencies, including UNESCO and UNICEF, and other partners sponsored the World Education Forum, held in Dakar, Senegal, to assess international progress in achieving the goal of Education for All and to adopt a strategy for further action (the 'Dakar Framework'), with the aim of ensuring universal basic education by 2015. The Dakar Framework, incorporating six specific goals, emphasized the role of improved access to education in the reduction of poverty and in diminishing inequalities within and between societies. UNESCO was appointed as the lead agency in the implementation of the Framework, focusing on co-ordination, advocacy, mobilization of resources, and information-sharing at international, regional and national levels. It was to oversee national policy reforms, with a particular focus on the integration of EFA objectives into national education plans. An EFA Global Action Plan was formulated in 2006 to reinvigorate efforts to achieve EFA objectives and, in particular, to provide a framework for international co-operation and better definition of the roles of international partners and of UNESCO in leading the initiative. UNESCO's medium-term strategy for 2008–13 committed the organization to strengthening its role in co-ordinating EFA efforts at global and national levels, promoting monitoring and capacity-building activities to support implementation of EFA objectives, and facilitating mobilization of increased resources for EFA programmes and strategies (for example through the EFA-Fast Track Initiative, launched in 2002 to accelerate technical and financial support to low-income countries).

UNESCO advocates 'Literacy for All' as a key component of Education for All, regarding literacy as essential to basic education and to social and human development. UNESCO is the lead agency of the UN Literacy Decade (2003–12), which aims to formulate an international plan of action to raise literacy standards throughout the world and to assist policy-makers to integrate literacy standards and goals into national education programmes. The Literacy Initiative for Empowerment (LIFE) was developed as an element of the Literacy Decade to accelerate efforts in some 35 countries where illiteracy is a critical challenge to development. UNESCO is also the co-ordinating agency for the UN Decade of Education for Sustainable Development (2005–14), through which it aims to establish a global framework for action and strengthen the capacity of education systems to incorporate the concepts of sustainable development into education programmes. The April 2000 World Education Forum recognized the global HIV/AIDS pandemic to be a significant challenge to the attainment of Education for All'. UNESCO, as a co-sponsor of UNAIDS, takes an active role in promoting formal and non-formal preventive health education. Through a Global Initiative on HIV/AIDS and Education (EDUCAIDS) UNESCO aims to develop comprehensive responses to HIV/AIDS rooted in the education sector, with a particular focus on vulnerable children and young people. An initiative covering the 10-year period 2006–15, the Teacher Training Initiative in sub-Saharan Africa, aims to address the shortage of teachers in that region (owing to HIV/AIDS, armed conflict and other causes) and to improve the quality of teaching.

A key priority area of UNESCO's education programme is to foster quality education for all, through formal and non-formal educational opportunities. It assists members to improve the quality of education provision through curricula content, school management and teacher training. UNESCO aims to expand access to education at all levels and to work to achieve gender equality. In particular, UNESCO aims to strengthen capacity-building and education in natural, social and human sciences and promote the use of new technologies in teaching and learning processes.

The Associated Schools Project (ASPnet—comprising some 7,900 institutions in 176 countries in 2008) has, since 1953, promoted the principles of peace, human rights, democracy and international co-operation through education. It provides a forum for dialogue and for promoting best practices. At tertiary level UNESCO chairs a University Twinning and Networking (UNITWIN) initiative, which was established in 1992 to establish links between higher education institutions and to foster research, training and programme development. A complementary initiative, Academics Across Borders, was inaugurated in November 2005 to strengthen communication and the sharing of knowledge and expertise among higher education professionals. In October 2002 UNESCO organized the first Global Forum on International Quality Assurance, Accreditation and the Recognition of Qualifications to establish international standards and promote capacity-building for the sustainable development of higher education systems.

Within the UN system UNESCO is responsible for providing technical assistance and educational services in the context of emergency situations. This includes establishing temporary schools, providing education to refugees and displaced persons, as well as assistance for the rehabilitation of national education systems. In Palestine, UNESCO collaborates with UNRWA to assist with the training of teachers, educational planning and rehabilitation of schools.

NATURAL SCIENCES

The World Summit on Sustainable Development, held in August–September 2002, recognised the essential role of science (including mathematics, engineering and technology) as a foundation for achieving the MDGs of eradicating extreme poverty and ensuring environmental sustainability. UNESCO aims to promote this function within the UN system and to assist member states to utilise and foster the benefits of scientific and technical knowledge. A key objective for the medium-term strategy 2008–13 was to mobilize science knowledge and policy for sustainable development. Throughout the natural science programme priority was to be placed on Africa, least developed countries and small island developing states. The Local and Indigenous Knowledge System (LINKS) initiative aims to strengthen dialogue among traditional knowledge holders, natural and social scientists and decision-makers to enhance the conservation of biodiversity, in all disciplines, and to secure an active and equitable role for local communities in the governance of resources.

In November 1999 the General Conference endorsed a Declaration on Science and the Use of Scientific Knowledge and an agenda for action, which had been adopted at the World Conference on Science, held in June–July 1999, in Budapest, Hungary. By leveraging scientific knowledge, and global, regional and country level science networks, UNESCO aims to support sustainable development and the sound management of natural resources. It also advises governments on approaches to natural resource management, in particular the collection of scientific data, documenting and disseminating good practices and integrating social and cultural aspects into management structures and policies. UNESCO's Man and the Biosphere Programme supports a world-wide network of biosphere reserves (comprising 531 sites in 105 countries at July 2008), which aim to promote environmental conservation and research, education and training in biodiversity and problems of land use (including the fertility of tropical soils and the cultivation of sacred sites). The third World Congress of Biosphere Reserves was held in Madrid, Spain, in February 2008. UNESCO also supports a Global Network of National Geoparks (57 in 18 countries at July 2008) which was inaugurated in 2004 to promote collaboration among managed areas of geological significance to exchange knowledge and expertise and raise awareness of the benefits of protecting those environments.

UNESCO promotes and supports international scientific partnerships to monitor, assess and report on the state of Earth systems. With the World Meteorological Organization and the International Council of Science, UNESCO sponsors the World Climate Research Programme, which was established in 1980 to determine the predictability of climate and the effect of human activity on climate. UNESCO hosts the secretariat of the World Water Assessment Programme (WWAP), which prepares the periodic *World Water Development Report*. UNESCO is actively involved in the 10-year project, agreed by more than 60 governments in February 2005, to develop a Global Earth Observation System of Systems (GEOSS). The project aims to link existing and planned observation systems in order to provide for greater understanding of the earth's processes and dissemination of detailed data, for example predicting health epidemics or weather phenomena or concerning the management of ecosystems and natural resources. UNESCO's Intergovernmental Oceanographic Commission serves as the Secretariat of the Global Ocean Observing System. The International Geoscience Programme, undertaken jointly with the International Union of Geological Sciences (IUGS), facilitates the exchange of knowledge and methodology among scientists concerned with geological processes and aims to raise awareness of the links between geoscience and sustainable socio-economic development. The IUGS and UNESCO jointly initiated the International Year of Planet Earth (2008).

UNESCO is committed to contributing to international efforts to enhance disaster preparedness and mitigation. Through education UNESCO aims to reduce the vulnerability of poorer communities to disasters and improve disaster management at local and national levels. It also co-ordinates efforts at an international level to establish monitoring networks and early-warning systems to mitigate natural disasters, in particular in developing tsunami early-warning systems in Africa, the Caribbean, the South Pacific, the Mediterranean Sea and the North East Atlantic similar to those already established for the Indian and Pacific oceans. Other regional partnerships and knowledge networks were to be developed to strengthen capacity-building and the dissemination of information and good practices relating to risk awareness and mitigation and disaster management. Disaster education and awareness were to be incorporated as key elements in the UN Decade on Education for Sustainable Development (see above). UNESCO is also the lead agency for the International Flood Initiative, which was inaugurated in January 2005 at the World Conference on Disaster Reduction, held in Kobe, Japan. The Initiative aimed to promote an integrated approach to flood management in order to minimize the damage and loss of life caused by floods, mainly with a focus on research, training, promoting good governance and providing technical assistance.

A priority of the natural science programme for 2008–09 was to promote policies and strengthen human and institutional capacities in science, technology and innovation. At all levels of education UNESCO aimed to enhance teaching quality and content in areas of science and technology and, at regional and sub-regional level, to strengthen co-operation mechanisms and policy networks in training and research. With the International Council of Scientific Unions and the Third World Academy of Sciences, UNESCO operates a short-term fellowship programme in the basic sciences and an exchange programme of visiting lecturers.

UNESCO is the lead agency of the New Partnership for Africa's Development (NEPAD) Science and Technology Cluster and the NEPAD Action Plan for the Environment.

SOCIAL AND HUMAN SCIENCES

UNESCO is mandated to contribute to the world-wide development of the social and human sciences and philosophy, which it regards as of great importance in policy-making and maintaining ethical vigilance. The structure of UNESCO's Social and Human Sciences programme takes into account both an ethical and standard-setting dimension, and research, policy-making, action in the field and future-oriented activities. One of UNESCO's so-called overarching objectives in the period 2008–13 was to address emerging ethical challenges.

A priority area of UNESCO's work programme on Social and Human Sciences for 2008–09 was to promote principles, practices and ethical norms relevant for scientific and technological development. It fosters international co-operation and dialogue on emerging issues, as well as raising awareness and promoting the sharing of knowledge at regional and national levels. UNESCO supports the activities of the International Bioethics Committee (IBC—a group of 36 specialists who meet under UNESCO auspices) and the Intergovernmental Bioethics Committee and hosts the secretariat of the 18-member World Commission on the Ethics of Scientific Knowledge and Technology (COMEST), established in 1999, which aims to serve as a forum for the exchange of information and ideas and to promote dialogue between scientific communities, decision-makers and the public.

The priority Ethics of science and technology element aims to promote intergovernmental discussion and co-operation; to conduct explorative studies on possible UNESCO action on environmental ethics and developing a code of conduct for scientists; to enhance public awareness; to make available teaching expertise and create regional networks of experts; to promote the development of international and national databases on ethical issues; to identify ethical issues related to emerging technologies; to follow up relevant declarations, including the Universal Declaration on the Human Genome and Human Rights (see below); and to support the Global

Ethics Observatory, an online world-wide database of information on applied bioethics and other applied science- and technology-related areas (including environmental ethics) that was launched in December 2005 by the IBC.

UNESCO itself provides an interdisciplinary, multicultural and pluralistic forum for reflection on issues relating to the ethical dimension of scientific advances, and promotes the application of international guidelines. In May 1997 the IBC approved a draft version of a Universal Declaration on the Human Genome and Human Rights, in an attempt to provide ethical guidelines for developments in human genetics. The Declaration, which identified some 100,000 hereditary genes as 'common heritage', was adopted by the UNESCO General Conference in November and committed states to promoting the dissemination of relevant scientific knowledge and co-operating in genome research. In October 2003 the General Conference adopted an International Declaration on Human Genetic Data, establishing standards for scientists working in that field, and in October 2005 the General Conference adopted the Universal Declaration on Bioethics and Human Rights. At all levels UNESCO aims to raise awareness and foster debate about the ethical implications of scientific and technological developments and promote exchange of experiences and knowledge between governments and research bodies.

UNESCO recognizes that globalization has a broad and significant impact on societies. It is committed to countering negative trends of social transformation by strengthening the links between research and policy formulation by national and local authorities, in particular concerning poverty eradication. In that respect, UNESCO promotes the concept that freedom from poverty is a fundamental human right. In 1994 UNESCO initiated an international social science research programme, the Management of Social Transformations (MOST), to promote capacity-building in social planning at all levels of decision-making. In 2003 the Executive Board approved a continuation of the programme but with a revised strategic objective of strengthening links between research, policy and practice. In 2008–13 UNESCO aimed to promote new collaborative social science research programmes and to support capacity-building in developing countries.

UNESCO aims to monitor emerging social or ethical issues and, through its associated offices and institutes, formulate preventative action to ensure they have minimal impact on the attainment of UNESCO's objectives. As a specific challenge UNESCO is committed to promoting the International Convention against Doping in Sport, which entered into force in 2007. UNESCO also focuses on the educational and cultural dimensions of physical education and sport and their capacity to preserve and improve health.

Fundamental to UNESCO's mission is the rejection of all forms of discrimination. It disseminates information aimed at combating racial prejudice, works to improve the status of women and their access to education, promotes equality between men and women, and raises awareness of discrimination against people affected by HIV/AIDS, in particular among young people. In 2004 UNESCO inaugurated an initiative to enable city authorities to share experiences and collaborate in efforts to counter racism, discrimination, xenophobia and exclusion. As well as the International Coalition of Cities against Racism, regional coalitions were to be formed with more defined programmes of action. An International Youth Clearing House and Information Service (INFOYOUTH) aims to increase and consolidate the information available on the situation of young people in society, and to heighten awareness of their needs, aspirations and potential among public and private decision-makers. Supporting efforts to facilitate dialogue among different cultures and societies and promoting opportunities for reflection and consideration of philosophy and human rights, for example the celebration of World Philosophy Day, are also among UNESCO's fundamental aims.

CULTURE

In undertaking efforts to preserve the world's cultural and natural heritage UNESCO has attempted to emphasize the link between culture and development. In December 1992 UNESCO established the World Commission on Culture and Development, to strengthen links between culture and development and to prepare a report on the issue. The first World Conference on Culture and Development was held in June 1999, in Havana, Cuba. In November 2001 the General Conference adopted the UNESCO Universal Declaration on Cultural Diversity, which affirmed the importance of intercultural dialogue in establishing a climate of peace. UNESCO's medium-term strategy for 2008–13 recognized the need for a more integrated approach to cultural heritage as an area requiring conservation and development and one offering prospects for dialogue, social cohesion and shared knowledge.

A priority element of UNESCO's draft work programme on Culture for 2008–09 was promoting cultural diversity through the safeguarding of heritage and enhancement of cultural expressions. In January 2002 UNESCO inaugurated the Global Alliance on Cultural

Diversity, to promote partnerships between governments, non-governmental bodies and the private sector with a view to supporting cultural diversity through the strengthening of cultural industries and the prevention of cultural piracy. In October 2005 the General Conference approved an International Convention on the Protection of the Diversity of Cultural Expressions. It entered into force in March 2007 and the first session of the intergovernmental committee servicing the Convention was convened in Ottawa, Canada, in December.

UNESCO's World Heritage Programme, inaugurated in 1978, aims to protect historic sites and natural landmarks of outstanding universal significance, in accordance with the 1972 UNESCO Convention Concerning the Protection of the World Cultural and Natural Heritage, by providing financial aid for restoration, technical assistance, training and management planning. At July 2008 the 'World Heritage List' comprised 878 sites in 145 countries, of which 679 had cultural significance, 174 were natural landmarks, and 25 were of 'mixed' importance. The organization is assisting in the preservation of numerous historical and natural sites in Eastern Europe and Central Asia, including the Monastery of Haghpat in Armenia, the Bialowieza Forest (Belarus/Poland), Bagrati Cathedral (Georgia), the Kremlin and Red Square in Moscow (Russia), Saint Sophia Cathedral (Ukraine) and the historic centres of Bukhara and Shakhrisyabz, and Samarkand (Uzbekistan). UNESCO also maintains a list of 'World Heritage in Danger', which at July 2008 included the Walled City of Baku (Azerbaijan); the site was damaged by an earthquake in November 2000 and remains endangered by modern urban development.

UNESCO supports the safeguarding of humanity's non-material 'intangible' heritage, including oral traditions, music, dance and medicine. An Endangered Languages Programme was initiated in 1993. By 2008 the Programme estimated that, of some 6,700 languages spoken world-wide, about one-half were endangered. It works to raise awareness of the issue, for example through publication of the *Atlas of the World's Languages in Danger of Disappearing*, to strengthen local and national capacities to safeguard and document languages and administers a Register of Good Practices in Language Preservation. In October 2003 the UNESCO General Conference adopted a Convention for the Safeguarding of Intangible Cultural Heritage, which provided for the establishment of an intergovernmental committee and for participating states to formulate national inventories of intangible heritage. The Convention entered into force in April 2006 and the intergovernmental committee convened its inaugural session in November. The second session was held in Tokyo, Japan, in September 2007. A List of Intangible Cultural Heritage in Need of Urgent Safeguarding was scheduled to be operational by 2009. In May 2001, November 2003 and November 2005 (i.e. before the Convention entered into effect) UNESCO awarded the title of 'Masterpieces of the Oral and Intangible Heritage of Humanity' to a total of 90 examples of intangible heritage deemed to be of outstanding value. UNESCO's culture programme also aims to safeguard movable cultural heritage and to support and develop museums as a means of preserving heritage and making it accessible to society as a whole.

In November 2001 the General Conference authorized the formulation of a Declaration against the Intentional Destruction of Cultural Heritage. In addition, the Conference adopted the Convention on the Protection of the Underwater Cultural Heritage, covering the protection from commercial exploitation of shipwrecks, submerged historical sites, etc., situated in the territorial waters of signatory states. UNESCO also administers the 1954 Hague Convention on the Protection of Cultural Property in the Event of Armed Conflict and the 1970 Convention on the Means of Prohibiting and Preventing the Illicit Import, Export and Transfer of Ownership of Cultural Property. In 1992 a World Heritage Centre was established to enable rapid mobilization of international technical assistance for the preservation of cultural sites. Through the World Heritage Information Network (WHIN), a world-wide network of more than 800 information providers, UNESCO promotes global awareness and information exchange.

UNESCO aims to support the development of creative industries and or creative expression. Through a variety of projects UNESCO promotes art education, supports the rights of artists, and encourages crafts, design, digital art and performance arts. In October 2004 UNESCO launched a Creative Cities Network to facilitate public and private sector partnerships, international links, and recognition of a city's unique expertise. At July 2008 nine cities were participating in the network. UNESCO is active in preparing and encouraging the enforcement of international legislation on copyright, raising awareness on the need for copyright protection to uphold cultural diversity, and is contributing to the international debate on digital copyright issues and piracy.

Within its ambition of ensuring cultural diversity, UNESCO recognizes the role of culture as a means of promoting peace and dialogue. Several projects have been formulated within a broader concept of Roads of Dialogue. In Central Asia a project on intercultural dialogue follows on from an earlier multi-disciplinary study of the ancient Silk Roads trading routes linking Asia and Europe, which illustrated many examples of common heritage. Other projects include a study of the movement of peoples and cultures during the slave trade, a Mediterranean Programme, the Caucasus Project and the Arabia Plan, which aims to promote world-wide knowledge and understanding of Arab culture. UNESCO has overseen an extensive programme of work to formulate histories of humanity and regions, focused on ideas, civilizations and the evolution of societies and cultures. These have included the *General History of Africa*, *History of Civilizations of Central Asia*, and *History of Humanity*. In 2008–09 UNESCO endeavoured to consider and implement the findings of the Alliance of Civilizations, a high-level group convened by the UN Secretary-General that published a report in November 2006.

COMMUNICATION AND INFORMATION

UNESCO regards information, communication and knowledge as being at the core of human progress and well-being. The Organization advocates the concept of knowledge societies, based on the principles of freedom of expression, universal access to information and knowledge, promotion of cultural diversity, and equal access to quality education. In 2008–13 it determined to consolidate and implement this concept, in accordance with the Declaration of Principles and Plan of Action adopted by the World Summit on the Information Society (WSIS) in November 2005.

A key strategic objective of building inclusive knowledge societies was to be through enhancing universal access to communication and information. At national and global levels UNESCO promotes the rights of freedom of expression and of access to information. It promotes the free flow and broad diffusion of information, knowledge, data and best practices, through the development of communications infrastructures, the elimination of impediments to freedom of expression, and the development of independent and pluralistic media, including through the provision of advisory services on media legislation, particularly in post-conflict countries and in countries in transition. UNESCO recognizes that the so-called global 'digital divide', in addition to other developmental differences between countries, generates exclusion and marginalization, and that increased participation in the democratic process can be attained through strengthening national communication and information capacities. UNESCO promotes policies and mechanisms that enhance provision for marginalized and disadvantaged groups to benefit from information and community opportunities. Activities at local and national level include developing effective 'infostructures', such as libraries and archives and strengthening low-cost community media and information access points, for example through the establishment of Community Multimedia Centres (CMCs). Many of UNESCO's principles and objectives in this area are pursued through the Information for All Programme, which entered into force in 2001. It is administered by an intergovernmental council, the secretariat of which is provided by UNESCO. UNESCO also established, in 1982, the International Programme for the Development of Communication (IPDC), which aims to promote and develop independent and pluralistic media in developing countries, for example by the establishment or modernization of news agencies and newspapers and training media professionals. the promotion of the right to information, and through efforts to harness informatics for development purposes and strengthen member states' capacities in this field.

UNESCO supports cultural and linguistic diversity in information sources to reinforce the principle of universal access. It aims to raise awareness of the issue of equitable access and diversity, encourage good practices and develop policies to strengthen cultural diversity in all media. In 2002 UNESCO established Initiative B@bel as a multidisciplinary programme to promote linguistic diversity, with the aim of enhancing access of under-represented groups to information sources as well as protecting under-used minority languages. UNESCO's Programme for Creative Content supports the development of and access to diverse content in both the electronic and audiovisual media. The Memory of the World project, established in 1992, aims to preserve in digital form, and thereby to promote wide access to, the world's documentary heritage. By July 2008 158 inscriptions had been included on the project's register, originating from 67 countries, one private foundation and one international organization (the archives of the ICRC's former International Prisoners of War Agency, 1914–1923, submitted by the ICRC in 2007). UNESCO also supports other efforts to preserve and disseminate digital archives and, in 2003, adopted a Charter for the Preservation of Digital Heritage.

UNESCO promotes freedom of expression, of the press and independence of the media as fundamental human rights and the basis of democracy. It aims to assist member states to formulate policies and legal frameworks to uphold independent and pluralistic media and infostructures and to enhance the capacities of public service broadcasting institutions. In regions affected by conflict UNESCO supports efforts to establish and maintain an independent media service and to use it as a means of consolidating peace.

UNESCO also aims to develop media and information systems to respond to and mitigate the impact of disaster situations, and to integrate these objectives into wider UN peace-building or reconstruction initiatives. UNESCO is the co-ordinating agency for 'World Press Freedom Day', which is held annually on 3 May. The theme for 2008 was 'Access to information and the empowerment of people'. It also awards an annual World Press Freedom Prize. UNESCO maintains an Observatory on the Information Society, which provides up-to-date information on the development of new ICTs, analyses major trends, and aims to raise awareness of related ethical, legal and societal issues. UNESCO promotes the upholding of human rights in the use of cyberspace. In 1997 it organized the first International Congress on Ethical, Legal and Societal Aspects of Digital Information ('INFOethics').

UNESCO promotes the application of information and communication technology for sustainable development. In particular it supports efforts to improve teaching and learning processes through electronic media and to develop innovative literacy and education initiatives, such as the ICT-Enhanced Learning (ICTEL) project. UNESCO also aims to enhance understanding and use of new technologies and support training and ongoing learning opportunities for librarians, archivists and other information providers.

Finance

UNESCO's activities are funded through a regular budget provided by contributions from member states and extrabudgetary funds from other sources, particularly UNDP, the World Bank, regional banks and other bilateral Funds-in-Trust arrangements. UNESCO co-operates with many other UN agencies and international non-governmental organizations.

UNESCO's proposed Regular Programme budget for the two years 2008–09 was US $631m.

Publications

(mostly in English, French and Spanish editions; Arabic, Chinese and Russian versions are also available in many cases)

Atlas of the World's Languages in Danger of Disappearing (online).

Copyright Bulletin (quarterly).

Encyclopedia of Life Support Systems (online).

International Review of Education (quarterly).

International Social Science Journal (quarterly).

Museum International (quarterly).

Nature and Resources (quarterly).

The New Courier (quarterly).

Prospects (quarterly review on education).

UNESCO Sources (monthly).

UNESCO Statistical Yearbook.

World Communication Report.

World Educational Report (every 2 years).

World Heritage Review (quarterly).

World Information Report.

World Science Report (every 2 years).

Books, databases, video and radio documentaries, statistics, scientific maps and atlases.

Specialized Institutes and Centres

Abdus Salam International Centre for Theoretical Physics: Strada Costiera 11, 34014 Trieste, Italy; tel. (040) 2240111; fax (040) 224163; e-mail sci_info@ictp.it; internet www.ictp.it; f. 1964; promotes and enables advanced study and research in physics and mathematical sciences; organizes and sponsors training opportunities, in particular for scientists from developing countries; aims to provide an international forum for the exchange of information and ideas; Dir KATEPALLI R. SREENIVASEN (India).

European Centre for Higher Education (CEPES): Str. Stirbei Vodà 39, 010102 Bucharest, Romania; tel. (1) 313-0839; fax (1) 312-3567; e-mail info@cepes.ro; internet www.cepes.ro; Dir Dr JAN SADLAK.

International Bureau of Education (IBE): POB 199, 1211 Geneva 20, Switzerland; tel. 229177800; fax 229177801; e-mail doc .centre@ibe.unesco.org; internet www.ibe.unesco.org; f. 1925, became an intergovernmental organization in 1929 and was incorporated into UNESCO in 1969; the Council of the IBE is composed of representatives of 28 member states of UNESCO, designated by the General Conference; the Bureau's fundamental mission is to deal with matters concerning educational content, methods, and teaching/learning strategies; an International Conference on Education is held periodically; Dir CLEMENTINA ACEDO (Venezuela); publs *Prospects* (quarterly review), *Educational Innovation* (newsletter), educational practices series, monographs, other reference works.

UNESCO International Centre for Technical and Vocational Education and Training: UN Campus, Hermann-Ehlers-Str. 10, 53113 Bonn, Germany; tel. (228) 8150-100; fax (228) 8150-199; e-mail info@unevoc.unesco.org; internet www.unevoc.unesco.org; f. 2002; promotes high-quality lifelong technical and vocational education in UNESCO's member states, with a particular focus on young people, girls and women, and the disadvantaged; Dir RUPERT MACLEAN.

UNESCO International Institute for Educational Planning (IIEP): 7–9 rue Eugène Delacroix, 75116 Paris, France; tel. 1-45-03-77-00; fax 1-40-72-83-66; e-mail info@iiep.unesco.org; internet www .unesco.org/iiep; f. 1963; serves as a world centre for advanced training and research in educational planning; aims to help all member states of UNESCO in their social and economic development efforts, by enlarging the fund of knowledge about educational planning and the supply of competent experts in this field; legally and administratively a part of UNESCO, the Institute is autonomous, and its policies and programme are controlled by its own Governing Board, under special statutes voted by the General Conference of UNESCO; a satellite office of the IIEP is based in Buenos Aires, Argentina; Dir MARK BRAY (United Kingdom).

UNESCO Institute for Information Technologies in Education: 8 Kedrova St, 117292 Moscow, Russia; tel. (495) 129-29-90; fax (495) 129-12-25; e-mail info@iite.ru; internet www.iite.ru; the Institute aims to formulate policies regarding the development of, and to support and monitor the use of, information and communication technologies in education; it conducts research and organizes training programmes; Dir Dr VLADIMIR KINELEV.

UNESCO Institute for Life-long Learning: Feldbrunnenstr. 58, 20148 Hamburg, Germany; tel. (40) 448-0410; fax (40) 410-7723; e-mail uil@unesco.org; internet www.unesco.org/education/uil; f. 1951, as the Institute for Education; a research, training, information, documentation and publishing centre, with a particular focus on adult basic and further education and adult literacy; Dir ADAMA OUANE (Mali).

UNESCO Institute for Statistics: CP 6128, Succursale Centre-Ville, Montréal, QC, H3C 3J7, Canada; tel. (514) 343-6880; fax (514) 343-6882; e-mail uis@unesco.org; internet www.uis.unesco.org; f. 2001; collects and analyses national statistics on education, science, technology, culture and communications; Dir HENDRIK VAN DER POL (Netherlands).

UNESCO Institute for Water Education: Westvest 7, 2611 AX Delft, Netherlands; tel. (15) 2151-715; fax (15) 2122-921; e-mail info@ unesco-ihe.org; internet www.unesco-ihe.org; f. 2003; activities include advisory and policy-making functions; setting international standards for postgraduate education programmes and professional training in the water sector; education, training and research; and co-ordination of a global network of water sector organizations; Dir Prof. RICHARD A. MEGANCK.

World Health Organization—WHO

Address: Ave Appia 20, 1211 Geneva 27, Switzerland.
Telephone: 227912111; **fax:** 227913111; **e-mail:** info@who.int;
internet: www.who.int.
WHO, established in 1948, is the lead agency within the UN system concerned with the protection and improvement of public health.

Organization

(October 2008)

WORLD HEALTH ASSEMBLY

The Assembly meets in Geneva, once a year. It is responsible for policy making and the biennial programme and budget; appoints the Director-General; admits new members; and reviews budget contributions.

EXECUTIVE BOARD

The Board is composed of 32 health experts designated by, but not representing, their governments; they serve for three years, and the World Health Assembly elects 10–12 member states each year to the Board. It meets at least twice a year to review the Director-General's programme, which it forwards to the Assembly with any recommendations that seem necessary. It advises on questions referred to it by the Assembly and is responsible for putting into effect the decisions and policies of the Assembly. It is also empowered to take emergency measures in case of epidemics or disasters.

Chairman: NIMAL SIRIPALA DE SILVA (Sri Lanka).

SECRETARIAT

Director-General: Dr MARGARET CHAN (People's Republic of China).

Deputy Director-General: Dr ANARFI ASAMOA-BAAH (Ghana).

Assistant Directors-General: DENIS AITKEN (United Kingdom) (Representative of the Director-General for Partnership and UN Reform), ALA ALWAN (Iraq) (Non-communicable Diseases and Mental Health), Dr CARISSA F. ÉTIENNE (Dominica) (Health Systems and Services), TIMOTHY G. EVANS (Canada) (Information, Evidence and Research), Dr DAVID L. HEYMANN (USA) (Health Security and Environment and Representative of the Director-General for Polio Eradication), Dr ERIC LAROCHE (France) (Health Action in Crises), DAISY MAFUBELU (South Africa) (Family and Community Health), HIROKI NAKATANI (Japan) (HIV/AIDS, TB, Malaria and Neglected Tropical Diseases), ANDREY V. PIROGOV (Russia) (Executive Director of the WHO Office at the UN), NAMITA PRADHAM (India) (General Management), SUZANNE WEBER-MOSDORF (Germany) (Executive Director of the WHO Office at the EU).

PRINCIPAL OFFICES

Each of WHO's six geographical regions has its own organization, consisting of a regional committee representing relevant member states and associate members, and a regional office staffed by experts in various fields of health.

WHO Centre for Health Development: I. H. D. Centre Bldg, 9th Floor, 5–1, 1-chome, Wakinohama-Kaigandori, Chuo-ku, Kobe, Japan; tel. (78) 230-3100; fax (78) 230-3178; e-mail wkc@wkc.who.int; internet www.who.or.jp; f. 1995 to address health development issues; Dir Dr JACOB KUMARESAN (India).

WHO Lyon Office for National Epidemic Preparedness and Response: 58 ave Debourg, 69007 Lyon, France; tel. 4-72-71-64-70; fax 4-72-71-64-71; e-mail oms@lyon.who.int; supports global capacity-building for detection of and response to epidemics of infectious diseases; provides bridging role between WHO headquarters, the regional offices and ongoing activities in the field; Dir Dr GUÉNAËL RODIER.

WHO Mediterranean Centre for Vulnerability Reduction (WMC): rue du Lac Windermere, BP 40, 1053 Les Berges du Lac, Tunisia; tel. (71) 964-681; fax (71) 764-4558; e-mail info@wmc.who.int; internet wmc.who.int; f. 1997; advocates globally for appropriate health policies; trains health professionals; supports capacity-building for community action at grassroots level; works closely with WHO's regional offices; Dir (vacant).

Activities

WHO's objective is stated in its constitution as 'the attainment by all peoples of the highest possible level of health'. 'Health' is defined as 'a state of complete physical, mental and social well-being and not merely the absence of disease and infirmity'.

WHO has developed a series of international classifications, including the *International Statistical Classification of Disease and Related Health Problems (ICD)*, providing an etiological framework of health conditions, and currently in its 10th edition; and the complementary *International Classification of Functioning, Disability and Health (ICF)*, which describes how people live with their conditions.

WHO acts as the central authority directing international health work, and establishes relations with professional groups and government health authorities on that basis.

It provides, on request from member states, technical and policy assistance in support of programmes to promote health, prevent and control health problems, control or eradicate disease, train health workers best suited to local needs and strengthen national health systems. Aid is provided in emergencies and natural disasters.

A global programme of collaborative research and exchange of scientific information is carried out in co-operation with about 1,200 national institutions. Particular stress is laid on the widespread communicable diseases of the tropics, and the countries directly concerned are assisted in developing their research capabilities.

It keeps diseases and other health problems under constant surveillance, promotes the exchange of prompt and accurate information and of notification of outbreaks of diseases, and administers the International Health Regulations. It sets standards for the quality control of drugs, vaccines and other substances affecting health. It formulates health regulations for international travel.

It collects and disseminates health data and carries out statistical analyses and comparative studies in such diseases as cancer, heart disease and mental illness.

It receives reports on drugs observed to have shown adverse reactions in any country, and transmits the information to other member states.

It promotes improved environmental conditions, including housing, sanitation and working conditions. All available information on effects on human health of the pollutants in the environment is critically reviewed and published.

Co-operation among scientists and professional groups is encouraged. The organization negotiates and sustains national and global partnerships. It may propose international conventions and agreements, and develops and promotes international norms and standards. The organization promotes the development and testing of new technologies, tools and guidelines. It assists in developing an informed public opinion on matters of health.

WHO's first global strategy for pursuing 'Health for all' was adopted in May 1981 by the 34th World Health Assembly. The objective of 'Health for all' was identified as the attainment by all citizens of the world of a level of health that would permit them to lead a socially and economically productive life, requiring fair distribution of available resources, universal access to essential health care, and the promotion of preventive health care. In May 1998 the 51st World Health Assembly renewed the initiative, adopting a global strategy in support of 'Health for all in the 21st century', to be effected through regional and national health policies. The new approach was to build on the primary health care approach of the initial strategy, but was to strengthen the emphasis on quality of life, equity in health and access to health services. The following have been identified as minimum requirements of 'Health for all':

Safe water in the home or within 15 minutes' walking distance, and adequate sanitary facilities in the home or immediate vicinity;

Immunization against diphtheria, pertussis (whooping cough), tetanus, poliomyelitis, measles and tuberculosis;

Local health care, including availability of essential drugs, within one hour's travel;

Trained personnel to attend childbirth, and to care for pregnant mothers and children up to at least one year old.

In the implementation of all its activities WHO aims to contribute to achieving by 2015 the UN Millennium Development Goals (MDGs) that were agreed by the September 2000 UN Millennium Summit. WHO has particular responsibility for the MDGs of: reducing child mortality, with a target reduction of two-thirds in the mortality rate among children under five; improving maternal health, with a specific goal of reducing by 75% the numbers of women dying in childbirth; and combating HIV/AIDS, malaria and other diseases. In addition, it directly supports the following Millennium 'targets':

halving the proportion of people suffering from malnutrition; halving the proportion of people without sustainable access to safe drinking water and basic sanitation; and providing access, in co-operation with pharmaceutical companies, to affordable, essential drugs in developing countries. Furthermore, WHO reports on 17 health-related MDG indicators; co-ordinates, jointly with the World Bank, the High-Level Forum on the Health MDGs, comprising government ministers, senior officials from developing countries, and representatives of bilateral and multilateral agencies, foundations, regional organizations and global partnerships; and undertakes technical and normative work in support of national and regional efforts to reach the MDGs.

The Eleventh General Programme of Work, for the period 2006–15, defined a policy framework for pursuing the principal objectives of building healthy populations and combating ill health. The Programme took into account: increasing understanding of the social, economic, political and cultural factors involved in achieving better health and the role played by better health in poverty reduction; the increasing complexity of health systems; the importance of safeguarding health as a component of humanitarian action; and the need for greater co-ordination among development organizations. It incorporated four interrelated strategic directions: lessening excess mortality, morbidity and disability, especially in poor and marginalized populations; promoting healthy lifestyles and reducing risk factors to human health arising from environmental, economic, social and behavioural causes; developing equitable and financially fair health systems; and establishing an enabling policy and an institutional environment for the health sector and promoting an effective health dimension to social, economic, environmental and development policy. WHO is the sponsoring agency for the Health Workforce Decade (2006–15).

During 2005 the UN's Inter-Agency Standing Committee (IASC), concerned with co-ordinating the international response to humanitarian disasters, developed a concept of organizing agency assistance to IDPs through the institutionalization of a 'Cluster Approach', comprising 11 core areas of activity. WHO was designated the lead agency for the clusters on Health.

COMMUNICABLE DISEASES

WHO identifies infectious and parasitic communicable diseases as a major obstacle to social and economic progress, particularly in developing countries, where, in addition to disabilities and loss of productivity and household earnings, they cause nearly one-half of all deaths. Emerging and re-emerging diseases, those likely to cause epidemics, increasing incidence of zoonoses (diseases or infections passed from vertebrate animals to humans by means of parasites, viruses, bacteria or unconventional agents), attributable to factors such as environmental changes and changes in farming practices, outbreaks of unknown etiology, and the undermining of some drug therapies by the spread of antimicrobial resistance are main areas of concern. In recent years WHO has noted the global spread of communicable diseases through international travel, voluntary human migration and involuntary population displacement.

WHO's Communicable Diseases group works to reduce the impact of infectious diseases world-wide through surveillance and response; prevention, control and eradication strategies; and research and product development. The group seeks to identify new technologies and tools, and to foster national development through strengthening health services and the better use of existing tools. It aims to strengthen global monitoring of important communicable disease problems. The group advocates a functional approach to disease control. It aims to create consensus and consolidate partnerships around targeted diseases and collaborates with other groups at all stages to provide an integrated response. In 2000 WHO and several partner institutions in epidemic surveillance established a Global Outbreak Alert and Response Network (GOARN). Through the Network WHO aims to maintain constant vigilance regarding outbreaks of disease and to link world-wide expertise to provide an immediate response capability. In March 2005 GOARN responded to an outbreak of Marburg haemorrhagic fever in Angola, which, by July, had killed more than 300 people. From March 2003 WHO, through the Network, was co-ordinating the international investigation into the global spread of Severe Acute Respiratory Syndrome (SARS), a previously unknown atypical pneumonia. From the end of that year WHO was monitoring the spread through several Asian countries of the virus H5N1 (a rapidly mutating strain of zoonotic highly pathogenic avian influenza—HPAI) that was transmitting to human populations through contact with diseased birds, mainly poultry. It was feared that H5N1 would mutate into a form transmissable from human to human. In February 2005 WHO issued guidelines for the global surveillance of the spread of H5N1 infection in human and animal populations. WHO urged all countries to develop influenza pandemic preparedness plans and to stockpile antiviral drugs, and in May, in co-operation with the UN Food and Agriculture Organization (FAO) and the World Organisation for Animal Health (OIE), it launched a Global Strategy for the Progres-

sive Control of Highly Pathogenic Avian Influenza. A conference on Avian Influenza and Human Pandemic Influenza that was jointly organized by WHO, FAO, OIE and the World Bank in November 2005 issued a plan of action identifying a number of responses, including: supporting the development of integrated national plans for H5N1 containment and human pandemic influenza preparedness and response; assisting countries with the aggressive control of H5N1 and with establishing a more detailed understanding of the role of wild birds in virus transmission; nominating rapid response teams of experts to support epidemiological field investigations; expanding national and regional capacity in surveillance, diagnosis, and alert and response systems; expanding the network of influenza laboratories; establishing multi-country networks for the control or prevention of animal trans-boundary diseases; expanding the global antiviral stockpile; strengthening veterinary infrastructures; and mapping a global strategy and work plan for co-ordinating antiviral and influenza vaccine research and development. An International Pledging Conference on Avian and Human Influenza, convened in January 2006 in Beijing, People's Republic of China (PRC), and co-sponsored by the World Bank, European Commission and PRC Government, in co-operation with WHO, FAO and OIE, requested a minimum of US \$1,200m. in funding towards combating the spread of the virus. By June 2008 a total of 385 human cases of H5N1 had been laboratory-confirmed, in Azerbaijan, Bangladesh, Cambodia, PRC, Djibouti, Egypt, Indonesia, Iraq, Laos, Nigeria, Pakistan, Thailand, Turkey and Viet Nam, resulting in 243 deaths. Cases in poultry had become endemic in parts of Asia, and recent outbreaks in poultry had been reported in some European and Middle Eastern countries, and in some countries in West, Central and Northeast Africa.

One of WHO's major achievements was the eradication of smallpox. Following a massive international campaign of vaccination and surveillance (begun in 1958 and intensified in 1967), the last case was detected in 1977 and the eradication of the disease was declared in 1980. In May 1996 the World Health Assembly resolved that, pending a final endorsement, all remaining stocks of the smallpox virus were to be destroyed on 30 June 1999, although 500,000 doses of smallpox vaccine were to remain, along with a supply of the smallpox vaccine seed virus, in order to ensure that a further supply of the vaccine could be made available if required. In May 1999, however, the Assembly authorized a temporary retention of stocks of the virus until 2002. In late 2001, in response to fears that illegally-held virus stocks could be used in acts of biological terrorism (see below), WHO reassembled a team of technical experts on smallpox. In January 2002 the Executive Board determined that stocks of the virus should continue to be retained, to enable research into more effective treatments and vaccines.

In 1988 the World Health Assembly launched the Global Polio Eradication Initiative, which aimed initially to eradicate poliomyelitis by the end of 2000; this target was subsequently advanced to 2005, and most recently to end-2008. WHO's regional office for Europe declared the continent to be 'polio-free' in June 2002.

WHO is committed to the elimination of leprosy (the reduction of the prevalence of leprosy to less than one case per 10,000 population). The use of a highly effective combination of three drugs (known as multi-drug therapy—MDT) resulted in a reduction in the number of leprosy cases world-wide from 10m.–12m. in 1988 to 259,017 in January 2007. The Global Alliance for the Elimination of Leprosy, launched in November 1999 by WHO, in collaboration with governments of affected countries and several private partners, including a major pharmaceutical company, aims to support the eradication of the disease through the provision until end-2010 of free MDT treatment. Most cases occur in Africa, Asia and South America.

The objective of providing immunization for all children by 1990 was adopted by the World Health Assembly in 1977. Six diseases (measles, whooping cough, tetanus, poliomyelitis, tuberculosis and diphtheria) became the target of the Expanded Programme on Immunization (EPI), in which WHO, UNICEF and many other organizations collaborated. As a result of massive international and national efforts, the global immunization coverage increased from 20% in the early 1980s to the targeted rate of 80% by the end of 1990. In 1992 the Assembly resolved to reach a new target of 90% immunization coverage with the six EPI vaccines; to introduce hepatitis B as a seventh vaccine; and to introduce the yellow fever vaccine in areas where it occurs endemically.

In June 2000 WHO released a report entitled 'Overcoming Antimicrobial Resistance', in which it warned that the misuse of antibiotics could render some common infectious illnesses unresponsive to treatment. At that time WHO issued guidelines which aimed to mitigate the risks associated with the use of antimicrobials in livestock reared for human consumption.

HIV/AIDS, TB, MALARIA AND NEGLECTED DISEASES

Combating the human immunodeficiency virus/acquired immunodeficiency syndrome (HIV/AIDS), tuberculosis (TB) and malaria are organization-wide priorities and, as such, are supported not only by their own areas of work but also by activities undertaken in other areas. TB is the principal cause of death for people infected with the HIV virus and an estimated one-third of people living with HIV/AIDS globally are co-infected with TB. In July 2000 a meeting of the Group of Seven industrialized nations and Russia, convened in Genoa, Italy, announced the formation of a new Global Fund to Fight AIDS, TB and Malaria (as previously proposed by the UN Secretary-General and recommended by the World Health Assembly) (see below).

The HIV/AIDS epidemic represents a major threat to human well-being and socio-economic progress. Some 95% of those known to be infected with HIV/AIDS live in developing countries, and AIDS-related illnesses are the leading cause of death in sub-Saharan Africa. It is estimated that more than 25m. people world-wide died of AIDS during 1981–2007. WHO supports governments in developing effective health-sector responses to the HIV/AIDS epidemic through enhancing their planning and managerial capabilities, implementation capacity, and health systems resources. The Joint UN Programme on HIV/AIDS (UNAIDS) became operational on 1 January 1996, sponsored by WHO and other UN agencies; the UNAIDS secretariat is based at WHO headquarters. Sufferers of HIV/AIDS in developing countries have often failed to receive advanced antiretroviral (ARV) treatments that are widely available in industrialized countries, owing to their high cost. (It was estimated in 2005 that only 15% of HIV/AIDS patients were receiving the optimum treatment.) In May 2000 the World Health Assembly adopted a resolution urging WHO member states to improve access to the prevention and treatment of HIV-related illnesses and to increase the availability and affordability of drugs. A WHO-UNAIDS HIV Vaccine Initiative was launched in that year. In June 2001 governments participating in a special session of the UN General Assembly on HIV/AIDS adopted a Declaration of Commitment on HIV/AIDS. WHO, with UNAIDS, UNICEF, UNFPA, the World Bank, and major pharmaceutical companies, participates in the 'Accelerating Access' initiative, which aims to expand access to care, support and ARVs for people with HIV/AIDS. In March 2002, under its 'Access to Quality HIV/AIDS Drugs and Diagnostics' programme, WHO published a comprehensive list of HIV-related medicines deemed to meet standards recommended by the Organization. In April WHO issued the first treatment guidelines for HIV/AIDS cases in poor communities, and endorsed the inclusion of HIV/AIDS drugs in its *Model List of Essential Medicines* (see below) in order to encourage their wider availability. The secretariat of the International HIV Treatment Access Coalition, founded in December of that year by governments, non-governmental organizations, donors and others to facilitate access to ARVs for people in low- and middle-income countries, is based at WHO headquarters. In 2006 WHO, UNAIDS and partner organizations negotiated a framework approach aimed at achieving universal access to HIV/AIDS prevention, treatment, care and support by 2010. The resulting document was entitled the '2007–10 Strategic Framework for UNAIDS support to countries' efforts to move towards universal access'. WHO supports the following *Three Ones* principles, endorsed in April 2004 by a high-level meeting organized by UNAIDS, the United Kingdom and the USA, with the aim of strengthening national responses to the HIV/AIDS pandemic: for every country there should be one agreed national HIV/AIDS action framework; one national AIDS co-ordinating authority; and one agreed monitoring and evaluation system.

At December 2007 1.6m. people in Eastern Europe and Central Asia were reported to have HIV/AIDS, of whom an estimated 150,000 were newly infected during that year. Russia and Ukraine (which has an estimated adult prevalence rate of 1.4%, the highest in Europe) have serious epidemics. Belarus, Moldova, Kazakhstan, Kyrgyzstan and Uzbekistan also have rising rates of HIV/AIDS prevalence.

In 1995 WHO established a Global Tuberculosis Programme to address the challenges of the TB epidemic, which had been declared a global emergency by the Organization in 1993. According to WHO estimates, one-third of the world's population carries the TB bacillus. In 2006 this generated 9.2m. new active cases (0.7m. in people co-infected with HIV), and killed 1.7m. people (0.7m. of whom were also HIV-positive). Some 22 high-burden countries account for four-fifths of global TB cases. The largest concentration of TB cases is in South-East Asia. WHO provides technical support to all member countries, with special attention given to those with high TB prevalence, to establish effective national tuberculosis control programmes. WHO's strategy for TB control includes the use of the expanded DOTS (direct observation treatment, short-course) regime, involving the following five tenets: sustained political commitment to increase human and financial resources and to make TB control in endemic countries a nation-wide activity and an integral part of the national health system; access to quality-assured TB sputum microscopy; standardized short-course chemotherapy for all cases of TB under proper case-management conditions; uninterrupted supply of quality-assured drugs; and maintaining a recording and reporting system to enable outcome assessment. Simultaneously, WHO is encouraging research with the aim of further advancing DOTS, developing new tools for prevention, diagnosis and treatment, and containing new

threats (such as the HIV/TB co-epidemic). Inadequate control of DOTS in some areas, leading to partial and inconsistent treatments, has resulted in the development of drug-resistant and, often, incurable strains of TB. The incidence of so-called Multidrug Resistant TB (MDR-TB) strains, that are unresponsive to at least two of the four most commonly used anti-TB drugs, has risen in recent years, and WHO estimates that about four-fifths are 'super strains', resistant to at least three of the main anti-TB drugs; of the 14.4m. prevalent cases of TB in 2006, some 0.5m. were reported to be MDR. WHO has developed DOTS-Plus, a specialized strategy for controlling the spread of MDR-TB in areas of high prevalence.

In 2006 Azerbaijan, Estonia, Moldova, Kazakhstan, parts of the Russian Federation, Tajikistan, Ukraine and Uzbekistan had the highest prevalence of MDR-TB infection in the world.

The 'Stop TB' partnership, launched by WHO in 1999, in partnership with the World Bank, the US Government and a coalition of non-governmental organizations, co-ordinates the Global Plan to Stop TB, which represents a 'roadmap' for TB control. The current phase of the plan, covering the period 2006–15, aims to facilitate the achievement of the MDG of halting and beginning to reverse by 2015 the incidence of TB by means of access to quality diagnosis and treatment for all; to supply ARVs to 3m. TB patients co-infected with HIV; to treat nearly 1m. people for MDR-TB; to develop a new anti-TB drug by 2010 and a new vaccine by 2015; and to develop rapid and inexpensive diagnostic tests at the point of care. The Global TB Drug Facility, launched by 'Stop TB' in 2001, aims to increase access to high-quality anti-TB drugs for sufferers in developing countries.

In September 2006 WHO expressed strong concern at the emergence of strains of Extensive Drug Resistant TB (XDR-TB) that are virtually untreatable with most existing anti-TB drugs. XDR-TB is believed to be most prevalent in Eastern Europe and Asia.

In July 1998 WHO declared the control of malaria a priority concern, and in October the organization, jointly with UNICEF, the World Bank and UNDP, formally launched the Roll Back Malaria programme, which aims by 2015 to achieve a 75% reduction in the prevalence of malaria morbidity and mortality over 2005 levels. The disease acutely affects at least 350m.–500m. people, and kills an estimated 1m. people, every year. Some 90% of all malaria cases occur in sub-Saharan Africa.

Global Fund to Fight AIDS, TB and Malaria: 6–8 chemin Blandonnet, 1214 Vernier-Geneva, Switzerland; tel. 227911700; fax 227911701; e-mail info@theglobalfund.org; internet www.theglobalfund.org; f. 2000 as a partnership between governments, civil society, private sector interests, UN bodies (including WHO, UNAIDS, the IBRD and UNDP), and other agencies to raise resources for combating AIDS, TB and malaria; the Fund supports but does not implement assistance programmes; US \$9,700m. was pledged by international donors at a conference convened in Sept. 2007 to replenish the Fund during 2008–10; by July 2008 the Fund had approved \$10,800m. (of which \$5,500m. had been disbursed) in respect of more than 550 grants supporting prevention and treatment programmes in 136 countries; by that time the cumulative allocation of grant funding by region was as follows: Africa (57%), the Middle East and North Africa and South Asia (15%), East Asia and the Pacific (13%), Eastern Europe and Central Asia (8%), and Latin America and the Caribbean (8%); while the approximate distribution by health sector was: HIV/AIDS (61%), malaria (25%), TB (14%) and strengthening of health systems (1%); Exec. Dir Dr MICHEL KAZATCHKINE.

Joint UN Programme on HIV/AIDS (UNAIDS): 20 ave Appia, 1211 Geneva 27, Switzerland; tel. 227913666; fax 227914187; e-mail communications@unaids.org; internet www.unaids.org; established in 1996 to lead, strengthen and support an expanded response to the global HIV/AIDS pandemic; activities focus on prevention, care and support, reducing vulnerability to infection, and alleviating the socioeconomic and human effects of HIV/AIDS; launched the Global Coalition on Women and AIDS in Feb. 2004; in June 2005 adopted a policy position paper for intensifying HIV prevention; co-sponsors: WHO, UNICEF, UNDP, UNFPA, UNODC, ILO, UNESCO, the World Bank, WFP, UNHCR; Exec. Dir PETER PIOT (Belgium) (until 31 Dec. 2008).

NON-COMMUNICABLE DISEASES AND MENTAL HEALTH

The Non-communicable Diseases and Mental Health group comprises departments for the surveillance, prevention and management of uninfectious diseases, such as those arising from an unhealthy diet, and departments for health promotion, disability, injury prevention and rehabilitation, mental health and substance abuse. Surveillance, prevention and management of non-communicable diseases, tobacco, and mental health are organization-wide priorities.

Addressing the social and environmental determinants of health is a main priority of WHO. Tobacco use, unhealthy diet and physical inactivity are regarded as common, preventable risk factors for the four most prominent non-communicable diseases: cardiovascular diseases, cancer, chronic respiratory disease and diabetes. WHO aims to monitor the global epidemiological situation of non-communicable diseases, to co-ordinate multinational research activities concerned with prevention and care, and to analyse determining factors such as gender and poverty. In 1998 the organization adopted a resolution on measures to be taken to combat non-communicable diseases; their prevalence was anticipated to increase, particularly in developing countries, owing to rising life expectancy and changes in lifestyles. For example, between 1995 and 2025 the number of adults affected by diabetes world-wide was projected to increase from 135m. to 300m. In 2005 chronic diseases reportedly accounted for nearly 30m. deaths globally.

The sixth Global Conference on Health Promotion, convened jointly by WHO and the Thai Government, in Bangkok, Thailand, in August 2005, adopted the Bangkok Charter for Health Promotion in a Globalized World, which identified ongoing key challenges, actions and commitments.

In February 1999 WHO initiated a new programme, 'Vision 2020: the Right to Sight', which aimed to eliminate avoidable blindness (estimated to be as much as 80% of all cases) by 2020. Blindness was otherwise predicted to increase by as much as twofold, owing to the increased longevity of the global population.

In May 2004 the World Health Assembly endorsed a Global Strategy on Diet, Physical Activity and Health; it was estimated at that time that more than 1,000m. adults world-wide were overweight, and that, of these, some 300,000 were clinically obese. WHO has studied obesity-related issues in co-operation with the International Association for the Study of Obesity (IASO). The International Task Force on Obesity, affiliated to the IASO, aims to encourage the development of new policies for managing obesity. WHO and FAO jointly commissioned an expert report on the relationship of diet, nutrition and physical activity to chronic diseases, which was published in March 2003.

WHO's programmes for diabetes mellitus, chronic rheumatic diseases and asthma assist with the development of national initiatives, based upon goals and targets for the improvement of early detection, care and reduction of long-term complications. WHO's cardiovascular diseases programme aims to prevent and control the major cardiovascular diseases, which are responsible for more than 14m. deaths each year. It is estimated that one-third of these deaths could have been prevented with existing scientific knowledge. The programme on cancer control is concerned with the prevention of cancer, improving its detection and cure, and ensuring care of all cancer patients in need. In May 2004 the World Health Assembly adopted a resolution on cancer prevention and control, recognizing an increase in global cancer cases, particularly in developing countries, and stressing that many cases and related deaths could be prevented. The resolution included a number of recommendations for the improvement of national cancer control programmes. WHO is a co-sponsor of the Global Day Against Pain, which is held annually on 11 October. The Global Day highlights the need for improved pain management and palliative care for sufferers of diseases such as cancer and AIDS, with a particular focus on patients living in low-income countries with minimal access to opioid analgesics, and urges recognition of access to pain relief as a basic human right.

The WHO Human Genetics Programme manages genetic approaches for the prevention and control of common hereditary diseases and of those with a genetic predisposition representing a major health importance. The Programme also concentrates on the further development of genetic approaches suitable for incorporation into health care systems, as well as developing a network of international collaborating programmes.

WHO works to assess the impact of injuries, violence and sensory impairments on health, and formulates guidelines and protocols for the prevention and management of mental problems. The health promotion division promotes decentralized and community-based health programmes and is concerned with developing new approaches to population ageing and encouraging healthy life-styles and self-care. It also seeks to relieve the negative impact of social changes such as urbanization, migration and changes in family structure upon health. WHO advocates a multi-sectoral approach—involving public health, legal and educational systems—to the prevention of injuries, which represent 16% of the global burden of disease. It aims to support governments in developing suitable strategies to prevent and mitigate the consequences of violence, unintentional injury and disability. Several health promotion projects have been undertaken, in collaboration between WHO regional and country offices and other relevant organizations, including: the Global School Health Initiative, to bridge the sectors of health and education and to promote the health of school-age children; the Global Strategy for Occupational Health, to promote the health of the working population and the control of occupational health risks; Community-based Rehabilitation, aimed at providing a more enabling environment for people with disabilities; and a communication strategy to provide training and support for health communications personnel and initiatives. In 2000 WHO, UNESCO, the World Bank and UNICEF adopted the joint Focusing Resources

for Effective School Health (FRESH Start) approach to promoting life skills among adolescents.

Mental health problems, which include unipolar and bipolar affective disorders, psychosis, epilepsy, dementia, Parkinson's disease, multiple sclerosis, drug and alcohol dependency, and neuropsychiatric disorders such as post-traumatic stress disorder, obsessive compulsive disorder and panic disorder, have been identified by WHO as significant global health problems. Although, overall, physical health has improved, mental, behavioural and social health problems are increasing, owing to extended life expectancy and improved child mortality rates, and factors such as war and poverty. WHO aims to address mental problems by increasing awareness of mental health issues and promoting improved mental health services and primary care.

The Substance Abuse department is concerned with problems of alcohol, drugs and other substance abuse. Within its Programme on Substance Abuse (PSA), which was established in 1990 in response to the global increase in substance abuse, WHO provides technical support to assist countries in formulating policies with regard to the prevention and reduction of the health and social effects of psychoactive substance abuse. PSA's sphere of activity includes epidemiological surveillance and risk assessment, advocacy and the dissemination of information, strengthening national and regional prevention and health promotion techniques and strategies, the development of cost-effective treatment and rehabilitation approaches, and also encompasses regulatory activities as required under the international drugs-control treaties in force.

The Tobacco or Health Programme aims to reduce the use of tobacco, by educating tobacco-users and preventing young people from adopting the habit. In 1996 WHO published its first report on the tobacco situation world-wide. According to WHO, about one-third of the world's population aged over 15 years smoke tobacco, which causes approximately 3.5m. deaths each year (through lung cancer, heart disease, chronic bronchitis and other effects). In 1998 the 'Tobacco Free Initiative', a major global anti-smoking campaign, was established. In May 1999 the World Health Assembly endorsed the formulation of a Framework Convention on Tobacco Control (FCTC) to help to combat the increase in tobacco use (although a number of tobacco growers expressed concerns about the effect of the convention on their livelihoods). The FCTC entered into force in February 2005. The greatest increase in tobacco use is forecast to occur in developing countries.

FAMILY AND COMMUNITY HEALTH

WHO's Family and Community Health group addresses the following areas of work: child and adolescent health, research and programme development in reproductive health, making pregnancy safer and men and women's health. Making pregnancy safer is an organization-wide priority. The group's aim is to improve access to sustainable health care for all by strengthening health systems and fostering individual, family and community development. Activities include newborn care; child health, including promoting and protecting the health and development of the child through such approaches as promotion of breast-feeding and use of the mother-baby package, as well as care of the sick child, including diarrhoeal and acute respiratory disease control, and support to women and children in difficult circumstances; the promotion of safe motherhood and maternal health; adolescent health, including the promotion and development of young people and the prevention of specific health problems; women, health and development, including addressing issues of gender, sexual violence, and harmful traditional practices; and human reproduction, including research related to contraceptive technologies and effective methods. In addition, WHO aims to provide technical leadership and co-ordination on reproductive health and to support countries in their efforts to ensure that people: experience healthy sexual development and maturation; have the capacity for healthy, equitable and responsible relationships; can achieve their reproductive intentions safely and healthily; avoid illnesses, diseases and injury related to sexuality and reproduction; and receive appropriate counselling, care and rehabilitation for diseases and conditions related to sexuality and reproduction.

In September 1997 WHO, in collaboration with UNICEF, formally launched a programme advocating the Integrated Management of Childhood Illness (IMCI). IMCI recognizes that pneumonia, diarrhoea, measles, malaria and malnutrition cause some 70% of the approximately 11m. childhood deaths each year, and recommends screening sick children for all five conditions, to obtain a more accurate diagnosis than may be achieved from the results of a single assessment. WHO's Division of Diarrhoeal and Acute Respiratory Disease Control encourages national programmes aimed at reducing childhood deaths as a result of diarrhoea, particularly through the use of oral rehydration therapy and preventive measures. The Division is also seeking to reduce deaths from pneumonia in infants through the use of a simple case-management strategy involving the recognition of danger signs and treatment with an appropriate antibiotic.

In 1990 the WHO Regional Committee for Europe established the EUROHEALTH programme in Central and Eastern Europe. The programme was to establish reforms in health care and environment, to control communicable and non-communicable diseases, and to improve the health of women and children.

SUSTAINABLE DEVELOPMENT AND HEALTHY ENVIRONMENTS

The Sustainable Development and Healthy Environments group focuses on the following areas of work: health in sustainable development; nutrition; health and environment; food safety; and emergency preparedness and response. Food safety is an organization-wide priority.

WHO promotes recognition of good health status as one of the most important assets of the poor. The Sustainable Development and Healthy Environment group seeks to monitor the advantages and disadvantages for health, nutrition, environment and development arising from the process of globalization (i.e. increased global flows of capital, goods and services, people, and knowledge); to integrate the issue of health into poverty reduction programmes; and to promote human rights and equality. Adequate and safe food and nutrition is a priority programme area. WHO collaborates with FAO, the World Food Programme, UNICEF and other UN agencies in pursuing its objectives relating to nutrition and food safety. An estimated 780m. people world-wide cannot meet basic needs for energy and protein, more than 2,000m. people lack essential vitamins and minerals, and 170m. children are estimated to be malnourished. In December 1992 WHO and FAO hosted an international conference on nutrition, at which a World Declaration and Plan of Action on Nutrition was adopted to make the fight against malnutrition a development priority. Following the conference, WHO promoted the elaboration and implementation of national plans of action on nutrition. WHO aims to support the enhancement of member states' capabilities in dealing with their nutrition situations, and addressing scientific issues related to preventing, managing and monitoring protein-energy malnutrition; micronutrient malnutrition, including iodine deficiency disorders, vitamin A deficiency, and nutritional anaemia; and diet-related conditions and non-communicable diseases such as obesity (increasingly affecting children, adolescents and adults, mainly in industrialized countries), cancer and heart disease. In 1990 the World Health Assembly resolved to eliminate iodine deficiency (believed to cause mental retardation); a strategy of universal salt iodization was launched in 1993. In collaboration with other international agencies, WHO is implementing a comprehensive strategy for promoting appropriate infant, young child and maternal nutrition, and for dealing effectively with nutritional emergencies in large populations. Areas of emphasis include promoting healthcare practices that enhance successful breast-feeding; appropriate complementary feeding; refining the use and interpretation of body measurements for assessing nutritional status; relevant information, education and training; and action to give effect to the International Code of Marketing of Breast-milk Substitutes. The food safety programme aims to protect human health against risks associated with biological and chemical contaminants and additives in food. With FAO, WHO establishes food standards (through the work of the Codex Alimentarius Commission and its subsidiary committees) and evaluates food additives, pesticide residues and other contaminants and their implications for health. The programme provides expert advice on such issues as food-borne pathogens (e.g. listeria), production methods (e.g. aquaculture) and food biotechnology (e.g. genetic modification). In July 2001 the Codex Alimentarius Commission adopted the first global principles for assessing the safety of genetically modified (GM) foods. In March 2002 an intergovernmental task force established by the Commission finalized 'principles for the risk analysis of foods derived from biotechnology', which were to provide a framework for assessing the safety of GM foods and plants. In the following month WHO and FAO announced a joint review of their food standards operations. In February 2003 the FAO/WHO Project and Fund for Enhanced Participation in Codex was launched to support the participation of poorer countries in the Commission's activities.

WHO's programme area on environmental health undertakes a wide range of initiatives to tackle the increasing threats to health and well-being from a changing environment, especially in relation to air pollution, water quality, sanitation, protection against radiation, management of hazardous waste, chemical safety and housing hygiene. In 2008 it was estimated that some 1,200m. people world-wide had no access to clean drinking water, while a further 2,600m. people are denied suitable sanitation systems. WHO helped launch the Water Supply and Sanitation Council in 1990 and regularly updates its *Guidelines for Drinking Water Quality*. In rural areas the emphasis continues to be on the provision and maintenance of safe and sufficient water supplies and adequate sanitation, the health aspects of rural housing, vector control in water resource management, and the safe use of agrochemicals. In urban areas assistance is provided to identify local environmental health priorities and to

improve municipal governments' ability to deal with environmental conditions and health problems in an integrated manner; promotion of the 'Healthy City' approach is a major component of the programme. Other programme activities include environmental health information development and management, human resources development, environmental health planning methods, research and work on problems relating to global environment change, such as UV-radiation. The WHO Global Strategy for Health and Environment, developed in response to the WHO Commission on Health and Environment which reported to the UN Conference on Environment and Development in June 1992, provides the framework for programme activities. In May 2008 the 61st World Health Assembly adopted a resolution urging member states to take action to address the impact of climate change on human health.

Through its International EMF Project WHO is compiling a comprehensive assessment of the potential adverse effects on human health deriving from exposure to electromagnetic fields (EMF). In June 2004 WHO organized a workshop on childhood sensitivity to EMF.

WHO's work in the promotion of chemical safety is undertaken in collaboration with ILO and UNEP through the International Programme on Chemical Safety (IPCS), the Central Unit for which is located in WHO. The Programme provides internationally evaluated scientific information on chemicals, promotes the use of such information in national programmes, assists member states in establishment of their own chemical safety measures and programmes, and helps them strengthen their capabilities in chemical emergency preparedness and response and in chemical risk reduction. In 1995 an Inter-organization Programme for the Social Management of Chemicals was established by UNEP, ILO, FAO, WHO, UNIDO and OECD, in order to strengthen international co-operation in the field of chemical safety. In 1998 WHO led an international assessment of the health risk from bendocine disruptors (chemicals which disrupt hormonal activities).

In September 2005 a forum comprising representatives of WHO, IAEA, UNDP, UNEP, FAO, OCHA, the World Bank and the UN Scientific Committee on the effects of Atomic Radiation, and the governments of Belarus, Russia and Ukraine, issued an assessment of the long-term health, environmental and socio-economic effects of the 1986 Chornobyl (Chernobyl) nuclear reactor accident.

Since the major terrorist attacks perpetrated against targets in the USA in September 2001, WHO has focused renewed attention on the potential malevolent use of bacteria (such as bacillus anthracis, which causes anthrax), viruses (for example, the variola virus, causing smallpox) or toxins, or of chemical agents, in acts of biological or chemical terrorism. In September 2001 WHO issued draft guidelines entitled 'Health Aspects of Biological and Chemical Weapons'.

Within the UN system, WHO's Department of Emergency and Humanitarian Action co-ordinates the international response to emergencies and natural disasters in the health field, in close co-operation with other agencies and within the framework set out by the UN's Office for the Co-ordination of Humanitarian Affairs. In this context, WHO provides expert advice on epidemiological surveillance, control of communicable diseases, public health information and health emergency training. Its emergency preparedness activities include co-ordination, policy-making and planning, awareness-building, technical advice, training, publication of standards and guidelines, and research. Its emergency relief activities include organizational support, the provision of emergency drugs and supplies and conducting technical emergency assessment missions. The Division's objective is to strengthen the national capacity of member states to reduce the adverse health consequences of disasters. In responding to emergency situations, WHO always tries to develop projects and activities that will assist the national authorities concerned in rebuilding or strengthening their own capacity to handle the impact of such situations. Under the UN's Consolidated Inter-agency Appeal Process (CAP) for 2008, launched in December 2007, WHO appealed for US $93.9m. to fund its emergency humanitarian operations.

Since October 1999 WHO has provided emergency humanitarian assistance (including co-ordination activities, strengthening primary care and health care management, improving communicable disease surveillance, TB control, HIV and STI prevention, and psycho-social rehabilitation) for some 500,000 people affected by the civil conflict in the Republic of Chechnya (the Chechen Republic of Ichkeriya, Russian Federation).

HEALTH TECHNOLOGY AND PHARMACEUTICALS

WHO's Health Technology and Pharmaceuticals group, made up of the departments of essential drugs and other medicines, vaccines and other biologicals, and blood safety and clinical technology, covers the following areas of work: essential medicines—access, quality and rational use; immunization and vaccine development; and world-wide co-operation on blood safety and clinical technology. Blood safety and clinical technology are an organization-wide priority.

In January 1999 the Executive Board adopted a resolution on WHO's Revised Drug Strategy which placed emphasis on the inequalities of access to pharmaceuticals, and also covered specific aspects of drugs policy, quality assurance, drug promotion, drug donation, independent drug information and rational drug use. Plans of action involving co-operation with member states and other international organizations were to be developed to monitor and analyse the pharmaceutical and public health implications of international agreements, including trade agreements. In April 2001 experts from WHO and the World Trade Organization participated in a workshop to address ways of lowering the cost of medicines in less developed countries. In the following month the World Health Assembly adopted a resolution urging member states to promote equitable access to essential drugs, noting that this was denied to about one-third of the world's population. WHO participates with other partners in the 'Accelerating Access' initiative, which aims to expand access to antiretroviral drugs for people with HIV/AIDS (see above).

WHO reports that 2m. children die each year of diseases for which common vaccines exist. In September 1991 the Children's Vaccine Initiative (CVI) was launched, jointly sponsored by the Rockefeller Foundation, UNDP, UNICEF, the World Bank and WHO, to facilitate the development and provision of children's vaccines. The CVI has as its ultimate goal the development of a single oral immunization shortly after birth that will protect against all major childhood diseases. An International Vaccine Institute was established in Seoul, Republic of Korea, as part of the CVI, to provide scientific and technical services for the production of vaccines for developing countries. In September 1996 WHO, jointly with UNICEF, published a comprehensive survey, entitled *State of the World's Vaccines and Immunization*. In 1999 WHO, UNICEF, the World Bank and a number of public and private sector partners formed the Global Alliance for Vaccines and Immunization (GAVI), which aimed to expand the provision of existing vaccines and to accelerate the development and introduction of new vaccines and technologies, with the ultimate goal of protecting children of all nations and from all socio-economic backgrounds against vaccine-preventable diseases.

WHO supports states in ensuring access to safe blood, blood products, transfusions, injections, and healthcare technologies.

INFORMATION, EVIDENCE AND RESEARCH

The Information, Evidence and Research group addresses the following areas of work: evidence for health policy; health information management and dissemination; and research policy and promotion and organization of health systems. Through the generation and dissemination of evidence the Information, Evidence and Research group aims to assist policy-makers assess health needs, choose intervention strategies, design policy and monitor performance, and thereby improve the performance of national health systems. The group also supports international and national dialogue on health policy.

WHO co-ordinates the Health InterNetwork Access to Research Initiative (HINARI), which was launched in July 2001 to enable relevant authorities in developing countries to access biomedical journals through the internet at no or greatly reduced cost, in order to improve the world-wide circulation of scientific information; by July 2008 more than 3,750 publications were being made available to health institutions in 113 countries.

Finance

WHO's regular budget is provided by assessment of member states and associate members. An additional fund for specific projects is provided by voluntary contributions from members and other sources, including UNDP and UNFPA.

A regular budget of US $3,745.1m. was proposed for the two years 2008–09, of which some 6.7%, or $250.8m., was provisionally allocated to Europe.

Publications

Bulletin of the World Health Organization (monthly).

Eastern Mediterranean Health Journal (annually).

International Classification of Functioning, Disability and Health—ICF.

International Statistical Classification of Disease and Related Health Problems.

Model List of Essential Medicines (every two years).

Pan-American Journal of Public Health (annually).

3 By 5 Progress Report.

Toxicological Evaluation of Certain Veterinary Drug Residues in Food (annually).

Weekly Epidemiological Record (in English and French, paper and electronic versions available).

WHO Drug Information (quarterly).

WHO Global Atlas of Traditional, Complementary and Alternative Medicine.

WHO Model Formulary.

World Health Report (annually, in English, French and Spanish).

World Malaria Report (with UNICEF).

Zoonoses and Communicable Diseases Common to Man and Animals.

Technical report series; catalogues of specific scientific, technical and medical fields available.

Other UN Organizations Active in the Region

OFFICE FOR THE CO-ORDINATION OF HUMANITARIAN AFFAIRS—OCHA

Address: United Nations Plaza, New York, NY 10017, USA.

Telephone: (212) 963-1234; **fax:** (212) 963-1312; **e-mail:** ochany@un.org; **internet:** ochaonline.un.org.

The Office was established in January 1998 as part of the UN Secretariat, with a mandate to co-ordinate international humanitarian assistance and to provide policy and other advice on humanitarian issues. It administers the Humanitarian Early Warning System, as well as Integrated Regional Information Networks (IRIN) to monitor the situation in different countries and a Disaster Response System. A complementary service, Reliefweb, which was launched in 1996, monitors crises and publishes information on the internet.

The IRIN–Central Asia Office, based in Islamabad, Pakistan, covers Afghanistan, Iran, Kazakhstan, Kyrgyzstan, Nepal, Pakistan, Tajikistan, Turkmenistan and Uzbekistan. A sub-office is located in Bishkek, Kyrgyzstan.

Under-Secretary-General for Humanitarian Affairs and Emergency Relief Co-ordinator: Sir JOHN HOLMES (United Kingdom).

UNITED NATIONS OFFICE ON DRUGS AND CRIME—UNODC

Address: Vienna International Centre, POB 500, 1400 Vienna, Austria.

Telephone: (1) 26060-0; **fax:** (1) 26060-5866; **e-mail:** unodc@unodc.org; **internet:** www.unodc.org.

The Office was established in November 1997 (as the UN Office of Drug Control and Crime Prevention) to strengthen the UN's integrated approach to issues relating to drug control, crime prevention and international terrorism. It comprises two principal components: the United Nations Drug Programme and the Crime Programme.

Executive Director: ANTONIO MARIA COSTA (Italy).

OFFICE OF THE UNITED NATIONS HIGH COMMISSIONER FOR HUMAN RIGHTS—OHCHR

Address: Palais Wilson, 52 rue de Paquis, 1201 Geneva, Switzerland.

Telephone: 229179290; **fax:** 229179022; **e-mail:** infodesk@ohchr.org; **internet:** www.ohchr.org.

The Office is a body of the UN Secretariat and is the focal point for UN human-rights activities. Since September 1997 it has incorporated the Centre for Human Rights. The High Commissioner is the UN official with principal responsibility for UN human rights activities.

High Commissioner: NAVANETHEM PILLAY (South Africa).

UNITED NATIONS HUMAN SETTLEMENTS PROGRAMME—UN-HABITAT

Address: POB 30030, Nairobi, Kenya.

Telephone: (20) 621234; **fax:** (20) 624266; **e-mail:** infohabitat@unhabitat.org; **internet:** www.unhabitat.org.

UN-Habitat was established, as the United Nations Centre for Human Settlements, in October 1978 to service the intergovernmental Commission on Human Settlements. It became a full UN programme on 1 January 2002, serving as the focus for human settlements activities in the UN system.

Executive Director: ANNA KAJUMULO TIBAIJUKA (Tanzania).

UNITED NATIONS CONFERENCE ON TRADE AND DEVELOPMENT—UNCTAD

Address: Palais des Nations, 1211 Geneva 10, Switzerland.

Telephone: 229171234; **fax:** 229070043; **e-mail:** info@unctad.org; **internet:** www.unctad.org.

UNCTAD was established in 1964. It is the principal organ of the UN General Assembly concerned with trade and development, and is the focal point within the UN system for integrated activities relating to trade, finance, technology, investment and sustainable development. It aims to maximize the trade and development opportunities of developing countries, in particular least-developed countries, and to assist them to adapt to the increasing globalization and liberalization of the world economy. UNCTAD undertakes consensus-building activities, research and policy analysis and technical co-operation.

Secretary-General: Dr SUPACHAI PANITCHPAKDI (Thailand).

UNITED NATIONS POPULATION FUND—UNFPA

Address: 220 East 42nd St, New York, NY 10017, USA.

Telephone: (212) 297-5020; **fax:** (212) 297-4911; **internet:** www.unfpa.org.

Created in 1967 as the Trust Fund for Population Activities, the UN Fund for Population Activities (UNFPA) was established as a Fund of the UN General Assembly in 1972 and was made a subsidiary organ of the UN General Assembly in 1979, with the UNDP Governing Council (now the Executive Board) designated as its governing body. In 1987 UNFPA's name was changed to the United Nations Population Fund (retaining the same acronym).

Executive Director: THORAYA A. OBAID (Saudi Arabia).

UN Specialized Agencies

INTERNATIONAL CIVIL AVIATION ORGANIZATION—ICAO

Address: 999 University St, Montréal, QC H3C 5H7, Canada.

Telephone: (514) 954-8219; **fax:** (514) 954-6077; **e-mail:** icaohq@icao.org; **internet:** www.icao.int.

ICAO was founded in 1947, on the basis of the Convention on International Civil Aviation, signed in Chicago, in 1944, to develop the techniques of international air navigation and to help in the planning and improvement of international air transport.

Secretary-General: TAÏEB CHÉRIF (Algeria).

Regional Office for Europe and the North Atlantic: 3 bis, Villa Emile-Bergerat, 92522 Neuilly-sur-Seine Cédex, France; tel. 1-46-41-85-85; fax 1-46-41-85-00; e-mail icaoeurnat@paris.icao.int; internet www.icao.int/eurnat; Dir KARSTEN THEIL.

INTERNATIONAL LABOUR ORGANIZATION—ILO

Address: 4 route des Morillons, 1211 Geneva 22, Switzerland.

Telephone: 227996111; **fax:** 227988685; **e-mail:** ilo@ilo.org; **internet:** www.ilo.org.

ILO was founded in 1919 to work for social justice as a basis for lasting peace. It carries out this mandate by promoting decent living standards, satisfactory conditions of work and pay and adequate employment opportunities. Methods of action include the creation of international labour standards; the provision of technical co-operation services; and training, education, research and publishing activities to advance ILO objectives.

Director-General: JUAN O. SOMAVÍA (Chile).

Regional Office for Europe and Central Asia: 4 route des Morillons, 1211 Geneva 22, Switzerland; tel. 227996666; fax 227996061; e-mail europe@ilo.org; internet www.ilo.org/public/english/region/eurpro/geneva/; Dir PETRA ULSHOEFER.

Sub-regional Office for Eastern Europe and Central Asia: 107031 Moscow, ul. Petrovka 15, Apt 23, Russia; tel. (495) 933-08-10; fax (495) 933-08-20; e-mail moscow@ilo.org; internet www.ilo.ru; Dir ELAINE FULTZ.

INTERNATIONAL MARITIME ORGANIZATION—IMO

Address: 4 Albert Embankment, London, SE1 7SR, United Kingdom.

Telephone: (20) 7735-7611; **fax:** (20) 7587-3210; **e-mail:** info@imo.org; **internet:** www.imo.org.

The Inter-Governmental Maritime Consultative Organization (IMCO) began operations in 1959, as a specialized agency of the UN to facilitate co-operation among governments on technical matters affecting international shipping. Its main aims are to improve the safety of international shipping, and to prevent pollution caused by ships. IMCO became IMO in 1982.

Secretary-General: EFTHIMIOS MITROPOULOS (Greece).

INTERNATIONAL TELECOMMUNICATION UNION—ITU

Address: Place des Nations, 1211 Geneva 20, Switzerland.
Telephone: 227305111; **fax:** 227337256; **e-mail:** itumail@itu.int; **internet:** www.itu.int.

Founded in 1865, ITU became a specialized agency of the UN in 1947. It acts to encourage world co-operation for the improvement and use of telecommunications, to promote technical development, to harmonize national policies in the field, and to promote the extension of telecommunications throughout the world.

Secretary-General: HAMADOUN TOURÉ (Mali).

UNITED NATIONS INDUSTRIAL DEVELOPMENT ORGANIZATION—UNIDO

Address: Vienna International Centre, POB 300, 1400 Vienna, Austria.
Telephone: (1) 260260; **fax:** (1) 2692669; **e-mail:** unido@unido.org; **internet:** www.unido.org.

UNIDO began operations in 1967 and became a specialized agency in 1985. Its objectives are to promote sustainable and socially equitable industrial development in developing countries and in countries with economies in transition. It aims to assist such countries to integrate fully into global economic system by mobilizing knowledge, skills, information and technology to promote productive employment, competitive economies and sound environment.

Director-General: KANDEH YUMKELLA (Sierra Leone).

UNIVERSAL POSTAL UNION—UPU

Address: Weltpoststr., 3000 Bern 15, Switzerland.
Telephone: 313503111; **fax:** 313503110; **e-mail:** info@upu.int; **internet:** www.upu.int.

The General Postal Union was founded by the Treaty of Berne (1874), beginning operations in July 1875. Three years later its name was changed to the Universal Postal Union. In 1948 UPU became a specialized agency of the UN. It aims to develop and unify the international postal service, to study problems and to provide training.

Director-General: EDOUARD DAYAN (France).

WORLD INTELLECTUAL PROPERTY ORGANIZATION—WIPO

Address: 34 chemin des Colombettes, 1211 Geneva 20, Switzerland.
Telephone: 223389111; **fax:** 227335428; **e-mail:** wipo.mail@wipo.int; **internet:** www.wipo.int.

WIPO was established in 1970. It became a specialized agency of the UN in 1974 concerned with the protection of intellectual property (e.g. industrial and technical patents and literary copyrights) throughout the world. WIPO formulates and administers treaties embodying international norms and standards of intellectual property, establishes model laws, and facilitates applications for the protection of inventions, trademarks etc. WIPO provides legal and technical assistance to developing countries and countries with economies in transition and advises countries on obligations under the World Trade Organization's agreement on Trade-Related Aspects of Intellectual Property Rights (TRIPS).

Director-General: FRANCIS GURRY (Australia).

WORLD METEOROLOGICAL ORGANIZATION—WMO

Address: 7 bis, ave de la Paix, 1211 Geneva 2, Switzerland.
Telephone: 227308111; **fax:** 227308181; **e-mail:** wmo@wmo.int; **internet:** www.wmo.int.

WMO was established in 1950 and was recognized as a Specialized Agency of the UN in 1951, aiming to improve the exchange of information in the fields of meteorology, climatology, operational hydrology and related fields, as well as their applications. WMO jointly implements, with UNEP, the UN Framework Convention on Climate Change.

Secretary-General: MICHEL JARRAUD (France).

WORLD TOURISM ORGANIZATION—UNWTO

Address: Capitán Haya 42, 28020 Madrid, Spain.
Telephone: (91) 5678100; **fax:** (91) 5713733; **e-mail:** omt@world-tourism.org; **internet:** www.world-tourism.org.

The World Tourism Organization was established in 1975 and was recognized as a Specialized Agency of the UN in December 2003. It works to promote and develop sustainable tourism, in particular in support of socio-economic growth in developing countries.

Secretary-General: FRANCESCO FRANGIALLI (France) (until Jan. 2009).

ASIAN DEVELOPMENT BANK—ADB

Address: 6 ADB Ave, Mandaluyong City, 0401 Metro Manila, Philippines; POB 789, 0980 Manila, Philippines.

Telephone: (2) 6324444; **fax:** (2) 6362444; **e-mail:** information@adb.org; **internet:** www.adb.org.

The ADB commenced operations in December 1966. The Bank's principal functions are to provide loans and equity investments for the economic and social advancement of its developing member countries, to give technical assistance for the preparation and implementation of development projects and programmes and advisory services, to promote investment of public and private capital for development purposes, and to respond to requests from developing member countries for assistance in the co-ordination of their development policies and plans.

MEMBERS

There are 48 member countries and territories within the ESCAP region and 19 others (see list of subscriptions below).

Organization

(October 2008)

BOARD OF GOVERNORS

All powers of the Bank are vested in the Board, which may delegate its powers to the Board of Directors except in such matters as admission of new members, changes in the Bank's authorized capital stock, election of Directors and President, and amendment of the Charter. One Governor and one Alternate Governor are appointed by each member country. The Board meets at least once a year. The 41st Bank Annual Meeting was held in Madrid, Spain, in May 2008.

BOARD OF DIRECTORS

The Board of Directors is responsible for general direction of operations and exercises all powers delegated by the Board of Governors, which elects it. Of the 12 Directors, eight represent constituency groups of member countries within the ESCAP region (with about 65% of the voting power) and four represent the rest of the member countries. Each Director serves for two years and may be re-elected.

Three specialized committees (the Audit Committee, the Budget Review Committee and the Inspection Committee), each comprising six members, assist the Board of Directors in exercising its authority with regard to supervising the Bank's financial statements, approving the administrative budget, and reviewing and approving policy documents and assistance operations.

The President of the Bank, though not a Director, is Chairman of the Board.

Chairman of Board of Directors and President: Haruhiko Kuroda (Japan).

Vice-Presidents: Ursula Schäfer-Preuss (Germany), Zhao Xiaoyu (People's Republic of China), Bindu Lohani (Nepal), C. Lawrence Greenwood, Jr (USA).

ADMINISTRATION

The Bank had 2,443 staff at 31 December 2007.

Five regional departments cover Central and West Asia, East Asia, the Pacific, South Asia, and Southeast Asia. Other departments and offices include Private Sector Operations, Central Operations Services, Regional and Sustainable Development, Strategy and Policy, Cofinancing Operations, and Economics and Research, as well as other administrative units.

There are Bank Resident Missions in Afghanistan, Azerbaijan, Bangladesh, Cambodia, the People's Republic of China, India, Indonesia, Kazakhstan, Kyrgyzstan, Laos, Mongolia, Nepal, Pakistan, Papua New Guinea, Sri Lanka, Tajikistan, Thailand, Uzbekistan and Viet Nam, all of which report to the head of the regional department. There are Extended Missions in Kerala and Tamil Nadu (India), Sumatra (Indonesia) and the Maldives. In addition, the Bank maintains a country office in the Philippines, a Special Office in Timor-Leste, a Pacific Liaison and Co-ordination Office in Sydney, Australia, and a South Pacific Regional Mission, based in Vanuatu (with a Sub-regional Office in Fiji). Representative Offices are located in Tokyo, Japan, Frankfurt am Main, Germany (for Europe), and Washington, DC, USA (for North America).

Managing Director-General: Rajat M. Nag.

INSTITUTE

ADB Institute (ADBI): Kasumigaseki Bldg, 8th Floor, 2–5 Kasumigaseki 3-chome, Chiyoda-ku, Tokyo 100-6008, Japan; tel. (3) 3593-5500; fax (3) 3593-5571; e-mail info@adbi.org; internet www.adbi.org; f. 1997 as a subsidiary body of the ADB to research and analyse long-term development issues and to disseminate development practices through training and other capacity-building activities; Dean Dr Masahiro Kawai (Japan).

FINANCIAL STRUCTURE

The Bank's ordinary capital resources (which are used for loans to the more advanced developing member countries) are held and used entirely separately from its Special Funds resources (see below). A fourth General Capital Increase (GCI IV), amounting to US $26,318m. (or 100%), was authorized in May 1994. At the final deadline for subscription to GCI IV, on 30 September 1996, 55 member countries had subscribed shares amounting to $24,675.4m.

At 31 December 2007 the position of subscriptions to the capital stock was as follows: authorized US $55,977.8m.; 'callable' subscribed $52,040.7m.

The Bank also borrows funds from the world capital markets. Total borrowings during 2007 amounted to US $8,854m. (compared with $5,576m. in 2006). At 31 December 2007 total outstanding debt amounted to $31,569m.

In July 1986 the Bank abolished the system of fixed lending rates, under which ordinary operations loans had carried interest rates fixed at the time of loan commitment for the entire life of the loan. Under the new system the lending rate is adjusted every six months, to take into account changing conditions in international financial markets.

Activities

Loans by the ADB are usually aimed at specific projects. In responding to requests from member governments for loans, the Bank's staff assesses the financial and economic viability of projects and the way in which they fit into the economic framework and priorities of development of the country concerned. In 1985 the Bank decided to expand its assistance to the private sector, hitherto comprising loans to development finance institutions, under government guarantee, for lending to small and medium-sized enterprises; a programme was formulated for direct financial assistance, in the form of equity and loans without government guarantee, to private enterprises. In 1992 a Social Dimensions Unit was established as part of the central administrative structure of the Bank, which contributed to the Bank's increasing awareness of the importance of social aspects of development as essential components of sustainable economic growth. During the early 1990s the Bank also aimed to expand its role as project financier by providing assistance for policy formulation and review and promoting regional co-operation, while placing greater emphasis on individual country requirements. During that period the Bank also introduced a commitment to assess development projects for their impact on the local population and to avoid all involuntary resettlement where possible and established a formal procedure for grievances, under which the Board may authorize an inspection of a project by an independent panel of experts, at the request of the affected community or group.

The currency instability and ensuing financial crises affecting many Asian economies in the second half of 1997 and in 1998 prompted the Bank to reflect on its role in the region. The Bank resolved to strengthen its activities as a broad-based development institution, rather than solely as a project financier, through lending policies, dialogue, co-financing and technical assistance. In mid-1999 the Bank approved a technical assistance grant to establish an internet-based Asian Recovery Information Centre, within a new Regional Monitoring Unit, which aimed to facilitate access to information regarding the economic and social impact of the Asian financial crisis, analyses of economic needs of countries, reform programmes and monitoring of the economic recovery process. In April 2005 the Unit was replaced by an Office of Regional Economic Integration, which aimed to promote economic co-operation and integration among developing member countries and to contribute to economic growth within the whole region. In September 2008 the Office organized a high-level conference, attended by representatives of multilateral institutions, credit rating agencies, regulatory and supervisory bodies and banks to discuss and exchange ideas on measures to strengthen the region's financial markets and contain the global financial instability evident at that time.

In November 1999 the Board of Directors approved a new overall strategy objective of poverty reduction, which was to be the principal consideration for all future Bank activities. The strategy incorporated key aims of supporting sustainable, grass-roots based economic growth, social development and good governance. During 2000 the

Bank began to refocus its country strategies, projects and lending targets to complement the poverty reduction strategy. In addition, it initiated a process of consultation to formulate a long-term strategic framework, based on the target of reducing by 50% the incidence of extreme poverty by 2015, one of the so-called Millennium Development Goals (MDGs) identified by the UN General Assembly. The framework, establishing the operational priorities and principles for reducing poverty, was approved in March 2001. A review of the strategy, initiated at the end of 2003, concluded that more comprehensive, results-oriented monitoring and evaluation be put in place, with reference to both country strategies and programmes and management systems. It also recommended a closer alignment of Bank operations with national poverty reduction strategies. The review determined to include capacity development as a new overall thematic priority for the Bank, in addition to environmental sustainability, gender and development, private sector development and regional co-operation. In mid-2004 the Bank initiated a separate reform agenda to incorporate the strategy approach 'Managing for development results' throughout the organization. In July 2006 the Bank adopted a strategy to promote regional co-operation and integration in order to combat poverty through collective regional and cross-border activities.

In June 2006 the Bank convened a panel of eminent persons to assess the Bank's future role within the region. The report of the panel, submitted in March 2007, prompted further wide-ranging consultations. In April 2008 the Bank published a new long-term strategic framework to cover the period 2008–20 ('Strategy 2020'), replacing the previous 2001–15 strategic framework, in recognition of the unprecedented economic growth of recent years and its associated challenges, including the effect on natural resources, inadequate infrastructure to support economic advances, and widening disparities both within and between developing member countries. The Bank determined to refocus its activities onto three critical agendas: inclusive economic growth; environmentally sustainable growth; and regional integration. It determined to initiate a process of restructuring its operations into five core areas of specialization: infrastructure; environment, including climate change; regional co-operation and integration; financial sector development; and education. Some 80% of Bank lending was to be allocated to these five areas by 2012. Under the strategy the Bank resolved to act as an agent of change, stimulating economic growth and widening development assistance, for example by supporting the private sector with more risk guarantees, investment and other financial instruments, placing greater emphasis on good governance, promoting gender equality and improving accessibility to and distribution of its knowledge services. It also committed to expanding its partnerships with other organizations, including with the private sector and other private institutions. The strategy was endorsed at the annual meeting of the Board of Governors, convened in Madrid, Spain, in May.

In 2007 the Bank approved 96 loans for 82 projects amounting to US $10,105.6m. Loans from ordinary capital resources in 2007 totalled $8,212.8m., while loans from the ADF amounted to $1,892.8m. The largest proportion of assistance, amounting to some 39% of total lending, was allocated to the transport and communications sector. The largest borrower was Pakistan, accounting for some 20% of total lending.

In 2007 the Bank approved 39 grants amounting to US $672.7m. financed by Special Funds (see below) and other bilateral and multilateral sources. It also approved 242 technical assistance projects, with funding of $243.3m., five equity investments amounting to $80.0m., and four multitranche financing facilities, totalling some $4,024.0m. The Bank's Operations Evaluation Office prepares reports on completed projects, in order to assess achievements and problems. In April 2000 the Bank announced that, from 2001, some new loans would be denominated in local currencies, in order to ease the repayment burden on recipient economies.

The Bank co-operates with other international organizations active in the region, particularly the World Bank group, the IMF, UNDP and APEC, and participates in meetings of aid donors for developing member countries. In May 2001 the Bank and UNDP signed a memorandum of understanding (MOU) on strategic partnership, in order to strengthen co-operation in the reduction of poverty, for example the preparation of common country assessments and a common database on poverty and other social indicators. Also in 2001 the Bank signed an MOU with the World Bank on administrative arrangements for co-operation, providing a framework for closer co-operation and more efficient use of resources. In May 2004 the Bank signed a revised MOU with ESCAP to enhance co-operation activities to achieve the MDGs. In early 2002 the Bank worked with the World Bank and UNDP to assess the preliminary needs of the interim administration in Afghanistan, in preparation for an International Conference on Reconstruction Assistance to Afghanistan, held in January, in Tokyo. The Bank pledged to work with its member governments to provide highly concessional grants and loans of some US $500m. over two-and-a-half years, with a particular focus on road reconstruction, basic education, and agricultural irrigation rehabilitation. In June 2008, at an international

donors' conference held in Paris, France, the Bank pledged up to $1,300m. to finance infrastructure projects in Afghanistan in the coming five years. A new policy concerning co-operation with non-governmental organizations (NGOs) was approved by the Bank in 1998. The Bank administers an NGO Center to provide advice and support to NGOs on involvement in country strategies and development programmes.

In June 2004 the Bank approved a new policy to provide rehabilitation and reconstruction assistance following disasters or other emergencies. The policy also aimed to assist developing member countries with prevention, preparation and mitigation of the impact of future disasters. At the end of December the Bank announced assistance amounting to US $325m. to finance immediate reconstruction and rehabilitation efforts in Indonesia, the Maldives and Sri Lanka, which had been severely damaged by a series of large waves, or tsunamis, that had spread throughout the Indian Ocean as a result of a massive earthquake that had occurred close to the west coast of Sumatra, Indonesia. Of the total amount $150m. was to be drawn as new lending commitments from the Asian Development Fund. Teams of Bank experts undertook to identify priority operations and initiated efforts, in co-operation with governments and other partner organizations, to prepare for more comprehensive reconstruction activities. In accordance with the 2004 policy initiative, an interdepartmental task force was established to co-ordinate the Bank's response to the disaster. In January 2005, at a Special ASEAN Leaders' Meeting, held in Jakarta, Indonesia, the Bank pledged assistance amounting to $500m.; later in that month the Bank announced its intention to establish a $600m. Multi-donor Asian Tsunami Fund to accelerate the provision of reconstruction and technical assistance to countries most affected by the disaster. In March 2006 the Bank hosted a high-level co-ordination meeting on rehabilitation and reconstruction assistance to tsunami-affected countries. In October the Bank, with representatives of the World Bank, undertook an immediate preliminary damage and needs assessment following a massive earthquake in north-west Pakistan, which also affected remote parts of Afghanistan and India. The report identified relief and reconstruction requirements totalling some $5,200m. The Bank made an initial contribution of $80m. to a Special Fund (see below) and also pledged concessional support of up to $1,000m. for rehabilitation and reconstruction efforts in the affected areas.

The Bank has actively supported regional, sub-regional and national initiatives to enhance economic development and promote economic co-operation within the region. The Bank is the main co-ordinator and financier of a Greater Mekong Sub-region (GMS) programme, initiated in 1992 to strengthen co-operation between Cambodia, the People's Republic of China, Laos, Myanmar, Thailand and Viet Nam. Projects undertaken have included transport and other infrastructure links, energy projects and communicable disease control. The first meeting of GMS heads of state was convened in Phnom-Penh, Cambodia, in November 2002. A Core Environment Programme was inaugurated in 2005. Other sub-regional initiatives supported by the Bank include the Central Asian Regional Economic Cooperation (CAREC), South Asia Sub-regional Economic Cooperation (SASEC) initiative, the Indonesia, Malaysia, Thailand Growth Triangle (IMT-GT), and the Brunei, Indonesia, Malaysia, Philippines East ASEAN Growth Area (BIMP-EAGA).

SPECIAL FUNDS

The Bank is authorized to establish and administer Special Funds. The Asian Development Fund (ADF) was established in 1974 in order to provide a systematic mechanism for mobilizing and administering resources for the Bank to lend on concessionary terms to the least-developed member countries. In 1998 the Bank revised the terms of ADF. Since 1 January 1999 all new project loans are repayable within 32 years, including an eight-year grace period, while quick-disbursing programme loans have a 24-year maturity, also including an eight-year grace period. The previous annual service charge was redesignated as an interest charge, including a portion to cover administrative expenses. The new interest charges on all loans are 1%–1.5% per annum. During 2007 36 ADF loans were approved, amounting to US $1,893m. In May 2008 30 donor countries pledged $4,200m. towards the ninth replenishment of ADF resources (ADF X), which totalled $11,300m. to provide resources for the four-year period 2009–12. The total amount included replenishment of the Technical Assistance Special Fund (see below).

The Bank provides technical assistance grants from its Technical Assistance Special Fund (TASF). By the end of 2007 the Fund's total resources amounted to US $1,361.3m. During 2007 $77.5m. was approved under the TASF project preparation and advisory activities. The Japan Special Fund (JSF) was established in 1988 to provide finance for technical assistance by means of grants, in both the public and private sectors. The JSF aims to help developing member countries restructure their economies, enhance the opportunities for attracting new investment, and recycle funds. The Japanese Government had committed a total of 111,000m. yen (equivalent to some \$956.4m.) to the JSF by the end of 2007. During 2007 the Bank approved 55 technical assistance projects for the JSF, amounting to \$43.1m., bringing a total of \$1,017.2m. approved since 1988. The Bank administers the ADB Institute Special Fund, which was established to finance the ADB Institute's operations. By 31 December 2007 cumulative commitments to the Special Fund amounted to 15,800m. yen (or \$133.0m.).

In February 2005 the Bank established the Asian Tsunami Fund, with funds of US \$600m., to accelerate the provision of reconstruction and technical assistance to countries most affected by the natural disaster that had affected several countries in the region in December 2004. At the end of 2007 the Fund's uncommitted resources amounted to \$40.0m. The Pakistan Earthquake Fund was established in November 2005, with a commitment from the Bank of \$80m., to help to deliver emergency grant financing and technical assistance required for immediate rehabilitation and reconstruction efforts following the massive earthquake that had occurred in October. Further contributions, amounting to \$51.4m., have been made by Australia, Belgium, Finland and Norway. In February 2007 the Bank established, with an initial \$40.0m., the Regional Co-operation and Integration Fund to fund co-operation and integration activities in the region. By the end of 2007 the Fund's total resources amounted to \$41.2 million, of which \$33.8m. was uncommitted.

TRUST FUNDS

The Bank also manages and administers several trust funds and other bilateral donor arrangements. The Japanese Government funds the Japan Scholarship Program, under which 2,235 scholarships had been awarded to recipients from 35 member countries between 1988 and 2007. In May 2000 the Japan Fund for Poverty Reduction was established, with an initial contribution of 10,000m. yen (approximately US \$92.6m.) by the Japanese Government, to support ADB-financed poverty reduction and social development activities. By the end of 2007 cumulative commitments to the Fund totalled \$360.4m. and 103 projects, amounting to \$266.3m., had been approved for implementation. A Japan Fund for Information and Communication Technology (ICT) was established in July 2001, for a three-year period (later extended by one year until mid-2005), to promote the advancement and use of ICT in developing member countries. In March 2004 a Japan Fund for Public Policy Training was established, with an initial contribution by the Japanese Government, to enhance capacity-building for public policy management in developing member countries.

The majority of grant funds in support of the Bank's technical assistance activities are provided by bilateral donors under channel financing arrangements (CFAs), the first of which was negotiated in 1980. CFAs may also be processed as a thematic financing tool, for example concerned with renewable energy, water or poverty reduction, enabling more than one donor to contribute. A Co-operation Fund for Regional Trade and Financial Security Initiative was established in July 2004, with contributions by Australia, Japan and the USA, to support efforts to combat money laundering and the financing of terrorism. Other financing partnerships facilities may also be established to mobilize additional financing and investment by development partners. In November 2006 the Bank approved the establishment of an Asia Pacific Carbon Fund (within the framework of a Carbon Market Initiative) to finance clean energy projects in developing member countries. In the following month the Bank established a Water Financing Partnership Facility to help to achieve the objectives of its Water Financing Program. In July 2008 the Bank established a new Future Carbon Fund to stimulate investment in clean energy projects beyond 2012 (when the Kyoto Protocol regulating trade in carbon credits was due to expire).

Finance

Internal administrative expenses totalled US \$325.5m. in 2007 and were budgeted at \$357.2m. for 2008.

Publications

ADB Business Opportunities (monthly).
ADB Institute Newsletter.
ADB Review (monthly).
Annual Report.
Asia Economic Monitor (2 a year).
Asian Development Outlook (annually).
Asian Development Review (2 a year).
Basic Statistics (annually).
Development Asia (2 a year).

Key Indicators for Asia and the Pacific (annually).
Law and Policy Reform Bulletin (annually).
Sustainability Report.
Studies and technical assistance reports, information brochures, guidelines, sample bidding documents, staff papers.

Statistics

SUBSCRIPTIONS AND VOTING POWER
(31 December 2007)

Country	Voting power (% of total)	Subscribed capital (% of total)
Regional:		
Afghanistan	0.325	0.034
Armenia	0.537	0.298
Australia	4.917	5.773
Azerbaijan	0.653	0.444
Bangladesh	1.114	1.019
Bhutan	0.303	0.006
Brunei	0.580	0.351
Cambodia	0.338	0.049
China, People's Republic	5.442	6.429
Cook Islands	0.301	0.003
Fiji	0.353	0.068
Georgia	0.571	0.341
Hong Kong	0.733	0.543
India	5.352	6.317
Indonesia	4.646	5.434
Japan	12.756	15.571
Kazakhstan	0.942	0.805
Kiribati	0.302	0.004
Korea, Republic	4.320	5.026
Kyrgyzstan	0.537	0.298
Laos	0.310	0.014
Malaysia	2.472	2.717
The Maldives	0.302	0.004
Marshall Islands	0.301	0.003
Micronesia, Federated States	0.302	0.004
Mongolia	0.310	0.015
Myanmar	0.733	0.543
Nauru	0.302	0.004
Nepal	0.416	0.147
New Zealand	1.524	1.532
Pakistan	2.037	2.174
Palau	0.301	0.003
Papua New Guinea	0.373	0.094
Philippines	2.200	2.377
Samoa	0.301	0.003
Singapore	0.570	0.340
Solomon Islands	0.304	0.007
Sri Lanka	0.761	0.579
Taiwan	1.168	1.087
Tajikistan	0.527	0.286
Thailand	1.385	1.358
Timor-Leste	0.306	0.010
Tonga	0.302	0.004
Turkmenistan	0.501	0.253
Tuvalu	0.300	0.001
Uzbekistan	0.836	0.672
Vanuatu	0.304	0.007
Viet Nam	0.571	0.341
Sub-total	65.040	63.390
Non-regional:		
Austria	0.570	0.340
Belgium	0.570	0.340
Canada	4.474	5.219
Denmark	0.570	0.340
Finland	0.570	0.340
France	2.156	2.322
Germany	3.752	4.316
Ireland	0.570	0.340
Italy	1.741	1.803
Luxembourg	0.570	0.340
Netherlands	1.117	1.023
Norway	0.570	0.340
Portugal	0.570	0.340
Spain	0.570	0.340

Country—*continued*	Voting power (% of total)	Subscribed capital (% of total)
Sweden	0.570	0.340
Switzerland	0.764	0.582
Turkey	0.570	0.340
United Kingdom	1.929	2.038
USA	12.756	15.571
Sub-total	34.960	36.610
Total	100.000	100.000

LENDING ACTIVITIES BY SECTOR

	2007		1968–2007
Sector	Amount (US $ million)	%	%
Agriculture and natural resources	146.3	1.4	12.5
Education	145.0	1.4	4.4
Energy	1,403.7	13.9	19.6
Finance	1,158.0	11.5	12.5
Health, nutrition and social protection	50.0	0.5	2.3
Industry and trade	95.0	0.9	4.2
Law, economic management and public policy	1,179.5	11.7	4.3
Transport and communications	3,925.8	38.8	24.3
Water supply, sanitation and waste management	408.2	4.0	5.2
Multi-sector	1,594.1	15.8	10.6
Total	10,389.3	100.00	100.00

LENDING ACTIVITIES BY COUNTRY, 2007
(US $ million)

Country	Ordinary Capital	ADF	Total
Armenia	—	66.6	66.6
Azerbaijan	246.0	10.0	256.0
Bangladesh	500.0	465.7	965.7
Cambodia	8.0	27.0	35.1
China, People's Republic	1,306.7	—	1,306.7
Georgia	25.0	—	25.0
India	1,386.4	—	1,386.4
Indonesia	995.0	50.0	1,045.0
Kazakhstan	100.0	—	100.0
Kyrgyzstan	—	15.0	15.0
Maldives	4.5	5.3	9.8
Malaysia	10.0	—	10.0
Mongolia	10.0	—	10.0
Pakistan	1,565.0	454.8	2,019.8
Papua New Guinea	60.0	40.0	100.0
Philippines	583.8	—	583.8
Samoa	—	26.6	26.6
Sri Lanka	327.5	115.0	442.5
Tajikistan	—	71.7	71.7
Uzbekistan	96.0	30.0	126.0
Viet Nam	968.9	515.0	1,483.9
Sub-regional (Central and West Asia)	20.0	—	20.0
Total	8,212.8	1,892.8	10,105.6

Source: *ADB Annual Report 2007.*

THE COMMONWEALTH OF INDEPENDENT STATES—CIS

Address: 220000 Minsk, Kirava 17, Belarus.

Telephone: (17) 222-35-17; **fax:** (17) 227-23-39; **e-mail:** postmaster@www.cis.minsk.by; **internet:** www.cis.minsk.by.

The Commonwealth of Independent States is a voluntary association of 11 states, established at the time of the collapse of the USSR in December 1991.

MEMBERS

Armenia	Moldova
Azerbaijan	Russia
Belarus	Tajikistan
Georgia	Ukraine
Kazakhstan	Uzbekistan
Kyrgyzstan	

Note: Azerbaijan formally became a member of the CIS in September 1993. Georgia was admitted to the CIS in December 1993. In August 2008 Georgia announced its intention to terminate its membership; this was to enter into effect after a 12-month delay, in August 2009. Ukraine ratified the foundation documents that established the CIS in 1991 but has not yet ratified the CIS Charter. Turkmenistan has associate membership, reduced from full membership in August 2005.

Organization

(October 2008)

COUNCIL OF HEADS OF STATE

This is the supreme body of the CIS, on which all the member states of the Commonwealth are represented at the level of head of state, for discussion of issues relating to the co-ordination of Commonwealth activities and the development of the Minsk Agreement. Decisions of the Council are taken by common consent, with each state having equal voting rights. The Council meets at least once a year. An extraordinary meeting may be convened on the initiative of the majority of Commonwealth heads of state. The chairmanship of the Council is normally rotated among member states.

COUNCIL OF HEADS OF GOVERNMENT

This Council convenes for meetings at least once every three months; an extraordinary sitting may be convened on the initiative of a majority of Commonwealth heads of government. The two Councils may discuss and take necessary decisions on important domestic and external issues, and may hold joint sittings.

Working and auxiliary bodies, composed of authorized representatives of the participating states, may be set up on a permanent or interim basis on the decision of the Council of Heads of State and the Council of Heads of Government.

EXECUTIVE COMMITTEE

The Executive Committee was established by the Council of Heads of State in April 1999 to supersede the previous Secretariat, the Inter-state Economic Committee and other working bodies and committees, in order to improve the efficient functioning of the organization. The Executive Committee co-operates closely with other CIS bodies including the councils of foreign ministers and defence ministers; the Economic Council; Council of Border Troops Commanders; the Collective Security Council; the Secretariat of the Council of the Inter-parliamentary Assembly; and the Inter-state Committee for Statistics.

Executive Secretary and Chairman of the Executive Committee: SERGEY N. LEBEDEV (Russia).

Activities

On 8 December 1991 the heads of state of Belarus, Russia and Ukraine signed the Minsk Agreement, providing for the establishment of a Commonwealth of Independent States. Formal recognition of the dissolution of the USSR was incorporated in a second treaty (the Alma-Ata Declaration), signed by 11 heads of state in the then Kazakh capital, Alma-Ata (Almaty), later in that month.

In March 1992 a meeting of the CIS Council of Heads of Government decided to establish a commission to examine the resolution that 'all CIS member states are the legal successors of the rights and obligations of the former Soviet Union'. Documents relating to the legal succession of the Soviet Union were signed at a meeting of Heads of State in July. In April an agreement establishing an Inter-parliamentary Assembly (IPA), signed by Armenia, Belarus, Kazakhstan, Kyrgyzstan, Russia, Tajikistan and Uzbekistan, was published. The first Assembly was held in Bishkek, Kyrgyzstan, in September, attended by delegates from all these countries, with the exception of Uzbekistan.

A CIS Charter was adopted at the meeting of the heads of state in Minsk, Belarus, in January 1993. The Charter, providing for a defence alliance, an inter-state court and an economic co-ordination committee, was to serve as a framework for closer co-operation and was signed by all of the members except for Turkmenistan and Ukraine; by 2008 Ukraine had still not signed the Charter.

In May 1994 the CIS and UNCTAD signed a co-operation accord. A similar agreement was concluded with the UN Economic Commission for Europe in June 1996. Working contacts have also been established with ILO, UNHCR, WHO and the European Union. In June 1998 the IPA approved a decision to sign the European Social Charter (see Council of Europe); a declaration of co-operation between the Assembly and the OSCE Parliamentary Assembly was also signed.

In November 1995, at the Council of Heads of Government meeting, Russia expressed concern at the level of non-payment of debts by CIS members, which was deemed to be hindering further integration. At the meeting of the Council in April 1996 a long-term plan for the integrated development of the CIS, incorporating measures for further socio-economic, military and political co-operation, was approved.

In March 1997 the then Russian President, Boris Yeltsin, admitted that the CIS institutional structure had failed to ameliorate the severe economic situation of certain member states. Nevertheless, support for the CIS as an institution was reaffirmed by the participants during the meeting. At the heads of state meeting held in Chişinău, Moldova, in October, Russia was reportedly criticized by the other country delegations for failing to implement CIS agreements, for hindering development of the organization and for failing to resolve regional conflicts. Russia, for its part, urged all member states to participate more actively in defining, adopting and implementing CIS policies. Meeting in April 1999 the Council of Heads of Government adopted guidelines for restructuring the CIS and for the future development of the organization. Economic co-operation was to be a priority area of activity, and in particular, the establishment of a free trade zone. In June 2000 the Councils of Heads of State and Government issued a declaration concerning the maintenance of strategic stability, approved a plan and schedule for pursuing economic integration, and adopted a short-term programme for combating international terrorism (perceived to be a significant threat in central Asia). An informal CIS 10-year 'jubilee' summit, convened in November 2001, adopted a statement identifying the collective pursuit of stable socio-economic development and integration on a global level as the organization's principal objectives. A summit of heads of state convened in January 2003 agreed that the position of Chairman of the Council of Heads of State (hitherto held by consecutive Russian presidents) should be rotated henceforth among member states. Leonid Kuchma, then President of Ukraine, was elected as the new Chairman. (In September 2004, however, Russia's then President Vladimir Putin was reappointed temporarily as the Chairman of the Council, owing to a perceived deterioration in the international security situation and a declared need for experienced leadership.) A summit meeting convened in September 2003, in Yalta, Ukraine, focused on measures to combat crime and terrorism, and endorsed an economic plan for 2003–10.

In September 2004 the CIS Council of Heads of State, meeting in Astana, Kazakhstan, was dominated by consideration of measures to combat terrorism and extremist violence, following a month in which Russia, including North Ossetia, had experienced several atrocities committed against civilian targets. As part of a wider consideration of a reorganization of the CIS, the Council resolved to establish a Security Council.

Member states of the CIS have formed alliances of various kinds among themselves, thereby potentially undermining the unity of the Commonwealth. In March 1996 Belarus, Kazakhstan, Kyrgyzstan and Russia signed the Quadripartite Treaty for greater integration. This envisaged the establishment of a 'New Union', based, initially on a common market and customs union, and was to be open to all CIS members and the Baltic states. Consequently these countries (with Tajikistan) became founding members of the Eurasian Economic Community (EURASEC), inaugurated in October 2001. In April 1996 Belarus and Russia signed the Treaty on the Formation of a Community of Sovereign Republics (CSR), which provided for extensive economic, political and military co-operation. In April 1997 the two countries signed a further Treaty of Union and, in addition, initialled the Charter of the Union, which detailed the procedures and institutions designed to develop a common infrastructure, a single currency and a joint defence policy within the CSR, with the eventual aim of 'voluntary unification of the member states'. The Charter was signed in May and ratified by the respective legislatures the following month. The Union's Parliamentary Assembly, comprising 36 members from the legislature of each country, convened in official session for the first time shortly afterwards. Azerbaijan, Georgia, Moldova and Ukraine co-operated increasingly from the late 1990s as the so-called GUAM group, which envisaged implementing joint economic and transportation initiatives (such developing a Eurasian Trans-Caucasus transportation corridor) and establishing the GUAM Free Trade Zone. Uzbekistan joined in April 1999, creating GUUAM. The group agreed in September 2000 to convene regular annual summits of member countries' heads of state and to organize meetings of ministers of foreign affairs at least twice a year. In May 2005 Uzbekistan left GUUAM; consequently, the group reverted to the name GUAM. Meeting in Kyiv, Ukraine, in May 2006 the heads of state of Azerbaijan, Georgia, Moldova and Ukraine adopted a charter formally inaugurating GUAM as a full international organization and renaming it Organization for Democracy and Economic Development—GUAM. The heads of state suggested that the GUAM countries might withdraw from the CIS. In April 2003 Armenia, Belarus, Kazakhstan, Kyrgyzstan, Tajikistan and Russia established the Collective Security Treaty Organization (see below). Russia, Armenia, Azerbaijan and Georgia convene regular meetings as the 'Caucasian Group of Four'. In 1994 Kazakhstan, Kyrgyzstan, Tajikistan and Uzbekistan formed the Central Asian Economic Community. In February 2002 those countries relaunched the grouping as the Central Asian Co-operation Organization (CACO), to indicate that co-operation between member states had extended to political and security matters. Russia joined the organization in 2004. In October 2005, at a summit of CACO leaders in St Petersburg, Russia, it was announced that the organization would be merged with EURASEC. This was achieved in January 2006 with the accession to EURASEC of Uzbekistan, which had hitherto been the only member of CACO that did not also belong to the Community.

The CIS regularly sends observer teams to monitor legislative and presidential elections in member states. In March 2005 Ukraine announced that it was to suspend its participation in the CIS Election Monitoring Organization (CIS-EMO, registered as a non-governmental organization in December 2003), owing to discrepancies in the findings of the observers of that body with those of the Organization for Security and Co-operation in Europe (OSCE) during the Ukrainian presidential election that was held in October and December 2004. The CIS-EMO's assessment had failed to concur with that of the OSCE on several previous occasions. The CIS Convention on Democratic Elections Standards, Electoral Rights and Freedoms in Member States, adopted in October 2002, had by 2008 been ratified by Armenia, Kyrgyzstan, Moldova, Russia and Tajikistan.

A number of multilateral meetings of senior representatives of CIS member states held during early 2005, including a meeting of foreign ministers convened in mid-March and a meeting of prime ministers in early April, discussed new recommendations for restructuring the organs of the CIS, with a view to increasing the overall efficiency of the organization. The recommendations were presented to the August 2005 summit of the Council of Heads of State, which was held in Kazan, Russia. Several declarations were signed at the Kazan summit, including a document on co-operation in humanitarian projects and combating illegal migration; however, a consensus on far-reaching reform of the organization failed to be reached by CIS leaders at that time.

The heads of state of Armenia, Georgia, Turkmenistan (which had downgraded its full membership of the CIS to associate membership in 2005) and Ukraine did not attend an informal summit of CIS leaders convened in Moscow in July 2006. Heads of state attending the regular summit meeting for 2006, convened in November, in Minsk, Belarus, urged CIS foreign ministers to submit during 2007 proposals for revitalizing the organization.

At the 2007 CIS summit meeting, held in Dushanbe, Tajikistan, in October, CIS heads of state (excluding those of Georgia and Turkmenistan) adopted the 'Concept for Further Development of the CIS' and an action plan for its implementation. Azerbaijan endorsed the document, but reserved the right to abstain from implementing certain clauses. The Concept cited the 'long-term formation of an integrated economic and political association' as a major objective of the Commonwealth, and determined that the multi-sector nature of the organization should be retained and that the harmonized development of its interacting spheres should continue to be promoted. Further goals detailed in the Concept included: supporting regional socio-economic stability and international security; improving the economic competitiveness of member states; supporting the accession of member states to the WTO; improving regional living standards and conditions; promoting inter-parliamentary co-operation; increasing co-operation between national migration agencies; harmonizing national legislation; and standardizing CIS structures and bodies. The state chairing the Council of Heads of State was to have responsibility for co-ordinating the implementation of the Concept. Leaders attending the Dushanbe summit also determined to establish a special body to oversee migration in the region and adopted an agreement aimed at promoting the civil rights of migrants.

In mid-August 2008, following a period of conflict between Georgian and Russian forces earlier in that month, Georgia announced its intention to leave the CIS; this was to come into effect in August 2009. The 2008 regular CIS summit meeting was convened in Bishkek, Kyrgyzstan, in October, without the participation of Azerbaijan, (outgoing) Georgia, or Ukraine. Leaders attending the summit meeting considered—and determined to send for revision—a draft CIS Economic Development Strategy until 2020. The CIS leaders also discussed means of alleviating the regional impact of the ongoing global financial crisis.

ECONOMIC AFFAIRS

At a meeting of the Council of Heads of Government in March 1992 agreement was reached on repayment of the foreign debt of the former USSR. Agreements were also signed on pensions, joint tax policy and the servicing of internal debt. In May an accord on repayment of inter-state debt and the issue of balance-of-payments statements was adopted by the heads of government, meeting in Tashkent, Uzbekistan. In July it was decided to establish an economic court in Minsk.

The CIS Charter, adopted in January 1993, provided for the establishment of an economic co-ordination committee. In February, at a meeting of the heads of foreign economic departments, a foreign economic council was formed. In May all member states, with the exception of Turkmenistan, adopted a declaration of support for increased economic union and, in September, agreement was reached by all states except Ukraine and Turkmenistan on a framework for economic union, including the gradual removal of tariffs and creation of a currency union. Turkmenistan was subsequently admitted as a full member of the economic union in December 1993 and Ukraine as an associate member in April 1994.

At the Council of Heads of Government meeting in September 1994 all member states, except Turkmenistan, agreed to establish an Inter-state Economic Committee to implement economic treaties adopted within the context of an economic union. The establishment of a payments union to improve the settlement of accounts was also agreed. In April 1998 CIS heads of state resolved to incorporate the functions of the Inter-state Economic Committee, along with those of other working bodies and sectional committees, into a new CIS Executive Committee.

In October 1997 seven heads of government signed a document on implementing the 'Concept for the Integrated Economic Development of the CIS'. The development of economic co-operation between the member states was a priority task of the special forum on reform held in June 1998.

Guidelines adopted by the Council of Heads of State in April 1999 concerning the future development of the CIS identified economic co-operation and the establishment of a free trade zone (see Trade) as priority areas for action. At the summit meeting held in September 2003 CIS foreign ministers approved a draft plan aimed at improving and enhancing economic co-operation until 2010. Improving the economic competitiveness of member states was a primary focus of the 'Concept for Further Development of the CIS' that was adopted by the organization's October 2007 summit meeting.

TRADE

Agreement was reached on the free movement of goods between republics at a meeting of the Council of Heads of State in February 1992, and in April 1994 an agreement on the creation of a CIS free trade zone (envisaged as the first stage of economic union) was concluded. In July a council of the heads of customs committees, meeting in Moscow, approved a draft framework for customs legislation in CIS countries, to facilitate the establishment of a free trade zone. The framework was approved by all the participants, with the exception of Turkmenistan. In April 1999 CIS heads of state signed a protocol to the 1994 free trade area accord, which aimed to accelerate co-operation. In June 2000 the Council of Heads of State adopted a plan and schedule for the implementation of priority measures related to the creation of the free trade zone, and at the September 2003 summit meeting Russia, Belarus, Kazakhstan and Ukraine

signed the Union of Four agreement establishing the framework for a Common Economic Space (CES, see below).

At the first session of the Inter-state Economic Committee in November 1994 draft legislation regarding a customs union was approved. The development of a customs union and the strengthening of intra-CIS trade were objectives endorsed by all participants, with the exception of Georgia, at the Council of Heads of Government meeting held in March 1997. In March 1998 Russia, Belarus, Kazakhstan and Kyrgyzstan signed an agreement establishing a customs union, which was to be implemented in two stages: firstly, the removal of trade restrictions and the unification of trade and customs regulations; followed by the integration of economic, monetary and trade policies. In February 1999 Tajikistan signed the 1998 agreement to become the fifth member of the customs union. In October 1999 the heads of state of the five member states of the customs union reiterated their political determination to implement the customs union and approved a programme to harmonize national legislation to create a single economic space. In May 2000 the heads of state announced their intention to raise the status of the customs union to that of an inter-state economic organization, and, in October, the leaders signed the founding treaty of EURASEC. Under the new structure member states aimed to formulate a unified foreign economic policy, and, taking into account existing customs agreements, collectively to pursue the creation of the planned single economic space. In the following month the five member governments signed an agreement enabling visa-free travel within the new Community. (Earlier in 2000 Russia had withdrawn from a CIS-wide visa-free travel arrangement agreed in 1992. Kazakhstan, Turkmenistan and Uzbekistan subsequently withdrew from the agreement, and Belarus announced its intention to do so in late 2005.) In December 2000 member states of the Community adopted several documents aimed at facilitating economic co-operation. EURASEC, governed by an inter-state council based in Astana, Kazakhstan, was formally inaugurated in October 2001. In October 2003 the Community was granted observer status at the UN. The Union of Four agreement on establishing the framework for a CES, adopted in September 2003 by the leaders of Belarus, Kazakhstan, Russia and Ukraine, envisaged the creation of a free trade zone and the gradual harmonization of tariffs, customs and transport legislation. While participation at each stage would remain optional, decisions would be obligatory and certain areas of sovereignty would eventually be ceded to a council of heads of state and a commission. The Union of Four accord entered into force in April 2004. Meeting on the sidelines of the CIS summit held in October 2007, EURASEC leaders determined to establish a fully operational customs union by 2011, with Belarus, Kazakhstan and Russia as the founding members, and Kyrgyzstan, Tajikistan and Uzbekistan to join at a later date, once they had achieved the requisite accession conditions. Ukraine, which was also committed to participation in the GUAM Free Trade Zone, was not at that time participating actively in the negotiating process on the CES. Also in May 2004, at a meeting between the prime ministers of the CIS member states, all participants except Ukraine signed a protocol to abolish all restrictions on trade by 2012. It is envisaged that the CES, which is open to accession by other CIS member states, will form the basis of the planned wider EURASEC economic integration. Despite significant growth in the gross domestic product of the poorer states of the CIS (Armenia, Azerbaijan, Georgia, Kyrgyzstan, Moldova, Tajikistan and Uzbekistan, known as the 'CIS-7'), in April 2005 the IMF called for greater harmonization of trade rules within the CIS, as well as liberalization of transit policies and the removal of non-tariff barriers.

The CIS maintains a 'loose co-ordination' on issues related to applications by member states to join the World Trade Organization (WTO). Supporting the accession of member states to the WTO was a primary focus of the Concept for Further Development of the CIS that was adopted by the October 2007 summit meeting of the Commonwealth.

BANKING AND FINANCE

In February 1992 CIS heads of state agreed to retain the rouble as the common currency for trade between the republics. However, in July 1993, in an attempt to control inflation, notes printed before 1993 were withdrawn from circulation and no new ones were issued until January 1994. Despite various agreements to recreate the 'rouble zone', including a protocol agreement signed in September 1993 by six states, it effectively remained confined to Tajikistan, which joined in January 1994, and Belarus, which joined in April. Both those countries proceeded to introduce national currencies in May 1995. In January 1993, at the signing of the CIS Charter, the member countries endorsed the establishment of an inter-state bank to facilitate payments between the republics and to co-ordinate monetary-credit policy. Russia was to hold 50% of shares in the bank, but decisions were to be made only with a two-thirds majority approval. In December 2000, in accordance with the CSR and Treaty of Union (see above), the Presidents of Belarus and Russia signed an agreement providing for the adoption by Belarus of the Russian currency from 1 January 2005, and for the introduction of a new joint Union currency by 1 January 2008; the adoption by Belarus of the Russian currency was, however, subsequently postponed.

In October 2004 Russia and Kazakhstan announced a proposal to establish a CIS Development Bank, with a capital of €1m.

DEFENCE

An Agreement on Armed Forces and Border Troops was concluded on 30 December 1991, at the same time as the Agreement on Strategic Forces. This confirmed the right of member states to set up their own armed forces and appointed Commanders-in-Chief of the Armed Forces and of the Border Troops, who were to elaborate joint security procedures. In February 1992 an agreement was signed stipulating that the commander of the strategic forces was subordinate to the Council of Heads of States. Eight states agreed on a unified command for general-purpose (i.e. non-strategic) armed forces for a transitional period of two years. Azerbaijan, Moldova and Ukraine resolved to establish independent armed forces.

In January 1992 Commissions on the Black Sea Fleet (control of which was disputed by Russia and Ukraine) and the Caspian Flotilla (the former Soviet naval forces on the Caspian Sea) were established. The formation of a defence alliance was provided for in the CIS Charter adopted in January 1993; a proposal by Russia to assume control of all nuclear weapons in the former USSR was rejected at the same time.

In June 1993 CIS defence ministers agreed to abolish CIS joint military command and to abandon efforts to maintain a unified defence structure. The existing CIS command was to be replaced, on a provisional basis, by a 'joint staff for co-ordinating military co-operation between the states of the Commonwealth'. It was widely reported that Russia had encouraged the decision to abolish the joint command, owing to concerns at the projected cost of a CIS joint military structure and support within Russia's military leadership of bilateral military agreements with the country's neighbours. In December the Council of Defence Ministers agreed to establish a secretariat to co-ordinate military co-operation as a replacement to the joint military command. In November 1995 the Council of Defence Ministers authorized the establishment of a Joint Air Defence System, to be co-ordinated largely by Russia. A CIS combat duty system was under development in the early 2000s. Russia and Belarus were also developing a joint air-defence unit in the context of the CSR (see above). In February 2006 Georgia withdrew from the Council of Defence Ministers, on the grounds that it intended to join NATO and did not wish to be a member of both groupings.

In September 1996 the first meeting of the inter-state commission for military economic co-operation was held; a draft agreement on the export of military projects and services to third countries was approved. The basic principles of a programme for greater military and technical co-operation were approved by the Council of Defence Ministers in March 1997. In April 1998 the Council proposed drawing up a draft programme for military and technical co-operation between member countries and also discussed procedures advising on the use and maintenance of armaments and military hardware. The programme was approved by CIS heads of state in October 2002. Draft proposals relating to information security for the military were approved by the Council in December. It was remarked that the inadequate funding of the Council was impeding co-operation.

In August 1996 the Council of Defence Ministers condemned what it described as the political, economic and military threat implied in any expansion of NATO. The statement was not signed by Ukraine. The eighth plenary session of the IPA, held in November, urged NATO countries to abandon plans for the organization's expansion. Strategic co-operation between NATO and CIS member states increased from the mid-1990s, particularly with Russia and Ukraine. In the late 1990s the USA established bilateral military assistance programmes for Azerbaijan, Georgia, and Uzbekistan. Uzbekistan and other central Asian CIS states played a support role in the US-led action initiated in late 2001 against the then Taliban-held areas of Afghanistan (see below).

During September 2004 the CIS Council of Heads of State determined to establish a Security Council, comprising the ministers responsible for foreign affairs and for defence, and heads of security and border control.

REGIONAL SECURITY

At a meeting of heads of government in March 1992 agreements on settling inter-state conflicts were signed by all participating states (except Turkmenistan). At the same meeting an agreement on the status of border troops was signed by five states. In May a five-year Collective Security Treaty was signed. In July further documents were signed on collective security and it was agreed to establish joint peace-making forces to intervene in CIS disputes. In April 1999 Armenia, Belarus, Kazakhstan, Kyrgyzstan, Russia and Tajikistan signed a protocol to extend the Collective Security Treaty (while Azerbaijan, Georgia and Uzbekistan withdrew from the agreement).

In September 1993 the Council of Heads of State agreed to establish a Bureau of Organized Crime, to be based in Moscow. A meeting of the Council of Border Troop Commanders in January 1994 prepared a report on the issue of illegal migration and drug trade across the external borders of the CIS; Moldova, Georgia and Tajikistan did not attend. A programme to counter organized crime within the CIS was approved by heads of government, meeting in Moscow, in April 1996. In March 2001 CIS interior ministers agreed to strengthen co-operation in combating transnational organized crime, in view of reportedly mounting levels of illicit drugs trafficking in the region.

An Agreement on the Co-operation of the CIS Member States in Combating Trafficking in Persons, Human Organs and Tissues was adopted in November 2005 and by 2008 had been ratified by Azerbaijan, Armenia, Belarus, Kyrgyzstan and Russia. In addition, a Decision on the Programme of Co-operation of the CIS Member States in Combating Trafficking in Persons covering 2007–10 was adopted by eight CIS states in November 2006.

The fourth plenary session of the IPA in March 1994 established a commission for the resolution of the conflicts in the secessionist regions of Nagornyi Karabakh (Azerbaijan) and Abkhazia (Georgia) and endorsed the use of CIS peace-keeping forces. In the following month Russia agreed to send peace-keeping forces to Georgia, and the dispatch of peace-keeping forces was approved by the Council of Defence Ministers in October. The subsequent session of the IPA in October adopted a resolution to send groups of military observers to Abkhazia and to Moldova. The inter-parliamentary commission on the conflict between Abkhazia and Georgia proposed initiating direct negotiations with the two sides in order to reach a peaceful settlement.

In December 1994 the Council of Defence Ministers enlarged the mandate of the commander of the CIS collective peace-keeping forces in Tajikistan: when necessary CIS military contingents were permitted to engage in combat operations without the prior consent of individual governments. At the Heads of State meeting in Moscow in January 1996 Georgia's proposal to impose sanctions against Abkhazia was approved, in an attempt to achieve a resolution of the conflict. Provisions on arrangements relating to collective peace-keeping operations were approved at the meeting; the training of military and civilian personnel for these operations was to commence in October. In March 1997 the Council of Defence Ministers agreed to extend the peace-keeping mandates for CIS forces in Tajikistan and Abkhazia (following much disagreement, the peace-keepers' mandate in Abkhazia was further renewed in October). The mandate of the CIS peace-keeping operation in Tajikistan was eventually terminated in June 2000. At a meeting of the Council in January 1998 a request from Georgia that the CIS carry out its decisions to settle the conflict with Abkhazia was added to the agenda. The Council discussed the promotion of military co-operation and the improvement of peace-making activities, and declared that there was progress in the formation of the collective security system, although the situation in the North Caucasus remained tense. In April President Yeltsin requested that the Armenian and Azerbaijani presidents sign a document to end the conflict in Nagornyi Karabakh; the two subsequently issued a statement expressing their support for a political settlement of the conflict. A document proposing a settlement of the conflict in Abkhazia was also drawn up, but the resolutions adopted were not accepted by Abkhazia. Against the wishes of the Abkhazian authorities, the mandate for the CIS troops in the region was extended to cover the whole of the Gali district. The mandate expired in July 1998, but the forces remained in the region while its renewal was debated. In April 1999 the Council of Heads of State agreed to a retrospective extension of the operation's mandate; the mandate subsequently continued to be renewed at six-monthly intervals until March 2003 when it was extended indefinitely. The CIS peace-keeping force in Abkhazia worked in close co-operation with the UN Observer Mission in Georgia (UNOMIG), and, from 2002, the two forces conducted regular joint patrols of the upper Kodori valley. In April 2008 it was reported that measures were to be taken to increase the numbers of personnel deployed to the CIS force in Abkhazia. However, at the beginning of September 2008 the Georgian Government decided to terminate the CIS peace-keeping operation in Abkhazia, following a period of violent insecurity between Georgia and Russia in August and, at the end of that month, Russia's recognition of Abkhazia and South Ossetia as independent states. UNOMIG remained operative following the termination of the CIS force.

In February 1995 a non-binding memorandum on maintaining peace and stability was adopted by heads of state, meeting in Almaty. Signatories were to refrain from applying military, political, economic or other pressure on another member country, to seek the peaceful resolution of border or territorial disputes and not to support or assist separatist movements active in other member countries. In April 1998 the Council of Defence Ministers approved a draft document proposing that coalition forces be provided with technical equipment to enhance collective security.

In June 1998, at a session of the Council of Border Troop Commanders, some 33 documents were signed relating to border co-operation. A framework protocol on the formation and expedient use of a border troops reserve in critical situations was discussed and signed by several participants. A register of work in scientific and engineering research carried out in CIS countries in the interests of border troops was also adopted. A programme aimed at enhancing co-operation between border troops was adopted by heads of state in October 2002. In February 2004 an expert group drafted regulations for the establishment of a common system to register foreign nationals and stateless persons.

In June 1998 CIS interior ministers, meeting in Tashkent, Uzbekistan, adopted a number of co-operation agreements, including a framework for the exchange of information between CIS law-enforcement agencies; it was also decided to maintain contact with Interpol.

An emergency meeting of heads of state in October 1996 discussed the ongoing conflict in nearby Afghanistan and the consequent threat to regional security. The participants requested the UN Security Council to adopt measures to resolve the situation. In May 2000 the six signatory states to the Collective Security Treaty pledged to strengthen military co-operation in view of the perceived threat to their security from the Taliban regime in Afghanistan. In October those countries signed an agreement on the Status of Forces and Means of Collective Security Systems, establishing a joint rapid deployment function. The so-called CIS Collective Rapid Reaction Force was to be assembled to combat insurgencies, with particular reference to trans-border terrorism from Afghanistan, and also to deter trans-border illegal drugs trafficking (see above). In June 2001 a CIS Anti-terrorism Centre was established in Moscow. The centre was to co-ordinate counter-terrorism activities and to compile a database of international terrorist organizations operating in member states. In October, in response to the major terrorist attacks perpetrated in September against targets in the USA—allegedly co-ordinated by militant fundamentalist Islamist leader Osama bin Laden—the parties to the Collective Security Treaty adopted a new anti-terrorism plan. In December 2002 the committee of the Collective Security Treaty member countries adopted a protocol on the exchange of expertise and information on terrorist organizations and their activities. In April 2003 the signatory states determined to establish the Collective Security Treaty Organization (CSTO); ratification of its founding documents was completed by September, when it applied for UN observer status. In early November CSTO co-ordinated an operation targeting drugs traffickers involving some 30,000 law enforcement officers. The signatory countries to the Collective Security Treaty participate in regular so-called 'CIS Southern Shield' joint military exercises. A CSTO joint anti-terrorism exercise, involving some 2,000 troops, was held in Kazakhstan and Kyrgyzstan in August 2004. A summit meeting of CSTO leaders held in October 2007 endorsed documents enabling the future establishment of CSTO joint peace-keeping forces and the creation of a co-ordination council for the heads of member states' emergency response agencies.

In October 2002 a Central Asian subdivision of the CIS anti-terrorism centre was established in Bishkek, Kyrgyzstan. The CIS summit in September 2003 approved draft decisions to control the sale of portable anti-aircraft missiles and to set up a joint co-ordination structure to address illegal immigration.

In November 2003, following a popular uprising against the Georgian regime, an emergency meeting of CIS foreign ministers was convened in Kyiv, Ukraine. The meeting issued a statement reaffirming Georgia's territorial integrity and calling for the restoration of the constitutional and democratic process; a CIS envoy was dispatched to the capital, Tbilisi, to mediate in a handover of power from the deposed President, Eduard Shevardnadze. In early January 2004 a team of some 70 CIS observers was present at elections to choose a new Georgian President.

In September 2004 CIS ministers of the interior, convened in Kyiv, Ukraine, agreed to draft joint programmes to combat crime and drugs trafficking in the period 2005–07. In October CIS directors of security agencies and intelligence services, meeting in Minsk, Belarus, discussed regional counter-terrorism measures, including efforts to exchange information and restrict sources of terrorist finance. The meeting adopted a new CIS programme on combating international terrorism and manifestations of extremism, to cover the period 2005–07.

LEGISLATIVE CO-OPERATION

An agreement on legislative co-operation was signed at an Inter-Parliamentary Conference in January 1992; joint commissions were established to co-ordinate action on economy, law, pensions, housing, energy and ecology. The CIS Charter, formulated in January 1993, provided for the establishment of an inter-state court. In October 1994 a Convention on the rights of minorities was adopted at the meeting of the Heads of State; by 2008 this had been ratified by Azerbaijan, Armenia, Belarus, Kyrgyzstan and Tajikistan. In May 1995, at the sixth plenary session of the IPA, several acts to improve co-ordination of legislation were approved, relating to migration of labour, consumer rights, and the rights of prisoners of war; revised legislation on labour migration and the social protection of migrant workers was adopted in November 2005. A CIS Convention on Human Rights and Fundamental Freedoms, adopted at that time, and incorporating the Statute of a proposed CIS Commission on Human Rights, had by 2008 been ratified by Belarus, Kyrgyzstan, Russia and Tajikistan. In November 2006 an agreement on the protection of participants in the criminal justice system was signed by eight member states.

The creation of a Council of Ministers of Internal Affairs was approved at the Heads of State meeting in January 1996; the Council was to promote co-operation between the law-enforcement bodies of member states. The IPA has approved a number of model laws, relating to areas including banking and financial services; charity; defence; ecology, the economy; education; the regulation of refugee problems; combating terrorism; and social issues, including obligatory social insurance against production accidents and occupational diseases.

OTHER ACTIVITIES

The CIS has held a number of discussions relating to the environment. In July 1992 agreements were concluded to establish an Inter-state Ecological Council. It was also agreed in that month to establish *Mir*, an inter-state television and radio company. In October 2002 a decision was made by CIS heads of government to enhance mutual understanding and co-operation between members countries through *Mir* radio and television broadcasts. In February 1995 the IPA established a Council of Heads of News Agencies, in order to promote the concept of a single information area. CIS leaders meeting in Moscow, Russia, in May 2005 agreed to sign a declaration aimed at enhancing co-operation between CIS members in the humanitarian, cultural and scientific spheres.

A CIS Electric Energy Council was established in 1992, and a Petroleum and Gas Council was created at a Heads of Government meeting in March 1993, to guarantee energy supplies and to invest in the Siberian petroleum industry. The Council was to have a secretariat based in Tyumen, Siberia. In October 2002 the Council of Heads of Government signed a co-operation agreement on energy effectiveness and power supply. In the field of civil aviation, the Inter-state Economic Committee agreed in February 1997 to establish an Aviation Alliance to promote co-operation between the countries' civil aviation industries.

THE COUNCIL OF EUROPE

Address: Ave de l'Europe, 67075 Strasbourg Cédex, France.
Telephone: 3-88-41-20-33; **fax:** 3-88-41-27-45; **e-mail:** infopoint@coe.int; **internet:** www.coe.int.

The Council was founded in May 1949 to achieve a greater unity between its members, to facilitate their social progress and to uphold the principles of parliamentary democracy, respect for human rights and the rule of law. Membership has risen from the original 10 to 47.

MEMBERS*

Albania	Lithuania
Andorra	Luxembourg
Armenia	Macedonia, former Yugoslav
Austria	republic
Azerbaijan	Malta
Belgium	Moldova
Bosnia and Herzegovina	Montenegro†
Bulgaria	Monaco
Croatia	Netherlands
Cyprus	Norway
Czech Republic	Poland
Denmark	Portugal
Estonia	Romania
Finland	Russia
France	San Marino
Georgia	Serbia†
Germany	Slovakia
Greece	Slovenia
Hungary	Spain
Iceland	Sweden
Ireland	Switzerland
Italy	Turkey
Latvia	Ukraine
Liechtenstein	United Kingdom

*Belarus is a state candidate for membership of the Council of Europe. Canada, the Holy See, Japan, Mexico and the USA have observer status with the Committee of Ministers. The parliaments of Canada, Israel and Mexico have observer status with the Parliamentary Assembly.

†Following the division of Serbia and Montenegro into separate sovereign states in June 2006, Serbia retained the seat hitherto held by Serbia and Montenegro. Montenegro was admitted as a member in May 2007.

Organization
(October 2008)

COMMITTEE OF MINISTERS

The Committee consists of the ministers of foreign affairs of all member states (or their deputies, who are usually ministers' permanent diplomatic representatives in Strasbourg); it decides all matters of internal organization, makes recommendations to governments and draws up conventions and agreements with binding effect; it also discusses matters of political concern, such as European co-operation, compliance with member states' commitments, in particular concerning the protection of human rights, and considers possible co-ordination with other institutions, such as the European Union (EU) and the Organization for Security and Co-operation in Europe (OSCE). The Committee meets weekly at deputy ministerial level and once a year (in May or November) at ministerial level. Six two-day meetings are convened each year to supervise the execution of judgments of the European Court of Human Rights (see below).

CONFERENCES OF SPECIALIZED MINISTERS

There are 20 Conferences of specialized ministers, meeting regularly for intergovernmental co-operation in various fields.

PARLIAMENTARY ASSEMBLY

President: LLÚIS MARIA DE PUIG (Spain).
Chairman of the Socialist Group: ANDREAS GROSS (Switzerland).
Chairman of the Group of the European People's Party: LUC VAN DEN BRANDE (Belgium).
Chairman of the Alliance of Liberals and Democrats for Europe: MÁTYÁS EÖRSI (Hungary).
Chairman of the European Democrat Group: MIKHAIL MARGELOV (Russia).

Chairman of the Unified European Left Group: TINY KOX (Netherlands).

Members are elected or appointed by their national parliaments from among the members thereof; political parties in each delegation follow the proportion of their strength in the national parliament. Members do not represent their governments, speaking on their own behalf. At October 2008 the Assembly had 318 members (and 318 substitutes): 18 each for France, Germany, Italy, Russia and the United Kingdom; 12 each for Poland, Spain, Turkey and Ukraine; 10 for Romania; seven each for Belgium, the Czech Republic, Greece, Hungary, the Netherlands, Portugal and Serbia; six each for Austria, Azerbaijan, Bulgaria, Sweden and Switzerland; five each for Bosnia and Herzegovina, Croatia, Denmark, Finland, Georgia, Moldova, Norway and Slovakia; four each for Albania, Armenia, Ireland and Lithuania; three each for Cyprus, Estonia, Iceland, Latvia, Luxembourg, the former Yugoslav republic of Macedonia, Malta, Montenegro and Slovenia; and two each for Andorra, Liechtenstein, Monaco and San Marino. The parliaments of Canada, Israel and Mexico have permanent observer status. (Belarus's special 'guest status' was suspended in January 1997.)

The Assembly meets in ordinary session once a year. The session is divided into four parts, generally held in the last full week of January, April, June and September. The Assembly submits Recommendations to the Committee of Ministers, passes Resolutions, and discusses reports on any matters of common European interest. It is also a consultative body to the Committee of Ministers, and elects the Secretary-General, the Deputy Secretary-General, the Secretary-General of the Assembly, the Council's Commissioner for Human Rights, and the members of the European Court of Human Rights.

Standing Committee: represents the Assembly when it is not in session, and may adopt Recommendations to the Committee of Ministers and Resolutions on behalf of the Assembly. Consists of the President, Vice-Presidents, Chairmen of the Political Groups, Chairmen of the Ordinary Committees and Chairmen of national delegations. Meetings are usually held at least twice a year.

Ordinary Committees: political affairs; legal and human rights; economic affairs and development; social, health and family affairs; culture, science and education; environment, agriculture, and local and regional affairs; migration, refugees and population; rules of procedure and immunities; equal opportunities for women and men; honouring of obligations and commitments by member states of the Council of Europe.

SECRETARIAT

The Secretariat incorporates the Secretariats and Registry of the institutions of the Council. There are Directorates of Communication and Research, Strategic Planning, Protocol and Internal Audit, and the following Directorates General: Political Affairs; Legal Affairs; Human Rights; Social Cohesion; Education, Culture and Heritage, Youth and Sport; and Administration and Logistics.

Secretary-General: TERRY DAVIS (United Kingdom).
Deputy Secretary-General: MAUD DE BOER-BUQUICCHIO (Netherlands).
Secretary-General of the Parliamentary Assembly: MATEO SORINAS BALFEGÓ (Spain).

EUROPEAN COURT OF HUMAN RIGHTS

The Court was established in 1959 under the European Convention on Human Rights. It has compulsory jurisdiction and is competent to consider complaints lodged by states party to the European Convention and by individuals, groups of individuals or non-governmental organizations claiming to be victims of breaches of the Convention's guarantees. The Court comprises one judge for each contracting state. The Court sits in three-member Committees, empowered to declare applications inadmissible in the event of unanimity and where no further examination is necessary, seven-member Chambers, and a 17-member Grand Chamber. Chamber judgments become final three months after delivery, during which period parties may request a rehearing before the Grand Chamber, subject to acceptance by a panel of five judges. Grand Chamber judgments are final. The Court's final judgments are binding on respondent states and their execution is supervised by the Committee of Ministers. Execution of judgments includes payment of any pecuniary just satisfaction awarded by the Court, adoption of specific individual measures to erase the consequences of the violations found (such as striking out of impugned convictions from criminal records, reopening of judicial proceedings, etc.), and general measures to prevent new similar violations (e.g. constitutional and legislative reforms, changes of domestic case-law and administrative practice, etc.). At its meeting in March 2008 the Committee of Ministers supervised the payment of just satisfaction awarded by the Court in 845 cases, the adoption, in 139 cases or groups of cases, of individual measures, and 178 cases or groups of cases requiring the adoption of new general measures. In addition, the Committee started examining 185 new judgments of the Court and draft final resolutions (concerning 121 cases). When the Committee of Ministers considers that the measures taken comply with the respondent state's obligation to give effect to the judgment, a final resolution is adopted that terminates the supervision of the case. In 2007 the Court delivered 1,735 judgments, and some 88,850 cases were pending at 1 June 2008.

President: JEAN-PAUL COSTA (France).

Registrar: ERIK FRIBERGH (Sweden).

CONGRESS OF LOCAL AND REGIONAL AUTHORITIES OF THE COUNCIL OF EUROPE (CLRAE)

The Congress was established in 1994, incorporating the former Standing Conference of Local and Regional Authorities, in order to protect and promote the political, administrative and financial autonomy of local and regional European authorities by encouraging central governments to develop effective local democracy. The Congress comprises two chambers—a Chamber of Local Authorities and a Chamber of Regions—with a total membership of 318 elected representatives (and 318 elected substitutes). Annual sessions are mainly concerned with local government matters, regional planning, protection of the environment, town and country planning, and social and cultural affairs. A Standing Committee, drawn from all national delegations, meets between plenary sessions of the Congress. Four Statutory Committees (Institutional; Sustainable Development; Social Cohesion; Culture and Education) meet twice a year in order to prepare texts for adoption by the Congress.

The Congress advises the Council's Committee of Ministers and the Parliamentary Assembly on all aspects of local and regional policy and co-operates with other national and international organizations representing local government. The Congress monitors implementation of the European Charter of Local Self-Government, which was opened for signature in 1985 and provides common standards for effective local democracy. Other legislative guidelines for the activities of local authorities and the promotion of democracy at local level include the 1980 European Outline Convention on Transfrontier Co-operation, and its Additional Protocol which was opened for signature in 1995; a Convention on the Participation of Foreigners in Public Life at Local Level (entered into force in 1997); and the European Charter for Regional or Minority Languages (entered into force 1998). In addition, the European Urban Charter (adopted 1992) defines citizens' rights in European towns and cities, for example in the areas of transport, urban architecture, pollution and security; the European Landscape Convention (entered into force in March 2004) details an obligation for public authorities to adopt policies and measures at local, regional, national and international level for the protection, management and planning of landscapes; and the Charter on the Participation of Young People in Municipal and Regional Life (adopted in 1992 and revised in 2003), sets out guidelines for encouraging the active involvement of young people in the promotion of social change in their municipality or region. In May 2005 the Congress concluded an agreement with the EU Committee of the Regions on co-operation in ensuring local and regional democracy and self-government.

President: YAVUZ MILDON (Turkey).

Activities

In an effort to harmonize national laws, to put the citizens of member countries on an equal footing and to pool certain resources and facilities, the Council of Europe has concluded a number of conventions and agreements covering particular aspects of European co-operation. Since 1989 the Council has undertaken to increase co-operation with all countries of the former Eastern bloc and to facilitate their accession to the organization. In October 1997 heads of state or government of member countries convened for only the second time (the first meeting took place in Vienna, in October 1993) with the aim of formulating a new social model to consolidate democracy throughout Europe. The meeting endorsed a Final Declaration and an Action Plan, which established priority areas for future Council activities, including fostering social cohesion; protecting civilian security; promoting human rights; enhancing joint measures to counter cross-border illegal trafficking; and strengthening democracy through education and other cultural activities. In addition, the meeting generated renewed political commitment to the Programme of Action against Corruption, which has become a key element of Council activities. A third meeting of heads of state or government was held in Warsaw, Poland, in May

2005. In a Final Declaration and an Action Plan the meeting defined the principal tasks of the Council in the coming years, i.e. promoting human rights and the rule of law, strengthening the security of European citizens and fostering co-operation with other international and European organizations. The Council's activities have three cross-cutting themes: children, democracy, and combating violence.

HUMAN RIGHTS

The protection of human rights is one of the Council of Europe's basic goals, to be achieved in four main areas: the effective supervision and protection of fundamental rights and freedoms; identification of new threats to human rights and human dignity; development of public awareness of the importance of human rights; and promotion of human rights education and professional training. The most significant treaties in this area include: the European Convention for the Protection of Human Rights and Fundamental Freedoms (European Convention on Human Rights) (which was adopted in 1950 and entered into force in 1953); the European Social Charter; the European Convention for the Prevention of Torture and Inhuman or Degrading Treatment or Punishment; the Framework Convention for the Protection of National Minorities; the European Charter for Regional or Minority Languages; and the Convention on Action against Trafficking in Human Beings.

The Steering Committee for Human Rights is responsible for inter-governmental co-operation in the field of human rights and fundamental freedoms; it works to strengthen the effectiveness of systems for protecting human rights and to identify potential threats and challenges to human rights. The Committee has been responsible for the elaboration of several conventions and other legal instruments including the following protocols to the European Convention on Human Rights: Protocol No. 11, which entered into force in November 1998, resulting in the replacement of the then existing institutions—the European Commission of Human Rights and the European Court of Human Rights—by a single Court, working on a full-time basis; Protocol No. 12, which entered into force in April 2005, enforcing a general prohibition of discrimination; No. 13, which entered into force in July 2003, guaranteeing the abolition of the death penalty in all circumstances (including in time of war); and No. 14, adopted in May 2004, which aimed to enhance the effectiveness of the Court by improving implementation of the European Convention on Human Rights at national level and the processing of applications, and accelerating the execution of the Court's decisions.

The Steering Committee for Human Rights was responsible for the preparation of the European Ministerial Conference on Human Rights, held in Rome in November 2000, to commemorate the 50th anniversary of the adoption of the European Convention on Human Rights. The Conference highlighted, in particular, 'the need to reinforce the effective protection of human rights in domestic legal systems as well as at the European level'.

The Council of Europe Commissioner for Human Rights (whose office was established by a resolution of the Council's Committee of Ministers in May 1999) promotes respect for human rights in member states.

Commissioner for Human Rights: THOMAS HAMMARBERG (Sweden).

European Committee for the Prevention of Torture and Inhuman or Degrading Treatment or Punishment (CPT)

The Committee was established under the 1987 Convention for the Prevention of Torture as an integral part of the Council of Europe's system for the protection of human rights. The Committee, comprising independent experts, aims to examine the treatment of persons deprived of their liberty with a view to strengthening, if necessary, the protection of such persons from torture and from inhuman or degrading treatment or punishment. It conducts periodic visits to police stations, prisons, detention centres, and all other sites where persons are deprived of their liberty by a public authority, in all states parties to the Convention, and may also undertake ad hoc visits when the Committee considers them necessary. After each visit the Committee drafts a report of its findings and any further advice or recommendations, based on dialogue and co-operation. By October 2008 the Committee had published 204 reports and had undertaken 256 visits (159 periodic and 97 ad hoc).

President: MAURO PALMA (Italy).

European Social Charter

The European Social Charter, in force since 1965, is the counterpart of the European Convention on Human Rights, in the field of protection of economic and social rights. A revised Charter, which amended existing guarantees and incorporated new rights, was opened for signature in May 1996, and entered into force on 1 July

1999. By October 2008 27 member states had ratified the Charter and 25 had ratified the revised Charter. Rights guaranteed by the Charter concern all individuals in their daily lives in matters of housing, health, education, employment, social protection, movement of persons and non-discrimination. The European Committee of Social Rights considers reports submitted to it annually by member states. It also considers collective complaints submitted in the framework of an Additional Protocol (1995), providing for a system which entered into force in July 1998, permitting trade unions, employers' organizations and NGOs to lodge complaints on alleged violations of the Charter. The Committee, composed of 15 members, decides on the conformity of national situations with the Charter. When a country does not bring a situation into conformity, the Committee of Ministers may, on the basis of decisions prepared by a Governmental Committee (composed of representatives of each Contracting Party), issue recommendations to the state concerned, inviting it to change its legislation or practice in accordance with the Charter's requirements.

President of the European Committee of Social Rights: POLONCA KONČAR (Slovenia).

FRAMEWORK CONVENTION FOR THE PROTECTION OF NATIONAL MINORITIES

In 1993 the first summit meeting of Council of Europe heads of state and government, held in Vienna, mandated the Committee of Ministers to draft 'a framework convention specifying the principle that States commit themselves to respect in order to assure the protection of national minorities'. A special committee was established to draft the so-called Framework Convention for the Protection of National Minorities, which was then adopted by the Committee in November 1994. The Convention was opened for signature in February 1995, entering into force in February 1998. Contracting parties (39 states at October 2008) are required to submit reports on the implementation of the treaty at regular intervals to an Advisory Committee composed of 18 independent experts. The Advisory Committee adopts an opinion on the implementation of the Framework Convention by the contracting party, on the basis of which the Committee of Ministers adopts a resolution. A Conference entitled 10 Years of Protecting National Minorities and Regional or Minority Languages was convened in March 2008 to review the impacts of, and the role of regional institutions in implementing, both the Framework Convention and the Convention on Minority Languages.

Executive Secretary: ALAIN CHABLAIS (acting).

RACISM AND INTOLERANCE

In October 1993 heads of state and of government, meeting in Vienna, resolved to reinforce a policy to combat all forms of intolerance, in response to the increasing incidence of racial hostility and intolerance towards minorities in European societies. A European Commission against Racism and Intolerance (ECRI) was established by the summit meeting to analyse and assess the effectiveness of legal, policy and other measures taken by member states to combat these problems. It became operational in March 1994. The European conference against racism, held in October 2000, requested that ECRI should be reinforced and, in June 2002, the Committee of Ministers of the Council of Europe adopted a new Statute for ECRI that consolidated its role as an independent human rights monitoring body focusing on issues related to racism and racial discrimination. Members of ECRI are appointed on the basis of their recognized expertise in the field; they are independent and impartial in fulfilling their mandate. ECRI undertakes activities in three programme areas: country-by-country approach; work on general themes; and relations with civil society. In the first area of activity, ECRI analyses the situation regarding racism and intolerance in each of the member states, in order to advise governments on measures to combat these problems. In December 1998 ECRI completed a first round of reports for all Council members. A second series of country reports was completed in December 2002 and a third monitoring cycle, focusing on implementation and 'specific issues', was initiated in 2003; it was envisaged that some 37 reports would have been published under the third cycle by the end of 2008. ECRI's work on general themes includes the preparation of policy recommendations and guidelines on issues of importance to combating racism and intolerance. ECRI also collects and disseminates examples of good practices relating to these issues. Under the third programme area ECRI aims to disseminate information and raise awareness of the problems of racism and intolerance among the general public.

EQUALITY BETWEEN WOMEN AND MEN

The Steering Committee for Equality between Women and Men (CDEG—an intergovernmental committee of experts) is responsible for encouraging action at both national and Council of Europe level to promote equality of rights and opportunities between the two sexes.

Assisted by various specialist groups and committees, the CDEG is mandated to establish analyses, studies and evaluations, to examine national policies and experiences, to devise concerted policy strategies and measures for implementing equality and, as necessary, to prepare appropriate legal and other instruments. It is also responsible for preparing the European Ministerial Conferences on Equality between Women and Men. The main areas of CDEG activities are the comprehensive inclusion of the rights of women (for example, combating violence against women and trafficking in human beings) within the context of human rights; the issue of equality and democracy, including the promotion of the participation of women in political and public life; projects aimed at studying the specific equality problems related to cultural diversity, migration and minorities; positive action in the field of equality between men and women and the mainstreaming of equality into all policies and programmes at all levels of society. In October 1998 the Committee of Ministers adopted a Recommendation to member states on gender mainstreaming; in May 2000 it approved a Recommendation on action against trafficking in human beings for the purpose of sexual exploitation; and in May 2002 it adopted a Recommendation on the protection of women from violence. Following a decision of the meeting of heads of state or government convened in Warsaw in May 2005, a Council of Europe Task Force to Combat Violence against Women, including Domestic Violence (EG-TFV) was established. In June 2006 the Committee of Ministers adopted the Blueprint of the Council of Europe Campaign to Combat Violence against Women, including Domestic Violence, which had been drafted by the EG-TGF.

MEDIA AND COMMUNICATIONS

Article 10 of the European Convention on Human Rights (freedom of expression and information) forms the basis for the Council of Europe's activities in the area of mass media. Implementation of the Council of Europe's work programme concerning the media is undertaken by the Steering Committee on the Media and New Communication Services (CDMC), which comprises senior government officials and representatives of professional organizations, meeting in plenary session twice a year. The CDMC is mandated to devise concerted European policy measures and appropriate legal instruments. Its underlying aims are to further freedom of expression and information in a pluralistic democracy, and to promote the free flow of information and ideas. The CDMC is assisted by various specialist groups and committees. Policy and legal instruments have been developed on subjects including: exclusivity rights; media concentrations and transparency of media ownership; protection of journalists in situations of conflict and tension; independence of public-service broadcasting, protection of rights holders; legal protection of encrypted television services; media and elections; protection of journalists' sources of information; the independence and functions of broadcasting regulatory authorities; and coverage of legal proceedings by the media. These policy and legal instruments (mainly in the form of non-binding recommendations addressed to member governments) are complemented by the publication of studies, analyses and seminar proceedings on topics of media law and policy. The CDMC has also prepared a number of international binding legal instruments, including the European Convention on Transfrontier Television (adopted in 1989 and ratified by 32 countries by October 2008), the European Convention on the Legal Protection of Services Based on or Consisting of Conditional Access (ratified by eight countries at October 2008), and the European Convention Relating to Questions on Copyright Law and Neighbouring Rights in the Context of Transfrontier Broadcasting by Satellite (ratified by two countries at October 2008).

In March 2005 the Council's Committee of Ministers adopted a declaration on freedom of expression and information in the media in the context of the fight against terrorism. A declaration on the independence and functions of regulatory authorities for the broadcasting sector was adopted by the Committee of Ministers in March 2008. In that month the Committee also adopted a Recommendation on the use of Internet Filters aimed at promoting a balance between freedom of expression and the protection of children against harmful material published on the internet.

SOCIAL COHESION

In June 1998 the Committee of Ministers established the European Committee for Social Cohesion (CDCS). The CDCS has the following responsibilities: to co-ordinate, guide and stimulate co-operation between member states with a view to promoting social cohesion in Europe, to develop and promote integrated, multidisciplinary responses to social issues, and to promote the social standards embodied in the European Social Charter and other Council of Europe instruments, including the European Code of Social Security. In 2002 the CDCS published the *Report on Access to Social Rights in Europe*, concerning access to employment, housing and social protection. The Committee supervises an extensive programme of work on children, families and the elderly. In March 2004 the Committee of Ministers approved a revised version of the Council's Strategy for Social Cohesion (adopted in July 2000).

The European Code of Social Security and its Protocol entered into force in 1968; by October 2008 the Code had been ratified by 20 states and the Protocol by seven states. These instruments set minimum standards for medical care and the following benefits: sickness, old-age, unemployment, employment injury, family, maternity, invalidity and survivor's benefit. A revision of these instruments, aiming to provide higher standards and greater flexibility, was completed for signature in 1990 and had been signed by 14 states at October 2008.

The European Convention on Social Security, in force since 1977, currently applies in Austria, Belgium, Italy, Luxembourg, the Netherlands, Portugal, Spain and Turkey; most of the provisions apply automatically, while others are subject to the conclusion of additional multilateral or bilateral agreements. The Convention is concerned with establishing the following four fundamental principles of international law on social security: equality of treatment, unity of applicable legislation, conservation of rights accrued or in course of acquisition, and payment of benefits abroad. In 1994 a Protocol to the Convention, providing for the enlargement of the personal scope of the Convention, was opened for signature; by October 2008 it had been ratified only by Portugal.

HEALTH

Through a series of expert committees, the Council aims to ensure constant co-operation in Europe in a variety of health-related fields, with particular emphasis on health services and patients' rights, for example: equity in access to health care, quality assurance, health services for institutionalized populations (prisoners, elderly in homes), discrimination resulting from health status and education for health. These efforts are supplemented by the training of health personnel. Recommendations adopted by the Committee of Ministers in the area of health cover blood, cancer control, disabilities, health policy development and promotion, health services, the protection of human rights and dignity of persons with mental disorder, the organization of palliative care, the role of patients, transplantation, access to health care by vulnerable groups, and the impact of new information technologies on health care.

A Partial Agreement in the Social and Public Health Field aims to protect the consumer from potential health risks connected with commonplace or domestic products, including asbestos, cosmetics, flavouring substances, pesticides, pharmaceuticals and products which have a direct or indirect impact on the human food chain, pesticides, pharmaceuticals and cosmetics; and also has provisions on the integration of people with disabilities. Two Euroepean treaties have been concluded within the framework of this Partial Agreement, the European Agreement on the Restriction of the use of Certain Detergents in Washing and Cleaning Products, and the Convention on the Elaboration of a European Pharmacopoeia (establishing legally binding standards for medicinal substances, auxiliary substances, pharmaceutical preparations, vaccines for human and veterinary use and other articles). The latter Convention entered into force in eight signatory states in May 1974 and, by October 2008 had been ratified by 37 states and the European Union. WHO and 21 European and non-European states participate as observers in the sessions of the European Pharmacopoeia Commission. In 1994 a procedure on certification of suitability to the European Pharmacopoeia monographs for manufacturers of substances for pharmaceutical use was established. A network of official control laboratories for human and veterinary medicines was established in 1995, open to all signatory countries to the Convention and observers at the Pharmacopoeia Commission. The sixth edition of the European Pharmacopoeia, in force since 1 January 2008, is updated regularly in its electronic version, and includes more than 1,800 harmonized European standards, or 'monographs', 268 general methods of analysis and 2,210 reagents.

The 1992 Recommendation on A Coherent Policy for People with Disabilities contains the policy principles for the rehabilitation and integration of people with disabilities. This model programme recommends that governments of all member states develop comprehensive and co-ordinated national disability policies taking account of prevention, diagnosis, treatment education, vocational guidance and training, employment, social integration, social protection, information and research. It has set benchmarks, both nationally and internationally. The 1995 Charter on the Vocational Assessment of People with Disabilities states that a person's vocational abilities and not disabilities should be assessed and related to specific job requirements. The 2001 Resolution on Universal Design aims to improve accessibility, recommending the inclusion of Universal Design principles in the training for vocations working on the built environment. The 2001 Resolution on New Technologies recommends formulating national strategies to ensure that people with disabilities benefit from new technologies. In April 2006 the Council of Europe Committee of Ministers

adopted a Recommendation endorsing a recently-drafted Council of Europe action plan for 2006–15, with the aim of promoting the rights and full participation of people with disabilities in society and of improving the quality of life of people with disabilities in Europe.

In the co-operation group to combat drug abuse and illicit drugs trafficking (Pompidou Group), 35 states work together, through meetings of ministers, officials and experts, to counteract drug abuse. The Group follows a multidisciplinary approach embracing, in particular, legislation, law enforcement, prevention, treatment, rehabilitation and data collection. In January 2007 the Group initiated an online register of ongoing drug research projects; a revised version of the register was launched in April 2008.

Improvement of blood transfusion safety and availability of blood and blood derivatives has been ensured through European Agreements and guidelines. Advances in this field and in organ transplantation are continuously assessed by expert committees.

In April 1997 the first international convention on biomedicine was opened for signature at a meeting of health ministers of member states, in Oviedo, Spain. The so-called Convention for the Protection of Human Rights and the Dignity of Human Beings with Respect to the Applications of Biology and Medicine incorporated provisions on scientific research, the principle of informed patient consent, organ and tissue transplants, and the prohibition of financial gain and disposal of a part of the human body. It entered into force on 1 November 1999 (see below).

POPULATION AND MIGRATION

The European Convention on the Legal Status of Migrant Workers, in force since 1983, has been ratified by Albania, France, Italy, Moldova, the Netherlands, Norway, Portugal, Spain, Sweden, Turkey and the Ukraine. The Convention is based on the principle of equality of treatment for migrant workers and the nationals of the host country as to housing, working conditions, and social security. The Convention also upholds the principle of the right to family reunion. An international consultative committee, representing the parties to the Convention, monitors the application of the Convention.

In 1996 the European Committee on Migration concluded work on a project entitled 'The Integration of Immigrants: Towards Equal Opportunities' and the results were presented at the sixth conference of European ministers responsible for migration affairs, held in Warsaw. At the conference a new project, entitled 'Tensions and Tolerance: Building better integrated communities across Europe' was initiated; it was concluded in 1999. During the period 1977–2005 an ad hoc committee of experts on the Legal Aspects of Territorial Asylum Refugees and Stateless Persons (CAHAR) assisted the Committee on Migration with examining migration issues at the pan-European level. In 2002 CAHAR prepared a Recommendation relating to the detention of asylum seekers. In May 2005 the Committee of Ministers adopted *Twenty Guidelines on Forced Return of Illegal Residents*, which had been drafted by CAHAR.

The European Committee on Migration was responsible for activities concerning Roma/Gypsies in Europe, in co-ordination with other relevant Council of Europe bodies. In December 2004 a European Roma and Travellers Forum, established in partnership with the Council of Europe, was inaugurated.

In May 2006 the Council of Europe adopted a Convention on the avoidance of statelessness in relation to State succession.

The European Population Committee, an intergovernmental committee of scientists and government officials responsible for population matters, monitors and analyses population trends throughout Europe and informs governments, research centres and the public of demographic developments and their impact on policy decisions. It compiles an annual statistical review of regional demographic developments and publishes the results of studies on population issues.

COUNCIL OF EUROPE DEVELOPMENT BANK

The Council of Europe Development Bank was established in April 1956 by the Committee of Ministers, initially as the Resettlement Fund, and later as the Council of Europe Social Development Fund, and then renamed again in November 1999. It is a multilateral development bank with a social mandate, promoting social development by granting loans for projects with a social purpose. Projects aimed at solving social problems related to the presence of refugees, displaced persons or forced migrants are a priority. In addition, the Bank finances projects in other fields that contribute directly to strengthening social cohesion in Europe: job creation and preservation in small and medium-sized enterprises; social housing; improving urban living conditions; health and education infrastructure, protection of the environment, and rural modernization; protection and rehabilitation of the historic heritage. At December 2007 the Bank had total assets of €18,509m. In 2007 the Bank approved new projects with a value of €2,414m. Its lending activities have been increasingly targeted at central and eastern European countries.

LEGAL AFFAIRS

The European Committee on Legal Co-operation develops co-operation between member states in the field of law, with the objective of harmonizing and modernizing public and private law, including administrative law and the law relating to the judiciary. The Committee is responsible for expert groups which consider issues relating to administrative law, efficiency of justice, family law, nationality, information technology and data protection.

Numerous conventions and Recommendations have been adopted, and followed up by appropriate committees or groups of experts, on matters which include: efficiency of justice, nationality, legal aid, rights of children, data protection, information technology, children born out of wedlock, animal protection, adoption, information on foreign law, and the legal status of non-governmental organizations.

In December 1999 the Convention for the Protection of Human Rights and the Dignity of Human Beings with Respect to the Applications of Biology and Medicine: Convention on Human Rights and Biomedicine entered into force, as the first internationally binding legal text to protect people against the misuse of biological and medical advances. It aims to preserve human dignity and identity, rights and freedoms, through a series of principles and rules. Additional protocols develop the Convention's general provisions by means of specialized texts. A Protocol prohibiting the medical cloning of human beings was approved by Council heads of state and government in 1998 and entered into force on 1 March 2001. A Protocol on the transplantation of human organs and tissue was opened for signature in January 2002 and entered into force in May 2006, and a Protocol concerning biomedical research opened for signature in January 2005 and entered into force in September 2007. Work on draft protocols relating to protection of the human embryo and foetus, and genetics is ongoing. A Recommendation on xenotransplantation was adopted by the Committee of Ministers in 2003.

In 2001 an Additional Protocol to the Convention for the protection of individuals with regard to automatic processing of personal data was adopted. The Protocol, which opened for signature in November, concerned supervisory authorities and transborder data flows. It entered into force in July 2004.

In 2001 the European Committee for Social Cohesion (CDCS) approved three new conventions on contact concerning children, legal aid, and 'Information Society Services'. In 2002 the CDCS approved a Recommendation on mediation on civil matters and a resolution establishing the European Commission for the Efficiency of Justice (CEPEJ). The aims of the CEPEJ are: to improve the efficiency and functioning of the justice system of member states, with a view to ensuring that everyone within their jurisdiction can enforce their legal rights effectively, increasing citizen confidence in the system; and enabling better implementation of the international legal instruments of the Council of Europe concerning efficiency and fairness of justice.

A Convention on Contact concerning Children was adopted in May 2003. It entered into force in September 2005 and by October 2008 had been ratified by five states. A new convention on the Protection of Children against Sexual Exploitation and Sexual Abuse was adopted in July 2007 and had 29 signatures by October 2008.

The Consultative Council of European Judges has prepared a framework global action plan for judges in Europe. In addition, it has contributed to the implementation of this programme by the adoption of opinions on standards concerning the independence of the judiciary and the irremovability of judges, and on the funding and management of courts.

A Committee of Legal Advisers on Public and International Law (CAHDI), comprising the legal advisers of ministers of foreign affairs of member states and of several observer states, is authorized by the Committee of Ministers to examine questions of public international law, and to exchange and, if appropriate, to co-ordinate the views of member states. The CAHDI functions as a European observatory of reservations to international treaties. Recent activities of the CAHDI include the preparation of a Recommendation on reactions to inadmissible reservations to international treaties, the publication of a report on state practice with regard to state succession and recognition, and another on expression of consent of states to be bound by a treaty.

With regard to crime, expert committees and groups operating under the authority of the European Committee on Crime Problems have prepared conventions on such matters as extradition, mutual assistance, recognition and enforcement of foreign judgments, transfer of proceedings, suppression of terrorism, transfer of prisoners, compensation payable to victims of violent crime, money-laundering, confiscation of proceeds from crime and corruption.

A Convention on Cybercrime, adopted in 2001, entered into force in July 2004 and by October 2008 had received 23 ratifications. In 2003 member states concluded an additional Protocol to the Convention relating to the criminalization of acts of a racist and xenophobic nature committed through computer systems; this entered into force in March 2006 and had been ratified by 13 countries at October 2008. A Council of Europe conference on cybercrime, convened in April 2008, with participation by around 200 experts on combating cybercrime, addressed emerging cyber-criminal threats and trends, reviewed the effectiveness of legislation on cybercrime, and adopted guidelines aimed at improving co-operation between crime investigators and internet service providers.

A Multidisciplinary Group on International Action against Terrorism, established in 2001, elaborated a protocol that updated the 1977 European Convention on the Suppression of Terrorism. In 2002 the Council's Committee of Ministers adopted a set of 'guidelines on Human Rights and the Fight against Terrorism'. In 2003 a Committee of Experts on Terrorism (CODEXTER) was inaugurated, with a mandate to oversee and co-ordinate the Council's counter-terrorism activities in the legal field. CODEXTER formulated the Council of Europe Convention for the Prevention of Terrorism, which was opened for signature in May 2005 and entered into force in June 2007. By October 2008 the Convention for the Prevention of Terrorism had been ratified by 15 member states. In 2006 the Council of Europe launched a campaign to combat trafficking, which seeks to raise awareness of the extent of trafficking in present-day Europe and to emphasize the measures that can be taken to prevent it. The campaign also promotes participation in the Convention on Action against Trafficking in Human Beings; the Convention entered into force in February 2008 and, by October of that year, had been ratified by 18 countries.

The Group of States Against Corruption (GRECO) became operational in 1999 and became a permanent body of the Council in 2002. At October 2008 it had 46 members (including the USA). A monitoring mechanism, based on mutual evaluation and peer pressure, GRECO assesses members' compliance with Council instruments for combating corruption, including the Criminal Law Convention on Corruption, which entered into force in July 2002 (and by October 2008 had been ratified by 41 states), and its Additional Protocol (which entered into force in February 2005). The evaluation procedure of GRECO is confidential but it has become practice to make reports public after their adoption. GRECO's First Evaluation Round was completed during 2001–02, and the Second Evaluation Round was conducted during 2003–06. The Third Evaluation Round, which was ongoing in 2008, was initiated in January 2007 and covered member states' compliance with, *inter alia*, requirements of the Criminal Law Convention on Corruption and its Additional Protocol, and the area of transparency of political party funding.

The Select Committee of Experts on the Evaluation of Anti-Money Laundering Measures (MONEYVAL) became operational in 1998. It is responsible for mutual evaluation of the anti-money-laundering measures in place in 28 Council of Europe states that are not members of the Financial Action Task Force (FATF). The MONEYVAL mechanism is based on FATF practices and procedures. States are evaluated against the relevant international standards in the legal, financial and law enforcement sectors. In the legal sector this includes evaluation of states' obligations under the Council of Europe Convention on Laundering, Search, Seizure and Confiscation of the Proceeds from Crime and on the Financing of Terrorism, which entered into force in May 2008. After the terrorist attacks against targets in the USA on 11 September 2001, the Committee of Ministers adopted revised terms of reference, which specifically include the evaluation of measures to combat the financing of terrorism. MONEYVAL undertook its first round of onsite visits during 1998–2000. Its second round, focusing even more closely on the effectiveness of national systems, began in 2001 and was completed in 2004. MONEYVAL's third evaluation round, covering the period 2005–10, was being conducted in accordance with a comprehensive global methodology agreed with the FATF, FATF-style regional bodies, IMF and World Bank, and was evaluating the effectiveness of enforcement measures in place to combat the financing of terrorism as well as money laundering. The evaluations of MONEYVAL are confidential, but summaries of adopted reports are made public.

A Criminological Scientific Council, composed of specialists in law, psychology, sociology and related sciences, advises the Committee and organizes criminological research conferences and colloquia. A Council for Penological Co-operation organizes regular high-level conferences of directors of prison administration and is responsible for collating statistical information on detention and community sanctions in Europe. The Council prepared the European Prison Rules in 1987 and the European Rules on Community Sanctions (alternatives to imprisonment) in 1992. A council for police matters was established in 2002.

In May 1990 the Committee of Ministers adopted a Partial Agreement to establish the European Commission for Democracy through Law, to be based in Venice, Italy. The so-called Venice Commission was enlarged in February 2002 and in mid-2008 comprised all Council of Europe member states in addition to Kyrgyzstan (which joined in 2004) Chile (joined in 2005), the Republic of Korea (2006), Algeria (2007) and Morocco (also 2007). The Commission is composed of independent legal and political experts, mainly senior academics, supreme or constitutional court judges, members of national parliaments, and senior public officers. Its main activity is constitutional assistance and it may supply opinions upon request, made through the Committee of Ministers, by the Parliamentary Assembly, the Secretary-General or any member states of the Commission. Other states and international organizations may request opinions with the consent of the Committee of Ministers. The Commission is active throughout the constitutional domain, and has worked on issues including legislation on constitutional courts and national minorities, electoral law and other legislation with implications for national democratic institutions. The creation of the Council for Democratic Elections institutionalized co-operation in the area of elections between the Venice Commission, the Parliamentary Assembly of the Council of Europe, and the Congress of Regional and Local Authorities of the Council of Europe. The Commission disseminates its work through the UniDem (University for Democracy) programme of seminars, the CODICES database, and the *Bulletin of Constitutional Case-Law*. In May 2005 Council Heads of State decided to establish a new Forum for the Future of Democracy, with the aim of strengthening democracy and citizens' participation.

The promotion of local and regional democracy and of transfrontier co-operation constitutes a major aim of the Council's intergovernmental programme of activities. The Steering Committee on Local and Regional Democracy (CDLR) serves as a forum for representatives of member states to exchange information and pursue co-operation in order to promote the decentralization of powers, in accordance with the European Charter on Local Self-Government. The CDLR's principal objective is to improve the legal, institutional and financial framework of local democracy and to encourage citizen participation in local and regional communities. In December 2001 the Committee of Ministers adopted a Recommendation on citizens' participation in public life at local level, drafted on the basis of the work conducted by the CDLR. The CDLR publishes comparative studies and national reports, and aims to identify guidelines for the effective implementation of the principles of subsidiarity and solidarity. Its work also constitutes a basis for the provision of aid to central and eastern European countries in the field of local democracy. The CDLR is responsible for the preparation and follow-up of Conferences of Ministers responsible for local and regional government.

Intergovernmental co-operation with the CDLR is supplemented by specific activities aimed at providing legislative advice, supporting reform and enhancing management capabilities and democratic participation in European member and non-member countries. These activities are specifically focused on the democratic stability of central and eastern European countries. The programmes for democratic stability in the field of local democracy draw inspiration from the European Charter of Local Self-Government, operating at three levels of government: at intergovernmental level, providing assistance in implementing reforms to reinforce local or regional government, in compliance with the Charter; at local or regional level, co-operating with local and regional authorities to build local government capacity; and at community level, co-operating directly with individual authorities to promote pilot initiatives. Working methods include: awareness-raising conferences; legislative opinion involving written opinions, expert round-tables and working groups; and seminars, workshops and training at home and abroad.

In February 2005 the 14th session of the conference of European ministers responsible for local and regional government adopted the Budapest Agenda for Delivering Good Local and Regional Governance in 2005–10, which identified challenges confronting local and regional democracy in Europe and actions to be taken in response to them. In October 2007 the 15th session of the conference adopted the Valencia Declaration, recommitting to the implementation of the Budapest Agenda and endorsing a new Council of Europe Strategy on Innovation and Good Governance at Local Level. The 15th session also determined to draft an additional protocol to the European Charter on Local Self-Government consolidating at European level the right to democratic participation, citizens' right to information, and the duties of authorities relating to these rights.

The policy of the Council of Europe on transfrontier co-operation between territorial communities or authorities is implemented through two committees. The Committee of Experts on Transfrontier Co-operation, working under the supervision of the CDLR, aims to monitor the implementation of the European Outline Convention on Transfrontier Co-operation between Territorial Communities or Authorities; to make proposals for the elimination of obstacles, in particular of a legal nature, to transfrontier and interterritorial co-operation; and to compile 'best practice' examples of transfrontier co-operation in various fields of activity. In 2002 the Committee of Ministers adopted a Recommendation on the mutual aid and assistance between central and local authorities in the event of disasters affecting frontier areas. A Committee of Advisers for the development of transfrontier co-operation in central and eastern Europe is composed of six members appointed or elected by the Secretary-General, the Committee of Ministers and the Congress of Local and Regional Authorities of Europe. Its task is to guide the promotion of transfrontier co-operation in central and eastern European countries, with a view to fostering good neighbourly relations between the frontier populations, especially in particularly sensitive regions. Its programme comprises: conferences and colloquies designed to raise awareness on the Outline Convention; meetings in border regions between representatives of local communities with a view to strengthening mutual trust; and legal assistance to, and restricted meetings with, national and local representatives responsible for preparing the legal texts for ratification and/or implementation of the Outline Convention. The priority areas outlined by the Committee of Advisers include South-East Europe, northern Europe around the Baltic Sea, the external frontiers of an enlarged European Union, and the Caucasus.

EDUCATION, CULTURE AND HERITAGE

The European Cultural Convention covers education, culture, heritage, sport and youth. Programmes on education, higher education, culture and cultural heritage are managed by four steering committees. During the second half of 2008 a new Council of Europe cultural governance observatory, CultureWatchEurope, was to become operational, mandated to monitor the follow-up to all relevant Council of Europe Conventions; to act as a forum for the exchange of information on culture, and on cultural and natural heritage; to observe ongoing relevant policies, practices, trends and emerging issues; to highlight good practice; and to analyse and advise on policy.

The education programme consists of projects on education for democratic citizenship and human rights, history teaching, intercultural dialogue, instruments and policies for plurilingualism, the education of European Roma/Gypsy children, teaching remembrance—education for the prevention of crimes against humanity, and the 'Pestalozzi' training programme for education professionals. The Council of Europe's main focus in the field of higher education is, in co-operation with the European Union, on the Bologna Process, which was launched in 1999 with the aim of establishing a European Higher Education Area by 2010, including education networks and student exchanges at all levels. In May 2007 the Council of Europe and the European Union signed a memorandum of understanding confirming mutual co-operation in the promotion of democratic citizenship and human rights education and reaffirming commitment to the Bologna Process. Other Council of Europe activities in the area of education include the partial agreement for the European Centre for Modern Languages located in Graz, Austria, the Network for School Links and Exchanges, and the European Schools Day competition, organized in co-operation with the European Union.

In December 2000 the Committee of Ministers adopted a Declaration on Cultural Diversity, formulated in consultation with other organizations (including the European Union and UNESCO), which created a framework for developing a European approach to valuing cultural diversity. A European Charter for Regional or Minority Languages entered into force in 1998, with the aim of protecting regional or minority languages, which are considered to be a threatened aspect of Europe's cultural heritage. It was intended to promote the use in private and public life of languages traditionally used within a state's territory. The Charter provides for a monitoring system enabling states, the Council of Europe and individuals to observe and follow up its implementation. The meeting of heads of state or government convened in Warsaw in May 2005 identified intercultural dialogue as a means of promoting tolerance and social cohesion; this was supported by the Faro Declaration on the Council of Europe's Strategy for Developing Intercultural Dialogue adopted by ministers of culture convened in Faro, Portugal, in October of that year. In May 2008 the Council of Europe organized, in Liverpool, United Kingdom, a conference on intercultural cities, which addressed replacing a multicultural approach to cultural diversity with an intercultural outlook, encouraging interaction between and hybridization of cultures, with a view to generating a richer common cultural environment. A new Council of Europe Intercultural Cities Programme was launched at the conference. In that month the Committee of Ministers adopted a *White Paper on Intercultural Dialogue* which stated that clear reference to the universal values of democracy, human rights, and the rule of law must underpin the use of intercultural dialogue as a means of addressing the complex issues raised by increasingly culturally diverse societies.

The Framework Convention on the Value of Cultural Heritage for Society (known as the Faro Framework Convention), which was adopted in October 2005 and had been ratified by four countries at October 2008, establishes principles underpinning the use and development of heritage in Europe in the globalization era.

The European Audiovisual Observatory, established in 1992, collates and circulates information on legal, production, marketing and statistical issues relating to the audiovisual industry in Europe, in the four sectors of film, television, video and dvd, and new media. The European Convention for the Protection of Audiovisual Heritage and its Protocol were opened for signature in November 2001; the first document entered into force in January 2008, and had been ratified by five countries at April of that year. The Eurimages support fund, in which 33 member states participate, helps to finance co-production of films. The Convention for the Protection of the Architectural Heritage and the Protection of the Archaeological Heritage provide a legal framework for European co-operation in these areas. The European Heritage Network is being developed to facilitate the work of professionals and state institutions and the dissemination of good practices in more than 30 countries of the states party to the European Cultural Convention.

YOUTH

In 1972 the Council of Europe established the European Youth Centre (EYC) in Strasbourg. A second residential centre was created in Budapest in 1995. The centres, run with and by international non-governmental youth organizations representing a wide range of interests, provide about 50 residential courses a year (study sessions, training courses, symposia). A notable feature of the EYC is its decision-making structure, by which decisions on its programme and general policy matters are taken by a Programming Committee composed of an equal number of youth organizations and government representatives. In May 2005 a European Youth Summit was convened, in Warsaw, to coincide with the summit of heads of state or government.

The European Youth Foundation (EYF) aims to provide financial assistance to European activities of non-governmental youth organizations and began operations in 1973. Since that time more than 300,000 young people have benefited directly from EYF-supported activities, including, in 2007, the participation of some 15,000 young people in around 300 projects. The Steering Committee for Youth conducts research in youth-related matters and prepares for ministerial conferences.

In 1997 the Council of Europe and the European Youth Information and Counselling Agency (EYRICA) concluded a partnership agreement on developing the training of youth information workers. In November 2007 the Council of Europe and EYRICA jointly convened a colloquy on 'The future of Youth Information in Europe'.

SPORT

The Committee for the Development of Sport, founded in November 1977, oversees sports co-operation and development on a pan-European basis, bringing together all the 49 states party to the European Cultural Convention. Its activities focus on the implementation of the European Sport Charter and Code of Sports Ethics (adopted in 1992 and revised in 2001), the role of sport in society, the provision of assistance in sports reform to new member states in central and eastern Europe, and the practice of both recreational and high level sport. A Charter on Sport for Disabled Persons was adopted in 1986. The Committee also prepares the Conferences of European Ministers responsible for Sport (usually held every four years) and has been responsible for drafting two important conventions to combat negative influences on sport. The European Convention on Spectator Violence and Misbehaviour at Sport Events (1985) provides governments with practical measures to ensure crowd security and safety, particularly at football matches. The Anti-Doping Convention (1989) has been ratified by 49 European countries (as at October 2008), and is also open to non-European states. In October 2004 the ministerial conference, convened in Budapest, Hungary, adopted principles of good governance in sport, and a resolution on European sports co-operation in 2004–08. In May 2007 the Committee of Ministers adopted the Enlarged Partial Agreement on Sport (EPAS), which aimed to develop a framework for a pan-European platform of intergovernmental sports co-operation and to set international standards.

ENVIRONMENT AND SUSTAINABLE DEVELOPMENT

In 1995 the Pan-European Biological and Landscape Diversity Strategy (PEBLDS), formulated by the Committee of Ministers, was endorsed at a ministerial conference of the UN Economic Commission for Europe, which was held in Sofia, Bulgaria. The Strategy is implemented jointly by the Council of Europe and UNEP, in close co-operation with the European Community. In particular, it provides for implementation of the Convention on Biological Diversity. It promotes the development of the Pan-European Ecological Network (PEEN), supporting the conservation of a full range of European ecosystems, habitats, species and landscapes, and physically linking core areas through the preservation (or restoration) of ecological corridors.

The Convention on the Conservation of European Wildlife and Natural Habitats (Bern Convention), which was signed in 1979 and entered into force in June 1982, gives total protection to 693 species of plants, 89 mammals, 294 birds, 43 reptiles, 21 amphibians, 115 freshwater fishes, 113 invertebrates and their habitats. The Convention established a network of protected areas known as the 'Emerald Network'. The Council awards the European Diploma for protection of sites of European significance, supervises a network of biogenetic reserves, and co-ordinates conservation action for threatened animals and plants. A European Convention on Landscape, to provide for the management and protection of the natural and cultural landscape in Europe, was adopted by the Committee of Ministers in 2000 and entered into force in July 2004.

Regional disparities constitute a major obstacle to the process of European integration. Conferences of ministers responsible for regional/spatial planning (CEMAT) are held to discuss these issues. In 2000 they adopted guiding principles for sustainable development of the European continent and, in 2001, a resolution detailing a 10-point programme for greater cohesion among the Regions of Europe. In September 2003 the 13th CEMAT, convened in Ljubljana, Slovenia, agreed on strategies to promote the sustainable spatial development of the continent, including greater public participation in decision-making, an initiative to revitalize the countryside and efforts to prevent flooding. The 14th meeting was held in Portugal, in October 2006, and the 15th was to be convened in 2009.

EXTERNAL RELATIONS

Agreements providing for co-operation and exchange of documents and observers have been concluded with the United Nations and its agencies, and with most of the European inter-governmental organizations and the Organization of American States. Relations with non-member states, other organizations and non-governmental organizations are co-ordinated by the Directorate General of Political Affairs. In 2001 the Council and European Commission signed a joint declaration on co-operation and partnership, which provided for the organization and funding of joint programmes.

Israel, Canada and Mexico are represented in the Parliamentary Assembly by observer delegations, and certain European and other non-member countries participate in or send observers to certain meetings of technical committees and specialized conferences at intergovernmental level. Full observer status with the Council was granted to the USA in 1995, to Canada and Japan in 1996 and to Mexico in 1999. The Holy See has had a similar status since 1970.

The European Centre for Global Interdependence and Solidarity (the 'North-South Centre') was established in Lisbon, Portugal, in 1990, in order to provide a framework for European co-operation in this area and to promote pluralist democracy and respect for human rights. The Centre is co-managed by parliamentarians, governments, non-governmental organizations and local and regional authorities. Its activities are divided into three programmes: public information and media relations; education and training for global interdependence; and dialogue for global partnership. The Centre organizes workshops, seminars and training courses on global interdependence and convenes international colloquies on human rights.

The partial European and Mediterranean Major Hazards Agreement (EUR-OPA), adopted in 1987, facilitates co-operation between European and non-European southern Mediterranean countries in the field of major natural and technological disasters, covering knowledge of hazards, risk prevention, risk management, post-crisis analysis and rehabilitation.

Since 1993 the Council of Europe and European Union have jointly established a co-operative structure of programmes to assist the process of democratic reform in central and eastern European countries that were formerly under communist rule. The majority of ongoing joint programmes are country-specific (for example, programmes focused on Albania (inaugurated in 1993), on Armenia, Azerbaijan and Georgia (1999), on Bosnia and Herzegovina (2003), Moldova (1997), Russia (1996), Serbia (2001), and Ukraine (1995). Sub-regional multilateral thematic programmes have also been implemented, for example on combating organised crime and corruption, and on the protection of national minorities. A scheme of Democratic Leadership Programmes for the training of political leaders has been implemented. Within the framework of the co-operation programme 21 information and documentation offices have been established in central and eastern European countries.

Finance

The budget is financed by contributions from members on a proportional scale of assessment (using population and gross domestic product as common indicators). The 2008 budget totalled €201m.

Publications

Activities Report (in English and French).

The Bulletin (newsletter of the CLRAE, quarterly).

Bulletin On Constitutional Case-Law (3–4 times a year, in English and French).

The Council of Europe: 800 million Europeans (introductory booklet).

Education Newsletter (3 a year).

The Europeans (electronic bulletin of the Parliamentary Assembly).

The Fight Against Terrorism, Council of Europe Standards (in English and French).

Human Rights and the Environment (in English, French and Italian).

Human Rights Information Bulletin (3 a year, in English and French).

The Independent (newsletter of the North-South Centre, 3 a year).

Iris (legal observations of the European audiovisual observatory, monthly).

Naturopa (2 a year, in 15 languages).

Penological Information Bulletin (annually, in English and French).

The Pompidou Group Newsletter (3 a year).

Recent Demographic Developments in Europe (annually, in English and French).

Social Cohesion Developments (3 a year).

Yearbook of Film, Television and Multimedia in Europe (in English and French).

ECONOMIC CO-OPERATION ORGANIZATION—ECO

Address: 1 Golbou Alley, Kamranieh St, POB 14155-6176, Tehran, Iran.

Telephone: (21) 22831733; **fax:** (21) 22831732; **e-mail:** registry@ecosecretariat.org; **internet:** www.ecosecretariat.org.

The Economic Co-operation Organization (ECO) was established in 1985 as the successor to the Regional Co-operation for Development, founded in 1964.

MEMBERS

Afghanistan	Kyrgyzstan	Turkey
Azerbaijan	Pakistan	Turkmenistan
Iran	Tajikistan	Uzbekistan
Kazakhstan		

The 'Turkish Republic of Northern Cyprus' has been granted special guest status.

Organization

(October 2008)

SUMMIT MEETING

The first summit meeting of heads of state and of government of member countries was held in Tehran in February 1992. Summit meetings are generally held at least once every two years. The ninth summit meeting was convened in Baku, Azerbaijan, in May 2006. The 10th summit meeting was scheduled to be held in Islamabad, Pakistan, during 2009.

COUNCIL OF MINISTERS

The Council of Ministers, comprising ministers of foreign affairs of member states, is the principal policy- and decision-making body of ECO. It meets at least once a year.

REGIONAL PLANNING COUNCIL

The Council, comprising senior planning officials or other representatives of member states, meets at least once a year. It is responsible for reviewing programmes of activity and evaluating results achieved, and for proposing future plans of action to the Council of Ministers.

COUNCIL OF PERMANENT REPRESENTATIVES

Permanent representatives or Ambassadors of member countries accredited to Iran meet regularly to formulate policy for consideration by the Council of Ministers and to promote implementation of decisions reached at ministerial or summit level.

SECRETARIAT

The Secretariat is headed by a Secretary-General, who is supported by two Deputy Secretaries-General. The following Directorates administer and co-ordinate the main areas of ECO activities: Trade and investment; Transport and communications; Energy, minerals and environment; Agriculture, industry and tourism; Project and economic research and statistics; Human resources and sustainable development; and International relations. The Secretariat services regular ministerial meetings held by regional ministers of agriculture; energy and minerals; finance and economy; industry; trade and investment; and transport and communications.

Secretary-General: KHURSHID ANWAR (Pakistan).

Activities

The Regional Co-operation for Development (RCD) was established in 1964 as a tripartite arrangement between Iran, Pakistan and Turkey, which aimed to promote economic co-operation between member states. ECO replaced the RCD in 1985, and seven additional members were admitted to the Organization in November 1992. The main areas of co-operation are transport (including the building of road and rail links, of particular importance as seven member states are landlocked), telecommunications and post, trade and investment, energy (including the interconnection of power grids in the region), minerals, environmental issues, industry, and agriculture. ECO priorities and objectives for each sector are defined in the Quetta Plan of Action and the Istanbul Declaration; an Almaty Outline Plan, which was adopted in 1993, is specifically concerned with the development of regional transport and communication infrastructure. The period 1998–2007 was designated as the ECO Decade of Transport and Communications. Meeting in October 2005, in Astana, Kazakhstan, the ECO Council of Ministers adopted a document entitled *ECO Vision 2015*, detailing basic policy guidelines for the organization's activities during 2006–15, and setting a number of targets to be achieved in the various areas of regional co-operation.

In 1990 an ECO College of Insurance was inaugurated. A joint Chamber of Commerce and Industry was established in 1993. The third ECO summit meeting, held in Islamabad, Pakistan, in March 1995, concluded formal agreements on the establishment of several other regional institutes and agencies: an ECO Trade and Development Bank, in Istanbul, Turkey (with main branches in Tehran, Iran, and Islamabad, Pakistan); a joint shipping company, airline, and an ECO Cultural Institute, all to be based in Iran; and an ECO Reinsurance Company and an ECO Science Foundation, with headquarters in Pakistan. In addition, heads of state and of government endorsed the creation of an ECO eminent persons group and signed the following two agreements in order to enhance and facilitate trade throughout the region: the Transit Trade Agreement (which entered into force in December 1997) and the Agreement on the Simplification of Visa Procedures for Businessmen of ECO Countries (which came into effect in March 1998). The sixth ECO summit meeting, held in June 2000 in Tehran, urged the completion of the necessary formalities for the creation of the planned ECO Trade and Development Bank and ECO Reinsurance Company. The ECO Cultural Institute was inaugurated in that year. The Shipping Company is now also operational. In May 2001 the Council of Ministers agreed to terminate the ECO airline project, owing to its unsustainable cost, and to replace it with a framework agreement on co-operation in the field of air transport. The ECO Trade and Development Bank, headquartered in Istanbul, was inaugurated in late 2006, and commenced operations in

2008; it was expected that branches would subsequently be opened in Iran and Pakistan. In May 2007 the draft articles of agreement for the establishment of the planned ECO Reinsurance Company were finalized.

In September 1996, at an extraordinary meeting of the ECO Council of Ministers, held in Izmir, Turkey, member countries signed a revised Treaty of Izmir, the Organization's founding charter. An extraordinary summit meeting, held in Ashgabat, Turkmenistan, in May 1997, adopted the Ashgabat Declaration, emphasizing the importance of the development of the transport and communications infrastructure and the network of transnational petroleum and gas pipelines through bilateral and regional arrangements in the ECO area. In May 1998, at the fifth summit meeting, held in Almaty, Kazakhstan, ECO heads of state and of government signed a Transit Transport Framework Agreement (TTFA) and a memorandum of understanding to help combat the cross-border trafficking of illegal goods. (The TTFA entered into force in May 2006.) The meeting also agreed to establish an ECO Educational Institute in Ankara, Turkey. In June 2000 the sixth ECO summit encouraged member states to participate in the development of information and communication technologies through the establishment of a database of regional educational and training institutions specializing in that field. ECO heads of state and government also reconfirmed their commitment to the Ashgabat Declaration. In December 2001 ECO organized its first workshop on energy conservation and efficiency in Ankara. The seventh ECO summit, held in Istanbul, Turkey, in October 2002, adopted the Istanbul Declaration, which outlined a strengthened and more proactive economic orientation for the Organization.

Convening in conference for the first time in March 2000, ECO ministers of trade signed a Framework Agreement on ECO Trade Co-operation (ECOFAT), which established a basis for the expansion of intra-regional trade. The Framework Agreement envisaged the eventual adoption of an accord providing for the gradual elimination of regional tariff and non-tariff barriers between member states. The so-called ECO Trade Agreement (ECOTA) was endorsed at the eighth ECO summit meeting, held in Dushanbe, Tajikistan, in September 2004. Heads of state and government urged member states to ratify ECOTA at the earliest opportunity, in order to achieve their vision of an ECO free trade area by 2015. The meeting also requested members to ratify and implement the Transit Transport Framework Agreement (see above), to support economic co-operation throughout the region.

ECO ministers of agriculture, convened in July 2002, in Islamabad, adopted a declaration on co-operation in the agricultural sector, which specified that member states would contribute to agricultural rehabilitation in Afghanistan, and considered instigating a mechanism for the regional exchange of agricultural and cattle products. In December 2004, meeting in Antalya, Turkey, agriculture ministers approved the Antalya Declaration on ECO Co-operation in Agriculture and adopted an ECO plan of action on drought management and mitigation. In March 2007, meeting in Tehran, ECO ministers of agriculture approved the concept of an ECO Permanent Commission for Prevention and Control of Animal Diseases and Control of Animal Origin Food-Borne Diseases (ECO-PCPCAD). In April 2007 an ECO experts' group convened to develop a work plan on biodiversity in the ECO region with the aim of promoting co-operation towards achieving a set of agreed biodiversity targets over the period 2007–15. An ECO Seminar on Ecotourism was held in Kastamonu Province, Turkey, in the following month. In September 2007 the ECO Regional Center for Risk Management of Natural Disasters was inaugurated in Mashhad, Iran; the Center was to promote co-operation in drought monitoring and early warning. An ECO International Conference on Disaster Risk Management was convened in the following month, in Islamabad, Pakistan. In February 2006 a high-level group of experts on health was formed; its first meeting, held in the following month, focused on the spread of avian influenza in the region.

A meeting of ministers of industry, convened in November 2005, approved an ECO plan of action on privatization, envisaging enhanced technical co-operation between member states, and a number of measures for increasing cross-country investments; and adopted a declaration on industrial co-operation. The first meeting of the heads of ECO member states' national statistics offices, convened in January 2008 in Tehran, adopted the ECO Framework of Co-operation in Statistics and a related plan of action. An ECO Trade Fair was staged in Pakistan, in July 2008. The Organization maintains ECO TradeNet, an internet-based repository of regional trade information.

ECO has co-operation agreements with several UN agencies and other international organizations in development-related activities. An ECO-UNODC Project on Drug Control and Co-ordination Unit commenced operations in Tehran in July 1999. In December 2007 the ECO Secretary-General welcomed, as a means of promoting regional peace and security, the inauguration of the UN Regional Centre for Preventive Diplomacy in Central Asia (UNRCCA), based in Ashgabat, Turkmenistan. In that month ECO and the Shanghai Co-operation Organization signed a memorandum of understanding on mutual co-operation in areas including trade and transportation, energy and environment, and tourism. ECO has been granted observer status at the UN, OIC and WTO.

In November 2001 the UN Secretary-General requested ECO to take an active role in efforts to restore stability in Afghanistan and to co-operate closely with his special representative in that country. In June 2002 the ECO Secretary-General participated in a tripartite ministerial conference on co-operation for development in Afghanistan that was convened under the auspices of the UN Development Programme and attended by representatives from Afghanistan, Iran and Pakistan. The ECO summit meeting in October authorized the establishment of a special fund to provide financial assistance for reconstruction activities in Afghanistan. Projects to be implemented by the fund were reviewed during the first mission of the ECO Secretariat to Afghanistan, led by the Secretary-General in June 2005.

Finance

Member states contribute to a centralized administrative budget.

Publications

ECO Annual Economic Report.
ECO Bulletin (quarterly).
ECO Environment Bulletin.

EUROPEAN BANK FOR RECONSTRUCTION AND DEVELOPMENT—EBRD

Address: One Exchange Square, 175 Bishopsgate, London, EC2A 2JN, United Kingdom.

Telephone: (20) 7338-6000; **fax:** (20) 7338-6100; **e-mail:** generalenquiries@ebrd.com; **internet:** www.ebrd.com.

The EBRD was founded in May 1990 and inaugurated in April 1991. Its object is to contribute to the progress and the economic reconstruction of the countries of central and eastern Europe which undertake to respect and put into practice the principles of multiparty democracy, pluralism, the rule of law, respect for human rights and a market economy.

MEMBERS

Countries of Operations:

Albania	Macedonia, former Yugoslav
Armenia	republic
Azerbaijan	Moldova
Belarus	Mongolia
Bosnia and Herzegovina	Montenegro
Bulgaria	Poland
Croatia	Romania
Estonia	Russia
Georgia	Serbia
Hungary	Slovakia
Kazakhstan	Slovenia
Kyrgyzstan	Tajikistan
Latvia	Turkmenistan
Lithuania	Ukraine
	Uzbekistan

Other EU members*:

Austria	Ireland
Belgium	Italy
Cyprus	Luxembourg
Czech Republic	Malta
Denmark	Netherlands
Finland	Portugal
France	Spain
Germany	Sweden
Greece	United Kingdom

EFTA members:

Iceland	Norway
Liechtenstein	Switzerland

Other countries:

Australia	Mexico
Canada	Morocco
Egypt	New Zealand
Israel	Turkey
Japan	USA
Republic of Korea	

* The European Community and the European Investment Bank are also shareholder members in their own right.

Organization

(October 2008)

BOARD OF GOVERNORS

The Board of Governors, to which each member appoints a Governor (normally the minister of finance of that country) and an alternate, is the highest authority of the EBRD. It elects the President of the Bank. The Board meets each year. The 2008 Annual Meeting was convened in Kyiv, Ukraine, in May.

BOARD OF DIRECTORS

The Board, comprising 23 directors, elected by the Board of Governors for a three-year term, is responsible for the organization and operations of the EBRD.

ADMINISTRATION

The EBRD's operations are conducted by its Banking Department, headed by the First Vice-President. Three other Vice-Presidents oversee departments of Finance; Risk Management, Human Resources and Nuclear Safety; and Administration and Environ-ment. Other offices include Internal Audit; Communications; and Offices of the President, the Secretary-General, the General Counsel, the Chief Economist and the Chief Compliance Officer. A structure of country teams, industry teams and operations support units oversee the implementation of projects. The EBRD has 32 local offices in 26 countries. At December 2007 there were 1,052 staff at the Bank's headquarters and 297 staff in the Resident Offices.

President: Thomas Mirow (Germany).

First Vice-President: Varel Freeman (USA).

Activities

In April 1996 EBRD shareholders, meeting in Sofia, Bulgaria, agreed to increase the Bank's capital from ECU 10,000m. to ECU 20,000m., to enable the Bank to continue, and to enhance, its lending programme (the ECU was replaced by the euro, with an equivalent value, from 1 January 1999). It was agreed that 22.5% of the new resources was to be paid-up, with the remainder as 'callable' shares. Contributions were to be paid over a 13-year period from April 1998. At 31 December 2007 paid-up capital amounted to €5,198m.

The Bank aims to assist the transition of the economies of central Europe, southern and eastern Europe and the Caucasus, and central Asia and Russia towards a market economy system, and to encourage private enterprise. The Agreement establishing the EBRD specifies that 60% of its lending should be for the private sector, and that its operations do not displace commercial sources of finance. The Bank helps the beneficiaries to undertake structural and sectoral reforms, including the dismantling of monopolies, decentralization, and privatization of state enterprises, to enable these countries to become fully integrated in the international economy. To this end, the Bank promotes the establishment and improvement of activities of a productive, competitive and private nature, particularly small and medium-sized enterprises (SMEs), and works to strengthen financial institutions. It mobilizes national and foreign capital, together with experienced management teams, and helps to develop an appropriate legal framework to support a market-orientated economy. The Bank provides extensive financial services, including loans, equity and guarantees, and aims to develop new forms of financing and investment in accordance with the requirements of the transition process. In 2006 the Bank formally began to implement a strategy to withdraw, by 2010, from countries where the transition to a market economy was nearing completion, i.e. those now members of the European Union (see below), and strengthen its focus on and resources to Russia, the Caucasus and central Asia. New operations in the Czech Republic were terminated at the end of 2007. Mongolia and Montenegro became new countries of operations in 2006.

In the year ending 31 December 2007 the EBRD approved 353 operations, involving funds of €5,583m., compared with €4,936m. for 301 operations in the previous year. During 2007 some 38% of all project financing committed was allocated to the financial sector, including loans to SMEs through financial intermediaries, while 34% was for the corporate sector, including agribusiness, manufacturing, property, tourism, telecommunications and new media. Some 42% of the Bank's commitments in 2007 was for 83 projects in Russia, compared with 38% in 2006. By the end of 2007 the Bank had approved 2,596 projects since it commenced operations, for which financing of €36,938m. had been approved. In addition, the Bank had mobilized resources amounting to an estimated €80,506m., bringing the total project value to €116,919m.

From 2002 EBRD, together with the World Bank, IMF and Asian Development Bank, sponsored the CIS-7 initiative which aimed to generate awareness of the difficulties of transition for seven low-income countries of the Commonwealth of Independent States (Armenia, Azerbaijan, Georgia, Kyrgyzstan, Moldova, Tajikistan, Uzbekistan), strengthen international and regional co-operation, and promote reforms to achieve economic growth. A review of the scheme was published in April 2004. In that month a new initiative was launched to increase activities in those CIS states, designated 'Early Transition Countries' (ETCs), in particular to stimulate private sector business development, market activity and financing of small-scale projects. In November the Bank established a multi-donor ETC Fund to administer donor pledges and grant financing in support of EBRD projects in those countries. In 2006 Mongolia was incorporated into the ETC grouping. In 2007 funding commitments for the ETCs amounted to some €416m. for 105 projects, compared with €290m. for 80 projects in the previous year. During that year the Bank's resident office in Tblisi, Georgia, was transformed into a regional focal point for specialized activities in the Caucasus and Moldova.

During 1999 the Bank participated in international efforts to secure economic and political stability in the Balkans, following the conflict in Kosovo. Subsequently the Bank has promoted the objectives of the Stability Pact for South-Eastern Europe by expanding its commitments in the region and by taking a lead role among international financial institutions in promoting private sector development. In July 2000 a US/EBRD SME Financing Facility was established for South East Europe and other early transition countries. In April 1999 the Bank and the European Commission launched a new EU/EBRD SME Finance Facility, to provide equity and loan financing for SMEs in countries seeking accession to the EU. The Facility was also to extend technical assistance in areas including financial regulation, competition policy and telecommunications. During 2003 an EU/EBRD Municipal Finance Facility became operational, with funds of €120m., to assist small municipalities to undertake infrastructure projects to meet EU standards. Following the accession of eight Central European and Baltic countries to the EU in May 2004 the Bank envisaged continuing to provide support in restructuring, encouraging private sector investment and the expansion of local businesses. In November 2006 a new Western Balkans Fund was established as a multi-donor facility to support economic growth and the business environment in Albania, Bosnia and Herzegovina, the former Yugoslav republic of Macedonia, Montenegro and Serbia (including Kosovo).

A Trade Facilitation Programme extends bank guarantees in order to promote trading capabilities, in particular for SMEs. An increasing number of transactions are intra-regional arrangements. By the end of 2007 115 issuing banks in the region, together with 640 confirming banks in countries world-wide, were participating in the Programme. During 2007 the Bank financed 1,056 trade transactions under the Programme, with a value of some €777m.

A high priority is given to attracting external finance for Bank-sponsored projects, in particular in countries at advanced stages of transition, from government agencies, international financial institutions, commercial banks and export credit agencies. The EBRD's Technical Co-operation Funds Programme (TCFP) aims to facilitate access to the Bank's capital resources for countries of operations by providing support for project preparation, project implementation and institutional development. Resources for technical co-operation originate from regular TCFP contributions, specific agreements and contributions to Special Funds. The Baltic Investment Programme, which is administered by Nordic countries, consists of two special funds to co-finance investment and technical assistance projects in the private sectors of Baltic states. The Funds are open to contributions from all EBRD member states. The Russia Small Business Fund (RSBF) was established in 1994 to support local SMEs through similar investment and technical co-operation activities. By the end of 2007 the Fund had disbursed more than 421,000 loans, with funding of some €3,500m. A new Western Balkans Local Enterprise Facility was established in 2006, and by the end of 2007 had donor funding of €65m. Other financing mechanisms that the EBRD uses to address the needs of the region include Regional Venture Funds, which invest equity in privatized companies, in particular in Russia, and provide relevant management assistance, and the Central European Agency Lines, which disburse lines of credit to small-scale projects through local intermediaries. A TurnAround Management (TAM) initiative provides practical assistance to senior managers of industrial enterprises to facilitate the expansion of businesses in a market economy. A Business Advisory Services scheme complements TAM by undertaking projects to improve competitiveness, strategic planning, marketing and financial management in SMEs. During 2007 more than 120 TAM and almost 950 BAS projects were initiated. A new strategy for the TAM/BAS programme for the period 2008–10 was approved in October 2007, envisaging greater focus on SME support in rural areas, in particular in Russia and Ukraine.

In 2001 the EBRD collaborated with other donor institutions and partners to initiate a Northern Dimension Environmental Partnership (NDEP) to strengthen and co-ordinate environmental projects in northern Europe. The Partnership, which became operational in November 2002, includes a 'nuclear window' to address the nuclear legacy of the Russian Northern Fleet. The Bank manages the NDEP Support Fund. At the end of 2007 donor funding to the NDEP amounted to €243m. The Bank administers a number of other funds specifically to support the promotion of nuclear safety. By the end of 2007 donor countries and the EU had pledged more than €2,000m. to funds including the Nuclear Safety Account (NSA), a multilateral programme of action established in 1993, the Chornobyl (Chernobyl) Shelter Fund (CSF), established in 1997, and International Decommissioning Support Funds (IDSFs). The funds have enabled the closure of nuclear plants for safety reasons in countries where this would otherwise have been prohibitively costly. In 1997 a CSF-financed Chornobyl Unit 4 Shelter Implementation Plan (SIP) was initiated to assist Ukraine in stabilizing the protective sarcophagus covering the damaged Chornobyl reactor. The first-stage Unit 4

shelter was completed in December 2006. A contract for construction of a new safe confinement of the destroyed unit 4 was signed in 2007.

The EBRD's founding Agreement specifies that all operations are to be undertaken in the context of promoting environmentally sound and sustainable development. It undertakes environmental audits and impact assessments in areas of particular concern, which enable the Bank to incorporate environmental action plans into any project approved for funding. An Environment Advisory Council assists with the development of policy and strategy in this area. In May 2006 the Bank launched a Sustainable Energy Initiative (SEI), which commits the Bank to doubling investments in energy efficiency and renewable energy projects to some €1,500m. within three years. By the end of 2007 €1,700m. had been already been committed under the SEI. As part of the Initiative a Multilateral Carbon Credit Fund was established, in December 2006, in co-operation with the European Investment Bank, providing a means by which countries may obtain carbon credits from emission-related projects. By the end of 2007 the Fund had resources totalling €190m.

Publications

Annual Report.
Economics of Transition (quarterly).
Law in Transition (2 a year).
Sustainability Report (annually).
Technical Co-operation—Donors Report (annually).
Transition Report (annually).
Voices of Change (annually).
Working papers, fact sheets.

Statistics

PROJECT FINANCING COMMITTED BY SECTOR
(€ million)

	2006	2007
Financial institutions		
Bank equity	321.5	120.2
Bank lending	1,078.8	1,084.7
Equity funds	199.6	400.0
Non-bank financial institutions	333.6	307.2
Small business finance	274.3	206.0
Energy		
Natural resources	11.8	212.5
Power and energy	389.8	402.2
Infrastructure		
Municipal infrastructure	307.1	317.7
Transport	529.2	617.9
Corporate sector		
Agribusiness	426.2	517.0
Manufacturing	714.7	841.9
Property and tourism	200.3	426.6
Telecommunications and new media	149.3	129.4
Total	4,936.2	5,583.3

PROJECT FINANCING COMMITTED BY COUNTRY
(in € million)

	2006	2007
Albania	48.2	45.1
Armenia	40.4	77.8
Azerbaijan	134.4	122.0
Belarus	23.7	45.8
Bosnia and Herzegovina	133.0	156.4
Bulgaria	155.0	203.0
Croatia	302.7	152.6
Czech Republic	47.0	39.8
Estonia	0.2	11.0
Georgia	114.0	192.0
Hungary	50.5	·38.7
Kazakhstan	242.0	531.6
Kyrgyzstan	18.8	11.7
Latvia	0.0	18.1
Lithuania	20.5	37.5

—*continued*	2006	2007
Macedonia, former Yugoslav republic .	35.1	26.2
Moldova	19.8	35.6
Mongolia	—	33.6
Montenegro	0.1	17.5
Poland	259.2	160.5
Romania	254.7	336.4
Russia	1,863.7	2,295.0*
Serbia	327.3	215.6
Slovakia	19.0	74.3
Slovenia	2.0	13.0

—*continued*	2006	2007
Tajikistan	19.0	26.2
Turkmenistan	0.0	2.6
Ukraine	797.0	646.8
Uzbekistan	5.3	14.7

Note: Operations may be counted as fractional numbers if multiple sub-loans are grouped under one framework agreement.
* Approximate figure.
Source: *EBRD Annual Report 2007.*

EUROPEAN UNION*

Permanent Missions to the European Union

(October 2008)

Armenia: 28 rue Montoyer, 1000 Brussels; tel. and fax (2) 348-44-01; e-mail armembel@skynet.be; internet www.armembassy.be; Ambassador Viguen Tchitetchian.

Azerbaijan: 464 ave Molière, 1050 Brussels; tel. (2) 345-26-60; fax (2) 345-91-58; e-mail office@azembassy.be; internet www.azembassy.be; Ambassador Emin Eyyubov.

Belarus: 192 ave Molière, 1050 Brussels; tel. (2) 340-02-70; fax (2) 340-02-87; e-mail embbel@skynet.be; internet www.belembassy.org/belgium/eng; Ambassador Vladimir L. Senko.

Georgia: 62 ave de Tervuren, 1040 Brussels; tel. (2) 761-11-90; fax (2) 732-85-47; e-mail info@georgia-embassy.be; internet www.belgium.mfa.gov.ge; Ambassador Konstantin Zaldastanishvili.

Kazakhstan: 30 ave Van Bever, 1180 Brussels; tel. (2) 374-95-62; fax (2) 374-50-91; e-mail kazakstan.embassy@swing.be; internet www.kazakstanembassy.be/DisplayPage.asp?PageId=30; Ambassador Konstantin V. Zhigalov.

Kyrgyzstan: 47 rue de l'Abbaye, 1050 Brussels; tel. (2) 640-18-68; fax (2) 640-01-31; e-mail kyrgyz.embassy@skynet.be; Ambassador Chinguiz Aitmatov.

Moldova: 54 rue Tenbosch, 1050 Brussels; tel. (2) 732-96-59; fax (2) 732-96-60; e-mail bruxelles@mfa.md; Ambassador Victor Gaiciuc.

Russia: 31–33 blvd du Régent, 1000 Brussels; tel. (2) 502-18-55; fax (2) 513-76-49; e-mail misrusce@coditel.net; internet www.russiaeu.mid.ru; Ambassador Vladimir A. Chizhov.

Tajikistan: 363–365 ave Louise, BP 14, 1050 Brussels; tel. (2) 640-69-33; fax (2) 649-01-95; e-mail tajemb-belgium@skynet.be; internet www.taj-emb.be; Ambassador Saimumin S. Yatimov.

Turkmenistan: 106 ave F. D. Roosevelt, 1050 Brussels; tel. (2) 648-18-74; fax (2) 648-19-06; e-mail turkmenistan@skynet.be; Ambassador Kakadjan Mommadov.

Ukraine: 99–101 ave Louis Lepoutre, 1180 Brussels; tel. (2) 340-98-60; fax (2) 340-98-79; e-mail pr_ec@mfa.gov.ua; internet www.ukraine-eu.mfa.gov.ua; Ambassador Andriy Veselovsky.

Uzbekistan: 99 ave F. D. Roosevelt, 1050 Brussels; tel. (2) 672-88-44; fax (2) 672-39-46; e-mail ambassador@uzbekistan.be; Ambassador Vladimir Norov.

European Neighbourhood Policy

In the late 1980s the extensive political changes and reforms in Eastern Europe led to a strengthening of links with the EC. In December 1989 EC heads of government agreed to establish the European Bank for Reconstruction and Development (EBRD) to promote investment in Eastern Europe, with participation by member states of the Organisation for Economic Co-operation and Development (OECD) and the Council for Mutual Economic Assistance (CMEA), which provided economic co-operation and co-ordination in the communist bloc between 1949 and 1991. The EBRD began operations in April 1991. In the same year the EC established the Technical Assistance to the Commonwealth of Independent States (TACIS) programme to assist in the development of successful

*The European Union (EU) was formally established on 1 November 1993 under the Treaty on European Union; prior to this it was known as the European Community (EC)

market economies in the CIS and to foster pluralism and democracy, by providing expertise and training to the 12 CIS countries of the former USSR, as well as to the Baltic states of Estonia, Latvia and Lithuania. The Baltic states left the programme in 1992 (being eligible, instead, for assistance under the 'Operation PHARE' programme—Poland/Hungary Aid for Restructuring of Economies). In 1993 Mongolia became eligible for TACIS assistance; from 2003, however, that country was incorporated into the EU's ALA aid programme for developing countries in Asia and Latin America.

In March 2003 the European Commission launched a European Neighbourhood Policy (ENP) with the aim of enhancing co-operation with countries adjacent to the enlarged Union. A new European Neighbourhood and Partnership Instrument (ENPI) replaced TACIS and MEDA (which was concerned with EU co-operation with Mediterranean countries) from 2007. All countries covered by the ENP (Armenia, Azerbaijan, Belarus, Georgia, Moldova, Ukraine and several Mediterranean countries) were to be eligible for support under the ENPI. Russia was not covered by the ENP, and the relationship between Russia and the EU was described as a Strategic Partnership, which was also to be funded by the ENPI. In accordance with the ENP, in December 2004 the EU agreed 'Action Plans' with Moldova and Ukraine, establishing targets for political and economic co-operation. These Plans were adopted by EU foreign ministers and the two countries concerned in February 2005. ENP Action Plans for Armenia, Azerbaijan and Georgia were developed in 2005 and published in late 2006. The EU did not enter into discussions on a Plan with Belarus, stating that it first required the country to hold free and fair elections in order to establish a democratic form of government (see below). The eventual conclusion of more ambitious relationships with partner countries achieving sufficient progress in meeting the priorities set out in the Action Plans (through the negotiation of European Neighbourhood Agreements) was envisaged.

Regional Relations

The EU has diplomatic relations with a number of countries in the region (see above). In 1992 EU heads of government decided to replace the agreement on trade and economic co-operation that had been concluded with the USSR in 1989 with new Partnership and Co-operation Agreements (PCAs), providing a framework for closer political, cultural and economic relations between the EU and the former republics of the USSR. The PCAs are preceded by preliminary Interim Agreements. An Interim Agreement with Russia on trade concessions came into effect in February 1996, giving EU exporters improved access to the Russian market for specific products, and at the same time abolishing quantitative restrictions on some Russian exports to the EU; a PCA with Russia came into effect in December 1997. In January 1998 the first meeting of the Co-operation Council for the EU-Russia PCA was held, and in July an EU-Russia Space Dialogue was established. In June 1999 the EU adopted a Common Strategy on Russia. This aimed to promote the consolidation of democracy and rule of law in the country; the integration of Russia into the common European economic and social space; and regional stability and security. At the sixth EU-Russia summit, held in October 2000, both parties agreed to initiate a regular energy dialogue, with the aim of establishing an EU-Russia Energy Partnership. However, the status of Kaliningrad, a Russian enclave situated between Poland and Lithuania, became an increasing source of contention as the EU prepared to admit those two countries. Despite opposition from Russia, the EU insisted that residents of Kaliningrad would need a visa to cross EU territory. In November 2002, at an EU-Russia summit meeting held in Brussels, a compromise agreement was reached, according to which residents of the enclave were to be issued with multiple-transit travel documentation; the new regulations took effect in July 2003. Also in November 2002, the EU granted Russian exporters market economy status, in recognition of the progress made by Russia to liberalize its economy. At a summit held in St Petersburg, Russia, in May 2003, the EU and Russia agreed to improve their co-operation by creating four 'common spaces' within the framework of the PCA. The two sides agreed to establish a common economic space; a common space for freedom, security and justice; a space for co-operation on external security; and for research, education and culture. However, relations between the EU and Russia remained strained by Russia's opposition to EU enlargement, partly owing to fears of a detrimental effect on the Russian economy, as some of its neighbouring countries (significant markets for Russian goods) were obliged to introduce EU quotas and tariffs. In February 2004 the European Commission made proposals to improve the efficacy of EU-Russia relations, given their increased dependence, the enlargement due to take place in May, and unresolved territorial conflicts in a number of countries close to the Russian and EU borders (Azerbaijan, Georgia and Moldova). In May, at a bilateral summit held in the Russian capital, Moscow, the EU agreed to support Russia's membership of the World Trade Organization (WTO), following Russia's extension in April of its PCA with the EU to the 10 accession states. The Russian President, Vladimir Putin, signed legislation ratifying the Kyoto Protocol of the UN Convention on Climate Change in November, following EU criticism of the country's failure to do so. The Kyoto Protocol entered into force in February 2005. Consultations on human rights took place between the EU and Russia for the first time in March of that year, in Luxembourg. At a summit held in Moscow in May the two sides adopted a single package of 'road maps', to facilitate the creation of the four common spaces in the medium term. A further summit, which took place in London, the United Kingdom, in October, focused on the practical implementation of the road maps. As part of the common space on freedom and justice, agreements on visa facilitation (simplifying the procedures for issuing short-stay visas) and on readmission (setting out procedures for the return of people found to be illegally resident in the territory of the other party) were reached in that month, and were signed at the EU-Russia summit held in Sochi, Russia, in May 2006. In July the Commission approved draft negotiating directives for a new EU-Russia Agreement to replace the PCA, which was to come to the end of its initial 10-year period in December 2007. The PCA remained in force pending the conclusion of a new agreement. In March 2007 the Commission published a Country Strategy Paper for EU-Russia relations in 2007–13. Associated with the paper was a National Indicative Programme for Russia for 2007–10, which envisaged that financial allocations from the EU to Russia during that period would amount to €30m. annually. Financial co-operation was intended to focus on the common spaces and the package of road maps for their creation. At an EU-Russia summit meeting held in Mafra, Portugal, in October 2007 it was agreed to establish a system to provide early warning of threats to the supply of natural gas and petroleum to the EU, following the serious disruption of supplies to EU countries from Russia, via Belarus, in previous years.

On 8 August 2008 Georgia launched a military offensive in the separatist republic of South Ossetia, prompting retaliatory intervention by Russia. A cease-fire agreement was brokered four days later, with the assistance of French President Nicolas Sarkozy, whose country held the rotating Presidency of the Council of the European Union. However, Russia's failure to withdraw its troops from Georgian territory by the end of August, and its decision to recognize the independence of the republics of South Ossetia and Abkhazia, resulted, at the beginning of September, in an agreement by EU leaders to postpone talks with Russia on the new PCA, which had been scheduled to commence later that month. Following further negotiations with Sarkozy, Russia subsequently agreed to withdraw its troops from Georgia by 10 October. Meanwhile, in early September EU ministers of foreign affairs reached agreement on the deployment of an EU Monitoring Mission (EUMM) to Georgia from 1 October. The EUMM comprised some 350 personnel from 22 countries, and had a mandate to remain in Georgia for a period of one year. An EU-Russia summit meeting was scheduled to take place in mid-November.

In February 1994 the EU Council of Ministers agreed to pursue closer economic and political relations with Ukraine, following an agreement by that country to renounce control of nuclear weapons on its territory. A PCA was signed by the two sides in June. In December EU ministers of finance approved a loan totalling ECU 85m., conditional on Ukraine's implementation of a strategy to close the Chernobyl (Chornobyl) nuclear power plant. An Interim Trade Agreement with Ukraine came into force in February 1996; this was replaced by a PCA in March 1998. In December 1999 the EU adopted a Common Strategy on Ukraine, aimed at developing a strategic partnership on the basis of the PCA. The Chernobyl plant closed in December 2000. The EU has provided funding to cover the interim period prior to the completion of two new reactors (supported

by the EBRD and the European Atomic Energy Community—Euratom) to replace the plant's generating capacity.

The EU welcomed the inauguration as President of the pro-Western candidate, Viktor Yushchenko, in January 2005, and the EU action plan for Ukraine adopted in the following month envisaged enhanced co-operation in many areas. At a summit held in the Ukrainian capital, Kyiv, in December, the EU and Ukraine signed agreements on aviation and on Ukraine's participation in the EU's 'Galileo' civil satellite navigation and positioning system and a memorandum of understanding on increased co-operation in the energy sector. Ukraine reiterated its strategic goal to be integrated fully into the EU, and the EU pledged support for Ukraine's bid to join the WTO. It was also announced at the summit that Ukraine had been granted market economy status. Meanwhile, an EU mission to monitor Ukraine's border with Moldova was deployed for an initial period of two years, at the request of both countries' Governments. It was hoped that the mission would help prevent trafficking in people, the smuggling of goods, the proliferation of weapons and customs fraud. A dispute between Russia and Ukraine over gas prices in January 2006 was of considerable concern to the EU, which relied on Russia for some 25% of its gas (with some member states entirely dependent on imports from Russia), most of which passed through Ukraine. In March 2007 negotiations began on an enhanced agreement between the EU and Ukraine, which was intended to supersede the PCA. In the same month it was announced that the EU was to increase substantially the amount of aid allocated to Ukraine for the implementation of the EU action plan. A total of €494m. was to be made available to Ukraine in 2007–10. In mid-February 2008 EU ministers of foreign affairs attended a conference on the EU's Black Sea Synergy programme, held in Kyiv, Ukraine. Following the accession to the EU of the littoral states Bulgaria and Romania, the programme aims to improve co-operation between countries bordering the Black Sea, as well as between members of the Black Sea region and the EU. In September, at an EU-Ukraine summit, held in Paris, France, the EU announced plans to sign an Association Agreement with Ukraine in 2009. However, although EU leaders welcomed Ukraine's desire to align itself with the Union, they failed to confirm that Ukraine might ultimately be invited to pursue full membership.

An Interim Agreement with Belarus was signed in March 1996. However, in February 1997 the EU suspended negotiations for the conclusion of the Interim Agreement and for a PCA in view of serious reverses to the development of democracy in that country. EU technical assistance programmes were suspended, with the exception of aid programmes and those considered directly beneficial to the democratic process. In 1999 the EU announced that the punitive measures would be withdrawn gradually upon the attainment of certain benchmarks. In 2000 the EU criticized the Government for failing to accept its recommendations on the conduct of the legislative elections held in October. In November 2002 EU member states imposed a travel ban on President Alyaksandr Lukashenka and other senior Belarusian officials, in protest against the lack of democracy and the declining human rights situation in the country; the ban was lifted in April 2003. In September 2004 the European Parliament condemned Lukashenka's attempt to gain a third term of office by scheduling a referendum to change the country's Constitution, which permitted a maximum of two terms. The EU subsequently imposed a travel ban on officials responsible for the allegedly fraudulent legislative elections and the referendum held in Belarus in October, which abolished limits on the number of terms that the President was permitted to serve. The Council, nevertheless, reiterated the EU's willingness to develop closer relations with Belarus if Lukashenka were to introduce fundamental democratic and economic reforms. In January 2005 the EU condemned the imprisonment of a former opposition presidential candidate on allegedly politically motivated charges. As part of efforts to support civil society and democratization, in September the European Commission initiated a €2m. project to increase access in Belarus to independent sources of news and information. In April 2006, following Lukashenka's re-election in the previous month, the EU extended the travel ban imposed in 2004 to include Lukashenka and 30 government ministers and other officials. In November 2006, in a communication to the Belarusian authorities, the EU detailed the benefits that Belarus could expect to gain, within the framework of the European Neighbourhood Policy, were the country to embark on a process of democratization and to show due respect for human rights and the rule of law. In mid-October 2008 EU ministers of foreign affairs agreed to soften sanctions against Belarus, which had released three high-profile political prisoners from detention in August, by suspending the travel ban on Lukashenka and other officials.

In May 1997 an Interim Agreement with Moldova entered into force; this was replaced by a PCA in July 1998. The first EU-Moldova Co-operation Council meeting was held in the same month in Brussels. Interim Agreements entered into force during 1997 with Kazakhstan (April), Georgia (September) and Armenia (December). An Interim Agreement with Azerbaijan entered into force in March

1999. A PCA with Turkmenistan was signed in May 1998 and an Interim Agreement with Uzbekistan entered into force in June. By the end of that year PCAs had been signed with all the countries of the CIS, except Tajikistan, owing to political instability in that country. All remaining Agreements had entered into force by 1 July 1999, with the exception of those negotiated with Belarus and Turkmenistan. A PCA with Tajikistan was eventually signed in October 2004.

In April 2008, following a visit to Turkmenistan by the Commissioner for External Relations and European Neighbourhood Policy, Turkmenistani President Gurbanguly Berdymuhamedov pledged to supply some 10,000m. cu m of natural gas per year to the EU from 2009 (thereby enabling EU member states to reduce their reliance on Russian gas supplies). A memorandum of mutual understanding and co-operation on energy issues was signed between the EU and Turkmenistan in May.

The EU's Northern Dimension programme covers the Baltic Sea, Arctic Sea and north-west Russia regions. It aims to address the specific challenges of these areas and to encourage co-operation with external states. The Northern Dimension programme operates within the framework of the EU-Russia PCA and the TACIS programme, as well as other agreements and financial instruments. An Action Plan for the Northern Dimension in the External and Cross-border Policies of the EU, covering the period 2000–03, was adopted in June 2000. The Plan detailed objectives in the following areas of co-operation: environmental protection; nuclear safety and nuclear waste management; energy; transport and border-crossing infrastructure; justice and internal affairs; business and investment; public health and social administration; telecommunications; and human resources development. The first conference of Northern Dimension foreign ministers was held in Helsinki, Finland, in No-vember 1999; a second foreign ministers' conference was convened in April 2001 and the third in August 2002. At a ministerial conference on the Northern Dimension held in October guidelines were adopted for a second Action Plan for the Northern Dimension in the External and Cross-border Policies of the EU, covering the period 2004–06. The second Action Plan, which was formally adopted in October 2003, set out strategic priorities and specific objectives in five priority areas: economy and infrastructure; social issues (including education, training and public health); environment, nuclear safety and natural resources; justice and home affairs; and cross-border co-operation. Under the Northern Dimension programme, priority was given to efforts to integrate Russia into a common European economic and social area through projects dealing with environmental pollution, nuclear risks and cross-border organized crime. At a Northern Dimension summit meeting held in Helsinki, Finland, in November 2006 the leaders of the EU, Iceland, Norway and Russia endorsed a new Policy Framework Document and Northern Dimension Political Declaration, replacing the three-year action plans hitherto in place with a new common regional policy. (Observer status was granted to Canada and the USA.)

Humanitarian Assistance

In 2006 the European Community Humanitarian Office (ECHO) granted €20.8m. in assistance to victims of the conflict in Chechnya; €3.0m. in support of those affected by drought in Moldova; and €2.0m. to assist vulnerable communities in the separatist republic of Abkhazia (Georgia).

ISLAMIC DEVELOPMENT BANK

Address: POB 5925, Jeddah 21432, Saudi Arabia.

Telephone: (2) 6361400; **fax:** (2) 6366871; **e-mail:** idbarchives@isdb .org; **internet:** www.isdb.org.

The Bank was established following a conference of Ministers of Finance of member countries of the Organization of the Islamic Conference (OIC), held in Jeddah in December 1973. Its aim is to encourage the economic development and social progress of member countries and of Muslim communities in non-member countries, in accordance with the principles of the Islamic *Shari'a* (sacred law). The Bank formally opened in October 1975. The Bank and its associated entities—the Islamic Research and Training Institute, the Islamic Corporation for the Development of the Private Sector, the Islamic Corporation for the Insurance of Investment and Export Credit, and the International Islamic Trade Finance Corporation—constitute the Islamic Development Bank Group.

MEMBERS

There are 56 members.

Organization

(October 2008)

BOARD OF GOVERNORS

Each member country is represented by a governor, usually its Minister of Finance, and an alternate. The Board of Governors is the supreme authority of the Bank, and meets annually. The 33rd meeting was convened in Jeddah, Saudi Arabia, in June 2008.

BOARD OF EXECUTIVE DIRECTORS

The Board consists of 14 members, seven of whom are appointed by the seven largest subscribers to the capital stock of the Bank; the remaining seven are elected by Governors representing the other subscribers. Members of the Board of Executive Directors are elected for three-year terms. The Board is responsible for the direction of the general operations of the Bank.

ADMINISTRATION

In addition to the President of the Bank, there are three Vice-Presidents, responsible for Operations, Trade and Policy, and Corporate Resources and Services.

President of the Bank and Chairman of the Board of Execut-ive Directors: Dr AHMAD MOHAMED ALI (Saudi Arabia).

Vice-President Operations: Dr AMADOU BOUBACAR CISSE (Niger).

Vice-President Trade and Policy: Dr SYED JAAFAR AZNAN (Malaysia).

Vice-President Corporate Resources and Services: Dr SYED JAAFAR AZNAN (Malaysia) (acting).

REGIONAL OFFICES

Kazakhstan: 050000 Almaty, Aiteki Bi Street 67; tel. (727) 272-70-00; fax (727) 250-13-02; e-mail ROAK@isdb.org; Dir HISHAM TALEB MAAROUF (acting).

Malaysia: Menara Bank Pembangunan Bandar Wawasan, Level 13, Jalan Sultan Ismail, 50250 Kuala Lumpur; tel. (3) 26946627; fax (3) 26946626; e-mail ROKL@isdb.org; Dir AHMAD SALEH HARIRI.

Morocco: Km 6.4, Ave Imam Malik Route des Zaers, POB 5003, Rabat; tel. (37) 757191; fax (37) 775726; Dir SIDI MOHAMED OULD TALEB.

Senegal: Dakar; Dir SAIDOU BERRY.

FINANCIAL STRUCTURE

The Bank's unit of account is the Islamic Dinar (ID), which is equivalent to the value of one Special Drawing Right (SDR) of the IMF (average value in 2007 SDR 1 = US $1.58025). In May 2006 the Bank's Board of Governors approved an increase in the authorized capital from ID 15,000m. to ID 30,000m. At January 2008 total committed subscriptions amounted to ID 13,870.01m.

SUBSCRIPTIONS

(million Islamic Dinars, as at 9 January 2008)

Afghanistan	. .	9.93	Maldives	. . .	9.23
Albania	. .	9.23	Mali	. . . .	18.19
Algeria	. .	459.22	Mauritania	. .	9.77
Azerbaijan	. .	18.19	Morocco	. . .	91.69
Bahrain	. .	25.88	Mozambique	. .	9.23
Bangladesh	. .	182.16	Niger	. . .	24.63
Benin	. . .	18.19	Nigeria	. . .	4.65
Brunei	. .	45.85	Oman	. . .	50.92
Burkina Faso	. .	24.63	Pakistan	. . .	459.22
Cameroon	. .	45.85	Palestine	. . .	19.55
Chad	. . .	9.77	Qatar	. . . .	97.73
Comoros	. .	2.50	Saudi Arabia	. .	3,685.13
Côte d'Ivoire	. .	4.65	Senegal	. . .	45.89
Djibouti	. .	4.96	Sierra Leone	. .	4.96
Egypt	. . .	1,278.67	Somalia	. . .	4.96
Gabon	. . .	54.58	Sudan	. . . .	72.77

The Gambia	9.23	Suriname	9.23
Guinea	45.85	Syria	18.49
Guinea-Bissau	4.96	Tajikistan	4.96
Indonesia	406.48	Togo	4.96
Iran	1,293.34	Tunisia	19.55
Iraq	48.24	Turkey	1,165.86
Jordan	73.50	Turkmenistan	4.96
Kazakhstan	19.29	Uganda	24.63
Kuwait	985.88	United Arab	
Kyrgyzstan	4.96	Emirates	1,045.96
Lebanon	9.77	Uzbekistan	2.50
Libya	1,478.24	Yemen	92.38
Malaysia	294.01		

Activities

The Bank adheres to the Islamic principle forbidding usury, and does not grant loans or credits for interest. Instead, its methods of project financing are: provision of interest-free loans, mainly for infrastructural projects which are expected to have a marked impact on long-term socio-economic development; provision of technical assistance (e.g. for feasibility studies); equity participation in industrial and agricultural projects; leasing operations, involving the leasing of equipment such as ships, and instalment sale financing; and profit-sharing operations. Funds not immediately needed for projects are used for foreign trade financing. Under the Import Trade Financing Operations (ITFO) scheme, funds are used for importing commodities for development purposes (i.e. raw materials and intermediate industrial goods, rather than consumer goods), with priority given to the import of goods from other member countries. In AH 1424 the Bank adopted a new group strategic framework, which identified three principal objectives: the promotion of Islamic financial industry and institutions; poverty alleviation; and the promotion of co-operation among member countries. To achieve these objectives, the Bank determined the following as priority areas of activity: human development; agricultural development and food security; infrastructure development; intra-trade among member countries; private sector development; and research and development in Islamic economics, banking and finance. In 2005 the Bank initiated a consultation process, led by a commission of eminent persons, to develop a new long-term strategy for the Bank. A document on the AH 1440 Vision was published in March 2006.

By 9 January 2008 the Bank had approved a total of ID 14,844.8m. (equivalent to some US $20,532.4m.) for project financing and technical assistance since operations began in 1976, ID 21,944.1m. ($29,799.1m.) for foreign trade financing, and ID 501.1m. ($640.8m.) for special assistance operations, excluding amounts for cancelled operations. During the Islamic year 1428 (20 January 2007 to 9 January 2008) the Bank approved a net total of ID 3,573.1m., for 327 operations.

The Bank approved 39 loans in the Islamic Year 1428, amounting to ID 239.2m. These loans supported projects concerned with the education and health sectors, infrastructural improvements, and agricultural developments. During that year the Bank's total disbursements totalled ID 2,307.5m., bringing the total cumulative disbursements since the Bank began operations to ID 26,089.2m. The Bank approved 73 technical assistance operations during that year in the form of grants and loans, amounting to ID 10.9m.

Import trade financing approved during the Islamic year 1428 amounted to ID 1,697.3m. for 67 operations. By the end of that year cumulative import trade financing amounted to ID 17,510.7m. During AH 1427 the Bank's export financing scheme was formally dissolved, although continued to fund projects pending the commencement of operations of the International Islamic Trade Finance Corporation (ITFC, see below). The Bank also finances other trade financing operations, including the Islamic Corporation for the Development of the Private Sector (ICD, see below), the Awqaf Properties Investment Fund and the Treasury Department. In addition, a Trade Co-operation and Promotion Programme supports efforts to enhance trade among OIC member countries. In June 2005 the Board of Governors approved the establishment of the ITFC as an autonomous trade promotion and financing institution within the Bank Group. The inaugural meeting of the ITFC was held in February 2007. In May 2006 the Board of Governors approved a new fund to reduce poverty and support efforts to achieve the UN Millennium Development Goals, in accordance with a proposal of the OIC. It was inaugurated, as the Islamic Solidarity Fund for Development, in May 2007; at that time 28 countries had pledged US $1,600m. to the Fund. The Fund became operational in early 2008.

In AH 1407 (1986–87) the Bank established an Islamic Bank's Portfolio for Investment and Development (IBP) in order to promote the development and diversification of Islamic financial markets and to mobilize the liquidity available to banks and financial institutions.

During AH 1427 the IBP approved eight operations amounting to ID 135.8m. During AH 1428 resources and activities of the IBP were transferred to the newly-established ITFC. The Bank's Unit Investment Fund (UIF) became operational in 1990, with the aim of mobilizing additional resources and providing a profitable channel for investments conforming to *Shari'a*. The initial issue of the UIF was US $100m., which has subsequently been increased to $325m. The Fund finances mainly private sector industrial projects in middle-income countries and also finances short-term trade operations. In October 1998 the Bank announced the establishment of a new fund to invest in infrastructure projects in member states. The Bank committed $250m. to the fund, which was to comprise $1,000m. equity capital and a $500m. Islamic financing facility. In November 2001 the Bank signed an agreement with Malaysia, Bahrain, Indonesia and Sudan for the establishment of an Islamic financial market. In April 2002 the Bank, jointly with governors of central banks and the Accounting and Auditing Organization for Islamic Financial Institutions, concluded an agreement, under the auspices of the IMF, for the establishment of an Islamic Financial Services Board. The Board, which was to be located in Kuala Lumpur, Malaysia, was intended to elaborate and harmonize standards for best practices in the regulation and supervision of the Islamic financial services industry. In August 2003 the Bank mobilized some $400m. from the international financial markets through the issue of the International Islamic Sukuk bond.

The Bank's Special Assistance Programme was initiated in AH 1400 to support the economic and social development of Muslim communities in non-member countries, in particular in the education and health sectors. It also aimed to provide emergency aid in times of natural disasters, and to assist Muslim refugees throughout the world. Operations undertaken by the Bank are financed by the Waqf Fund (formerly the Special Assistance Account). By the end of AH 1428 some US $640.8m. had been approved under the Waqf Fund Special Assistance Programme for 1,185 operations, of which 465 were in member countries and 720 were for Muslim organizations and communities in non-member countries. Other assistance activities include scholarship programmes, technical co-operation projects and the sacrificial meat utilization project (see below). In January 2005 the Bank allocated $500m. to assist the survivors of the Indian Ocean earthquake and tsunami which struck coastal areas in 14 countries in late December 2004. The Bank dispatched missions to provide emergency relief to Indonesia, the Maldives and Sri Lanka, and planned to send further teams to assess the requirements for reconstruction. The Bank approved an assistance programme amounting to $501.6m. following a massive earthquake in north-west Pakistan that occurred in October 2005. The funds aimed to support recovery, rehabilitation and reconstruction efforts. The Bank increasingly has worked to assist post-conflict member countries in rehabilitation and reconstruction. It is a member of the management committee of the Afghanistan Reconstruction Trust Fund, which was established in 2001; during 2003 the Bank approved an operation to assist Afghan refugees. In December 2003 the Bank approved a Programme for Reconstruction of Iraq, with funding of ID 365.5m. ($500m.) to be implemented over a five-year period. In October 2002 the Bank's Board of Governors, meeting in Burkina Faso, adopted the Ouagadougou Declaration on the co-operation between the Bank group and Africa, which identified priority areas for Bank activities, for example education and the private sector. The Bank pledged $2,000m. to finance implementation of the Declaration over the five years 2004–08. A new IDB Special Programme for the Development of Africa was endorsed at a summit meeting of the OIC held in March 2008.

In AH 1404 (1983–84) the Bank established a scholarship programme for Muslim communities in non-member countries to provide opportunities for students to pursue further education or other professional training. The programme also assists nine member countries on an exceptional basis. By the end of the Islamic year 1428 5,237 people had graduated and 2,640 were undertaking studies under the scheme, at a cost of ID 50m. The Merit Scholarship Programme, initiated in AH 1412 (1991–92), aims to develop scientific, technological and research capacities in member countries through advanced studies and/or research. A total of 392 scholarships had been awarded, at a cost of ID 11m., by the end of AH 1428. In AH 1419 (1998–99) a Scholarship Programme in Science and Technology for IDB Least Developed Member Countries became operational for students in 20 eligible countries. By the end of AH 1428 205 students had been selected under the programme to study in other Bank member countries, of whom 92 had graduated under the Programme.

The Bank's Programme for Technical Co-operation aims to mobilize technical capabilities among member countries and to promote the exchange of expertise, experience and skills through expert missions, training, seminars and workshops. In December 1999 the Board of Executive Directors approved two technical assistance grants to support a programme for the eradication of illiteracy in the Islamic world, and one for self-sufficiency in human vaccine production. The Bank also undertakes the distribution of meat sacrificed by

Muslim pilgrims. The Bank was the principal source of funding of the International Centre for Biosaline Agriculture, which was established in Dubai, UAE, in September 1999.

BANK GROUP ENTITIES

International Islamic Trade Finance Corporation: Jeddah, Saudia Arabia; f. 2007; commenced operations Jan. 2008; aims to promote trade and trade financing in Bank member countries, to facilitate access to public and private capital, and to promote investment opportunities; auth. cap. US $3,000m.; subs. cap. $750m.; CEO Dr WALID AL WOHAIB.

Islamic Corporation for the Development of the Private Sector (ICD): POB 54069, Jeddah 21514, Saudi Arabia; tel. (2) 6441644; fax (2) 6444427; e-mail icd@isdb.org; internet www.icd-idb .org; f. 1999; to identify opportunities in the private sector, provide financial products and services compatible with Islamic law, mobilize additional resources for the private sector in member countries, and encourage the development of Islamic financing and capital markets; the Bank's share of the capital is 50%, member countries 30% and public financial institutions of member countries 20%; p.u. cap. US $330.1m. (Jan. 2008); mems: 44 countries, the Bank, and five public financial institutions (a further seven countries have signed the Articles of Agreement and are in the process of ratification); CEO and Gen. Man. KHALID M. AL-ABOODI.

Islamic Corporation for the Insurance of Investment and Export Credit (ICIEC): POB 15722, Jeddah 21454, Saudi Arabia; tel. (2) 6445666; fax (2) 6379504; e-mail idb.iciec@isdb.org.sa; internet www.iciec.com; f. 1994; aims to promote trade and the flow of investments among member countries of the OIC through the provision of export credit and investment insurance services; auth. cap. ID 100m., subscribed cap. ID 97.24m. (Jan. 2008); mems: 35 member states and the Islamic Development Bank (which contributes 50% of its capital); Gen. Man. Dr ABDEL RAHMAN A. TAHA.

Islamic Research and Training Institute: POB 9201, Jeddah 21413, Saudi Arabia; tel. (2) 6361400; fax (2) 6378927; e-mail irti@ isdb.org; internet www.irti.org; f. 1982 to undertake research enabling economic, financial and banking activities to conform to Islamic law, and to provide training for staff involved in development activities in the Bank's member countries; the Institute also organizes seminars and workshops, and holds training courses aimed at furthering the expertise of government and financial officials in Islamic developing countries; Acting Dir BASHIR ALI KHALLAT; publs *Annual Report, Islamic Economic Studies* (2 a year), various research studies, monographs, reports.

Publication

Annual Report.

Statistics

OPERATIONS APPROVED, ISLAMIC YEAR 1428
(20 January 2007–9 January 2008)

Type of operation	Number of operations	Amount (million Islamic Dinars)
Total project financing . . .	183	1,737.8
Project financing	110	1,726.8
Technical assistance . .	73	10.9
Trade financing operations* .	82	1,818.3
Special assistance operations .	62	17.0
Total†	327	3,573.1

* Including operations by the ICD, the Islamic Bank's Portfolio, the UIF, and the Awqaf Properties Investment Fund.
† Excluding cancelled operations.

DISTRIBUTION OF PROJECT FINANCING AND TECHNICAL ASSISTANCE BY SECTOR, ISLAMIC YEAR 1428
(20 January 2007–9 January 2008)

Sector	Number of operations	Amount (million Islamic Dinars)	%
Agriculture and agro-industry	6	30.2	
Industry and mining .	7	89.6	12.9
Transport and communications . .	21	407.1	27.1
Public utilities . . .	24	463.2	29.1
Social services . . .	51	226.9	22.4
Financial services/Other .	38	155.3	0.8
Total*	147	1,372.3	100.0

* Excluding cancelled operations.

Source: *Islamic Development Bank: Annual Report 1428 H.*

NORTH ATLANTIC TREATY ORGANIZATION—NATO

Address: blvd Léopold III, 1110 Brussels, Belgium.

Telephone: (2) 707-41-11; **fax:** (2) 707-45-79; **e-mail:** natodoc@hq .nato.int; **internet:** www.nato.int.

The Atlantic Alliance was established on the basis of the 1949 North Atlantic Treaty as a defensive political and military alliance of a group of European states (then numbering 10) and the USA and Canada. The Alliance aims to provide common security for its members through co-operation and consultation in political, military and economic fields, as well as scientific, environmental, and other non-military aspects. The objectives of the Alliance are implemented by NATO. Since the collapse of the communist governments in Central and Eastern Europe, from 1989 onwards, and the dissolution, in 1991, of the Warsaw Treaty of Friendship, Co-operation and Mutual Assistance (the Warsaw Pact), which had hitherto been regarded as the Alliance's principal adversary, NATO has undertaken a fundamental transformation of its structures and policies to meet the new security challenges in Europe.

Secretary-General: JAKOB GIJSBERT (JAAP) DE HOOP SCHEFFER (Netherlands).

Regional Relations

At a summit meeting of the Conference on Security and Co-operation in Europe (CSCE, now renamed as the Organization for Security and Co-operation in Europe—OSCE) in November 1990, the member countries of NATO and the Warsaw Pact issued a Joint Declaration, stating that they were no longer adversaries and that none of their weapons would ever be used 'except in self-defence'. The two groups also signed an agreement limiting Conventional Armed Forces in Europe (CFE), whereby conventional arms would be reduced to within a common upper limit in each zone. Following the dissolution of the USSR in December 1991, the eight former Soviet republics with territory in the area of application of the CFE Treaty committed themselves to honouring its obligations in June 1992. The Treaty entered retroactively into full force from 17 July (Armenia was unable to ratify it until the end of July, and Belarus until the end of October). In March 1992, under the auspices of the CSCE, the ministers of foreign affairs of NATO and of the former Warsaw Pact countries (with Belarus, Georgia, Russia and Ukraine taking the place of the USSR) signed the 'Open Skies' treaty. Under this treaty, aerial reconnaissance missions by one country over another were to be permitted, subject to regulation. At the summit meeting of the OSCE in December 1996 the signatories of the CFE Treaty agreed to begin negotiations on a revised treaty governing conventional weapons in Europe. In July 1997 the CFE signatories concluded an agreement on Certain Basic Elements for Treaty Adaptation, which provided for substantial reductions in the maximum levels of conventional military equipment at national and territorial level, replacing the previous bloc-to-bloc structure of the Treaty. In accordance with a series of agreements, or Commitments, approved at an OSCE meeting held in Istanbul, Turkey, in November 1999, Russia was required to withdraw forces from and reduce levels of military equipment in Georgia and Moldova, a process being monitored by NATO. In April 2007 NATO ministers of foreign affairs held immediate discussions following an announcement by the Russian President that his government intended to suspend unilaterally implementation of CFE obligations. An extraordinary conference of parties to the CFE was convened in June to consider Russia's security concerns relating to the final document on adaptation of the Treaty. In July NATO expressed its concern following Russia's confirmation that it was to suspend obligations under the Treaty, with effect from mid-December. In April 2008 NATO heads of state and government urged Russia to resume its implementation of the Treaty.

An extensive review of NATO's structures was initiated in June 1990, in response to the fundamental changes taking place in Central and Eastern Europe. In November 1991 NATO heads of government, convened in Rome, Italy, recommended a radical restructuring of the organization in order to meet the demands of the new security environment, which was to include further reductions in military forces in Europe, active involvement in international peace-keeping operations, increased co-operation with other international institutions and close co-operation with its former adversaries, the USSR and the countries of Eastern Europe. The basis for NATO's new force structure was incorporated into a new Strategic Concept, which was adopted in the Rome Declaration issuing from the summit meeting. The concept provided for the maintenance of a collective defence capability, with a reduced dependence on nuclear weapons. Substantial reductions in the size and levels of readiness of NATO forces were undertaken, in order to reflect the Alliance's strictly defensive nature, and forces were reorganized within a streamlined integrated command structure. A new Strategic Concept, which confirmed NATO to be the principal generator of security in the Euro-Atlantic area, was approved at a special summit meeting, convened in Washington, DC, USA, in April 1999, to commemorate the 50th anniversary of the Alliance. A separate initiative was approved to assist member states to adapt their defence capabilities to meet changing security requirements, for example improving the means of troop deployment and equipping and protecting forces.

The enlargement of NATO, through the admission of new members from the former USSR and Eastern and Central European countries, was considered to be a progressive means of contributing to the enhanced stability and security of the Euro-Atlantic area. In December 1996 NATO ministers of foreign affairs announced that invitations to join the Alliance would be issued to some former Eastern bloc countries during 1997. The NATO Secretary-General and member governments subsequently began intensive diplomatic efforts to secure Russia's tolerance of these developments. It was agreed that no nuclear weapons or large numbers of troops would be deployed on the territory of any new member country in the former Eastern bloc. In May NATO and Russia signed the Founding Act on Mutual Relations, Co-operation and Security, which provided for enhanced Russian participation in all NATO decision-making activities, equal status in peace-keeping operations and representation at the Alliance headquarters at ambassadorial level, as part of a recognized shared political commitment to maintaining stability and security throughout the Euro-Atlantic region. A NATO-Russian Permanent Joint Council (PJC) was established under the Founding Act, and met for the first time in July; the Council provided each side the opportunity for consultation and participation in the other's security decisions, but without a right of veto. In March 1999 the Czech Republic, Hungary and Poland became members of NATO. In the following month the NATO summit meeting, held in Washington, DC, USA, initiated a new Membership Action Plan (MAP) to extend practical support to aspirant member countries and to formalize a process of reviewing applications. In March 2003 protocols of accession, amending the North Atlantic Treaty, were adopted by the then 19 NATO member states with a view to admitting Bulgaria, Estonia, Latvia, Lithuania, Romania, Slovakia and Slovenia to the organization. They acceded to the Treaty in March 2004.

In May 1997 NATO ministers of foreign affairs, meeting in Sintra, Portugal, concluded an agreement with Ukraine providing for enhanced co-operation between the two sides; the so-called Charter on a Distinctive Relationship was signed at the NATO summit meeting held in Madrid, Spain, in July. In May 1998 NATO agreed to appoint a permanent liaison officer in Ukraine to enhance co-operation between the two sides and assist Ukraine to formulate a programme of joint military exercises. The first NATO-Ukraine meeting at the level of heads of state took place in April 1999. A NATO-Ukraine Commission met for the first time in March 2000. In November 2002 a NATO-Ukraine Action Plan was adopted, which provided for a structured programme of activities. In February 2005, at a NATO-Ukraine summit meeting, NATO leaders expressed support for Ukraine's reform agenda and agreed to strengthen co-operation with the country. As a token of its commitment to strengthened co-operation, NATO announced that it would launch a project, the largest of its kind ever undertaken, to assist Ukraine in the decommissioning of old ammunition, small arms and light weapons stockpiles. In April NATO invited Ukraine to begin an 'Intensified Dialogue' on its aspirations to NATO membership and on the relevant reforms that it would be required to undertake. In the same month NATO and Ukraine effected an exchange of letters preparing the way for Ukraine to support 'Operation Active Endeavour' (see below). In June talks held between NATO ministers of defence and their Ukrainian counterpart focused on NATO's assistance to Ukraine in the reform of its defence and security sectors. In October the NATO-Ukraine Commission held its first meeting within the framework of the Intensified Dialogue. Ukraine reaffirmed its wish to join the Membership Action Plan for aspirant NATO mem-

bers. A meeting of the NATO-Ukraine Commission held at foreign ministerial level in December acknowledged Ukraine's support for NATO's operations and missions, including the UN-mandated International Security Assistance Force in Afghanistan, the Kosovo Peace Implementation Force in Kosovo and 'Operation Active Endeavour'. The meeting agreed to explore the possibility of a Ukrainian contribution to the NATO Training Mission–Iraq and to the logistical support offered by NATO to the African Union in Darfur, Sudan. A meeting of the ministers of defence of the NATO-Ukraine Commission held in June 2006 discussed Ukraine's defence policy and the ongoing transformation of the Ukrainian armed forces. In this context, ministers confirmed that the NATO-Ukraine Joint Working Group on Defence Reform should remain a key mechanism. In April 2008 NATO heads of state and government, meeting in Bucharest, Romania, approved, in principle, Ukraine's future membership of the Alliance. Georgia was also invited to apply for MAP status.

In August 2008 an extraordinary meeting of the NAC was convened to discuss an escalation of conflict in Georgia. The meeting expressed solidarity with Georgia's actions to counter attacks by separatist forces in Abkhazia and South Ossetia and deplored as disproportionate the use of force by Russia. Several days later the NAC held a special ministerial meeting to demand a peaceful, lasting solution to the conflict based on respect for Georgia's independence, sovereignty and territorial integrity. The meeting agreed that NATO would support Georgia in assessing damage to civil infrastructure, as well as in re-establishing an air traffic system and advising on cyber defence issues. Ministers also determined to establish a NATO-Georgia Commission, to strengthen co-operation and political dialogue between the two sides and to oversee Georgia's future application for NATO membership. A Framework Document to establish the Commission was signed by NATO's Secretary-General and Georgia's Prime Minister in the Georgian capital, Tbilisi, in September; the inaugural session of the Commission was convened immediately.

EURO-ATLANTIC PARTNERSHIP COUNCIL (EAPC)

The EAPC was inaugurated on 30 May 1997 as a successor to the North Atlantic Co-operation Council (NACC), which had been established in December 1991 to provide a forum for consultation on political and security matters with the countries of Central and Eastern Europe, including the former Soviet republics. The Partnership for Peace (PfP) programme, which was established in January 1994 within the framework of the NACC, was to remain an integral element of the new co-operative mechanism, incorporating practical military and defence-related co-operation activities that had originally been part of the NACC Work Plan. In June 1994 Russia, which had previously opposed the strategy as being the basis for future enlargement of NATO, signed the PfP framework document, which included a declaration envisaging an 'enhanced dialogue' between the two sides. Despite its continuing opposition to any enlargement of NATO, in May 1995 Russia agreed to sign a PfP Individual Partnership Programme, as well as a framework document for NATO-Russian dialogue and co-operation beyond the PfP. During 1994 a Partnership Co-ordination Cell (PCC), incorporating representatives of all partnership countries, became operational in Mons, Belgium. The PCC, under the authority of the North Atlantic Council (NAC), aims to co-ordinate joint military activities and planning in order to implement PfP programmes. The first joint military exercises with countries of the former Warsaw Pact were conducted in September. In December 1997 NATO ministers of foreign affairs approved the establishment of a Euro-Atlantic Disaster Response Co-ordination Centre (EADRCC), and a non-permanent Euro-Atlantic Disaster Response Unit. The EADRCC was inaugurated in June 1998. During 2000 ad hoc working groups were convened to consider EAPC involvement in global humanitarian action against mines, addressing the challenge of small arms and light weapons, and prospects for regional co-operation in South-Eastern Europe and in the Caucasus. The EAPC Action Plan for 2002–04 aimed to promote new approaches to co-operation in the combating of international terrorism. The Istanbul summit meeting in June 2004 agreed to strengthen co-operation with partner countries in the Caucasus and Central Asia. A Special Representative of the Secretary-General to the two regions was appointed in September. In October the first Individual Partnership Action Plan (IPAP) was signed with Georgia, with the aim of defining national security and defence objectives and reforms and country-specific NATO assistance. IPAPs were concluded with Azerbaijan in May 2005, Armenia in December, Kazakhstan in January 2006 and with Moldova in May. In 2008 Bosnia and Herzegovina and the former Yugoslav republic of Macedonia determined to develop IPAPs.

In September 2001 the EAPC condemned terrorist attacks against targets in the USA, perpetrated by militant Islamist fundamentalists. Meanwhile the NAC, for the first time in the history of the Organization, invoked Article 5 of the founding treaty, concerning collective self-defence, which stipulates that an armed attack against one NATO member on European or North American territory is considered as an attack against all the allies. In December NATO ministers of defence initiated a review of military capabilities and defences with a view to strengthening the Organization's ability to counter international terrorism.

In October 2001 NATO launched 'Operation Active Endeavour' to undertake surveillance and monitoring of maritime trade in the Mediterranean area and to detect and deter terrorist activity, including illegal trafficking. In March 2004 the Operation was expanded to include active participation by countries in the Euro-Atlantic Partnership Council and the Partnership for Peace programme. An Exchange of Letters between NATO and Russia, concluded in December 2004, facilitated the implementation from February 2006 of joint training activities. In September 2006 NATO authorized the participation of a Russian naval ship in the Operation. Ukraine participated in the Operation for the first time in June 2007.

NATO-RUSSIA COUNCIL

In December 2001 an agreement was concluded by NATO ministers of foreign affairs and their Russian counterpart to establish a successor body to the Permanent Joint Council (PJC), with a greater decision-making role. The NATO-Russia Council, which replaced the PJC, was inaugurated in May 2002 at a meeting of heads of state and of government. The Council was to provide a framework for consultation, consensus-building, co-operation, joint decisions and joint actions on a range of issues of common interest, with NATO member states and Russia working as equal partners. The Council was to meet at ambassadorial level each month, and at the level of ministers of foreign affairs and of defence twice a year. The following were identified as priority areas for co-operation: measures to combat terrorism, including joint assessments of specific terrorist threats; crisis management; non-proliferation of weapons of mass destruction and other arms control and confidence-building measures; consideration of theatre missile defence; search and rescue at sea; enhanced military-to-military co-operation and defence reform; and a strengthened joint approach to civil emergencies. In October a joint NATO-Russia conference, focusing on aspects of defence reform, was held at the NATO Defense College in Rome, Italy. The third NATO-Russia conference on the role of the military in combating terrorism

was convened in April 2004. In September the Council issued a joint statement condemning recent atrocities committed against civilians in North Ossetia and other parts of the Russian Federation. In December the Council approved an Action Plan on Terrorism as a framework for co-operation in evaluating and responding to threats posed by terrorism and the proliferation of weapons of mass destruction. In April 2005, at an informal meeting of the ministers of foreign affairs of the NATO-Russia Council, Russia signed the PfP Status of Forces Agreement that provides a legal framework for the movement to and from Allied countries, partner countries and Russia of military personnel and support staff. (It was ratified by the Russian Parliament in May 2007.) In June 2005 a meeting of the Council endorsed Political-Military Guidance towards Enhanced Interoperability between Russian and NATO forces, thereby facilitating the preparation of those forces for possible joint operations. In April 2006 an informal meeting of the Council's ministers of foreign affairs reviewed NATO-Russia co-operation to date and adopted recommendations identifying interoperability, an Afghanistan counter-narcotics project, a co-operative airspace initiative (CAI) and intensified political dialogue as the priority areas for future co-operation. The fifth anniversary of the Council and the 10th anniversary of the NATO-Russia Founding Act were commemorated by ambassadors of both sides, meeting in Moscow, Russia, in June 2007, and by military representatives of the Council, convened in Naples, Italy, in September. In April 2008 the NRC, meeting at the level of heads of state, determined to extend on a permanent basis the joint project on counter-narcotics training of Afghan and Central Asian personnel and to accelerate the CAI project to ensure it reaches full operational capability by the end of 2009. In August 2008 meetings of the NRC were temporarily suspended owing to Russia's military action in Georgia. The NAC determined that normal relations with Russia could not be continued until Russia demonstrated commitment to the NRC's basic principles of peace and security.

NATO Information Office in Moscow: 119049 Moscow, ul. Mytnaya 3, Russia; tel. (495) 937-36-40; fax (495) 937-38-09; e-mail office@nio-moscow.nato.int; internet www.nato.int/structur/oip/niom/niom.htm; opened Feb. 2001.

ORGANIZATION FOR SECURITY AND CO-OPERATION IN EUROPE—OSCE

Address: Wallnerstrasse 6, 1010 Vienna, Austria.
Telephone: (1) 514-36-0; **fax:** (1) 514-36-96; **e-mail:** info@osce.org; **internet:** www.osce.org.

The OSCE was established in 1972 as the Conference on Security and Co-operation in Europe (CSCE), providing a multilateral forum for dialogue and negotiation. It produced the Helsinki Final Act of 1975 on East–West relations (see below). The areas of competence of the CSCE were expanded by the Charter of Paris for a New Europe (1990), which transformed the CSCE from an ad hoc forum into an organization with permanent institutions, and the Helsinki Document 1992. In December 1994 the summit conference adopted the new name of OSCE, in order to reflect the organization's changing political role and strengthened secretariat.

PARTICIPATING STATES

Albania	Greece	Portugal
Andorra	Hungary	Romania
Armenia	Iceland	Russia
Austria	Ireland	San Marino
Azerbaijan	Italy	Serbia
Belarus	Kazakhstan	Slovakia
Belgium	Kyrgyzstan	Slovenia
Bosnia and	Latvia	Spain
Herzegovina	Liechtenstein	Sweden
Bulgaria	Lithuania	Switzerland
Canada	Luxembourg	Tajikistan
Croatia	Macedonia, former	Turkey
Cyprus	Yugoslav republic	Turkmenistan
Czech Republic	Malta	Ukraine
Denmark	Moldova	United Kingdom
Estonia	Monaco	USA
Finland	Montenegro	Uzbekistan
France	Netherlands	Vatican City (Holy
Georgia	Norway	See)
Germany	Poland	

Organization
(October 2008)

SUMMIT CONFERENCES

Heads of state or government of OSCE participating states convene periodically to set priorities and political orientation of the organization. The most recent conference was held in Istanbul, Turkey, in November 1999.

MINISTERIAL COUNCIL

The Ministerial Council (formerly the Council of Foreign Ministers) comprises ministers of foreign affairs of member states. It is the central decision-making and governing body of the OSCE and meets every year in which no summit conference is held. The 16th Ministerial Council was scheduled to take place in Helsinki, Finland, in December 2008.

PERMANENT COUNCIL

The Council, which is based in Vienna, is responsible for day-to-day operational tasks. Members of the Council, comprising the permanent representatives of member states to the OSCE, convene weekly. The Council is the regular body for political consultation and decision-making, and may be convened for emergency purposes.

FORUM FOR SECURITY CO-OPERATION (FSC)

The FSC, comprising representatives of delegations of member states, meets weekly in Vienna to negotiate and consult on measures aimed at strengthening security and stability throughout Europe. Its main objectives are negotiations on arms control, disarmament, and confidence- and security-building; regular consultations and intensive co-operation on matters related to security; and the further reduction of the risks of conflict. The FSC is also responsible for the implementation of confidence- and security-building measures (CSBMs); the preparation of seminars on military doctrine; the holding of annual implementation assessment meetings; and the provision of a forum for the discussion and clarification of information exchanged under agreed CSBMs.

CHAIRMAN-IN-OFFICE (CIO)

The CIO is vested with overall responsibility for executive action. The position is held by a minister of foreign affairs of a member state for a one-year term. The CIO is assisted by a Troika, consisting of the preceding, current and incoming chairpersons; ad hoc steering groups; or personal representatives, who are appointed by the CIO with a clear and precise mandate to assist the CIO in dealing with a crisis or conflict. In June 2008 an informal 'Quintet of Chairmanships' was inaugurated, comprising the Troika and the next two countries holding the office.

Chairman-in-Office: ALEXANDER STUBB (Finland) (2008).

SECRETARIAT

The Secretariat comprises the following principal units: the Conflict Prevention Centre, the Action against Terrorism Unit, the Anti-trafficking Assistance Unit, the Office of the Co-ordinator of OSCE Economic and Environmental Activities, External Co-operation, the Strategic Police Matters Unit, the Training Section, a Department of Human Resources, and the Department of Management and Finance, responsible for technical and administrative support activities. The OSCE maintains an office in Prague, Czech Republic, which assists with documentation and information activities.

The position of Secretary-General was established in December 1992 and the first appointment to the position was made in June 1993. The Secretary-General is appointed by the Ministerial Council for a three-year term of office. The Secretary-General is the representative of the CIO and is responsible for the management of OSCE structures and operations.

Secretary-General: MARC PERRIN DE BRICHAMBAUT (France).

Co-ordinator of OSCE Economic and Environmental Activities: BERNARD SNOY (Belgium).

Director of Conflict Prevention Centre: HERBERT SALBER (Germany).

Special Representative and Co-ordinator for Combating Trafficking in Human Beings: EVA BIAUDET (Finland).

OSCE Specialized Bodies

HIGH COMMISSIONER ON NATIONAL MINORITIES

POB 20062, 2500 EB The Hague, Netherlands; tel. (70) 3125500; fax (70) 3635910; e-mail hcnm@hcnm.org; internet www.osce.org/hcnm.

The office of High Commissioner on National Minorities was established in December 1992, with the first High Commissioner appointed in January 1993. The High Commissioner is an instrument for conflict prevention, tasked with identifying ethnic tensions that have the potential to develop into conflict, thereby endangering peace, stability or relations between OSCE participating states, and to promote their early resolution. The High Commissioner works in confidence and provides strictly confidential reports to the OSCE CIO. The High Commissioner is appointed by the Ministerial Council, on the recommendation of the Senior Council, for a three-year term.

High Commissioner: KNUT VOLLEBAEK (Norway).

OFFICE FOR DEMOCRATIC INSTITUTIONS AND HUMAN RIGHTS (ODIHR)

Aleje Ujazdowskie 19, 00-557 Warsaw, Poland; tel. (22) 520-06-00; fax (22) 520-06-05; e-mail office@odihr.pl; internet www.osce.org/odihr.

Established in July 1999, the ODIHR has responsibility for promoting human rights, democracy and the rule of law. The Office provides a framework for the exchange of information on and the promotion of democracy-building, respect for human rights and elections within OSCE states. In addition, it co-ordinates the monitoring of elections and provides expertise and training on constitutional and legal matters.

Director: JANEZ LENARČIČ (Slovenia).

OFFICE OF THE REPRESENTATIVE ON FREEDOM OF THE MEDIA

Wallnerstrasse 6, 1010 Vienna, Austria; tel. (1) 512-21-450; fax (1) 512-21-459; e-mail pm-fom@osce.org; internet www.osce.org/fom.

The office was founded in 1998 to strengthen the implementation of OSCE commitments regarding free, independent and pluralistic media.

Representative: MIKLÓS HARASZTI (Hungary).

PARLIAMENTARY ASSEMBLY

Radhusstraede 1, 1466 Copenhagen K, Denmark; tel. 33-37-80-40; fax 33-37-80-30; e-mail osce@oscepa.dk; internet www.oscepa.org.

The OSCE Parliamentary Assembly, which is composed of 320 members from 55 parliaments, was inaugurated in July 1992, and meets annually. The Assembly comprises a Standing Committee, a Bureau and three General Committees and is supported by a Secretariat in Copenhagen, Denmark.

President: JOAO SOARES (Portugal).

Secretary-General: R. SPENCER OLIVER (USA).

OSCE Related Bodies

COURT OF CONCILIATION AND ARBITRATION

Villa Rive-Belle, 266 route de Lausanne, 1292 Chambésy, Geneva, Switzerland; tel. 227580025; fax 227582510; e-mail cca.osce@bluewin.ch; internet www.osce.org/cca.

An OSCE Convention on Conciliation and Arbitration, providing for the establishment of the Court, was concluded in 1992 and entered into effect in December 1994. The first meeting of the Court was convened in May 1995. OSCE states that have ratified the Convention may submit a dispute to the Court for settlement by the Arbitral Tribunal or the Conciliation Commission.

President: ROBERT BADINTER (France).

JOINT CONSULTATIVE GROUP (JCG)

The states that are party to the Treaty on Conventional Armed Forces in Europe (CFE), which was concluded within the CSCE framework in 1990, established the Joint Consultative Group (JCG). The JCG, which meets in Vienna, addresses questions relating to compliance with the Treaty; enhancement of the effectiveness of the Treaty; technical aspects of the Treaty's implementation; and disputes arising out of its implementation. There are currently 30 states participating in the JCG.

OPEN SKIES CONSULTATIVE COMMISSION

The Commission represents all states parties to the 1992 Treaty on Open Skies, and promotes its implementation. Its regular meetings are serviced by the OSCE secretariat.

Activities

In July 1990 heads of government of the member countries of the North Atlantic Treaty Organization (NATO) proposed to increase the role of the CSCE 'to provide a forum for wider political dialogue in a more united Europe'. The Charter of Paris for a New Europe, which undertook to strengthen pluralist democracy and observance of human rights, and to settle disputes between participating states by peaceful means, was signed in November. At the summit meeting the Treaty on Conventional Armed Forces in Europe (CFE), which had been negotiated within the framework of the CSCE, was signed by the member states of NATO and of the Warsaw Pact. The Treaty limits non-nuclear air and ground armaments in the signatory countries. In April 1991 parliamentarians from the CSCE countries agreed on the creation of a pan-European parliamentary assembly. Its first session was held in Budapest, Hungary, in July 1992.

The Council of Foreign Ministers met for the first time in Berlin, Germany, in June 1991. The meeting adopted a mechanism for consultation and co-operation in the case of emergency situations, to be implemented by the Council of Senior Officials (CSO; subsequently renamed the Senior Council, which was dissolved in 2006, with all functions transferred to the Permanent Council). A separate mechanism regarding the prevention of the outbreak of conflict was also adopted, whereby a country can demand an explanation of 'unusual military activity' in a neighbouring country. These mechanisms were utilized in July in relation to the armed conflict in Yugoslavia between the Republic of Croatia and the Yugoslav Government. In mid-August a meeting of the CSO resolved to reinforce considerably the CSCE's mission in Yugoslavia and in September the CSO agreed to impose an embargo on the export of armaments to Yugoslavia. In October the CSO resolved to establish an observer mission to monitor the observance of human rights in Yugoslavia.

In January 1992 the Council of Foreign Ministers agreed that the Conference's rule of decision-making by consensus was to be altered to allow the CSO to take appropriate action against a participating state 'in cases of clear and gross violation of CSCE commitments'. This development was precipitated by the conflict in Yugoslavia, where the Yugoslav Government was held responsible by the majority of CSCE states for the continuation of hostilities and was suspended from the grouping. It was also agreed at the meeting that the CSCE should undertake fact-finding and conciliation missions to areas of tension, with the first such mission to be sent to Nagornyi Karabakh, the largely Armenian-populated enclave in Azerbaijan.

In March 1992 CSCE participating states reached agreement on a number of confidence-building measures, including commitments to exchange technical data on new weapons systems; to report activation of military units; and to prohibit military activity involving very large numbers of troops or tanks. Later in that month at a meeting of the Council of Foreign Ministers, which opened the Helsinki Follow-up Conference, the members of NATO and the former members of the Warsaw Pact (with Russia, Belarus, Ukraine and Georgia taking the place of the USSR) signed the Open Skies Treaty. Under the treaty, aerial reconnaissance missions by one country over another were permitted, subject to regulation. An Open Skies Consultative Commission was subsequently established (see above).

The summit meeting of heads of state and government that took place in Helsinki, Finland, in July 1992, adopted the Helsinki Document, in which participating states defined the terms of future CSCE peace-keeping activities. Conforming broadly to UN practice, peacekeeping operations would be undertaken only with the full consent of the parties involved in any conflict and only if an effective cease-fire were in place. The CSCE may request the use of the military resources of NATO, the CIS, the EU, Western European Union (WEU) or other international bodies. The Helsinki Document declared the CSCE a 'regional arrangement' in the sense of Chapter VIII of the UN's Charter, which states that such a regional grouping should attempt to resolve a conflict in the region before referring it to the Security Council. In 1993 the First Implementation Meeting on Human Dimension Issues (the CSCE term used with regard to issues concerning human rights and welfare) took place. The Meeting, for which the ODIHR serves as a secretariat, provides a now annual forum for the exchange of news regarding OSCE commitments in the fields of human rights and democracy. Also in 1993 the first annual Economic Forum was convened to focus on the transition to and development of free-market economies as an essential aspect of democracy-building. It was renamed the Economic and Environment Forum in 2007 to incorporate consideration of environmental security matters. The 2008 Forum was convened in Prague, Czech Republic, in May.

In December 1993 a Permanent Committee (later renamed the Permanent Council) was established in Vienna, providing for greater political consultation and dialogue through its weekly meetings. In December 1994 the summit conference redesignated the CSCE as the Organization for Security and Co-operation in Europe (OSCE) and endorsed the role of the organization as the primary instrument for early warning, conflict prevention and crisis management in the region. The conference adopted a 'Code of Conduct on Politico-Military Aspects of Security', which set out principles to guide the role of the armed forces in democratic societies. The summit conference that was held in Lisbon, Portugal, in December 1996 agreed to adapt the CFE Treaty, in order to further arms-reduction negotiations on a national and territorial basis. The conference also adopted the 'Lisbon Declaration on a Common and Comprehensive Security Model for Europe for the 21st Century', committing all parties to pursuing measures to ensure regional security. A Security Model Committee was established and began to meet regularly during 1997 to consider aspects of the Declaration, including the identification of risks and challenges to future European security; enhancing means of joint co-operative action within the OSCE framework in the event of non-compliance with OSCE commitments by participating states; considering other new arrangements within the OSCE framework that could reinforce security and stability in Europe; and defining a basis of co-operation between the OSCE and other relevant organizations to co-ordinate security enforcement. In November 1997 the Office of the Representative on Freedom of the Media was established in Vienna, to support the OSCE's activities in this field. In the same month a new position of Co-ordinator of OSCE Economic and Environmental Activities was created.

In November 1999 OSCE heads of state and of government, convened in Istanbul, Turkey, signed a new Charter for European Security, which aimed to formalize existing norms regarding the observance of human rights and to strengthen co-operation with other organizations and institutions concerned with international security. The Charter focused on measures to improve the operational capabilities of the OSCE in early warning, conflict prevention, crisis management and post-conflict rehabilitation. Accordingly, Rapid Expert Assistance and Co-operation (REACT) teams were to be established to enable the organization to respond rapidly to requests from participating states for assistance in crisis situations. The REACT programme became operational in April 2001. The 1999 summit meeting also adopted a Platform for Co-operative Security as a framework for co-operation with other organizations and institutions concerned with maintaining security in the OSCE area. At the Istanbul meeting a revised CFE Treaty was signed, providing for a stricter system of limitations and increased transparency, which was to be open to other OSCE states not currently signatories. The US and EU governments determined to delay ratification of the Agree-

ment of the Adaptation of the Treaty until Russian troop levels in the Caucasus had been reduced.

In April 2000 the OSCE High Commissioner on National Minorities issued a report reviewing the problems confronting Roma and Sinti populations in OSCE member states. In April 2001 the ODIHR launched a programme of assistance for the Roma communities of south-eastern Europe. The OSCE and the then UN Office for Drug Control and Crime Prevention (ODCCP) jointly organized a conference in October 2000, supported by the Governments of Kazakhstan, Kyrgyzstan, Tajikistan, Turkmenistan and Uzbekistan and attended by representatives of 67 states and 44 international organizations, which aimed to promote co-operation, democratization, security and stability in Central Asia and to address the threat of drugs-trafficking, organized crime and terrorism in the sub-region. In November an OSCE Document on Small Arms and Light Weapons was adopted, aimed at curtailing the spread of armaments in member states. A workshop on implementation of the Document was held in February 2002. In mid-November 2000 the Office of the Representative on Freedom of the Media organized a conference, staged in Dushanbe, Tajikistan, of journalists from Kazakhstan, Kyrgyzstan, Tajikistan and Uzbekistan. In February 2001 the ODIHR established an Anti-Trafficking Project Fund to help to finance its efforts to combat trafficking in human beings. In July the OSCE Parliamentary Assembly adopted a resolution concerned with strengthening transparency and accountability within the organization.

In September 2001 the Secretary-General condemned terrorist attacks perpetrated against targets in the USA, allegedly by militant Islamist fundamentalists. In early October OSCE member states unanimously adopted a statement in support of the developing US-led global coalition against international terrorism. In December the Ministerial Council, meeting in Romania, approved the 'Bucharest Plan of Action' outlining the organization's contribution to countering terrorism. An Action against Terrorism Unit was established within the secretariat to co-ordinate and help to implement the counter-terrorism initiatives. A Personal Representative for Terrorism was appointed by the CIO in January 2002. Also in December 2001 the OSCE sponsored, with the ODCCP, an International Conference on Security and Stability in Central Asia, held in Bishkek, Kyrgyzstan. The meeting, which was attended by representatives of more than 60 countries and organizations, was concerned with strengthening efforts to counter terrorism and providing effective support to the Central Asian states. In October 2002 the ODIHR and the Government of Azerbaijan organized an international conference on religious freedom and combating terrorism. At a Ministerial Council meeting held in Porto, Portugal, in December, the OSCE issued a Charter on Preventing Terrorism, which condemned terrorism 'in all its forms and manifestations' and called upon member states to work together to counter, investigate and prosecute terrorist acts. The charter also acknowledged the links between terrorism, organized crime and trafficking in human beings. At the same time, a political declaration entitled 'Responding to Change' was adopted, in which member states pledged their commitment to mutual co-operation in combating threats to security. The OSCE's first Annual Security Review Conference was held in Vienna, in July 2003. The meeting elaborated a range of practical options for addressing the new threats and challenges, including the introduction of common security features on travel documentation, stricter controls on manual portable air defence systems and the improvement of border security and policing methods. Security issues were also the subject of the Rotterdam Declaration, adopted by some 300 members of the Parliamentary Assembly in July, which stated that it was imperative for the OSCE to maintain a strong field presence and for field missions to be provided with sufficient funding and highly trained staff. It also recommended that the OSCE assume a role in unarmed peace-keeping operations.

During July 2003 the first OSCE conference on the effects of globalization was convened in Vienna, attended by some 200 representatives from international organizations. Participants called for the advancement of good governance in the public and private sectors, the development of democratic institutions and the creation of conditions that would enable populations to benefit from the global economy. At a meeting of the Ministerial Council, convened in Maastricht, Netherlands, in December, member states endorsed a document that aimed to address risks to regional security and stability arising from stockpiles of conventional ammunition through, inter alia, detailing practical steps for their destruction. In December 2004 the Ministerial Council, held in Sofia, Bulgaria, condemned terrorist attacks that had been committed during the year, including in Madrid, Spain, in March, and in Beslan, Russia, in September. The meeting issued a statement expressing determination to pursue all measures to prevent and combat international terrorism, while continuing to protect and uphold human rights. In order to consider OSCE's capacity to address new security challenges, and to provide a new strategic vision for the organization, the Council resolved to establish a Panel of Eminent Persons on Strengthening the Effectiveness of the OSCE. The Panel presented its report, comprising some 70 recommendations, to the Permanent Council in June 2005.

In July 2003 the Permanent Council adopted a new Action Plan to Combat Trafficking in Human Beings. The Plan was endorsed by the Ministerial Council, held in Maastricht, Netherlands, in December. The Council approved the appointment of a Special Representative on Combating Trafficking in Human Beings, mandated to raise awareness of the issues and to ensure member governments comply with international procedures and conventions, and the establishment of a special unit within the secretariat. In July 2004 the Special Representative organized an international conference to consider issues relating to human trafficking, including human rights, labour, migration, organized crime, and minors. Participants agreed to establish an Alliance against Trafficking in Persons, which aimed to consolidate co-operation among international and non-governmental organizations.

OSCE provides technical assistance to the Southeast European Co-operative Initiative.

OSCE MISSIONS AND FIELD ACTIVITIES

In 2008 there were OSCE missions in Bosnia and Herzegovina, Georgia, Kosovo, the former Yugoslav republic of Macedonia, Moldova, Montenegro and Serbia. The OSCE was also undertaking field activities in Albania, Armenia, Azerbaijan, Belarus, Croatia, Kazakhstan, Kyrgyzstan, Tajikistan, Turkmenistan and Uzbekistan. The OSCE has institutionalized structures to assist in the implementation of certain bilateral agreements. In 2008 there was also an OSCE representative to the Russian-Latvian Joint Commission on Military Pensioners. During 1994–2006 the OSCE sent a representative to the Estonian Government Commission on Military Pensioners (terminated in September 2006).

In January 1995 Russia agreed to an OSCE proposal to send a fact-finding mission to assist in the conflict between the Russian authorities and an independence movement in the Chechen Republic of Ichkeriya (Chechnya). The mission criticized the Russian army for using excessive force against Chechen rebels and civilians; reported that violations of human rights had been perpetrated by both sides in the conflict; and urged Russia to enforce a cease-fire to allow the delivery of humanitarian supplies by international aid agencies to the population of the city. An OSCE Assistance Group to Chechnya mediated between the two sides, and, in July, brokered a cease-fire agreement between the Russian military authorities in Chechnya and the Chechen rebels. A further peace accord was signed, under the auspices of the OSCE, in May 1996, but the truce was broken in July. A more conclusive cease-fire agreement was signed by the two parties to the conflict in August. In January 1997 the OSCE assisted in the preparation and monitoring of general elections conducted in Chechnya. The Assistance Group remained in the territory to help with post-conflict rehabilitation, including the promotion of democratic institutions and respect for human rights. In December 1998, however, the Assistance Group relocated from its headquarters in Groznyi (also known as Dzokhar from March of that year) to Moscow, owing to security concerns. It continued to co-ordinate the delivery of humanitarian aid and implementation of other assistance projects. In September 1999, in response to resurgent separatist activity, Russia launched a military offensive against Chechnya. In early November an OSCE mission arrived in the neighbouring Republic of Ingushetiya to assess the condition and needs of the estimated 200,000 refugees who had fled the hostilities; however, the officials were prevented by the Russian authorities from travelling into Chechnya. The issue dominated the OSCE summit meeting held in İstanbul, later in that month. The meeting insisted upon a political solution to the conflict and called for an immediate cease-fire. An agreement was reached with the Russian President to allow the CIO to visit the region, and on an OSCE role in initiating political dialogue. In February 2000 the CIO welcomed the Russian Government's appointment of a Presidential Representative for Human Rights in Chechnya. In June 2001 the Assistance Group to Chechnya resumed operations inside the territory from a new office in Znamenskoye. An OSCE/ODIHR delegation visited Chechnya during that month to evaluate the prevailing humanitarian and human rights situation. In December the mandate of the OSCE in Chechnya was extended for one year; the mission was withdrawn on 31 December 2002, owing to failure by the OSCE and Russia to agree on a further extension of the mandate.

In August 1995 the CIO appointed a Personal Representative concerned with the conflict between Armenia and Azerbaijan in the Nagornyi Karabakh region. The OSCE provided a framework for discussions between the two countries through its 11-nation Minsk Group. In October 1997 Armenia and Azerbaijan reached agreement on OSCE proposals for a political settlement; however, the concessions granted by the Armenian President, Levon Ter-Petrossian, which included the withdrawal of troops from certain strategic areas of Nagornyi Karabakh, precipitated his resignation in February 1998. The proposals were rejected by his successor, Robert Kocharian. Nevertheless, meetings of the Minsk Group continued in 1998 and

both countries expressed their willingness to recommence negotiations. The then CIO, Bronisław Geremek, met with the leaders of both countries in November and persuaded them to exchange prisoners of war. In 2005/06 the Minsk Group undertook intensive negotiations to formulate a set of basic principles for a peaceful settlement of the conflict, including proposals for the redeployment of Armenian troops, demilitarization of formally occupied territories and a popular referendum to determine the final legal status of the region. In spite of continued diplomatic efforts, in July 2007 the Co-Chair of the Minsk Group (the ministers of foreign affairs of France, Russia and the USA) expressed concern at the lack of agreement on the basic principles. In November the Co-Chair presented a Document of Basic Principles for the Peaceful Settlement of the Nagornyi Karabakh Conflict to be considered by both sides. In April 2008 the Co-Chair, with the CIO Personal Representative, met with the heads of state of Armenia and Azerbaijan, and secured agreement by all sides to continue negotiations based on the current proposals.

In July 1999 the OSCE Permanent Council approved the establishment of an Office in Yerevan (Armenia), which began operations in February 2000. The Office works independently of the Minsk Group to promote OSCE principles within the country in order to support political and economic stability. It aims to contribute to the development of democratic institutions and to the strengthening of civil society. An Office in Baku (Azerbaijan) opened in July 2000 with a mandate to undertake activities in democratization, human rights, economy and the environment, and media. In November 2001 the Office in Yerevan presented a report on trafficking in human beings in Armenia, which had been compiled as a joint effort by the OSCE, IOM and UNICEF. In March 2002 the CIO visited the region to discuss prospects for peace, and the OSCE's role in the process. In that year a programme on military and security issues was initiated in Armenia which was to enhance the OSCE's role in police-related activities in conflict prevention, crisis management and post-conflict rehabilitation. In July 2003 the Armenian police service signed a Memorandum of Understanding with the OSCE, launching a major police assistance programme. The first phase of the programme, the renovation of a police training centre, was initiated in March 2005; the centre opened, in Yerevan, in March 2007. In 2007–08 the Office in Yerevan supported the establishment of four anti-corruption centres, located across the country. In March 2008 the CIO sent a Special Envoy to help to restore political stability following a disputed presidential election, held in the previous month which had led to a state of emergency being declared. In October the Office signed agreements with a parliamentary committee and with the country's Ombudsman to promote effective and democratic monitoring of the country's security forces. In February 2005 the OSCE and Azerbaijani authorities agreed to increase co-operation in judicial and legal reform, after consideration of a report on trial monitoring compiled by the Office in Baku and ODIHR in 2003 and 2004. Other activities undertaken by the Office in 2006 and 2007 included assisting the establishment of public environmental information centres and supporting the development of small and medium-sized enterprises. In February 2007 a national voter register was inaugurated, having been established with the support of the Office. A public anti-corruption centre was opened in the capital, in April, and two regional centres were established in Martuni and Stepanavan in May. In that month an OSCE/ODIHR election observation mission noted considerable progress in democratic processes during the recently-conducted legislative elections. During 2008 the Office in Baku worked to secure democratic principles in the preparation of a presidential election, held in October, including initiatives to encourage the freedom of assembly, media impartiality, and non-interference by executive agencies in the work of election commissions.

The OSCE Mission to Georgia was established in 1992 to work towards a political settlement between disputing factions within the country. Since 1994 the Mission has contributed to efforts to define the political status of South Ossetia and has supported UN peacekeeping and human rights activities in Abkhazia. In 1997 the Mission established a field office in Tskhinvali (South Ossetia). In December 1999 the Permanent Council, at the request of the Government of Georgia expanded the mandate of the existing OSCE Mission to Georgia to include monitoring that country's border with the Chechen Republic of Ichkeriya (Chechnya). The first permanent observation post opened in February 2000 and the monitoring team was fully deployed by July. In December 2001 the Permanent Council approved an expansion in the border monitoring mission to cover the border between Georgia and Ingushetia. A further expansion, to include monitoring Georgia's border with Dagestan, was effected from January 2003. A special envoy of the OSCE Chairman visited Georgia in July 2004 following a deterioration in the security situation. In November the Mission assisted the Georgian Government to develop an Action Plan to combat trafficking in human beings. In the same month the Mission helped to organize a national workshop on combating money-laundering and suppressing the financing of terrorism. In April 2005 the OSCE Permanent Council established a Training Assistance Programme for some 800 Georgian border guards. In June 2006 OSCE participating states pledged more than €10m. in support of projects for social and economic rehabilitation in the zone of the Georgian–Ossetian conflict. The donors' conference was the first of its kind to be organized by the OSCE. During 2007 the Mission continued to support activities concerned with police reform, human rights monitoring and education, munitions disposal, border control and management, counter-trafficking, and strengthening local democracy. OSCE observers participated in an international election observation mission to monitor parliamentary elections held in May 2008. In July the Mission signed a memorandum of understanding with the Georgian Ministry of Defence to implement a three-year plan to strengthen local capacity for the dismantling and disposal of munitions. In the same month the Mission organized a training course for officials on the protection of human rights and fundamental freedoms. At that time the OSCE expressed concern at escalating tensions between the Georgian and Ossetian authorities. In August intensive fighting broke out when Georgian forces entered the territory and attempted to seize control of Tskhinvali. The resulting counter-attack by Ossetian troops, supported by additional Russian land and air forces, contributed to extensive civilian casualties, population displacement and damage to the region's infrastructure. The OSCE participated in diplomatic efforts to secure a cease-fire and convened a special meeting of the Permanent Council to discuss the organization's contribution to stabilizing the post-conflict situation. Members agreed to expand the Mission to Georgia by 100 military monitoring officers, of whom 20 were to be deployed immediately to the areas adjacent to South Ossetia. In late August the CIO and the Head of the Mission to Georgia visited the worst affected areas. In the following month the Head of Mission met the Russian Minister for Foreign Affairs to discuss issues relating to the freedom of movement of the Mission's monitors and the need for the effective delivery of humanitarian aid. In October the OSCE met with senior representatives of the UN and EU, in Geneva, Switzerland, to consider the stability and security of the region and the situation of displaced persons.

In September 1997 the Permanent Council determined to establish an OSCE Advisory and Monitoring Group in Belarus to assist with the process of democratization; the Group commenced operations in February 1998. It was subsequently active in strengthening civil society, organizing training seminars and workshops in electoral practices, monitoring the human rights situation, including the registration of political parties and the development of an independent media, and in mediating between the President and opposition parties. The OSCE/ODIHR declared legislative elections staged in Belarus in October 2000 not to have been conducted freely and fairly, and pronounced that presidential elections held in September 2001 had not met the standards required by the organization. In December 2002 the decision was taken to terminate the Group and to establish in its place an OSCE Office in Minsk with a mandate to promote institution-building, strengthen relations with civil society, and development economic and environmental activities. The Office was opened in January 2003. In September the ODIHR entered into dialogue with the Belarus authorities on reforming electoral legislation. In the same month the Minsk Office expressed its concern at the recent closure of NGOs in Belarus for alleged violations of the law. In October 2004 some 270 observers from 38 countries participated in a joint mission of the ODIHR and the OSCE Parliamentary Assembly to monitor parliamentary elections in Belarus. The mission concluded that several fundamental democratic principles had not been adhered to during the electoral process. In June 2005 the Minsk Office expressed concern at sentences of 'restricted freedom' passed on two prominent Belarusian opposition figure after they had been charged with organizing group activities which violated public order. In December the Office likewise voiced its disquiet at the adoption by the House of Representatives of the Belarusian National Assembly of legal amendments 'that could deal a serious blow to civil society and individuals'. In March 2006 the OSCE CIO expressed his profound concern over detentions and arbitrary court proceedings that had occurred in the aftermath of a presidential election held earlier in the month, urging the Belarusian authorities 'immediately to put an end to the persecution of their opponents'. In April the CIO criticized a prison sentence passed on Belarus's principal opposition leader, Alyaksandr Milinkevich, and called for his immediate release. In July the CIO condemned the sentence passed on another opposition candidate in the presidential election, after he had been arraigned on charges of 'hooliganism' and 'organizing and participating in group activities that gravely violated public order'. In August the CIO expressed concern at sentences passed on four members of a local organization charged with intending to act as observers in the March election. In November 2007 the Office in Minsk organized a workshop on best practices in combating money-laundering and the financing of terrorism. Other activities were concerned with environmental issues, including renewable sources of energy and transboundary water management. In October 2008 the Office organized a workshop to discuss best practices in border crossing control across the central and eastern European region.

An OSCE Mission to Moldova was established in February 1993, in order to assist conflicting parties in that country to pursue negotia-

tions on a political settlement, as well as to observe the military situation in the region and to provide advice on issues of human and minority rights, democratization and the repatriation of refugees. In December 1999 the Permanent Council, with the approval of the Russian Government, authorized an expansion of the Mission's mandate to ensure the full removal and destruction of Russian ammunition and armaments and to co-ordinate financial and technical assistance for the withdrawal of foreign troops and the destruction of weapons. In June 2001 the Mission established a tripartite working group, with representatives of the Russian Ministry of Defence and the local authorities in Transnistria to assist and support the process of disposal of munitions. Destruction of heavy weapons began in mid-2002, under the supervision of the Mission. In 2005 observers from the ODIHR and OSCE Parliamentary Assembly participated in international missions to monitor parliamentary and local elections in Moldova, conducted in March and July, respectively. In March 2006 the OSCE Mission to Moldova initiated a Trial Monitoring Programme to observe court proceedings and judicial processes. In May 2003 a seminar on federalism, organized by the OSCE Parliamentary Assembly, was held further to promote negotiations between Moldova and the Transnistrian region on the development of a new Moldovan constitution, based on the principles of federalism. A second parliamentary conference on federalism was convened in September. In September 2004 the OSCE Mission financed a workshop as part of a two-year project concerned with 'strengthening protection and assistance to victims of trafficking, adults and minors'. During 2005 the OSCE Mission hosted negotiations which resulted in the Transnistrian authorities extending permanent registration to four Moldovan schools. In March 2006 the OSCE CIO expressed concern at the situation along the Transnistrian section of the Moldovan–Ukrainian state border and instructed the Mission to pursue a solution by consulting with all relevant parties. During a visit to Moldova in May the CIO urged all parties to the Transnistrian issue to resume negotiations. In January 2007 representatives of the OSCE, Russia and Ukraine met, with observers from the EU and USA, to consider the future of the settlement process and invited chief negotiators from the Moldovan and Transnistrian authorities to initiate mediated discussions in the following month. In June an ODIHR/Council of Europe electoral observation mission, monitoring local elections, noted shortcomings in international standards, including the intimidation of candidates. In October the OSCE Mission organized a high level seminar on confidence- and security-building measures, in support of peace negotiations between Moldova and Transnistria. In April 2008 the Head of Mission welcomed the resumption of direct dialogue between the leaders of the two sides. In the same month the Mission organized a seminar on economic and environmental confidence-building measures, held in Odessa, Ukraine, which was attended by representatives of both sides, the international mediators (Russia, Ukraine and OSCE) and international observers (EU and USA). The Special Envoy of the CIO visited the region in July to pursue settlement discussions with representatives of both sides.

In 1999 an OSCE Project Co-ordinator in Ukraine was established, following the successful conclusion of the OSCE Mission to Ukraine (which had been established in November 1994). The Project Co-ordinator is responsible for pursuing co-operation between Ukraine and the OSCE and providing technical assistance in areas including legal reform, freedom of the media, trafficking in human beings, and the work of the human rights Ombudsman. In April 2002 an ODIHR Election Observation Mission monitored parliamentary elections held in Ukraine. In July 2003 the Project Co-ordinator and the Ukrainian defence ministry launched a joint programme to assist former military personnel to adapt to civilian life. In September 2004 an ODIHR mission was deployed to observe forthcoming presidential elections. More than 300 short-term observers monitored the first and second round polls, which were held in October and November respectively. In December the country's Supreme Court ruled that, owing to electoral irregularities, the second round voting should be re-run at the end of that month. The OSCE/ODIHR mission remained in the country to observe the process, and produced preliminary recommendations on the conduct of the re-run. In late January 2005 the CIO attended the inauguration of the newly-elected President, Viktor Yuschchenko. During 2005 activities of the Project Co-ordinator included supporting the establishment of a new investment promotion agency, organizing a conference on gender equality and law enforcement, training courses for judges in the new court system, a seminar to draft a national programme to combat human trafficking and a forum on media and election law, and hosting an international conference on strengthening the rule of law in the country. In June 2006, during a visit to Ukraine, the OSCE CIO expressed his support for the Ukrainian authorities' active engagement in negotiations with Moldova over the so-called Transnistrian border question. In a meeting with Ukraine's President and the country's foreign minister the CIO commended 'democratic advances' that had been made in parliamentary elections held in March. In 2007 the OSCE organized workshops and other initiatives to strengthen efforts to counter trafficking in humans among government officials, judges, consular officials and NGOs. In September the OSCE led an international election observation mission to oversee the conduct of parliamentary elections. During 2008 the Project Co-ordinator organized a series of training courses, for the judiciary, police officers and government officials, to help to combat trafficking in human beings. Other courses were also organized on implementing the rule of law.

The OSCE Mission to Tajikistan was established in December 1993, and began operations in February 1994. The Mission worked with the UN Mission of Observers to Tajikistan (UNMOT) to promote a peace process in that country, and was a guarantor of the peace agreement concluded in June 1997. The Mission remained actively concerned with promoting respect for human rights, assisting the development of the local media, locating missing persons, and the fair distribution of humanitarian aid. Following multi-party parliamentary elections, held in February 2000, the Mission's focus was to be on post-conflict rehabilitation. In October 2002 the Permanent Council, taking into account the progress made in Tajikistan since the end of the civil conflict, decided to adapt the OSCE's mandate in the country and to replace the mission with a Centre in Dushanbe, with effect from the beginning of November. On 1 January 2004 the Centre initiated a two-year Mine Action Programme. In February 2005 an ODIHR mission observed parliamentary elections in Tajikistan, and reported a failure to meet certain OSCE commitments and other international standards. In November the Centre opened an explosive ordinance disposal training centre and demolition ground as the first stage in implementing a programme on small arms and light weapons and conventional ammunition. The activities of the Centre in 2006 included facilitating conferences and meetings on the establishment of a national human rights institution in Tajikistan and on democratic principles in the country's electoral process. In June 2008 the Centre was renamed the OSCE Office in Tajikistan, with an expanded mandate to support the country in efforts to maintain peace and security, counter crime and implement other OSCE commitments.

In December 2000 the Permanent Council renamed the OSCE Liaison Office in Central Asia the OSCE Centre in Tashkent. The Centre aimed to promote OSCE principles within Uzbekistan; it also functioned as an information exchange between OSCE bodies and participating Central Asian states and as a means of liaising with OSCE presences in the region. In July 1998 the Permanent Council determined to establish OSCE Centres in Bishkek (Kyrgyzstan), Almaty (Kazakhstan), and Ashgabad (Turkmenistan), all of which opened in January 1999. The Centres were to encourage each country's integration into the OSCE, and implementation of its principles, and to focus on the economic, environmental, human and political aspects of security. In January 2000, for the first time, the OSCE refused to dispatch official observers to monitor presidential elections in a member state, owing to concerns about the legitimacy of elections held in Kazakhstan. Subsequently the Centre in Almaty, with the ODIHR and the OSCE Parliamentary Assembly, initiated a roundtable-on-elections project to improve electoral legislation, thus strengthening the political system. The project concluded in January 2002, when participants presented a list of recommendations to the national parliament. In September 2004 a joint OSCE/Council of Europe mission, observing parliamentary elections, declared concern at procedural standards in relation to election legislation in that country. In mid-October the OSCE Centres in Bishkek and Almaty organized a roundtable concerned with the electoral processes in Kazakhstan and Kyrgyzstan attended by participants from state institutions and civil society organizations. A joint ODIHR and OSCE Parliamentary Assembly mission observed legislative elections held in Kyrgyzstan in February and March 2005. The mission reported many procedural and democratic shortcomings in the election process. Following an escalation of civil and political tensions after the polls, the Centre in Bishkek offered to provide a forum for dialogue between the authorities and opposition groups. Some improvements to the electoral process were reported by the ODIHR misson that monitored an early presidential election in July. During 2005 the Centre in Bishkek supported a police assistance programme, an election assistance programme, good governance projects, economic development initiatives, and conflict prevention activities. In that year the Centre in Almaty assisted the Kazakh authorities to develop a national action plan on combating human trafficking, to implement efforts to control small arms and lights weapons, to develop a pollution control register, and to combat money-laundering and other illegal financial activities. Some 450 international observers participated in a mission to monitor a presidential election, held in December. The ODIHR subsequently reported a failure to meet certain OSCE and international standards. In March 2006 the Centre in Almaty organized a roundtable discussion of draft Kazakh legislation to combat money-laundering and terrorism. In the same month, on the occasion of talks with President Niyazov of Turkmenistan in Ashgabad, the OSCE CIO emphasized the importance of political reforms and democratization. In June the Centre in Bishkek organized a meeting to review progress made towards OSCE commitments during presidential and local elections in 2005 and parliamentary elections in 2006. In November the OSCE Centre in Almaty organized an international conference on the development of democratic processes in Kazakhstan. In June 2007 the Centre was renamed the OSCE Centre in Astana. In December the Centre organized two regional seminars on international standards and practices in efforts to combat trafficking in humans. In the first half of 2008 the Centre organized roundtable discussions on a range of issues, including the reform of media legislation, transparency in police activities, and parliamentary development. In July the Centre held a workshop on combating money-laundering and organized crime throughout Central Asia. In the same month the Centre in Bishkek hosted a workshop on border-related activities and co-operation between the Central Asian states. In July 2006 an OSCE Project Co-ordinator was established in Uzbekistan as a new form of co-operation between the OSCE and that country. The office has subsequently been involved with developing and promoting the institution of Ombudsman, raising awareness of OSCE human rights standards, training police officers and supporting socio-economic development. In September 2008 the Project Co-ordinator hosted an OSCE workshop on promoting co-operation within Central Asia to counter international terrorism.

By 2004 all five Central Asian OSCE Centres launched a Central Asian Youth Network to promote collaboration among the region's students and study of OSCE's fundamental principles. An OSCE Academy in Bishkek was inaugurated in December 2002 as a regional centre for training, research and dialogue, in particular in security-related issues.

Japan, the Republic of Korea, Thailand and Afghanistan have the status of 'partners for co-operation' with the OSCE, while Algeria, Egypt, Israel, Jordan, Morocco and Tunisia are 'Mediterranean partners for co-operation'. Regular consultations are held with these countries in order to discuss security issues of common concern. In October 2004 OSCE deployed a team of observers to monitor the presidential election in Afghanistan, representing the organization's first election mission in a partner country.

OSCE Offices in Eastern Europe and Central Asia

OSCE Centre in Aşgabat: 744005 Ashgabat, Turkmenbashy Shayoly 15, Turkmenistan; tel. (12) 35-30-92; fax (12) 35-30-41; e-mail info_tm@osce.org; internet www.osce.org/ashgabad/; Head of Centre IBRAHIM DJIKIC (Bosnia and Herzegovina).

OSCE Centre in Astana: 010000 Astana, Beibitshilik 10, Kazakhstan; tel. (7172) 32-68-04; fax (7172) 32-83-04; internet www.osce .org/astana; Head of Centre ALEXANDRE KELTCHEWSKY (France).

OSCE Centre in Bishkek: 720001 Bishkek, Toktogula 139, Kyrgyzstan; tel. (312) 66-50-15; fax (312) 66-31-69; e-mail pm-kg@osce .org; internet www.osce.org/bishkek/; Head of Centre ANDREW TESORIERE (United Kingdom).

OSCE Mission to Georgia: 0114 Tbilisi, Kristanisi Governmental Residence 5; tel. (32) 20-23-03; fax (32) 24-42-03; e-mail pm-ge@osce .org; internet www.osce.org/georgia/; Head of Mission TERHI HAKALA (Finland).

OSCE Mission to Moldova: 2012 Chișinău, str. Mitropolit Dosoftei 108; tel. (22) 22-34-95; fax (22) 22-34-96; e-mail secretary-MD@osce .org; internet www.osce.org/moldova/; Head of Mission PHILIP N. REMLER (USA).

OSCE Office in Baku: 1004 Baku, 4 Magomayev Lane, 2nd Floor, Azerbaijan; tel. (12) 497-23-73; fax (12) 497-23-77; e-mail office-az@ osce.org; internet www.osce.org/baku/; Head of Office JOSÉ-LUIS HERRERO (Spain).

OSCE Office in Minsk: 220116 Minsk, pr. Gazety Pravda 11, Belarus; tel. (17) 272-34-97; fax (17) 272-34-98; e-mail office-by@ osce.org; internet www.osce.org/belarus/; Head of Office HANS JOCHEN SCHMIDT (Germany).

OSCE Office in Tajikistan: 734017 Dushanbe, Zikrullo Khojaev 12, Tajikistan; tel. (372) 24-33-38; fax (372) 24-91-59; e-mail cid-tj@ osce.org; internet www.osce.org/tajikistan/; Head of Office VLADIMIR PRYAKHIN (Russia).

OSCE Office in Yerevan: 375009 Yerevan, ul. Teryan 89, Armenia; tel. (10) 54-58-45; fax (10) 54-10-61; e-mail yerevan-am@osce.org; internet www.osce.org/yerevan/; Head of Office SERGEY KAPINOS (Russia).

OSCE Project Co-ordinator in Ukraine: 01054 Kyiv, vul. Striletska 16; tel. (44) 492-03-82; fax (44) 492-03-83; internet www.osce .org/ukraine/; Project Co-ordinator L'UBOMÍR KOPAJ (Slovakia).

OSCE Project Co-ordinator in Uzbekistan: 700015 Tashkent, ul. Afrosiyob 12B, 4th Floor; tel. (71) 140-04-70; fax (71) 140-04-66; e-mail osce-cit@osce.org; internet www.osce.org/tashkent/; Project Co-ordinator ISTVAN VENCZEL (Hungary).

Personal Representative of the OSCE Chairman-in-Office on the Conflict Dealt with by the OSCE Minsk Conference (Nagornyi Karabakh): Tbilisi, Zovreti 15, Georgia; tel. (32) 37-61-61; fax (32) 98-85-66; e-mail persrep@access.sanet.ge; Personal Rep. ANDRZEJ KASPRZYK (Poland).

Finance

All activities of the institutions, negotiations, ad hoc meetings and missions are financed by contributions from member states. The budget for 2008 amounted to €164.2m.

Publications

Annual Report of the Secretary-General.
The Caucasus: In Defence of the Future.
Decision Manual (annually).
OSCE Handbook.
OSCE Newsletter (monthly, in English and Russian).
Factsheets on OSCE missions, institutions and other structures are published regularly.

ORGANIZATION OF THE BLACK SEA ECONOMIC CO-OPERATION—BSEC

Address: Sakıp Sabancı Cad., Müşir Fuad Paşa Yalısı, Eski Tersane 34460 İstinye-İstanbul, Turkey.
Telephone: (212) 229-63-30; **fax:** (212) 229-63-36; **e-mail:** info@bsec-organization.org; **internet:** www.bsec-organization.org.

The Black Sea Economic Co-operation (BSEC) was established in 1992 to strengthen regional co-operation, particularly in the field of economic development. In June 1998, at a summit meeting held in Yalta, Ukraine, participating countries signed the BSEC Charter, thereby officially elevating BSEC to regional organization status. The Charter entered into force on 1 May 1999, at which time BSEC formally became the Organization of the Black Sea Economic Co-operation, retaining the same acronym.

MEMBERS

Albania	Georgia	Russia
Armenia	Greece	Serbia
Azerbaijan	Moldova	Turkey
Bulgaria	Romania	Ukraine

Note: Observer status has been granted to Austria, Belarus, Croatia, Czech Republic, Egypt, France, Germany, Israel, Italy, Poland, Slovakia, Tunisia and the USA. The Black Sea Commission, the BSEC Business Council, the European Commission, the International Black Sea Club, and the Energy Charter Conference also have observer status. Iran, the former Yugoslav republic of Macedonia, Montenegro and Uzbekistan have applied for full membership.

Organization
(October 2008)

PRESIDENTIAL SUMMIT

The Presidential Summit, comprising heads of state or government of member states, represents the highest authority of the body.

COUNCIL

The Council of Ministers of Foreign Affairs is BSEC's principal decision-making organ. Ministers meet twice a year to review progress and to define new objectives. Chairmanship of the Council rotates among members; the Chairman-in-Office co-ordinates the activities undertaken by BSEC. The Council is supported by a Committee of Senior Officials. Upon request of the Chairman-in-Office a Troika, comprising the current, most recent and next Chairman-in-Office, or their representatives, is convened to consider BSEC's ongoing and planned activities.

PERMANENT INTERNATIONAL SECRETARIAT

The Secretariat's tasks are, primarily, of an administrative and technical nature, and include the maintenance of archives, and the preparation and distribution of documentation. Much of the organization's activities are undertaken by 15 working groups, each headed by an Executive Manager, and by various ad hoc groups and meetings of experts.

Secretary-General: LEONIDAS CHRYSANTHOPOULOS (Greece).

Activities

In June 1992, at a summit meeting held in Istanbul, heads of state and of government signed the summit declaration on BSEC, and adopted the Bosphorus statement, which established a regional structure for economic co-operation. The grouping attained regional organization status in May 1999 (see above). The Organization's main areas of co-operation include transport; communications; trade and economic development; banking and finance; energy; tourism; agriculture and agro-industry; health care and pharmaceuticals; environmental protection; science and technology; the exchange of statistical data and economic information; collaboration between customs authorities; and combating organized crime, drugs-trafficking, trade in illegal weapons and radioactive materials, and terrorism. In order to promote regional co-operation, the Organization also aims to strengthen the business environment by providing support for small and medium-sized enterprises; facilitating closer contacts between businesses in member countries; progressively eliminating obstacles to the expansion of trade; creating appropriate conditions for investment and industrial co-operation, in particular through the avoidance of double taxation and the promotion and protection of investments; encouraging the dissemination of information concerning international tenders organized by member states; and promoting economic co-operation in free trade zones. A Working Group on Culture was established in November 2006 to promote and protect the cultural identity of the region.

A BSEC Business Council was established in Istanbul in December 1992 by the business communities of member states. It has observer status at the BSEC, and aims to identify private and public investment projects, maintain business contacts and develop programmes in various sectors. A Black Sea Trade and Development Bank has been established, in Thessaloníki, Greece, as the Organization's main funding institution, to finance and implement joint regional projects. It began operations on 1 July 1999 (see below). A BSEC Co-ordination Centre, located in Ankara, Turkey, aims to promote the exchange of statistical and economic information. An International Centre for Black Sea Studies (ICBSS) was established in Athens, Greece, in March 1998, in order to undertake research concerning the BSEC, in the fields of economics, industry and technology.

In recent years BSEC has undergone a process of reform aimed at developing a more project-based orientation. In April 2001 the Council adopted the so-called BSEC Economic Agenda for the Future Towards a More Consolidated, Effective and Viable BSEC Partnership, which provided a roadmap for charting the implementation of the Organization's goals. In 2002 a Project Development Fund was established and a regional programme of governance and institutional renewal was launched. Under the new orientation the roles of BSEC's Committee of Senior Officials and network of country co-ordinators were to be enhanced. In April 2008 the BSEC Council inaugurated a new €2m. BSEC Hellenic Development Fund to support regional co-operation. The Council also adopted the modalities for BSEC fast-track co-operation, aimed at enabling subgroups of member states to proceed with policies that other member states were unwilling or unable to pursue. A meeting of the Council scheduled for late October 2008 was to adopt new guidelines on improving the efficiency of the grouping.

BSEC aims to foster relations with other international and regional organizations, and has been granted observer status at the UN General Assembly. In 1999 BSEC agreed upon a Platform of Co-operation for future structured relations with the European Union. The main areas in which BSEC determined to develop co-operation with the EU were transport, energy and telecommunications infrastructure; trade and the promotion of foreign direct investment; sustainable development and environmental protection, including nuclear safety; science and technology; and combating terrorism and organized crime. BSEC supports the Stability Pact for South-Eastern Europe, initiated in June 1999 as a collaborative plan of action by the EU, the Group of Seven industrialized nations and Russia (the G8), regional governments and other organizations concerned with the stability of the region. The Declaration issued by BSEC's decennial anniversary summit, held in Istanbul in June 2002, urged that collaboration with the EU should be enhanced. In April 2005 representatives of BSEC and the EU met in Brussels, Belgium, to address possibilities for such co-operation, focusing in particular on the EU's policy in the Black Sea region and on the development of regional transport and energy networks (see Alexandroupolis Declaration, below). In June 2007 BSEC heads of state confirmed their commitment to an enhanced relationship with the EU, based on a communication of the European Commission, published in April, entitled 'Black Sea Synergy—a New Regional Co-operation Initiative'. In November 2006 BSEC signed a Memorandum of Understanding with the International Road Federation.

BSEC has supported implementation of the Bucharest Convention on the Protection of the Black Sea Against Pollution, adopted by Bulgaria, Georgia, Romania, Russia, Turkey and Ukraine in April 1992. In October 1996 those countries adopted the Strategic Action Plan for the Rehabilitation and Protection of the Black Sea (BSSAP), to be implemented by the Commission of the Bucharest Convention. In March 2001 the transport ministers of BSEC member states adopted a Transport Action Plan, which envisaged reducing the disparities in regional transport systems and integrating the BSEC regional transport infrastructure with wider international networks and projects. In April 2007 BSEC governments signed an agreement for the co-ordinated development of a 7,000 km-long Black Sea Ring Highway. A memorandum of understanding relating to the development of 'Motorways of the Sea' was also signed. In March 2005 ministers of BSEC member states responsible for energy adopted the Alexandroupolis Declaration, approving a common framework for future collaboration on the creation of a regional energy market, and urging the liberalization of electricity and natural gas markets in accordance with EU directives as a basis for this.

Finance

BSEC is financed by annual contributions from member states on the following scale: Greece, Russia, Turkey and Ukraine each contribute 15% of the budget; Bulgaria, Romania and Serbia contribute 7.5%; the remaining members each contribute 3.5%.

Publication

Black Sea News (quarterly).

Related Bodies

Parliamentary Assembly of the Black Sea: 1 Hareket Kösku, Dolmabahçe Sarayi, Besiktas, 80680 İstanbul, Turkey; tel. (212) 227-6070; fax (212) 227-6080; e-mail pabsec@pabsec.org; internet www.pabsec.org; f. 1993; the Assembly, consisting of the representatives of the national parliaments of member states, aims to provide a legal basis for the implementation of decisions within the BSEC framework; comprises three committees concerning economic, commercial, technological and environmental affairs; legal and political affairs; and cultural, educational and social affairs; the presidency rotates every six months; Sec.-Gen. ALEXEY KUDRIAVTSEV.

Black Sea Trade and Development Bank: 1 Komninon str., 54624 Thessaloniki, Greece; tel. (2310) 290400; fax (2310) 221796; e-mail info@bstdb.org; internet www.bstdb.org; f. 1999; the Bank supports economic development and regional co-operation by providing trade and project financing, guarantees, and equity for development projects supporting both public and private enterprises in its member countries; auth. cap. SDR 3,000m. (Oct. 2008); Sec.-Gen. GEORGE KOTTAS.

BSEC Business Council: Müsir Fuad Pasa Yalisi, Eski Tersane, 80860 Istinye, İstanbul, Turkey; tel. (212) 229-1144; fax (212) 229-0332; e-mail info@bsec-business.org; internet www.bsec-business .org; f. 1992; aims to secure greater economic integration and to promote investment in the region; Sec.-Gen. Dr COSTAS MASMANIDIS.

International Centre for Black Sea Studies: 4 Xenophontos Str., 10557 Athens, Greece; tel. (210) 3242321; fax (210) 3242244; e-mail icbss@icbss.org; internet www.icbss.org; f. 1998; aims to foster co-operation and promote research and knowledge-sharing among BSEC mems and partner countries; administers a Black Sea Research Network; convenes an Annual Conference and Annual Lecture; Dir Gen. Dr DIMITRIOS TRIANTAPHYLLOU; publs *Black Sea Monitor* (quarterly), Policy Briefs.

ORGANIZATION OF THE ISLAMIC CONFERENCE—OIC

Address: Kilo 6, Mecca Rd, POB 178, Jeddah 21411, Saudi Arabia.
Telephone: (2) 690-0001; **fax:** (2) 275-1953; **e-mail:** info@oic-oic .org; **internet:** www.oic-oci.org.

The Organization was formally established in May 1971, when its Secretariat became operational, following a summit meeting of Muslim heads of state at Rabat, Morocco, in September 1969, and the Islamic Foreign Ministers' Conference in Jeddah in March 1970, and in Karachi, Pakistan, in December 1970.

National Liberation Front (MNLF) of the southern Philippines, the United Nations, the African Union, the Non-Aligned Movement, the League of Arab States, the Economic Co-operation Organization, the Union of the Arab Maghreb and the Co-operation Council for the Arab States of the Gulf. The revised OIC Charter, endorsed in March 2008, made future applications for OIC membership and observer status conditional upon Muslim demographic majority and membership of the UN.

MEMBERS

Afghanistan	Indonesia	Qatar
Albania	Iran	Saudi Arabia
Algeria	Iraq	Senegal
Azerbaijan	Jordan	Sierra Leone
Bahrain	Kazakhstan	Somalia
Bangladesh	Kuwait	Sudan
Benin	Kyrgyzstan	Suriname
Brunei	Lebanon	Syria
Burkina Faso	Libya	Tajikistan
Cameroon	Malaysia	Togo
Chad	The Maldives	Tunisia
Comoros	Mali	Turkey
Côte d'Ivoire	Mauritania	Turkmenistan
Djibouti	Morocco	Uganda
Egypt	Mozambique	United Arab
Gabon	Niger	Emirates
The Gambia	Nigeria	Uzbekistan
Guinea	Oman	Yemen
Guinea-Bissau	Pakistan	
Guyana	Palestine	

Note: Observer status has been granted to Bosnia and Herzegovina, the Central African Republic, Russia, Thailand, the Muslim community of the 'Turkish Republic of Northern Cyprus', the Moro

Organization

(October 2008)

SUMMIT CONFERENCES

The supreme body of the Organization is the Conference of Heads of State, which met in 1969 at Rabat, Morocco, in 1974 at Lahore, Pakistan, and in January 1981 at Mecca, Saudi Arabia, when it was decided that ordinary summit conferences would normally be held every three years in future. An extraordinary summit conference was convened in Doha, Qatar, in March 2003, to consider the situation in Iraq. A further extraordinary conference, held in December 2005, in Mecca, Saudi Arabia, determined to restructure the OIC. The 11th ordinary Conference was held in Dakar, Senegal, in March 2008. The summit conference troika comprises member countries equally representing OIC's African, Arab and Asian membership.

CONFERENCE OF MINISTERS OF FOREIGN AFFAIRS

Conferences take place annually, to consider the means for implementing the general policy of the Organization, although they may also be convened for extraordinary sessions. The ministerial conference troika comprises member countries equally representing OIC's African, Arab and Asian membership.

SECRETARIAT

The executive organ of the organization, headed by a Secretary-General (who is elected by the Conference of Ministers of Foreign Affairs for a five-year term, renewable only once) and four Assistant Secretaries-General (similarly appointed).

Secretary-General: Prof. Dr EKMELEDDIN IHSANOGLU (Turkey).

At the summit conference in January 1981 it was decided that an International Islamic Court of Justice should be established to adjudicate in disputes between Muslim countries. Experts met in January 1983 to draw up a constitution for the court; however, by 2008 it was not yet in operation.

EXECUTIVE COMMITTEE

The third extraordinary conference of the OIC, convened in Mecca, Saudi Arabia, in December 2005, mandated the establishment of the Executive Committee, comprising the summit conference and ministerial conference troikas, the OIC host country, and the OIC Secretariat, as a mechanism for following-up resolutions of the Conference.

STANDING COMMITTEES

Al-Quds Committee: f. 1975 to implement the resolutions of the Islamic Conference on the status of Jerusalem (Al-Quds); it meets at the level of foreign ministers; maintains the Al-Quds Fund; Chair. King MUHAMMAD VI OF MOROCCO.

Standing Committee for Economic and Commercial Co-operation (COMCEC): f. 1981; Chair. ABDULLAH GÜL (Pres. of Turkey).

Standing Committee for Information and Cultural Affairs (COMIAC): f. 1981; Chair. ABDOULAYE WADE (Pres. of Senegal).

Standing Committee for Scientific and Technological Co-operation (COMSTECH): f. 1981; Chair. ASIF ALI ZARDARI (Pres. of Pakistan).

Other committees comprise the Islamic Peace Committee, the Permanent Finance Committee, the Committee of Islamic Solidarity with the Peoples of the Sahel, the Eight-Member Committee on the Situation of Muslims in the Philippines, the Six-Member Committee on Palestine, the Committee on United Nations reform, and the ad hoc Committee on Afghanistan. In addition, there is an Islamic Commission for Economic, Cultural and Social Affairs, and there are OIC contact groups on Bosnia and Herzegovina, Kosovo, Jammu and Kashmir, Sierra Leone, and Somalia. A Commission of Eminent Persons was inaugurated in 2005.

Activities

The Organization's aims, as proclaimed in the Charter (adopted in 1972, with revisions endorsed in 1990 and 2008), are:

(i) To promote Islamic solidarity among member states;

(ii) To consolidate co-operation among member states in the economic, social, cultural, scientific and other vital fields, and to arrange consultations among member states belonging to international organizations;

(iii) To endeavour to eliminate racial segregation and discrimination and to eradicate colonialism in all its forms;

(iv) To take necessary measures to support international peace and security founded on justice;

(v) To co-ordinate all efforts for the safeguard of the Holy Places and support of the struggle of the people of Palestine, and help them to regain their rights and liberate their land;

(vi) To strengthen the struggle of all Muslim people with a view to safeguarding their dignity, independence and national rights;

(vii) To create a suitable atmosphere for the promotion of co-operation and understanding among member states and other countries.

The first summit conference of Islamic leaders (representing 24 states) took place in 1969 following the burning of the Al Aqsa Mosque in Jerusalem. At this conference it was decided that Islamic governments should 'consult together with a view to promoting close co-operation and mutual assistance in the economic, scientific, cultural and spiritual fields, inspired by the immortal teachings of Islam'. Thereafter the foreign ministers of the countries concerned met annually, and adopted the Charter of the Organization of the Islamic Conference in 1972.

At the second Islamic summit conference (Lahore, Pakistan, 1974), the Islamic Solidarity Fund was established, together with a committee of representatives which later evolved into the Islamic Com-

mission for Economic, Cultural and Social Affairs. Subsequently, numerous other subsidiary bodies have been set up (see below).

ECONOMIC CO-OPERATION

A general agreement for economic, technical and commercial co-operation came into force in 1981, providing for the establishment of joint investment projects and trade co-ordination. This was followed by an agreement on promotion, protection and guarantee of investments among member states. A plan of action to strengthen economic co-operation was adopted at the third Islamic summit conference in 1981, aiming to promote collective self-reliance and the development of joint ventures in all sectors. In 1994 the 1981 plan of action was revised; the reformulated plan placed greater emphasis on private-sector participation in its implementation. Although several meetings of experts were subsequently held to discuss some of the 10 priority focus areas of the plan, little progress was achieved in implementing it during the 1990s and early 2000s. In October 2003 a meeting of COMCEC endorsed measures aimed at accelerating the implementation of the plan of action.

The fifth summit conference, held in 1987, approved proposals for joint development of modern technology, and for improving scientific and technical skills in the less developed Islamic countries. The first international Islamic trade fair was held in Jeddah, Saudi Arabia, in March 2001.

In 1991 22 OIC member states signed a Framework Agreement on a Trade Preferential System (TPS-OIC) among the OIC Member States; this entered into force in 2003, following the requisite ratification by more than 10 member states, and was envisaged as representing the first step towards the eventual establishment of an Islamic common market. A Trade Negotiating Committee (TNC) was established following the entry into force of the Framework Agreement. The first round of trade negotiations on the establishment of the TPS-OIC, concerning finalizing tariff-reduction modalities and an implementation schedule for the Agreement, was held during April 2004–April 2005. In November 2006, at the launch of the second round of negotiations, ministers adopted a road-map for establishing the TPS-OIC by 1 January 2009. In June 2007 the TNC adopted rules of origin for the TPS-OIC.

The first OIC Anti-Corruption and Enhancing Integrity Forum was convened in August 2006 in Kuala Lumpur, Malaysia.

CULTURAL CO-OPERATION

The Organization supports education in Muslim communities throughout the world, and was instrumental in the establishment of Islamic universities in Niger and Uganda. It organizes seminars on various aspects of Islam, and encourages dialogue with the other monotheistic religions. Support is given to publications on Islam both in Muslim and Western countries. The OIC organizes meetings at ministerial level to consider aspects of information policy and new technologies.

HUMANITARIAN ASSISTANCE

Assistance is given to Muslim communities affected by wars and natural disasters, in co-operation with UN organizations, particularly UNHCR. A resolution on the status of refugees in the Muslim world that was adopted by the 10th OIC summit meeting, held in October 2003, urged all member states to accede to the 1951 UN Convention on the Status of Refugees. In March 2008 a conference of OIC leaders and Islamic non-governmental organizations determined to establish an OIC centre for the analysis of humanitarian requirements in OIC member states. The countries of the Sahel region (Burkina Faso, Cape Verde, Chad, The Gambia, Guinea, Guinea-Bissau, Mali, Mauritania, Niger and Senegal) receive particular attention as victims of drought. OIC member states have provided humanitarian assistance to the Muslim population affected by the conflict in Chechnya, and to Darfur, southern Sudan. In 2008 the OIC and Islamic Development Bank were planning an international conference on the rehabilitation and reconstruction of Darfur. The OIC has established trust funds to assist vulnerable people in Afghanistan, Bosnia and Herzegovina, and Sierra Leone. In March 2008 the OIC launched a humanitarian support operation for Palestinians in Gaza; an initial 'assistance caravan' transported medical supplies and equipment to the area. In October 2008 the OIC Secretary-General urged OIC member states and other interested donors to provide humanitarian assistance to Algeria, in response to recent devastating torrential rains, and to Kyrgyzstan, in support of survivors of a recent earthquake in that country's Alai region.

POLITICAL CO-OPERATION

Since its inception the OIC has called for vacation of Arab territories by Israel, recognition of the rights of Palestinians and of the Palestine Liberation Organization (PLO) as their sole legitimate representative, and the restoration of Jerusalem to Arab rule. The 1981 summit conference called for a *jihad* (holy war—though not necessarily in a military sense) 'for the liberation of Jerusalem and the occupied territories'; this was to include an Islamic economic boycott of Israel. In 1982 Islamic ministers of foreign affairs decided to establish Islamic offices for boycotting Israel and for military co-operation with the PLO. The 1984 summit conference agreed to reinstate Egypt (suspended following the peace treaty signed with Israel in 1979) as a member of the OIC, although the resolution was opposed by seven states.

In August 1990 a majority of ministers of foreign affairs condemned Iraq's recent invasion of Kuwait, and demanded the withdrawal of Iraqi forces. In August 1991 the Conference of Ministers of Foreign Affairs obstructed Iraq's attempt to propose a resolution demanding the repeal of economic sanctions against the country. The sixth summit conference, held in Senegal in December, reflected the divisions in the Arab world that resulted from Iraq's invasion of Kuwait and the ensuing war. Twelve heads of state did not attend, reportedly to register protest at the presence of Jordan and the PLO at the conference, both of which had given support to Iraq. Disagreement also arose between the PLO and the majority of other OIC members when a proposal was adopted to cease the OIC's support for the PLO's *jihad* in the Arab territories occupied by Israel, in an attempt to further the Middle East peace negotiations.

In August 1992 the UN General Assembly approved a non-binding resolution, introduced by the OIC, that requested the UN Security Council to take increased action, including the use of force, in order to defend the non-Serbian population of Bosnia and Herzegovina (some 43% of Bosnians being Muslims) from Serbian aggression, and to restore its 'territorial integrity'. The OIC Conference of Ministers of Foreign Affairs, which was held in December, demanded anew that the UN Security Council take all necessary measures against Serbia and Montenegro, including military intervention, in order to protect the Bosnian Muslims.

A report by an OIC fact-finding mission, which in February 1993 visited Azad Kashmir while investigating allegations of repression of the largely Muslim population of the Indian state of Jammu and Kashmir by the Indian armed forces, was presented to the 1993 Conference. The meeting urged member states to take the necessary measures to persuade India to cease the 'massive human rights violations' in Jammu and Kashmir and to allow the Indian Kashmiris to 'exercise their inalienable right to self-determination'. In September 1994 ministers of foreign affairs, meeting in Islamabad, Pakistan, agreed to establish a contact group on Jammu and Kashmir, which was to provide a mechanism for promoting international awareness of the situation in that region and for seeking a peaceful solution to the dispute. In December OIC heads of state approved a resolution condemning reported human rights abuses by Indian security forces in Kashmir.

In July 1994 the OIC Secretary-General visited Afghanistan and proposed the establishment of a preparatory mechanism to promote national reconciliation in that country. In mid-1995 Saudi Arabia, acting as a representative of the OIC, pursued a peace initiative for Afghanistan and issued an invitation for leaders of the different factions to hold negotiations in Jeddah.

A special ministerial meeting on Bosnia and Herzegovina was held in July 1993, at which seven OIC countries committed themselves to making available up to 17,000 troops to serve in the UN Protection Force in the former Yugoslavia (UNPROFOR). The meeting also decided to dispatch immediately a ministerial mission to persuade influential governments to support the OIC's demands for the removal of the arms embargo on Bosnian Muslims and the convening of a restructured international conference to bring about a political solution to the conflict. In December 1994 OIC heads of state, convened in Morocco, proclaimed that the UN arms embargo on Bosnia and Herzegovina could not be applied to the Muslim authorities of that Republic. The Conference also resolved to review economic relations between OIC member states and any country that supported Serbian activities. An aid fund was established, to which member states were requested to contribute between US $500,000 and $5m., in order to provide further humanitarian and economic assistance to Bosnian Muslims. In relation to wider concerns the conference adopted a Code of Conduct for Combating International Terrorism, in an attempt to control Muslim extremist groups. The code commits states to ensuring that militant groups do not use their territory for planning or executing terrorist activity against other states, in addition to states refraining from direct support or participation in acts of terrorism. In a further resolution the OIC supported the decision by Iraq to recognize Kuwait, but advocated that Iraq comply with all UN Security Council decisions.

In July 1995 the OIC contact group on Bosnia and Herzegovina (at that time comprising Egypt, Iran, Malaysia, Morocco, Pakistan, Saudi Arabia, Senegal and Turkey), meeting in Geneva, declared the UN arms embargo against Bosnia and Herzegovina to be 'invalid'. Several Governments subsequently announced their willingness officially to supply weapons and other military assistance to the Bosnian Muslim forces. In September a meeting of all OIC ministers of defence and foreign affairs endorsed the establishment of an 'assistance mobilization group' which was to supply military, economic, legal and other assistance to Bosnia and Herzegovina. In a

joint declaration the ministers also demanded the return of all territory seized by Bosnian Serb forces, the continued NATO bombing of Serb military targets, and that the city of Sarajevo be preserved under a Muslim-led Bosnian Government. In November the OIC Secretary-General endorsed the peace accord for the former Yugoslavia, which was concluded, in Dayton, USA, by leaders of all the conflicting factions, and reaffirmed the commitment of Islamic states to participate in efforts to implement the accord. In the following month the OIC Conference of Ministers of Foreign Affairs, convened in Conakry, Guinea, requested the full support of the international community to reconstruct Bosnia and Herzegovina through humanitarian aid as well as economic and technical co-operation. Ministers declared that Palestine and the establishment of fully-autonomous Palestinian control of Jerusalem were issues of central importance for the Muslim world. The Conference urged the removal of all aspects of occupation and the cessation of the construction of Israeli settlements in the occupied territories. In addition, the final statement of the meeting condemned Armenian aggression against Azerbaijan, registered concern at the persisting civil conflict in Afghanistan, demanded the elimination of all weapons of mass destruction and pledged support for Libya (affected by the US trade embargo). Ministers determined that an intergovernmental group of experts should be established in 1996 to address the situation of minority Muslim communities residing in non-OIC states.

In December 1996 OIC ministers of foreign affairs, meeting in Jakarta, Indonesia, urged the international community to apply pressure on Israel in order to ensure its implementation of the terms of the Middle East peace process. The ministers reaffirmed the importance of ensuring that the provisions of the Dayton Peace Agreement for the former Yugoslavia were fully implemented, called for a peaceful settlement of the Kashmir issue, demanded that Iraq fulfil its obligations for the establishment of security, peace and stability in the region and proposed that an international conference on peace and national reconciliation in Somalia be convened. In March 1997, at an extraordinary summit held in Pakistan, OIC heads of state and of government reiterated the organization's objective of increasing international pressure on Israel to ensure the full implementation of the terms of the Middle East peace process. An 'Islamabad Declaration' was also adopted, which pledged to increase co-operation between members of the OIC. In June the OIC condemned the decision by the US House of Representatives to recognize Jerusalem as the Israeli capital. The Secretary-General of the OIC issued a statement rejecting the US decision as counter to the role of the USA as sponsor of the Middle East peace plan.

In early 1998 the OIC appealed for an end to the threat of US-led military action against Iraq arising from a dispute regarding access granted to international weapons inspectors. The crisis was averted by an agreement concluded between the Iraqi authorities and the UN Secretary-General in February. In March OIC ministers of foreign affairs, meeting in Doha, Qatar, requested an end to the international sanctions against Iraq. Additionally, the ministers urged all states to end the process of restoring normal trading and diplomatic relations with Israel pending that country's withdrawal from the occupied territories and acceptance of an independent Palestinian state. In April the OIC, jointly with the UN, sponsored new peace negotiations between the main disputing factions in Afghanistan, which were conducted in Islamabad, Pakistan. In early May, however, the talks collapsed and were postponed indefinitely. In September the Secretaries-General of the OIC and UN agreed to establish a joint mission to counter the deteriorating security situation along the Afghan–Iranian border, following the large-scale deployment of Taliban troops in the region and consequent military manoeuvres by the Iranian authorities. They also reiterated the need to proceed with negotiations to conclude a peaceful settlement in Afghanistan. In December the OIC appealed for a diplomatic solution to the tensions arising from Iraq's withdrawal of co-operation with UN weapons inspectors, and criticized subsequent military airstrikes, led by the USA, as having been conducted without renewed UN authority. An OIC Convention on Combating International Terrorism was adopted in 1998. An OIC committee of experts responsible for formulating a plan of action for safeguarding the rights of Muslim communities and minorities met for the first time in 1998.

In early April 1999 ministers of foreign affairs of the countries comprising OIC's contact group met to consider the crisis in Kosovo. The meeting condemned Serbian atrocities being committed against the local Albanian population and urged the provision of international assistance for the thousands of people displaced by the conflict. The group resolved to establish a committee to co-ordinate relief aid provided by member states. The ministers also expressed their willingness to help to formulate a peaceful settlement and to participate in any subsequent implementation force. In June an OIC Parliamentary Union was inaugurated; its founding conference was convened in Tehran, Iran.

In early March 2000 the OIC mediated contacts between the parties to the conflict in Afghanistan, with a view to reviving peace negotiations. Talks, held under OIC auspices, ensued in May. In

November OIC heads of state attended the ninth summit conference, held in Doha, Qatar. In view of the significant deterioration in relations between Israel and the Palestinian (National) Authority (PA) during late 2000, the summit issued a Declaration pledging solidarity with the Palestinian cause and accusing the Israeli authorities of implementing large-scale systematic violations of human rights against Palestinians. The summit also issued the Doha Declaration, which reaffirmed commitment to the OIC Charter and undertook to modernize the organization's organs and mechanisms. Both the elected Government of Afghanistan and the Taliban sent delegations to the Doha conference. The summit determined that Afghanistan's official participation in the OIC, suspended in 1996, should not yet be reinstated. In early 2001 a high-level delegation from the OIC visited Afghanistan in an attempt to prevent further destruction of ancient statues by Taliban supporters.

In May 2001 the OIC convened an emergency meeting, following an escalation of Israeli–Palestinian violence. The meeting resolved to halt all diplomatic and political contacts with the Israeli government, while restrictions remained in force against Palestinian-controlled territories. In June the OIC condemned attacks and ongoing discrimination against the Muslim Community in Myanmar. In the same month the OIC Secretary-General undertook a tour of six African countries—Burkina Faso, The Gambia, Guinea, Mali, Niger and Senegal—to promote co-operation and to consider further OIC support for those states. In August the Secretary-General condemned Israel's seizure of several Palestinian institutions in East Jerusalem and aerial attacks against Palestinian settlements. The OIC initiated high-level diplomatic efforts to convene a meeting of the UN Security Council in order to discuss the situation.

In September 2001 the OIC Secretary-General strongly condemned major terrorist attacks perpetrated against targets in the USA. Soon afterwards the US authorities rejected a proposal by the Taliban regime that an OIC observer mission be deployed to monitor the activities of the Saudi Arabian-born exiled militant Islamist fundamentalist leader Osama bin Laden, who was accused by the US Government of having co-ordinated the attacks from alleged terrorist bases in the Taliban-administered area of Afghanistan. An extraordinary meeting of OIC ministers of foreign affairs, convened in early October, in Doha, Qatar, to consider the implications of the terrorist atrocities, condemned the attacks and declared its support for combating all manifestations of terrorism within the framework of a proposed collective initiative co-ordinated under the auspices of the UN. The meeting, which did not pronounce directly on the recently-initiated US-led military retaliation against targets in Afghanistan, urged that no Arab or Muslim state should be targeted under the pretext of eliminating terrorism. It determined to establish a fund to assist Afghan civilians. In February 2002 the Secretary-General expressed concern at statements of the US administration describing Iran and Iraq (as well as the Democratic People's Republic of Korea) as belonging to an 'axis of evil' involved in international terrorism and the development of weapons of mass destruction. In early April OIC foreign ministers convened an extraordinary session on terrorism, in Kuala Lumpur, Malaysia. The meeting issued the 'Kuala Lumpur Declaration', which reiterated member states' collective resolve to combat terrorism, recalling the organization's 1994 code of conduct and 1998 convention to this effect; condemned attempts to associate terrorist activities with Islamists or any other particular creed, civilization or nationality, and rejected attempts to associate Islamic states or the Palestinian struggle with terrorism; rejected the implementation of international action against any Muslim state on the pretext of combating terrorism; urged the organization of a global conference on international terrorism; and urged an examination of the root causes of international terrorism. In addition, the meeting strongly condemned Israel's ongoing military intervention in areas controlled by the PA. The meeting adopted a plan of action on addressing the issues raised in the declaration. Its implementation was to be co-ordinated by a 13-member committee on international terrorism. Member states were encouraged to sign and ratify the Convention on Combating International Terrorism in order to accelerate its implementation. In June 2002 ministers of foreign affairs, meeting in Khartoum, Sudan, issued a declaration reiterating the OIC call for an international conference to be convened, under UN auspices, in order clearly to define terrorism and to agree on the international procedures and mechanisms for combating terrorism through the UN. The conference also repeated demands for the international community to exert pressure on Israel to withdraw from all Palestinian-controlled territories and for the establishment of an independent Palestinian state. It endorsed the peace plan for the region that had been adopted by the summit meeting of the League of Arab States in March.

In June 2002 the OIC Secretary-General expressed his concern at the escalation of tensions between Pakistan and India regarding Kashmir. He urged both sides to withdraw their troops and to refrain from the use of force. In the following month the OIC pledged its support for Morocco in a territorial dispute with Spain over the small island of Perejil, but called for a negotiated settlement to resolve the issue.

An extraordinary summit conference of Islamic leaders convened in Doha, Qatar, in early March 2003, to consider the ongoing Iraq crisis welcomed the Saddam Hussain regime's acceptance of UN Security Council Resolution 1441 and consequent co-operation with UN weapons inspectors, and emphatically rejected any military strike against Iraq or threat to the security of any other Islamic state. The conference also urged progress towards the elimination of all weapons of mass destruction in the Middle East, including those held by Israel. In May the 30th session of the Conference of Ministers of Foreign Affairs, entitled 'Unity and Dignity', issued the Tehran Declaration, in which it resolved to combat terrorism and to contribute to preserving peace and security in Islamic countries. The Declaration also pledged its full support for the Palestinian cause and rejected the labelling as 'terrorist' of those Muslim states deemed to be resisting foreign aggression and occupation. The 10th OIC summit meeting, held in October, in Putrajaya, Malaysia, issued the Putrajaya Declaration, in which Islamic leaders resolved to enhance Islamic states' role and influence in international affairs. The leaders adopted a plan of action that entailed: reviewing and strengthening OIC positions on international issues; enhancing dialogue among Muslim thinkers and policy-makers through relevant OIC insitutions; promoting constructive dialogue with other cultures and civilizations; completing an ongoing review of the structure and efficacy of the OIC Secretariat; establishing a working group to address means of enhancing the role of Islamic education; promoting among member states the development of science and technology, discussion of ecological issues, and the role of information communication technology in development; improving mechanisms to assist member states in post-conflict situations; and advancing trade and investment through data-sharing and encouraging access to markets for products from poorer member states.

In mid-May 2004 the OIC Secretary-General urged combat forces in Iraq to respect the inviolability of that country's holy places. Shortly afterwards he condemned the ongoing destruction of Palestinian homes by Israeli forces, and consequent population displacement, particularly in Rafah, Gaza. He urged international organizations to condemn Israel's actions and appealed to the UN Security Council to intervene promptly in the situation and to compel Israel to respect international law. In June the Secretary-General welcomed progress achieved by a round of expert-level talks on nuclear confidence-building measures conducted during that month by India and Pakistan. An observer mission dispatched by the OIC to monitor presidential elections held in the Palestinian territories in early January 2005, at the request of the PA, was rejected by Israel. Later in that month the inaugural meeting of an OIC Commission of Eminent Persons was convened in Putrajaya, Malaysia. The Commission was mandated to finalize recommendations in the following areas: the preparation of a strategy and plan of action enabling the Islamic community to meet the challenges of the 21st century; the preparation of a comprehensive plan for promoting enlightened moderation, both within Islamic societies and universally; and the preparation of proposals for the future reform and restructuring of the OIC system. An OIC Digital Solidarity Fund was inaugurated in May 2005. In December the third extraordinary OIC summit, convened in Mecca, Saudi Arabia, adopted a 'Ten-Year Programme of Action to Meet the Challenges Facing the Umma in the 21st Century', a related Mecca Declaration and a report by the Commission of Eminent Persons. The summit determined to restructure the OIC, and mandated the establishment of an Executive Committee, comprising the summit conference and ministerial conference troikas (equally reflecting the African, Arab and Asian member states), the OIC host country, and the OIC Secretariat, as a mechanism for following-up Conference resolutions.

In January 2006 the OIC strongly condemned the publication in a Norwegian newspaper of a series of caricatures of the Prophet Muhammad that had originally appeared in a Danish publication in September 2005 and had caused considerable offence to Islamists. In August 2006 the OIC convened a meeting of humanitarian bodies in Istanbul, Turkey, to address means of collecting donations for and delivering assistance to victims of the ongoing crises in Lebanon and the Palestinian territories. Shortly afterwards a meeting of the newly-formed Executive Committee, held in Kuala Lumpur, Malaysia, agreed to form a Contact Group for Lebanon, to be co-ordinated by Malaysia. In October a meeting of Iraqi Islamic scholars from all denominations issued the Makkah Declaration on the Iraqi situation, in which they urged unity between different Islamic factions in that country. The first OIC Conference on Women was held in the following month, on the theme 'the role of women in the development of OIC member states'.

In December 2007 the OIC organized the first International Conference on Islamaphobia, aimed at addressing concerns that alleged instances of defamation of Islam appeared to be increasing world-wide (particularly in Europe). These were being observed by an Islamic Observatory on Islamophobia, established in September 2006. The 11th OIC heads of state summit meeting, held in Dakar, Senegal, in March 2008, endorsed a revised OIC Charter. The summit welcomed recent contacts between the Israeli and Palestinian leaders. Participation by OIC member states in the OIC Digital Solidarity Fund was promoted, and the meeting also requested each member state to establish a board to monitor national implementation of the Tunis Declaration on the Information Society, adopted by the November 2005 second phase of the World Summit on the Information Society. In view of a reported rise in anti-Islamic attacks in western nations, OIC leaders denounced stereotyping, profiling and discrimination, and urged the promotion of Islam by Islamic states as a 'moderate, peaceful and tolerant religion'.

Finance

The OIC's activities are financed by mandatory contributions from member states.

Subsidiary Organs

Islamic Centre for the Development of Trade: Complexe Commercial des Habous, ave des FAR, BP 13545, Casablanca, Morocco; tel. (2) 314974; fax (2) 310110; e-mail icdt@icdt.org; internet www .icdt.org; f. 1983 to encourage regular commercial contacts, harmonize policies and promote investments among OIC mems; Dir-Gen. ALLAL RACHDI; publs *Tijaris: International and Inter-Islamic Trade Magazine* (bi-monthly), *Inter-Islamic Trade Report* (annually).

Islamic Jurisprudence (Fiqh) Academy: POB 13917, Jeddah, Saudi Arabia; tel. (2) 667-1664; fax (2) 667-0873; internet www .fiqhacademy.org.sa; f. 1982; Sec.-Gen. Sheikh MOHAMED HABIB IBN AL-KHODHA.

Islamic Solidarity Fund: c/o OIC Secretariat, POB 178, Jeddah 21411, Saudi Arabia; tel. (2) 680-0800; fax (2) 687-3568; f. 1974 to meet the needs of Islamic communities by providing emergency aid and the finance to build mosques, Islamic centres, hospitals, schools and universities; Chair. Sheikh NASIR ABDULLAH BIN HAMDAN; Exec. Dir ABDULLAH HERSI.

Islamic University in Uganda: POB 2555, Mbale, Uganda; tel. (45) (772) 616337; fax (45) 4433502; e-mail info@iuiu.ac.ug; internet www.iuiu.ac.ug/; f. 1988 to meet the educational needs of Muslim populations in English-speaking African countries; second campus in Kampala; mainly financed by OIC; Rector Dr AHMAD KAWESA SENGENDO.

Islamic University of Niger: BP 11507, Niamey, Niger; tel. 723903; fax 733796; e-mail unislam@intnet.ne; internet www .universite_say.ne/; f. 1984; provides courses of study in *Shari'a* (Islamic law) and Arabic language and literature; also offers courses in pedagogy and teacher training; receives grants from Islamic Solidarity Fund and contributions from OIC member states; Rector Prof. ABDELALI OUDHRIRI.

Islamic University of Technology (IUT): Board Bazar, Gazipur 1704, Dhaka, Bangladesh; tel. (2) 980-0960; fax (2) 980-0970; e-mail vc@iut-dhaka.edu; internet www.iutoic-dhaka.edu; f. 1981 as the Islamic Centre for Technical and Vocational Training and Resources, named changed to Islamic Institute of Technology in 1994, current name adopted in June 2001; aims to develop human resources in OIC mem. states, with special reference to engineering, technology, tech. and vocational education and research; 135 staff and 646 students; library of 26,500 vols; Vice-Chancellor Prof. Dr IMTIAZ HOSSAIN; publs *News Bulletin* (annually), *Journal of Engineering and Technology* (2 a year), annual calendar and announcement for admission, reports, human resources development series.

Research Centre for Islamic History, Art and Culture (IRCICA): POB 24, Beşiktaş 80692, İstanbul, Turkey; tel. (212) 2591742; fax (212) 2584365; e-mail ircica@ircica.org; internet www .ircica.org; f. 1980; library of 60,000 vols; Dir-Gen. Prof. Dr HALIT EREN; publs *Newsletter* (3 a year), monographical studies.

Statistical, Economic and Social Research and Training Centre for the Islamic Countries: Attar Sok 4, GOP 06700, Ankara, Turkey; tel. (312) 4686172; fax (312) 4673458; e-mail oicankara@sesrtcic.org; internet www.sesrtcic.org; f. 1978; Dir-Gen. S. ALPAY; publs *Journal of Economic Co-operation among Islamic Countries* (quarterly), *InfoReport* (quarterly), *Statistical Yearbook* (annually).

Specialized Institutions

International Islamic News Agency (IINA): King Khalid Palace, Madinah Rd, POB 5054, Jeddah 21422, Saudi Arabia; tel. (2) 665-8561; fax (2) 665-9358; e-mail iina@islamicnews.org.sa; internet www.islamicnews.org.sa; f. 1972; distributes news and reports daily on events in the Islamic world, in Arabic, English and French; Dir-Gen. ERDEM KOK.

Islamic Educational, Scientific and Cultural Organization (ISESCO): BP 2275 Rabat 10104, Morocco; tel. (37) 772433; fax (37) 772058; e-mail cid@isesco.org.ma; internet www.isesco.org.ma; f. 1982; Dir-Gen. Dr ABDULAZIZ BIN OTHMAN ALTWAIJRI; publs *ISESCO Newsletter* (quarterly), *Islam Today* (2 a year), *ISESCO Triennial*.

Islamic States Broadcasting Union (ISBU): POB 6351, Jeddah 21442, Saudi Arabia; tel. (2) 672-1121; fax (2) 672-2600; internet www.isboo.org; f. 1975; Sec.-Gen. HUSSEIN AL-ASKARY.

Affiliated Institutions

International Association of Islamic Banks (IAIB): King Abdulaziz St, Queen's Bldg, 23rd Floor, Al-Balad Dist, POB 9707, Jeddah 21423, Saudi Arabia; tel. (2) 651-6900; fax (2) 651-6552; f. 1977 to link financial institutions operating on Islamic banking principles; activities include training and research; mems: 192 banks and other financial institutions in 34 countries; Sec.-Gen. SAMIR A. SHAIKH.

Islamic Chamber of Commerce and Industry: POB 3831, Clifton, Karachi 75600, Pakistan; tel. (21) 5874910; fax (21) 5870765; e-mail icci@icci-oic.org; internet /iccionline.net/en/; f. 1979 to promote trade and industry among member states; comprises nat. chambers or feds of chambers of commerce and industry; Sec.-Gen. Dr MOSTAFA HODIEB.

Islamic Committee for the International Crescent: POB 17434, Benghazi, Libya; tel. (61) 95824; fax (61) 95829; internet www.uhik .org/en/index.php; f. 1979 to attempt to alleviate the suffering caused by natural disasters and war; Pres. ALI MAHMOUD BUHEDMA.

Islamic Solidarity Sports Federation: POB 5844, Riyadh 11442, Saudi Arabia; tel. (1) 480-9253; fax (1) 482-2145; e-mail issf@awalnet .net.sa; f. 1981; Sec.-Gen. Dr MOHAMMAD SALEH GAZDAR.

Organization of Islamic Capitals and Cities (OICC): POB 13621, Jeddah 21414, Saudi Arabia; tel. (2) 698-1953; fax (2) 698-1053; e-mail webmaster@oicc.org; internet www.oicc.org; f. 1980; aims to preserve the identity and the heritage of Islamic capitals and cities; to achieve and enhance sustainable development in member capitals and cities; to establish and develop comprehensive urban norms, systems and plans to serve the growth and prosperity of Islamic capitals and cities and to enhance their cultural, environmental, urban, economic and social conditions; to advance municipal services and facilities in the member capitals and cities; to support member cities' capacity-building programmes; and to consolidate fellowship and co-ordinate the scope of co-operation between members; comprises 147 capitals and cities as active members, eight observer members and 15 associate members, in Asia, Africa, Europe and South America; Sec.-Gen. OMAR KADI.

Organization of the Islamic Shipowners' Association: POB 14900, Jeddah 21434, Saudi Arabia; tel. (2) 663-7882; fax (2) 660-4920; e-mail mail@oisaonline.com; internet http://www.oisaonline .com; f. 1981 to promote co-operation among maritime cos in Islamic countries; in 1998 mems approved the establishment of a new commercial venture, the Bakkah Shipping Company, to enhance sea transport in the region; Sec.-Gen. Dr ABDULLATIF A. SULTAN.

World Federation of Arab-Islamic Schools: 2 Wadi el-Nile St, Maadi, Cairo, Egypt; tel. (2) 358-3278; internet www.wfais.org; f. 1976; supports Arab-Islamic schools world-wide and encourages co-operation between the institutions; promotes the dissemination of the Arabic language and Islamic culture; supports the training of personnel.

OTHER REGIONAL ORGANIZATIONS

Agriculture, Food, Forestry and Fisheries

(for organizations concerned with agricultural commodities, see Commodities)

International Centre for Agricultural Research in the Dry Areas (ICARDA): POB 5466, Aleppo, Syria; tel. (21) 2213433; fax (21) 2213490; e-mail icarda@cgiar.org; internet www.icarda.org; f. 1977; aims to improve the production of lentils, barley and faba beans throughout the developing world; supports the improvement of on-farm water-use efficiency, rangeland and small-ruminant production in all dry-area developing countries; within the West and Central Asia and North Africa region promotes the improvement of bread and durum wheat and chick-pea production and of farming systems; undertakes research, training and dissemination of information, in co-operation with national, regional and international research institutes, universities and ministries of agriculture, in order to enhance production, alleviate poverty and promote sustainable natural resource management practices; member of the network of 15 agricultural research centres supported by the Consultative Group on International Agricultural Research (CGIAR); Dir-Gen. Dr MAHMOUD MOHAMED BASHIR EL-SOLH; publs *Annual Report, Caravan Newsletter* (2 a year).

International Food Policy Research Institute (IFPRI): 2033 K St, NW, Washington, DC 20006, USA; tel. (202) 862-5600; fax (202) 467-4439; e-mail ifpri@cgiar.org; internet www.ifpri.org; f. 1975; co-operates with academic and other institutions in further research; develops policies for cutting hunger and malnutrition; committed to increasing public awareness of food policies; Chair. Dr ROSS GARNAUT (Australia); Dir Gen. JOACHIM VON BRAUN (Germany).

> **International Service for National Agricultural Research (ISNAR):** IFPRI, ISNAR Division, ILRI, POB 5689, Addis Ababa, Ethiopia; tel. (11) 646-3215; fax (11) 646-2927; e-mail ifpri-addisababa@cgiar.org; fmrly based in The Hague, Netherlands, the ISNAR Program relocated to Addis Ababa in 2004, under the governance of IFPRI; Dir Dr WILBERFORCE KISAMBA-MUGERWA.

North Pacific Anadromous Fish Commission: 889 W. Pender St, Suite 502, Vancouver, BC V6C 3B2, Canada; tel. (604) 775-5550; fax (604) 775-5577; e-mail secretariat@npafc.org; internet www.npafc.org; f. 1993; mems: Canada, Japan, Republic of Korea, Russia, USA; Pres. DOHYUNG KOO; publs *Annual Report, Newsletter* (2 a year), *Statistical Yearbook, Scientific Bulletin, Technical Report.*

World Organisation of Animal Health: 12 rue de Prony, 75017 Paris, France; tel. 1-44-15-18-88; fax 1-42-67-09-87; e-mail oie@oie.int; internet www.oie.int; f. 1924 as Office International des Epizooties (OIE); objectives include promoting international transparency of animal diseases; collecting, analysing and disseminating scientific veterinary information; providing expertise and promoting international co-operation in the control of animal diseases; promoting veterinary services; providing new scientific guidelines on animal production, food safety and animal welfare; launched in May 2005, jointly with FAO and WHO, a Global Strategy for the Progressive Control of Highly Pathogenic Avian Influenza (H5N1), and, in partnership with other organizations, has convened conferences on avian influenza; experts in a network of 156 collaborating centres and reference laboratories; 172 mems; Dir-Gen. BERNARD VALLAT; publs *Disease Information* (weekly), *World Animal Health* (annually), *Scientific and Technical Review* (3 a year), other manuals, codes etc.

Arts and Culture

Baltic Music Network: Willemoesgade 52, 2100 Copenhagen Ø, Denmark; tel. 35-26-49-07; fax 33-93-44-13; f. 1991 to encourage the international exchange of culture, particularly music, in the Baltic Sea region; mems: orgs and individuals in nine countries; Co-ordinator IB JENSEN.

European Cultural Foundation: Jan van Goyenkade 5, 1075 HN Amsterdam, Netherlands; tel. (20) 5733868; fax (20) 6752231; e-mail eurocult@eurocult.org; internet www.eurocult.org; f. 1954 as a non-governmental organization, supported by private sources, to promote activities of mutual interest to European countries on aspects of culture; maintains national committees in 23 countries and a transnational network of institutes and centres: European Institute of Education and Social Policy, Paris; Institute for European Environmental Policy, London, Madrid and Berlin; Association for Innovative Co-operation in Europe (AICE), Brussels; EURYDICE Central Unit (the Education Information Network of the European Community), Brussels; European Institute for the Media, Düsseldorf; European Foundation Centre, Brussels; Fund for Central and East European Book Projects, Amsterdam; Institute for Human Sciences, Vienna; East West Parliamentary Practice Project, Amsterdam; and Centre Européen de la Culture, Geneva; also manages a grants programme for European co-operation projects; Chair. Dr KATHINKA DITTRICH VAN WERINGH (Germany); Dir GOTTFRIED WAGNER; publs *Annual Report, Newsletter* (monthly).

International Centre for the Study of the Preservation and Restoration of Cultural Property (ICCROM): Via di San Michele 13, 00153 Rome, Italy; tel. (06) 585531; fax (06) 58553349; e-mail iccrom@iccrom.org; internet www.iccrom.org; f. 1959; assembles documents on the preservation and restoration of cultural property; stimulates research and proffers advice; organizes missions of experts; undertakes training of specialists; mems: 117 countries; Dir-Gen. Dr MOUNIR BOUCHENAKI (Algeria); publ. *Newsletter* (annually, in Arabic, English, French and Spanish).

Organization of World Heritage Cities: 15 rue Saint-Nicolas, Québec, QC G1K 1M8, Canada; tel. (418) 692-0000; fax (418) 692-5558; e-mail secretariat@ovpm.org; internet www.ovpm.org; f. 1993 to assist cities inscribed on the UNESCO World Heritage List to implement the Convention concerning the Protection of the World Cultural and Natural Heritage (1972); promotes co-operation between city authorities, in particular in the management and sustainable development of historic sites; holds an annual General Assembly, comprising the mayors of member cities; mems: 233 cities world-wide; Sec.-Gen. LEE MINAIDIS (interim); publ. *OWHC Newsletter* (2 a year, in English, French and Spanish).

Commodities

International Cadmium Association: 168 ave Tervueren, 1150 Brussels, Belgium; tel. (2) 777-05-60; fax (2) 777-05-65; e-mail info@cadmium.org; internet www.cadmium.org; f. 1976; covers all aspects of the production and use of cadmium and its compounds; includes almost all producers and users of cadmium.

International Cotton Advisory Committee (ICAC): 1629 K St, NW, Suite 702, Washington, DC 20006-1636, USA; tel. (202) 463-6660; fax (202) 463-6950; e-mail secretariat@icac.org; internet www.icac.org; f. 1939 to observe developments in world cotton; to collect and disseminate statistics; to suggest measures for the furtherance of international collaboration in maintaining and developing a sound world cotton economy; and to provide a forum for international discussions on cotton prices; mems: 44 countries; Exec. Dir Dr TERRY TOWNSEND (USA); publs *Cotton This Week!* (internet/e-mail only), *Cotton This Month, Cotton: Review of the World Situation* (every 2 months), *Cotton: World Statistics* (annually), *The ICAC Recorder, World Textile Demand* (annually), other surveys, studies, trade analyses and technical publications.

International Grains Council (IGC): 1 Canada Sq., Canary Wharf, London, E14 5AE, United Kingdom; tel. (20) 7513-1122; fax (20) 7513-0630; e-mail igc@igc.org.uk; internet www.igc.org.uk; f. 1949 as International Wheat Council, present name adopted in 1995; responsible for the administration of the International Grains Agreement, 1995, comprising the Grains Trade Convention (GTC) and the Food Aid Convention (FAC, under which donors pledge specified minimum annual amounts of food aid for developing countries in the form of grain and other eligible products); aims to further international co-operation in all aspects of trade in grains, to promote international trade in grains, and to achieve a free flow of this trade, particularly in developing member countries; seeks to contribute to the stability of the international grain market; acts as a forum for consultations between members; provides comprehensive information on the international grain market; mems: 25 countries and the EU; Exec. Dir ETSUO KITAHARA; publs *World Grain Statistics* (annually), *Wheat and Coarse Grain Shipments* (annually), *Report for the Fiscal Year* (annually), *Grain Market Report* (monthly), *IGC Grain Market Indicators* (weekly).

International Lead and Zinc Study Group (ILZSG): Rua Almirante Barroso 38, 5th Floor, Lisbon 1000-013, Portugal; tel. (21) 3592420; fax (21) 3592429; e-mail root@ilzsg.org; internet www .ilzsg.org; f. 1959 for intergovernmental consultation on world trade in lead and zinc; conducts studies and provides information on trends in supply and demand; mems: 27 countries and the European Commission; Chair. V. K. THAKRAL (India); Sec.-Gen. DON SMALE; publ. *Lead and Zinc Statistics* (monthly).

International Organisation of Vine and Wine (Organisation Internationale de la Vigne et du Vin—OIV): 18 rue d'Aguesseau, 75008 Paris, France; tel. 1-44-94-80-80; fax 1-42-66-90-63; e-mail contact@oiv.int; internet www.oiv.int; f. 2001 (agreement establishing an International Wine Office signed Nov. 1924, name changed to International Vine and Wine Office in 1958); researches vine and vine product issues in the scientific, technical, economic and social areas, disseminates knowledge, and facilitates contacts between researchers; mems: 41 countries and five countries with observer status; Dir-Gen. FEDERICO CASTELLUCCI (Italy); publs *Bulletin de l'OIV* (every 2 months), *Lexique de la Vigne et du Vin*, *Recueil des méthodes internationales d'analyse des vins*, *Code international des Pratiques oenologiques*, *Codex oenologique international*, numerous scientific publications.

International Silk Association: 34 rue de la Charité, 69002 Lyon, France; tel. 4-78-42-10-79; fax 4-78-37-56-72; e-mail isa-silk .ais-sole@wanadoo.fr; f. 1949 to promote closer collaboration between all branches of the silk industry and trade, develop the consumption of silk, and foster scientific research; collects and disseminates information and statistics relating to the trade and industry; organizes biennial congresses; mems: employers' and technical organizations in 40 countries; Gen. Sec. X. LAVERGNE; publs *ISA Newsletter* (monthly), congress reports, standards, trade rules, etc.

International Sugar Organization: 1 Canada Sq., Canary Wharf, London, E14 5AA, United Kingdom; tel. (20) 7513-1144; fax (20) 7513-1146; e-mail exdir@isosugar.org; internet www.isosugar.org; administers the International Sugar Agreement (1992), with the objectives of stimulating co-operation, facilitating trade and encouraging demand; aims to improve conditions in the sugar market through debate, analysis and studies; serves as a forum for discussion; holds annual seminars and workshops; sponsors projects from developing countries; mems: 81 countries producing some 83% of total world sugar; Exec. Dir Dr PETER BARON; publs *Sugar Year Book*, *Monthly Statistical Bulletin*, *Market Report and Press Summary*, *Quarterly Market Outlook*, seminar proceedings.

Organization of the Petroleum Exporting Countries (OPEC): 1020 Vienna, Obere Donaustrasse 93, Austria; tel. (1) 211-12-279; fax (1) 214-98-27; internet www.opec.org; f. 1960 to unify and co-ordinate members' petroleum policies and to safeguard their interests generally; holds regular conferences of member countries to set reference prices and production levels; conducts research in energy studies, economics and finance; provides data services and news services covering petroleum and energy issues; mems: Algeria, Iran, Iraq, Kuwait, Libya, Nigeria, Qatar, Saudi Arabia, United Arab Emirates, Venezuela; Sec.-Gen. ABDULLA SALEM EL-BADRI (Libya); publs *Annual Report*, *Annual Statistical Bulletin*, *OPEC Bulletin* (monthly), *OPEC Review* (quarterly), *Monthly Oil Market Report*.

Development and Economic Co-operation

Asia-Pacific Mountain Network (APMN): c/o International Centre for Integrated Mountain Development, GPO Box 3226, Khumaltar, Lalitpur, Nepal; tel. (1) 5003222; fax (1) 5003299; e-mail apmn@ mtnforum.org; internet apmn.icimod.org; f. 1995; forum for the production and dissemination of information on sustainable mountain development, reducing the risk of mountain disasters, economic development, the elimination of poverty, and cultural heritage; mems: about 2,000.

Barents Euro-Arctic Council: c/o Ministry of Foreign Affairs, 119200 Moscow, Smolenskaya-Sennaya pl. 32/34; internet www .beac.mid.ru; f. 1993 as a forum for Barents regional intergovernmental co-operation; mems: Denmark, Finland, Iceland, Norway, Russia, Sweden, European Commission; chairmanship of the Council rotates on a two-yearly basis between the member states (Nov. 2007–Nov. 2009: Russia).

Central Asia Regional Economic Co-operation (CAREC): CAREC Unit, ADB, POB 789, 0980 Manila, Philippines; tel. (2) 6325857; fax (2) 6362387; internet www.adb.org/Carec; f. 1997; a sub-regional alliance supported by several multilateral institutions (Asian Development Bank, European Bank for Reconstruction and Development, International Monetary Fund, Islamic Development Bank, United Nations Development Programme, and World Bank) to promote economic co-operation and development; supports projects in the following priority areas: transport, energy, trade policy, trade facilitation; mems: Afghanistan, Azerbaijan, Kazakhstan, Kyrgyzstan, Mongolia, Tajikistan, Uzbekistan, Xinjiang Uygur Autonomous Region (of the People's Republic of China).

Council of Baltic Sea States (CBSS): Strömsborg, POB 2010, 103 11 Stockholm, Sweden; tel. (8) 440-19-20; fax (8) 440-19-44; e-mail cbss@cbss.org; internet www.cbss.org; f. 1992 as a forum to strengthen co-operation between countries in the Baltic Sea region, including Russia; Dir Dr GABRIELLE KÖTSCHAU (Germany); publ. *Newsletter* (monthly).

Eurasian Economic Community (EURASEC): 105066 Moscow, 1-i Basmannyi per. 6/4, Russia; tel. (495) 223-90-00; fax (495) 223-90-24; e-mail evrazes@evrazes.ru; internet www.evrazes.com; f. 2000; formerly a Customs Union agreed between Belarus, Kazakhstan, Kyrgyzstan, Russia and Tajikistan in 1999; the merger of EURASEC with the Central Asian Co-operation Organization (CACO) was agreed in Oct. 2005, and achieved in Jan. 2006 with the accession to EURASEC of Uzbekistan, which had hitherto been the only mem. of CACO that did not also belong to EURASEC; aims to create a common economic space with a single currency; a free trade zone was established at the end of 2002; in Oct. 2007 EURASEC leaders approved the legal basis for establishing a new customs union, initially to comprise Belarus, Kazakhstan and Russia, with Kyrgyzstan, Tajikistan and Uzbekistan expected to join by 2011; mems co-operate on issues including customs tariff harmonization, migration, border security and negotiating admission to the WTO; Armenia, Moldova and Ukraine have observer status; Sec.-Gen. TAIR A. MANSUROV.

Pacific Basin Economic Council (PBEC): 900 Fort St, Suite 1080, Honolulu, HI 96813, USA; tel. (808) 521-9044; fax (808) 521-8530; e-mail info@pbec.org; internet www.pbec.org; f. 1967; an asscn of business representatives aiming to promote business opportunities in the region, in order to enhance overall economic development; advises governments and serves as a liaison between business leaders and government officials; encourages business relationships and co-operation among members; holds business symposia; mems: 20 economies (Australia, Canada, Chile, People's Republic of China, Colombia, Ecuador, Hong Kong, Indonesia, Japan, Republic of Korea, Malaysia, Mexico, New Zealand, Peru, Philippines, Russia, Singapore, Taiwan, Thailand, USA); Pres. and CEO ROBERT LEES; Pres. STEPHEN OLSEN; publs *Pacific Journal* (quarterly), *Executive Summary* (annual conference report).

World Economic Forum: 91–93 route de la Capite, 1223 Cologny/ Geneva, Switzerland; tel. 228691212; fax 227862744; e-mail contact@weforum.org; internet www.weforum.org; f. 1971; the Forum comprises commercial interests gathered on a non-partisan basis, under the stewardship of the Swiss Government, with the aim of improving society through economic development; convenes an annual meeting in Davos, Switzerland; organizes the following programmes: Technology Pioneers; Women Leaders; and Young Global Leaders; and aims to mobilize the resources of the global business community in the implementation of the following initiatives: the Global Health Initiative; the Disaster Relief Network; the West-Islamic World Dialogue; and the G-20/International Monetary Reform Project; the Forum is governed by a guiding Foundation Board; an advisory International Business Council; and an administrative Managing Board; regular mems: representatives of 1,000 leading commercial companies world-wide; selected mem. companies taking a leading role in the movement's activities are known as 'partners'.

Economics and Finance

Bank for International Settlements (BIS): Centralbahnplatz 2, 4002 Basel, Switzerland; tel. 612808080; fax 612809100; e-mail email@bis.org; internet www.bis.org; f. pursuant to the Hague Agreements of 1930 to promote co-operation among national central banks and to provide additional facilities for international financial operations; provides secretariat for the Basel Committee on Banking Supervision; representative offices in Hong Kong and Mexico; mems: central banks in 55 countries, incl. Russia; Chair. JEAN-PIERRE ROTH (Switzerland); Gen. Man. MALCOLM D. KNIGHT (Canada); publs *Annual Report*, *Quarterly Review: International Banking and Financial Market Developments*, *The BIS Consolidated International Banking Statistics* (every 6 months), *Joint BIS-IMF-OECD-World Bank Statistics on External Debt* (quarterly), *Regular OTC Derivatives Market Statistics* (every 6 months), *Central Bank Survey of Foreign Exchange and Derivatives Market Activity* (every 3 years).

European Federation of Financial Analysts Societies (EFFAS): Einsteinstr. 5, 63303 Dreieich, Frankfurt-am-Main, Germany; tel. (6103) 583348; fax (6103) 583335; e-mail claudia.stinnes@ effas.com; internet www.effas.com; f. 1962 to co-ordinate the activities of European asscns of financial analysts; aims to raise the standard of financial analysis and improve the quality of information given to investors; encourages unification of national rules and draws up rules of profession; holds biennial congress; mems: asscns in 25 European countries; Chair. FRITZ H. RAU; Gen. Sec. CLAUDIA STINNES.

Group of 20 (G20): internet www.g20.org; f. Sept. 1999 as an informal deliberative forum of finance ministers and central bank governors representing both industrialized and 'systemically important' emerging-market nations; aims to strengthen the international financial architecture and to foster sustainable economic growth and development; in 2004 participating countries adopted the G20 Accord for Sustained Growth and stated a commitment to high standards of transparency and fiscal governance; the IMF Managing Director and IBRD President participate in G20 annual meetings (Nov. 2008: São Paulo, Brazil); mems: ministers of finance and central bank governors of Argentina, Australia, Brazil, Canada, People's Republic of China, France, Germany, India, Indonesia, Italy, Japan, Republic of Korea, Mexico, Russia, Saudi Arabia, South Africa, Turkey, United Kingdom, USA and the European Union.

International Bank for Economic Co-operation (IBEC): 107996 Moscow, ul. Masha Poryvaeva 11, Russia; tel. (495) 975-38-61; fax (495) 632-95-80; e-mail info@ibec.ru; f. 1963; provides credit and settlement facilities for member states, and also acts as an international commercial bank, offering services to commercial banks and enterprises; mems: nine states, incl. Bulgaria, Czech Republic, Poland, Romania and Slovakia; Chair. VITALII S. KHOKHLOV; Man. Dirs V. SYTNIKOV, E. BOURDAKOV.

International Investment Bank: 107078 Moscow, ul. Masha Poryvaeva 7, Russia; tel. (495) 975-40-08; fax (495) 975-20-70; e-mail if@iibbank.com; internet www.iibbank.com; f. 1970; regional development bank focusing on project financing and providing credit facilities for construction and modernization projects and other activities; following the decision in 1989–91 of most member states to adopt a market economy, the Bank conducted its transactions (from 1 Jan. 1991) in convertible currencies, rather than in transferable roubles; cap. €214.5m., reserves €431.2m. (31 Dec. 2002); mems: Bulgaria, Cuba, Czech Republic, Mongolia, Romania, Russia, Slovakia and Viet Nam.

Nordic Investment Bank (NIB) (Nordiska Investeringsbanken): Fabianinkatu 34, POB 249, 00171 Helsinki, Finland; tel. (10) 618001; fax (10) 6180725; e-mail info@nib.int; internet www.nib.int; f. 1975; provides finance and guarantees for the implementation of investment projects and exports in the Nordic and Baltic regions; the main sectors of the Bank's activities are energy, infrastructure development, transport and communications, and manufacturing; also manages an Environmental Loan Facility which facilitates environmental investments in the Nordic Adjacent Areas (north-west Russia); mems: Governments of Denmark, Estonia, Finland, Iceland, Latvia, Lithuania, Norway and Sweden; Pres. and CEO JOHNNY ÅKERHOLM.

Education

Comparative Education Society in Europe (CESE): Institut für Augemeine Pädagogik, Humboldt-Universität zu Berlin, Unter den Linden 6, 10099 Berlin, Germany; tel. (30) 20934094; fax (30) 20931006; e-mail juergen.schriewer@educat.hu-berlin.de; internet www.cese-europe.org; f. 1961 to promote teaching and research in comparative and international education; organizes conferences and promotes literature; mems: in 49 countries; Pres. Prof. ROBERT COWEN (United Kingdom); Sec. and Treas. Prof. HANS-GEORG KOTTHOFF (Germany); publ. *Newsletter* (quarterly).

European Association for Education of Adults (EAEA): 60 rue de la Concorde, 1050 Brussels, Belgium; tel. (2) 513-52-05; fax (2) 513-57-34; e-mail gina.ebner@eaea.org; internet www.eaea.org; f. 1953; aims to create a 'learning society' by encouraging demand for learning, particularly from women and excluded sectors of society; seeks to improve response of providers of learning opportunities and authorities and agencies; mems: 114 orgs in 41 countries; Pres. JÁNOS TÓTH; Gen. Sec. GINA EBNER; publs *EAEA Monograph Series*, newsletter.

European Union of Arabic and Islamic Scholars (Union Européenne des Arabisants et Islamisants—UEAI): c/o Bernadette Martel-Thoumian, Université de Grenoble, BP 47, 38040 Grenoble, Cedex 9, France; e-mail Bernadette.Martel-Thoumian@upmf-grenoble.fr; f. 1964 to organize congresses of Arabic and Islamic Studies; holds congress every two years; mems: 300 in 28 countries; Pres. Prof. SILVIA NAEF (Switzerland); Sec. Prof. BERNADETTE MARTEL-THOUMIAN (France).

European University Association (EUA): 13 rue d'Egmont, 1000 Brussels, Belgium; tel. (2) 230-55-44; fax (2) 230-57-51; e-mail info@eua.be; internet www.eua.be; f. 2001 by merger of the Association of European Universities and the Confederation of EU Rectors' Conferences; represents European universities and national rectors' conferences; promotes the development of a coherent system of European higher education and research through projects and membership services; provides support and guidance to mems. mems: 775 in 45 countries; Pres. GEORG WINCKLER; Sec.-Gen. LESLEY WILSON; publs *Thema, Directory, Annual Report*.

Environmental Conservation

Baltic Marine Environment Protection Commission (Helsinki Commission)—HELCOM: Katajanokanlaituri 6B, 00160 Helsinki, Finland; tel. (9) 6220220; fax (9) 62202239; e-mail firstname.lastname@helcom.fi; internet www.helcom.fi; f. 1980 to combat regional pollution; governing body of the Convention on the Protection of the Marine Environment of the Baltic Sea Area; responsibilities include the prevention of airborne, sea and land-based pollution; a new Convention was signed in 1992 and entered into force in 2000; in November 2007 adopted a Baltic Sea Action Plan to reduce pollution in the area by 2021; mems: Denmark, Estonia, European Community, Finland, Germany, Latvia, Lithuania, Poland, Russia and Sweden; Exec. Sec. ANNE CHRISTINE BRUSENDORFF; publ. *Baltic Sea Environment Proceedings*.

Caspian Environment Programme: 63 Golestan Alley, Valiasr Ave, 1966733413 Tehran, Iran; tel. (21) 22042285; fax (21) 22051850; e-mail cep.pcu@undp.org; internet www.caspianenvironment.org; f. 1998 by Azerbaijan, Iran, Kazakhstan, Russia and Turkmenistan with the aim of halting the deterioration of environmental conditions in the area of the Caspian Sea and also with a view to promoting sustainable development in the region.

Commission on the Protection of the Black Sea Against Pollution: Dolmabahçe Saray II. Hareket Köxkü, 34353 Bexiktax, Istanbul, Turkey; tel. (212) 2279927; fax (212) 2279933; e-mail ahmet.kideys@blacksea-commission.org; internet www.blacksea-commission.org; established under the 1992 Convention on the Protection of the Black Sea Against Pollution (Bucharest Convention) to implement the Convention and its Protocols; also oversees the 1996 Strategic Action Plan for the Rehabilitation and Protection of the Black Sea; Exec. Dir Prof. AHMET KIDEYS.

Consortium for Oceanographic Research and Education (CORE): 1201 New York Ave, NW, Suite 420, Washington, DC 20005, USA; tel. (202) 332-0063; fax (202) 332-9751; e-mail coml@coreocean.org; internet www.comlsecretariat.org; f. 1999 to launch and host the International Steering Committee and Secretariat for the Census of Marine Life, a 10-year initiative to assess the diversity, distribution and abundance of marine life being implemented by a network of researchers from more than 70 countries; aims to promote, support and advance the science of oceanography; Pres. RICHARD WEST.

IUCN—International Union for Conservation of Nature: 28 rue Mauverney, 1196 Gland, Switzerland; tel. 229990000; fax 229990002; e-mail webmaster@iucn.org; internet www.iucn.org; f. 1948, as the International Union for Conservation of Nature and Natural Resources; supports partnerships and practical field activities to promote the conservation of natural resources, to secure the conservation of biological diversity as an essential foundation for the future; to ensure wise use of the earth's natural resources in an equitable and sustainable way; and to guide the development of human communities towards ways of life in enduring harmony with other components of the biosphere, developing programmes to protect and sustain the most important and threatened species and eco-systems and assisting governments to devise and carry out national conservation strategies; incorporates the Species Survival Commission (SSC), a science-based network of volunteer experts aiming to ensure conservation of present levels of biodiversity; compiles annually-updated Red List of Threatened Species, comprising in 2008 some 44,838 species, of which 16,928 were threatened with extinction; maintains a conservation library and documentation centre and units for monitoring traffic in wildlife; mems: more than 1,000 states, government agencies, non-governmental organizations and affiliates in some 140 countries; Pres. MOHAMMED VALLI MOOSA (South Africa); Dir-Gen. JULIA MARTON-LEFÈVRE (USA); publs *World Conservation Strategy, Caring for the Earth, Red List of Threatened Plants, Red List of Threatened Species, United Nations List of National Parks and Protected Areas, World Conservation* (quarterly), *IUCN Today*.

Nordic Environment Finance Corpn (NEFCO): Fabianinkatu 34, POB 249, 00171 Helsinki, Finland; tel. (9) 18001; fax (9) 630976; e-mail info@nefco.fi; internet www.nefco.org; f. 1990; finances environmentally beneficial projects in Central and Eastern Europe with transboundary effects that also benefit the Nordic region; MAGNUS RYSTEDT.

Regional Environmental Centre for Central and Eastern Europe: 2000 Szentendre, Ady Endre ut. 9–11, Hungary; tel. (26) 504-000; fax (26) 311-294; e-mail rec-info@rec.org; internet www.rec.org; f. 1990; aims to assist in the solution of environmental problems in Central and Eastern Europe through the promotion of co-operation between non-governmental organizations, governments and businesses, the free exchange of information and public participation in decision-making; provides grants and training and facilitates networking; 16 local offices; Exec. Dir MARTA SZIGETI BONIFERT.

World Ocean Observatory: c/o Open Space Institute, 1350 Broadway, Rm 201, New York, NY 10018, USA; tel. (212) 356-4295; e-mail info@theW2O.net; internet www.thew2o.net; f. 2004; recommendation of the final report of the Independent World Commission on the Oceans; serves as a focal point for ocean-related information from governments, non-governmental organizations and other networks; aims to enhance public awareness of the importance of oceans and facilitate the dissemination of information; maintains an online radio station and organizes other online events; Dir PETER NEILL; publ. *World Ocean Observer* (monthly).

WWF International: 27 ave du Mont-Blanc, 1196 Gland, Switzerland; tel. 223649111; fax 223648836; e-mail info@wwfint.org; internet www.panda.org; f. 1961 (as World Wildlife Fund), name changed to World Wide Fund for Nature in 1986, current nomenclature adopted 2001; aims to stop the degradation of natural environments, conserve bio-diversity, ensure the sustainable use of renewable resources, and promote the reduction of both pollution and wasteful consumption; addresses six priority issues: forests, freshwater, marine, species, climate change, and toxics; has identified, and focuses its activities in, 200 'ecoregions' (the 'Global 200'), believed to contain the best part of the world's remaining biological diversity; actively supports and operates conservation programmes in more than 90 countries; mems: 54 offices, five associate orgs, c. 5m. individual mems world-wide; Pres. Chief EMEKA ANYAOKU (Nigeria); Dir-Gen. JAMES P. LEAPE; publs *Annual Report, Living Planet Report*.

Government and Politics

Central European Initiative (CEI): CEI Executive Secretariat, Via Genova 9, 34121 Trieste, Italy; tel. (040) 7786777; fax (040) 360640; e-mail cei-es@cei-es.org; internet www.ceinet.org; f. 1989 as 'Quadragonal' co-operation between Austria, Italy, Hungary and Yugoslavia, became 'Pentagonal' in 1990 with the admission of Czechoslovakia, and 'Hexagonal' with the admission of Poland in 1991, present name adopted in 1992, when Bosnia and Herzegovina, Croatia and Slovenia were admitted; the Czech Republic and Slovakia became separate mems in January 1993, and Macedonia also joined in that year; Albania, Belarus, Bulgaria, Romania and Ukraine joined the CEI in 1995 and Moldova in 1996; the Federal Republic of Yugoslavia (now the separate sovereign states of Montenegro and Serbia) admitted in 2000; encourages regional political and economic co-operation with a focus on the following nine areas of activity: climate, environment and sustainable energy; enterprise development (incl. tourism); human resource development; information society and media; intercultural co-operation (incl. minorities); multimodal transport; science and technology; sustainable agriculture; interregional and cross-border co-operation; economic forum held annually since 1998 (11th economic forum: Chisinau, Moldova in Oct. 2008); Sec.-Gen. PIETRO ERCOLE AGO; publ. *Newsletter* (monthly).

Collective Security Treaty Organization (CSTO): 103012 Moscow, Varvarka 7, Russia; tel. (495) 606-97-71; fax (495) 625-76-20; e-mail odkb@gov.ru; internet www.dkb.gov.ru; f. 2003 by signatories to the Treaty on Collective Security (signed Tashkent, Uzbekistan, May 1992); aims to co-ordinate and strengthen military and political co-operation and to promote regional and national security; maintains a joint rapid deployment force; the Oct. 2007 leaders' summit endorsed documents enabling the establishment of CSTO joint peace-keeping forces and the creation of a co-ordination council for the heads of member states' emergency response agencies; the leaders' summit convened in Sept. 2008 issued a joint declaration stating that conflicts should be settled preferably through political and diplomatic means in line with international law and stating the following as immediate priorities: strengthening efforts to promote nuclear non-proliferation; to combat terrorism, drugs-trafficking and weapon-smuggling; to expand co-operation with international bodies; and to promote international efforts to establish 'anti-drug and financial security belts' around Afghanistan; the CSTO became an observer in the UN General Assembly in 2004; in April 2006 it signed a protocol with the UN Office on Drugs and Crime to develop joint projects to combat drugs-trafficking, terrorism and transborder

crime; mems: Armenia, Belarus, Kazakhstan, Kyrgyzstan, Russia, Tajikistan, Uzbekistan; Sec.-Gen. NIKOLAY BORDYUZHA.

Global Elders: POB 49785, London WC2H 7WQ, United Kingdom; e-mail info@theelders.org; internet www.theelders.org; f. 2001; aims to alleviate human suffering world-wide by offering a catalyst for the peaceful resolution of conflicts, seeking new approaches to unresolved global issues, and sharing wisdom; comprises: Kofi Annan (Ghana), Ela Bhatt (India), Lakhdar Brahimi (Algeria), Gro Brundtland (Norway), Jimmy Carter (USA), Fernando H Cardoso (Brazil), Graça Machel (Mozambique), Nelson Mandela (South Africa), Desmond Tutu (South Africa), Mary Robinson (Ireland), Aung San Suu Kyi (Myanmar), Muhammad Yunus (Bangladesh), Li Zhaoxing (People's Republic of China).

Group of Eight (G8): an informal meeting of developed nations, then comprising France, Germany, Italy, Japan, the USA and United Kingdom, first convened in Nov. 1975, at Rambouillet, France, at the level of heads of state and government; Canada became a permanent participant in 1976, forming the Group of Seven major industrialized countries—G7; from 1991 Russia was invited to participate in the then G7 summit outside the formal framework of co-operation; from 1994 Russia contributed more fully to the G7 political dialogue and from 1997 Russia became a participant in nearly all of the summit process scheduled meetings, excepting those related to finance and the global economy; from 1998 the name of the co-operation framework was changed to Group of Eight—G8, and since 2003 Russia has participated fully in all scheduled summit meetings, including those on the global economy; the European Union is also represented at G8 meetings, although it may not chair fora; G8 heads of government and the President of the European Commission and President of the European Council convene an annual summit meeting, the chairmanship and venue of which are rotated in the following order: France, USA, United Kingdom, Russia, Germany, Japan, Italy, Canada (2008: Hokkaido Toyako, Japan); G8 summit meetings address and seek consensus, published in a final declaration, on social and economic issues confronting the international community; the following ('+8') nations: Australia, Brazil, People's Republic of China, India, Indonesia, Mexico, Republic of Korea and South Africa were guest participants at the June 2008 G8 summit; G8 sectoral ministerial meetings (covering areas such as energy, environment, finance and foreign affairs) are held on the fringes of the annual summit, and further G8 sectoral ministerial meetings are convened through the year; mems: Canada, France, Germany, Italy, Japan, Russia, the USA and United Kingdom; European Union representation.

International Federation of Resistance Movements (FIR): Lassallestr. 40/2/2/6, 1020 Vienna, Austria; tel. (1) 726-30-91; f. 1951; supports the medical and social welfare of former victims of fascism; works for peace, disarmament and human rights, and against fascism and neo-fascism; mems: 76 national organizations; Pres. MICHEL VANDERBORGHT; Sec.-Gen. OSKAR WIESFLECKER (Austria).

International Institute for Democracy and Electoral Assistance (IDEA): Strömsborg, 103 34 Stockholm, Sweden; tel. (8) 698-3700; fax (8) 20-2422; e-mail info@idea.int; internet www.idea.int; f. 1995; aims to promote sustainable democracy in new and established democracies; provides world-wide electoral assistance and focuses on broader democratic issues in Africa, the Caucasus and Latin America; 25 mem. states; Sec.-Gen. VIDAR HELGESEN (Norway).

International Institute for Peace: Möllwaldplatz 5, 1040 Vienna, Austria; tel. (1) 504-64-37; fax (1) 505-32-36; e-mail secretariat@iip.at; internet www.iip.at; f. 1957; non-governmental organization with consultative status at ECOSOC and UNESCO; studies conflict prevention; new structures in international law; security issues in Europe and world-wide; mems: individuals and corporate bodies invited by the executive board; Pres. ERWIN LANC (Austria); Dir PETER STANIA (Austria); publ. *Peace and Security* (quarterly).

International Peace Bureau (IPB): 41 rue de Zürich, 1201 Geneva, Switzerland; tel. 227316429; fax 227389419; e-mail mailbox@ipb.org; internet www.ipb.org; f. 1891; promotes international co-operation for general and complete disarmament and the non-violent solution of international conflicts; co-ordinates and represents peace movements at the UN; conducts projects on Disarmament for Development and the abolition of nuclear weapons; mems: 300 peace orgs and 150 individual mems in 70 countries; Pres. TOMAS MAGNUSSON; Sec.-Gen. COLIN ARCHER (United Kingdom); publs *IPB News* (every 2 weeks, by email), *IPB Geneva News*.

Inter-Parliamentary Union (IPU): 5 chemin du Pommier, CP 330, 1218 Le Grand-Saconnex/Geneva, Switzerland; tel. 229194150; fax 229194160; e-mail postbox@mail.ipu.org; internet www.ipu.org; f. 1889 to promote peace, co-operation and representative democracy by providing a forum for multilateral political debate between representatives of national parliaments; mems: national parliaments of 146 sovereign states, incl. Armenia, Azerbaijan, Belarus, Georgia, Kazakhstan, Kyrgyzstan, Russia, Tajikistan, Ukraine and Uzbekistan; seven assoc. mems; Sec.-Gen. ANDERS B. JOHNSSON

(Sweden); publs *Chronicle of Parliamentary Elections* (annually), *The World of Parliaments* (quarterly), *World Directory of Parliaments* (annually).

Non-aligned Movement (NAM): c/o Permanent Representative of Cuba to the UN, 315 Lexington Avenue, New York, NY 10016; tel. (212) 689-7215; fax (212) 779-1697; e-mail cuba@un.int; internet www.canada.cubanoal.cu; f. 1961 by a meeting of 25 Heads of State, with the aim of linking countries that had refused to adhere to the main East/West military and political blocs; co-ordination bureau established in 1973; works for the establishment of a new international economic order, and especially for better terms for countries producing raw materials; maintains special funds for agricultural development, improvement of food production and the financing of buffer stocks; South Commission promotes co-operation between developing countries; seeks changes in the United Nations to give developing countries greater decision-making power; holds summit conference every three years; 15th conference (July 2008): Tehran, Iran; mems: 118 countries.

Northern Forum: 716 W 4th Ave, Suite 100, Anchorage, Alaska, USA; tel. (907) 561-3280; fax (907) 561-6645; e-mail NForum@northernforum.org; internet www.northernforum.org; f. 1991; aims to improve the quality of life of Northern peoples through support for sustainable development and socio-economic co-operation throughout the region; Exec. Dir Priscilla P. Wohl.

Organisation for the Prohibition of Chemical Weapons (OPCW): Johan de Wittlaan 32, 2517JR The Hague, Netherlands; tel. (70) 4163300; fax (70) 3063535; e-mail media@opcw.org; internet www.opcw.org; f. April 1997, on the entry into force of the Chemical Weapons Convention (CWC)—an international, multilateral disarmament treaty banning the development, production, stockpiling, transfer and use of chemical weapons—to oversee its implementation; verifies the irreversible destruction of declared chemical weapons stockpiles, as well as the elimination of all declared chemical weapons production facilities; OPCW member states undertake to provide protection and assistance if chemical weapons have been used against a state party, or if such weapons threaten a state party, and together with OPCW inspectors, monitor the non-diversion of chemicals for activities prohibited under the CWC and verify the consistency of industrial chemical declarations; CWC states parties are obligated to declare any chemical weapons-related activities, to secure and destroy any stockpiles of chemical weapons within the stipulated deadlines, as well as to inactivate and eliminate any chemical weapons production capacity within their jurisdiction; mems: states party to the Convention (183 at Jan. 2008); 2008 budget: €75m; Dir-Gen. Rogelio Pfirter.

Organization for Democracy and Economic Development (GUAM): vul. Melnykova 36/1, 04119 Kyiv, Ukraine; tel. (44) 4837457; fax (44) 4837457; e-mail office@guam.org.ua; internet www.guam.org; f. 1997 as a consultative alliance of Georgia, Ukraine, Azerbaijan and Moldova (GUAM); Uzbekistan joined the grouping in April 1999, when it became known as GUUAM, but withdrew in May 2005, causing the grouping's name to revert to GUAM; formally inaugurated as a full international organization and current name adopted by heads of state at a summit held in Kyiv in May 2006; objectives include the promotion of a regional space of democracy, security, and stable economic and social development; strengthening relations with the EU and NATO; developing a database on terrorism, organized crime, drugs-trafficking, and related activities; establishing a GUAM energy security council; creating the GUAM Free-Trade Zone, in accordance with an agreement signed by heads of state at a meeting in Yalta, Ukraine, in July 2002; further economic development, including the creation of an East–West trade corridor and transportation routes for petroleum; and participation in conflict resolution and peace-keeping activities, with the establishment of peace-keeping forces and civilian police units under consideration; Sec.-Gen. Valeri Chechelashvili (Georgia).

Shanghai Co-operation Organization (SCO): 41, Liangmaqiao Road, Chaoyang District, Beijing, People's Republic of China; tel. (10) 65329806; fax (10) 65329808; e-mail sco@sectsco.org; internet www.sectsco.org; f. 2001, replacing the Shanghai Five (f. 1996 to address border disputes); comprises People's Republic of China, Kazakhstan, Kyrgyzstan, Russia, Tajikistan and Uzbekistan; aims to achieve security through mutual co-operation; promotes economic co-operation and measures to eliminate terrorism and drugs-trafficking; agreement on combating terrorism signed June 2001; a Convention on the Fight against Terrorism, Separatism and Extremism signed June 2002; Treaty on Long-term Good Neighbourliness, Friendship and Co-operation was signed August 2007; maintains an SCO anti-terrorism centre in Tashkent, Uzbekistan; holds annual summit meeting (Aug. 2008: Dushanbe, Tajikistan); Sec.-Gen. Bolat Nurgaliyev (Kazakhstan).

Unrepresented Nations and Peoples Organization (UNPO): POB 85878, 2508 CN The Hague, Netherlands; tel. (70) 3646504; fax (70) 3646608; e-mail unpo@unpo.org; internet www.unpo.org; f. 1991; an international, nonviolent, and democratic membership organization representing indigenous peoples, minorities, and unrecognised or occupied territories united in the aim of protecting and promoting their human and cultural rights, preserving their environments, and finding nonviolent solutions to conflicts that affect them; mems: 60 orgs representing occupied nations, indigenous peoples and minorities; Gen. Sec. Marino Busdachin; publ. *UNPO Yearbook*.

Western European Union (WEU): 15 rue de l'Association, 1000 Brussels, Belgium; tel. (2) 500-44-12; fax (2) 500-44-70; e-mail secretariatgeneral@weu.int; internet www.weu.int; f. 1955, within the terms of the Brussels Treaty (1948), as the main organization for European co-operation in the field of defence and security; in December 1991 WEU agreed that the organization be developed as the defence component of the EU and as the means of strengthening the European pillar of the Atlantic Alliance; in June 1992 ministers agreed upon an operational role for WEU, by supporting international humanitarian, peace-keeping and crisis management missions ('Petersburg Tasks'); mid-1992–mid-1996 undertook a joint monitoring operation with NATO in the Adriatic sea; May 1997–May 2001 maintained a Multinational Advisory Police Element (MAPE) in Albania; greater co-operation with the EU and possible integration of WEU into the EU was incorporated into the Amsterdam Treaty (1997); WEU's crisis management responsibilities were transferred to the EU by July 2001; mems: Belgium, France, Germany, Greece, Italy, Luxembourg, Netherlands, Portugal, Spain, United Kingdom; six Associate Members, seven Associate Partners and five Observers; Sec-Gen. Javier Solana Madariaga (Spain)

Assembly of Western European Union (European Security and Defence Assembly): 43 ave du Président Wilson, 75775 Paris Cédex 16, France; tel. 1-53-67-22-00; fax 1-53-67-22-01; e-mail info@assembly.weu.int; internet www.assembly-weu.org; composed of the representatives of the Brussels Treaty powers to the Parliamentary Assembly of the Council of Europe; it meets at least twice a year, and may proceed on any matter regarding the application of the Brussels Treaty and on any matter submitted to the Assembly for an opinion by the Council; may adopt resolutions or recommendations, which can be transmitted to international organizations, governments and national parliaments; since 2000 has acted as the Interparliamentary European Security and Defence Assembly, focusing on the development of a European Security and Defence Policy and the EU's civil and military crisis-management capabilities; Pres. Jean-Pierre Masseret (France).

Industrial and Professional Relations

General Confederation of Trade Unions (GCTU): 119119 Moscow, 42 Leninsky Prospekt, Russia; tel. (495) 938-79-15; fax (495) 938-21-55; e-mail mail@vkp.ru; internet www.vkp.ru; f. 1992; congress convenes every five years (4th congress: Moscow, Russia, Sept. 2002); mems: 48 trade union organizations from CIS countries, comprising about 75m. workers; Pres. Vladimir Scherbakov.

World Federation of Trade Unions (WFTU): 40 Zan Moreas St, 11745 Athens, Greece; tel. (210) 09236700; fax (210) 09214517; e-mail info@wftucentral.org; internet www.wftucentral.org; f. 1945 on a world-wide basis; mems: 132m. in 121 countries; Gen. Sec. George Mavrikos (Greece); publ. *Flashes from the Trade Unions* (every 2 weeks).

Law

International Institute of Space Law (IISL): 8–10 rue Mario Nikis, 75015 Paris, France; tel. 1-45-67-42-60; fax 1-42-73-21-20; e-mail president@iafastro-iisl.com; internet www.iafastro-iisl.com; f. 1959 at the XI Congress of the International Astronautical Federation; organizes annual Space Law colloquium; studies juridical and sociological aspects of astronautics; makes awards; Pres. Dr Nandasiri Jasentuliyana (USA); publs *Proceedings of Annual Colloquium on Space Law*, *Survey of Teaching of Space Law in the World*.

International Nuclear Law Association (INLA): 29 sq. de Meeûs, 1000 Brussels, Belgium; tel. (2) 547-58-41; fax (2) 503-04-40; e-mail info@aidn-inla.be; internet www.aidn-inla.be; f. 1972 to promote international studies of legal problems related to the peaceful use of nuclear energy; holds conference every two years; mems: 460 in 38 countries; Sec.-Gen. Patrick Reyners; publs *Congress reports*, *Une Histoire de 25 ans*.

Medicine and Health

Association of National European and Mediterranean Societies of Gastroenterology (ASNEMGE): Hollandstr. 14/Mezzanine, 1020 Vienna, Austria; tel. (1) 219-91-80; fax (1) 219-91-80-29; e-mail info@asnemge.org; internet www.asnemge.org; f. 1947 to facilitate the exchange of ideas between gastroenterologists and to disseminate knowledge; organizes International Congress of Gastroenterology every four years; mems: in 43 countries, national societies and sections of national medical societies; Pres. Prof. ROLF HULTCRANTZ (Sweden); Gen. Sec. F. BAZZOLI (Italy).

Council for International Organizations of Medical Sciences (CIOMS): c/o WHO, ave Appia, 1211 Geneva 27, Switzerland; tel. 227913467; fax 227914286; e-mail cioms@who.int; internet www.cioms.ch; f. 1949 to serve the scientific interests of the international biomedical community; aims to facilitate and promote activities in biomedical sciences; runs long-term programmes on bioethics, health policy, ethics and values, drug development and use, and the international nomenclature of diseases; maintains collaborative relations with the UN; holds a general assembly every three years; mems: 66 orgs; Pres. Prof. MICHEL B. VALLOTTON; Sec.-Gen. Dr GOTTFRIED KREUTZ; publs *Reports on Drug Development and Use*, *Proceedings of CIOMS Conferences*, *International Nomenclature of Diseases*, *International Ethical Guide-lines for Biomedical Research Involving Human Subjects*.

European Association for Palliative Care: National Cancer Institute Milano Via Venezian 1, 20133 Milan, Italy; tel. (02) 2390-3390; fax (02) 2390-3393; e-mail amelia.giordano@istitutotumori.mi.it; internet www.eapcnet.org; f. 1988; aims to promote palliative care in Europe and to act as a focus for all of those who work, or have an interest, in the field of palliative care at the scientific, clinical and social levels; mems: 42 national asscns in 25 countries; Pres. LUKAS RADBRUCH (Germany); Sec.-Gen. TINE DE VLIEGER (Belgium); publs *European Journal of Palliative Care* (6 a year), *Palliative Medicine* (8 a year).

European Health Management Association (EHMA): 4 rue de la Science, 1000 Brussels, Belgium; tel. (2) 502-65-25; e-mail info@ehma.org; internet www.ehma.org; f. 1966; aims to improve health care in Europe by raising standards of managerial performance in the health sector; fosters co-operation between managers, academia, policy makers and educators to understand health management in different European contexts and to influence both service delivery and the policy agenda in Europe; mems: 225 institutions in 30 countries; Pres. Dr NAOMI CHAMBERS; Dir JENNIFER BREMNER; publs *Newsletter*, *Eurobriefing* (quarterly).

World Medical Association (WMA): 13 chemin du Levant, CIB-Bâtiment A, 01210 Ferney-Voltaire, France; tel. 4-50-40-75-75; fax 4-50-40-59-37; e-mail wma@wma.net; internet www.wma.net; f. 1947 to achieve the highest international standards in all aspects of medical education and practice, to promote closer ties among doctors and national medical asscns by personal contact and all other means, to study problems confronting the medical profession, and to present its views to appropriate bodies; holds an annual General Assembly; mems: 83 national medical asscns; Pres. Dr JON SNAEDAL (Iceland); Sec.-Gen. Dr OTMAR KLOIBER (Germany); publ. *The World Medical Journal* (quarterly).

Posts and Telecommunications

European Conference of Postal and Telecommunications Administrations: Federal Ministry of Economics and Labour, Scharnhorststr. 34–37, 10115 Berlin, Germany; e-mail kai.ulrich@bmwa.bund.de; internet www.cept.org; f. 1959 to strengthen relations between member administrations and to harmonize and improve their technical services; set up Eurodata Foundation, for research and publishing; mems: 26 countries; Sec. KAI ULRICH; publ. *Bulletin*.

European Telecommunications Satellite Organization (EUTELSAT): 70 rue Balard, 75502, Paris Cédex 15, France; tel. 1-53-98-47-47; fax 1-53-98-37-00; internet www.eutelsat.com; f. 1977 to operate satellites for fixed and mobile communications in Europe; EUTELSAT's in-orbit resource comprises 18 satellites; commercialises capacity in three satellites operated by other companies; mems: public and private telecommunications operations in 47 countries; Chair. and CEO GIULIANO BERRETTA.

Internet Corporation for Assigned Names and Numbers (ICANN): 4676 Admiralty Way, Suite 330, Marina del Rey, CA 90292-6601, USA; tel. (310) 823-9358; fax (310) 823-8649; e-mail icann@icann.org; internet www.icann.org; f. 1998; non-profit, private-sector body; aims to co-ordinate the technical management and policy development of the internet; comprises three Supporting Organizations to assist, review and develop recommendations on internet policy and structure relating to addresses, domain names, and protocol; Pres. and CEO PAUL TWOMEY (Australia).

Press, Radio and Television

Asia-Pacific Broadcasting Union (ABU): POB 1164, 59700 Kuala Lumpur, Malaysia; tel. (3) 22823592; fax (3) 22844382; e-mail info@abu.org.my; internet www.abu.org.my; f. 1964 to foster and co-ordinate the development of broadcasting in the Asia-Pacific area, to develop means of establishing closer collaboration and co-operation among broadcasting orgs, and to serve the professional needs of broadcasters in Asia and the Pacific; holds annual General Assembly; mems: 194 in 54 countries and territories; Pres. ABDUL RAHMAN HAMID (Malaysia) (acting); Sec.-Gen. DAVID ASTLEY (Australia); publs *ABU News* (every 2 months), *ABU Technical Review* (every 2 months).

European Alliance of News Agencies: Norrbackagatan 23, 11341 Stockholm, Sweden; tel. and fax (8) 301-324; e-mail erik-n@telia.com; internet www.pressalliance.com; f. 1957 as European Alliance of Press Agencies (name changed 2002); aims to promote co-operation among members and to study and protect their common interests; annual assembly; mems: in 30 countries; Man. Dir. Dr WOLFGANG VYSLOZIL (Austria); Sec.-Gen. ERIK NYLÉN.

European Broadcasting Union (EBU): CP 45, 17A Ancienne-Route, 1218 Grand-Saconnex, Geneva, Switzerland; tel. 227172111; fax 227474000; e-mail ebu@ebu.ch; internet www.ebu.ch; f. 1950 in succession to the International Broadcasting Union; a professional asscn of broadcasting organizations, supporting the interests of members and assisting the development of broadcasting in all its forms; activities include the Eurovision news and programme exchanges and the Euroradio music exchanges; mems: 74 active (European) in 54 countries, 48 associate mems; Pres. FRITZ PLEITGEN; Sec.-Gen. JEAN RÉVEILLON (France); publs *EBU Technical Review* (annually), *Dossiers* (2 a year).

Organization of Asia-Pacific News Agencies (OANA): c/o Bernama News Agency, 38 Jalan 1/65A, 50400 Kuala Lumpur, Malaysia; tel. (3) 26939933; fax (3) 26981102; internet www.oananews.org; f. 1961 to promote co-operation in professional matters and mutual exchange of news, features, etc. among the news agencies of Asia and the Pacific via the Asia-Pacific News Network (ANN); 13th General Assembly: Bangkok, Thailand, 2007; mems: 40 news agencies in 33 countries; Pres. SYED JAMIL JAAFAR (Malaysia); Sec.-Gen. AZMAN UJANG.

Religion

ACER–Russie (l'Action Chrétienne des Etudiants Russes): 91 rue Olivier de Serres, 75015 Paris, France; tel. 1-42-50-53-46; fax 1-42-50-19-08; e-mail courrier@acer-russie.org; internet www.acer-russie.org; f. 1961 as Aid to Believers in the Soviet Union; supports Christianity, in particular the Russian Orthodox Church, in the countries of the former USSR; Pres. ALEXANDRE VICTOROFF; publ. *Bulletin de l'Aide aux Chretiens de Russie*.

Conference of European Churches (CEC): POB 2100, 150 route de Ferney, 1211 Geneva 2, Switzerland; tel. 227916111; fax 227916227; e-mail cec@cec-kek.org; internet www.cec-kek.org; f. 1959 as a regional ecumenical organization for Europe and a meeting-place for European churches, including members and non-members of the World Council of Churches; holds assemblies every six years; mems: 125 Protestant, Anglican, Orthodox and Old Catholic churches in all European countries; Gen. Sec. The Ven. COLIN WILLIAMS; publs *Monitor* (quarterly), CEC communiqués, reports.

European Baptist Federation (EBF): Nad Habrovkou 3, Jeneralka, 164 00 Prague 6, Czech Republic; tel. 296392250; fax 296392254; e-mail office@ebf.org; internet www.ebf.org; f. 1949 to promote fellowship and co-operation among Baptists in Europe; to further the aims and objects of the Baptist World Alliance; to stimulate and co-ordinate evangelism in Europe; to provide for consultation and planning of missionary work in Europe and elsewhere in the world; mems: 51 Baptist Unions in European countries and the Middle East; Pres. HELARI PUU (Estonia); Gen. Sec. TONY PECK (United Kingdom).

Federation of Jewish Communities of the CIS: 127055 Moscow, 5A 2nd Vysheslavtzev Pereulok, Russia; tel. (495) 737-82-75; fax (495) 783-84-71; e-mail info@fjc.ru; internet www.fjc.ru; f. 1998 to restore Jewish society, culture and religion throughout the countries of the fmr Soviet Union through the provision of professional assistance, educational support and funding to member communities; Pres. LEV LEVIEV.

Muslim World League (MWL) (Rabitat al-Alam al-Islami): POB 537, Makkah, Saudi Arabia; tel. (2) 5600919; fax (2) 5601319; e-mail info@themwl.org; internet www.themwl.org; f. 1962; aims to advance Islamic unity and solidarity, and to promote world peace and respect for human rights; provides financial assistance for education, medical care and relief work; has 45 offices throughout the world; Sec.-Gen. Prof. Dr ABDULLAH BIN ABDUL MOHSIN AL-TURKI; publs *Al-Aalam al Islami* (weekly, Arabic), *Dawat al-Haq* (monthly, Arabic), *Muslim World League Journal* (monthly, English), *Muslim World League Journal* (quarterly, Arabic).

Slavic Gospel Association: 6151 Commonwealth Dr., Loves Park, IL 61111, USA; tel. (815) 282-8900; fax (815) 282-8901; e-mail info@sga.org; internet www.sga.org; f. 1934; runs Regional Ministry Centres in Belarus, Russia and Ukraine; sponsors bible and ministry training to church pastors and workers in CIS countries; provides Russian-language bibles and Christian literature; sponsors national church-planting missionaries and humanitarian aid; Pres. Dr ROBERT W. PROVOST; publs *Insight* (monthly newsletter), *Prayer and Praise* (calendar).

Union of Councils of Soviet Jews: POB 11676, Cleveland Park, Washington, DC 20008, USA; tel. (202) 237-8262; fax (202) 237-2236; e-mail mnaftalin@ucsj.com; internet www.ucsj.com; f. 1970; supports the Jewish community in the former USSR through eight bureaux in Moscow, St Petersburg, Almaty, Bishkek, Lviv, Riga, Tiblisi and Minsk; co-ordinates the Yad L'Yad partnership programme, linking Jewish communities in the former USSR with participating schools and synagogues in the USA; Pres. YOSEF I. ABRAMOWITZ; Sec. MICHA H. NAFTALIN.

World Council of Churches (WCC): 150 route de Ferney, Postfach 2100, 1211 Geneva 2, Switzerland; tel. 227916111; fax 227910361; e-mail info@wcc-coe.org; internet www.wcc-coe.org; f. 1948 to promote co-operation between Christian Churches and to prepare for a clearer manifestation of the unity of the Church; activities are grouped under the following programmes: The WCC and the ecumenical movement in the 21st century; Unity, mission, evangelism and spirituality; Public witness: addressing power, affirming peace; Justice, *diakonia* and responsibility for creation; Education and ecumenical formation; and Inter-religious dialogue and co-operation; mems: 349 Churches in more than 110 countries; Gen. Sec. Rev. Dr SAMUEL KOBIA (Kenya); publs *Current Dialogue* (2 a year), *Ecumenical News International* (weekly), *Ecumenical Review* (quarterly), *International Review of Mission* (quarterly), *WCC News* (quarterly), *WCC Yearbook*.

Science

European Association of Geoscientists and Engineers (EAGE): POB 59, 3990 DB Houten, Netherlands; tel. (30) 6354055; fax (30) 6343524; e-mail eage@eage.org; internet www.eage.org; f. 1997 by merger of European Asscn of Exploration Geophysicists and Engineers (f. 1951) and the European Asscn of Petroleum Geoscientists and Engineers (f. 1988); these two organizations have become, respectively, the Geophysical and the Petroleum Divisions of the EAGE; aims to promote the applications of geoscience and related subjects and to foster co-operation between those working or studying in the fields; organizes conferences, workshops, education programmes and exhibitions; seeks global co-operation with organizations with similar objectives; mems: approx. 8,500 in more than 100 countries; Exec. Dir A. VAN GERWEN; publs *Geophysical Prospecting* (6 a year), *First Break* (monthly), *Petroleum Geoscience* (quarterly).

Federation of European Biochemical Societies: c/o Institute of Cancer Biology and Danish Centre for Human Genome Research, Danish Cancer Society, Strandboulevarden 49, 2100 Copenhagen Ø, Denmark; tel. 35-25-73-64; fax 35-25-73-76; e-mail secretariat@febs.org; internet www.febs.org; f. 1964 to promote the science of biochemistry through meetings of European biochemists, advanced courses and the provision of fellowships; mems: approx. 40,000 in 36 societies; Chair. Prof. JOLANTA BARANSKA; Sec.-Gen. Prof. JULIO E. CELIS; publs *The FEBS Journal*, *FEBS News*, *FEBS Letters*, *FEBS Newsletter*.

International Council for Science (ICSU): 51 blvd de Montmorency, 75016 Paris, France; tel. 1-45-25-03-29; fax 1-42-88-94-31; e-mail secretariat@icsu.org; internet www.icsu.org; f. 1919 as International Research Council; present name adopted 1931; new statutes adopted 1996; to co-ordinate international co-operation in theoretical and applied sciences and to promote national scientific research through the intermediary of affiliated national organizations; General Assembly of representatives of national and scientific members meets every three years to formulate policy. The following committees have been established: Cttee on Science for Food Security, Scientific Cttee on Antarctic Research, Scientific Cttee on Oceanic Research, Cttee on Space Research, Scientific Cttee on

Water Research, Scientific Cttee on Solar-Terrestrial Physics, Cttee on Science and Technology in Developing Countries, Cttee on Data for Science and Technology, Programme on Capacity Building in Science, Scientific Cttee on Problems of the Environment, Steering Cttee on Genetics and Biotechnology and Scientific Cttee on International Geosphere-Biosphere Programme. The following services and Inter-Union Committees and Commissions have been established: Federation of Astronomical and Geophysical Data Analysis Services, Inter-Union Commission on Frequency Allocations for Radio Astronomy and Space Science, Inter-Union Commission on Radio Meteorology, Inter-Union Commission on Spectroscopy, Inter-Union Commission on Lithosphere; national mems: academies or research councils in 98 countries; Scientific mems and assocs: 105 nat. scientific bodies and 29 int. scientific unions; Pres. GOVERDHAN MEHTA; Exec. Sec. THOMAS ROSSWALL; publs *ICSU Yearbook*, *Science International* (quarterly), *Annual Report*.

Nuclear Threat Initiative: 1747 Pennsylvania Ave NW, 7th Floor, Washington, DC 20006, USA; tel. (202) 296-4810; fax (202) 296-4810; e-mail contact@nti.org; internet www.nti.org; f. 2001 to help strengthen global security by reducing the risk of use of and preventing the spread of nuclear, biological and chemical weapons; promotes the objectives of the Nuclear Non-Proliferation Treaty; Pres. and CEO CHARLES B. CURTIS (USA).

Social Sciences

Association for the Study of the World Refugee Problem (AWR): internet www.awr-int.de; f. 1951 to promote and co-ordinate scholarly research on refugee problems; Pres. RAINER WIESTNER (Italy); Gen. Sec. Dr JENS LÖCHER; publs *AWR Bulletin* (quarterly, in English, French, Italian and German), treatises on refugee problems (17 vols).

European and Mediterranean Network of the Social Sciences: c/o Foundation for International Studies, St Paul St, Valletta VLT07, Malta; tel. 237547; fax 230551; e-mail aspiteri@arts.um.edu.mt; f. as successor to the European Co-ordination Centre for Research and Documentation in Social Sciences; aims to provide a forum for discussion and exchange of research towards greater understanding of issues affecting the well-being of the region's peoples; publ. *Mediterranean Social Sciences Review*.

European Association for Population Studies (EAPS): POB 11676, 2502 AR The Hague, Netherlands; tel. (70) 3565200; fax (70) 3647187; e-mail contact@eaps.nl; internet www.eaps.nl; f. 1983 to foster research and provide information on European population problems; organizes conferences, seminars and workshops; mems: demographers from 40 countries; Exec. Sec. GYS BEETS; publ. *European Journal of Population/Revue Européenne de Démographie* (quarterly).

International Peace Institute: 777 United Nations Plaza, New York, NY 10017-3521, USA; tel. (212) 687-4300; fax (212) 983-8246; e-mail ipi@ipinst.org; internet www.ipacademy.org; f. 1970 (as the International Peace Academy) to promote the prevention and settlement of armed conflicts between and within states through policy research and development; educates government officials in the procedures needed for conflict resolution, peace-keeping, mediation and negotiation, through international training seminars and publications; off-the-record meetings are also conducted to gain complete understanding of a specific conflict; Chair. RITA E. HAUSER; Pres. TERJE ROD-LARSEN.

Social Welfare and Human Rights

European Federation of Older Persons (EURAG): Wielandgasse 9, 8010 Graz, Austria; tel. and fax (316) 81-4608; e-mail office@eurag-europe.org; internet www.eurag-europe.org; f. 1962 as the European Federation for the Welfare of the Elderly (present name adopted 2002); serves as a forum for the exchange of experience and practical co-operation among member organizations; represents the interests of members before international organizations; promotes understanding and co-operation in matters of social welfare; draws attention to the problems of old age; mems: orgs in 33 countries; Pres. Dr EVELINE HÖNIGSPERGER; Sec.-Gen. JAAP VAN DER SPEK (Netherlands); publ. (in English, French, German and Italian) *EURAG Information* (monthly).

Global Humanitarian Forum: 9 ave de la Paix, 1202 Geneva, Switzerland; tel. 229197500; fax 229197519; e-mail ghf-geneva@ghf-geneva.org; internet www.ghf-geneva.org; f. 2007 to support dialogue and encourage partnerships to focus international attention on and generate increased investment towards addressing key humanitarian concerns; also seeks to place international migration issues on the global agenda; CEO WALTER FUST (Switzerland).

Global Migration Group (GMG): f. 2003, as the Geneva Migration Group; renamed as above in 2006; mems: ILO, IOM, UNCTAD, UNDP, United Nations Department of Economic and Social Affairs (UNDESA), UNFPA, OHCHR, UNHCR, UNODC, and the World Bank; holds regular meetings to discuss issues relating to int. migration, chaired by mem. orgs on a six-month rotational basis.

International Federation of Red Cross and Red Crescent Societies: 17 chemin des Crêts, Petit-Saconnex, CP 372, 1211 Geneva 19, Switzerland; tel. 227304222; fax 227330395; e-mail secretariat@ifrc.org; internet www.ifrc.org; f. 1919 to prevent and alleviate human suffering and to promote humanitarian activities by national Red Cross and Red Crescent societies; conducts relief operations for refugees and victims of disasters, co-ordinates relief supplies and assists in disaster prevention; Pres. JUAN MANUEL SUÁREZ DEL TORO RIVERO (Spain); Sec.-Gen. MARKKU NISKALA (Finland); publs *Annual Report*, *Red Cross Red Crescent* (quarterly), *Weekly News*, *World Disasters Report*, *Emergency Appeal*.

International Organization for Migration (IOM): 17 route des Morillons, CP 71, 1211 Geneva 19, Switzerland; tel. 227179111; fax 227986150; e-mail info@iom.int; internet www.iom.int; f. 1951 as Intergovernmental Committee for Migration; name changed in 1989; a non-political and humanitarian organization, activities include the handling of orderly, planned migration to meet the needs of emigration and immigration countries and the processing and movement of refugees, displaced persons etc. in need of international migration services; mems: 120 states; observer status is held by 20 states and 71 intergovernmental and non-governmental organizations; Dir-Gen. WILLIAM LACY SWING (USA); publs include *International Migration* (quarterly), *Migration* (quarterly, in English, French and Spanish), *World Migration Report* (every 2 years, in English).

International Society for Human Rights: 60388 Frankfurt-am-Main, Borsigallee 9, Germany; tel. (69) 420108-36; fax (69) 420108-29; e-mail info@ishr.org; internet www.ishr.org; f. 1972; promotes fundamental human rights and religious freedom; mems: 30,000 in 26 countries (incl. Azerbaijan, Belarus, Moldova, Russia, Ukraine, Uzbekistan); Pres. ALEXANDER FRHR. VON BISCHOFFSHAUSEN (Germany); Dir Gen. KARL HAFEN; publs *Für die Menschenrechte* (every two months), *Newsletter* (quarterly).

Médecins sans frontières (MSF): 78 rue de Lausanne, CP 116, 1211 Geneva 21, Switzerland; tel. 228498400; fax 228498404; internet www.msf.org; f. 1971; independent medical humanitarian org. composed of physicians and other members of the medical profession; aims to provide medical assistance to victims of war and natural disasters; operates longer-term programmes of nutrition, immunization, sanitation, public health, and rehabilitation of hospitals and dispensaries; awarded the Nobel peace prize in 1999; mems: national sections in 21 countries in Europe, Asia and North America; Pres. Dr CHRISTOPHE FOURNIER; publ. *Activity Report* (annually).

World Social Forum (WSF): Support Office: Rua General Jardim 660, 7th Floor, São Paulo, Brazil 01223-010; e-mail forumsocialmundial.org.br; internet www.forumsocialmundial.org; f. 2001 as an annual global meeting of civil society bodies; the first WSF was held in Porto Alegre, Brazil, in Jan. 2001; a Charter of Principles was adopted in June 2002; the WSF is a permanent global process which aims to pursue alternatives to neo-liberal policies and commercial globalization; its objectives include the development and promotion of democratic international systems and institutions serving social justice, equality and the sovereignty of peoples, based on respect for the universal human rights of citizens of all nations and for the environment; the sixth (2006) Forum was polycentric, held in Bamako (Mali), Caracas (Venezuela), and Karachi (Pakistan), and the seventh (2007) Forum was convened in Nairobi, Kenya; an International Council, comprising 129 civil society organizations and commissions, guides the Forum and considers general political questions and methodology; the Support Office in São Paulo, Brazil, provides administrative assistance to the Forum process, to the International Council and to the specific organizing committees for each annual event; mems: civil society organizations and movements world-wide.

Sport and Recreations

International Gymnastic Federation (Fédération internationale de Gymnastique): 10 rue des Oeuches, CP 359, 2740 Moutier 1, Switzerland; tel. 324946410; fax 324946419; e-mail info@fig-gymnastics.org; internet www.fig-gymnastics.com; f. 1881 to promote the exchange of official documents and publications on gymnastics; mems: 129 affiliated Federations; Pres. BRUNO GRANDI; Gen. Sec. ANDRÉ GUEISBUHLER; publs *FIG Bulletin* (3 a year), *World of Gymnastics* (3 a year).

International Olympic Committee (IOC): Château de Vidy, 1007 Lausanne, Switzerland; tel. 216216111; fax 216216216; internet www.olympic.org; f. 1894 to ensure the regular celebration of the Olympic Games; the IOC is the supreme authority on all questions concerning the Olympic Games and the Olympic movement; Olympic Games held every four years (summer games 2008: Beijing, People's Republic of China; winter games 2010: Vancouver, Canada); mems: 115 representatives; Dir-Gen. URS LACOTTE; publ. *Olympic Review* (quarterly).

International Skating Union (ISU): 2 chemin de Primerose, 1007 Lausanne, Switzerland; tel. 216126666; fax 216126677; e-mail info@isu.ch; internet www.isu.ch; f. 1892; holds regular conferences; mems: 78 national federations in 61 countries; Pres. OTTAVIO CINQUANTA; Gen.-Sec. FREDI SCHMID; publs Judges' manuals, referees' handbooks, general and special regulations.

International Ski Federation (Fédération Internationale de Ski—FIS): Marc Hodler House, Blochstr. 2, 3653 Oberhofen am Thunersee, Switzerland; tel. 332446161; fax 332446171; e-mail mail@fisski.ch; internet www.fis-ski.com; f. 1924 to further the sport of skiing; to prevent discrimination in skiing matters on racial, religious or political grounds; to organize World Ski Championships and regional championships and, as supreme international skiing authority, to establish the international competition calendar and rules for all ski competitions approved by the FIS, and to arbitrate in any disputes; mems: 108 national ski asscns; Pres. GIAN FRANCO KASPER (Switzerland); Sec.-Gen. SARAH LEWIS (United Kingdom); publs *Weekly Newsflash*, *FIS Bulletin* (2 a year).

International Tennis Federation: Bank Lane, Roehampton, London, SW15 5XZ, United Kingdom; tel. (20) 8878-6464; fax (20) 8878-4744; e-mail communications@itftennis.com; internet www.itftennis.com; f. 1913 to govern the game of tennis throughout the world, promote its teaching and preserve its independence of outside authority; produces the Rules of Tennis; organizes and promotes the Davis Cup Competition for men, the Fed. Cup for women, the Olympic Games Tennis Event, wheelchair tennis, 16 cups for veterans, the ITF Sunshine Cup and the ITF Continental Connelly Cup for players of 18 years old and under, the World Youth Cup for players of 16 years old and under, and the World Junior Tennis Tournament for players of 14 years old and under; organizes entry-level professional tournaments as well as junior and senior circuits; mems: 141 full and 57 associate; Pres. FRANCESCO RICCI BITTI; publs *World of Tennis* (annually), *Davis Cup Yearbook*, *ITF World* (quarterly), *ITF This Week* (weekly).

Olympic Council of Asia: POB 6706, Hawalli, 32042 Kuwait City, Kuwait; tel. 5734972; fax 5734973; e-mail info@ocasia.org; internet www.ocasia.org; f. 1981; organizes Asian Games and Asian Winter Games (held every 4 years), and Asian Indoor Games and Asian Beach Games (held every 2 years); mems: 45 national Olympic committees; Dir Gen. HUSAIN AL-MUSALLAM.

Union of European Football Associations (UEFA): 46 route de Genève, 1260 Nyon 2, Switzerland; tel. 848002727; fax 848012727; e-mail info@uefa.com; internet www.uefa.com; f. 1954; works on behalf of Europe's national football asscns to promote football; aims to foster unity and solidarity between national asscns; mems: 53 national asscns; Pres. MICHEL PLATINI (France); Gen. Sec. DAVID TAYLOR; publ. *Magazine* (available online).

World Chess Federation (Fédération internationale des echecs—FIDE): 9 Syggrou Ave, Athens 11743, Greece; tel. (210) 9212047; fax (210) 9212859; e-mail office@fide.com; internet www.fide.com; f. 1924; controls chess competitions of world importance and awards international chess titles; mems: national orgs in more than 160 countries; Pres. KIRSAN ILYUMZHINOV; publ. *International Rating List* (2 a year).

Technology

Regional Council of Co-ordination of Central and East European Engineering Organizations: c/o MTESZ, 1055 Budapest, Kossuth Lajos tér 6–8, Hungary; tel. (1) 353-4795; fax (1) 353-0317; e-mail mtesz@mtesz.hu; f. 1992; Hon. Pres. JÁNOS TÓTH.

World Association of Industrial and Technological Research Organizations (WAITRO): c/o SIRIM Berhad, 1 Persiaran Dato' Menteri, Section 2, POB 7035, 40911 Shah Alam, Malaysia; tel. 55446635; fax 55446735; e-mail info@waitro.sirim.my; internet www.waitro.org; f. 1970 by the UN Industrial Development Organization to organize co-operation in industrial and technological research; provides financial assistance for training and joint activities; arranges international seminars; facilitates the exchange of information; mems: 161 research institutes in 75 countries; Pres. Dr DIETER R. FUCHS (Germany); Sec.-Gen. Dr ROHANI HASHIM; publ. *WAITRO News* (quarterly).

World Association of Nuclear Operators (WANO): Cavendish Court, First Floor, 11–15 Wigmore St, London, W1U 1PF, United Kingdom; tel. (20) 7478-9200; fax (20) 7495-4502; internet www.wano.org.uk; f. 1989 by operators of nuclear power plants; aims to improve the safety and reliability of nuclear power plants through the exchange of information; operates four regional centres (in Paris, France; Tokyo, Japan; Moscow, Russia; and Atlanta, USA) and a Co-ordinating Centre in the United Kingdom; mems: in 35 countries; Pres. S. K. Jain; Man. Dir Lucas Mampaey.

Tourism

International Tourist Association (ASTOUR): 113532 Moscow, Ozerkovskaya 50, Russia; tel. (495) 235-36-88; fax (495) 230-27-84; f. 1992; promotes travel to Russia and other member countries of the CIS; Exec. Dir Janne Andrianova; publ. *Journal* (monthly).

Trade and Industry

Association of European Chambers of Commerce and Industry (EUROCHAMBRES): The Chamber House, 19 ave des Arts, 1000 Brussels, Belgium; tel. (2) 282-08-50; fax (2) 230-00-38; e-mail eurochambres@eurochambres.be; internet www.eurochambres.eu; f. 1958 to promote the exchange of experience and information among its members and to bring their joint opinions to the attention of the institutions of the European Union; conducts studies and seminars; co-ordinates EU projects; mems: 44 nat. asscns of Chambers of Commerce and Industry, 2,000 regional and local Chambers and 18m. mem. enterprises in Europe; Pres. Jörg Mittelsten Scheid (Germany); Sec.-Gen. Arnaldo Abruzzini (Italy).

European Federation of Tile and Brick Manufacturers: c/o Cérame-Unie, 18–24 rue des Colonies, BP 17, 1000 Brussels, Belgium; tel. (2) 511-30-12; fax (2) 511-51-74; e-mail sec@cerameunie.net; internet www.cerameunie.net; f. 1952 to co-ordinate research between members of the industry, improve technical knowledge and encourage professional training; mems: asscns in 23 European and east European countries; Sec.-Gen. Rogier Chorus.

International Co-operative Alliance (ICA): Regional Office for Europe (Co-operatives Europe): 105 ave Milcamps, 1030 Brussels, Belgium; tel. (2) 743-10-33; fax (2) 743-10-39; e-mail office@coopseurope.coop; internet www.ica.coop/europe/; f. 1994; promotes the role of co-operatives and supports their development in Central and Easten Europe, and aims to establish centres to process data and to provide expertise, training and other resources; in 1998 a Plan of Action on Gender Equality was adopted; a Regional Assembly is usually held every two years; mems: 84 orgs in 37 countries; Regional Dir Rainer Schlüter (Germany).

World Trade Organization: Centre William Rappard, 154 rue de Lausanne, 1211 Geneva 21, Switzerland; tel. 227395111; fax 227314206; e-mail enquiries@wto.org; internet www.wto.org; f. 1 Jan. 1995 as the successor to the General Agreement on Tariffs and Trade (GATT); aims to encourage development and economic reform among developing countries and countries with economies in transition participating in the international trading system; mems: 153 countries at Oct. 2008, incl. Armenia, Georgia, Kyrgyzstan and Moldova; Observer countries include Azerbaijan, Belarus, Kazakhstan, Russia, Ukraine and Uzbekistan, all of which have applied to join the Organization; Dir-Gen. Pascal Lamy (France); publs *Annual Report* (2 volumes), *World Trade Report*, *International Trade Statistics*.

Transport

Danube Commission: Benczúr utca 25, 1068 Budapest, Hungary; tel. (1) 352-1835; fax (1) 352-1839; e-mail secretariat@danubecom-intern.org; internet www.danubecom-intern.org; f. 1948; supervises implementation of the Belgrade Convention on the Regime of Navigation on the Danube; approves projects for river maintenance; supervises a uniform system of traffic regulations on the whole navigable portion of the Danube and on river inspection; mems: Austria, Bulgaria, Croatia, Germany, Hungary, Moldova, Montenegro, Romania, Russia, Serbia, Slovakia, Ukraine; Pres. Milovan Božinović; Dir-Gen. Dr István Valkár; publs *Basic Regulations for Navigation on the Danube*, *Hydrological Yearbook*, *Statistical Yearbook*, proceedings of sessions.

European Civil Aviation Conference (ECAC): 3 bis Villa Emile-Bergerat, 92522 Neuilly-sur-Seine Cédex, France; tel. 1-46-41-85-44; fax 1-46-24-18-18; e-mail secretariat@ecac-ceac.org; internet www.ecac-ceac.org; f. 1955; aims to promote the continued development of a safe, efficient and sustainable European air transport system; mems: 42 European states; Pres. Luis Fonseca de Almeida; Exec. Sec. Gerry Lumsden.

International Transport Forum: 2 rue André Pascal, 75775 Paris Cédex 16, France; tel. 1-45-24-97-10; fax 1-45-24-97-42; e-mail itf.contact@oecd.org; internet www.internationaltransportforum.org; f. 2006 by a decision of the European Conference of Ministers of Transport (f. 1953) to broaden membership of the org; aims to create a safe, sustainable, efficient, integrated transport system; provides an annual Forum in Liepzig, Germany; holds round tables, seminars and symposia; shares Secretariat staff with OECD; mems: 51 member countries; Sec.-Gen. Jack Short; publs *Annual Report*, various statistical publications and surveys.

Organisation for the Collaboration of Railways: Hozà 63–67, 00681 Warsaw, Poland; tel. (22) 6573654; fax (22) 6219417; e-mail osjd@osjd.org.pl; internet www.osjd.org; f. 1956; aims to improve standards and regulations in railway traffic between countries of Europe and Asia; promotes co-operation on issues relating to traffic policy and economic and environmental aspects of railway traffic; ensures enforcement of a number of rail agreements; aims to elaborate and standardize general principles for international transport law. Conference of Ministers of mem. countries meets annually; Conference of Gen. Dirs of Railways meets at least once a year; mems: ministries of transport of 27 countries world-wide; Chair. Tadeusz Szozda; publ. *OSShD Journal* (every 2 months, in Chinese, German and Russian).

Youth and Students

WFUNA Youth: c/o WFUNA, 1 United Nations Plaza, Room DC1-1177, New York, NY 10017, USA; tel. (212) 963-5610; fax (212) 963-0447; e-mail coordinating.committee@qmail.com; internet www.wfuna-youth.org; f. 1948 by the World Federation of United Nations Associations (WFUNA) as the International Youth and Student Movement for the United Nations (ISMUN), independent since 1949; an international non-governmental organization of students and young people dedicated especially to supporting the principles embodied in the United Nations Charter and Universal Declaration of Human Rights; encourages constructive action in building economic, social and cultural equality and in working for national independence, social justice and human rights on a world-wide scale; maintains regional offices in Austria, France, Ghana, Panama and the USA; mems: asscns in over 100 mem. states of the UN.

World Federation of Democratic Youth (WFDY): 1139 Budapest, Frangepán u. 16, Hungary; tel. (1) 350-2202; fax (1) 350-1204; e-mail wfdy@wfdy.org; internet www.wfdy.org; f. 1945; promotes the unity, co-operation, organized action, solidarity and exchange of information and experiences of work and struggle among the progressive youth forces; campaigns against imperialism, fascism, colonialism, exploitation and war and for peace, internationalist solidarity, social progress and youth rights under the slogans Youth unite! and Forward for lasting peace!; mems: 152 members in 102 countries; publ. *World Youth*.

RESEARCH INSTITUTES

ASSOCIATIONS AND INSTITUTES STUDYING EASTERN EUROPE, RUSSIA AND CENTRAL ASIA

ARGENTINA

Centro de Estudios Internacionales para el Desarrollo (CEID) (International Research Centre for Development): Juan Bautista Alberdi 6043, 8°, C1440AAL Buenos Aires; tel. and fax (11) 4686-0212; e-mail admin@ceid.edu.ar; internet www.ceid.edu .ar; f. 1998; civil society, education, ecology and international relations in the Russian Federation and the Commonwealth of Independent States (CIS), Central and Eastern Asia, Africa and Central America; international electronic symposiums; Pres. Lic. MARCELO JAVIER DE LOS REYES; publ. *El Periódico del CEID* (quarterly).

ARMENIA

Armenian Centre for National and International Studies: 0033 Yerevan, Yerznkian St 75; tel. (10) 52-87-80; fax (10) 52-48-46; e-mail root@acnis.am; internet www.acnis.am; f. 1994; research on foreign and public policy issues; Pres. RAFFI K. HOVANNISIAN; publ. *Hayatsk Yerevanits* (monthly).

Institute of Economics: 0009 Yerevan, Abovian St 15; tel. (10) 58-19-71; attached to the Armenian Nat. Acad. of Sciences; Dir M. KOTANIAN.

International Centre for Human Development (ICHD): Yerevan, Sayat Nova St 19; tel. (10) 58-26-38; fax (10) 52-70-82; e-mail mail@ichd.org; internet www.ichd.org; f. 1999; research and public-policy institution, with a particular focus on regional co-operation; Chair. ARMEN R. DARBINIAN; Exec. Dir TEVAN POGOSIAN.

AUSTRALIA

Centre for Arab and Islamic Studies (CAIS): Australian National University, Bldg 127, Canberra, ACT 0200; tel. (2) 6125-4982; fax (2) 6125-5410; e-mail cais@anu.edu.au; internet arts.anu .edu.au/cais/default.asp; focuses on the Middle East and Central Asia; Dir Prof. AMIN SAIKAL.

Contemporary Europe Research Centre (CERC): University of Melbourne, 2nd Floor, 234 Queensberry St, Carlton, VIC 3052; tel. (3) 8344-9502; fax (3) 8344-9507; e-mail cerc@cerc.unimelb.edu.au; internet www.cerc.unimelb.edu.au; f. 1989; interdisciplinary research on Europe and the former USSR; library and database; Dir Prof. PHILOMENA MURRAY; Deputy Dir Prof. LESLIE HOLMES; publ. *CERC Working Paper Series*.

Ukrainian Studies Association of Australia: Ukrainian Section, Dept of European Languages, Division of Humanities, Macquarie University, NSW 2109; tel. (2) 9850-7034; fax (2) 9850-7054; e-mail halyna.koscharsky@mq.edu.au; internet www.eurolang.mq.edu.au/ukrainian; Pres. Dr HALYNA KOSCHARSKY; publ. *Biuleten / Newsletter*.

AUSTRIA

Institut für Osteuropäische Geschichte, Universität Wien (Institute for East European History): 1090 Vienna, Spitalgasse 2/Hof 3, Universitätscampus; tel. (1) 427-74-11-01; fax (1) 427-79-41-1; e-mail osteuropa-geschichte@univie.ac.at; internet www.univie.ac .at/iog; f. 1907; education and research; Chief Profs H. HASELSTEINER, A. KAPPELER, A. SUPPAN.

International Institute for Applied Systems Analysis (IIASA): 2361 Laxenburg, Schlossplatz 1; tel. (2) 236-80-70; fax (2) 236-71-31-3; e-mail volker@iiasa.ac.at; internet www.iiasa.ac.at; f. 1972; scientific studies on environmental, social and technological issues and economics, incl. the transition of Eastern European economies; Dir Prof. STEN NILSSON; publ. *Options*.

Internationales Institut für den Frieden (International Institute for Peace—IIP): 1040 Vienna, Möllwaldplatz 5; tel. (1) 504-64-37; fax (1) 505-32-36; e-mail secretariat@iip.at; internet www.iip.at; f. 1957; peace research and studies on interdependence as a strategy for peace, future tasks for the UN, the security structure of Europe in the post-Cold War era, reconstruction of countries in Central and Eastern Europe, and prevention of conflict; Pres. ERWIN LANC; Dir PETER STANIA; publs *IIP Occasional Papers*, *Peace and Security* (quarterly), other publications and reports.

Österreichische Ukrainistenverband: Universität Wien, Institue für Slawistik, Spitalgasse 2–4, 1080 Vienna; tel. (1) 4277-42-680; e-mail alois.woldan@univie.ac.at.

Österreichisches Institut für Internationale Politik (OIIP) (Austrian Institute of International Affairs): 1040 Vienna, Oper-ngasse 20B; tel. (1) 581-11-06; fax (1) 581-11-06-10; e-mail info@oiip .at; internet www.oiip.at; f. 1978; independent research studies on national and international foreign and security policy, European integration, Central and Eastern Europe, Russia, the Near East and the Balkans; international environmental and development policies; foreign-policy conferences and workshops; library; Dir Prof. OTMAR HOELL; publs working paper series and *Wiener Schriften zur Internationalen Politik*.

Österreichisches Ost- und Südosteuropa-Institut (Austrian Institute of East and South-East European Studies): 1010 Vienna, Josefsplatz 6; tel. and fax (1) 512-18-95; e-mail office@osi.ac.at; internet www.osi.ac.at; f. 1958; research and information centre; educational and cultural politics, ecology, geography, history, nationality and minority studies; library of 47,000 vols and 2,400 periodicals and documents; Dir Dr ELISABETH VYSLONZIL; publs *OSI-Aktuell* (newsletter), *Österreichische Osthefte* (quarterly), *Schriftenreihe des Österreichischen Ost- und Südosteuropa-Instituts*, *Wiener Osteuropastudien*, *Atlas of Eastern and Southeastern Europe*.

Wiener Institut für Internationale Wirtschaftsvergleiche (WIIW) (Vienna Institute for International Economic Studies): 1010 Vienna, Oppolzergasse 6; tel. (1) 533-66-10; fax (1) 533-66-10-50; e-mail wiiw@wsr.ac.at; internet www.wiiw.ac.at; f. 1974; focuses on Central and Eastern Europe, the CIS and the Balkans; analyses economic devts of countries in transition, studies East-West European integration and the comparative aspects of global economic trends; reference library of over 13,000 vols and 350 periodicals; Dir MICHAEL LANDESMANN; Administrative Dir ELISABETH HAGEN; publs research reports, working papers and a monthly database.

AZERBAIJAN

Institute of Economics: 1000 Baku, Narimanov pr. 31; tel. (12) 39-34-57; attached to Azerbaijan Acad. of Sciences; researches domestic and international economics; Dir SHAHBAZ MURADOV.

Institute of History: 1000 Baku, H. Javid pr. 31; tel. (12) 39-36-15; fax (12) 39-36-19.

BELARUS

Association of Political Science of Belarus: 200672 Minsk, pr. Partizanski 26; tel. (17) 249-41-34; fax (17) 227-83-05; f. 1993; conducts research in the fields of economics, industrial relations, politics and social affairs; Pres. V. A. BOBKOV; Vice-Pres. A. V. SHARAPO.

Belarusian Association for Ukrainian Studies: 220002 Minsk, vul. Starozhovskaya 8/175; tel. (17) 233-64-51; Dir TETIANA KOBRZHYTSKA.

Development and Security Research Institute of Belarus: 220050 Minsk, vul. Babruiskaya 11.

Economic Research Institute of the Ministry of the Economy: 220086 Minsk, vul. Slavinskaga 1; tel. (17) 264-02-78; fax (17) 264-64-40; internet www.main.gov.by/bel_site/economy.nst; f. 1962; preparation of reports on scientific research activities; library of 53,439 vols; Dir POLONIK STEPAN STEPANOVICH.

Independent Institute of Socioeconomic and Political Studies (NISEPI): 220030 Minsk, POB 219; tel. and fax (17) 622-80-49; e-mail iiseps@iiseps.org; internet www.iiseps.org; f. 1992; supports democracy and a transition to a market economy; research into political, economic and social issues, foreign affairs, employment and security in Belarus and neighbouring states; in April 2005 the Supreme Court of Belarus ordered the closure of the institute; library of 300 books and 30 periodicals; Dir Prof. OLEG T. MANAYEV; Deputy Dir Dr ALYAKSANDR SOSNOV; publs *IISEPS News* (4 a year, in Russian and English), *Analytical Bulletin of Belarusian Think Tanks* (4 a year, in Belarusian and Russian).

Institute of Economics of the National Academy of Sciences of Belarus: 220072 Minsk, ul. Surganova 1, Bldg 2; tel. (17) 284-24-43; fax (17) 284-07-16; e-mail directorship@economics.basnet.by; internet economics.avilink.net; f. 1931; areas of interest include the dynamics and structure of the Belarusian transition economy, industrial economics and policy, international economic relations, privatization of state enterprises, and regional and urban economics and policy; Dir Prof. PETR G. NIKITENKO.

BELGIUM

Centre for the New Europe (CNE): 23 rue de Luxembourg, bte 1, 1000 Brussels; tel. (2) 506-40-00; fax (2) 506-40-09; e-mail info@cne .org; internet www.cne.org; f. 1993; conducts research to develop and promote policies favouring a market-orientated economy and individual, rather than collectivist, values; Pres. STEPHEN POLLARD; Man. Dir JAMES ROGERS; publs *CNE Health Bulletin* (monthly), *Monatsmagazin* (monthly, in German), research papers.

Centre de Recherches Interdisciplinaires sur la Transition des Pays de l'Est vers l'Economie de Marché (CRITEME) (Centre for Interdisciplinary Research on the Transition of Eastern Countries to a Market Economy): Université Libre de Bruxelles, Institut de Sociologie, 44 ave Jeanne, bte 124, 1050 Brussels; tel. (2) 650-33-60; fax (2) 650-34-27; research on socio-economic devts in Central and Eastern Europe and the former USSR.

EGMONT—Institut Royal des Relations Internationales (EGMONT—Royal Institute of International Relations): 69 rue de Namur, 1000 Brussels; tel. (2) 223-41-14; fax (2) 223-41-16; e-mail info@egmontinstitute.be; internet www.egmontinstitute.be; f. 1947; research on international relations, economics, politics and international law, particularly with regard to the European Union, the World Trade Organization and European security; library of 700 vols and 200 periodicals; Dir-Gen. RAF VAN HELLEMONT; Chair. Vicomte ÉTIENNE DAVIGNON.

BULGARIA

Bulgarian Association for Ukrainian Studies: 1403 Sofia, St Clement of Ohrid University of Sofia, Faculty of Slavonic Philology, Blvd Tsar Osvoboditel 15, Rm 130; tel. (2) 85-83-07; fax (2) 946-02-55; e-mail ter@slav.uni-sofia.bg; Dir Dr LIDIA TERZIISKA.

CANADA

Canadian Institute of Ukrainian Studies: University of Alberta, 450 Athabasca Hall, Edmonton, AB T6G 2E8; tel. (780) 492-2972; fax (780) 492-4967; e-mail cius@ualberta.ca; internet www.cius.ca; f. 1976; Dir ZENON E. KOHUT.

Canadian International Council (CIC): 45 Willcocks St, POB 210, Toronto, ON M5S 1C7; tel. (416) 977-9000; fax (416) 976-7319; e-mail mailbox@canadianinternationalcouncil.org; internet www .igloo.org/canadianinternational; f. 1928 as Canadian Institute of International Affairs; renamed in 2007; 8,000 vols; Chair. JIM BALSILLIE; publs *Behind the Headlines* (quarterly), *International Journal* (quarterly), *International Insights* (online).

Centre for European, Russian, and Eurasian Studies: University of Toronto, c/o Munk Centre for Int. Studies, 1 Devonshire Place, Toronto, ON M5S 3K7; tel. (416) 946-8938; fax (416) 946-8939; e-mail ceres@utoronto.ca; internet www.utoronto.ca/ceres; f. 1963; conducts research to promote a broad and integrated understanding of the nations and peoples of the region, past and present; forms part of the School of Graduate Studies and Faculty of Arts and Sciences; Russian and East European library collection of c. 400,000 vols; Dir Prof. JEFFREY KOPSTEIN; publs newsletters (3 a year), working papers, *Bulletin on Current Research in Soviet and East European Law* (3 a year).

PEOPLE'S REPUBLIC OF CHINA

China Institute of International Studies: 3 Toutiao, Taijichang, Beijing 100005; internet www.ciis.org.cn; comprises divisions of: American studies; Asia-Pacific studies; Western European studies; South Asian, Middle Eastern and African studies; East European, Russian and Central Asian studies; International Politics; and World Economy; Pres. MA ZHENGANG; publ. *Journal of International Studies* (every 2 months).

Chinese Association for Ukrainian Studies: 48 Xintaicang Yixiang Donzhimen, Beijing 100007; tel. (10) 4031547; fax (10) 4074077; Dir Prof. JIANG CHANGBIN.

Institute of East European, Russian and Central Asian Studies (IEERCAS): Chinese Academy of Social Sciences, POB 1103, Beijing 10000; tel. (10) 64014006; fax (10) 64014008; f. 1965 as the Institute of Soviet and East European Studies; current name adopted in 1992; four research sections, on: Russia; Central Asia; Ukraine; and East Europe; more than 60,000 volumes and 280 periodicals; Dir Prof. ZHANG WENWU; publs *East European, Russian and Central Asian Studies*, *Studies on the East European, Russian and Central Asian Market*.

CHINA (TAIWAN)

Graduate Institute of Russian Studies: National Chengchi University, 64 Chih-nan Rd, Sec. 2, Wen-Shan District, Taipei 116; tel. (2) 29363413; fax (2) 29387124; e-mail russia@nccu.edu .tw; internet www.cc.nccu.edu.tw/nccucd/263/index.htm; f. 1994;

research on international politics and economics, to further diplomatic and economic relations; Associate Prof. WU-PING KWO.

Institute of International Relations: 64 Wan Shou Rd, Wen Shan 116, Taipei 11625; tel. (2) 82377277; fax (2) 29382133; e-mail iir@ nccu.edu.tw; internet iir.nccu.edu.tw/english0315.htm; f. 1953; research on: the USA, Europe and Africa; Asia, Oceania and the Pacific Rim; and mainland Chinese affairs; affiliated to National Chengchi University; library of more than 100,000 vols and 985 periodicals; Dir TUAN Y. HO; publs *Wenti yu yanjiu (Issues & Studies)* (quarterly, in Chinese), *Montai to Kenkyu* (every 2 months, in Japanese).

Institute of Russian and Slavic Studies: Tamkang University, Taipei 25137,; tel. (2) 26215656-2710; fax (2) 26209908; e-mail tisx@ www2.tku.edu.tw; internet www2.tku.edu.tw/~tisx; f. 1990; historical research, as well as diplomacy, economics, military issues, politics and society in Russia and the other independent states of the former USSR, with particular emphasis on the devt of Sino-Russian bilateral relations; library of 4,500 vols; Dir V. V. MALIAVIN.

COLOMBIA

Instituto de Estudios Políticos y Relaciones Internacionales (IEPRI) (Institute of Political Studies and International Relations): Universidad Nacional de Colombia, Edificio Manuel Ancizar 3°, Of. 3026, Ciudad Universitaria, Bogotá, DC; tel. and fax (1) 316-5217; e-mail maeep_bog@unal.edu.co; internet www.unal.edu.co/ institutos/iepri; international relations, incl. European Studies; Dir LUIS ALBERTO RESTREPO; Co-ordinator of European Section HUGO FAZIO VENGOA.

CROATIA

Institut za Međunarodne Odnose (IMO) (Institute for International Relations): 10000 Zagreb, POB 303, ul. Ljudevita Farkaša Vukotinovića 2/2; tel. (1) 4877460; fax (1) 4828361; e-mail ured@ mairmo.irmo.hr; internet www.imo.hr; f. 1963; attached to the University of Zagreb; principal fields of research include economic devt and transformation, international economic and cultural co-operation, and international relations; library of 10,700 vols and 400 periodicals; Dir Dr MLADEN STANIČIĆ; publs *Croatian International Relations Review* (quarterly, in English), *Culturelink* (quarterly, in English), *Euroscope* (6 a year), *Euroscope Reports*.

CUBA

Centro de Estudios Europeos: Avda 3, No 1805, entre 18 y 20, Miramar, Apdo 11300, Havana; tel. (7) 206-3098; fax (7) 204-1435; e-mail cee@cee.co.cu; internet www.cee.cubaweb.cu; f. 1987; organizes annual conference; Dir ALBERTO DENNYS GUZMÁN PÉREZ; publ. *Revista de Estudios Europeos* (quarterly, in English and Spanish).

CZECH REPUBLIC

Czech Association for Ukrainian Studies: Benediktsa 16, 110 00 Prague 1; tel. 222318302; Pres. Dr VACLAV ZIDLICKY.

Institute for East-West Studies: Rasinova náb. 78/2000, 120 00 Prague 2; tel. 2296759; fax 2297992; f. 1981; research into East-West relations, incl. economic and devt questions; Pres. JOHN EDWIN MROZ; Dir STEPHEN HEINTZ; publs annual report, conference reports.

Ústav mezinárodních vztahů (Institute of International Relations): Nerudova 3, 118 50 Prague 1; tel. 251108111; fax 251108222; e-mail umv@iir.cz; internet www.iir.cz; f. 1957; research on international relations and foreign and security policy, publishing, training and education; Dir Ing. Dr PETR DRULÁK; Deputy Dir Ing. Dr PETR KRATOCHVÍL; publs *Mezinárodní politika / International Politics* (monthly, in Czech and English), *Perspectives—The Central European Review of International Affairs* (2 a year, in English).

DENMARK

Center for East European Studies (CEES): Copenhagen Business School, Porcelænshaven 24, 2000 Frederiksberg; tel. 38-15-25-15; fax 38-15-25-00; e-mail nm.cees@cbs.dk; internet www.cbs.dk/ cees; f. 1996; transition in Eastern Europe; Dir NIELS MYGIND.

Center for Russiske og Østeuropæiske Studier (Dept of Russian and East European Studies): Syddansk Universitet, Campusvej 55, 5230 Odense; tel. 65-50-10-00; fax 65-15-78-92; e-mail bro@litcul .sdu.dk; internet www.sdu.dk/hum/studier/slavisk/index.html; f. 1966; Soviet-Danish relations, history of Soviet/Russian society, culture and literature, Russian language; library of 15,000 vols; Dirs Prof. ERIK KULAVIG, Prof. BENT JENSEN.

Danish Centre for International Studies and Human Rights: Strandgade 56, 1401 Copenhagen K; tel. 45-32-69-86-86; fax 45-32-69-86-00; internet fusion.humanrights.dk; f. 2003 through merger of existing research institutes; Chair. of Bd UFFE ELLEMANN-JENSEN; comprises:

Danish Institute for Human Rights: Strandgade 56, 1401 Copenhagen K; tel. 32-69-88-88; fax 32-69-88-00; e-mail center@humanrights.dk; internet www.humanrights.dk; Chair. of Bd CLAUS HAAGAN JENSEN.

Danish Institute for International Studies: Strandgade 56, 1401 Copenhagen K; tel. 32-69-87-87; fax 32-69-87-00; e-mail diis@diis.dk; internet www.diis.dk; f. 2003; library of some 100,000 vols and 100 periodicals; Chair. of Bd Prof. GEORG SØRENSEN.

Institute of History and Area Studies: Aarhus University, Slavic and Hungarian Dept, Ndr. Ringgade, 8000 Aarhus C; tel. 89-42-64-70; fax 89-42-64-65; e-mail slavisk@au.dk; internet www.hum.au.dk/slavisk/web.

Institute of Political Science: University of Copenhagen, Rosenborggade 15, 1130 Copenhagen K; tel. 35-32-33-66; fax 35-32-33-99; e-mail polsci@ifs.ku.dk; general and comparative political science, information technology, international relations and organization, public administration, policy studies, sociology and statistics.

Thorkil Kristensen Institutett (TKI) (Thorkil Kristensen Institute): Sydjysk Universtitetcenter, Niels Bohr Vej 9, Esbjerg 6700; tel. 79-19-11-11; fax 79-14-11-99; e-mail fla@suc.suc.dk; f. 1971; research into events in Central and Eastern Europe, the former USSR and the People's Republic of China, and their effects on Western Europe; also concerned with relations between the European Union and Central and Eastern European countries, incl. the CIS; centre for East-West research; Dir Prof. FINN LAURSEN; publs working papers.

ESTONIA

Eesti Välispoliitika Instituut (Estonian Foreign Policy Institute): Islandi väljak 1, 15049 Tallinn; tel. 646-6376; fax 631-7599; e-mail evi@evi.ee; internet www.evi.ee; principal areas of research include regional security, EU integration and enlargement, and developments in Russia; Dir ANDRES KASEKAMP; Chair. of Council URMAS PAET.

Estonian Institute for Futures Studies: Lai 34, Tallinn 10133; tel. 641-1760; fax 641-1759; e-mail eti@eti.online.ee; devt scenarios for Estonia and its neighbouring areas; Dir ERIK TERK.

FINLAND

Aleksanteri Institute, Finnish Centre for Russian and Eastern European Studies (FCREES): University of Helsinki, POB 42, Unioninkatu 33A, 00014 Helsinki; tel. (09) 19124175; fax (09) 19123615; e-mail aleksanteri@helsinki.fi; internet www.helsinki.fi/aleksanteri; f. 1996; national co-ordinating unit and research institute; Dir Prof. MARKKU KIVINEN.

Bank of Finland Institute for Economies in Transition (BOFIT): POB 160, 00101 Helsinki; tel. (10) 8312287; fax (10) 8312294; e-mail bofit@bof.fi; internet www.bof.fi/bofit; f. 1998; specializes in high-level study and academic analysis of individual national economies involved in the transition from a command to a market economy; Dir Dr PEKKA SUTELA; publs *BOFIT Weekly*, *BOFIT Discussion Papers*, *BOFIT Online*, *BOFIT Russia Forecast*, *BOFIT Russia Statistics*, *BOFIT China Forecast*, *BOFIT China Statistics*.

Institute for East-West Trade: Pan-European Institute, Turku School of Economics and Business Administration, Rehtorinpellonkatu 3, 20500 Turku; tel. (2) 481481; fax (2) 4814268; e-mail viestinta@tse.fi; internet www.tse.fi/en/units/specialunits/pei/Pages/default.aspx; f. 1987; research focuses on the foreign economic relations of the Eastern part of the European Union and in neighbouring countries, in particular Belarus, Russia and Ukraine; Dir Prof. KARI LIUHTO.

Ulkopoliittinen instituutti (UPI) (Finnish Institute of International Affairs—FIIA): POB 400, Kruunuvuorenkatu 4, 00160 Helsinki; tel. (02) 06111700; fax (02) 06111799; e-mail etunimi.sukunimi@upi-fiia.fi; internet www.upi-fiia.fi; f. 1961; research into Russia-European Union (EU) relations, Chinese society, European foreign affairs and security issues, EU expansion, the Middle East, terrorism, transatlantic relations; Dir RAIMO VÄYRYNEN; publs *Ulkopolitiikka/Finnish Journal of Foreign Affairs* (quarterly), UPI working papers, UPI Briefing Papers.

Venäjän ja Itä-Euroopan Instituutti (Finnish Institute for Russian and East European Studies—FIREES): Antinkatu 44, 00100 Helsinki; tel. (9) 22854434; fax (9) 22854431; e-mail bibliotek@rusin.fi (library); internet www.rusin.fi; research into Russia and Eastern Europe; focuses on basic and applied research in social sciences and humanities, especially culture, population and social structures; library of more than 90,000 vols, 300 journals and maps; Dir WALDEMAR MELANKO; publ. *Finlyandskiye tetradi* (in Russian, irregular).

FRANCE

Association d'études et d'informations politiques internationales (Association for International Political Study and Information): 86 blvd Haussman, 75008 Paris; f. 1949; Dir G. ALBERTINI; publs *Est et Ouest/Este y Oeste* (2 a month), *Documenti sul Comunismo*.

Centre d'études des mondes russe, caucasien et centre-européen (Centre of Russian, Caucasian and Central European Studies): Ecole des Hautes Etudes en Sciences Sociales (EHESS), 54 blvd Raspail, 75006 Paris; tel. 1-49-54-25-58; fax 1-49-54-24-83; e-mail centre.russe@ehess.fr; internet cercec.ehess.fr; f. 1995; history of Russia, the USSR, the Caucasus, Central Asia and Central Europe from the 17th century; history, social and demographic studies, diplomacy and cultural contacts between Russia, the West and the rest of the world, and ethnography, historiography, social sciences and statistics; library of 22,000 vols, 115 periodicals and 700 microfilms; Dir ALAIN BLUM; publs *Bibliographie Européenne des Travaux sur l'ex-URSS et l'Europe de l'Est*, *Cahiers du Monde Russe*, *Revue d'Etudes Comparatives Est-Ouest*.

Institut d'études slaves: 9 rue Michelet, 75006 Paris; affiliated to Centre nationale de la recherche scientifique; publs *Revue d'études slaves* (in French and Russian), *La Revue russe* (in French and Russian).

Association française des études ukrainiennes (French Association of Ukrainian Studies): e-mail fouchard@ehess.fr; internet www.ukraine-europe.info/afeu; Pres. PHILIPPE DE SUREMAIN; publ. *Bulletin de l'Association Française des Etudes Ukrainiennes*.

Institut français des relations internationales (Ifri) (French Institute of International Relations): 27 rue de la Procession, 75740 Paris Cedex 15; tel. 1-40-61-60-00; fax 1-40-61-60-60; e-mail accueil@ifri.org; internet www.ifri.org; f. 1979; international politics and economy; security issues; regional studies; library of 33,000 vols, 200 periodicals; Pres. Prof. THIERRY DE MONTBRIAL; Exec. Dir PIERRE LEPETIT; publs *Politique étrangère* (quarterly, in French), *Notes de l'Ifri*, *Publications du CFE à l'Ifri*, *Travaux et recherches de l'Ifri*, *Rapport annuel mondial sur le système économique et les stratégies (RAMSES)* (annually, in French), *Cahiers du Centre asie ifri cahiers et conférences de l'Ifri*.

GEORGIA

Caucasian Institute for Peace, Democracy and Development (CIPDD): 0108 Tbilisi, POB 101; tel. (32) 33-40-81; fax (32) 33-41-63; e-mail cipdd@cipdd.org; internet www.cipdd.org; f. 1992 to promote democratic and free-market values and to encourage the impartial theoretical analysis of the post-communist transition process in Georgia and the Caucasus region.

Centre for Peace and International Relations Studies (CPIRS): 0100 Tbilisi; e-mail cpirs@ip.osgf.ge; internet www.cpirs.org.ge; f. 1998 to promote democratic and free-market values and to encourage peace and international co-operation in the Caucasus region.

Georgian Foundation for Strategic and International Studies: 0108 Tbilisi, Chitadze 3A; tel. (32) 47-35-55; fax (32) 98-52-65; e-mail gfsis@gfsis.org; internet www.gfsis.org; f. 1999.

International Centre for Geopolitical and Regional Studies (ICGRS): 0100 Tbilisi, POB 158, M. Aleksidze 3; tel. (32) 98-40-34; fax (32) 93-26-70; e-mail vasitar@caucasus.net; Dir GIORGE TARKHAN-MOURAVI.

Research Centre of National Relations: 0107 Tbilisi, Leselidze 4; attached to Georgian Acad. of Sciences; Dir G. V. ZHORZHOLIANI.

GERMANY

Deutsche Gesellschaft für Osteuropakunde eV (German Society for East European Research): 10719 Berlin, Schaperstr. 30; tel. (30) 21478412; fax (30) 21478414; e-mail info@dgo-online.org; internet www.dgo-online.org; f. 1913; concerned with research into all areas of Central and Eastern Europe, with particular emphasis on political issues; Pres. Prof. Dr RITA SÜSSMUTH; Dir Dr HEIKE DÖRRENBÄCHER; publs *Osteuropa* (monthly), *Osteuropa-Recht*, *Osteuropa Wirtschaft* (quarterly).

European Centre for Minority Issues: 24939 Flensburg, Schiffbrücke 12; tel. (461) 141-490; fax (461) 141-4919; e-mail info@ecmi.de; internet www.ecmi.de; relations between minority ethnic and cultural groups with states and with majority groups; publ. *European Yearbook of Minority Issues*; Dir MARC WELLER.

Forschungsstelle Osteuropa an der Universität Bremen (Research Centre for East European Studies at Bremen University): 28359 Bremen, Klagenfurter Str. 3; tel. (421) 2187891; fax (421) 2183269; e-mail anlorenz@osteuropa.uni-bremen.de; internet www.forschungsstelle-osteuropa.de; f. 1982; concentrates mainly on culture, politics and society in the Czech Republic, Poland, Russia, Slovakia and Ukraine; recent research projects have focused on political decision-making processes, economic culture and identity formation; library includes approx. 300 Russian periodicals; Dir Prof. Dr WOLFGANG EICHWEDE; publs *Russian Analytical Digest* (in asscn with Center for Security Studies at the Swiss Federal Institute of Technology Zürich), *Dokumentationen zu Kultur und Gesellschaft im Östlichen Europa, Analysen zu Kultur und Gesellschaft im Östlichen Europa*, catalogues, working papers and e-mail newletters (more than 10,000 subscribers).

Frankfurt Institute for Transformation Studies (FIT): European University Viadrina, 15207 Frankfurt (Oder), POB 1786; tel. (335) 55342861; fax (335) 55342807; e-mail elange@euv-frankfurt-o .de; internet fit.euv-frankfurt-o.de; research on cultural dimensions of political and economic systems in Eastern Europe; transformation, and capital markets and banking reform; Exec. Dir Prof. Dr DETLEF POLLACK; publs *Annual Report*, discussion papers.

George C. Marshall Center for Security Studies: 82467 Garmisch-Partenkirchen, Gernackerstr. 2; fax (8821) 7502452; e-mail webpage@marshallcenter.org; internet www.marshallcenter.org; f. 1993; includes College of International and Security Studies and a conference centre; long-term interdisciplinary research on transatlantic-Eurasian security and defence; a German-US joint initiative; library of 40,000 vols and 500 periodicals; Dir Dr JOHN ROSE; publs *Marshall Center Papers Series, Quarterly Update*.

Institut für Friedensforschung und Sicherheitspolitik (IFSH) (Institute for Peace Research and Security Policy): Universität Hamburg, 22587 Hamburg, Falkenstein 1; tel. (40) 8660770; fax (40) 8663615; e-mail ifsh@ifsh.de; internet www.ifsh.de; f. 1971; focuses on the establishment of security structures and projects dealing with conflict settlement and prevention; library of 24,000 vols and 150 periodicals; Dir Dr REINHARD MUTZ; publs *Hamburger Beiträge zur Friedensforschung und Sicherheitspolitik, Hamburger Informationen zur Friedensforschung und Sicherheitspolitik, IFSH Aktuell, Pädagogische Informationen zur Friedensforschung und Sicherheitspolitik, OSCE Yearbook*.

Institut für Slavistik (Institute for Slavonic Studies): University of Regensburg, 93053 Regensburg, Universitätsstr. 31; tel. (941) 9433362; fax (941) 9431988; internet www.uni-regensburg.de/ Fakultaeten/phil_Fak_IV/Slavistik/; research on the culture, languages and literature of Central and Eastern Europe.

Osteuropa-Institut (OEI) der Freien Universität Berlin (Institute for Eastern European Studies of the Free University Berlin): 14195 Berlin, Garystr. 55; tel. (30) 53380; fax (30) 53788; e-mail oei@ zedat.fu-berlin.de; internet www.oei.fu-berlin.de; f. 1951; engaged in contemporary and historical cultural studies, economics, history, jurisprudence, philosophy, political science and sociology; library of 360,000 vols; Dir Prof. WOLFRAM SCHRETTL; publs *Berliner Osteuropa Info* (2 a year), *Forschungen zur Osteuropäischen Geschichte*, working papers.

  Deutsche Assoziation der Ukrainisten eV: tel. and fax (30) 8231006; Pres. Prof. BOHDAN OSADCZUK.

Osteuropa-Institut München (Munich Institute of East European Studies): 81679 München, Scheinerstr. 11; tel. (89) 9983960; fax (89) 9810110; e-mail oeim@oei-muenchen.de; internet www .oei-muenchen.de; f. 1952; observation and analysis of economic devt in Eastern Europe and the former USSR; library of over 160,000 vols and 600 periodicals; Dir Prof. Dr JOCHACHIM MUELLER; publs *Economic Systems* (quarterly, in English with German abstracts), *Jahrbücher für Geschichte Osteuropas* (quarterly), working papers (irreg.).

Ost-West Institut an der Universität Koblenz-Landau (East-West Institute at the University of Koblenz-Landau): 56016 Koblenz, Postfach 201 602, Abteilung Koblenz; tel. (261) 2871590; fax (261) 2871591; e-mail owi@uni-koblenz.de; internet www.uni-koblenz.de; f. 1996; focuses on Central and Eastern Europe, incl. the Asian states of the former USSR.

Stiftung Wissenschaft und Politik (SWP) (German Institute for International and Security Affairs): 10719 Berlin, Ludwigkirchplatz 3–4; tel. (30) 880070; fax (30) 88007100; e-mail swp@swp-berlin.org; internet www.swp-berlin.org; f. 1962; Dir Prof. Dr VOLKER PERTHES.

Zentralinstitut für Mittel- und Osteuropastudien (ZIMOS) der Katholischen Universität Eichstätt (Central Institute for the Study of Central and Eastern Europe of the Catholic University of Eichstätt): 85072 Eichstätt, Ostenstr. 27; tel. (8421) 931717; fax (8421) 931780; e-mail zimos@ku-eichstaett.de; internet www .ku-eichstaett.de/zimos/body.htm; f. 1994; research includes the study of the history of communism in Russia and the former USSR, the Czech Republic, Hungary, Poland and Slovakia; library of approx. 4.5m. vols; Dir Prof. Dr NIKOLAUS LOBKOWICZ; publs *Forum für Mittel- und Osteuropäische Zeit- und Ideengeschichte* (2 a year), book series.

GREECE

Hellenic Foundation for European and Foreign Policy (ELIA-MEP): Odos Xenophontos 4, 105 57 Athens; tel. (1) 3315022; fax (1) 3642139; e-mail eliamep@eliamep.gr; internet www.eliamep.gr; f. 1988; forum for the understanding of issues relating to foreign and security policy, European affairs and international relations; Pres. PARIS KYRIAKOPOULOS; Dir-Gen. THEODORE COULOUMBIS; publs *Agora Choris Synora / Market without Frontiers* (quarterly), *ELIA-MEP Newsletter, Journal of Southeast European and Black Sea Studies, Greece and the World* (annually).

HUNGARY

Institute for Strategic and Defence Studies: Miklós Zrínyi National Defence University, 1241 Budapest, POB 181; tel. (1) 432-9092; fax (1) 432-9058; e-mail ssvki@mltc.hu; internet www .svki.hu; 3,000 vols; Dir Prof. FERENC GAZDAG; publ. *Defence Studies* (6 a year).

Ukrán és Ruszin Filológiai Tanszék (Dept of Ukrainian and Rusyn Philology): 4400 Nyíregyháza, Nyíregyházi Főiskola, Sóstói u. 31B; tel. (42) 599-400; fax (42) 404-092; e-mail udvarii@nyf.hu; f. 1992; the history of Ukraine, Rusyn-Hungarian interethnic relations, and Ukrainian-Hungarian lexicography and word formation; library of 5,000 vols; Dir Dr UDVARI ISTVÁN; publs *Glossarium Ukrainicum 1–7, Studia Ukrainica et Rusinica Nyíregyháziensia, Dimensiones Culturales et Urbanales Regni Hungariae, Vice Versa*.

INDIA

International Institute for Non-Aligned Studies (IINS): A-2/59 Safdarjung Enclave, New Delhi 110 029; tel. (11) 26102520; fax (11) 26196294; e-mail iins@iins.org; internet www.iins.org; f. 1980; has consultative status (general category) with the UN Economic and Social Council (ECOSOC); works in the fields of international relations, social devt and human rights, and has a Centre for Human Rights; Dir-Gen. Dr PRAMILA SRIVASTAVA; publs *News from the Non-Aligned World* (every 2 weeks, in English and Hindi), *Non-Aligned World* (quarterly).

IRAN

Centre for the Study of Central Asia and the Caucasus (CSCAS): Institute for Political and International Studies, POB 19395-1793, Shahedd Aghaei St, Tehran; tel. (21) 230267175; fax (21) 22802649; e-mail centerlasia@ipis.ir; f. 1983; research and information on economics, international relations, Islamic studies and law; library; Dir MANOUCHEHR GHADERI; publs *Amu Darya: Iranian Journal of Central Asian Studies, Caucasus Review* (quarterly), *Central Asia*.

International Centre for Caspian Studies: POB 19395-7177, Tehran; tel. and fax (21) 2293799; e-mail info@caspianstudies.com; internet www.caspianstudies.com/E-home.htm; f. 1998; non-governmental research organization, which examines economic, political, environmental, cultural and social issues in the Caspian Sea region.

ISRAEL

Cummings Center for Russian and East European Studies: Tel-Aviv University, Ramat Aviv, Tel-Aviv 69978; tel. 3-6409608; fax 3-6409721; e-mail crees@post.tau.ac.il; internet www.tau.ac.il/ ~russia; f. 1971; carries out research, study and documentation, and publishes information on the history and current affairs of Russia, the former Soviet republics and the countries of Eastern Europe; Dir GABRIEL GORODETSKY; publs *Cummings Center Series* of monographs, collections of essays and original documents on the history of Russia, the USSR and Central Asia (2 a year).

Israeli Association of Ukrainian Studies: Centre of Slavic Languages and Literatures, Hebrew University of Jerusalem, POB 7823, Jerusalem 91078; tel. and fax 2-5634073; e-mail jeremy@vms.huji.ac.il; Pres. Prof. WOLF MOSKOVICH.

Marjorie Mayrock Center for Russian, Eurasian and East European Research: Faculty of Social Sciences, Hebrew University of Jerusalem, Mount Scopus, Jerusalem 91905; tel. 2-5883180; fax 2-5882835; e-mail msrussia@mscc.huji.ac.il; internet pluto.huji .ac.il/~msrussia/home.htm; f. 1969; holds seminars and conferences; Dir STEFANI HOFFMAN; publ. *CIS Environment and Disarmament Yearbook*.

ITALY

Associazione Italiana di studi Ucraini (Italian Association of Ukrainian Studies): Dipartimento di Studi Letterari, Linguistici e Filologici (Sezione Slavistica), Università di Milano, Piazza S. Alessandro, 20123 Milan; tel. (02) 50313628; fax (02) 50313632; e-mail giovanna.brogi@unimi.it; internet www.aisu.it; f. 1993; colloquia and conferences devoted to Ukrainian culture; approx. 60 mems; Pres. Prof. GIOVANNA BROGI BERCOFF.

Istituto di studi e documentazione sull'Europa comunitaria e l'Europa orientale (ISDEE) (Institute for the Study and Documentation of the European Community and Eastern Europe): Corso Italia 27, 34122 Trieste; tel. (040) 639130; fax (040) 634248; e-mail isdee@spin.it; internet www.isdee.it; f. 1969; documentation, study and research on economic, institutional, political and social devt in Europe and on relations between Western Europe and Central and Eastern Europe; Chair. TITO FAVARETTO; Man. Dir SERGIO GOBET; Scientific Dir CORRADO CAMPOBASSO; publ. *Est-Ovest* (6 a year, in English, French and Italian).

Osservatorio sull'evoluzione nei paesi dell'Europa orientale (EUROEST) (Centre for the Study of the Development of the Countries of Eastern Europe): c/o Dipartimento di Economia, Università degli Studi di Trento, Via Inama 5, 38100 Trento; tel. (0461) 882162; fax (0461) 882222; e-mail euroest@risc1.gelso.unitn.it; internet euroest.gelso.unitn.it; f. 1992; monitors and analyses devts in Eastern Europe, in particular economic transformation; Dirs Prof. GIOVANNI PEGORETTI, Prof. BRUNO DALLAGO, GIANMARIA AJANI, RICARDO SCARTEZZINI; publs *Blue Series* and *Green Series* of working papers.

JAPAN

Centre for European Studies: Nanzan University, 18, Yamazatocho, Showa-ku, Nagoya 466-8673; tel. (52) 832-3111; fax (52) 831-2741; e-mail cfes@ic.nanzan-u.ac.jp; internet www.nanzan-u.ac.jp/EUROPE; f. 1991; the study of contemporary European affairs (incl. Belarus, Russia and Ukraine), primarily in the field of social sciences; library of 4,126 vols and 189 periodicals; Dir Prof. TAKAHIROI MARUOKA; publ. *Nanzan Daigaku Yoroppa Kenkyu Senta-ho/Bulletin of the Nanzan Centre for European Studies* (annually).

Centre for Northeast Asian Studies: Tohoku University, 41 Kawauchi, Aoba-ku, Sendai, Miyagi Prefecture 980-8576; tel. (22) 795-6009; fax (22) 795-6010; e-mail contasia@cneas.tohoku.ac.jp; internet www.cneas.tohoku.ac.jp/index_e.html; f. 1996; integrated area studies on culture, economics, environment, resources and society in the North-East Asia region (North Asia, from Siberia to the Bering Strait, East Asia and Japan); library of 12,000 vols; Dir SEGAWA MASAHISA; publs *Northeast Asian Alacarte, Northeast Asian Studies, Northeast Asian Study Series*.

Centre for Russian Studies: Japan Institute of International Affairs, 11th Floor, Kasumigaseki Bldg, 3-2-5, Kasumigaseki, Chiyoda-ku, Tokyo 100-6011; tel. (3) 3503-7261; fax (3) 3503-7292; e-mail info@jiia.or.jp; internet www.jiia.or.jp; comprehensive research concerning the former USSR, the CIS and Eastern Europe; library of 20,000 vols and 470 periodicals; Pres. HISASHI OWADA; Dir TOSHIRO OZAWA (acting); publs *Japan Review of International Affairs* (quarterly, in English), *JIIA Newsletter, Kokusai Mondai/International Affairs, Roshia Kenkyu/Russian Studies* (2 a year).

Economic Research Institute of Northeast Asia (ERINA): 6th Floor, Nihonseimai Masayakoji Bldg, 6-1178-1, Kamiokawamae, Niigata 951-8068; f. 1993; focuses on north-eastern China, Japan, the Democratic People's Republic of Korea, the Republic of Korea, Mongolia and Far Eastern Russia; Chair. HISAO KANAMORI; publs *ERINA Report, Journal of Econometric Study of Northeast Asia, Northeast Asia White Paper*.

Hokkaido Daigaku Surabu Kenkyu Senta (Slavic Research Centre, Hokkaido University): Kita-9, Nishi-7, Kita-ku, Sapporo 060-0809; tel. (11) 706-2388; fax (11) 706-4952; e-mail src@slav.hokudai.ac.jp; internet src-h.slav.hokudai.ac.jp; f. 1955; national centre for interdisciplinary research activities on Slavic Eurasian countries; areas of research include economics, ethnology, geography, humanities, international relations and political-social systems; library of 167,000 vols and 1,600 periodicals; Dir SHINICHIRO TABATA; publs *Acta Slavica Iaponica* (annually), *Suravu Kenkyu/Slavic Studies* (annually), *SRC Newsletter, SRC Occasional Paper Series*.

Japanese Association for Ukrainian Studies: University of Tokyo, 3-8-1, Komaba, Meguroku, Tokyo 153; tel. (3) 5454-6487; fax (3) 5454-4339; e-mail nakai@waka.c.u-tokyo.ac.jp; Pres. Prof. KAZUO NAKAI; publ. *Ukuraina Tsushin*.

Shadan Hojin, Russia To-Oh Boekikai (ROTOBO) (Japan Association for Trade with Russia and Central and Eastern Europe): Kaneyama Bldg, 1-2-12, Shinkawa, Chuo-ku, Tokyo 104-0033; tel. (3) 3551-6215; fax (3) 3555-1052; e-mail rotobo@root.or.jp; internet www.root.or.jp/rotobo_inst.

KAZAKHSTAN

Central Asia Agency of Political Research: 050000 Almaty, Dostyk 85A/309; tel. (727) 291-12-78; fax (727) 291-15-09; e-mail apr@lorton.com; internet www.caapr.kz; independent, non-governmental research institution.

Institute of Economics: 050000 Almaty, Kurmangazy 29; tel. (727) 293-01-75; fax (727) 262-78-19; e-mail ieconom@academset.kz; f. 1952; research and training; attached to the Ministry of Education and Science; library of 900 vols; Dir M. B. KENZHEGUZIN; publ. *Izvestiya NAS Republiky Kazakhstana* (annually).

REPUBLIC OF KOREA

Institute for Far Eastern Studies (IFES): Kyungnam University, 28-42, Samchung-dong, Chongro-ku, Seoul 110-230; tel. (2) 735-3202; fax (2) 735-4359; f. 1972; affiliated to the Institute of Oriental Studies (Russian Federation); research programmes on developing countries; annual conference on Korean-Russian relations; research seminars; library of 10,000 vols; Dir Dr JO YUNG-HWAN; publs include *Asian Perspective* (2 a year), *Korea and World Politics* (2 a year), *Research Series of North Korea* and *Research Series of the Third World* (annually).

KYRGYZSTAN

Centre for Economic Research: 720071 Bishkek, pr. Chui 265A; tel. (312) 25-53-90; fax (312) 24-36-07; e-mail tdyikanbaeva@hotmail.com; f. 1956; researches the mechanisms of forming, and the devt of, the market economy, analyses the limits, structure and legalization of the shadow economy and macroeconomic aspects of social economic policy, and advises the Kyrgyz Govt; library of the Acad. of Sciences of some 1m. vols; Dir TOKTOBIUBIU S. DYIKANBAEVNA.

Institute for Regional Studies: 720000 Bishkek, POB 1880; e-mail ifrs@elcat.kg; internet www.ifrs.elcat.kg; f. 1994 as the Kyrgyz Peace Research Centre; supports democratization in Central Asia; runs Programme on Sustainable Development in Central Asia, the Civic Education and Training Programme, and a Gender Studies Unit; research, seminars and conferences; library.

LITHUANIA

Institute of International Relations and Political Science: Vilnius University, Vokieciu g. 10, Vilnius 1130; tel. (5) 251-4130; fax (5) 251-4134; e-mail tspmi@tspmi.vu.lt; internet www.tspmi.vu.lt; f. 1992; research on international relations and political science, including regional security and foreign policy issues, democratization during transition, nationalism, the rule of law and the free-market economy; publ. *Politologija* (Political Science) (4 a year); Dir Prof. RAIMUNDAS LOPATA.

Lietuvos Ukrainistu Asociacija (Lithuanian Association of Ukrainian Studies): Vysniu 4–6, Vilnius 2038; tel. (2) 265-513; e-mail jaroslava@takas.lt; Pres. NADIA NEPOROZHINA.

MOLDOVA

Academia de Studii Economice (Academy of Economic Studies): 2005 Chişinău, str. Bănulescu-Bodoni 61; tel. (2) 22-41-28; fax (2) 22-19-68; e-mail ase_info@ase.md; internet www.ase.md; f. 1991; Rector BELOŞTECINIC GRIGORE; publ. *Economica*.

Institutul de Cercetari Economice (Institute of Economic Research): 2012 Chişinău, bd Ştefan cel Mare 1; tel. (2) 26-24-01; e-mail 231sii@math.moldova.su; f. 1960; attached to the Acad. of Sciences of Moldova; conducts research on economic devt in Moldova; Dir V. CIOBANU; publs research reports.

MONGOLIA

Institute of Oriental and International Studies: c/o Acad. of Sciences, Sühabaataryn Talbay 3, 210000 Ulan Bator 11; f. 1968; research on oriental and international affairs, in particular Mongolia's relations with the People's Republic of China and the Russian Federation; Dir A. OCHIR; publs *Dorno-Örno* (2 a year), *Mongolian Journal of International Affairs* (annually).

NETHERLANDS

Instituut voor Oost-Europees Recht en Ruslandkunde (Institute of East European Law and Russian Studies): Leiden University, Faculty of Law, Steenschuur 25, POB 9520, 2300 Leiden; tel. (71) 5277814; fax (71) 5277600; e-mail e.h.uiterweerd@law.leidenuniv.nl; internet www.law.leidenuniv.nl; f. 1953; from 1993 involved in assisting the legal community of Eastern Europe to draft legislation and new civil codes; library of 40,000 vols and 350 periodicals; publs *Law in Eastern Europe Series, Review of Central and East European Law* (quarterly).

Slavische Talen en Culturen (Russisch): Rijksuniversiteit Groningen, POB 716, 9700 AS Groningen; tel. (50) 3636061; fax (50) 3635821; e-mail cet@let.rug.nl; internet www.rug.nl/let/onderwijs/talenenculturen/slavischeTalenCulturen/index.

NORWAY

Forum 18: POB 6663, Rodeløkka, 0502 Oslo; e-mail f18news@editor.forum18.org; internet www.forum18.org; f. 2000; research into and promotion of religious freedom, particularly in post-communist states, seeking to promote the implementation of Article 18 of the Universal Declaration of Human Rights; Chair. ED BROWN.

Fridtjof Nansen Institute (FNI): Fridtjof Nansens vei 17, POB 326, 1326 Lysaker; tel. 67-11-19-00; fax 67-11-19-10; e-mail post@fni

.no; internet www.fni.no; f. 1958; social-science research on international issues concerning energy, the environment and resource management; research programmes on European energy and environment, multilateral assistance; Dir PETER JOHAN SCHEI; publs *FNI Reports*, *Nansen News*.

Institutt for Forsvarsstudier (IFS) (Norwegian Institute for Defence Studies): Tollbugata 10, 0152 Oslo; tel. 23-09-31-05; fax 23-09-33-79; e-mail info@ifs.mil.no; internet www.ifs.mil.no; f. 1980; research programmes on military theory and strategic studies; Norwegian security and defence policy; patterns of international conflict and co-operation; transatlantic studies; library of over 8,000 vols; Dir Prof. Dr ROLF TAMNES; publs *Defence and Security Studies* (4 a year), *Oslo Files on Defence and Security* (6 to 8 a year).

International Peace Research Institute, Oslo (PRIO): Hausmanns Gate 7, 0186 Oslo; tel. 22-54-77-00; fax 22-54-77-01; e-mail info@prio.no; internet www.prio.no; f. 1959; independent foundation; the research programme follows four broad themes: conflict resolution and peace-building; ethics, norms and identities; security; the study of civil war; library of 13,000 vols and 400 periodicals; Dir STEIN TØNNESSON; publs *Journal of Peace Research* (6 a year), *Security Dialogue* (4 a year).

Norsk Utenrikspolitisk Institutt (NUPI) (Norwegian Institute of International Affairs): POB 8159, 0033 Oslo; tel. 22-99-40-00; fax 22-36-21-82; e-mail info@nupi.no; internet www.nupi.no; f. 1959; research and information on political and economic issues, focusing on international security policy, the long-term political devt of Europe and Russia, international economic and devt issues, conflict resolution and peace operations; library of 25,000 vols and 400 journals; Pres. KJETIL M. STULAND; Dir JAN EGELAND; Head of Centre for Russian Studies HELGE BLAKKISRUD; publs *Hvor Hender Det* (weekly newsletter), *Internasjonal Politikk* (quarterly), *Nordisk Ostforum* (quarterly), *Forum for Development Studies* (2 a year), *NUPI Rapport* (research report) and monographs.

PAKISTAN

Institute of Regional Studies: 12, St 84, Embassy Rd, G-6/4, Islamabad; tel. (51) 9203974; fax (51) 9203974; e-mail irspak@comsats.net.pk; internet www.irs.org.pk; f. 1982; covers a wide range of research into economics, industry, international and internal affairs, science and technology, and security-related and socio-cultural issues relating to South and South-West Asia, extending studies to include Central Asia and the People's Republic of China; Pres. Maj.-Gen. (retd) JAMSHED AYAZ KHAN; Editor ABUL BARAKAT; publs include *Regional Studies* (quarterly), *Selections from Regional Press* (fortnightly), *Spotlight on Regional Affairs* (monthly).

Pakistan Institute of International Affairs: Aiwan-e-Sadar Rd, POB 1447, Karachi 74200; tel. (21) 5682891; f. 1947 to study international affairs and to promote the scientific study of international politics, Pakistani foreign policy, economics and jurisprudence; library of 32,430 vols, 43 microfilms, 135 tapes; Chair. FATEHYAB ALI KHAN; publ. *Pakistan Horizon* (4 a year).

POLAND

Central and East European Economic Research Centre (CEEERC): Joint Graduate Instruction Centre, Dept of Economics, University of Warsaw, 02-097 Warsaw, ul. Banacha 2B; tel. (22) 8227404; fax (22) 8227405; e-mail pkaczmarczyk@wne.uw.edu.pl; internet www.wne.uw.edu.pl; f. 1998; centre for policy-relevant issues critical to the devt of open and competitive economies in the post-communist countries of Central and Eastern Europe; Dir Dr PAWEŁ KACZMARCZYK.

Instytut Slawistyki, Polska Akademia Nauk (PAN) (Slavonic Institute, Polish Acad. of Sciences): 00-337 Warsaw, ul. Bartoszewicza 1B m. 17; tel. and fax (22) 8267688; e-mail iwona@ispan.waw.pl; internet www.ispan.waw.pl; f. 1954; research into, and study of, Slavonic history, literature and linguistics; library of 120,000 vols; Dir Prof. Dr Hab. ZBIGNIEW GREN; publs *Acta Baltico-Slavica*, *Slava Meridionalis* (annually), *Studia Literaria Polono-Slavica* (annually), *Studia z Filologii Polskiej i Slowanskiej* (annually), *Slavica* (annually).

Instytut Studiów Politycznych (Institute of Political Studies): 00-625 Warsaw, ul. Polna 18/20; tel. (22) 8255221; fax (22) 8252146; e-mail politic@isppan.waw.pl; f. 1990 to develop theoretical work and empirical studies of post-communist societies; attached to Polish Acad. of Sciences; library of over 17,000 vols and over 40 periodicals (titles); Dir Prof. WOJCIECH MATERSKI; publs *Culture and Society* (quarterly), *Civitas* (annually), *Political Studies* (annually), *Polish-German Yearbook*.

Ośrodek Studiów Wschodnich (Centre for Eastern Studies): 00-564 Warsaw, ul. Koszykowa 6A; tel. (22) 5258000; fax (22) 6298799; e-mail info@osw.waw.pl; internet www.osw.waw.pl; f. 1990; monitors and analyses the political, economic and social situation in the countries of the CIS and in Central and South-Eastern Europe; Dir

JACEK CICHOCKI; publs *Annual Report*, *CES Studies* (every 2 months), *Week in the East* (weekly), *Policy Briefs* (occasional).

Ośrodek Studiów Wschodnich przy Uniwersytetu Warsawskiego (Centre of Eastern Studies at the University of Warsaw): 00-046 Warsaw, ul. Nowy Swiat 69; tel. (22) 6200381; fax (22) 267520; f. 1990; an interdisciplinary science and research unit on subjects relating to the Baltic Republics, Belarus, the Russian Federation and Ukraine, in particular questions of economics, ethnicity, law, sociology and socio-political systems; Dir Prof. MICHAŁ DOBROCZYŃSKI; publ. *Polityka Wschodnia / Eastern Politics* (2 a year).

Polski Instytut Spraw Międzynarodowych (PISM) (Polish Institute of International Affairs): 00-032 Warsaw, ul. Warecka 1 A; tel. (22) 5568000; fax (22) 5568099; e-mail pism@pism.pl; internet www.pism.pl; f. 1996; research, courses, conferences; library of 150,000 vols; Dir Prof. RYSZARD STEMPLOWSKI; publs *Polski Przeglad Dyplomatyczny* (every two months), *Polish Digest of International Affairs* (quarterly), *Europe* (quarterly, in Russian), *Raporty* (in English and Polish), *Conferences* (in English and Polish), *Collections* (in English and Polish), *Polskie Dokumenty Dyplomatyczne* (in English and Polish).

Polskie Towarzystwo Ukrainoznawcze (Polish Association for Ukrainian Studies): University of Warsaw, 02-678 Warsaw, ul. Szturmowa 4; Pres. Prof. Dr STEFAN KOZAK; publ. *Yearbook Warszawskie Zeszyty Ukrainoznawcze-Varshavki Ukrainoiznavchi Zapyski*.

RUSSIA

Carnegie Endowment for International Peace Center for Russian and Eurasian Programs: 103051 Moscow, ul. Sadova-Samatechnaya 24–27; tel. (495) 258-50-25; fax (495) 258-50-20; e-mail info@carnegie.ru; internet www.carnegieendowment.org/programs/Russia; f. 1993; promotes intellectual collaboration between academics in Russia, the USA and the successor states of the USSR on issues of international peace and understanding; research programmes on conventional arms control and security, and ethnicity and nationality; Dir ROSE GOTTEMOELLER; Dir of Russian and Eurasian Programs ANDREW KUCHINS; publs *Nuclear Non-Proliferation: A Compilation of Materials and Documents* (6 a year), *Nuclear Successor States of the Soviet Union* (2 a year).

Central Economics Research Institute: 119898 Moscow, Smolenskii bul. 3/5; tel. (495) 246-84-63.

Centre for Black Sea and Mediterranean Studies: Russian Acad. of Sciences, 103873 Moscow, ul. Mokhovaya 8/3, tel. (495) 203-73-43; fax (495) 200-42 08, f. 1989 under the auspices of the Institute of Europe of the Russian Acad. of Sciences; research into Black Sea and Mediterranean countries and into Russian policy towards those countries; Dir NIKOLAI A. KOVALSKI.

Centre for Caucasian Studies: 117133 Moscow, ul. Ak. Vargi 24/9; tel. and fax (495) 339-13-23; e-mail iskand@glas.apc.org; f. 1992; research on political and economic issues of the North Caucasian and Transcaucasian regions; projects include the effects on Europe of the instability in the Caucasus and democratic institutions and systems in the region; Dir ALAN C. KASAYEV.

Centre for National Security and International Relations: 121069 Moscow, per. Khlebnyi 2/3; tel. (495) 291-20-52; fax (495) 202-90-00; e-mail srogov@rambler.ru; f. 1992; research into Russian civil-military relations, ethnic conflicts in Eastern Europe, peace-keeping and US and Russian strategy; Dir SERGEI M. ROGOV; publ. bulletin on security issues in countries of the former USSR (monthly).

Centre for Political and International Studies: 129090 Moscow, pr. Mira 36, Office 505; tel. (495) 680-34-41; fax (495) 680-02-45; e-mail an@inno.mgimo.ru; internet www.cpis.su; f. 1989; non-governmental, non-profit org.; holds conferences, publs books on international security and international relations, and has undertaken more than 60 international research projects; Dir ALEKSANDR NIKITIN.

Centre for Strategic and Global Studies: Russian Acad. of Sciences, 103001 Moscow, ul. Spiridonovka 30/1; tel. (495) 290-63-85; fax (495) 202-07-86; e-mail csgs@inafr.msk.su; f. 1991; conducts research on economic and political issues, incl. global and political economic trends, environmental issues, geopolitical issues, the new world order, the devt of the CIS, and Mediterranean and Black Sea Studies; Dir Prof. Dr LEONID L. FITUNI.

Gorbachev Foundation—International Non-governmental Foundation for Socio-economic and Political Studies: 125167 Moscow, Leningradskii pr. 39/14, Russia; tel. (495) 945-64-99; fax (495) 945-78-99; e-mail gf@gorby.ru; internet www.gorby.ru; f. 1992; research on the economic and political problems faced by the countries of the former USSR during the transition to democracy, incl. national and regional politics, European security and arms control; Pres. MIKHAIL S. GORBACHEV.

INDEM (Informatika dlya Demokratii—Information for Democracy) Centre for Applied Political Studies: 101000

Moscow, per. B. Zlatoustinskii 3/7; tel. and fax (495) 206-81-72; e-mail fond@indem.org; internet www.indem.ru; Pres. GEORGII A. SATAROV; publ. *Russian Monitor: Archive of Contemporary Politics* (quarterly).

Institut Aktualnykh Mezhdunarodnykh Problem (Institute for Contemporary International Studies): 119021 Moscow, ul. Ostozhenka 53/2; tel. (495) 208-09-50; fax (495) 208-91-96; e-mail iamp@dipacademy.ru; internet www.dipacademy.ru; f. 1994; attached to the Diplomatic Academy of the Ministry of Foreign Affairs; Dir ERAST A. GALUMOV; publ. *Diplomatic Yearbook*.

Institut Ekonomiki (Institute of Economics): Russian Acad. of Sciences, 117218 Moscow, Nakhimovskii pr. 32; tel. and fax (495) 129-52-28; e-mail vopreco@opc.ru; internet www.inst-econ.org.ru; Dirs L. I. ABALKIN, D. YE. SOROKIN, YU. G. PAVLENKO, S. V. KLIMENKO; publs *Voprosy Ekonomiki / Problems of Economics* (monthly), *Federalizm (Federalism)*.

Institut Ekonomiki Perekhodnogo Perioda (IEPP) (Institute of the Economics of Transition): 103918 Moscow, Gazetnyi per. 5/3; tel. (495) 629-64-13; fax (495) 203-88-16; e-mail mslobod@iet.ru; internet www.iet.ru; f. 1990; Dir Dr YEGOR GAIDAR; publ. *Russian Economy: Trends and Prospects*.

Institut Mirovoi Ekonomiki i Mezhdunarodnykh Otnoshenii (IMEMO) (Institute of World Economics and International Relations): 117997 Moscow, ul. Profsoyuznaya 23; tel. (495) 120-43-32; fax (495) 913-65-75; e-mail imemoran@imemo.ru; internet www.imemo.ru; f. 1956; attached to Russian Acad. of Sciences; research into issues of global economy and international relations, including economic relations and the conversion of military economies, arms control and disarmament; library; Dir N. A. SIMONIYA; publs *Disarmament and Security Yearbook* (monthly), *Mirovaya Economika I Mezhdunarodnye Otnosheniya* (monthly), *Economic Barometer* (in Russian, monthly, and in English, quarterly).

Institut Natsionalnoi Modeli Ekonomiki (Institute for the Study of the Russian Economy): 121854 Moscow, ul. B. Nikitskaya 44/2/26; tel. (495) 290-51-08; fax (495) 291-15-95; e-mail economic@clcp.co.ru; internet www.inme.ru; f. 1992.

Institut Slavianovedeniya i Balkanistiki (Institute of Slavonic and Balkan Studies): 125040 Moscow, pr. Leninskii 32A; tel. (495) 938-17-80; fax (495) 938-22-88; f. 1946; part of the Russian Acad. of Sciences; the major centre of Slavic and Balkan research in the Russian Federation, it also studies the relationship of the Slavs and other neighbouring ethnic groups with the Russian people; Dir VLADIMIR K. VOLKOV; publs monographs and periodicals.

Institut Sotsialno-Politicheskikh Issledovanii (Institute of Socio-Political Research): Russian Acad. of Sciences, 119991 Moscow, pr. Leninskii 32A; tel. (495) 938-19-10; fax (495) 938-18-86; e-mail info@ispr.ru; internet www.ispr.ru; f. 1991; Dir VYACHESLAV N. KUZNETSOV.

Institut Sravnitelnoi Politologii (Institute for Comparative Political Studies): 101990 Moscow, Kolpachnyi per. 9 A/1; tel. (495) 925-53-53; fax (495) 923-86-10; e-mail ispran@hotmail.ru; internet ispran.pskovcity.ru; f. 1966; attached to Russian Acad. of Sciences; library of 50,000 vols; Dir G. YU. SEMIGIN; publs *Forum* (annually), *Polis* (6 a year).

Levada Centre (Levada Analytical Centre): 125319 Moscow, ul. Chernyakovskogo 16; tel. (495) 229-38-10; fax (495) 229-38-25; e-mail direct@levada.ru; internet www.levada.ru; f. 2003; fmrly VTsIOM-A; research into social development, poverty, public opinion in Russia, marketing research; Dir Dr LEV D. GUDKOV.

Moskovskii Gosudarstvennii Institut Mezhdunarodnykh Otnoshenii (Universitet) MID Rossii (MGIMO) (Moscow State Institute of International Relations—University—of the Ministry of Foreign Affairs of Russia): 119454 Moscow, pr. Vernadskogo 76; tel. (495) 434-00-89; fax (495) 434-90-66; internet www.mgimo.ru; f. 1944; studies international political and economic relations; areas of interest include Central Asian security, Russian policy in Central Asia and Moldova, CIS affairs and nuclear non-proliferation; Rector Prof. ANATOLII V. TORKUNOV; publ. *Moscow Journal of International Law*.

Otdeleniye Mezhdunarodnych Ekonomicheskikh i Politicheskikh Issledovanii, Institut Ekonomiki (Dept for International Economic and Political Studies, Institute of Economics): 117418 Moscow, Novocheremushkinskaya 42A; tel. (495) 128-91-35; fax (495) 120-83-71; e-mail imepi@transecon.ru; internet www.transecon.ru; f. 1960 as the Institute for the Economy of the World Socialist System; forms part of the Russian Acad. of Sciences; research on political and economic reform, and international relations in post-communist countries of Central and Eastern Europe, in particular the former Soviet republics; Dir Prof. SVETLANA GLINKINA; publs *Bulletin of Research Information*, *The World of Transformations*, scholarly articles and monographs.

PIR Center for Policy Studies in Russia (PIR Center): 123001 Moscow, Trekhprudnyi per. 11/13, Bldg 1, Office 025; tel. (495) 234-25; fax (495) 234-95-58; e-mail reception@pircenter.org; internet www.pircenter.org; f. 1994; non-profit, independent research and public education organization, which focuses on international security and arms control, and non-proliferation issues linked directly to Russia's internal situation; Chair. of Bd Prof. ROLAND M. TIMERBAYEV; publs *Security Index Journal* (quarterly, in Russian and English) and *Yadernyi Kontrol (Nuclear Control)* (weekly, in Russian).

Reforma—International Foundation for Economic and Social Reforms (Reforma): 109240 Moscow, nab. Kotelnicheskaya 17; tel. (495) 926-77-52; fax (495) 975-23-73; f. 1990; research into economic transition, CIS integration, ethnic conflict and the Russian Constitution; several brs thoughout the Russian Federation and the rest of the CIS; publ. *Reforma Monthly*.

Russian Association for Ukrainian Studies: Institute of Slavonic and Balkan Studies, 117334 Moscow, Leninskii pr. 32; Pres. Dr LIUDMILA A. SOFRONOVA.

Russian Foreign Policy Association: 103064 Moscow, ul. Yakovoapostolskii per. 10; tel. (495) 298-10-53; fax (495) 975-21-90; e-mail fpa.moscow@public.mtu.ru; f. 1992; includes the Centre for Ethnopolitical and Regional Studies.

Tsentr Strategicheskikh i Politicheskikh Issledovanii Mezhdunarodnyi (Centre for Strategic and International Political Studies): 103753 Moscow, ul. Rozhdestvenka 12; tel. (495) 924-51-50; fax (495) 256-84-58; f. 1991; research and training on Central Asia and Transcaucasia, ethnic relations, Eurasian studies, international relations, Islamic studies, the Middle East and North Africa, military and strategic studies, and politics; holds conferences and undertakes consultancy work; Pres. Prof. VITALII V. NAUMKIN; Exec. Dir Dr ALEKSANDR FILONIK.

SLOVAKIA

Asociatsia Ukrainistiv Slovachchyny (Slovakian Association for Ukrainian Studies): Filozofická Fakulta Prešovskej Univerzity, 17 Novembra c. 1, 08078 Prešov; tel. (51) 7570-841; fax (91) 7570-824; e-mail babotova@unipo.sk; internet www.unipo.sk; f. 1991; studies Slovak-Ukrainian cultural and historical relations; Head of Section MIKULÁŠ MUŠINKA; publs monographs.

SLOVENIA

Slavistično društvo Slovenije (Slovene Slavonic Studies Society): 1000 Ljubljana, Aškerčeva 2/II; tel. (1) 2411306; fax (1) 4259337; f. 1935; a forum for professional Slavists to provide a link between research and professional practice and to organize support for, and to publish, Slavic research; Pres. MARKO JESEMVĖR; publs *Jezik in slovstvo* (6 a year), *Slavistična revija* (quarterly).

SWEDEN

Central Asia and the Caucasus Centre for Social and Political Studies: Hubertusstigen 9, 97 455 Luleå; tel. and fax (920) 62-016; e-mail murad@communique.se; internet www.ca-c.org; f. 1998 to study and review the social and political situation in Central Asia and the Caucasus from an academic point of view, to create a database and to distribute information; Dir Dr MURAD ESENOV; publ. *Central Asia and the Caucasus: Journal of Social and Political Studies*.

Centre for Russian and East European Studies: Centre for European Research, Göteborg University, Pilgaten 19, 1st Floor, POB 720, 405 30 Göteborg; tel. (31) 773-43-16; fax (31) 773-44-61; e-mail crees@crees.gu.se; internet www.host.gu.se/crees; f. 1991; cross-disciplinary centre to promote contacts between the University, the public sector, the business communities of western Sweden and the countries of the region; Dir Prof. RUTGER LINDAHL.

Silk Road Studies Program: Institute for Security and Development Policy, Västra Finnbodavägen 2, 131 30 Nacka; tel. (18) 471-63-35; fax (18) 10-63-97; e-mail jpopjanevski@silkroadstudies.org; internet www.silkroadstudies.org/new/index.htm; forms part of the joint transatlantic Central Asia-Caucasus Institute (USA) and Silk Road Studies Program; Chair. Dr S. FREDERICK STARR; Research Dir Dr SVANTE E. CORNELL; publs *Silk Road Papers* (occasional), *Central Asia-Caucasus Analyst* (every 2 weeks).

Stockholm Institute of Transition Economics (SITE): Stockholm School of Economics, POB 6501, 113 83 Stockholm; tel. (8) 736-96-70; fax (8) 31-64-22; e-mail site@hhs.se; internet www2.hhs.se/SITE; f. 1989; conducts economic research on issues facing countries in transition and contributes to the development of economic research institutions in those countries; Dir Dr TORBJÖRN BECKER; publs *Transition Economics Abstract Series (TEASE)*, *Economics of Transition*, working papers, newsletters and reports.

Stockholm International Peace Research Institute (SIPRI): Signalistgatan 9, 169 70 Solna; tel. (8) 655-97-00; fax (8) 655-97-33; e-mail sipri@sipri.org; internet www.sipri.org; f. 1966; scientific research into the conditions for peaceful solutions to international conflicts and a stable peace focusing, in particular, on arms control and disarmament; library of 44,000 vols; Dir ALYSON J. K. BAILES; publs *SIPRI Yearbook*, monographs, occasional papers and research reports.

SWITZERLAND

Center for Security Studies at the Swiss Federal Institute of Technology Zürich (Center for Security Studies der Eidgenössische Technische Hochschule—ETH—Zürich): internet www.css .ethz.ch; international and national security policy, with particular emphasis on Switzerland, the USA, Russia and Europe; Dir Prof. ANDREAS WENGER; publs *Russian Analytical Digest* (in asscn with Forschungstelle Osteuropa an der Universität Bremen, Germany), *CSS Studies in Security and International Relations*, monographs, occasional papers and research reports.

Institut Suisse de Recherche sur les Pays de l'Est (Swiss Eastern Institute): Jubiläumsstr. 41, 3000 Bern 6; tel. (31) 431212; fax (31) 433891; f. 1959; study of, and information on, the devt of former communist countries; library; Dir Dr GEORG J. DOBROVOLNY; publs *Le Périscope* (monthly), *Schwejzarskij Vestnik* (monthly, in Russian), *SOI-Bilanz* (monthly), *Swiss Press Review* (every 2 weeks), *Zeit-bild* (every 2 weeks).

TAJIKISTAN

Institute of World Economics and International Relations: 734000 Dushanbe, ul. Aini 44; tel. (372) 23-27-32; fax (372) 22-57-65; f. 1964; attached to Acad. of Sciences; conducts research into economic devt in Tajikistan and other countries, with particular attention to transitional economies and the process of integration into the global economy; Dir RASHID K. RAKHIMOV; publ. *Ekonomiko-Matematicheskie Metody v Planirovanii Narodnogo Khozyaistva*.

TURKEY

Karadeniz ve Orta Asya Ülkeri Arastirma Merkez (Black Sea and Central Asian Countries Research Centre): Orta Dogu Teknik Üniversitesi, Ismet Inönü Bul., 06531 Ankara; tel. (312) 2101204; fax (312) 2101105; e-mail kora@rorqual.cc.metu.edu.tr; internet www .metu.edu.tr/home/wwwkora; f. 1992; data analysis and economic and political forecasting; Dir Dr ALI RIZA GÜNBAK.

TURKMENISTAN

Institute of Economics: 744032 Aşgabat, Bikrova sad keşi 28; tel. (12) 24-02-52; Dir G. M. MURADOV.

UKRAINE

Institute for Economic Research: 01023 Kyiv, bulv. Druzhby Narodiv 28; tel. (44) 269-96-33; e-mail sas@niei.kiev.ua; areas of research have included analysis of the most important trends in Ukrainian economic and social devt and the state of Ukraine's economy during the transition to a market economy.

Institute of Economics: 01011 Kyiv, vul. P. Mirnoho 26; tel. (44) 290-84-44; fax (44) 290-86-63; f. 1992; attached to the Acad. of Sciences; conducts research into transitional economies, theory of political economy and the devt of agro-industrial complexes in Ukraine; library; Dir I. I. LUKINOV; publs *Ekonomika Ukrainy* (monthly), *Istoriya Narodnoho Hospodarstvo Ta Ekonomichnoi Dumki Ukrainy* (annually), research reports.

Institute of International Relations of Kyiv T. Shevchenko National Univ.: 04119 Kyiv, vul. Melnikova 36/1; tel. (44) 213-09-90; fax (44) 213-07-67; e-mail long@iir.kiev.ua; internet www.iir.kiev .ua; Dir Prof. Dr LEONID GUBERSKY.

Institute of the World Economy and International Relations: Nat. Acad. of Sciences, 01030 Kyiv, vul. Leontovicha 5; tel. (44) 235-70-22; fax (44) 235-51-27; f. 1992; research and studies on European and national economic, political and social problems; transitional societies and world civilization processes; global, national and regional interdependence in the contemporary world; US and transatlantic economic and policy studies; political culture of African and Asian societies; Dir A. N. SHLEPAKOV.

Mizhnarodna Asotsiatsiya Ukrainistiv (International Association of Ukrainian Studies): 01001 Kyiv, vul. Hrushevskoho 4; tel. and fax (44) 229-76-50; e-mail iaus@gilan.uar.net; Pres. Prof. YAROSLAV ISEYEVICH; publ. *Biuleten Respublikans'koi Asotsiatsii Ukrainoznavtsiv*.

Ukrainian Centre for International Security Studies (UCISS): 02023 Kyiv, POB 541; tel. and fax (44) 212-58-37; e-mail globus@uciss.freenet.kiev.ua; internet www.isn.ethz.ch/uciss/uciss .htm; f. 1991 to study national, regional and global security issues; Pres. Dr LEONID BELOUSOV; Exec. Dir OLEKSANDR PARFIONOV; publs occasional papers.

Ukrainian Institute for Social Research: 04112 Kyiv, vul. Degtyarivska 52, 5th Floor; tel. (44) 211-38-91; e-mail uisr@ukrnet

.ua; internet www.uisr.org.ua; f. 1991; Chair. of Bd OLEKSANDR O. YAREMNKO.

UNITED KINGDOM

Centre for Central and East European Studies: University of Liverpool, Liverpool L69 7WZ; tel. (151) 794-2422; fax (151) 794-2366; e-mail swainnj@liverpool.ac.uk; internet www.liv.ac.uk/ history/research/ccees.htm; f. 1990; Deputy Dir Dr NIGEL SWAIN.

Centre for Defence and International Security Studies (CDISS): PO Box 801, Lancaster, LA1 9DX; tel. and fax (1524) 221585; e-mail info@cdiss.org; internet www.cdiss.org; f. 1990 as a unit of the University of Lancaster; independent from 2004; European security and transatlantic relations; revolutionary warfare; space security; missile threats and responses; maritime security; military integrity and professionalism; holds conferences and seminars; Dir Dr MARTIN EDMONDS.

Centre for Economic Reform and Transformation (CERT): School of Management and Languages, Heriot-Watt University, Riccarton, Edinburgh EH14 4AS; tel. (131) 451-3485; fax (131) 451-3498; e-mail s.a.ashby@hw.ac.uk; internet www.som.hw.ac .uk/cert/; f. 1990; tracks and analyses economic transformation in Central and Eastern Europe and the CIS; Dir Prof. MARK E. SCHAFFER; publ. *CERT Discussion Papers*.

Centre for Research into Post-Communist Economies (CRCE): 57 Tufton St, London SW1P 3QL; tel. and fax (20) 7233-1050; e-mail crce@trident-net.co.uk; internet www.crce.org.uk; f. 1984; research into issues affecting communist economies and those economies making the transition from communism to a market economy; publ. *Post-Communist Economies*; Exec. Dir LISL BIGGS-DAVISON.

Centre for Russian, Central and East European Studies (CRCEES): Dept of Central and East European Studies, University of Glasgow, 8 Lilybank Gdns, Glasgow G12 8RZ; tel. (141) 330-8539; fax (141) 330-5594; e-mail ceeswebmaster@lbss.gla.ac.uk; internet www.gla.ac.uk/departments/centralandeasteuropeanstudies/ crcees/; aspects of identity and culture and their social, political and economic implications, political transformation and economic relations; Dir RICHARD BERRY.

Centre for Russian and East European History: University of Aberdeen, King's College, Aberdeen AB24 3FX; tel. (1224) 272465; fax (1224) 272203; e-mail p.dukes@abdn.ac.uk; f. 1989; specializes in Siberia and the Russian Far East, comparative Russian-US studies, Russian-Scottish connections; Dir Prof. PAUL DUKES; publs occasional papers.

Centre for Russian and East European Studies: European Research Institute, School of Social Sciences, University of Birmingham, Edgbaston, Birmingham B15 2TT; tel. (121) 414-6346; fax (121) 414-3423; e-mail crees@bham.ac.uk; internet www.crees.bham.ac .uk; f. 1963; a multidisciplinary centre focusing on the social sciences and history, incl. studies of Central European, Russian and Ukrainian politics and society, post-communist economic transformation, the history of Russia and the USSR, security studies, Russian language and literature, Polish and Ukrainian languages; Baykov Library of 90,000 vols; Dir Dr DEREK AVERRE; publs *Research Papers on Russian and East European Studies (ResPREES)*, *Birmingham Slavonic Monographs*.

Centre for Russian, Soviet and Central and East European Studies: University of St Andrews, St Andrews, Fife KY16 9AL; tel. (1334) 462907; fax (1334) 462927; e-mail pghist@st-andrews.ac.uk; internet www.st-and.ac.uk/institutes/crscees; f. 1990; Dir Dr FRANCES NETHERCROFT.

Centre for the Study of Public Policy: Edmund Wright Bldg, University of Aberdeen, Aberdeen AB24 3QY; tel. (1224) 272275; fax (1224) 273442; e-mail cspp@abdn.ac.uk; internet www.abdn.ac.uk/ cspp; f. 1976; undertakes international policy research, with particular emphasis on sample surveys of mass-behaviour and public opinion in Central and Eastern Europe and Russia; Dir Prof. RICHARD ROSE; publ. *Studies in Public Policy* (16 a year).

Centre for the Study of Terrorism and Political Violence (CSTPV): School of International Relations, University of St Andrews, New Arts Building, Library Park, The Scores, St Andrews, Fife KY16 9AL; tel. (1334) 462935; fax (1334) 461922; e-mail gm39@ st-andrews.ac.uk; internet www.st-andrews.ac.uk/~wwwir/ research/cstpv/index.php; f. 1994; Chair. Prof. PAUL WILKINSON; Dir Prof. ALEX P. SCHMID; publ. *Terrorism and Political Violence* (quarterly).

Centre of International Studies: First Floor, 17 Mill Lane, Cambridge CB2 1RX; tel. (1223) 767235; fax (1223) 767237; e-mail intstudies@lists.cam.ac.uk; internet www.intstudies.cam.ac.uk; f. 1967; research and postgraduate courses on international studies; Dir Prof. CHRISTOPHER HILL; publ. *Cambridge Review of International Affairs* (3 a year).

Chatham House (Royal Institute of International Affairs): Chatham House, 10 St James's Sq., London SW1Y 4LE; tel. (20) 7957-5716; fax (20) 7957-5710; e-mail jnixey@chathamhouse.org.uk; internet www.chathamhouse.org.uk/russiaeurasia; f. 1920; an independent body, which aims to promote the study and understanding of international affairs, incl. international security and economics; the Russia and Eurasia Programme serves as a forum for debate and research on the foreign and domestic policies of Russia and the CIS, focusing specifically on security, peace-keeping, conflict prevention, energy and economics; publishes extensively and holds regular seminars and study groups to address topical issues; library of 140,000 vols and 650 periodicals; Chair. Dr DeANNE JULIUS; Dir Dr ROBIN NIBLETT; Man., Russia and Eurasia Programme JAMES NIXEY; publs *International Affairs* (5 a year), *The World Today* (monthly).

International Institute for Strategic Studies: Arundel House, 13–15 Arundel St, Temple Place, London, WC2R 3DX; tel. (20) 7379-7676; fax (20) 7836-3108; internet www.iiss.org; f. 1958; conducts research and analysis, and provides a forum for contacts on military and political developments relevant to the prospects, course and consequences of conflict world-wide; c. 2,500 individual mems and 450 corporate and institutional mems; Chair. Prof. FRANÇOIS HEISBOURG; Dir-Gen. and Chief Exec. Dr JOHN CHIPMAN; publs include *The Military Balance* (annual), *Strategic Survey* (annual), *Strategic Comments* (10 a year), *Survival* (quarterly), *Adelphi Papers* (monograph series).

Keston Institute: POB 752, Oxford OX1 9QF; tel. (1865) 792929; fax (1865) 240042; e-mail admin@keston.org.uk; internet www.keston.org.uk; f. 1969 as the Centre for the Study of Religion and Communism; non-governmental organization studying religious affairs and promoting religious freedom in post-communist and communist countries; Pres. Canon Dr MICHAEL BOURDEAUX; Chair. XENIA DENNEN; publs *Frontier* (quarterly), *Religion, State and Society: the Keston Journal* (quarterly).

Nottingham Institute of Russian, Soviet and East European Studies: Dept of Russian and Slavonic Studies, University of Nottingham, University Park, Nottingham NG7 2RD; tel. (115) 951-5824; fax (115) 951-5834; e-mail nirees@nottingham.ac.uk; internet www.nottingham.ac.uk/nirees; f. 1986; interdisciplinary research activity in Russian and East European studies; seminars, workshops and conferences; Chair. Dr ADAM SWAIN.

Russian and Eurasian Studies Centre: St Antony's College, Oxford University, 62 Woodstock Rd, Oxford OX2 6JF; tel. (1865) 284728; fax (1865) 274526; e-mail richard.ramage@sant.ox.ac.uk; internet www.sant.ox.ac.uk/russian; f. 1953; multidisciplinary research; maintains close links with the Oxford Society for the Caspian and Central Asia (TOSCA); library of 24,000 vols; Dir ROBERT SERVICE.

School of Central and East European Studies: Hetherington Bldg, Bute Gardens, Glasgow, G12 8RS; tel. (141) 330-5585; fax (141) 330-5594; e-mail m.baister@socsci.gla.ac.uk; internet www.arts.gla.ac.uk/Slavonic/School.htm; f. 1999 as Institute of Central and East European Studies; absorbed by the School of Central and East European Studies in 2002–03; research on culture, economics, history, politics and society in Central and Eastern Europe, Russia and other CIS member states; host to the website of the British Association for Slavonic and East European Studies (BASEES) and the European Centre for Occupational Health, Safety and the Environment (ECOHSE); Glasgow University Library holds 75,000 to 80,000 vols on Central and Eastern Europe and Russia; Head of School Prof. JAMES D. WHITE.

School of Oriental and African Studies (SOAS): University of London, Thornhaugh St, London WC1H 0XG; tel. (20) 7637-2388; fax (20) 7436-3844; e-mail mo2@soas.ac.uk; internet www.soas.ac.uk; f. 1916; library of approx. 1.2m. vols; Dir Prof. PAUL WEBLEY; publ. *SOAS Bulletin*.

School of Slavonic and East European Studies (SSEES): UCL, 16 Taviton St, London WC1H 0BW; tel. (20) 7679-8700; fax (20) 7679-8755; e-mail ssees@ssees.ac.uk; internet www.ssees.ac.uk; f. 1915; multidisciplinary research into the culture, economics, geography, history, international relations, language, politics and sociology of Eastern Europe and Russia; has a Centre for Russian Studies and a Centre for South-East European Studies; library of 350,000 vols and 1,200 periodicals; Dir Dr ROBIN P. AIZLEWOOD; publs *Slavonic and East European Review* (quarterly), *Slovo: An Inter-disciplinary Journal of Russian, East European and Eurasian Affairs* (2 a year).

USA

American Association for the Advancement of Slavic Studies: 8 Story St, 3rd Floor, Cambridge, MA 02138; tel. (617) 495-0677; fax (617) 495-0680; internet www.aaass.org; f. 1948; Exec. Dir DMITRY GORENBURG.

American Association for Ukrainian Studies: 34 Kirkland St, Cambridge, MA 02138; tel. (617) 495-4053; fax (617) 495-8097; e-mail dillon@ukrainianstudies.org; internet www.ukrainianstudies.org; f. 1989; Pres. ALEXANDRA HRYCAK.

American Enterprise Institute for Policy Research (AEI): 1150 17th St, NW, Washington, DC 20036; tel. (202) 862-5800; fax (202) 862-7177; e-mail vrodman@aei.org; internet www.aei.org; f. 1943; conducts research into economic policies, Eastern European affairs, international trade and finance, regional devt, and social and political issues; Pres. CHRISTOPHER C. DeMUTH; publs *AEI Newsletter* (monthly), *The American*.

Brookings Institution: 1775 Massachusetts Ave, NW, Washington, DC 20036-2103; tel. (202) 797-6000; fax (202) 797-6004; e-mail communications@brookings.edu; internet www.brookings.edu; f. 1916; research and publishing in the fields of economics, development, the politics of energy, US foreign policy, and domestic reform and foreign policy, with an emphasis on Russia, the Caucasus and Central Asia; library of 80,000 vols; Pres. STROBE TALBOTT; publs *Brookings Papers on Economic Activity* (3 a year), policy briefs, and individual reports and books.

Center for East Asian Studies (CEAS): Monterey Institute of International Studies, 460 Pierce St, Monterey, CA 93940; tel. (831) 647-4100; fax (831) 647-4199; e-mail info.ceas@miis.edu; internet www.miis.edu/centers-ceas.html; projects examine issues such as: the role of Pacific Rim countries in the devt of the Russian Far East; the regional security implications of North-East Asian economic devt; and cross-border migration in North-East Asia; library of 77,000 vols and 565 periodicals; Dir Dr TSUNEO AKAHA.

Center for Eurasian, Russian and East European Studies (CERES): Georgetown Univ., ICC 111, POB 571031, Washington, DC 20057-1031; tel. (202) 687-6080; fax (202) 687-5829; e-mail guceres@georgetown.edu; internet ceres.georgetown.edu; f. 1959; interdisciplinary research on relevant regions; approx. 2,000 vols and online periodicals; Dir Dr ANGELA E. STENT; Assoc. Dir Dr JENNIFER E. LONG; publ. regular newsletter.

Center for European and Russian Studies (CERS): University of California, 11367 Bunche Hall, POB 951446, Los Angeles, CA 90095-1446; tel. (310) 825-4060; fax (310) 206-3555; e-mail vwheeler@isop.ucla.edu; internet www.isop.ucla.edu/euro/; library of over 250,000 vols and 1,000 periodicals; Dir IVAN BEREND; publs *Communist and Post-Communist Studies* and working papers.

Center for Foreign Policy Development: Watson Institute for International Studies, Brown University, 2 Stimson Ave, POB 1948, Providence, RI 02912; tel. (401) 863-3465; fax (401) 863-7440; e-mail cfpd@brown.edu; f. 1981; global security issues; particularly concerned with relations between the USA and countries of the former USSR; Dir P. TERRENCE HOPMANN; publ. *Watson Institute Briefings Newsletter*.

Center for Nations in Transition (CNT): University of Minnesota, 230 Hubert H. Humphrey Center, 301 19th Ave S, Minneapolis, MN 55455; tel. (612) 625-3073; fax (612) 626-9860; e-mail thageman@hhh.umn.edu; internet www.hhh.umn.edu/centers/cnt/main.htm; involved in research and institutional design for sustainable devt, and educational activities in Central and Eastern European countries; Russian and Central European Area Studies library, available online at www.lib.umn.edu/rce; Dir ZBIGNIEW BOCHNIARZ.

Center for Nonproliferation Studies (CNS): Monterey Institute of International Studies, 460 Pierce St, Monterey, CA 93940; tel. (831) 647-4154; fax (831) 647-3519; e-mail cns@miis.edu; internet www.cns.miis.edu; f. 1989; library of 77,000 vols and 565 periodicals; Dir Dr WILLIAM C. POTTER; publs *CNS Forum, Inventory of International Nonproliferation Organizations and Regimes, Nonproliferation Review, Status Report: Nuclear Weapons, Fissile Material and Export Controls in the Former Soviet Union*, occasional papers.

Center for Russian and East European Studies: University of Kansas, 1440 Jayhawk Blvd, Lawrence, KS 66045-7574; tel. (785) 864-4236; fax (785) 864-3800; e-mail crees@ukans.edu; internet www.ukans.edu/~crees; f. 1960; language and area studies in Polish, Russian, Ukrainian and general Central and Southern European affairs; special programmes for US Army Foreign Area Officers; library of 350,000 vols and 3,000 periodicals (current and out of print); Dir Dr MARIA CARLSON.

Center for Russian and East European Studies (CREES): University of Michigan, 1080 South University Ave, Suite 3668, Ann Arbor, MI 48109-1106; tel. (734) 764-0351; fax (734) 763-4765; e-mail crees@umich.edu; internet www.ii.umich.edu/crees; f. 1959; US Dept of Education National Resource Center for Eastern Europe, Russia and Central Asia; Dir DOUG NORTHROP.

Center for Russian and East European Studies (REES): University of Pittsburgh, 4G15 Posvar Hall, Pittsburgh, PA 15260; tel. (412) 648-7407; fax (412) 648-7002; e-mail crees@ucis.pitt.edu; internet www.ucis.pitt.edu/crees; f. 1965; a US Dept of Education Title VI National Resource Center; areas of research include contemporary Russian culture, societies in transition, foreign policy, Balkan and Slovak studies; library of 361,000 vols; Dir Dr ROBERT M.

Research Institutes

HAYDEN; publs *Carl Beck Papers, Pitt Series in Russian and East European Studies, East European Politics and Societies*.

Center for Russian and East European Studies (CREES): University of Virginia, 223 Minor Hall, POB 400180, Charlottesville, VA 22904-4167; tel. (434) 924-3033; fax (434) 924-7867; e-mail crees@virginia.edu; internet minerva.acc.virginia.edu/~crees; Dir ALLEN C. LYNCH.

Center for Russian and Eurasian Studies (CRES): Monterey Institute of International Studies, 460 Pierce St, Monterey, CA 93940; tel. (831) 647-4100; fax (831) 647-4199; e-mail info@miis.edu; internet www.miis.edu/rcenters-cres.html; f. 1986; interdisciplinary study and research on Russia and the newly independent states, in the fields of contemporary politics and society, regional security and Russian foreign policy; library of 8,000 vols and 130 periodicals; Pres. CLARA YU; publs *NIS Environmental Watch* and occasional papers.

Center for Russian, East European and Central Asian Studies (CREECA): University of Wisconsin-Madison, 210 Ingraham Hall, 1155 Observatory Dr., Madison, WI 53706-1397; tel. (608) 262-3379; fax (608) 890-0267; e-mail events@creeca.wisc.edu; internet www.creeca.wisc.edu; f. 1993; a US Dept of Education Title VI National Resource Center; forms part of the Int. Institute, University of Wisconsin-Madison; library of 600,000 vols; Dir TED GERBER.

Center for Russian, East European and Eurasian Studies (CREEES): University of Iowa, Int. 22, Iowa City, IA 52242-1802; tel. (319) 335-3584; fax (319) 353-2033; e-mail uicreees@uiowa.edu; internet www.uiowa.edu/~creees; f. 1997; the centre provides support to the schools of business, education, law and medicine, and in the fields of humanities and social sciences for the devt of courses focusing on Eastern Europe, Russia and Central Asia; Russian, East European and Eurasian Studies collection of approx. 140,000 vols; Dir RUSSELL SCOTT VALENTINO.

Center for Russian, East European and Eurasian Studies: Stanford University, Bldg 40, Main Quad, Stanford, CA 94305-2006; tel. (650) 723-3562; fax (650) 725-6119; internet creees.stanford.edu; f. 1966; the promotion and support of the interdisciplinary study of the region; Dir Prof. NANCY S. KOLLMANN; publs newsletter and conference papers.

Center for Russian, East European and Eurasian Studies (REENIC): University of Texas at Austin, Geography 106 A1600, Austin, TX 78712; tel. (512) 471-7782; fax (512) 471-3368; internet reenic.utexas.edu/reenic/online.html; Dir JOAN NEUBERGER.

Center for Slavic and East European Studies (CSEES): Ohio State University, 303 Oxley Hall, 1712 Neil Ave, Columbus, OH 43210-1219; tel. (614) 292-8770; fax (614) 292-4273; e-mail csees@osu.edu; internet slaviccenter.osu.edu; f. 1965; Dir YANA HASHAMOVA (acting).

Center for Slavic, Eurasian and East European Studies (CSEEES): FedEx Global Education Center, University of North Carolina at Chapel Hill, POB 5125, Chapel Hill, NC 27599-5125; tel. (919) 962-0901; fax (919) 962-2494; e-mail jmolich@email.unc.edu; internet www.unc.edu/depts/slavic; f. 1991; operates jointly with Duke University; a US Dept of Education Title VI National Resource Center; undergraduate education, graduate student and faculty research, conferences and seminars; Dir Dr ROBERT M. JENKINS; publ. *Connections* (quarterly newsletter).

Center for Strategic and International Studies (CSIS): 1800 K St, NW, Washington, DC 20006; tel. (202) 887-3200; fax (202) 775-3199; e-mail rep@csis.org; internet www.csis.org; f. 1962; public-policy research institute dedicated to analysis and policy impact; Russian and Eurasian programme; Pres. and Chief Exec. JOHN HAMRE; Chair. SAM NUNN; publs *Washington Papers* (monographs), *Washington Quarterly*, newsletters.

Central Asia-Caucasus Institute: Nitze School of Advanced International Studies, Johns Hopkins University, 1619 Massachusetts Ave, Washington, DC 20036; tel. (202) 663-7723; fax (202) 663-7785; e-mail caci2@jhu.edu; internet www.silkroadstudies.org/new/index.htm; f. 1996; forms part of the joint transatlantic Central Asia-Caucasus Institute and Silk Road Studies Program (also based at the Institute for Security and Development Policy, Stockholm, Sweden); Chair. Dr S. FREDERICK STARR; publs *Silk Road Papers, Central Asia-Caucasus Analyst* (every 2 weeks).

Davis Center for Russian Studies: Harvard University, CGIS South Bldg, 3rd Floor, 1730 Cambridge Street, Cambridge, MA 02138; tel. (617) 495-4037; fax (617) 495-8319; e-mail daviscenter@fas.harvard.edu; internet www.daviscenter.fas.harvard.edu; f. 1948, renamed the Kathryn W. and Shelby Cullom Davis Center for Russian Studies in 1996; adopted current name in 2002; advanced study of the experiences and problems of Russia and adjacent regions of Europe and Asia; library; Dir TIMOTHY J. COLTON; publ. monograph series (100 vols).

Ukrainian Research Institute: 34 Kirkland St, Cambridge, MA 02138; tel. (617) 495-4053; fax (617) 495-8097; e-mail huri@fas.harvard.edu; internet www.huri.harvard.edu; f. 1973; Dir MICHAEL S. FLIER.

EastWest Institute: 700 Broadway, 2nd Floor, New York, NY 10003; tel. (212) 824-4140; fax (212) 824-4149; e-mail mwashington@ewi.info; internet www.iews.org; f. 1981; the study of conflict prevention and democracy; Chair. GEORGE F. RUSSELL, Jr; Pres. JOHN EDWIN MROZ.

Ellison Center for Russian, East European and Central Asian Studies: University of Washington's Jackson School of International Studies, POB 353650, Seattle, WA 98195-3650; tel. (206) 543-4852; fax (206) 685-0668; e-mail reecas@u.washington.edu; internet jsis.washington.edu/ellison; a US Dept of Education Title VI National Resource Center; Dir STEPHEN HANSON.

The Harriman Institute: Columbia University, 420 West 118th St, 12th Floor, New York, NY 10027; tel. (212) 854-4623; fax (212) 666-3481; e-mail harriman@columbia.edu; internet www.harriman.columbia.edu; f. 1946; runs programmes on Central Asian, Georgian, Ukrainian and Balkan studies; also Georgian Studies centre and Russian Practicum; Dir CATHARINE NEPOMNYASHCHY; publ. *Harriman Review* (quarterly).

Hudson Institute: 6th Floor, 1015 15th St, NW, Washington, DC 20005; tel. (202) 974-2400; fax (202) 974-2410; e-mail info@hudson.org; internet www.hudson.org; f. 1961; studies Eastern Europe, global food issues and US strategic issues; library of 13,000 vols; Pres. HERBERT (HERB) I. LONDON; Chief Exec. KENNETH R. WEINSTEIN.

Institute for Democracy in Eastern Europe (IDEE): 1718 M St, NW, No. 147, Washington, DC 20036; tel. (202) 466-7105; fax (202) 387-6466; e-mail idee@idee.org; internet www.idee.org; f. 1985; supports independent human rights, political and social movements, and publications independent of government control, in Central and Eastern Europe and the countries of the former USSR; library of 1,000 vols; Pres. IRENA LASOTA.

Institute for East-West Studies: 700 Broadway, 2nd Floor, New York, NY 10003; tel. (212) 824-4100; fax (212) 824-4149; e-mail newyork@ewi.info; internet www.iews.org; f. 1981; has a particular focus on economic and regional devt, international security, the Russian regions, and transfrontier co-operation; Chair. GEORGE F. RUSSELL, JR; Pres. JOHN EDWIN MROZ.

Institute for European, Russian and Eurasian Studies: George Washington University, Elliott School of International Affairs, 1957 E St, NW, Suite 412, Washington, DC 20052; tel. (202) 994-6340; fax (202) 994-5436; e-mail ieresgwu@gwu.edu; internet ieres.org; f. 1961 as the Institute of Sino-Soviet Studies; name changed as above 1992; Dir Dr HOPE M. HARRISON.

Institute of Slavic, East European and Eurasian Studies: University of California, Berkeley, 260 Stephens Hall, POB 2304, Berkeley, CA 94720-2304; tel. (510) 642-3230; fax (510) 643-5045; e-mail iseees@berkeley.edu; internet socrates.berkeley.edu/~iseees; f. 1957; Berkeley main library includes Slavic and East European collections comprising 750,000 vols and 10,000 serial titles; Dir YURI SLEZKINE; publs *ISEEES Newsletter* (3 a year), *BPS Working Paper Series*.

Institute for the Study of Conflict, Ideology and Policy (ISCIP): Boston University, 141 Bay State Rd, Boston, MA 02215; tel. (617) 353-5815; fax (617) 353-7185; e-mail buiscip@bu.edu; internet www.bu.edu/iscip; f. 1988; focuses on conflict-prone societies in crisis, especially Russia and other post-Soviet republics, paying particular attention to destabilizing factors of a political, ethnic or international nature; Dir Prof. URI RA'ANAN; publs *The ISCIP Analyst* (every 2 weeks), *Perspective* (every 2 months), *ISCIP Update* and *Behind the Breaking News*; database of political and security devts in the post-Soviet republics.

Kennan Institute: Woodrow Wilson International Center for Scholars, 1 Woodrow Wilson Plaza, 1300 Pennsylvania Ave, NW, Washington, DC 20004-3027; tel. (202) 691-4100; fax (202) 691-4247; e-mail kennan@wilsoncentre.org; internet www.wilsoncentre.org/kennan; f. 1974; Russia, Ukraine and neighbouring countries; Dir BLAIR A. RUBLE.

Matthew B. Ridgway Center for International Security Studies: University of Pittsburgh, 3930 WWPH, Pittsburgh, PA 15260; tel. (412) 624-7884; fax (412) 624-7291; e-mail brizzi@gspia.pitt.edu; internet www.ridgway.pitt.edu; research into organized crime; the non-proliferation of weapons of mass destruction; regional conflict; and new dimensions of international security, including the environment, chemical and biological weapons, terrorism, information warfare, etc.; Dir Dr DONALD GOLDSTEIN (acting); publ. *Ridgway Newsletter*.

The National Bureau of Asian Research (NBR): 1215 4th Avenue, Suite 1600, Seattle, WA 98161; tel. (206) 632-7370; fax (206) 632-7487; e-mail nbr@nbr.org; internet www.nbr.org; f. 1989; research on politics and security, economics and trade, and health and society issues affecting US relations with East, Central and South Asia, and Russia; publs *NBR Book Series, NBR Analysis, NBR*

Briefing, *NBR Bulletin*, *NBR Special Reports*, *Asia Policy*; Pres. RICHARD ELLINGS.

National Council for Eurasian and East European Research (NCEEER): 2601 4th Ave, Suite 310, Seattle, WA 98121; tel. (206) 441-6433; fax (206) 753-0066; e-mail danochka@nceeer.org; internet www.nceeer.org; f. 1978; covers economic, political and social developments and trends in the post-communist countries of Asia and Europe; Chair. MARK BEISSINGER; Pres. and Editor ROBERT HUBER.

Princeton Institute for International and Regional Studies: Princeton University, Aaron Burr Hall, Princeton, NJ 08544-1022; tel. (609) 258-4851; fax (609) 258-3988; e-mail piirs@princeton.edu; internet www.princeton.edu/~piirs; f. 2003; fmrly Center of International Studies (f. 1951); international relations and international and regional development research; Dir KATHERINE S. NEWMAN; publs *World Politics* (quarterly), *PIIRs News* (2 a year), books, occasional papers.

Russian, East European and Eurasian Center (REEC): University of Illinois at Urbana-Champaign, 104 Int. Studies Bldg, 910 S Fifth St, Champaign, IL 61820-6216; tel. (217) 333-1244; fax (217) 333-1582; e-mail reec@uiuc.edu; internet www.reec.uiuc.edu; f. 1959; US Dept of Education-designated national research centre; interdisciplinary research; Slavic and East European Library of 683,960 vols and 117,000 periodicals; Dir RICHARD TEMPEST; publ. *Slavic Review*.

Russian and East European Institute: Indiana University, 1020 E Kirkwood Ave, 565 Ballantine Hall, Bloomington, IN 47405-6615; tel. (812) 855-7309; fax (812) 855-6411; e-mail reei@indiana.edu; internet www.indiana.edu/~reeiweb/index.html; f. 1958; interdisciplinary training and research; main library holds 600,000 vols on Slavic and East European issues; Dir DAVID L. RANSEL; publ. *REEIfication* (quarterly newsletter).

Russian and East European Studies Center (REESC): University of Oregon, Eugene, OR 97403-1262; tel. (541) 346-5052; fax (541) 346-5041; e-mail hessler@uoregon.edu; internet darkwing .uoregon.edu/~reesc; f. 1968; Knight Library of 180,000 vols and 100 serial titles; Dir JULIE HESSLER.

Shevchenko Scientific Society (Naukove Tovarystvo im. Shevchenka): 63 Fourth Ave, New York, NY 10003-5200; tel. (212) 254-5130; fax (212) 254-5239; e-mail info@shevchenko.org; internet www .shevchenko.org; f. 1873; dissolved in 1939 and re-established in 1947; Pres. OREST POPVYCH; publ. *Ukranian Literature: a Journal of Translation* (every 2 years).

UCLA Center for European and Eurasian Studies (CEES): 11367 Bunche Hall, POB 951446, Los Angeles, CA 90095-1446; tel. (310) 825-4060; fax (310) 206-3555; e-mail cees@international.ucla .edu; internet www.international.ucla.edu/euro/; f. 1993; multidisciplinary teaching and research, especially concerned with the European Union in the framework of the new East-West connection.

US Institute of Peace: 1200 17th St, NW, Suite 200, Washington, DC 20036-3011; tel. (202) 457-1700; fax (202) 429-6063; e-mail usip_requests@usip.org; internet www.usip.org; f. 1984 by US Congress; aims to promote conflict resolution by peaceful means; Chair. J. ROBINSON WEST; Pres. RICHARD H. SOLOMON.

World Association of International Studies: Hoover Institution, Stanford University, Stanford, CA 94305-6010; tel. (650) 322-2026; fax (650) 723-1687; e-mail wais@adrian.edu; internet cgi.stanford .edu/group/wais/cgi-bin/?page_id=164; f. 1965; performs a continuous online discussion of international affairs (www.stanford.edu/ group/wais); Pres. WILLIAM RATCLIFF (acting); Chair. PHYLLIS GARDNER.

UZBEKISTAN

Institute of Economics: 100060 Tashkent, ul. Borovski ko'ch 5; tel. (71) 33-86-03; fax (7) 33-14-78; internet econ.uzsci.net; attached to Uzbek Acad. of Sciences; Dir AMAN KH. KHIKMATOV.

SELECT BIBLIOGRAPHY (BOOKS)

For books on individual countries see the Bibliography at the end of each Country Survey.

Acar, F., and Gries-Ayata, A. (Eds). *Gender and Identity Construction: Women of Central Asia, the Caucasus and Turkey*. Leiden, Brill, 2000.

Adshead, S. A. M. *Central Asia in World History*. London, Macmillan, 1993.

Akiner, S. *Islamic People of the Soviet Union: an Historical and Statistical Handbook, with an Appendix on the non-Muslim Turkic peoples of the Soviet Union*. 2nd edn, London, Kegan Paul International, 1986.

Akiner, S. (Ed.). *Cultural Change and Continuity in Central Asia*. London, Kegan Paul International, 1991.

The Caspian: Politics, Energy and Security. London, Routledge-Curzon, 2004.

Alexander, C., Buchli, V., and Humphrey, C. *Urban Life in Post-Soviet Asia*. London, UCL Press, 2007.

Alleg, H. *Etoile rouge et croissant vert, l'Orient sovietique/Red Star and Green Crescent*. Moscow, Progress Publishers, 1985.

Allen, W. E. D., and Mouratoff, P. *Caucasian Battlefields: History of the Wars on the Turco-Caucasian Border 1828–1921*. Cambridge, Cambridge University Press, 1953.

Allison, R., and Bluth, C. *Security Dilemmas in Russia and Eurasia*. London, Royal Institute of International Affairs, 1998.

Allison, R., Light, M., and White, S. *Putin's Russia and the Enlarged Europe (Chatham House Papers)*. Blackwell, London, 2006.

Allworth, E. (Ed.). *Central Asia: 130 Years of Russian Dominance, a Historical Overview*. Durham, NC, Duke University Press, 1994.

Amineh, M. P., and Houweling, H. (Eds). *Central Eurasia in Global Politics: Conflict, Security and Development*. Leiden, Brill, 2004.

Amirahmadi, H. *The Caspian Region at a Crossroad: Challenges of a New Frontier of Energy and Development*. Basingstoke, Macmillan, 2000.

Anderson, J. *The International Politics of Central Asia*. Manchester, Manchester University Press, and New York, St Martin's Press, 1997.

Andrew, C., and Gordievsky, O. *KGB, the Inside Story*. London, Hodder and Stoughton, 1990.

Apor, B., Behrends, J. C., Jones, P., and Rees, E. A. *Leader Culture in Communist Dictatorships: Stalin and the Eastern Bloc*. Basingstoke, Palgrave Macmillan, 2005.

Applebaum, A. *Between East and West: Across the Borderlands of Europe*. New York, Pantheon, 1995.

Gulag: A History of the Soviet Camps. London, Allen Lane, 2003.

Aras, B. *The New Geopolitics of Eurasia and Turkey's Position*. London, Frank Cass, 2002.

Åslund, A. *How Capitalism Was Built: the Transformation of Central and Eastern Europe, Russia, and Central Asia*. Cambridge, Cambridge University Press, 2007.

Atabaki, T., and Mehendale, S. (Eds). *Central Asia and the Caucasus: Transnationalism and Diaspora*. Abingdon, Routledge, 2006.

Atabaki, T., and O'Kane, J. (Eds). *Post-Soviet Central Asia*. London, Tauris Academic Studies (in association with the International Institute for Asian Studies), 1998.

Auer, M. R. *Restoring Cursed Earth: Appraising Environmental Policy Reforms in Eastern Europe and Russia*. Lanham, MD, Rowman and Littlefield, 2004.

Aves, J. *Post-Soviet Transcaucasia*. London, Royal Institute of International Affairs, 1993.

Baldick, J. *Animal and Shaman: Ancient Religions of Central Asia*. London and New York, I. B. Tauris, 2000.

Batalden, S. K., and Batalden, S. L. *The Newly Independent States of Eurasia: Handbook of Former Soviet Republics*. 2nd edn, Phoenix, AZ, Oryx, 1997.

Berg, A., and Kreikemeyer, A. (Eds). *Realities of Transformation: Democratization Policies in Central Asia Revisited*. Baden-Baden, Nomos, 2006.

Bertsch, G. K. *Crossroads and Conflict: Security and Foreign Policy in the Caucasus and Central Asia*. New York, Routledge, 1999.

Bertsch, G. K., and Potter, W. C. (Eds). *Dangerous Weapons, Desperate States: Russia, Belarus, Kazakhstan and Ukraine*. London, Routledge, 1999.

Betz, D. *Civil-Military Relations in Russia and Eastern Europe*. London, Routledge, 2004.

Blum, D. W. *National Identity and Globalization: Youth, State and Society in Post-Soviet Eurasia*. New York, Cambridge University Press, 2007.

Boobbyer, P. *The Stalin Era*. London, Routledge, 2000.

Boramy, Z., and Moser, R. G. *Ethnic Politics after Communism*. New York, Cornell University Press, 2005.

Bourdeaux, M. (Ed.). *The Politics of Religion in Russia and the New States of Eurasia*. Armonk, NY, M. E. Sharpe, 1995.

Bregel, Y. *An Historical Atlas of Central Asia*. Leiden, Brill, 2003.

Bremmer, I., and Taras, R. (Eds). *New States, New Politics: Building the Post-Soviet Nations*. Cambridge, Cambridge University Press, 1997.

Breyfogle, N., Schrader, A., and Sunderland, W. *Peopling the Russian Periphery: Borderland Colonization in Eurasian History*. Abingdon, Routledge, 2007.

Brower, D. R. *Turkestan and the Fate of the Russian Empire*. London, RoutledgeCurzon, 2003.

Brown, A. (Ed.). *The Soviet-East European Relationship in the Gorbachev Era*. Boulder, CO, Westview Press, 1990.

Brown, A., Kaser, M., and Smith, G. (Eds). *The Cambridge Encyclopaedia of Russia and the Former Soviet Union*. Cambridge, Cambridge University Press, 1994.

Brzezinski, Z., and Sullivan, P. (Eds). *Russia and the Commonwealth of Independent States: Documents, Data and Analysis*. Armonk, NY, M. E. Sharpe, 1996.

Buckley, M. (Ed.). *Post-Soviet Women from the Baltic to Central Asia*. Cambridge, Cambridge University Press, 1997.

Buttino, M. (Ed.). *In a Collapsing Empire: Underdevelopment, Ethnic Conflicts and Nationalisms in the Soviet Union*. Milan, Feltrinelli, 1993.

Cambridge International Reference on Current Affairs. *A Political and Economic Dictionary of Eastern Europe*. London, Europa Publications, 2002.

Capisani, G. R. *The Handbook of Central Asia: a Comprehensive Survey of the New Republics*. London, I. B. Tauris, 2000.

Carrère d'Encausse, H. *The End of the Soviet Empire: The Triumph of the Nations*. New York, Basic Books, 1994.

Carter, H., and Ehteshami, A. *The Middle East's Relations With Asia and Russia*. London, RoutledgeCurzon, 2004.

Chervonnaya, S. M. *Conflict in the Caucasus: Georgia, Abkhazia and the Russian Shadow*. Glastonbury, Gothic Image Publications, 1995.

Christian, D. *A History of Russia, Central Asia and Mongolia: Inner Eurasia from Pre-history to the Mongol Empire*. Oxford, Blackwell Publishers, 1999.

Chuvin, P., and Gentile, P. *Asie Centrale: l'Indépendance, le Pétrole et l'Islam*. Paris, Le Monde Poche, 1998.

Clarke, R. A., and Matko, D. J. I. *Soviet Economic Facts, 1917–81*. London, Macmillan, 1983.

Cockerham, W. C. *Health and Social Change in Eastern Europe*. London, Routledge, 1999.

Collins, K. *Clan Politics and Regime Transition in Central Asia*. Cambridge, Cambridge University Press, 2006.

Combs, D. *Inside the Soviet Alternate Universe: The Cold War's End and the Soviet Union's Fall Reappraised*. University Park, PA, Penn State University Press, 2008.

Cox, M. (Ed.). *Rethinking the Soviet Collapse: Sovietology, the Death of Communism and the New Russia*. London, Pinter, 1998.

Crandall, M. S. *Energy, Economics, and Politics in the Caspian Region: Dreams and Realities*. Westport, CT, Greenwood, 2006.

Crockatt, R. *The Fifty Years War: The United States and the Soviet Union in World Politics, 1941–1991*. London, Routledge, 1996.

Crosston, M. *Fostering Fundamentalism: Terrorism, Democracy and American Engagement in Central Asia*. Aldershot, Ashgate, 2006.

Cummings, S. N. *Power and Change in Central Asia*. London, Routledge, 2001.

Cummings, S. N. (Ed.). *Oil, Transition and Security in Central Asia*. London, RoutledgeCurzon, 2003.

D'Agostino, A. *Gorbachev's Revolution 1985–1991*. Basingstoke, Macmillan, 1998.

Dahrendorf, R. *After 1989: Morals, Revolution and Civil Society*. Basingstoke, Macmillan (in association with St Antony's College, University of Oxford), 1997.

Danber, R. *The Soviet Nationality Reader: The Disintegration in Context*. Boulder, CO, Westview Press, 1992.

Daniels, R. V. *The End of the Communist Revolution*. London, Routledge, 1993.

D'Anieri, P. *Economic Interdependence in Ukrainian-Russian Relations*. New York, State University of New York Press, 1999.

Danilovich, A. *Russian-Belarusian Integration: Playing Games Behind the Kremlin Walls*. Aldershot, Ashgate, 2006.

Dannreuther, R. *Creating New States in Central Asia: The Strategic Implications of the Collapse of Soviet Power in Central Asia*. London, Brassey's (for the International Institute for Strategic Studies), 1994.

Darden, K. A. *Economic Liberalism and its Rivals: The Formation of International Institutions among the Post-Soviet States*. Cambridge, Cambridge University Press, 2008.

Dawisha, K. *Eastern Europe, Gorbachev and Reform: The Great Challenge*. 2nd edn, Cambridge, Cambridge University Press, 1988.

Dawisha, K. (Ed.). *The International Dimension of Post-Communist Transitions in Russia and the New States of Eurasia*. Armonk, NY, M. E. Sharpe, 1997.

Dawisha, K., and Parrott, B. (Eds). *Democratic Changes and Authoritarian Reactions in Russia, Ukraine, Belarus and Moldova*. New York, Cambridge University Press, 1997.

The End of Empire? The Transformation of the USSR in Comparative Perspective. Armonk, NY, M. E. Sharpe, 1997.

Conflict, Cleavage and Change in Central Asia and the Caucasus. Cambridge, Cambridge University Press, 1997.

Democratisation and Authoritarianism in Post-Communist Societies. 4 vols. Cambridge, Cambridge University Press, 1998.

Dawisha, K., and Valdes, J. 'Socialist Internationalism in Eastern Europe', in *Problems of Communism*, Vol. 36, No. 2 (March/April), 1987.

Desai, P. *The Soviet Economy*. Oxford, Basil Blackwell, 1987.

Dienes, L. *Soviet Central Asia: Economic Development and National Policy Choices*. Boulder, CO, Westview Press, 1987.

Diuk, N., and Karatnycky, A. *New Nations Rising: the Fall of the Soviets and the Challenge of Independence*. New York and Chichester, John Wiley and Sons, 1993.

Djalilli, M.-R., and Kellner, T. *Géopolitique de la Nouvelle Asie Centrale*. Paris, Presse Universitaires de France, 2001.

Drobizheva, L. (Ed.). *Ethnic Conflict in the Post-Soviet World: Case Studies and Analysis*. Armonk, NY, M. E. Sharpe, 1996.

Dudoignon, S., and Komatsu, H. (Eds). *Islam in Politics in Russia and Central Asia (Early Eighteenth to Late Twentieth Centuries)*. London, Kegan Paul International, 2001.

Dunlop, J. B. *The Rise of Russia and the Fall of the Soviet Empire*. Princeton, NJ, Princeton University Press, 1994.

Ebel, R. E., and Menon, R. (Eds). *Energy and Conflict in Central Asia and the Caucasus*. Lanham, MD, Rowman and Littlefield, 2000.

Edwards Economic Research Inc. *The Middle East and Central Asia Economic Databook*. London, Europa Publications, 2002.

Ehteshama, A. (Ed.). *From the Gulf to Central Asia: Players in the new Great Game*. Exeter, University of Exeter Press, 1994.

Eickelman, D. F. *Russia's Muslim Frontiers: New Directions in Cross-cultural Analysis*. Bloomington, IN, Indiana University Press, 1993.

Elgie, R., and Moestrup, S. *Semi-presidentialism Outside Europe: A Comparative Study*. Abingdon, Routledge, 2007.

Erturk, K. A. (Ed.). *Rethinking Central Asia: Non-Eurocentric Studies in History, Social Structure and Identity*. Reading, Ithaca Press, 1999.

Esposito, J. L. *Oxford History of Islam*. Oxford, Oxford University Press, 2000.

Ewans, M. (Ed.). *The Great Game: Britain and Russia in Central Asia*. New York, Routledge, 2003.

Fedorov, Y. *Lands of Discord: Central Asia and the Caspian Between Russia, China and the West (Chatham House Papers)*. Oxford, Wiley-Blackwell, 2008.

Ferdinand, P. (Ed.). *The New Central Asia and its Neighbours*. London, Royal Institute of International Affairs/Pinter, 1994.

Fitzpatrick, S. (Ed.). *Stalinism*. London, Routledge, 2000.

Forbes Manz, B. *The Rise and Rule of Tamerlane*. Cambridge, Cambridge University Press, 1999.

Fowkes, B. *The Disintegration of the Soviet Union: a Study in the Rise and Triumph of Nationalism*. Basingstoke, Macmillan, 1997.

Fritz, V. *State-building: A Comparative Study of Ukraine, Lithuania, Belarus and Russia*. New York, Central European University Press, 2007.

Frucht, R. (Ed.). *The Encyclopedia of Eastern Europe—From the Congress of Vienna to the Fall of Communism*. New York, Garland Publishing, 2000.

Gafurov, B. G. *Central Asia: Pre-Historic to Pre-Modern Times*. 2 vols. Delhi, Shipra, 2005.

Galeotti, M. *Gorbachev and His Revolution*. London, Macmillan, 1997.

Gammer, M. (Ed.). *The Caspian Region*. 2 vols. London, Routledge, 2004.

Ethno-nationalism, Islam and the State in the Caucasus: Post-Soviet Disorder. Abingdon, Routledge, 2007.

Gleason, G. *The Central Asian States: Discovering Independence*. Boulder, CO, Westview Press, 1997.

Glenn, J. *The Soviet Legacy in Central Asia*. New York, St Martin's Press, 1999.

Gokay, B. *Soviet Eastern Policy and Turkey, 1920–1991: Soviet Foreign Policy, Turkey and Communism*. Abingdon, Routledge, 2006.

Goldenberg, S. *Pride of Small Nations: The Caucasus and Post-Soviet Disorder*. London, Zed Books, 1994.

Gorbachev, M. *Perestroika*. 2nd edn, London, Fontana Collins, 1988.

Grancelli, B. *Soviet Management and Labor Relations*. Boston, MA, Unwin Hyman, 1988.

Gray, K. R. (Ed.). *Soviet Agriculture: Comparative Perspectives*. Ames, IO, Iowa State University Press, 1990.

Grousset, R. *The Empire of the Steppes: A History of Central Asia*. Piscataway, NJ, Rutgers University Press, 1989.

Hagendoorn, L., Linssen, H., and Tumanov, S. *Intergroup Relations in the States of the Former Soviet Union*. London, Psychology Press, 2001.

Haghayeghi, M. *Islam and Politics in Central Asia*. Basingstoke, Macmillan, 1995.

Hahn, G. M. *Russia's Islamic Threat*. New Haven, CT, Yale University Press, 2007.

Hanson, P. *Trade and Technology in Soviet-Western Relations*. London, Macmillan, 1981.

Haugen, A. *The Establishment of National Republics in Central Asia*. Basingstoke, Palgrave Macmillan, 2003.

Hedlund, S. *Private Agriculture in the Soviet Union*. London, Routledge, 1990.

Herzig, E. *The New Caucasus: Armenia, Azerbaijan and Georgia*. London, Royal Institute of International Affairs, 1999.

Hewett, E. A. *Reforming the Soviet Economy: Equality versus Efficiency*. Washington, DC, Brookings Institution Press, 1989.

Hiro, D. *Between Marx and Muhammad: The Changing Face of Central Asia*. London, HarperCollins, 1994.

War Without End: The Rise of Islamist Terrorism and Global Response. London, Routledge, 2002.

Holden, G. *The Warsaw Pact: Soviet Security and Bloc Politics*. Oxford, Basil Blackwell, 1989.

Hopkirk, P. *Setting the East Ablaze: Lenin's Dream of an Empire in Asia*. Oxford, Oxford University Press, 1986.

The Great Game. 2nd edn, Oxford, Oxford University Press, 2001.

Hosking, G. *Russia: People and Empire*. London, HarperCollins, 1997.

Hosking, G., and Service, R. (Eds). *Russian Nationalism, Past and Present*. Basingstoke, Macmillan, 1997.

Hudson, G. E. (Ed.). *Soviet National Security Policy under Perestroika*. Boston, MA, Unwin Hyman, 1990.

Humphrey, C. *The Unmaking of Soviet Life: Everyday Economies After Socialism*. New York, Cornell University Press, 2002.

Hunter, S. *Central Asia since Independence*. Westport, CT, Praeger, 1996.

Strategic Developments in Eurasia After 11 September. Abingdon, Routledge, 2004.

Ito, T., and Tabata, S. (Eds). *Between Disintegration and Reintegration: Former Socialist Countries and the World Since 1989*. Sapporo, Slavic Research Centre, Hokkaido University, 1994.

Jackson, N. J. *Russian Foreign Policy and the CIS: Theories, Debates and Actions*. London, Routledge, 2003.

Jeffries, I. *The Caucasus and Central Asian Republics at the Turn of the Twenty-First Century: A Guide to the Economies in Transition*. New York, Routledge, 2003.

The Countries of the Former Soviet Union at the Turn of the Twenty-First Century: the Baltic and European States in Transition. New York, Routledge, 2004.

Jones Luong, P. *The Transformation of Central Asia: States and Societies From Soviet Rule to Independence.* Ithaca, NY, Cornell University Press, 2004.

Jonson, L. *Keeping the Peace in the CIS: The Evolution of Russian Policy.* London, Royal Institute of International Affairs, 1999.

Jonsson, A. *Human Trafficking and Human Security.* Abingdon, Routledge, 2008.

Kaariainen, K. *Religion in Russia After the Collapse of Communism: Religious Renaissance or Secular State?* Lewiston, NY, Edwin Mellen Press, 1998.

Kagarlitsky, B. *Empire of the Periphery: Russia and the World System.* Ann Arbor, MI, Pluto Press, 2008.

Kaiser, R. J. *The Geography of Nationalism in Russia and the USSR.* Princeton, NJ, Princeton University Press, 1994.

Kalyuzhnova, Y., Jaffe, A. M., Lynch, D., and Sickles, R. C. *Energy in the Caspian Region: Present and Future.* Basingstoke, Palgrave Macmillan, 2002.

Kaminski, B. (Ed.). *Economic Transition in Russia and the New States of Eurasia.* Armonk, NY, M. E. Sharpe, 1996.

Kanet, R. E. (Ed.). *The New Security Environment: the Impact on Russia, Central and Eastern Europe.* Aldershot, Ashgate, 2005.

Karny, Y. *Highlanders: A Journey to the Caucasus in Quest of Memory.* New York, Farrar, Straus and Giroux, 2000.

Kazemzadeh, F. *The Struggle for Transcaucasia (1917–1921).* Westport, CT, Hyperion Press, 1981.

Keep, J. *Last of the Empires: A History of the Soviet Union 1945–1991.* Oxford, Oxford University Press, 1996.

Keller, S. *To Moscow, not Mecca: the Soviet Campaign Against Islam in Central Asia, 1917–41.* Westport, CN, Praeger, 2001.

Kelley, D. R. (Ed.). *After Communism: Perspectives on Democracy.* Fayetteville, AR, University of Arkansas Press, 2003.

Kempe, I., et al. *Direct Neighbourhood: Relations Between the Enlarged EU and the Russian Federation, Ukraine, Belarus and Moldova.* Gütersloh, Bertelsmann Foundation Publishers, 1998.

Kenez, P. *A History of the Soviet Union from the Beginning to the End.* 2nd edn, Cambridge, Cambridge University Press, 2006.

Kennedy-Pipes, C. *Stalin's Cold War: Soviet Strategies in Eastern Europe, 1943 to 1956.* Manchester, Manchester University Press, 1996.

Khazanov, A. M. *After the USSR: Ethnicity, Nationalism and Politics in the Commonwealth of Independent States.* Madison, WS, University of Wisconsin Press, 1995.

Kittrie, N., and Volgyes, I. (Eds). *The Uncertain Future: Gorbachev's Eastern Bloc.* New York, Paragon House, 1988.

Kleveman, L. *The New Great Game: Blood and Oil in Central Asia.* New York, Atlantic Monthly Press, 2003.

Knight, A. W. *Spies Without Cloaks: The KGB's Successors.* Princeton, NJ, Princeton University Press, 1996.

Kolstoe, P. *Russians in the Former Soviet Republics.* London, Hurst, 1995.

Kostecki, W., Zukrowska, K., and Goralczyk, B. J. *Transformations of Post-Communist States.* Basingstoke, Macmillan, 2000.

Kotkin, S. *Armageddon Averted: The Soviet Collapse, 1970–2000.* Oxford, Oxford University Press, 2001.

Kötzinger, P. *Frontiers and Horizons of the EU: the New Neighbours Ukraine, Belarus and Moldova.* Hamburg, Körber-Stiftung, 2005.

Kozlov, V. I. *The Peoples of the Soviet Union.* London, Hutchinson, 1988.

Krag, H., and Funch, L. *The North Caucasus: Minorities at a Crossroads.* London, Minority Rights Group International, 1995.

Kuehnast, K., and Nechemias, C. (Eds). *Post-Soviet Women Encountering Transition: Nation Building, Economic Survival, and Civic Activism.* Baltimore, MD, Johns Hopkins University Press, 2004.

Kulchik, Y., Fadin, A., and Sergeev, V. *Central Asia After the Empire.* London, Pluto Press (in association with the Transnational Institute), 1996.

Laird, R. F., and Hoffman, E. P. (Eds). *Soviet Foreign Policy in a Changing World.* New York, Aldine de Gruyter, 1986.

Laitlin, D. G. *Identity in Formation: the Russian-speaking Populations in the Near Abroad.* Ithaca, NY, Cornell University Press, 1998.

Landau, J. M., and Kellner-Heinkele, B. *Politics of Language in the Ex-Soviet Muslim States: Azerbaijan, Uzbekistan, Kazakhstan, Kyrgyzstan, Turkmenistan, Tajikistan.* Ann Arbor, MI, University of Michigan Press, 2001.

Lapidus, G. W., and Zaslavsky, V. (Eds). *From Union to Commonwealth: Nationalism and Separatism in the Soviet Republics.* Cambridge, Cambridge University Press, 1992.

Laruelle, M. *Russian Eurasianism: An Ideology of Empire.* Baltimore, MD, Johns Hopkins University Press, 2008.

Lee, R. W. *Smuggling Armageddon: The Nuclear Black Market in the Former Soviet Union and Europe.* New York, St Martin's Press, 1998.

Lee, S. J. *Stalin and the Soviet Union.* London, Routledge, 1999.

Lewis, D. C. *After Atheism: Religion and Ethnicity in Russia and Central Asia.* New York, St Martin's Press, 1999.

Lewis, D. W. P., and Lepesant, G. (Eds). *What Security for Which Europe?* New York, Peter Lang, 1999.

Lieven, A. *Ukraine and Russia: A Fraternal Rivalry.* Washington, DC, Carnegie Endowment for International Peace, 1997.

Light, M. *The Soviet Theory of International Relations.* Brighton, Wheatsheaf, 1988.

Lightbody, B. *The Cold War.* London, Routledge, 1999.

Linden, R. H. (Ed.). *Studies in East European Foreign Policy.* New York, Praeger, 1980.

Litvin, V. *The Soviet Agro-Industrial Complex.* Boulder, CO, Westview Press, 1987.

Longworth, P. *Russia's Empires: Their Rise and Fall—from Prehistory to Putin.* London, John Murray, 2005.

Lubin, N. *Central Asians take Stock: Reform, Corruption and Identity.* Washington, DC, US Institute of Peace, 1995.

Luong, P. *Institutional Change and Continuity in Post-Soviet Central Asia: Power, Perception and Pacts.* Cambridge, Cambridge University Press, 2002.

Luong, P. J. (Ed.). *The Transformation of Central Asia: States and Societies From Soviet Rule to Independence.* Ithaca, NY, Cornell University Press, 2004.

Lynch, A. *The Soviet Study of International Relations.* Cambridge, Cambridge University Press, 1988.

Lynch, D. *Russian Peacekeeping Strategies in the CIS: the Cases of Moldova, Georgia and Tajikistan.* Basingstoke, Macmillan, 2000.

Engaging Eurasia's Separatist States: Unresolved Conflicts and De Facto States. Washington, DC, US Institute of Peace, 2004.

Mackinnon, M. *The New Cold War: Revolutions, Rigged Elections and Pipeline Politics in the Former Soviet Union.* Ontario, Vintage Canada, 2008.

McCauley, M. *Afghanistan and Central Asia: A Modern History.* Harlow, Longman, 2002.

McChesney, R. D. *Central Asia: Foundations of Change.* Princeton, NJ, Darwin Press, 1996.

McGwire, M. *Perestroika and Soviet National Security.* Washington, DC, Brookings Institution, 1991.

McKee, M., Healy, J., and Falkingham, J. *Health Care in Central Asia.* Maidenhead, Open University Press, 2002.

McLoughlin, B., and McDermott, K. (Eds). *Stalin's Terror: High Politics and Mass Repression in the Soviet Union.* Basingstoke, Palgrave Macmillan, 2004.

McMann, K. M. *Economic Autonomy and Democracy: Hybrid Regimes in Russia and Kyrgyzstan.* Cambridge, Cambridge University Press, 2006.

Malcolm, N. *Soviet Policy Perspectives on Western Europe (Chatham House Papers).* London, Routledge (for the Royal Institute of International Affairs), 1989.

Mandelbaum, M. (Ed.). *Central Asia and the World: Kazakhstan, Uzbekistan, Tajikistan, Kyrgyzstan and Turkmenistan.* New York, Council on Foreign Relations Press, 1994.

The Rise of Nations in the Soviet Union: American Foreign Policy and the Disintegration of the USSR. New York, Council on Foreign Relations, 1991.

Mason, J. W. *The Cold War—1945–1991.* London, Routledge, 1996.

Medvedev, Z. A. *Soviet Agriculture.* New York and London, Norton, 1977.

Mellor, R. E. H. *The Soviet Union and its Geographical Problems.* London, Macmillan, 1982.

Melvin, N. *Russians beyond Russia: The Politics of National Identity.* London, Royal Institute of International Affairs, 1995.

Melvin, N., and King, C. (Eds). *Nations Abroad: Diaspora Politics and International Relations in the Former Soviet Union.* Boulder, CO, Westview Press, 1998.

Menashri, D. (Ed.). *Central Asia Meets the Middle East.* London, Frank Cass, 1998.

Menon, R., and Nelson, D. (Eds). *Limits to Soviet Power.* Lexington, MA, Lexington Books, 1989.

Menon, R., Fedorov, Y. E., and Nodia, G. (Eds). *Russia, the Caucasus, and Central Asia: the 21st Century Security Environment*. Armonk, NY, M. E. Sharpe, 1999.

Merridale, C. *Ivan's War: The Red Army 1941–45*. London, Faber & Faber, 2005.

Mesbahi, M. (Ed.). *Central Asia and the Caucasus after the Soviet Union: Domestic and International Dynamics*. Gainesville, FL, University Press of Florida, 1994.

Metge, P. *L'URSS en Afghanistan, de la Coopération á l'Invasion: 1947–1984*. Paris, Cirpes, 1984.

Mickiewicz, T. M. *Economic Transition in Central Europe and the Commonwealth of Independent States*. Basingstoke, Palgrave Macmillan, 2005.

Miller, E. A. *To Balance or Not to Balance: Alignment Theory and the Commonwealth of Independent States*. Aldershot, Ashgate, 2006.

Miller, J. *Mikhail Gorbachev and the End of Soviet Power*. New York, St Martin's Press, 1993.

Milor, V. (Ed.). *Changing Political Economies: Privatization in Post-Communist and Reforming Communist States*. Boulder, CO, Lynne Rienner, 1994.

Minorsky, V. F. *Studies in Caucasian History*. London, Cambridge Oriental Series, 1953.

The Turks, Iran and the Caucasus in the Middle Ages. London, Variorum Reprints, 1978.

Montefiore, S. S. *Young Stalin*. London, Wiedenfeld & Nicolson, 2007.

Moskoff, W. (Ed.). *Perestroika in the Countryside: Agricultural Reform in the Gorbachev Era*. Armonk, NY, M. E. Sharpe, 1990.

Mozaffari, M. (Ed.). *Security Policies in the Commonwealth of Independent States: The Southern Belt*. Basingstoke, Macmillan, and New York, St Martin's Press, 1997.

Mullerson, R. *International Law, Rights and Politics: Developments in Eastern Europe and the CIS*. London, Routledge, 1994.

Nahaylo, B., and Swoboda, V. *Soviet Disunion: A History of the Nationalities Problem in the USSR*. London, Hamish Hamilton, 1990.

Naumkin, V. V. *Radical Islam in Central Asia: Between Pen and Rifle*. Lanham, MD, Rowman and Littlefield, 2005.

Naumkin, V. V. (Ed.). *State, Religion and Society in Central Asia*. Reading, Ithaca Press, 1993.

Central Asia and Transcaucasia: Ethnicity and Conflict. Westport, CT, Greenwood, 1994.

Nichol, J. P. *Diplomacy in the Former Soviet Republics*. Westport, CT, Praeger, 1995.

Nielsen, J. S. (Ed.). *The Christian–Muslim Frontier: Chaos, Clash, or Dialogue?* London, I. B. Tauris, 1998.

Nogee, J. L., and Donaldson, R. H. (Eds). *Soviet Foreign Policy since World War II*. 3rd edn, Oxford, Pergamon, 1988.

Nove, A. *An Economic History of the USSR*. Revised edn. Harmondsworth, Penguin, 1982.

Nygren, B. *The Rebuilding of Greater Russia: Putin's Foreign Policy Towards the CIS countries*. Abingdon, Routledge, 2007.

O'Ballance, E. *Wars in the Caucasus, 1990–1995*. New York, New York University Press, 1997.

Odom, W. E., and Dujarric, R. *Commonwealth or Empire? Russia, Central Asia and the Transcaucasus*. Indianapolis, IN, Hudson Institute, 1995.

Olcott, M. B. *Central Asia's New States: Independence, Foreign Policy and Regional Security*. Washington, DC, US Institute of Peace, 1996.

Central Asia's Second Chance. Washington, DC, Carnegie Endowment for International Peace, 2005.

Olcott, M. B., Åslund, A., and Garnett, S. *Getting it Wrong: Regional Co-operation and the Commonwealth of Independent States*. Washington, DC, Carnegie Endowment for International Peace, 1999.

Olson, J. S. (Ed.). *Ethnohistorical Dictionary of the Russian and Soviet Empires*. Westport, CT, and London, Greenwood Press, 1994.

Organisation for Economic Co-operation and Development (OECD). *Assistance Programmes for Central and Eastern Europe and the Former Soviet Union*. Paris, OECD, 1996.

Painter, D. *The Cold War—An International History*. London, Routledge, 1999.

Painter, D., and Leffler, M. (Eds). *The Origins of the Cold War—An International History*. London, Routledge, 1994.

Paksoy, H. B. (Ed.). *Central Asia Reader: the Rediscovery of History*. Armonk, NY, M. E. Sharpe, 1994.

Parrott, B. (Ed.). *State Building and Military Power in Russia and the New States of Eurasia*. Armonk, NY, M. E. Sharpe, 1995.

Peimani, H. *Regional Security and the Future of Central Asia: The Competition of Iran, Turkey and Russia*. Westport, CN, Praeger, 1998.

Failed Transition, Bleak Future?: War and Instability in Central Asia and the Caucasus. Westport, CN, Praeger, 2002.

Pentikaïnen, J. (Ed.) *'Silent As Waters We Live': Old Believers in Russia and Abroad: Cultural Encounter With the Finno-Ugrians*. Helsinki, Finnish Literature Society, 1999.

Pipes, R. *The Formation of the Soviet Union: Communism and Nationalism, 1917–23*. Cambridge, MA, Harvard University Press, 1964.

Communism: A History. New York, Modern Library, 2001.

Plokhy, S. *The Origins of the Slavic Nations: Premodern Identities in Russia, Ukraine, and Belarus*. Cambridge, Cambridge University Press, 2006.

Polokhalo, V. (Ed.). *The Political Analysis of Post-Communism: Understanding Post-Communist Societies*. Kyiv, Political Thought, 1995.

Pomfret, R. W. T. *The Economies of Central Asia*. Princeton, NJ, Princeton University Press, 1995.

Asian Economies in Transition: Reforming Centrally Planned Economies. Cheltenham, Edward Elgar Publishing, 1996.

Ponton, G. *The Soviet Era: Soviet Politics from Lenin to Yeltsin*. Oxford, Basil Blackwell, 1994.

Pope, H. *Sons of the Conquerors: the Rise of the Turkic World*. London, Duckworth, 2005.

Prizel, I. *National Identity and Foreign Policy: Nationalism and Leadership in Poland, Russia and Ukraine*. Cambridge, Cambridge University Press, 1998.

Pryce-Jones, D. *The War That Never Was: The Fall of the Soviet Empire, 1985–1991*. London, Weidenfeld and Nicolson, 1995.

Quester, G. (Ed.). *The Nuclear Challenge in Russia and the New States of Eurasia*. Armonk, NY, M. E. Sharpe, 1995.

Raack, R. C. *Stalin's Drive to the West 1938–45: The Origins of the Cold War*. Cambridge, Cambridge University Press, 1996.

Ramet, S. P. (Ed.). *Religious Policy in the Soviet Union*. Cambridge, Cambridge University Press, 2005.

Rashid, A. *Taliban: Islam, Oil and the New Great Game in Central Asia*. Revised edn. London, I. B. Tauris, 2002.

Jihad: The Rise of Militant Islam in Central Asia. New Haven, CT, and London, Yale University Press, 2002.

Reese, R. R. *The Soviet Military Experience—A History of the Soviet Army, 1917–1991*. London, Routledge, 1999.

Remnick, D. *Lenin's Tomb: The Last Days of the Soviet Empire*. London, Viking, 1993.

Renata, D. (Ed.). *Building Security in the New States of Eurasia: Subregional Co-operation in the Former Soviet Space*. Armonk, NY, M. E. Sharpe, 2000.

Richmond, W. *The Northwest Caucasus: Past, Present, Future* (Central Asian Studies). Abingdon, Routledge, 2008.

Roberts, G. *The Soviet Union in World Politics—Co-existence, Revolution and Cold War 1945–1991*. London, Routledge, 1998.

Roberts, J. *Pipeline Politics: The Caspian and Global Energy Security*. London, Chatham House, forthcoming.

Roeder, P. G. *Red Sunset: The Failure of Soviet Politics*. Princeton, NJ, Princeton University Press, 1994.

Ro'i, Y. (Ed.). *Democracy and Pluralism in Muslim Eurasia*. New York, Frank Cass, 2004.

Ronnas, P., and Sjoberg, O. (Eds) *Economic Transformation and Employment in Central Asia*. Ankara, International Labour Office, 1994.

Roux, J.-P. *L'Asie Centrale, Histoire et Civilizations*. Paris, Fayard, 1997.

Roy, O. *The New Central Asia: The Creation of Nations*. 2nd edn, London, I. B. Tauris, 2007.

Rubin, B. R., Lubin, N., and Martin, K. *Calming the Ferghana Valley*. New York, Century Foundation, 2000.

Rubin, B. R., and Snyder, J. (Eds). *Post-Soviet Political Order*. London, Routledge, 1998.

Ruffin, M. H., et al. *Post-Soviet Handbook: a Guide to Grass-roots Organisations and Internet Resources*. 2nd edn, Seattle, WA, Center for Civil Society International, 1999.

Ruffin, M. H., and Waugh, D. C. *Civil Society in Central Asia*. Seattle, WA, University of Washington Press, 1999.

Rumer, B. *Soviet Central Asia: 'A Tragic Experiment'*. Boston, MA, Unwin Hyman, 1989.

Rumer, B. (Ed.). *Central Asia: A Gathering Storm?* Armonk, NY, M. E. Sharpe, 2002.

Central Asia At The End Of The Transition. Armonk, NY, M. E. Sharpe, 2005.

Rumer, B., Trenin, D., and Zhao, H. *Central Asia: Views From Washington, Moscow, and Beijing*. Armonk, NY, M. E. Sharpe, 2007.

Rumer, B., and Zhukov, S. (Eds). *Central Asia: The Challenge of Independence*. Armonk, NY, M. E. Sharpe, 1998.

Sabahi, F., and Warner, D. *The OSCE and the Multiple Challenges of Transition: The Caucasus and Central Asia*. Aldershot, Ashgate, 2003.

Sadri, H. A., and Hall, G. O. *Geopolitics and Security in the Caspian Sea Region*. London, Saqi, 2007.

Sagdeev, R. Z., and Eisenhower, S. (Eds). *Islam and Central Asia*. Washington, DC, Eisenhower Institute, 2000.

Saideman, S. M. *For Kin or Country: Xenophobia, Nationalism and War*. New York, Columbia University Press, 2008.

Sakwa, R. *Soviet Politics in Perspective*. 2nd edn, London, Routledge, 1998.

The Rise and Fall of the Soviet Union. London, Routledge, 1999.

Sandle, M. *A Short History of Soviet Socialism*. London, UCL Press, 1998.

Schmidtke, O., and Yekelchyk, S. *Europe's Last Frontier?: Belarus, Moldova and Ukraine Between Russia and the European Union*. Basingstoke, Palgrave Macmillan, 2008.

Service, R. *Stalin: a Biography*. Basingstoke, Macmillan, 2004.

Shalin, D. N. (Ed.). *Russian Culture at the Crossroads: Paradoxes of Post-Communist Consciousness*. Boulder, CO, Westview Press, 1996.

Shlapentokh, V. *Public and Private Life of the Soviet People*. New York, Oxford University Press Inc, 1989.

A Normal Totalitarian Society: How the Soviet Union Functioned and How it Collapsed. Armonk, NY, M. E. Sharpe, 2001.

Smith, A., and Pickles, J. (Eds). *Theorizing Transition*. London, Routledge, 1998.

Smith, G. (Ed.). *The Nationalities Question in the Soviet Union*. 2nd edn, London, Longman, 1996.

Smith, G., et al. *Nation-Building in the Post-Soviet Borderlands: The Politics of National Identities*. New York, Cambridge University Press, 1998.

The Post-Soviet States: Mapping the Politics of Transition. London, Arnold, 1999.

Snyder, J. C. (Ed.). *After Empire: The Emerging Geopolitics of Central Asia*. Washington, DC, National Defence University Press, 1995.

Soucek, S. *A History of Central Asia*. Cambridge, Cambridge University Press, 2000.

Spoor, M. *The Political Economy of Rural Livelihoods in Transition Economies: Land, Peasants and Rural Poverty in Transition*. Abingdon, Routledge, 2008.

Srivastava, V. N. *The Separation of the Party and the State: Political Leadership in Soviet and Post Soviet Phases*. Aldershot, Ashgate, 1999.

Starr, F., and Cornell, S. (Eds). *The Baku-Tbilisi-Ceyhan Pipeline*. Washington, DC, and Uppsala, Central Asia-Caucasus Institute and Silk Road Studies Programme, 2005.

Stefes, C. H. *Understanding Post-Soviet Transitions: Corruption, Collusion and Clientelism*. Basingstoke, Palgrave Macmillan, 2006.

Stern, L. *Western Intellectuals and the Soviet Union, 1920–40: From Red Square to the Left Bank*. Abingdon, Routledge, 2006.

Suny, R. G. (Ed.). *Transcaucasia, Nationalism and Social Change: Essays in the History of Armenia, Azerbaijan and Georgia*. Ann Arbor, MI, Michigan Slavic Publications, 1983.

Suny, R. G., and Kennedy, M. D. (Eds). *Intellectuals and the Articulation of the Nation*. Ann Arbor, MI, University of Michigan Press, 1999.

Swietochowski, T. *Russia and Azerbaijan*. New York, Columbia University Press, 1995.

Szelenyi, I. (Ed.). *Privatizing the Land: Rural Political Economy in Post-Communist and Socialist Societies*. London, Routledge, 1998.

Szporluk, R. (Ed.). *National Identity and Ethnicity in Russia and the New States of Eurasia*. London, M. E. Sharpe, 1994.

Russia, Ukraine and the Breakup of the Soviet Union. Stanford, CA, Hoover Institution Press, 2000.

Taras, R. *Post-Communist Presidents*. New York, Cambridge University Press, 1997.

Taubman, W. *Krushchev: The Man and His Era*. New York, W. W. Norton, 2003.

Terry, S. M. *Soviet Policy in Eastern Europe*. New Haven, CT, Yale University Press, 1984.

Thubron, C. *The Lost Heart of Asia*. London, Penguin, 1995.

Shadow Of The Silk Road. London, Chatto & Windus, 2007.

Tolz, V., and Elliot, I. (Eds). *The Demise of the USSR: From Communism to Independence*. Basingstoke, Macmillan, 1995.

Turnbull, M. *Soviet Environmental Policies and Practices: The Most Critical Investment*. Aldershot, Dartmouth, 1991.

Turnock, D. (Ed.). *East Central Europe and the Former Soviet Union*. London, Hodder Arnold, 2001.

Urban, G. R. *End of Empire: The Demise of the Soviet Union*. Washington, DC, American University Press, 1993.

Van Wie Davis, E., and Azizian, R. (Eds). *Islam, Oil, and Geopolitics: Central Asia After September 11*. Lanham, MD, Rowman and Littlefield, 2006.

Vassiliev, A. *Central Asia: Political and Economic Challenges in the Post-Soviet Era*. London, Saqi, 2001.

Wädekin, K.-E. (Ed.). *Communist Agriculture*. London, Routledge, 1990.

Wagener, H.-J. (Ed.). *Economic Thought in Communist and Post-Communist Europe*. London, Routledge, 1998.

Waller, M., Coppieters, B., and Malashenko, A. (Eds). *Conflicting Loyalties and the State in Post-Soviet Russia and Eurasia*. London, Portland, 1998.

Warikoo, K. K. (Ed.). *Central Asia: Emerging New Order*. New Delhi, Har-Anand Publications/Himalayan Research and Cultural Foundation (India), 1995.

Way, L. *Pluralism By Default: Challenges of Authoritarian State-Building in Belarus, Moldova and Ukraine*. Glasgow, Centre for the Study of Public Policy, 2003.

Wegren, S. K. (Ed.). *Land Reform in the Former Soviet Union and Eastern Europe*. London, and New York, Routledge, 1998.

Weisbrode, K. *Central Eurasia: Prize or Quicksand? Contending Views of Instability in Karabakh, Ferghana and Afghanistan*. Oxford, Oxford University Press (for the International Institute for Strategic Studies), 2001.

Weller, R. C. *Rethinking Kazakh and Central Asian Nationhood: A Challenge To Prevailing Western Views*. Los Angeles, CA, Asia Research Associates, 2006.

Wheeler, G. *The Modern History of Soviet Central Asia*. Westport, CT, Greenwood Press, 1975.

White, S. *Gorbachev in Power*. Cambridge, Cambridge University Press, 1990.

Communism and its Collapse. London, Routledge, 2000.

White, S., Gill, G., and Slider, D. *The Politics of Transition: Shaping a Post-Soviet Future*. Cambridge, Cambridge University Press, 1993.

Whiting, A. S. *Siberian Development and East Asia*. Stanford, CA, Stanford University Press, 1981.

Whitlock, M. *Beyond the Oxus*. London, John Murray, 2003.

Williamson, J. (Ed.). *Economic Consequences of Soviet Disintegration*. Washington, DC, Institute for International Economics, 1993.

Wilson, A. *Virtual Politics: Faking Democracy in the Post-Soviet World*. New Haven, CT, Yale University Press, 2005.

Woff, R. *The Armed Forces of the Former Soviet Union: Evolution, Structure and Personalities*. 3 vols. London, Brassey's, 1996.

Wöll, A., and Wydra, H. *Democracy and Myth in Russia and Eastern Europe*. Abingdon, Routledge, 2007.

Wood, A. *Stalin and Stalinism*. London, Routledge, 1990.

Zevelev, I. *Russia and its New Diasporas*. Washington, DC, United States Institute of Peace, 2001.

SELECT BIBLIOGRAPHY (PERIODICALS)

American Bibliography of Slavic and Eastern European Studies (ABSEES): University of Illinois Library at Urbana-Champaign, 128 Observatory, 901 South Mathews Ave, Urbana, IL 61801, USA; tel. (217) 333-0284; fax (217) 333-7011; e-mail absees@uiuc.edu; internet www.library.uiuc.edu/absees; f. 1956 under the auspices of the American Asscn for the Advancement of Slavic Studies; covers US and Canadian scholarship on Central and Eastern Europe and the former USSR; contains bibliographic records, book extracts and reviews, dissertations, online resources and selected government publs; Man. Editor KRISTEN HILL; in English.

Annual Report of the East-West Institute: 700 Broadway, 2nd Floor, New York, NY 10003, USA; tel. (212) 824-4100; fax (212) 824-4149; e-mail iews@iews.org; internet www.iews.org; f. 1981; East-West relations and economics; Editor ELIZABETH BELFER; in Russian and English; circ. 3,000.

Anthropology & Archaeology of Eurasia: M. E. Sharpe Inc, 80 Business Park Dr., Armonk, NY 10504, USA; tel. (914) 273-1800; fax (914) 273-2106; e-mail custserv@mesharpe.com; internet www.mesharpe.com; Editor MARJORIE MANDELSTAM BALZER; 4 a year; in English.

A-P Blitz: Asia-Plus Information Agency, 734002 Dushanbe, ul. Bokhtar 35/1, 8th Floor, Tajikistan; tel. (372) 21-72-20; fax (372) 21-78-63; e-mail info@asiaplus.tj; internet www.asiaplus.tj; f. 1996; Gen. Dir UMED BABAKHANOV; 250 a year (in Russian and in English).

Armenian Review: Armenian Review Inc, 80 Bigelow Ave, Watertown, MA 02172, USA; tel. (617) 926-4037; fax (617) 926-1750; internet www.armenianreview.org; f. 1948; Editor Dr HAYG OSHAGAN; quarterly.

Armeniya Segodnya (Armenia Today): Armenian Society for Friendship and Cultural Relationss, Yerevan, Abovian St 3, Armenia; tel. (2) 56-45-14; Armenian international relations and foreign affairs; 2 a month.

Asia-Plus: Dushanbe, pr. Sherozi 16, 3rd Floor, Tajikistan; tel. and fax (372) 21-72-20; e-mail newspaper@asiaplus.tajik.net; internet www.asiaplus.tajik.net; f. 2000; culture, economics, education, health care, politics, reform, regional news and social security; Dir UMED BABAKHANOV; weekly.

Ayna: Sita Politik Tanitim Danismanlik Hizmetleri AŞ, Abide-I-Hürriyet Cad. 78-15, 80260 Sisli, İstanbul, Turkey; tel. (212) 2472157; fax (212) 2255623; f. 1993; issues concerning the Turkic-speaking nations of Central Asia; Editor O. SUAT OZCELEBI; quarterly; in English and Turkish.

Azerbaijan International: POB 5217, Sherman Oaks, CA 91413, USA; tel. (818) 785-0077; fax (818) 997-7337; e-mail ai@artnet.net; internet www.azer.com; f. 1993; an independent magazine committed to the discussion of issues relating to Azerbaijanis around the world; features culture, language, music, art, literature, international relations and petroleum; Editor BETTY BLAIR; quarterly.

Aziya I Afrika Segodnya (Asia and Africa Today): Institute of Oriental Studies, Russian Acad. of Sciences, 103777 Moscow, ul. Rozhdestvenka 12, Russia; tel. (495) 925-29-42; fax (495) 975-23-96; f. 1957; Russian policy in the Asia-Pacific region; affiliated to the Institute of Africa; Editor MICHAEL L. KAPITSA; monthly; in Russian; circ. 2,000.

Belarusian Review: Belarusian-American Association, Inc, POB 1347, Highland Park, NY 08904, USA; tel. and fax (732) 222-1951; e-mail belarusianreview@hotmail.com; internet www.belreview.cz; f. 1989; quarterly; in English.

Biuletyn Kaliningradzki (Kaliningrad Bulletin): Centre for Eastern Studies, 00-564 Warsaw, ul. Koszykowa 6A, Poland; f. 1993; information on economic, political and social policy in the successor states to the USSR, in particular Belarus, the Russian Federation and Ukraine; monthly; in Polish.

BNA's Eastern Europe Reporter: Bureau of National Affairs, 1231 25th St, NW, Washington, DC 20037, USA; internet www.bna.com; current news arranged by country, industry and topic; monthly.

BOFIT Weekly: Bank of Finland Institute for Economies in Transition, POB 160, 00101 Helsinki, Finland; tel. (10) 8312268; fax (10) 8312294; e-mail bofit@bof.fi; internet www.bof.fi/bofit_en/seuranta/viikkokatsaus/index.htm; f. 2004 to replace *Russian and Baltic Economies—Week in Review*; two-page review of the previous week's focal events in Russia and the People's Republic of China, distributed by e-mail and also published online; Editor TIMO HARELL; weekly; in English; circ. 1,500.

Bulletin of the Asia Institute: 3287 Bradway Blvd, Bloomfield Hills, MI 48301, USA; e-mail bai34@aol.com; internet www.bulletinasiainstitute.org; publishes studies in the art, archaeology, history, languages and numismatics of ancient Iran, Mesopotamia and Central Asia; Editor CAROL ALTMAN BROMBERG.

Business Eastern Europe: Economist Intelligence Unit, Economist Bldg, 111 West 57th St, New York, NY 10019, USA; tel. (212) 554-0600; fax (212) 586-0248; e-mail newyork@eiu.com; internet www.eiu.com; articles dealing with running businesses in Eastern Europe; Editor JOHN REED; weekly; in English.

Business New Europe (BNE): Berlin, Germany; tel. (30) 54710222; fax (30) 54710223; e-mail editor@businessneweurope.eu; internet www.businessneweurope.eu; f. 2007; business, economics, finance and politics in Central and South-Eastern Europe; weekly; published in electronic format and distributed by e-mail; daily supplements include: *BNE: Daily Eastern Europe*; *BNE: Daily Russia*; and *BNE: Daily Ukraine*; monthly supplements: *BNE: Banker*; *BNE: Deal*; *BNE: Stocks/BNE: IPO*; and *BNE: Investor*; Editor-in-Chief BEN ARIS; Managing Editor NICHOLAS WATSON.

Business and Politics: Russian Foreign Policy Foundation, 107078 Moscow, per. B. Kozlovskii 4, Russia; tel. (495) 924-72-70; fax (495) 208-08-06; Russian business, economic relations and foreign policy; monthly; in English.

Business Russia: Economist Intelligence Unit, Economist Bldg, 111 West 57th St, New York, NY 10019, USA; tel. (212) 554-0600; fax (212) 586-0248; e-mail newyork@eiu.com; internet www.eiu.com; articles dealing with running businesses in the former USSR; monthly; in English.

Business Week—Russia: McGraw-Hill Inc, 1221 Ave of the Americas, New York, NY 10020, USA; tel. (212) 512-2000; fax (212) 512-6111; f. 1991; articles on business, economics and industry of particular interest to the Russian Federation; monthly; in Russian; circ. 50,000.

Cahiers d'études sur la Méditerranée orientale et le monde turcoiranien (CEMOTI) (Journal of Studies on the Eastern Mediterranean and Turkish-Iranian World): 56 rue Jacob, 75006 Paris, France; tel. 1-58-71-70-56; fax 1-58-71-70-90; e-mail vaner@ceri.sciences-po.org; internet www.ceri-sciencespo.com/publica/cemoti/presente.htm; f. 1985; published by l'Association française pour l'étude Méditerranée orientale et du monde turcoiranien (AFE-MOTI); covers the geographical zone from the Balkans to ex-Soviet Central Asia, incl. the Caucasus; utilizes all aspects of political science, among other disciplines, to analyse the complexity of the region's current affairs, as well as looking to other disciplines; Editor SEMIH VANER; 2 a year; in French and English.

Canadian-American Slavic Studies: Charles Schlacks, Jr, POB 1256, Idyllwild, CA 925-1256, USA; tel. (951) 659-4641; e-mail info@schlacks.com; internet www.schlacks.com; Editor CHARLES SCHLACKS, Jr; quarterly; in English, French, German and Russian.

Canadian Slavonic Papers: Canadian Association of Slavists, University of Alberta, Dept of Modern Languages and Cultural Studies, 200 Arts Bldg, Edmonton, AL T6G 2EG, Canada; tel. (780) 492-2566; fax (780) 492-9106; e-mail csp@ualberta.ca; internet www.ualberta.ca/~csp; Editor OLEH S. ILNYTZKYJ.

Central Asia and the Caucasus: Journal of Social and Political Studies: Central Asia and the Caucasus Center for Social and Political Studies, Hubertusstigen 9, 974 55 Luleå, Sweden; tel. and fax (920) 62-016; e-mail murad@communique.se; internet www.ca-c.org; f. 1995; covers economics, human rights, parties and movements, politics, religion and society, and culture and the arts; Editor Dr MURAD ESENOV; every 2 months; in English and Russian.

Central Asia-Caucasus Analyst: Nitze School of Advanced International Studies, Johns Hopkins University, 1619 Massachusetts Ave, NW, Washington, DC 20036, USA; tel. (202) 663-7723; fax (202) 663-7785; e-mail caci2@jhu.edu; internet www.cacianalyst.org; f. 1999; journal of the Central Asia-Caucasus Institute and Silk Road Studies Program Joint Center; Editor Dr SVANTE E. CORNELL; every 2 weeks.

Central Asian Survey: Routledge, Taylor & Francis, 4 Park Sq., Milton Park, Abingdon, Oxfordshire, OX14 4RN, United Kingdom; tel. (20) 7017-6000; fax (20) 7017-6336; e-mail casurvey@soas.ac.uk; internet www.tandf.co.uk/journals/titles/02634937.asp; f. 1982; economics, history, politics and religions of the Central Asian and

Caucasus region; Editor DENIZ KANDIYOTI; quarterly; in English; circ. 600.

Central Asiatic Journal: Harrassowitz Verlag, 65174 Wiesbaden, Germany; tel. (611) 530899; fax (611) 530570; e-mail verlag@ harrassowitz.de; internet www.harrassowitz-verlag.de; f. 1955; archaeology, history, languages and literature of Central Asia; Editor Prof. GIOVANNI STARY; 2 a year; in English, French and German; circ. 320.

CEU Political Science Journal: Central European University, 1051 Budapest, Nádor u. 9, Hungary; e-mail ceu_polsci@yahoo.com; internet www.personal.ceu.hu/PolSciJournal; f. 2006; politics and economics of Central and Eastern Europe; in English; Man. Editors SERGIU GHERGHINA, ARPAD TODOR; 5 a year.

Chechnya Weekly: Jamestown Foundation, 4516 43rd St NW, Washington, DC 20016, USA; tel. (202) 483-8888; fax (202) 483-8337; e-mail pubs@jamestown.org; internet chechnya.jamestown .org/pub-chweekly.htm; Editor LAWRENCE A. UZZELL; weekly; in English.

Chinese Communist Affairs Monthly: Institute of Int. Relations, 64 Wan Shou Rd, Mucha, Taipei 11625, Taiwan; tel. (2) 9394921; fax (2) 9378609; countries of the former USSR and East European issues, in addition to Chinese affairs.

CIS Environment and Disarmament Yearbook: Marjorie Mayrock Centre for Russian, Eurasian and East European Research, Faculty of Social Sciences, Hebrew University of Jerusalem, Mount Scopus, Jerusalem 91905, Israel; tel. 2-5883180; fax 2-5882835; e-mail msrussia@mscc.huji.ac.il; internet pluto.huji.ac.il/~msrussia; focuses on the ecological aspects of nuclear and chemical disarmament and examines other areas of environmental concern in the former USSR; Editor ZE'EV WOLFSON; annually; in English.

CIS Yearbook: Institute for Contemporary International Studies, 119021 Moscow, ul. Ostozhenka 53/2, Russia; tel. (495) 208-9461; fax (495) 208-9466; e-mail iamp@rol.ru; international affairs and politics of the countries of the CIS; monthly; in Russian.

Classical Russia 1700–1825: Charles Schlacks, Jr, POB 1256, Idyllwild, CA 925-1256, USA; tel. (951) 659-4641; e-mail info@schlacks .com; internet www.schlacks.com; Editor ELENA MARASSINOVA; annually; in English, French, German and Russian.

Communist and Post-Communist Studies: Center for European and Russian Studies (CERS), University of California, 405 Hilguard Ave, Los Angeles, CA 90095-1446, USA; tel. (310) 825-4060; fax (310) 206-3555.

Contemporary Security Policy: Routledge, Taylor & Francis, 4 Park Sq., Milton Park, Abingdon, Oxfordshire, OX14 4RN, United Kingdom; tel. (20) 7017-6000; fax (20) 7017-6336; e-mail tf.enquiries@ informa.com; internet www.tandf.co.uk/journals/titles/13523260 .asp; f. 1979; a forum to discuss the broadening spectrum of security issues emerging in the post-Cold War world and the security implications of economic decline, ethnic conflict, environmental degradation, nationalism and underdevt, etc.; Editors AARON KARP, REGINA KARP; 3 a year; in English.

Controversia: A Journal of Debate and Democratic Renewal: International Debate Education Association, Open Society Institute, 400 West 59th St, New York, NY 10019, USA; tel. (503) 370-6620; fax (503) 370-6171; e-mail alathrop@willamette.edu; f. 2002; Editors DAVID CRATIS WILLIAMS, MARILYN J. YOUNG.

Country Profiles: Economist Intelligence Unit, 26 Red Lion Square, London WC1R 4HQ, United Kingdom; tel. (20) 7576-8000; fax (20) 7830-1023; e-mail london@eiu.com; internet www.eiu.com; individual reports on each of the member countries of the CIS; annually; frequently updated online; in English.

Country Reports: Economist Intelligence Unit, 26 Red Lion Square, London WC1R 4HQ, United Kingdom; tel. (20) 7576-8000; fax (20) 7830-1023; e-mail london@eiu.com; internet www.eiu.com; reports on each of the member countries of the CIS; quarterly; frequently updated online; in English.

Current Digest of the Post-Soviet Press: East View Information Services, Inc, 10601 Wayzata Blvd, Minneapolis, MN 55305, USA; tel. (952) 252-1201; fax (952) 252-1202; e-mail periodicals@eastview .com; internet dlib.eastview.com/sources/publication .jsp?id=6765&uid=612; f. 1949; translations and abstracts from Russian-language press materials; Editor GORDON LIVERMORE; weekly; in English; circ. 1,000.

Current Politics and Economics of Russia, Eastern and Central Europe: Nova Science Publishers, 400 Oser Ave, Suite 1600, Hauppauge, NY 11788, USA; tel. (631) 231-7269; fax (631) 231-8175; e-mail novaeditorial@earthlink.net; internet www.novapublishers .com; f. 1990; changing political and social issues; Editor G. T. SHALTILIS; quarterly; in English.

Defence Studies: Institute for Strategic and Defence Studies, 1241 Budapest, POB 181, Hungary; tel. (1) 262-1920; fax (1) 264-9623; e-mail h9315gaz@ella.hu; the armed forces, conflict resolution and security; 6 a year; in English.

Defense and Security Analysis: Centre for Defence and Int. Security Studies (CDISS), PO Box 801, Lancaster, LA1 9DX, United Kingdom; tel. and fax (1524) 221585; e-mail medmonds@cdiss.org; internet www.cdiss.org; f. 1985; defence theory and analysis; Editor-in-Chief Dr MARTIN EDMONDS; quarterly; in English.

Democratization: Routledge, Taylor & Francis, 4 Park Sq., Milton Park, Abingdon, Oxfordshire, OX14 4RN, United Kingdom; tel. (20) 7017-6000; fax (20) 7017-6336; e-mail tf.enquiries@informa.com; internet www.tandf.co.uk/journals/titles/13510347.asp; f. 1994; contemporary emphasis and a comparative approach, with special reference to democratization in the developing world and in post-communist societies; Editors JEFFREY HAYNES, GORDON CRAWFORD; 5 a year.

Demokratizatsiya (Demography and Democracy in Russia): Heldref Publications, 1319 18th St, NW, Washington, DC, 20036-1802, USA; tel. (202) 687-0100; e-mail dem@heldref.org; internet www .demokratizatsiya.org; Exec. Editors MICHAEL A. McFAUL, FIONA HILL, NIKOLAI V. ZLOBIN.

Diplomatic Yearbook: 119021 Moscow, ul. Ostozhenka 53/2, Russia; tel. (495) 246-18-44; e-mail yuri.fokine@dipacademy.ru; internet dipacademy.ru; international relations and diplomatic history; publ. by Diplomatic Academy of Ministry of Foreign Affairs; Editor-in-Chief YURI FOKINE.

Disarmament and Security Yearbook: Institute of World Economy and Int. Relations, Russian Acad. of Sciences, 117859 Moscow, ul. Profsoyuznaya 23, Russia; tel. (495) 120-43-32; fax (495) 310-70-27; e-mail ineir@sovam.com; f. 1987; foreign policy, international relations and strategic studies; in English.

Donald W. Treadgold Studies in Russian and East European and Asian Studies: HMJ School of Int. Studies, University of Washington, POB 353650, Seattle, WA 98195-3650, USA; tel. (206) 221-6348; fax (206) 685-0668; e-mail treadgld@u.washington.edu; internet jsis .washington.edu/ellison/outreach_treadgold.shtml; f. 1969 as *Publications on Russia and Eastern Europe*; present name adopted 1993; Editor GLENNYS YOUNG.

East Central Europe: Charles Schlacks, Jr, POB 1256, Idyllwild, CA 925-1256, USA; tel. (951) 659-4641; e-mail info@schlacks.com; internet www.schlacks.com; f. 1974; 2 a year; in English, French and German.

East Europe Monographs: Governmental Research Bureau, Park College, Kansas City, MO 64152, USA; tel. (816) 741-2000; f. 1969; Editors JERZY HAUPTMANN, GOTTHOLD RHODE; irreg.; in English.

East European Politics and Societies: University of California Press, 2000 Center St, Suite 303, Berkeley, CA 94704-1223, USA; tel. (510) 643-7154; fax (510) 642-9917; e-mail journals@ucop.edu; internet www.ucpress.edu/journals/eeps; f. 1986; economic, political and social issues in Eastern Europe; Editor VLADIMIR TISMANEANU; 3 a year; in English; circ. 650.

East European Quarterly: Regent Hall, University of Colorado, POB 29, Boulder, CO 80309, USA; tel. and fax (941) 753-4782; e-mail eeqeem@web.tv.net; f. 1967; publishes articles on the civilization, culture, economics, history and politics of Eastern Europe; Editor STEPHEN FISCHER-GALATI; quarterly; in English; circ. 1,000.

East European Jewish Affairs: Routledge, Taylor & Francis, 4 Park Sq., Milton Park, Abingdon, Oxfordshire, OX14 4RN, United Kingdom; tel. (20) 7017-6000; fax (20) 7017-6336; e-mail tf.enquiries@ informa.com; internet www.tandf.co.uk/journals/titles/13501674 .asp; f. 1970; fmrly *Soviet Jewish Affairs*; published under the aegis of the Dept of Hebrew and Jewish Studies of UCL (fmrly University College London), and the Oxford Institute for Yiddish Studies; interdisciplinary journal dealing with the position of Jews in the former USSR and East-Central Europe, from an historical perspective and in the context of general, social, economic, political and cultural developments in the region; Man. Editor SAM JOHNSON; 3 a year; in English.

East-West Business and Trade: Welt Publishing LLC, Suite 1400, 1413 K St, NW, Washington, DC 2005, USA; tel. (407) 279-095; fax (407) 278-8845; f. 1972; business relations, economic devt, political stability and international organizations; Editor JOHN JUSTIN FORD; 2 a month; in English; circ. 3,500.

Eastern European Consensus Forecasts: Consensus Economics Inc, 53 Upper Brook St, London W1K 2LT, United Kingdom; tel. (20) 7491-3211; fax (20) 7409-2331; internet www.consensuseconomics .com; f. 1998; economic forecasts for the East European region, incl. Turkey; Editor CHE-WING PANG; 6 a year; in English.

Eastern European Constitutional Review: 161 Ave of the Americas, 5th Floor, New York, NY 10013, USA; tel. (212) 998-6562; fax (212) 995-4769; e-mail ar55@is8.nyu.edu; internet www.law.nyu.edu/ eecr/volumes.html; published by New York University Law School and Central European University (Budapest, Hungary); East European constitutional law and post-communist politics; Editors STEPHEN HOLMES, ALISON ROSE, AVIEZER TUCKER; quarterly; in English and Russian; circ. 7,000.

Eastern European Economics: M. E. Sharpe Inc, 80 Business Park Dr., Armonk, NY 10504, USA; tel. (914) 273-1800; fax (914) 273-2106; e-mail custserv@mesharpe.com; internet www.mesharpe.com; f. 1962; macroeconomic and microeconomic analysis of Eastern European transitional economies; Editor JOSEF C. BRADA; 6 a year; in English; circ. 400.

Economic Change and Restructuring: Kluwer Academic Publishers BV, van Godewijckstraat 30, POB 17, 3300 AA Dordrecht, Netherlands; tel. (78) 6576116; fax (78) 6576377; e-mail services@wkap.nl; internet www.kluweronline.com/issn/0013-0451; fmrly *Economics of Planning*; Editors ROBERTA BENINI, WOJCIECH W. CHAREMZA.

Economic Survey of Europe: Economic Commission for Europe, United Nations, Palais des Nations, 1211 Geneva 10, Switzerland; tel. (22) 9172606; fax (22) 9170027; e-mail unpubli@unog.ch; economic analysis, incl. statistical information; 2 a year; in English and Russian.

Economic Systems: Osteuropa-Institut München, 81679 München, Scheinerstr. 11, Germany; tel. (89) 9983960; fax (89) 9810110; e-mail rfrensch@lrz.uni-muenchen.de; internet www.lrz-muenchen.de/~econsys; f. 1970; international economics, the theory of economic systems and comparative economics; published in collaboration with the European Association for Comparative Economic Studies; Man. Editor R. FRENSCH; quarterly; in English with German abstracts; circ. 450.

Economics of Transition: Blackwell Publishing Ltd, 9600 Garsington Rd, Oxford OX4 2DQ, United Kingdom; tel. (1865) 776868; fax (1865) 714591; e-mail cs-journals@wiley.com; internet www .blackwellpublishers.co.uk; published for the European Bank for Reconstruction and Development (EBRD); transition economies; Man. Editors PHILIPPE AGHION, WENDY CARLIN; 4 a year; in English.

Ekho Planety (Echo of the Planet): 125993 Moscow, Tverskoi bul. 10–12, Russia; tel. (495) 202-67-48; fax (495) 290-59-11; e-mail echotex@itar-tass.com; internet www.explan.ru; f. 1988; cultural, economic and social international affairs; Editor VALENTIN VASILETS; weekly; in Russian; circ. 12,000.

Ekonomika i Matematicheskiye Metody (Economics and Mathematical Methods): Central Mathematical Economics Institute, Russian Acad. of Sciences, 117418 Moscow, ul. Krasikova 32, Russia; tel. (495) 129-16-44; fax (495) 310-70-15; f. 1965; journal of the Central Mathematical Economics Institute and of the Institute of Market Problems; theoretical and methodological problems of economics and econometrics; Editor V. L. MAKAROV; quarterly; in Russian; circ. 3,500.

Ekonomika Ukrainy (The Economy of Ukraine): 01015 Kyiv, vul. Moskovska 37/2, Ukraine; tel. (44) 280-32-71; fax (44) 280-31-10; f. 1958; published by the Ministry of the Economy, Ministry of Finance and National Academy of Sciences of Ukraine; credit policy, management, state of the national economy in sectoral and territorial aspects, taxes, and theoretical and applied economics; Editors Prof. SERHIY I. PYROZHKOV, I. P. VUSYK; monthly; in Ukrainian and Russian; circ. 3,236 (2005).

Ekonomika i Zhizn (Economics and Life): 127994 Moscow, pr. Bumazhnyi 14, Russia; tel. (495) 250-57-93; fax (495) 200-22-97; e-mail gazeta@ekonomika.ru; internet www.akdi.ru; f. 1918; fmrly *Ekonomicheskaya Gazeta*; international and domestic economic and business activity in the former USSR; Editor YURII YAKUTIN; weekly; in Russian; circ. 1,100,000.

Ekspert (Expert): 125866 Moscow, ul. Pravdy 24, Novyi Gazetnyi kor., Russia; tel. (495) 789-44-65; fax (495) 228-00-78; e-mail ask@expert.ru; internet www.expert.ru; f. 1995; business news from Russia and the CIS, financing, politics, privatization, science and technology, and the stock market; Editor-in-Chief VALERII FADAYEV; weekly; circ. 60,000 (2002).

Emerging Europe Monitor: Business Monitor International, Mermaid House, 2 Puddle Dock, London EC4V 3DS, United Kingdom; tel. (20) 7246-5100; fax (20) 7248-0467; e-mail subs@businessmonitor .com; internet www.businessmonitor.com; macroeconomic performance, outlook and political risk; Marketing Man. JENNIE BEEBEE; monthly; in English.

Emerging Markets Finance and Trade: M. E. Sharpe Inc, 80 Business Park Dr., Armonk, NY 10504, USA; tel. (914) 273-1800; fax (914) 273-2106; e-mail custserv@mesharpe.com; internet www.mesharpe.com; f. 1965; tracks the most critical questions facing emerging market economies; Editor ALI M. KUTAN; 6 a year; in English.

Est-Ovest (East-West): Istituto di Studi e Documentazione sull'Europa Comunitaria e l'Europa Orientale (ISDEE), Corso Italia 27, 34122 Trieste, Italy; tel. (040) 639130; fax (040) 634248; e-mail isdee@spin.it; internet www.isdee.it; f. 1970; institutional, political and socio-economic aspects of Eastern Europe and of East-West relations; 6 a year; in Italian, English and French; circ. 400.

Eurasia Daily Monitor: Jamestown Foundation, 4516 43rd St NW, Washington, DC 20016, USA; tel. (202) 483-8888; e-mail pubs@jamestown.org; internet www.jamestown.org/edm; f. 2004; daily e-mail journal.

Eurasian Geography and Economics: Bellwether Publishing Ltd, 8640 Guilford Rd, Suite 200, Columbia, MD 21046-2612, USA; tel. (410) 290-3870; fax (410) 290-8726; e-mail subs@bellpub.com; internet www.bellpub.com/psge; f. 1960 as *Soviet Geography*, and subsequently renamed *Post-Soviet Geography and Economics*; economics, geography and urban affairs in the countries of Central and Eastern Europe, the former USSR and the socialist countries of Asia; Editors ANDERS ASLUND, C. CINDY FAN, ALEXANDER B. MURPHY; 6 a year; in English.

Eurazja (Eurasia): Centre for Eastern Studies, 00-564 Warsaw, ul. Koszykowa 6A, Poland; f. 1994; economic, political and social issues, in particular in Central Asia; in Polish.

Europe-Asia Studies: 8–9 Lilybank Gardens, Glasgow G12 8RZ, United Kingdom; tel. (141) 330-5259; fax (141) 330-5594; e-mail europe-asia@gla.ac.uk; internet www.tandf.co.uk/journals/titles/09668136.asp; f. 1949; politics, economics, society and history of the former USSR and communist-ruled Eastern Europe; characteristics and processes in the post-communist period; transnational political and economic relations; comparative studies between countries in the region; Editor Prof. TERRY COX; 10 a year; in English; circ. 1,400.

European Education: M. E. Sharpe Inc, 80 Business Park Dr., Armonk, NY 10504, USA; tel. (914) 273-1800; fax (914) 273-2106; e-mail custserv@mesharpe.com; internet www.mesharpe.com; discusses education issues in the member countries of the Council of Europe; Editor HANS J. LINGENS; 4 a year, in English.

European Security: Routledge, Taylor & Francis, 4 Park Sq., Milton Park, Abingdon, Oxfordshire, OX14 4RN, United Kingdom; tel. (20) 7017-6000; fax (20) 7017-6336; e-mail tf.enquiries@informa.com; internet www.tandf.co.uk/journals/titles/09662839.asp; f. 1992; reviews new concepts, institutions, problems and prospects for European security in the wake of the end of the Cold War, to explore the possibilities and dangers of creating an alternative security system for Europe; includes cultural, economic, environmental, ethnic, political and social dimensions; Editor-in-Chief ANDREA ELLNER; quarterly; in English.

Experiment: A Journal of Russian Culture: Charles Schlacks, Jr, POB 1256, Idyllwild, CA 925-1256, USA; tel. (951) 659-4641; e-mail info@schlacks.com; internet www.schlacks.com; Editor JOHN E. BOWLT; annually; in English and Russian.

Ferghana.ru: 113191 Moscow, POB 90, Russia; tel. (495) 955-2950; fax (495) 955-2927; e-mail ferghana@ferghana.ru; internet www .ferghana.ru; f. 1998; publ. by the Ferghana.ru Central Asia Humanitarian-Informational Centre; covers politics and culture of post-Soviet Central Asia, particularly Kyrgyzstan, Tajikistan and Uzbekistan; online only; in Russian and English.

Forschungen zu Osteuropa (Research into Eastern Europe): Edition Temmen, 28209 Bremen, Hohenlohestr. 21, Germany; tel. (421) 348430; fax (421) 348094; e-mail info@edition-temmen.de; internet www.edition-temmen.de; f. 1986; publication of Forschungstelle Osteuropa an der Universität Bremen; Editor HOLST TEMMEN; irreg.; in German.

Forschungen zur Osteuropäischen Geschichte: Osteuropa-Institut der Freien Universität Berlin (Institute of East European Studies of the Free University Berlin), 14195 Berlin, Garystr. 55, Germany; tel. (30) 83852076; fax (30) 83854036; e-mail oei@zedat.fu-berlin.de; internet www.oei.fu-berlin.de; f. 1954; Editor HOLM SUNDHAUSSEN.

Forum 18 News Service: POB 6603, Rodeløkka, 0502 Oslo, Norway; e-mail f18news@editor.forum18.org; internet www.forum18.org; f. 2003; religious freedom, particularly in post-communist countries; weekly and daily e-mail bulletins; Editor FELIX CORLEY.

From the Other Shore: Russian Writers Abroad, Past and Present: Charles Schlacks, Jr, POB 1256, Idyllwild, CA 925-1256, USA; tel. (951) 659-4641; e-mail info@schlacks.com; internet www.schlacks .com; Editor LEONID LIVAK; annually; in English, French and Russian.

Global Crime: Routledge, Taylor & Francis, 4 Park Sq., Milton Park, Abingdon, Oxfordshire, OX14 4RN, United Kingdom; tel. (20) 7017-6000; fax (20) 7017-6336; e-mail tf.enquiries@informa.com; internet www.informaworld.com/smpp/title~content=t714592492~db=all; f. 1995; fmrly *Transnational Organized Crime*; a multidisciplinary journal that identifies and explores cross-border criminal activities, the threats posed by such crime to national and international security, and govt responses to it; Man. Editor FEDERICO VARESE; 4 a year; in English.

Global Newsline: Former Soviet Union and Central Asia: BBC Monitoring, Caversham Park, Reading RG4 8TZ, United Kingdom; tel. (118) 948-6289; fax (118) 946-3823; e-mail marketing@mon.bbc .co.uk; internet www.monitor.bbc.co.uk; political and economic e-mail news service; in English.

Global Studies: Russia, the Eurasian Republics, Central and Eastern Europe: McGraw Hill/Dushkin Publishing Group, 2460 Kerper Blvd,

Dubuque, IA 52001, USA; tel. (563) 588-1451; fax (563) 589-1385; e-mail jill_peter@mcgraw-hill.com; internet www.dushkin.com; f. 1990; Man. Editor LARRY LOEPPKE; every 2 years; in English.

Harriman Review: Harriman Institute, Columbia University, 420 West 188th St, New York, NY 10027, USA; tel. (212) 854-6218; fax (212) 666-3481; e-mail harriman@columbia.edu; internet www .columbia.edu/cu/sipa/regional/hi; f. 1994; Eastern and Central Europe; Editor RONALD MEYER; quarterly; in English; circ. 1,500.

Indeks Bezopasnosti (Security Index): PIR Center for Policy Studies (Russia), 119049 Moscow, Dobryninsky per. 4-yi, Bldg 8 (m. Oktyabrskaya), Russia; tel. (495) 987-19-15; fax (495) 987-19-14; e-mail petelin@pircenter.org; internet www.pircenter.org; f. 1994; international security, arms control, nuclear non-proliferation and dual-use technologies; Editor VLADIMIR A. ORLOV; quarterly; in Russian and English; circ. 1,000.

International Affairs: Royal Institute of International Affairs, Chatham House, 10 St James's Sq., London SW17 4LE, United Kingdom; tel. (20) 7314-3662; fax (20) 7957-5710; e-mail ktaylor@ chathamhouse.org.uk; internet www.chathamhouse.org.uk; contemporary world politics; extensive book reviews; 6 a year.

International Affairs: Russian Foreign Policy Foundation, 107078 Moscow, pr. Bolshoi Kozlovski 4, Russia; tel. (495) 924-72-70; fax (495) 208-08-06; internet www.mosinfo.ru/news/int-aff/subintaf .html; f. 1992; 5 a year; in English.

International Journal: Canadian International Council, 45 Willcocks St, POB 210, Toronto, ON M5S 1C7, Canada; tel. (416) 487-6830; e-mail mailbox@canadianinternationalcouncil.org; internet www.igloo.org/canadianinternational; f. 1946; commentary and articles on international affairs; quarterly; in English.

International Peacekeeping: Routledge, Taylor & Francis, 4 Park Sq., Milton Park, Abingdon, Oxfordshire, OX14 4RN, United Kingdom; tel. (20) 7017-6000; fax (20) 7017-6336; e-mail tf.enquiries@informa .com; internet www.tandf.co.uk/journals/titles/13533312.asp; f. 1994; examines the theory and practice of peace-keeping; Editor MICHAEL PUGH; 5 a year; in English; circ. 1,500.

Internet Resources for Eurasia: Civil Society International, 2929 NE Blakeley St, Seattle, WA 98105, USA; tel. (206) 523-4755; fax (206) 523-1974; e-mail ccsi@u.washington.edu; internet www .friends-partners.org/~ccsi.

Istoriya narodnoho hospodarstvo ta ekonomichnoi dumki Ukrainy (History of the National Government and Economic Thought of Ukraine): Institute of Economics, Ukrainian Acad. of Sciences, 01011 Kyiv, vul. P. Mirnoho 26, Ukraine; tel. (44) 290-84-44; fax (44) 290-86-63; f. 1965; economic history, systems and theories; Editor I. I. DEREVYANKIN; annually; in Ukrainian.

Izvestiya NAS Republiky Kazakhstana (News): Institute of Economics of the Ministry of Science and Higher Education, Kazakhstan Acad. of Sciences, 050010 Almaty, Kurmangazy 29, POB 137, Kazakhstan; tel. (727) 262-87-88; fax (727) 263-12-07; e-mail adm@econ.academ.south-capital.kz; social science and economic issues; Editor Prof. A. K. KOSHANOV; annually; in Kazakh; circ. 500.

Johnson's Russia List: World Security Institute, 1779 Massachusetts Ave, NW, Suite 615, Washington, DC 20036-2109, USA; tel. (301) 942-9281; fax (202) 478-1701; e-mail davidjohnson@starpower.net; internet www.cdi.org/russia/johnson/default.cfm; f. 1996; daily e-mail digest on Russian and post-Soviet politics, culture and society; in English; monthly Research and Analytical Supplement (Editor Stephen D. Shenfield); Dir DAVID JOHNSON.

Journal of Communist Studies and Transition Politics: Routledge, Taylor & Francis, 4 Park Sq., Milton Park, Abingdon, Oxfordshire, OX14 4RN, United Kingdom; tel. (20) 7017-6000; fax (20) 7017-6336; e-mail tf.enquiries@informa.com; internet www.tandf.co.uk/ journals/titles/13523279.asp; f. 1985; devotes particular attention to the process of regime change and also to the effects of this upheaval on communist parties, ruling and non-ruling, in Europe and the wider world; Man. Editor STEPHEN WHITE; quarterly; in English.

Journal of East-West Business: Int. Business Press (IBP), POB 399, Middletown, PA 17057, USA; tel. (717) 566-3054; fax (717) 566-8589; e-mail k9x@psu.edu; f. 1994; business studies, devt, practice and strategies, focusing on Russia, the CIS and Central and Eastern European countries; Editor-in-Chief Dr ERDENER KAYNAK; quarterly; in English; circ. 500.

Journal of European Integration: European Institute of Public Administration, Onze Lieve Vrouweplein 22, POB 1229, 6201 Maastricht, Netherlands; fax (43) 3296296; e-mail jei@eipa-nl.com; internet www.tandf.co.uk/journals/titles/07036337.html; f. 1978; publishes articles with a focus on pan-European integration from an interdisciplinary perspective, integrating economics, history, law, politics and sociology; Exec. Editors THOMAS CHRISTIANSEN, SIMON DUKE; 6 a year (from 2009).

Journal of Islamic Studies: Oxford Centre for Islamic Studies, George St, Oxford OX1 2AR, United Kingdom; tel. (1865) 278730; fax (1865) 248942; e-mail publications@oxcis.ac.uk; internet www

.oxfordjournals.org/islamj; all aspects of Islam; Editor Dr FARHAN AHMAD NIZAMI.

Journal of Muslim Minority Affairs: Routledge, Taylor & Francis, 4 Park Sq., Milton Park, Abingdon, Oxfordshire, OX14 4RN, United Kingdom; tel. (20) 7017-6000; fax (20) 7017-6336; e-mail tf .enquiries@informa.com; internet www.tandf.co.uk/journals/titles/ 13602004.asp; Editor SALEHA S. MAHMOOD; 3 a year.

Journal of Power Institutions in Post-Soviet Societies: c/o 15 rue Charlot, 75003 Paris, France; e-mail contact@pipss.org; internet www.pipss.org; f. 2004; multidisciplinary online journal devoted to the armed forces and power institutions of post-Soviet societies; Chief Editor ELISABETH SIECA-KOZLOWSKI; in French, English, Russian and German.

Journal of Russian and East European Psychology: M. E. Sharpe Inc, 80 Business Park Dr., Armonk, NY 10504, USA; tel. (914) 273-1800; fax (914) 273-2106; e-mail custserv@mesharpe.com; internet www .mesharpe.com; f. 1962; translations of both new and published academic articles; Editor PENTTI HAKKARAINEN; 6 a year; in English.

Journal of Slavic Military Studies: Routledge, Taylor & Francis, 4 Park Sq., Milton Park, Abingdon, Oxfordshire, OX14 4RN, United Kingdom; tel. (20) 7017-6000; fax (20) 7017-6336; e-mail tf .enquiries@informa.com; internet www.tandf.co.uk/journals/titles/ 13518046.asp; f. 1988; investigates all aspects of military affairs in the Slavic nations of Central and Eastern Europe, in an historical and geopolitical context; Editors Col DAVID M. GLANTZ (retd), CHRISTOPHER DONNELLY; quarterly; in English.

Journal of Southeast European and Black Sea Studies: Routledge, Taylor & Francis, 4 Park Sq., Milton Park, Abingdon, Oxfordshire, OX14 4RN, United Kingdom; tel. (20) 7017-6000; fax (20) 7017-6336; e-mail tf.enquiries@informa.com; internet www.informaworld.com/ fbss; f. 2001; covers the politics, political economy, international relations and modern history of South-Eastern Europe and the Black Sea region; Editors FRANZ-LOTHAR ALTMANN, THEODORE COULOUMBIS, SHIREEN HUNTER, THANOS VEREMIS, SUSAN WOODWARD; 4 a year; in English.

Journal of Ukrainian Studies: CIUS Press, 430 Pembina Hall, University of Alberta, Edmonton, T6G 2H8, Canada; tel. (780) 492-2972; fax (780) 492-4967; e-mail jus@ualberta.ca; internet www.utoronto.ca/cius/webfiles/jus.htm; f. 1976; publ. by Canadian Institute of Ukrainian Studies; Editor (vacant); 2 a year; in English.

Main Economic Indicators: Organisation for Economic Co-operation and Development (OECD), 2 rue André Pascal, 75775 Paris Cedex 16, France; tel. 1 45-24-16-93; fax 1-45-24-17-13; e-mail oecdrow@ turpin-distribution.com; internet www.oecdbookshop.org/oecd/ display.asp?sf1=identifiers&st=04745523; f. 1999; covers Russia, Ukraine, the Baltic states (Estonia, Latvia and Lithuania), Bulgaria, Romania and Slovenia; available online and in print; monthly; in English.

Medunarodni problemi (International Problems): 11000 Belgrade, ul. Makedonska 25, Serbia; tel. (11) 3373824; fax (11) 3373835; e-mail branam@eunet.yu; internet www.diplomacy.bg.ac.yu; f. 1948; review of the Institute of International Politics and Economics; covers international law, international organizations, international political relations and the world economy; Editor BRANA MARKOVIĆ; quarterly; in Serbian and English; circ. 1,000.

Mezhdunarodnaya Zhizn (International Life): 103064 Moscow, pr. Gorokhovski 14, Russia; tel. (495) 265-37-81; fax (495) 265-37-71; e-mail inter_affairs@mid.ru; f. 1954; foreign policy concerns of Russia and other countries; Editor-in-Chief BORIS PYADISHEV; monthly; in English and Russian; circ. 30,000.

Military Thought: A Russian Journal of Military Theory and Strategy: East View Information Services, Inc, 10601 Wayzata Boulevard, Minneapolis, MN 55305, USA; tel. (952) 252-1201; fax (952) 252-1202; e-mail periodicals@eastview.com; internet www.eastview .com/evpj/evjournals_new.asp?editionid=555; f. 1918 in Russian; English version from 1992 (Russian version now published by Russian Ministry of Defence); global military devts, issues affecting the Russian Armed Forces, military theory and planning in Russia; Editor S. RODIKOV; 4 a year; in Russian and English; circ. 200.

Mirovaya Ekonomika i Mezhdunarodnye Otnoshenii (World Economy and International Relations): Institute of World Economy and Int. Relations, Russian Acad. of Sciences, 117859 Moscow, ul. Profsoyuznaya 23, Russia; tel. (495) 128-08-83; fax (495) 120-14-17; e-mail ineir@sovam.com; f. 1957; world economy and international relations, and political and economic devt of the contemporary Russian Federation; Editor GERMAN G. DILIGENSKII; monthly; in Russian; circ. 5,000.

Moldovan Economic Trends: Ministry of Economy, Govt Bldg, 2033 Chişinău, Rm 219, Piaţa Marii Adunări Naţionale, Moldova; tel. (2) 23-40-13; fax (2) 23-40-57; e-mail currie@moldova.md; internet www .met.dnt.md; published by the Govt of Moldova and the European Expertise Service; quarterly.

Monitor: Centre for Eastern Studies, 00-564 Warsaw, ul. Koszykowa 6A, Poland; f. 1991; responsible to the Ministry of Foreign Economic Relations; economic, political and social information and analysis on the countries of the former USSR, in particular Belarus, the Russian Federation and Ukraine; in English.

Moscow Journal of International Law: Moskovskii Gosudarstvennii Institut Mezhdunarodnykh Otnoshenii (MGIMO—Moscow State Institute of Int. Relations), 119454 Moscow, pr. Vernadskogo 76, Russia; tel. and fax (495) 434-93-13; e-mail mjil@mgimo.ru; internet www.mjil.ru; f. 1990; all branches of international law, in connection with contemporary international relations and foreign policy of Russia and other members of the CIS; Editor-in-Chief YURII M. KOLOSOV; quarterly; in Russian, with summaries in English; circ. 1,000.

Moscow Times Business Review: 125212 Moscow, ul. Vyborgskaya 16, Russia; tel. (495) 937-33-99; fax (495) 937-33-93; e-mail businessreview@imedia.ru; internet www.businessreview.ru; business and current affairs; Editor-in-Chief EDMUND HARRIS; Editor FLORENCE GALLEZ; monthly.

Moskovskii Universitet Vestnik, Seriya 7: Ekonomika (Moscow University Herald, Volume 7: Economics): Moscow M. V. Lomonosov State University, 103009 Moscow, ul. Gertsena 5–7, Russia; tel. (495) 939-53-40; f. 1966; one of 14 volumes, which cover a wide range of academic subjects; includes bibliographical information, book reviews and indexes; 6 a year; in Russian; circ. 2,200.

Nationalities Papers: Routledge, Taylor & Francis, 4 Park Sq., Milton Park, Abingdon, Oxfordshire, OX14 4RN, United Kingdom; tel. (20) 7017-6000; fax (20) 7017-6336; e-mail tf.enquiries@informa .com; internet www.tandf.co.uk/journals/titles/00905992.asp; publ. of the Association for the Study of Nationalities; non-Russian nationalities of the former USSR and national minorities in Central and Eastern Europe; Editor-in-Chief and Man. Editor Dr STEVE SABOL; 5 a year; in English.

NEP Era: Literature and Culture 1921–28: Charles Schlacks, Jr, POB 1256, Idyllwild, CA 925-1256, USA; tel. (951) 659-4641; e-mail info@schlacks.com; internet www.schlacks.com; Editor ALEXIS POGORELSKIN; annually; in English, French, German and Russian.

New Zealand Slavonic Journal: Russian School of Languages and Cultures, University of Canterbury, POB 4800, Christchurch, New Zealand; tel. (3) 366-7001; fax (3) 364-2522; e-mail evgeny.pavlov@ canterbury.ac.nz; internet www.lanc.canterbury.ac.nz/russ/nzsj/ nzsjindex.shtml; f. 1967; culture, history, language and literature of Russia and other countries; Editor Dr YEVGENII PAVLOV; annually; in English and Russian.

Novoye Vremya (New Times): 127994 Moscow, M. Putinkovskii per. 1/2, POB 4, Russia; tel. and fax (495) 980-87-20; e-mail mail@ newtimes.ru; internet www.newtimes.ru; f. 1943; foreign and Russian affairs; Editor ALEKSANDR PUMPYANSKII; weekly; in Russian and English; circ. 25,000 (2002).

Novyi Zhurnal (New Review): 611 Broadway, Suite 842, New York, NY 10012, USA; tel. and fax (212) 353-1478; e-mail newreview@msn .com; internet magazines.russ.ru/nj; f. 1942; covers general cultural topics, incl. literature; Editor-in-Chief Prof. MARINA ADAMOVITCH; quarterly; in Russian; circ. 600.

Obshchestvennye nauki v Uzbekistane (Social Sciences in Uzbekistan): Fan (Science) Publishers, 700047 Tashkent, Ya. G'ulomov ko'ch. 70/102, Uzbekistan; tel. (71) 133-69-91; fax (71) 133-49-01; f. 1957; publication of the Uzbek Acad. of Sciences; fields covered include economics and oriental studies; monthly; in Russian.

Occasional Papers of the Institute for Contemporary International Studies: Institute for Contemporary International Studies, 119021 Moscow, ul. Ostozhenka 53/2, Russia; tel. (495) 208-9461; fax (495) 208-9466; e-mail iamp@rol.ru; Russian foreign policy and international diplomacy; monthly; in Russian.

Ost-Wirtschaftsreport (Eastern Economic Report): Verlagsgruppe Handelsblatt GmbH, 40213 Düsseldorf, Kasernenstr. 67, Germany; tel. (211) 8870; fax (211) 326759; f. 1973; Editor JULIANE LANGEN-ECKER; every 2 weeks; in German; circ. 1,200.

Osteuropa (Eastern Europe): Aachen, Germany; tel. (241) 32707; fax (241) 405879; e-mail oe@rwth-aachen.de; internet osteuropa .dgo-online.org; f. 1925; information about Central and Eastern Europe, incl. culture, economy, education, literature, new trends and devts in politics and society; Editor Dr A. STEININGER; monthly; in German; circ. 2,350.

Osteuropa-Wirtschaft (Eastern Europe Economy): German Soc. for East European Research, Güllstr. 7, 80336 München, Germany; tel. (89) 74613321; fax (89) 74613333; e-mail u9511aa@mail .lrz-muenchen.de; f. 1956; economic issues relevant to Central and Eastern Europe, incl. new trends and devts, and problems of transformation; also includes book reviews, indexes and statistical information; Editor Dr F.-L. ALTMANN; quarterly; in German and with abstracts in English; circ. 750.

Oxford Slavonic Papers: Oxford University Press, Great Clarendon St, Oxford OX2 6DP, United Kingdom; tel. (1865) 267907; fax (1865) 267485; e-mail enquiry@oup.co.uk.

Perspectives on European Politics and Society: Routledge, Taylor & Francis, 4 Park Sq., Milton Park, Abingdon, Oxfordshire, OX14 4RN, England; tel. (20) 7017-6000; fax (20) 7017-6336; e-mail c.z.ross@ dundee.ac.uk; internet www.tandf.co.uk/journals/titles/15705854 .asp; f. 2000; covers all aspects of European politics, including Russia; Editor Dr CAMERON ROSS; 4 a year.

Political Crossroads: James Nicholas Publishers, POB 5179, South Melbourne, Vic 3205, Australia; tel. (3) 9696-5955; fax (3) 9699-2040; e-mail custservice@jnponline.com; internet www .jamesnicholaspublishers.com.au/pcjrnl.htm; cultural ideology, economic and administrative organizations, international relations, leadership and political theory; Man. Editor JOSEPH ZAJDA; 2 a year; in English.

Politychna Dumka / Politicheskaya Mysl / Political Thought: 01030 Kyiv, vul. Leontovycha 5, Ukraine; tel. and fax (44) 235-02-29; e-mail politdumka@bigmir.net; internet www.politdumka.kiev.ua; f. 1993; current affairs and political analysis; Ukrainian, Russian and English editions; Editor-in-Chief VOLODOMYR POLOKHALO.

Polityka i Chas / Politics and the Times: 02160 Kyiv, pr. Vozyednannya 15–17, Ukraine; tel. and fax (44) 550-31-44; f. 1994 to replace *Pid praporam Lenina* (Under the Banner of Lenin); organ of the Ministry of Foreign Affairs; Ukrainian international relations and foreign affairs; Editor-in-Chief LEONID BAIDAK; monthly, in Ukrainian; quarterly, in English; circ. 6,000.

Polityka Wschodnia (Eastern Politics): Centre for Eastern Studies of the University of Warsaw, 00-046 Warsaw, ul. Nowy Swiat 69, Poland; tel. (22) 6200381; fax (22) 267520; relations between Belarus, the Russian Federation, Ukraine and the former Soviet Baltic states (Estonia, Latvia and Lithuania); 2 a year; in Polish.

Post-Communist Economies: Centre for the Study of Post-Communist Economies (CRCE), 57 Tufton St, London SW1P 3QL, United Kingdom; tel. and fax (20) 7233-1050; e-mail tf.enquiries@informa .com; internet www.tandf.co.uk/journals/titles/14631377.asp; f. 1989; transformation economics of communist and former communist countries, in particular in Eastern Europe, Russia and Central Asia; fmrly *Communist Economies and Economic Transformation*; Editor ROGER CLARKE; quarterly; in English.

Post-Soviet Affairs: Bellwether Publishing Ltd, 8640 Guilford Rd, Suite 200, Columbia, MD 21046, USA; tel. (410) 290-3870; fax (410) 290-8726; e-mail bellpub@bellpub.com; internet www.bellpub.com; f. 1985; economics, foreign policy, nationality issues and political science in the countries of the former USSR; Editor GEORGE W. BRESLAUER; quarterly; in English.

The Prague Watchdog: Saratovská 33, 100 00 Prague 10, Czech Republic; tel. 602565074; e-mail mail@watchdog.cz; internet www .watchdog.cz; f. 2000; weekly; in Czech, English and Russian; website, and weekly e-mail bulletin covering the conflict in Chechnya; also publishes a monthly magazine in Russian for Chechens; Editor-in-Chief TOMÁŠ VRŠOVSKÝ.

Pro et Contra: Carnegie Moscow Center, Carnegie Endowment for International Peace, 125009 Moscow, ul. Tverskaya 16/2, Russia; tel. (495) 935-89-04; fax (495) 935-89-06; e-mail editor@carnegie.ru; internet www.carnegie.ru/ru/pubs/procontra; f. 1996; policy journal; every 2 months; in Russian.

Problems of Economic Transition: M. E. Sharpe Inc, 80 Business Park Dr., Armonk, NY 10504, USA; tel. (914) 273-1800; fax (914) 273-2106; e-mail custserv@mesharpe.com; internet www.mesharpe.com; f. 1958; translation of selected articles from economic journals in the former USSR; includes indexes and statistical information; Editor BEN SLAY; monthly; in English.

Problems of Post-Communism: National Council for Eurasian and East European Research, 910 17th St, NW, Suite 300, Washington, DC 20006, USA; tel. (202) 822-6950; fax (202) 822-6955; e-mail popc@ nceeer.org; internet www.nceeer.org; f. 1951; edited at the National Council for Eurasian and East European Research; covers economic, political and social devts and trends in the post-communist countries of Asia and Europe; Editor ROBERT T. HUBER; 6 a year; in English.

Reforma Monthly: Int. Foundation for Economic and Social Reforms (Reforma), 109240 Moscow, nab. Kotelnicheskaya 17, Russia; tel. (495) 926-77-52; fax (495) 975-23-73.

Religion in Eastern Europe: Christians Associated for Relations with Eastern Europe, AMBS, 3003 Benham Ave, Elkhart, IN 46517, USA; tel. (219) 296-6209; fax (219) 295-0092; e-mail waltersawatsky@cs .com; internet ree.georgefox.edu; f. 1981; insight into the religious situation in Eastern Europe; Editors Dr WALTER SAWATSKY, Dr PAUL MOJZES; 4 a year; circ. 450.

Religion, State and Society: Routledge, Taylor & Francis, 4 Park Sq., Milton Park, Abingdon, Oxfordshire, OX14 4RN, United Kingdom; tel. (20) 7017-6000; fax (20) 7017-6336; e-mail editor@rssjournal.org .uk; internet www.tandf.co.uk/journals/journal

.asp?issn=0963-7494; f. 1973 as *Religion in Communist Lands*; name changed as above in 1992; interdisciplinary coverage of all aspects of religious life and religion-state relations, maintaining a traditional focus on communist and post-communist countries, but treating themes of world-wide concern, with a comparative approach where appropriate, to reveal similarities and differences in the historical and current experience of countries, regions and religions, in stability or in transition; Editor Dr Philip Walters; quarterly; in English.

Review of Russian Periodic: Continent (Kontinent), 217 Fourth Ave, Garwood, NJ 07027, USA; e-mail continent@comcast.net; politics, history, philosophy, religion; also *Continent* (quarterly); Representative Marina Adamovich; 2 a year; in English.

Revolutionary Russia: Routledge, Taylor & Francis, 4 Park Sq., Milton Park, Abingdon, Oxfordshire, OX14 4RN, United Kingdom; tel. (20) 7017-6000; fax (20) 7017-6336; e-mail tf.enquiries@informa.com; internet www.informaworld.com/frvr; f. 1988; concentrates on the revolutionary period of Russian history, from approx. 1880–1932, with an interdisciplinary and international approach; Editor Jonathan Smele; 2 a year; in English.

Revue d'Etudes Comparatives Est-Ouest: Centre National de la Recherche Scientifique, 44 rue de l'Amiral Mouchez, 75014 Paris, France; tel. 1-43-13-56-69; fax 1-43-13-56-70; e-mail receoo@ivry.cnrs.fr; f. 1970; economics, history of ex-communist and communist countries, law, politics and sociology; Editor Marie-Claude Maurel; 4 a year; in French, with summaries in French and English; circ. 800.

RFE/RL Russian Political Weekly: Radio Free Europe/Radio Liberty, 110 00 Prague 1, Vinohradská 1, Czech Republic; tel. (2) 21123628; fax (2) 21122012; e-mail corwinj@rferl.org; internet www.rferl.org; Editor Julie Corwin.

Romantic Russia: Literature and Culture 1815–1855: Charles Schlacks, Jr, POB 1256, Idyllwild, CA 925-1256, USA; tel. (951) 659-4641; e-mail info@schlacks.com; internet www.schlacks.com; Editor (vacant); annually; in English, French, German and Russian.

Rossiiskii Ekonomicheskii Zhurnal (Russian Economic Journal): 109542 Moscow, pr. Ryazanskii 99, Russia; tel. (495) 377-25-56; e-mail rem@energosvjaz.ru; f. 1958; theory and practice of economics and economic reform; Editor A. Y. Melentev; monthly; in Russian; circ. 6,000.

Rusia Hoy (Russia Today): Institute of Latin American Studies, Russian Acad. of Sciences, 113035 Moscow, ul. B. Ordynka 21, Russia; tel. (495) 233-43-40; fax (495) 233-40-70; monthly; in Spanish.

Russia and Eurasia Review: Jamestown Foundation, 4516 43rd St, NW, Washington, DC 20016, USA; tel. (202) 483-8888; e-mail pubs@jamestown.org; internet russia.jamestown.org/pubs_russia.htm; f. 2002; Editor Peter Rutland; fortnightly.

Russia and Euro-Asia Bulletin: Contemporary Europe Research Centre, University of Melbourne, 2nd Floor, 234 Queensberry St, Carlton, Vic 3052, Australia; tel. (3) 9344-9502; fax (3) 9344-9507; e-mail cerc@cerc.unimelb.edu.au; internet www.cerc.unimelb.edu.au/bulletin; f. 1994; economic trends; every 2 months; in English.

Russia Profile: 119021 Moscow, Zubovskii bul. 4, Russia; tel. (495) 981-64-86; fax (495) 201-30-71; e-mail info@russiaprofile.org; internet www.russiaprofile.org; publ. by Independent Media/Sanoma (Finland) in asscn with RIA-Novosti; in-depth analysis of Russian politics, business, culture and society; Editor Andrei Zolotov, Jr; monthly.

Russian Analytical Digest: ETH Zentrum, Leonhardhalde 21, 8092 Zürich, Switzerland; internet www.res.ethz.ch/analysis/rad; publ. by Center for Security Studies at the Swiss Federal Institute of Technology Zurich (ETH Zurich) in asscn with Forschungstelle Osteuropa an der Universität Bremen (Research Centre for East European Studies), Bremen Univ., Germany; f. 2006 to replace *Russian Regional Report*; political, economic, and social developments in Russia and its regions, and Russia's role in international relations; Editor Jeronim Perovich; every 2 weeks; online only.

Russian Economy: Trends and Prospects: Institute of Economic Transition, 103918 Moscow, ul. Ogareva 5/3, Russia; tel. (095) 202-42-74; e-mail e40102@sucemi.bitnet.

Russian Education and Society: A Journal of Translations: M. E. Sharpe Inc, 80 Business Park Dr., Armonk, NY 10504, USA; tel. (914) 273-1800; fax (914) 273-2106; e-mail custserv@mesharpe.com; internet www.mesharpe.com; f. 1958; post-Soviet writing on pedagogical theory and practice, education policy, youth and the family; Editor Anthony Jones; monthly; in English.

Russian Film, Past and Present: Charles Schlacks, Jr, POB 1256, Idyllwild, CA 925-1256, USA; tel. (951) 659-4641; e-mail info@schlacks.com; internet www.schlacks.com; annually; in English, French, German and Russian.

Russian History: Charles Schlacks, Jr, POB 1256, Idyllwild, CA 925-1256, USA; tel. (951) 659-4641; e-mail info@schlacks.com; internet

www.schlacks.com; f. 1974; Editor Richard Hellie; 4 a year; in English and Russian.

Russian Monitor: Archive of Contemporary Politics: Centre for Applied Political Studies (INDEM), 121914 Moscow, ul. Novyi Arbat 15, Russia; tel. (495) 202-32-14; fax (495) 202-31-69; e-mail indemglas@apc.org; quarterly.

Russian Music, Past and Present: Charles Schlacks, Jr, POB 1256, Idyllwild, CA 925-1256, USA; tel. (951) 659-4641; e-mail info@schlacks.com; internet www.schlacks.com; Editor Ruth Rischin; annually; in English, French, German and Russian.

Russian Politics and Law: M. E. Sharpe Inc, 80 Business Park Dr., Armonk, NY 10504, USA; tel. (914) 273-1800; fax (914) 273-2106; e-mail custserv@mesharpe.com; internet www.mesharpe.com; f. 1962; analysis of past and contemporary issues, such as constitutionalism, foreign relations, ideology, imperialism, nationalism, party devt and state-building; Editor Nils H. Wessell; 6 a year; in English.

Russian Review: Blackwell Publishing Inc, 350 Main St, Malden, MA 01248, USA; tel. (781) 388-8599; fax (781) 388-8232; e-mail customerservices@blackwellpublishing.com; internet www.blackwellpublishing.com; Editor Eve Levin; quarterly.

Russian Social Science Review: a Journal of Translations: M. E. Sharpe Inc, 80 Business Park Dr., Armonk, NY 10504, USA; tel. (914) 273-1800; fax (914) 273-2106; e-mail custserv@mesharpe.com; internet www.mesharpe.com; f. 1960; presents essays and studies in a range of fields, incl. anthropology, economics, education, history, literary criticism, political science, psychology and sociology, for insights into the problems of post-Soviet society; Editor Patricia A. Kolb; 6 a year; in English.

Russian Studies in History: M. E. Sharpe Inc, 80 Business Park Dr., Armonk, NY 10504, USA; tel. (914) 273-1800; fax (914) 273-2106; e-mail custserv@mesharpe.com; internet www.mesharpe.com; f. 1962; translations of Russian history articles; Editors Joseph Bradley, Christine Ruane; 4 a year; in English.

Russian Studies in Literature: M. E. Sharpe Inc, 80 Business Park Dr., Armonk, NY 10504, USA; tel. (914) 273-1800; fax (914) 273-2106; e-mail custserv@mesharpe.com; internet www.mesharpe.com; f. 1964; translations of Russian literary criticism and scholarship; Editor John Givens; 4 a year; in English.

Russian Studies in Philosophy: M. E. Sharpe Inc, 80 Business Park Dr., Armonk, NY 10504, USA; tel. (914) 273-1800; fax (914) 273-2106; e-mail custserv@mesharpe.com; internet www.mesharpe.com; f. 1962; translations of Russian articles on philosophy; Editor Marina F. Bykova; 4 a year; in English.

Sankt-Peterburgskii Universitet Vestnik, Seriya 5: Ekonomika (St Petersburg University Herald, Edition: Economics): St Petersburg University, 192194 St Petersburg, ul. Chaikovskogo 62, Russia; tel. and fax (812) 272-59-93; e-mail vestnik@econ.pu.ru; f. 1946; one of eight editions; quarterly; in Russian, with summaries in English.

Science and Global Security: the Technical Basis for Arms Control and Environmental Policy Initiatives: Harwood Academic Publishers, POB 32160, Newark, NJ 07102-0301, USA; tel. (973) 643-7500; fax (973) 643-7676; internet www.gbhap.com/science_global_security; f. 1989; scientific analyses relating to arms control and global environment policy; Editors H. A. Feiveson, Stanislav N. Rodionov; quarterly; in English and Russian.

Short-Term Economic Indicators: Organisation for Economic Co-operation and Development, 2 rue André-Pascal, 75775 Paris Cedex 16, France; tel. 1-45-24-82-00; e-mail stat.contact@oecd.org; internet www.oecd.org.

Silver Age: Russian Literature and Culture 1881–1921: Charles Schlacks, Jr, POB 1256, Idyllwild, CA 925-1256, USA; tel. (951) 659-4641; e-mail info@schlacks.com; internet www.schlacks.com; Editor (vacant); annually; in English, French, German and Russian.

Slavic and Eastern European Journal: c/o the Editor, University of Kentucky, Lexington, KY 40506, USA; tel. (859) 257-9854; fax (859) 257-3743; e-mail seej@uky.edu; internet www.aatseel.org/see_journal; publ. by the American Association of Teachers of Slavic and Eastern European Languages; research studies in all areas of Slavic culture, language and literature; Exec. Dir Patricia L. Zody; Editor-in-Chief Dr Gerald Janecek.

Slavic Review: An Interdisciplinary Journal of Russian, Eurasian, and East European Studies: University of Illinois at Urbana-Champaign, 57 E Armory Ave, Champaign, IL 61820-6601, USA; tel. (217) 333-3621; fax (217) 333-3872; e-mail slavrev@illinois.edu; internet www.slavicreview.uiuc.edu; f. 1941 as *American Slavic and East European Review*, name changed 1961; covers art, history, humanities, literature, linguistics and social sciences in Eastern Europe, Eurasia and Russia; publ. by the American Association for the Advancement of Slavic Studies; Editor Mark D. Steinberg; quarterly; in English; circ. approx. 4,500.

Slavonic and East European Review: School of Slavonic and East European Studies, UCL, Gower St, London WC1E 6BT, United

Kingdom; tel. (20) 7679-8724; fax (20) 7679-8755; e-mail seer@ssees .ucl.ac.uk; internet www.ssees.ucl.ac.uk/seer.htm; f. 1922; quarterly; Deputy Editor Dr BARBARA WYLLIE.

Slavonica: Maney Publishing, Suite 1C, Joseph's Well, Hanover Walk, Leeds, LS3 1AB, United Kingdom; tel. (113) 243-2800; fax (113) 386-8178; e-mail maney@maney.co.uk; internet www.maney .co.uk/search?fwaction=show&fwid=214; f. 1983 as *Scottish Slavonic Review*; name changed in 1994; culture, history, language and literature in Central and Eastern Europe and Russia; Editor JEKATERINA YOUNG; 2 a year; in English; circ. approx. 150.

Slovo: School of Slavonic and Eastern European Studies, UCL, Gower St, London WC1E 6BT, United Kingdom; tel. (20) 7862-8619; fax (20) 7862-8641; e-mail slovo@ssees.ucl.ac.uk; internet www.ssees.ac.uk/slovo.htm; interdisciplinary journal concerned with Central and East European, Russian and Eurasian affairs; Man. Editor KATHERINE O'NEILL; in English; 2 a year.

Socialist Realism: Literature and Culture 1928–1953: Charles Schlacks, Jr, POB 1256, Idyllwild, CA 925-1256, USA; tel. (951) 659-4641; e-mail info@schlacks.com; internet www.schlacks.com; Editor (vacant); annually; in English, French, German and Russian.

Solanus. International Journal for Russian and East European Bibliographic, Library and Publishing Studies: c/o Dr Christine Thomas, Slavonic and East European Collections, British Library, 96 Euston Rd, London NW1 2DB, United Kingdom; tel. (20) 7412-7587; fax (20) 7412-7554; e-mail cgthom@yandex.ru; internet www.ssees .ac.uk/solanus/solacont.htm; publ. of the School of Slavonic and East European Studies, University College London; Editor Dr CHRISTINE THOMAS; annually.

Soviet and Post-Soviet Politics and Society: Ibidem-Verlag, Melchiorstr. 15, 70439 Stuttgart, Germany; tel. (711) 9807954; fax (711) 8001889; e-mail info@ibidem-verlag.de; internet www .ibidem-verlag.de/spps.html; f. 2004; analysis of the contemporary politics and society of the countries of the former Eastern bloc, and of the social and cultural history of the Tsarist empire and Soviet Union after 1905; Editor Dr ANDREAS UMLAND; in English, German and Russian.

Soviet and Post-Soviet Review: Charles Schlacks, Jr, POB 1256, Idyllwild, CA 925-1256, USA; tel. (951) 659-4641; e-mail info@ schlacks.com; internet www.schlacks.com; f. 1974; Editor VLADIMIR BULDAKOV; 3 a year; in English, French, German and Russian.

Stanford Slavic Studies: Dept of Slavic Languages and Literature, Stanford University, c/o Berkeley Slavic Specialities, POB 3034, Oakland, CA 94609-0034, USA; tel. (510) 653-8048; fax (510) 653-6313; Editors LAZAR FLEISHMAN, GREGORY FREIDIN, RICHARD SCHUPBACH.

Statistical Co-operation with Central and Eastern Europe and Central Asia: Dept for Int. Development, Statistics, 94 Victoria St, London SW1E 5JL, United Kingdom; tel. (20) 7917-7000; fax (20) 7917-0019; e-mail enquiry@dfid.gov.uk; internet www.dfid.gov.uk.

Statutes and Decisions: the Laws of the USSR and its Successor States: M. E. Sharpe Inc, 80 Business Park Dr., Armonk, NY 10504, USA; tel. (914) 273-1800; fax (914) 273-2106; e-mail custserv@ mesharpe.com; internet www.mesharpe.com; f. 1964; translations from the Russian; Editor SARAH J. REYNOLDS; 6 a year; in English.

Steppe Magazine: A Central Asian Panorama: Manor Farm, Nettlebed, Oxfordshire, RG9 5DA, United Kingdom; tel. (1491) 641914; e-mail info@steppemagazine.com; internet www.steppemagazine .com; f. 2006; arts, culture, history, landscape and people of Central Asia; illustrated; Editors and Publrs SUMMER COISH, LUCY KELAART; 2 a year; in English.

Symposium: A Journal of Russian Thought: Charles Schlacks, Jr, POB 1256, Idyllwild, CA 925-1256, USA; tel. (951) 659-4641; e-mail info@schlacks.com; internet www.schlacks.com; annually; in English, French, German and Russian; Editor (vacant).

Teatr: Russian Theatre, Past and Present: Charles Schlacks, Jr, POB 1256, Idyllwild, CA 925-1256, USA; tel. (951) 659-4641; e-mail info@ schlacks.com; internet www.schlacks.com; f. 2000; Editor (vacant); annually; in English, French, German and Russian.

Tracking Eastern Europe—Executive Business Guide: AMF Int. Consultants, 812 N Wood Ave, Suite 204, Linden, NJ 07036, USA; tel. (098) 486-3534; fax (098) 486-4084; f. 1990; foreign investment in Eastern Europe and the former USSR; Editor FRED T. ROSSI; 2 a month; in English.

Transcultural Studies: a Series in Interdisciplinary Research: Charles Schlacks, Jr, POB 1256, Idyllwild, CA 925-1256, USA; tel. (951) 659-4641; e-mail info@schlacks.com; internet www.schlacks .com; Co-Editors SLOBODANKA M. VLADIV-GLOVER, EVERT VAN DER ZWEERDE; annually.

Transition Report: European Bank for Reconstruction and Development, 1 Exchange Sq., London EC2A 2JN, United Kingdom; tel. (20) 7338-6000; fax (20) 7338-6100; e-mail pubsdesk@ebrd.com; internet www.ebrd.com; annually.

Transitions: Institut de Sociologie, Université Libre de Bruxelles, 44 ave Jeanne, CP 124, 1050 Brussels, Belgium; tel. (2) 650-34-42; fax (2) 650-35-21; e-mail adesmarl@ulb.ac.be; internet www.ulb.ac.be/is/ revtrans.html; f. 1960; 2 a year; in French and English.

Transitions Online (TOL): Chlumova 22, 130 00 Prague 3, Czech Republic; tel. (2) 222780805; fax (2) 222780804; e-mail transitions@ tol.org; internet www.tol.org; f. 1999; culture, economy, media and politics in Central and Eastern Europe, the Balkans, and the former USSR; online only; daily; in English; Editor JEREMY DRUKER.

The Ukraine List: c/o Dept of Ukrainian Studies, University of Ottawa, 559 King Edward Ave, Ottawa, ON K1N 6N5, Canada; tel. (613) 562-5800 ext. 3692; fax (613) 562-5351; e-mail darel@ uottawa.ca; internet www.ukrainianstudies.uottawa.ca/ ukraine_list; f. 1998; weekly; e-mail digest on Ukrainian politics, including articles translated from Ukrainian and other languages; in English; Dir DOMINIQUE AREL.

Ulkopolitiikka (Finnish Journal of Foreign Affairs): Ulkopoliittinen Instituutti (UPI—Finnish Institute of Int. Affairs), Mannerheimintie 15A, 00260 Helsinki, Finland; tel. (9) 4342070; fax (9) 43420769; e-mail ulkopolitiikka@upi-fiia.fi; internet www.ulkopolitiikka.fi; f. 1962; presents recent research findings and background discussions relevant to foreign-policy and security-policy issues; Editors Dr TAPANI VAAHTORANTA, UNNA LEHTIPUU, MAARIKA TOIVONEN; quarterly; in Finnish; circ. 2,000.

Venäjän aika: Novomedia Oy, Kaupintie 16B /16, 00440 Helsinki, Finland; tel. (9) 8545320; fax (9) 85453250; e-mail novomedia@ novomedia.fi; internet www.novomedia.fi; Editor ALEKSANDER BORODAVKIN.

Vneshnyaya Torgovlya (Foreign Trade): 121108 Moscow, ul. Minskaya 11, Russia; tel. (495) 145-68-94; fax (495) 145-51-92; e-mail vneshtorg@mtu-net.ru; f. 1921; Editor Y. M. DEOMIDOV; every 2 months; in Russian and English; circ. 8,000.

Voprosy Ekonomiki (Questions of Economics): Institute of Economics, Russian Acad. of Sciences, 117218 Moscow, Nakhimovskii pr. 32, Russia; tel. and fax (495) 124-52-28; e-mail mail@vopreco.ru; internet www.vopreco.ru; f. 1929; covers problems of economic theory, monetary and fiscal policies, social issues, structural and investment policy, technological change, transitional economics; Editor L. I. ABALKIN; monthly; in Russian; circ. 6,500 (2004).

World Policy Journal: Q Corpn, 49 Sheridan Ave, Albany, NY 12210, USA; tel. (212) 229-5808; fax (212) 807-1294; e-mail wpj@newschool .edu; internet www.worldpolicy.org/journal/index.html; f. 1983; published by the World Policy Institute; international affairs; Man. Editor LINDA WRIGLEY; quarterly.

Zeitschrift für Ostmitteleuropa-Forschung (Journal of East Central European Studies): 35037 Marburg, Gisonenweg 5-7, Germany; tel. (6421) 184125; fax (6421) 184139; e-mail vertrieb@mailer .uni-marburg.de; internet www.uni-marburg.de/herder-institut; f. 1952; history of East Central Europe (the geographical area covered by Poland, Estonia, Latvia, Lithuania, the Czech and Slovak Republics, western Belarus and western Ukraine); Editors Dr WINFRIED IRGANG, MARKO WAUKER; quarterly; in German and English; circ. 650.

INDEX OF REGIONAL ORGANIZATIONS

(Main reference only)